THE
GREAT BOOK
OF WINE

CREATED AND PRODUCED
BY
EDITA LAUSANNE

THE GREAT BOOK OF WINE

Galahad Books • New York

Originally published in Switzerland by Edita Lausanne

First English Printing by World—1970

© Copyright 1969, 1970 by Edita Lausanne

Library of Congress Catalog Card Number: 74-80064

ISBN 0-88365-252-8

Printed in Hong Kong by Mandarin Publishers Ltd.

CONTENTS

WINE AND CIVILIZATION

THE GREAT WINE REGIONS OF THE WORLD

THE WAYS OF WINE AND MAN

FOREWORD

The fact that millions of human beings have from earliest times regarded wine as a noble drink is due to an unusual sequence of events. When a comparison is made with other crafts and customs that have not survived the rough passage of history, the story of wine is remarkable. Without such a fortuitous succession of events, neither vine nor wine would ever have become so widely and so highly esteemed throughout the world.

In the beginning, the only grape capable of producing a pleasant-tasting drink grew wild all over the Middle Eastern countries. It was precisely here that men first began to cultivate the soil, select plants, and live in organized communities. Had the vine been just an ordinary plant, it would probably have shared the same fate as the Middle Eastern and Egyptian civilizations. It was the wine that saved the vine. This subtle beverage was found to possess extraordinary virtues; the intoxication it produced was attributed to divine powers. Consequently, the vine was held to be a gift from the heavens and wine a drink associated with the worship of the gods and the celebration of those favourites of the gods: heroes, poets and artists. Men offered wine in homage to the deity; in their turn, through wine, the gods endowed men with strength, inspiration and a liberating sense of well-being. Wine was at that time as much appreciated as it was rare.

Carried on the tide of the expansion of the Roman Empire, the vine spread and flourished far beyond the boundaries of its native land. Leather bottles, amphoras and butts, all filled with wine, found their way back to Rome from the heart of Gaul, Germania, Africa and the Iberian Peninsula. This wide-flung empire finally crumbled before the onslaught of the Barbarians, who knew nothing of wine, but the art of viniculture had been already handed on and the succeeding chapter in wine's history ensured not only its survival but its spectacular revival. Indeed, since the evening when Jesus Christ shared the bread and wine of the Lord's Supper with his disciples, wine has been an indispensable part in the cult of the new religion which was destined to spread throughout the world. Wherever Christianity was adopted, men endeavoured to cultivate vines and, either by indigenous production or importation, to obtain wine. Monks, bishops and missionaries promoted and encouraged viticulture. Nor were the nobility by any means indifferent to the prestige of a drink so closely associated with holy rites and one, moreover, that promoted gaiety and enthusiasm. Wine became their chosen drink for ceremonial occasions and victory celebrations.

Through the centuries, wine became more popular, and more democratic too. Industrial revolutions, social changes, the gradual breakdown of class barriers and the increasing economic power of the bourgeoisie were all responsible for this development. The luxury of a private cellar was no longer the prerogative of lords spiritual or temporal. Improvements in vine cultivation and vinification methods helped further this new turn of events.

As its religious symbolism and associations have evolved, so wine has developed an almost mystical reputation in everyday life. It endows every occasion with a special significance, whether a family gathering, lover's tryst or merely when friends meet. At the present time, we have the good fortune to enjoy the welcome traditions bequeathed to us. We must understand and appreciate this gift of the gods before we, too, pass it on.

What is the best way to cultivate a palate for wine? How and when should different wines be served? What are the finer points of wine? The answers to these and many other questions will be found in this book which provides a comprehensive range of information to put you at your ease whenever conversation turns to vine and wine. And never forget that you do not really taste a wine unless you look at it, nose it and talk about it.

Joseph Jobé

The names of wines are printed in small capitals and the species of vine in italics. British weights and measures are used throughout. The publishers have selected the illustrations in this book without being influenced in any way by commercial or publicity considerations. The same holds true for the some 6,500 wines in the lists.

WINE
AND CIVILIZATION

HISTORICAL OUTLINE

"And Noah began to be an husbandman, and he planted a vineyard: and he drank of the wine, and was drunken." This is the first biblical mention of that illustrious plant to which Old and New Testaments continually allude in countless allegories, parables, symbolic references and stories.

The history of the vine in actual fact, however, goes back much farther. From the very earliest times, it is linked with that of Eastern mythology and particularly with the legend of Dionysus which spread from Asia to Egypt, through Thrace and the Mediterranean lands.

The worship of Dionysus, or Bacchus, by his initiates went far beyond mere veneration for the creator and patron of the vine. In the earliest Orphic concept, Dionysus was considered a supreme deity. Soon, however, his character was defined more sharply: the cult of Dionysus developed into the celebration of vine and wine. In Athens, it furnished occasions for large-scale festivities, called the Dionysia, with processions, carousing and plays. In Rome, one day every year was dedicated to Bacchus. As for the Bacchanalia, in which more limited numbers indulged, they probably originated in Egypt. Thence they spread to Greece and finally to Rome where they degenerated into outrageous displays of debauchery and disorder. The public authorities at last banned the Bacchanalia, not without stormy arguments, in 186 B.C.

Thus wine, quite literally, had its own god. As a result, it enjoyed an almost sacred reputation, was featured in many religious ceremonies and pagan rituals even before the dawn of Christianity, and continued to play a prominent part in biblical writings. It is hardly surprising, therefore, that wine has inspired a wealth of pictorial representation, a symbolism of real documentary value. An Assyrian bas-relief shows two figures drinking against a setting of vine branches and grapes, while an Egyptian tomb decoration accurately depicts the order of viticultural tasks, the grape harvest and the cellar work in the presence of the scribe responsible for keeping the books. Writing tablets uncovered in Carthage, Tunis and Morocco supply us with similar information, and innumerable other relics and traces, whether buried underground or on the sea bed, are constantly coming to light. All these discoveries swell the already great volume of records with which museums, palaces, ancient temples, cathedrals, monasteries and castles are so plentifully stocked, so that archaeological remains alone could provide virtually all the information necessary to trace the history of wine cultivation back to remotest antiquity.

Wine occupies a regal place in the literature of every age. Centuries before Christ, Homer refers to the most famous vineyards in ancient Greece. He gives details concerning cellaring and drinking customs. Innume-

Almost always trained upwards, the Egyptian vine, claimed by Diodorus, the Greek historian, to have been imported by the god Osiris, served to embellish gardens. At this period, no royal or princely domain nor temple was without its vine-arbour and, accordingly, its wine.

The vine was also cultivated from a very early date in the basin of Mesopotamia and is frequently featured in Assyrian decoration during the time of the Sargonides. In this bas-relief from the seventh century B.C., King Assurbanipal enjoys a cup of wine under a vine-bower.

rable poets throughout the centuries have drawn on wine for their inspiration and some of them, notably Virgil, have made a valuable contribution to its history. On the other hand, accurate and comprehensive information can also be found in treatises on agriculture such as the *De re rustica* by Columella, a Latin agronomist born in Cadiz during the first century. He describes all the viticultural practices which are still applied today, such as tilling, planting, fertilizing, propagation by cuttings, grafting, layering, dressing, as well as winemaking.

Thanks to the works of such writers as the poet Hesiod, the historians Herodotus and Xenophon and the geographer Strabo, we know exactly where the vineyards were located in ancient times. In Asia, they flourished on the shores of the Persian Gulf, in Babylonia, in Assyria, on the shores of the Caspian, the Black Sea and the Aegean, in Syria and Phoenicia. Palestine, the homeland of the legendary Canaan grape, possessed a whole range of renowned wines. These wines were produced from plants that were selected and cultivated with the utmost care and in accordance with the methods prescribed by Hebrew law.

Flourishing in Egypt and Asia, the cultivation of the vine reached the heights of glory in Europe. It gained a foothold in Greece, particularly in those islands with the evocative names of Lemnos, Lesbos, Chios, Samos, Kos, Tenos and Naxos. On the latter the magnificent ruins of a huge portico, the last remains of the temple of Dionysus, still rise majestically above the sea. The chain of vineyards stretches on through Rhodes, Crete

Cythera, Leucadia and Corcyra. Suspended, as it were, between the two azure seas, these vines yielded wines which were shipped to the Mediterranean cities, chiefly to Rome, where good Greek wines, sometimes fetching exorbitant prices, long enjoyed unrivalled prestige. Meanwhile, the Italian vintage wines of Mamertine, Falernian and many others soon began to acquire comparable esteem. These were left to age for ten, twenty, thirty years, and sometimes even longer.

Great wine-drinkers as they were, the imbibing of the ancients frequently developed into inveterate drunkenness. The example was set at the highest social levels. The imperial orgies of Nero, Caracalla and Tiberius, to mention only a few, have remained famous. It was solely due to their bacchic exploits that many individuals won favour with Tiberius or other emperors and were thus invested with important offices. In Rome, for a very long time, women were forbidden to drink wine, yet certain Egyptian bas-reliefs depict women of high society clearly in a state of inebriation.

So it seems that drunkenness was not unknown in ancient times, but there were also those enlightened drinkers who knew how to appreciate, respect and to recognize wine as one of the finest gifts of nature and the gods. Wine was and remains one of the basic elements, even one of the motivating forces, of Mediterranean civilizations.

Reaching Gaul in the wake of the Roman armies, viticulture spread up the banks of the Rhône as far as Lyons, swept beyond to Burgundy, and on to the Rhine which it also reached via Helvetia. (Wine was known

This Greek jug, called an *oinochoe*, was used in the second half of the sixth century B.C. The only ornamentation on the black ground is a narrow red strip with the inscription "Lysias made me".

The Greeks used this striking high-handled jug, which was called a *cyathos*, to draw wine from the mixing-bowls and pour it into the drinkers' cups.

already in these regions. As soon as they had tasted it, the Gauls, the Cimbri and the Germans had began to import it in large quantities.) At the same time, travelling along the banks of the Garonne, the vine reached Bordeaux. In the third century it occupied the same areas in Europe as it does today, including the districts around the Danube, thanks to the Emperor Probus who willingly converted his legionaries into vinegrowers when there was no fighting to be done.

But Rome suffered the repercussions of this expansion. The overproduction of Italian vintages and the competition of wines from the Empire resulted in falling prices. The slump led the Emperor Domitian to order vines to be pulled up in some regions, particularly those that produced only mediocre wines. Such measures were not dissimilar to those put into practice much later, in the Middle Ages and even in modern times. For the same reason there developed laws, regulations and prohibitions regarding winemaking, trading and shipping, and even the economics of viticulture itself. Cato the Elder is known to have calculated the depreciation over a certain period of his slaves, who were to him no more than the machines of his time.

In spite of these crises and hazards, viticulture prospered, reaping the benefit of the Pax Romana, nor was it unduly affected by the fall of the Roman Empire and the disturbed period that ensued. The Church had taken affairs in hand. The bishop, master of the city, was its vinegrower and cellarman. Not only must enough wine be produced for Holy Communion but also to pay homage to the monarchs and high-ranking dignitaries who broke their journeys at the town. Most important of all, there were the episcopal funds to be kept supplied. This secular viticulture, flourishing throughout the Middle Ages, ran parallel to another branch of viticulture practised by the monks, with the abbeys serving as hostelries. Situated on the main highways, they welcomed men of power—who, in their turn, showed their generosity—as well as the poor and pilgrims. Both monks and travellers appreciated wine.

Kings, dukes and feudal lords were not long in following the example set by the monks and the Princes of the Church. Vines bordered the castle as they did the monastery. Wine retained all its former prestige.

With the growth of the bourgeoisie, many of the vineyards around the towns passed into the hands of rich citizens. The wine trade benefited from an ever increasing clientele in northern countries, particularly Holland, Flanders and England, to which there flowed a steady stream of ports, Madeiras, sherries and certain Mediterranean wines, wines from Bordeaux and Burgundy and, later, from Champagne. Bordeaux belonged to England from the twelfth to the fifteenth century and quite a number of Lord Mayors of London

In ancient times, the wine jugs used in Mediterranean countries assumed a great variety of shapes. This Etruscan *olpe* with its round mouth and high handle is reminiscent of the Greek jug *oinochoe*.

This Roman amphora, fashioned in a lustrous polychrome glaze, bears testimony to the great progress achieved in the workmanship and styling of wine vessels by the time of Alexander the Great.

were natives of Bordeaux. Flanders, however, recognized the Duke of Burgundy as its sovereign lord.

A great deal of wine was drunk in the countries to the north. In fact, their inhabitants proved far more intemperate than the natives of winegrowing countries, where the taster of ancient times, like his counterpart today, preserved an almost sacerdotal sobriety.

In 1579, the Dutch acquired independence and began concentrating all their efforts on commerce. They boasted a large and superlatively well organized navy, warehouses and stores. Systematically they applied themselves to a study of the market and succeeded in creating demand and controlling consumption. At the time of Louis XIV, they were buying vast quantities of "small" wines which they proceeded to blend, adulterate and resell at a large profit, openly defying the wine-exporting countries where the integrity of the vintages was scrupulously observed and where the wine trade was subjected to the close surveillance of the guilds and the authorities. It was also the Dutch who, initially for purely lucrative purposes, instigated the production and heavy consumption of spirits.

From the early Middle Ages, especially in France but also in Italy and the regions bordering on the Rhine, viticulture and the wine business played an important part in the extensive development of the communities, the sovereign granting various rights, franchises and privileges to the wineproducers and hence to the municipal authorities. This explains why the pages of the history of wine are often turned by political events. For instance, among the leaders of the Paris uprising in July 1789, when the Bastille was destroyed, were certain wine merchants who hoped to capitalize on the riots and bring about the abolition of the very unpopular taxes levied on wines imported into the capital.

As early as the Renaissance, the map of European vineyards corresponded very closely to that of today. Colonization and the spread of Christianity brought viticulture to countries overseas, such as Latin-America, Mexico, California, South Africa; or gave it new impetus, as in Algeria. There, as in all other Moslem countries, viticulture had been curbed by the teachings of the Koran which forbade the use of alcohol. Nonetheless, twelve centuries after Mohammed Algeria was among the leading wineproducing countries.

Among the many vicissitudes in the history of the vine and wine, the cryptogamic diseases and the parasites brought from America in the middle of the last century were the most deadly. But man's ingenuity and perseverance invariably found a way to overcome all such calamities. During the nineteenth century, winemaking methods were greatly improved, and today they have reached an almost scientific degree of perfection. In this age of space flights and nuclear science, wine has retained all its former prestige. Closely linked with the origin of our civilization, it represents one of its proudest and most pacific achievements. Wine is still the most gracious and the noblest drink of all.

THE VINE SPECIES

"Plant your vineyard from good stock." The old French adage proclaims a fundamental truth and underscores the all-important part played by the species of vine in determining the success of the end result, whether this be the wine glinting in our glass, the unfermented grape juice faithfully echoing the original flavour of the fruit, or the ripe young cluster of grapes decorating the dining-table.

The knowledge of the countless varieties of vine, their distant origins, their types, and their history linked to the history of civilization itself, is a many-sided science, embracing botany, biology, anthropological geography, and even paleontology. The layman, however, has barely ever heard such words as *Merlot, Gamay* or *Riesling*. Little does he care if the northern vineyards are descended from wild vines, as some specialists would have us believe, or if these vineyards were planted with vines brought from southern climes by those migrating north. The true wine-lover, on the other hand, is well informed in such matters.

Among the species yielding red wine that are cultivated in France, he will award the palm to the *Pinot Noir* from Burgundy, the *Gamay* from Beaujolais, the *Cabernet-Sauvignon* from Bordeaux, and the *Grenache* which thrives along the banks of the Rhône, in Provence, Languedoc and Roussillon. He will also award honourable mentions to the *Malbec* and the *Merlot*, grapes which are often blended with *Cabernet*, as well as to *Cinsaut, Mourvèdre, Carignan, Savagnin* from the Jura, the *Black Muscat* from Frontignan, the Savoyard *Mondeuse* and the *Tannat* cultivated in the Hautes-Pyrénées.

The range of white grapes is equally wide. There is the *Chardonnay*, responsible for the excellence of the wines from Champagne and the vintage wines from Burgundy, the *Sauvignon Blanc* and *Chenin* which produce the wines from the Loire and Anjou, *Semillon* from the famous vineyards in the Gironde, *Muscadet, Clairette*, the *White Muscats* and, finally, the *Chasselas* with which most of the vineyards in the French-speaking cantons of Switzerland are planted.

All these species of grape yield a great variety of different wines, alternately full-bodied, fruity, robust or rich, but this is not the place to start a glossary of the subtle and innumerable nuances so readily distinguished by the professional palate.

Several French grape species have been introduced into other wineproducing countries, such as Spain, Italy, Russia and California, whilst the *Sylvaner, Riesling* and *Traminer* which yield the Rhine and Moselle wines can also be found as far afield as Hungary and Czechoslovakia, and notably in Alsace and Switzerland.

In Italy, a variety of *White Muscat* yields the Asti. *Barbera* originates in Piedmont, *Nerello* in Sicily. *Soave* prospers from Verona to the Adriatic. Spanish sherry, Portuguese port and Madeira also have their own species of grape while California, a large wineproducer, has adopted the wines from this hemisphere.

Sometimes a wineproducer will content himself with one particular species of grape; but then again, after due consideration, he may decide to combine two or more different varieties. Thus, the wine from Médoc owes its scent and spiciness to the *Cabernet*, its well-balanced richness to the *Merlot*. Similarly, the grape species *Grenache, Mourvèdre, Syrah* and *Clairette* blend their different virtues and temperaments in the opulent Châteauneuf-du-Pape, the leading Côtes du Rhône.

Apart from the vines cultivated for wine grapes, there are all those that yield dessert grapes: the French *Gros-Vert* and *Chasselas*, the Italian *Regina* and *Ignea*, the Spanish *Almeria* and *Malaga*, the *Rish Baba* from Persia, the *Emperor* from California, and many more besides, without forgetting the widely cultivated *Zante* and *Muscat* and other varieties whose grapes are usually dried and eaten in the form of raisins.

This brief summary has only skimmed the surface of a major chapter in the study and lore of wine. Albeit rudimentary, its aim has been to evoke the wondrous riches and diversity of this complex and universally famous plant which seems truly to have been, together with corn, one of the earliest and most ancient products of cultivation.

The botanist Linné conferred the name of *vitis vinifera* on the vine which provides us with both dessert grapes and wine grapes. Its origin can be traced back to the Tertiary period, some forty-five million years ago. Today, several thousand species of this plant are known to man.

Dessiné d'après Nature par Apelle De Fontaine.

17

The *Chardonnay* (below) is also called *Pinot Blanc Chardonnay*. Widely grown in Champagne and particularly in the famous "Côte des Blancs" region, this grape endows Champagne with all its piquant freshness and delicacy, and also accounts for the fame of the great white wines of Burgundy. Californian winegrowers use it to produce a light, white table wine.

For a long time, the *Pinot Blanc* (above) was confused with the *Chardonnay* (above right). *Pinot Blanc* is found in Burgundy, Champagne, Alsace and in Germany, where it is known by the name of *Weissburgunder*. It is also grown in Hungary, Yugoslavia and California. This is one of the great species.

The *Harslevelü* (lime leaf) is of Hungarian origin and has never left its native soil. Blended with another grape, the *Furmint*, it produces the famous Tokay wine which, incidentally, has no connection with the *Tokay* from Alsace, a wine made from the *Pinot Gris*.

The *Grenache* appears to have originated in Spain where it is known as *Garnacha* or *Alicantina*. After having been somewhat spurned, it has now acquired great popularity on both sides of the eastern Pyrenees and as far as the lower Rhône valley.

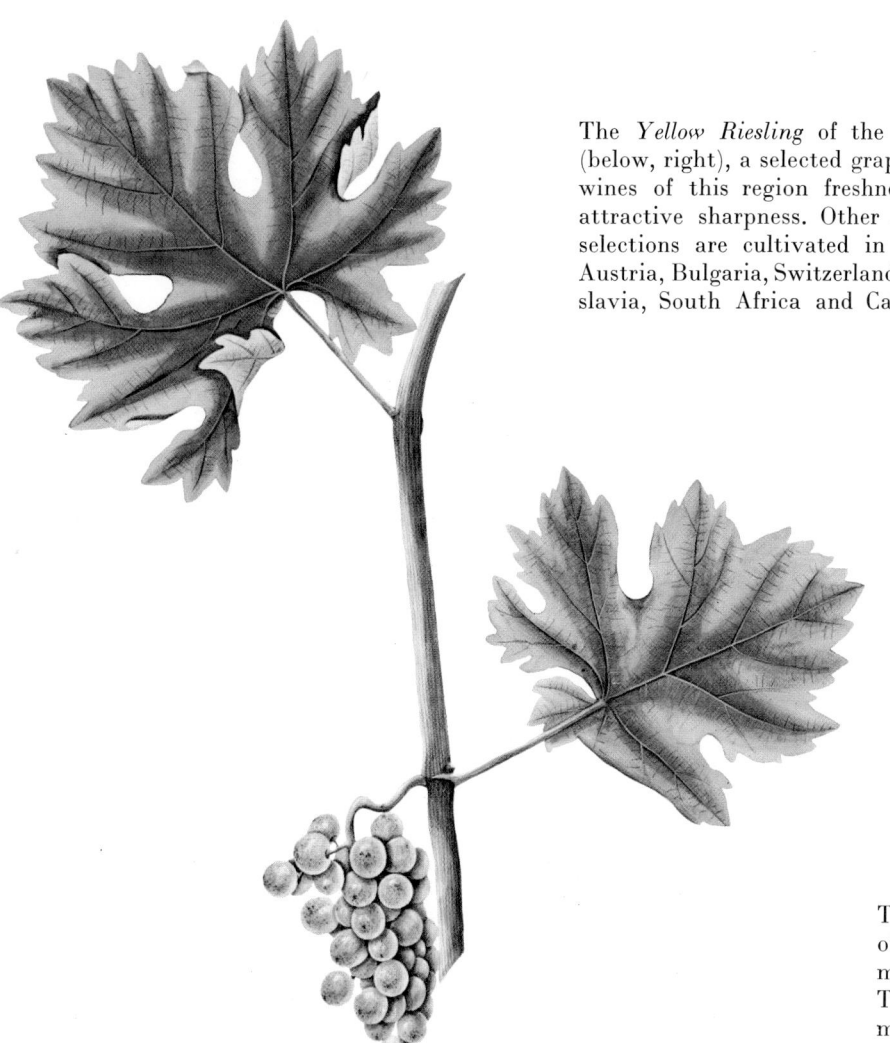

The *Yellow Riesling* of the Moselle (below, right), a selected grape, gives wines of this region freshness and attractive sharpness. Other *Riesling* selections are cultivated in Alsace, Austria, Bulgaria, Switzerland, Yugoslavia, South Africa and California.

The *Pinot Noir* (below) probably originated in Burgundy. One of the great varieties, it is found in regions having the same climate as its native province. Its German name is *Blauburgunder*. The juice of the *Pinot Noir* is colourless and it is the colouring matter in the grape skins which, during fermentation in the vat, brings to the wine the brilliant ruby hue so extolled by the poets.

The *Riesling* (above) is pre-eminently a species originating on the banks of the Rhine and the Moselle, but it adapts perfectly to various other regions. The *Riesling* from Rheingau has its own very positive character and should on no account be confused with the *Riesling Italico* which is produced from another species of grape and thus yields an altogether different type of wine.

The *Chenin Noir* (opposite, left) was the original vine of Anjou. A hardy and fertile species when young, it yields a delicate, clear wine of a fine red colour. Its cultivation is confined exclusively to the valley of the Loire.

19

Ous auons dit
plusieurs choses
des plantes des
vignes par de
uant quant nous traictics
de la commune nature des
plantes. Et a present en ce
quart liure nous voulons
parler de la nature ⁊ de la
couraige des vignes et de
toutes manieres de vignes
et de tou le prouffit du fruit
en particulier. ▭
De la naturture de la vig

ne en soy et de la vertu des
fueilles ⁊ des cendres et de
sa larme. ▭
Vascun a congnois
sance des vignes que
cest fors que es froides con
trees ou le fruit ne puet
croistre Si conclus que est
vne humble et ployante
arbreillon moult tortue ⁊
noeuse et rongneuse qui
a larges conduis ⁊ pertuis
et pores grant moelle: lar
ges et entretrenchees fueilles

VINES, WINE AND WORK

My grandfather was a vinegrower. I remember seeing him using the sulphur spray which was carried on one's back and worked by means of a pump. In those days he wore an old straw hat, old jacket, old trousers and ancient laced boots, all tinged with the blue of the Bordeaux mixture which also stained his moustache and his heavy eyebrows. I remember, too, the wine harvests. In those days, they used to press the grapes, in the vineyards, into containers which were then emptied into a large barrel securely fixed on to a cart. It was quite a long journey to the wine-press. There, in the open, waited an enormous vat. The barrel was rolled on to two stout planks and spewed the grapes into the vat whose contents were subsequently transferred to the wine-press.

The wine-press was worked by an enormous wooden beam called a yoke. At one end there was a rope whose other end was wound round a second vertical beam, turned on its own axis by means of meshed cogs and driven by a crank which was operated by hand. All night long, the creaking of the beams, the groaning of the stretched ropes and the metallic rhythm of the ratchets could be heard, while the must, in its natural state, free from additives and rich in its own yeasts, trickled through pipes into the cellar. And two or three days later the fanstastic work of the fermentation began.

This is not ancient history; it happened less than fifty years ago. Yet in those days, men still seemed to take real pleasure in performing these humble and manual tasks, in practising this craft which perpetuated the time-honoured traditions to which the vinegrower was profoundly attached but which, frequently, were very localized and accepted as routine. Then, too, almost everything depended on the efforts and the skill of man, that highly developed, intelligent machine, that very inexpensive source of power.

Today, my grandfather's vines are cultivated in much the same way as they were fifty years ago. They still occupy terraces laid out on steep slopes, are still planted in relatively close rows. This is the custom in nearly all northern vineyards planted on the sides of hills. Elsewhere, in the plains, where the vine can spread out at its ease and where it is encouraged to stretch to medium or full height, machines have long since made their appearance. Subsoil ploughs break up the ground and turn it over, work that can also be carried out with explosives.

Tractors now clatter along between the well-spaced rows, pulling machines behind them that clean the soil and lay the second dressing. Lightening the labours of today's vinegrower are improved sprays, usually machine-driven, atomizers and other accessories, sometimes airborne on airplanes or helicopters, which spread insecticides, fungicides and other substances.

If the cultivator of vines in the days of yore could be compared to a foot-soldier, he now belongs to the ranks of a motorized army of far greater efficiency. As for the production of wine, it has increasingly become the business of oenologists, scientifically trained, who spend much of their time bent over test-tubes, microscopes and other equipment, converting the mysteries of wine into chemical formulae. However, they do not disdain the vinicultural experience handed down through countless generations nor neglect visits to the cellars to inspect the wine in its own habitat, tasting it critically, guiding its progress and nurturing it to maturity as has been done from time immemorial.

Indeed, even if methods have been modernized and the vinegrower, in order to secure his livelihood, has resorted to technical advances and to rationalization of work, the responsible tasks involved in the cultivation of vines and production of wines have remained basically and essentially the same.

Naturally, practices may vary, depending on the region, climate and species of grape. But, by and large, the vinegrower in France performs the same tasks and goes through very much the same motions as his counterpart in Bessarabia or California, experiencing the same hopes and anxieties, the same satisfactions and disappointments. Dependent on his vines he is, himself, subject to the eternal rhythm of the seasons. While today machines have taken over so many viticultural and vinicultural processes, there are still many tasks, such as dressing the vines, that still require, and will always require, the experience and unique manual dexterity of men.

The new year for the vines begins in November when, the grapes all gathered in, the vinegrower thoroughly sluices and scrubs his wine-press, utensils, appliances, vats and casks, not forgetting to use the sulphured wick to prevent mildew. The last leaves drop away from the vine stems after a final glorious display of rich autumnal colours: every shade of gold and yellow in the case of the white grape plants, the resplendent spec-

This illuminated design from the fifteenth century, taken from the *Livre des profits champêtres* by Pierre de Crescens, illustrates the stages in vine cultivation during the Middle Ages: hoeing, weeding, training plants on trellises, grape-gathering, pressing by foot and broaching the cask.

trum of crimsons and purples for those which bear the black grape. Thus stripped of its working apparel, the vine obtains to all outward appearances a brief respite.

But if the vine may sleep, the vinegrower can take no rest. This is the time of year when, not so very long ago, the women and children pulled out the vine-props, laying them in orderly groups of six, well spread out between the rows of vines. Today, it is increasingly the practice to leave the vine-props in position as metal vine stakes have long since come into use. Moreover, vines trained into the shape of a goblet, the stem supported by a central prop, seem gradually to be ceding ground to vines trained on wire.

Under the obliging sun of an Indian summer, earth that has gradually slipped downhill is transported by the vinegrower back to the top of his sloping vineyard. This arduous task was performed with the aid of a basket harnessed on the back in times gone by, so that after a few years of this work the same man could truthfully claim to have carried the entire vineyard on his

back. Nowadays, this burden and other heavy work has been taken over by power-driven machines, whose sputtering fills the air. But first of all, the digging had had to be done, trenches to be made at the base of the vines all along the walls. And if the walls had shown signs of wear or damage, the vinegrower had to take up his trowel and perform a mason's work, repairing and repointing. "Mortar of winter, mortar of iron", so runs an old French saying.

Earth to carry uphill, walls to reinforce are jobs to be done in terraced vineyards spread over the hillsides and not in vineyards on the plains. However, whether on the hills or plains, autumn is the time for tilling and ridging, worked by ploughs which lift and turn over the earth all along between the rows. The old vine-plants must also be grubbed out and their gnarled, blackened and twisted stumps sometimes feed their owner's fire.

Naturally, all this time, down in the cellar, the new wine requires care and constant attention. At ground level, the vinegrower takes shelter from the cold and inclement weather, repairs his tools, puts his equipment in order, cuts new vine-props, sharpening them into points and impregnating them with tar or sulphur. It is also in winter that he prepares the straw used for tying the vine shoots, although this is being replaced more by metal or plastic fasteners.

Once Christmas is past, time rushes by. At the end of January, with the days stretching out, the vinegrower feels a compulsive urge to take up his pruning shears. "If we would drink," runs an old French proverb, "we must dress the vine before St. Gregory's day", St. Gregory's day falling on March 12th.

Dressing the vine necessitates long experience and the greatest care. The olant must be trained and the root stock kept to a reasonable size. Most important of all, production must be controlled, next year's fruit

Vigneron

Vinegrowers of every age were strenuous workers. In 1351, the King of France required that they perform "their day's work loyally, from sunrise to sunset", which left little time for drinking the product.

growing on the young shoots that sprout from last year's vine stock. Therefore, these root stocks must be judiciously dressed and, following the example of Janus, the god whose two faces looked in opposite directions and who gave his name to the year's first month, the future judged while paying due consideration to the past.

The vinegrower knows that an overly sturdy vine stock yields fewer fruit than one of less strength that produces a generous quantity but runs the risk of becoming spent. He also knows that the young shoots farthest from the stock bear the most. All his knowledge is behind the apparently casual wielding of his pruning shears. Every cut displays experience and foresight, guiding the development of each branch. If he cuts short, leaving only two or three buds, he wishes to husband the vine stock and not force it to an immoderate yield. If he cuts long, leaving three or four buds to a branch, he aims at a more plentiful harvest. It is up to the vinegrower to decide whether the vine is capable of such output. A wise master, he decides nothing without due consideration and as a result the vine, originally a highly fertile plant, is made to comply obediently with the prescribed directions. These directions vary according to region, species of grape, soil and climate whether the vine must have low, medium or tall growths, single stem, lattice-work or "goblet" shaped branches. Dressing vines may be a highly specialized technique but it is also an art and involves a kind of complicity between the man and the plant.

When winter is over, the dressed shoots weep, each horn bearing its glittering pearl. The buds, still muffled in their fleecy down, are ready to open. The vinegrower experiences his first qualms. At any moment, the frost can cut down the young shoots. If this happens, the vines will have to be faithfully tended throughout the year without hope of a satisfactory yield. In northern vineyards, this threat hangs over

the vinegrower's head until the end of April, and sometimes even into May the beginning of which month is notorious for its treacherous weather.

Before dressing, the vinegrower has been attending to grafting, essential since the arrival of the phylloxera, a minute plant louse which found its way to Europe from America in the middle of the last century. This terrible little creature attacked the roots and wrought the most appalling havoc; it would have brought about the annihilation of European vineyards had not the appropriate remedy been found and applied. It was discovered that the roots of the American vines were immune to phylloxera and so now almost every European vine is grafted on to an American root. When this has been done the vinegrower lays out the grafts in boxes full of damp sawdust, which are then stacked in some overheated place. In May, they will be planted in nurseries. Since this job requires considerable care and skill, the vinegrower sometimes prefers to entrust it to the nurseryman.

With winter well and truly behind, and a warm haze rising in the morning sun, the first small flowers venture timidly along the foot of the wall while machines resume their humming and all nature begins to stir. The spring ploughings leave behind a clean and tidy vineyard, a joy to behold with its tautened and refurbished wires stretching out as far as eye can see, or with its vine props standing to attention like the pikes of a vast army of footsoldiers drawn in battle array. The soil, as yet innocent of weeds, conceals the ploughed-in manure, unless dried manure or mineral fertilizers have been spread, which is increasingly the practice.

From now until the end of summer, unless the vinegrower relies entirely on weed-killers, the motorized hoe will regularly travel between the rows of vines, replacing men who, not long since, still raked away the weeds with pathetic doggedness from spring to autumn. Each vinegrower's descendants emancipate themselves more and more from this drudgery, acquiring machines that do the job just as well and much more quickly.

In the spring, the grafts in the nursery must be lifted, their roots trimmed and paraffin wax applied. They are then put in sand in a cool place, to prevent them shooting before they are planted in their permanent vineyard. It is also in the spring, as soon as the buds open, that the vinegrower begins the treatments against parasites, insects and cryptogams. This battle with disease continues without respite until a few weeks before the grape harvest.

The red spider is first on the scene, followed shortly afterwards by the first batch of caterpillars and the first fluttering swarms of dancing butterflies. The mushrooms and other fungi are not far behind. The drama has begun, and the vinegrower is all too grimly

This miniature from the *Tacuinum sanitatis*, a medical book translated from the Arabic in the fourteenth century, portrays in the most natural and unaffected manner grape-picking as it was carried out during that time in Italy. Worthy of note is the grape-treading, a primitive method of pressing now abandoned; and the use of composite crops, still widely practised in some parts of Italy even to this day.

commonly known as vine-worms, ravage the leaves or bunches of grapes before, during and after flowering.

The fungoid growths are equally destructive. The oidium's fibres spread over leaves and branches, their sinister suckers infiltrating everywhere. Mildew is the enemy of leaf, branch and grape, which it withers, darkens and dries out. Black rot, also from America, and the fungi causing white rot or excoriose, which sets in after hail, are allies of those fungi causing root rot and a grey rot, a disease of the grape; and finally there is apoplexy, the ultimate and fatal phenomenon of a stock disease. These pests could claim their right to exist as being granted by the Creator but, if allowed to proliferate, they could quickly put an end to the cultivation of the vine.

The vinegrower, once again enlisting the aid of the scientist, relies on his laboratory to produce all kinds of washes and powders for spraying and on the technologist to devise all manner of machines from the humble bellows and the old hand-operated spray, carried on the back, to self-propelled sulphurators, powered diffusers and atomizers. The arsenal includes flowers of sulphur, liquid sulphur, copper sulphate, lime, carbonate of soda, acids, perchlorides, oxides, hydrates, dioxides, arsenic and nicotine. Finally, there are multi-purpose concentrated products called synthetic fungicides, each combining several remedies to simplify the vinegrower's work. All these chemicals are administered to the vines, with the same care and foresight as a mother tends her child, in order to ensure their satisfactory growth and development.

familiar with the plot and the leading players with their outlandish names, although he is never sure about what will happen in the last act.

Among the animal parasites, of which the phylloxera is the most deadly, there is a large cast of coleoptera. The larva of the leaf-hopper devour the undersides of leaves. The common vinegrub is also dubbed "the writer" because it busies itself cutting out fine strips on the leaves, resembling writing, while its larva attack the vine roots. The leaf-roller, which rolls up the leaves into cigar shape, inside which its grubs snugly nest, joins with weevils of various kinds to complete this unwelcome throng.

The pyralis, the two annual generations of cochylis or vine-moth, the four generations of leaf-roller moths or endemis are very attractive fly-by-nights, waking at dusk or dancing in the moonlight, but their caterpillars,

The artists of the Middle Ages, who were so fond of depicting the various crafts, have bequeathed us faithful pictorial representations in richly illustrated prayer books. The cooper's art was not forgotten. Here are vat-makers, jug-makers, shook-makers, and hogshead binders busy before the approaching wine harvest. After chamfering and turning over the staves, they fit and bind them together with wooden hoops.

26

Great precision, perseverance and endless patience are required. There can be no clock-watching when the work is pressing; during these long summer days the time for sleep is all too short. Arduous work indeed, spurred on by the hope of due rewards, but also accompanied by the philosophical acceptance of possible frustration. Then, patience and hope give way to resignation which is neither weakness nor despair but courageous wisdom, for the vinegrower can always hope for better fortune next year, as the same vine lives on through many years, good, bad or indifferent.

The battle against parasites, launched in the spring, is waged alongside the other viticultural tasks, particularly those concerned with the leaves. Called "thinning out" in certain regions, this is the first dressing carried out on the young shoots at the time the dry branches are pruned. First of all, as soon as the vine has flowered, the leaves are thinned out and the unwanted buds cut away. The shoots appearing at the foot of the vine and others which do not contribute to the growth of the plant, sprouting elsewhere than on the dressed branches—all such parasite growth is removed. This delicate task, requiring almost specialist skill, prepares for and facilitates the next winter's dressing. The strength of each plant is taken into account. Carried out early in the season in vineyards to the south, this operation is left until later in those regions subject to frost. But the vine will not wait so this work must be done quickly and perhaps extra labour employed.

Next the tips of the herbaceous shoots are removed, thus controlling future growth. Later and up until

August, new toppings or clippings are carried out, although the usefulness of this practice seems questionable. Completing this stage of the work the vine shoots are attached to their props or guide-wires with straw or raffia ties, or rings.

For ten to fifteen days or more the buds in each cluster flower one by one and an exquisite perfume floats over the vineyard, reminiscent of mignonette or incense. Sunny, warm weather gives the vines the chance to blossom and set quickly and in the best conditions. Rain and cold retard the flowering and hamper fertilization. Under these conditions, the pollen may be washed away or the crop may fail because of degenerative phenomena or even by excessive vigour of the plant.

If everything goes according to plan, the buds come out well, the plant has flowers in good weather, there is no loss of pollen and all the parasites are eradicated.

The year's labours are rewarded. This scene from the mid-fifteenth century comes from the prayer book which belonged to the Duchess of Burgundy. The seasonal grape pickers, hired in market-places, are paid in cash or in kind by the owner of the vines. It has been a good harvest and everybody, well content, goes off to the wine-press, which is the property of the local lord of the manor or of the local council.

CRIEUR DE VIN . 1586.

Sworn public officials, the wine criers were commissioned to promote the sale of wine on behalf of the inn-keepers.   Jug and glass in hand, they vaunted their wares round the streets or outside the inns.   Patronized by the King of France, their guild grew to great power in the thirteenth and fourteenth centuries.

This ink and wash sketch by Leonar Bramer of Delft, entitled "Halt before the Inn", deftly portrays a pastoral scene of the seventeenth century. The wine shop of those days was often no more than a casually converted farmhouse where, in summer months, passers-by stopped for a few refreshing moments. A barrel serves as a table. Who cares? Life is for living, there is music and companionship and the wine is cool.

The small, hard grapes that the young bunch proudly held out towards the sun now droop towards the ground. Gradually, they become translucent. They are beginning to ripen. About this time, the shoots begin to turn brown and lignify. The owner walks round his vines, carrying brush and pot of paint, marking the stocks from which, in a few months time, he will take grafts for future nurseries.

While the vine, now ripening, passes through its third phase, the vinegrower can at last obtain a brief respite. However, right up to harvest time, a danger hangs over his head. One sudden shower of hail may crash down with a storm, despite all the artillery the vinegrowers can muster in the shape of rockets that explode into the very heart of the clouds—the result is ruthless destruction of leaves, shoots and bunches of grapes.

Whatever the summer may have been, there comes at last a time when in the wide autumnal skies vast, wheeling flocks of starlings appear, avid for the ripe grapes, only momentarily frightened off by the fire-crackers exploded by alert vintners among the vines. High time now for the harvest!

First comes a thorough clean-up of all the implements to be used, which are subsequently left to dry in the sun. As soon as the grapes are ripe, the pickers spread out across the vines. The grapes are heaped in crates and loaded on lorries which are quickly driven to the press. Bearing little resemblance to a wine-press of my grandfathers' day on its stone pedestal, with its beam and huge vertical screw, the modern version is a horizontal cylinder into which the harvested grapes are poured after first being crushed in another machine. In fact, especially in large enterprises such as the wine co-operatives, the press has become a kind of small factory where everything is carried out faster, more reliably and where there is very much less manual work than in the past. Knobs and levers are pressed to bring electric, hydraulic and pneumatic forces into play.

In some enterprises, the red grapes are no longer vatted, the process which gives the wine its colour. This operation, extending over several days, necessitates considerable equipment which obviously takes up far more space than the cylinder where the grapes are simply heated to achieve the same result.

This progress and these new methods have in no way altered or detracted from the extraordinary phenomenon of fermentation which the ancients attributed to some superhuman spirit and whose mystery was at last explained by Louis Pasteur.

The yeasts responsible for fermentation are present on the grapes, carried by the winds and insects—supplied, in fact, by nature. But once again that dispenser of the good as well as the bad has been tamed and harnessed to suit man's requirements. Careful observation, selection and judicious training have resulted finally in the production of fine, good yeasts, free from such bacterial maladies as the *tourne*, acescence and other vine diseases. Strong, healthy, honest yeasts prevent sluggish, incomplete fermentation. They are incorporated in the must after being rendered aseptic.

When fermentation is finally complete, the yeasts have finished their work and fall to the bottom of the vat where they form the wine lees. After depositing its lees, the young and troubled milky new wine, saturated with carbonic gas, will clear of its own accord, but usually man lends a helping hand. Clarifying the wine, by adding gelatine-based products, white of egg or separated milk which draw the lees and other impurities down to the bottom of the vat is a long-established craft, now replaced by the more efficient and less hazardous filtering process which also rids the wine of any doubtful germs it may still contain. Among these are the germs which, needing air, proliferate on the surface: the bacteria of acescence which can change the wine into vinegar, and the surface fungoid growths which spread a thin, whitish film over the wine, reducing its alcoholic strength and value.

To avoid such dangers, the cellarman shields his wine from contact with the air by filling his vats right up to the top, or by burning a sulphured wick to use up any oxygen left in the empty space over the liquid.

Even more dangerous are the germs breeding in the depths of the wine and not requiring air. The *tourne* readily attacks badly fermented wine, making it extremely unpalatable, while the dreaded grease disease makes the wine ropy, oily and insipid. Red wines, poor in tannin and acids, are vulnerable to another disease that turns them bitter.

So much for the bacteria. But there are still various chemical actions to contend with. Brown casse yellows and sweetens new wines and gives them an artificial taste of age. Black casse gives the wine an unpleasant, leaden colour while white casse makes it cloudy and milky. Again, the wine may acquire musty, earthy smells and stagnant, mouldy tangs, reminiscent of iron or bad egg: these are nearly always the result of faults or negligence, carelessly picked grapes, badly maintained vats or cellars, and are seldom met with in the cellar of the conscientious and enlightened vinegrower.

Such mishaps and diseases can generally be prevented by ensuring the utmost cleanliness from the grape harvest to the time of bottling. A good cellarman should also keep his eye on the thermometer. Wine appreciates warmth while it is coming up to its second fermentation, during which it loses its excess acidity, but it needs cool surroundings to clarify itself. Unless these conditions are fulfilled, the wine becomes capricious and unpredictable. In actual fact, the producer could confine himself to certain essential tasks: thorough preparation of his casks, the judicious management of yeats, careful cellaring and the intelligent use of the sulphurated wick; ensuring that his vats are constantly full; heating, cooling and airing the cellars when the wine demands it and, finally, filtering and decanting at the right moment. Given these and good weather, and if the wine contains the correct elements in the right proportions, all should be well.

However, within the limits of statutory regulations, which clearly stipulate that wine is pure, fermented grape juice, oenology prescribes various methods to remedy various deficiencies, defects or lack of balance, to accelerate or retard various vinicultural processes.

The vinegrower's cellar is a hallowed place, jealously guarded, secret and reserved for the initiated who form a kind of fraternity. Highest in rank is the wine-taster. Often the diplomatic envoy from some customer, he takes his responsibilities seriously. On other occasions, he may be just a favoured guest. At all times, he is an artist, endowed with enviable physical attributes, the first being excellent sight in order to detect anything that may dim or cloud the crystal transparency of the wine. His nose is a finely-tuned instrument, capable of capturing and analysing every nuance of the bouquet. His taste buds are particularly acute. Having examined and critically sniffed the wine, he rolls it round his mouth, chops it up and down against his palate, rests it on his tongue and contemplates, allowing his senses to appeal to his memory. And at last he lets the noble liquid slip gently down inside him, feels the warm glow, savours its strength and flavour and then, and only then, pronounces judgement.

This elaborate ritual in honour of the wine is perfectly understandable. When the glass is raised in the cellar, the wine gleams as though it held captive the fugitive summer long past, bequeathing us some of its lingering light and splendour. At this moment, the vinegrower reaps the full recompense for his efforts. He now finds justification for the pride that never leaves him throughout the long seasons and his entire working life which he has dedicated to this hard and unremitting task, constantly renewing his confidence in nature and his faith in what the future holds in store.

WINE AND THE ARTS

Throughout the viticultural regions of Europe, vine and wine have always provided sources of inspiration for popular art. For centuries, craftsmen have embellished all kinds of workaday articles which play a part in the making and selling of wine, ranging from the wine-press itself to the sign above the tavern. In the Middle Ages, popular art reflected, above all, the vision of a profoundly religious man with a keen sense of symbolism. Christ was frequently represented on or around the wine-press. The wine-press itself is an allegory of Christ's sufferings and a symbol of the prophecy of Isaiah (lxiii,3): "Alone I have trodden at the wine-press and no man from among the peoples was with me. I have trampled them in my wrath, I have crushed them in my fury; their blood has spattered my apparel and all my raiment is stained withal."

All through the Middle Ages the Bible, which mentions vine and wine in more than two hundred passages, proved a virtually inexhaustible source of inspiration.

One of the most frequently used themes was that of Joshua and Caleb. The two scouts sent by Moses to explore Palestine brought back a gigantic bunch of Canaan grapes, a sign of the anticipated plenty of the Promised Land. The vine symbolized Christ and life eternal; hence the bunch of grapes held by Jesus, Mary and various saints always alludes to the sacrifice of Christ and the Last Supper. In medieval art, the shape of the vine, symbol of God's people in the Bible, was often borrowed to represent Christ's genealogical tree. Down the centuries, vinegrowers naïvely entrusted the destiny of their vines to popular saints. As rough weather, parasites and disease have always menaced the vine, it is not surprising that when a saint performed a miracle that favoured the vines or the wine he was quickly adopted as protector of the vineyard. In Switzerland, for instance, St. Othmar and St. Theodule were both credited with increasing the quantity of wine during bad harvests; hence they were accorded, as

Billhook in hand, St. Vernier patronizes the vineyards of the Rhine and Burgundy. St. Vincent, attired in deacon's vestments, is also a patron of Burgundy wine. St. Urban, the thirteenth-century Pope, protected Alsace and many German wineproducing regions from hail.

Joshua and Caleb, sent to Canaan to reconnoitre the country, discovered grapes which grew to an unbelievable size. They hoisted one of the giant bunches on to a pole and carried it back together.

From the sixteenth century onwards, almanacs and record books began to appear, containing symbols of the months as well as pictures of the vinegrower's principal tasks, weeding, dressing the vines, harvesting or making wine casks. These printed pictures brought themes hitherto only found in the prestigious prayer books owned by the great feudal lords within reach of a much wider audience.

Again from the same period, and taking into account the increasing skill of contemporary craftsmen, various articles and guild emblems connected with viticulture proliferated. Local customs began to spring up. In addition to their round-topped chests and guild flags, the vinegrowers, like the coopers, had their own domestic figurines. A favourite subject was the vintager, bowed under the weight of the narrow wooden tub full of grapes on his back. In German-speaking countries these figurines were known as *Buttenmännchen* and were often very attractively worked in wood or metal, gracing the table at social gatherings.

Even today at the carnival that marks the end of the grape harvests in Lower Austria, very unusual types of decorative emblems, peculiar to the region, can still be seen in the traditional processions. These are either wheels made from plaited straw, indicating that the vinegrower is selling his new wine on the spot, or painted wooden suns, drawing attention to the fact that the vineyard is being looked after by guardians. Another interesting local custom is the parading of the "vineyard goat", a frame of wood with a carved goat's head, laden with fruit and generally considered as the symbol of fertility. At the end of the festival, it is either sold at auction or presented to the mayor.

In all wineproducing districts, the architecture of the vinegrower's house is a compromise between work requirements and economic necessity. Naturally, the style varies from one region to another, and according to the social and financial status of the individual, but it is always noticeably different from the farmhouses and other country dwellings. The byre and the barn lose ground to the preponderance of vinegrowing over other kinds of cultivation. The cellar, forming the very foundation of the entire building, not only influences the appearance of the house but often indicates the financial circumstances of the owners by its decoration, borrowed from town residences. Sometimes its wide, arched door is the main ornamental feature of the façade. Whatever kind of building it may be, brick or stone, its cellar is always constructed in a similar way. It is made as deep and thick as possible and usually from natural stone. Symbolic grapes and vine-shoots often decorate the doors, beams and even the implements. The same decorative motifs are also seen on crucifixes, particularly at the boundaries of vineyards.

a symbol, a small wine cask. St Vernier was always depicted as a vinegrower and was worshipped in the Rhineland, in Burgundy and the Auvergne. The martyrology of the French Church has this to say about St. Urban: "His patronage in the sight of God often protected the vines from bad weather and destruction. More than once, by his prayers, he drove away the rains, scattered the winds, preserved the vines from storms which threatened: it is because of this that vinegrowers invoke his aid against the vagaries of inclement weather and he is always portrayed with a bunch of grapes." This particular St. Urban was Bishop of Langres. His rôle seems to have been confused with that of his namesake, the more famous Pope Urban, so much so that today it is the celebrated Pope who is recognized as the patron saint of vinegrowers. Many saints became protectors of vineyards simply because their feast-days happened to fall during the flowering of the vine or the ripening of the grapes. As for St. Vincent, very popular throughout Burgundy, he was probably adopted by vinegrowers as a result of a play on the French words *sent le vin*, in other words, *Vincent*. An old saying, still quoted in Santenay, maintains that any vinegrower not keeping St. Vincent's day will have his buttocks eaten by ants while he is having tea. St. Vincent is generally shown as a deacon, holding a palm leaf and a bunch of grapes.

The armorial bearings of many families and municipalities depict the vinegrower's work, with pruning-knife and wine-press in evidence as well as the ubiquitous bunch of grapes and twining vines. More than any other activities, the tasks involved in making wine, storing it, carrying and distributing it have encouraged the development of popular art. Everyday articles, traditional in kind and shape, are favourite subjects for decoration. The wooden wine-press is often richly decorated, as it is part of the patrimony, handed down from one generation to the next. Wine casks as well may have their own decoration. Valuable family possessions, these enormous wooden barrels were carved with the names of the vinegrower and his wife for whom they were built, with armorial bearings, monograms and even, like a house, the year of construction, and were often inaugurated at a wedding.

The front of these sometimes richly carved tuns is particularly characteristic of viticultural art. No doubt these casks, containing special wines from the large vineyards belonging to religious communities or princes, were first carved and ornamented in the wine cellars of monasteries and castles. The great chapters like those of Speyer or Würzburg exercised widespread influence throughout southern Germany, and this custom of decorating the huge casks was revived in the cellars of Austrian monasteries in the baroque period. Clearly, it was the monks who set the fashion for embellishing casks with pictures of saints or the patriarch Noah, considered as the father of viticulture. Occasionally, the abbeys engaged their own wood-carvers, but the work was more usually entrusted to the coopers themselves. During the eighteenth century and into the early part of the nineteenth, a cooper would spend countless, devoted hours carving and painting religious motifs, such as the patron saints of the guild. In the course of the nineteenth century, traditional designs were gradually superseded by simpler or more down-to-earth imagery, carvings of family names or portrayals of everyday scenes. The large casks, fitted with a trap-door through which a lad could clamber to clean the inside, were particularly well suited to carvings, even on the door itself. Now usually a plain piece of wood, this door was often carved in a very special manner in times gone by. The designs frequently featured fishes, naiads, tritons and other legendary creatures, symbolizing the great volume of liquid contained within the barrel. The richest collections of carved tuns are probably those now in the Wine Museum at Speyer, in the Palatinate, at the Julius Hospice in Würzburg in Bavaria, and in the Wine Museums of Beaune in Burgundy and of Kreme in Lower Austria.

Considering their size, so far above average, these giant casks represent significant monuments to the craftsmen of those days. They were constructed as much for the supply of some stronghold as to nourish the vanity of some great personage. Their real function, however, was usually to combine the different wines contributed as tithes into one blend so that all the officials entitled to perquisites in the form of wine received the same quality, thereby eliminating all grounds for complaint.

Most of these giant casks of the baroque period have now disappeared. Among the most richly decorated that of Königstein in Saxony should be mentioned. It was built for King Ausgustus the Strong. Other notable examples were the second Heidelberg tun, built in 1664 for the Grand Elector Charles-Louis of the Palatinate, and that of Ludwigsburg, built between the years 1717-20 for the Duke Eberhard Louis of Württemberg. The master-cooper Michael Werner of Landau in the Palatinate constructed the first Heidelberg tun for Jean Casimir in 1589; as a result he became famous and was given orders for similar casks from many other potentates. In old engravings, Werner and his helpmates can be seen at work on these enormous casks, proving that even in those days such an undertaking was considered an extraordinary feat and worthy of wide renown. One of these mammoth casks, with

Little figures in painted wood, the *Büttenmännchen* were characteristic of popular Germanic art and were often used for decorations at social gatherings.

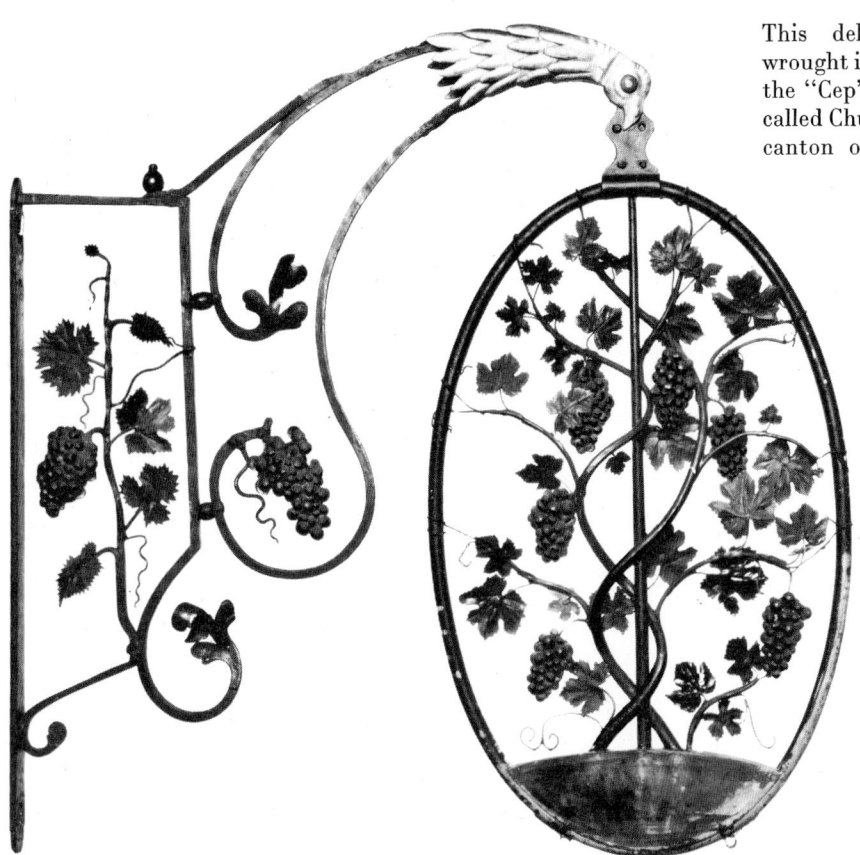

This delicate sign in wrought iron once graced the "Cep" inn at a town called Chur, in the Swiss canton of the Grisons.

Even the bung-hole of a cask provides an excuse for adding an amusing design in carved wood.

This "goat" was a symbol of fertility. Carved in wood and laden with grapes it formerly played a leading rôle in the processions at the wine festivals that ended the grape harvests in Lower Austria.

The elaborate fronts of many casks have now taken their places in collections. On this tun, which is dated for 1880, the carved decoration is still strictly traditional.

The New World also had its inn signs in the last century. Some were very simple, representing merely a symbolic object such as a bunch of grapes, a bottle or a drinking glass. Others, like this one, are genuine pictorial descriptions of life in days gone by. Errors in perspective were held to be of little consequence, as long as the subject was reasonably well-proportioned and the colours bright enough to attract attention. The wine, served in decanters and prominently displayed, seems to have been in plentiful supply at the "Strangers' Resort". Although vineyards already existed at this time in the New World, much wine was imported from Europe and, when good, was both scarce and expensive.

a capacity of nearly 53,000 gallons, can be seen to this day by visitors to the cellars of Heidelberg Castle.

Along with the big casks, the coopers produced small barrels for a great variety of purposes. One might be used by the vinegrower to carry his daily ration of wine when he was going to spend all day working in the vines. Another might be presented to the abbot at the time of his election. Still another would be used, year after year, to hold the Midwinter wine. This was a new wine, blessed on December 27th on the occasion of the festival of St. John the Apostle and devoutly treasured, to be drunk only on rare occasions, at a wedding, for instance, or before setting out on a long journey, being credited with beneficial virtues.

Amusing little casks, enabling three different wines to be drawn off by working a disc, are further examples of the coopers' art. They were very much in keeping with the spirit of the baroque age when games and tricks of every kind were much in vogue. After decades of apparent neglect, this craft is now being revived in various regions, notably in Lower Austria, and seems

to be in great demand by publicans, wine merchants and affluent private individuals. Created purely for decoration, these casks come almost exclusively from vinegrowing regions: the South Tyrol, Lower Austria, the banks of the Rhine and the Moselle.

The cultivation of the vine and wine gave rise to a multitude of smaller receptacles. Almost until the end of the eighteenth century, the bottle as a means of preserving wine was still unknown in German-speaking territories. The wine was stored in casks in the cellar, simply drawn off into jugs and then poured into glasses or goblets. The bottle, a French innovation, only appeared in these regions towards the end of the eighteenth century and only with the introduction of sparkling wines. Flasks which slipped easily into the pocket or into saddlebags were used to carry wine when travelling and these first flat, pouch-shaped bottles began to make their appearance around 1820, together with the wood or leather cases which were designed to hold them. This shape of bottle can still be found today in the typical flasks of Franconia called *Bocksbeutel*.

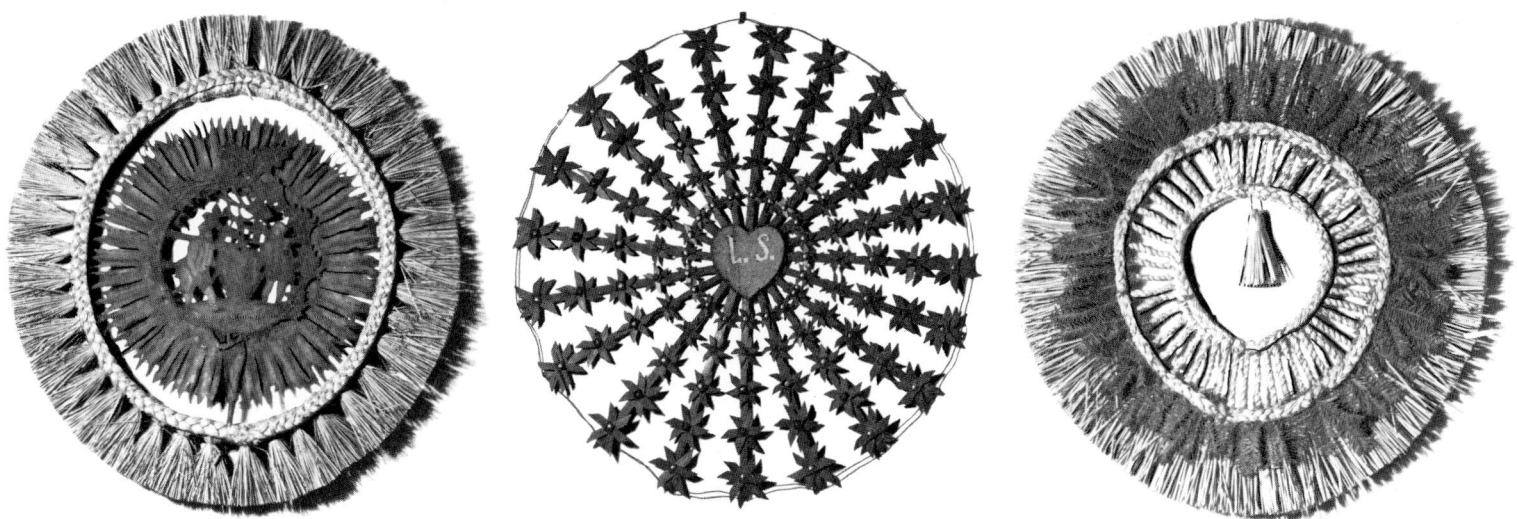

To the left and right are two *Heurigen Kränze*, wheels of plaited straw. Following an edict by Empress Maria Theresa, Austrian vinegrowers have hung these wheels over their doors to show passers-by that there is new wine in their cellar. In the centre is one of the wooden suns which, rising above the vineyards of Wachau, warned that they were guarded against trespassers and helped to frighten away unwelcome birds.

Other longer bottles, also flat and generally fluted, were designed to be carried on the person. All had screw stoppers in pewter or, in the case of gentlemen of rank, even in silver or gold. Humbler versions in wood, earthenware or even fashioned from gourds and used by farm workers, have also been discovered. Many such receptacles, fitted with a strap, were intended for carrying to work in the fields. Whenever possible, they were left in a spring or stream to keep the wine cool. They might be decorated with proverbial inscriptions, simultaneously bacchic and biblical, such as "Wine gladdens the heart of he who drinks in moderation, but it is harmful to the man who drinks too much", or "What is life without wine?" Innumerable small potteries turned out various types of pitchers, usually with handles, decorated with vine leaves, coats-of-arms and bacchic quotations while elsewhere pewter flagons were popular drinking vessels.

The tavern signs in small towns and in the countryside can also be considered as picturesque and characteristic examples of contemporary art. Those carved in wood have become extremely rare today. Magnificent specimens of hanging signs with their decorative supporting brackets testify to the high standard of wrought-iron work achieved in the eighteenth century. Depicting the vine and a bunch of grapes, as well as a variety of other motifs, these are for the most part the work of long-forgotten village craftsmen.

Our age is one of unceasing change. Like so many other crafts and professions, those associated closely or remotely with vines or wine have developed rapidly over the last few decades. Everywhere, glass or synthetic materials have replaced wood while implements and recipients whose design seemed to have attained near-perfection are rapidly disappearing from the scene of the cultivation of the vine and are taking their places in museums and auction rooms.

The same tasks engendered the same types of implements all over Europe, but each region endowed them with its own characteristic style. The cooper, the basket-worker and the maker of edged tools all worked to order and to local requirements. In one district, the grape-baskets borne on the back and the harvesting panniers might be made in wicker and, in another, wood. They might be round and deep in one province, oval and shallow in the next. Methods of cultivation, harvesting and wine-making influenced the shape and design of every article. Notwithstanding the fact that their ultimate purpose was the same, they differed from vineyard to vineyard in the same way that their owners differed. Vinegrowers they all may be, but distinguished one from the other by their traditions and working habits. Today, all these tools and implements form part of a common heritage and bear witness to a highly productive art that can be admired in museums devoted to the vine and to wine.

Active promoters of the European vineyards in the Middle Ages, the monks often boasted famous cellars, the forerunners of our inns and public houses. The casks were broached and the wine, mercifully not reserved exclusively for divine service, was drunk on the premises.

THE GREAT
WINE REGIONS OF
THE WORLD

THE VINE
CONQUERS THE WORLD

The great botanical family of Ampelidaceae, to which the vine belongs, is very widely represented in all cultivated regions of the world. All plants belonging to the genus *vitis* bear grapes but out of the forty-odd known species only one, the European *vitis vinifera*, produces the edible grapes used to make wine. *Vitis labrusca*, a species of American origin, is sometimes cultivated for wine but produces poor results. *Vitis vinifera* thrives only within the temperate zones of the two hemispheres, between latitudes 50 and 30 degrees North and 30 and 40 degrees South. This vine does not stand up well to excessive heat or rigorous cold, nor does it tolerate overly abundant rains or severe drought. Furthermore, it is difficult to make wine when the ambient temperature is above 15º C. (about 60º F.).

A rapid look at history shows that the regions where *vitis vinifera* has developed are also the regions where various civilizations reached the peak of their development. This is scarcely surprising, for of all plants which have been improved and transformed by the genius of man, the vine—even more than wheat or rice—is a silent witness to his patience and his untiring work over many generations.

The original or autochtonous vineyards were in the Caucasus (Georgia and Armenia), on the isles of the Aegean Sea and in Egypt. It was these that gave birth to the present-day vineyards. Other natural vineyards in China, Japan, and the eastern and central parts of North America, did not benefit from conditions suitable for their development and they have remained more or less in an embryonic state. But starting out from the Eurasian regions, *vitis vinifera* spread widely, for many and very different reasons.

Some of the vineyards owe their existence to the brutal facts of military conquest: a good many French vineyards began to appear as the Roman legions established themselves in the country. Sometimes it was the political supremacy or ideology which sufficed to propagate the vine cultures—this was the case with the Greek vineyards when, at the dawn of modern history, Continental Greece was under the influence of the Aegean powers. Nearer home, colonial conquests have resulted in the vine being transplanted to Australia, New Zealand, South Africa and South America.

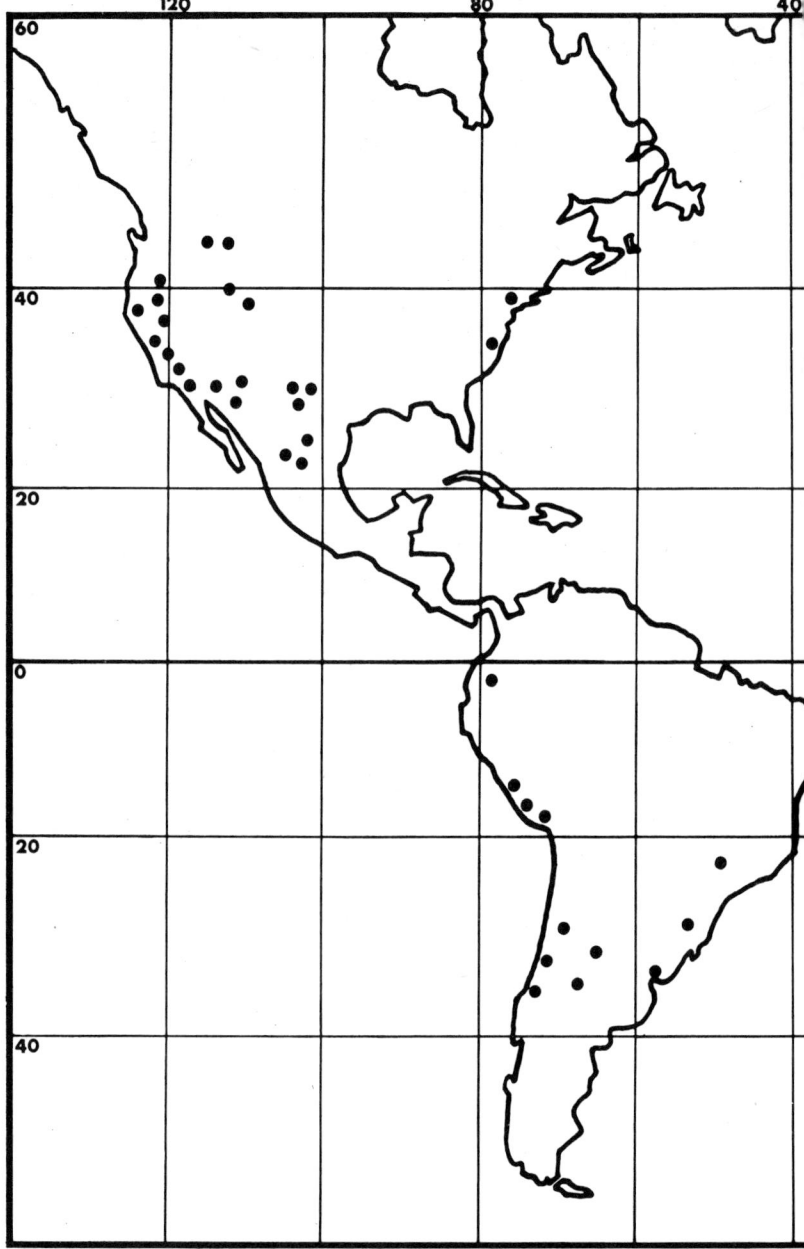

The missionary zeal of the Christians has often been reflected in a vine culture derived from their liturgical needs for altar wine: thus it was that the Spanish, after the Islamic interlude in the Iberian Peninsula, reintroduced the cultivation of the vine and the use of wine in southern Spain. Similarly, the first vines in California were planted by Franciscan missionaries. Elsewhere, it was the victims of religious persecution who spread a type of culture with which they were closely connected, as in South Africa, where the first vinegrowers, well versed in their calling, were the French Protestants who emigrated there after the Repeal of the Edict of Nantes in 1685. Some of the vineyards of southern Russia were created, at the end

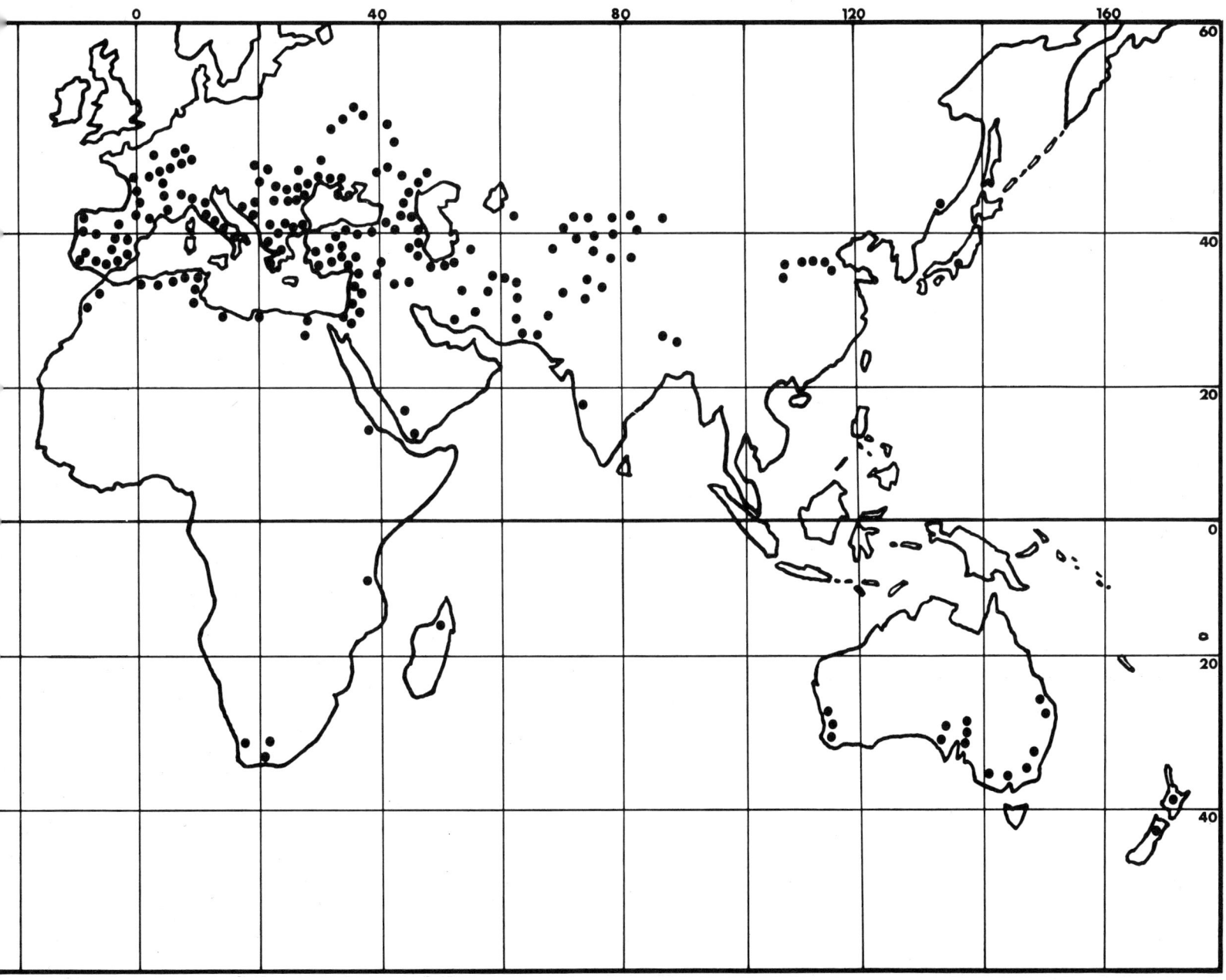

of the nineteenth century, by the snobbery of an aristocracy which wanted to produce on its own estates wines to which it then gave such famous names as Sauternes or Vougeot. Now Russia is the fifth largest wineproducer in Europe.

The expansion or reduction of the viticultural areas depended also—as is increasingly the case today—on economic fluctuations. In Brazil, following a slump in coffee, plantation owners did not hesitate to lease out part of their lands to vinegrowers of Italian origin. And before the First World War, in the former Austro-Hungarian Empire the areas cultivated to vines varied in direct relation to the economic and political situation of the various parts of the Empire.

The present state of the viticultural regions of the world is therefore the result of very numerous factors, which in turn depend on many facets of human activities. It is for this reason that the vineyards of the world vary to a marked degree within the climatic limits that are suitable for them.

The *Office International de la Vigne et du Vin* (O.I.V.) (International Office of Vine and Wine) in Paris has been collecting, studying and publishing, for the best part of half a century now, all the information possible on the vine and on wine in the world. The office functions as a centre of co-ordination and also of scientific, technological, economic and legal information for most of the viticultural countries.

THE WINES
OF BURGUNDY

PIERRE FORGEOT

The Bible relates that the vine was created on the third day with the other plants (Genesis i. 2). But how long did it take to reach Burgundy after Noah and his Ark came to rest on Mount Ararat? No written evidence can possibly tell us. It is generally thought that, long before the Christian era, there were vines, albeit wild, growing in the present Burgundy wine area in the middle of eastern France, north of the Côtes du Rhône region and south-west of Champagne and Alsace. It was only through a slow process of change, doubtless beginning about the third century B.C. and advancing as their skill in the art grew, that our ancestors were able to improve the quality of the grape. Roman rule lasted five centuries and was vital to the development of the vineyards of Burgundy. Many of the Roman legionaries came from the wineproducing areas of Italy, and they brought to the Eduans—as the inhabitants of this region of Gaul were then known—their experience in the cultivation of the vine and in winemaking.

With the clearing of suitable vineyard land and the planting of better selected vine-stock in the first century A.D., it became possible to expand the vineyards and begin to produce the types of wines best suited to the province. The results were spectacular. By the fourth century, Numene was able to report: "The wines of this region are the subject of foreigners' admiration." Somewhat later, in 570, Gregory of Tours proclaimed: "There is no liquor preferable to the wine of these vineyards—it is a noble Falernian." About the year 456, the Burgundians proper arrived

on the scene. They may rightly be called a migrant people, having apparently left the distant plains of Asia several millennia before the Christian era. By about 900 B.C., they had reached what is now called Norway and spread through Sweden, Germany and Switzerland before replacing the Romans in the fifth century in south-eastern Gaul, where they created their vast kingdom. In 534 the Burgundians were defeated by the Franks, but though their passage was brief, they had none the less imprinted their personality on the character, habits and customs of the region, and they gave their name to the province.

During this period and through the Middle Ages, Christianity became firmly established. Large religious estates were created through endowments made to churches, convents, abbeys and other institutions, rivalling and soon surpassing those of princes. This state of affairs continued until the French Revolution secularized religious orders and divided their land.

Burgundy was not spared the various disasters of the Middle Ages—invasions (Arab, Norman etc.), civil wars, pillaging, famines, plagues. In his history of Beaune, Rossignol writes: "The archives contain but a few vague words which bear witness to that universal desolation." It is not difficult to imagine that the cultivation of the vine made little progress in those times. Its rise began only in the tenth century with the creation of two monastic orders that were to exert an immense influence on the whole of Europe. The monks cleared the ground, replanted vine-stock and did much for the vineyards of Burgundy, putting them on the road to becoming what they are today. The research carried out first at the Abbey of Cluny and later at Cîteaux led to methods of cultivation and winemaking that, by and large, were the same as those we now employ. The spiritual and physical expanse of these two abbeys was immense—was not one of the abbots, St. Mayeul, called in his own lifetime "the prince of monastic religion and the arbiter of kings"? Cluny possessed two thousand dependencies and Cîteaux more than three thousand. In other words, their power was an important factor in the spreading growth both of Burgundy wines and of their fame.

In fact, the quality of Burgundy wines was even the cause of serious diplomatic incidents! Petrarch tells us: "The cardinals [then in Avignon] no longer wish to return to Rome, since there are no Burgundy wines in Italy. Our prelates believe that their lives will not be happy without this liquor—for them, wine is the fifth element." For his part, Pope Urban V said: "I am little concerned to see again those transalpine lands where there is no Beaune wine."

These were the fourteenth and fifteenth centuries, auspicious times for Burgundy, both because of the monastic orders of which we have just spoken and because of the growth of the court of the Grand Dukes of the West, as the dukes of Burgundy then preferred to be called—Philip the Bold, John the Fearless, Philip the Good and Charles the Bold. For over a century, from 1364 to 1477, these four dukes, "the immediate lords of the best wines in Christendom", raised their duchy to such heights of power as to intimidate the kings of France and the princes of Europe. At the death of Charles the Bold, their power extended beyond the duchy of Burgundy (Dijon, Beaune, Mâcon) to the county of Burgundy (Besançon) and across a large part of Holland, Belgium, Luxemburg, Alsace and the counties of Nevers, Artois and Picardie. They cared much for their wines and gifts of them were greatly esteemed, as this letter from Pope Innocent VII testifies: "My son . . . Greetings. . . . This Beaune wine that you have sent Us has a good and agreeable taste. It is quite pleasing to Our palate and constitution. We have made almost regular use of it as a curative during Our recent illness. Therefore, We call upon your Lordship and request that you send Us more as soon as the possibility arises. We shall be very pleased to receive it and your Lordship will thus be doing Us a very great favour."

Cultivation of the vineyards gradually became more democratic as first the bourgeoisie and then the peasant vintager received greater freedom. The vines were no longer the exclusive property of the nobility and the clergy; the latter, in fact, frequently indulged in such excesses that decent folk were obliged to react. The competence of the monks in the subject of wine and their taste for the beverage caused many a ribald comment. As they said at the time:

Boire en Templier, c'est boire à plein gosier,
Boire en Cordelier, c'est vider le cellier.

To drink like a Templar is to drink heartily,
To drink like a Franciscan is to empty the cellar.

The vineyards were finally and totally democratized in the eighteenth century by the French Revolution. The sale of the property of the clergy and the nobility divided up their immense estates and initiated the process of fragmentation, which subsequently increased through successive splits caused, in particular, by inheritances. This fragmentation characterizes the vineyards of Burgundy even today—quite unlike the large estates of Bordeaux. There are twice as many vinegrowers in Burgundy as in Bordeaux, in a cultivated area one-third the size, and very few vineyards are wholly owned by a single person. Moreover, towards the end of the last century, the whole area was nearly lost to the notorious pest, phylloxera, an insect from America which attacked the roots and killed off the vine-stock. The whole industry was facing collapse, for no practical and effective remedy could be discovered. In the end, the only way to save the vineyards was to graft old vine-stocks on to American phylloxera-resistant stock. This cure did not affect the quality of the product; quite the contrary, it made possible the creation of improved varieties, better suited to the consumers' requirements.

There are certain conditions that must be fulfilled if a really fine wine is to be produced—and we shall only be discussing fine wines here. To the old saying: "The finest gesture a person can make is to fill his neighbour's glass", folk-wisdom will immediately add: "Tell me what you drink and I'll tell you who you are." It being understood, of course, that, as M. de Borose remarked: "good things are made for good people; otherwise we should be obliged to believe that God created them for bad people . . . which is unthinkable !"

Five specific factors must coincide if a Burgundy is to be able to develop its best qualities:

THE SOIL. Vines are not planted just anywhere but generally on the slopes of hills. The soil on flat country is too rich; the grape absorbs too much water and the wine is diluted. On hilltops the soil is poor; the vine does not grow properly, the grape does not take in all the elements it requires and the wine is incomplete.

In the words of Gaston Roupnel: "Before wine can even be conceived, its chosen soil must be very old and its cradle a tomb replete with the ashes of years and the dust of centuries." One is often surprised to

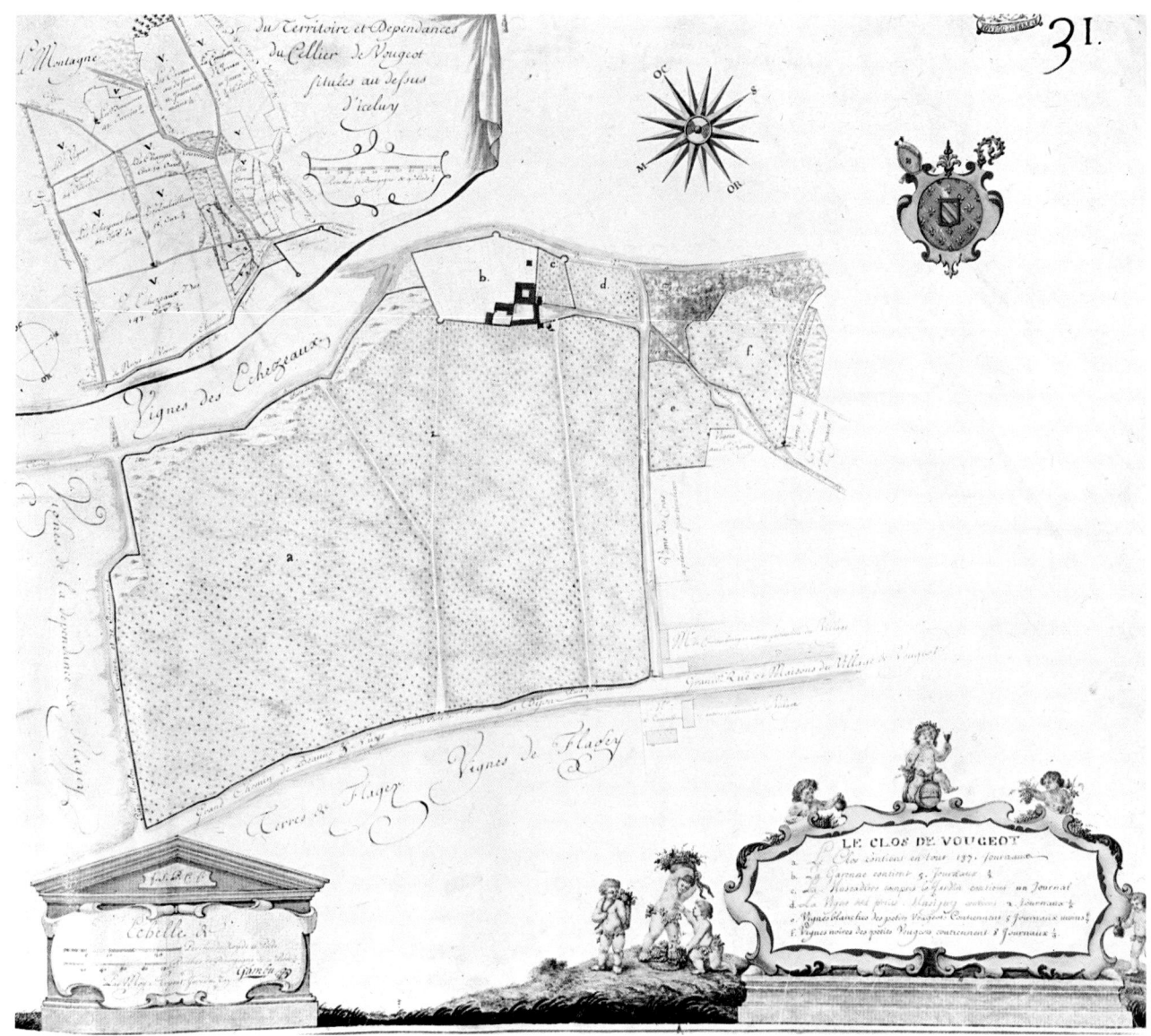

Created in about 1150 by the Bernardine monks of Cîteaux, the Clos-Vougeot estate very soon became a model vineyard. It has quite accurately been called the navel of Burgundy. Despite the many vicissitudes of its early history, it grew steadily until the fourteenth century. Its 128 acres are today divided among 60 different owners.

see in this land of great growths so many different names side by side but, nevertheless, possessing significant differences in quality. The mystery of the extremely complex composition of the soil affecting the final result is mentioned by Maurice Constantin-Weyer in his book *L'âme du vin* ("The Soul of Wine"): "A secret alchemy works upon even the least of the soil's riches to produce an elixir beyond compare."

THE VINE. To plant a "hybrid" on the slope of a hill is a little like bandaging a wooden leg. The great wines of Burgundy demand two types of vine-stock: for red wines, the *Pinot*—the finer the grape the better the result—the juice of which is colourless and very sweet; for white wines, the *Chardonnay* grape is used, to which the same applies.

There are two main secondary types that go with the two "greats". One is the *Gamay*, a red grape with white juice which produces the remarkable wines of the granite soil of the Beaujolais. As two writers of the region have commented: in order to savour their excellence to the full "you would need a *corniole* [gullet] as long as a swan's to make the pleasure last longer". The other is the *Aligoté*, a white grape, very old, which gives one single wine, the BOURGOGNE ALIGOTÉ.

THE CARE OF THE VINE. Tilling, pruning, looking after the vines, pest control—all these are decisive factors in the proper cultivation of the vine and the production of healthy, promising grapes. The work is done throughout the year, thus justifying an ancient saying: "The vine grows in the vintner's shadow."

The vintage itself is also part of the "care of the vine", for to gather the grapes at the correct stage of ripeness is vital and the date, always chosen with great care, is very important.

Of course, many imponderables can upset the patient vintner's work. Spring frosts, around the beginning of May, may occur in any year, resulting in the loss of up to three-quarters of the crop. *Coulure* (premature dropping of the fruit) is feared when rain or cold in June inhibit fecundation. Hail is a formidable danger to the vine; where it falls, all or most of the crop may be destroyed. The final unforseeable factor beyond man's control is the proper sequence of rain and sun. To produce a great vintage, rain is needed at the right times, and sun is needed in large amounts especially in the two months before harvesting.

VINIFICATION. It is often said that the rules of hygiene are like unattractive women—nobody follows them. To which strong-minded people add without hesitation the following maxim: "Lean heavily on your principles—they'll always give way in the end." Neither of these maxims can be applied to winemaking, especially since Burgundy adopted the shorter vinification method in 1938 in order to produce more flexible wines which matured much earlier while still maintaining their former high standards. And this is where the splitting up of vineyards mentioned above is regrettable, since strict rules have to be followed and the vintner often finds it difficult to keep up with the progress made and adopt the new methods.

STORAGE AND TREATMENT. The French word *elevage*, which loosely translated means "upbringing", is much misunderstood when applied to the winegrowing profession. It has been remarkably well explained by two nineteenth-century authors, Danguy and Aubertin: "Once made, red wine must, through constant and unceasing care, be brought to the point at which it possesses all the necessary qualities for it to be tasted with pleasure." In 1885, Dr Lavalle wrote: "Precisely because of all its perfection, the wine of Burgundy demands intelligent care and, like those splendid

The Burgundy wine area, of which just under half lies in the Beaujolais, consists of 105,000 acres unevenly scattered among four departments. Only the Chablis region in the north between the Yonne and the Armançon seems to hold itself aloof from the natural continuity provided for these glorious vineyards by the river Saône. The other regions on its right bank form an almost continuous belt between Dijon and Villefranche. The Côte de Nuits from Fixin to Corgoloin and the Côte de Beaune from Ladoix-Serrigny to Santanay have shared the benefits of the prestige gained by their vineyards with the whole of Burgundy. The vineyards of Mercurey, more widely scattered than the rest, provide a link with the compact southern group of the Mâconnais and the Beaujolais, linked to the Burgundy area by many geographical and commercial bonds.

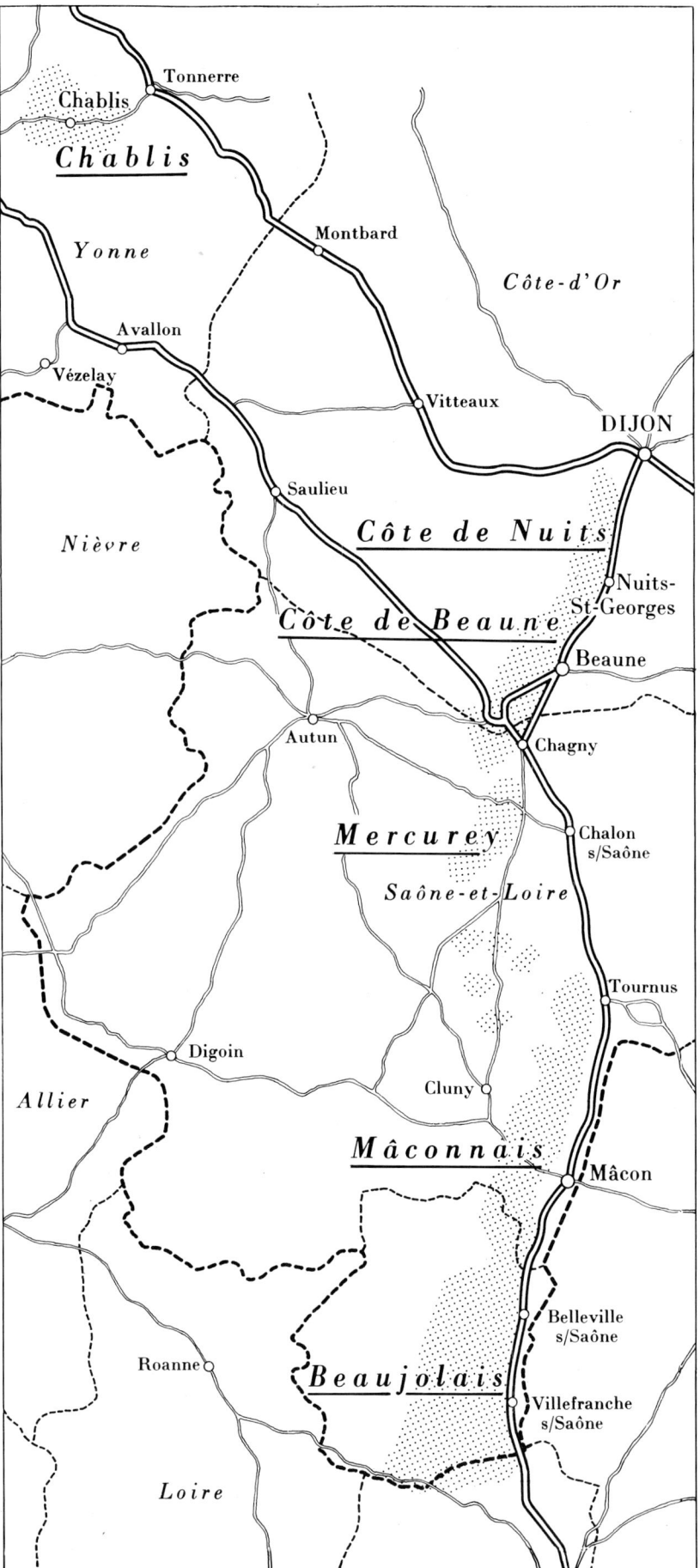

flowers that must be painstakingly cultivated for several years before they will open their marvellous blooms, full of brightness and perfume, it requires a knowing hand to lead it skilfully and patiently to the point at which it is worthy to be offered to a man of taste."

In Burgundy, it is the buyer-shipper who, over the last few centuries, has lovingly prepared the necessary sanctuaries: cellars vaulted or built so as to maintain a relatively even temperature. The fact is that the vintner, once again because of the fragmentation of property, and the small number of large estates, quite frequently confines himself to the growing side, and his job ends as soon as the wine is made. Furthermore the investment is considerable—a large amount of space, installations (always interesting to visit), capital to build up large stocks of bottles and barrels for the ageing period and sufficient qualified personnel are all necessary. Finally, a sales organization must be set up in France and abroad to dispose of the product. These are circumstances that have made the Burgundian wine shippers, though few in number, very important people. There are two hundred of them, to be found mainly in the large wine centres.

France accounts for about 50 per cent of the buyers of the great wines of Burgundy. They are distributed through three types of buyers—wholesalers from outside the Burgundy area who sell them in their own particular markets and also to a significant number of retailers; hotel, restaurant and café owners, and individual wine merchants; and private individuals, who buy in barrels or assortments of bottles.

In 1967, exports went to 138 different countries throughout the world—11,844,300 gallons of wines with an *appellation contrôlée*, produced in Burgundy. For several years, Burgundy has ranked first among all the production areas of French *appellation contrôlée* wines by value and by volume of wines sold outside France. Quite an achievement, as the official statistics will show. For, again in 1967, Burgundy produced 12.5 per cent of all French wines entitled to an A.O.C. label

(A.O.C. = Appellation d'Origine Contrôlée = Registered Designation of Origin), while its exports accounted for 39.4 per cent of French A.O.C. wines exported (excluding Champagne and sparkling wines). To be precise, exports were 8,250,640 gallons of wines in casks and 3,593,220 gallons in bottles. These figures do not include non-A.O.C. (but labelled) wines crossing the frontier since the customs statistics do not go into sufficient detail. But here too, Burgundy is at the head of the list by a wide margin.

Exports of bottled wines are limited by higher selling prices, due to the special processes involved, to customs duties and the considerable costs of transport. Even so, the United States buys only bottled wines. Canada's imports are 90 per cent bottled and other countries are yearly increasing their import percentages in this category.

Among the chief importers of A.O.C. Burgundy wines in terms of volume, Switzerland ranks first. Though a small country in terms of population, it is closely linked to the province and absorbs over one-third of its exports. Next comes the United States, which now takes 14 per cent of Burgundy's foreign sales and, in terms of value is becoming its biggest customer (25 per cent of the total). For, besides from the ordinary wines, Americans are buying fine and great wines, but solely in the bottle. West Germany's position is uncertain because of its present regulations. With the opening of the frontiers, this market, taking 13.4 per cent at present, may be completely transformed. Next comes Belgium, traditionally a lover of Burgundy wines, with 12.3 per cent. Great Britain follows next with very little concern as to A.O.C.s; Britons still tend to drink wine *à la tasse*, i.e. by the glass. Imports are, as in the past, piecemeal, and therefore frequently consist of "labelled wines" lacking an A.O.C. but meeting the desired quality requirements. Further principal importers of A.O.C. Burgundy wines are Sweden, Canada, Denmark, the Netherlands and Italy, where sales are increasing rapidly.

THE WINE AREAS

Over the centuries the kingdom, duchy or province of Burgundy has been like a balloon, swelling and shrinking as circumstances dictated. Its frontiers were always vague, varying hugely around a central kernel consisting of a few hundred square miles centring on the cities of Beaune and Dijon. The only definite and undisputable characteristic of Burgundy is that it has always been a crossroads, a fact that throughout

its history has brought more trouble than benefits.

No feature in its geographical shape is sufficiently precise for us to be able to describe its shape. Only in the east did the Saône River clearly mark part of the boundary between the duchy (Beaune-Dijon) and the county of Burgundy (Besançon), that is between the present Haute Bourgogne and the Franche-Comté. The very nature of the terrain confirms these differences—the plain of the Saône, the vineyard slopes, the forests of the mountainous Morvan and of the Châtillonnais, a maze of fields, meadows and different crops. The twentieth century has not improved matters much, even though the division of France into departments, often arbitrarily welded together, should have given Burgundy, along with the soul which it has always had, at least a clearly defined territory. But no—and this is true of a number of other French provinces—according to the various civil, military and religious authorities there is not one Burgundy, but several, the land they cover differing quite inexplicably.

When the need arose to define the Burgundy wine area, the official attempt to do so was frankly an innovation. Ignoring history and thankfully taking into account more realistic and practical considerations, the Civil Tribunal of Dijon, in a decree dated April 29th, 1930, defined the production areas authorized to use the title Burgundy as follows: "Local, consistent and time-honoured usage, has it that the Burgundy wine area is exclusively composed of the Côte-d'Or, Yonne and Saône-et-Loire departments, plus the Villefranche-sur-Saône *arrondissement* in the Rhône department."

The Villefranche-sur-Saône district, or to call it by its better-known name, the Beaujolais, has never been politically a part of Burgundy at any time in its history. As the writer, A. Julien said in 1816: "There is cause for astonishment in my joining the Beaujolais and Burgundy, since the first is part of the Rhône department. But my intention is to present and group together wines of the same type, and the wines of the Beaujolais have very little in common with those of the Lyonnais."

It is, therefore, solely on the basis of its geographical situation, the nature of its wines and its commercial traditions that this great wine area has been adopted as an integral part of the Burgundy area. There have never been any complaints about it.

Turning to the north, we find, just above the Beaujolais, the vineyards of the Mâconnais in Saône-et-Loire, quite close to the hills and a little away from the Route Nationale 6 in the south of the department, which narrows towards the north. There it meets the Mercurey region, which lies mainly on the hillside and is sometimes called the Côte Chalonnaise, a comparison with the famous wine areas farther north.

Next we enter the Côte-d'Or and follow Route Nationale 74, a triumphal procession of all the most glorious names in Burgundy. It is a narrow belt of vines, about 200 to 900 yards wide and 30 miles long; the first part is called the Côte de Beaune and the other the Côte de Nuits, after which we reach the administrative capital, Dijon. Finally, right at the top of the map, in the Yonne, we find a small patch of 7,000 acres of vines mainly around the village of Chablis,

We shall return to discuss in greater detail the structure of these various regions of the Burgundy wine area as officially defined by the law.

DESIGNATIONS OF ORIGIN

Someone once wrote: "Good wine warms the heart, revives the brain and overhauls the machinery." It should come as no surprise to learn that a beverage with such powers has been strictly controlled since the very earliest times.

We must return to the beginning of the fifteenth century to find a document which, by its very tone, bears a certain similarity to our modern designations of origin. It is the edict of Charles VI, in February 1415, which states that: "the wines of Burgundy shall be those that are produced above the Pont de Sens, whether in the region of Auxerrois or in that of Beaulne". It further divided the wines of Burgundy into two categories—Basse-Bourgogne (Lower Burgundy) for parishes from the Pont de Sens to Cravant, including, in particular, the Auxerrois; and Haute-Bourgogne (Upper Burgundy), which was sub-divided into four regions: the Beaunois, the Mâconnais, the Tournus and the Dijonnais, in that order. The king

seems to have had good advisers, since the divisions he established have been respected to this day.

Over two hundred years later, we come to the repression of fraud. On April 27th, 1622, Louis XIII prohibited, with suitable penalties, the sale, "as Burgundies, of wines of the Lyonnais and the Beaujolais".

For many years to come, the *tastevin*, or sampling cup, was to be the sole judge in disputes. "Beaune wine" was, for a very long time, the name given to all the fine wines of the Côte-d'Or and "Auxerre wine" to the wines (then mainly red) of the Yonne.

However, a basic law was enacted on August 1st, 1905 to repress "fraud or attempted fraud as regards the nature, quality, type, origin and denomination of the product". This was supported by the law of May 6th, 1919 which defined the designations and production areas, and the decree-law of July 30th, 1935 which dealt with designations of origin and established the A.O.C. system.

Thus were defined the areas in each wineproducing commune that, according to ancient custom, were entitled to call their produce quality wine, *ceteris paribus*. Thus we now have A.O.C.s bearing the names of the villages of Fleurie, Pouilly-Fuissé, Meursault, Beaune, Nuits, Chablis, etc.

This region, in fact, is made up of small-holdings, called *climats*, the names of which often refer back to quite ancient title deeds. According to local, consistent and time-honoured usage, a number of these *climats* have been selected in an official document as being most likely to produce the best wines. They are, generally speaking, halfway up the hillside and are called the *Premiers Crus* (First Growths). On labels, price lists and bills, the name of the *climat* or vineyard always comes after the name of the village, as in the cases of BEAUNE-GRÈVES, MEURSAULT-CHARMES, POMMARD-RUGIENS, NUITS-VAUCRAINS, CHAMBOLLE-MUSIGNY AMOUREUSES, etc.

Then, from these First Growths, the law has selected what used to be called *têtes de cuvée* (best of the vintage), which really had to be the best of the best. These are now called the *Grands Crus* (Great Growths) whose names stand out alone on labels and in documents. For example—CHAMBERTIN, MONTRACHET, CLOS VOUGEOT, CORTON, CORTON-CHARLEMAGNE, etc.

Within any commune that is not so selected, wines may be produced but they are entitled only to a more general designation—and then under certain conditions, e.g. BOURGOGNE, BOURGOGNE ALIGOTE, BOURGOGNE-PASSE-TOUT-GRAINS and BOURGOGNE GRAND ORDINAIRE, or a regional designation such as BEAUJOLAIS, MACON, PETIT CHABLIS.

Furthermore, as we have already noted above, the types of vine-stock upon which the right to an A.O.C. depends are also strictly controlled.

Since it is quite difficult to assess quality officially, one way around the problem was thought to be the supervision of two factors—the yield per hectare and the level of alcohol in the wine. The first of these may have a direct bearing on the quality. Nevertheless, it is all quite relative and frequently, if all the necessary conditions have been fulfilled throughout the year, quantity and quality may not be incompatible. This is why the law allows the yield (in the villages of the Côte-d'Or, for example, it is 35 hectolitres per hectare i.e. about 300 gallons per acre) to vary from year to year, according to the quantity and quality of the crop. The procedure is, of course, very complicated and is determined by a decree from the Minister of Agriculture.

The degree of alcohol specified is, in each case, a minimum level and an indifferent standard at that. As Georges Duhamel said during a chapter of the Brotherhood of the Knights of the Tastevin: "Though alcohol is the vital spirit of wine, it is certainly not its soul." Nobody would dream of buying a great Burgundy wine on the basis of its alcoholic content, as though it were a table wine.

This quite complicated procedure is but a small beginning, since the movement of wine in France is not unrestricted, but governed by a whole series of legal documents as well as all the decrees on wine production. For example, every year before the harvest, the vintner must declare all the wine he possesses. After the harvest, he must declare the amount produced in every one of his vineyards. These two statements are kept by the appropriate services of the indirect taxation authority. If the wine leaves the wineproducer's cellars, whether for sale or as a gift, it must be accompanied by an official document, the excise papers delivered by the above-mentioned authority. Its function is to "release" from bond wines destined for bars, hotels, restaurants, retailers, middlemen and private persons, where the duties must be paid at the outset. If the wine is for a wholesaler or exporter, these papers act as a sort of permit for payment of duties to be deferred in the case of wholesalers or not to be levied at all in the case of exporters.

It is, therefore, easy to check on remaining stocks, which is done by the indirect taxation authority twice a year and also by the fraud and quality control brigade, which may make spot checks at any time.

Further explanation is needed of a number of well known Burgundy A.O.C.s which are difficult to find on any wine map. For example—CÔTE DE BEAUNE-VILLAGES. The fact is that the A.O.C. given by law may, in some cases, be changed, but always downwards. This is called *déclasser* (to downgrade) a wine.

It is often a voluntary process, generally to meet commercial requirements. Thus the wines of many little-known villages are sometimes hard to sell under their own names and are, therefore, downgraded to a more regional A.O.C.—CÔTE DE BEAUNE-VILLAGES or BOURGOGNE, for example. Or a shipper who has created a trade name puts it under a simple regional A.O.C., the highest common denominator of all the wines sold under the name.

Downgrading may, of course, also be compulsory. For example, two or several wines from different A.O.C.s may, for one reason or other, be mixed. In principle, the resulting wine may not use either or any of the original A.O.C.s, but must use one common to them all. Thus, the blending of a CHAMBERTIN with a CHARMES-CHAMBERTIN gives a plain GEVREY-CHAMBERTIN; a BEAUNE and an ALOXE-CORTON gives an ordinary BOURGOGNE. Downgrading is also compulsory if the grower exceeds the allotted maximum yield of any particular A.O.C.

4 BOUCHARD PÈRE & FILS
1 CHAMBERTIN
3 1959
2 APPELLATION CHAMBERTIN CONTROLÉE

MIS EN BOUTEILLES PAR
5 BOUCHARD PÈRE & FILS, NÉGOCIANTS A BEAUNE (COTE-D'OR)

4 BOUCHARD PÈRE & FILS
1 CHAMBERTIN
3 1961
1a CLOS DE BÈZE
2 APPELLATION CHAMBERTIN CONTROLÉE

MIS EN BOUTEILLES PAR
5 BOUCHARD PÈRE & FILS, NEGOCIANTS A BEAUNE (COTE-D'OR)

4 BOUCHARD PÈRE & FILS
1 CHARMES-CHAMBERTIN
3 1959
2 APPELLATION CHARMES-CHAMBERTIN CONTROLÉE

MIS EN BOUTEILLES PAR
5 BOUCHARD PÈRE & FILS, NÉGOCIANTS A BEAUNE (COTE-D'OR)

CHAMBERTIN

1. Chambertin – the name of the wine. This simple title should never be confused with the A.O.C. Gevrey-Chambertin (see opposite page). Chambertin is one of the Great Growths of the commune of Gevrey-Chambertin. – 2. The compulsory inclusion of the A.O.C. ensures that the wine is from the 33 acres of the Chambertin *climat* and no other. – 3. The vintage. The fact that it is on the label and not on the neck band is an additional guarantee of authenticity. – 4. The name of the shipper, compulsory in the case of A.O.C. wines. – 5. Bottled by the shipper – ano

CHAMBERTIN - CLOS DE BÈZE

1. Chambertin – the name of the wine. At first glance, no difference between this label and the above. One thing, then, is certain – it is a Chambertin and therefore a great wine. – 1a. Clos de Bèze provides an additional clue. This *climat* is also a Great Growth of the commune of Gevrey-Chambertin (see map on page 84). However, although a Chambertin-Clos de Bèze may be called Chambertin, the reverse is not possible. On some labels, the Clos de Bèze comes immediately below Chambertin in the same type-face. – 2. The compulsory inclusion of the A.O.C. has Chambertin alone; it could equally mention Chambertin-Clos de Bèze. – 3. 4. 5. As above.

CHARMES-CHAMBERTIN

1. Charmes-Chambertin – the name of the wine. In this case, a different name comes before the word Chambertin. It is not the name of the commune but of the *climat* (see map on page 84). Such a label designates a Great Growth, albeit of lesser repute than the two above. Similar labels are used by other *climats*: Chapelle-Chambertin, Griotte-Chambertin, Latricières-Chambertin, Mazis-Chambertin and Ruchottes-Chambertin. All these are Great Growths from the commune of Gevrey-Chambertin. – 2. The A.O.C. may not mention Chambertin alone but must by law cover both – Charmes-Chambertin. – 3. 4. 5. As above.

GEVREY-CHAMBERTIN "LES CAZETIERS"

1. Gevrey-Chambertin – the name of the wine. Here we have the name of the commune; it is therefore not a great wine but a village A.O.C. – 1a. Under the village A.O.C. comes the *climat* concerned – "Les Cazetiers". Since this name is in the list of First Growths (see page 76), the full title, "Gevrey-Chambertin Les Cazetiers" indicates a First Growth from Gevrey-Chambertin. That is to say, a wine whose precise geographical origin guarantees its quality. The name of the vineyard must be mentioned on the label in letters no higher or wider than those of the A.O.C. of the commune. – 2. Note that the A.O.C. mentions Gevrey-Chambertin; it might also have been in full – "Gevrey-Chambertin Les Cazetiers". – 3. 4. 5. As above.

GEVREY-CHAMBERTIN

1. Gevrey-Chambertin – the name of the wine. This label bears only the village A.O.C. It is, therefore, a wine from somewhere in the commune of Gevrey-Chambertin other than a vineyard producing Great or First Growths, except where the latter may have been downgraded to Gevrey-Chambertin. – 2. The A.O.C. guarantees that the wine is exclusively from the commune of Gevrey-Chambertin. This is not necessarily a guarantee of quality. – 3. The vintage. – 4. 5. More than in the previous cases, the name of the shipper is the real guarantee of quality. By clearly indicating his name, the shipper stakes his reputation.

BOURGOGNE (BURGUNDY)

1. 1a. Bourgogne – the generic name and "La Vignée", a trade name. This label is very different from the previous ones, firstly because it does not bear the name Chambertin or Gevrey-Chambertin. The generic classification as Burgundy means that the wine is from different places in Burgundy. It may even be Gevrey-Chambertin alone. The shipper is not satisfied with the generic description alone and has added his trade name "La Vignée". This means he attaches great importance to the quality of this wine. – 2. The Burgundy A.O.C. only means that the wine was made in Burgundy. In judging its quality, the trade name and the name of the shipper will be decisive factors. – 3. Bottling by the shipper himself also indicates that he attaches a great deal of importance to the quality of the wine. N.B. – It will be seen that the vintage is not mentioned on the label. In this case, it will be on the neck of the bottle or there may be no vintage indicated at all.

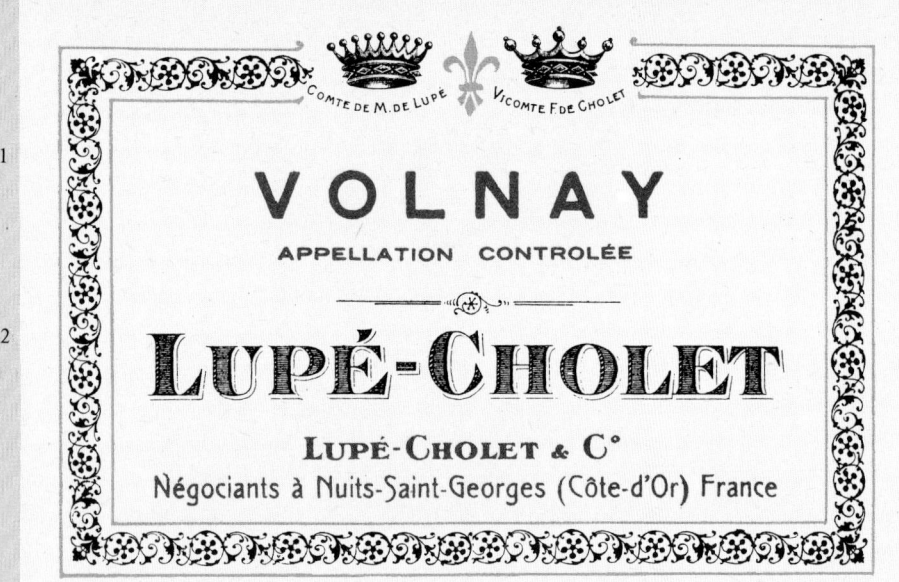

VOLNAY

1. Volnay – the A.O.C. This is a village growth in the Côte de Beaune. A simple A.O.C. guaranteeing quality. – 2. In such cases, the name of the shipper is decisive in any *a priori* judgement of quality.

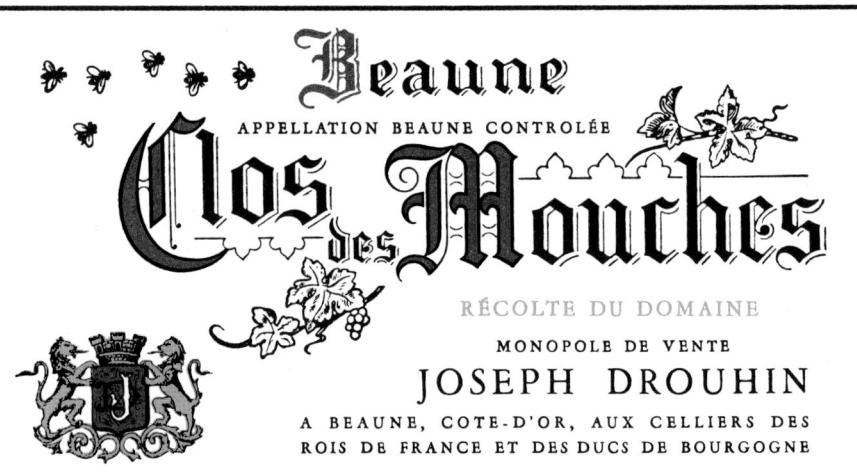

BEAUNE CLOS DES MOUCHES

1. Beaune – the A.O.C. – 2. The name of the vineyard is "Clos des Mouches". Since it is written in larger type-face than the A.O.C., it must be a First Growth. If it were not, the type-face of the name of the vineyard would have to be no more than half the height and width of that of the A.O.C. – 3. The name of the shipper. His sales monopoly *(monopole de vente)* should be taken as a guarantee of authenticity and quality.

GRANDS ÉCHÉZEAUX

1. Grands Echézeaux – the name of the wine, immediately followed by the A.O.C. At first sight, we see it is not a village A.O.C. It is probably a Great Growth. The connoisseur will then identify it as one of the seven Great Growths of the commune of Vosne-Romanée. – 2. The indication of how many bottles were made and the individual bottle number leave no room for doubt; we have ample proof that this is a very great wine, nicely confirmed by the date of the vintage. – 3. The name of the proprieter is enough to convince even the most cautious. – 4. That it is estate-bottled is a logical conclusion from the fact that the number of bottles made has already been mentioned.

MERCUREY

1. Mercurey – the A.O.C. This is not a great growth or a village A.O.C. but that of a region following the Côte de Beaune (see page 78). Mercurey wines are not unlike the Côte de Beaune wines. – 2. In the case of communal or regional A.O.C.s, the good name of the shipper is the guarantee of quality.

BROUILLY

1. Brouilly – the A.O.C. Only a Beaujolais fan would know that this is a First Growth Beaujolais, for the word Beaujolais is not on the label. Thus *a minimum knowledge* of the wines of this region is required to tell what wine a Brouilly is. The same type of label is used for the following names: Chénas, Chiroubles, Côte de Brouilly, Fleurie, Juliénas, Morgon, Moulin-à-Vent and Saint-Amour. – 2. Bottling by the shipper is an additional guarantee of authenticity.

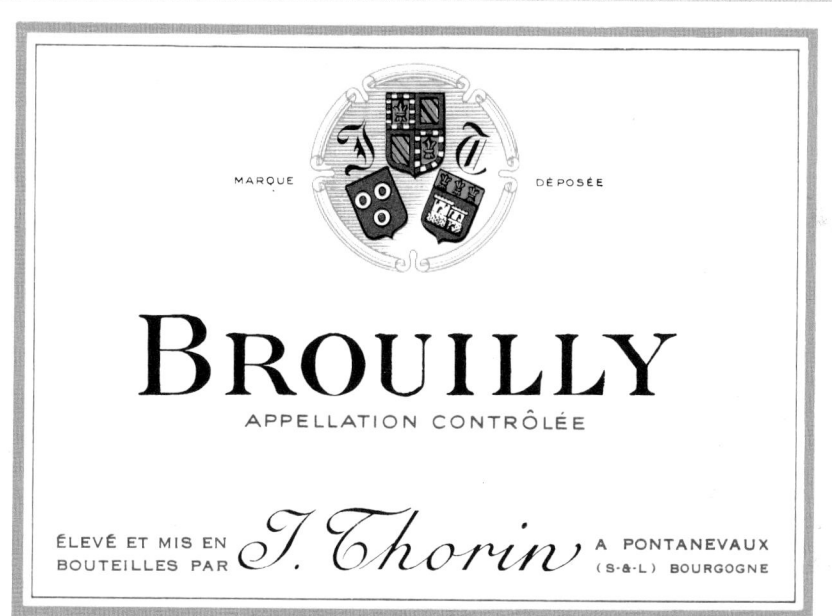

BEAUJOLAIS

1. Beaujolais – the A.O.C. This is a regional name. A clear distinction should be made between Beaujolais, Beaujolais Superieur and Beaujolais-Village, which are three quite separate A.O.C.s. The first is the most common. – 2. The shipper's name here is very important, for there are as many types of Beaujolais as there are producers.

THE CHABLIS REGION

Let us now study the regions of Burgundy in detail, starting in the north and finishing far to the south.

The vines of Chablis go far back in time. They were first widely grown under the Roman occupation. Their home is in the department of Yonne, which takes its name from the river passing through it on its way to Montereau, where it meets the Seine.

The capital of the department is Auxerre, known in the ancient chronicles as Autissiodurum, Autricidurum and Alciodurum, and later Auceure or Aucerre. It is a very ancient town which already existed in the time of the Celts and flourished in Roman times. It was by then a "city"—*civitas Autissiodorum*—and gave its name to a vast region stretching as far as the Loire —the *Pagus Autissodorensis*. Although St. Pilgrim first christianized the inhabitants in the third century, the sixth bishop of the region, St. Germain, who owned vineyards there, contributed equally to the spread of the faith. His youth was eventful and his public life dubious until he was appointed to this important post. At that time he changed suddenly and completely; his conduct became exemplary and he well deserved his eventual canonization. All the while, he carefully tended his extensive vineyards, and though he could not enjoy his wines himself, he unstintingly offered them to his guests who, as an ancient writer records, greatly appreciated them. Together with St. Martin, he was one of the most popular saints.

The wines of the region were then known as the wines of Auxerre. They were red wines and kept their name until the eighteenth century. Meanwhile the wines of Chablis were gaining a reputation of their own. This came through a long-established monastery, founded in 510 by St. Sigismund, and subsequently through a junior branch at the Abbey of Cîteaux, at Pontigny, built in 1114, which created a *clos* (vineyard) like the Clos de Vougeot. Benefiting, as we have seen, from the reputation of the parent branch, it is not surprising that the quality of the wines it produced became known throughout Europe. The vine spread across the whole region and by the twelfth century "the number of presses had to be increased considerably", as the Abbot Leneuf tells us.

It is true that these vineyards had one great advantage; while land transport was difficult because of the vehicles used and the bad condition of the roads, to say nothing of the robbers, brigands and other unsavoury characters so popular at the time, the two waterways of the Yonne and the Saône enabled the wines to reach Paris easily. The capital had "French" wines—that is local wines from the Ile de France—but the better wines were supplied by Auxerre. This enabled production to increase so that by the nineteenth century it was the largest in Burgundy. In 1788, 79,487 acres were under vines; by 1866, 93,235 acres were planted and in 1888, when the phylloxera struck, 100,323 acres were producing wine. The bourgeois and the nobility of Paris also contributed: they liked, as they do today, to have a country residence and vineyards in the region. In 1527, there were an estimated 700 or so. By the end of the sixteenth century, Olivier de Serres could write: "One sees the great towns vacated by presidents, councillors, bourgeois and other notables, who retire to their rustic farms for the wines, preferring to take so much trouble to drink well rather than to drink badly and avoid the discomforts of their rustic seats."

The development of the vineyards was abruptly halted by the invasion of phylloxera at the close of the nineteenth century. At the same time, its once so favourable situation was changed for the worse by progress. The birth of the railways opened up new areas to modern transportation. The completion of the Paris-Marseilles line made it possible to ship the wines of the Midi easily to Paris. The vines of the south grew in better conditions and, in particular, were not threatened by frost. Yields were higher and prices lower in spite of transport costs. The winegrowers of the Yonne, faced with this competition and defeated by the ravages of phylloxera, did not believe expensive restocking to be worthwhile. Almost the only area to be restocked was the Chablis, where the great white wines were grown. That is why, in 1967, the official figures for the Yonne were: 8,542 harvest declarations for 6,973 acres under cultivation—consisting of 3,931 acres for ordinary wine (for everyday consumption) and 3,042 acres for A.O.C. wines; the average production of the latter is 770,000 gallons of which 5 per cent is red.

Chablis is a small town that has preserved many facets of the past. It was once a fortified town but the Porte Noël is almost the last vestige of those times. The town is almost exactly halfway between Auxerre (Route Nationale 6) and Tonnerre (Route Nationale 5) and is divided by the river Serein, which is a tributary of the Yonne.

The importance of the Serein is that it has cut a valley at an altitude of about 450 feet through low hills (the average height of which is 900 feet) on which the Chablis vines grow.

On the right hand bank of the Serein, facing Chablis, grow the vines that produce the great wines sold under the name of CHABLIS GRAND CRU, followed sometimes by the name of the vineyard. There are seven of these vineyards: LES BLANCHOTS, exactly opposite the town near the road going up to Fyé: then, to the north, LES CLOS, VALMUR, GRENOUILLES, VAUDÉSIR, LES PREUSES and BOUGROS. Altogether, these Great Growths produce an average of 18,150 gallons a year on about 112 acres.

Other wines produced are the CHABLIS PREMIER CRU, in scattered vineyards on both sides of the river. The main vineyards entitled to this A.O.C. are on the right bank—with MONT DE MILIEU and MONTÉE DE TONNERRE to the south of the Great Growths and to the north FOURCHAUME, with VAUCOUPIN in the commune of Chichée. On the left bank, we find such names as FORÊTS, MONTMAINS, VAILLONS, MÉLINOTS, CÔTES DE LECHET, BEAUROY and others, and in Chichée, VAUGIRARD and VOSGROS. The average yield of this designation is 148,500 gallons from 680 acres.

The third A.O.C. is CHABLIS, used by various vineyards in the region, still on the same hills as mentioned above. The average production is 141,900 gallons on about 766 acres.

The fourth A.O.C. of the region is PETIT CHABLIS, a name given to white wines grown in a larger area but on quite scattered vines. The average is 68,200 gallons on 300 acres.

If we add all these figures together we have an average production of 376,750 gallons, as against the 770,000 gallons mentioned above. The difference is made up by more general types grown throughout the region—BOURGOGNE (red or white), BOURGOGNE GRAND ORDINAIRE (red or white), BOURGOGNE ALIGOTÉ (white). The same occurs in the other wineproducing communes, especially those of the Côte d'Or.

In sum, the least and the most one can say about the white wines of Chablis is that this name is synonymous, throughout the world, with dry white wine, positive proof of their great fame.

In 1759, Canon Gaudin wrote to Madame d'Epinay: "My Chablis wine has body to it. Its fragrance caresses the throat and leaves a delicate aftertaste of mushrooms." Under the Restoration, the Chevalier de Piis, presiding over an epicurean dinner, sang its praises thus:

> *Qui pourra mettre en oubli*
> *Le limpide et sec CHABLIS*
> *Qui joint à tant d'autres titres,*
> *L'art de faire aimer les huîtres?*

> Who could ever forget
> The clear and dry CHABLIS
> Which adds to its many virtues
> That of inducing a love for oysters?

In the nineteenth century a wine expert called Jules Guyot passed the following judgement: "The wines of Chablis occupy one of the front ranks of the white wines of France. Spirited without the spirit being felt, they have body, subtlety and a delightful fragrance. They are, above all, outstanding for their cleanness and digestibility as well as the stimulating, warming and clear effect on the intellect. Despite their justly deserved reputation of long standing, their real value is, for me, far higher than their fame."

It is scarcely necessary to add further praise after the passages quoted above. Since the last century the white wines of the Chablis region of Burgundy have been irreproachable. It delights all winelovers when drunk with fish and seafoods during the first part of a well-planned meal.

THE CÔTE DE NUITS

We now leave the region of Chablis and turn west. After 22 miles of many different landscapes, in which there are but a few insignificant vineyards, we reach the Côte d'Or and the administrative capital of Burgundy, Dijon. It is a town with many interesting monuments, such as the former palace of the dukes of Burgundy, La Chartreuse de Champmol, the cathedral of St. Benigne, the churches of St. Michael and Our Lady, old buildings, a magnificent fine arts museum etc., but little to do with the great wines of Burgundy. However, there are large manufacturers of liqueurs —including Crême de Cassis, the famous blackcurrant liqueur and such specialities of the town as mustard and gingerbread. In the past there were many vine-

yards around Dijon which formed the "Côte Dijonnaise". But first phylloxera and then the growth of the town itself gradually wiped them out.

Dijon was once reputed for its *vins de garde* (wines worth laying down) that took some little time to "settle down" but that aged well and could be kept for many years. Since the short vinification process has been used, these wines are, like all Burgundies, ready earlier. They develop all their qualities much sooner but must also be drunk much sooner.

In order to visit the Côte de Nuits and the Côte de Beaune, we must head due south along Route Nationale 74 which will take us into Saône-et-Loire and on the way show us all the most famous growths of Upper

Burgundy. This road is about 720 feet above sea level and to the right of Dijon we can see the small hills that overlook the plain from between 450 and 900 feet. Their summits are almost always denuded or covered with Austrian black pine. On their slopes grow the vines that produce the A.O.C. wines, the Route Nationale almost forming their farthest limit. In the plain that continues to the Saône and the Jura grow scattered vineyards producing a number of ordinary wines but not sufficient to supply the needs of the department. Before beginning our visit of the Côte de Nuits, let us look at a few figures. In all the Côte d'Or there are 14,000 acres of vineyards producing an average 4,500,000 gallons of A.O.C. wines and 6,000 acres producing about 3,300,000 gallons of ordinary wines. All these wines are made by 13,000 vintners—which once again goes to show how far the land has been split up and the disadvantages this brings.

THE COMMUNE OF CHENÔVE

This is the first of the winemaking villages to come into view, at the foot of a hill 2 ½ miles from Dijon. Here can be visited the great vineyard of the dukes of Burgundy, which contains two magnificent thirteenth-century presses, one of which, used mainly for white wine, was in use until 1926. The names CLOS-DU-ROI and CLOS-DU-CHAPITRE recall their ancient masters. The A.O.C. wines are sold under regional A.O.C.s.

THE COMMUNE OF MARSANNAY-LA-CÔTE

Two miles farther on, south of Chenôve, lies this commune, famous for its rosé wines. They have become its speciality, since rosé wines are rare in Burgundy where the preference is for great red or white wines, unless catastrophic weather conditions have wiped them out—fortunately a rare occurrence. Rosé wines, obtained by crushing red grapes without vatting them, can only be sold under a regional A.O.C.—BOURGOGNE, for example, followed in the case of Marsannay by the name of the commune.

THE COMMUNE OF FIXIN

This village gives us our first A.O.C. bearing the local name—Fixin. It is an ancient village and was once attached to the abbey of Bèze. Apart from its wines, it is also famous for a statue by the sculptor Rude, *The Awakening of Napoleon*, set up in a park in 1847 by Noisot, the commander of the grenadier guards.

The vineyards of Fixin cover 316 acres. Under this A.O.C. about 50,000 gallons of red wine are made. However, other wine is sold under the more general A.O.C.—CÔTE DE NUITS-VILLAGES and other regional A.O.C.s. In the nineteenth century, the wine experts Danguey and Aubertin wrote as follows about the wines of Fixin: "These wines have a spirit, colour and bouquet that develops with age, as well as a great ability to keep a long time." We might mention in passing the classed First Growths of the commune: LA PERRIÈRE, named after a formerly famous quarry, the CLOS-DU-CHAPITRE, near the old buildings of the Chapter of Langres, LES ARVELETS, the name of which derives from *arbelaie* (place where maples grow), AUX CHEUSOTS, today called the CLOS-NAPOLÉON, LES MEIX-BAS and finally LES HERVELETS.

THE COMMUNE OF BROCHON

This village, about half a mile to the south of Fixin, was famous in former times as the home of Dijon's tragic poet, Prosper Jolyot de Crébillon (1674-1762). It now produces wines of which the best are sold as GEVREY-CHAMBERTIN and others as CÔTE-DE-NUITS-VILLAGES or as regional A.O.C.s. The area under cultivation is 116 acres. Some inexpensive wines are also produced from the *Gamay*, but are not exported.

THE COMMUNE OF GEVREY-CHAMBERTIN

Quite nearby, some eight miles from Dijon, lies the very important wine village of Gevrey, which by royal decree added the name of its best vineyard, Chambertin, to its own in 1847. In the Rue Haute the ruins of a castle belonging to the abbots of Cluny can still be seen. There are a great many vineyards producing a range of very great red wines. Let us consider first of all the Great Growths of which the following first two are the most famous.

CHAMBERTIN-CLOS-DE-BÈZE owes its name to the monks of the abbey of Bèze, who owned this land from the seventh century, through an endowment made by

The imposing château of the Clos-Vougeot lies in the hearth of the famous vineyard. Built in 1551 by the forty-eighth abbot of Cîteaux, Dom Jean Loisir, it was confiscated by the decree of February 13th, 1790, passed through many hands, lay uninhabited for a long time, and was finally rejuvenated in 1944 when it was taken over by the illustrious brotherhood of the Knights of the Tastevin of Burgundy.

Amalgaire, the Duke of Lower Burgundy. The area under cultivation is 37 acres and the average yield of this designation 7,722 gallons.

Immediately next to it lies the vineyard of CHAMBERTIN, named after a vinegrower named Bertin who originally owned land adjacent to that of the monks of Bèze, on which he planted the same wine-stock and produced an excellent wine. It became known locally as the *champ du Bertin* (Bertin's field), and has since become one of the most celebrated wines of Burgundy. Its area is 32 acres and it produces an average of 6,600 gallons. Gaston Roupnel said of this wine: "It blends grace with vigour. It joins firmness to delicacy and subtlety. All these contrary qualities produce in it an admirable synthesis of unique generosity and absolute virtue. It is in itself as great a Burgundy as it is possible to have."

CHARMES-CHAMBERTIN. Part of this vineyard was formerly called Mazoyères-Chambertin. Charmes apparently comes from *chaume* meaning "fallow land". Area—78 acres: Average yield—17,600 gallons.

CHAPELLE-CHAMBERTIN. This vineyard once held a chapel dedicated to Our Lady, built in 1155 and razed to the ground in the time of the French Revolution. Area—13 acres: Average yield—3,200 gallons.

GRIOTTE-CHAMBERTIN. This name signifies either a place planted with cherries (*griottes*), or an area of rock called, in the local dialect, *criot*. Area—13 ½ acres: Average yield—1,540 gallons.

LATRICIÈRES-CHAMBERTIN. Area—17 acres: Average yield—3,520 gallons.

MAZIS-CHAMBERTIN. Area—31 acres: Average yield 4,620 gallons.

RUCHOTTES-CHAMBERTIN. Area—8 acres: Average yield—1,672 gallons.

The difference in quality among these Great Growths is slight. Gaston Roupnel said of these wines, which all add the name Chambertin to their own: "Nothing is more appropriate than this ancient usage. Between Chambertin on one hand and Latricières and Charmes on the other hand, the difference lies in a toning down of vigour and robustness, often compensated for in good years by a more clearly tangible delicateness that is more sensitive, more mature."

Apart from these Great Growths, there are about 171,600 gallons of great red wines entitled to the A.O.C. GEVREY-CHAMBERTIN. Many vineyards are classified as First Growths. These, too, were praised by Gaston Roupnel, who valued highly "these firm, ruddy wines, of full and flavoured body".

This village, 2 ½ miles away from Gevrey-Chambertin, followed somewhat tardily the fashion of the Côte and in 1927 added to its own name that of one of the most famous vineyards. It was, perhaps, commercially a mistake, since Morey is easier to pronounce in every language and therefore a better market prospect.

Its remarkable wines, though relatively little known, were sold as Chambolle-Musigny or Gevrey-Chambertin before the law on A.O.C.s was passed. Nevertheless, among its vineyards are four Great Growths (red), of which the Burgundy expert Dr Ramain said in the last century that they were "powerful nectars, full-bodied, sappy, with their own special savour and a strong fragrance of strawberries or violets". These Great Growths are four in number, although most of one of them, the vineyard of Les Bonnes-Mares, lies in Chambolle-Musigny and will therefore be dealt with under the next heading.

Clos-Saint-Denis. This name was given because the vineyard once belonged to the abbey of St. Denis of Vergy, founded in 1623 by the archdeacon of Autun near Nuits-Saint-Georges. Area—16 acres: Average yield—3,366 gallons.

Clos-de-la-Roche is the near neighbour of the Great Growths of Gevrey-Chambertin. Area—38 acres: Average yield—7,172 gallons.

Clos-de-Tart. This once belonged to the Bernadine nuns of the convent of Our Lady of Tart, which received it in 1260 from the Chevalier Etienne Dojon. During the Revolution it was sold for 68,000 pounds. Area—18 acres: Average yield—3,300 gallons.

Apart from these Great Growths, about 40,000 gallons of Morey-Saint-Denis (including First Growths) are produced, almost all red, of which Danguy and Aubertin gave the following appreciation: "A fine colour, a bouquet developing with age, full-bodied and winy."

THE COMMUNE OF CHAMBOLLE-MUSIGNY

About a mile and a quarter to the south, quite far away from Route Nationale 74 and some three miles from Gevrey-Chambertin, huddled in a coomb, we find the tiny village of Chambolle-Musigny. The name of its most famous vineyard, Musigny, was added to it in 1878. Dr Lavalle, the nineteenth-century writer on Burgundy wines, wrote: "Many people are of the opinion that this commune produces the most delicate wines of the Côte de Nuits". There are two great wines:

Musigny. "The wine of silk and lace, the supreme delicateness of which knows no violence but can veil its vigour", as Gaston Roupnel put it. The name of the vineyard is very ancient; it is already found in an Act of 1110. It produces a few gallons of white wine —quite exceptional in this area and for a Great Growth—about 180 on the average, as against 6,500 for red in a total area of 26 acres.

Les Bonnes-Mares. As we have seen, this vineyard lies partly in Morey-Saint-Denis (4 ½ acres) and partly in Chambolle (34 acres). Its name recalls perhaps the *Maires*, the goddesses who protected the harvests in many ancient nations, or possibly the word *marer*, to plough. An average of 8,580 gallons is produced here.

Apart from these two Great Growths, Chambolle-Musigny has First Growths entitled to the village A.O.C. Danguy and Aubertin said about them: "They have a fine delicate bouquet and several wine experts have said they are the finest, most perfumed and most. delicate in the Côte de Nuits. They are extremely winy, beautifully coloured and pungent." Area—427 acres: Average yield under the Chambolle-Musigny A.O.C. (including First Growths) is 92,664 gallons. The following are some of the First Growth vineyards: Les Amoureuses, Les Charmes, Les Cras, Les Borniques, Les Baudes, Les Hauts-Doix, Derrière-la-Grange, Les Fousselottes, Les Plantes, Les Chatelots, Les Gruenchers, Aux Beaux-Bruns and Aux Combottes.

THE COMMUNE OF VOUGEOT

About half a mile from Chambolle, beside the Route Nationale, lies the smallest village in the Côte but certainly one of the best known throughout the world, especially since the brotherhood of the Knights of the Tastevin began inviting wine-lovers from every country to its "Chapters" held in the château on the property. Apart from these and official guests, representatives of the press, radio, television and cinema —the modern means of communications—are parti-

cularly fond of the place. It is not surprising that its name is on everybody's lips. The Clos-de-Vougeot is "a solemn and beautiful thing, powerful yet not overpowering", said Gaston Roupnel.

The property was first developed by the monks of Cîteaux, early in the twelfth century. There followed a patient task of regrouping, since, apart from endowments, several parcels of land had to be incorporated before it reached its present size of 124 acres.

At first, the monks built a modest chapel, a shelter for their presses and a cellar for their new wines. The wines, when ready, were taken to a safer refuge and better cellars in the Château of Gilly-les-Vougeot, a few miles away in the plain. During the Renaissance, in 1551, the 48th abbot, Dom Jean Loisir, had the château built. It remained the property of Cîteaux until the Revolution, when it was sold as a "national asset". Thus began the subdivisions that only stopped when 65 owners shared the vines and the Brotherhood owned the building.

The wine produced at the Clos-Vougeot, classified as a Great Growth, has always enjoyed the very best of reputations and even received military honours. Stendhal tells us how Colonel Bisson, while passing on his way to join the army on the Rhine, halted his troops and made them present arms before the Clos to the sound of bugles and drums. The Duke of Aumale apparently did the same.

An average of 28,600 gallons of wine with the A.O.C. CLOS-VOUGEOT or, to give it its modern form, CLOS-DE-VOUGEOT A.O.C., is produced yearly. Another nineteenth-century wine-lover, Dr Morelot, defined it as follows: "With ROMANÉE and CHAMBERTIN and a few others, it shares the first position among the wines of the Côte d'Or and even the whole of France."

The commune of Vougeot yields, from just over 30 acres, various other red wines entitled to the VOUGEOT A.O.C., but not to be confused with the Great Growth. The First Growth vineyards are: the CLOS-DE-LA-PERRIÈRE, LES CRAS, LES PETITS-VOUGEOTS and the CLOS-BLANC.

THE COMMUNE OF VOSNE-ROMANÉE

Courtépée wrote in the eighteenth century: "There are no common wines in Vosne." This little village, two miles from Vougeot, has no fewer than seven Great Growths, of which two are produced in the neighbouring commune of Flagey-Echézeaux but are legally linked with Vosne-Romanée.

The name ROMANÉE recalls ancient deeds and perhaps the beginnings of these vineyards during the Roman occupation.

Three different wines carry this name:

LA ROMANÉE. About 550 gallons produced from just over two acres of land.

ROMANÉE-CONTI. This vineyard became the property of the princes of Conti in 1760. So generously did they spread the fame of their "velvet and satin" wine, as Mgr. de Juigné described it, that their name became forever linked to the property. On 4 ½ acres, an average of 1,100 gallons (just over 6,500 bottles) are produced of this wine, which Ramain called "magnificent, with a penetrating bouquet of violets, mingling with a perfume of cherries, the colour of sparkling rubies and an extremely delicate softness". This vineyard was also the last to resist phylloxera. During the last war, however, the shortage of carbon disulphide led to the vine's destruction. New grafted vine-stock had to be planted and the first vintage took place in 1952.

ROMANÉE-SAINT-VIVANT, another vineyard to bear the Romanée name, harks back to the monastery of St. Vivant, founded at the beginning of the tenth century a few miles from Nuits-Saint-Georges (24 acres producing an average 3,650 gallons).

RICHEBOURG is a wine of which Camille Rodier once said: "This splendid growth with its incomparable velvetiness and wealth of bouquet is one of the most sumptuous of Burgundy." Part of its 20 acres belonged to the monks of Cîteaux before the Revolution. Average yield—5,300 gallons.

LA TACHE. With an area of 15 acres this vineyard produces an average 3,740 gallons.

LES GRANDS ECHÉZEAUX and LES ECHÉZEAUX. These vineyards, the south-east neighbours of the Clos-Vougeot, are in the commune of Flagey-Echézeaux. The first—Area 23 acres: Average yield 6,600 gallons. The second—76 acres and 12,100 gallons.

A final appreciation: "Burgundy has produced nothing better than this little corner, which epitomizes its enchantments and whose wines express the tender generosity of its spirit."

THE COMMUNES OF NUITS-SAINT-GEORGES AND PREMEAUX

Nuits-Saint-Georges (Saint-Georges, the name of its best vineyard, was added in 1892) is the little Burgundian village that gave its name to this part of the Côte. Little remains of its past except the church of St. Symphorien, founded in the thirteenth century. But it was here that the Brotherhood of the Knights of the Tastevin was founded by Georges Faiveley and Camille Rodier. The first chapter was held on November 16th, 1934 in the Caveau Nuiton. This soon became too small as success followed success, and today it is the Château of Clos-Vougeot, a more imposing structure, that shelters the hosts and guests at the numerous events organized by the Brotherhood.

Many important wine shippers are to be found at Nuits, together with firms specialized in the manufacture of sparkling Burgundy, of which more than one million bottles are made each year. In 1882, one of the shippers, a much travelled man and long a student of the wines of the region, had the idea of using the Champagne method. The result was a white, a rosé and a red sparkling wine, the latter of which is in particularly great demand in the Nordic countries, Great Britain, the United States and other English-speaking countries. There are also several liqueur manufacturers and two large fruit juice firms in Nuits-Saint-Georges. This all goes to make the town a thriving commercial centre. As Paul Cazin remarked: "The only thing you don't see in Nuits is water."

The two communes in the title of this section produce wines sold under the A.O.C.s of NUITS or NUITS-SAINT-GEORGES (which is the same thing) on an area of 928 acres, averaging 171,600 gallons of red and 660 gallons of white wines.

Dr Lavalle once wrote: "Generally speaking, the wines of Nuits are less firm, less harsh than the wines of Gevrey and mature more quickly. They have more body and colour than those of CHAMBOLLE-MUSIGNY."

Nuits has a civic hospice, founded in 1692. Through the centuries, endowments have led to its possessing considerable property solely in vineyards producing the First Growths of the town. Every year its wines are sold by public auction, usually the Sunday before Palm Sunday. There are fourteen vintages and in 1968, for example, 102 batches were sold in 37 lots.

THE COMMUNES OF PRISSEY, COMBLANCHIEN AND CORGOLOIN

A.O.C. CÔTE DE NUITS-VILLAGES

These three communes are the last of the Côte de Nuits. The last two are mainly famous for their large quarries which yield a stone which is easy to polish and used to cover floors. The wines are partly covered by the A.O.C. CÔTE DE NUITS-VILLAGES.

The wines sold under this A.O.C. do not come from all the villages of the Côte de Nuits, but solely from the following five: Brochon and Fixin, mentioned at the beginning of the chapter; Prissey, Comblanchien and Corgoloin. The more famous A.O.C.s—GEVREY-CHAMBERTIN, MOREY-SAINT-DENIS, CHAMBOLLE-MUSIGNY, VOSNE-ROMANÉE and NUITS-SAINT-GEORGES may never be sold as CÔTE DE NUITS-VILLAGES. The average amount declared under the A.O.C. CÔTE DE NUITS-VILLAGES is 86,592 gallons, all being red wines.

We shall now leave the Côte de Nuits with its very great red wines. Recalling what we said at the beginning of this chapter, our advice is not to let them get too old. René Engel, that reputed wine expert and Grand Cardinal of the Brotherhood of the Knights of the Tastevin, is fond of saying: "Old wines are unfortunately not always the best.... To have very old wines in one's cellar is a little like having a centenarian grandmother in the family. She is proudly presented to the guests, but they must be apologized to in advance in case she has a dewdrop on the end of her nose or if she is only half awake."

THE CÔTE DE BEAUNE

The second part of the great vineyards of the Côte d'Or begins after the stone quarries of Comblanchien.

The wines here are more varied and though there is only one Great Growth, CORTON, among the red wines, all the Great Growths in the white wines are in this area. It used to be said that all the wines of the Côte de Beaune were "early" wines (vins de primeur) as opposed to the "laying down" wines (vins de garde) of the Côte de Nuits. In other words, they could be enjoyed much younger. Today, however, all wines are ready sooner than in the past.

Let us then follow the south-westerly road that leads from Ladoix-Serrigny in the direction of Mâcon as far as Cheilly. Some names are not always well-known, but if one day the wine-lover can spare a few moments to make the acquaintance of these wines he will have some agreeable surprises. As Guy Faiveley, Grand Master of the Brotherhood of the Knights of the Tastevin, once remarked: "There are some wines that are poets, others that are prose-writers. There are those that are performers or lithe acrobats and others that are overpowering boxers."

THE COMMUNE OF LADOIX-SERRIGNY

This winegrowing commune produces red and white wines sold under various A.O.C.s including CORTON. The area under vine is 335 acres. The reds are sold, apart from under the appellation CORTON—which is the only red Great Growth of the Côte de Beaune—mostly as CÔTE DE BEAUNE-VILLAGES. There is an average yield of about 1,100 gallons of white wine and 26,400 gallons of red sold as LADOIX.

Aloxe is a pretty village on a small hillock. In 1862, the name of its most famous vineyard was added to it. Throughout the ages, it has been graced by the exalted. The Emperor Charlemagne owned many *ouvrées* (about one-ninth of an acre) of vineyards. The Emperor Otho was also an owner: he seems to have given his name to CORTON—the *curtis* ("estate" or "garden") *Othonis* ("of Otho"). The large abbeys, including Cîteaux, possessed land in this corner of Burgundy. Two Great Growths are produced here. CORTON was mentioned by Voltaire when writing to Gabriel le Bault, president of the Parliament of Burgundy: "The older I become, Sir, the more I value your kindness. Your excellent wine is becoming indispensable to me." Especially as he did not want to pay for it ! The dukes of Burgundy and later the kings of

Founded in 1443 by Nicolas Rolin, chancellor to Philip the Good, the Hôtel-Dieu in Beaune is an architectural jewel of Burgundy. Together with the Hospice de la Charité, it makes up the illustrious group of the "Hospices de Beaune". Their vineyards, increased throughout the centuries by endowments, now cover 130 acres. Every November the traditional sale of their wines takes place, the proceeds being used to maintain the institutions.

France owned 110 *ouvrées* (about 12 acres) of one of the vineyards in this A.O.C. It is still called *Le Clos du Roy*, "the king's vineyard". CORTON produces about 52,800 gallons of red and 1,460 gallons of white wine. "The CORTONS of good years are perfect wines, worthy of the most delicate gourmet's table," said Dr Lavalle.

The second Great Growth is CORTON-CHARLEMAGNE, a white wine, the name obviously recalling the Emperor Charlemagne. He loved the region and made numer-ous gifts to the churches in the province, especially those of St. Vincent at Chalon-sur-Saône, Saulieu and other places. The annual yield averages 17,600 gallons, of which Camille Rodier said: "A white wine of great bearing, rich in alcohol, forceful, golden, sappy, smelling of cinnamon and tasting of gun flint."

Aloxe-Corton produces an average of 77,000 gallons sold under its name, 99 per cent of the yield being red. Dr Lavalle said of them in the last century: "They are the firmest and frankest wines of the Côte de Beaune."

THE COMMUNE OF PERNAND-VERGELESSES

Behind the Aloxe hillock, at the bottom of a coomb in a very pretty setting, the village of Pernand-Vergelesses produces part of the CORTON and CORTON-CHARLEMAGNE wines. As well as the CORTON, red wines are sold under the village name or as CÔTE DE BEAUNE-VILLAGES. There are 3,256 gallons of white and 27,940 gallons of red wine produced on 353 acres. Danguy and Aubertin wrote: "These wines are a little firmer than those of Savigny: they have fire and strength and are worth laying down."

THE COMMUNE OF SAVIGNY-LÈS-BEAUNE

Away from the Côte and at the mouth of a deep valley lies this ancient village which, for a very long time, was the home of important wine shippers. In more recent times they have tended to pass over Savigny in favour of Beaune and Nuits, but this village is still quite busy, for its wines are famous. Under the SAVIGNY A.O.C., 5,390 gallons of white and 125,400 gallons of red wines are produced. Camille Rodier said of them: "These perfumed, mellow, young and healthy wines are rich in bouquet."

THE COMMUNE OF CHOREY-LÈS-BEAUNE

Facing Savigny from the other side of Route Natio-nale 74 is Chorey-lès-Beaune. Its 300 or so acres produce 33,000 gallons of red wine sold under the village name or under the name of CÔTE DE BEAUNE-VILLAGES. In 1828, Dr Morelot wrote: "The good Chorey wines are used when the best quality wines are passing through a bad period. They improve them and make them agreeable to drink."

THE COMMUNE OF BEAUNE

Beaune, which has given its name to this part of the Côte since the Roman occupation, is the real capital of Burgundy. Its life is centred around the disposal of fine wines. Over sixty shippers use the numerous cellars which through the centuries were dug into its ramparts. Convents, churches and abbeys in the town and surrounding area have also used them to keep their wines well protected. Many lords have had the same idea, not to mention the militant religious orders.

The imposing bastions that rise from the ramparts and are visible from a great distance, have been and still are used to store the bottles and barrels in the deep shelter of their seven-yard thick walls. For this very reason, the shippers' installations are extremely inter-esting to visit, as the tourists know full well. Beaune is, therefore, an extremely ancient town still almost completely surrounded by walls which guard the many historical monuments—the Basilica of Our Lady, the ancient church of St. Nicolas, the palace of the dukes of Burgundy, which has been made into a wine museum that no enthusiast should miss, the belfrey, the old houses, etc., and towering above the rest, the *Hôtel-Dieu*, a marvel of the fifteenth century. It was founded in 1443 by Nicolas Rolin, then chancellor to Philip the Good, Duke of Burgundy, and his wife, Guigone de Salins, to aid the destitute. It has managed to con-tinue its ancient role, a rare achievement. The "ladies of charity" still go from room to room caring for and comforting the sick, as they have done uninterruptedly for nearly five and a half centuries. Although the old hospital now has a modern neighbour, it has not suffered as a result. Its own life flourishes, as can be attested by the tens of thousands of tourists who visit it every year. Over the centuries, many donations have been made to the *Hôtel-Dieu* and the *Hospice de la Charité*, which are kept under joint management. Some

125 acres of vineyards have gradually accumulated to the estate of the Hospice de Beaune: in Corton-Charlemagne and Meursault for white wines and in Aloxe-Corton, Auxey-Duresses, Beaune, Corton, Monthelie, Pommard, Savigny and Volnay for red wines. The auctioning of the Hospice's wines on the third Sunday in November is renowned throughout the world as being "the world's greatest charity sale". And it is a fact that it enables the work of Nicolas Rolin to be continued year after year in support of the old and sick and the needy. In 1966, 752 casks brought to the estate 2,312,033 new French francs.

The vineyards of Beaune cover a large area: 1,329 acres are contained within the area allowed to sell wines under this designation. The average yield is 196,900 gallons, of which 95 per cent is red. Dr Lavalle, the famous wine expert of the last century,

whom we have already quoted, gave this appreciation of them: "I think that the great wines of Beaune are worthy of the greatest praise. The best vintages, in good years, reach a point at which they cannot be distinguished from the most outstanding wines, except by well-practised experts; and are more often than not they are sold at the highest prices. The second best vintages are the everyday wines of princes."

The vineyards of Beaune that give the best wines are: LES MARCONNETS, LES FÈVES, LES BRESSANDES, LES GRÈVES, LES TEURONS, LE CLOS-DES-MOUCHES, LE CLOS-DU-ROI, LES AVAUX, LES TOUSSAINTS, LES BOUCHEROTTES, LES VIGNES-FRANCHES, LES AIGROTS etc.: there are too many to mention them all.

A look around the cellars and a visit to the Hôtel-Dieu is the normal programme of more than 300,000 tourists who visit Beaune every year.

THE COMMUNE OF POMMARD

Who does not know the name of this village two miles south of Beaune? Nevertheless, to reach it you must leave Route Nationale 74 and take Route Nationale 73 towards Autun, passing through several miles of vineyards.

Pommard, a name easy to pronounce in any language, was for this very reason long a synonym for the wines of the Côte de Beaune. The law on A.O.C.s

restricted the use of its name to those wines produced on the 838 acres in the commune. Many wines from neighbouring villages were affected by this measure, since they lost a traditional and easy marketing channel. About 209,000 gallons of "firm, ruddy, frank and long-lasting wines", to quote Dr Morelot, are now produced under the POMMARD A.O.C. These wines were steady favourites of the great lords and abbeys.

THE COMMUNE OF VOLNAY

En dépit de Pommard et de Meursault,
C'est toujours Volnay le plus haut.

In spite of Pommard and Meursault,
It's still Volnay that's the highest.

This Burgundy saying does not refer to the relative qualities of the wines but to the geographical situations of these villages, with Volnay on top of the hill above its vineyards and Meursault and Pommard below.

On an area of 530 acres are produced an average of 135,850 gallons, all of red wine. The wines of Volnay are qualified by Camille Rodier as being "less ruddy than BEAUNE or Pommard, noted especially for their elegance, smooth taste, perfect balance and quite delicate bouquet. After MUSIGNY, they are the finest wines in all Burgundy." It should be noted that VOLNAY-CAILLERETS are produced in Meursault.

THE COMMUNE OF MONTHELIE

A mile and a half from Volnay, with its back to the Côte, this village is made picturesque by its ancient houses that rise like steps up the hill. Its vines grow on a little over 230 acres which produce an average 880 gal-

lons of white wine and 30,800 gallons of red. A technical advisor to the I.N.A.O. (National Institute for Designations of Origin) had expressed the opinion that these wines are not as well known as they ought to be.

THE COMMUNE OF AUXEY-DURESSES

At the foot of Monthelie, deep in a large valley, lies the little village of Auxey-Duresses. The area was much frequented by the Gauls, who built a camp on the mountain overlooking the countryside. On about 370 acres under the village name an average of 16,170 gallons of white wine and 30,800 gallons of red

are produced. The red wines are *forts gravains*, meaning not lacking in colour, body or bouquet. Pierre Léon Gauthier wrote: "On the vines of Duresses ripens a wine that was long sold under the VOLNAY and POMMARD labels—this was before A.O.C.s—without any detriment to the good name of those great wines."

THE COMMUNE OF SAINT-ROMAIN

At the foot of the magnificent cliffs that surround the valley of Auxey-Duresses the houses of Saint-Romain climb like stepping stones up the slope. The village once possessed a castle, the ruins of which are still to be seen. Now its 358 acres produce an average 10,780 gallons of white wine and 46,922 gallons of red under the village name. Roland Thévenin, poet and mayor of the village, sang its praises thus:

> *O SAINT-ROMAIN hardi, robuste et si fruité,*
> *Nous aimons ta fraîcheur ainsi que ta finesse.*
>
> O SAINT-ROMAIN, forthright, robust and so fruity,
> We love your freshness and delicacy.

THE COMMUNE OF MEURSAULT

We now return to the Côte, to the little town of Meursault which covers the entry to the valley leading to Auxerre. It was probably the first place occupied by the Romans when they penetrated this region. The vineyards of Meursault cover 1,030 acres and have always been famous for their white wines. For four miles the soil becomes quite unlike that of Beaune or Volnay, and the *Chardonnay* grape is king. There are some 9,200 gallons of red wine produced here but the 209,000 gallons of white wine are better known by far. Camille Rodier wrote: "MEURSAULT white wines have the following special characteristic—they are both dry and mellow, which is quite unusual. They are rich in alcohol, a beautiful golden green in colour, bright and clear, they keep well and have the frank taste of ripe grapes and a touch of hazelnut. They are among the most famous white wines of France."

Meursault is also famous for its *Paulée*, which takes up the last of the Three Glorious Days devoted to the wines of Burgundy. The *Paulée* was created in 1923 by Count Lafon and is the official dinner closing the vintage. It is given by the vineyard owners for all those who worked in the vintage with them. Nowadays, about four hundred persons attend this joyous banquet, which is not too official, since custom has it that everyone brings a bottle of his greatest and rarest wine to pass around the table—and that does not tend to dampen the celebrations !

THE COMMUNES OF PULIGNY-MONTRACHET AND CHASSAGNE-MONTRACHET

At the northern end of the Côte d'Or, in the commune of Gevrey-Chambertin and the neighbouring villages are the Very Great Growths of red wines. In the south, we find the Great Growths of white wines. Puligny-Montrachet, like the Côte de Meursault, produces almost nothing but white wines. There are five Great Growths in this region which we shall describe in descending order of merit.

MONTRACHET sits astride two communes: two-thirds in Puligny and one-third in Chassagne. Both added its name to theirs towards the end of the nineteenth century. In 1878, Bertall wrote: "this admirable white wine is the first among the white wines of Burgundy, as CHÂTEAU-YQUEM is the first among the white wines of Bordeaux. Let us not compare the two, say enthusiasts, let us merely say that they are both the first among the white wines of the world." This goes hand in hand with Dr Lavalle's comment in 1855: "The wine of Montrachet must be considered as one of those marvels whose perfection can only be appreciated by a small number of the elect." Only 20,000 or so bottles are produced annually on an area of 18 ½ acres. There is very little true Montrachet and the enthusiast must be careful not to confuse it with all the other wines that include the word Montrachet in their A.O.C.s.

CHEVALIER-MONTRACHET is geographically just above MONTRACHET and is about the same size. The wine can be drunk a little earlier than its neighbour, but it rarely attains the same perfection. It is, therefore, classified just below MONTRACHET. The average yield is 2,662 gallons or about 15,000 bottles.

BÂTARD-MONTRACHET grows on 29 acres just below Montrachet; the two are separated by a path. The vineyard sits astride Puligny and Chassagne and produces an average 6,710 gallons.

BIENVENUE-BÂTARD-MONTRACHET (Area—5 ½ acres, average yield—2,046 gallons) and CRIOTS-BÂTARD-MONTRACHET, situated in Chassagne, producing an average 880 gallons, are the last of the Great Growths of white wines.

The origin of these names is often debated. One story, which we summarize here although we cannot guarantee its authenticity, has it that during the Crusades, the governor of the castle of Montrachet had a son who departed for the Holy Land. Meanwhile, the old lord was bored at the castle and took to passing near the Clos des Pucelles, where the young maidens of the region disported themselves. The Devil tempted him and nine months later a blessed event took place. The Duke of Burgundy, who was not amused, decreed

The name Corton Charlemagne recalls the ownership of the Emperor, who once held many acres here. And Corton is a reminder of another Emperor—Otho, for the name is said to have come from *Cortis Othonis*—the garden of Otho.

The pretty village of Aloxe-Corton nestles on the slopes of a wooded hillock overlooking the road from Beaune to Dijon. The name Corton was added to the village name of Aloxe to honour the only red Great Growth of the Côte de Beaune.

Meursault stands at the entry of the valley leading to Auxerre, and is, of course, famous for its delicious dry and mellow white wines. It is also known for its *Paulée*, the vintage dinner.

that in the line of the Montrachets, the old lord was henceforth to be known as Montrachet the Elder, the Crusader as the Chevalier Montrachet and the child as the Bâtard Montrachet. The crusader was killed in battle so the bastard inherited and was welcomed at the castle with cries of "welcome to the bastard of Montrachet". But the lord, already an old man, could not bear to hear the baby crying and protested in patois: *a crio l'Bâtard* (the bastard is crying). When the castle was destroyed, these names were given to the vineyards in their memory.

Puligny-Montrachet produces 73,480 gallons of white and 5,830 gallons of red wine on nearly 580 acres under the village name. Camille Rodier says of them: "These fruity, distinguished and sweet-smelling white wines are related to the better MEURSAULTS." And, in fact, LES CAILLERETS, LES COMBETTES, LES PUCELLES, LES FOLATIÈRES, etc. are very distinguished wines.

Chassagne-Montrachet produces much more red wine than Puligny, averaging 924,000 gallons. These are among the best on the Côte. Camille Rodier had no hesitation in saying: "The red CHASSAGNES are undeniably like certain good vintages of the Côte de Nuits." There is also a good deal of white wine—53,900 gallons on average, resembling all the others produced on this part of the Côte, relatively dry and extremely subtle.

THE COMMUNE OF SAINT-AUBIN

Just behind Chassagne, towards Paris on Route Nationale 6, we cross this little winegrowing village whose area under vine is about 300 acres. Under its name, or more generally under the appellation CÔTE DE BEAUNE-VILLAGES, an average of 12,760 gallons of white and 19,140 gallons of red wine are produced. The hamlet of Gamay, where the vine of the same name was born, is part of Saint-Aubin.

THE COMMUNE OF SANTENAY

Santenay is the last winegrowing commune of the Côte d'Or. It has been inhabited since time immemorial and its grottoes contain many traces of their neolithic and iron-age inhabitants. Although a wine village, Santenay has distinguished itself further by possessing, of all things a mineral water spring! The villagers tend to avoid it, however, and leave it to the "city folk" to enjoy. The 939 acres under vine produce, under the SANTENAY label, an average 83,400 gallons of red and only 2,200 gallons of white wines. Minimum alcohol content for the red wines is 10.5° and for the white wines 11°. Dr Lavalle describes these wines as follows: "They are firm, mellow and always keep well. With age, they acquire a very delicate bouquet." The best are from the *climat* of Les Gravière, the only one in the commune with a *tête de cuvée* classification. Some wines are blended with those of other communes and sold under the A.O.C. CÔTE DE BEAUNE-VILLAGES.

THE COMMUNES OF CHEILLY, DEZIZE AND SAMPIGNY-LES-MARANGES

After the Côte d'Or, we enter Saône-et-Loire through these villages. As their vineyards are next to Santenay, they are included in the Côte de Beaune, but are sold either under their own names or under the A.O.C., CÔTE DE BEAUNE-VILLAGES. The area under vine is about 300 acres in Cheilly, 100 acres in Dezize and 150 acres in Sampigny-les-Maranges. Very little wine is declared under this appellation and the villages are producing an average of 4,500 gallons, 2,600 gallons and 2,500 gallons of red wine respectively.

THE CÔTE DE BEAUNE-VILLAGES A.O.C.

This is an A.O.C. that is used a great deal and that is well-known to consumers. The preceding tour of the Côte de Beaune villages reveals many names that are not familiar to the wine-buying public. The CÔTE DE BEAUNE-VILLAGES appellation allows these lesser known villages to come together under the same title, thus avoiding any difficulties they might otherwise have in selling their excellent wines. (They nevertheless retain the right to produce wines under their own names if they wish to do so.) CÔTE DE BEAUNE-VILLAGES always indicates a red wine, and comes from the villages or parts of the villages in the following list: Auxey-Duresses, Chassagne-Montrachet, Cheilly-lès-Maranges, Chorey-lès-Beaune, Côte de Beaune, Dezize-lès-Maranges, Ladoix-Serrigny, Meursault rouge, Meursault-Blagny, Monthelie, Pernand-Vergelesses, Puligny-Montrachet, St-Aubin, Sampigny-lès-Maranges, Santenay, Savigny.

THE REGION OF MERCUREY

We now leave the Côte d'Or for Saône-et-Loire, but, in a sense, we are still in the Côte de Beaune of which Mercurey is traditionally a continuation through its methods of cultivation and vinification, the character of its wines and its trading customs.

These vineyards were named the Côte Chalonnaise after the town of Chalon-sur-Saône, a busy trading centre in the first few centuries of our era since it was well situated for both land and river transport. At a later date, it became an important wine centre for the region, but this has gradually been eroded by industry, which is now master of the town.

We shall travel from north to south in dealing with the four A.O.C.s in the region—RULLY, MERCUREY, GIVRY and MONTAGNY.

RULLY. This is an ancient village, 14 miles from Beaune, near Chagny and Route Nationale 6. It dates back to Roman times. Its caves were even inhabited during the stone ages. It was originally on the hill, but the plague of 1347 forced the inhabitants to resettle farther down. The village still has a thirteenth-century feudal castle, which was altered in the fifteenth century.

The vineyards of the RULLY A.O.C. give 18,832 gallons of white wine and 5,170 gallons of red. This white wine is very individualistic, heady and perfumed and lending itself to the Champagne method. It was the original reason for the considerable trade in sparkling Burgundy wines which developed in this village.

MERCUREY. The wines permitted to use this A.O.C. are produced in a large vineyard situated within several communes. Mercurey is reminiscent of the Roman occupation through its very name; Saint-Martin-sous-Montagne is one of the many villages named after the most popular saint in Burgundy; and finally, across the Orboise River from Mercurey, there is Bourgneuf-Val-d'Or. These wines are in all respects similar to those of the Côte de Beaune. "They differ from the Santenays only by an imperceptible degree," said Claude Bonvin. A. Jullien wrote: "The red wines of Mercurey are distinguished by their perfume: they are honest and may be kept for a long time." The average yield is 220,000 gallons of reds and 15,000 of whites. The First Growths take the names of the five following vineyards: CLOS-DU-ROY, CLOS-VOYEN, CLOS-MARCILLY, CLOS-DES-FOURNEAUX, CLOS-DES-MONTAIGUS.

GIVRY. The ancient township of this name goes back to Gallo-Roman times. It produces, in its confines, the wines allowed to use this A.O.C. Once upon a time they were in great demand, but since the law on A.O.C.s, few enthusiasts have heard their name—a great pity. In the nineteenth century, A. Jullien said that the privileged growths of this commune were superior to those of Mercurey. Frank, strong and perfumed, they are the wines of connoisseurs. Nowadays, the average yield under the GIVRY name is 30,470 gallons of red wine and 4,840 gallons of white.

MONTAGNY. The wines sold under this A.O.C. come from the communes of Montagny, Buxy, Saint-Vallerin and Jully-les-Buxy, with a total area of 754 acres producing 51,150 gallons of white wine alone. It is said they "keep the mouth clean and the head clear".

THE MÂCONNAIS

This is the most important wine area of the Saône-et Loire, taking its name from its capital. Mâcon, "the queen of the Saône", is called thus because it lies beside a magnificent stretch of water, which makes it a metropolis for boat lovers as well. Known in Roman times as *Matisco in Aeduis*, the city was part of the Eduens, the same Gallic province as the future Côte d'Or. The town was important in Roman times. It possessed grain stores and a factory producing arrows and javelins "because the wood in the region was excellent for the purpose". At that time, it was built at the foot of the Roman Castrum, but gradually the city slipped down towards the Saône, especially after being devastated by the Barbarians in the fifth century and the Saracens in the eighth. It still possesses many Gothic and Renaissance remains, including a famous wooden house and various aristocratic residences of the eighteenth century.

The Mâconnais is, therefore, a very ancient region, with magnificent vineyards and remarkable Romanesque churches in many of its tiny villages. There were more vineyards before the phylloxera plague than today. In the north of the region, for example, lies Tournus, a very ancient town with the famous Romanesque church of St. Philibert and some very old houses. The vineyards surrounding it were mentioned by the poet Ausonus and were increased in size by the abbey of Cluny. It was even said that "Tournus produced a *Pinot* wine at the end of the sixteenth century as good as the most famous." However, there remain today but a few scattered vineyards producing mainly white wines. One must go down to the south of the Mâconnais to find a very important vineyard at the foot of a hill, where, according to Lamartine "the autumn grapes distill their balmy liqueur". Lamartine considered himself "a vintner rather than a poet" and his memory is kept all along the "Circuit Lamartinien", through Milly-Lamartine where he lived as a child, the château of Monceau, one of his favourite residences, and the château of Pierreclos, home of Marguerite, the Laurence of his *Jocelyn*. This area contains the various A.O.C.s we are about to look at.

POUILLY-FUISSÉ. The white wine sold under this A.O.C. is too well known throughout the world to need a lengthy description. It comes from the communes of Pouilly, Fuissé, Solutré, Vergisson and Chaintré. This region is easy to locate because of the two spurs of rock that stick up like saw teeth at Vergisson and Solutré. At the foot of the latter lies the prehistoric site after which the Solutrian epoch of paleology was named. A large number of human skeletons and the bones of thousands of horses have been found there. The view from the top of these rocks is magnificent, with vineyards surrounding them on all sides and stretching, to the east, as far as Mâcon and the Beaujolais on the horizon. POUILLY-FUISSÉ charms the eye before the palate. Its colour is golden shot with emerald: it is as vigorous as the greatest growths of Burgundy; its thoroughbred delicacy is perfumed with a particularly delightful bouquet. An average 462,000 gallons of this wine are produced.

POUILLY-VINZELLES and POUILLY-LOCHÉ. These two A.O.C.s, also applicable to white wines, are different from the previous ones. POUILLY-LOCHÉ may be called POUILLY-VINZELLES but not vice versa. The vineyards are near those of POUILLY-FUISSÉ and the quantity is very similar, but not much is produced under these two A.O.C.s—33,000 gallons of POUILLY-VINZELLES and only 11,000 of POUILLY-LOCHÉ.

MÂCON. The vineyards of the Mâconnais are too extensive to permit giving all the details of the various A.O.C.s. Some villages have been singled out and are allowed to append their names to the word Mâcon (these are white wines) or are allowed to sell their wines as MÂCON-VILLAGES.

The difference between MÂCON SUPÉRIEUR and MÂCON white wines is mainly a matter of yield per acre and minimum alcoholic strength. As for the red and rosé wines, usually made from the *Gamay* grape, some villages may append their names to Mâcon, but their wines may never be sold as MÂCON-VILLAGES, which is strictly for white wines. These Mâconnais wines hold an important position in the Burgundy wine selection. White wines that may be sold as MÂCON-VILLAGES or MÂCON SUPÉRIEUR are often sold as BOURGOGNE BLANC and have a worldwide reputation under this general A.O.C. The red wines, without claiming the qualities of the Côte d'Or wines, honourably fulfil their role as the vanguard of the fine wines of Burgundy. They are quite full-bodied and agreeably fruity early wines, to be drunk young but unlikely to turn vinagery even if kept for a long time.

THE BEAUJOLAIS

We are now in the south of Burgundy, in this great and beautiful vineyard of the Rhône department whose northern tip overlaps the Saône-et-Loire department.

The region gets its name from the château of Beaujeu, built in the middle of the ninth century and very important under the first family of the house of Beaujeu until 1265. One of the lords, Humbert III, built a new village in 1110 nearer the Saône, then the major artery of communications. He little realized that the new village, Villefranche, would gradually assume the position and influence of Beaujeu in the management of the affairs of the Beaujolais until, in 1532, it became the capital of the region.

The province, at first a buffer state between the Mâconnais and the Lyonnais, was later joined to the kingdom of France, where it remained until 1560. Then it fell into the hands of the Bourbon-Montpensiers and still later, in 1626, into the hands of the Orleans family.

The revolutions of 1789, 1830 and 1848 passed almost unnoticed in the Beaujolais, which throughout its existence has known events of greater local impact —invasions, pillages, famines and plagues. In 1790, the province was integrated into the newly created departments—first Rhône-Loire, then Rhône from November 1793 when Lyons, its capital, revolted against the Convention.

The present vineyards, 32 miles long and between seven and ten miles wide, have 37,065 acres of fine wines, reaching an altitude of over 1,600 feet towards the Monts-du-Beaujolais that crowd the western horizon. To the east, Route Nationale 6, following the Saône at several hundred yards distance, marks the far boundary of the vineyards. It is necessary for the traveller to leave the main road if he wants to further his acquaintance with this beautiful region. The vineyards of the Beaujolais were not always admired as they are today. Their history and development are quite unlike those of the other regions of Burgundy. Although some names are indubitably Roman in origin—Jullié, Juliénas, Romanèche, for example—the first document known to speak of vineyards, the Cartulary of St. Vincent, goes back to the end of the tenth century. The next is of a vineyard at Brulliez, now called Brouilly, mentioned in an endowment made in 1160. Another ancient document referring to the existence of vines tells of a canon of Lyon, Odon Rigaud, who, in 1282, gave his cathedral church a great bell called the "Rigaud" and a vine, the produce of which was to be kept for the persons who rang the bell. This is the origin of the expression, well known throughout Burgundy, "to drink by ringing the Rigaud" or "to drink like a bell-ringer".

The wines of Beaujolais were originally used to quench the thirst of Lyons. Even now there is still a saying that three rivers flow into the town—the Rhône, the Saône and the Beaujolais. They were very often in competition with the vintners of the Mâconnais, who had to pay extremely high duties before their produce was allowed into the town.

Furthermore, since the Beaujolais is not part of the duchy of Burgundy, its wines could not be sold there. An ordinance of 1446 stated that in Dijon "provisions may include the wines of Tournus, the Chalonnais and the Beaunois and this side of the mountains as far as Messigny, but not those of the lowlands such as the Lyonnais, the Viennois, Tournon and other places".

It was purely by chance that the wines of the Beaujolais, towards the seventeenth century, became known outside their own area. Some merchants from the Lorraine, while in Mâcon, tasted some wines unknown to them. They were taken to where they were produced and bought several cellars. The news was heard by two other shippers, this time from Paris, and business rapidly expanded between the Beaujolais and the French capital.

However, when it came to taking the wines to the north the means of transport were found to be all but non-existent. The opening of the Briare canal made it easier to reach Paris via the Monts-du-Beaujolais and the Loire—a very important event for the wines of the Mâconnais as well, since they also benefited.

After the royal edict of 1776, which at Turgot's instigation established unrestricted transport and trade of wines throughout the kingdom, the difficulties of transporting the wines of the Mâconnais and especially those of the Beaujolais diminished and the region really began its rapid development. During the nineteenth century, the Beaujolais became more and more a part of Burgundy and through its constant development the first among the Burgundian vineyards.

The region is traditionally divided into two halves, Lower and Upper Beaujolais, which are no more than geographical terms. Taken as a whole, they look like a great expanse of hills and dales descending from west to east, which offer every variety of exposure to the sun. The region is scattered with a great number of isolated vineyards, often featuring the very beautiful houses of the masters or small châteaux and their outhouses, the historical successors to the Roman *villae*. The tiny villages are also very scattered. The overall effect of the setting, the scattered villages and the variety of exposures of the soil is quite unusual and extremely pleasant.

Lower Burgundy begins about 12 miles from Lyons, just before Saint-Jean-des-Vignes, an evocative name. It continues to the north through the districts of Anse, the Bois-d'Oingt and Villefranche-sur-Saône. It includes very many villages and a beautiful landscape of vines, fields and woods, varying according to the altitude and exposure. It produces what is called *vins de comptoir*—over the counter wines sold in the bars of the Lyonnais to refresh the thirsty and tired citizens. They are doubtless less delicate and less complete than their northern neighbours, but then they are modest wines and lay no claims to perfection.

Upper Beaujolais consists of the districts of Belleville-sur-Saône and Beaujeu in the Rhône department, and La Chapelle-de-Guinchay canton to the south in the Saône-et-Loire. It would be very much worth the unhurried tourist's while to spend a few hours looking around the area. There are two well-signposted routes—the quick route, marked by red signposts which will take him from Villefranche to Crèches-sur-Saône, almost missing the hills but passing through all the "growths" of the Beaujolais; or the tourist route, mapped out in green, which is very much to be recommended. When you reach Beaujeu, you are well advised to leave it and take departmental road 136 up through spectacular scenery and remarkable views of the whole region. Then come down the Fût-d'Avenas Pass with its panoramic observation platform. On a clear day the view embraces a good deal of the Beaujolais and the Saône plain right up to the Jura and the Alps. We can guarantee that none who tries it will regret this detour, which enables the traveller to get a better idea of the size and variety of this district.

In the Upper and Lower Beaujolais, the wines are permitted to use three A.O.C.s—Beaujolais, Beaujolais-Supérieur and Beaujolais-Villages. There are, further, nine "growths". They are almost entirely red wines, since the 55,000 gallons of white Beaujolais amounts to 0.4 per cent of the total average yield and are, in fact, produced in vineyards that border on the white Mâcon area.

BEAUJOLAIS is the basic A.O.C. and the difference between it and BEAUJOLAIS-SUPÉRIEUR is the minimum alcoholic content which is a degree higher for the latter. The average yield for both A.O.C.s, 7,480,000 gallons, is as vast as is the area under production.

Victor Rendu wrote that: "The fine and almost fine Beaujolais wines are delicate, light and sappy. Though they are not so rich in bouquet as the great wines of Upper Burgundy, they do not lack fragrance. They are, in general, not deeply coloured; or, to be more accurate, they settle quickly and come rapidly to maturity. Precociousness is one of their main features."

Let us say, then, that the Beaujolais is a good unpretentious wine to be drunk with friends, their full glasses clinking merrily in the bar or wine cellar but always far from any formal occasion. It fosters sudden friendships because it is a wine that inspires those who appreciate its intrinsic qualities—friendliness, tenderness and generosity.

The wines that may use the A.O.C. BEAUJOLAIS-VILLAGES come from 28 wine communes in the Rhône department and eight in the Saône-et-Loire: Juliénas, Jullié, Emeringes, Chénas, Fleurie, Chiroubles, Lancié, Villié-Morgon, Lantigné, Beaujeu, Régnié, Durette, Cercié, Quincié, Saint-Lager, Odenas, Charentay, Saint-Etienne-la-Varenne, Vaux, Le Perréon, Saint-Etienne-des-Oullières, Rivolet, Arbuissonnas, Salles, Saint-Julien, Montmelas, Blacé and Denicé in the Rhône; and Leynes, Saint-Amour-Bellevue, La Chapelle-de-Guinchay, Romanèche, Pruzilly, Chânes, Saint-Vérand and Saint-Symphorien-d'Ancelles in the Saône-et-Loire. These wines may also be sold under their own names, often tacked on to the word BEAUJOLAIS.

From this list we should mention Vaux, not so much for its excellent wines as for the reputation it has gained through the second name given it by the writer Gabriel Chevalier—Clochemerle.

The average yield under this A.O.C. is 3,300,000 gallons. Louis Orizet, the poet of the region, wrote: "BEAUJOLAIS-VILLAGES, we love you because you are not quite great. If you were we would have to wait many months to drink you, which would be a pity. . . . A boon to the mistress of every household, a Beaujolais goes with all sauces. . . . It has that rare privilege for a red wine—to be drunk cool. . . ." The late Georges Rozet, historiographer of the Brotherhood of the Knights of the Tastevin, wrote: "They do not overwhelm the drinker and their basic quality is their smoothness. They are soft, fruity, tasty, inviting, etc. . . . There is no end to the list of adjectives used to define them. I should like to see them placed in three columns like litanies, like the flowing epithets that poured once upon a time from the inexhaustible pen of the creator of Pantagruel."

BEAUJOLAIS-VILLAGES is an extremely agreeable wine and, at a modest price, will accompany any dish without disappointing. It will not be browbeaten by strong dishes and, in spite of everything, always manages to guard its own flavour intact. It need not be drunk by the thimbleful either. "Let me refill your glass" was the watchword of the inn-keepers of yore when they saw their customers' glasses rapidly emptying. One can do that with this wine and still abide by the rule of Burgundy: Drink well (never let a wine unworthy of you pass your lips) and to your own measure (never drink too much—it is inadvisable and nothing to be proud of).

Since we have to begin somewhere, let us begin our discussion of the nine "growths" of the Beaujolais from the southernmost of these—it would be too difficult to classify them by quality.

BROUILLY and CÔTE-DE-BROUILLY. At about the level of Belleville-sur-Saône, 5 miles towards the hills from this town, the Mont-Brouilly reaches up to an altitude of some 1,300 feet. On top is a chapel, built in 1857, which can be seen from anywhere in the region and is a place of pilgrimage for the winemakers. The wines using the BROUILLY A.O.C. are produced in six communes huddled around the hill. The average production is 792,000 gallons on about 2,000 acres of land. BROUILLY is typical of Beaujolais wines—halfway between the light wines and the Great Growths. It loses nothing by ageing.

CÔTE DE BROUILLY comes from vines that cling to the sides of the hill and cover about 500 acres. The average yield is 18,532 gallons.

The above two A.O.C.s are entirely different and should not be confused.

MORGON. A few miles to the north, the little hamlet of Morgon, with its narrow, winding streets, has given its name to the 1,360 acres of vineyards in the Villié-Morgon. It is a very sturdy wine which can be kept for a very long time. Average yield—616,000 gallons.

CHIROUBLES. The village bearing this name is much nearer the hills, and high up. Thanks to Pulliat, the writer on vines, it was the first to plant the grafted vine after the phylloxera plague.

The total area under the CHIROUBLES A.O.C. is about 3,000 acres, producing 209,000 gallons of a distinguished wine, halfway between MORGON and FLEURIE.

Continuing along the road beyond Chiroubles we reach, just before the Fût-d'Avenas Pass, the lookout point mentioned earlier, which offers a fine view of most of the Beaujolais and the Mâconnais.

FLEURIE. The name is aptly chosen for "the queen of Beaujolais", as this scented wine is called. A little more versatile than the rest, it is more delicate and finely perfumed. This commune, its name redolent of spring, lies near Romanèche-Thorins. Its slender clocktower looks down upon the many châteaux and masters' houses, some quite old, scattered around the countryside. The area under the FLEURIE A.O.C. is one of the largest in the Beaujolais, about 1,730 acres producing an average 517,000 gallons.

MOULIN-à-VENT. This growth, without doubt the best known and most sought after in the Beaujolais, is produced on part of the Chénas (Rhône) and on Romanèche-Thorins (Saône-et-Loire). There are about 1,730 acres of vineyards. Its name comes from an ancient windmill, the only one of its kind in the region, of which only the tower remains. A writer once stated that: "No one has ever contested the excellence of these vines. They are the realm of Bacchus, and Moulin-à-Vent and Thorins form the very heart of it. The soil is so precious to the vine that none is spared for the larger trees." The wine was formerly known as THORINS—Romanèche, the bearer of a Roman name, appended the name of its best vineyard to itself. The average yield is 484,000 gallons of fine, ruddy wine—full-bodied, firm and, after a few years, very much like some of the wines of the Côte d'Or.

CHÉNAS. Once again a vineyard straddling two communes, Chénas (Rhône) and La-Chapelle-de-Guinchay (Saône-et-Loire). It overlooks the Moulin-à-Vent vineyard, with its hillock that was formed, according to legend, by the giant Gargantua unloading his basket.

It is also said that the name of Chénas cames from the oak trees *(chênes)* that formerly covered the district and indeed most of the Beaujolais.

The area of this A.O.C. is 457 acres producing an average of 132,000 gallons of generous, perfumed wine.

JULIÉNAS. The wine that may use this A.O.C. is produced within the commune of Juliénas—named after Julius Caesar, it is said, as well as Jullié, Emeringes and Pruzilly, covering 1,310 acres. The first grapes of the Beaujolais are said to have ripened along the Roman road, on vines planted in this soil which so resembles the one that Claudel described as: "dry and lumpy like curdled milk and full of tiny pebbles that retain the heat like firebricks so that the plump and sleepy grapes cook through on both sides". It gives 374,000 gallons of full, fruity, warm wine that matures well.

SAINT-AMOUR. We conclude our trip around the nine growths of the Beaujolais with this A.O.C. produced in the commune of the same name situated in the Saône-et-Loire. If this name did not exist, it would have to be invented—"holy love of the vine, holy love of the wine that flows for the holy love of mankind". This vineyard lies between Juliénas and Pouilly-Vinzelles, 8 miles south of Mâcon. Its vines now belong with the Beaujolais, though for a long time they were one of the gems of the Mâconnais. They used to belong to the Chapter of Saint-Vincent-de-Mâcon. Area approximately 530 acres and average yield 167,200 gallons of fresh, frank, agreeable wine.

Emile Vuillermoz said that these growths provided "all the chromatic scale, from the velvety notes of the delightful FLEURIE, though the more mysterious sounds of BROUILLY, the resonance of JULIÉNAS, the arpeggios of MOULIN-à-VENT, the frank impact of MORGON and the harmonies of CHÉNAS, to the clear sounds of SAINT-AMOUR and CHIROUBLES".

This ends our journey in this vast area that gives us Beaujolais, the wine that used to be drunk in all the taverns from "pots"—stone jugs painted blue. We have also reached the end of our pilgrimage around the different growths of Burgundy—CHABLIS, CÔTE DE NUITS, CÔTE DE BEAUNE, the regions of Mercurey and the Mâconnais. Henri Béraud's comment would apply to many of them: "This wine is not a *nouveau riche*. It remains and shall remain what it has always been. Its clear flow will bring us a little of the soul of the vintagers who have brought it into existence on their hillsides, a soul full of strength, wisdom and joviality."

LIFE IN BURGUNDY

It has been written of the Burgundians that they are "deep-thinking, even calculating, moderate like their country in all ways, active and energetic but loving logical order and reasoned practicality, greatly preferring life as it is and its material benefits, genial observers, formidable scoffers, often ingenious and witty".

We might add a few touches to this quite realistic portrait as regards their eating and drinking habits. And here everyone agrees with Clément Vautel: "There can be no lasting pleasure nor possible harmony in a house where the lunch is a failure and the dinner bankrupt."

How can one not enjoy good food when it is accompanied by "that divine juice that its lovers drink pure in the morning and unadulterated at night" and which, apart from all its other merits, "is pleasant to wives when their husbands have drunk it"?

But let us finish our portrait by remembering that Burgundy has been called, among other things, "a hospitable land". Why not? One need scarcely ask on seeing the pleasure on the faces of those returning from this region. Nor do they stint their numbers: Beaune, as already noted, has 300,000 visitors a year.

The daily round in Burgundy is quiet and unspectacular. The vintner's work requires a good deal of patience throughout the year and the cellarman remains always underground. From time to time, however, the calm surface breaks and the sound of laughter, songs and dances fills the air. Harvest time and the Vine and Wine Festival organized every September in Dijon by the Burgundian Committee are two such occasions.

Life in Burgundy is also punctuated by other events—we have already mentioned the sale of wines at the Hospices of Beaune, the oldest of the three known as *Les Trois Glorieuses*. In connection with this famous sale, which, let us recall, takes place on the third Sunday in November, there are various events in Beaune on the Saturday, such as the general exhibition of the wines of Burgundy and, in the evening, at the Château of the Clos-Vougeot, the "extraordinary" chapter of the Brotherhood of the Knights of the Tastevin. On Sunday, the exhibition continues and the wines of the Hospices of Beaune are sold. The day ends with a dinner by candlelight in one of the bastions of the town belonging to the Hospices. On Monday, the last day, there is the *Paulée* of Meursault, which is the traditional dinner marking the end of the vintage.

In all the regions of Burgundy that we have visited only briefly in this book, there are special celebrations attractive to follow and pleasant to participate in.

In the north, Chablis houses the Brotherhood of the Piliers Chablisiens (Pillars of Chablis), which holds its chapters in the wine-cellar of Vaucorbeil several times a year, usually on St. Vincent's day. This is the occasion for the exhibition and tasting of the wines of the Yonne and for the traditional event in the region —*le repas du cochon* ("the feast of the pig"). The singing and dancing of a chorus lends added charm to these candlelight banquets.

In Dijon, we have the Burgundian Committee which holds its rites in the magnificent thirteenth-century cellar of Clairvaux and organizes the Vine and Wine Festival. The rites are accompanied by folklore groups and recall the dubbing ceremonies of the Middle Ages. New distinctions are conferred in the Order of the Grand Dukes of the West, a reminder of the four great dukes of Burgundy.

Continuing south, we pass by the Clos-de-Vougeot, to greet the institution that is so much admired and copied everywhere—the Brotherhood of the Knights of the Tastevin—who were the first to establish contacts

Lifting his *tastevin*, the wine-taster prepares to pass judgement. This shallow cup, solid silver or silver-plated, has two sets of facets, with different reliefs to help the wine-taster in his examination.

Vintage time in Burgundy. Armed with their shears the vintagers (*layots* in the Burgundian patois) gather the grapes into their wicker baskets. The baskets are then carried on carts along the paths between the vines and their contents are emptied into large barrels for conveyance to the wine-press. Unlike in the Burgundy vineyards, planted to the *Pinot Noir*, in the Beaujolais the *Gamay* grape is used.

between wine-lovers and the wines of a province. "To invite someone is to assume responsibility for his well-being for as long as he is under your roof," said Brillat-Savarin, and this is the rule of the Brotherhood during its chapters. They have proved so successful that they have had to organize additional chapters, splendid banquets during which the sponsors instill their spirit of gaiety, humour and the wit that is the mark of companionable people. They are assisted by the Cadets of Burgundy, created by the Brotherhood, and they have attained the necessary skill in folklore throughout the years as well as the much more complex arts of music and diction.

Let us remember, in passing, the Saint-Vincent-Tournant, created by the Brotherhood, which brings together all the winegrowing communes of the Côte in a religious and secular ceremony for the feast of the patron saint of vintagers. There is also the *Taste-vinage*, at which good wines are selected for the wine-lover—this has become a famous ceremony. Any wineproducer or shipper wishing to participate must possess a given number of bottles of the same vintage. He then must send in samples—one to be tasted and the others for subsequent checks. In the cellar of the Château of the Clos-Vougeot, the specialists meet the press and, of course, consumer representatives. The

tasters are always very severe: between 30 and 35 per cent of the wines are rejected each year, not because they are bad, but because they do not attain the level of distinction required. These two events have been very successful and well attended from the start.

About 12 miles farther south, in the little village of Savigny-lès-Beaune, the *Cousinerie de Bourgogne* (Cousinhood of Burgundy) meets under the sign of hospitality that is legendary in the province. "Bottle on the table and heart in hand" is its guiding principle and "all gentlemen are cousins" is its motto.

The headquarters of the Brotherhood of the Vintagers of Saint-Vincent is in Mâcon, in the Saône-et-Loire. During its chapters, distinguished guests and wine-lovers, if their conduct in wine matters is irreproachable, are received as knights or officers. These chapters are enlivened by a choir which sings all the traditional songs of the region.

Finally there is the Brotherhood of the Companions of the Beaujolais, created in 1947 and now holding its own vattings at Lacenas, after being received into all the most important cellars in the Beaujolais. The Companions swear an oath of wine to promote the wines of the Beaujolais in every way and to love and assist other companions. He who breaks his oath is "for all time unworthy to drink with an honest man".

The Chapters of the Brotherhood of the Knights of the Tastevin are held regularly in the ancient cellar of the Château of Clos-Vougeot. When their "wine education" is complete, the new members of the Brotherhood are initiated by a ceremony that combines humour and the picturesque.

WINES OF BURGUNDY

CHABLIS • WHITE WINES

Regional appellation : Chablis, Petit Chablis.

Principal first growths

Chablis-Mont de Milieu, Chablis-Montée de Tonnerre, Chablis-Fourchaume, on the right bank of the Serein.
Chablis-Forêts, Chablis-Vaillons, Chablis-Mélinots, Chablis-Côte de Léchet, Chablis-Beauroy, on the left bank of the Serein.
Chablis-Vaucoupin, Chablis-Vaugros, Chablis-Vaugiraud, in the commune of Chichée.

Great growths

Chablis-Vaudésir, Chablis-Preuses, Chablis-Les Clos, Chablis-Grenouilles, Chablis-Bougros, Chablis-Valmur, Chablis-Blanchots.

CÔTE DE NUITS • RED WINES

Generic appellation :

a) Bourgogne ordinaire, Bourgogne grand ordinaire • *b)* Bourgogne Passe-tout-grains • *c)* Bourgogne, Bourgogne Marsannay, Bourgogne Hautes Côtes de Nuits • *d)* Vins fins de la Côte de Nuits or Côte de Nuits-Villages (Communes of Fixin, Brochon, Prissey, Comblanchien, Corgoloin).

Appellation of communes	*Appellation of first-growth communes*	*Great growths*	*First great growths*
Fixin . . . . (only red wine)	La Perrière, Les Hervelets, Les Meix-Bas, Aux-Cheusots, Le Clos du Chapitre, Les Arvelets.		
Gevrey-Chambertin . . . (only red wine)	Les Véroilles, Village Saint-Jacques called "Le Clos Saint-Jacques", Aux Combottes, Bel-Air, Cazetiers, Combes-aux-Moines, Estournelles, Lavaut, Poissenot, Champeaux, Les Goulots, Issarts, Les Corbeaux, Les Gémeaux, Cherbaudes, La Perrière, Clos-Prieur (only upper part), le Fonteny, Champonnets, Au Closeau, Craipillot, Champitonnois called "Petite Chapelle", Ergots, Clos-du-Chapitre.	Charmes-Chambertin Chapelle-Chambertin Griotte-Chambertin Latricières-Chambertin Mazis-Chambertin Ruchottes-Chambertin	Chambertin Chambertin-Clos-de-Bèze
Morey-Saint-Denis . . . (red wine and 1·6% white wine)	Les Larrets or "Clos-des-Lambrays", Les Ruchots, Les Sorbés, Le Clos-Sorbés, Les Millandes, Le Clos-des-Ormes, Meix-Rentiers, Monts-Luisants, Les Bouchots, Clos Bussières, Aux Charmes, Les Charrières, Côte Rôtie, Calouères, Maison Brûlée, Chabiots, Les Mauchamps, Les Froichots, Les Fremières, Les Genévrières, Les Chaffots, Les Chenevery, La Riotte, Le Clos-Baulet, Les Gruenchers, Les Faconnières.	Clos-de-Tart Clos-St.-Denis Clos-de-la-Roche	Bonnes-Mares
Chambolle-Musigny . . . (only red wine)	Les Bonnes-Mares, Les Amoureuses, Les Charmes, Les Cras, Les Borniques, Les Baudes, Les Plantes, Les Hauts Doix, Les Chatelots, Les Gruenchers, Les Groseilles, Les Fuées, Les Lavrottes, Derrière-la-Grange, Les Noirots, Les Sentiers, Les Fousselottes, Aux Beaux-Bruns, Les Combottes, Aux Combottes.		Musigny (2% white wine)
Vougeot . . . . (only red wine)	Le Clos Blanc, Les Petits-Vougeot, Les Cras, Clos de la Perrière.		Clos-de-Vougeot
Vosne-Romanée . . . . . (only red wine)	Aux Malconsorts, Les Beaux-Monts, Les Suchots, La Grand'Rue, Les Gaudichots, Aux Brûlées, Les Chaumes, Les Reignots, Le Clos des Réas, Les Petits-Monts.	Romanée Romanée-St-Vivant Grands-Echezeaux Echezeaux	Romanée-Conti Richebourg La Tâche
Nuits-Saint-Georges . . . (red wine; 0·4% white wine)	Les Saint-Georges, Les Vaucrains, Les Cailles, Les Porets, Les Pruliers, Les Hauts-Pruliers, Aux Murgers, La Richemonne, Les Chabœufs, La Perrière, La Roncière, Les Procès, Rue-de-Chaux, Aux Boudots, Aux Cras, Aux Chaignots, Aux Thorey, Aux Vignes-Rondes, Aux Bousselots, Les Poulettes, Aux Crots, Les Vallerots, Aux Champs-Perdrix, Perrière-Noblet, Aux Damodes, Les Argillats, En la Chaîne-Carteau, Aux Argilats, Clos de la Maréchale, Clos-Arlots, Clos des Argillières, Clos des Grandes Vignes, Clos des Corvées, Clos des Forêts, Les Didiers, Aux Perdrix, Les Corvées-Paget, Le Clos-Saint-Marc.		

CÔTE DE BEAUNE • RED WINES

Generic appellation :

a) Bourgogne ordinaire, Bourgogne grand ordinaire • *b)* Bourgogne Passe-tout-grains • *c)* Bourgogne • *d)* Côte de Beaune • *e)* Côte de Beaune-Villages

Appellation of communes	Appellation of first-growth communes	Great growths
Aloxe-Corton . . . . . . (1 % white wine)	Les Valozières, Les Chaillots, Les Meix, Les Fournières, Les Maréchaudes, En Pauland, Les Vercots, Les Guérets, La Maréchaude, La Toppe-au-Vert, La Coutière, Les Grandes-Lolières, Les Petites-Lolières, Basses-Mourettes.	Corton
Pernand-Vergelesses . . . (11 % white wine)	Ile-des-Vergelesses, Les Basses-Vergelesses, Creux-de-la-Net, Les Fichots, En Caradeux.	Corton
Savigny-lès-Beaune . . . (4 % white wine)	Aux Vergelesses, Aux Vergelesses dit Bataillière, Les Marconnets, La Dominode, Les Jarrons, Basses-Vergelesses, Les Lavières, Aux Gravains, Les Peuillets, Aux Guettes, Les Talmettes, Les Charnières, Aux Fourneaux, Aux Clous, Aux Serpentières, Les Narbantons, Les Hauts-Marconnets, Les Hauts-Jarrons, Redrescuts, Aux Guettes, Les Rouvrettes, Aux Grands-Liards, Aux Petits-Liards, Petits-Godeaux.	
Chorey-lès-Beaune . . .	Chorey-lès-Beaune.	
Beaune. . . . . (5 % white wine)	Les Marconnets, Les Fèves, Les Bressandes, Les Grèves, Les Teurons, Le Clos-des-Mouches, Champs-Pimont, Clos-du-Roi, Aux Coucherias, En l'Orme, En Genêt, Les Perrières, A l'Ecu, Les Cent-Vignes, Les Toussaints, Sur-les-Grèves, Aux Cras, Le Clos-de-la-Mousse, Les Chouacheux, Les Boucherottes, Les Vignes-Franches, Les Aigrots, Pertuisots, Tielandry ou Clos-Landry, Les Sisies, Les Avaux, Les Reversées, Le Bas-des-Teurons, Les Seurey, La Mignotte, Montée-Rouge, Les Montrevenots, Les Blanches-Fleurs, Les Epenottes.	
Pommard	Les Rugiens-Bas, Les Rugiens-Hauts, Les Epenots, Les Petits-Epenots, Clos-de-la-Commaraine, Clos-Blanc, Les Arvelets, Es-Charmots, Les Argillières, Les Pézerolles, Les Boucherottes, Les Sausilles, Les Croix-Noires, Les Chaponnières, Les Fremiers, Les Bertins, Les Garollières ou Jarollières, Les Poutures, Le Clos-Micot, La Refene, Clos-du-Verger, Derrière-Saint-Jean, La Platière, Les Chanlins-Bas, Les Combes-Dessus, La Chanière.	
Volnay	En Caillerets, Caillerets-Dessus, En Champans, En Chevret, Fremiets, Bousse-d'Or, La Barre or Clos-de-la-Barre, Le Clos-des-Chênes, Les Angles, Pointe-d'Angles, Les Mitans, En l'Ormeau, Taille-Pieds, En Verseuil, Carelle-sous-la-Chapelle, Ronceret, Carelle-Dessous, Robardelle, Les Lurets, Les Aussy, Les Brouillards, Le Clos-des-Ducs, Les Pitures-Dessus, Chanlin, Les Santenots, Les Petures, Village-de-Volnay.	
Monthélie . . . . (2.5 % white wine)	Sur Lavelle, Les Vignes-Rondes, le Meix-Bataille, Les Riottes, La Taupine, Le Clos-Gauthey, Le Château-Gaillard, Les Champs-Fulliot, Le Cas-Rougeot, Duresse.	
Auxey-Duresses . . . . . (32 % white wine)	Les Duresses, Les Bas-des-Duresses, Reugne, Reugne called La Chapelle, Les Grands-Champs, Climat-du-Val called Clos-du-Val, Les Ecusseaux, Les Bretterins called La Chapelle, Les Bretterins.	
Santenay . . . . (2 % white wine)	Les Gravières, Clos-de-Tavannes, La Comme, Beauregard, Le Passe-Temps, Beaurepaire, La Maladière.	
Cheilly, Dezize, Sampigny-lès-Maranges	Le Clos-des-Rois, La Boutière, Les Maranges, Les Plantes-de-Maranges.	
Chassagne-Montrachet . .	Clos-Saint-Jean, Morgeot, Morgeot called Abbaye-de-Morgeot, La Boudriotte, La Maltroie, Les Chenevottes, Les Champs-Gain, Grandes-Ruchottes, La Romanée, Les Brussolles, Les Vergers, Les Macherelles, En Cailleret.	
Other appellations . . . . *of communes*	Saint-Romain, Meursault-Blagny or Blagny, Puligny-Montrachet, Ladoix, Saint-Aubin.	
Saint-Aubin . . . . . . (4 % white wine)	La Chatenière, Les Murgers-des-Dents-de-Chien, En Remilly, Les Frionnes, Sur-le-Sentier-de-Clou, Sur Gamay, Les Combes, Champlot.	

CÔTE DE BEAUNE • WHITE WINES

Generic appellation: **a)** Bourgogne ordinaire, Bourgogne grand ordinaire • **b)** Bourgogne aligoté • **c)** Bourgogne • **d)** Côte de Beaune.

Appellation of communes	*Appellation of first-growth communes*	*Great growths*	*First great growths*
Aloxe-Corton		Corton-Charlemagne	
Pernand-Vergelesses		Corton-Charlemagne	
Chorey-lès-Beaune . . .	Chorey-lès-Beaune.		
Saint-Romain			
Meursault . . . . (4 % red wine)	Aux Perrières, Les Perrières-Dessus, Les Perrières-Dessous, Les Charmes-Dessus, Les Charmes-Dessous, Les Genevrières-Dessus, Les Genevrières-Dessous, Le Poruzot-Dessus, Le Poruzot-Dessous, Le Poruzot, Les Bouchères, Les Santenots-Blancs, Les Santenots-du-Milieu, Les Caillerets, Les Petures, Les Cras, La Goutte-d'Or, La Jennelotte, La Pièce-sous-le-Bois, Sous-le-Dos-d'Ane.		
Puligny-Montrachet . . . (6·4 % red wine)	Le Cailleret, Les Combettes, Les Pucelles, Les Folatières, Clavoillons, Le Champ-Canet, Les Chalumeaux, Les Referts, Sous-le-Puits, La Garenne, Hameau-de-Blagny.	Chevalier-Montrachet, Bâtard-Montrachet, Bienvenues-Bâtard-Montrachet, Criots-Bâtard-Montrachet.	Montrachet
Chassagne-Montrachet . .	Morgeot, Morgeot called Abbaye-de-Morgeot, La Boudriotte, La Maltroie, Clos-Saint-Jean, Les Chenevottes, Les Champs-Gain, Grandes-Ruchottes, La Romanée, Les Brussoles, Les Vergers, Les Macherelles, Chassagne or Cailleret.	Bâtard-Montrachet Criots-Bâtard-Montrachet	Montrachet
Other appellations . . . . *of communes*	Ladoix, Meursault-Blagny or Blagny, Saint-Aubin, Cheilly-Dezize-les-Maranges, Sampigny-lès-Maranges.		

MERCUREY REGION

Generic appellation: Bourgogne.

Appellation of communes	*First growths*
Mercurey (red 95 %) . .	Clos-du-Roy, Clos-Voyens or Les Voyens, Clos-Marcilly, Clos-des-Fourneaux, Clos-des-Montaigus.
Givry (red 87 %)	
Rully (white 80 %) . . .	Margotey, Grésigny, Vauvry, Mont-Palais, Meix-Caillet, Les Pierres, La Bressande, Champ-Clou, La Renarde, Pillot, Cloux, Raclot, Raboursay, Ecloseaux, Marissou, La Fosse, Chapitre, Préau, Moulesne.
Montagny (white) . . .	

MÂCONNAIS

Generic appellation: Bourgogne • Mâcon supérieur (red wine 37 % and white) • Mâcon-villages (white wine) • Mâcon (red wine 76 %) Pinot-Chardonnay-Mâcon (white wine).

Appellation of communes   Pouilly-Fuissé (white), Pouilly-Vinzelles (white), Pouilly-Loché (white).

BEAUJOLAIS

Generic appellation: **a)** Bourgogne ordinaire, Bourgogne grand ordinaire • **b)** Bourgogne Passe-tout-grains • **c)** Bourgogne aligoté **d)** Bourgogne • **e)** Beaujolais • **f)** Beaujolais supérieur • **g)** Beaujolais-Villages.

First growths . . . . . .   Brouilly, Chenas, Chiroubles, Côte de Brouilly, Fleurie, Juliénas, Morgon, Moulin-à-vent, Saint-Amour. (red wine)

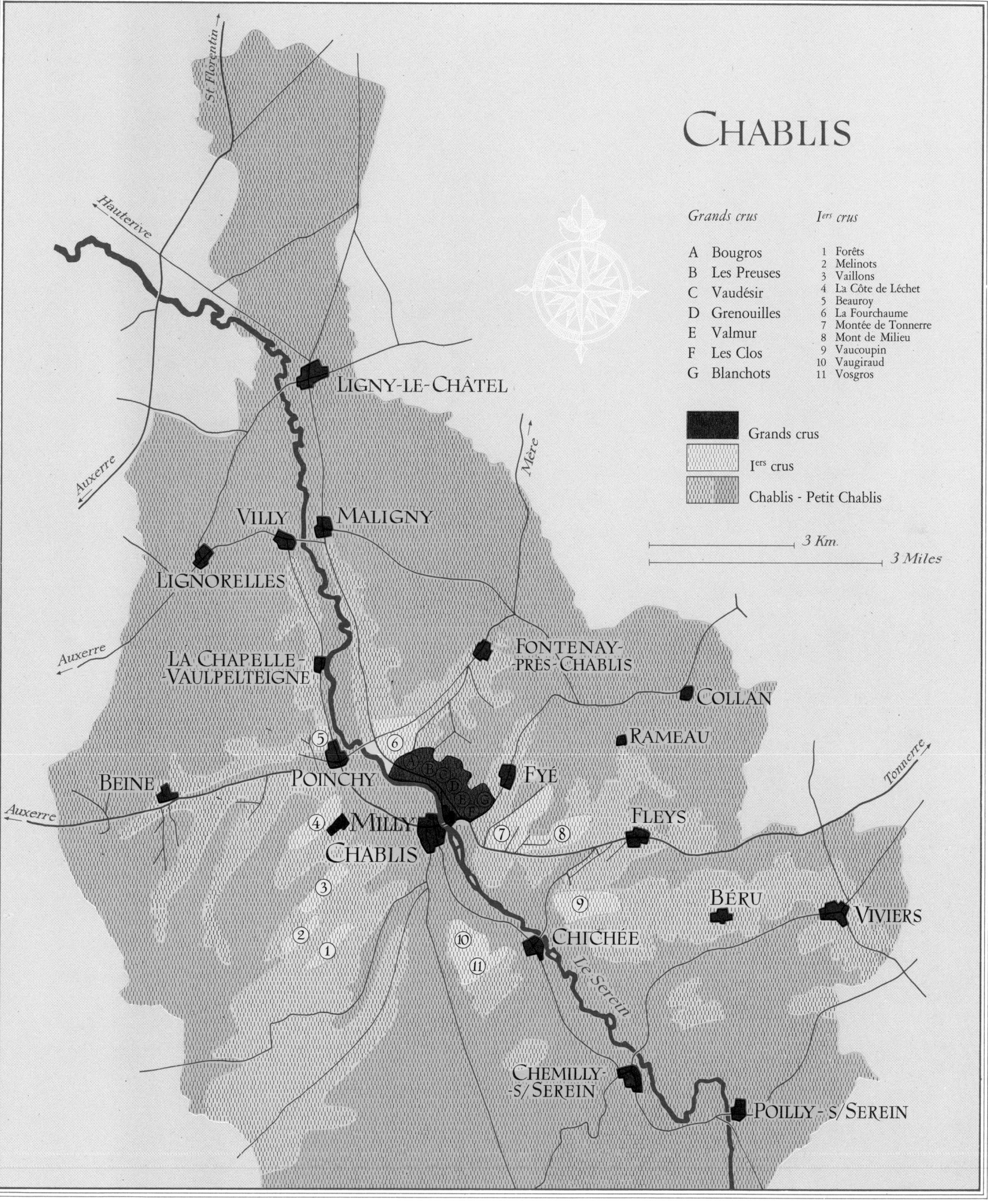

CHABLIS

Grands crus

A Bougros
B Les Preuses
C Vaudésir
D Grenouilles
E Valmur
F Les Clos
G Blanchots

Iers crus

1 Forêts
2 Melinots
3 Vaillons
4 La Côte de Léchet
5 Beauroy
6 La Fourchaume
7 Montée de Tonnerre
8 Mont de Milieu
9 Vaucoupin
10 Vaugiraud
11 Vosgros

Grands crus

Iers crus

Chablis - Petit Chablis

3 Km.

3 Miles

LIGNY-LE-CHÂTEL

VILLY   MALIGNY

LIGNORELLES

LA CHAPELLE-
VAULPELTEIGNE

FONTENAY-
PRÈS-CHABLIS

COLLAN

RAMEAU

POINCHY

FYÉ

BEINE

MILLY-
CHABLIS

FLEYS

BÉRU

VIVIERS

CHICHÉE

CHEMILLY-
S/SEREIN

POILLY-S/SEREIN

Hauterive

St Florentin

Auxerre

Auxerre

Auxerre

Mère

Tonnerre

Le Serein

Grands crus

1 La Tache
2 Romanée
3 Romanée-Conti
4 Romanée-Saint-Vivant
5 Richebourg
6 Echezeaux
  Grands-Echezeaux   7 Clos-de-Voug

Appellations de commune   NUITS-SAINT-GEORGES   VOSNE-ROMANÉE   VOUGEOT

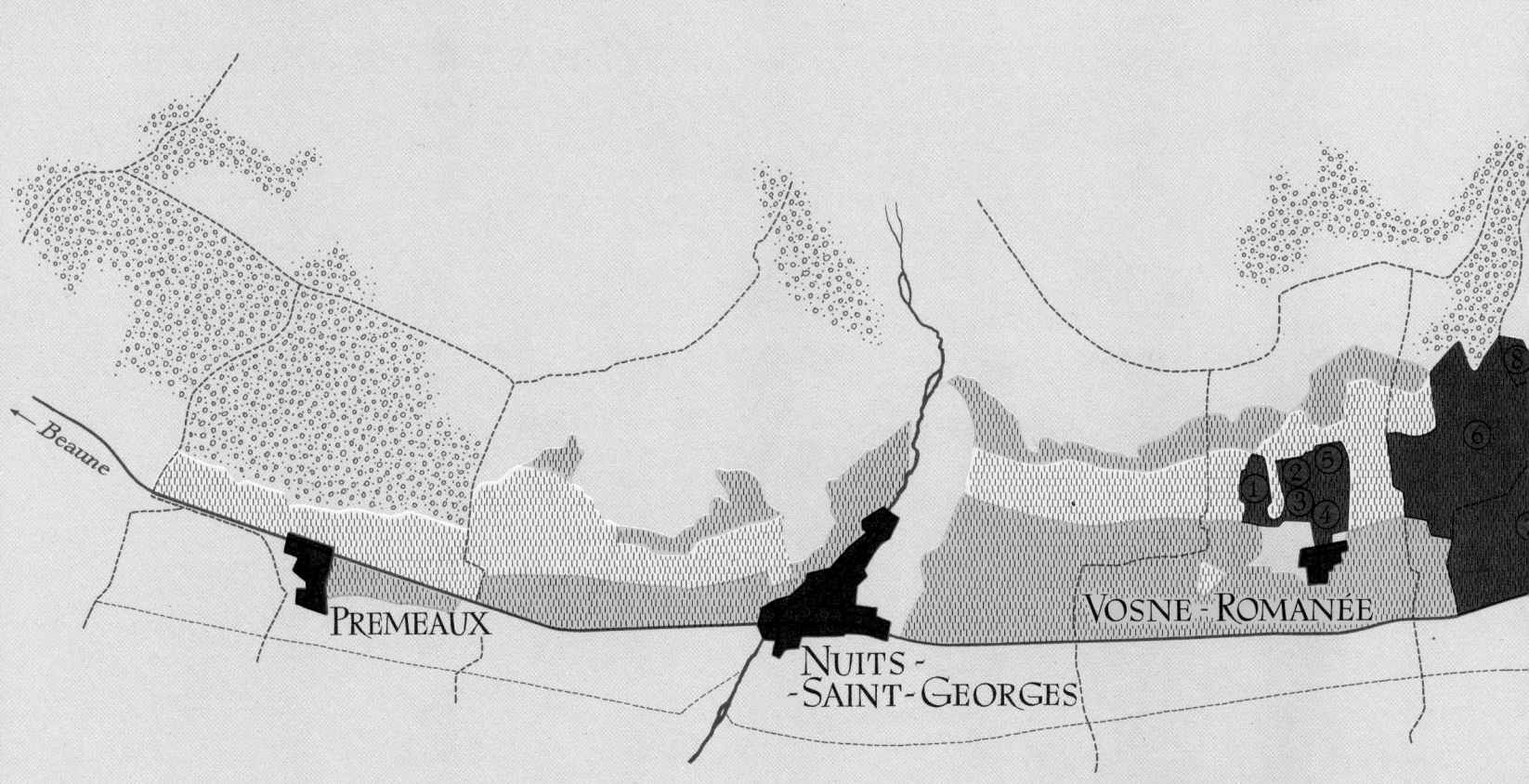

PREMEAUX

NUITS-
-SAINT-GEORGES

VOSNE-ROMANÉE

← Beaune

2 Km.

2 Miles

LA CÔTE DE NUITS

14 Mazoyères-Chambertin
15 Latricières-Chambertin
16 Charmes-Chambertin
17 Chambertin
18 Chambertin-Clos-de-Bèze
19 Griotte-Chambertin
20 Chapelle-Chambertin
21 Mazis-Chambertin
22 Ruchottes-Chambertin

10 Bonnes-Mares
11 Clos-de-Tart
12 Clos-Saint-Denis
13 Clos-de-la-Roche

8 Musigny
9 Bonnes-Mares

CHAMBOLLE-MUSIGNY   MOREY-SAINT-DENIS   GEVREY-CHAMBERTIN   FIXIN

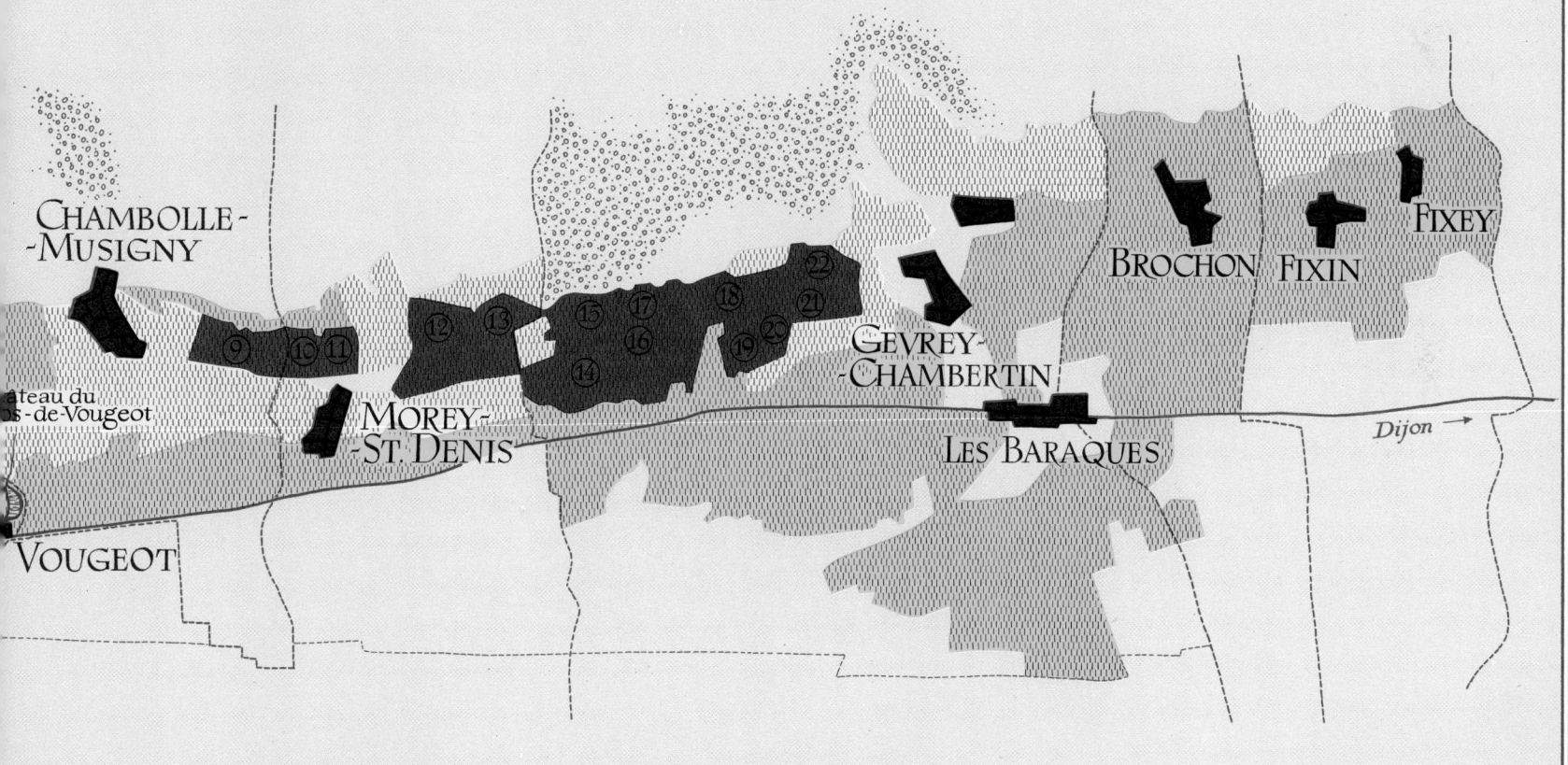

Grands crus   I^{ers} crus   Appellations de commune

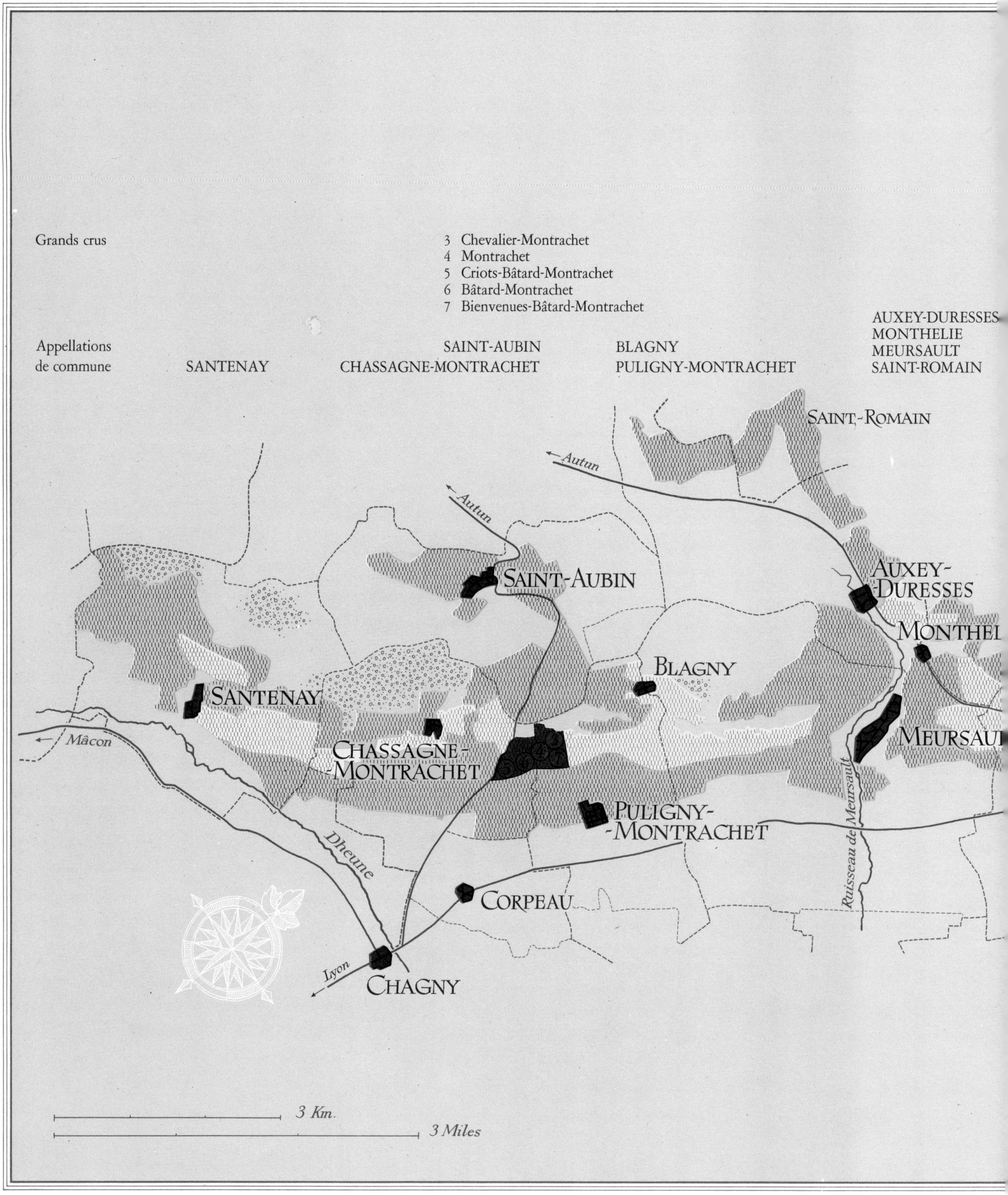

Grands crus

3 Chevalier-Montrachet
4 Montrachet
5 Criots-Bâtard-Montrachet
6 Bâtard-Montrachet
7 Bienvenues-Bâtard-Montrachet

Appellations
de commune

SANTENAY

SAINT-AUBIN
CHASSAGNE-MONTRACHET

BLAGNY
PULIGNY-MONTRACHET

AUXEY-DURESSES
MONTHELIE
MEURSAULT
SAINT-ROMAIN

SAINT-ROMAIN

Autun

Autun

SAINT-AUBIN

AUXEY-
DURESSES

MONTHEI

BLAGNY

SANTENAY

Mâcon

CHASSAGNE-
-MONTRACHET

MEURSAUL

PULIGNY-
-MONTRACHET

Ruisseau de Meursault

Dheune

CORPEAU

Lyon

CHAGNY

3 Km.

3 Miles

LA CÔTE DE BEAUNE

1 Corton (rouge - red)
2 Corton-Charlemagne (blanc - white)

PERNAND-VERGELESSES
ALOXE-CORTON
LADOIX

SAVIGNY-LÈS-BEAUNE
CHOREY-LÈS-BEAUNE

OLNAY   POMMARD   BEAUNE

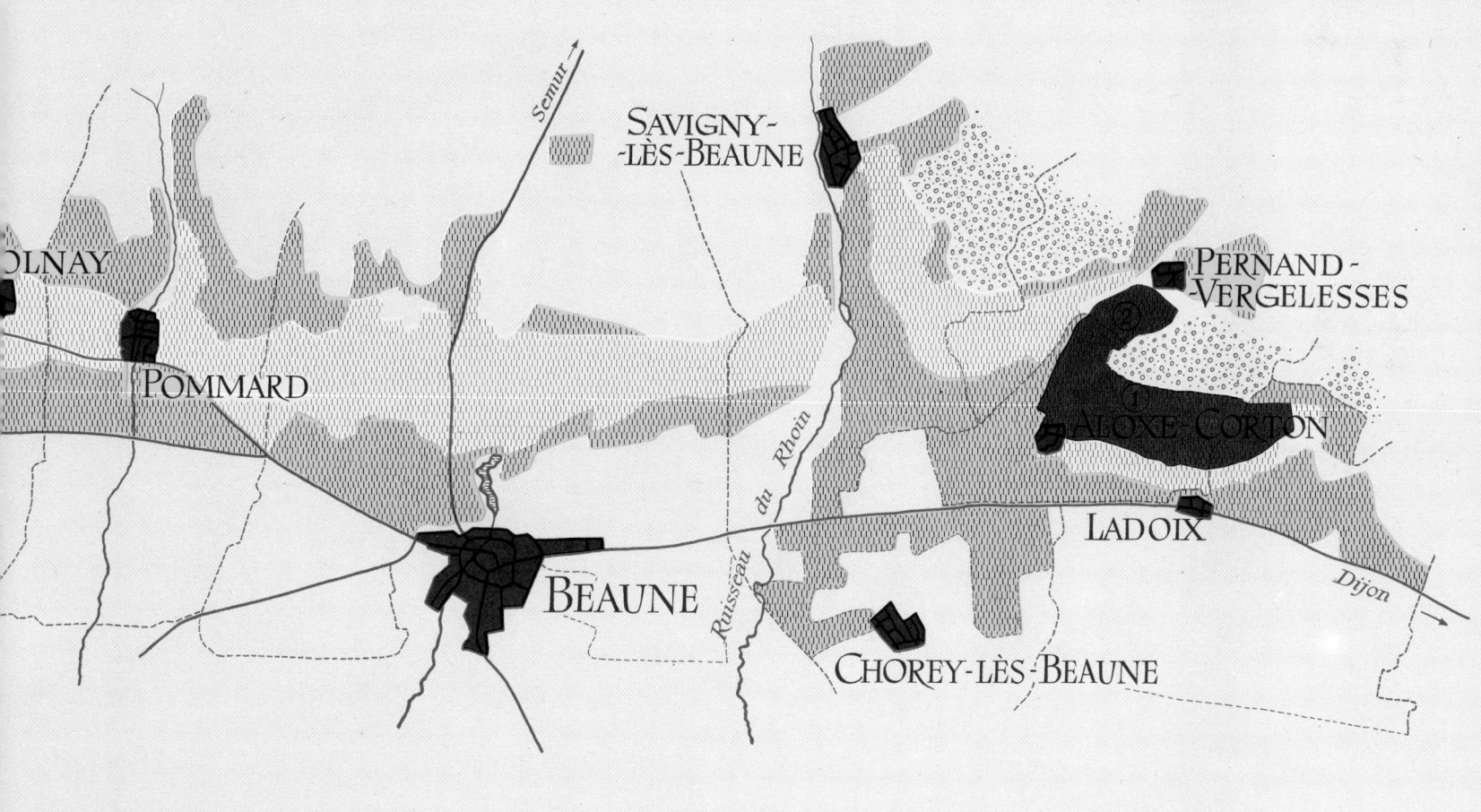

Grands crus   I^{ers} crus   Appellations de commune

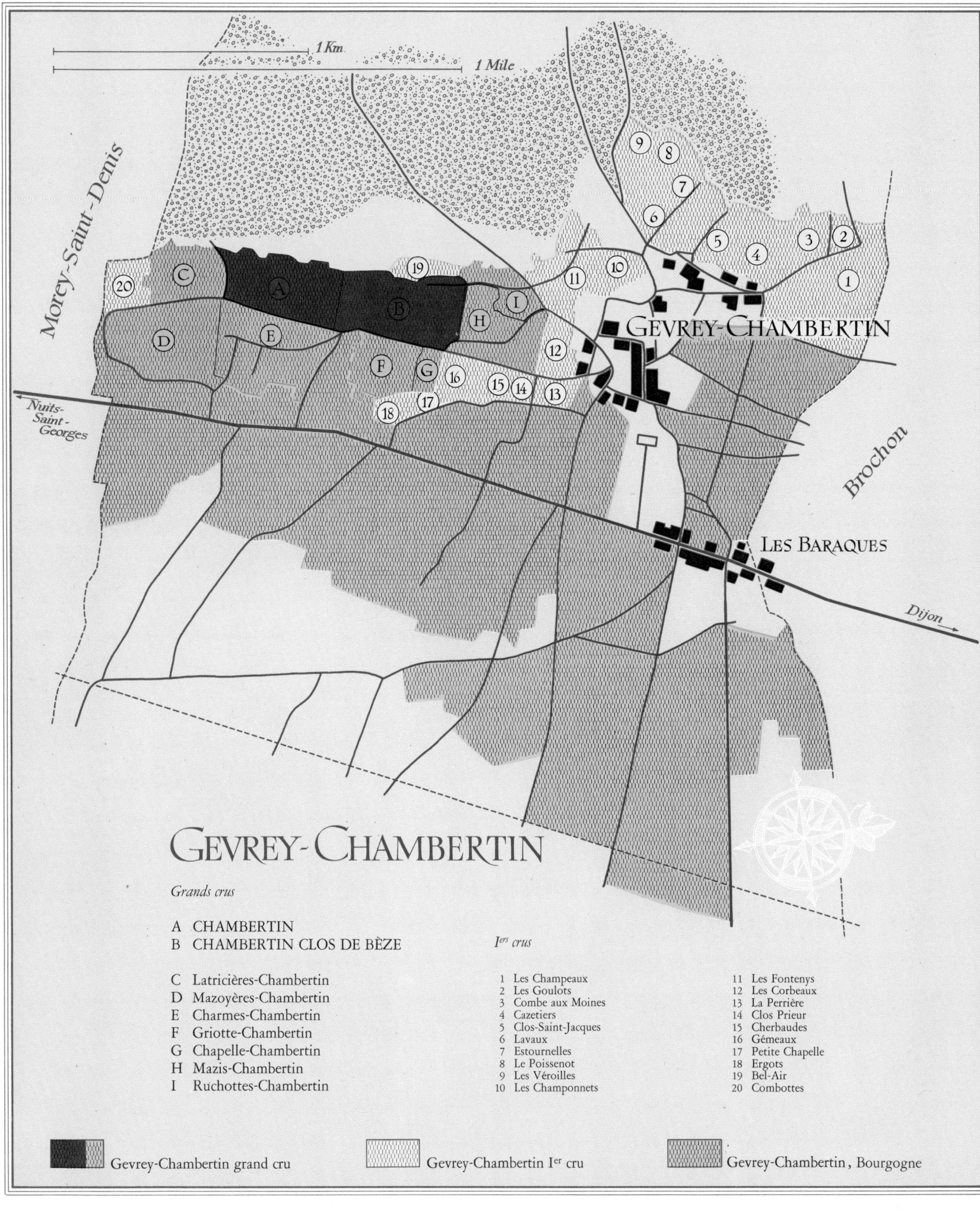

GEVREY-CHAMBERTIN

Grands crus

A CHAMBERTIN
B CHAMBERTIN CLOS DE BÈZE

C Latricières-Chambertin
D Mazoyères-Chambertin
E Charmes-Chambertin
F Griotte-Chambertin
G Chapelle-Chambertin
H Mazis-Chambertin
I Ruchottes-Chambertin

Iers crus

1	Les Champeaux	11	Les Fontenys
2	Les Goulots	12	Les Corbeaux
3	Combe aux Moines	13	La Perrière
4	Cazetiers	14	Clos Prieur
5	Clos-Saint-Jacques	15	Cherbaudes
6	Lavaux	16	Gémeaux
7	Estournelles	17	Petite Chapelle
8	Le Poissenot	18	Ergots
9	Les Véroilles	19	Bel-Air
10	Les Champonnets	20	Combottes

Gevrey-Chambertin grand cru   Gevrey-Chambertin Ier cru   Gevrey-Chambertin, Bourgogne

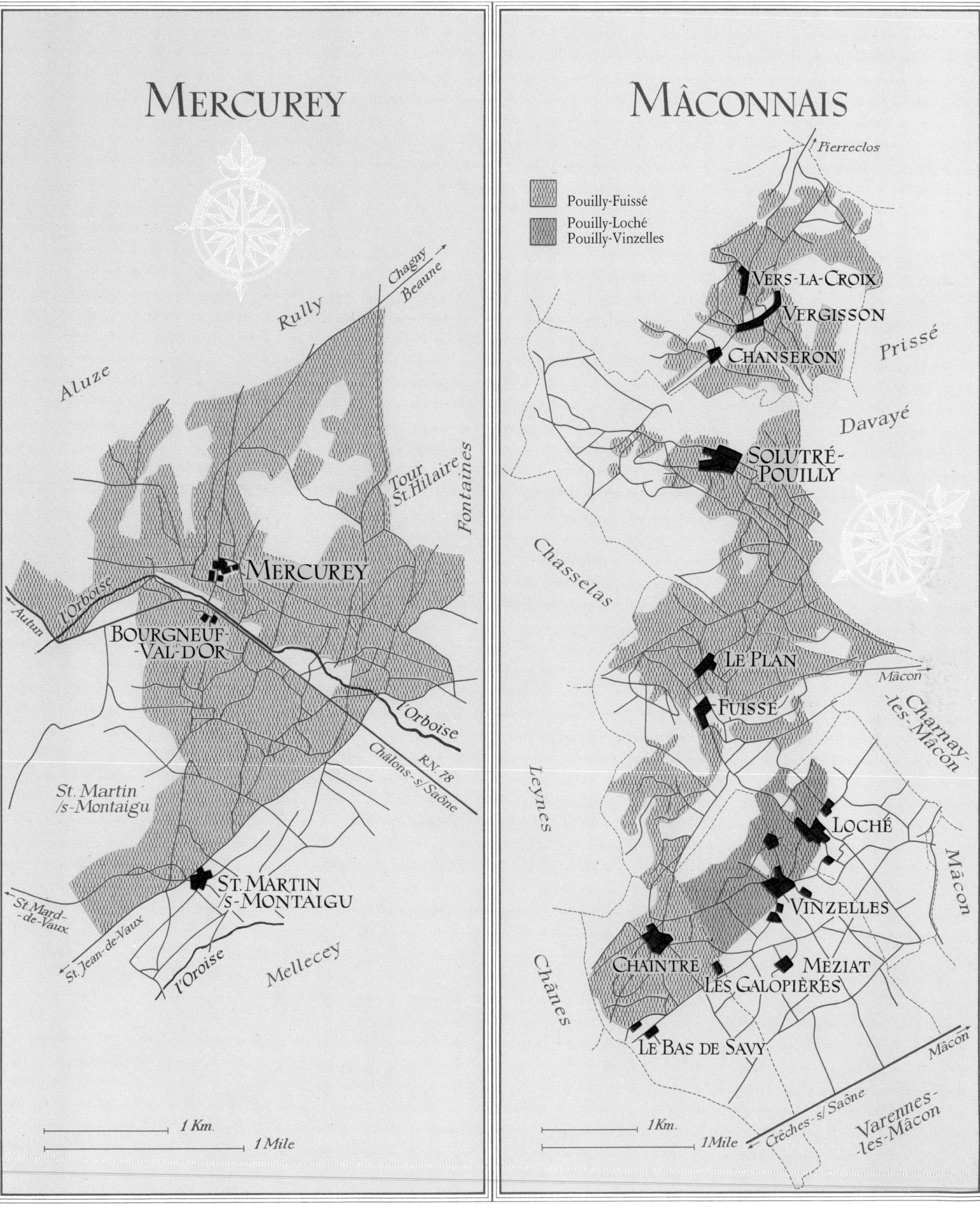

MERCUREY

Chagny
Beaune

Rully

Aluze

Tour
St. Hilaire

Fontaines

l'Orboise

MERCUREY

Autun

l'Orboise

BOURGNEUF-
VAL-D'OR

l'Orboise

Châlons-s/Saône

R.N. 78

St. Martin
/s-Montaigu

St. Mard
-de-Vaux

St. Jean-de-Vaux

l'Oroise

ST. MARTIN
/s-MONTAIGU

Mellecey

1 Km.

1 Mile

MÂCONNAIS

Pierreclos

Pouilly-Fuissé

Pouilly-Loché
Pouilly-Vinzelles

VERS-LA-CROIX

VERGISSON

Prissé

CHANSERON

Davayé

SOLUTRÉ-
POUILLY

Chasselas

LE PLAN

Mâcon

FUISSÉ

Charnay-
-les-Mâcon

Leynes

LOCHÉ

Mâcon

VINZELLES

CHAINTRÉ

MEZIAT

LES GALOPIÈRES

Chânes

LE BAS DE SAVY

Mâcon

1 Km.

1 Mile

Crêches-s/Saône

Varennes-
-les-Mâcon

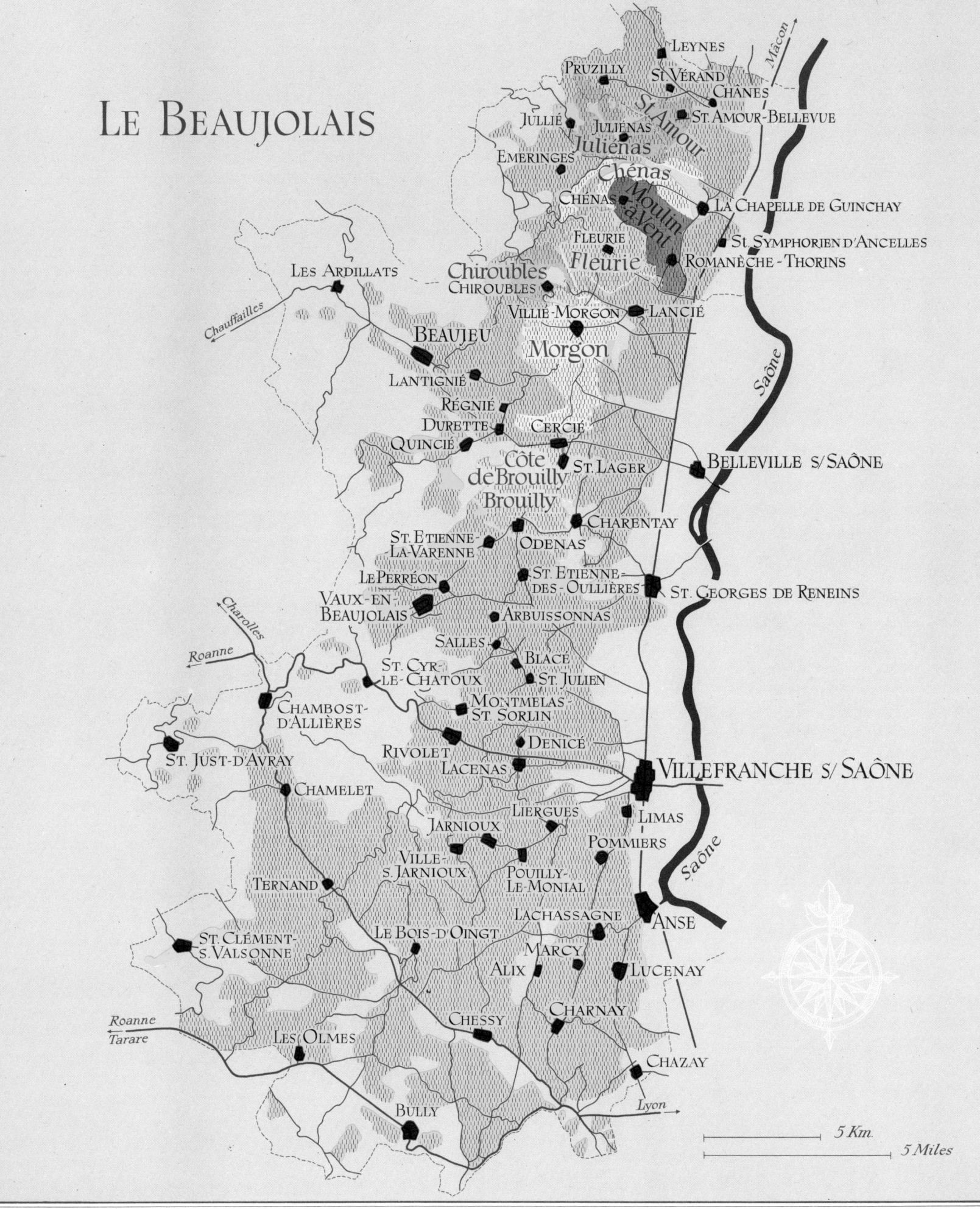

Le Beaujolais

LEYNES

PRUZILLY

St. Vérand

CHÂNES

Julié

St. Amour-Bellevue

Juliénas

St. Amour

Emeringes

Juliénas

Chénas

Chénas

Moulin à Vent

La Chapelle de Guinchay

Fleurie

St. Symphorien d'Ancelles

Les Ardillats

Fleurie

Romanèche - Thorins

Chiroubles

Chiroubles

Villié-Morgon

Lancié

Beaujeu

Morgon

Lantignié

Régnié

Durette

Cercié

Quincié

Côte de Brouilly

St. Lager

Belleville s/Saône

Brouilly

Charentay

St. Etienne-La-Varenne

Odenas

Le Perréon

St. Etienne-des-Oullières

St. Georges de Reneins

Vaux-en-Beaujolais

Arbuissonnas

Salles

Blacé

St. Cyr-le-Chatoux

St. Julien

Montmelas-St. Sorlin

Chambost-d'Allières

Rivolet

Denicé

St. Just-d'Avray

Lacenas

Villefranche s/Saône

Chamelet

Liergues

Limas

Jarnioux

Pommiers

Ville-s/Jarnioux

Pouilly-Le-Monial

Ternand

Lachassagne

Anse

Le Bois-d'Oingt

Marcy

St. Clément-s/Valsonne

Alix

Lucenay

Chessy

Charnay

Les Olmes

Chazay

Bully

Mâcon

Chauffailles

Charolles

Roanne

Roanne
Tarare

Lyon

Saône

5 Km.

5 Miles

THE WINES OF THE RHÔNE

PHILIPPE CHERIX and JEAN BERTIN-ROULLEAU

In the course of history, some rivers have divided the land through which they flowed, while others, much more rarely, have united and held together the peoples of each bank. Few rivers have done this to such lasting effect and over such a long period as has the river Rhône. Since time immemorial, it would seem, Nature has drawn man's attention to this vast furrow of fertility so propitious to peaceful relations: and when the vine crept in, right behind the first Greek merchants and the Roman legions, it was at home from the beginning. For close on six hundred years, the plant lingered in the plains of the Lower Rhône, fruitful in what was then Gaul around Narbonne, reaching the town of Lyons only in the first century of our era. From there, part of the vine escaped up the river Saône to conquer Burgundy, and it is surely one of the Rhône's claims to glory that it thus facilitated this bewitching viticultural colonization. Savoy and the Pays Romand saw in their turn this wine of the Rhône, and the vine-shoots of Dionysus reached even farther—as far, indeed, as they could go, until the great Alps stopped them and they reached the river's very source.

What an astonishing destiny for that thin trickle of limpid-clear water that springs from the unending fountain-head of the Furka glacier! Jostled from all sides in the rocks, the infant river drops dizzily to where, some 1,640 feet lower at Visperterminen (altitude 4,260 feet), the vine awaits. From here onwards to the sea, these plants will never leave the river's banks. In this rocky region, the vines must struggle for life under a sun that is often harsh: but the winegrower of the Valais canton, his face dried like parchment by the winds, the burning *fœhn* and the chilling *bise* in turn, is a hard and tenacious man. His task is a veritable gamble, yet the result is admirable: a range of wines, mostly whites and mostly dry, of which some are real works of art. The plants lie on the slopes in asymmetrical plots, giving the landscape a curiously mottled effect. Almost all the planting is on the river's right bank, facing the sun, or in the lateral valleys.

The river continues its flow down towards the plain, its waters more and more cloudy, swollen with the rivers feeding it from north and south.

Suddenly, at Martigny, the Rhône appears to change its mind. It forms a sharp right-hand turn and seems about to betray its southern destiny as it tries to return to a Germanic land. But then the plain opens wide and the river hurls itself forward: laden with mud and silt, it digs its bed deeply between the cantons of Vaud and Valais. The vines thin out on the left bank but spread profusely on the other.

The Rhône is still a great grey torrent full of fury when it meets Lake Leman. The soothing lake disciplines, warms and cleans the river in a series of operations that the eye does not even suspect: the Rhône seems to have disappeared completely. Yet it is but hidden, mysteriously, in the waves and the vine has not ceased to follow the river. It spreads in steeply terraced rows along the shores to Lausanne, the Lavaux region where begins that marvellous land of La Côte in which the living seems so easy. The plants, lined up neatly as though on shelves, give every sign of opulence.

Across the lake lies France. On the slopes of the Savoy mountains (Chablais and Faucigny), cultivation is much more sparse, and winters harsh. Here in this hard, tormented countryside, dominated by the forerunners of the mighty Alps, the vineyards produce a vigorous white wine: CRÉPY.

Farther west, the vineyards close up against each other between the lake and the Jura mountains. Geneva is not far away, where the lake is usually called Lake of Geneva. And the river, bursting at the very gates of Calvin's city out of the deep waters, can once again appear between its own banks and run, flirting, through the vineyards of the Mandement and the Upper-Savoy Genevois.

From Seyssel to Vienne, across the frontier now, in France, for about 110 miles the vineyards are scarce, and the Rhône, fortified with the waters of the Saône, rolls on towards Dauphiné, widening as it goes. The vine is not stubborn to the point of trying to grow in soils that do not suit it, but this momentary self-effacement of the Rhône vineyards is already preparing a special awakening. Only a few miles from Vienne, at Ampuis, where the vines are grown in little bow-like arches, with the plants tied together three-by-three, there is a cultivation of CÔTE RÔTIE. This is the threshold of an enormous vineyard stretching for almost 125 miles southward. The CÔTES DU RHÔNE, which include about one hundred varied communes, form two distinctly different agglomerates: one near Tournon, the other near Orange. The first is concentrated around HERMITAGE, while the second is around that illustrious CHÂTEAUNEUF so loved by the popes.

The whole of this very picturesque region has a wild, tormented surface, with marls, molasse and alluvial deposits forming stony slopes and high dry terraces where the red grape dominates. The river Rhône, here gorged with the waters of the Isère and the Drôme, has on occasion some formidable floods, but fortunately a hot sun makes haste to comfort the unfortunate vinegrower.

This is now the Pays de Vaucluse, that which formerly was the Comtat Venaissin: it is already part of the Provence, that region of extremes *par excellence*, where brutal rains and parching drought, cutting *mistral* wind and northern *tramontane* alternate with each other. Eternal Provence, with its perfume of plants and fruit, its heavy silence scarcely rippled by the chirping of the grasshoppers or the solid swearing of the winegrowers. The flavour of the western language pleases the Rhône and reminds it of other tongues of other folk of the vineyards: the roughness of the Valais and Savoy *patois*, the slowness of the accent of the Leman, the dry rhythm of the man from Lyons and then, from Valence on, the French that the people of Provence sing so well.

The Rhône, now become enormous, is preparing itself majestically to flow into the all-absorbing sea. But the vineyards along its banks will stop near Avignon. From there, taking full advantage of the wonderful richness of the southern soil, yet wishing to avoid the humid Camargue, the vines spread to east and west so that, from Saint-Raphaël to Perpignan, other vineyards are formed: those of the Côtes de Provence, Languedoc and Roussillon. It was in these regions that the Greeks and the Romans first transmitted to France that wondrous heritage of wine which later winegrowers were able to exploit so well.

Thus the river Rhône has given the vineyards, along the almost 500 miles of land traversed, a thousand-year-old birthright to bring man pleasure. True, the winegrowers of Languedoc, Provence, Savoy and Valais must battle with various problems in order to succeed: the sun, so necessary to breathe life into the wine, is not always kindly; the vine-plants do not feed everywhere on the same soils; the geography of the area often brings a disordered layout to the winegrower's plans for planting. But the river itself has managed to smooth out many of these diversities of cultivation. Man, guided quite naturally by that flowing water, has been able to bring Mediterranean wine into the heart of Europe. Then, by dint of constant and profitable exchanges with his neighbours, he has striven to increase and improve his wines. The great fraternity of a common language, from Sierre to Marseilles, has joined that other fraternity of the wine to create an authentic Rhône mentality, as sung by Frédéric Mistral and Charles Ferdinand Ramuz.

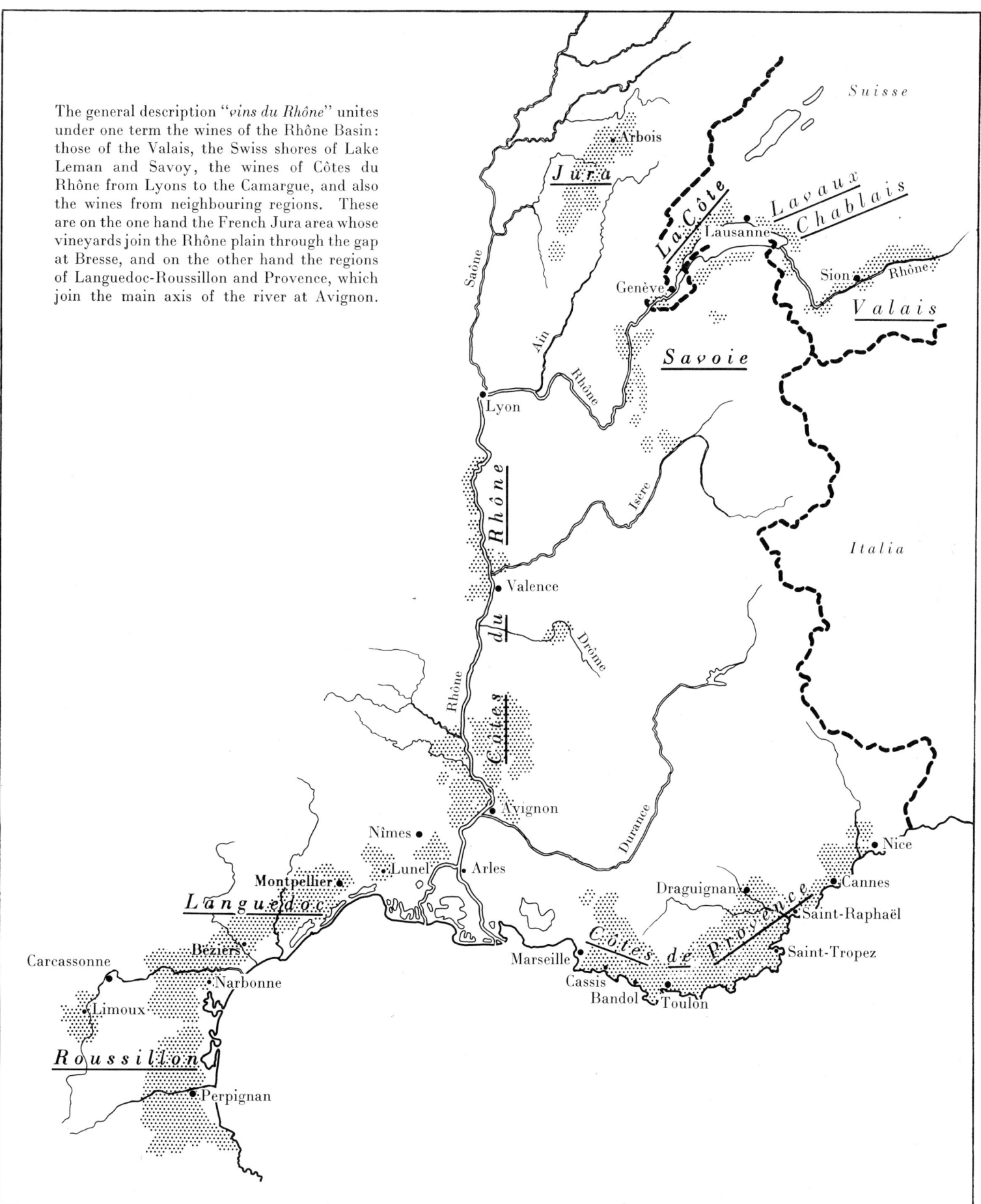

The general description *"vins du Rhône"* unites under one term the wines of the Rhône Basin: those of the Valais, the Swiss shores of Lake Leman and Savoy, the wines of Côtes du Rhône from Lyons to the Camargue, and also the wines from neighbouring regions. These are on the one hand the French Jura area whose vineyards join the Rhône plain through the gap at Bresse, and on the other hand the regions of Languedoc-Roussillon and Provence, which join the main axis of the river at Avignon.

Suisse

Jura

Arbois

La Côte *Lavaux* *Chablais*

Lausanne

Genève

Sion *Rhône*

Valais

Saône

Ain

Rhône

Savoie

Lyon

Isère

Italia

Rhône

Valence

Drôme

du

Côtes

Rhône

Durance

Avignon

Nîmes

Nice

Lunel Arles

Draguignan Cannes

Montpellier

Saint-Raphaël

Languedoc

Côtes de Provence

Saint-Tropez

Béziers

Marseille

Carcassonne

Narbonne

Cassis

Bandol Toulon

Limoux

Roussillon

Perpignan

THE SWISS WINES OF THE RHÔNE VALLEY

French-speaking Switzerland stands out as having the largest production of wine of all Swiss viticultural regions. The vineyards are for the most part planted on the slopes along the Rhône, in the level area of the river plain and on the more or less steep slopes alongside Lake Leman. There is an important production of white wines, while that of red wine, about 25 per cent of its total, is constantly increasing. Geographically, politically, and qualitatively too, three characteristic regions are prominent along the Swiss run of the Rhône: the cantons of Geneva, Valais and Vaud.

The method of cultivation used is generally the low cultivation *en gobelet*, as practised in the Canton of Vaud. A few timid attempts have been made to introduce the semi-high and high methods of cultivation, usually on flat or almost-flat land. But the desire always to bring out the natural richness of the wines generally keeps the winegrowers faithful to techniques, well-tried and cheap, which they have used over the years, both for working the land and for thinning and preparing the vines. This latter is very delicate work, carried out during the month of June, and consists of tying the vine-shoots and stems to the vine-props. In former times, this work was done by the girls of the Aosta Valley (in Italy), Savoy (in France) and Valais (in Switzerland), who used to come into the Canton of Vaud for the occasion, but this custom is dying out now. Dressed in their beautiful local costumes, the girls left their neighbouring regions and, for ten or twelve days, worked the vines *en tâche*, that is, by small plots of just over an acre each.

Cultivating *en gobelet* allows the grapes, growing closer to the ground, to benefit from a more complete maturing and an optimal enrichment in natural sugar. Plants trained in this way have a single vertical trunk terminating in several arms following the shape of a goblet. The advantages of such a method are its simplicity and that no vine support is needed.

Canton of Valais

The traveller descending the Rhône valley sees the first vines appear soon after Brig, alongside the river and up in the lateral valleys. The land in Valais used for vine cultivation has usually a poor soil which has been improved over the centuries only by tremendous effort. Patient maintenance work is needed to maintain the little terrace walls which alone hold back the soil clinging to the mountainside. In this valley bordered by mountain peaks with eternal snow, the sun brings its warmth and blessing with great generosity.

The people of Valais are a sturdy race, proud of many traditions, who have known how to get the best results from the almost Mediterranean climate of the Rhône valley. The vine is queen in a canton where excellent fruit orchards produce apricots, asparagus and strawberries. It must have existed there since earliest times, but the vines which were cultivated in those far-off days have been almost completely abandoned in favour of varieties perfectly suited to the valley's soil and climate. The extent of the vineyard in Valais, which is still expanding, is about 10,000 acres, of which about 8,500 are on slopes and hillsides. To reap the full benefit of the sun the vines are mostly planted on the right bank of the river; and the vine-growers cover the soil, or mix gravel or crushed shale into it, to catch and hold the warmth still more. The vinegrower of this land has an endless patience: he has gone close to the great mountain glaciers to seek the water source for the essential irrigation of his plants, and has led the precious liquid down to the vineyards by artificial canals or *bisses* along the mountainside, distributing it by trickling or sprinkling.

This is a deeply religious land, but one that is very realistic too. A famous vinegrower, now dead, liked to tell the following tale: "Back in the days when the Bishop of Sion, today the cantonal capital, was both spiritual and temporal prince of the Valais, an angel of the Lord appeared to him in his prayers and spoke as follows: 'The Lord has been touched by the great troubles of the people of Valais, whose vines dry up in the sun, while the people of Bern [the neighbouring canton, separated from Valais by a chain of mountains] receive a plentiful rain to produce beautiful green and lush grazings. Therefore my Master, in order to distribute better his blessings, will cause it to rain on Valais as on other parts of Helvetia. Its people will be able to abandon their costly and dangerous *bisses* and instead of killing themselves in this work of leading the water to the vines and watering, they will be able to relax and have a good time.' The bishop, deeply moved, thanked the angel profusely but asked leave for eight days before giving his assent to this generous celestial proposition, in order to be able to submit it to his dear brethren. Eight days later the angel, punctual at the rendezvous, received the following answer: 'My brethren thank the Lord for all his blessings, but as far as the matter of watering is concerned, they would prefer to look after it themselves, for they know better than anyone else what needs doing.' Since that time the sun shines for everyone, with special care for this rather privileged canton."

The steeply terraced vineyards of the Valais.

High above Lake Leman, the famous Riex-Epesses vineyards chequer the slopes of the lake. This general view shows the vineyards following the indentations of the lake. In the centre background, the Rhône enters the lake near Villeneuve.

Between Lausanne and Geneva lie the vineyards of La Côte. Benefitting from the sun and the microclimate of the Lake Leman, La Côte is the most important viticultural region of the Canton of Vaud.

The wines which are harvested in Valais and which have gained it fame carry the name of FENDANT for the white wines produced from *Chasselas* (*Fendant Roux* and *Fendant Vert*), and that of DÔLE for the reds. The latter is a harmonious mixture of wines derived from the *Pinot Noir*, which originates from Burgundy, and the *Gamay*, a typical Beaujolais vine-stock. Each year, some 7,700,000 gallons of FENDANT, DÔLE and other wines from special stock are harvested, to bring to sagacious drinkers fresh strength, a delight to the palate, warmth of heart and a flowering of the spirit.

The white wines of the Valais are very numerous and very different from each other, depending on the stock which produced them. But the best-known and most widely sold is certainly FENDANT; harvested for probably about a century, it comes from vine-stocks which originated in the neighbouring canton of Vaud, where they were already well acclimatized. It is an admirable wine which pleases at all hours by its balance, its restrained strength and even, in hot years, by its hidden violence; it is a dry wine without any residual sugar in suspension. It is chosen as the friend and companion of those evenings for eating the *raclette*, a well-known cheese dish typical of Valais.

It is JOHANNISBERG which occupies the second place of importance among the white wines. Produced from *Sylvaner* or *Plant du Rhin*, whose grape-bunches are recognizable by their small size and closely-packed clusters, this wine is warmer than FENDANT. It is selected with special care, is remarkable for its strength, but nevertheless combines a great distinctiveness with an exquisite and attractive charm. This wine makes a good companion to the locally grown asparagus.

The art of guiding the wine, of leading it to its perfect flowering, is very well-known here, and the concern and respect for the profession of oenologist have brought a wide fame to the wines of Valais. As with FENDANT, one must drink JOHANNISBERG while it is still young; it is not a wine that should be allowed to age too much.

Beside these two well-known wines, one must mention a few other specialities whose quantities are, however, very small, at the most not more than 5 per cent of the entire harvest of Valais.

PINOT GRIS or MALVOISIE (Malmsey) is a heady and strong wine which, in good years, does not manage to change all the natural sugar it contains into alcohol. It is especially a dessert wine, mellow and flavoursome, with its bright colour shining brilliantly in the glass like molten gold. MALVOISIE therefore charms the drinker as much by its beauty as by its taste and its bouquet, bringing a note of agreeable bliss to the conclusion of a meal that was perhaps full of extravagances, pomp and pageantry.

ERMITAGE is a firm, powerful and strongly-alcoholic wine, capable of being kept for a long time and with a bouquet which sings all the beauties of Valais.

Then there are PETITE ARVINE, AMIGNE and HUMAGNE, typical local wines which have not emigrated elsewhere. ARVINE is a virile and lively wine which sometimes has some bite; it resists the ravages of time thanks to its natural liveliness. AMIGNE (*vinum amoenum*) is a more delicate, more pleasant wine with a light bouquet; it holds its own at the beginning of a meal as well as at the end. HUMAGNE (*vinum humanum*), which is gradually disappearing, could be said to resemble certain old winegrowers of Valais: it not only has their brusqueness and sharpness, but also shares their frankness and nobility.

Some other wines also deserve mention, notably MUSCAT. Very little is harvested but it is vinified as a dry wine and then fermented to have more savour and bouquet: it is a wine which, if drunk while still young, flatters the most exacting noses and taste-buds by its aroma. Finally, one can mention two local specialities which are not commercialized and which one must be lucky enough to drink on the spot in order to appreciate fully their true qualities: PAYEN, made from a very old vine-stock, *Sauvagnin*, and VIN DU GLACIER, also from an old plant, *Rèze*. All these wines are specialities of Valais which are much discussed but which it is unfortunately very difficult to encounter, owing to their extreme rarity.

Among the red wines, DÔLE deserves a special mention: it is a wine which has body and mellowness yet which is nevertheless not heavy nor tiring. A delightful blending of *Pinot Noir* and *Gamay*, DÔLE can only carry this name if it contains a minimum amount of natural sugar, which is very closely checked and if the entire crop has been supervised by the Cantonal laboratory. If the alcohol content is not high enough, the wine will be named GORON: lighter and very pleasant, this never leaves the Valais.

Canton of Vaud

As far as Saint-Maurice, the Rhône valley is relatively narrow, but then it widens suddenly to form the vast Lake Leman, along all of which stretches the Canton of Vaud. To simplify, one may say there are three different viticultural regions in this canton; Chablais, Lavaux and La Côte.

In a general way, Vaud produces chiefly white wines, marketed under the name DORIN, although a production of red wines under the name SALVAGNIN has been increasing over the past ten years. This canton produces about 6,600,000 gallons each year, harvested from 8,000 acres of vines. All wines bearing the name

DORIN come from the *Chasselas* (*Fendant Roux* and *Fendant Vert*), a vine that has kept its name when commercialized.

DORIN, CHABLAIS, YVORNE and AIGLE have, in particular, built up a big reputation: these dry wines, true-bred, warm and of a great finesse—a major quality in wine—are much sought after. Among them, one must single out for special notice OVAILLES D'YVORNE, one of the best sites in the canton.

In the Lavaux region, the Dézaley wines are excellent; coming from vineyards hanging on steep slopes, these wines—aristocratic, rich, full—are dry with all the delicacy and exquisite bitterness needed to assure them a long life, and the slight hint of a flinty taste is a characteristic flavour. These are once more wines from the *Chasselas* grape, which because of its large yield and sturdiness and the earthy taste of the wine is still preferred by the conservative Swiss vinegrowers to the more noble vines that the vineyard would seem to favour. The Dézaley is a big terraced southern slope with glacial moraine overlying the original mollasse. It lies between Vevey and Lausanne and obtains its excellent microclimate mainly because of its proximity to Lake Leman. This vineyard was created around 1100, together with the other famous vineyards mentioned above, thanks to the untiring efforts of Cistercian monks. After the desecularization of the clergy it fell under Bern sovereignty and today belongs to the Wine Estates of the City of Lausanne.

In the canton of Vaud, wines are presented with the name of their commune of origin, so that one has for the region of Lavaux such famous labels as EPESSES, RIVAZ, SAINT-SAPHORIN (usually abbreviated to SAINT-SAPH), among others. The white wines of Vaud are, as a general rule, less tender than those of Valais, but also less lively than the wines of Geneva. These shades of meaning were much clearer in olden times, and winegrowers of Vaud, great ones for picturesque speech, liked to say that the wines of Geneva were *raides et pointus* ("stiff and pointed") like the North Wall of the Eiger, only to hear the Genevese Calvinists reply that the Vaud wines were as flat as the pages of the psalm-book! But progress in oenology has erased all these faults, so that today these wines are delicate, fruity, fresh and pleasant, as much at home during a meal as on any other occasion.

The slopes of La Côte, the most important viticultural region of the Canton of Vaud, are gentler, and if the wines harvested there are also less full-bodied and warm, they are nevertheless also appreciated for their remarkably fresh bouquet.

Large co-operative cellars and big firms have made the wines of this region well known, with such names as the famous VINZEL, MONT, FÉCHY, LUINS, TARTEGNIN and MORGES. There are, in addition, numerous châteaux along La Côte, rich in history and hiding in their cellars the inviting and exhilarating wines from the vineyards which surround them.

The red wines of Vaud carry the name SALVAGNIN (from the name of this old vine-stock); but only reds from noble stock (*Pinot* and *Gamay*) may in fact carry it, for this name is only given after a severe quality test. Elegant, balanced, velvety, flattering, well-bred, these slightly dark-coloured wines are warm enough and rich enough in alcohol to accompany spiced and seasoned foods. The ceaseless search for fresh markets leads some proprietors to offer their wines by separating the vine-stock used; the *Pinot Noir* can then do full justice to all its real magnificence and, as Latin-speaking winegrowers might be tempted to say, *in Pinot veritas*.

Red wines which do not have the SALVAGNIN name are sold under various trade names. In very great demand, these wines are served cool like Beaujolais wines and should also be drunk while young, unlike the PINOT which reveals itself, after a few years of ageing, as a wine of high class.

Special vine-stocks are much less cultivated in the Canton of Vaud than in Valais or Geneva; one does, however, find generous JOHANNISBERGS, sweet white PINOT-CHARDONNAYS, and RIESLING-SYLVANERS with a strongly muscat bouquet. But on the whole, these wines are rare as much by their high quality as by their small quantity, although they may well carry to a seventh heaven those who partake of them.

Canton of Geneva

Leaving the Canton of Vaud, the traveller arrives in Geneva, the site not only of a great international city with many attractions but also of a rich and flourishing vineyard of about 2,500 acres. One-fifth of this area is planted to red stock, and *Gamay*, which comes especially from Beaujolais, is the most-used vine-stock; *Pinot Noir*, however, of Burgundian origin, is carving for itself an increasing large share of the canton's wine production. The white wines come from different vine-stocks of which the most important, *Chasselas*, covers an area of 1,235 acres. About 740 acres produce wines which are original and full of personality; they come from special, well-acclimatized vine-stocks: *Riesling-Sylvaner*, *Sylvaner* and *Aligoté*. Some other plants, such as *Pinot Gris*, *Chardonnay* or *Pinot Blanc*, in particular, produce exquisite and well-bred wines in, alas, only small quantities. About 500 acres are planted to red vine-stock, producing, in a year and for an average total of 2,640,000 gallons, as much red wine as white.

On the banks of Lake Leman, above the village of Saint-Saphorin, the terraced vines of Lavaux turn towards the south-west to benefit from a triple share of the sun's warmth: that of the heavenly body itself, that received from the lake by reflection and, in the cool of the day, that returned to the soil from the little walls of sun-baked stones. In this vineyard, the most widely grown vine-stock is the *Chasselas*.

The winegrowers of Geneva are proud to be the descendants and the worthy successors of very long lines of antecedents. These vineyards, in fact, date back to the time of the Roman conquest, and several emperors have left their mark in various decrees. Domitian, trying to prevent the expansion of the vine, ordered the uprooting of half of those not belonging to Romans; Probus, on the other hand, favoured its cultivation and kept his soldiers busy in their spare time spreading the noble plant to numerous regions.

The vineyard of Geneva had a very chequered history over the centuries and the vinegrowers needed a firmly rooted faith to persevere in their work. Having survived the pillaging, pilfering and general murdering characteristic of, in particular, the sixteenth and seventeenth centuries, they saw towards the end of the nineteenth century two new pests emerge, as elsewhere in Europe: phylloxera and mildew. Powerless to fight against these two calamities, they suffered the disappearance of half their vineyards; but the

vineyards were re-planted and now extend in gentle folds between the Jura mountains and the Salève ridge.

The wines produced from *Chasselas* and called PERLAN have gained for themselves an enviable place over the past few years: generally light, they are usually sold *sur lie*, that is, they have not been decanted. They have kept their natural carbonic acid gas, have a delicate perfume and rejoice the eye of the connoisseur as they sparkle gently in the glass. It has been said they are much like the Genevese: not very biting at one's first meeting, they turn out to be the most joyous and friendly of companions. These wines can be drunk still milky, before they have finished fermenting, although it is preferable to allow them to reach full maturity. However, they are not rich enough in alcohol to gain much by being kept for several years.

The success of the wines produced from special vine-stocks must be mentioned here. Talented winegrowers in this region offer, for example, RIESLING-SYLVANER with a slightly musky perfume; dry and strong, this is much drunk as an aperitif. SYLVANER or JOHANNISBERG take the richness of the vine from which they come and deserve encouragement from the drinker; thanks to the little-known *Muscat* plant, and also to *Aligoté* and *Chardonnay*, which are very high-class stocks, excellent and harmonious wines can be offered to the consumer.

The greater part of the wines of Geneva are very well produced, with modern methods and the large cellars grouped together under a single trade name. A few well-equipped individual proprietors produce, on their own, wines which are becoming better known.

A final mention must be made of the red Geneva wines GAMAY and PINOT NOIR: the former are produced in some quantity and are supple and friendly wines, not heavy, and excellent in company; the PINOT is a richer wine which has already brought joy to a few connoisseurs in good years.

The Bacchic Brotherhoods

Everywhere, be it in Geneva, Valais or Vaud, one sees the marvels and the gifts that wine brings in its train. One must admire not only the wine itself, but also the manner in which the ideas of the land are enriched, the customs strengthened and even the thoughts and way of life of Rhône-side dwellers heightened—wherever wine is present.

Recently, between the years 1950 and 1960, several brotherhoods of wine were formed in these three Swiss cantons, with the sole aim of making the varieties of wealth offered by the Rhône vineyards better known and more appreciated. The Académie du Cep in Geneva, the Channe in Valais and the Confrérie du Guillon in Vaud all organize great gastronomic dinners, usually in the château de Dardagny in Geneva, the château de Chillon (immortalized by the poet Byron) in Vaud, or a number of other famous places in Valais. The dishes and the wines are presented, served and commented upon with love, humour and competence. These well-dressed occasions see the friends of wine come running from just about everywhere, to meet *ce fils sacré du soleil* ("this sacred son of the sun") as Baudelaire put it, in order to prove that this drink mentioned in the Bible is admirably adept at forging faithful friendships, opening hearts, broadening the spirit and giving the final proof that wine throughout the world is the ambassador of civilization.

THE WINES OF SAVOY

Two writers of ancient Rome, Pliny the Younger and Columella, made famous the wines of Allobroge, the Savoy of today. The prince of Roman gourmets, Lucullus, had Savoy wines served at his table and the vinegrowers of Savoy are proud of the title of seniority that history has conferred on them.

With the exception of the local table wines drunk in the region, the wines of Savoy make up that honourable company called *vins délimités de qualité supérieure*, or more simply "V.D.O.S.". There is no outstanding vintage wine; there are simply good, honest wines which are, none the less, well known outside their place of birth.

The vineyard of Savoy can be divided into three zones:

1. To the north, the southern shores of Lake Leman, from Evian to Annemasse; the right bank of the river Arve from Annemasse to Bonneville, and the area along the Swiss frontier to Saint-Julien-en-Genevois. These make up a relatively homogeneous zone which is chiefly planted, as across the border in Switzerland, with *Chasselas*. The winegrowers produce fresh, light white wines, such as MARIN, RIPAILLE and MARIGNAN. First place, however, must go to COTEAUX-DE-CRÉPY and PETIT CRÉPY, both of them clear, semi-sparkling wines with a delicate perfume of almond, reputed also to be the most diuretic wines in France.

2. In the centre, the region of the Lake of Bourget, Seyssel and the left bank of the Rhône gives a very characteristic wine called Savoy ROUSSETTE, the principal vintages of which are FRANGY, MARESTEL, MONTHOUX and SEYSSEL. These wines have a good bouquet; fruity and full-bodied, they are the product of *Altesse*, a vine brought back, it is said, by the Count of Mareste from a crusade. Seyssel also produces a pleasant sparkling wine.

3. To the south, the vineyard encompasses the region of Chambéry, the right bank of the river Isère from Saint-Pierre-d'Albigny to Sainte-Marie-d'Alloix, and the Arc valley up to Saint-Michel.

Apart from the local wines, a few white wines have emerged from anonymity; these are the wines of Monterminod, Apremont, Abymes, Chignin, Cruet, Montmélian and Saint-Jean-de-la-Porte. To these white wines one can add a few reds and rosés, light, easy to drink and which, it is said, do not upset the drinker's temper.

The total production of the wines of Savoy is about 4,400,000 gallons.

THE WINES OF THE FRENCH JURA

The Roman naturalist Pliny, who also served in the armies of Germania, recalled "this grape needing no special preparations which produces the pitch-flavoured wine recently bringing pleasure to Sequani the area of the river Seine". If one is to believe this statement, the vine was established on the western edge of the Jura mountains right at the beginning of our historic age. There it prospered and the resulting VIN D'ARBOIS gained wide renown.

In the year 1885 occurred the first attack of phylloxera, which within the next ten years was to destroy the entire vineyard. The pre-phylloxera vines were cultivated with the aid of props and with no particular order or symmetry. The new vines were planted in lines and trained on to wire supports, a method allowing the use of a plough to work the land wherever it does not slope too much and an arrangement which also enables the grapes to soak up the maximum warmth of the sun. The first harvests of the twentieth century bear witness to the rebirth of this vineyard.

Today, the vineyard of the Jura, well situated and with a cold, humid climate in winter, extends from Salins in the north to Saint-Amour in the south, a stretch of some 50 miles in length by 8 miles at its widest part. It is planted to *Ploussard* or *Poulsard*, *Trousseau* and *Gros Noirin* for the red wines, and to *Naturé* or *Savagnin*, *Chardonnay* or *Pinot Blanc* for the white wines. Apart from the local table wines, the Jura produces three well-known wines:

The CÔTES-DU-JURA are full-bodied, heady red wines, earthy rosés, and dry whites which, although lively and fruity, are sometimes found to be a little acid when young.

The VINS D'ARBOIS are finer and more generous than the above-mentioned ones; the reds and rosés come from the *Ploussard* and, to a lesser degree, from the *Trousseau* and *Pinot Noir*. It is interesting to recall, in passing, that it was in Arbois, where he was born and where he owned a vineyard, that the illustrious Louis Pasteur worked on his study of fermentation.

The CHÂTEAU-CHALON is the wine *par excellence* of the Jura vineyards. This amber-coloured wine—hence its name *vin jaune*—is unusual in its production and handling. In the spring of the second year, after a normal vinification, it is transferred to a cask already impregnated with *vin jaune*. There it is left to age, without being touched in any way—not even the skin on its surface is disturbed—and it is bottled only after six years. This *vin jaune* is a truly original wine and one of the best white wines in France. Some of it is also produced under the name CÔTES-DU-JURA or ARBOIS, but it is the CHÂTEAU-CHALON which is the undisputed leader. It is the only white wine which must not be served chilled but slightly *chambré*, nearly at room temperature, in its specially shaped bottle called a *clavelin*.

The Jura vinegrowers also produce, apart from a sparkling wine processed by the *méthode champenoise* around Arbois, the so-called *vin de paille*, or straw wine. It is a wine of the winter frosts, made from grapes harvested at the end of the autumn which have been stored carefully on trays of straw until February; the grapes are then pressed, and the wine is kept in little oaken barrels. The *vin de paille* is a beautiful burned-topaz colour, a dessert wine with an unctuous bouquet.

Among the unusual Jura wines, one should not forget MACVIN, an aperitif produced by cooking the must from white grapes, infusing spices and, after filtering, adding *eau-de-vie de marc* (white brandy)

The annual production of the wines of the French Jura is now only about 660,000 gallons, not one-tenth of what it was before the advent of phylloxera.

THE WINES OF THE CÔTES DU RHÔNE

An infinite variety of locations and an infinite variety of wines—such are the characteristic features of the Côtes du Rhône region, stretching 125 miles along the majestic river, from Vienne-la-Romaine to Avignon, city of the Popes. In a few short hours by train or car, one passes from a northern world to a southern world, from forests of chestnuts to forests of olive trees. The wines produced in the various parts of the Rhône valley are different for reasons of variations of climate, of soil and also of vine-stocks.

The Côtes du Rhône region can be divided into two parts, separated by non-viticultural areas: the northern part from Vienne to Valence, and the southern part from Bourg-Saint-Andéol (just opposite Pierrelatte) as far as Avignon.

The cultivation of the vine has developed particularly in the vineyards of the CÔTES-DU-RHÔNE *appellation d'origine contrôlée*, but perhaps principally in the vineyards producing the basic type of wine. Thus, between 1956 and 1967, the area planted to vine increased from 31,085 acres to 60,330 acres, and wine production (including vintage wines) from 8,030,000 gallons to more than 22,000,000 gallons today (1967: 19,800,000 gallons of basic CÔTES-DU-RHÔNE, 4,400,000 gallons of vintage wines). As for the marketing side of wine production, the domestic demand has followed the increase in production, while exports have leaped ahead, from 1,386,000 in 1960 to about 3,216,400 gallons in 1967.

The basic regional name of the wine, which includes all types, is CÔTES-DU-RHÔNE. Within this vineyard, however, there are the following *appellations d'origine contrôlée* established by special decree of the French authorities: CHÂTEAUNEUF-DU-PAPE, CÔTE-RÔTIE, CONDRIEU, CORNAS, HERMITAGE, SAINT-PÉRAY, TAVEL, CHÂTEAU-GRILLET, CROZES-HERMITAGE, LIRAC and SAINT-JOSEPH.

CÔTE-RÔTIE: The vineyard of CÔTE-RÔTIE lies 22 miles south of Lyons and almost opposite Vienne, on precipitous slopes where the soil must be held in place by small walls. Two vine-stocks, *Viognier* and *Syrah*, produce a wine with a great fragrance and a delicate perfume which recalls violets and raspberries.

This red wine, harvested at Ampuis, develops its qualities to the full after ageing in casks for three or four years; it can be kept in the bottle for more than 20 years. The average production is 26,400 gallons.

CONDRIEU: This white wine comes solely from the white vine *Viognier* and must have an alcohol content of at least 11°. Its area of production includes the three communes of Condrieu (Rhône), Vérin and Saint-Michel (Loire). This gives an average production of about 4,400 gallons from the 17 acres of vineyards that the fifteen or so producers cultivate. Cultivation is carried out solely on small, stone-walled terraces, a type of exploitation of the land that is extremely difficult because it is impossible to employ mechanical aid. This difficulty accounts for the fact that these vineyards are being gradually abandoned.

The fermentation of Condrieu wines is allowed to proceed more or less slowly according to the prevailing temperature; it continues up to the end of the year when the rigorous winter stops the process. Fermentation re-starts in the spring and continues until some time in summer, if dry wines are being produced. To obtain the sweet wines, which contain 15-30 grammes of sugar per litre and represent 80 per cent of the total production here, fermentation is stopped by successive racking, combined with blending.

This wine is not drunk when it is old, because although it stands up to ageing very well, it loses that special fruitiness which has made its name. Bottling is therefore carried out, depending on the type of wine, during the first or the second year.

CHÂTEAU-GRILLET: This vintage wine is not cultivated very extensively and is confined to a few plots of land in the communes of Verin and Saint-Michel-sous-Condrieu (Loire).

The granite hillsides of Château-Grillet, facing south and dominating the Rhône, have a climate which is dry and hot during the summer and mild during the autumn, allowing the vine *Viognier* to attain over-maturity. The character of this tiny vineyard lies in its topography: the whole is made up of small, stepped terraces planted to not more than two rows of plants, and sometimes to only a few individual plants.

Harvested in late October, the must from these white grapes is put in casks and allowed to ferment very slowly over several months. It is racked a number of times to ensure a perfect clarification, and forms a very particular bouquet of violets. After two years of constant care, it is bottled, and it can then be kept for many years. Dry and fairly heady, it has some resemblance to Rhine wine, although it has more body and gives off a better developed perfume.

CROZES-HERMITAGE: This wine is produced in the communes of Serves, Erome, Gervans, Larnage, Crozes-Hermitage, Tain-l'Hermitage, Mercurol, Chanos-Curson, Beaumont-Montreux, La Roche-de-Glun and Pont-de-l'Isère.

The red wines are produced solely from the *Syrah* grape; the whites from the *Roussanne* and *Marsanne* varieties. However, the addition of *Marsanne* and *Roussanne* white grapes within the limits of 15 per cent is authorized for the production of red wine.

The hilly nature of the terrain makes cultivation here an extremely arduous affair. On the stepped-up terraces, all work must be done by hand, and fertilizers as well as the entire harvest can be carried only on the backs of men. The average production from 865 acres is 312,000 gallons.

These red wines are lighter and more purplish than the HERMITAGE wines which follow in these pages, and they retain a tang of the soil, although they are less mellow or fine.

The white wines are very slightly coloured and sometimes lack a certain flavour and strength; they are, however, fine and light, with a perfume of hazelnut.

L'HERMITAGE: The hillside of l'Hermitage, which produces the wine of that name, lies in the northern part of the Côtes du Rhône region, in the department of Dauphiné. It commands the little town of Tain-l'Hermitage, in the department of Drôme, situated beside the Rhône on Route Nationale No. 7 between Vienne and Valence.

The earliest vineyards here date back to the tenth century, but legend has it that Henri Gaspart de Sterimberg, a knight returning from the Crusades under Louis VIII and weary of wars, sought from Queen Blanche de Castille a corner of land to which he could retire. This would explain the origin of the name "Hermitage". HERMITAGE obtained its titles to nobility as a wine under Henry IV and Louis XIII and especially under Louis XIV. Up to the time of the phylloxera disaster at the end of the last century, this was universally considered to be one of the foremost wines of France, being the favourite vintage wine of the Czar's court in Russia. It was also much esteemed in nineteenth-century England.

The HERMITAGE vineyard is blessed with a quite exceptional geographical position: it faces south-west at an altitude of 894 feet above sea-level, only 6 ¼ miles from the 45° parallel of latitude.

The red wine is produced entirely from the vine *Syrah*, while the white wine comes from *Marsanne* with the addition of a small quantity of *Roussanne*. The 400 acres under cultivation are spread among 70 small viticultural properties. The wines of Hermitage are no longer the wines of the Lyons region, following on from those of Burgundy, nor are they wines of Provence yet; they are strictly Rhône wines.

SAINT-JOSEPH: The name of Saint-Joseph is a relatively recent one, since it was authorized by a decree dated June 15th, 1956. It had had, nonetheless, its "letters patent of nobility" for many years: according to Elie Brault in the book *Anne and her time*, Louis XII would allow on his table only the wines from his property at Beaune, his land at Tournon or his vineyards at Chenoves.

Six communes in the department of Ardèche are entitled to produce this wine, with the exception of lands which are unsuitable on account of their soil or their position are: Glunn, Mauves, Tournon, Saint-Jean-de-Muzols, Lemps and Vion.

For the red wines the *Syrah* grape is used while the *Marsanne* and *Roussanne* produce the whites.

The vine is cultivated on the steep slopes overlooking the right bank of the Rhône. Most of the work is done by hand, and the vintage is carried in on the grape-pickers' backs. The maximum yield permitted is 350 gallons per acre. The mean annual production is 33,000 gallons from 200 acres.

The SAINT-JOSEPH reds are fine wines with a perfumed bouquet although they are, perhaps, rather less full-bodied than the HERMITAGE wines. They have a fine ruby colour and are agreeable to drink after a few years in the bottle. The whites are fruity, supple and mellow; they should be drunk young while they retain their full perfume.

CORNAS. Every day throughout the centuries, as the rising sun sheds its rays on the Rhône valley, the first communes to benefit from them have been Châ-teaubourg and Cornas, situated as they are with their backs to the Cévennes. The commune of Cornas has a Provençal type of climate, as witness the olive, fig and almond trees which flourish in many a garden there. This privileged situation has encouraged the cultivation of the vine for more than a thousand years. A document of the time of Charles V reveals that the Great Companies halted at Cornas for far longer than was scheduled in their marching programme since they could not resist the good wine in the inns of this tiny piece of countryside.

The A.O.C. CORNAS covers the area around the village and the granite slopes; the alluvial soils in the Rhône valley are excluded. The vineyard has an area of only 300 acres.

The grapes grown in the vineyard are the *Syrahs*. Since they are not very productive, long shoots are permitted and this means that the shoots must be fastened to the props before the spring. All the work of cultivation on the terraces must be done by hand and the harvest seldom exceeds 44,000 gallons.

The best wine comes from the grapes ripened on the slope. It is richer and fuller bodied, fruitier and heavier with a characteristic taste of the soil due to its richness in tannin. In its first year, CORNAS may be a little sour and astringent; it reaches its peak of quality after three winters in the wood and two years in the bottle.

SAINT-PÉRAY. At the foot of Mount Crussol and in the latitude of Valence, we find the village of Saint-Péray. It would seem that the department of Ardèche has always been a favourite winegrowing country and, with CORNAS and SAINT-JOSEPH, SAINT-PÉRAY forms the trinity of fine Vivarais wines.

The vineyard, which is one of the oldest in the northern Côtes du Rhône area, is quite limited in area: 193 acres with 90 owners. The soil is tilled by hand because of the narrowness of the space between the rows of vines. In the parcels where the slope is less steep it is sometimes possible to use horse-ploughs or hand-ploughs.

The only white grapes permitted are the *Roussette* (or *Roussanne*) and the *Marsanne*. The *Roussette* is a fine grape variety and produces a high-class wine with a strong perfume, but since it is not very productive and is sensitive to disease, it is gradually being abandoned. Because of the soil type lighter wines are produced than on the other side of the Rhône.

Until the beginning of the nineteenth century, the Saint-Péray wines were served *nature*, i.e. as still wines. Attempts by local wine-merchants in 1828 to convert them into sparkling wines produced excellent results, and since then Saint-Péray has been available in that form also. Classical white-wine vinification is used. After pressing and drawing off, the must is fermented in 50-gallon hogsheads called *pièces*. The fermentation must be completed before winter. The dry white wines are usually bottled after two or three years.

The wines produced are marketed, therefore, either as still wines, as dry SAINT-PÉRAY, or as sparkling wines. It is the latter form—SAINT-PÉRAY MOUSSEUX—which is now the better known.

CHÂTEAUNEUF-DU-PAPE. This is the "Pontiff" of the Côtes du Rhône wines. In addition to possessing all the warmth of the Provençal sun, this wine is perfumed by the full aroma of that region's sparse soil. Between Orange and Avignon, dominating one of the widest and most breath-taking landscapes of Provence, an abrupt hill bears a picturesque village crowned by an imposing medieval ruin. The place was formerly selected by the popes as their summer residence. Climbing up the sides of the hill, the impressive vineyard of Châteauneuf-du-Pape reveals that the local winegrowers have lost nothing of the traditional renown attached to this soil. The wine produced is still in every way worthy of the pontifical table. The territory entitled to the A.O.C., i.e. the commune of Châteauneuf-du-Pape and parts of the communes of Orange, Courthezon, Beddarides and Sorgues, has been strictly limited since 1923. Incidentally, the national regulations on A.O.C.s, promulgated in December 1936, were inspired by what had been achieved at Châteauneuf-du-Pape.

The methods of cultivation, vinification and conservation have been fixed both by law and by the strong force of local tradition.

CHÂTEAUNEUF-DU-PAPE comes from thirteen grapes, seven of which, *Grenache, Clairette, Mourvèdre, Picpoul, Terret, Syrah* and *Cinsault*, are regarded as principal grapes, while the other six, *Counoise, Muscadin, Vaccarèse, Picardan, Roussanne* and *Bourboulenc*, are regarded as ancillary. Each of these grapes contributes its own special note to the wine produced: the *Grenache* and the *Cinsault* give it warmth, sweetness and mellowness; the *Mourvèdre*, the *Syrah*, the *Muscadin* and the *Vaccarèse* contribute colour, solidity and staying-power; the *Counoise* and the *Picpoul* supply wininess, taste, freshness and a special bouquet, while the *Clairette, Bourboulenc, Roussanne* and *Picardan* give it elegance, fire and brilliance.

The wines of Châteauneuf-du-Pape are always highly coloured and very warm. They have a powerful bouquet reminiscent of oriental spices. They are very varied in type: the pebbly soils give a great deal of strength while the sandy and sandy-clayey soils produce a wine of great finesse and elegance.

The vineyard covers over 6,000 acres which produce 176,000 gallons (15,400 gallons only of white wine). It has virtually doubled in the last twenty years.

Side by side with the great vineyards we have just mentioned, there is a host of small villages whose names strike no particular chord but which are excellent producers of wine with the A.O.C. CÔTES-DU-RHÔNE. This wine comes from no less than 138 communes with an average annual production of 13,200,000 gallons. Some of the areas involved are entitled to a stricter commune regulation, the place-name being granted to their wine after compulsory tasting. Cases in point are Cairanne, Gigondas, Vacqueyras etc.

Although the *Grenache* and the *Carigan* form the framework of the CÔTES-DU-RHÔNE wines, any or all of the following grape varieties can be used to distinguish one wine from another: *Clairette, Syrah, Mourvèdre, Terret Noir, Counoise, Picpoule, Muscardin, Bourboulenc, Ugni Blanc, Roussanne, Marsanne* and *Viognier*. It should be added that there are also variations due to the soil, the exposure, and individual cultivation which give each growth its originality. Everything is carefully regulated: the grape variety, the soil, the pruning of the plant, the degree of alcohol and the yield.

CAIRANNE. This is one of the oldest of winegrowing terrains. Almost all the Clairanne vineyard, which covers 3,000 acres, consists of slopes and terraces facing due south.

VACQUEYRAS and GIGONDAS. The main GIGONDAS grape is the *Grenache* while VACQUEYRAS is still largely based on the *Carignan*, which is gradually being replaced by the *Cinsault* and the *Syrah*. The red wines of the A.O.C. are of great quality and approach those of CHÂTEAUNEUF-DU-PAPE.

LIRAC. The LIRAC wines, whether red, rosé or even white, have each their own special type.

The principal grape, the *Grenache*, must make up at least 40 per cent of the planting for Lirac reds and rosés, the other 60 per cent consisting of *Cinsault* and *Mourvèdre*. Secondary grapes such as *Syrah* and *Picpoul* are permitted. In the case of the whites, 30 per cent of the planting must be the *Clairette* grape.

All these old local grapes, distributed throughout each vineyard in judiciously determined proportions and mixed together in the same vat at the harvest, produce these charming Lirac wines with such a pronounced bouquet and particular perfume.

TAVEL. A little village 8 miles from Avignon, Tavel, harvests from a particularly arid soil about 462,000 gallons on the average of a light red wine obtained from such old grape varieties as: *Clairette, Cinsault, Grenache* etc. This wine was very much appreciated by the Popes of Avignon, and by Philippe le Bel who claimed that "the only good wine is that from Tavel". It has an incomparable bouquet and, although strongly alcoholic, is light to the taste. Tavel can be taken as an aperitif or with red meat; it develops its full savour when it is put as an accompaniment to a young partridge or when served with a thrush with juniper berries.

RASTEAU. In this case, a single grape, the *Grenache*, has given birth to an excellent natural sweet wine. The must is vinified according to the classical method of obtaining naturally sweet wines. During fermentation, a certain amount of alcohol is added and this prevents the sugar from being completely transformed into alcohol. The wine thus retains a certain amount of sugar, which is the reason for its sweetness, while at the same time developing a high alcohol content.

BEAUMES-DE-VENISE. This is a natural sweet wine produced from various white *Muscats* with a special taste which are among the finest of their type. These wines are aged in casks or demijohns; when exposed to the sunlight, they develop a beautiful golden colour.

THE WINES OF THE CÔTES DE PROVENCE

The wines of the Côtes de Provence are of very ancient origin; under the name of "Provence wines", they were already known to the Romans. According to a statement by Justinian, it was the Gauls who cultivated the first vines brought from Italy and the near East by the Phocaeans, and they were already honoured during the reign of Caesar, who speaks of them in his Commentaries. The fame of the Provence wines continued through the Middle Ages and into the Renaissance; the Cartulary of Lérins mentions them and lords and abbots began to fix the rules for their production and marketing through such decrees as the Act of King Charles II in 1292, and the authorization by Queen Mary in 1391, both sovereigns of Provence.

In the seventeenth and eighteenth centuries, they were in high repute at the Court of the Sun King, where Madame de Sévigné became their best ambassadress. From this period dates the foundation by Louis de Vauvray, Naval Intendant at Toulon, of one of the first baccanalian orders, that of the "Knights of Medusa". In the nineteenth century and at the beginning of the twentieth, the *appellation contrôlée* and even the fame of the Côtes de Provence wines were in decline; under various names, some of these wines were used for blending and others for making vermouth. Only a few owners, proud of their growths and strong in the markets they had conquered, kept aloft the flag of this A.O.C.: under the auspices of the Syndical Association of the Winegrowing Landowners of the Var, established in 1931, they were to form the basis for the resurrection of the CÔTES-DE-PROVENCE.

The area of production is the result of a delimitation based on the geological, hydrological and climatic study of the land by a commission nominated by ministerial decree and composed of representatives of the National Institute of Place-Name Descriptions of Origin *(appellation d'origine)*, the General Inspectorate of the Ministry of Agriculture and the Science Faculties of the Universities of Marseilles and Montpellier. The area of production is limited to the following zones: the coastal zone of Provence from La Ciotat to Saint-Raphael; the Permian depression which stretches from Sanary through Toulon to Carnoules and Leluc; the triassic plateau of Lorgues-Carces; the terraces of the valley of the Var and the area described by geologists as the Eubeau Basin in the Alpes-Maritimes. A card index has been established for each producing commune and an individual card index per producer. They are all minutely followed.

The delimitation of the area of production, the fixing of a minimum production per acre and the determination of the grapes did not, in the eyes of the producers, constitute a sufficiently strict selection and they consequently imposed upon themselves the obligation to submit their produce, which already met the standards laid down, to an organoleptic analysis followed by examination by a tasting commission to decide if the wine were worthy of the *appellation contrôlée* CÔTES-DE-PROVENCE. In 1953 the wines were granted a statue allowing those of a sufficiently high standard to be sold as CÔTES DE PROVENCE V.D.Q.S. *(Vins Délimités de Qualité Supérieure)*, which is a secondary quality guarantee, and some wines are permitted to be sold as Classified Growths.

GRAPES. The varieties making up the CÔTES-DE-PROVENCE are fairly numerous. Some of them, however, play only a secondary part and occupy a limited area; everywhere the same basic grape varieties are cultivated.

Among the red grapes, the *Carignan* clearly heads the field, occupying as it does 25 per cent or more of the area of the vineyard. Late in budding, of average productivity but sensitive to oïdium, it gives full-bodied alcoholic wines which are sometimes rather sour in their youth. This bitterness rapidly disappears with age. A certain proportion of this grape is required.

The *Cinsault*, like the *Grenache* elsewhere, contributes suppleness, mellowness and bouquet. The same is true of the *Tibouren*, which is cultivated in a substantial area of the Maures mountains.

The *Mourvèdre*, an élite grape, formerly held a much more important place than at present; the irregularity of its production has caused it to lose ground. However, under the impulse of a few progressive winegrowers, it is once again gaining a certain favour and is now definitely extending its sway. If it is included in suitable proportions, it should ensure that the wines age well and should distinctly improve their quality.

Among the white grapes, the *Ugni* and the *Clairette*, together with the *Rolle* in the Alpes-Maritimes, have an almost complete monopoly. To these principal grapes, however, are sometimes added some other high-quality varieties including the *Syrah*, the *Cabernet*, the *Barbaroux*, the *Picpoul*, the *Roussanne* and the *Pecoultouar*.

It is by a judicious association of grapes, each contributing its particular characteristics, that the CÔTES-DE-PROVENCE acquire their balance and their special quality. There is a growing trend toward increasing the proportion of high-quality grapes, and rapid progress is being made. We should mention that the law imposes a minimum alcohol content of 11° for the red and rosé wines and of 11.5° for the white wines.

VINIFICATION. On their arrival in the cellars, whether private or co-operative, the vintages are carefully selected so that only grapes entitled to the A.O.C. will be introduced into the vats. Since the use of the mustimeter and the refractometer have become generalized, the winegrowers wait until the grapes have reached complete maturity so as to have the maximum number of degrees.

Fermentation usually takes place in concrete vats; some owners of classed growths, however, vinify in wooden vats. On the other hand, wood is always used when storing the wine for any length of time; this is obligatory for producers who sell in the bottle. A frequent practice is to remove the stalks. Vatting is generally quite short: 4 to 5 days for red wines but somewhat longer for the white wines, which ferment for about a fortnight; and only 24 hours for the rosé wines which are the natural result of the first 100 per cent pressing of rosé grapes. The white wine is usually obtained by the so-called "bleeding" method. It consists in leaving open the drainage tap of the vat which contains the trodden vintage and withdrawing a certain proportion of the must.

The environmental conditions and the grapes cultivated make it possible to obtain, by rational vinification and careful storage, wines of the very first quality.

CLASSED GROWTHS. The Commission on Boundaries noted that, among the mass of producers, there were some who were organized to vinify in the best conditions and to store part of their harvest every year which was later sold, after ageing, in bottles. The Commission therefore adopted the idea of Classed Growths for any estate which had formerly practised ageing. It considered whether the fame of the wines from such-and-such a holding was justified on the basis of the environmental conditions, the grapes used, the cultivation methods, the vinification and growing processes used and the quality of the wines obtained. Moreover, it demanded a minimum ageing of 15 months for the red wines and 8 months for the rosé and white wines. Of more than 60 vineyards visited, the Commission decided that only 30 merited selection as CÔTES-DE-PROVENCE Classed Growths.

The fact that Provençal wines adapt easily to almost any dish might have accounted for the expansion of the A.O.C. to the detriment of certain wines.

The rosé, the great speciality of the CÔTES-DE-PROVENCE, is fruity and full-flavoured and has an irridescent robe. A choice companion to all dishes, it adds a note of high-quality, which is much appreciated by the epicures, to the festive board.

The white wine is generally dry, sometimes sparkling, but always full of the savour of the Provençal hills and proves a most happy foil to the fish and shellfish of the Mediterranean coast. The dace of the gulf of Saint-Tropez, the crayfish of the Corsican creeks, the red mullet from the rocky depths of the Var coast as well as the Mediterranean shell-fish take on their full gustatory value when set off by the bouquet of a bottle of CÔTES-DE-PROVENCE.

The red wine, which is very full-flavoured, is at its best when accompanying pâtés, pasties, game and roasts. It is the perfect foil to venison and brings out still further the delicate aroma of woodcock flamed in old armagnac.

As in the case of a number of other wines, a special shape of bottle has been created for CÔTES-DE-PROVENCE. It is derived from the original form of the Provençal bottle.

Wine Confraternity

Faithful to their tradition, the winegrowers of the Côtes-de-Provence, like those of many other wine-producing regions, have created a wine society or, more exactly, have revived a very ancient confraternity, founded in 1690, the Confraternity of the Knights of Medusa, from the name of one of the classical gorgons. Its first Grand Master was M. Dantan, its chief founder being the Naval Intendant at Toulon, M. Louis Girardin de Vauvray, who was named a benefactor member of the Order in 1697.

The rituals of the Order unfold in the sumptuous setting of the Château de Sainte-Roseline, at Arcs-de-Provence, in its cloisters and in its park, and they are presided over by Baron de Rasque de Laval and his Grand Council.

THE WINES OF LANGUEDOC AND ROUSSILLON

In Languedoc-Roussillon we find a very large wine-growing area which flourishes under extremely favourable natural conditions. The cultivation of the wine is at present the dominant activity of the region. In certain districts it is combined with other activities such as market gardening and fruit-growing on the Garde bank of the Rhône, cattle-raising in the region of Garrigues and the lower Montagne Noire, industry in the coalfields of Alès and near the urban centres of Montpelliers, Nîmes and Béziers and fishing along the coast, but it remains the sole activity for most of the communes in spite of the changeover which has begun.

Although 85 per cent of the wines are ordinary wines for current consumption, produced from the best grapes and vinified under first-class conditions, it should not be forgotten that 12 per cent are wines of simple *appellation d'origine* while 3 per cent are wines of *appellation contrôlée*. Over the last five years, wines for current consumption coming from vineyards free of hybrids and obtained from recommended grapes, which have satisfied a series of analyses and been passed by a tasting commission, can use the title of "selected wines" and be sold as such without blending.

These selected wines are beginning to take their places besides the growths of good repute such as Saint-Chinian, Coteaux-du-Languedoc, Cabrières, Faugères, Mejanelle, Mont-Peyroux, Picpoul de Pinet, Pic Saint-Loup, Saint-Christol, Saint-Drezery, Saint-Georges d'Orques, Saint-Saturnin and Vesargues, all delimited wines of superior quality (V.D.Q.S.) produced in the department of Hérault. It should not be forgotten that the Hérault plain also produces some very aromatic muscat wines such as Frontignan, Muscat de Lunel, Mireval and Clairette du Languedoc.

In the department of the Gard, as well as the Côtes-du-Rhône wines with an *appellation d'origine contrôlée* —particularly the Rosé de Chusclan, Tavel and Lirac—the V.D.Q.S. Costières-du-Gard, with a production of 6,600,000 gallons from 15,000 acres, are agreeably fruity and palate-pleasing wines.

The second largest French department in terms of wines produced, with an average production of 154,000,000 gallons, the Aude produces about 48,400,000 gallons of guaranteed place-name description wines, including 20,900,000 gallons of Corbières and 8,800,000 gallons of Minervois, as well as 1,540,000 to 1,760,000 gallons of A.O.C. wines, including 990,000 gallons of natural sweet wines. It should be added that, in the case of wines for ordinary consumption, there is a growing tendency to improve the grapes used (Gre-nache and *Cinsault*). Vinification is also being very appreciably improved. The 141 co-operative cellars in the department vinify between 55 per cent and 56 per cent of the wine production. The winegrowers to an increasing degree are producing wines which are drinkable "as they stand".

In the range of quality wines there are, in addition to Corbières and Minervois, the names of Fitou, Clape, Quatourze, Blanquette de Limoux (374,000 gallons) and the natural sweet wines, with a comparable production, which have ensured the wine-growing reputation of the department.

Coming solely from the delimited Limousin slopes in the Upper Valley of the Aude, the Blanquette de Limoux is a sparkling white wine, prepared according to a very ancient method with *Mauzac* and *Clairette* grapes. For many centuries, Blanquette de Limoux has been favoured for its sparkle, elegance and fruitiness. It should be mentioned that the wine was granted an *appellation contrôlée* in 1938.

The Corbières vineyard, most of which is located in the department of the Aude, covers 74,130 acres. The vine is cultivated there according to careful and time-honoured local methods, with a respect for tradition calculated to maintain the specific characteristics of the wines. Judicious regulations have gone far to establish a balance between the necessary progress in technology and the improvement of the quality of the wines. These wines should have a minimum alcohol content of 11° and similar regulations are found in all French areas producing wines entitled to an *appellation d'origine* (delimitations of the parcels of land, grapes, degree, yield and viticultural practises). The annual production exceeds 22 million gallons.

The Corbières are, for the most part, red wines with a few rosé wines. White Corbières are much rarer.

The reds are substantial, complete wines whose quality improves with age. After a year, they lose a great deal of colour; after the second winter, their quality begins to blossom and they can be bottled. This produces a wine whose bouquet harmonizes well with pork, fowl, roasts, game and cheese.

The rosé wines are distinguished by their fruitiness, their elegance and their nervousness. They form a perfect accompaniment to fish and shell-fish; generally speaking, they have the advantage of being drinkable with all dishes.

As for the natural sweet wines of Roussillon and the Midi, the origin of the titles of nobility of which they are so proud is very ancient. The vineyards from which these wines come are to be found on steep terraces, on sunny slopes that overhang the sea as at Banyuls, or clinging to the last buttresses of the Pyrenees.

It is in the Pyrénées-Orientales, for the most part, that the BANYULS, MAURY, RIVESALTES, CÔTES-D'AGLY and CÔTES-DE-HAUT-ROUSSILLON wines are harvested. The southern winegrowing part of the Corbières of Aude, adjacent to Roussillon, also produces some of them but in much smaller quantities.

At Banyuls, the *Grenache Noir* predominates. It is cultivated under the direct influence of the winds from the sea, on the abrupt flanks of the last foothills of the Albères, in the small amount of arable land left by the slow crumbling of a bedrock of primary schists which has a rust-like colour and the appearance of old timber.

In the Fenouillèdes, near Maury, the *Grenache Noir* prevails once again in conjunction with an exceptional soil. The vineyard clings to rounded hillocks of dark flakey marls. Boxed in between two high white cliffs of hard limestone, the vineyard in its arid corridor profits by a particularly favourable concentration and a great intensity of sunshine. The first preoccupation of the purchaser and consumer should be carefully to verify the origin of the bottles he is buying. If it comes from Banyuls or Maury it will be a dark red or brick-coloured wine. Ageing brings reflections of purple and gold; when very old, the BANYULS and the MAURY often acquire the special taste described as *rancio* which is much appreciated by Catalan epicures. The experienced taster will recognize the special bouquet of the *Grenache Noir* in the BANYULS and the MAURY and will appreciate all the warmth and charm of these wines which are vinified by the maceration process. During fermentation, the must remains in more or less prolonged contact with the pulp and skin; macerated in this way, it acquires the most subtle of its qualities.

In the Côtes-d'Agly, as well as a large number of plantations of *Grenache Noir*, we find the *Grenache Gris* and the *Grenache Blanc* mixed together and supplemented by the *Maccabéo*. These grapes are planted mostly on secondary soils, but also on prime holdings constituted by the breaking up of primary ferruginous schists and black schists, the latter of which are appropriately called "grape schists"—schists which were once used to improve the soil of the vineyards.

At Rivesaltes, besides parcels of land completely planted to *Muscat*, the *Grenache Blanc* and the *Malvoisie* give wines of great elegance; most of the wine is established on terraces of ancient, very pebbly, alluvium between Salses, Rivesaltes and the "Crest" of Pia.

In the Côtes-de-Haut-Roussillon, the Aspres region, the *Grenaches* still have priority but they are giving way more and more to *Muscat* and *Maccabéo*, which contribute their very special bouquet. The ranks of the vines are planted on white gravelly or pebbly alluvial hills, red in colour, which were deposited at the tertiary period and then furrowed by erosion. This area is also very arid, hence its name Aspres.

White wines with a golden tint are also produced at Rivesaltes, the Côtes-d'Agly and the Côtes-de-Haut-Roussillon; in ageing, they often take on a beautiful burnt "topaz" tint. Once vinification is complete, these wines should have a minimum total potential alcohol content of 21.5° and titrate at least 15°.

The consumer should take care to cool his bottles to between 5° and 10° C; these are the ideal temperatures for consuming the natural wines. It should not be forgotten that the *Muscats* are always very sweet and should be ranked with the sweetest of natural sweet wines but that, under the other descriptions, several more or less sweet types can be found. Natural sweet wines based on *Malvoisie* and, particularly, on *Grenache* will, when aged in certain ways, acquire the much sought-after *Rancio* taste.

In their country of origin, the wines of Perpignan are regarded as the essential concomitant to various regional gastronomic manifestations. They prepare or conclude the *cargolades* at which the whole menu (snails, sausages, cutlets etc.) is grilled in the embers of a vine-shoot fire; they are used to accompany fruit dishes as well as Catalan pastries such as *bougnettes*, *rousquilles* and aniseed cakes.

The Catalan, settling himself firmly, drinks his wine through open lips from the *porrón*, a glass carafe with a finely drawn out conical spout which is held up at arm's length: a very fine jet of golden amber describes a harmonious and scintillating curve. In this skilful way of drinking *à la régalade*, the wine splashes out over the tongue, the palate and the taste buds. These natural sweet wines can be served as aperitifs. In this case, however, the drier types such as BANYULS and MAURY should be sought out. The wines of Perpignan are also particularly suitable as dessert wines or *digestifs*. Whether white, brick-coloured or of the muscat type, they should all be served very cold but not iced.

SWISS WINES OF THE RHÔNE VALLEY

CANTON OF VALAIS

WHITE WINES

Types of wine	Appellation of the growth and commercial appellation
Fendant	Fendant, Les Riverettes, Grand-Schiner Le Père du Valais, Brûlefer, Combe d'Enfer, Trémazières, Sur Plan d'Uvrier, Rives du Bisse, Réserve de Tous-Vents, Vieux Sion, La Guérite, Les Murettes, Etournailles, Vieux Sierre, Clos de Balavaud, Rocailles, Solignon, Montibeux, Grand Baillif, Pierrafeu, Vin des Chanoines, Etoile de Sierre, Ste-Anne, Réserve du Procureur, Fendant du Ravin.
Johannisberg	Johannisberg, Burgrave, Le Grand-Schiner Prince de l'Eglise, Johannisberg de Chamoson, Ravanay, Rives du Bisse, Brûlefer, Novembre, Salgesch, Mont d'Or, St-Théodule, Rhonegold, Grand Bouquet, Johannisberg Balavaud, Johannestrunk, Vin des Chevaliers.
Malvoisie	Malvoisie, Marjolaine, Combe d'Enfer, Malvoisie mi-flétrie, Rives du Bisse, Côte Dorée, Vieux Sierre, Rawyre, Vieux Plants, Brindamour, Malvoisie de la Fiancée, Malvoisie Pinot gris.
Amigne	Belle Valaisanne, Rives du Bisse, Raisin d'Or.
Arvine	Belle Provinciale, Petite Arvine de Chamoson.
Ermitage	Ermitage, Rives du Bisse, Hermitage, Ermitage « Cuvée réservée », Vieux Plants, Ermitage Vétroz, Les Chapelles.
Humagne	Humagne Vétroz.
Païen	Vin du Glacier.
Rèze	Vin du Glacier.
Riesling	Riesling, Goût du Conseil « Mont d'Or », Colline des Planzettes Sierre.

RED WINES

Dôle	Le Grand-Schiner Chapeau Rouge, Clos du Château, Combe d'Enfer, Dôle de Chamoson, Dôle-Pinot noir sur Plan d'Uvrier, Dôle von Salgesch (La Chapelle), Dôle Ravanay, Rives du Bisse, Hurlevent, Les Mazots, Dôle du Mont, Dôle de Salquenen, Vieux Sierre, Soleil de Sierre, Sang de l'Enfer, Clos de Balavaud, Dôle de Balavaud, Girandole, Crêta Plan, Chanteauvieux, Gloire du Rhône, Dôle-Pinot noir, Vieux Villa, Vieux Salquenen, Romane.
Merlot	Colline des Planzettes Sierre.
Pinot noir	Pinot noir de Chamoson, Le Sarrazin, Le Grand Schiner Saint Empire, Pinot noir du Valais, Rives du Bisse, Uvrier, Vendémiaire, Rhoneblut, Römerblut, Oeil-de-Perdrix, Millésime, Beau Velours, Colline des Planzettes Sierre, La Tornale, Ste-Anne, Vieux Cellier, Le Préféré, Chapelle de Salquenen, Johannestrunk, Pinot noir de Salquenen, Vin des Chevaliers, Crête de l'Enfer.
Rosé	Oeil-de-Perdrix, Rosé d'Eros.

CANTON OF VAUD

WHITE WINES • Dorin (Chasselas)

Appellation of communes	Appellation of the growth and commercial appellation
CHABLAIS	
Bex	Chêne.
Ollon	Côtes de Verschiez.
Aigle	Clos de Beauregard, Clos du Paradis, Clos de la Vineuvaz, Les Forteresses, Clos du Cloître, Crosex-Grillé, Aigle Royal, Hospices Cantonaux, Domaine de la Commune, Les Cigales, Merveilles des Roches, Les Murailles, Réserve du Vidôme.
Yvorne	Château Maison blanche, Vieux Collège, Clos de la George, Clos des Rennauds, Clos du Rocher, L'Ovaille, Le Chant des Resses, Les Fornets, Les Portes Rouges, Le Petit Vignoble, Plan d'Essert, Près Roc, Domaine de la Commune.
Villeneuve	Sur la Tour, Clos du Châtelard, De nos Domaines, Caves des Hospices cantonaux, Les Terrasses, Vin de l'Empereur.
Villeneuve (pinot gris)	Ovaille, Jeu du Roy.
LAVAUX	
Montreux	Rossillion, Château de Châtelard, Côtes de Pallens, Coteaux du Haut-Léman.
La Tour-de-Peilz	Clos des Mousquetaires.
Vevey	Caves de l'Hôpital.
Corsier	Cure d'Attalens.
Corseaux	Clos Châtonneyre, Clos sur la Chapelle.
Chardonne	Clos des Berneyses, Château de Chardonne, Cave des Allours, le Chantey, Le Fin de la Pierraz, Burignon, Clos de la Chenalettaz, Petite Combe.
Saint-Saphorin – Rivaz	Faverges, Les Rueyres, Blassinges, Charmus de la Cure, Château de Glérolles, Larchevesque, Les Fosses, Planète, Roches Brûlées, La Riondaz, Roche Ronde, Roc Noir, Pierre Noire, Grand Vigne, Domaine d'Ogoz, Le Grillon, Clos des Plantaz.

Appellation of communes	Appellation of the growth and commercial appellation
Dézaley	Chemin de Fer, L'Evêque, L'Arbalète, Chapotannaz, Clos des Abbayes, Dézaley de la Ville, Embleyres, Clos des Moines, Clos de l'Ermite, Clos du Philosophe, Château Marsens, Sous-Marsens, De la Tour, La Borne, La Gueniettaz, Mousquetaires, Renard, Pertuizet, Sur les Abbayes, La Médinette.
Epesses	Boux d'Epesses, Braise d'Enfer, Calamin, Chanteperdrix, Coup de l'Etrier, Crêt-dessous, Crêt-brûlé, La République, Terre à Boire.
Cully	Les Blonnaises, Chenaux, St-Amour, La Perle.
Riex	Maison Blanche.
Villette-Grandvaux	Bouton-d'Or, Belletaz, Bien-Venu, Clos des Echelettes, Clos des Roches, Daley Villette, Treize Vents, Domaine du Daley, En Genévaz, Côtes de Courseboux, Clos de la Cour.
Lutry	Bolliattaz, Grandchamp, Montagny, Clos de Chamaley, Joli Cœur, Ma Réserve, Boutefeu, Clos des Cloîtres, Châtelard, Clos des Brûlées, Bertholod.

LA CÔTE

Morges	Bravade, Clos des Abbesses, Marcelin, Domaine de la Commune.
Nyon	Château de Crans, Château de Duillier, Banderolle.
Aubonne	Curzille.
Allaman	Clos du Château, Ville de Lausanne.
Féchy	Clos des Bayels, Clos du Martheray, Vieux Coteaux, Mon Pichet, Joli Site.
Bougy	Domaine de Riencourt, Cave de Fischer, Château de Bursinel.
Gilly	Château de Vincy, Coteau de Gilly.
Perroy	Malessert, Clos de la Dame, Clos de la Donery, Abbaye de Mont Ville de Lausanne, Cave du Prieuré, Clos de l'Augmendaz.
Mont	Autecour, Haute-Cour, Crochet, Montbenay, Clos des Truits, Château de Mont, La Viborne, Chatagnéréaz, Mont-Crochet, Les Pierrailles, La Montoise, Beau-Soleil, Domaine de la Bigaire, Famolens, Beauregard.
Tartegnin	Clos du Rousillon, Clos des Panissières.
Vinzel	Domaine de la Bâtie, Château de Vinzel, Clos du Château de Bursins.
Luins	Château de Luins, La Capite, Domaine de Sarraux-dessous, Sarraux.

RED WINES

CHABLAIS	Salvagnin Eminence, Salvagnin Mille pierres, Clos de l'Abbaye, Clos du Châtelard, Clos de la George, Côtes de Verschiez, Bex, Pinot noir Monseigneur, Pinot noir le Notable.
LAVAUX	Salvagnin des Caves de l'Hôpital, Salvagnin de l'Hôpital des Bourgeois de Fribourg, Salvagnin Cep d'Or, Salvagnin Chevron rouge, Salvagnin Coteaux du Haut-Léman, Salvagnin Forban, Salvagnin Grain rouge, Pinot noir Coin des Serpents, Pinot noir Cuvée du Docteur, Pinot noir Grand-Croix, Pinot noir Sept Murs, Pinot-Gamay Montorgueil, Pinot-Gamay Roche rouge, Pinot-Gamay Saint-Saphorin printanier, Pinot-Gamay sous l'Auvent, Pinot-Gamay Burignon, Dôle d'Epesses.
LA CÔTE	Salvagnin Commune de Morges, Salvagnin Château de Saint-Saphorin, Salvagnin Domaine de Valmont, Salvagnin du Baril, Salvagnin Chapeau rouge, Salvagnin Croix du Val, Salvagnin Licorne, Salvagnin Piganot, Clos des Abbesses Clos du Paradis, Pinot noir Clos du Satyre, Pinot noir Grand Brocard.

ROSÉ WINES

Gamay	Bellarosa, Busard, La Caille, Perle Rose, Roussard, St-Martin, Vieux Murs.
Pinot	Oeil-de-Perdrix, Oeil-de-Perdrix - Clos du Terraillex, Oeil-de-Perdrix - Chantemerle.

CANTON OF GENEVA

WHITE WINES

Types of wine	Appellation of the growth and commercial appellation
Chasselas	Les Contamines, Chasselas Genève, Clos des Curiades, Clos de la Donzelle, Perle du Mandement, Coteau de Lully, Bouquet Royal.
Riesling-Sylvaner	Riesling-Sylvaner Satigny, Les Argoulets.
Aligoté	Lully, Clos des Curiades.
Pinot blanc	Les Curiades.

RED WINES

Gamay	Gamay de Gondebaud, Les Clefs d'Or, Gamay-Lully, Domaine des 3 Etoiles.
Gamay rosé	Rose Reine.
Gamay Pinot	Gamay Pinot, Pinogamay.
Pinot noir	Clos des Curiades, Le Damoiseau, Pinot noir Lully.

106

FRENCH WINES OF THE RHÔNE VALLEY

WINES OF SAVOY

Generic appellation	*Appellation of the growth or of the commune*
Vins de Savoie	Marin, Ripaille, Marignan, Coteaux de Crépy, Petit Crépy, Monterminod, Apremont, Abymes, Chignin, Cruet Montmelian, Saint-Jean-de-la-Porte
Roussette de Savoie . .	Frangy, Marestel, Monthoux, Seyssel.

WINES OF THE JURA

Generic appellation	Côtes-du-Jura, Château-Chalon, L'Etoile, Arbois.

CÔTES DU RHÔNE

WHITE WINES

Generic appellation	*Appellation of the growth or of the commune*
Saint-Péray	Amour de Dieu, Arboisset, Château de Beauregard, Bellevue, La Beylesse, Biguet, Biousse, Blaches, Bouzigues, Le Bret, Buissonnet, La Cacharde, Cerisier, La Chaume, Le Chêne, Combette, Coste Claude, La Côte, Coteau-Caillard, Coudiol, La Crozette, Déseret, Fauterie, Fourniers, La Gamone, Le Géant, Grand-Champ, Hongrie, Issartel, Jirane, Lubac, Maison Blanche, Malgazon, Marcale, Mois de Mai, Moulin-à-vent, Pateaud, Perrier, Pinchenas, La Plantier, Prieuré, Putier, Aux Putiers, Rochette, Ruines de Crussol, Sainte Fleurie, Les Sapettes, Soulignasses, Thioulet, Tourtousse, La Venance, Vergomars.
Château-Grillet	
Condrieu	Chéri, La Garenne, Vernon, Boucher, Château-Grillet, Laboye, Le Colombier.

ROSÉ WINES

Tavel	Aqueria, Blaise d'arbres, Bouvettes, Cabanette, Campey, Carcenies, Comeyre, Cravailleu et Alexandre, La Genestière et Fourcadure, Manissy, Montezardes et Trinquevedel, Olivet, Les Patus, Plaine de Vallongue, Plans et Palus, Les Prés, Roc Crispin et Malaven, Romagnac, Tavelet et les Oliviers, Vau et Clos, Vaucroze, Vaucroze et Vacquières, La Vaussière, La Vaute, Vestides, Le Village.
Côte-du-Rhône Chusclans	

WHITE WINES AND RED WINES

Châteauneuf-du-Pape . .	L'Arnesque, Barbe d'Asne, Bas-Serres, Beau Renard, La Bigote, Les Blaquières, Bois de Boursan, Bois de la Vieille, Bois Senescau, Les Bosquets, Le Boucou, Les Bourguignons, Les Brusquières, Cabrières, Cansaud, Castelas, La Cerise, Charbonnières, Chemin de Sorgues, Le Clos, Colombis, Combes d'Arnavel, Combes Masques, Coste-Froide, Coteau de l'Ange, Les Coulets, La Crau, La Croze, Devès d'Estouard, Les Esqueiron, Farguerol, La Font du Loup, La Fortisse, Four à Chaux, Les Galimardes, La Gardine, Grand chemin de Sorgues, Grand Devès, Grand Pierre, Les Grands Galiguières, Grandes Serres, La Grenade, Jaquinotte, Le Lac, Le Limas, Les Marines, Les Mascarrons, Mont de Viès, Montolivet, Mont Pertuis, Mont Redon, Moulin à Vent, La Nerthe, Le Parc, Les Parrans, Pelous, Petite Bastide, Petites Serres, Pied-de-Baud, Pied-Redon, Les Pielons, Pierre-à-Feu, Pignan, Les Plagnes, Les Pradels, Relagnes, Les Revès, La Roquette, Roumiguières, Saint-Joseph, Les Serres, Terres-Blanches, Les Tresquous, Vaudieu, Cabane Saint-Jean, Cansaud, La Chartreuse, Chemin de Châteauneuf, Les Combes, Le Coulaire, Coteau de Saint-Jean, La Crau, Croix de Bois, Duvet, Les Escondures, La Font de Michelle, La Font du Loup, Les Garrigues, Le Grand Plantier, Marron, Patouillet, La Petite Crau, Pied-Redon, Piegeoulet, Ras-Cassa, Reveirores, Sauvines, Terre-Ferme. La Barnuine, Barratin, Les Bédines, Chapouin, Coucoulet, La Crau, Le Cristia, Font du Loup, La Gardiole, Le Grès, Guigasse, La Jamasse, Le Mourre de Gaud, Le Mourre de Vidal, Le Mourre des Perdrix, Palinteau, Pignan, Le Pointu, Le Rayas, Saint-Georges, Saintes-Vierges, Les Saumades, Valori, La Bertaude, Boidauphin, Boilauzon, Cabrières, Maucoil, Palestor, Chafeune, Franquizons, Le Grand Collet, La Lionne.
Crozes-Hermitage	Bourret, Les Habrards, Martinet, Les Mejeans.
Hermitage or Ermitage . .	Beaumes, Les Bessards, La Croix, La Croix de Jamot, Les Diognères, Les Diognères et Torras, Les Greffieux, Les Gros des Vignes, L'Hermite, L'Homme, Maison Blanche, Le Méal, Les Murets, Péléat, La Pierrelle, Les Rocoules, Les Signaux, Varogne.
Lirac	
Saint-Joseph	
Côtes-du-Rhône	Rochegude, Saint-Maurice-sur-Eygues, Vinsobles, Cairanne, Gigondas, Rasteau, Roaix, Séguret, Vacqueras, Valréas, Visan, Laudun.

RED WINES

Côte Rôtie . . . .   Les Arches, Basseron, La Blanchonne, Les Bonnevières, La Brocarde, Le Car, Chambre-tout, La Chatillonne, Les Chavaroches, La Chevalière, Chez Gaboulet, Chez Gueraud, Les Clos et Claperonne, Le Cognet, Le Combard, Combe de Calon, Corps des Loups, La Côte Baudnin, Le Crêt, Fontgent, Lefouvier, La Frizonne, Les Gagères, La Garde, Les Germines, La Giroflarie, Grande Plantée et la Garelle, Les Grandes Places, Le Grand Taillé, Grosse Roche et la Balayat, La Guillambaule, Janville, Les Journaries, Lancement, La Landonne, Les Lézardes, Le Mollar, Montmain, Montuclas, Le Moulin, Les Moutonnes, Nève, Le Pavillon Rouge, La Pommière, Les Prunelles, Les Rochains, Rosier, Les Sévenières, Thramon de Gron, Les Triottes, Le Truchet, La Turque, La Viallière, La Viria.

Cornas

PROVENCE AND THE SOUTH-EASTERN REGION

Generic appellation or appellation of communes   Bandol, Bellet, Clairette de Die, Palette, Coteaux d'Aix-en-Provence, Coteaux des Baux, Côtes du Lubéron, Coteaux de Pierrevert, Côtes-de-Provence, Coteaux du Tricastin, Côtes de Ventoux, Haut-Comtat, Châtillon-en-Diois.

LANGUEDOC AND ROUSSILLON

Generic appellation, appellation of the growth or of the commune   Corbières, Minervois, Costières du Gard, Coteaux du Languedoc, Coteaux de la Méjanelle, Saint-Saturnin, Montpeyroux, Coteaux de Saint-Christol, Quatourze, La Clape, Saint-Drézéry, Saint-Chinian, Faugères, Cabrières, Coteaux de Verargues, Pic Saint-Loup, Saint-Georges-d'Orques, Picpoul de Pinet, Fitou, Roussillon dels Aspres, Corbières du Roussillon, Corbières Supérieures du Roussillon.

108

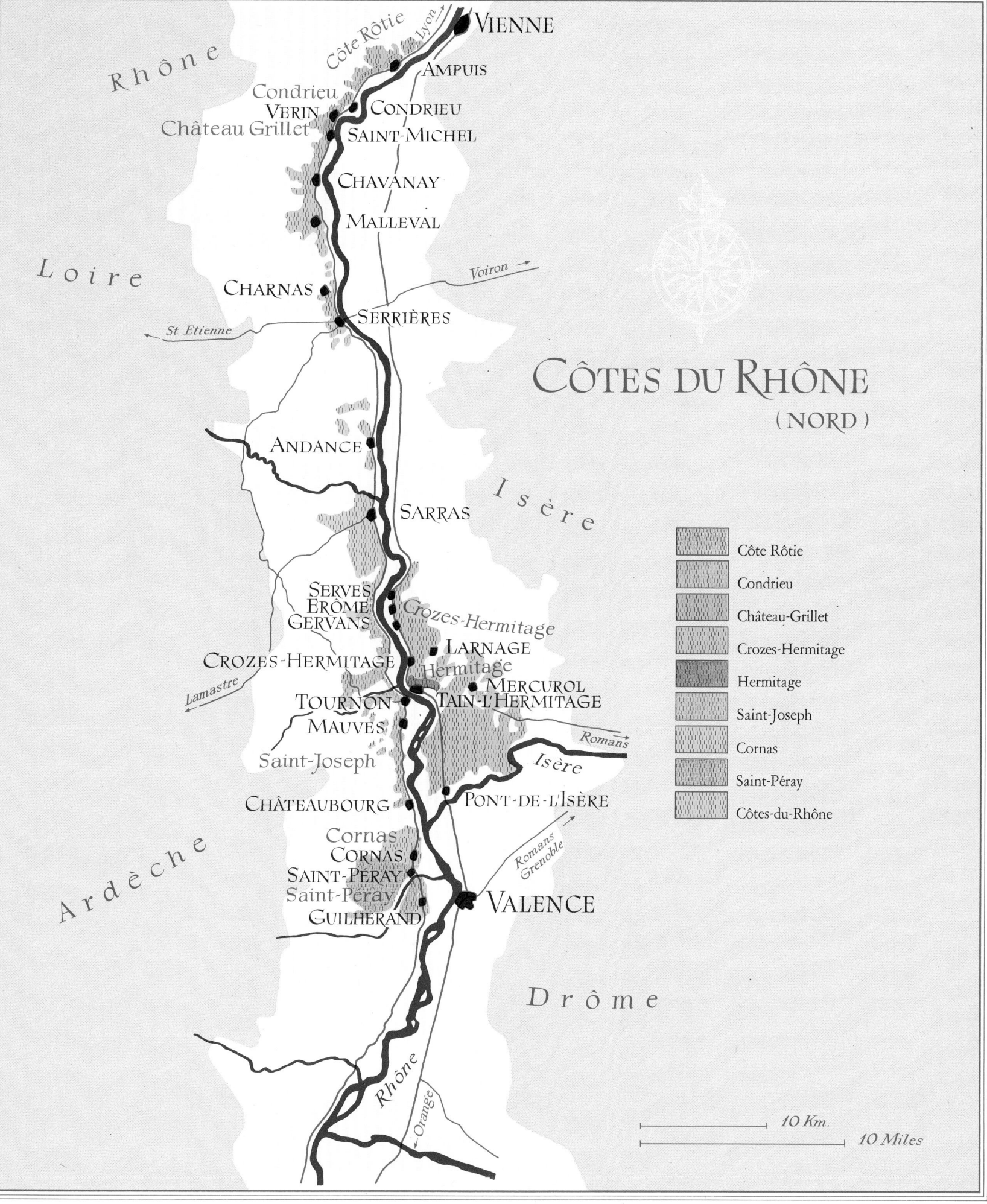

Rhône

VIENNE

Côte Rôtie

Lyon

AMPUIS

Condrieu
VERIN   CONDRIEU
Château Grillet   SAINT-MICHEL

                         CHAVANAY

                         MALLEVAL

Loire

                                        Voiron

CHARNAS
                         SERRIÈRES

St. Etienne

                                        Isère

                                                CÔTES DU RHÔNE
                                                (NORD)

ANDANCE

SARRAS

SERVES
ERÔME   Crozes-Hermitage
GERVANS

                         LARNAGE | | Côte Rôtie
CROZES-HERMITAGE | | Condrieu
                         Hermitage | | Château-Grillet
Lamastre   MERCUROL | | Crozes-Hermitage
                         TAIN-L'HERMITAGE | | Hermitage
TOURNON- | | Saint-Joseph
MAUVES   Romans | | Cornas
Saint-Joseph   Isère | | Saint-Péray
                                                  | | Côtes-du-Rhône
CHÂTEAUBOURG   PONT-DE-L'ISÈRE

Cornas
CORNAS   Romans
SAINT-PÉRAY   Grenoble
Saint-Péray
GUILHERAND   VALENCE

Ardèche

                         Drôme

                         Rhône

                         Orange

                                        10 Km.
                                        10 Miles

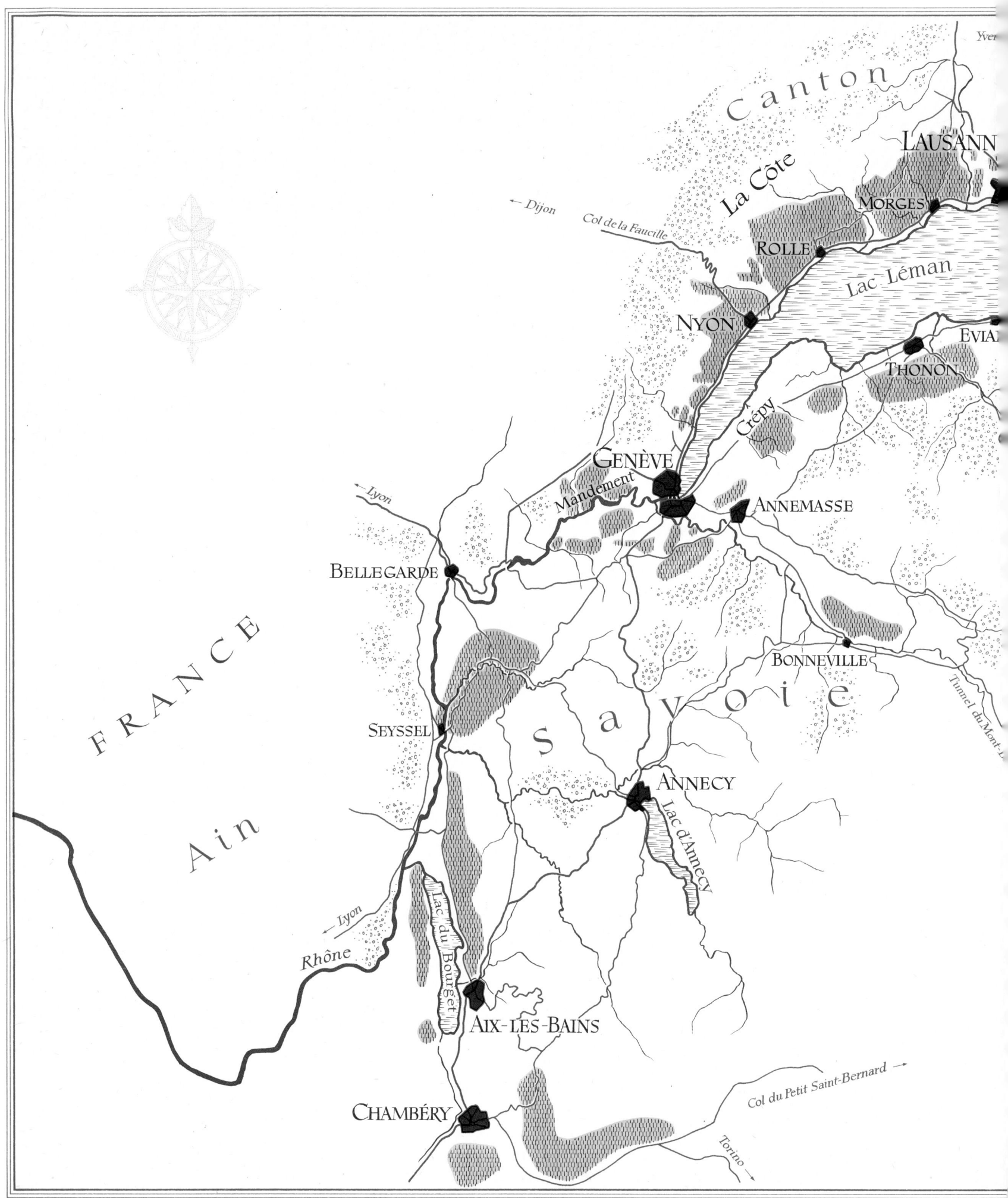

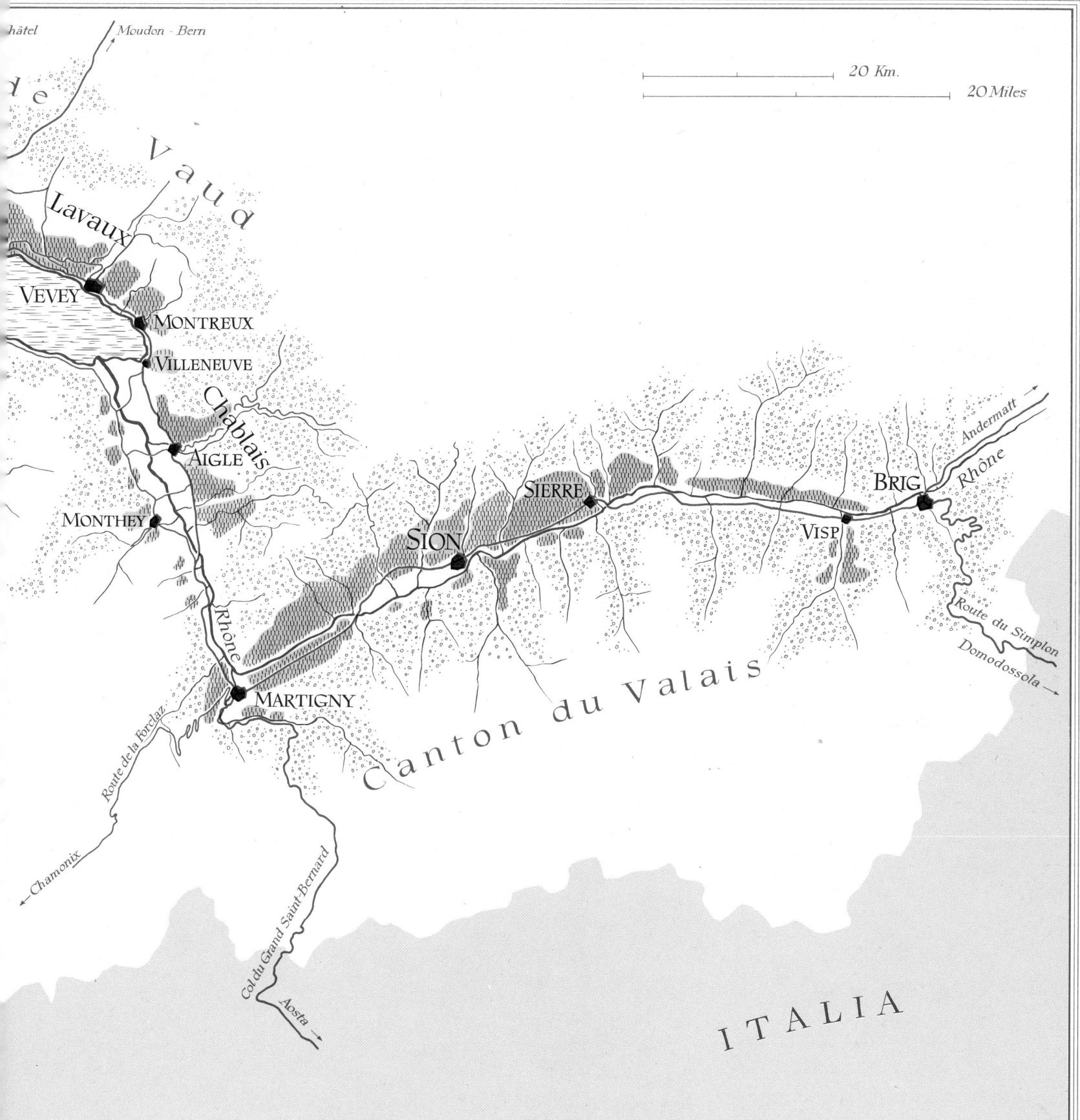

châtel   Moudon - Bern

20 Km.

20 Miles

V a u d

Lavaux

VEVEY

MONTREUX

VILLENEUVE

Chablais

AIGLE

MONTHEY

SIERRE

SION

BRIG

VISP

Rhône

Andermatt

Rhône

Route du Simplon

Domodossola

Rhône

MARTIGNY

C a n t o n   d u   V a l a i s

Route de la Forclaz

Chamonix

Col du Grand Saint-Bernard

Aosta

I T A L I A

RHÔNE SUISSE · SAVOIE

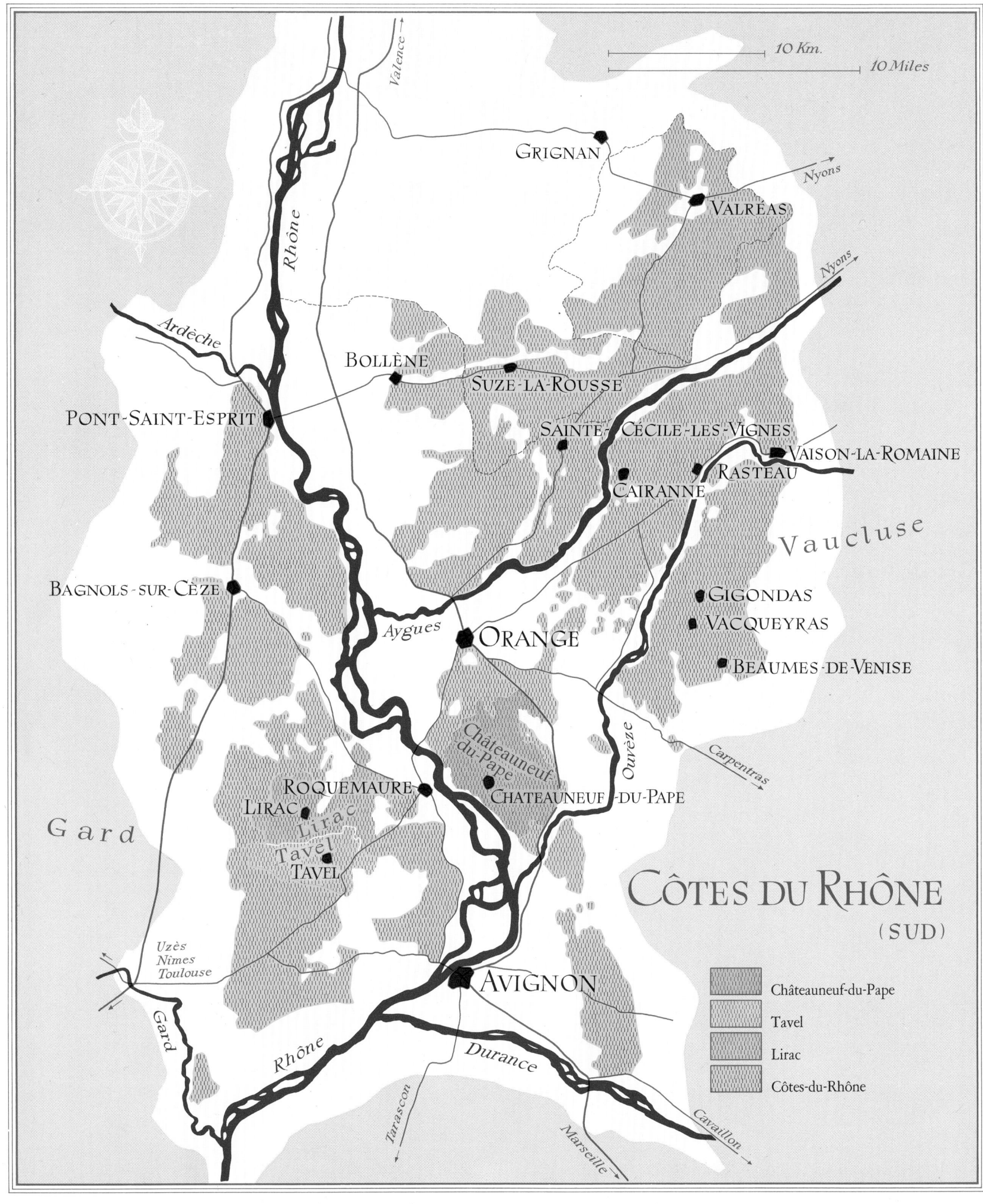

CÔTES DU RHÔNE

(SUD)

	Châteauneuf-du-Pape
	Tavel
	Lirac
	Côtes-du-Rhône

THE WINES OF THE LOIRE

ALEXANDER FRESNEAU

Long before the invasion of the Gauls the vine existed on the banks of the Loire. The Romans invaded this region 22 years after Christ, and probably found it growing wild. Its first cultivation, according to a popular legend, began in A.D. 380 when St. Martin and his disciples planted vines in the Abbaye de Marmoutier near Tours, which was founded at that time. These events are recounted by the historian Gregory, Bishop of Tours from 573 to 595, in his *Ecclesiastical History of France*, and by Fredegarius in his chronicles of the year 757. The vine flourished and spread rapidly; but in the thirteenth century it was restricted to the hillsides where it produced wines of a superior quality.

The first viticultural region along the Loire is the Massif Central, which contains the vineyards of Auvergne, Saint-Pourçain-sur-Sioule and Chateaumeil-lant. A little farther on the river crosses the chalky and flinty hills between Pouilly-sur-Loire, Sancerre and Menetou-Salon. Then come the two vineyards of Quincy and Reuilly, situated one near the other with identical soil, then the Val de Loire which one may consider as being on the very edge of the Loiret. This department also harbours the Giennois and Orléanais vineyards which have lost much of their importance in the last fifty years.

It is at Blois, the gateway to the Touraine, that the chalky soil has its beginning. It then stretches for miles and miles, following the course of the Loire and fertilizing the vineyards of Monts-Près-Chambord, Vendômois, Coteaux du Loir, Jasnières, Touraine,

Vouvray, Montlouis, Bourgueil, Chinon and Saumurois, as far as the Angevine schists which introduce the Armorican Massif. The Angevine vineyard is the most important, and is responsible for nearly all the wines produced in this region. Aubance and Lyons bring one to the maritime zone of the Loire, and leaving Anjou behind one comes next to the MUSCADET vineyard in Basse-Bretagne. Special mention should be made of the Ancenis vineyard and the *Gros Plant* so sought after by tourists. From Orléanais to the ocean, the Val de Loire presents a soft and gentle spectacle to the traveller, with its sumptuous châteaux and variety of viticultural treasures. Other landscapes may offer fairer sights, but there is none more harmonious nor more compelling than these banks of the Loire.

In order to obtain choice wine, winegrowers have constantly taken pains to improve their vine-plants either through selection, by developing new varieties, or by importing well known grapes from distant parts.

It is possible that the vine-stocks developed by the monks in Touraine and elsewhere are derived from a particular type of vine which produced black grapes found growing wild in the forests. It is perhaps to this same wild lambrusca that the sixteenth-century poet Ronsard refers in his ode to Aubepin. This red vine was called *Pineau d'Aunis*, Aunis being a small village in Saumur. It deserves our gratitude, for it is thought that on some unknown date it produced, after selection, the white variety, *Chenin Blanc*, or *Pineau de la Loire*, a wonderful plant found in Touraine and Anjou. It is impossible to know exactly when this vine-plant was given the name *Chenin*, but it was already known as such in the early sixteenth century.

The *Sauvignon*, a noble plant found in Pouilly-sur-Loire, Sancerre, Quincy and Reugny is, however, of unknown origin. There is no document to show whether it is a plant indigenous to the region or whether it was imported.

On several occasions, numerous vines taken from foreign or other French viticultural regions were planted in these parts. It is not known exactly how or when the *Muscadet* grape came to the region of Nantes, but it would seem to date from the seventeenth century. When the frozen vines were replanted following the terrible winter of 1709, the *Muscadet* grape was introduced on a wide scale into the region. It would appear to have been brought from Burgundy, where it was known as *Melon*.

The *Gros Plant*, cultivated in the Atlantic Loire, originally came from Charentes through an exchange with Poitou, an intermediary province. Its wine was at first distilled, but today it produces a highly sought-after dry wine. It is of the same grade as the Muscadet.

The *Cabernet Franc*, which is cultivated in Touraine and in the regions of Bourgueil and Chinon as well as in Anjou, has a much disputed origin. According to some, it came from Rhuis, in Bretagne. According to others, and this seems more logical, the Bordelais grape was brought to the Loire valley either by Abbot Breton,

an administrator of Richelieu, when he inherited the property of the Abbey of Saint-Nicolas-de-Bourgueil; or even before, if we believe Rabelais when he speaks of "the good Breton wine, which does not grow in Bretagne but in this worthy land of Verron".

The *Côt* grape is cultivated in various places, but it certainly originated in Bordelais. The *Groslot de Cinq-Mars* or *Grolleau* was obtained around 1810 through the selection process in the region of Chinon.

Other grapes, such as the *Pinot Noir*, *Pinot Beurot*, and *Meunier* are thought to have come from Burgundy.

It is difficult to give any precise figures as to the number of fine quality vineyards in the *appellation contrôlée* category along the Loire. The *Chenin Blanc* or *Pineau de la Loire* covers about 37,000 acres, the *Muscadet* 21,000, the Sauvignon grape—which is constantly expanding—5,000, and the *Cabernet* 10,000. Other red grapes, apart from the *Cabernet*, probably cover a total area somewhat larger than that of the *Chenin Blanc (Groslot, Côt, Gamay, Pinot Noir, Pinot Meunier, Pineau d'Aunis)*. White grapes other than the *Muscadet*, the *Sauvignon* and the *Chenin* cover around 5,000 acres of ground.

The vine region which produces the *appellation contrôlée* wines of the Loire Valley is about 74,000 acres in area. However the actual surface under cultivation is in fact bigger as part of the harvest is reserved for making table wines.

POUILLY-SUR-LOIRE - SANCERRE - QUINCY
REUILLY - MENETOU-SALON

The staple grape of these vineyards is the *Sauvignon*, blended at times with another variety.

POUILLY-SUR-LOIRE. Under this classification come all the wines produced in the communes of Pouilly-sur-Loire, Saint-Andelain, Tracy-sur-Loire, Saint-Laurent, Saint-Martin-sur-Nohain, Garchy and Mesvres-sur-Loire.

Depending on what grape variety they are made from, the wines of Pouilly-sur-Loire are known under one or the other of the following two categories: POUILLY FUMÉ (which should not be confused with another white wine, the POUILLY FUISSÉ produced in Burgundy) or BLANC FUMÉ DE POUILLY for those wines made from the *Sauvignon* grape alone; POUILLY-SUR-LOIRE in the case of wines derived from the *Chasselas* grape, whether blended with the *Sauvignon* grape or not. Only the communes of Pouilly-sur-Loire, Saint-Audelain and Tracy are true viticultural regions, although the actual area under cultivation is notably smaller. At present it includes about a thousand acres.

The commune of Saint-Audelain, larger than Pouilly-sur-Loire, has the most important vineyards, more so than those of Pouilly and Tracy. Other communes have a smaller area under cultivation. Since only about a thousand acres are capable of being harvested, it follows that each holding is quite small; there is one of more than 32 acres, but a dozen are on the order of 7 ½ acres each. The average production figure for POUILLY FUMÉ is about 46,200 gallons; for POUILLY-SUR-LOIRE about 154,000 gallons. POUILLY FUMÉ has a distinct and even sometimes pronounced bouquet; it is musky and smoky at the same time, a long-lived wine which ages well. The POUILLY-SUR-LOIRE, on the other hand, is considered to be best when drunk within the year.

SANCERRE. Thirteen communes come under this heading: Sancerre, Saint-Satur, Bué, Suvry-en-Vaux, Menetou, Ratel, Ménétréol Thauvenay, Vinon, Verdigny, Cresancy and some isolated parcels of land at Bannay and Veaugues.

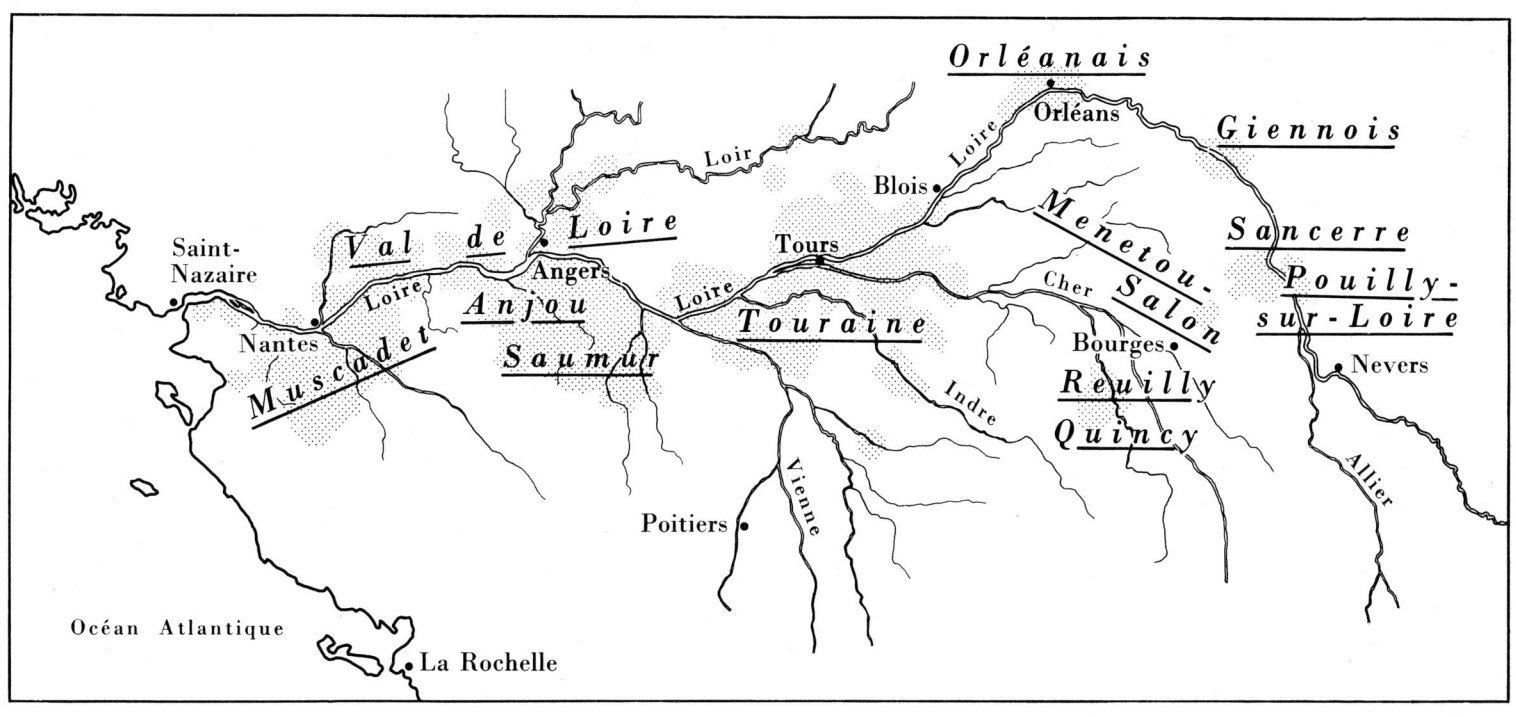

Spread across some fifteen viticultural departments, from the Massif Central to the Atlantic Ocean, the famous vineyards of the Loire are ranged in tiers on the slopes which dominate the "royal river" and its tributaries. The wines of this charming valley are mainly produced in four major regions: the Centre (around Nevers, Giens, Bourges and Orleans), in Touraine, in Anjou-Saumur and in the region of Nantes.

The area under cultivation is some 1,500 acres, of which 1,300 acres grow the *Sauvignon* grape and the rest the *Pinot Noir*. Production has developed in the last ten years. During this time, the average yield was 143,000 gallons while present production, which is still increasing, gives an average yield of more than 330,000 gallons annually.

As in Pouilly-sur-Loire, the soil in which the vine grows is a calcerous-clay deposit, or sometimes mass formations of calcium formed on the slopes in the same geological era. The plains that dominate these slopes are clay-like and unsuitable for winegrowing. Each type of soil produces wine of a different character. The blended vines are sometimes of a higher quality than that of the components. SANCERRE is somewhat more mellow than the POUILLY FUMÉ and generally matures sooner than the latter.

These are pleasant, very fruity wines, though they cannot be compared to Burgundies made from the *Pinot Noir* grape. The red and rosé varieties have only recently qualified for the *appellation contrôlée*.

QUINCY. This vineyard is situated about 12 miles to the west of Bourges, along the right bank of the Cher. It is a small vineyard, of about 600 acres, which will probably develop in the next few years. It comprises the communes of Quincy and Brinay. The average wine-harvest is about 110,000 gallons, worked by 250 growers. The average grower cultivates about 2 acres and there are about twenty properties of 5 to 8 acres each and one of about 25 acres. QUINCY, which is nearly always dry, gets its fine quality from the grand soil which serves as its cradle and which makes it an excellent companion to oysters.

REUILLY. This name is given to the wine of four communes, two in the Indre, Reugny and Diou regions, and two in the Cher, Chery and Lazenay. Their vineyards are situated along the banks of the Arnon, 6 miles to the west of Quincy.

The area planted with the *Sauvignon* grape is definitely getting smaller. At present it is about 62 acres, almost entirely in Reuilly and Diou. Production is very much lower here: about 1,300 to 1,800 gallons yield a dry and semi-dry wine for local consumption.

MENETOU-SALON. Some 16 miles to the west of Vierzon is Menetou-Salon which has given its name to the youngest of the *appellation d'origine* wines of the Loire, created by decree in 1959. It is cultivated on a very small scale as its vineyard covers only 1,500 acres. It grows two grapes, the *Sauvignon* which produces a wine similar to that of Sancerre, though not nearly as well-balanced or as fine in flavour; and the *Pinot Noir* from Burgundy whose red and rosé wines have a most agreeable taste. The total production of this category varies yearly from 132,000 to 220,000 gallons.

TOURAINE

Touraine, so peaceful and welcoming, has been planted to vines since the fourteenth century, and the fame of its wines has grown with the years. Rabelais and Ronsard sang their praises, Alfred de Vigny and Balzac knew how to appreciate them and the beauties of their birthplace, and Alexander Dumas had the King's Musketeers drink them. Here, then, are the wines of which Jules Romain said "they are the very essence of French wit".

Their production is more varied than abundant. The white wines, whether dry, semi-dry or dessert wines, are fresh with full bouquets; the best of them are to be found in the lovely village of Vouvray. The delicate red wines of Bourgueil, Saint-Nicolas and Chinon are followed by a cheerful group of gay companions: red wines and rosés from the Côtes du Cher, white wines made from the *Pineau* or *Sauvignon* grape, which one must taste when visiting the châteaux.

A classic definition of Touraine describes this province as "a rough tweed trimmed with gold". The plains covered with forests, sandy moors and ploughed fields give the land an impression of sadness. There are the forests of Montrichard, Amboise, Chinon, Champeigne between Cher and the Indre, the Richelais and the Gâtine. But cutting across these unproductive regions are smiling valleys whose rich culture, sumptuous castles, white villas, and harmonious landscapes present such an enticing picture as to make a man believe that this is the very place where it would be wonderful to live.

The climate of Touraine is neither unbearably hot in summer nor excessively cold in winter, as the sea breeze modifies the differences in temperature.

Along the border, where the plains meet the valleys, on chalky slopes or terraced embankments pebbled by the Loire and the Vienne—this is where the Touraine winegrowers planted the present vineyards some fifteen centuries ago. The soil which nourishes the vine is often supported by yellow chalk or "Touraine tufa", in which the magnificent Vouvray caves have been carved. This immense blanket of chalk is covered with granitic sand sometimes mixed with silex clay which occurs when the chalk decalcifies.

The soil at the bottom of the slopes contains flinty sand, clay and chalk; it is the *aubuis* so perfectly suited to the *Pineau de la Loire*. It produces the finest and by far the most full-bodied wines.

On both banks of the Loire and the Vienne, in the Bourgueil and Chinon regions, the gravelly beds, brushed by the waters and mixed with sand clay, offer a soft and fertile soil for the *Cabernet Franc* grape.

The region of the white wines made from the *Pineau* grape extends from Tours to Blois, where the vines are cultivated on chalky slopes covered with the mixture locally known as *aubuis*. The vineyard of Vouvray is situated at the head of this region, near Tours.

In Loir-et-Cher, the Mesland region, with identical soil, offers excellent rosés and red wines produced from the *Gamay* grape, side by side with the clear fruity wines made from the *Pineau* grape. Farther south, along the chalky banks of the Cher and the Oisly plain where the ground is composed of sand over clay, red wines grow in the company of fine white wines made from the *Pineau* and *Sauvignon* grapes. In Touraine, the vine spreads over some 15,000 acres, producing wines of the *appellation contrôlée* category in the amount of 4,400,000 gallons per annum.

THE GREAT WHITE WINES. In Touraine as in Anjou, these are derived almost entirely from a single grape, the *Pineau de la Loire*. It alone is responsible for the reputation of the great wine of Touraine. The *Menu Pineau*, also called *Arbois*, gives more delicate wines and has decreased in quantity in Vouvray and Montlouis, but it still flourishes in Loir-et-Cher, the Contres plain, and Pontlevoy, as well as along the banks of the Cher. The *Sauvignon* grape in these regions has, in the past ten years, become more and more popular. Today it covers around 750 acres.

There are differences in pruning methods for the *Pineau de la Loire* and the *Sauvignon* which have important implications for their wines.

When pruning the *Pineau de la Loire*, it is desirable to cut well back into the stalk so as to produce wines with rich bouquets. However, this is not always possible, for this single most important operation in vine culture must take into account the strength on the vine-shoot, its stock and the nature of soil in which it is planted. The *Sauvignon*, on the other hand, need not be cut back too far, but should be dressed long, in the *Guyot double* manner with two long spurs and from six to eight buds.

The *Pineau de la Loire* grape is always cultivated close to the ground, at a density of about 2,240 plants per acre. *Sauvignon* vines, being taller (4 feet as against 3) are planted less densely, only 1,800 plants per acre. Attempts to raise the height of cultivation of the vine have proved inconclusive and unsatisfactory. The vine does not mature so well and has a stronger acid content; the wine is less robust and full-bodied.

The *Sauvignon* grape is picked before it reaches full maturity, usually towards the end of September. The *Pineau de la Loire*, however, is harvested according to

The Loire, that flows through the heartland of France, is naturally the link between many and various wine centres. Mentioned by Rabelais, the growths have a long history. Right, the fresh-picked grapes are poured into the press in a cellar hewn out of the rock.

Above: Typical of the Loire region is this two-wheeled cart, used to bring in the newly-picked grapes.

Right: A meeting of the *Confrérie des "Sagavins d'Anjou"*. At one time the Anjou region concentrated on the production of sparkling wine, but the demand has fallen off recently.

117

A ruined windmill stands guard over the widely-spaced rows of vines in Anjou. The wine harvest is here again, and whole families spend their days in the vineyards until the crop is picked.

the destination of its grape. If the wine-harvest is to be made into sparkling wines, the grapes must be picked before they are completely ripe, when their acid content is from seven to eight grams. If the proprietor wishes to produce a natural wine he must wait until the grape has become fully mature and then select his grapes. This can only be done in very good years. But these wines have a particularly fine bouquet, they are very sweet and at the same time fresh, delicate, robust, and of an exceptionally high quality.

GREAT RED WINES. The best of these, from Bourgueil and Chinon, are made from a grape cultivated in Gironde, especially in the Saint-Emilion region: the *Cabernet Franc* which must be pruned so as to leave a long stalk and a branch bearing seven to eight buds. The grower grafts a piece of bark containing sap on to the vine stalk so that the stem can grow. This stock is common but not extensive. It is considered exceptional to produce more than 400 gallons from an acre. The soil has a great influence on the wine. It might be difficult for the uninformed to distinguish a BOURGUEIL from a CHINON, but connoisseurs can easily tell the difference between a wine which has been planted in gravelly soil and one from a tufa soil.

The wines from grapes grown in gravelly soil are fine wines with good bouquets. They acquire their full qualities reasonably quickly, while the grapes planted in tufa are harder, do not bear fruit until a year later, and conserve admirably.

The wine of Bourgueil charms with its bouquet, its raspberry flavour and its invigorating freshness. It is a fruity, delicate wine, pleasant when young, but at its best after three or four years in a bottle. Some wines which are hard in the first years lighten with age.

CHINON differs from BOURGUEIL in its bouquet —which invokes violets—and its mellow warmth. It is particularly good when drunk young, full of a delicious sweetness. Demand for these wines seems to be growing. For some ten years the vineyards seem to have been developing, especially in the communes of Cravant and Chinon.

It should be mentioned, moreover, that these wines are made from stalked grapes. The stalks are removed as the clusters are picked from the vines by a special machine (known locally as a *rapoire* or *égrenoir*). It consists of a rotating funnel-shaped barrel with a wicker or wooden frame and a screen. The grater or stalker stirs the harvest with a long wooden paddle to separate the grapes from the stalks. Grapes are mechanically stalked by only one co-operative and six wineries, which represents less than 30 per cent.

Most wineries ferment wine in wooden vats with loose lids. Big wineries, however, ferment their wine in cement vats.

Contrary to the practice of many viticultural regions, the period of fermentation here is long, from 18 to 20 days. For example, in the wooden vats where the storage temperature is more than 17º-18º, the secondary fermentation takes place on the twelfth to thirteenth day, and thus the wine can be marketed quickly without any risk to the buyer afterwards. The alcohol content must not be below 9.5º for the wine to be entitled to the *appellation contrôlée* CHINON.

OTHER WINES OF THE TOURAINE. Aside from VOUVRAY, MONTLOUIS, BOURGUEIL and CHINON, Touraine has some other very charming wines which often equal these famous growths, but they are rarely to be found outside the region. Among these are:

AZAY-LE-RIDEAU. This region is better known for its castle than its wines. The communes around the area—especially Saché, where Balzac wrote *Le Lys dans la Vallée*—have always enjoyed a reputation for dry and semi-dry white wines, which are fruity and fresh and of which they produce 22,000 to 26,500 gallons. Unfortunately, since the Second World War, production of these wines has decreased, as the producers have replaced a considerable number of vines with apple orchards. They are also trying to orient their production towards sweet wines.

AMBOISE. The canton of Amboise, situated at the eastern tip of the department of Indre-et-Loire, is as famous for its castle as Azay-le-Rideau; however, it also produces fine quality wines which keep well. This is not surprising as both banks of the Loire form an extension of the vineyards of Vouvray and Montlouis. As always in Touraine, the wines are cultivated in a subsoil of calcareous tufa. This region also produces pleasant red and rosé wines made from the *Côt* grape, sometimes from the Beaujolais *Gamay* and less often from the *Cabernet* variety.

MESLAND. The Mesland region in Loir-et-Cher continues the Touraine vineyard along the right bank of the Loire, with Monteaux, Onzain and Chouzy-sur-Cisse. It produces from 330,000 to 440,000 gallons which is almost half the wine produced under the *appellation* TOURAINE in Loir-et-Cher.

All these wines are very agreeable when young, but the rosés made from the *Gamay* grape are the most successful, which perhaps accounts for the fact that more of them are produced. They get their fruitiness, lightness and fine texture from the granite sands which cover the chalky subsoil of Touraine.

JASNIÈRES and COTEAUX DU LOIR. At the far end of the three provinces, Touraine, Maine and Anjou, some 25 miles to the north, the valley of the river Loir offers the same favourable conditions for the vine as can be found in Touraine. The position of this little river, the nature of the soil, as well as the climate, are all the same here as above and below Tours. This region is at the northern tip of the viticultural zone and only in those years when the sun has been particularly generous does the *Pineau de la Loire* produce white wines of quality, and the *Pineau d'Aunis* become sufficiently ripe to give good red wines. This vineyard used to be far more important than it is today, but the wines have retained their reputation. Ronsard sang the praises of the wines of the Loir, and in *Pantagruel* Rabelais informs us joyfully that the little town of La Chartre was full of wine merchants and had at least twenty-seven inn-keepers.

SAUMUR AND ANJOU

The Saumur region used to be known as "Haut-Anjou". The Saumur wines at that time were the most prominent of this region. At the end of the eighteenth century, as Dr Maisonneuve tells us in his study of Anjou wines, a large quantity of white wine from Saumur were exported, the red wines being reserved for local consumption.

In those days, the winegrowers neglected natural wines somewhat in favour of sparkling wines, which were highly sought after. There, as in Vouvray, several wine-merchants or companies would produce some 7 million bottles of sparkling wine, 20 per cent of which were for export. In the last twenty years, however, this trade has undergone a slump, and today's figure is barely 3 ½ million bottles.

The sparkling wines made in Saumur have an advantage over those of Vouvray. The latter can only be produced from a single grape, the *Pineau de la Loire*, or *Chenin Blanc*. In Saumur, however, the regulations allow for a certain percentage of white wines made from red grapes to be added—up to as much as 60 per cent. This, as well as refining the froth, adds to the quality of the *cuvée* and reduces the somewhat objectionable tang of the soil. The *Cabernet* and the *Groslot* are the grapes which are used for this purpose. The former is of a higher quality and is sought after for the large vats.

The sparkling wines made in Saumur have distinguished qualities—fine, with agreeable bouquets, and a distinct, even personal character—which they owe to a privileged climate and soil as well as to selected grapes.

Apart from the sparkling wines, there are also some slightly effervescent white and rosé wines which are constantly growing in quantity and importance. The amount produced for commercial purposes has increased within the last fifteen years, and now equals that of sparkling wines. The bottling is similar to that of "still" wines; the cork is held by a thin wire fastener, as there is very little pressure.

Rosés of Cabernet. The Saumur region produces rosé only from the *Cabernet* grape, while elsewhere in Anjou rosés are also made from *Groslot*. The *Cabernet Franc* and *Cabernet Sauvignon* grape varieties cover more than 6,000 acres which in turn produce an average of more than 2,200,000 gallons of wine per year.

The Saumur rosé made from the *Cabernet* grape is of a very light colour, as it is usually made from a white vinification, that is to say from grape pressings which have not been crushed, but allowed to ferment from their own weight. Their very pale colour means that they can be added without any difficulty to sparkling white wines.

Some rosé wines which have been slightly crushed have a stronger colour and a richer bouquet.

The other centres of production for rosé wines made from the *Cabernet* grape are the regions of Layon and Brissac in Aubance. In these regions the grapes are crushed and allowed to soak for a few hours. The cells of the broken skin of the grapes mix with the fermenting must, a more or less important part of coloration. The skins are broken and added for colour at the same time as the grapes are pressed. This process is carried out rapidly in order to achieve the finest quality wine. The pressure should not be too great in order to avoid breaking the stalks, which would make the wine astringent.

Wines which have fermented in a vat where the skins of the *Cabernet* grape were added are light pink; those which are pressed and go through a rapid vinification have a characteristic slightly yellow colour. If they have a strawberry hue, this means that a richly coloured juice was added afterwards.

These wines should only contain small quantities of anhydrous sulphur, to avoid discoloration. They should not have more than 11° to 12° in order to remain fruity and fresh. A drop of sweetening does them no harm and helps to cover slight faults. These wines are best when young, otherwise they lose some of their fruitiness and life.

Rosés of Groslot. Before the war, these were almost the only wines cultivated in the area. They are fresh, light, and should be drunk within the year.

If there is only a little wine made from the *Groslot* grape, say about 350 to 450 gallons to an acre, then the wine is very pleasant with an alcohol content from about 9° to 10.5° or exceptionally 11°. The *Groslot* likes gravelly soils as well as clay or calcareous sands, and produces a special seed. The rosé it makes is much better dry; when sweet the wines tend to be heavy. To produce a very fruity, well-balanced, full-bodied rosé, one should add a small amount of *Gamay*, *Cabernet*, or *Pineau d'Aunis*.

ANJOU. The wines of Anjou have been praised by the poets of the Pléiade and enjoy a reputation which dates back to the sixth century when Apollinius praised the town of Angers as having been blessed by Bacchus. In the thirteenth century these wines gained great fame during the reign of the Plantagenets, who imported them to England. Still later, the Dutch and Belgians were good customers for more than two centuries. Boats laden with wine would travel up the Loire to depots at Chalonnes, Rochefort, and Ponts-de-Cé. The wine was brought to the river either by water (Layon, Thouet) or by land. In *Eugénie Grandet*, Balzac recounts an incident where "Père" Grandet tries to sell his wine-stock.

Boats no longer go up the Loire, but wine has found a new means of transport and has conquered new markets—a tribute to its quality and to the efforts made by winegrowers and wine-merchants. There is an infinite variety of Anjou wines. There are white wines made from the *Chenin* and *Pineau* grapes, reds and rosés from the *Cabernet* grape and rosés from the *Groslot* grape variety. There are also dry wines, semi-dry, sweet and dessert wines, still wines, slightly sparkling and sparkling wines, light or robust wines, which have been harvested in several stages by picking grapes which have attained the *pourriture noble* or "noble rot" category.

The Anjou wines are harvested throughout most of the south-east area of Maine-et-Loire, along the slopes which border the Loire below Angers, as well as from the land of the seventeen communes of Deux-Sèvres, from the area surrounding Bouillé-Loretz, and from eight communes along the Vienne River to the south of Saumur.

The largest wineproducing cantons are Thouarcé and Rochefort-sur-Loire where the vine covers 20 per cent of the area. Then come the viticultural regions that lie to the south of Saumur: Montreuil, Bellay, Doué-la-Fontaine, where the land under cultivation is 14 per cent.

The charm of Anjou lies in its climate—the deep blue sky, softened by a slight haze from the sea, the gentle winters, the early spring. Anjou is not a natural geographical region, but the focal point of several provinces which have widely diverging characteristics: the Vendean and Armorican mountain massifs, the mountain passes of Poitou and Touraine. Owing to this lack of homogeneity in its geographical make-up,

Anjou offers a varied soil which reflects almost every geological era: schists, sandstone, primitive calcareous rock, sands, clay, diorite-sand and especially calcareous tufa, chalky sands and a flinty, gravelly soil. To the west of Saumur, in the valley of Layon, the slopes are rich in calcareous sands which nourish a fertile vineyard which produces rosé and white wines. About 40,000 acres are covered in fine quality grapes. The white wines are produced from a single grape, the *Chenin Blanc*, which is planted over about 22,000 acres. A recent law has permitted, in certain circumstances, a small quantity of *Sauvignon* or *Chardonnay* grapes to be added. The best red grape is, as in Touraine, the *Cabernet Franc*. For about twelve years now, however, it has been either replaced to a certain extent by the *Cabernet Sauvignon* grape, which in the selection procedure produces a higher quality of wine, or else the two varieties are mixed. These two grapes are the ones most frequently used to produce red and rosé wines of superior quality. They cover more than 7,500 acres. The other grape varieties are used to produce rosés only. The *Groslot* grape, much cultivated during the reconstruction period, has now been replaced by the *Cabernet Sauvignon*, the *Gamay* and the *Pineau d'Aunis*. The red grapes, which ripen before the *Pineau*, are harvested earlier, usually from September 20th on. To make a rosé wine, the grapes are pressed immediately, without being crushed, in order to obtain a must with a very light colour. The must always ferments without any stalks. The grapes which go to make red Champignys are only pressed when all the stalks have been removed. Fermentation in open vats with unhinged lids or in cement vats lasts from eight to ten days. The wine is then preserved for a year in a large wooden barrel. For some years now, quite a significant amount of red wine has been produced by means of carbonis fermentation, a method yielding light, fruity wines which are most certainly considered to be at their best when young, rather than when aged. The *Pineau de la Loire* and *Chenin* grapes are picked first towards the beginning of October, but only in small quantities, for the grapes are still fresh and ripe. Later, when the *pourriture noble* (noble rot) sets in, they are picked again in larger and larger quantities. Often the harvest continues into the middle of November.

Fermentation takes place in wooden barrels, each of which contains 50 gallons. The temperature of the wine-cellars is from 10° to 35°, which enables these wines, through a slow fermentation, to attain the bouquet and finesse which is characteristic of them. Often the producer is obliged to heat the underground cellars during the first cold spells in order to bring them up to a temperature of 16° to 18°. In Anjou, as in all the other regions of the Loire, the wine benefits from being bottled in the early spring after having been racked, clarified and sometimes even filtered several times. When the wine is bottled later in the year, from May to September, the character of the wine changes, and the freshness and lightness which give it its essential quality are diminished.

Sulphur dioxide is indispensable. It acts both physiologically, since it stops fermentation, and chemically in that its anti-oxygen properties prevent premature ageing, the unwanted sweetness and colouring of maderization, and the spread of oxidasic casse. The anhydride is then eliminated by oxidation which leaves the wine clear and pure but retaining all its freshness and bouquet.

The average harvest of fine quality wines from the Anjou and Saumur regions is some 12,100,000 gallons.

Within Anjou there are two regional *appellations*: ANJOU and SAUMUR. The Saumur region is in fact considered a part of Anjou, according to provisions of legislation passed by the Angers tribunal, and following decrees controlling both *appellations*: a wine made in Saumur may be sold as an ANJOU, but not vice versa. The sub-regional *appellations are*: COTEAUX DU LAYON, COTEAUX DE LA LOIRE, COTEAUX D'AUBANCE, COTEAUX DU LOIR. The *appellations* of individual communes or vineyards are: BONNEZEAUX and QUARTS DE CHAUME, along the slopes of Layon; SAVENNIÈRES, along the Loire, as well as the CULÉE DE SENANT and ROCHE AUX MOINES varieties.

THE MUSCADET REGION

To leave Anjou at Ingrandes is to leave behind all the grape varieties discussed so far and to discover two new ones. Since 1955 a new trend has manifested itself in the Ancenis area: planting and propagating a *Gamay* grape for the production of red and rosé wines. In Basse-Bretagne, the area under vine cultivation at the time of the Romans was for a long time of small importance. In fact only the grounds belonging to the Abbey and its fortified enclosures were reserved for the vine.

When did the *Muscadet* grape first make its appearance in the Loire-Atlantique? Certain documents in Nantes disclose that in 1639, on numerous small farms, the red grapes were pulled out to be replaced by a good grape-stock from Burgundy. The terrible winter of 1709, however, almost entirely wiped out the vineyards. It was necessary therefore to replant completely, which required great effort. Leases provided that the replanting be in *Muscadet de Bourgogne* grapes. Thus it was in the year 1735 that the *Muscadet* grape of today was first known.

At the end of the last century, the *Muscadet* grape occupied approximately a third of the land reserved for the vine, the rest being taken up mainly by the *Gros Plant* grape, a variety of the *Folle Blanche* stock, a staple grape of the Cognac region.

When the vineyards were replanted again after the phylloxera epidemic, the *Gros Plant* lost out to the *Muscadet* grape.

The entire vineyard area here is situated on crystalline schists, on layers of gravelly soil, and on rare calcareous islets which in no way alter the lay of the land. The vine is planted on the gravelly slopes facing the south-west. The vineyards are concentrated in the

regions to the south of the Loire, Sèvres and Maine. This region produces three-quarters of the MUSCADET stock. It is also cultivated to the north of the Loire, mainly in the area between Nantes and Ancenis and around Grand-Lieu Lake.

The *Muscadet* grape ripens early. It is picked very early in the season, towards the beginning of September. Usually, already towards the 15th of this month, the harvesters are in full swing. The flat countryside offers no natural underground cellars; winecellars in this region consist of small buildings with tile roofs.

The wine is fermented in casks or tuns which hold a maximum of six litres (over 10 ½ pints). The process of fermentation is slow, in order that it may acquire a fine bouquet and fruity texture. The wine must be bottled in haste, in fact only a few months after the grapes have been picked. When bottled in its lees, with a small amount of carbonic gas, it retains a finesse and charm which make it very agreeable and much sought after as a companion to sea-food.

MUSCADET generally has a slight acid content, is of a pale yellow colour and light character. It is very difficult to define its bouquet and flavour. The niceties are infinite, and vary considerably from commune to commune and even vineyard to vineyard.

It is possible, however, to distinguish other characteristics peculiar to each type of MUSCADET. The wine comes from the hillsides along the Loire is particularly full-bodied, often with a higher acidity; this is not a fault since a lack of acidity would make this wine spiritless and sharp in character.

The area covered by the *Muscadet* grape is nearly 25,000 acres, producing an average of about 6,600,000 gallons per annum.

WINES OF THE LOIRE

CENTRAL REGION

Name of the wine	*Principal growths*		
White wines . . . . . Pouilly Fumé.	Château du Nozet	La Loge aux Moines	Côteau des Girarmes
	Coteaux des Loges		
Pouilly-sur-Loire	Les Berthiers	Le Bouchot-du-Haut	Le Grand Bouchot
	Bois-Fleury	Les Cassiers	Le Grand Puizac
	Boisgibaud	Château du Nozet	Mezières
	Bouchot	Les Chétives-Maisons	Le Petit Soumard
	Le Bouchot-du-Bas	Les Girarmes	
Ménetou-Salon			
Quincy	Bourg	Les Chavoches	Les Gravoches
	Les Brosses	Cornançay	Rimonet
White, red and rosé	Bruniers	Le Grand Chaumoux	Villalin
wines . . . . Sancerre	Amigny	La Côte	La Perrière
	Coteau de Bannon	La Côte-de-Verdigny	Les Plantes
	Beauregard	Les Côtelins	La Porte du Clos
	Les Belletins	Les Coudebraults	La Poussie
	Chambraste	Les Crilles	Reigny
	Champtin	Clos de l'Epée	Les Rochons
	Les Chassaignes	Fricambault	Saint-Martin
	Château de Sancerre	La Grande Côte	Les Terranges
	Chavignol	Les Groux	Château de Thauvenay
	Chemarin	Lare	Le Thou
	Chêne Marchand	Les Montachins	Côte de la Vallée
	Les Chevillots	Les Monts-Damnés	Les Vicairies
	Les Coinches	La Moussière	Les Vignes-Chatton
	La Comtesse	Le Paradis	Les Vignes de Ménetou
Reuilly	Beaumont	Les Couagnons	Les Marnais
	Les Beauregards	Le Figuier	Clos des Messieurs
	Les Bossières	Les Lignys	Les Varennes
	Chatillons		

TOURS REGION

Name of the wine	*Commune*	*Principal growths*	
White wines . . . . . Touraine — Azay-le-Rideau	Azay-le-Rideau		
Montlouis	Montlouis.	Clos de la Barre	Clos Renard
		Clos de la Frelonnerie	Les Sicots
		La Milletière	
	Lussault	Cray	Pintray
	Saint-Martin-le-Beau . . .	Château du Boulay	Clos de Mosny
		Cange	
Jasnières (in the Sarthe, a			
fairly rare wine)	Jasnières	L'Aillerie	Les Hussières
		Les Beduaux	Les Jasnières
		La Bonatière	Les Longues Vignes
		Les Côtières	Les Mollières
		Les Fleuries	La Mule
		Les Gargouilles	Le Paradis
		La Gidonnière	Saint-Jacques
		Les Haurières	Sous-le-Bois
		Les Héridaines	Les Verboisières

VOUVRAY

Commune	Principal growths		
White wines . . . . . Vouvray	Les Argouges	La Fontainerie	La Muscadelle
	Domaine de l'Auberidière	Les Fouinières	Clos Naudin
	Clos des Barguins	La Gaillardière	Clos de Nouis
	Clos de la Barre	Clos de Gaimont	Perrets de Minuze
	Clos Baudoin	Château Gaudrelle	Clos du Petit-Mont
	Clos Bel-Air	Clos des Girardières	Le Portail
	Clos des Bidaudières	Grand Echeneau	La Renardière
	Clos du Bois-Rideau	Clos des Gues d'Amant	Clos des Roches
	Les Bois Turmeaux	Le Haut-Lieu	Clos Saint-Come
	Clos Le Bouchet	Coteau J.-Jouffroy	Clos Saint-Mathurin
	Clos du Bourg	Clos des Lions	Sauzelles
	Clos de la Brianderie	La Loge	Clos Toulifaut
	Coteaux des Brosses	Clos la Lucassière	Vallée Coquette
	Les Brosses	Clos de Marigny	Clos de Val-Roche
	Les Brûlées	Monaco	Clos Vaufuget
	Coteau Chatrie	Château Montcontour	Clos les Verneries
	Clos Dubois	Clos le Mont	Clos le Vigneau
	L'Epinay		
Chançay	Clos des Augustins	Croix-de-Vaux	La Pirée
	Clos Baguelin	Clos de la Forêt	Château Valmer
	Coteau de Chançay	Grand Bathes	Clos de Vau
	Clos de Charmigny	Château Gaillard	Coteau de Vaux
	La Croix-de-Bois	Petites Bastes	Veaux
Noizay	Clos d'Anzou	Le Grand Coteau	La Roche-de-Cestres
	Les Barres	La Grotte	Clos de la Rochère
	Coteau de Beaumont	Les Hauts-Bois	Coteau de la Rochère
	Clos de Beauregard	Clos Hure	Roquefort
	Clos du Bois d'Ouche	Clos Marteau	La Tremblaie
	Bois Guyon	Molaville	Clos de Venise
	Clos de la Bretonnière	Château d'Ouche	Coteau de Venise
	Goguenne	Clos de la Roche	
Rochecorbon	Clos de l'Alleau	Clos de la Bourdonnerie	Clos de l'Olivier
	Château les Armuseries	Les Chapelles	Clos des Pentes
	Château des Basses-Rivières	Clos de la Chasse-Royale	Clos de Sens
		Clos Château-Chevrier	Clos de la Taisserie
	Clos des Batonnières	Château de la Lanterne	Le Clos Vaufoinard
	Bois-Soleil	Château de Montgouverne	
Sainte-Radegonde	Clos de l'Archerie	Clos Mon-Baril	Clos Saint-Georges
	Clos de la Hallotière	Clos de Rougemont	
Vernou-sur-Brenne. . . .	Les Batailleries	Hardilliers	Perrets-de-Fou-Joint
	Bel-Air	Haut-Cousse	Les Pichaudières
	La Carte	L'Hermineau	Poupine
	Le Cassereau	La Joubardière	Clos de Pouvray
	Clos de Chaillemont	Clos des Longs-Reages	Clos Roc-Etoile
	Clos Chauvin	Clos des Madères	Rue Baffert
	Chopet	Clos Mauguin	Clos des Surins
	Le Clos	Clos de la Meslerie	Tabourneau
	La Coudraie	Mialet	Terne
	Les Deronières	Les Morandières	Clos Thenot
	Château de l'Etoile	Le Mortier	Clos des Thierrières
	Le Feau	La Neurie	Tortemains
	La Folie	Noyer-de-Cens	Vau-Louis
	La Follière	Pain-Perdu	Vaux-Barres
	Clos de Fougerai	Pâtureaux	Vignes-Morier
	Clos Franc	Peu-de-Cartes	Clos de Vilmier

CHINON

Name of the wine		Commune	Principal growths	
White, red and rosé wines	Chinon	Chinon	Les Aubuis	Repos de Saint-Martin
			Les Bruneau	La Rochelle
			Les Closeaux	Rochette
			Montrobert	Saint-Jean
			Clos du Parc	Saint-Louand
			Clos du Pin	La Vauzelle
		Avoine	Les Lignes	
		Beaumont-en-Veron . . .	Château de Dauzay	Les Peuilles
			Les Gresilles	Les Picasses
			Clos du Langon	Les Pineaux
			Le Martinet	Roche-Honneur
		Cravant-les-Coteaux . . .	Les Battereaux	Clos de la Haie-Martel
			Bel-Air	Les Quatre-Ferrures
			Les Coutures	La Semellerie
			La Gresille	Coteaux de Sonnay
		Rouzilles	Pelivet	
		Huismes	Bauregard	Clos Marie
			La Colline	Le Pin
		La Roche-Clermault . . .	Les Aiguillons	Les Rosettes
			Les Bessardières	Sassay
		Ligré	Clos de Galonnes	Clos du Saut-du-Loup
			La Noblaie	Saute-aux-Loups
			Le Paradis	Le Vau-Breton
		Panzoult	La Galippe	Clos Queron
			La Haie-Martel	Ronce
		Rivière	La Croix-Marie	Les Harrassons
			Les Croulards	Clos Saint-Hilaire
Red and rosé wines . .	Bourgueil	Bourgueil	Chevrette	Clos de l'Oie-qui-casse
			Les Galuches	Les Pins-Les Sablons
			Clos des Geslets	La Salpetrerie
		Benais	Beauvais	Petit-Mont
			La Chanteleuserie	Les Raguenières
		Chouzé-sur-Loire	Les Goutierreries	Les Grandes Ouches
		Ingrandes-de-Touraine . .	Clos de Blottières	La Gallotière
			Cru des Brunetières	Minière-Château
		Restigné	Les Evois	Château Louys
			Fougerolles	La Philebernière
			Domaine de la Gaucherie	Clos de la Platerie
			Les Grands-Champs	Les Rosaies
			Les Hauts-Champs	Clos du Vendôme
		Saint-Nicolas-de-Bourgueil	Beaupuy	La Jarnoterie
			La Contrie	La Martellière
			Clos de l'Epaisse	Port-Guyet
			Les Fondis	Clos de la Torrillère
			Forcine	Clos du Vigneau
			La Gardière	La Villatte

SAUMUR REGION

Name of the wine		Commune	Principal growths	
White wines	Coteaux de Saumur	Montsoreau	Clos des Rotissants	Clos des Pères
		Bizay	Clos des Treilles	
		Brézé	Les Clos du Château de Brézé	Château La Ripaille
				Clos des Carmes
		Parnay	Clos des Murs	Clos des Saints-Pères
		Saint-Cyr	Butte de Saumoussay	
		Turquant	Château Gaillard	
		Dampierre	Clos des Morains	
		Souzay	Champ Chardon	Clos de la Bienboire
		Saumur	Château de la Fuye	

Name of the wine	Commune	Principal growths

Red wines . . . . . . Cabernet de Saumur

Souzay	Champigny-le-Sec	
Saumur	Souzay	Varrains
	Parnay	Allonnes
	Saumoussay	Brain-sur-Allones

Rosé wine . . . . . . Cabernet de Saumur

ANGERS REGION

White wines

Name of the wine	Commune		
Coteaux de la Loire	Savennières	Principal growths	La Coulée de Serrant / Château d'Epire	La Roche-aux-Moines / Clos du Papillon

La Possonnière, La Pommeraye, Ingrandes, Montjean, Bouchemaine, Saint-Barthélemy, Andard, Brain-sur-l'Authion.

Coteaux du Loir	Huillé	Principal growths	Clos des Tertres / Clos Pilate	Clos du Pineau / Clos la Patrie

Lézigné, Durtal, Baugeois.

Coteaux du Layon	Rochefort-sur-Loire	Principal growths	Quart de Chaume / Clos de Sainte-Catherine	Les Guimonières
	Beaulieu-sur-Layon	Principal growths	Château du Breuil	Les Mullonnières
	Saint-Aubin-de-Luigné	Principal growths	La Roulerie / Château La Fresnaye	Plaisance
	Rablay	Principal growths	L'Argonette / Le Clos de la Roche / Les Gonnordes	La Touche / Les Sablonnettes / Les Celliers
	Faye-sur-Layon	Principal growths	Château de Chanze / Château de Mongeneau / La Madeleine / Les Noëls	La Saillanderie / La Pierre-Gauderie / Les Jouets / Le Miroir
	Thouarcé	Principal growth	Bonnezeaux	

Other vine-growing communes Saint-Lambert-du-Lattay, Le Champ, Chaudefonds, Martigné-Briand, Chavagnes, Brigné, Concourson.

Coteaux de l'Aubance   Murs-Erigné, Vauchrétien, Sainte-Melaine-sur Aubance, Quincé, Brissac, Juigné-sur-Loire, Saint-Saturnin-sur-Loire, Saint-Jean-des-Mauvrets.

Rosé wines

Rosé d'Anjou	Dampierre, Varrains
Cabernet d'Anjou	Chacé, Bagneux, Martigné-Briand, Tigné, Le Thoureil, Vauchrétien, Murs, Notre-Dame-d'Alençon, Brissac.

NANTES REGION

White wines . . . . . Name of the wine	Principal growths	
Muscadet de Sèvre-et-Maine	Vallet / Mouzillon / Le Pallet	La Chapelle-Heulin / La Regrippière / Saint-Fiacre-sur-Maine
Muscadet des Coteaux de la Loire	Saint-Herblon / Ancenis / Saint-Géréon	Liré / Drain

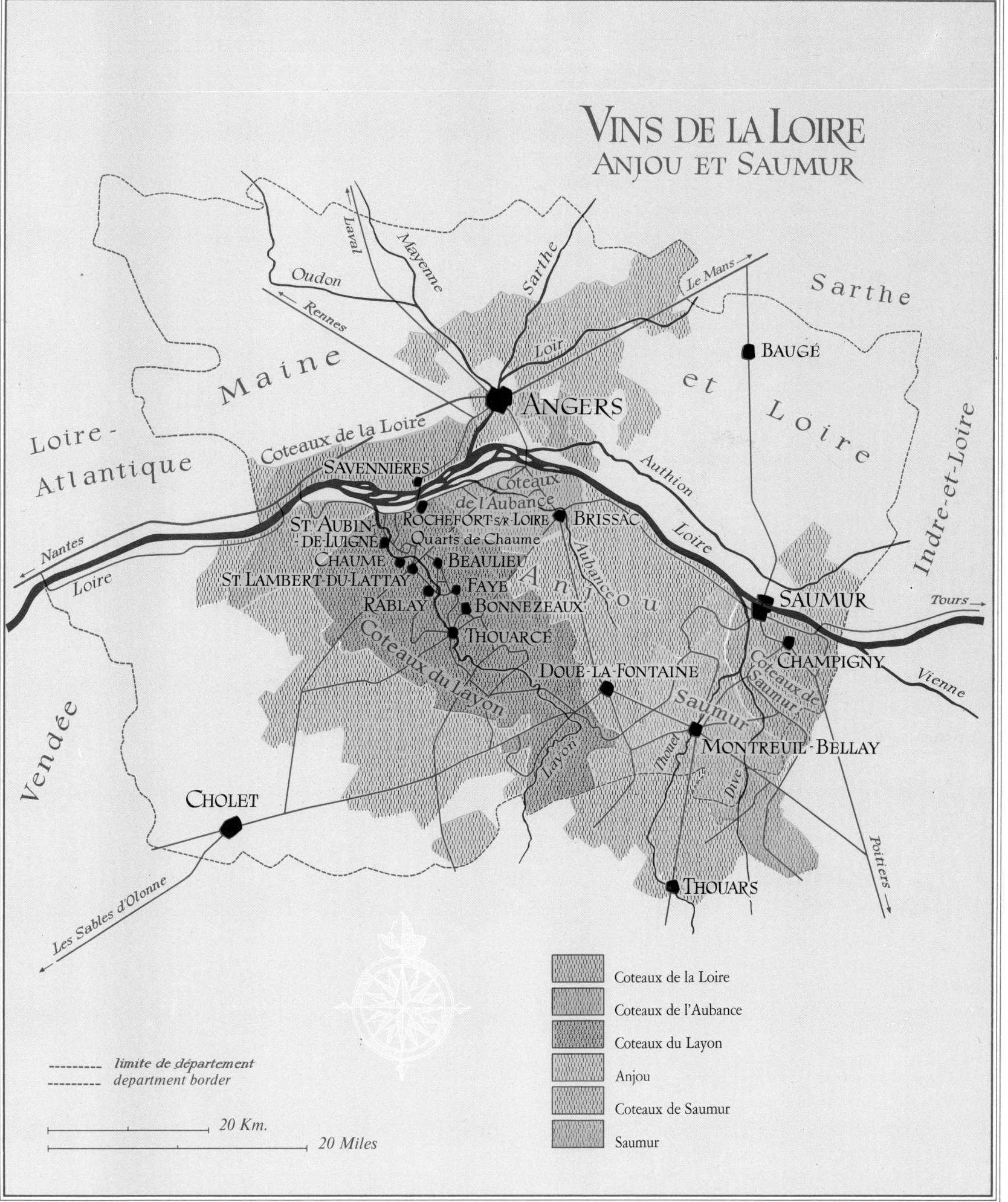

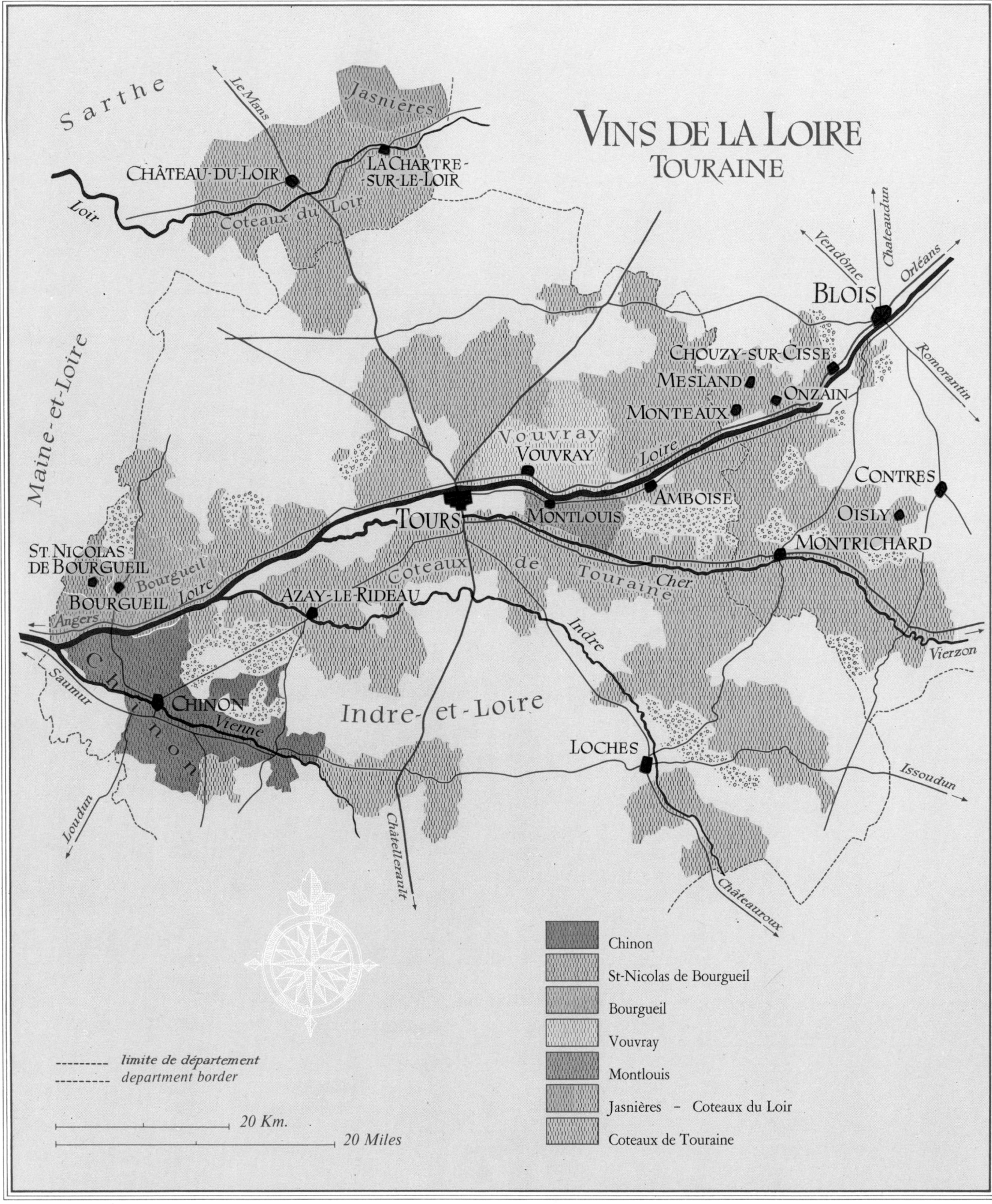

VINS DE LA LOIRE
TOURAINE

Sarthe

Jasnières

CHÂTEAU-DU-LOIR LA CHARTRE-SUR-LE-LOIR

Le Mans

Loir

Coteaux du Loir

Vendôme

Châteaudun

Orléans

BLOIS

CHOUZY-SUR-CISSE

MESLAND ONZAIN

Romorantin

MONTEAUX

Maine-et-Loire

Vouvray
VOUVRAY

Loire

AMBOISE

CONTRES

OISLY

TOURS Montlouis

MONTRICHARD

ST·NICOLAS
DE·BOURGUEIL

Coteaux   de   Touraine

Cher

Bourgueil Loire

Vierzon

BOURGUEIL

AZAY·LE·RIDEAU

Angers

Indre

Saumur

Chinon

CHINON

Vienne

Indre-et-Loire

Loudun

Châtellerault

LOCHES

Issoudun

Châteauroux

20 Km.

20 Miles

- - - - - - - - - *limite de département*
- - - - - - - - - department border

	Chinon
	St-Nicolas de Bourgueil
	Bourgueil
	Vouvray
	Montlouis
	Jasnières – Coteaux du Loir
	Coteaux de Touraine

THE WINES
OF BORDEAUX

GASTON MARCHOU

Between the first and third centuries of the Christian era, the Bordeaux countryside witnessed the triumph of the medium-sized estate. The large Gallic domain, hitherto indivisible under the authority of the chieftain of the clan, began to break up. In most cases, the chief was anxious to obtain the title of "Roman citizen", which obviously implied an obligation to accept the conqueror's legal system. Since Roman Law did not recognize the right of inalienability, land was bought, sold and sub-divided. It became a matter for speculation, a means of self-enrichment and a way of paying debts. It could be bequeathed by will.

Agrarian reform, though almost imperceptible, was rendered inevitable by the interaction of customs and vested interests. When great landowners reappeared, even before the break-up of the Empire, the large domain was not re-established. Wealth no longer meant the ownership of a single immense territory but of a number of adjoining estates, each having its own economy. In some cases, in fact, there were no means of communication between such land-holdings.

The cultivation of the vine and the preparation of wine were much better suited to this sub-division than to the vast expanses of territory under a single head. Where necessary, in fact, it encouraged the process.

In A.D. 92, Domitian inaugurated a policy which was to continue until the present day, despite successive repulses and the harmful consequences it was to produce. This emperor, who has been harshly judged by history for other reasons, tried to remedy the shortage of wheat by prohibiting the planting of new vines on Italian soil and ordering that half those that existed in the western provinces should be uprooted. Montesquieu, it is true, gives another reason for Domitian's decision: "This weak and timid prince," he said, "caused the vines in the two Gauls to be grubbed up lest the wine should attract the barbarians." Possibly the author of the *Spirit of the Laws* was loath to leave a Roman emperor, even a mediocre one, in the company of the mid-eighteenth-century economists who advocated pulling up vines. Nevertheless, he was wrong to state as a fact that the Gallic vineyards even partly disappeared under Domitian. The governor of the province was obliged to grant official privileges and exemptions. Incidentally, the winegrowers of Bordeaux often dispensed with them both. They simply bribed the officials responsible for applying the edict.

Even in Rome itself, the winegrowing interests of Bordeaux were defended with typically Gascon asperity and irony. By means of clandestinely distributed pamphlets, the vine, condemned to death by Domitian but still very much alive, addressed the Emperor: "Eat me down to the roots," it said, "I shall still bear enough grapes for great libations to be poured on the day that Caesar is slain !"

Domitian was assassinated four years later. One cannot attack the vineyards of Bordeaux with impunity. The great French administrator Tourny was also to discover the fact. Although he sacrificed his fortune for the city and lavished his affection on it, he was disgraced because he forgot that the fame of its wine was more important than his own.

If the vine, which climbs in serried ranks up the slopes of the right bank of the Médoc, drives back the forest from the left bank and rushes through the sands of the delta to the ocean, has succeeded in defending itself against arbitrary central power, this is most clearly explained by the medium- and small-holding system. It would have been much easier for the officials to ensure that the vines were uprooted in the domains covering the area of a canton or several communes, it would have been far more serious for anyone to disobey the Emperor and the landowners would have been more vulnerable.

At the time of Domitian, the vineyards were grouped around the city; but Burdigala, as it was than known, was built on a very simple plan and was still rustic. The proprietor lived on his land, in his Gallo-Roman villa. He preferred the scent of new-mown hay and the strong perfume of his wine-cellar to the frenzied habit of writing verse which he was to contract at the time of Ausonius, when he was completely latinized. This final latinization of Aquitaine, incidentally, in the twilight of the Empire, coincided with a decline of Latin influence in the East.

While awaiting his conversion to poetry, the master of the villa trembled for his flowering vine if the nights of May were clear. In his short hood and gaiters, he would rise early in the morning to go and see it. He would take the fragile corollas delicately between index finger and middle finger and regard them with a paternal eye. He would meet his workmen, unless he was up before them. He would talk to them, ask the advice of the most experienced, look up at the sky, observe the colour of the river, sometimes shining like a silver lake, sometimes restless and yellow if heavy rain was approaching from the uplands. From his garden-neat vineyard, laid out in tasteful and human geometrical patterns, he had banished the fruit trees which were grown elsewhere. He personified the ageless proverb that Olivier de Serres was to borrow from the land of the Gironde:

The shadow of a good master
Makes the vine grow much faster

However, this good master was not only a wine-grower whose ear was the first to hear the cuckoo heralding the certain arrival of fine summer days. Since the villa had to provide for all its own needs, he was also an artisan or even an engineer. He brought to life the lost dream of self-sufficiency which is still evoked in Olivier de Serres' *Theatre of Agriculture and Field Management*. Every villa possessed a forge, a carpentry shop and a pottery kiln. It manufactured earthenware pottery, tools and instruments. The owner supervised everything, like a paterfamilias who,

living close to the land, was well aware of the limits of productive efforts and the precariousness of their results.

He stamped an impression on the soil of the Gironde which successive invasions were unable to efface. It is to the credit of the first Gallo-Roman landowner, to his peasant mentality, and the care he bestowed on his vine which he cherished like a queen, that the region, when the Gallic system of serfdom was renounced, refrained from introducing the despicable Roman custom of slave labour.

The seeds of what the all-embracing goodness of a Younger Pliny had attempted in Italy and what Christianity was to achieve in due course, were already present in the Bordeaux vineyards by the middle of the third century A.D. The Gironde landowner of the fifth century was thus appreciably better off than the debt-ridden Italian farmer of whom Columella tells us. He was a man who lived well from his free labour and harvested the fruits of the earth, at least partly to his own advantage. The famous wine which was drunk from silver cups in the palaces was also drunk by him from his rustic earthenware goblet. He caught the echo of the praises lavished on the "liquor of the Gods" like a father hearing a tribute to his infant prodigy.

The wine of Bordeaux was to become the sole preoccupation of a whole population. Thanks to it, the social classes, so well-marked elsewhere, were intermingled in a common faith. Beyond the narrow compartmentation of feudalism, it opened up new horizons so attractive that archbishop and cobbler, noble and burgher were assembled together in a kind of superior guild. In the centuries to come, a singular wine-born aristocracy was to arise, in the eyes of which all other products of human activity, including politics and war, would be negligible or secondary.

In the first half of the eighth century, Bordeaux found itself briefly under Arab domination, the only régime which could definitely endanger the vine, since the Moors were conquerors who did not drink it. When deliverance came with Charles Martel, the city still had to face twenty years of war during which the dukes of Aquitaine defended their inheritance against the successors of Clovis. Finally, the Bordeaux country became a march of the Carolingian empire. A noble procession now passes by, a glittering interlude in the mediocrity of those remote ages. Charlemagne comes first, mounted upon his battle charger, holding his sword "Joyeuse" with its ruby-encrusted hilt, with which he will touch the sarcophagus of St. Seurin. Four pages on horseback hold a canopy above his head. Next come his three sons, then the bishops, the dukes, the Twelve Peers, the counts and the knights. The Emperor is interested in the winegrower's way of life; he visits the wineries. He forbids the custom of

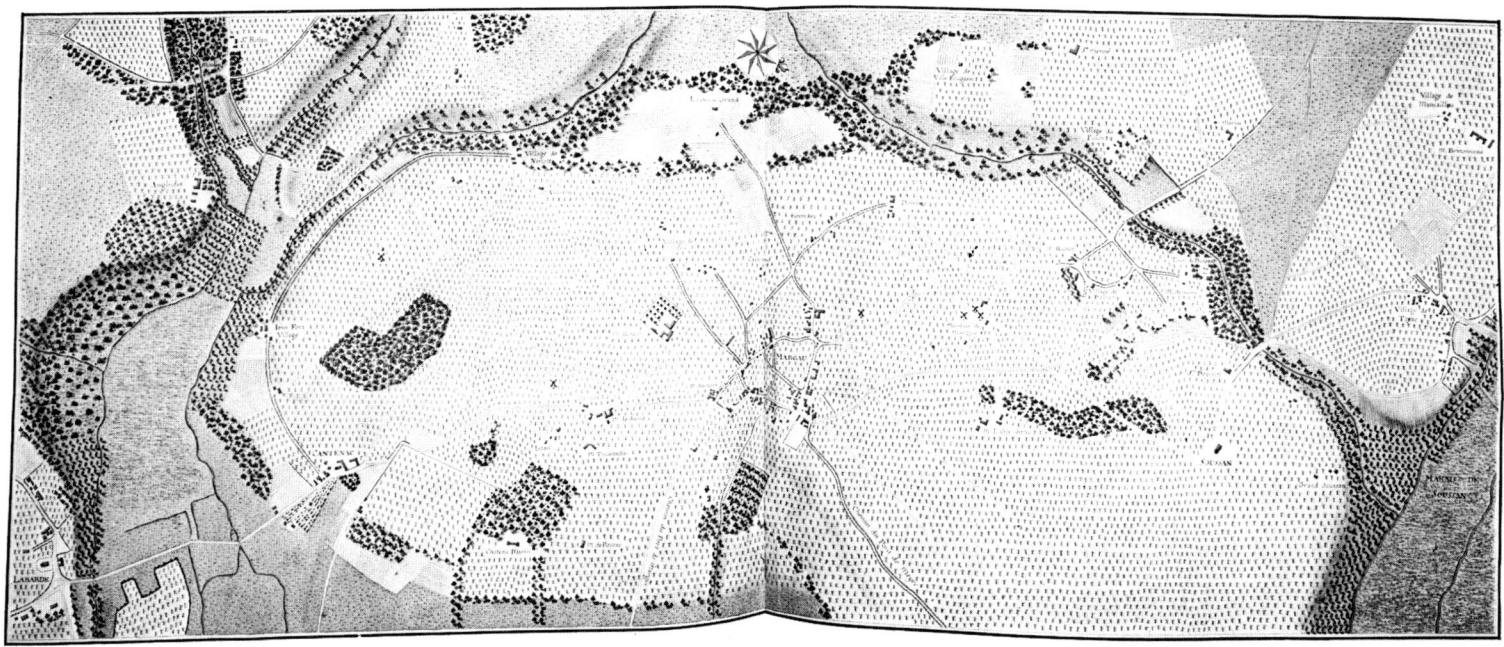

Situated in the Haut-Médoc, on the left bank of the Gironde, the commune of Margaux owes its world-wide renown to Château Margaux, one of the great lords of the Bordeaux wine-country. In the middle of the eighteenth century, Monsieur de Fumel, the military Governor of Bordeaux, planted it with fine, carefully selected vines which quickly made the estate's name. It is shown here on a contemporary plan.

carrying Bordeaux wine in leather bottles and prescribes the use of hooped casks. He discusses vintages with the merchants and orders good years to be aged in jars.

The eternal wine of Bordeaux is a continuous creation; not only as regards winegrowing and viticultural techniques, in which scientific innovations must constantly be controlled by references to tradition, but also at the prestige level, where promotion efforts are ineffective unless constantly renewed. Hence, in the Middle Ages, after the marriage of the beautiful Eleanor of Aquitaine to Henry Plantagenet of England, the *Jurade* or City Council of Bordeaux based the whole of its foreign policy on the need to keep and develop the English market, the sole outlet for claret. After the reunion of Guienne with France, Bordeaux wine could no longer depend exclusively upon exports. Continental consumers had to be found. From the sixteenth century onwards, the city fathers carried out a systematic campaign to find them.

In 1555, the Mayor of Bordeaux visited the French Court, taking with him twenty *tonneaux* (four hogsheads) of wine for presentation to noblemen who were favourably disposed to the city and its trade. A year later, twenty *tonneaux* of Graves were sent to the Cardinal of Lorraine and to Marshal Saint-André for the same reason. In 1559, the Duke of Alba, while passing through Bordeaux, was visited by the *Jurats* or aldermen who offered him a present of wine. In 1596,

a Bordeaux *Jurat* named Pierre de Brach, on a mission to Paris, was instructed to distribute several *tonneaux* of wine to the best effect. He recounts the difficulty he had in bringing the wine into the capital: "An hundred times I wished the wine back on its vine, for truly I believe it less troublesome to bring a king into Paris than a little wine. There are fifty formalities, routines and prescripts." On June 3rd, 1681, the Muscovite Ambassador arrived in Bordeaux and, having greeted him, the *Jurats* presented him with several dozen bottles of fine wine and some brandy. It is noteworthy that bottled Bordeaux thus made its official appearance at the end of the seventeenth century, even if bottling was not yet the standard commercial practice. It was not until the following century that the establishment of the first industrial glass-works gave birth to the Bordeaux fine-wine business which was to produce the first classification by parishes and then by châteaux or estates.

In 1728, twelve years before Tourny was appointed intendant of Bordeaux, the Duke of Antin was able to write to Robert de Cotte: "The Bordelais prefer to sell their wine rather than to put up fine buildings." The fine buildings were not, in fact, to be put up (as later events were to prove) until the area became closely dependent on the central power. The Bordeaux wine trade, on the other hand, was still to remain for a long time yet the privilege of the people of Bordeaux.

The "Great Privilege" or "Wine Privilege" remained in force until the Revolution, when it was abolished as an unjust feudal institution. In fact, the privilege was perfectly justified. Quite apart from the guarantees it gave of quality production, the beneficiaries were responsible for maintaining the city and its ramparts. This very complex legal monument was the *Jurade's* masterpiece. Its purpose was to restrict access to the port of Bordeaux to wines produced in the seneschalcy.

In addition, everything connected with wine—brokerage, retail sale in the Bordeaux taverns and pot-houses, the shape and capacity of the *barrique* (a barrel containing about 50 U.K. gallons, the standard model for which was installed in the City Hall in 1597), everything was regulated and the regulations were scrupulously observed. Every *barrique* had to carry, at both ends, the growth mark, burnt in with a hot iron. This mark was removed once the *barrique* was empty, unless it was returned to the vineyard of origin. Its owner had to obtain a certificate ("stamp") from the local mayor or parish priest that the cask had been duly returned. The text of the "stamp" stipulated that "it is enjoined upon all merchants' masters of the wine-stores to erase immediately, under penalty of a fine of three thousand livres [about £600 or $1,440] and corporal punishment, the marks on *barriques* which have been broached in their stores whether for consumption, ullaging, fine bottling or cutting down."

This affair of the "stamp" brought the constant conflict between traders and producers to a height of tension. It aroused so many protests among the traders of Chartrons, the trading quarter of Bordeaux, that the regulation was annulled. It should be realized, incidentally, that the chief result of the "stamp" system, as elaborated by the *Jurats*, was not only to prevent the dilution of the wine but also to turn the merchants into habitual lawbreakers, since all normal work in a winestore became impossible. The sovereign power of the *Jurade*, no longer able to assert itself in grand designs, was degenerating into officiousness.

The quarter of a century between the treaty of 1763, which ended the Seven Years War, and 1789 was, roughly speaking, the period of the "Trade with the Isles". Never had the flame of enterprise burned more brightly in the "Port of the Moon". With a rapidity comparable to the lightning development of the towns of the American West in the nineteenth century, Bordeaux carried out the programme outlined by Tourny. The society which was to die under the knife for the crime of "merchandizing" was certainly the gayest and most artistic that the City of Montaigne had ever known. It had subtlety, poetry and a very lively taste for nature, though without the dialectic bent so dear to Rousseau. Each year when autumn

came the whole of that fashionable society, counsellors of the *Parlement* at its head, left the "Follies" of the suburbs embalmed in the fragrance of the wine-vat; Pomona's sleep began, and the port of Bordeaux awoke. The crescent-shaped roadstead was immense. It stretched from the old Salinières quarter to the more modern quarter of Chartrons, making a semi-circle in front of the classical perspective of the house-fronts.

Breaking the medieval records of which Froissart had spoken, the port was filled with as many as 300 ships, not counting brigs and brigantines. The vessels flew the flags of England, Holland, the Hanseatic towns, Denmark, the Baltic countries, Spain and the distant American republic. At that time, Bordeaux was the greatest distribution centre for colonial goods in all Europe and monopolized a quarter of France's foreign trade.

In fact, if the time of the "Trade with the Isles" is reduced to the period during which it was brilliant and stable, it will be realized that it lasted no longer than fifteen years! Fifteen years during which the *barriques* from those parishes of Médoc and Graves whose growths had, for the first time, been arranged in a hierarchy in 1755, were lined up and modestly concealed behind piles of exotic wealth.

The Jacobin incursion plunged Bordeaux into the same stupor as the arrival of the Barbarians had done. For that happy-go-lucky city, the Napoleonic wars were a long and sombre tunnel. When peace was restored, the port for a long time remained deserted and the "Trade with the Isles" became a shadowy memory. Happily, however, during those fifteen years the wine of Bordeaux had become a "European creation", as Gabriel Delaunay well put it. English, Germans, Dutch, Belgians and Scandinavians could no longer do without it. It was their fidelity to this unique product that saved Bordeaux. Stripping off the white gloves they had worn to handle samples of indigo, the people of Bordeaux had no recourse but to return to their vines and their winestores, and this they did. Since then, whatever the economic climate, however enticing the promise of an industrial future might be, the Bordeaux winegrowers have known where they are going. They will never again depart from their vine-bordered road.

I remember, during the war, a honey-sweet morning draped in a luminous, velvety mist. It was at a spot in that immense Central European plain where the very shape of a vine-stock is unknown. That morning, for the first time in months, I felt my distant birthplace refilling my void. Like many another, I knew that extraordinary, almost painful moment when the wearisome dizziness of captivity suddenly becomes fixed in a blinding revelation. By undreamt-of approaches, our lost France reclaimed her anonymous flock and gave each of us back his provincial identity. With the help of a sign, expressly given to us, marvellous images of the past rose up under our closed eyelids with a force, a truth, a wealth of detail which the seeing eyes can never achieve.

It needed that dawn in the early Silesian autumn, the melancholy of a desolate grassland on which innumerable rain-puddles reflected clouds driven by the West wind, the misty prospect of the huts and strange quality of the sounds in the atmosphere, to give me back the soft and magnificent "grape-gathering weather" in the middle of Elsterhorst Camp.

This well-known phenomenon of exile turned me into one of those naïve travellers of ancient times who would suddenly discover an unknown city from the brow of a hill. But my discovery was a symbolic one.

It gave me a destiny. I realized that the glory of Bordeaux both siezes upon the senses and obtrudes upon the intellect, for even before encountering the miraculous life of Joan of Arc, translating Voltaire or sending its women to Paris for their frocks, a civilized nation makes the acquaintance of Bordeaux wine.

On the other hand, there is a vine epic in the Bordeaux country. Through wine, the vine presides over the social, moral and political activities of every day; it regulates life, of which it is the essential framework. A child born on the banks of the Garonne cannot conceive of a countryside without vineyards.

Throughout the centuries, the vine has been the friend of man in every country where the grape ripens. But once and once alone, in the history of mankind, it hat been a whole people's reason for living; and that was in Bordeaux.

THE REGIONS OF BORDEAUX

If you look at a map of France, your eye will be caught by the blue indentation of the Gironde estuary. It is a vast gateway to the ocean, the longest and widest along the whole coastline. From Ambès Bill, where the Garonne and the Dordogne meet, to the sea is a distance of some 60 miles and, at that point, the river is 2 miles wide. Downstream, the two banks are more than 6 miles apart. This expanse of water is subject to tidal action. When the ocean rises, its irresistible mass pours into the estuary, hurling back the current. This is the phenomenon known as the "bore" which is more or less violent according to season. The tidal wave moves with the speed of a galloping horse, raising in front of it a wall of seething, yellowish water. The bore does not slacken off before reaching Bordeaux and the violent agitation is still visible well above the city.

In the age of wooden ships, the mouth of the Gironde, although it had not yet achieved its present configuration, was an excellent route for penetrating into the continent. No other European river could carry ships so far inland. If, however, the reader follows the course of the Garonne in an atlas, he will realize that the river is not only the "maryne-lyke waie to the see of Biscaye and the noble and puyssante citie of Bourdeaulx" as the old portulan maps put it. Crossing the Limogne, you reach the Naurouze plateau which connects the basin of the Garonne to that of the Aude. This is the easiest and most agreeable route between the Mediterranean and the Atlantic. Long before the conquest, the Romans of Narbonne used to send their merchants down the Garonne, whence they took ship for the British Isles and the ports of the north.

Although the right bank of the estuary, which is bordered by a succession of cliffs, has been unchanged for thousands of years, this is not true of the left bank. Even as late as the historical period, this was a confused jumble of dunes and marshes through which the waters of the river made their way, depositing silt. Not more than six or seven centuries ago, the river embraced part of the long riparian plain now called the Médoc before losing itself in the Atlantic. The island thus formed was, at high tide, crossed by other arms of the river which, although a true estuary to the east, opened out into a delta in the west.

The department of the Gironde, the limits of which more or less coincide with the frontiers of the ancient Guienne, is the largest in France and covers more than 2 ½ million acres. It can be divided into two distinct regions. The first, covering about 1,500,000 acres, is bordered by the ocean on the one side and, on the other, by the left banks of the Gironde, the Garonne, the Ciron and the Barthus. It is a well-wooded countryside which belongs to the great Landes forest. Near the river, however, an outcrop of quaternary gravels forms a ridge on which are found the most famous vineyards in the world. The second region consists of a succession of hills and plateaus on the right banks of the Gironde and the Garonne. Their soil varies considerably. Starting from the south, we come to the Réolais, consisting of more or less argillaceous sandstones, the Entre-Deux-Mers and, on the right bank of the Dordogne, the very characteristic sub-regions of the Fronsadais and the Saint-Emilionnais where the gravel becomes more and more clayey and gives birth to several Great Growths. The Blayais-Bourgeais region, which is opposite the Médoc, across the Gironde, borders the right bank of the estuary, like a predominantly limestone wall.

Even nowadays, despite the vine which reigns on both banks, despite the links forged between all the inhabitants of the Bordeaux country over two millenia, the great river still separates two different worlds. To the west, the impenetrable curtain of coniferous forest shuts off the horizon behind the vineyards. To the east, there rise up hills so steep that the whiteness of limestone outcrops can be seen on their flanks.

The mild winters of the Gironde are due to the Gulf Stream. The temperate summers with their golden light, which will be entrapped in the liquid prison of the grape, are saved from excessive heat by a protective bank of clouds. The wine of Bordeaux is as much the offspring of a climate as of a soil.

THE "APPELLATIONS CONTRÔLÉES"

What is meant by the three words: "Wine of Bordeaux"? Speaking at Nogent-sur-Marne one day, the late-lamented Jean Valmy-Baysse replied to that question with as much elegance as simplicity: "the wine of Bordeaux, gentlemen, is France personified!"

To the foreign consumer, the trademark "Bordeaux" does, in fact, mean the rarest and most sought-after of products, regular consumption of which is a sign of good taste and distinction.

Bordeaux wine is, as someone once put it, "something quite other than merchandise". It is a product which, according to Aristotle's definition, may be classified among the great universals. If, however, the universal makes the unity of the species, the particular makes its number. The legal descriptions of origin Bordeaux and Bordeaux Supérieur belong to the number.

Here we shall have to indulge in a little more history. These "descriptions of origin" are so loaded with references, they express the idea of collective heritage and ownership so well that, not so long ago, their delimitation gave rise to a hot dispute which was finally settled only by a decree published in the *Official Gazette* of February 19th, 1911.

Before they came to their decision, the legislators were bombarded with more or less justified claims that the description Bordeaux should be extended to wines which were sometimes far removed from the city of that name.

The archivist Brutails helped them to decide on the limits by bringing his historical knowledge to bear and making a clear distinction between the wines of the seneschalcy and those of the Uplands (Haut-Pays) in accordance with traditions dating from the Middle Ages.

In that distant era, the only wines entitled to the description Bordeaux were those harvested in the immediate vicinity of the city by winegrowers who were freemen of the city and dwelt *intra muros*. To guard the privilege King John had stated on April 15th, 1214: "We desire that all the wines of our citizens of Bordeaux, which come from the vines of their city, should travel freely on the river." In other words, all other wines were subject to a blockade and were discriminated against fiscally.

Like waves spreading out from a stone splashing in water, the description—or, more exactly, the privilege—was then extended to the 350 parishes of the seneschalcy of Guienne. Such was the legal position of the vineyards in 1789. It was not too critical.

The new administrative division of France into departments, on the threshold of the nineteenth century, once again extended the area of the description Bordeaux. Instead of the 350 parishes of the seneschalcy, it covered almost all the 554 communes of the Gironde. It was only a strike by the Council General that prevented the description being also extended to 63 communes of the Dordogne and Lot-et-Garonne.

After the decree of 1911, the winegrowers of the Lot-et-Garonne tried to call their wines "wines of the Bordeaux Uplands". This attempt was rejected by the courts since the description *Haut-Pays bordelais* was not a traditional one. Quite the contrary, in fact, since the term "Haut-Pays" was used to identify wines other than those known by the trademark Bordeaux. So much so, indeed, that cutting the city wines with wines from the Haut-Pays had always been prohibited, as is evidenced by numerous fiats of the Bordeaux *parlement* down the centuries. The Act of 1911 was thus perfectly straightforward. Its purpose was to fit the place-of-origin concept into the framework of modern law and to protect the description Bordeaux from the concept of "provenance" with all the possibilities of generalized fraud it entailed.

At this stage of regulation, however, the name "Bordeaux" covered all the growths of the Bordeaux region without distinction, including the Great Growths which had been the beneficiaries of the 1855 classification and which had made use of all their prestige to obtain the decree.

In early 1919, the problem of descriptions of origin came up again with a new urgency owing to the Peace

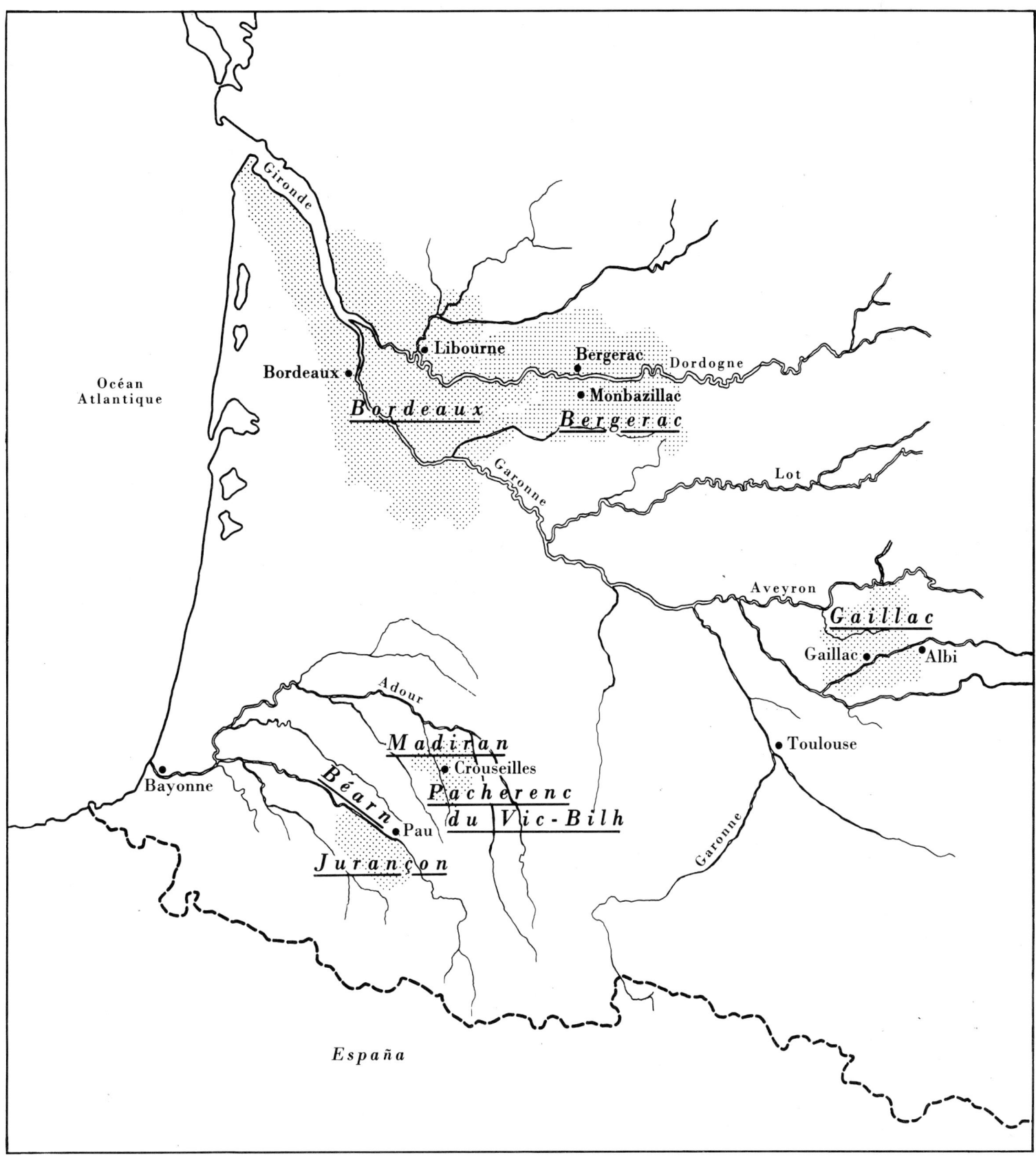

The Aquitaine basin is one of the principal winegrowing regions in France. The vine is mainly cultivated in the departmnt of the Gironde which groups, around the proud name of Bordeaux, a great number of famous designations such as Médoc, Graves, Sauternes, Barsac and St.-Emilion. Other vineyards are to be found around Bergerac and Monbazillac, in the middle reaches of the Dordogne; around Gaillac in the Albigeois and, finally, in the former province of Béarn, to the south of the Adour and the Gave de Pau.

Conference being held at Versailles. If respect for descriptions of origin was to be imposed upon Germany, internal regulations had to be set up. The Descriptions of Origin Act was promulgated on May 6th, 1919. From then on, legislation proliferated. The most decisive laws were the Capus Act of 1927 and the Decree-Act of 1935. The fact was that the winegrowers were unable to accept geographical origin as the sole criterion entitling to a "description". The 1919 Act was supplemented therefore by others which took account of new factors such as soil, vine species, degree of alcohol and yield per acre. Thus were born the *appellations d'origine contrôlée* (A.O.C.), the guaranteed descriptions of origin.

In the case of the Bordeaux region, the result of these provisions was a sort of hierarchy. It may, perhaps, have been a mistake to put the most limited description at the top and gradually descend to more and more general descriptions with an increasingly large production. Thus, in order of descent, a Pauillac growth was entitled to the descriptions PAUILLAC, MÉDOC and BORDEAUX.

To put it another way, a Pauillac wine which was considered to be unworthy of its name of origin and which lacked the characteristics required of a good Médoc could always be marketed as a BORDEAUX. This use of the description BORDEAUX as a catch-all was to produce great confusion in view of the world-wide renown of the greatest fine-wine producing region in France. However famous some celebrated châteaux or a few restricted descriptions might be, the foreign wine-lover had great difficulty in understanding that the word BORDEAUX standing alone indicated the more modest products of the Bordeaux region. The most recent example of this regrettable confusion was given by the world press when commenting on a speech made by the then French Minister of Agriculture, Mr. Edgard Pisani, during a visit to Bordeaux. He said: "I have been and still am struck by the fact that the 'Bordeaux' flag is fast reaching the stage when it waves over the most mediocre goods and that so much disorder has been created in this winegrowing area that the first care of every winegrower is to put on a château label instead of the Bordeaux one."

Being badly informed about the A.O.C. legislation, all that some journalists gleaned from his statement was the inference that Bordeaux wine was mediocre in general. Nonetheless the Minister's criticism was perfectly justified and the reluctance of some Girondin producers to use the name BORDEAUX was quite understandable. It does not mean, however, that they were entirely in the right. Although the descriptions BORDEAUX and BORDEAUX SUPÉRIEUR were used to denote the more mediocre products, the great mass of BORDEAUX wines in terms of the Capus Act were of excellent quality and widely used to improve growths better placed economically.

It was necessary to escape from that blind alley and take up the challenge to logic. The question was who would take the first step on the way back to a sound tradition. One solution would have been for the Great Growths to meet their historic responsibilities and once more inscribe the name of Bordeaux on the pediment of their fame. In that way, they would have taken up anew their centuries-old mission and, like true nobles, would have returned to the head of their troops and imposed discipline amongst them. The hesitation to sign such a blank cheque, however, was quite understandable. The other solution, more in keeping with the style of our era, was for those involved to take the revaluation of the description BORDEAUX into their own hands and that, in fact, was what they did.

Thanks to Mr. Pierre Perromat, President of the National Institute of Descriptions of Origin but who never abandoned the presidency of the BORDEAUX and BORDEAUX SUPÉRIEUR wine syndicate, these wines have, since 1967, enjoyed full descriptions of origin. They are subject to tasting and analytical tests like most of the other Gironde descriptions and have recovered their independence. There is no longer a catch-all description. Henceforth, the only refuge for disinherited Bordeaux descriptions is the category: "wines for everyday consumption".

The description BORDEAUX CLAIRET, which derives from the description BORDEAUX, has been highly fashionable in recent years. It is a rosé wine from any red grape already covered by the regional description and is obtained by "bleeding" the vat before the must has taken on its full colour. BORDEAUX CLAIRET has nothing in common with the old claret, which was a briefly fermented red wine. It is none the less a charming, fruity wine, both delicate and cheerful.

THE WINES OF THE LEFT BANK
OF THE GIRONDE AND THE GARONNE

MÉDOC

In 1855, a patriot of the Médoc, Mr. Saint-Amant, could write: "The Médoc appears rich and sumptuous: yet it both is and it isn't. A great year lavishes abundance there, but such a year arrives but once every three or four years. In other years, it is difficult to meet expenses, which are much greater on the large domains where people talk unceasingly of restricting their size without ever taking any measure to that end. The owner of a great growth of Médoc should not sink all his fortune in it, but half at most, in order to support the costs and be able to await the favourable moment to sell his wines. The revenue from the vines is precarious and unequal. Such a domain should be held as a subsidiary and its owner should glory in it."

A century ago, the great Bordeaux wines had reached their zenith. What would Mr. Saint-Amant write now about the wonderful vocation of an area which is noble among the noblest?

It will be realized that the period in which Mr. Saint-Amant was defining the viticulture of Médoc was also that of the celebrated "classification". The idea of the "parish" (which dated from 1755) gave place to that of the "château", the "manor-house", thereby marking a dual evolution in the vineyard: a technical evolution as the practice of château bottling developed and an economic evolution whereby the exploitation of the Médoc was improved by an injection of business capital. In 1855, Médoc viticulture was beginning to reveal a veritable humanism. A great Médoc wine-grower proved it not so long ago by showing us his "book of reason". It was the treasured wealth of a long experience of husbandry. In it we find, indeed, traces of events which shook the world throughout the century: wars, revolutions and massacres; but what our venerable friend noted down was, perhaps, more important. It was the creation of that masterpiece, an eminent bottle of wine. Nothing but short remarks, dates and figures, but these notes have a Homeric quality, the flavour of an epic constantly rolled up and unrolled to the rhythm of the seasons and the rhythm of work. The patriarch had recorded, for future generations, the softness of a morning, the freshness of an evening, the time taken by a wagon to come from the vine to the wine-store, the song of the first cuckoo or the flight of the symbolic blackbirds which formed part of the folklore of the domain.

In Médoc, viticulture is first and foremost an act of faith. If the earth were to explode tomorrow, the justification of our existence would be that we are able to present to our Creator this book of reason in which a wise man questioned the whole of nature to discover the right moment for "pouring", bottling or ploughing.

To the extent that Médoc is unquestionably a work of art, its production, like that of the other great wines of Bordeaux, involves an irreducible minimum of traditional husbandry. This does not mean that, as Paul Valéry put it, the Médoc winegrower "backs into the future". He is by no means filled with nostalgia for the past. He refuses to subject the traditional vineyard to an experimental aspect of technology, but no one is more delighted when technology performs some function which is of service to the vineyard. If, for example, our planners clear away the spider's web of electricity and telephone wires from the Médoc skies, we shall see this "husbandman" immediately adopt the aircraft or the helicopter to spread insecticides or fungicides. If the agricultural machinery industry manages to supply him with a reasonable engine for his ploughing, he will abandon animal traction which, in some places, is still indispensable.

Over a distance of fifty miles in the direction of the river, with a depth inland of six to ten miles, the vineyards of Médoc produce wines which, though different, are all remarkable, even in years which are poor in alcohol content. There are no finer, more thoroughbred, more intellectualized wines. This nobility proceeds from their bouquet and aroma which are unique among the great French wines.

The truth is that a Médoc can hold its peak of perfection for a very long time. When President Albert Lebrun came to Pauillac to open the first of the famous festivals to longevity, it was not only the centenarian winegrowers who were fêted. An 1834 growth was tasted and that, too, was in excellent health.

The northern part of the Médoc Peninsula constitutes the generic place-name description MÉDOC.

This region stretches from Saint-Seurin-de-Cadourne to the Pointe de Grave and skirts the Gironde estuary over a distance of twelve miles, its width being from four to five miles.

At the very edge of the river, vineyards cover a strip of gravelly land, cut by shallow valleys, which is from one to two miles wide. It is this tongue of land which produces the best wines. On the other soils (clayey limestones), the wines produced are more commonplace but are held worthy of the name "Great Ordinary".

In the 1855 classification, Médoc was not allotted any classed or "Superior Bourgeois" growths but only "Bourgeois" growths. There were quite a number of these, however, and they often fetched prices well above their position in the Médoc hierarchy. Eleven communes possessed such "Bourgeois" growths: Saint-Germain-d'Esteuil, Ordonac-et-Potensac, Saint-Yzans, Couquèques, Blaignan, Saint-Christoly-de-Médoc, Bégadan, Lesparre, Valeyrac, Civrac and Prignac.

To the south of this region, towards Bordeaux, is the area which has earned the place-name description of origin HAUT-MÉDOC. It covers a number of sub-descriptions which are well-known throughout the world and are among the brightest jewels in the Bordeaux crown, MARGAUX glowing in their midst like a royal ruby. Since the dawn of time, several neighbouring parishes have shared in its ancient renown but nowadays four communes, in addition to that of Margaux, are entitled to the description, namely Cantenac, Soussans, Arsac and Labarde. CHÂTEAU MARGAUX, whose nobility is equalled only by the historic memories attached to the domain and the magnificent mansion of the same name, is a *Premier Cru Classé*, or "First Growth". The description MARGAUX as a whole connotes a great, sometimes very great, fine, full-bodied and elegant wine with a world-wide reputation.

Moulis is situated in the centre of the Haut-Médoc. At the end of the Hundred Years War, this little area was still more sylvan than viticultural and Pey Berland, the future Archbishop of Bordeaux, used to graze his father's flocks there. Moulis, however, with its good-quality gravel soils, clearly had a winegrowing vocation. Moulis growths are mentioned in the list drawn up by the Intendancy of Guienne in 1767 but, according to the 1855 classification, it contained only "Superior Bourgeois" growths.

The wines of MOULIS, which are very much appreciated in Germany, Belgium and the Netherlands, have the rare advantage that they will keep in perfect safety. In addition to the delicacy, bouquet and elegance of the great Médocs, they have also a balanced constitution which guarantees them a happy old age.

The Listrac vineyards occupy one of the highest hill-tops in the Haut-Médoc. The growths of this place-name description are reminiscent of the MOULIS in their body and vinosity. For centuries, this parish has also produced white wines, which strongly resemble the best white GRAVES. The 1855 classification gave no classed growths to Listrac but it had several "Superior Bourgeois" growths.

"Passers-by, you are now entering the ancient and celebrated vineyard of Saint-Julien, bow low...." Such is the proud inscription at the boundary of Saint-Julien-Beychevelle. It is now applied to an excellent vineyard, one of the richest dependencies of the Haut-Médoc. It refers, however, to the sailors' custom of striking their sails in salute when passing the Château de Beychevelle, residence of the Duke of Epernon, Grand Admiral of France. SAINT-JULIEN can be distinguished from the other famous wines of the Haut-Médoc by its beautiful purple colour, its great elegance and its mellowness. More full-bodied than MARGAUX, less hearty than PAUILLAC; it can also be recognized by a very personal bouquet that develops quickly.

Encouraged by its winegrowing mayor, Saint-Julien is steadily increasing its fame. There is so much competition among the producers in this commune that several "Superior Bourgeois" or "Bourgeois" growths, which were formerly almost unknown, have become as much valued as a "classified growth".

Situated about thirty miles from Bordeaux, Pauillac is the most important of the winegrowing communes of the Médoc. It has a House of Wine and is the headquarters of the *Commanderie du Bontemps-Médoc*. This fraternity uses the town as a starting point for all its ceremonies, the most important of which, the Flower Festival, is the occasion for a gathering of lovers of Bordeaux wine from all over the world. The place-name description PAUILLAC also applies to the wines harvested in certain of the lands of Saint-Sauveur, Saint-Estèphe and Cissac. The Lesparre Decree, one of the most detailed instruments of viticultural jurisprudence, lists the vineyards, plot by plot, in which PAUILLAC is grown. In some cases, even the rows of vine-stocks are measured and numbered. This description, the most representative of the Gironde winegrowing region, is the only one which possesses two first growths, three seconds, one fourth, eleven fifths and a whole train of "Superior Bourgeois" and "Bourgeois" growths, the nobility and brilliant qualities of which are often very close to the Great Growths.

PAUILLAC wines, whether they have a great coat of arms or a simple shield, are the most masterful of the wines of the Médoc. The great years give them characteristics which can be rather surprising if they are drunk before the ageing process which develops their incomparable charms. Nevertheless a PAUILLAC, even when it is too young and astringent, charms the experienced palate. This wine is always promising and has never lied.

The place-name description SAINT-ESTÈPHE is reserved solely for growths from the commune of that name, one of the largest in the Médoc. The SAINT-ESTÈPHE wines have an individual bouquet, and are delicate, mellow and distinguished. The soil, which is gravelly over an iron-pan subsoil, produces five classified growths, two of them being seconds; numerous "Bourgeois" growths, and a whole series of "artisan" and "peasant" growths. This rather byzantine hierarchy is very often pushed aside, however, by the great reputation for quality of all the SAINT-ESTÈPHE wines.

The time has now come to speak of the famous "classification". To what extent did the grandeur and luxury of the Châteaux of Médoc affect the judgement passed on their growths? It would be difficult to say. It is certain, however, that the first Bordeaux labels using a château name were always adorned with the picture of a genuine château. It must also be admitted that great mansions are to be found throughout the Médoc area. For the most part, they reflect the taste of the early nineteenth century when they were built. They are reminiscent of the neo-Gothic style popularized by Sir Walter Scott in 1812, when he built his Abbotsford manor on the south bank of the Tweed.

The main factors taken into account in establishing a hierarchy of quality were, it is true, the taste of the wine, the price it fetched, the more or less cared-for appearance of the vineyard, technical details of wine-making equipment and a few historical references. Nevertheless, since the initiative for classification came from a Chartrons firm of wine merchants, then at the zenith of its power, which either owned or was closely connected with the largest domains in the Médoc, we may well think that the 1855 classification reflected a vague notion of "caste" (at least to the extent that subjectivity inevitably played its part).

Hence, the châteaux of the Médoc have, from the very beginning, been a commercial factor as well as an architectural one. They formed the backbone of the classification system and spread the fame of Bordeaux wine far and wide. Consequently, a château label was desired for every growth of any quality in the Bordeaux area, even if the winegrower lived in the simplest of dwellings. The multiplicity of châteaux in the Gironde is by no means a product of Gascon ostentation, of a rather childish arrogance; it is the result of hard economic facts. It became necessary, therefore, to regulate the legal use of the word château. The Decree of September 30th, 1949 fixed the following conditions for its use:

1. The wine must be entitled to a place-name description of origin.

2. The wine must come from an agricultural holding, designated by the word château or by an equivalent word, which must genuinely exist as an agricultural holding and be already precisely designated by these words and expressions.

3. The name of the château or its equivalent must be restricted to the produce of the agricultural holding designated by the proposed words.

Legal usage, by its interpretation of the word château, had already prepared the way for the evolution implicit in the Decree. A ruling by the Bordeaux Civil Court, dated May 8th, 1939, had declared that the word château denoted a given agricultural or viti-cultural holding.

It should not be hastily concluded, however, that the majority of the châteaux in the Bordeaux region are of recent construction or that they exist only in the official register of wine growths. The ancient seneschalcy of Guienne, with its fascinating history and wealth of legend, is a veritable goldmine for the archaeologist and the art-lover. Noble mansions abound, often surrounded by famous vineyards.

Thus we find in the Médoc, for example, the Château d'Angludet which, although rebuilt in the eighteenth century, was the lair of a notorious robber baron during the Hundred Years War. The Château d'Issan at Margaux also dates from the Anglo-Gascon alliance. With its nine pavilions and pyramid-topped towers, it has a fairy-tale appearance. The present buildings have succeeded two or three earlier structures at one time inhabited by famous French families.

Ornamented by its Grecian façade, Château Margaux is rather more than the most famous "label" in the world. It once belonged to King Edward III of England. In the twelfth century, it was known by the name of La Mothe. At that time it was, of course, a fortified castle. It was successively the property of the d'Albret, de Montferrand and de Durfort families. Towards the middle of the eighteenth century, its then owner, Monsieur de Fumel, assisted the Marquis de Lafayette to embark for America, despite the opposition of the Court. The present owner of Château Margaux is Mr. Pierre Ginestet, Grand Chancellor of the Bordeaux Wine Academy.

A little to the north, at Pauillac, Château Mouton-Rothschild has known four generations of the Barons de Rothschild since 1853. In the more remote past, the great winegrowers of Mouton were the Seigneur de Pons (1350), the Duke of Gloucester (1430), Jean Dunois, Gaston de Foix, the Dukes of Joyeuse and the Dukes of Epernon. Baron Philippe de Rothschild, the present proprietor, has established a superb wine museum adjacent to the wine-sheds of the Château. The objects on display are rich beyond compare but give not the slightest impression of ostentation. They include a Mycenean goblet of the thirteenth century B.C., masterpieces of the German goldsmith's art and paintings by Picasso, Giacometti and Juan Gris.

Since time immemorial, the lands of Graves have surrounded Bordeaux, except on the east where the ancient city is bounded by the river. Since the vineyards of Bordeaux are primarily a creation of the city, Graves has always been their focal point. It was not the vineyard which gave birth to the town but the citizens of Bordeaux who, having planted the civilizing grape, lavished the most constant and attentive care upon it and honoured it as a divinity. In the Middle Ages, the grape was still being harvested *intra muros*, in the very centre of Bordeaux. The Gascon terriers (land-holding registers) have revealed the existence of a vineyard entirely within the town, the harvest from which was sufficient to stock the cellars of the *Jurats* and the chapters. By the end of September, baskets were being filled with grapes in the Rue de Saint-Genès, near St. Nicholas' Church, at the Croix-Blanche, at Terre-Nègre, in the Place Dauphine, at the Palais-Gallien and the Rue des Capérans, charming spots which the ravages of urbanization have not spared. Nowadays, the vineyard of Graves begins at the Jalle de Blanquefort, the southern boundary of the Médoc. To the south, it extends as far as Langon, having left the river at Virelade to encircle the Cérons and Sauternes-Barsac areas as, to the north, it once encircled the former Burdigala. Its total length is 38 miles and its average width does not exceed six miles.

It was for the wine of Graves (and not for the others which were then too far from Bordeaux) that the collegiate government of the city proclaimed the edicts forming the basis of the most extraordinary legal monument of all time: the famous *Privilège des Vins*, as evidenced by the highly secret records of the deliberations of the *Jurade*, otherwise called the *Livre des Bouillons* from the copper bosses—*boullons*—which protected its cover.

Halfway through the Middle Ages, with the same eagerness to regulate everything, the *Jurade* of Bordeaux set up the official corps of Taverners. Although this seemed, at first sight, an attempt to introduce a police force into the wineshops and keep them orderly, the main objective of the *Jurats*, in this case, was to control frauds within the municipal jurisdiction. For example, to help sales of nondescript wines, it had been customary to cry "a very drinkable wine of Graves". This commercial misrepresentation now became impossible, and much too dangerous for an official clothed in all the majesty of the municipality.

Moreover, all the control measures applied at both the production and distribution stages and which had such a favourable effect on the reputation of Bordeaux wines, originated from the desire felt by the wine-growing burghers to protect their urban growths, i.e. the place-name description GRAVES. That is why the Bordeaux archives for the sixteenth, seventeenth and eighteenth centuries reveal the names and activities of the inspectors of urban vineyards, an office that was already of very ancient foundation.

Today, in our mind's eye, we can see these velvet-clad burghers jogging on horseback across the vineyards. The warm, juicy bunches are presented to them on white cloths and we see them, having brushed away a greedy wasp with a gloved and beringed hand, tasting a grape thoughtfully and then, raising their heads, gazing wisely and reflectively at the vine.

In permanent session throughout the harvest time, the *Jurade* would listen to the reports of its itinerant experts and, after debate, would fix the day on which the grape pickers, the *laborador de vinhas* could begin picking with the best chance of obtaining a wine of quality. The great bell of the City Hall would then "ring in the wine-harvest".

The period when there was no Bordeaux wine other than Graves was, *par excellence*, the time of CLARET. The English gave the name to the produce of a region much smaller than the Bordeaux region of today but the antiquity of which, as compared with the Bordeaux winegrowing area as a whole, is unquestionable.

Much closer to us, in the middle of the eighteenth century, any red Bordeaux exported to Germany became, for the importing wine merchant, Pontac wine, the name of the then owner of Château Haut-Brion, the uncrowned king of Graves. The future member of the "big four" served as an insignia for the whole vineyard, a century before the 1855 classification.

During the whole nineteenth century the place-name description GRAVES was predominantly "red". Nowadays, in the second half of the twentieth century, the grape distribution has virtually returned to what it was in its hey-day, namely, the era when the harvests of La Brède and Martillac were gathered by Charles Secondat de Montesquieu. This new balance between whites and reds is, perhaps, mainly due to the fact that the city of Bordeaux for the last two hundred years has been extending its limits, intensifying building operations and swallowing up communes which were formerly famous for their production of red wine: Caudéran, Talence, Mérignac etc. Moreover, ten miles to the south of Bordeaux, in centres such as Léognan which had been entirely devoted to red grapes before the phylloxera crisis, whole estates have been replanted with white grapes. At present, the figures for the production of GRAVES are 880,000 gallons of white wine and 330,000 gallons of red.

However that may be, the white GRAVES have often reflected great glory on the place-name and have been deservedly fashionable, as has once again been the case during the last twenty years. But this fashion has never been the result of a snobbish insistence that white GRAVES should be this or that, that it must be dry or semi-dry. It is what it has to be, whatever a few professional food-pundits may say. The white GRAVES harvested in the north of the region are naturally dry with a charming touch of acidity. At Martillac, La Brède, Saint-Morillon, Saint-Sèlve, Saint-Médard and Cadaujac, they are still dry but already softened by the suave bouquet characteristic of the soil of Léognan. Speaking of these thoroughbred wines, Rabelais described them as "gay and fluttering". At Portets, Arbanats, Landiras and Budos, they became more unctuous, trickling down the inside of the glass. The brokers distinguish these wines by saying they are fat. Lastly, the nearer we come to Langon, the more the wines are reminiscent of CÉRONS mellowness. In the Graves country, therefore, some less dry wines are found alongside the more numerous dry wines, all of them being admirable because they are quite natural.

Leaving aside all personal preference, however legitimate it might be, the soul of Bordeaux is undoubtedly to be found in a glass of red GRAVES.

As often happens in the case of the eldest of a large family, GRAVES bears the most striking resemblance to its father. MÉDOC, with its subtle and complex bouquet, or SAINT-EMILION, with its reckless gallantry, need envy their elder brother in nothing except the dominating fragrance which follows a red GRAVES everywhere like an invisible escutcheon. It is the perfume which has been transmitted from stock to stock and from vat to vat for over 2,000 years. One has to experience this privilege of the red GRAVES in order to become convinced.

That is what I must have perceived at a very early age when my grandfather first gave me a small piece of goatsmilk cheese (to clean my palate) and after it a finger of HAUT-BRION 1888. In that already remote period, the growth was not called a red GRAVES, as it is today, but a GRAVES DE BORDEAUX. The memory of that initiation and of that inward resplendence has, once and for all, enabled me to identify a Bordeaux wine, whether noble or artisan, red or white, from the left bank or the right bank of the Garonne.

Of course, one has to be up-to-date. It must be realized that there has been, not a development of taste—taste has not developed since the Parthenon—but a certain depravation of taste. Some will claim that henceforth the general public will be looking for supple, round red wines; in other words, wines stripped of their authentic character. With respect to some products without breeding or which have been badly vinified, the general public may be perfectly right. It may well be that agreeable mediocrity is preferable to decayed and aggressive nobility. This is a valid point of view but for anyone who tasted his first GRAVES three or four years after his last feeding bottle, the criterion could never be that of the wine-canning industry.

A good GRAVES remains "as eternity itself has shaped it". It is food for the body and the soul. It has a luminous robe the colour of those rustic window-panes through which our childhood reveries recreated a summer twilight in the midst of winter. It is as elegant as the solution to a Euclidian theorem. Above all, since it is from Graves, it has that bracing and discreet bitterness that makes it kin to all the savours of the Bordeaux soil.

Direct in its taste, frank in its attack, though full of mysteries and chaste aromas, GRAVES rises from the depths of memory like a promise of happiness and peace, so needful in this anguish-stricken world.

THE CÉRONS REGION

Situated 22 miles to the south-east of Bordeaux, on the left bank of the Garonne, the Cérons region is made up of three communes: Cérons, Illats and Podensac. The boundaries of this place-name description are slightly fictional. There are dry CÉRONS wines which possess the characteristics of the finest GRAVES, the only distinction being a particularly fruity aroma, while other CÉRONS are closely related to SAUTERNES-BARSAC. The sweet CÉRONS are, however, lighter than the growths obtained in the soil of Barsac.

The soil of Cérons, silicious gravel over clayey limestone, is virtually the same as in Sauternes. To obtain sweet CÉRONS, picking is carried out (as in Sauternes) by successive stages and the must, which is comparatively less rich, nevertheless produces wines with a strength of 12º to 15º of alcohol and, in addition, 1º to 3º of liqueur. The CÉRONS type is distinguished by its nervousness, elegance and extremely fine bouquet. All these qualities, combined with the ambiguous position of the Cérons region, have caused its produces to be described as a link between the best dry white wines and the most famous of the great sweet wines.

In Cérons more than elsewhere, we thus encounter those imponderables which make white Bordeaux so variable. The place-name description produces annually between 330,000 and 396,000 gallons.

The essential originality of the winemaking process in the Sauternes area consists, first of all, in the method of harvesting.

Normal ripening is insufficient. The winegrower has to wait for the grape to become "overripe" and develop a rot which is so special, so peculiar to the microclimate that it is described as "noble". It is caused by a characteristic mycoderm, which flourishes only in certain winegrowing regions and which is called *botrytis cinerea*, a minute fungus which, in great years, produces the famous "roast" that can be recognized in old bottles.

It is not always easy to turn the *botrytis* to best account. Its effect on a given bunch of grapes is not uniform. Hence the need to harvest by picking individual grapes. If it rains, picking has to be suspended until the grapes dry out. The result is that the harvest has to be staggered over a period of up to two months, and quantity is sacrificed to quality, yields being less than 170 gallons per acre.

Thanks to this process, which is quite unique in viticultural technology (it amounts to a veritable concentration of the vintage on the vine), the musts have a sugar content of between 15° and 20° or even more on leaving the press. In 1929, 25° were found while, in 1959, some musts were recorded which attained 30°.

In an average year, the ideal is to obtain a balance after fermentation between the alcohol content (14°) and the unconverted sugar content (4° of *liqueur*). In a very great vintage year, the divergence can be considerable. The care lavished on the wine-store is mainly aimed at activating alcoholic fermentation. As will be realized, the glory of Sauternes-Barsac is an expensive one. There can never be any question, in this soil, of sacrificing the supreme, the "extravagant" quality to considerations of cost.

The wine of Sauternes-Barsac is still and will always remain one of the few things in this world whose inimitable nobility brushes aside the notion of "productivity", as conceived of by economists dealing in large quantities of ordinary consumer goods rather than rare products.

The Sauternais can best be compared, therefore, to a dream country ruled over by a wizard, the wizard being the most famous wine on earth, the wine of kings and the king of wines. The region must be entered deliberately, but once we are there, time seems to lose its meaning and the ordinary world, humming with cares and duties, drifts far away from our eyes and from our memories. All the enchantments of this magic land weave round us a fairy net which holds us willing prisoners in a life of rarest pleasure.

I can remember a fine afternoon in June. The park of the Château of Suduiraut appeared, under a thrilling sky, to be rising out of the vaporous haze which bathes Fragonard's *Fête de Saint-Cloud* or Jean-Baptiste Pater's *Garden Party*, or was it the slight mist of the *Embarkation for Cythera*? Maurice Chevalier was singing, clutching a jeroboam of Château d'Yquem to his breast, proving that there are mysterious affinities between the most varied forms of art. The only condition to be fulfilled is that, however appearances may change, artistic creation must remain faithful to the classic standards of quality. What music, painting and song offer us in their highest forms is also to be found in the subtle bouquet of a Sauternes-Barsac. That is why you should make the circuit of the Sauternes country (which is well signposted for the visitor) at a slow speed with the engine barely ticking over, just as you move slowly and appreciatively past the masterpieces in the Uffizi Gallery.

There are some discoveries that are worthless unless you make them for yourself. In the Palazzo Vecchio in Florence, for example, I came across the most intelligent of guides. He watches visitors coming, going, dreaming, strolling and sometimes retracing their steps (which is so important). Then, smiling, he intervenes, simply because someone has overlooked something he loves. I should like to imitate him and not drag the reader by main force to the entrance of a vineyard if he is attracted by the slate-crowned roof of a tower. Let it suffice that, en route, you do not neglect a growth which, once known, will have a permanent place in your heart and in your memory. Whether you approach the Sauternais circuit from the beginning or from the end, you will find only one road marked "No Entry": the road to mediocrity. It is a magic carpet straight out of a fairy-tale and, if the turnings appear frequent, it could be that your head might be turning round a little.

THE WINES BETWEEN
THE GARONNE AND THE DORDOGNE

PREMIÈRES CÔTES DE BORDEAUX

When the contemporaries of Ausonius visited him, they did so languorously stretched out in boats furnished with carpets and cushions, under canopies of laurel branches and with pennants streaming. This patrician luxury which was shared by winegrowers and poets, men of the world and philosophers in an intimate society marks the zenith of the region now called the Premières Côtes de Bordeaux. This place-name description covers thirty-four communes along the right bank of the Garonne, between Bassens and Saint-Macaire. It is essentially an area of abrupt slopes which dominate the river for 38 miles. The plateaux of Entre-Deux-Mers (Between the Two Seas) forms its hinterland as far as the left bank of the Dordogne.

Despite its exceptional length and the size of its production (3,300,000 gallons), the Premières Côtes region produces growths which head the list at international exhibitions. Although the northern part of the region is almost exclusively devoted to red wines, the southern part, beyond Gambes, covers what are usually called the great white wines of the right bank.

The red Premières Côtes de Bordeaux were undoubtedly among the first Bordeaux wines regularly exported. Pey Berland, the last Gascon Archbishop of Bordeaux, possessed an important red vineyard in the Parish of Bouillac. Under the archiepiscopal privileges, therefore, it was a Premières Côtes de Bordeaux growth which the English, on their arrival with the "wine fleet", would purchase as a first priority.

When young, these wines are robust, fruity, rich in tannin and very tonic. With age, they acquire considerable delicacy and the bouquet characteristic of the Bordeaux soil. As for the white, semi-dry or sweet Premières Côtes de Bordeaux, they sometimes reach such a degree of delicacy and elegance that their nobility requires some specific place-name descriptions in the form of enclaves: such is the case with Cadillac and Gabarnac.

LOUPIAC AND SAINTE-CROIX-DU-MONT

Loupiac and Sainte-Croix-du-Mont are also enclaves in the Premières Côtes de Bordeaux but have no legal connection with the latter place-name description.

Both Loupiac and Sainte-Croix-du-Mont belong to the kingdom of the *Semillon, Sauvignon* and *Muscadelle* grapes. Apart from this triumvirate, no other grape is permitted to enter into the composition of these illustrious sweet growths. On the abrupt and sunny slopes, the bunches of grapes are not picked until they have reached a subtle degree of over-ripeness. And yet, what delicacy, what tang of the soil is to be found in a Loupiac or a Sainte-Croix !

What gaiety is to be found in one or another of these bottles ! Without wearing the sumptuous garb of a Sauternes, they too evoke the bronze satin in which Watteau dresses the beauties in his enchanted parks.

The sweet warmth of these wines, their bouquet, their topaz robe go beyond the vocabulary of the gourmet; it would need the music of a Verlaine poem to give an adequate impression of so much grace.

The boundary of the place-name description Loupiac is a little to the south of Cadillac, whose best growths are in no way inferior to those of the two gems of the Premières Côtes de Bordeaux.

HAUT-BENAUGE

The place-name description Haut-Benauge is restricted to white wines produced by the communes of Arbis, Cantois, Escoussans, Ladaux, Soulignac, Saint-Pierre-de-Bat and Targon. This region, although much smaller than the former county of Benauge, has nevertheless retained as its centre the enormous and majestic castle built by the redoubtable Lords of Benauge on the hill of Arbis. In former times, the county was called "Black Benauge" and was darkened by the oak forests from which was obtained the timber for the manufacture of the *barriques*. But the winegrowers cleared the land and, ever since, the serried ranks of vine-stocks have occupied the flanks of the valleys. Black Benauge is one of the world's most beautiful viticultural areas. It produces a white, semi-dry wine which has harvested awards and medals.

CÔTES DE BORDEAUX-SAINT-MACAIRE

The place-name description Côtes de Bordeaux-Saint-Macaire extends the Premières Côtes de Bordeaux towards the south. It covers the communes of Saint-Macaire, Pian, Saint-Pierre-d'Aurillac, Saint-Martin-de-Sescas, Caudrot, Saint-André-du-Bois, Saint-Martial, Saint-Laurent-du-Bois, Saint-Laurent-du-Plan and Sainte-Foy-la-Longue. Few white wines are so adaptable as Côtes de Bordeaux-Saint-Macaire. Robust and fine, they form an agreeable accompaniment to sea-food as well as to desserts and even certain roasts.

GRAVES DE VAYRES

In the vicinity of Libourne, on the ancient road which once linked Burdigala to Lutetia, the communes of Vayres and Arveyres, on the left bank of the Dordogne, constitute the winegrowing territory entitled to the place-name description Graves de Vayres. This designates a colourful and subtle red wine, of great delicacy, reminiscent of the second growth of Pomerol and endowed with the precious commercial quality of being drinkable at an early age. The white wines from the same soil can be distinguished from the excellent products of Entre-Deux-Mers by their mellowness and their very typical aroma.

ENTRE-DEUX-MERS

Entre-Deux-Mers is a name which really appeals to the imagination. It evokes all kinds of ideas of distant voyages and unknown lands. People who are unfamiliar with the place-names of these great winegrowing regions are generally disappointed to learn that "Between the Two Seas" refers to the territory between the right bank of the Garonne and the left bank of the Dordogne. The place-name description does not, of course, include those which have just been defined but it nevertheless extends over the largest and most productive part of the Bordeaux vineyard, and in fact, covers one-fifth of the area of the department. The spontaneous luxuriance of the vegetation in Entre-Deux-Mers and the survival of large tracts of oak, hornbeam and elm are relics of the ancient forest cleared by the Romans to plant the civilizing vine. After the Barbarian invasions, immense tracts of these woodlands reappeared and, this time, it was the monks who launched a new attack on the hardy forest mass. The Abbey of Saint-Girard, at La Sauve, was founded in 1090. For centuries, this community shared, with the monks of Sainte-Croix, at Bordeaux, the privilege of supervising the winegrowing destiny of Entre-Deux-Mers. In 1547, a wine of the region was selling for 20 to 25 crowns the *tonneau* as against only 18 to 22 crowns for a Libournais-Fronsadais product. The place-name description of origin Entre-Deux-Mers, which has been defined since 1924, became a guaranteed description by the decree of July 31th, 1937. According to this legal instrument, the place-name description can only be applied to white wines made exclusively from the noble grapes: *Sauvignon, Semillon, Muscadelle,* and *Merlot,* harvested within the area delimited. Red wines of the same origin must carry the place-name descriptions Bordeaux or Bordeaux Supérieur.

In the last few years, spurred on by the youthful officers of its viticultural syndicate, Entre-Deux-Mers has regained its ancient fame. This was achieved through a policy strongly emphasizing quality which is intended to give this dry white wine back its natural characteristics. Fifteen years ago, the persons responsible for the place-name description decided to increase the proportion of *Sauvignon* in the vineyards. As this trend has continued ever since whenever new vines were being planted, Entre-Deux-Mers has once again become a very fruity and recognizable wine, both fresh and nervous, which meets the requirements of the consumer of today. It should not be forgotten, however, that Entre-Deux-Mers is a Bordeaux wine. In other words, it is an hygienic wine, a healthy wine, just like the red wines of similar origin. In addition to the incomparable satisfaction to the taste buds, it possesses other important qualities which should be mentioned: its richness in vitamin P and its high bactericidal power which is completely independent of its alcoholic content. Invigorating, tonic and diuretic, it is just the wine for people who have difficulty in taking other white wines. It is an unfailing destroyer of the pathogens which are found in raw vegetables and well-informed doctors do not hesitate to attribute to it therapeutic virtues also. All this has been known empirically for a very long time, but serious studies carried out by learned professors and their pupils in the laboratories and universities on Entre-Deux-Mers have made it possible to formulate the benificent action of this growth in scientific terms.

After many years of endeavour, Baron Philippe de Rothschild at last achieved the reclassification of Mouton Rothschild from Second Growth to First. This was achieved in 1973, and crowns a lifetime's work in improving and cultivating the wine. In the background to this harvesting scene can be seen Château Mouton, which contains the famous wine museum.

The canton of Sainte-Foy-la-Grande comprises only fifteen communes, but the controlled place-name description SAINTE-FOY-BORDEAUX has nineteen. They have been detached from the north-eastern part of the vast Entre-Deux-Mers region to delimit a sweet or semi-dry white wine, the dominant characteristics of which are suppleness and elegance. Coming from the Périgord confines of the Bordeaux country, this white wine is, if dry, a perfect foil for the oysters, shellfish and delicious shad caught in the Dordogne.

THE WINES OF THE RIGHT BANK OF THE DORDOGNE AND THE GIRONDE

SAINT-EMILION

On the right bank of the Dordogne, Saint-Emilion and its vineyards are high places where the wind of the spirit blows free. The whole of France and a good part of the civilized world can testify to that.

The "great" little city—with apologies for the paradox—has known a cosmopolitan animation every year since very ancient times. In fact, Camille Jullian, in his history of the Gauls, states that Saint-Emilion was one of the ritual stages on the journey to Compostella. A pious and motley crowd always filled the monolithic church. An extraordinary vitality and spirituality overflowed from those narrow streets and corbelled houses, and faith in a world in which men were brothers was proclaimed from all the towers in joyous peals of bells and in solemn fanfares of trumpets.

At Saint-Emilion, the tumultuous heartbeat of French history can be felt. Here and there, as you walk about the town, you suddenly encounter an astonishingly fresh vision of the past, whether it be the Tour du Roi or the Grotte des Girondins. But in this acropolis where all the friends of wine come to worship together in the high traditions of the past, there are other voices than those of stones, vigorous human voices raised in eloquent testimony of the centuries which have passed.

Today as yesterday, the vine and wine are the reason for living, the cause of happiness and, sometimes, suffering for the viticultural peoples of the eight communes which make up the place-name description: Saint-Emilion, Saint-Laurent-des-Combes, Saint-Hippolyte, Saint-Christophe-des-Bardes, Saint-Etienne-de-Lisse, Saint-Sulpice-des-Faleyrens, Saint-Pey-d'Armens and Vignonet. The area of the place-name description amounts to 11,250 acres.

In our days, the poets have glorified the powerful and noble wine of SAINT-EMILION, as did Henri d'Andeli in the eleventh century. In our days, we may compare SAINT-EMILION to the nectar of the gods, as did Louis XIV in 1650. It is not only the town of stone which is immutable. As well known in the past as the wines of Graves, the wines of Saint-Emilion continue their royal career without any artificial vinification. When the weight of years has broken down the other wines and has left in the bottles nothing but a tasteless and colourless water, then it is that SAINT-EMILION develops all its wealth and all its perfume. "The wine of Saint-Emilion," wrote Victor Rendu, "has body, a beautiful colour, an agreeable delicacy, generosity and a special bouquet which is found in particular in the best sections of this distinguished vineyard. Good Saint-Emilion wine should, after its early years, have a dark, brilliant and velvety colour and a touch of bitterness which flatters the palate. In addition, it must have body which does not prevent it from becoming very smooth at a later stage. It becomes very much finer after six months in bottle but does not reach its full perfection until it is from 6 to 10 years old."

The most prestigious domains of the place-name description have recently been granted a classification but are still subject to the rigorous quality control exercised by the illustrious *Jurade* and the Saint-Emilion Viticultural and Agricultural Syndicate, which is alone entitled to bestow upon the wine a "certificate of approval" for marketing.

In addition to the communes entitled to the simple place-name description, the following five others have obtained the right to add Saint-Emilion to their own names: SAINT-GEORGES-SAINT-EMILION, MONTAGNE-SAINT-EMILION, LUSSAC-SAINT-EMILION, PUISSEGUIN-SAINT-EMILION, PARSAC-SAINT-EMILION.

As for the special place-name description SABLES-SAINT-EMILION, this refers to a small part of the commune of Libourne, between Saint-Emilion and Pomerol, which produces excellent red wines which are subtle and fragrant and mature quite quickly.

POMEROL AND ITS REGION

The commune of Pomerol, which covers 1,550 acres, is a few miles to the north-east of Libourne. It is bordered by the vineyards of Saint-Emilion to the east and of Fronsac to the west.

As far back as history records, the existence of Pomerol is evidenced by memorials of every kind. This clayey-gravel plateau was crossed by a Roman road which the winegrower poet Ausonius had to take when travelling from the port of Condat, on the Dordogne, to his magnificent villa of Lucaniacus in the Saint-Emilion region.

In the Middle Ages, the Knights Hospitallers of St. John established their first commandery at Pomerol. From the twelfth century onwards, therefore, the famous borough was endowed with a fortified manor, a hospital and a Romanesque church which has now, unfortunately, disappeared.

With the Knights Hospitallers, as in the time of the Romans, the vine was in high honour in Pomerol. But the Hundred Years War which, of course, lasted three centuries, was not very kind to this ancient countryside. Time and time again, French and Anglo-Gascons turned the parish into a battlefield. Moreover, as long as Pomerol remained under the fleur-de-lis, its wine could not take the Bordeaux road, i.e. they could not be sold to its good and faithful English customers. However, after the decisive French victory at Castillon in 1453, which entailed the surrender of Guienne, the wines of Pomerol made rapid progress in gaining a reputation and soon became one of the most precious jewels in the Bordeaux crown.

For these are complete wines which gladden both the nose and the palate. These growths have a fine and generous vinosity which comes from grapes such as the *Bouchet* and the *Merlot*. While retaining the delicacy of the SAINT-EMILION wines, they also approach the wines of the Médoc. POMEROL wines go extremely well with red meat, game and cheese.

The guaranteed place-name description LALANDE DE POMEROL (about 1,250 acres), with its soil varying from siliceous clay to clayey gravel, produces fine red wines comparable with those of its famous neighbour. Next door, the commune of Néac, which corresponds exactly to the area of the place-name description, contains a 675-acre vineyard. The NÉACS are generally supple, velvety, full-bodied and have a strong bouquet. Although it is impossible to establish any absolute rule in this field, it is agreed that the First Growths of NÉAC are roughly comparable in quality with the second First Growths of POMEROL.

CÔTES DE FRONSAC

When crossing the Bordeaux country on his return from Spain, Charlemagne had fortifications built on the knoll of Fronsac which commands the Dordogne. This fortress became the bastion *par excellence* of the strategic region. The enormous castle still existed in the fifteenth century, but it could not survive three days of battering by the artillery of Jean Bureau, Master of Artillery of France under Charles VII. Even genius is powerless to control the future. If Fronsac with its knoll deserves to be called a high place, it is not because of its military history. Fronsac is glorious for its red wines. High-coloured, robust and plump, with age they gain an exquisite distinction. They have never betrayed the attention given them by the flower-bearded emperor and, in more modern times, by the Duke of Richelieu (1706-1788), who was as famous for his knowledge of wine as for his amorous successes. Richelieu, who also held the title of Duke of Fronsac, built on the knoll one of those charming "follies" that the eighteenth century sprinkled throughout the Bordeaux region. In that house, he gave fashionable parties. It was about the same time that Richelieu introduced the wine of Bordeaux to the Court of France.

On the legal plane, the description FRONSAC does not exist. The name forms part of two separate place-name descriptions: CÔTES DE CANON-FRONSAC, which includes the best slopes, particularly that of Canon; and CÔTES DE FRONSAC.

CÔTES DE CASTILLON

The Côtes de Castillon comprise the territory of Castillon-sur-Dordogne (recently rebaptized Castillon-la-Bataille) and of several neighbouring communes. This is not only an ancient winegrowing region but also an historic site. Castillon-sur-Dordogne became Castillon-la-Bataille in 1953 when the commune celebrated the fifth centenary of the last battle of the Hundred Years War. It was at Castillon that Talbot, the English general, fell and Albion's continental ambitions melted away in the smoke of Charles VII's mor-

CHÂTEAU CHEVAL BLANC

1. 1a. Trade name "Château Cheval Blanc". This name is well-known to wine-lovers but the merchant-viniculturist gives further details on his label and indicates that the wine is a "first great growth". The vintage is also mentioned on the label. – 2. 2a. Place-name description of origin: Saint-Emilion, which is confirmed by the reference to "Saint-Emilion, first great growth". Nothing could be more explicit, therefore, than this label, and the knowledgable wine-lover will also be aware that the Cheval Blanc is one of the two "first great growths classed as (a)" in the area. – 3. Name of the merchant-viniculturist. – 4. The reference to bottling at the Château is compulsory for the great growths of Bordeaux; it is a guarantee of both quality and authenticity.

CHÂTEAU HAUT-MARBUZET

1. Trade name "Château Haut-Marbuzet". This growth did not appear in the list of growths classified in 1855 but was mentioned in the syndicate merit-list of March 3rd, 1966 with the annotation "exceptional great-bourgeois" (see page 158). – 2. Guaranteed descriptive name: Saint-Estèphe. The Saint-Estèphe area is in the Haut-Médoc near the border of the Bas-Médoc.

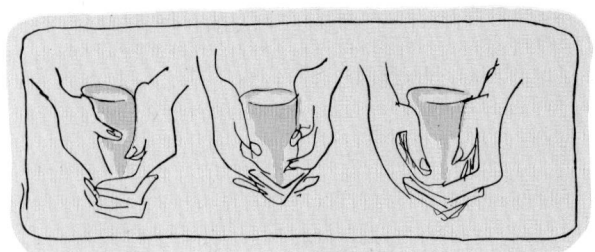

CHÂTEAU MOUTON-ROTHSCHILD

1. Trade name "Château Mouton-Rothschild". This label is laconic and, apart from its more elegant style, nothing distinguishes it from its next-door neighbour. As a great noble, Château Mouton-Rothschild does not mention its rank in the 1855 classification in which it was one of the eminent second growths (see page 158). – 2. Place-name description of origin: Pauillac. Some people will find it difficult to place Pauillac in the Haut-Médoc and to realize, at first glance, that Mouton-Rothschild is a Bordeaux wine. – 3. Name of the merchant-viniculturist. – 4. 4a. Careful details of the château bottling process are given, the bottle being numbered after the word "Ci". Confirmation of this operation is given in 4a.

CHÂTEAU RIEUSSEC

1. Trade name "Château Rieussec". We are immediately informed that it is a first great growth. – 2. 2a. Place-name description of origin: Sauternes. This is a great dessert wine. The year gives the knowledgeable wine-lover an indication of quality. The description of origin is in the prescribed form. – 3. Name of the merchant-viniculturist. – 4. Reference to bottling at the Château.

1

2

2a

4/3

CHÂTEAU PÉTRUS

1. Trade name "Pétrus". The indication "great wine" is not very explicit. – 2. Place-name description of origin: Pomerol. – 2a. This area has no official classification like those of the Médocs and Saint-Emilions, but Pétrus is regarded as the best of the Pomérols. The description is repeated in the prescribed form. – 3. Reference to bottling at the Château. – 4. Name of the merchant-viniculturist.

CHÂTEAU LA MISSION HAUT BRION

1. Trade name Château la Mission Haut Brion. The reference to "classified great growth" make it immediately clear that this is a great wine; it should not, however, be confused with Château Haut Brion which is a "first classed great growth". – 2. Place-name description of origin: Graves. Since there are both red and white Graves, I should, perhaps, mention that Château la Mission Haut Brion is a red wine. – 3. Reference to bottling at the Château. – 4. Name of the merchant-viniculturist.

1

2

4

3

2a

1

2

4

3

tars. A dreary plain? No, indeed! The symmetrical rows of the vines are interrupted by fields of clover, alfalfa and maize in which tractors and a last few patient oxen carry out their manoeuvres. In this fertile countryside, the ghosts of the past are imprisoned in a small circle traced out, from dawn to dusk, by the shadow of the cenotaph erected in memory of the illustrious defeated. Anyone, according to his sense of history, can put whatever he likes into an empty tomb. Filling one's glass is a much more serious procedure. Hence, no one should ever go to Castillon without taking the opportunity of tasting for himself the excellent wines which are entitled to carry this famous name. The red wines (80 per cent of the harvest) have a richly tinted robe, a generous fragrance and a full body which does not prevent them from acquiring great suppleness from at least the third racking onwards. In the spring following the vintage, they deserve a respectable place on the connoisseur's table. The white wines, which represent only a small part of the harvest, come from the north-west part of the area. Fine and delicate, they keep perfectly. (The recognition of CÔTES-DE-CASTILLON by I.N.A.O., the National Institute of Descriptions of Origin, is fairly recent.)

BOURGEAIS

The general appearance of the town of Bourg-sur-Gironde is that of a small fortified medieval city. It bears some resemblance to Saint-Emilion overhanging the valley of the Dordogne, but its origins may be even more ancient. Discoveries of the greatest interest dating from the palaeolithic and neolithic eras have been made in twenty-eight different spots at Bourg. Thousands of objects and tools have been found, tons of chipped flints and wall-carvings of great beauty. Many caves have yet to be explored. Such are the unquestionable proofs of the presence of prehistoric humanity in this large village.

It is clear that the first inhabitants of Bourg came from the Eyzies region through Rouffignac, the forest of La Double, the Entre-Deux-Mers and the Fronsac region. According to the theory dear to the heart of André Siegfried, they had quite naturally followed the "fall of the waters" and had halted in front of the immense estuary (which they took for the ocean itself), finally settling down to plant the vine on the slopes dominating its bank.

Some time ago, an English archaeological journal published an article on the villa of Ausonius at Bourg. It was situated on the outskirts of the town, towards the present Blaye-du-Bourg, on the slope facing the sea. Very comfortable and luxurious, like the other villas which the poet-consul possessed in Guienne, it was also the centre of an important vineyard. Ausonius himself speaks of it in clear and precise terms when singing the praises of the wine of Bourg. There seems good reason to believe that this vineyard had already been in existence for several centuries, since it takes much longer for a vine to produce a famous wine than for a poet to compose a poem!

From the Gallo-Roman epoch to the Middle Ages and the present day, the history of Bourg has been closely linked with that of Bordeaux. The two cities have the same love for the vine and for freedom.

Without a break since 1273, the winegrowers and burghers of Bourg have elected their mayor and corporation. The last *Jurats* (wearing a hood and a livery of red and white damask) were elected two years before the Revolution. This proud commune was never the vassal of any lord apart from the greatest lord of all, the King. When the king was English, Bourg took advantage of his remoteness to stretch its liberties and privileges as far as possible.

Thus the burghers of Bourg, unlike Archbishop Pey Berland, have felt the "wind of history" caress their walls and shiver among the vine shoots. They opposed no resistance to Charles VII. Basically animated by the same municipal passion as Bordeaux but more rural and less torn by Italian-style factions, Bourg was able to keep its unity and follow a single line of conduct while the metropolis of Aquitaine saw its cohesion break up under the pressure of events.

It is hardly possible to say whether the virtues and wisdom of the Bourg vintners were responsible for the fame of the wine of this region, or vice-versa. Anyway, the fact is that this fame, which goes back to the dawn of history, was confirmed once again at the end of the eighteenth century by the chronicler Abbé Baurein: "The wines of Bourg were so esteemed in the last century that private individuals with property in the Bourgeais and in the Médoc would only sell their Bourg wine on condition that the purchaser also agreed to take the Médoc." This evidence has been much contested in modern times but there are still proprietors with vineyards on both sides of the water.

The red wines of the Bourgeais are rich in vitamins, have a very agreeable bouquet and age excellently. As for the white wines, whether semi-dry or sweet, they are sturdy, nervous and full-bodied. It should be noted that some of the white wines do not have the right to carry the appellation BORDEAUX because of the types of grapes used to produce them.

A former staging point on the way to Compostella, the citadel of Blaye, built by Vauban in 1652 on the remains of a Roman *castrum*, is haunted by the ghost of Jauffré Rudel, the twelfth-century troubadour and poet of the Distant Love, and the more tragic shade of the Duchess of Berry, imprisoned in 1832 for attempting to organize an uprising against Louis Philippe.

The whole countryside is bathed in the poetry of the sea. It was selected as the locale for the film *Moderato Cantabile* with the 2 ½-mile wide estuary providing the backdrop. But the slopes overhanging the Gironde are covered with vines. "Opulent plains with gentle hillocks, sumptuous hills, abrupt spurs which defended Bordeaux against the Saracen and Norman invasions," so wrote E. Lacroix, "the lands of Blaye, coveted by the conquerors of the north and the south, still remain one of the finest flowers of the soil of France. Since the most ancient times, the vine, under a temperate sky, has occupied this privileged earth in which the limestones reluctantly surrender to the silicas and red clays which already announce the truffle-perfumed slopes of Périgord."

The wineproducing area of the place-name descriptions BLAYE and CÔTES-DE-BLAYE covers the cantons of Blaye, Saint-Savin and Saint-Ciers-sur-Gironde.

The simple description BLAYE deals expressly with both red and white wines. The first must come from the following grapes which, incidentally, are not all to be found elsewhere in the appellation BORDEAUX: *Cabernet, Béquignol* and *Verdot*. The use of any other grape cancels the right to the place-name description.

The white wines must be made from the following grapes: *Semillon, Sauvignon, Muscadelle, Merlot Blanc, Folle Blanche, Colombard, Pineau de la Loire* and *Frontignan*. The last four grapes are not encountered anywhere else in the place-name description BORDEAUX. In the place-name description CÔTES-DE-BLAYE, there is still some tolerance regarding grapes, at least as far as the red wines are concerned. In the case of the whites, only the classic trilogy of *Sauvignon, Semillon* and *Muscadelle* is permitted.

The reds are colourful, fruity and sweet, and gain by early bottling. The tannin and iron they contain recommend them as tonic wines. Of all the wines of the Gironde, they are perhaps the only ones whose savour recalls the good growths of Burgundy. The white wines are nervous and delicate. By one of nature's happy juxtapositions, they make an ideal accompaniment to the delicious oysters of Marennes whose beds are established on the near-by Seudre.

WINES OF THE NEIGHBOURING REGIONS

The basins of the Garonne, Dordogne and Adour are devoted to viticulture. We shall not go back to the problems which arose, at the beginning of the present century, with respect to these "marginal" vineyards when it was a question of marking out the boundaries of the production area of Bordeaux wine. In the long run, the autonomy granted to the "marginal" wines turned out to their advantage in that it made it possible for them to bring out their individuality.

Thus, the wine of Cahors, before being marketed in the "Port of the Moon" under the name of VIN DE HAUT-PAYS, had been sung by Horace and Virgil. Like the wines from the slopes of the Isle and the Lot and from around Bergerac, it is a powerful, highly-coloured red wine which, though rough in its youth, has a remarkable vinosity after a few years in the bottle. Its basic grape is the *Malbec* which gives it a very agreeable bouquet. The slopes of Marmandais, an area of mixed farming with an abundance of fertile orchards, also supply some agreeable red wines from near the great place-name descriptions of the Gironde. The CÔTES DE BUZET, also in Lot-et-Garonne, are

V.D.Q.S. red wines (delimited wines of superior quality) which are fruity and light, supple and round. The VILLAUDRIC are red wines harvested a few miles from Montauban which have the same qualities and also the advantage that they can be drunk young. On the Côte d'Argent and in the Basque country, the *gastronomade* (gourmet) takes pleasure in the growths of IROULEGUY, SAINT-ETIENNE-DE-BAIGORRY and ANHAUX. These are delicately fruity and act as an excellent foil to the local ham. The wines of Béarn are often vinified as rosé and are accommodating enough to go equally well with fish and with white meat. Astride two departments (Landes and Gers), the vineyard of Tursan was formerly quite famous and produces white and red wines as well as a few rosés with a very elegant bouquet. On the borders of Languedoc, Fronton also produces red, white and rosé wines, the principal outlet for which is Toulouse. Elegance and delicacy characterize the LAVILLEDIEU, red and white growths from Tarn-et-Garonne.

The wines of MONBAZILLAC can, in good years, compete with the best of the luscious white wines of

Bordeaux, although their aroma is rather less complex. In this soil, which has long been famous, the wine-growers must, as in Sauternes and Barsac, await the "noble rot" before harvesting. In the first two or three years after picking, the MONBAZILLAC wines are very attractive and run like liquid gold. It would be wrong, however, to yield to temptation. As they age, they acquire a deeper but no less luminous colour and, above all, develop their full character which then differs appreciably from that of a great luscious white wine of Bordeaux of similar age.

Without aspiring to the heights of the MONBAZILLAC, the dry, semi-dry or semi-sweet wines of BERGERAC have charm and a distinguished bouquet which, as André Lamondé wrote, make one celebrate the food-stuffs of that "land of Périgord paved with truffles and heavenly with *foie gras*". However, a type of BERGERAC of higher and more constant quality is to be found in the place-name descriptions CÔTES DE SAUSSIGNAC and CÔTES DE BERGERAC.

The Périgord poet Armand Got glorified MONTRAVEL in the following terms:

Montravel ! Montravel !
Les sucs fruités, moelleux, d'un bouquet non pareil,
Les vins "de bonne foi" comme un "dict" de Montaigne,
Qui font "vivre à propos" et sont de bon conseil.

Montravel ! Montravel !
Mellow, fruity juices of a fragrance clear and wise,
Doughty wines which savour of a saying of Montaigne,
Conducive to right living and magnanimous advice.

The simple place-name description MONTRAVEL is reserved for wines harvested in the plain. The place-name descriptions CÔTES DE MONTRAVEL and HAUT-MONTRAVEL cover less fertile soils and produce growths of a greater distinction. They are remarkably fruity and elegant. The best white wines of the Lot-et-Garonne are from the Côtes de Duras: less sweet than the MONTRAVEL wines, but fresh and delicate.

Decked in pale gold, ardent and heady, ROSETTE comes from the white grapes used in the Bordeaux country: *Semillon*, *Sauvignon* and *Muscadelle*.

The winegrowers of Gaillac were among those who, not so long ago, fought the most bitterly for inclusion in the place-name description BORDEAUX. Their wine is now managing very well on its own, thanks to the Confraternity of Bacchus to which part of their élite belongs. The sweet GAILLAC is a rough wine drunk very soon after the harvest. However, the guaranteed place-name description of origin GAILLAC indicates a dry white wine without excess acidity which is light and very drinkable. GAILLAC PREMIÈRES CÔTES has a fine colour and a great frankness of taste which it keeps in its age and which it owes to its dominant grape, the *Mauzac*, which has the peculiarity of pro-

ducing a thick-skinned fruit which can ripen fully despite the rains of September. GAILLAC PERLÉ is a perfectly natural sparkling wine, no product other than the grape being used to obtain it. Without acidity or tartness, gushing with savoury cream, it is an exquisite "lady's wine", as the saying went half a century ago, in its lusciousness, delicacy and relatively low alcohol content. The red wines are unequal in quality but the best of them have body, a fine colour and travel well.

Surrounded by a large area which produces only white wines, Madiran has a shrine sheltering a small wooden Virgin of great antiquity named Our Lady of the Vines. The vines in question are red. The chief growths of this Bigorre soil are ANGUIS, LE PARSAN, LES TUILERIES, LES TURCOS and HECHACQ. They are made from the noble grapes: *Cabernet Sauvignon* and *Cabernet Franc* which are used in the best holdings of the Bordeaux country. These wines have an aroma which is reminiscent of that of the grape-flower, a spare, very fluid scent which is obviously due to the *Cabernet*. Unfortunately, more fertile grapes have been introduced into the vineyards on the pretext of productivity. In the context of the new outlets offered by the Common Market, it would no doubt be a wise policy to eliminate these intruders. Tonic and digestive, MADIRAN keeps for a very long time. However, a sediment forms which adheres to the side of the bottle and the wine must therefore be decanted.

Portet is the tiny capital of a winegrowing area which may, perhaps, be more ancient than that of Jurançon. It produces a white wine from a grape called *Pacherenc* with which the *Mansenc*, a Jurançon plant, is sometimes mixed. The harvest is late. Formerly, picking was still being carried out at Christmas. Nowadays, it is just about finished before the end of November. Hence the winegrowers of this countryside have been rather resistant to the benefits of modern oenology. The savours of their wine give themselves without evasion "like the virgins of Béarn" as Paul de Cassagnac, who admired this growth and its countryside, once wrote.

Caring little for fashion, PORTET is luscious, sweet or dry according to the caprices of nature. It maderizes readily but the winegrower is indifferent to this. He does not mind the maderized taste and he produces his wine for himself, not for the wine-merchant.

Some very interesting wines resembling the PORTET have been obtained at Lambeye, Montpezat and Crouzeilles, which are communes of the Vic-Bilh.

Even if there is no historic proof that Henry IV had his lips moistened at birth with Jurançon wine, this legendary episode continues to shed an immortal glory on the slopes in front of which the town of Pau was built. What is more, the scene is part of the spiritual heritage of our civilization. Whether authentic or not, it generally annoys and irritates the enemies of wine in France. It it by no means necessary, however, to resort to this reference to prove the nobility of a growth harvested at the end of autumn in the communes of Jurançon, Gan, Laroin, Saint-Faust, Aubertin and Monein. It owes nothing to anyone. None of the grapes which compose it has been identified in any other viticultural region. Very sensitive to oïdium, the large and small *Mansencs*, the *Cruchen* and the *Courbu* produce tight bunches of juice-heavy grapes which are naturally reduced, dried and candied on the vine, producing a veritable concentration of the must before picking. The richness in sugar of this must is transformed into liquid without altering the delicacy of the bouquet which characterizes the finished product.

JURANÇON is in the first rank of the most famous sweet wines. It involves both the senses and the spirit and lends itself to that famous "after-taste" of which the great connoisseurs speak.

Around that great queen—a vintage bottle of Bordeaux—we find a host of noble companions and maids of honour which, according to protocol, may be less beautiful but are sometimes so pretty that, in a sense, they become her equal. The wines of the south-west form the retinue without which there could, of course, be no sovereign.

THE LIFE OF THE WINE PEOPLE
IN THE BORDEAUX COUNTRY

In the last fifteen years or so, something has changed in the hearts and spirits of the Bordeaux winegrowers. They have not lost sight of the fact that the area of production is of paramount importance as regards the quality of the growth, but they have remembered that the origin of a wine is not enough to make it good, any more than the highest birth and impeccable ancestry will make a gentleman if his education be defective.

The rebirth of the three great pilot-confraternities of the Bordelais (*Jurade de Saint-Emilion, Commanderie du Bon-Temps Médoc et des Graves* and *Connétablie du Guyenne*) is due to this new viticultural psychology, although, in some cases, it has been the cause of it. The confraternities, by bringing together the wine professionals on a more human and humanist level than could be achieved by the trades unions, by reviving ancient handicraft and corporative traditions and by excluding all demagogy and disputes from their meetings, have restored to a place of honour that comradely mentality which, in the past, was the glory of the guilds, even though the guilds were also syndicates which fought the authorities to retain their "privileges".

The modern Bordeaux confraternities have taken from these old associations only their noblest and most disinterested features and have left for the trades unions the technological and contentious aspects which all modern viticulture must entail, even if it has a thousand years of history behind it.

THE JURADE DE SAINT-EMILION

The development and prosperity of the Jurade de Saint-Emilion date from the twelfth century when Richard the Lionheart accorded it various privileges and freedoms. The most ancient document known concerning the town of Saint-Emilion is the Charter of Falaise, dated July 8th, 1199, in which on the death of his brother Richard, John Lackland confirmed the privileges granted by his predecessor. The great concessions made by the English kings were, of course, designed to create conditions under which the Bordeaux vintners could provide the best wine possible for the ever-thirsty English market.

This was the origin of the *Jurade*, composed, as the old writings put it, of "honest folk" elected by their fellow-citizens to administer with sovereign power the interests of the commune. As regards the cultivation of the vine and vinification, the *Jurats* displayed a tireless and scrupulous vigilance. They held the "vintner's mark" (a branding iron with the arms of the town), proclaimed the "ringing in" of the harvest, banned the sale of insufficiently "fine" wine and dealt rigorously with abuses and fraud.

From the tunning stage onwards, they watched over the quality of the growths, visited the wine-stores and cellars and checked the *barriques*. After which the "vintner" branded the casks of "good wine" with the coat of arms of the town. "Unworthy" wine was destroyed by fire. Lastly, the *Jurats* issued certificates without which it was forbidden to transport wine. These measures, which may appear excessively authoritarian, ensured the prosperity of the region through the resounding fame of SAINT-EMILION, which the English then called the king of wines.

The men of goodwill who, on September 13th, 1948, with due solemnity and authenticity reconstituted the *Jurade*, did not aspire to the political powers of their ancestors but limited themselves to the immense task of placing the wine of Saint-Emilion once again on the throne of its ancient splendours.

The *Connétablie de Guyenne*, here shown being solemnly received in the City Hall of Gouda in the Netherlands, in 1952 revived the title if not the administrative functions of an institution which in the Middle Ages had extensive influence in the Bordeaux country.

The first pressing operations often take place on the picking site. The baskets of the wine-pickers are emptied into the *baste*, a little tub of light wood containing about 5 ½ gallons. The grapes are rammed down in the rudimentary manner shown in the picture.

The most illustrious of the Bordeaux whites comes from the Château d'Yquem (above); among the reds, that of the Château Lafite-Rothschild (below) is one of the top prestige wines of the Médoc area.

THE COMMANDERIE DU BON-TEMPS MÉDOC ET DES GRAVES

Likewise, in October 1951, the men of the Médoc desired one thing and one thing only: to establish an organization which, in modern society, could really serve the cause of their wine, irrespective of classification or privilege, great growths and modest artisan growths alike, with the sole proviso that they were the good Médoc wines on which the universal glory of Bordeaux was founded.

Thus, under the distant patronage of a winegrowing religious order formerly active in Médoc, this utterly unique society was formed. It comprises the winegrowers, whether owners of famous châteaux or simple "bourgeois" growers, the wine-brokers (the link between production and trade) and, lastly, the wine-merchants who for centuries have been exporting Médoc throughout the whole world.

The *Commanderie* has taken as its emblem the wooden bowl which was well-known to the image-carvers of the gothic churches. This *bontemps*, or *lou desquet* as it is called in the local dialect, is a tiny piece of winemaking equipment used for beating the whites of eggs which are then "whipped" in the *barrique* of new wine to

154

clarify it. The commanders' hats are shaped like the *desquet* and are topped by a white cover reminiscent of the beaten egg-whites. It is also with *lou desquet* that, in the wine-stores of the Médoc, when summer has come again, the happy marriage between the new harvest and the wine ready for bottling is achieved.

For some years now, the Médoc *Commanderie* has had two offshoots in the white-wine country: the *Commanderie du Bontemps de Sauternes-Barsac* (dressed in golden velvets) and the *Commanderie du Bontemps de Sainte-Croix-du-Mont* (in light-yellow linen).

THE CONNÉTABLIE DE GUIENNE

The *Connétablie de Guienne*, much referred to throughout the Middle Ages in the Bordeaux country, was the link which bound to the great mother-city the small winegrowing daughter towns which are still dotted along the banks of the Garonne and the Gironde. The important administrative functions of the Constable, with his headquarters in the Palais de l'Ombrière, though carefully distinguished from the attributions vested in the *Jurats* of Bordeaux, were inspired by the same concern: to serve the viticultural interest of the seneschalcy by controlling the origin and the quality of the wines. Memory of those past ages aroused enthusiasm in the hearts of those who founded the contemporary *Connétablie*, in 1952. They were winegrowers from the Premières Côtes de Bordeaux, Entre-Deux-Mers, Benauge and part of Graves who were later joined by those of the Côtes de Bourg, Blaye and Saint-Macaire.

As the *Connétablie* marches by torchlight under the porticos of the quasi-royal Château of Cadillac-sur-Garonne, dressed in majestic black robes stamped with the golden cross, the moving rite of the enthronement unfolds in the barrel-vaulted crypt. While prominent personalities listen to the indictment which will open to them the gates of the Privy Council, the spectators feel themselves enveloped in ten centuries of history.

THE HOSPITALLERS OF POMEROL

It was at the beginning of the twelfth century that the powerful Hospitallers of St. John of Jerusalem chose Pomerol as the site for their first Commandery in Libournais. In the post-Roman era, it was they who, for nearly five centuries, cultivated the vine in that parish. From it they produced a wine regarded as a wonder for the comfort of pilgrims and the cure of the sick. In the spring of 1968, with the permission of the Sovereign Order of Malta, the winegrowers of Pomerol reconstituted the Commandery which joined the other confraternities in the Grand Council of Bordeaux.

GRAND COUNCIL OF BORDEAUX

The Grand Council of Bordeaux is not still another confraternity but a high assembly which, during the Middle Ages, presided over the destiny of the city and of the province. At times of crisis, all the corporate bodies of Bordeaux and Guienne met in the Great Council for joint deliberation as to the decisions which should be taken with respect, chiefly, to the production of and trade in wine. That is what still happens today. Although it is true that the city among the vines reigns over a great variety of soils, it has but one soul as it has but one history.

While respecting the personality of each of the viticultural regions of the Bordeaux country, the Grand Council is thus responsible for safeguarding and strengthening the idea of unity contained in the three words: wines of Bordeaux.

It has a dual significance. Within the limits of the Bordeaux country, it makes a reality of the necessary idea of association. Outside, particularly in new markets where the name of Bordeaux takes precedence over the numerous place-name descriptions of the Gironde, it makes it possible to fix the attention on a product whose great variety should not cause one to forget its unique provenance.

When all the confraternities are met together, the Grand Council holds chapters either at Bordeaux, in the House of Wine, headquarters of the Inter-Professional Wine Council of Bordeaux, or in great foreign cities during which, according to an ancient ritual, it awards to some rarely privileged persons the title of "Companion of Bordeaux".

THE BORDEAUX WINE ACADEMY

The Bordeaux Wine Academy, which is not a confraternity either, is entitled to a seat in the Grand Council. It is an academy in the full sense of the word. Around a few celebrated writers who are members of the French Academy, it groups in all 40 life members belonging to Letters, Science and the Arts, the owners of Great Growths, winegrower merchants etc. It sits either in the city of Bordeaux itself or in the great châteaux of the region.

The aims of the Academy are noble in their humanism. The company puts in the forefront of its work the defence and the glorification of Bordeaux wine by the exact observance of refined tasting usage and the study of viticultural and winegrowing dialectics. It publishes annually a code of vintages which is not a simple scale of values applied to Bordeaux growths but a mass of information concerning the development of a number of harvests since 1920.

WINES OF BORDEAUX
LEFT BANK OF THE GARONNE AND OF THE GIRONDE

SAUTERNES AND BARSAC REGIONS • WHITE WINES

CLASSIFICATION OF THE GREAT GROWTHS OF 1855

Superior first growth . . . Château d'Yquem . . . Sauternes

First growths

Château La Tour-Blanche . . .	Bommes	Château Rabaud-Sigalas	Bommes	Château Climens	Barsac
Château Lafaurie-Peyraguey . .	»	Château Rabaud-Promis	»	Château Guiraud	Sauternes
Clos Haut-Peyraguey	»	Château de Suduiraut	Preignac	Château Rieussec	Fargues
Château Rayne-Vigneau	»	Château Coutet	Barsac		

Second growths

Château de Myrat	Barsac	Château Filhot	Sauternes	Château Romer	Preignac
Château Doisy-Daene	»	Château Broustet	Barsac	Château Lamothe	Sauternes
Château Doisy-Védrines	»	Château Caillou	»	Château Nairac	Barsac
Château Doisy	»	Château Suau	»		
Château d'Arche	Sauternes	Château de Malle	Preignac		

OTHER GREAT GROWTHS OF SAUTERNES AND BARSAC

Château Raymond-Lafon . . .	Sauternes	Château du Mayne	Barsac	Château Montjoie	Barsac
Château Lafon	»	Château Camperos.	»	Château Lapeloue	»
Château Lanère	»	Château Saint-Marc	»	Château Moura	»
Domaine du Coy	»	Château Gravas	»	Château des Rochers.	Preignac
Château Comarque	»	Château Latrézotte	»	Château Bastor-Lamontagne . .	»
Château d'Arche-Vimeney . . .	»	Château Villefranche.	»	Château d'Arche-Pugneau . . .	»
Château Haut-Bommes	Bommes	Clos des Princes	»	Château du Pick	»
Château Mauras	»	Clos du Roy	»	Domaine de Lamothe-Vigneau,	
Cru Bel-Air	»	Château Petit-Mayne	»	château des Remparts	»
Château Cameron	»	Château Brassens-Guiteronde . .	»	Domaine de la Forêt	»
Cru Bergeron	»	Château Fleury	»	Château Jonka	»
Château Le Hère	»	Château Simon	»	Château Saint-Amand	»
Château Lamourette	»	Château Jacques-le-Haut . . .	»	Château de Veyres	»
Domaine de Souba	»	Château Bouyot.	»	Château d'Armajan-des-Ormes .	»
Château Cantegril	Barsac	Cru Hournalas	»	Château Guimbalet	»
Château Baulac.	»	Château du Roc	»	Château Monteils	»
Château Piada	»	Château Grand-Mayne Guy-né-		Cru Peyraguey	»
Château Piot	»	Marc	»	Château Laribotte	»
Château Grillon	»	Château Simon Carrety	»	Château Fontebride	»
Château Mathalin	»	Château Menauta	»	Château du Mayne	»
Château Dudon	»	Château Coustet	»	Clos de l'Ecole	»
Château de Carles	»	Cru La Pinesse	»	Château Gilette	»
Château Guiteronde	»	Château Ducasse	»	Château Haut-Bergeron	»
Château La Clotte et Cazalis . .	»	Château Péchon	»	Château de Pleytegeat	»
Château Roumieu	»	Château Saint-Robert	»	Clos du Pape	Fargues
Château Massereau	»	Château Massereau-Lapachere .	»	Château de Fargues	»
Château Rolland	»	Château Mercier.	»	Cru Fillau	»
Château Pernaud	»	Château La Bouade	»	Cru Mothes	»
Château Prost	»	Château Grand Carretey	»	Château Paillon-Claverie	»
Château Luziès	»	Château L'Haouilley	»	Château Portarrieu	»
Château Liot	»	Château Jany	»	Château de Touilla	»
Château Hallet	»	Château Menate	»		

CÉRONS REGION • WHITE WINES

Château de Cérons et de Calvi-		Château Mayne-Binet	Cérons	Château Haut-Mayne	Cérons
mont	Cérons	Cru Larrouquey.	»	Clos Barail	»
Grand enclos du Château de Cérons	»	Château Sylvain.	»	Domaine des Moulins à Vent . .	»
Lalannette-Ferbos	»	Château Lamouroux	»	Cru de Peyroutène.	»

Domaine de Freyron	Cérons	Crus des Grands-Chênes	Cérons	Domaine de Castagnaou	Podensac
Château Beaulieu	»	Crus Ferbos-Lalanette	»	Château du Hau-Rat	Illats.
Château Grand Chemin	»	Cru des Moulins à Vent	»	Château Archambaud	»
Château Barthez	»	Clos des Moulins à Vent	»	Clos du Tauzin	»
Cru du Moulin-à-Vent	»	Domaine de Caillou	»	Château Cantau	»
Château des Bessanes	»	Château Méric	»	Château Beaulac	»
Cru Haut-Mayne	»	Cru du Moulin	»	Château Haut-La-Huntasse	»
Clos Bourgelat	»	Cru Haut-Belloc	»	Château Le Huzet	»
Château de l'Emigré	»	Cru Voltaire	»	Domaine de Calbet	»
Château Balestey	»	Clos Avocat	»	Château Thôme-Brousterot	»
Château du Seuil	»	Cru Larrouquey	»	Domaine de Prouzet	»
Cru de Du Peyrat	»	Cru Majans	»	Château Despeyrères	»
Clos de l'Avocat	»	Cru Cravaillas	»	Château Haut-Gravier	»
Château La Salette	»	Cru du Freyron	»	Domaine de Jaussan	»
Cru Dauphin	»	Cru Le Mayne	Podensac	Clos des Roches	»
Cru La Liste	»	Château d'Anice	»	Cru Navarot	»
Cru des Magens	»	Cru des Cabanes	»	Château Haut-Bourdat	»
Cru Menaut-Larrouquey	»	Château de Madère	»	Château Cazès	»
Cru Chacha	»	Cru Le Bourdieu	»	Clos du Bas Lançon	»
Cru de Pineau	»	Cru Boisson	»	Cru de Brazé	»
Clos Cantemerle	»	Cru Maucouade	»	Cru Haut-Boutoc	»
Cru Cleyrac	»	Cru du Brouillaou	»	Château Tinan	»
Château Lalanette	»	Cru Madérot	»	Cru de Lionne	»
Domaine du Salut, Château Hura-din	»	A Mayne d'Imbert	»	Domaine de Gallier	»
		Domaine Le Cossu	»	Domaine de Menjon	»

GRAVES REGION • WHITE WINES AND RED WINES

CLASSIFIED GROWTHS • I.N.A.O. classification officially recognized by the decree of February 16, 1959

RED WINES

Château Haut-Brion	Pessac	Château de Fieuzal	Léognan	Château Malartic-Lagravière	Léognan
Château Bouscaut	Cadaujac	Château Haut-Bailly	»	Château Olivier	»
Château Carbonnieux	Léognan	Château La Mission-Haut-Brion	Talence	Château Pape-Clément	Pessac
Domaine de Chevalier	»	Château La Tour-Haut-Brion	»	Château Smith Haut-Lafitte	Martillac
		Château La-Tour-Martillac	Martillac		

WHITE WINES

Château Bouscaut	Cadaujac	Château Couhins	Villenave-d'Ornon	Château Laville Haut-Brion	Talence
Château Carbonnieux	Léognan			Château Malartic-Lagravière	Léognan
Domaine de Chevalier	»	Château La-Tour-Martillac	Martillac	Château Olivier	»

The above classification is in alphabetical order, except for the Château Haut-Brion, classified in 1855

LIST OF THE PRINCIPAL GROWTHS

Château Haut-Brana	Pessac	Château Lespault	Martillac	Château des Fougères	La Brède
Château Haut-Carré	Talence	Château La Solitude	»	Château Guillaumot	»
Château Pique-Caillou	Mérignac	Château Lafargue	St-Médard-	Domaine de Lasalle	»
Château Chêne-Vert	»	Château Lamothe	Eyrans	Cru de Magneau	»
Château Baret	Villenave-	Château de La Prade	»	Cru de Méric	»
Château Cantebau-Couhins	d'Ornon	Château Lusseau	Aygue-	Clos du Pape	»
Château Pontac-Monplaisir	»	Château du Méjan	morte	Château Bel-Air	St-Morillon
Château Bardins	Cadaujac	Château Saint-Jérôme	»	Château Belon	»
Château Malleret	»	Château Boiresse	»	Domaine de Gravette	»
Château Lamothe-Bouscaut	»	Château de Beauchêne	Beautiran	Domaine du Jau	»
Château Poumey	Gradignan	Château Grand Bourdieu	»	Château Piron	»
Château de France	Léognan	Château de Tuquet	»	Château du Bonnat	St-Selve
Château Gazin	»	Château Ferrande	Castres	Domaine du Barque	»
Domaine de Grand-Maison	»	Château Foucla	»	Domaine de La Peyrère	»
Château La Louvière	»	Château Bas-Pommarède	»	Château Bernard-Raymond	Portets
Château Larrivet-Haut-Brion	»	Château Pommarède de Haut	»	Château Cabannieux	»
Château Le Pape	»	Château Lognac	»	Château Crabitey	»
Château Chaviran	Martillac	Domaine de Sansaric	»	Château de Doms	»
Château Ferran	»	Château de La Brède	La Brède	Château Jean-Gervais	»
Château Lagarde	»	Cru de Bichon	»	Château des Graves	»
Château Malleprat	»	Château La Blancherie	»	Château Les Gravières	»
Château Haut-Nouchet	»	Château de l'Espérance	»	Domaine de La Girafe	»
Château La Roche	»	Cru d'Eyquem	»	Château de Graveyrion	»

Château Lagueloup	Portets	Château de Virelade	Virelade	Domaine d'Ordonnat	Langon
Château Lhospital	»	Château de Gayon	»	Clos Léhoul	»
Château Madelis	»	Château des Tilleuls	»	Château Ludeman	»
Château Millet	»	Château d'Arricaud	Landiras	Château Péran	»
Château Le Mirail	»	Château Batsères	»	Domaine de Toumilot	»
Château Moulin	»	Château Pessille	»	Château Bellefontaine	St-Pierre-
Château Pessan	»	Cru de Baylen	Budos	Clos Cantalot	de-Mons
Château du Pingoy	»	Château de Budos	»	Clos Cazebonne	»
Château de Portets	»	Château des Charmettes	»	Château des Jaubertes	»
Château Rahoul	»	Cru de l'Hermitage	»	Clos La Magine	»
Château La Tour-Bicheau	»	Domaine de Courbon	Toulenne	Château Magence	»
Domaine de Videau	»	Château de la Gravère	»	Clos du Moulin-à-Vent	»
Château Vieille-France	»	Clos Louloumet	»	Château Peydebayle	»
Cru du Bérot	Arbanats	Château Respide	»	Château des Queyrats	»
Château Mamin	»	Château La Tourte	»	Château de Respide	»
Domaine des Places	»	Château Tustoc	»	Château Toumillon	»
Château Tourteau-Chollet	»	Château Chanteloiseau	Langon	Clos d'Uza	»
Domaine de Teychon	»	Domaine des Gluchets	»		

MÉDOC REGION • RED WINES

GREAT GROWTHS OF THE 1855 CLASSIFICATION

First growths

Château Lafite-Rothschild, Pauillac   Château Margaux, Margaux   Château Latour, Pauillac   Château Mouton-Rothschild, Pauillac

Second growths

Château Brane-Cantenac	Cantenac	Château Léoville-Lascases	St-Julien	Château Rausan-Ségla	Margaux
Château Cos-d'Estournel	St-Estèphe	Château Léoville-Poyféré	»	Château Rauzan-Gassies	»
Château Montrose	»	Château Léoville-Barton	»	Château Pichon-Longueville	Pauillac
Château Ducru-Beaucaillou	St-Julien	Château Dufort-Vivens	Margaux	Château Pichon-Longueville-La-	
Château Gruaud-Laroze-Sarget	»	Château Lascombes	»	lande	»

Third growths

Château Kirwan,	Cantenac	Château Palmer	Cantenac	Château La Lagune	Ludon
Château Calon-Ségur,	St-Estèphe	Château Desmirail	Margaux	Château Giscours	Labarde
Château Cantenac-Brown	Cantenac	Château Ferrière	»	Château Lagrange	St-Julien
Château Boyd-Cantenac	»	Château Malescot-Saint-Exupéry	»	Château Langoa	»
Château d'Issan	»	Château Marquis-d'Alesme-Becker	»		

Fourth growths

Château Beychevelle	St-Julien	Château Talbot	St-Julien	Château Prieuré-Lichine	Margaux
Château Branaire-Ducru	»	Château Duhart-Milon	Pauillac	Château Pouget	Cantenac
Château Saint-Pierre	»	Château La Tour-Carnet	St-Laurent	Château Marquis-de-Therme	Margaux
				Château Lafon-Rochet	St-Estèphe

Fifth growths

Château Pontet-Canet	Pauillac	Château Haut-Bages-Libéral	Pauillac	Château Pédesclaux	Pauillac
Château Batailley	»	Château Lynch-Bages	»	Château Clerc-Milon	»
Château Haut-Batailley	»	Château Lynch-Moussas	»	Château Belgrave	St-Laurent
Château Croizet-Bages	»	Château Dauzac	Labarde	Château Camensac	»
Château Grand-Puy-Ducasse	»	Château Mouton-Baron-Philippe	Arsac	Château Cantemerle	Macau
Château Grand-Puy-Lacoste	»	Château Le Tertre	Pauillac	Château Cos-Labory	St-Estèphe

EXCEPTIONAL GROWTHS

Château Angludet	Cantenac	Château Bel-Air, Marquis d'Aligre	Sousans	Château Moulin-Riche	St-Julien
Château La Couronne	Pauillac	Château Chasse-Spleen	Moulis	Château Ville-Georges	Avensan

LIST OF THE PRINCIPAL BOURGEOIS GROWTHS ACCORDING TO THE SYNDICAL PRIZE-LIST OF MARCH 3, 1966

EXCEPTIONAL GREAT BOURGEOIS GROWTHS

Château Agassac	Ludon	Château La Closerie	Moulis	Château Houissant	St-Estèphe
Château Andron-Blanquet	St-Estèphe	Château Citran	Avensan	Château Lanessan	Cussac
Château Beausite	»	Château Le Crock	St-Estèphe	Château de Marbuzet	St-Estèphe
Château Le Boscq	»	Château Dutruch-Gd-Poujeaux	Moulis	Château Meyney	»
Château Capbern	»	Château du Glana	St-Julien	Château Phélan-Ségur	»
Château Caronne-Ste-Gemme	St-Laurent	Château Haut-Marbuzet	St-Estèphe	Château Villegeorge	Avensan

GREAT BOURGEOIS GROWTHS

Château Belle-Rose	Pauillac	Château Hanteillan	Cissac	Château Paveil-de-Luze	Soussans
Château Bel-Orme	St-Seurin	Château Labégorce-Zédé	Margaux	Château Pibran	Pauillac
Château Bibian-Darriet	Listrac	Château Lafite-Canteloup	Ludon	Château Pomeys	Moulis
Château Le Bourdieu	Vertheuil	Château Lamarque	Lamarque	Château Potensac	Potensac
Château Le Breuil	Cissac	Château Laujac	Bégadan	Château du Raux	Cussac
Château La Cardonne	Blaignan	Château Lestage	Listrac	Château Rolland	Pauillac
Château Canteloup	St-Estèphe	Château Lestage-Darquier	Moulis	Château Saransot-Dupré	Listrac
Château du Castera	St-Germain	Château Liversan	St-Sauveur	Château Ségur	Parem-
Château Coufran	St-Seurin	Château Loudenne	St-Yzans		puyre
Château Coutelin-Merville	St-Estèphe	Château Mac-Carthy	St-Estèphe	Château Sénéjac	Le Pian
Château Cissac	Cissac	Château Malleret	Le Pian	Châteaux Sociando-Mallet et Pon-	
Château Fonbadet	Pauillac	Château Morin	St-Estèphe	toise-Cabarrus	St-Seurin
Château Fonréaud	Listrac	Château Moulin à Vent	Moulis	Château du Taillan	Le Taillan
Château Fontesteau	St-Sauveur	Château Moulis	»	Château La Tour-de-By	Bégadan
Château Fourcas-Dupré	Listrac	Château Patache-d'Aux	Bégadan	Château Verdignan	St-Seurin
Château Grandis	St-Seurin				

BOURGEOIS GROWTHS

Château Bel-Air-Lagrave	Moulis	Château Haut-Padarnac	Pauillac	Château Romefort	Cussac
Château Bonneau	St-Seurin	Château Larrivaux	Cissac	Château Roquegrave	Valeyrac
Château Bellegrave	Listrac	Cru Lassalle	Potensac	Château La Rose-Anseillan	Pauillac
Château de Come	St-Estèphe	Château Mac-Carthy-Moula	St-Estèphe	Château Saint-Bonnet	St-Christoly
Château Chambert	»	Château Malescasse	Lamarque	Château Saint-Christoly	»
Château Donissan	Listrac	Château Maurac	St-Seurin	Château Tayac et Siamois	Soussans
Château Grand-Duroc-Milon	Pauillac	Château Monthil	Bégadan	Château Les Ormes-Sorbet	Couquèques
Château La Fleur-Saint-Bonnet	St-Christoly	Clos du Moulin	St-Christoly	Château La Tour-Blanche	St-Christoly
Château La Fleur-Milon	Pauillac	Château Moulin-Rouge	Cussac	Château La Tour-des-Termes	St-Estèphe
Château Fonpiqueyre	St-Sauveur	Château Pabeau	St-Seurin	Château La Tour-St-Bonnet	St-Christoly
Château Fort-de-Vauban	Cussac	Château Le Privera	St-Christoly	Château Victoria	Vertheuil
Château Gallais-Bellevue	Potensac	Château Labatisse	St-Sauveur	Château Vieux-Moulin	Cussac
Château Grand-Saint-Julien	St-Julien	Château Renouil-Franquet	Moulis		

SOME OTHER BOURGEOIS GROWTHS

Château Dillon	Blanquefort	Château Barreyre	Arcins	Château La Tour-Milon	Pauillac
Château Fongravey	»	Château Poujeaux	Moulis	Château La Tour-d'Anseillan	»
Château Grand-Clapeau	»	Château Duplessis Hauchecorne	»	Château La Garosse	St-Sauveur
Château de Parempuyre	Parem-	Château La Closerie Gd Poujeaux	»	Château Peyrabon	»
Cru Ségur-Fillon-isle-d'Arès	puyre	Château Robert-Franquet	»	Château La Tour du Mirail	Cissac
Château La Dame-Blanche	Le Taillan	Château Gressier-Grand-Poujeaux	»	Château La Tour Saint-Joseph	»
Domaine de Chalet-de-Germignan	»	Château Duplessis-Fabre	»	Château Le Roc	St-Estèphe
Château Ludon-Pomiès-Agassac	Ludon	Château Ruat-Petit-Poujeaux	»	Château Tronquoy-Lalande	»
Château La Providence	»	Château La Morère	»	Château Fonpetite	»
Château d'Arche	»	Château Médrac	»	Château de Pez	»
Château « Trois-Moulins »	Macau	Château du Testeron	»	Château La Haye	»
Château Maucamps	»	Château l'Ermitage	Listrac	Château Pomys	»
Château Fellonneau	»	Château Semeillan-Mazeau	»	Château Les Ormes de Pez	»
Château Larronde-Desormes	»	Château Semeillan Balleu-Faulat	»	Château Ladouys	»
Château Larrieu-Terrefort	»	Château Lafon	»	Château Saint-Roch	»
Château d'Arsac	Arsac	Château Fourcas-Hosten	»	Château Clauzet	»
Château Montbrison	»	Château Rose-Sainte-Croix	»	Château Grand-Village-Capbern	»
Le Moulin-Avensan	Avensan	Château Granins	»	Château Domeyne	»
Château Rosemont	Labarde	Château La Bécade	»	Château Picard	»
Château Siran	»	Château du Cartillon	Lamarque	Château Mac-Carthy	»
Château Martinens	Cantenac	Château Cap-de-Haut	»	Château Laffitte-Carcasset	»
Château Montbrun	»	Château Moulin-Rose	»	Château Latour de Marbuzet	»
Château Rouge Port-Aubin	»	Château Lanessan	Cussac	Château Faget	»
Château Pontac-Lynch	»	Château Beaumont	»	Domaine de Pez	»
Château de Labegorce	Margaux	Château Lamothe-Bergeron	»	Château Reysson	Vertheuil
Château L'Abbé-Gorsse-de-Gorsse	»	Château Larose-Trintaudon	St-Laurent	Château La Gravière-Couerbe	»
Château La Gurgue	»	Château Larose-Perganson	»	Château Charmail	St-Seurin-
Domaine de Clairefont	»	Château Galan	»	Château du Haut-Carmail	Cadourne
Château La Tour-de-Mons	Soussans	Château Corconnac	»	Château Livran	St-Germ.-
Château La Bégorce	»	Château La Tour Marcillanet	»	Château Beaulieu	d'Esteuil
Château Haut-Breton	»	Château Gloria	St-Julien	Château Carcanieux-les-Graves	Queyrac
Château Marsac-Séguineau	»	Château Haut Bages Monpelou	Pauillac	Château La Croix-Landon	Begadan
Château de l'Aiguillette	»	Château Malécot	»	Château Bellegrave	»
Château La Tour-du-Roc	Arcins	Château Balogues	»	Château Bellerive	»
Château d'Arcins	»	Château Latour-L'Aspic	»	Château Les Lesques	Lesparre

REGION BETWEEN GARONNE AND DORDOGNE

CÔTES DE BORDEAUX SAINT-MACAIRE • WHITE WINES

Château Cordeliers	St-Macaire	Domaine de Flous	St-Pierre-d'Aurillac	Château Machorre	St-Martin-de-Sescas
Domaine de Belle-Croix	»			Château La Serre	Caudrot
Domaine des Charmettes	St-Martial	Château Perrayne	St-André-du-Bois	Domaine de Jacob	St-Laurent-du-Pian
Château Haut-Bardin	»	Château Malromé	»		
Cru Terrefort	Le Pian	Château d'Arche-Lassalle	»	Domaine de Beaulieu	Ste-Foy-la-Longue
Château Fayard	»				
Cru Rigal	»				

SAINTE-CROIX-DU-MONT • WHITE WINES

Château Loubens	Ste-Croix-du-Mont	Domaine de Morange	Ste-Croix-du-Mont	Château Terfort	Ste-Croix-du-Mont
Château de Tastes	du-Mont	Château La Gravière	du-Mont	Château Les Marcottes	du-Mont
Château Bouchoc	»	Château Labory	»	Domaine de Roustit	»
Château Lafüe	»	Château Coullac	»	Cru des Arroucats	»
Château Laurette	»	Château Loustauvieil	»	Clos Belle-Vue	»
Château Bel-Air	»	Château Roustit	»	Château La Graville	»
Château de L'Escaley	»	Domaine du Tich	»	Cru de La Gravière du Tich	»
Château du Grand-Peyrot	»	Domaine des Sorbiers	»	Château Lapeyreyre	»
Château La Rame	»	Château Jean Lamat	»	Château Copis	»
Château La Mouleyre	»	Château du Pavillon	»	Château La Caussade	»
Château Médouc	»	Château Bertranon	»	Château du Verger	»
Château des Mailles	»	Clos de Verteuil	»		

LOUPIAC • WHITE WINES

Château de Ricaud	Loupiac	Château Lanusse-Couloumet	Loupiac	Château La Yotte	Loupiac
Château Mazarin	»	Château du Vieux-Moulin	»	Cru de Montallier-Lambrot	»
Château Dauphiné-Rondillon	»	Clos Champon-Ségur	»	Domaine du Chay	»
Château du Cros	»	Domaine de Turon-Lanere	»	Domaine de Barbe-Maurin	»
Château de Loupiac-Gaudiet	»	Château des Roches	»	Château Terrefort	»
Château Pontac	»	Domaine de Rouquette	»	Château Le Portail Rouge	»
Château Tarey	»	Château Le Tarey	»	Château de Martillac	»
Domaine de Malendure	»	Cru du Couloumet	»	Cru du Merle	»
Clos Jean	»	Domaine de Pasquet	»	Clos de Giron	»
Château de Rondillon	»	Château Pageot-Couloumet	»	Domaine de Miqueu-Bel-Air	»
Château La Nère	»	Château Peyruchet	»	Château Roustin	»
Domaine du Noble	»	Domaine de Roby	»	Domaine de Guinot	»
Cru de Couloumet-Les Boupeyres	»	Domaine du Rocher	»	Château de Beaupuy	»
				Château Margès-Dusseau	»

PREMIÈRES CÔTES DE BORDEAUX • WHITE WINES

Château Laurétan	Langoiran	Château Terrasson	Langoiran	Château de Plassans	Tabanac
Château Sauvage	»	Cru Baylibelle	»	Château Lucques Bessan	»
Château La Tour Maudan	»	Château Lagareyre	»	Château Lamothe	»
Château Pommarède	»	Domaine du Pin	»	Château Sentour	»
Château Biac	»	Château Barrère	»	Château Renon	»
Château Le Gardera	»	Domaine du Gourdin	»	Château La Providence	»
Château Tanesse	»	Domaine de Côte-Rôtie-Lamothe	»	Domaine d'Armaing	»
Château Faubernet	»	Château Dutoya	»	Château Laroche	Baurech
Château du Vallier	»	Château Chauvin	»	Domaine de Melin	»
Domaine de Bellevue	»	Domaine de Lagaloche	»	Château Puygueraud	»
Château Gourran	»	Château La Ronde	Le Tourne	Château de Lyde	»
Château Lapeyruche	»	Château Pic	»	Château Gaussens	»
Château Langoiran	»	Domaine de Moutons	»	Château Pressac	»
Château de l'Eglise	»	Château Le Mesnil	»	Château de Haux	Haux
Château La Ligassonne	»	Domaine de la Côte Rôtie	Tabanac	Château du Juge	»
Domaine Crassat-Gramman	»	Château Lagarosse	»	Château La Gorce	»

Château Peneau	Haux	Château Mony	Rions	Château Faugas	Gabarnac
Château Gréteau	»	Clos du Monastère du Broussey	»	Domaine de La Cure	»
Château Brigaille	»	Domaine de la Bastide	»	Cru du Bourdieu	Monprimblanc
Château Lamothe de Haux	»	Château des Remparts	»	Château Beau-Site Monprimblanc	blanc
Château du Grava	»	Château Peironnin	»	Domaine de Lagrange	»
Château de La Bézine	»	Clos de Ricouet	»	Clos La Burthe	»
Domaine de Bernadon	»	Domaine de Carsin	»	Domaine Lambert	»
Château du Courreau	»	Château La Roque	La Roque	Château de Teste	»
Château Jeanganne-Préfontaine	»	Château Peller	»	Cru de Vigneyre	»
Château Bellegarde	Paillet	Clos Dezarneauld	»	Domaine de la Frairie	»
Château Paillet	»	Château Haut-Laroque	»	Domaine de Poncet	Omet
Château l'Ermitage	»	Château Lassalle	»	Domaine des Biscarets	»
Château de Marsan	Estiac-sur-	Château Birot	Béguey	Domaine de Camelon	»
Au Moulin des Graves	Garonne	Domaine du Pin	»	Clos du Boudeur	»
Château du Peyrat	Capian	Château Peyrat	»	Domaine de La Bertrande	»
Château de Caillavet	»	Château Boisson	»	Château Mont-Célestin	Verdelais
Château Suau	»	Domaine de la Marquise	»	Château Pomirol le Pin	»
Château Barakan	»	Château de Garreau	Cadillac	Cru Cantegrit	»
Domaine de Sainte-Anne	»	Château du Juge	»	Domaine de Grava	»
Château de Grand-Mouëys	»	Château des Tourelles	»	Château Gravelines-Semens	»
Château Ramondon	»	Château Arnaud-Jouan	»	Domaine de Joffre	»
Domaine de Potiron	»	Château Fayau	»	Domaine de Lescure	»
Château de Grand-Branet	»	Château de Beaulieu	»	Cru du Haut-Roudey	»
Château Lezongard	Villenave-	Clos des Capucins	»	Cru de Nazareth	»
Château Fauchey	de-Rions	Château Lardiley	»	Domaine de Boustit	»
Domaine de Lamarque	Cardan	Château Côte-Belle	»	Château La Prioulette	St-Maixant
Château Janisson	»	Château Justa	»	Château du Point-de-Vue	»
Château Videau	»	Clos Saint-Cricq	»	Château Chante-l'Oiseau	»
Domaine de Bourgalade	»	Château de la Passonne	»	Château Malagar	»
Domaine de Lhoste	»	Château du Gard	»	Château Montonoir	»
Domaine de Mespley	»	Cru Peytoupin	»	Château Pique-Caillou	»
Château du Payre	»	Cru La Gravette	»	Château Lavison	»
Château Mageot	»	Domaine de Chasse-Pierre	»	Château Saint-Germain	St-Germain-
Château de l'Espinglet	Rions	Domaine de Saint-Cricq	»	Domaine de la Maroutine	de-Graves
Domaine du Broussey	»	Château du Pin	»	Château Génisson	»
Domaine de Hautes-Graves	»	Château Marcelin-Laffitte	Gabarnac	Clos de Millanges	»
Domaine de Cholet	»	Clos Pierre-Jean	»	Domaine de Goursin	»
Château Jourdan	»	Domaine du Moulin de Ballan	»	Château Saint-Germain	»
Domaine de Cardonne	»	Clos du Grand-Bonneau	»	Domaine du Fihl	Donzac
Château Caïla	»	Château Latour Feugas	»	Domaine du Haurin	»
				Domaine de Prentigarde	»

PREMIÈRES CÔTES DE BORDEAUX • RED WINES

Château Bassaler Castanède	Bassens	Château Léon	Carignan	Château La Rigaudière	Camblanes
Château Favols	Carbon-	(Domaine de Camelon)	»	Château de Courtade	»
	Blanc	Château Malherbes	Latresne	Château Damluc	»
Château La Croix	Lormont	Château Gassies	»	Domaine de Cluseau	»
Château de Cypressat	Cenon	Domaine de Pardaillan	»	Château Lestange	Quinsac
Château Costeriou	Bouliac	Domaine du Grand-Parc	»	Château Péconnet	»
Château Montjon-Le-Gravier	Ste-Eulalie	Château Pascot	»	Château de Pranzac	»
Château La Tour-Gueyraud	»	Château Rauzé-Sybil	Cénac	Domaine de Chastelet	»
Château de Chelivette	»	Château Haut-Brignon	»	Domaine de Castagnon	»
L'Abbaye de Bonlieu	»	Château Materre	»	Château Montaigne	»
Château Larose	»	Château Saint-Sève	»	Château Bel-Air	»
Château Malbec	»	Château La Mouline	»	Château Bellevue	»
Château d'Intrans	»	Château Duplessis	»	Château du Peyrat	Cambes
Château du Grand Jour	Yvrac	Château Rauzé	»	Château La Navarre	»
Château Bellevue	»	Domaine de Roquebrune	»	Château Maran	»
Domaine de Bouteilley	»	Château Latour	Camblanes	Château Puy-Bardens	»
Château Maillard	»	Château Bel-Air	»	Château Brémontier	»
Château Canteloup	»	Château Brethous	»	Château Lardit	»
Château Labatut	»	Château Courtade Dubuc	»	Château Roubric	»
Château Cayre	»	Château Lafitte	»	Château La Chabanne	»
Château Miraflorès	»	Château Lagarette	»	Clos de Gourgues	St-Caprais-
Château Tertre du Renard	»	Château Tapiau	»	Château Campet	de-
Château de Carignan	Carignan	Château du Tasta	»	Domaine de Luc	Bordeaux
Château Roqueys	»	Clos Haut-Forcade	»	Domaine des Conseillants	»

ENTRE-DEUX-MERS • WHITE WINES AND RED WINES

HAUT-BENAUGE

Château du Vert	Arbis	Domaine de Fongrane	Gornac	Domaine de la Grangeotte	Gornac
Domaine de Gouas	»	Château Cazeau	»	Château d'Ories	»
Clos de Terrefort	»	Château Martinon	»	Domaine de Pédebert	»
Château de Benauge	»	Château Pouly	»	Domaine de Troubat	»
Domaine de Meyssau	Cantois	Château d'Hauretz	»	Domaine de Peyrines	Mourens-
Domaine de Fermis	»	Domaine de la Gaborie	»	Domaine de Mondain	Monpezat
Domaine de Talusson	»	Domaine de Terrefort	»	Domaine du Ferron	Soulignac
Domaine de Pasquet	Escoussans	Domaine du Houre	»	Château de Toutigeac	Targon
Domaine de Nicot	»	Château La Mazerolle	»	Domaine de Brufanno	»

CANTONS OF BRANNE, OF PUJOLS, OF SAUVETERRE AND OF PELLEGRUE

Domaine de Fauchey	Branne	Domaine de Vignolles	St-Quentin-	Château de Pressac	Daignac
Château de Blagnac	Cabara	Clos Picard	le-Baron	Château Mauros	Guillac
Château du Grand Puch	St-Germain-	Château de Bellefontaine	Baron	Château de Vidasse-Pessac	Pessac-s.-
	Puch	Château Raymond	»	Domaine Le Mayne	Dordogne
Domaine Le Pin	St-Aubin-	Château Ramonet	»	Domaine de Glayse	»
	de-Blaignac	Domaine du Grand-Canteloup	Nérigean	Domaine de la Rivière	Pujols
Domaine de la Girolatte	Naujan-et-	Château Martouret	»	Château de la Salle	Rauzan
Château Beaufresque	Postiac	Château de Montlau	Moulon	Château Villotte	»
Château de Naujan	»	Château Mouchac	Génissac	Château du Bedat	Blasimon
Domaine de la Rouergue	»	Château Rambaud	»	Château de Roques	Mauriac
Château Bonnet	Grézillac	Château du Burg	»	Château de Courteillac	Ruch
Domaine de Cabirol	Camiac	Château Fantin	St-Jean-	Château de Grand-Champs	St-Sulpice-
Domaine de Balestard	St-Quentin-		de-Blaignac		de-Pomiers
	le-Baron				

CANTONS OF CARBON-BLANC AND OF CRÉON

Château du Burk	Ambès	Château La Mothe	Montussan	Clos de Dominge	Camarsac
Château Sainte-Barbe	»	Château La Tour	Sallebœuf	Château Seguin	Lignan
Château Parabelle	Ambarès	Château Grand-Monteil	»	Clos Saint-Jean	»
Château du Tillac	»	Château Pontac-Gasparini	»	Château de Tustal	Sadirac
Château Formont	»	Château de Lesparre	Beychac-	Domaine de Calamiac	»
Château du Gua	»	Château Quinsac	et-Cailleau	Château Guillaumet	»
Château du Peychaud	»	Domaine de La Grave	»	Château Lestage	»
Château Lagraula	St-Sulpice-	Château Senailhac	Tresses	Domaine de Landreau	»
Château Beauval	Cameyrac	Château Bel-Air	»	Château de Bergerie	St-Genès-
Château Quantin	»	Château Lestrilles	Artigues		de-
Château de Reignac	St-Loubès	Château Lafitte	»		Lombaud
Château Lescart	»	Château Landeron	Pompignac	Château Beauduc	Créon
Château Labatut	»	Château Rivasseau	»	Château Patrouilleau	La Sauve
Château Chelivette	»	Château des Arrouches	»	Domaine de Castebelle-	»
Château Les Dauphins	»	Château Beaulé	»	des-Praud	
Château La Tour-Puymirand	Montussan	Domaine des Carmes	»	Château Chateauneuf	»
Château Lavergne	»	Château de Camarsac	Camarsac	Château de Goélane	St-Léon
Château Fonchereau	»	Château Beauséjour	»	Château Le Cugat	»
				Château du Bedat	Blasimon

SAINTE-FOY-BORDEAUX REGION • RED WINES AND WHITE WINES

Château de Courauneau	Ligueux	Château de Langalerie	St-Quentin-	Château de La Tour Beaupoil	Pessac-sur
Château La Roche	Les Lèves	Domaine de Mayne	de-Caplong		Dordogne
Château des Vergnes	»				

GRAVES-DE-VAYRES • RED WINES

Château Bel-Air	Vayres	Château Bussac	Vayres

RIGHT BANK OF THE DORDOGNE AND OF THE GIRONDE

SAINT-ÉMILION REGION • RED WINES

GREAT GROWTHS OF THE 1955 CLASSIFICATION

First great classified growths (a)

Château Ausone . . . . St-Emilion   Château Cheval-Blanc . . . . . St-Emilion

First great classified growths (b)

Château Beauséjour . . . . . . St-Emilion	Clos Fourtet . . . . St-Emilion	Château Magdelaine . . . . . . St-Emilion
Château Bel-Air . . . . »	Château Figeac . . . . »	Château Pavie . . . . »
Château Canon . . . . »	Château La Gaffelière . . . . . »	Château Trottevieille . . . . . »

Great classified growths

Château l'Angélus . . . . St-Emilion	Château Le Grand-Corbin- Pécresse . . . . St-Emilion	Château Le Couvent . . . . . St-Emilion
Château l'Arrosée . . . . »	Château Grand-Mayne . . . . . »	Château Le Prieuré Saint-Emilion . . . . »
Château Balestard-la-Tonnelle . »	Château Grand-Pontet . . . . . »	
Château Bellevue . . . . »	Château Les Grandes-Murailles . »	Château Mauvezin-La- Gommerie . . . . »
Château Bergat . . . . »	Château Guadet-Saint-Julien . . »	Château Moulin du Cadet . . . »
Le Cadet Bon . . . . »	Château Jean-Faure . . . . . . »	Château Pavie-Decesse . . . . »
Château Cadet-Piola . . . . . . »	Clos des Jacobins . . . . »	Domaine Pavie-Macquin . . . . »
Château Canon-La-Gaffelière . . »	Château La Carte . . . . »	Pavillon Cadet . . . . »
Château Cap de Mourlin . . . . »	Château La Clotte . . . . . . »	Château Petit-Faurie-de-Soutard »
Château Chapelle-Madeleine . . »	Château La Cluzière . . . . . . »	Château Ripeau . . . . »
Château Chauvin . . . . »	Château La Couspaude. . . . . »	Château Sansonnet . . . . . . »
Château Corbin . . . . »	Château La Dominique . . . . »	Château Saint-Georges- Côtes-Pavie . . . . »
Château Corbin-Michotte . . . »	Clos La Madeleine . . . . . . »	
Château Coutet . . . . »	Château Larcis-Ducasse . . . . »	Clos Saint-Martin . . . . »
Château Croque-Michotte. . . . »	Château La Marzelle . . . . . . »	Château Soutard . . . . »
Château Curé-Bon-la-Madelaine . »	Château Larmande . . . . . . »	Château Tertre-Daugay . . . . »
Château Fonplégade . . . . . . «	Château Laroze . . . . »	Château Trimoulet . . . . . . »
Château Fonroque . . . . . . »	Château La Serre . . . . »	Château des Trois Moulins . . . »
Château Franc-Mayne . . . . . »	Château La Tour-du-Pin-Figeac »	Château Troplong-Mondot . . . »
Château Grand-Barrail- Lamarzelle-Figeac. . . . . . »	Château La Tour-Figeac . . . . »	Château Villemaurine . . . . . »
Château Grand Corbin Despagne	Château Le Châtelet . . . . . »	Château Yvon-Figeac . . . . . »

Principal other growths

Château Badette . . . . St-Emilion	Château Dassault . . . . St-Emilion	Château Haut-Simard . . . . . St-Emilion
Clos Badon . . . . »	Château Daugay . . . . »	Domaine de Haut-Veyrac . . . »
Domaine de Badon-Patarabet . »	Domaine De Rey . . . . »	Château Hermitage-Mazerat . . »
Château Baleau . . . . »	Château De Rol . . . . »	Château Jacquemeau . . . . . »
Château Beau-Mazerat . . . . »	Château Etoile-Pourret . . . . »	Château du Jardin-Saint-Julien . »
Château Belles-Plantes . . . . »	Château Fongaban-Bellevue . . »	Château du Jardin-Villemaurine. »
Château Berliquet . . . . . . »	Château Fonrazade . . . . . . »	Château Jaugue-Blanc . . . . . »
Château Bézineau . . . . »	Château Franc-Patarabet. . . . »	Château Jean de Mayne . . . . »
Château Bord-Ramonet . . . . »	Château Franc-Pourret. . . . . »	Château Jean Voisin . . . . . »
Château Bragard . . . . »	Clos du Grand-Châtelet . . . . »	Clos Jean-Voisin . . . . »
Château Cadet-Soutard . . . . »	Domaine du Grand-Faurie . . . »	Château La Clotte-Grande-Côte . »
Château Cadet-Fonroque. . . . »	Château Grand Mirande . . . . »	Château La Croix-Chantecaille . »
Château Cantenac . . . . »	Château Guadet-Le-Franc-Grâce- Dieu . . . . »	Château La Fleur-Mérissac . . . »
Château Cardinal-Villemaurine . »		Château La Fleur-Pourret . . . »
Château Cartau . . . . »	Château Gueyrot . . . . »	Château La Fleur-Vachon . . . »
Château Cassevert . . . . . . »	Château Haut-Berthonneau. . . »	Domaine La Gaffelière . . . . . »
Château Cauzin . . . . »	Château Haut-Cadet . . . . . . »	Château La Gommerie . . . . . »
Château Champion . . . . . . »	Château Haut-Fonrazade . . . . »	Château La Grâce-Dieu . . . . »
Domaine du Châtelet . . . . . »	Château Haut-Grâce-Dieu . . . »	Château La Madeleine . . . . . »
Domaine de Chante-Grive-Badon »	Château Haut-Grand-Faurie . . »	Château Le Manoir . . . . . . »
Château Châtelet-Moléonne . . »	Château Haut-La Rose. . . . . »	Clos La Marzelle . . . . »
Château Cheval-Noir. . . . . . »	Château Haut-Mazerat . . . . »	Château Laniotte . . . . »
Château du Clocher . . . . . . »	Domaine Haut-Patarabet . . . »	Château Laplagnotte-Bellevue . »
Château Cormey . . . . »	Château Haut-Pontet . . . . . »	Château Laporte . . . . »
Château Cormey Figeac . . . . »	Château Haut-Pourret . . . . . »	Château La Rose . . . . »
Couvent-des-Jacobins . . . . . »	Clos Haut-Pourret . . . . . . »	Château La Rose Pourret . . . »
Château Cravignac . . . . . . »	Château Haut-Sarpe . . . . . »	Château La Rose-Rol . . . . . »
Château Croix-de-Chantecaille . »	Château Haut-Segotte . . . . . »	Château La Tour-Fonrazade . . . »

Château La Tour-Pourret ...	St-Emilion	Château Vieux-Ceps ...	St-Emilion	Château Puy-Blanquet	St-Etienne
Château La Tour-Saint-Pierre .	»	Château Villebout ...	»	Château du Rocher ...	de-Lisse
Château Magnan ...	»	Château Vieux-Grand-Faurie ..	»	Château du Vieux-Guinot ...	»
Château Magnan-La-Gaffelière .	»	Château Vieux-Moulin-du-Cadet.	»	Château Baladoz ...	St-Laurent-
Château Malineau ...	»	Château Vieux-Pourret. ...	»	Clos La Barde ...	des-Combes
Château Martin ...	»	Domaine de Yon ...	»	Château de La Barde ...	»
Château Matras ...	»	Château Yon-Figeac ...	»	Château de Béard ...	»
Château Matras-Côte-Daugay ..	»	Château Barde-Haut ...	St-Christophe	Château Bellefont-Belcier ...	»
Château Mazerat ...	»	Château Les Basiliques ...	des-Bardes	Château Belle-Isle-Mondotte ..	»
Château des Menuts ...	»	Château Brun ...	»	Château La Bouygue ...	»
Clos des Menuts ...	»	Château du Cauze ...	»	Château Godeau ...	»
Côte Mignon-Lagaffelière	»	Château Coudert ...	»	Château Haute-Nauve ...	»
Château Montlabert ...	»	Château Fombrauge ...	St-Emilion	Château Pipeau ...	»
Château Moulin-Saint-Georges .	»	Château Gaubert ...	»	Château du Sable ...	»
Château Petit-Figeac ...	»	Château Grangey ...	»	Château Villebout ...	»
Château Mouton-Blanc	»	Château Guillemot ...	»	Château Larcis-Ducasse	»
Château Clos de l'Oratoire ...	»	Château Haut-Sarpe ...	»	Château Capet ...	St-Hippo-
Château Le Palat ...	»	Château Lapelletrie ...	»	Château de Ferrand ...	lyte
Château Patris ...	»	Château Laroque ...	»	Château Capet-Guillier	»
Château Petit-Cormey ...	»	Château Larquet ...	»	Château Haut-Plantey	»
Château Petit-Faurie-Trocard .	»	Château Marrin ...	»	Château Lassègue ...	»
Domaine Petit-Val ...	»	Château Panet ...	»	Château Maurens ...	»
Château Peyraud ...	»	Clos des Moines ...	»	Château Monlot-Capet ...	»
Château Peygenestou ...	»	Château Quentin ...	»	Château Pailhas ...	»
Clos Picon-Cravignac	»	Château Rol-de-Fombrauge ...	»	Château Pipeau-Ménichot ...	»
Château Pindefleurs ...	»	Château Saint-Christophe ...	»	Clos des Sarrazins ...	»
Château Pontet ...	»	Château Sarpe-Grand-Jacques .	»	Château Gros ...	St-Pey-
Château Pontet-Clauzure ...	»	Clos de Sarpe ...	»	Château Fourney ...	d'Armens
Château Pontet-Fontlabert ...	»	Château Sarpe Pelletan ...	»	Château Jean-Blanc ...	»
Château Puygenestou ...	»	Château La-Tour-St-Christophe .	»	Château La Chapelle-de-Lescours	»
Château Régent ...	»	Château Vieux-Sarpe ...	»	Cru Peyrouquet ...	»
Château Royland ...	»	Château Bel-Air-Ouy ...	St-Etienne	Château de Saint-Pey	»
Clos Saint-Emilion ...	»	Domaine du Calvaire ...	de-Lisse	Château Saint-Pierre ...	»
Château Saint-Julien	»	Château Canterane ...	»	Château Le Castelot ...	St-Sulpice-
Domaine de la Salle	»	Château Côte Bernateau ...	»	Château Grand-Pey-Lescours ..	de-Faleyrens
Château Simard ...	»	Château de Lisse ...	»	Château Lande de Gravet ...	»
Château Soutard-Cadet	»	Château La Fagnouse ...	»	Château de Lescours ...	»
Enclos de Soutard	»	Domaine de Haut-Bruly ...	»	Château Monbousquet ...	»
Château La Tour-Pourret ...	»	Château du Haut-Rocher ...	»	Château de Faleyrens ...	»
Château Trianon ...	»	Domaine de Haut-Veyrac ...	»	Château Saint-Martial ...	»
Cru Troquart ...	»	Château Jacques-Blanc ...	»	Château Trapeau ...	»
Château Truquet ...	»	Château Lamartre ...	»	Château Quercy ...	Vignonet
Château Vachon ...	»	Château Mangot ...	»	Château Peyroutas ...	»
Clos Valentin ...	»	Château Mont-Belair. ...	»	Château Rouchonne-Vignonet .	»
Château de la Vieille-Cloche ..	»	Château de Pressac ...	»		

SABLES-SAINT-ÉMILION • RED WINES

Château Martinet ...	Sables-	Château Garde-Rose ...	Sable-	Château Cruzeau ...	Sable-
Clos de la Bordette ...	St-Emilion	Château Doumayne ...	St-Emilion	Château Gueyrosse ...	St-Emilion
Château de la Capelle	»	Clos Froidefond ...	»	Château Quinault ...	»

MONTAGNE-SAINT-ÉMILION • RED WINES

Château Bayard. ...	Montagne-	Château Haut-Plaisance	Montagne-	Château La Tour-Montagne...	Montagne-
Château Beauséjour ...	St-Emilion	Château Jura-Plaisance	St-Emilion	Château La Tour-Paquillon ..	St-Emilion
Château Bellevue ...	»	Château La Bastienne ...	»	Château Maison-Blanche	»
Château Calon ...	»	Château La Bichaude ...	»	Château des Moines ...	»
Château Corbin ...	»	Château Lafleur ...	»	Château Montaiguillon ...	»
Château Coucy ...	»	Château La Papeterie ...	»	Château Mouchet-Montagne ..	»
Château de Fontmurée ...	»	Château La Picherie ...	»	Château Moulin-Blanc ...	»
Château Gay-Moulin ...	»	Château La Tête-du-Cerf	»	Clos des Moulins-de-Calon ...	»
Château Haut-Goujon	»	Château La Tour-Calon ...	»	Château Négrit ...	»
Château Les Hautes-Graves ..	»	Château La Tour-Corniaud ...	»	Château Paradis ...	»

Château Petit-Clos	Montagne-	Château Les Tuileries-de-Bayard	Montagne-	Domaine de Faizeau	Montagne-
Château Pierrot-Plaisance . . .	St-Emilion	Château Vieille-Maison	St-Emilion	Domaine de Fontmurée	St-Emilion
Château Plaisance	»	Château Le Vieux-Logis	»	Domaine de Gillet	»
Château Rocher-Corbin	»	Vieux Château Goujon	»	Domaine de La Barde	»
Château Roudier	»	Domaine de Beaudron	»	Domaine de Labatut.	»
Château Saint-André-Corbin . .	»	Domaine de Cazelon	»	Domaine de La Clotte	»
Château Saint-Jacques-Calon . .	»	Domaine Croix-de-Mission . . .	»	Domaine de La Vieille	»
Château des Tours.	»				

SAINT-GEORGES SAINT-ÉMILION • RED WINES

Château Bellevue	St-Georges-	Château La Tour du Pas-Saint-	St-Georges-	Château Samion.	St-Georges-
Château Calon	de-Montagne	Georges	de-Montagne	Château Tourteau	de-Montagne
Château Bel-Air Haut-Mont-		Château Macquin	»	Château Troquard	»
guillon	»	Château Saint-André-Corbin . .	»	Château Vieux-Guillou	»
Château du Châtelet	»	Château Saint-Georges	»	Domaine de Maisonneuve . . .	»
Château Guillou	»	Château Saint-Georges Cap-d'Or.	»	Domaine de Grimon	»
Château Haut-Troquard	»	Château Saint-Louis	»		

LUSSAC SAINT-ÉMILION • RED WINES

Château Belair	Lussac	Domaine de Lagrange	Lussac	Château Petit-Refuge	Lussac
Château Bellevue	»	Château La Tour-de-Ségur . . .	»	Château Poitou-Lussac	»
Clos Blanchon	»	Château Lion-Perruchon	»	Château Souchet-Piquat	»
Domaine du Courlat.	»	Château de Lussac	»	Château Taveney	»
Château Croix-de-Blanchon . .	»	Château du Lyonnat	»	Château Terrien	»
Château Haut-Larose	»	Clos du Lyonnat	»	Château Tiffray-Guadey	»
Château Haut-Piquat	»	Domaine de Rambaud	»	Château La Tour-de-Grenet. . .	»
Château La Fleur-Perruchon . .	»	Château La Ferrière	»	Château Les Vieux-Chênes . . .	»

PUISSEGUIN SAINT-ÉMILION • RED WINES

Château Beauséjour	Puisseguin	Château Guibot-la-Fourvieille .	Puisseguin	Château de Puisseguin	Puissseguin
Cru Belair	»	Château Haut-Bernon	»	Château du Roc de Boissac . . .	»
Château Chêne-Vieux	»	Château La Clotte	»	Clos du Roy	»
Château Durand	»	Château des Laurets	»	Château Teyssier	»
Château Guibaud	»	Château du Mayne	»		

PARSAC SAINT-ÉMILION • RED WINES

Château Langlade	Parsac	Château Malagin	Parsac	Château Piron	Parsac
Château Lestage	»	Château Musset.	»		

POMEROL • RED WINES

Château Beauchêne (former Clos		Clos du Clocher	Pomerol	Château Grandchamp	Pomerol
Mazeyres)	Pomerol	Château Conseillante.	»	Domaine des Grands-Champs . .	»
Château Beauregard	»	Château La Croix-Saint-Georges.	»	Château Grate-Cap	»
Clos Beauregard.	»	Clos l'Eglise	»	Château Guillot	»
Château Belle-Brise	»	Domaine de l'Eglise	»	Clos des Hautes Graves	»
Château Bourgneuf-Vayron . .	»	Clos l'Eglise-Clinet	»	Domaine de Haut-Pignon . . .	»
Château Brun-Mazeyres	»	Château l'Enclos	»	Château Haut-Plateau	»
Château Le Caillou	»	Château L'Evangile	»	Domaine Haut-Pomerol	»
Château de Cantereau	»	Château Ferrand	»	Château Enclos Haut-Mazeyres .	»
Château Carillon	»	Château Feytit-Clinet	»	Château La Cabanne	»
Château Certan-Demay	»	Château Gazin	»	Château La Croix	»
Château Certan-Marzelle	»	Château Gombaude-Guillot et		Château La Commanderie . . .	»
Château du Chêne-Liège	»	Grandes Vignes Clinet réunis .	»	Château Lacroix-de-Gay	»
Château Clinet	»	Château Gouprie	»	Château Lafleur	»

La Fleur du Gazin.	Pomerol	Clos Mazeyres.	Pomerol	Château Saint-André	Pomerol
Château La Fleur-Petrus	»	Château Monbran	»	Château Saint-Pierre.	»
Château La Ganne	»	Château Monregard La Croix . .	»	Château de Sales	»
Château Lagrange	»	Château Moulinet	»	Château Samson	»
Château La Grave-Trigant-de-Boisset.	»	Château Mouton-Mazeyres . . .	»	Château Sudrat-Boussaton . . .	»
Château La Pointe	»	Château Nenin	»	Château du Tailhas	»
Château Latour à Pomerol et Grandes Vignes réunies . . .	»	Cru de La Nouvelle-Eglise . . .	»	Château Taillefer	»
		Château Petit-Bocage	»	Clos des Templiers.	»
Château La Violette	»	Château Petit-Village	»	Clos Toulifaut	»
Château La-Vraye-Croix-de-Gay.	»	Château Petrus	»	Château Tristan	»
Château Le Gabachot	»	Château Plince	»	Château Trotanoy	»
Château Le Gay.	»	Château La Providence	»	Château de Valois.	»
Château Le Prieuré La Croix . .	»	Clos René	»	Château Vieux-Certan	»
Château Mazeyres	»	Clos du Roi.	»	Vieux Château Cloquet.	»
		Château Rouget	»		

LALANDE-DE-POMEROL • RED WINES

Clos des Arnaud.	Lalande-de-Pomerol	Clos l'Etoile	Lalande-de-Pomerol	Château de Musset	Lalande-de-Pomerol
Château de Bel-Air		Domaine de Grand-Moine . . .		Château Perron	
Château Bourseau	»	Château Grand-Ormeau	»	Sabloire du Grand Moine . . .	»
Petit Clos de Brouard	»	Château La Gravière.	»	Château Sergant	»
Château de la Commanderie . .	»	Clos Haut Cavujon	»	Château Templiers	»
Château La Croix-Saint-Jean . .	»	Château Laborde	»	Château de Viaud	»
Château Les Cruzelles	»	Château des Moines	»	Domaine de Viaud	»
Clos de l'Eglise	»	Clos des Moines	»	Clos de la Vieille-Forge.	»

NÉAC LALANDE-DE-POMEROL • RED WINES

Domaine du Bourg	Néac	Château Garraud	Néac	Domaine de Machefer	Néac
Château Canon Chaigneau . . .	»	Château Gachet	»	Château Moulin-à-Vent	»
Clos du Castel	»	Domaine des Grands-Bois-Chagneau	»	Château Moulin-Blanc	»
Château Chaigneau-Guillon . . .	»			Château Moncets	»
Château Châtain	»	Domaine du Grand-Ormeau . .	»	Château Nicole	»
Clos du Châtain	»	Château Haut-Ballet.	»	Domaine du Petit-Bois	»
Domaine du Châtain	»	Château Haut-Chaigneau . . .	»	Château Saint-André	»
Vieux Château Chevrol.	»	Château Lacroix	»	Château Siaurac.	»
Château Les Chaumes	»	Château La Croix-Saint-André .	»	Domaine de Surget	»
Château Chevrol-Bel-Air	»	Château Lafaurie	»	Château de Teysson	»
Château Drouilleau-Belles-Graves	»	Château Lafleur-Lambaret . . .	»	Château Tournefeuille	»
Château Fougeailles	»	Château Lavinot-la-Chapelle . .	»	Château Yveline	»

CANON FRONSAC • RED WINES

Château Vray-Canon-Boyer . .	St-Michel-de-Fronsac	Cru Gros-Bonnet	Fronsac	Château Capet-Bégaud	Frousac
Château Canon		Château de Toumalin	»	Clos Lariveau	St-Michel-de-Fronsac
Château Vrai-Canon-Bodet-La Tour.	»	Château Barrabaque	»	Château Pey-Labrit	
		Domaine de Trepesson	St-Michel-de-Fronsac	Cru La Tour-Ballet	»
Château Vrai-Canon-Bouché . .	»	Domaine de Trepesson-Lafontine		Domaine de Roulet	Fronsac
Château Canon-Lange	Fronsac	Château Bodet	Fronsac	Domaine de Bourdieu-Panet . .	»
Château Junayme	»	Château Panet	»	Château Toumalin-Jonquet . . .	»
Château Canon	»	Domaine du Haut-Caillou . . .	»	Domaine de Margalis	»
Château Comte	»	Château Gaby	»	Château Coustolle	»
Château Belloy	»	Château Moulin-Pey-la-Brie . .	»	Château Pichelèvre	»
Château Mazeris-Bellevue . . .	St-Michel-de-Fronsac	Cru Casi-Devant	St-Michel-de-Fronsac	Cru Combes-Canon	St-Michel-de-Fronsac
Château La Fleur-Canon		Domaine du Haut-Mazeris . . .		Clos Nardon	
Château du Pavillon-Haut-Gros-Bonnet	Fronsac	Château Cassagne	»	Clos Toumalin	Fronsac
		Château La Marche-Canon . . .	Fronsac	Clos Haut-Cailleau	»
Château Mazeris	St-Michel-de-Fronsac	Château Vincent		Château Canon-Bourret	»
Château des Combes-Canon . .		Château Haut-Ballet.	St-Michel-de-Fronsac	Château Canon de Brem	»
Château Grand-Renouil	»	Crus Moulin-à-Vent		Château La Tour-Canon	»
Château Maussé	»	Château du Gazin	»	Château Lamarche-Candelayre .	»
Château Lariveau	»	Château Cassagne	»	Château Roulet	»
Château La Chapelle-Lariveau .	»	Château Larchevesque	Fronsac		

166

CÔTES DE FRONSAC • RED WINES

Château des Trois-Croix	Fronsac	Château La Tour Beau-Site	Fronsac
Château Gagnard	»	Domaine de la Croix	»
Château de Pontus	»	Clos Bellevue	St-Michel-
Château La Dauphine	»	Château Queyreau-de-Haut	de-Fronsac
Château La Valade	»	Château Tasta	St-Aignan
Château La Fontaine	»	Château Tasta-Guillier	»
Château Arnauton	»	Château Jeandeman	»

Château de Carles	Saillans
Châteaux de Malgarni et Coutreau	»
Château Mayne-Viel	Galgon
Cru Vincent	St-Aignan
Château Vincent	»
Domaine de Vincent	»

BOURGEAIS REGION • RED WINES AND WHITE WINES

Château du Bousquet	Bourg	Château de Blissa	Bayon	Château Mendoce	Villeneuve
Domaine du Boucaud	»	Clos Nodot	»	Château Peychaud	Teuillac
Château du Haut-Gravat	»	Château Rousset	Samonac	Château Cottière	»
Château Croûte-Charlus	»	Château Barrieux	»	Domaine de Rivereau	Pugnac
Château Croûte-Mallard	»	Château Macay	»	Domaine de Viaud	»
Château Mille-Secousses	»	Domaine de Bel-Air	»	Château Lamothe	Lansac
Château Lalibarde	»	Domaine de Bouche	»	Château de Taste	»
Château Rider	»	Château de Thau	Gauriac	Château La Barde	Tauriac
Château Cambes-Kermovan	»	Château du Domaine de Desca-		Domaine de Guerrit	»
Château de la Grave	»	zeaux	»	Château Nodoz	»
Château Rebeymond-Lalibarde	»	Château Poyanne	»	Château de Maco	»
Domaine de Paty	»	Domaine de Bujan	»	Château Grand-Jour	Prignac et
Château Rebeymont	»	Domaine de Peyror	»	Château Le Mugron	Gazelles
Château Belleroque	»	Clos du Piat	»	Château de Grissac	»
Domaine de Noriou-Lalibarde	»	Clos de Seillas	»	Domaine de Christoly	»
Château Gros-Moulin	»	Domaine de Bonne	»	Château Laureusanne	St-Seurin
Château Lagrange	»	Château La Grolet	St-Ciers-	Château Berthou	Comps
Domaine de Lalibarde	»	Château Rousselle	de-Canesse	Domaine des Augiers	»
Château Tayac	Bayon	Château Guiraud	»	Domaine de Fonbonne	Teuillac
Château Eyquem	»	Château La Tour-Seguy	»	Château des Richards	Mombrier
Château Falfas	»	Domaine de Grand-Chemin	»	Château Guienne	Lansac
Château de la Croix (Millorit)	»	Château de Barbe	Villeneuve		

BLAYAIS REGION • RED WINES AND WHITE WINES

Château Cazeaux	St-Paul	Château Breuil	St-Martin-	Château Meneau	Mazion
Château Lescadre	Cars	Château La Brousse	Caussade	Château La Cure	Cars
Château Crusquet	»	Château Petit-Trou	»	Château Les Alberts	Mazion
Château Barbet	»	Château La Garde	St-Seurin-	Château Le Virou	St-Girons
Château Bellevue	Plassac		Cursac	Château Chasselauds	Cartelègue
Château Les Chaumes	Fours	Château Clos d'Amières	Cartelègue	Château Le Coudeau	Cars
Domaine du Chai	»	Château Le Cone Moreau	Blaye	Château Dupeyrat	St-Paul
Château Pardaillan	Cars	Château Le Cone Sebilleau	»	Château Guillonnet	Anglade
Château Gontier	Blaye-Plassac	Château Berthenon	St-Paul	Château Gordat	Cars
Château Monconseil	Plassac	Château Perreyre	St-Martin	Château Haut-Cabat	»
Château Le Cone Taillasson	Blaye		Caussade	Château Lagrange Marquis de	
Château Gigault	Mazion	Château Pinet La Roquete	Berson	Luppe	Blaye
Château Le Menaudat	St-Androny	Château Lamothe	St-Paul	Château Puy Beney	Mazion
Château Les Petits-Arnauds	Cars	Château Ricadet	Cartelègue	Château La Garde Roland	St-Seurin-
Château Sociondo	»	Château Rebouquet	Berson		Cursac
Château Charron	St-Martin	Château La Girouette	Fours	Château La Hargue	Plassac
Château Saugeron	Blaye	Château Pinet	Berson	Château Gadeau	»
Château Les Moines	»	Château La Bertonnière	Cartelègue	Château Lafont	Cartelègue
Château Le Mayne Gozin	Plassac	Château Peybrune	Plassac	Château Pomard	St-Martin
Château Lassale	St-Genès	Château La Perotte	Eyrans	Château Boisset	Berson
Ancien Manoir de La Valette	Mazion	Château Le Mayne Boye	Cars	Château Cantemerle	St-Genès
Château Puy Beney Lafitte	»	Château La Cave	Blaye	Château Perrein	Mazion
Château Segonzac	St-Genès-	Château Chaillou	St-Paul	Château Mazerolles	Cars
	de-Blaye	Domaine de Graulet	Plassac	Château Les Bavolliers	St-Christ.-
Château La Cabane	St-Martin-	Château Les Ricards	Cars		de-Blaye
	Caussade	Château La Tour Gayet	St-Androny	Moulin de la Pitance	St-Girons
Château La Taure Sainte-Luce	Blaye	Château Mayence	Mazion		

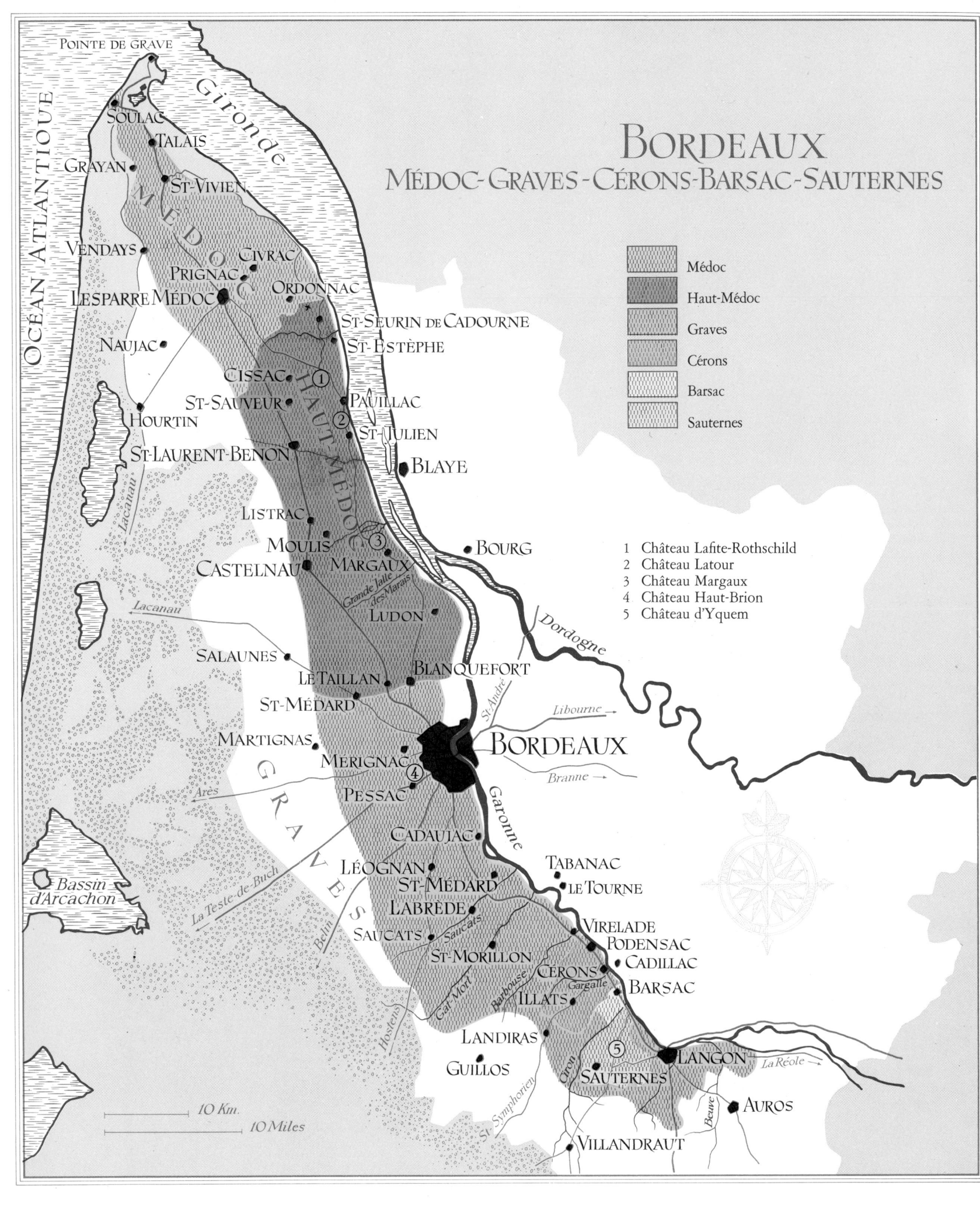

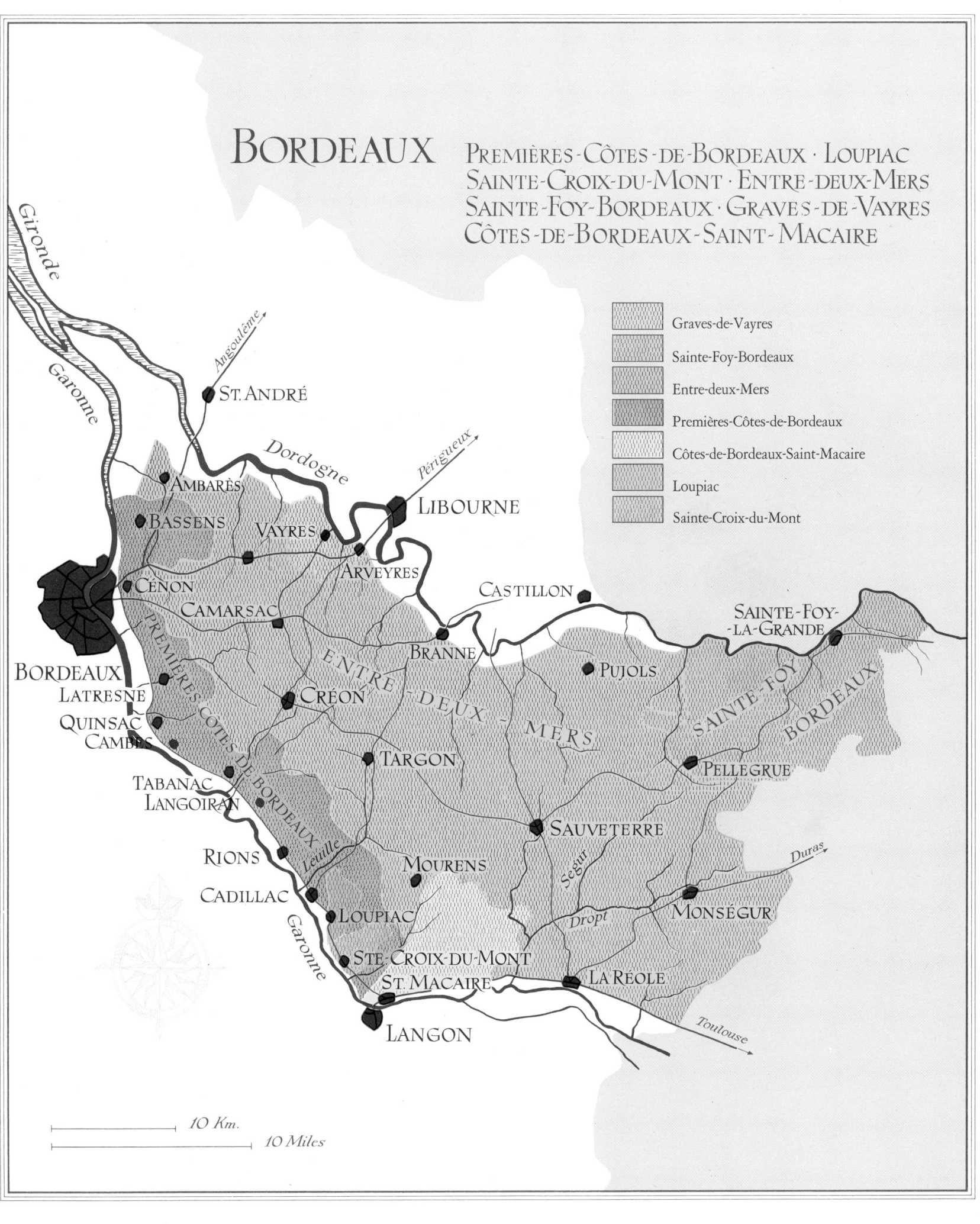

BORDEAUX

PREMIÈRES-CÔTES-DE-BORDEAUX · LOUPIAC
SAINTE-CROIX-DU-MONT · ENTRE-DEUX-MERS
SAINTE-FOY-BORDEAUX · GRAVES-DE-VAYRES
CÔTES-DE-BORDEAUX-SAINT-MACAIRE

Graves-de-Vayres

Sainte-Foy-Bordeaux

Entre-deux-Mers

Premières-Côtes-de-Bordeaux

Côtes-de-Bordeaux-Saint-Macaire

Loupiac

Sainte-Croix-du-Mont

Gironde

Garonne

Angoulême

ST. ANDRÉ

Dordogne

Périgueux

AMBARÈS

BASSENS   VAYRES

LIBOURNE

CÉNON

ARVEYRES

CAMARSAC

CASTILLON

SAINTE-FOY-
LA-GRANDE

BORDEAUX

BRANNE

LATRESNE

PUJOLS

ENTRE-DEUX-MERS

CRÉON

SAINTE-FOY

QUINSAC
CAMBES

PREMIÈRES CÔTES DE BORDEAUX

BORDEAUX

TARGON

PELLEGRUE

TABANAC
LANGOIRAN

Leuille

SAUVETERRE

Duras

RIONS

Ségur

MOURENS

CADILLAC

Dropt

MONSÉGUR

LOUPIAC

Garonne

STE·CROIX·DU·MONT

ST. MACAIRE

LA RÉOLE

Toulouse

LANGON

10 Km.

10 Miles

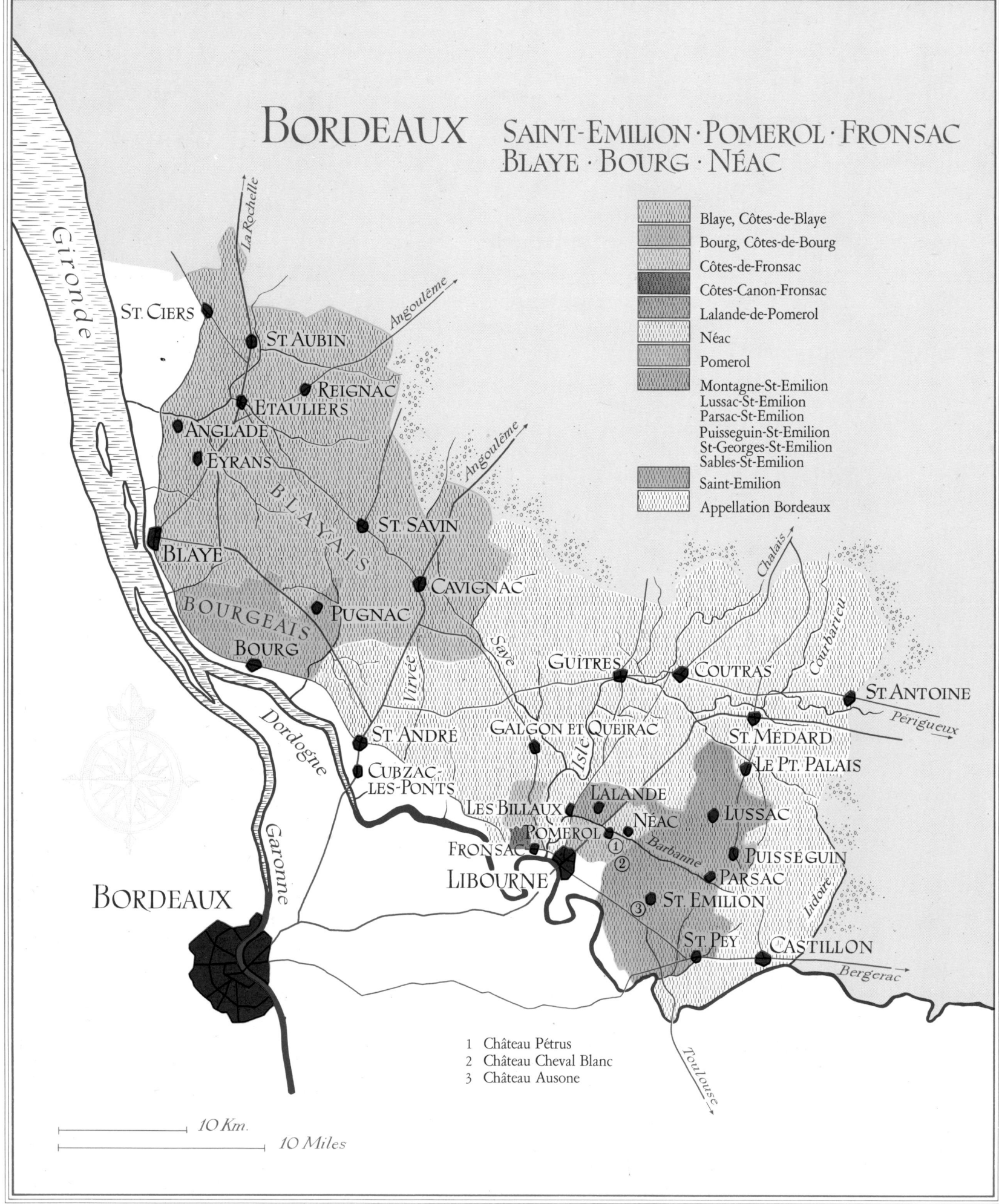

BORDEAUX

SAINT-EMILION · POMEROL · FRONSAC
BLAYE · BOURG · NÉAC

	Blaye, Côtes-de-Blaye
	Bourg, Côtes-de-Bourg
	Côtes-de-Fronsac
	Côtes-Canon-Fronsac
	Lalande-de-Pomerol
	Néac
	Pomerol
	Montagne-St-Emilion
	Lussac-St-Emilion
	Parsac-St-Emilion
	Puisseguin-St-Emilion
	St-Georges-St-Emilion
	Sables-St-Emilion
	Saint-Emilion
	Appellation Bordeaux

Gironde

La Rochelle

Angoulême

ST. CIERS

ST. AUBIN

REIGNAC

ETAULIERS

ANGLADE

EYRANS

BLAYAIS

Angoulême

ST. SAVIN

BLAYE

Chalais

Courbarieu

BOURGEAIS

CAVIGNAC

PUGNAC

BOURG

Saye

GUÎTRES

COUTRAS

ST. ANTOINE

Dordogne

Virvée

Isle

Périgueux

ST. ANDRÉ

GALGON ET QUEIRAC

ST. MÉDARD

CUBZAC-LES-PONTS

LE PT. PALAIS

LALANDE

LUSSAC

LES BILLAUX

NÉAC

Barbanne

POMEROL

①

FRONSAC

②

PUISSÉGUIN

Garonne

LIBOURNE

PARSAC

Lidoire

BORDEAUX

③

ST. EMILION

ST. PEY

CASTILLON

Bergerac

Toulouse

1 Château Pétrus
2 Château Cheval Blanc
3 Château Ausone

10 Km.

10 Miles

THE WINES OF SPAIN

ELADIO ASENSIO VILLA

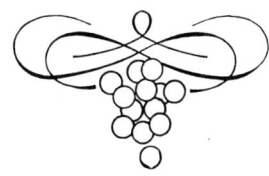

Legend says the vine was first brought into Spain under some very ancient civilization. Indeed, in some parts of southern Spain it is even said that the Phoenicians came to Spain, in the course of their Mediterranean trading, to buy the wine grown there. Historically, however, it has been proved irrefutably that it was the Romans who introduced winegrowing into Spain under the Empire. Thereafter, it spread over the northeastern provinces, the coast of the Spanish Levante (the east coast from Tarragona to Alicante) and to Andalusia, where it flourished exceedingly, especially under the Arab rulers. Later, the vine began to be cultivated in the temperate zones farther inland. Gradually the large number of varieties of vine which Spain produces today began to be planted in the valleys, on the slopes and on the foothills (up to 3,000 feet) and in the coastal area of the Spanish Levante. The geographical distribution of the vine in Spain is as varied as the character of the regions. Another factor is the widespread existence of small-holdings, since, originally at any rate, winegrowing was particularly suited to one-family farming. There are a number of other special features, notably the fact that winegrowing is carried on side-by-side with the cultivation of the olive, the other great Mediterranean crop, and in some cases vineyards and olive groves are inextricably mingled.

Wine was one of Spain's largest resources in the Middle Ages, as it was in other Mediterranean countries. The trade in Spanish wines really began to flourish in the tenth century, carried by sea and river to the north-ern European countries and to some areas in eastern Europe. This prosperity continued until the end of the eleventh century. In the twelfth century the economic, and one might even say cultural, renaissance of wine took place. Consumption increased in the wealthiest northern and central European countries as well as in the Mediterranean countries, where it was already the usual beverage and where the wines produced in Spain were well known.

Because of its geographical location, Spain was to some extent outside the main flow of European trade, and this placed it in a very special position. Under these conditions, wine could not be exported, and so it came to be consumed domestically. But once it was possible to establish normal trade from the ports of Barcelona and Valencia, Spain made a great effort to conquer the foreign markets and sell its most typical commodities, especially its wines, which already enjoyed a great reputation.

The Spanish wine trade, however, like the trade in other Spanish commodities, suffered greatly from the repercussions of economic crises in several European countries. This state of affairs was reflected in the measures taken by several of the Spanish kingdoms before the unification of Spain. This continued until 1868, the year in which the great French vineyards were invaded and ruined by the phylloxera, for this opened up new outlets for Spanish wines throughout the world. Spanish winemaking techniques also profited, for a great many French growers settled in the best Spanish winegrowing districts after their own vineyards had been destroyed and introduced their skills and practices. But, as always happens when success comes too suddenly, disorganization prevailed in the Spanish markets abroad and Spain neglected to consolidate the markets it had gained as a result of the disappearance of French wines. Winegrowing in Spain, too, underwent a severe crisis when the phylloxera crossed the Pyrenees and made its appearance there in turn, wiping out numerous vineyards and leading to very serious economic and social consequences which left deep traces on the history of the vine in Spain and indeed on Spanish agriculture in general.

Over the past forty years Spanish wine production has been very unequal in quantity. It has been influenced not only by climate but also by unfavourable natural phenomena occurring in other countries. It may, however, look forward to a more promising future, since the public authorities are taking a greater interest in it and the trade itself is eager for more effective organization. According to the official statistics of the Ministry of Agriculture for 1965, the total area planted to vines was 4,273,000 acres, of which 485,960 were also planted to mixed crops; but since the vine in fact covers 75 per cent of the area of mixed cultivation, it can be said that the actual area of the Spanish vineyards is about 4,151,300 acres. It is estimated that about 3,953,600 acres are planted to wine grapes and the rest to table grapes and raisins. In area, therefore, the Spanish vineyards are the largest in the world, more extensive even than the French and Italian.

The importance of wine and grape production to Spanish agriculture and the economy of Spain is due to the fact that the area planted to vine accounts for 3.73 per cent of the total cultivated area, and especially to the fact that the area planted to the wine grape accounts for 3.62 per cent of it. A comparison of the winegrowing area with that under other crops shows that it is exceeded only by grain and olives.

Average production in 1963-1966 was 63,230,000,000 gallons. This is a significant figure which may be taken as representing the potential of Spanish grape production. The 1964 harvest can be considered a record; it was due to a combination of favourable climatic conditions in that year.

As we have seen, the Spanish vineyards are distributed all over the Peninsula, since its climatic conditions are everywhere favourable to the vine, which requires above all long periods of unbroken sunshine. The roots remain in the ground for fifty years, sometimes longer, and this is a factor contributing to keeping the population on the land.

A glance at the map of the agricultural regions in Spain shows that every province, including the Balearic and Canary islands, has its winegrowing districts. As to area, La Mancha and the region of Utiel and Requeña (province of Valencia) take first place, followed by Catalonia and the area between Alicante and Jumilla (province of Murcia), where over 30 per cent of the land is planted to vine. Classifying groups of provinces by the area of vineyards, the order is:

Group I (over 250,000 acres per province): Ciudad Real, Toledo, Valencia and Albacete; the four provinces total 1,542,000 acres, or over one-third of the total area planted to vine in Spain.

Group II (from 123,550 to 247,100 acres): Saragossa, Tarragona, Cuenca, Badajoz, Alicante, Barcelona and Murcia; these seven provinces have 1,290,000 acres of vineyards.

Group III (61,775 to 123,550 acres): Zamora, León, Malaga, Navarre, Madrid, Logroño and Valladolid; the vineyards in these seven provinces cover 551,033 acres.

Group IV (24,710 to 61,775 acres): Cadiz and Cordoba, two provinces with wines of a high quality.

Group V (12,355 to 24,710 acres): Pontevedra, Gerona, Granada, Segovia, Seville, Almeria, Álava, Lugo and Guadalajara. The vineyards in these nine provinces cover 67,000 hectares. Winegrowing is less important here, but the province of Álava should be mentioned for its wines of exceptionally good quality and the provinces of Gerona and Pontevedra, which produce very acceptable wines.

Lastly, in Group VI (under 13,000 acres) are the provinces in which winegrowing is only of secondary importance: Balearic Islands, Santa Cruz de Tenerife, Jaen, Soria, Las Palmas, Corunna, Oviedo, Santander, Vizcaya and Guipuzcoa.

To sum up, the area of the winegrowing districts varies between a maximum of 646,000 acres in the province of Ciudad Real and a minimum of 64 acres in Guipuzcoa. Average yields and number of plants per acres vary a great deal from region to region in accordance with the climate, the grape varieties and the categories of the wines.

The total area of grape growing in irrigated regions is only 96,430 acres, 66,250 of which only are planted to wine grapes. Planting is forbidden by law nowadays on land that is not irrigated. The vineyards that existed on this land at the time when they became restricted areas are liable to a graduated tax.

Wines are classified according to their colour (red, white, other). Production (official figures for 1965) is: red wines 40.5 per cent, white wines 41 per cent, other 18.5 per cent. In the "other" class are musts, fortified wines, rosé wines, vermouths and aperitifs blended

Enjoying as it does a splendid climate, the Spanish winegrowing region is one of the largest in the world and few provinces do not produce wines of their own. The principal wine regions include the Rioja, Navarre, the province of Saragossa, the east coast from Barcelona to Alicante, La Mancha and the southern provinces with Malaga and Jerez de la Frontera, and the Canary and Balearic Islands.

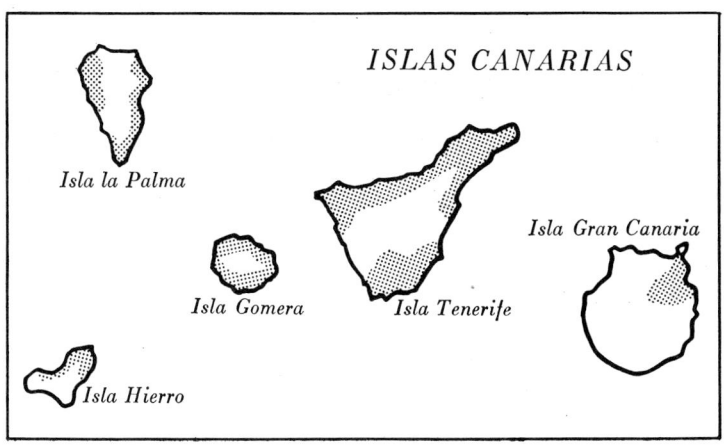

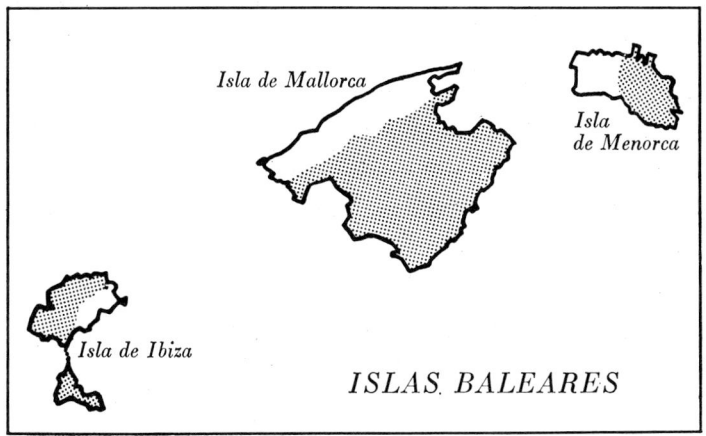

173

with quinquina. White wines predominate in New Castile, Andalusia and Catalonia, red wines elsewhere. Comparing the regions by vineyards which bottle in their own cellars, we find that in the north-west (Galicia and Asturias) there is a definite breakdown into very small properties so far as winegrowing is concerned. Western and eastern Andalusia, the Spanish Levante and New Castile have a more rational and consequently more profitable structure. In general, the co-operative movement is continuously expanding, speedily rationalizing the sectors in which reforms are most urgently needed. It promotes the concentration of cellar-bottling, which is essential from the economic point of view, and likewise an improved quality, for the small growers do not possess the skills and technical equipment necessary to guarantee at least a minimum of quality, classification and presentation. Vinification is carried out practically in the vineyard itself, as the grape does not travel well to the vat, even in co-operatives. As a rule, the larger co-operatives are no more than some six miles away from the vineyards. The wines may be classified as, first, the ordinary *(corrientes)* for immediate national consumption, and, second, the better wines for maturing.

The wines, of course, differ from each other owing to the differences inherent in the climate, nature of the soil, exposure, variety of grape and method of vinification, so that the wines from different regions have from the outset very marked characteristics of their own. Different methods of vinification within the regions produce further variations, as can be seen from the many different types of sherry.

THE WINES OF THE RIOJA

The winegrowing region of the Rioja covers the region of that name comprising the provinces of Logroño and Álava and some communes in Navarre. It is the region of quality wines; they are some of the most sought-after of the wines of guaranteed origin, the Spanish equivalent of the French *appellation d'origine contrôlée*. It stretches from around Haro to Alfaro in the valley of the Ebro and beyond its banks. It may be divided into three main districts: the Lower Rioja between the Yregua and the right bank of the Ebro; the Upper Rioja, a more humid area, the centre being Haro and taking in the north-western part of the province of Logroño on both sides of the Ebro; and the Rioja Alavesa, formed by the valleys of several tributaries of the Ebro, the Oja, Tirón, Najerilla, Leza and Cidacos; it is a transitional land in which the natural characteristics of the Basque provinces, Castile and Navarre all blend.

In most of the districts in the Rioja winegrowing is extremely important. The area planted to vine in the provinces of Logroño, Álava and Navarre is 203,000 acres, 188,300 solely to vines and the rest mixed cultivation.

The region produces a very wide range of wines, all of them differing in strength, taste and bouquet. This is due to the large number of grape varieties and the proportions in which they are used, which differ from district to district. All of them, however, obviously belong to the same family because of the characteristics they have in common.

In the Upper Rioja the red varieties are the *Tempranillo*, *Mazuela*, *Graciano* and *Garnacha* and the white the *Viura* and *Malvasia*. The red wines, mostly from the *Tempranillo*, are very well-balanced, robust, well built, with a good acidity and a prominent bouquet, well suited for maturing. They run from 10.5° to 12° in strength, according to their origin. The white wines are rather lower in alcohol content; they are dry and have a fair bouquet.

The Lower Rioja is the largest district, stretching from the town of Logroño to Alfaro. The *Garnacha* predominates, and so most of the wines are red. They are very full-bodied with an extremely high alcohol content, ranging from 14° to 16°; they are thick, hardly acid at all and rather sweet. Co-operatives are very common in this region.

The Rioja Alavesa, a long narrow strip north of the Ebro, is protected by the Cantabrian Mountains and, owing to its exposure, gets more sun than the Upper Rioja. The wines are typically very well-balanced, very full-bodied, very heavy and excellent for maturing. Their taste and bouquet have a character all their own, and their average strength may be as high as 14°.

Ageing of the wines is considered of great importance in the Rioja: they must be matured within a carefully delimited zone for a period of at least two years, one year of this in oak casks.

RIOJA is aged in fairly small oak Bordeaux casks (225 litres—about 50 gallons) in underground cellars called *calados*. The must and grapes are carefully selected, since not all the wines are suitable for ageing. With some varieties of grape the colour is not stable enough and the wines therefore do not keep. The *Tempranillo* variety ages best.

The first stage (maturing in Bordeaux casks) should last from two to five years, according to the character of the wine and the type of wine desired. The necessary racking is done during this period and slow oxidation occurs in the cellar, which is kept at a constant and cool temperature. This stabilizes the wine.

The second stage consists in reduction. The wine is bottled and kept for a period that depends on the results of the first stage. This is the stage in ageing during which the aroma begins to develop. The red wines acquire a ruby tint and are quite clear, with an intense and characteristic bouquet.

The Rioja wines most widely sold are usually first-year wines that are shipped by the growers or co-operatives themselves. The wines called *corrientes*, or ordinary light carafe wines, are wines which have been stabilized and bottled during their first year.

Stabilized wines bottled and kept for two years are commonly known as harvest wines or second-year wines, and are white, red or rosé. Wines of a light-red colour (darker than rosés, but lighter than reds) are called Rioja Claretes. These are the wines that generally reach the foreign market and are served in the better Spanish restaurants.

Lastly, wines aged in oak casks before bottling are designated as third, fourth, etc. year wines, or *viejas reservas* (old reserve). They include reds, claretes, dry whites, sweet whites and rosés. Unfortunately some of these lose much of their charm from being over-aged.

Switzerland imports a great deal of Rioja, some 1,430,000 gallons. The U.S. market is promising and the Cuban market is fairly promising but irregular.

THE WINES OF NAVARRE

In the province of Navarre, adjacent to the Rioja, the valley of the Ebro broadens and the river receives as tributaries the Ega, Arga and Aragón. Navarre stretches along the foothills south of the Pyrenees and the region is one of fertile valleys and slopes with a very good exposure, moderately sunny and sheltered from the prevailing winds, two ideal conditions for winegrowing. The wine district comprises roughly the southern half of the province, hence the name guaranteeing the origin. The principal grape variety is the *Garnacha*; the *Tempranillo* is also used, but to a lesser degree, like the *Viura* and the *Malvasia*. The *Moscatel* is used for making dessert wines.

Climatic conditions, which are quite different in northern and southern Navarre, obviously influence the characteristics of the vineyards and consequently the wines. In the north, where the rainfall ranges from 30 to 40 inches, the wines are not as high in alcohol content as in the Ribera district, where the rainfall is 20 inches at most. Both districts produce very tolerable wines, allowing for their special characteristics.

The wines produced on 8,055 acres of vineyards within the province of Navarre and in the communes adjacent to the province of Logroño are entitled to carry the Rioja label.

The winegrowing area producing Navarra wines may be divided into three quite different regions: the Lower Ribera, made up of the area near the Ebro in the south of the province, which produces very strong red wines, sometimes as high as 18°, and very good fortified wines; the district of Valdizarbe, where the wines are not so strong (from 11° to 15°) and more acid than the Ribera wines; and the district of Montaña, whose wines do not sell as well as those from the other two districts. Some of the better Navarre wines are the light wines of Estella, on the banks of the Ega, the reds and claretes of Peralta, Salces and Artajona in the valley of the Arga, the reds of Olite and Tafalla on the banks of the Cidacos and the reds and claretes of Murchante, Cintruénigo and Cascante on the banks of the Ebro. Most of the wines are sold for local consumption, although a proportion is exported each year.

THE WINES OF CARIÑENA

The board of directors in charge of awarding guarantees of origin has recently awarded the label to Cariñena, defining its production area as a fairly small one in the province of Saragossa south of the former capital of Aragon. It is made up of the communes of Aguaron, Alfamén, Almonacid de la Sierra, Alpartir, Cariñena, Cosuenda, Encinacorba, Tosos, Langares, Paniza and Villanueva de Huerva. In this area, whose name

covers the reputedly best regional vineyards, various types of wine are made, very typical of those harvested all over the province of Saragossa.

The traditional grape varieties are the *Cariñena*, *Black Garnacha* and *White Garnacha*, which produce very full-bodied, heavily coloured wines with a high degree of dry extract. The first variety produces wines of a strength ranging from 14° to 17°, seldom less than

13º and sometimes rising to as much as 18º. This is the same as the maximum strength obtained experimentally in the laboratory. The dry extract ranges from 20º to 32º according to the type of wine. The wine is fermented in underground wells and in spite of the advent of co-operatives with their modern techniques some treading still goes on. There are red table wines, dry table *claretes* and various kinds of sweet and fortified dessert wines.

The communes of Alfamén, Alpartir, Almonacid de la Sierra and the lower part of the commune of Sariñena produce wines for blending. The communes of Langares, Cosuenda, Aguaron, Tosos and Villanueva de Huerva produce *corrientes*. The higher parts of these communes and of the communes of Encinacorba and Paniza make wines which, aged by well-tested techniques, display the characteristics of fine table wines: they are very well-balanced, they have an agreeable and delicate flavour and their alcohol content does not run much above 14º.

The whole region produces the classic Aragon *claretes*, which are somewhat like the light-coloured red wines from some other regions. Brilliant in colour, these are highly appreciated table wines; they have a high alcohol content similar to that of the usual red wine. Both the red wines and the *claretes* are very suitable for blending, the reds especially, because of their deeper colour.

THE WINES OF THE EAST COAST

TARRAGONA. The region which produces Tarragona wines, comprising part of the province of that name, is made up of a large number of communes. The most characteristic varieties of grape are the *Cariñena*, *Garnacha* and *Picapoll* for the reds, and the *Macabeo*, *Malvasia*, *Moscatel*, *White Picapoll* and *Pansa* for the whites. Mixed cultivation is sometimes practised.

The TARRAGONA CAMPO wines should be distinguished from the TARRAGONA CLASICO. They are red and white sweet dessert wines, from 2.5º to 7º Beaumé, with an alcohol content ranging from 14º to 23º. The very typical Tarragona vinification process is rapid oxidation of the must at very high temperatures. The cellars are not underground, but very well-aired and subject to abrupt changes in temperature. The wine is stored in glass containers. With the current trend towards dry wines and spirits the sweet TARRAGONA CAMPOS are not as widely seen as they used to be.

PRIORATO. The name of this region derives from the priory of a fifteenth-century Carthusian monastery, the ruins of which are still to be seen. These wines are produced in an enclave within the region covered by the TARRAGONA guaranteed origin label. The region is made up of several communes and the towns of Reus, Valls and La Secuita where the maturing is done. The permitted grapes are the *Cariñena*, the *Garnachas*, the *Macabeo* and the *Pedro Ximénez*.

The Priorato wines make excellent table wines and are good for blending. They have a high alcohol content, from 14º to 18º, while the fortified and aged dessert wines may run as high as 22º.

PANADÉS. The district which produces the Panadés wines, which are good table wines, mostly white—is made up of parts of the provinces of Barcelona and Tarragona. The wines enjoy the guarantee of origin and are derived from the *Macabeo*, *Xerel-lo*, *Parellada*, *Sumoll*, *Merseguera*, *Moscatel*, *Garnacha* and *Malvasia* grape varieties for the whites; the main varieties for the reds are the *Black Sumoll*, *Cariñena*, *Morastrell*, *Black Garnacha* and *Tempranillo*. The first-year wines have a low dry extract, a moderate alcoholic content (10º to 12º in general), but a high acidity, so that they are very suitable for making sparkling wines.

These cellar-bred wines are matured with the greatest biochemical care. The first-year wine is bottled with the yeast and the racking liquor to produce the second fermentation characteristic of wines made by the Champagne method. The bottles are laid flat in underground cellars to enable the added sugar to ferment and produce the carbonic acid gas characteristic of wines of this type, which escapes when the bottle is uncorked. The maturing of the sparkling wine really begins after the second fermentation. The quality of the sparkling Panadés wines has been constantly improved. More and more different varieties of this wine are being produced and the market is continuously expanding.

ALELLA (370 acres). This small district, with two quite different slopes, the larger with a southern exposure towards the sea, the other facing north, is part of the province of Barcelona. It produces delicate table wines, very pale whites, light reds and rosés. The drier wines run to between 11º and 13º. The grape varieties used are the *Pansa*, *Garnacha*, *Picapoll*, *Macabeo* and *Malvasia* for the whites and the *Black Garnacha*, *Tempranillo* and *Sumoll* for the reds.

MALVASIA DE SITGES. This wine comes from a very small district planted solely to the *Malvasia* grape. Sweet, very agreeable to the taste, old gold in colour, it is greatly appreciated as a dessert wine but it has a very small yield.

CONCA DEL BARBARÁ. The winegrowing district of this name is situated in the south of the province of Tarragona below the Priorato; there are some very good table wines similar to those coming from Alella and Panadés. Together with two other East Coast regions, Barcelona and Malvasia de Sitges, Conca del Barbará comes under the official place-name control (denominacion de origen) regulations, a programme for which was established some years ago.

ALICANTE. The Alicante winegrowing district may be divided into two parts. The first, running west from Alicante itself, produces wines for blending and some table wines; the second, in the north-east of the province where the soil varies considerably and the main variety of grape is the *Moscatel*, supplies mostly fortified wines. The deeply coloured red wines, which are used for blending, have an alcohol content between 14° and 18° and their dry extract titrates between 25° and 35° Beaumé. The alcohol content of the *clarete* and red table wines does not exceed 14°, while that of the fortified wines varies between 14° and 17°, with a Beaumé measurement ranging from 7° to 10°.

VALENCIA, UTIEL-REQUENA and CHESTE. These three wines of guaranteed origin are regulated by the Board and are divided into three sections corresponding to the three growing districts.

The Utiel-Requena district is in the west of the province of Valencia. The Cheste district is an enclave in the centre, and the Valencia district proper covers the remainder of the province.

The Utiel-Requena district is the highest-lying and most rugged, and so the reds, *claretes* and rosés have a lower alcohol content (10° to 13°). They are very suitable for ageing owing to their high fixed acidity. Grapes used are the *Bobal*, *Garnacha* and *Crujidera*.

The Cheste wines are made from a wide range of varieties, the *Pedro Ximénez*, *Planta Fina*, *Moscatel*, *Merseguera*, *Macabeo* and *Planta Nova*. All of them are white wines running between 11° and 15°. The wines in the third district, Valencia, are very varied. The grape varieties are the same as for the Cheste wines, with, in addition, the *Malvasia* for the whites and the *Garnacha Tintorera* and *Monastrell* for the reds. This district produces red table wines, fortified and dessert wines and sweet wines named after the grape from which they are derived: *Malvasia*, *Pedro Ximénez* or *Moscatel*. The alcohol content of the dessert wines can be as high as 23°.

THE WINES OF THE CENTRE AND THE SOUTH-EAST

The districts that produce the wines of the central and south-eastern part of Spain are part of the provinces of Ciudad Real (the MANZANARES and VALDEPEÑAS) and Toledo (the NOBLEJAS), which, with the provinces of Cuenca and Albacete, make up La Mancha. Vines take up the greater part of the arable land in this region. The province of Ciudad Real comes first with 645,000 acres, or 23.6 per cent of the cultivated area; then Toledo with 332,450 acres, or 12.8 per cent, followed by Albacete with 247,100 acres (12.9 per cent) and Cuenca with 221,033 acres (12 per cent). The vineyards of these four provinces account for about 35 per cent of the total Spanish winegrowing area. The figures show the vast importance of grape and winegrowing in this part of Castile. Here, as in the Catalan and Andalusian regions, whites predominate, though the few red wines produced are very good.

La Mancha is a broad plain between 1,500 and 2,400 feet above sea-level. The climate is dry and semi-arid, which accounts for the comparatively low yields of the vines. Indeed, La Mancha is a name that has derived from the Moorish word *marzo*, meaning "dry land". The wines from all the communes in La Mancha have certain characteristics in common, due both to identical climatic conditions and to the fact that the processes of vinification used are fairly similar.

Most of the grape varieties are white, like the wines themselves; the *Airen* is by far the most common, the *Pardillo*, *Verdencho*, *Albillo* and *Macabeo* less widely grown. The most characteristic red varieties are the *Cencibel*, with some *Garnacha*. The varieties with the largest yields are the *Airen* among the whites and the *Cencibel* among the reds. In the province of Ciudad Real the average yield is about 6 hundredweight per acre, slightly higher in Cuenca. La Mancha is the main region producing *corrientes*, dry wines with an alcohol content of 11.5^o to 13°, with a moderate degree of fixed acidity. They are used all over Spain as table wines and aperitifs, especially in the capital, Madrid. Most of the La Mancha wines are vinified in *tinajas*, the large vats of baked clay typical of the region. Although more modern vats are to a certain extent taking over from the *tinajas*, the old-fashioned clay pots are still widely used and are generally preferred by the vintners. Each vessel is made by hand and may hold as much as 2,500 gallons of wine.

The most characteristic of the La Mancha wines is the VALDEPEÑAS from the *Cencibel* grape. It is ruby-coloured with fine shadings and up to 14º alcohol content. The wines called ALOQUE, from the same district, are pleasant-tasting *claretes* which are almost rosés. The generic guaranteed origin label MANCHA covers growths from a wide area made up of a large number of communes, the principal being Alcazar de San Juan, Campo de Criptana, San Martin de Valdiglesias, Socuellamos, Ciudad Real, Manzanares, Méntrida, Tarancón, Ocaña, Noblejas, El Bonillo and Villarobledo. To be entitled to the label the wines must be at least two years old and have been matured for at least one year in oak casks. The wines of Manchuela and Almansa, which also are entitled to a guaranteed origin label, deserve a mention here.

By far the majority of the commonest regional white wines are derived from the *Airen* grape. Their alcohol content is 12º to 14º. They are golden, clear, but not very brilliant, and their fixed sulphuric acidity is low (2.40º). They are usually drunk in their first year. The wines made from the *Pardillo* grape at Tarancón and the red wines of Belmonte, the *claretes* of Noblejas and the wines from Yepes, Ocaña and Esquivias are well liked in some parts of the country, especially in the province of Cuenca, and have a strong local following. Excellent local wines are produced in this central region, in the provinces of Toledo and Madrid. Very deep-coloured wines with a high alcohol content and a high dry extract are produced in the districts of Méntrida (province of Toledo) and Navalcarnero (province of Madrid) and in the communes of Arganda and Colmenar. The Méntrida wines are entitled to the guaranteed origin label.

The grape varieties are the Madrid *Red Garnacha* and some *Cencibel* for the reds, and the *Jaen, Torrentes* and *Pardillo* for the whites. The red wines of Arganda, Colmenar and San Martin de Valdeiglesias run to 15º and are slightly astringent, low in acid and usually with a good taste. Some dessert wines are made, notably the MOSCATEL.

The very reputable wines from the province of Avila, north-west of the province of Madrid, may also be included in this region. The *Garnacha* and *Tempranillo* grapes are most used for the reds and mainly the *Jaen, Malvar, Torrentes* and *Verdejo* for the whites. The village of Cebreros produces the best known of the Avila wines, red wines without much colour, almost *claretes* in fact, and white wines with a good taste but little body. Quite agreeable dessert wines are made from the reds. The white table wines are golden in colour, light and generally dry.

THE WINES OF JUMILLA (MURCIA)

The province of Murcia is not part of Andalusia, even though it is in southern, or rather south-eastern, Spain. It produces wines which are highly spoken of, mostly from the *Monastrell* grape, with some from the *Garnacha*. They are entitled to the JUMILLA label. The JUMILLA-MONASTRELL wines range from 14.5º to 18º alcohol content, and this strength is wholly natural, since no alcohol is added during fermentation. There are some other types of wine also entitled to the label, running between 12.8º and 15º, made from grape varieties of which the *Monastrell* accounts for at least 50 per cent. This, of course, tends to promote the growing of this variety, for, even though its yield is small, its quality is excellent. The Board is therefore quite right in keeping the wine under control. The reds and *claretes* from this district are greatly liked in Spain and abroad. They have a high dry extract and their deep, rich red colour reflects the amount of tannin in them. They age very well, though they are very often drunk young as *corrientes*.

THE WINES OF SOUTHERN SPAIN

In the Montilla-Moriles district the first-year wines are rather insipid but are very suitable for maturing, which gives them a remarkable aroma and other fine qualities. They are produced all over the province of Cordoba from the vineyards on the limestone of the Sierra of Montilla and Moriles Altos. Their guaranteed origin labels are MONTILLA ALBERO and MORILES ALBERO. They are matured in a district made up of Montilla, Los Moriles, Aguilar de la Frontera, Lucena, Cabra and Doña Mencia, Puente-Genil and Cordoba.

By far the largest proportion of the wines of the Montilla and Moriles district are made from *Pedro Ximénez* grape; the *Lanren, Baladi, Baladi-Verdejo* and *Moscatel* are also cultivated but in far smaller amounts. The continental climate, the soil and the slopes are very well suited to these varieties. The traditional types of these wines, all of them white, are known as *fino, fino viejo* (or *amontillado*), *oloroso* and

This painting by Velasquez (1595-1660) is entitled the Triumph of Bacchus. A good jug of wine has made these wretched Castilian peasants forget their worst misfortunes and at the culminating point of their joyful drunkenness they render solemn homage to Bacchus and to wine.

oloroso viejo. The first-named has an alcohol content of 16º to 16.5º, the *fino viejo* 17º to 17.5º, the *oloroso* 18º to 19º and the *oloroso viejo* 19º to 21º. Although these wines are blended to match the standard sherry grades no alcohol at all is added, whereas in the sherry vinification process grape alcohol is used to stabilize and fortify the wine. The wines are pale greenish-gold in colour, limpid and transparent, with a very prominent bouquet and a special taste which marks them out from the sherries (q.v.) of the same name. Light and dry, they have a delicate bitter-almond flavour.

MALAGA. Wine has been grown in this district from remote ages. The winegrowing district of 89,000 acres of vineyards covers the whole province, with a definite predominance of the *Moscatel* and the *Pedro Ximénez*. The *Moscatel* makes raisins, the *Pedro*

Ximénez produces sweet and semi-sweet wines, old gold in colour, with an alcohol content of 14º to 23º. This type is known as the LACHRYMA CHRISTI. With their low acidity, Malaga wines are famous throughout the world for their incomparable bouquet and taste.

HUELVA. This province is in western Andalusia and its winegrowing district was once known as the Condado de Niebla (County of Fog). The main winegrowing districts are Niebla, Bollullos del Condado, Paterna, Almonte, Bonares and Moguer. The main varieties are the *Palomino*, *Garrido Fino*, *Mantuo de Sanlucar* and *Listan*. The wines are golden and very fragrant, and they are sweeter in the Moguer district than elsewhere. The wines are something like those of Jerez owing to the similarity of climate, soil and grape, but do not in general have such a delicate flavour.

OTHER WINE DISTRICTS

RIBEIRO. There are three separate winegrowing districts in the Galician province of Orense. The largest is Ribeiro in the western part of the province, west of the town of Orense. The *Treixadura* is most used for the white wines, and to a lesser extent the *Albariño*; the *Garnacha, Caiño* and *Brancellao* for the reds. The alcohol content of the white wines run to 10º to 11º, the reds to 10º to 12º. These sharp, clean, light wines with their slight sparkle are appreciated locally. The red wines are deeply coloured and acid.

VALDEORRAS. The second district is Valdeorras, a region of gently sloping hills where the vine is always planted above 2,500 feet and trellised against cryptogamic diseases. White wines are made from the *White Godello* and the red wines from the *Garnacha, Alicante* and *Mencia*.

MONTERREY. In the third district, the valley of Monterrey, the vines are grown on gentle slopes, not above 2,500 feet. The rainfall is nearly 40 inches and the vine is usually trellised. The grape varieties are the same as in the other districts. The red wines are rather more full-bodied than elsewhere in the province.

ESTREMADURA. In the provinces of Badajoz and Caceres, which make up Estremadura, *corrientes* are produced among which that from Almendralejo is notable. In the Barros district the vineyards cover 20 per cent of the cultivated area. The wines are drunk locally or taken elsewhere to mature. Most of the whites come from the *Unite Jaen*, but the *Airen* is also grown. The *Garnacha* and the *Morisca* are used for the reds. The *Pedro Ximénez, Palomino* and *Macabeo* are grown as table grapes.

The white wines of Almendralejo are light, sweet and golden, not very acid and run to 13º. Those of Villanueva de la Serena are rather more straw-coloured and also rather stronger, about 15º, and are often drunk as aperitifs. The red wines of Guarena are pleasantly fresh and almost purple in colour. Stronger red wines are made in the Salvatierra de los Barros district, and rosés in Fregenal. In the province of Caceres the *Jaen, Cayetana* and *Airen* are used for the whites, and the *Garnacha* and *Negra de Almendralejo* for the reds. Both the reds and whites are of very unequal quality. The best are the whites from Cañamero, the *claretes* from Montehermoso and the reds from Montanchez.

RUEDA and TORO. The Castilian province of Valladolid and the provinces of León and Zamora produce a great deal of *corrientes* and a few wines with some character. In the province of Valladolid the best wines come from Rueda, La Nava, Peñafiel, Cigales and La Seca, in León from La Bañeza and in Zamora from Toro. The *White Verdejo* and the *Red Garnacha* are the main varieties in the Rueda district. The climate is dry, the mean rainfall 16 inches. The alcohol content of the Rueda wines is 13º, sometimes higher; they are straw-coloured and are drunk locally. The white wines of La Seca and Nava del Rey are well spoken of. The *clarete* of Cigales and the wines from Mucientes and Fuensaldaña, which enjoy a deserved reputation, are not quite so strong. Very full-bodied, thick, purple red wines are produced around Peñafiel. Besides these *corrientes* there are some special wines which, when matured and bottled, are much sought after in the domestic market. Light, sharp, slightly acid, pleasant-tasting wines are made from the *Red Mencia* and *Prieto Picudo* grapes in the province of León. Lastly, in the north of the province of Zamora, the district known as Tierra del Vino (Wineland) produces the Toro wines, *corrientes* of good quality which, however, unfortunately do not age.

THE WINES OF JEREZ

The town of Jerez de la Frontera (province of Cadiz), situated in the centre of the district which has given its name to sherry, was founded by the Phoenicians. The name Xera, "a town situated close to the Pillars of Hercules", is found in documents dating from the fourth century B.C. Martial (A.D. 40-104) mentions the wines of Ceret in some of his epigrams. When the Moors occupied Andalusia, they called the town Sherisch, from which comes the English "sherry", the name by which the Jerez wines are generally known. In 1894 the phylloxera destroyed almost all the vineyards, but there were luckily enough vine stocks left to re-establish vineyards with qualities similar to the pre-phylloxera ones.

The wine known as JEREZ or SHERRY, the label of origin being legally protected, is made exclusively from grapes gathered within a restricted area in the north-west of the province of Cadiz comprising the communes of Jerez de la Frontera, Puerto de Santa Maria, Sanlucar de Barrameda, Chiclana, Puerto Real, Chipiona, Rota and Trebujena. The outstanding vineyards are those on the calciferous soils of the communes of Jerez

180

de la Frontera, Puerto de Santa Maria and Sanlucar de Barrameda. These communes, together with the neighbouring communes of Rota and Chipiona, make up the district of Upper Jerez.

GRAPE VARIETIES. The two varieties best suited to sherry-making are the *Palomino* and the *Pedro Ximénez*. The two sub-varieties of the *Palomino*, the *Palomino Fino* and the *Jerez*, are white, and account for more than 70 per cent of the vineyards in the district. The *Palomino* is particularly well suited to the local soil and climate, and its shoots take very well on the stock of the *Berlianderi*, the best American vine for calciferous soil. The *Pedro Ximénez* supplies first-rate 13º to 14º musts, and with enough exposure to sun the grapes can produce wines with an alcohol content running as high as 30º to 32º. When semi-fermented, these musts produce the PEDRO XIMÉNEZ, a natural sweet wine with very special organoleptic characteristics.

The cultivation of the vineyards in all its details is far too vast and specialized a subject to go into here, but it may be noted that throughout the district the vines are treated with as much loving care as a great and stately garden.

HARVESTING and PRESSING. The vintage usually starts in the first two weeks of September, but the date, of course, varies with the weather. The grapes are never gathered until they are fully ripe, for it is only then that they produce the maximum quantity of juice and, as their sugar content is at its height, they give the alcoholic strength desired. The ideal time to begin the vintage is shown by the changes in the grapes' colour from green to a dark tobacco brown and in the stalks, which become woody.

The grapes are picked in stages, since only the fully-ripened bunches are gathered. They are then placed in baskets which hold about 25 pounds each and are transported to the *almijar* with which all large vineyards are equipped.

The *almijar* is a very clean platform of beaten earth on which the bunches of grapes are spread in the sun on woven esparto mats and left for varying periods according to the type of wine to be made. The grape throws off any remaining humidity. At night the grapes are covered with mats to protect them from the dew. This age-old practice causes certain changes in the grape and must which affect the character of the wine. In the first place, the evaporation of the humidity reduces the weight; this brings about a concentration of the juice and consequently gives the must a higher sugar content, an increased total acidity and an increase in the alkaline content of the cinders. It is interesting that despite the increase in overall acidity, part of the malic acid disappears, so that its concentration is halted or even reduced. This should be borne in mind, for this acid affects the wine's aroma and flavour. The grapes are then taken from the *almijar* to the presses. The must is expressed by various methods ranging from the classic grape-treading by men in spiked leather boots to mechanical presses. In every case the juice which exudes naturally from the press before pressure is applied is kept separate from the juice extracted from the mush after pressing. In other words the first juice is expressed by light pressure on the grapes (the weight of the man who treads them, for instance). The presses may either be screw-presses, the oldest and best-known type, or modern variable-pressure machines. The juice from the mush alone will make lower-quality wines, which are generally used for distilling.

Besides exposing the picked grapes to the sun, another very typical process it used from time immemorial in the Jerez de la Frontera district. This is "plastering", which is the addition of gypsum or calcium sulphate to the musts to induce the necessary degree of acidity. There is a great deal of controversy about this method with regard to the way calcium sulphate acts on the musts. They become brighter, fining is speeded up, the colour brightens too, large deposits are formed and the alcohol content rises because of the completer fermentation. The amount of gypsum that is used in this method is about 26 ounces to 32 ounces in an 110-gallon cask. Plastering, however, is subject to strict regulation, since the limits are fixed by law in a number of countries, including Spain itself. But broader limits are tolerated for sherry and other fortified wines. The wine-making equipment and containers are normally sterilized with sulphuric acid (sulphur anhydride or sulphur dioxide) or with potassium bisulphite or liquefied pure SO_2. The purpose of this sterilization is to prevent infection by microbic flora which may damage the musts or wines. Though this method is lethal to micro-organisms if enough sulphur is used, it does not damage the yeasts most suited to vinification.

VINIFICATION AND MATURING. If a wine is to be entitled to bear the label SHERRY with its guarantee of origin, it must undergo a process of maturing and ageing in wood within a district defined by regulation, that is to say, in cellars situated within the communes of Jerez, Puerto de Santa Maria and Sanlucar de Barrameda. It may not be matured in any of the other communes. The maximum permitted production is 700 gallons per acre in the Upper Jerez district and 900 gallons elsewhere. The purpose, of course, is to protect the wine's quality.

Maturing sherry is a delicate affair, for it has to be geared to the musts each year, since owing to the factors set out earlier in this section each vintage produces different musts. The Jerez cellarers are past masters in the art of maturing their wines and are able to co-ordinate the various factors which continually affect it at this stage of its vinification so as to obtain sherries of such uniform and constant quality that they live up to their brand name.

The must obtained by one of the processes described above is drawn off straight into casks holding 30 *arrobas*—about 110 gallons—which are immediately taken to the cellar.

A few hours after treading and pressing, the first fermentation, called "lively fermentation", begins. It is therefore essential to transport the casks as quickly as possible to the cellars (which are usually close to the towns) since too high a temperature may damage the normal proliferation of the yeasts which are to convert the glucose into alcohol. Disease germs may also develop at this stage, reducing the sugar content which, in turn, would reduce the alcohol content and could even produce acetic acid.

The cellars in the Jerez de la Frontera district are not constructed underground, as in the other winegrowing districts. They are long buildings made up of several cellars some twenty feet high, separated by long galleries. The casks are stacked lengthwise one above the other, in several rows, usually three, on either side of the cellars, leaving access corridors down the middle of each cellar. To get as much fresh air as possible and, above all, ensure a stable temperature, the cellars are built some miles from built-up areas, with thick walls and in an open space facing south-west or south, where they catch the sea-breeze. Since a great deal of oxygen is needed in maturing sherry, the cellars have small windows some way up the walls and they are always left open in order to set up a constant draught. The floor of the cellar is of beaten earth and is frequently watered to keep the air fresh and the temperature even. It is covered with small oak squares at places where the casks are rolled or any work is to be done.

Since the climate in this region is temperate in September, there is no need to fear any sudden rise in temperature during the fermentation, which might have a harmful effect on the wine, in particular a reduction in the alcohol content. This danger is further mitigated by the fact that the casks hold so little. Nevertheless, a constant strict watch is kept to prevent any accidents. When the lively fermentation is completed, the cellarer inspects the wine-musts (the local name for musts less than a year old) to see whether they have kept dry; if so, the fermentation is completed. He then waits until January, February, or March at the latest, to start the racking in order to separate the wine-musts from the deposits or lees formed at the bottom of the cask. During the racking he engages in one of the most delicate of the operations which are to determine the future wine: an initial classification of the contents of each cask by its special characteristics, such as delicacy of flavour, aroma and colour. A mark is then placed on the bottom of each cask: one or more *palmas* (stylized palms) if the wine is likely to be fit for *finos*; one or more *rayas* (stripes) if it is fuller-bodied; one or more stripes barred diagonally, whence the name *palo cortado* (cut stick) when it is sweeter and sharper, though still fairly full-bodied. After the classification has been made, the next stage, in March, is fortification, consisting in adding a certain amount of alcohol. The casks are then transferred to the ageing cellar where the real sherry process takes place. This process gives the wine the strength it lacks and raises the alcohol content to 15.5°, or slightly more for the wines of the *rayas* and *olorosos* type.

One of the most interesting things in the making of sherry is the action of certain micro-organisms which live in the wine and feed on its components. They cause chemical reactions which liberate aldehydes and free acids; these determine the aroma and taste peculiar to sherry. They are known as *flor*, or flower. The flor is composed of yeasts which form a very thin film on the top of the wine at the beginning of the second stage in their development, and this film gradually thickens if the temperature and humidity are right. While the flor is forming, the casks are examined frequently to watch the characteristics—consistency, colour and so on—and at the same time to see whether the wine is still in the same class as it was—*palmas*, *rayas* or *palo cortado*—or if its classification has changed. The flor does not act continuously in the maturing of sherry, but only when the temperature and humidity are favourable, i.e. first about April and then in August or September. During these two periods white spots appear on the surface of the wine and spread till they form irregular patches resembling small flowers—hence the name. The patches gradually expand until they form a species of thin white coating which finally attains the thickness and consistency of cream. The chemical and biological transformations of these yeasts which live and grow on the wine combine to make up one of the major characteristics of maturing sherry.

With the type of wine called *finos* (pale dry) of the *amontillados*, the formation and development of the flor is allowed to proceed during the first years of ageing until the wine is bottled. With the *olorosos* (sweet, dark), *paloscortados* (midway between the *finos* and the *amontillados*) and in the final stage of the *amontillados* the development is muted by the addition of a little wine alcohol, which raises their alcoholic content slightly. This and fortifying are the only things added in the course of maturing the wine.

Ageing by the *solera* system works differently. Its purpose is to keep indefinitely a specified type of wine which will always have exactly the same characteristics no matter when it is drunk. Losses either by racking and filtering or from natural causes are made up by adding younger wines. In this method of ageing a number of casks are used, all of them containing wines which may be old or young, but are invariably of the same type and in the same classification while maturing.

In the cellars of Jerez the casks are ranged above each other in three or four rows. The lowest are the casks called *sole*, the row nearest the ground—hence the term *solera*. To avoid confusion, it should be explained that this term is also applied to very old and noble dark wines, since all the dark sherries, whether *finos* (fine), *palidos* (pale) or *añejos* (aged), come from the *sole* casks. Above the row of *sole* casks are ranged two or three rows of casks known as *criaderas* (breeders).

The wines to be marketed are drawn from the *sole* row; they are the oldest. Great care is taken not to draw off more than half the contents of each cask. The *solera* casks are filled up with slightly younger wine from the *criaderas* row. The *criaderas* in turn, are filled up with younger wine from the third row. The number of *criaderas* varies with the types of wine; there are usually more for the *finos* than for the *olorosos* and *amontillados*. In blending care is taken to add a smaller amount of young wine than the amount of old wine left in the cask, so that the older wine may act on the younger, imparting to it its better qualities. The cellarers are very skilled in making these careful blends and in adapting each type of new wine to the wine of previous years and the result is that the oldest casks remain always the same in quality.

The maturing of Manzanilla must be described separately, as it has features of its own. The general process is similar to that we have just described, but in the Sanlucar de Barrameda district the harvest is brought in fairly early, about the first week in September. Exposure to the sun, which raises the alcohol content of the wine-must to 12º-13º, does not take place, nor are the musts for making Manzanilla given the *añada* treatment for more than twelve months. The *solera* and *criadera* casks must never be full; a void corresponding to at least 22 gallons is essential. There should be ten or twelve casks in the *sole* row. Too much wine should not be drawn off in the racking, but it should be racked frequently; four or five cellar jugs (capacity about 20 pints) should be drawn off monthly or even every five days. The alcohol content should not exceed 15.5º while the dry Manzanilla are maturing. If it does, it has to be lowered with young wine; but if it falls below 14.8º, it must be raised by adding wine with a higher alcohol content or an admixture of sherry or alcohol known as *miteado* or *combinado*. The dry Manzanillas become Manzanillas *pasadas* if the process is prolonged, the alcohol content gradually increasing to 17º or 20º. Owing to this high alcohol content, the flor dies, but the wine already has all the qualities to which it owes its great reputation.

When the wines from the *soleras* are drawn, they are clarified to stabilize them and to keep them perfectly clear and bright. This is done with beaten egg-whites, five to twenty per 500-litre (about 110 gallons) cask.

The regulations for the Sherry guarantee require four groups of cellars: vinification cellars, production cellars, maturing and storage cellars, and maturing and shipping cellars. This last group is sub-divided into cellars for shipping to Spain and shipping abroad.

The regulations also prescribe that no cellar to which they apply may sell or export more than 40 per cent at the most of its reserves in hand at the beginning of each crop year. No wine may use the guaranteed origin label unless it is at least three years old. A Board exists to see that the regulations are observed.

Export sales of sherry to the United Kingdom in barrel are by far the largest, with some 6,600,000 gallons, increasing fairly regularly each year (by an average of 374,000 gallons). Annual shipments to Denmark and Sweden are also increasing; they are 550,000 and 330,000 gallons respectively. Sherry exports to the United States have doubled since 1961.

The following general characteristics of sherry should be particularly born in mind:

1. There is no such thing as a vintage sherry, that is a sherry produced from the wine harvested in one particular year. The year of bottling is sometimes seen marked on the cork, but since this does not indicate a "vintage" it is of no special interest.

2. An eighty-year-old sherry does not mean a wine that is eighty years old, but a sherry from a cask first filled eighty years ago. It is possible that traces of the original wine are still present in the sherry but the usual interpretation is that the particular blend has been maintained unchanged for eighty years.

3. The longevity of sherries in the bottle is very hard to determine and depends on the quality. A good quality sherry from a well-reputed house can be kept in the bottle for many years. Since this wine is fortified it travels much better than fine wines and the consumer can buy it when he needs it.

4. The sherry bouquet is produced by the oxidizing effect of certain varieties of yeast that form a film on top of the wine which "blossoms" into flors twice a year. This flor is carefully watched by the cellar masters and the casks are only part-filled to give the air access to it.

MANZANILLA

**MANZANILLA
SHERRY**

"Para conservar el conocimiento,
vete al vino con tiento;
pero, si el vino es de Jerez,
perderás el tiento alguna vez".

Produced and Bottled by

WILLIAMS & HUMBERT

JEREZ and LONDON

PRODUCE OF SPAIN

Registered Trade Mark

RGTO. EMB. No. 206   PRINTED IN SPAIN

MANZANILLA

1. Name of wine; Manzanilla. Manzanilla is a very pale, dry light sherry with a special bouquet and an alcohol content between 15.5º and 17º. – 2. Reminder: Manzanilla comes from the restricted region of Jerez. – 3. Origin. – 4. Grower and shipper's name.

DON ZOILO
(lower left)

1. Trade name "Don Zoilo". – 2. "Very Old Dry Sherry" describes the wine; it has no vintage year, so the shipper has to produce a sherry that will be precisely the same year after year. Actually, the real name is Don Zoilo Dry. – 3. Origin. – 4. Grower and shipper's name. The wine's quality is bound up with the shipper's reputation.

PEDRO DOMECQ

1. Trade name "Primero". – 2. Type of sherry: amontillado. The wine has a more pronounced bouquet and taste than Manzanilla and is older. "Medium Dry Nutty" are details of the wine. This is the most typical sherry; alcohol content ranging from 16º to 18º, old amontillados from 22º to 24º. – 3. Origin. – 4. Grower and shipper's name.

DON ZOILO

VERY OLD

DRY

SHERRY

PRODUCE OF SPAIN

ZOILO RUIZ-MATEOS, S.A.

JEREZ

LIT. HURTADO JEREZ

Pedro Domecq

ESTABLISHED 1730

MACHARNUDO CASTLE PROPERTY OF THE FIRM

Primero

AMONTILLADO SHERRY

MEDIUM DRY NUTTY

PRODUCED AND SHIPPED BY PEDRO DOMECQ

JEREZ DE LA FRONTERA, SPAIN

S.B. 74- 69098

"BROWN BANG" SHERRY
(GOLDEN OLOROSO)

SANDEMAN BROS. & Cº
JEREZ DE LA FRONTERA SPAIN

Sandeman Bros. & Co.

(REGISTERED TRADE MARK)
SANDEMAN
ESTABLISHED IN THE YEAR 1790

BROWN BANG SHERRY

1. Trade name "Brown Bang Sherry". – 2. Oloroso has more body and bouquet than amontillado; this wine is golden; some olorosos may be slightly lighter in colour (tawny). – 3. Origin. – 4. Grower and shipper's name. – 5. This shows that this wine was served to King George VI.

SOLDADO
SELECTED OLD BROWN
SHERRY

Sis justus nec timeas

PRODUCE OF
SPAIN

BODEGAS DE SAN PATRICIO
ESTABLISHED 1780
JEREZ DE LA FRONTERA (SPAIN)

GARVEY

SOLDADO

1. Trade name "Soldado". – 2. "Old Brown" sherry is sometimes called "Raya"; it is dark brown and sweeter than oloroso, stronger, 18º to 20º, but with less bouquet. – 3. Origin. – 4. The shipper mentions the "bodega" where the sherry was matured. – 4. Grower and shipper's name.

PRODUCE OF SPAIN

Gonzalez Byass
Jerez

CREAM SHERRY

EMB 222

DIAMOND JUBILEE
REGISTERED TRADE MARK
CREAM

DIAMOND JUBILEE

1. Trade name "Diamond Jubilee". – 2. This sherry of the "cream" type is sweet, with a very strong flavour and great vigour. – 3. General origin. – 4. Grower and shipper's name. This name should not be confused with the name of the sherry; this is not quite clear from the label.

TYPES OF SHERRY

FINOS. Drier, less full-bodied and not so strong as the *olorosos*. There are two types.

– the *finos* proper, straw-coloured, pale, with a sharp and delicate aroma, which may be compared to that of almonds; they are light, dry and not very acid; the alcohol content is between 15.5° and 17°.

– the *amontillados*, amber-coloured, very dry, with less bite, soft and full in flavour, nutty; alcohol content 16° to 18°.

OLOROSOS. Darker, heavier and stronger than the *finos*. There are several types:

– the *rayas* are lower-class *olorosos*, old gold in colour, fuller-bodied and less delicate in aroma. They sometimes taste somewhat sugary, possibly because fermentation was not completed; strength 18° and over.

– the *olorosos* proper, dry, dark golden, with great aroma, though less bite than the *finos*. Their delicate taste may be compared to that of the walnut. They are called *amorosos* when they are sugary and rather fuller-flavoured. The alcohol content is the same as the above.

– the *paloscortados*, midway between the *amontillados* and *olorosos* proper; they may be called the higher-class *oloroso* type. They have the aroma of *amontillados* and the flavour of *olorosos*; colour and alcohol content similar to the latter.

– the "creams", rather sweet, with the body of *olorosos*. A judicious blend of dry *olorosos* with some PEDRO XIMÉNEZ. The blends are matured in *soleras* before they are sold.

DULCES. These are deep-coloured sweet wines from various grape varieties:

– PEDRO XIMÉNEZ is a natural sweet wine, its sweetness due to the exposure to the sun of *Pedro Ximénez* grapes after they are picked in order to obtain a must at nearly 30° Beaumé which is subjected to partial fermentation. In some cases, the grapes intended for this type of wine are exposed for as long as twenty days, so that complete fermentation is not possible. The wine is dark, with an alcohol content between 10° and 15°.

– MOSCATEL, a natural sweet wine from grapes of this variety, between 10° and 20° Beaumé.

MANZANILLA. A dry wine produced in the Sanlucar de Barrameda district. It comes under the Sherry Regulation Board, but has a different label from SHERRY. The two types of MANZANILLA come from the same district and the same variety of grape. The difference begins at the maturing stage. MANZANILLAS must by law be matured in cellars at Sanlucar de Barrameda. MANZANILLA is a delicate, light, very pale and very aromatic, dry and only slightly acid wine with a slightly bitter taste and an alcohol content between 15.5° and 17°. There are two types: MANZANILLA FINA is smooth and slightly bitter and does not age; MANZANILLA PASADA acquires a special taste by ageing and has a more prominent aroma, somewhat like that of the *olorosos*, but the taste is dry and has the characteristics of MANZANILLA FINA.

The sherries that are produced in California or in the South African Republic are wines produced in the same way as those of the Jerez region. But the differences in soil and climate give wines of the sherry type, wines that are analogous but not identical to the original sherries. To taste and compare for oneself is the only means by which one can form a judgement on this subject. The same comparison can be made between the true Champagne vinified in France and the innumerable sparkling wines that sometimes carry the name of Champagne.

Sherry is believed to have been introduced into what is now the United States of America by the Spanish explorer Álvaro Núñez who discovered Florida in 1528 and who came from a long line of vintners and cellar owners in Jerez. Something is even known of the price of sherry in Spain during those epic days of discovery since there is an account of a certain gentleman paying sixteen golden pesos (8 ½ dollars, 70 shillings) for a *botija* or jar of wine.

In conclusion let us move forward a few years to Shakespeare's time and repeat what he had to say in Henry IV Part 2 about the "sherris" drunk in England in the sixteenth and seventeenth centuries: "A good sherries-sack hath a twofold operation in it. It ascends me into the brain; dries me there all the foolish and dull and crudy vapours which environ it; makes it apprehensive, quick, forgetive, full of nimble, fiery and delectable shapes; which delivered o'er to the voice,—the tongue,—which is the birth, becomes excellent wit. The second property of your excellent sherries is,—the warming of the blood; which, before cold and settled, left the liver white and pale, which is the badge of pusillanimity and cowardice; but the sherries warms it and makes it course from the inwards to the parts extreme; it illumineth the face; which, as a beacon, gives warning to all the rest of this little kingdom, man, to arm: and then the vital commoners and inland petty spirits muster me all to their captain, the heart, who great and puffed up with this retinue, doth any deed of courage; and this valour comes of sherries...."

(Act IV, Scene III)

WINES OF SPAIN

NORTH-WESTERN SPAIN

RIBEIRO

Dry white wines	Pazo	Albariño

NORTHERN SPAIN

RIOJA

Dry red wines	Banda Azul	Castillo Ygay	Royal	Viña Tondonia
	Banda Roja	Imperial	Viña Monty	Viña Vial
	Bordon	Marques Riscal	Viña Pomal	Viña Zaco
	Castillo de las Arenas	Reserva Yago	Viña Real	
Dry white wines	Castillo Ygay Reserva	Marques Riscal	Rinsol	Viña Sole
	Corona	Monopole	Viña Paceta	Viña Tondonia
	Etiqueta Blanca			
Medium-sweet white wines . .	Diamante	Monte-Haro	Viña Zaconia	
Dry rosé wines	Brillante	Castillo de las Arenas		

RIOJA ALTA

Red wines	El Siglo	Monte Real	Viña Ardanza	Viña del Perdon
	Glorioso reserva	Viña Albina Vieja reserva	Viña Ercoyen	
White wines	Canchales	Metropol		
Rosé wines	Viña Ercoyen			

NAVARRE

Red wine	Castillo de Tiebas

CARIÑENA

Dry red wine	Cariñena

EASTERN SPAIN

ALELLA

Dry red wine	Marfil	
Sweet red wine	Lacre Violeta	
Dry white wines	Lacre Gualda	Marfil	Super Marfil reserva
Red wines	Oro Viejo	Zumilla	
Dry rosé wine	Marfil	

PRIORATO

Dry red wines	Falset Garnacha Priorato	High Priorato	Priorato Reserva especial
Sweet red wines	Priorato extra Rancio Solera 1918		Vicosa Generoso Priorato

PANADÉS

Sweet white wines	Malvasia	Moscatel
Red wine	Sumoll	

TARRAGONA

Dry red wines	Spanish Red Wine 1955	Viña Vinlo
Red wines	Aureo	Tarragona-Tawny
Dry white wines	Dry Grand Solera	

JUMILLA

Dry red wine	Solera
White wine	Oro Viejo Solera 1902

CENTRAL SPAIN

NOBLEJAS

Red wine	Noblejas	
White wine	Ocaña	Yepes

VALDEPEÑAS

Red wines	Cencibel (Tinto fino)	Garnacha	Tinto Basto
Dry white wines	Airen (Lairén)	Cirial	Pardillo

SOUTHERN SPAIN

MORILES-MONTILLA

Dry wines	*Amontillado*	Alvear Montilla	
	Amontillado pasado . .	Flor de Montilla	
	Fino	Moriles extra san Joaquin	Los Palcos
	Moriles	Seneca	Tercia
	Oloroso	Oloroso Alvear	
	Oloroso viejo	Diogenes	
	Blanco seco	Solera 1906	

MALAGA

Sweet wines	*Moscatel*	Moscatel Delicioso
	Moscatel dorado	Cariño
	Extra viejo	Pedro Ximenez FP
	Lágrima selecte	Los Frailes
	Dulce	Lacrimae Christi
	Dulce añejo	Malaga
Medium-sweet wine	*Vieja solera*	Pajarete 1908

Manzanillas	Aris	Eva	La Piconera	Pochola
	Atalaya	Fina	Macarena	Rayito
	Bertola	Garbosa	Mari-Paz	Rechi
	Bone Dry	Gloria	Merito	Regina
	Caricia	Greta	Montana	Sirena
	Carmelita	Hilda	Olorosa Angelita	Solear
	Carmen	La Ballena	Osborne	Torre Breva
	Carola	La Capitana	Papirusa	Varela
	Clasica	La Especial	Pemartin	Villamarta
	Cochero	La Goya	Petenera	Viva la Pepa
	Deliciosa	La Jaca Andaluza	Piedra	Wisdom & Warter
	Duff Gordon	La Lidia		

Finos	Agustinito	Deportivo	Jardin	Pedro Dry
	Alvaro	Don Algar	La Ina	Pemartin
	Apitiv	Don Zoïlo « Dry »	La Condesa	Pinta
	Banquete	Ducal	La Panesa	Preferido
	Barbadillo	Eco	Loredo	Quinta
	Benito	El Catador	Los Compadres	Quisquilla
	Bergantin	Faena	Mantecoso	Redoble
	Betis	Fajardo	Marinero	Rivero
	Bombita	Feria Sherry	Marismeño	Sancho
	Camborio	Finito	Matador Pale Dry	San Patricio
	Campero	Fino F.M.	Menesteo	Tio Mateo
	Canto	Flamenco	Merito	Tio Pepe
	Casanovas	Gaditano	Micalet	Tres Palmas
	Clarita	Hernan Cortés	Olivar	Varela
	Chiquilla	Hidalgo	Palma	Victoria
	Coronel	Inocente	Pando	Viña del Carmen
	Cuesta Alta	Jarana	Pavon	Viña del Cuco

Amontillados	Abolengo	Dry Pale	John Peter	Principe
	Algar	El Botanico	King Alfonso	Rosa
	Amontillado 50	El Cid	La Capilla	Salinera
	Amontillado S.S.S.	El Duque	La Uvita	Salvador
	Anticuario	El Gallo	Lord Sherry	Sancho
	Ataulfo	El Navio	Luque	Santa Cruz
	Barbadillo	El Tresillo	Martial	Siglo de Oro
	Baroness Cocktail	Escogido	Matador	Solito
	Benito	Escuadrilla	Merito	Tio Diego
	Botaina	Fairyland	Millonario	Tio Guillermo
	Buleria	Finest	Miranda	Tito Jaime
	Carta Blanca	Fino Ideal	Nila	Tocayo
	Carta Real	Fino Zuleta	N.P.U.	Tulita
	Casanovas	Florido	Old Dry Classic	Ultra
	Chambergo	Guadalupe	Oñana	Varela
	Club	Guapito	Pemartin	Viejo M.M.M.
	Coquinero	Guerrero	Pizarro	Viña AB
	Del Abuelo	Imperial	Predilecto	Viño del Virrey
	Diestro	Jauna	Primero	Vintners Choice
	Dry Don			

Olorosos	Alfonso	Cacique	Don Quijote	España
	Almirante	Capitan	Don Zoïlo « Medium »	Fandango
	Autumn Leaves	Cartujo	Doña Juana	Favorito
	A Winter's Tale	Casanovas	Double Century	Fenecio
	Bailen	Chambelan	Dry Sack	Galarza
	Barbadillo	Diestro	D.S.	Gran Señor
	B.C. 200	Dique	Duque	Harmony
	Black Tom	Don Gonzalo	El Cesar	La Espuela
	Blazquez	Don Nuño	El Patio	La Infanta

	La Merced	Molino	Regio	Solera P.J.
	La Novia	Montado	Rio Viejo	Solera Tizon
	La Raza	Navigator	Royal Double	Solera Victoria Regina
	Long Life	Nina	Sancho	Tercios
	Los Flamencos	Nº 10 R.F.	Solariego 1807	Torrecera
	Martial Golden	Nº 28	Solera E	Trafalgar Solera 1805
	Mayoral	Nutty Solera	Solera Florido	Valdespino
	Medium Golden	Ochavico	Solera Granada	Varela
	Mercedes	Orrantia	Solera 1842	Viña Isabel
	Merito	Pemartin	Solera 1865	Wisdom's Choice
	1874	Real	Solera Misa V.O.B.S.	Zuleta

Palos cortados	Deportivo	Don José	Ojo de Gallo	Superior
	Diestro	Eva	Romate	Tres Cortados

Pedro Ximenez	Bobadilla	El Abuelo	Niños	Solera 1847 (Brown)
	Cardenal Cisneros	Gonzalez	Osborne	Solera Superior
	Carla	La Goleta	Pemartin	Superior
	Cartago (Brown)	Legionario	Procer	Superior
	Cob-Nut (Brown)	Martial (Brown)	Reliquia	Valderrama
	Consejero	Matador (Brown)	Romate	Venerable
	Diestro	M.G.L.	Royal (Brown)	Vintners (Brown)
	Diestro (Brown)	1827	Soldado (Brown)	Wisdom
	Ducha	1870		

Moscatel	Ambrosia	Evora	Padre Lerchundi	San Pedro
	Atlantida	Fruta	Payaso	Tambora
	Baron	Gran Fruta	Pico Plata	Toneles
	Duquesa	Laura	Polca	Triunfo
	Evangelio	1870	Promesa	Vitoria

Creams	Abraham	Dalgar	Harmony	Real Tesoro
	Armada	Descarado	Infanta	Reverencia
	Benito	Diamond Jubilee	Laurel	Romate
	Bertola Cream	Diestro	Luque	Royal
	Blazquez	Don Zoïlo « Cream »	Matador Cream	Sancho
	Carlton House	El Monasterio	Meloso	San Rafael
	Carmela	El Tutor	Merito	Sherry Joselito
	Casanovas	Eva	Nectar	The Dome
	Celebration	Felicita	Orleans 1886	To-Night
	Coronation	Flor de Jerez	Osborne	Varela
	Cream 201	Gentileza	Palomino	Vintners
	Cream Sherry	Grape Cream	Pemartin	Wisdom's Cream
	Cristina			

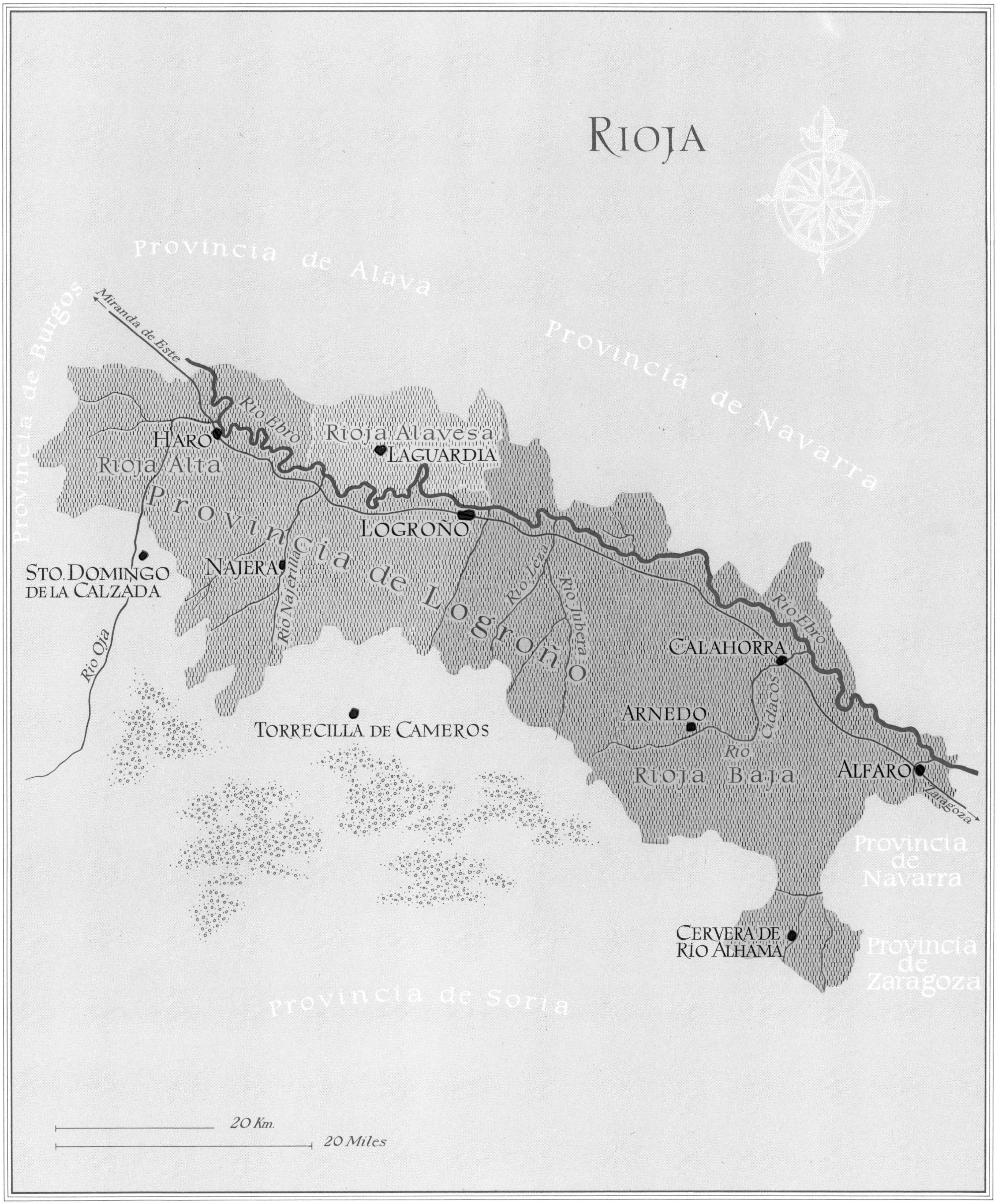

RIOJA

Provincia de Alava

Provincia de Burgos

Provincia de Navarra

Miranda de Este

Río Ebro

HARO

Rioja Alta

Rioja Alavesa

LAGUARDIA

Provincia de Logroño

LOGROÑO

STO. DOMINGO
DE LA CALZADA

NAJERA

Río Najerilla

Río Leza

Río Iregua

Río Oja

Río Ebro

CALAHORRA

Río Cidacos

ARNEDO

TORRECILLA DE CAMEROS

Río

Rioja Baja

ALFARO

Zaragoza

Provincia
de
Navarra

CERVERA DE
RÍO ALHAMA

Provincia
de
Zaragoza

Provincia de Soria

20 Km.

20 Miles

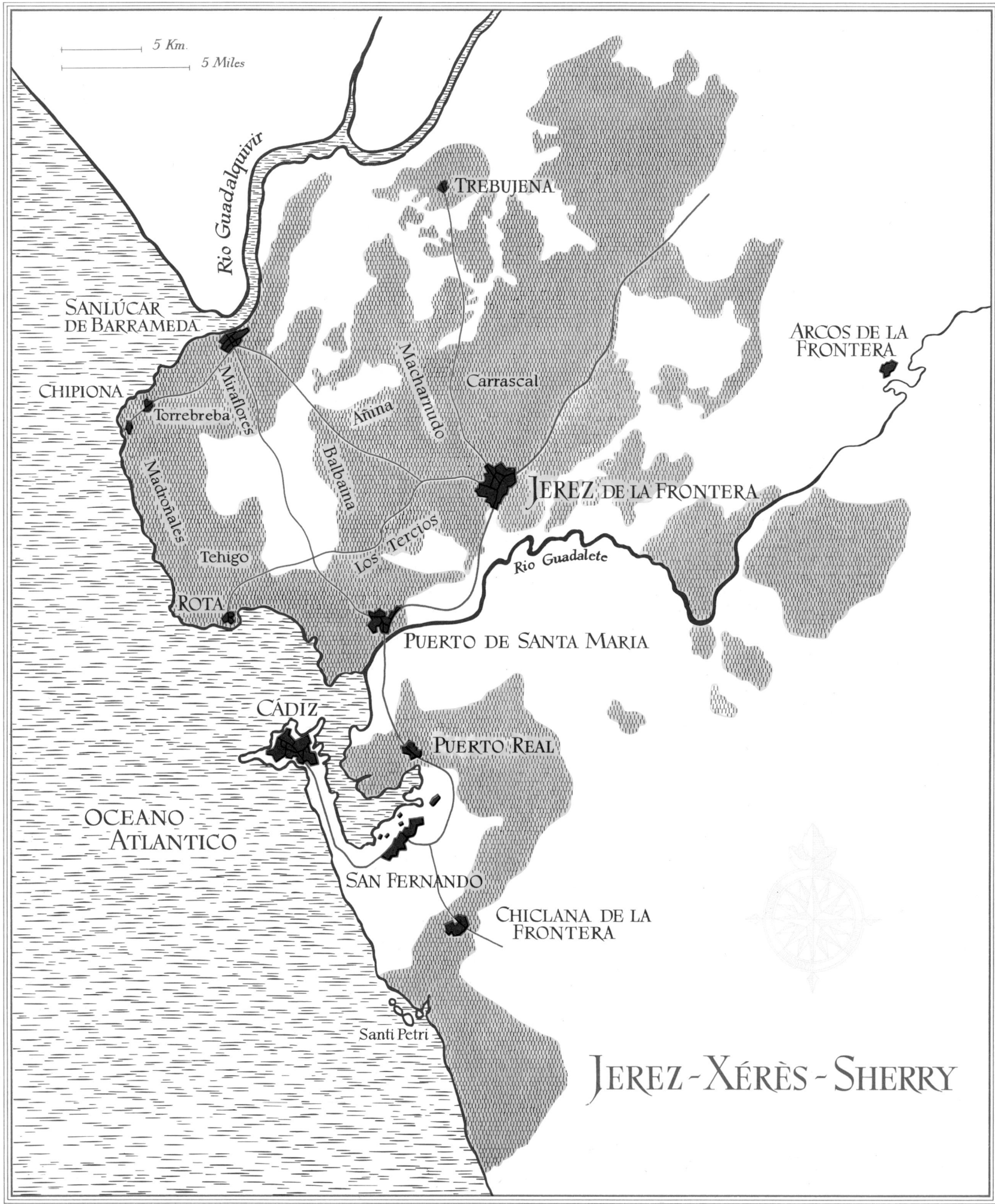

5 Km.

5 Miles

Rio Guadalquivir

TREBUJENA

SANLÚCAR
DE BARRAMEDA

ARCOS DE LA
FRONTERA

CHIPIONA

Miraflores

Carrascal

Torrebreba

Añina

Machamudo

JEREZ DE LA FRONTERA

Balbaina

Madroñales

Los Tercios

Tehigo

Rio Guadalete

ROTA

PUERTO DE SANTA MARIA

CÁDIZ

PUERTO REAL

OCEANO
ATLANTICO

SAN FERNANDO

CHICLANA DE LA
FRONTERA

Santi Petri

JEREZ·XÉRÈS·SHERRY

THE WINES
OF PORTUGAL

SUZANNE CHANTAL DOS SANTOS

Although in world ranking Portugal stands in only sixth position for the total quantity of wine produced annually—behind Italy, France, Spain, the U.S.S.R. and Argentina—she is in fact the world's number one producer when one relates the density of production to the total area of land (metropolitan and insular) under cultivation. The Portuguese is a great drinker of wine, with an average annual consumption of 25 gallons per head. Despite this, he remains a sober citizen, for he has always known how to drink his wine; also, although flavoursome, it has a low alcohol content and it is as rare to see any drunkenness in the countryside as it is in the towns.

Portugal is a country conditioned by the extreme changeableness of its sky and by the great geological variety of its soils. This diversity is reflected in the some 330,000,000 gallons of wine that she drinks or exports each year. The country is very much under the influence of the great ocean winds, which favour a climate not unduly dry, except in the plains south of the river Tagus where, in any case, wheat is grown and not vines. Blessed with sunshine, the climate favours viticulture quite outstandingly. One can find traces of the vine in the very earliest history of the land: for example, on the sarcophagus of Reguengos, dating from two thousand years ago, can be seen the detailed figures of men treading the grape. Much has been said and written on the subject of who first introduced the vine-plant into Portugal, one argument being that it came from Gaul with the Romans, another that it was brought by the Greeks and Phoenicians who, from

earliest times, had navigated along the shores of Portugal and had eventually established trading here.

This Lusitania of Roman times was famous for its oil and its wines, since its olive-groves and vineyards made excellent neighbours. So much so that Rome became alarmed at the popularity of the wines, which were competing seriously with those of Italy. The Emperor Domitian decreed severe laws forbidding the cultivation of the vine in the provinces under Roman occupation, often even going as far as having it uprooted and replaced by cereal crops. The vine nevertheless survived this treatment, while both the Barbarians, who drank beer, and the Moors, who tolerantly would allow local customs to be continued in the territories they dominated, left it to prosper and develop. At the time of modern Portugal's birth, in the twelfth century, when young Afonso Henriques was recruiting troops for the Crusades to the Holy Land—as well as to chase the occupying Arab armies out of his future kingdom—we find one of these knight-errants making a prophetic statement: Arnulfo, an Englishman, in a letter which has come down to us, praised highly the merits of the wine from Douro. It was a precursor of what was to be seen, centuries later, as a root of one of the oldest alliances in the world, that of the Portuguese, who make the wine, and the English, who like to drink it. When Afonso Henriques captured Lisbon in 1147, vine-plants were found under the defensive walls of the future capital. As the young kingdom became more populated, the monks planted vineyards in the vast domains which were entrusted to them; and this not merely to

193

obtain their altar wine. The wonderful illustrations of the Apocalypse by Lorvao show the wine harvest and the grape-presses. The Burgundian dynasty, also, was so conscious of the richness that viticulture represented for this country which it dominated for more than two centuries that a decree by Sancho I, at the beginning of the thirteenth century, prescribed that "whomsoever shall destroy with premeditation a vine-plant shall be brought in judgement as it were for the death of a man".

One of the earliest and the most successful commercial exchanges between Portugal and the northern countries of Europe (England, Germany and The Netherlands) was with wine, which was shipped from Viana do Castelo. The cultivation of the vine, in which the Portuguese excel both by nature and by taste, then took on a new importance. The vineyards spread to the banks of the rivers and into the harshest regions: the sea-shore sands of Colares as well as the rocky ravines of Douro. But of course the day came when wine was over-produced at the expense of its quality, and viticulture, far from nourishing people in Portugal, almost condemned them to die of hunger. Strict measures had again to be taken, as in the days of Rome: wine production was limited, and thousands of inferior-quality vine-stocks were uprooted, to be replaced by more useful crops. In fact, all through its history, the Portuguese vineyard has known a series of crises and successes, and one of the constant factors of its evolution has been the anxiety of the authorities to safeguard the quality of the wine used for export. Divergent claims have been made as to whether this policy has been to the detriment or to the benefit of the wines or vineyards considered of secondary importance, since in this sector conditions of production are up to the local growers and there is no outside control.

World events have also had a marked influence on Portuguese viticulture. The sixteenth century seemed almost to be dedicated to the desertion and neglect of the vineyards, as all the fever and ambition of the Portuguese adventurers and explorers was diverted overseas to the newly-discovered foreign lands. Within a very few years, the vines were taken over by heaths and waste-lands. After the wars with Louis XIV of France, England prohibited the importation of the wines of Aquitania and signed, in 1703, the Treaty of Methuen with Portugal which guaranteed a vital exchange—that of a monopoly in Portuguese wines for one in English wools. The wine trade picked up

again: from 632 casks (of about 120 gallons each) exported in 1687, it rose spectacularly to 17,000 casks in 1757. England drank mostly the wines from Douro, and a large number of English wine merchants moved to the Continent and established themselves at Porto, where they could buy the standing harvests and closely supervise the shipment of the casks. From the very special conditions of this collaboration was to be born the most famous of Portuguese wines: port.

Although the nineteenth century saw improvements in cultivation and in the processes of vinification, successive disasters descended on the unfortunate Portuguese vineyards. In 1832, during the fratricidal warring between the rival kings Pedro and Miguel, Pedro landed in Porto and drew the chaos and horrors of battle into that region. Crops were neglected or pillaged, the winemaking plant in Porto set afire and the wine stocks destroyed.

In 1846, an insidious illness appeared: oïdium. It was necessary to clean out the vineyards, replacing most of the plants with new stock. Then twenty years later came another catastrophe, which was at first attributed to abnormally hot and dry summers and cold and humid winters. Vinegrowers wore themselves out in ineffectual and unorganized battle until it was discovered that this was an epidemic caused by an insect then unknown in Europe: phylloxera. Many growers gave up, discouraged by the terrifying devastation it had wrought. But others persevered, imported American plants to restock and by dint of years of courage, patience and hard work gradually rebuilt the kingdom's vineyards.

Today, vineyards account for more than 10 per cent of the total agricultural area under cultivation (excepting forestry regions) in Portugal; and the vine, which by its very nature is already diversified, has become even more so under the local methods of cultivation and vinification. But this suits the Portuguese agricultural system, parcelled out as it is into small-holdings, dependant on the family unit, where everyone likes to grow the wheat, rye or maize for his bread, the olives for his oil and the grapes for his wine. This means that many winegrowers drink their own wine—which does not therefore appear in any official production statistics—and have an annual production which is too small to be marketable. Under present conditions, the majority of winegrowers belong to co-operatives, working under the direction and supervision, and also with the assistance, of special organizations.

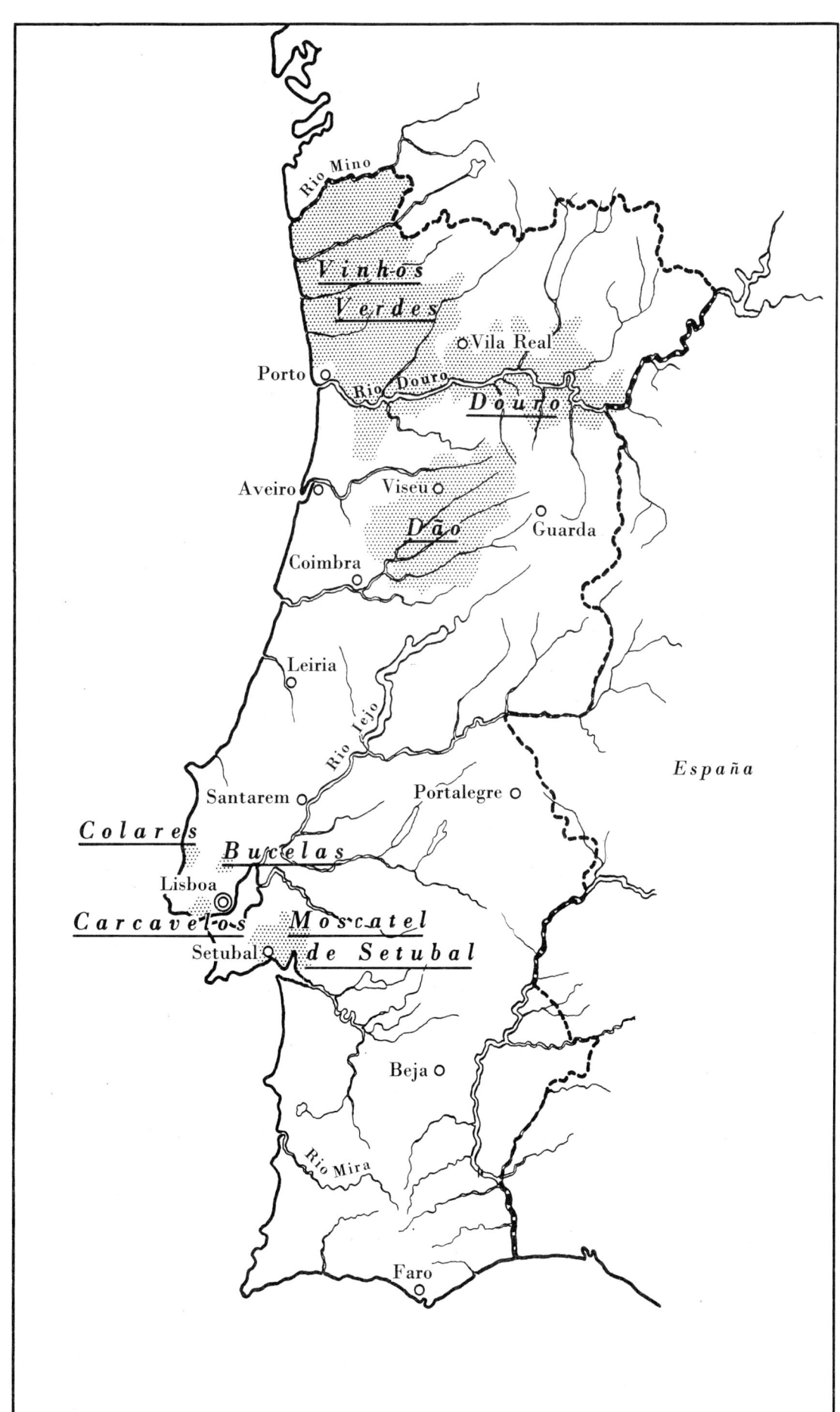

The great majority of the Portuguese vineyards lie to the north of Lisbon. The most important are those of the Upper Douro region, home of the celebrated port wine. Those of the Minho region produce the *vinhos verdes* ("green wines"); then come the vineyards of Dão, Colares and Bucelas. South of the capital, only the vineyards in the region of Setúbal are of any size.

COCKBURN'S
REGISTERED TRADE MARK

PORT
"Vintage Character"

ESTABLISHED 1815

SHIPPED BY
COCKBURN SMITHES & CO LTD
OPORTO

PRODUCE OF PORTUGAL

QUINTA DO NOVAL
1963
VINTAGE PORT

This wine has been produced on the **150**th anniversary
of the Shipper ANTÓNIO JOSÉ DA SILVA
VINHOS, S. A. R. L.
VILA NOVA DE GAIA – PORTUGAL
and bottled in 1965, **250** years after the first known
records of the Quinta do Noval - **1715**

VINTAGE PORT
1. Type of port: "Vintage Port". This is a good red port, from the best growth of a good year. Free of any blending additive, it has been bottled after 2-3 years in the wood. Caution! It is probably necessary to decant it. – 2. Date of vintage. This mention is obligatory for every true vintage port. – 3. This mention indicates the vineyard of origin. – 4. Name of the merchant-producer. – 5. This port was bottled in 1965.

PORT: VINTAGE CHARACTER
1. Name of the wine: "Port". This generic term seems to suffice. – 2. The mention "Port" is here amplified by the expression "Vintage Character". This means that although not vintage nor free from any blending, this port wine has been treated in the manner of a vintage port, i.e. bottled after a few years in the wood and sold while still fairly young. One can therefore expect a good red semi-sweet port. – 3. Name of origin. There is no exact or obligatory formula. – 4. Name of the merchant. The connoisseur will give his preference to a particular firm, or to a particular port from a particular firm and another port from another firm. In this realm, there is nothing to beat experience.

ROYAL OPORTO WINE C.º
FOUNDED BY ROYAL CHARTER IN 1756

WHITE PORT
EXTRA
(DRY)
PRODUCT OF THE ALTO DOURO

REAL COMPANHIA VELHA

COMPANHIA GERAL DA AGRICULTURA DAS VINHAS DO ALTO DOURO
V. N. DE GAIA – PORTUGAL

O VINHO DO PORTO É UM VINHO NATURAL, SUJEITO A CRIAR DEPÓSITO COM A IDADE
RECOMENDA-SE QUE SEJA SERVIDO COM O CUIDADO INDISPENSÁVEL PARA NÃO TURVAR.

WHITE PORT
1. Name of the wine: "White Port". Here again, this mention seems sufficient, particularly as it will be appraised in relation to the name of the merchant. – 2. The mention "extra dry" draws attention to the fact that this white port is very dry; it is in fact an aperitif wine. – 3. Another version of the name of origin. – 4. Name of the merchant. The Real Companhia Velha was, from 1756 onwards, behind the origin of the regulations for port wine.

2
1
3
2a
4

SIBIO

1. Trade name: "Sibio". – 2. 2a. This name is amplified: dôce = sweet; tinto = deep red; tipo vintage = vintage type (in other words, not aged in the wood). This is therefore a young port, deep-red coloured, with violet reflections. – 3. Name of origin. – 4. Name of the merchant.

EL-REI D. JOSÉ

1. Trade name: "El-Rei D. José". – 2. "Alourado" gives the colour (tawny in English). This type of port will be 15-20 years old. Meio dôce = semi-sweet, this is therefore a dessert wine. – 3. Name of origin. – 4. Name of the merchant.

PARTNERS' PORT

1. Trade name: "Partners' Port". – 2. In the mention "Finest rich ruby", the word ruby holds the attention and indicates not only its colour but also its age of the wine. "Ruby" also indicates that this port has a beautiful red colour, with reflections as in a precious stone, and an age of 10-15 years. – 3. Name of origin. – 4. Name of the merchant. The connoisseur will appraise the label as a whole when judging the quality of a port, since the name of the merchant cannot be dissociated from the trade name.

1
2
4/3
4

4
4
1
2/3

THE GREAT WINEGROWING REGIONS OF PORTUGAL

Certain regions have types of wines with such clear-cut characteristics that their zone of cultivation has been legally, and severely, delimited; by the same token, this has given them the right to an *appellation contrôlée*. This is the case with eight of the fourteen great wineproducing regions of Portugal: Bucelas, Carcavelos, Colares, Dão, Douro, Entre-Douro-e-Minho, Madeira and Setúbal.

WINES OF DÃO: Dão is a green and fertile region, both thickly wooded and intensely cultivated, which rises in tiers from the foothills of the two mountainous "spines" of Portugal: the Serra d'Estrela and the Caramulo. The farmer of these parts is stubborn, vigorous, resistant; his wine tends to resemble him, being strong and full-bodied. It ages well, possesses a good and velvety aroma and a deep colour that seems to come from the rolling landscapes with their low-toned tints, pines, purple heather and rocky outcrops.

This wine, long cultivated as a family affair and pressed in the open-air, is rightly considered to be Portugal's best table wine. Several varieties exist, as a result of the great diversity of soils (where sometimes shale is mixed with granite) and of the vineyards' varying exposures to the sun. One can find the vine-plant at an altitude of more than 1,600 feet on the heights of Tarouca and Castro Daire, or tumbling along the banks of the Mondego (SANTA COMBA, TABOA, MORTAGUA) and on to the plain (MANGUALDE, VISEU). All these wines are therefore quite distinct, although at the same time related through a common stock: *Tourigo*, a vine which provides a high sugar content and a slightly astringent taste. By mixing red grapes and white grapes, a naturally oily, sweet wine is obtained. The red wines, although having a low alcohol content, are full-bodied, with beautiful deep-ruby reflections, while the whites are light, fresh, clear and very perfumed. In 1966, the area of the vineyard was 46,386 acres, producing 19,712,000 gallons.

WINES OF COLARES: It is really astonishing to see, between Cintra and the coast, within almost a stone's throw of Lisbon, the vine being cultivated along the sea-shore and on sandy lands now left high-and-dry by a retreating sea, particularly in the silted-up estuary of the old river Galamares. Yet the vineyards of Colares are among the very oldest in Portugal. Stretching to the south of Cabo da Roca, the westernmost point of the European continent, through the regions of Turcifal and Fontanelas and right on to Azenhas do Mar, they have the noteworthy distinction of having survived the terrible phylloxera epidemic, simply because this insect was not able to live in the sand.

The cultivation of these vineyards is extremely difficult and sometimes even dangerous, for the first step entails digging trenches five to ten yards deep in light, running soil in order to get down to the more solid clay layers where the vine-plants can take root. Each plant spreads its roots sideways along the trenches, which are gradually filled in as new shoots appear. The vinegrower carefully layers his stock, enabling each layered shoot, once covered over, to become the basis of still more new shoots. But the extraordinary intricacy of the procedure in encouraging these last shoots means that, in reality, they are still part of the original vine-plant. Sometimes whole rows of vine-plants are thus made up of one solitary vine-plant at the bottom of the original trench, while up above ground, sheltered by heather or leafy screens and cut back very hard to stand up against the strong Atlantic winds, the vines twist and stretch on their way like strange muscular serpents.

With the arrival of summer, the bunches of grapes must be propped up so that they are not dried by the burning sand. The harvest is brief but picturesque and even in these times it is often carried on the backs of donkeys. In present days, too, a local *adega* weighs the grapes on the spot, and they are treated at once. Periods of rest in the cask before and after the press enriches the must in tannin and colouring matter. COLARES wine must be kept in the cask for two years, and attains its best form from the age of five years onwards. The site of the vineyard, the influence of the sea fogs and winds and of course more particularly the *Ramisco* (vine-plant of the sands) all give COLARES a special flavour, full-bodied yet velvety. Even the red wine is extremely light because of its low alcohol content, while the white is highly perfumed. The production of this unusual wine is very small: only 88,000 gallons for a vineyard of 620 acres which, alas, is getting ever smaller as amenities for tourists gradually invade the Lisbon Peninsula.

WINES OF CARCAVELOS: The Carcavelos region is composed of alluvial deposits on the banks of the Tagus estuary, a soil much less dry and sandy than that of the Colares and producing a wine which is quite different.

The vine *Galego Dourado* gives a quick-fermenting must of a clear colour; the wineproducer adds a completely fermented wine called *abafado* which lends a certain velvety texture to this liqueur, dry rather than sweet, with a rather surprising almond flavour and an alcohol content of at least 19° to 10°. Much appreciated in the seventeenth and eighteenth centuries, CARCAVELOS has now become a rare wine (an area of

77 acres produce no more than 5,500 gallons) which is bought up almost entirely by Great Britain and the Scandinavian countries.

WINES OF SETÚBAL: Scarcely 25 miles from the capital but on the southern bank of the Tagus lies the region of Setúbal, with its pines and rice-fields.

A centuries-old reputation enhances MOSCATEL DE SETÚBAL: this was the wine—along with GARNACHE and MALVASIA, both wines from plants of those same names—that was so lauded among the *vins étranges* appreciated in the Paris of the fifteenth century. Rabelais mentions it when describing the *Temple de la Dive Bouteille*, Louis XIV insisted on having it in his cellars at Versailles and Voltaire had it brought to his property at Ferney.

The stalks of the grapes are left in the must, which gives the MOSCATEL its lively perfume, its strong colour and its characteristic taste. The wine is never drunk until it is at least five or six years old, and there are some MOSCATEL, called "museum wines", which are very old indeed and quite unexcelled: the 1920 vintage is perhaps the best of these. This MOSCATEL DE SETÚBAL, particularly appreciated in Canada, has been called by experts "the quintessence of liqueur wines"; it is sweet, light, fruity yet less musk-scented than FRONTIGNAN and lively enough to be excellent when drunk as an aperitif provided it is iced. It goes very well with second courses and desserts or, better still, with cheese, especially Azeitao ewe's cheese with its original flavour and taste of aromatic herbs.

The Estremadura Transtagana (south of the Tagus) produces other good wines: for example, the region of Palmela has light-red clarets and red table wines, notably PIRIQUITA, which is silky, supple yet robust. And Azeitao is the home of FAISCA, a very pleasant rosé which is extremely popular abroad: its delightful colour and thirst-quenching freshness (for it must, of course, be drunk iced) attract the drinker without startling him. Under the trade-name LANCERS, it is one of the best-selling wines in the United States.

WINES OF BUCELAS: The wines of the region of Bucelas, which are produced from the *Arinto* vine of the Tagus estuary, are dry and somewhat acid wines the colour of yellow straw. Much appreciated by Wellington's officers and men during his Peninsula War against Napoleon, they afterwards found a great success in England. Charles Dickens mentions them as among his favourite wines, along with SAUTERNES and sherry, and Lord Byron praises their qualities, to which George III of England adds that of having cured him of a troublesome kidney disease.

VINHOS VERDES: While such wines as DAO, COLARES, BUCELAS, CARCAVELOS and even MOSCATEL have their imitators in other countries, the noted VINHOS VERDES ("green wines") are 100 per cent Portuguese all along the line. Their unusual name does not come from their colour (they are in fact red or white) but from the amount of ripening, for these wines are produced from plants in northern Portugal which are pruned espalier fashion and whose grapes never reach maturity.

These VINHOS VERDES, lively, slightly acid and always extremely young, have a very long history behind them and seem to have been known to Strabon.

Minho, home of VINHOS VERDES, is at the same time Portugal's most densely-populated province and that with perhaps the most difficult land, for its granite-like soil is unforgiving and unrelenting. Centuries-old parcelling of the land has resulted in an infinite number of tiny properties each hardly able to support a family—this is the region of traditional emigration to seek new hope, even though the vineyards hold man close through the unceasing cares which they demand and the joys and benefits they return. Human wisdom over the years has dictated that these vineyards must not be given a soil so dearly needed to feed so many mouths, and by law the vine may be cultivated only on waste ground, along the edges of fields or by paths and roads. So the farmer of Minho plants his vines in espaliers, as high hedges or even, very frequently, on living supports such as chestnuts, sycamores, poplars, cherry-trees or alders. The vine-plant is tied to the tree by fine willow stalks and the vine-shoots are allowed to hang down. These "grape-bearing trees" which delighted Jean Giraudoux, these "hanging vines", these paths of trellis give the landscape a gentle shade and cut up the country roads with a lace-like pattern of chiaroscuro. Their tart grapes come from very old selected vine-stocks: *Vinhão*, *Borracal* and *Espadeira* for the black grapes and *Azal* or *Dourado* for the white grapes.

The vines of the Minho basin remain undisturbed for long years and the plants become almost arborescent. The roots descend deep into a soil dug and fertilized with green heather and animal manure, while above ground, the knotted and muscled stem and the long supple vine-shoots often reach a height of 15 feet. The humidity of this region encourages plant sickness, which means an unrelenting struggle with long sprays, using special products against the mildew and phylloxera. Harvested in September and racked at the end of the year six weeks after they have been bottled, these VINHOS VERDES are already a sparkling wine—and there is one of their characteristics, even one of their charms. The white wines are thirst-quenching, light and harmless, admirably suited to picnics and summer lunches, with an alcohol content of only 6° to 9°. The red VINHOS VERDES are also of low alcohol content, but these full-bodied wines are of a dark purple colour, with a crimson foam which stains the glass.

199

The VINHOS VERDES have been long appreciated for their refreshing taste of fruit and their lively youthfulness, but for many years they were drunk only locally, for it was said they travelled badly. Rich in lactic acid and malic acid, they were volatile and lacked body. More recently, it has been possible to stabilize them and they are now exported to Belgium, Africa and Great Britain, not to mention even to France where an equivalent wine does not exist. The price of modern progress has to be paid, however, and today bottles of uniform contents have replaced the attractive little stoneware jugs, the shape and size of which were seldom quite uniform.

There are 90,000 producers of VINHOS VERDES; of these, only 33,000 produce more than 11,000 gallons each a year, while 54,000 of them produce only about 200 gallons! The success of these wines has seen exports rise to 1,320,000 gallons out of a total production of 66,000,000 gallons, the balance being drunk in the country and making up 33 per cent of the home consumption of Portuguese wine.

OTHER WINEPRODUCING REGIONS: Several other regions of Portugal are of quite some interest to viticulture, particularly eight of them which are expected to become delimited zones, with the production of their wines strictly controlled. These are the wines of Pinhel, light and pleasant clarets; the wines of Lafoes, nonsparkling but otherwise similar to the VINHOS VERDES and grown on trellises (these *verdascos* are usually red wines and total about 1,540,000 gallons a year); the wines of Bairrada, semi-sparkling whites or reds which come not far from Dão with its ANADIA wines; the wines of Buçaco, rich and strong yet smooth; wines from the region of Sangalhos with reds which come close to the best of those from Dão, and whites which rival those of Anadia; the wines of Alcobaça, where Cistercian monks in the twelfth century cleared the barren lands to plant the vineyards; the wines of Ribatejo, where the plants stand high to escape the periodical floodings of the Tagus, with notably ALMEIRIM, CARTAXO and several ordinary wines, including the full-flavoured "ordinary" red wine, of a low alcohol content but keeping its quality well, which flows freely during the *festas bravas* that accompany the bullfights and the popular feasting on roast kid; finally, the wines of Torres Vedras, full-bodied tannin-rich ordinary red wines used for blending and also simple wines for café-restaurants and family tables; over towards Obidos, the GAEIRAS and especially the white type is very worthy.

It is noticeable that, with the exception of MOSCATEL DE SETÚBAL, all these good quality wines are grown north of the Tagus, although the southern provinces do have some of their own. In Alentejo, for example, the names of such places as Cuba, Vidigueira, and so on, would seem to indicate that the vine was once cultivated there, but the region, which is thinly populated, was devoted to other crops—cereals, cork oak and olives, all better adapted to large seasonal monocultures. A few vineyards of Alentejo which escaped the oïdium infection were able to produce, around the end of the nineteenth century, some strong and aromatic wines which were practically unknown outside the region, although one should mention the wine of Borba.

The province of Algarve, in the extreme south, long had the unfair reputation of producing the country's most mediocre wine. It was unfair because here too the vine had to give way to other crops such as almonds, figs and locust-beans, although the local population is considerable and well used to the multiple tasks of small cropping and make good winegrowers. The grapes grown are excellent: the black grapes from *Pauferros* produce a wine with a very good bouquet and the white grapes from *Tamarez* produce a very sweet wine, of which Lagõa is the main producer. The Portuguese government is encouraging viticulture in the province of Algarve and various schemes are in progress for reviving once-popular wines.

Fuzeta and Moncarapacho produce a Malaga-type dessert wine while AFONSO III, a liqueur wine, is a good aperitif with the warmth of sherry.

In the far north of the country, Chaves offers a wine with many connoisseurs called "wine of the dead" because it is sometimes buried to hasten its ageing.

Finally, Portugal produces some natural sparkling wines, notably at Lamego, with also some much appreciated rosés such as the already-mentioned FAISCA. MATEUS ROSÉ is also exported in the whole world—Europe, the United States, Canada, Australia, Hong Kong—and demand for the wine is so high (13 million bottles in 1967) that it absorbs the entire harvest, from its home province of Trás-os-Montes to around Anadia.

This abundance (304,681,828 gallons in 1966), this diversity, this often exceptional quality, this long and solid reputation mean that wine is a major trump-card for Portugal in the international market-place. Many of these wines are, however, enjoyed locally, perhaps particularly by the French, whose country sets restrictive measures with very limited quotas to protect the French national wine trade against imports of all wines, except those which have no equivalent in France, such as port, Madeira, VINHOS VERDES and some rosés. Portuguese wines exported in the bottle (only 7 per cent of the total, however, because of transport costs) carry a seal of guarantee, but the remainder of the production is exported in casks. In 1967, the total of wine exports exceeded 7,920,000 gallons, or a value of 1,350 million escudos.

PORT WINES

This famous wine owes to Porto only its name, for the vineyards which produce it are stepped along the ravine sides of the Upper Douro valley, and it is the town of Vila Nova de Gaia (across from Porto itself) where the wine is treated and aged, over many years, in the shade and silence of the great winemaking plants.

But it is from Porto, since time immemorial, and from Porto alone that this famous wine has been shipped to the four corners of the world, and it is the name Porto that one reads today, as one did a hundred years ago, on the casks rolled so gaily along the riverside quays. Some relate the tale that the name *rio douro* means "river of gold" and that this heavy and slow-running water does indeed run over nuggets of gold. The truth, however, is elsewhere and quite different, and one can perhaps remember Jean de La Fontaine: the treasure of the Douro, he maintained, must be wrenched from it with grit, with hard sweat, with faith and with love. For this most generous of wines is born of the most ungenerous and avaricious of lands, and throughout its long life it remains at the mercy of a thousand different perils: drought, wind, frost, fog, storms and all the illnesses of the vine. Just one week, if conditions go wrong at the moment the grape is ripe, is sufficient to ruin a whole harvest.

The port must is also a fragile substance, which must be observed and handled with loving and knowing care if one is to extract the very best qualities from it. It is sensitive to heat, to air currents, to odours, to any delay in pressing the grapes or in fermentation. It passes long years maturing in large casks where it sheds its skin and absorbs enrichment at the same time, yet this very sojourn reduces also its vitality, for the rate of evaporation can reach as much as 4 per cent a year. Port wine demands a great deal of vigilance and care and costs its producer much. In Douro, from the vinegrower to the consumer, the whole world lives a veritable cult of the wine.

Many people claim that the plants which produce port wine came originally from Burgundy. However that may be, it is known that, at the end of the eleventh century, Henry, grandson of Robert I, Duke of Burgundy, had won fame at the side of El Cid in the fighting against the infidels. As a reward, he was given the lands of Douro and Minho and he later married a natural daughter of Alfonso VI, King of Leon and of Castille, receiving also the title of Count of Portugal. As Henry then settled down in his property and seems to have had few other worries than to make the most of his land, it is quite probable that he cultivated the vine and preferred the vine-stock of his home. In any case, it was to be many years before the vineyards of Douro became famous, for in reality their history begins only with the eighteenth century.

The wines at this time were very full-bodied, heavy and loaded with tannin; furthermore, in an effort to heighten their colour, elderberries were added, while various methods of stabilization were attempted so that the wine might survive the voyage to the English shores. It can be admitted outright: the wines were abominable and the English would certainly have preferred the wines of Bordeaux had not their endless quarrels with the French led to a complete ban on the import of the wines of Aquitania. Yet the English soldiers and sailors remembered very well having drunk some very satisfactory local wines in the harbour bars and other places during their campaigns.

The demand for the wines, as a result of the Treaty of Methuen in 1703, encouraged farmers without any experience to try cultivating vine-plants, and the prospect of easy gains had already incited the winegrowers to cut corners on wine production. One must bear in mind, too, that at this time wines were everywhere drunk very young and the secret of ageing the great vintage wines had been lost over the years in the same way as the use of impervious jars. The wine quickly went bad in the barrels and survived no better in the skin containers.

Since they were in any case obliged to drink this unpleasant wine, bought, understandably, at the nearest point to their land, in northern Portugal, the English decided to go and see on the spot how it was made. Merchants established themselves at Porto, although at first they opened only transport offices, later risking their capital by buying the standing harvest. In this way, they discovered the Douro and became winegrowers: they had the necessary capital and made the law of the vineyards, and they could also choose the best musts. But overproduction very rapidly brought the prices down and the valley lived wretchedly.

The REAL COMPANHIA: Bartholomeu Pancorvo, a man richer in ideas than in gold, was the first to understand the vital need to take the whole production of wine in hand in Douro, in order to keep a check on quality and prices. The English, however, caused his plan to fail and the poor man did not survive his ruin. But the idea was now in the air and a monk, Brother Mansilha, in high favour at Court, developed a scheme to win the game. He had the backings of the great Duke of Pombal. He instigated the founding of the *Real Companhia dos Vinhos do Alto Douro* (Royal Company of the Wines of Upper Douro) in 1756 and took up both the monopoly of trade with England and Brazil and the production of wine-based spirits.

Brother Mansilha began by countering the manoeuvres of the English, who were baulked in their attempted take-over of the vineyard. But, as is often the case, he was opposed even more violently by the very people he hoped to help, for in 1759, three years after the foundation of the Royal Company and at the time of the great popular drinking feasts and carnivals, the price of wine had gone up a few pence in the bars. There was a riot in Porto and the mob, feeding on its own fury, pillaged the premises of the Royal Company and burned all the books. The repression was brutal—people were jailed, hanged, quartered—but order was finally restored.

One of the first jobs for the Royal Company, henceforth sovereign in the field, was to mark out the best region for producing a high quality wine. The exceptional qualities of the wine meant that, with appropriate treatment and ageing, it could become not merely a table wine but a vintage wine. Many mediocre vine-plants were sacrificed and on the confined space remaining, experiments were patiently carried out with more and more rigid methods of vinification.

At the same time, success was achieved in developing mass production of glass vessels in which the wine could rest sheltered from the air. Inaugurated in Portugal, this procedure was to permit the whole world to find again the powerful yet delicate flavour of the ancient wines, while the Upper Douro was to discover the secret of its incomparable port. This wine very rapidly met an immense popularity in England for, warm, comforting, tonic, it brought into the humid mists of the long English winters the living light and the warmth of a beautiful fire in the hearth. Even today port is more popular in colder countries than in its native Portugal, where a lighter wine is preferred,

Porto benefited from the wealth of the vineyards. Always hardworking, thrifty and valiant, the old town had never been very smart. But the gold from port wine now gave her palaces and churches in which one might see, as in San Francisco, vine-shoots and grape-clusters stretching right on to the altars. Roads and bridges were built for transporting the wine, and soon, too, appeared more winemaking plants, official and private offices, and spacious and beautiful houses. English merchants established themselves in a road which was named Street of the English, and built, at great expense, a *factorerie* where they could discuss their business. The Portuguese, for their part, had become aware of their national heritage: proprietors of lands set their estates (called *quintas*) in order and established firms to produce and sell their own wines.

Thus two groups, with the same aims, associated yet at the same time competitors, and living even in the heart of a relatively small town two absolutely separate existences, were working side by side—in the vineyards of Douro, in the winemaking plants of Vila Nova de Gaia and in the offices in Porto.

From this comes something of the special physiognomy of Porto. It is certain that its pearly skies, its frequent mists, its freshly cool climate were already making it a "northern capital". And one can understand that the English felt at home, for the natives of Porto were, by nature, hard-working, provident, enemies of waste and false manifestations, to which qualities this contact with the English added efficiency and exactness, as well as a taste for elegant and family comfort. In Porto, behind the austere granite of the house façades, one finds beautiful mahogany, fine carpets, precious silverware, added to the dignity of old port decanted in crystal flasks.

THE VINEYARDS OF DOURO

Any good vine-plant, once acclimatized to Douro, would give port wine, but a vine-plant of Douro transplanted elsewhere would cease to produce port wine. This strange alchemy which, it is believed, presides over the making of this wine is the work of Nature, which has brought together on the banks of the Upper Douro and its tributaries (Corgo, Torto, Tua) conditions which are special, exceptional, mysterious and delicate. Here the vinegrower comes to grips with lava terrains, rugged and rocky. He plants his vine on a chaotic accumulation of eroded, crumbled and broken-up land, the work of the torrents and rivers, for it is true that for a long time there have grown on these ungrateful slopes only scrub brush and the aromatic grasses that the mountain goats feed on.

Down in the deep river gorges, the winter air currents are icy and fog collects like thick cottonwool. When summer comes, the storms build up and their effects are felt from valley to valley, until, finally, the sun begins to heat the stone. The valleys become ovens of 40º C. and even 50º, enveloping without a breath of air the whole "land of wine", the region so minutely and strictly laid out in vineyards whose product can be turned into *approveitado* (approved) port wine. The part of the Douro production not used for port will give table wines or wine alcohol.

In 1966, the total production of these vineyards, an area of nearly 60,000 acres, was 33,000,000 gallons, of which only 6,930,000 gallons were *approveitado*.

This goes to show that apart from the position of the lands, their soil composition and their exposure to the sun, one must also count the local conditions, meteo-

This view of the site of Cachao de San Salvador da Pesqueira, near Beira, shows us the landscape of the Upper Douro valley as it was about the middle of the eighteenth century. This is the period that saw, under the impulse of the institute of the *Real Companhia dos Vinhos do Alto Douro*, the restoration of the vineyards and the birth of port wine, a wine which was to extend its reputation across the entire world.

rological or otherwise, which increase or reduce the quality of the must each year. And even before the harvest, it was necessary to create the vineyard—with the hand of man and on the back of man. The hard, laminated, slated rock had to be broken up with the hand-pick, crumbled and laid out in terraces, open to the maximum amount of sun and rain. These terraces held by small stone walls, climb the steepest slopes, with the lowest plants at water-level: it is said that the best grapes are picked where they have ripened "listening to the creaking of the river boats' heavy rudders". The plants do not grow above an altitude of 1,000 feet; any higher and ripening cannot take place satisfactorily.

The terraces give the landscape a strange and imposing aspect. As far as the eye can see, the hillsides are striped and patterned as if with giant fingerprints, and everywhere one looks, the plants line up rank on rank, held by vine-props and wires. The shoots hang fairly close to the ground, benefiting from all the emanations of the soil, but care has been taken also to see that the grape-bunches are neither soiled nor damaged by contact with the ground. To conserve the

rains of winter and keep a reserve of freshness during the heat of summer, a large ditch is dug and filled with rough stones at the foot of each plant, whose roots go six feet under ground. No secondary crops; the entire vitality of this soil is dedicated to the vine. The leguminous plants between the vine-plants are mulched in as additional fertilizer. The whole winter is spent clearing, cleaning and tidying the vineyard. Working under enormous capes of maize straw for protection against the frequent rain between October and March, the vintners repair the little walls, disinfect and consolidate the vine-props, layer, graft and prune the vine, until along the lines not a dead leaf nor a stone is to be seen. The vine-shoots turn green, the grape-bunches begin to lengthen. It is the perilous time when a morning frost can turn it red and kill it. Throughout the workers must fight parasites, be prepared for storms, watch the sky; and then comes the summer, with its terrible dryness and burning winds. The harvest, in September, is at once a task, a ritual, a feast. It is a final effort, crowning a whole year of hard labour and bringing its reward or, sometimes, withholding it.

THE HARVEST AND THE PRESSING

The ideal moment of ripening of the grapes has to be seized on, a moment that varies for each *quinta* and even for each slope of the hillside. Then the women, with their scissors and baskets, crouch beside the vine-plants, cut the grape-bunches and check each to make sure that not a single spoiled or unripe bunch goes to the press. Under the slight shade of the leaves, the workers suffocate in the heat mirrored by the stones, too hot to rest a hand on them. The baskets are emptied into hods at the end of each row, collected by groups of *barracheiros*, the stalwarts who can carry a load of 165 pounds of grapes well balanced on the nape of the neck with a leather strap and steadied with a steel hook. They walk in a long single file, with a heavy step, in time to the rhythm of the stick of the leader, who guides them down the stone steps and steep paths of the vineyards. The presses are set up as low down the hills as possible, yet high enough to escape the danger of the sudden and violent floods of the often torrential rivers.

In the vastness of the landscape, men trudge onwards like ants, glistening with sweat. The sticky juice glues to their skin the jute sacking with which they protect their backs. These *barracheiros* are irreplaceable, because no other method of transporting the grapes has been found which can be used in these steep vineyards.

At the presses, everything has been made ready. Over the past months, new barrels have been carved and the old ones cleaned. For centuries, the grape was pressed with the feet, because this was believed to be the only way of extracting all the goodness from the pulp and skin of the grape without crushing the grape-pips. Tiring work, in the vats filled with wet and slippery grapes, which had to be pressed till they were crushed and split open and were transformed into a gluey porridge-like mass. The pressers had to bring air down into the mass too, by constantly lifting their knees high, in order to break up the crust that the waste products formed on the surface of the liquid. A team of six men would take twenty hours to extract some 200 gallons of must. But a joyous exaltation seemed to lie over this work, reminiscent of a birth: the pressers, already a little dizzy with the vapours rising from the vat, were encouraged with songs and music, and the womenfolk danced all night long around the stone vats by the light of lanterns. Today, this pressing with the feet has become difficult because of lack of seasonal labour, and is being replaced more and more by a mechanical process, called the Ducellier process, which gives, after a mechanical stoning, excellent results: a system of valves, set in action by the fermentation, simultaneously stirs and aerates the must.

Another critical moment comes with the decision of how much wine alcohol should be added to the must in order to stop the transformation of sugar into the alcohol which results from fermentation. The quantity depends itself on the richness of the must: too much rain, before or during the harvest, swells the grapes but may reduce their sugar content by several degrees, while drought and dry periods give a rich but rarer grape. In Douro, nothing ever seems to be given in quite the right quantities. The measured addition of wine alcohol will therefore give a wine which is more or less dry or sweet.

Suitably "dosed" in this way and allowed to settle, the must is left in the freshness of the cellars of the *quinta*, until in the springtime it is transported to the winemaking plants of the estuary. For many years a curious type of boat was used for this, with a flat bottom and a high poop on which an experienced helmsman ruled. The Douro is treacherous, even impetuous here, seamed with hidden reefs or shoals, and the old-fashioned *barcos rabelos* have given way little by little, first to trains and then to heavy road transport. The valley's charm is the loser, for nothing was more picturesque than this sight of the sailing boats or the *rabelos*, sometimes towed by oxen, sometimes beating against the wind.

TYPES OF PORT

Until its arrival at Vila Nova da Gaia, the wine is still young and a little rash, but it will now undergo a long retirement, during which it will learn the best of wisdom. Depending on the characteristics which they show right at the start of their life, that is to say when they leave the presses, the new wines will belong to one or other of the two great port "families": that of the "blends", which are the more numerous, or that of the highly prized "vintages".

The blends, which cover the majority of the port wines, are as their names indicate, blends aged in the wood. Once the must has settled, after two years in the cask, it is again weighed, tasted and appraised. Other types of must are then sought which can be added, bringing with them characteristics of their own which will underline or complement those of the original must. Some of the blending musts may bring strength, others colour, others again bouquet. Any port worthy of the name is made up of at least sixteen varieties of vine-stock. Like a florist making up a display, or a painter mixing the colours on his palette, or a perfumer dosing out the essences, the port experts compose, mix and dose the different port wines.

They work surrounded by retorts, test-tubes, bottle-racks, note-books, in veritable laboratories that the

All along the Douro, thanks to centuries of work by the vinegrowers, the vines climb across the steep hillsides and give the landscape the aspect of some enormous staircase fashioned by giants. Even today, springtime still sees the wine moved by boat along the river. The old-fashioned *barcos rabelos* transport the barrels of must to the famous winemaking plants at Vila Nova da Gaia, opposite Porto.

Above: A view of the terraces that produce Port, laboriously hacked out of the stony ground by hand in the valley of the Douro, Portugal. Left: Labourers plant and tend the vines with loving care, planting each in a sort of basin surrounded by big stones to conserve the water. Below: In the Douro valley, where extremes of heat and cold are known, the vintners wear capes of maize straw in bad weather.

winemaking firms have fitted out. To inspiration must be linked experience. For it is not purely a question of inventing a new port, but of establishing a successful formula which can be followed and above all maintained, in order that a trade product can be confidently and successfully marketed.

Listed, their composition carefully analysed, the blends are then put into enormous wooden casks, in order to prevent both their oxydation and too rapid an evaporation. The wines remain there under constant supervision. They are measured, sounded, tasted, and the attentive ear of the master winemaker watches out for and notices the noises, deep or light, which come from the immense *cuvée*. This latter remains alive and moving for, as it takes on greater age, the wine is enlivened and enriched with the careful addition of young and strong musts. No port wine may be drunk before it has aged five to six years in the wood. It reaches its fullness after about thirty years, but one can drink ports of sixty years and more which have remained absolutely marvellous. It is impossible and in fact a vain effort to try to date the different blends; one can merely say that they are *cuvées spéciales*.

For reasons of convenience and economy, the blends are usually exported in barrels and bottled by the importers. The importers of a few large brands, to ensure the unbroken quality of their chosen *cuvée*, insist on bottling in the winemaking plants before the wines are sold, and in this case, the bottle is sealed by the Port Wine Institute. This institute works with two other bodies, the Port Wine Shippers Guild and Douro House, to control and regulate the cultivation, vinification and exporting of port.

Contrary to the blends, the port vintages always have a birth certificate. It is always a *very* good year. When a harvest has been outstandingly good in quality, a vintage year is decided. The must, which is usually treated and kept in the wood for two years, is put straight into bottles without any blending, and the bottle, hermetically sealed, is put in the winemaking plant. There, the wine ages, in austere and silent solitude, for ten, twenty, thirty years or even more. It skins and enriches itself by natural means. It is a *millésimé* port. The vintage ports are more appreciated in England, or at any rate were so in earlier days: the old connoisseurs of Thackeray and Dickens' times valued them more than any other. But the vintage ports, one can well imagine, are fragile: they demand a lot of care in the conservation, transport and even in the drinking. Furthermore, even if their fine uprightness is admirable, they do not have the clever complexity that enchants the connoisseurs of the blended ports. Great vintage years are very rare; one can mention the years 1890, 1900 (still to be found on the market), 1908, 1927, 1931, 1945 and 1947. According to the vine-plant used in their production, vintage ports are more or less light or dark, and with age, darken or lighten, although most vintage ports gradually become "tawny", that is to say, the colour of light mahogany.

In addition to this fundamental difference between blends and vintages, port is divided into extra-dry, dry (usually white port), semi-dry and sweet (red). Ageing, by decanting the colouring matter, touches all with gold, and the shades of colour spread out from light topaz to bronze. The official colours are: deep red, red, ruby (these are the "fulls"), light gold, onion peel (the "tawnies"), pale white, pale straw and golden.

The "fulls" are fairly young port wines, rich, full-bodied, ruby-coloured or deep garnet. The "tawnies" are old wines which have taken on the colour of amber or wild honey. A good port can be recognized first by its aroma, and secondly because it "weeps", that is to say it lets slide down the sides of the glass a long, slow unctuous tear.

PORT IN THE WORLD

England, for some time, has been no longer the world's major importer of port: between 1900 and 1919, the British drank each year 13,200,000 gallons but in 1939 they bought only 6,380,000 gallons.

Up to the war of 1914-1918, port, with Madeira, was intimately linked with the daily life of the upper-class English. It was the sole wine judged worthy of using for the Sovereign's Toast, at the end of a meal. Chosen with the greatest care—and tastes in port could be discussed all night—a bottle was served to the gentlemen, while the ladies "withdrew", going to the drawing-room (or withdrawing-room) for infusions of herbs or tea and light conversation. The men emptied the bottle between them while chatting. Each gentleman's club knew exactly the preferences of its eminent members and kept in reserve a suitable supply of their port and cigars. The great families had their cellars, where reserves were built up, either as a financial investment or for sentimental reasons. A similar custom, still preserved in Douro, established for each child born into a family a stock of bottles which was increased from year to year. The lucky child who came into the world the year of a vintage port could be assured of an outstanding wine with which to celebrate its coming-of-age or its wedding.

But while England began reducing its consumption of port, others, France among them, began to discover it. Or rather, re-discover it, for this wine had been much appreciated long ago, especially after the Napoleonic invasions at the beginning of the nineteenth century. The archives of the region of Douro hold the requisition orders signed by the general occupying Porto, be he the English ally or the French enemy. It is amusing to note that some of these carry the same date: for example, March 29th, 1809 was the day that Wellington, landing unexpectedly, interrupted the lunch of Marshal Soult.

Despite its relatively limited area, the Douro vineyard presents a rich variety of vine-stocks. One remembers, too, that the blends, spread out over ten years or more, obey subtle and supple rules. This is why port wines are so varied and why they suit all tastes and all climates.

HOW AND WHEN TO DRINK PORT

One must first know just what one expects of port. If it is a question of serving a refreshing aperitif which at the same time sets an "ambiance", one should choose a dry white port, and serve it chilled, either by chilling the glasses with an ice-cube or by putting the glasses themselves in a chilling recipient. This is the way the French usually drink port wine. For an afternoon refreshment, a five-to-seven reception or the end of a meal, a "tawny" or a "full" is preferable. A semi-dry or a sweet port makes a delightful accompaniment to dessert pastries and to certain fruits, but not citrus varieties.

One should not, moreover, neglect to serve port with the cheese. It is no doubt to enhance the taste of the port that the English brought into fashion savouries or hot dishes, usually with cheese and spiced and offered right at the end of the meal, when the bottles or decanters are going round. It is also the English who put port into their famous Stilton cheese, cutting into the centre and filling the hole with good port as cutting proceeds, which allows the wine to permeate the creamy mass. All the cheeses in the world—Danish, Dutch or Swiss cheese, Portuguese, Spanish or Italian cheese, and of course the inexhaustible *plateau* of French cheese—have a common denominator: they enhance the port which, in its turn, exalts the cheese.

In Douro and in Portugal in general, port is drunk according to a certain ritual. It must never, even in a public establishment, be served open; the law requires that the bottle be presented. In private homes, the wine is not brought in its bottle; it is considered more elegant, and shows a better knowledge of port itself, to transfer it a few hours beforehand into a decanter, where it may rest and take the air. A vintage port is never uncorked, for in the ten or twenty years of its life, the best of corks would have spoiled and mildewed and thus, inevitably, cork dust would fall in the wine. Real connoisseurs therefore, to open a bottle of a really great port, use a pair of special pliers heated red-hot in a fire, with which they decapitate the bottle.

Although such refinements have largely fallen into disuse, both port wine and the mistress of house who intends to offer it have everything to gain in observing the niceties. There is a wide choice of decanters, some old, engraved, cut, filled gold, others modern, heavy, belted with leather. They usually carry a metal medallion round the neck marked with the word "Port" in more or less fancy letters. The glass, on the other hand, should be very simple, in fine crystal, with a foot, and all in one piece in the shape of a tulip or a balloon. One can thus better appraise the colour of the wine, and the bouquet is more concentrated. Connoisseurs say port should be "chewed" before it is swallowed, after having lengthily held the glass (except in the case of the fresh white ports) in the hollow of the hand. Thus port gratifies all the senses.

These days one can forget the old rule that port is always served in a clockwise direction; but remember that connoisseurs never re-cork a bottle: once opened, it is drunk. If, however, one should wish to keep an opened bottle and not be able to finish it in the following days, it should be decanted into a smaller flask where it will be free from air.

Port for anniversaries and tête-à-tête meals; as a pick-me-up for grandfather or the overworked student; port to warm the hunter after the stalk or the traveller after the long trip; prelude and conclusion of a large banquet; port in a reducing diet; port drunk with friends informally at a bar or at an important ceremony in an official reception—in brief, port, the truly grand *seigneur*, is everywhere at home.

On the official level, port is also the Portuguese wine which is most carefully watched over by the authorities. Several official organizations watch to ensure that it is cultivated, vinified and marketed according to very strict rules. The *Casa do Douro* supports, advises and sometimes finances the vinegrowers; the *Gremio dos Exportadores*, at Porto, organizes and co-ordinates the trade in wine; and the *Instituto do Vinho do Porto* heads all these other activities, checking and controlling all the wines which will be put on the market and which may not be sold in Portugal without a guarantee seal. This small seal, marked "I.V.P.", seen on a bottle is a sign which does not mislead. Many wines are exported in casks, with a certificate of origin. Some frauds can be carried out when the wine is bottled, but fortunately many countries, including France, have enough respect for great wines, of whatever origin, to punish fraud energetically and effectively. It is therefore possible anywhere to drink a port wine which is just as good as in the cellars of Gaia, where Portugal likes to greet visitors and let them taste these jewel-shaded wines.

THE WINES OF MADEIRA

The equerries of Henry the Navigator landed in Madeira in 1419 after years of searching for the Fortunate Isles. Stranded after a terrible storm on an almost barren island which out of gratitude they had baptized Porto Santo, the voyagers had for months seen a misty silhouette appearing and disappearing on the horizon, a real "enchanted" island. They landed there at last, disembarking in a rocky creek occupied by sea animals and which they describe in their portulan as *Camara de Lobos*. All around were dense forests, made up of trees whose odour was so strong that men became dizzy when cutting them down. They called the island Madeira, which means wood in Portuguese.

As a result of the travellers' reports men were sent to colonize the islands and they planted both European-style and tropical crops. In this way, Madeira grew and side by side flourished cane sugar and grape-vines.

Right from the start, the Madeira wine proved to be excellent. Ca da Mosto, the celebrated Venitian navigator, in 1455 praised the wine drunk in these new isles. The whole of Europe became enthused. The Duke of Clarence, locked up in the Tower of London, chose to drown himself in a barrel of Malmsey wine to escape the vengeance of his brother. Falstaff, as Shakespeare claimed, sold his soul one Friday for a glass of good Madeira and a cold leg of chicken. François I insisted on always having some in his castles in Touraine. Portugal granted special privileges to the English merchants established at Funchal, where trade was brisk, and the wines of the island, which were traded against wheat and dairy produce of Ireland, wood and rice from America, and fish from Newfoundland, provisioned the long-haul sailing ships.

William Bolton, the British Consul at Funchal, a shipowner and banker, played an important role in the development of the Madeira vineyard, and in 1699, complained that the supply could not meet the demand, particularly from the American colonists. The future George IV, the first gentleman of Europe, lent them his prestige in England: nothing else was drunk at Carlton House and 22,000 pipes (a pipe was large-size cask) of wines were exported to Great Britain in 1813. But there was another side to the coin.

In 1852, a terrible disease attacked the island's vineyards: oïdium. Whole plants were decimated. Twenty years later, phylloxera struck. The plants would have been abandoned had it not been for the stubborn work of enlightened winegrowers, who managed to save a part of the vineyard and rebuilt some stocks. Thanks to their patience and devotion, Madeira wine little by little took its place in trade again. Today its role in the country's economy is important: Portugal in 1966 exported 1,017,786 gallons of Madeira out of a total production of 2,200,000 gallons.

THE VINES OF MADEIRA

The island of Madeira is very small—only 30 miles long by 16 miles wide—and one-third of it is hardly suitable for cultivation. It is an old volcano, jutting up out of the ocean, defending itself with high cliffs and caves as deep as 2,400 feet. As in Douro, arable land must be created out of nothing, patiently, tenaciously, by breaking up the lava with the pick. The farmer of Madeira cultivates the smallest patch of ground that can be reached, even if it hangs out into space. The vine is his little luxury, his joy and his pride, so that one sees it growing on trellises along the edges of paths and covering the tiled roofs shadowing the little courtyards where the women sit and embroider. Those grapes are for the family table. But the great wines of Madeira come from the land with the best exposure, in the south-west. The plots are so narrow that the regions are called *estreitos* (straitened). Among the most famous are Campanario, Ponta do Pargo and Madalena.

In order to make use of this area so meagerly awarded, the winegrowers *roll* the vines in numerous tight coils, held up by wires, and strip off the leaves from the vine-shoots so that the grape-bunches may drink in the sun all day long. The sun gilds them, ripens them, gives them their sugar: the grapes must be picked when very ripe, but not one shrunken or spoiled grape must reach the press.

THE HARVEST AND THE TYPES OF WINE

The harvest is a festival. For the same reasons as in Douro, everything must be carried on the backs of men, even the must, which is brought to the winemaking plants in goatskins or in small 80-100 pint barrels.

This must is kept in a barrel open to the sun; there, it gradually reduces and caramelizes (the method particularly used for sweet wines). Nowadays, a system of hot-baths heats the must to 50°. The fermented must gives the *vinho claro* which is then left to rest in order to obtain the *vinho trasfugado*.

As with the wine of Porto, Madeira includes two family types: the vintage wine, which is must from an outstanding harvest, aged in closed bottles and with nothing added; and the Madeira *solera* (from the Portuguese for sun), which is a wine aged always in the

Harvest time on the isle of Madeira. The vinegrower works standing, picking at his own height the bunches of grapes swollen with sugar. These are collected in baskets and sorted on the spot, before being carried down to the presses. As in the Douro region, the must is transported by *borracheiros*, carrying goatskins with capacities of about eleven gallons.

same barrel. But in the latter, the inevitable evaporation is compensated for each year by filling the barrel to the brim with wine of the same type but one year younger. The date of a vintage *solera* is therefore that of the original must. There still exist on the island a few flasks of a venerable wine called MADÈRE DE NAPOLÉON, produced in 1792. The British Consul at Funchal offered some to Napoleon in 1815 on his way to St. Helena. The exiled emperor was ill and did not touch any of the precious barrels, which were returned after his death to the Consul; the latter sold the Madeira to Charles Blandy, who had it bottled in 1840. One can still sample some of this old Madeira today, although this is indeed an exceptional case. Normally, one is advised to choose from Madeiras of between twenty and thirty years old.

In contrast to port, which demands peace and quiet in its life, Madeira seems all the better for long voyages. This was established in the seventeenth century, on sampling MALVASIAS which had been shipped to America: the rocking of the ships and the heat of the tropics seemed to be so advantageous to the ageing of Madeira that the custom developed of "sending it out on a voyage": so much so that a shipment of wine which had made the round trip to India was very much sought after by connoisseurs. A cargo of MALVASIA was a great prize for pirates and certain shipments are known to have changed the colours under which they were sailing three of four times during the course of a voyage.

The English, during the eighteenth and nineteenth centuries, were great connoisseurs of Madeira. Ladies used it to perfume their handkerchieves and officers on campaigns demanded fifteen bottles a month. The truth is that, in addition to the pleasures it brings, Madeira has great tonic qualities; from 1785 on, it was much recommended for sick or over-worked people and was nicknamed the "milk of the old".

Madeira is also a marvellous wine for cooking, and sets off admirably such dishes as consommés, filet of beef, game, liver and lights, dishes in aspic, punches; and of course it is the essential ingredient of the well-known garnish, Madeira sauce. For cooking, one should use young Madeiras, above all never confusing those used in the kitchen and those drunk in the drawing-room.

A happy and very fashionable innovation consists of giving a reception where only two types of Madeira are served: one very dry, the other sweet and velvety. The first accompanies canapés and salted biscuits, the second, sweets.

There are four great Madeiras, of which the first is MALVASIA or MALMSEY obtained from pressing the ripest of the grapes. This was the very first to be cultivated on the island and was produced from vine-plants which came from Candia. Cultivated in the hottest part of the isle, its grapes are long, conical and very golden. The juice from these grapes is full of the sun's warmth; it is velvety and takes on the appearance of liquid gold, with a smoothness of honey.

MALVASIA has long been the great favourite among the wines of Madeira, for it expresses all the sensual, intoxicating and slightly mysterious charm of this island of perfumes. It is especially suitable as a dessert wine and is drunk at room temperature. On the other hand, SERCIAL, which is produced from vine-plants originating in the Rhine valley, is dry, amber and strong. It evokes quite another aspect of the island: the abysses, the peaks which pierce the clouds, the wild and grandiose landscapes. The best SERCIAL wines come from the vineyard where the soil is the most barren, not far from the abyss above which perches the *Curral das Freiras*, a convent built to escape the pillaging of barbarians. SERCIAL should never be drunk until it has at least eight to ten years of age, and should be served chilled as an aperitif.

VERDELHO, a semi-dry, and BOAL, a semi-sweet, are stronger wines than MALVASIA but do not have its mellowness; on the other hand, if they lack the haughty austerity of SERCIAL, they are more pleasant, more complete and more suitable for every occasion.

Madeira must be served with the same care as port, decanted into a flask before being drunk from fine and transparent glasses.

Finally, one must say a word about the wine of Porto Santo, the neighbouring island of Madeira, and especially the wine of Pico, in the Azores, which also had its moment of glory in the eighteenth and nineteenth centuries at the Russian Court. The vineyards —destroyed by an epidemic and only now just beginning to re-establish themselves—grow on soil which is as black as charcoal. The region is called the Land of Mystery, at the foot of a volcano which is the highest peak in Portugal. Walls of pumice-stone protect the plants, which grow, stunted and clinging to the very stone, never more than a few together. The wine of Pico is dry, lively, a little rough: it could be described as a sort of wild sherry.

In the very strange church of Jesus, at Setúbal, a panel of *azulejos* (Moorish tiles) represents the Tree of Jesse: the tree is a vine-plant which sprouts from the abdomen of the patriarch and then, spreading out, represents the Son of God. Nothing could better express the vital and sacred character of this most noble crop which, in Portugal, reunites the two most precious things: bread and wine. The vine nourishes man, and brings him joy, strength and hope.

WINES OF PORTUGAL

DRY WHITE WINES

Bucelas
Bucelas Velho
Dão Cabido
Dão Caves Império
Dão Grão Vasco
Dão Monástico
Dão Real Vinícola

Dão U. C. B.
Douro Favaios
Vinho Verde Agulha
Vinho Verde Alvarinho-Cepa Velha
Vinho Verde Amarante
Vinho Verde Aveleda — 1 R
Vinho Verde Casa do Landeiro

Vinho Verde Casal Garcia
Vinho Verde Casal de Pejeiros
Vinho Verde Casal da Seara
Vinho Verde Casalinho
Vinho Verde Casal Miranda
Vinho Verde Deu-la-Deu
Vinho Verde Lagosta

Vinho Verde Quinta da Aveleda
Vinho Verde Quinta do Tamariz
Vinho Verde Reserva da Aveleda
Vinho Verde Valverde
Vinho Verde Verdeal
Vinho Verde Lafões
Vinho Verde Sico

SWEET WHITE WINES

Arealva
Borlido

Casalinho
Corveta

Emir
Grandjó

Monte Serves
Murtelas

ROSÉ WINES

Aliança
Dom Silvano

Faísca
Isabel

Mateus
Grandélite

Spiral
Barros

RED WINES

Aliança
Arealva
Carvalho, Ribeiro & Ferreira
Colares M. J. C.
Colares V. S.
Dão Cabido
Dão Caves Aliança
Dão Caves Império
Dão Grão Vasco

Dão Monástico
Dão Real Vinícola
Dão Sóvida
Dão U. C. B.
Dão Vale da Fonte
Evel
J. M. da Fonseca
Lagoa
Lagos

Messias
Palmela-Clarete
Periquita
Quinta do Seminário
Reserva Sogrape
Romeira
Serradayres
Solar
Vinho Verde Casal da Seara

Vinho Verde C. Mendes
Vinho Verde Casal Garcia
Vinho Verde Folgazão
Vinho Verde Moura Basto
Vinho Verde Quinta do Tamariz
Vinho Verde Verdeal
Vinho Verde Lafões
Vinho Verde São Gonçalo
Vinho Verde Valverde

VARIOUS GENEROSOS WINES

Carcavelos-Quinta do Barão
Carcavelos-Quinta da Bela Vista

Estremadura Silveira
Estremadura Lezirão

Moscatel de Setúbal - Setúbal
    superior

Moscatel de Setúbal - Setúbal Roxo
Palmela superior

NATURAL SPARKLING WINES

Assis Brasil
Danúbio

Grande Natal
Monte Crasto

Neto Costa
Principe Real

Raposeira
Companhia Velha

MADEIRA

Sercial   Verdelho   Boal   Malmsey (Malvoisie)   Rainwater   Solera

PORT WINES

VERY DRY WHITE WINES (BRANCOS)

Casino Dry White
Dow's Dry White Aperitif Port
Dry Tang
Branco Extra Seco
Chip Dry

D. Fernando Extra Dry White
Prince Henry
Cocktail Port
Revisec Extra Seco

Porto Aperitivo
Porto Fino
Golden Crown White Extra Dry
Extra Dry White

Port Dry White Estoril
Carito
Dry Tua
Souza Port Dry White

DRY WHITE WINES (BRANCOS)

Very Dry, Old
Very Dry White Port
Rainha Santa Dry White
Top Dry
Secco Branco
Brig's Port White Dry

Superior Alto Douro Dry White Port
Porto Imperial Dry White
Argonauta Dry White
Dry Finish White Port

Dry Port
Aperitive
Dry White Port
Dry Old Port
Clipper

Special White Dry
Porto Dry White Estoril
Dalva's Dry White Port
Dryor
Porto Triunfal (White Dry Port)

DRY RUBY WINES (ALOIRADOS-CLAROS)　　DRY TAWNY WINE (ALOIRADO)　　MEDIUM-DRY WHITE WINE (BRANCO)

D. Velhissimo　　　　Gotas de Ouro (seco)　　　　　　　Velho Seco　　　　　　　　　　Special Pale Dry

MEDIUM-DRY TAWNY WINES (ALOIRADOS)

Directors Reserve　　　　Dow's Boardroom Port　　　　Choco　　　Commendador　　　Victória　　　Dalva's Port

SWEET LIGHT TAWNY WINES (ALOIRADOS-CLAROS)

Fine Royal Choice　　　　Warre's Nimrod Port　　　　Quinta do Bom Retiro　　　　Fine Port　　　　Duque de Bragança

SWEET TAWNY WINES (ALOIRADOS)

Douro Velho
Royal Diamond
Senex
Medieval Port
Top Honours
Particular
Noval 20 Anos
Directorial
Special Reserve
54 Port

Imperial
Quinta do Junco
Royal Port No. 3
Cintra Grand Corona
Vintners Choice
Emperor
Boa Vista
His Eminence's Choice
Rodo
Acordo Finest Old Tawny Port

Superb Old
Shippers
Old Lodge
Lança 2 Coroas
Revinor
Imperial Tawny Doce
Tawny Superior
Very Old Superior
Royal Port No. 1

Porto Clube
Very Superior Old Port
Royal Delicate
Porto Antonat Tawny
Porto Nogueira Genuíno
Ultra Tawny
Porto Cruz
Atlantic
Vasconcellos

SWEET WHITE WINE　　　　VERY SWEET TAWNY WINES (ALOIRADOS)　　　　WHITE LAGRIMA (BRANCO)

Lacrima Christi　　　　　Porto V V　　　Royal Esmeralda　　　　　　Lacrima Christi

SWEET RUBY WINES (TINTOS-ALOIRADOS)

Quinta das Quartas　　　　Marquês de Pombal　　　　Crasto V. O. R.　　　　Century Port　　　　Abelha

SWEET RED WINES (TINTOS)

Rainha Santa 840　　　Imperial Crown

DOURO

Mirandela

Bragança

MURÇA

Chaves

VILA REAL

ALIJÓ

PENAGUIÃO

MESÃO FRIO

← *Porto*

Rio Douro

Aveiro →

LAMEGO

ARMAMAR

Moimenta

TABUAÇO

Moimenta

S. JOÃO DA PESQUEIRA

Penedono

QUINTAS

1	Quinta do Roco	26	Sernadelo Baranda
1A	» Pedregal	27	» Val do Locaio
2	Sernadelo	28	» Mourão
2A	» Telhada	29	» Varaes
3	» Pitarrela	30	» Abraham
4	» Loureiro	31	» Couto
5	» Osorio	32	» Val dos Sapos
6	» Lagares	33	Quinta do Terrão
7	» Travassos	34	» Marrocos
8	» Bairro	35	» Sta Barbara
9	» Partelo	36	» Covaes
10	» Gervide	37	» Garcia
11	» S. Gonçalo	38	» Torre
12	» Boavista	39	» Bouca
13	» Gonte	40	» Matta
14	» Forrester	41	» Val de Lagea
15	» Val de Fogo	42	» S. Joaninho
16	» Loureiro	43	» Deveza
17	» Mourisca	44	» Fonte do Peso
18	» Garcia	45	» Val Bom
19	» Romarigo	46	» Canal
20	» Retorta	47	» Zambujal
21	» Firveda	48	» Enxudreiro
22	» Vacaria	49	» Cabanas
23	» Valado	50	» Bagauste
24	» Carneiro	51	» Foz de mil lobos
25	» Pacheca	52	» Barrilar

53	Quinta do Portelo
54	» Frades
55	» S. Joaninho
56	» Ferrader
57	» Carvalhosa
58	» Val Moreira
59	» Val Mór
60	» Antonio de Melo
61	» Costa
62	» Caleiro
63	» Pasteleira ou Sobreira
64	» Bom Dia
65	» Crasto
66	» Lagoa Alta
67	» Borges
68	» Napoles
69	» Tedo
70	» Alegria
71	» Lobata
72	» Figueiredo
73	» Pessanha
74	» Trancada
75	» Serra
76	» Jocozelo
77	» de la Rosa
78	» Cachuxa
79	» Nova

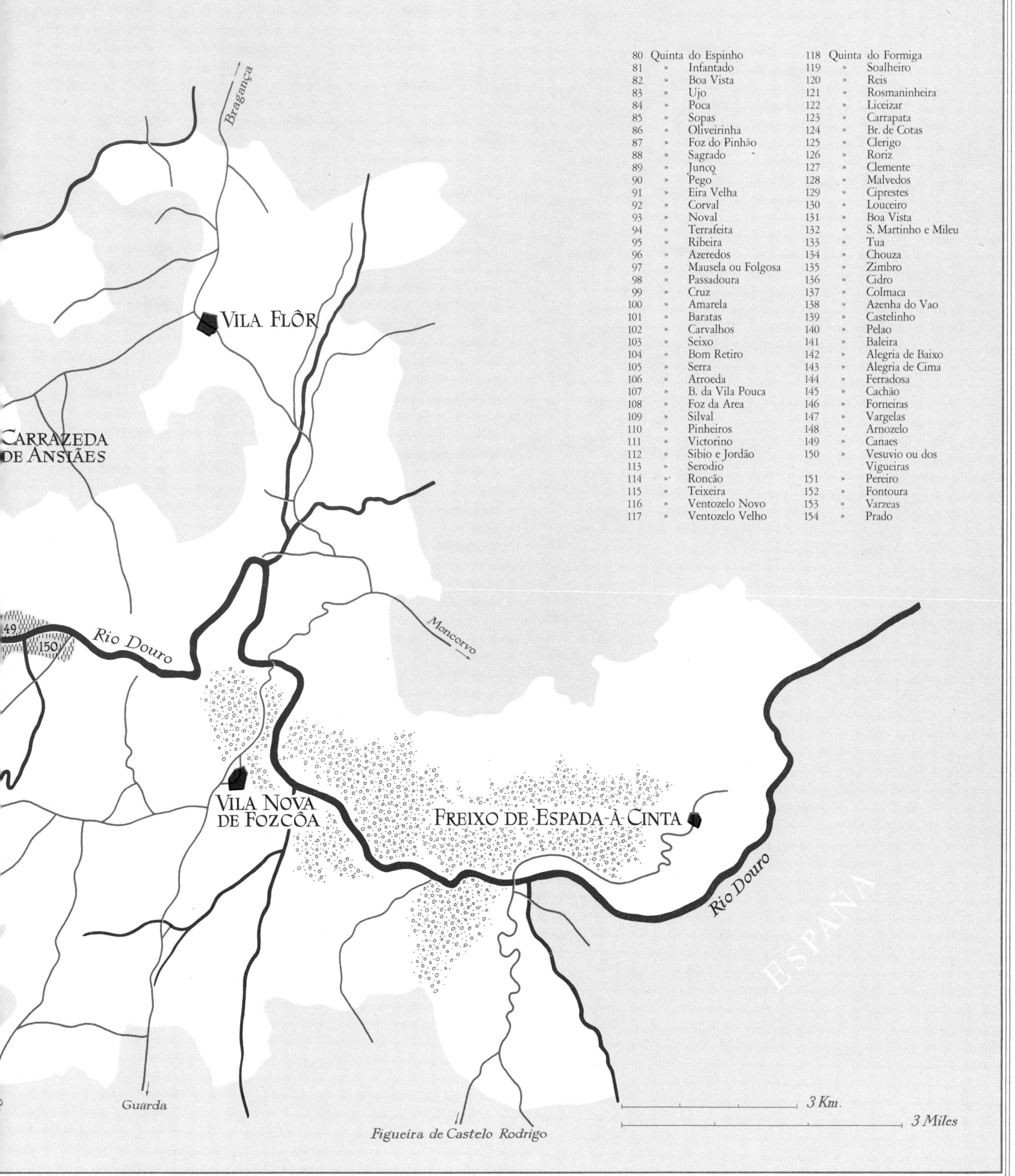

80	Quinta	do Espinho	118	Quinta	do Formiga
81	»	Infantado	119	»	Soalheiro
82	»	Boa Vista	120	»	Reis
83	»	Ujo	121	»	Rosmaninheira
84	»	Poca	122	»	Liceizar
85	»	Sopas	123	»	Carrapata
86	»	Oliveirinha	124	»	Br. de Cotas
87	»	Foz do Pinhão	125	»	Clerigo
88	»	Sagrado	126	»	Roriz
89	»	Junco	127	»	Clemente
90	»	Pego	128	»	Malvedos
91	»	Eira Velha	129	»	Ciprestes
92	»	Corval	130	»	Louceiro
93	»	Noval	131	»	Boa Vista
94	»	Terrafeita	132	»	S. Martinho e Mileu
95	»	Ribeira	133	»	Tua
96	»	Azeredos	134	»	Chouza
97	»	Mausela ou Folgosa	135	»	Zimbro
98	»	Passadoura	136	»	Cidro
99	»	Cruz	137	»	Colmaca
100	»	Amarela	138	»	Azenha do Vao
101	»	Baratas	139	»	Castelinho
102	»	Carvalhos	140	»	Pelao
103	»	Seixo	141	»	Baleira
104	»	Bom Retiro	142	»	Alegria de Baixo
105	»	Serra	143	»	Alegria de Cima
106	»	Arroeda	144	»	Ferradosa
107	»	B. da Vila Pouca	145	»	Cachão
108	»	Foz da Area	146	»	Forneiras
109	»	Silval	147	»	Vargelas
110	»	Pinheiros	148	»	Arnozelo
111	»	Victorino	149	»	Canaes
112	»	Sibio e Jordão	150	»	Vesuvio ou dos Vigueiras
113	»	Serodio			
114	»	Roncão	151	»	Pereiro
115	»	Teixeira	152	»	Fontoura
116	»	Ventozelo Novo	153	»	Varzeas
117	»	Ventozelo Velho	154	»	Prado

Bragança

VILA FLÔR

CARRAZEDA DE ANSIÃES

Rio Douro

49

150

Moncorvo

VILA NOVA DE FOZCÔA

FREIXO DE ESPADA-À-CINTA

Rio Douro

ESPAÑA

Guarda

Figueira de Castelo Rodrigo

3 Km.

3 Miles

THE WINES OF ITALY

GIOVANNI DALMASSO

Tracing the origins of winegrowing and winemaking is not an easy undertaking. History from its very beginning often accumulates legends, myths and traditions; reality is distorted by poetry, folklore or fantasy. In Italy this is particularly true. There the cultivation of the vine goes back to very ancient times. Man apparently discovered in the Neolithic age the quasi-magic properties of the fermented grape, which conferred on the moderate drinker the "wise forgetfulness of life" of which Dante speaks. The vine in those times grew freely in its wild state in the forests, winding itself around the trees and climbing to a considerable height. Man learned to cultivate it and produce the still-mysterious process of alcoholic fermentation.

One point remained in dispute for a long time: should our vine, commonly called the European vine (the plant *vitis vinifera*) be considered as a native plant or was it on the other hand imported into Italy on the tide of the great human migrations from Asia Minor or North Africa? Doubtless both theories have a basis in fact. The crossing of the different vine-plants gave birth to the innumerable varieties of vines which led Virgil to exclaim in his *Georgics*: *Quem scire velit, Libyci velit aequoris idem* ("He who would know [the infinite variety of vines] would just as well [count] the grains of sand in the Lybian desert").

Certainly even in Homeric times Sicily was producing abundant quantities of wine. One episode in the *Odyssey* seems to point to this: when, near Etna, the Cyclops Polyphemus, whom Ulysses had blinded, falls stupefied by drink into a deep sleep. The Etruscans, who had settled in Italy perhaps about 1000 B.C., must certainly have contributed to disseminating the vine. They came from the East, where agriculture had already reached a certain stage of evolution, which no doubt included vinegrowing and winemaking. But when the Etruscans landed on the Tyrrhenian sea coast they probably found old and sturdy vines already growing there, since Pliny had asserted that a statue in Populonia was carved from a single vine plant.

There is no doubt that in the time of Pliny the Elder, Italy already led the world in the quantity and excellence of her wines, outstripping even Greece, whose pupil she had been in winegrowing. In his *Naturalis Historia* Pliny speaks of 195 kinds of wine, of which over half were produced in Italy. What were some of the wines of ancient Italy? The MAMERTINO around Messina, the TAUROMENITANUM from the region of Taormina, the POTULAMUM, the SIRACUSANUM, the wines of Agrigente and Selinonte and the BIBLINO in the region of Syracuse. In Calabria the most appreciated were the BRUTIUM and, moving northwards to Lucania, the wines of Consentia, Tempio, Rhegium and Buxentium. Apulia also produced well-reputed wines, notably those of Tarente, Babia, Brindisi, Canosa and Aulon. However the region which in the times of the Empire produced the wines praised most highly by the Latin poets was the area dominated by Naples, Campania, which could boast its FALERNO, its CECUBO, its CALENO, its FORMIANO and the wines of Vesuvius.

Latium supplied numerous wines to the capital of the ancient world, but none was of outstanding quality.

The same could be said, moving north, of the wines of Umbria, the Marches and even Tuscany, which today is such an important wineproducing area. It is not until one comes to the Upper Adriatic, around the Gulf of Trieste, that one finds one of the most famous wines of Antiquity: the PUCINUM, produced near the mouth of the Timaro, not far from Aquileia.

The north of Italy produced another great wine, the RETICO, which Virgil himself claimed was rivalled only by the FALERNO. It is nevertheless difficult to know for certain whether it resembled the excellent wines of today from the region of Verona, or those of the Valtelino or even the Trentino.

The fame of Italian wines has in no way diminished over the centuries. Italy today has the world's second largest winegrowing area and is the biggest producer of wine and of dessert grapes. Her average annual production over the last decade (1958-1967) was 1,408,000,000 gallons. In 1967 it even reached 1,650,000,000 gallons. Apulia headed the list of regional harvests in 1967 and has done so for several years; this province alone produces more than 264,000,000 gallons of wine. In second place comes Veneto, with some 220,000,000 gallons: third, Sicily, 198,000,000; fourth Emilia-Romagna (187,000,000) and fifth Piedmont (154,000,000); sixth comes Latium (110,000,000); seventh Tuscany (88,000,000); eighth Campania (72,600,000); ninth Lombardy (66,000,000) and tenth the Marches (59,400,000), followed by the Abruzzi, the Trentino-Upper Adige, Sardinia and Calabria. One of the essential characteristics of Italian winegrowing is its repartition in two forms: monoculture and mixed culture. Italy is the only country in the world where the cultivation of vines alongside other plants, either climbing or herbaceous, is still very widespread. In 1967, for 3,075,000 acres of vineyards under monoculture there were 5,137,500 acres under mixed culture.

As for the distribution of vineyards according to altitude, the Virgilian precept *Bacchus amat colles* ("Bacchus loves the hills") is still true today in Italian agricultural economy and continues to give a very typical appearance to the countryside of peninsular Italy. In many regions, for example the Monferrato and the Langhe of Piedmont, or the region of Pavia in Lombardy, the hills which stretch as far as the eye can see are often entirely covered by a mantle of vineyards which seem almost to have been etched there by a calligrapher of olden days.

In many places the way of life and social standards have changed, accompanied inevitably by a progressive reduction in the rural population, which is increasingly attracted by the salary of the urban worker. The labour shortage has brought about a marked change in Italian winegrowing. Mechanization has been introduced almost everywhere. Machines have been tried out for the wine harvests, but sometimes the whole appearance of vineyards on the plains had to be changed. This is why vines "married" to trees (elms, maples, poplars) are gradually giving way to close-set, regular rows of plants which make possible much more rational methods of cultivation.

NORTHERN ITALY

Northern Italy, which in all produces around 660,000,000 gallons of wine (almost half the national production) has a great variety of reds, whites and rosés. They are mainly ordinary, fine or superior wines, but they also include special wines such as sparkling wines and aromatized or *passiti* wines.

It would take too long to list them all; better to limit oneself to a few notes on the best ones, on a geographical basis, taking the winegrowing regions in order from west to east.

PIEDMONT. Although, as mentioned earlier, other regions of Italy are bigger producers of wine, there is probably not one which surpasses Piedmont in the variety of quality wines yielded by the vineyards which cover its hillsides as far as the eye can see.

In general red table wines predominate, classed according to quality as ordinary (for everyday consumption), fine and superior. But there is no lack of whites—dry table wines or luxury wines, sparkling, aromatized or not, and there are even some dessert wines.

Beginning with the red wines and passing over the ordinary wines, which are often produced by mixing various grapes, the *uvaggi*, we find that one of them outclasses all the others: it is referred to as "the king of Italian wines" and "the wine of kings": BAROLO. It wins such praise both because of its intrinsic quality and because in the nineteenth century it was the favourite of the monarchs of the House of Savoy, who even envisaged growing it on their estates. Its production zone (quite a small area) is found in the Langhe district, a region of hills around Alba (the ancient Albe la Langhe, rival of Rome) and which includes, besides Barolo, a dozen other districts. The grape that produces this superb wine is the NEBBIOLO, a vine which was already under cultivation about A.D. 1300, not only in this region but in other areas of Piedmont and

In Italy, where vines are cultivated in all twenty administrative regions, the system of naming wines varies from one region to another and even from one district to another. Sometimes the name of the wine is derived from that of the vine, such as the Barbera and the Dolcetto, or the district where it is produced, as with Marsala. Other names, such as Sangue de Giuda or Lacryma Christi, evoke the legendary past.

under other names, as in Lombardy and Valtelino. This aristocratic plant requires a carefully chosen climate and soil. It is not a prolific plant, yet it is capable of producing wines of a very high quality. BAROLO is an excellent *da arrosto* wine, in other words a wine to drink with roasted or grilled meats. It is a superior quality red with a strong alcohol content (13º-14º), a lot of body, a harmonious flavour and a rich and fine bouquet. When young it has a sharp taste, due to its acid and tannin content; it requires a long ageing process. Today its authenticity is guaranteed by the regulation on production that forms part of the Presidential Decree of May 6th, 1966. This law stipulates that the name BAROLO may be given to wine produced in the above-mentioned region only if it has been kept at least three years in oak casks; this gives it a beautiful orange-red colour. Its delicate bouquet has overtones of violets, mixed with a slight odour of tar; it has a somewhat dry flavour, which is always rather austere yet at the same time harmonious and velvety. All this makes for a wine particularly well-suited to red meats, such as game, roasts and braised beef (sometimes accompanied by truffles). It is served at a temperature of 20º C. and should be opened an hour beforehand, to allow a slight oxydation.

A wine which has a great deal in common with BAROLO is the BARBARESCO, which also comes from the *Nebbiolo* vine. It derives its name from the district where it is produced, land clinging to the steep slope of a hill on the right bank of the Tanaro, not far from Alba and overlooked by a Roman tower. It also must be aged in oak but matures more quickly than BAROLO.

In Piedmont the *Nebbiolo*, also called *Spana*, yields other good quality *da arrosto* wines, produced in even smaller quantities than the two named above. They are GATTINARA, LESSONA, MOTTALCIATA, GHEMME, SIZZANO, FARA and BOCA, found in the provinces of Vercelli and Novarro, at the foot of the Biella Alps. All these wines have a sharp taste when young and take a long time to mature. With time, however, they take on an admirably harmonious flavour.

On the rocky slopes of the hills which lie on the borders of the province of Turin and the Aosta Valley it is once more the *Nebbiolo*—which changes its name yet again, to become this time the *Picotener*—which produces another much sought after *da arrosto* wine: the CAREMA. Slightly lighter in colour, it is, once suitably aged, an outstandingly fine wine.

Another Piedmontese wine, produced on a much wider scale, is the BARBERA, which takes its name from the vine. The size of the area producing it and the quantities in which it is produced make it the most representative of Piedmont's wines. At an estimate, half the wine production in Piedmont is made up of BARBERA. It originates in the Astigiano, but is also found in a large part of the province of Alessandria and in the provinces of Cuneo and Turin. Genuine BARBERA D'ASTI, if correctly matured (not less than three to four years), is looked on as an excellent quality wine which with time acquires a harmonious flavour.

Many of the characteristics of BARBERA may also be attributed to another wine, the FREISA, which also takes its name from its vine. It is produced in large quantities and comes, in part, from the same wine-producing area. It is grown in the Astigiano and on the hills which reach from Asti almost to the outskirts of Turin. The centre of this area is Chieri. Two quite distinct types of FREISA are made: one is dry, the other a more popular speciality. If sufficiently matured the former improves greatly (for a shorter time, however, than the BARBERA). It develops a delicate violet flavour and loses much of the acid taste of its youth.

A third red table wine, produced in large quantities in another part of Piedmont, is the DOLCETTO. It takes its name from a vine bearing a very sweet grape which matures very rapidly. The wine, however, is a dry one. It has developed all its qualities by the first or at the latest the second year. It has body and a moderate amount of acidity. It has an agreeable, well-rounded aroma, slightly but pleasantly bitter. A slightly sparkling variety, best appreciated outside meal-times, is also produced. The DOLCETTO vineyards go as far as the Langhe region, which is made up of a series of hills. These divide in two, part of them lying between Alba and Mondori in the province of Cuneo, the other centred on Acqui in the province of Alessandria. Since the *Dolcetto* matures so quickly, it is also grown above 1,800 feet.

Another wine that improves with age is the GRIGNOLINO, produced in a very small area lying for the most part in the province of Asti, but also to a lesser extent in the province of Alessandria (near Casalemonferrato). Many consider it to be the best of Piedmont's table wines because of its fresh, delicate and harmonious flavour, its fragrant aroma, its fine, light ruby colour and its moderate alcohol content (11º-12º).

As has already been pointed out, there are, in comparison to the red wines, very few white wines. The best-known and most prevalent of these is the CORTESE, produced almost entirely in the province of Alessandria. It is a very pleasant wine, with a reasonable alcohol content (10º-11º), a fine straw-yellow colour and a flavour which is dry, light, fresh and delicately perfumed and goes very well with fish.

Another fine white wine comes from the Canavese region in the province of Turin, principally from Caluso, the centre of the area. The vine used for this wine is the *Erbaluce*, hence the name ERBALUCE DI CALUSO.

The same vine also yields small quantities of a famous dessert wine, the CALUSO PASSITO, obtained after a lengthy fermentation of the grapes.

But Piedmont is also proud, and rightly so, of its "special" wines, of which the best examples are the MOSCATO D'ASTI and the ASTI SPUMANTE. The grape from which they are made is the *Yellow Muscat* also called *Muscat di Canelli* after a small town in the centre of the production area and the industrial zone. Here are produced the famous sparkling wines that have won such favour on the national and international markets. These wines are subjected to a complex and detailed treatment, now perfected, and acquire a distinctive personality much prized by the general public.

Among the other special wines of Piedmont is the BRACHETTO, grown on a small strip of land between Asti and Acqui. It is a wine with a delicious aroma recalling both the *Muscat* and roses; it is one of the rare good-quality sparkling red wines. Finally, a red MALVASIA SPUMANTE, produced in the province of Asti, has quite recently come to the fore.

LOMBARDY. Lombardy is certainly not one of the main wineproducing regions of Italy, but it can lay claim to several quality wines. The vineyards are divided into three distinct areas: the Oltrepò of Pavia, the Valteline and the western shores of Lake Garda.

The first of these would seem to be the prolongation of the hills of Piedmont, or more precisely of the hills of Monferrato. It lies in the province of Pavia and appears to be an endless series of hills, covered with magnificent vineyards producing excellent red and white wines. Of the red wines, the majority are produced from the Piedmontese *Barbera* and local vines: *Ovattina* (also called *Bonarda*), *Uva Rara* or "rare grape", and *Ughetta*. Their names are well known to connoisseurs today: BUTTAFUOCO ("fire-propagator") BARBACARLO ("Charles' beard") SANGUE DI GIUDA ("blood of Judas") CLASTIDIO, FRECCIAROSSA, MONTENAPOLEONE. Brilliant ruby red in colour, with a good bouquet and a dry flavour, they are on the whole mellow, well-constituted table wines which if matured correctly ripen into good *da arrosto* wines appreciated in particular by the Milanese. Their alcohol content reaches 11º-13º and their rather pronounced acidity is yet not excessive. Besides these dry wines, there are other agreeable wines, such as the CANNETO DOLCE, the BONARDA AMABILE, the NEBBIOLO DI RETORBIDO, held in great esteem for drinking between meals.

In the white wines of the Oltrepó of Pavia, the most outstanding come from the *Riesling* vine (mainly Italian, to a lesser extent Rhenish) the *Pinots* or the *Cortese*, such as the FRECCIAROSSA, the white CLASTIDIO or the white CANNETO. All are good dry white wines with a delicate bouquet.

Another major winegrowing area of Lombardy producing excellent quality wines is the Valtelino, in the province of Sondrio. The quality of its wines has been acknowledged for centuries, though it is open to doubt whether the famous RETICO of the Rhaetian vines which was such a favourite of the Emperor Augustus is in fact the ancestor of today's Valtelino wines.

The work of the vinegrowers of the valley of the Adda, in the province of Sondrio, who crawl on to narrow vertiginous terraces to tend their vines, deserves to be admired. From these exposed sites they obtain first quality *da arrosto* wines. These are *Nebbiolo* vines, which we have mentioned before, but here they change their name to *Chiavennasca*. They produce lively, rich, smooth and harmoniously flavoured wines, deep and intense in colour, dry, with a subtle bouquet and rather full-bodied. They are identified by the names of the districts where they are grown. The best-known are the SASSELLA, GRUMELLO, INFERNO, FRACIA, VALGELLA, and VILLA. These are wines which are particularly sought-after by the Swiss, many of whom are moreover proprietors of vineyards in Valtelino, which is a sort of natural prolongation of their own lands.

One particular type of Valtelino wine whose prestige has revived recent years is the SFURZAT. It is a wine which responds to a long maturing process, when it changes into a real dessert wine (with an alcohol content of 15º-16º). It tastes rather sweet at first, then takes on a smooth, well-rounded, rich flavour and turns almost orange in colour.

The third well-known winegrowing area in Lombardy is the western bank of Lake Garda, in the province of Brescia. It has been famous for many years for its excellent red and rosé fine table wines. The most popular, in Lombardy principally but also abroad, are those from the Valtenesi. A sixteenth-century sage, A. Bacci, declared that the wines of Saló on Lake Garda were sold as far away as Germany; he mentioned the SCHIAVA and GROPELLO. Confining ourselves to the present day, we find a predominance of red and rosé wines. These are made principally from the *Gropello* and *Merzemino* vines. The red wine is ruby coloured, with an aroma which develops progressively and a slightly bitter but harmonious and velvety flavour. The rosé is cherry-coloured and both its bouquet and its flavour are sweeter.

Another wine which comes from this same province of Brescia, near the southern slopes of Lake Garda, is the LUGANA, a dry, high quality white wine. It is produced in limited quantities on the clay lands of the plain from the *Lugana*, a particular type of *Trebbiano*. It has an almost green straw colour, a delicate bouquet, a fresh and harmonious flavour and goes extremely well with fish. The same region also produces the

PUSTERLA, a fine wine which is found as red, white and rosé. It comes from quite a small vineyard which lies to the north of the castle of Brescia.

LIGURIA. Although winegrowing plays only a small role in the economy of this region, Ligurian wines nevertheless have a very good reputation. Among the most important is the VERMENTINO, a good quality dry white wine found on the western Riviera between Genoa and Ventimiglia. It has a fine dark straw-yellow colour, a pleasant bouquet and a moderate alcohol content. Close to the same area, the red vine *Rossese* yields the DOLCEACQUA, a particularly well-known wine, which improves with age. Garnet-red in colour, it is particularly pleasant, very slightly alcoholic and with a delicate bouquet.

Along the Eastern Riviera the most famous wines are those of the CINQUETERRE ("Five Lands") which take their name from a picturesque part of the province of Spezia. Winegrowing here is quite an extraordinary process, carried out according to tradition on the dizzy slopes which rise above the sea. The vines cling to the rock-face, producing, very sparingly, small clusters of white grapes of the *Rosco*, *Albarolo* and *Vermentino* varieties. These vines ripen perfectly, giving a must with a very high sugar content which is turned into dry wine, or after a brief fermentation period, into dessert wines which go by the curious local name of SCIACCHETRA.

THREE VENETIAS. This large area of northern Italy today competes with Apulia for first place as the biggest producer of wine. It can also pride itself on possessing an extremely large number of quality wines of all categories. Moving still from west to east in this rapid survey one arrives, after Lombardy, in the neighbouring province of Verona. Here one must first of all go up the River Adige as far as Tridentine Venetia in the provinces of Trentino and Bolzano.

In the province of Trentino are found both white and red table wines qualifying for the "fine" or "superior quality" label. One of the most characteristic fine wines is the TEROLDEGO. It comes from a vineyard lying at the junction of the Noce and the Adige rivers called the "Campo rotaliano" which is almost entirely covered with the famous "Trentino trellises". This wine, produced from the *Teroldego* vine, is quite different from the other Trentino wines. It has a bright ruby colour, with a strong bouquet, which, as the wine ages, takes on a hint of raspberries and violets. The MARZE-MINO is a noticeably different wine, light ruby in colour, with a delicate aroma which asserts itself very gradually; it is subtly full-bodied with a refined flavour.

Besides these two local wines the Trentino also produces from imported vines wines such as the CABERNET, the MERLOT and the PINOT NOIR. All are wines which after a short ageing period can be reclassed as "superior quality" wines. First place among the whites must be given to the TRAMINER: it is a very fine wine which takes its name from a vine from the Tridentine district of Termeno. It has a delicate aroma and a dry and velvety taste. Another superior quality white wine with a great deal of distinction is made from a species of *Riesling* which grows in Trentino, the *Riesling Italico*. Finally, the *Pinot Blanc* gives excellent semi-sparkling and sparkling wines.

The province of Bolzano (Upper Adige) produces a wide variety of quality wines, especially superior quality red table wines. Of these the most outstanding is the SANTA MADDELENA, obtained from the *Schiave*. This vine is cultivated on the abrupt and picturesque slopes that tower above the town of Bolzano and behind which rises the magnificent silhouette of the Dolomites. CALDARO, produced in great quantity, originates in the terraced vineyards bordering the Lago Caldaro, part of which moreover belongs to the province of Trentino. It is a wine with a very slight alcohol content and an extremely agreeable taste: at once dry and mellow, it gives off a light aroma of almonds. Finally there is the LAGREIN rosé wine, coming from the grape of the same name, which is a delicately perfumed wine with a dry, fresh and harmonious flavour.

Among the most reputed of the whites are the TERLANO, a dry, light, greenish-yellow wine, and those mentioned already, such as the TRAMINER, the PINOT —especially the BORGOGNA (WEISSBURGUNDER) and the PINOT GRIS (RULÄNDER)—the RIESLING RENANO and the SYLVANER VERDE, which is a speciality of the Bressanone vineyard. All these local wines benefit from extremely painstaking production and cultivation techniques which give each a distinct personality.

Turning back down the Adige river one arrives in Veneto proper, or "Euganea" Venetia, a vast and varied region with many vineyards, producing charming wines of all categories including excellent fine or superior quality reds and whites.

The BARDOLINO, VALPOLICELLA and VALPANTENA red wines come from the most famous vineyards. They are produced from a mixture of various native vines, especially the *Molinara* (or *Rosara*) the *Corvina Veronese* and the *Negrera* with *Rondinella* and *Rossignola*. All these wines are ready for consumption after only a few months of fermentation, but improve greatly if aged for two to three years. They then acquire characteristics which raise them into the category of superior quality wines. Generally, however, they are less robust and less austere, as well as lighter in colour, than the Piedmontese wines.

A very well-known quality white wine from Verona is the SOAVE, the product of a small vineyard on the

The Oltrepò of Pavia is an extension of the Piedmont hills, and produces excellent red and white wines from vineyards that climb the hills and descend the slopes.

The grapes are being povred into this traditional cart, usually hauled by two white oxen, in this scene at Asti, home of the famous spaskling Asti spumante.

frontier of the province of Vicenza. It is made from two vines, the *Garganega* and the *Trebbiano*. Straw-yellow, with a dry harmonious flavour and a delicate bouquet, it is a light-bodied wine with a low alcohol content. Nor should one overlook the RECIOTO, a famous, special, almost liqueur-like red wine, whose production is an ancient tradition in the province of Verona—some even seek to trace it back to Theodoric the Great, King of the Ostrogoths (A.D. 454-526). It comes from the same vines as the VALPOLICELLA and undergoes a long period of fermentation.

A wine similar to the SOAVE, the GARGANEGA DI GAMBELLARE, is produced in the province of Vicenza in an area bordering on the preceding one. Other excellent white wines, such as the PINOT (white or *gris*) or the VESPAIOLA are found in the same region. Just recently the production of fine red table wines has been developed, especially in the region of Breganza. These are obtained from imported vines such as the *Merlot, Cabernet* and *Pinot Noir*, and from the *Tokay*.

We now come to the province of Padua. Ten years ago it could boast of only a small number of fine and superior quality table wines, produced on an unusual hill formation of volcanic origin, the Colli Euganei, which rise from the immense plain characteristic of most of the province. These wines have a very ancient reputation, which today has been reinforced by the introduction, side by side with the old local vines *(Gargenaga, Pinella Serpina)*, of foreign vines such as the *Pinot Blanc*, the *Sauvignon* and the *Riesling*. Formerly vines such as the *Pattaresco* and the *Corbinella* and another variety, the unassuming *Friularo*, used for producing red blending wines, flourished in this region. Today cultivation is concentrated on quality vines such as the *Cabernet Franc* and the *Merlot* which can yield good and even excellent red wines.

The province of Venice, which is the natural continuation of Padua, is a plain where, thanks to the introduction of rigorously selected foreign vines, good red wines are produced from the *Cabernet* and *Merlot* and reasonably fine white wines from the *Riesling Italico* or the *Sauvignon*.

It is worth pausing a moment in the province of Treviso: this is one of the most varied and pleasant of the Venetias. Its claim to fame lies in having founded, in 1877, Italy's first school specializing in winegrowing and oenology, the School of Conegliano, which has made a considerable contribution to the development of these subjects. It was next to this school that in 1923 an experimental laboratory opened that has made a decisive contribution to vinegrowing and the wine industry in the Venetias.

The province of Treviso has acquired a solid reputation for the white wines grown on its hills and the few red wines produced in the plain. Among the white wines, those produced on the hills of Conegliano and others from the hills of Valdobbiadene are deservedly famous: the former are golden-yellow in colour and come mostly from the *Prosecco*; the latter, paler in colour, come from the *Verdiso*. The best of them are used to make excellent sparkling wines.

Besides white wines this region also produces good fine red table wines, especially from the *Merlot*, to a lesser degree from the *Cabernet Franc* and a very old local plant, the *Marzemino*. Formerly the RABOSO DI PIAVE, an extremely acid and deeply coloured wine, was also much-prized, especially as a wine to mix with others. It has been largely replaced by the RABOSO VERONESE, which is in itself an honest table wine.

Now for the easternmost region of northern Italy, where the Friuli and the Julian Venetia meet. The people of Friuli have always been extremely proud of their wines, even if in the past they were not always of very good quality. Among the traditional wines made from local plants should be mentioned the REFOSCHI among the reds, and the VERDUZZO among the whites. Of the latter the one most worthy of mention is the TOCAI FRIOLANO, made from a plant which has been grown widely for a long time in part of the plain (towards Portogruaro) where it yields an exquisite wine, harmonious in flavour, fresh and extremely pleasant. It should be stressed that this wine has no connection with the famous Hungarian TOKAY, which is produced from quite different vines. Nevertheless the vintners of Friuli still produce (as did the great lords of the past) a liqueur-like wine, resembling the TOKAY ASZU, which takes its name from the vine, the *Piccolit*, so called because its grape seeds, due to a malformation, are very small in size. The fruit is left to decay before being pressed, in order to give a wine with a high alcohol content, but which is also deliciously sweet and perfumed and of a golden-yellow colour.

Towards the east we come to the province of Gorizia, which suffered severely during the last war. Today its winegrowing is limited to the Collio Goriziano, a small hilly area bordering the Friuli. Its vineyards produce, albeit in limited quantities, a variety of white and red wines of undeniable quality. Among the whites: the RIESLING ITALICO, the TOCAI, the PINOT BLANC, the PINOT GRIS, the SAUVIGNON, the TRAMINER, the MALVASIA (a non-aromatic Malmsey, probably coming from Istria); and among the reds the MERLOT, the CABERNET FRANC, the PINOT NOIR. A white wine which is no longer very common but was formerly well-known is the RIBOLLA GIALLO (from the name of the vine); a red wine, the old TERRANO, produced in limited quantities on the Karst de Gorizia from red *Refoso*, should also be mentioned here.

EMILIA ROMAGNA. As far as production is concerned, Emilia Romagna is one of the most important wine-growing regions of Italy. Here the vines stretch across a plain whose climate is eminently suitable to their growth. The red wines grown here belong to the LAMBRUSCHI family and are widely appreciated. All these wines have some characteristics in common: a very bright colour, a very pronounced bouquet and flavour, a typical acid taste, often tempered by a slight sweetness and, finally, an abundant but shortlived froth. They all fit perfectly with Emilian cooking, which is highly flavoured and rather greasy, based as it is largely on pork. The LAMBRUSCHI come from different varieties of the *Lambrusca* vine grown on the Emilian plain in the province of Parma above all, but also in Reggio Emilia, Modena and Bologna. They are not all of the same quality. The best wine is certainly the SORBARA, named for the district of Modena where it predominates. While possessing the same characteristics as the others, it is a finer, more graceful and undoubtedly superior wine. It turns sparkling if produced carefully by the appropriate technique. However, a fault in the flowers of the sapling considerably reduces its productivity and restricts its cultivation.

Other good LAMBRUSCHI are the SALAMINO (or LAMBRUSCO DI SANTA CROCE) and the GRASPAROSSA (or LAMBRUSCO DI CASTELVETRO). Finally the LAMBRUSCO MAESTRI and the LAMBRUSCO DI MONTERICCO should also be mentioned.

Besides the LAMBRUSCHI, Emilia produces several red wines for everyday consumption and for blending purposes. Only the part of the province of Plaisance bordering on Lombardy and Piedmont produces fine table wines. One of these is the GUATTURNIO of the Colli Piacentini, produced from the Piedmontese *Barbera* and *Croatina* vines grown in the foothills of the Apennines. Among the white table wines are those derived from the *Otrugo, Trebbiano, Romagnolo, Sauvignon, Pinot,* and some special aromatic wines obtained from the *Malvasia di Candia* and the *Yellow Muscat.*

If we go from Modena to Bologna and from there to the provinces of Forli and Ravenna (and so enter Romagna), we find, beside the extensive cultivation of the vine on the plain, winegrowing in the hills. Among the vines of the plain a white vine predominates, the *Trebbiano Romagnolo* which gives everyday wines. Of the hillside vines, another white grape vine, the *Albana,* grown most of all between Imola and Cesena, has given a top quality wine for centuries. The most famous is the BERTINORO, an excellent dry white wine, golden yellow, with a delicate, fruity flavour, which can take on the agreeable personality of a dessert wine.

CENTRAL ITALY

The six regions of Central Italy (Tuscany, the Marches, Umbria, Latium, Abruzzi and Molise) produce in all only 242,000,000 gallons of wine (about one sixth of the country's total production). Two of these regions have a very old reputation as winegrowers.

TUSCANY. Of Tuscany, one could say the same as of Piedmont: although it is not one of the biggest wineproducers in the country (it maintains an average of 88,000,000 gallons), the proportion of fine wines and superior table wines certainly exceeds that of other regions of Italy. About 80 per cent of these wines are reds. The most important and the best known internationally—it is often taken as a synonym for "Italian wine"—is CHIANTI. Its name comes from a small area in the centre of Tuscany, between the provinces of Sienna and Florence. The name CHIANTI appears in very reliable documents as early as 1260, but old texts refer most frequently to a CHIANTI of 1378, when the "CHIANTI League" was instituted (by an official Act of the Republic of Florence). It comprised the present districts of Gaide, Radda and Castellina. The production zone has, however, slowly been extended with the passage of time to include the districts of Poggibonsi, San Sasiano, Val di Pesa, Castelnuevo Berardenga and other Tuscan vineyards more or less bordering on it, all of which have produced for a long time a wine which has the same biochemical qualities as the original CHIANTI. As the demand for this wine keeps on growing both in Italy and abroad and it becomes increasingly difficult to refuse the right to the name CHIANTI to wines grown in these neighbouring vineyards, the problem has been discussed on many occasions and was even taken up by Parliament. The result was a ministerial decree in 1932, followed by a decree of the President of the Republic in 1967 which brought the controversy to an end. The latter decree stipulated that the name CHIANTI belonged to all the wines produced in a clearly defined area. This area was subdivided into six strictly defined sub-areas which use in addition to the name CHIANTI CLASSICO for the whole area, the names MONTALBANO, RUFINO, COLLI FIORENTINI, COLLI SENESI, COLLI ARETINI and COLLINE PISANE.

The predominant vines remain the traditional ones. The regulation on the production of CHIANTI lays down that the basic vines must be: 50-80 per cent *Sangiovese,*

10-30 per cent *Canaiolo Nero* and 10-30 per cent *Malvasia del Chianti*. Among the complementary vines are the *Colorino*, the *Mammolo* and the *Bonamico*.

There is one traditional and characteristic practice in the winemaking process of Chianti, called the *governo* ("government"). It consists of adding to the new wine during the month of November a small quantity (5 to 10 per cent) of must made from grapes which have been specially conserved on trellises or hung up on hooks. If the cellar is kept at the right temperature this grape ferments and if the casks are hermetically sealed, the carbon dioxide dissolves in the wine, giving it a characteristic tang and adding a surprising but agreeable taste to the young Chianti. Tuscans say it "kisses and bites". Chianti can be drunk in its first year, at the latest in late spring. But the best is aged in casks for two or three years. After at least two years it can be labelled Chianti Vecchio, and after three years of ageing it earns the right to the description *réserve*.

The characteristics of Chianti are: a very bright ruby-red colour which tends to garnet as it ages; a strong bouquet when young but which turns with time to an aroma of violets or iris; a dry flavour, slightly impregnated with tannin, which becomes delicate, mild and velvety with age. The alcohol content of Chianti must be at least 11.5°; that of the wine entitled to the label Chianti Classico 12°.

Most Chianti is sold commercially in *fiaschi* with a straw covering. These *fiaschi* formerly contained around two litres. Then one-litre half-fiaschi were introduced, followed by half-litre bottles and finally quarter-litre ones. The oldest Chiantis, the "reserves" of very famous houses (such as Ricasoli, Antinori, Frescobaldior, the more modern ones of Rufino and Melini) are always put in dark glass bottles.

Chianti is not, however, the only highly-prized wine of Tuscany. To mention only those superior red table wines most closely resembling Chianti, there is first and foremost the Brunello di Montalcino from the gentle countryside of the same name near Sienna. It too is produced from the *Sangiovese*; its alcohol content is between 12.5° and 13°. It has more body than Chianti and needs maturing for at least three years before becoming smooth and perfectly harmonious and acquiring its delicious aroma of violets. It is unfortunate that this wine cannot be produced in larger quantities.

Next comes the Nobile di Montepulciano (which also takes its name from a small area in the province of Sienna). It is a wine with a rather dark, almost garnet colour and a very slightly bitter taste. It too requires ageing for at least two years. It was an extremely popular wine in the seventeenth century.

Some other famous red wines should also be mentioned which often bear the names of families of the Tuscan nobility; the Brioli of Ricasoli, the Antinori, the Pomino, the Nippozano of Frescobaldi, the Artimino and the Carmignano. Nor should one forget the Montecarlo, a light red wine produced on the hillsides of the province of Lucques, which was already well-known in the thirteenth century.

Although produced in much smaller quantities than the red wines, some of the whites deserve mention; above all the Vernaccia di S. Gimignano. It is an excellent dry white wine which comes from a small area of the same name in the province of Sienna and from a vine which also has the same name. It should be pointed out here that the Vernaccia of Tuscany bears no relation to the more famous Vernaccia of Sardinia and Oristano. This is a wine whose praises were sung by poets and minstrels as long ago as the fourteenth century. It is never more than 12° and has a very slight acidity.

Chianti also takes the form of good dry white wines (in small quantities) which are often rather loosely termed Chianti Bianco. One of the best is the Arbia Bianco of Ricasoli. But dry white wines are produced in greater quantities in the province of Arezzo: for instance those called the Bianchi Vergini ("virgin whites"), which are only slightly alcoholized, but have a very strong acid content. There is also a Montecarlo Bianco which was highly prized by the Medici when they were masters of Florence.

Even better known are the white wines of the Isle of Elba. Associated with the memory of Napoleon's exile, this iron-bearing island in the Tyrrhenian Sea, the largest of the Tuscan archipeligo, produces several quality wines in the vineyards which cling in dizzy flights of terraces to its mountainsides. The vines grown there are the *Biancone di Portoferraio* and the *Procanico*, a sub-species of the *Trebbiano Toscano*. Suitably treated, they yield wines which are highly esteemed as an accompaniment to fresh seafood or the island's delicious crayfish.

Besides the Elba Bianco a red wine is also produced from a base of *Sangiovese*, mixed with a little *Canaiolo* and the white grapes spoken of earlier. These are wines with a very slight alcohol content and which have relatively little acidity.

The Isle of Elba also produces some good special wines: chief of these is the Aleatico di Portoferraio. Ruby-red, with a bouquet and flavour which become more pronounced with the passage of time, it brings to mind the sweet, velvety, highly-alcoholized *Muscat*. There is in fact a Moscato dell'Elba, golden-yellow, sweet and wonderfully aromatic, made from the semi-dried grapes of the *Moscato* plant.

The amount of Tuscan wine for sale has grown progressively smaller over the last 50 years, partly because of the ravages of phylloxera, but also because of serious economic difficulties, arising chiefly from high production costs. However, for the last ten years production has again been on the increase, due to the slow but fundamental transformation of the traditional mixed culture into monoculture. Thanks also to the effect of a new law protecting the nomenclature of the better-known wines, production should soon reach its original level, with the added benefit of a guarantee to the consumer that the wines bearing such impressive labels are authentic.

THE MARCHES. In this province, on the Adriatic side of Tuscany, mixed culture still outweighs the specialized methods, but as the old plantations of climbing vines disappear they are replaced by short vine-stocks.

On the whole the proportion of white wines produced in the Marches is higher than in other regions of Italy. At an estimate, about 50 per cent of its production is taken up by red wines, 47 per cent by whites and the rest by rosés. Without a doubt, the best and the most characteristic wines are to be found among the whites. First comes the VERDICCHIO DEI CASTELLI DI JESI, produced in the province of Ancona. The hills it grows on and the vine it comes from bear the same name. It is one of Italy's most pleasant dry whites.

Another very similar wine is the VERDICCHIO DI MATELICA. The same grapes are used as for the first VERDICCHIO, but they are generally mixed with a small proportion of *Trebbiano Toscano* and *Malvasia Toscana*. It, too, is a straw-yellow, dry-tasting wine, but with a slightly bitter after-taste. Its alcohol content is usually around 12º, which is quite high for a dry white wine.

Another good wine from the Marches is the BIANCHELLO DEL METAURO, produced in the undulating countryside of the province of Pesaro from a mixture of white grapes in which the *Bianchello* (or *Biancame*) predominates. Usually it is a wine for everyday consumption; it can rise to heights if it comes from the best vines and undergoes very careful vinification.

In general the reds of the Marches are looked on as good ordinary wines, but some are of a quality which enables them to challenge the most famous Tuscan wines. The best-known is the ROSSO CONERO, named after the mountain which rises above the town of Ancona and the corresponding area along the Adriatic coast. The basic vine used is the *Montepulciano*, which should not be confused with the Tuscan vine mentioned in connection with the NOBILE. The area where it is produced comprises various districts lying between Ancona and Osimo-Castelfiardo to the south and

Falconara to the north. It is a pleasant, fine dry wine, with a brilliant ruby colour, a pleasing bouquet and a delicate flavour. It has a moderate alcohol content (in general 11.5º) and a reasonable acidity level.

The province of Ascoli Piceno produces another red wine known as the PICENO which is made from a mixture of grapes in which the *Sangiovese* and the *Montepulciano* predominate. It closely resembles the preceding wine but has in addition just a slight suspicion of bitterness.

Although it is impossible to list all the wines of the Marches, many of which are produced in very small quantities from imported vines such as the *Barbera*, the *Merlot*, the *Cabernet Franc*, the *Carignan* or the *Pinot Noir*, one special wine cannot be omitted: the VERNACCIA DI SERRAPETRONA, from the province of Macerata, a sweetish sparkling red which is made from slightly fermented grapes.

UMBRIA. Wine production in Umbria exceeds 17,600 gallons only in the very best years. And, what is extremely rare in Italy, it produces more white wine than red (respectively 60 and 40 per cent). Generally its wines are of an ordinary quality. Of course, some quite fine products can be found among the old-established firms or from the most advantageously sited vineyards: for instance the FONTESEGALE, the MONTECASTELLI and the AMELLA in the upper valley of the Tiber; the wines from the hills of Perugia; or the white GRECO DI TODI and the SACRANTINO DI MONTEFALCO, a sort of fermented red wine, very sweet and strongly alcoholized. But these are without any claims to a premier quality rating.

There is, however, one wine which on its own earns a well-deserved reputation for the wine production of Umbria: the ORVIETO, one of the most famous of Italian white wines. It is made from grapes grown in the tiny vineyard of the district of Orvieto, where the soil is mainly tuff mixed with volcanic materials. The main plant is the *Procanico* (which is simply the *Trebbiano Toscano* combined with other vines such as the *Grechetto* and the *Verdello*). Two types of wine are produced from this ORVIETO; one, a dry wine, is the best known today; the other, a pleasant wine which can be drunk at any time of the day, with a very distinguished golden colour, was very popular in days gone by. In the sixteenth century it was the favourite of Pope Paul III Farnese, who was a great lover of good wine. To prepare this type of wine it was customary in those days, much more than today, to put the must of very ripe grapes (sometimes they were even allowed to start rotting) to ferment in small vats inside deep, cool caves which had been hollowed out of the tuff. This encouraged the development of the very finest bouquet and flavours.

Italy, where artists find inspiration in the limpid light, where historians and archaeologists explore ancient ruins and sweethearts admire each other to the sound of love songs and mandolins. But Italy would not of course be Italy without the abundantly flowing wine, uniting young and old, men and women, as in this romantic painting of an Italian wine shop by Pietro Lucatelli (1634-1710).

But apart from the vineyards of Orvieto, it must infortunately be concluded that winegrowing in Umbria will remain as it is, due to the rather unfavourable ecopedological conditions in the region.

LATIUM. The fame of the wines of Latium goes back in time to the heydays of the Roman Empire. At that period Latium extended into the present-day Campania and the wines most highly praised by the Latin poets came in fact from this region.

Latium is today looked on as one of the most important winegrowing regions of Italy. Its annual production averages around 88,000,000 gallons (but in 1967 it was more than 110,000,000). A particularly outstanding feature is the marked predominance of white wines over the reds: in the provinces of Rieti, Frosinone and Latina, some 65 per cent of the wines are white; in Rome and Viterbo white wines make up 90 per cent

of the total! And a large number of these are good enough to be classed as quality wines; today most of them qualify for an *appellation d'origine*.

The most famous wines of Latium are those known by the generic name of DEI CASTELLI ("castles"). All are wines produced in the unusual region of volcanic hills to the south of Rome (more precisely the Colli Albani) which are practically covered with flourishing vineyards growing almost nothing but white grapes. They are chiefly: the *Malvasia di Candia*, the *Malvasia del Lazio*, the *Trebbiano Giallo* (or *Greco*) and, to a lesser extent, the *Trebbiano Toscano*, the *Bellone* and the *Bonvino*. The vines are all short bushes and the vineyards often stretch beyond the horizon. Although the appellation DEI CASTELLI is a generic one applying to an area of about 50 square miles, there are particular appellations according to the districts of production.

Among the best known and appreciated wines of the region is the FRASCATI—produced mostly in the district of the same name, but also throughout its designated region. In most cases it is made from the grapes of the *Malvasia del Lazio*, the *Greco* (or *Trebbiano Giallo*), the *Trebbiano Toscano* and also from a little of the *Bellone* and the *Bonvino*. It has always been quite an agreeable wine and when it is sweet it is called *cannellino*. In olden times it was dark yellow in colour because the musts were left to ferment at length on the grape marc and the grapes were picked when they were over-ripe and already starting to decay. They were then called *uve infavate*. Today however, thanks to more rational techniques, wines are produced with a straw-yellow, slightly golden colour and a very low tannin content. Their bouquet and flavour may be less pronounced but they have gained in subtlety.

Two other Roman CASTELLI which have recently won legal recognition of their *appellation d'origine* are the MARINO and the COLLI ALBANI. Their name is now officially acknowledged by the National Committee for the Protection of "Appellations d'Origine". The MARINO is made from a mixture of grapes of *Malvasia di Candia*, of *Malvasia del Lazio*, of green and yellow *Trebbiano Toscano* and of *Bonvino* in an area close to the Lake of Albano and Castelgandolfo. Straw yellow in colour, it is a rich, sweet wine with a delicate bouquet and a pleasant dry flavour. The COLLI ALBANI wine comes from much the same plants, grown in a region close by the preceding one. It resembles the MARINO very closely and their chemical composition is practically the same. Both are agreeable fine table wines which are much appreciated not only by local consumers but also by the numerous visitors to Rome.

The Latium also produces a whole category of quite different wines, several of which can claim an impressive and long-established reputation. One of them most frequently mentioned, because of its strange name, is the EST ! EST !! EST !!! of Montefiascone. It is a dry white wine which, though it lacks any bouquet, has a pleasant taste and a fine gold colour. It has a moderate alcohol content (11º) and acidity level. The grapes which between them produce this wine are the *Procanico* (or the *Trebbiano Toscano*), the *Malvasia di Candia* and the *Rosetto (Trebbiano Giallo)*.

The most widely produced of Latium's red wines is the CESANESE, which comes from a vine of the same name. The most popular is the wine of Affile, a small area some 50 miles from Rome. This dark-red wine comes in two varieties, dry and sweet; it has a full-bodied flavour and characteristic agreeable bouquet. Equally popular is the red wine CESANESE DEL PIGLIO, which is grown not only in the district of the same name but also in neighbouring districts to the south-east of Rome. Ruby-red, with a very strong bouquet, it is full of flavour and body. It is both dry and smooth to the taste, well alcoholized (11º to 12.5º) but with a moderate acid content. Sometimes it is left to age, to produce an even better quality wine.

A naturally sweet wine is the beautiful garnet-coloured ALEATICO of Gradoli (province of Viterbo) which comes from a vine of the same name. To keep it sweet, the must undergoes various filtrations which prevent it fermenting. When it is ready for sale it has an alcohol content of 10º and 9 per cent of sugar. Another, sweeter variety is more alcoholic. In flavour the ALEATICO is reminiscent of *Muscat*.

Among the outstanding wines of Latium of relatively recent date (in contrast to so many others whose history goes back to pre-Christian times), the wines of Aprilia ought to be mentioned. This name was given to one of the settlements which followed the draining of the Pontine Marshes a few years before the Second World War. It was a bold venture: flourishing towns and villages, gentle countryside, orchards and vineyards sprang up where once had been only evil-smelling marshland. The wines of Aprilia, to speak of just these wines, come from an area south of the Roman CASTELLI some seven miles from the Tyrrhenian Sea coastline (close to Anzio and Netturo). The soil there is volcanic in origin, part sand, part clay and part what is clearly volcanic matter. Several *appellation contrôlée* wines come from there: TREBBIANO DI APRILIA, SANGIOVESE DI APRILIA and MERLOT DI APRILIA. All are fine table wines which stand up very well to comparison with wines of much older ancestry.

The TREBBIANO DI APRILIA comes from the *Trebbiano Giallo* or *Trebbiano Toscano* vines. It is straw-yellow, with a very definite bouquet and a delicate, dry and agreeable flavour. It is a pleasant wine, which like the other wines of Latium, is suitable for all kinds of meals. The SANGIOVESE DI APRILIA, made from the *Sangiovese* vine (the same basic vine as for CHIANTI) is a rosé wine with an orange tinge; it has a personable aroma and a dry, well-balanced flavour.

The MERLOT DI APRILIA (from the *Merlot* vine) has met with a great deal of success in Venezia. A garnet-red wine with a very pronounced aroma, it is dry and full-bodied, though not excessively so.

Another designated area producing good red and white wines known by the appellation CORI, after the wineproducing centre of the region, is to be found on the hills of Aprilia. The vines here grow in volcanic soil and enjoy a mild climate, thanks to the Lepini hills which shelter them from the cold winds, a combination of natural circumstances particularly conducive to the production of quality wines. The CORI BIANCO is made from the grapes of the *Malvasia di Candia, Bel-*

lone, *Trebbiano Toscano*, and the *Trebbiano Giallo;* the Cori Rossi from the *Montepulciano*, the *Sangiovese* and other local vines. Neither of these table wines is lacking in quality; the white may be dry or sweet, with an alcohol content of around 11°. The red is always dry, but smooth, fresh and with a moderate degree of alcohol.

After the draining of the marshes a model wine-growing centre was established, the Maccarese estate, which produces highly-reputed red and white wines sold under the name of Castel San Giorgio, as well as other, more ordinary wines.

Abruzzi and Molise. This is a predominantly mountainous region containing the highest peaks of the Appennines (Gran Sasso and Maiella); at the other extreme it is practically at the level of the Adriatic Sea. In between stretches a succession of hills, a constantly changing countryside of picturesque villages each with their architectural peculiarities and folklore.

The first point to note about winegrowing and production in this region is that here, contrary to the regions north of the Abruzzi (the Marches), specialized culture far outstrips mixed culture. In addition, more than half of the grapes produced are grown as a fruit crop and not for wine. The average wine production of the past few years was around 50,600,000 gallons, of which some 30 per cent was white wine, 40 per cent

red wine and 30 per cent rosé wine, among which are some classified as "fine" wines. One of the most typical is the Cerasuolo d'Abruzzo, so-called because of its cherry-red colour. It is produced mainly in the provinces of L'Aquila, Chieti and Pescara. Its colour comes from a technical peculiarity of the winemaking process; the must (of black grapes) is fermented away from the grape marcs. It is made almost entirely from the *Montepulciano d'Abruzzo* vine, which is the most widespread in the region. It is essentially dry, but it is often smooth, agreeable and quite strongly alcoholized. It should not be confused with another wine which is produced in larger quantities and takes its name from the same vine: the Montepulciano d'Abruzzo. In contrast to the Cerasuolo, its must is fermented on the marc, giving a full-bodied ruby-coloured wine, with a good bouquet. Dry or slightly mellow, with a good alcohol content (12°-13°), it is capable of turning into a notable *da arrosto* wine after a short period of ageing.

The most typical white wine is the Trebbiano d'Abruzzo from the *Trebbiano* vine, produced mostly at Francavilla, Ortona, Città Sant'Angelo and Monte-silvano. It is usually quite a dark straw-yellow colour, with a pleasant bouquet, a dry flavour and around 11° to 12° of alcohol. Another good white wine is the Peligno, from Pratola Peligna, a village of L'Aquila.

SOUTHERN ITALY

Oenologically speaking, southern and insular Italy have many similarities. According to the most recent official statistics (those of 1967), out of a total area of 2,840,000 acres of vineyards under monoculture, 1,635,000 were in southern or insular Italy. It should be added that most of the lands under viticulture in these vast regions have a very clear "winegrowing vocation" and could hardly be used for any other crop.

Apulia. Even disregarding the particularly good wine harvest of 1967 (278,630,000 gallons), wine production exceeded 220,000,000 gallons in four of the seven past years. The five provinces which make up the region of Apulia—Foggia, Bari, Brindisi, Tarento and Lecce—all produce wine; the most important are Bari and Lecce. Whites, reds and rosés are all represented. Superior red table wines have been produced for a long time in some of the centres of the province of Foggia, for example at Cerignola, where the Santo Stefano is produced from a mixture of local vines —*Troia, Montepulciano* and *Lascirma*—or such other varieties as *Alicante* and *Barbera*. The red Castel del Monte, produced in the area of the Murgi hills

from the *Bombino Nero, Troia* and *Montepulciano* grapes, has an alcohol content of 12° to 13°. If aged a little it turns into an excellent table wine.

Today, the production of quality wines is spreading to a remarkable extent in Apulia, partly because of the introduction of better vine plants and partly due to a change from the traditional methods of pruning the vines (a system of low, heavily pruned bushes recalling the "goblet" shape of the South of France) into the cultivation of taller, more productive plants. These have been introduced wherever the depth, fertility and moisture, either natural or irrigation-produced, of the soil have made it possible. Much better grape harvests are obtained by these methods, and because of their very low sugar content, the grapes can be used to make table wines of every-day quality.

The rosé wines of Apulia have increased in number, especially since the last war. A rosé type of the Castel del Monte mentioned earlier is made, with an unusual bouquet and a dry but delicate and velvety taste. Another agreeable rosé wine is produced in the area of the Castellana hills, in the province of Bari,

231

while still others, such as the GIGLIANO rosé, produced at Copertino from the *Malvasia Nera* and the *Negro di Amaro* vines, come from Cerignolo and the Salentino.

Of the white wines, the SANSEVERO, from the province of Foggia, deserves to be mentioned; it comes from the district of the same name and others close by. Made from the *Bombino Bianco* and the *Trebbiano Toscano* in almost equal quantities, it is a straw-yellow colour, with a pleasant bouquet and a fresh, dry, harmonious flavour. It has been granted an *appellation d'origine contrôlée*. There is also a red and a rosé SANSEVERO. The LOCOROTONDO and the MARTINAFRANCA are made from a mixture of two plants, the *Verdeca* and the *Bianco d'Alessano*.

An important centre for the production of white wines is Ostuni-Cisternino-Ceglie, bordering on the district of Martina. It provides a good white wine which goes by the name of OSTUNI and is made from a combination of the *Verdeca* and *Bianco d'Alessano* vines.

The hilly region of Conversano in the province of Bari produces another white wine from a mixture of *Verdeca*, *Malvasia* and *Bianco d'Alessano*: it too is a dry, well-balanced wine.

Finally Apulia itself produces a number of special wines, mainly sweet wines, but also some aromatic varieties. Among these latter is the MOSCATI DI TRANI, made from the *Muscat Blanc*, the same vine which produces the famous ASTI SPUMANTE and the COLLI EUGANEI, as well as the *Muscats* of the Isle of Elba, of Syracuse in Sicily and Tempio in Sardinia.

The Trani wine is a true sweet wine, golden-yellow, with a delicious aroma. Prepared from slightly rotten grapes, it not infrequently has an alcohol content as high as 17°. A very similar wine is the MOSCATO DI SALENTO, which is also called SALENTO BIANCO LIQUOROSO. The ALEATICO DI PUGLIA is made from the

In olden days, vines in Italy frequently grew up trees. This made for wine harvests as picturesque as this one painted by Philip Hackert at the end of the eighteenth century in the countryside around lovely Sorrento.

232

same vine which produces the ALEATICO of the Isle of Elba. It is produced in small quantities in the provinces of Bari, Brindisi, Lecce and Tarento and bears a slight resemblance to *Muscat* with its warm, slightly sweet flavour. It may have as much as 15º to 17º alcohol and generally it is left to age for two or three years.

CAMPANIA. The vineyards of this very rugged and picturesque region are shrinking noticeably, particularly in the provinces of Naples and Salerno. The most northerly part of the region, bordering on Latium in the province of Caserta, produces a wine which was famous in olden times: the FALERNO, described as fiery by Horace, fuming by Tibullus and immortal by Martial. The vine which produces this illustrious wine is the *Aglianico*, also called *Ellanico*. Today's FALERNO is a heavy, dull-red, full-bodied wine with a rather bitter taste due to its high tannin content (which comes from the prolonged fermentation of the must with the skins). A warming wine because of its high alcohol content (from 13º to 16º) it is slightly acidified and often retains a certain amount of non-decomposed sugar, which introduces a sweet note into the bitterness. This wine should undergo quite a long ageing process to bring out all its qualities and it deserves to be produced in a more rational manner.

Equally famous is the LACHRYMA CHRISTI, which originates on the slopes of Mount Vesuvius. This is the legendary symbol of the tears which Our Lord is supposed to have shed on Capri, land of sin, after Lucifer, banished by God, stole the island from Paradise and let it fall in the Gulf of Naples. It is a fine dry white wine notable for its golden-yellow colour, its subtle, perfumed bouquet, its velvety flavour and its moderate alcohol content. It is made from the *Falanghina*, *Greco di Torre* and *Fiano* vines. There is also a red LACHRYMA CHRISTI, but it is quite an ordinary wine.

Moving down to the peninsula of Sorrento, we come to a very well-known red wine, the GRAGNANO, produced in a hilly region near Castellamare di Stabia. It is made from the *Aglianico*, *D'Olivella* and *Piè di Palumbo* vines. It is an excellent table wine, full-bodied and rather tart, a quality which increases its appeal for Neapolitan consumers. Among the other wines of Sorrento, the RAVELLO deserves a brief mention. There exists a white type, a rosé type and a red which is obtained by mixing the grapes of the *Bianca di Sorrento*, the *Pinot Blanc* and the *Pinot Noir*. All these wines are around 12º.

One should not leave the Gulf of Naples without mentioning the principal wines of its islands. The white CAPRI wine was long sought after as one of the best dry Italian wines. The main vines used to produce it are the *Greco* and the *Fiano*. Present-day production of this wine is on a considerably smaller scale. On the next island a white ISCHIA is made from a mixture of *Forastera* (predominantly), *Biancolella* and *San Leonardo*. It has a straw-yellow or slightly golden colour, an agreeably delicate bouquet and a dry, harmonious flavour. Red ISCHIA is made from *Guarnaccia*, *Piedirosso* and a little *Barbera*.

Among the wines of the province of Salerno are the wine of Corbera and those of Monte Julio and of Cilento, which if suitably aged may well turn into superior quality red table wines. They are exported in large quantities for blending with South American wines.

The province of Avellino (or Irpinia) is almost entirely covered by hills and mountains, which form three distinct winegrowing areas: the del Sabato valley, the region of Taurasino and the Colle del Partenio. The most important and the most popular of the red wines is the TAURASI, produced in the district of the same name and in the districts adjacent to it. It is without a doubt one of the best superior Italian table wines. It is made from the *Aglianico*, which is one of the most widely grown vines both in Campania and the adjoining Basilicato, mixed with 20 per cent of other vines (*Piedirosso, Montonico, Barbera*). Among the white wines the GRECO DI TUFO (or GRECO DEL VESUVIO) should be mentioned; it is also to be found in the Benevento and the province of Naples. The vine of the same name is centuries old; it is even thought to be the *Aminea Gemella* of Columella. The FIANO is a similar white wine made from a vine which the Latin people called *Vitis Apiana* because it was such a favourite with the bees.

The neighbouring province of Benevento produces quality white and red wines, particularly in the areas of Solopaca, in the Telesina valley and towards the borders of Campania and Molise. The white wines are made from a mixture of *Greco Bianco*, *Trebbiano* and *Malvasia Bianca*; they are light golden-yellow in colour, with a very pleasant bouquet and a dry, velvety and harmonious flavour. The red wines come from a mixture of *Olivella*, *Montepulciano*, *Sangiovese*, *Aglianico* and *Mangiaguerra*. They are bright red, with a strong bouquet and pleasing, harmonious flavour.

Another wine of Campania which deserves mention is the ASPRINIO DELL'AVERSANO, made from a vine which grows up the very tall poplars of the plain. It has a very light alcohol content (7º to 8º) but is on the other hand quite acid. To protect it from the summer heat it is stored in deep caves and served very cold.

BASILICATO. This region lies between Apulia to the east and Campania to the west. It is mainly mountainous woodland and only a limited area can be used for winegrowing. Most of the wine production of the region is carried out in the district of Vulture, an old volcanic mountain chain in the north of the region.

Here vines grow at heights of as much as 2,400 feet above sea level. The districts of Barile, Rionero, Rapolla, Melfi, Maschito, Venoso and others, all land of volcanic origin, are covered with vineyards yielding quality wines. The most outstanding of these is the AGLIANICO DEL VULTURE, one of the best fine red wines of southern Italy. When young it is a splendid ruby-red which turns to garnet with age. It is a generous wine with a very pronounced acidity. Suitable ageing for three to four years develops its bouquet and lends it a sweeter taste.

CALABRIA. This region is almost entirely surrounded by the sea and is an essentially mountainous, wooded land. Vines grow in a very scattered fashion in only a small part of the region. Calabria's wines were famous even in antiquity and the wines of Sybaris, the BALBINO and the AMINEI, were equally well known.

One of the wines which has remained famous for its excellent quality throughout the centuries is the CIRO, produced in the province of Catanzaro. It is made from the black grapes of the *Gaglioppo* and a small proportion of *Greco Bianco* and *Greco Nero*. The POLLINO and the SAVUTO DI ROGLIANO, which come from much the same vines, have similar qualities to the CIRO. But in the past Calabria also produced good sweet wines, now limited to the Muscat of Cosenza and Salento and the Malvasia of Brindisi. Steps should be taken to prevent their disappearance.

SICILY

In the days of Pliny, Sicily could pride itself on possessing several of the most highly prized wines of Roman Italy. Among these were the MAMERTINO which was so popular with the court of Caesar, the TAUROMENITANUM, the POTULASUM and the BIBLINUM. Today Sicily ranks third among the wineproducing regions of Italy. Its expansion has been considerably fostered by aid from the Regional Institute of Vines and Wine, set up in Palermo in 1950.

Because of its southerly latitude and the fact that it is an island, Sicily generally has a hotter climate than any other region of Italy. Vines are not only grown all along its splendid beaches with their rich crops of citrus fruits, but are also cultivated inland to quite an altitude, as, for instance, on the slopes of Mount Etna. Every province of the island can boast the production of quality wines. From the province of Messina comes a wine with a particularly well-established reputation: the FARO, made from the *Nerello Cappuccio, Mascalese, Nocera, Nerello d'Avala*, etc. It is a generous, harmonious, ruby-red wine. After ageing, it takes on all the qualities of an excellent *da arrosto*. The MAMERTINO, which has such a distinguished name, is produced on the heights above Messina from white grapes, especially the *Cataratto*, mixed with *Inzolia, Grillo* and other vines. It is in fact more of a dessert wine than a table wine, and is produced in very small quantities.

The wineproducing area of the province of Catania is made up of a strip of land running around the cone of Mount Etna from the north to the south and the east. It includes all or a part of the districts of Paternó, Nicolosi, Viagrande, Zafferana, Milo and Linguaglossa. The vines from which its wines are made are principally: the *Carricante* and the *Cataratto Bianco* for white wines; the *Nerello Mascalese* and the *Nerello Mantellato* for the reds and the rosés. White ETNA is dry and straw-yellow in colour. After a brief ageing period it matures into a *da arrosta* wine.

The province of Syracuse offers a wide variety of wines, either for direct consumption, or, more often, for blending with other wines. The best blending wines come from Pachino in the far south of the island. They are strong, richly coloured, full-bodied wines which never have less than a 15° of alcohol content. This province also produces some very reputable, fine and superior-quality wines such as the white or red ELORO. The white is made from *Cataratto, Inzolia, Grillo* and *Albanello*; the red comes from the *Calabrese*.

The adjoining province of Ragusa produces another excellent wine, which goes by the name of FRAPPATO DI VITTORIA, made from the *Frappato* and *Calabrese* vines; and a special wine called the CERASUOLO DI VITTORIA because of its cherry colour. It is strongly alcoholic (15° to 16°) and is frequently exported to other parts of the country as a blending wine.

In western Sicily the white CORVO, a wine served with entrées, is made from 40 per cent of *Cataratto* and the remainder from *Inzolia*; the red is made from *Perricone* and *Catanese*. Well matured, CORVO becomes a wonderful *da arrosto* wine. Western Sicily is, however, primarily the land of MARSALA. For close on two centuries it has been by far the best known and most prized of Sicilian wines. Its origins go back to 1773, when an Englishman, John Woodhouse, who exported the produce of western Sicily to England, discovered the quality of the wines of the Marsala vineyards, cultivated in those days by somewhat primitive methods. He developed the production of these wines and was responsible for their rise in popularity. MARSALA is made from the *Grillo* and *Cataratto* vines and, to a lesser extent from the *Inzolia* and *Catanese*: all bear grapes with a high sugar content and little acidity. The vineyards of Marsala, which jut out into the provinces of Palermo and Agrigente but lie otherwise almost entirely in the province of Trapano, enjoy a hot climate. MARSALA is made by adding cooked concentrated must to fermented must. The different types of MARSALA, varying in sweetness and alcohol content are the result of variations in the proportions of this mixture. The alcohol content ranges from 17º to 20º and the sugar content from 5 to 10 per cent. One of the most highly rated MARSALAS is the SUPERIOR OLD MARSALA (S.O.M.) with 18º of alcohol. A prerequisite for obtaining the best quality MARSALA is to let it mature in wooden casks. A remarkable thing is that this process takes place in large buildings, even on the ground floor, where the wine is subject to sudden changes in temperature.

Among the many "special" wines of Sicily is the MOSCATO DI SIRACUSA, made from the white *Muscat*, the *Inzolia*, the *Cataratto* and the *Albanello*, whose grapes are gathered only when they begin to show the first signs of decay. It is a true sweet wine, dry, delicious, full-bodied, with an alcohol content of about 14º to 17º. Other liqueur-like Muscats are produced in western Sicily, especially in the province of Palermo. One of the best is the LOZUCCO, originally named after a vast property belonging to the House of Orleans, but which today is almost non-existent. On the other hand large quantities of an aromatic Muscat are still produced on the picturesque island of Pantelleria. The vines which grow on its mountainous and volcanic terrain yield some excellent wines. The most important variety is the *Zibbibo* whose fruit is left to rot for the purpose of making either raisins or wine.

Another outstanding liqueur-like wine is the MALVASIA DI LIPARI. It is produced in the archipelago of the same name on the small islands of Salina and Stromboli. The grapes are left to decay for a week, in order to make a very alcoholic wine (from 15º to 16º).

SARDINIA

Sardinian oenology was always particularly noted for its special wines, but several table wines in the ordinary, fine and superior classes have also long claimed attention. Among the superior wines should first be mentioned a white from the province of Cagliari with the historic name of NURAGUS. The *Nuragus* vine from which it is made is in fact reputed to be the oldest of all vines, going back to prehistoric times. It produces an excellent fine table wine, with a light bouquet and a dry, fresh, subtle taste. The VERMENTINO, from the province of Sassari, is another fine dry white wine, with an amber-like colour, a delicate bouquet and a very slightly bitter taste. There are some quite respectable, if slightly sweet, red wines made in the Ogliastra from the *Cannonau* vine. Among the superior quality wines, pride of place should go to the VERNACCIA DI ORISTANO, "the most Sardinian of Sardinian wines", whose austere taste is well-suited to the fierce temperament of the island's inhabitants. It is a dry, strongly alcoholic wine. The vine it comes from is grown in the deep cool soils of the Tirso Valley, the only place where it gives really good wine. Light amber-yellow in colour, with a powerful and distinctive bouquet, its mellow flavour has just a hint of bitterness. Its alcohol content varies between 15.5º and 17º. Lengthy ageing in oak casks enables its much-prized qualities to develop to the full. Among the special white wines should be mentioned the famous

Sardinian MALVASIA, with its golden hue and bouquet reminiscent of almond flowers. Another sweet white wine is the typically Sardinian NASCO from the province of Cagliari, which is undoubtedly one of the most delicious of Italian sweet wines. Lastly there is the MOSCATO DEL CAMPIDANO of Cagliari. In contrast to the *Muscats* of northern Italy, it is produced by a special technique: once the must has reached a 10º to 12º alcohol content fermentation is stopped by the addition of very pure ethyl alcohol. This method gives a delicious wine of 15º to 16º.

Among Sardinia's range of special red wines is the famous OLIENA which Gabriele D'Annunzio hailed as the "Nepenthe of Oliena". It is a strongly alcoholic wine (from 15º to 17º) but not at all sweet; it has a strong bouquet and a mellow, slightly bitter taste. As it ages it turns somewhat orange in colour. The *Cannonau*, which is the main vine used in the production of OLIENA, also supplies another special red wine, the CAMPIDANO DI CAGLIARI. Ruby-red when young, it takes on an orange hue with age, and at the same time acquires a pleasant bouquet and a smooth, generous flavour. It is held to be one of the most tonic of dessert wines. Two other sweet wines should also be mentioned: the MONICA and the GIRO, both probably of Spanish origin. Some, in fact, compare the Sardinian sweet wines to the same type of wines produced in Spain, in particular to MALAGA and MADEIRA wines.

WINES OF ITALY

PIEDMONT

Dry red wines	Barolo	Boca	Barbera d'Alba
	Nebbiolo d'Alba	Barbaresco	Barbera del Monferrato
	Carema	Ghemme	Dolcetto delle Langhe e d'Ovada
	Gattinara	Sizzano	Freisa di Chieri e d'Asti
	Lessona	Barbera d'Asti	Grignolino d'Asti
Medium-sweet red wines	Brachetto d'Acqui	Barbera d'Asti	Freisa di Chieri
	Malvasia di Casorso	Barbera d'Alba	Freisa d'Asti
	Nebbiolo Piemontese	Barbera del Monferrato	Grignolino d'Asti
Dry white wines	Cortese di Gavi	Erbaluce di Caluso	
Sweet white wines . . .	Moscato d'Asti	Asti spumante	Caluso Passito

LOMBARDY

Dry red wines	Barbacarlo dell'Oltrepo pavese	Grumello	Riviera del Garda
	Buttafuoco dell'Oltrepo pavese	Inferno	Franciacorta
	Sangue di Giuda Oltrepo pavese	Sassella	Botticino
	Freccia Rossa di Casteggio	Valgella	Cellatica
Medium-sweet red wines .	Barbacarlo dell'Oltrepo pavese	Canneto	Clastidium
	Sangue di Giuda dell'Oltrepo pavese	Bonardo amabile	Nebbiolo di Retorbido
Dry white wines	Riesling dell'Oltrepo pavese	Frecciarossa di Casteggio	Tocai di San Martino della Battaglia
	Cortese dell'Oltrepo pavese	Lugana	Pusterla
Medium-dry white wine .	Clastidium di Casteggio		
Sweet white wines . . .	Spumante di S. Maria della Versa	Moscato di Casteggio	
Dry rosé wines	Chiaretto del Garda	Pusterla	

LIGURIA

Dry red wine	Rossese di Dolceacqua		
Dry white wines	Vermentino	Polcevera	Cinqueterre
	Coronata		
Sweet white wine	Cinqueterre passito (Sciacchetrà)		

TRENTINO-ALTO ADIGE

Dry red wines	Lago di Caldaro (or Caldaro)	Marzemino	Cabernet
	Santa Maddalena	Lagrein	Merlot
	Terodelgo	Termeno	Pinot
Dry white wines	Pinot	Riesling renano	Sylvaner verde
	Ruländer	Traminer	Terlano
Sweet white wines . . .	Moscato trentino	Moscato atesino	
Rosé wines	Lagarino rosato (Lagrein)	Mazermino d'Isera	

VENETIA

Dry red wines	Bardolino	Valpolicella	Merlot delle Venezie
	Valpantena	Cabernet delle Venezie	Rosso dei Colli veronesi
Sweet red wines	Recioto della Valpolicella	Recioto Veronese	
Dry white wines	Soave	Bianco dei Colli Berici	Valdobbiadene
	Bianco di Breganze	Bianco dei Colli Euganei	Verduzzo
	Bianco di Gambellara	Prosecco di Conegliano	Pinot
Medium-dry white wines	Bianco dei Colli Berici	Colli Trevigiani	

236

FRIULI AND JULIAN VENETIA

Dry red wines	Rossi dei Colli Friulani Rossi del Collio Goriziano	Cabernet friulano Tocai friulano	Merlot friulano Refoschi
Dry white wines	Bianchi dei Colli Friulani	Bianchi del Collio Goriziano	Tocai Friulano

EMILIA AND ROMAGNA

Dry red wines	Lambrusco di Sorbara Lambrusco Salamino di S. Croce	Lambrusco grasparossa di Castelvetro Guatturnio dei Colli Piacentini	Sangiovese di Romagna Grasparossa
Dry white wines	Albana di Romagna	Trebbiano di Romagna	Bertinoro
Sweet white wine	Albana di Romagna		

TUSCANY

Dry red wines	Chianti Chianti classico Chianti Colli Aretini Chianti Colli Fiorentini Chianti Colli Senesi Chianti Montalbano	Chianti Rufino Chianti Colline Pisane Brunello di Montalcino Vino nobile di Montepulciano Antinori Brolio	Nipozzano Artimino Carmignano Monte-Carlo Rosso delle Colline Lucchesi Elba
Sweet red wine	Aleatico di Porto-Ferraio		
Dry white wines	Vernaccia di San Gimignano Bianchi vergini dell'Aretino	Arbia Moscadello di Montalcina	Bianco dell'Elba Monte-Carlo
Sweet white wines . . .	Moscato dell'Elba	Vino Santo toscano	

THE MARCHES

Dry red wines	Rosso Conero	Rosso Piceno	
Sweet red wine	Vernaccia di Serrapetrona		
Dry white wines	Verdicchio dei Castelli di Jesi	Verdicchio di Matelica	Bianchello del Metauro

UMBRIA

Red wines	Torgiano	Sacrantino de Montefalco	
Dry white wines	Orvieto	Torgiano	Greco di Todi
Sweet white wine	Orvieto		

LAZIO

Dry red wines	Ceasanese Ceasanese del Piglio	Sangiovese di Aprilia Falerno	Merlot di Aprilia Castel San Giorgio
Medium-dry red wine . .	Ceasanese del Piglio		
Sweet red wine	Aleatico viterbese		
Dry white wines	Est ! Est !! Est !!! Colli Lanuvini Colli Albani Colonna	Frascati Marino Velletri Montecompatri	Cori Trebbiano di Aprilia Falerno
Medium-dry white wines	Est ! Est !! Est !!! Colli Albani Colli Lanuvini	Colonna Frascati Marino	Malvasia di Grotta-ferrata (or Grotta-ferrata) Cori
Sweet white wines . . .	Moscato di Terracina	Colonna	Frascati

ABRUZZI

Dry red wines	Cerasuolo di Abruzzo	Montepulciano di Abruzzo
Medium-sweet white wine	Cerasuolo di Abruzzo	
Medium-dry white wines .	Trebbiano di Abruzzo	Peligno

CAMPANIA

Dry red wines	Aglianico	Taurasi	Ischia
	Lacrima Christi del Vesuvio	Vesuvio	Ravello
	Falerno		
Medium-sweet red wines	Conca	Gragnano	Solopaca
Dry white wines	Capri	Lacrima Christi del Vesuvio	Furor divina Costiera
	Ischia	Ravello	Asprinio
	Greco di Tufo	Falerno	Bianco d'Avellino
		Greco di Tufo	
Medium-dry white wines	Solopaca		
Dry rosé wine	Ravello		
Medium-dry rosé wine	Solopaca		

APULIA

Dry red wines	Castel del Monte	Primitivo di Gioia e Manduria	Barletta
	Santo Stefano di Cerignola		
Medium sweet red wine	Castel Acquaro		
Sweet red wine	Aleatico di Puglia	Moscato del Salento (or Salento)	Zagarese
Dry white wines	Sansevero	Martinafranca Locorotondo	Torre Giulia
		Ostuni	
Sweet white wines	Moscato di Salento (or Salento liquoroso)		Moscato di Trani
Dry rosé wines	Castel del Monte	Gigliano	

BASILICATA

Dry red wine	Aglianico del Vulture	
Dry white wine	Provitaro	
Sweet white wines	Malvasia del Vulture	Moscato del Vulture
Medium-dry rosé wine	Malvasia di Lucania	

CALABRIA

Dry red wines	Cirò di Calabria	Pollino	Lacrima di Castrovillari
	Savuto di Rogliano		
Dry white wines	Provitaro	Balbino	
Sweet white wines	Greco di Gerace	Moscato di Cosenza	Malvasia di Cosenza
Rosé wine	Pellaro		

SICILY

Dry red wines	Faro	Eloro	Frappato di Vittoria
	Etna	Corvo di Casteldaccia	Cerasuolo di Vittoria
Dry white wines	Corvo di Casteldaccia	Eloro	Bianco di Alcamo
	Etna	Lo Zucco	
Medium-dry white wines	Mamertino	Marsala vergine	
Sweet white wines	Malvasia di Lipari	Moscato Lo Zucco	Moscato Passito di Pantelleria
	Mamertino	Moscato di Siracusa	Cerasuolo di Vittoria
	Marsala	Moscato di Noto	
Dry rosé wines	Eloro	Etna rosato	

SARDINIA

Dry red wines	Oliena	Cannonau del Campidano	Campidano di Cagliari
Sweet red wines	Cirò di Sardegna	Monica di Sardegna	
Dry white wines	Nuragus	Vermentino di Gallura	Malvasia di Bosa
	Vernaccia di Oristano	Vernaccia di Sardegna	
Sweet white wines	Nasco	Moscato del Campidano	Moscato di Tempio

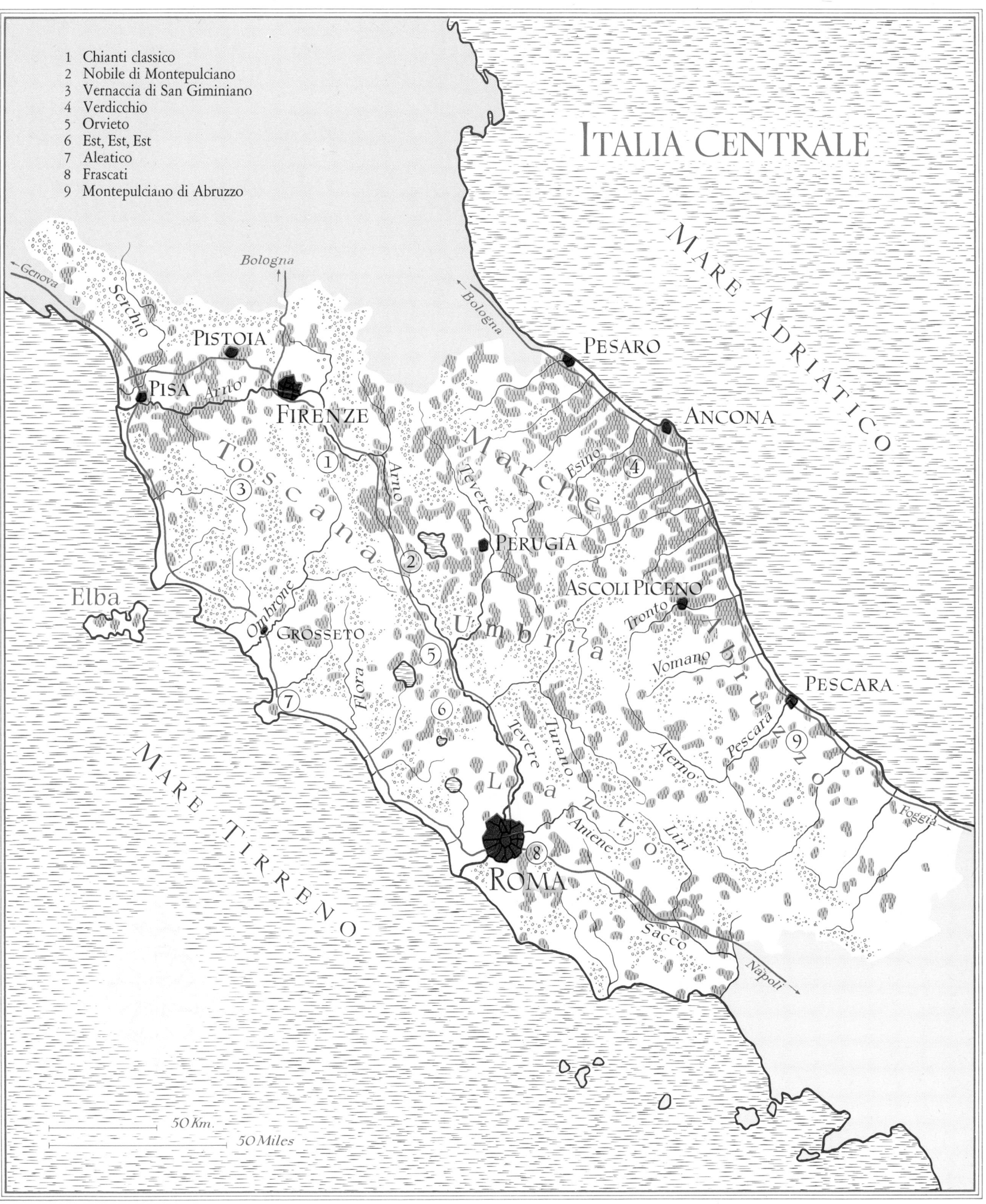

ITALIA CENTRALE

1 Chianti classico
2 Nobile di Montepulciano
3 Vernaccia di San Gimignano
4 Verdicchio
5 Orvieto
6 Est, Est, Est
7 Aleatico
8 Frascati
9 Montepulciano di Abruzzo

MARE ADRIATICO

MARE TIRRENO

Genova

Bologna

Bologna

Serchio

PISTOIA

PISA

Arno

FIRENZE

Toscana

Elba

Ombrone

GROSSETO

Flora

Arno

Tevere

Marche

Esino

PESARO

ANCONA

Umbria

PERUGIA

ASCOLI PICENO

Tronto

Vomano

Tevere

Turano

Aterno

Pescara

Abruzzo

PESCARA

Liri

Foggia

Lazio

Aniene

Sacco

Napoli

ROMA

50 Km.

50 Miles

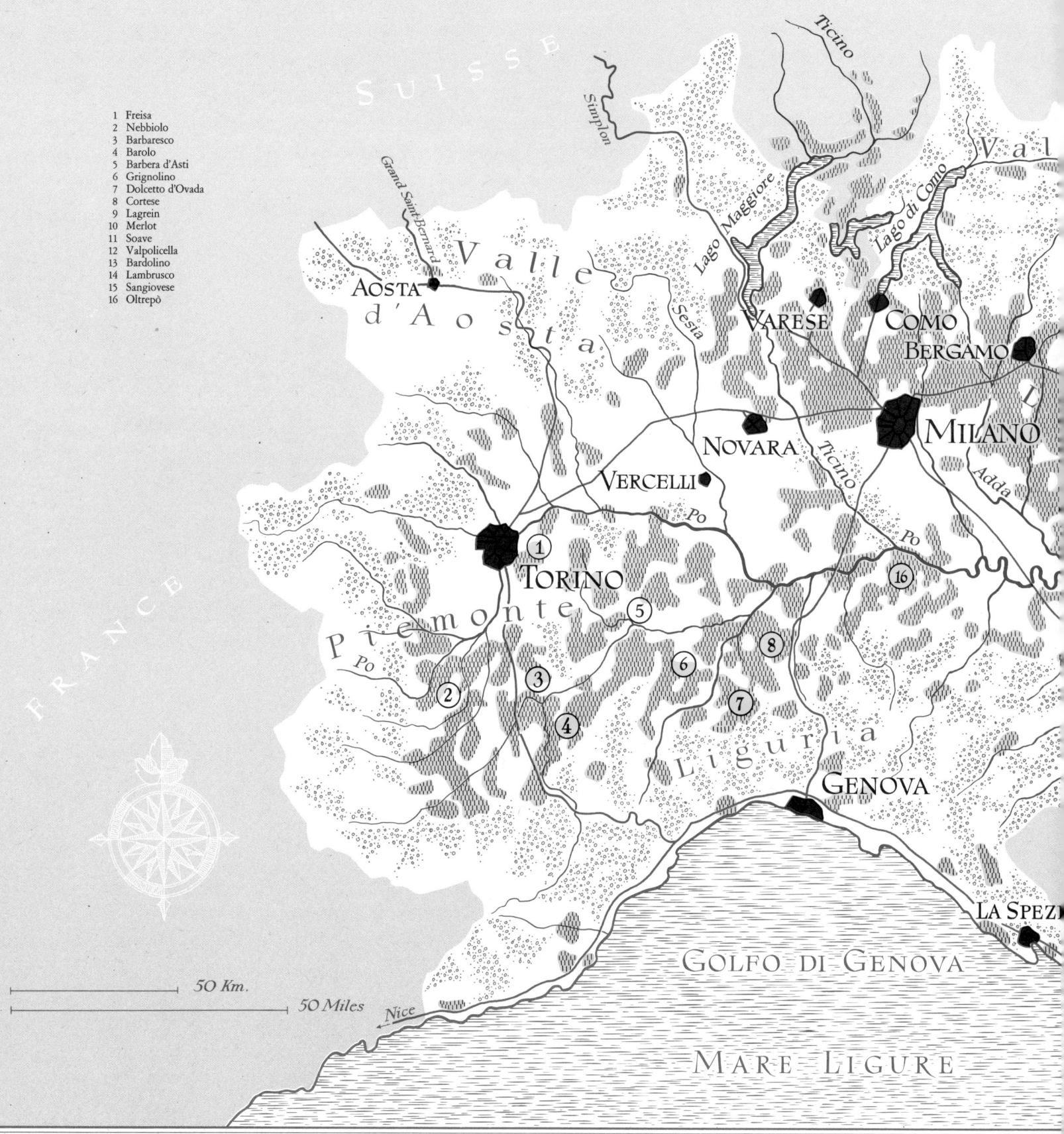

ITALIA SETTENTRIONALE

1 Freisa
2 Nebbiolo
3 Barbaresco
4 Barolo
5 Barbera d'Asti
6 Grignolino
7 Dolcetto d'Ovada
8 Cortese
9 Lagrein
10 Merlot
11 Soave
12 Valpolicella
13 Bardolino
14 Lambrusco
15 Sangiovese
16 Oltrepò

SUISSE

FRANCE

Ticino

Simplon

Grand Saint-Bernard

Valle d'Aosta

AOSTA

Lago Maggiore

Lago di Como

VARESE

COMO
BERGAMO

Val

MILANO

NOVARA

Adda

VERCELLI

Sesia

Ticino

Po

Po

TORINO

① ⑯

Piemonte

⑤

⑧

⑥

③

⑦

②

④

Liguria

Po

GENOVA

LA SPEZ

GOLFO DI GENOVA

Nice

MARE LIGURE

50 Km.

50 Miles

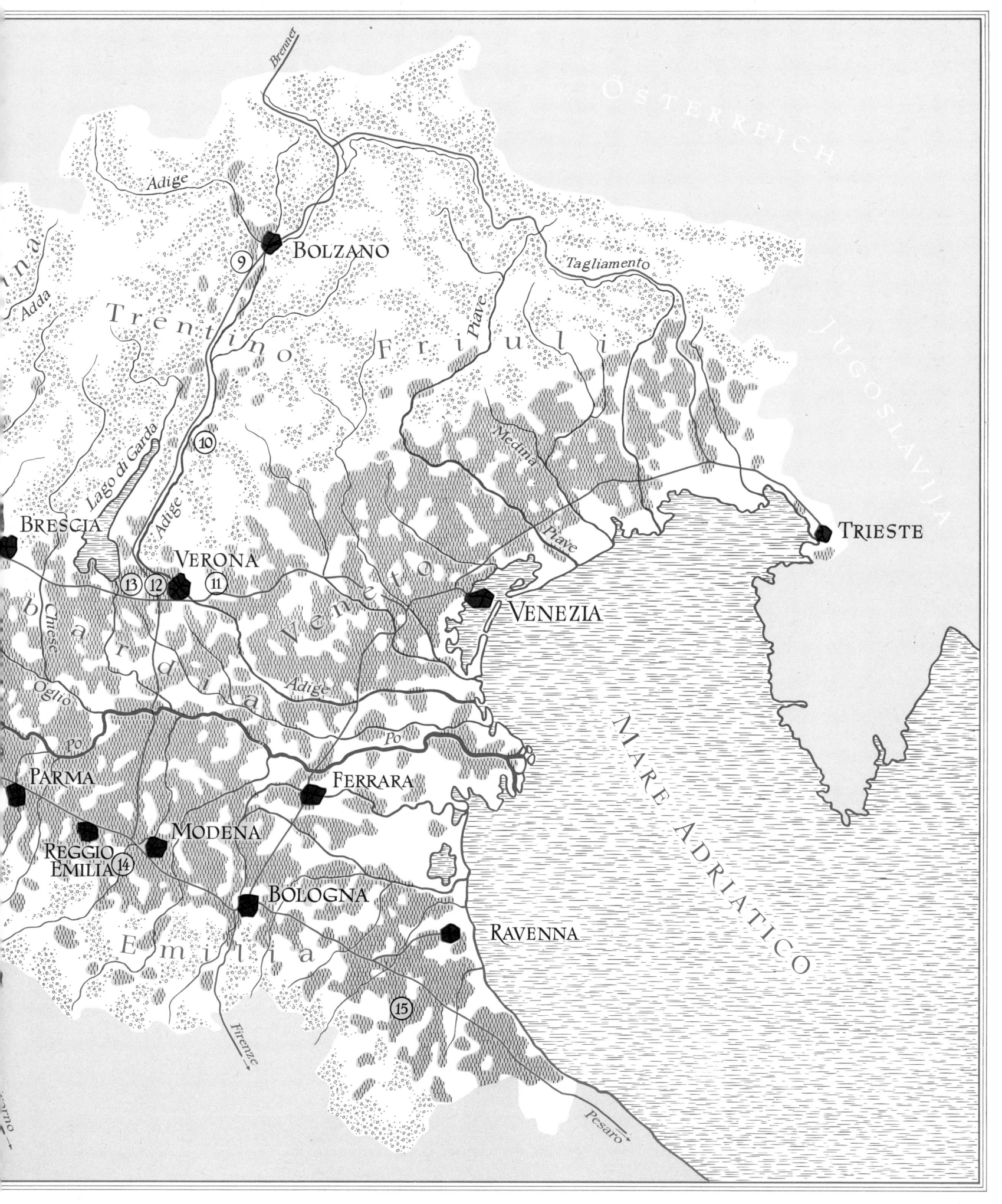

50 Km.
50 Miles

1 Falerno
2 Lacryma Christi
3 Malvasia
4 Etna
5 Corvo
6 Alcamo
7 Pachino
8 Faro
9 Marsala

MARE ADRIATICO

Roma

Pescara

Candelaro

Celone

FOGGIA

Volturno

① NAPOLI

② SALERNO

Ofanto

BARI

MATERA

Bradano

Basento

BRINDISI

TARANTO ③

LECCE

GOLFO DI TARANTO

Sele

Calore

Agri

Sinni

Basilicata

Puglia

Campania

SASSARI

Mannu

NUORO

Tirso

Sardegna

Mannu

Fluminendosa

Cixerri

CAGLIARI

MARE TIRRENO

Crati

Trionto

Savuto

Calabria

MARE IONIO

PALERMO

Messina ⑧

REGGIO CALABRIA

TRAPANI

⑥

⑤

⑨

Sicilia

Simeto

④

CALTANISSETTA

ENNA

Platani

Salso

CATANIA

AGRIGENTO

Acate

SIRACUSA

⑦

MARE MEDITERRANEO

ITALIA MERIDIONALE E INSULARE

THE WINES
OF THE RHINE

JOSEPH JOBÉ, JOSEPH DREYER and HELMUT ARNTZ

Had not the Rhine river carried its civilizing influences northward, the vine would have remained confined to the basin of the Rhône. As early as the fourth century B.C. Greek adventurers pushed their way up the Rhône to the Swiss plateau and very probably made contact with the Celts along the Jura as far as Basel long before the Romans arrived. They probably introduced vines which they had acclimatized in Gaul. The process was completed by the gradual Romanization and, later, the Christianization of Central Europe. Once the vine had crossed the barrier of the Alps, it became established in the east wherever the altitude permitted, and permanent vineyards grew up round the veterans' colonies and the earliest monastic establishments on the Rhine until at last a new chain of vineyards stretched from Chur to Bonn.

The source of the Rhine, or at least of the larger of its two branches known as the Upper Rhine, is not very far from the source of the Rhône. The stream issuing from Lake Tuma is only a few miles from the Furka glacier; but the two rivers flow in different directions, turning, as it were, their backs on each other. The Rhine, starting higher up, goes farther and is slower to decide on its final course. The vine in the Grisons grows lower down than the vine in the Valais—not above 1,800 feet—where the Rhine first definitely flows northwards. It favours the red grape, which, indeed, is the predominating variety all along the Upper Rhine. The landscape, with the Alps in the background, often verges on the sublime. The language along the river moves on from Romanche to the various dialects of eastern Switzerland, while the impetuous stream is tamed by man and becomes international. The right bank borders the Austrian Vorarlberg and the tiny Principality of Liechtenstein, where the vine is scanty, but where the inhabitants, looking to Switzerland, have always felt that the Rhine brings them closer to the Swiss rather than separating them.

Now the river comes to Lake Constance, where, like the Rhône in Lake Leman, its waters slow down and disappear in the broad expanse. To the north, the first German vineyards shimmer on the foothills of the Black Forest. Opposite, the red grapes of the Rheintal in St. Gallen and the Untersee in Thurgau counterbalance the whites of Baden. The town of St. Gallen, a far-famed bulwark of medieval culture, is not far away—one more link in the chain of episcopal and university towns of the Middle Rhine, like Constance, Basel, Freiburg-in-Breisgau and Strasbourg.

Flowing through Lake Constance the river makes a deep bend, turning sharply east and west; and it maintains this course as far as Basel. Over a hundred yards wide here, it flows past the vineyards of the Klettgau in the Canton of Schaffhausen and narrows somewhat in the loom of the Swabian Jura just before it makes an impressive leap of over sixty feet that sends it hurtling through the Cantons of Zurich and Aargau. There, as it flows past the vineyards of Baden to the north, its tributary, the Aare, which links it to most of the Swiss lakes, flows in from the left. The vineyards of Zurich, the Bernese Jura, Fribourg and Neuchâtel are thus connected up with the Rhine.

Indeed, the connection has always been very close, as is shown by the alliance concluded in the sixteenth century between the people of Strasbourg and the people of Zurich. The good burghers of Zurich, to show how speedily they could come to Strasbourg's, aid, rowed down the Limmat, the Aare and the Rhine and reached the city in less than eighteen hours, "before a dish of millet had time to cool". Neuchâtel, it should be noted, was subject to French influence; here the *Riesling*, the traditional variety of the Rhine, yields to a stock brought in from the west, the *Chasselas*.

The Rhine achieves its maturity at Basel. Meeting the buttress of the Jura's eastern end, it turns definitely north along the passage formed by the parallel ranges of the Black Forest and the Vosges. It is still seven hundred and fifty feet above sea-level and it takes it some five hundred miles to descend to the sea. The wine road, continuous on the right bank, does not start again to the west until Mulhouse, where the famous Alsatian winegrowing region begins. The vineyards on the French bank, carefully terraced on the last outcroppings of the Vosges, exposed to the rising sun and with an extremely favourable climate, are parcelled out in very small lots. Their wines have been distributed for ages throughout Europe by the Rhine itself and, in medieval times, many a boat carried the precious SYLVANERS and RIESLINGS to the courts of Swabia, Bavaria, Sweden and England.

To the east the vineyards of Baden and Württemberg are separated by the Black Forest, joined nowadays in a single *Land* of the Federal Republic of Germany. The wines of the Neckar were as celebrated in feudal Europe as those of the Main, the Moselle and the Aare.

Although the vineyards are so densely concentrated, this has in no way detracted from the personality of each region. The Rhine wines are derived from a very few varieties of grape and would seem to be closely akin, but each vineyard has a pronounced character of its own and its neighbour has no wish to imitate it. The Palatinate, to which the river now brings us, is simply a natural extension of Alsace, and yet the soil has changed. Our hearts were won by the GEWURZTRAMINER, but now we are enchanted by the celebrated growths of Forst and Deidesheim. It is hard to choose between them, for it is very true that "the sky, the climate and the land are all in every glass" of these delightful wines.

The landscape gradually changes from Karlsruhe to Mainz, becoming less abrupt; the rapids gradually disappear, as do the alluvial deposits between its many branches, and the river spreads in a broad stream over a deep and stable bed, with firm banks: it becomes navigable. The towns, which hitherto seemed to shun the banks, are now situated closer to the river, like Worms, whose lofty Romanesque cathedral surveys the ripening Palatinate wines to the south and the wines of Rheinhesse to the north.

From Mainz the vineyards follow the winding route of the Main, threading eastward through Franconia to successfully invade Bavarian territory, despite its apparent total occupation by the hop. At Bingen, on the other bank, at the very moment when the Rhine at last emerges from the vast curve it had described downstream from Worms, the Nahe takes over the vine and carries it up into Rheinhesse.

Now we come to the heart of the romantic Germany, the fantastic stage-setting of marauding Burgraves and elves, massacres and sorceries, Fürstenberg, Gutenfels, the Pfalz, that lowering pile jutting out of the waters, the Cat and the Mouse, still defying each other, and Rheinfels—ruined towers, jagged keeps, massive and disturbing shades, and among them on either bank the vineyards of the Lower Rhineland, a miracle of life amidst all this ancient death.

At Koblenz, at the junction with the Moselle, and not far from the junction with the Lahn, the wine road becomes a three-pronged fork, the middle prong going as far as Bonn. Thereafter, reaching the northern limit of the area dictated by nature, the vine becomes scarce. Rotterdam and the sea are too far away for wine to reach them except by import. But, if only along one half of its course, the story of the vines of the Rhine gives us a convincing example of what a natural means of communication can bestow upon man by way of increasing his pleasure and his profit. Despite many bloody episodes, the Rhine has been more than a left and a right bank; there has been an upstream and a downstream as well, a flowing route which, as the centuries passed, spread the art of printing, the humanism of Erasmus, the fantasies of Romanticism and, more recently, the European spirit. More celebrated here than anywhere, the vine has, through undisclosed channels, contributed to an awareness of the Rhine's high mission.

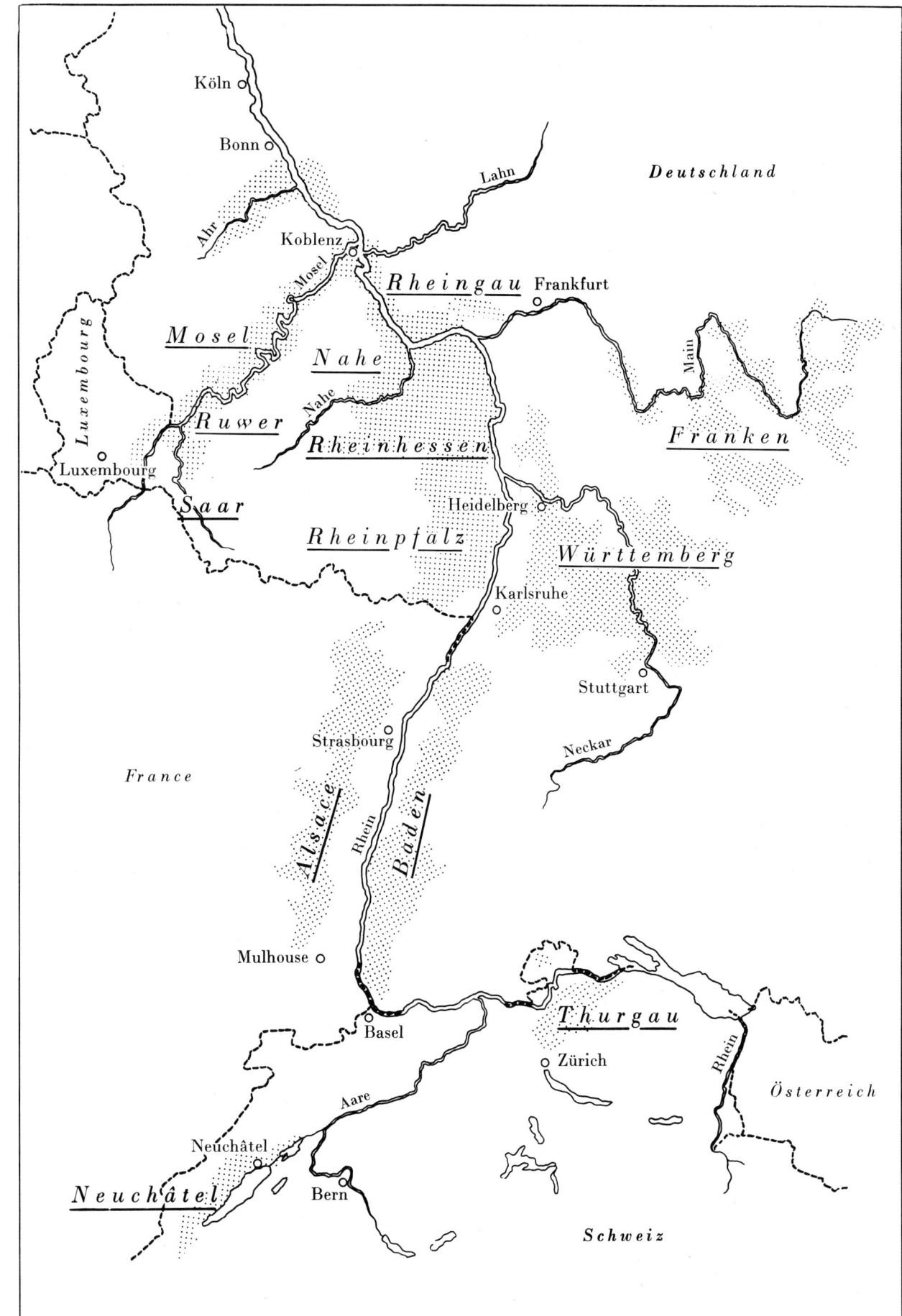

"Wines of the Rhine" covers the wines of the Upper Rhine (the wine-growing cantons of German Switzerland), the wines from the shores of the Lake of Neuchâtel, those of Alsace, and the German wines of Baden, Württemberg, the Palatinate, Rheinhesse, the valley of the Nahe, Franconia, the Rheingau, the valleys of the Moselle, Saar and Ruwer, and of the Ahr and the Middle Rhine (or Mittelrhein).

245

THE WINES OF THE UPPER RHINE

The wine districts of eastern and northern Switzerland are all part of the Rhine basin. It seems to suit them less well than the Valais and the shores of Lake Leman, though the winegrowing tradition is quite as ancient. The growers formerly produced mainly white wines, but the reds predominate nowadays, except in the vineyards of the Lakes of Biel and Neuchâtel.

In this part of Switzerland the vine seems more threatened than in the Rhine Valley, for various reasons, including the constant growth of industrialization and urbanization and competition from foreign wines. Some vineyards are now mere fossils, such as those of Basel-City, Lucerne, Solothurn and Schwyz, none of which exceeds 20 acres.

Of the old white varieties, the *Elbling* has practically disappeared and the *Raüschling* and *Completer* are merely curiosities; they have been replaced by the *Riesling-Sylvaner*, which is as preponderant in these areas as the *Chasselas* in western Switzerland. The *Riesling-Sylvaner* was produced in 1882 from a cross between the *Riesling*, a late-ripening grape with a high acid content, and the green *Sylvaner* (or *Johannisberg*), also a late ripener. In Germany this variety has kept the name of its inventor, *Müller-Thurgau*. After several years of experiment and improvement, he produced a new variety, stable, prolific, rather low in acid and not exacting about soils. It is the variety best suited to the local climatic and soil conditions. The *Riesling-Sylvaner* gives a wine with a fine bouquet, light-bodied and fresh, with a slight muscat flavour.

The commonest red variety is the *Pinot Noir*, called here the *Blauburgunder*, or *Blue Burgundy*. It was introduced into the Grisons between 1630 and 1635 by the Duc de Rohan who was in command of French troops at Maienfeld. The variety became common in other regions later, especially in regions with a good exposure and a deep, rich, loose soil. The *Pinot Noir* wines produced in the Grisons are, together with the wines of Neuchâtel, the best in Switzerland, but do not give the highest yields.

CANTON OF THE GRISONS. Travelling down the Upper Rhine, we come to vineyards downstream from Chur, those of Còstamser, Trimmis and Zizers. Here the *Pinot Noir* produces a light red wine and the *Riesling-Sylvaner* a white with a strong bouquet.

After the junction with the River Landquart, the Lower Rhine Valley seems more suited to the vine, and the vineyards of the Grisons Seigneury—the Bündner Herrschaft—spread over the communes of Malans, Jenins, Maienfeld and Fläsch. By far the commonest variety (99 per cent) is the *Pinot Noir*, which was introduced during the Thirty Years War. This region of the Grisons, less frequented by tourists than the Engadine, enjoys a very pleasant climate, especially in September and October; fog is virtually unknown and though the *fœhn*, the warm south wind, is unpleasant to man, it is beneficial to the grape, which thus ripens in conditions more favourable than those in many other parts of German Switzerland.

Most of the vineyards are owned by smallholders who trellis the vine and devote to its care about 400 to 600 hours per acre per year. Though this vine has never been afflicted with the phylloxera, it is being gradually replaced with resistant stocks. A variety of unknown origin, the *Completer*, is still to be found in the commune of Malans; it produces a white wine which is a local speciality. The best Grisons growths are the reds, which are fragrant and well-balanced. They are drunk young and preferably on the spot. The yield is very variable, but averages 132,000 gallons.

CANTON OF ST. GALLEN. Further down the Rhine we enter the Canton of St. Gallen. The area under wine cultivation may be divided into three regions:

1. The southern region, with the vineyards lying between the districts of Bad Ragaz, Sargans and Lake Walen. The wines are mainly red, and the best-known growths include the SCHLOSS WERDENBERG and the PORTASER from Pfäfers.

2. The northern region comprises the vineyards situated between Hub and the entry of the Rhine into Lake Constance. As in the northern part of the Grisons, the valley of the Rhine is suitable here for vine-growing, but the area under cultivation has shrunk by three-quarters since the end of the last century. The best red wines bear the names of BALGACHER, SONNENBURGER, REBSTEINER, MARBACHER, PFAUENHALDE, ROSENBERG, EICHHOLZ, MONSTEINER, BERNERKER and BUCHENBERG, the latter known as "the pearl of the Rheintal". The FORSTWEIN from Altstätten fetches remarkable prices. All these wines are from the *Pinot Noir* grape, locally known as *Blauburgunder*. The two winegrowing communes of the Canton of Appenzell, Wolfhalden and Lutzenberg, may be added to this region; they produce, half and half, red and white wines for local consumption.

3. The small vineyards in the north-west of the Canton, Bronschhofen and Wil, where the WILBERG is highly appreciated. Growers in this region make a wine from red grapes after removing the stalks, known as BEERLIWEIN; it is full-bodied and fragrant and has a heavy bouquet.

CANTON OF THURGAU. The vineyards of Thurgau lie between the lower arm of Lake Constance, the Rhine and the Thur. Most of them (80 per cent) produce a red wine from the *Pinot Noir*, the remainder being a white from the *Riesling-Sylvaner*.

The ARENENBERG DOMANE is worth bearing in mind and tasting locally. Further south, the vineyards of Stettfurt produce the famous SONNENBERG, a growth of admirable consistency.

Almost all the wines in this region are drunk locally. The tourist will certainly drink them with the local dishes—*féra*, a fish from Lake Constance, with a white wine from the Untersee; and slices of liver pâté, Thurgau style, with a red from Warth.

CANTON OF SCHAFFHAUSEN. In the Schaffhausen region, the vine crosses the Rhine to the right bank. The foothills at the end of the Jura form a protecting screen. The *Pinot Noir* is grown on the heavier soils, the *Riesling-Sylvaner* on the chalk regions.

In 1900, the area grown to vine was 2,710 acres; it has stabilized in recent years at between 890 and 940 acres.

Some 90 per cent of the area produces red wines from the *Pinot Noir*. The whites come from the *Riesling-Sylvaner* and are distinguished by a very strong bouquet. Some other varieties (*Pinot Gris* and *Elbling*) are rarely to be found. Hallau is the largest winegrowing commune, and its most notable wine is the HALLAUER "IM HINTERE WAATELBUCK", a red of first-rate quality. Passing through Schaffhausen, where the traveller will visit the Zu Allerheiligen Museum or the Falls of the Rhine, according to his taste, he will be able to sample a full-bodied red, the MUNOT, which takes its name from the squat keep which dominates the town and the Rhine valley.

CANTON OF ZURICH. Further south again, in the Canton of Zurich, residential and industrial areas have gradually encroached upon the winegrowing area, which has shrunk from some 12,400 acres at the beginning of the century to 740 today. The climate is less suited to the vine in this region than on the banks of the Rhine, particularly because of the spring frosts. The vine clings, however, to the most sheltered and sunniest slopes. This winegrowing area may be divided into three regions:

1. In the north: the Zurich vineyards—the district is called the *Weinland*, or wine country—follow on from those in Thurgau and, like them, produces red wines from the *Pinot Noir* and whites from the *Riesling-Sylvaner* and the *Raüschling*, full-bodied wines which are suitable for laying down.

2. Farther to the west, the Zurich Unterland is still part of the Jura and produces a great variety of wines, mostly reds from the *Pinot Noir* and whites from the *Riesling-Sylvaner*. These are local wines for local consumption.

3. In the south: the shores of the Lake of Zurich and the banks of the Limmat, downstream from Zurich, produce wines which are well reputed. Stäffa, the largest winegrowing commune in the canton, is proud of its STERNENHALDE and its LATTENBERG; Herliberg produces a CLEVNER SCHIPFGUT, well-reputed among local connoisseurs. Other wines are APPENHALDE, CHORHERRENHALDE, ÄBLETEN and TURMGUT. Weiningen, on the slopes of the Limmat, is the second largest winegrowing commune in the canton.

The people of Zurich have many local dishes and it is not hard to find a range of wines worthy to go with them. However, these pleasures of the table are confined to those who can take advantage of an undisturbed sojourn in the canton, since none of the wines grown under what are called "regional agreements" may be exported.

CANTON OF AARGAU. The course of the Limmat takes us quite naturally into the Canton of Aargau. Here the vine spreads along the slopes of the Aare and its tributaries, the Limmat and the Reuss, on the sheltered slopes of the Jura and the north-eastern shore of Lake Hallwil. The area covers no more than 740 acres. The *Riesling-Sylvaner* (27 per cent) and the *Pinot Noir* (55 per cent) are the two main varieties. The wines are light and fragrant, with a low alcohol content. The white wines, such as the SCHINZNACHER RÜHBERG, have a bouquet that is highly appreciated; the reds, especially the NETTELER, GOLDWAND and BRESTENBERGER, are excellent table wines.

The vineyards in the Canton of Lucerne, an extension of the Aargau vineyards southwards, are certainly more of a curiosity than anything else, since they cover only 4 acres (171 ares).

CANTON OF BASEL. From the border of the Canton of Schaffhausen to Basel there are no vineyards along the Rhine. The twin cantons of Basel-City and Basel-Country each possess some vineyards. That of Basel-City—there is only one—is on the other side of the Rhine at Riehen, is called *Im Schlipf* and is only about 2 ½ acres in area. Basel-Country is rather better off (about 125 acres), particularly on the end slopes of the Jura and along the Birs. Very little but white wines are produced, from the *Chasselas* and the *Riesling-Sylvaner*, and they are curiosities more for the local fancier than the passing tourist.

CANTON OF SOLOTHURN. Going up the Aare from Basel we cross the Canton of Solothurn, which produces local wines with an alcoholic content varying from 9° to 11°. The white wines are from the *Chasselas*, locally known as the *Gutedel,* and the reds from the *Burgunder.* The winegrowing area in Solothurn has been greatly reduced in less than a century and today covers only about ten acres.

CANTON OF BERN. We now come to the Lake of Biel, the north shores of which, backed by the Jura, form a winegrowing district from Vingelz-Biel to La Neuveville, extending westwards into the Canton of Neuchâtel. It is planted almost entirely with *Pinot Noir* and *Chasselas,* the latter greatly predominating. These wines are light, fragrant and sharp, and are best drunk young. The best-known are the TWANNER and the SCHAFISER. A long way upstream, at the very threshold of the Alps, there lie the vineyards of Spiez and Oberhofen, which produce white wines from the *Riesling-Sylvaner* and reds from the *Pinot Noir.*

THE WINES OF NEUCHÂTEL

Although they are part of the Rhine basin, the vineyards along the shores of the Lake of Neuchâtel are in French Switzerland, a Latin country. That is perhaps why a local poet has asserted that "The land of Neuchâtel is not yet of the South, but is by no means any longer of the North."

In this region, transitional both geographically and historically, the vine seems to have been known even before the coming of the Romans. Winegrowing in this district has been established with certainty by a document dating from A.D. 998; Rodolphe, Lord of Neuchâtel, donated a vineyard at Bevaix to the Abbey of the Benedictines at Cluny. Today, the winegrowing region of the Lake of Neuchâtel extends along the lower foothills of the Jura from the Lake of Biel to the banks of the Orbe; the western part, in fact, lies within the Canton of Vaud. This region takes the form of a long ribbon some 30 miles in length by less than a mile in breadth. Along the lake it is about 1,300 feet above sea-level; the highest vineyards are at 1,800 feet, but most lie between 1,300 and 1,600 feet. These benefit from the lake's heat and stabilizing influence; at Neuchâtel itself the mean winter temperature is 1 to 1.5 degrees higher than at Fribourg or Bern. In summer the vine receives light and heat reflected from the lake, but it is subject to spring frosts despite the range of the Jura which protects it from the cold north winds. The area under vine cultivation is at present 1,560 acres in the Canton of Neuchâtel and 500 acres in the Canton of Vaud.

The markets for Neuchâtel wine trade have varied greatly. At times the trade was mainly with Bern, at others with Solothurn when that city received the foreign ambassadors accredited to the Federal Diet. There is a story that the boatmen carrying barrels of Neuchâtel to Solothurn sometimes succumbed to the temptation to sample the goods, replenishing the casks with the same volume of water.

The wines of Neuchâtel are well known today far beyond the frontiers of Switzerland. They are now sold under the generic name of NEUCHÂTEL, since the quality of the vineyards is remarkably homogeneous. Some growers and estate-bottlers add a place or growth name. The knowledgeable wine-lover may well choose a NEUCHÂTEL-SAINT-BLAISE or a NEUCHÂTEL-CORTAILLOD, denoting communes, or a NEUCHÂTEL-CHÂTEAU D'AUVERNIER or NEUCHÂTEL-HÔPITAL DE POURTALÈS, denoting a growth. Bottlers and shippers undertake to sell only Neuchâtel wines. There is an official inspection for quality and production. For over twenty-five years the State of Neuchâtel has exercised a control over the alcohol content at harvest time, and this induces growers to defer the picking and pay special attention to quality. The inspectors are paid by the State, must hold themselves available to the bottler and inspect every *gerle* (about 22 gallons) as it reaches the vat.

The Neuchâtel red wines are some of the best in Switzerland. They are splendidly rich in colour and have a strong bouquet, they are fragrant and fairly sharp and develop a delicate and well-bred aroma. One of the best is that of Cortaillod. All are derived from the *Pinot Noir.* The ŒIL DE PERDRIX (partridge eye) also comes from the *Pinot Noir,* but is slightly fermented in the vat; it is a light wine of an intriguing shade and one which is drunk young.

All the white wines (about three times as many as the reds) come from the *Chasselas.* Bottled while they are still on the lees, they retain enough carbonic acid gas to make them slightly sparkling. Locally they are said "to make the star"—i.e. they show the sparkle. They are light and fresh, with a very delicate floweriness. Some may find they have a flinty taste. Besides the wines from the *Chasselas* it is possible to find—but in limited quantities only—whites from the green *Sylvaner,* delicate and well-balanced, from the *Riesling-Sylvaner,* with a strong muscat flavour; from the grey *Pinot,* flowery, supple and bland; and from the white *Pinot,* very delicate indeed. Throughout the region the *Chasselas* whites go extremely well with the fish which are characteristic of the Lake of Neuchâtel, notably those called *palée* and *bondelle.* The reds from

This print of the Romantic period shows the Neuchâtel winegrowing district seen from the south-west near Colombier, looking towards Auvernier and Neuchâtel. The vineyards stretch in a ribbon some 30 miles in length and an average of less than one mile wide. The lake mitigates the harsh climate and the range of the Jura protects the vineyards from the north winds; but frost can do a great deal of damage.

the *Pinot Noir* go very well with red meat or game. Total production year in and year out stands at between 1,320,000 and 1,540,000 gallons.

The westernmost part of the region, which is in the Canton of Vaud, is also planted to *Chasselas* and *Pinot Noir*, as well as some special local varieties. Some growers make the wine "Neuchâtel style", i.e. on the lees, and produce wines comparable to the true Neuchâtel. Others vinify "Vaudois style", by racking, and produce a more supple wine, which, however, in the opinion of some people, loses something of its original quality. Most of these wines are sold under the name BONVILLARS. Both the reds and the whites are typical local wines *(vin du pays)*.

Whereas the Vaudois wines of La Côte, Lavaux and the Chablais (see chapter on wines of the Rhône) usually have an alcohol content of 10.5º to 13º, these run from 9.5º to 11º, occasionally to 12º. They are wines which sparkle gaily, but are not treacherous; and they are believed to encourage liveliness and wit in those who drink of them.

In the Rhine basin, too, we should mention the winegrowing district on the southern slopes of Mont-Vully, between the Lake of Neuchâtel and the Lake of Morat. The white *Chasselas* wines are light, acid and fresh; the few red wines from the *Pinot Noir* or the *Gamay* have a fine colour and a distinctly agreeable bouquet. These, too, are local wines.

THE WINES OF ALSACE

Alsace lies in a rift-valley running north and south, originating in an ancient massif the remains of which form the Vosges on the west and the Black Forest on the east. Shut in by the Jura on the south and the hills of Lower Alsace on the north, it forms a "punch-bowl" with a continental climate, cold in winter and hot in summer, with its maximum rainfall in July and August and its minimum in winter.

The Alsatian winegrowing district covers the foot-hills of the Vosges from Thann in the south to Marlen-heim in the north. Here, between the Belfort Gap and the Col de Saverne are the only breaches in the mountain wall through which air flows in from the west, to disturb the thermal and climatic balance of the part of Alsace centring on Colmar. This area is practically on the 48th parallel, the same latitude as Orleans. The prevailing winds are south in winter and north in summer. On an average computed over fifty years there are about sixty days of frost annually at Colmar; they occur even at the beginning of May, on the three days known as the *saints de glace* ("the ice saints"). Serious damage is, however, comparatively rare and remains localized. The reason is that the vineyards are situated at a height between about 550 and 1,200 feet, above the fogs that form in the flatlands, and the exposure to the sun and the geological conditions for heat storage are far more favourable than they are in the flatlands. The mean annual temperature at Colmar is 10.8° C.; on the slopes it is several tenths of a degree higher. Since the Vosges themselves catch most of the rain, the rainfall in the foothills is slight, from 20 to 28 inches annually.

The climatic conditions of the Alsatian winegrowing district are therefore extremely favourable. The annual cycle usually follows the same rhythm: budding in mid-April, flowering in mid-June, ripening in mid-August and harvest about October 10th; this gives the grapes about 115 days to develop, spread over a spring which is usually fine, a hot and thundery summer and a sunny autumn. The Alsatian vineyards also benefit from exceptional geological conditions. The foothills of the Vosges are the outcrop of the rift-valley and have a very complex geological structure; triassic, liassic and tertiary jurassic rock lie side-by-side and are blended with modern alluvial deposits, partly covered by older gravelly layers, with scree talus of glacial origin or surface deposits of loess from the flatlands. These climatic and geological conditions are the key to the special characteristics of the wines of Alsace, as compared with other wines, and the key to the principles of Alsatian winegrowing.

CHARACTERISTICS OF THE WINES OF ALSACE

Wine is, of course, produced by the fermentation of the juice of grapes; and grape juice possesses in a latent state all the qualities which the wine may later aspire to. A wine can never be improved; all that can be done is to preserve the qualities it already possesses. The heat stored up during the process of ripening comes out in the sugar concentration and determines the subsequent strength of the wine; the soil forms its body, and the variations in temperature caused by the inflow of continental or oceanic cold air modulate its fragrance. Therefore, as we move from a warm to a cooler region, the sugar content lessens and the strength diminishes; conversely, the acidity increases and reaches the maximum permissible limit near the northerly limit of winegrowing, while the fruity aromas thin out and are finally lost in an acid tartness. This may be demonstrated by following the white wines from south to north and examining the relationship between their two antagonistic components, acidity and sugar. A white wine from the south naturally has an excess of natural sweetness and an inconsistent acidity (Bordeaux wines, MONBAZILLAC, etc.). North of a certain latitude all the sugar can be fermented; this produces a dry wine. If the acidity is comparatively low, the wine takes on fragrance by developing the body (Burgundies, MACON in particular); as it increases, the aromas of the fruit become more prominent and more delicate and the wines become fruity (Alsatian and Austrian wines). Again, if there is a great deal of natural acidity in the grape juice, vinification becomes difficult, for simultaneously to lessen the concentration of acidity and to accentuate the compensating sweetness requires great technical skill and knowledge of vinification.

In Alsace vinification is simple: it is designed purely to keep the wine in its natural state. The alcohol content is usually between 11° and 14°, and in good years many growths retain a few grammes of residual sugar per litre. The tartaric acid content of the matured wines ranges from 5 to 7 grammes per litre. The prerequisites for producing a well-balanced wine are therefore excellent. But to preserve the original and special character of an Alsatian wine it is essential to preserve the taste of the fruit, that is its fruitiness and its youth. Hence oxidation must be prevented at all costs, since that would mean vinifying in the Burgundy manner, and this would completely change the wine's type. This technical detail of winemaking is a very delicate matter and requires constant vigilance, which accounts for the fact that the winegrowers of

Alsace refuse to deliver in cask and bottle their own wines in their own cellars as early as the month of May.

To sum up, the wines of Alsace have three basic characteristics: freshness, fruitiness and youth, owing to the triple balance between body, acidity and the taste of the fruit. They therefore give an impression of freshness, delicacy and "race", varying with the variety of the grape and the relation between the three components. People accustomed to the creamy quality called *moelleux* are somewhat startled by their first taste of an Alsatian wine, since the threefold balance typical of it is almost unique among the French wines and even among the German; but they speedily acquire a taste for these attractive and well-bred wines which conceal a relatively luxuriant substance behind a cool approach; they are always natural, frank and genuine.

THE PRINCIPLES OF ALSATIAN WINEGROWING

Alsatian winegrowing is governed by climatic and geological imperatives and by tradition.

Except for a few climatically similar districts in Central Europe, there is no winegrowing district where the vine grows as densely as in Alsace. Mounted on stakes, the vines usually grow to about 7 feet 8 inches (2.4 metres) and consequently bear a high yield. The district, therefore, is naturally propitious to quantity production, and efforts have always been made to push it in that direction, whereas the Alsatian grower in his wisdom, taking advantage of the extreme geological variety of the soil, has devoted all his attention to finding the variety of grape that will enable him to combine satisfaction of the market demand with the essential maintenance of the quality of his wines.

It has been stated in various works on the subject that the Alsatian winegrowing region has been considerably reduced in area. In actual fact it has remained practically the same for centuries, but it must be understood that "the winegrowing district of Alsace" means the traditional winegrowing region on the foothills of the Vosges, about 30,000 acres under production and 5,000 to 7,500 acres fallow or being readied, in accordance with the normal growing cycle. Since 1961 the whole of this region has been officially recognized as a winegrowing district entitled to the so-called *appellation d'origine contrôlée* (A.O.C.). It produces some 15,400,000 gallons annually, 99 per cent of it white wine. This delimitation is the outcome of constant efforts over many years to recover the stability and quality control which was formerly customary in the towns and villages in the district, which did their utmost to reduce or even eliminate winegrowing on the flatlands and to prevent the planting of coarse varieties with excessively large yields.

A ministerial decree with force of law issued in 1945 defined the varieties permitted. There are now considerably fewer, only those which furnish the most dependable quality having been retained. A distinction is drawn between the noble varieties—*Riesling, Muscat, Gewürztraminer,* the *Pinots* (white, grey, or Alsatian *Tokay,* and red) and *Sylvaner*—and the ordinary varieties, the *Chasselas, Knipperlé* and *Goldriesling.* All the others listed in the older classifications have disappeared.

These varieties are of very ancient stock; most of them, mentioned from the sixteenth century onward, have been selected by centuries-old tradition and long deliberation. Each requires the appropriate soil, the limestone supplying lightness and elegance and the clay body and solidity. Whereas the *Sylvaner* is fairly indifferent to the type of soil, the *Pinots* prefer chalk and the *Muscat* and the *Gewürztraminer* soil rich in clay; the *Riesling,* on the other hand, does best on primary formations. Given the extreme variety of the soils, each commune is able—some, of course, more successfully than others—to grow most of the varieties.

THE WINES OF ALSACE

The ZWICKER is a light and pleasant wine with no great pretentions, generally served as a carafe wine. It comes from several varieties of grape, usually the *Chasselas,* and legally must be from a noble variety.

The SYLVANER is fruitier and sharper, with an apparent sparkle, and is very pleasing to drink. It is of good quality at Barr; very full-bodied in the Haut-Rhin; and really appetizing at Westhalten.

The PINOT BLANC is a very well-balanced wine which could be described as discreet and distinguished. It is currently very popular.

The ALSATIAN TOKAY, from the grey *Pinot,* is a wine of rare elegance with a regal build; it is the richest of the Alsatian growths and has a most attractive velvety flavour. It is called Tokay because of the tradition embodied in an ancient legend that General Lazare de Schwendi, warring against the Turks in Hungary around 1560, brought back some roots which he cultivated in his conservatory at Kientzheim. This wine is still grown around Kientzheim in the central district of the Haut-Rhin area, between Eguisheim and Bergheim, where the best-known Alsatian vineyards are situated.

The ALSATIAN MUSCAT is the wine with the strongest but also the freshest bouquet in the whole range of Alsatian wines. Its fruitiness is very characteristic; it faithfully reproduces the savour of the fresh grape.

The GEWÜRZTRAMINER, which is known outside Alsace sometimes simply as "Gewürz" and sometimes as "Traminer", is the great Alsatian speciality. This wine is clothed in velvet, it is perfumed, it is brilliant and it seduces the ladies, for it is potent and enchanting.

The RIESLING is an elegant and distinguished wine, with a great deal of discretion. Delicate and fragrant, it has a fine and subtle bouquet. Many Alsatians call the RIESLING the emperor of Alsatian wines. The RIESLINGS of Turckheim and Bergheim in the Haut-Rhin and Dambach in the Bas-Rhin are highly spoken of. These wines age extraordinarily well.

FROM PRESS TO TABLE

Until a few years ago the whole grape harvest was pressed by the grower and the wine was sold by the barrel in the grower's own cellar after tasting, comparing and discussing the price with the shipper, innkeeper or private buyer through a local expert broker. Since 1945 the Alsatian wine district has undergone a great, though necessary, change; but a change that is rather to be regretted nevertheless. Formerly all the growers used to keep their own wines in their own cellars and people visited them there, tasted, laughed, spent whole nights among the vats, sang, emptied glasses and ate bacon or smoked ham with the wine.

This atmosphere is now to be found only at the cellars of a few large growers. The handlers, who bring in their own grapes, vinify their wines and sell them direct to the consumer. Many of the growers' cellars are empty and the magnificent oak barrels ring hollow; the grapes are sold to the trade or taken to the cooperative, which does the winemaking and marketing. Some of the poetry is lost, but quality is gained.

Growers, co-operatives and handlers very seldom sell their wines by the barrel, but in bottles known as Alsace *flûtes*, holding 72 centilitres (about 24 fluid ounces) for quality wines or a litre for carafe wines. The ordinary wines are bottled in March and the better wines in May or June. All these bottles bear a label which must state *Appellation Alsace Contrôlée*, usually with the addition of the name of the grape variety and the shipper. Sometimes such qualifications as *grande réserve, grand vin* or *vin fin* are added; these are conventional terms for wines which must by law be over 11º in strength. The consumer thus receives wines which are absolutely reliable.

All that the buyer has to do, therefore, is to lay the bottles down in a cool and slightly damp cellar kept in the dark at a temperature of about 12º C. If this is done, a quality wine will keep from five to ten years depending on whether it is a full-bodied wine, that is to say, of a sunny vintage year, or a lighter wine of a year in which there was not much sun. The Confrérie Saint-Etienne, the main selling and connoisseur organization, even has bottles of the 1834 and 1865 vintages, over a century old but still in perfect condition; actually, 1834 was a fairly difficult year but 1865 was the great year of the century.

Alsace wine is drunk cool, but not iced, at a temperature of about 12º C. If the chill is taken off slightly, it develops its bouquet deliciously, but keeps its youthful flavour. It may, of course, be drunk by itself as a thirst-quencher; the CHASSELAS, ZWICKER and SYLVANER are wines of which one can never grow tired. Even better, for sipping, are the PINOT BLANC or the EDELZWICKER, while on great occasions one of the Big Four, RIESLING, MUSCAT, TOKAY or GEWÜRZTRAMINER, with a slight preference for a fine MUSCAT.

The Alsatians always take some rather out-of-the-way snack with their wine, such as walnuts and wholemeal bread with a new wine, or unsweetened tarts with cheese puff paste or almonds or olives, before they sit down to a board amply stocked, but not as groaning as it was in the old days. Alsace, despite its many misfortunes, has always been a wealthy region and for centuries the granary and cellar of a large part of Europe. It had everything—fish, fowl, meat of all kinds, game, frogs, snails, white bread, cheese, and, above all, splendid wines which were exported in all directions from as early as the seventh century to stock the tables of prince and wealthy merchant.

Alsace has the reputation of always keeping a decent balance from every point of view, and all excess at table is frowned upon. Libations are copious, true, but never to excess; the Alsatian knows by nature how to drink decently, and he never fails to stop before laughter degenerates into imbecility. At table the wines are married to the dishes in accordance with simple rules conforming to the methodical Alsatian nature. An ordinary carafe wine is adequate with a good choucroute, a baeckaeffa or cold meats for a modest meal. Or, if something rather better is wanted, a PINOT BLANC or a modest RIESLING. For a more elaborate meal, with cheese and dessert, a bottle of TRAMINER is opened towards the end of the meal. The number of glasses beside each place increases for a banquet, for each dish calls for its own wine. Thus, a RIESLING is proper—or, going down the scale, a PINOT or a SYLVANER—with dishes which are not highly seasoned, such as asparagus, shell-fish, trout *au bleu* or white meat. The GEWÜRZTRAMINER is essential with a lobster *à l'américaine* or a well-ripened, strong munster or roquefort cheese, for it marries with them inimitably. For rich food, such as Strasbourg foie gras, the TRAMINER, and especially the TOKAY, is essential for the marriage. For the main dish the choice is wide open, though a really good vintage TOKAY is not to be sneezed at on occasion.

Alsatian women are excellent cooks, but a bottle of wine beside the pot is needed, for plenty of wine used in cooking a country dish makes it far more digestible.

The Alsatian philosophy of the table is that you must never eat purely for eating's sake nor drink simply to drink; but you should eat to drink better and drink to eat better. And the Alsatians take great care to stick to this maxim.

The Alsatian vineyards are among the oldest in France; they appeared soon after those around Narbonne. They experienced great prosperity from the seventh century onward, growing with that of Strasbourg, long the largest river port on the Rhine and the most famed wine market in central Europe; and this lasted until the Thirty Years War, which brought endless disturbances in its train. The winegrowing district was rich, but not opulent; it was and still is bourgeois; there are no châteaux, only cities and affluent market towns with a rigid sense of duty.

The Alsatian winegrower is a bourgeois; he is his own master; serfdom and share-cropping have never existed. He buys his land, never rents it; he makes his wine and he ensures that it is good enough for himself and his friends. This accounts for his character, and, too, the degree to which in Alsace, a wealthy and generous land, everything is imbued with balance.

THE WINES OF GERMANY

Germany, together with Canada and the U.S.S.R., is the most northerly winegrowing country in the world. Comparatively weak sunlight lasting over a long period creates the ideal conditions for white wines with a low alcohol content, an acid freshness and a bouquet not blurred by a high sugar content.

Winegrowing reached the Celtic area on the left bank of the Rhine before the Roman era, and excavations in the valleys of the Moselle, the Ahr and the Middle Rhine have demonstrated conclusively that the Romans cultivated the vine on the left bank. On the right bank in Roman times there was some trade in wine, and it has been proved that in the Frankish period (about A.D. 800) winegrowing was carried on everywhere where the vine still grows, while during the warm period of the Middle Ages it extended in a most remarkable way throughout the territory of the Germanic Holy Roman Empire. In the twelfth century the vine was grown in East and West Prussia and in Mecklenburg, and even in parts of Schleswig-Holstein and in Denmark.

A regression began in the sixteenth century and has not yet been halted. The deterioration of the climate after 1550 was only one factor. Imports of better quality at moderate prices by the League of Hanseatic towns and the dissolution by the Reformation of the monasteries which had hitherto been the main centres of winegrowing were disastrous to North Germany. In other regions, such as Württemberg, winegrowing never recovered from the Thirty Years War.

In addition, consumers' tastes changed. Wine had conquered regions whose climate was generally unfavourable to the slow ripening of grapes. It would hardly be true to say that the Germans of the Middle Ages preferred bitter drinks as well as having a documented predilection for bitter foods. The wine often produced nothing but alcohol; it was sweetened with honey, spiced and very often heated and drunk as a sort of hot punch. Until the end of the sixteenth century the consumption of wine must have been ten times higher than it is now. Bavaria, nowadays considered to be wholly devoted to beer, grew wine in the fifteenth to seventeenth centuries even in the Upper Bavarian regions.

But around 1500 the art of winning alcohol by distilling other fruits became widespread in Germany, and beer, which was dearer than wine till about 1550, became much cheaper. All these reasons, not to speak of the huge burden of customs duties and excise, account for the fact that the winegrowing area today is considerably less than half what it was around 1550.

In recent years the yield of must has been some 132,000,000 gallons. The greater proportion of this, 90,200,000 gallons, is supplied by three adjacent regions: the Palatinate, Rheinhesse and the valleys of the Moselle, Saar and Ruwer. Comparatively insignificant districts such as the Ahr (74,000 acres) and the Middle Rhine, including Siebenbergen (173,000 acres), remind us that the vine was once grown much farther to the north until the competition from wines imported from southern Europe, through Hamburg especially, became so fierce that German wine production fell off steeply, a decline hastened by the devastations of the last of the great religious wars. Present-day consumption amounts to an average of 28 pints per capita; 36.4 per cent of it is met out of imports.

GRAPE VARIETIES. Some of the whites—*Riesling, Sylvaner, Traminer, Ruländer*—do not give of their best except in good years and in very sunny exposures. This is notably the case with *Riesling*. Others, however, like the *Müller-Thurgau*, ripen more quickly and produce an agreeable wine even if there is not much sun.

The soil also makes a great deal of difference; indeed, it and the variety together determine the wine's character. This particular feature distinguishes Germany sharply from the other winegrowing countries. It is due to the low alcohol and sugar content; since neither of these two components are present in large quantities to affect the wine's smell and taste, the delicate qualities derived from the rocks in the sub-soil which do affect nose and palate come into their own.

Germany leaves the pre-eminence in the red varieties to her neighbour to the west. But the *Spätburgunder*, the German version of the Burgundian *Pinot Noir* grape, grown on red sandstone and schist, gives a ruby wine of a firm ripeness, outstanding in quality, deep burgundy in shade, with a character that yields nothing to wines from other countries. This is true, too, of the garnet-coloured *Frühburgunder*; the wine is first-rate, full-bodied, sometimes velvety; the *Portugieser* produces a paler wine, which has little bouquet and is lighter; it is sensitive to frost and early-ripening, and it is drunk young. In good years it is warm and velvety and its colour becomes dark red.

The better German wines have a character all their own—fruity acidity, balanced, flowery bouquet, a low alcohol content and lightness—and are thus a type of wine for which there is an evergrowing demand.

BADEN

The winegrowing region of the Upper Rhine, incorporated by referendum since 1952 in the *Land* of Baden-Württemberg, is divided up into six completely different winegrowing districts. In the south-west, on the shores of Lake Constance—at Meersburg to be exact—there is the SEEWEIN. This sharp and full-bodied wine from the *Ruländer*, *Traminer* and *Burgunder* varieties grown on moraines suffers from the altitude, and this is only partly counterbalanced by the southern climate and the broad stretch of water. Here, as elsewhere in Baden, is the famous WEISSHERBST, derived from a *Burgunder* vinified as a white wine. It is full-bodied with a fine bouquet.

On the deep clayey soils, partly covered with loess, of the Margraviate, between Basel and Freiburg-in-Breisgau, the *Gutedel*, or *Chasselas*, imported from Geneva in 1780, produces a soft, perfumed wine of low acidity. Between Freiburg and Baden-Baden three regions share the warmth of the upper valley of the Rhine and the protection of the range of the Black Forest against the east winds: Breisgau, the vineyards of the Kaiserstuhl and Ortenau. On the Kaiserstuhl the vine grows on volcanic tuff, in Breisgau on loess, in Ortenau on granite, near Freiburg and in the valley of the Glotter on gneiss.

A wide range of grape varieties are grown on this variety of soils, no one of them predominating. The 20,600 acres of the winegrowing area in Baden are planted 23.4 per cent to *Müller-Thurgau* and 21 per cent to *Blue Spätburgunder*; *Gutedel (Chasselas)* 16.2 per cent, *Ruländer* (grey *Pinot*) 13.5 per cent, *Sylvaner* 8 per cent and *Riesling* 6.8 per cent. But 11 per cent is still left for the *Traminer*, *Portugieser*, old varieties such as the *Elbling* and *Raüschling*, and new selections such as the *Freisamer*. The must harvest amounts to an average of 154,000,000 gallons a year.

At Neuweier and in neighbouring areas the MAUERWEIN is bottled in flagons, or *Bocksbeutel*, as in Franconia; elsewhere in long bottles, as in the Moselle. One sixth of the 400,000 farms cultivate the vine as well as other crops. Baden is a *Land* of wine co-operatives; there are about 110 of them and they account for two-thirds of the production. They are managed by an organization called the Central Federation of Wine-Growers' Co-operatives.

Among the Breisgau wines the GLOTTERTÄLER is famed and, indeed, rather feared for its effects.

The best wines come from the Kaiserstuhl, which dominates the plain of the Rhine. The principal places are Achkarren (SCHLOSSBERG), Ihringen (WINKLER BERG, FOHRENBERG, ABTSWEINGARTEN), Bickensohl (STEINFELSEN, EICHBERG, HOCHSTATT), Oberrottweil (HENKENBERG, KIRCHBERG, EICHBERG), Bischoffingen (STEINBRUCK, ROSENKRANZ) and the State domains of Blankenhornsberg. The vine grows everywhere on the eroded basaltic tuff of the old volcano, producing wines of a *Sylvaner* type, full and ripe, the *Riesling*, acid and elegant, the *Spätburgunder*, outstanding, and the *Ruländer*, ardent and impetuous with a soft and exquisite fruity flavour.

In the Ortenau, where the *Riesling* is called *Klingelberger* after the castle around which it was first planted in 1776, there are also some wines of quality at Durbach, Ortenberg, Neuweier and Oberkirch, for instance; the best red wines of the Ortenau are derived from the *Blauer Spätburgunder*. The MAUERBERG at Neuweier and the SONNENBERG, the KLOSTERBERG and the NÄGELSFÖRST at Varnhalt are wines of repute. This district also produces perfumed TRAMINERS reminiscent of the Alsatian wine.

In the Bühlertal red wines predominate, such as WALDULM, KAPPELRODECK, BÜHLERTAL and AFFEN-

TALER, the label of the latter being decorated with a monkey, although the name really comes from the Latin greeting *Ave*.

Northern Baden up to Heidelberg once had extensive vineyards, but in many places they have been reduced to insignificance by industrialization. But on the slopes of the Kraichgau and the Odenwald, BERG-STRASSENWEINE (wines of the mountain road) are still produced, as well as table wines from north of Heidelberg. Lastly, at the north-eastern end, the Taubergrund produces a wine which is almost contiguous at Wertheim-am-Main with the Franconian wines, which it closely resembles.

The Badeners' "wine road" is considerably longer than the Palatines', for Baden extends for 125 miles. A Baden label guarantees the quality of the wine.

WÜRTTEMBERG

The vineyards are terraced in the valleys of the Neckar and its tributaries, the Jagst, Kocher, Rems, Enz, Murr, Bottwar and Zaber. The soil is partly triassic and partly conchiferous limestone. The triassic soils are heavy and chalky, especially where they are broken down by deposits of marl. The conchiferous lime is lighter and warmer.

Until the Thirty Years War the Swabian wine district covered a million acres. Today it has only 15,750 acres producing 10,120,000 gallons of wine. The main variety is the *Trolinger* (28.4 per cent), which is found only in Württemberg and produces a brick-red, full-bodied wine; 24.8 per cent is planted to *Riesling* and 13.1 per cent to *Sylvaner*. The remainder is divided between the *Portugieser* (10.6 per cent), the *Müller-Thurgau* (6.3 per cent), the dark red *Limberger* (6 per cent), the *Samtrot* and the *Schwarzer Urban*.

Near Reutlingen the vineyards climb to over 1,700 feet. The cultivation is a typical co-operative enterprise. In 1920 the co-operatives took over a district which had gone completely out of cultivation for many years and have brought it to a level which can bear comparison with other districts. The Württemberg wines are hard to find on the market; apparently, the growers drink their wine themselves, usually very young, in the first two years.

One of the Württemberg specialities is the SCHILLER-WEIN, something like the French rosé. It is made either by blending red and white grapes in the press or by leaving the skins of red grapes in the must for a short time (which is how the WEISSHERBST is produced in Baden). Another Württemberg speciality is a young wine which has not completed the fermentation process; it is called SUSER and is a very good and easy wine to drink. The communes of Cannstatt, Unter-türckheim and Feuerbach produce excellent growths.

Stuttgart, the capital of Baden-Württemberg, is not only a large centre of the wine trade but still has an 2,000-acre vineyard. A French saying of about 1630 claimed that "if the grape of Stuttgart were not picked, the city would drown in wine".

The *Sylvaner* grape produces fresh green wines in the upper valley of the Neckar. There are fragrant, full-bodied Rieslings in the valley of the Rems as well as luscious Sylvaners. The Rems valley produces the famous STETTENER BROTWASSER. The valleys of the Murr and the Bottwar shelter Steinheim, Kirchheim, Murr, Kleinbottwar, Grossbottwar, Lombach and Marbach, the home of the poet Schiller, whose family is said to have given its name to the SCHILLERWEIN.

There is another place with the name of Stetten in the red wine district of Heuchelberg and, farther on, Schwaigen. In the valley of the lower Neckar there is Lauffen, where the vine grows on conchiferous lime, as at Heilbronn and Flein. It is on this soil too that the *Riesling* and *Sylvaner* of Taubergrund ripen. Maulbronn and Gundelsheim, as well as Schnait in the valley of the Rems, produce wines which are well spoken of.

THE PALATINATE

The Palatinate in the *Land* Rhein-Pfalz has 45,000 acres of vineyards and produces 37,400,000 gallons of must on an average; it is the largest wine-growing region in Germany. The *Sylvaner* is the principal variety of vine-plant grown in this district, with 39.6 per cent of the total area, followed by the *Müller-Thurgau* with 20.4 per cent, the red *Portugieser* with 17.7 per cent and the *Riesling* with 13.6 per cent. As early as the period of the Holy Roman Empire the Palatinate was known as "the wine-cellar of the Empire". This region is particularly favoured by nature; it gets an average of 1,875 hours of sunshine and the winter lasts less than three months. The vineyards are mostly on the flatlands and are easy to farm mechanically; only in a few places are they situated as high as 900 feet. The Haardt mountain range, which is an extension of the Vosges, protects the Palatinate plain from the bitter north winds and from the rain and snow from the west. Indeed, so sheltered is the district and so mild the climate that oven figs and lemons, apricots and peaches can flourish there. The vine stretches in a ribbon 50 miles long by some two to four miles wide from the Alsatian border northwards to the edge of the Rheinhesse along the *Weinstrasse* (wine road) from the Wine Gate at Schweigern to Grünstadt.

The region is rich in archaeological finds which prove that the Romans cultivated the vine here on a large scale. Many of these finds are to be seen in the Wine Museum at Speyer, the largest in Germany. The importance of this winegrowing district at the time of the Frankish kingdoms was due to the fact that by the Treaty of Verdun in A.D. 834 which parcelled out the empire of Charlemagne, the region of Speyer, Worms and the Nahe was given to Germania because of its wealth of wine *(propter vini copiam)*.

The Palatinate comprises three winegrowing regions: the Oberhaardt, the Mittelhaardt and the Unterhaardt. The Oberhaardt, or Upper Haardt, is covered with fertile loess on which the *Sylvaner* produces a fresh and generous table wine for ordinary consumption *(Konsumwein)* in more than 50 communes between the Alsatian border and Neustadt. The *Traminer*, with its noble and discreet bouquet, also prospers. Hambach, Maikammer and Edenknoben are noted for their high yields. The best growths are to be found between Gleisweiler and Hasbach; Edenknoben and Diedesfeld are the best-known communes, producing sound and characteristic wines.

Farther north, the transition to the Mittelhaardt, or Central Haardt, is virtually imperceptible; the best-known communes are Deidesheim, Ruppertsberg, Forst and Wachenstein. The district extends to Dachenheim and Weisenheim-am-Berg. The soils are lighter on the whole, compounded of sand and warm gravel; the rainfall is slight. The Forst and Deidesheim vineyards are improved with powdered basalt, which makes them even warmer.

On the escarpments of the Haardt range there are triassic, red sandstone and schist outcrops, besides granite, gneiss and schist, and chalky and clayey alluvial deposits at the foot of the range. The *Riesling* is not much grown, but produces a vigorous and fruity wine here, with the very prominent tang of the local soil called *Schmeck*; but the *Sylvaner* is also represented by soft and rather sweet wines of a high quality—as, indeed, are the *Gewürztraminers*, which produce wines that are both fiery and round.

The Mittelhaardt produces the heaviest must in Germany. In 1959, a hot year, the must of the Haardt wines sometimes titrated at over 300° Ochsle. In the large vineyards which produce these selected and dried-out grapes they remain on the stem until as late as mid-November even in average years.

The nearly 3,500 different types of wine are being systematically reduced. Besides the great internationally famous estates (such as Bassemann-Jordan, von Buhl and Bürklin-Wolf) there are co-operatives which own huge vineyards. A large percentage of vinegrowers vintage their wines at these co-operatives, of which there are usually two in each village, divided as they are by their religious or by their political leanings.

A list of the most famous names in the Central Haardt would certainly include the following growths (classified by commune): at Forst DOPP, GRAINHÜBEL, HOCHENMORGEN, KIESELBERG, LEINHÖHLE, MÄUSHÖHLE, MÜHLE, MÜHLE UND GEHEU and RENNPFAD; at Ruppertsberg HOFSTUCK, HOHEBURG and NUSSBIEN; at Wachenheim BÖHLIG, GOLDBÄCHEL, LUGINSLAND and RECHBÄCHEL; and at Bad Dürkheim HOCHMESS, MICHELSBERG and SPIELBERG.

Second only to these great wines there comes a group which includes some other first-rate wines. For example: at Forst KRANICH, LANGENBÖHL, MUSENHANG, PECHSTEIN, WALSHÖHLE and SCHNEPPENPFLUG; at Deidesheim BILDSTÖCKL, HAHNENBÖHL, HERRGOTTSACKER, HOFSTÜCK, LANGENBÖHL and LANGENMORGEN; at Königsbach IDIG, ROLANDSBERG and BENDER; at Wachenheim DREISPITZ, FUCHSMANTEL, GERÜMPEL and SCHENKENBÖHL; at Bad Durkheim FROHNHOF, HOCHBENN, KLOSTERBERG and NONNENGARTEN.

There are also wines of quality at Gimmeldingen (MEERSPINNE and SCHILD), Kallstadt (NILL and SAUMAGEN), Ungstein (HERRENBERG, HÖNIGSÄCKEL and SPIELBERG) and at Freinsheim, Herxheim-am-Berg and Mussbach.

The Unterhaardt, or Lower Haardt, which stretches as far as Rheinhesse and the Nahe, supplies *Konsumwein* and table wines, the ZELLER SCHWARZER HERRGOTT being the best of them. The Unterhaardt accounts for about 13 per cent of the Palatinate production, the Mittelhaardt for about 35 per cent and the Oberhaardt for 52 per cent. A poet has said of Palatinate wine that in combining maturity with gentleness it is the maternal female among wines, and another has described it thus: "The wine of the Palatinate has the advantage over its two brothers (the Rheingau and the Rheinhesse) of having its own very special temperament, which ranges from the gracious levity of adolescence to the impetuous passion of the grown man, from blooming, perfumed and frivolous youth to noble, polite and dignified maturity."

The Rheingau, where some of the best-known vineyards of Germany line the right bank of the Rhine, which here flows east and west, giving the vines a southern, sunny aspect.

The Kaiserstuhl, the remains of an old volcano, dominates the Rhine plain and produces some of the best wine of Baden from its tufa soil.

RHEINHESSE

From the name one would suppose that Rheinhesse was the old *Land* lying between the Imperial Cathedral Cities of Worms and Mainz, but that disappeared from the political map in 1945. Rheinhesse is now a region of the Rheinpfalz, a *Land* of the Federal Republic, with Mainz as its capital. In the south the Palatinate vineyards near Worms merge into the Rheinhesse. In the north and east the border follows the bend of the Rhine from Bingen to Worms, and in the west it extends up the valley of the Nahe. Legend is fond of associating the cultivation of the vine in the Rheinhesse with Charlemagne, but, as in other regions, there is evidence that it existed there as early as A.D. 753.

The Rheinhesse is the second-largest winegrowing district in Germany. Extending over 176 communes, 40,500 acres are planted to vines, 8.5 per cent to red varieties (almost all *Portugieser*). The *Sylvaner* predominates among the whites (with 47 per cent), followed by the *Müller-Thurgau* (33.2 per cent) and the *Riesling* (6.2 per cent). The harvest of must amounts to one quarter of the entire German yield.

The *Sylvaner* grows best on heavy soils, producing a sweet wine with a rich bouquet. This valley country has chalky and marly soils as well as clayey soils which, though none too good in wet years since the water does not drain off easily, are very favourable to the grape in hot summers. Loess and friable sandstone are also common, particularly between Worms, Osthofen and Oppenheim. On the mountain slopes in the south-eastern part of the region the vineyards are set on porphyritic quartz with a high potassium content. On the other hand, around Nachenheim and Nierstein there are surface outcrops of red sandstone and sandy clay of the Permian period. Near Bingen the vineyards are set on quartz shales, the soil best suited to the *Riesling*, and produce a light, luscious wine with a natural sweatness smacking of the grape.

The Rheinhesse wine best known abroad is not a growth. Large vineyards cultivated by monks stretch round the church of Our Lady of Worms. "Monk" is *minch* in the local dialect and becomes *milch*, and this is the origin of the name Liebfrauenmilch, which has been adopted for all the sweet wines of the Rheinhesse that have the fine qualities of Rhine wine. Even the neighbouring wines of the Palatinate claim the right to sell under the LIEBFRAUENMILCH label.

The quality wines in the strict sense come from the district along the Rhine. The hinterland to Alzey and the valley of the Nahe supplies *Konsumwein*. Mainz and Worms are the capitals of the German wine trade. The vineyards are mostly owned by small-holders, medium-sized holdings and co-operatives, but, for all that, Bingen, Nierstein and Oppenheim have estates which enjoy a world-wide reputation.

Oppenheim, with its chalk and marl, produces *Auslese* (wines from carefully selected bunches of grapes) and *Beerenauslese* (selected berries, i.e. wines made from overripe grapes that have acquired the noble rot—the *Edelfaüle*—picked immediately after the harvest and pressed separately). These wines can attain great age. The Oppenheim wines are heavy and ripe, particularly such great growths as KREUZ and KRÖTENBRUNNEN, together with the world-renowned REISEKAHR.

On the red sandstone spur which crops out at Nierstein white wines are produced which are indubitably among the best-known in the world; they have a fruity bouquet and great elegance. Thirty years ago an attempt was made to reduce the vast number of names which had led to a great deal of confusion, especially abroad. A single name was selected for each growth to include all the others, but this necessary reform is still only a project. The names of the wines with a world-wide reputation are AUFLANGEN, REHBACH, BRUDERSBERG, ÖLBERG, GLÖCK, PETTENTAL and FLÄSCHENHALL. Just behind them come HEILIGENBAUM, ORBEL, FUCHSLOCH, KRANSBERG, FLOSS, HIPPING, KEHR and SANKT KILIANSBERG.

But Rheinhesse is, of course, more than the OPPENHEIM, NIERSTEIN and LIEBFRAUENMILCH names combined, although the ROTTENBERG from Nackenheim and the STEIG from Dalsheim are perhaps the only other "internationally reputed growths" besides those already listed. Above Bingen the Rochusberg—with the SCHLOSSBERG, SCHWÄTZERCHEN and ROCHUSBERG—and the Scharlachberg produce very high quality wines; and the following are also certainly worth mentioning: HOCH SANKT ALBAN, WESTRUM and SILBERBERG from Bodenheim; ENGELSBERG and FENCHELBERG from Nackenheim; and STEIG and RODENSTEIN from Dalsheim.

We come at length to Ingelheim, where the blue *Burgunder* produces the famous reds of SONNENBERG, PARES and GRAVER STEIN.

Shortly after 1800 the Romantic poet Ludwig Tieck described the Rheinhesse wines in the following terms: "These excellent spritely waves which range from the light LAUBENHEIM to the strong NIERSTEINER in whetting your whistle flatter the palate, purifying, refreshing and toning up the senses. To what should they be compared but to the tranquil steadiness of good writers, to generosity and fullness devoid of chimeras and gothick allegory?"

THE VALLEY OF THE NAHE

The winegrowing valley of the Nahe stretches from Bingerbrück at the junction of the Nahe and the Rhine to Martinstein, with the lateral valleys of Guldenbach, Trollbach, Grafenbach, Alsenz and Glan. An area of 7,500 acres is planted to the vine, almost entirely of white varieties. The *Sylvaner* predominates with 40 per cent; the rest is half-and-half *Riesling* and *Müller-Thurgau*. The annual yield is some 5,280,000 gallons. Politically, the Nahe region was part of Rhenish Prussia until 1940; it is now a region of the Rheinpfalz.

The soil in the upper Nahe valley, terraced between the Hunsrück and the Soonwald, is Devonian, whereas the deeper and narrow valleys are mostly schist. The wines are fresh and metallic, something like those of the Saar. This is the country of Monzingen, whose wines were lauded by Goethe, and the Ebernburg, "the asylum of justice", where Franz von Sickingen gave refuge to the exiles of the Reformation.

The soil of the Middle Nahe is clayey and sandy, composed of calcareous sand and porphyry. Where the valley widens along the prehistoric Rhenish sea the vine springs up on clay, marl and loess. The variety of soils is reflected in the great variety of the wines, unexampled in such a small area.

The KUPFERGRUBE of Schlossböckelheim, the KAUTZENBERG, BRUCKES, KRONENBERG, KRÖTENPFUHL and NARRENKAPPE of Bad Kreuznach, the ROTENFELS of Münster-am-Stein and the HERMANNSBERG, HERMANNSHÖHLE, ROSSEL and ROSENBERG of Niederhausen are internationally renowned. The other growths from Schlossböckelheim, Waldböckelheim, Kreuznach, Münster-am-Stein, Niederhausen and Norheim are well spoken of, and the Alsenz and Glan valleys produce equally good wines, especially those from Altenbamberg, Ebenburg and Dielkirchen.

The State lands around Schlossböckelheim and Niederhausen originated on land cleared of forest. The area was later extended by taking over abandoned farms and by buying up vineyards near Altenbamberg which had long lain fallow after the ravages of the phylloxera. The nobel wines come from the State domain of Niederhausen, between Schlossböckelheim and Bad Kreuznach, and the volcanic soils near Münster-am-Stein. They are fruity and luscious, at times oncoming and vigorous, at times gently mature, with a special and attractive character all their own.

For centuries the pun was repeated (in German) that the *Weine bei der Nahe* (wines beside the Nahe) were *beinahe Weine* (almost wines). In 1816 only 2,500 acres were planted to the vine. The area has multiplied three fold in 80 years when many other winegrowing districts were diminishing.

FRANCONIA

At the beginning of the nineteenth century there were still some 27,000 acres planted to vines in Franconia in the Free State of Bavaria; today, there are only 5,700 acres, with an average annual yield of 2,640,000 gallons of must.

The Franconian vineyards stretch from Hanau in the west to Bamberg in the east, and in the north from a line running from Bad Kissingen to Hammelburg to near Ansbach in the south. The climate is oceanic west of the Spessart range and continental east of it. Geologically, Franconia is Triassic marl from Zeil-am-Obermain to the Aichgrund, conchiferous lime from Schweinfurth to Ochsenfurth and variegated sandstone on the western slopes of the Spessart. The pebbly soils are in many places covered with loess and sand. The yield per acre is only 350 to 1,100 gallons, but this means that the wine has all the more body and bouquet. The bouquet and not the alcohol content has given it the reputation of a heady wine. The *Sylvaner* predominates, with 55.2 per cent.

The *Müller-Thurgau* accounts for 31.7 per cent and the *Riesling* is inconsiderable, with only 4 per cent, though it should be said that the *Riesling* is the variety that produces the best growths from Würtzburg, the capital, namely the sweet and round LEISTE and the STEIN, sharp and perfumed, the wine which has lent its name to the typical wine of Franconia, the STEINWEIN. The wines from Eschendorf, Randersacker and Iphofen are equally good. Eschendorf produces the best, LUMP, KIRCHBERG, EULENGRUBE and HENGSTBERG; the vines grow on chalk-and-clay strata here, with loam and silt. Randersacker has the PFÜLBEN, a wine with a world-wide reputation, and the HOHBURG, SPIELBERG and TEUFELSKELLER; Iphofen produces the JULIUS-ECHTERBERG and KRONSBERG KALB UND KAMMER. But Hörstein and Frickenhausen also produce wines of the best quality, as does Klingenberg, where the *Burgunder* grows on variegated sandstone.

Besides such celebrated vineyards as the Juliusspital and Bürgerspital there are several co-operatives. The

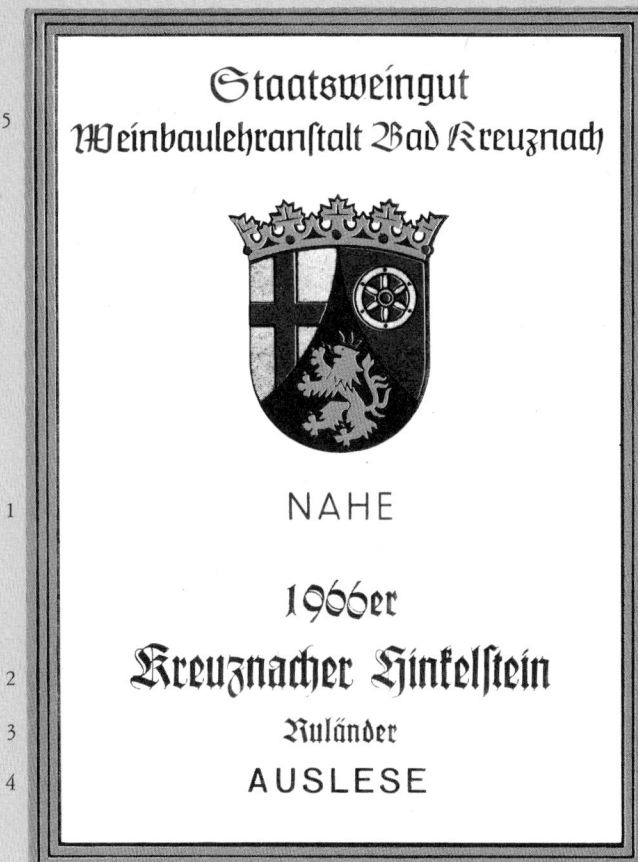

KREUZNACHER HINKELSTEIN

This straightforward label gives the following details: 1. Name of region: valley of the Nahe. – 2. Name of growth and vintage. – 3. Grape variety: Ruhländer, the German name for the grey Pinot. – 4. Auslese means that the grapes were specially selected at harvesting. – 5. Grower's name.

RAUENTHALER GEHRN

This is a rather more elaborate label. – 1. Wine from the Rheingau. – 2. Name and vintage of wine. – 3. Grape variety: Riesling. – 4. Spätlese: late-gathered, therefore a fairly sweet wine. – 5. Grower's name. – 6. Naturrein – i.e. natural wine with no sugar added. – 7. Cabinet: special reserve. – 8. Estate-bottled.

IHRINGER WINKLERBERG

The Baden vineyards lie in German territory opposite Alsace. This is a wine of the Oberrhein-Baden region, situated along the Rhine north of Basel. – 1a. The Kaiserstuhl vineyards lie on the slopes of the volcanic mountain of that name in Breisgau. – 2. Growth: Winklerberg from the village of Ihringen. – 3. Grape variety and vinification: Pinot Noir pressed to produce a rosé. – 4. Auslese: specially selected grapes. – 5. Grower's name. – 6. Estate-bottled.

IPHÖFER KAMMER

The Franconian wines are put up in broad-beamed flagons called "Bocksbeutel", hence the unusual shape of the label. – 1. Region: Franconia. – 2. Growth: Kammer from the village of Iphofen, and vintage. – 3. Grape variety: Sylvaner; special reserve; no sugar added. – 4. Estate-bottled and grower's name.

WEINSBERGER SCHEMELSBERG

This label denotes a type of red wine very popular in Germany. – 1. Wine from Württemberg. – 2. Growth: Schemelsberg from the village of Weinsberg, and vintage. – 3. Grape variety: Spätburgunder. – 4. Grower's name.

FORSTER JESUITENGARTEN

The Palatinate wines have a great reputation and this is a very celebrated label. – 1. Name of region: Rheinpfalz, or Palatinate. – 2. Growth: Jesuitengarten from the village of Forst, and vintage. – 3. Grape variety: Riesling; Trockenbeerenauslese – selected grapes gathered when overripe and dried out, therefore a sweet wine. – 4. Grower's name. – 4a. The grower is sole proprietor of this growth. – 5. Estate-bottled.

WEHLENER SONNENUHR

Moselle is so well known for its Riesling grapes that the grape variety is not mentioned on this label. – 1. Region: Mosel-Saar-Ruwer. – 2. Growth: Sonnenuhr from the village of Wehlen, and vintage. – 3. Eiswein Auslese means a wine made from grapes caught by an early frost, carefully gathered and immediately pressed. This is therefore, an "ice wine", rare and with a very special bouquet. – 4. Grower's name. – 5. Estate-bottled. – 6. The grower is a member of growers associations to promote the sale of wines of high quality.

largest State domain in Germany is in Franconia, covering about 400 acres. The Carolingians bestowed large donations of vineyards upon the monasteries scattered throughout the region. After the separation of Church and State, all the Church property reverted to the Free State of Bavaria. The properties include some of the most famous Franconia wines, especially the STEIN at Würzburg, the SCHALKSBERG and the LEISTE on the other bank of the Main and, farther upstream, the RANDERSACKER, and downstream the THÜNGERSHEIM. The Bavarian Wine Institute, of which the former Royal Bavarian Cellars at Würzburg and the State Wine Institute at Veitshochheim are branches, has a great reputation for experimental cultivation. With few exceptions, the wines of Franconia are put up in the special flagon called *Bocksbeutel*.

The wine of Franconia smacks of the soil that produces it. It can be full-bodied and down to earth, but it may also be well-bred and fresh. In any particular year, its quality greatly depends on the weather. This wine has all the variations of cold steel, from the supple Damascene blade to the Turkish scimitar.

THE RHEINGAU

The 7,584 acres of the Rheingau vineyards are divided up among no more than twenty communes and stretch for some 30 miles along the right bank of the Rhine between Wiesbaden and the valley of the Wisper near Lorch (Hochheim-am-Main also belongs to the Rheingau). The region was part of Rhenish Prussia until 1946, after which it was included in the *Land* of Hessen, the capital being Wiesbaden, itself a winegrowing commune of the Rheingau. The Rhine, which elsewhere flows north and south, here flows east and west. The vineyards in the "elbow of the Rhine" enjoy a full southern exposure, so that they have a truly southern winegrowing climate, especially as the Taunus range of hills protects the Rheingau from the cold north winds and the river bends enough to cut off most of the wind from the east or the west.

An inland geological sea and its deposits which were covered with a layer of clayey loess in the Diluvian epoch gradually built up the Upper Rheingau in terraces from Hochheim to Rüdesheim. The southern slopes, which rise to 600 feet, draw additional warmth from the sun's reflection from the Rhine, which is some 800 yards wide in this part. The warm summers and the humidity from evaporation make up for the frequently inadequate warmth of the soil.

Upstream from Rüdesheim the river flows between high cliffs and its bed is 600 feet deep. The shores are no longer gentle slopes, as in the Upper Rheingau, but sheer drops, terraced with innumerable low walls climbing from the river to the top of the cliffs some 900 feet above. The Rhine flows through Assmannshausen, which produces from the *Spätburgunder* a red wine with a strong flavour of almonds. But white varieties are grown in the rest of the Rheingau.

In area the Rheingau is only the seventh-largest German winegrowing district, but in quality its wines rank with the best in the world. The Hochheim wines have such a reputation in Britain that all Rhine wines are called hock there. The saying "a good hock keeps the doctor away" was probably coined at the time Queen Victoria visited Germany, but the wines from the Rheingau had been celebrated since the sixteenth and seventeenth centuries, owing particularly to the highly skilled viniculture practised at the Abbeys of Johannisberg and Eberbach. It was here that the first *Spätlese* wines were made, from overripe grapes picked after the ordinary harvest, and especially the *Trockenbeerenauslese*, wines made from overripe grapes which have acquired the "noble rot" and have been left to dry on the vine, somewhat like corinth currants. Ten women have to work for two whole weeks to gather enough grapes to make 20 bottles of these wines. It is no accident that such wines are found only here, for the autumn mist that rises from the Rhine, known as the *Traubendrücker*, or grape-presser, causes the grapes to become overripe and to acquire the noble rot *(Edelfäule)* and, if the weather is suitable, the grapes may be picked as late as the second fortnight in November. One of the regional specialities is the EISWEIN ("ice wine") which comes from sudden frosts; the frozen water remains in the press and the vat collects only an extract of the ethers of sugared oils and perfume.

All the best growths are produced by the *Riesling*, which accounts for 77 per cent of the area planted to vines; the remainder is partly *Müller-Thurgau* (17.9 per cent) and partly *Sylvaner* (7.6 per cent). The average yield is about 4,620,000 gallons. The vineyards, because of the inheritance laws, are mostly smallholdings. The large properties, however, are also very productive. There are hardly any co-operatives.

The wines from the *Riesling* combine an elegant fruitiness and sweetness with acidity in a noble harmony which the connoisseur calls *finesse*, meaning something like "supreme delicacy". The bouquet is flowery and

elegant. Though made from overripe grapes, the wines of the Rheingau are light, considerably lighter, for instance, than the fine wines of Baden or the Palatinate. This is due in great part to the soils. On the terraces above the Rhine the vine grows on sericite and clayey shale and often, too, on quartz. The eroded rocks have broken down into clayey and loamy soil and the alluvial loess has a high lime content.

It is hard to choose among so many very great wines. Of those with a world-wide reputation Hochheim would undoubtedly be represented primarily by the DOMDECHANEY, KIRCHENSTÜCK, RAUCHLOC and STEIN. Eltville produces the KALBSPFLICHT, KRUMBCHEN, MONCHHANACH, SONNENBERG, TAUBENBERG and the ELSFELD, Elsfeld being the former name of the place at the time when the Archbishops of Mainz resided there. The wines from Eltville, like those from the large vineyards owned by the Graf von Eltz and the Barons Langwerth von Simmern, are of great character.

Erbach too has wines with a world-wide reputation, such as the famous MARKOBRUNN from a vineyard bordering Erbach and Hattenheim, and the BRÜHL, HOHENRAIN, RHEINHELL and SIEGELSBERG; Hattenheim can boast of the ENGELMANNSBERG, HASSEL, MANNBERG, NUSSBRUNNEN and WISSELBRUNN; Östrich the DOOSBERG, EISERWEG, KELLERBERG and LENCHEN. The EDELMANN and OBERBERG are the two main growths from Mittelheim. All these are wines of the *Riesling* type, full-bodied and with a magnificent bouquet.

Immediately thereafter comes Winkel; Goethe esteemed its noble wines, such as the DACHSBERG, HASENSPRUNG, JESUITENGARTEN and OBERBERG. In the commune of Winkel, too, there is Schloss Vollrads, which has been in the possession of the Greiffenklaus family since the fourteenth century, and nearby is Schloss Johannisberg, presented by the Emperor of Austria to Prince von Metternich in 1816. Some connoisseurs consider the SCHLOSS JOHANNISBERGER the king of German wines, but the HOLLE, MITTELHOLLE, KLAUS and KLAUSER BERG are equally magnificent.

Geisenheim produces the ROTHENBERG, DECKER, HOHER DECKER, KOSACKENBERG, LICKERSTEIN and MÄUERCHEN; and the next town, Rüdesheim, boasts internationally reputed wines: the RÜDESHEIMER BERG, BRONNEN, BURGWEG, DICKERSTEIN, HAUPTMANN, HELLPFAD, LAY, MÜHLSTEIN, PAARES, ROSENECK, ROTTLAND, STUMPFENORT and ZOLLHAUS and the BISCHOFSBERG and SCHLOSSBERG growths. The Rüdesheim wines are reputed to be particularly full-bodied.

Assmannshausen is known for its red wines from the *Spätburgunder* grape, the main growths being the HÖLLENBERG and HINTERKIRCH. Some connoisseurs consider that the red wines of Assmannshausen are the best in Germany. The most important vineyard in the region, the ancient Höllenberg, was already under cultivation at the beginning of the twelfth century. Rauenthal produces the BAIKEN, GEHRN, HERBWEG, ROTHENBERG, WÜLFEN and WIESHELL. These upland wines have a remarkable body and bouquet, and some people say they are for gentlemen only, but their velvety suppleness and delicate perfume recommend them to the ladies too.

Of the wines of Kiedrich we may mention the GRÄFENBERG, WASSEROS, SANDGRUBE and TURMBERG. A few miles farther on grows the STEINBERG, the vineyard, like the Abbey of Eberbach, being State property. The name alone has such a reputation that the grower adds only the description of the method used—*Kabinett* (or "special reserve"), *Spätlese* (late picking), *Auslese* (specially selected berries, or grapes), *Beerenauslese* (specially selected berries, or grapes) or *Trockenbeerenauslese* (selected overripe grapes left on the vine till dried in order to achieve the maximum sugar content possible). There only remains Hallgarten,

with its DEUTELSBERG, HENDELBERG, JUNGFER and SCHÖNHELL; its clayey marl produces wines highly esteemed for their great elegance and full-bodied character. The vineyards here rise to 900 feet.

The State domains in the Rheingau date back to 1866, when the Duke of Nassau had to cede his possessions to the King of Prussia. The Steinberg, the largest single vineyard, is 125 acres in extent. The domain also includes vineyards at Rüdesheim, Hattenheim, Rauenthal, Kiedrich and Hochheim, as well as the Assmannshausen vineyards, which produce mainly red wines. The State owns in all over 350 acres, almost all the whites coming from the *Riesling* grape.

The Institute for Tree, Wine and Horticultural Research, founded at Geisenheim in 1872, is in the forefront of wine research in Germany, while the former Cistercian Abbey at Eberbach is a kind of pilgrims' shrine for wine-lovers.

An English poet who compared the German wines to people called the Rheingau wine "a noblewoman". It should be respected accordingly.

MOSELLE - SAAR - RUWER

The three valleys of the Moselle and two of its tributaries, the Saar and the Ruwer, extend for some 190 miles. The winegrowing district of the Moselle stretches from Perl to Koblenz for 125 miles. From the ancient and fairy-tale-like village of Serrig to the junction with the Moselle near Konz the Saar district spreads for some 30 miles, and Waldrach-Sommerau is some 75 miles from the junction of the Moselle with the Ruwer. There are also some good vineyards along such tributaries of the Moselle as the Dhron and the Lieser. Most of the district is in the Rheinpfalz, and only a very small part of it, with 125 acres of vineyards, encroaches upon the Saar.

The three valleys form a unit, though their wines have characteristics all their own. All of them share the typical *Riesling* bouquet and have a fine and fruity acidity. The Saar wines are sparkling and well-bred; the Ruwer wines are noted for their so-called smoky taste and elegant acidity. The Moselles are usually fuller-bodied. The district is divided into the Upper, Middle and Lower Moselle. The vineyards are protected by the cliffs of the Hunsrück and the Eifel. They follow the windings of the river, which wanders so much that, especially in the Middle Moselle, the loops seem to cross their own course and the river triples its length. Hence the exposure keeps changing, so that many sunny slopes facing east and south give way without transition to shady woods and pastures. The canalization of the Moselle has proved advanta-

geous because of the intenser reflection of the sun due to the uniform raising of the water level.

Unlike the vineyards in the Palatinate and the Neckar valley, the vineyards here are situated on the slopes. They are so steep in the Lower Moselle that all farming has to be done by hand. As at Bremm, the growers have to carry back in hods the earth washed down by the rains. Here the vineyards can no longer compete within the Common Market with vineyards that can be worked by machine.

The banks of the Moselle between the Lorraine border and the junction with the Saar are made of white chalk; thence to the junction with the Ruwer they are the red sandstone of the Trier basin. Only thereafter begin the blueish banks of shale.

Winegrowing in the valley of the Moselle is the oldest in Germany. It may well have been introduced into the Trier region, then Celtic, by Greek colonists from Massilia (Marseilles) before the Roman conquest of Gaul.

The old grape variety *Elbling*, which was the only one grown along the Moselle before the Thirty Years War, now covers only 11 per cent of the 25,000 acres of vineyards, which produce only whites. The *Riesling* is ahead with 79 per cent; the remainder is *Müller-Thurgau*. The average yield is 19,800,000 gallons.

The Upper Moselle, stretching from the Luxembourg border to the junction with the Saar near Trier, produces lesser table wines, which are also used for the manufacture of sparkling wines. The Lower Moselle between Boulay and the junction with the Rhine produces ordinary *Konsumwein*, but in places some very decent table wines, at Bremm, Ediger, Beilstein, Valwig, Pommern and Winningen. Sometimes they have some of the characteristics of Rhine wines. The growers gather them with some difficulty from the parcels terraced steeply above each other.

The Middle Moselle is one great vineyard from the old Imperial Roman City of Trier to Alf and Bullay. The most famous villages are Trittenheim with its ALTÄRCHEN, APOTHEKE and LAURENTIUSBERG; then Neumagen (ROSENGÄRTCHEN, ENGELGRUBE and LAUDAMUSBERG), Dhron (HOFBERG, ROTERD and SÄNGEREI) and Piesport (GOLDTRÖPFCHEN, GÜNTERSLAY and FALKENBERG). Piesport is world-famous for the unequalled *finesse* of the perfume of its wines. After Wintrich, with the Ohligsberg and Geierslay, we very soon come to Brauneberg, which until only fifty years ago was still called Dusemont (from the Latin *in dulce monte*—"on the sweet hill"), a very appropriate name for it, for all the Great Growths, such as the FALKENBERG, HASENLAUFER and JUFFER, have a southern exposure and produce a very delicate bouquet. The following villages produce wines with a world-wide reputation: Lieser (NIEDERBERG), Bernkastel, Kues, Wehlen, Graach, Zeltingen, Erden, Ürzig and Traben-Trabach. The BERNKASTLER DOKTOR, also sold under the name of DOKTOR UND GRABEN, and facing it, at Bernkastel-Kues the JOHANNISBRÜNCHEN, KARDINALSBERG and PAULINUSHOFBERG open the way to the culminating point of the Moselle vineyards, Ürzig. The famous wines of Wehlen are the LAY, NONNENBERG and SONNENUHR; at Graach the ABTSBERG, DOMPROBST and HIMMELREICH; at Zeltingen the HIMMELREICH and SONNENUHR again and the SCHLOSSBERG; at Erden the BUSSLAY, HERRENBERG, PHÄLAT and TREPPCHEN; at Ürzig the WÜRTZGARTEN; and at Traben the GAISPFAD, GEIERSLAY, KRÄUTERHAUS and WÜRTZGARTEN.

The Saar produces wine on its lower stream after emerging from the industrial region. It then becomes a narrow picturesque valley in which the vine roots bristle from the steep and rocky slopes. The vineyards begin near Staadt, and there are decent wines at Serrig, Saarburg and Irsch (HUBERTUSBERG), and especially

The painter Janscha produced this watercolour in 1789; it shows the village of Oestrich beside the Rhine and, on the far right, Schloss Johannisberg. The Emperor Francis II of Austria presented this property to Prince von Metternich in 1816 in gratitude for his restoration of Austrian power in Europe. Today, Schloss Johannisberg produces the greatest and the most famous wines of the Rheingau district.

The commune of Zeltingen, in the central part of the valley of the Moselle, contains three of the greatest growths in this district: Zeltinger Rotlay, Zeltinger Himmelreich and Zeltinger Schlossberg. These vineyards, with a fine sunny exposure and a very considerable yield, were a source of contention between the Archbishops of Trier and Cologne for centuries; neither would yield these fine wines to the other.

good ones at Ayl (KUPP), Ockfen (BOCKSTEIN, GEISBERG and HERRENBERG), Wavern (HERRENBERG) and Wiltingen (SCHARZHOFBERG, BRAUNE KUPP and DOHR). Wiltingen is the largest viticultural commune in the Saar valley. Its most famous vineyard, the Scharzhofberg, was not planted until 1750.

Some of the best wines from Oberemmel are the AGRITIUSBERG, SCHARZBERG and HÜTTE. The ALTENBERG, SONNENBERG and HÖRECKER are the best from Kretnach; Filzen produces a HERRENBERG; and, lastly, the FALKENSTEIN, from Konz, like the SCHARTZHOFBERGER from Wiltingen, needs no commune name.

The Ruwer produces great wines at Waldrach (HAHNENBERG, HUBERTUSBERG, JESUITENGARTEN, JUNGFERNBERG and KRONE), at Kasel (NIES'GEN, KERNAGEL and KÄULCHEN) and from the two large vineyards at Grünhaus (MAXIMIN GRÜNHÄUSER) and Karthaüserhof, which belonged to the Carthusian Order from the fourteenth century on (EITELSBACHER KARTHÄUSER HOFBERG). There is also the vineyard at Avelsbach (ALTENBERG, HERRENBERG and HAMMERSTEIN). All over the Moselle, Saar and Ruwer districts one is struck by the abundance of ecclesiastical names. The Bishop of Trier and the monasteries, which have done so much for the cultivation of the vine since the establishment of Christianity in these parts, still own the best vineyards, such as the Bernkastel Hospital, founded at Küs by Cardinal Nicolas de Cusa.

The State domain in the Moselle was founded at the beginning of this century. It did not acquire existing

266

vineyards, but planted new ones, originally as a social measure. As the tanners' bark from the oak forests had been replaced by chemicals in the tanneries, the plantations of oak on the slopes of the Saar and the Ruwer ceased to be profitable. But good quality wines could prosper here, and so 198 acres were planted at Ockfen in 1896 and more later at Avelsbach and Servig.

Moselle wines cleanse the palate and stimulate the appetite. They go best with fish, hors-d'œuvres and salads. Lively, a soft green in colour, they are of invigorating freshness. When young, Moselle contains a little carbonic acid gas and pricks the tongue; it is slightly sparkling. It is drunk young, for its freshness and character are liable to go off with age. Moselle needs sun; it does not attain its natural sweetness in years when there is not much sun and has to be improved artificially. "Nowhere else," Baudelaire said, "is so much hard work, so much sweat and so much ardent sun needed to bring the grapes to life and to imbue the wine with soul."

THE VALLEY OF THE AHR

The Ahr virtually follows the northern border of the Rheinpfalz. Winegrowing is restricted to a strip some 15 miles long in the lower valley, where the vine is set on shale. It grows on rocky terraces, very narrow in places, where a thin layer of earth often holds only a few roots. With its 16 winegrowing communes and 1,312 acres, producing 660,000 gallons of wine at most, at the most northerly limit of winegrowing in the world, the Ahr wine district is romantic. Moreover, it is the largest red wine district in Germany, though the 31.1 per cent of *Portugieser* and 23.2 per cent of *Spätburgunder* are supplemented by 43 per cent of white grapes, 23 per cent *Riesling* and 16 per cent *Müller-Thurgau*. It is to be hoped the region will remain faithful to the *Spätburgunder*, which derives a warmth and special fineness from the sun-drenched schist. Especially round the State domain, the former monastry of Marienthal, noble, velvety and soft red wines are produced in good years. The winegrowing district begins at Altenahr, where the Ahr finishes its romantic course between cliffs, continues via Rech, Mayschoss and Dernau to Ahrweiler, Marienthal and Walportz-heim, and ends at Bad Neuenahr and Heimerzheim.

Co-operatives first arose in the Ahr district, which formerly experienced great difficulty in marketing its wines, and spread throughout Germany; the fact that holdings were only about an acre in extent made it necessary to regroup them if they were to survive.

THE MIDDLE RHINE

All the wines from north of a line running from Bingen to Lorchhausen—except the valleys of the Moselle and the Ahr—are designated as coming from the Mittelrhein, or Middle Rhine. The region is part of the Rheinpfalz, except the northern part, which encroaches upon Rhein-Westfalen. The winegrowing area, stretching for more than 75 miles and containing 104 communes, totals 2,412 acres. It has constantly diminished over the past few centuries; in 1883 it was still 7,907 acres. As late as 1828 there were 2,903 acres of vineyards in the district of Neuwied; there were no more than 534 in 1949. Red wine exists in any quantity only in the Siebenbergen district. The *Riesling* predominates in the Middle Rhine proper (87.7 per cent). The *Müller-Thurgau* accounts for as much as 34.6 per cent in the Siebenbergen, but elsewhere for only 6.2 per cent. The total yield is some 1,540,000 gallons.

This decline is not due only to a falling-off in quality. Industry has drained off labour from winegrowing, and on the flatlands other kinds of fruit are more profitable. The phylloxera, too, was a decisive factor in this reconversion. Faced with such economic risks, most of the Mittelrhein growers decided not to replant vines. On the left bank there are no vineyards north of Koblenz. The main winegrowing districts on the left bank lie south of Koblenz at Steeg, Bachrach, Oberwesel and Boppard, while Kaub and Braubach are on the right bank. On the right bank the vineyards stretch to Königswinter and Niederdollendorf via Leutesdorf, Hammerstein and Leubsdorf. Bachrach was a famous German wine centre until the eighteenth century, mainly because it was the place where the wines from the Palatinate and the Rheinhesse were transhipped because they could not pass the falls upstream from Bingen.

The rock was formed by the erosion of clayey shales, carboniferous sandstones and, in places, quartzite soils which generally warm up readily. The wines have great body and may be described as sturdy, but have a rather high acidity.

THE WINES OF THE RHINE

SWISS WINES OF THE UPPER RHINE

CANTON OF THE GRISONS

White wines . . . . . . Malanser Completer, Malanser Tokayer, Tokayer Eigenbau, Churer Tokayer aus dem Lochert

Red wines . . . . Malanser Blauburgunder, Malanser Blauburgunder Fuchsen, Malanser Blauburgunder Rüfiser, Churer Süssdruck Lürlibader, Churer Costamser Beerli, Süssdruck Duc de Rohan, Süssdruck Bündner Rheinwein, Malanser Rüfiwingert, Schloss Freudenberg, Maienfelder Blauburgunder Kuoni-Wii, Maienfelder Schloss Salenegg, Jeninser Chüechler Beerliwein, Malanser Beerli Weisstorkel

CANTON OF ST. GALLEN

White wines . . . . . . Tokayer Hoch Chapf Eichberg, Balgacher Riesling-Sylvaner

Red wines . . . . Altstätter Forst, Altstätter Rebhaldner Blauburgunder, Balgach Beerli Blauburgunder, Rebsteiner Süssdruck Blauburgunder, Hoch Chapf Eichberg, Bernecker Blauburgunder, Sarganser Langstrich Blauburgunder, Bernecker Rosenberger, Balgacher Buggler, Walenstadt Beerli Felixer am Ölberg, Melser Beerli Ritterweg, Portaser Blauburgunder, Baccastieler-Beerli Sevelen, Freudenberger Beerli

CANTON OF THURGAU

White wines . . . . . . Kalchrainer Tokayer, Arenenberg Domaine

Red wines . . . . Nussbaumer, Götighofer, Kalchrainer Blauburgunder, Hüttwiler Stadtschryber

CANTON OF SCHAFFHAUSEN

White wines . . . . . . Löhningen, Munötler Tokayer

Red wines . . . . Buchberger, Gächlinger, Osterfinger, Trasadinger, Steiner, Wilchinger Beerli, Hallauer Blauburgunder, Siblingen Eisenhalder, Osterfinger Blauburgunder, Osterfinger-Beerli Badreben, Hallauer Beerli Graf von Spiegelberg, Blauburgunder Beerli Munötler, Löhninger Clevner Beerli, Chäfer-Steiner Blaurock, Hallauer Süssdruck vom Schälleweg

CANTON OF ZURICH

White wines . . . . . . Riesling-Sylvaner Berg am Irchel, Riesling-Sylvaner Meilen, Meilener Räuschling, Riesling-Sylvaner Stäfner, Tokayer Weiningen, Riesling-Sylvaner Weinigen, Eglisauer Riesling-Sylvaner, Eglisauer Tokayer, Weininger Räuschling, Flurlinger Tokayer, Räuschling Küsnacht, Riesling-Sylvaner Sternenhalde

Red wines . . . . Blauburgunder Oberembach, Blauburgunder Schlosshof Berg am Irchel, Birmenstorfer Klevner, Eglisauer Blauburgunder, Stammheimer Blauburgunder, Eglisauer Stadtberger Beerli, Weiniger Klevner, Worrenberger Blauburgunder Rebhüsli, Blauburgunder Burg Schiterberger, Blauburgunder Schloss Goldenberg, Clävner Sternenhalde, Rudolfinger Beerli Blauburgunder, Stammheimer Beerli Blauburgunder, Clevner Sternhalden Stäfa

CANTON OF AARGAU

White wines . . . . . . Zeininger Riesling-Sylvaner, Bözer Riesling-Sylvaner, Tokayer Schlossberg Villingen, Mandacher Riesling-Sylvaner, Riesling-Sylvaner Würenlingen, Schinznacher Riesling-Sylvaner, Schinznacher Rütiberger

Red wines . . . . Birmenstorfer Klevner, Blauburgunder Klingnauer Kloster Sion, Blauburgunder Schlossberg Villigen, Brestenberger Klevner, Döttinger Clevner Auslese, Döttinger Süssdruck, Elfinger Blauburgunder Schlotterboden, Ennetbadener-Beerli, Goldwändler, Klevner Villiger Steinbrüchler Beerliwein, Rütiberger, Wettinger Herrenberg Blauburgunder, Wettinger Kläfner, Wettinger Scharten, Zeininger Clevner

CANTON OF LUCERNE

White wine . . . . . . Riesling-Sylvaner Schloss Heidegg

Red wine . . . . Schloss Heidegg Clevner

CANTON OF BASEL

White wine . . . . Arlesheimer Schlossberg Gutedel

Red wines . . . . Arlesheimer Blauburgunder, Benkener Blauburgunder, Liestaler Blauburgunder

WINES OF LAKES BIEL AND NEUCHÂTEL

CANTON OF BERN

White wines . . . . . . Ligerzer, Ligerzer Kirchwein, Schafiser, Schafiser Bois de Dieu, Schafiser Engel, Schafiser Stägli-Wy, Schafiser Schlössliwy, Twanner, Twanner Engelwein, Twanner Engelwein pinot gris, Twanner Kapfgut Clos des Merles, Twanner Kapfgut Sous la roche, Twanner Steinächt, Twanner Auslese Johanniter, Der edle Twanner Chroshalde, Twanner Closer, Tschugger, Erlach Chasselas Lamperten, Schlossberg Erlach Gutedel

Red wines . . . . La Neuveville Oeil-de-Perdrix, Twanner Blauburgunder, Schafiser Pinot noir, Tschugger Pinot noir, Schlossberger Erlach Blauburgunder

CANTON OF NEUCHÂTEL
Compulsory generic trade name : Neuchâtel

White wines . . . . . . Pinot gris, Cortaillod, Auvernier, Cressier, Domaine de Champréveyres, Champréveyres de la Ville, Château d'Auvernier, Domaine de Chambleau P.H. Burgat, Goutte d'or, Domaine du Mas des Chaux, Chasse-Peines, Cru des Gravanys, Hôpital Pourtalès, Cressier La Rochette, La Grillette, Clos des Sous-Monthaux, Francœur, Cru des Bourguillards, Cru des Chair d'Ane, Cru des Merloses

Red wines . . . . Pinot noir, la Béroche, Oeil de Perdrix, Cru d'Hauterive, Francarmin, Cru des Gravanys, Hôpital Pourtalès, Pinot noir Cru des Chanez, Cru de la Ville, La Grillette, Clos des Sous-Monthaux, Tour de Pierre

CANTON OF VAUD

Red wines . . . . Salvagnin Clos du Manoir, Salvagnin Grand Nef, Clos Chenevières, Domaine du Château de Valeyres, Pinot noir Clos du Terraillex, Pinot noir Vin des Croisés

WINES OF ALSACE

Zwicker, Edelzwicker, Sylvaner, Pinot blanc-clevner, Riesling, Muscat, Gewürztraminer, Tokay d'Alsace

WINES OF GERMANY
BADEN

Munzingen	Lindenberg, Berg, Kapellenberg, Steinern
Tiengen	Rebtal, Hauser
Oberrimsingen	
Niederrimsingen . . .	Bürkele, Scheibenbuck, Attila Felsen, Sonnenberg
Opfingen	Vogler, Kessler, Biergarten
Merdingen	Bühl, Mättenziel, Abbeureben
Gottenheim	Kriegacker, Ober-Kirchtal, Hahlen, Unterrain, Oberrain, Besteurein
Wasenweiler	Berg, Kreuzhalde-Staig, Eichen, Bösselsberg-Wanne, Kinzgen-Lot, Grub-Höge, Mamberg, Görn, Flanzer, Schlichten
Breisach	Eckartsberg, Schlossberg, Augustinerberg, Münsterberg
Ihringen	Winklerberg, Fohrenberg, Abtsweingarten, Himmelburg, Vorderer Winklerberg
Blankenhornsberg	Blankenhornsberger
Achkarren	Schlossberg, Büchsenberg, Bömisberg, Traubengarten, Rittersprung, Steinfelsen
Bickensohl	Steinfelsen, Eichberg, Bitzenberg, Käferhalde, Erlenhalde, Roggenberg, Hochstadt
Oberrotweil	Eichberg, Henkenberg, Kirchberg, Käselberg, Steingrubenberg, Wittel, Badenberg, Blindstöckle
Bötzingen	Weingarten, Eckberg, Kirchberg, Ganghalde, Laiere
Eichstetten	Lerdenberg, Mühlenberg, Eichenlaub, Rutzenhalden, Silbern
Burkheim	Burgberg, Käsleberg, Feuerberg, Schlossgarten, Haselberg
Bischoffingen	Enselberg, Hüttenberg, Rosenkranz, Steinbuck
Jechtingen	Eichert, Hochberg
Sasbach	Limberg
Endingen	Herzen, Steingrube, Buchberg
Ortenberg	Schlossberg, Freudentaler Berg, Im Silberlöchle, Im Rot, Im Käfersberg, Im Sonnenschein, Messerschmitt, Trottberg, Im Köpfle, Himmelsleiter, Käfersberger, Gottesacker
Zell-Weierbach	Abtsberg, Bittigrain, Stein, Riesenberg, Schmiedenbrünnle, Kohlenberg, Steinberg
Durbach	Schlossberg, Plauelrain, Herrenberg, Steinberg, Schwarzloch, Annaberg, Staufenberg, Josephberg
Schloss Staufenberg . . .	Schlossberg, Klingelberg
Waldulm	Pfarrberg, Russhalde
Neuweier	Mauerberg, Altenberg

WÜRTTEMBERG

Region of Stuttgart and Essling

Esslingen	Neckarhalde, Schenkenberg, Burgberg
Esslingen-Mettingen . . .	Mettinger Schenkenberg, Mettinger Lerchenberg
Esslingen-Sulzgriess . . .	Sulzgriesser Rosenholz
Stuttgart-Obertürkheim .	Obertürkheimer Kirchberg, Obertürkheimer Ailenberg
Stuttgart-Rotenberg . . .	Rotenberger Schlossberg, Rotenberger Hinterer Berg
Stuttgart-Untertürkheim .	Untertürkheimer Blick, Untertürkiehmer Mönchsberg, Untertürkheimer Goldberg, Untertürkheimer Altenberg, Untertürkheimer Hetzen, Untertürkheimer Semlis, Untertürkheimer Diethof
Stuttgart-Uhlbach . . .	Uhlbacher Steingrube, Uhlbacher Haldenberg, Uhlbacher Götzenberg
Stuttgart-Rohracker . . .	Rohrackerer Edenberg
Stuttgart-Hedelfingen . .	Hedelfinger Linsenberg
Stuttgart-Bad Cannstatt .	Cannstatter Zuckerle, Cannstatter Steinhalde, Canstatter Wolfersberg, Cannstatter Berg
Stuttgart-Mühlhausen . .	Mühlhäuser Berg, Mühlhäuser Wolfersberg
Stuttgarter Stadtgebiet. . (the town of Stuttgart)	Neue Weinsteige, Mönchshalde, Kriegsberg, Lenzhalde, Obere Weinsteige, Feuerbacher Lehmberg

REMSTAL

Fellbach	Lämmler, Wetzstein, Berg, Vorderer Berg, Hinterer Berg
Schait	Sonnenberg, Sandmorgen, Halde, Altenberg
Stetten	Häder, Lindhälder, Pfaffenberg, Pulvermächer, Brotwasser
Beutelsbach	Burghalde, Kappelberg, Rossberg
Endersbach	Klinge, Wetzstein
Grossheppach	Wanne, Klingenberg, Altenberg
Kleinheppach	Greiner, Sonnenberg
Korb	Kopf, Sommerhalde, Wanne
Strümpfelbach	Sonnenbühl, Fronklinge
Hanweiler	Berg, Bubenhalde, Kelterweinberg
Grunbach	Halde, Berg, Klingle
Winnenden	Holzenberg, Stöckach

MIDDLE NECKAR

Besigheim	Wurmberg, Neckarhälde, Niedernberg, Enzhälde
Mundelsheim	Mühlbächer, Käsberg, Rozenberg, Himmelreich, Pfaffenklinge, Steig
Hessigheim	Felsengarten, Wurmberg, Katzenöhrle
Walheim	Schalkstein, Eichquell
Gemmrigheim	Niedernberg
Kircheim	Kapellenberg
Höpfigheim	Königsberg
Hofen	Berg
Erligheim	Kirschgarten, Lerchenberg
Asperg	Berg

LOWER NECKAR

Neckarwestheim	Schlossberg, Herrlesberg
Lauffen	Katzenbeisser, Krappenfelsen, Mauerseugen, Nonnenberg
Talheim	Haigern, Geigersberg, Schlossberg
Schozach	Blauer Berg, Roter Berg, Mühlberg
Klingenberg	Schlossberg
Heilbronn	Stiftsberg, Wartberg, Staufenberg, Stahlbühl, Hundsberg, Riedenberg
Flein.	Altenberg, Eselsberg, Sonnenberg, Staufenberg, Kirchenweinberg, Grafenberg, Klosterberg
Neckarsulm	Scheuerberg, Haag, Hägelich
Erlenbach	Petersbühl, Schönbühl, Herzgrüble, Sommerberg, Kay
Gundelsheim	Himmelreich, Hoheneck, Wolkenstein

BOTTWARTAL

Grossbottwar	Harzberg, Wunnenstein, Schmiedberg, Köchersberg
Kleinbottwar	Götzenberg, Linsenberg, Brüssele
Oberstenfeld	Forstberg
Hof und Lembach	Lichtenberg
Winzerhausen	Wunnenstein
Unterheinriet	Sommerberg, Nährnberg
Beilstein	Wartberg, Vogelsang, Steinberg, Burgberg
Burg Wildeck	Burg Wildecker

WEINSBERG VALLEY AND ÖHRINGEN REGION

Weinsberg	Burgberg, Schemelsberg, Ranzenberg, Wildenberg, Glückenhälde
Ellhofen	Berg
Lehrsteinfeld	Rosengarten, Steinacker, Althälde
Grantschen	Wildenberg, Rosenberg, Altenberg
Willsbach	Dieblensberg, Beerlesberg, Zeilberg, Rosenberg
Wimmental	Freudenberg, Eselsberg
Sülzbach	Altenberg, Ranberg
Affaltrach	Salzberg, Dorfberg
Eschenau	Salzberg, Paradies
Hösslinsülz	Weinhalde
Hölzern	Berg, Weinsteige
Gellmersbach	Dezberg, Kirchberg
Weiler	Berg, Schlierbach
Eberstadt	Eberfürst, Nonnenberg
Eichelberg	Hundsberg
Löwenstein	Wohlfahrtsberg, Eulenberg, Lerchenbühl
Verrenberg	Goldberg
Heuholz-Harsberg	Dachsteiger, Spielbühl
Geddelsbach	Schneckenhof
Siebeneich	Himmelreich
Adolzfurt	Berghäusle
Michelbach	Rosenberg

ZABERGAU AND LEINTAL

Bönnigheim	Steingrube, Kapellenberg, Pfaffenwerg, Kirchweg, Spiegel
Brackenheim	Mäusekammer, Zweifelberg, Burg
Haberschlacht	Dachsberg, Langhälde, Gaisengrund
Neipperg	Burgwengert, Schlossberg, Seeberg, Altenberg, Steingrube
Stockheim	Schöllkopf, Altenberg
Dürrenzimmern	Feuer, Mönchsberg, Kehle
Hausen	Vogelsang, Staig, Seeberg, Steinhalde
Grossgartach	Annung, Sonntagsberg, Ehrenberg, Grabensgrund
Schwaigern	Grafenberg, Sonntagsberg, Vogelsang, Ruthe, Breiten
Stetten a. H.	Sonnenberg, Vorderer Berg, Hinterer Berg
Nordheim	Sonntagsberg, Auerberg, Sommerberg, Gräfenberg
Kleingartach	Leinburg
Cleebronn	Michaelsberg, Ruith
Güglingen	Hummelsberg, Hegnach
Hohenhaslach	Kirchberg
Knittlingen	Reichshalde
Eilfingerberg	Eilfingerberg
Oberderdingen	Brehmich, Wilfenberg, Kupferhalde, Hagenrain
Steinbachhof	Steinbachhöfer
Ochsenbach	Rohrsteig
Sternenfels	Sandberg, Schiedberg
Rosswag	Halde
Mühlhausen	Mönchsberg, S chlossweinberge, Felsen
Horrheim	Rieser, Röckenberg
Maulbronn	Scheuelberg, Klosterberg

KOCHERTAL – JAGSTTAL – TAUBERTAL

Bad Ingelfingen	Schlossberg, Hoher Berg
Criesbach	Burgstall
Niedernhall	Burgstall, Heyerberg, Bromberg, Engweg
Forchtenberg	Haardt, Kocherberg
Weikersheim	Karlsberg, Schmecker
Markelsheim	Mönchsberg, Probstberg, Tauberberg
Laudenbach	Heimberg, Schafsteige

UPPER NECKAR

Neuffen	Schlosssteige
Linsenhofen	Sand
Beuren	Fels
Weilheim	Limburg
Metzingen	Berghalde, Florian

THE PALATINATE

Neustadt	Erkenbrecht, Grain, Vogelsang, Guckinsland, Mandelgarten, Ritterberg, Mandelgewann
Hardt	Bürgengarten, Kirchenstück, Herrenletten, Herrengarten, Herzog, Mandelring, Hofstück, Kalkgrube, Aspen, Knappengraben, Schlossberg
Mussbach	Räppel, Eselshaut, Hundsrück, Hohlbaum, Katzenhauer, Glockenzehnt, Hundertmorgen, Knappengraben
Deidesheim	Leinhöhle, Grainhübel, Kalkofen, Kieselberg, Mäusehöhle, Hohenmorgen, Grain, Geheu, Kränzler, Vogelsang, Linsenbusch, Hofstück, Reiss, Paradiesgarten, Hahnenböhl, Rennpfad, Klostergarten, Langenböhl, Langenmorgen, Petershöhle, St. Michelsberg, Sonneneck, Herrgottsacker
Gimmeldingen	Schild, Kapelle, Meerspinne, Bienengarten, Hofstück, Kirchenstück
Königsbach	Idig, Mückenhaus, Ölberg, Jesuitengarten, Reiterpfad, Hitzpfad, Bender
Ruppertsberg	Hoheburg, Nussbien, Mandelgarten, Reiterpfad, Linsenbusch, Goldschmied, Hofstück, Geisböhl, Kreuz, Mandelacker
Forst	Kirchenstück, Jesuitengarten, Kranich, Ungeheuer, Freundstück, Pechstein, Ziegler, Langenmorgen, Mäuerchen, Linsenstück, Musenhang, Mariengarten, Schnepfenflug, Hellholz, Hahnenböhl, Elster, Altenburg, Fleckinger, Langenacker, Langenböhl
Wachenheim	Goldbächel, Rechbächel, Gerümpel, Luginsland, Böhlig, Königswingert, Mandelgarten, Oberstnest, Schenkelböhl, Fuchsmantel, Wolfsdarm
Gönnheim	Sonnenberg, Mandelgarten
Friedelsheim	Schlossgarten, Tiergarten, Neuberg
Bad Dürkheim	Michelsberg, Spielberg, Hochbenn, Hochmess, Schenkelböhl, Fronhof, Proppelstein, Feuerberg, Fuchsmantel, Forst, Klosterberg
Ungstein	Herrenberg, Michelsberg, Spielberg, Weilberg, Kreuz, Kobnert, Nussriegel, Bettelhaus, Osterberg, Honigsäckel
Leistadt	Annaberg, Kalkofen, Spiessberg, Frohnberg, Kirchenstück, Herzfeld, Herrenmorgen
Kallstadt	Saumagen, Nill, Horn, Kobnert, Steinacker, Kreuz, Kirchenstück, Kreidkeller
Herxheim	Himmelreich, Steinberg, Felsenberg, Honigsack, Kirchenstück, Goldberg, Berg, Steinberg, Sommerseite
Freinsheim	Oschelkopf, Gross, Rosenbuhl, Hochgewann, Liebfrauenberg, Musikantenbuckel, Mandelgarten, Goldberg, Gottesacker, Hahnen
Weisenheim/Berg	Feinerde, Mandelgarten, Sonnenberg
Kircheim	Römerstrasse, Schwarzerde
Dirmstein	Hochgewann, Mandelpfad
Bockenheim	Burggarten, Dom, Sonnenberg
Zell	Schwarzer Herrgott
Bissersheim	Goldberg
Kieln-Karlbach	Hofstück, Herrenberg
Gross-Karlbach	Orlenberg
Sausenheim	Hochgewann, Klostergarten
Laumersheim	Kirchgarten
Grünstadt	Bergel
Kindenheim	Burgweg
Schweigen	Sonnenberg, Vogelsang
Bergzabern	Altenberg, Steinbühl
Billigheim	Pfaffenberg
Eschbach	Hasen, Schlossberg
Wollmesheim	Mütterle
Mörzheim	Schreckenberg
Ranschbach	Seligmacher
Birkweiler	Kastanienbusch, Herrenberg, Mandelberg
Siebeldingen	Starkenberg, Sonnenschein, Forst
Nussdorf	Kaiserberg
Burrweiler	Schäwer
Flemlingen	Zechpeter
Edesheim	Forst
Edenkoben	Blücherschanze, Heiligkreuz
Rhodt	Rosengarten, Herrengarten
St. Martin	Schlossberg, Ritter v. Dalberg
Maikammer	Heiligenberg, Alsterweiler Kapellenberg
Diedesfeld	Brühl, Johanniskirchel
Duttweiler	Mandelberg
Hambach	Schlossberg, Grain

Worms	Katterloch, Stiftsgarten, Kirchenstück, Liebfrauenstift
Osthofen	Rosstal, Goldberg, Klosterberg, Hasenbiss, Wölm, Liebenberg
Westhofen	Kirchspiel, Gries, Roterde, Ring
Dalsheim	Steig, Rodenstein, Sauloch, Bürgel, Wingertsstätte
Oppenheim	Reisekahr, Kreuz, Krötenbrunnen, Kreuzkugel, Schützenhütte, Herrenberg, Zuckerberg, Goldberg, Daubhaus, Herrenweiher, Kehrweg, Kugel, Sacktärger, Schlossberg, Steig
Nierstein	Auflangen, Rehbach, Brudersberg, Ölberg, Glöck, Pettental, Fläschenhahl, Heiligenbaum, Orbel, Fuchsloch, Kranzberg, Floss, Hipping, Kehr, St. Kiliansberg, Rehbach, Schnappenberg, Streng, Gutes Domtal, Domtal, Paterberg, Findling, Schmitt, Spiegelberg, Flockenberg
Nackenheim	Rotenberg, Engelsberg, Fenchelberg, Kreuz, Fritzenhölle, Kapelle, Kirchberg, Spitzenberg
Mettenheim	Michelsberg, Schlossberg, Goldberg
Dienheim	Tafelstein, Hofstück, Goldberg, Gumben, Ebenbreit, Guldenmorgen
Bodenheim	Hoch, St. Alban, Westrum, Silberberg, Kahlenberg, Burgweg, Johannisberg, Heitersbrünnchen, Kapelle, Mönchpfad, Leidhecke, Neuberg, Leistenberg
Laubenheim	Damsberg, Neuberg, Hitz, Kalkofen, Klosterberg, Vogelsang
Gau-Bischofsheim	Herrenberg, Brühl, Pfaffenberg, Kellerberg, Kirscheck, Glockenberg, Gickelsberg, Kreuzwingert, Pfaffenweg
Ingelheim	Sonnenberg, Horn, Pares, Grauer Stein
Bingen	Schlossberg, Schwätzerchen, Scharlachberg, Rochusberg, Ohliger Berg, Auberg, Mainzerweg, Rosengarten
Alsheim	Frühmesse, Rheinblick, Fischerpfad
Guntersblum	Bornpfad, Himmeltal, Sonnenberg, Eiserne Hand, Wohnweg, Vögelsgärten, Steig, Hasenweg
Bechtheim	Hasensprung, Geyersberg, Pilgerpfad, Gotteshilfe
Pfaffenschwabenheim . .	Hölle
Alzey	Sibillenstein
Gau-Odernheim	Petersberg
Nieder-Saulheim.	Goldberg, Probstei
Uffhofen	Laroche

NAHE

Bingerbrück	Schloss Leyer, Pittermännchen
Münster-Sarmsheim . . .	Kapellenberg, Langenberg, Daubenpflänzer, Pittersberg
Winzenheim	Rosenheck, Berg
Bretzenheim	Kreuzberg, Schützenhöll, Steinweg
Dorsheim	Burgberg
Windesheim	Fels
Bad Kreuznach	Brückes, Narrenkappe, Kauzenberg-Stübchen, Krötenpfuhl, St. Martin, Kahlenberg, Steinberg, Hinkelstein, Mönchberg, Osterhölle, Gutental, Mollenbrunnen, Forst, Monart, Rosengarten, Vogelsang, Kauzenberg, Belz
Ebernburg	Erzgrube, Schlossberg, Götzenfels, Feuerberg
Roxheim	Birkenberg, Mühlenberg, Höllenpfad, Hüttenberg, Neueberg, Wiesberg
Norheim	Dellchen, Kafels, Kirscheck, Hinterfels, Schmalberg
Altenbamberg-Alsenz . .	Kehrenberg, Rothenberg, Laurentiusberg, Treuenfels, Pfarrwingert, Bangert
Schlossböckelheim . . .	Königsfels, Kupfergrube, Felsenberg, Mühlberg, Königsberg, In den Felsen, Pühläcker, Heimberg
Niederhausen	Hermannshöhle, Felsensteyer, Mönchberg, Hermannsberg, Mfingstweide, Rosenheck, Rossel, Fels
Odernheim	Weinsack, Disibodenberg
Monzingen	Frühlingsplätzchen, Lay, Rosenbaum, Gabelstich, Kronenberg, Halenberg
Meddersheim	Altenberg
Waldböckelheim.	Mühlberg
Langenlonsheim	Löhr, Sonnenborn
Wallhausen	Pastorenberg, Johannesberg

FRANCONIA

Volkach	Ratsherr, Berg, Kirchberg
Obereisenheim	Höll
Escherndorf	Lump, Eulengrube, Fürstenberg, Hengstberg, Berg, Kirchberg
Nordheim	Vögelein, Kreuzberg
Sommerach	Katzenkopf, Engelsberg, Wilm
Dettelbach	Berg, Rondell
Abtswind (Steigerwald) . .	Schild, Altenberg
Castell	Schlossberg, Hohnart, Bausch
Wiesenbronn	Wachhügel
Rödelsee	Küchenmeister, Schlossberg, Schwanleite, Hoheleite

Iphofen	Julius Echterberg, Kammer, Kronsberg, Kalb, Burgweg
Einersheim	Vogelsang
Hüttenheim	Tannenberg
Bullenheim	Paradies
Ippesheim	Herrschaftsberg
Kitzingen	Eselsberg, Buchbrenner Berg
Sulzfeld	Cyriakusberg, Altenberg, Maustal
Marktbreit	Sonnenberg
Frickenhausen	Kapellenberg, Babenberg, Fischer
Sommerhausen	Steinbach, Altenberg
Randersacker	Pfülben, Teufelskeller, Hohbug, Spielberg, Sonnenstuhl, Marsberg, Kapellenberg, Ewig Leben, Lämmerberg
Würzburg	Stein, Jesuitenstein, Harfe, Schalksberg, Felsenleiste, Innere Leiste, Leiste, Neuberg, Rossberg, Abtsleite, Schlossberg, Pfaffenberg, Guthentahl, Lindleinsberg
Veithöchsheim	Abtsberg, Neuberg, Fachtel, Wölflein
Thüngersheim	Scharlach, Ravensburg, Johannisberg
Stetten	Im Stein, Loch, Rosstal
Schloss Saaleck	Schloss Saalecker
Hammelburg	Liebental, Fürstenberg, Bach
Homburg	Kallmuth
Bürgstadt	Mainhölle, Martinskirch, Hohenlinde
Grossheubach	Bischofsberg, Engelsberg
Klingenberg	Schlossberg, Felsenrot
Erlenbach	Altenberg, Krähenschnabel
Hörstein	Reuschberg, Abtsberg, Schwalbenwinkel

RHEINGAU

Hochheim	Domdechaney, Kirchenstück, Stein, Rauchloch, Stiehlweg, Königin-Viktoria-Berg, Hölle, Neuberg, Sommerheil, Steinern Kreuz, Daubhaus
Wiesbaden-Schierstein . .	Dachsberg, Hölle, Homberg, Marschall, Schäferberg
Wiesbaden-Frauenstein. .	Mühlberg, Herrenberg, Sand
Niederwalluf	Walkenberg, Berg-Bildstock, Oberberg, Mittelberg, Unterberg, Steinritz, Rötherweg
Oberwalluf	Sonnenberg, Langenstück
Eltville.	Sonnenberg, Taubenberg, Langenstück, Mönchhanach, Kalbspflicht, Klümbchen, Siebenmorgen
Rauenthal	Baiken, Gehrn, Wieshell, Rothenberg, Herberg, Langenstück, Pfaffenberg, Burggraben, Siebenmorgen, Steinmächer
Martinsthal	Steinberg, Langenberg, Pfaffenberg, Wildsau, Heiligenstock, Mauer, Kirchgarten, Rödchen
Kiedrich	Gräfenberg, Sandgrub, Wasserros, Heiligenstock, Klosterberg, Scharfenstein
Erbach	Marcobrunn, Siegelsberg, Honigberg, Michelmark, Pellet, Kahlig, Steinmorgen, Hohenrain
Hattenheim.	Nussbrunnen, Wisselbrunn, Hassel, Mannberg, Steingberg, Hinterhaus, Pfaffenberg, Schützenhaus, Engelmannsberg, Heiligenberg, Klosterberg
Hallgarten	Jungfer, Schönhell, Kirschenacker, Deutelsberg, Sandgrub, Hendelberg, Rosengarten, Mehrhölzchen, Geiersberg, Würzgarten
Oestrich	Doosberg, Lenchen, Pfaffenpfad, Hitz, Deez, Hölle, Eiserberg, Klosterberg, Mühlberg, Räucherberg
Mittelheim	Edelmann, Honigberg, Sonnenberg, St. Nikolaus, Rheingarten
Winkel	Hasensprung, Bienenberg, Honigberg, Dachsberg, Guthenberg, Jesuitengarten, Steinchen, Hellersberg, Erntebringer
Johannisberg	Schloss Johannisberg, Kochsberg, Hölle, Steinstück, Hansenberg, Vogelsang, Schwarzenstein, Kerzenstück, Nonnenhöhle, Goldatzel, Erntebringer
Geisenheim	Rothenberg, Kläuserweg, Fuchsberg, Mäuerchen, Morchberg, Kosakenberg, Katzenloch, Lückerstein, Hinkelstein, Mönchpfad
Rüdesheim	Berg Bronnen, Berg Rottland, Zollhaus, Berg Schlossberg, Berg Burgweg, Berg Roseneck, Berg Ramstein, Bischofsberg, Drachenstein, Sonnenberg, Kirchenpfad, Backhaus, Klosterlay, Magdalenenkreuz, Dechaney, Klosterberg
Assmannshausen	Höllenberg, Frankenthal, Bohren, Steil, Hinterkirch, Kapellenberg, Assmannshäuser Berg, Silberberg
Aulhausen	Kaisersteinfels, Orleans, Frenz
Lorch/Rheingau	Bodenthal, Lehn, Pfaffenwies, Kapellenberg, Schlossberg, Krone, Niederflur
Lorchhausen	Seligmacher, Rosenberg, Schönberg, Galgenpfad, Kapellchen

MOSELLE

Winningen	Uhlen, Röttgen, Hamm, Rosenberg
Müden	Hohenlay, Rotenburg, Himmelsberg
Pommern.	Rosenberg, Goldberg, Greisenmund, Kapellenberg
Cochem	Pinnerberg, Langenberg, Schloss, Schlossberg, Kreuzberg, Tummetchen
Valwig	Herrenberg, Schwarzenberg

Bruttig	Kuckucksberg, Siebenköpfchen, Brandenberg, Johannisberg, Kreuz, Rathausberg
Senheim	Kirchrech, Wahrsager, Bienengarten, Lay, Rosenberg, Schwarzberg
Ediger	Feuerberg, Osterlämmchen, Pfaffenberg, Elzoberg, Hasensprung
Bremm	Kalmont
Alf	Herrenberg, Astasberg, Frauenberg, Kapellenberg, Kronenberg
Bullay	Domherrenberg
Merl	Stefansberg, Königslay, Klosterberg, Fettgarten, Schafenstein, Münchslay, Adler
Zell	Burglay, Domherrenberg, Schwarze Katz, Nussberg, Petershorn, Heiligenhäuschen, Kapertchen
Reil	Vom heissen Stein, Falkly, Goldlay, Weingrube, Görlay, Mauseberg, Mulley-Hofsberg, Pfefferberg, Sorrent, Staaden
Enkirch	Steffensberg, Monteneubel, Herrenberg, Edelberg, Weinkammer, Hinterberg
Traben-Trarbach	Schlossberg, Würzgarten, Geisspfad, Kräuterhaus, Ungsberg, Königsberg, Burgberg, Halsberg, Hühnerberg, Backhaus, Bergpächter, Rickelsberg, Steinbacher
Kröv	Steffensberg, Herrenberg, Engelberg, Paradies, Petersberg, Letterlay, Halsbach, Heislay, Niederberg, Petersberg, Nacktarsch
Kinheim/Kindel	Rosenberg, Hubertusberg, Eulenlay, Hubertushofberg, Löwenberg, Petrusberg
Erden	Treppchen, Prälat, Busslay, Himmelreich, Herrenberg, Herzlay, Filisberg, Frankenlay, Hötlay, Kaufmannsberg, Rotkirch, Schönberg
Ürzig	Würzgarten, Urlay, Schwarzlay, Lay
Zeltingen	Sonnenuhr, Rotlay, Himmelreich, Schlossberg, Kirchenpfad, Bickert, Kirchlay, Stefanslay, Steinmauer, Schwarzlay, Welbersberg
Graach	Josephshöfer, Himmelreich, Domprobst, Abtsberg, Obstberg, Goldwingert, Bistum, Kirchlay, Lilienpfad, Petrus, Rosenberg, Stablay, Heiligenhaus, Hömberg, Münich, Münzlay, Tirlei
Wehlen	Sonnenuhr, Lay, Abtei, Münzlay, Nonnenberg, Klosterlay, Rosenberg, Wertspitz
Kesten	Paulinshofberger, Herrenberg, Niederberg
Bernkastel	Doktor, Doktor und Graben, Badstube, Olk, Kirchgraben, Graben, Schlossberg, Rosenhang, Königsstuhl, Lay, Bratenöfchen, Pfaffenberg, Pfalzgraben, Schwanen, Altenwald, Held, Eich, Lay, Johannisbrünnchen
Kues	Kardinalsberg, Weissenstein, Herrenberg, Kalbrech, Lay, Rosenberg
Lieser	Niederberg, Schlossberg, Kirchberg, Paulsberg, Pfaffenberg, Rosenberg
Brauneberg	Juffer, Hasenläufer, Bürgerslay, Burgenberg, Falkenberg, Nonnenlay, Kammer, Mandelgraben, Lay, Obersberg, Sonnenuhr
Maring	Römerpfad, Brauneberg, Klosterberg, Schwarzlay, Rosenberg, Sonnenuhr
Mülheim	Sonnenlay, Mühlheimer, Johannisberg, Elisenberg, Bitsch, Kloster
Veldenz	Geisberg, Kirchberg, Bitsch, Elisenberg, Neuberg
Wintrich	Grosser Herrgott, Rosenberg, Olk, Sonnenseite, Simonsberg, Geierslay, Ohligsberg, Geyerskopf, Neuberg
Minheim	Grauberg, Rosenberg, Lay, Christenlay
Piesport	Goldtröpfchen, Hubertuslay, Güterslay, Grafenberg, Falkenberg, Taubengarten, Treppchen, Lay, Bildchen, Hohlweid Pichter, Michelsberg
Niederemmel	Lay, Taubengarten, Gunterslay
Dhron	Dhronhofberger, Roterd, Sängerei, Kandel, Pichter, Grosswingert, Hengelberg
Neumagen	Laudamusberg, Engelsgrube, Rosengärtchen, Sonnenuhr, Hengelberg, Layenberg, Pichter, Pfaffenberg, Thierlay, Kirchenstück, Lasenberg
Trittenheim	Apotheke, Altärchen, Laurentiusberg, Clemensberg, Fahrsfels, Falkenberg, Laurentiusberg, Neuberg, Sonnenteil, Vogelsang, Weierbach, Olk
Leiwen	Klostergarten, Laurentiuslay
Klüsserath	Bruderschaft, Königsberg, St. Michael
Thörnich	Ritsch, Engass, Ley, Schiesslay
Detzem	Würzgarten, Klosterlay, Königsberg, Maximiner Klosterlay, Stolzenberg
Mehring	Zellerberg, Plattenberg, Goldkupp, Huxlay, Kuckuckslay
Schweich	Annaberg, Herrenberg, Marienpichter
Longuich	Herrenberg, Probstberg, Maximiner Herrenberg, Kirchberg
Eitelsbach	Karthäuser Hofberg
Trier	Römerberg, Rotenburg, Vogelsang, Deutschherrenköpfchen, Pichter, Augenscheiner, Geisberg, Johannisberg, Neuberg, Herrenberg, Klosterberg

THE SAAR

Konz-Karthaus	Zuckerberg, Jesusberg, Kelterberg, Falkensteiner
Obermenning	Zuckerberg
Filzen	Urbelt, Herrenberg, Neuberg, Pulchen, Vogelberg
Wawern	Herrenberg, Jesuitengarten, Ritterpfad, Goldberg
Kanzem	Berg, Altenberg, Hörecker, Sonnenberg, Unterberg, Kelterberg, Wolfsberg
Wiltingen	Braune Kupp, Scharzhofberger, Dom Scharzhofberger, Kupp, Gottesfuss, Braunfels, Scharzberg, Klosterberg, Johannislay, Rosenberg, Schlangengraben, Schlossberg, Dohr, Neuberg
Oberemmel	Hütte, Agritinsberg, Karlsberg, Altenberg, Eltzerberg, Junkersberg, Lauterberg, Raul, Rosenberg, Scharzberg, Scharzberger
Schoden	Herrenberg
Ayl	Kupp, Herrenberg, Neuberg, Euchariusberg, Junkerberg, Scheiderberg, Silberberg, Sommerberg
Ockfen	Bockstein, Herrenberg, Geisberg, Heppenstein, St. Irminer

Saarburg Beurig	Mühlenberg, Layenkaul, Rausch, Antoniusbrunnen, Klosterberg, Berggarten
Irsch.	Hubertusberg, Sinnenberg, Wolfsberg
Serrig	Vogelsang, Kupp, Würzberg, Saarstein, Trutzberg, Antoniusberg, Schloss Saarfelser, Hindenburglay, Wingertsheck, Würzburger Helenenberg, Würzburger Marienberg

RUWER

Mertesdorf	Maximin Grünhäuser Herrenberg, Maximin Grünhäuser Bruderberg, Mertesdorfer, Lorenzberg, Spielberg, Treppchen
Eitelsbach	Karthäuserhofberg, Sonnenberg, Grossenberg, Sang, Burgberg, Kronenberg, Marienberg, Rothenberg, Marienholz
Kasel	Kernagel, Pichter, Herrenberg, Hitzlay, Niesgen, Taubenberg, Hiesgen, Steininger, Kohlenberg, Katharinenberg, Käulgen, Lorenzberg, Paulinsberg
Waldrach.	Jesuitengarten, Krone, Ehrenberg, Kloserberg, Meisenberg, Schloss Marienlay
Pölich/Mosel	Held, Südlay

AHR

Altenahr	Eck, Zapfenberg, Übigberg
Rech.	Herrenberg, Schieferstein
Reimerzhoven.	Ravenley
Laach	Berg
Mayschoss	Mönchberg, Silberberg
Dernau.	Hardtberg, Goldkaul, Sondersberg, Burgberg
Ahrweiler.	Rosental, Daubhaus, Silberberg, Berg
Walporzheim	Domberg, Kräuterberg, Gärkammer, Himmelchen
Marienthal	Jesuitengarten, Klosterberg, Trotzenberg, Klostergarten, Klosterley
Bad Neuenahr	Schieferley, Sonnenberg
Heimersheim	Landskroner Berg
Bachem	Karlskopf, Sonnenberg

MIDDLE RHINE

ST. GOAR REGION

Alken	Bleidenberg, Lay, Kölscheberg, Burgberg, Hunnenstein, Sonnenring
Bacharach	Posten, Hahn, Wolfshöhle, Kloster Fürstental, Mühle, Dell, Schlossberg, Bill
Bad Salzig	Römerberg, Sazbornberg, Altlay
Boppard	Hamm, Ewig Bach, Gietel, Feuerlay, Wiesborn, Mandelstein, Kerler, Hetz, Ohlenberg
Breitscheid	Steeger Mühlberg, Breitscheid und Rechtel
Brodenbach.	Hunnenstein, Neuwingert, Burgberg, Geisseberg, Schlossberg
Burgen/Mosel	Bischofsteiner, Klopplay, Kuckucksberg
Damscheid	Goldemund, Geissberg, Schippen, Frankenhöll
Dellhofen	Hambach, Sayen
Hirzenach	Staat, Probsteiberg, Röttgen
Langscheid	Pützbach
Manubach	Retz, Mühle, Mönchwingert, St. Oswald, Grube, Langgarten
Niederburg	Knüppelberg, Kohlgrube, Büttenberg
Niederfell.	Rotmauer, Grub, Fächern, Kochlay, Goldlay, Münichsberg
Niederheimbach . . .	Raifersley, Löwenhell, Soonecker Schlossberg, Fron-Weingarten
Niederspray	Bopparder Hamm, Niederspray
Oberdiebach	Fürstenberg, Mittelberg, Mühlberg, Bischofstube, Glasten, Kräuterberg
Oberfell	Ringmauer, Brauneberg, Kebelberg, Marienberg
Oberheimbach	In der Sonne, Brückenstück, Wahrheit, Anweg
Oberspray	Bopparder Hamm
Oberwesel	Rheinhell, Ölsberg, Bernhell, Hangestein, Engehell, Hardthell, Lauerbaum, Bernstein, Würgehöll
Perscheid	Mittelhöll, In und ober der Hartel, Niedersagen
St. Goar	Hasenflöz, Bank Riesling, Kuhstall
Steeg	St. Jost, Kripp, Flur, Bocksberg, Hambuch, Mühlberg
Trechtingshausen	Morgenbach, Kieslau, Bodental
Urbar	Beulsberg, Oelsberg
Weiler bei Bad Salzig . .	Mühlenberg, Ziehberg, Rheinberg
Werlau	Ameisenberg, Frohwingert, Hasenflöz

ST. GOARSHAUSEN REGION

Bornich	Rieslingberg, Rothenack, Vordere Reste, Hintere Reste
Braubach	Mühlberg, Kapellenberg, Koppelstein, Walkenberg, Liebedell, Marmorberg, Jagenstiel, Stiel
Dürscheid	Rosengarten, Mühlenstein, Hochstadt, Kolben
Fachbach	Sommerberg
Kamp-Bornhofen	Schlossberg, Bornhofertal, Hohenstock, Gies, Schädert
Kaub	Schlossberg, Blüchertaler, Silbernagel, Pfalzgrafenstein, Backofen, Sonnenberg
Kestert	Liebensteiner, Kirchköppel, Nadenkopf, Im Stenner
Nochern	Hohe Lay, Rabenack, Am Brünnchen, Im Kanzler, Fensel
Oberlahnstein	Koppelstein, Karstel, Helmestal
Ostersprai	Bopparder-Hamm
Patersberg	Herschelberg, Schützenhaus, Herzenhöll, Mittelpfad
St. Goarshausen	Hessern, Loreley-Edel, Hühnerberg, Heiderstein, Burg Katz
Wellmich	Auf Roth, Hietzert, Oberberg, Auf der Mauer, Ohlenberg

UNTERLAHN REGION

Nassau	Haniob, Plattenstück, Niederberg
Obernhof	Goetheberg, Schreiberlay
Weinähr	Giebelhölle, Ackerbergen, Bollwerk, Rother-Pfad

KOBLENZ REGION

Dieblich	Fahrberg, Heilgraben, Fächer
Güls	Pattig-Heyerberg, Bienengarten
Kobern	Uhlen, Pappenscheren, Weissenberg, Rossenberg
Koblenz-Stadt	Moselweisser-Hamm, Römerheg, Aveberg, Kreuzberg
Lay	Hamm, Ankelspfad, Kützenberg
Rhens	Obersberg, Sonnenlay, König Wenzel
Urbar	Besselicher Klostermauer, Besselicher lange Zeilen
Vallendar/Rhein	Rheinnieder
Winningen	Rosenberg, Weinhex, Kirchenberg, Sternberg, Brückstück, Röttgen, Hamm, Uhlen

NEUWIED REGION

Bad Hönningen	Schlossberg, Feigenberg, Burgberg, Elsberg
Dattenberg	Domtaler, Tempelberg, Gertrudenberg
Erpel	Hühner-Berg, Karrenweg, Strohberg, Müdersgass, Leitzberg, Schwalkaul
Hammerstein	Schlossberg, Vorderberg, Hölle, Leyfelsen
Leubsdorf	Stehleberg, Daufenberg, Oberau
Leutesdorf	Laurentiusberg, Rosenberg, Martinsley, Gartenley, Forstberg, Olterberg
Linz	Rheinheller, Kaiserberg
Rheinbrohl	Monte Jupp, Römerberg, Pflanzenberg, Rheinbrohler Ley
Unkel	Unkeler-Berg, Mannberg, Sonnenberg

SIEBENGEBIRGE

Oberdollendorf	Laurenziusberg, Sülzenberg, Rosenhügel, Grafenberg
Niederdollendorf	Kellerberg, Longenburgerberg, Heisterberg
Königswinter	Drachenley, Kuckstein
Rhöndorf	Domley, Ulananeck, Mönchenberg

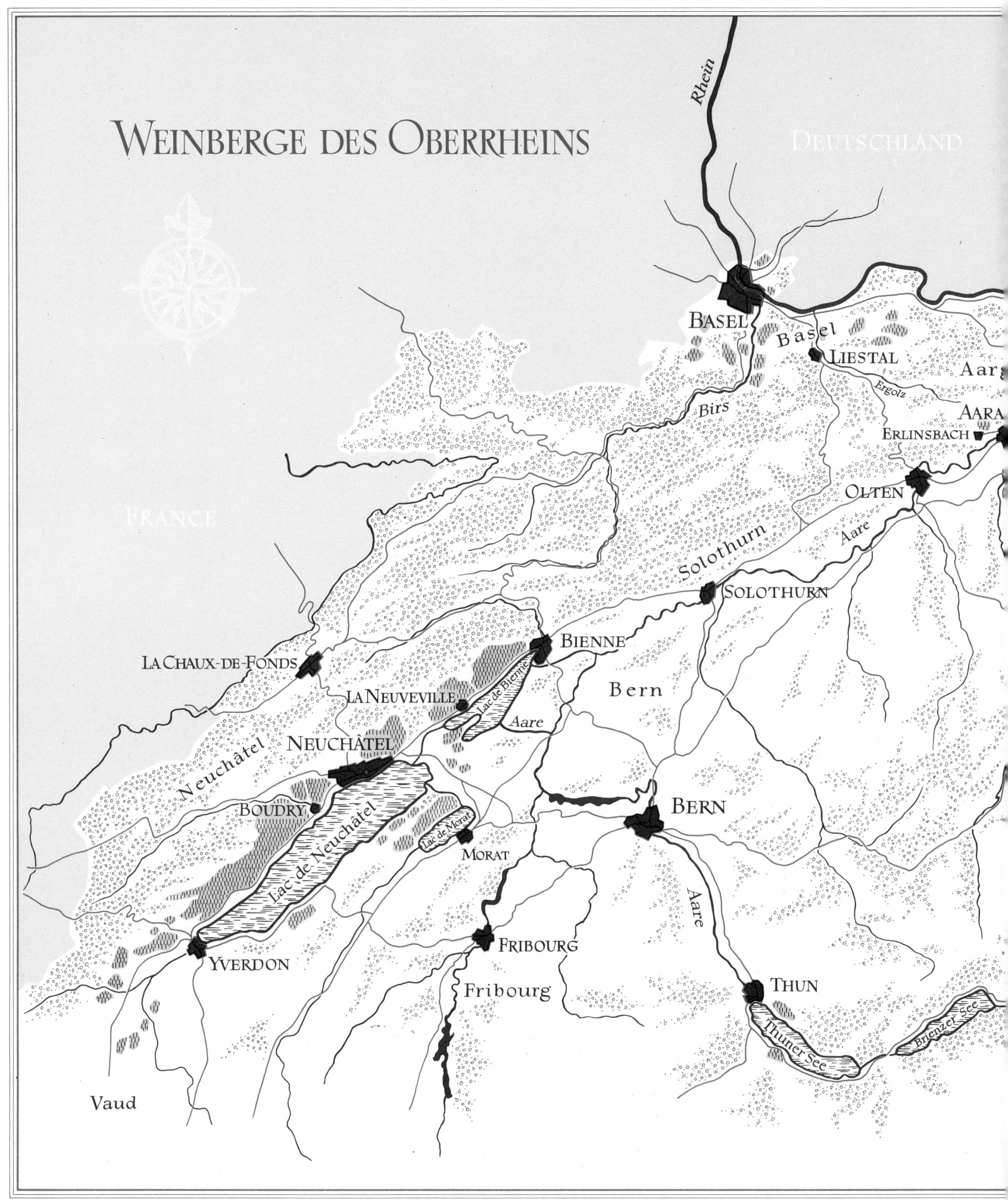

WEINBERGE DES OBERRHEINS

DEUTSCHLAND

Rhein

BASEL

Basel

LIESTAL

Aarg

Ergolz

AARA

Birs

ERLINSBACH

FRANCE

OLTEN

Aare

Solothurn

SOLOTHURN

LA CHAUX-DE-FONDS

BIENNE

Bern

LA NEUVEVILLE

Lac de Bienne

Aare

NEUCHÂTEL

Neuchâtel

BOUDRY

Lac de Neuchâtel

Lac de Morat

BERN

MORAT

YVERDON

FRIBOURG

THUN

Fribourg

Aare

Thuner See

Brienzer See

Vaud

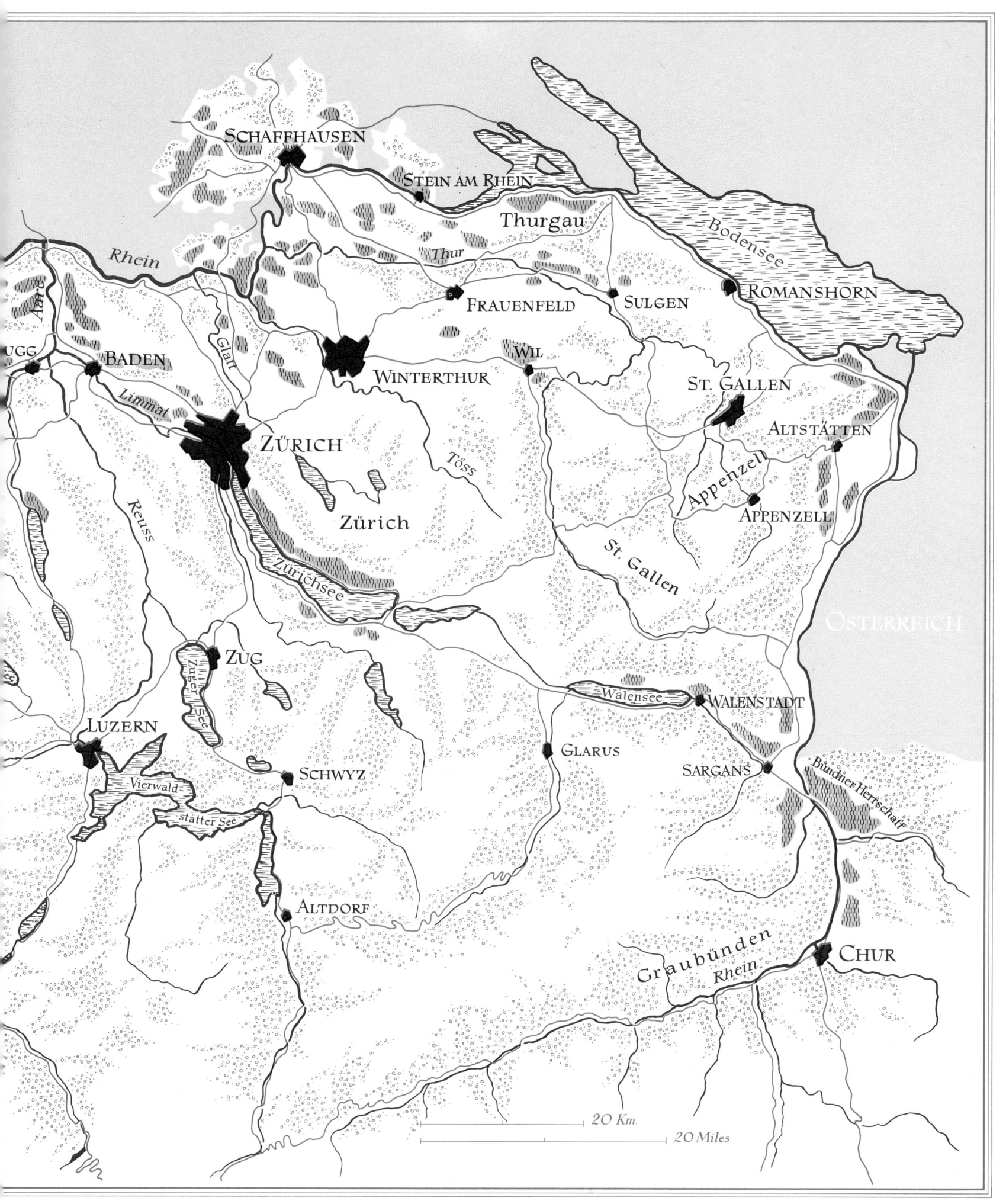

SCHAFFHAUSEN

STEIN AM RHEIN

Thurgau

Bodensee

Rhein

Thur

FRAUENFELD

SULGEN

ROMANSHORN

UGG

Aare

BADEN

Glatt

WINTERTHUR

WIL

ST. GALLEN

ALTSTÄTTEN

Limmat

ZÜRICH

Töss

Appenzell

APPENZELL

Reuss

Zürich

St. Gallen

ÖSTERREICH

Zürichsee

ZUG

Walensee

WALENSTADT

Zuger See

LUZERN

GLARUS

SARGANS

Bündner Herrschaft

Vierwald-

SCHWYZ

stätter See

ALTDORF

Graubünden

CHUR

Rhein

20 Km.

20 Miles

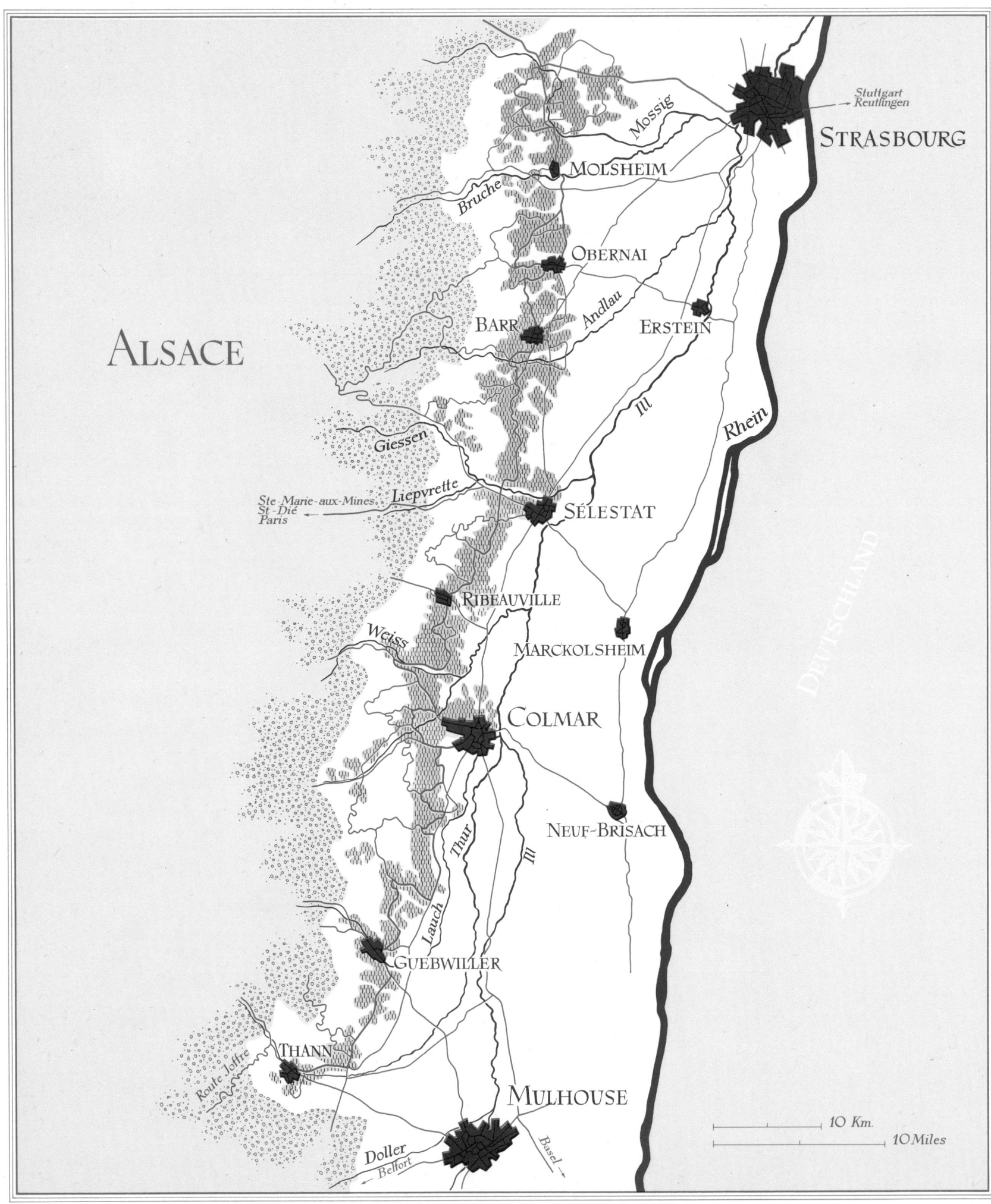

ALSACE

STRASBOURG

Stuttgart
Reutlingen

MOLSHEIM

OBERNAI

BARR

ERSTEIN

Mossig

Bruche

Andlau

Ill

Rhein

Giessen

Liepvrette

Ste.-Marie-aux-Mines
St.-Dié
Paris

SÉLESTAT

RIBEAUVILLE

Weiss

MARCKOLSHEIM

COLMAR

DEUTSCHLAND

NEUF-BRISACH

Thur

Ill

Lauch

GUEBWILLER

THANN

Route Joffre

MULHOUSE

Doller
Belfort

Basel

10 Km.

10 Miles

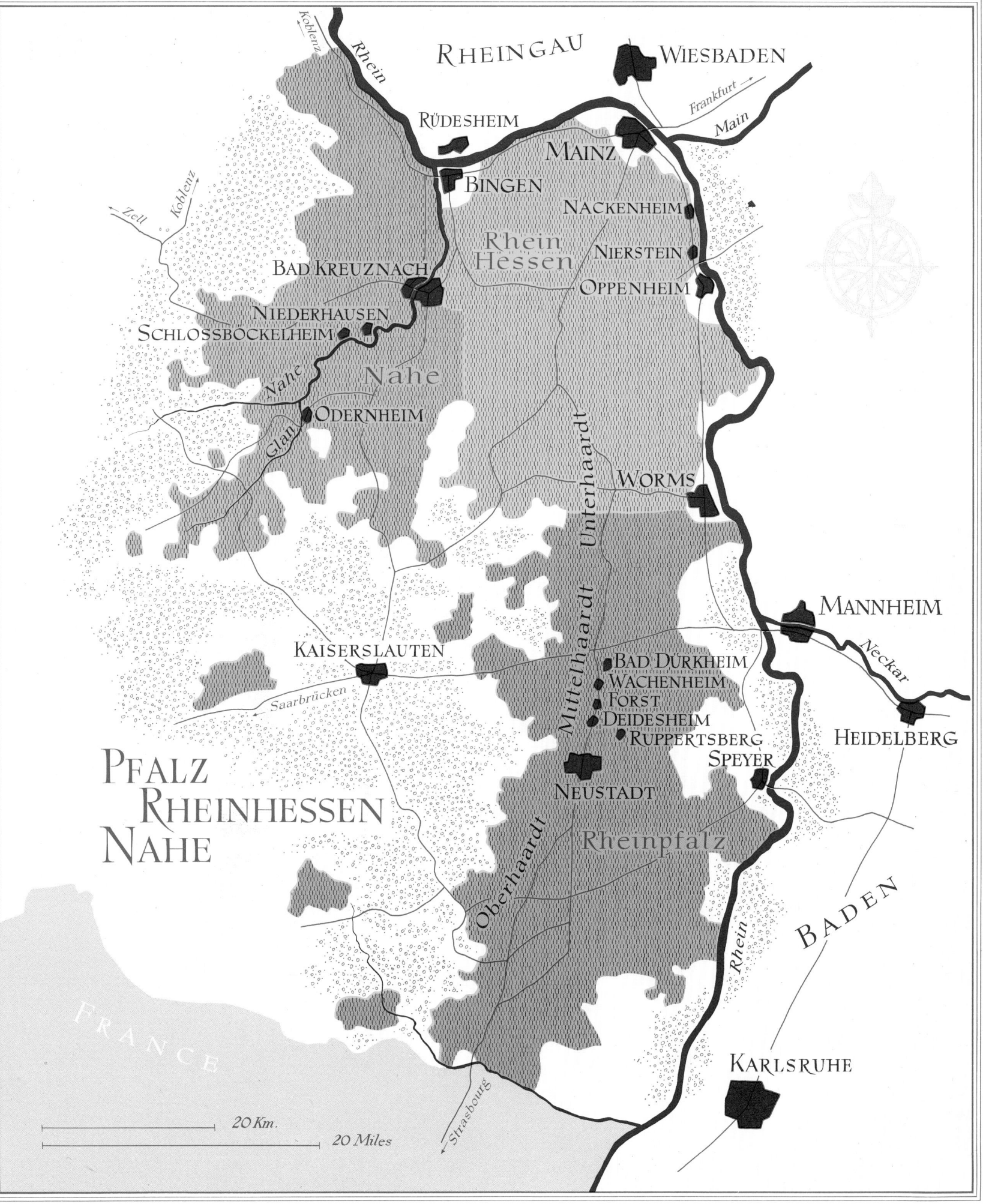

RHEINGAU

WIESBADEN

Koblenz

Rhein

RÜDESHEIM

Frankfurt

Main

MAINZ

Zell

Koblenz

BINGEN

NACKENHEIM

Rhein
Hessen

NIERSTEIN

BAD KREUZNACH

OPPENHEIM

NIEDERHAUSEN

SCHLOSSBÖCKELHEIM

Nahe

Nahe

Unterhaardt

Glan

ODERNHEIM

WORMS

MANNHEIM

Neckar

KAISERSLAUTEN

Mittelhaardt

BAD DÜRKHEIM

Saarbrücken

WACHENHEIM

FORST

DEIDESHEIM

RUPPERTSBERG

SPEYER

HEIDELBERG

PFALZ
RHEINHESSEN
NAHE

NEUSTADT

Rheinpfalz

Oberhaardt

Rhein

BADEN

FRANCE

KARLSRUHE

20 Km.

20 Miles

Strasbourg

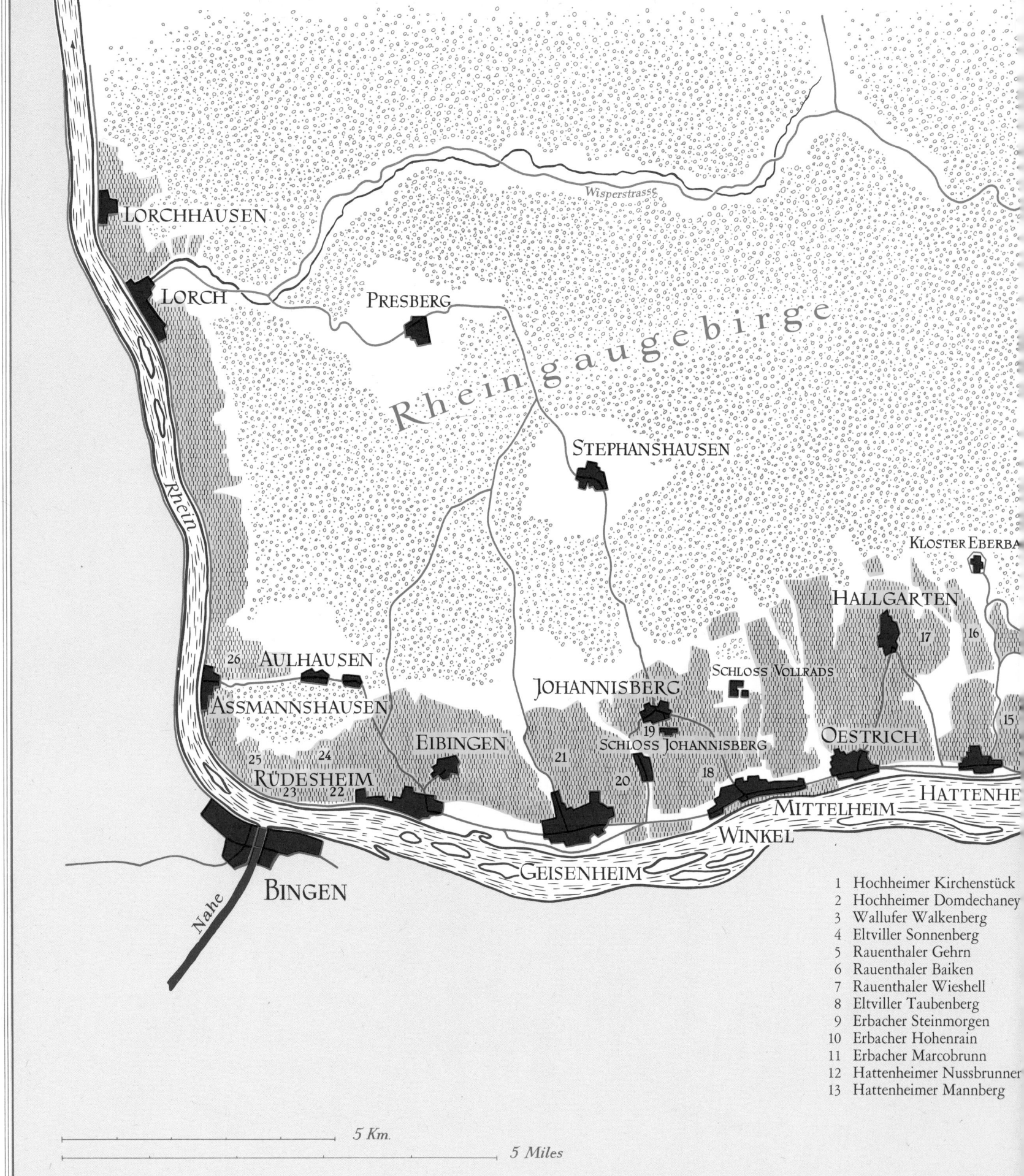

LORCHHAUSEN

LORCH

PRESBERG

Wisperstrasse

R h e i n g a u g e b i r g e

STEPHANSHAUSEN

Rhein

KLOSTER EBERBA

HALLGARTEN

17   16

26   AULHAUSEN

Schloss Vollrads

JOHANNISBERG

15

ASSMANNSHAUSEN

19

EIBINGEN

Schloss Johannisberg

OESTRICH

25   24

21   20   18

RÜDESHEIM

23   22

HATTENHE

MITTELHEIM

WINKEL

GEISENHEIM

Nahe

BINGEN

1   Hochheimer Kirchenstück
2   Hochheimer Domdechaney
3   Wallufer Walkenberg
4   Eltviller Sonnenberg
5   Rauenthaler Gehrn
6   Rauenthaler Baiken
7   Rauenthaler Wieshell
8   Eltviller Taubenberg
9   Erbacher Steinmorgen
10   Erbacher Hohenrain
11   Erbacher Marcobrunn
12   Hattenheimer Nussbrunner
13   Hattenheimer Mannberg

5 Km.

5 Miles

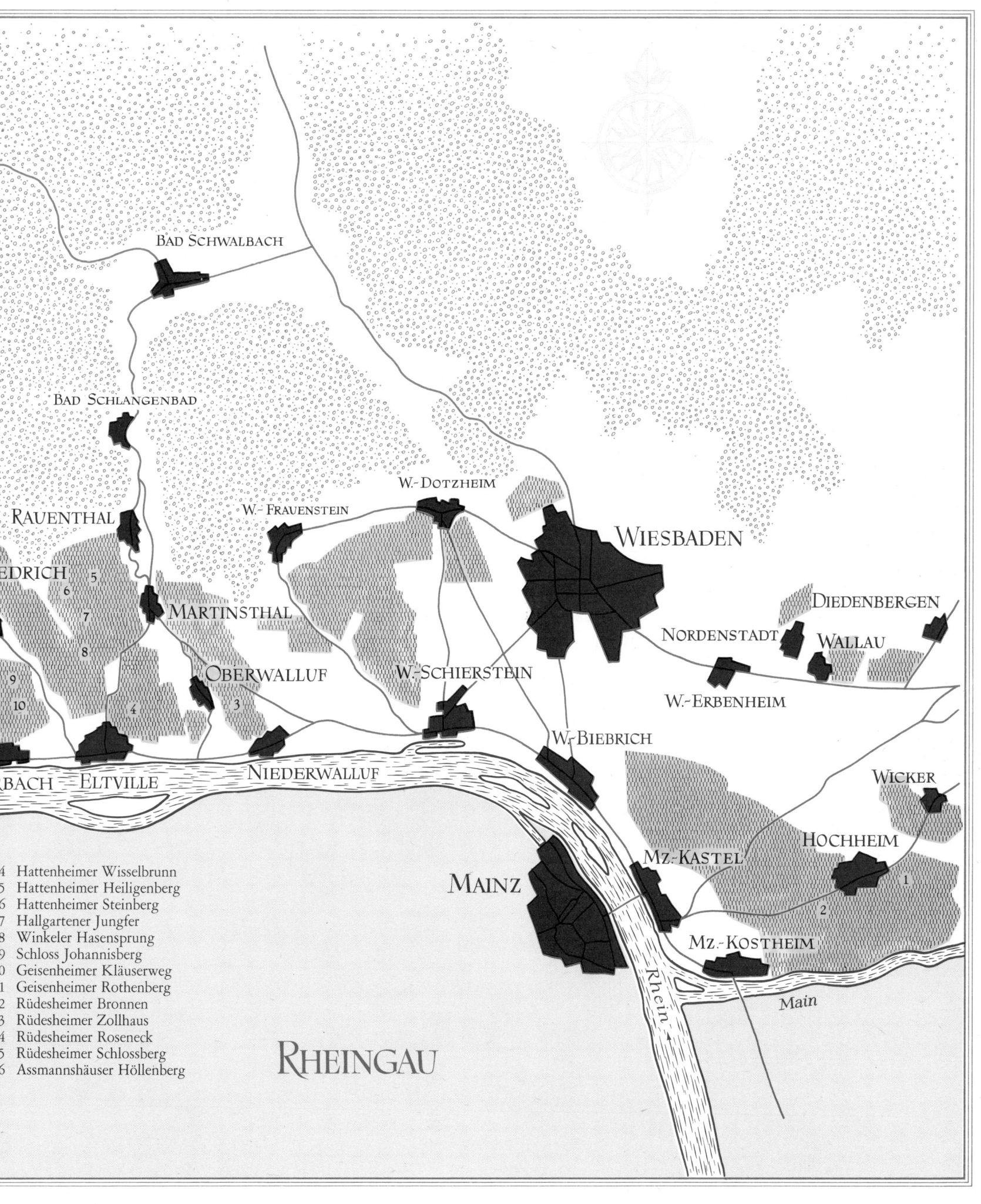

BAD SCHWALBACH

BAD SCHLANGENBAD

W.-DOTZHEIM

RAUENTHAL

W.-FRAUENSTEIN

WIESBADEN

...EDRICH

5

6

7

8

9

10

MARTINSTHAL

OBERWALLUF

4

3

W.-SCHIERSTEIN

DIEDENBERGEN

NORDENSTADT

WALLAU

W.-ERBENHEIM

W.-BIEBRICH

WICKER

...RBACH   ELTVILLE   NIEDERWALLUF

HOCHHEIM

Mz.-KASTEL

MAINZ

1

2

Mz.-KOSTHEIM

Rhein

Main

14 Hattenheimer Wisselbrunn
15 Hattenheimer Heiligenberg
16 Hattenheimer Steinberg
17 Hallgartener Jungfer
18 Winkeler Hasensprung
19 Schloss Johannisberg
20 Geisenheimer Kläuserweg
21 Geisenheimer Rothenberg
22 Rüdesheimer Bronnen
23 Rüdesheimer Zollhaus
24 Rüdesheimer Roseneck
25 Rüdesheimer Schlossberg
26 Assmannshäuser Höllenberg

RHEINGAU

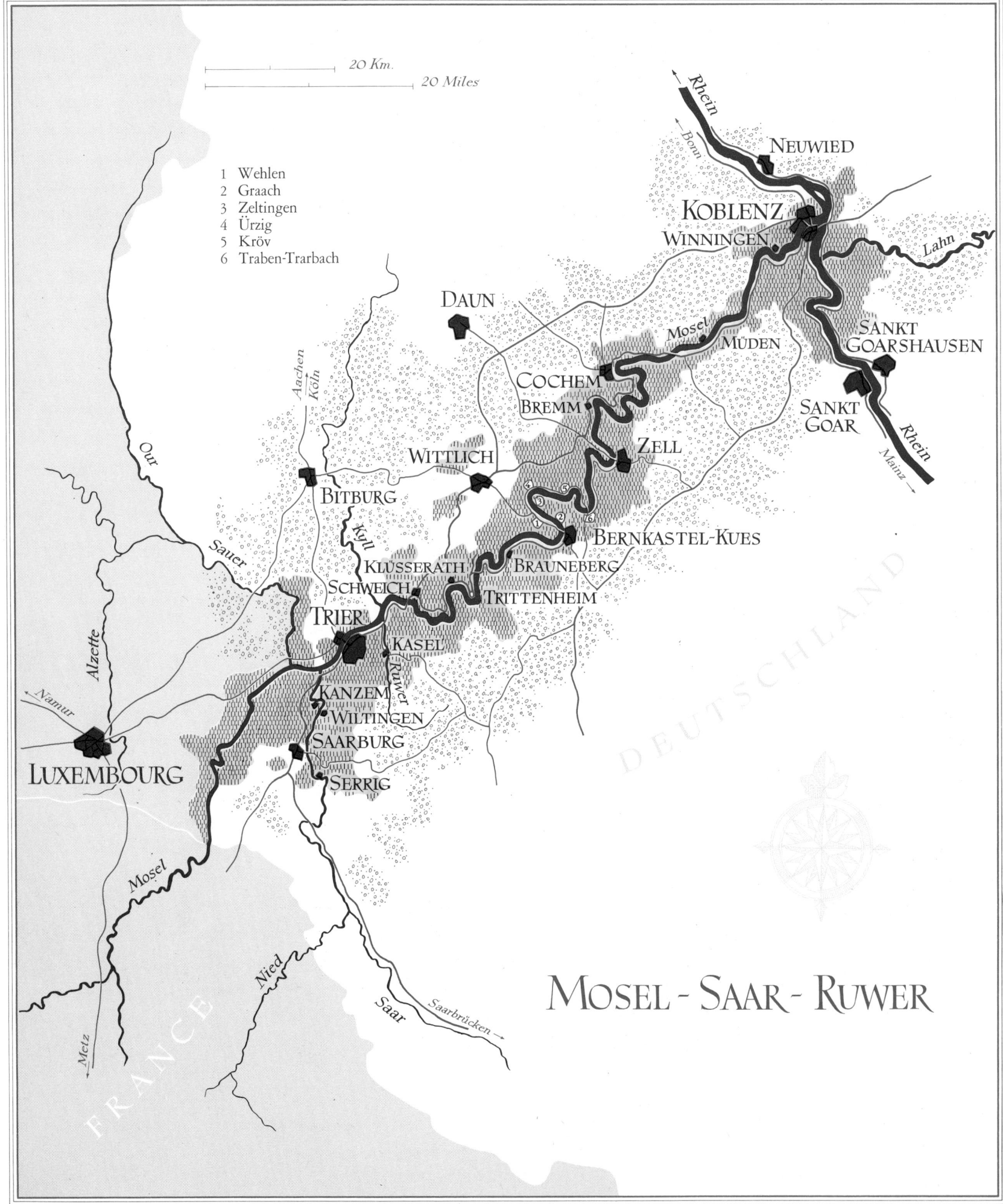

1 Wehlen
2 Graach
3 Zeltingen
4 Ürzig
5 Kröv
6 Traben-Trarbach

20 Km.
20 Miles

Rhein
Bonn
NEUWIED
KOBLENZ
WINNINGEN
Lahn
DAUN
Mosel
MÜDEN
SANKT GOARSHAUSEN
COCHEM
BREMM
SANKT GOAR
Rhein
WITTLICH
ZELL
Mainz
BITBURG
Aachen
Köln
Kyll
BERNKASTEL-KUES
KLÜSSERATH
BRAUNEBERG
SCHWEICH
TRITTENHEIM
TRIER
KASEL
Ruwer
KANZEM
WILTINGEN
SAARBURG
SERRIG
Our
Sauer
Alzette
Namur
LUXEMBOURG
Mosel
DEUTSCHLAND
Nied
Metz
Saar
Saarbrücken
FRANCE

MOSEL - SAAR - RUWER

THE WINES
OF CENTRAL EUROPE,
THE BALKANS, THE USSR

JOSEPH JOBÉ and BORIS POGRMILOVIC

At the time of the Roman Empire, the vine was cultivated in Spain, Gaul and Helvetia as well as along the frontiers of the Empire, on the Rhine and on the Danube. In the Middle Ages, all the countries of central Europe produced some wine. However the climate and geological conditions as well as the economic and political fluctuations were less favourable to wine production in these countries than, for example, in France and Italy.

Today Czechoslovakia, of all the central European countries, is the one where the least wine is produced and drunk; just over a gallon per person per year. It is easy to understand this: the vineyards, situated at the farthest point north of the viticultural zone, are only cultivated on a marginal basis. However, at the beginning of the seventeenth century, before the Thirty Years War, even Bohemia, and in particular the area around Prague, was a country of vineyards and rich in wine. Before phylloxera attacked the stock, the Czech vineyards were as important as those of the present republic of Austria. It is true that the last few centuries have seen a slight change in climate which has adversely affected the vine, but there are other reasons for this regression. Czechoslovakia, Austria, Hungary and part of Yugoslavia all once belonged to a single large conglomeration of which Austria was the predominant element. Within this Empire, an increase or a reduction in the amount of land allotted to the cultivation of the vine depended not only on climatic conditions but also on historical events. Moreover, certain provinces, especially Hungary, suffered from the influence and invasion of the Moslem Turks, who were not wine drinkers. As wine was sometimes scarce in the most highly productive areas, a greater effort was required from the wine-growers in other regions of the Empire. At the end of First World War, each of the new states born of the fall of the Austro-Hungarian Empire had to view the future in a new light.

The Austrian vineyards, more ancient than the name of the country, have made very little progress. The vine here is cultivated on a very small scale and is confined to the eastern part of the country.

In Czechoslovakia, however, the vine covered 42,000 acres in 1917 and 25,000 acres in 1947; today it covers about 61,800 acres. The Hungarian vineyards have developed on quite a different scale. Here, apart from the years 1955 to 1958, production has always been maintained at around 495,000 acres. Hungarians drink from 5 ½ to 6 ½ gallons of wine per person per year, and export 20 per cent of their production.

The Greeks as much as the Romans were responsible for the introduction of the vine to Yugoslavia, where its development was further encouraged by the lords of the land and the monasteries. Under Turkish domination, the actual area under cultivation dwindled, but it did not disappear entirely. Since the beginning of this century, the area under vines has doubled. Consumption *per capita* is on a par with the neighbouring countries of Austria, Hungary and Bulgaria.

In Rumania and Bulgaria it would seem the vine was first introduced by the Greeks and later by the Romans. These two countries have better climatic conditions than Czechoslovakia, and in Rumania especially, the influence of the Black Sea does much to temper the excesses of the continental climate. In this country, the vine grows wherever the soil is favourable and the sun shines sufficiently. Despite a long period of submission to the Turkish Empire, the Rumanians continued to grow the vine though their overlords cared little for the fruits of their labour.

In 1913, Rumania had only 178,000 acres of soil under cultivation; today it has about 740,000. It produces more white wine than red, while in Bulgaria the opposite is the case. The increase of production continues under the incentive of the co-operatives and of the research institutes set up by the Government.

In Bulgaria, the soil planted to vines in 1913 was 131,000 acres; today it is about 445,000 acres and consumption has more than doubled in the last ten years. It is now 3 to 5 gallons per person per year.

A similar situation exists in southern Russia: in 1914 the vineyards were spread over 526 acres, while today they have developed to cover about 2 ½ million. It is true that the Russians are not great consumers of still wines; they prefer sparkling wines to the extent of about 200 bottles a year per thousand inhabitants.

Throughout the whole area, which stretches from Prague to the Black Sea and the Adriatic, there is only one wine as famous as the "great" wines: TOKAY.

AUSTRIA

Today Austria produces much less wine than it once did. The ebb and flow of history are responsible for this decrease. The Romans most probably introduced the vine to the banks of the Danube 2,000 years ago. After the invasion of the Barbarians who destroyed the Roman colonies, the vines were replanted under Emperor Otto I, from the year 955 onwards. Towards the end of the Middle Ages, the vine covered 200,000 acres in Lower Austria alone. When neighbouring Hungary was occupied by the Turks in 1526, the whole wine trade—and the competition in wines—between the two countries came to an end. As one result, for one and a half centuries the amount of land under cultivation in Austria increased greatly. The present area under cultivation is only a tenth of what it used to be at its zenith. Today, some 99,000 acres of vineyards produce 33,000,000 gallons of wine. As the country imports 11,000,000 gallons, it may be deduced that every Austrian drinks an average of 6 ½ gallons of wine a year, as against 15 gallons of beer. Austria exports 330,000 gallons of wine a year, nearly all in white wines.

In fact, most of the wine produced (85 per cent) is white wine made from various grape-stocks. The best known are the *Riesling*, the *Traminer*, the *Sylvaner*, as well as the *Grüner Veltliner*. Sometimes the *Sauvignon*, *Rotgipfler* and *Muskat-Ottonel* are also used.

Austrian wines have been much appreciated for many years. Nearly four centuries ago, in 1580, Johannes Rasch wrote an important work on viticulture in this country. At the end of the seventeenth century wines were already classified according to their quality, and the classification was ratified by the Imperial Court in 1673.

In 1780, the Empress Maria Theresa promulgated a law on wine which still affects the industry today. Certain provisions of this law stated that every vineyard had the right to sell the wine from its vines without paying taxes. When a wine-merchant had wine in his cellar, he would place a crown of leaves or straw above his cellar-door to indicate to the passer-by that he was welcome within. Here, he might rest himself and partake of some liquid refreshment. This was the origin of the famous *Heurigen*, where every year the Viennese and countless numbers of tourists go to enjoy a few moments of laughter and merry-making. Under the shady bowers, amidst a lovely countryside and preferably in good company, the lover of white wine can savour the best local products such as GRINZING, SIEBERING and NUSSDORF, as well as WIENER NUSSBERG, probably the best of all. Let us hasten to add that the vineyards around Vienna are neither the only ones, nor even the best in the country.

The winegrowing area of Burgenland includes the banks of Lake Neusiedel and, farther south, the area around the town of Eisenberg. Usually, local wines are drunk in such places as Oggau, Mörbisch, Rust, St. Margarethen, Eisenstadt, Mattesburg and Oberpullendorf. Some wines, naturally, are better than others: among the white wines these are the RUSTER GREINER, RUSTER SATZ, RUSTER TURNER, while among the red wines there are the RUSTER BAUMGARTEN, RUSTER G'MÄRK, RUSTER MITTELKRÄFTEN, and especially the RUST LIMBERGER, a *Pinot Noir*. Styria, in the Mur valley, near the lower part of Graz and Sulm, mainly produces white wines. The best-known vineyard is situated in the commune of Klöch, and some consider the KLÖCHER BERG one of the best *Traminers*

In this painting by Lucas van Valckenborgh (1530-1597) peasants gather apples, coopers prepare barrels, some winegrowers harvest the grapes while others trample the vintage. The mildness of these last fine days, the abundance of the earth's gifts and the promise of good wine has incited their masters to pass the day in the country: at midday they assemble to eat lunch to the strains of a violin.

in Europe. Other local wines highly-thought of by the Austrians are the HARTBERGER RING, the HARTBERGER LÖFFELBACH, the GRASSNITZBERG, the OTTENBERGER WITSCHEINBERG and the KOBELBERG.

In the Baden region to the south of Vienna—a region also called Südbahn—the best-known white wines are those of Gumpoldskirchen, in particular the GUMPOLDSKIRCHNER SPIEGEI, the GUMPOLDSKIRCHNER WIEGE and the GUMPOLDSKIRCHNER SONNBERG. Of the red wines, which are fewer, the VÖSLAUER ROTWEIN deserves particular mention.

The winegrowing areas, which produce local wines, white for the most part, are north of the Danube in the Weinviertel, which along the length and the western side runs from Vienna to Czechoslovakia, as well as along the banks of the Danube from Vienna to the confluence of the river Kamp, including Klosternberg, the Kamp valley and Langenlois.

However, it is especially the region of Krems and of Wachau above Krems that produce the best Austrian wines. In the past, these wines were not so well thought of because of their somewhat high acid content—in fact a well-known saying had it *sauer wie der Wachauer* ("as sour as Wachauer wine"). The winegrowers of Krems, a dynamic and pretty little town, were however able to produce Rieslings with a full-flavoured bouquet. The best of these may be compared to the Moselle Rieslings. To name but a few, the KREMSLER KÖGL, KREMSER KREMSLEITEN and KREMSER WACHTBERG may be recommended.

Farther up-stream is Dürnstein, a very picturesque place with the ruins of a feudal castle. It is well-known for its DÜRNSTEINER LIERENBERG, and for the DÜRNSTEINER HOLLERIN, which was served in 1955 at the time of the signing of the Austrian State Treaty which proclaimed Austria's independence. Yet farther up-stream, the Stein vineyards produce the STEINER GOLDBERG, made from the best *Müller-Thurgau* grape in Wachau. The Loiben wines are some of the best white wines to come from the banks of the Danube: wines such as the LOIBENER KAISERWEIN and the UNTERLOIBENER BRUGSTALL.

The traveller faced with a list of Austrian wines is often puzzled, as the names by which these wines are known are not always mentioned as fully or as systematically on the wine-list as is the practice elsewhere. For some wines only the place of origin is given—for example, WACHAUER 1959, a wine produced in Wachau in the year 1959. Others are known by the name of the grape used, without mentioning the place of origin, as in the case of VELTLINER 1959; this simply designates a wine produced from the *Grüner Veltliner* grape in the year 1959. Yet others mention the grape used preceded by the name of the commune; for example, the STEINER VELTLINER 1959, produced from the *Grüner Veltliner* grape in the commune of Stein in the year 1959. It should be noted, however, that the best wines, especially those we have referred to, mention the name of the commune or the village, followed by the name of the vineyard. For example: DÜRNSTEINER LIEBENBERG, designating a wine grown in the vineyard of Liebenberg in the commune of Dürnstein. A wine-lover who choses any of these wines will be sure to have chosen from among the best wines of Austria.

Austrian wines are little known abroad; for the most part they must be drunk in the country itself. The white wines are considered the best, but they should not be compared to the German wines made from the same stock. Those drunk in the "Heurigen" near Vienna have a low alcohol content; they are pale-coloured wines, sometimes of a milky white hue, fresh wines which are sometimes slightly effervescent.

HUNGARY

The most famous Hungarian wine is TOKAY. Associated with the names of emperors and kings, lords and poets, it has overshadowed all the other wines of the country. For Hungary is a country rich in vineyards and wines; it has 543,600 acres of vine and produces nearly 88,000,000 gallons of wine, which places it in about tenth position among the wineproducing countries of Europe.

The Romans introduced the vine to the Hungarian plains. Since those days, the vine there has undergone many vicissitudes. First cultivated by the Magyars, it was neglected when the Tartars laid the country waste in 1241. Later again, settlers from the west brought with them a new vine-plant, *Furmint*, from which TOKAY was produced. Afterwards, when for 173 years (from 1526 to 1699) the country was occupied by Moslem Turks, the vine was once again neglected. In the eighteenth century, however, the Hungarian wine-cellars were among the best-stocked in Europe, thanks to Count István Szecheny.

Today Hungarian production fluctuates around 88 million gallons of wine, a quarter of which, at the most, is for export. Hungary produces mainly white wines (60 per cent). It also produces rosés (25 per cent) and a little red wine (15 per cent). These wines are usually known by a compound name; the first indicates the place of origin, the second the grape. For example, BADACSONYI KEKNYELÜ means that the wine is made from the *Kéknyelü* ("blue stalk") grape, in the Badacsony region. The white wines of Sopron, Somló, Villány-Pécs, Gyöngyös-Visonta are ordinary wines mainly for local consumption.

Red wine can be found in Sopron, which is near the Austrian border, in particular in the district of Szek-szárd, to the south of Lake Balaton. Most of the reds come from an original Balkan grape, the *Kadarka*.

The western bank of Lake Balaton, on the slopes of Mount Badacsony, is particularly favourable to the cultivation of grapes such as *Kéknyelü*, *Furmint*, and *Szürkebarát (Pinot Gris)*. BADACSONY KEKNYELÜ is a dry white wine with a pleasant bouquet and an attractive colour bordering on green, while BADACSONY SZÜRKEBARAT is a semi-sweet white wine which, when mature, has a rich amber colour. Nevertheless, it does not have the distinction of the *Pinot Gris* wines in other parts of Europe. RIESLINGS are cheap white wines of Italian origin, very different from those produced in the Rhine districts.

The Mór region, farther to the north, is one of Hungary's oldest viticultural areas. The MÖRI EZERJO, which means "the one-thousandfold good Mor", is a dry wine with a very lovely light green colour and an agreeably sharp tang.

The DEBRÖI HÁRSLEVELÜ is another typical Hungarian white wine. The grape *Hárslevelü* ("lime-blossom") is cultivated in the mountainous region of the north; it produces a sweet wine which is highly thought of by the Hungarians.

The EGRI BIKAVER, or "Bull's Blood of Eger" is the only Hungarian red wine known abroad, no doubt because of its name. The Eger region is situated between Budapest and the Tokay region. The EGRI BIKAVER has a dark rich colour and a slightly bitter taste. It is made from a mixture of several vines: the *Kadarka*, *Médoc Noir* and *Bourguignon*. In Hungary it is much recommended during convalescence owing to its tonic properties. The EGRI LEANYKA is a white wine made from an indigenous grape, the *Leanyka*.

TOKAY is by all odds the best-known. The town which gave its name to the wines of this region is situated on the Bodrog, at the foot of the Hégalja, which dominates the Tisza plain. This is an area of orchards and vineyards where only 28 villages have the right to call the wine they produce TOKAY. (It should be stated quite clearly that the name TOKAY does not cover the whole range of wines produced in this region.) The excellence of this wine springs from a wonderful harmony that exists between the soil and the climate, the grape and the process of vinification. The soil consists of a layer of crumbled lava which covers alluvial mountain deposits on a bed of volcanic rocks. The climate is varied; the summers are very hot and very dry, the autumns long and sunny, but the winters are harsh. The altitude of the vineyard varies from 500 to 650 feet above sea-level. The grape which gives TOKAY its special character is the *Furmint*. Students of the vine are divided in their opinions as to its origin, but agree that in this country it has found the soil and the climate most suitable for it. It is believed that settlers coming from the west brought the *Furmint* to prominence. Its name is probably derived from the French *froment* (wheat) which has become *Furmint* in Magyar; no doubt it has to do with the colour of the grapes. To this grape, which is always the predominant one in TOKAY, are sometimes added small quantities of *Hárslevelü* and *Muscat Jaune*. The third factor responsible for its success is the process of vinification and the special cellars in which it is stored.

First, there is the TOKAY FURMINT, or FURMINT DE TOKAY, a wine made according to traditional methods, by pressing the juice of the *Furmint* grape-clusters without using the dry grapes. This is a full-flavoured, fruity wine. Often the year of manufacture is mentioned on the label.

The TOKAY SZAMARODNI or SZAMARODNI DE TOKAY is made from the fermentation of grapes which have not been specially selected but picked late and so have clusters which are dry or have reached a stage of *pourriture noble* (noble rot). Its alcohol content is higher than that of the TOKAJI FURMINT; it can be sweet, as it is in sunny years, but when dry makes an excellent aperitif. The label on the bottle will indicate the year and type of wine.

The TOKAJI ASZU or ASZU DE TOKAY is the most famous of all the TOKAYS and is usually the one referred to when speaking simply of TOKAY. It is said to owe its origin to a seventeenth-century local war, which caused a delay in the vine-harvest; the winegrowers thus rediscovered the advantages of a late wine-harvest which had already been known to their forefathers. Late in the season, sometimes even after the first snow has fallen, when the grapes are overripe and

have reached a *pourriture noble*, the wine-harvesters pick them one by one. The grapes are then crushed and stirred together until they form a kind of crust. When this process has been completed, 2 to 6 basketfuls (puttonos) weighing 33 pounds each of the final mixture are added to every hogshead of 30 gallons of must or wine, whether it is young or old, which is produced in the same region.

The sugar and aroma from the pressing of dried grapes dissolves in the must or wine, which after a second slow fermentation produces the world-famous TOKAY ASZU. The number of basketfuls poured into each hogshead depends on several factors: on the one hand on the quality of the must or wine which is being used—this varies from year to year—on the other hand on the type of TOKAJI ASZU one wishes to produce. For this wine can be sweet or semi-sweet.

The TOKAJI ASZU maintains essentially the same degree of excellence from year to year largely owing to the art of the master winemakers. The TOKAJI FURMINT and the TOKAJI SZAMARODNI, however, vary from year to year depending on the quality of the wine-harvest. When buying TOKAJI ASZU, one should know that the label on the bottle always mentions how many basketfuls of concentrated grapes have been put into each hogshead. For example: "3 puttonos" means that the wine is sweet, yet not nearly as sweet as a wine with a label reading "6 puttonos". This is the maximum. Moreover, the TOKAJI ASZU bottle has a traditional shape; it is pot-bellied like a Burgundy bottle, with a well-defined neck longer than that of the claret bottle. The wine will keep for a long time, like a sherry or Madeira. It is a wine known the world over, made famous by Voltaire, Goethe and Burns, while Louis XIV is said to have called it "the wine of Kings and the King of wines".

The TOKAJI MASLAS is produced by fermenting must or wine on the lees of TOKAY, usually on the lees of the ASZU or the SZAMARODNI. In order to produce the desired results the must stands for several months in small barrels called *Gönci*.

The TOKAJI ESZENCIA, or ESSENCE OF TOKAY is made by fermenting a thick must made from overripe grapes or those which have reached a state of *pourriture noble*. It is a very sweet, liqueur-like dessert wine.

TOKAY is produced in several countries (Alsace, northern Italy and eastern Switzerland), but only those wines referred to here come from Hungary and are authentic TOKAYS. They are exported by the Hungarian Board of Foreign Trade (Monimpex). Rarely, one does find a very old bottle of TOKAY, a delight to the connoisseur or anyone nostalgic for the charm of the gay nights in Budapest at the time of the Austro-Hungarian monarchy or between the two wars.

CZECHOSLOVAKIA

Czechoslovakia, of all the countries which were part of the former Austro-Hungarian Empire, is certainly the one which produces the least wine. Its output is about 6,600,000 gallons a year, half as much as Alsace alone produces, and even if some years happen to be more abundant, such as 1964 when production reached 16,479,716 gallons, Czechoslovakia has nevertheless not recovered from the ravages of phylloxera.

Bohemia, in the Melnik region, Roudnice and Litomerice, to the north of Prague, produce an ordinary white wine called LUOMILLA, made from the *Sylvaner* and *Traminer* grapes. The red wines are made from *Bourguignon Bleu*, *Portugais* or *Saint-Laurent* grapes. Because of its geographical position Bohemia produces wines similar to those of certain German wine regions.

Morovia has little wine, and almost all of it comes from the region near the Austrian frontier: the Rhine Rieslings, the Italien Rieslings and the Veltline.

Of the three main regions in the country, Slovakia is the best developed from the point of view of viticulture and gives about three-quarters of the national yield. Near the Hungarian frontier, to the north of the Tokay region, the Mala Trna and Nove Mestro vineyards also produce so-called TOKAY. Elsewhere, in the Bratislava area, they make the usual wines: Veltliner, Riesling or Sylvaner.

Czechoslovakia has to import a certain amount of wine: in 1965 it imported 9,752,468 gallons, and 4,110,876 gallons in 1966. Wine here is by no means a national drink; the average Czech drinks only about ten pints of wine a year. As there are no great wines, the tourist must console himself with the local white wines. These are light, fruity, and of low alcohol content and may be enjoyed in charming surroundings. The Czech wines have much improved since the establishment of a control over their quality.

RUMANIA

The Rumanian winegrowers have for centuries managed to maintain a difficult balance between the soil, the climate and the art of cultivating the vine. Although the country geographically belongs in a temperate zone considered favourable for the vine, its climate is nevertheless extreme: very hot in the summer, very cold and windy in winter. Yet wine has been produced in this country since before the seventh century B.C. When the Greeks founded their Black Sea colonies they cultivated the vine here in order to produce wine which they then stored in huge pot-bellied amphoras and sent throughout the civilized world.

By the development of the nurseries and the application of modern scientific methods of viticulture and viniculture the area of Rumania's winegrowing districts has been greatly enlarged in the past few years. The present Rumanian vineyard covers more than 741,300 acres and produces more than 132,000,000 gallons of wine, most of it white wine.

The principal vineyards are the Cotnari and the Murfatlar, producing dessert wines; the Tirnave; the Dealul-Mare, the Focsain and the Banat, producing both red and white table wines. The best-known and the most renowned of the Rumanian white wines come from the Tirnave Mare and Tirnave Mica valleys, in the centre of the country. The TIRNAVE PEARL, a wine made from a mixture of several grapes which give it a very well-balanced bouquet, is well known outside Rumania.

Other white wines are made from a single vine-plant whose name they carry; for example, the FETEASCA DE TIRNAVE, RIESLING DE TIRNAVE, or RIESLING DE DEALUL-MARE, near Ploesti in Munténie.

The KADARKA is the most common red wine in the Balkans; the wine from Teremia, near the Yugoslav border, is often referred to; and there is also the SEGARCEA CABERNET, made from the *Cabernet* grape. It comes from the vineyards of the *Valea Calugaresca* (Valley of the Monks) which lies to the east of Ploesti. The SADOVA is a slightly sweet rosé from the Dragasani region, where the vine is often more than a century old. The white dessert wines from these parts are very highly thought of. In the north, the COTNARI wine is sweet and fruity. The MURFATLAR, from near the Black Sea, has a fine orange-blossom bouquet which is probably unique.

Rumanian wines are exported mainly to Germany, Austria and the Eastern European countries, although the Focsani Fructexport also sells a certain amount of wine to such countries as Switzerland, Belgium, Holland, Sweden, Denmark, France and Great Britain. Rumania has many indigenous stocks, but is making a real effort to improve the quality of its wines through a progressive elimination of hybrids and a selection of vine types. The new co-operatives have also done much to improve the standard in vine culture and turn the country's great wine potential to the best account.

BULGARIA

Before World War II, the vineyards of Bulgaria spread over an area of 331,200 acres; in 1968 they covered 494,200 acres. This increase is due on the one hand to a major change in the system of ownership, and on the other to a systematic reconstruction of the vineyards so that mechanization could be introduced on a large scale. The country today produces 66,000,000 gallons of wine per year; 52 per cent red wines, 48 per cent white wines. Although it is divided into viticultural regions, it would not be correct to attribute a particular wine to a given region. It might also be practical to mention only the better-known Bulgarian wines.

The *Dimiat* is the best-known grape. It grows near the Black Sea, in the Choumen regions and farther west in the province of Tarnovo. It produces a dry but fruity wine of a rich golden-green colour. Wines are named by their grape or by regional names, and sometimes by a combination of both. (WARNENSKI DIMIAT means a DIMIAT from Warna.) These wines recall the Rieslings, while the wines from the *Misket* grapes, in particular the MISKET KARLOVA or the MISKET DE KARLOVO, bring to mind the Sylvaner, as does the SONGURLARE MISKET which is produced on the coast. Other, more common white wines are the BALGARSKE SLANTSE or BULGARIAN SUN made from the *Furmint* grape; the DOUNAVSKA PERLA or PEARL OF THE DANUBE, and the SLANTCHEV BIRAG or SUNSHINE COAST, made from a Georgian grape, the *Rehaziteli*. The SLAVIANKA is a wine made from the *Muscat* grape; it is golden and full-flavoured, with the characteristic savour of the grape.

Although there are many more red wines, they are much less varied. Usually they are known by their grape. PAMID is purely for domestic consumption. GAMSA (the Bulgarian name for KADARKA) is an agreeable wine, with a pleasant bouquet, especially when young. Sometimes it is known by a local name such as KRAMOLINSKA, or wine from Kramoline.

MAVROUD, produced in the Assennovgrad region, has a rich dark red colour, and is somewhat acid, with an alcoholic content of 11 to 12 degrees. This wine is often used for blending with lighter red wines.

MELNIK is a wine from the north-west region. It is dark red, somewhat full-bodied, but of good quality. The *Melnik* grape variety has been cultivated in Bulgaria since ancient times and is probably a plant of French origin. The CABERNET is another Bulgarian wine made from the *Cabernet-Sauvignon* grape, which was introduced into the country.

YUGOSLAVIA

The history of Yugoslav vine culture and wines is similar to that of Italy, France and Spain. They all use the same vinification methods and even the same grapes: the *Burgundac* or *Pinot Noir*, the *Cabernet*, the *Merlot* and the *Riesling*. The Yugoslav climate and soil give a particular character to its wines. The vineyards cover 640,000 acres and produce, apart from table grapes, 110 to 132 million gallons of wine. The vine is cultivated throughout the country, from north to south in the following six regions: Slovenia, Istria, Crotia, Dalmatia, Serbia and Macedonia.

Slovenia has a flourishing vineyard situated in the Save and Drave valleys, including the districts of Ljutomer, Ormoz, Ptuj, Radgona and Maribor, as well as along the Adriatic to the Italian frontier. In this area, most of the white wines are made from the grapes of the *Traminer, Riesling Rhenan, Riesling Laski*, the *Sauvignon, Pinot Blanc* and *Sipon*, the local counterparts of the Hungarian *Furmint*. The Slovenia region produces 486,000 bottles of wine annually, about 9 per cent of the national output.

Istria is known for its red wines made from the grapes of the *Feran, Bogonja (Gamay), Merlot* and *Cabernet* varieties. Two white wines are also produced here, one made from the *Pinot* grapes, the other from the *Malvasia* or Malmsey grape. The Istrian growers employ the Italian methods of mixed cultivation, so that other plants can be seen growing side by side with the vines.

Croatia is one of the most important winegrowing regions in Bulgaria. The north produces white wines, light but somewhat acid, or wines with a rich bouquet and very high alcohol content. *Traminer, Riesling, Sauvignon* and *Semillon* grape varieties are greatly cultivated in this area. The coastal wines are red, similar to the full and heady wines from the Mediterranean. This area produces 5,038,000 gallons of wine, 35 per cent of the national yield.

The most famous grape-vine in Dalmatia is the *Plavac*, which produces a red wine of the same name. It is a full-bodied, ruby-red wine with a very special bouquet. Dalmatia also makes some semi-dry red wines known as DINGNAC and POSTUP. An unusual type of sweet wine called PROSEK can be found in this area but it rarely appeals to the taste of foreigners.

The Serbian vineyard is the largest of all the Yugoslav vineyards and is responsible for half the wine produced in Yugoslavia. It makes mainly white wines and just a few red wines such as the ZUPA. The area around the town of Smederevo grows a white wine called SMEDEREVKA, similar to CHABLIS from Burgundy. Other celebrated white wines are the FRUSKA GORA, the VRSAC and the SUBOTICA. Elsewhere in Serbia, an indigenous grape, the *Prokupac*, is cultivated. It makes a very good table wine. Macedonia mainly produces ordinary red wines. Yugoslavia also exports wines from Herzegovina: the ZILAVKA, a dry white wine from Kosovo and Metohija. This is known in West Germany as AMSELFELDER SPÄTBURGUNDER.

Since the end of World War II, the establishment of co-operative underground-cellars has done much to improve methods of vinification and wine-storage. Yugoslavian wine (8,800,000 to 11,000,000 gallons per year) is exported mainly to East Germany, Czechoslovakia, Poland and Italy.   B. POGRIMILOVIC

THE SOVIET UNION

Russia is the fifth largest wineproducing country in the world, after Italy, France, Spain and Argentina. Whether it be a good or a bad year, it produces 330 to 396 million gallons of wine. The viticultural zone forms a large semi-circle in the south of the country, stretching from the Rumanian frontier to the borders of Iran, India, Turkestan and Mongolia. However the most important ones are going from the west to the east: Moldavia, the Ukraine, the Crimea, the lower waters of the Don, the Krasnodar region, Russian Georgia and Usbekistan.

Vine culture in these region goes back for many years. Long before the emergence of man, the vine itself existed in a wild state in the land now occupied by the Soviet Union. Russian botanists have discovered on the shores of the Black Sea at least sixty varieties of wild vine, several of which were probably domesticated as far back as the stone age. Viniculture was developed in the bronze age in Georgia at least, where objects dating from this period and representing drinking scenes have been discovered. Much later Homer, Xenophon and Heroditus refer to it in their works.

Moldavia, which was formerly Bessarabia and was part of Rumania, produces mainly table wines. PINOT and ALIGOTÉ are among the white wines, BORDO is a red, no doubt made from the *Cabernet-Sauvignon* of the Bordeaux type. Some Moldavian wines may be found on the markets of Western Europe: the NEGRI DE PURKAR and the CABERNET, both reds, and the FETYSK, a white wine. Ukrainian white wines are made from the *Riesling* and *Aligoté* grapes, the red wines from the *Cabernet* grape variety.

The Crimea has a wide range of wines. Dry white wines are the SEMILLON OREANDA, the RIESLING MASSANDRA and the ALIGOTÉ AY-DANIL. Dry red wines are the CABERNET LIVADIA, the SAPERAVI MASSANDRA, and the BORDO AY-DANIL. There is also a wide range of dessert wines: white, rosé or red. Among the white wines, the mòre celebrated are the MUSCAT MASSANDRA and the MUSCAT LIVADIA, the rosé MUSCAT ALUPKA and, of the reds, the MUSCAT KUCHUK-LAMBAT. The Crimea also produces wines known as PORT, MADEIRA and TOKAY. Of course these wines are named by type, not by origin.

The subtropical climate of Georgia is ideal for cultivating the vine. It produces white wines such as NAPUREOULI and TSINANDALI, and red wines like the MUKUZANI and SAPERAVI which are to be found on sale, for example, in Great Britain.

Armenia, where the vine is said to have originated, produces TOKAY and dessert wines. Uzbekistan, on the border with Iran, has mainly dessert wines, red or white, and port-type wines.

Sparkling wines, whether red or white, such as the TZYMLIANSK and rosé, are produced today by the so-called *en continu* method from the vineyards of the Crimea, Krasnodar and the Kouban valley. The well-known "DONSKI" is a sparkling wine made along the banks of the Don. Sparkling wines made from the *Muscat* grape also deserve a mention.

It is strange but true that the U.S.S.R. produces six times more sweet and dessert wines than dry wines —this is partly because in Russia wine is consumed mainly on festive occasions rather than every day.

WINES OF CENTRAL EUROPE

AUSTRIA

WACHAU

White wines . . . .

Loibener Kaiserwein
Unterloibener Rotenberg
Unterloibener Burgstall
Kremser Kögl
Steiner Goldberg
Kremser Kremsleiten
Kremser Wachtberg

Dürnsteiner Liebenberg
Kremser Pfaffenberg
Steiner Pfaffenberg
Steiner Schreck
Dürnsteiner Hollerin
Dürnsteiner Himmelsstiege
Weissenkirchner Klaus

Weissenkirchner Achleiten
Undhof Wieden-
    Weissburgunder
Weisser Burgunder
Ruländer
Neuburger

Undhof Wieden Spät- und
    Auslese Grüne Veltliner
Dürnsteiner Muskat-Ottonel
Zöbinger Muskat-Ottonel
Sonnenkönig
Heiligensteiner Sauvignon
Undhof Goldberg

Red wines . . . . .

Alter Knabe - Saint Laurent

VIENNA-SÜDBAHN

White wines . . .

Wiener Nussberg
Gumpoldskirchner Spiegel
Gumpoldskirchner Sonnberg
Gumpoldskirchner
    Goldknöpfel
Gumpoldskirchner Rasslerin
Gumpoldskirchner
    Grimmling
Gumpoldskirchner
    Stocknarrn

Klosterneuburger
    Rheinriesling
Nussberger Schwarze Katz
Original Gumpoldskirchner
    Rheinriesling
Neuburger
Neuburger Spät-
    und Auslesen
Badener Lumpentürl-
    Neuburger

Kahlenberger Traminer
Sauvignon
Weisser Burgunder
Klostercabinet
Franzhauser Kabinett-
    Neuburger
Grüner Veltliner
Jungherrn Müller-Thurgau
Königswein Zierfandler
Zierfandler

Kavalier-Zierfandler
Zierfandler Ried Kramer
Gumpoldskirchner
    Zierfandler
Goldknöpferl-Rotgipfler
Rotgipfler Spät- und
    Auslesen
Kreuzweingarten-Spätlese
Zierfandler-Rotgipfler
    Sonnberg
Spätrot-Rotgipfler

Red wines . . . . .

Blauburgunder
Soosser Blauer Burgunder

Saint Laurent
Sooser Blauer Portugieser

Saint-Laurent-Ausstich

Vöslauer Rotwein

BURGENLAND

White wines . . . .

Ruster Greiner
Ruster Satz
Ruster Turner
Ruster Vogelsang
Muskat-Traminer

Ruster Ruländer
Original Joiser Ruländer
Ruster Muskateller
Muskat-Ottonel
Welschriesling-Spätlesen

Original Golser
    Welschriesling
Weisser Storch Ruster
    Welschriesling

Ruster Ausbruch
Müller-Thurgau
    Beerenauslese
Oggauer Ambrosi

Red wines . . . . .

Ruster Baumgarten
Ruster G'märk
Ruster Mittelkräften

Rust Limberger
Ruster Blauburgunder
Blauer Burgunder Spätlese

Oggauer Blaufränkisch
Blaufränkisch
Pöttelsdorfer Bismarckwein

Schützenberger Rotkelch
Blaufränkisch Spätlesen

STEIERMARK

White wines . . . .

Klöcher Berg
Hartberger Ring
Hartberger Löffelbach
Grassnitzberg
Ottenberger Witscheinberg

Köbelberg
Sulztal
Glanzer Berg
Steinbach
Schlossberg

Silberberg
Hochkittenberg
Morillon
Ruländer
Muskateller

Hochbrudersegg
Muskat-Sylvaner
Sausaler Welschriesling
Müller-Thurgau

Red wine . . . . .

Schilcher

CZECHOSLOVAKIA

Furmint   Harchlevelu   Lipouvina   Muskat de Lunel   Muskat Ztly

HUNGARY

White wines . . . .

Tokaji Szamorodni (dry)
Tokaji Furmint

Badacsonyi Kéknyelü
Badacsonyi Szürkebarát

Balatonfüredi
Móri Ezerjó

Debröi Hárslevelü
Léanyka

Red wines . . . . .

Egri Bikavér

Soproni Kékfrankos

Dessert wines . . . .

Tokaji Aszu (3-5 puttonos)

Tokaji Szamorodni (sweet)

WINES OF THE BALKANS

YUGOSLAVIA

White wines	Banatski rizling (Kreaca) — dry Belan — dry Graševina (Italian Riesling) — dry	Grk Malvazija — dry and sweet Maraština — dry and medium-dry Muskat Ottonel — medium-dry and sweet	Pošip — dry Rebula — dry Silvanac — dry and medium-dry Smederevka — dry	Traminac — dry and medium-dry Vugava Žilavka — dry
Rosé wines	Cviček — dry	Opol dalmatinski — dry	Ruzica — dry	
Red wines	Burgundac crni (pinot noir) — dry Dingač — medium-dry Frankovka — dry	Kavčina (Žametna črnica) — dry Kraski teran — dry Kratošija — dry	Muskat ruza (Moscate rosa) — medium-sweet and sweet Plavac — dry Postup — medium-dry	Prokupac — dry and medium-sweet Refošk — dry and medium-sweet Vranac — dry

BULGARIA

White wines	Pomoria Dimiat Preslav Dimiat Tchirpan Dimiat	Varna Dimiat Euxinograd Hemona	Songurlaré Misket Liaskovetz Riesling	Riesling of the Valley of Roses
Red wines	Chipka Novosseltzi Gamza Pavlikeni Gamza	Soukhindol Gamza Kalouger Kramolin	Loud Guidia Assénovgrad Mavroud Melnik	Pamid Pirgovo
Dessert wines	Bisser Hebros	Kadarka "Valley of Roses" Vratza Misket	Pomoria Slavianka	Tarnovo Varna

ROUMANIA

White wines	Dealul Mare Diosig Drâgâsani	Husi Murfatlar Muscel	Nicoresti Teremia-Tomnatic-Comlos Valea lui Mihai	Valea Târnavelor Cotnar
Red wines	Sarica-Niculitel	Cotnar		

WINES OF THE SOVIET UNION

White wines of the Crimea	Aligoté Ay-Danil Riesling Massandra	Riesling Alkadar	Semillon Oreanda
White wines of Krasnodar	Riesling Abraou	Riesling Anapa	
White wines of Georgia	Gurdjurni Manadis Mukuzani	Myshako Riesling Mzvane	Napureouli Tsinandali
Red wines of Azerbaidjan	Chemakha	Kurdamir	Matrassa
Red wines of the Crimea	Bordo Ay-Danil	Cabernet Livadia	Saperavi Massandra
Red wines of Krasnodar	Cabernet Abraou		

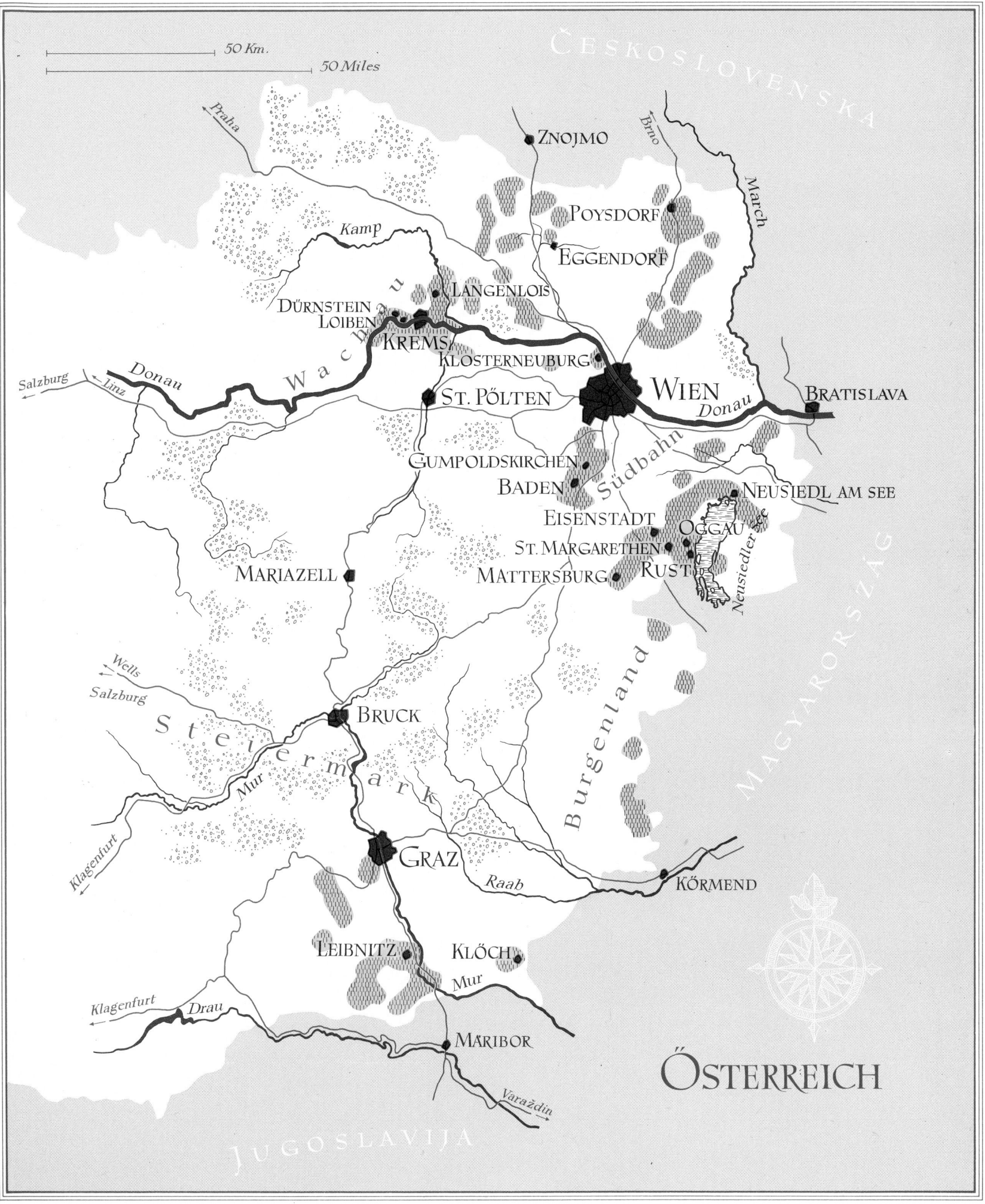

ČESKOSLOVENSKA

Praha

Brno

March

ZNOJMO

POYSDORF

EGGENDORF

Kamp

LANGENLOIS

DÜRNSTEIN
LOIBEN

Wachau

KREMS

KLOSTERNEUBURG

WIEN

BRATISLAVA

Salzburg — Linz — Donau

Donau

ST. PÖLTEN

GUMPOLDSKIRCHEN

Südbahn

BADEN

NEUSIEDL AM SEE

EISENSTADT

OGGAU

ST. MARGARETHEN

Neusiedler See

MARIAZELL

MATTERSBURG

RUST

Burgenland

MAGYARORSZÁG

Wells
Salzburg

S t e i e r m a r k

Klagenfurt

BRUCK

Mur

GRAZ

Raab

KÖRMEND

Klagenfurt

LEIBNITZ

KLÖCH

Mur

Klagenfurt

Drau

MARIBOR

Varaždin

ÖSTERREICH

JUGOSLAVIJA

50 Km.

50 Miles

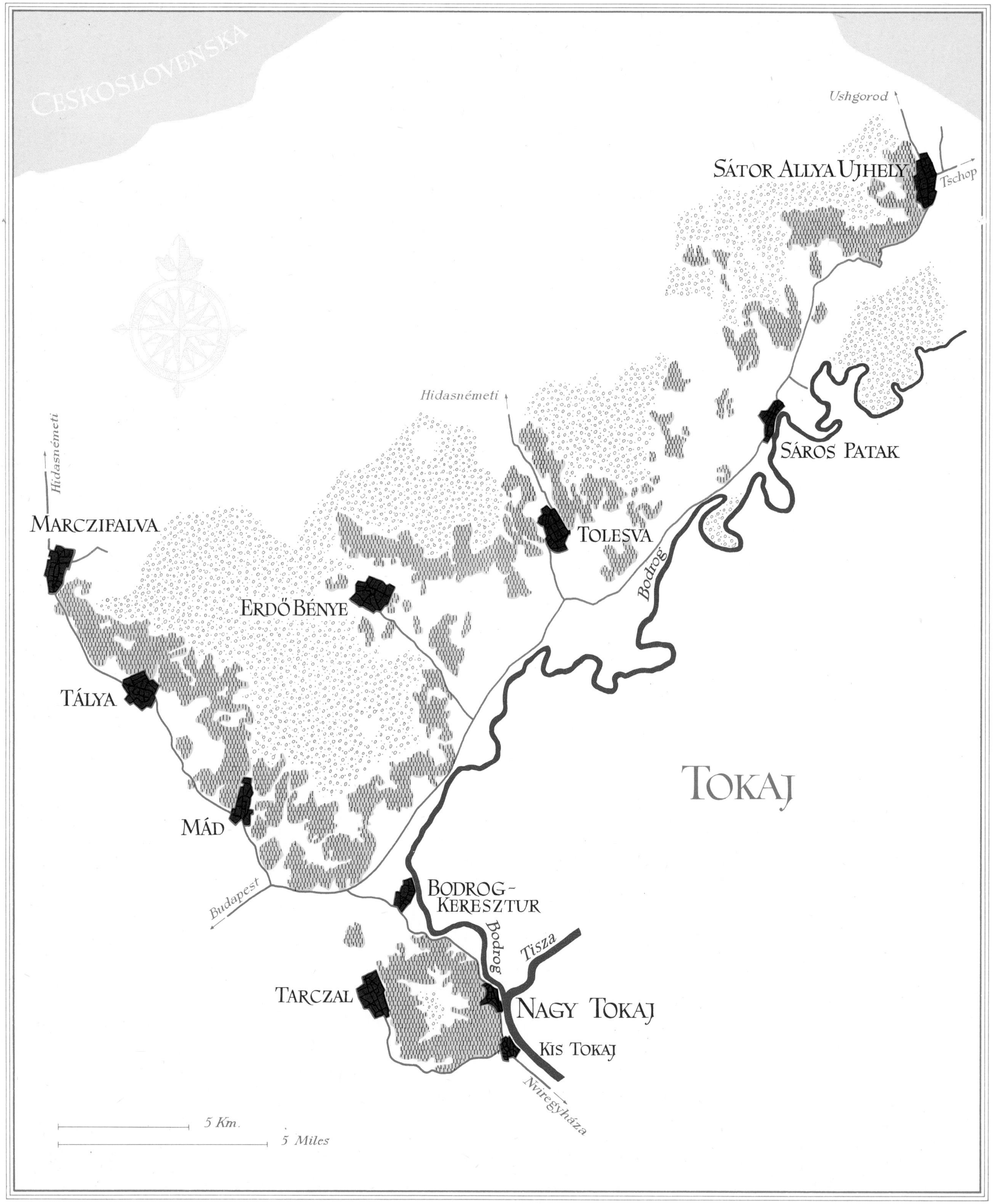

CESKOSLOVENSKA

Ushgorod

SÁTOR ALLYA UJHELY

Tschop

Hidasnémeti

SÁROS PATAK

MARCZIFALVA

Hidasnémeti

TOLESVA

Bodrog

ERDŐ BÉNYE

TÁLYA

TOKAJ

MÁD

Budapest

BODROG-
KERESZTUR

Bodrog

Tisza

TARCZAL

NAGY TOKAJ

KIS TOKAJ

Nyiregyháza

5 Km.

5 Miles

THE WINES OF THE EASTERN MEDITERRANEAN

JOSEPH JOBÉ

All the countries of the Eastern Mediterranean basin have cultivated the vine since ancient times. The Egypt of the Pharaohs, the Promised Land of the Hebrews, the vast Persian Empire as well as the ancient Greek cities all produced wine. Under the benevolent eyes of the gods, the poets sang its praises, artisans and artists immortalized it on bas-reliefs and frescoes. The aged Homer celebrated "wine that gives us a manly heart"; Archilochus put the following truculent lines into the mouth of a galley-slave:

> One cannot mount guard
> While dying of thirst

The gentle Anachreon had a more melancholy turn of phrase:

> When I drink wine
> My pain is driven away
> And my dark thoughts
> Fly to the ocean winds

Like an echo come the words from the Book of Proverbs (xxxi, 6-7): "Give strong drink unto him that is ready to perish, and wine unto those that be of heavy hearts. Let him drink, and forget his poverty, and remember his misery no more."

When paganism gave way to Christianity the people of the Mediterranean basin continued to cultivate the vine and to produce wine right up to the Moslem era.

The later history of the vine in these regions may be explained in part by the ebb and flow of Christianity and Islam. Even today, Moslem influence is predominant in Egypt and Jordan; it is also felt in Moslem Turkey and, more surprisingly, in Christian Greece through the marketing of a considerable part of the vine-harvest, not as wine but as dried grapes or raisins (more than a hundred thousand tons are produced per year in each country).

After World War I, cultivation of the vine in this part of the world increased at a phenomenal rate. The surface under cultivation in Greece multiplied fifteenfold and production of wine rose ten times. Cyprus, on the other hand, made somewhat slower progress. But in Turkey, between 1939 and 1966, the number of vineyards doubled and wine production rose by four times. The evolution of the vineyard in Israel shows remarkable variations: the area under cultivation rose from 30,000 acres in 1936 to 45,000 acres in 1946, only to decrease in 1948 to 13,500 acres, rising again between 1956 and 1966 to 25,000 acres. However, despite these fluctuations, the actual production of wine has been constantly on the increase. From 506,000 gallons in 1936 it rose to 8,095,120 gallons in 1966. This means that from approximately the same area of vines as were under cultivation in 1936, sixteen times as much wine was being produced 30 years later. Egypt and the Lebanon have also increased their viticultural areas and their production of wine, but to a lesser degree. At present Egypt produces about 990,000 gallons and the Lebanon 836,000 gallons of wine; these are negligible amounts in comparison with the large viticultural regions of France. The Greeks and the Cypriots are, needless to say, the heaviest wine-drinkers of all these peoples.

GREECE

In Greece, vineyards and wine are as old as the gods, the land and the poets. Dionysus cultivated the vine and Homer sang the praises of wine in the Iliad and the Odyssey. More important still, the Greeks transplanted the vine to their colonies. Thus it is that many famous vineyards like those of Sicily, Malaga, Jerez and the Rhône valley are of Greek origin.

The present viticultural area is 500,000 acres which produce 83,600,000 gallons of wine, 150,000 tons of dessert grapes and as many dried grapes. The Greek likes his wine, and drinks about 50 to 70 pints a year. The country exports nearly 11,000,000 gallons a year.

The Peloponnese is the most important viticultural region. Its wines are mentioned on most wine-lists in hotels. They are dry white wines, such as the DEMESTICHA, the SANTO HELENA, the ANTIKA or the SANTA

"Let us drink wine, the wine of noble Bacchus; when we drink it our troubles sleep." The words of the Greek lyricist Anachreon convey exactly the spirit of this scene decorating an antique vase.

LAOURA. The Peloponnese vineyard may be divided into three regions. The central part produces a well-balanced white wine, the MANTINEIA, around the ruins of the same name. The Patras region produces excellent dessert wines, such as the MAVRODAPHNE (red) or the MUSCAT DE PATRAS (white). In the third part, along the banks of the Gulf of Corinth and in particular at Nemea, a red full-bodied wine is made, the NEMEA or the HIGH NEMEA, depending on the altitude of the vineyard; these start at sea-level and reach up to about 2,500 feet in the interland.

On the mainland, Attica, already a land of wines and olives in ancient times, today produces a whole range of white wines made from the *Saviatiano* grape. The PALLINI is the best wine in these parts, though it is not the best-known. Attica is also famous for its RETSINA, which in the opinion of many is the best wine in the land. The tourist who likes to taste the local wines will find something to satisfy his curiosity almost everywhere. For the benefit of those who visit the beautiful ruins of the site dedicated to Apollo, there is the wine of Arakhova, a village near Delphi. Macedonia offers the best red wine, NAOUSSA, made from the *Popolka* grape which is also known as the *Noir de Naoussa*. Thessalia has two red wines, the RAPSANI and the AMBELAKIA; Epirus makes only one semi-sweet white wine, the ZITSA.

The soil and climate of the Greek islands are usually favourable to the vine, and nearly every island has its own vineyard. Crete, for example, has a very important growth. In the east, there are fortified red table wines, wines of substance though not much spirit, made from the *Leatiko* grape; farther west, the Heraklion region produces red wines made from the *Ketsifali* and *Mandilari* grape varieties; these are full-bodied, rich wines with a heavy bouquet. At the farthest point west, in the region of Canea, only the red grape *Romeikon* is cultivated. On the other hand, the little island of Santonni is very fertile thanks to its volcanic soil, and produces such dry white wines as the NYCHTERI or sweet white wines like the VINO SANTO. The island of Samos offers a whole range of white wines, dry wines, resinated wines and sweet dessert wines, known as MUSCAT DE SAMOS. The islands of Rhodes and Zakinthos also have dry white wines, while the island of Leucadia produces red wines.

Greece is, of course, also the country of the RETSINA, a wine which has a very special taste. It is a bitter taste, acquired by flavouring the wine with resin during the process of fermentation. The resin comes from a pine-tree—the *calitris quadrivalvis*—which grows in that region. As the RETSINA takes on a bitter taste only after it has aged one year, those who are tasting it for the first time are advised to try a youthful RETSINA, preferably from the Attica area; the resin flavour is not to the liking of all visitors.

Well-known and highly thought of are the dessert wines of Greece, starting perhaps with the MUSCAT DE SAMOS already mentioned, and going on to the MAVRODAPHNI, a very sweet red wine, a type of Malaga. We might also mention that the *Malvasia*, or Malmsey grape, originated in Peloponnisos. Today, the grape can be found in many other countries, Italy, France, Spain and Madeira for instance, where it has adapted well to local conditions and gives excellent white wines.

Greece can legitimately be proud of its viticultural history—was not Homer, 2,800 years ago, already singing the praises of the wine of his country? "There is no moment more pleasurable than when the guests, sitting around a well-laden table, lend their ear to the voice of a singer, whilst the cup-bearer, having drawn wine from the amphoras, moves round the table to pour into each and every cup in turn."

CYPRUS

Thanks to its privileged geographical situation, Cyprus not only cultivated the vine at a very early date but participated throughout ancient times in the flourishing wine trade between Egypt, Greece and Rome. After the fall of the Roman Empire in the west in A.D. 476, there followed a long night of seven centuries for the vine.

The Crusaders and the Knights Templars were responsible for the revival of viniculture in Cyprus. But again, when the Turks arrived in 1571, the vine suffered another period of neglect although it did not disappear completely. It survived in the south-west part of the isle on the sunny slopes of Mounts Troghodhus and Makhera. From the grapes which grow in these parts, the Cypriot winegrowers make mainly ordinary table wines: red full-bodied wines, with a high tannin content, such as AFAMES and OTHELLO. There are fewer white wines. The driest and the best are APHRODITE and ANSINOE. A rosé, KOKKINELLI, is a fresh, semi-sweet wine, although it is somewhat darker in colour than most rosés. The best Cypriot wine is a dessert wine called COMMANDARIA. Named after the Knights Templars who guarded the Temple of Colossus, it is made from white or red grapes, specially dried in order to increase their sugar content. Usually the red grapes are used as they are more abundant. Only about twenty villages (Kalokhono, Zoopiyi, Yerass, Ayias and Mancas are the better known) are authorized to produce COMMANDARIA, and experts can distinguish the qualities which each village gives to the COMMANDARIA just as a connoisseur of Burgundy can tell from which particular vineyard along the Côte de Nuits or Beaune the Burgundy he is tasting has come.

Cyprus exports a good third of its wines, in particular red wines and COMMANDARIA.

As a final point of interest, one should mention that it was vine-shoots from Cyprus that produced, in the fifteenth century, the first Madeira wine.

TURKEY

If one believes, as many do, that Anatolia is the mother-country of the European vine, then Turkey has indeed a long heritage of viticulture. For as long as there were non-Moslem peoples living within the Turkish frontiers in Europe, there were Turkish wines for sale on the domestic and foreign markets. At the beginning of the twentieth century, following a period of political unrest, wine production went into a steep decline, but the whole picture changed with the establishment in 1928 of a Monopolies Board. From its lowest ebb in 1928 of 590,000 gallons, production reached 9,556,000 gallons in 1966. However, only 2 to 3 per cent of the grapes grown are used to make wine. Turkey has white wines *(beyez)* and red wines *(kirmizi)* which are found mainly in Thrace and along the shores of the Sea of Marmara, in Izmir (Smyrna) and in Anatolia. The best of the dry white wines usually come from the *Hasandede, Narince* and *Emir* grape varieties. The best red wines are made from the *Oküzgüzö-bogazkere, Papaskarasin* and *Kalecikkarasi* grape varieties; these wines have a very dark colour.

Well known on the international market is BUZBAG, a wine from Anatolia made from the *Bogazkere* grape, and TRAKYA, a dry red or white wine from the European part of Turkey. Sweden imports BEYAZ, a semi-dry white wine, which comes from Tekirdag in Thrace.

Other wines of quality are the red ADABAG and KALEBAG. The Turks like sweet wines and the term "sarap" on a label indicates a very sweet wine, too sweet for the Western palate. Among the best of the dessert wines can be named the TEKEL GAZIANTEP and the TEKEL KALEBAG ANKARA, which are both red wines, and a white wine the TEKEL MISBAG IZMIR. There are also some ordinary local wines: for example, in Istanbul there is the GÜZEL MARMARA, either a red or a white dry or semi-dry wine; Ankara has the GÜZELBAG, which is also either a red or dry or semi-dry white wine; Izmir produces the IZMIR, once again a red or dry white wine and from Central Anatolia comes both red and white ÇUBUK.

ISRAEL

The Bible attests that the people of Israel cultivated the vine. If ever a cluster of grapes was famous, it is surely the one brought back by the Hebrew scouts from Canaan. And if there ever was a famous drunkard, albeit an involuntary one, it is certainly Noah.

In the same way that Palestine has a turbulent history, so too was the history of its viticulture, for the vine was destroyed by some, replanted by others; reintroduced by the Crusaders, only to be finally abandoned for many centuries.

When the first Zionists started to filter into Palestine around 1882, they planted, on the advice of the Rothschilds, French vine-plants. With time, the surface under cultivation increased, and today it reaches about 25,000 acres. Vineyards which produce grapes for making wine are planted in different regions of the country stretching from the south to the north: in the Negev, along the coast-line and on the foothills of Judea, in the mountains around Jerusalem, in the Sharon valley, on the hills of Samaria as well as in Upper and Lower Galilee. The average rainfall varies from 8 inches a year in the Negev to 27 inches in the mountains of Upper Galilee.

The *Cargnan* (41 per cent) and the *Alicante Grenache* (32 per cent) are the most common grape varieties. The winegrowers and viticultural co-operatives produce every conceivable type of wine, even sparkling Champagne-like wine made by the *méthode champenoise*. To name a few: The AVDAT WHITE (dry) and the CARMEL HOCK (semi-dry) are white wines; the MIKWE ISRAIL (dry) and the ADOM ATIC (semi-dry) are red wines, and the BINAYMINA is a rosé. There are also some white dessert wines (MUSCATEL) or reds (INDEPENDENCE WINE). Annual production reaches a total of about 7,920,000 gallons of which about 330,000 are for export.

An Israeli drinks only seven to nine pints of wine a year but he eats 26 to 28 pounds of table grapes.

The viticultural area in the neighbouring countries of Syria, the Lebanon and Jordan is much larger than in Israel. But as these three countries are of the Moslem faith, the produce of their vineyards is marketed, locally or abroad, in the form of table grapes or dried grapes; very little is made into wine. Jordan produces from 22,000 to 330,000 gallons of wine; Syria about 550,000 gallons, and the Lebanon 836,000 gallons, while the State of Israel produces more than five times as much from an area which is ten times smaller than that of her three neighbours put together. There is also a small vineyard in Iran, in the Azerbaijan and Teheran regions. Kurdistan is noted for its wine which on pressing acquires the scent of violets. Even in the best years, however, this country does not produce more than 88,000 gallons of wine.

EGYPT

The paintings on the tombs of the Pharaohs bear witness to the antiquity of the vine in this country (see page 12). However, after the arrival of the Arabs on the scene, vine cultivation fell into a decline, and wines became either very rare or very bad. Towards the beginning of this century, however, the vines were replanted, and after thirty years of hard work, Egyptian wines have once again found their qualities of yesteryear. And even if Egypt does not figure in many books on viticulture and wine, nor is usually referred to in statistical data, the country of the Pharaohs nonetheless produces each year an average of about 990,000 gallons of wine, and excellent wine at that.

The Maryat region, west of the Nile delta, was already famous for its wine in ancient times: Cleopatra offered Caesar a wine from Mareotide when he came to pay her a visit. This region produces two white wines, the CLOS MARIOUT and the CRUS DES PTOLÉMÉES, as well as a red wine, the CLOS MATAMIR.

As Egypt is a Moslem country, its consumption of wine is very low and its imports are negligible. A third of its production is exported.

WINES OF GREECE

DRY WHITE WINES

Agrylos	Gerania	Lindos de Rhodes	Pallini	Verdes
Arcadia	King Minos	Mantineia	Samos	Votrys
Demesticha	Lefkas	Marco	Santa Helena	Ymettos
Peza				Santa Laoura

MEDIUM-SWEET WHITE WINES

Gerania	Pallini	Samos	Zitsa

SWEET WHITE WINES

Samos	Muscat Rion de Patras	Muscat de Limnos	Paros	Rhodes Kair (or Chevalier
Muscat de Samos	Muscat Achaïa de Patras	Vino Santo de Santorin	Pilion	de Rhodes)
Muscat de Rhodes				Ymettos

DRY RED WINES

Agrylos	Halkidiki	Demesticha	Lefkas	Nadussa
Archanès	Castel Danielis	Peza	Marco	Nemea

SWEET RED WINE

Mavrodaphni

SPARKLING WINE

Zitsa

WINES OF ISRAEL

DRY WHITE WINES

Askalon Blanc 1963	Avdat White	Binyamina Blanc	Ein Guedi White	Mikwe Israel Blanc

MEDIUM-DRY WHITE WINES

Carmel Hock	Doron	Ein Guedi	Hock d'Askalon	Hock Patron

DESSERT WINES

Ashdod	Golden Cream	Muscat Supérieur	Muscatel - 19°	Topaz Ein Guedi

ROSÉ WINES

Binyamina Rosé	Mikwe Israel	Pink (dry)	Rose of Carmel (medium-dry)	Vin Rosé d'Askalon

DRY RED WINES

Arad	Avdat Red	Ben-Ami 1965	Binyamina Red	Mikwe Israel

MEDIUM-DRY RED WINES

Adom Atic	Askalon Rouge 1965	Château Binyamina	Ein Guedi Red	Mont Rouge

DESSERT WINES

Château Richon Red	Hadar	Mikwe Israel-Dessert	Porath Atic	Poria
Ein Guedi Red Wine	Independence Wine			

WINES OF CYPRUS

DRY WHITE WINES	RED WINES	ROSÉ WINES	DESSERT WINES
Aphrodite	Cyprus	Othello	Commandaria
Arsinoe	Afames	Kokkineli	Muscat de Chypre

WINES OF EGYPT

RED WINES

Clos Mariout   Cru des Ptolémées

WHITE WINES

Clos Matamir

WINES OF TURKEY

DRY WHITE WINES

Barbaros	Doluca	Kulüp beyaz	Merih	Tekel ürgüp
Diren	Kalebag	Marmara Incisi	Quakaya yildizi	Trakya

MEDIUM-DRY WHITE WINES

Beyaz   Narbag

SWEET WHITE WINES

Tekez Misbag izmir   Adabag

RED WINES

Buzbag   Kalebag   Kulüp   Merih   Trakya   Yakut Damcasi

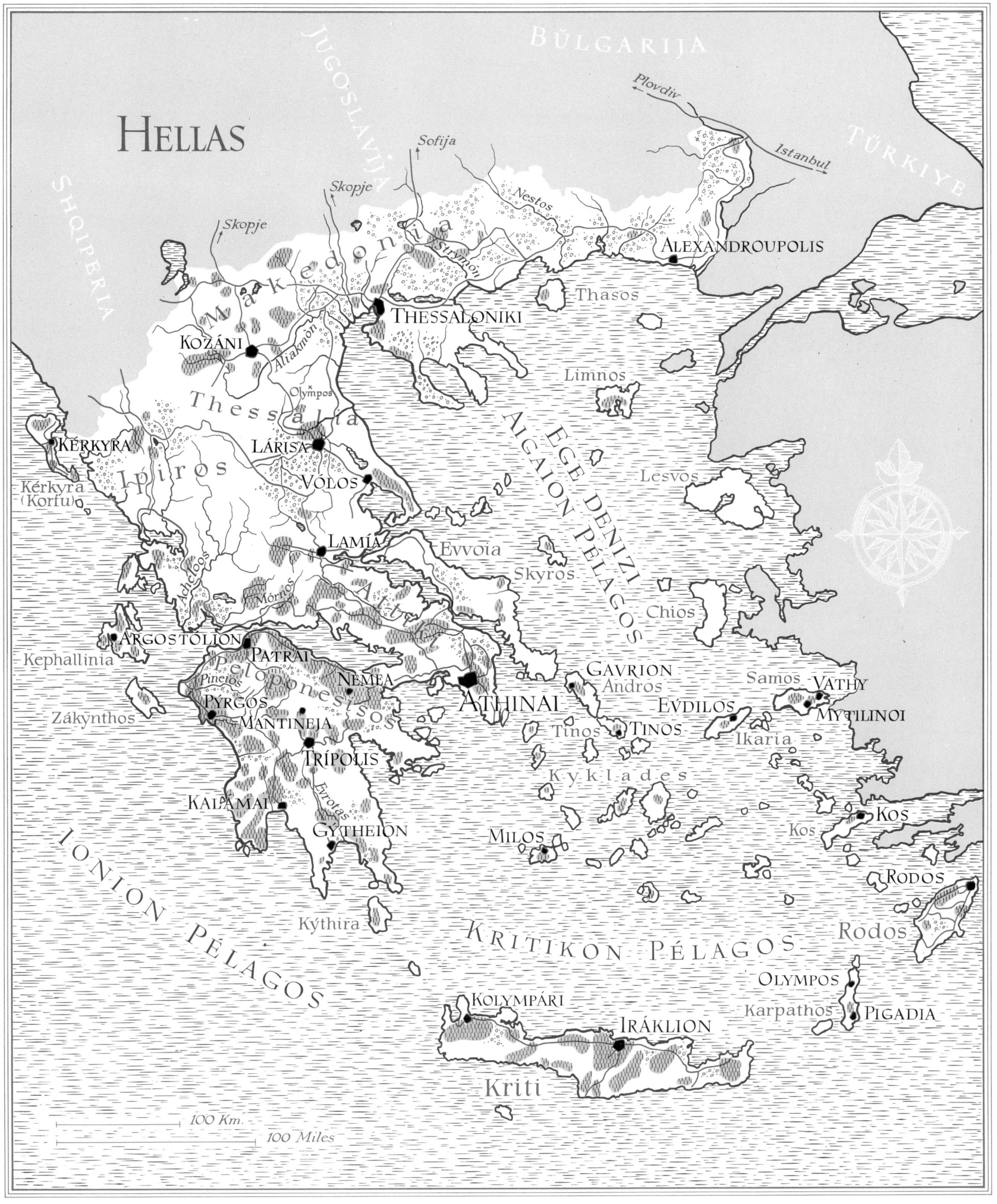

HELLAS

SHQIPËRIA

JUGOSLAVIJA

BŬLGARIJA

TÜRKIYE

Skopje →

Sofija →

Skopje

Plovdiv →

Istanbul →

Nestos

ALEXANDROUPOLIS

Makedonija

Strimón

THESSALONIKI

Thasos

KOZÁNI

Aliakmón

Limnos

Thessalia

Olympos

KÉRKYRA

LÁRISA

Lesvos

Ipiros

VÓLOS

Kérkyra
(Kérku)

EGĒ DENIZI
AIGAION PÉLAGOS

LAMÍA

Evvoia

Akhelóos

Skyros

Mórnos

Chios

Aitō...

ARGOSTÓLION

Peloponnisos

PATRAI

Kephallinia

Pineiós

NEMEA

GAVRION

Andros

Samos

VATHY

PÝRGOS

ATHINAI

EVDILOS

MYTILINOI

Zákynthos

MANTINEJA

Tinos

TINOS

Ikaria

TRÍPOLIS

Kyklades

Evrotas

KALÁMAI

KOS

GYTHEION

Kos

MILOS

RODOS

IONION PÉLAGOS

Kýthira

KRITIKON PÉLAGOS

Rodos

OLYMPOS

Karpathos

PIGADIA

KOLYMPÁRI

IRÁKLION

Kriti

100 Km.

100 Miles

THE WINES OF AFRICA

DENIS BOUVIER and KENNETH MAXWELL

NORTH AFRICA

In the nature of its soil and its climate as much as the affinity of its distant past to Latin antiquity, North Africa resembles much more closely the European shores of the Western Mediterranean than the rest of the African continent. The Africans themselves, in fact, call it *djezira el Maghreb,* meaning "the Western Isle". The vine, like some messenger running ahead to announce the arrival of Mediterranean civilization, first saw life in the south, on the spurs of the mountains of Daïa, at the very doors of the Sahara. On this side, towards the north, begins the outer desert, which girdles the Mediterranean. From east to west, the vine runs along the coastal plains, up the hillsides and on the mountains, up to an altitude of about 3,600 feet, stretching from Kelibia in Tunisia as far as Bou Assida in Atlantic Morocco.

Here, as elsewhere, the vine has periodically appeared and disappeared throughout its history. There are many reasons for this, among them the continuous rivalries of nomadic and non-nomadic peoples, the conflicts between Christianity and Islam, and—nearer to our own times—the compelling demands of changing economics and politics.

No trace remains today to show whether the vine existed before the arrival of the Tyrians, who came to found Carthage. It is more than likely that they planted it themselves, in the valley of Medjerdah, before developing it further in their coastal colonies of

Northern Africa. But it was Rome who first undertook to colonize this province of Africa which she had taken over from Carthage. The legions sent by Caesar and later by Augustus put to good use their talents as builders, farmers and winegrowers. From Carthage, restored from its ashes, to Lixus, near today's Larache in Morocco, where legend has situated the Garden of the Hesperides, the very end of their world, Rome turned Mauritania into the cellar of its empire. The vine grew near the ports or, farther inland, on the slopes around Roman farms such as we see, for example, on the mosaics of Tabarka. This wine of Africa, so much appreciated in Rome, was equally appreciated in Byzantium, which gave a new impulse to the vine by converting the Berber tribes to Christianity and so spreading the influence of wine right into the mountainous regions of the Atlas.

This agricultural and vinicultural life, however, had soon to give way to a pastoral existence when the Moslem hordes from Arabia undertook, in the seventh century, to conquer North Africa and convert its people to Islam. The former Roman Empire fell then into total chaos. The winegrowing gave way before the increasing, often forced conversion to Islam of the Christian or Israelite populations, and the vine was almost totally wiped out. It would be a mistake, nevertheless, to believe that as a result of the many fights inside the country and the invasions which followed each other, all contact ceased between the Maghreb and Christian Europe. There still existed in the Algeria of the tenth century nearly 40 cathedral cities, and there is every reason to think that cultivation including that of the vine was continued around them. In other regions more under Arab influence, as in Tunisia, Christian colonies began to spring up after the Eighth Crusade and, although they were very much spread out, wine trading could be established by Tunis between these colonies and Marseilles. In the *fondouk* of Tunis—the fondouk being the walled area reserved for Europeans outside a Moslem town—wine was sold both wholesale and retail, using hall-marked measures. In this way, the "presence" of wine was maintained, incredible as it may seem in a period when Christianity was finding itself in an almost continuous battle with Islam.

This presence was maintained until the arrival of the Turkish sultan's Janissaries who, in their turn, stained the history of the Maghreb with blood. Winegrowing died out rapidly, to revive only at the beginning of the eighteenth century. At this time, and notably in Tunisia during the Hussein Dynasty, a more settled way of life developed: the stone-built house reconquered the ground where previously nomads had pitched their tents. A few vineyards were recreated then, chiefly for consumption of the fruit: Tunisia possessed more than 5,000 acres of vines before the French began administrating the land.

The first colonists to follow the conquest into this land cared little about this local cultivation, although a few did take the risk of trying to produce wine in the African climate and with methods not yet adapted to local conditions. They soon ran into the problem of the musts, for in Mediterranean North Africa autumn is still a hot season. The temperature of the winemaking plants is still very high, fermentation takes place too rapidly, and the quality of the wine suffers. Several factors, however, contributed later to the development of this winegrowing, notably the arrival from 1871 on of settlers from Alsace and Lorraine, after the Franco-Prussian War. Others followed who had been defeated at home by the phylloxera epidemic of 1880. They came from all the vineyards of France, bringing with them a wide variety of vine-plants which they were able to exploit fully on this immense land, in a climate ideal for viticulture. To this could be added the opportunity of winning the French mainland market, where phylloxera had wiped out entire harvests. These winegrowers seized the chance of increasing the volume of production, both in Algeria and in Tunisia. But soon, the situation changed. In France, the vineyards were replanted with phylloxera-resistant American stock, while North Africa saw the disease reach its own shores, although its spread was quickly stopped. France thus found herself, within a very few years, in possession of two important winegrowing regions, and it became essential to take steps to prevent a dangerous over-production. Vines producing only an ordinary wine were uprooted on a large scale. Fortunately, the Algerian wines—heavy, full-bodied, richly-coloured—harmoniously complemented the lighter and more acid wines of Languedoc-Roussillon of southern France. A permanent organization to export Algerian blending wines to France could thus be established. The North African vineyard was modernized and developed; the wines improved in quality, thanks also to planting new vines such as *Alicante-Bouschet*, *Cinsault*, *Carignan*, *Clairette* and *Grenache*. Better methods of vinification, more suited to the climate, were also introduced.

From 1919 to 1955, the North African vineyard progressed by leaps and bounds. Cultivation methods were rationalized and winegrowing became an industry, with increased mechanization, new transport and modern distribution methods. Even the actual vinification was now viewed as an industrial operation: the work, from the harvest to the bottling, was simplified to a maximum degree to make up for a lack of qualified labour. Some care was taken, too, to train the local inhabitants as vineyards workers by giving them agricultural instruction in specialized centres. While this effort was only limited in scope, a number of local winegrowers, in Oran especially, began to cultivate the vine for wineproduction, and began selling their produce, either direct to the market, or through the numerous agricultural co-operatives.

It is true that troubles due to over-production were never lacking and rivalry never disappeared in the various parts of the Mediterranean. But North Africa had acquired, with its vineyards, a new-found economic dimension of considerable importance.

Can one now look at the future of the North African vineyard more optimistically, after all the political upheavals which Morocco, Tunisia and Algeria have seen in turn? While that question perhaps cannot be answered yet, it would seem that wine production can be kept up provided two main conditions are borne in mind. The first is that the vines must not monopolize land in areas where the government would like to develop food production or industry. The second is that wine exports to foreign markets must be solidly covered by bilateral agreements with European countries and, more particularly, with France. This latter point clearly demonstrates how closely the North African viticultural industry is linked to and indeed controlled by economic and political contingencies.

TUNISIA

When one looks at a map of the Mediterranean around Tunisia, the little port of Kelibia appears like an island, surrounded by the sea on one side and by fields of olives and vines on the other. It is the first vineyard one meets in Tunisia when arriving from the east. Its wine grapes, *Muscat d'Alexandrie*, give a wine full of savour, as if impregnated with the perfumes of the Orient. But one must reach Carthage to be really in the heart of the great Tunisian vineyard. Here some Punic sculptor of long-ago has cut wine-grapes into the stonework of a monument to the goddess Tanit. In its modern form, this vineyard of 111,200 acres is the work of European colonists. To supplement the few local vines of table grapes spread along the coast, new vine-plants were introduced, such as *Grenache, Carignan, Alicante-Bouschet, Mourvèdre, Morastel, Vocéra, Pinot Noir* for red wines, and *Pedro-Ximenez, Sémillon, Sauvignon, Clairette de Provence, Beldi, Ugni, Merseguera, Muscat d'Alexandrie* and *Terracina* for whites.

The Tunisian vineyard, hit by phylloxera only in 1936, faced ten catastrophic years from 1943 to 1953. It managed to make a fresh start with regular expansion of production, despite the departure of many European winegrowers after Tunisia's Declaration of Independence in 1956. Today, 900 small concerns have regrouped themselves into well-equipped co-operatives; the cellars can hold more than ten million gallons of a wine which, thanks to the care given it by qualified workers, can be of a very good quality. But this already considerable stock of wine could be doubled, even tripled, for the French market, which is still the main customer. Home consumption of wine is dropping and new commercial outlets are urgently needed.

Going from west to east, the Tunisian vineyard is located in the regions of Bizerte, Mateur and Raf-Raf in the north; Tebourba, Massicault, Sedjourni and Carthage around Tunis; Khanguet, Grombalia, Bou Arkoub, Bir Drassen and Kelibia on Cape Bon. It thus forms a giant crescent around the Gulf of Tunis. Farther south, there are smaller vineyards, those of the Gulf of Hammamet and Zaghouan in the north, and Thibar at the foot of the Teboursouk mountains in the Caidate of the same name.

Tunisian law protects three types of wine. First of all, the VIN SUPÉRIEUR DE TUNISIE, a red, rosé or white wine with an alcohol content of 11º to 13º, depending on the region and the yield, and aged at least one year. Muscat is next, either with a simple *appellation d'origine* MUSCAT DE TUNISIE, or else with an *appellation d'origine contrôlée*, in which case it is sold under the name of the commune where it was produced, such as MUSCAT DE RADÈS or MUSCAT DE THIBAR. Finally, there are the vintage wines, with an *appellation d'origine contrôlée* but where the name of the vine does not appear, such as RADÈS and KELIBIA.

Most Tunisian wines are exported, but one can sample on the spot and with much pleasure a good SAINT-CYPRIEN or a THIBAR from the St. Joseph property.

ALGERIA

The colonization of Algeria was certainly responsible for the proper exploitation of its soil, the development of techniques for production, vinification and sale of their wines, all of which have placed Algeria among leading wineproducing countries.

Seven years after it gained its independence, the young state has kept alive its viticulture, despite the departure of its qualified European workers and the consequent disappearance of its non-Moslem domestic market. All honour to the nation. It is in any case absolutely essential for Algeria to maintain its viticulture: more than 50 per cent agricultural employment comes from the vineyards. The latter are in an even more important position when one realizes that not only do they produce the wine which provides, when sold, half of Algeria's total exports and cargoes for her merchant ships, the vineyards also supply the raw materials for a number of industries born of vinicultural side-products, such as the manufacture of alcohol, tartrates, oil, fertilizers and fodder. This trade requires costly and extensive equipment and installations, and the economic and social importance of the vini-viticultural production becomes even clearer. The government thus has not only the first preoccupation of making sure this colonial heritage produces profitably, but they must at the same time increase professional training and put a brake on the exodus from the countryside, which has been noticeable since 1962. A certain preference can understandably be seen, however, in favour of the conversion of the viticultural regions to cultivation of some product more independent of the French market, for the shipments of wine are at present only saleable in the former mother country, and the government must remember also that these sales are made thanks largely to commercial agreements which French vintners would be only too happy to see go.

The Algerian vineyard lies between La Calle in the east and Nemours (today called Ghazaouet) in the west, extending also from north to south, from the shores of the Mediterranean to the slopes of the Atlas upper plateau. Its total area is about 865,000 acres but its distribution has no uniformity, for Algeria is a very undulating land.

Apart from a few plants of local origin (*Hasseroum, Grilla, Farhana*), all the vine-plants grown in Algeria come from Europe, and have been grafted with American stocks to combat phylloxera. The red wines are usually wines for blending, full-bodied, with a high alcohol content and a good deal of tannin, although they can also be good vintage wines classified as of superior quality, or given a simple *appellation d'origine*. They come from vine-plants such as *Carignan, Cinsault, Alicante-Bouschet, Morastel, Mourvèdre, Gamay, Pinot Noir* and *Cabernet*. The white wines, which are usually of good quality, full-bodied, rather perfumed, and well alcoholized, come from plants such as *Clairette, Grenache, Ugni Blanc, Faramon, Macabéo* and *Merseguera*, although *Alicante* or *Cinsault* are also used. The climate, the nature of the soil, the exposure to the sun and type of vine-plant all have the usual influence on the wine produced, but here the altitude of the vineyards appears to play a particularly important role. The wines of the plain are usually light and do not keep well; the wines from the mountains are usually full-bodied, rich, heavy and thick, and the wines of the slopes, between the plains and the mountains, are of an intermediate type, fine, lively and with a delicate bouquet. Annual yield is about 198,000,000 gallons.

EASTERN ALGERIA

DEPARTMENT OF ANNABA (BÔNE). Coming in from Tunisia by the Medjerdah Valley, one meets the first mountain vineyards around Souk Ahras, at an altitude of about 2,100 feet. Their wine is supple but full-bodied, with a good colour. Continuing west from Souk Ahras on towards Medjez Sfa, one enters the Wadi Seybouse which leads, northwards, to the Bône plain and, westwards, to the region of Guelma. There are some very fine vineyards here, stretched along the flanks of the valley at an altitude varying between 300 and 900 feet, near Guelma, Heliopolis and Petit. They produce full-bodied but supple wines with a slightly earthy tang. Up towards Bône itself, vines are much rarer and one must edge over to Aïn Mokra, west of Seybouse Valley, to find them again, or else run eastwards along the valley to La Calle, where the wine is clean-tasting, light and with a good body.

DEPARTMENTS OF CONSTANTINE, BATNA AND SÉTIF. Returning from the Wadi Seybouse and following, beyond Guelma, the Wadi Bou Hamdane and the Wadi Zenati, the traveller passes the Kroub to reach Constantine in the north, and Lambèse and Batna in the south. The region just around Constantine produces excellent wines, those of Lambèse and Batna being rather more full-bodied and supple. Beyond Constantine and the Col des Oliviers, the region of Azzaba (Jemmapes) produces very honest table wines. But the palm of victory for the wines of the Constantine region must go, along with those of Souk Ahras, to the wines of BÉNI MELEK, with its vineyards laid out along the Eocene slopes of Skikda (Philippeville). The white wines of this part are much sought for their vigour and robustness. Still farther west of Constantine, one meets the vineyards of Petite-Kabylie and their light, lively and almost colourless wines, lacking somewhat in acidity and body; they are to be found around Djidjelli, Chefka, the foothills of Djebel Seddets and in the Wadi Djinedjerre. Finally, there are two vineyards encircling Petite-Kabylie: Sétif, in the south, at an altitude of 3,300 feet, and Akbou-El Maten-El Kseur in the Wadi Soummam which separates Petite-Kabylie from Grande-Kabylie in the west. The savour and bouquet of these wines is very fine.

CENTRAL ALGERIA

DEPARTMENTS OF ALGIERS AND TIZI OUZOU. The central region of Algeria has immense vineyards and is certainly the second most important of the country's viticultural areas. But here the estates formerly owned by Europeans have passed into the management of the Algerians themselves, and the inexperience of these new winegrowers, who took over from the colonists from one day to the next, shows in the many vines, notably in Mitidja, which were worn out before their time and are now abandoned. Viticulture nevertheless remains one of the primary agricultural activities here, in Mitidja and Sahel d'Alger, from Thénia to Ténès.

Following the Mediterranean shore, one finds east of the capital the vineyards of Thénia, Rouïba, Bou Bérah and Abbo, followed, south-east of Reghaïa, by those of St.-Pierre and Arbatache, then those of Souk el Haad, Chabet-et-Ameur, Isserville-les-Issers and Les Isserts in the Department of Tizi Ouzou. This region produces very well-balanced wines. Nearer Algiers stretch the vineyards of Aïn Taya, Dar el Baida (Maison-Blanche) and El Harrache (Maison Carrée). In the coastal region are the vinegrowing communes of Boufarik, Hadjout, Sidi Moussa, then Mouzaïa, Blida and El Affroun and, along the slopes, Bouzaréa, Montebello, Beni Mered, Guyotville, Cheragas, Zeralda, Douera, Mahelma,

Kolea, Bou Aroun, and so one. Their wines are cool and fruity, with an alcohol content of 10° to 12°.

DEPARTMENT OF EL ASNAM (ORLÉANSVILLE). The vineyards in this Department are in the north, in Sahel; Villebourg, Novi, Gouraya and Ténès; then in Dahra, west of Hadjout, Meurade and Bou Yersen. They produce "wines of the slopes" that are solid, lively and well-coloured. The best-known wines of this Department are, in fact, the Côtes du Zaccar, produced above Miliana and along towards Rouïan and Orléansville; they are fairly full-bodied wines, robust and lively and with an alcohol content of 11° to 13°. Many people do not hesitate to compare them with the French Côtes de Rhône wines.

DEPARTMENT OF MÉDÉA. There are vineyards at an altitude of 2,100 feet around the towns of Médéa, Damiette, Hassen ben Ali and Lodi, and farther east at an altitude of 1,800 feet, in the region of Sour el Gozlan, Bir Rabalou and Aïn Bessem. The reputation of the MÉDÉA and AIN BESSEM wines is already firmly established and they can be compared to those of Bouïra at the foot of Djurdjura in the Department of Tizi Ouzou. All are classified as of superior quality.

WESTERN ALGERIA

DEPARTMENT OF MOSTAGANEM. This region still has very many private estates which, up to the time of independence, made up part of the vast Department of Oran, producer of two-thirds of the country's total wine harvest and undoubtedly of the best wines in Algeria.

Going down the right bank of the Wadi Cheliff and leaving behind the vineyards of the Zaccar slopes, one finds not far from the mouth of the watercourse, on the slopes of Dahra, wines which are fine yet fruity and which keep well. South of the Wadi, vineyards of the plains on argillo-siliceous soil, around Mohammédia and Relizane, criss-cross those of the slopes near Mostaganem, Mesra, Rivoli, Mazagran, Aïn Tédelès and so on. Their wines have an alcohol content of only 10° to 12°, but they are honest and robust types, while those of Mostaganem have the right to the appellation V.D.Q.S.,

as do also those of Mascara, the large viticultural area south of the Beni Chougran mountains. The wines known under the appellation COTEAUX DE MASCARA have probably the finest reputation of any in Algeria. The wines called MASCARA, on the other hand, produced from vines at a lower altitude, are of a lesser quality.

DEPARTMENT OF ORAN. The vineyard of this Department is divided into four large regions. East of the provincial capital, in a magnificent plain reminiscent of the French landscapes of Languedoc, the vines stretch as far as the eye can see from Sidi Chami to Arzew, past Assi Bou Nif, Fleurus, Gdyel, Renan and Ste. Léonie. Farther south is the little vineyard area of St. Lucien, in the Wadi Tlélat. West of Oran, facing the sea on both sides of Sahel, are the vines of Aïn el Turk and Bou Sfer; then those of Misserghin and Brédéah, turned towards Sebkra d'Oran and the slopes of M'silah. These vines produce lively wines with a pronounced bouquet. South-west of Sahel d'Oran is the area producing the Aïn Témouchent and Aïn Kial wines, while those of Rio Salado and Hammam bou Hadjar come from the Metla plain, at an average altitude of 1,200 feet. Finally, the last viticultural region of this department is that of the Tessalah mountains, which produces excellent reds, whites and rosés deserving the classification of "superior quality". The main centres are Sidi bel Abbès, Sidi Daho, Sidi l'Hassen, Sidi Khaled, Lamtar and Wadi Imbert.

DEPARTMENTS OF TLEMCEN AND SAIDA. Adjoining the frontiers of Morocco, the Department of Tlemcen produces vintage wines of which the best is COTEAUX DE TLEMCEN. Outside of Tlemcen, there are vines in the communes of Bréa, Négrier, Mansourah, Aïn Fezza, Lamoricière and Wadi Chouly. There is a small vineyard at Marnia, north-west of the Tlemcen mountains and near the Moroccan frontier, which produces the same type of wine as the preceding areas.

This tour of the vineyards of Oran and Alger ends in the Department of Saïda, where, backed up against the Daïa mountains and facing the great Sahara, is the vineyard of Saïda, while at the westernmost point of Algeria is Aïn el Hadjar and its excellent wine.

MOROCCO

Tingitan Mauretania, the name given by the Romans to their colony in Morocco, has known the vine since earliest antiquity. Today, the most up-to-date vineyards rub shoulders with the traditional vine which produces grapes for the table. There are in all some 185,000 acres planted to the vine, of which four-fifths produce wine, to the extent of 55,000,000 gallons.

Most Moroccan wines are either reds or rosés, with only a small quantity of whites being produced. The red wines are generous, supple and rich, well-balanced but perhaps lacking a little in spirit, with an alcohol content of 12° to 14°. The rosés are clear, limpid and lively, with an agreeable fruitiness. The whites are distinguished as elegant, warm but a little heavy, with a good bouquet. At Boulaouane, El Jadida (south of Casablanca) and Demnate in the area of Marrakech, there is a production of "grey" wines, which are dry and fruity, and also of table wines made from the *Muscat d'Alexandrie*. The most commonly met vines are *Cinsault*, *Carignan*, *Grenache* and *Alicante-Bouschet* for the red wines, and *Pedro Ximenez*, *Plant X*, *Clairette* and *Grenache* for the white wines. The main viticultural areas are Oujda, Berkane, Anged El Aioum and Taourirt in the east; around Taza, Fez and Meknès (whose red wines, fairly light, are the best in Morocco) in the centre; and around Rabat and the Chaouïa Plain towards the west. Other vineyards are spread across southern Morocco between Safi and Mogador, and farther east along the Wadi Tensift up to Sidi Addi, and finally at Bou Assida, on the south-west slopes of the High Atlas, where the vineyards are rather few and far between.

SOUTH AFRICA

In the fertile soil of the Cape of Good Hope, the vine has found superb conditions for growth, and it has prospered there for more than three centuries. Today, the vineyards stretch across the hillsides and valleys of the hinterland, from the foot of the mountain which rises above Table Bay to the chain of purple peaks whose imposing stature confers on the Cape such magnificence and such beauty.

Against this backdrop of hills and mountains, the vineyards of the Cape survey one of the most enchanting panoramas in the world. The farms with their gabled-ends and their whitewashed façades are pure history, the history of the first colonists, and they reflect the perseverance and character of the people who conceived this famous Dutch-style Cape architecture.

Three years after the first Dutch settlement was established at the Cape of Good Hope, in February 1655, a packet of the Dutch East India Company sailed into Table Bay, carrying a few European vine-plants. Johan van Riebeeck, Governor of the Colony, had these plants set out in the gardens of the Company, at the foot of Table Mountain. Four years later, South Africa's viticulture was born when grapes from those vine-plants were pressed to make the first Cape wine. Some twenty years after that, Governor Simon van der Stel himself set out 100,000 roots of vine in a model-farm in Constantia Valley, thus encouraging the colonists to develop cultivation of the vine. And at the end of the seventeenth century, a large number of French Huguenot refugees poured into the Cape, bringing with them the experience and the secrets of winemaking. They settled in the valleys of Stellenbosch, Paarl, Drakenstein and Franschhoek, building up the viticulture there and greatly improving the quality of the region's wines. Some of these farms and workings carry their original French names to this day.

The harvests increased and wine could soon be exported to Batavia. For one must remember that the original reason for the Dutch settlement at the Cape was as a port of call where ships could take in fresh supplies on the voyage from the Netherlands to India. Nevertheless, as the Cape wine became known and appreciated in Europe, considerable quantities were shipped to Great Britain and the Continent of Europe.

Most of the South African wine was at that time being produced in the Constantia Valley by the Groot-Constantia farm, which was then the property of the Cloete family. The Muscat from Constantia was, in fact, described as "undeniably a dessert wine, strong but delicate, and having in its bouquet something singularly agreeable". In 1805, Great Britain, then fighting against Napoleon, occupied the Cape for the second time: her vessels came to take on supplies there, being no longer able to do so in France. The wine-growers were encouraged to produce vintage wines for export, and an official wine-taster was appointed to sample the export wines and ensure that they had the required quality and ageing. The British Government wished to stimulate the export of wines still more, and in 1813 introduced a preferential customs tariff for imported colonial wine. The result of this colonial preference was absolutely staggering. The production of wines of all kinds, both natural wines and sweet and liqueur wines, shot up. From 930,000 gallons in 1813, the South African wine production rocketted in 1824 to 2,442,000 gallons, of which nearly one-half (1,011,000 gallons) were exported. These preferential tariffs were, however, progressively cut back in later years, until they were finally abolished in 1861 by William Gladstone's government.

Phylloxera ravaged the vineyards of the Cape in 1885, leaving the winegrowers in a very poor situation. The disease was finally eliminated in the same way as in Europe, by grafts on American stock resistant to the parasite. But after this cure, the revitalized wines met a fresh problem in the first part of the twentieth century—over-production. Their yield was so generous that in 1916 winegrowers had to be content with a one-penny profit per bottle of good quality wine. To cope with this overabundance and avoid a recurrence of the crisis, a co-operative organization was formed. The principal vinegrowers had already met several times in 1916 to discuss the advisability of setting up a central organization which would protect their interests. No one who saw this body founded realized that it would become an all-powerful apparatus of control, directing and ruling the activities of vinegrowers and wineproducers alike. A proposal for a central co-operative body was drawn up, and presented at a huge assembly at Paarl. The result was the foundation, in 1918, of the body known as the *Kooperatieve Wijnbouwers van Zuid-Africa* (K.W.V.), or Wine-Growers Co-operative of South Africa. It was then and still is today mainly made up of Afrikanders, and had as its principal aim the conduct, control and regulation of the sale and disposal of its members' production; it also guaranteed or tried to guarantee that their profits would be consistent with their production. Today, nobody can produce wine without the authorization of the K.W.V., which decides the maximum annual production of each vineyard and the minimum prices of good wines and distillation wines, and also calculates the "surplus" factor or proportion of each wineproducer which then has to be delivered free of charge to the K.W.V. No producer may sign a sales contract with a merchant without the prior approval of the K.W.V., which receives the payments due, nor may a producer sell any part of their harvest to individuals without the express consent of this governing body.

WINEGROWING REGIONS

The South African vineyard is situated in the south-west part of Cape Province, and is divided into two distinct zones. The first part includes the areas around Stellenbosch, Paarl and Wellington, then the area from Malmesbury to Tulbagh, and finally the Cape Peninsula and the famous Constantia Valley. The climate there is temperate: mild in spring, hot and even very hot in summer, either mild or hot in autumn, cold and humid in winter. This comparatively small region —very small, in fact, when one compares it with the regions which produce the many types of European wine—can produce most of the well-known wines thanks to the wide variety of soil and land; most of the South African natural wines of everyday type are to be found there.

The other major wine-producing zone is at a higher altitude. Known as the Little Karoo, it extends from Ladysmith to Outshoorn, between the Drakenstein and the Swartberg, and includes Worcester, Robertson,

Bonnievale and Swellendam. The climate here is much more severe than in the coastal region—less rain and more heat, hence the need to irrigate the land—but there is a good production, largely in the domain of dessert wines, sherries or ports.

Types of Vine-Plant. A wide variety of grape grows in these two regions, with the vine-plants used for white wines (*Riesling, Stein, Blanc Français, Clairette Blanche*) doing well along the coast. The *Hermitage, Cabernet Sauvignon* and *Shiraz* give light red wines, while the *Pinot, Gamay, Cabernet, Hermitage, Shiraz* and *Pinotage* give full-bodied reds. As far as the wines themselves are concerned, the strongest are produced in the regions close to the coast (Constantia, Somerset-West and certain parts around Stellenbosch), with the better wines coming from Paarl, Stellenbosch and Tulbagh; the light red wines come from around Paarl and Durbanville. A vine called *Pinotage*, developed by one of K.W.V.'s research workers who crossed *Hermitage* with *Pinot*, is very well known in South Africa and is planted quite extensively. Its wine combines the best qualities of the two separate species: a full-bodied red of good quality, with a fruity and perfumed bouquet which somehow recalls the French Beaujolais. In the Little Karoo region, the *Blanc Français, Hermitage, Hanepoot, Muscat* and *Sultana* vines produce dessert wines.

The Climate. Although in the southern hemisphere, the whole calendar of vine growth is, naturally, entirely different from that of Europe, the influence of each season is nevertheless very similar. Spring, from September to November, is the busiest time of the year for the vinegrower. In summer, from December to February, the grape ripens; the harvest is carried out in the southern autumn, between March and May. The cold, humid winter is in the middle of the year.

The South African climate is almost over-generous; in fact, the sun presents some serious problems for the vinegrowers. While in Europe the harvest ripens in the cool of autumn after a relatively short summer, in South Africa it ripens during the heat of midsummer, which creates special problems in the fermentation and ageing. On the other hand, grapes that ripen under a strong sun always contain a high proportion of sugar, which does not always balance out the natural acidity. One can say, too, that the South African winegrower is much less bothered by the capricious moods of the weather than his European counterpart. In the Cape, *every* wine-year is a good year. There is, however, a constant search to profit from what little amount of freshness can be found or engineered during the ripening of the grape, for it facilitates the conservation of the bouquet and aroma in the wine, particularly in the white wines. An interesting difference of opinion is seen in this connection: some farmers use vine-props to lift the vine clear of the ground during the torrid midsummer period, while other farmers take quite the opposite viewpoint and leave the vine close to the ground, claiming that the vine leaves protect the grape from the sun's strength. A great deal of attention is paid to the orientation of the vineyards. It has been proved that the vines which are grown on the cooler southern slopes (remembering that this is the southern hemisphere) produce better white wines, while for good red wines the winegrowers prefer the sites facing north, that is, towards the prevailing sun.

GENERAL CHARACTERISTICS OF THE WINES

The products of the Cape vineyards can never be the same as the European wines of similar type, however much the South African growers may simulate European production methods by using modern refrigeration and modern control systems during the fermentation and ageing processes. And even were the vine and the soil identical to those in Europe, the sheer heat of the Cape climate raises the sugar content, reduces the acidity, and consequently gives an entirely different wine. In this respect, wine-lovers who attempted to find in the Cape wines the exact replicas of the European wines they know, would be depriving themselves of a rare chance for enjoyment: the Cape wines possess their own aroma and characteristics, despite their apparent resemblance to European wines.

The production of Cape vintage wines has been made possible by the introduction of temperature control in the cellars. By using great stainless-steel or steel containers, the winegrower can now control the speed of fermentation at a low temperature, and can thus re-create the fresh European climate which is needed if the wine is to retain its delicate perfume and its taste. This can be achieved in one of three ways. The required low temperature can be maintained by pumping cold water through pipes which pass through the must, or the must itself can be circulated through a refrigerating circuit, or the temperature of the air in the cellar itself can be lowered by air-conditioning.

The slightly-sweet wines so popular in South Africa are obtained by cutting short the fermentation, either by using a sulphureous gas, or else by compressing or chilling the must so that the wine, which already contains the authorized 2 per cent amount of sugar, keeps in addition a part of its natural sweetness. After ageing in cool cellars, the wine is clarified by being racked and filtered. In South Africa, white wines are bottled and drunk while they are still very young, sometimes after a mere six months and while they are still fresh, sparkling and deliciously fruity.

RIESLING is probably the best Cape white wine, followed closely by STEIN. The RIESLING wine tends to be the drier of the two; yet it is not, as the Cape climate might lead one to suppose, as dry as the German RIESLING. The STEIN wine is usually semi-sweet but it can be dry on occasion, in much the same way that the RIESLING can be semi-dry or semi-sweet. These wines, which have such an agreeable taste, fruitiness and aroma, tend, however, to be more full-bodied than the semi-sweet European wines. The wines made from *Clairette Blanche* vines are more delicate, and when drunk young, have an admirably mordant freshness and perfumed aroma.

The alcohol content of the Cape white wines, at 11º to 12º by volume, is slightly higher than the European white wines. These growers now also produce a SPÄTLESE, a white *mi-flétri*, which by virtue of letting the grapes dry longer before pressing them has a distinctly higher alcohol content. Good wines of a deep yellow colour, they are made from *Steen, Riesling,* or even *Hanepoot* vines.

As for the Cape red wines, they are usually aged for two or three years before being bottled, at which stage they are very drinkable, since most of them are dry and have a very pleasant perfume. To improve their quality still more, connoisseurs keep them yet another two or three years. There are, unfortunately, only a very few wineproducers who take the trouble to indicate the harvest-year on the bottle labels, and even then, these are wines from small winegrowers whose vines are renowned for their quality. A few experienced *restaurateurs* are careful to cellar the wine for two years or so, to avoid the possibility of any disagreeable surprises and to allow it to assert its best qualities.

It is the red wines of the Cape which come closest to European wines. The full-bodied reds, made from *Cabernet, Pinot Noir, Gamay* and *Hermitage* vines in the regions of Paarl, Stellenbosch and Durbanville, are of a Burgundy type, with all the qualities which that can imply. The light reds tend more towards the Bordeaux type and come from vines in Constantia Valley, around Stellenbosch and Somerset-West. The *Shiraz* vine does very well in the Cape climate, producing a red wine with a rich bouquet; blended with *Hermitage* or *Cabernet,* it gives a full-bodied wine of a certain distinction if it has been allowed to age. The red wine made from the crossed vine *Pinotage,* with its bright colour, its fruitiness and its pronounced bouquet, is one of the best full-bodied reds in the country.

The rosé wines, which are much lighter, are finding increasing approval, their freshness being particularly welcome in the South African heat. They have the colour of red wines but the main characteristics of whites; they tend to be astringent and to lack body.

APPELLATIONS. There are no provisions in South African law covering the use of the term *appellation d'origine contrôlée*. In point of fact, such a definition is not suitable for the wines of South Africa. Very many wines are described as "bottled" on such-and-such an estate, but most often they certainly do not come from vines harvested on one single estate; they may even come from a mixture of wines of quite different origins. One can also add that any mention on the label of the A.O.C. would probably not interest the South African consumer, who has more confidence in the guarantee of a standard quality offered in wine coming from the big estates. The name of the vine is sometimes given on the label, an advantage for the lover of good wine who is able to make his choice between wines from *Riesling* or *Cabernet* or *Pinotage*. As so many wines carry only the name of a winegrower, the only really reliable method of investigating their quality is by the tried and trusted one of tasting them. Some labels, however, carry the word "selected", which is usually an indication either that the grape was carefully selected before pressing, or the wine, while still young and before being treated and aged, was picked out as being of excellent quality. This solitary one-word mention is by no means negligible when it comes to judging the quality of the bottle's contents. The year of the wine-harvest is, as already pointed out, very rarely given: the South African consumer seldom pays any attention to it and the winegrowers claim that since the climatic conditions are always constant and perfect the quality of the wine is equally so !

On this ticklish point of appreciation of the quality of wines, one can mention that the foreign consumer might consider as too sweet or too heavy certain wines which are highly appreciated by the South Africans. Conversely, of course, the connoisseur of European wines might very well find happiness in a wine considered very "so-so" by the South African standards. More than 90 per cent of the wines which have some *appellation d'origine* are produced and sold by only four firms. These establishments, which are both wineproducers and merchants and are equipped with enormous cellars and the latest modern machinery, obtain their grapes either in their own vineyards or from neighbouring estates, and their wine either from their own production of from other wineproducers or co-operatives, in which case they buy young wine.

The Stellenbosch Farmer's Winery (S.F.W.), which also includes the Monis group, has the largest choice of wines. Those from Zonnebloem are its first line and are excellent white wines made from *Riesling*, with a dry and full-bodied CABERNET of delightful bouquet. There is also a semi-sweet, well-ripened ZONNEBLOEM *mi-flétri*.

Another branch of the S.F.W.'s activities concerns the so-called Lanzerac, whose origins date back to 1692. A magnificent and well-preserved Dutch-style farmhouse has been converted into a hotel which today has an international reputation. Here the wines of Lanzerac may be enjoyed, sold in bottles shaped like a dew-drop. They comprise two whites, a dry wine made from *Riesling* called RIESENSCHON and a semi-sweet made from *Stein* called GRÜNMÄDCHEN; while the red wines of Lanzerac are a full-bodied CABERNET and a good specimen of PINOTAGE, lighter than the Cabernet but still fairly full-bodied. There is also a light and semi-sweet rosé.

From the "Oude Libertas" cellars of the S.F.W., dating back to 1707, come very popular moderate-priced wines: GRATITUDE, a type of dry Chablis, and TASHEIMER GOLDTRÖPFCHEN, which is like a semi-sweet Rhine wine. Their CHÂTEAU LIBERTAS, carrying the name of these famous cellars, is a very well-known Burgundy-type wine.

The Stellenbosch Farmer's Winery also produces a whole series of ordinary wines which are very widely distributed. These include a Burgundy-type, TASSENBERG, and a semi-sweet wine called ZONNHEIMER which has a taste of *Hanepoot*. Probably the most popular of their wines is LIEBERSTEIN, a semi-sweet white wine which has been highly publicized.

The Nederburg property, which has recently linked up with the S.F.W., was the first concern in the Cape to experiment with German methods of vinification for fermentation and low-temperature ageing. Furthermore, this property will only plant and develop vines of pure stock. A very nice choice of white wines comes from their cellars. HOCHHEIMER, a Rhine riesling type, and MI-FLÉTRI, for those who prefer the rather sweeter *Spätlesen*, are both outstanding. SYLVANER-NEDERBURG is a pleasant and fairly dry white, but SELECTED RIESLING and RIESLING are the best-selling moderate-priced white wines. The CABERNET from this cellar is full-bodied with a nutty taste. One should note that the Nederburg winery does not produce any ordinary wines.

Gilbey-Santhagens, at Stellenbosch, offer wine drinkers several wines labelled TWEE JONGEZELLENS ("the two young bachelors")—for example, RIESLING "39", a dry Rhine-type wine with a very pleasant bouquet, and the semi-dry STEIN SUPERIOR. The cheapest wines in this series are the dry RIESLING, the semi-dry STEIN, the semi-sweet LIEBFRAUENMILCH, and a sweet rosé.

The Distillers Corporation of South Africa markets two medium quality wines which come from the Clos de la Résidence and which are much appreciated by those who seek inexpensive refreshment. THEUNIS-KRAAL, pleasantly dry and with a good taste, is a

313

Riesling, while ALTO ROUGE is a tasty dry wine made from *Cabernet*. GRÜNBERGER, a semi-dry stein-type wine contained in bottles of a special shape, VILLA BIANCA and VILLA ROSA, both semi-dry, all come from these same cellars. The Corporation also offers ordinary wines from the well-known WITZENBERG series.

The Castle Wine and Brandy Company of Capetown offers a range of white wines under the name VLOTTENHEIM ESTATES OF VLOTTENBERG. One finds a very pleasant semi-dry SYLVANER, a SCHLOSSBERG, a good quality dry RIESLING KABINETT and a semi-sweet HONIGBERG. Apart from these wines, the best known is ROUGEMONT, a very popular mellow Burgundy. For the rest, the firm's products are mostly very ordinary kinds of wines.

There are a certain number of private vineyards whose wines are worth searching for, although their combined production is very small compared with that of the big concerns. One can find these wines only in their home region, for their producers do not need to find other markets. Taking them in alphabetical order, the list begins with Alphen, the two-centuries old property in Constantia Valley. Alphen produces an ALPHEN RIESLING SELECTED and two light Burgundies, as well as good sherries and good dessert wines. The Bellingham property (Groot-Drakenstein) is trying to match European A.O.C. wines with a balanced range of high quality products, and offers a remarkable BLANC SEC PREMIER GRAND CRU, a semi-dry JOHANNISBERG, a delicious SHIRAZ, a STEIN and a rosé. The Delheim vineyard at Koelenhof produces a *mi-flétri* SPATZENDRECK for those who like a rather sweeter wine, and very worthy red wines which include a full-bodied PINOTAGE and a Burgundy-type wine, CABERNET-SAUVIGNON.

From Muratie, also at Koelenhof, come some very attractive red table wines: their CABERNET-SAUVIGNON is a light and perfumed Burgundy, the full-bodied GAMAY PINOT-NOIR has Burgundy-like qualities and their BORDEAUX brings a light taste of *Hermitage*. The Schoongezicht property, near Stellenbosch, produces two wines much sought after by wine-lovers, particularly the RUSTENBERG, a dry and full-bodied wine made from *Cabernet* which has many of the characteristics of a Médoc and has crowned many a harvest with excellent success. The other is a Schoongezicht white wine full of taste and with a rich bouquet which takes it name from the property where it is harvested; *Clairette Blanche* grapes are also used for this wine. The Uitkyk vineyard, at Mulders in Vlei, produces two wines which should be better known: the first is a dry white wine sold under the name of CARLSHEIM, the other is CARLONET CABERNET, a full-bodied and very fresh red wine.

In sparkling wines, GRAND MOUSSEUX from the Stellenbosch Farmer's Winery, ranging from extra-dry to sweet, is by far the most popular. These wines have a very fruity taste and are just a little sweeter than European sparkling wines.

South Africa has without any doubt really excellent products in the field of *liquoreux* wines. The range of dessert wines is simply immense, and covers all types. As examples one might mention MOOIUITSIG WYNKELDERS, from Bonnievale; MONIS MARSALA. an excellent product from the S.F.W., and the same firm's delicious MUSCADINE. Two firms offer from their cellars wines which, it seems, are identical to that famous eighteenth-century wine of Constantia: CONSTANTIABERG from Bertrams of Constantia and the SCHOONGEZICHT FRONTIGNAC.

The range of ports to be found in the Cape is also very large. The *topazes ambrés* are the lightest, going from very light reds to deep reds; the rubies are of a richer colour and more full-bodied. The vintage ports, which are produced only in limited quantities, are a deep red and full-bodied, their mellowness coming from ten to fifteen years of ageing in the bottle.

The best South African ports are made in the coastal region around Paarl and Stellenbosch. Most of the vines come originally from the Portuguese district of Douro, where port wine itself originated. *Pontac*, *Mataro* and *Shiraz* vines are used in order to be able to blend better, and care is taken to age the port sufficiently, even though the length of time needed in the South African climate is shorter than in Europe.

South African sherries come from authentic *xérès flor* vines, and the South African sherry vineyards are in the same southern latitude as the Spanish sherry vineyards are in the northern hemisphere. Furthermore, the principally used vine is *Palomino*, the "foundation stone" of Spanish sherries. The vines giving light sherries grow at Paarl, Stellenbosch, Tulbagh and Goudini in the south-western part of the Cape, while the more full-bodied sherries come from Worcester, Robertson, Mongatu and Bonnievale. The K.W.V. organization is quite certainly the largest producer and exporter of Cape sherries; many millions of gallons of stock are in the process of ageing.

Although the very dry and pale sherry sought in Europe is unknown in South Africa, there are nevertheless other very excellent sherries. The driest sherries —although even these are much less dry than their Spanish cousins—are the *finos* and the *amontillados*, fairly pale in colour and of a delicate flavour. The *oloroso* are darker, much sweeter and more full-bodied. As for the sherries aged by the *solera* system, they have a much darker colour and a much sweeter taste than the European varieties.

WINES OF AFRICA

ALGERIA

Aïn Bessem-Bouira	Coteaux de Médéa	Côtes du Zaccar	Miliana
Aïn El Hadjar	Coteaux de M'Silah	Haut-Dahra	Monts du Tessalah
Coteaux de Mascara	Coteaux de Tlemcen	Mascara	Mostaganem-Dahra

TUNISIA

Cap Bon	Kélibia	Muscat de Thibar	Sidi-Tabet
Carthage	Muscat de Kélibia	Radès	Thibar
Coteaux de Khanguet	Muscat de Radès	Saint Cyprien	Tébourba

SOUTH AFRICA

SUPERIOR QUALITY WINES

Dry white wines . . . .
Bellingham Premier Grand Cru — Lanzerac Riesenschön — Nederburg Selected Riesling
Carlsheim 8 — Nederburg Riesling — Twee Jongegezellen Riesling « 39 »

Medium-dry white wines . . .
Bellingham Late Vintage — Nederburg Sylvaner — Twee Jongegezellen Stein Superior
Bellingham Vintage Johannisberger — Twee Jongegezellen Stein — Vlottenheimer Sylvaner

Medium-sweet white wines . . .
Bellingham Selected Steinwein — Delheim Selected Stein Goldspatz — Nederburg Stein
Blumberger Late Harvest — Kupferberger Auslese — Tulbagher
Charantelle — Lanzerac Grünmädchen — Twee Jongegezellen Spätlese
Delheim Late-Harvest — Nederburg Hochheimer — Vlottenheimer Schlossberg
« Spatzendreck » — Nederburg Late Harvest — Zonnebloem Late Harvest

Dry red wines . . . .
Lanzerac Pinotage — Nederburg Selected Cabernet — Zonnebloem Cabernet
Lanzerac Cabernet — Stellenrood — Alphen Special Old Vintage

Medium-dry red wines . . . .
Bellingham Shiraz — Carlonet Cabernet

Dry rosé wines . . . .
Bellingham Rosé — Nederburg Rosé Sec

Medium-dry rosé wine . . . .
Bellingham Almeida

Medium-sweet rosé wines . . .
Lanzerac Rose — Nederburg Rose

VERY GOOD QUALITY WINES

Dry white wines . . . .
Alphen Dry White — La Gratitude — Schoongezicht
Alphen Selected Riesling — La Residence Theuniskraal — Stellenvale Selected Riesling
Bellingham Riesling — J.C. le Roux Mont Pellier — Stellenvale Selected Stellenblanche
Constantia Riesling — Molenburg Riesling — Theuniskraal
Culemborg Selected Riesling — Muratie Riesling — Twee Jongegezellen Liebfraumilch
Delheim Riesling — Muratie Stein — Twee Jongegezellen Riesling
Delheim White-French — Paarl Valley Old Riesling — Vlottenheimer Riesling Kabinet
De Rust Riesling — Prestige Selected Riesling — White Leipzig
Huguenot Riesling — Prestige Selected Stellenblanche — Witzenberg

Medium-dry white wines . . .
Delheim Selected Riesling — Tafelheim — Vlottenheimer Selected Riesling
De Rust Stein — Villa Bianca — Witzenberg Grand
Grunberger Stein

Medium-sweet white wines . . .	Amaliensteimer	Liebfrauborg	Stellenvale Estate Riesling
	Bruderberg Na Œs (late harvest)	Lombards Liebfraumilch	Tasheimer Goldtröpfchen
	Capinella	Molenberg Stein	Vlottenheimer Honigberg
	Constantia Valley Stein	Molenhof Stein	Volson
	Culemborg Selected Stein	Monis Steinheimer	Winterhock Stein
	Gezellen Liebfraumilch	Stellenvale Hochheimer	Witzenberg Spatlese
	Kloosterberg		

Slightly sparkling white wines .	Culemborg Perlé	La Provence	Nauheimer

Dry red wines	Bodenheim	Delheim Pinotage	Rustenburg
	Bruderberg Selected Cabernet	La Résidence Alto Rouge	St. Augustine
	Château Alphen	Muratie Claret	Valais Rouge
	Château Constantia	Muratie Pinot noir-Gamay	Vredenburg
	Château Le Roux	Nederburg Cabernet	Alphen Red
	Château Libertas	Province Red	Muratie Cabernet Sauvignon
	Château Monis	Rougemont	Vlakkenberg
	Delheim Cabernet-Sauvignon		

Medium-sweet red wines . . .	Back's Claret (light-bodied)	Stellenvale Cabernet (light-bodied)

Dry rosé wine	Valrosé

Medium-dry rosé wine	Villa Rose

Medium-sweet rosé wines . . .	Culemborg Rose	Rosala	Witzenberg Grand Rose
	La Provence	Twee Jongegezellen Rose	

DESSERT AND APERITIF WINES

Dessert wines	Amarella	Malvasia	Mooiuitsig White Muscadel
	Consanto	Miranda	Liqueur Wine
	Constantia Berg	Monis Barbola	Morilos Marsala
	Golden Bonwin	Monis Marsala	Muscadine
	Golden Mantilla	Monis Moscato	Ruby Bonwin
	Kloovendal	Mooiuitsig Red Muscadel Liqueur	Rynilla
	La Rhone	Wine	Stellenvale Marsala
	Malaga Red		

Port wines	Castelo Port	Government House Port	Mooiuitsig Fine Old Port
	Devonvale Port	Libertas	Muratie Port
	D.C. Vintage Port	Monis Cardinal Port	Santyis Old Ruby Vintage Port

Very dry sherries	Gonzales Byass Dry

D.G. Flor No. 1 sherries . . .	Harvey's Extra Dry	Old Master Amontillado	Libertas
	Karroo Sherry	Devonvale Solera Dry « Flor »	Monis Palido Sherry
	Mattersons Fine Dry	Harvey's Dry Sherry	Tayler's Pàle Dry Sherry

Medium-dry sherries	Bertrams Biscuit Sherry	Monis Dry Cream Sherry	Tudor Medium Cream Sherry
	D.G. Flor No. 2	Tayler's Mmooth Medium Sherry	

Medium-sweet sherries	Bertrams Oloroso Sherry	Gonzales Byass Medium	Sedgwick's Medium Cream
	Devon Cream Sherry	Roodezand Sherry	Vlei Sherry

Sweet sherries	D.G. Olorose	Harvey's Full Cream Sherry	Tayler's Full Cream Sherry
	Gonzales Byass Sweet	Libertas	Tayler's Rich Brown Sherry

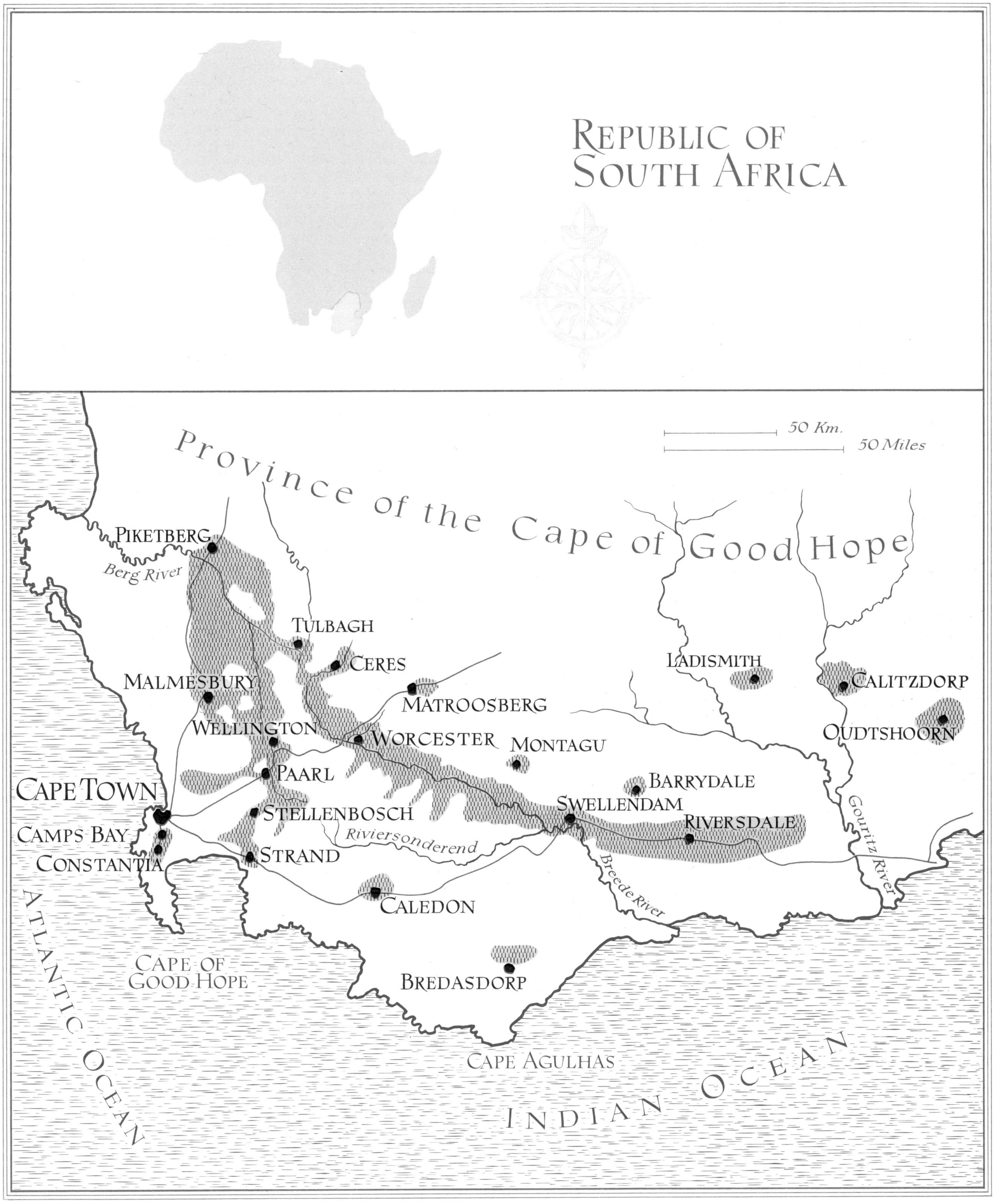

REPUBLIC OF SOUTH AFRICA

50 Km.

50 Miles

Province of the Cape of Good Hope

PIKETBERG

Berg River

TULBAGH

CERES

MALMESBURY

MATROOSBERG

LADISMITH

CALITZDORP

WELLINGTON

WORCESTER

MONTAGU

OUDTSHOORN

CAPE TOWN

PAARL

BARRYDALE

STELLENBOSCH

SWELLENDAM

RIVERSDALE

CAMPS BAY

Riviersonderend

CONSTANTIA

STRAND

Breede River

Gouritz River

CALEDON

CAPE OF
GOOD HOPE

BREDASDORP

ATLANTIC OCEAN

CAPE AGULHAS

INDIAN OCEAN

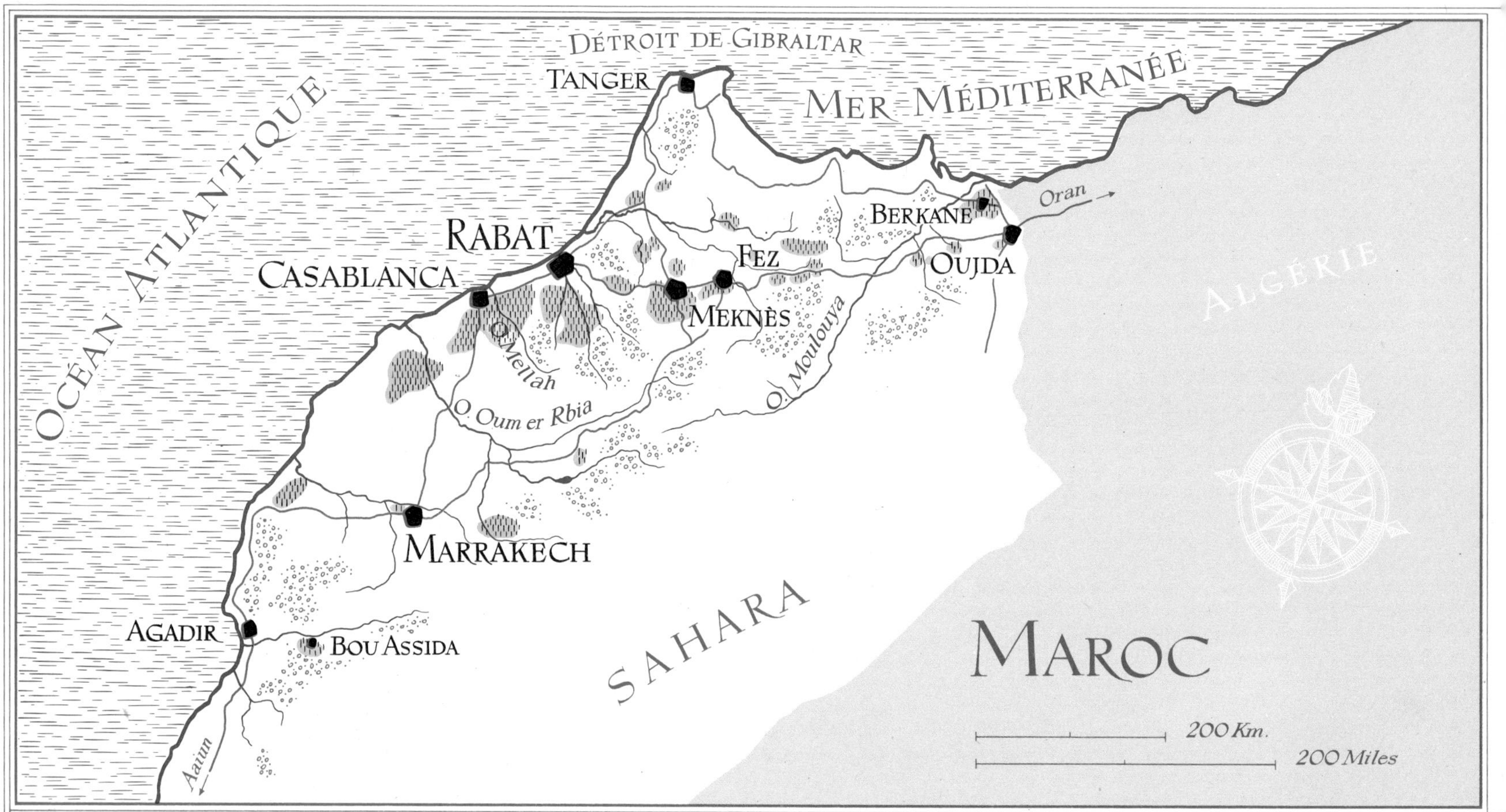

MAROC

DÉTROIT DE GIBRALTAR

TANGER

MER MÉDITERRANÉE

OCÉAN ATLANTIQUE

RABAT

CASABLANCA

Fez

BERKANE

OUJDA

ALGÉRIE

MEKNÈS

O. Mellah

O. Oum er Rbia

O. Moulouya

MARRAKECH

SAHARA

AGADIR

BOU ASSIDA

Aaiun

200 Km.

200 Miles

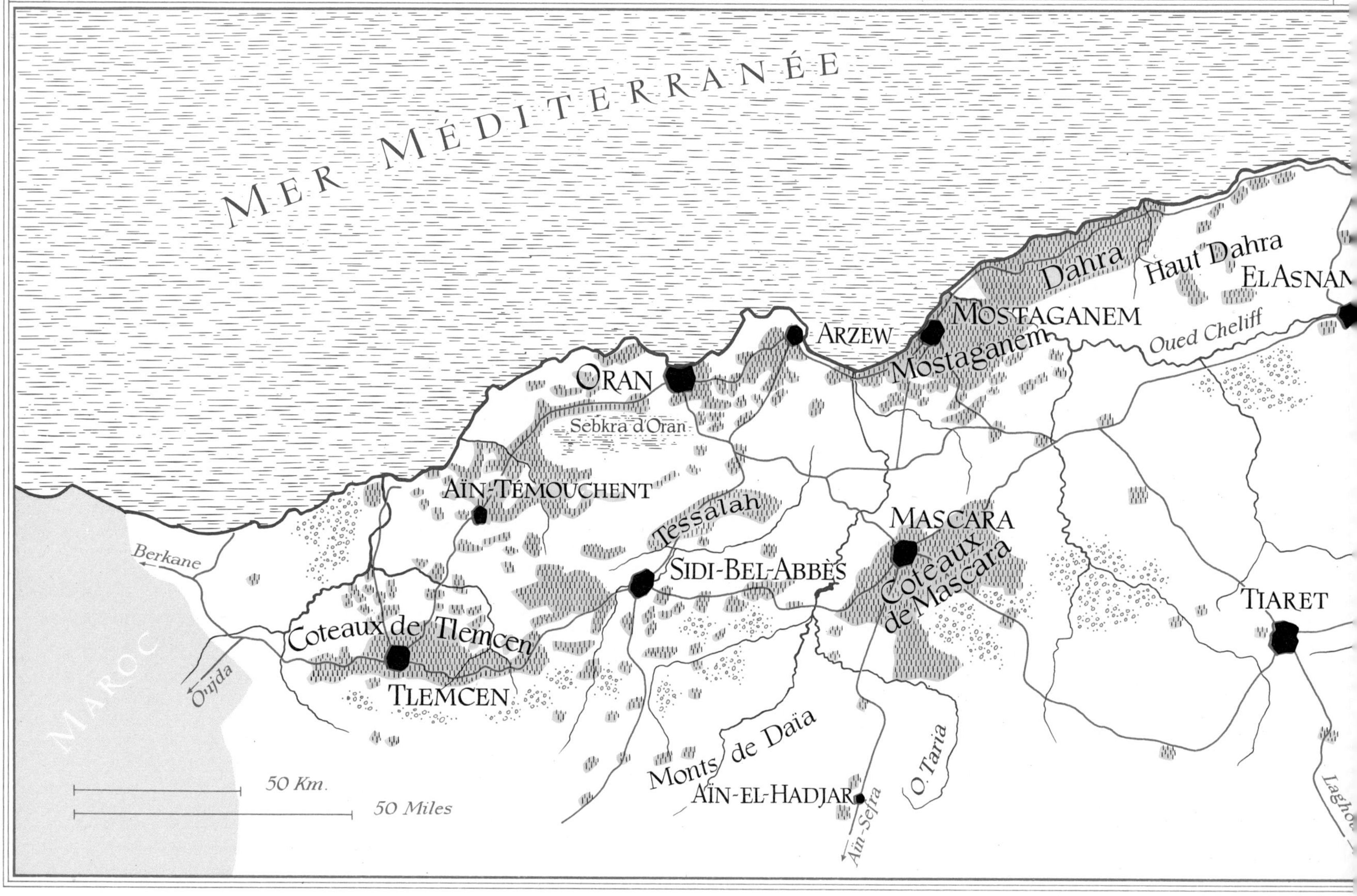

MER MÉDITERRANÉE

MAROC

Berkane

Oujda

Dahra

Haut Dahra

EL ASNAM

MOSTAGANEM

ARZEW

Mostaganem

Oued Cheliff

ORAN

Sebkra d'Oran

AÏN-TÉMOUCHENT

Tessalah

MASCARA

Coteaux de Mascara

SIDI-BEL-ABBÈS

TIARET

Coteaux de Tlemcen

TLEMCEN

Monts de Daïa

O. Taria

AÏN-EL-HADJAR

Aïn-Sefra

Laghouat

50 Km.

50 Miles

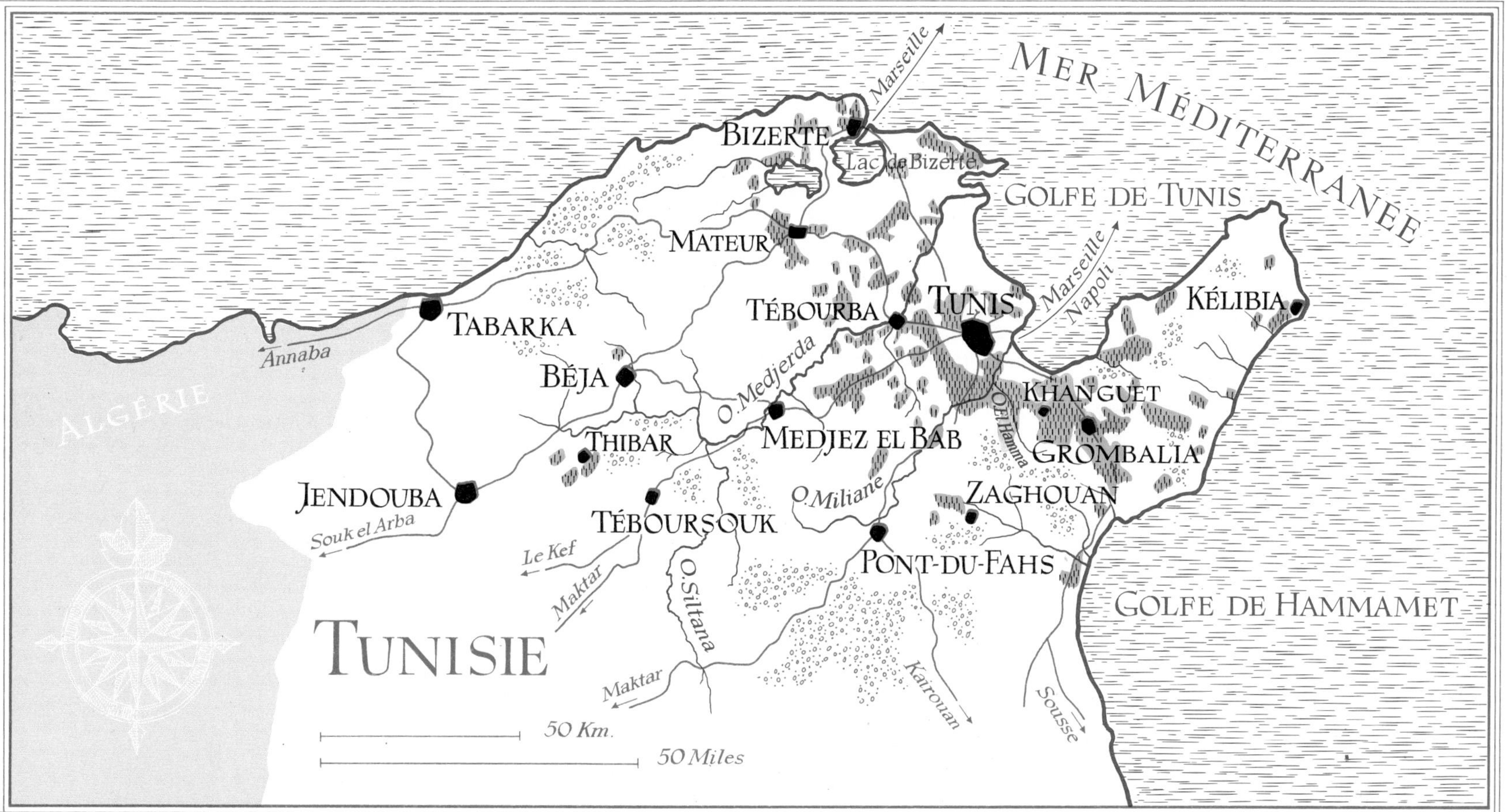

TUNISIE

MER MÉDITERRANÉE

GOLFE DE TUNIS

BIZERTE
Lac de Bizerte
Marseille

MATEUR

TÉBOURBA
TUNIS
Marseille
Napoli

KÉLIBIA

TABARKA
Annaba

BÉJA

O. Medjerda

KHANGUET
O. el Hamma

GROMBALIA

THIBAR

MEDJEZ EL BAB

ALGÉRIE

JENDOUBA
Souk el Arba

TÉBOURSOUK

ZAGHOUAN

O. Miliane

Le Kef

Maktar

O. Siliana

PONT-DU-FAHS

GOLFE DE HAMMAMET

Maktar

Kairouan

Sousse

50 Km.

50 Miles

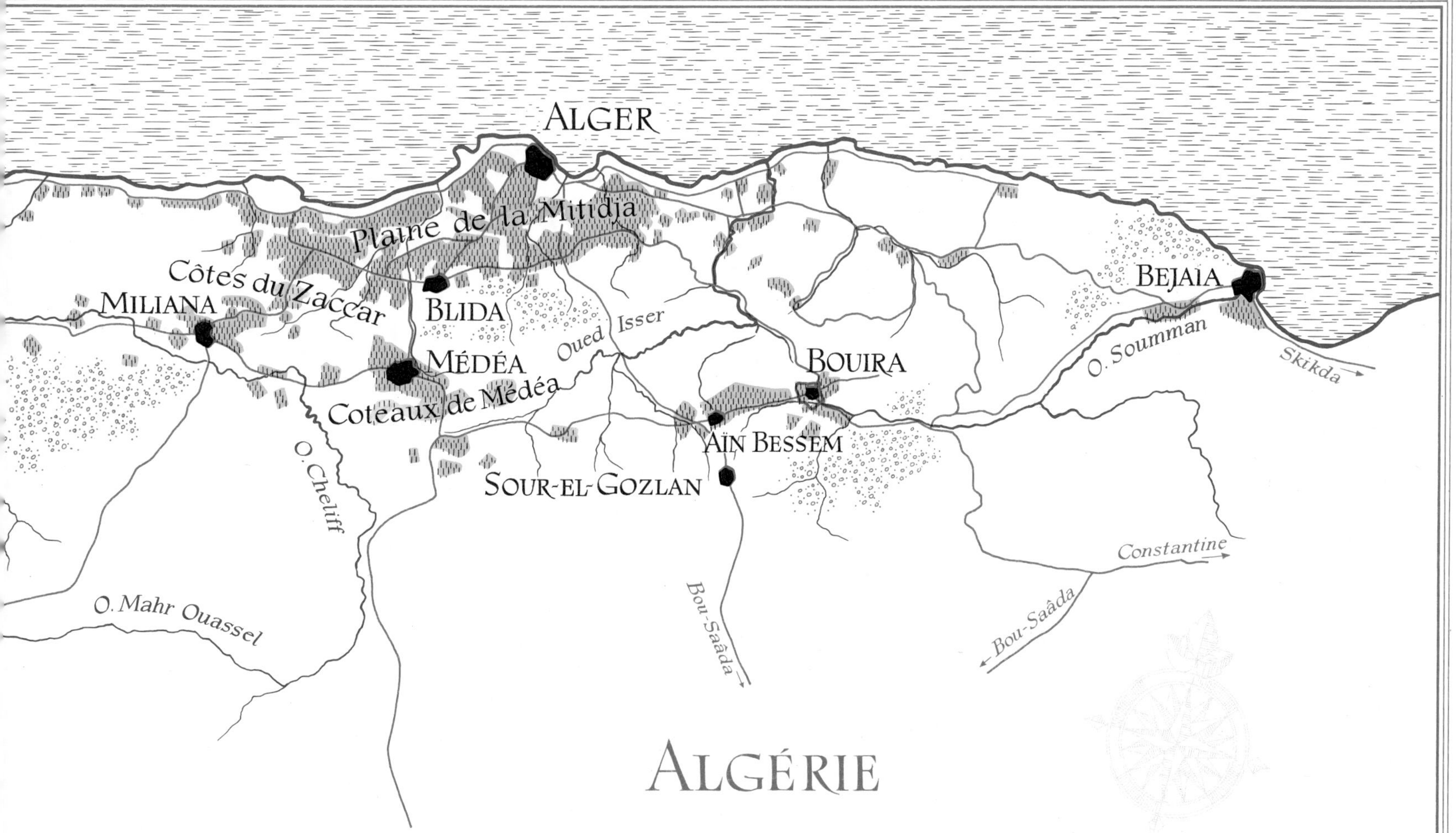

ALGÉRIE

ALGER

Plaine de la Mitidja

BEJAIA

Côtes du Zaccar

MILIANA

BLIDA

Oued Isser

O. Soumman

Skikda

MÉDÉA

BOUIRA

Coteaux de Médéa

AÏN BESSEM

O. Chelliff

SOUR-EL-GOZLAN

Constantine

O. Mahr Ouassel

Bou-Saâda

Bou-Saâda

THE WINES OF NORTH AMERICA

ROBERT THOMPSON

When considering the wines of the United States of America one must invariably divide them into two categories: those of California and those from other states. This is because Californian wines derive almost exclusively from the European *vitis vinifera* vines, whereas the eastern and northern states, with climate and conditions unsuitable for the growing of European vines, produce wines from native American or hybrid grapes. The *vitis vinifera* grape vines were introduced to Mexico by the Spaniards in the sixteenth century and from there went northwards to California. In 1769 Franciscan missionaries planted the first vines (probably of Spanish origin) in San Diego and in 1824 the first commercial vineyard was started in Los Angeles. Thereafter came a stream of fortune-seeking settlers. Among them were important contributors to Californian viticulture such as the Frenchman Jean Louis Vignes, who introduced French vines in the 1830s and subsequently expanded his vineyards to such an extent that within a generation winegrowing was the principal industry of the Los Angeles area.

In 1851 a Hungarian nobleman, Agoston Haraszthy —now called the father of Californian viticulture—followed Vignes' example and imported over 100,000 cuttings from 300 foreign varieties. With the boom caused by the Gold Rush of 1849 wine consumption rose, as did the number of enthusiasts like Haraszthy. From then onwards the wine industry fluctuated between slumps and outbreaks of phylloxera (between 1870 and 1876) and prosperous periods, with the formation in 1880 of the California State Board of Viticultural Commissioners doing much to stabilize winemaking.

By the end of the nineteenth century the main outlines of the present-day industry had emerged. The coastal districts north and south of San Francisco were concentrating their efforts on table wines, while the warmer regions of the interior were producing dessert wines. But just forty years later American viticultural progress received a severe blow in the form of the Prohibition Law. In 1919 the making of wine was declared unlawful in the United States and so it remained until the Repeal in 1933. Wine was legal, however, for medicinal and sacramental uses and the head of the house could make up to 200 gallons a year for himself and his family's consumption. Within five years of this date California had nearly 800 bonded wineries, the greatest number in its history. Most of them were small and lacked financial backing. Others, alas, were more anxious to make good profits than good wines; not until about 1938 did the market settle down to its present level of some 212 wineries. Regulations were passed to safeguard the industry and, under the guidance of the University of California, it was led to a highly skilled wine technology.

In other states, colonists spent two fruitless centuries attempting to grow imported vines. Only in the 1820s did winegrowers turn to the native grapes. With varieties such as *Isabella, Catawba* and *Norton* purely American wines were produced; then in 1852 the first hybrid, *Concord*, was established and thereafter, until the Prohibition Law, hybrids dominated. In fact, the Law was a greater hardship to the eastern states than to California. The native industry never quite regained full stride after the Repeal: of the many thriving states only New York's viticultural concern remains sound and vigorous. Others, such as Ohio, Maryland, New Jersey and Washington, lag behind.

There is, in fact, a continuous struggle between the American winegrowers who advocate the production of native grapes and the growing ranks of those who believe that only French-American hybrids based on European-type and native American parent vines will bring the market level with European competition (from which native American wines, with their distinctive and unusual flavour, have so far been kept). It should be remembered that native American and European wines are extremely dissimilar. If judged on its own particular merits, native American wine has many qualities which could bring it farther into the mainstream of world appreciation, a goal that attempts at imitating French or German wines cannot achieve.

Facts are significant: each year a greater number of connoisseurs add Californian wines to their cellars. And each year the total production rises. In 1952 the figure was 120 million gallons and in 1968 172 million (although dessert wines have lost some ground over the same period). These successes encourage more men to enter the winegrowing scene; so it is that a new name such as Heitz Cellars could be established in 1961 and by 1968 already enjoy a fine reputation.

It is this continuing atmosphere of change that lends much of the excitement to wine in California. One critic said it well: California offers the same sense of discovery that Burgundy must have offered before men know the Clos of Vougeot and of Tart were better than their neighbours. Will the example be followed?

CALIFORNIA

There are nine winegrowing regions in California. Of these, five ring San Francisco Bay; three far larger ones inland occupy the length of the San Joaquin Valley; the ninth lies to the east of Los Angeles.

The five districts near San Francisco are Sonoma-Mendocino (with the sub-districts of the Valley of the Moon and North Sonoma) and Napa to the north, Livermore to the east and Santa Clara-San Benito and Santa Cruz-Monterey to the south. Together they form the North Coast Counties or North Coast Districts. The relatively cold climate of these regions is suited to grapes of European origin: *Cabernet Sauvignon* from Bordeaux, *Pinot Noir* and *Chardonnay* from Burgundy, *Sauvignon Blanc* from Sauternes, *Barbera* from Piedmont, and so forth.

Each of the wine types is likely to be grown in each of the five districts, and with success: most wineries produce eight to twelve different wines, although perhaps two or three afford especial pride. To the uninitiated the fact that more than one wine comes from a single cellar may seem mystifying. However, after the Prohibition Repeal of 1933 every winery offered a wide selection of wines in order to survive the competition and this practice has continued. In addition, the climate of western America is so diverse and changes so subtly within each region (a reliable summer sun can be tempered from one mile to the next by cool, frequently foggy ocean breezes) that growers mostly own small, widely-scattered vineyards in order to take full advantage of the natural diversity of climate and soil.

The San Joaquin Valley districts are Lodi, Modesto and Fresno. Traditionally winemakers in these uniformly hotter and more spacious parts have concentrated on sweet grapes such as *Palomino*, the *Tinta* varieties of Portugal and several grapes of the *Muscat* family. But in order to keep up with the increasing demand for table wines (and counteract the falling dessert wine figures) growers are gradually turning to table wines to boost the limited capacity of the North Coast Counties. New agricultural techniques and grape types developed by research centres and at the University of California at Davis have helped with this.

The ninth region, Cucamonga, is named after a crossroads in the plain east of Los Angeles, and under the hot sun grapes producing a light, sweet wine are cultivated.

In California wines are named by three methods. The first group, known as "generics", covers the names brought over with the vines by immigrant settlers in the late nineteenth century; some of these names are still in use today, like CHABLIS and SHERRY. Then, since the late 1940s, there has been a growing tendency to call wines after their predominating grape variety, for example, CHARDONNAY and PALOMINO, and these are collectively termed "varietals". Thirdly, some wineries use proprietary names of their own coinage.

WHITE WINES

Several varietal wines offer themselves as light, fresh-flavoured types best drunk young with subtly flavoured poultry or shellfish: EMERALD RIESLING, GEWÜRZTRAMINER, GREEN HUNGARIAN, GREY RIESLING, JOHANNISBERG or WHITE RIESLING and SYLVANER. Of these six wines, only occasional bottlings of JOHANNISBERG RIESLING and GEWÜRZTRAMINER are expected to age; each has shown ability to remain fresh for five years, sound for ten. In California, JOHANNISBERG RIESLING makes a richly fruity, even robust wine.

323 Previous page:

The fertile hills of California have proved excellent for the growing of the grape, and a steadily increasing number of wineries are establishing a high reputation for their products.

The first commercial wineries were founded in the Napa Valley, California in 1861. The Beringer Brothers' winery, top, was started in 1876, and is still operated by the family. Inglenook, above, was in business in 1879, and was sold in 1963 by a descendant of the founder. Weinberger, left, seems to have vanished from the bottle labels—but as the estate combined a ranch as well, perhaps this side triumphed.

A second group of fuller-bodied varietal white wines includes CHARDONNAY (or PINOT CHARDONNAY), CHENIN BLANC, SEMILLON and SAUVIGNON BLANC, of which CHARDONNAY and SAUVIGNON BLANC command the greatest interest. The former, at its richest in California, evokes associations with ripe, sun-warmed fruit, apples or peaches. It has a lush, velvet smoothness that recommends it as an accompaniment to the buttery Maine lobster. A Napa Valley or Sonoma bottling from a favourable vintage will gain with age for up to six or seven years. SAUVIGNON BLANC just as intensely flavoured as CHARDONNAY, but it is less full and more austere. It ranks among the best of Californian wines as a companion to Pacific Ocean fish.

Californian vintners offer a roughly parallel series of white generics. Rhines are light and sweet; SAUTERNE (the final "s" of the French spelling is usually omitted) can be either sweet or dry, and have a more intensely fruity character than the Rhines. CHABLIS and MOUNTAIN WHITE are dry and the most intensely flavoured of the generics. Nearly all are offered as *vins de consommation* and are priced accordingly. Some come as press or blend wines from North Coast County cellars, but the great majority are made in the San Joaquin Valley.

RED WINES

The lighter and fruitier of Californian varietal red wines include: GAMAY, GRIGNOLINO, PINOT ST. GEORGE, RUBY CABERNET and ZINFANDEL. California has no wine quite so frivolous as French Beaujolais; its light reds have to be considered more vinous than that. But they are fresh and appealing, eminently suited to informal meals, or to summertime when a light chilling enhances them. RUBY CABERNET deserves special note. It is a University of California hybrid, descended from

Cabernet Sauvignon on one side and *Carignane* on the other, designed to produce distinctive red wines in warm districts. *Zinfandel* (a grape unique to California) is incredibly adaptable. It makes relatively good wines in each of the five climate zones of California, and in each of the nine geographic districts; its best showing, however, is in Napa and Sonoma, where it produces a highly distinctive red wine capable of ageing for ten years and often described as raspberry-like.

The more robust varietal reds of California are BARBERA, CABERNET SAUVIGNON, PETITE SIRAH and PINOT NOIR. PINOT NOIRS have a highly characteristic flavour. The failing—frequent but not inevitable—is a lack of that velvety smoothness associated with this grape in Burgundy. Most California PINOT NOIRS peak within five years, a few have needed ten years and some have required twenty. CABERNET SAUVIGNON, on the other hand, can almost always be expected to age twenty years with some grace. A spate of cool years since 1960 has even led to the wine from this grape being aged longer in barrels in California than it is in Bordeaux. The CABERNET SAUVIGNON is highly tannic, strongly marked by the instantly recognizable flavour of its grape, yet readily able to draw nuances through ageing.

Of California's generic reds BURGUNDYS are the most popular at present and are usually dry with pronounced fruitiness. MOUNTAIN REDS are an equable alternate, CHIANTIS are quite tart and VINO ROSSOS are sweeter.

ROSÉS

The great majority of Californian rosés are generics, although a few are made as varietals. The grape giving the best results is the GRENACHE, although the GRIGNOLINO, CABERNET SAUVIGNON, ZINFANDEL and GAMAY have been used successfully for rosé wines.

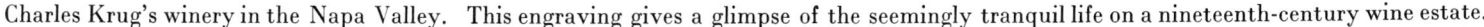

Charles Krug's winery in the Napa Valley. This engraving gives a glimpse of the seemingly tranquil life on a nineteenth-century wine estate.

ESTATE BOTTLED

Buena Vista

HARASZTHY ZINFANDEL

ESTATE GROWN AND BOTTLED BY
HARASZTHY CELLARS
BUENA VISTA VINEYARDS, SONOMA, CALIF

ALCOHOL 12½% BY VOLUME

4

2

1

3

5

HARASZTHY ZINFANDEL

1. Name of the wine and of the grapevine. The grapevine was imported into California from Europe around the middle of the nineteenth century by Count Agoston Haraszthy. The exact place of origin has never been definitely established. The grape gives a fragrant and fruity red wine characteristic of California. – 2. Name of the vineyard. – 3. Address and registered name of the vineyard. – 4. Indication of place of original bottling. – 5. Statement of alcohol content.

CABERNET SAUVIGNON

1. Name of the wine and of the grapevine. This grape, the same as that which gives Bordeaux claret, was imported into California. It gives a red wine of a beautiful deep ruby colour and with a most agreeable flavour. – 2. Name of the vineyard. – 3. Geographical origin of the wine and registered name of the vineyard. – 4. Indication of place of original bottling. – 5. Statement of alcohol content.

Beaulieu Vineyard

BV

ESTATE BOTTLED

NAPA VALLEY

CABERNET SAUVIGNON

PRODUCED & BOTTLED BY BEAULIEU VINEYARD
AT RUTHERFORD, NAPA COUNTY, CALIFORNIA

ALCOHOL 12.5% BY VOLUME

4

3

1

3

5

2

Vineyards Established 1852

ALMADÉN

California Mountain
PINOT NOIR

A distinguished, authentic Pinot Noir, velvety and fine, made entirely from grapes of this illustrious Burgundian variety, grown in Mountain Vineyards at Paicines, California

PRODUCED AND BOTTLED BY
Almadén Vineyards, Los Gatos, California

Alcohol 12½% by volume   0-67

4

2

1

2

3

5

PINOT NOIR

1. Name of the wine and of the grapevine. The grape is the same as that grown in Burgundy and which gives the famous red wines. – 2. Name of the vineyard and of the region. – 3. Name and address of the vineyards. – 4. Date of the foundation of the vineyard. – 5. Statement of alcohol content.

PINOT CHARDONNAY

1. Name of the wine and of the grapevine. This grape is very widespread in Champagne and Burgundy and gives a white wine resembling the dry white wine of Champagne that is much appreciated today. – 2. Name of the region. – 3. Name of the proprietor. – 4. Vintage date. – 5. Statement of alcohol content.

GEWÜRZ TRAMINER

1. Name of the wine and of the grapevine. This grape, which gives a white wine with a spicy scent and flavour, was imported from Alsace. – 2. Name of the region. – 3. Name of the proprietor. – 4. Date of the foundation of the vineyard. – 5. Statement of alcohol content.

SAUTERNE

1. Name of the wine. The name does not indicate the grapevine but the type of wine, which is a sweet white variety similar to French Sauternes. This wine can be made from grapes coming from several different regions of California. – 2. Name of the wine-merchant. – 3. Statement of alcohol content.

DINNER WINES

VARIETALS
Named for the grapes from which they are made.

White Wines

Serve chilled with fish, shellfish or poultry.
Light, crisp white wines, pale golden, or slightly green-gold in colour. Most are pleasantly dry. Some may have a hint of sweetness.
> Johannisberg Riesling – Grey Riesling – Traminer – Sylvaner

Rich, fuller-flavoured wines. These are usually dry wines, pale to light golden in colour. Some may have a hint of sweetness.*
> Pinot Chardonnay – Folle Blanche – Pinot Blanc – Dry Semillon – *Chemin Blanc

Medium to pronounced sweetness in these wines. They can be enjoyed most with dessert, fruit, fruit salad, and sweet food.
> Semillon – Sauvignon Blanc

Rosé Wines

Serve chilled with ham, pork, veal, lamb, poultry.
These are light, fruity wines, sometimes dry, sometimes slightly sweet*, with a cheerful pink colour, ranging in tone from deep rose to a pale, orange tinted hue.
> *Grenache Rosé – Gamay Rosé – Grignolino Rosé

Red Wines

Serve at cool room temperature with steaks, roasts, game, spaghetti, cheeses, stews, casseroles.
Fresh, fruity, red wines, dry and aromatic, light to medium in body.
> Zinfandel – Ruby Cabernet

Rich, red wines with distinctive flavour and appealing ruby colour, medium to full in body.
> Pinot Noir – Cabernet Sauvignon – Barbera

APPETIZER AND DESSERT WINES

Appetizer Wines

Aperitif or appetizer wines are usually dry and are drunk before meals or with the soup course. Chill them, or serve at room temperature, or pour over ice.
> Sherry: *dry :* Solera Cocktail – Pale Dry – Ultra Dry – Dry Watch
> *medium dry :* Solera Golden – Flor Sherry
> Vermouth – dry or sweet

Dessert Wines

Pour dessert wines after dinner, either with dessert or later. They are all sweet, rich wines that are particularly good with fruit, nuts, cheese, cake. Serve at room temperature.
> Sweet and cream Sherry: Solera Cream – Triple Cream – Rare Cream – Cream Flor
> Port: Solera Ruby – Solera Tawny – Vintage Port – Tawny Port – Rare Tawny – Tinta Port

Sauterne and sweet Semillon are also served as dessert wines.

Sparkling Wines

These festive wines are appropriate at any time, with food as by themselves. They range from extremely dry to quite sweet, from pale gold to deep red. Sparkling wines are best well chilled.
> *Champagne type :* Natural: very dry – Brut: dry – Extra dry: with just a hint of sweetness – Dry: medium sweet – Sec: noticeably sweet – Demi-Sec: very sweet

| *Rosé :* | *Muscat :* | *Red :* |
| Pink Champagne | Sparkling Muscat | Sparkling Burgundy |

APERITIF AND DESSERT WINES

California sherries are usually made after the fashion of Madeiras, although some are produced by the traditional flor method and aged and blended in a solera system. Ports are made in much the same way as those of Oporto, but rarely from the same grape.

THE WINEGROWERS OF CALIFORNIA

All told, California has around 212 licensed wineries within its capacious boundaries. The wineries that are of more than passing interest are noted in this section, with some incidental description of the districts in which they are found. Very nearly all of California's cellars welcome visitors, which encourages first-hand exploration in some of the state's handsomest countryside.

NAPA

Viticulture in the Napa Valley centres round the timeless little town of St. Helena toward the northern end of the valley.

A German named Charles Krug founded Napa's first commercial winery at St. Helena in 1861, and was soon followed by others; the valley has remained in the forefront of Californian winemaking since that era. Krug's name continues, although the cellars he built are now owned and operated by the family of the late Cesare Mondavi, who restored the estate after Prohibition. Beringer (1876) continued under its founding family. Beaulieu (1900) was sold to Heublein Inc. in 1969, although it still operates as a separate company. Inglenook (1879) was sold in 1963 by a descendant of the founder, Nybom. The Christian Brothers, although they came to this valley only in 1930, have a history dating back to 1882. Otherwise, the names are much newer: Heitz Cellar (1961), Hanns Kornell (1952), Louis M. Martini (1933, after a start elsewhere in 1923), Mayacamas (1947), Robert Mondavi (1966), Souverain (1953) and Stony Hill (1953). New or old, the cellars in the valley are among the most colourful in California and those who make wine in this valley now have made its name familiar in the world of wine far beyond state or even national borders. Its reputation rests with its red wines, especially the CABERNET SAUVIGNONS.

SONOMA

The Valley of the Moon in Sonoma is a focal point of Californian history. It is here that the first revolt against the Mexican government started California on the way to United States statehood. It continues to bear a marked resemblance to its Spanish beginnings.

Buena Vista, Hanzell and Sebastiani in the Valley and Korbel and Pedroncelli in North Sonoma are responsible for the district's reputation. Journalist Frank Bartholomew restored Buena Vista to operation in 1943, long after Agoston Haraszthy had made it famous in the 1860s and in 1906 left it to fall into oblivion. Korbel dates from the 1880s, Sebastiani from 1905. Hanzell was founded in 1956 to see how close California could come to classic Burgundies, both red and white.

LIVERMORE-ALAMEDA COUNTY

Most of the vines of Livermore belong to two old winegrowing families of California: Karl Wente, a German, came to Livermore in 1883, and James Concannon, indisputably Irish, arrived a year later. Other pioneer vinicultural families of Charles Wetmore and Louis Mel have disappeared. Mel had connections with the Château d'Yquem and obtained cuttings from its vineyards to plant in the similar soil of Livermore. The Wente family acquired Mel's vineyards and have retained a small block of those now-ancient vines.

Urban pressure grows steadily in Livermore but Wente has guarded against the future by planting sizeable new vineyards in an unpopulated part of Monterey County, a hundred miles south.

On the San Francisco Bay side of Alameda County lie the vinegrowing centres of Mission San José and Irvington. Here the red wine is almost as good as the white, and sparkling and Champagne-type wines, aperitifs and dessert wines are also produced.

SAN JOAQUIN VALLEY

To meet the growing demand for table wines, winemakers are taking two approaches. One is the use of newly developed grape varieties and climate-modifying vineyard practices to make dry and in some cases distinctive table wines by traditional vinification and ageing methods. The other is the perfection of techniques for handling enormous volumes of wine for mass appeal on the American market. Most of the traditional wines are made at Lodi, northernmost of the districts, especially by Acampo and East-Side.

At Modesto, the firm of E. & J. Gallo stands unmatched in the making of wines in great volume. Using modern equipment and every new technique, the brothers Ernest and Julio Gallo make table wines to carefully established standards in lots of half a million gallons at a time. Guild, United Vintners and several other wineries have taken to using similar methods. This new trend has not come entirely at the expense of aperitif and dessert wines long associated with the valley: they continue to be made as well or better than

before. At Fresno, a tiny cellar named Ficklin produces an outstanding dessert wine from four of the major grape varieties of the Douro, calling it TINTA PORT. The larger Cresta Blanca has two dry sherry types from *Palomino* grapes. Many of the sweet grapes of the sherry type grown and made into wines here are sold under the labels of North Coast wineries such as Novitiate of Los Gatos in Santa Clara, the Christian Brothers in Napa, Weibel in Alameda County.

SANTA CLARA

Urban pressure has affected the Santa Clara-San Benito district even more dramatically than the Livermore district. In fact, these two counties and the Santa Cruz-Monterey region have been blurred into a single four-county district in which the old Santa Clara wineries are completely dominant.

Almaden and Paul Masson, both descendants of the founder Etienne Thee (1852), have gone separate but similar ways in the post-Prohibition era. Both maintain their original cellars near the city of San José, but are growing elsewhere. Almaden has become the largest winegrowing estate devoted to classic table wine types in the world. Paul Masson has proceeded on a scale only slightly lower at another site a few miles away, at Soledad in Monterey County.

Harvest time on a Californian vineyard. Skilled vintagers come to the wine country each vintage season to select and gather the ripe grapes.

CUCAMONGA

Southernmost of California's wine districts is Cucamonga. One of the oldest districts, it is now being inundated by an eastward-sweeping wave of suburban residential communities. In spite of its declining size, the region has nearly 17,000 acres in vineyards, so it is hoped that it will survive for some years to come.

A full range of wines is produced in this region, from red table wines and sparkling "Champagnes" to aperitifs and dessert wines. The hot desert climate is not conducive to full-bodied wines and the light Cucamonga growths should be drunk when still young. Connoisseurs with a modest experience of Californian vintages can inevitably identify wines from Cucamonga owing to a *goût de terroir* (a special quality of wine which is attributable chiefly to soil-type) which transcends all grape varieties and methods of vinification. It is the only Californian district with so pronounced an individual characteristic.

OTHER STATES

More than half of the fifty American states have local wine industries, all but a few of them being planted to native grapes. Five of the states are of special importance for their winegrowing achievements.

New York State has several winegrowing districts, but owes its reputation to vintages from vineyards lying along the Finger Lakes, in the northern reaches of the state. The five Finger Lakes, each of them long and extremely narrow, are set in steepsided hills with lower slopes that favour winegrowing.

Local wineries have an average of seventy flourishing years behind them, and reason to be optimistic about a growing audience in the eastern and midwestern population centres of the United States. The largest winery, Taylor-Great Western, is large by any standards with its nine million gallon capacity. Widmers and Gold Seal are much smaller; Konstantin Frank's is a tiny cellar, but everybody in New York knows about it.

Traditionally the emphasis among the Finger Lakes cellars has been on sparkling wines and sherry types. There are sound reasons for this. The vineyards were planted to native American grapes, primarily of the genus *vitis labrusca*, for much of their history. Whenever these grapes are talked about in international wine circles, it is for their "foxy" taste: the flavour is imparted by a substance called methyl anthranilate, unmistakable in table wines, but less obvious in sparkling wines and oxidized sherry types.

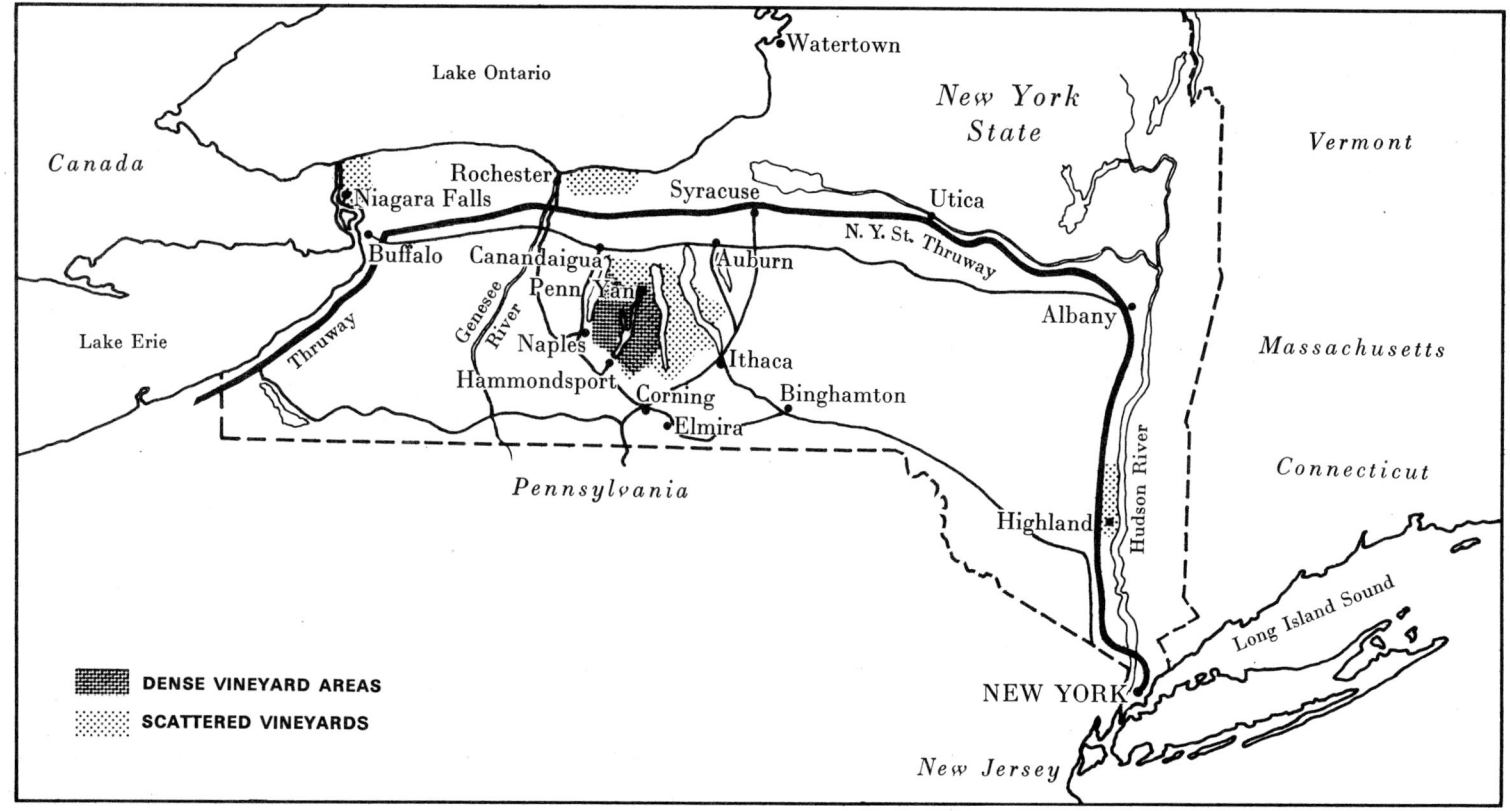

330

In recent years wine companies and growers, notably Taylor (founded 1880), have begun to experiment with hybrids such as *Seibel*, *Seyve-Villard* and so forth, and others, in particular Konstantin Frank, have begun experiments with European *vitis vinifera* varieties. In the case of his *Johannisberg Riesling*, Frank modestly claims to have achieved the perfect *auslese*. Gold Seal (1865) maintains both *vitis vinifera* and hybrid plantings in addition to native grapes; Widmeras (1888) also has experiments underway in both.

The distinctive wines of the district are from vineyards of the American *vitis labrusca* varieties, notably *Concord*, *Niagara*, *Elvira*, *Catawba*, *Delaware* and *Ives*. Usually these are softened by blending with hybrids.

Washington State makes very nearly as much wine as New York State, with many of the same grape varieties. But it has never approached the Finger Lakes wine for quality and has not won a following outside its boundaries. The great majority of vineyards in Washington are near the town of Yakima, a famous region of fruit orchards at the eastern foothills of the Cascade Mountain Range. Some growers are experimenting with such *vitis vinifera* as *Pinot Noir* and *Johannisberg Riesling*, but results to date are either inconclusive or discouraging: the primary difficulty appears to be a short season.

Oregon, between Washington and California, has several small vineyards of *Johannisberg Riesling*, *Traminer* and *Pinot Noir* growing in its Willamette Valley south of Portland. A few growers are attempting to found a new wine region based on the Napa or Sonoma lines. Almost no wines have reached the market after the first few years of experiment, but scientists from the Department of Viticulture and Enology of the University of California regard the beginning as propitious.

In the eastern half of the country, Maryland has won widespread recognition as a wine district through the efforts of one man, journalist and viticulturist Philip Wagner. Wagner has spent two decades experimenting with the French-American hybrids in an attempt to diversify and upgrade wines from the native American districts. Work at his Boordy Vineyards has had substantial effect on the New York winegrowing regions.

Ohio was among the earliest of the colonial American winegrowing states, but now its production is waning steadily. The climate remains favourable for the growing of native grapes, but increasing population is crowding the vineyards along Lake Erie into the neighbourhood of Sandusky. Sparkling wines, especially from the *Delaware* grape, continue to be regarded favourably by many wine drinkers in the midwest and east: Meier's is the best known.

THE WINES OF CANADA

Of all the wines on the North American continent those from Canada are perhaps the least known. The Canadians have two small and persistent wine districts. The largest, the Niagara Peninsula, Ontario, produces about 90% of Canada's grapes. Here, most of the grapes are native American varieties, but some *vitis vinifera*

vineyards are in bearing. The other district is in British Columbia. Its Okanagan Valley lies directly north of Washington's Yakima district, and produces a range of wines from native grape varieties. The Ontario district is the larger, and its wines are found more widely across Canada than British Columbians.

THE WINES OF MEXICO

Mexico is famous throughout the North American Continent for its beers, and unknown even within its borders for wine. The beers deserve their excellent reputation; the wines, although they are not rated by international standards, deserve slightly greater recognition than they receive.

Winemaking began in Mexico with the Spanish missionaries of the mid-eighteenth century, but its development was retarded by a combination of hot climate and poorly trained viticulturists and enologists. Large-scale plantings of vineyards did not take place until after 1920; even today the total acreage is only 25,000. The largest winegrowing district is Aguascalientes, the

most promising one Ensenada in Baja California. Here, technological skills are advanced, and the wineries are properly equipped.

Mexico's most distinctive wines to date have been sweet fortified ones, especially some of the Muscat types from Ensenada. Because of the hot climate, such wines no doubt will continue to surpass table wines in quality. Some of the latter are agreeable *ordinaires*, priced as such and served in Mexico City as well as in their districts of origin. It does not appear likely, however, that Mexican wines will gain great favour at home in the near future. The competition from beer is too great for the wines to expand beyond their small clientele.

Vineyards of the California valley extended in parallel lines as far as the eye can see. The grapes from these vines contribute to the millions of gallons which flow from California vineyards.

WINES OF CALIFORNIA

Red wines	Claret types . .	Cabernet Sauvignon . . .	Almadén, Beaulieu, Inglenook, Charles Krug, Louis Martini, Mirassou, Robert Mondavi, Sebastiani, Souverain
		Zinfandel	Buena Vista, Charles Krug, The Christian Bros., Louis Martini, Mirassou, Robert Mondavi, Pedroncelli
		Ruby Cabernet	East-Side
	Burgundy types.	Pinot Noir	Almadén, Beaulieu, Hanzell, Heitz Cellar, Inglenook, Louis Martini, Paul Masson, Martin Ray, Wente Bros.
	Italian types. .	Barbera	Louis Martini, Sebastiani
		Grignolino	Beringer, Heitz Cellar
		Chianti	Gallo, Italian Swiss Colony
White wines	Sauternes types .	Sauvignon Blanc . . .	Almadén, Concannon, Robert Mondavi, Wente Bros.
		Semillon	Concannon, Charles Krug, Louis Martini, Wente Bros.
	Burgundy types.	Pinot Chardonnay . . .	Almadén, Beaulieu, Hanzell, Heitz Cellar, Paul Masson, Mayacamas, Robert Mondavi, Souverain, Stony Hill, Weibel, Wente Bros.
		Pinot Blanc.	Heitz Cellar, Paul Masson, Mirassou, Wente Bros.
		Chenin Blanc	Charles Krug, Souverain
		Folle Blanche	Louis Martini
		Chablis	Beaulieu, The Christian Bros.
	Rhine types . .	Johannisberger Riesling .	Almadén, Beaulieu, Charles Krug, Louis Martini, Souverain
		Grey Riesling	Almadén, Charles Krug, Wente Bros.
		Traminer	Charles Krug, Louis Martini, Mirassou, Stony Hill
		Sylvaner	Buena Vista, Inglenook, Louis Martini
Aperitif and dessert wines .	Sherry types . .	dry	Solera Cocktail (Almadén) Pale dry (Beaulieu, Louis Martini) Ultra Dry (Buena Vista) Dry Watch (Cresta Blanca)
		medium dry	Solera Golden (Almadén) Flor Sherry (Novitiate of Los Gatos, Weibel)
		Sweet and Cream Sherry .	Solera Cream (Beaulieu) Triple Cream (Cresta Blanca) Rare Cream (Paul Masson) Cream Flor (Weibel)
	Port types . . .	Solera Ruby	Almadén
		Solera Tawny	Almadén
		Vintage Port	Buena Vista
		Tawny Port	Louis Martini
		Rare Tawny	Paul Masson
		Tinta Port	Ficklin
	Champagne types	Champagne	Almadén, Korbel, Hanns Kornell, Paul Masson, Weibel
		Pink Champagne	Almadén, Korbel, Paul Masson, Weibel
		Sparkling Burgundy . . .	Almadén, Korbel, Hanns Kornell, Paul Masson, Weibel
		Sparkling Muscat	Hanns Kornell
Rosé wines		Grenache rosé	Almadén, Beaulieu, Novitiate of Los Gatos
		Gamay rosé	Louis Martini, Robert Mondavi
		Grignolino rosé	Heitz Cellar

WINES OF NEW YORK STATE

Red wines	Burgundy	Delaware	Lake Country Red
	Claret	Isabella	Niagara
White wines	Catawba	Johannisberger Riesling Spätlese	Pinot Chardonnay
	Delaware	Lake Niagara	Rhine Wine
	Gewürztraminer	Muscat Ottonel	White Tokay

THE WINES
OF SOUTH AMERICA

DENIS BOUVIER

Within hours of their first landings on the cost of South America, the galleons flying the flags of Spain discharged upon the beaches two very disparate cargoes: barrels of gunpowder for their arms, and barrels of wine for the altar set up in the name of Their Very Catholic Majesties. But the supply of wine soon grew short, and the missionaries who landed with the *conquistadores* found themselves obliged to become winegrowers. In this way wine came to South America.

The aim of the emissaries sent out by Ferdinand of Spain and Manuel the Fortunate of Portugal was to conquer the "Western Indies". The sole purpose of the conquest was to appropriate for themselves the gold and wealth of these new countries which stretched from the Atlantic across the Andes to the "Great Ocean" beyond. But neither the cross, nor the royal standard, nor even the quantities of glass beads they brought could persuade the natives to let invaders plunder the riches of their land. The *conquistadores* then used more summary methods, which the Indians answered in their own way: they tortured their prisoners in original fashion, quenching their thirst by giving them molten gold to drink as a reprisal for the wine which the Franciscan and Jesuit Fathers had forced them to drink with the Host. And what remains today of this immense Empire after it was split up into the separate nations of Chile, Argentina, Brazil and Peru? The gold mines are long since empty, the art treasures shamelessly melted down into bullion; the people, decimated by war and bled dry by taxation, are reduced to poverty. The only living thing remaining

of what the conquerors brought to South America is, here and there, a vineplant, a thriving symbol of eternity.

This vine-plant gave birth to the immense South American vineyard of today, which spreads along the coastline, in the valleys of the Andes right at the foot of the Great Cordillera, and then up on the high plains into the Pampas region and to Uruguay. Wine, which at the heroic time of the *Conquista* was considered to be the perquisite of the new Crusaders, grew to be more appreciated as the Spanish influence came to dominate the people. Viticulture was further intensified when settlers flocked from across the seas; they came from France, Italy and Germany, often bringing with them as their sole possession the love of vineyards and wine as well as the knowledge acquired from centuries of winemaking in Burgundy, the Basque provinces, Tuscany or the banks of the Rhine. Thus viniculture spread through the new land of South America, which previously had only seemed capable of harbouring the sisal plant, or maté, maize and coffee. True, it was first necessary to make the soil suitable for cultivation, for it had been allowed to lie fallow for centuries. Canals were dug to irrigate the land, and experiments made to find the vine-plant best suited to the varied and often capricious climate of the area. Then it was necessary to develop new methods of vinification and culture. Here, the vinegrowers drew on their experiences in the African vineyards.

The South American vineyard has developed well, and it is today of respectable dimensions. The quality of its produce continues to improve, even though the wine it exports (at competitive prices) cannot hope to rival in quality the great wines of Western Europe. These are wines which compare more favourably with those of North Africa.

Not all countries cultivate the vine: Ecuador, Venezuela, Guiana and Paraguay do not. Of those that do, the following are listed in order of importance both as regards the area under cultivation and the production of wine: Argentina, Chile, Brazil, Uruguay, Peru, Bolivia and Columbia. It is interesting to note that until now no South American Government has introduced any official system of classification or control of the proprietary name in South America there is no *appellation d'origine contrôlée*.

ARGENTINA

Argentina, fourth largest wineproducer in the world, is the first in South America. Its wine, however, is grown solely for domestic consumption, not for world markets. How better could an Argentinian accompany the excellent meat of his abundant live-stock than with a bottle of his own wine?

The vine was introduced to Argentina in the sixteenth century, when the Spaniards first conquered the Pampas. Coming down from the high plains and mineral regions of Bolivia, they looked for new treasures in the foothills of the Andes. By comparison with the gold being sought by Don Pedro de Castillo and Juan Jupe, who founded the towers of Mendoza and San Juan, the humble vine planted by the Franciscans and Jesuits did not seem to promise a great future. However, despite the obstacles the kings of Spain brought to the development of viticulture in this part of the American continent, the Cuyo region grew rich in vineyards thanks to the patience and industry of its winegrowers. Alas, as Philip II's coffers grew heavy with rare and precious metals, the Spanish economy, mortally paralysed, came to a standstill.

The first vines planted in the provinces of Mendoza and San Juan would probably not have yielded any grapes unless the fallow soil had been previously irrigated. The Italian immigrants were the first to find a method of using the water which came down in torrents from the Andes and was rich in lime. Thus the vine could be cultivated even in desert-like conditions, and so began the famous "viticultural oases". Later this water brought the deadly phylloxera disease which drastically reduced wine-harvests; but in its turn the water helped, for the same network of irrigation canals which was responsible for spreading the disease later aided the method used to cure it. By plugging and overflowing the canals, it was possible to flood the infected vines and drown out the tiny plant lice that destroyed them.

The South American wine, which at first was produced only for local consumption, gradually began to infiltrate the whole country as new routes were opened up into the interior. In the nineteenth century, considerable progress was made in the field of vinification and viticulture, mainly owing to the influx of European immigrants. Today viticulture in Argentina is flourishing, having developed hand in hand with the demographic growth of the country. The winegrowers could doubtless pay more attention to the quality of their product, which is often the weak point in vinification when practised on too large a scale.

Grape varieties. *Criollo* is the first vine-plant cultivated in Argentina. It came, in fact, from Mexico and Peru, but can be considered an indigenous grape. It is probably from this stock that Brother Cedron made the first wine in Argentina 450 years ago. Today it produces white wines. White wines are also made from grapes introduced by French, Italian and Spanish growers, grapes such as the *Pedro Ximenez*, *Semillon*, *Pinot Blanc*, *Malvoisie* and the *Riesling*. Two-thirds of the red wines are made from the *Malbec* grape variety, and the remainder from various other European grape varieties.

Vinicultural provinces. In order of importance the chief wineproducing provinces are Mendoza, San Juan and Rio King, which between them provide 96 per cent of Argentina's wine-harvest. Then come the regions of Buenos Aires, Santa Fé, Córdoba, La Rioja, Catamarca, Salta, Jujy and Entrerios.

Mendoza. This province is by far the most important. It alone produces 70 per cent of Argentina's wine crop: in 1966, the wine-harvest there was 304,304,000 gallons. The area under cultivation is 488,900 acres, or 40 per cent of the entire South American vineyard. There are about 40,000 vintners in this region alone, but 16 per cent of the production is in the hands of only nine large companies. These firms have their own wine-cellars, and a distribution network throughout Argentina. Most of the wines produced here are red, but there is also a small quantity of white and sparkling wines. Very few winegrowers, however, try to produce quality wines; most are only interested in quantity, which they get by mechanizing production. Their well-equipped farms dot the far-flung vineyards which reach far beyond the horizon.

OCEANO PACIFICO

CHILE

Antofagasta

BRAZIL

LA RIOJA

Río Salado

Río Paraná

Río Uruguay

BENTO-GONÇALVES

JESÚS MARÍA

Córdoba

Santa Fe

Concordia

CAXIAS DO SUL

Porto Alegre

RIO GRANDE DO SUL

SAN JUAN

Salto

Pelotas

VILLA DOLORES

PAYSANDÚ

Valparaíso

MENDOZA

Rosario

SAN-NICOLÁS

URUGUAY

SANTIAGO

SAN RAFAEL

FLORIDA

O'HIGGINS

SAN JOSÉ

COLONIA

CANELONES

TALCA

BUENOS AIRES

Río de la Plata

MALDONADO

MONTEVIDEO

LINARES

CONCEPCIÓN

CHILLÁN

ARGENTINA

BÍO-BÍO

Bahía Blanca

Valdivia

Río Colorado

Osorno

RIO NEGRO

Río Negro

OCEANO ATLANTICO

MAPA VITICOLA
AMERICA DEL SUL

Among South American countries Chile produces the wine best known on the export market. Argentina is the largest wineproducer and after Chile, which holds second place, comes Brazil with an annual yield of about fifteen million gallons, most of which is sold abroad. Uruguay, although the smallest of the South American states, produces a great deal of wine, most of which is consumed locally.

337

Everything here is done on a very large scale. The Bodega Giol, in Mendoza, for example, can store about 19,140,000 gallons; and it is merely one of many.

SAN JUAN. Farther along the Great Cordillera, past the province of Mendoza, is San Juan, whose vineyard is one-quarter the size of Mendoza. But acre for acre, its yield is greater: it produces an average of 132,000,000 gallons of wine a year. Here the wine is richer, with more body, although the reason for this might be merely that San Juan is somewhat nearer to the Equator and thus enjoys a warmer climate.

RIO AND OTHER REGIONS. Rio is situated at the southern tip of the viticultural zone of the Republic of Argentina. It produces light red wines, excellent whites and also sparkling wines. These are considered Argentina's best wines. Other wineproducing areas are La Rioja, Salta and Buenos Aires, whose vineyards are being extended. Santiago del Estero is in the process of planting a vineyard.

WINE TYPES. The International Institute of Viti-Viniculture *(El Instituto Internacional de la Viti-vini-cultura)* has classified Argentinian wines into two groups: *comunes* (ordinary wines) and *no comunes* (the better grades). The *comunes* wines, which account for 90 per cent of the total production, are those sold as *vinos de mesa* or table wines. They are mostly red, very full-bodied wines, with an alcohol content ranging from 11º to 12.5º. The whites are ordinary wines with a higher alcohol content. Ordinary wine from the provinces of La Rioja, San Juan, Catamarca, Córdoba, Jujuy and Salta enjoys a form of regional appellation. These are unblended wines *envasado en origen* (bottled by the producer), or mixed with other wines (provided that the other wine used was made from grapes grown on the territory of the corresponding regional vineyard); these are known as *vinos de corte* (blended wines). The third category of wine known as *comunes* is that of special wines labelled *vinos de postre* (dessert wines) or *moscato*. *Vinos de mesa* and *vinos de postre* can be *seco* (dry), *dulce* (sweet) or *abocado* (a mild wine). The *vino de postre abocado* is made by adding a concentrated must to the wine whilst it is fermenting, and is very highly thought of by Argentinians.

The best Argentinian wines are the *vinos no comunes*. They come in four different categories: *finos* (fine wines), *reservas* (wines in reserve), *reservados* (reserved) and *especiales* (special wines). The fine wines are made mainly from the *Semillon*, *Pedro Ximenez*, *Cabernet*, *Barbera*, *Malbec* and *Torrentes* grapes. According to their colour they are known as: *tinto*, *blanco*, *clarete*, *rosado* or *criollo*. The reds are well-balanced, dry, strong and full-bodied wines, with an alcohol content from 12° to 13°. The white wines, whose alcohol content is slightly lower than the red, have a rich bouquet; they are well-balanced and have a very pleasant taste. The rosés are also well-balanced, with an alcohol content of from 12º to 13º. ESCORHUELO, RIO NEGRO and the well-known EL TRAPICHE are some of the best wines of Argentina.

Argentina also produces sparkling wines of the Champagne or Asti type as well as aerated wine, as mediocre here as anywhere else in the world. There are also vermouths and quinine waters.

A few Argentinian wines have adopted foreign names, such as Porto, Jerez, Champagne, Marsala, Médoc and Burgundy. It is interesting to note that although in Argentina there is a strict control on the production and quality of wine, there is none on the brand names.

CHILE

Chilean wines are by far the best in South America, and have established the highest reputation on the continent. However, Chile exports very little wine to the world market: only 1.25 per cent from an annual production of about 99,000,000 gallons. Most of the wines for export are honest table wines, and one must visit Chile, or more particularly the Santiago region, to taste the best the country has to offer.

As elsewhere in South America, the Europeans implanted the *vitis vinifera* in Chile, whose climate proved to be very favourable to the cultivation of the vine. The vineyard was modernized in the nineteenth century by Italian, French and German immigrants. The French techniques in viniculture and vinification were the most successful, hence French methods came to be generally accepted and practised in all the *haciendas* and these techniques are still employed today.

An attempt was made to extend viticulture to the drier and less suitable regions, but irrigation proved to be an inseparable problem. A Chilean, Silvestre Ochagavia, imported and planted French vines, and brought the *Cabernet*, *Sauvignon* and *Pinot* grapes into the central valley in Chile; then, following his example, the Government took measures to encourage the development of viticulture in that area.

Chile has three large viticultural regions. The biggest in area is the southern vineyard. Herein are contained the regions of Linares, the banks of the Maule river, Nuble, Conception and the Bío-Bío valley, where the production is mainly red wines (70 per cent), with a small quantity of white wines (30 per cent). These wines, originating for the most part from humid and cold areas, are light, with a low alcohol content; they are made from *Malbec, Cabernet, Semillon* and *Riesling* grapes.

The second largest viticultural region—Curico, Talca, Santiago, O'Higgins and Colchaga—has a dry, warm climate, but thanks to irrigation produces excellent wines. Red wines are made from the *Cabernet Franc, Cabernet Sauvignon, Merlot, Malbec* and *Petit Verdot* grapes; the white wines, from the *Semillon* and *Sauvignon* grapes. A few *Pinot Blanc* and *Pinot Noir* grapes can be found here and there, as well as the *País* or *Uva del País*, the national grape, one of the first vines to be planted on Chilean soil.

The third principal vineyard is farther north, near Coquimbo in the Aconcaga valleys and along the banks of the Maipo river, as well as up to the fringes of the Atacama desert. Here the *Muscat* grape flourishes and gives wines of a very high alcohol content: rich and full-bodied, similar to Madeira, ports or sherry. They are often blended with the southern varieties. The climate here in the northern part of the country does not favour viniculture, for it is either too dry or too humid, depending on the season.

Chilean wines are classified into four different categories according to their age. The first category is for ordinary table wines of one year; the second is the *especiales*, which are two-year-old wines; the third, the *reservados*, have been in the bottle for four years, and are often high quality wines; and finally, the *gran vino* wines are recognized as being the best. Their quality is guaranteed by the State, and they are left to mature in barrels for at least six years.

BRAZIL

Brazil is the third largest wineproducer in South America, with vineyards covering 170,500 acres and producing about 33,000,000 gallons. Planted at the time of the Portuguese conquest, the vine came into its own only at the beginning of the last century. It made some progress between the two wars and is still being developed today: within rather less than fifty years, the area under cultivation increased sevenfold. This development was above all the work of Italian immigrants, who knew how to bring the best out of a soil which until then had been neglected. However, as the average Brazilian only drinks about four pints a year, the rest is sold on the international market, where the main customers are the U.S.A., Argentina and Germany.

THE GRAPE VARIETIES. The *Isabella* is the grape most frequently used; it is an American hybrid which produces an ordinary table wine. The other grapes used are the *Duchesse, Merlot, Cabernet, Barbera, Niagara, Folha de Figos, Black July, Siebel* and such varieties as the *Delaware, Jacques Gaillard, Concord, Gothe, Trebbiano,* and *Moscatel.*

WINES. The Brazilian wine industry is controlled by a series of very simple regulations, which merely distinguish between table, dessert and blended wines. These wines can be called by their grape—BARBERA, MOSCATEL, TREBBIANO, MALVASIA, RIESLING and MERLOT—provided they consist of these varieties in an authorized proportion. As a result, one can find good quality ordinary wines, but never great wines. The ordinary table wines are of a red Burgundy or claret type, rosés, or dry, semi-dry and sweet white wines. Good table wines include those of the *Barbera, Cabernet* and *Merlot* grapes, which produce reds; or those of the *Trebbiano, Poverella, Malvasia* and *Riesling* grape which produce whites. Other good wines have their own trade names. Brazil also produces sparkling wines, made in the bottle or in any of several types of closed containers. These *espumante* (effervescent) wines are from the juice of the *Moscatel* and *Malvasia* grapes.

The Rio Grande do Sul represents the biggest viticultural area, for its climate is the most favourable to vine cultivation. Other wineproducing areas are São Paulo, Santa Caterina, Rio de Janeiro and Minas Gerias, with vineyard altitudes varying from 2,100 to 5,400 feet; surely a record.

Caxias do Sul and Bento-Concalves are the main areas of production in Rio Grande do Sul. Having abandoned the *Lambrusca grape*, which produced a very mediocre growth, the winegrowers here turned mainly to the *Concord, Isabella, Tercy* and *Herbemont* grapes, and to hybrids of the *Seibel* grape. The best alternative grapes used to make red wines are the *Sangiovesi, Barbera* and *Cabernet*; while for white wines, there are the *Merlot, Riesling, Malvasia* and *Trebbiano* grapes. The wines produced in this State, especially the reds, are usually of a very high quality.

In the State of São Paulo, the vine is concentrated around the regions of Jundiai and São Roque, but the best wine comes from Pardo, São José do Rio, Serra Negra, Salto de Itu, Ararquara, Campinas and Guararema. These vines are more or less the same varieties as those in the Rio Grande do Sul.

There are other viticultural centres in Brazil, notably Videira in Santa Catarina and Recife in Pernambuco.

URUGUAY

Viniculture was first introduced into Uruguay towards the end of the last century from the Montevideo region. Smallest of all South American States (apart from French and Dutch Guiana), it produces 18,700,000 gallons of wine per annum, which puts it fourth among the viticultural countries on this continent. But wine stocks are insignificant and almost exclusively for domestic consumption. Production just about meets the demand, which is nevertheless eight times greater than in the United States, while production is about one-tenth! This underlines the importance of viticulture which, despite competition from *maté*, the national drink, almost doubled in the years 1958 to 1963, when it reached almost 27,500,000 gallons. Wine is drunk more and more frequently with meals, especially with lamb roasted on the spit, a choice dish in Uruguay.

A country with a temperate climate and heavy rainfall, Uruguay has several winegrowing regions, mainly in the south. The Canelones region is the most important; there the vines cover more than 24,500 acres, divided into small-holdings. Montevideo follows, with 13,400 acres shared between 1,874 winegrowers; then San José, Colonia, Paysandu, Florida, and Maldonado in order of production. Although there are quite a few vintners—some 7,300 for the whole country—there are also many large co-operatives, or *bodégueros*, which have their own underground cellars with all the most modern equipment for pressing and vinification. The most common vine in Uruguay is one which is rarely met anywhere else in the world; here it is called *Harriague*. In the Hautes-Pyrénées of France, where it comes from, it is better known as *Tannat*. It gives a good quality red wine. The best wines however, are made from grapes such as *Alicante*, *Carignan*, *Grenache* and *Cinsault*. Other grapes used are *Vidiella*, whose origin is unknown; *Cabernet*, here used to make an ordinary wine; *Barbera* and *Niebbiolo*. Often the quality of the wine is improved through judicious blending. Most white wines are made from *Semillon* and *Pinot Blanc* grapes as well as the American *Isabella*, while some hybrids also produce a very poor quality wine.

Uruguay thus produces the usual variety of wines: *tinto*, *rosado* and *blanco*, of both ordinary and better quality. But there is no methodical classification of wines which would guarantee its quality for the consumer. It seems clear that the wines of the *gran reserva* are better than others, so that an *appellation d'origine* shown on the label might help to distinguish between the local wines and the blended wines. The latter may be blended from a mixture of grapes or with foreign wines. There are also a great many wines which state the name of the grape from which they are made. Finally, Uruguay also produces special wines such a *sherry-quinquina*, dessert wines and sparkling wines.

PERU, BOLIVIA AND COLOMBIA

Peru. Francisco Carabantes, the Spanish conqueror of Peru, introduced the vine there about the middle of the sixteenth century. Peru today has a vineyard of 20,560 acres producing 5,830,000 gallons of wine, making it the fifth wineproducing country on the Latin-American continent. The main wine areas are Lima, Ica, Chincha, Moquegua, Tacana and Lacumba.

The climate here is not at all favourable to the production of great wines and some regions are completely unable to support vine cultivation. The Andes are for the most part too cold and rugged and other regions are too hot and arid for good wine culture.

The white Peruvian wines are, nevertheless, pleasant, light, and have an agreeable bouquet. The red wines, however, are more ordinary, heavy with tannin and of a very poor quality. All the wine in Peru is produced for domestic consumption. Besides wine and *chicha*, a national drink made from sweet maize, some sweet wine such as Madeira or sherry is also drunk. The wines here are usually known by their place of origin: Locumba, Moquegua, Chincha, Ica, and so on.

Bolivia. The vine was probably brought to Bolivia from varieties originating in the Canaries. Today, the Bolivian vineyard covers some 5,000 acres and produces about 132,000 gallons a year, concentrated in the province of La Paz. There are also an additional 4,000 acres on which table grapes are cultivated. The wines produced are reds or whites, with an alcohol content from 13º to 15º; they are usually heavy. The country also produces some wines similar to sherry.

Colombia. Colombia is the smallest wineproducer in South America, with a mere two thousand or so gallons. The vinicultural conditions here are exceptional owing to the torrid climate of the country, which allows the grape to mature several times a year, thus upsetting the usual wine-harvest cycle. Colombia produces mainly white sherry, port-type wines and light table wines which are decidedly sweet.

THE WINES OF AUSTRALIA

JOHN STANFORD

Modern civilization came late to Australia. In 1788 the establishment of a British colony at Sydney was followed by the planting of European *vitis vinifera* vines at Parramatta in the early 1790s in the garden of the Reverend Samuel Marsden. By 1820, James Busby, working with a grant of money from the new Government, had established commercial vineyards near Newcastle in the Hunter Valley, a hundred miles north of Sydney. This is still one of Australia's premier wine-producing areas.

During the next twenty years vineyards were established around the southern city of Melbourne at Lilydale and Geelong, at Rutherglen and Corowa on the Victoria-New South Wales border, in South Australia near Adelaide, and in Western Australia near Perth. In the next two decades political and religious persecution in Silesia brought settlers to the Barossa Valley who planted vines and founded the settlements of Tanunda, Lyndoch, Nuriootpa, Angaston, Seppeltsfield, Watercale and Clare. In the Swan Valley of Western Australia, vines originally planted for table grapes in the 1820s began to produce wine in the 1880s. The Chaffey brothers came from California in 1887 and established the irrigated vineyards around Mildura on the Murray River in Victoria.

Later development in irrigated districts followed down the Murray into South Australia (Renmark, Berri, Loxton, Waikerie, Nildottie) and upstream along the Victoria border. One most important development was the creation of the Riverina irrigation area around the towns of Griffith, Leeton and Yenda in south-western New South Wales with water from the Murrumbidgee River in 1912.

The climate for vine cultivation in Australia is even, warm during the growing period, with a tendency to too much rather than to too little sunlight, and too little rather than too much rain. Vintage variations are less noticeable than in the colder areas of Europe, but the same grapes are used for the basic wine styles.

Names such as CLARET, BURGUNDY, HOCK, CHABLIS, WHITE BURGUNDY, MOSELLE, CHAMPAGNE, SHERRY, PORT, and MADEIRA indicate wines of very similar style to European counterparts, but with flavours differing with the influence of soil types and warmer ripening conditions. Varietal labels indicating grape varieties and districts are taking over from these traditional wine style names: CABERNET, SAUVIGNON, HERMITAGE, CABERNET SHIRAZ, MALBEC, RIESLING, TRAMINER-RIESLING, SEMILLON, GREAT WESTERN PINOT, COONA-WARRA CLARET, HUNTER RIVER DRY RED etc.

Many brand labels indicate skilful blending, usually specified on the label, of wines from different districts with similar style but different flavours. This established technique has been developed by wine families owning vineyards and wineries in similar climatic conditions up to a thousand miles apart. Table wines made in this way have proved their ability to develop and improve for more than twenty years in the bottle.

Australian winemakers are extremely anxious for the quality of their products. Each year a wine fair is held in the principal towns (Melbourne, Sydney, Adelaide, Perth and Brisbane) and an average of 550 samples coming from all the wine districts are judged for awards. Australians wines presented at the fairs in France, Poland and Yugoslavia are very well received.

The volume of production, at around 40 million gallons of base wine per year is small by world standards. Winemaking methods are sound and imaginative. Most winemakers are graduates of the Oenology School at Roseworthy, South Australia or of French, German or American Schools of Oenology. In conjunction with the Australian Wine Research Institute and the Commonwealth Scientific and Industrial Research Organization (C.S.I.R.O.) they have developed their own techniques of cultivation, vine breeding, winemaking methods, chemical research and analysis to suit the conditions imposed by isolation and climate. Wine production is increasing by 10 to 12 per cent per year and is mainly consumed within Australia.

HUNTER VALLEY DISTRICTS. This small but expanding wine region is a hundred to a hundred and fifty miles north of Sydney in New South Wales. The older established area is at Pokolbin, near Cessnock. Recent development has been around Muswellbrook in the Upper Hunter Valley, seventy miles farther north. Production is almost entirely red and white table wines.

Principal plantings: mainly *Shiraz (Hermitage)* and *Semillon* with some *White Hermitage, Mataro, Pinot Noir, Cabernet* and *Traminer*.

Wine styles: soft, round, aromatic Burgundy wines, white and red, with a characteristic district flavour. They develop and mature for long periods in the bottle.

CENTRAL AND NORTH EASTERN VICTORIA. This district was once famous for its gold digging and then, around 1900, it became for a while Australia's largest wineproducing area. But phylloxera destroyed large areas of vines and South Australia then became the producers of 70 per cent of the country's wine.

Principal plantings: *Shiraz, Grenache, Cabernet Sauvignon* (red), *Semillon, White Hermitage, Verdeilho, Muscatel, Marsanne, Riesling* (white).

Wine styles: rich, full-flavoured, sweet dessert wines (Muscat, Madeira, and port styles) and big, full-bodied dry red with some light Riesling and other dry white.

WESTERN VICTORIA. These cool, elevated vineyards situated in the foothills of the Grampian Mountains were established by Swiss settlers in 1853.

Principal plantings: *Shiraz, Cabernet Sauvignon, Malbec, Pinot Meuniere, Mataro, Ouillade, Riesling, Semillon, Chardonnay*.

Wine styles: light, delicate Champagne and Riesling styles, crisp and more robust dry whites from *Semillon* and *Chardonnay*, aromatic dry reds from *Shiraz, Cabernet, Pinot* and *Malbec*.

SOUTH-EASTERN SOUTH AUSTRALIA. This cool, low-lying region 250 miles from Adelaide, near the Victorian border, was originally planted as adjuncts to large pastoral homesteads but later developed as an important district for the production of dry red wines.

Principal plantings: *Shiraz, Cabernet Sauvignon, Riesling*.

Wine types: crisp, full-bodied dry red wines of claret style of high quality.

ADELAIDE AND SOUTHERN VALES. This cool, moist, even-temperature coastal district lies between the suburban foothills near Adelaide, along the south coast of St. Vincent's Gulf to Reynella, McLaren Vale and Langhorne Creek and contains some of the earliest planting established in South Australia (1838).

Principal plantings: *Shiraz, Cabernet Sauvignon, Grenache* (red), *Riesling, Semillon, White Hermitage, White Sauvignon*.

Wine styles: crisp, full-flavoured dry red wines, similar to the French Bordeaux; light, delicate dry white; flor sherry; sweet red (vintage and tawny style ports).

BAROSSA VALLEY - EDEN VALLEY - CLARE. This is one of the largest winegrowing regions of Australia. It ranges from the Clare-Watervale Plateau, eighty miles north of Adelaide, through the main Barossa Valley, around Tanunda, Nuriootpa and Angaston to the high, colder districts of Springton, Eden Valley and Pewsey Vale, forty to fifty miles from Adelaide. It is famous for its Vintage Festival and produces all types of wine.

Principal plantings: *Shiraz, Cabernet, Mataro, Grenache, Malbec, Clare Riesling, Riesling, Semillon, White Hermitage*.

Wines styles: light, fragrant, crisp Rieslings from Clare, Watervale, Eden Valley, Rowland Flat and Angaston. Soft, full-flavoured dry reds from Angaston, Keyneton, Springton, Kalimna, Seppeltsfield and Tanunda. Rich, sweet dessert wines from Tanunda, Lyndoch and Nuriootpa. Sherries and brandy from the main bed of the valley.

SWAN VALLEY. This old winemaking district is between six and twenty miles from Perth, Western Australia. There are many very small makers but only four to five significant companies.

Principal plantings: *Shiraz, Grenache, Cabernet, Malbec, Ouillade*.

Wine styles: because rain seldom falls at all in January and February, during the ripening period for grapes immediately preceding vintage, many wines are full, rich and low-acid Burgundy styles. There is in all the Swan Valley wines, just as in those of the Hunter Valley, a characteristic flavour evident to a greater or lesser degree and determined by the nature of the soil.

MURRAY VALLEY. The Murray River rises in the Australian Alps from rain and snow waters. It runs inland from the eastern seaboard, through the dry plains along the Victoria-New South Wales border into South Australia. Near Waikerie, 150 miles north of Adelaide, it swings south and joins the Southern Ocean about sixty miles south of Adelaide—a total distance of 1,609 miles. Irrigated vineyards are spaced along the whole of its length. The largest winegrowing centres are: Mildura, Robinvale, Renmark, Berri, Loxton, Waikerie-Cadell, Nildottie and Langhorne Creek.

A large proportion of Australian brandy originates in this extended area. Base wines are made mainly from *Sultana*, *Waltham Cross* and *Doradillo* grapes. Here also originate many of the sweet dessert wines made from *Muscat* and similar varieties, which form the blending base of the white dessert and sweet sherry styles for Australian, English and Canadian markets. The same vineyards and wineries produce high quality flor sherry,

base wines and light, soft dry and sweet table wines (hock, Moselle, Sauterne styles) and a growing output of rosé and light, dry red table wines.

In many districts, particularly Cadell, Nildottie, Langhorne Creek, Mildura and Loxton, new plantings of recent years have been in premium wine varieties—*Cabernet*, *Shiraz*, *Riesling*, *Semillon*, etc.

RIVERINA DISTRICT. This vineyard was founded in 1912 when water was reticulated sixty miles overland from Narrandera to water a dry basin of rich, heavy soil around the towns of Griffith, Yenda and Leeton.

The area produces fruit of all types, but almost all the vines are winemaking varieties. Fourteen wineries process these grapes for dry red, dry and sweet white table wines, sherries, sweet dessert wines and brandy. Controlled irrigation techniques developed and used in this area have produced table wines of high quality.

THE WINES OF NEW ZEALAND

New Zealand's two islands lie across the moist trade winds between 35° and 41° south latitude. The South Island has a few experimental vineyards—at Otago and Nelson—but is too cold for commercial planting. On the other hand the North Island climate, which varies between the extreme of sub-tropical forest and volcanic activity in the far north and the cold south, supports the wine industry. In the northern districts of Henderson and Kumeu (near Auckland), the Te Kauwhata Viticultural Research Station and the Coromandel Peninsula, and southward at Hawkes Bay, are the two main areas where the majority of New Zealand's vines grow. There is only slightly more sunlight than in the cooler Australian districts, but the rainfall is much higher—in some areas over fifty inches per year.

Two famous figures in the founding of Australian vineyards, James Busby and the Reverend Samuel Marsden, settled in the far north at the Bay of Islands in the early 1830s. When the seat of Administration was moved farther south to Auckland, these vineyards died out and were never replanted.

Around 1835 priests of the Marist Order planted vineyards at Hawkes Bay. Henderson and Hawkes Bay are now the two most important producing districts, each with about five to six hundred acres planted. The smaller districts of Thames and Te Kauwhata will probably expand with the current increasing demand for wine in New Zealand.

The art of winemaking had not noticeably progressed until the late 1950s. Recent investment by the Australian companies of Penfolds, McWilliams and Seppelts has lent impetus to the New Zealand wine pioneers.

The winemaking region of Henderson is situated on the edge of the city of Auckland and was formed by a few large families of vintners and a larger number of Yugoslav and Dalmatian settlers who have established small wineries for the production of fortified wines.

White wines can be made to a good quality standard from the European varieties *Müller-Thurgau* (*Riesling-Sylvaner* hybrid) and some *Chardonnay* and *Chasselas*. *Palomino* grows well and is used for dry sherries.

Red wines are light and thin. The best styles come from the *Pinotage* (*Pinot-Hermitage* hybrid), *Cabernet Sauvignon*, and one of the better hybrids, *Seibel 5437*, which has good colour but less flavour.

The Mission Vineyard of the Marist Order is the oldest, but its wines do not reach the open market. McWilliams, Glenvale and Vidal are the main producers. The vineyards are near Napier, extending to Hastings through the Taradale-Greenmeadows districts.

Grape varieties similar to those of the Henderson district are used, mainly *Müller-Thurgau* for white wines with some *Cabernet* and *Pinotage* for red. *Seibel 5437* is the best of several varieties of red hybrids used.

The addition of cane sugar to the must is an accepted winemaking principle owing to the short ripening period and low natural sugar content at normal maturity.

The New Zealand wine industry is still small, but it is expanding. The wine consumed by the population of 2 ½ million has trebled in fifteen years to about 2 million gallons. In its early years nearly all its wines were sweet, fortified dessert wines and sherries. However, the recent increases have been largely to table wines, the best of which are light, crisp, dry whites.

TABLE OF WINE QUALITIES
BY REGIONS AND YEARS, TAKING INTO ACCOUNT THE EVOLUTION OF THE WINES
compiled by La Compagnie des Courtiers-Gourmets Piqueurs de Vins de Paris

YEARS	Red Bordeaux	White Bordeaux	Red Burgundy	White Burgundy	Côtes du Rhône	Alsace	Pouilly-s./Loire Sancerre	Anjou Touraine
1928	★	•••	•••	•••				
1929	••••	••••	★	••				
1934	••••	•••	••••	•••	•••			••••
1937	••	★	••••	•••	••••			••••
1943	••	•••	•••	•••	•••			•••
1945	••••	••••	•••	•••	••••			
1947	••••	••••	••••	•••	•••	(STOCKS EXHAUSTED)	(STOCKS EXHAUSTED)	★
1948	••••	••						•••
1949	•••	••••	••••	•••	••••			••••
1950	•••	••		•••	•••			
1952	•••	•••	•••	•••	••••			•••
1953	★	•••	•••	•••				•••
1955	★	••••	••••	•••	•••			•••
1957	••	•••	•••	•••	•••			•••
1959	•••	••••	••••	•••	•••			••••
1961	★	••••	★	•••	••••			•••
1962	••••	••••	••••	•••	•••			•••
1964	••••	••	••••	•••	•••	•••		•••
1966	••••	•••	••••	•••	•••	••••		•••
1967	•••	••••	•••	•••	•••	••••	••	••
1969	•••	••	••••	••••	••	•••	•••	•••
1970	••••	••••	•••	••••	•••	•••	••••	•••
1971	••••	•••	••••	•••	•••	★	•••	•••
1972	••	••	•••	••	••	•	•	••
1973	A year of abundance: some quality wines certain.							

• Medium Year   •• Good Year   ••• Very Good Year   •••• Great Year   ★ Exceptional Year

CHAMPAGNE
Vintage: vary according to brands; notable years 1966 and 1969. – Non-vintage: blend of different vintages.

These appreciations are on an average basis, the exception confirming the rule.

THE WINES
OF CHAMPAGNE

JEAN ARNABOLDI

It may be said, without fear of contradiction, that Champagne is one of the most celebrated wines in the world. But if man in his wisdom has raised it to such eminence, he must also admit that its origins have been lost in the mists of time. It is perhaps not an exaggeration to speak of predestination. For when the inland sea which in pre-history covered the Champagne region disappeared, it left in its place a chalky subsoil which was gradually covered by a layer of fertile soil wherein plants might prosper. Recent discoveries made near Sézanne have shown that the vine must have existed there as far back as the tertiary period. Fossilized leaves which were excavated have been judged to be very close to the *vitis rotunda folia*, also known as the *plant américain*. What an extraordinary coincidence this proved to be was seen thousands of years later, when this very same grape was to save the Champagne vineyard from the devastations of phylloxera.

The first real facts about Champagne wine to emerge from history date from the Roman conquest, for when the legions reached the banks of the Marne, they found a flourishing viticulture already in existence. Bringing fresh knowledge and new methods, these legions were to contribute to the development of the vine here as they had previously done in the other provinces of Gaul. The Romans already knew arboriculture as it was then practised in Italy, but they were quick to appreciate the advantages of the methods used by the Gauls. On the other hand, they introduced a new concept, the idea of stock selection. They even imported from Narbonne a quick-growing variety of vine. The reputation of

Champagne wines travelled quickly to Rome, as Pliny himself bears witness: "Other wines from Gaul which have been recommended as fit for the King's table are those from the land of Rheims, known as Ay."

The decree passed by Domitian in A.D. 92 was to prove almost fatal to the future expansion of the vineyards of Gaul and in particular to those around Champagne. The Emperor decreed that all the vines were to be pulled out. Fortunately for posterity, his orders were not everywhere obeyed. It is clear, of course, that occupation troops must live off local produce, and that an army has greater need of cereals and dairy produce than of liquids whose consumption does not always favour military discipline or heroic behaviour. Perhaps other, more worldly commercial reasons crept in too, for the wines of Gaul competed with those of the Mediterranean shores. Be that as it may, the fact remains that for two hundred years the vine had to be cultivated in secret, until that day when another, better-inspired emperor, Probus, raised the ban, and, furthermore, required his troops to help in the reconstruction of the vineyards, a task which the Gauls themselves undertook with much enthusiasm. From Rheims down south to Chalons, the work was quickly done, and memories of Domitian were forgotten.

The advent and spread of Christianity had a marked influence on viticulture, for the monks were obliged to procure locally the wine they used to celebrate Mass. Monasteries also served as inns where travellers sought food, shelter and a welcoming table. The quality of Champagne was noteworthy from this period.

The soil of Champagne has delivered up many proofs of the importance of its vineyard: earthenware jars, coins imprinted with symbols taken from the vine, and even glasses whose elongated shape foreshadows the flute-shaped Champagne glasses of today.

In the fifth and sixth centuries, Champagne became part of the history of France and perhaps even of Heaven, for Clovis was crowned King of France at Rheims by St. Remi, the apostle to the Franks. The chronicles of the time recount the miracles the good saint accomplished: how he caused wine to flow from a barrel of water, and how he gave Clovis, when the latter was warring with Alaric, "a flask filled with holy wine, and recommended him to continue the war for as long as the flask supplied wine for him and others of his train to whom he wished to offer it. The King as well as several of his officers drank the wine, but the jug remained full." From a more practical point of view, the testament of St. Remi is an irrefutable document which portrays faithfully the economic situation and morals of his time. For example, it relates how wine is often offered by the winegrowers as a gift to the king or to the archbishopric of Rheims. Other chronicles speak of the growing expansion of the Champagne vineyard, and enlighten us as to the quality of its wines and how they were used. In those days, Champagne was a still wine *de qualité, pur et fruité* (fine, pure and fruity), excellent for the sick. The decorations and sculptures on monuments, notably those of Rheims Cathedral and Ay Church, have been inspired directly by the wine and depict some part of the life of those who have given their lives to viniculture.

Flodoard, in his history of the church of Rheims, tells us that the wine harvest of 929 was completed by the month of August, which shows that in those days the grapes ripened much earlier. In the eleventh century, Pope Urban II, who had been at one time Canon of Rheims, preached in favour of the Second Crusade at Châtillon-sur-Marne, where a huge statue perpetuates his memory. A kind of redistribution of land took place then, when the Lords leaving for the Holy Land entrusted their property to the Church. During their absence, which sometimes became permanent, the monks reorganized and nationalized viniculture, and it is in fact from this period onwards that their influence on the destiny of the Champagne wines became decisive.

Later invasions and battles only served to increase the fame of these wines. It is said that the Emperor of Germany, Wenceslas, when he met the King of France, Charles VI at Rheims in 1398, indulged in such libations that he was ready to sign "whatsoever was desired".

The consecration of the King of France at Rheims heightened the prestige of the wines of Champagne still further. On February 13th, 1575, for the first time, Champagne was the only wine to be served on the occasion of the coronation of Henry III. Its power of seduction seemed so great that emperors and monarchs, Charles V, François I, Henry VIII and a Pope, Jean de Medicis who later became Leon, all had to own a house in Ay. Henry IV was pleased to think of himself as "Sire of Ay" and valued very highly this *vin de Dieu*, light, fruity, and sacred to boot.

Favoured by kings, Champagne soon captured the Court. Poets sang its praises. Winegrowers multiplied their efforts to satisfy the demand and noticed that for some obscure reason, the wine from time to time would become effervescent. But they were never able to fathom the mystery. Louis XIV was a great lover of the wine of Ay, but even more fervent admirers were the Marechal de Bois-Dauphin, the Marquis Charles de Saint-Evremond and the Count of Olonne, who would drink no other wine with their meals. In 1672, St. Evremond wrote to Count Olonne: "Don't spare yourself any cost to have the wine of Champagne, be you so far as two hundred leagues from Paris. No other province can produce such excellent wines for all seasons as Champagne. It offers us the wines of Ay, Avenet and Auville until the spring; and Tessy, Sillery and Verzenay for the rest of the year. Were you to ask me which of these wines I prefer, without having recourse to tastes in fashion which introduce false delicacies, I would tell you that the good wine of Ay is the most natural of all wines. It is by far the healthiest, and is purged of any objectionable tang of the soil. The peach flavour, which characterizes it, gives one a most exquisite feeling."

This analysis and this delicacy of palate shows that already in those times Champagne had attained a position of eminence. It is said that St. Evremond, having fallen into disgrace with the king in 1661, had to flee to Holland, and later to England where he introduced the Court of Charles II to the delicacies of the table and to fine wine. He easily convinced the court, which soon gave Champagne the place of honour.

At this point in time, one should look more closely into the details of the production of Champagne wines and more particularly into a fundamental change that came about, and which can be said to have ensured their place in history, forever distinctive from other wines. These already famous wines have until this time been still—or almost-still—wines. The black grapes, placed in vats for only a short time or even not vatted at all, produced a grey wine, and were dominated by the red wines, even though it was not possible to conserve the latter for more than a short time and their transportation was somewhat hazardous. In the middle of the seventeenth century (1640 or

Dom Perignon, a Benedictine monk from the Abbey of Hautvillers, had the brilliant idea of blending the produce of different vineyards in the Champagne region so as to obtain a stock whose quality would be superior to any of the individual elements from which it was composed. José Frappa has painted him here, old and blind, tasting grapes with the sensitivity and knowledge that enabled him to distinguish each of the varieties brought in the baskets. There never was a man, said one of his contemporaries, more gifted than he in the secrets of wine-making. Although Dom Perignon died over two centuries ago his name is still honoured and will ever be associated with Champagne.

1660, the date is disputed) the Champagne winegrowers increased their efforts to "produce wines of a finer quality than anywhere else in the kingdom". They succeeded in making pale wines which, in some years, produced in the bottle a certain effervescence which was most agreeable and enhanced their bouquet. This effervescence seemed to occur more often in white wines made from *Pinot* grapes, when the must was fermented separately from the marc, and thus the idea evolved to let this fermentation take place in the bottle. The *vin de Dieu* became *vin Diable* or *saute-bouchon* without,

however, losing any of its original qualities or appeal. On the contrary, it has stood the test of time and change, as history has shown.

Dom Perignon was its man of destiny. It is common knowledge that though the wine's merits are acknowledged, its originator is sometimes disputed. It seems a shame to demolish idols, the more so as every inventor always owes something to his predecessors.

Born in the same year as Louis XIV, Dom Perignon (1638-1715) was also to die in the same year. Brought up in a bourgeois family from St. Menehould, he took

347

his vows in the Benedictine Order and entered the Royal Abbey of Saint-Vanne at Verdun, where he distinguished himself by his great knowledge and devout charity. In 1668 he became cellarer of the Benedictine Abbey at Hautvillers, in the diocese of Rheims. His duties were to supervise the supplies of food and other goods, to check the sources of revenue, the running expenses and generally to keep the accounts. The cellars were therefore also in his care. The village of Hautvillers lies on slopes above the Marne valley, and its situation is therefore particularly favourable for the cultivation of the vine. The domain belonging to the Abbey was quite considerable and several other vineyards were adjacent to it. For these reasons, Dom Perignon concentrated his intelligence on winemaking, in which capacity he was well served by his extraordinary gifts as a wine-taster. His first great idea was to bring together the vines in such a way that by intermarrying they would benefit from each other's better qualities, harmoniously, without any one dominating the others. He had such a delicate palate that by tasting a grape he was able to tell which variety it came from. He decided which grapes to use early in the year, and this procedure came to be acknowledged as essential to the production of sparkling wines. Dom Perignon was also the first in Champagne to seal bottles with cork, which soon replaced the old wooden pegs.

He organized wine production and studied the phenomenon of the rise of foam in the bottle by the rule-of-thumb means at his disposal. No one really knows, however, whether he obtained fermentation in the bottle as a result of the natural sugar content in the wine, that is to say not yet transformed into alcohol, or if he was the first to add a suitable amount of cane sugar.

His body lies at rest in the church at Hautvillers and this epitaph is engraved on his tombstone. "Here lies Dom Perignon, for 47 years cellarer of this Monastery who, after administering the property of our community with a care and dignity that merits praise, blessed with many virtues, the greatest of which was his paternal love for the poor, died in the 77th year of his life, in 1715." His name is remembered to this day.

Henceforth all the humble force of the Benedictine brothers was bent towards the making of Champagne. From this time on, the foam process was "controlled", the wine gained in popularity, and the beginning of the eighteenth century witnessed a great increase in demand. The still wines were neglected for the benefit of the sparkling wines. At the Court, the Marquis of Sillery, well known for his good taste, was an ardent protagonist of the new sparkling wine. The Regent was also convinced of the excellence of Champagne, as were later Louis XV and Louis XVI, though somewhat less flamboyantly. Madame de Pompadour paid it the

highest of feminine compliments by declaring "it is the only wine that makes a woman more beautiful after drinking", and the Comtesse de Parabère was accused of drinking like a *lansquenet* (a German mercenary soldier)! In 1739 the city of Paris gave a brilliant ball at which 1,800 bottles of Champagne wine were drunk.

At about this time wine-merchants set up the first wine-shops in Champagne, some of which still exist today. Their wine cellars were built on the chalky soil which favours the preservation of wine, but there remained two problems which had to be solved: the study of the fermentation process and the breakage of bottles. The latter was solved before the former by an apothecary from Châlons known as François and whose name merits eternal fame. The breakage of bottles affected some 40 per cent of the production, but François learned through his research work to control excessive fermentation by fixing the correct sugar dosage. At the same time, the glass-works made great progress in the quality of their glass. Between the two, the distressing problem of breakage was very considerably decreased. In 1858, Maumené, a professor at Rheims, seems to have been the first to study the action of the yeasts which influence fermentation, but it was not until Pasteur's work in this field became known that Champagne was produced scientifically.

Since then, the history of Champagne has been one of victory and success, if still sometimes acquired the hard way, through a disease of the wine or folly of man. The new techniques and the progress achieved, allied to the tenacity, the skill and the knowledge of the wine-growers and wine-merchants of the Champagne area, found their just recompense in a constant expansion of demand throughout the world.

THE CHAMPAGNE VINEYARD

The Champagne country, whose origins are founded on the same chalky subsoil as the Ele de France, a region which carries through to the Ardennes, forms the eastern part of the Parisian basin. Its landscapes have the same peacefulness, the same harmony born of gently undulating plains, dipping sometimes towards shallow valleys. The slopes dominate by a few hundred feet the rivers whose waters flow peacefully on, and their average altitude is never more than 600 feet.

Its geological make-up and its geographical position have always given the Champagne a singular identity. At the time of the *Ancien Régime*, the region covered 6,177,500 acres, or almost one-twentieth of the whole of France. Under the Revolution, it was divided into four separate *départements*—Aube, Marne, Haute-Marne, Ardennes—while the remainder of its land was given to Yonne and Aisne.

Its subsoil consists of a chalky sediment from which, in thicker or thinner layers, calcareous, clay and flint sands detach themselves.

The viticultural zone was clearly defined by the law of July 22nd, 1927, which marked it out in accordance with its natural boundaries: only those vineyards which came within its confines have the right to the appellation CHAMPAGNE.

The viticultural area is not all in one block. It covers 86,485 acres, which were planted to the wine in their entirety by the last century. The invasion of phylloxera, however, destroyed a great number of the vines; at the present time, 44,500 acres are fully productive. They are divided up in the following manner: 38,500 acres in Marne, 4,000 in Aube and 2,000 in Aisne. This whole represents slightly more than one-hundredth of the entire area given over to viticulture in France.

There are four distinct zones within the Champagne vineyard: the Montagne de Rheims, the Vallée de la Marne, the Côte des Blancs and the vineyards of Aube. The first three are situated in the districts of Rheims and Epernay, and constitute the most important vineyards, the very heart of the Champagne region. It is they that produce the most illustrious growths. The vines, planted in rows along the sides of the slopes, form a ribbon about 75 miles long, but whose width varies from only about 300 yards in some parts to little more than a mile.

Apart from still wines which have their own very specific *appellation d'origine*, Champagne wines do not mention their vineyard of origin in the general classification, for Champagne is, by its very nature, a combination of musts from several varieties of grapes. The particular growth referred to here is therefore called a *cru de raisin*.

THE MONTAGNE DE REIMS. The Montagne de Reims forms the southern side of the Vesle valley, whilst its eastern tip joins up with the Marne valley, which it dominates at Epernay. The Great Growths of the main Champagne vineyard were classified according to very old usage. Verzenay, Mailly, Sillery and Beaumont-sur-Visle are the Great Growths of Montagne de Reims, which is situated to the north at the very edge of Rheims forest. Ludes, Chigny-les-Roses, Rilly-la-Montagne, Villers-Marmery, Verzy, Villers-Allerand and Trépail are some of the best growths.

To the south of the town, Petite Montagne also has some good growths worth mentioning, such as Ville-Dommange, Ecueil, Sacy, Pargny-sur-Saulx, Jouy-lès-Reims.

THE MARNE VALLEY. The slopes of the Marne valley stretch the length of the river between Tours-sur-Marne and Dormans, extending towards Château-Thierry and beyond to Aisne. Its leading vineyard is Ay, framed by Mareuil-sur-Ay and Dizy, followed in a less elevated rank in the classification of vineyards by Cumières and Hautvillers, the region in which Dom Perignon earned his fame.

On the right bank of the river, the vineyards of Damery, Venteuil, Châtillon-sur-Marne, Vandières, Verneuil and Vincelles deserve mention. For quite a different reason, however, the name of the little hamlet of Tréloup is linked with the history of the Champagne area, for it was here that the first sign of phylloxera was seen in 1890. On the left bank, the valley of Cubry, which ends at Epernay, offers a number of interesting varieties made from the *Pinot Fin* grape, in the vineyards of Epernay and Pierry. Other localities such as Moussy, Vinay and Saint-Martin-d'Ablois grow the *Pinot Meunier* grape, which produces wines noted for their fruitiness. Other well-known vineyards are those in the regions of Mardeuil, Boursault, Leuvrigny, Festigny, Troissy and Dormans.

THE CÔTE DES BLANCS AND OTHER VINEYARDS. The Côte des Blancs is situated directly to the south of the Marne. Its great names ring melodiously in the minds of all connoisseurs of Champagne: Cramant, Avize, Oger and Le-Mesnil-sur-Oger. Chouilly, at the junction of two zones, also recalls happy memories, and its vineyards produce very fine quality white grapes, of which the *Chardonnay* is king.

The Côte des Blancs stretches south to the outskirts of Petit Morin, where it gains an extra slope of black and white grapes, considered to be some of its best. The Petit Morin valley is flanked by several vineyards growing the *Meunier* grape, which produces very fruity wines.

These zones, here rapidly reviewed, make up practically the whole of the Champagne area. There is, however, one other zone of a transitional nature whose geological characteristics are no longer quite as well-defined, but which nevertheless produces wine still entitled to be known by the same appellation. From amongst its vineyards, one can mention these of Côte de Château-Thierry, the Sézanne region and those in the vicinity of Vitry-le-François.

Between the region of Sézanne and the Aube vineyard there is quite a large gap, as it is not until Bar-sur-Aube and Bar-sur-Seine that one finds slopes which form a part of the same viticultural zone.

THE SOIL. The soil, as already indicated, has a chalky subsoil—an essential element. The great vineyards are usually planted halfway up the slopes on a fine layer of loose earth left over from slopes of the tertiary period, rich in chalk of the Senonian stratum, a single block of which can be more than 600 feet thick.

The chalky subsoil assures perfect drainage, stabilizes the infiltration of water and so maintains the ideal amount of humidity. Moreover, this geological composition offers another great advantage; it retains the heat from the sun and emits it again in a regular and constant manner. Finally, the light, which plays a very important role in the ripening of the grapes, is stronger here than the climate would lead one to believe, owing to the reflected whiteness of the chalky soil.

THE CLIMATE. The climate of the Champagne area is practically identical to that of the Parisian basin. Usually it is moderate, and the winters are seldom severe. In spring the weather is uncertain but mild, the summers are hot and the autumns are often good, all of which is of great importance to vine culture. The winds blowing from the sea soften the continental climate characteristics, which at their harshest are often too harsh for the vine, and the average annual temperature is about 50° F.

The wine, moreover, benefits from the surrounding forests and groves, which not only shield it from harsh weather but also provide a most desirable humidity. The altitude at which the vineyard is planted, from about 500 to 600 feet, also serves to protect it to a certain extent from spring frosts and cold early morning mists, which are naturally much worse in the valleys below. The vintner has learned to protect himself from these natural enemies of viticulture, and the modern methods at his disposal have enabled him practically to eliminate their often disastrous effects. This, of course, is equally applicable to hail.

GRAPE VARIETIES. Very strict legal provisions define which grapes may be used to produce Champagne. The varieties permitted are the *Pinot Noir* and the *Pinot Meunier*, both black grapes, and the *Chardonnay*, a white grape. Apart from these, the law permits the use of a few local stocks such as the *Petit Meslier* and the *Arbanne*; these, however, are slowly becoming extinct. It should be noted that following the invasion of phylloxera, the indigenous long-rooted plants were naturally replaced by grafted stock.

This law has but sanctioned centuries-old methods of vinification which winegrowers had practised, by confirming the perfect harmony of these plants with the soil and the climate. The influence of these grapes on the quality of the wine is, needless to say, considerable. Each brings its own quality, and the dosage, the intermarriage, the perfect harmonizing of all these qualities give to Champagne its essential character. Its delicate quality, its bouquet and its mellow warmth are derived from the various grapes, and the different proportions in which they are used decided by the dictates of sensitive palates. This forms a highly complicated and delicate process which will be examined in more detail, although it can be said here that no explanation can take the place of human experience.

The *Pinot Noir* grape (with its varieties) predominates in Champagne (it is also used, more than any others, to produce the great red wines of Burgundy). It makes a wine with a full bouquet, generous, powerful and robust. It produces a white wine by a process which we will study later.

The *Pinot Meunier* is a variety of the *Pinot Noir* grape. More hardy, it plays an important role in second quality Champagnes. The *Chardonnay*, which is a white grape, is found mainly on the Côte des Blancs. When blended with other grapes, it gives forth its essential finesse and elegance.

All these grapes have certain common characteristics: they are precocious, vigorous, quick to mature, produce very sweet musts rich in sugar and have unrivalled finesse and bouquet.

After the phylloxera invasion, all the stocks were grafted to the *American Plant*. It is well known that it is the graft which imparts its character to the stock, from which it derives new strength to enable it to resist any future attacks of the pest.

A vine lives for about thirty years, and only begins to produce fruit four years after it has been planted. The density in the Champagne vineyards reaches a closely-packed and regular thickness of 3,000 to 4,000 plants per acre, the yield (usually about 6,500 pounds per acre) is kept down in order to maintain the quality. This legal requirement is administered by a body called the Institut National des Appellations d'Origine (I.N.A.O.), which sees to it that the law is strictly carried out.

The pruning of the vine is also rigidly regulated by law: all the vines of Champagne must be pruned short, according to the accepted methods of the systems of "Royat", "Chablis", "Guyot" or "Vallée de la Marne".

A WINE-HARVEST TO CONQUER THE WORLD

After a long year of labour, care, anxiety, and hope, harvest-time arrives at last. This penultimate act of the great annual spectacle is performed with extraordinary care and concern, especially in the Champagne region. One might even venture to say that nowhere else in the world are the grapes picked with so much attention paid to each and every detail.

The fruit will have blossomed some hundred days before the date of picking is officially proclaimed by Prefectorial order. Laboratories have carried out tests to establish the exact sugar and acid content of the grapes now attaining their full maturity in the gentle rays of a mid-September sun. Work begins, and it is clear that local labour is not sufficient. The winegrowers get help from all the regions of France, especially miners from the North and from Lorraine. From one

The sumptuous "Oyster Dinner" painted by Jean-François de Troy (1679-1752) also renders homage to champagne. Some of the guests watch the cork blown high in the air, while others appreciatively sip the sparkling wine.

year to the next the growers try to find the "flying squads" of temporary workers who are already familiar with the delicate work of fruit picking and well versed in the habits of the Champagne winegrowers. Split up into small groups called *hordes* or *hordons*, they work methodically and conscientiously, their bright clothes forming multi-coloured patches which bob and weave among the tightly packed green vines. The wine-harvesters receive free board and lodging. Their wages are fixed by the joint committee of the C.I.V.C. according to their age and qualifications. This is to distinguish the pickers (aged from 12, 13, 14 years and up), the carriers of small baskets, the unloaders of big baskets, the general labourers, the group leaders—all these people making up the "foreign" workers.

Then come the press-men, who are also classified by jobs: hand press, hydraulic press, hand dryer, hydraulic dryer and so on. Every army, even a peaceful one, requires a rear-echelon staff, and the kitchen staff must be added too. The grape pickers, men, women and children, pick the clusters from the root of vines with great care, using shears, make a preliminary sorting of the grapes (if necessary); and they place the grape-bunches in small baskets, each of which holds about eleven pounds.

Then it is the turn of the carriers. They collect the baskets and pour their contents on to large wicker-work hurdles under the watchful eye of the "sorters", who are responsible for a final careful sorting. It is necessary to take out the green grapes or those not sufficiently ripe, as otherwise they would reduce the alcohol content of the wine, as well as the bad and overripe grapes which would spoil the quality of the wine. This work is very burdensome, and some argue as to its necessity. The Champagne winegrowers certainly believe in it.

Those grapes considered good enough for vinification are *placed*—not poured—in large wicker-work baskets, quaintly named *mannequins*, or in similar receptacles, often made of plastic, which can hold some 110 to 180 pounds, and which are then placed with great care by the carriers in vehicles with springs—a peculiarity of this region for a long time—which are driven very carefully to the press-house, with care to avoid bumps that might damage the grapes.

The vine-presses are in *vendangeoirs* which belong either to wine-merchants, local co-operatives, vineyard-owners or to wine-brokers. Except in the case of the *récoltant-manipulant*, the work of the vineyard is now completed. This is a special characteristic of vinicultural Champagne. The grapes are weighed and then paid for, according to the price fixed each year by the C.I.V.C., after bargaining between winegrowers and wine-merchants. The sale is completed when the buyer has the grapes poured into the wine-press.

PRESSING THE GRAPES. The grapes are pressed as soon as possible. Champagne vintners use special presses, low and squat, so the must can flow out quickly without dissolving the colouring matter from the stalks, and without any risk of the flavour being spoiled by the wood. Some 9,000 pounds of grapes are placed on the floor of the press. The CHAMPAGNE appellation is given only to those wines whose must has been obtained by pressing not more than a hectolitre of juice per 150 kilos of grapes or about 20 gallons from 300 pounds. For this reason, the limit is fixed at 2,666 litres of must per marc which makes 13 barrels of 45 gallons each.

Then the first pressing takes place, or better, the first *serre* (squeeze). Usually electrically-controlled, the *plancher* (ceiling) held by a *mouton* (stock) is lowered on to the grapes, with a pressure attaining as much as 40 tons per square metre.

The must filters through the mass of grapes being pressed and flows through a spout with a filter into a 220-gallon vat called a *bélon*. The operation is repeated. The grapes must be pressed in one and a half hours, or two hours at the most.

The first ten barrels or 450 gallons are the cuvée from which the great Champagnes will be made. The next three pressings are known as *tailles* (cuts), so-called because it is necessary to cut up the compressed marc with a spade before it is squeezed again. One thus has a first and second pressing of poorer quality.

The must remains for only a short time in the graduated vats, of oak or cement, in which it was first collected. It is very quickly transferred to other types of vats known as *débourbage* (settling) vats where it stays for 10 to 12 hours, time enough for it to settle out all the foreign bodies it still contains: stones, skin and any other impurities.

When the wine has fully settled, the must is drawn off in barrels which hold 45 gallons each and is labelled according to origin. This operation is often carried out with mobile vats. Whatever the method, the wine is then transferred to the cellars where the delicate process of vinification commences.

VINIFICATION. Champagne is the product of two successive fermentations, whose essential elements are yeasts. These micro-organisms appear on the skin of the grape just before it ripens, and they are what changes the must into wine.

THE FIRST FERMENTATION. The first fermentation is also known by the evocative name of *bouillage* (boiling). It takes place either in oaken barrels, or in vats made of glazed cement, enamelled steel or stainless steel. The ambient temperature is maintained at 20° or 22°C., and the must seethes. For several days, fermentation is tumultuous, then its violence slackens and calm follows. Three weeks pass before the first clarifying racking takes place. The wine is next left cold in order to let its deposits settle and the liquid become limpid clear. Then it is drawn off for the second time.

Formerly, Christmas would find the cellar doors wide open to the chill air. Alas, the poetry has gone, giving way to sheer efficiency, and today, in many cellars, modern air-conditioning plants turn this part of the vinification process into an example of precision which is at the same time a guarantee of quality and consistency. For it is now that preparations for making Champagne differ from those for other wines.

LA CUVÉE. This operation is also known as *cuvée de tirage* (draught cuvée), and both its preparation and its carrying out require a careful combination of talent and technical know-how.

At the first racking or drawing-off, usually wines from the same growth are assembled in order to produce a homogeneous vatful which can then be used for later blending operations.

Right from the beginning of the year, specialists from each house taste the harvested wines, for they will be obliged to produce a wine, whatever the variations of that particular harvest may have been, which carries on the qualities and is faithful to the character that has made it known. It is therefore only after the second racking that the different growths are blended.

The vintner is now faced with two possibilities. If he wishes to produce a *millésime* (a wine showing the year of manufacture) it is clear that only wines of the same year may be blended. If he does not wish to produce a *millésime*, the shortcomings in the vintage of a particular year may be compensated for by adding wines from previous years which have been specially kept for this purpose. Needless to say, a successful blending requires several trials before the formula is applied to whole casks. The essential characteristics one must bear in mind in order to achieve an ideal result are: vinosity (flavour and strength), bouquet, aroma, elegance, delicacy, spirit and conservation ability. The latter characteristic will have been confirmed by a complex analysis.

The different wines are mixed in huge casks or in vats equipped with mixers which permit a perfect blending. Traditionally, Champagne is made from a blend of both black and white grapes. There are some varieties, however, made from white grapes alone: these are known as *Blanc de Blancs*. There is also a rosé Champagne, usually made by adding to the original mixture red wine from the Champagne vineyards, although sometimes the rosé Champagne is prepared as a rosé from the time it first goes to the press.

By the beginning of March, the exact composition of the *cuvée* must be ready, so that the producer can proceed with clarifying by filtering or by thinning down.

RACKING. At this stage, the wine in the vat is a still wine, but with the coming of spring, when it is racked, its whole destiny will change. To get the wine into the condition to become frothy, it is now transferred into special clearing vats, at the same time adding natural ferments and a liqueur. This liqueur is in fact a solution of pure cane sugar dissolved in wine. The wine is then stirred so that all the ingredients are well blended.

If one is trying to produce a *crémant* type of Champagne, one adds a smaller quantity of the sweet solution to the wine. The next step is to draw off the wine into bottles, where the mysterious transformation will take place. What seems to happen is that the sugar solution changes into alcohol and carbonic acid gas, which provokes the effervescence. Imprisoned within the bottle, which is now firmly corked and wired, the carbonic acid gas remains dissolved in the liquid and only starts to bubble when the bottle is uncorked.

THE SECOND FERMENTATION. This is the slow continuation of the process just outlined above. Taken immediately into cellars dug out of the chalk subsoil, the bottles are laid carefully on special wooden battens. They are constantly under close surveillance, as there is still a risk of bottle-breakage, despite the great improvements made in glass manufacture: the pressure of the gas can sometimes rise to 5 or 6 atmospheres. The corks also might be faulty and let some wine leak.

When the second fermentation is completed, the wine is clear, with all the deposits at the neck of the bottle, and its alcohol content is 12º. It is now necessary to remove the deposit and extract the sediment-coated cork.

REMUAGE, OR SETTLING THE DEPOSIT. The bottles are stacked *sur pointe* (with the cork pointing downwards) in wooden frames designed in such a way that the bottle can be inclined in different positions whilst the deposit is working its way down on to the cork. Every day, skilled cellarists give the bottle a sharp turn whilst also shaking it. At the same time, they rotate it one-eighth of a turn to the right or to the left, according to a guide mark painted at the bottom of the bottle, while the frames are tilted a little more downward. This process needs not only a dexterous hand but a rapid one; a good worker can *passer* 30,000 bottles a day.

Finally, the deposit will have all collected at the neck of the bottle, which reaches a vertical position in from six weeks to three months. By then, all the bottles are in the same position.

DÉGORGEMENT, OR REMOVAL OF THE CORK. It is now necessary to remove the deposit whilst at the same time allowing the minimum amount of gas and wine to escape. Disgorging, which is entrusted only to experts, is a manœuvre which used to depend on great speed to avoid spillage. Today, this delicate operation is more and more frequently being carried out by freezing the

1

2

3

2

1

3

1

2

3

PERRIER-JOUET

1. Trade name "Champagne Perrier-Jouet". – 2. Type of Champagne: *Extra Brut*. This indicates that no liqueur was added to this wine, which is therefore a very dry Champagne. Bottles marked "Finest Quality" and "Reserve cuvée" mean that the *négociant-manipulant* attributes particular importance to this type of Champagne. In other words, the quality of this Champagne may be judged by the reputation of its *négociant-manipulant* or by one's own experience. – 3. In the reference N.M. 3.624.332, the letters N.M. indicate that this is a vintage of first importance produced by a *négociant-manipulant*. The letters M.A. would signify a wine of secondary quality. The number that follows is the index number of the vintage on the register of the *Comité Interprofessionnel du Vin de Champagne* (C.I.V.C.).

MERCIER

1. Trade name: "Champagne Mercier". – 2. Type of Champagne: *Brut*. This indicates that only a small amount (about 1.5 per cent) of liqueur was added to the wine, or possibly none at all. – 3. The initials N.M. indicate that this is a primary vintage wine produced by a *négociant-manipulant*.

MUMM DOUBLE CORDON

1. Trade name: "Double Cordon de G. H. Mumm", commonly known as "Mumm Double Cordon". – 2. Type of Champagne: *Sec*. This indicates that between 2.5 per cent and 5 per cent of liqueur was added to the wine. This Champagne is therefore not as dry as the *Brut* and *Extra-Brut* Champagnes. – 3. The initials N.M. indicate that this is a primary vintage wine produced by a *négociant-manipulant*.

TAITTINGER

1. Trade name: "Champagne Taittinger". – 2. Type of Champagne: *Demi-sec.* This is a wine to which between 5 per cent and 8 per cent of liqueur has been added. It is therefore a slightly sweet wine. – 3. Here the initials N.M. again indicate a primary vintage wine produced by a *négociant-manipulant*.

CLICQUOT-PONSARDIN

1. Trade name: "Champagne Veuve Clicquot Ponsardin". – 2. Type of Champagne: *Brut* 1962. This is a *Brut* vintage Champagne. Only the very best years are indicated on Champagne labels. – 3. This is also a primary vintage Champagne produced by a *négociant-manipulant*.

DOM PÉRIGNON

1. Trade name: "Dom Pérignon". This is one of the rare occasions where the name of the wine itself has replaced the name of the *négociant-manipulant*. Dom Pérignon is always a vintage (*millésimé*) Champagne, but conversely not every harvest produces a Dom Pérignon. It is always made from the juice of the first pressings of selected grapes, using white grapes only; it is therefore a *Blanc de Blancs*. – 2. Name of the *négociant-manipulant*. – 3. Primary vintage wine of a *négociant-manipulant*.

neck of the bottle. The necks of the bottles are inserted in a brine freezing solution at a temperature of minus 20°; very rapidly, ice forms near the cork, trapping the impurities. When the cork is removed, the ice is immediately blown out, along with a small quantity of froth and wine. The bottle is then examined, and a dosage, liqueur consisting of pure cane sugar dissolved in old and high-class Champagne, is added to make up the lost wine. The strength of the liqueur depends on the type of Champagne desired: *brut*, *sec* (dry), *demi-sec* (semi-dry) or *doux* (sweet). *Extra-brut* means that the Champagne has no sugar content at all.

CORKING. After such a lengthy and delicate operation, it is understandable that corking is very important. The bottles must be hermetically sealed so only the finest quality cork is chosen for this purpose. The cork is 1 ¾ to 2 ¼ inches long and 1 ¼ to 1 ½ inches wide, and must, by law, have certain information printed on it. Once the cork is in place, a metal capsule is put over it and the whole is encircled by a wire-mesh, so that the pressure of gas in the bottle does not blow the cork out again. The bottles are then put back in the cool cellars to age, some for as long as six or seven years, before they set out to conquer the world.

RANGE OF CHAMPAGNE WINES

Champagne, as has been seen, is obtained by blending wines from three different grapes: the *Pinot Noir* and the *Pinot Meunier*, both black grapes, and the *Chardonnay*, a white grape. Many people are surprised to learn that this wine, so pure and clear, is made to a large extent from black grapes.

As in other vineyards, grapes from the same stocks do not necessarily have the same flavour or qualities, since these are influenced by the soil and place where they are grown. A connoisseur can easily tell the difference between the varieties. But with Champagne it is more difficult to distinguish the range of wines and their varieties because of the grape marriages which initiated the fame of Champagne and contributed so much to its glory. The different firms possess their own particular characteristics, and long experience is needed to distinguish between them.

The soil and a favourable location are so important and make for such a difference in the final variety of the grapes that certain coefficients have been granted to the producing regions, by commune and according to the quality of their produce. It is true that these basic coefficients are liable to change every year, depending on the results of the wine-harvests.

The coefficients range from 77 per cent to 100 per cent; those of 100 per cent are traditionally known as "*grands crus*", while those of 90 to 99 per cent are entitled "*premiers crus*". These titles are rarely carried on the label, because the guarantee of quality is, in most cases, given by the great names of the firms who absorb 80 per cent of the production. The opposite is true for most other wines, which normally are only too pleased to be able to announce "grand cru".

Before examining the various types of Champagne, it is useful to recall the legal protection of the *appellation d'origine contrôlée*, which benefits producers and consumers alike.

Only the following is recognized as Champagne:

1. wine produced from vines planted from authorized stocks, within the limits of the viticultural Champagne region, pruned to the required height, of a limited yield per acre;

2. wine of an assured quality guaranteed by a limited yield in must and by a minimum alcohol content;

3. wine prepared in accordance with the natural procedure known as *méthode champenoise*, in premises within the Champagne region where only wines from this region may be stored;

4. wine stored in bottles prior to shipping for at least one year (but for three years after the harvesting, in the case of wines with a *millésime*).

These principles, which have been progressively sanctioned by French law, are applied and controlled, to avoid any fraud, by the C.I.V.C. in the name of the public authority, vinegrowers and wine-merchants.

After the final stage, the dosing of the wine, the various types of Champagne can be classified as follows:

Brut without mention of year. This is a wine that is usually light and lively, very suitable as an aperitif as it prepares both the mind and the palate.

Brut millésimé. This is a very good wine which comes from a good vintage year, since only wines of the same year may be blended together in order to produce a first-grade bottle. In some years it might even be a collector's bottle. This type of wine is often more full-bodied and more generous; it deserves to be savoured with particular care. To mention a few of the old vintage wines very difficult to find nowadays: 1928, 1933, 1934, 1937, 1943, 1945, 1949 and 1953. Their merits vary, but one should be wary of those which have been aged too long. Here again, one might ask: should Champagne be drunk young or old? Several things must be considered. First, although the carbonic acid gas in the Champagne gives it a certain resistance to bacteria and assures its conservation, it does not mean that the wine is impervious to everything and can remain in optimum condition forever. It is as much alive as any other wine and must receive the same attention and care. It ages and may change. After ten years or so, it may take on a slight colour and begin to maderize; this will continue with the years. It is then said to have become a *renarde* (a vixen). It remains drinkable, of course, but its essential qualities fade, just as a beautiful flower fades. Moreover, the pressure of the gas decreases and little by little the wine loses its life. There is no point, therefore—except as an experiment and perhaps in the case of a particularly good vintage year—in keeping Champagne for a long time. It is put on the market at the time in its life when it is suitable for comsumption; this is one of the rules which control the quality of Champagne.

Dry and semi-dry Champagne. The present trend is towards the *brut* or extra dry variety, and the sweeter type of Champagne, possessing perhaps a little less character, is certainly much less in demand today. These are wines which are very pleasant with desserts; they must, however, be served at a cooler temperature than the others.

Rosé. This remains an amusing exception, but does not lack attraction nor admirers. A very fruity wine with an excellent colour, it is coming more and more into favour and the big firms have no hesitation in offering it. Its bouquet varies according to the way it has been made. Some are produced by adding a small amount of red wine from Champagne; others—and this is preferable—are produced as a rosé from the start. It cannot compete with great classical Champagnes.

It should be added that the shippers also prepare wines for specific foreign markets, to meet specific preferences of their clients. The fruitiness and sweetness of these vary according to their destination.

There remain two other effervescent wines of Champagne which should be mentioned, both of which are very pleasant to drink:

The *crémant*, whose gas content is lower than that of Champagne. This is done by reducing the amount of liqueur added to the wine before the second fermentation. These lithe, light, fruity wines go down very well, but they can never match their superiors. They have, nevertheless, their own place in the Champagne family.

The *Blanc de Blancs* is made solely from white grapes, using the *Chardonnay* variety. It is a very elegant, light wine, with a particularly fine bouquet.

Finally, the Champagne region also produces non-effervescent, so-called "still wines".

THE STILL WINES OF CHAMPAGNE

The still white wines of Champagne are an excellent introduction to a better knowledge of Champagne. There is a *Blanc de Blancs* which has not been *champagnisé* (given a Champagne sparkle), and also a *Blanc de Noirs*, this latter a much more full-bodied wine. The big firms market it. It offers the dominant characteristics of the Champagne vineyards, with its own particular spirit, colour and charm. The still red wines are simple and excellent, but somewhat fragile. Their flavour and strength remind one of the wines of Burgundy, whilst their tannin content recalls those of Bordeaux. The best known among them is the incomparable Bouzy, but Cumières, Ambonnay, Verzenay, Sillery, Mailly, Saint-Thierry also have excellent wines. The appearance of a red wine from Champagne on the table is always greeted with surprise and interest. These amazing red wines have a very special fruity flavour, while their mischievousness is more apparent than real. They are great wines produced with care and should not be drunk at room temperature; they are at their best when cooled. In great vintage years, they are very full-bodied and may be kept for a long time. There is a limit, however: wine of the year 1959, for example, is of a very different order, far removed from the lightheartedness of other years. These red wines at a certain age would seem to become almost too robust and to lose much of their original appeal.

Bouzy is marketed independently of the large Champagne producers by the individual growers since it is not a wine requiring the skilled blending of the sparkling Champagnes.

THE MARKETING OF CHAMPAGNE

The grape has ripened, the Champagne is born. Now it must be marketed—and it has long been known that the people of Champagne are as prudent as they are smart. The whole structure of commercialization and marketing in the Champagne area is as special as the wines. The marketing structure includes:

– *Négociants-manipulants* who themselves vinify the wines from their own vines, or from the must which they buy from individual vinegrowers. They blend and marry, bottle and market the wine themselves.

– *Négociants non manipulants:* companies or individuals marketing Champagne but not making it.

– *Récoltants-manipulants:* vintners who produce and then market their own wine.

– *Co-opératives de manipulation* who press, vinify and blend wines brought to them by member growers. The co-operatives also market the wine themselves.

In the English-speaking countries these terms are rarely met since almost all Champagne is exported by the *grande marque* houses such as Moët et Chandon, Heidsick, G.H. Mumm and Veuve Clicquot, who belong to the first category, the *négociants-manipulants*.

Certain indications must figure on Champagne labels in order to protect the consumer against possible fraud:

N.M. for a first-quality Champagne belonging to a *négociant-manipulant*.

M.A. (B.O.B.—buyer's own brand—in English) for a lesser Champagne belonging to a *négociant-manipulant* or a *négociant non manipulant* and which he can market under his own chosen name, changing his supplier but not his label should he so wish.

C.M. for a brand from a *récoltant-manipulant*.

R.M. for a brand from a *co-operative-manipulante*.

Another requirement for Champagne labels is for the number accorded to the product by the C.I.V.C. to be indicated after the category initials.

An extraordinary network of cellars dug out of the limestone rock twists and turns its way through the subsoil of Champagne. Some of these chalk cellars can be traced back to Gallo-Roman times, but their continued development required—and still requires—continual maintenance. Today, there are about 125 miles of underground tunnels, sheltering millions of bottles, at a constant temperature of 10º to 11º. Some cellars are up to 45 yards deep, and many of the large Champagne firms feel it a duty, as well as a pleasure, to show people around them. Without these cellars, their wine could not be what it is. In 1970, a total of 102,224,090 bottles left the cellars of Champagne, an increase of 8.77 per cent over the sales for 1966.

This increase, moreover, reflects a steady growth. Only one year, 1958, had sales figures showing a sharp decline, as seen in the statistics kept since 1955. In fifteen years, from 1955 to 1970, the number of bottles to leave the cellars rose from 37,706,826 to more than 102 million per annum. During the same period, the increase in sales was higher for *récoltants-manipulants* than for merchants. The latter nevertheless hold their own and sold 75,509,933 bottles in 1970 as against the 26,714,157 bottles sold in the same year by the *récoltants-manipulants*.

The increase in the sales by the growers can be explained by the fact that they can step up production as much as they wish, while the wine-merchants must set a limit to their trade ambitions. Being directly responsible for their own production, the growers can increase direct sales to clients. The wine-merchants, on the other hand, must rely on purchases from vineyards and on the state of the grape market, the latter being directly influenced by the vintage. The wine-merchant must constantly bear in mind that the vines he owns directly meet only one-fifth of his needs; he thus has to buy the remaining four-fifths. The amount of capital he must invest may be judged by the fact that in 1971 a kilogramme (about 2 lb.) of grapes was selling for around 5.41 French francs.

Sales abroad are increasing, which is attracting great interest. Nevertheless, the domestic French market remains far and away the most important: 71,169,802 bottles sold there as against 31,054,288 for export. In 1967, the twelve main markets, in decreasing order of importance, were: Great Britain, Italy, United States, Belgium, Germany, Switzerland, Venezuela, Canada, Holland, Sweden, Denmark, Germany-NATO.

WHAT ONE SHOULD KNOW IN ORDER TO BUY WELL. When buying Champagne, first of all, look carefully at the label on the bottle that is the object of your heart's desire, unless it is a particularly well-known name in which you know you can have full confidence. There is practically no fraud in Champagne, but that is not to say that all Champagnes are equally good.

The word "Champagne", as well perhaps as the *millésime* or year of production, should be written either on the main label or on the neck of the bottle, in clearly legible letters. This information is also printed on the side of the cork, which is of course inside the bottle's neck. Note next the signs just describe in detail, bearing in mind the different categories of merchants in the Champagne trade, the C.I.V.C. index number and the initials indicating the category.

Most people know a good wine-merchant whom they feel they can trust. But never allow him to sell a bottle which has been on display, for it has naturally suffered from this. The bottle must be brought up from the cellar, or at least from a bottle-rack in which it was lying flat, for the cork must always be moistened.

There is no point in building up large stocks of Champagne, and in any case, everything depends of course on how much one consumes. One should set up a Champagne cellar with various types of bottles, going from the ordinary to the best vintage Champagne, and including full-bodied vintage Champagne.

The following selection is given as an example:

Fresh wines: Laurent-Perrier, Lanson, Piper Heidsieck, Mercier, Canard Duchêne, Jeanmaire, etc.

Better-balanced wines with more character: Mumm, Perrier-Jouet, Pommery, Ruinart, Taittinger, etc.

Older and stronger wines: Bollinger, Krug, Pal Roger, Veuve Clicquot, Roederer, etc.

It must be stressed that this list is given purely as an indication, not as a recommendation for buying.

THE PRESTIGE WINES. In recent years, a number of the large firms have tended to establish *cuvées spéciales*, or very special selections of Champagnes. This has been done in a move to meet the requirements for an even higher quality, which would satisfy the taste of the most demanding of connoisseurs, and also from a desire to establish still more solidly the renown of their names. These wines are usually presented with a luxurious refinement, albeit inspired by the simple and seductive shapes of old flasks which thus find a new youth. These are growths of great character. Some of the most famous are: Dom Perignon, by Moët et Chandon, which started this trend; the Cuvée Grand Siècle by Laurent-Perrier; the Comtes de Champagne by Taittinger; the Florens Louis by Piper-Heidsieck; the Cuvée Charles VII by Canard Duchêne; the Cuvée Elysée by Jeanmaire; the Cuvée de L'Empereur by Mercier, and the Roederer sold in crystal bottles. Bollinger presented a 1961 vintage Champagne, which was not uncorked until 1971, as the top-quality product of their firm.

Still on the subject of bottles, one can use the opportunity to detail their great variety. Their names are: split (half-pint), pint (1/10 gallon), quart (1/5 gallon), magnum (2 quarts), jeroboam (4 quarts), rehoboam (6 quarts), methuselah (8 quarts), salmanasar (12 quarts), balthazar (16 quarts) and nebuchadnezzar (20 quarts).

It should be said at once that the bottles with resounding biblical names, from magnum on, are only show pieces, derived from folklore. On the other hand, for some inexplicable reason, Champagne in magnums is always first-rate. This also applies to any other first quality wine.

As a general rule, it is a good idea to furnish one's cellar with bottles of various sizes, suitable for different occasions, bearing in mind that one bottle is usually adequate to serve six or seven guests, unless they are real lovers and connoisseurs of Champagne. The half-pint bottles, or "splits" should be avoided, as they are rather too small to warrant cellar-space.

CHAMPAGNE AND SPARKLING WINES

Champagne is so very special that, of all the effervescent wines, it is the only one not to be known as a "sparkling wine" or *mousseux*. Here, usage and time have gone against etymology. Yet the term "sparkling wine" is applied to all wines which, after a second artificial fermentation, froth when poured into a glass. Depending on the amount of froth, they are called *perlants* (pearly), *pétillants* (effervescent), or *mousseux* (sparkling). *Crémant* is reserved for Champagne.

Sparkling wines are made in three different ways: the rural or natural method; the *méthode champenoise*, and the method known as *cuve close*.

The rural or natural method. The wine is vinified by its natural fermentation without anything being added to it. It is its natural sugar, which has not been turned into alcohol during the first fermentation, which activates the second fermentation. The wine having been bottled after the first fermentation, a second fermentation now takes place in the bottle which gives the wine its effervescence. Modern processes of analysis and vinification enable the vintner to control the effervescence throughout the whole procedure, and thus to produce at his pleasure either a pearly or an effervescent wine.

This method is used in France, especially in Gaillac, Limoux (Blanquette) and in Die, whose yellowish-gold Clairette is reputed.

"Methode Champenoise". This method has been described already in detail, but the main principles are recalled here.

The first fermentation, aptly called "tumultuous", in former times took place in wooden casks. Nowadays, through modern progress, it usually takes place in vats. The process becomes calmer after three weeks, and up to that point, vinification is more or less the same as in all vineyards. The preparation of the *cuvée* (contents of the vat), however, is characteristic of Champagne, for in this region the blending of grapes is far more subtle than anywhere else. Racking follows, then the natural ferments, plus a liqueur made from a mixture of older wine and sugar, bring about the conditions that lead the wine's becoming frothy in the bottle during the second fermentation.

It is in fact this second, very precisely controlled fermentation which brings that fine quality to the wine, for its sparkle and froth must be enduring as well as light. The work of the vintners is not ended when the bottles are cellared, for there remain all those intricate steps which are peculiar to the Champagne vineyards and the *méthode champenoise*: remuage (moving the deposit towards the cork), uncorking or *dégorgement* (removing the cork with its wad of sediment), *dosage* (addition of more liqueur) and so on.

The "cuve close" method. This differs from the two previous ones in that the second fermentation does not take place in bottles but in enormous vats. The wine is inferior when produced by this method and is certainly no substitute for the *méthode champenoise*. French law forbids Champagne made in *cuve close* to be sold as an A.O.C. wine.

These methods are the only ones used in France, and are followed more or less closely, in other countries producing sparkling wines. In Italy, for example, Asti Spumante is made by the *méthode champenoise* up to a certain stage of its development; that is, until the second fermentation in the bottle has taken place. To avoid the *remuage* and the operation of uncorking, the wines are transferred from the bottles into enormous closed vats where they are clarified and filtered.

Finally, and purely for the record, sparkling wine can also by produced simply by adding carbonic acid gas. It need hardly be said that such wines are of a very inferior quality.

LIFE IN THE CHAMPAGNE REGION

Life in the Champagne region follows the rhythm of the work in the vineyards. Although the history of the province is particularly rich in facts and fables, its folklore today has fallen into disuse. One must not be too harsh in blaming the people of Champagne; rather, it should be recognized that the nature of their soil and climate is less propitious to popular festivities than that of the large vineyards to the south. This is the land, moreover, that has been rocked and torn by cruel wars over the centuries, tragedies which have contributed to the disappearance of pleasant customs and joyous occasions which are very difficult to keep up when the heart has gone out of them.

On the other hand, one should not conclude that the vinegrowers of Champagne are a sad people. Everywhere that wine is to be found, the people are warm-hearted and generous.

In former days, when the winegrower poured the grapes into the vat or wooden barrel, he never failed to pronounce a revered formula which expressed all hopes: *Saint Martin, bon vin* ("Saint Martin, make the wine good"). Having thus satisfied his religious beliefs, he did not hesitate to turn to other practices in which piety had no part! A case of "better safe than sorry", no doubt. To take care of superstitions, he also placed a steel knife between the wood of the barrel and the first metal ring.

The Feast of St. Vincent is celebrated on January 22nd here as in all vineyards. Once the simple religious ceremonies have been concluded, including blessing the vines, a propitiatory bottle of good wine is enjoyed.

On the patron saint's day, as well as at all other festivities, whether religious or secular, the sole joy comes from the wine, and the festival of Mardi Gras or *Feux de la Saint-Jean*, in summer, with their maypoles, dances and chorus-singing, are now of the past. The hard work at harvest time does not prevent the workers from enjoying themselves, but workers brought in from other places to help in the harvest are not the ones to bring back the habits and customs of long ago.

If the *Vigneronne* is no longer danced around the wine-press, the last day of harvesting is still celebrated by the *Cochelet*. This consists mainly of a sumptuous meal, with plenty of Champagne, followed by a local ball and *farandole* dances born from the imaginations of the participants.

Modern times have also killed off the friendly *cavées*, or cellar parties, when each vinegrower brought a log to help keep the fire going and joined in the hearty singing before sharing the *queugnots* (a type of biscuit), united with all his friends under the sign of the vine.

THE COMMANDERY OF THE CHAMPAGNE SLOPES. As in other wine regions, an influential brotherhood has pledged itself to spread the fame of Champagne wines. Its origins date back to the seventeenth century when the founders, the Count of Olonne, the Marquis of Saint-Evremond and the Marquis of Mortemart, practising what they preached, formed a group of famed epicures. In those days they were called les *marquis friands* ("the sweet-toothed marquises"), but the irreverant found them another title wherein could be detected some envy: les *fins débauchés* ("the first-class rakes"). In fact, they shared a common love for a good life and had a predilection for the wines of Champagne, which surely absolves them from any sin. Years passed, and it was only after the war that the brotherhood was brought back from its deep sleep by a winegrower from Champillon, Roger Gaucher, and François Taittinger.

The brotherhood is headed by a Commander (at present, Georges Prade, former vice-president of the Municipal Council of Paris) who is helped by a *Conseil Magistral*. The most prominent members of this Council are the *Capitaine Chambellan* (Captain Chamberlain), the *Connétable Premier officier* (High Constable First Officer), the *Grand Chancelier* (Great Chancellor), the *Gardien de la Constitution* (Guardian of the Constitution), and others of lesser mark.

The objectives of the brotherhood are to propagate the noble wine, to defend its prestige and its quality, and to battle relentlessly against malpractice and fraud.

Caps on their heads and swords at their sides, the high dignitaries often go from place to place, organizing or attending important national and international occasions. They insist strictly on remaining an independent group, and though in close contact and on excellent terms with the firms and wine-merchants, they will not accept any protection, nor admit any exclusive rights.

The brotherhood, which today has more than 4,000 members, holds its chapters in the cellars of the most illustrious houses of Rheims and Epernay. It turns out in the vineyards to celebrate St. Vincent's Day, the feast of the patron saint of vinegrowers.

SPARKLING WINES THROUGHOUT THE WORLD

Sparkling wines are produced in nearly all the large viticultural regions in the world, and can be either white, red or rosé, with a very wide range of quality.

THE SPARKLING WINES OF FRANCE

France is the largest producer of sparkling wines in the world, including Champagne: in 1960, 110 million bottles were produced, of which 50 million were Champagne. In 1970, Champagne alone accounted for 102 million bottles.

Burgundy and Bordelais also produce sparkling wines of the *appellation contrôlée* category, but which cannot pretend to compete with the celebrated growths of the Champagne region. The Rhône basin produces the following sparkling wines: ARBOIS MOUSSEUX, L'ETOILE MOUSSEUX or CÔTES DU JURA MOUSSEUX; and farther south there are the sparkling wines of SAVOIE AYSE (Ayse is the name of the growth), the SEYSSEL MOUSSEUX, the SAINT-PERAY MOUSSEUX and the CLAIRETTE DE DIE MOUSSEUX which carry an A.O.C. In the Loire valley, almost every viticultural region has its own sparkling wine: MONT-LOUIS MOUSSEUX, VOUVRAY MOUSSEUX, TOURAINE MOUSSEUX, SAUMUR MOUSSEUX, ANJOU MOUSSEUX, all of which are popular. BLANQUETTE DE LIMOUX and GAILLAC MOUSSEUX, produced in the south-west, deserve more than passing mention.

All French sparkling wines are obliged by law to state on their labels how they have been made, whether by the *méthode champenoise*, *vin mousseux produit en cuve close*, or *vin mousseux gazéfié*.

THE SPARKLING WINES OF GERMANY

After France, Germany is the next largest producer of sparkling wines. They are known either as *Sekt* or *Schaumwein*, the latter being generally inferior to the *Sekt*. The wines sell at a wide range of prices; the best *Sekt* can cost up to ten times more than an ordinary *Schaumwein*. Most German sparkling wines are not made from German but from imported wines, and purchases of foreign wines can sometimes reach as high as three-quarters of the whole German production of sparkling wines. In 1967, only 23.4 per cent of the country's sparkling wines were of German origin.

There are two types of sparkling wine: "Riesling", which retains the fruity bouquet and the original flavour of the grape, and "Champagne" which is more like a traditional aperitif or dessert wine. Both types have the usual range of tastes, varying from the driest to the sweetest, with the same terms being used as those of Champagne. The law obliges the producer to specify on the label in which country the wine was first bottled. Thus a label which says *Französischer Schaumwein* indicates that it is a French sparkling wine, produced in France, while a label *Deutscher Schaumwein* signifies that the wine was prepared and bottled in Germany. However, the origin of the wine used might be German or foreign. The German equivalent for the French *vin mousseux gazéifié* is *mit Zusatz von Kohlensäure*, indicating that CO_2 has been injected. In order to avoid any misunderstandings, one should note that labels with the name *Beeren-Schaumwein* have nothing in common with labels such as *Trockenbeerenauslese* or *Beerenauslese*; "Beeren-Schaumwein" or "Obst-Schaumwein" simply means "sparkling wine made from currants," or "sparkling wine made from fruit". These are therefore not sparkling wines, but aerated fruit juices.

Most producers of German sparkling wines are in the central viticultural region of Hesse in the Rhineland or the Palatinate. The largest producer, Henkell, is at Wiesbaden. Some of the best and oldest producers are Söhnlein at Wiesbaden-Schierstein, Mattheus Müller (MM) at Eltville, Kupferberg at Mainz, Kessler at Esslingen, Burgeff at Hochheim, and Deinhard at Koblenz. Some German sparkling wines carry the name of their growths and a year. The consumption of sparkling wines has greatly increased in the last few years, rising from 50 million bottles in 1956 to 144.2 million bottles in 1965.

THE SPARKLING WINES OF THE SOVIET UNION

The Russians seem to have a partiality for sparkling wines: in 1965, they produced 50 million bottles. The SOWJETSKOJE SCHAMPANSKOJE is produced by a second fermentation either in the bottle in *cuve close* or in double vats. If it is kept for three years before being marketed, the qualification "old" is added. This sparkling wine, when made from red wines, is known as "Soviet Red Champagne". However, if it is made with red wines from Tzymlyansk, it is distinguished by the label ZYMLJANSKSJE. A wine which is artificially injected with carbonic acid gas is known as "aerated wine", and must be so described on the label. The Soviet sparkling wines offer the whole range of varieties, from *brut* to sweet wines with a 10 per cent to 10.5 per cent sugar content. The best Soviet Champagnes are probably KAFFIA in the Crimea, and that produced by Abraou Dursso in the Kouban valley.

Champagne's famous vineyard of Côte d'Hautvillers basks on its Marne valley hillside (above). Here, in harvest time, *porteurs* carry the grapes in small baskets (left) from the vines to the sorters. Time is precious, and the grape-pickers—most of them seasonal workers—eat their midday meal on the spot, among the vines (below).

Once selected, the best grapes are placed in baskets called *mannequins* containing from 150 to 180 pounds of grapes. The *débardeurs* (unloaders) then transport them to the wine-press in horse-drawn carts (right).

The foreman of the vineyard (above) keeps a beady eye on all stages of the harvest, from picking to the presses. In all their various handlings, it is vital that the grapes should never be crushed or even bruised.

Deep in the cellar, a skilled workman performs the delicate task of *remuage*—a slight shake and a twist to every bottle so that the sediment will gradually work its way down and settle near the cork (below).

THE SPARKLING WINES
OF THE UNITED STATES OF AMERICA

The United States produces various types of sparkling wines. There is the wine commonly known in that country as Champagne: it is a light, sparkling wine whose second fermentation takes place in glass containers holding not more than one gallon (about 3.8 litres), and whose appearance and taste tends to resemble true Champagne as closely as possible. French Champagne producers have always fought against the use of the name of their province and of their product by the producers of American sparkling wines. A certain amount of control does, however, exist, since by Californian law the word "Californian" or "American" must appear on the label as well as a statement defining the vinification method used and the place of production.

There is also the "sparkling grape wine" which is made by the *cuve close* method. If this wine has a Champagne-like taste, it is then called "sparkling wine—Champagne type". "Crackling wine" is an effervescent wine, and "carbonated wine" is an aerated sparkling wine. The total United States production of sparkling wine is about 70 million bottles in 1970.

There is not room in these few brief comments on American sparkling wines to permit a fair judgement of their quality. Here, as in many other regions, all the different varieties in all the various prices ranges may be found. The connoisseur of Champagne is, however, always surprised to find the name "Champagne" on the bottles of certain American sparkling wines which are very highly priced and have quite a different taste from true Champagne. In New York State many sparkling wines are made from native grape varieties such as *Catawba*, *Delaware*, *Elvira* and *Isabella* and have often to be blended with Californian wines to reduce the penetrating foxy taste of the eastern grapes. In California the best Champagne-type wines are produced from the *Pinot Noir* and *Pinot Chardonnay* grapes. The *Semillon*, *Sauvignon Blanc*, *White Riesling*, *Pinot Blanc* and *Folle Blanche* also give good results. The Californian Champagnes go through the same *dosage* process as do their French models and have the dry to sweet range, although a really dry Champagne is not often found in this country. The best sparkling wines are produced by F. Korbel and Brothers, Hanns Kornell Cellars, and Almadén Vineyards in California, and Great Western Producers and Gold Seal Vineyards in New York State.

The American connoisseurs of true Champagne are quite numerous: in 1970, 4,509,626 bottles of Champagne were imported into that country.

THE SPARKLING WINES
OF OTHER COUNTRIES

Sparkling wine is called *spumante* in Italy, *espumoso* in Spain and *espumante* in Portugal. Italy has only a small variety of sparkling wines: ASTI SPUMANTE is very well known even outside of Italy's frontiers, but there are also its cousins BARBERA D'ASTI SPUMANTE, GRIGNOLINO D'ASTI SPUMANTE and MOSCATO D'ASTI SPUMANTE. ASTI SPUMANTE is made by the *méthode champenoise* from a muscat wine. It is a sweet wine but the bubbles prevent the sweetness from being disagreeable and if served very cold this drink is even refreshing. The sweetness is not produced by the addition of sugar or by over-ripening of the grapes but from the natural sweetness of the grape itself. In Lombardy, MOSCATO DI CASTEGGIO SPUMANTE is also drunk, and PROSECCO DI CONEGLIANO SPUMENTE in Venetia; both of these wines, however, are less well known than the ASTI.

Spain's centre of production of sparkling wines is San Sandurni de Noya, near Villafranca del Panadès. These wines are clear with a bouquet which savours of honey. Spanish wines are made quite often by the classic Champagne method and the phonetic equivalent, Xampan, often appears on the labels. One of the Catalonian Champagne-type wines once lost a High Court case in London and thenceforth Spanish sparkling wines were not allowed to be sold in England as Spanish Champagnes. The fact that the defendant firm was not one that used the traditional *méthode champenoise* did not help their case. Besides the *méthode champenoise* two other processes are used to make wine sparkle in Spain. One is the *cuve close* method and the other is the regrettable carbonizing method which turns many still wines into unpalatable drinks of the fizzy lemonade order. There are only about forty firms that make a sparkling wine by the *méthode champenoise* and these are the only ones that are entitled to call themselves *cavas*. Many of these *cavas* welcome the casual visitor and are pleased to explain the complicated process used to make their sparkling wines. The visitor may be invited to taste the produce, which he can enjoy in the knowledge that it has been made the right way.

In Portugal, sparkling wines are made in the regions of Bairrada and Lamego, and are often named after the viticultural company which produced them.

Other countries, such as Argentina, Brazil, Israel, South Africa, Switzerland and Uruguay produce some sparkling wines by one or the other of the established methods. Throughout the world, at all latitudes, sparkling wine is a drink for festive occasions, synonymous with happiness, gaiety and joy.

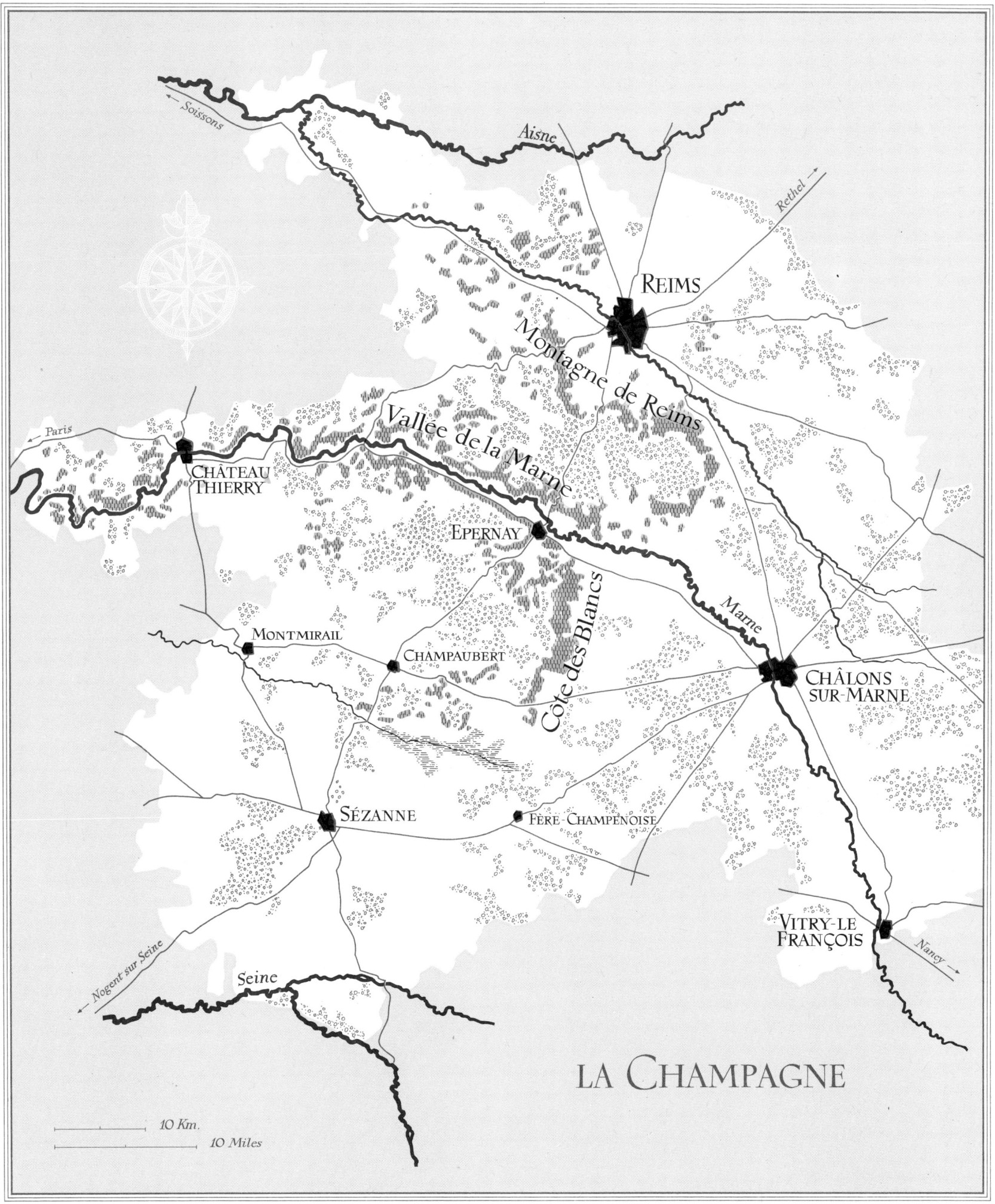

LA CHAMPAGNE

10 Km.

10 Miles

THE WAYS
OF WINE AND MAN

WINE AND HEALTH
A DOCTOR'S GUIDE

GÉRARD DEBUIGNE

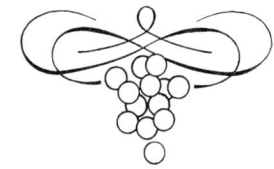

Wine has been for a very long time considered as one of the basic elements of human nourishment. In fact, Olivier de Serres, the French agronomist, was only confirming an already widely held opinion when he wrote, in his famous *Théâtre de l'Agriculture* published in 1600: "After bread comes wine, the second nutriment given by the Creator to sustain life and the first to be famed for its excellence." Long before him, the famous words in Ecclesiastes (ix, 7), "Go thy way, eat thy bread with joy, and drink thy wine with a merry heart" proved that even a thousand years before the dawn of Christianity wine was held to be as essential an item of human sustenance as bread.

All this apart, water was actually considered unhealthy to drink during the seventeenth and eighteenth centuries. Sydenham, the English doctor who discovered laudanum, claimed that the poor people who drank water managed to remain in good health only because their organisms were adapted to wretched conditions. Buffon, the French naturalist, expressed a similar opinion when he declared: "Pure water is not sufficient to keep up the strength of working men." From time immemorial, man has sought more in his food than the mere satisfaction of a physical need. He has always looked also for a combination of physical and spiritual gratifications, a means to combat worry and fatigue and a mild and pleasant stimulant.

In addition to its hygienic and dietetic properties, wine is the only source of nourishment that ideally fulfils this inherent desire of the human species. No other earth-grown product occupies its singular place of honour; none other speaks more eloquently to our hearts, tastes, memories and dreams. Neither grain, which makes the allegorical "daily bread" a nourishing reality for millions, nor rice, which forms the staple diet of an entire continent, nor coffee, nor tea, both much-loved in some countries, can replace it.

This is why wine, whose history is inseparable from that of mankind and even civilization itself, will undoubtedly always retain its special, privileged place in our minds and on our tables.

THE PROPERTIES OF WINE

Wine's qualities are invaluable, innumerable, irreplaceable. It goes without saying, however, that in order to benefit from wine's wonderful virtues, the maximum daily quantities advocated by authorities on the subject, and confirmed by laboratory experiments, should not be exceeded.

Professor Trémolières provided a good guide during the last European Congress on alcoholism: "For healthy adults whose diet is sufficient and well-balanced, the organism can normally oxidise a maximum of one litre of wine in the case of men, and three-quarters of a litre in the case of women. If these measures are exceeded, and if one of the above conditions is not met, as for example in cases of insufficient nourishment, the alcohol is oxidized by toxic processes, and thereby produces a pernicious effect." To which it may be added that, providing reasonable care is taken to distribute the daily intake over the two main meals, wine will not inebriate but contribute its tonic and beneficial properties to the diet of the consumer.

It is worth pointing out that the amount of wine consumed by the average, healthy individual usually falls quite naturally within the specified limits. Alcoholism, so long regarded as a deadly passion and a vice, is increasingly coming to be considered in medical pathology as an illness. The theory of the "alcoholic disease", championed by Jellinek, was introduced into French medical circles around 1956. According to this theory, alcoholism is a "physical compulsion complicated by a mental obsession", its victims being those who suffer from a particular kind of emotional disorder. Only specific types of people, therefore, become alcoholics and there is no reason whatever to stigmatize wine, nor to spoil the pleasure of worthy, decent folk who drink it in moderation by instilling in them a fear that they may become alcoholics.

It is moreover a surprising but accepted fact that the ravages of alcoholism are most marked in those unfortunate regions where no vines are grown. This is not to say that hearty wine drinkers are exempt from the consequences of over-indulgence. But it is primarily those who, already suffering from various nervous or emotional derangements, habitually swallow aperitifs, cocktails, manufactured spirits or anything, good or bad, containing alcohol who are most prone to alcoholism and who have to be treated in the psychiatric wards of hospitals, and rarely those congenial and reasonable imbibers of good wine.

The Nutritional Value of Wine

Since wine is almost 90 per cent water, it is an old and gleeful joke that "any wine drinker is an unwitting drinker of water". Be that as it may, wine also contains many other valuable elements making it a real liquid food with incomparable qualities. But although the most advanced methods of quantitative analysis have succeeded in determining the various proportions of the different constituents of wine, they have yet to reveal the mysterious ingredient which gives wine its reputation of a symbolic and sacred sustenance. The sense of well-being and pleasant euphoria that pervades body and soul while downing a good wine can hardly be expressed in milligrams of one element or another.

We must therefore content ourselves with what information wine itself chooses to divulge as to its own properties and ingredients which, in any case, vary from one wine to another, depending on the kind of soil, the species of grape, the year of harvesting, the length of time the wine has been bottled and, above all, the care and attention it receives during the time it is growing to maturity.

Wine's Calorific Value

This depends on two factors: alcoholic strength and sugar content. Even ignoring all its other ingredients and assuming that wine is merely a dilution of alcohol in water, it would still be a food or, at the very least, a dietary supplement.

As the research carried out by Atwater in 1902 has proved, alcohol is immediately utilized by the body —unlike sugar, fats and amino acids—and it thereby supplements to a certain extent the other energizing foods. However, the work of Schaeffer, Le Breton and Dontcheff has shown that wine can only supply 50 per cent of the body's basic requirements, in other words 600 to 800 calories.

But it cannot be stressed enough that the ten cubic centimetres of alcohol contained in one litre of wine have no relation to the same quantity of alcohol absorbed neat. Wine is not merely and simply a solution of one per cent ethylic alcohol! Intimately blended with a multitude of other living elements, alcohol, an inert substance, enhances the entire complex of wine with its valuable qualities.

The number of calories contained in a litre of wine varies between 600 and 1,000, with an average of 600 to 700 in the case of red wine. Sweet, soft white wines of the Sauternes type with their high sugar content contain more calories than dry white wines. Naturally sweet wines and dessert wines, rich in both sugar and alcohol, contain the most calories of all. In countries enjoying a high standard of living, the calorie content of a wine may seem of trifling importance, and most people are more concerned with reducing an already excessive general intake. Nevertheless, where the source of this body fuel is wine, it certainly seems to possess quite remarkable powers to generate well-being, enthusiasm and intellectual activity.

Vitamins

Wine supplies the body with all the vitamins in the grape. Even on the basis of its wealth of vitamins, wine can be described without exaggeration as a "living drink".

Wine contains the following vitamins:

Vitamin C. This has well-known effects on general physical tone, physical fitness, resistance to cold and fatigue. Athletes need two to three times as much Vitamin C as persons with sedentary occupations.

Vitamin P (or C_2). In association with Vitamin C, this vitamin increases physical resistance and has a very definite effect in certain cases of debility with low blood pressure. Lavollay and Sevestre attribute wine's tonic effect to its Vitamin P content.

Vitamin B_2 or riboflavine. Considered by some to be of nutritive value, this vitamin is active in the metabolism of the glucides, proteins, irons, vitamins A, B_1, PP and the adrenocorticotrophic hormones.

Vitamin B_3 or PP. This is a powerful stimulant of the cell functions. Andross has demonstrated that productivity increased when substantial amounts of this vitamin were included in the diet of a group of workmen.

Mineral Salts and Trace Elements

Without certain minerals, the human system cannot survive. Sulphur, phosphorus, chlorine, sodium, potassium, magnesium, calcium and iron are all essential to life. The system can assimilate these substances only in the form of organic salts, in other words combined with vegetable or animal matter. It cannot assimilate them in their natural state or in the form of mineral salts, except for a few substances such as kitchen salt. In wine, the mineral salts are incorporated with other substances and can be assimilated readily. Although total deficiency in mineral salts is rare, relative deficiency is quite common and wine therefore constitutes a far from negligible source of these valuable substances.

BIOCHEMICAL EFFECTS OF WINE ON THE SYSTEM

If only on account of the calories, vitamins and mineral salts which it supplies in a highly palatable and easily assimilated form, wine can be considered one of the most valuable foods. Yet these are only a few of the virtues which were proved by our ancestors' instinctive physical need.

Wine Aids Digestion

St. Paul needed no converting to this virtue. He exhorted Timothy: "Stop drinking only water. Take a little wine for your stomach's sake and for your frequent discomforts." Even at that time it was recognized that wine's natural acidity increased the secretions of saliva. Wine thus makes an excellent aperitif, the first few sips preparing the organs for digestion. Furthermore, it is the only good, natural and healthy aperitif which does not "whet the appetite the way that the wrong key opens a lock, by breaking it," as a famous doctor once wittily remarked.

The secretion of gastric juices is also stimulated and increased. Furthermore, wine also contains enzymes similar to those present in the digestive juices, thus facilitating the work of tired or deficient stomachs. Its tannin stimulates the fibres of the entire alimentary canal. The regular use of good wine also stimulates intestinal secretions and thus helps to combat the constipation with which so many people nowadays seem to be plagued.

But, first and foremost, wine has been found to greatly facilitate the digestion of proteins contained in meat, fish, oysters and cheese. Genevois even went so far as to say that it was the only drink which, because of its ionic acidity and low osmotic pressure, allowed proteins to be easily digested. With today's increased standard of living, the modern diet is particularly rich in proteins of animal origin, formerly luxuries in which only the well-to-do could regularly indulge. Wine, combining excellently with these proteins, achieves a perfect gastronomic harmony and subsequently facilitates their digestion. Thus the well-planned marriage of meats, fish, shellfish or cheese with an eligible wine is not only an epicurean refinement but a sensible and scientifically proven aid to healthy digestion.

Wine as an Antiseptic

The bactericidal power of wine has long been recognized. Even the Sumerians used balms and ointments with a wine base, and our forbears instinctively reached for wine to cleanse and asepticize wounds. The bactericidal action of wine is due not only to the alcohol it contains but also to its acids, tannin, sulphurous acid and ethers.

It has been proved that one cubic centimetre of white wine, mixed with one cubic centimetre of culture medium, kills 99 per cent of the colon bacilli and the bacilli of cholera and typhoid. So it is not surprising that armies were sometimes issued with wine during epidemics of dysentery, as we learn from the *Journal* written by a certain Percy during the Prussian campaign in 1807: "The dysentery is improving. The army is only slightly the worse for it now. Wine is being distributed to the troops: it is the best preventative."

Similarly, the custom of sprinkling oysters or other shellfish with white wine not only adds to their delectability but is a prudent health precaution into the bargain. The wine that children can be seen drinking in restaurants in Europe, albeit well diluted, also serves, at least in part, a hygienic purpose.

The Antitoxic Properties of Wine

Wine has proved an effective therapeutic agent in the prevention of infectious and feverish diseases and in certain toxic-infections such as influenza. Despite the ever-widening range of modern medicines, a glass of good mulled wine is still a sovereign remedy for incipient flu' and one that it would be foolish to relegate to the store of "old wives' tales". The antitoxic action of wine has even prevented certain cases of alkaloid poisoning, such as sparteine and strychnine.

In the same way, marinading and cooking game in wine has shown itself to be a wise precaution. Obviously, wine is primarily used to tenderize rather tough meat and to bring out its flavour. But in the case of beasts or fowl whose bodies may have accumulated a considerable amount of toxins, due to fatigue, or whose wounds may be unclean, wine safeguards against possible food poisoning.

The Anti-Allergic Properties of Wine

These have been demonstrated by Weissenbach who advises crushing strawberries in red wine fifteen minutes before serving, to safeguard against the risk of an allergic reaction to which some people are prone.

WINE AND MODERN MAN

Naturally, wine is no longer the indispensable nutriment of those days when nourishment was very much less rich and varied than today. Nevertheless, it still plays a useful role and remains an ideal drink.

Not only does wine provide stimulating sensations to jaded palates, it also gives our frequently abused systems the necessary tonic to resist the stresses of modern life. Wine meets a pressing contemporary need: to keep the mind alert and the body in top physical condition. The vitamins it contains happen to be those best suited to combat the fatigue and weariness of a world and age increasingly dominated by the rhythm of machines.

Tannin contributes still further to the bracing properties of wine. Red wines, richer in tannin, are more tonic than white and have a more marked stimulant effect. Red wine is therefore preferable to white when energy flags and the organism has need of a fillip. The habit of drinking a "stirrup-cup" before vaulting into the saddle, so popular in times past, proves the value of this tonic to mind and muscles, the cheering qualities of a stimulant so ideally suited to sustain the horseman on his tiring rides. As long as it is taken in moderate quantities, wine never produces depressing after-effects, the penalty of so many modern drugs.

But although it is an ideal tonic, wine is also the best and healthiest promoter of relaxed well-being. More than ever before, modern man needs "tranquillizers" to help him shoulder his cares, resolve the problems that beset him and cope with the discouraging aura of anxiety about him. Wine promotes optimism and *joie de vivre* and even produces a marked mental improvement in cases of anxiety.

Natural, harmless and nearly as old as the world itself, good wine in reasonable quantities is infinitely better than all the "pep pills" with their dangerous artificial happiness. The sense of well-being that comes from good food and wine naturally and spontaneously produces the state of relaxation with which modern man is so obsessed but which our ancestors had much less need to seek. Furthermore, this method calls for no tiresome procedures, no special equipment —all that is needed is a wine list!

Finally, the infectious euphoria created by good wine gives human relations a friendliness and gaiety which are often all too lacking in the modern world. In an age when worries, overwork and jangled irritation beset the world with strangers and enemies, a quiet glass of wine between friends helps to restore those forgotten qualities of comradeship and human warmth.

WINE AND SPORTSMAN

Sport = no alcohol. This is the unequivocal equation advocated by sportsmen and their trainers who believe in rigorous self-denial and who even go so far as to include wine in their uncompromising verdict. However, the latest studies on the subject, far from extolling the special diets formerly in fashion, agree that the ideal diet for an athlete is quite simply the ideal, healthy and well-balanced diet of an ordinary man engaged in a strenuous physical occupation. Spirit-based or manufactured aperitifs and liqueurs, except for special occasions, should indeed be excluded from the athlete's menu and forbidden during training, but to condemn wine would be a sad exaggeration.

Wine, which Pasteur described as "the healthiest and most hygienic of drinks" has shown itself to be ideal for sportsmen, even more so than for those with sedentary occupations.

All drinks other than wine have various disadvantages. Fruit juices, especially those of citrus fruits, are not always well tolerated. Although pleasant enough to drink between meals, they hardly make good gastronomic partners with a well-cooked meal. Beer dulls the mind, burdens the stomach and produces unwelcome belching and flatulence. Cider can provoke gastric troubles and has an irritant, laxative effect on the intestine. Too much coffee or tea lead to insomnia and excitability, and athletes are already quite nervous enough. Milk, usually badly tolerated by most adults, is a food not a drink. Continual consumption of waters with a high mineral or soda content is not recommended for athletes. What else remains, save slightly aerated mineral water or plain tap water?

More than anyone else, the sportsman, dependent on top physical and mental condition to put out his best effort, needs wine, a valuable mixture which stimulates cell functions and whose beneficial and soothing properties can hardly be denied.

Particularly during training, and when the sport in question involves considerable muscular effort, the athlete is advised to adopt a diet very rich in proteins, such as meats, fish, eggs and cheese. Wine, it will be remembered, is a powerful aid to the digestion of these substances. Its vitamins help to counter muscular and nervous fatigue and keep the athlete in good shape.

The mineral salts contained in wine help to prevent deficiencies which may seriously upset the delicate balance of the athlete's physical form. Iron is an essential element in training, increasing the volume of blood and aiding in its aeration. Similarly, sulphur is needed to eliminate the toxins produced by fatigue from intensive training. Both sulphur and iron are found in wine.

Finally, the tonic and calming properties of wine are most beneficial to the general morale of the athlete, whose strict discipline, often fanatically intensive training and obsession with optimum performances often result in a delicate and even precarious mental state. In these conditions, it is in the athlete's interest to drink a reasonable amount of wine. When he is exerting considerable muscular effort, his pulmonary activity speeds up and he can eliminate alcohol more easily than persons leading a sedentary life.

In fact, authorities on sport are by no means against a reasonable consumption of good wine. Doctor Mathieu, medical adviser to Olympic teams, declares: "For a normal subject, if the quantity of wine does not exceed half a litre a meal, or one litre a day, the alcohol is entirely burned up by the organism and wine then becomes an excellent nutritional drink." Boigey, whose work on exercise as a form of therapy is now universally recognized, considers that "natural wine is the most commendable of alcoholic drinks. It contains a wonderful range of useful and well-balanced substances which nothing else can replace."

Doctor Encausse, medical officer of the High Commission for Youth and Sport in France, advocates that consumption of wine should be limited to three-quarters of a litre per day for a healthy adult weighing approximately 150 pounds, wisely concluding that the medical profession should recommend temperance rather than abstinence.

Nevertheless, allowing for a certain flexibility of interpretation, not all wines can be recommended for athletic activities. This applies to robust or fortified wines, rich in bouquet and highly coloured. Burgundies and wines from the Côtes du Rhône should, alas, be reserved for Sundays and holidays and forgotten during training. The same applies to white wine which has the unfortunate reputation, especially among mountain guides, of going straight to the legs. However, the athlete still has an entire range of light, attractive red and rosé wines to choose from. He needs no commiseration.

WINE AND YOUTH

Obviously, nobody would think of giving a young child undiluted wine. However, in the traditional Italian family, children do drink very limited quantities of wine at the table, wine being considered as an integral part of the Italian meal. And it is interesting to note that Italy has a lower rate of alcoholism *per capita*, for example, than the United States.

In France, too, well-diluted wine is served with school meals and this is, in fact, far healthier than the fizzy drinks so liberally dispensed to their offspring by English and American parents.

During adolescence, a small quantity of good, undiluted wine, drunk with meals, can do no harm. It should be remembered that many tonics recommended for "the awkward age" have a wine base, yet nobody worries about the dangers of alcoholism in prescribing them. A healthy respect for wine, moderation in its use and discernment for its quality, instilled at an early age, will do much to prevent livers and mental processes from being damaged in later life by the imbibing of dubious or indifferent mixed drinks based on spirits.

WINE AND THE ELDERLY

The virtues of wine for older people are well known. The Médoc, famous as a wineproducing and wine-drinking region, is justly proud of its record for the longevity of its inhabitants.

Diminishing digestive secretions often result in old people having poor appetites. Lack of nourishment and vitamin deficiency may result, aggravated by additional factors such as ill-fitting dentures, sometimes mistaken dietary fads or, quite simply, a restricted budget. Good wine, being easily assimilated and pleasant to drink, stimulates old people's appetites and facilitates digestion. Its stimulant and tonic properties are valuable at an age when there is increasing debility. Especially in the case of dessert wines or naturally sweet wines, it also contributes valuable calories and comforting warmth to the system. Attention should also be drawn to the fact that there are many good but quite modestly priced wines. Despite all the care taken in its production, wine is still fairly reasonable in price when compared to the other alcoholic drinks on the market.

WINE AND ILLNESS

Old Hippocrates, the Father of Medecine, who lived from 460 to 377 B.C., taught that "wine is wonderfully suitable for man if, in sickness as in health, it is administered in proper and fair measure".

As long ago as the Carolingian era, the ordinary diet that the sick and elderly received in the monasteries included strengthening and savoury wine soups. In later history, Joan of Arc was also said to be very partial to them.

The bactericidal and antitoxic properties of wine that make it an excellent agent in the prevention of infection have already been mentioned. And Nature, generously providing man with the remedies for the ills she herself inflicts, has foreseen all eventualities by providing different wines for different ailments.

Thus naturally sweet or dessert wines, those delicacies of the vine, are particularly recommended for convalescents, the emaciated and those suffering from debility. On the other hand, diabetics should on no account be given these wines because their diet does not permit food with a high sugar content.

Light, dry white wines, pleasantly sharp and with their low sugar and alcohol content, stimulate the appetite and digestive processes. They are eminently suitable for dyspeptic subjects. They are also recommended in cases of obesity, their calorific value being very modest and their diuretic properties well known: the white wines of Savoy sustain the morale of those heroes who submit to the cure at Bride-les-Bains.

Sparkling wines are recommended for some kinds of dyspepsia, their carbonic acid being an effective remedy for vomiting. Champagne is the prerogative of convalescents, raising the morale as well as helping the system to recover. It is a wonderful "steadier" after a shock and is even useful in cases of low blood pressure.

Wines light in body and alcoholic strength, whatever their colour, are suitable for all invalids and should be chosen for everyday use. Full-bodied wines with rich bouquets should be kept in the cellar to celebrate the time of recovery.

The last word on the subject could very well be left to Sir Alexander Fleming, who once so wisely remarked: "Penicillin may cure human beings, but it is wine that makes them happy."

DOCTOR'S ORDERS

Wines that may be drunk—and those that may not be—by persons sufferings from certain bodily disorders:

Ailment	Wines Permitted	Wines Prohibited
Hyperchlorhydria (excess hydrochloric acid in the gastric juices)	Light red wines in small quantities.	Full-bodied red wines, very dry white wines, young and acid wines (beware of white and rosé wines in general), dessert wines.
Hypochlorhydria (inadequate secretion of hydrochloric acid in the stomach)	Light red wines or slightly acid dry white wines of low alcoholic content, young wines, Muscadet, Crépy, Fendant, Champagne, Beaujolais.	Wines of high alcoholic strength, dessert wines.
Various gastric disorders	Light red wines in small quantities, old Médoc.	White and rosé wines, sparkling and semi-sparkling wines.
Ulcers	No wine.	All wines.
Between attacks	No limitation.	None.
Intestinal troubles	All red wines when not acute.	White wines, sparkling wines and those of high alcoholic content, Burgundy, Côtes-du-Rhône. Never drink iced wines.
Constipation	All light wines, white, red or rosé.	Wines of high alcoholic strength, Burgundies, Côtes-du-Rhône.
Serious hepatic deficiencies (alcoholism, precirrhosis, cirrhosis resulting from hepatitis and jaundice)	No alcoholic drinks whatever, not even diluted wine.	
Vesicular lithiasis (biliary dyskinesia, abdominal migraine)	Red or white wine diluted with water (no more than ¼ litre per day).	Neat wine, dessert wines.

Hypercholesterolemy (excess cholesterol) and arteriosclerosis	All wines but in limited quantities.	
Cardiac deficiency	All wines allowed: white, red, rosé, dry or sweet.	Avoid very full-bodied wines of high alcoholic strength.
Hepatobiliary disease (biliary lithiasis, family cholemia)	Light wine, particularly red, in small quantities or preferably diluted with water, very little white wine.	Full-bodied, fortified wines rich in mineral extracts, dessert wines, Champagne and sparkling wines, iced wines.
High blood pressure (salt-free and soda-free diets)	Use wine and spirits for flavouring in cooking.	Limit the quantity in cases of inadequate blood circulation.
Renal deficiency (acute nephritis and Bright's disease)	All wines but in small quantities.	
Bladder stones	White, red and rosé wines, dry or sweet.	Avoid Bordeaux rich in mineral extracts, Burgundies and full-bodied wines.
Nutritional disorders (arthritis, gout, uric lithiasis, excess of uric acid in the blood, isolated albuminuria)	Young or old red Bordeaux in limited quantities, very little light white wine, local wines of low alcoholic strength.	Burgundies, Côtes-du-Rhône, Saint-Emilion, Champagnes and sparkling wines, ports, Madeira, dessert wines, all full-bodied, highly coloured, noble wines.
Obesity (crash diet)	No wine.	All wines are forbidden, the food intake being insufficient and unbalanced, the alcohol will be oxidized in the body by toxic processes. In addition, wine would add undesirable extra calories.
Obesity (continuous treatment)	Very dry white wines, young and of low alcohol content, Muscadet, Savoy and Alsace wines, light Bordeaux, local red and rosé wines. ¼ to ½ litre per day at the maximum. Remember that the calories contained in wine should be counted in the daily calorie allowance.	Sweet white wines, full-bodied and strong wines, naturally sweet and dessert wines.
Diabetes	Very dry white wine, extra-dry Champagne, red wines of low alcohol content.	Liqueur-like white wines, white Bordeaux, Vouvray, wines of high alcoholic content, Burgundy, Saint-Emilion, dessert wines, naturally sweet wines and fortified French and other wines (muscat, port, Malaga, Madeira and Samos).
Dermatitis	Dry, young and light wines, local red and rosé wines of low alcoholic content.	Full-bodied wines of high alcoholic content, sweet white wines, naturally sweet and liqueur wines.
Emaciation	Sweet white wines, wines made from grapes with "noble rot", dessert wines, naturally sweet and liqueur wines. Médoc, generous Burgundy, Côtes-du-Rhône, old Cahors; a little at frequent intervals through the day, drunk with meals.	Drink as little as possible while eating. Attractive, light wines should thus be avoided.
Convalescence	Champagne, sweet white wines, wines made from grapes with "noble rot", Médoc, old red Burgundy, high-class white Burgundy.	
Low blood pressure	Champagne, full-bodied and aromatic red wines, high-class white wines from Burgundy.	
Nervous breakdown	Champagne, red wines rich in tannin, Bourgueil, Madiran, old Médoc.	Wines with high alcoholic content. Avoid white wines.
Pregnancy	Dry white wines, red Bordeaux (particularly Médoc), Champagne and sparkling wines.	Absolutely no strong wines whatever, particularly fortified wines such as sherry and vermouth.

Should children drink wine?

It is certainly not advisable to give children alcoholic drinks. As far as wines are concerned, heavy or fortified wines should be particularly avoided. At the end of the meal, children may safely be given a little young or light wine, diluted with four times its volume of water, the quantity of wine depending on the child's age. As a rough guide, children between 5 and 7 years could be given a quarter to half a wineglassful, those between 7 and 10 half a glassful, 10 to 12 year olds two-thirds to three-quarters of a glass, while from the age of thirteen onwards a child can quite safely be given a full glass of wine.

YOUR OWN CELLAR

BERNARD GRENOUILLEAU

The first essentials for a good wine cellar are constant temperature, darkness and adequate ventilation. The temperature should be about 11º C., or 52º F. The cellar should be neither too dry nor too humid; ideally it should be cut out of rock or vaulted in mortared stone and always facing north. In certain wineproducing regions, as elsewhere, houses are naturally built with underground cellars. These days, however, in the provinces as well as in metropolitan areas, those who have a good, large cellar under the house can consider themselves as very fortunate.

If the cellar already meets these basic requirements, all that remains is to equip and arrange it to the best possible advantage. If, on the other hand, it is over-dry or over-humid, these disadvantages can be partly remedied by modern materials. An effective and traditional touch is achieved by spreading river-bed sand over the floor and watering it when the weather becomes too hot. If the cellar is equipped with air-shafts or other means of ventilation these should always be kept closed during periods of extreme cold or heat. Condensation should be guarded against as variations in temperature can result in streaming walls and dripping ceilings. Any cellar should be as free as possible from vibrations, something not always easy to achieve for those who live in the city.

Naturally, the cellar must be clean, tidy and well kept and perishables should be prohibited. This can be a delicate problem when the housewife sees this attractive, clean, cool place which is so ideal for storing things. Nevertheless, no fruit or vegetables which might decay should be allowed in the cellar, nor any old clothes, papers and the like as, with time, they can give off a musty smell which is likely eventually to permeate and spoil the wine.

THE APARTMENT CELLAR

From the traditional interpretation of the word, a cellar in an apartment seems a paradox. Yet with a reasonable amount of skill and imagination, what could be called an "apartment cellar" can be easily arranged. Even in a smallish flat, a closet or wall cupboard can serve, providing this is sufficiently far away from the kitchen or a heat source of any kind. If needs be, one can use the recess of a blocked-up door. Ventilation is necessary but this is quite simply achieved with wire mesh at the top and bottom and a lining of fibre glass, necessary for good thermal insulation. Obviously a small cellar of the kind in question cannot contain a large stock of wine, but it should easily hold between fifty and a hundred bottles. If these are choice wines, that is a fair number and also represents a substantial cash investment.

Whatever the size, shape or location of the cellar, once it is ready it is just a matter of filling it. Racks for bottles can be of wood, cement, brick or iron, depending on individual tastes and means. If small barrels of wine are to be stored, then stands of wood, stone or cement must be installed.

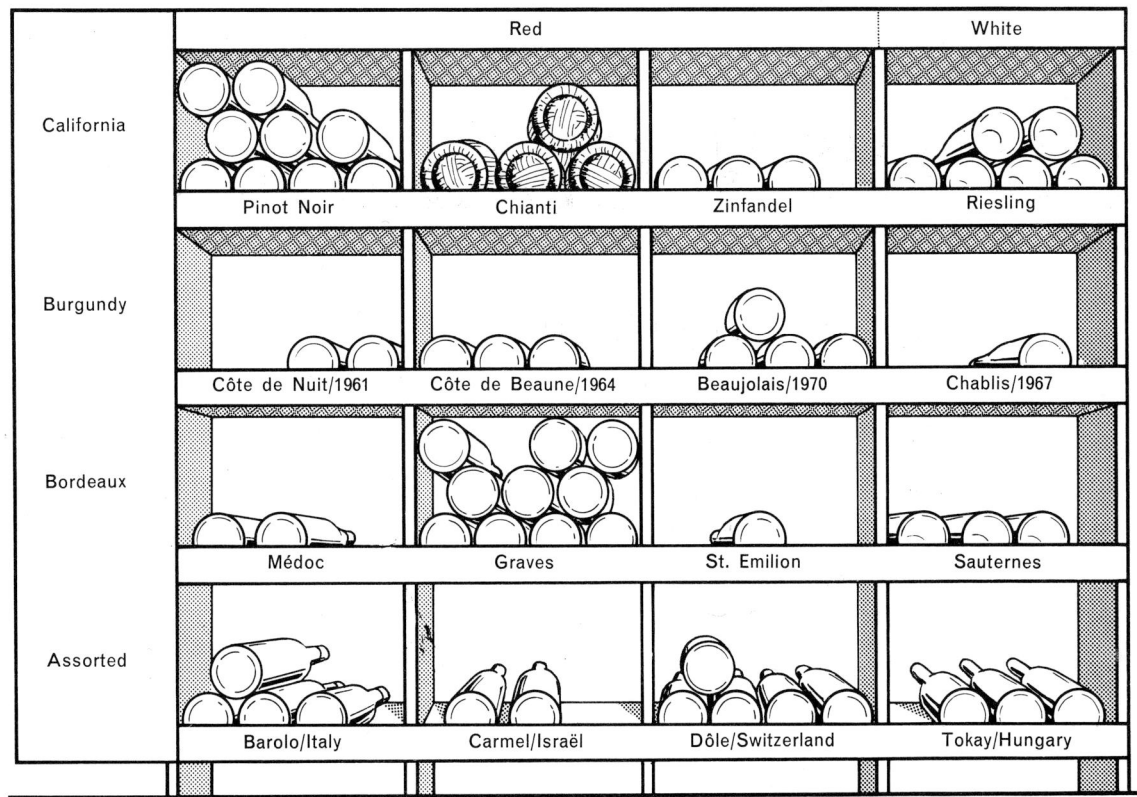

	Red			White
California	Pinot Noir	Chianti	Zinfandel	Riesling
Burgundy	Côte de Nuit/1961	Côte de Beaune/1964	Beaujolais/1970	Chablis/1967
Bordeaux	Médoc	Graves	St. Emilion	Sauternes
Assorted	Barolo/Italy	Carmel/Israël	Dôle/Switzerland	Tokay/Hungary

In a real cellar intended to hold several hundred bottles the most rational method is to have one compartment for each wine. There are many ways of arranging the bottles; by region and by *cru*, the reds on the left (diagram); chronologically, the oldest on the left; for lovers of wines of a particular region, one compartment to the wine of each sub-region; in adjoining compartments wines from regions or countries with nothing in common. The important thing is to have an orderly and logical system that facilitates periodic sampling and stock-taking and the replenishing of stocks when necessary. The name and vintage of the wine should be specified on each compartment.

Arranging a stock of fine wines is not necessarily a complicated undertaking. Here are a few suggestions, although there are many other equally good solutions: *(left to right, top)* racks placed one on top of the other; lengths of clay piping; wooden or plastic packing cases; *(bottom)* a gaily painted box divided diagonally; a ready-made bottle holder (available on the market); a converted set of small, deep shelves.

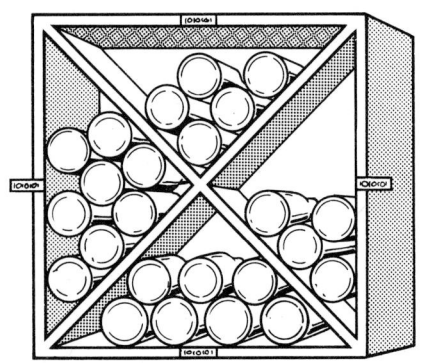

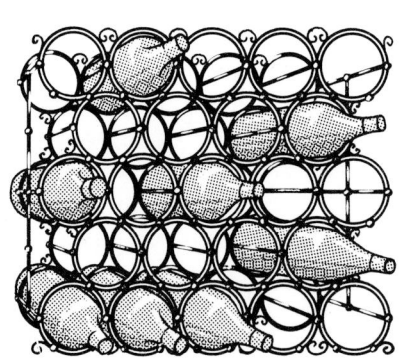

Not surprisingly, the most difficult part of setting up a private cellar is knowing what wine to buy and this, precisely, is the most difficult advice to give. It depends primarily on how much money is available, but also, of course, on personal tastes and preferences and whether or not a wineproducing region is near at hand. In this chapter, some general guidelines will be given as to how cost, personal preference and availability may best be combined.

For private individuals, buying in barrels is recommended only for local wines. For those fortunate enough to have access to such wines, it is often a very good idea to buy a barrel, or even a hogshead, depending on the size of the family and the amount of entertaining that is done. Before ordering wine in barrel, it is most important to find out whether it is ready for bottling or if it requires special attention beforehand. Such a wine will probably be a standard type and the attention needed very simple and straightforward. The most important thing is for the wine to be allowed time to settle. If it has not previously been treated, it is perhaps even advisable to clarify it. There is no need for professional filtering equipment or procedures. The old method of clarifying with white of egg is perfectly adequate and is still practised by reputable wineries producing high-class wines. For a cask containing approximately 50 gallons, two or three egg whites are whisked with a pinch of coarse salt, using an earthenware—but never a metal—bowl. The mixture is then poured into the cask through the bung-hole in the top, stirred with a special whisk or a clean stick and left to settle for a few days. The albumin draws all impurities down to the bottom of the cask. If it is a sound and well-constituted wine, it can be bottled several days later, after ensuring that the tap is placed high enough off the bottom of the barrel so that only perfectly clear wine pours out. If it is considered preferable to siphon the wine out with a rubber tube, a stick should be attached whose end projects about an inch below the end of the tube, so that the tube will not touch the bottom.

If the wine is stored in the cask for any length of time, the cask should be lying down on its stand with the bung on the top; otherwise, when the level of the wine drops, it will be necessary to ullage it frequently to ensure a good wine when bottled. Normally, the cask is not kept in this way until the wine is at least a year old. Should ullage prove absolutely necessary, the traditional method can be used. This consists of putting enough carefully washed and dried pebbles into the liquid to bring the surface of the wine flush with the bung-hole. Obviously, if the wine is very young it must be racked periodically to draw off the clear wine from the lees, but this requires special kinds of vessels. It should be borne in mind that casks are very difficult to keep in good condition. An empty cask quickly spoils and filling it later can be disastrous.

Bottles should be very carefully washed so that not the slightest trace of smell can be transferred to the wine. They must be drained thoroughly on a proper rack, protected from dust. As for corks it is a mistake to economise, particularly in the case of wines which will be kept for a considerable time. For ordinary wines to be drunk in the course of the year, or the following one at the latest, conical corks are available which can be inserted by hand. However, whether conical or any other shape, they must be of good quality. Nothing is more disagreeable than to find that a good wine has been spoilt by a bad cork. Corks should be dipped in boiling water, seasoned in wine or, better still, moistened with a neutral alcohol of the brandy spirit type.

Once the bottles are filled and corked it only remains to lay them carefully in their racks. In some countries, when the bottles are to be kept for a long time, they are buried in sand, temperamental white wines being buried standing up.

As for sealing the wine, it is better to use sealing wax rather than the familiar metal foil for bottles which are to be stored for a long time. Apart from its efficiency, this lends the bottle a good seal, if the pun may be excused, with a touch of old-fashioned charm and craftsmanship. The wax is melted with a spoonful of oil in any kind of small, deep pot, over a gentle heat just sufficient to keep the sealing wax liquid. The necks of the bottles should first be carefully wiped free of any moisture to prevent cracking, then dipped into the wax and removed with a quick turn.

For those people who insist on foil caps, these can actually be applied without a machine, but there is a knack to it. A piece of string should be attached to a hook or some point on the wall, the other end being held in one hand. The capsule is firmly pressed on to the neck of the bottle and the string is then looped round it. The string is pulled as tight as possible and the neck of the bottle twirled up and down the entire length of the string. With a bit of practice the caps are firmly fixed in place.

Bottling and maturing wine is not recommended for amateurs. If a good, clear, filtered local wine can be found and they wish to bottle it themselves, this can be an amusing pastime providing they have enough patience and time. It can also be an economic proposition as bulk wine costs less. But whether the wine is in cask or bottle it is well worth while purchasing it at least several months before drinking.

Even with the humblest of cellars, the average wine-lover should take good care to have at least 50 bottles of *vin ordinaire* in stock for everyday use, and to replenish his supplies before they run really low. This practice makes it easier for purchaser and merchant alike to maintain the same quality. It is a wise and well-known French saying that "it is always a pleasure to change bread, but never the wine". The quantity of 50 bottles only serves as an example for those with limited cellar space, although even the amateur aspires to greater things. Apart from all the pleasure and satisfaction derived from owning a private cellar, laying down a stock of choice wines can also be a financial investment, inasmuch as prices increase as wines age. There is ample proof of this in the astronomical prices fetched by bottles auctioned from private cellars.

A cellar of fine wines with any pretension to being well-stocked should contain, on the average, a thousand bottles covering a variety of wines. The following suggestions give some idea of how the stock would be divided up.

- 25 to 50 bottles of Champagne, to be renewed at least every two years. 50 bottles of SAUTERNES or vintage sweet wines, bought during a good year and laid down for future use.

- 200 bottles, at least, of good red Bordeaux such as MÉDOC, GRAVES, SAINT-EMILION, as many as possible of good vintages, which should be replaced from time to time so that stocks are never exhausted.

- 200 bottles of red and white Burgundy for drinking within three, four or five years.

- 50 bottles of special aperitif or dessert wines such as port, Madeira, SAMOS, BANYULS, MALVASIA, MARSALA and MAVRODAPHNI.

- 100 bottles of assorted whites from such districts as the Rhine and Moselle, from Hungary, Alsace, Switzerland, Italy and Central Europe, including CHABLIS, POUILLY, MUSCADET, GRAVES, HUELVA.

The remainder, about a third of the total, can be made up from miscellaneous or informal red wines, suitable for drinking at any time of day and not necessarily with meals. They will almost certainly include Beaujolais, except for the best vintages which should be laid down for future use; CÔTES-DU-RHÔNE, rosé wines from Provence and elsewhere in France, notably Anjou, fruity red wines from Spain, VALPOLICELLA from Italy, and so on.

This fulfils the basic requirement for a good cellar stock: a good selection of important French wines for drinking with special meals; a range of aperitif and dessert wines; a range of local or unusual foreign wines, depending on the owner's taste; young, delicate white wines of any origin and a good light table wine with a low alcohol content and a clean, fresh taste.

SUGGESTIONS FOR A CELLAR OF MODERATE SIZE

The proportion of white wines to red is obviously a matter of personal preference. Perhaps a good balance would be 12 different kinds of red wine and 10 different white wines, allowing for twelve bottles of each as the minimum. The suggestions below merely provide a guide to constituting a well-balanced cellar, a theme for endless, individual variations.

CHOICE OF WHITE WINES

4 *dry white wines* to serve with fish and seafood and, occasionally, to drink as an aperitif.

2 *medium-dry, mellow white wines* for rice dishes, various entrées and vegetable dishes.

2 *sweet wines* to accompany desserts.

2 *Champagnes* or, failing this, 2 first-class sparkling wines.

Dry white wines

Germany:	Riesling from the Moselle, Rheingau or Palatinate. These should be tasted before ordering.
Alsace:	Riesling, Pinot Gris, Tokay.

CHOICE OF RED WINES

2 *light red wines* to serve with roast fowl, veal and lamb.

4 *full-bodied red wines* to accompany red meat, roast meat of any kind and cheese.

6 *good vintage red wines* kept in reserve for special occasions and banquets.

Light red wines

Burgundy:	Beaujolais.
Côtes du Rhône:	Châteauneuf-du-Pape, Crozes, Hermitage.

WHITE WINES

Italy:	Orvieto, Vino del garda, Frascati, Vernaccia, Est ! Est !! Est !!!, Trevigiani, Garganega di Ganbellara.
Loire:	Sancerre, Anjou, Muscadet.
Portugal:	Vinho verde (branco).
Savoy:	Roussette de Savoie.
Switzerland:	Neuchâtel, Dorin, Fendant.
Yugoslavia:	Smederevka, Zilavka.
U.S.A.:	Chablis, Riesling and Sylvaner from California.

All these wines should be gradually restocked at the rate they are consumed. On the average they can only be kept for four years.

Mellow or medium-dry white wines

Alsace:	Gewürztraminer.
Germany:	Riesling Spätlese from the Moselle or Rhine, also Sylvaner Spätlese from Franconia and the Rheinhesse.
Bordeaux:	Graves de Vayres, Premières Côtes de Bordeaux, Saint-Foy, Saint-Macaire.
Touraine:	Vouvray.
Italy:	Castelli Romani, Frascati, Orvieto, Verdicchio with the mention *abbocato* or *semi-seccho*.
Switzerland:	Malvoisie, Petite Arvine.
Austria:	Riesling, Zierfandler and Rotgipfler "Spätlese".
Hungary:	Badacsonyi Kéknyelu, Badacsonyi Szurkebarat.

These wines should be gradually restocked at the rate they are consumed. They will not keep in prime condition longer than an average of four years.

Sweet white wines and dessert wines

Bordeaux:	Sauternes, Cérons, Loupiac, Barsac, Montbazillac.
Anjou:	Vouvray.
Hungary:	Tokay aszu (3 to 6 puttonyos).
Spain:	Malaga or Priorato extra rancio, sweet sherry.
Italy:	Cinqueterre (sweet), Malvasia di Lipari, Moscato, Vino santo, Caluso passito.
Greece:	Mavrodaphni, Samos.
Portugal:	Port.
Germany:	Moselle or Rhine wines with the mention "Trockenbeerenauslese".
Yugoslavia:	Spalato prosecco, Stolacer Ausbruch.
Roumania:	Cotnari Grase, Murfatlar-Muskat.
America:	Tokay from California.

These wines can usually keep for five years or more and some of them for about ten years. Their condition can best be judged by periodic tasting.

Champagnes

Champagne brut, dry or demi-sec.

A high-class sparkling wine can replace Champagne if preferred. Champagne can usually be kept for four to five years.

RED WINES

Bordeaux:	Light Médoc or Graves.
Italy:	Chianti, Bardolino, Barbusco, Grignolino Valpolicella.
Spain:	Priorato tinto.
Portugal:	Vinho verde (tinto).
Switzerland:	Salvagnin.
Austria:	Blauburgunder (Pinot Noir).
Germany:	Spätburgunder (Pinot Noir).
California:	Zinfandel.
Bulgaria:	Kramolin.

There is no reason why really good local wines, if available, should not replace the wines in the above list. As in the case of medium-dry or dry white wines, these should gradually be replaced as stocks are depleted. On average, these wines should be drunk within five years.

Full-bodied red wines

Burgundy:	From known regional vineyards or *Premiers Crus* from the Côtes de Nuits and Côtes de Beaune.
Côtes du Rhône:	Hermitage, Côte Rôtie.
Switzerland:	Dôle from the Valais.
Italy:	Barbera, Nebbiolo, Reciotto, Veronese, Falerno.
Bordeaux:	From the best vineyards in the Médoc, Saint-Emilion and Pomerol.
Algeria:	Wines from Médéa and Tlemcen.
Spain:	The best Rioja (Rioja Imperial, Rioja Marquès de Riscal), Vina Pomal.
Chile:	Wines from Curico and Talca.
Portugal:	Dao or Colares wines.
Yugoslavia:	Plavac.
Hungary:	Egri Bikaver.

These wines can be kept six to eight years; certain Bordeaux and Burgundies keep even longer. Only tasting can determine the condition and maturity of the wine.

Great red wines

This list is limited to wines from the best vineyards. They are generally quite costly but have the advantage of keeping longer.

Burgundy:	Chambertin or one of the other great wines from the Gevrey-Chambertin region; Bonnes Mares (Côte de Nuits); Corton (Côte de Beaune); Musigny; Clos-de-Vougeot; Romanée Conti or one of the other great wines from Vosné-Romanée.
Bordeaux:	Château Margaux or one of the great classified wines from Margaux; Château Lafitte or one of the great classified wines from Pauillac; Château Montrose or one of the great classified wines from Saint-Estèphe; Château Ausone or another superior Saint-Emilion; Château Haut-Brion or another superior red Graves.
Italy:	Barolo, Vino Nobile de Montepulciano.
Austria:	Oggauer Blaufränkisch Alte Reserve.
Germany:	Ihringer Blankenhornsberg.

The great red wines can be kept for over ten years but, apart from very exceptional wines, not longer than fifteen. The best vintages should be chosen, bearing in mind that these vary from one wineproducing region to another.

1. Those who like vin rosé should choose from the following list

Germany:	Assmannhäuser Höllenberg, Durbacher Schlossberg Weissherbst Auslese, Ihringer Jesuitengarten, Burgunder Weissherbst Auslese.
Austria:	Schloss Kirchberg.
France:	Tavel (rosé), Sancerre (rosé), Cabernet d'Anjou, Brégançon (Provence).
Italy:	Chiareto del Garda, Cagarino, Ravello.
Switzerland:	Œil-de-Perdrix (Neuchâtel).

All these wines should be drunk young as they rarely keep longer than three years.

2. For those who like Pinot

Here is a selection of wines made from the famous Pinot grape which is cultivated throughout Europe as well as in South Africa and California.

a) Pinot Noir (Blauburgunder, Spätburgunder)

Germany:	Oberingelheimer Sonnenberg Spätburgunder (Rheinhesse), Ihringer Winklerberg (Baden), Assmannshäuser Höllenberg (Rheingau).
Switzerland:	Dôle (Valais), Duc de Rohan Pinot Noir (Bündner Herrschaft), Auvernier Pinot Noir (Neuchâtel).
France:	All the red Burgundies from Côte de Nuits and Côte de Beaune (see lists on pages 90-91).
Italy:	Pinot Nero (Trentino).
Roumania:	Dealne Mare.
Yugoslavia:	Burgundac crni.
California:	Pinot Noir or Red Pinot.

b) Pinot Gris

(Ruländer in Germany and Austria), Tokay in Alsace and eastern Switzerland, Szürkebarat in Hungary, Malvoisie in Valais.

Germany:	Durbacher Herrenberg (Baden), Bickensohler Steinfelsen (Kaiserstuhl).
Austria:	Ruster Ruländer (Burgenland).
Switzerland:	Malvoisie (Valais), Malauser Tokajer (Grisons).
Italy:	Pinot grigio (Trentino).
Hungary:	Badacsonyi Szürkebarat (Lake Balaton).
Yugoslavia:	Ljutomer Rulendac sivi (Slovenia).

c) Pinot Blanc

(Weisser Burgunder in Germany) or Pinot Chardonnay.

Germany:	Blankenhornsberger Weissburgunder (Kaiserstuhl), Ihringer Winklerberg (Ihringen).
Austria:	Undhof Wieden Weissburgunder (Wachau), Kloster-Cabinet Weissburgunder (Klosterneuburg).
France:	Montrachet, Meursault, Chablis and Pouilly-Fuissé.
Italy:	Pinot bianco (Trentin).
Yugoslavia:	Collio, Burgundac Bijeli (Slovenia).
South Africa:	White Pinot.

3. A cellar for Riesling enthusiasts

Germany:	Rüdesheimer Schlossberg (Rheingau), Wehlener Sonnenuhr (Moselle), Diedesheimer Leinhöhle (Rheinpfalz), Oppenheimer Sackträger (Rheinhesse), Durbacher Schlossberg (Baden).
Austria:	Kremser Kögl, Dürnsteiner Hollerin.
Switzerland:	Goût du Conseil (Valais).
France:	Riesling d'Alsace.
California:	Johannisberg-Riesling.
South Africa:	Paarl-Riesling.
Chile:	Coquinto-Riesling.
Australia:	Quelltaler Hock.

4. A cellar for those specializing in rare or unusual wines

Each wineproducing area has its specialities whose fame sometimes never crosses local boundaries. Travellers and gourmets often appreciate these rarities, choosing them according to the countries they visit and the discoveries made.

Some of these delightful and little-known wines are listed below as a starting point for those who will doubtless add discoveries of their own.

Germany:	Wines with the mention "Trockenbeerenauslese" or "Eiswein", Durbacher Herrenberg (Baden), Assmannshäuser Höllenberg Rotwein Edelbeerenauslese (Rheingau).
Austria:	Ruster Ausbruch (Burgenland): very sweet.
Switzerland:	Réze (vin de glacier, Valais), Malanser Completer (Grisons), Païen (Traminer de Visperterminen, Valais).
France:	Château-Chalon (young wine from the Jura). Romanée (the rarest of the great red wines from Burgundy, only 2,500 litres produced each year). White Musigny (the rarest of the great white wines from Burgundy, only 800 litres produced each year).
Italy:	Falerno (red), the wine extolled by Horace. Cinqueterre (white), praised by Pliny, Petrarch and D'Annunzio. Marsala vergini.
Spain:	A wine from Los Moriles (sherry type with a nutty flavour).
Portugal:	An authentic vintage port of 1921, 1927, 1931, 1935, 1943, 1945 or 1947.
Cyprus:	Commandaria (a sweet wine).

5. Other Suggestions

Some people favour specializing in wines from a certain geographical region. A cellar can be stocked with Rhône wines, ranging from the Canton of Valais to the Côtes du Rhône, or Rhine wines coming from the Swiss Canton of Grisons to the Rheingau. Some people concentrate on wines from Italy, as they are readily available in most places. Further suggestions are given in the second part of this book.

Apart from a conventional basic stock, it is a good idea to lay in a few bottles of some wine that is relatively unknown locally. It makes a good conversation piece as well as a pleasant change for visitors to have something different from the well-known bottles seen every day in the main street windows or the supermarket.

TASTING WINE

Without some kind of basic plan and a few tips from the experts it is difficult to envisage stocking up a cellar, however humble the outlay may be. Beginners should not let themselves be daunted by the prospect for, although in terms of commercial investment the buying price will not grow very quickly, the pleasure of drinking a wine which has been bought and nurtured until it is ready and fully matured is beyond price.

Despite the work of oenologists and the studies of renowned scientists on the inherent properties of wines, particularly great wines, and notwithstanding the results of intensive research by eminent biologists and even mathematicians, wine still retains a good part of its mystery and wine-tasting has not yet been elevated to the level of a science or even a technique. It is still essentially an art.

Nonetheless, the professional wine-taster is guided by certain established and accepted rules and codes. He is ethically bound to subdue his own personal tastes and preferences and endeavour to be as objective as is humanly possible, for his is the duty of pronouncing judgements which could have far-reaching consequences, and for which he will be held personally and professionally responsible. Such strict measures of quality and criticism are the only means by which a norm or standard can be made acceptable to producers and tasters alike.

All the considerations taken into account by the professional, exaggerated as they may appear to the uninitiated, are distilled here into simple, practical hints. The professional aids to wine selection are interesting to know but not absolutely necessary to someone who merely wishes to discover a good wine to his liking. This chapter only aims to guide the amateur through the maze of intricate but infinitely evocative and pleasurable paths that lead to familiarity with wine. As Boileau, Provost of Paris in the thirteenth century, observed, "He who knows not how to drink knows nothing."

TOUCH AND HEARING

It has been argued that the effects of touch and hearing are due more to imagination than anything else, although the pleasant feeling of a fine crystal glass or a silver goblet held between the fingers, and the sound of its delicate ring in the half-light of an echoing cellar, undoubtedly enhance the drinker's pleasure. Actually, touch does in fact play a very real part in the appreciation of wine. It is neither pretentious nor exaggerated to talk of "tactile tasting" in describing the sensations perceived by the various parts of the mouth which are capable of judging the wine's consistency, its fluidity or viscosity, both valuable clues to quality described as the "architectural relief of wine". And as a certain Monsieur Orizet, well known for his appreciation of the elixirs of the grape and of his own eloquence, once remarked "To what else but our sensations of touch can we attribute our reactions when we describe a wine as harsh, round, supple, tender, thin or velvety?" In a more modest way, hearing also contributes to determining the quality of wine, if only in detecting latent fermentation by holding the glass up to the ear.

SIGHT TEST

The first gesture the wine-taster makes is to raise his filled glass to the light of day. This inspection yields valuable insight into the quality of the wine.

White wine, which should be bottled young and not have been exposed to coloration from a prolonged sojourn in wood, should appear clear and gleam with a whiteness tinted slightly green. There are exceptions to the rule, of course, such as the yellow wines from Arbois and the pale amber of Sauternes. It is also recognized that all the great white wines assume a delicate golden hue over the years. As far as young wines are concerned, an indefinite or murky colour always denotes the presence of some disease or defect while a yellowish tint betrays oxidization, resulting in a sweet, pervasive flavour which only very few people consider as a virtue. But the taster should not attach too much importance to clarity alone: a non-filtered wine can still be of excellent quality.

Sight as well as hearing can detect the tiny gas bubbles which, if they cloud the wine to any appreciable extent, are probably due to a second fermentation. On the other hand, there are some naturally slightly sparkling wines, known as such, whose mild effervescence does not affect their clarity. Many Swiss white wines have this slight effervescence, often depending on how long they have been bottled, as do some of the wines from France and neighbouring countries. Agreeable though it may be, this sparkle can sometimes conceal a certain mediocrity. In the case of red wines, it is rarer and less highly esteemed, although it certainly gives some wines, such as the delicious Valpolicella, a very special charm.

As far as rosé is concerned, the appearance of the wine is very important. From the rose-pink Tavel to the pale red of Côtes de Toul, the colour range is infinite, the more so because with the growing fashion for this wine, many vineyards are now beginning to produce rosé. It should not be too pale in colour as this is both unattractive and often indicates dubious production methods.

None of these observations applies to very new wines which are naturally clouded by a large quantity of lees. Even at this stage, however, a great deal can be learned by visual examination. Moreover, any healthy wine will clear rapidly if allowed to do so.

As far as red wines are concerned, visual inspection is very important and provides valuable hints to quality, age and even origin. The depth of colour, dependent on the species of grape and the length of time the grapes were left to ferment, decreases with time. But whether it be muted, as in the case of Beaujolais, or deep ruby as in Châteauneuf-du-Pape, or even richer in colour for a young Bordeaux, the colour should be pure and true. A good bright red, tending towards cherry-red, usually denotes good quality. Tints of purplish blue, on the other hand, can be a sign of hybrid or mixed wine. The "robe" of a red wine, to use the experts' term for colour, is of the greatest significance. Visual examination also enables the trained eye to detect various diseases, such as casse, and even to differentiate between the various kinds of the disease—brown, blue, ferrous and so on. An experienced taster will be able to diagnose the grease disease, which makes wine oily and ropy, or the *tourne* which betrays its presence by silky ripples when the liquid is agitated. Especially in the case of red wines, a sight test also gives a good indication of whether or not a wine is mature or on the decline.

A GOOD NOSE

"A good nose for wine" should not always be interpreted as a derogatory expression. One of the classic gestures of the wine-taster is to swirl the wine around the glass before raising it to his nostrils. There is good reason for this ritual. The wine, gently swirling, spreads a thin coating of liquid over the upper walls of the glass so that a greater surface of the wine is exposed to the air, resulting in maximum evaporation of the odoriferous substances. This procedure is of paramount importance for, as everyone knows, a wine's "bouquet" determines its character.

At this stage, great powers of discernment and a good memory are required by the taster to recall the characteristics of all the wines he has ever tasted before and all the aromas that have ever been encountered by his nasal passages. It is by smell that he can recognize native tangs and the approximate region of the vineyard, the aroma being closely linked to the type of grape planted in a specific soil.

The primary aroma of a must before aromatic fermentation is essentially a product of the type of grape: it is particularly distinctive, for instance, in the juice from muscat grapes. After fermentation is complete, good new wines exude a multitude of scents constituting the secondary aromas, some flowery, some fruity. These fragrances of iris, violet, rose, lime, blackcurrant, apple, cherry, strawberry and raspberry have led to the designation of new wines as "fruity". Subsequently, through the slow and mysterious alchemy that nature brings to bear, first in the casks and later in the bottle, the wine gradually becomes transformed, the primary and secondary perfumes dwindling, becoming less identifiable, and mingling at last into the final "bouquet", more discreetly floral in character and exuding a whole new range of aromas whose synthesis enables the connoisseur to recognize the wine, its origin and its year. In this final bouquet, which lingers on until the wine begins to deteriorate, the wine-lover will recall many familiar odours such as coffee, Russian leather, amber, truffles and even fowl droppings, as described by vinegrowers of the Médoc.

It is sometimes as well to reserve judgement on those wines which seem to flatter the palate at the first sip but which may, like new-found friends, reveal a lack of sincerity on deeper acquaintance. Most of the great wines only slowly and gradually divulge their true characters as the bottle empties, which explains why producers of red Graves used to declare that their wines should only be judged after the third glass. Although perhaps exaggerated, this sentiment was the sincere distillation of long years of experience.

THE TASTE

Tasting is actually the last and most important stage in judging a wine. The most logical one of all, indeed, since wine is intended to be consumed. After the wine-taster has examined the wine and explored its aromas, he sips and rolls the wine around his mouth.

Strictly speaking, the tongue plays the leading rôle in tasting, but the tongue can only distinguish between the four basic tastes, namely acidity, bitterness, saltiness and sweetness, all other nuances of tastes being but variations of these primary four. Schools of wine-tasting test their trainees' natural aptitudes by presenting them with these four basic tastes.

Bitterness is detected at the back of the tongue; saltiness and sweetness by the tongue's tip and sides. Acidity is recognized by the centre and the sides of the tongue. Simultaneously, fragrance and the subtleties of flavour are discerned by the olfactory cells and swell the harmonic symphony of sensations experienced by the taster who should, by now, be ready to pronounce judgement. If he is a well-trained expert, he will be able to determine the alcoholic strength of the wine, define the amount of reducing sugars, the total acidity and the volatile acidity, if this is present to any marked degree, with only a small margin of error. He should be able to express his opinion as to the wine's quality although subjective factors will inevitably colour his judgement, however objective he may strive to be.

Many are the tales extolling the extraordinary tasting powers of certain palates. Paul Mounet, member of the Comédie-Française, brother of Mounet-Sully and a native of Bergerac, the Dordogne town famed for its wine and truffles, was said to be capable of telling the age and vineyard of any great wine even when blindfolded. It is a pity to debunk such stories but this one is scarcely credible. The worthy gentleman may well have successfully performed such a feat once, or even on several occasions, but the wines in question were very likely those of a distinctive type and ones with which Mounet was already reasonably familiar. Furthermore, probably only one or two wines were submitted to him at any one time, thus husbanding the sensitivity of his palate.

Correct and unerring recognition of the origin and year of a wine is really only possible on a local or, at the most, a regional scale by an inhabitant of the region. Obviously a wineproducer in Beaujolais, accustomed to sampling all the different local wines each season, is able to recognize wines from the various vineyards in his area and even to distinguish between those of individual producers which, although made from the same type of grape, can differ to a considerable extent. Although identification of new wines is relatively simple, the process becomes very much more difficult in the case of fully matured ones.

In any case, as a certain Monsieur de la Palice once so rightly remarked, a wine must be tasted to be known. And who can possibly have tasted every wine? Hence the necessity for the professional taster to specialize in only various types of wines.

PRACTICAL ADVICE

A few words are in order concerning the physical and material circumstances surrounding the ritual of tasting. It has been established beyond doubt that the taster's state of health, the time of day and even the general ambiance will all affect his reactions. His state of health is particularly important and even so slight an indisposition as a cold can seriously impair the judgement. In my early days, I remember that I would often seek the advice of an old wine merchant whose sureness of palate I had always admired. After several years it seemed to me that the old man's judgements

were less accurate, until one day we found ourselves in complete contradiction on certain points. Extremely awed by the old gentleman and not daring to contradict him outright, I solicited the opinions of his acquaintances and learned that for some time he had had diabetes, undoubtedly the cause of his failing acumen.

The best time for tasting is usually at the end of the morning, just before the midday meal, when most people begin to feel the first stirrings of appetite. The mental state as well as the general surroundings are of great importance. Some interesting experiments have been made on the effects of external influences such as light, temperature and even ambient noise and it has been found that the same taster can experience different reactions depending on the colour of the light, the temperature of the room and whether tasting took place in silence or to the accompaniment of music.

As far as the amateur is concerned, the essential requirement for serious tasting is total concentration and any noise should be discouraged. Tasting should take place in daylight or, if this is not possible, the light should be white and non-fluorescent. In a cellar, the clarity and brilliance of the wine is best judged by candlelight. If the wine-lover is seriously interested in determining the wine's quality for future reference, he should abstain from eating all those tempting titbits such as cheese, nuts and canapés which are habitually offered round on such occasions. The least of all evils is a small piece of dry bread.

The importance of the type of glass cannot be overestimated. It should preferably be of crystal with a very fine rim, barrel-shaped or in the form of a chalice. The washing of the glasses is a very important factor and one that gives rise to many difficulties. The increasing habit of putting everything into dishwashing machines which use detergents can result in a pervasive taste clinging to the glass which can fundamentally affect the taste of the wine. Certain tasters insist on their glasses being rinsed in distilled water while professionals always carry their own silver tasting cup, although this is definitely less acceptable than a fine crystal glass, especially for white wines.

Wine should not be tasted in an over-heated or a very cold room. The ideal temperature is between 20º and 22º centigrade (around 68º to 70º F.). Naturally, any manufactured or natural perfumes must be avoided and even vases of flowers should be abandoned on the day of the tasting. A strongly flavoured toothpaste or tobacco smoke can be ruinous.

Tasting may be a complicated art but it is also much more pleasant and rewarding than is generally thought. As Paul Claudel, French diplomat and writer, so eloquently proclaimed, "... wine is the professor of taste, the liberator of the spirit, and the light of intelligence..."

GLOSSARY OF WINE-TASTING TERMS

Acid . . . . excessively sharp taste

Aromatic . . . . smooth, subtle and pleasant aroma, usually "grapey"

Astringent . . . excessive tannin, harsh on the palate

Attractive . . . . light, fresh, easy to drink

Austere . . . . . under-developed; often applicable to bouquet of a fine wine expected to develop

Bitter . . . . flavour sometimes met in the aftertaste; usually a sign of ill health in the wine

Body . . . . the weight of a wine in the mouth

Bouquet . . . . . scent or smell of good wine; often characteristic

Clean . . . . fresh, unalloyed taste

Complete . . . . well-built and balanced, fragrant and agreeable

Corked . . . . . . tasting of cork, unpleasantly musty

Dainty . . . . . . fresh and fruity

Delicate . . . . . of good quality; just short of distinguished

Distinguished of the highest quality in all respects

Dumb . . . . under-developed as yet

Fading . . . . . . deteriorating in quality but still drinkable

Fiery . . . . . . goes to the head quickly, often a sign of too much alcohol for true balance

Fine . . . . elegant, distinguished, with a delicate bouquet

Firm . . . . rather hard and pungent but well-built

Flabby . . . . . . unattractive, lacking in body and natural acidity

Flat . . . . dull, lifeless, insipid flavour

Fleshy . . . . . . full-bodied, rich with good general consistency

Fresh . . . . having the fruitiness and qualities of young wine

Fruity . . . . . . mellow, fragrant; fleshy quality derived from, but not generally tasting of, ripe grapes

Full . . . . rich, fleshy, well-knit with a clean taste

Generous . . . . strong, robust, invigorating, full of flavour

Goût de terroir a characteristic earthy taste of wine from specific vineyards

Green . . . . young, sharp and acid (not vinegary)

Hard . . . . excessive tannin, lacking in smoothness and fruit

Harsh . . . . . . rough, astringent, catches the tongue

Heady . . . . . . fiery and aromatic, high alcohol content

Heavy . . . . . . unctuous and full-bodied, containing much "extract"

Light . . . . pale in colour, moderate strength, well-balanced

Lively . . . . . . vigorous, acid, pleasantly pungent effect on nose and palate

Long . . . . descriptive of a great wine, well-sustained flavour and aroma

Madérisé . . . . having acquired the yellowish-brown tint and smoky, burnt taste of Madeira, due to heat and oxygen

Massive . . . . . full-bodied, powerful, spirited, rich

Mellow . . . . . soft and smooth, mature

Noble . . . . with the distinctive characteristics of its origin

Nose . . . . term applied to a wine with a fine bouquet

Ordinary . . . . undistinguished, of indefinite origin

Perfumed . . . powerfully scented

Rich . . . . silky, smooth, well rounded

Robust . . . . . rich, full, good consistency and alcoholic strength

Round . . . . . . full-bodied, well balanced and mellow

Sharp . . . . . . slightly over acid with a tartness that stings the palate

Short . . . . ephemeral taste, lacking in persistence

Sinuous . . . . . lively, fresh, vigorous, promising to mature well

Sound . . . . . . a healthy wine with good lasting qualities

Sweet . . . . . . very sugary, full, noticeable glycerine quality but pleasant in taste

Thin . . . . lacking in body and strength (usually wines from poor years)

Unbalanced . . lack of harmony between physical constituents and aesthetic elements

Velvety . . . . . fine, full, silky and particularly soft in texture

Vinous . . . . . full-bodied, good alcoholic strength, plenty of grip, fruit and strength of character

Well-knit . . . . balanced, robust and harmonious in all respects

Young . . . . . raw, harsh and under-developed (not a fault)

USEFUL TERMS FOR DESCRIBING WINE

	Qualities	Defects
General Character	Robust, well-built, rich, full, fleshy, velvety, clean, well-knit, dainty, rugged.	Thin, harsh, ill-balanced, acid, sour, austere, short, mediocre.
Colour	Sumptuous, ruby, amber-coloured, clear, lively, brilliant.	Faded, cloudy, over-strong.
Flavour and Strength	Lively, sinuous, noble, massive, full, heady, stout, robust.	Flabby, flat, light, cold.
Sugar Content	Dry, sweet, mellow, liqueurish.	Ill-balanced, flat, raw, rugged, insipid.
Bouquet	Fruity, fine, flowery, scented.	Short, dull, corked, fading.

FOR DRINKING

PIERRE ANDRIEU

The drinking glass appears only relatively late in the history of mankind. It was certainly known by the Egyptians and Phoenicians; the glass-works of Sidon and Alexandria were famous. The origin of glass itself is obscure. A French authority on the subject, J. Girardin, once wrote, "Chance played a considerable rôle in the invention of glass. However, it is difficult to believe the writings of Pliny the Elder in this connection. According to him, the Phoenician soda merchants, having landed on the banks of the River Balus, there prepared their meals. For lack of anything better, they used slabs of natron with which to steady the cooking pots. But during the cooking process the slabs melted and the sand underneath was turned into glass. Obviously, considering the high temperatures required, glass as we know it today could never have been produced in the circumstances reported by Pliny."

Whatever its origins, the Persians were already using glass receptacles during the reign of Alexander the Great, and archaeologists have discovered ancient Egyptian flasks containing evidence of their use for wine. It was probably around 1800 B.C. that the Phoenicians started to make the glassware that graced Roman tables during the reign of Nero, and in the first century A.D. glass-works were established in Gaul and Spain. Egypt, especially the region around Alexandria, supplied most of the very expensive and sometimes coloured crystal glass during this period. It is very surprising to discover in ancient writings that these crystal glasses and goblets did not break when they were dropped. François Carnot, a noted glass

expert, has drawn attention to the fact that these were probably the first blow-moulded glass articles. "They were very slowly cooled in the mould," he wrote, "thereby producing a toughened glass." Manufacture developed rapidly and, all over the territory occupied during the Roman Conquest, small cups, flasks and other glass vessels are found interred in graves with the ashes of their owners.

Apart from the jewel-encrusted goblets or wine cups in gold and silver, served at the palace tables of emperors and kings, the first tableware made for a prosperous clientele was in copper. The designs on the Greek and Roman vessels were admirably wrought and featured heads of contemporary gods such as Bacchus, vine leaves, bunches of grapes and similar appropriate designs in relief.

On the other hand, the metal specimens remaining from the pre-Roman era in Gaul, such as bronze and pottery vessels, are much simpler in design although their shape is not without elegance. At Celtic feasts, beer, mead or wine were served in horns. Wild ox horns, often richly ornamented with gold and silver trimmings, were particularly favoured and continued in use throughout the Merovingian era; they are even mentioned up to the fifteenth century. Another somewhat macabre drinking vessel was made from a human skull, either, so the historians claim, that of an enemy killed in battle or of some ancestor. It was considered a great honour for a guest to be invited to drink from a skull, and in order to qualify for such a privilege he had to have killed an enemy in battle.

Glass-making was already flourishing in Roman times, as may be seen from this carafe, goblet and drinking glass, all vessels made for wine.

For less ceremonial, family gatherings, earthenware cups or bowls were used, each guest serving himself by dipping his cup into an earthenware pot placed on the table or on the ground, a custom not far removed from our punch bowl.

From King Dagobert's solid gold wine cup to the gilded silver ostrich egg facsimile belonging to Charles V, many bizarre, opulent or unusual drinking vessels were created according to the fashion of the day or to satisfy the whims and wit of those who ordered these personal expressions of their eccentricities.

Among these memorable historic vessels was the richly decorated goblet encrusted with diamonds belonging to Good King René of Anjou. It held three pints, a fair draught of wine in any age. As curios or merely specimens of extremely fine craftsmanship, these examples of early glass now fetch very high prices as collectors' pieces on the world's markets, on those rare occasions when they change hands.

During the Middle Ages, glass drinking vessels, oddly enough, disappeared for several centuries from some regions, becoming so rare that two guests often shared

Roman wine receptacles were very varied as may be seen from these exhibits in the Mouton-Rothschild Museum in the Bordeaux region of France. In the background, on the right, a Syro-roman "bubble" flagon; on the left, a Turkish jug (fifteenth to sixteenth century) and, below it, a Persian earthenware bottle (twelfth to thirteenth century). In the foreground are two examples of twelfth-century Persian pottery.

one glass. At this period, the window-glass makers, producers of a coarse green glass, occasionally turned out a few small goblets with inverted conical bases, but these were rather rare. The outside surfaces carried ornamental tracery and arabesque patterns, decoration achieved by sticking coarse glass threads on to the first blown shape.

Glassware certainly proliferated during the Renaissance, when the craft attained its peak under the Italian influence. Glass-makers established themselves over all the wooded regions of France such as Normandy, Lorraine, Nevers, Orleans, Poitou, Dauphiné and Provence. Although recognized as Guilds of Gentlemen, they were inclined to be nomadic, moving on when their local fuel supply of wood or bracken ran out. From the sixteenth century onwards, they often intermarried with glass-making families from Murano and Altare brought from Italy by the French nobility. The glass they made differed markedly from region to region. Amber glass came from Provence; a bluish variety from the Margeride region, marbled in appearance and lined with white, pale blue or dark red enamel; and rose-coloured glasses from Burgundy and Nevers, although these unfortunately often "threw out their salt and spoilt the wine". From each place came glasses of different shape, colour and design with simple or elaborate decoration in jewels or multi-coloured enamels. "Bell-shaped goblets" and the hanaps made in the forests of Chamborant around 1340 by a certain Guionet are no longer to be found, and rare indeed are examples of pre-Renaissance glassware.

Renewed interest in the use of glass drinking vessels stemmed from the Arabs and, to a great degree, the glass-makers of Damascus who produced very fine enamelled glasses from the thirteenth to the fifteenth century. Contrary to the generally accepted belief, the Venetians copied the delightfully designed glasses which their seafarers brought from the far coasts. Famous as shrewd merchants and shippers, the burghers of Venice traded in this glassware and established the celebrated Venetian glass industry. They had greater success than their counterparts in other countries, since they were able to improve on the original production methods. They were also more skilled in applying gold, and their enamelling was more delicate. The Venetian pearl-workers, accustomed to working with minute pearls, wielded the sticks of enamel with a light and delicate touch. The beautiful Venetian goblets or decanters are superb works of art and were reserved for the tables of sovereigns and high dignitaries.

Two specimens of seventeenth-century glasses from the Lower Rhine. The one on the right is reminiscent of the *Römer* in general shape and by the superposition of two elements, in this example a cone on a cylinder, moulded separately. The drinking vessel on the left is made of green glass in the form of a small barrel.

388

By the sixteenth century the Venetians' skill in making glass had progressed to the point of producing white glass so pure and clear that it was called "crystalline" or "Venetian crystal". During the same period they manufactured a more ordinary "fern glass", so called because of the engraved design on its sides. It is only fair to mention that the famous works of Murano were founded by Greek workers who took refuge in Venice, after the fall of Constantinople.

These ordinary glasses were not always highly esteemed and pedlars, heedless of possible breakages, hawked their wares through town and countryside, the streets echoing to the refrain,

> Lovely glasses, pretty glasses,
> Beer glasses, a penny a pair.

In the sixteenth century the influence of the Venetian glass-makers spread to Holland. Here, as in most other countries, the glass-works were installed by natives from the City of the Doges. In Holland, already recognized as the home of the diamond cutter, glassware was decorated with fine engravings of arms and other heraldry, cut into the glass with a diamond point. During the eighteenth century some of these engravers perfected a new type of stippling.

Silver drinking mugs were very practical when travelling, hunting or eating out of doors, a whole set easily nesting one inside the other. These were German cups personalized with engravings of the owners' names and with various decorative motifs.

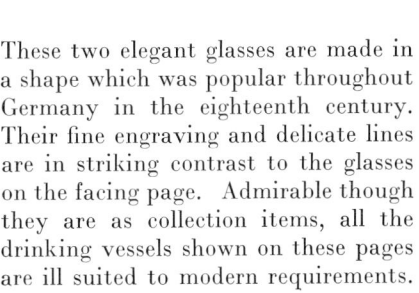

These two elegant glasses are made in a shape which was popular throughout Germany in the eighteenth century. Their fine engraving and delicate lines are in striking contrast to the glasses on the facing page. Admirable though they are as collection items, all the drinking vessels shown on these pages are ill suited to modern requirements.

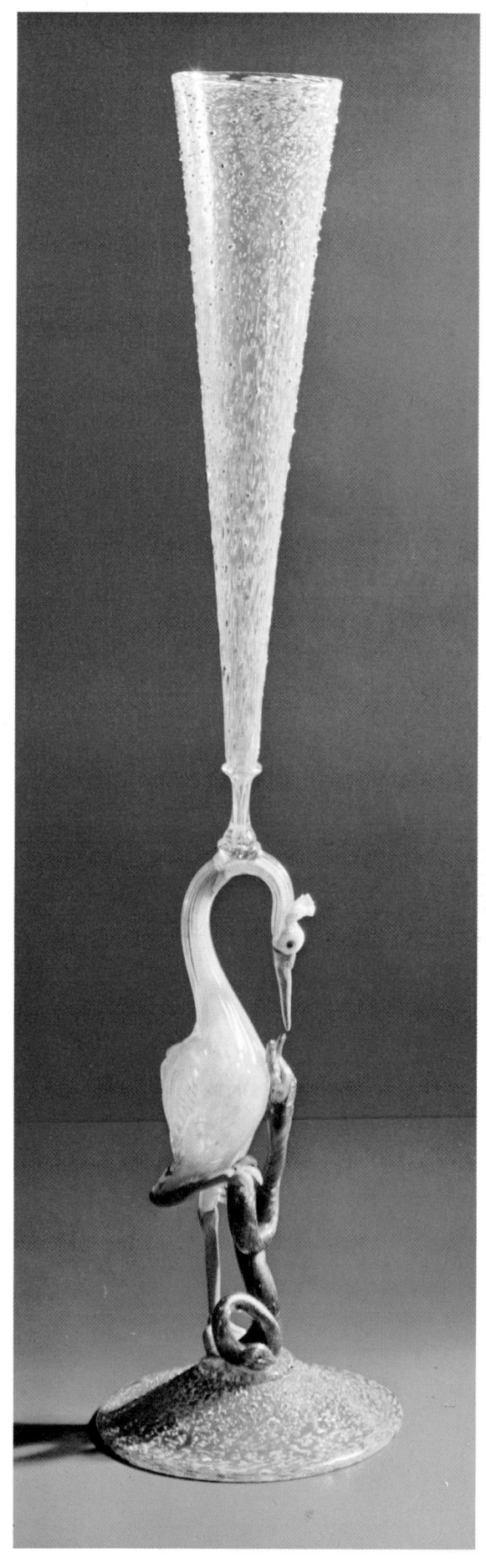

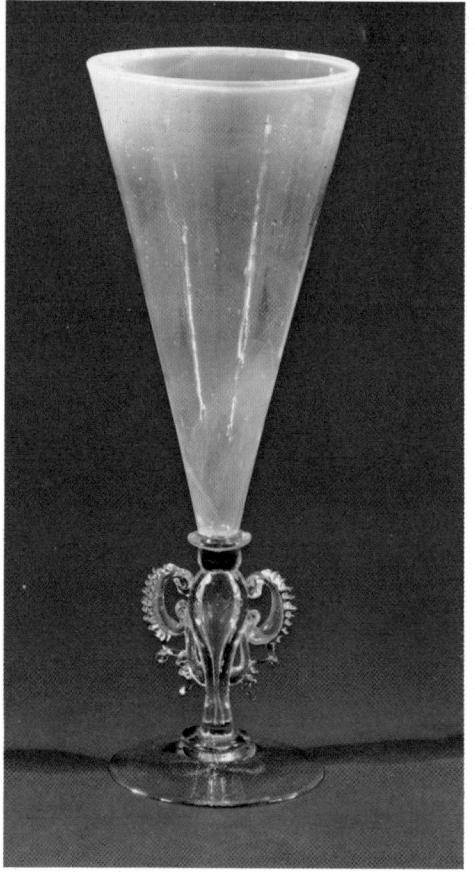

From the sixteenth century on, the Venetians were past masters in the art of glass-making, enamelling and relief ornamentation. The oval drinking cup, above, in engraved agate dates from the late sixteenth century. Emeralds set in enamelled gold and silver give it a regal air. The seventeenth-century Venetian flute glasses (left) are worthy of any collector's pride—or envy.

The two nautilus cups on the facing page bear witness to the consummate artistry of German goldsmiths and silversmiths in the seventeenth century. Splendid show pieces as they may be, they are scarcely suitable as vessels for drinking wine.

390

Across the Channel, glasses were designed with a very heavy cap-shaped base, but the stem became finer as time went on. Small bubbles of air were sometimes purposely trapped inside the crystal, resulting in an original effect in the play of light. Some of the glasses were also ornamented with filigree work. Towards the end of the seventeenth century the English discovered their own special type of crystal by adding barium of lead to the glass. Compared to Venetian glass, crystal produced in Britain was heavy, but fickle fashion, perennial follower of the newly created or novel, developed a taste for the heavy, pure glass, with dire effects on the Venetian glass-making industry. The English shipped their glass to Holland for engraving, not by the diamond method but with a small wheel, a technique demanding considerable solidity in the glass.

Jacobean engraved glasses, glasses for religious ceremonies and those used on board sailing vessels were particularly conspicuous because of their short stem and their solid, heavy base.

In Silesia, as in Bohemia, crystal with a potash base was generally used, while engraving was replaced by mouldings on the outside of glasses which were lavishly ornamented in gold and often delicately etched. Occasionally landscapes were painted in black, and all over Germany examples of enamelled glassware, not without artistic merit, could be found. In Bohemia the method of tinting glass with purple by means of gold salts was discovered and these glasses were often further enhanced by designs interwoven with purple and gold.

At the invitation of Catherine the Great, the Silesian glass-makers set up a factory near Moscow, bringing

Passglas: to reduce the measures of wine staked during card games, these glasses were divided into sections, each corresponding to one game.

The numerous fiefs that split Germany during the seventeenth century gave rise to endless disputes over inheritances. On these emblazoned glasses, the feudal lord asserted his properties, his territorial claims and even the territory he hoped to acquire.

The best glasses are those that allow the maximum development and appreciation of the wine's qualities. A clear white tulip glass is ideal for most wines. It should be slightly larger for red Burgundies than for red Bordeaux and in general rather larger for red wines than for whites. For sparkling wines some prefer the *flûte* but for Champagne the tulip glass is better. The wines of Alsace and Anjou are drunk from traditionally shaped glasses set on high stems, white Swiss wines from glass tumblers and the wines of the German Rhineland from the *Römer*.

with them experience and skill acquired in Bohemia, which could again be traced back to the Venetians.

Spanish glass was not unnaturally first influenced by that from the Arab countries resulting in glassware with garish, ill-assorted colours. Venetian craftsmen subsequently transformed the yellow Spanish glass by giving it a delicate crackle finish and enlarging the coloured scrolls favoured by their predecessors.

During the sixteenth century, Venetian glass-makers installed their first works at Antwerp, in Flanders. Early in the seventeenth century they opened another in the Principality of Liége. These yellowish glasses were usually tall, decorated with masks and blue beaded designs. The enamelled varieties always bore the distinctive sign of a lily of the valley.

Although Louis XIV owned five magnificent goblets in rock crystal, this noble material fell from favour during the eighteenth century and was replaced on royal and lordly tables by Bohemian glass which was also produced in France. At Tourlaville in the region of Cherbourg, at Saint-Louis, Montcenis, Baccarat and Sèvres, still renowned today for its fine table-ware, crystal-works sprang up and thrived. Cafés and *bistros* had also to be supplied and so bar or counter glasses for serving spirits were produced — "trick" glasses, really, as their shape and thickness gave the impression of holding much more than they actually did.

The well-known "hock" glasses with their graceful long stems surmounted by a bulbous cup, the *Römer* as they are called in German, were manufactured at Cologne. Here, the other typical glasses were also made with scrolls and enamelled serpents' heads.

Bavarian enamelled glasses were well suited to the renowned capacity of their users. They provided ample space for portraying the full Imperial Eagle as well as the armorial bearings of all the states under the Emperor. In celebration of the Augsburg peace treaty, glasses were designed bearing the portraits of the French, German and Swedish monarchs, Catholics on one side of the glass and Protestants on the other, all receiving the Lord's blessing and embrace. All such occasions gave rise to commemorative glassware and the family arms or those of the great dynasties were often used to decorate these expansive surfaces.

No discussion of European glassware is complete without mention of Saint-Louis crystal. Reported in print as long ago as 1673, the Saint-Louis glass-works were in existence under the name of Münsthal as far back as 1586. During the Thirty Years' War they were destroyed, then reborn as the "Royal Glass Works of Saint-Louis" when Lorraine came once more under French rule. "The Company of Crystal Makers of Saint-Louis", as it has been known since 1829, is the birthplace of the first crystal in France.

BOTTLES AND DECANTERS

Wine bottles are taken so much for granted today that scarcely a thought is given to their history. Actually, the custom of storing wine in glass bottles only goes back to the fifteenth century.

Glass vessels were certainly known earlier, as far back as Alexandria, Athens and Rome, but they were usually reserved for perfumes. If glass was employed at all to hold wine the vessels had an intermediate use — similar to that of our decanters — and brought the wine from wherever it was stored for serving.

Before glass bottles came into general use, ceramic or metal pots and jugs of varying artistic merit were provided by the potters or metal workers, and archaeologists have uncovered proof of their existence in Gallo-Roman time. A silver pot dating back to the first century B.C., glass goblets and bottles together with medals and coins bearing the effigy of the Emperor Trajan, a wine cup in red clay with the words *Reims Feliciter* and dating from the second or third century, a clay carafe, the lower part of its handle ornamented with a bunch of grapes, have all been excavated in the province of Champagne.

In homes in Gaul, servants brought wine to the table in earthenware or silver receptacles which resembled cooking pots. Each guest helped himself in turn with a small cup called a *cyathe*.

Froissart, the French chronicler, records that when the Earl of Douglas carried the heart of the King of Scotland to the Holy Sepulchure in 1328, there was little else in his baggage save gold bottles—though posterity is not informed as to the contents of these opulent flasks. Two silver bottles are listed in the inventory of the personal belongings of Charles V after his death. In the Louvre Museum in Paris are two beautiful gilt silver bottles bearing the arms of Henry III, exquisite in their simplicity of form and decoration, their general shape seemingly inspired by the gourd. Even King John of England used bottles in 1360, as shown by the following entry in a list of the royal expenses: "To Jehan Petit Fay, the sum of sixty sous minted at Tours for four leather bottles in which to carry water and wine for the said Sire when he is going to the country." When travelling, wine was also carried in metal flasks, usually made in silver.

In many ways, the silversmith made a considerable contribution to the development of the common wine bottle's illustrious ancestors. During the ninth century their powerful guild was granted a charter by King Charles the Bald. Previous to this, silver work appears to have been almost entirely confined to the monastery workshops. Fourteenth-century records show that

glass receptacles were beginning to compete for favour with those in precious metals. The last will and testament of a certain Jehanne of Burgundy in 1352 mentions "two small bottles in glass mounted with silver".

From the sixteenth century onwards, glass receptacles began to appear in well-to-do homes and the word "bottle" began to assume the bacchic implications which it has enjoyed ever since. Pierre de l'Estoile, in his "Diary of a Parisian Bourgeois", dubbed the Cardinal of Guise "Cardinal of the Bottles", remarking that ". . . he loved them so dearly and hardly concerned himself with anything but the delights of the kitchen of which he had so much greater knowledge and understanding than affairs of Church and State." It is better to gloss over the unhappy end of this epicurean prelate whose afflictions were so prolonged as to allow him ample time to reflect on his self-indulgent past and to be scourged with pain.

During this period, glass-making was the only manual craft to which a gentleman could turn his hand without any loss of dignity. In the glass-works, strange to relate, only the nobility had the right to blow bottles. When the glass was melted, the nobleman took the iron blow-pipe and started the operation. Savary, a duke, general and high functionary under the First Empire, noted "It behoves only a gentleman glassmaker to blow glass." This tradition can be traced back to the fourteenth century and there is evidence to prove that even the haughty Louis XIV blew glass on December 19th, 1655.

In the province of Anjou, mounted travellers used a kind of leather bottle, placed beside them on the saddle, containing a small quantity of wine for the journey. This receptacle was called a *boutille*, an early form of the French word *bouteille*. Changes in pronunciation and spelling during the gradual but wider adoption of the English language in the British Isles gave rise to that comforting form of the well-worn word, bottle. While the bottle was emerging as a form of practical packaging, most farmers and agricultural workers used earthenware receptacles or those made from other forms of fired clay. These shapes, too, were probably inspired by the gourd. Others carried their wine ration in small barrels of the same materials, decorated with pastoral or allegorical scenes.

It was only around the fifteenth century that the bottle began to assume a more elegant and practical shape, similar to that of today; but glass bottles had not yet supplanted those in metal or leather used until then. Silver bottles, engraved with the arms of the owner, were still being made in the sixteenth century.

Towards the seventeenth century, glass containers came into everyday use. They were called flagons, carafes, decanters, flasks and so on, the word *bouteille* being strictly reserved for receptacles containing wine. Although other forms of containers abounded, bearing heraldic devices or decorative emblems, in the wine cellar and the church the bottle reigned supreme. Such bottles were designed with a broad base and, in order to minimize the effect of sediment on the contents, the bottom of the bottle was recessed inwardly, a device that had already been employed by goldsmiths and silversmiths in the Middle Ages.

Until the end of the eighteenth century, goblets and drinking glasses did not form part of the table setting, but remained on the sideboard together with whatever contained the wine. It was customary to signal to a servant who filled the glass, brought it to the table on a small tray, waited while it was drunk and then returned

Despite the gradual appearance of glass, earthenware containers for wine have never altogether disappeared. Light wine regains the freshness of the cellar when reposing in the hollow of a cool earthenware pitcher. Shapes have altered little since ancient times. In the centre can be seen a small Roman jug dating from the third century. On the right, a rustic German pot, turned on a wheel at the beginning of the sixteenth century.

Imported or produced locally by the Romans between the years A.D. 50 and 75, this flagon was discovered in a cemetery at Barnwell in Great Britain. It was the custom in those days to bury familiar objects in the grave with the deceased. On a moulded base, the craftsman has fashioned the neck and body, blown from a single piece. Then a ball of molten glass was stuck to the body and drawn up to form a handle. The spiral decorations were applied later.

The family of Champagne bottles shown below has many members. The smallest, the split (7 oz), corresponds to a quarter of a standard bottle; the pint (14 oz) corresponds to half a standard bottle, a standard bottle (third from right) containing a quart (1 pt 11 oz) of Champagne. Next comes the magnum (2 quarts), the jeroboam (4 quarts), the rehoboam (16 quarts) and the mighty nebuchadnezzar (20 quarts). Champagne is always better from the standard or magnum bottle than from one of the smaller sizes. The bottle should be placed in an ice-bucket an hour before serving but not in the freezing compartment of the refrigerator since wine cooled too abruptly will lose its flavour. The cork should be removed gently and gradually so that the only sound one hears is a light sigh, and the wine poured into a glass shaped like a tulip or a rugby ball.

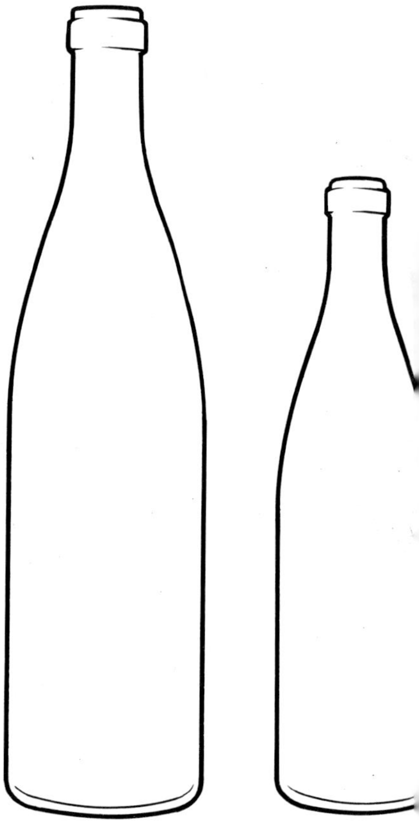

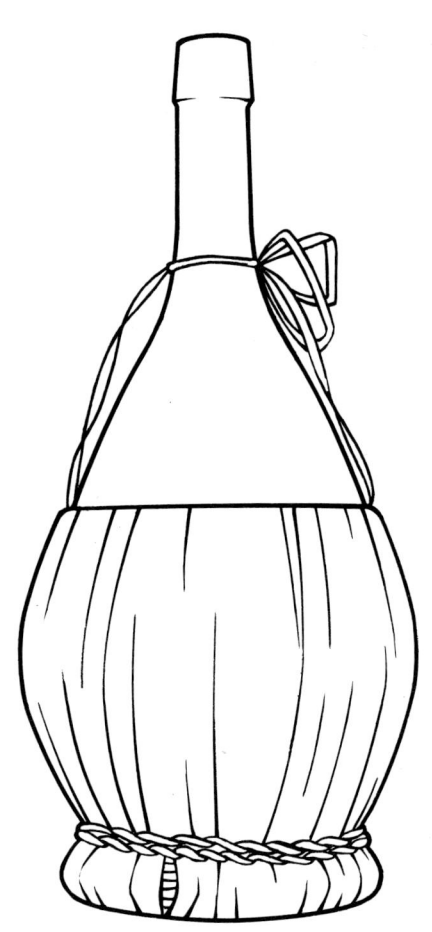

The bottles shown above belong to several different families. Starting from the left there is the Burgundy shape (bottle and half-bottle) and then the Bordeaux shape (bottle and half-bottle). A bottle contains 1 pint 9 ounces of red or white wine, a half-bottle 13 ounces. The bulging, straw-covered *fiascho* originates from Central Italy and has a capacity of about 3 ½ pints. Although usually associated with Chianti, this bottle is also used for the white wines of Orvieto. The Boxbeutel, a flat, oval bottle used in Franconia in Germany and Styria in Austria, is best-known abroad as the container for the pale green-gold coloured Steinwein.

The half-litre bottle on the left of this pair has a long neck and prominent shoulders; it is used exclusively for the Hungarian Tokay. Most other Hungarian export wine is sold in the slender bottle shown on the right, a shape now widely used but principally identified with the wines of the Moselle and the Rhine, its areas of origin. Standard Rhine and Moselle bottles have a capacity of 1 pint 5 ounces.

it to the sideboard. In surroundings of great luxury, two servants performed this service, standing on the left of the diner, one holding the glass while the other filled it from a decanter of carafe. The unconventional Marquis de Rouillac, who died in 1662, was the first member of high society to have the idea of dismissing the servants and eating in peace. Few dared to imitate him, so bottles and glasses did not cross the hallowed gap between sideboard and dining table until about 1760.

In the region of Montreuil-Bellay in Anjou, a certain number of highly interesting old bottles have been collected, such as a seventeenth-century half-bottle, called a *fillette*, and others dating from the same period in dark glass, varying in capacity and irregular in shape with the shoulder sometimes wider than the base. There are also some amusing specimens such as the "priest's bottle". These ecclesiastical gentlemen were entitled to levy a tithe in kind on the year's wine harvest, and with this in mind of course took good care to select bottles of generous cubic capacity.

In the eighteenth century, bottle shapes began to assume more slender, graceful lines, similar to those we recognize and accept today. About this time, too, French crystal began to face serious competition from England, the popularity of whose lead-glass was fast spreading, and French glass-makers were obliged to turn their production over to other products, including bottles and flagons. Owners of estates ordered their heraldic arms to be emblazoned on bottles especially blown for them, and various vintners, notably those from Liége, had their coats-of-arms represented on the bottles coming from their own cellars. By 1775, the fame of the glass-works in Ingrandes-sur-Loire, in the province of Anjou, was widespread. Its bottles were exported as far afield as America and the Indies.

In the seventeenth century it had already been discovered that the inverted conical recess in the bottom of the bottle facilitated precipitation of the sediment which forms after bottling. Being heavier than the liquid, it remained at the lowest level with little risk

At the beginning of the eighteenth century, flagons still lacked grace and slenderness. The silhouette of the English bottle on the right is still similar to that of the twelfth century. The shape of the Dutch bottle (left) was much seen at the end of the seventeenth century.

Up until the last century, merchants did not always supply the exact quantity of wine for which they charged and the buyer was often tricked by the shape of the bottle. Certainly, the "weights and measures" system of those days was rather rudimentary.

of it contaminating the wine if care is taken in handling the bottle. The bottle's neck gradually tapered up, to a certain point, leaving very little surface exposed to the air and thus helping to prevent evaporation. So the evolution of the bottle's shape was not arbitrary, but determined by good sense and experience.

In the extremely rare *Treatise on the Cultivation of Vines and the Art of Making Wine*, many notes are found relating to bottles, whose shape varied from country to country. " In England," it is noted, "the neck is short and flattened out, the body practically the same width all the way down. In France, its capacity varies, thus encouraging knavery. Some bottles have a very elongated neck, short body and deeply recessed base. All these bottles are more or less in the shape of a pear. It would be desirable that the regulations drawn up for Champagne were enforced throughout France; one would thus be sure of the quantity of wine one orders, for the buyer often sees only the shape of the bottle and is misled as to its contents. For example, the ordinary bottle does not even hold three-quarters of a pint whereas, according to the law of equity, it should contain a pint. Therefore the buyer is always cheated to a greater or lesser extent, as he cannot be in Champagne."

During the eighteenth century the bottle came into general use. While Louis XV was on the throne, one thousand one hundred and four bottles, large and small, with or without coats-of-arms, were counted at the house of Mlle Desmares, evidence that the bottle had, at last, been granted the "freedom of the city" on the tables of the world, in the homes of rich and poor alike.

During the greater part of the nineteenth century, the shrewder wine merchants turned topical events and personalities to good account by having special bottles designed in unexpected shapes. Among the more popular were a cockerel, an umbrella, a grenadier, the Eiffel Tower, a pipe, a lantern, a dwarf holding a pistol,

The bottles of times past were heavier yet more fragile than the containers of today and perhaps even more handsome and attractive.

the heads of eminent French politicans such as Gambetta and General Boulanger and a beatified Joan of Arc.

The famous Belgian wine connoisseur, Maurice des Ombiaux, however, seemed to care little what shape the bottle might be when he wrote, "I like to see a bottle of Médoc or Pauillac with its stamped cork, a dusty bottle of old Vougeot over which several generations of spiders have spun their gossamer, or the bottle covered with tide-marks from the winter's floods. But, also, I like to contemplate the ruby of a St. Emilion, the purplish-brown of a Nuits, the sea-green of a Pouilly, the corn yellow of a Sauternes, the gold of a Meursault or the straw yellow of an Arbois through the faceted crystal of a decanter. What greater pleasure for the eyes can there be than the tints which Bacchus has bestowed on his nectars?"

LABELS

In the first century, during the time when Gaius Petronius was proconsul in Bethany, wine was kept in two-handled jugs called amphoras. Corks being as yet unknown, the neck was closed with a plaster stopper or a plug of oil-soaked cloth. But even these primitive amphoras bore a mention not only of the vineyard but also of the consul in office at the time of filling.

So far, extensive research has failed to reveal any examples of labels, even handwritten ones, prior to the eighteenth century. The earliest specimens were very plain. Bereft of coats of arms or any kind of decorative design, they were simply bordered with a thin line, often drawn with pen and ruler, and stated their contents with matter-of-fact succinctness: "Vins Mousseux—1741—Claude Moët" or "Rozé—Claude et J.-R. Moët—Epernay", or "Vins vieux—1743—Claude Moët —Epernay", nothing more enlightening than that.

Later in the eighteenth century, the form of the label became more elaborate. A certain Commander Quenaidit supplies the following description: "Generally in the shape of a vertical rectangle, or trapezoid with the shorter side at the base, some with the tops rounded to a lesser or greater degree. They were very ordinary and nondescript with floral borders, like most chemists' labels of the same era. This type is still used to label samples of wine, the year and the name of the vineyard being written in the centre by hand."

The art of labelling reached its prime in the nineteenth century. Such was the proliferation of rich and luxurious symbols that they have been described as "the orchestration of a triumphant hymn to the glory of the vineyards of the world". Up until the twentieth century, liqueur labels of the same period reflected changing tastes and fashions, whereas wine labels never busied themselves, one might say, with such trivia, loftily contenting themselves, with very few exceptions, to indicating the year, the vineyard and its owner, and occasionally the wine's name.

A full study of wine labels is an immense undertaking requiring far greater space than is available here and so those used on Champagne bottles over the ages must serve as representatives of the gradual evolution.

Researchers are universally grateful to an anonymous municipal employee, long since unmindful of such earthly things, who collected Champagne labels in his youth, sticking them into an old school exercise book. Together with other collections, the fruits of his youthful zeal give us a good idea of the type of labels in use during the first half on the nineteenth century. The earliest appears to date from about 1820 and carries the name of the Chanoine brothers who decorated this label according to contemporary taste with silver lettering on a black ground. Shortly afterwards, Moët and Chandon followed suit with a similar design featuring blue lettering on white. Although this was designed for their Ay rosé wine by the painter J.-B. Isabey, it was to be the forerunner of their famous *carte bleue*. All these labels were lithographed. Early in the nineteenth century, Moët and Chandon also used a shield-shaped label which was later redesigned for their famous 1928 vintage.

In certain wineproducing areas, where vineyards were owned by individuals rather than syndicates, little attempt was made for a very long time to distinguish the produce of one vineyard from another, hence those labels so uniform and alike in appearance.

Towards 1835, the sparkling wines from Champagne were decked with labels having a coloured ground with a white or gold ornamental border composed of parallel hatchings which gradually developed into ornamental foliage, garlands and Renaissance-style fleurons. In Rheims, around 1830, the first labels for Pommery and Greno appeared. These were extremely simple, featuring only the name in black on a white ground. Roederer bordered their labels with vine leaves while Clicquot-Ponsardin favoured beautiful ornamental script. Some wineproducers believed in small labels, such as those used by Ruinart Père et Fils for their sparkling Œil de Perdrix or that chosen by Jacquesson & Fils for the sparkling Ay at about the same time. Apart from surmounting their name with a crown they seemed to think their wine needed no further introduction.

Most wine merchants at this time considered that the function of the label was merely to indicate the nature of the contents. In consequence, labels simply and unceremoniously read: "Sparkling Burgundy", "Volnay", "Vosne", "Beaune", "Romanée" with the renowned Chambertin which was spelt as "Chambetin".

This assortment of labels from the last century demonstrate how little importance producer and merchant alike attached to the appearance of the bottle, even in the case of great wines. Granted the public of those days was probably less enlightened, easier to please and placed greater trust in their suppliers. The label of Château d'Yssan, the oldest of the three, is very reticent as to the origin of its contents. The Margaux label is slightly more forthcoming, although the description is still vague. The label below suggests that the innkeeper was the only guarantor for the wine.

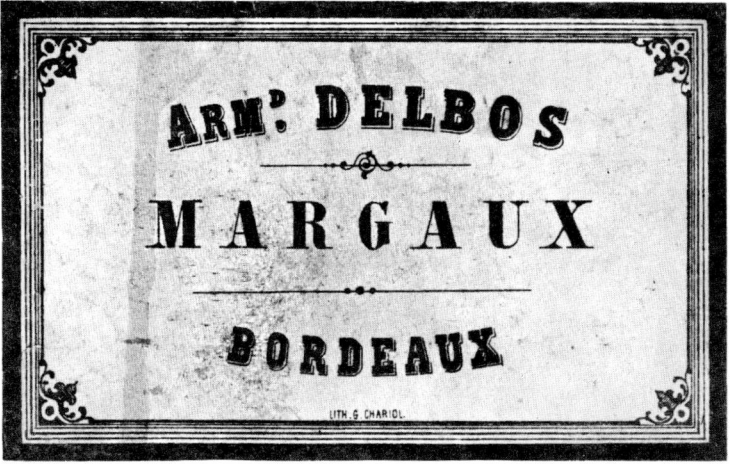

The name Meursault was boxed in with vine leaves or occasionally appeared, like those of Volnay and Pommard (spelt at that time with only one "m"), below a small oval picture showing the imposing gateway to a château in Burgundy.

With the Second Empire came a great variety of decorative labels, but copper-plate engraving and lithography were often abandoned in favour of rather carelessly produced glossy lithographs in colour.

Since the laws and other special legislation concerning *appellations d'origine* came into force in the 1930s the wording on most labels has been strictly controlled. However, this by no means prevented printers and designers from giving free rein to their imagination; landscapes, scenes from the grape harvest, costumes or symbolic emblems resulted in a colourful fresco, gay as the bubbles in wine, blending pictorial skills and the needs of sales promotion. Some printers specializing in labels produced what can legitimately be considered works of art. Perhaps this progress in label design was responsible for the expression that a bottle was *bien habillée*, or "well-dressed".

In Burgundy, various viticulturists and wine merchants now vie with one another to produce labels in the old-fashioned style, while taking advantage of modern techniques. In the region around Bordeaux the great number of vineyards has given rise to a plethora of labels, most of which have "the château" represented in varying degrees of importance. Some are excellent, others still content themselves with the old conventional style.

Baron Philippe de Rothschild is to be commended for his initiative in approaching the greatest artists of the day to design labels for his famous vintages. Artists like Jean Cocteau (1947), Marie Laurencin (1948), Dignimont (1949), Vertès (1951), Leonor Fini (1952), Carzou (1954), Georges Braque (1955), Salvador Dali (1958), Jacques Villon (1960) and Georges Mathieu (1961) contributed to the value of the Rothschild vintages. The labels on wines from Alsace, Provence, Roussillon, the Côtes du Rhône, the Jura and the province of Béarn also deserve honourable mentions while those from Champagne maintain a lordly grandeur. The label serves as a visiting card for the bottle's contents. It is both an advertisement and a pedigree, an indication of status, and an invitation to better acquaintance. It should attract yet impress, reflect the quality within and provide a visual foretaste of the gastronomic delights that lie in store. But, above all, it must be in keeping with the type of wine inside. It would scarcely be appropriate for a modest red wine to bear the glowing label of a vintage port, nor would a costly Chambertin be fittingly attired with the rough-and-ready label of a *vin ordinaire* to wash down a simple snack.

Labels also reflect national characteristics. The Swiss dress their bottles with typical reserve and delicacy. In France, character varies from one region to another. Alsace labels are restrained in colour, Champagne labels shine with gold, a splash of colours lights up those from Provence and Roussillon. Pouilly-Fumé, Muscadet and wines from the Loire reflect the clear sky above their homes and are circumspect in their attire. The labels of Côtes-du-Rhône shimmer with the sunshine of their birthplace, while Burgundies and Bordeaux maintain a non-committal dignity.

Spanish labels with their bright colours and bold lettering display a flamboyant nobility and Moorish richness. Rich as the wine from Oporto and sparkling as the "green wines" of their country, the Portuguese labels are as illuminated as old manuscripts. They feature saints and holy figures on stained glass windows, conquistadores portrayed in flame, blood-red and gold, as if to remind one of the accumulated riches in the treasure houses of Villanova de Gaya.

Italy surrounds its vermouths and chiantis in bright but less subtle colours. Sometimes its labels are unexpectedly quiet and subdued but this is more the exception than the rule. Those from Naples and Piedmont, Venice and Florence exude an extrovert, meridional flavour. Luxembourg labels are similar to those from Alsace and share, with the Rhine wines, the soft tints of their local skies.

Around the world, similar relationships exist between each country, its national characteristics, its wine and its labels to which, one hopes, artists will continue to contribute all their skills and imagination. They need have no fear of belittling their reputation.

WINE AND FOOD

FLAVIEN MONOD

Few housewives who pride themselves in the appearance of their home will leave it without flowers, however modest the bouquet. For very similar reasons, the master of the house will see to the proper care and stocking of his wine cellar. In both cases, it is knowledge and skill in selecting that makes the difference between an ordinary home and one brightened by a touch of colour and harmony—and the reward is the pleasure of sharing one of the joys of life.

A man's home may be his castle, as is frequently heard in Britain, but a house anywhere is a meeting place where friends and relations gather. The inside as well as the outside aspect reflects the taste of those who live there, reveals their personalities and shows to what extent they have acquired the art of living. A quick glance at the books on the shelves or the wines on the racks in the cellar can divulge many secrets. One meal may not reveal all, but it will serve to show whether the guest is made the object of special attention, with spontaneous gaiety and warmth, or whether he is merely the object of dutiful obligation.

Quite often, a posy of wild flowers or, as on the European Continent, a bunch of dried aromatic herbs is more appreciated than a sumptious basket of flowers arranged by strange, impersonal hands, or an overflowing store-bought cornucopia. Better often the warm, lively embrace of unsophisticated family repartee and sincere cordiality than the strained conventional social conversations. In the same way, a friendly little wine with its clean, simple taste and fresh colour in a humble bottle is sometimes better received than a famous vintage, heavily labelled and pretentious, decorated with the arms of some distant nobility.

THE DAILY TABLE WINE

How would you choose an "everyday" wine to drink with the family or share with an intimate friend? What is "a wine for everyday"? And what kind of wine is suitable for drinking with meals, every day, and to offer occasionally to those friends who don't need to be impressed with a showy label? Such a wine should quench the thirst, be light enough to drink deeply from brimming glasses and have a consistently reliable quality. Above all, it should be friendly and unpretentious. There is no need here to flatter a creation from the kitchen, or raise a meal to olympian heights; but at the same time, the wine should not quarrel with a dish. It should be accommodating, jovial, sympathetic and, above all, without after effects. Therefore it will not suffice to choose just any little *vin rosé* or red wine for this purpose without prior trial or testimonial. That innocent pink blush often conceals unpleasant surprises: drowsiness, heavy heads, and confused thoughts.

A light wine does not always mean a mediocre wine, just as simplicity does not always mean foolishness. A wine without frills can be a good companion to a quick meal. It can help work go smoothly, inspire goodwill and a genial disposition, all important qualities in our age of frenzied activity.

For everyday wines, we shall consider only light young red wines here. White wines and those of famous vintages are for other occasions. Naturally, personal taste plays its part here as in everything else. Anyone who lives in a wine-producing region does not have far to look for suitable, often even excellent wines.

Nor should hybrid wines be spurned. If they are chosen carefully they can reveal many attractive qualities. As a rough guide to local taste an Italian would probably opt for a light wine from Piedmont, the Spaniard for one from Galicia, while the favourite with a Portuguese would be a Colares.

SOME SUGGESTIONS

From the wines of France, one would choose a light MÉDOC, POMEROL, a Beaujolais of the current year, a CÔTES DU VENTOUX, a CHÂTILLON EN DIOIS, a BOURGUEIL or a CHINON. From Italy, CHIANTI or VALPOLICELLA would fit the bill. From Spain, the choice would be one of the light reds of Galicia. If you know where to find a Swiss wine you cannot do better than ask for a SALVAGNIN.

FEASTS, FRIENDS AND FAMILY

Wine is the best of friends on any occasion. All over the world, the gathering of friends and family around the table on Sundays is synonymous with relaxation of body and freedom of the spirit. A family table is a friendly table and its preparation is inspired more by love, affection and friendship than by respect for form or etiquette. And to choose a wine for friends and relatives is one of those truly unselfish pleasures; pleasurable in itself, it gives pleasure to others.

In discussing the choice of wines, a few words on food are necessary. The passing years have happily eroded the habit of confusing quantity with quality, which often left guests so overstuffed as to be apoplectic and weak at the knees. A well-planned meal with a properly chosen wine should leave the wits clear and the shanks firm. Consider, for instance, a meal of hors-d'œuvres, a light entrée, a meat dish, vegetables, cheese and dessert. If the main dish is rich and heavy—a meat with a rich cream sauce, or game—then one of the other courses can be left out. Some people may also appreciate a light salad, and there is no need to fear the truism that salad does not go well with wine—this is the moment to serve a glass of fresh (but not iced) water. It is refreshing to the palate and makes a "taste interval" between the main wine and the wine served with the cheese. The dessert does not have to be a heavy dish but can be a pastry or, possibly, fresh fruit.

A simply chosen menu will influence the choice of wines. On the other hand, a very good way of choosing a menu is to plan it around some well-known wine which has reached its full and glorious maturity and thus becomes the focal point for the whole meal. The main dish is decided upon first and from this point one can go backwards and forwards through the menu. The wine can be from Burgundy, Bordeaux, Tuscany, Douro, Rioja or of even more exotic origins such as the Romanian Kadarka, the Yugoslavian Plavac, Naonassa from Greece or one of many others from all over the old and new worlds.

The most generally accepted and popular choice for the main wine is a red and if this be so then the main course should be red meat, a meat with rich sauce or a fowl. But this does not mean that a classic dry white wine cannot be served beforehand as a piquant overture. The tried and true belief that such a wine goes with such-and-such a dish still holds good. A more comprehensive guide to compatible wines and dishes can be found on pages 431-32.

FAMILY REUNIONS

Family reunions usually fall into two main classifications; those with religious overtones and those which are simply social get-togethers. In the Anglo-Saxon world families naturally gravitate together at Christmas, for New Year celebrations, wedding anniversaries, birthdays and on other traditional occasions, but in Continental Europe families meet on any pretext, even if only to enjoy a good old unrestrained gossip. Wedding breakfasts and lunches, the receptions which follow, christenings and similar celebrations are traditionally formal, restrained and discreet. Although they should not be the occasion for gastronomic over-indulgence, the food may nevertheless be excellent and the wines of top quality. In such solemn circumstances the wines should be limited to three, a white wine and two reds. The classic rule still applies: progression in strength and richness throughout the meal.

Many changes can be rung on these three basic choices. If, for example, all the wines are to be from Burgundy then a dry white and two reds, the second being of greater body, can be chosen. All the wines can be from Bordeaux or from one cellar, in which case the host's pocket and knowledge guide his choice.

MENU BASED ON BURGUNDY

Concentrating on Côtes de Beaune

White . . . MEURSAULT, MONTRACHET
First red . . POMMARD, SAVIGNY
Second red . PERNAND-VERGELESSE, ALOXE-CORTON

Concentrating on Côtes de Nuits

White . . . CLOS VOUGEOT BLANC
First red . . CHAMBOLLE-MUSIGNY, FIXIN
Second red . ROMANÉE-CONTI, CLOS-VOUGEOT

MENU BASED ON BORDEAUX

White . . .	DRY GRAVES
First red . .	MÉDOC, POMEROL
Second red .	PAUILLAC, ST-ESTÈPHE, ST-EMILION

A MENU FROM YOUR OWN CELLAR

Balancing three wines from your own stock depends on the size and variety of your cellar. At times like these one wishes one had been more courageous by investing in a few more bottles! But one should not be afraid to mix the vintages. There is no reason why a Swiss or German white cannot be followed by, say, a red Italian and then a Portuguese or Spanish red.

For special occasions when an unexpected meal with wine is required (and these can occur quite frequently), the meal may well be preceded by a good *brut* Champagne; but, it must be repeated, this should be served before the meal. In exceptional circumstances, Champagne could possibly be drunk before the coffee, but to serve it immediately afterwards would be bad taste and one of the few existing deadly sins left in this permissive age.

FORMAL DINNERS OR RECEPTIONS

Wine can make or break a formal dinner. Without its noble presence the whole affair would be much less memorable or spectacular. Its inherent prestige, the way it is handled, the care with which it is chosen, sets the seal on the dignity and the importance of the occasion. The most valuable wines play their regal part in a setting of good taste, impeccable manners and a relaxed if formal atmosphere. The house is a stage set to impress the guests and establish the mood. Serving plates, dishes, and glasses, silver and linen are all proudly on view. The food has been chosen and cooked with patience and care and now the guests have assembled. When they have had time enough to make or renew aquaintanceships they proceed to their places at the table. The memory of the pre-dinner drinks fades from the fickle mind as the first wine makes its impressive entrance.

Bottles, opened beforehand, are brought from a cool store; the reds that have been breathing in the *chambré* atmosphere are brought to the fore. The term *chambré* can, as a reminder, bear some explanation here. It was adopted by our forbears and is somewhat of an anachronism today. Inside the thick stone walls of ancient and unheated houses, dining-rooms were much cooler in olden times. Today, with very rare exceptions, no wine can bear the temperature of a room where men may be wearing tropical weight suits or women can sit comfortably in topless evening or dinner dresses. It is as unthinkable to put a lump of ice into a glass of white wine as it is to serve an over-warm red wine.

It is taken for granted that most of the guests, if not experts, will be at least reasonably knowledgeable about wine. Their comments or even criticisms will not be judged out of place. Pertinent remarks will be appreciated by the host who will gladly reveal the wine's origin and pedigree as far as he knows it.

Professional tasting terms should be used with caution and accuracy. The technical vocabulary should simplify conversation and not complicate it. One can say, for example, that a great red wine has a beautiful colour, a strong bouquet of well-blended aromas, that it leaves a clean taste on the palate, that it is long with a lingering flavour. Never say that it is well-dressed (that means the label), that it has an agreeable perfume or a delicious taste. Say, if you must, that it has body and bouquet and that it will age well. Best of all, say that it has been selected by a true connoisseur and that little as you profess to know about the subject, you can appreciate its qualities. Everyone will then marvel at your modesty!

Returning to the first bottle on the menu, a white wine makes a good introduction to most meals. The quality must be carefully taken into account observing the golden rule which demands that no wine must ever make the palate regret the wine which precedes it. Thus the triumphant entry of a great white wine should not make the first red wine that follows it appear too modest in comparison. Wine, in all its nobility, has an inborn courtesy and should never intrude or attract attention to itself. A dinner should never be allowed to turn into a tiresome wine-tasting; there is a time and place for both. Like a well-mannered friend the wine's presence should not compete with, but should complement the subtle tastes produced in the kitchen, or even ennoble them.

When four wines complement a meal they should progress from lightest to fullest in body, from humblest to noblest, from youngest to most mature, from first to last or, in other words, from better to better.

WHEN FRIENDS DROP BY

There is no doubt that the very appearance of a bottle of wine creates an atmosphere of relaxation. It creates a level on which people of like tastes can meet and informally pass the time. If the weatherman permits, then eating and drinking in the open air, having a picnic or a barbecue adds to the informality. Here all pretence is abandoned and a simple friendly meal is as enjoyable as something cooked with great care after many hours of preparation. Wine can even be served at a sausage party, preferably with the Vienna variety, as the grease on fried or grilled sausages does not combine well with wine.

Wines on these occasions should be able to stand up to unwonted extremes of temperature. There is no reason why such a party cannot be held with snow on the ground providing there is shelter from the wind. If one lives near or by a vineyard it is only a matter of buying what the local producers drink themselves in the same circumstances. These wines only need to be attractive, lively, gay, young and pleasant. Light whites, light reds, authentic *vin rosé* but not *pelure d'oignon*, fruity or "flinty" wines, dry white wines are good choices. Highly alcoholic wines should be avoided.

Popular wines for drinking in this open atmosphere are French white wines from the Loire or those from the Swiss canton of Vaud, the light SYLVANERS and the REISLINGS from Alsace, or wines from the Rhine and Moselle districts. A *rosé* from Provence in France might be chosen, as would the pinkish wines of the Balearic Islands, the MAVROD from Bulgaria, or the CVICEK from Slovenia. There are innumerable reds of almost every nationality to choose from. They should be light in colour, fruity, and clean on the palate. They can come from places as far apart as Beaujolais and Austria, Périgod and California, where SANTA ROSA is a good example. Slightly sparkling natural wines are ideal at such times, whether they come from Anjou, Saumar, Touraine, Seyssel or Neuchâtel. The RIESLING ITALICA or LAMBRUSCO would be excellent.

Modern technology has come to the aid of the wine-lover: the portable ice-box or insulated container should be used whenever possible to carry the wines and to store them while they are being served. The wine warms up only too quickly in glasses held between the fingers, or in the sun. Of course, if you can lay hands on one, a small cask is a worthy centre-piece for any meal in the open, even if covered with old wet sacks soaked in brine to keep it cool or nestling on a bed of crushed ice. There is nothing like the sensation of drawing off a glass of wine from a wooden barrel.

WINE IN RESTAURANTS

A business lunch or a restaurant meal with friends is an important part of the eating-out habits of the modern male. For business lunches, most people want to order a contradiction in terms; a good meal, a light meal, and a quick meal. Accordingly, the special delights of the kitchen must sometimes be sacrificed. To make up for this, the wine may be carefully selected. The golden rule is, the simpler the better. Work in the afternoon prohibits the choice of wines that are too rich. Most wine waiters now appreciate this and have a good light wine which does not tend to put a client or an associate to sleep over his desk during the afternoon. Such after-effects are inclined to make the guest think twice before accepting another invitation.

It is just as well, however, to know how to read the wine list and not only the right-hand column! Those "little white wines" which "go down just like milk" can sometimes have a treacherous delayed action, whilst light red wines, for instance those with a high tannin content, are often more open and less insidious.

Dining with friends or entertaining a guest who is just passing through is quite a different matter. There is usually more time, and the whole night following for the constitution to recover. In these circumstances that favourite showplace of a restaurant or popular country inn can be just as important as the local architecture or the natural scenic beauty. Fewer limitations are imposed and a wide choice of carefully selected wines can show the guest he is not only welcome but appreciated. Of course, knowing the guest's tastes beforehand makes everything simpler. Knowing the restaurant and its cellar is a great help, too, as it is not always the most expensive or most well-known shipper's or château label which is best suited to the guest's palate or the host's pocket.

TALKING OVER WINE

When a friend drops in for a gossip, to put the world to rights or just to renew old aquaintance, wine can be a splendid change from the old, tired, spirit-based concoction of the cocktail era. As a matter of fact, some hosts, especially when dining out or even at business lunches, have taken to seating their guests at the table instead of standing by the bar, and serving them a light wine instead of an aperitif. The wine blends better with whatever is to follow and is less of a shock to the system than a potent iced mixture.

With a private cellar, following the habit of the continental European, it is a delightful practice to invite visitors to make their own choice of wine guided by a few words of expertise. The welcome offering of a bottle of wine, too, is always a compliment to the caller who brings it. For the casual visitor, the wine should be chosen from its personal history, such as one brought back from an interesting journey, or a particularly good year which is maturing in a bin; but whatever it is, it should be something special.

To talk over a bottle of wine is an experience. Conversation flows, stimulated by the quiet genie in the bottle which relaxes the mind and soothes the way to near-forgotten conversational delights. Choose wines that bring mental pictures of grapes harvested in distant places. Serve wines that have been bought for the cellar and not yet tasted. A new wine on a strange palate is a good opening for conversation.

This is the time to find out if the year fulfils its expected promise. These are the times to try the wines from Israel or Turkey, from Yugoslavia and Hungary. Their names sing an invitation to taste; TEKIGRAD, BOZCAADA, MÜREFTE, ELAZIG, and KOKINELLI from Cyprus, KOONAWARA from Southern Australia, STELLENBOSCH from South Africa, and EL TRAPICHE from the Argentine. It is the time when you can test out your guests' knowledge, their recognition of the wine regions, and their tastes for future occasions. You might even imbue them with your own enthusiasm for this fascinating subject, wine.

CHEESE AND WINE

It is well known that the taste of wine is at its most glorious with cheese. There are so many cheeses and so many wines that it would require an encyclopedic work to marry them all. However, there is a general rule that certain cheeses go with certain wines, just as with other dishes, and classic partners are cited in this chapter, well-established after long aquaintance. Roquefort with a great red wine? Most certainly, but there are esoteric connoisseurs who sing the praises of Roquefort combined with MONTBAZILLAC. Who is to say? There is ample choice and the field is open for all tastes. Here is a general guide to the marriage of wines and cheeses:

Great, strong, robust and well-knit red wines from all regions: Danish blue, Gorgonzola, Roquefort, and Stilton.

Red wines of high to medium strength from all regions: Brie and Camembert.

Red wines of medium body and bouquet from Dalmatia, Médoc, Morgon, The Palatinate, and Tuscany: Maroilles, Livarot and Munster.

White wines and robust red wines from Bordeaux, Burgundy, Andalusia, Piedmont and Tunisia: Cheddar and Gruyère.

White wines, rosés, dry or fruity red wines from Beaujolais, Galicia, the Loire, Umbria, Savoy and Serbia: Cantal, Gouda, Hervé and Port-Salut.

Light and dry wines, local wines from the cheese-producing regions: goat cheese and dry cheese made from ewes' milk.

Apart from these, there are those cream and curd cheeses like Petits-Suisse which are served sprinkled with salt or sugar. Sweetened cheeses come to the table as desserts or with salads. White wines, rosé or light red wines on the dry side should be drunk with such world-famous cheese dishes as *fondue* or *raclette*.

There is little complication with cheese soufflés as the wine is chosen to suit the cheese on which the dish is based. Cheese savouries, most common on the Anglo-Saxon table and usually eaten at the end of the meal, can be accompanied by a sherry or a dry port.

The main wine served with the meat or game, can equally well accompany the cheese, bearing in mind that it should not interfere with the good order of the hierarchy of the wines as the meal progresses.

SWEETS, DESSERTS AND WINES

As a general rule, wines are not desirable with sweet dishes. There are exceptions which are listed here, and they should be studied to complete a knowledge of wines and food. Under no circumstances should wine be served with aciduous fruits or any desserts containing chocolate in any form. Although this law should really not be transgressed, a little cheating is forgivable in some cases and authorities on the subject reluctantly admit there may be something to be said for the following combinations:

Soft and sweet wines: ALICANTE, BARSAC, LACHRYMA CHRISTI, MOSCATI DI PANTELLERIA, MARSALA ALEATICO, SAUTERNES, VINO SANTA.

Slightly sparkling sweet wines: ASTI SPUMANTE, BLANQUETTE DE LIMOUX, medium-dry CHAMPAGNE, CLAIRETTE DE DIE, may be drunk with cakes, biscuits, petits fours and tarts.

Red wines of medium body with a fruity bouquet with strawberries, raspberries and peaches.

Sweet, unfortified wines: FRONTIGNAN, MALVOISIE, MAVRODAPHI DE PATRAS, MOSCATEL with pastries without much cream.

It is not always possible to prevent someone from finishing their wine with the dessert, but with careful management the meal can be arranged so that the glass can be finished earlier. A good way around the problem is to provide a cool, but not iced, glass of fresh water and then, immediately after the sweet course, serve a dessert wine when the palate has been cleared. Frequently, those delicious dessert wines are forgotten: the good ports, Madeiras, Malaga and oloroso sherry, while the taste of a great MONTBAZILLAC is a pleasure and an experience not to be missed.

WINE IN FOOD

Countless recipes prescribe wine in making a sauce or for including in the cooking, as in casseroles or marinades. If a cheap *vin ordinaire* is not obtainable it always seems a pity to raid the cellar, but the accepted rule demands that the wine used in the cooking should be the same as that served on the table. However, here too a little cheating is permissible, and normally, a Riesling, a cheap Burgundy or a simple Côtes du Rhône will do well enough.

407

Old menus have more value as comparative history than as practical hints for the modern kitchen. Many explanations have been put forward for the continued decrease in the quantity of food consumed by guests at table. It may not be necessary but perhaps just as well to point out that in the days of the great banquets guests were only helped to a choice of the fifty or so courses served and were not obliged to eat their way through them all. However, it must be understood that social class structures were totally different from those of today and such menus were only served in baronial castles, in the palaces of royalty and the clergy, and the mansions of the rich leisured classes whose pleasures were mainly active and out of doors and entailed quite a lot of physical exercise and expenditure of energy.

Modern society has produced different pressures and the demands of work and hygiene have developed a more balanced, simplified and cleaner diet gradually to replace the gluttonies of yesteryear. However, it is to be hoped that our modern physical condition still allows us to do justice to the menu of a banquet.

ANCIENT MENUS

In the year 1656, a certain Madame la Chancelière invited Louis XIV to dinner at her château at Pont-chartrain. The first course was composed of twenty-four dishes, including sixteen warm hors-d'œuvre, and eight rich soups. This was followed by eight plates bearing the meat that had been cooked in the soup and sixteen dishes of lean meat. The third course was made up of eight platters of roasts and sixteen dishes of vegetables prepared in the meat gravy. The fourth course offered the choice of eight pies, cold meat or fish and sixteen kinds of salads with oil, cream and butter. Last of all, twenty-four different pastries, twenty-four dishes of fresh fruit, twenty-four dishes of sweetmeats, preserves and sweet sauces. In all, 168 dishes or prepared plates were served, without counting the different desserts.

In this account by Prosper Montagné no mention is made of the wines served with the dinner. It does, however, give an indication of the abundance of the food served at the time of the Sun King, who was himself reputed to have an extraordinarily large appetite. The following menu, served to three great nineteenth-century figures, is nearer our subject and less shocking to our modern tastes:

Menu for the dinner of the "Three Emperors"
served to Alexander II, the Czar
and the King of Prussia at the Café Anglais, Paris,
June 7, 1867

Soups
Imperatrice, Fontanges

Removes
Soufflé à la Reine
Sole filets à la vénitienne
Turbot steaks au gratin
Saddle of mutton

Entrées
Poulets à la portugaise
Hot quail pie
Lobster à la parisienne
Champagne sorbet

Roasts
Duck à la rouennaise
Canapés of bunting

Wines
MADEIRA, RETURN FROM INDIA 1846
XÉRÈS 1821
CHÂTEAU YQUEM 1847
CHAMBERTIN 1846
CHÂTEAU MARGAUX 1847
CHÂTEAU LATOUR 1847
CHÂTEAU LAFITE 1848

Desserts
Aubergines à l'espagnole
Asparagus
Cassolettes princesse
Bombe glacée

In this example the wines are mentioned, but the question arises as to what dish was served with which wine. Was the Château Yquem served with the soufflé, the buntings or the *bombe glacée*? One can guess or, better still, try them out. In the next menu there are still no details but the combinations are easier to guess.

Banquet held in the honour of
Emile Loubet, President of the French Republic,
on his return from Russia,

May 27, 1902, at the invitation of
the Conseil général du Nord, at Dunkirk.

Hors-d'œuvre à la Russe

Dunkirk salmon à la Flamande

Filet de Bœuf à la Parisienne

Jellied duck

Poularde du Mans à l'Estragon

Salade Jean-Bart

Suprêmes de Pêches and Greengage plums
à la Montmorency

Desserts

Wines

BARSAC

MÉDOC

CHÂTEAU GRUAUD-LAROSE

MONTEBELLO FRAPPÉ

LIQUEURS

GREAT MENUS OF TODAY

WITH BURGUNDY

A meal based on Burgundy wines alone can combine all possible and imaginable variations. The choice of food can, as previously suggested, be guided by the wines. The MONTRACHET goes just as well with another fish entrée, while the Côte de Beaune wines, because of their good colour and reputation, marry well with strongly flavoured meats.

Salmon mousse
CHEVALIER-MONTRACHET
Ham à la Villandry
SAVIGNY-LÈS-BEAUNE
Fowl stuffed with truffles
Timbales Agnès Sorel
Mimosa Salad
RICHEBOURG
Sabayon au Madère
MADEÏRA

For an official or intimate dinner it is sometimes preferable to order according to the established gastronomic rules. A first-class and reputable restaurant can always provide a small separate room with service,

WITH BORDEAUX

The great white wines of Bordeaux are not very well known but similar wines can be found outside France and have been mentioned in this book. In the following menu salmon mousse has been included for Bordeaux as well as, previously, for Burgundy. As for drinking a soft and sweet wine with *foie gras*, just try it and you will be convinced that it is an excellent combination.

Salmon mousse
CÔTES-DE-BLAYE
Crawfish tails au gratin
SAINTE-CROIX-DU-MONT SEC
Saddle of lamb
CHÂTEAU LAFITE
Parfait au foie gras
Crêpes fourrées
CHÂTEAU YQUEM

and will supply all the needs from its kitchens and cellars. A good head waiter will be able to guide you in creating a symphony of wine and food which will enchant the guests so do not hesitate to consult him.

MENU WITH CHAMPAGNE

Champagne wines are either liked or disliked—it is as simple as that. If they are enjoyed then there is no further comment to be made and the following dishes are well-married to the wine.

Jellied filets of sole
AVIZE
Truffles in pastry
CRAMANT
Pheasant à la Bohémienne
MAREUIL-SUR-AY
Cardons à la moelle
Salade Aïda
BOUZY
Biscuit glacé Lyrique
MAILLY-CHAMPAGNE

MENUS WITH DIFFERENT WINES

Before dinner: CHAMPAGNE BRUT
Foie gras en croûte
CHAMPAGNE NATURE
Soufflé de truites Beauvilliers
ENTRE-DEUX-MERS-HAUT-BENAUGE
Prague Ham à la Chablisienne
POMMARD
Nest of Quails
Pommes Bonne-femme
Salades Béatrix
NUITS-SAINT-GEORGES
Nut cake
CHÂTEAU-CHALON

Médaillons de jambon Polignac
BLANC DE L'ETOILE
Crawfish tails à la mode du couvent de Chorin
MEURSAULT
Poulet de grain Jaqueline garniture Marie-Louise
Salade Orloff
POMEROL
Charlotte Royale
QUART-DE-CHAUME

Lobster and coconut salad
MÂCON BLANC
Timbale Sully
MARGAUX
Filets de bœuf Wellington
Samade Rachel
CHAMBOLLE-MUSIGNY
Diplomate chaud
VIN DE PAILLE

Langouste en Bellevue
PALETTE
Selle de chevreuil Grand Veneur
Timbales Maréchale
Salade Belle Hélène
GEVREY-CHAMBERTIN
Croûte à l'ananas
PINEAU DES CHARENTES

410

Unfortunately, not many people nowadays have the time, the means or the inclination to set off on a purely gastronomic journey. However, it may just be possible to arrange a business trip, a cultural or educational tour even a relaxing holiday which takes in places famous for their blend of cellar and kitchen, whether they be towns, provinces or countries.

The itineraries suggested here are based on personal experiences and include some memorable possibilities. The choice of localities has been dictated more by the wines than food. If French provinces predominate, this is because France is the mother of wines, and there are many different regions which have their own typical vintages. All in all the names represent an imaginary journey across the Continent of Europe and a sampling of regional delicacies and specialities encountered all too rarely elsewhere.

Many of these specialities and wines, listed alphabetically to spare regional and national jealousies, are not widely known or acclaimed. Simple and exquisite, each dish is accompanied by a special wine and they are minor poems in casseroles and carafes.

Region	Wine	Colour	Dish
ALSACE	Tokay from Alsace	White	Braised ham and apple crumble
	Gewürztraminer	White	Pheasant *à la Strasbourg*
ANJOU	Champigny	Red	*Bouilleture* (fish stewed in red wine and herbs)
AUSTRIA	Prälatenwein	White	Quetsche plums with almonds in pastry
AUVERGNE	Chanturgue	Red	Besse-en-Chandesse *coq au vin*
BEARN	Irouléguy	Red	Wild goat with mushrooms
BERRY	Chateaumeillant	Red	Pancakes with pork cracklings
BORDEAUX	Pomerol or Lalande de Pomerol	Red	Lamprey *à la bordelaise*
BOURBONNAIS	Saint-Pourçain	Red	*Truffat* (potato pie)
BURGUNDY	Passe-tout-grain	Red	Pigeon stew
	Beaujolais	Red	*Pot-au-feu* or *Boeuf-gros-sel*
BRITTANY	Muscadet	White	Rabbit cooked in Muscadet wine
BUGEY	Charveyron	Red	Bernardine ragout of woodcock
CORSICA	Sciaccarello	Red	*Coppa, figatello, lonzo* (cold meat specialities)
DAUPHINÉ	Jarjayes	White	*Poulet roussille*
FRANCHE-COMTÉ	Hypocras	Red	Baume-les-Dames quince cheese
GASCONY	Madiran	Red	*Sanguète de poulet*
GERMANY	Schloss Böckelsheimer Kupfergrube	White	Goose breasts grilled over vine shoots, sautéed potatoes and cranberry sauce
ITALY	Rocca-di-papa	White	Mozzarella in carrozza (toasted cheese and ham sandwich)
	Chianti	Red	Beefsteak *alla Fiorentina*
	Vino Nobile di Montepulciano	Red	*Osso buco*
LANGUEDOC	Minervois	Red	Mourtayrol (boiled beef, chicken and ham with saffron)
LORRAINE	Gris de Pagny-sur-Moselle	White	Boulay frogs *au gratin*
LYONS	Beaujolais of the year	Red	Stuffed veal
ORLEANS	Cour Cheverny	White	Montargis mushrooms on toast
PÉRIGORD	Côtes de Duras	Red	Goat's cheese
PORTUGAL	Moscatel de Setubal	White	*Doce d'ovos* (dessert made from egg yolks)
PROVENCE	Taradeau	White	Snails *à la suçarelle*
SAVOY	Princess-Rocheray	Red	Pork cooked in wine with a cream sauce
SPAIN	Ribeiro	White	Octopus stewed in its own ink
SWITZERLAND	Dézaley	White	Liver sausage
	Abbaye de Mont	White	Filet of perch

LIST OF COLOUR MAPS

WINE MUSEUMS

GERMANY

Weinbaumuseum
MEERSBURG/LAKE CONSTANCE

Historisches Museum der Pfalz
mit Weinmuseum
Gr. Pfaffengasse 7
SPEYER

Museum für die Geschichte des Weines
RÜDESHEIM

GREAT BRITAIN

Harvey's Winemuseum
BRISTOL

AUSTRIA

Museum der Stadt Krems
Theaterplatz 9
KREMS AN DER DONAU

SPAIN

Museo del Vino
Plaza Jaime Iº
VILAFRANCA DEL PANADÉS

FRANCE

Musée du Vin
ANGERS

Musée du Vin
Hôtel des Ducs de Bourgogne
BEAUNE

Château d'Entrecasteaux
Ile de Bendor (off Bandol)

Maison du Vin
1, cours du 30-Juillet
BORDEAUX (GIRONDE)

Musée du Vin
CÉRONS (GIRONDE)

Musée du Vin de Champagne
ÉPERNAY

Château-Lascombes
MARGAUX (GIRONDE)

Musée Rothschild
Domaine Mouton-Rothschild
par PAUILLAC (GIRONDE)

Musée d'Espelosin
ROCHECORDON (I.-et-L.)

Musée de la Mission Haut-Brion
TALENCE (GIRONDE)

ITALY

Museo del Vino
Castello Ringberg
CALDERO (BOLZANO)

Musée du Vin Martini
PESSIONE (TURIN)

SWITZERLAND

Musée de l'Areuse
BOUDRY/NE

PHOTOGRAPHIC ACKNOWLEDGEMENTS

Graphische Sammlung Albertina, Vienna, p. 11. Archives départementales, Dijon: Yves Debraine, Lausanne, p. 45. Archives Nationales, Paris: Patrick Guilbert, Saint-Brice, p. 131. Archives photographiques, Paris, p. 224. Badisches Landesmuseum, Karlsruhe: Willi Moegle, Leinfelden-Oberaichen, p. 395 centre. Bavaria-Verlag, Munich: Ruth Hallensleben, p. 34 at right. Bibliothèque de l'Arsenal, Paris: Patrick Guilbert, Saint-Brice, p. 20. Bibliothèque cantonale et universitaire, Lausanne, p. 22, 24, 26 top, 27 top; Scope, Lausanne, p. 95. Bibliothèque du Muséum d'Histoire naturelle, Paris: Patrick Guilbert, Saint-Brice, p. 17. Bibliothèque Nationale, Cabinet des Estampes, Paris: Patrick Guilbert, Saint-Brice, p. 23, 30. British Museum, London, p. 388, 392 at left, 395 at left. Companhia Geral da Agricultura das Vinhas do Alto Douro, Vila Nova de Gaia, p. 203. Confrérie des Chevaliers du Tastevin, Nuits-Saint-Georges, p. 31 centre. J. Decker, Saumur, p. 117, 118. Edita, Lausanne, p. 92 top, 223, 249. Ami Guichard, Lausanne, p. 146. Historisches Museum, Basle, p. 32. Historisches Museum der Pfalz, Speyer, p. 15 at right. Instituto do Vinho do Porto, Porto, p. 197, 206. Juliusspital Keller, Würzburg: Gundermann, Würzburg, p. 34 bottom right. Kunsthistorisches Museum, Vienna: Erwin Meyer, Vienna, p. 287. Kunstmuseum, Düsseldorf, p. 265, 392 at right; Walter Klein, Düsseldorf, p. 389 at left; Carlfred Halbach, Mettmann, p. 389 at right; Willi Moegle, Leinfelden-Oberaichen, p. 395 at right. Luftverkehr Strähle, Schorndorf, p. 262, 266. Pierre Mackiéwicz, Aix-en-Provence, p. 57, 61, 65, 66, 74, 154 top left, 362 top, 363 bottom left. Mainfränkisches Museum, Würzburg: Alfred Burkholz, Würzburg, p. 31 at right. The Mansell Collection, London, p. 13. Gaston Marchou, Cambes: National Foto Persbureau, Amsterdam, p. 154 bottom right. Martini & Rossi, Turin, p. 15 at left. Moët & Chandon, Epernay: Yves Debraine, Lausanne, p. 347, 400. Musée des Beaux-Arts, Orléans: Yves Debraine, Lausanne, p. 229. Musée Condé, Chantilly: Giraudon, Paris, p. 26 bottom, 27 bottom. Musée du Louvre, Cabinet des Dessins, Paris: Patrick Guilbert, Saint-Brice, p. 14. Musée de Mouton-Rothschild, Pauillac: Pierre Berdoy, Morainvilliers, p. 387, 391. Museo Nacional del Prado, Madrid: Edita, Lausanne, p. 191. Museó Nazionale, Naples: Scala, Florence, p. 298. Museum für die Geschichte des Weines, Rüdesheim: Ami Guichard, Lausanne, p. 399. National Gallery of Art, Washington, p. 35. Oriental Institute, University of Chicago, p. 10. Österreichisches Museum für Volkskunde, Vienna: Ritter, Vienna, p. 34 at right. Österreichische Nationalbibliothek, Vienna, p. 25, 36. Charles Page, Vevey, p. 92 bottom, 145. Perestrello's Photographos Ltda., Funchal, p. 210. Abbé Perrodin, Conliège, p. 31 at left. Photo Giraudon, Paris, p. 351. Römisch-Germanisches Museum, Cologne: Willi Moegle, Leinfelden-Oberaichen, p. 386. O. Ruppen, Sion, p. 91. Roger Schall, Paris, p. 73, 154 top right, 362 bottom right and left, 363 top left, at right. Schweizerisches Landesmuseum, Zurich, p. 33, 34 top left. Victoria and Albert Museum, London, p. 398, 402. Wallraff-Richartz-Museum, Cologne: Heinz Doppelfeld, Cologne-Ehrenfeld, p. 232. Weinbaumuseum, Krems: K. Gartler, Krems, p. 37, 401. Wine Institute, San Francisco, p. 323, 324, 325, 326, 327, 329, 332. Dr. Wolff & Tritschler, Offenburg, p. 257. Württembergische Landesbibliothek, Stuttgart: Hermann Schnepf, Stuttgart, p. 18-19. Zähringer Museum, Baden-Baden: Willi Moegle, p. 390.

ACKNOWLEDGEMENTS

The Publisher extends his warmest thanks to the Curators of Museums and libraries, the Directors and Administrators of official organizations or private societies and the Collectors who have helped in the preparation of this work. Special thanks are due to:

Israelian Embassy, Bern; Pierre Androuët, Paris; Piero Antinori, Florence; François des Aulnoyes, Centre National de Coordination, Paris; Dr von Bassermann-Jordan'sches Weingut, Deidesheim; Ferdinando de Bianchi, Madeira Wine Association Ltd., Funchal; Bouchard Père & Fils, Beaune; Louis Philippe Bovard, Office de propagande pour les vins vaudois, Lausanne; Carlos Cavero Beyart, Presidente del Sindicato Nacional de la Vid, Madrid; Champagne Mercier, Epernay; Champagne Perrier-Jouët, Epernay; Champagne Taittinger, Reims; Jacques Chevignard, Grand Chambellan de la Confrérie des Chevaliers du Tastevin, Nuits-Saint-Georges; Cockburn Smithes & Co. Lda, Vila Nova de Gaia; Comité Interprofessionnel du Vin d'Alsace, Colmar; Comité Interprofessionnel des Vins à Appellation Contrôlée de Touraine, Tours; Companhia Geral da Agricultura das Vinhas do Alto Douro "Real Companhia Velha", Vila Nova de Gaia; Confrérie Saint-Etienne d'Alsace, Colmar; Confrérie des Vignerons de Saint Vincent, Mâcon; Confrérie des Vignerons Vevey; Conseil Interprofessionnel des Vins d'Anjou et de Saumur, Angers; Consejo Regulador de la Denominación de Origen Jerez, Jerez de la Frontera; Consejo Regulador de la Denominación de Origen Panadés, Vilafranca del Panadés; Consejo Regulador de la Denominación de Origen Rioja, Logroño; Il Corriere Vinicolo, Rome; J. M. Courteau, Conseil Interprofessionnel du Vin de Bordeaux, Bordeaux; J. Dargent, Comité Interprofessionnel du Vin de Champagne, Epernay; Kemalettin Demirer, Turkish Embassy, Bern; Manuel Cotta Dias, Junta Nacional lo Vinho, Lisbon; Pedro Domecq S.A., Jerez; Joseph Drouhin, Beaune; H. Duboscq, Saint-Estèphe; J. Faiveley, Nuits-Saint-Georges; F.A.O., Rome; Héritiers Fourcaud-Laussac, Saint-Emilion; P. Fridas, sous-directeur Office International de la Vigne et du Vin, Paris; Pierre Galet, Ecole Nationale Supérieure Agronomique de Montpellier, Montpellier; Garvey S.A., Jerez Gonzalez, Byass & Co. Ltd., Jerez; Dr Heger, Ihringen; Juliusspital-Weingut, Würzburg; A. S. Hogg, Peter Dominic Limited, London; Dr. Harry Kühnel, Archivdirektor, Krems a.d. Donau; Restaurant Ledoyen, Paris; Henri Leyvraz, Station fédérale d'essais agricoles, section de viticulture, Lausanne/Pully; Madame Edmond Loubat, Pomerol; Henri Maire, Arbois; Manuel & Cie S.A., Lausanne; Dr A. Miederbacher, Unione Italiani Vini, Milan; Moët & Chandon, Epernay; Jean Mommessin, Mâcon; Monimpex, Budapest; G. H. Mumm & Co., Reims; New Zealand High Commission, London; H.F.M. Palmer, Adelaide; Dr Adolf Paulus, Museum für die Geschichte des Weines, Rüdesheim; Americo Pedrosa Piros de Lima, Instituto do Vinho do Porto, Porto; Porcelaine Limoges-Unic, Paris; R. Protin, Directeur de l'Office International de la Vigne et du Vin, Paris; Joh. Jos. Prüm, Wehlen; C. Quittanson, Inspecteur Divisionnaire du Service de la Répression des Fraudes et du Contrôle de la Qualité, Ministère de l'Agriculture, Dijon; Real Companhia Vinicola do Norte de Portugal, Vila Nova de Gaia; Représentation Commerciale de l'U.R.S.S. en Suisse, Bern; Gilbert Rohrer, Lausanne; Roth & Sauter, Lausanne; Baron Philippe de Rothschild, Mouton-Rothschild; Fritz Salomon, Präsident des Österreichischen Weininstituts, Vienna; Sandeman Bros. & Co., Jerez; José Augusto dos Santos, Casa de Portugal, Paris; Francisco Sanz Carnero, Dirección General de Agricultura, Madrid; Antonio Carlos Sarmento de Vasconcellos, Instituto do Vinho do Porto, Porto; Dr Karl Schultz, Konservator, Historisches Museum der Pfalz, Speyer; Antonio José da Silva Vinhos, S.A.R.L., Vila Nova de Gaia; Jean-Louis Simon, Station fédérale d'essais agricoles, section de viticulture, Lausanne/Pully; Société Civile du Domaine de la Romanée-Conti, Vosne-Romanée; Société Vinicole Perroy S.A., Epesses; Société des Domaines Woltner, Bordeaux; Staatliche Lehr- und Versuchsanstalt für Wein- und Obstbau, Weinsberg; Staatsweingut, Weinbaulehranstalt, Bad Kreuznach; Syndicat régional des Vins de Savoie, Chambéry; Szende László, Orszagos Borminösitö Intézet, Budapest; J. Thorin, Pontanevaux; E. Tomov, Embassy of the Republic of Bulgaria, Bern; Johann Traxler, Österreichisches Weininstitut, Vienna; Verwaltung der Staatsweingüter im Rheingau, Eltville; Veuve Clicquot-Ponsardin, Reims; Wente Bros., Livermore, California; Fred Wick, Vevey; Dr Robert Wildhaber, Basel; Williams & Humbert Ltd., Jerez; Terence McInnes, The Wine Institute, San Francisco; Leo Wunderle, Lucerne; Zoilo Ruiz-Mateos S.A., Jerez.

The colour maps were drawn by Robert Flach, from documents and information provided by:

Pierre Forgeot, Beaune; Office International de la Vigne et du Vin, Paris; Office de propagande pour les vins vaudois, Lausanne; Fédération des Vins de Savoie, Chambéry; Comité Interprofessionnel des Vins des Côtes du Rhône, Avignon; Comité Interprofessionnel des Vins à Appellation Contrôlée de Touraine, Tours; Conseil Interprofessionnel des Vins d'Anjou et de Saumur, Angers; Conseil Interprofessionnel des Vins de Bordeaux; Comité Interprofessionnel du Vin d'Alsace, Colmar; Consejo Regulador de la Denominación de Origen Jerez, Jerez de la Frontera; Consejo Regulador de la Denominación de Origen Rioja, Logroño; Dirección General de Agricultura, Madrid; Instituto do Vinho do Porto, Porto; Verkehrsverein Rüdesheim; Österreichisches Weininstitut, Vienna; Wine Institute, San Francisco; Comité Interprofessionnel du Vin de Champagne, Epernay.

The English translation is by Michael and Angela Kelly, Pully, Switzerland and Peter Dewhirst, I.T.E.S., Geneva.

INDEX OF WINES

418

420

426

431

432

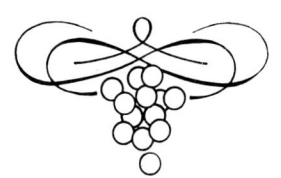

This book is published under the direction of
AMI GUICHARD

Editorial responsibility and supervision by
JOSEPH JOBÉ
in collaboration with Percy Knauth and Valerie Green

Production under the direction of
CHARLES RIESEN

This book is published under the direction of
AMI GUICHARD

Editorial responsibility and supervision by
JOSEPH JOBÉ
in collaboration with Percy Knauth and Valerie Green

Production under the direction of
CHARLES RIESEN

200,000 B.C.

Homo sapiens—
modern humans—
appear (according
to archaeological
evidence).

10,000 B.C.

Humans turn from
hunting and gathering
to agriculture.

CHAPTER 1

THE RISE OF CIVILIZATION

PREHISTORY – 2500 B.C.

A ziggurat in the Sumerian city of Ur

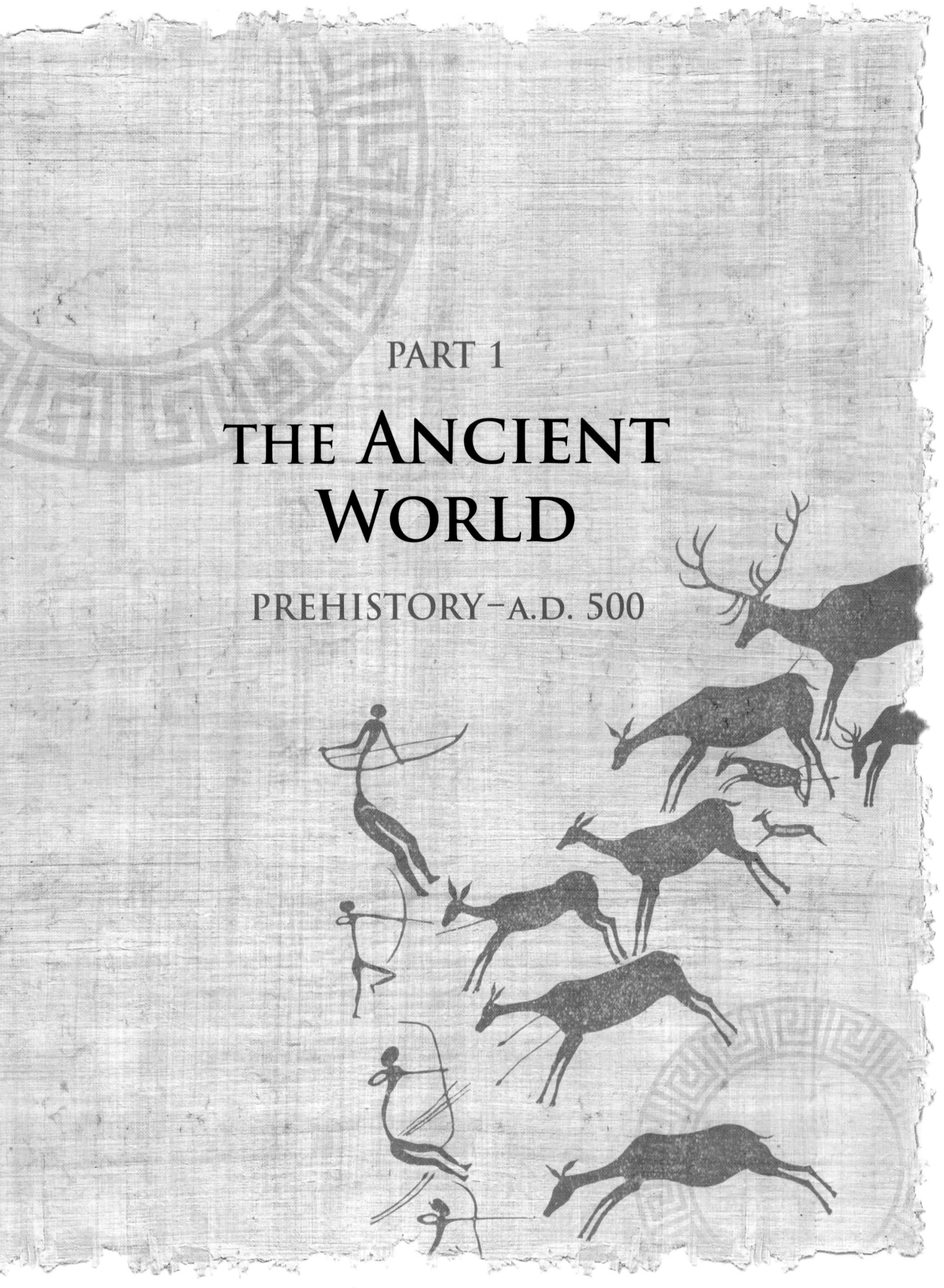

PART 1

THE ANCIENT WORLD

PREHISTORY–A.D. 500

World History
Our Human Story

EDITED BY PATRICIA O'CONNELL PEARSON AND JOHN HOLDREN

The Contemporary World

Part 3

Entering the Modern Era

Part 2

Early Civilizations and Empires

Contents

Front Cover Illustration Credits

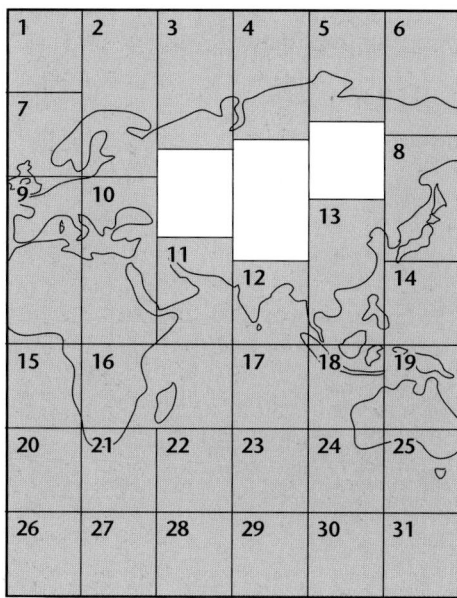

1 Confucius, © Gautier Willaume/iStockphoto. 2 Minoan painting of The Blue Ladies, © Kevin Schafer/Corbis. 3 Sigiriya fresco, © Holton Collection/SuperStock 53-2227-A-P38C. 4 Cleopatra, The Art Archive/Ragab Papyrus Institute Cairo/Gianni Dagli Orti. 5 Venus of Brassempouy, © Gianni Dagli Orti/Corbis. 6 Cave painting at Tassili N'Ajjer, © Kazuyoshi Nomachi/Corbis. 7 Alexander the Great, © Getty Images/Thinkstock. 8 Julius Caesar, © Paolo Gaetano Rocco/iStockphoto. 9 Frieze of The Immortals, © Getty Images/Thinkstock. 10 Cizhou ware, seated woman, © Philippe Michel/AGE Fotostock. 11 Nok head, Werner Forman/Art Resource, NY. 12 Ashanti gold mask, Werner Forman/Art Resource, NY. 13 Moche head, The Art Archive/Archaeological Museum Lima/Gianni Dagli Orti. 14 Genghis Khan, James L. Stanfield/National Geographic Stock. 15 Teotihuacan mask, Michel Zabé/Art Resource, NY. 16 Buddha at Wat Mahathat, © Thom Lang/Corbis. 17 Mona Lisa, Dover Publications. 18 Statue of David, Asier Villafranca/123RF Limited. 19 Galileo Galilei, Galleria degli Uffizi, Florence, Italy/The Bridgeman Art Library. 20 Queen Elizabeth, Photos.com/Thinkstock. 21 Ludwig van Beethoven, © W.J. Baker/Library of Congress, Prints and Photographs Division, LC-USZC4-9589. 22 Simón Bolívar, The Art Archive. 23 Karl Marx, Photos.com/Thinkstock. 24 Amelia Earhart, © Bettmann/Corbis. 25 Spinners in a cotton mill, Library of Congress, Prints and Photographs Division, LC-DIG-nclc-02119. 26 Albert Einstein, Library of Congress, Prints and Photographs Division, LC-USZC4-4940. 27 Eleanor Roosevelt, © Getty Images. 28 Mohandas Gandhi, © Dinodia Photos/Alamy. 29 Nelson Mandela, © Louise Gubb/The Image Works. 30 Mother Teresa, © Matthew Polak/Sygma/Corbis. 31 Astronaut, Dover Publications.

ISBN: 1-60153-123-0

Printed by RR Donnelley, Roanoke, VA, USA, June 2011, Lot 062011

World
History
Our Human Story

EDITED BY PATRICIA O'CONNELL PEARSON AND JOHN HOLDREN

k12

Editors

Patricia O'Connell Pearson
John Holdren

Associate Editor

Alan Fraker

Contributors

Tamim Ansary
Lydia Bjornlund
Kevin Cantera
Mary Beth Klee
Michael Stanford

Parts of *World History: Our Human Story* have been adapted from these K12 publications:

The Human Odyssey: Our Modern World, 1400 to 1914, ed. Mary Beth Klee, John Cribb, and John Holdren (K12 Inc., 2005)

The Human Odyssey: From Modern Times to Our Contemporary Era, ed. Mary Beth Klee, John Cribb, and John Holdren (K12 Inc., 2007)

Book Staff and Contributors

Mary Beck Desmond *Senior Text Editor*
Jeff Burridge *Text Editor*
Allyson Jacob *Associate Text Editor*
Suzanne Montazer *Creative Director, Print*
Stephanie Shaw Williams *Print Visual Designer*
Charlotte Fullerton *Illustrations Editor*
Meredith Condit *Associate Illustrations Editor*
Jean Stringer *Rights Specialist*
Kevin Cantera *Research Editor*
Sheila Jordan *Research Editor*
Connie Moy *Research Editor*
David Swanson *Map Editor*
Candee Wilson *Senior Project Manager*

John Holdren *Senior Vice President for Content and Curriculum*
Maria Szalay *Senior Vice President for Product Development*
David Pelizzari *Vice President, Content and Curriculum*
Amelia Jackson-Zaremba *Senior Instructional Designer*
Kim Barcas *Vice President, Creative*
Sally Russell *Creative Director, Media*
Chris Frescholtz *Director Project Management, High School*

Lisa Dimaio Iekel *Production Manager*
John Agnone *Director of Publications*

About K12 Inc.

K12 Inc., a technology-based education company, is the nation's leading provider of proprietary curriculum and online education programs to students in grades K–12. K¹² provides its curriculum and academic services to online schools, traditional classrooms, blended school programs, and directly to families. K12 Inc. also operates the K¹² International Academy, an accredited, diploma-granting online private school serving students worldwide. K¹²'s mission is to provide any child the curriculum and tools to maximize success in life, regardless of geographic, financial, or demographic circumstances. K12 Inc. is accredited by CITA. More information can be found at www.K12.com.

World History
Our Human Story

EDITED BY PATRICIA O'CONNELL PEARSON AND JOHN HOLDREN

6000 B.C.

2000 B.C.

c. 7000 B.C.
Thousands of people settle in the village of Çatalhüyük (in what is now Turkey).

c. 4500 B.C.
Villages and towns grow rapidly in Sumer.

c. 3000 B.C.
Sumerian city-states develop the elements of civilization.

*T*he study of world history begins with **prehistory**, the long period before the invention of writing, extending back to the time of the earliest humans and beyond. Prehistory is much longer than history. Prehistory reaches far back in time, perhaps millions of years, and encompasses all that happened before human beings first invented a system of writing some five thousand years ago.

Over the past century and a half, scientists have unearthed physical evidence that has led to widespread agreement about when, where, and how human beings appeared around the world. Yet despite this widely shared view of prehistory, our knowledge of the distant past is tentative. As new evidence comes to light, historians and scientists revise their theories.

The evidence reveals a picture of the distant past in which early humans, at different times and in various places, faced similar challenges: meeting basic needs, adapting to changing environments, expressing themselves in practical, creative, and spiritual ways—and, eventually, organizing their societies and establishing the first civilizations.

Evidence of the Distant Past

On a hot July day in 1959 in eastern Africa, a sharp-eyed woman named Mary Leakey unearthed a treasure. It was not a chest of gold or a religious relic, but a small piece of a bone. This little object would help scientists and historians answer a question that had long puzzled them: Where did we come from?

Finding the Past

Mary Leakey and her husband Louis Leakey were both experienced **archaeologists**, scientists who study **artifacts**, which are objects left behind by humans or human ancestors. Together with a team of native East Africans, they had spent the past twenty-five years hunting for artifacts among the rocks of the Olduvai (OHL-duh-WAY) Gorge, a 30-mile-long (48.3 km) gash in the earth on Africa's windswept Serengeti Plain.

On that day in July 1959, Mary Leakey noticed what looked like "a scrap of bone" half buried in the dirt. "I carefully brushed away a little of the deposit, and then I could see parts of two large teeth in place in the upper jaw," she later recalled. "Though we were not immediately aware of it, the whole nature of our research was about to alter drastically, and we ourselves were going to be profoundly affected."

Over the next months, the Leakeys worked painstakingly to reconstruct a nearly complete skull from more than four hundred fragments and **fossils**, the remains or traces of living organisms preserved in the earth's crust

Key Questions

- How do historians, archaeologists, and other researchers reconstruct prehistory?

- Why are scholars' conclusions about the distant past tentative?

- What are the most widely accepted theories on when and where the earliest humans lived and how they migrated?

Eastern Africa holds clues to humanity's early history.

Archaeologists Louis and Mary Leakey search for clues to humanity's distant past.

A modern-day paleontologist performs a CT (computerized tomography) scan to learn more about a Neanderthal skull.

over long periods of time. The task was much like putting together a jigsaw puzzle. That's a big part of what archaeologists like the Leakeys do—discover and assemble pieces of the puzzle of the past.

Archaeologists provide some of the evidence that helps historians understand the distant past. Other evidence comes from **paleontologists**, who study the fossil remains of ancient animals and plants. Historians also turn to **anthropologists**, who study human **culture**, a people's way of living, including their knowledge, beliefs, and values. As historians piece together a picture of humanity's distant past, the picture can change when scientists discover new puzzle pieces and offer new interpretations of the evidence.

Dating Prehistory

The small piece of fossilized bone that Mary Leakey discovered in 1959 turned out to be nearly two million years old. Scientists use a number of modern technologies to determine the age of artifacts. For example, radiocarbon dating, developed in the late 1940s, allows scientists to estimate the age of fossils from about a thousand to fifty thousand years old by measuring the quantity of carbon-14 atoms, which are known to decay at a constant rate.

For older fossils, archaeologists can use a variety of methods, including paleomagnetic dating, which examines mineral evidence of changes in the earth's magnetic field. Potassium-argon dating allows scientists to measure the rate of decay of atoms in volcanic rock. And now, scientists can analyze human DNA, the molecular blueprint of life, to track evolutionary changes over time. Together, these technologies have given those who investigate prehistory new ways to answer their questions about human origins.

Ancient Hominids: Human Ancestors

In 1974, fifteen years after Mary Leakey's discovery, another alert archaeologist was working in a parched portion of Ethiopia in eastern Africa. After a disappointing day of fossil hunting, Donald Johanson spotted a fossilized human-like elbow. It turned out to be a small part of a nearly complete skeleton belonging to an ancient female **hominid**, that is, a member of a family of beings that includes modern humans and many ancient human ancestors. Later, as Johanson and his team were celebrating the discovery, music was playing, including a song by the popular rock band, The Beatles. From the title of the song, "Lucy in the Sky with Diamonds," the roughly three-million-year-old skeleton got her nickname, Lucy.

From the shape of Lucy's leg bones and pelvis, investigators could determine that she walked on two legs. Yet her brain was relatively small. Lucy may have been a direct ancestor of modern humans or just a cousin on a branch of the family tree. She belonged to the hominid species *Australopithecus afarensis*, which scientists think roamed Africa beginning about four million years ago.

Scientists are not sure if *A. afarensis* or some other species gave rise to a new group of hominids with a bigger brain, a quicker gait, and agile hands. Scientists call this new group *Homo*, which means "man," a term that includes all of us.

Fossil footprints found in East Africa indicate that a human-like primate walked there more than three million years ago.

The Handy Man

An early species of *Homo* lived near a salty lake in what is today an African desert. Long ago, fresh-water rivers ran into that lake, attracting ancestors of modern animals such as gazelles, rhinos, and elephants. The area also attracted human ancestors who resembled *Australopithecus* but had a higher, rounder forehead, a less protruding face, and a smaller jaw.

One of these hominids died beside that giant lake about two million years ago, and was unearthed in the early 1970s by Richard Leakey, Mary and Louis Leakey's son. Scientists had already coined a name for the new species, *Homo habilis*, or "handy man," because of their ability to make tools by chipping at stones to create a sharp edge.

That simple technology gave *Homo habilis* a major advantage, allowing them to kill and butcher large animals and add meat to their diet. Many experts believe that members of *Homo habilis* formed some of the first organized social groups by working together to hunt wild game.

Homo Erectus

Scientists have identified another group that lived after *Homo habilis*, called *Homo erectus*, which means "upright man." Skeletal remains suggest that these hominids walked fully upright and first appeared about 1.8 million years ago. Like other hominids, *Homo erectus* appears to have originated in Africa. Scientists think that from Africa they moved north into Asia and Europe, perhaps in response to changes in their environment.

With a bigger brain, *Homo erectus* created a variety of stone tools, including hand axes, cleavers, scrapers, and sharp-bladed knives. They lived in caves or built simple shelters and hunted big game. They made a great step forward when they learned how to use fire. Fire provided protection, warmth, and a way to cook meat. It would also come in handy for later hominids.

The Neanderthals

Neanderthals (nee-AN-dur-TAWLZ)—named for the Neander Valley in Germany, where their fossil remains were discovered in 1856—flourished in Europe for about two hundred thousand years. Neanderthals had stout bodies suited to the cold. Contrary to comic book caricatures, they were not dull, clumsy hunchbacks. Their brains were about the same size as ours. They were skilled big-game hunters who used a wide variety of stone tools, and they crafted shells and stones into jewelry. Neanderthals lived across Europe and as far east as central Asia.

When archaeologists unearthed a Neanderthal boy who died about seventy thousand years ago, they found his body lying in a grave surrounded by six pairs of goat horns, perhaps placed there by his family and friends. Some archaeologists think that such a careful funeral arrangement indicates a concern among Neanderthals for spiritual matters, perhaps even a belief in a soul and an afterlife.

By about twenty-eight thousand years ago, Neanderthals had disappeared completely. Maybe they couldn't survive the rapid swings in temperature that accompanied the last ice age. Perhaps other hominids took over Neanderthal hunting grounds. Whatever the reasons, by about thirty thousand years ago, Neanderthals were all but gone, replaced by a newcomer who was taller and better suited to **adapt**, or adjust, to a changing environment. This newcomer was the latest and most successful hominid—our own subspecies, *Homo sapiens*, which means "wise man."

Homo Sapiens

Modern-day humans belong to the species *Homo sapiens*. For many years, scientists thought that Neanderthals were a subspecies of *Homo sapiens*. Recent genetic tests of a Neanderthal skeleton, however, have led most scientists to consider Neanderthals close ancestors of modern humans but a separate species.

Ice Ages

From a variety of evidence, scientists have concluded that during the last 570 million years, the climate of the earth has gone back and forth between warm periods and cool periods. The cooler periods are called ice ages because glaciers (huge sheets of ice) covered large areas of the planet. Ice ages have sometimes lasted several million years. The last major ice age, which began about two million years ago and ended about eleven to twelve thousand years ago, is often called "*the* Ice Age." During this time, glaciers repeatedly advanced over much of northern Europe, North America, South America, and parts of Asia.

This reconstruction of an early human hunter—a Cro-Magnon man—is based on remains discovered in France.

We know about prehistoric *Homo sapiens* from the artifacts they left behind. One population of early humans is called *Cro-Magnon*, after a rock shelter near a village in southwestern France where archaeologists first discovered their remains. Evidence suggests that Cro-Magnons lived in small groups, or clans, of twenty to thirty extended family members.

Cro-Magnons lived as **hunter-gatherers**. The men formed hunting groups and the women foraged for nuts, roots, berries, and seeds. They lived in caves or simple huts and wore tunics made of hides or fur. They worked bones into slender needles and carved antlers into spearheads. They chipped flint into specialized blades and chisels.

Cro-Magnons also used fire to harden spear tips and cook food. They built stone fire pits around which clan members could gather—perhaps to plan the next hunt, explain the moon

Cave Paintings in Lascaux

One day in September 1940, four boys ran through the woods near the town of Montignac in southwest France. Suddenly their small dog disappeared into a crack in the ground. The boys went after the dog, squeezing into the narrow crevice. The crevice opened into a cave. Lighting matches, the boys saw images of bulls, stags, and horses painted in red, brown, and black on the cave walls. The boys had stumbled upon the largest collection of prehistoric art yet discovered in the world.

The Lascaux Caves stretch more than 325 feet (99 m) underground and include more than 1,500 drawings and 600 realistic paintings. These artworks were created over a span of 5,000 years, beginning more than 15,000 years ago. While the Lascaux cave paintings are among the most famous, Stone Age people around the world painted on cave walls. The efforts of these prehistoric artists provide a wealth of information about how the earliest humans lived.

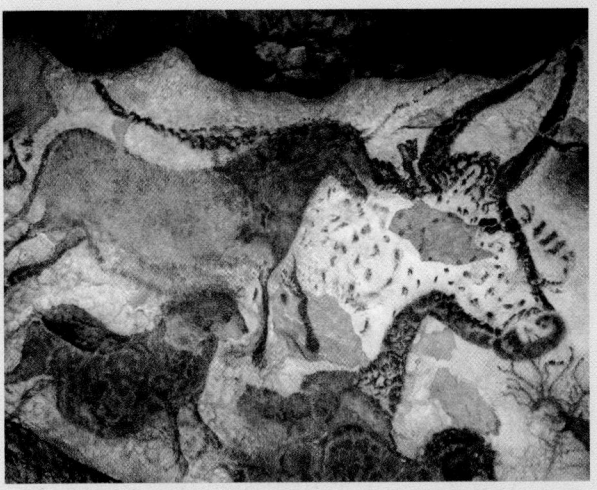

Ancient paintings of horses and a great bull adorn the wall of a cave in southwestern France.

and stars, or tell stories. Cro-Magnons also found time for artistic expression. They carved figures out of stone and ivory, and they painted animals and symbols on the walls of caves.

Out of Africa?

When and where did modern humans first appear? Some scientists have suggested a **multiregional** theory, which states that modern humans evolved independently in various parts of the world. Most scientists, however, now agree that the evidence supports the **out-of-Africa theory**, which states that the earliest *Homo sapiens* originated in Africa and then migrated to other parts of the world.

As recently as the year 2000, investigators of prehistory vigorously debated these two theories. But the data currently available—including very recent archaeological finds, new studies of human anatomy, and persuasive evidence from DNA analysis—has led most scholars to support the idea of humanity's African origins.

The Neolithic Revolution

The hunter-gatherers who used stone tools and mastered the use of fire lived in an era of prehistory called the **Paleolithic period**, or the Old Stone Age, which lasted from about 2,000,000 B.C. to about 11,000 B.C. Beginning about 11,000 B.C., the Old Stone Age gradually gave way to the New Stone Age, or the **Neolithic period**, when stone tools were increasingly used for farming.

Key Questions

- Why did some early peoples make the transition from hunter-gatherers to pastoral and agricultural societies?
- What kinds of changes occurred as people settled in one place to farm?

The Agricultural Revolution

Over the long course of human history, there are key turning points when life changed so dramatically that the impact is still felt today. These moments of dramatic change are often described as **revolutions**. One such revolution occurred during the Paleolithic period when, more than a million years ago, human ancestors first learned to make use of fire.

As the Ice Age ended around 11,000 B.C., the Paleolithic period gave way to the Neolithic. As the glaciers retreated, changes in climate created changes in the life patterns of Neolithic people. In western Europe, for example, hunters who for centuries had fed their clans by following massive herds of reindeer found the game increasingly scarce as the global temperature warmed.

To adapt and survive, these people had to find new sources of food. Groups in some parts of the world made innovations so dramatic that historians call it the **Neolithic Revolution**. The Neolithic Revolution is also referred to as the **agricultural revolution**. It marked a great shift, as humans turned from hunting and gathering to farming—from food getting to food producing.

The Beginnings of Agriculture

Great changes seldom take place all at once. The agricultural revolution was more of a series of hits and misses than a single event. Human beings were not hunters and gatherers one day, then farmers and herders the next. That change took place very slowly and almost always near river valleys, where the first producers of food had a helping hand from Mother Nature.

The first people to produce food were probably women. Well before 8000 B.C. in the Middle East, women learned to cut the wheat and barley grasses growing wild along the hillsides. Next, the women made an important discovery. They learned that if they let some of the ripe grain seeds drop to the ground, more grasses would grow in that place the next year. Eventually, the women learned that they could sow those seeds in fields where such grasses did not usually grow. Using sharp-pointed digging sticks, they could break the ground and plant the seeds. With plentiful water and good luck, they could harvest the life-giving grain to make bread or porridge at season's end.

Keeping Track of the Years

Various initials can be used to designate dates. The initials B.C. ("before Christ," that is, before the birth of Jesus) are interchangeable with B.C.E. ("before the common, or current, era"). The initials A.D. (*anno Domini*, Latin for "in the year of the Lord") are interchangeable with C.E. ("common era" or "current era"). The bigger the number B.C., the earlier the date; thus, 1500 B.C. is earlier than 150 B.C.

This new endeavor—deliberately planting seeds—was the beginning of the agricultural revolution. Agriculture was a momentous change indeed. It meant that human beings were beginning to control their physical environment.

People soon tried to improve the way they farmed, expanding the areas they could plant. For example, some farmers learned that fire could help them grow more grain. They cleared land by cutting trees, bushes, and grass, and then burning them. The remaining ashes left the soil rich in nutrients. This kind of farming is called slash-and-burn agriculture, and it helped early people maintain fertile soil.

The first farmers used simple wooden sticks to plant their crops. People soon invented new tools, including sharp-bladed hoes of wood or stone. The growth of farming also led to advances in pottery. Early humans learned to make clay jars and storage containers to stockpile the grain harvest. Farming also led to new human relationships, because growing enough crops to feed an entire clan required cooperation and organization.

Domesticating Animals

With the development of agriculture, the human population grew, thriving on plentiful harvests of wheat and barley. But the area around the grain fields was not good for wild animals. When people cleared a piece of land, the gazelles, red deer, wild boar, and goats that once roamed there lost much of their natural food supply, and so they moved on. As time passed, hunters found fewer and fewer animals to hunt. Hunting had always required great skill. Now hunters needed even greater skill if they wanted to eat meat.

Some men chose to remain hunters, and they followed the animals into different regions. Other men, however, began to share in the work of agriculture. For many, farming was a more reliable way to get food than hunting. Still others began to catch some of the wild animals that had stayed behind. Instead of killing them, they *domesticated* them—they tamed the animals and kept them in herds.

Like agriculture, the domestication of animals was another significant change in human history. By keeping a small herd of goats, sheep, or cattle, people could be sure of having meat

Where Is the Middle East?

The area that today is known as the Middle East is situated at the crossroads of three continents—Europe, Asia, and Africa.

The "Middle East" is a general and unofficial label. It is usually considered to include the extensive region that stretches from Turkey in the north to Yemen in the south, and from Egypt in the west to Iran in the east.

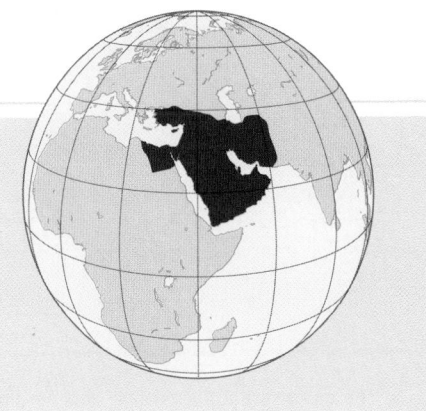

close at hand. As these early herders watched the tame goats and cattle feed their young with milk, they learned to milk the goats and cattle. They learned to use the sheep's woolly skin to make clothing.

In some places, the wolves that traveled along with people, scavenging bones and growling over scraps, became less fierce with each generation. Tamed descendants of those wild wolves became dogs. Domesticated dogs accompanied people on hunts, providing companionship and a way to ward off enemies.

Agriculture Around the World

It took time for people to become farmers, and that transformation occurred at different times under different environmental conditions around the world. As early as 40,000 B.C., foragers in the African rain forest may have planted and harvested yams simply by cutting the top off the plant and burying it in the soil. However, true agriculture—the purposeful act of planting seeds and then cultivating and harvesting the plants—is thought to have originated in the Middle East about twelve thousand years ago, when the first farmers cultivated wheat and barley.

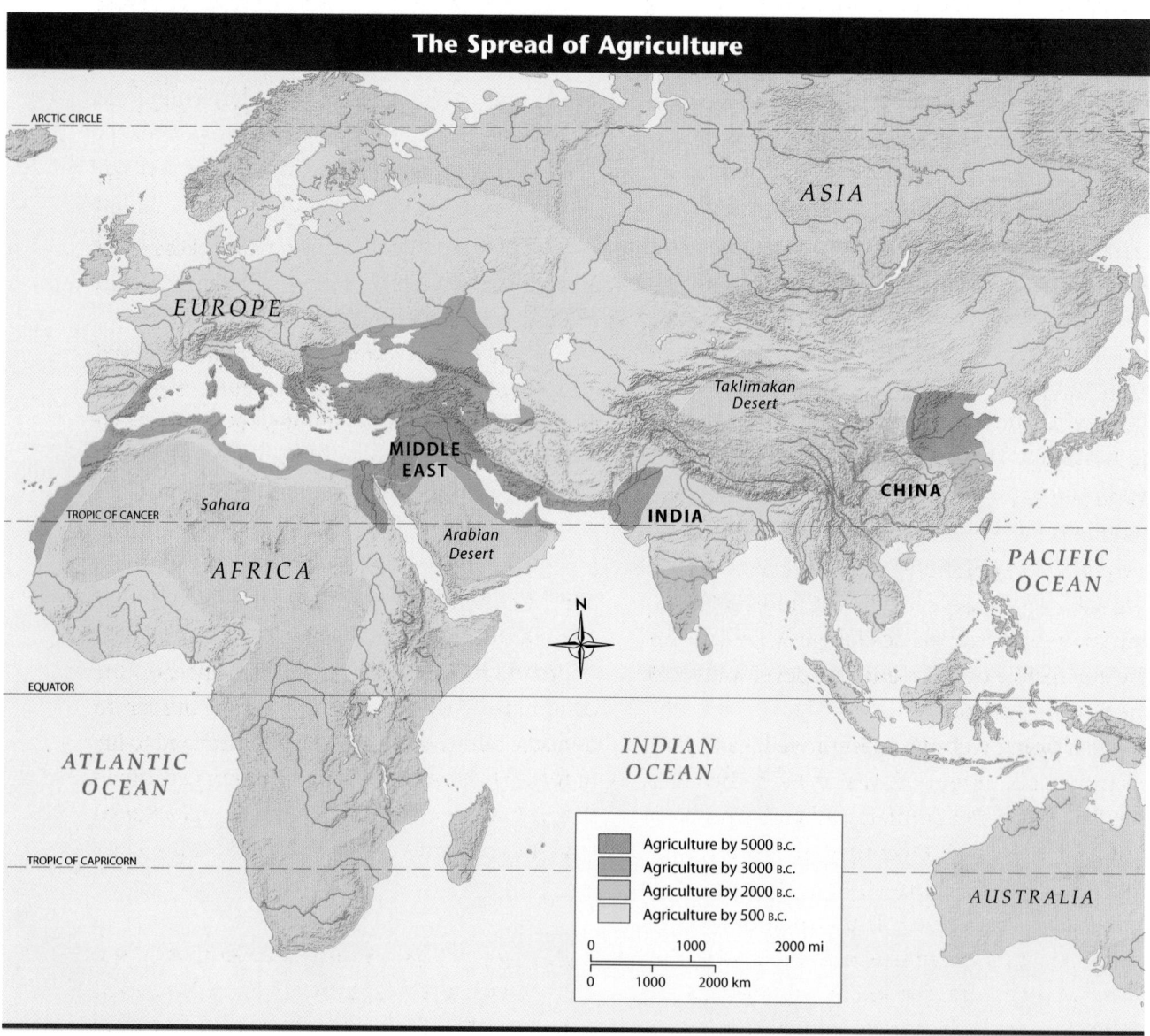

The Spread of Agriculture

Agriculture by 5000 B.C.
Agriculture by 3000 B.C.
Agriculture by 2000 B.C.
Agriculture by 500 B.C.

The rapid spread of farming and herding made it possible for large numbers of people to live in permanent settlements with a dependable food supply.

In recent years, archaeologists have excavated the sites of early human settlements, many of them in caves, where they have found seeds, pieces of rinds, plant stems, and other evidence of farming. New technologies allow scientists to date these remnants of the past. Findings in a cave in Oaxaca, Mexico, for example, suggest that people were farming there about ten thousand years ago.

In Asia, sometime before 6000 B.C., farmers cultivated rice in fertile valleys along major rivers in what is now China. Agriculture also developed independently in the Americas, where, beginning around 8000 B.C., early farmers cultivated sweet potatoes, chili peppers, beans, and maize (corn).

By about 3000 B.C., agriculture was common in many parts of the world. There were farmers in Europe, along the northern coast of Africa, and also in India and China. Nearly all these farmers planted along the banks of rivers or in fertile valleys watered by springs.

Agriculture Brings Great Changes

With the rise of agriculture, humans now had the power to transform nature for their own benefit. As once-nomadic hunter-gatherers began to rely more and more on farming, some settled down and built the first villages near their fields. As the revolution in agriculture rolled forward, it brought changes to almost every aspect of human life. You will soon learn how these changes would lead to the emergence of cities and the development of the first civilizations.

As farming techniques improved, early farmers produced more food, which led to healthier populations, higher birthrates, and more people to cultivate more land. Over time, these early farmers produced a **surplus**—that is, they produced more than they needed. The surplus of food left some men and women free to do other jobs. They no longer had to till the soil or tend herds. Some people focused their attention on making pottery, others on weaving baskets. Some made bricks of dried mud and used them to build houses.

The invention c. 5000 B.C. of the wooden plow, depicted in this sculpture, was a great step forward for farming.

Human beings were beginning to divide the work. Everyone did something important, but not everyone had to do the same thing. This **division of labor** led to higher productivity and larger surpluses.

In farming communities, social roles changed according to gender and age. Over time, men took over most of the work of farming, especially after the invention of a heavy wooden plow around 5000 B.C. Women were the principal caregivers for young children because most of their tasks kept women closer to home, where they turned milk into cheese or yogurt, collected eggs, or wove fabric to make clothes.

Young children and the elderly members of the community—who would have been a burden to nomadic hunter-gatherers—also contributed to life in the early farming villages. Children performed simple but helpful tasks, while older folks shared wisdom and kept vital skills and traditions alive.

Early Village Life

Archaeologists have found the remains of several settlements dating from the Neolithic period. Around 7000 B.C., in the southern part of what is now Turkey, thousands of people settled in the village of Çatalhüyük (chah-TAHL-hoo-YOOK).

Dwellings in Jericho, as depicted in this model, were constructed of mud bricks, straw, and branches.

The people lived in hundreds of closely packed rectangular dwellings made of mud brick. Archaeologists have unearthed the remains of shrines with paintings on the walls. These paintings suggest that the people of Çatalhüyük engaged in religious practices.

An even older settlement, Jericho, sits near a natural spring a few miles from the Jordan River (near what is now the city of Jerusalem). Today, Jericho is a city of twenty thousand inhabitants. In 10,000 B.C., humans camped by the waters of the spring to harvest wild grains. The fertile soil around the spring proved well suited to agriculture, and by 9000 B.C., nearly a thousand people occupied the site. They lived in more than seventy mud-brick dwellings. Their village was surrounded by a large stone wall. The existence of the wall suggests that the people of Jericho had a leader or governing body that could organize such a large-scale building project.

Though spread far and wide, these early farming villages shared knowledge and technology with each other, giving rise to early systems of trade. The farmers of Çatalhüyük, for example, grew varieties of crops from hundreds of miles away and made tools from stones they could not obtain locally—evidence of trade with distant regions. The people of Jericho used obsidian (a dark volcanic glass) from Turkey, turquoise from Sinai, and seashell ornaments from the Red Sea. Meanwhile, a **pastoral** people who tended flocks of goats and sheep founded Jarmo, a cluster of two dozen mud huts in the foothills of what is now northeastern Iraq, using building

Pastoral people are shepherds or herdsmen whose lives depend on their flocks.

techniques pioneered by people living many hundreds of miles away.

Trade and interaction between villages led to greater knowledge, refined technologies, and larger populations. This interchange helped set the stage for the first human civilizations to develop in a land between two rivers.

Mesopotamia: The Land Between the Rivers

A large swath of land stretches from the eastern shores of the Mediterranean Sea in the west to the Persian Gulf in the east. In this region, called the **Fertile Crescent**, the land and climate favored agriculture, which encouraged the growth of new settlements.

The eastern half of the Fertile Crescent is dominated by two great rivers, the Tigris (TIY-gruhs) and Euphrates (yoo-FRAY-teez). Both rivers have

The Euphrates River and rich soil drew a growing population to the land near the waterway.

Sumer and the Fertile Crescent

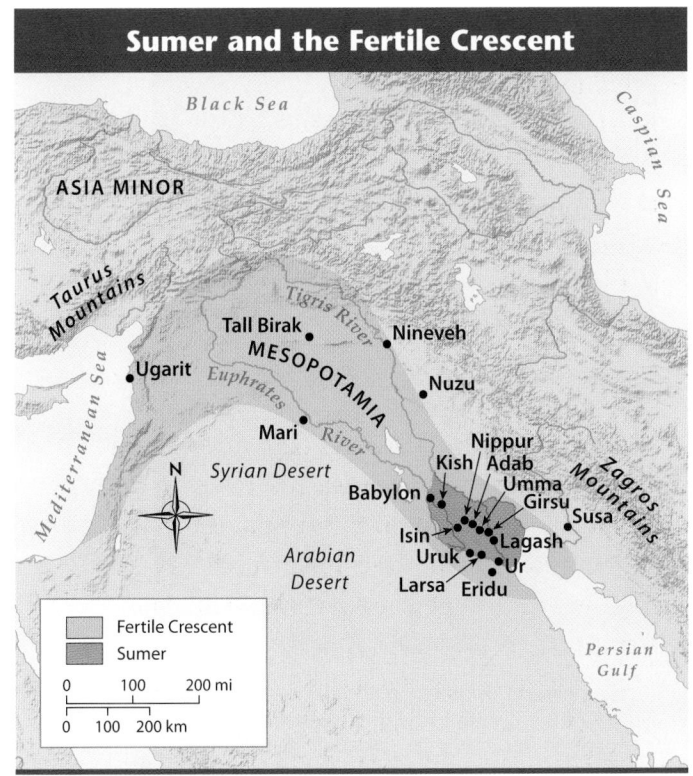

In Mesopotamia, the first cities arose on fertile river plains, surrounded by deserts and mountains.

their sources in the rugged mountains of southern Turkey. From there they meander for more than a thousand miles to the Persian Gulf.

Ancient Greek travelers gave a name to the region between the Tigris and Euphrates. They called it Mesopotamia, from Greek words that mean "between the rivers."

The land between the rivers was a floodplain. Every year in the spring, as snows from the surrounding mountains melted, the rivers flooded. The receding floodwaters deposited a layer of silt—nutrient-rich sand and soil that is excellent for planting—along the riverbanks. Since some of the low-lying land was swampy, many kinds of waterfowl and fish lived there. That made for good hunting. Such abundance attracted a growing population to the river valleys.

Irrigating the Land

Nobody knows for sure when people first inhabited Mesopotamia. By 5800 B.C., farming communities had been established along channels carved out by

the Euphrates. To survive, the people of the farming villages of Mesopotamia had to work together to overcome many obstacles posed by the natural world. To coax crops out of the land, inhabitants had to control the rivers' floodwaters. Year after year, as the floodwaters receded, the silt built up on the riverbanks to form natural levees (LEH-veez), or banks of soil. The people learned to build up these natural levees. They worked with their neighbors to make the levees higher and stronger to protect the fields from severe spring floods.

In the land of southern Mesopotamia, known in ancient times as Sumer (SOO-mur), the people enjoyed rich soil, but they needed more water. If they planted wheat and barley in the fall, winter rains would help, but even those rains were not enough. When crops needed additional water in the winter, farmers could poke holes in the levees to let the water pour out, and then dig little channels in the earth to guide the water to their crops. As the years passed, the men and women of Sumer dug bigger channels to carry more water. Eventually, the channels became canals that ran for miles, bringing water from the levees to the crops. This way of bringing water to the land is called **irrigation**.

As his ancestors did long ago, this farmer uses irrigation ditches—and the Euphrates River—to water his dry fields.

15

The Decline of Hunter-Gatherers

As agriculture caught on, many formerly nomadic people settled down to a sedentary life—that is, they remained in one place. While most people settled down, hunting and gathering as a way of life did not disappear entirely. Until the late 1800s, some native peoples of North America lived by hunting bison. In the far north, native Inuit people still hunt whales, seals, and fish. In the Amazon region of South America, the Txicao people continue to exist as hunter-gatherers. Groups of hunter-gatherers also persist in portions of southern Africa and in parts of Australia. The hunter-gatherer way of life became more difficult to maintain as the size and number of farming communities reduced the land available to wild animal and plant life.

A cave painting of bowmen and deer, c. 9000 B.C., illustrates the hunting way of life.

Irrigation provided the key to successful farming in Mesopotamia, where the soil was rich but little rain fell. Because of irrigation, the Sumerians (soo-MEHR-ee-uhnz) did not have to depend entirely on rain to water their crops. The effort to construct a system of canals required cooperation and organization, the roots of government.

Sumer: From Villages to the First Cities

The towns of Sumer grew rapidly between 4500 and 4000 B.C. Large farming villages absorbed smaller settlements. The largest towns developed around temples overseen by priests who made offerings to various deities in hopes of ensuring good harvests. Surrounding the temple were clusters of mud-brick houses. Farther away, closer to the fields, lived the farmers who grew the crops on which the entire town depended.

In Sumer, the agricultural revolution led to an advanced, complex civilization. In time, the towns of Sumer grew to become the first cities. Eridu, in what is now Iraq, boasted a massive temple complex in its city center. Uruk covered more than six hundred acres, with a dense tangle of houses and narrow alleyways surrounding the temple, plus a number of outlying villages many miles away, each with its own irrigation system.

Other cities dotted the irrigated lowlands near the place where the Tigris and Euphrates approached the Persian Gulf. Sometimes fighting, sometimes cooperating, and always eager to trade with each other, these cities in Sumer became the world's first civilization.

Civilization Begins in Sumer

By 3200 B.C., the patchwork of urban centers and their surrounding farming communities in lower Mesopotamia formed a recognizable civilization known as Sumer. The English word *civilization* comes from the Latin *civitas*, which means "city." Though definitions vary, historians and other scholars generally agree on the features that are common to all civilizations:

- City life, with complex social organizations
- Trade and economic activity, which encourage innovation and spread knowledge
- Governance, through which social order is maintained
- Division of labor, in which different people take on specialized tasks
- Record keeping of some kind

Together, these characteristics may have developed first in Sumer, but they are displayed by every civilization everywhere.

Key Questions

- What are the essential conditions that define a people as a *civilization*?
- How does civilization differ from other kinds of social organization?
- Where did the first civilizations begin?

A Network of Trade

Lower Mesopotamia lacked natural resources apart from the clay that people used to build their dwellings. But Sumerian farmers grew a surplus of grain, and this surplus gave Sumerians the ability to obtain what they needed through trade, especially stones, metals, and wood.

Sumerian trading ships, made of animal skins sewn tightly around a wooden frame, sailed south down the rivers to the open sea, hugging the coastline toward trading posts on the Persian Gulf. These ships, laden with many tons of grain, might return with a load of copper, or with gold and precious stones from a thousand miles away in Turkey, or with bright blue lapis lazuli, popular among well-to-do Sumerians, from faraway Afghanistan.

Sumerians also traded by land, bringing supplies of timber hundreds of miles from Lebanon. Eventually Sumer found itself in the middle of an active economic network—over land, rivers, and sea—that stretched from the Indus Valley in the east to the Nile River in the west, and as far north as the Black Sea.

A bull's head of gold and lapis lazuli, c. 2500 B.C., from the city of Ur

New Ideas and Inventions

The cities of Sumer exchanged more than goods. Along the networks of trade flowed new ideas.

It was probably Sumerian artisans, or skilled workers, who, sometime around 3500 B.C., first used the wheel to make pottery. It was not until a few hundred years later that someone attached a wheel to a wagon or cart. Until then, Sumerians had hitched animals to large sleds to move cargo over dusty land. The wheel transformed land travel and gave Sumerians a new way to move imports and exports over great distances.

Because lower Mesopotamia had no naturally occurring metals, Sumerians had long imported copper, gold, and raw ore from lands that today are Turkey and Iran. By about 3000 B.C., Sumerians had become experts at combining copper with tin to produce a new metal that changed the world, bronze. Bronze was harder and more durable than simple copper, and easier to forge into tools. With bronze the Sumerians could make better farming implements, including tougher plows, which led to larger harvests. The new metal was also used to make jewelry, ceremonial objects, and, perhaps most significant, weapons and armor. The era when people began to use bronze rather than stone to make tools and weapons is called the **Bronze Age**. The Bronze Age, which began in Sumer in about 3000 B.C., started later in other parts of Asia and Europe.

A small bronze chariot shows the use of wheels c. 2600 B.C. The wheel greatly improved travel for the Sumerians.

Social Structure in Sumer

As the cities of Sumer grew, so did the number of mud-brick dwellings that surrounded the temple. Some homes were almost palaces—two stories tall with a half-dozen rooms, constructed around open, airy courtyards. Most Sumerian dwellings, however, were little more than clay huts. As the population of the cities increased, houses grew more cramped. Alleyways became narrower and dirtier. Pigs and dogs rooted through garbage dumped in the streets. Because no sewer system existed, people faced illness or death from polluted water.

By 2500 B.C., among the thousands of people who lived in cities in lower Mesopotamia, only a small portion enjoyed the benefits of prosperity. A **social hierarchy** (HIY-uh-rahr-kee) developed, in which a few wealthy and powerful people formed an upper class of society, while most other people fell into the lower classes. In the social hierarchy of Sumer, a select few benefited from the hard work of the many.

> A *hierarchy* is a system of organizing people or things within ranked groups.

At the very top of the social hierarchy was the king, a ruler who might govern one Sumerian city or many. The king was often a military conqueror who had forcibly taken control of key trade routes.

Below the king were the priests, who led temple rituals and worship of the gods. Then came wealthy landowners, the upper-class folks who lived in the big homes near the temple and wore gold and jewels to display their wealth. Soldiers, merchants, and skilled artisans occupied the next level of the Sumerian social hierarchy. Last came free laborers, the majority of the people. Free laborers worked in the fields growing crops, usually beside the landowner's slaves. Together, they did most of the work that made civilization run.

At the very bottom of the Sumerian social hierarchy were the slaves. People captured in war usually became slaves, but individuals could also be sold into slavery, sometimes by parents who were deeply in debt. People could also become slaves if they did not repay loans, or if they were born to slaves. In many Sumerian cities, slave women

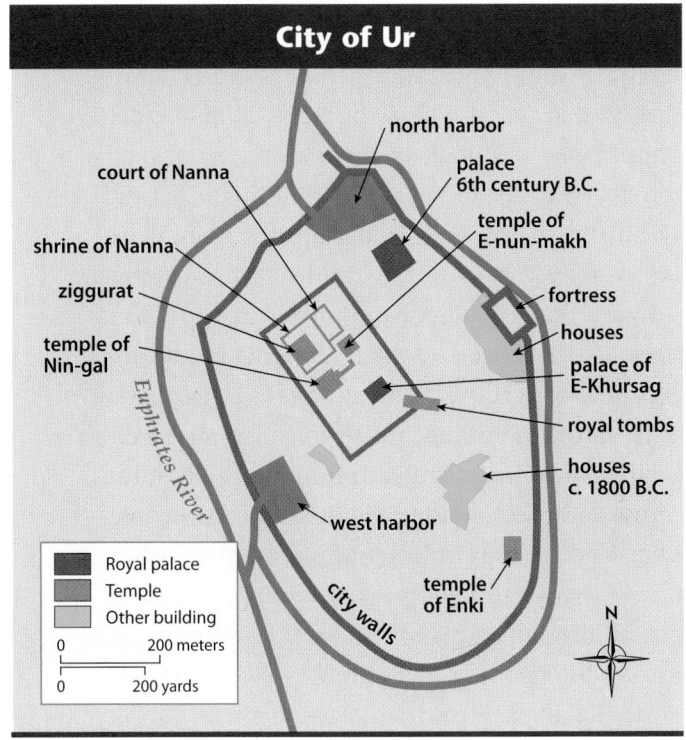

City of Ur

north harbor
court of Nanna
palace
6th century B.C.
temple of
E-nun-makh
shrine of Nanna
ziggurat
fortress
temple of
Nin-gal
houses
palace of
E-Khursag
royal tombs
houses
c. 1800 B.C.
west harbor
Euphrates River
temple
of Enki
city walls
N

- Royal palace
- Temple
- Other building

0   200 meters
0   200 yards

produced the cloth that Sumerian traders sold for profit. Although some slaves managed to purchase their own freedom, and a few obtained positions of power, most lived desperate lives. They could be bought and sold at any moment, beaten, and sometimes killed.

Religion in Sumer: Worshipping Many Deities

Regardless of where they lived, early humans viewed the natural world as a place full of powerful spirits and magical beings. Early people lived among dangerous wild animals and under constant threat from storms, floods, and natural disasters. In response, they explained the world by filling it with strange and mysterious powers. Over time, people came to think of these powers as gods or goddesses in human or animal form.

The people of Sumer practiced **polytheism**—that is, they worshipped many deities, or gods and goddesses. They believed the gods controlled every aspect of life, from making bricks to milling grain. In the minds of the Sumerians, their gods were immortal but looked and acted like humans, with human weaknesses and desires. The gods

could be kind or cruel. They could bring victory in war or a bountiful harvest. Or they could make human beings miserable with disease, drought, famine, and floods.

The Sumerians thought their role was to serve the gods, just as slaves served their masters. To understand what the gods had in store for humanity, Sumerian priests looked to the stars, the sun, and the moon for clues, a practice that gave rise to the study of astronomy. Sumerian kings used belief in the gods to justify their authority.

Ziggurats: Temples to the Gods

Each Sumerian city had its own special god or goddess who was believed to provide protection and prosperity. The temple, the home of the city's god, was called a **ziggurat** (ZIH-guh-rat). In the most powerful Sumerian cities, ziggurats were high, terraced pyramids, with each story smaller than the one below. Without much available stone or timber, the Sumerians used sun-dried mud bricks for the core and baked brick for the exterior of their ziggurats.

Some Sumerian Deities

An	the chief god who presided over all others
Enlil	the supreme ruler who sent a flood to destroy humankind, and who took An's place as chief god
Nanna	the god of the moon, the master of the months and seasons
Inanna	(later called Ishtar) the goddess of both love and war
Shamash	the god of the sun, and the source of justice
Ninhursag	"Mother Earth," the source of life
Enki	"Lord Earth," the god of earth and water
Nergal	the god of the underworld

One hundred mud-brick steps lead up the great ziggurat in Ur, built c. 2100 B.C. to honor the moon god Nanna.

Three long staircases led to the temple at the very top. There, high above the din of business activity that surrounded the ziggurat, and flanked by temple slaves bearing the finest food—fish, mutton, honey, cakes—the priests offered gifts to the gods with hope for a good harvest.

Such enormous temples took many years to build. The great ziggurat of Ur measured about 30,000 square feet (9,144 square m) at its base, and reached as high as 120 feet (36.6 m). It could be seen for miles around, and reminded the people of Sumer that they lived only to serve the gods.

Government in Sumer

In the 1920s and 1930s, the British archaeologist Sir Leonard Woolley excavated an ancient royal cemetery in the ruins of Ur. Along with a wealth of priceless artifacts, Woolley unearthed a series of tombs belonging to powerful kings and queens of Sumer.

Buried along with the dead monarchs were their living attendants. One tomb contained the remains of fifty-nine people, each wearing official government attire, who had sat down to die in order of rank, apparently after taking a dose of poison. Elsewhere, Woolley found a wagon with the bones of a driver and the bones of oxen lying in front. He found musical instruments lying beside dead musicians, and dead soldiers still armed with copper daggers.

To understand why loyal subjects would willingly follow their kings and queens to death requires an understanding of Sumerian government. Ancient Sumer was a **theocracy** (thee-AH-kruh-see), a government ruled by a deity or, more precisely, by a human ruler who was believed to be guided by the gods. In Sumer, the king claimed to draw his authority from Enlil, the most powerful deity. The people viewed their king as an earthly representative chosen by the gods.

In the earliest years of Sumerian civilization, a different king ruled over each **city-state**, the area including the city itself as well as the fields and villages surrounding it. Over time, as some city-states made alliances and others fought bloody wars, the most powerful kings came to rule over many city-states. The king was expected to bring the favor of the gods to all the cities he controlled.

Most kings gathered a group of older men to serve as advisers. Kings also gave power to the priests and priestesses who worked in the temples. The king, along with his advisers and the priests, controlled the people by controlling agriculture and trade. Sumerian queens were revered and respected, but enjoyed no formal power. They influenced the government through their husbands and by rearing royal children.

The Invention of Writing

The most significant of all Sumerian innovations was the development of a system of writing. The invention of written language signaled the end of prehistory and ushered in a new age in human existence.

The development of writing was partly motivated by the need to record economic transactions. As early as 8000 B.C., Mesopotamian traders began using small clay tokens with distinctive shapes to keep track of grain, animals, and other

A terra-cotta tablet with Sumerian writing recorded the sale of a field and house, paid in silver.

goods. By 5000 B.C., this system had evolved into a series of **pictograms**, simple drawings representing specific things, such as a plow, a bull, or a boat.

If a harvest was good, farmers would transport their surplus crops to storehouses or sell them to merchants. Trained city officials called **scribes** created a record or a receipt by molding a small lump of raw clay into a square and scratching out some pictograms. In the hot air of Mesopotamia, the clay tablets dried quickly. Scribes also kept records, in the form of clay tablets, of the entire community's grain reserves. Archaeologists have unearthed thousands of these clay tablets, offering insight into the development of pictograms into true writing.

Over time, scribes changed the meaning of the pictograms. Instead of simply representing individual things, the pictures came to stand for categories, ideas, or actions. For example, the pictogram for "foot" could also mean "to stand." The pictograms themselves became smaller until they could be drawn with just a few simple lines. Eventually these groups of lines came to represent the sounds of language.

To write, Sumerian scribes pressed sharpened reeds into soft clay tablets, creating a series of wedgelike impressions. This method gave Sumerian writing its name, *cuneiform* (kyoo-NEE-uh-form), a Latin word meaning "wedge shaped."

Literature in Sumer: The Epic of Gilgamesh

Sumerian writing helped spread information and culture, from helpful hints for farmers to myths that explained the origins of the world. The world's earliest literature included Sumerian stories, love poems, hymns, proverbs, and, most famously, the *Epic of Gilgamesh* (GIL-guh-mesh).

An *epic* is a long poem about the deeds of a great hero or heroes.

Math in Sumer

Along with written language, Sumerians devised a method for keeping track of numbers with a system based on 60. You can still see evidence of this ancient system today. For example, modern math measures a circle as having 360 degrees (6×60), and modern clocks measure hours and minutes in increments of 60. Innovations in mathematics led to breakthroughs in other areas of Sumerian science, including astronomy, engineering, and design.

Originating as a story told aloud, *Gilgamesh* was first written down in about 2100 B.C. It tells the tale of Gilgamesh, a king in ancient Sumer who began his reign as a fierce, cruel ruler. To help the oppressed people, the gods send a wild man, Enkidu (EN-kee-doo), to Sumer.

The two men fight at first but later become best friends. They embark on a series of adventures together, and their friendship helps Gilgamesh learn to be a good king. The story was

A gold panel depicts Gilgamesh taming lions.

21

FROM THE EPIC OF GILGAMESH

Gilgamesh and Enkidu travel to the Land of the Cedars (possibly modern Lebanon) on the eastern edge of the Mediterranean Sea. With help from the gods, they vanquish their foe and return home, triumphant.

One day, the restless Gilgamesh began to worry about his fame. "I am known here, but not elsewhere," he complained to his friend Enkidu. "We will go to the Land of the Cedars and destroy the evil Watchman, and I will raise a monument with my name on it."

"That land is a forest, surrounded by a giant ravine," warned Enkidu. "The Watchman guards it from a house made of strong cedar."

"We will travel together," argued Gilgamesh. "Shamash, god of the sun, will protect us. We will also protect each other, and if we fall in battle, our names will be known forever."

So the men set out with heavy weapons. For days they journeyed, until they came to the Green Mountain where cedars spread their shade. Gilgamesh took hold of his axe and felled a towering tree. When the Watchman heard the noise from far away, he came roaring out of his house. "Who has trespassed these woods?" he bellowed.

Through miles of trees he crashed, and when he came to the place where the cedar was felled, he cast an evil eye upon Gilgamesh.

"Oh, Shamash," Gilgamesh prayed, "how will we escape?"

The god of the sun then sent thirteen winds—an ice wind, a sandstorm, a south wind, a north wind, and many more—to cover the eyes of the Watchman. Unable to see, the evil one fell under Enkidu's blows. The mountains shook, and all the trees of the forest quivered. Gilgamesh cut down the trees of the forest, while Enkidu followed behind to clear the roots. The men turned toward Uruk, victorious....

Gilgamesh gazed upon the city he had built. "These walls are strong," Gilgamesh observed. "Here is a place of well-built houses, of pleasurable gardens, and fertile fields. Here is a palace and a high temple for the gods. Long after I die," he thought, "here my deeds will live on."

Thus, Gilgamesh, the mighty king, had grown wise. He had traveled far and come to understand secret things. Upon a stone monument he engraved his story so that all might know it, and he lived as a great hero for the rest of his days.

popular in Sumer four thousand years ago for the same reasons that people enjoy good books and movies today—it explores human themes like love and friendship, and it illustrates the courage with which mortals face challenges and loss.

Sumer's Decline and Legacy

Civilization in Sumer reached its height in the third millennium B.C. By about 1700 B.C., however, the civilization that existed in lower Mesopotamia was no longer recognizably Sumerian. New civilizations in northern Mesopotamia overcame the city-states of the south, while embracing their gods and literature, as well as much of their wealth of culture, knowledge, and innovation.

> A *millennium* is a period of one thousand years.

Sumerian civilization declined for many reasons, including one that illustrates how human activities, such as agriculture, can have unintentional destructive effects on the natural environment. The water that Sumerian farmers used to irrigate their fields contained varying levels of salt. Over many centuries, as small amounts of salt accumulated, the soil was poisoned through a process known as *salinization*. Beginning as early as 2400 B.C., crops no longer grew as well in what had once been a fertile plain. Within another five hundred years, salinization led to a dramatic drop in grain production.

Much as the earliest human hunter-gatherers had sought the most productive land, the members of the first civilization were also constantly on the lookout for more productive land and more wealth. This led to conflict between the different city-states within Sumer. The rulers of the various city-states became rivals for territory. Some city-states built canals to divert water from the fields of other city-states to their own, which led to more fighting. These wars between the city-states were often long, hard, and brutal.

Even as the Sumerian city-states fought among themselves, they also faced threats from outside. Nomadic people who lived on the edges of Sumer sometimes attacked and robbed Sumerian cities. Sumer, located on the low-lying floodplain of the Tigris and Euphrates rivers, had few natural defenses, which made it easy for bands of warriors to attack.

North of Sumer in Mesopotamia, another early civilization developed in a land known as Akkad (AK-ad). By 2350 B.C., the Akkadians (uh-KAY-dee-uhnz), aided by new Bronze Age weapons, had grown powerful enough to conquer the great Sumerian cities.

Even as geographic and political changes led to the decline of Sumer, the basic model of civilization established in Sumer was taking shape in distant lands. We will see how other peoples planted and nourished the roots of civilization: city life, trade, governance, division of labor, and record keeping.

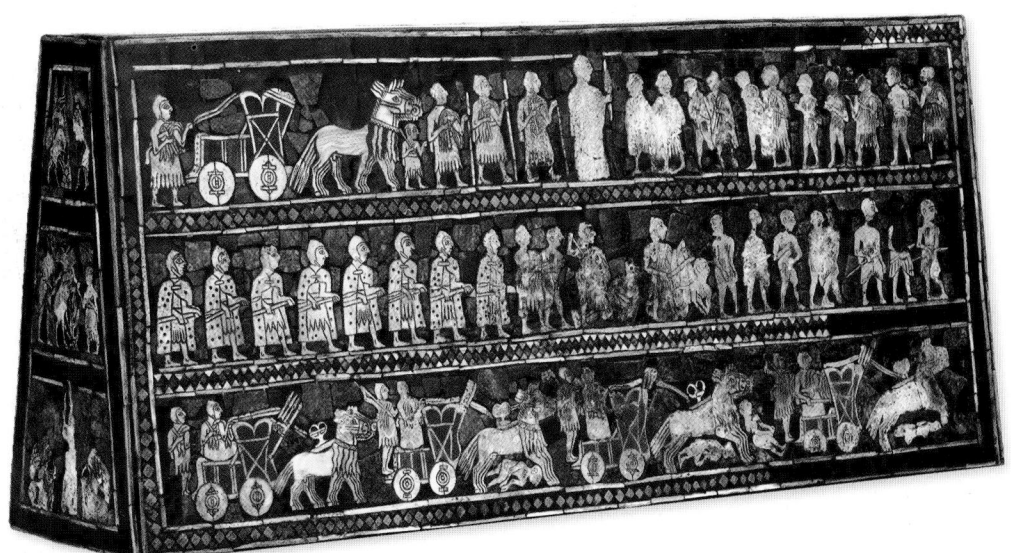

This hollow wooden box inlaid with a mosaic of shell, red limestone, and lapis lazuli is one of the earliest representations of a Sumerian army, c. 2500 B.C.

Chapter 2
Early River Valley Civilizations 3100–1000 B.C.

3000 B.C.

2500 B.C.

c. 2100 B.C.
After a period of strife,
Egypt is reunited; the
Middle Kingdom begins.

c. 3100 B.C.
Narmer unites Upper
and Lower Egypt.

Civilization emerges
in the Indus Valley.

The majestic Egyptian pyramids at Giza

1500 B.C.

1000 B.C.

c. 1700 B.C.
The Shang establish
China's first dynasty.

*T*he earliest civilizations began in river valleys where small Neolithic farming villages evolved into complex urban centers. In North Africa, the Nile Valley provided the setting for Egyptian civilization. In South Asia, civilization developed in the Indus Valley. And in East Asia, China's civilization grew along two great rivers.

In the fifth century B.C., the Greek historian Herodotus wrote that Egypt was "the gift of the Nile." By "Egypt" he meant the Nile Valley, for indeed, then as now, almost every Egyptian lived within ten miles of the river. This ancient Egyptian civilization produced a system of writing as well as wonders of architecture and art.

Our understanding of early civilization in the Indus Valley is partial because the discovery of evidence is limited and recent. Archaeological remains reveal an organized civilization with prosperous farming.

Egypt: The Gift of the Nile

The Nile is the world's longest river, flowing more than 4,000 miles (about 6,600 km) out of the east African highlands down to the Mediterranean Sea. Of those 4,000 miles, only a small portion can be easily traveled because the river has six cataracts, stretches of thundering rapids and waterfalls squeezed between steep cliffs.

Key Questions

- Why was ancient Egypt called "the gift of the Nile"?
- What are the distinguishing characteristics of ancient Egyptian culture?

The Nile River Valley

Ancient Egyptian civilization took shape along the last 650 miles (1,046 km) of the Nile, past the First Cataracts. Here, the current smooths out and the river flows between high hills in a narrow shoestring of a valley more than 500 miles (800 km) long but never more than 10 miles (16 km) wide. About 125 miles (201 km) from the sea, the river splits into several streams that fan out across a flat triangle of land made up of the silt the Nile carries so abundantly. This area is the Nile Delta. (The word *delta* comes from the triangular Greek letter Δ.)

The Attractions of the River

In ancient times, people settled along the Nile mainly because yearly floods kept spreading new layers of fertile, black silt over the land. Floods are feared in some places, but here the waters rose at the same time every

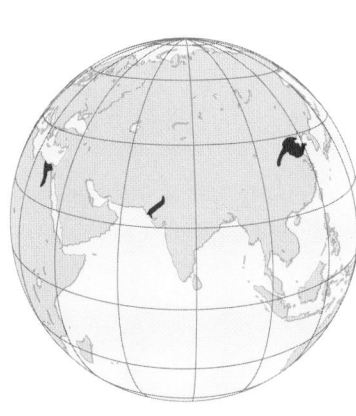

The Nile, Indus, and Huang He and Yangtze river valleys

Yearly summer floods brought rich life-giving soil to the Nile River valley.

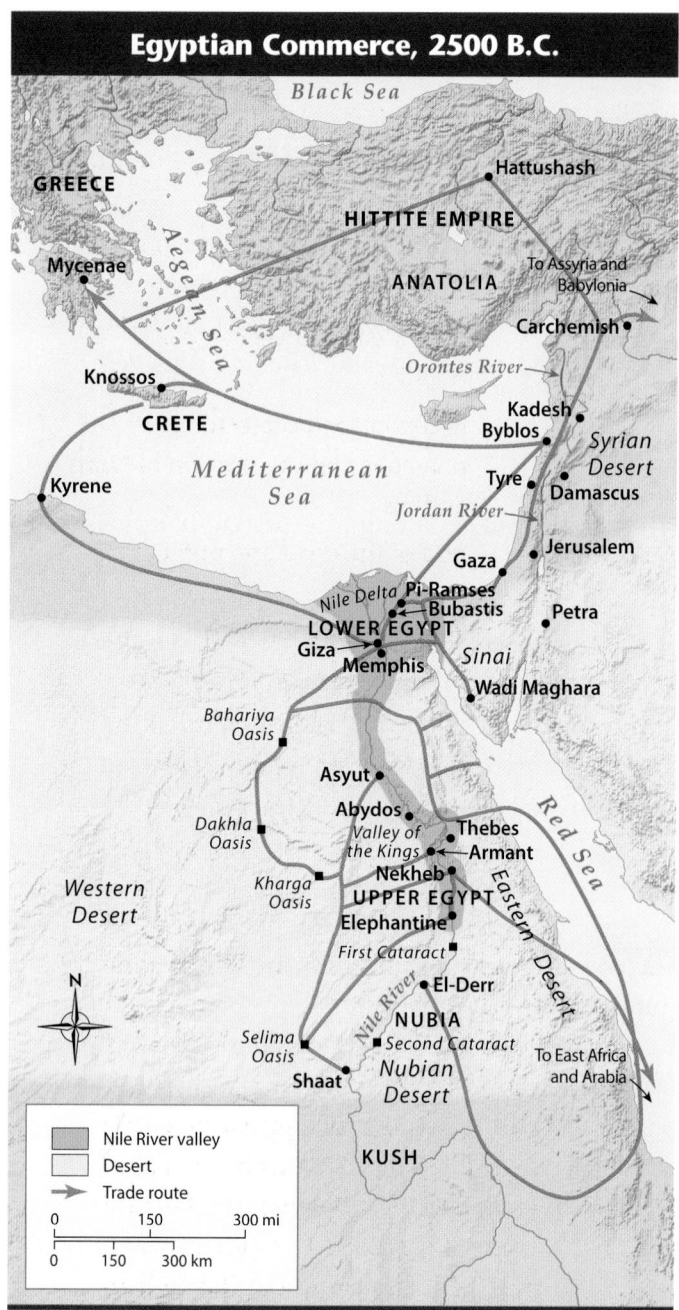

Egyptian Commerce, 2500 B.C.

Egyptian merchants traded extensively with other civilizations around the Mediterranean, along the coast of East Africa, and eastward into Babylonia.

the cataracts. The prevailing winds blew south while the current ran north, so boats could go either way by putting up or taking down sails. Up and down this watery highway, travelers and messages flowed, helping to weave the Egyptians into a unified people.

A Sheltered Valley

Unlike the settlements in Sumer, Egyptian villages had no walls because geography protected them from enemies. Deserts to the east and west of the Nile Valley discouraged invaders from attempting to cross. The First Cataracts provided a barrier against invasions from the south. Only the north lay open to the outer world, and through that portal Egyptians traded with other peoples.

Among the villages in Egypt, there was little conflict because there was little to fight over. All villages had access to the river and all were well situated for trade. Besides, food was plentiful. The river provided fish, and the fields produced barley, wheat, leeks, onions, beans, vegetables, and fruit, as well as flax from which the Egyptians made linen.

The ancient Greek historian Herodotus (hih-RAHD-uh-tuhs) wrote that the Egyptians "gather in fruit from the earth with less labor than any other men.... When the river has come up of itself...and after watering has left them again, then each man sows his own field, and turns into it swine [pigs], and when he has trodden the seed into the ground by means of the swine...he waits for the harvest."

Harnessing the Waters

Reaping the bounties of the Nile took more work than Herodotus reckoned. The Egyptians built extensive irrigation systems to manage the floodwaters. They constructed levees to hold some floodwaters in reserve, and dug canals to direct the waters through their fields.

The entire Nile Valley was a single system, so it made no sense for each village to build its own irrigation works. Villages banded together

year. The waters began to rise in June shortly after a star called Sirius appeared above the horizon. They peaked in August, and receded in September. Egyptians could plan their lives around these predictable floods. The floods brought life-giving soil for farming.

The river also provided an excellent natural transportation system, easily navigable below

to undertake shared projects. Such efforts took much coordination, so leaders and specialists emerged to organize the work. Slowly a **bureaucracy** (byur-AH-kruh-see) took shape, a hierarchy of workers with defined jobs. Managing the river therefore led Egyptians to develop a government, a writing system, and other advanced skills.

Religion in the Nile Valley

Year after year, life in the Nile Valley followed a recurring pattern: a dry season was followed by floods, which were followed by an abundant harvest. Like the Sumerians, the Egyptians owed their harvests to a flooding river and the bounty of nature. Also like the Sumerians, the Egyptians worshipped many gods—more than 1,500 gods and goddesses, most associated with elements of nature. Many were pictured as having human bodies with animal heads that expressed their main traits.

The Egyptians believed that, like people, their gods married, gave birth, ate, drank, and fought. While each village had its favorite protectors, certain deities were revered throughout the land,

Egyptian Deities

Re	god of the sun; creator of the gods
Osiris	god of the afterlife and plants; ruler of the underworld
Isis	goddess of motherhood, magic, and healing; wife of Osiris
Seth	god of chaos and evil; brother of Osiris
Horus	falcon-headed protector of pharaohs and the sky; son of Osiris and Isis
Anubis	god of the dead attempting to enter the underworld; Osiris's assistant
Wadjet	protector of Lower Egypt as a cobra; nurse to Horus
Iusas	protector of Upper Egypt as a vulture; partner of a god

such as Re (ray), the sun god, and Thoth, the god of wisdom.

Perhaps most beloved of all was Osiris (oh-SIY-rus), god of the underworld and vegetation. According to the ancient story, Osiris was killed and dismembered by his brother Seth, the god of chaos. But Isis (IY-sus), the faithful wife of Osiris and the goddess of mothering and magic, collected his parts and bandaged him together. When their son, the falcon-headed sky god Horus, defeated Seth in an epic battle, Osiris came back to life. This myth—with its depiction of life, death, and rebirth—took on special meaning for the ancient Egyptians, as it reflected the cycle of crop planting and harvesting in the Nile Valley.

Death and the Afterlife

The ancient Egyptians buried their dead in the Red Land, as they called the desert on either side of the fertile Nile Valley (known as the Black Land). West

An elaborate piece of jewelry depicts the falcon-headed Egyptian god Horus, protector of pharaohs and the sky.

The Great Sphinx was carved out of bedrock near the pyramid of the pharaoh Khafre.

of the Nile lay vast "cities of the dead" containing countless tombs, as well as monumental sculptures, such as the Sphinx, a statue the size of a building with the body of a lion and a human face.

Because the Egyptians believed that life continued beyond the grave, they put great effort into preparing for a life after death. Unlike the Sumerians, they did not picture the afterlife as a gloomy existence in a shadowy underworld. Instead, they anticipated a joyful continuation of the life lived *before* death.

Achieving that afterlife required help from the living. The Egyptians believed that the soul had several parts. One part, the *ka*, was a twin of the earthly body and stayed with the corpse after death. Another part, the *ba*, flew around by day but came back to the *ka* each night. If the *ba* could not recognize its body, it might get lost. So Egyptians embalmed the bodies of their important dead to preserve them as mummies.

Mummification involved removing the internal organs (which were kept in jars nearby) and filling the body cavity with a type of salt that drew the moisture out of flesh. This process protected the body from decay. The dried body was wrapped in layers of strips of linen. The resulting mummy was placed in a body-shaped coffin with the person's

Modern scanning technology shows what a 3,000-year-old Egyptian mummy sealed inside a wooden coffin probably looks like.

THE BOOK OF THE DEAD

The Book of the Dead is a collection of prayers, hymns, and spells that the ancient Egyptians believed would aid them in their passage to the afterlife. This prayer, written on a papyrus scroll and buried with the deceased inside a coffin, offers a vision of the afterlife for an Egyptian nobleman who hopes for an eternity of continued prosperity and power.

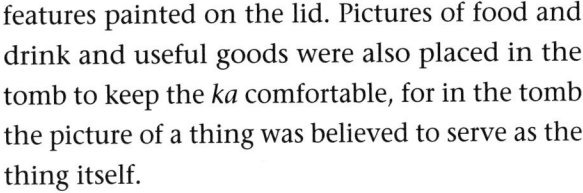

The doors of heaven are opened for me, the doors, of earth are opened for me....

I shall live upon cakes made of white grain, and my ale shall be made of the red grain of [the Nile]. In a clean place shall I sit on the ground beneath the foliage of the date-palm....

I have gained the mastery over my heart; ...I have gained the mastery over my mouth; I have gained the mastery over my two hands; I have gained the mastery over the waters; I have gained the mastery over the canal; I have gained the mastery over the rivers; I have gained the mastery over the furrows; I have gained the mastery over the men who work for me; I have gained the mastery over the women who work for me in the underworld; I have gained the mastery over all things which were ordered to be done for me upon earth and in the underworld. I shall lift myself up on my left side, and I shall place myself on my right side; I shall lift myself up on my right side, and I shall place myself on my left side. I shall sit down, I shall stand up, and I shall place myself in the path of the wind like a guide who is well prepared.

features painted on the lid. Pictures of food and drink and useful goods were also placed in the tomb to keep the *ka* comfortable, for in the tomb the picture of a thing was believed to serve as the thing itself.

Facing Judgment

Plentiful historical evidence provides a good idea of what the Egyptians expected in the next world. They believed that eventually a dead person traveled across a river to the kingdom of Osiris, ruler of the dead. There were many obstacles on the way, but the Egyptians had many prayers, hymns, and spells to help. This information was sometimes carved on tomb walls. By about 1550 B.C., it was written down and placed in tombs. Known as *The Book of the Dead*, it offered a route to follow, chants for protection, and answers to questions the dead might be asked in the Hall of the Two Truths, where judgment took place.

There, the Egyptians believed, the jackal-headed god Anubis (uh-NOO-bus) weighed the person's heart against a feather representing virtues such as truth and justice, while the person gave testimony to prove that he or she had earned an afterlife. If the scales balanced, the soul could merge with Osiris and live forever. For example, as this passage from *The Book of the Dead* shows, a dead person facing judgment might say:

"I gave bread to the hungry, …clothes to the naked, and a boat to him who was boatless. I have not deprived the orphan of his property. I have not killed; I have not commanded to kill…."

Egyptian Society

By 3000 B.C., Egyptian society was organized as a hierarchy, with a single ruler at the top and about 90 percent of the people at the bottom. At the peak of the social pyramid sat the king, whom the Egyptians considered a living incarnation of the god Horus, and thus directly responsible for the seasons, floods, and harvests. Below the king were leading priests and officials, many of them members of the royal family. Then came tax collectors, bookkeepers, and skilled professionals such as doctors. Below them were merchants and artisans such as masons, painters, and metalworkers.

At the bottom of the ancient Egyptian social order were the peasants, who labored to feed and serve all those above them. They had the lowest status and the hardest lives—on average, they lived less than half as long as people in the higher classes. Slaves ranked even lower, but early Egypt had few slaves.

Scribes, who could read and write, made up a privileged class, working mostly for the government and the

Statues of servants were buried with the dead, to attend them in the afterlife.

A wooden model depicts how ancient Egyptian farmers plowed their fields.

temples. They listed, counted, and recorded everything from the sizes of fields to taxes owed and paid. Any man could be a scribe if he could learn to write, but in practice few could afford the years of schooling needed to learn the complex Egyptian writing system. Very few Egyptians were literate.

While a few Egyptian women served as high priestesses in charge of temples, most women worked in the home. Nevertheless, custom and law gave Egyptian women many of the same rights as men. Women could divorce, own property, inherit and bequeath wealth, and enter most occupations. Herodotus was shocked to note that in Egypt "women attend the markets and trade, while the men sit at home at the loom."

To *bequeath* is to leave property behind to one's survivors.

Everyday Life

What was everyday life like for Egyptians? Scenes preserved in tomb paintings portray a busy, stable, hardworking society. We see fishermen casting nets, farmers grinding barley to make beer, women kneading dough with their feet, and workers laboring on monumental tombs for the kings.

While the peasants labored, the upper classes enjoyed life to the fullest. Hunting, boxing, and archery were popular sports. Both men and women enjoyed swimming. Young and old alike played board games such as senet, similar to backgammon. Professional dancers entertained at parties, where musicians played flutes, harps, clappers, rattles, and drums.

The masses lived mainly on onions, bread, and beer, but might sometimes add fish and vegetables to their diet. Elite Egyptians enjoyed fine banquets, feasting on antelope meat, beef, figs, melons, dates, and oatcakes dipped in honey.

Elite (ay-LEET) means belonging to a select or privileged group.

Whatever their social status, all Egyptians wore similar clothes—an off-white linen sheath for women, a knee-length kilt for men—but the upper classes' garments were of a finer, softer linen. Since linen does not dye well, the Egyptians added color with beads and bangles. They considered well-oiled hair attractive, so upper-class women placed a pat of perfumed grease on their wigs and let it melt down over their faces in the course of an evening.

Two Kingdoms Unite

Long before written history, Egypt began organizing into kingdoms, known in ancient times as the Two Lands, because they were two very different regions. Over time, one king came to rule the entire delta region, known as Lower Egypt. Another ruled the long, narrow valley called Upper Egypt.

One of the two sides of a carved flat stone called the Narmer Palette, which dates from about the thirty-first century B.C., shows Narmer smiting his enemies.

Upper and Lower Egypt

If you look at the map on page 28, Lower Egypt is near the Nile Delta, apparently "above" Upper Egypt. Why? Did the Egyptian mapmakers make a mistake? Not quite. The Nile, like all rivers, flows downhill. Its source is high in the mountains of central and eastern Africa, where the river was called the Upper Nile and the land Upper Egypt. The river flows towards its mouth, where it eventually branches out to form the Nile Delta and empties into the Mediterranean Sea. Because the elevation here is very low, at or near sea level, the river was called the Lower Nile, and the land it flowed through, Lower Egypt. So, even though north is the "upper" direction on the map, the river and the land of Lower Egypt are both lower than the highlands at the Nile's source to the south.

The ruler of Lower Egypt wore a red crown, while the king of Upper Egypt wore a white crown. Around 3100 B.C., a ruler named Menes Narmer united the two kingdoms. There is no written record of his feat, but we can guess how he did it from figures carved on each side of a flat stone, called a palette. One side shows a gigantic Narmer wearing a white crown and getting ready to club a king wearing a red crown. The other side shows Narmer wearing the red crown and gazing over the beheaded bodies of many smaller kings.

With Narmer, the king of Egypt became known as the Ruler of the Two Lands and wore a double crown, both red and white. He ruled from Memphis, a city on the border between the Two Lands.

As a unified kingdom, Egypt went on to enjoy more than two thousand years of stability and prosperity. Twice in that time, however, unity broke down and the kingdom went through a century or two of turmoil. Historians use these markers to divide the history of ancient Egypt into three time periods: the Old Kingdom, the Middle Kingdom, and the New Kingdom.

The Old Kingdom

In the Old Kingdom (from about 2660 to 2180 B.C.), Egyptians saw their monarch as a supreme god who loomed so far above his subjects that they dared not even speak his name. Many referred simply to the "Great House" or *pharaoh*. By the sixteenth century B.C., *pharaoh* had become the official title that Egyptians used to refer to their god-king.

Why Build Pyramids?

Many people think of pyramids as the very emblem of ancient Egypt, though in fact the pyramids were mostly built in the Old Kingdom, and all the great ones went up during the reigns of just a few kings. Khufu (whom the Greeks called Cheops) built the biggest of them all. The Great Pyramid of Giza towers more than 450 feet (137 m) above its surrounding plain and has a base measuring 756 feet (230 m) per side.

It took twenty to thirty thousand people at least six years to build this monument—which was quick, considering what they had to do. They cut more than two million blocks of limestone out of the cliffs, hauled each 2.5-ton block several miles on sleds without wheels, and then lifted each block into place.

This whole huge mass of stone was constructed to protect one tiny chamber deep inside the pyramid, where the king's coffin rested, along with the goods he needed after death. It seems an almost unbelievable amount of labor for the sake of a single man, but the Egyptians felt they all had a stake in this one man's fate. In their eyes, the pharaoh protected the eternal order that made survival possible for all. By securing eternal life for their king, they believed they were ensuring, for example, the regular flooding of the Nile and the continuation of plentiful harvests.

Towering over the landscape, the Great Pyramid of Giza was built to protect the resting place of the pharaoh Khufu.

The pyramids' every detail embodied power and perfection. Their four sides formed precise triangles. Their four corners marked the four directions. They were precisely square at the bottom, and they stood on carefully leveled ground. Numerous mathematical properties were coded into them. For example, a circle whose radius equals the height of Khufu's pyramid would have a circumference exactly equal to the perimeter of the pyramid's base. If you find that hard to follow, imagine the mind that could conceive of such an idea and then build it.

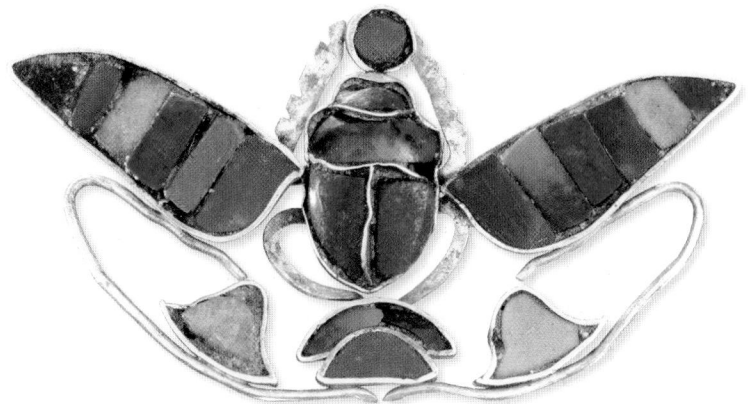

A scarab decorated with lapis lazuli, a stone not native to Egypt, shows that early Egyptians traded far and wide.

The Middle Kingdom

In the later days of the Old Kingdom, the kings started building smaller tombs, while the governors of outlying regions built ever larger monuments for themselves. This transformation was a sign that Egypt was coming apart. When a series of dry years led to crop failures, faith in the pharaoh eroded and rebellions broke out. Egypt fragmented into dozens of separate kingdoms, each headed by a chieftain who claimed to be the king of the Two Lands but really ruled only his own local region. "The land is full of gangs," one writer lamented. "All is in ruin. A man smites his brother, plague is throughout the land...."

This time of strife ended in the mid- to late-twentieth century B.C., when the Theban king Amenemhet I (AHM-uhn-ehm-HEHT) conquered all his rivals and reunified Egypt. Still, Amenemhet and later monarchs of the Middle Kingdom never quite regained the grandeur of earlier pharaohs. Instead of thinking of their king as a living god, the Egyptians now considered him partly divine but also human.

A Vigorous Society

The pharaohs of the Middle Kingdom managed to make Egypt in many ways more dynamic than ever. Literature thrived and the arts flourished. The government bureaucracy operated like a well-oiled machine. Thousands of well-educated officials were organized into departments and worked busily to carry out the pharaoh's will, under the direction of the **vizier** (vuh-ZEER), the highest government official serving the pharaoh.

With the government humming so efficiently, trade flourished as never before. Egyptian ports welcomed ships from places like Crete, an island near Greece. Cities on the Sinai (SIY-niy) Peninsula served as entry points for caravans coming overland from Mesopotamia, bringing goods such as lapis lazuli from lands as distant as Afghanistan.

Since the Nile Valley has no forests, Egyptians imported timber from what is now Lebanon. They traded grain, glassware, linen, and fine furniture for cedar and juniper wood. Egyptian merchants traveled south and west for ebony, ivory, ostrich eggs, and feathers. Egyptian armies also went south and west, into Nubia and Libya, to control the trade routes.

Trade brought prosperity to the Middle Kingdom. But when rival nobles began fighting among themselves and a series of weak pharaohs came to the throne, Egypt declined into disunity. In this weakened condition, the kingdom was vulnerable to invaders who pressed into northern Egypt. The following chapter tells how these invaders, called the Hyksos (HIHK-sohs), dominated Egypt for decades, until Egypt once again triumphed and enjoyed another golden age during the New Kingdom.

Science, Art, Writing and Literature

Ancient Egyptian civilization enjoyed a continuous existence at least twenty times longer than the entire history of the United States to date. During those many centuries, the Egyptians made great achievements in various fields, including mathematics, science, art, and literature.

Math and Science

The ancient Egyptians identified some basic principles of arithmetic and geometry. For example, they discovered how to work with fractions. Early on, Egyptians created an accurate solar calendar. They were the first to calculate that a solar year was exactly 365¼ days long. They divided the year into twelve months of thirty days each and set five days aside for a festival.

Their technical advances included smelting metals and blowing glass. They also perfected the science of embalming bodies, which they used when making mummies.

To *smelt* metals is to melt and refine them.

While Egyptian doctors relied mainly on magical ideas that have long since been discarded, they did have a basic understanding of how to prevent disease. They also explored the medicinal properties of many plants, and were the first to recommend castor oil as a remedy. Later, the Greeks built on ancient Egyptian findings as a basis for more sophisticated medical discoveries.

Ancient Egyptian Art

The ancient Egyptians made especially striking achievements in art and architecture. The earliest Egyptian artists established elements of style that later artists carried on through the centuries. For example, they almost always painted faces in profile, while portraying bodies from the front.

The Egyptians created not only colossal statues and monumental buildings but also delicate figurines, intricate miniature models, and exquisite glassware, furniture, and jewelry. Like many ancient artists, Egyptian painters focused on their gods but also created detailed scenes of everyday life.

Writing and Literature

Shortly after the Sumerians invented cuneiform, the Egyptians developed their own system of writing. At first, the Egyptians used simple pictograms representing specific things—a picture of a sun meant "sun." Over time, these pictograms evolved into **hieroglyphics** (hiy-ruh-GLIH-fiks), or "sacred carvings." These stylized but still pictorial marks stood for broad ideas. A sailboat, for example, could mean "sailboat" but could also mean "south," the direction of travel for a sailboat on the Nile. Later, some signs came to stand for sounds.

The Egyptians needed an efficient writing system because their complex society depended on long-distance communication, record keeping, and accurate accounting. The ancient Egyptians also created an extensive literature of songs, prayers, spells, hymns, wisdom books, instruction manuals, religious stories, and love poems.

Egyptian picture writing, or hieroglyphics, embellished a pharaoh's tomb.

Unearthing Ancient Egypt

Howard Carter, a British archaeologist, devoted his life to chasing what many regarded as a legend about the lost tomb of a pharaoh named Tutankhamen (too-tahng-KAH-muhn). In 1922, digging in the Valley of the Kings on the west bank of the Nile, Carter and his crew found a staircase leading down into the earth. That year, on November 26, Carter knocked a hole in the door he found at the bottom of those stairs and peered into a room no one had seen for more than three thousand years. Behind him, one of his partners whispered, "Do you see anything?"

"Yes," said Carter, "I see wonderful things."

Tombs like the one Carter discovered were preserved from wind, weather, heat, and light. Today, they are a major source of information about life in ancient Egypt, as they reveal glimpses of that long-ago time in colors as vivid as the day they were painted.

The Egyptians invented a paperlike writing material called *papyrus* (puh-PIY-rus), made from the stalks of papyrus plants that grew in the marshes along the Nile. The papyrus reeds were cut into strips and soaked to release gluelike sugars, then laid crisscross and pressed flat to dry. The scribes could roll their sheets of papyrus into cylinders for storage when they weren't using them. Eventually, the Egyptians filled many libraries with their writings. A famous library in the city of Alexandria had more than seven hundred thousand papyrus scrolls about history, astronomy, geography, and many other subjects.

Hieroglyphics were beautiful but so complicated to write that simpler scripts were developed for more informal uses. Eventually, Egyptians began using Greek letters to write Egyptian words, and hieroglyphics were forgotten.

The Rosetta Stone

For centuries, the history of ancient Egypt was locked away in hieroglyphics that no one could read. Then, in 1799, near the town of Rashid, called Rosetta by Europeans, French soldiers found a slab of black rock on which the same text had been carved in three different kinds of writing. Some scholars soon recognized the writing on one part of the stone as a form of ancient Greek. The other two parts were covered with ancient Egyptian symbols.

Scholars who could read ancient Greek used that writing to help decipher the remaining two sets of Egyptian symbols. This breakthrough enabled scholars to produce dictionaries to guide the translation of hieroglyphics on ancient papyrus scrolls, monuments, and pyramid walls. The Rosetta Stone helped reveal the stories, beliefs, and history of ancient Egypt.

The Rosetta Stone, found in Egypt in 1799, unlocked clues to a lost language.

EXCAVATING A LOST TOMB

Before he discovered the tomb of Tutankhamen, the young Howard Carter accompanied the Swiss archaeologist Edouard Naville on an excavation of the long-lost tomb of Hatshepsut, the first queen of Egypt. Carter, a skilled artist, made many drawings and managed the excavation of the burial chamber. In the following passage, Naville describes reaching the burial chamber, and credits Carter for his active role in the grueling and dangerous work.

Long before we reached this chamber the air had become so bad, and the heat so great, that the candles carried by the workmen melted, and would not give enough light to enable them to continue their work; consequently we were compelled to install electric lights,…with lamps attached as needed.

…As soon as we got down about 50 meters [164 ft], the air became so foul that the men could not work. In addition to this, the bats of centuries had built innumerable nests on the ceilings of the corridors and chambers, and their excrement had become so dry that the least stir of the air filled the corridors with a fluffy black stuff, which choked the noses and mouths of the men, rendering it most difficult for them to breathe. To overcome these difficulties, we installed an air suction pump at the mouth of the tomb, to which was attached a zinc pipe, which before the burial chamber was reached extended about 213 meters [700 ft].

…The serious danger of caving ceilings throughout the entire length of the corridors and chambers was a daily anxiety, and in some places required either bracing or taking down. Happily…no accidents occurred, though many of the men and boys were temporarily overcome by the heat and bad air. Braving all these dangers and discomforts, Mr. Carter made two or three descents every week, and professed to enjoy it.

We all looked forward to the finding of the burial chamber,…but our hopes were frustrated when we found this chamber also filled with small stones and fallen ceilings, through which we "entered" at the rate of 2 meters [6.5 ft] a day, and which required a month's work to clear entirely.

Queen Makare Hatshepsut by Howard Carter

Early Civilization in the Indus River Valley

Key Questions

- Why is our knowledge of the ancient Indus Valley civilization limited?

Sumer and Egypt were not the only areas where civilization emerged in river valleys. In other parts of the world, other peoples followed a similar pattern. The river valleys of India and China, like those in Egypt and Mesopotamia, also became cradles of human civilization. Along the banks of the Indus River, city builders were at work by 2500 B.C.

The Geography and Economy of the Indus Valley

The Indus River lies at the northwestern edge of a huge landmass that geographers call the Indian subcontinent—it is part of the continent of Asia, and has its own distinctive geographic and political features. This area contains the modern-day countries of India, Pakistan, Bangladesh, Nepal, and Bhutan. Today, the Indian subcontinent is home to nearly one and a half billion people—more than one-fifth of the people living on earth.

Half of the diamond-shaped Indian subcontinent extends down into the Indian Ocean, forming a giant peninsula, while the rest thrusts up into Asia. Scientists estimate that more than fifty million years ago, this whole mass was a separate continent surrounded by ocean. But over a vast expanse of time, the continent drifted northward, little by little, year by year, until it pushed into Asia. Where the two land masses met, the earth buckled to form the world's highest mountains, the Himalayas, and their craggy western spur, the Hindu Kush. The massive Himalayan ranges wall off the Indian subcontinent from the rest of Asia.

> A *peninsula* is an area of land nearly surrounded by water.

Monsoon Winds: Blessing and Curse

The climate of India is shaped by the effects of seasonal winds called **monsoons**. Every year, heavy winds blast across much of the subcontinent. The winter monsoons blow dry air from the northeast. Then, during the warmer months, the winds reverse direction. The summer monsoons blow from the southwest and carry moisture from the Indian Ocean toward land.

For the civilization that developed along the Indus River, the summer monsoons were a blessing and a curse. The heavy rains caused the river to flood, and as the Indus overflowed its banks, it deposited rich silt, turning the floodplain into fertile fields. But the floods were unpredictable. Sometimes the monsoon winds brought too much rain, and the flooding caused great destruction. Sometimes there was too little rain, which could lead to drought and famine. This unpredictable

> A *famine* is a severe shortage of food.

When the Indus floods, it deposits rich silt, turning the floodplain into fertile fields.

cycle of wet and dry continues to dominate the climate of the Indian subcontinent today.

The area stretching across the subcontinent from northern India into southern Pakistan gets less than ten inches (25.5 cm) of rain per year. This land, the Thar Desert, is one of the largest deserts in the world.

Indus Valley Civilization

Out of the snow-packed peaks of the high Himalayas come three mighty rivers. Two of them, the Brahmaputra and the Ganges (GAN-jeez), meander down through central and eastern India to the Bay of Bengal. The third, the Indus, flows to the Arabian Sea. Here in the Indus River system, another of the world's great urban civilizations was born more than four thousand years ago.

In 1900, no one even knew this ancient civilization had ever existed. Traces of it remained, but no one recognized what they were seeing. Some large mounds, about six hundred miles (965 km) upriver from the sea, looked like ordinary hills to the local people. During the nineteenth century, British engineers building a railroad found hundreds of thousands of fire-baked bricks littering this area. They did not recognize them as artifacts from an ancient civilization, so they used the bricks to strengthen the railway beds they were building.

The First Urban Planners

In 1921, a team of archaeologists decided to dig in the mounds near a place called Harappa (huh-RA-puh). They soon uncovered the remains of a thick platform of mud brick, and a massive brick wall encircling the area. Further digging revealed that the walls enclosed many buildings, including a citadel—a fortress.

In time, the archaeologists unearthed a whole city, laid out in a precise grid, with streets as straight as rulers. The houses were made of baked

In the 1920s, archaeologists unearthed the remains of an entire ancient city near Harappa in the Indus Valley.

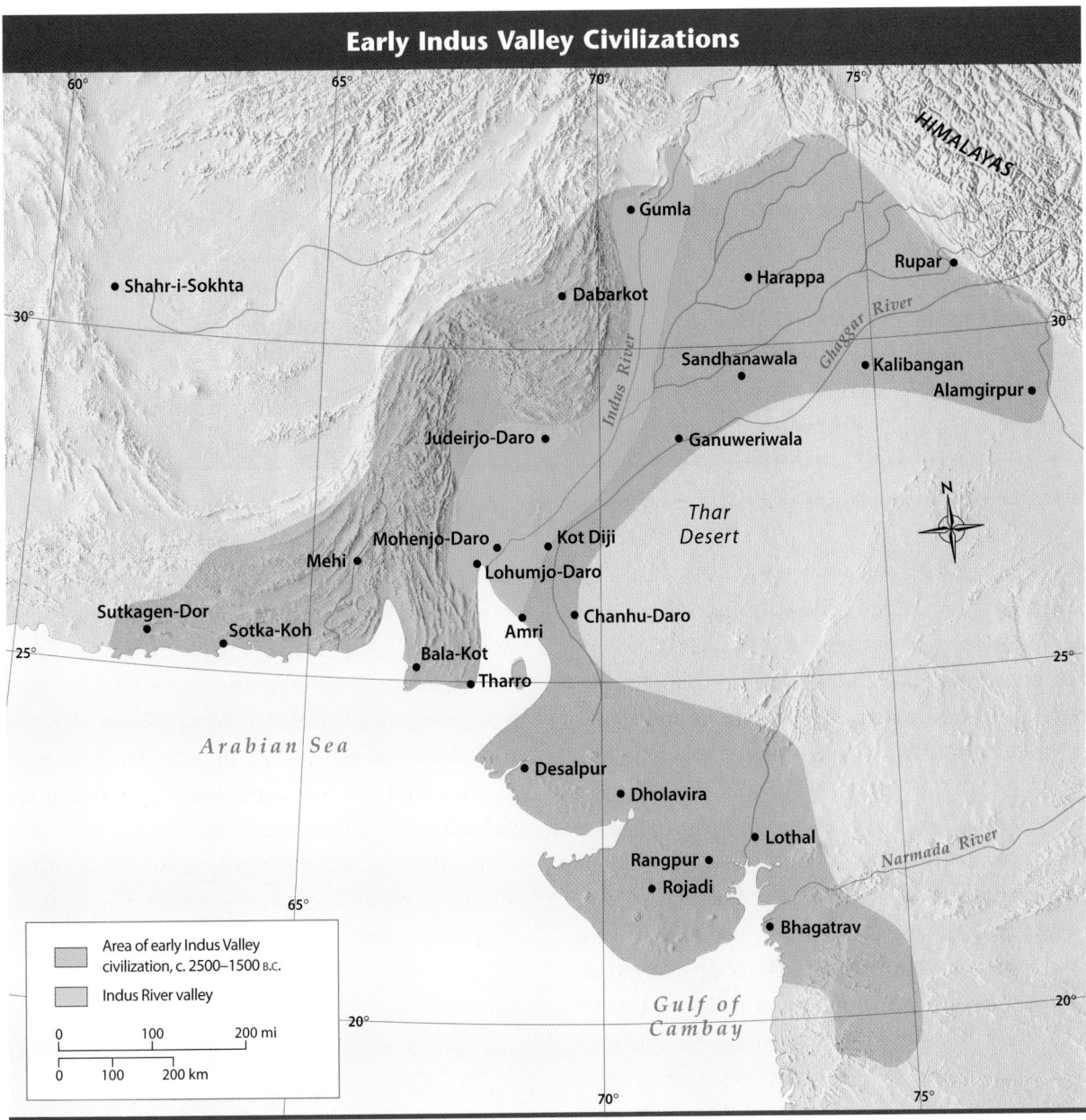

Early Indus Valley Civilizations

Area of early Indus Valley
civilization, c. 2500–1500 B.C.

Indus River valley

| 0 | 100 | 200 mi |
| 0 | 100 | 200 km |

More than a hundred towns and cities grew along the banks of the Indus River and its tributaries.

bricks and equipped with bathrooms, indoor plumbing, and drains as sophisticated as anything to be found in Europe as late as the 1800s.

Archaeologists' dating techniques revealed that this city had flourished between 2300 B.C. and 1750 B.C. At its peak, it must have housed more than thiry-five thousand people. Who were they? No one knows.

Soon, 400 miles (644 km) south of Harappa, another ancient city came to light at Mohenjo-Daro (moh-HEN-joh DAHR-oh), a name meaning

"Mound of the Dead." This city was as big as Harappa and laid out in the same orderly way. Its bricks were exactly the same shape and size as those in Harappa, as if the two cities had been built from one set of plans. Since then, many more sites have been found.

A Powerful Culture

Apparently, these people of the Indus once had a kingdom covering some half-million square miles—geographically, it was the biggest of the

How Cities Vanish over Time

Cities disappear from history for many reasons. A city might be destroyed by a conqueror or a natural catastrophe, such as an earthquake or flood. Sometimes a slower disaster, such as a long drought, forces the inhabitants to move away because they can no longer feed themselves. Once the population of a city drops too low or the people become too weak or disorganized to keep up repairs, natural forces begin to act. Wind, water, and plants can crumble stone, reducing buildings to rubble.

ancient river-valley civilizations. It must have been well-organized, for only a powerful and efficient government could build such complex cities and enforce standards for weights and measures, as these people must have done.

We know they were productive farmers because they built large granaries (storage houses for wheat and rice). We know they were expert craftspeople and fine artists. Archaeologists have found tools, mirrors, and jewelry, as well as thousands of carved soapstone seals, which merchants probably used to stamp their wares. The seals show animals that had been domesticated in

Archaeological finds, like this gold and bead necklace from Harappa and this stone animal seal from Mohenjo-Daro, show the skill of Indus Valley craftsmen.

the region, such as chickens, water buffalo, and hump-backed bulls called zebus. The seals also show wild beasts that roamed the area—tigers, elephants, and rhinoceroses—as well as mythical beasts such as unicorns.

The people of the Indus certainly had a writing system, because the seals are covered with a form of picture writing. No one yet has been able to decode this ancient writing. We know these people were energetic traders, because their mysterious seals have turned up as far away as Mesopotamia.

The End of the Indus Civilization

The ruins of Mohenjo-Daro and other Indus Valley cities hint at a great civilization that flourished for seven or eight hundred years. Though these people didn't build huge ziggurats or imposing pyramids, their cities bustled with activity. But by about 1500 B.C., their civilization had largely faded away. Why?

Scholars once assumed that Harappan civilization was wiped out by warlike tribes from the north, which invaded India around 1500 B.C. But recent evidence suggests that the Indus civilization collapsed before the invading tribes arrived. There are signs that a series of natural catastrophes occurred. Perhaps disease brought about this civilization's demise. In Mohenjo-Daro, archaeologists found a few skeletons lying in the street, as though the last people there died with no one to bury them.

Archaeologists have also found houses that were apparently abandoned suddenly, as well as the skeletons of people killed by falling rubble as they fled. Some scientists suspect that a series of earthquakes set off ruinous floods.

The Indus is not a predictable river like the Nile. It floods unexpectedly and has changed course drastically at times, drowning some towns and leaving others stranded far from water. Perhaps the very river that gave birth to this civilization helped to destroy it. Perhaps—there is much we simply do not know.

Early Civilization in China

The fourth of the early river valley civilizations emerged in China. Although civilization in China began a little later than in Sumer, Egypt, and India, the historical evidence suggests that it began without contact with those other civilizations.

Geographic features made China in some ways a world apart. To the north stretched a vast desert called the Gobi (GOH-bee). In the west were the high Himalayas and other mountainous lands. To the south and east lay bodies of water—the South China Sea, the East China Sea, and the Yellow Sea. These barriers kept the people of China mostly isolated for thousands of years.

How Two Rivers Shaped Early China

Civilization in China first took root between two great river systems, the Huang He (hwahng huh) and the Yangtze (YANG-see). Between these rivers lies the North China Plain, China's major farmland. In all the vast landscape of China, only a small percentage of the land is good for farming, and much of this land lies in the North China Plain.

In ancient China, the Huang He was the cradle of civilization, for it was here that nomadic herders settled down some seven thousand years ago to build villages and try farming. They chose this plain because it is covered with a layer of fine-grained, wind-blown yellow soil, called *loess* (lehs). The Huang He—also called the Yellow River—is loaded with loess, and its floods deposit a layer of it in which some crops thrive.

The Huang He is also called the Yellow River because of the silt that it carries.

43

Not Much Meat

The people of ancient China kept few herd animals, for these beasts, especially cows, require lots of land for grazing, and fertile land was limited. The Chinese villagers ate more vegetables than meat, which is still true of the Chinese diet. What meat they did eat came from pigs, not cattle.

The Huang He is dangerously swift and one of the muddiest rivers in the world. The yellow silt it carries tends to build up, which can raise the river bed. In some places, the river actually runs above the surrounding plains, and the waters have to be held back by man-made dikes. If the dikes break, water explodes across the land, washing away whole villages. No wonder, then, that the Chinese have long called the river that gave birth to their civilization "China's Sorrow."

Even so, villages sprouted in this floodplain long ago. Since the country is quite hilly, the people cut terraces into the yellow slopes to create level land. In the Huang He Valley, inhabitants grew millet, a grain good for making crackers and porridge.

Farther south, early Chinese civilization also developed along the Yangtze River. The Yangtze is sometimes called Chang Jiang (chahng jee-yahng), which means "long river," an appropriate name for the third-longest river in the world. The climate in this region was warmer than in the north, and the land was green and lush. Every spring, melting snow poured waters into the Yangtze and its many tributaries. In the marshy land of the well-watered valleys, farmers learned to grow rice.

In this warm southern climate, Chinese farmers could grow a surplus of food. With that surplus, people were free to do other jobs besides farming—weaving baskets, making cloth, or fashioning pots to store grain. They began building simple wooden homes along the rivers and fields. Before long, there were villages, and then cities—the beginnings of civilization in ancient China.

Scratching a living from the soil was back-breaking work for these early Chinese villagers. They had to stay on guard against not only natural disasters but also nomads who would swoop down from the north to pillage their homes and steal their crops. Archaeologists can trace the incidence of warfare in the broken bones of skeletons and the number of stone weapons found in the prehistoric villages they have excavated.

Early Chinese Society

China's geography did little to promote interaction among villages. The Huang He is too wild for boat traffic, and the rugged landscape made foot travel difficult. People in one village might speak a different language from those in a nearby village. They also went to war with one another over land and resources, for there were spots along the Huang He that offered advantages such as more fertile soil, better protection from floods, and greater shelter from the wind.

Home Life and Culture

From earliest times, the Chinese put home and family at the center of life, but life in the home had a hierarchy, an organization in which some were clearly ranked higher than others. The guiding rule in the Chinese family was respect for parents and elders. Chinese fathers instilled in their children a sense of filial piety—that is, of respectful duty and unquestioning obedience to one's parents. In the family, women held an inferior position and were subservient to men.

The most honored members of the family were the ones who had died—the ancestors. The Chinese believed that the spirits of their ancestors lived on in some realm between heaven and earth, where they continued to take a keen interest in the affairs of the family. Because the ancestors' spirits were considered part of the household, the Chinese offered them food and drink and practiced rituals to keep them happy. While the Chinese did not worship their ancestors, they did believe the ancestors might influence the gods on their behalf.

As Chinese society developed, the hierarchy of the home extended to the larger society. In the home, children owed utmost obedience to a stern father whose absolute authority was almost godlike. In the larger society, ordinary citizens owed utmost obedience to the king, who reigned as a stern, godlike father to the whole society. And just as women had low status in the home, they also held a low position in Chinese society.

Early Chinese villagers made sophisticated pottery and created artifacts out of a precious stone called jade, using strings soaked in sandy glue to file shapes into the hard stone. They also worked out the length of a year and developed a calendar that is still used to determine the date of the Chinese New Year. The calendar associates each year in a repeating twelve-year cycle with one of twelve animals, each of which was thought to represent a different character trait.

The Chinese also learned how to use the silkworm to produce silk—a process that some evidence suggests dates back to prehistoric times in China. The cocoons of silkworms have been found in excavated Chinese villages. In the years ahead, as China grew and developed, silk would become one of the most desired products from China.

China's Dynasties Begin

The history of Chinese civilization is marked by the rule of several **dynasties**. A dynasty is a single family that rules for many years. In ancient Egypt, when a pharaoh died, his son usually became the new pharaoh. Power stayed in the family and passed from generation to generation. The same sort of thing happened in China. When a Chinese king died, power usually passed to someone else in the family, sometimes a brother, but usually a son.

According to Chinese tradition, the Xia (shyah) Dynasty was China's first ruling family. Many historians, however, consider the Xia as mythical, because no trace of them has been found. Instead, historians generally identify the Shang as China's first dynasty.

The Shang Dynasty: Evidence in the Bones

Archaeological evidence suggests that the rule of the Shang Dynasty began about 1600 B.C. and lasted hundreds of years. Scholars once thought the Shang were, like the Xia, a legendary dynasty, until evidence proved the legend to be based in fact.

Traces of the Shang Dynasty existed all around but long went unnoticed. For years, peasants in northern China had been plowing up what they called "dragon bones" and selling them to apothecaries, who ground them up to make medicine. Without knowing it, the Chinese were grinding their history into dust.

> An *apothecary* makes and sells drugs and medicines.

In 1889, two scholars saw one of the bones *before* it was ground up. They recognized the scratches on the bone as writing of some kind. The scholars asked to be taken to where the bones

The rich farming region between the Huang He and Yangtze rivers was home to the Shang Dynasty.

China's "Legendary" First Dynasty

The legend of the Xia Dynasty goes back to Ssu-ma Ch'ien's *Historical Records*, written around 100 B.C. He tells of a hero named Yu, who tamed China's floods and then founded the Xia Dynasty. Ssu-ma Ch'ien names the Shang as China's second dynasty. His list of Shang kings almost exactly matches the thirty names found on artifacts by archaeologists. If he was right about the Shang Dynasty, could the Xia Dynasty have been real as well?

had come from. They were guided to a village near the city of Anyang, where peasants had collected hundreds of such bones.

The bones, it turned out, were oracle bones, dating back to the Shang Dynasty—a real dynasty after all. Shang priests used these oracle bones to consult the ancestors. The priests would scratch a question into a piece of oxen bone or tortoise shell—for example, the priests would ask the gods whether a battle would succeed, or what was causing the king's disease. The priests would then push a red-hot metal rod into the bone until a crack appeared. They believed that the direction of the crack revealed the answer to the question.

Archaeologists found one oracle bone that asks whether a hunt would be successful: "We are going to hunt at Ch'iu. Any capture?" On the same bone is an inscription, added later, that tells how the prediction came out: "The hunt on this day actually captured 1 tiger, 40 deer, 164 foxes, 159 hornless deer."

The Shang as Builders and Soldiers

Archaeologists have dug up the ancient capital of the Shang at Anyang and several other cities. The Shang built palaces and cities with earthen walls around them. Much like the ziggurats of Mesopotamia, the pyramids of Egypt, and the citadels of the Indus Valley, the city walls built by the Shang

were huge **public works** projects, carried out by the government for public use.

The enormous walls surrounding Shang cities were made not of brick or stone but of pounded earth. Workers poured soil into a wooden frame, stamped it hard as cement, then poured in another layer and pounded that down. The walls were more than 60 feet (18.3 m) thick and 30 feet (9 m) high. They ran for miles, surrounding and protecting palaces, workshops, public buildings, and homes.

Clearly, the kings of the Shang Dynasty had enormous armies of workers at their command. Many were slaves captured in war, but the Chinese monarch could and did conscript farmers out of their fields to serve in his armies or labor on his huge construction projects.

> To *conscript* is to compel someone into required service.

By inscribing questions on oracle bones, priests of the Shang Dynasty asked their ancestors to foretell the future.

The Shang kings were also military commanders, often at war with the nomadic invaders from the north, and always pushing to gain more territory and resources from small Chinese states. The king was surrounded by noble relatives who went to war with him in two-wheeled chariots, wearing bronze armor and fighting with bronze weapons.

When a king died, his body and treasures were placed in a burial chamber at the bottom of an enormous pit. A warrior was killed and placed by the door to guard him. Members of the king's household were sacrificed and placed above the chamber in careful patterns. More human sacrifices—probably slaves and prisoners of war—were laid on the ramps leading out of the pit. The whole pit was then overfilled to create a mound.

An 8.5-foot bronze statue, c. 1150 B.C., likely depicts a Shang ruler.

Chinese Culture Emerges

Much of what we know about Shang culture comes from more than eighty thousand oracle bones found with writing on them. Scholars could decipher the writing on these bones because the characters are early versions of ones still used in Chinese writing today.

The invention of this script might have been the greatest achievement of the Shang Dynasty. Although the spoken language differed in various parts of China, people in all parts of China could learn the same system of writing. The written language helped unify China. It enabled a single government to communicate with a multitude of people despite the differences in their spoken languages.

Only a small class of people, however, could read the complex Chinese script, which had thousands of different characters. Thus literacy was limited to the few among the upper classes who had the resources to master the complicated writing system. While the Chinese script served to unify China politically, it also further separated those of noble rank from the masses of peasants, and put power in the hands of a class of literate scholars and officials.

The Continuity of Chinese Culture

Artists of the Shang era made bronze pots, vessels, and other artifacts that they stamped with stylized images of people and animals, such as dragons. These styles and themes endured through the ages of Chinese history. For example, the dragon remains a symbol of kindly power and wisdom in China.

The Shang Dynasty came to an abrupt end in 1046 B.C. when a rebel leader named Wu Wang conquered their capital. He put the last Shang king to death and founded the Zhou (djoh) Dynasty.

Modern Chinese culture can be traced back in a continuous line through the Shang Dynasty to those first villages in the Huang He and Yangtze valleys. The civilizations that built Sumer's ziggurats, Egypt's pyramids, and ancient India's citadels all came to an end. China, however, is the world's oldest living civilization. The people of China today can trace their writing, history, art, and philosophy further back in time than people in any other modern nation.

Shang Dynasty artistry is evident in this bronze knife handle created in the shape of a dragon.

CHAPTER 3
THE FIRST EMPIRES

2300–500 B.C.

2500 B.C.

2000 B.C.

c. 2350 B.C.
Sargon of Akkad
establishes the
world's first empire.

c. 1790 B.C.
King Hammurabi
introduces the first
written code of law.

Decorated wooden back panel of Tutankhamen's royal throne, c. 1346 B.C.

1000 B.C.

500 B.C.

c. 1400 B.C.
Egypt's New Kingdom reaches the height of its power.

c. 600 B.C.
Nebuchadnezzar rebuilds the ancient city of Babylon.

Persia rules the world's largest empire at the time.

*I*n the small city-states of Sumer, the people were united by language, ancestry, and the gods they worshipped in common. Around 2350 B.C., however, the rulers of some city-states began to conquer their neighbors and build **empires**. An empire brings different peoples or formerly independent states together under the control of one ruler.

The rise and fall of empires marked a new stage of human history. By uniting many different peoples, the early empires led to further exchange of goods, ideas, information, and technologies. With power concentrated in their hands, the early empire builders constructed massive public works that changed their societies. New ideas of government emerged, and the first codes of law were written.

The First Empires Appear in Mesopotamia

Key Questions

- How do empires differ from other structures of government?

- What characteristics did the early empires of western Asia share? How did they differ?

- Why was Hammurabi's code significant?

As you've learned, in ancient times the land of southern Mesopotamia was known as Sumer. To the north of Sumer lay the land of Akkad. For many years, the Akkadians and Sumerians lived side by side as entirely different peoples. Over time, however, the Akkadians adopted many Sumerian ways, a result of **cultural diffusion**, the spread of ideas, products, and practices from one society to another.

The Akkadian Empire

From Akkad came Sargon, a ruler destined to conquer Sumer and build a great empire in Mesopotamia—indeed, he established what is generally acknowledged as the world's first empire. Sargon is one of the first people in history whose life we know about in some detail, though much of that detail is from legends and stories written after his lifetime.

Sargon the Conqueror

Sargon was born in Akkad around 2300 B.C., into a poor family. Legends say he was raised by a gardener who found him as a baby floating in a reed basket on the Euphrates River. He grew up as a servant in the royal palace of Kish, where he became the king's trusted cupbearer, and then became king himself.

While we have little reliable evidence about Sargon's personal life, we know a good deal about his career as a ruler. As king, he organized a strong Akkadian army and headed south on a military campaign unlike any the world had seen. He attacked the wealthy Sumerian cities, conquering them one by one, until he controlled the entire Fertile Crescent.

Sargon did not simply conquer. He also tried to blend Sumer and Akkad into one realm. He made Akkadian the official language of his empire but adopted the cuneiform script of the Sumerians to write it. He supported the worship of both Sumerian and Akkadian gods. As the years passed, the process of cultural diffusion

Some of the world's earliest empires rose and fell in Mesopotamia.

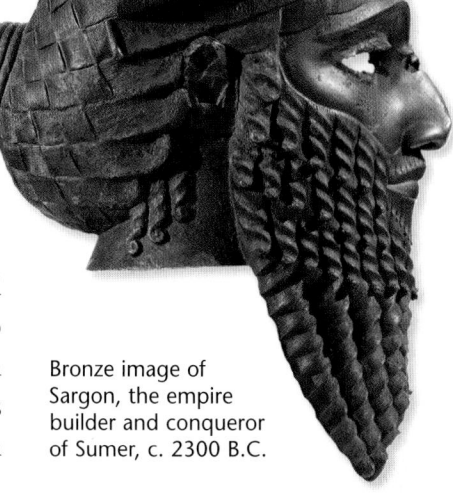

Bronze image of Sargon, the empire builder and conqueror of Sumer, c. 2300 B.C.

Anatolia— Where Continents Meet

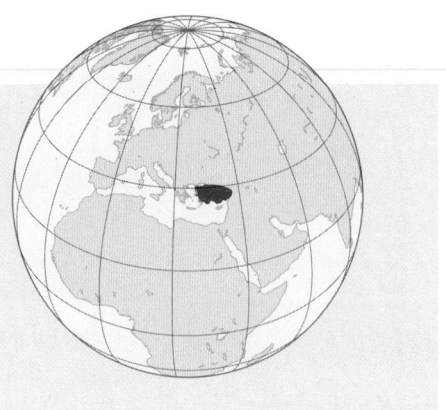

Anatolia, also called Asia Minor, is part of modern-day Turkey. It is a huge peninsula lapped by the waters of the Mediterranean and Black seas.

Anatolia is located where the continents of Asia and Europe meet. Over time, as many different peoples moved through and into the region, it became a crossroads of trade and diverse cultures.

continued—the two cultures interacted, borrowed from each other, and gradually produced something new.

Sargon was mainly interested in controlling the trade routes linking the Fertile Crescent to Syria, Egypt, and **Anatolia** (A-nuh-TOH-lee-uh). Along these routes, traders carried such highly valued goods as timber, grain, and, above all, copper and tin, the two metals needed to make bronze. Armies equipped with bronze weapons enjoyed a crucial advantage because bronze was the hardest metal known to people of the time.

By controlling the trade routes, Sargon could funnel wealth into his treasury. He could then buy the loyalty of his supporters and pay men to fight for him. His force of more than 5,400 men was the world's first, full-time professional army. Sumerian merchants accepted Sargon's rule (and taxes) because his army protected them and kept trade goods moving.

As it grew, Sargon's empire became harder to control. The Sumerians often tried to revolt. Sargon fought more than thirty wars to keep his empire united. Once Sargon died, the Sumerians rebelled against Akkadian rule. By about 2190 B.C., Sargon's empire had come apart.

The Babylonian Empire

After Sargon's empire crumbled, the cities of Mesopotamia fell to fighting one another. Nomadic tribes who roamed the surrounding deserts began to attack. One of these tribes, the Amorites, raided the cities and eventually seized control, replacing Sargon's empire with a collection of separate city-states.

Hammurabi and the Babylonian Empire

The most powerful Amorite city-state was Babylon, situated where the Tigris and Euphrates come closest together, near the site of what is now Baghdad in Iraq. Around 1790 B.C., the Amorite king Hammurabi came to power in Babylon. He employed not only conquest but also skillful deal making to unite the Amorite cities. Hammurabi's Babylonian Empire, often called Babylonia, was even bigger than Sargon's.

Hammurabi appointed officials throughout his empire to carry out the policies he set in the capital city. He organized a system for collecting

Sargon's Lost Capital

Sargon ruled from a city called Agade (uh-GAH-day). After Sargon's empire fell, invaders destroyed this city, and today historians don't know where its ruins are buried. We know about Agade only from ancient texts, which describe a city of crowded streets where one might expect to be jostled by monkeys, elephants, and other beasts, as well as people of many lands, reflecting the range of Sargon's conquests.

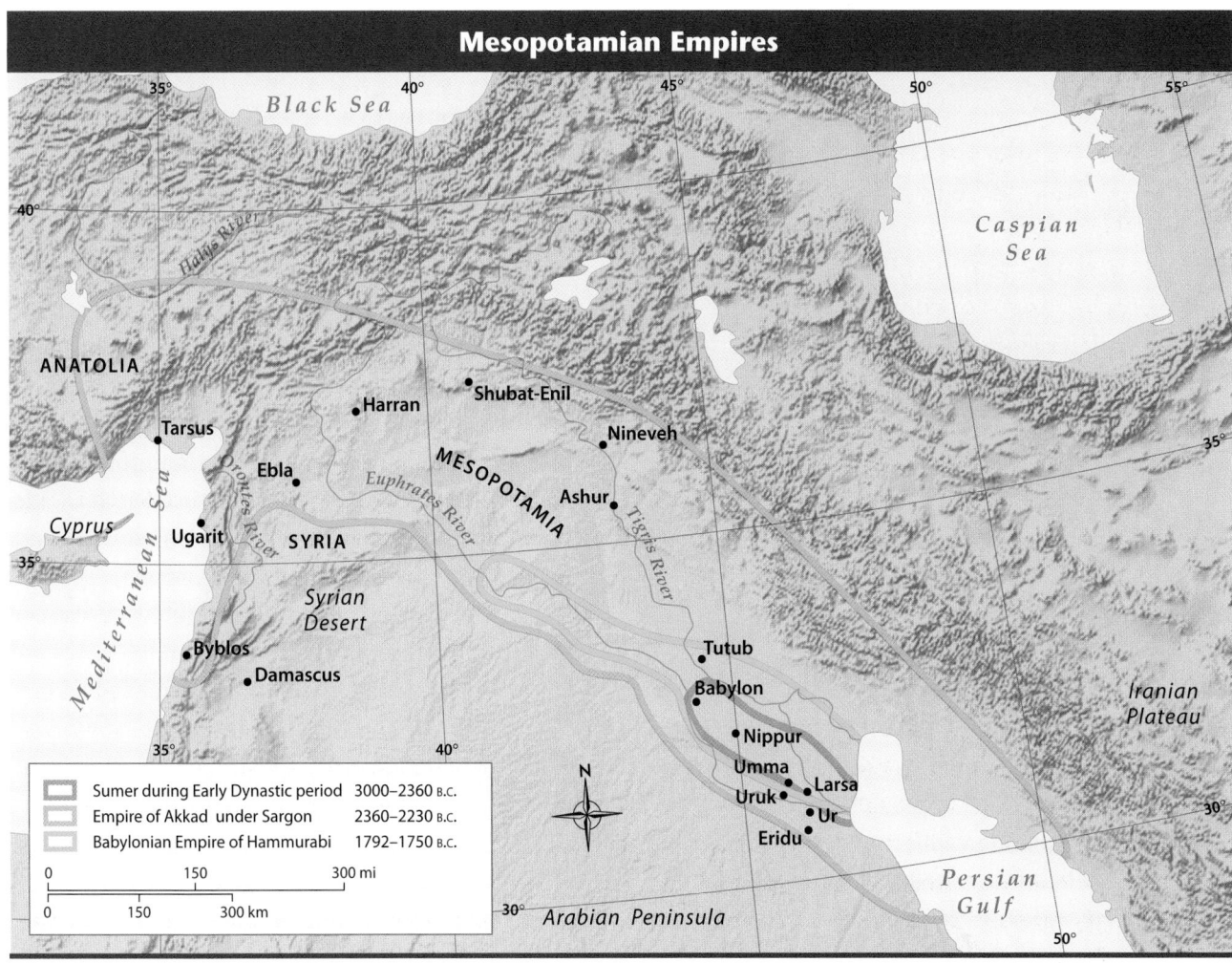

Mesopotamian Empires

Map legend:
- Sumer during Early Dynastic period 3000–2360 B.C.
- Empire of Akkad under Sargon 2360–2230 B.C.
- Babylonian Empire of Hammurabi 1792–1750 B.C.

Empires rose and fell as rulers fought for control of the wealthy city-states of Mesopotamia.

taxes from his subjects. He built many temples. He constructed irrigation systems to improve farming. He oversaw the markets to make sure business ran smoothly. Thanks to Hammurabi's policies, more people began trading a greater variety of goods across greater distances.

Hammurabi's Code

Hammurabi's greatest achievement was the **Code of Hammurabi**, a set of 282 laws carved on a seven-foot (2 m) *stele* (steel), or stone pillar, set in a public square. This was the first time a government had posted an organized set of laws for all to see. Copies of the code were also distributed throughout the empire on clay tablets. Hammurabi's code set forth for his empire a body of laws covering a wide variety of matters such

as prices, contracts, stealing, kidnapping, debt, and slavery. The laws told Babylonians what they could and couldn't do, and what punishment they faced for breaking a law.

Hammurabi's code shows the importance of commerce in Babylonian society because so many of the laws dealt with contracts, payments, and business disagreements. We get a picture of family life from the many laws that address marriage, divorce, and parental rights.

Hammurabi's code did not ensure equal treatment for all. Babylonia was divided into unequal social classes. Some people were slaves, and some were nobles with special privileges. Men had more rights than women. The laws Hammurabi posted include the following:

Atop the stele of Hammurabi, the king is depicted receiving the code from Shamash, the Sumerian god of justice.

- If someone carelessly floods his neighbor's field while watering his own crop, he shall pay for his neighbor's loss with corn.
- If a son strikes his father, his hands shall be cut off.
- If a man knocks out the teeth of his equal, his teeth shall be knocked out.
- If a man puts out another man's eye, his own eye shall be put out.
- If he puts out the eye of another man's slave, he shall pay one-half the slave's value.
- If someone strikes the body of a man higher in rank, he shall receive sixty blows with an ox whip in public.
- If a man strikes a free-born woman so that she loses her unborn child, he shall pay ten shekels for her loss.
- If the woman dies, his own daughter shall be put to death.

Laws that demand "an eye for an eye and a tooth for a tooth" seem harsh and unforgiving. In Hammurabi's day, however, one man blinding another could start a feud between clans and lead to years of bloodshed. Hammurabi's code was meant to curb violence by establishing limits. Hammurabi himself stated that his laws were meant "to cause justice to prevail in the land, [and] to destroy the wicked and the evil, that the strong may not oppress the weak." In a world that was often chaotic and brutal, and in a time when kings could change laws to suit their whims, the Code of Hammurabi must have brought a sense of order and stability to many Babylonians.

Babylonia flourished under Hammurabi but it began to crumble after he died. In 1595 B.C., the Hittites (HIH-tiyts), a rising power from Asia Minor, attacked the city. After sacking Babylon, the Hittites withdrew, but they left the wounded city open to new attacks. Raiders from the hills moved in, and Mesopotamia fell into turmoil. The Babylonian Empire was no more.

> To *sack* a city is to raid, pillage, and plunder it.

Indo-European Migrations

When a large group of people leaves one place, travels a long distance, and settles in another place, we say they have **migrated**. One of the most important migrations in history came to light because of the work of linguists—scholars who study languages and the ways they change over time.

Beginning in the late 1700s, linguists noticed that some of the ancient languages of Europe, such as Greek and Latin, showed resemblances to ancient languages of Asia, such as Persian and Sanskrit (an Indian language). For example, in Sanskrit the word for the number "two" is *dva*. In Persian, it is *du*, while in both Greek and Latin it is *duo*. Why, the linguists wondered, did languages spoken in such widely separated lands have such similar words?

Later, historians decided that there must have been a group of peoples who spoke a language from which many other languages evolved. These peoples, called **Indo-Europeans**, probably lived north of the Black Sea on the steppes—vast dry

Language Similarities				
English	**Sanskrit**	**Persian**	**Spanish**	**German**
mother	mātár	muhdáhr	madre	Mutter
father	pitár	puhdáhr	padre	Vater
daughter	duhitár	dukhtáhr	hija	Tochter
new	návas	now	nuevo	neu
six	sát	shahsh	seis	sechs

grasslands—of what is now southern Russia. Beginning around 3000 B.C., the Indo-Europeans began a great series of migrations that lasted more than two thousand years and covered many thousands of miles.

Some of the Indo-European groups migrated south and east. One group, the Aryans, settled in present-day Iran. Later, some of the Aryans broke away and migrated farther east, to India. Other Indo-Europeans migrated west, toward Europe. Among them were the Hittites, who settled in Asia Minor. Another group, the Celts, kept moving through western Europe until they reached the British Isles. The Irish of today are descended from the Celts.

As the Indo-Europeans divided and moved in different directions over vast distances, their languages grew apart. But linguists say that these languages belong to the same language family, which includes the main languages spoken today in Europe, Iran, and India. The family resemblances between words in hundreds of different languages allow us see the routes of one of history's great migrations.

Push and Pull Factors

Migrations are usually caused by what historians call *push* and *pull* factors. Push factors drive people away from a place. Pull factors are what attract them to another place.

The pull factor for the Indo-Europeans became the wealthy cities of the settled south. What was the push factor? It probably wasn't some

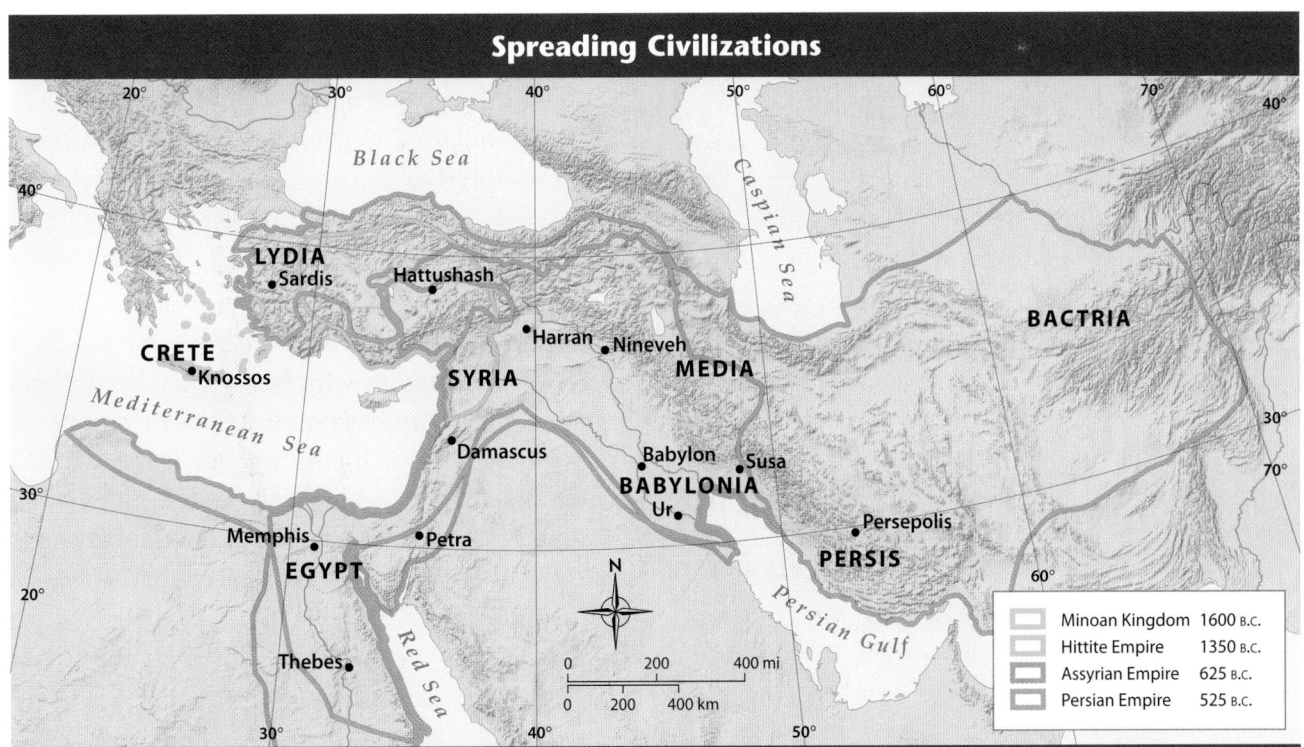

Spreading Civilizations

Minoan Kingdom	1600 B.C.
Hittite Empire	1350 B.C.
Assyrian Empire	625 B.C.
Persian Empire	525 B.C.

Smaller city-states and kingdoms were conquered and consolidated into increasingly larger empires that eventually extended from Europe to India.

sudden catastrophe, since these migrations continued for about two thousand years. More than likely it was due to increasing population.

Instead of competing for pasture for their herds, some clans roamed away in search of new grazing grounds. They moved rapidly and far because they may have been the first people to domesticate and ride horses, perhaps as long ago as 3500 B.C.

The Hittites

Sometime before 1700 B.C., the warlike Indo-European tribe, the Hittites, migrated into Asia Minor and built their capital in the highlands. They knew how to make iron, a secret they guarded closely because it gave them a technological advantage over their rivals. With their iron weapons, the Hittites could win most battles. Hittite warriors drove horse-drawn two-wheeled chariots, each of which could carry three soldiers into battle—one to drive, one to fight, and another to fight or shield his comrades. Most chariots of this time carried only two soldiers, so the Hittites had an edge.

A stag-shaped Hittite drinking vessel made of silver

In the sixteenth century B.C., Hittite soldiers marched to Babylon and plundered the city. Later, they built an empire between the Black Sea and the Syrian coast.

The Hittites were great cultural borrowers. From earlier inhabitants of Asia Minor they learned to make ceramic vases shaped like animals. From the Sumerians they borrowed cuneiform, which they adapted to their own written language. They developed a code of laws similar to Hammurabi's. Like the Mesopotamians, they decorated their public buildings with rows of figures carved into rock. They worshipped hundreds of gods because they accepted all the local deities they came across.

A golden figure of a Hittite goddess, seated with a child

Around 1275 B.C., the Hittites' aggressive empire building faltered when they battled to a standstill against the Egyptian pharaoh Ramses II. (You'll read more about him later in this chapter.) Soon after that, Hittite power began to fade, in part because by this time many other people had learned how to make iron, so the Hittites no longer had an advantage.

The Hittite Empire crumbled around 1200 B.C., although historians aren't sure why. The Hittites might have been conquered by a wave of invaders from lands west of the Aegean Sea. These so-called Sea People were sacking many coastal cities at the time. Because few records from the time exist, we know little about the Sea People who toppled the Hittite Empire.

Invasion and Empire in Egypt

As Mesopotamian empires rose and fell, the world's oldest kingdom continued to thrive. By the sixteenth century B.C., Egypt had grown rich from trade with Nubia, Mesopotamia, and the Indus River valley. Egypt's wealth had attracted throngs of people from poorer lands to its northern cities.

Key Questions

- How did Egypt expand and gain power during the New Kingdom?

- Why did some pharaohs of Egypt's New Kingdom undertake enormous public building projects? How were they able to carry out these projects?

- What aspects of Egyptian culture did the rulers of Kush adopt and preserve?

The Hyksos Invade

During the period known as the Middle Kingdom, Egypt grew prosperous from trade. But when a series of weak pharaohs came to the throne, a group of nomads from western Asia pushed into the Nile Delta. Egyptians called them Hyksos, which meant "rulers of foreign lands," and considered them barbarians. The Hyksos, however, possessed advanced war technology brought by the Indo-Europeans, including horse-drawn chariots, iron armor, and composite bows made of strips of bone and wood glued together. With these advantages, the Hyksos defeated the Egyptians.

Beginning in about 1630 B.C., Hyksos kings ruled much of Egypt for a little more than a hundred years. Egyptian dynasties continued to rule in the southern city of Thebes (theebz), but they had to give the Hyksos a **tribute**, a payment one people makes to another as a gesture of submission. The Hyksos maintained Egyptian temples and adopted some Egyptian customs, but the Egyptians always saw them as outsiders and enemies.

After decades of Hyksos domination, the rulers of Thebes rebelled. It took two generations of fighting, but in the early 1500s B.C. they drove out the last of the Hyksos. Ahmose I of Thebes declared himself king of a united Egypt. His reign marked the beginning of the New Kingdom (1550–1070 B.C.), during which Egypt reached new heights of glory.

The New Kingdom

The first pharaohs of the New Kingdom were aggressive conquerors. They marched north, armed with military technology adopted from the Hyksos. They took over most of Syria and a small strip of land on the Mediterranean Sea called Palestine. From the people of these lands, they demanded tribute. The new wealth pouring in encouraged them to push west to conquer Libya and south to take over Nubia. The Egyptian pharaoh now ruled many people who didn't consider themselves Egyptians. Egypt had become an empire.

A regent is someone who rules when the monarch is absent, disabled, or too young to rule.

Hatshepsut and Thutmose

The fifth ruler of the New Kingdom was the powerful female pharaoh, Hatshepsut (hat-SHEP-soot). She started out as a regent for

On one of the sphinxes that guarded her temple, Hatshepsut had herself depicted as a bearded pharaoh.

her stepson Thutmose III, the official male heir to the throne. She ruled on his behalf because he was a child. Around 1480 B.C., however, Hatshepsut boldly declared herself Egypt's pharaoh. She had statues made that depicted her as a man wearing the ceremonial false beard that male pharaohs wore.

Hatshepsut's reign is best remembered for the great trade expeditions she sent to Punt, an African kingdom near the southern end of the Red Sea. Punt was the source of luxury goods such as incense, myrrh, and exotic animal skins.

When Thutmose came of age, he took over from his stepmother and proved to be the most aggressive pharaoh of all. He went to war every year for twenty years. By the time he died, his armies had crossed the Euphrates in the north and penetrated deep into Nubia in the south.

Akhenaten's New Religion

During the mid-1300s B.C., Amenhotep IV (ahm-uhn-HOH-tep) became one of the most disruptive rulers Egypt had ever seen. He outlawed the worship of the many gods of ancient Egypt. He did not end the practice of religion, but established a new religion that replaced the old gods with one new, all-powerful god.

The one god, he said, was not Amen, Egypt's most popular god, but the sun god Aten, represented only by a radiant disk. The pharaoh changed his own name to Akhenaten (ahk-NAH-tn), meaning "the spirit of Aten." He outlawed the worship of all other gods, shut their temples, and stripped their priests of power. He then built a new capital city devoted to Aten.

Historians consider Akhenaten one of the earliest practitioners of a **monotheistic** religion—a religion that promotes the worship of one god. Nevertheless, the pharaoh failed to convert his people. When Akhenaten died after ruling for seventeen years, a new pharaoh, still a boy, mounted the throne. This boy-king was born Tutankhaten but he changed his name to Tutankhamen, to honor the god Amen-Re.

During Tutankhamen's ten-year reign, it was probably the priests and generals who wielded the real power. Using the boy-king as their instrument, they restored the temples of the many gods,

Akhenaten makes an offering of lotus flowers to the sun god Aten, which he established as Egypt's only deity.

The solid gold death mask of Tutankhamen

demolished Akhenaten's city, removed his name from all monuments, and moved the capital back to Thebes. Later, they revised the written accounts of the pharaohs to skip thirty years of Egyptian history, erasing the memory of both Akhenaten and Tutankhamen.

Tutankhamen's existence was not rediscovered until 1922, when the archaeologist Howard Carter found his tomb. Grave robbers had never plundered the tomb because they never knew the boy-king existed.

Ramses the Great

Once the old gods were restored, the stage was set for one of the giants of Egyptian history, Ramses II, known as Ramses the Great. He ruled for more than sixty years, about twice as long as most Egyptians lived. With his highly trained army of charioteers, archers, and foot soldiers, the pharaoh put down revolts and fended off invaders who threatened Egypt's vast empire.

The major challenge Ramses II faced came from the Hittites. The Hittites, with their chariots and strong bows, had forged an empire in central Asia Minor. Seeking to expand their empire, the Hittites took part of Syria, which had long been an Egyptian possession. Ramses marched north with twenty thousand troops to drive out the Hittites.

Around 1275 B.C., the two sides clashed at Kadesh (KAY-desh) in Syria. Later accounts of the battle vary. Egyptian records celebrate a victory for Ramses, while Hittite accounts claim the Egyptians went down in defeat. Historians think that the Hittite king drew Ramses into a trap by sending out false reports that made Ramses think the Hittites had withdrawn to the north. When Ramses reached Kadesh and set up camp, the Hittite troops came out of hiding.

The startled Egyptians found themselves facing thirty-five thousand Hittite soldiers and thousands of war chariots. Against terrible odds, Ramses managed to avoid defeat, though he fell short of victory. The Egyptians ended up pulling back. The Hittites stayed where they were and came no farther.

Later, the two kings negotiated a complex peace agreement involving trade deals, cultural exchanges, and a marriage between Ramses and a Hittite princess. Both kings' copies of this document still exist. It is believed to be the world's oldest written peace treaty, and it set the border between the two empires, bringing stability to the region.

Ramses II, known for his building programs, had many monuments built to himself, this one at the Luxor Temple.

59

The Hebrews in Egypt

The Hebrews were among the many people enslaved in Egypt during the New Kingdom. The Hebrews were a nomadic people from Palestine who probably migrated into Egypt around 1400 B.C. They came in search of pastures and economic opportunities, but over two centuries they sank into slavery and ended up working on the pharaoh's building projects. Biblical accounts report that Moses, who led the Hebrews out of Egypt, was raised as an Egyptian at the pharaoh's court. This pharaoh may have been Ramses II, but historians can't be sure because Egyptian sources make no mention of the Hebrews.

Monuments, Temples, and Tombs

Ramses and his successors carried out an ambitious building program that dwarfed anything seen since the days of the Old Kingdom. These pharaohs didn't build pyramids but carved their tombs right into the cliffs overlooking the Nile or lining the valley's canyons.

Near Thebes, one narrow gorge called the Valley of the Kings contains sixty-two known tombs and perhaps more yet to be discovered. At nearby Karnak, Ramses built a great hall about the size of a modern-day football field, with 134 stone pillars, each one about 70 feet (21 m) tall and 40 feet (12 m) around. Here, other pharaohs of the New Kingdom completed a temple complex covering almost two square miles. About 250 miles (402 km) south of Thebes, at Abu Simbel (ah-boo SIM-bull), Ramses built a massive temple with four seated statues of himself, each more than 60 feet (18 m) tall, flanking the doorway. Ramses built more monuments to himself than any other pharaoh.

The pharaohs could build such monuments because they had plenty of labor at their command. They put prisoners of war to work as slaves. Stones and supplies were costly, but the pharaohs had wealth pouring in from tribute, plunder, and trade.

Decline of the New Kingdom

Even as the great tombs and temples were going up, Egypt was losing its grip. After Ramses, weaker pharaohs came to the throne. Their weakness tempted local governors to take matters into their own hands, which weakened the pharaohs even more.

The people Egypt had conquered saw their chance to break away. The people north of Egypt

Ramses II had a massive temple built at Abu Simbel, which featured four 67-foot-high (20.4 m) seated statues of himself.

rebelled. From the west of Egypt came the Libyans, who attacked their one-time masters and established a dynasty that ruled Egypt for a while. Nomadic tribes came out of the western desert to raid the riches along the Nile. By about 1070 B.C., Egypt had broken into many small kingdoms.

Nubia and the Kingdom of Kush

South of Egypt, two rivers, the Blue Nile and the White Nile, flow together to form the Nile. The land called Nubia stretched roughly from the rivers' meeting point northward to the First Cataract, which marked the southern boundary of Egypt. Nubia's rocky landscape was not good for farming, but the region was rich in minerals, including gold and emeralds. Nubia's location also made it a center of trade, as goods from central Africa passed through the region on their way to Egypt.

During the Middle Kingdom, Egypt conquered and ruled over much of northern Nubia. In southern Nubia (part of present-day Sudan), however, the kingdom of Kush was growing more powerful. Around 1700 B.C., when the Middle Kingdom collapsed, the Kushites took advantage of Egypt's weakness to extend their power into northern Nubia. As the Hyksos took over Egypt, the Kushites formed a loose alliance with the Hyksos, and trade between Kush and Egypt increased greatly.

After driving out the Hyksos and beginning the New Kingdom, around 1550 B.C., the Egyptians were eager to punish any Hyksos allies, so they marched south into Nubia. They built fortresses throughout the northern part of Nubia. The Kushites had to bow to Egypt's greater power.

Kushite Rule in Egypt

As the New Kingdom weakened, the power of Kush began to grow again. By this time, however, many Kushites admired Egyptian culture. For example, the Kushites had started using

An artist's interpretation of a Kushite festival shows the king Taharka, son of Piankhi, leading a procession.

hieroglyphics and making Egyptian-looking art. When the Egyptian government broke down and fell prey to invaders, Kushite armies marched north to protect the art, temples, and cities of Egypt—and to expand their own power.

Kushite armies marched into Egypt led by a king named Piankhi (PYAHNG-kee), also called Piye (PEE-yeh). Around 750 B.C., Piankhi took over the city of Memphis, Egypt's first capital, and went on to conquer much of Egypt.

The Kushites continued to rule Egypt for about a century. These Nubian pharaohs linked themselves to Egypt's oldest traditions. They encouraged artists to revive the classic styles of the Old Kingdom. For example, in Kush they revived the practice of mummifying the bodies of dead leaders and burying them in pyramids (though smaller than the pyramids built during Egypt's Old Kingdom).

The Kushite pharaohs went on ruling Kush as well as Egypt. To keep control of Kush, they spent much time in their southern capital city, Napata, and left day-to-day administration of Egypt to local officials. In the mid-600s B.C., new imperial powers rising in Mesopotamia would push the Kushites out of Egypt.

Expanding Empires in Mesopotamia

Key Questions

- How did Cyrus and Darius maintain control of the Persian Empire?

- What are some major legacies of the Persian Empire?

The earliest empires in Mesopotamia—Sargon's and then Hammurabi's—gave way over time to much larger empires in southwestern Asia. By 900 B.C., empires centered in Mesopotamia were expanding far beyond the Fertile Crescent.

The Assyrians

Around 1750 B.C., the fall of Hammurabi's Babylon launched a period of disorder during which many groups wrestled for power. Out of that turmoil, the Assyrians managed to build a powerful kingdom in northern Mesopotamia, covering part of what is now northern Iraq and southeastern Turkey. In the following centuries, the Assyrians went on to build the biggest empire of the age.

Assyrian armies had iron weapons, a technology they learned from the Hittites. Assyrian kings led their armies west to the Mediterranean coast and east into what is now Iran. They struck south through Babylonia, extending their power to the Persian Gulf.

As their power increased so did their arrogance. After each crushing victory, they posted inscriptions boasting of their triumph. After beating a rival, one king crowed, "On his royal neck I trod with my foot as on a footstool."

From every campaign the Assyrians brought home loot, but soon they moved past plundering. They divided their conquests into provinces run by Assyrian governors, who kept the tribute flowing. They established a network of officials to run their territory efficiently. They set up a communication system to stay informed about rebellions and other events within their empire.

To crush revolts, Assyrian kings often drove whole populations to new regions far from their original homes. They calculated that people living in unfamiliar territory among strangers would be less able to organize rebellions against Assyrian rule.

To put down the frequent revolts, the Assyrians maintained a standing army of professional charioteers, cavalry, bowmen, lancers, and military engineers equipped with iron-headed battering rams and other siege weaponry. This feared military machine could fight on any terrain, from plains to mountains to fortified cities.

From about 850 to 650 B.C., Assyrian kings carved out a huge empire. They defeated Syria, Palestine, and Babylonia, and in time their conquests stretched far beyond the Fertile Crescent. Around 700 B.C., when Babylon revolted, the Assyrian king Sennacherib (suh-NA-kuh-rub) crushed it and bragged, "From its foundation to its top, I destroyed, I devastated, I burned with fire."

Art and Learning

Despite their brutal methods of ruling, the Assyrians loved art and learning. Sennacherib, who laid waste to Babylon, built the great walled city of Nineveh along the Tigris River. In its time, Nineveh, Assyria's capital, became the biggest and perhaps the most beautiful city in the world. Huge statues of bulls stood outside its gates. Rivers were diverted to flow through the city, serving as as cool streams watering many parks. Assyrian palaces were built of cypress, cedar, boxwood, and pistachio wood, and their grounds were adorned with sculptures of alabaster and white limestone.

This sculpture of a human-headed winged bull, which once adorned a temple, is an iconic example of the art of ancient Mesopotamia.

The greatest of the Assyrian kings was also among its last. Ashurbanipal (ah-shur-BAH-nuh-pahl), who reigned from 668 to 627 B.C., was not only a warrior but also a scholar and a patron of learning. His library at Nineveh contained more than twenty thousand clay tablets ranging from historical records (sometimes more legendary than factual) to books on subjects such as foretelling the future. Nineveh was later destroyed, but the library and the tablets survived.

The Chaldeans

As the Assyrian Empire expanded, it grew too big to defend, and it embraced too many people who hated the Assyrians and their harsh ways. At the end of the seventh century B.C., two groups formed an alliance against Assyria: the Chaldeans (kal-DEE-uhnz), who lived within the empire, and the Medes (meedz), who lived east of it. In 612 B.C., these two groups toppled the hated Assyrian Empire and demolished Nineveh, to the relief of the many people Assyria had been oppressing.

Nineveh was never rebuilt. The Chaldeans, however, held much of the Assyrian Empire together, and ruled it from the ancient city of Babylon. For about seventy-five years this Chaldean Empire—also called the New Babylonian Empire— flourished as brilliantly as any culture since the first Babylonia ruled by Hammurabi a thousand years earlier.

The most famous ruler of this powerful empire was Nebuchadnezzar II (neb-yuh-kud-NEH-zur). In 586 B.C., he destroyed Jerusalem, burned Solomon's Temple to the ground, and brought the Hebrews back to Babylon as slaves.

Like the Assyrians, however, Nebuchadnezzar loved beauty as much as war. He made Babylon the wonder of the age. Its enormous walls were glazed with red, blue, and cream-colored bricks. The city had more than a thousand temples, including an almost 300-foot (91 m) tall ziggurat that, in biblical literature, is likely the structure the Hebrews called the Tower of Babel.

63

The stunning Ishtar Gate, decorated with figures of dragons and bulls, marked the entrance to the city of Babylon.

Nebuchadnezzar surrounded his capital city with a double wall running more than ten miles. Nine gates led through the walls and into the great city. Each was named for one of Babylon's gods. Grandest of all was the stunningly beautiful Ishtar Gate.

To please one of his wives, Nebuchadnezzar built the famous Hanging Gardens of Babylon, which were like artificial cliffs with vines and flowers spilling down their faces. These elegantly terraced gardens, watered by the Euphrates, have long since vanished, but the Greek historian Herodotus described them as one of the wonders of the ancient world.

Medicine and Stargazing

The Chaldeans made impressive advances in science. They had some understanding of how illness spread and how to relieve many symptoms with medicinal plants.

They believed the gods lived in the sky, so they studied and recorded the movements of the stars. Their motivations for studying the sky lay in astrology—using the stars to predict events on earth—but their precise observations helped lay the basis for scientific astronomy.

The Persian Empire

The Chaldeans gave way to the Persians, a people from the east. The story of the Persian Empire begins with the great Indo-European migrations. Around 1000 B.C., two Indo-European tribes, the Persians and Medes, came south between the Black and Caspian seas to inhabit the Iranian plateau. The Medes settled around the Zagros Mountains while the Persians settled farther south along the Persian Gulf. Both groups spoke dialects of Persian.

A *plateau* is a broad, level, elevated expanse of land.

The Iranian plateau was too dry for productive farming, so these new settlers made their living from their herds, and from selling horses and mules to the Mesopotamians. They also mined minerals such as silver, iron, and precious stones. And they profited from trade passing through their region.

A *dialect* is a form of a language spoken by a particular group or in a specific region.

Cyrus the Great

A powerful leader emerged among the Persians, a man known to history as Cyrus the Great. Cyrus was the son of a lesser Persian king, and the Persians as a whole accepted the Medes as their masters. Yet around 550 B.C., Cyrus became king of all the Persians and Medes. The Medes yielded to him because their army would not fight Cyrus.

In 539 B.C., Cyrus led an army of Persians and Medes down to Babylon. The city's walls were supposedly too high to climb and too thick to break through. Cyrus, however, drained a river that ran under the walls and marched through the resulting tunnel.

Cyrus took the city without a fight because some people in Babylon preferred Persian to

Primary Source

TRAINING YOUNG WARRIORS

From their mid-twenties until old age, all sons of the Persian elite, including Cyrus himself, served the empire as military officers. Before they could join a military campaign, however, they trained for ten years as members of the royal hunt, learning how to travel long distances on foot with little to eat except what they could kill. These endurance and survival skills served them well in battle and helped make the Persian armies among the most feared in the ancient world. The following passage, from a study of Cyrus written by the Greek historian Xenophon (who lived c. 430 to 350 B.C.), describes the rigorous training of Persian youths.

The lads follow their studies till the age of sixteen or seventeen, and then they take their places as young men. After that they spend their times as follows. For ten years they are bound to sleep at night round the public buildings...to guard the community.... During the day they present themselves before the governors for service to the state, and, whenever necessary, they remain in a body round the public buildings. Moreover, when the king goes out to hunt, which he will do several times a month, he takes half the company with him, and each man must carry bows and arrows, a sheathed dagger... slung beside the quiver, a light shield, and two javelins, one to hurl and the other to use, if need be, at close quarters.... The king leads just as he does in war, hunting in person at the head of the field, and making his men follow, because it is felt that the exercise itself is the best possible training for the needs of war. It accustoms a man to early rising; it hardens him to endure heat and cold; it teaches him to march and to run at the top of his speed; he must perforce learn to let fly arrow and javelin the moment the quarry is across his path.... Such is the life of the youth. But when the ten years are accomplished they are classed as grown men.

Persian bronze statuette, 5th–4th century B.C.

THE **FORTRESS OF BABYLON**

In the following passage, the Greek historian Herodotus describes the magnitude of the walled fortress of Babylon. He refers to two ancient units of measurement, the stade and the royal cubit. A stade was the length of a Greek footrace in a stadium, or 200 yards. The distance around the fortress of Babylon was 480 stades, or 55 miles. Its thickness was equally impressive. A royal cubit is almost two feet, so a wall "fifty royal cubits in breadth, and in height two hundred" was approximately 90 feet thick and 350 feet high. It is no wonder that when Cyrus, the Persian conqueror, brought his armies to Babylon, he chose to drain the moat around the fortress rather than scale the walls themselves.

Now Assyria contains many large cities, but the most renowned and the strongest, and where the seat of government was established after the destruction of Nineveh, was Babylon, which is of the following description: the city stands in a spacious plain, and is quadrangular, and shows a front on every side of one hundred and twenty stades; these stades make up the sum of four hundred and eighty in the whole circumference. Such is the size of the city of Babylon. It was adorned in a manner surpassing any city we are acquainted with. In the first place, a moat, deep, wide, and full of water, runs entirely round it; next, there is a wall fifty royal cubits in breadth, and in height two hundred…. And here I think I ought to explain how the earth, taken out of the moat, was consumed, and in what manner the wall was built. As they dug the moat they made bricks of the earth that was taken out; and when they had molded a sufficient number, they baked them in kilns….They first built up the sides of the moat, and afterward the wall itself in the same manner; and on the top of the wall, at the edges, they built dwellings of one story, fronting each other, and they left a space between these dwellings sufficient for turning a chariot with four horses. In the circumference of the wall there are a hundred gates, all of brass….

Chaldean rule. Ancient Greek and Persian historians claimed that many cities opened their gates to Cyrus for this reason. It wasn't that Cyrus rejected the use of force. He was a warrior who used conquest to forge the biggest empire the world had yet seen, stretching from the Indus River to the gates of Europe. All of Assyria would have fit inside it twice over. To govern his empire, however, Cyrus enforced policies very different from those of the Assyrians.

Cyrus relied on tolerance more than terror. He allowed the people he conquered to keep their customs, worship their own gods, and follow their own ways. His soldiers had orders not to loot,

A Median officer pays homage to the imperial King Darius.

in Babylon as slaves, but Cyrus let them return to Judea and rebuild their temple.

Governing the Persian Empire

After Cyrus died, his son took the throne peacefully, but when this son died, trouble broke out. After some confusion, Darius (duh-RIY-uhs) I, a Persian nobleman unrelated to Cyrus, ended up as king. He claimed that he and Cyrus shared a distant ancestor.

On the face of a cliff, Darius—later known as Darius the Great—had his story carved in three languages. Twenty-five centuries later, this inscription gave scholars the key to decoding cuneiform, unlocking the archives of Mesopotamian culture going back to Sumerian times.

Darius probably seized the throne illegally, but he proved to be as great a leader as Cyrus. He built a vast army around a core of ten thousand elite professional bodyguards. These were called the Immortals because as soon as one fell ill, he was replaced, thus keeping the group at exactly ten thousand men in the peak of fitness.

and he protected the temples in each place he conquered. He did this to win the good will of local priesthoods. Through them, he believed, he could keep conquered populations obedient. Instead of deporting whole populations to strange lands, he allowed exiled populations to return home. The Hebrews, for example, were still living

The Persian king Darius built a vast army of bodyguards, depicted here on part of an ancient citadel.

Darius kept close watch on his officials, who in these carved figures are shown paying homage to their king.

galloped from location to location carrying pouches full of letters. These letters were written in ink on thin sheets of leather. To move the mail quickly, the carriers worked in relays. One rider galloped a short distance and then handed his bag to another rider, who took it at top speed another short distance. These couriers could carry a letter 200 miles (322 km) in a day. (In the early nineteenth-century United States, a similar system would be used to move the mail; it was called the Pony Express.)

Darius divided his vast territory into about twenty provinces, each governed by a Persian nobleman called a *satrap*. Darius kept the satraps under control by requiring them to report to him constantly and receive his orders. Darius's spies, unofficially called the "eyes and ears of the king," kept a close watch on the satraps and all others who might cause trouble.

Darius devoted great effort to building the enormous city of Persepolis. He established what was, at the time, the world's best **infrastructure**, a system of roads, bridges, and lodgings needed for travel and communication. The Persian Royal Road between the cities of Susa and Sardis was the wonder of its time.

The Royal Road was just one part of a system of roads connecting the king to every corner of his realm. On the major highways, stations spaced about a day's travel apart provided travelers with food and places to rest. Local people kept each station stocked with supplies, as part of the tribute they owed the king. In exchange, they enjoyed the stability and safety his government guaranteed.

Ancient Persia had the world's first real postal service, a network of mounted mail carriers who

Persia Meets Its Match

For all his benevolence, Darius tolerated no disobedience. When the Ionians of Asia Minor rebelled, he struck them down harshly. Then he sent both an army and a navy to punish the Athenians of Greece for having sided with the rebels. The Greeks, however, defeated both his forces.

Darius's son, Xerxes (ZURK-seez), vowed to avenge his father's humiliation. Upon inheriting the throne, Xerxes led an even larger army to Greece, but he, too, was defeated. (In a later

The Mail Carriers' Unofficial Motto

Carved in stone above the entrance to the main New York City post office building is a famous statement: "Neither snow nor rain nor heat nor gloom of night stays these couriers from the swift completion of their appointed rounds." The sentence comes from a book written sometime around 450 B.C. by the Greek historian Herodotus. He was writing about the Persian mail couriers.

chapter, you will read more about these famous Greek victories over the Persians.)

After two defeats at the hands of the Greeks, the Persian Empire went into a long decline. Xerxes was less gifted than Darius, and worse kings followed him. Fights for the throne broke out within the royal family. The satraps lost respect for the squabbling monarchy and stopped following orders. Government services broke down, the roads grew less safe, and trade decreased, which led to widespread poverty.

When a new king and conqueror, Alexander, known as Alexander the Great, invaded the country in 334 B.C., Persia looked powerful but it had already rotted on the inside. Alexander defeated it easily and burned down Persepolis. The last of the Persian monarchs was murdered by his own nobles as he fled.

The Legacy of the Persian Empire

For more than two hundred years, the Persians had established peace from Asia Minor to modern-day Pakistan. They knitted a vast territory together with an unparalleled system of roads. They secured their subjects' loyalty by allowing them to follow their own ways.

The Persians adopted whatever they found useful from the many cultures they ruled. From the Lydians, for example, they took the idea of minting coins. Persian art combined themes and styles from Greece, Mesopotamia, Egypt, and other lands.

Persepolis, their capital, was a city of enormous palaces full of huge halls with high pillars like those in Egypt. The city's broad boulevards were lined with statues of lions and bulls with human heads that looked Assyrian. The workers and materials came from places as distant as Afghanistan, India, Lebanon, and Egypt.

Patterns of Early Empire

Within the space of a few pages, you have read about happenings that took place over about two thousand years, years that witnessed the rise and

Zoroastrianism: Light Versus Darkness

One legacy of the Persian Empire was the religion of its royal family, Zoroastrianism (zawr-uh-WAS-tree-uh-nih-zuhm), which still survives.

Zoroastrians follow the teachings of the ancient sage Zoroaster (zawr-uh-WAS-tuhr). These teachings are recorded in scriptures called the Avesta. Zoroastrians see the world as a battleground between Ahriman, god of darkness, and Ahuramazda, god of light. They believe that people can choose either side and must face judgment for their choices after death. In the seventh century, Zoroastrianism gave way to the new religion of Islam. Today, Zoroastrianism has followers worldwide, most of them in India.

fall of many early empires. The conquerors who founded these empires were driven by similar goals—all wanted to control trade routes, resources, and land. Through conquest they gained wealth, which they used to build stronger armies. Stronger armies in turn helped them grow even wealthier and more powerful.

Different rulers tried different tactics for holding onto power and administering their vast territories. Some used harsh force to bend conquered peoples to their will, while others allowed conquered peoples to maintain many of their own ways.

None, however, had the means to unify many diverse groups of people and maintain their loyalty to a distant central government over long periods of time. Often, when weak rulers came to the throne, loyalties shifted and conquered people seized the opportunity to rebel. Sometimes, outside powers would take advantage of the fighting among the rulers and launch an invasion. These early empires set the stage for empires yet to come in this and other parts of the world.

CHAPTER 4

PEOPLE AND IDEAS ON THE MOVE

1500–300 B.C.

1800 B.C.	1600 B.C.	1400 B.C.

Abraham leads the Hebrews from Ur to Canaan; Judaism emerges.

On the island of Crete, Minoan civilization reaches its height.

1500 B.C.
Aryans move into the Indian subcontinent; Hinduism emerges.

Minoans traded goods and spread ideas as they sailed the waters of the Mediterranean.

1000 B.C.

800 B.C.

600 B.C.

1100 B.C.
Phoenicians
dominate trade in
the Mediterranean.

596 B.C.
Babylonians conquer
Jerusalem; the Jewish
Diaspora begins.

*S*argon's Akkadia. Hammurabi's Babylon. Egypt's New Kingdom. Nebuchadnezzar in Assyria. Cyrus and the Persians. While these ancient empires rose and fell, other groups made a mark on history as well.

Through migration and trade, distinct groups spread their cultures, ideas, and languages over vast distances. Trade between two seafaring nations—the Minoans and the Phoenicians—tied the different cultures of the Mediterranean region together. Around the same time, a group of Indo-European nomads, the Aryans, migrated to India where they established a society based on the caste system and founded one of the major world religions, Hinduism.

Meanwhile, another group of nomads, the Hebrews, wandered from Mesopotamia to the shores of the Mediterranean Sea, where they developed a new religious idea—that the universe was ruled by a single, all-powerful God who held high ethical expectations of humanity.

Mediterranean Trading Kingdoms

In the period after 1500 B.C., many different peoples lived in southwest Asia and the Mediterranean region, though our knowledge of them is limited. We do know that during the times of powerful empires and in times of turmoil, some of these peoples—including the Minoans (mih-NOH-uhnz) and the Phoenicians (fih-NEE-shunz)—prospered as a result of extensive trade. They also left lasting legacies.

The Minoans

In the year 1900, Sir Arthur Evans, a British archaeologist, discovered the buried ruins of a huge palace at Knossos (NAH-suhs), on the Mediterranean island of Crete (kreet). Evans had stumbled on the remains of the earliest civilization in Europe, one that flourished from about 3000 to 1100 B.C. Evans named it the Minoan civilization, after King Minos (MIY-nuhs), a mythical ruler of Crete.

As Evans dug up the ruins of the palace, he was astonished to find how wealthy and advanced the Minoan culture had been. Among the dozens of rooms, he discovered a storeroom with huge jars designed to hold thousands of gallons of olive oil. He uncovered the remains of a sophisticated plumbing system that piped fresh water into the palace. His most striking discovery, however, was a series of frescoes—wall paintings made by applying colors to wet plaster. Some of the frescoes depicted plants and animals. Others showed Cretan men and women dressed in elegant clothes. Later archaeologists

Key Questions

- Why is our knowledge of Minoan culture limited?

- How did trade affect the spread of ideas in the ancient world?

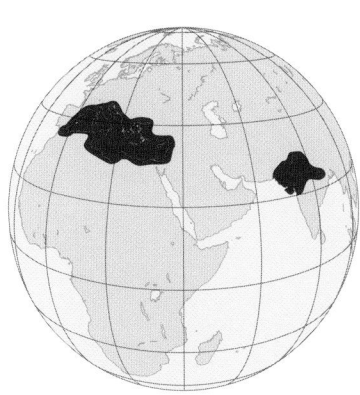

Trade and ideas changed the Mediterranean and India.

A fresco from c. 1600 B.C. depicts splendidly dressed women of the Minoan court.

The Real Atlantis?

According to an ancient Greek legend, an island called Atlantis supported a rich and powerful culture until it was torn apart by an earthquake and sank beneath the sea. Some scholars think that this myth reflects the destruction of the Minoan cities by earthquakes and tsunamis (giant sea waves) after the eruption of a volcano on a nearby island.

discovered other Minoan palaces and cities on both Crete and mainland Greece.

Minoan civilization reached its height around 1600 B.C. Great seafarers, the Minoans traded with Egypt and other countries around the Mediterranean. Protected by the sea from invasion, they lived peacefully in open cities without walls.

Still, much about the Minoans remains mysterious. No one has yet figured out their system of writing. We cannot read their records, and we don't know what religion they followed. However, since they depicted snakes and bulls so often in their art, some historians think they may have worshipped those animals. Some Minoan paintings show men and women somersaulting over the backs of charging bulls. Were these bull-leapers taking part in a religious ritual or just practicing a very dangerous sport? Scholars don't know for sure.

Equally mysterious are the reasons for the decline of the Minoan culture. We know only that some time after 1500 B.C., the great Minoan cities were destroyed—perhaps by a huge earthquake, or maybe by foreign invaders.

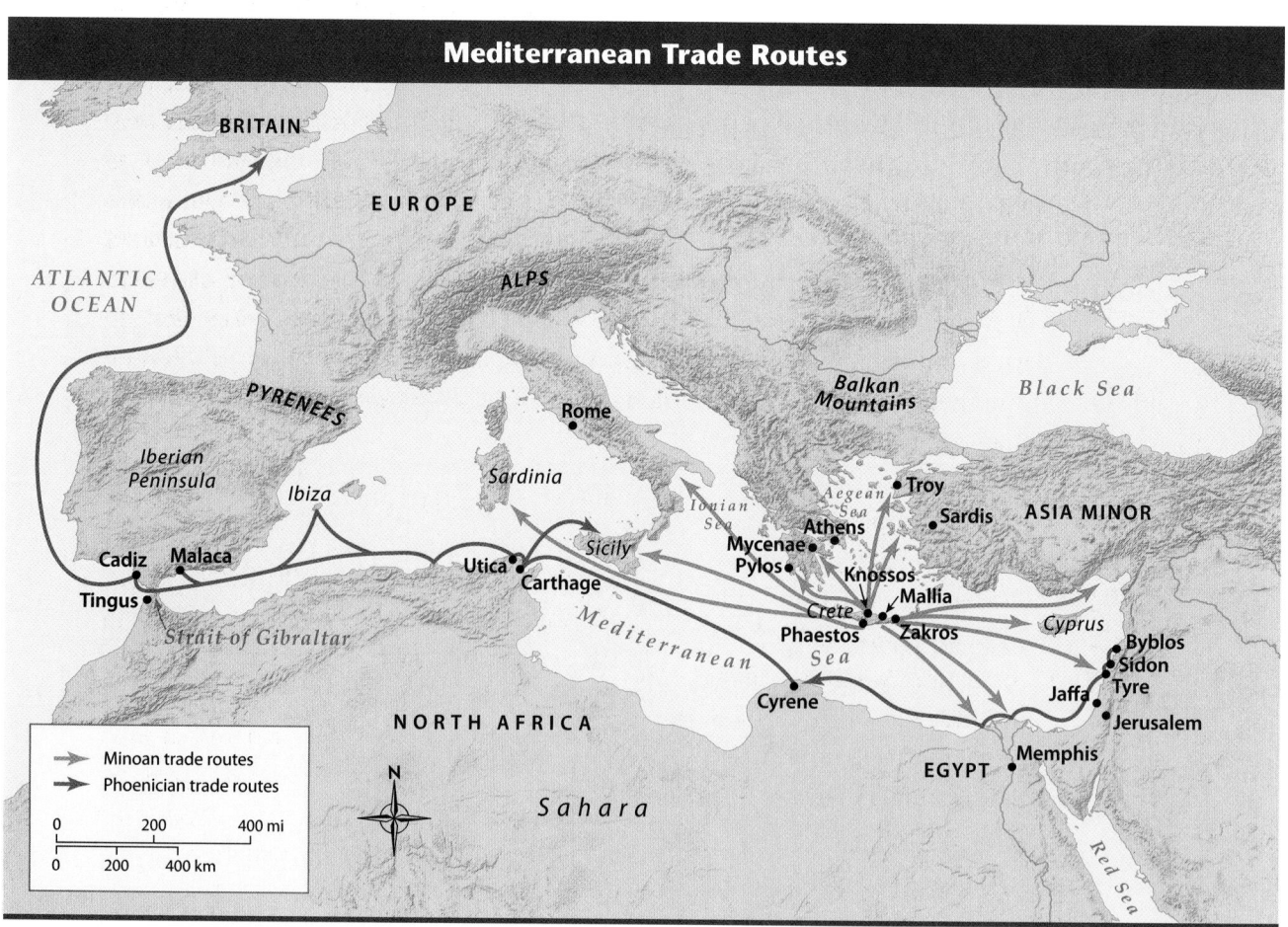

Mediterranean Trade Routes

The Minoans and Phoenicians were seafaring peoples whose merchants built trade networks across the Mediterranean and out into the Atlantic Ocean, linking three continents.

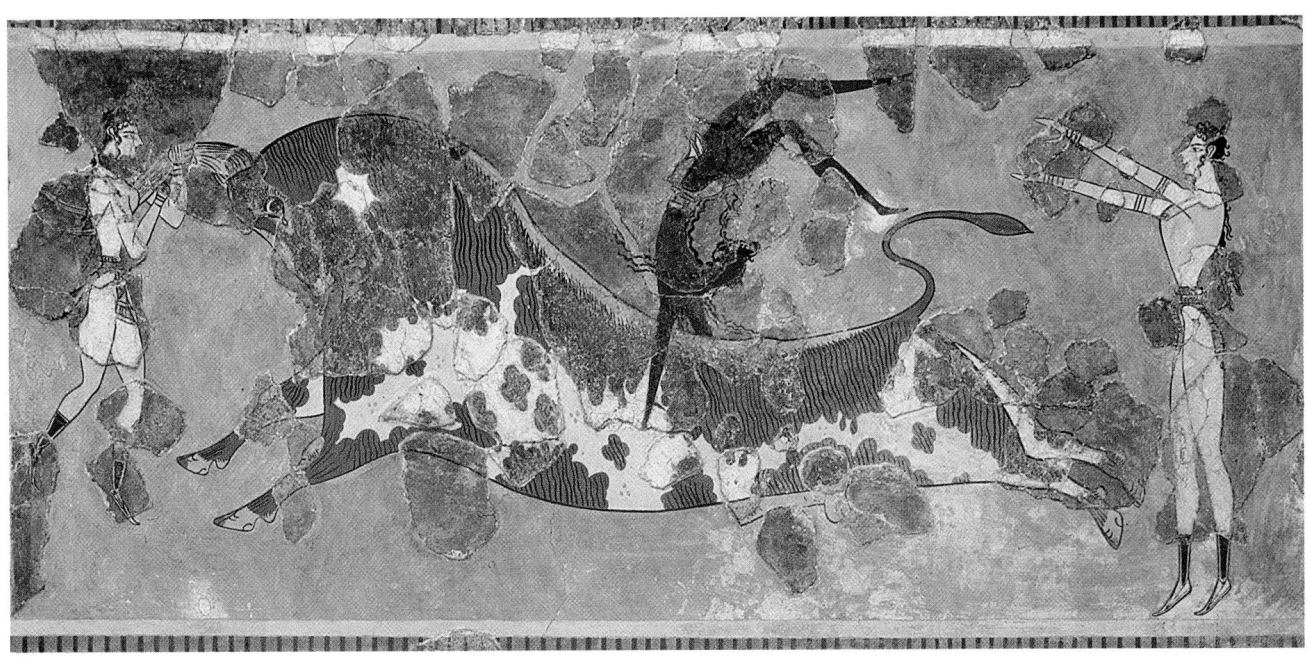

A skilled acrobat somersaults over the back of a charging bull in this vivid Minoan wall painting, c. 1500 B.C.

Phoenician Seafarers

After the decline of the Minoan culture, a new group of seafarers came to dominate trade in the Mediterranean. They lived in cities on the coast of what is now Lebanon. They traded in glass, metals, jewelry, and lumber with other peoples across southwest Asia, southern Europe, and northern Africa. One of their products was especially prized—a purple dye made from shellfish, which is why their neighbors called them Phoenicians, meaning "the Purple People."

The most daring seafarers of their time, the Phoenicians sailed all over the Mediterranean and into the stormy Atlantic Ocean, possibly reaching Britain. According to an ancient Greek historian, around 600 B.C. a Phoenician fleet even managed to sail all the way around the continent of Africa, a feat not achieved again until A.D. 1498.

The seafaring Phoenicians traded objects like this glass jar.

At key places along their trade routes, the Phoenicians established colonies, settlements subject to the rule of the Phoenician homeland. Among the most important of these colonies were the cities of Cadiz (kuh-DIHZ) in Spain, and Carthage in northern Africa. While the Phoenicians dominated their colonies, they were dominated by larger empires around them—first the Assyrians, then the Babylonians, and finally the Persians. To avoid being conquered, they paid tribute to the rulers of those empires.

The Color Purple

To the peoples of the ancient Mediterranean, the special purple dye produced by the Phoenicians was worth more than its weight in gold. Only the wealthy and powerful could afford to use it to color their clothes. Later, under the Roman Empire, a law was passed decreeing that only the emperor himself could wear the color. Afterward, when an emperor came to power in Rome he was said to "assume the purple."

The Phoenicians' most lasting contribution was their invention of an alphabet, a system of writing in which each symbol stood for a particular sound. Through Phoenician traders, the alphabet spread to Greece. The Greeks modified the Phoenician alphabet, which used only consonants, to include vowel sounds. Later, the Greek alphabet was modified by the Romans, who wrote in letters very much like the ones we use today. Thus, the Phoenician system of writing is the distant predecessor of the alphabet used by speakers of English and the other Western languages.

A Region of Many Peoples

The Phoenicians lived in a region of many peoples and cultures, all influencing each other through trade. To the northwest, along the Aegean Sea in present-day Turkey, was the land of the Lydians—probably the first people to have made their money out of metal. (Previously, peoples had used various things for money, including seashells, salt, grain, and bars of gold.)

South of Phoenicia lived the Philistines (FIH-luh-steenz), who fought a series of wars

On ships like this one, drawn in cutaway view, Phoenicians traded goods and spread ideas to distant lands.

against the Hebrews. To the west lay the country of the Aramaeans (A-ruh-MEE-uhnz). Their language, Aramaic (A-ruh-MAY-ihk), became the main language of the region, and their system of writing later gave rise to the Hebrew and Arabic alphabets.

What Do We Mean by "Western"?

What do we mean when we refer to "Western languages" or "Western civilization" or "the Western world"? Geographically, west is a direction—the sun sets in the west. To a historian, "west" is also an idea, or rather, a vast set of ideas and attitudes. Today, when historians refer to Western civilization, they are thinking of a body of ideas generally shared in Europe and the Americas. Western civilization, embracing the ideas of Europe and the Americas, is sometimes contrasted with Eastern civilization, made up of the ideas of India, China, Japan, and other countries. But this is a broad general contrast, as there are many commonly shared ideas across both East and West.

The Hebrews and the Origins of Judaism

Key Questions

- What are the basic beliefs of Judaism?

- How did the beliefs of the Hebrew people differ from the beliefs of other early peoples?

- How did the beliefs of Judaism influence later legal and religious systems?

Among the Phoenicians' neighbors was a small group of people who had an enormous impact on the history of the world. These people, the ancient Israelites, were called Hebrews. The earliest Hebrews are thought to have been nomadic herdsmen in Mesopotamia. Historians think that around 1800 B.C., they migrated with their flocks to the shores of the Mediterranean, settling south of Phoenicia in an area called Canaan (KAY-nuhn).

In ancient Egypt, during the mid-1300s B.C., the pharaoh Akhenaten had decreed the worship of a single sun god, but the Egyptians resisted the decree and quickly returned to the worship of many gods. The ancient Hebrews are generally acknowledged by historians as having founded the first monotheistic religion. Later the religion of the Hebrews would become known as Judaism, and the followers of Judaism would be called Jews.

The Ancient Hebrews

Our understanding of the Hebrews differs from our understanding of other ancient peoples. We know about the Minoans and the Phoenicians mostly through the discoveries of archaeologists, but most of what we know of the ancient Hebrews comes from their own religious writings, gathered into a work called the Tanakh (tah-NAHK), or Hebrew Bible. The Hebrews were the first people to write their history. Today the Hebrew Bible is considered sacred not only by Jews but also by Christians, who call it the Old Testament.

The Torah (TOHR-uh) consists of the first five books of the Hebrew Bible—Genesis, Exodus, Leviticus, Numbers, and Deuteronomy. The Torah is considered especially sacred by Jews. It contains the basic religious ideas of Judaism, and also gives a version of the early history of the Hebrews. We do not know how accurate this history is, however, because it was written down many centuries after the events it describes.

According to the Torah, Abraham lived in the city of Ur in Mesopotamia around 2000 B.C. The Torah says that God spoke to Abraham, saying, "Get thee out of thy country, and from thy kindred, and from thy father's house, unto the land that I will show thee. And I will make of thee a great nation, and I will bless thee." Abraham, the Torah recounts, moved his followers and his flocks across more than a thousand miles of desert, to the land of Canaan. Because of his obedience to God, and his role in the great migration, Abraham would be remembered as the father of the Hebrew people.

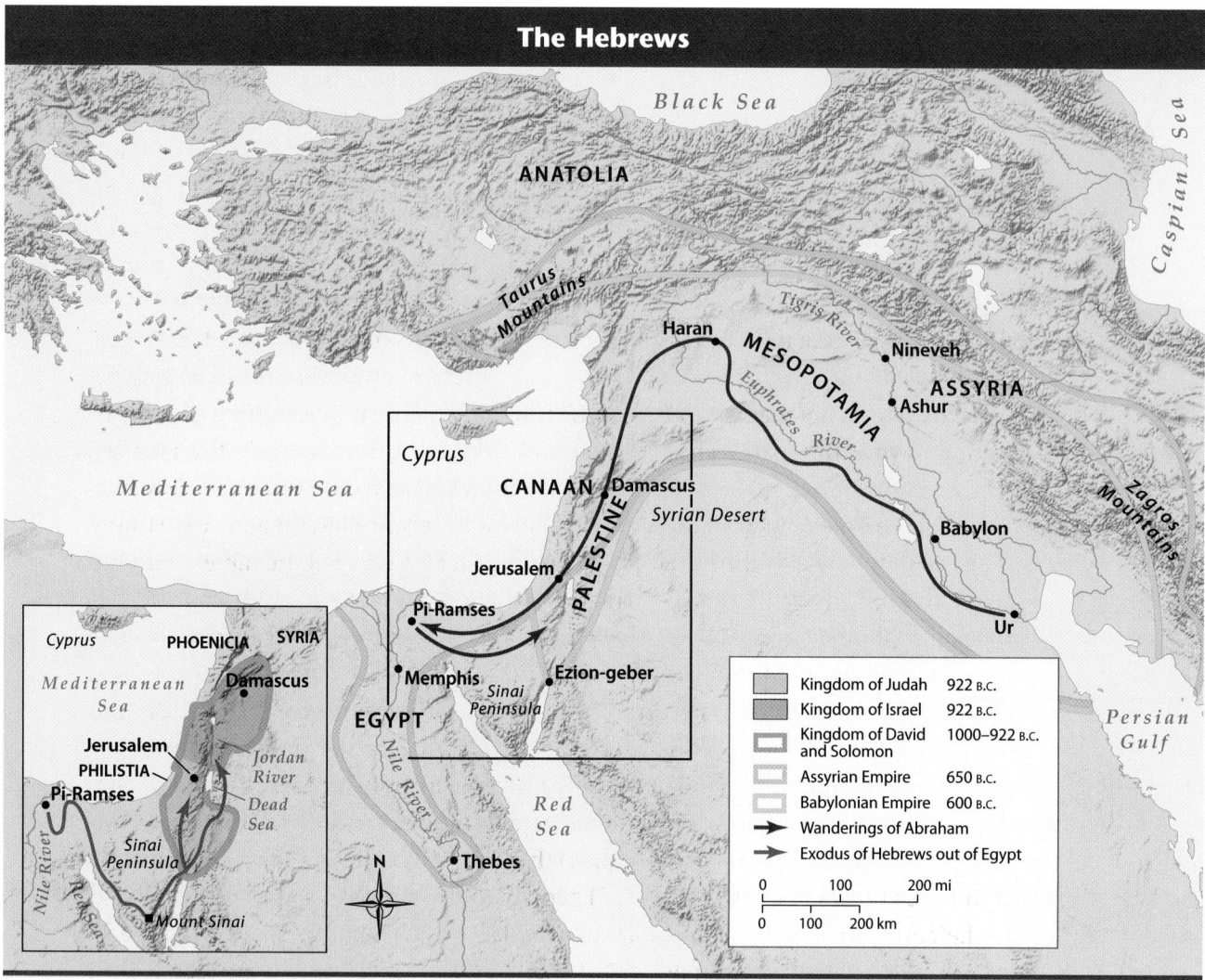

The Hebrews

Judaism, one of the world's major monotheistic religions, had its beginnings in a narrow, fertile strip of land on the eastern edge of the Mediterranean Sea.

Covenant and Commandments

Monotheism is the belief that there is one all-powerful God. Unlike other ancient peoples, who were polytheists—worshippers of many gods—the Hebrews worshipped one God, whom they at first called Yahweh (though they later came to consider the name of the divinity too sacred to be spoken).

The Hebrews believed that God had created the world and everything in it. He was both all-powerful and omnipresent (present everywhere). By contrast, most polytheists believed that the gods had only limited powers, with each god presiding over a particular place or a specific part of nature, such as the sky or the sea.

The Hebrews believed that God had a special relationship to the Hebrew people. According to the Torah, God made a **covenant**—a sacred agreement—with Abraham, after Abraham settled in Canaan. In this covenant, says the Torah, God promised that Abraham's descendants would possess the land of Canaan and become a "great and mighty nation." This biblical promise gave rise to the idea of the Hebrews as a "chosen people."

According to the Torah, Abraham had a grandson named Jacob, and God gave Jacob a special name, "Israel," meaning "God rules." Jacob himself had twelve children, whose descendants became the twelve tribes of a new nation, Israel. In later years, the Hebrews would be called Israelites.

The Hebrews, in traditional striped robes, asked for permission to enter and trade with Egypt, as depicted on this ancient tomb mural.

The line of leaders stretching from Abraham to the sons of Jacob would be known as the "patriarchs," or "fathers."

The Torah says that in the time of Jacob, famine broke out in Canaan. To escape starvation, the Hebrews moved south to the wealthy land of Egypt. At first they prospered there, but then the Egyptians turned against them and enslaved them. The Hebrews remained in slavery, says the Torah, until God appeared to Moses and commanded him to lead his people out of Egypt.

At first, the Torah says, the Egyptian pharaoh refused to let the Hebrews go free, so God afflicted the Egyptians with a series of horrible plagues, and then destroyed their army by drowning it in the sea. Finally, Moses was able to lead the people out of Egypt and back toward their homeland in Canaan—a journey referred to as the Exodus, which means "the going-out." Thus, according to the biblical account, God had proven his power and his loyalty to his chosen people by crushing the Egyptians.

According to the Torah, the Hebrews under Moses wandered in the wilderness for forty years before they made it back to Canaan. At one point in the journey, God called Moses up to the top of a tall mountain. The Torah recounts that there, on Mount Sinai, God gave Moses two stone tablets containing laws that every Hebrew had to obey. These laws have since become widely known as the Ten Commandments.

Among other things, the commandments forbade the Hebrews to steal, to commit murder, or to lie about their neighbors. The very first commandment stressed absolute loyalty to God: "I am the LORD thy God, who brought thee out of the land of Egypt…. Thou shalt have no other gods before Me." The Hebrews believed that they deserved God's blessings only as long as they obeyed his laws.

Moses led the Hebrews out of Egypt, in a journey known as the Exodus (as envisioned here in a painting from the mid-1800s). According to the Torah, the Hebrews wandered in the wilderness for forty years before reaching Canaan.

THE **TEN COMMANDMENTS**

The commandments widely known as the Ten Commandments make up a small part of the more than six hundred commandments in the Torah. The Ten Commandments are the ones that, according to the Torah, were written by God on two stone tablets and brought down from Mount Sinai by Moses. The Hebrew phrase for these commandments refers more precisely to ten "statements" or "declarations." Early Christian scholars adopted these commandments, numbered them, and called them the Decalogue, Greek for "ten words."

There are slight variations in the order and wording of the commandments as adopted by Judaism, Catholicism, Protestantism, and various denominations. For example, one of the commandments is variously translated as "Thou shalt not kill" or "Thou shalt not murder." These variations in part result from different ways of translating and organizing the text that provides the basis for the Ten Commandments, the Book of Exodus, Chapter 20. (The following text is from an English translation of the Hebrew Bible published in the early 1900s.)

And God spake all these words, saying:

I am the LORD thy God, who brought thee out of the land of Egypt, out of the house of bondage. Thou shalt have no other gods before Me.

Thou shalt not make unto thee a graven image, nor any manner of likeness, of anything that is in heaven above, or that is in the earth beneath, or that is in the water under the earth; thou shalt not bow down unto them, nor serve them; for I the LORD thy God am a jealous

Israelite Kingdoms

The Torah relates that Moses died on the way to Canaan, and his followers continued on to resettle the land. Historians believe that the account in the Torah may reflect a migration that occurred in about 1200 B.C. From this point on, the Hebrews are more often referred to as Israelites, after the twelve tribes that descended from the twelve sons of Jacob.

The Torah tells the story of the resettling of Canaan. Later parts of the Hebrew Bible relate more of Israelite history. These writings report that,

several generations after the return to Canaan, the Israelites came into conflict with a people called the Philistines. The Philistines were a warlike people who fought against the Israelites for possession of Canaan. Palestine, meaning "land of the Philistines," became another name for Canaan.

To resist the Philistines, the twelve tribes united under a leader named Saul, making him their king. When Saul died in battle, probably around 1000 B.C., he was succeeded by a warrior named David, who, the Hebrew Bible says, was especially favored by God. A famous biblical story

God, visiting the iniquity of the fathers upon the children unto the third and fourth generation of them that hate Me; and showing mercy unto the thousandth generation of them that love Me and keep My commandments.

Thou shalt not take the name of the LORD thy God in vain; for the LORD will not hold him guiltless that taketh His name in vain.

Remember the Sabbath day, to keep it holy. Six days shalt thou labor, and do all thy work; but the seventh day is a Sabbath unto the LORD thy God, in it thou shalt not do any manner of work, thou, nor thy son, nor thy daughter, nor thy man-servant, nor thy maid-servant, nor thy cattle, nor thy stranger that is within thy gates; for in six days the LORD made heaven and earth, the sea, and all that in them is, and rested on the seventh day; wherefore the LORD blessed the Sabbath day, and hallowed it.

Honor thy father and thy mother, that thy days may be long upon the land which the LORD thy God giveth thee.

Thou shalt not murder. Thou shalt not commit adultery. Thou shalt not steal. Thou shalt not bear false witness against thy neighbor.

Thou shalt not covet thy neighbor's house; thou shalt not covet thy neighbor's wife, nor his man-servant, nor his maid-servant, nor his ox, nor his ass, nor any thing that is thy neighbor's.

tells how the young David, with a single stone from his slingshot, killed a gigantic Philistine warrior named Goliath.

David proved to be a great king, defeating the Philistines and conquering the lands of other neighboring peoples. After he seized the city of Jerusalem, it became the Israelites' political capital. When David's son and successor, Solomon, built a great temple in the city, Jerusalem became the Israelites' center of religious worship as well. During and after Solomon's time, however, came a period of disunion. The Israelite nation split in two, dividing into a northern kingdom called Israel and a southern kingdom called Judah.

Defeat and Diaspora

During this period, the Hebrew Bible tells us, many Israelites started worshipping foreign gods. Some religious teachers angrily warned the people that God would punish them for their disloyalty. These warnings seemed to come true when the land of the Israelites fell prey to powerful foreign empires.

Around 720 B.C., the northern kingdom of Israel was conquered by the Assyrians. More than a century later, the Babylonian king Nebuchadnezzar conquered Judah. His soldiers plundered Jerusalem, destroying Solomon's temple, and carried off most of its inhabitants to Babylon as slaves.

The period of the Babylonian Exile, as it is known, lasted until the Persians conquered Babylon fifty years later. Many of the inhabitants of Judah then returned to their homeland, but a large number stayed behind in Mesopotamia. Meanwhile, the Assyrian conquest of the kingdom of Israel had scattered its inhabitants among many different countries. The **Diaspora** (diy-AS-puh-ruh)—from the Greek word for "scattering"—of the Jewish people had begun.

Judaism and Ethical Monotheism

By insisting that there was only one God, Judaism made a dramatic break from the polytheistic religions of the ancient world. Judaism was also

With battering rams and torches, the Assyrians assaulted and conquered the Hebrew town of Lachish, c. 701 B.C.

The Diaspora, Then and Now

The people first known as Hebrews were later called Israelites. Today they are generally known as Jews, followers of the religion called Judaism. After the conquest of their country by the Assyrians and Babylonians, the Jews were scattered around southwest Asia and the Mediterranean region. By the first century A.D., more Jews were living outside Israel than within it. Later, even more Jews were forced out of their homeland by Roman conquests. The term *diaspora* refers both to this dispersion of the Jews and to the body of Jews living outside Israel.

In 1948, Israel again became an independent nation, and many Jews moved there. But there are still far more Jews in the Diaspora. Of the roughly fourteen million Jews worldwide, about five million live in Israel. Today, Jews live all around the world. Apart from Israel, more live in the United States than in any other country.

radically different from other religions of its time in its understanding of the nature of God. Other peoples, such as the ancient Egyptians and the Greeks, thought that the gods sometimes acted selfishly, carelessly, or cruelly. By contrast, the Hebrews believed their God to be just and loving. In the words of one biblical poem, "The Lord is good to all, and his compassion is over all that he has made."

The God of the Jews demanded more than worship from his followers. He also demanded that they act in the world with honesty, fairness, and mercy. This idea of a single God laying down *moral* rules for his followers is sometimes called **ethical monotheism**. As a teacher named Micah put it in the Hebrew Bible, "What does the Lord require of you, but to do justice, and to love kindness, and to walk humbly with your God?"

This ancient Hebrew idea of God's ethical expectations of humanity was a new idea in the history of religion. The Sumerians and Egyptians believed that their gods cared mainly about the offerings people made to them. But the Hebrews came to believe that their God cared not just about how people worshipped him but also about how they treated each other.

As part of this new emphasis on people as ethical beings with social responsibilities, the authors of the Torah included hundreds of specific laws that all Hebrews were expected to follow. These laws—which the Hebrews believed were handed down by God—covered everything from diet and hygiene to rules for farming, lending money, and punishing crimes. Many laws stressed the need for helping the poor. Furthermore, the Hebrews believed that God's laws were meant to apply not just to a select group but to everyone—man or woman, young or old, rich or poor.

It turned out that the Hebrews did not always follow the laws. Some of them even broke away from their religion and worshipped foreign gods. In the time of the divided kingdoms, some fervent religious teachers, called prophets, spoke out against what they condemned as corruption and disloyalty to God. The writings of prophets such as Isaiah and Jeremiah became an important part of Jewish tradition, reminding Jews of their duties to God and mankind.

Judaism's Lasting Influence

Over the last two thousand years, most Jews have lived in countries far from their biblical homeland. Often, as part of a small, distinct minority, they have met with persecution. Yet most have clung strongly to their religious traditions.

Around the world, Jews meet for worship in religious centers called synagogues. They keep the Sabbath (from sundown Friday to sundown Saturday) as a day devoted to rest and worship. Jews study the Tanakh, or Hebrew Bible, which is made up of a large number of writings of many kinds, including law, history, prophecy, and poetry. Scholars believe that most of the Hebrew Bible was composed between 1200 B.C. and 100 B.C.

Many Jews also study a huge collection of later writings called the Talmud. This collection conveys the ideas of a number of rabbis (religious teachers) over many centuries. The Talmud helps Jews understand the laws and ideas of the Bible, and how to apply them to their own lives.

For Jews, the holiest of scriptures is the Torah, the first five books of the Bible, including the story of the Hebrews from Abraham through Moses. Every synagogue has a Torah scroll, a copy of the Torah handwritten on a special material made of animal skins and then rolled around two pieces of wood. The scroll is treated with the greatest reverence and stored in a beautifully decorated container called the ark. Every Sabbath service includes a reading from the Torah.

The ideas of Judaism have had a tremendous and lasting impact on world history. Abraham is considered the patriarch of three monotheistic religions—Judaism, Christianity, and Islam. Christianity adopted the Tanakh as the first part of its own scriptures, renaming it the Old Testament. From the Jews, Christians learned the principle of ethical monotheism—the idea that there is only one God, and that he demands just behavior from his followers. Islam also centers on the concept of ethical monotheism, and builds on other ideas from Judaism. Judaism influenced the development of later Western political ideals by emphasizing the importance of law and insisting that everyone should be equal under the law.

The Dead Sea Scrolls—so called because they were found in caves on the northwest shore of the Dead Sea—constitute one of the most significant archaeological discoveries of all time. About 900 documents, written in Hebrew, Aramaic, and Greek, include some of the only known copies of biblical texts made before 100 B.C.

India: The Vedic Age

You have learned that the Indian subcontinent, a vast, wedge-shaped peninsula, is watered by a system of great rivers, including the Indus and the Ganges. (The Indus is mostly in modern-day Pakistan.) From ancient times, Indians have revered the Ganges as a goddess, "Mother Ganga," whose life-giving waters fertilize the fields along her banks. In the south, which lacks the great rivers of the north, farmers rely on seasonal rain-bearing winds, the monsoons, for water. In the central part of southern India, the Deccan Plateau gets much less rainfall than the coastal plains. On these plains, the lush, wet climate is perfect for growing pepper, nutmeg, and other highly valued spices that, through much of India's history, have played a large part in its trade with the outside world.

On the subcontinent of India, more than four thousand years ago, some of the world's earliest civilizations thrived along the Indus River. At Harappa and Mohenjo-Daro, archaeologists have unearthed the remains of two thriving cities. This advanced culture flourished for eight hundred years and then, for reasons that remain mysterious, passed out of history. By 1800 B.C., most of the great cities of the Indus Valley had been abandoned. Around three hundred years later, a new chapter of Indian history opened with the arrival of the Aryans.

The Aryans

The Aryans belonged to the group of peoples known as Indo-Europeans, who had been migrating out of Central Asia for centuries. Nomadic cattle herders, the Aryans may have been searching for better grazing land when they crossed the mountain passes and arrived on the north Indian plains. Gradually, the Aryans mingled with the local people and, as they spread eastward along the plain of the Ganges, abandoned their lives as nomads and turned to farming.

The Aryans spoke a language called Sanskrit, a version of the original Indo-European tongue that later evolved into hundreds of different languages, including Greek, Latin, and English. At first, the Aryans had no system of writing, and instead organized their culture through **oral tradition**—the handing down of laws, ideas, and stories by word of mouth.

Many Aryans reached the north Indian plains by way of the Khyber Pass, a mountain pass that links modern Pakistan and Afghanistan.

Key Questions

- How did migrating peoples affect the civilizations of southern Asia?
- What literary works provide information on early Indian society?
- What are the basic beliefs of Hinduism? With what country is Hinduism most closely associated?

Aryan Settlement of India, 1200 B.C.

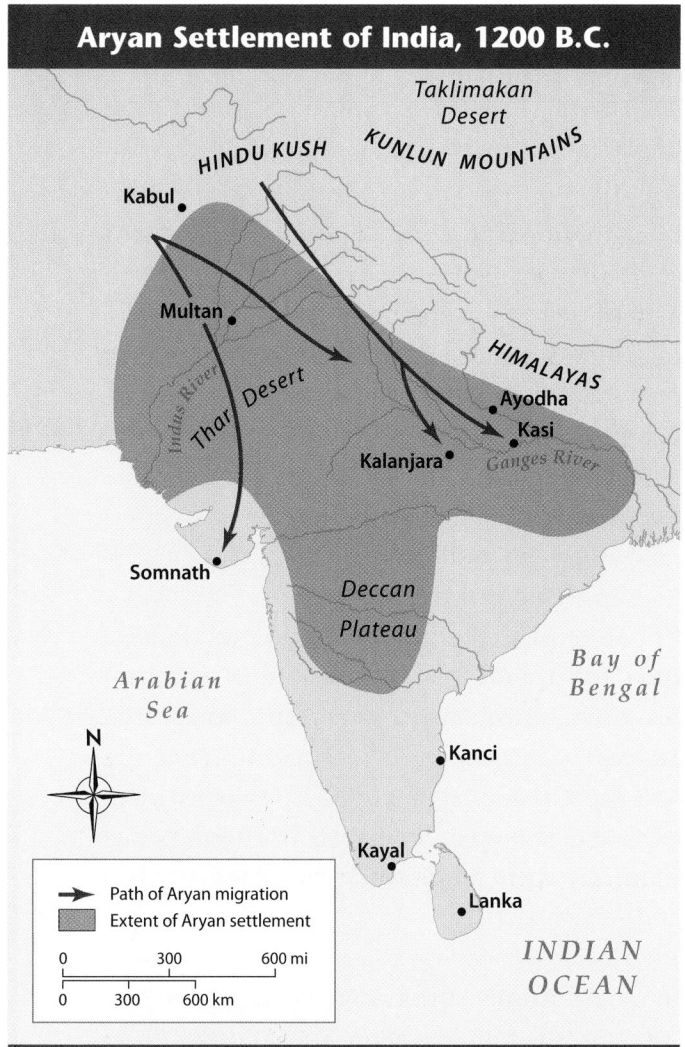

Taklimakan Desert

HINDU KUSH KUNLUN MOUNTAINS

Kabul

Multan

Indus River

Thar Desert

HIMALAYAS

Ayodha

Kasi

Kalanjara

Ganges River

Somnath

Deccan Plateau

Arabian Sea

Bay of Bengal

N

Kanci

Kayal

Lanka

INDIAN OCEAN

→ Path of Aryan migration

Extent of Aryan settlement

0   300   600 mi

0   300   600 km

Aryan herders moved onto the plains of India over hundreds of years and formed farming communities.

The most important of the works passed on by oral tradition were the Books of Knowledge, or **Vedas** (VAY-duhz). Though scholars are not sure precisely when the Vedas were composed, the probable years of composition, ranging from about 1500 to 500 B.C., are often called India's Vedic Age. The Vedas, which consist of hymns to the Aryans' many gods, later became the first sacred writings of Hinduism, the dominant religion of India.

The Caste System

It is through the Vedas that we learn that Aryan society was rigidly divided into four classes, or varnas. Today we use a later European term, **castes**, to refer to these traditional classes.

The highest, most honored caste consisted of the Brahmans, the priests who kept the sacred writings and performed sacrifices to the gods. Next came the caste of warriors, the Kshatriyas (KSHA-tree-ahz). Lower down were the Vaishyas (VIYSH-yuhz), the caste of merchants and farmers. The fourth and lowest caste, the Shudras, consisted of ordinary workers. Even lower than the Shudras, and outside the four classes, were the "outcastes" or "untouchables," who did work considered unclean and disgusting, such as sweeping animal dung from the streets or tanning animal hides. Every person in Vedic India was born into one of these groups and remained within it for life.

Over time, the caste system became even more complex, as thousands of subcastes developed within the four-caste structure. These subcastes, known as jatis (JAH-teez), from a term meaning "birth," consisted of people belonging to the same extended family group or practicing the same occupation. Marriage between members of different jatis was forbidden.

Aryan society, like most warrior societies, was **patriarchal**—that is, men held the authority. As the caste system developed, it reinforced inequality between men and women. The Vedas mention women taking part in religious ceremonies and sacrifices, but by the early centuries A.D., women were forbidden even to read the Vedas. Husbands expected absolute obedience from their wives. One lawgiver decreed, "A virtuous wife should constantly serve her husband like a god, even if he behaves badly."

Hindu Caste System

Caste	Membership
Brahmans	Priests and highly educated individuals
Kshatriyas	Warriors
Vaishyas	Merchants and farmers
Shudras	Workers
Untouchables	Menial laborers

The Beliefs of Hinduism

The peoples and cultures of the Indus Valley mixed with the Aryans who gradually migrated into India from central Asia and settled on the Ganges plain. From this mixture emerged the traditions of Hinduism, one of the world's oldest living religions. Hinduism incorporates a wide range of beliefs, including a belief in many gods as well as in one universal essence. Hindu ideas have profoundly influenced people in Asia and around the globe.

Reincarnation and Release

One of the central ideas of Hinduism is dharma (DUHR-muh), the notion that each person has a particular religious and social duty, whether as a warrior, farmer, or servant. It was only by devotedly fulfilling his dharma that a person might hope to ascend through the rigid class structure.

Any rise in class, however, would not take place in a person's current lifetime. As Hinduism developed, the idea evolved that after a person dies, he or she is **reincarnated**—reborn into a different life-form, either human or animal. "Those whose conduct has been good," says an early Hindu text, "will quickly attain some good birth, the birth of a Brahman, a Kshatriya, or a Vaishya. But those whose conduct has been evil will quickly attain an evil birth, the birth of a dog, or a hog, or a Chandala [an untouchable]."

That passage comes from one of the works called the Upanishads (oo-PAH-nih-shahdz), philosophical writings that were added to the Vedas after about 1000 B.C. According to the Upanishads, while people can hope to be reborn into a higher caste, a fortunate few are able to escape the endless, wearying cycle of death and rebirth. By living intensely pure and spiritual lives, these people are able to achieve *moksha* (MOHK-shuh), or liberation, a state of serene release from the cycle of reincarnation.

Two Epics of Hinduism

Not all of the basic works of Hinduism are scriptures like the Vedas or philosophical writings like the Upanishads. Two great epic poems, the *Mahabharata* (muh-HAH-BAHR-uh-tuh) and the *Ramayana* (rah-MAH-yuh-nuh), have helped mold the religious and social beliefs of Hindus since they were written down between about 400 B.C. and A.D. 400.

The *Mahabharata* is a sprawling poem of more than one hundred thousand lines. It tells the story of two families who fight a long, brutal war for control of northern India. The *Ramayana*, only about one-fourth as long as the *Mahabharata*, relates the tale of Prince Rama, a wise and noble ruler whose wife, Sita (SEE-tuh), is kidnapped by a demon king. The demon takes Sita away to his home on an island surrounded by sea monsters. Rama enlists the aid of the friendly monkey-god Hanuman (HUN-oo-mahn), who orders his army of monkeys to build a bridge to the island. After a terrific battle, Rama and Hanuman defeat the demon and rescue Sita.

While both epics tell exciting stories, they also illustrate the moral ideas of Hinduism, in particular the principle of dharma. Even today, Hindu children are as familiar with the stories in the epics as Jewish or Christian children are familiar with the stories of Abraham, Moses, or King David.

A scene from the *Ramayana* (in this 18th-century painting): Rama and the monkey king Hanuman defeat Ravana.

Other Beliefs of Hinduism

Hinduism, unlike many other religions, had no one founder and it follows no single sacred scripture. Instead, it evolved over thousands of years. Furthermore, Hindus themselves differ considerably in some of their beliefs and in the way they put them into practice. Some scholars describe Hinduism as a collection of related religions—all rooted in the land of India—rather than a single religion.

In general, however, Hindus share a belief in reincarnation and the closely related idea of **karma**. The law of karma says that every good act a person performs results in something good, and every bad act in something bad. Often, however, the good or bad effects do not show up until the person has died and been reincarnated. Thus, if a person is reborn in some lowly form—say, as a hog or as an untouchable—it is because he is carrying bad karma from a previous life. But, according to Hindu belief, a person's good karma will be rewarded by rebirth into one of the higher castes.

Hindus worship many gods. The three main gods are Brahma, who created the world; Vishnu (VISH-noo), who preserves it; and Shiva (SHIH-vuh), god of both destruction and regeneration. Different groups of Hindus pay special reverence to different gods. Hindus believe these deities might sometimes take human form. For example, Prince Rama, the hero of the *Ramayana*, is thought to have been an avatar, or incarnation, of Vishnu.

The Upanishads also describe an eternal spiritual force called Brahman, which is greater than all the gods. "All works, all desires, all scents, all tastes belong to [Brahman]: it encompasses all this universe. ...When I depart from [here] I shall merge into it." Hindus who focus more on Brahman than on individual gods have much in common with followers of monotheistic religions like Judaism.

Hindus differ, too, in their ways of worship. Some worship in groups by chanting, praying, and offering gifts of food and flowers to the gods. Others engage in the solitary practice of yoga, an intense form of meditation. Devoted practitioners

The image of Shiva, the Hindu god of destruction and regeneration, adorns an Indian temple mural that dates to the eighth century A.D.

of yoga, called yogis, learn to control their breathing and to stretch their bodies into difficult positions. This physical discipline allows them to focus their minds on spiritual matters. Hindus believe the most determined yogis may achieve *moksha*, the release from the cycle of rebirth.

Hindus also differ in their attitudes toward violence. The religion had its roots in the warlike Aryan tribes, and the warrior (Kshatriya) caste is one of the most honored. But Hinduism also developed the principle of ahimsa, or noninjury to living things. Many Hindus follow a vegetarian diet because they think that the killing of animals is wrong.

More than anything else, Hinduism is the religion of a single nation—India. It is practiced almost exclusively by Indians and the descendants of Indians living in other parts of the world. Because India is such a populous nation, Hinduism remains one of the world's major religions, with hundreds of millions of followers.

1027 B.C.
The Zhou Dynasty
establishes the "mandate
of heaven."

c. 500 B.C.
Buddhism emerges;
Confucius teaches his ethical
principles in China.

A.D. 1

A.D. 400

269 B.C.
Asoka begins his rule
of India's Mauryan
Dynasty.

c. 100 B.C.
China enters a golden
age under the Han
Dynasty.

C. A.D. 400
India enjoys a
golden age under the
Gupta Empire.

Chapter 5
Classical India and China
1000 B.C. – A.D. 500

The Great Stupa, a stunning third-century B.C. Buddhist place of worship

*S*ome periods of civilization are considered *classical*. These are times when a society makes extraordinary achievements in art, science, religion, philosophy, and politics. Classical ages often exert a strong influence over later generations.

The classical periods of the two great Asian civilizations of India and China gave rise to influential religions and philosophical systems—Buddhism, Confucianism, and Daoism. In China, a system of government emerged that would last nearly two thousand years. In India, advances in mathematics and astronomy furthered understanding of the way the world works.

Both civilizations produced artistic and literary works that served as models for hundreds of years and are still studied and admired today.

India and the Birth of Buddhism

Key Questions

- What characterizes a *classical* period in civilization?

- How and where did Buddhism begin, and what are its central beliefs?

- In what ways was India under the Gupta Empire a classical civilization?

The dominant religion of India, Hinduism, was born among the Aryans who migrated to the subcontinent around 1500 B.C. The earliest Hindu scriptures, the Vedas, contain hymns to the Aryans' many gods. The Vedas also describe the beginnings of the caste system that divided Indian society into four groups, with priests (Brahmans) at the top, followed by warriors, merchants, and ordinary workers.

Between 800 and 500 B.C., a new set of Hindu religious writings appeared. These new scriptures, the Upanishads, questioned some of the ideas in the Vedas. The Upanishads shifted the emphasis from many gods to a universal spiritual force called Brahman. The Upanishads also introduced the doctrine of reincarnation—that after death, everyone will be reborn in another form of life.

The idea of reincarnation helped take away some of the harshness of the caste system. A poor person of low caste, by acting well in his present life, could hope to be reborn as a wealthy, powerful person of high caste. A few especially holy people might achieve a state called *moksha*—release from the cycle of death and rebirth.

The Buddha's Path

Around 500 B.C., traditional Hindu ideas were challenged by an Indian prince who gave up a life of wealth and power to become a religious teacher. His followers broke away from Hinduism to form a new religion. They called their teacher the Buddha (BOO-duh), which means "the Enlightened One" or "the Awakened One." The religion he founded is called Buddhism.

Siddhartha Gautama

The prince who came to be known as the Buddha was named Siddhartha Gautama (sid-DAHR-tuh GOW-tuh-muh). What we know of his life comes from stories told in the Buddhist scriptures.

According to these stories, Siddhartha's father ruled a small state in northern India, where the prince grew up in wealth and luxury. He lived in three different palaces, where he was so sheltered that he never encountered unhappiness or suffering.

One day, the young prince decided to leave the palace and take a chariot ride through the city. As he rode through the streets, he was startled to see a bent-over man leaning on a stick. The prince asked his charioteer what was wrong with the man. The charioteer replied that the man was

The world still feels the influence of classical Asian civilizations.

91

simply old, and that everyone, even the prince, would grow old. Shaken, the prince returned to the palace.

The next day he rode out again. This time he saw a sick man. The charioteer explained that everyone, even Siddhartha, would eventually get sick. The troubled prince returned to the palace, only to ride out again the next day. This time he was shocked by the sight of a corpse. The charioteer explained that the man had died, and that all people, even the prince, must die.

According to the accounts of Siddhartha's life, the troubled prince then returned to the palace. What is the point of living, he wondered, if life leads to nothing more than old age, sickness, and death? He decided that he had to discover the meaning behind the suffering that all people experience.

Leaving the luxury of the palace, Siddhartha set off on a spiritual quest. He wandered the countryside for six years, talking and studying with holy men. For a time, he became an ascetic—a person who practices extreme self-denial to attain spiritual insight. He cut off his hair. He ate almost nothing, sometimes only a single pea in a day.

Still Siddhartha found himself no closer to an answer. He gave up his ascetic practices and instead began to meditate. One night, as he meditated beneath a tree, he experienced a great flash of understanding. He saw into the roots of human suffering and he realized how to escape it. He had become the Buddha—the Enlightened One. Now, he set out to teach his message of enlightenment to others. He soon gathered a group of disciples, who were attracted by his gentleness and wisdom.

The Teachings of Buddhism

In the first sermon he preached to his followers, the Buddha described what came to be called the Four Noble Truths. First, said the Buddha, all life is suffering, because it involves physical and mental discomforts—not only old age, sickness, and death, but also unfulfilled longings, loss, and grief.

Second, suffering is caused by desire—the cravings that everyone experiences, including desires for pleasure, love, wealth, and power. Desire, said the Buddha, causes the endless, wearying cycle of birth and rebirth.

The third noble truth is that desire and suffering only end when a person has achieved Nirvana—that is, when he or she has eliminated the cycle of desire that leads to reincarnation. One who reaches Nirvana will never be reborn, and is free from the suffering that comes with life. Over time, the followers of the Buddha would interpret Nirvana differently. Some saw it as a kind of non-being—the word *Nirvana* means something like "blowing out," as a candle is blown out. Others saw it in more positive terms, as a state of the highest bliss.

An Indian sculpture portrays the Buddha, the Enlightened One, sitting with legs crossed in the posture known as the lotus position, used in the practice of meditation.

The fourth noble truth, said the Buddha, is that the way to achieve Nirvana is through following the Noble Eightfold Path:

- Right understanding (seeking accurate knowledge)
- Right intention (avoiding destructive thoughts and desires)
- Right speech (saying nothing untrue or harmful to others)
- Right action (acting virtuously)
- Right livelihood (doing work that does not harm others)
- Right effort (resisting evil and negative states of mind)
- Right mindfulness (maintaining a true awareness of the world)
- Right concentration (training thoughts through meditation)

The Buddha spent decades traveling around India, gathering many followers. He taught them to seek enlightenment by following the Noble Eightfold Path. He said they must show compassion to all living things, including animals. The Buddha also taught his followers to ignore the caste divisions of Hinduism. "No one is an outcaste by birth," he declared, "nor is anyone a Brahman by birth. It is by deeds that a person becomes a Brahman."

The Spread of Buddhism

After the Buddha's death, the religion he founded spread far beyond the borders of India. Beginning in the third century B.C., Buddhist missionaries, traveling by sea, took their faith to the island of Sri Lanka, south of India, and from there to the southeast Asian countries of Burma, Thailand, and Cambodia. Several centuries later, a new wave of missionaries took the Buddhist message eastward to China, Korea, and Japan. Later still, Buddhism spread northward, becoming the dominant religion of Tibet.

As Buddhism spread, it split into three main branches. The earliest branch, called Theravada

This painted cotton cloth depicts a mandala, a symbolic diagram that represents the universe. Both Buddhists and Hindus use mandalas in sacred rites and as instruments of meditation.

(ther-uh-VAH-duh), became dominant in Southeast Asia. This branch tried to remain close to the simplicity of the Buddha's original teachings. The Mahayana branch, which became the main form of Buddhism in China, Korea, and Japan, was a more complicated version of the faith. It stressed the importance of *bodhisattvas* (boh-dih-SUHT-vuhz), saintlike figures who, having reached enlightenment, choose to be reborn on earth in order to enlighten others. A third form of Buddhism, the Tibetan or Vajrayana, held that by becoming enlightened, a believer could acquire almost supernatural powers.

Buddhism had an enormous influence on the art and architecture of the countries to which it spread. In India and Southeast Asia, Buddhists erected stupas, great domed buildings to serve as places of worship. In Japan and China, they built tall, multileveled towers called pagodas. Everywhere in Buddhist countries, sculptors carved or cast statues of the Buddha. Most often, he is

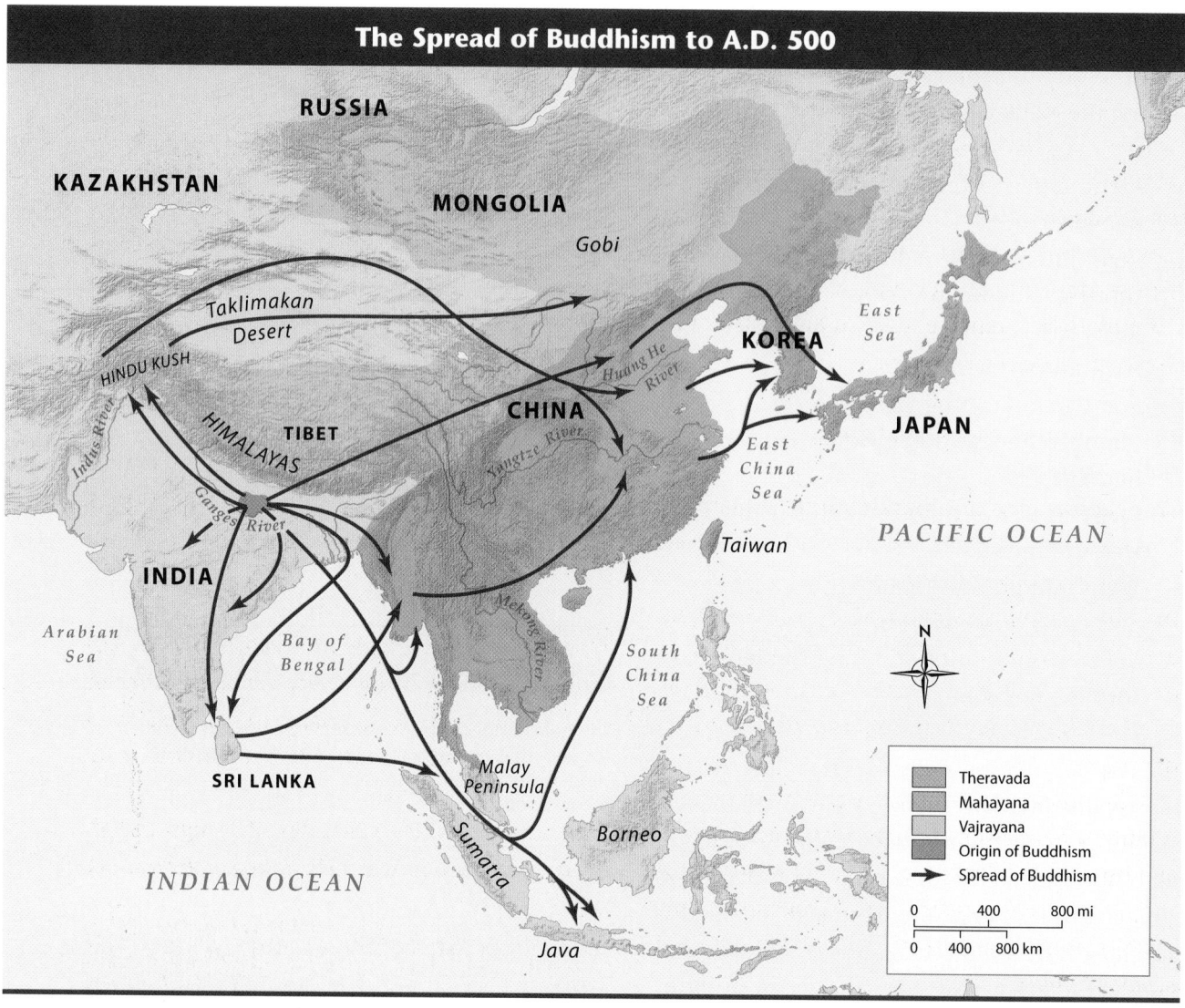

The Spread of Buddhism to A.D. 500

RUSSIA

KAZAKHSTAN

MONGOLIA

Gobi

Taklimakan Desert

HINDU KUSH

Indus River

HIMALAYAS

TIBET

CHINA

Huang He River

Yangtze River

KOREA

East Sea

JAPAN

Ganges River

INDIA

Arabian Sea

Bay of Bengal

Mekong River

East China Sea

Taiwan

PACIFIC OCEAN

SRI LANKA

Malay Peninsula

Sumatra

South China Sea

Borneo

INDIAN OCEAN

Java

N

Theravada
Mahayana
Vajrayana
Origin of Buddhism
Spread of Buddhism

| 0 | 400 | 800 mi |
| 0 | 400 | 800 km |

In the centuries following the Buddha's death, missionaries carried his teachings throughout eastern Asia and won millions of converts to Buddhism.

depicted sitting serenely, as if in meditation. The size of these statues ranges from tiny to enormous. One stone statue of the Buddha in China is over two hundred feet (61 m) tall.

Even as Buddhism spread around Asia, it largely died out in India. The hold of Hinduism, the native religion, proved too strong. But just as Buddhism took many of its central ideas, such as reincarnation, from Hinduism, so Hinduism was influenced by Buddhism's values of compassion and nonviolence. Buddhism became the dominant religion of eastern Asia. Today it is one of the world's most widespread religions, with about 350 million followers. The largest groups of Buddhists

live in the nations of Tibet, Sri Lanka, Burma, Thailand, Cambodia, Vietnam, China, Korea, and Japan.

India's Great Empires

Aryan India was divided into many small states that often fought each other. This lack of unity left the subcontinent vulnerable to foreign powers. In 518 B.C., the emperor Darius I of Persia conquered northwestern India. The Persians ruled the region for more than two centuries until they were defeated by another set of foreign conquerors—the Greeks. Alexander the Great, from Macedonia in Greece, led the Greeks to conquer northwestern India.

Alexander stayed in India only briefly before withdrawing back to the west. Into the power vacuum left by his retreat came a fiercely warlike Indian king named Chandragupta (chuhn-druh-GOUP-tuh), whose reign began in about 325 B.C. He seized control of the northern part of the subcontinent, as well as much of what is now Afghanistan. In doing so, he established the first Indian empire, named after his family, the Maurya (MOWR-ee-uh).

The Mauryan Empire and the Reign of Asoka

The capital city of Chandragupta's Mauryan Empire sprawled along the banks of the Ganges River. It may have been the world's largest city at the time. Chandragupta's well-organized government was divided into different departments—for example, one department focused on taxation, another on commerce, and another on the upkeep of temples.

Chandragupta did not hesitate to use force to maintain his power. He kept a vast army as well as a huge network of spies to detect anyone who might be plotting against him. One of Chandragupta's ministers declared, "Government is the science of punishment."

Chandragupta's grandson, Asoka (uh-SOH-kuh),was an even greater warrior than Chandragupta, but a gentler ruler. Under Asoka's leadership, the Mauryan armies conquered most of the rest of India. After one especially bloody battle, however, Asoka was seized by remorse at the loss of life. He converted to Buddhism and resolved to follow the Buddha's path of nonviolence. The emperor renounced fighting, along with hunting and eating meat.

Asoka promoted the Buddhist faith throughout India. He built tens of thousands of stupas. He sent the first Buddhist missionaries abroad, to Sri Lanka and Burma. At the same time, he preached tolerance for other religions. "All sects deserve reverence for one reason or another," he declared.

Asoka also dedicated himself to the welfare of his subjects, whom he called "my children." He built a network of roads to improve communication throughout his empire. Along the roads, he erected tall stone pillars with sayings and proclamations inscribed on them. Some of these pillars encouraged his subjects to live righteously. Others recorded Asoka's good works: "On the roads…I have had mango groves planted and I have had wells dug and rest houses built every eight miles. And I have had many watering places made everywhere for the use of beasts and men."

Asoka died in 232 B.C. He would be remembered as the wisest and kindest of India's kings, and an inspiration to its future rulers.

Prosperity Through Trade

After Asoka's death, the Mauryan Empire began to disintegrate. Lacking his strength and wisdom, Asoka's successors were unable to control such a vast territory. India fractured once again into small competing kingdoms.

In the following centuries, although India's political unity dissolved, the country grew more

Carved lions stand watch atop a stone column built by Asoka, inscribed with Buddhist teachings and royal edicts.

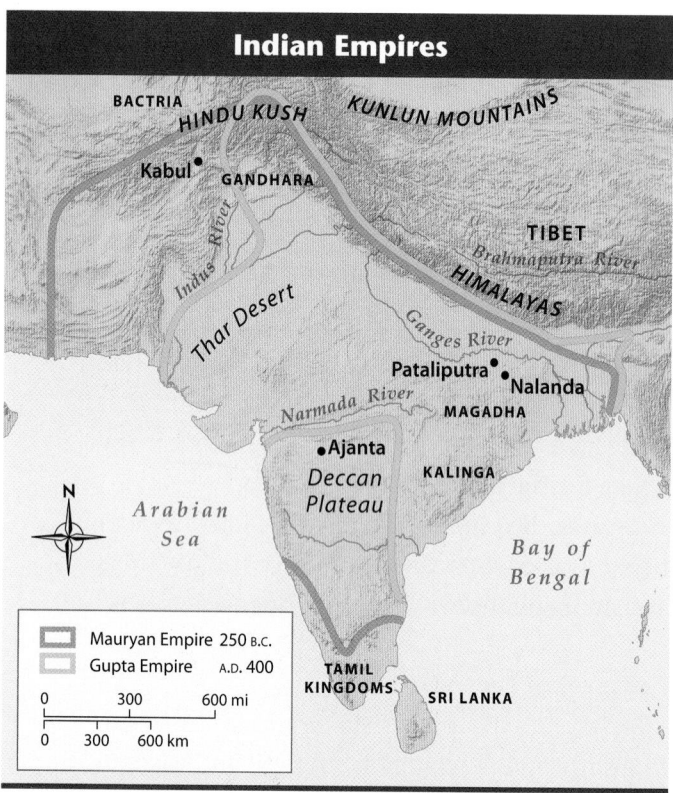

Indian Empires

BACTRIA
HINDU KUSH
KUNLUN MOUNTAINS
Kabul
GANDHARA
Indus River
TIBET
Brahmaputra River
HIMALAYAS
Thar Desert
Ganges River
Pataliputra
Nalanda
Narmada River
MAGADHA
Ajanta
Deccan
Plateau
KALINGA
N
Arabian
Sea
Bay of
Bengal
TAMIL
KINGDOMS
SRI LANKA

Mauryan Empire 250 B.C.
Gupta Empire A.D. 400

0   300   600 mi
0   300   600 km

The imposing Hindu Kush and Himalayan mountain ranges contained both the Mauryan and Guptan empires within the boundaries of the Indian subcontinent.

prosperous, largely because of thriving foreign trade. From India, traders went east to China and west to Mesopotamia and the Mediterranean. India exported luxury goods—pepper, spices, ivory, and textiles—to please the wealthy citizens of the Roman Empire. In exchange, the Romans sent wine, olive oil, and, most valuable of all, gold coins. Modern-day archaeologists have found hoards of Roman coins buried throughout India.

Asoka's encouragement of Buddhism also encouraged trade, since Buddhist merchants could do business with anyone, regardless of caste. As trade expanded, so did a new middle class of merchants and bankers. Most Indians, however, still clung to Hindu practices, and most still lived in small villages, farming or working in traditional occupations defined by their caste.

The Gupta Empire and a Golden Age

After five hundred years of disunity, a new empire, the Gupta, emerged in northern India around the year A.D. 320. Its founder was a king who called himself Chandragupta, after the ruler of the Mauryan Empire, although he bore no relation to him. On his deathbed, he told his son Samudra Gupta to "rule the whole world." Samudra Gupta went on to conquer most of northern India.

The Gupta Empire never reached the size of Asoka's. But it achieved so much in the realms of art and learning that the reign of the Guptas is remembered as India's golden age.

The greatest of the Gupta emperors was Chandragupta II, the son of Samudra Gupta. His reign from A.D. 376 to 415 was a period of peace and prosperity throughout the empire. Chandragupta II identified himself as a Hindu monarch and built Hindu temples throughout the country. Like Asoka, he showed great tolerance for other religions.

A Visitor to the Gupta Empire

In about A.D. 400, a Chinese Buddhist monk named Fa-hsien (sometimes spelled Faxian) traveled to the realm of the Guptas to view holy sites associated with the Buddha. He stayed in India for about ten years, recording his impressions. In his travels, Fa-hsien experienced no hostility toward his Buddhist beliefs. He noted with approval that, like Buddhists, most higher-caste Hindus were vegetarians. He praised the humanity of Chandragupta's rule: "The king," Fa-hsien noted, "governs without decapitation or corporal punishments." The inhabitants of the empire's cities were "rich and prosperous," he wrote, but also full of "benevolence and righteousness." In the capital city, he found free hospitals to which "the poor of all countries, the destitute, crippled, and diseased, may repair."

The Gupta emperors ordered Hindu temples to be built out of stone rather than wood. Artists decorated the new temples with lifelike statues of gods and goddesses. These statues, which show fluidly moving bodies in gracefully swaying clothes, set a standard for Hindu sculptors throughout the centuries to come.

Gupta rulers also sponsored the work of authors writing in the classical language of Sanskrit. Literary contests were held at court, with poets competing to produce the best verses on a theme chosen by the king. The poet and playwright Kalidasa, later known as the "Shakespeare of India," was a member of the court of Chandragupta II.

An ancient collection of animal fables, the *Panchatantra* (PUHN-chuh-TUHN-truh), seems to have reached its final form in the Gupta period. The stories of the *Panchatantra* gradually spread westward, showing up as folktales in many languages of the Middle East and Europe.

In this lively illustration from the *Panchatantra*, a raven addresses assembled animals.

Arabic Numerals

A numeral is a symbol used to represent a number. Today, most people in the world use the numerals 1, 2, 3, 4, 5, 6, 7, 8, 9, and 0, which can be combined to represent any number. These numerals were first invented by Indian mathematicians of the Gupta period, and later adopted by the Arabs, who changed some of their shapes. Because Europeans learned of the numerals from Arabic sources, the numerals became known as *Arabic* numerals.

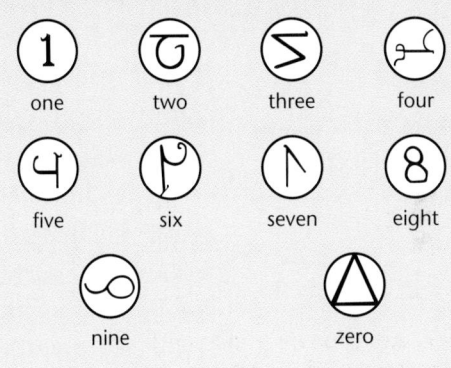

The Gupta period also saw major achievements in science and technology. Indian metallurgists refined techniques for producing iron and steel. Indian astronomers, among the most advanced in the world at the time, understood that the earth is round and that it rotates on its axis. In mathematics, the thinkers of Gupta India made important innovations. Indian mathematicians invented both the zero and the numbering system usually known as Arabic numerals, which is in use today throughout the world.

After Chandragupta II's death in A.D. 415, the Gupta Empire began a slow decline. Chandragupta's successors struggled with the problem of holding together such a large territory. Wars against invading nomadic tribes depleted the empire's wealth. By A.D. 550, the Gupta Empire had fragmented once again into a collection of small warring kingdoms. But it left behind a strengthened Hinduism and a memory of cultural achievement that continues to inspire Indians today.

China: The Age of Confucius

The history of China is usually organized into dynasties, periods in which the country was ruled by a single family. The earliest Chinese dynasty, the Shang, began around 1600 B.C. The Shang built palaces and walled cities. Shang craftsmen produced beautiful artifacts of bronze. The Shang Dynasty also saw the invention of the Chinese system of writing.

Key Questions

- How did China become more unified under the Zhou Dynasty?
- What are the key tenets of Confucianism?
- What is Daoism and how does it differ from Confucianism?

The Zhou Dynasty and the Mandate of Heaven

In 1027 B.C., the Shang Dynasty was overthrown by the Zhou, a warlike group from western China. Less culturally advanced than the Shang, the Zhou adopted the Shang Dynasty's system of writing and its method of casting bronze.

The Zhou sought to justify their takeover of the country. The new rulers explained that a dynasty ruled only with the blessing of the many gods known collectively as "heaven." According to the Zhou, a king had the right to rule because he had been given a mandate—an authorization—by heaven. The king kept this authority only as long as he acted well and governed justly. If he failed to do so, then heaven would take back its mandate and confer it on another ruler. By this reasoning, when a dynasty lost favor with heaven, it deserved to fall.

The Zhou rulers claimed that the last Shang king had been cruel and tyrannical, while the new Zhou king embodied the highest virtue. Thus the Zhou justified the change of dynasty as a return to the proper order rather than a disruption. This notion that history is organized into dynasties, each one ruling with a "mandate of heaven," took root in Chinese culture.

Economic Growth Under the Zhou

The Zhou Dynasty lasted longer than any other in Chinese history—more than eight hundred years, from about 1050 to 250 B.C. In reality, however, the Zhou rulers controlled China for less than half that time. In 771 B.C., a Zhou king suffered a severe defeat at the hands of a tribe of nomads. He was forced to move his capital to a city to the east. During the remainder of the Zhou Dynasty, called the Eastern Zhou period, China divided into a number of competing city-states whose individual leaders held the real power.

Although China was politically fragmented in this period, it enjoyed growing prosperity. The Chinese learned to smelt and cast iron, and in the ensuing centuries they made great advances in iron technology. They fashioned iron axes to clear new lands for farming and iron plows that dug more deeply than wooden ones. These innovations helped the Chinese produce a larger food supply, which led to a growth in population. By the end of the

The calligraphic tradition begun during the Zhou Dynasty continues today. Each character represents a word.

Zhou Dynasty, China had about twenty million people, making it the most populous country in the world at the time, and it remains so today.

Trade as well as agriculture flourished in the Eastern Zhou period. Helped by the expansion of roads and canals, merchants transported goods such as grains, salt, and metals around the country. Their jobs were made easier by a new, more portable form of money—copper coins with holes in the center, so that they could be carried on strings. These coins would remain in use in China until the nineteenth century.

Not everyone shared in the country's growing prosperity. Large landowners grew wealthy, but the peasants who worked their land paid heavy taxes, having to give up a large portion of the crops they grew. Peasants also suffered by being drafted into the armies of the warring nobles.

Zhou Achievements

China became more culturally unified during the later Zhou Dynasty, partly due to improvements in transportation and communication. The system of writing that the Zhou adopted from the Shang, and further refined, proved another unifying force.

Unlike an alphabet, in which each letter stands for a particular sound, in the Chinese system each character stood for a whole word. A character could represent two words that sounded different but meant the same thing. China was a vast country with many different languages and dialects. Since the words of different dialects could all be represented in the same characters, the written script helped unify the country. At the same time, because it was so difficult to memorize thousands of characters, few people became literate.

The basic educational text of the Zhou upper classes was a collection of poems titled *Shi Jing*. The title may be translated as the *Classic of Poetry* or the *Book of Songs*. The book is still considered the first masterpiece of Chinese literature. Its 305 poems show great variety, speaking of noble princes, weary warriors, hardworking farmers, dutiful spouses, and broken-hearted lovers.

The Teachings of Confucius

The political chaos and social unrest of the later Zhou Dynasty led to a revolution in philosophy. Chinese scholars and thinkers tried to envision a more just and orderly way of life. They questioned the basic premises of society and government. Their questions gave rise to a large number of competing philosophies called the "hundred schools" of thought. Two of these philosophies would prove far more lasting than the rest—Confucianism (kuhn-FYOO-shuh-nih-zuhm) and Daoism (DOW-ih-zuhm).

Confucius Offers His Wisdom

K'ung-fu-tzu, who lived from about 551 to 479 B.C., is better known outside China as Confucius, a

A painting on silk depicts the Chinese philosopher Confucius teaching his students how to be exemplary people.

states could become men of virtue like these kings, Confucius believed, then China's many divisions could be healed. So Confucius began to wander from state to state, offering himself as an adviser to political leaders. But he discovered no rulers willing to take his advice and change their corrupt or selfish ways.

Along the way, however, Confucius attracted many young disciples eager to learn from his ideas. He was willing to teach anyone, rich or poor, as long as they showed eagerness to learn. "I teach only those who burst with enthusiasm," he declared. "If I explain one corner of a subject, I expect the student to discover the other three for himself."

Confucian Teachings

Confucianism is not a religion but a system of ethics, dealing with morals and values in human conduct. Confucius did not deny the existence of gods, but as a philosopher he focused instead on how people should live in the world. He said, "To keep one's distance from the gods and spirits while showing them reverence can be called wisdom."

Confucius emphasized the importance of what are often called the Five Relationships—the relationship between parent and child, between elder brother and younger brother, between husband and wife, between ruler and subject, and between friends. Confucius believed that the

form of his name coined much later by European missionaries. According to tradition, he was the son of a minor official in the state of Lu, who died while Confucius was still a boy. Despite his difficult early years, Confucius yearned to be a scholar. "At fifteen, I set my heart on my learning," he remembered.

Confucius spent years studying works on religion, ritual, and history, as well as the *Book of Songs*. His reading led him to admire the early kings of the Zhou Dynasty. If the rulers of China's warring

Teachers Who Never Wrote

Confucius never wrote his ideas. Instead, his sayings were handed down orally, first by his students and then by later generations. Several hundred years after his death, the teachings of Confucius were gathered into a book called the *Analects*.

Confucius is not the only great teacher who never wrote down his ideas. We know the ideas of the Greek philosopher Socrates mainly through the writings of his student Plato. The Gospels—the biographies of Jesus of Nazareth, which include his teachings—were written one and two generations after his death. Similarly, the words of the Buddha were passed down by word of mouth long before being gathered into books.

FROM THE
ANALECTS OF CONFUCIUS

After Confucius died, his students wrote down what they remembered from their conversations with the great teacher. Their own students continued the process, as did later generations. So the book we know as the *Analects*, which contains the sayings of Confucius, is the work of perhaps three centuries of scholarship.

"First put yourself in order. Then be sure you act justly and sincerely toward others, and you will be a happy man."

To those working in government, Confucius said: "Go before the people with your own good example and work hard for their sake."

"An exemplary person helps bring out what is beautiful in other people and discourages what is ugly in them. A petty person does just the opposite."

"Let the ruler be as a ruler ought to be. Let the official be as an official ought to be. Let the father be as a father ought to be. Let the son be as a son ought to be. Then there will be good life and good government."

"It is the wiser person who gives rather than takes."

"He who studies but does not think is lost; he who thinks but does not study is dangerous."

"Is it not pleasant to learn with a constant perseverance and application?"

"He who wishes to secure the good of others has already secured his own."

first relationship—between parent and child—is the most important of all. He thought that people first become good by respecting and obeying their parents, a virtue sometimes called filial piety.

In the same way, said Confucius, the younger brother should respect and obey his elder brother, and the wife should respect and obey her husband. (Confucius seems to have agreed with the view that women were inferior to men, an attitude long held in China and elsewhere.) Similarly, Confucius stated, the subject should respect and obey the ruler.

But Confucius stressed that these relationships should be *mutual*. In exchange for respect and obedience, the parent, elder brother, husband, and ruler should act justly and generously, in a way that is worthy of respect. As Confucius saw it, the fifth relationship—that of friends—is an equal one. Each should treat the other with respect.

The Ideal Ruler

For Confucius, the ideal ruler was one who maintained tradition. He should know the literary classics like the *Book of Songs* and perform the rituals of governing in the time-honored way. By doing so, Confucius thought, the ruler could create a better, more orderly society, like the one that Confucius believed had existed in the time of the first Zhou kings.

It was not enough, however, for the ruler to follow the forms of tradition. It was also necessary, Confucius said, that the ruler set a moral example. When one leader asked Confucius if he should execute those who broke the law, the philosopher replied, "In administering your government, what need is there for you to kill? Just desire the good yourself and the common people will be good."

Confucius urged his followers to strive to become "gentlemen." In Confucius's eyes, a "gentleman" lived a moderate, well-balanced life, displayed perfect manners, and treated others with fairness and compassion. He advised, "When [traveling] abroad behave as though you were receiving an important guest. When employing the services of the common people behave as though you were officiating at an important sacrifice." Confucius also stated the earliest known form of what is often called the Golden Rule: "Do not impose on others what you yourself do not desire."

Confucian Ideas Take Root

Confucius died believing himself a failure because he never found the ideal ruler willing to govern according to his teachings. After his death, however, his ideas took deep root, in part because they built on feelings already strong among the Chinese, such as the importance of family relationships.

A few centuries later, under the Han Dynasty, Confucianism became the official philosophy of the Chinese government. For hundreds of years afterward, young men who wanted to serve in government would study the sayings of Confucius in the *Analects*, as well as the ancient literary works he had revered as classics.

Confucianism had a broader influence as well, shaping attitudes toward family and tradition among millions of Chinese people. Later, Confucian ideas made their way to other east Asian nations, including Korea, Japan, and Vietnam. Today, Confucianism remains a dominant philosophy in nearly one-third of the world.

Daoism

The late Zhou Dynasty also saw the birth of a philosophy that contradicts Confucianism in some ways and complements it in others. Tradition holds that this philosophy, called Daoism, was founded by a philosopher known as Laozi (low-dzuh), who may never have existed. Legend says that Laozi once met Confucius. When Confucius spoke about the importance of revering the ancestors and keeping up their ways, Laozi responded dismissively, "The bones of the men you are speaking of have long since turned to dust." By implying that it made no sense to follow tradition, Laozi was presenting a view at odds with Confucianism.

As a philosophy, Daoism is less concerned with the individual's place in society than with his place in nature and the universe. The main Daoist

Chinese tradition holds that the philosopher Laozi (depicted here riding a water buffalo) founded Daoism.

work, the *Dao de Ching* (DOW duh JING) (also spelled *Tao-te Ching*), speaks of the Dao, or the "Way," a mysterious order beneath all things that people should strive to live in harmony with.

"Through not desiring," says the *Dao de Ching*, "one becomes tranquil." Much more mystical than the *Analects* of Confucius, the *Dao de Ching* is a difficult work to understand. Over time, many people interpreted it to mean that they could escape the conflicts and turmoil of society by submitting to the simple rhythms of nature.

Daoism came to have a large influence on Chinese culture. Many poems and paintings depict scholars and officials who have retired from life's struggles to embrace the Dao among beautiful lakes and mountains. By stressing nature over society, the individual over the group, and spontaneity over tradition, Daoism provided Chinese culture with an important balance to Confucian ideals.

Yin and Yang

One famous symbol connected with Daoism is the yin-yang circle. Each half of the circle stands for an opposing set of qualities or ideas. *Yin* represents things that are supposedly female, dark, weak, and passive. *Yang* represents things that are supposedly male, bright, strong, and active. The two halves of the *yin-yang* circle lock together in a way that shows how these opposing principles depend on each other. Their dependence creates the underlying harmony of the universe, according to Daoist principles.

Daoism's famous symbol, the yin-yang circle

The Sanquingshan Mountains in east China have long been a destination for those who embrace the Dao.

103

China: New Dynasties and a Golden Age

Key Questions

- What were the major achievements of the Qin and Han dynasties?
- How was China under the Han Dynasty a classical civilization?

Late in the Zhou Dynasty, when China was fragmented into many competing city-states, the western state of Qin (chin) was the most warlike. The Qin cavalry was famed and feared for its skill at fighting on horseback. Gradually, Qin conquered its neighbors until, in 221 B.C., it united all of China under its rule. To confirm his power over the country, the Qin leader ordered all weapons not belonging to Qin soldiers to be melted down. He also took the ambitious title Shi Huangdi (shur hwahng-dee), meaning "The First Emperor."

The Qin Dynasty

Qin Shi Huangdi united the vast land of China into an empire. As emperor, he would become known as the Tiger of China for his bold and ruthless way of governing. He took power away from local landowners and warlords. He divided the empire into dozens of districts, each with an administrator appointed to make sure the emperor's orders were carried out. To knit the country together after the long period of disunion, Qin Shi Huangdi built a network of roads radiating from the capital city that eventually stretched for thousands of miles.

To protect against invasion, Qin Shi Huangdi had hundreds of thousands of workers build a wall of earth and stone along China's northern frontier. Later emperors also built stronger, more extensive walls. All these fortifications form part of what we know as the Great Wall of China, most of which was constructed many centuries after the Qin Dynasty.

Qin Shi Huangdi worked to unify China economically as well as politically. To encourage trade, he built a series of canals reaching into China's far south. He standardized weights and measures so that merchants everywhere could receive a fair price for their goods. He also standardized coinage, ordering everyone to use the same coins. He even decreed that all carts for hauling goods be built to the same width.

As a leader, Qin Shi Huangdi was not only efficient but also brutal. He

Shi Huangdi, a title meaning "First Emperor," united China into an empire.

Unification of Imperial China

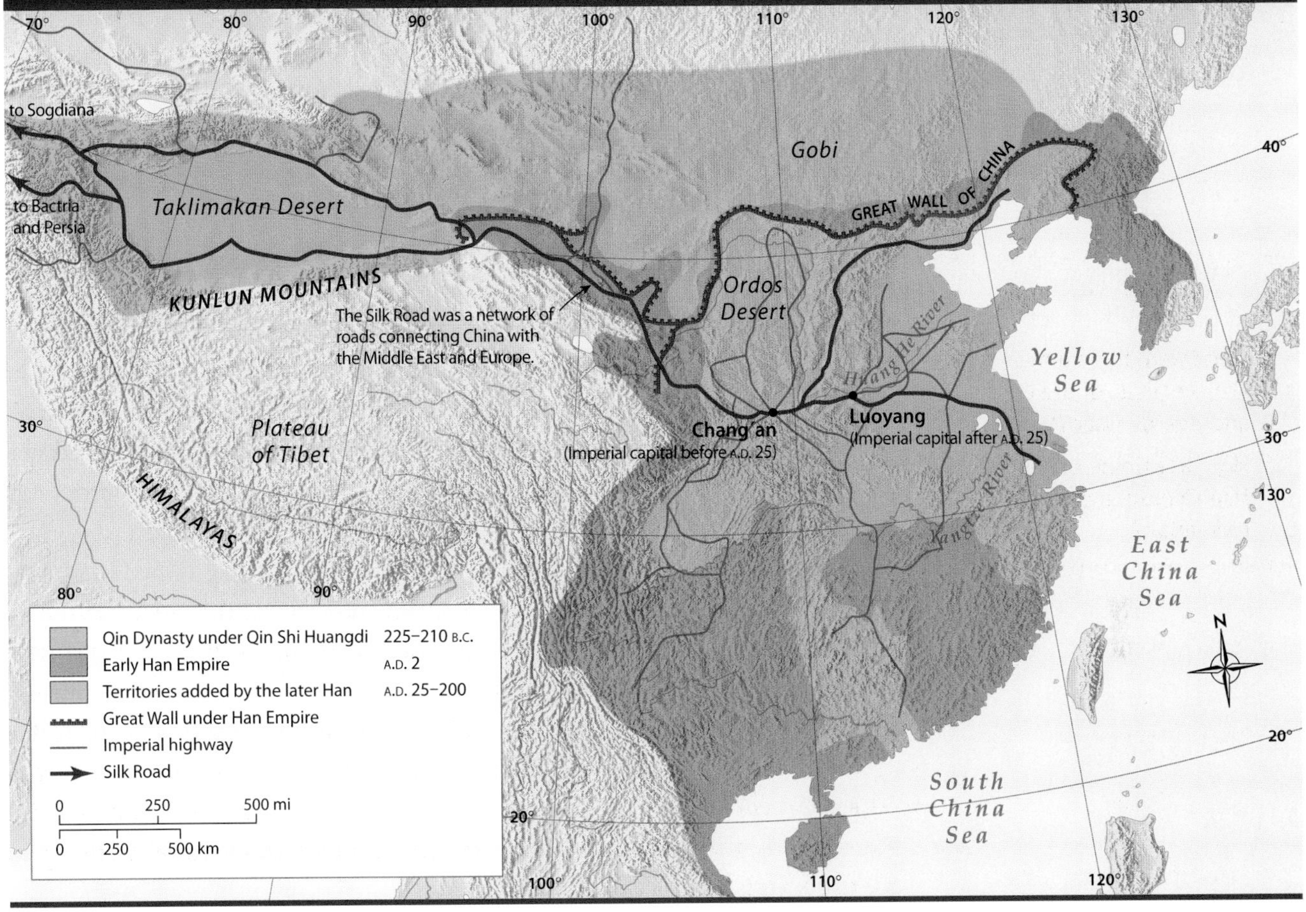

to Sogdiana

to Bactria
and Persia

Taklimakan Desert

KUNLUN MOUNTAINS

The Silk Road was a network of
roads connecting China with
the Middle East and Europe.

Gobi

GREAT WALL OF CHINA

*Ordos
Desert*

Hwang He River

*Yellow
Sea*

*Plateau
of Tibet*

HIMALAYAS

Chang'an
(Imperial capital before A.D. 25)

Luoyang
(Imperial capital after A.D. 25)

Yangtze River

*East
China
Sea*

Qin Dynasty under Qin Shi Huangdi	225–210 B.C.
Early Han Empire	A.D. 2
Territories added by the later Han	A.D. 25–200

Great Wall under Han Empire
Imperial highway
Silk Road

0   250   500 mi
0   250   500 km

*South
China
Sea*

N

Qin armies united warring Chinese states into one empire and began an expansion that would continue into the
Han Dynasty that followed.

surrounded himself with advisers known as Legalists, who believed that rulers should govern by
making harsh laws and applying them strictly. The
Legalists spoke of rewards and punishments as the
"two handles" of the law. One of the emperor's
Legalist ministers declared, "If you glorify the
good, errors will be hidden; if you put scoundrels
in charge, crime will be punished."

This attitude was contrary to
Confucius's idea that government should be in the hands
of upright men who lead by
moral example.

The emperor refused to
tolerate any ideas opposed to
his own. In 213 B.C., he issued
a remarkable command. He

A *banliang*, a Chinese
half-ounce bronze coin

ordered that all books throughout the empire be
burned, except those on practical matters such as
medicine and farming. When scholars protested,
he had hundreds of them executed.

When Qin Shi Huangdi died in 210 B.C., many
rejoiced. The emperor had been hated and feared.
Peasants resented the high taxes he had imposed
to raise money for his roads and canals. Scholars resented his book burning. Too many people
of every class had suffered punishment under
his harsh laws. Now the opponents of the Qin
declared that the dynasty had lost the mandate of
heaven and no longer possessed the moral authority to rule. A series of rebellions broke out until, in
206 B.C., the last Qin ruler was overthrown. The
dynasty that created a great Chinese empire had
lasted a mere fifteen years.

An Army for the Afterlife

In the year 1974, farmers digging a well in central China made an astonishing discovery— a vast tomb filled with thousands of lifelike statues made of terra-cotta, each one different from the others. The tomb was that of Qin Shi Huangdi. Each statue represented a soldier in the emperor's army. The figures were presumably placed in the emperor's tomb to protect him in the afterlife.

Terra-cotta soldiers stand guard at the tomb of Qin Shi Huangdi, as they have for more than two millennia.

The Han Dynasty

The rebel general who overthrew the Qin, Liu Bang (lee-oo BAHNG), founded a dynasty called the Han, which would last more than four hundred years, a period remembered as the most glorious in Chinese history. The first commoner to rule China, Liu Bang understood how important it was for a ruler to have the affection of the people he ruled. He took to heart this philosopher's saying: "The prince is the boat; the common people are the water. The water can support the boat, or the water can capsize the boat."

Liu Bang understood that the Qin Dynasty had been "capsized" by the people's hatred. So he abolished the harsh laws of Qin Shi Huangdi and established himself instead as a lenient ruler. Unlike Qin Shi Huangdi, Liu Bang was open to advice. He tried to rule according to Confucian ideals. At the same time, however, he valued the centralized government that the Qin had set up. Throughout the Han Dynasty, China would remain strong and unified.

Expansion Under Han Rule

Liu Bang's great-grandson Wudi (woo-dee), known as the Martial Emperor, came to the throne at the age of sixteen and ruled for fifty-four years. During his long reign, Wudi expanded the empire in every direction, until it almost reached the borders of present-day China.

Wudi reorganized and strengthened the imperial army so that it was capable of fighting in numerous campaigns at once. His generals defeated the nomads that had been threatening the empire's northern frontiers, and led expeditions into the neighboring countries of Manchuria and Korea. Sweeping south, Wudi's armies invaded Vietnam. Meanwhile, officers returning from the western frontier brought the emperor news of markets to the west for Chinese goods, especially silk.

Unlike his ancestor Liu Bang, Wudi ruled China with a heavy hand. He tightly controlled the actions of his officials, and tolerated little dissent. But he appointed able ministers and generals, and his military exploits appealed to the patriotism of most Chinese people. In spite of his high-handed ways and occasional cruelty, Wudi was generally respected. He would be remembered as one of the most energetic and effective of Chinese emperors.

China's Golden Age Under the Han

Under the Han, China's economy prospered. Agriculture boomed, helped by technology. For example, the collar harness distributed weight evenly around a horse's shoulders, making plowing the ground more effective. Waterwheels captured the power of rivers and streams to crush grain

Detail on a Chinese vase reveals the complicated process of spinning silk from silkworm cocoons.

Han Society

In Han China, the government tightly controlled the economy. It restricted the rights of merchants, forbidding them to own land or become officials. By contrast, in a land so dependent on agriculture to feed so many, farmers were honored. But most peasant farmers remained poor, while many merchants grew rich.

In every class, Chinese women had little power and limited roles. Throughout their lives, they were expected to be subservient to men—first to their fathers and then to their husbands. They rarely received an education, and, except for farm women, were not expected to work outside the home. Yet one of the jobs most important to China's prosperity—silk making—was performed exclusively by highly skilled women.

The Han Dynasty produced the first female historian in Chinese history, Ban Zhao (bahn jow), who lived from about A.D. 45 to 115. Her writings expressed traditional ideas about women's roles. In one book, she urged women to always be humble: "Humility means yielding and acting respectfully, putting others first and oneself last, …[and] enduring insults and bearing with mistreatment."

in mills. A larger food surplus led to a growth in population, which in turn led to the building of new cities.

For the first time in Chinese history, trade with distant nations flourished. Imported goods, including wool and glass, came from as far away as the Roman Empire. These goods were exchanged most often for China's most precious export, silk. The Chinese, who had invented the complicated technology of making the fabric from the cocoons of silkworms, kept their method secret, so that China had a monopoly on silk production.

> To hold a *monopoly* is to have the exclusive power or right to sell or trade in certain goods.

The Han Dynasty saw the opening of the Silk Road, a series of trade routes extending across western China and central Asia. Caravans of camels transported silk and other Chinese goods to Persia, where they were shipped by sea to Mediterranean ports. Buddhist missionaries from India also traveled the Silk Road, bringing their faith eastward to China.

Camel caravans, loaded with Chinese silk and other highly prized goods, traveled the Silk Road, a vital trade network.

107

Han Government

The Han rulers used taxation to influence the behavior of their subjects. For example, to encourage marriage, they heavily taxed unmarried women. They also tried to encourage agriculture by only lightly taxing farmers. However, many peasant farmers were sharecroppers who had to give up as much as half of their crop yield to the owners of the land they worked. Peasants were also required to serve the government for one month out of the year, for example, by building roads. These burdens on peasants would eventually lead to unrest.

The Han Dynasty, like the Qin Dynasty that preceded it, emphasized the unity of the empire. A single set of laws applied throughout China. The currency remained uniform. The Han simplified the Qin system of writing to make it an even more effective means of communication.

> To *assimilate* is to merge people into the ways of the larger society.

As China expanded, the government tried to assimilate conquered peoples into the Chinese way of life. But former nomads often balked at becoming farmers or paying taxes. Their resistance sometimes flared into rebellion.

The Han emperors placed great emphasis on the careful selection of government officials. In most countries in the ancient world, people got government positions because they were born into powerful families, or knew those who were. In Han China, however, civil service was based on education and scholarship. In one famous proclamation, the emperor Wudi declared that for his generals and government officials, he wanted only "men of brilliant and exceptional talents."

Candidates for government positions had to be schooled in the Confucian classics. After being recommended by local officials, they traveled to the capital, where they took written examinations. Only hardworking and determined job-seekers successfully completed this process. The Han method of selecting officials for civil service by competitive examination survived in China until the last emperor lost his throne in 1912.

Han Culture

One new invention during the Han Dynasty, paper, would revolutionize culture in China, and eventually around the world. Previously, the Chinese had written mostly on silk or strips of bamboo. With the invention of paper, documents could be produced far more easily and distributed more widely. Along with official documents, Han emperors encouraged the publication of books, particularly copies of the Confucian classics. But no one knows how accurate these copies were.

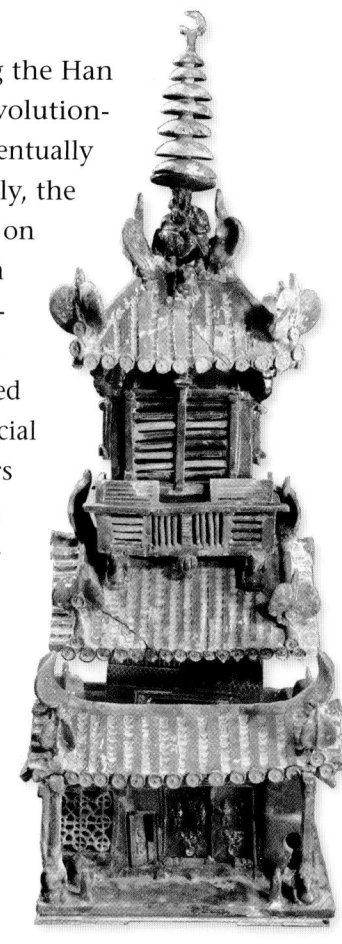

A model of a typical Han Dynasty house of the wealthy

Han writers produced some notable poetry. The most celebrated literary work of the time was a history of China called *The Historical Records*. Its author, Ssu-ma Ch'ien (suh-muh chee-en), served in the court of the emperor Wudi. In a letter to a friend, Ssu-ma Ch'ien outlined the boldness of his ambition: "I have gathered up and brought together the old traditions of the world which were scattered and lost....I wished to examine into all that concerns heaven and man." His book includes biographies of the emperors, while at the same time covers subjects as varied as music, astrology, and economics. Today Ssu-ma Ch'ien's work is considered a classic of literature as well as history.

During the Han Dynasty, artists adorned the walls of tombs with paintings of historical figures or lively scenes from everyday life, including pictures of jugglers, charioteers, horsemen, and people enjoying a feast. Other artists produced figurines in jade or elaborately decorated lacquer boxes—pieces destined for the households of wealthy officials or merchants. Potters produced elegant cups, plates, and bowls covered with colorful glaze. In later centuries, China's pottery would be among its most highly valued exports.

Decline and Legacy

The Han Dynasty began to decline in the first century B.C. The empire's many wars of conquest drained the treasury. Rich landowners often refused to pay taxes. Meanwhile, the growing tax burden on the peasants provoked rebellions around the country.

In the midst of this unrest, a government official seized the throne and deposed the Han emperor. He tried to pacify the country by seizing farms from large landowners and giving the land to the peasants. But disorder increased in the wake of disastrous floods that destroyed crops and left people starving. In A.D. 23, the rebellious official was assassinated and a new member of the Han family restored the dynasty.

The next two centuries are known as the Later or Eastern Han period. In the first decades of the Eastern Han period, strong emperors brought back the country's former prosperity. Once again, Chinese armies marched off to conquer peoples living on the edges of the empire. Trade on the Silk Road revived.

Soon, however, the throne passed into the hands of less effective emperors. Seeing the weakness of the new rulers, officials at court tried to grab power for themselves. Conspiracies and plots broke out. Members of different factions murdered each other. Large landowners in the countryside, defying the emperor, raised their own armies.

By the end of the second century A.D., the central government was seriously weakened. When large-scale revolts broke out among the peasants, the emperor sent three armies to different parts of the country. The soldiers put down the revolts, but the generals who led them stayed to rule the regions where they had been sent. In A.D. 220, the last Han emperor was deposed. For the next sixty years, China would be divided into three kingdoms.

Despite this turmoil, in later centuries the Chinese would look back on the Han Dynasty as a golden age. Under the Han emperors, China became more unified while vastly expanding its size. It dominated its neighbors, both militarily and economically. The Silk Road opened China to the outside world, linking it to lands as far away as Europe. Most of the Han emperors attempted to govern wisely, according to the principles of Confucius. They were assisted by officials drawn from the most talented and best educated of their subjects. The prestige of the dynasty remains so great that today's Chinese often refer to themselves as "the people of Han."

Two bronze warrior statues of the Eastern Han Dynasty were unearthed in 1969 in Wu-Wei, Kansu, China.

Minoan civilization
flourishes in Crete.

Ancient Greece
enters a dark age.

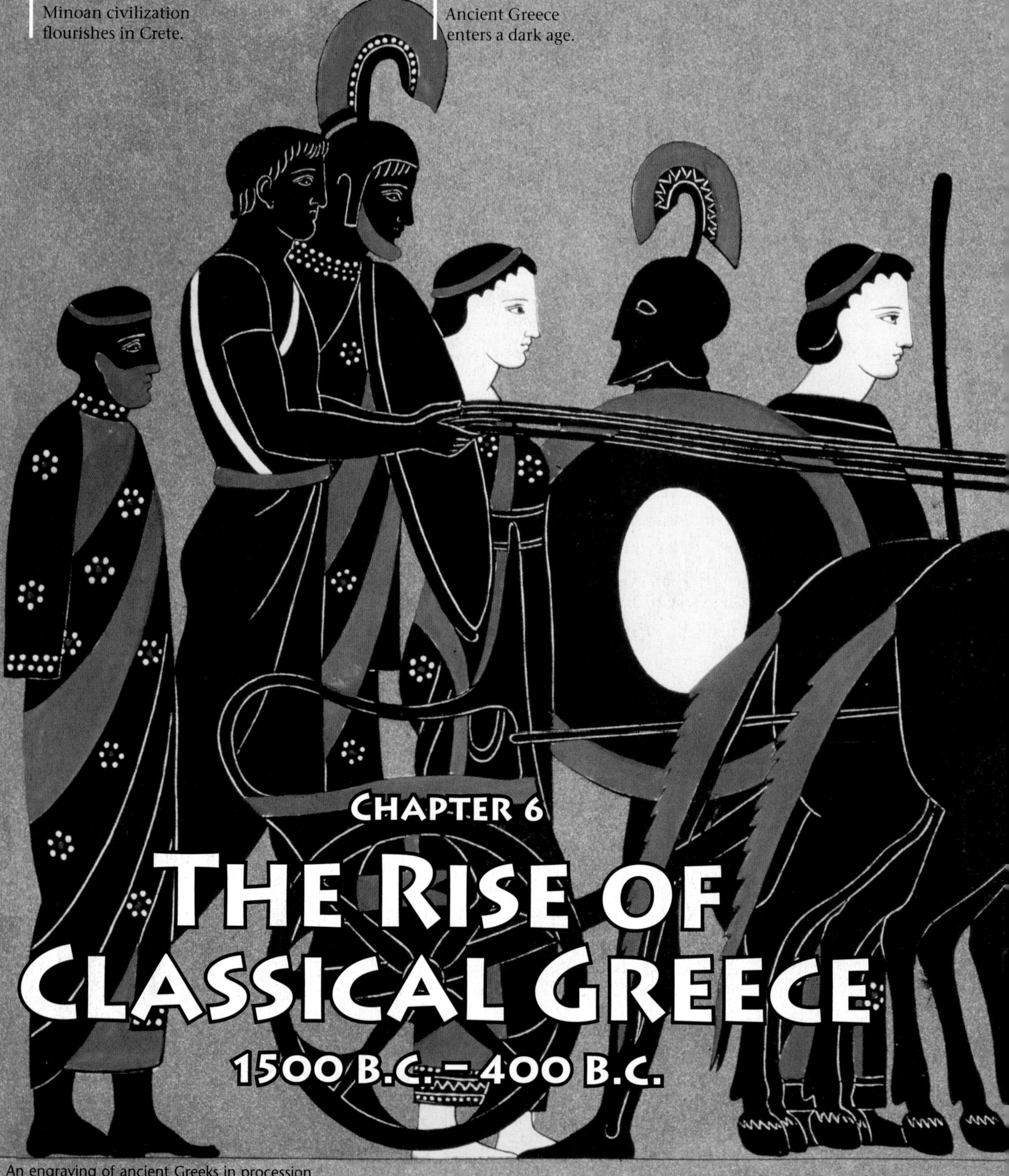

CHAPTER 6
THE RISE OF
CLASSICAL GREECE
1500 B.C. – 400 B.C.

An engraving of ancient Greeks in procession

800 B.C.

600 B.C.

c. 480 B.C.
The Persian Wars end
in a Greek victory.

461 B.C.
Pericles expands
democracy as Athens
enjoys a golden age.

776 B.C.
The first Olympic
Games are held in
Greece.

500 B.C.
Democracy begins
in Athens.

404 B.C.
Sparta's victory in
the Peloponnesian
War brings disaster
to Athens.

*B*eginning about 500 B.C., Greece, a small country in southeastern Europe, would exert an enormous influence on history. Linked by trade to the ancient civilizations of the Near East, Greece developed its own rich and distinctive culture. The country remained divided into dozens of small city-states, with different forms of government. One of these city-states, Athens, was the birthplace of a new political system, *democracy*, or "rule by the people."

Twice the Greek city-states joined together to fight off invading forces of the mighty Persian Empire. Greek victories in the Persian Wars ushered in the most glorious period of Greek culture. This golden age ended, however, when rivalry between Athens and Sparta brought on a disastrous war.

Greek Beginnings

In 1876, a German archaeologist, Heinrich Schliemann (HIYN-rik SHLEE-mahn), was digging in the ruins of the ancient Greek fortress of Mycenae (miy-SEE-nee). There he discovered tombs containing bodies dating from ancient times. Along with the bodies, Schliemann uncovered a gigantic hoard of precious metal—plates and drinking cups, brooches and sword handles, all fashioned of silver and gold. Several of the bodies had golden masks fitted to their skulls. Gazing on one of the masks, Schliemann imagined that he might have found the tomb of Agamemnon, a legendary king of Mycenae.

Who Were the Mycenaeans?

The people who buried their rulers in these treasure-filled graves were Indo-Europeans who had migrated into Greece around 1900 B.C. They built hilltop fortresses ringed with stone walls so massive that later generations thought they had been built by giants. Later the people became known as Mycenaeans (miy-suh-NEE-uhnz), after the most impressive of these fortress cities. By about 1400 B.C., the increasingly wealthy and powerful Mycenaeans were building palaces decorated with vivid wall paintings illustrating scenes of hunting and warfare.

The Mycenaeans became wealthy both by trading with peoples around the Mediterranean and by launching seaborne raids against their neighbors. Around 1450 B.C., they invaded Crete, capturing the wealthy cities of the advanced Minoan civilization.

By 1150 B.C., however, Mycenaean society began to decline. Many of the great palaces were destroyed—perhaps by internal warfare, perhaps by foreign invasion, or perhaps by natural disaster. Soon the Mycenaeans had passed out of history, leaving to later Greeks a lasting memory of cultural brilliance and military might.

Geography Shapes Greek Life

Historians believe that the Mycenaeans never united politically. Instead, each fortress town was probably the center of its own small kingdom. This lack of unity was due in part to the geography of Greece.

Greece occupies a peninsula jutting into the Mediterranean Sea. Rugged mountains cover almost four-fifths of the landscape. Although most Greeks in ancient times lived by farming, only the valleys between the mountains were favorable for agriculture. Thus, each valley, walled off by surrounding hills, tended to support

Key Questions

- How did the geography of Greece influence the development of independent city-states?

- What elements of shared culture and values bound together the diverse Greek city-states?

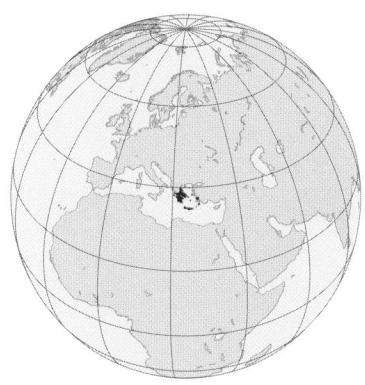

Greece lies in southeastern Europe on the Mediterranean.

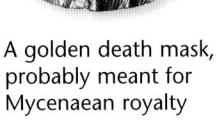

A golden death mask, probably meant for Mycenaean royalty

113

a separate society. The geography of Greece—with its rocky terrain and isolated valleys—differed significantly from other centers of ancient civilization. In Mesopotamia and Egypt, for example, large rivers and broad floodplains helped rulers mold vast regions into single kingdoms.

Greece's mountainous landscape made inland travel difficult. For most Greeks, however, there was an easier way to travel—by water. In the southern half of Greece, no place is far from the sea, so it was easy to sail from one part of Greece to another.

East of Greece, the Aegean Sea contains many small islands. From early times, Greeks occupied these islands and used them as stepping-stones in trade with other lands. This seaborne commerce connected the Greeks to other advanced civilizations in the Middle East and Egypt.

Troubled Times

After the decline of the Mycenaean kingdoms, a new group of Greeks, the Dorians, came to dominate much of the country. They never achieved a culture as advanced as that of Mycenae. Instead, beginning about 1200 B.C., Greece entered a bleak period known as its Dark Age.

For the next three centuries, from 1200 to 900 B.C., the Greeks built no great palaces or fortresses. Archaeologists have found no wall paintings dating from this period, or any precious artifacts like those uncovered at Mycenae. Perhaps more significant, they have found no writing of any kind. While the Mycenaeans kept detailed government records, during the Dark Age the Greeks seem to have lost the knowledge of writing.

In the chaotic conditions of the Dark Age, agriculture suffered. In parts of Greece, the population declined as people migrated in search of richer land to farm or safer places to live. Some of these migrants settled on the Aegean islands. Others set up colonies on the coast of Asia Minor (today's Turkey). In later times, these settlements, collectively known as Ionia (iy-OH-nee-uh), would be among the most prosperous of Greek cities.

Shared Language, Legends, and Beliefs

Although scattered widely, the Greeks were still bound by the cultural ties of common language and shared religious beliefs. Like most peoples of the ancient world, the Greeks were polytheists.

The mountainous landscape of southern Greece meets the vivid blue waters of the Mediterranean Sea.

This bronze statue most likely shows the sea god Poseidon in the act of throwing his trident (a spear, now gone).

They believed that their many gods were immortal and far more powerful than men. But the Greek gods behaved as unpredictably as human beings. Like people, the gods could be honest or devious, kind or cruel, generous or selfish.

The Greeks explained many of the workings of nature as actions of the gods. For example, a lightning flash meant that the sky god Zeus was angrily hurling thunderbolts. Earthquakes happened when the sea god Poseidon stamped his feet.

The Greeks believed that a god named Hades (the brother of Zeus and Poseidon) ruled the underworld, which was populated by the souls of the dead. The Greeks envisioned this underworld as a dark and gloomy place. Thus the Greek religion encouraged people to seek fulfillment in earth life rather than look forward to a reward after death.

The Greeks told stories about their gods, stories that we call *myths*. One of the most famous myths recounts how a Greek queen named Helen—the most beautiful woman in the world—is kidnapped by a prince of Troy, a city in Asia Minor. A great Greek army sails to Troy to win Helen back and avenge her kidnapping. It takes ten years of brutal warfare before the city of Troy finally falls to the Greeks. In the course of this conflict, known as the Trojan War, the gods fight alongside the humans, some taking the side of the Greeks, some fighting for the Trojans.

During the Dark Age, stories of the Trojan War were told and retold in epic poems handed down by word of mouth. Toward the end of the Dark Age, a poet known as Homer took the traditional poems and shaped them into two great epics, the *Iliad* and the *Odyssey*. We know nothing about Homer's life, although later Greeks said that he was blind, since a blind poet is mentioned in the *Odyssey*.

The *Iliad* focuses on the deeds of the Greek warriors at Troy, especially Achilles (uh-KIH-leez), the greatest fighter among the Greeks. The *Odyssey* tells the story of Odysseus, a Greek chieftain, and his long, adventure-filled voyage home after the fall of Troy.

Hellenic Civilization

Both the *Iliad* and the *Odyssey* look back from the Dark Age to the civilization of Mycenaean times. The epics fostered pride among the Greeks by recalling the glorious deeds of their ancestors. More and more, Greeks celebrated the common

Some Gods and Goddesses

Zeus	king of the gods
Hera	(wife of Zeus) goddess of women and marriage
Poseidon	god of the seas
Athena	goddess of wisdom
Apollo	god of music and poetry
Aphrodite	goddess of love and beauty
Artemis	goddess of the moon and of hunting
Ares	god of war
Hermes	god of commerce and travel
Hestia	goddess of hearth and home
Hades	god of the underworld

Today's Olympic Games

The first Olympic Games, held in Olympia, Greece, were limited to male athletes, and consisted simply of foot races. In time, more events were added, such as wrestling and discus throwing. The original Olympics were held from 776 B.C. to A.D. 394 and then faded into a distant past. In the 1870s, when German archaeologists uncovered evidence of the ancient games, people began to think about reviving the Olympics, this time as an international competition. The Olympics resumed in Athens in 1896 with participants from Greece, France, the United States, Britain, and other lands. Today's Olympic Games bring together athletes from all over the globe, both men and women, to prove what the human body and spirit can accomplish— an idea the ancient Greeks would have applauded.

A fifth-century statue of a Greek discus thrower

farmland. The spread of agriculture meant a surplus of food, which led to a rise in population. Trade revived, and with it came the reinvention of writing.

Greek merchants who traded across the Aegean Sea borrowed the alphabet used in Phoenicia. The Greeks added letters representing vowel sounds, which the Phoenician alphabet lacked. Thus the Greeks created a system of writing using twenty-four letters, the forerunner of the alphabet we use today. Because this alphabet was easy to learn and use, literacy spread among the Greeks. The development of a literate civilization eventually encouraged the growth of the world's first democracy. The new alphabet preserved the epics of Homer in written form and provided the means to capture the words of the great Greek poets, historians, and philosophers of later times.

culture of Hellas—their name for Greece. Around the time of Homer—roughly in the eighth century B.C.— Greeks from all over began gathering to celebrate Panhellenic festivals (*panhellenic* means relating to all Greek peoples). One of the most important of these gatherings, the Olympic Games, drew athletes from different Greek cities to compete against each other in sports such as wrestling, boxing, and javelin throwing.

By Homer's time, the Dark Age in Greece was ending. Landowners were converting pasture to

The Greek Polis

Although Greeks became more culturally unified, they never united under a single ruler. By the end of the Dark Age, the Greeks organized into separate

Schliemann and the Search for Troy

Before he found the treasure-filled graves of Mycenae, the German archaeologist Heinrich Schliemann made an even more momentous discovery. Most scholars of his time thought that the city of Troy described in Homer's epics had never actually existed. But Schliemann, using Homer's *Iliad* as a guide and building on the findings of an amateur geologist, dug for the remains of Troy at a site in the country of Turkey. Today most scholars agree that the city Schliemann found was the one the Greeks called Troy. In his eagerness, Schliemann destroyed valuable historical evidence as he dug to the lower levels of the excavation site, where he was convinced the ruins of Troy were to be found. Schliemann boasted that his discovery of Troy was "an event which stands alone in archaeology."

The ruins of the Parthenon, a magnificent temple, sit atop the Acropolis in Athens, recalling the glory of Greece.

city-states. The Greeks called a city-state a *polis* (PAH-luhs). Each polis consisted of a capital city with its surrounding countryside and villages. Some had only a few hundred inhabitants, while Athens had hundreds of thousands. Eventually Greece would be divided into some two hundred *poleis* (PAH-lays—the plural form of *polis*).

Although the city-states differed in size and power, they shared common characteristics. The capital cities were walled to defend against enemies. In most cities, if invaders attacked, residents could retreat to a central fortified hill called an *acropolis* (literally, a "high city"). The acropolis often served as a center for religious worship. Other gatherings took place in the lower town, in a square called the *agora* (A-guh-ruh). In the bustling agora, merchants peddled their wares, politicians gave speeches, and athletes competed in games.

As their populations expanded, city-states often found themselves running out of good farmland. In order to feed their inhabitants, they looked for land abroad. As early as the eighth century B.C., city-states sent sailors to establish colonies throughout the Mediterranean region. Soon, Greek settlements appeared as far away as Italy, northern Africa, and the shores of the Black Sea.

The Root of Politics

Our word *politics* is related to the root, *polis*. Politics originally meant "the art of governing the city state." Other English words relating to government, such as *policy* and *police*, also derive from *polis*.

117

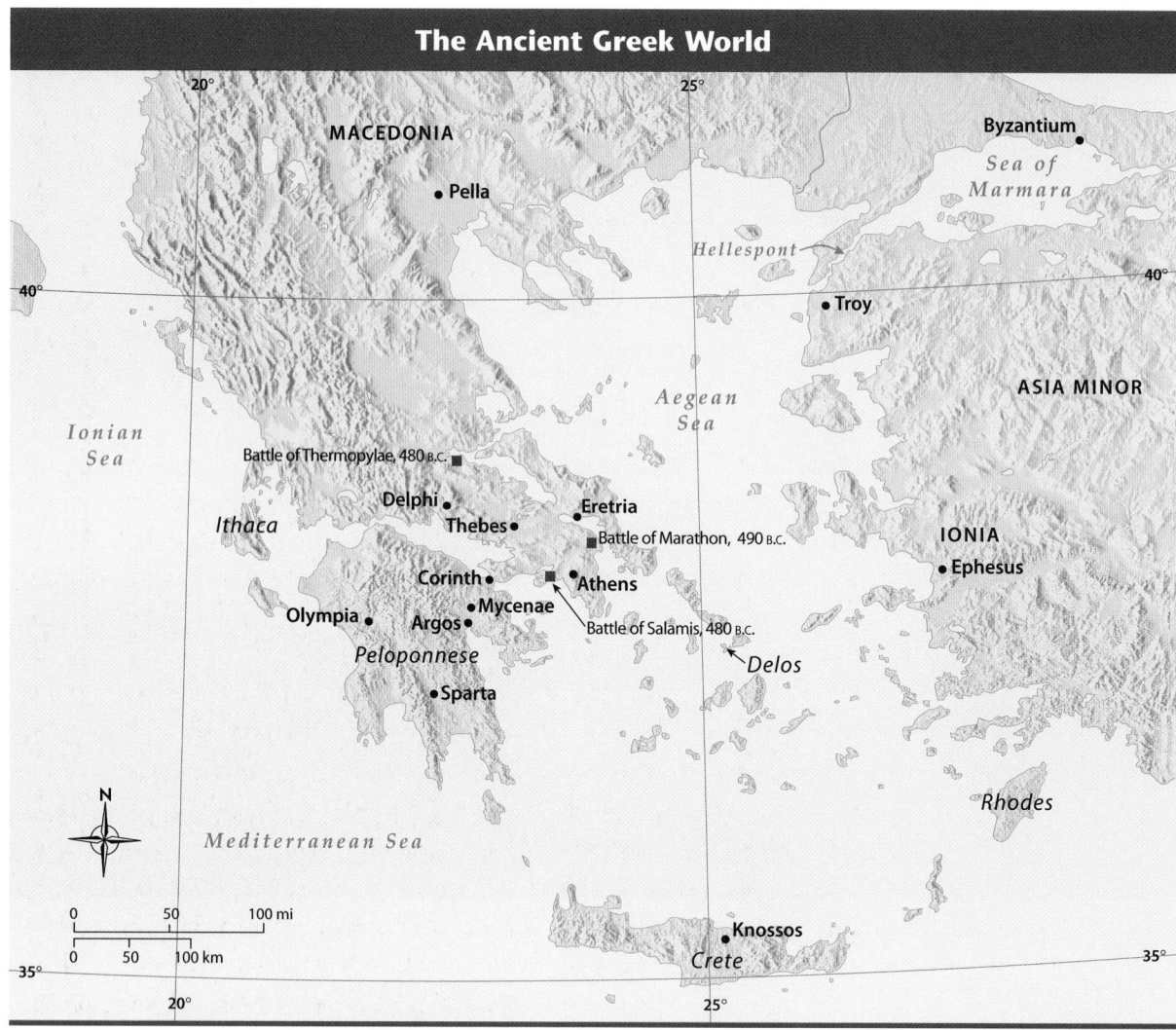

The Ancient Greek World

The Greeks, because of their mountainous homeland, turned to the Mediterranean Sea, and the lands in and around it, for their economic and political expansion.

Each polis, along with its colonies, proudly proclaimed its independence and the right to run its own affairs. Thus, different city-states developed different forms of government. No polis was ruled by an absolute monarch who, like the kings of Egypt and Persia, claimed godlike powers. The Greeks believed instead in sharing power among a wider group of citizens. The modern ideal of citizenship—that people should be involved in both serving and running the government—has its origins in the city-states of ancient Greece.

In these city-states, however, only citizens could participate in running the polis and only some people were citizens. Women and slaves were excluded from citizenship. In some cities, only property owners could be citizens. Foreigners who came to live and work in Greek cities, such as Athens, could never become citizens.

For a while, many city-states were dominated by a few families of wealthy landowners. In some city-states, strong leaders overthrew the leading families and established themselves as single rulers, called "tyrants." Today the word *tyrant* means a cruel and unjust ruler. The tyrants of the early Greek city-states made themselves popular by seizing the property of the rich and finding work for poor citizens. By about 500 B.C., however, the rule of these tyrants had come to an end, because rule by a single man went against the Greeks' basic principles of citizenship.

Athens and Sparta: Rival City-States

Sparta and Athens, the two largest city-states in ancient Greece, developed starkly different forms of government. Their rivalry would eventually lead to a disastrous decades-long war.

Sparta: A Military State

The southern part of Greece, called the Peloponnese (PEH-luh-puh-neez), is a large peninsula shaped like a hand with outstretched fingers. In ancient times, the most powerful polis on the Peloponnese was Sparta. In Sparta, every citizen spent his life either fighting or training for war. The Spartans were famed and feared as the mightiest warriors in Greece.

During the Dark Age, the Spartans conquered the territories around their city. They enslaved the conquered people, whom they called *helots*. The Spartans forced the helots to farm the land to provide food for the polis. Since the conquered area was so large, the helots greatly outnumbered the Spartan citizens, possibly by as much as seven to one. The Spartans became an almost purely military society, in part because they feared that the helots might revolt.

The Spartan Life

Sparta was unusual among Greek city-states in that it had a king. In fact, it had two of them. One king could lead the army to war while the other stayed behind to run the city's affairs. But the kings shared authority with a council elected by the citizens.

In Sparta, as in other Greek city-states, only men were considered citizens. In Spartan society, each citizen trained from childhood to be a soldier. At the age of seven, boys left their families to live in military barracks. They went barefoot and wore only thin cloaks in even the coldest weather. They were fed small meals that kept them constantly hungry. Their teachers then encouraged the boys to try to steal food. If caught, they were beaten—not for stealing, but for being foolish enough to get caught. This harsh treatment

Armored Greek soldiers and a chariot adorn the rim of an ancient bronze jar.

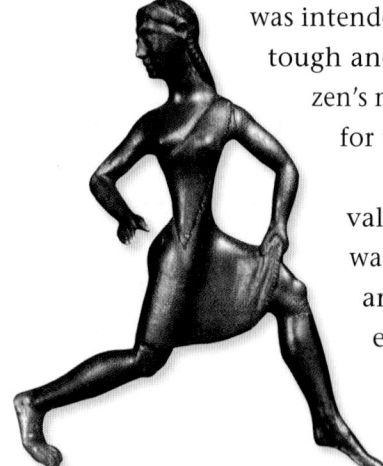

A bronze running figure illustrates the freedom enjoyed by Spartan girls.

was intended to turn each boy into a tough and cunning warrior. A citizen's military training continued for the rest of his life.

Above all, the Spartans valued the virtues of the warrior—courage, endurance, and unquestioning obedience to orders. Spartans prided themselves on their toughness and looked down on other Greeks as soft and luxury-loving. Today the word *spartan* has come to mean a way of life that is deliberately simple and strict.

Spartan women took no part in government. Yet in some ways, they enjoyed more freedom than other Greek women. They had broader rights to own property. Women in other city-states were often restricted to their homes, but in Sparta, girls and young women exercised outdoors, strengthening themselves so that they could bear strong sons. When a Spartan warrior marched off to fight, his wife or mother would warn him, "Return with your shield or on it." In other words, come back from battle in glory, proudly holding your shield—or be carried back upon it, dead.

Spartans focused so exclusively on war that they had little time for cultural pursuits such as art and literature. Unlike their rivals in Athens, they produced no great poets, sculptors, or architects. Other Greeks feared the Spartans, and sometimes admired them, but none copied their harsh, demanding way of life.

Athens: Birthplace of Democracy

The polis of Athens—named for Athena, the goddess of wisdom—lay northeast of the Peloponnese in a region called Attica. It would become the largest, richest, and most culturally brilliant of the Greek city-states.

Athens, known as the birthplace of democracy, was not always democratic. Early on, like most city-states, Athens was dominated by an aristocracy of wealthy landowners. Around 620 B.C., an Athenian official named Draco wrote a new set of laws, laying down fixed punishments for specific crimes. In theory at least, the same laws applied to all Athenians. But Draco's laws were so severe, ordaining the death penalty for many minor crimes, that today we call an overly harsh law "draconian."

Beginning in 594 B.C., a leader named Solon initiated a series of reforms. An aristocrat himself, he understood that the aristocracy's grip on power was causing unrest among Athens' other classes. At Solon's urging, wealthy merchants, as well as landowners, were allowed to hold government office. Solon also created a body called the Assembly to represent the interests of the lower classes and balance the power of the aristocrats. Solon became so famous for his reforms that even today a wise legislator is sometimes referred to as a "solon."

Even after the changes brought by Solon, many in Athens resented the power and wealth of the aristocrats. Around 560 B.C., Peisistratus (piy-SIHS-truht-uhs) seized power and made himself tyrant of Athens. Peisistratus won popularity by giving land to poor farmers and employing impoverished city-dwellers to work on public buildings. After Peisistratus died in 527 B.C., his son took charge but proved a far less effective ruler. He was overthrown in 510 B.C., and one-man rule in Athens came to an end.

Athenian Democracy

After the rule of Peisistratus and his son, the old aristocratic families struggled for control of Athens. A politician named Cleisthenes (KLIYS-thuh-neez) decided that the only way to end this conflict was to take power out of the hands of the aristocrats for good. The reforms he put in place mark the birth of democracy in Athens and in the history of the world.

Cleisthenes divided the Athenian population into ten tribes. Each tribe sent fifty members to participate in a council of five hundred, and this council administered the government. More dramatically, every citizen, no matter how poor, was entitled to cast his vote in the Assembly. The Assembly decided important matters, such as whether the city should go to war. Nowhere else in the world did the common man have so direct a say in government.

But, as in less democratic Greek cities, citizenship was limited. Women, slaves, and resident foreigners, who together made up the majority in Athens, were not citizens. Citizenship was limited to adult males whose fathers had also been citizens. Consequently, less than 20 percent of the population was ever entitled to participate in the workings of Athenian democracy.

Still, Athens gave the world its first democracy. While Spartans relied on military might, Athenians embraced the rule of the people. Politics had become the business of every man, not just the privileged few.

Democracy Then and Now

Democracy means "rule by the people." While democracy in ancient Athens was limited to male citizens, modern nations that we call democracies, such as the United States, generally grant the right to vote to all adults, male and female. However, like Athens, many modern democracies make it difficult for foreigners to gain citizenship.

In one way, too, the Athenian system represented a purer form of democracy than any we see today. In the *direct* democracy of Athens, each citizen cast his vote directly on the great issues facing the city. By contrast, in a *representative* democracy, or *republic*, citizens vote for representatives who then vote on the issues and enact laws. Representative democracy is the system that prevails today in the United States and other republics. Direct democracy would be unworkable in a modern nation like the United States, with a population more than a thousand times that of ancient Athens.

An artist's portrayal of an assembly shows the lawmaking body of Athens that was open to all citizens of the city-state.

War, Glory, and Decline

By the fifth century B.C., the Greek city-states had become prosperous, largely by trading with other countries and with their own colonies around the Mediterranean. Like Athens and Sparta, each polis was proud of its independence and was convinced of the superiority of its own form of government. But a powerful empire to the east was determined to end the independence of the Greeks and lay claim to their wealth.

The Persian Wars

While the city-states of Greece pursued their separate destinies, the nation of Persia—today's Iran—had conquered an enormous empire. By 500 B.C., the Persian Empire stretched from Libya in northern Africa all the way to India. Among its subjects were the Greek cities of Ionia, on the coast of Asia Minor. In 499 B.C., some of the Ionian cities rose in revolt against the Persians. The Athenians sent forces to Ionia to fight alongside their fellow Greeks.

After several years of fighting, the Persians succeeded in crushing the Ionian rebellion. But the Persian emperor, Darius I, was enraged at the Athenians for supporting the revolt. He vowed never to forget that the inhabitants of the small city-state had challenged him. Darius even commanded a servant to stand by his table while he ate, repeating, "Master, remember the Athenians."

The Battle of Marathon

In 490 B.C., Darius sent a large army to punish the Athenians and subdue all of Greece. The Persian fleet landed near Marathon, a plain twenty-four miles (38.6 km) north of Athens. The Athenians sent a messenger to Sparta to ask for help. The Spartans told him that they were celebrating a religious festival and were forbidden to fight during that time. The Athenians would have to face the Persians on their own.

The Athenians who marched out to meet the Persians were not professional soldiers but farmers, merchants, and craftsmen who furnished their own weapons and armor. These citizen-soldiers went into battle not as mounted aristocrats but as foot soldiers, called *hoplites* (HAHP-liyts).

The Athenians were outnumbered by the Persians. But the Athenian hoplites had some advantages over their enemies. First, they were battling for their homeland. Most of Darius's troops, by contrast, had been forced to join his army. Second, the Athenians had an effective way of fighting, in a formation called a *phalanx* (FAY-langks). Each phalanx contained multiple rows of warriors standing shoulder to shoulder, each carrying a long spear. When a tightly packed phalanx, bristling with spears, charged toward an enemy, it made a terrifying sight.

Key Questions

- What was the significance of the Persian Wars in Greek history?

- What are the major cultural and political achievements of the Golden Age of Athens under Pericles?

- How did Greek democracy influence later Western political thought?

- What were the major causes and consequences of the Peloponnesian War?

In the Battle of Marathon, the Athenians advanced in a phalanx, a tight formation of spear- and shield-bearing soldiers.

In battle, the Persians relied heavily on their archers. But at Marathon, as the Greeks rushed toward the enemy, their long shields protected them from the Persians' arrows. When the phalanxes crashed into the Persian lines, the Greeks drew their swords and fought the Persians hand-to-hand.

Miltiades (mil-TIY-uh-deez), a Greek general, knew that the Persians placed their strongest soldiers in the center of their lines. So he ordered his men to attack the ends of the Persian lines first. Once the Greeks had beaten the weaker Persian soldiers, they turned toward the center, surrounding Darius's finest warriors and cutting them down. The surviving Persians soon panicked and ran back toward their boats. The Greek historian Herodotus reported that 6,400 Persians and only 192 Greeks died at Marathon.

According to a famous legend, after the battle the Greeks told a runner named Pheidippides (fiy-DIP-uh-deez) to carry the news of victory to Athens on foot. Pheidippides ran the twenty-five miles (40 km) to Athens without stopping. Reaching the city, he declared, "We have won!"—and then fell dead of exhaustion. (The modern-day twenty-six-mile [42 km] footrace known as a marathon is named for the legendary run made after the Battle of Marathon.)

Although the story of Pheidippides may be mythical, the Greeks had clearly won a great victory. With superior tactics and courage, the Athenians defeated a much larger enemy force. They preserved their independence and their democracy. Later ages would come to see the Battle of Marathon as an inspiring example of free men resisting oppression.

Victory at Salamis

Ten years after their defeat at Marathon, the Persians attempted a second invasion of Greece. The emperor Xerxes, son of Darius, sent a huge force—more than three hundred thousand soldiers, some historians estimate—to avenge his father's defeat. Each city-state realized that it could not face the Persian onslaught alone. So thirty city-states came together to form an alliance under Sparta.

The Persians advanced through Greece's mountainous north. At a narrow pass in the mountains called Thermopylae (thuhr-MAH-puh-lee), a Greek force of six or seven thousand met the Persians. After several days of battle, the Greek leader, King Leonidas (lee-AHN-ih-duhs) of Sparta, feared that his army would be encircled and destroyed. He sent most of the soldiers south toward their homes. Leonidas himself—along with three hundred Spartans and several

123

In the Battle of Salamis, the seafaring Athenians sailed their triremes to victory against the Persians' larger ships.

hundred troops from the cities of Thespiae and Thebes—remained behind to hold the pass. All were overwhelmed and slaughtered. But they had managed to delay the enemy advance, and so showed all of Greece a striking example of Spartan bravery.

The Persians marched south to Athens and found the city deserted. The Spartan stand at Thermopylae had bought time for the inhabitants to flee to safety. The vengeful Persians set fire to the sacred buildings on the Acropolis. Unknown to the Persians, the Athenian army had gathered on ships offshore of Athens.

When referring to the Acropolis of Athens, it is customary to capitalize *Acropolis.*

The Athenians had always been seafarers. In the years before the second Persian invasion, they had constructed a large fleet to defend against invasion. The Athenian ships were light, swift vessels called triremes (TRY-reems). Each trireme had a metal spike on its bow, designed for ramming enemy ships.

The Athenians decided to fight the Persians on the sea rather than on land. They stationed their ships at one end of a narrow passageway between the mainland and an island called Salamis (SA-luh-muhs). As Persian ships squeezed through the passageway, the Athenians attacked. Again and again the swift, nimble Athenian triremes rammed and sank the larger, heavier Persian ships. Seated on a nearby hill, the emperor Xerxes watched in dismay as more than two hundred of his ships were lost.

The Athenian victory at Salamis turned the tide of the war. A few months later, a combined Greek army led by the Spartans defeated the remainder of the armies of Xerxes. For a second time, the mighty Persian empire had failed to conquer Greece.

The Golden Age of Athens

The Greeks rejoiced in their victory over the Persians, a victory that seemed to defy all odds. They had kept their independence. Furthermore, the city-states, despite their differences, had shown that they could pull together in the face of a foreign threat. Nowhere was this sense of pride and confidence stronger than among the Athenians, the victors of Marathon and Salamis.

Democracy in the Age of Pericles

Historians refer to the five decades following the Persian Wars as the Golden Age of Athens, a time of prosperity and unparalleled cultural achievement. Through most of this period, the city was led by Pericles (PER-uh-kleez), who served as a member of a group of ten generals elected once a year to oversee the city's defenses.

A brilliant politician, Pericles was so respected that, beginning in 461 B.C., he was returned to office almost every year for three decades. Concerned with much more than military matters, Pericles sponsored public building programs and encouraged the work of playwrights, artists, and architects. Under Pericles, Athens became the most beautiful and richly cultured city in Greece. In a famous speech, Pericles proclaimed, "Future ages will wonder at us, as the present age wonders at us now."

Pericles also supported the expansion of democracy. Before his time, poor citizens had the right to vote in the Assembly, but they rarely held public office. Officials were unpaid, and the poor could not afford to give up working to serve in government. After helping to defeat the Persians, citizens of the lower classes demanded a stronger voice in the affairs of the city. Pericles helped change the laws so that officials received pay for their services.

Statesman, general, democrat, and builder, Pericles led Athens during its Golden Age, one of the most inventive and creative periods in history.

To safeguard their democracy, the Athenians instituted a practice called *ostracism*. If a prominent person seemed too greedy for power, the Assembly could vote to exile him. Citizens voted by scratching the person's name on a piece of broken pottery called an *ostrakon*. Anyone receiving at least six thousand votes would be banished from the city for ten years. (Today, to ostracize someone is to shun or expel him.)

Athenian democracy did not extend to the female half of the population. Unlike Spartan women, the wives and daughters of Athenian citizens mostly stayed at home, taking care of their households. Often, several slaves would help a citizen's wife with her work. In the time of Pericles, as much as one-third of Athens' population may have consisted of slaves. These slaves were often foreigners captured in battle. They did all sorts of jobs, from farming to mining to highly skilled work as potters and blacksmiths.

Although the privileges of democratic citizenship extended to only a minority of the city's residents, Athens nevertheless achieved the world's first democracy. Nowhere else in the ancient world did so large a group of people have a share in political power. To later generations, Athens handed down the idea that, under democracy, a citizen's participation in government is both a right and a duty. "We do not say," proclaimed Pericles, "that a man who takes no interest in politics is a man who minds his own business; we say that he has no business here at all."

The Delian League

After the Persian Wars, Athens convinced more than a hundred other city-states to join an alliance known as the Delian League. The league's aim was to unite against Persian threats. Each city-state gave ships and money to the league, which became powerful and rich. Athens gave the most ships, so it was chosen to command the fleet and lead the league. Athens also prospered more than any other city-state in the league.

Pericles used money from the Delian League's treasury to help fund many building projects, including the magnificent temple to Athena called the Parthenon. (In the next chapter, you'll read more about the Parthenon and other great architectural and cultural achievements of the Greeks.)

Over time, other cities began to question Athens' leadership. In 465 B.C., when the island of Thasos tried to leave the Delian League, the Athenians blockaded the island and forced it to give up its fleet. Soon Athens began demanding more tribute from the other city-states and meddling more and more in their affairs. The league evolved from a defensive alliance into an Athenian empire.

The Peloponnesian War and Greek Decline

The only city-state in Greece powerful enough to challenge Athens was Sparta. In response to Athenian expansion, the Spartans formed their own defensive league of cities located on the Peloponnese. Both Sparta and Athens interfered in the affairs of each others' allies. Tensions between the two sides grew until, in 431 B.C., war broke out. Because Sparta and many of its allies came from the Peloponnese, the conflict is called the Peloponnesian War. Pitting the powerful navy of the Athenians against the mighty land forces of Sparta, the Peloponnesian War would last for decades and engulf much of the Greek world.

City-States at War

Early in the war, the Spartans attacked the Athenian homeland. People from the countryside flocked to Athens to escape the Spartan onslaught. Overcrowding and a lack of sanitation caused a deadly plague that swept through the city. The Greek historian Thucydides (thoo-SID-uh-deez) recalled that "the bodies of the dying were heaped one on top of the other." In the end, perhaps one-third of the city perished. Among the victims of the plague was Pericles.

Fearful of catching the plague themselves, the Spartans eventually retreated. But the war ground on for decades, with savage battles fought all over Greece and as far away as Sicily, an island off the Italian coast. Meanwhile, in many city-states, civil war broke out between supporters of the Spartans and supporters of the Athenians.

The tide began to turn against Athens in 412 B.C., when the Spartans made a treaty with their old enemies the Persians. With Persian help, the Spartans built a fleet of ships powerful enough to challenge the mighty Athenian navy. In 405 B.C., the Spartan fleet defeated the Athenians in a sea battle fought in the Hellespont (HEH-luh-spahnt), the channel between Asia Minor and Europe. Almost all the Athenian ships were captured or sunk.

After crushing the Athenian navy, the Spartans blockaded the city, keeping out food and supplies. In 404 B.C., the starving Athenians finally surrendered. Some of the embittered enemies of Athens demanded that the city be destroyed. The Spartans refused, out of respect for Athens' heroic role in the Persian Wars. But the victorious Spartans went on to abolish the Athenian democracy. They replaced it with a council of thirty men known to sympathize with Sparta. To keep their hold on power, the Thirty Tyrants, as they were called, executed hundreds of prominent Athenians.

In 403 B.C., Athenians rebelled. They overthrew the Thirty Tyrants and reestablished their democracy. But Athens remained a devastated city. After three decades of war, the city had lost its empire and its influence as a model of democracy. The government could no longer afford to improve and beautify the city as it had under Pericles.

With the Golden Age behind them, Athenians lost the energy and self-confidence that had brought prosperity to the city and inspired the work of great architects, artists, and dramatists. Instead, they were left with questions. Why had their city been defeated? Had the gods deserted them? Was democracy truly the best form of government? And if not, what was? As you'll see in the next chapter, in seeking answers to such questions, the newly humbled and skeptical Athenians would further enrich the intellectual heritage of the world.

THE **FUNERAL ORATION** OF **PERICLES**

In his *History of the Peloponnesian War*, the Greek historian Thucydides (who had fought in the war) reports one of the greatest speeches in history, delivered around 430 B.C. by Pericles, to honor Athenian soldiers who had died in the war. This part of the speech is known as the Funeral Oration of Pericles. Pericles emphasizes not the war or the fallen soldiers, but what they died for.

I will not talk about the battles we have won.... Instead I will talk about our spirit and our way of life. I will talk about those things that have made us great.

Our government does not copy those of our neighbors. Instead, ours is a model for them. Ours is a democracy because power is in the hands not of a minority, but of the whole people. Everyone is equal before the law....

Our political life is free and open. So is our day-to-day life. We do not care if our neighbor enjoys himself in his own way. We are free and tolerant in our private lives. But in public affairs, we obey the laws. We especially obey the ones that protect the lowly.

When our work is done, we are in a position to enjoy all kinds of recreation for our spirits. There are ceremonies and contests all year.... Our city brings us good things from all over the world.

And our city is open to the whole world. We never keep people out for fear they will spy on us. That is because we do not rely on secret weapons. We rely on our own real courage and loyalty. The Spartans, now, train hard from childhood on. We live without all their controls. But we are just as brave in facing danger as they are! Our love of beauty does not lead to weakness. Our love of mind does not make us soft.

Everyone here is interested in the polis. *We do not say a man who is not interested in politics is minding his own business. We say he has no business here at all!*

Looking at everything, I say Athens is a school for the whole of Greece. Future ages will wonder at us. The present age wonders at us now....

I could tell you what we gain by defeating our enemies. Instead, I would rather have you gaze on the greatness of Athens every day. Then you would fall in love with her. You would realize her greatness.

Our happiness depends on our freedom. And our freedom depends on our courage. Because of that, I will not mourn the dead. In their lives, happiness and death went hand in hand.

CHAPTER 7
GREEK GLORY AND THE

475 B.C.   **450** B.C.   **425** B.C.   **400** B.C.

c. 470 B.C.
Aeschylus,
Athens' first great
dramatist, writes
powerful tragedies.

449 B.C.
Pericles becomes
the leader of Athens.

438 B.C.
The Parthenon, the
temple of Athena, is
dedicated in Athens.

Hippocrates, "the
Father of Medicine,"
practices and
teaches medicine.

399 B.C.
Socrates, charged
with corrupting the
youth of Athens, is
sentenced to death.

The magnificent ruins of the Parthenon atop the Acropolis in modern-day Athens

HELLENISTIC AGE
500 B.C.–300 B.C.

350 B.C. **325 B.C.** **300 B.C.** **275 B.C.**

343 B.C.
Aristotle becomes
the tutor of
Alexander.

336 B.C.
Alexander becomes
king of Macedonia
and begins building
an empire.

We use the terms *classic* or *classical* to refer to something that is timeless, and of lasting value and surpassing excellence. When historians refer to "classical civilization," they often mean, in particular, the civilizations of ancient Greece and Rome between about 500 B.C. and A.D. 500. Ideas and institutions from ancient Greece and Rome have continued to influence people for more than two thousand years.

In this chapter we focus on classical civilization in Greece. What we call the West—the civilization of Europe and the Americas—has been deeply influenced by the literary, artistic, and scientific achievements of ancient Greece. Even before Greek culture spread westward into Europe, it spread east across vast regions of Asia, where it was carried by the armies of one of history's most ambitious conquerors, Alexander the Great.

Art and the Written Word in the Golden Age of Greece

Key Questions

- What qualities define classic works of Greek art and architecture?

- Who were the great Greek playwrights of the classical age? What major themes did they explore?

Much of Western art as we know it was born in the prosperous and democratic Athens of the fifth century B.C. Greek sculpture and architecture reached their peak of excellence during the Golden Age of Athens. The city's artists and architects, supported by leaders like Pericles, created standards of beauty that would shape Western culture for thousands of years. Athens also supported theater, and Greek writers made lasting contributions to the art of drama.

Greek Architecture and Sculpture

In an enormous number of works—from the statues and paintings of the Renaissance artist Michelangelo to the Statue of Liberty that looms over New York Harbor—we can see the influence of Greek sculpture. In structures ranging from local banks to the U.S. Supreme Court Building, modern architects have copied the features of ancient Greek temples. In doing so, these later artists and architects have sought to capture the artistic qualities most admired by the ancient Greeks themselves—harmony, symmetry, and balance.

The Parthenon

Temples were the most important and impressive buildings in any Greek city-state. Unlike today's churches or mosques, they did not serve as gathering places for worshippers. Instead, the Greeks thought of a temple as the home of a particular god. The ancient Greeks usually built their temples clustered on a fortified hill called an acropolis.

In 480 B.C., the invading Persians under Xerxes burned the buildings on the Acropolis in Athens, a flat-topped hill that rises dramatically three hundred feet (91 m) above the city. After Pericles became leader of Athens in 449 B.C., he convinced the Assembly to fund a massive rebuilding program. The buildings constructed on the Acropolis under Pericles' leadership include what is generally considered the greatest masterpiece of Greek architecture, the temple of Athena known as the Parthenon.

It took fifteen years and twenty-two thousand tons of marble to build the massive structure. Today the Parthenon lies partly in ruins, its roof blown off by an explosion in the seventeenth century A.D. The columns surrounding the temple remain, along with the entablature (the band of stone between the columns and the now-missing roof). Even in its ruined state, the building dazzles visitors with its beauty.

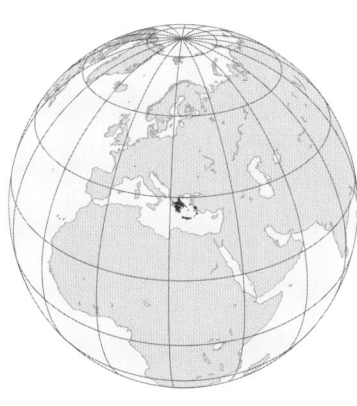

Classical Greece's influence is still felt in the West today.

A model of the Parthenon, left, shows how the temple might have looked in ancient times, and, at right, how it looks today.

To lend a sense of harmony and balance, the ancient Greek architects carefully designed the number and arrangement of columns, eight in the front and back and seventeen on the sides. The builders of the Parthenon knew that the thick marble columns might look clumsy if they made them perfectly straight. So, to make the columns look graceful rather than heavy, the Greeks designed them to swell slightly in the middle and taper at the top.

Greek Columns

Different styles of Greek architecture are characterized by the different kinds of columns supporting buildings. A building built in the Doric style, like the Parthenon, has thick columns with capitals (tops) that are simple and round. Ionic columns have scroll-shaped capitals. Corinthian columns have ornate capitals carved into clusters of leaves.

Doric, Ionic, and Corinthian columns

The Parthenon exemplifies the Greek artistic ideals of balance and proportion. In its combination of strength and elegance, the Parthenon also reflects the cultural confidence of Athens' Golden Age. Pericles might have been thinking of the Parthenon when he proudly proclaimed in a speech, "Mighty indeed are the marks and monuments...which we have left."

Greek Sculpture: Idealizing the Human Form

A masterpiece of architecture, the Parthenon also served as a setting for masterworks of art. Pericles appointed Phidias (FID-ee-uhs), the greatest sculptor of his time, to decorate the Parthenon with scenes from Greek mythology and the life of the city. Lifelike sculptures adorned the building's entablature as well as its pediments (the triangular areas below the roof).

One of the pediments illustrated the newborn goddess Athena. According to myth, Athena sprang fully grown and armed from the head of her father, Zeus. Other sculptures showed Greek warriors fighting mythical female warriors called the Amazons, as well as half-human, half-horse beings called the Centaurs.

On the entablatures the sculptors depicted a procession of Athenian citizens, with some on horseback. The horsemen and their mounts are represented so vividly that they seem ready to spring from the marble.

Bronze *Warrior of Riace*, attributed to Phidias

After Phidias, the most important sculptor of the time was Myron, who worked mostly in bronze and became famous for his statues of athletes. No sculptor before Myron had so realistically rendered the human body in art. At the same time, Myron and other Greek artists expressed their admiration of the human form by idealizing it—that is, they chiseled perfectly shaped athletes, powerful heroes, and beautiful women in order to show the human form in all its glory. The human figures in their statues had the same perfect proportions as the gods they carved lounging on Mount Olympus. The smooth-muscled warriors and thinly draped goddesses of Greek sculpture set a standard of beauty that would endure for thousands of years.

Greek Painting

Like sculpture, painting was a respected art form in the Golden Age of Greece. Greek artists, like those of ancient Crete and Mycenae, decorated the walls of houses and palaces with colorful paintings, though few of these wall paintings have survived. What has remained, however, are many smaller works painted on pottery.

Greek artists decorated jugs, cups, and vases with figures of gods and humans. Unlike the sculptors of the Parthenon, pottery painters often illustrated scenes from everyday life—cobblers making shoes, blacksmiths forging weapons, housewives spinning wool.

During the Golden Age, Greek potters developed a dramatic style of painting brick-red figures on a black background. The artists added features

The Greeks believed that Helios, the god of the sun, drove his chariot across the sky from east to west every day, as depicted on this ancient vase.

such as eyes and mouths in black so that the figures show a range of emotions. Artists of this period also made their paintings more realistic by using the technique known as foreshortening (making distant things appear smaller, as they seem to the naked eye). In a humbler way than the great sculptors, the pottery painters captured the Greek belief in the importance of the individual and the joy of physical existence.

Classical Greek Literature

During the Golden Age of ancient Greece, Greek writers produced lasting masterworks of literature. Later generations of Europeans would revere the literature of the classical Greek period as models of reason, elegance, and formal perfection.

Greek Drama

The Western idea of drama was invented by the Greeks. Drama had its origins in religious festivals in which a priest sang or recited the deeds

133

The ancient Greek theater at Delphi is set on the natural slopes of Mount Parnassus.

of a god. Gradually these rituals evolved into a sort of show in which a single actor impersonated one of the gods or heroes. In the early fifth century B.C., a playwright named Aeschylus (ES-kuh-luhs) thought to add a second actor to the performance, and drama as we know it was born.

Although theaters were built throughout Greece during the Golden Age, our knowledge of Greek drama is limited mostly to Athens, where the greatest playwrights lived, and where the city encouraged the development of drama. Going to plays was considered almost a civic duty. Grants were given to those who could not afford tickets.

While plays were performed year-round, every March Athens put on a major drama festival in a theater at the foot of the Acropolis. Thousands of people sat on stone benches that curved around a semicircular acting area. Each play had a cast of two or three actors who interacted with each other and with a group of men called the chorus, who commented on the action. All the actors wore clay masks with exaggerated expressions and mouthpieces to make their voices louder so that the large audience could hear.

Three serious plays, or trage-dies, were produced during each day of the festival. The day's enter-tainment was rounded out in the evening by a single comedy, per-haps so the audience could go home in a lighthearted mood. The tragedies usually focused on traditional tales of gods and heroes, while the comedies were often drawn from everyday life.

Greek actors wore masks with exaggerated expressions to convey their characters' emotions to the audience.

Three Great Tragedians

In the Golden Age of Greece, Athens produced three great tragedians—Aeschylus, Sophocles (SAHF-uh-kleez), and Euripides (you-RIP-uh-deez). Between them, they wrote hundreds of plays, of which only thirty-three have survived.

In his works, Aeschylus is often concerned with the theme of *hubris* (HYOO-bruhs), or excessive pride. The Greeks believed in competition and achievement, but they also thought that the gods punished men who grew too proud and overreached themselves. In *The Persians*, Aeschylus, who as a young man had fought in the Battle of Marathon, depicts the Persian defeat at Salamis as punishment for the hubris of the emperor Xerxes. In *Agamemnon*, he attributes the murder of the mythical king Agamemnon as the result of the arrogance the king displayed after conquering Troy.

Sophocles' most famous play, *Oedipus the King*, also tells the story of the downfall of a great man. Unlike Xerxes and Agamemnon, Oedipus (ED-uh-puhs), king of Thebes, is a just and popular ruler, though he can be hot-tempered and arrogant. He unwittingly commits two terrible crimes when he kills his father and marries his mother, not knowing the true identity of either. When he discovers the truth, he blinds himself in despair. At the end of the play, the chorus says of Oedipus:

> *Who could behold his greatness without envy?*
> *Now what a black sea of terror has overwhelmed him.*
> *Now as we keep our watch and wait our final day,*
> *count no man happy till he dies, free of pain at last.*

The third great tragedian of the time, Euripides, wrote provocative plays that questioned the values of his fellow citizens. At the height of the Peloponnesian War, Euripides wrote *The Trojan Women*, a play lamenting the destruction that warfare brings. His most famous play, *Medea*, tells of a mythical woman who kills her children out of rage against her unfaithful husband. Euripides gives Medea lines that sound like a protest against the restrictions imposed on women by Athenian society: "Of all things living and which can form a judgment," Medea laments, "we women are the most unfortunate creatures."

The greatest Athenian writer of comedy was Aristophanes (air-uh-STAHF-uh-neez). In his rollicking, sometimes obscene works, he satirizes prominent figures in Athenian life. In *The Clouds*, he mocks the philosopher Socrates. In *The Frogs*, he makes fun of tragedy itself, showing Aeschylus and Euripides (who by then had both died) squabbling in the underworld over who was the better playwright.

The tragedies and comedies of ancient Athens continue to be performed in theaters around the world. In particular, the great tragedies retain their hold on modern audiences because they deal so profoundly with enduring questions about the human condition, such as: Do we have free will or are things fated to happen? Which is more important, the individual or the community? And, how should we deal with the inevitable fact of suffering?

Greek Poetry

Homer, who composed the *Iliad* and the *Odyssey*, was considered the greatest poet of ancient Greece. Every educated Greek could quote lines from Homer's epics about the Trojan War and its aftermath.

Besides Homer's great epics, many shorter poems from ancient Greece have survived as well. Pindar, a poet of the Golden Age, became famous for his poems in praise of various rulers and victorious athletes.

Sappho (SAF-oh), the only female writer from ancient Greece whose name we know, composed a very different kind of poetry. Sappho is the first great love poet of the Western world. Her poems, which survive mainly in fragments, express the power of love to inflict both joy and pain.

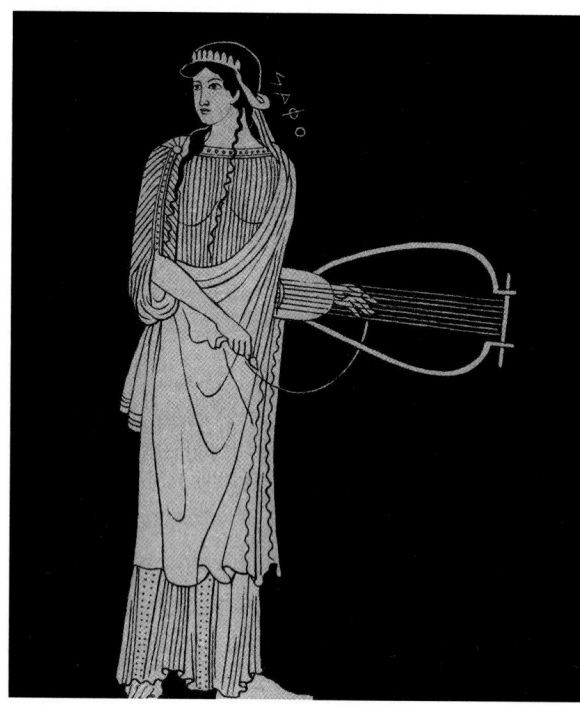

Sappho, depicted here on an ancient Greek vase, was the first great love poet of the Western world.

Writing a century and a half before the Golden Age, she declared that love, not war or glory, was the greatest subject for a poet:

> *Some say a cavalry corps,*
> *Some, infantry, some, again,*
> *will maintain that the swift oars*
>
> *of our fleet are the finest*
> *sight on dark earth; but I say*
> *that whatever one loves, is.*

The Writing of History

Along with other features of our civilization, the study of history as we understand it was born in the Athens of Pericles. Before this time, people in different cultures had handed down stories of the past. These stories usually mixed fact and legend in an effort to justify the ways of the existing culture. Herodotus, a Greek of the Golden Age, is known as the "father of history" because he was the first writer who sought to do research to determine the *facts* about past times. He called his work *historia*, a word meaning "inquiry," which gives us our word *history*.

Herodotus set out to tell the tale of the Persian Wars, which meant that he had to describe events that occurred not only in Greece but throughout the vast Persian Empire. In search of facts and insight, he traveled through Greece, the Near East, and Egypt, reading records, studying monuments, and listening to stories. While proud to be Greek, Herodotus nevertheless wrote admiringly about other cultures. He introduced his history of the Persian Wars by saying, "I hope...to preserve the memory of the past by putting on record the astonishing achievements both of our own and of the Asiatic peoples."

For all his objectivity, Herodotus did include some legends and fanciful stories in his work. A younger historian named Thucydides practiced a more purely factual history. His book about the Peloponnesian War (in which Thucydides had served as a commander) is a masterpiece of historical writing. Unlike the work of Herodotus, which is full of colorful details about the customs of people in different lands, Thucydides focuses on the motives and deeds of politicians and generals. His *History of the Peloponnesian War* stands as the first great work of political history.

Lovers of Wisdom

"The activity of our intelligence," declared the Greek philosopher Aristotle, "constitutes the complete happiness of man.... Intelligence, above all else, is man." The ancient Greeks believed in the power of the human intellect to answer all kinds of questions—from the reasons for disease to the nature of the universe to the most desirable form of government. Their probing curiosity produced the first philosophers and scientists of the Western world.

The Great Philosophers

Today we use the word *science* to mean the organized study of the universe and the laws of nature. The Greeks used a different word. They called it *philosophy*. The word philosophy comes from two Greek words—*philo*, meaning "love," and *sophia*, meaning "wisdom." So *philosophy* literally means the "love of wisdom." To the Greeks, loving wisdom, studying the laws of nature, and thinking about man's place in the world were all one and the same.

Ancient Greece produced a long line of thinkers whose ideas form the basis of philosophy in the West. Probably the first man to call himself a philosopher was Pythagoras (puh-THAG-uh-ruhs), who lived in the sixth century B.C., about a hundred years before Athens' Golden Age. Pythagoras speculated widely on everything from music to astronomy to mathematics. When asked whether he was wise, he replied, "No, I am only a lover of wisdom." Like later philosophers, Pythagoras thought that the search for truth was more important than any final answers.

The Sophists

During the Golden Age, one group of philosophers came to prominence. These were the Sophists (SAH-fists), traveling teachers who made their living by instructing young men in the practice of debate. Their services were especially prized in democratic Athens, where success often depended on the ability to win arguments in the Assembly.

The Sophists were known not only for their skill as teachers but also for their skepticism toward traditional ideas. The greatest of the Sophists, Protagoras (proh-TAG-uh-ruhs), argued that people had no way of knowing whether the gods existed. He also declared, "Each individual person is the measure of all things—of things that are, that they are, and of things that are not, that they are not." In other words, according to Protagoras, truth changes according to the perspective of the individual. This view, known as relativism, probably shocked many ancient Athenians, but has been influential in modern times.

Key Questions

- How did Socrates, Plato, and Aristotle influence the course of thought in Western civilization?

- What were the major achievements of the ancient Greeks in science and mathematics?

As he prepares to drink hemlock, Socrates consoles his followers, as depicted in Jacques-Louis David's famous painting from 1787, *The Death of Socrates*.

The great age of Greek philosophy came during and after the Peloponnesian War. That conflict ended in a Spartan victory and disastrous defeat for Athens, diminishing the once mighty city's power and shattering its lofty self-confidence. The polis never regained its former glory. Its wealth had been spent on war, its fleet no longer controlled the sea, and its best soldiers and leaders were dead. New leaders tried to make the citizens feel proud and confident again, but Athenians felt their failures deeply.

During this troubled time, a handful of great thinkers emerged—brilliant men who thought intensely about what had gone wrong and what was truly important in life. In the twilight of Athens, some of the greatest philosophers in history lived and taught, including Socrates (SAHK-ruh-teez), Plato, and Aristotle (AIR-uh-stah-tl).

Socrates: The Gadfly of Athens

Socrates was born around 470 B.C. Like the Sophists, Socrates taught his students to question traditional values. Unlike the Sophists, however, he refused to take money for his teaching. He also rejected the relativism of the Sophists. Socrates believed that philosophy could discover universal moral truths. He wanted to make his students not merely successful but *good*. He challenged them to look closely at all of their thoughts and actions. "The unexamined life is not worth living," he declared.

Socrates never wrote anything down. We know of his teachings through the writings of others, especially his student Plato. Seated in the bustling Athenian agora, Socrates taught by posing questions. "What is justice?" he might ask, or "What is love?" When someone gave a confident answer, Socrates would ask further questions, probing his student's ideas. Usually, the person would wind up realizing that he knew much less than he thought he did. Socrates compared himself to a gadfly— a pesky, stinging insect. He wanted to prod people to question their assumptions and think more clearly.

For his probing, questioning way of teaching, Socrates earned many followers, and just as many enemies. In 399 B.C., at the age of seventy, he was put on trial for corrupting the youth of Athens and showing disrespect to the gods. His defiant and mocking answers to the charges angered the jury, and he was sentenced to die by drinking hemlock, a powerful poison. He met death bravely, assuring his followers that "no evil can happen to a good man, either in life or after death."

Socrates' influence lives on in many ways. Many modern teachers—especially professors in American law schools—use the Socratic method of teaching by asking questions. Above all, however, Socrates molded the thought of the greatest of all Greek philosophers, Plato and Aristotle.

A SOCRATIC DIALOGUE

Here is an example of how Socrates questioned people to make them examine and question their own ideas. When the Athenians placed Socrates on trial, they accused him of teaching dangerous ideas to young people. Socrates defended himself by asking his chief accuser, Meletus (muh-LEE-tus), a series of questions. The account of the trial of Socrates was written by the philosopher Plato, a student of Socrates, in a work called the *Apology*.

Socrates: Come here, Meletus, and let me ask a question. You think a great deal about the improvement of young people?

Meletus: Yes, I do.

Socrates: Tell the judges, then, who improves the young. For you must know, as you have taken pains to discover who corrupts them, and are accusing me. Speak up, friend, and tell us who their improver is.

Meletus: The laws.

Socrates: But that, my good sir, is not my meaning. I want to know who the person is who, in the first place, knows the laws.

Meletus: The judges, Socrates, who are present in court.

Socrates: What, all of the judges, or some only and not others?

Meletus: All of them.

Socrates: That is good news! There are plenty of improvers, then. And what do you say of the audience here—do they improve young people?

Meletus: Yes, they do.

Socrates: And the senators?

Meletus: Yes, the senators improve them.

Socrates: But perhaps the members of the citizen Assembly corrupt them? Or do they too improve them?

Meletus: They improve them.

Socrates: Then every Athenian improves and elevates the young, with the exception of me. I alone corrupt them? Is that what you affirm?

Meletus: That is what I stoutly affirm.

Socrates: I am very unfortunate if that is true. But suppose I ask you a question: Would you say that this also holds true in the case of horses? Does one man do them harm, and the rest of the world do them good? Is not the exact opposite true? One man—the horse trainer—is able to do them good, while others rather injure them. Is not that true, Meletus, of horses, or any other animals? Yes, certainly. Happy indeed would be the condition of youth if they had one corrupter only, and all the rest of the world were their improvers.

Plato and the Ideal Republic

Plato was born in the year 427 B.C. into a wealthy and aristocratic Athenian family. At the age of twenty, he became a student of Socrates. After the death of Socrates, Plato established his own school, called the Academy, in a grove of olive trees outside the city. Students at the Academy studied philosophy, mathematics, astronomy, and other subjects. Sometimes called Europe's first university, the Academy would last for centuries.

A brilliant writer, Plato composed dozens of philosophical works collectively known as the *Dialogues*. Each dialogue takes the form of an imagined or remembered conversation between Socrates and his students. However, scholars believe that many of the ideas in the dialogues were first conceived by Plato rather than Socrates.

The most influential of all the dialogues is *The Republic*, in which Plato analyzes different forms of government in order to determine which is best. Plato had become skeptical about democracy when a jury in democratic Athens condemned his revered teacher Socrates. Plato became convinced that the uneducated, undisciplined masses could not make good decisions. In *The Republic*, Plato argued that the ideal government is one ruled not by the people but by philosopher-kings, men whose wisdom and sense of justice have been formed by decades of intellectual training. In expressing his vision of the ideal state, Plato became the first of many Western writers to describe what later writers would call a *utopia*, an imaginary perfect society.

Plato wrote about much more than government. The subjects of his dialogues range from the origin of languages to the nature of love to the fate of the soul after death. To this day, thinkers continue to grapple with questions first posed by Plato. A modern philosopher remarked that all of Western philosophy is only "a series of footnotes to Plato."

Aristotle the Authority

Socrates had educated Plato, and Plato, in turn, schooled a brilliant young man who became the leading philosopher of ancient Greece. His name was Aristotle, and he was born in 384 B.C. in Macedonia, a few hundred miles to the north of Athens. His father served as physician to Macedonia's king. At the age of seventeen, Aristotle was sent south to study at Plato's Academy. The young man's brilliance so impressed the older philosopher that he called him "the intelligence of the school." Aristotle would remain at the Academy for twenty years.

Aristotle later returned to Macedonia for a time to tutor the king's son, Alexander. (You will learn more about Alexander later in this chapter.) In 335 B.C., Aristotle founded his own school in Athens, the Lyceum (liy-SEE-uhm). Like the Academy, the Lyceum lasted for many years, and gave a word to later languages. In many parts of Europe today, what Americans call a high school is known as a *lyceum*.

Aristotle taught and wrote on a staggering array of subjects, including physics, chemistry, astronomy, ethics, politics, and literature. He gathered information carefully and systematically, anticipating the methods of modern-day scientists. When he wanted to study zoology, he

A detail from Raphael's *The School of Athens*, painted in 1510, shows Plato, at left, walking with Aristotle.

had gamekeepers put tags on wild animals so he could follow their movements. When he wanted to study politics, he had his students collect the constitutions from city-states all over Greece.

The field of study called political science began with Aristotle's *Politics*, in which he divides governments into three different types: monarchy (rule by one person), oligarchy (rule by a few for the benefit of a ruling minority), and democracy (rule by the many). Each form of government, he argued, can be either good or bad, depending on circumstances. Aristotle was less opposed to democracy than Plato, but he worried that rule by the people could break down into mob rule.

Aristotle's influence extended far beyond the fields of science and politics. He invented logic, a step-by-step method of reasoning that almost all later scientists and philosophers would use to organize their thoughts. He also gave people a new standard for living a good life, by following what he called a "mean," or middle course. For example, a soldier afraid to fight is cowardly. A soldier too eager to fight is foolhardy. For Aristotle, the ideal soldier would be prudent—brave yet cautious, because prudence is the mean (the middle point) between cowardice and foolhardiness. Later generations admired this idea so much that they referred to it as the doctrine of the golden mean.

Aristotle wrote so much on so many subjects, and had such persuasive ideas, that for almost two thousand years he would be considered the authority on almost everything. Hardly a branch of science, philosophy, religion, or art developed without feeling his influence. His works on science were relied on for centuries.

So great was Aristotle's authority that even when he was wrong—such as his view of the universe as a series of spheres—it was difficult for people to accept new facts or evidence that contradicted him. Because Aristotle had said so, people believed for generations that flies had only four legs, and that women had fewer teeth than men, even though they could have disproved these "facts" by simply looking and counting.

Aristotle's Logic

Like other Greeks, Aristotle was very interested in the ability of humans to reason. He was the first philosopher to analyze how people can use logic to reason well and be certain of their conclusions. Here is a simple example of the kind of Aristotelian logic called a syllogism (SIH-luh-jih-zuhm):

Fact: All mammals are warm-blooded.
Fact: A cat is a mammal.
From those two facts, we can conclude that a cat is warm-blooded.

Here is another example of such logic:

Fact: All men are mortal.
Fact: Socrates was a man.
Conclusion: Socrates was mortal.

For Aristotle, that kind of logic was just the beginning. His organized study of logic and its rules set Western thought on a path toward scientific understanding.

Science and Mathematics

The word *science* comes from a Greek word meaning "knowledge." Today, by *science* we mean the study of the physical world, including such fields as biology, zoology, and astronomy. Even before Aristotle, Greek thinkers were engaged in scientific pursuits. In the early sixth century B.C., an Ionian Greek named Thales (THAY-leez) studied astronomy and predicted a total eclipse of the sun. He also declared that the whole world was composed of a single substance, water. Although this idea was incorrect, it showed the fundamental scientific attitude that the universe could be understood through reason.

Through the years, Greek scientists continued to speculate on the building blocks of matter. Democritus (dih-MAHK-ruht-uhs), a scientist of the Golden Age, built on the ideas of his teacher, Leucippus (lou-SIP-uhs) and theorized that everything is made of tiny particles called *atoms*, too small to be seen by the naked eye. Modern

Greek Mapmakers

Geography compelled the ancient Greeks to become innovators in mapmaking. Because they lived in a mountainous, rocky land, the Greeks turned to the sea for their livelihood. As they traded and set up colonies throughout the Mediterranean region, the Greeks required knowledge of the sea and the surrounding area. Many Greek scholars included mapmaking among their pursuits. Eratosthenes (ehr-uh-TAHS-thuh-neez), a mathematician who lived in the third century B.C., created a map of the world and worked out a fairly accurate calculation of the circumference of the earth. Perhaps the most famous Greek mapmaker was Ptolemy (TAH-luh-mee), a geographer and astronomer who lived later during the time of the Roman Empire.

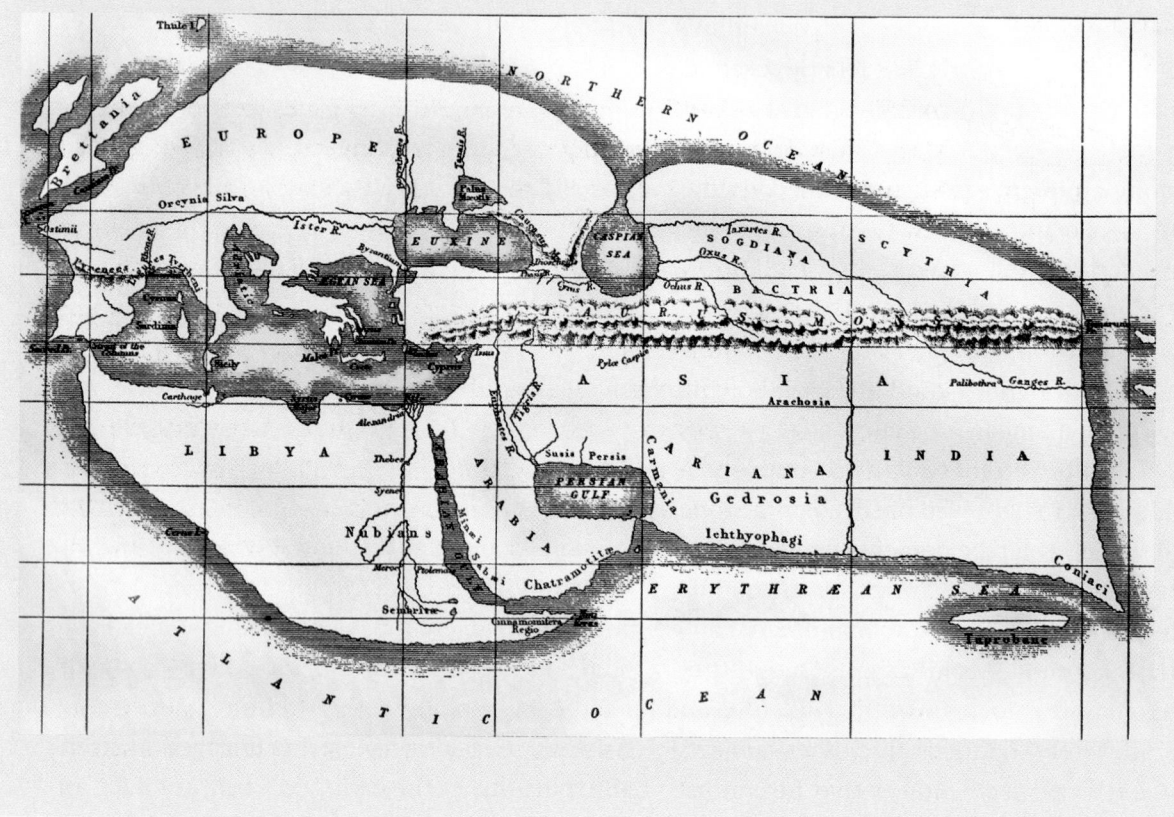

chemistry accepts the existence of atoms and even smaller particles.

Other scientists of ancient Greece pursued more practical subjects. A physician named Hippocrates (hip-AHK-ruh-teez) became known as "the Father of Medicine" for insisting that disease was a natural phenomenon rather than a punishment sent by the gods. Hippocrates is best remembered today for setting down ethical standards for physicians. Even today, many doctors swear a Hippocratic oath, pledging to treat their patients ethically and humanely, and to respect their privacy.

In ancient Greece, the study of mathematics was closely allied with both philosophy and science. Mathematical calculations allowed Thales to predict the eclipse. The philosopher Pythagoras came up with a formula for determining right angles, which enabled Greek architects to build walls that stood absolutely upright. The Pythagorean theorem, as it is now known, is still studied in high school geometry classes today. An inscription over the door of Plato's Academy read, "Let no one ignorant of geometry enter here."

Alexander and the Hellenistic Age

Key Questions

- How did Alexander the Great build an empire? What was his vision for the empire?

- What were the major cultural characteristics and achievements of the Hellenistic Age?

The long Peloponnesian War weakened all of the Greek city-states. Even after the war's end, the city-states continued to fight among themselves. Meanwhile, to the north of Greece, Macedonia was growing in power and influence.

Alexander of Macedonia

In 359 B.C., an ambitious king named Philip II came to the throne of Macedonia, determined to conquer the quarrelsome cities to the south. For the next two decades, Philip tried to bully the city-states into submission. Few Greeks took seriously the threat of conquest by Macedonia, a country they considered backward. But in Athens, an orator named Demosthenes (dih-MAHS-thuh-neez) warned his countrymen: "[Philip] cannot rest content with what he has conquered; he is always taking in more, everywhere casting his net round us, while we sit idle and do nothing."

Demosthenes' fears came true in 338 B.C., when the Macedonian army defeated a combined force from Athens and Thebes. Philip now controlled all of the city-states except Sparta. In the decisive battle, Philip's cavalry had been led by his eighteen-year-old son and heir, Alexander, afterward known as "the Great."

Young Alexander

From the first, Alexander stood out as exceptional. Before his birth, his mother dreamed that lightning struck her womb, presumably an omen of Alexander's future greatness.

According to the ancient historian Plutarch (PLOO-tahrk), when Alexander was ten years old he saw his father's men trying without success to mount a massive black horse named Bucephalus (byoo-SEH-fuh-luhs). After watching the powerful steed throw one man after another, the boy declared that *he* could tame the horse. Alexander, who had observed that Bucephalus was bucking in fear at his own shadow, grasped the animal's halter and turned his head to face the sun. Having calmed the horse, Alexander mounted it and rode away to the cheers of Philip's men. Bucephalus and Alexander rode together for the next twenty years.

To tutor his young son in Greek literature and culture, Philip summoned the best Greek teachers, including Aristotle. The philosopher taught Alexander to love the works of Homer, especially the *Iliad*, with its story of the Trojan War. According to legend, Aristotle gave the young prince a copy of the *Iliad*, and Alexander slept with it under his pillow for the rest of his life, determined to become an even greater warrior than Homer's hero, Achilles.

In 337 B.C., Philip gathered representatives of the Greek states to announce an ambitious plan. He would lead the Greeks in conquest of the vast Persian empire, in revenge, he said, for the Persian attacks on Greece a century and a half before. But the following year, Philip was assassinated by political enemies. It was left to Alexander to fulfill his father's dreams of conquest.

The Empire of Alexander the Great

The assassination of his father thrust Alexander suddenly into the role of king. Although only twenty, he was already an excellent soldier and an experienced leader, having stood in for the king when Philip was away on military campaigns. Furthermore, Alexander inherited an experienced and well-trained army, and with it, his father's ambition to conquer the Persian Empire.

In 334 B.C., with a combined force of Greeks and Macedonians, Alexander crossed the Hellespont into Asia Minor. Leaping off his ship, he hurled his spear into the ground, thus symbolically proclaiming his right to all territory he would win through force of arms. For the next year, Alexander's troops fought their way across Asia Minor. In 333 B.C., at the Battle of Issus in Syria, Alexander smashed a large Persian army. The Persian emperor fled, and Alexander captured his family, a severe humiliation for the Persians.

Next, Alexander marched his army south to Egypt, where the Persian forces surrendered without a fight. Many Egyptians, who had never accepted Persian domination, welcomed Alexander as a liberator. To celebrate his claiming of this ancient land, Alexander founded a new city, which he called Alexandria, on the coast of northern Egypt. Then he led his troops eastward, toward the heart of Persia itself. In 330 B.C., Alexander captured and burned the Persian capital of Persepolis, to avenge, he said, the burning of the Acropolis of Athens one hundred and fifty years before.

Shortly after the burning of Persepolis, the Persian emperor was assassinated by one of his

A Roman mosaic shows Alexander the Great leading a charge against the Persian army at the Battle of Issus in 333 B.C.

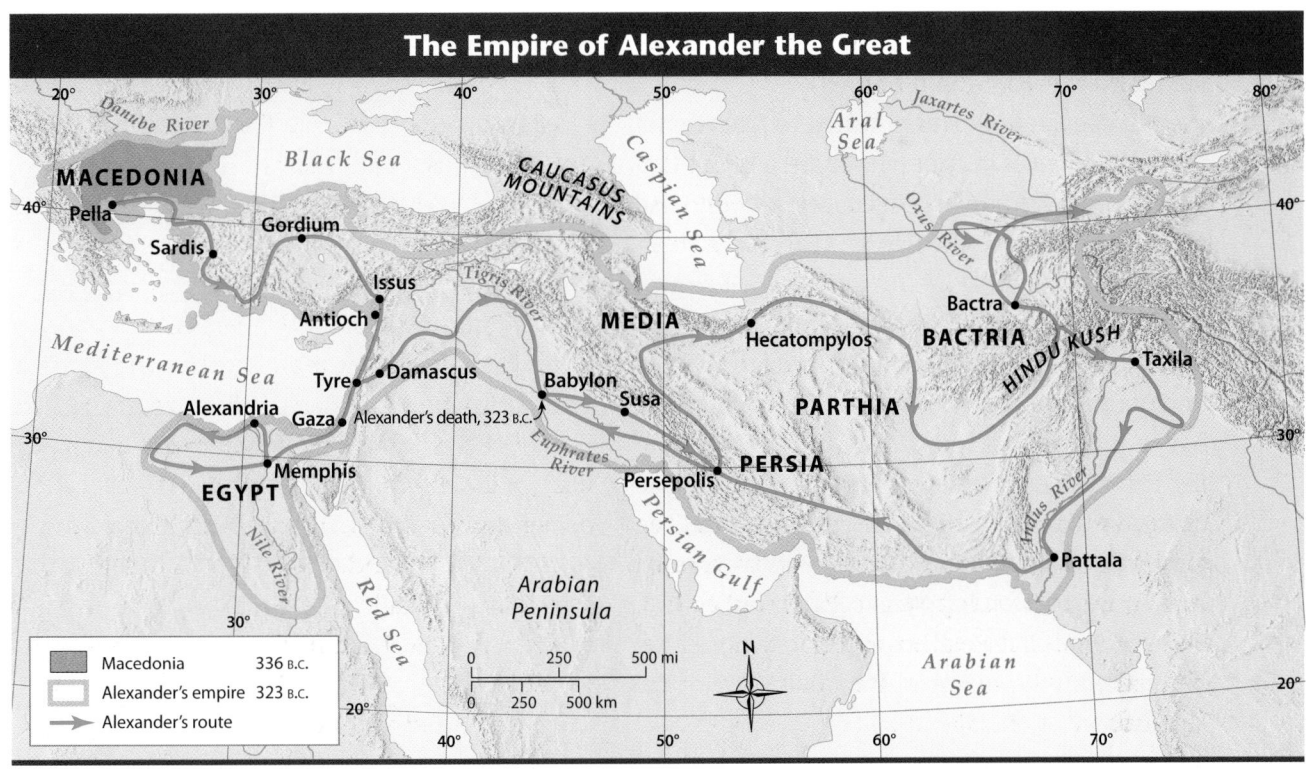

The Empire of Alexander the Great

Macedonia 336 B.C.

Alexander's empire 323 B.C.

Alexander's route

It took only thirteen years for Alexander the Great and his armies to conquer an enormous empire linking Europe and Asia.

own officials. Alexander, who now considered himself the legitimate ruler of the Persian Empire, began a process of blending Persians and Greeks. He dressed in a way that combined the royal robes of Macedonia with those of Persia. He accepted Persian soldiers into his army. He encouraged his men to marry women from the lands they had conquered, and in 327 B.C., he himself married a Persian noblewoman named Roxana, said to be the most beautiful woman in Asia.

Some of Alexander's Greek and Macedonian followers resented his turn to Persian ways, especially his demand that they prostrate themselves—lie flat on the ground—in his presence. The Greeks had always seen themselves as free men, unwilling to worship kings as if they were gods.

Alexander's army had grown weary after almost a decade of marching and fighting. Still, Alexander pushed them to make further conquests. In 326 B.C., Alexander led his troops farther eastward, into India, where they won a battle against natives fighting from the backs of elephants. At this point, however, Alexander's exhausted men

Alexander led his men as far east as India, where he was victorious over Indian troops who rode elephants into battle.

145

refused to follow him any farther. Reluctantly, he turned westward, toward home.

But Alexander never returned to Macedonia. He died of a fever in Babylon, in present-day Iraq, having conquered the largest empire the world had yet known. He was thirty-three years old.

The Hellenistic Age

The three centuries following the death of Alexander the Great are known as the Hellenistic Age, a term that comes from the Greeks' name for themselves, Hellenes. This period saw the diffusion of Greek culture through much of the ancient world, including all the lands conquered by Alexander, from Egypt to India. In many ways, however, the Greek culture of the Hellenistic Age differed from the culture of the Golden Age of the city-states.

The Legacy of Ancient Greece	
Humanities and Culture	Greek language and mythology
	Philosophy—seeking truth and wisdom
	History as a discipline of study
	The Olympiad
Fine Arts	Lifelike sculptures of idealized human forms
	Classical architecture—symmetry and balance
	Drama (comedy and tragedy)
Politics and Government	Direct democracy
	Trial by peers
	The concept of citizenship
Science and Technology	Habits of scientific observation and inquiry
	Advancements in geometry and physics
	Insights in geography and mapmaking

Alexander's Empire Splits

When Alexander died in 323 B.C., his generals fought over who would succeed him. None was strong enough to maintain the empire, and the conflict ended with three generals—Ptolemy, Seleucus, and Antigonus—dividing it up. Each founded a dynasty that lasted for generations before falling to Rome's power. The Antagonid kingdom consisted of Macedonia and northern Greece and fell to the Romans in 168 B.C.

The Seleucid kingdom was the largest and included much of the Near East and Persia. Its diversity of cultures made it hard to control. The Maccabees, Jews in the province of Judea, revolted against the Seleucids in 165 B.C. and eventually set up their own kingdom. The Seleucids finally lost all their territory but Syria, which became a province of Rome in 64 B.C.

The Ptolemaic kingdom included Egypt, Palestine, and Libya. In 30 B.C., Cleopatra IV, the last of the Ptolemies, committed suicide when Egypt was conquered by Rome.

Plutarch, Alexander's biographer, says that in the course of Alexander's conquests, he founded seventy cities, and named many of them Alexandria. By far the most famous of the Alexandrias was the one on the Mediterranean coast of Egypt. This city, made wealthy through trade, attracted a diverse population including Greeks, Egyptians, and Jews. The city was also famous for the Pharos, a lighthouse more than four hundred feet (122 m) tall.

Even more remarkable was the city's library, the greatest in the ancient world. Designed to contain a copy of every book ever written in Greek, it may have housed 700,000 papyrus scrolls. Next to the library was a research center known as the Museum, after the nine Muses, the goddesses of the arts. Here scholars lived and studied in luxurious surroundings, supported by the city's government.

One of the scholars who worked at Alexandria was the mathematician Euclid (YOO-kluhd). His *Elements* would serve as the main textbook of geometry from his own to modern times. Also working in Alexandria was the scientist Archimedes (ahr-kuh-MEE-deez), who made major advances in mathematics and physics. Archimedes invented remarkable machines and weapons, including a rotating screw-shaped device to raise water from lower to higher levels, and an array of huge mirrors to catch the sun's rays and set fire to enemy ships.

Ambitious and energetic men flocked from Greece to the new Hellenistic cities to take jobs in business or government, since most government posts were reserved for Greeks. These cities offered new opportunities for women as well. Education became common for upper-class women, leading some to practice philosophy and music. Some cities even allowed women to hold minor public offices, which would have been unheard of in the traditional city-states.

Philosophy and Art in the Hellenistic Age

In the Hellenistic Age, a new individualism flourished in philosophy. Philosophers called Stoics argued that emotion causes suffering, and that men should therefore live strictly according to reason. The Epicureans defended pleasure (of a moderate kind) as the highest goal in life. The more radical Cynics—from the Greek word for "dog"—disdained civilization itself, wandering from town to town and living in the streets like animals.

Although very different in some ways, these schools of philosophy were similar in focusing on the needs of the individual rather than the communal ties of the city-state. The philosopher Epicurus declared, "Man is not by nature adapted for living in civic communities"—a far cry from Aristotle's definition of man as a "political animal."

Artists, too, broke with earlier traditions. For example, sculptors embraced more varied and realistic subjects. In place of the idealized young athletes and warriors chiseled by sculptors of the Golden Age, artists in the Hellenistic Age depicted more realistic figures, including aged women, battered boxers, and suffering slaves.

Greek Culture Goes On

By 150 B.C., the Hellenistic world was in decline. The separate kingdoms could not sustain their strength, especially in the face of a new power—Rome.

The Hellenistic world came to an end in 30 B.C., with the suicide of Cleopatra, the last of the Ptolemies. By then, a new empire, led by Rome, dominated the Mediterranean world. Although the Greeks had lost their political sway, they exerted an enormous cultural influence over their conquerors. The Romans would base much of their art, literature, and philosophy on Greek models. The conquests of Rome would carry the influence of Greece across Europe, and far forward into the future.

The ruins of a temple dedicated to the sea god Poseidon overlook the Aegean Sea.

CHAPTER 8
ROME REPUBLIC AND EMPIRE
700 B.C.–A.D. 200

800 B.C.

600 B.C.

400 B.C.

753 B.C
Rome is founded
(according to Roman
tradition).

509 B.C.
Rome establishes
a republic.

451 B.C.
The Twelve Tables
establish uniform
written law in Rome.

A re-creation of the Roman Forum, c. A.D. 200

200 B.C.

A.D. 1

A.D. 200

146 B.C.
In the Third Punic War,
Rome destroys Carthage
and gains control of the
western Mediterranean.

44 B.C.
Julius Caesar is made
dictator for life.

27 B.C.
Octavian becomes
Rome's first emperor. The
Roman Republic ends.

*I*n the years following the decline of Athens and the breakup of Alexander's empire, the center of power and culture in the Mediterranean world shifted west from Greece to Italy, in particular to the city of Rome.

The ancient Romans established a republic, which became an early model for representative government. Through trade and warfare, Rome expanded its territory and influence across the Mediterranean. In time, the Roman Republic gave way to dictatorial rule, at first under Julius Caesar.

During the first two centuries of the Roman Empire, a series of emperors helped maintain a long period of relative peace and, at least for the upper classes, prosperity. During this time, the Romans made tremendous achievements in law, government, engineering, architecture, and the arts. The achievements of the ancient Romans exert influence to this day.

The Birth of the Roman Republic

Key Questions

- What is a republic?
- What were the key features of government in the early Roman Republic?
- How did the Roman Republic evolve over time to become more representative?

Rome began as a small village on the narrow, boot-shaped Italian Peninsula that juts into the Mediterranean Sea, forming an important crossroads between the eastern and western Mediterranean. Livy (LIHV-ee), a Roman historian born in 59 B.C., wrote that "gods and men chose this site for good reasons: all its advantages make it the best place in the world for a city destined to grow great."

Rome's location was indeed ideal. To the north, the rugged Alps offered protection from invaders. Also to the north, the Po River valley provided rich farmland. To the east of Rome lay a mountain range, the Apennines (A-puh-niynz), that divide the peninsula. Compared to the mountainous terrain of Greece, however, the Apennines were less rugged and easier to cross, thus permitting travel and trade between east and west on the peninsula.

Rome is not a coastal city but sits about fifteen miles (24 km) inland on the Tiber River. The distance to the Tyrrhenian (tuh-REE-nee-uhn) Sea was far enough to discourage pirates and invading fleets but close enough to allow Roman traders to join busy networks of trade across the Mediterranean Sea.

Climate also gave Rome an advantage. The inhabitants enjoyed the sunny summers and mild winters of central Italy. Generous rainfall fed meandering rivers, making the area ideal for growing wheat in the lowlands. Shepherds grazed cattle, goats, and sheep on lush hillsides.

The Early People of Rome

Like Livy, many Romans believed their city was destined for greatness. They believed the gods had favored Rome since its founding. A much-loved Roman myth linked the city's origin to Romulus and Remus, who were said to be twin sons of Mars, the Roman god of war.

According to the legend, Romulus and Remus, abandoned as infants, were rescued and fed by a she-wolf. The babes were soon found by a local shepherd. The shepherd and his wife raised the boys as their own. Years later, says

Rome's empire: Egypt to Britain, Spain to Mesopotamia, and north to the Danube River

The mild Italian climate makes the hillsides outside Rome ideal for growing grapes.

151

the myth, Romulus and Remus came upon a land of seven hills above the Tiber River. They agreed it was a good location to build a city, as it would be easy to defend. So they enlisted help and began the work of founding a new city. But the brothers argued over who should rule. In a fit of rage, Romulus killed Remus. Romulus established his town on the Palatine (PA-luh-tiyn), one of the seven hills, and, in his own honor, named the settlement Rome.

Ancient Roman historians recorded the legend as fact, setting the date of the founding of Rome at 753 B.C. Archaeological evidence indicates that Rome is older. Its seven hills were settled around 1000 B.C. by a people known as Latins, who spoke Latin, an Indo-European language.

The Latins farmed the land or raised livestock. They thrived in the hospitable climate. In the surrounding countryside, known as Latium, they built simple villages of mud huts. Some of these villages eventually grew into towns and cities.

The Etruscans

To the south, Greek colonies dotted the Italian Peninsula. To the north of Rome, in a region called Etruria, lived a people called the Etruscans. Around 650 B.C., the Latins fell under the control of the Etruscans.

During the seventh century B.C., the Etruscans controlled much of central Italy, including Latium. We know little about the Etruscans because we have limited evidence of their culture beyond some ancient burial sites. What we know suggests that Greek culture inspired the Etruscans, and that the Etruscans in turn heavily influenced early Rome.

The early Romans adapted their alphabet from the Etruscans, which the Etruscans had learned from the Greeks. The Romans borrowed the Etruscan style of dress called a toga, a long robe draped over the body. The Romans learned military strategies from the Etruscans, as well as architectural innovations, including the use of the arch as an element in construction.

The Roman Republic

According to ancient historians, Rome's Etruscan kings ruled the city with almost total power, controlling the army, the courts, and religious worship. Draped in purple-fringed togas, these kings could confiscate property, control travel, and collect taxes on all trade. Some of the early kings used their power wisely, while others were cruel and selfish.

The king's power irritated the richest Roman citizens, a group known as **patricians**. The proud patricians claimed descent from legendary Roman families, and passed their noble positions from one generation to the next. Most patricians relied on trade for their wealth, and they resented the king's power to tax what they bought and sold. In 509 B.C., the Romans rebelled and overthrew the Etruscan king Tarquin (TAHR-kwin).

Establishing a Republic

The year 509 B.C., when the last Etruscan king was overthrown, is traditionally accepted as the year of the founding of a new government, the **Roman Republic**. The word *republic* comes from the Latin *res publica*, which means "public thing" or "public affairs."

A republic is a government in which citizens elect their leaders. The leaders have the authority

A Symbol of Power

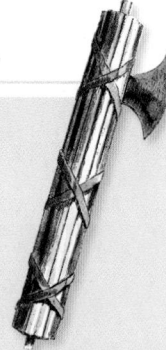

Early Rome was ruled by powerful kings. The fasces (FAS-eez) was the symbol of the Roman king. It was a bundle of rods tied tightly together, with an axe in the center. The rods were a sign that the king could beat or punish the people, while the axe signified that the king could sentence people to death.

When the king appeared in public, attendants carried fasces to remind people of the king's power.

Fasces, symbol of Roman authority

A procession of patricians, members of Rome's aristocratic ruling families

to make important decisions on behalf of the people. The real power still belongs to the citizens, however, for in a republic the people can vote to replace leaders who put their own interests ahead of those of the community.

When the Romans overthrew the king and established a republic, they set up a democratic government. But it was not like the *direct* democracy of Athens, in which every free male citizen had a vote in passing laws and electing leaders. Rome's republic was a *representative* democracy, in which eligible citizens elected leaders who represented them with a vote in the assembly.

Patricians and Plebeians

In the new Roman Republic, patricians made up less than 10 percent of the total population, but they held virtually all the power. The patricians were mainly wealthy landowners. When the republic was established, only patricians could hold important political offices, or vote in the citizen assembly, a group of eligible males that elected leaders and enacted laws.

For many years, patricians controlled the government and largely excluded the **plebeians** (plih-BEE-uhnz), the merchants, craftsmen, farmers, and others who made up the majority of the Roman population. (In Latin the word *plebs* means "the common people.") The plebeians were citizens but for a long time had little power or influence in government. Many plebeians found themselves in debt to moneylenders, and the moneylenders were usually patricians.

The plebeians baked bread and built roads. Plebeian farmers worked all day to produce food for the republic. When wars came, they put down their plows and picked up swords. Rome's success relied on them, yet they enjoyed few rewards.

After years of suffering in silence, in 494 B.C. the plebeians began to resist. To show patricians how much Rome needed them, plebeians refused to serve in the army. The plebeians formed their

153

Cicero, one of Rome's most eloquent orators, speaks before the Senate.

own assembly and elected their own leaders, called **tribunes**.

Gradually, political representation in the Roman Republic expanded to include more of the population. To be sure, sharp contrasts remained between rich and poor, while women, non-Romans, and slaves remained excluded from citizenship. Still, by about 290 B.C., the plebeians had gained political equality with patricians.

Laws for All

Dissatisfied plebeians also called for written laws to establish the duties and benefits of Roman citizenship. They hoped such laws would help protect debtors from slavery and prevent farmers from losing their land. Facing another uprising by plebeians, the patricians gave in. Around 450 B.C., Rome created its first set of written laws, the **Twelve Tables**.

Inscribed in bronze, the Twelve Tables were posted for everyone to see. They listed the rights and responsibilities of all citizens, and spelled out criminal and religious laws. These laws were not

all to the plebeians' advantage—for example, one law prohibited marriage between plebeians and patricians. Nevertheless, the Twelve Tables, like the Code of Hammurabi in ancient Babylon, applied to rich and poor alike. Because the laws were made public, patrician judges had to base their decisions on laws rather than whims.

Over the centuries, as Roman society expanded and grew more complex, the Twelve Tables were replaced by more and better laws. Indeed, the Roman system of law was one of its lasting contributions to the Western world.

Rome's Republican Government

Rome's constitution—its plan for government—was not a single written document but a collection of practices and traditions developed over many years. Cato, an influential Roman statesman in the early second century B.C., is reported to have said that "in other states a single man had established the constitution," while "the constitution of our [Roman] republic was not the work of one, but of many; and had not been established in the life of one man, but during several generations and ages."

The Roman Republic, while by no means perfect, was still a remarkable achievement. The republic lasted for about five hundred years. As the Roman Republic developed, the government was divided into three branches that roughly distributed legislative, executive, and judicial functions to different bodies and officials.

Legislative power—the power to make laws—belonged to the Senate and the citizen assemblies. The Senate had existed long before the republic, originally as a group of advisers to the king, drawn from Rome's most important patrician families. During the republic, the Senate grew and became the most powerful body in the government.

Senators came from wealthy, landowning families, so the Senate often ignored the interests of the poor. Not all senators were patricians, but most were. The senators were chosen from the aristocracy for life terms. For a long time the Senate's three hundred members had the authority to approve laws passed by the citizen assemblies. The Senate's importance was marked by initials stamped on every public building in Rome: SPQR—*Senatus populusque Romanus*, Latin for "Senate and people of Rome."

Over time, the republic developed various assemblies, bodies of citizens that helped make laws and run the republic. The powerful Centuriate Assembly consisted mainly of wealthy men capable of furnishing armed troops in groups of a hundred if needed. The Centuriate Assembly elected various government officials, and also served a judicial function as the highest court of appeal in cases involving capital punishment.

The Tribal Assembly included all citizens and was set up in such a way that the wealthiest could not determine its course. One responsibility of the Tribal Assembly was to elect tribunes, who helped safeguard the rights of plebeians against patrician abuses of power. In time, the tribunes gained the power of the *veto*—from the Latin word meaning "I forbid"—over acts of the Senate.

Executive power was mainly in the hands of various officials called magistrates. The two highest magistrates were called **consuls**. They were elected by the Centuriate Assembly and were responsible for overseeing much of the government and the army. Together the consuls shared the *imperium*, or power to govern. The two consuls executed laws approved by the Senate and the assemblies. In the fourth century B.C., Romans decided that one of the consuls must always be a plebeian. The consuls were powerful men, but there were limits to their authority. They were elected to serve terms of just a single year. Either consul could forbid the actions of the other, so that no single man would hold too much power.

Other elected magistrates included the censors and praetors (PREE-tuhrz). The censors held great power because they selected new senators when a vacancy opened. The praetors, chosen by the Centuriate Assembly for one-year terms, mainly served a judicial function, acting as judges in civil and criminal cases.

Appointing a Dictator

In times of serious trouble, the consuls, with approval of the Senate, could appoint a **dictator**, a single leader with absolute power whose rule was limited to six months or less. The dictator's job was to save Rome from disaster, and then return power to the people.

Such a crisis occurred in 458 B.C., when enemies surrounded a Roman army and threatened to destroy it. A distressed Senate summoned Cincinnatus to act as dictator. Cincinnatus was a former senator who had lost his wealth and become a simple farmer. When asked to serve Rome again, he readily accepted.

It took Cincinnatus just two weeks to rescue the beleaguered army. Then, his job done, he promptly resigned. He returned power to the Senate and people of Rome, and went back to his farm. Over the years, the actions of Cincinnatus took on almost legendary status. His name has since become a synonym for a shining example of selfless citizenship and public service.

The American Cincinnatus

After the American Revolution, the example of Cincinnatus inspired George Washington, who had led the Continental Army to victory over the British. General Washington was so popular among his soldiers that he very likely could have claimed supreme power in the new United States. Instead, he resigned his military command and returned to his land in Virginia. For these actions, some have called him the "American Cincinnatus."

CHECKS AND BALANCES IN THE ROMAN REPUBLIC

Polybius, a Greek who lived in the second century B.C., was brought to Rome as a captive, where he rose to become a prominent historian. He praised the virtues of Roman government, which he saw as superior to that of the Greeks. In this passage, he discusses the three branches of government in the Roman Republic. He explains what we now call "checks and balances"—the idea, as Polybius put it, that if one branch of government attempted "to exceed its proper limits," the others would respond to ensure that it was "reduced again within its own just bounds." The Constitution of the United States is based in part on these ancient Roman ideas.

The three kinds of government—monarchy, aristocracy, and democracy—were all found united in the commonwealth of Rome. And so even was the balance between them all, and so regular the administration that resulted from their union, that it was no easy thing to determine with assurance whether the entire state was to be estimated an aristocracy, a democracy, or a monarchy. For if they turned their view upon the power of the consuls, the government appeared to be purely monarchial and regal. If, again, the authority of the senate was considered, it then seemed to wear the form of aristocracy. And, lastly, if regard was to be had to the share which the people possessed in the administration of affairs, it could then scarcely fail to be denominated a popular state....

Such are the parts of the administration, which are distinctly assigned to each of the three forms of government that are united in the commonwealth of Rome. It now remains to be considered, in what manner each...is enabled to counteract the others, or to cooperate with them....

For whenever either of the separate parts of the republic attempts to exceed its proper limits, excites contention and dispute, and struggles to obtain a greater share of power than that which is assigned to it by the laws, it is manifest that...no one single part...is in itself supreme or absolute.... On the contrary...the part which thus aspires must soon be reduced again within its own just bounds, and not be suffered to insult or depress the rest. And thus the several orders of which the state is framed are forced always to maintain their due position....

The Roman Republic Grows and Changes

Key Questions

- How did Rome expand and maintain control of its territory?

- As Rome undertook its Mediterranean conquests, how did its society and government change?

- What crises threatened the Roman Republic after 100 B.C.?

Under the republic, Rome's power grew. So did the population. For this growing population, Rome needed more land. Rome set out to expand its territory, sometimes at the expense of its neighbors. Some Italian city-states formed alliances with Rome. Others feared Roman dominance and launched wars against the city.

In 396 B.C., Roman armies marched north and conquered an Etruscan city-state. Over the next hundred years, Rome conquered central Italy, and then turned to take the wealthy Greek cities in the south. By about 270 B.C., Rome controlled most of the Italian Peninsula, including the Greek colonies in the south, which had fiercely resisted Roman rule.

The Roman Army

Roman conquests were made possible by a powerful and well-disciplined army. Most of the fighting was done by plebeians who became citizen-soldiers during times of war. The plebeians formed the backbone of the Roman army, and ancient historians praised them as models of civic duty.

The Roman army was made up of highly mobile units called *legions*. Each legion consisted of 3,600 to 4,500 infantry soldiers. A legion was divided into centuries—units of roughly one hundred soldiers—with each century under the command of an officer called a *centurion*.

Early Roman armies used the Greek phalanx, and adapted the formation for the hills and mountains of Italy. On the battlefield, legions maneuvered in three-row squares, with cavalry (troops on horseback) protecting the flanks. The foot soldiers on the front row battled the enemy, first with long spears called javelins, and then with short iron swords. As the front line sagged, troops from the second and third rows stepped in to support it.

The Roman army succeeded not only because of effective tactics but also because of constant training, strict discipline, and fierce

Elite military officers are depicted with an eagle (upper left), a symbol of Roman power.

A Pyrrhic Victory

During Rome's war against Greek colonies in the southern Italian Peninsula, the Greek king Pyrrhus (PIHR-uhs) defeated the Romans twice. But the victories were costly, for Pyrrhus lost many men in the bloody fighting and was unable to replenish his troops. Today, any success that comes at a ruinous cost is sometimes called a "pyrrhic (PIHR-ik) victory."

loyalty. The qualities that made one a good soldier, the Romans believed, also made one a good citizen.

The Punic Wars

Across the Mediterranean from Rome lay Carthage (KAHR-thij), a powerful North African city-state and a wealthy center of trade. With their powerful navy, the Carthaginians (kahr-thuh-JIN-ee-uns) controlled much of North Africa's Mediterranean coast and dominated the western Mediterranean Sea. Carthage also controlled the islands of Corsica and Sardinia, as well as the western half of Sicily. Roman ships could sail certain parts of the Mediterranean only with the permission of Carthage.

During Rome's conquest of the Italian Peninsula, Carthage and Rome had formed an alliance against the Greeks. But when a Carthaginian army occupied part of Sicily, Romans began to worry that Carthage might be planning to extend its empire into Italy.

In 264 B.C., the Romans decided to stop Carthaginian advances in Sicily and seek the rich plunder that a war with Carthage might bring. After a few years of successful fighting, the Romans fixed on the goal of driving the Carthaginians out of Sicily altogether. That was the start of a long series of fights between Rome and Carthage known as the Punic (PYOO-nik) Wars.

Writing about two hundred years after the Punic Wars, the historian Livy said that "no two more powerful countries ever made war against each other than Rome and Carthage." Rome had

a powerful army but a weak navy. In contrast, Carthage was a great naval power without much of a land-based army.

The Romans went to work building a fleet modeled on a Carthaginian ship that had run aground in Italy. They equipped each ship with a twelve-foot (4 m) gangplank with a heavy iron spike at one end. During sea battles, these Roman ships could pull alongside the enemy and swing out the gangplanks, sending the spikes crashing through the other vessels' decks. Roman foot soldiers would then run across the planks to fight hand to hand.

After two bloody decades, the Romans finally drove the Carthaginians out of Sicily. It was a great victory, and all of Rome celebrated. But the struggle with Carthage was far from over.

The Second Punic War: Hannibal Crosses the Alps

Over the next several years, the Carthaginians raised a powerful army under the command of a brilliant general named Hannibal. It was said that as a child Hannibal had taken an oath to destroy Rome. In 218 B.C., Hannibal launched the Second Punic War with one of the most famous military expeditions in history. Because he knew

In the First Punic War, Roman ships were equipped with gangplanks and iron spikes for boarding Carthaginian vessels.

A sixteenth-century painting shows the Battle of Zama, in which Scipio defeated Hannibal, ending the Second Punic War.

that the Romans thought of Carthage as a naval power, and so would expect an invasion by sea, he set out instead to cross the formidable Alps and attack Rome by land.

Hannibal set out from Spain with a massive army. Historical accounts vary, but by most estimates Hannibal started with an army of from forty to fifty thousand infantrymen and eight to nine thousand cavalry, along with thirty-seven war elephants. Trained elephants had been used in warfare for centuries. With thick hides that offered protection from arrows and javelins, the raging creatures thundered down upon the battlefield, striking terror into the hearts of enemy soldiers who watched as their comrades were crushed and trampled.

Hannibal's army crossed the Pyrenees Mountains and the Rhone River. Then they faced the rugged, snowy Alps. The journey over the high peaks of the Alps took two weeks. Thousands of soldiers died, and by the time he reached the green

plains of northern Italy, Hannibal had lost almost half his army, and as many as twenty elephants.

Despite his losses, Hannibal launched one attack after another. Roman legions broke under ferocious assaults by unrelenting Carthaginian soldiers who swept into battle accompanied by trumpeting war elephants. After one battle, it was said that every woman in Rome wept for a dead son, husband, father, or brother.

For fifteen years Hannibal continued to raid Italy, destroying crops and burning villages. He aimed to shatter the Romans, both physically and in spirit. The Romans, however, were not easily crushed. They turned to attack Hannibal's homeland, Carthage. When Rome sent a force to North Africa under the command of its own extraordinary general, Scipio (SIP-ee-oh) the Elder, Hannibal rushed home to defend Carthage. In 202 B.C., at the African town of Zama, Scipio defeated Hannibal, and Rome emerged victorious in the Second Punic War.

The Third Punic War

Carthage was forced to surrender most of its territory and suffer the humiliation of Roman rule. By 150 B.C., however, Carthage began to grow powerful again. Some Romans felt threatened. A Roman statesman known as Cato the Censor began to insert a phrase into every speech he made: *"Delenda est Carthago"*—"Carthage must be destroyed."

War broke out once more, but the Third Punic War, which lasted from 149 to 146 B.C., favored Rome from the start. Rome triumphed again, and the victors made sure there would be no fourth war. The Romans went from house to house, killing Carthaginians throughout the city. The unhappy survivors were sold into slavery. The Romans burned the city and cursed the site.

North Africa became a Roman province. Now Rome controlled all the western Mediterranean and most of Spain. Rome was no longer a city-state fighting to fend off rivals and protect its trade routes. It was becoming a sprawling empire.

Controlling the Eastern Mediterranean

In the same year that they destroyed Carthage, Roman legions also sacked Corinth, one of the richest cities in Greece. The conquest was the culmination of Rome's expansion in the eastern Mediterranean. Eventually, all Greek territory in the Mediterranean world fell to the Roman legions.

By 146 B.C., the Roman Republic controlled immense territory from Asia Minor to North Africa and Greece to Spain. For Rome, the Mediterranean had become *Mare Nostrum*, "our sea."

Roman expansion brought new people under the control of Rome. Some former enemies became citizens, while others gained limited citizenship. All conquered people were expected to send soldiers to serve in the Roman legions. Rome allowed these men to maintain their own religious and cultural identities. In fact, Romans often adopted customs of people they had defeated in battle.

The Republic Threatened

Rome had once enjoyed a reputation for treating conquered people mercifully. But after ruthlessly destroying the cities of Carthage and Corinth, the Romans came to be feared as brutal conquerors.

To maintain its new status as the most powerful force in the Mediterranean world, Rome organized its conquered territories into provinces. Throughout the provinces, aristocrats often got lucrative jobs collecting rents and taxes, and many simply pocketed most of what they gathered. Powerful offices were sold to the highest bidder. Once in office, provincial officials often took bribes in exchange for favors. Ordinary Romans grew angry over such abuses of power. To them, it seemed that only the wealthy and powerful enjoyed the rewards of expansion.

> *Lucrative* means highly profitable.

Changes at Home

Roman expansion also created difficulties for ordinary citizen-soldiers. With the men off at war, many poor farming families relied on hired hands or slaves to run the family farm. Women had to take on farm work in addition to their domestic duties. Many farmers could not pay rents, and thousands were driven from their farms. Since the beginnings of the republic years before, Romans had idealized hardworking farmers as the foundation of society and success. Now, however, those farmers were suffering.

Trouble for small farmers meant a great opportunity for Rome's upper classes. Rich landowners could purchase the small plots of land abandoned by bankrupt farmers. Others illegally snatched public lands. Combining many small fields into large farms, wealthy Romans established enormous estates called **latifundia**. These vast farms were owned by patricians and worked primarily by slaves. The latifundia produced grain, olive oil, and wine—items in great demand that could be traded across the expanding Roman domains. The owners made huge profits, but those riches created a growing divide between wealthy Romans and the resentful poor.

An ancient mosaic shows an elaborate Roman estate at Carthage, in North Africa.

Reform and Violence

Over time, landless farmers and unemployed veterans—homeless, poverty-stricken, and desperate—crowded into the city of Rome. Riots broke out. Elsewhere, slaves launched revolts against their wealthy masters. Conquered cities grew restless, and tribes on Rome's northern borders harassed the already thinly stretched Roman legions.

All around, it seemed, the republic was in disarray. An enormous gap widened between a small wealthy class and a large poor class. Wealthy senators lamented the collapse of the traditional virtues that had made Roman citizens such hardworking farmers and loyal soldiers. But few did anything to improve the lot of those in need.

Two brothers, known as the Gracchi (GRAK-iy), acted to help the poor and calm the growing social unrest. The elder brother, the tribune Tiberius Gracchus, pushed for land-reform laws to redistribute public lands to poor soldiers and small farmers.

Tiberius's reforms threatened patricians in the Senate and other wealthy landowners. They had come to depend on the riches derived from the public lands that Tiberius wanted to give to plebeians. Tiberius further angered his enemies by announcing his desire to be reelected tribune, when reelection had not been practiced for hundreds of years. In 133 B.C., a group of senators started a riot in the plebian assembly, during which Tiberius was beaten to death and many of his followers killed as well.

Ten years later, Tiberius's brother Gaius (GAY-uhs) Gracchus revived land reform and extended Roman citizenship, actions that again angered wealthy landowners. In 121 B.C., after hundreds of his supporters had been killed, Gaius Gracchus took his own life. Murder and violence had become part of Roman politics.

Meanwhile, problems continued within the Roman legions. Because so many farmers had lost their land, there were not enough citizens to meet the minimal landholding qualifications for service. In 107 B.C., the consul Gaius Marius tried to solve this problem by raising an enormous army from the masses of unemployed. He armed them and paid their salaries at public expense, promising gifts of land to his soldiers at the end of their service.

As a result of these reforms, the loyalty of Marius's soldiers belonged to him, not to the republic. Soon, other politicians raised their own armies of loyal troops. What had once been republican armies of citizen-soldiers loyal to Rome were now personal armies with troops pledging allegiance only to their immediate commander. These armies would become a potent political tool for a new generation of ambitious leaders.

From Republic to Empire

Around the first century B.C., Rome's system of law and its republican institutions were on shaky ground. The Roman Republic was threatened by ambitious leaders who placed personal interests above the good of the community. Rome suffered through bitter civil wars as powerful leaders with personal armies battled to govern Rome's vast territory. One such leader was Julius Caesar.

Julius Caesar Gains Power

Julius Caesar was a well-educated member of a proud patrician family. He became consul in 59 B.C. and formed an alliance with two political rivals—Pompey (PAHM-pee), a well-known general, and Crassus, a wealthy patrician. Together, they ruled as the First Triumvirate (triy-UHM-vuh-ruht). Caesar knew that true power could only come at the head of a loyal army. He worked to have himself appointed governor and military leader in Gaul, made up of present-day France and neighboring lands.

In Gaul, Caesar demonstrated brilliant generalship during eight years of fighting. He instilled loyalty in his soldiers and demonstrated cunning and bravery in battle, with methods that continue to be studied by generals today. A gifted writer, Caesar recorded his conquests in a book, *The Gallic War*. Casting himself as a hero, Caesar's tale of military adventure brought the young general fame and popularity back in Rome.

By 50 B.C., Caesar had built a loyal personal army. Nearly fifty thousand battle-hardened troops stood ready to follow their general wherever he led. To the Senate, the popular general posed a political threat. It ordered Caesar to return to Rome without his army.

Camped with his army near a bridge at the Rubicon (ROO-bih-kahn) River, Caesar pondered his future. If he resigned, he would be at the mercy of his enemies in Rome. If he led his men across the Rubicon, there would be no going back. He would be asking for war. The river marked the boundary that divided Italy from the provinces. For Caesar to cross the river with his army would be an act of treason against the state.

Caesar hesitated only a moment—then marched his troops across the Rubicon. He had openly defied the Senate and chosen civil war—and he knew it. "The die is cast," Caesar said, as his troops splashed across the river. To this day, the expression "to cross the Rubicon" means to take an action from which there is no turning back.

As Caesar's army marched toward Rome, his enemies in the Senate panicked. They fled the city, but Caesar followed. He swept through Spain and Greece before heading off to Egypt and Asia Minor. One by one, he defeated his enemies. *"Veni, vidi, vici"* (WAY-nee, WEE-dee, WEE-kee), Caesar declared

- What role did Julius Caesar play in the end of the Roman Republic?
- How did Rome become an empire under Caesar Augustus?
- What was the Pax Romana?

A PORTRAIT OF JULIUS CAESAR

Suetonius (swee-TOH-nee-uhs), a Roman biographer born in A.D. 69, wrote a series of accounts of Roman emperors, titled *Lives of the Caesars*. In this work, Suetonius mingled historical narrative with personal details and tidbits of gossip. Here are some brief passages from his account of Julius Caesar.

He was tall, of a fair complexion, round limbed, rather full faced, with eyes black and piercing; he enjoyed excellent health except toward the close of his life when he was subject to sudden fainting fits and disturbances in his sleep....

He was extremely nice in the care of his person, and kept the hair of his head closely cut and had his face smoothly shaved. His baldness gave him much uneasiness, having often found himself on that score exposed to the jibes of his enemies. He used therefore to brush forward the hair from the crown of his head, and of all the honors conferred on him by the Senate and People, there was none which he either accepted or used with greater pleasure than the right of wearing constantly a laurel crown....

He liked his residence to be elegant and his entertainments sumptuous. He pulled down entirely a villa near the grove of Aricia, which he built from the foundation, and finished at heavy cost, because it did not meet his taste, although at that time he had only limited means, and was in debt....

It is said he actually invaded Britain in hopes of finding pearls there. He was accustomed to compare the size of these and ascertain their weight merely by poising them in his hand. At any cost he would purchase gems, carved work, statues, and pictures, executed by eminent masters of antiquity....

He was perfect in the use of arms, an accomplished rider, and able to endure fatigue beyond all belief. On a march he used to go at the head of his troops, sometimes on horseback, but oftener on foot, with his head bare in all kinds of weather. He would travel post in a light carriage without baggage, at the rate of one hundred miles per day; and if he was stopped by floods in the rivers, he swam across.... Often he rallied his troops by his own personal exertions, stopping those who fled, keeping others in their ranks, and seizing men by the throat, turned them again towards the enemy....

He always treated his friends with such kindness and good nature, that when Gains Oppius, in traveling with him through a forest, was suddenly taken ill, he resigned to him the only place there was to shelter them at night, and lay on the ground in the open air....

Hail Caesar!

Caesar, the family name of Julius Caesar, eventually became the title adopted by all Roman emperors. Indeed, political rulers many centuries removed from the Roman Empire also adopted the name. In Russia, the supreme leader was called the *tsar* (zahr; also spelled *czar*), and in Germany for a time, the ruler was called *kaiser* (KIY-zur). Both titles come directly from the name "Caesar."

after one of his victories—"I came, I saw, I conquered." Senators remaining in Rome now relied on Caesar to survive. In 44 B.C., they declared him "dictator for life."

Caesar's Rome

As dictator, Caesar enjoyed nearly absolute power. He allowed elections to continue, but controlled results by putting forward hand-picked candidates and packing the assembly with loyal supporters. Caesar maintained other republican traditions, but, like a king, he governed from a golden throne.

Although Caesar ruled with a firm hand, he won the praises of the people. He celebrated public holidays with splendid parades. With great energy, he tackled a huge number of problems. He organized the administration of the provinces. He lowered taxes and gave land and food to the poor. He established a new calendar with a 365-day year, and a leap year every four years. This calendar—called the Julian calendar, after Julius

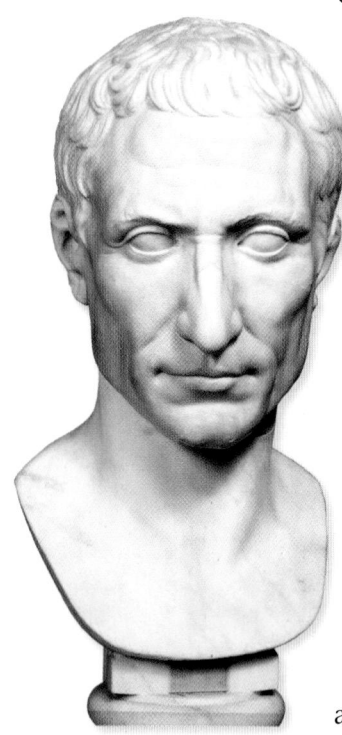

Julius Caesar, "dictator for life"

Caesar—remains, with small changes, the one we still use today.

Caesar's power and popularity alarmed many members of the Senate. They called Caesar a tyrant, and wondered if he would soon declare himself king. A group of senators, led by Marcus Brutus, a longtime friend of Caesar's, began plotting to assassinate him.

On March 15, 44 B.C.—the day the Romans called the Ides of March—the plotters surrounded the dictator on the floor of the Senate and stabbed him to death. When he saw his friend Brutus lift a dagger, ready to strike, Caesar is said to have cried out in dismay, *"Et tu, Brute?"* (et TOO, BROO-teh) meaning, "You, too, Brutus?" Brutus drove in the dagger.

The great Julius Caesar was dead, stabbed twenty-three times. Rome and the world remember him as a brilliant military leader and ruthless politician whose own ambitions led to his eventual downfall.

Octavian Triumphs

Caesar's assassins called themselves "liberators" who had saved the republic from a would-be king. But after Caesar's death, little changed. Rome still faced the difficulties of governing vast territory. Farmers struggled to get by. Problems plagued the army, and cities teemed with discontented mobs. Rome needed a strong leader.

Caesar's great-nephew and adopted son, Octavian, provided that leadership. Only eighteen years old when Caesar died, Octavian seemed to many Romans a mere boy. But he was wise beyond his years.

Octavian rallied troops loyal to the name of Caesar. With the help of two allies, Marc Antony and Marcus Aemilius Lepidus, Octavian hunted down and defeated Caesar's assassins. For a time, Octavian and his two allies ruled together as the Second Triumvirate, dividing Rome's vast provinces among them.

Octavian sought to expand his power. He pressured Lepidus to resign, and accused Marc

Queen Cleopatra

Cleopatra was a shrewd leader and a cunning politician. As ruler of Egypt she was the last monarch in the dynasty established by Ptolemy, a general and close friend of Alexander the Great. According to legend, when she and Antony committed suicide in 30 B.C., Cleopatra let herself be bitten by a poisonous snake, the symbol of Egyptian royal authority.

An ancient Egyptian statue of Cleopatra

Antony of treason. Antony, who ruled his territory from Egypt, had forged an alliance with Cleopatra, queen of Egypt. Octavian accused Antony of plotting to make Cleopatra the queen of Rome, and the two sides went to war. Octavian's forces defeated the combined forces of Antony and Cleopatra at the battle of Actium in 31 B.C. Shortly thereafter, Antony and Cleopatra took their own lives.

Octavian now ruled supreme. Rome was poised to enter a new period in the history of civilization, one that would launch new achievements in art, government, law, engineering, and peace.

The Augustan Age

Two years after his victory at Actium, Octavian declared that he had successfully restored the republic. In fact, after eliminating his competition, Octavian took supreme control of Rome, much like his great-uncle had. Unlike Julius Caesar, however, Octavian was determined to make a show of returning power to the Senate and people of Rome. The Senate responded by declaring Octavian *Augustus*, or "favored by the gods." From then on, Octavian would be known as Caesar Augustus, or simply by the title, Augustus.

Augustus called himself *princeps*, or "first citizen." In truth, he was the first Roman emperor. With his rule, the Roman Republic was no more.

Augustus gained new powers bestowed by a Senate willing to do his bidding. Initially, the emperor's authority rested upon his immense wealth, his popularity, and his command of a loyal army. Over the span of his forty-one-year reign, however, Augustus secured his supremacy through wise political decisions and popular reforms.

Augustus built roads and aqueducts (AK-wuh-dukts), stone channels that carried water to the city from the surrounding hills. He built cities that he populated with his former soldiers. He turned Egypt into a Roman province

Octavian took the title "Caesar Augustus" and launched Rome on the road to empire.

Lit at dusk, the ruins of the Roman Forum, in ancient times the city's hub of economic, religious, and judicial life

and dredged parts of the Nile irrigation system that had become clogged with silt, thus helping to produce enough grain to feed an empire. He brought peace to troubled provinces and expanded Rome's northern border.

Augustus also helped clean up the messy Roman tax system by taking a **census**, a count of the entire population. The census allowed the emperor to know the number of people living in the provinces, how much they owed in taxes, and how many soldiers they owed Rome.

Augustus fixed roads, set up an organized fire brigade in the city, built a police force, and appointed capable administrators to run the city government. His construction projects included majestic temples and grand public buildings. In Rome, Augustus claimed, "I found a city built of bricks; I leave her clothed in marble." (In the next chapter you will read about life and culture in Rome's Augustan Age.)

Emperors After Augustus

In 2 B.C., the Senate declared Augustus "Father of his Country," prompting him to declare, "I have at last achieved my highest ambition!" As father of a line of emperors, however, Augustus had little success. Because "first citizen" was not an official office, it could not simply be handed down to an heir. Instead, Augustus planned to select one of his relatives as a successor and have the Senate confirm his choice.

Unfortunately for Augustus, he outlived all of his preferred successors, including his own grandsons. Finally, he decided upon a stepson, Tiberius. When the great Augustus died at age seventy-five, Tiberius took over, the second of five emperors of what is called the Julio-Claudian Dynasty. All the emperors in this dynasty were—by marriage, adoption, or birth—members of a family established by Julius Caesar.

Tiberius ruled for twenty-three years. Where Augustus had been loved, Tiberius was deeply unpopular. When Tiberius died in A.D. 37, there were parties in the streets of Rome, and people called for his body to be tossed into the Tiber River.

The successor to Tiberius, Emperor Gaius Caligula Caesar, was even more hated. The Roman historian Suetonius called Caligula a "monster," and reported that the emperor once nominated his horse for consul. Caligula was killed by his own guards in A.D. 41, after ruling less than four years. He was succeeded by Claudius, who had a reputation as a fool but ran the empire smoothly during his thirteen-year reign.

In A.D. 54, a new emperor, Nero, took the throne at age sixteen. It was widely rumored

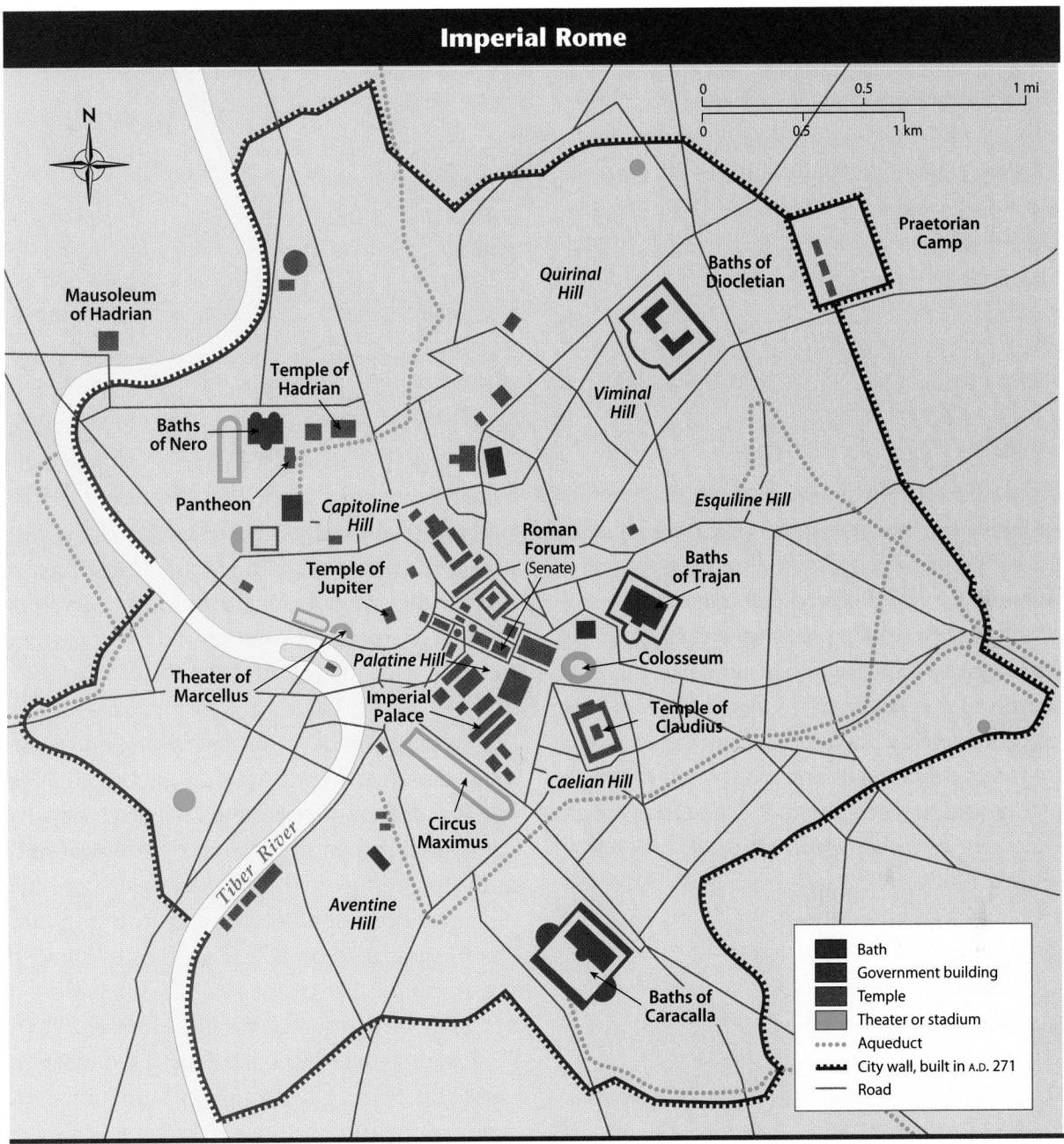

Imperial Rome

Mausoleum of Hadrian

Temple of Hadrian

Baths of Nero

Pantheon

Capitoline Hill

Temple of Jupiter

Theater of Marcellus

Imperial Palace

Palatine Hill

Circus Maximus

Aventine Hill

Tiber River

Quirinal Hill

Viminal Hill

Baths of Diocletian

Praetorian Camp

Esquiline Hill

Roman Forum (Senate)

Baths of Trajan

Colosseum

Temple of Claudius

Caelian Hill

Baths of Caracalla

■	Bath
■	Government building
■	Temple
■	Theater or stadium
⋯	Aqueduct
▪▪▪	City wall, built in A.D. 271
—	Road

Scale: 0 0.5 1 mi / 0 0.5 1 km

that his mother had poisoned Claudius. A great-great-grandson of Augustus, Nero ruled competently for the first half of his reign, thanks to the help of skilled advisers. In time, however, Nero used his power for his own pleasure rather than for the good of Rome. He became brutal and ruthless—he ordered his own mother put to death. When a great fire swept through Rome in A.D. 64, rumors spread among the people that Nero had set the blaze himself. While the rumors were almost certainly untrue, they suggest the contempt with which the Roman people viewed their emperor.

In A.D. 68, Nero's military commanders rose against him. Nero, under threat of death, took his own life by enlisting a servant to cut his throat. The Julio-Claudian line of emperors died with him.

A year-long civil war followed, in which four men battled to become emperor. Vespasian (veh-SPAY-zhee-uhn) ultimately won, ruling until A.D. 79 and establishing the Flavian Dynasty, which included his sons Titus and Domitian

167

Hadrian's Wall

Hadrian, who ruled as emperor from A.D. 117–138, liked to travel through his vast realm. In 122, he visited Britain and ordered the construction of a massive wall to act as a defensive barrier between Roman territory to the south and invaders to the north. Roman soldiers built an eighty-mile (129 km) stone wall that stretched from coast to coast and included towers, forts, and gates. Sections of this impressive structure can still be seen today.

The massive structure known as Hadrian's Wall guarded the north of Britain from invaders.

(duh-MISH-uhn). The Flavian Dynasty ended in A.D. 96 with the murder of Domitian. It was followed by a long period of wise leadership by five rulers known as the Good Emperors.

During this period, the emperor Trajan, who ruled until 117, expanded Roman territory in the east. His adopted son Hadrian shored up the empire's defenses by building military fortifications as far away as Britain.

Marcus Aurelius, the last of the Good Emperors, ruled until his death in A.D. 180. He is

A statue of Marcus Aurelius shows the emperor with raised hand, a gesture of authority. A thoughtful philosopher, he was considered the last of the Good Emperors.

remembered for his book, *Meditations*, a collection of thoughts from throughout his career that reveal his passion for the Stoic philosophy of the Greeks, which argued that, in the pursuit of wisdom, calm reason must prevail over emotion.

The Pax Romana

The long period of prosperity and relative calm between Augustus and Marcus Aurelius is called the **Pax Romana**, or "Roman Peace." Despite the name, the period was marred by war and strife, including conflicts on the border and the violent suppression of a Jewish revolt in Jerusalem. Nevertheless, because it was mostly a time of peace and prosperity, the Pax Romana is viewed as the high point of the Roman Empire.

Rome's vast empire stretched from Egypt to Britain, Spain to Mesopotamia, and north to the Danube River in Europe. As many as seventy million people lived within the boundaries of the Roman Empire, with nearly one million in the city of Rome itself. Some 10 percent of people under Roman rule enjoyed the benefits of citizenship, an important status that brought legal protections and privileges. Throughout the empire, wealthy people often received citizenship in exchange for service to the government, such as the collection of taxes, the maintenance of public facilities, and the administration of Roman law. In all the provinces, Roman legions kept the peace.

Expansion of the Roman Empire

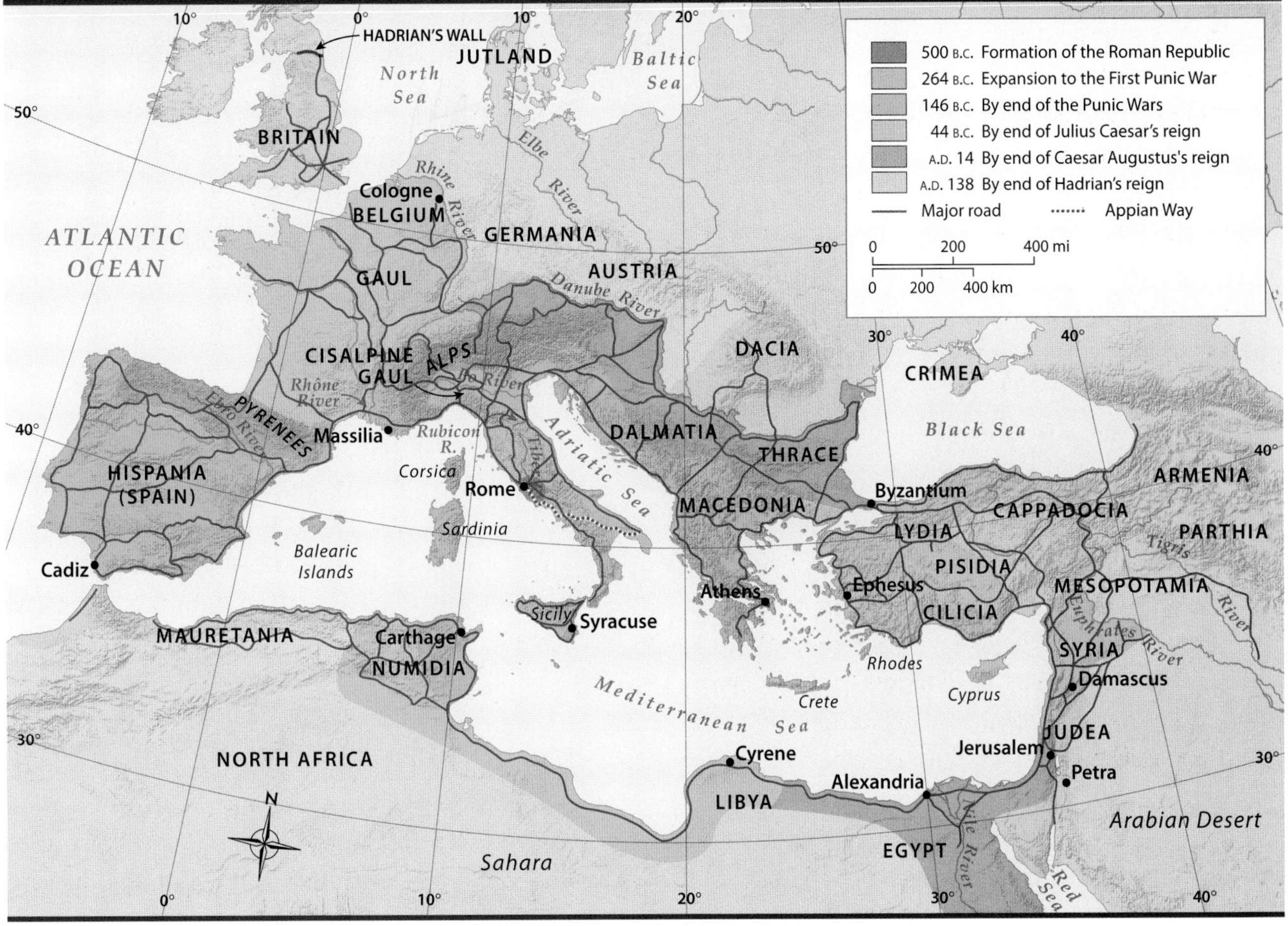

500 B.C.	Formation of the Roman Republic
264 B.C.	Expansion to the First Punic War
146 B.C.	By end of the Punic Wars
44 B.C.	By end of Julius Caesar's reign
A.D. 14	By end of Caesar Augustus's reign
A.D. 138	By end of Hadrian's reign
——	Major road
·······	Appian Way

0   200   400 mi
0   200   400 km

HADRIAN'S WALL
JUTLAND
North Sea
Baltic Sea
BRITAIN
Cologne
Rhine River
Elbe River
BELGIUM
GERMANIA
ATLANTIC OCEAN
GAUL
AUSTRIA
Danube River
CISALPINE GAUL
ALPS
Rhône River
DACIA
CRIMEA
PYRENEES
Massilia
Rubicon R.
Corsica
DALMATIA
Black Sea
ARMENIA
HISPANIA (SPAIN)
Rome
THRACE
Byzantium
CAPPADOCIA
PARTHIA
Tigris
Sardinia
MACEDONIA
LYDIA
Cadiz
Balearic Islands
Adriatic Sea
PISIDIA
MESOPOTAMIA
Euphrates River
Athens
Ephesus
CILICIA
Sicily
Syracuse
SYRIA
MAURETANIA
Carthage
Damascus
NUMIDIA
Rhodes
Cyprus
Crete
JUDEA
NORTH AFRICA
Mediterranean Sea
Cyrene
Jerusalem
Petra
Alexandria
Arabian Desert
LIBYA
EGYPT
Nile River
Sahara
Red Sea

Over the course of six hundred years, the Romans built a vast, interconnected empire.

Roman coins, the currency of the empire

Across this vast realm there was one official language. There was one system of coinage, weights, and measures. There was one government administration and one body of laws. A busy network of trade connected the vast world of the Pax Romana, bringing luxury goods such as silk and spices from faraway China and India. Roads and bridges eased travel through the empire, and the general peace enforced by the Roman legions brought a sense of order and stability.

Despite the wealth generated by trade, a huge gap remained between rich and poor in Roman society. The cities were home to many unemployed citizens, many of whom relied on handouts of free food, called the "dole." During the reign of Augustus, more than a half million people relied on such government assistance for their survival.

Roman culture thrived and spread throughout the empire during the general calm of the Pax Romana. Roman traditions, already strongly influenced by the Hellenic world, fused with local customs. The legacy of the Pax Romana is a varied tapestry of law, society, religion, and culture. In the following chapter, you will learn more about this rich legacy, and about how Roman society changed in response to outside forces as well as pressures from within.

169

A.D. 1

100

200

c. 30
Jesus Christ is crucified
in Jerusalem.

c. 64
Emperor Nero orders
persecution of Christians.

c. 130
The Roman Empire reaches
its greatest extent.

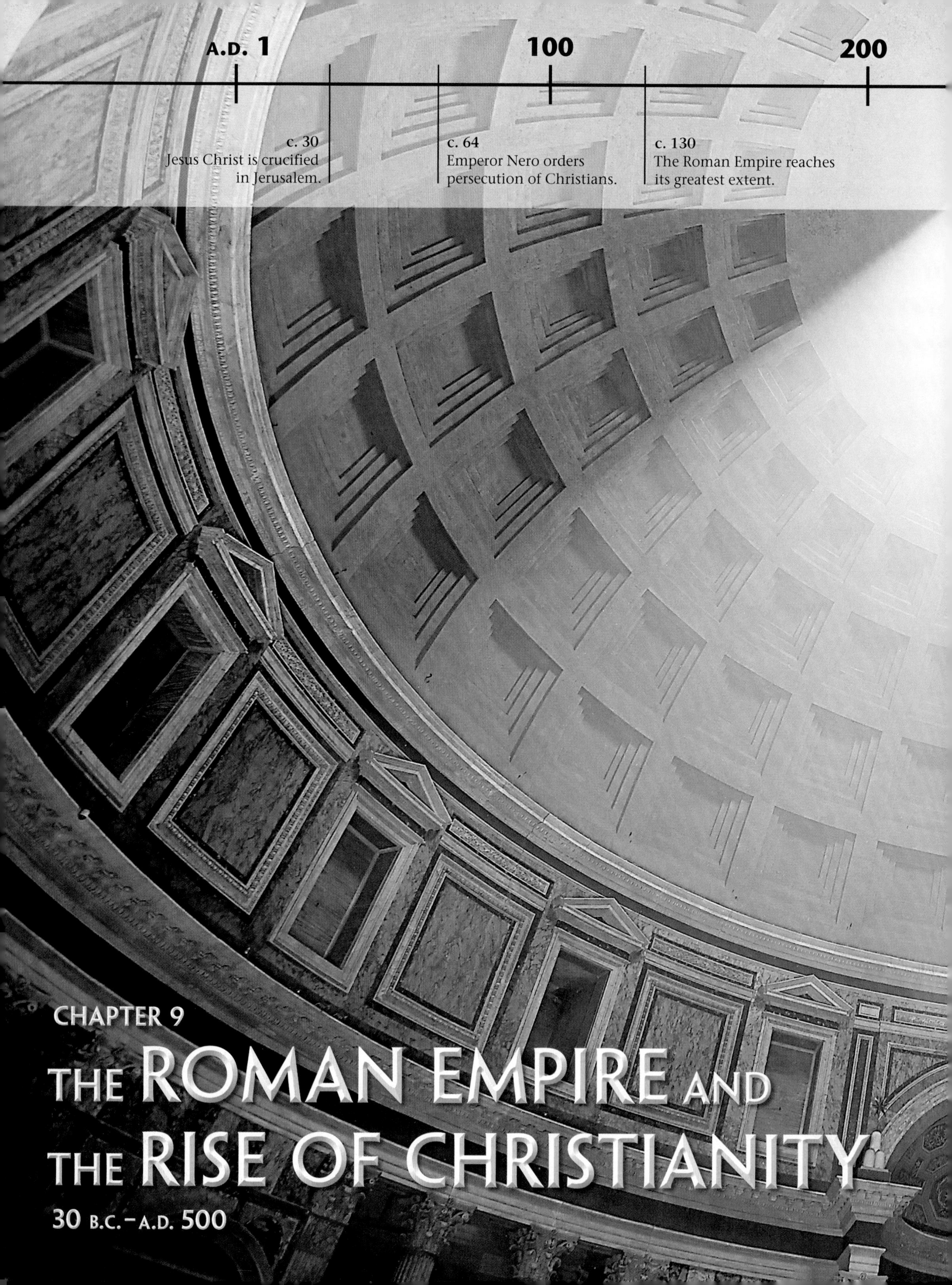

CHAPTER 9

THE ROMAN EMPIRE AND THE RISE OF CHRISTIANITY

30 B.C.–A.D. 500

300

400

500

313
Emperor Constantine legalizes Christianity in the Roman Empire.

330
Constantine moves the capital of the Roman Empire east to Byzantium, later called Constantinople.

410
The Visigoths sack Rome as Germanic tribes invade Roman lands.

Sunlight streams through the open-air oculus (a circular opening) in the dome of the Pantheon in Rome.

For more than two centuries, the Pax Romana brought prosperity and stability to the Roman Empire. Never before had so many people enjoyed such a long period of relative peace. Trade flourished, and Rome achieved monumental feats in law, engineering, and architecture.

But old problems persisted. Rich and poor lived dramatically different lives. Slave labor replaced the work of common people. Many wondered what had become of traditional Roman values like hard work, selfless service, and respect for family.

At the same time, a new movement emerged that would eventually grow into the world's largest religion. Based on the simple yet powerful message of a Jewish carpenter, Jesus of Nazareth, Christianity grew from a tiny community of worshippers to the most powerful force in the Roman Empire during the fourth century.

By that time, Rome had changed greatly from the empire founded by Augustus. Facing serious problems on its frontiers, inside its government, and among its people, the Roman Empire gradually declined and fell. It left behind a rich legacy that remains influential to this day.

Society and Culture in the Roman Empire

Key Questions

- What were the major social and cultural characteristics of the Roman Empire?

- In what ways did Roman culture borrow from and build on the achievements of the Greeks?

Imperial Rome prospered during the Pax Romana. Upper-class Roman land-owners amassed great wealth by selling the produce of their estates. Some Romans worked their way out of poverty to become merchants and crafts-people in Rome's active trading network, forming a middle class that lived in comfort. But despite the wealth generated by trade, a huge gap remained between rich and poor in Roman society.

The Gap Between Rich and Poor

Sometime around the year A.D. 100, Pliny the Younger, a wealthy Roman, threw a party. His letters tell us that he served snails, eggs, "barley-cake, wine with honey chilled with snow, and any number of similar delicacies." After dinner, his guests enjoyed a comic play.

For wealthy Romans like Pliny, life was good. They built large homes, often on hilltops away from the noise and filth of the city. They hosted parties where guests might recline on sofas to eat delicacies such as ostrich brains or flamingo tongues. In beautiful countryside locations, many rich Romans owned vacation homes, or villas. Pliny owned a seaside villa, complete with running water, heated baths, and a gymnasium.

Among ordinary Romans, a lucky few had good jobs. They worked as farmers, bakers, builders, merchants, or craftspeople. But in cities all over the empire, many people had no work or only seasonal work. To survive, the poor relied on the dole, handouts of free grain from the government. Poor families typically boiled the grain to make gruel, which they might flavor with onions and wash down with watery wine.

In Roman cities, poor families often lived in ill-maintained apartment buildings called **tenements**. Cramped and dingy, the tenements of Rome outnumbered private homes by more than twenty to one. Fortunate residents on the bottom floor might enjoy running water, but those in upper levels had no

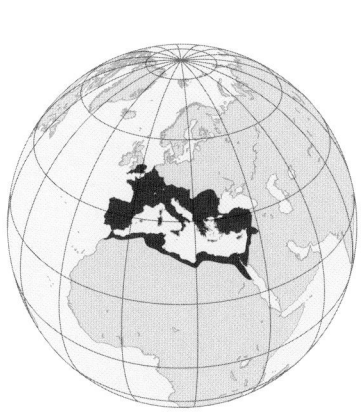

The Roman Empire, surrounding the Mediterranean

An artist's rendering depicts a street scene with crowded tenements, home to the poor of ancient Rome.

plumbing. They lugged buckets of water upstairs and carried them down filled with waste. Some simply emptied their buckets out the windows. In parts of the city, flies buzzed above open pits of filth. Dead animals decomposed in alleyways. City life was not only dirty but dangerous. Poorly constructed tenements often collapsed. Fires were common. Robbery and murder plagued the streets.

Public Entertainments: "Bread and Circuses"

Augustus and the emperors that followed him knew they had to keep the people happy. If the many poor and unemployed in the city became restless, they might riot and threaten the peace. So, to divert them, the emperors provided the people with all kinds of games, races, and spectacles, many of them bloody and cruel.

In Rome, people flocked to the Circus Maximus, the largest of Rome's U-shaped stadiums enclosing long racetracks. Here the empire's finest charioteers competed against each other in four-horsed, two-wheeled chariots. The Circus Maximus could hold about two hundred fifty thousand spectators, who cheered wildly for their favorite teams and drivers. As many as twelve chariots might run in a single race. Drivers were regularly thrown from their chariots and trampled to death.

Rich and poor alike poured into Rome's fifty-thousand-seat Colosseum to witness the contests

A Roman mosaic portrays gladiators battling each other in a scene played out thousands of times in the Colosseum.

between trained fighters known as gladiators. Before each bout, gladiators marched past the emperor's box and cried, *"Morituri te salutamus"*— "We who are about to die salute you."

Some gladiators carried a heavy shield and short sword, while others wielded a trident, dagger, and net. Thus armed, they met in the arena and sometimes battled each other to the death. Some bouts pitted man against beast. Lions, tigers, leopards, and even elephants were hunted to death in the Colosseum.

Sometimes, the hunted became the hunter. Wild beasts were set upon unarmed criminals or slaves, who were torn apart and devoured for the sport of the watchers. The greater the slaughter, the more the people seemed to love it. The first-century writer Seneca called gladiator contests "butchery plain and simple."

Like modern sports heroes, successful gladiators could become celebrities. A small number were free citizens seeking fame and fortune, but most were condemned criminals, prisoners of war, or slaves, forced to fight.

In addition to bloody and cruel public entertainments, Rome's rulers also provided monthly rations of free grain, oil, and wine. The leaders

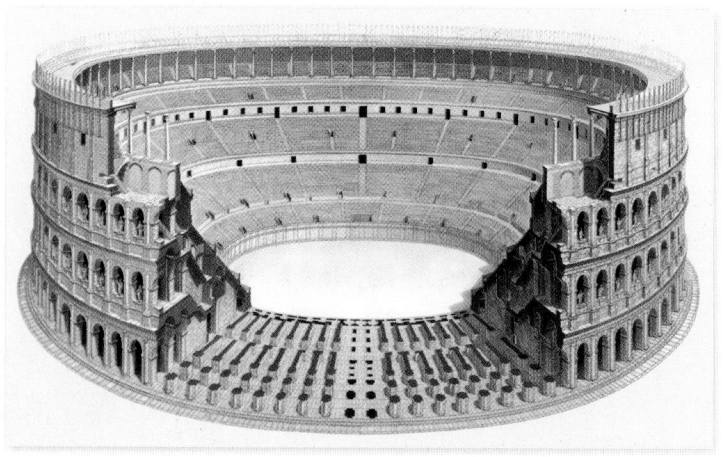

A cutaway model of the Colosseum shows the huge oval amphitheater, venue of many Roman games.

reasoned that a well-fed and entertained public would be a peaceful one. "These people want only two things—bread and circuses," a Roman writer complained.

Slaves in the Empire

During republican times, Roman citizens had provided much of the labor needed to keep Roman society functioning. During the Pax Romana, however, more and more of that work was done by slaves. By the second century, nearly one-third of the inhabitants of the Roman Empire were slaves. Some historians think that slavery weakened Roman society by creating unemployment among the poor and idleness among the rich.

Slaves might be captives of battle or former Roman citizens unable to pay their debts. The lives of Roman slaves varied widely. In private households, some slaves ran businesses for their masters. Others, such as well-educated Greeks taken in conquest, became tutors and teachers and enjoyed significant influence on Roman culture. Some domestic slaves could earn enough money to buy their freedom. Rome granted citizenship to most freed slaves, and the hope of freedom gave many slaves a reason to work hard.

Slaves on farms or in mines lived much harder lives. A Roman writer of the second century described slaves in a flour mill: "You could see scars from whippings all over their bodies…. Letters had been branded on their foreheads and shackles bound their ankles."

Family in Early Rome

In nearly every Roman home, good citizens maintained a sacred shrine that housed tiny statues of dead ancestors. The spirits of these departed loved ones were thought to watch over the household, protecting family members and preserving their values.

Romans honored their ancestors because families formed the fundamental unit of Roman society. The family was ruled by the **paterfamilias** (pa-tuhr-fuh-MIH-lee-us), a term meaning "father

Slaves in Revolt: Spartacus

Sometimes entire communities of slaves rose in revolt against their masters. A famous slave revolt occurred in 73 B.C., led by a gladiator named Spartacus. A veteran of the Roman legions, Spartacus had fallen on hard times and ended up a slave. He was sent to a gladiator training camp in southern Italy, where he led a revolt that spread panic throughout the peninsula. Leading some ninety thousand rebels, Spartacus initially defeated Rome in battle after battle. In the end, it took eight legions to put down the rebellion led by Spartacus, more forces than Rome needed to defeat Hannibal.

of the family." The paterfamilias was the male head of the household, and by Roman law he was the absolute ruler of the family. One of the laws in Rome's Twelve Tables said, "To a father…shall be given over a son the power of life and death." Fathers even had the right to sell children into slavery, although this rarely occurred.

Husbands did not have the same power over wives, because in most cases the women they married remained under the control of their own paterfamilias. Roman women raised their children, managed household finances, and oversaw the family's slaves. Roman children were expected to honor family elders and display filial piety—respect and obedience to parents, the paterfamilias, and the republic.

Boys in well-to-do families were educated in literature, history, geography, and Greek. Lessons in public speaking and law helped many young men prepare for prestigious and well-connected careers in government.

Roman Culture

According to Sallust, a Roman historian of the first century B.C., Julius Caesar had observed that when confronted by excellence, the Romans "preferred to imitate, rather than envy." The more the Romans learned of Greek culture, the more they imitated it and adapted it to suit Roman needs, forming a mix of Greek and Roman traditions often called **Greco-Roman** culture.

The Romans had long admired Greek achievements in art, architecture, literature, and philosophy. They read Homer's *Iliad* and *Odyssey*, as well as the works of Plato and Aristotle. Many Roman families sent their sons to school in Athens or hired Greek tutors. Greek craftsmen and teachers traveled to Rome. The Romans modeled their plays and theaters after the Greeks.

During the Pax Romana, Rome expanded its rule into areas of the Mediterranean world where Greek culture already thrived. Greek city-states came under Roman control, as did vast territories conquered centuries earlier by Alexander the Great. As Roman rule spread, Greco-Roman culture created a bond between people separated by many miles.

Juno, queen of the Roman gods

Roman Religion: Borrowing from the Greeks

When it came to religion and the gods, the Romans borrowed heavily from the Greeks. They adopted Greek deities and gave them Roman names. Zeus, king of the Greek gods, became Jupiter, king of the Roman gods. Aphrodite, the Greek goddess of love, became known as Venus. Ares, the Greek god of war, became the god Mars, who was believed to lead Roman armies to victory.

One important religious ritual remained uniquely Roman. The temple of Vesta, goddess of hearth and family, kept the ceremonial flame of

Roman Deities and Greek Origins

Greek God	Roman Name	Description
Zeus	Jupiter	king of the gods
Hera	Juno (JOO-noh)	queen of the gods
Poseidon	Neptune	god of the sea
Hades	Pluto	god of the underworld
Athena	Minerva (muh-NUR-vuh)	goddess of wisdom
Aphrodite	Venus	goddess of love
Ares	Mars	god of war
Apollo	Apollo	god of light, music, and poetry
Artemis	Diana	goddess of the moon and hunting
Demeter	Ceres (SEER-eez)	goddess of agriculture
Hermes	Mercury	messenger of the gods
Hephaestus	Vulcan	blacksmith of the gods
Hestia	Vesta	goddess of the hearth
Dionysus	Bacchus (BA-kus)	god of wine

Jupiter, king of the Roman gods

Virgil's Aeneid

Virgil modeled his masterwork, the *Aeneid*, after the great Greek epic of the Trojan War, Homer's *Iliad*. Every educated Roman knew the story of the Trojan War—a Trojan prince, Paris, seized the beautiful wife of the Greek king Menelaus and took her to Troy. Thousands of Greek soldiers then sailed to Troy for vengeance and to take back the lovely Helen.

In the *Aeneid*, Virgil describes how the war ends with a deceptive plan thought up by the Greek hero Odysseus, whom the Romans called Ulysses. Ulysses devises the plan of the Trojan Horse. Greek soldiers hide inside a gigantic wooden horse, which the Trojans drag through the gates into their city. In the dark of night, the Greek warriors emerge from the horse and set fire to Troy.

When the Greeks attack, the sound of roaring flames awakens Aeneas, a prince of Troy and, according to legend, a son of Venus. A loyal son, Aeneas thinks first of his father, but decides he must first save Priam, the king of Troy, who is like a father to all Trojans. But Aeneas arrives too late, only to see the king stabbed to death by a Greek.

Virgil's epic relates how, after the Trojan War, Aeneas escapes from Troy and sails west. After many adventures, he leads the Trojan exiles to settle in Latium, where they became the ancestors of the Romans.

Greek warriors emerge from hiding inside the Trojan Horse.

the city burning day and night. The fire, thought to guarantee the strength of the republic, was tended by priestesses called the Vestal Virgins.

Other Roman religious ceremonies and rituals were designed to earn the favors of the gods and ensure a good life. Because they connected virtually every aspect of daily life to a higher power, many Romans performed small rituals throughout the day. They also looked forward to taking part in public religious festivals, such as the popular Saturnalia (sa-tuhr-NAYL-yuh) held every December, during which masters and slaves temporarily switched places.

A Literary Golden Age

Much of what historians know about Rome comes from ancient writers who described the society around them. During the reign of Augustus, Roman writers produced so many enduring works that the time is remembered as the golden age of Latin literature.

Augustus encouraged poets to celebrate Rome's greatness. The poet Horace pleased the emperor with verses that described the joys of Roman life. One of his poems offers this advice: *carpe diem* (KAHR-peh DEE-em), or "seize the day."

Born in 70 B.C., Rome's greatest poet, Virgil (VUR-juhl), wrote early works that idealized the hardworking farmers who made Rome's greatness possible. Caesar Augustus called on Virgil to compose a new story about the founding of Rome. The emperor wanted an epic poem to rival those of the Greeks, Homer's *Iliad* and *Odyssey*. In response, Virgil produced his masterpiece, the *Aeneid* (uh-NEE-id), which tells the story of Aeneas (ih-NEE-us), a Trojan prince and early ancestor of the Roman people. Unlike Greek heroes who seek fame and glory, Virgil's hero personifies the Roman ideals of self-sacrifice and loyalty to the paterfamilias.

Other Roman poets had less success pleasing the emperor. Ovid (AHV-uhd) wrote poetry poking fun at Roman virtues, and an infuriated Augustus exiled him. But irreverent writing remained popular. Petronius and Juvenal, for example, wrote

This fresco painted on the bedroom wall of a wealthy Roman's home depicts an elaborate window and garden scene.

satires, which used humor to criticize aspects of Roman social life, including the indulgent ways of rich Romans.

Some Roman writers chose to follow the example of the great Greek historian Herodotus. Livy, born in 59 B.C., wrote more than a hundred books on the history of Rome, from its founding to his own day. Throughout, Livy glorified what he saw as the unique destiny of the Romans.

Tacitus (TAS-uh-tuhs), who became consul of Rome in A.D. 97, wrote his *Annals*, a history of the empire during the first century. Writing about emperors who were already dead, Tacitus felt free to describe unflattering details about Rome's past leaders. Many modern historians think that Tacitus exaggerated the worst deeds of the first-century

emperors to emphasize his belief that Rome was declining as it strayed from its traditional values.

Like the Greeks, the Romans valued oratory, the art of public speaking. The great Roman orator Cicero (106–43 B.C.) excelled in the spoken word. Cicero was called a "new man" because none of his ancestors had held office. Because of his brilliant public speaking, Cicero became a leading citizen of Rome.

The Visual Arts

Roman artists admired Greek sculptures that depicted idealized human forms. They copied Greek statues and created their own sculptures celebrating Roman accomplishments. One artist portrayed Augustus as a near-god, muscular and brimming with vitality. In reality, Augustus was over forty and unhealthy when the statue was made.

Over time, Roman sculpture became less idealized and increasingly realistic. Roman artists created works that portrayed subjects with human flaws and emotions. For example, a late third-century sculpture of the emperor Aurelian shows a man with droopy eyes and a sad, careworn face.

Roman artists created many **frescoes** by painting directly onto wet plaster. Frescoes often covered entire walls in Roman homes. Most frescoes were painted in bright colors and portrayed scenes from Greek and Roman mythology. Some featured family portraits.

In the homes of wealthy Romans, as well as in many public buildings, the floors were decorated with **mosaics** (moh-ZAY-iks). In a mosaic, tiny

Pompeii: A Buried City

On August 24, in A.D. 79, life in the Roman city of Pompeii (pom-PAY) was violently interrupted by the eruption of Mount Vesuvius, a volcano in southern Italy. As poisonous gases filled the air and molten ash rained down, Pompeii, a city of ten to twenty thousand residents, was buried. The city was lost for more than 1,600 years until it was rediscovered in the mid-1700s. Modern archaeologists have uncovered homes and public buildings with well-preserved frescoes and mosaics. Artifacts collected from the ash—pots and pans, elegant sculptures, and even graffiti—help paint a picture of the everyday lives of Roman people.

pieces of colored tile are arranged to form a picture or a design. Mosaics often featured scenes from famous battles or popular legends. Some offered practical messages. For example, one mosaic at the entry of a Roman home spelled out the words *cave canem*—"beware of the dog."

Roman Architecture and Engineering

Centuries before the Pax Romana, the Romans had learned from the Etruscans how to build arches. They adapted what they learned, and also used concrete—a mix of lime, water, and sand—to create stunning structures, such as the Circus Maximus and the Colosseum.

A magnificent temple called the Pantheon, dedicated to the Olympian gods, still stands in Rome today, nearly two thousand years after it was built. The temple features a 140-foot (43 m) dome built using concrete, as well as the technology of the arch. The Pantheon's dome remained the largest in the world until the 1800s.

Mastery of the arch also gave Romans the know-how to build aqueducts, which carried water into the city from the surrounding hills. Some aqueducts ran along the ground, while others rose overhead, supported by brick arches. Rome itself

The two-thousand-year-old Pantheon, a temple dedicated to the Roman gods, still stands in Rome.

had eleven aqueducts, carrying about 300 million gallons (1.4 billion l) of water a day. Some of the water was channeled to public fountains on each city block. Much of it went to supply Rome's *thermae* (THUHR-mee), huge public baths and centers of social life, where friends met to chat and conduct business. Visitors to the baths went through a series of bathing rituals in steam rooms, dry heat rooms, hot pools, and cold pools.

Across the empire, Romans looked with pride on their aqueducts as a symbol of Rome's ingenuity and practicality. A section of a massive aqueduct still stands in southern France, its three

This magnificent Roman aqueduct in southern France rises in three tiers of arches above a river gorge.

tiers of arches climbing 160 feet (49 m) above a river gorge.

Roman Roads

The Romans built a system of roads, the best in the ancient world, to connect the territories they controlled. In 312 B.C., the Romans started building their first great road, the Appian (A-pee-uhn) Way, also known as the *regina viarum*, or "queen of roads." (See map, p. 169.) Over time, more roads spread out from Rome like the spokes of a great wheel, linking the city to the farthest reaches of its empire—to Britain, Spain, North Africa, Asia Minor, and other lands. The Romans eventually built fifty thousand miles (80,467 km) of roads.

The Appian Way was the main highway leading south out of Rome. It is paved with stones that were polished and then carefully fitted together.

Roman engineers oversaw the construction of the highways. The work was often done by soldiers between military campaigns. The roads were built so well that they could last decades without repair. Some portions of Roman roads are still used today.

These well-built roads allowed Roman armies to move swiftly throughout the empire. Good roads also increased travel, communication, and trade. Carts loaded with goods such as wool, timber, corn, and wheat creaked along the imperial highways. Luxury goods such as silk, jewels, and spices came from as far away as China and India. Roman roads allowed travelers to carry goods, ideas, and innovations from one end of the empire to the other, speeding the spread of Greco-Roman culture.

Advancements in Medicine and Astronomy

In science and mathematics, the Romans were more interested in practical application than theory. Mostly they used what others—especially the Greeks—had discovered, and adapted it to their own needs.

During the last half of the second century, significant advancements in medicine were made by Galen (GAY-luhn), a physician and philosopher born in Greece. As a young man, Galen studied medicine at Alexandria in Egypt. Later he moved to Rome, where he gained fame for curing patients that other physicians had given up on.

Galen's medical advancements were based on his studies in anatomy—the study of the parts of the body and how they function. Because the dissection of human corpses was forbidden, Galen based most of his insights on dissecting the bodies of dogs, pigs, monkeys, and other animals. One of his most important findings was that blood—not air, as had long been assumed—flows through arteries. Galen's many writings on human anatomy remained the authority for medicine in Europe until the 1600s.

As Galen was advancing knowledge of the human body, Ptolemy was developing his ideas about the motions of celestial bodies. A mathematician and astronomer of Greek descent who lived in Egypt, Ptolemy erroneously placed the earth at the center of the universe. Despite this error, he accurately predicted the paths of the planets and stars across the sky. His insights made travel safer and more predictable. He also wrote an eight-volume geography treatise with a detailed world map that was acclaimed throughout the ancient world.

The Rise of Christianity

During the reign of Caesar Augustus, the Roman Empire covered more than half of Europe, most of North Africa and Asia Minor, and parts of the eastern Mediterranean. Historians estimate that the empire included between fifty and seventy million subjects.

Within so vast a realm, there lived a variety of people with diverse religious beliefs and practices. In the provinces, Roman leaders usually allowed local people to worship their own gods as long as they also honored the Roman gods. In some cases, the Romans adopted the religious beliefs of the people they conquered. Just as Romans had embraced Greek deities, they also adopted other foreign religious practices, including worship of the Egyptian goddess Isis and the Persian sun god Mithras.

Despite their tolerance and, in some cases, acceptance of other religious practices, the Romans remained committed to the worship of their own gods. In the words of the Roman orator Cicero, religion was "the foundation of our state." He believed Rome's success relied on pious worship and observance of time-honored traditions. Good Romans actively sought the favor of the gods through daily rituals and temple ceremonies.

In the provinces, while Roman subjects were allowed to maintain their traditional worship, they were expected to honor the Roman gods as well. For most inhabitants of the empire, who were accustomed to worshipping multiple gods, this posed no great problem. The demand to honor the Roman gods, however, did prove a great problem for the people of Judea, a province east of Rome that was home to the Jewish people.

Hellenism in Judea

The Jewish people of Judea inherited the traditions of their Hebrew forefathers. Their neighbors in the region believed in many gods, but the Jews placed their faith in only one God. They followed the laws and teachings of the Torah, the first five books of the Hebrew Bible. And according to the Torah, the worship of any other gods was strictly forbidden.

Judea had been conquered several times before coming under Roman control. Before Roman rule, Judea had been part of the empire of Alexander the Great. With Alexander's conquest came a steady flow of Greek people, ideas, and art into Judea. Some Jews admired the art and philosophy of the Greeks. They liked the comforts of Greek life. They decided they could enjoy these benefits without giving up Judaism. Gradually, they became Hellenized—that is, they began to adopt and imitate Greek ideas and customs.

After the death of Alexander, the Jews revolted. For a brief time, they lived without foreign rule. During this time, two parties grew powerful in Judea.

Key Questions

- What were the major teachings of Jesus of Nazareth?

- How did Christianity survive early persecution and spread to become a major world religion?

One party wanted to rid the region of Hellenistic ways. The other wanted to keep them. Civil war broke out, and the Hellenized Jews asked Rome for help. The Romans lost no time in coming to the aid of the Hellenized Jews. But when the civil war was over, Rome ruled Judea.

Judaism in the Empire

Judea came under Roman rule in 63 B.C. The Jewish community remained divided. On one side, wealthy and influential Jews admired Greco-Roman culture. They benefited from trade with the wide Roman world, and many adopted Rome's fashions, if not its religion. On the other side were Jews who strictly interpreted the Torah and rejected any kind of compromise. To them, the adoption of a foreign culture meant losing their identity as God's chosen people.

One small group of Jews was especially opposed to Hellenism and Roman rule. This group, called the Zealots (ZEH-luhts), regarded rule by foreigners as an offense to God. The Zealots reminded the Jews of a message from their prophets of old. The prophets had predicted the coming of the Messiah (meh-SIY-uh), a mighty king who would liberate the Jews and drive any foreign rulers from the promised land.

The Zealots urged the immediate and forceful overthrow of Roman rule. In A.D. 6, they started a rebellion against Rome, which was quickly crushed. To punish the rebels, the Romans enforced a cruel but common practice of the time—they crucified many hundreds of Zealots, nailing them to wooden crosses and leaving them to hang until dead.

The Zealots did not give up. They rebelled again in A.D. 66, after a Roman official stole gold from the Jewish temple in Jerusalem. The Zealots drove Romans from the capital, but after three years Rome again routed the rebels and destroyed their temple. A final Zealot uprising occurred in A.D. 132, after which the Romans banned all surviving Jews from Jerusalem.

The Life and Teachings of Jesus

Between the first and second Zealot uprisings, new ideas came from Judea, ideas that would change the Roman Empire and eventually sweep across much of the world. In this out-of-the-way Roman province, the religion of Christianity was born.

The Early Life of Jesus

Just north of Judea, Galilee was a land of shepherds and olive orchards surrounding a freshwater lake called the Sea of Galilee. In Nazareth, a village in southern Galilee, lived a Jewish carpenter named Jesus.

Jesus' life was short, only about thirty-three years, and we know little about him. The writings that tell us about his life and teachings were recorded many years after his death. These writings are known as the **Gospels**, from two old English words meaning "good news." The Gospels—the books of Matthew, Mark, Luke, and John—were later collected into the Christian Bible.

The Birthday of Jesus

As you have learned, the calendar used by much of the world is based on a system that divides years into B.C. (before Christ) and A.D. (*anno Domini*, Latin for "in the year of our Lord"). This system, devised in the sixth century, designated the year of Jesus' birth as A.D. 1. Modern-day scholars believe that the sixth-century monks who reckoned the date of Jesus' birth were off by several years. Thus, most current scholars think that Jesus was actually born earlier than A.D. 1—perhaps in the year 4 B.C. He died around the year A.D. 29.

The Gospels, which sometimes vary in their accounts of the life of Jesus, say little about Jesus' childhood, but as a Jewish boy he would have studied the Torah. The Gospels do not say if Jesus encountered Zealots while growing up, but Galilee was a well-known stronghold of anti-Roman sentiment. As a child, Jesus likely overheard adults complaining about Roman rule and wondering aloud about the arrival of the Messiah.

The Message of Jesus

According to the Gospels, when Jesus was about thirty he heard that his cousin John, known throughout Galilee as John the Baptist, was preaching and

A sixth-century artwork depicts the Sermon on the Mount.

urging Jews to prepare for the Messiah's coming. Those who listened and promised to reform their lives were immersed by John in the Jordan River. This ritual, called baptism, was a symbol of washing away old sins or offenses against God. Jesus asked John to baptize him. Afterward, the Gospels say, Jesus went into the wilderness to pray and be alone. When he returned, he began a new life as a wandering preacher, traveling from village to village to spread his message.

Jesus taught that the kingdom of God was open to all people—rich or poor, free or slave. He said that the kingdom of God that the Jews awaited was not a kingdom of marble temples decked with gold and silver. Rather, it was a spiritual kingdom, a way of living in harmony with God's will. Jesus taught that God loved all people and wanted people to love each other. The Gospel of Luke reports that Jesus said, "Love your enemies; do good to them which hate you, bless them that curse you."

During the brief years during which Jesus spread his message, he chose twelve men to be his closest companions. They became his **apostles**. It would be their task to carry on Jesus' work when he was gone.

To many, Jesus must have seemed revolutionary. He encouraged people to give their money to the poor. He promised that the meek would inherit the earth. He spent time with criminals and lepers. While some found his message disturbing, others were inspired by it, and many flocked to hear him speak. Word spread that Jesus performed miracles, such as healing the sick, bringing sight to the blind, and even raising the dead. People began calling Jesus the promised Messiah. Some hoped he would lead a revolt against Rome.

Crucifixion and Resurrection

In Jerusalem, some Jewish leaders saw Jesus as a troublemaker who challenged their authority. According to the Gospels, some of these Jewish leaders plotted to turn Jesus over to the Romans, who were always quick to punish rabble-rousers.

The Gospels report that Jesus traveled to Jerusalem to observe the holiday of Passover, the time when the Jews celebrated their ancestors' liberation from bondage in Egypt. He shared the traditional Passover supper with his twelve apostles. As he served them bread and wine, Jesus told his apostles that the simple meal would be a way to

183

Primary Source

THE SERMON ON THE MOUNT

In the Christian Bible, the Gospel of Matthew recounts how Jesus sat down with some of his followers on a high place and taught them about the message he wanted them to spread. His words have come to be known as the Sermon on the Mount. Here is a part of the Sermon on the Mount, known as the Beatitudes (bee-A-tuh-toodz), from a Latin term meaning "blessed."

Blessed are the poor in spirit, for theirs is the kingdom of heaven.

Blessed are those who mourn, for they shall be comforted.

Blessed are the meek, for they shall inherit the earth.

Blessed are those who hunger and thirst for righteousness, for they shall be satisfied.

Blessed are the merciful, for they shall obtain mercy.

Blessed are the pure in heart, for they shall see God.

Blessed are the peacemakers, for they shall be called sons of God.

Blessed are those who are persecuted for righteousness' sake, for theirs is the kingdom of heaven.

remember him when he was gone. He said that the bread represented his body, while the wine symbolized his blood. Later, as Jesus prayed in a nearby garden, a group of armed men seized him and turned him over to Pontius Pilate (PAHN-shuhs PIY-luht), the Roman governor of Judea.

According to the Gospels, Jewish leaders accused Jesus of calling himself the king of Judea and inciting revolt against Rome. They knew that the Romans regularly put to death anyone suspected of treason. Pilate handed Jesus over to be put to death by crucifixion, the typical punishment for treason. The Gospels say that Roman soldiers beat Jesus and spit on him. Then they took him to a hill in Jerusalem, nailed him to a cross, and left him to die. According to the Gospel of Luke, before dying, Jesus asked God to forgive his executioners.

The Gospels report that Jesus was buried in a garden tomb, which was sealed with a rock. But when some of his followers visited the tomb, the rock had been rolled away. Proclaiming the resurrection, his followers said that Jesus had risen from the dead, which they took as proof that he was the Messiah. Over the next weeks, the Bible says, Jesus appeared to his apostles and prepared them to go

An ancient Roman ivory carving depicts Jesus' crucifixion.

out and preach his "good news." Then, according to the Gospels, Jesus was taken up to heaven, an event called the Ascension, which is still celebrated by Christians.

Immediately following Jesus' death, many of his followers went into hiding. They were afraid they might face punishment for their devotion to him. But as the immediate danger passed, they resumed sharing stories about Jesus. They called him "Christ," from the Greek word *Christos*, which means "anointed one" and roughly translates as "Messiah." His followers began calling themselves Christians.

Jesus' followers described his death on the cross. They said he had risen from the dead, and predicted that some day he would return to complete the work he had begun. More and more people listened, and many believed what they heard. The number of Christians began to grow.

The Spread of Christianity

Jesus had appointed his apostle Peter to lead his followers after he was gone. Peter, a fisherman, was not well-educated, and had never traveled far from Judea. But under his guidance, the community of Jesus' followers flourished. Peter established a Christian church in Jerusalem, and later traveled up and down the Mediterranean coast, spreading Jesus' message and organizing Christian communities. Peter went to Rome to lead a small and growing Christian community.

The apostle who did the most to spread the message of Jesus, Paul, had in fact never met Jesus. Paul helped transform what was a Jewish movement into a religion that appealed to **gentiles**, or non-Jews.

Originally named Saul, he came from Tarsus, a prosperous city in Asia Minor. Saul, who grew

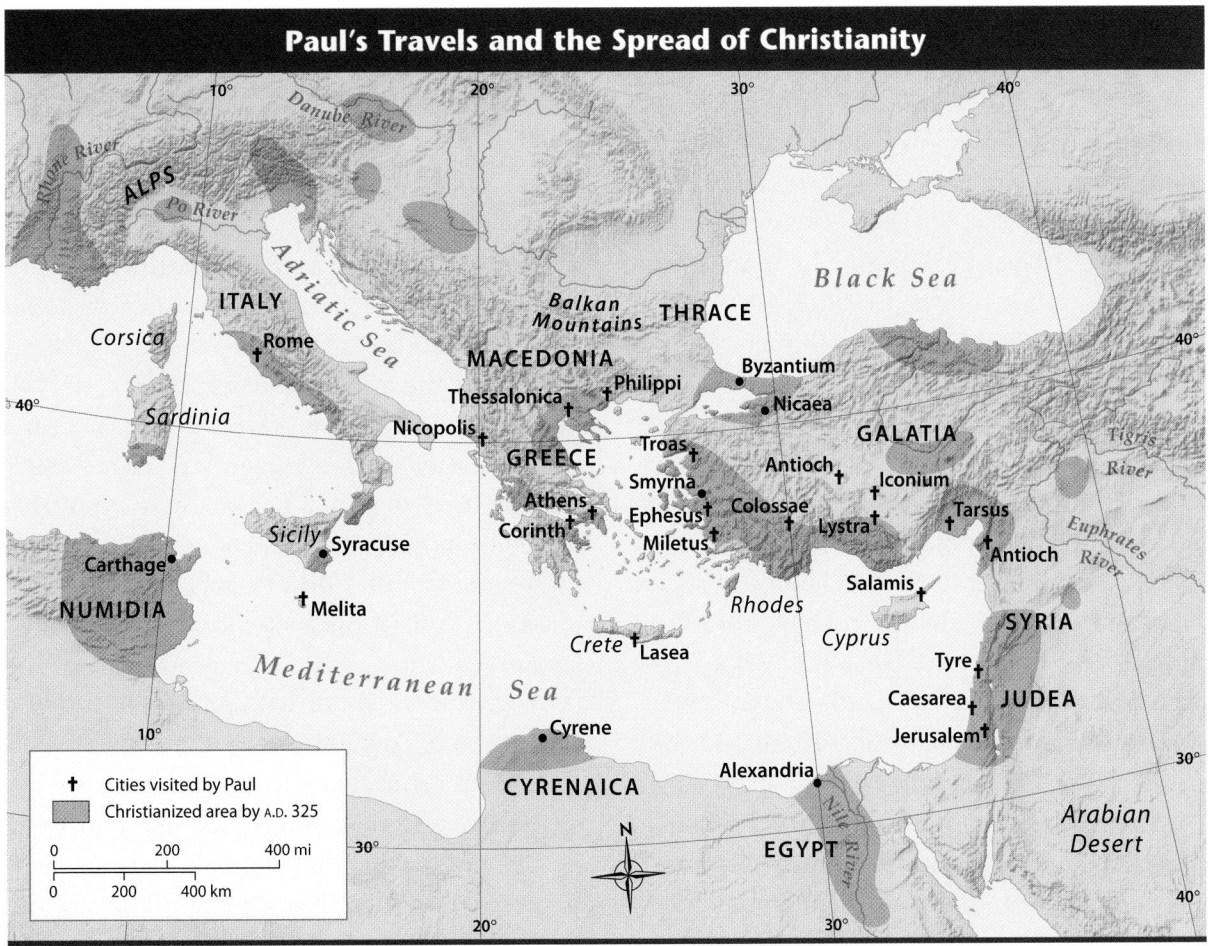

Paul's missionary travels throughout the eastern Mediterranean region began the rapid spread of Christianity.

185

up speaking Greek and surrounded by Greek culture, was nevertheless devoted to his Jewish faith. When he first came to Jerusalem to study, Saul despised the new Christian movement. He saw it as a threat to Jewish law, and he resolved to destroy all Christians. Then Saul had a life-changing experience. One account in the Christian Bible says he was blinded by a great light, fell to the ground, and heard the voice of Jesus asking why Saul persecuted him. After that, the Bible says, Saul came to believe in Jesus.

Saul changed his name and his mission. As Paul, he went from being one of Christianity's most determined enemies to one of its most fervent advocates. For the next twenty years, Paul traveled throughout the empire, preaching the message of Jesus. Since Paul spoke and wrote Greek, he could communicate with gentiles in a language they understood.

During his long travels, Paul stayed in touch with distant Christian communities by writing long letters, or **epistles** (ih-PIH-suhlz). The epistles explained Jesus' message and offered practical guidance. Many of Paul's epistles became part of the Christian Bible. Through Paul's efforts, the message of Jesus spread from a handful of Jews in the area near Jerusalem to gentiles throughout the eastern Mediterranean and finally even to Rome itself.

Persecution and Acceptance

At first, most Romans viewed Christianity as simply an odd offshoot of the Jewish religion. They paid little attention to the wandering preachers who talked of a Jew who had risen from the dead. After all, the vast Roman Empire was full of people who held various beliefs in different gods. So at first the Romans saw no threat from this new faith called Christianity. But that was about to change.

During the reign of the emperor Nero, Roman officials organized persecutions against Christians. They burned scriptures and crucified those who refused to worship Roman gods. Soon, Roman leaders found it useful to blame Christians for

The catacombs were used as burial places but also as hideaways for those who faced religious persecution.

everything from plagues to earthquakes. In A.D. 64, when a great fire swept through Rome, Nero blamed the catastrophe on the Christians and sent many to painful deaths.

In the face of persecutions, Christians began worshipping in secret. They met in **catacombs**, underground chambers beneath Rome that also served as burial halls. Christians decorated the underground walls with symbols of their faith, including a simple fish symbol, which represented Jesus. (The Greek word for fish was made of the initial letters of Jesus' name and title—"Jesus Christ, Son of God and Savior.")

After Nero's death in A.D. 68, Christians enjoyed periods of tolerance. The new faith grew rapidly. By the year 300, Christians made up about 10 percent of the empire's population. They came from all walks of life. Some held important positions within Roman society.

The last great persecution began shortly after the year 300, when the emperor Diocletian (diy-uh-KLEE-shun) tried to stamp out Christians once and for all. Roman soldiers began seizing Christian property and arresting and executing Christian leaders. They burned an entire town in which everyone professed to be Christian, killing all the inhabitants. In other places, they tortured believers before putting them to death.

The killing and torture of Christians during the reign of Diocletian came to be known as the Great Persecution. But killing its believers did not stamp out Christianity. In fact, it had the opposite effect. People who died for the faith were known as **martyrs**, from a Greek word for "witness." Christian martyrs—men, women, and children—endured terrible punishments, and their bravery inspired some to embrace the teachings of Jesus. Diocletian's attempts to wipe out the Christians actually strengthened their numbers.

Constantine and the Edict of Milan

During Diocletian's time, the Roman Empire fell into civil war. (You'll read more about these conflicts later in this chapter.) In 312, Constantine (KAHN-stuhn-teen) emerged as the victor and new emperor. According to various accounts, before one key battle, Constantine—who was not himself a Christian—saw a vision of a flaming cross in the sky, and under it fiery letters spelling out the Latin phrase *In hoc signo vinces*—"In this sign [you shall] conquer." Constantine won this battle and others after it. Soon after he became emperor, he sent out an edict, or order.

Constantine, emperor of Rome from A.D. 312 to 337

It was called the Edict of Milan (muh-LAHN) because the emperor issued the order after a meeting in Milan, Italy.

The Edict of Milan said that all religions were free to exist in Rome. It said that Christians were no longer to be persecuted, and that any property that had been taken from them must be returned. Constantine's edict made Christianity a legally recognized faith. Christians were allowed "open and free exercise of their religion," and could enjoy the full rights of Roman citizens.

Only when he was on his deathbed did Constantine convert to Christianity. He died in 337, the first Christian emperor of the Roman Empire. His actions had a lasting impact. During his reign, large numbers of Romans converted. In 380, the emperor Theodosius made Christianity the official religion of the empire and banned the public ceremonies of other religions.

The Early Christian Church

The early Christians came from many backgrounds, but they shared certain key beliefs and practices. To them, Jesus was the Messiah, the savior who had risen from the dead and whom they believed would someday return. New converts entered the Christian community through the ritual of baptism. They were submerged in or sprinkled with water, following the example of Jesus, who had been baptized by John. In remembrance of Jesus' body and blood, early Christians celebrated the Eucharist, or Holy Communion, a ritual meal of bread and wine that recalled Jesus' final meal with his apostles.

Organizing the Church

As Christian communities spread across the Roman world, they faced internal challenges. There was no agreement on how Christian churches should be run and no coherent **theology**, that is, no organized expression of the fundamental principles of the faith.

As Christians gradually organized, they began to define the functions of the **clergy**—the church leaders—in relation to the **laity** (LAY-uh-tee), the

187

Augustine of Hippo

During a time of uncertainty within the Roman Empire, influential Christian thinkers helped unify the church. Among these early "church fathers," as they are called, none had more impact on Christian theology than Augustine, the bishop of Hippo, a town in North Africa.

Born in 354 to a Christian mother and a polytheist father, Augustine converted to Christianity in 386 and became bishop within a decade. His book, *City of God*, examines differences between earthly laws and the law of God. Expounding on the philosophy of Plato, Augustine argues that earthly distractions prevent human beings from achieving spiritual purity.

Governments, said Augustine, had the responsibility to help people remain pure through the power of the church. This idea offered a religious foundation for powerful Christian kingdoms that would later rise in western Europe. Augustine's philosophy helped the church survive long after the Roman Empire had disintegrated.

members of the church who were not part of the clergy. The local leaders were called bishops, from a Greek word meaning "overseer." The bishops were assisted by deacons, while priests led religious services. Over time, bishops from the most important Roman cities, such as Antioch, Alexandria, and Rome, developed great prestige. They became known as patriarchs.

The bishop of Rome enjoyed special esteem as head of the Christians in the empire's capital. He became known as the **pope**. Eventually, the pope started to claim authority over all other bishops, which (as you will see in a later chapter) led to controversy and division in the church.

Defining the Faith: The Council of Nicaea

The structure of the church was taking shape, but it proved difficult to create an organized Christian theology. The followers of Jesus had different ideas about who Jesus was. For example, was he God himself, or the son of God? There were arguments over what Jesus had preached and exactly what his teachings meant.

To resolve the arguments, in 325 Constantine called some three hundred bishops and other church leaders from all over the empire to attend the Council of Nicaea (niy-SEE-uh). In an effort to organize and unify the Christian faith, the council issued the first version of what is known as the Nicene Creed, which set out some basic tenets of Christian faith.

Now that Christians had an officially approved version of their theology, they could also identify **heresy** (HAIR-uh-see), any belief or practice at odds with officially recognized doctrines. Heretics (HAIR-uh-tiks)—persons who held beliefs in conflict with approved beliefs—could face severe punishment.

Around the year 400, Christian bishops agreed on the writings that should be included in the Christian Bible. The result is called the **New Testament**. The first four books of the New Testament—the Gospels of Matthew, Mark, Luke, and John—recount the life and teachings of Jesus Christ.

The Roman Empire: Decline and Fall

What caused the Roman Empire to fall? There was no single cause, and no sudden fall. Rome's decline took place over many years, and was the result of many factors, including (but not limited to) external enemies, internal conflicts, economic hardship, disease, and natural disaster.

Political Turmoil

After the death of the emperor Marcus Aurelius in 180, the period historians call the Pax Romana came to an end. Although the people of Rome could not know it, the empire's best days were behind it. Invasions on the frontier, decreased trade, social unrest—the empire faced problems that would take a strong leader to fix. But after the death of Marcus Aurelius, strong leadership was hard to find.

Marcus Aurelius's son Commodus ruled for twelve years, during which he showed more interest in training as a gladiator than in solving Rome's problems. After he was killed in 192, civil war wracked Rome. Military leaders battled to become emperor. For nearly a century, Rome was governed by whoever had the strongest army.

Between 235 and 284, about fifty different men claimed the title of emperor, and only one of them died a natural death. With so many men vying for the throne, emperors spent most of their time eliminating enemies and protecting themselves from assassination attempts. They had little time to address the empire's problems, such as attacks on the Roman frontiers.

Military Turmoil

Beginning in the first century, Roman emperors had been forced to station troops on the empire's northern border to repel invading Germanic warriors. When these bands of fighters launched raids across the Rhine and Danube rivers, they caused panic and disrupted trade. In the third century, Rome faced a new threat as a powerful Persian dynasty began to attack from the east. To meet this threat, Rome's leaders were forced to transfer legions that had been defending the northern frontier against Germanic tribes.

With fewer Roman troops to defend the northern borders, emperors began paying Germanic warriors not to fight, or even hiring them to defend the frontier. Meanwhile, emperors protected themselves against rivals by employing **mercenaries**, professional soldiers for hire. In earlier times, most Roman troops had been citizen-soldiers who willingly took up arms

Key Questions

- What social, political, and economic factors contributed to the fall of the Roman Empire?
- What is Rome's cultural and political legacy?

TACITUS ON THE GERMANS

The Roman historian Tacitus wrote extensively about other peoples and cultures, with attention to the details of everyday life. In his *Germania*, written in A.D. 98, Tacitus describes the Germanic tribes on the frontiers of the empire. Most likely, he did not observe these peoples firsthand but instead relied on imperial documents and accounts from citizens and soldiers recently returned from the provinces.

Tacitus finds much to condemn about the Germanic peoples' ways of life, but he also presents their rough virtues as a contrast to the moral looseness—as he saw it—of his Roman contemporaries. The Fennians mentioned in the following excerpt may be the ancestors of the modern-day Irish, although most of the tribes Tacitus described lived near the Rhine.

In wonderful savageness live the nation of the Fennians, and in beastly poverty, destitute of arms, of horses, and of homes; their food, the common herbs; their apparel, skins; their bed, the earth: their only hope in their arrows, which for want of iron they point with bones. Their common support they have from the chase, women as well as men....

> The *chase* is the hunt.

Nor other shelter have they even for their babes, against the violence of tempests and ravening beasts, than to cover them with the branches of trees twisted together.... Such a condition they judge more happy than the painful occupation of cultivating the ground, than the labor of rearing houses, than the agitations of hope and fear attending the defense of their own property or the seizing that of others. Secure against the designs of men, secure against the malignity of the gods, they have accomplished a thing of infinite difficulty; that to them nothing remains even to be wished.

to defend Rome. But as the empire expanded, Rome increasingly relied on mercenaries or paid soldiers from outside the empire. By the third century, Rome's mighty army relied largely on paid soldiers.

In the early third century, the emperor Septimius Severus rewarded his loyal soldiers with a raise, increasing military pay by a third. Although this move depleted the treasury and created economic hardship for tax-paying Romans, the emperor did not seem to care. On his deathbed he advised his sons, "Be generous to your soldiers and take no heed of anyone else."

Economic and Social Decline

During the days of Rome's expansion, military conquests had filled the treasury with gold and other riches. Now, with Rome fighting defensive wars, the army no longer made money. It cost money—and lots of it.

The fighting on Rome's frontiers made trade and travel dangerous and expensive. Armies trampled farmers' fields, severely damaging agricultural production. Across the empire, prices went up on everything from grain to jewelry. To make matters worse, epidemics of smallpox and other diseases ravaged populations, killing as many as seven million people during the third century.

Rome's leaders dealt with the economic crisis by minting more coins, while at the same time reducing the amount of precious silver in the coins and increasing the amount of worthless metals. By the year 200, imperial coins had lost more than 50 percent of their value since the days of Augustus. As money declined in value, one result was severe **inflation**, a rapid and steady rise in prices.

In 212, the emperor increased the number of taxpayers by extending citizenship to all free inhabitants of the empire. But Roman citizenship was no longer the great honor it once had been. During the republic, Roman citizenship carried the right to have a say in the government. Now, in the face of so many problems, citizenship carried the burden of paying taxes to support a crumbling empire.

Attempts to Reform

In the 260s and 270s, the crises gripping Rome seemed to be resolved when powerful and competent emperors managed to push back invaders on the frontiers. With order partially restored, in 284 the emperor Diocletian took control.

Dividing the Empire

Diocletian—one of the emperors who persecuted Christians—recognized that the empire had grown too large for one man to govern. He attempted to solve the problem by dividing the empire into two sections—east and west. Instead of a single emperor, now there would be two, one to govern the west and another to lead the east. Under the new system, the two emperors had equal authority and shared the same title—Augustus. Each Augustus was assisted by a junior emperor, called Caesar. When an Augustus died, the Caesar would become emperor in his place, an arrangement that Diocletian hoped would solve conflicts over succession.

In theory, Rome remained a single empire. Over time, however, east and west took on separate identities. The Western Roman Empire, which included the city of Rome, faced its own issues, while the Eastern Empire faced others.

Although Diocletian's reforms brought relative stability, people remained unhappy. Diocletian levied heavy taxes. To control inflation he set prices for all kinds of goods. He also ordered that workers be tied to their professions for life, which locked many Romans into permanent poverty.

Constantine Moves the Capital

In 305, Diocletian stepped down from the throne. Within a few years, the other emperors were fighting for supreme control. Constantine emerged victorious from these civil wars. As you've learned, Constantine made the momentous decision to legalize Christianity. He also made another very important change when he decided to move the capital of the empire from Rome to a city farther east.

For many years, the Eastern Empire had been stronger and richer than the Western Empire. There was more trade and business in the east, and more opportunity, so Constantine decided to move the capital to the ancient Greek city of Byzantium (buh-ZAN-tee-um).

Byzantium was renamed *Novo Roma*, or "New Rome," but soon everyone simply called the city Constantinople (kahn-stant-n-OH-puhl), or "the city of Constantine." (The city is now called Istanbul, in Turkey.)

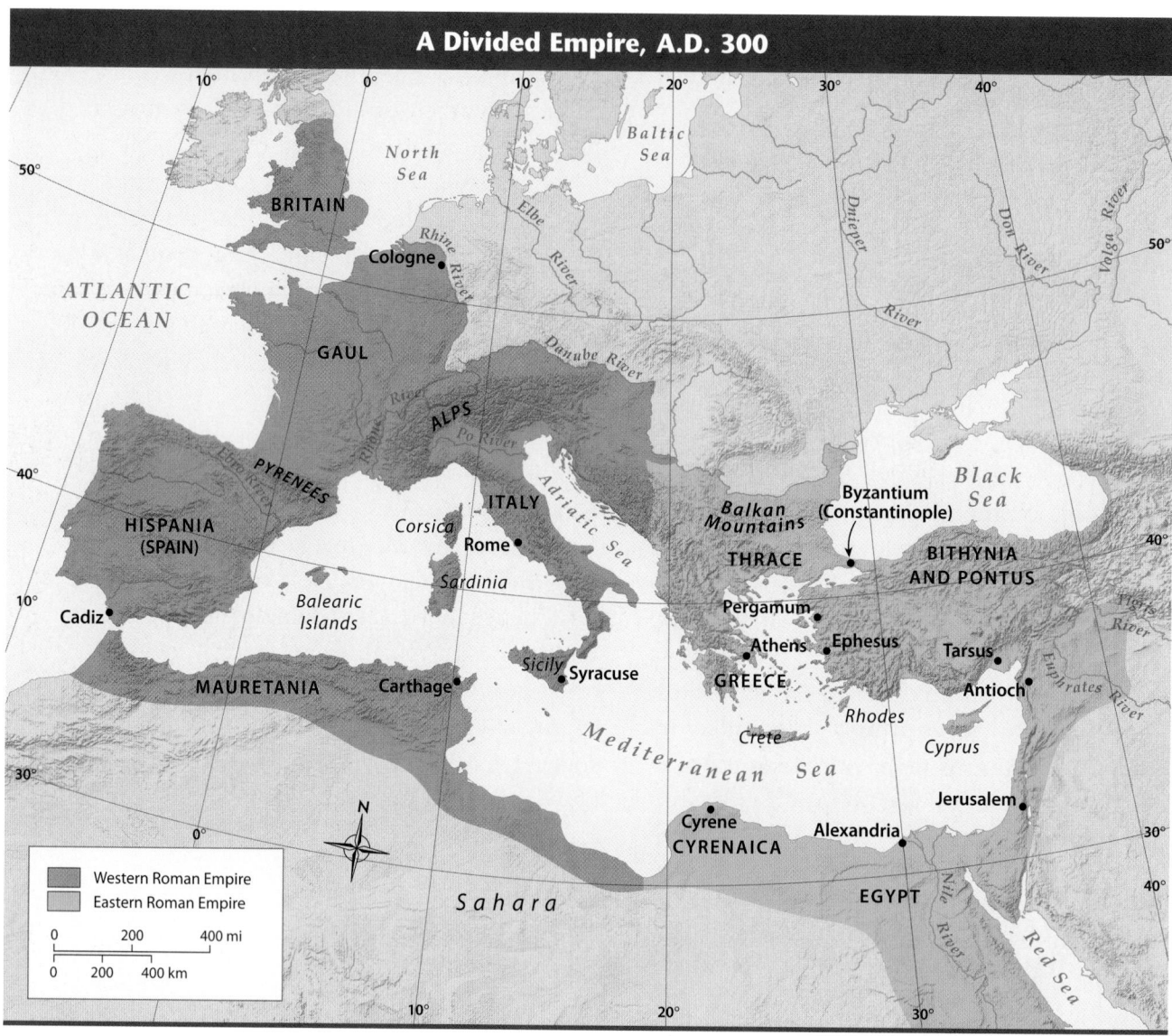

A Divided Empire, A.D. 300

To improve the administration and defense of the vast Roman Empire, the emperor Diocletian divided it into the Eastern Empire and the Western Empire.

Constantine wanted his new capital to be a second Rome. He built theaters, baths, forums, and Christian churches. Constantinople became the center of the Eastern branch of the Christian church. For the next eleven centuries, the city prospered.

The End of the Western Empire

As the Eastern Empire grew stronger, the Western Empire struggled. In Italy, roads and buildings fell into disrepair. War, famine, and disease took many lives. In many ways, the most serious threat came from the invading tribes, whom the Romans called "barbarians." Today people use the word *barbarian* to describe someone who is crude, coarse, or brutal. But in the study of history, the term refers to the tough, hard-fighting tribes perched along the Roman Empire's borders.

Barbarians Sack Rome

In the second half of the fourth century, the Huns, a nomadic people from central Asia, swept violently into Europe from the east. Under pressure from the Huns, Germanic tribes, such as the Visigoths, crossed the Danube River and moved into Roman territory.

192

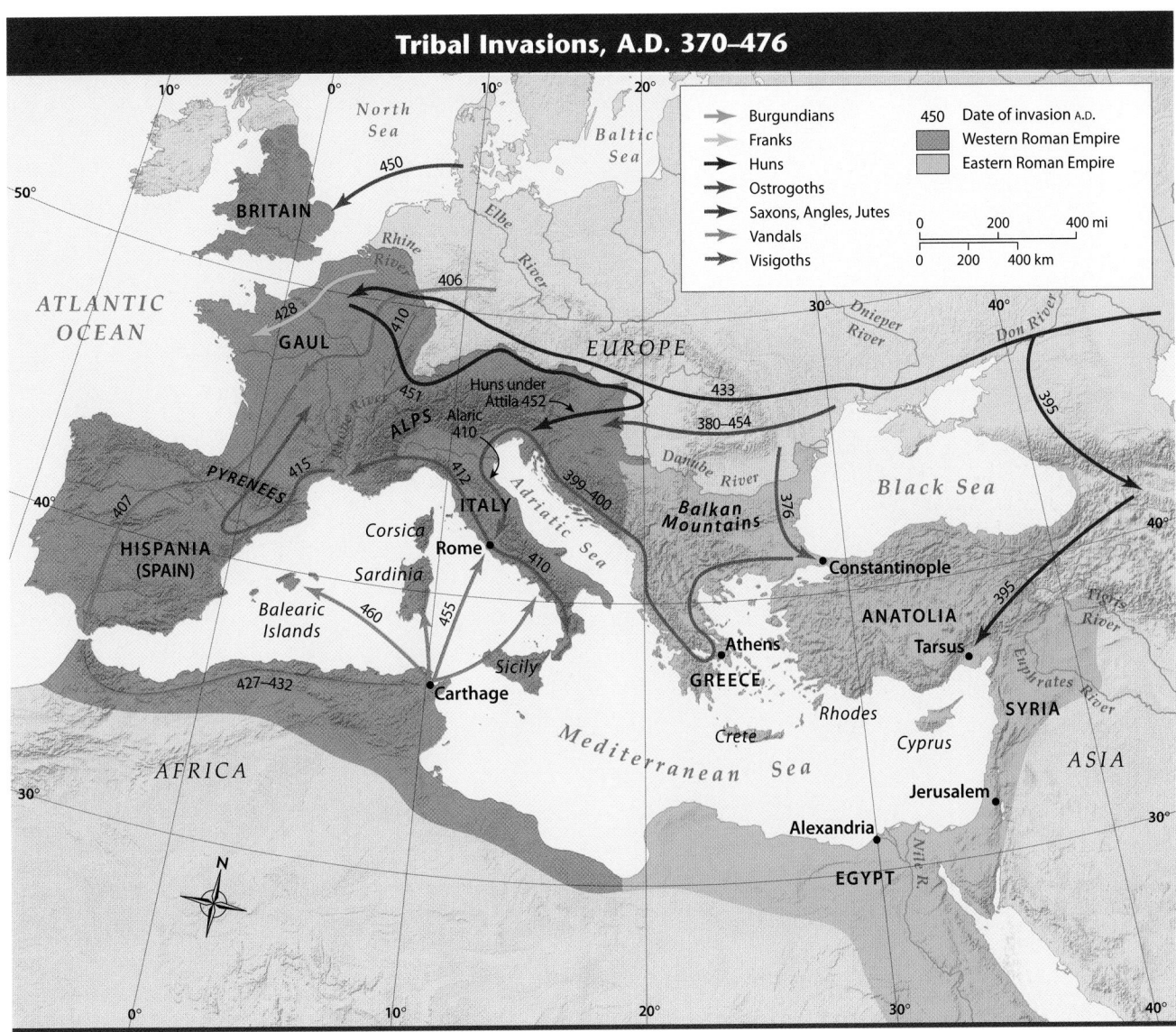

Tribal Invasions, A.D. 370–476

More than a century of invasion by Germanic tribes and Huns weakened both the Eastern and Western Roman Empires and led to the collapse of the Western Empire in A.D. 476.

The Roman emperor Valens allowed the Visigoths to settle on the south bank of the Danube. Valens hoped to enlist the Visigoths as allies and get tough new recruits for his army from among their ranks. When a famine broke out, however, the Romans refused to offer promised aid, and the Visigoths, desperate and starving, revolted. In 378, the Visigoths annihilated a Roman army at Adrianople and killed the emperor Valens.

In 410, the Visigoths captured Rome. They swarmed into the city and took everything they could lay their hands on. They toppled and

The Roots of "Barbarian"

Like many words in the English language, the word *barbarian* comes from the Greeks. The ancient Greeks used the word *barbaros* to describe anyone whose language they couldn't understand. To Greek ears, such people were making a noise that sounded like "ba, ba, ba" when they spoke. The Romans later picked up the term and used the word *barbarus* to describe people who couldn't speak Greek or Latin.

This ancient stone carving shows the once-invincible Roman soldiers battling fierce Germanic warriors. In the 400s, Rome's army found it increasingly difficult, and finally impossible, to withstand barbarian attacks.

melted down Rome's beautiful golden statues. They loaded their horses with bag after bag of Roman jewelry. When they had finished sacking the city, they burned a few buildings and marched away.

In the years that followed, waves of barbarian tribes swept back and forth across what were once Roman lands. The Vandals, driven from their lands by the Huns, invaded Gaul and fought their way to the Spanish coast. They left such devastation in their path that the modern word *vandal* means "destroyer of property."

In 429, Vandals conquered North Africa. In 455, they pushed into Italy and sacked the city of Rome. Meanwhile, the Franks occupied Gaul, while Angles and Saxons invaded Britain. The Huns, under their most ambitious leader, Attila, continued to ravage Europe.

The Last Emperor

As barbarian tribes crisscrossed Europe, battling each other and what was left of the once-feared Roman army, the Western Empire went through a series of mostly incompetent emperors. In 475, a powerful Roman general named Orestes announced a new emperor—his son, who was still just a boy.

Orestes dressed the child in imperial purple, and gave him the name Romulus Augustulus, the "little Augustus." For less than a year, the boy reigned as the last emperor of the west. In 476, Orestes' soldiers rebelled and murdered him. Taking pity on the child emperor, they sent Romulus Augustulus to live in southern Italy.

The year 476, when the last Roman emperor fell, is often cited as the date of the fall of the Western Roman Empire. But as you have seen, the

The ruins of the triumphal arch of the emperor Trajan (c. A.D. 100) in North Africa recall the glory and reach of the Roman Empire.

fall was gradual. It took place over many years, and was the result of multiple causes. Even as the Western Empire declined, people continued for years to speak Latin and follow Roman laws and customs. Only over time did Germanic culture become dominant as Roman cities and roads fell into ruin. And during these many centuries, the Eastern Empire continued to flourish, with its thriving center at Constantinople.

Rome's Legacy

The sprawling Roman Empire brought civilization to more people than ever before. After the fall of the Western Roman Empire, the European world went through a gradual transformation. As Germanic and other barbarian peoples established kingdoms with their own cultural identities, they continually looked backward, trying to match the glories achieved by the Roman Empire.

Rome's legacy remains powerful and evident to this day. Rome's influence permeates the modern world in language, law, architecture, engineering, government, and even sports.

Latin, the language of Rome, evolved into the modern languages known as Romance languages—Italian, French, Spanish, Portuguese, and Romanian. For fifteen hundred years or more, Latin persisted as the language of scholars and the Catholic Church. English, which is not a Romance language, was strongly influenced by Latin.

Rome's greatest legacy may be its ideas about law that still inform modern legal thinking and practice. The creation of the Twelve Tables enshrined Rome's commitment to law applied equally to all members of society. Many of today's legal protections originated as Roman laws, such as the idea that one is innocent until proven guilty. It is difficult to overstate the importance of these principles in democratic systems of government around the world, particularly in the West.

Many modern governments draw on examples of representative government pioneered during the Roman Republic. Modern legislative bodies, such as the U.S. Senate, were built on Roman models.

Modern Western civilization owes a great deal to Rome. The history of the Roman Empire is a study of both human potential and human weakness, an inspiring example of what a dedicated people can accomplish, and a somber warning of the dangers of unfettered power, unchecked ambition, and widespread corruption.

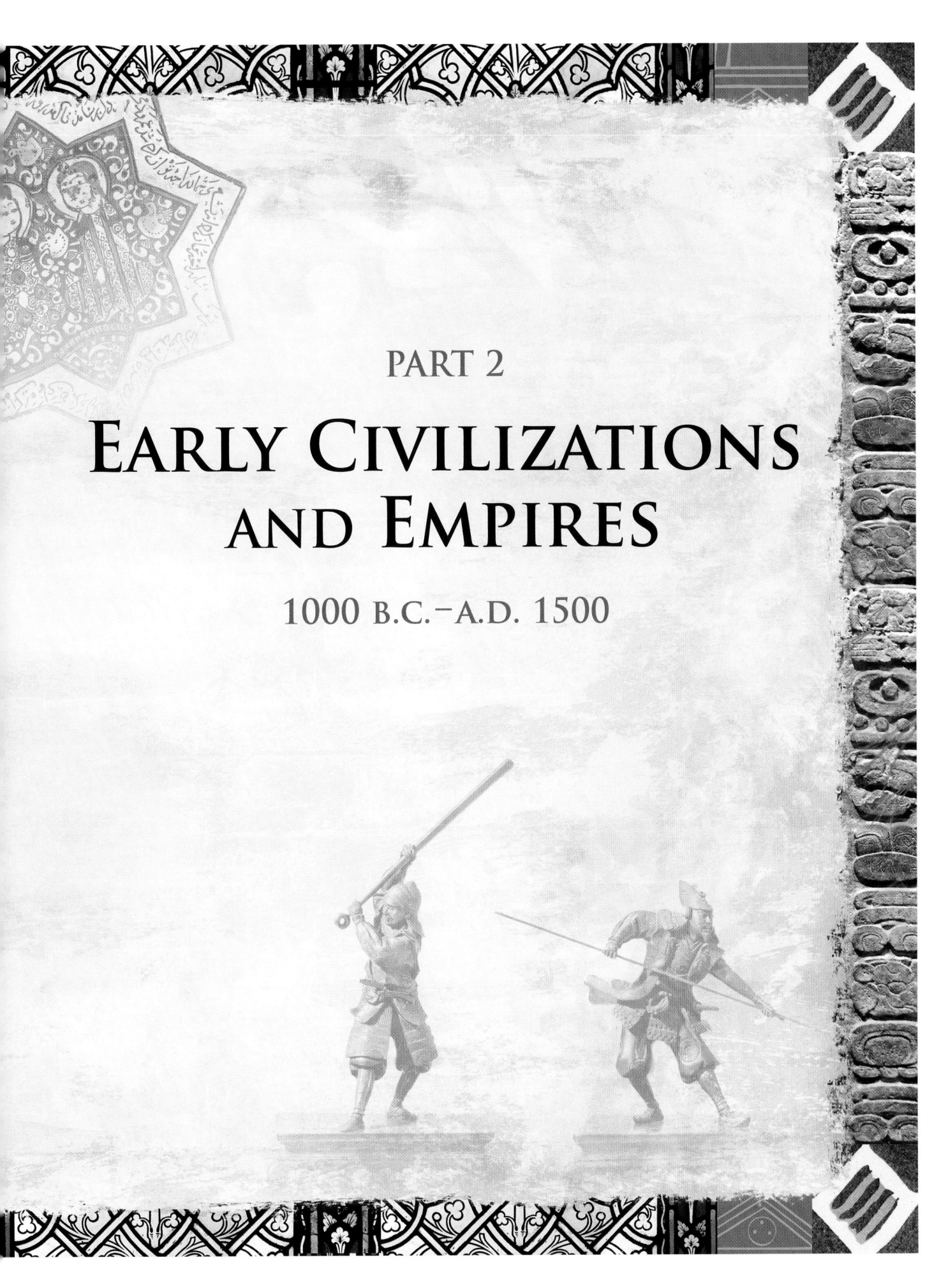

PART 2

EARLY CIVILIZATIONS AND EMPIRES

1000 B.C.–A.D. 1500

1000 B.C.

500 B.C.

c. 1200 B.C.
Olmec civilization
flourishes in Mesoamerica.

c. 1000 B.C.
Bantu migrations begin
from West Africa.

c. 450 B.C.
Meroë becomes the capital
of Kush in East Africa.

Buildings, artifacts, and artworks from the ancient civilizations of Africa, North America, and South America

Africa and the Americas

1000 B.C.–A.D. 700

A.D. 1

A.D. 500

C. A.D. 320
King Ezana declares
Christianity the official
religion of Aksum.

C. A.D. 500
Mayan civilization
reaches its height
in Mesoamerica.

*C*ivilization developed in different parts of the world at different times. Each civilization had its unique characteristics, but all civilizations followed a similar pattern as they evolved from simple agricultural villages to complex cities and societies. In some places, civilizations grew rapidly. Elsewhere, it took many thousands of years for people living in scattered villages to come together and form a civilization.

Long after the earliest complex societies developed in river valleys in Mesopotamia and along the Nile, civilizations arose in parts of Africa and the Americas. These civilizations built majestic monuments and splendid cities. Because few written records survive, our knowledge of these civilizations is limited mostly to archaeological evidence. As civilizations grew in Africa and the Americas, people had to adapt to different physical environments, just as earlier civilizations had done in other parts of the world. Over time, these new civilizations changed through contact with other cultures.

Diverse Land and Peoples in Africa

Key Questions

- How did the diverse geography of sub-Saharan Africa shape the lives of the early people living there?

- How did the Bantu migrations influence economies and cultures in eastern and southern Africa?

- How did Kush and Aksum become major trading centers? Why did they lose power?

Africa, the second-largest continent after Asia, covers a land surface three times larger than the United States. The vast continent is a land of diverse terrains and climates.

Africa's Diverse Geography

The largest desert in the world, the **Sahara**, dominates the northern third of Africa. The Sahara stretches from the Atlantic coast to the Red Sea. Only a few plants and animals can survive in the dry, hot conditions.

Immediately south of the Sahara, the barren desert gives way to a narrow band of dry, flat, scrubby grasslands that stretch across the continent. This region is called the **Sahel** (sah-HEL), from an Arabic word meaning "shore," perhaps because the Sahara seemed like an ocean of sand. The Sahel marks the southern boundary of the Sahara.

Farther south, beyond the Sahel, the land rises slightly and becomes the African **savanna**. The savanna covers about 40 percent of the continent. Much of the savanna consists of open, grassy plains dotted by trees, but the region also includes mountainous areas and tropical swamplands. The savanna attracts huge herds of grazing animals, such as gazelles and zebras. They in turn attract predators, such as lions, leopards, and humans.

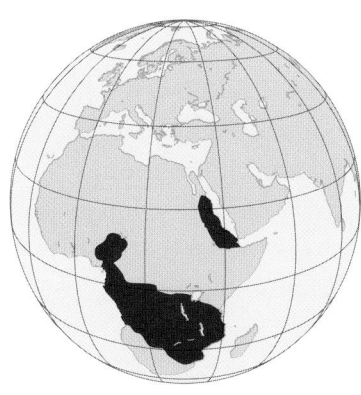

Africa's early peoples adapted to many environments.

The Serengeti Plain in East Africa, now a national park, is home to a wide variety of wildlife.

201

Most people in Africa live on the savanna, where the land and climate support agricultural production. Many people also live in the coastal areas on the extreme northern and southern coasts of Africa. There, the mild climate and fertile soil favor settlement and population growth.

In East Africa, the Serengeti (sehr-uhn-GET-ee) Plain covers over 5,700 square miles (14,763 square km). It is home to an annual migration of wildebeests that began when the first humans hunted them some thirty thousand years ago.

Also in East Africa, the Great Rift Valley runs along the continent from north to south. Formed by powerful geologic forces, the Rift Valley stretches for 3,480 miles (5,600 km) from Jordan in the Middle East to South Africa. The deepest parts of the Rift Valley have filled with water, creating Lake Victoria, the second-largest freshwater lake in the world, and Lake Tanganyika (tan-guhn-YEE-kuh), one of the deepest. Up and down the Rift Valley, archaeologists have discovered numerous fossils of early human ancestors, especially in places like Olduvai Gorge, where geologic upheaval has exposed layers of ancient rocks.

Africa is home to some of the world's great rivers, including the world's longest river, the Nile, which is 4,160 miles (6,690 km) long. The Congo River stretches 2,880 miles (4,630 km) through central Africa. The main river in western Africa, the Niger (NIY-jur), runs for 2,550 miles (4,100 km). With the important exception of the Nile, many African rivers are not navigable as they approach the coast. For example, along the Congo and Niger rivers, rapids, waterfalls, and silted shallows hamper travel. Nevertheless, Africa's rivers provided the life-giving water that attracted early humans to settle and take the first steps toward building civilizations.

Surrounding the Congo River in the heart of Africa is a tropical **rain forest**. With a thick canopy of trees, creeping vines, shrubs, and other plants, Africa's rain forest is home to more than half of the continent's animal species. Rain forests also once covered much of the West African coast, but in recent decades human activity has destroyed large expanses of these forests.

In the southern part of the continent is another vast desert, the Kalahari (kah-lah-HAH-ree). Unlike the Sahara, parts of the Kalahari receive a small amount of rain each year. This moisture allows an assortment of scrubby plants to grow in parts of the desert. The Kalahari is home to a variety of animals, including hyenas, jackals, lions, meerkats, giraffes, and several kinds of antelope.

Early Peoples of Africa

Africa is an enormous continent whose diverse geography has long influenced where and how its people live. Africa's earliest people were hunter-gatherers. Over time, many turned to nomadic, pastoral herding.

The Changing Land

If you were to look out over the Sahara now, you would see a barren landscape of sand dunes and vast gray expanses of rock and gravel. Ten thousand years ago, however, you would have seen lakes, rivers, and grasslands. Back then, rain fell plentifully in North Africa, and the environment supported humans who lived by herding and farming.

These early peoples left their mark on the region by painting on thousands of massive stones

Older than Lucy

In 2009, archaeologists announced a major new discovery in the study of human origins. Working in Africa's Great Rift Valley, researchers uncovered the partial skeleton of a female who stood under four feet (1.2 m) tall and lived 4.4 million years ago, more than one million years earlier than "Lucy," the oldest hominid found previously. Scientists dubbed the skeleton "Ardi," and refer to her as "Lucy's older sister."

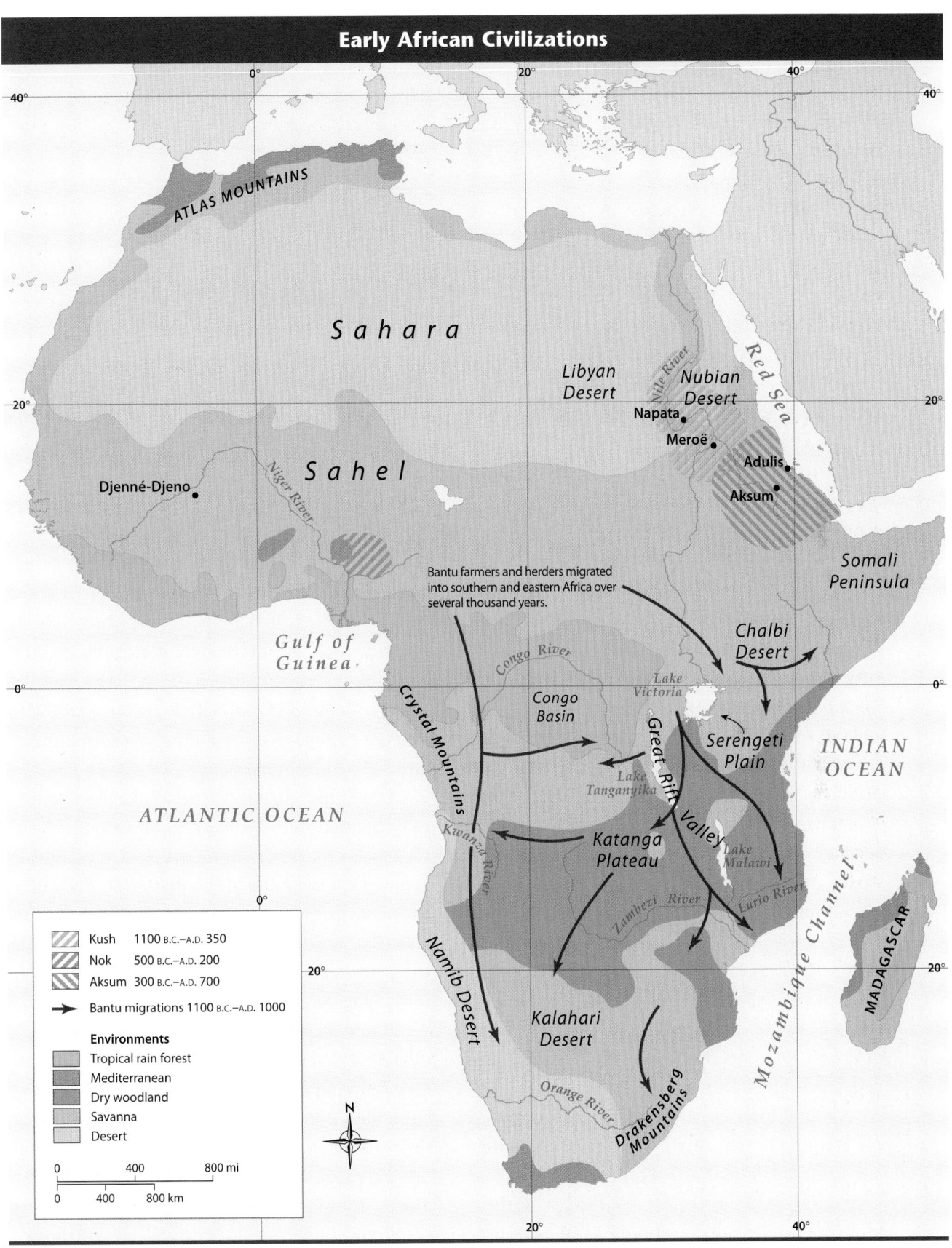

Early African Civilizations

ATLAS MOUNTAINS

Sahara

Libyan Desert

Nubian Desert

Napata

Meroë

Adulis

Aksum

Red Sea

Nile River

Sahel

Djenné-Djeno

Niger River

Somali Peninsula

Bantu farmers and herders migrated into southern and eastern Africa over several thousand years.

Gulf of Guinea

Congo River

Congo Basin

Chalbi Desert

Lake Victoria

Serengeti Plain

INDIAN OCEAN

Crystal Mountains

Lake Tanganyika

Great Rift Valley

ATLANTIC OCEAN

Kwanza River

Katanga Plateau

Lake Malawi

Zambezi River

Lurio River

Mozambique Channel

MADAGASCAR

Namib Desert

Kalahari Desert

Orange River

Drakensberg Mountains

Legend:

Kush	1100 B.C.–A.D. 350
Nok	500 B.C.–A.D. 200
Aksum	300 B.C.–A.D. 700
→	Bantu migrations 1100 B.C.–A.D. 1000

Environments
- Tropical rain forest
- Mediterranean
- Dry woodland
- Savanna
- Desert

0   400   800 mi

0   400   800 km

N

Early African civilizations, through migration and trade, spread their culture and technology across the diverse topography of Africa.

203

Prehistoric paintings on massive rock outcroppings depict herds of cattle and human hunters.

jutting up from the land. The paintings, made over a period of three to four thousand years, date back to about 8000 B.C., with the largest number of paintings dating from 3500 to 2500 B.C. The paintings show hunters stalking buffalo and elephants, animals now gone from the Sahara. The paintings also illustrate that these ancient inhabitants of Africa herded sheep, goats, and cattle on the rain-fed plains.

About five thousand years ago, the rains over the Sahara began to decline. Over the next centuries, the grasslands slowly gave way to desert. The people moved to more welcoming terrain. Some headed east, toward the fertile floodplains of the Nile. Others headed south, to what is now called sub-Saharan Africa.

As they journeyed, different groups of people adapted to the different environments they encountered. Some settled on rivers and inland lakes and became expert fishermen. Others moved into the rain forest and lived as hunter-gatherers. But the rain forest, though rich in plants and animals, was too dense to support large human populations. Eventually human civilizations would arise in the Sahel and on the plains of the savanna, where grasses grew wild and the land proved more hospitable for farming and human settlement.

The earliest African farmers followed a pattern that occurred all over the world. At first, they gathered grains that grew wild and used these grains to supplement their diet of fish and game. Over time, they learned to plant and cultivate the grains. By 1000 B.C., agriculture in Africa had spread from the Upper Nile (the southern stretch of the river) to the edge of the western rain forest.

Farmers grew sorghum and millet, two types of grasses that produce nourishing grain. In West Africa, around the wetlands of the Niger River, they cultivated rice. As farming techniques advanced, people settled, formed communities, and developed traditions as diverse as the land. In some places, these farmers relied on rainfall to water their crops, unlike the river-valley civilizations (such as in ancient Mesopotamia and Egypt) that relied on flooding rivers and irrigation.

Family and Religion

The early people who moved south of the Sahara shared many common ideas about their communities and the world. For all of them, the extended family was the foundation of society. Some families who shared ancestors formed groups called **clans**. Africa's earliest villages likely included members from one or more clans. As villages grew, some clan members moved off to establish new settlements, but remained connected to neighboring villages through kinship and shared traditions.

These early Africans had a deep respect for their family elders, both male and female. In religious rituals they honored dead ancestors, whom they believed watched over the living.

In addition to worshipping ancestors, most early African peoples believed in a god who had created the world. To many early people, the creator god was distant and remote, too far removed to have much impact on people's lives. Thus most early people focused their religious practices not on the creator but rather on the many spirits that they believed inhabited the world.

The idea that spiritual and supernatural forces act through all aspects of nature is called **animism**. Early African peoples believed that powerful spirits resided in trees, rivers, plants, animals, and even rocks. They believed these invisible powers acted in everyday life, and that they might do good or evil. Some people wore charms to ward off evil spirits. They consulted priests whom they believed could influence the spiritual powers working through nature.

Telling Stories

Most early African peoples had no system of writing. To transmit their culture from one generation to the next, they used memory and storytelling. In West Africa, they relied on oral tradition as embodied in important members of society called **griots** (GREE-ohs).

Some modern historians describe griots as "talking books." Griots passed on stories from times long past. They told myths that explained

Hunter-Gatherers Today

Some African hunter-gatherer societies never settled down in agricultural communities. As in other areas of the world, some of their descendants continue to follow their ancient nomadic ways of life. On the savanna of modern-day Kenya and Tanzania, the Dorobo live off the land, gathering wild fruits and hunting small game. In the Kalahari Desert, the people called the San still live as hunter-gatherers. Similarly, in the rain forests of the Congo, the Baka people survive by hunting, fishing, and collecting plants such as yams and palm nuts.

A modern-day San bushman stalks his prey.

the world around them. They shared proverbs that instructed people on how to live.

Using rhythmic music to accompany their storytelling, griots also kept recent history alive, sometimes offering commentary on current events. They helped people understand themselves and the world around them by conveying knowledge and traditions from one generation to the next.

The Nok

In 1928, while working near the tiny village of Nok (nahk) in the West African nation of Nigeria, a group of miners dug up a finely crafted piece of pottery. It was made from a baked clay called terra-cotta and shaped like a monkey's head. The miners had unearthed the first artifacts from a previously unknown African culture. Archaeologists have since discovered hundreds more pieces of terra-cotta sculpture made by the ancient people called the Nok, named after the village where they lived.

The Nok left no written records, so all we know of them comes from the artifacts they left behind. The Nok occupied an area northeast of the Niger River, in what is now Nigeria. They lived along streams in the grasslands where the Sahel meets the savanna. They grew sorghum and built homes of brick made from clay, straw, and mud, which is why their villages have long since disappeared.

As early as 500 B.C., the Nok forged iron, which they used to make weapons for hunting and tools for farming. Archaeologists have found the remains of specialized ovens in which the Nok melted rocks to extract iron. Historians remain unsure if the Nok learned ironworking from people in North Africa, or if they invented it independently. Nevertheless, iron technology helped Nok culture to thrive for more than eight hundred years.

Djenné-Djeno

Some nine hundred miles (1450 km) up the Niger River from the center of Nok culture, in what is now the country of Mali, another people who specialized in ironmaking built a large and prosperous city, Djenné-Djeno (jeh-NAY- jeh-NOH). Archaeological evidence suggests that the area was first occupied around 300 B.C., when nomadic herders on the Sahel settled on the fertile floodplain of the Niger to grow rice.

This terra-cotta sculpture dates to the ancient Nok culture.

By the third century B.C., the people in Djenné-Djeno had learned to smelt iron. Archaeologists have found iron knives, as well as pottery, jewelry, and toys. By A.D. 800, the city was the center of a flourishing trade network. Djenné-Djeno inhabitants traded iron, copper, and pottery up and down the Niger River as far as five hundred miles (805 km) away. At its peak, the city was home to perhaps fifty thousand people.

Djenné-Djeno began declining around A.D. 1100, possibly as a result of diseases that arrived from Europe. After A.D. 1400, the city was all but empty.

The Bantu Migrations

Human history is shaped by the movement, settlement, and interaction of different peoples. You have learned how the human story has been influenced by migrations, when large groups of people leave one place and travel a long distance to settle in another place. Early humans migrated for many reasons. Some migrated for reasons related to environmental changes—a changing climate might lead to a dwindling food supply. Some migrated for political reasons, such as the desire to flee from invaders. In later times, especially in our modern industrial age, people have migrated for economic reasons, leaving impoverished homelands to find work and a better life in some distant place.

One of the largest human migrations in history occurred over many centuries in Africa. Historians vary in their estimates of the time of these migrations, but beginning at least two thousand years ago, and continuing for more than a thousand years, the Bantu-speaking peoples began to migrate. These were not a single people but various groups who spoke one of the hundreds of languages that linguists categorize as Bantu.

From a region just south of the Sahara (part of present-day Nigeria), various Bantu-speaking peoples migrated to the south and east, spreading over much of the African continent below the equator. Like the movement of Indo-Europeans out of central Asia (see chapter 4), the long migration from western Africa was the result of push and pull factors.

One factor that pushed some groups of Bantu-speaking peoples to migrate was their use of slash-and-burn agriculture. Using this method, people cleared forests by cutting down trees, burning them, or both. Farmers cultivated the cleared land until the nutrients in the soil were depleted. Then they had to move on to new land, where they would again clear the forests, plant crops, and again move on when the soil was no longer productive. Because much of Africa's soil is relatively poor in nutrients to begin with, slash-and-burn agriculture pushed farming communities to move often.

Another push factor in the migrations of Bantu-speaking peoples was **desertification**, the process by which a desert expands. As the Sahara became drier and more barren, the desert grew larger. It pushed south, transforming once-fertile areas of the Sahel into uninhabitable wasteland. The desertification that enlarged the Sahara pushed the farmers who saw their cropland

Ongoing Desertification

The gradual expansion of the Sahara that began about five thousand years ago has not stopped. In fact, the continual desertification of agricultural land in Africa is one of the biggest challenges facing the continent today. While the expansion of the desert has been driven by climate change over many thousands of years, human activities have also sped up the process. For example, domesticated herds of grazing animals continue to add to desertification in Africa.

swallowed up by sand. The relatively fertile areas of the African savanna provided a pull to help launch the long migrations.

An early wave of migration brought Bantu-speaking peoples to the edges of the great rain forest surrounding the Congo River, where many settled in small villages. The dense forest did not allow for large farms. Some Bantu-speaking groups continued southeast, drawn to the open savanna, which was better suited for agriculture. Other groups migrated south and settled along the west coast of southern Africa, where they raised goats, sheep, and cattle on the grassy plains above the Kalahari.

At times the migrations advanced rapidly. At other times, they slowed almost to a halt as people stayed in the same villages for generations, before being pushed to move by an increasing population and the need for more land and food.

Bantu-speaking peoples had spread out across almost all of sub-Saharan Africa by A.D. 400. They brought more than just their languages and

Even today, the process of desertification continues to expand the Sahara, with its vast windswept dunes and rocky stretches.

Bantu Languages

The Bantu-speaking peoples brought their languages with them on their journeys, and these languages changed over time. Hundreds of modern African languages evolved from an original Bantu language, which no longer exists. Today, mainly in countries on the east coast of Africa, many millions of people still speak a Bantu language called Swahili (swah-HEE-lee) or Kiswahili. Over time, the Swahili language has been influenced by Arabic, the language most commonly spoken in Africa.

cultures. They carried iron tools and weapons that allowed them to dominate the nomadic bands of hunter-gatherers they displaced. Over time, the Bantu migrants established permanent settlements and developed distinct cultural traditions. Their descendants still live throughout sub-Saharan Africa today.

East African Kingdoms

In about 1400 B.C., Egyptian traders headed south to the land called Nubia, in what is now Sudan, where they bartered for goods from the African heartland. According to one ancient stone tablet, the traders returned to Egypt with gold, ivory, ebony (a dark wood used for ornamental sculpture), leopard skins, and more than a hundred enslaved people.

Unlike West African farming societies, East African civilizations supported themselves mainly through trade. Nubia's location made it a busy center of trade, as goods and resources from central and sub-Saharan Africa

passed through the region on their way to Egypt and the people of the Mediterranean world. Nubian traders grew rich and powerful by controlling nearly all the commerce up and down the southern half of the Nile.

The Kingdom of Kush

As Nubia thrived through trade, the people of Nubia created a powerful kingdom that the Egyptians called Kush. The rulers of Kush modeled themselves on Egyptian pharaohs. They built enormous pyramids for burial, and decorated tombs with Egyptian-style art. The people of Kush also embraced Egyptian culture and religion, and wore Egyptian fashions. As you have learned, around 750 B.C., the Kushites, led by a king named Piankhi, marched north and conquered Egypt. Kushite pharaohs continued to rule Egypt for nearly a century (see chapter 3). In Nubia, the leaders of Kush established their capital city at Napata.

In the mid-600s B.C., Assyrian conquerors pushed the Kushites out of Egypt. In Nubia, Kush continued to control the Upper Nile for hundreds of years. Around 450 B.C., the Kushites moved their capital from Napata to

Statues show Nubian pharaohs who modeled themselves on Egyptian rulers by building gigantic burial pyramids and assuming Egyptian fashion, culture, and religion.

The steep-sided pyramids at Meroë were built over the burial chambers of Kush rulers, c. 300 B.C.–A.D. 300.

Meroë (MEHR-oh-ee), a city between the Fifth and Sixth cataracts of the Nile. Meroë was located on a fertile plain. Nearby forests provided plenty of timber, essential fuel for forging iron. In Meroë, the Kushites produced great quantities of iron weapons and tools. Archaeologists working at the site of the ancient city have unearthed huge heaps of slag, a by-product of smelting iron.

The Greek historian Herodotus described the magnificence of Meroë in the fifth century B.C.: "There gold is obtained in great plenty, huge elephants abound, with wild trees of all sorts, and ebony; and the men are taller, handsomer, and longer lived than anywhere else."

As Meroë's fame spread, so did the variety of goods the people traded—ivory, gold, ebony, fine jewels, fragrances, and enslaved people. In time, Kush not only controlled the profitable trade moving down the Nile, but also the sea routes to the east and land routes west. By the first century B.C., the Kushites were sending caravans of camels across the Sahara to the North African coast, and shipping goods across the sea to India.

The Rise of Aksum

Kush thrived for many centuries. But the Roman Empire's conquest of Egypt in the first century B.C. led to disaster for Kush. The Romans devastated Kushite territory and carried thousands off to slavery. Though Kush continued to trade with Rome and other peoples for the next two hundred years, the

The Early Slave Trade in Africa

Much like early civilizations in other parts of the world, early African societies relied on slaves to perform hard labor on farms, in mines, and in mills. Slaves might be warriors captured in battle, or people kidnapped from hunter-gatherer tribes or farming villages. Beginning in the seventh and eighth centuries A.D., the slave trade expanded as Arab merchants in North Africa sold enslaved people from the African heartland to buyers throughout the Mediterranean world.

defeat greatly diminished its power. By the third century A.D., power and wealth shifted from Kush to another East African kingdom, Aksum (AHK-sum).

The kingdom of Aksum was located in what are now the countries of Eritrea and Ethiopia, in an area known as the Horn of Africa. The capital city, also called Aksum, lay southeast of Meroë, in the high country of modern-day Ethiopia. Historians believe the city of Aksum was founded as a trading outpost by Arabs from across the Red Sea, probably sometime during the sixth century B.C.

The city grew and prospered as a busy hub on the trade routes from Egypt and Meroë to the bustling port city of Adulis (AHD-uh-luhs) on the Red Sea. The location of Adulis gave traders access to routes up the Red Sea to the Mediterranean, or through the Gulf of Aden to the Arabian Sea, and from there to the Persian Gulf and all the way to India.

During the second and third centuries A.D., as Aksum took greater control of trade once controlled by Kush, the kingdom's wealth and power grew. As Aksum expanded, it became an increasingly cosmopolitan kingdom, attracting diverse people from various lands.

Greeks, Romans, Egyptians, Persians, Arabs, Indians, and more came to do business. All wanted to buy salt and gold from West Africa, as well as luxuries including ivory, rhinoceros horn, and frankincense (an aromatic product from tree resins). Roman traders especially sought gold to meet the needs of their growing empire's monetary system. In turn, the Aksumite merchants bought silk and spices, glass, wine, olive oil, and goods made of brass and copper. Amid the many tongues spoken, Greek was the main language of business.

King Ezana Adopts Christianity

The kingdom of Aksum reached its height in the mid-300s A.D. under a strong king named Ezana (AY-zah-nah). Ezana expanded Aksum's territory. He conquered the southern part of the Arabian Peninsula (what is now the country of Yemen). He invaded Kush, and in A.D. 350, his troops burned the once-thriving city of Meroë.

King Ezana is perhaps best remembered for making Christianity the official religion of Aksum. The cosmopolitan population of Aksum held a variety of beliefs. Most Aksumites were animists who also worshipped a creator god. Trade brought Jews and Buddhists to the kingdom. Many Christians also came, especially from the Roman Empire, where Christianity was rapidly gaining converts in the early to mid-300s.

Around A.D. 320, King Ezana converted to Christianity and declared it the official religion of Aksum. Some historians think that his conversion was motivated by a desire to maintain trading relationships with the Mediterranean world. Nevertheless, Ezana established an important religious tradition for Ethiopia. While many religions are practiced in Ethiopia today, the majority of the people are Christian. More than twenty million Ethiopians belong to the Ethiopian Orthodox Church, a branch of Christianity with some distinct beliefs and practices of its own.

Innovation and Decline

Among the ancient African kingdoms, Aksum was unusual in some ways. Besides Egypt and Meroë, Aksum is the only ancient African kingdom we

The wealthy kingdom of Aksum lay in the high country that is modern-day Ethiopia.

A sixth-century religious manuscript from an Aksum monastery is evidence of Ethiopia's Christian traditions.

know of that had a system of writing. The written language of Aksum was called Geez (gee-EHZ), brought by early Arab inhabitants. The New Testament was translated into Geez.

Aksum was also the first sub-Saharan kingdom to mint its own coins. The Aksumites minted coins of gold, silver, and copper, which helped them facilitate trade and control commerce.

In agriculture, the Aksumites found ways to adapt to the rugged, hilly terrain where they lived. They used terrace cultivation, a method of growing crops on hillsides by planting on flat ridges, resembling a staircase, built into the slopes. The terraces helped retain water and prevented soil erosion.

As Aksumite kings grew increasingly wealthy and powerful, some erected giant stone monuments called *stelae* (STEE-lee). Some stelae still stand in Ethiopia today. More than 140 stelae were erected in the city of Aksum. These tall stone obelisks marked the graves of rulers or commemorated important events. The largest stele—standing over a hundred feet (30 m) tall and weighing more than seven hundred tons (635 metric tons)—was carved from a single block of granite that had been

moved more than two miles (3 km) through the mountains.

Aksum prospered for eight hundred years, until the eighth century, when Arab and Persian traders took over the commerce flowing out of Africa. Aksum fell to invaders who followed a new and rapidly spreading religion, Islam. (You will read more about Islam in an upcoming chapter.) In A.D. 710, Islamic invaders destroyed the port city of Adulis. Aksum's leaders moved their capital to the north, and soon found themselves isolated as a Christian outpost in an increasingly Islamic region. Like other African civilizations, Aksum at its height enjoyed great wealth and influence, but its influence did not expand beyond a limited geographic region.

The tallest of the giant stelae monuments of Aksum was created around the time the court adopted Christianity.

211

Primary Source

Trading for Gold in Aksum

In the sixth century A.D., Cosmas, a Greek merchant and geographer, traveled in Asia and Africa. His travels took him to the empire of Aksum. In his writings, Cosmas includes the following description of the highly ritualized trade for gold that took place in what he calls "the country known as that of Sasu," in the far south of the Aksum, part of what is now Ethiopia.

The country known as that of Sasu is itself near the ocean, just as the ocean is near the frankincense country, in which there are many gold mines. The King of the Aksumites…sends thither special agents to bargain for the gold, and these are accompanied by many other traders—upwards, say, of five hundred—bound on the same errand as themselves. They take along with them to the mining district oxen, lumps of salt, and iron, and when they reach its neighborhood they make a halt at a certain spot and form an encampment, which they fence round with a great hedge of thorns. Within this they live, and having slaughtered the oxen, cut them in pieces, and lay the pieces on the top of the thorns, along with the lumps of salt and the iron.

Then come the natives bringing gold in nuggets like peas, called tancharas, and lay one or two or more of these upon what pleases them—the pieces of flesh or the salt or the iron, and then they retire to some distance off. Then the owner of the meat approaches, and if he is satisfied he takes the gold away, and upon seeing this its owner comes and takes the flesh or the salt or the iron. If, however, he is not satisfied, he leaves the gold, when the native seeing that he has not taken it, comes and either puts down more gold, or takes up what he had laid down, and goes away.

Such is the mode in which business is transacted with the people of that country, because their language is different and interpreters are hardly to be found. The time they stay in that country is five days more or less, according as the natives more or less readily coming forward buy up all their wares. On the journey homeward they all agree to travel well armed, since some of the tribes through whose country they must pass might threaten to attack them from a desire to rob them of their gold. The space of six months is taken up with this trading expedition, including both the going and the returning.

The Earliest Civilizations in the Americas

You have learned about early civilizations in Asia, Africa, and Europe. Now we turn to the development of civilization in the Americas—the continents of North and South America, and the land called Mesoamerica (meh-zoh-uh-MER-ih-kuh), which includes much of Mexico and Central America.

The Earliest Americans

Recent archaeological research suggests that the first humans arrived in North America some twelve to thirteen thousand years ago, and perhaps much earlier than that. Scholars think that these people were hunters from Asia who arrived in North America by crossing a land bridge, a huge swath of solid ground connecting the continents of Asia and North America. This land bridge, known as Beringia (buh-RIHN-jee-uh), now lies beneath the Bering Sea. During the last Ice Age, however, sea levels were lower than they are today, thus exposing land that is now underwater.

The land bridge that once linked Siberia to Alaska was some 750 miles (1207 km) wide from north to south. It was covered with grassy plains that attracted large grazing mammals such as woolly mammoths and bison. When these animals began migrating across the land bridge into North America, they were followed by nomadic hunter-gatherers from Asia. (Some recent

Key Questions

- What were the earliest civilizations in the Americas? How were they like older civilizations in Europe and Asia? How were they different?

- Why is so little known about the early peoples of South America?

The sites of early civilizations in the Americas

Archaeologists think that hunters from Asia followed big game into North America.

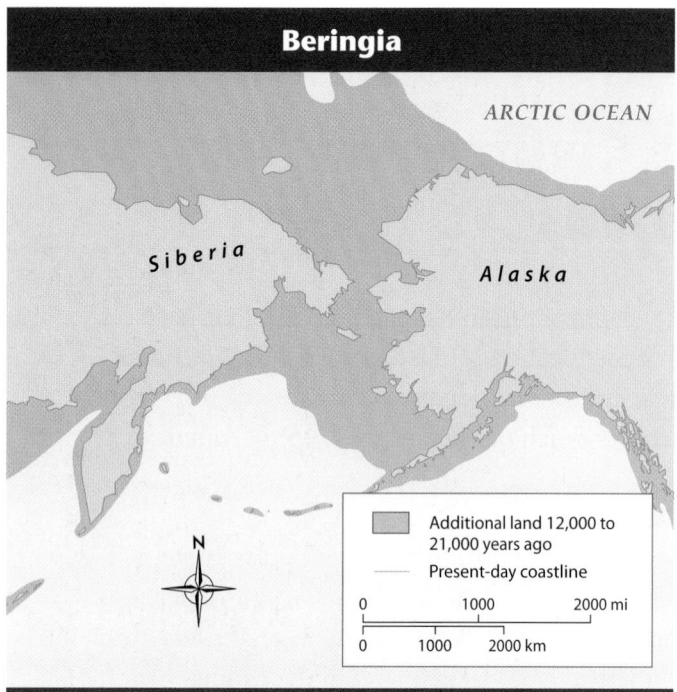

Beringia

ARCTIC OCEAN

Siberia

Alaska

Additional land 12,000 to 21,000 years ago

Present-day coastline

| 0 | 1000 | 2000 mi |
| 0 | 1000 | 2000 km |

N

Historians think that 12,000–13,000 years ago, nomadic hunter-gatherers crossed Beringia to North America.

archaeological findings suggest that some of these people may have sailed rather than walked.) Over time, some of these nomads followed the herds southward along the eastern edge of the Rocky Mountains. Some moved east into the Great Plains. Others trekked farther south.

Settling in Mesoamerica

As the earth slowly warmed and the oceans rose, the descendants of the earliest migrants populated the continents of North and South America. Some settled in Mesoamerica. The name *Mesoamerica* means "middle America" (*meso* means "middle" in Greek and Latin). Mesoamerica stretches from central Mexico south to northern Central America. Geographers consider Mesoamerica part of the North American continent.

The terrain of Mesoamerica varies from tropical rain forests in the eastern lowlands to pine forests atop the mountains of central Mexico. Desert covers vast stretches of the north. Early migrants were drawn to central Mesoamerica by the region's fertile soils and a wide variety of plants and animals.

Early inhabitants of Mesoamerica hunted deer and small game, such as rabbits. They fished and collected wild fruits, seeds, and nuts. Beginning around 7000 B.C., they cultivated squash and chili peppers.

At first, the people relied more on hunting and foraging for food than on farming. Over time, they learned to cultivate new crops, such as sweet potatoes, beans, and manioc, a starchy root vegetable. Sometime around 3000 B.C., the early inhabitants of Mesoamerica began growing **maize**, or corn. This crop would transform their lives and help make possible the rise of the first true civilizations in the Americas.

Maize grew in a variety of climates, from the highlands to the lowlands. Maize provided excellent nutrition. It could be harvested, dried, and stored in large amounts, enough to feed a large population throughout the year. By 2000 B.C., maize cultivation had spread throughout Mesoamerica.

The early settlers in Mesoamerica followed a pattern common to agricultural societies all over the world. They came together to form villages. The farmers among them were able to grow a surplus of maize. Surpluses led to specialized work. Complex social relationships developed, along with advanced forms of government, art, and architecture. Archaeologists generally agree that by 1200 B.C.—about the time the Egyptians were building their temples and the Greeks were fighting their Trojan Wars—civilization was taking shape in the Americas.

The Olmec

In the late 1850s, a farmer in southern Mexico was clearing land for a cornfield when his shovel clanged against something hard. At first he thought he had discovered a large upside-down iron cauldron. As he unearthed the object, however, he was surprised to find a giant human head carved from volcanic stone. The sculpture weighed nearly forty tons (36.3 metric tons), with a circumference over twenty feet (6 m).

Who crafted the enormous head? For many decades, the answer remained a mystery. Then, in the 1930s and 1940s, archaeologists discovered more colossal sculptures in the area, as well as other artifacts including lifelike figurines, intricate jewelry, and fragments of pottery dating back some three thousand years. These artifacts gave researchers a glimpse into the world of the Olmec (OHL-mehk), sometimes called America's first civilization.

Living in the land south of Mexico's Gulf coast, the Olmec flourished between 1200 and 400 B.C. Fertile soil meant plentiful harvests of maize, the chief Olmec crop. As populations increased, villages built along the numerous rivers grew into towns, and some of these grew into cities.

By 1000 B.C., one important Olmec city covered almost three square miles (7.75 square km).

The "Rubber People"

Historians remain unsure what name the Olmec used for themselves. The name, which means "rubber people," comes from the language of a later people in Mexico. The Olmec were the first people to make rubber, which they derived from the sap of a tree that grew in the rain forest. They turned the rubber into hard balls used to play a traditional game in which two teams competed on a long court. Players tried to score points by hitting the ball through a goal without using their hands or feet. Even after Olmec civilization faded away, the game remained important to Mesoamerican culture. A later version of the game was called *juego de pelota* (WAY-goh thay pay-LOH-tuh), which is Spanish for "ball game."

Archaeologists discovered this nine-foot-tall (2.75 m) stone head in Mexico. The Olmec left behind many such heads.

It was home to an enormous palace complex, hundreds of residences, and an underground aqueduct that provided clean drinking water. Another Olmec city featured a pyramid one hundred feet (30 m) high, completed around 400 B.C., that likely served as a center of religious ceremonies.

The Olmec built irrigation canals, ditches, and dams. They cleared forests, constructed roads, and polished iron ore to create brilliant mirrors for use in religious worship. Throughout Mesoamerica, the Olmec traded for goods such as jade, a precious green stone from hundreds of miles away. Olmec traders also dealt in iron ore, obsidian (a dark volcanic glass), jaguar pelts, rubber, salt, and cacao beans, from which chocolate is made.

The power of Olmec rulers is suggested by the massive carved heads, like the one discovered on the Mexican farm. Although some of the colossal heads may depict Olmec gods, archaeologists think that most of the sculptures honor powerful Olmec rulers. The heads were carved from massive pieces of basalt, a dark volcanic stone, which had to be transported dozens of miles through the rain forest and across muddy swamps. It required the work of hundreds of people to move such mighty rocks, each of which weighed many tons.

Olmec artists carved exquisite jade figurines. Olmec astronomers devised an intricate calendar. The Olmec also had a system of writing. Scholars used hieroglyphs to create books made of tree bark or deerskin.

Olmec religion recognized many deities, including a jaguar-like god and a snake with feathers, gods that the people of Mesoamerica would continue to worship for centuries. Like many other cultures, the Olmec kept shrines to the memories of dead ancestors.

It remains unclear what happened to the Olmec people, but by 300 B.C. many of their cities had been abandoned. Some historians think the Olmec may have been devastated by the eruption of a nearby volcano. Others blame the decline on newcomers taking over the Olmec's profitable trading routes.

Other Mesoamerican Civilizations

Mesoamerica was home to a number of civilizations that rose and declined over the centuries. Founded in central Mexico by an unknown people, the city of Teotihuacán (tay-oh-tee-wah-KAHN) rose to prominence around A.D. 400. Located about thirty miles (50 km) northeast of modern-day Mexico City, Teotihuacán at its peak was home to an estimated 125,000 to 200,000 people. The city's buildings included apartment-like dwellings, palaces, and temples. The central city was dominated by the Pyramid of the Sun, an elaborate structure that rises more than two hundred feet (60 m) above the ground.

The Pyramid of the Sun towered over Teotihuacán, once the largest city in the Americas.

In 1942, the Mexican artist Diego Rivera painted this mural depicting the people of the ancient Zapotec civilization engaged in various activities—panning for gold in a river, working in a gold foundry, making feather headdresses, and more.

Another people, the Zapotec, flourished in a region farther south, in what is now the Mexican state of Oaxaca (wah-HAH-kah). On a mountaintop near the center of the Oaxaca Valley, the Zapotec built the city of Monte Albán. At the center of the city was a giant plaza, surrounded by stone temples, palaces, and pyramids. The Zapotec built pyramids with stair-step sides and flat tops, where religious ceremonies were likely performed. Monte Albán thrived from about A.D. 200 to 700, but then Zapotec civilization began to decline, for reasons that still remain unclear to historians.

The Maya

While Olmec sculptors created colossal works of art, a people called the Maya (MIY-uh) still lived in primitive villages. But as the Olmec declined, the Maya developed an advanced civilization in Mesoamerica that thrived for over seven hundred years. The Maya would keep alive many cultural traits they inherited from the Olmec. From about A.D. 200 to 900, Maya culture spread across a region that today includes southern Mexico, Belize, the Yucatán Peninsula, much of Guatemala, and parts of El Salvador and Honduras.

The territory encompassed many environments, including tropical lowlands, dense rain forests, mild shorelines, and high country. The Maya adapted their farming techniques to various landscapes. On steep hillsides they created flat terraces to plant crops. In swamps they moved soil to make raised planting areas. In the rain forest they practiced slash-and-burn agriculture.

The Maya grew beans, sweet potatoes, squash, and chilies. They gathered wild plants, including avocados, pears, and vanilla beans. They hunted turkeys, deer, rabbits, and monkeys, and netted shellfish on the coast. But their main food source was maize. As Maya farms produced a surplus of maize, their civilization grew.

Maya Cities and Government

In the late 1830s, the American traveler and archaeologist John Lloyd Stephens explored an ancient city in southern Mexico. He discovered crumbling stone palaces and majestic pyramids choked by jungle vines. After reading his descriptions, some people wondered if the impressive buildings and wide streets belonged to the mythical lost continent of Atlantis. Future archaeologists would find that it was one of many impressive cities built by the Maya.

Maya cities were well-planned urban centers, with roads, reservoirs, palaces, temples, and private residences. The city of Tikal (tee-KAHL), in the jungle of Guatemala, may have been home to as many as sixty thousand people at its peak. Tikal had five enormous pyramids, which served as centers of

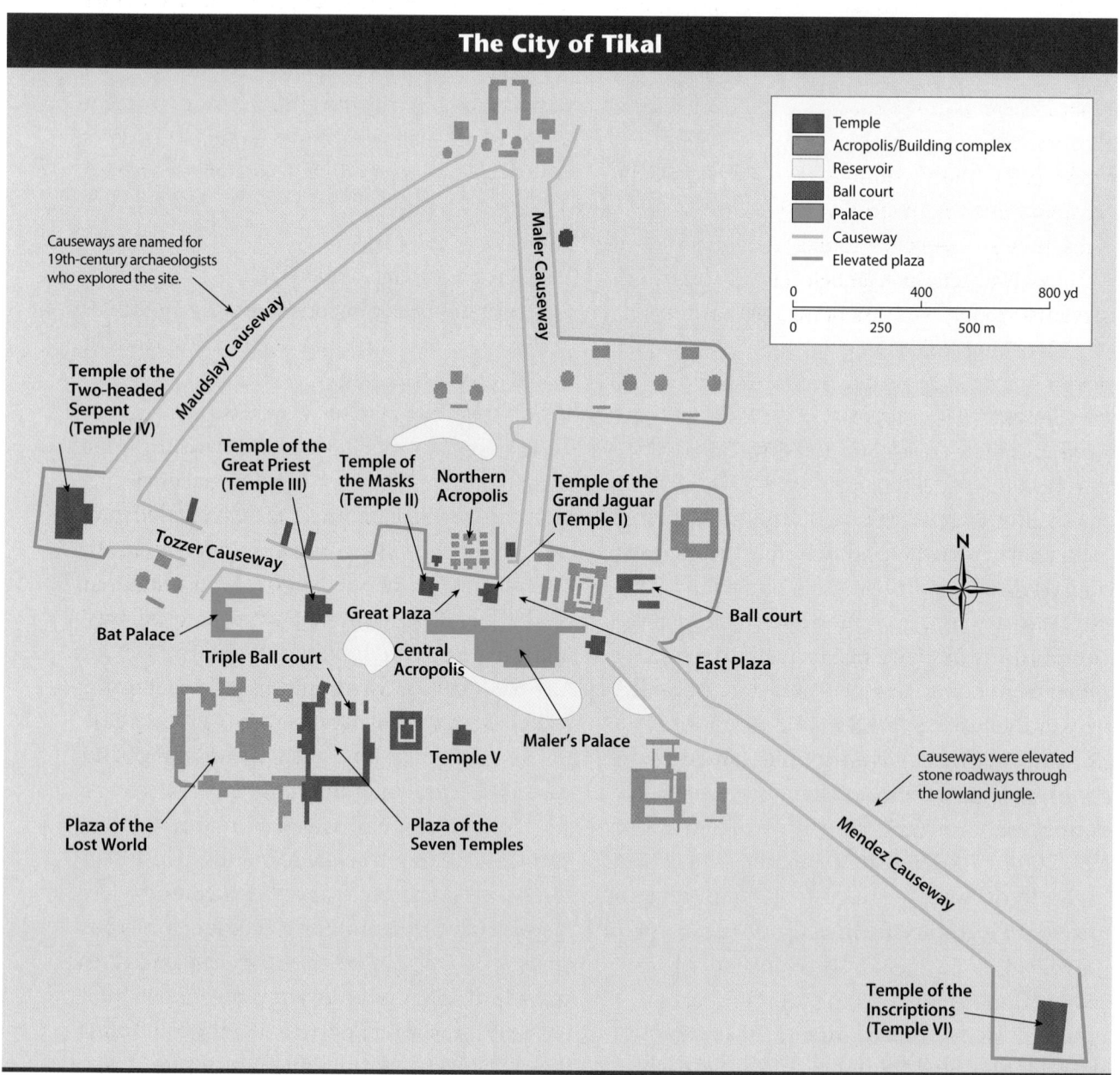

The City of Tikal

Legend:
- Temple
- Acropolis/Building complex
- Reservoir
- Ball court
- Palace
- Causeway
- Elevated plaza

Causeways are named for 19th-century archaeologists who explored the site.

Maler Causeway

Maudslay Causeway

Temple of the Two-headed Serpent (Temple IV)

Temple of the Great Priest (Temple III)

Temple of the Masks (Temple II)

Northern Acropolis

Temple of the Grand Jaguar (Temple I)

Tozzer Causeway

Bat Palace

Great Plaza

Ball court

Triple Ball court

Central Acropolis

East Plaza

Temple V

Maler's Palace

Causeways were elevated stone roadways through the lowland jungle.

Plaza of the Lost World

Plaza of the Seven Temples

Mendez Causeway

Temple of the Inscriptions (Temple VI)

N

0   400   800 yd
0   250   500 m

Tikal is one of the largest archaeological sites of Maya civilization, situated in modern-day northern Guatemala.

worship. But these pyramids were more than just temples. Like the pyramids of the ancient Egyptians, they also served as tombs where rulers were buried with their favorite belongings—and their servants—to take with them into the next world.

Maya kings ruled the cities and led a complex government run by aristocrats. Kings surrounded themselves with influential priests and military leaders who were often relatives. Lower-level government officials helped maintain the king's power over the wider territory controlled by the city. They collected tributes and controlled religious observances in the name of the king.

Maya kingdoms, or city-states, enjoyed the prosperity that came from trading with each other. But that commerce suffered when city-states grappled in war. Such conflicts flared up regularly, as rival kings battled over territory and prestige. Captives of battle were usually sacrificed to the gods in bloody rituals.

Maya Society

The Maya believed their rulers possessed powers that allowed them to communicate with the gods and thus bring blessings or curses upon the city-state. Below the king in the Maya social order were wealthy elites. Within this upper class there

were two groups. The first enjoyed high status as extended members of the royal family. The other, less-powerful group of elites included priests, scribes, merchants, warriors, artists, and landowners.

The majority of Maya were common people who farmed the land. Unskilled workers and craftspeople built pyramids, temples, and other public projects. Maya custom forbade marriage between common people and the elites.

Like other ancient civilizations, the Maya relied on slaves to do much of the hardest work. Slaves might be convicted criminals, or captives taken in war who had not been sacrificed. In rare instances, desperate parents might try to avoid poverty by selling their children into slavery. Most slaves were owned by the government or by members of the elite class. Slaves performed a variety of tasks, from farming to performing religious rituals.

Maya Religious Beliefs

The Maya worshipped many gods and goddesses, each believed to have important powers. The priests performed many rituals to keep the gods happy. It would be disastrous, the Maya thought, if the sun god or the rain god refused to bless the fields

Maya religion held that there were three realms in the universe: the heavens, where the gods lived; the earth, where the Maya lived; and, the underworld, where humans went after death. The Maya believed the heavens and the underworld were divided into many levels, each ruled by a different god.

Religion unified Maya society. From the king to the poorest farmer, all believed in the power of rituals to please the gods. In some rituals, a Maya king would cut himself and offer his blood to the gods. Other rituals included animal and human sacrifice.

The popular ball game introduced by the Olmec also had an important place in Maya religion. For the Maya, the game enacted a religious myth in which two heroes played against the gods of death. In some cases, members of the losing team were beheaded as a sacrifice to those gods.

Exploring Maya Ruins

The American archaeologist John Lloyd Stephens was intrigued by reports of ancient ruins on the Yucatán Peninsula and in Central America. In 1839 and into the early 1840s, Stephens and Frederick Catherwood, an English illustrator, made their way through an almost impenetrable jungle, and managed to avoid the dangers of local fighting along the way, to be rewarded at last by finding many magnificent ruins. Stephens and Catherwood published accounts with vivid descriptions and illustrations that helped to spark worldwide interest in Mesoamerican archaeology and the long lost civilization of the Maya. In the following passage, Stephens describes what he found in the ancient city of Uxmal.

The first object that arrests the eye on emerging from the forest is...this lofty structure.... From its front doorway I counted sixteen elevations, with broken walls and mounds of stones, and vast, magnificent edifices, which at that distance seemed untouched by time and defying ruin. I stood in the doorway when the sun went down, throwing from the buildings a prodigious breadth of shadow, darkening the terraces on which they stood, and presenting a scene strange enough for a work of enchantment....

This building is sixty-eight feet long.... Its form is not pyramidal, but oblong and rounding, being two hundred and forty feet long at the base, and one hundred and twenty broad, and it is protected all around, to the very top, by a wall of square stones....

On the east side of the structure is a broad range of stone steps between eight and nine inches high, and so steep that great care is necessary in ascending and descending; of these we counted a hundred and one in their places.... The whole building is of stone; inside, the walls are of polished smoothness; outside, up to the height of the door, the stones are plain and square; above this line there is a rich cornice or molding, and from this to the top of the building all the sides are covered with rich and elaborate sculptured ornaments....

The designs were strange and incomprehensible, very elaborate, sometimes grotesque, but often simple, tasteful, and beautiful. Among the intelligible subjects are squares and diamonds, with busts of human beings, heads of leopards, and compositions of leaves and flowers.... The ornaments, which succeed each other, are all different; the whole form an extraordinary mass of richness and complexity, and the effect is both grand and curious.

A color lithograph based on a drawing by Frederick Catherwood offers a glimpse of the Maya ruins that he and archaeologist John Lloyd Stephens encountered.

Maya Numbering System

The Olmec and Maya mathematics system used dots and bars to represent units. A dot stood for one unit, a bar for five. The Maya added the concept of zero, represented by a shell.

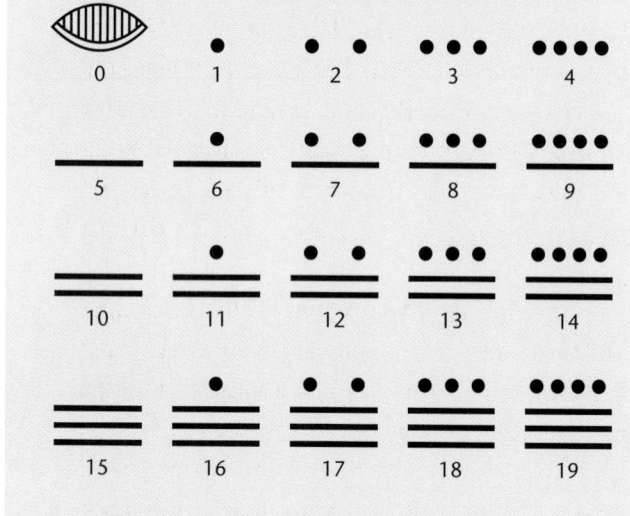

Maya Science and Writing

The Maya adopted the Olmec system of counting, which they improved by adding the idea of zero. Some historians credit the Maya with inventing the concept of zero as a number, although it was also devised independently by the Gupta in India. The zero allowed Maya mathematicians to make calculations with large quantities.

Maya calendars continue to intrigue people today. With precise astronomical observations, the Maya developed a 365-day calendar that was more accurate than any used in Europe at the time. In addition, the Maya devised calendars to track cycles of the moon, planets, and stars. They also created a "Long Count" calendar that recorded a cycle of nearly two million days. Maya astronomer-priests could predict eclipses, which were viewed as momentous events performed by the gods.

The Maya developed a system of writing, an important requirement of civilization. The Maya wrote in hieroglyphs, pictures that stood for words or sounds that made up words. On towering stone stelae, sculptors carved hieroglyphs describing the deeds of leaders and heroes. The Maya wrote books made of folded strips of bark, called codices (KOH-duh-seez; plural form of *codex*). Only four codices have survived, because invaders from Spain destroyed most of them in the sixteenth century. Modern-day scholars have been able to translate some Maya hieroglyphs, but much of their complex writing system remains a mystery.

Beginning around A.D. 800, Maya civilization declined. Recent evidence suggests that a long drought in the region may have prompted people to abandon the cities and retreat upland. Some

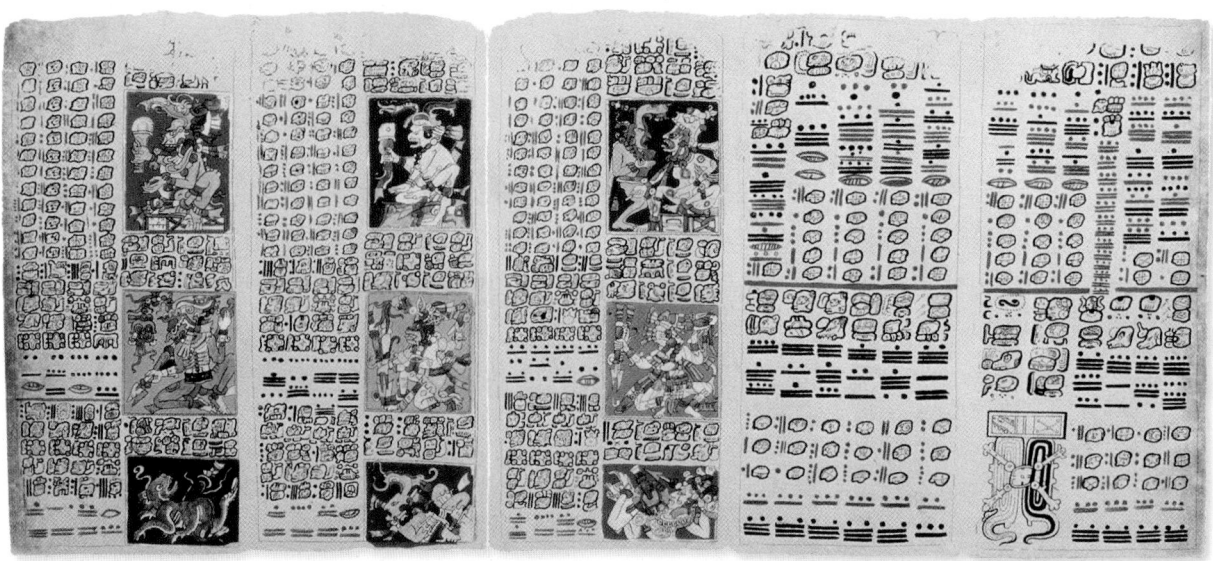

The Maya made remarkably precise astronomical calculations, as shown in this ancient book.

historians think that disease may have wiped out Maya populations. By 900, many Maya cities sat abandoned, though a few were still actively populated when the Spanish invaded in the 1520s. Today, some descendants of the Maya continue to occupy their traditional homeland in Mesoamerica, growing maize and maintaining some traditions of a once-mighty civilization.

Civilizations in the Andes: Early Peoples of South America

As the Olmec, the Maya, and other civilizations developed in Mesoamerica, complex societies were forming in South America. These early South American civilizations took shape in the challenging terrain of the Andes Mountains, in what is now the country of Peru.

The Geography of the Andes

The Andes form the world's second-highest mountain range, after the Himalayas in Asia. The Andes stretch north to south from Venezuela to southern Chile. While the highest summits reach over 22,200 feet (6,705 m) and remain permanently snow covered, the Andes also contain many green valleys. East of the mountains, streams run down to the Amazon rain forest, forming the world's largest river drainage system.

In general, agriculture is difficult in the Andes region. In Peru, between the Andes and the Pacific Ocean, lies a coastal plain, much of which is arid desert. In some places, rivers cut across the desert as they flow down from the Andes to the Pacific Ocean. These rivers create narrow strips of fertile land, where early humans first farmed and settled in South America.

These rivers allowed the cultivation of maize, which was a staple crop by 1500 B.C. The first South American farmers also grew potatoes, squash, and beans. In time, farming villages spread from the desert lowlands into the higher country to the east, where farmers grew crops in fertile valleys and, in the high country, raised animals such as llamas and alpacas. As populations increased,

the people built cities and religious centers high in the Andes.

The Chavín

One of the earliest South American cities was built at an elevation above 10,300 feet (3,150 m). The city, Chavín de Huántar (chah-VEEN thay WAHN-tahr), thrived from about 900 to 200 B.C. From the name of the city, archaeologists have taken the name for the earliest known civilization in South America, called the Chavín. The Chavín flourished during the same period that Olmec culture reached its height in Mesoamerica.

Little is known about Chavín life, but archaeologists at the site of Chavín de Huántar have discovered ruins left by highly advanced builders. A massive temple complex in the city housed an enormous pyramid. Beneath it, builders created a network of canals. When water rushed through the canals, it caused the entire temple to roar and vibrate, perhaps suggesting the presence of the gods to worshippers.

Chavín de Huántar may have housed some three thousand residents at its height, but most historians believe it served as a center of worship that attracted many visitors who attended ceremonies held there. By 200 B.C., the Chavín had begun to decline, but their culture influenced future civilizations that grew in the mountains of Peru.

Mysteries of the Nazca

In southwestern Peru, the coastal desert grows especially hot and dry on a high flat plain called the Nazca Plateau. Except for two rivers cutting through the barren country, the area is waterless. Sharp rocks and pebbles cover the ground. It seems an unlikely place for human settlement. Nevertheless, on this arid plateau the Nazca people thrived between 200 B.C. and A.D. 600. The Nazca urged crops out of the arid land with an underground irrigation system built with precise angles to draw water from the high country.

The Nazca were expert potters and weavers. They created colorful ceramics depicting animals

Early American Civilizations, 1100 B.C. to A.D. 600

Gulf of Mexico

● Uxmal

● Teotihuacán

Yucatan Peninsula

Monte Albán ●

● Tikal

The city of Teotihuacán was larger than imperial Rome.

● Copán

CENTRAL AMERICA

Caribbean Sea

PACIFIC OCEAN

ANDES MOUNTAINS

SOUTH AMERICA

Gulf of Guayaquil →

Amazon River

Tumbes River

Marten River

Chavin de Huántar ●

Central America

Olmec 1200–400 B.C.

Zapotec A.D. 200–700

Maya A.D. 200–900

South America

Chavin 900–200 B.C.

Nazca 200 B.C.–A.D. 600

Moche 200 B.C.–A.D. 700

N

Nazca Plateau ■

Gigantic Nazca line drawings were etched into the earth over a 130-square-mile area.

ANDES MOUNTAINS

0   200   400 mi

0   200   400 km

Although people lived throughout North and South America, the first complex civilizations and population centers were concentrated in Mesoamerica and along a narrow coastal strip of South America.

A hummingbird discernible only from the air is one of the giant pictures created by the Nazca on this rocky plateau.

The Nazca had created these giant images—but why? Some think the images on the plateau serve as a kind of giant calendar. Others speculate that the pictures were made as tributes to the gods. For now, the real reasons for their existence remain a mystery.

The Moche

Around the same time that the Nazca flourished in the harsh desert of southern Peru, the civilization of the Moche (MOH-chay) developed in the desert of the northern coast. At its height, the realm of the Moche extended for 300 miles (483 km) along the coast. The Moche settled by rivers that cascaded down from the Andes. They built a system of irrigation canals to channel water flowing down from the Andes into their fields, where they grew maize, beans, and other crops.

The Moche built flat-topped pyramids that towered over the bleak countryside. Some pyramids housed the lavish tombs of Moche kings. These tombs contain thousands of pieces of finely crafted pottery. Although the Moche left no written records, we get a picture of their lives from images painted on pottery by Moche artists. The paintings show scenes of people working the land, soldiers returning from battle, women weaving cloth, and more.

and mythic creatures. They also produced fine cloth made from alpaca wool, which came through long-distance trade with herders some 125 miles (200 km) away.

The most intriguing Nazca legacy is an unsolved puzzle that first came to light in the 1920s when planes began flying above the Nazca Plateau. On the rocky ground lay an array of enormous shapes and patterns that could only be seen from above. Long straight lines ran for miles, while the space between was filled with the outlines of geometric designs and plants and animal shapes, such as a spider, a hummingbird, a whale, a monkey (about 360 feet [110 m] long), and a pelican (about 930 feet [283 m] across).

Both the Nazca and the Moche civilizations began to decline around the year 600. Many historians believe that climate change may have led to their fall. Others point to the arrival of newcomers in both northern and southern Peru who likely encroached on Nazca and Moche land. As is the case with many early civilizations, while their achievements are remarkable, our knowledge of them remains tentative and incomplete, awaiting new insights from archaeologists and historians.

A gold and turquoise Moche ornament

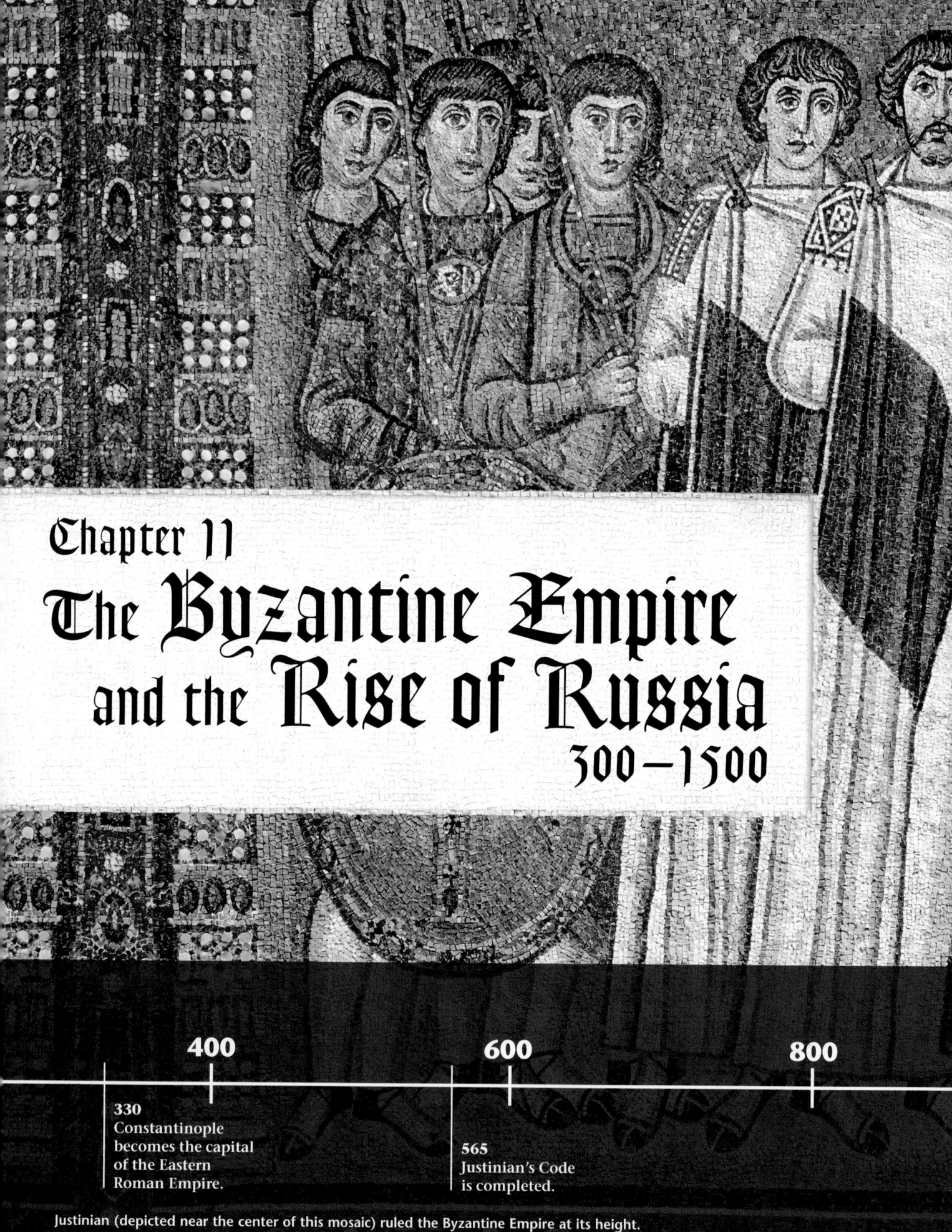

Chapter 11
The Byzantine Empire and the Rise of Russia
300–1500

400

600

800

330
Constantinople becomes the capital of the Eastern Roman Empire.

565
Justinian's Code is completed.

Justinian (depicted near the center of this mosaic) ruled the Byzantine Empire at its height.

MAXIMIANVS

1054
A schism divides
Christianity into the
Eastern Orthodox and
Roman Catholic churches.

1462
Ivan the Great
becomes tsar
of Russia.

1000

1200

1400

987
Prince Vladimir adopts
Orthodox Christianity
for Kievan Russia.

c. 1236
Mongol warriors
conquer Russia.

1453
Constantinople falls
to the Ottoman Turks,
marking the end of the
Byzantine Empire.

In the third century A.D., the emperor Diocletian divided the vast Roman Empire into two parts—the Western Empire and the Eastern Empire. As the Western Empire declined, the Eastern Empire grew stronger. In the fourth century, the emperor Constantine decided to move the imperial capital from Rome to a city in the Eastern Empire called Byzantium (later called Constantinople). Byzantium gave its name to an empire that would endure long after the Western Roman Empire was gone—the Byzantine Empire, which flourished for more than a thousand years.

The Byzantines preserved the legacy of Greece and Rome. They blended that legacy with influences from Persia to forge a new civilization with its own distinctive achievements in art, architecture, law, and other fields. Byzantine Christianity branched away from the Christianity practiced in the West, gradually taking shape as the Eastern Orthodox Church.

The cultural influence of Byzantine civilization spread north and helped shape a vast new country emerging there, Russia. When the Byzantine Empire fell, the Russians declared themselves the heirs of the Byzantines, and saw their land as both the embodiment of a new Rome and the capital of Orthodox Christianity.

Byzantium: A Thousand Years of Empire

Key Questions

- Why did the emperor Constantine choose the ancient city of Byzantium for his new capital?

- How did the Byzantine Empire and its influence expand under Justinian?

- What is the significance of Justinian's Code? What are some of the other great achievements of Byzantine civilization during the reign of Justinian?

As emperor, Constantine made two decisions with far-reaching and lasting consequences. First, in A.D. 313 he issued the Edict of Milan, giving equal status to all religions in the Roman Empire, and making Christianity an accepted religion. Christianity grew so rapidly that by 392 it had become the official religion of the Roman Empire.

Constantine's second pivotal decision was to move the imperial capital from Rome to Byzantium in the east, where his empire's wealth was now centered. He considered several sites for his new capital, including Jerusalem and ancient Troy. But in 330, he chose Byzantium, a thousand-year-old Greek town, because of its strategic location.

Constantine's City

Byzantium was advantageously located at the crossroads of Europe and Asia, the center of two vast trade networks. The city sat on a thumb of land controlling access to the Bosporus (BAHS-puh-ruhs), a strait linking the Sea of Marmara to the Black Sea. Another strait, the Dardanelles (dahrd-uhn-ELZ), linked the Sea of Marmara to the Aegean Sea. The Aegean Sea in turn led to the Mediterranean. Byzantium was strategically located to control trade between the regions surrounding the Mediterranean and Black seas. All ships sailing between the two seas had to pass through the Bosporus at Byzantium. Almost all land traffic between Asia and Europe passed through Byzantium as well.

A *strait* is a narrow channel of water linking two larger bodies of water.

Constantine transformed Byzantium into a capital worthy of the world's biggest empire. He gave the city a new name, in his own honor—Constantinople, "the city of Constantine." Because of its new status as the capital of the empire, the city was also known as the "New Rome."

With water on three sides, Constantinople was easy to defend. Constantine built sea walls on the city's three sides facing water. On the fourth side he built a stout wall to protect against land attacks. Within the city, he constructed palaces, forums, fountains, and sports arenas. The city featured a **hippodrome** (from Greek words meaning "horse track"), an imposing stadium for chariot racing that also housed circuses and theaters.

The Mese (MEHS-ee), a long road running through the heart of Constantinople, became the world's busiest market. The avenue was lined with shops that sold goods from across the world—porcelain and silks from China; spices and precious stones from India; cosmetics and perfumes from Arabia; grain from Egypt; and honey, fur, and hides from Russia. Merchants also sold sweet

The Byzantine, or Eastern Roman, Empire at its height

An artist's rendition of the walled city of Constantinople shows the Hagia Sophia and the hippodrome in the center foreground.

grapes and other local produce. In this cosmopolitan market, Arabs, Africans, Greeks, Syrians, and Jews might bump elbows with merchants from lands as distant as Gaul (now France) and Britain.

By the time Constantine died in 337, he left a busy, thriving capital in the east. Constantinople remained the capital of a dynamic Greek-speaking Christian empire for 1,100 years. Although its citizens called themselves Romans to the end, later historians named it the Byzantine Empire after the town that had served as its seed.

Justinian's Reign

The fate of the Roman Empire's two parts would prove the wisdom of Constantine's choice of a capital. In the fifth century, invading tribes began carving the Western Empire into Germanic kingdoms. In 476, they ousted the last emperor in Rome. But the Eastern Empire—the Byzantine Empire—would rise to great heights, reaching a peak of splendor under Justinian, who reigned from 527 to 565.

The Emperor Who Never Slept

Justinian was born into a peasant family. As a young man he went to live in Constantinople, where his uncle was a powerful military commander. Justinian's uncle, named Justin, made sure the young man received a first-class education. When Justin became emperor in 518, his rule was largely guided by his favorite nephew, whom he legally adopted. By the time his uncle died in 527,

Justinian was ready to rule as the new emperor.

And rule he did. A forceful man who slept little—according to legend, he *never* slept— Justinian was determined to extend Byzantine power across the Mediterranean. He was no warrior, but he had a brilliant general, Belisarius (bel-ih-SAIR-ee-uhs), to lead his armies.

A mosaic of Emperor Justinian with royal crown and scepter

Guided by Belisarius, Justinian's armies reconquered the lost provinces of the west. They took North Africa back from the Vandals, wrestled Italy away from the Ostrogoths, and later defeated the Visigoths in Spain. These campaigns strained the Byzantine economy, but they gave Justinian an empire that stretched from Syria to Spain. During his reign, Justinian doubled the size of his empire until Constantinople ruled much of the Mediterranean world.

Within this realm, Justinian wielded greater power than any of the early emperors. As head of both state and church, he titled himself **autocrat**, which meant "sole ruler" and implied absolute authority. Those who came to see the emperor, even foreign envoys, had to bow before him in homage, their faces pressed to the floor.

An *envoy* (EHN-voy) is an official sent by a government to transact business (such as negotiating a treaty) with another government.

The Empress Theodora

Justinian achieved much as emperor, but his reign would not have been as brilliant without the actions of a woman whose name is forever linked with his—his wife and trusted adviser, the empress Theodora (thee-uh-DOR-uh).

Theodora came from even humbler roots than Justinian. Her father was a bearkeeper in the circus and her mother was an actress, which was considered a disreputable profession at the time. Theodora herself performed onstage at a theater in the hippodrome. Justinian, it seems, fell in love with her at first sight. Byzantine law prohibited emperors from marrying actresses, but Justinian pushed to get the law changed.

As the emperor's most trusted adviser, Theodora wielded extraordinary influence. She appointed those she favored to government posts and dismissed those she disliked. She negotiated with foreign envoys. She secured greater rights for Byzantine women in marriage. She had laws passed to protect divorced women and to prohibit the sale of young girls.

The Nika Revolt

In 532, an outburst of mob violence almost toppled Justinian. Two competing groups, known as the Blues and the Greens, temporarily joined forces to oppose the emperor. The two groups originated as fans of rival chariot-racing teams but evolved into political factions. Many resented the high taxes imposed by Justinian's administration. Some, especially among the aristocratic class, opposed Justinian's efforts to strengthen his power and make himself more independent of the will of the senators.

In January 532, an incident led these simmering resentments to boil over. During chariot races at the hippodrome, the restless crowd began to shout *"Nika!"* or "Conquer!" Rioters rampaged through the city, setting fire to buildings and even attacking the royal palace.

In the following days, the leaders of what came to be called the Nika Revolt named a new emperor. As the uprising

A mosaic of Empress Theodora adorns a church Justinian built in Italy.

An icon of the Virgin and Child (Mary holding the infant Jesus) is one of many artworks adorning the Hagia Sophia, the magnificent cathedral Justinian built in Constantinople.

spread, much of Constantinople was in flames. Justinian prepared to flee the city, but Theodora persuaded him to stay and take a stand. Theodora is reported to have said:

> On the present occasion, if ever, flight is inexpedient even if it should bring us safety.... For one who has reigned it is intolerable to be an exile. May I never exist without this purple robe and may I never live to see the day on which those who meet me shall not address me as "Queen." If you wish, O Emperor, to save yourself, there is no difficulty.... Yonder is the sea, and there are the ships. Yet reflect whether, when you have once escaped to a place of security, you will not prefer death to safety.

Justinian decided to suppress the riot. He sent troops to the hippodrome, where many of the rioters were assembled. Soldiers poured into the stadium and slaughtered some thirty thousand rebels. Through grim and bloody means, the rebellion was put down, and Justinian remained in power.

A New Constantinople

Justinian took the devastation caused by the Nika Revolt as an opportunity to rebuild Constantinople. Augustus, the first emperor of Rome, had boasted of transforming his capital from brick to marble. Justinian resolved to do the same with Constantinople. He expanded his palace complex on the city's eastern hills. He constructed new aqueducts and public baths, and granaries, theaters, hospitals, and forums. Above all, he restored old churches and built new ones.

The most awe-inspiring of the churches was the cathedral known as Hagia Sophia (HAH-juh soh-FEE-uh), Greek for "Holy Wisdom." Like other Byzantine churches, Hagia Sophia was crowned by a great dome that symbolized heaven. Rising high above the floor, the dome spanned a seemingly impossible distance. To support the dome's great weight, the builders erected a system of interlocking marble piers and arches. Below, on the cathedral's walls, were panels of marble of varying hues: purple, pink, crimson, green, speckled, and white.

Hagia Sophia dominated the skyline of Constantinople. Surpassing in size any church in western Europe for a thousand years, it sat like an enormous crown on a slope above the busy waters of the Bosporus. Hagia Sophia was an achievement

Topped by a magnificent dome, Hagia Sophia once dominated the skyline of the city of Constantinople.

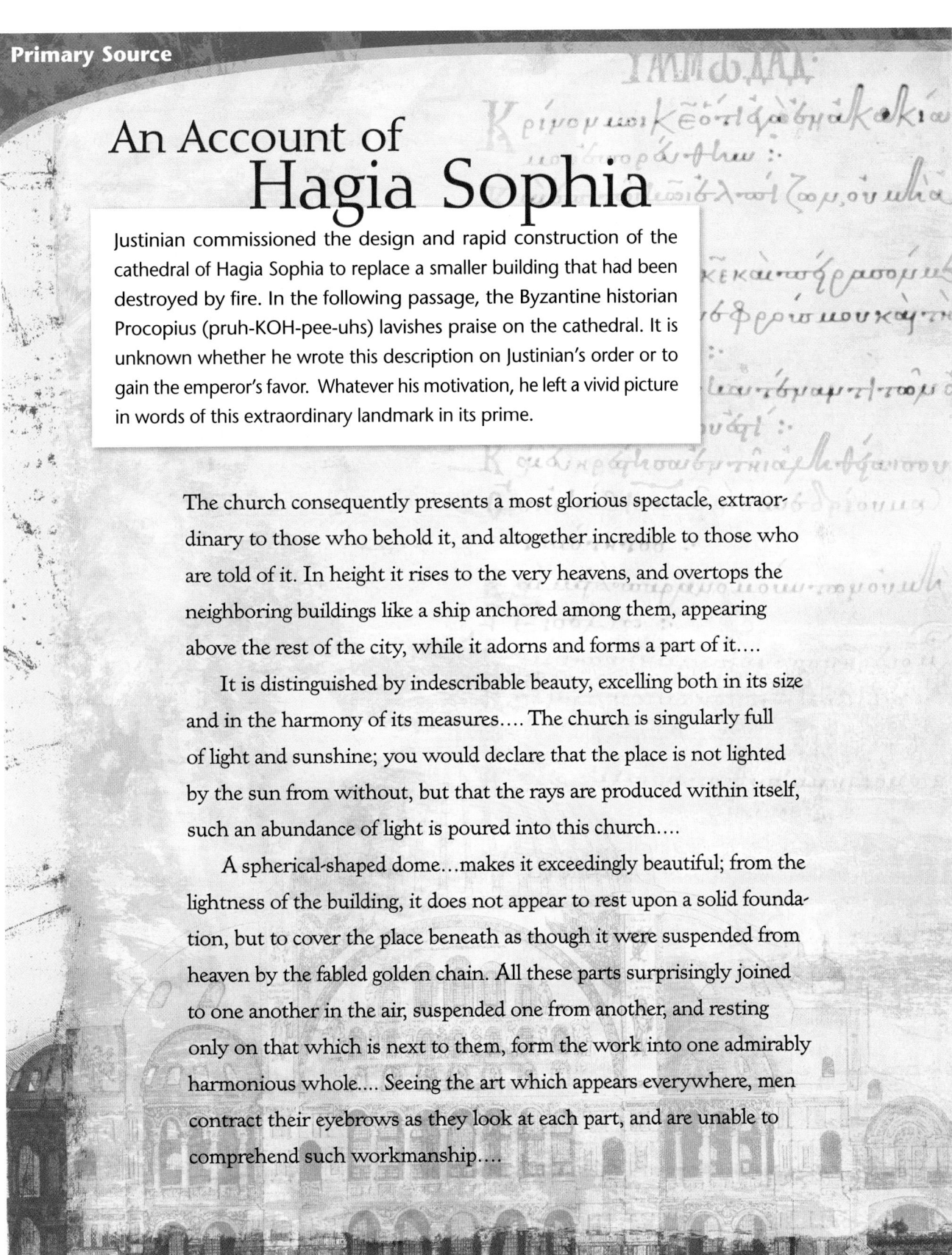

An Account of Hagia Sophia

Justinian commissioned the design and rapid construction of the cathedral of Hagia Sophia to replace a smaller building that had been destroyed by fire. In the following passage, the Byzantine historian Procopius (pruh-KOH-pee-uhs) lavishes praise on the cathedral. It is unknown whether he wrote this description on Justinian's order or to gain the emperor's favor. Whatever his motivation, he left a vivid picture in words of this extraordinary landmark in its prime.

The church consequently presents a most glorious spectacle, extraordinary to those who behold it, and altogether incredible to those who are told of it. In height it rises to the very heavens, and overtops the neighboring buildings like a ship anchored among them, appearing above the rest of the city, while it adorns and forms a part of it....

It is distinguished by indescribable beauty, excelling both in its size and in the harmony of its measures.... The church is singularly full of light and sunshine; you would declare that the place is not lighted by the sun from without, but that the rays are produced within itself, such an abundance of light is poured into this church....

A spherical-shaped dome...makes it exceedingly beautiful; from the lightness of the building, it does not appear to rest upon a solid foundation, but to cover the place beneath as though it were suspended from heaven by the fabled golden chain. All these parts surprisingly joined to one another in the air, suspended one from another, and resting only on that which is next to them, form the work into one admirably harmonious whole.... Seeing the art which appears everywhere, men contract their eyebrows as they look at each part, and are unable to comprehend such workmanship....

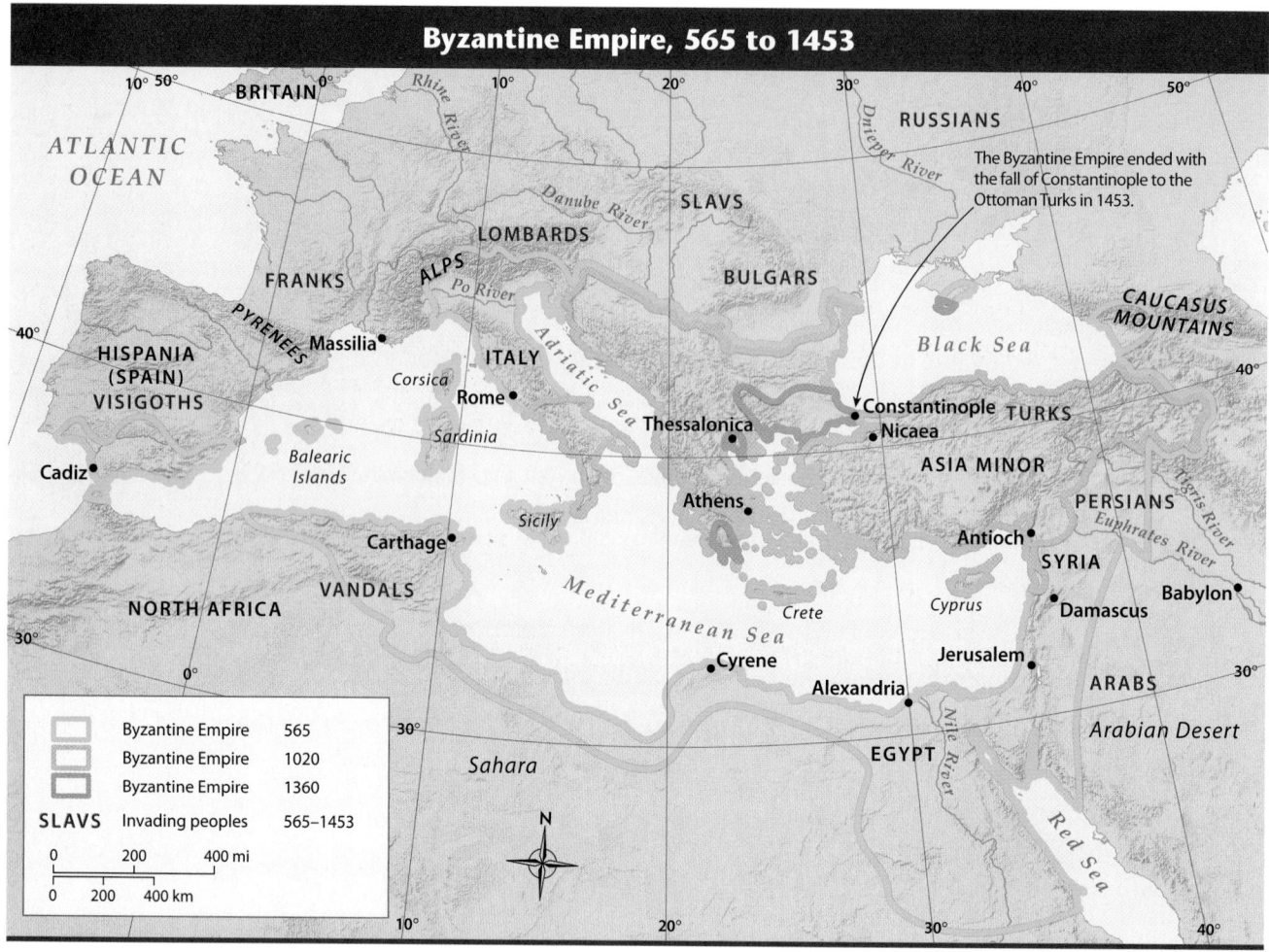

Byzantine Empire, 565 to 1453

The Byzantine Empire ended with the fall of Constantinople to the Ottoman Turks in 1453.

	Byzantine Empire	565
	Byzantine Empire	1020
	Byzantine Empire	1360
SLAVS	Invading peoples	565–1453

After the military success of Justinian, the Byzantine Empire steadily lost territory to invading armies over the next nine hundred years.

Reshaping the Laws

Justinian's finest achievement may have been his reshaping of Roman law. The Romans had established an effective legal system. Over time, however, emperors, judges, and senators had added so many confusing laws to the books that no one could make sense of them anymore. Sometimes one law repeated another, and sometimes two laws might say opposite things. The many commentaries written to interpret the laws only added to the confusion.

Justinian told his advisers that a single empire needed a single and consistent set of laws. He wanted all his subjects to obey the same laws, no matter where they lived. The laws should be easy to understand and, he insisted, they should not contradict each other.

Justinian appointed teams of legal scholars to simplify and organize the existing laws and commentaries. In 529, these scholars issued a list of more than four thousand clearly stated laws. They then published a volume that condensed all previous interpretations of the laws into a single consistent set. They also issued a book that explained the underlying logic of the legal system. Justinian himself added new laws designed to close gaps and address issues unique to his time.

The work took decades, but in 565 the job was finished. The new laws and commentaries were officially called *The Body of Civil Law,*

Justinian's Code

Like their Western Roman ancestors, the Eastern Romans took great pride in their laws. Justinian thought that a single empire needed a single set of laws. He appointed a commission to organize and simplify the existing laws and commentaries in order to produce a consistent body of laws. The result, known as Justinian's Code, influenced lawmakers for centuries. The laws addressed a variety of issues and situations, some very practical and specific, for example:

The sea and seashore belong to everyone. Every person in the empire is allowed to go to the beach.

Rivers belong to everyone. Anyone in the empire can fish in the rivers without being told to leave.

He who finds a jewel or other treasure washed up on the seashore may keep it for himself.

A thief who steals something valuable must pay the owner four times the worth of the stolen object.

If someone is trimming a tree near a road, he must call out a warning to anyone passing by. "Be careful!" he should say. "Limbs might fall on you!" If there is no warning, and a falling limb injures a traveler, it is the tree trimmer's fault. But if the traveler ignores the warning and is injured, it is not the tree trimmer's fault.

but they were unofficially known as Justinian's Code. The code enabled the many diverse groups within Byzantine society to live together, and it worked so well that it remained in force until the empire fell almost nine hundred years later. When historians assert that modern European law is based on Roman law, the Roman law they refer to includes Justinian's Code, which served as a model for the codes of law in many modern nations.

Justinian's Plague

Just as Justinian reached the peak of his power, disaster struck his city. Around 540, a devastating disease broke out in Constantinople. The disease was probably spread by fleas from infected rats on merchant ships bringing grain from Egypt. From the docks, it spread throughout and beyond the city.

Most historians think the disease was the bubonic plague. Victims grew melon-sized lumps in their groins and armpits. For a time, thousands

Disease and Historical Change

Recent scientific discoveries have given historians new insights into the dramatic effect of disease on civilizations. The role of disease has become a new field of historical study. Many historians believe disease has altered the course of history as much as battles, leaders, and profound ideas.

In ancient Greece during the Peloponnesian War, as many as one-third of the people of Athens, including Pericles, died of a plague, perhaps hastening the city's fall. Historians now believe that plague was typhus, smallpox, or measles.

Disease might have hastened the fall of the Roman Empire. Millions of Romans came down with malaria, a disease whose name comes from a phrase meaning "bad air." The Romans did not know the disease was carried by mosquitoes. Recent scholarship suggests the epidemic may have initiated a long population decline and severely weakened the Roman army attempting to defend the empire's frontiers.

Justinian's plague halted the expansion of the Byzantine Empire and hampered the economy of the region for many decades. Some historians argue that the plague helped shift the center of European power from the Mediterranean to areas farther north and west.

In later chapters, you will learn about the dramatic impact of other diseases, including the bubonic plague in Europe, and smallpox and chicken pox in the Americas. Our understanding of how disease shapes history continues to grow and change as historians and biologists uncover new evidence and debate its significance.

of people fell ill each day, and most of them died within a week. Corpses piled up so fast that survivors could do little more than haul them to the city walls and dump them into the sea.

Within months, the plague wiped out from one-third to one-half of the city's population. Over the next century and a half, the disease continued to flare up from time to time. In Constantinople, the plague hampered trade and devastated business. So many local farmers died that food supplies to the city were reduced to the point that some citizens starved.

Disease weakened Justinian's armies as well. Invaders began punching through the ill-defended borders. The Byzantine Empire had reached its greatest size under Justinian, but the plague reversed that expansion.

Territorial Gains and Losses

By the time Justinian died, the western lands he had conquered were breaking away or falling to barbarian invaders. The Byzantines spent the next nine hundred years fending off attacks. From the northwest came the Goths, from the northeast the Magyars, Bulgars, and Avars. In the seventh century, the Arabs marched out of the Arabian Peninsula under the banner of a new religion called Islam. They took Egypt and Syria, before falling to the Seljuk (sel-JOOK) Turks from Central Asia, who conquered most of Asia Minor and threatened Constantinople itself. (You will read more about Islam and the Seljuks in upcoming chapters.)

After the Turks arrived, the Byzantines lost territory, though the empire survived and even thrived as long as it held the dynamic trading center of Constantinople. Also, through their skill in diplomacy, the Byzantines often won at the negotiating table what they could not win in battle.

By the fifteenth century, however, under pressure from constant attacks that strained the military and drained resources, the Byzantine Empire dwindled to little more than the city of Constantinople. At last, even that remnant fell. In 1453, a rising new power, the Ottoman Turks, breached the city's walls with cannon fire. Constantinople became Istanbul, capital of a new Muslim empire.

Byzantine Civilization

The Byzantine Empire lasted for almost eleven centuries. For more than a thousand years, it stood as the inheritor and guardian of the legacies of Greece and Rome. As Germanic tribes overran western Europe, the Byzantines kept literacy and learning alive. They preserved Hellenistic and Latin culture. They improved Roman law. They continued to apply Roman engineering by building roads, bridges, aqueducts, stadiums, and theaters throughout their realm.

But the Byzantines did more than preserve. By blending the Greco-Roman legacy with influences from Eastern societies such as Persia, they developed a new culture that flourished within a framework of a distinctly Byzantine form of Christianity.

Eastern Orthodox Christianity

After Constantine issued the Edict of Milan in 313, Christianity began to take hold throughout the Roman Empire. When the empire split into East and West, however, just as the two regions diverged politically and culturally, so the practice of Christianity in the East began to branch apart from the West. Slowly but surely two distinct churches emerged.

Differences Between East and West

The two branches of the church were divided by language. In the West, the language of the church was Latin. In the East, it was Greek. Between East and West, differences emerged in the **liturgy**, the rites used by priests in public worship. Byzantine priests, for example, spoke about the Holy Spirit emanating from God the Father, while Western priests included God the Son as well. In the Byzantine world, these issues aroused heated discussion.

In A.D. 325, the emperor Constantine had convened the Council of Nicaea to resolve various disputes

Key Questions

- Why did Christianity split into Eastern and Western branches? What were the consequences of the division?

- What are some distinctive features and major achievements of Byzantine culture?

This container for religious relics, made c. 955, is an elaborate example of Byzantine enamelwork.

237

and forge an **orthodox doctrine**—that is, an established and accepted body of official teachings. Afterward, bishops continued to meet occasionally in councils to clarify Christian doctrine and resolve differences about church organization. Some differences, however, could not be resolved.

As you've learned, the bishops of the leading cities in the Roman Empire were called patriarchs, and the bishop of Rome became known as the pope (from the Latin word for "father"). In the 400s, the pope started to claim authority over all the patriarchs and bishops. Christians in the Latin-speaking Western Empire acknowledged the authority of the pope. But Christians in the Greek-speaking Eastern Empire did not accept the pope as the ruler of their churches. Over time, the patriarch of Constantinople emerged as the spiritual leader of the Eastern branch of Christianity.

The Iconoclastic Controversy

As decades and then centuries passed, the Eastern and Western churches developed different religious practices. In the power struggle between the pope in Rome and the patriarch in Constantinople, every difference between Eastern and Western Christianity turned into a bone of contention.

One of the most serious controversies concerned religious imagery. Religious images in Christian churches helped educate many illiterate people about biblical events. In the East, highly stylized paintings and statues of Jesus, Mary, and other holy figures were called **icons**. People often used icons to help them focus their worship. Some Byzantines, however, thought the use of icons came dangerously close to idol worship. To ban the use of icons, they forged a movement known as **iconoclasm** (iy-KAH-nuh-KLA-zuhm) or "icon breaking."

In the eighth century, an iconoclastic emperor went so far as to ban the use of icons and to order their destruction. Most Byzantine clergy and lay people protested the ban on icons. Western Christians, whose churches were filled with statues and paintings, supported the protests against iconoclasm. The Roman pope condemned the iconoclast movement, which only added to the tensions between East and West. Some Byzantine leaders resented what they saw as a Roman attempt to interfere in matters internal to the Byzantine church.

> Today, an *iconoclast* is one who tries to tear down traditional ideas or institutions.

The iconoclastic controversy ended in 843 when a church council officially allowed the use of icons. One unfortunate outcome of the iconoclast movement was the destruction of thousands of remarkable works of art dating back to the third century.

The Church Divides

The religious tensions between East and West kept mounting until at last, in 1054, the pope sent a representative to Constantinople to negotiate with the patriarch. The meeting went badly. In fact, the pope in Rome and the patriarch in Constantinople ended up **excommunicating** each other. That is, each declared the other unfit to receive Christian communion, and cast him out of the church, in effect denying each other the possibility of salvation. (Not until 1965 did Pope Paul VI and the Patriarch Athanagoras lift the excommunications.)

Thus began a great and lasting **schism** (SKIH-zuhm)—a rift, split, or division—in Christianity. The Byzantine branch of Christianity became a separate church, eventually known as the **Eastern Orthodox Church**. The Western branch became the **Catholic** (or Roman Catholic) **Church**. This division had far-reaching cultural and religious consequences.

Marble mosaic icon of Saint Eudocia

The Monastery of St. Catherine in modern-day Egypt was secluded from the attacks of iconoclasts. Its collection of icons and books remains a unique source of information about Byzantine art.

The Influence of Byzantine Culture

Even after the Byzantine Empire began to shrink, Byzantine culture, spreading north from Constantinople, remained a powerful and lasting influence. Above all, the Byzantine Empire was, as Constantine had intended, a Christian empire, and the church shaped much of the empire's lasting cultural influence.

Monasticism and Missionaries

Monasticism was the decision by some Christians to renounce worldly activities, deny bodily comforts, and devote themselves to contemplation of God. The movement was born in the Eastern Roman Empire in the late third century, and later spread to the West. Men who followed this course were called monks, and women nuns.

The first monastics lived as hermits in the deserts of Egypt and Syria. Eventually, however, monks and nuns formed communities, called **monasteries** and **convents**, where they lived by strict religious rules, cultivated gardens, and made their own clothing. Over time, monasteries and convents took on new tasks—educating young people, running hospitals, providing travelers' aid, and distributing charity.

Monks also did missionary work. By drawing new souls into their church, Orthodox monks helped spread Byzantine influence. Orthodox missionaries made many converts among the eastern European people called Slavs (slahvz), particularly among Slavic peasants who had worshipped pagan gods.

In the ninth century, two Greek brothers, Cyril and Methodius, enjoyed great success in converting

239

Greek brothers Cyril and Methodius helped invent the Cyrillic alphabet, which helped spread Orthodox Christianity.

many Slavs. Both spoke Slavic languages and helped invent an alphabet in which Slavic speech could be written down. Their followers later developed this writing system into the Cyrillic (suh-RIH-lik) alphabet, so called because early tradition credited Cyril with inventing it. The brothers translated key works of Orthodox Christianity and made them available to the Slavs. (Cyrillic is still used in Russia and some neighboring countries.)

Byzantine Art and Architecture

As old influences from the West began to blend with others from the East, a new culture—a unique Byzantine culture—took shape. Striking new forms of art and architecture emerged in Constantinople, largely inspired by the church. The Byzantine style in religious art and architecture was marked by bold, vibrant colors, precise geometric designs, and elaborate ornamentation.

The Greeks and Romans had favored elegant simplicity, but the Byzantines embraced the sumptuous extravagance of the East. Influenced by Persian and Egyptian architecture, Byzantine churches acquired dramatic domes. This architectural style eventually spread to the Slavic north. On church walls, Byzantine artists painted **frescoes**, water colors applied directly to moist plaster.

Byzantine artisans worked with marble, ivory, enamel, and glass. They covered statues with gold leaf and studded ceremonial objects with precious jewels. Beautifully painted icons depicted religious figures in rigid poses gazing straight ahead to express spiritual intensity. From the West, Byzantine artists learned to make **illuminated manuscripts** about sacred subjects, books with illustrations and page borders rendered in inks so vivid they seemed to glow.

The most spectacular works of Byzantine art were mosaics. On a surface of wet plaster, gifted craftsmen carefully pressed into place small stones and glass pieces of different hues—whites and pinks, grays and greens, reds and browns, glittering golds—each placed at a slight angle to best reflect the light. Adorning the vaults, walls, and domes of churches, most mosaics represented Christian themes. In the bright sunshine of midday or the candlelight of evening, Byzantine churches glowed with the reflected light of mosaics.

Colorful frescoes adorn the Dark Church, a monastic compound built in the early twelfth century.

The mosaic-covered ceiling of a Byzantine church features Christ with lambs, prophets, and the cross.

Byzantine Literature and Learning

In literature, the Byzantine devotion to religion led to a focus on hymns, religious poems, and the lives of saints. The most enduring Byzantine literary works are histories. Much of our knowledge of the wars and deeds of Justinian comes from his court historian Procopius. More entertaining is his *Secret History*. Found long after his death, it is an account of the imperial family filled with nasty gossip about scandalous misdeeds. Another historian, Anna Comnena, daughter of the twelfth-century emperor Alexius, wrote an epic biography of her father, *The Alexiad*, which gives a vivid picture of the Byzantine court.

Perhaps the greatest Byzantine contribution to literature was not writing but copying. In Constantinople, Byzantine scholars copied and taught the works of great Greek and Latin authors. Had these books not been preserved in Constantinople, they might have perished.

In the Byzantine world, the Orthodox Church established schools to train priests. The curriculum included not just religion but all the classical subjects, including mathematics, music, philosophy, science, and grammar. This scholarship was crucial to the survival and spread of Greco-Roman knowledge and culture throughout Byzantine territory and far beyond.

In the 1300s and 1400s, when the empire was crumbling, many Byzantine scholars moved to Italy. Their learning and knowledge of Greco-Roman culture helped nourish a cultural rebirth called the Renaissance (which you will explore in detail in a later chapter).

Society, Trade, and Cultural Diffusion

While most citizens of the Byzantine Empire made their living as farmers or herders, at its height the empire had nearly a thousand cities and towns, including such major urban centers

241

as Antioch and Alexandria. Constantinople was among the largest cities west of China, with a population that at times exceeded half a million.

Trade flourished in and among these cities. In Constantinople, many people earned their living as merchants or as laborers hauling cargo or loading ships. Others worked as masons and skilled artisans on government building projects. Still more were craftspeople, making finished goods. Since these jobs depended on skills that could be learned, even poor Byzantine citizens had some chance of moving up in the world by mastering a marketable skill.

After Byzantine monks smuggled silkworms out of China, silk-making became a highly profitable Byzantine industry. The techniques for making silk remained a closely guarded government secret because it was the most lucrative industry of ancient times. By A.D. 600, the sale of silk brought more riches to the Byzantine Empire than any other product.

Although the plague of the mid-sixth century stunned Constantinople, the city slowly recovered its role at the crossroads of world trade, in part because the *bezant*, the Byzantine gold coin, remained the world's most dependable form of currency. Thanks to heavy traffic through the city, Byzantine society absorbed influences from east, west, north, and south, and continued to export not only goods but also lasting cultural influences.

A Byzantine mosaic depicts builders at work.

Russia Rises

Around the ninth century, a new country began to form north of the Byzantine Empire. It was called Russia, and Byzantine civilization was the most important influence on its early development.

Geography and Early Peoples

Today, Russia is the largest country in the world. Its borders enclose about one-eighth of the earth's surface. It sprawls from eastern Europe over the Ural Mountains and across the treeless Asian grasslands known as the **steppes**. It extends through the barren region called Siberia eastward to the Pacific Ocean. North to south, Russia stretches from the Arctic Ocean to the shores of the Black and Caspian seas.

This immense country was born in the wooded plains between the Byzantine Empire and the Baltic Sea. Before the ninth century, the region was sparsely populated. Summers were short, and winters long and dark. Growing crops was difficult because farmers had to clear trees before they could plow. The thick forests hampered land travel, and slow-moving rivers discouraged water travel.

Slavic clans inhabited small villages in clearings along the rivers, scratching out a bare subsistence from the soil and supplementing their diet with

Key Questions

- How did Byzantine civilization shape Russia's religious, cultural, and political development?

- How did the Mongol invasions affect Russia?

- What role did Ivan the Great play in early Russian history?

Byzantine civilization shaped the development of early Russia.

Livestock graze on the steppes near the snowcapped Altai Mountains in Russia.

Where Is Scandinavia?

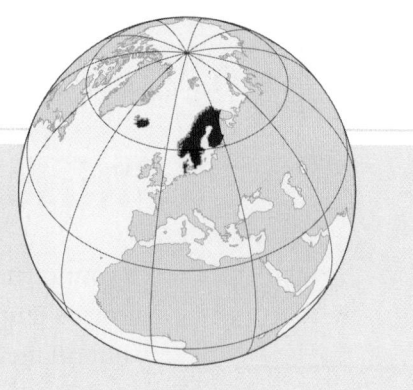

Scandinavia is the region of northern Europe occupied by present-day Sweden, Norway, and Denmark. Often the region is more broadly defined to include Finland, Iceland, and the Faroe Islands as well. The *Scandinavian Peninsula* refers to Norway and Sweden.

hunting. Much of what we know of the early history of these people comes from a source called the Russian Primary Chronicle. This historical work was long known as Nestor's Chronicle, because scholars once thought it was the work of a monk named Nestor. Modern scholars, however, think that the work compiles various sources, including early Byzantine accounts, official records, religious texts, and traditional legends. The earliest surviving manuscript of the Primary Chronicle, which dates from the late 1300s, shows the work of many hands.

According to the Primary Chronicle, these early eastern Slavs lived as scattered groups, obeying no common law and warring constantly with one another. Finally, says the Chronicle, "They said to themselves, 'Let us seek a prince who may rule over us and judge according to the law.'" So they sent an appeal to Rurik, leader of a northern

tribe called the Rus (roos). They told Rurik, "'Our whole land is great and rich, but there is no order in it. Come....'"

That account probably mixes legend with fact. We do know that sometime in the ninth century, bands of Varangians (vuh-RAN-jee-uhnz)—seafaring warriors from Scandinavia—crossed the Baltic Sea. Known to western Europe as Vikings, the Varangians were roaming the world at this time in dragon-headed longboats, plundering cities and wreaking havoc. (You'll read more about the Vikings in a later chapter.) The Varangians found the great rivers that flowed south through the Slavic homeland and began to use them as trade routes.

One Varangian tribe, the Rus, built great wooden fortresses along the rivers. By the eleventh century, they had established control over the Slavs in the region. Over time, they blended with their subjects, and a new group emerged, more Slavic than Scandinavian—these were the Russians.

Kievan Rus

Because their land was so ill-suited for farming, the Russians made their living mainly from commerce. They traded furs, timber, honey, beeswax, and other products of the forest—anything they could hunt, trap, fish, or gather—for grains and goods from the south.

The town of Novgorod (NAWV-guh-rahd), near the Baltic Sea, grew rich by linking north European commerce to markets in China, but it made a poor base for trade with the Byzantines. Better located for Byzantine trade was a city

Arguing over Sources

Modern scholars sometimes disagree in their interpretations of ancient sources. For example, how great was the role of the Varangian Rus in the early development of Russia? European scholars who rely on the Russian Primary Chronicle tend to emphasize the importance of the Varangians. Many modern-day Russian scholars, however, consider the Primary Chronicle unreliable, and insist on the greater importance of the eastern Slavs in early Russian history.

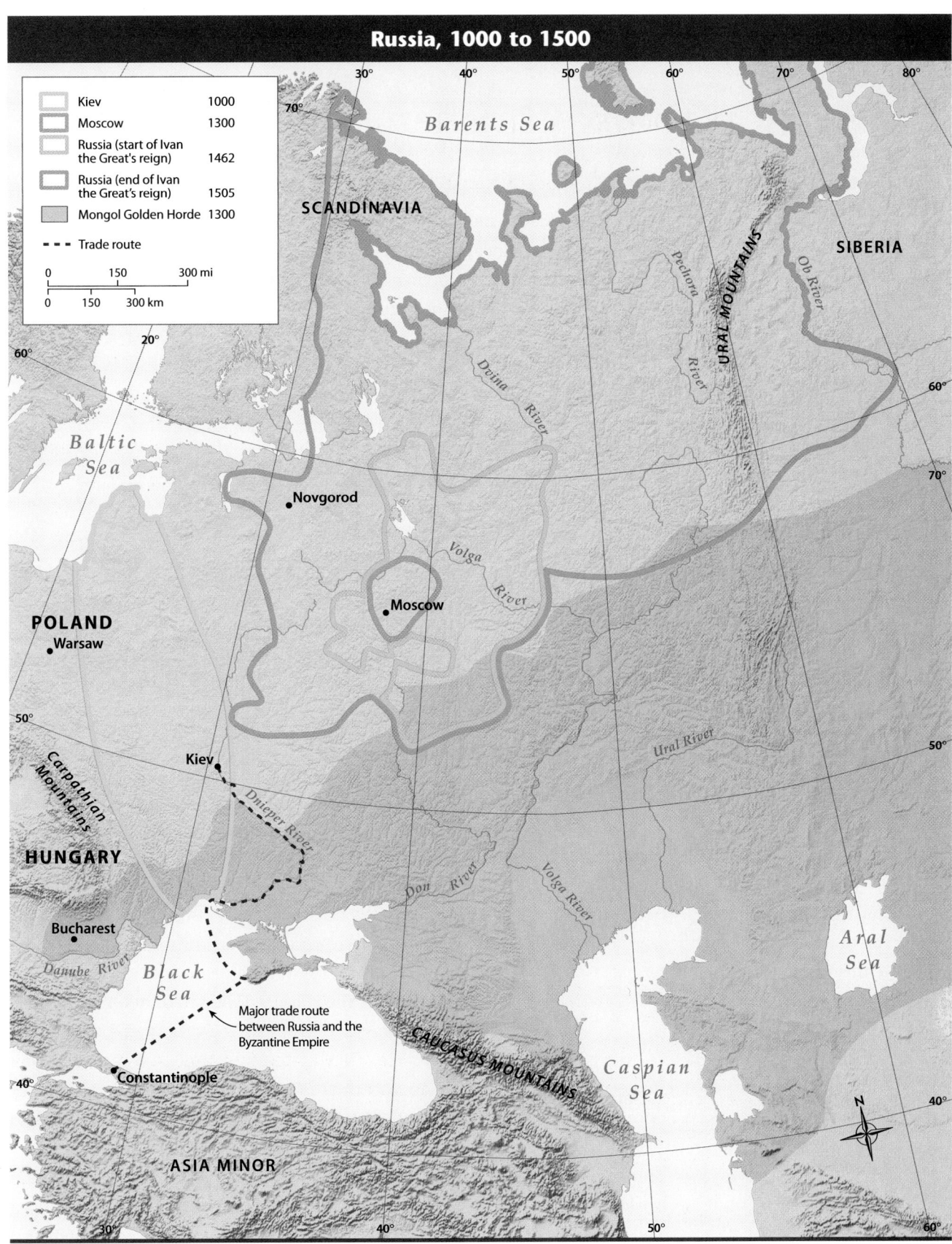

Russia, 1000 to 1500

Kiev	1000
Moscow	1300
Russia (start of Ivan the Great's reign)	1462
Russia (end of Ivan the Great's reign)	1505
Mongol Golden Horde	1300
- - - Trade route	

0   150   300 mi

0   150   300 km

Barents Sea

SCANDINAVIA

SIBERIA

URAL MOUNTAINS

Pechora River

Ob River

Dvina River

Baltic Sea

Novgorod

Volga River

POLAND

Warsaw

Moscow

Ural River

Carpathian Mountains

Kiev

Dnieper River

HUNGARY

Don River

Volga River

Aral Sea

Bucharest

Danube River

Black Sea

Major trade route between Russia and the Byzantine Empire

CAUCASUS MOUNTAINS

Caspian Sea

Constantinople

ASIA MINOR

N

Russia grew rapidly after the capital was moved from Kiev to Moscow and, later, after Ivan the Great successfully fought off the attacking Golden Horde.

245

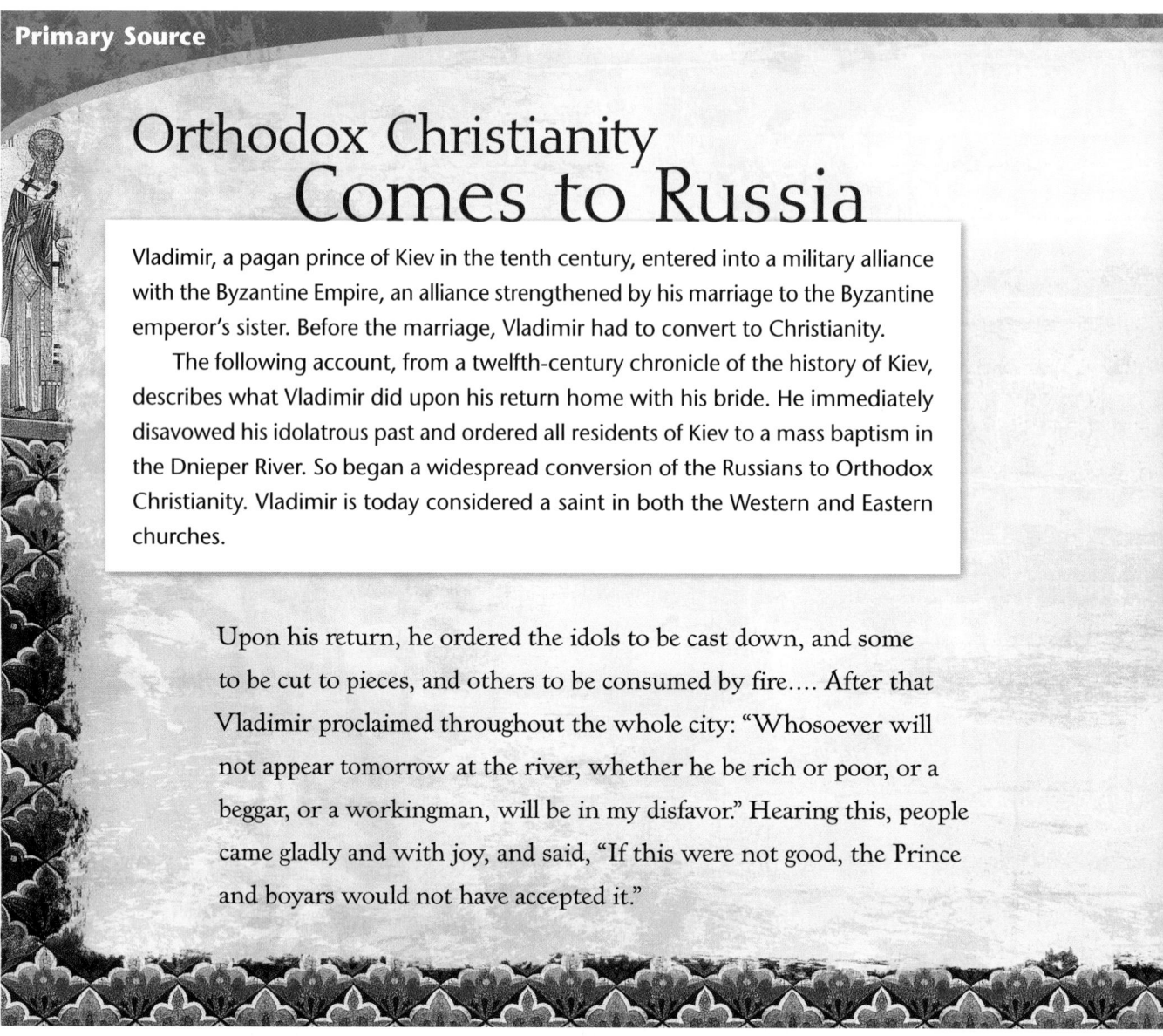

Orthodox Christianity
Comes to Russia

Vladimir, a pagan prince of Kiev in the tenth century, entered into a military alliance with the Byzantine Empire, an alliance strengthened by his marriage to the Byzantine emperor's sister. Before the marriage, Vladimir had to convert to Christianity.

The following account, from a twelfth-century chronicle of the history of Kiev, describes what Vladimir did upon his return home with his bride. He immediately disavowed his idolatrous past and ordered all residents of Kiev to a mass baptism in the Dnieper River. So began a widespread conversion of the Russians to Orthodox Christianity. Vladimir is today considered a saint in both the Western and Eastern churches.

Upon his return, he ordered the idols to be cast down, and some to be cut to pieces, and others to be consumed by fire…. After that Vladimir proclaimed throughout the whole city: "Whosoever will not appear tomorrow at the river, whether he be rich or poor, or a beggar, or a workingman, will be in my disfavor." Hearing this, people came gladly and with joy, and said, "If this were not good, the Prince and boyars would not have accepted it."

farther south, Kiev (KEE-ef). Kiev became the capital of Russia, and here the key elements of Russian culture first took shape.

Early Kiev

Kiev is now the capital of a country called Ukraine (yoo-KRAYN), and the language spoken there is a dialect of Russian. Kiev started as a trading post on the Dnieper (NEE-pur) River, which flows into the Black Sea. From Kiev, ships had access to the Mediterranean trade network and all the goods available in Constantinople.

According to the Primary Chronicle, Rurik's kinsman Oleg was the first to make Kiev his capital.

Oleg was not so much a king as head of a group of Russian princes, each ruling an area called a **principality**. In each principality, wealthy landowners called *boyars* dominated the mass of Slavic peasants.

Converting to Orthodox Christianity

One day in 941, a fleet of Russian warships appeared in the harbor of Constantinople. They could not breach the walls, but they pillaged the surrounding villages for several years, until at last Byzantine officials agreed to meet with them and work out a treaty. The two sides agreed that the Byzantines and Russians would trade as equal

Next morning Vladimir went out with the priests...to the Dnieper, and there came together people without number. They went into the water, and stood there up to their necks, and some up to their breasts, but the younger nearer the shore, and others held the younger ones, while the grown people waded into the water. And the priests stood there and said the prayers....

The people having been baptized, they all went to their homes, and Vladimir ordered churches to be built, and to place them there where formerly stood the idols. He built the church of St. Basil on the hill where stood the idol...to whom the Prince and others used to bring sacrifices. And he began to locate churches and priests over the towns, and to lead people to baptism in all towns and villages.

Vladimir, prince of Kiev, was baptized with his entire court in 988.

partners. From then on, Russians became regular visitors to Constantinople.

Around the year 957, Constantinople welcomed a royal visitor from Russia, the princess Olga, who had come to the Byzantine capital to be baptized. Princess Olga was the first ruler of Kiev to adopt Christianity. She had come to power in 945 when her husband was assassinated and her son was too young to rule. Her people continued to worship the old pagan gods, but when Olga's grandson Vladimir came to the throne, he decided a new religion might help unify his people.

An account in the Primary Chronicle, possibly legendary, reports that Vladimir sent agents to learn more about various religions, including Islam, Judaism, and Catholic Christianity. The group that visited Constantinople brought back the most impressive report. After seeing Hagia Sophia, they wrote: "We knew not whether we were in heaven or on earth. For on earth there is no such splendor or such beauty.... We only know that God dwells there among men...."

Vladimir joined the Orthodox Church and commanded all his subjects to convert. One twelfth-century account says that Vladimir ordered his subjects to come to the Dnieper River, where Orthodox priests performed a mass baptism.

Kiev's Height and Decline

Kiev prospered as an Orthodox Christian kingdom, benefiting from close ties with the Byzantine Empire. Vladimir extended his control from the Black Sea to the Baltic, an area that became known as Kievan Rus.

Vladimir's son Yaroslav led Kiev to its greatest period of glory. He built the city into a trading center that drew merchants from societies as distant as China. At the same time, he forged new political ties by having his daughters marry into the royal families of western Europe.

In Yaroslav's day, Kiev was a city of churches. More than four hundred structures beautifully built of wood graced the city. They were modeled along the lines of Byzantine architecture and decorated with Byzantine-style art, including mosaics and painted icons.

Yaroslav founded the first Russian school. He built the region's first library and filled it with Slavic translations of Greek and Latin texts. He also had scholars draft the first Russian law code, called "Russian Truth," based on Justinian's Code. It is no wonder his people called him Yaroslav the Wise.

After Yaroslav died, however, Kiev declined. Russian rulers had an unfortunate custom of dividing their realm among their sons. In just a few generations, this process transformed Kievan Rus from a powerful unified state into a collection of squabbling city-states. The discord left Kiev and all of Rus vulnerable to a fierce new enemy from the East.

Yaroslav the Wise guided Kiev to its greatest political and cultural heights.

Mongol Invasions

In the early thirteenth century, fierce horsemen came thundering out of the grassy plains of Mongolia, a land in central Asia, just north of China. Led by their chieftain, Genghis Khan (JEHNG-gihs KAHN), the Mongols set out on a campaign of plunder and conquest. Genghis Khan's sons and grandsons continued the campaign until they had built the largest land empire the world has known.

In the 1230s, the Mongols began pushing west. They charged into Russia, destroying whole towns in their path. The Russians called these invaders Tatars (TAH-tuhrz). The Tatars utterly destroyed Kiev, burning its churches and killing its inhabitants. The Tatars sowed such terror that no one dared to rebel, even after most of the Mongol army had moved on to eastern Europe.

Eventually, the Mongols divided their enormous empire into four **hordes** or military divisions, each ruled by a different branch of Genghis Khan's descendants. One group was known as the Golden Horde, perhaps because of the palace-sized golden tent that their leader put up wherever he went. The Golden Horde held Russia in its grip for over two centuries.

In time, the Mongol Tatars slightly loosened their grip on Russia. As long as a Russian prince paid tribute to his Tatar rulers and drafted soldiers for their armies, they left him alone. Although the Tatars had converted to Islam, they did not care what religion their Russian subjects followed. They left local Russian rulers in place to manage their own territories, so long as they paid the tribute.

A *tribute* is a payment one people makes to another as a gesture of submission.

For more than two centuries, Tatar domination separated Russia from the West. When western Europe was beginning to make major advancements in art and learning, Russia was left behind, with significant consequences for its later history.

The Tatars of the Golden Horde collect tribute from the Russian people.

Ivan the Great

The destruction of Kiev sent a flood of refugees north. Many settled in the principality called Muscovy (MUHS-kuh-vee), northeast of Kiev. Its capital, Moscow, near the ancient Russian city of Novgorod, was a thriving center of trade.

In the 1300s, the princes of Moscow were the Tatars' most loyal servants. To pay the tribute demanded by the Tatars, one Muscovite prince collected so much from his fellow Russians that he was nicknamed "Moneybags."

In 1462, a prince named Ivan III came to the throne of Muscovy. Ivan had no intention of remaining under Mongol rule. To the Russians, he became known as Ivan the Great.

Ivan Takes Charge

Ivan wanted to rule more than Muscovy. He wanted to rule all of Russia. Two obstacles stood in his way: the rival Russian princes and the Tatar overlords. To defeat his rivals, Ivan used any means he could to bring their territories under his control. Sometimes he bought their land, but most often he waged war.

Through war, Ivan won the important city of Novgorod. Unlike the Tatars, he was not content to let local rulers keep their power as long as they paid tribute. He killed the city's mayor and tore down the bell used to call citizens to public meetings. They would no longer need the bell or the meetings, for Ivan announced that he was "Protector of all Russia." By this, he meant that he was the absolute ruler, an autocrat in the mold of the great Byzantine emperors, and his will was law.

Ivan took land away from the aristocratic boyars and gave it to his own supporters and military officers, thereby creating a new Russian

249

A bronze statue of Ivan the Great stands as part of a larger monument erected in Russia in 1862.

aristocracy that was loyal only to him. All who resisted were sent into exile.

Through forceful, often ruthless means, Ivan gained control of much of northern Russia. He also worked to free Russia from the Tatars. He stopped sending tribute to the Tatar court. In 1480, Ivan announced that he would no longer give his allegiance to the Tatars.

The Tatars sent an army to crush Ivan. Ivan met them with his own army. The two armies sat for weeks on opposite sides of a broad river, neither daring to attack. Finally, the river froze. Expecting the enemy to charge, the Russian forces waited. To their surprise, the Tatars turned and rode away. Russia was free of its foreign masters.

Ivan Establishes the "Third Rome"

To unify his realm, Ivan used the pride that Russians took in their religion as a way to make them feel like one people. Two and a half centuries of Tatar rule had limited communication with Eastern Orthodox Christians in other regions, so the Russians had gradually developed their own version of Christianity. They conducted church services and read scripture in Russian, rather than in the Greek used in the Eastern Orthodox Church. They came to see the Russian Orthodox Church, as they called it, as the one true church, especially after Constantinople fell to the Turks in 1453, an event that left Orthodox Christianity with no capital.

Built in 1165, the white stone Church of the Intercession of the Holy Virgin is typical of Russian Orthodox churches of the time.

Ivan the Great rebuilt Moscow's kremlin, which became a symbol of Russia's new power.

Ivan the Great encouraged his people to believe that Moscow had replaced Rome and Constantinople as the new center of Christianity. In Ivan's view, Moscow was the "Third Rome" that would fill the place left vacant by the fall of Constantinople (which had been the "Second Rome").

Ivan assumed the traditional title of Roman emperors—he called himself the *tsar* (also spelled *czar*) of all Russia. The word comes from the Latin word *Caesar*. Later Russian rulers also called themselves tsars.

Ivan adopted the double-headed eagle, long a symbol of Byzantine power, as his own emblem. He married a Byzantine princess, the niece of the last Byzantine emperor. Her name was Zoe, but after her marriage she changed it to the more Russian-sounding Sophia. All these actions helped Ivan win the enthusiastic support of the Russian Orthodox Church.

A Fortress Rebuilt, a Legacy Preserved

Under Ivan the Great, Moscow became the capital of the independent kingdom of Muscovy and the center of Orthodox Christianity. Ivan wanted a place to stage royal ceremonies and spectacular religious festivals. He set out to rebuild Moscow's old and crumbling kremlin—in Russian, the word *kremlin* means "fortress."

Moscow's kremlin had fallen into disrepair. Ivan summoned the most talented builders in Russia, as well as famed architects and engineers from Italy. The Italian architects designed a majestic palace, which has come to be known as *the* Kremlin. Three great stone cathedrals rose inside the Kremlin's walls. It was all that Ivan could have hoped for: a mighty fortress, a center of learning, and a symbol of Russia's new power.

Ivan the Great shook off Tatar domination, made Moscow the center of both the Russian church and state, and extended his rule far beyond the bounds of Muscovy. In doing all this, he also preserved and extended the Byzantine legacy.

On the death of Ivan the Great in 1505, his son Vasily III ordered a new bell tower built in Moscow as a monument to his father.

251

At left, a stylized map to guide Muslims to Mecca; at right, a diagram of the Great Mosque at Mecca

700

900

622
Muhammad
leads the Hijrah
from Mecca to
Medina.

c. 680
Conflicts
within Islam
divide Sunni
and Shia.

732
Muslim expansion
into western Europe is
halted in France at the
Battle of Tours.

c. 1000
Ibn Sina begins his
Canon of Medicine, which
becomes a standard for
medical texts.

1100

1300

1071
Seljuk Turks defeat
the Byzantines at the
Battle of Manzikert.

1258
Mongols sack
Baghdad, ending the
Abbasid Caliphate.

*I*slam, one of today's major world religions, began on the Arabian Peninsula in the seventh century and grew within centuries to become a major spiritual, cultural, and political force. It grew out of the teachings of Muhammad, whose revelations were recorded in a book called the Qur'an. Followers of Islam, called Muslims, revere Muhammad as a prophet, the last in a long line of prophets from Moses to Jesus.

Muhammad, a monotheist, built a religious community around the worship of a single all-powerful God, and his teachings spread rapidly. Not long after his death, the religion of Islam branched into two major rival groups, the Sunni and the Shia.

Muhammad's successors forged a massive empire. In this vast realm, a distinctive Islamic civilization emerged. Muslim scholars preserved ancient Greek, Persian, and Indian learning while making remarkable advances of their own in fields as wide-ranging as medicine, mathematics, architecture, and philosophy.

The Rise of Islam

At the crossroads of three continents—Africa, Asia, and Europe—sits the Arabian Peninsula. This land was the birthplace of one of the world's major religions, Islam (iss-LAHM).

Key Questions

- Where and how did Islam begin?

- What do the Five Pillars of Islam require of all Muslims?

- How is Islam historically related to Judaism and Christianity?

Geography and Peoples of the Arabian Peninsula

The Arabian Peninsula is a huge landmass wedged between the Red Sea, the Persian Gulf, and the Arabian Sea. The southern coast has pastures and farmland but the rest of the peninsula is a blistering desert, much of it filled with shifting yellow sands piled into huge dunes by the wind. In this arid landscape, the only fresh water is to be found at occasional springs called **oases**.

Since the days of the Roman Empire, a people called the Bedouin (BEH-duh-wuhn) have made a home of the Arabian deserts. The Bedouins of ancient times were nomads who, with their herds of livestock, continually moved from place to place in search of sparse vegetation and water. They sheltered in the oases and their flocks supplied them with meat, milk, and wool. They rode camels, hearty animals that could go for days, even weeks, without water. The Bedouins were able to earn money as traders, hauling spices, dates, and other cargo across the peninsula.

The Bedouins were organized into families, clans, and tribes, but they recognized no single ruler or king. The tribes fought constantly. They disputed

At its peak, the Islamic Empire stretched from the Atlantic Ocean to India.

An oasis provides a rare source of fresh water in the desert sands near Riyadh, Saudi Arabia.

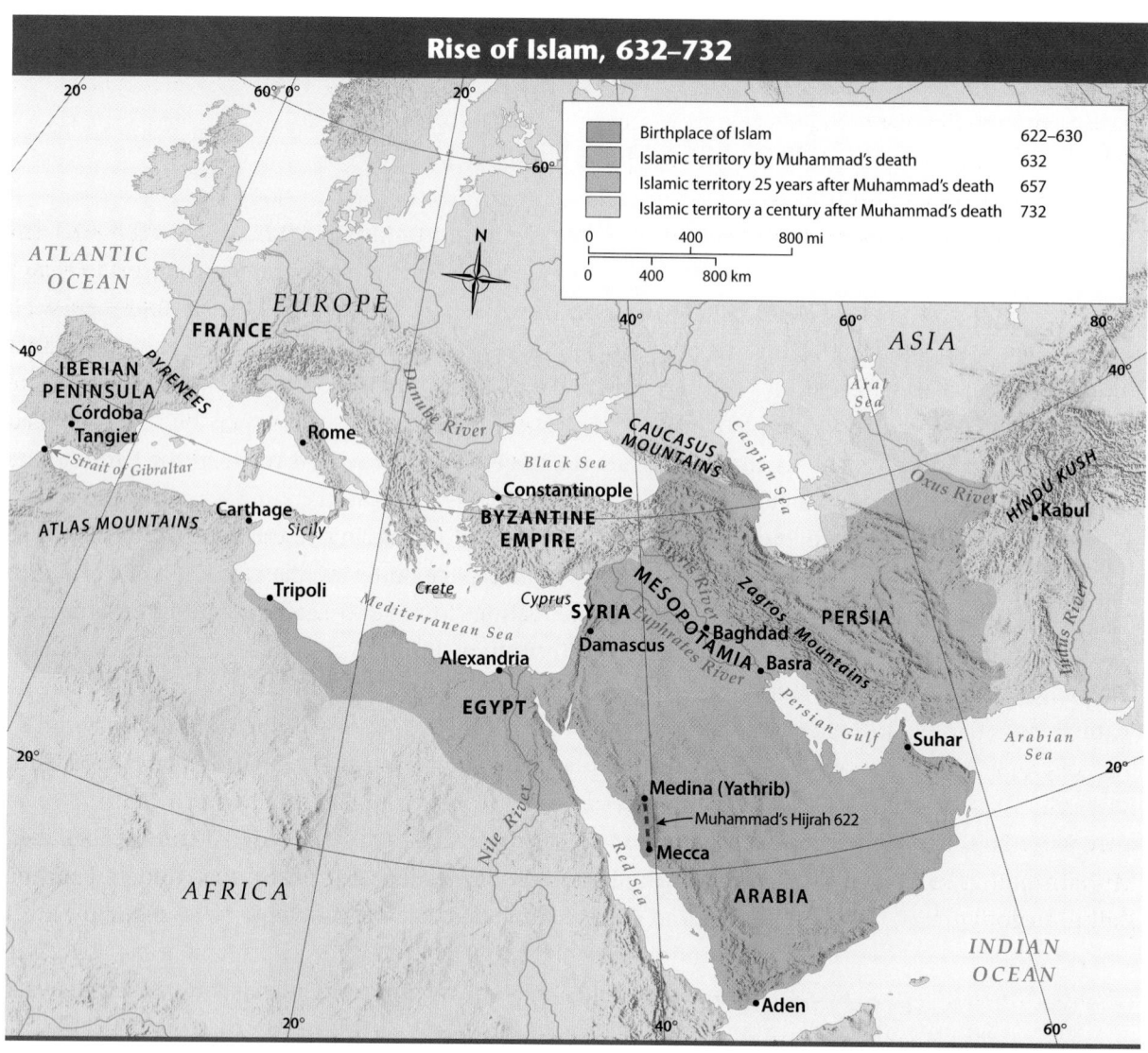

The influence of Islam grew rapidly during Muhammad's lifetime and in the century after his death, extending over five thousand miles from Spain to India.

over trade routes, oases, and matters of honor. They regularly raided one another's caravans.

Mecca and the Ka'bah

By the early 600s, ships from India and southern Africa were sailing up the Red Sea to trade with Egypt. Bustling Arabian towns emerged along the coast. One of the largest of these towns was Mecca (also spelled *Makkah*).

Trade, however, was only a side business for Mecca. The town's main attraction was a square stone temple called the **Ka'bah** (KAH-buh, meaning "the Cube"; also spelled *Kaaba*). The Ka'bah had a mysterious black stone built into its

foundation. Arabs believed that their ancestor Abraham had once restored this shrine after it had fallen into disrepair. Although Abraham had worshipped one God, most Arabs in the sixth century worshipped a multitude of nature gods, and they dedicated the Ka'bah to some of these nature gods.

The shrine attracted so many pagan pilgrims that temples to hundreds of other gods sprang up nearby. Mecca became an international center of both pilgrimage and trade, crowded with pagans, Christians, Jews, and others. People came to Mecca from places as distant as Ethiopia and the Byzantine Empire.

A *pilgrimage* is a journey to a religious shrine or other place considered sacred.

The Prophet Muhammad

Muhammad (moh-HAM-uhd; sometimes spelled *Mohammed*), the founder of Islam, was born around 570 into Mecca's most powerful tribe, the Quraysh (koo-RIYSH). Although his tribe was powerful, his clan was poor, and he rose from humble roots.

Muhammad's Early Years

Muhammad's father died before he was born, and his mother died when he was only six. The boy was raised by an uncle. As a young man, he got a job with a wealthy, older widow, Khadijah (kah-DEE-juh), who owned a trading business. Muhammad led her caravans and managed the business.

According to most historical sources, when he was twenty-five Muhammad married Khadijah. It was common practice at the time for a man to have more than one wife; and after Khadijah's death, Muhammad had several more wives. But while Khadijah lived, she was Muhammad's only wife. The couple's business prospered, and Muhammad gained a reputation as an honest, skillful negotiator.

A Changing Society

Despite his success in business, Muhammad was troubled by the state of the world around him. Arabia was going through unsettling changes at this time. In cities such as Mecca, most people were only a few generations removed from their nomadic past, when most families had been roughly equal in wealth, owning few possessions. In that not-so-distant past, clans took care of their old and sick and helped those in need.

But in Mecca in Muhammad's day, much had changed. Some people were grossly rich, others shockingly poor. Widows and orphans were often abandoned. The streets were noisy with drinking, fighting, and lewd conduct. Across Arabia, tribes continued to fight each other.

Perhaps worst of all, Mecca's prosperity had attracted the attention of dangerous neighbors. The powerful Byzantines and Persians, who had been struggling for control of Mediterranean trade, began to eye the rich towns along the Arabian coast.

Muhammad's Revelations

According to Muslim tradition, when Muhammad was about forty, he began to retreat to a cave near Mecca to meditate on the troubles he saw all around him. One day, the traditional accounts say, he came home trembling with fright. He told Khadijah that a powerful being had seized him in the cave and ordered him three times to "Recite!"

As Muhammad fled the cave, he heard a voice saying, "Thou art the messenger of God and I am Gabriel." In the end, Muhammad found that he could recite the angel Gabriel's message, which began, "Recite in the name of your Lord." The words seemed to flow from Muhammad's mouth as he received the first of what Muslims believe were many revelations from God.

Muhammad's wife told him she believed that the angel was real and that God had chosen Muhammad as his messenger to humankind. Heartened by her support, Muhammad began preaching. He urged Meccans to give up their uncaring ways and start practicing justice, charity, and peace. He preached that there was only one God, and that people must surrender their whole, unmixed loyalty to Allah (AH-luh or ah-LAH). *Allah* is the Arabic word for "God." From Muhammad's message came a new religion, Islam, the followers of which are called Muslims.

Muhammad spent the rest of his life preaching to the Arabs. He did not start out with the idea of establishing a new religion. At first he simply wanted the Arabs to give up their many idols and worship the one God—the same God that Jews and Christians worshipped. Gradually, Muhammad came to the conclusion that his mission was to be the prophet of Allah, and to bring a message from Allah to a world full of strife and bloodshed.

For a while, the people of Mecca considered Muhammad harmless. But the more he preached,

Depicting the Prophet

In religious art, Muslims avoid depicting the faces of religious figures, because to do so, they believe, is to encourage people to worship images instead of Allah alone. If a Muslim artist depicts Muhammad or another important religious figure, he will cover the face with a veil or with the image of a flame. For example, in the image below, by a Muslim artist of the fourteenth century, a veil covers the face of Muhammad, who is shown receiving a command from Allah delivered by the angel Gabriel.

Muslim artists always cover the faces of Muhammad and other important religious figures.

the more the Arab leaders turned against him. They didn't like being told their gods were not real. Besides, Meccans made a great deal of money from the thousands who journeyed every year to worship their tribal idols at the Ka'bah. All that business would disappear if pilgrims stopped coming to honor the old gods.

As Muhammad began to attract a band of believers, Mecca's rulers worried that they might lose their power and riches, so they came up with a plan to kill Muhammad and be rid of him forever.

The Hijrah

In 622, Muhammad barely escaped an assassination attempt by leading his followers to Yathrib (YA-thrub), a town more than two hundred miles (322 km) north of Mecca. Their journey is known as the **Hijrah** (HIJ-ruh; sometimes spelled *Hegira*), from the Arabic word for "migration."

The Hijrah marked a turning point in the history of Islam. In Mecca, Muhammad had been a preacher, but in Yathrib he became the leader, lawmaker, judge, and military commander of the whole town.

Muhammad told his followers that the Hijrah ended their ties to clan and tribe; they now belonged to a new group, the Muslim community. When Muslims later adopted a calendar of their own, they chose the year of the Hijrah as year one. The town of Yathrib became known as **Medina**, from the Arabic *Madinat al-Nabi*, which means "City of the Prophet."

In Medina, Muhammad encountered many Jews and Christians. He thought they would be eager to hear his message. After all, didn't they worship the same God that he worshipped? But many Christians felt little need to heed the prophet from Mecca. While some of Medina's Jews supported Muhammad, others did not, and some helped the Meccans try to oust Muhammad. Muhammad drove them out of the city and divided their lands among his followers.

The Return to Mecca

The Muslims began raiding the caravans of the Quraysh, the tribe that had driven them from Mecca. The Quraysh leaders of Mecca were angered by these raids. The result was several long years of war between Medina and Mecca. The Meccans attacked Medina several times, but Muhammad's forces always drove them back.

During this period, Muhammad's political power grew as the number of followers of Islam increased rapidly. In 630, Muhammad marched on Mecca with ten thousand soldiers and took it with scarcely a struggle. He called on Meccans to renounce their old gods and devote themselves to Allah. The Quraysh leaders could only watch as Muhammad marched to the Ka'bah, carried out hundreds of idols and destroyed them one by one. Muhammad then dedicated the cube-shaped shrine to the worship of Allah.

The man who had fled Mecca with his life in danger was now the city's undisputed leader. Muhammad proclaimed Mecca the holiest city in Islam. Mecca has since been the spiritual center of Islam, and to this day, when Muslims pray, wherever they may be, they turn to face in the direction of Mecca.

Muhammad's rule over Mecca would not last long. Soon after his triumph, he grew ill. He suffered from fatigue and fever. One day in 632, he took to his bed and spoke of his readiness to leave this world and join Allah. A few hours later, Muhammad breathed his last.

Muhammad's Teachings

Muhammad taught his followers a set of values and showed them a way to live. The principles he taught his followers continue to guide Muslim life today.

Above all, Muhammad preached that there is only one God, Allah, which means "God" in Arabic. Muhammad said that Allah wants people to choose right over wrong. People are free, Muhammad explained, but God, who is omnipotent (all-powerful), will hold people responsible for their choices.

Muhammad warned that people should submit to Allah and his commandments. In fact, *Islam* is the Arabic word for "submission," or surrendering one's whole self to God, and *Muslim* means "one who submits." Muslims believe they should submit their lives and thoughts to the will of Allah.

Muhammad insisted he was not founding a new religion but was the last of a long line of prophets. Among these prophets Muslims include Abraham, Moses, and Jesus from the Jewish and Christian traditions, though Muslims do not see Jesus as the son of God.

The Qur'an

Muhammad declared that he himself was an ordinary, mortal man, but that sometimes God spoke through him, and the words he spoke were not his but Allah's. Muslims called these words the *Qur'an* (kuh-RAN), an Arabic word meaning "recitations." Muhammad's followers passed on what he said, and some later collected his words as a single written book, which is the Qur'an that Muslims read today.

The Qur'an tells people to worship only Allah, to practice charity and justice, and to live in fear of Allah's judgment. It praises Allah's creations, gives vivid descriptions of heaven and hell, and recounts stories about earlier prophets such as Noah, Abraham, and Jesus. Some verses set forth specific rules for living as a member of the Muslim community. For example, the Qur'an specifies exactly how an inheritance should be divided among sons, daughters, wives, and

"People of the Book"

Judaism, Christianity, and Islam are all monotheistic religions. The Qur'an says that Allah is the same God that Jews and Christians worship. Muslims see Judaism and Christianity as, in effect, precursors of Islam. Muslims consider Muhammad the last prophet in a line that includes figures from the Jewish and Christian traditions, such as Abraham and Jesus. While Muslims see Muhammad as the last prophet, and the Qur'an as God's final and complete revelation, they are taught to respect Jews and Christians as "people of the book," that is, people who share the tradition of God's revelation to the prophets.

parents. In such passages, the Muslim scriptures read like a legal code.

The Five Pillars of Islam

Muhammad set forth five religious duties for Muslims to observe. He compared these duties to pillars holding up a roof, so they have become known as the Five Pillars of Islam.

- **The profession of faith:** Muslims must proclaim their faith in Allah and Muhammad's mission by reciting Arabic words that mean, "There is no god but God [Allah], and Muhammad is God's messenger."
- **Prayer:** At five prescribed times each day, Muslims must stop whatever they are doing, wash themselves, face Mecca, and pray. (In the desert, Muslims can use sand to cleanse themselves.)
- **Giving alms:** Muslims must give a portion of whatever wealth they have to those in need. The Qur'an says, "Be good to the poor and to your neighbors, whether they are friends or strangers."
- **Fasting:** During a month called Ramadan (RAH-muh-dahn), Muslims may not eat, drink, or smoke during the daylight hours. The Qur'an says that such sacrifices should help Muslims learn to fight temptation and have compassion for the poor and hungry. Ramadan, besides being a month of fasting, is also a time of additional prayer and religious study.
- **The pilgrimage to Mecca:** At least once in a lifetime, if they can, Muslims must travel to Mecca and perform certain rituals at the Ka'bah. The pilgrimage itself is called the **hajj** (haj). Today, many Muslims make the pilgrimage to Mecca each year. Although Muslims can make the pilgrimage at any time, one particular five-day period is recommended. During the hajj, the men all dress alike, in plain white robes, signifying that all are equal before Allah. The women

must be covered in modest Islamic dress. After circling the Ka'bah seven times, the pilgrims move on to several days of rituals.

Islamic Law: The Sharia

While Mecca was the holiest city in Islam, Medina remained the political center. In Medina, Islam became more than a religion. It became a community in which no line separated government and religion—indeed, the religious law was the only law. This law, known as the **Sharia** (shuh-REE-uh), or "the path," was derived in part from the Qur'an. Sharia law also came from the **Sunna**, a record of Muhammad's actions and advice, since Muhammad's life was considered an example of behavior for all Muslims.

Since they regarded Muhammad as a model for right living, early Muslims recorded everything they could remember about his words and deeds. They specified not only religious practices, such as prayer and pilgrimage, but also personal behaviors, such as refusing to eat pork. Over time, Muslim scholars added their own commentaries on traditional practices and customs, and their rulings joined the growing body of Sharia law.

By the ninth century, the Sharia had developed into a comprehensive framework for Muslim life, covering not only legal issues but also ethical standards for individual behavior. The laws applied to everything from crimes and punishments to diet, hygiene, dress, ethics, family life, community relations, and business practices. The Sharia not only outlawed theft, fraud, and murder, it also forbade gambling, eating pork, drinking intoxicating beverages, and charging interest on loans. The Sharia was considered to be not just a legal system but an expression of Allah's will. For those who follow the Sharia, Islam is not just a religion but a complete way of life.

The Practice of Islam Today

About 1.5 billion people now regard themselves as Muslims. Five times a day, the melodic call to prayer sounds from religious centers called

Muslims worship at sunset at the Grand Mosque in Mecca, the holiest city of Islam.

mosques (mahsks). Every Friday, faithful Muslims gather at these mosques for communal prayer. Religious leaders called **imams** (ih-MAHMZ) lead the prayers and give sermons.

Muslims live throughout the world but form the majority of the population in a belt of countries running from Morocco to Indonesia, and from tropical Africa to Kazakhstan. Although Islam started among Arabs, fewer than 20 percent of today's Muslims are Arab. Nearly half—more than six hundred million—of the world's Muslim population lives in Indonesia, Pakistan, India, and Bangladesh.

Most Muslim countries, with the notable exception of Saudi Arabia, now follow laws in a constitution written by political leaders. Even in these countries, however, the Sharia profoundly influences social values, and Islam still shapes daily life.

A Muslim Empire

On his death, Muhammad's community expanded into a state. Within a century, his successors had built an empire stretching from India to Spain. How did this remarkable expansion happen?

The Expansion Begins

During Muhammad's lifetime, almost all the pagan tribes on the Arabian Peninsula converted to Islam, which helped end warfare among them. But Muhammad never constructed a formal government. He named no successor nor left any instructions on how one should be chosen.

Muhammad's death divided Medina. One group thought his charismatic young cousin Ali should be their next leader. After all, Ali was married to Muhammad's daughter, Fatimah, and his children would be the Prophet's descendants. The majority, however, rallied around Muhammad's close friend and adviser, Abu Bakr (uh-BOO BAK-uhr).

A *charismatic* person has an extraordinarily appealing, magnetic personality.

Abu Bakr was chosen as the new leader and assumed the modest title of caliph (KAY-luhf), which means "successor." He said he could not replace the Prophet and would make no new laws. He would only administer the laws Muhammad had established.

Abu Bakr faced an immediate crisis. Many tribes that had pledged loyalty to Muhammad now declared their independence. Abu Bakr went to war to bring them back. He lived only two years as caliph, but in that time he defeated the rebels and established an Islamic state headquartered in Medina.

Abu Bakr attempted to extend Muslim influence even farther. He sent Muslim warriors into Mesopotamia, Syria, and lands along the eastern Mediterranean coast. These troops fought with zeal, because they believed they were carrying out the will of Allah.

Abu Bakr spread Islam across the Arabian Peninsula and beyond. The caliphs who followed set their sights to the north and west, on the empires of the Persians and the Byzantines.

Both empires were vulnerable when the Muslims attacked. The Byzantines and Persians had just fought an exhausting war. The Persians were rebelling against their rulers, and the plague was still ravaging the Byzantine world. Muslim armies easily toppled the Persian Empire. They brought all the eastern territories of the Byzantine Empire under Muslim rule.

Conflict and Division

After Abu Bakr's short reign, Muslims disagreed about how to choose the next caliph. One group believed that the caliph should always be someone from

Key Questions

- How and where did Islam spread after Muhammad's death?

- What led to the division between Sunni and Shia Muslims? What are the long-term consequences of this split?

Muhammad's family. Muhammad left no son, so this group rallied around his cousin and son-in-law, Ali, and Ali's descendants. Ali's supporters were called the Shia Ali ("the party of Ali"), or Shia (SHEE-ah) for short. They are often referred to as Shiites (SHEE-iyts).

Many followers of Abu Bakr, on the other hand, did not want the leadership of Islam to stay in Muhammad's family. They said the most capable Muslim should be the caliph, and that he should rule following the Qur'an and the example of Muhammad. These Muslims are called Sunni (SOU-nee), from *sunna*, the Arabic word for "example."

The Shia—the supporters of Ali—were pleased when Ali was chosen as the next caliph. But some Muslims rejected the decision. The governor of Syria, a man named Mu'awiya (moo-AH-wee-yuh), blamed Ali for the murder of the previous caliph. Mu'awiya claimed the caliphate (KAY-luh-fayt or KAL-uh-fayt) for himself. Ali spent much of his five years as caliph fighting Mu'awiya and other rebels. In 661, an assassin killed Ali and Mu'awiya immediately took charge.

> A *caliphate* is the office or government of a caliph.

The Meaning of Jihad

The early Muslims saw their wars of conquest as a **jihad** (jih-HAHD). In Arabic, *jihad* simply means "struggle." The Qur'an refers to jihad only in connection with self-defense, but the first caliphs expanded the term to include wars of conquest, which they viewed as holy wars against enemies of Islam. Many Muslims believed that those who died fighting to destroy the enemies of Islam would win a great reward in paradise, or the heavenly afterlife.

Some later scholars have emphasized the idea of a "greater jihad," that is, jihad as an internal spiritual struggle to overcome one's own faults and thus live a good life. Many Muslims now understand jihad as an internal struggle to better oneself. Some, however, still embrace the idea of jihad as war against enemies of Islam.

Ali's death marked the end of an era. The first four caliphs had been chosen by the community, and many Muslims later called them the "rightly guided ones." Mu'awiya, by contrast, established a dynasty known as the Umayyad (oo-MAH-yahd), and, like many ancient dynasties, the Umayyads followed the practice of passing authority from father to son. When an Umayyad caliph died, his son automatically inherited the throne.

Most Muslims accepted this new order, but not Ali's followers. In 680, Ali's son Husayn (hoo-SAYN; also spelled *Hussein*) marched into Iraq with a small band of followers, vowing to incite a revolt. An imperial army trapped him near the Euphrates River and killed him and his entire family.

The deaths of Ali and Husayn deeply moved the Shias and

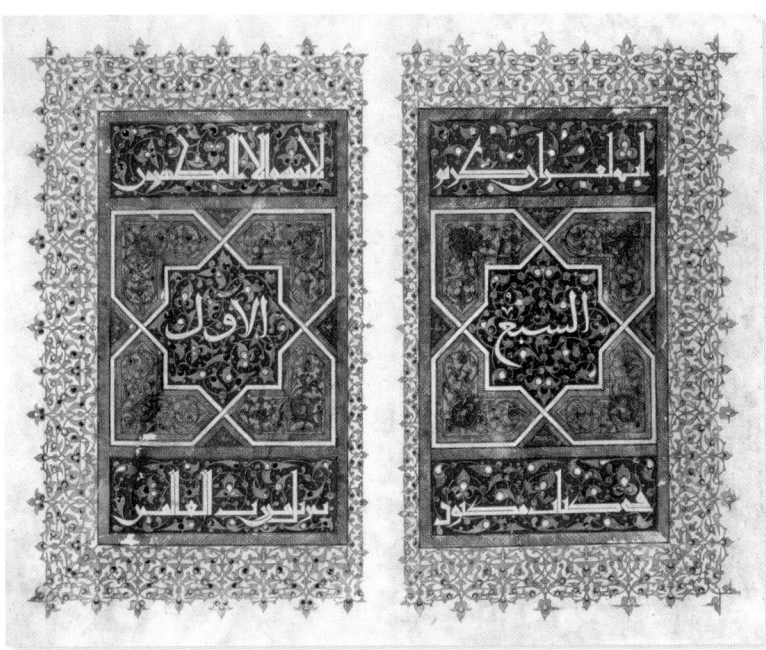

The elaborately decorated frontispiece, or opening pages, of a Qur'an, Islam's holy book, dating from about 1300

Shia and Sunni

The split between Shia and Sunni persists to this day, and has sometimes caused bitter struggles within Islam, even though their practices do not differ greatly. Both revere Muhammad and see the Qur'an as the word of God. Both observe the same religious festivals, but Shias also observe the anniversary of Husayn's death as a day of mourning. Compared to the Sunni, Shia Muslims invest their imams with more authority in religious matters, which has led to great political power for some Shia imams. Despite their similarities, the legacy of earlier conflicts continues to divide the two communities.

About 90 percent of Muslims today are Sunni. The rest are Shia. Most of the world's Shia population lives in Iran, where more than 90 percent of the Muslims are Shia.

Within Islam, a third and smaller group developed, called Sufis (SOO-feez). Sufis are mystics who seek a direct personal experience of God.

shaped their sense of themselves and their destiny. More than ever, the Shias passionately embraced the idea of a divinely inspired leader, descended from Ali, guiding the entire Islamic community.

In contrast, the Sunnis—by far the majority among Muslims—believed the era of divine guidance had ended with Muhammad. They accepted the idea of an ordinary man administering Sharia, the law derived from the Qur'an and from the Prophet's Sunna, his example and traditions.

The Umayyad Dynasty

The Umayyads moved their capital to Mu'awiya's base of power, the city of Damascus in Syria. They built a professional army and kept expanding their territory. By 715, Umayyad power extended beyond the Indus River in the east.

In the west, Muslim armies swept across North Africa. As they conquered, the Arab armies converted many Berbers—the pastoral people of North Africa—to Islam. Around 710, an army of both Arab and Berber soldiers crossed the Strait of Gibraltar and conquered much of Spain. Then they began to cross the Pyrenees and press into France.

In 732, however, near the city of Tours in west-central France, a Christian army led by Charles Martel stopped the Muslim advance. The Battle of Tours, as it is now known, is often considered a historical turning point because, had the battle gone the other way, Muslim armies might have continued their expansion into western Europe.

Charles Martel went on to found an important European dynasty. The Muslim commander died at Tours, and his army fell back to southern Spain, where a Muslim state had developed in the region called Al-Andalus (al-AN-duh-luhs).

Despite the defeat at Tours, in the century from 632 to 732, Muslim forces achieved enormous victories. A hundred years after Muhammad's death, the Muslim caliphs ruled a sprawling Islamic Empire.

A colorful and elaborate mosaic adorns the Great Mosque in Damascus, Syria, built c. 705–715.

In 691, the Umayyad caliphs completed the Dome of the Rock in Jerusalem, one of the three most holy sites for Muslims.

An Efficient Empire

At its greatest extent, the Muslim empire stretched from the Atlantic Ocean to India. The Umayyads ran an efficient empire. They built public wells, irrigation works, mosques, roads, bridges, and a postal system. Trade flourished, as Muslim merchants could travel safely over an extensive network of roads. Textiles from India found eager buyers in Spain, and Spanish silver was valued in faraway Afghanistan.

Arabic replaced Greek and Persian as the language of government, but the Umayyads kept the Persian and Byzantine administrative systems in place. The Umayyads welcomed anyone with useful skills, and did not force conquered peoples to convert to Islam. Under Umayyad rule, Jews, Christians, and Zoroastrians could not carry weapons but were allowed to practice their religions freely, so long as they paid a special tax. Many of those who could not afford to pay the tax eventually converted to Islam.

Tolerance of other religions did not mean social equality. Muslims had greater social and economic opportunities than non-Muslims, and Arab Muslims enjoyed more opportunities than non-Arab Muslims.

The Abbasid Dynasty

Despite the prosperity they helped create, the Umayyads had many enemies. In 750, Muslims who opposed the Umayyads united against them and went to war. They crushed the Umayyad army and then proceeded to massacre every Umayyad they could find. The most powerful of these rebel groups proclaimed one of their own as the new caliph. He was descended from an uncle of Muhammad named Abbas, and thus the new rulers were known as the Abbasids (uh-BA-sids).

The Splendors of Baghdad

In central Iraq, the Abbasids established their capital in Baghdad, near the site of ancient Babylon. By

265

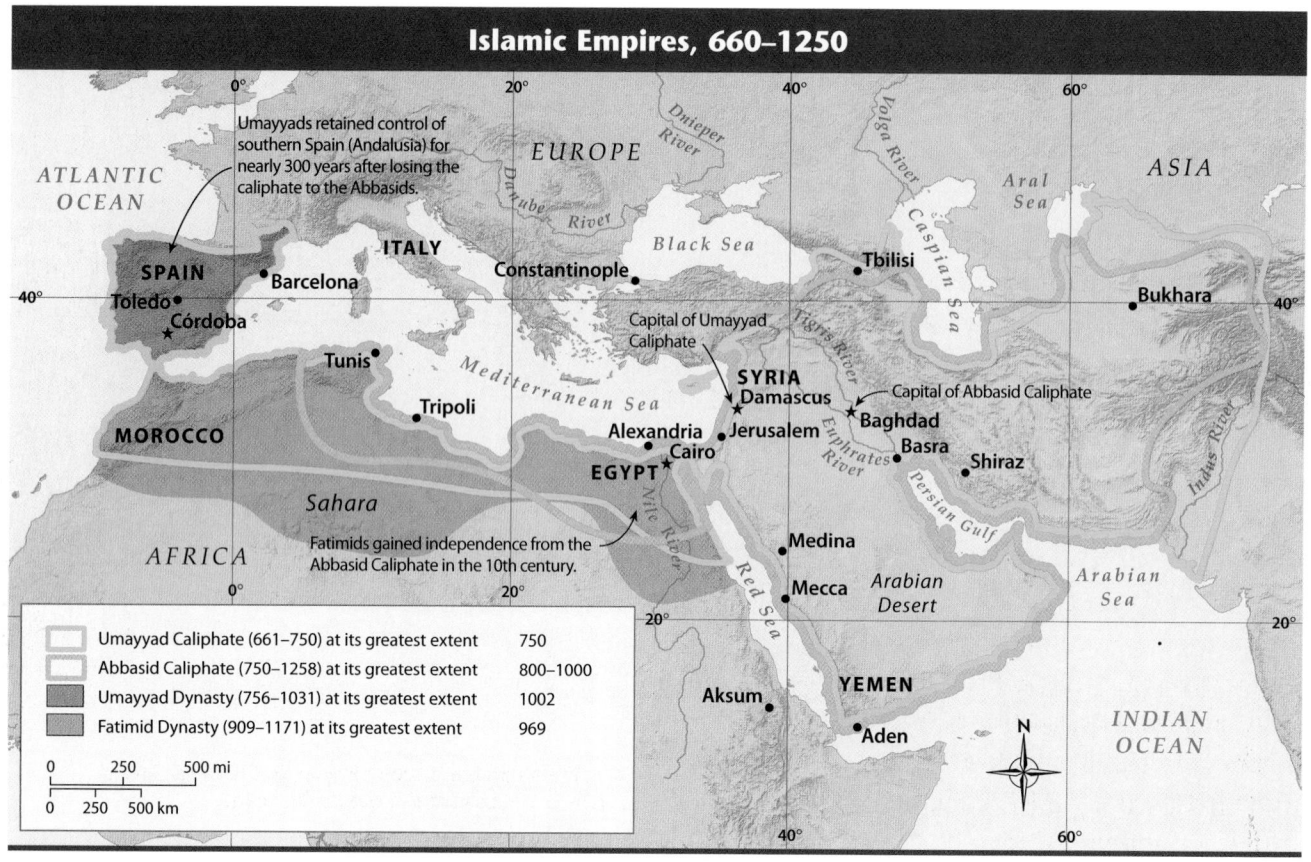

Islamic Empires, 660–1250

Umayyads retained control of southern Spain (Andalusia) for nearly 300 years after losing the caliphate to the Abbasids.

Capital of Umayyad Caliphate

Capital of Abbasid Caliphate

Fatimids gained independence from the Abbasid Caliphate in the 10th century.

	Umayyad Caliphate (661–750) at its greatest extent	750
	Abbasid Caliphate (750–1258) at its greatest extent	800–1000
	Umayyad Dynasty (756–1031) at its greatest extent	1002
	Fatimid Dynasty (909–1171) at its greatest extent	969

After four hundred years of expansion, the Islamic caliphate went on the defensive and ultimately succumbed to invading armies in the thirteenth century.

800, Baghdad was the first city in history with over a million people. Because ships from the Indian Ocean could sail up the Tigris River to Baghdad, the city became a hub of global trade.

Baghdad was also situated on caravan routes running east and west, from the Mediterranean coast and Asia Minor to India, China, and central Asia. "All the people of the world have their own neighborhoods there," one geographer wrote. "Merchandise comes from India, Sind, China, Tibet, the land of the Turks, ...[and] the Abyssinians...." In this thriving city, more than a hundred shops sold a recent Chinese invention, paper.

> *Sind* (also spelled *Sindh*) is part of what is now southeastern Pakistan.

A Diverse Society

Under the Abbasids, Arabs had to share power with Muslims of other origins. Arabic remained the language of law, prayer, and scholarship.

Persians held many positions in government, the arts, and professions such as medicine. The vizier, a powerful official who ran the empire's day-to-day business, was usually a Persian.

The Turks also rose to hold a share of power. The Turks were originally brought to the empire as slaves. The caliphs bought them as boys in central Asia and raised them in Baghdad to serve as elite bodyguards. The custom spread until even minor governors in outlying provinces were using Turkish slaves as bodyguards. Eventually, the Turks became a military aristocracy within the empire.

Under Abbasid rule, the Islamic Empire grew even more prosperous than it had been in Umayyad times. Scholarship and learning thrived. In this era, Muslims studied the great books of the past, developed new philosophies, and explored the natural world.

The Abbasids ruled for over five hundred years. Though their power waned after the first two

centuries, Muslims continued to make impressive cultural advances even as their political unity was fragmenting.

Islamic Rule in Spain

In 750, when the Abbasid revolutionaries were killing the Umayyads, one young Umayyad prince, Abd al-Rahman (uhb-DAHL-rahk-MAHN), managed to escape to Spain. There, in a region already conquered by Muslims, he managed to take control of the independent state of Al-Andalus, or Andalusia (AN-duh-LOO-zhuh). Abd al-Rahman established an Umayyad caliphate, and his descendants eventually claimed to be the true caliphs of Islam. Andalusia remained a Muslim kingdom until 1492, when its Christian neighbors overran it.

The Court of the Lions, at the Alhambra palace complex in Granada, Spain, features twelve carved lions at the base of the central fountain.

Abd al-Rahman followed the original Umayyad Empire's policy of religious toleration—a practical policy, since the people he ruled were mostly Christian, and included a significant number of Jews. While Muslims held the top political positions, Jews and Christians were protected as "people of the book," and were free to follow their own religious practices as long as they paid the required tax. They could enter any profession, and some achieved high positions in the government.

Splendid Cities in Spain

The Umayyads in Spain made the city of Cordoba their capital. By the tenth century, Cordoba was the biggest, richest city in Europe, famous for its well-lit streets, clean hospitals, beautiful mosques, and majestic public buildings. Above all, it was a center of learning—the largest of its seventy libraries housed more than four hundred thousand volumes.

Andalusia had other centers of culture as well. Granada, a later Muslim capital, was renowned for brilliant architecture, especially a palace complex known as the Alhambra, mainly constructed between the mid-1200s and the mid-1300s. Surrounded by high red walls and towers, the palace is a calm, beautiful site on a plateau overlooking Granada. Some of the walls feature intricate carvings in the shapes of flowers, stars, or Arabic writing. There are dozens of halls and gardens in the Alhambra, as well as grand courtyards, including the Court of the Lions, so called because of a central fountain with twelve carved lions forming the base.

Decline of the Abbasids

The Abbasid Empire reached a peak of wealth and splendor under the rule of its fifth caliph, Harun al-Rashid. Even during his reign, however, there was unrest and revolt in parts of the empire. When he died in 809, his two sons fought over who should become the next caliph. Their battles wreaked great damage on the city of Baghdad.

By the eleventh century, Abbasid power was waning. More and more, the central government in Baghdad lost control of the provinces, where governors did as they pleased.

267

In Egypt and North Africa, the Fatimid (FAT-uh-mid) Caliphate challenged the rule of the Abbasids. The Fatimids were Shia Muslims who claimed descent from Fatimah, the revered daughter of Muhammad. From their capital in Cairo, the Fatimids grew wealthy by controlling the network of trade from the Mediterranean to the Red Sea.

The Seljuk Turks

As the Abbasids grew weaker, a nomadic people from central Asia, the Seljuk Turks, grew stronger. The Seljuk Turks had converted to Islam, and for years they were hired to serve as soldiers in the armies of the Abbasid caliphs. In 1055, the Seljuks took control of Baghdad. They left the Abbasid caliph in place as the highest religious authority. The political power, however, was in the hands of the Seljuk leader, who took for himself the title of "sultan," a title that would later be used in much of the Islamic world.

The Seljuk Turks pushed into the Anatolian Peninsula (Asia Minor) and threatened the Byzantine Empire. In 1071, the Seljuks crushed the Byzantines at the Battle of Manzikert. Eventually they gained control of much of Asia Minor.

As Seljuk expansion threatened the city of Constantinople, the Byzantine emperor asked the Christian states of western Europe for help. Thus in 1095 began the first of a series of wars called the **Crusades**. Christian knights and others from western European lands streamed east to fight the Turks, halt Muslim expansion, and gain control of what they called the Holy Land, consisting of Jerusalem and its surroundings. These wars had little impact on the larger Islamic world, but the Crusaders took back stories about Muslim wealth that deeply impressed the West. (You will read more about the Crusades in a later chapter.)

The Mongols Attack

The final blow for the Abbasid Caliphate came from the Mongols. You've learned how, in the early thirteenth century, these fierce nomadic people, led by Genghis Khan, swept out of central Asia on a campaign of plunder and conquest. In 1258, Hülegü (hoo-LAH-goo), a grandson of Genghis Khan, burned down Baghdad—its libraries, mosques, and palaces were all reduced to rubble and ashes. The Mongols slaughtered the city's inhabitants—possibly as many as a million people.

The Abbasid Caliphate was no more. With the destruction of Baghdad, the center of Islamic civilization shifted to Cairo, in Egypt. Islam remained a powerful force, though the great Islamic Empire established by the Arabs in the seventh and eighth centuries was left fragmented.

The Abbasid Caliphate ended when Mongol forces stormed and captured Baghdad in 1258, reducing the city to rubble.

Islamic Life and Culture

The Sharia, you recall, was more than a legal code. It was also a comprehensive guide about how to live. It set down rules for individual behavior, business practices, family life, and more. Thus, for most Muslims, to practice Islam was a way of life as well as a religion.

Family and Society

The Sharia had a great deal to say about family life. It commanded that the young honor the old, children obey parents, and parents care for their children. Men could have several wives, and wives were expected to obey their husbands.

The Sharia did give women rights to own and control their own property, as well as some limited ability to seek divorce. As years passed and the Sharia evolved, some laws strictly separated the public and private spheres for women in Islamic society. For example, Sharia scholars declared that pious women must not show their faces to strangers, so Muslim homes were built with high surrounding walls. Women lived mostly in the private sphere of the home, but when they went out in public most women wore veils to cover their faces.

Social Structure

In the Islamic Empire, people associated with the court enjoyed top status as wealthy aristocrats. Religious scholars known as **ulama** acquired immense power, because they alone had authority to interpret the Sharia. They worked as judges and teachers, ran mosques, and advised the government.

In Muslim society, merchants enjoyed high respect since Muhammad himself had been a merchant. Those who worked the land, however, were mostly peasant farmers. They owned small plots or worked for landlords. These farmers were not tied to the land but could move freely to other districts if they had the means.

Most household labor was done by slaves. Slaves also worked in mines, on farms, and in the army. When Islam was founded, slavery was common throughout the world. The Qur'an placed some restrictions on slavery but, like the Bible, it did not ban slavery outright. Islam did teach that it was a virtuous act to free a slave.

While Muslims could own slaves, the law specified that those slaves could not be fellow Muslims. Most slaves came from non-Muslim lands, including non-Muslim parts of Africa, central and eastern Europe, and central Asia. The slave trade eventually formed a substantial part of the economy in parts of the Islamic Empire.

Key Questions

- What are some of the major achievements of Muslim scholars and artists?
- How did Muslim scholars preserve ancient Greek and Roman learning?

Trade and Urban Life

Since merchants enjoyed prestige in Islamic society, Muslim boys gladly went into trade. The empire was knit together by a vast network of land and sea routes. Ships crossed the Mediterranean hauling silver, copper, timber, and leather from Spain. They sailed back loaded with gems, incense, handcrafted goods, and other products from the East. Muslim traders sailed across the Indian Ocean to the islands of Indonesia for spices. They headed south to Africa for gold and slaves.

Caravans of camels and donkeys loaded with cargo crossed Persia, moving between central Asia, China, India, and Mesopotamia on the Silk Road, which was not a single highway but a complex network of roads.

Along the trade routes, Muslim scholars and writers often traveled with the merchants, since Muslims considered travel educational. During their travels, Muslims spread Islam as themselves absorbed the legacies of Greek, Chinese, and Indian thought.

In towns and cities, merchants traded goods in crowded, noisy **bazaars**, markets with rows of shops open to the street. Here, buyers and sellers from many lands exchanged news, stories, gossip, and ideas. These teeming marketplaces fueled the diffusion of culture and ideas.

Cities in the Islamic Empire

Many great cities grew and thrived in the Islamic Empire. New cities such as Kufa and Basra grew

The prayer hall of the Great Mosque at Cordoba, Spain, features a grand double-arched arcade.

up around Arab garrisons in conquered territory. Ancient centers such as Alexandria grew huge and rich. At their height, Baghdad, Cairo, and Cordoba were among the world's biggest cities, rivaled only by Constantinople and one or two cities in China.

In Muslim cities, neighborhoods clustered around mosques. The mosques served not just as places for public worship but as schools, meeting centers, and housing for travelers. Every city had at least one major mosque, usually set in the midst of a spacious public square. Private homes, mostly made of sun-dried bricks, lined narrow streets that snaked between high walls.

This lively portrayal of an Islamic bazaar, c. 1250, depicts a jeweler, an herbalist, a butcher, and a baker in their open-air shops.

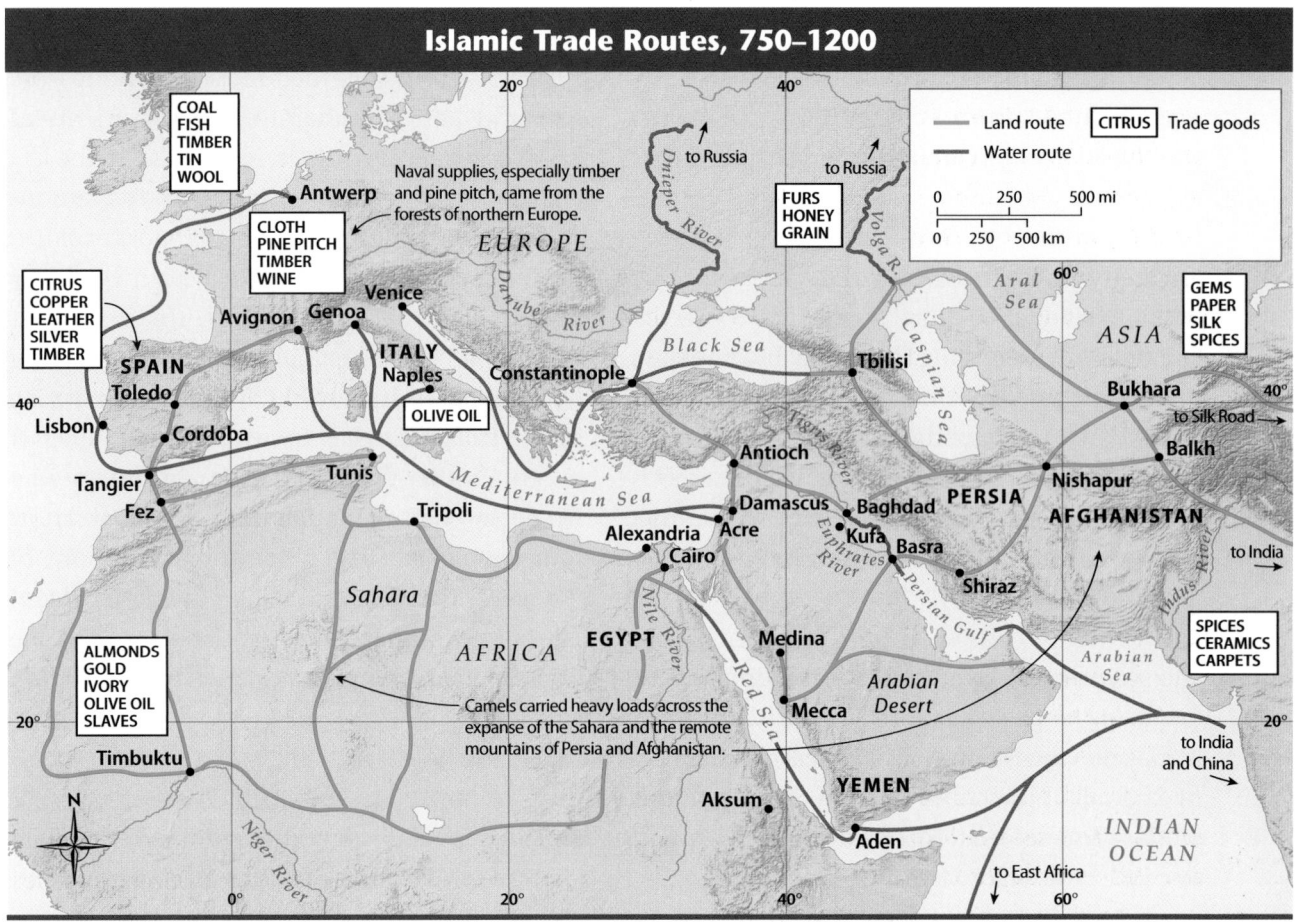

Islamic Trade Routes, 750–1200

Legend:
— Land route | CITRUS Trade goods
— Water route

0   250   500 mi
0   250   500 km

COAL
FISH
TIMBER
TIN
WOOL

Naval supplies, especially timber and pine pitch, came from the forests of northern Europe.

to Russia

to Russia

FURS
HONEY
GRAIN

GEMS
PAPER
SILK
SPICES

Dnieper River

EUROPE

Danube River

CLOTH
PINE PITCH
TIMBER
WINE

Antwerp

Volga R.

Aral Sea

ASIA

Venice

Avignon Genoa

CITRUS
COPPER
LEATHER
SILVER
TIMBER

ITALY
Naples

Black Sea

Tbilisi

Caspian Sea

Bukhara

to Silk Road

SPAIN
Toledo

Constantinople

Balkh

Lisbon

Cordoba

OLIVE OIL

Mediterranean Sea

Antioch

Tigris River

Baghdad PERSIA Nishapur

Tangier

Tunis

Damascus

Kufa

AFGHANISTAN

to India

Fez

Tripoli

Acre

Basra

Euphrates River

Alexandria

Shiraz

Cairo

Indus River

Sahara

Nile River

Medina

Persian Gulf

SPICES
CERAMICS
CARPETS

ALMONDS
GOLD
IVORY
OLIVE OIL
SLAVES

AFRICA **EGYPT**

Camels carried heavy loads across the expanse of the Sahara and the remote mountains of Persia and Afghanistan.

Mecca

Arabian Desert

Arabian Sea

to India and China

Timbuktu

Niger River

Aksum

Red Sea

YEMEN

INDIAN OCEAN

N

Aden

to East Africa

Trade along a network of strategic land and sea routes helped the Islamic caliphate prosper for nearly five centuries.

Portions of every city were set aside for bazaars. Businesses were separated by type, with butchers on one block, goldsmiths on another, and so on. Bazaars were busy social centers, filled with tea houses and restaurants where traveling merchants, local craftsmen, nomads, and others could chat, strike deals, and discuss ideas.

Islamic Scholarship

Muslim tradition holds that Muhammad could not read or write. Nevertheless, he greatly valued learning. "Seek knowledge even unto China," he told his followers. The early caliphs took him seriously. They set up schools so that young pupils could learn to read the Qur'an. They used state funds to pay a group of scholars to devote themselves entirely to learning and teaching. In Arab society, scholars were familiar and respected figures.

The Quest for Knowledge

As Muslims conquered new territories, they discovered and preserved the learning of older civilizations. Around the year 830, the Abbasid caliph built a massive library and research center in Baghdad. The center was called the House of Wisdom. It was filled with Arabic translations of great Persian, Indian, and Greek books. In other Muslim cities as well, scholars flocked to libraries to study the books, and students came to learn from the scholars.

In Egypt, scholars and students gathered in Cairo at Al-Azhar, a leading *madrassa* (a center of learning, like a university). Al-Azhar was established around 970 by the Fatimid Caliphate, mainly for the study of Islamic law and theology.

In Islamic Spain, the city of Toledo was a center of scholarship, where ancient Greek works were translated into Arabic and from Arabic into Latin.

271

The Latin books eventually found their way to Europe, where they helped fuel the revival of classical learning known as the Renaissance (which you'll read about in an upcoming chapter).

Science in the Muslim World

Inspired by the ancient Greeks, some Muslims began to study the natural world. They observed and classified everything from rocks and rainbows to stars and diseases. Unlike the Greeks, they conducted practical experiments to test their ideas. These curiosity-driven scholars called themselves philosophers, but they were really early scientists, laying the basis for such fields as physics, chemistry, and biology.

For religious reasons, the measurement of time and space was of great interest to Muslims. They frequently needed to know the precise time because Islamic rites such as praying, pilgrimage, and fasting must occur at prescribed times of the day or year. Muslims also needed to know their relative location since they must face Mecca when at prayer.

Arabs perfected the **astrolabe**, an instrument for determining the position of the sun, moon, and stars from any given spot. This instrument helped Muslim sailors and merchants, as it proved extremely useful for navigation. The astrolabe was also useful for surveying and mapping territory. Muslim geographers mapped the eastern hemisphere and were the first to estimate the approximate size of the earth.

Muslims built observatories to track the movement of heavenly bodies. They corrected the star charts and tables of the great Greek astronomer, Ptolemy. Based on these corrections, in the late eleventh century a panel of astronomers headed by the Persian mathematician Omar Khayyam (kiy-YAHM) devised a calendar so accurate it is still used in the Islamic world.

Astrolabe, c. 1300

Muslim Mathematical Advances

Islamic scientists did their most important work in mathematics. Muhammad al-Khwarizmi (al-KHWAHR-iz-mee) was born in Baghdad in the late eighth century and later studied in the famous House of Wisdom there. One of his books explored the numbering system that had been invented by Indian mathematicians of the Gupta period. Al-Khwarizmi's book, later translated into Latin, introduced to the Western world the Indian numbering system still used today, known as Arabic numerals.

In another book, al-Khwarizmi invented a whole new field of mathematics, which we know today as algebra. The name comes from one of the words in the Arabic title of the book, *al-jabr*. The book's complete title, translated, means "The Compendious Book on Calculation by Completion and Balancing."

Muslim Contributions to Medicine

Muslims made great contributions to the early study of medicine. They started by compiling and sorting the findings of the past. For example, the tenth-century Persian scholar al-Razi, perhaps the greatest physician of his time, wrote an encyclopedia comparing what Syrian, Greek, Indian, and Persian doctors had said about hundreds of illnesses.

Around the year 1000, the Persian philosopher Ibn Sina (IB-uhn SEE-nah), who was known to the West as Avicenna, began work on his masterpiece, *The Canon of Medicine*, in which he summarized the medical knowledge of his time and showed how to diagnose and treat every known illness. His book would later be translated and used for centuries in Europe. Medical schools as far away as Paris used Ibn Sina's *Canon* as their core textbook until the seventeenth century.

The word *canon* has many meanings, including an accepted body of rules and principles.

To apply this medical knowledge, the Abbasid caliphs built public hospitals that provided free care to all. Patients could benefit from effective medicines that Muslim doctors made from plant and animal extracts. Students traveled thousands

A detail from the Dome of the Rock mosque in Jerusalem features abstract and geometric patterns called arabesques.

of miles to study medicine at Muslim centers of learning. Some Europeans sent their sons to study medicine with Islamic scholars. The achievements of Ibn Sina and others made Muslim medicine a wonder of the age.

Islamic Art

A famous Islamic saying declares, "Allah is beautiful and loves beauty." Muslim artists tried to fill the world with beautiful things that pleased the eye and reminded the faithful of Islamic teachings. As Muslims expanded their empire, they encountered artwork in Egypt, Syria, Persia, Mesopotamia, and beyond. They learned from the lands they conquered and wove new ideas into their own distinctive style of art.

Because Muhammad had taught that Allah alone could create life, Muslims believed that it was a sin of arrogance to draw living creatures, for that would be imitating Allah. So Muslim artists usually did not make pictures or statues of lifelike beings. Instead, they decorated objects with complex patterns called **arabesques** (air-uh-BESKS), designs based on the intertwined forms of stems, vines, and flowers. Eventually, arabesques became more abstract and geometric.

Muslims admired **calligraphy** (kuh-LIH-gruh-fee), the art of beautiful writing. The elegant Arabic letters lent themselves

to intricate patterns. Muslims cherished copies of the Qur'an created by great calligraphers. Many of these books were artistic treasures, with vividly painted arabesques around the text. Muslim artists covered walls, floors, carpets, vases, swords, and more with elaborate letter-patterns, often working in passages from the Qur'an. For the Muslims, the art of calligraphy was yet another way to proclaim the glory of Allah.

Mosques and Muslim Architecture

Islamic civilization created many architectural masterpieces. As the Islamic Empire grew, Muslims adopted architectural features from different lands. The Byzantines—who had built the Hagia Sophia in Constantinople, with its enormous light-filled dome—inspired Muslim architects to build mosques with domes. In 691, the Umayyad caliphs completed a massive mosque in Jerusalem called the Dome of the Rock.

From the Persians, Muslims learned to construct mosques with pointed arches. When North African Muslims built mosques, they added towers called minarets (min-uh-RETS). Men climbed to the top of these minarets to call people to prayer.

The Sultan Ahmed Mosque, also called the Blue Mosque, in Istanbul, Turkey, features a dome and minarets from which the call to prayer goes out five times a day.

273

A decorated Persian mihrab marks the direction of Mecca.

In the prayer halls, rugs cover the floor. A decorated niche called a *mihrab* (mih-RAHB) marks the direction of Mecca, which worshippers face to pray.

Muslim Literature

Before Islam, the Arabs had a tradition of oral literature, including eloquent poems of love, lamentation, and praise for heroes. After Islam was founded, Arabs improved their alphabet to make sure the Qur'an would be preserved sound for sound, and the language itself gained power from the rhythmic, musical quality of the scriptures. The Arabic language soon came to dominate the Muslim world. When Persian, the older literary language of the region, began to flourish again in the eleventh century, it was written in Arabic script.

Muslim mystics, the Sufis, founded a tradition of love poetry addressed to Allah. Among the first of these Sufi poets was the Arabic poet Rabia of Basra, but few of her poems have survived. The greatest Sufi poet, Rumi, wrote in Persian. His poetry, translated into many languages, remains popular around the world.

The mathematician Omar Khayyam was also a poet. He wrote thoughtful, sometimes melancholy four-line stanzas, called "rubaiyat" (ROO-bee-aht), which are still well known in the West because of a nineteenth-century translation by the English writer Edward FitzGerald. Perhaps the best-known lines in *The Rubaiyat of Omar Khayyam* speak of "A Book of Verses underneath the Bough, / A Jug of Wine, a Loaf of Bread—and Thou."

Throughout the Muslim world, people told fables and stories filled with magic. These were written down later as a single book, in which the individual stories are framed by the tale of a king who, betrayed by his wife, sets out to marry and kill a new wife each day. But when he marries Scheherazade (shuh-hehr-uh-ZAHD), each night she tells him the beginning of a story, and he spares her to hear the end the next day—at which time she begins a new story. The book became world famous after it was translated and published

Before long, Muslims in other parts of the empire were building minarets on their mosques.

Mosques were frequently decorated with colorful mosaics. One caliph is said to have imported thousands of Byzantine artisans to work on mosaics for the Umayyad mosque in Damascus.

Mosques varied greatly in design. Some were humble buildings in small areas, while others were monumental structures spread over acres. Still, most mosques shared (and still share) some common features. The minaret forms the highest point, from which the call to prayer goes out five times a day. A dome often covers some part of the building. Inside, a courtyard provides a place to meditate or read. A fountain, well, or other source of water often stands in the courtyard, because it is the Muslim ritual to wash oneself before praying.

in Europe in the sixteenth century as *The Thousand and One Nights*. The collection, sometimes called *The Arabian Nights*, includes tales of now widely familiar figures such as Ali Baba, Sindbad, and Aladdin.

Philosophy and History

For religious reasons, the early Muslims recorded every detail of Muhammad's life and times, which gave rise to a general interest in historical writing. For example, the historian Tabari wrote the multivolume *History of the Prophets and Kings*, which begins with Adam and ends with the Abbasids.

The Arabs learned much from classical Greek philosophy. Some Muslim thinkers developed

An eleventh-century tile features a verse of Persian poetry: "Last night the moon came to your house, filled with envy. I thought of chasing him away. Who is the moon to sit in the same place as you?"

schools of Greco-Muslim philosophy. In Aristotle's logic, they saw a method for proving the Muslim revelations. In Plato's philosophy, they found ideas anticipating the Muslim doctrine about the oneness of God.

In Cordoba, the Muslim philosopher Ibn Rushd—known in the Western world as Averroës (uh-VEER-uh-weez)—wrote influential commentaries on Greek philosophy. His ideas on the relation between reason and faith were controversial in his time but influenced later religious thinkers, Jewish and Christian as well as Muslim.

Within the Islamic Empire, some non-Muslim thinkers drew similar inspiration from the Greeks. The twelfth-century Jewish philosopher Moses Maimonides (miy-MAHN-uh-deez) applied Greek logic to Jewish religious doctrine in a book titled *The Guide for the Perplexed*, which he wrote in Arabic. Later translated into Hebrew, the *Guide* had an enduring influence on Jewish thought.

One of the greatest Muslim philosophers, al-Ghazali, stoutly opposed philosophy because he thought it weakened faith. Yet he was the greatest logician of his age. His book about Aristotle, translated into Latin, helped introduce the Christian West to the great Greek philosopher. The knowledge preserved by al-Ghazali and other Muslim scholars would play a key role in bringing Greek thought to Europe.

Muslim civilization, which had begun on the Arabian Peninsula in the seventh century, had far-reaching influence. Muslim culture, as you have seen, drew upon diverse influences from many lands. Even as the Islamic Empire began to fragment, Muslim culture would persist.

Chapter 13 *East Asian*

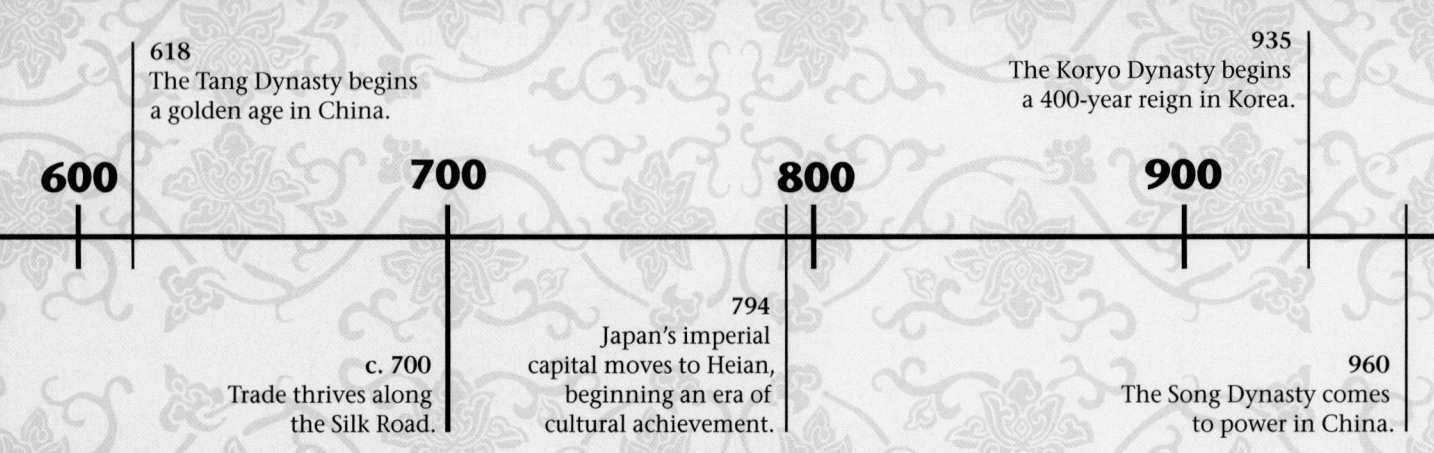

618
The Tang Dynasty begins
a golden age in China.

935
The Koryo Dynasty begins
a 400-year reign in Korea.

600   **700**   **800**   **900**

c. 700
Trade thrives along
the Silk Road.

794
Japan's imperial
capital moves to Heian,
beginning an era of
cultural achievement.

960
The Song Dynasty comes
to power in China.

A painting on silk from the early twelfth century depicts a busy city in China during the Song Dynasty.

Empires 500–1400

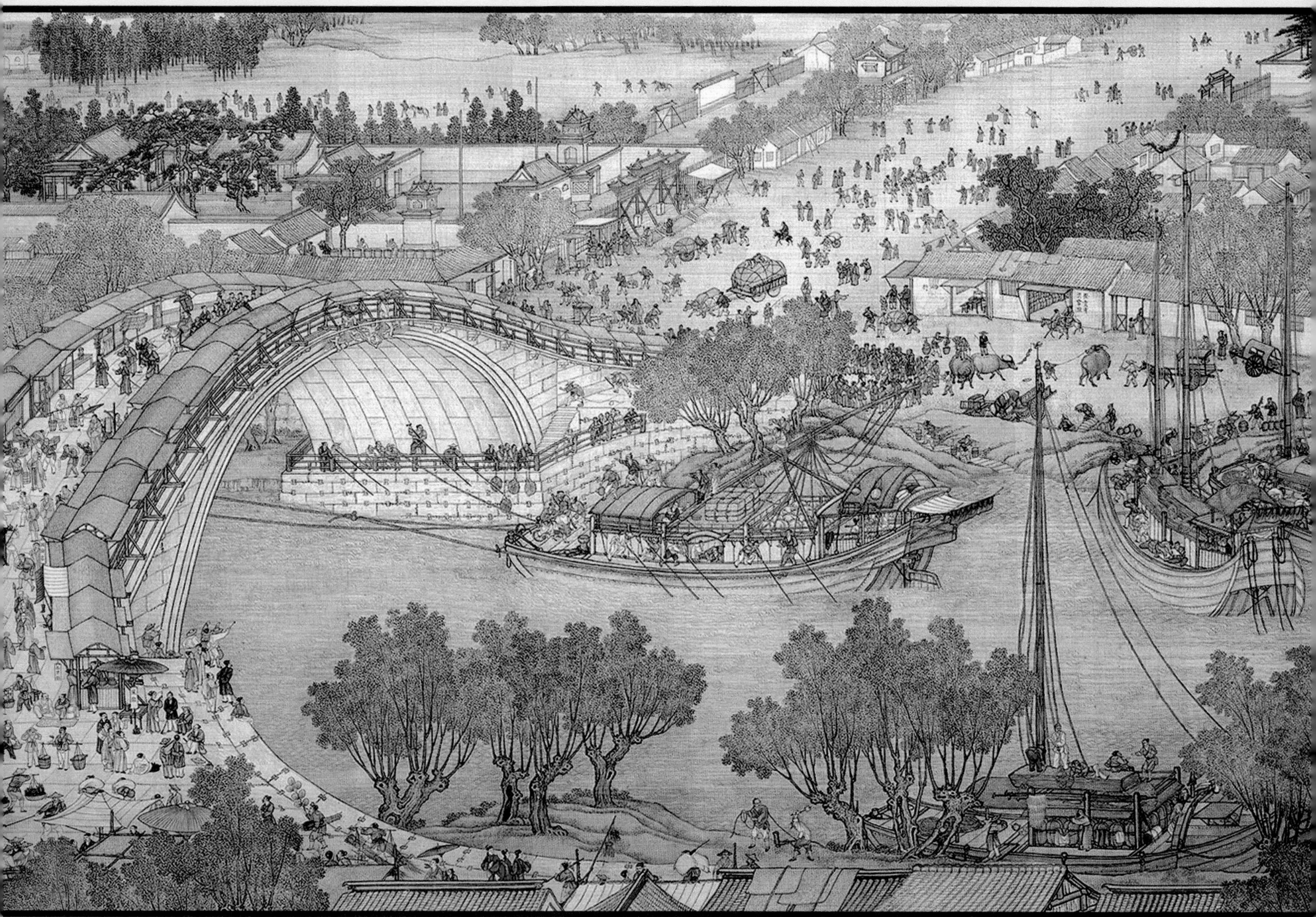

1100 — 1200 — 1300 — 1400

c. 1040
Chinese printers begin using movable type.

1279
The Mongol ruler Kublai Khan controls the largest contiguous land empire in history.

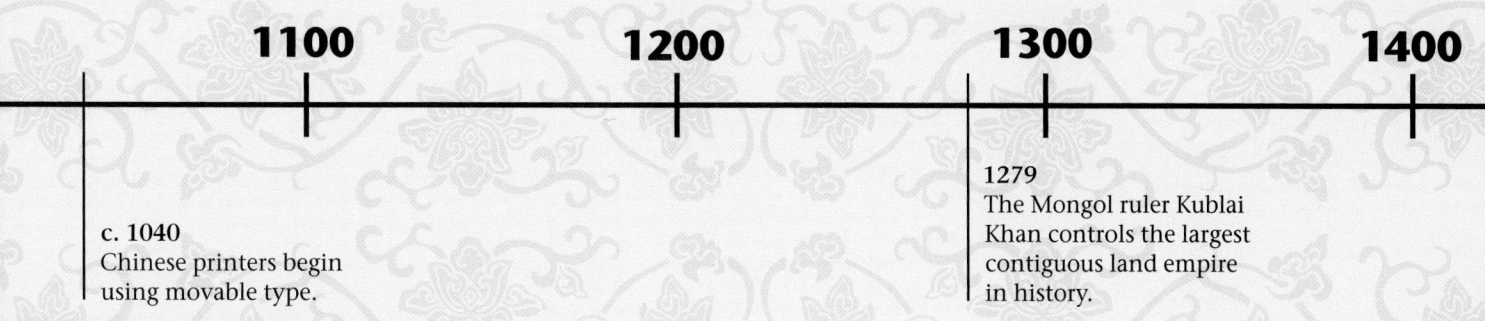

After the fall of the Han Dynasty in 220 A.D., China experienced a long period of conflict and division. But under the Tang and Song dynasties, which extended from the seventh to the thirteenth centuries, China enjoyed a period of unparalleled cultural accomplishment and technological innovation.

In the thirteenth century, the Song Dynasty, along with other civilizations across Asia, fell to fierce nomadic invaders from Mongolia. China briefly became part of a vast Mongol empire stretching from the Pacific to Europe. During this time, China's cultural interchange with the West accelerated. Meanwhile, two smaller countries to the east, Korea and Japan, built on Chinese influences to develop their own distinct cultures.

Tang and Song China

The powerful Han Dynasty, which had brought peace and stability to China, fell to rebellious generals in 220 A.D. For the next four centuries, China experienced disunity and turmoil. At first the country was divided among the three generals who had overthrown the Han. Then, in the early fourth century, nomadic peoples from the north and west conquered much of northern China.

Many Chinese fled to the south. But southern China was troubled by fighting among different groups who wanted to rule. For the next two centuries, a succession of different dynasties ruled southern China, none for very long.

Throughout this turbulent era, trade continued, as merchants brought goods and ideas from lands to the south and west. Also during this time, Buddhist missionaries who had traveled along the Silk Road from India converted enormous numbers of Chinese people to Buddhism.

The Sui Reunite China

The Han Dynasty had always placed special emphasis on the need for a unified China. In 589, the Han ideal of Chinese unity was achieved again by a general who took control of both northern and southern China. He established a new dynasty, the Sui (sway). He took the name Wendi (wen-DEE), and was known as the "Cultured Emperor."

As emperor, Wendi added to his own power by taking away the authority of local officials to hand out government jobs. To guard against invasions from the north, he ordered extensive repairs and improvements to the long series of fortifications known as the Great Wall of China.

Wendi's successor, Yangdi (YAHNG-dou), ordered the construction of an inland waterway, the Grand Canal, linking China's two longest rivers, the Yellow (or Huang He) and the Yangtze (or Chang Jiang). The canal provided a vital route for trade between northern and southern China.

Along the canal, rice traveled from southern fields to feed the army and government in the north. The thousand-mile Grand Canal remains the longest man-made waterway

Key Questions

- What were the major technological and cultural achievements of China's Tang and Song dynasties?

- What was the significance of the Silk Road in trade and cultural diffusion?

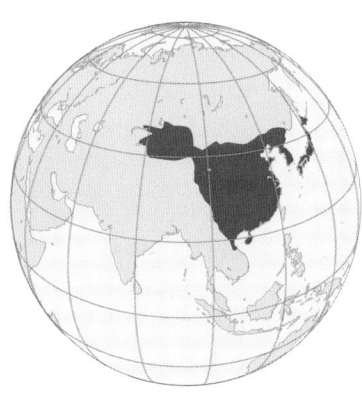

China, Japan, and Korea, c. 1000

Chinese laborers toil along the Huang He, or Yellow River.

on earth. But it was built at great human cost. For years, tens of thousands of peasants were forced to toil on the construction of the waterway, and many thousands died.

Yangdi led military campaigns into Vietnam and Korea in an attempt to expand the empire. But the invasion of Korea ended in a humiliating defeat for the Chinese. Afterward, rebellions broke out as generals jockeyed for power. Yangdi himself was assassinated in 618.

The Tang Dynasty

In 618, the year of Yangdi's death, an army general seized the capital and declared himself emperor. Thus began the Tang (tahng) Dynasty, which

China's Only Woman Emperor

Throughout Chinese history, a number of women wielded political influence in the imperial court through their husbands or sons. Only once, however, did a woman claim ultimate power for herself. In the late seventh century, when one of the Tang emperors died, his widow, Wu Zhao (woo joh), assumed power and eventually claimed the title of emperor for herself. China's only female emperor ruled for almost two decades.

Wu Zhao

would rule for the next three centuries. Tang emperors greatly expanded the Chinese empire. They took control of much of central Asia. In the east, they extended their influence into Korea. Under the Tang, China entered a golden age, a time of harmony, stability, and achievement.

The Tang emperors ruled from their capital at Chang'an (chahng-en). Chang'an was a carefully planned city with a chessboard pattern of broad, straight streets that became a model for capital cities in other eastern Asian countries.

Under the Tang, Chang'an became the biggest city on earth, with a population that, by some estimates, reached two million—about twice the population of Rome at the height of the Roman Empire. In the capital's crowded streets, merchants and Chinese residents mingled with travelers and Buddhist pilgrims from Japan, Korea, Vietnam, and other countries.

Establishing a Meritocracy

To select officials for the government, the Tang revived the civil service examination system first used by the Han. Young men spent years studying for these demanding examinations. Candidates had to demonstrate detailed knowledge of the Confucian classics as well as the ability to write original poetry and essays. In the provinces as well as the capital, the government established schools to help students prepare for the tests.

The Tang aimed to establish a *meritocracy*—a society led by those who have achieved authority through their talents and efforts rather than by birth into a wealthy or powerful family. With some changes, this system of choosing officials by examination would prevail in China until the overthrow of the last emperor in 1911.

The examination system helped conserve the traditional values of Confucianism. It also allowed talented and industrious members of the lower classes to rise in Chinese society, though in practice only men with at least moderate wealth could afford the years of education required to prepare for the exams.

The Tang Lose Power

The Tang Dynasty reached its height under the emperor Xuanzong (shoo-en-dzawng), who ruled from 712 to 756. A gifted poet and musician, Xuanzong welcomed talented artists of all kinds to the imperial court. Toward the end of his long reign, however, the weary emperor turned more and more to religion and neglected his administrative duties.

In 751, Arab warriors from the expanding Muslim empire defeated a Chinese force near Samarkand (SAHM-uhr-KAHND), shutting down much of China's trade with the West. Four years later, a rebellious general seized the city of Chang'an, forcing the emperor Xuanzong to flee.

The Tang eventually took back the capital city, but the dynasty never fully recovered. During the next century and a half, one weak emperor followed another. By the middle of the ninth century, regional warlords largely ignored the authority of the central government. Bandits roamed the countryside, plundering towns at will. Drought and famine led to peasant uprisings. In 907, the last Tang emperor was forced from the throne.

The Song Dynasty

Half a century of anarchy followed the fall of the Tang, as local warlords fought each other for power. Finally, as so often happened in the past, a military leader seized power in the south and set up a stable government. Eventually, north and south China were again united. By 960, a new dynasty had come to power, known as the Song (soong).

The Song would rule for another three hundred years, though they would never recapture

Anarchy is a state of social disorder and lawlessness, usually due to the breakdown or absence of government.

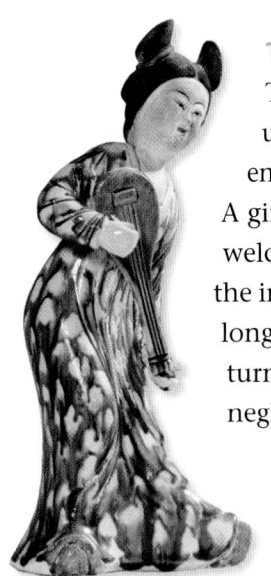

Tang porcelain figure

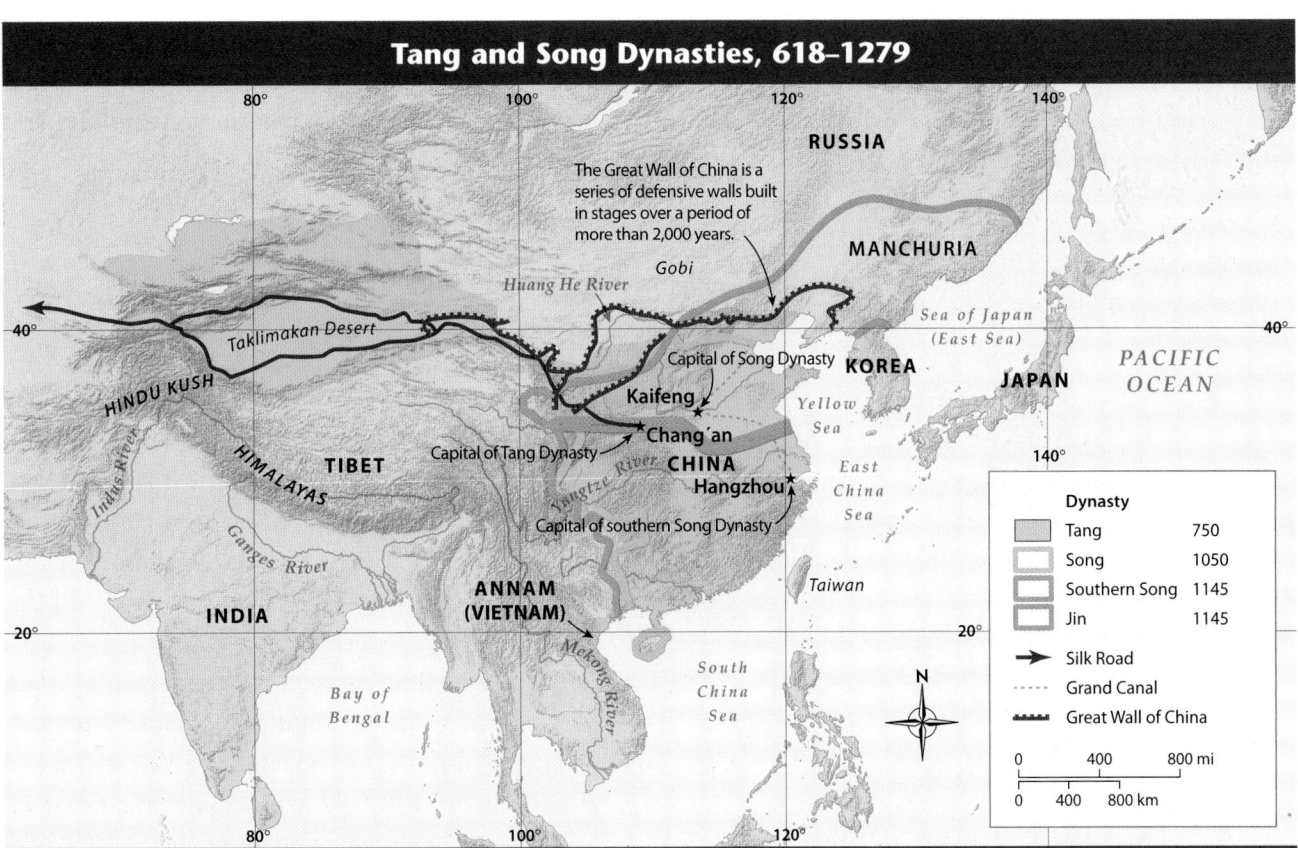

China enjoyed nearly six centuries of remarkable cultural and scientific growth during the Tang and Song dynasties before Mongol horsemen from the steppes overran their empire.

281

Feeding a Populous Land

The Tang and Song dynasties ruled China for a combined six hundred years. During these centuries, the population almost doubled. Advances in agriculture helped feed this rapidly growing population. The introduction of early-ripening rice allowed the farmers of southern China to produce two to three crops a year. By about 1100, China had a population of almost a hundred million, making it the most populous country in the world (as it remains today).

the military glory of the Tang, and their empire would be far smaller. During the dynasty's second half, the Song ruled only southern China, and lost the north to nomadic invaders. Nevertheless, the Song presided over a period of economic prosperity and dramatic innovations in technology.

Prosperity Under the Song

The Song emperors encouraged both agriculture and trade. Previously, peasant farmers had been required to pay their taxes in the form of a share of their crops, but Song rulers allowed farmers to use money to pay their taxes. This policy enabled farmers to sell their crops, pay their taxes, and then, with any money left over, buy products such as charcoal, tea, and wine.

The Song government encouraged merchants to trade with countries as far away as the Middle East and Africa. Large Chinese ships called junks sailed across the China Sea and the Indian Ocean. They carried finished goods, such as porcelain, that merchants traded for raw materials, such as pepper and cotton.

Chinese Society Under the Song

During the prosperous Song Dynasty, the gentry—the landowning upper class—grew in China. Among the gentry were many government officials who had attained their posts by passing the civil service examinations that demanded extensive knowledge of Confucian philosophy. The Song rulers strongly emphasized the Confucian values of loyalty to authority and respect for tradition.

As in Han times, these Confucian officials looked down on merchants, whom they considered greedy and lacking in public spirit. But thanks to the thriving economy, many merchants lived very comfortable lives. Although the mass of the people remained peasant farmers, they also benefited from the general rise in the standard of living.

Changes in society under the Song affected the status of women as well. With the spread of education, more women learned to read, and some devoted themselves to literary pursuits. One woman, Li Qingzhao (lee ching-jow), became one of the most celebrated Song poets. For the most part, however, women's lives were still restricted. As in the past, they were taught the Confucian ideal of subservience to their fathers and husbands.

A silk painting depicts an elaborate pavilion from the prosperous Song Dynasty, c. 1000.

The Custom of Foot Binding

The Song Dynasty saw the beginning of a custom called foot binding. In upper-class families, mothers would tie up the feet of their very young daughters, with the toes bent under the balls of the feet. This practice would bend the feet into a shape considered attractive by Chinese men. But women with bound feet were able to walk or stand only with difficulty. At first practiced only by the upper classes, foot binding gradually spread throughout Chinese society. The practice was banned in the early twentieth century.

Centuries of Achievement

The art and literature of China reached a high point under the Tang and Song dynasties. Especially under the Song, a remarkable number of technological innovations added to the prosperity, power, and influence of the Chinese empire.

Tang and Song Arts and Literature

Under the Tang Dynasty, Chinese poetry flourished. The two greatest poets of the period, Li Bai (lee baw) and Du Fu (doo foo), held very different views of life. Li Bai challenged traditional Confucian morality and urged his readers to pursue pleasure:

> For satisfaction in this life
> taste pleasure to the limit,
> And never let a goblet of gold
> face the bright moon empty.

In contrast, Du Fu, a deeply Confucian poet, wrote poems focused on the problems of society, especially the plight of the poor:

> Brooding on what I have lived through, if
>   even I know such suffering,
> The common man must surely be rattled
>   by the winds....

Artists of the Song Dynasty achieved new levels of excellence in landscape painting. On silk scrolls, Song painters depicted landscapes with finely detailed lakes, waterfalls, craggy mountains, and twisted trees. When these artists illustrated human figures or signs of civilization, such as houses, they were likely to render them in miniature, reflecting the traditional Chinese idea of the beauty and harmony of nature dwarfing the individual. In this, the Chinese painters differed from many Western artists, who, since the time of the Greeks, have focused on the human form as a central subject of their work.

Song Dynasty artists embraced nature, as illustrated by this lush, snowy landscape.

Tang and Song Innovations		
Porcelain	8th century	This hard and durable earthenware grew so popular that it came to be called *china*.
Mechanical clock	8th century	Water-propelled machinery created the clock's movement.
Gunpowder	9th century	The Tang and Song applied this explosive powder—originally used to make fireworks—to warfare.
Movable type	11th century	The Chinese developed movable type four hundred years prior to the same printing innovation in Europe.
Paper money	11th century	Paper currency stimulated the Chinese economy and enabled monetary transfers to take place over long distances.
Magnetic compass	12th century	Chinese sailors adapted the magnetic compass from land navigation to seafaring, an advance that accelerated global commerce and exploration.

While some writers and artists of the Tang and Song gained fame for their work, anonymous craftsmen were producing ceramic vessels—pots, jars, vases, and bowls—of stunning beauty and delicacy. Throughout Asia, Chinese porcelain and other ceramics became sought-after luxury goods. Porcelain, a highly valued commodity, eventually became known as china, since it was so closely associated with the country that invented it.

Song Innovations

Under the Song, the Chinese economy flourished in part because of a large number of technological innovations. One of the most important was the invention of movable type, which revolutionized printing.

Before this time, Chinese printers worked by carving characters into a wooden block, then covering the block with ink in order to transfer the characters to paper—a time-consuming process. Around 1040, however, printers began using movable characters made of wood, porcelain, or copper. Each character could be arranged in a frame, and then removed and reused. Song China became the first society

Chinese porcelain, like this vase, was highly prized throughout Asia.

with printed books. (Movable type would be independently developed in Europe in the mid-1400s.)

To make trade more convenient, the Song issued the first paper money in history, a form of currency eventually adopted around the world. Additionally, Chinese sailors under the Song were the first to use the magnetic compass. The compass had been invented centuries before, but Chinese sailors were the first to use it for navigation, which enabled them to sail farther than other seafarers.

Gunpowder—an explosive powder made from sulfur, charcoal, and saltpeter (potassium nitrate)—had been invented during the Tang Dynasty and was originally used for fireworks. By the time of the Song, it was being used for weapons as well. Although Song leaders banned the sale of gunpowder or its components to foreign traders, the technology of gunpowder spread rapidly, and it would revolutionize warfare.

Trading Goods and Ideas on the Silk Road

As early as 100 B.C., during the Han Dynasty, Chinese traders were transporting goods along the Silk Road, which, as you have learned, was not a single roadway but a vast network of trade routes stretching across Central Asia. The routes crossed sparsely populated deserts and mountain ranges in western China and the modern-day nations of Tajikistan, Afghanistan, and Turkmenistan, before reaching the ancient cities of Iran and the Middle East.

Along these routes, Chinese goods such as silk, ivory, and ceramics flowed westward, while gold, wine, glass, and horses from the west traveled to China. The Chinese may have acquired wheat, the chariot, and domesticated horses from their neighbors in central Asia. Most goods were carried by long caravans of camels—the only animals tough enough to survive the grueling journey in climates of extreme heat and cold.

The Silk Road remained an active network for trade for many centuries. Under the Tang Dynasty, trade along the Silk Road reached its height, with Chinese merchants exchanging goods and ideas with distant cultures of Asia. For example, in what is now Iraq, at their capital of Baghdad, the Muslim rulers of the Abbasid Empire cherished Chinese silks and ceramics. The Chinese themselves adopted musical instruments and even the game of polo from Persia (present-day Iran).

Ceramic camel figurine from the Tang, who were great traders

Along the Silk Road, traders carried not only material goods but also inventions and ideas. For example, in the first centuries A.D., Buddhism came to China by merchants and missionaries traveling the Silk Road. By the time of the Tang Dynasty, Buddhism, supported by the emperors, was flourishing in China. Throughout China, Buddhist monasteries provided important social services, including education for children, lodging for travelers, and banking for merchants.

Perilous Journey on the Silk Road

In 629, at the beginning of the Tang Dynasty, a Buddhist monk named Xuanzang (shoo-AHND-ZAHNG) traveled the Silk Road to India. It took him three years to reach his destination. Along the way, he was blinded by sandstorms, attacked by bandits, and nearly shot by frontier guards. At one point, Xuanzang found himself riding alone through the searing heat of the Gobi, observing the bones of former travelers. He would have died of thirst if his horse had not instinctively led him to an oasis.

Later, traveling with a group across the snowy Taishan Mountains, Xuanzang saw many of his fellow travelers buried by avalanches or killed by falling chunks of ice. After three years, he finally reached India, where he studied and translated Buddhist texts.

On his return to China, he was encouraged by the emperor to write an account of his travels. Xuanzang's book, *Great Tang Records on the Western Regions*, recounts both the perils of his journey and the customs of the many lands through which he passed.

Traders braved the perils of the Silk Road for various riches like gorgeously embroidered silk.

The Mongols

In earlier chapters, you have briefly encountered the Mongols on their campaigns of conquest in Russia and the Islamic Empire. Here, you will learn more about the Mongols—their background, their leaders, the massive empire they forged, and their legacy.

Horsemen from the Steppes

North of China lies the nation of Mongolia, the largest landlocked country on earth. Today it is also the world's most sparsely populated nation. The barren desert called the Gobi stretches across the southern part of the country. Much of the rest consists of grassy, treeless plains known as steppes. In this inhospitable land, rainfall is rare and the winters bitterly cold.

The native people of this land, known as Mongols, lived nomadic lives as herdsmen, following their sheep, goats, and yaks between summer and winter pastureland. Rather than settle in towns or villages, they carried their dwellings with them, in the form of tents known as yurts. (The Mongolian word for yurt is *ger*.) Because resources were scarce, Mongol tribes fought among themselves and sometimes raided the cities of Korea and northern China.

Mongol warriors were superb horsemen. Riding short, muscular horses, they charged into battle, firing arrows from their bows at full gallop. Mongol raiding parties could strike quickly and then rush back to the steppes, evading the less agile forces of their victims.

Key Questions

- Who were the Mongols, and how did they establish the largest land empire in history?

- What lasting impact did the Mongol conquests have on the lands they conquered?

The Mongol Empire was the largest empire in history.

Cliffs rise over the barren landscape of the Gobi in Mongolia.

286

An artist captures the fierceness of a Mongol warrior charging full speed into battle on horseback.

Genghis Khan

Around the year 1160, a boy named Temujin (TEHM-yuh-juhn) was born to the chieftain of a small Mongol tribe. While Temujin was still a child, his father was poisoned by enemies. The family fled to the wilderness, where they lived by hunting and foraging for berries and roots. Temujin grew into a ruthless young man. When he and his half-brother quarreled over some birds they had killed, Temujin shot his brother dead.

At the age of sixteen, Temujin returned from exile to marry a chieftain's daughter. He soon gained a reputation as a strong leader, brave in battle and fiercely loyal to his men. Gradually, he set about building alliances among the Mongol tribes. In 1206, at a gathering of tribal leaders, Temujin was proclaimed the khan—the ruler—of all the Mongols, and given the title Genghis Khan.

A bronze plaque believed to depict Genghis Khan

Under the leadership of Genghis Khan, Mongol armies swept across northern China, burning and looting cities. In 1215, they sacked the city of Beijing (bay-zhing), today the capital of China.

After conquering much of China, Genghis Khan looked toward Afghanistan and Persia. Thundering westward, the Mongol horsemen destroyed towns all along the ancient Silk Road. When the shah (king) of Persia refused to submit to Mongol rule, Genghis Khan invaded his country and drove him from the throne.

The Mongols were fierce warriors. It was said that they could ride for two days without dismounting, even sleeping in the saddle. Rather than stopping to cook food, they ate dried meat and kept moving.

The Mongols were not only tough, they were also skilled tacticians who quickly adopted new military technologies from their neighbors. When they laid siege to cities, they used catapults borrowed from Afghanistan and gunpowder-propelled rockets developed by the Chinese.

But perhaps the Mongols' most effective weapon was terror. Genghis Khan let it be known that cities that opened their gates to him would be spared destruction, while those that resisted would suffer the wholesale slaughter of men, women, and children.

The Mongol Empire

After Genghis Khan died in 1227, his empire was divided into four realms, or khanates, all owing allegiance to the new Great Khan, Genghis's son Ögödei (OH-goh-day).

Under Ögödei and his successors, the Mongols continued their wars of conquest. They seized much of Russia and pushed westward as far as Poland and Hungary, countries some six thousand miles from the Mongol homeland. In 1258, Baghdad, the greatest city of the Islamic world, fell to the Mongols, who destroyed its magnificent palaces, mosques, and libraries, and massacred much of its population. The captured caliph was sewn into a carpet and trampled to death by Mongol horses.

In 1260, Genghis's grandson Kublai (KOO-bluh) became the Great Khan. He completed the

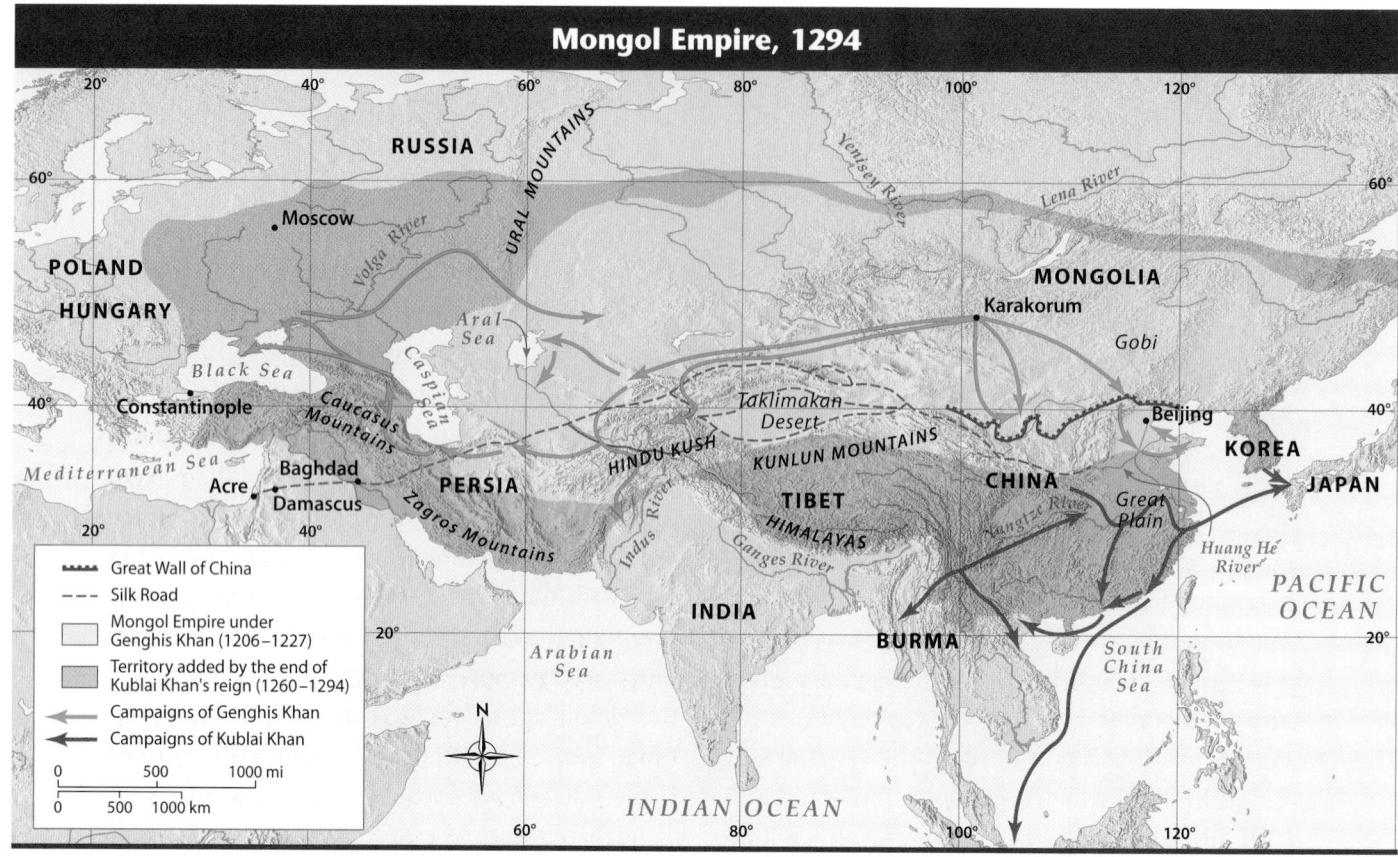

Mongol Empire, 1294

Great Wall of China
Silk Road
Mongol Empire under Genghis Khan (1206–1227)
Territory added by the end of Kublai Khan's reign (1260–1294)
Campaigns of Genghis Khan
Campaigns of Kublai Khan

The Mongols ruled most of Asia and the Middle East from the mid-twelfth to the mid-thirteenth centuries, encouraging trade and enforcing political stability throughout the region.

Contiguous means connected, touching along a boundary.

conquest of China, and reduced the neighboring land of Korea to a subject state. By 1279, Kublai Khan ruled the largest contiguous land empire in history, which stretched from the Pacific Ocean to eastern Europe. The Mongols would dominate this immense territory for another century.

There was a great contrast between the way the Mongols conquered and the way they ruled. The Mongols let conquered peoples serve in their armies and work as government officials. They built roads and encouraged trade across their lands. The Mongols often adopted local customs and religions. In the early fourteenth century, in the western part of the Mongol Empire, Islam became the official religion of the khanate of the Golden Horde. Kublai Khan welcomed Buddhist, Daoist, Christian, and Muslim clergy to his court.

Kublai Khan and the Yuan Dynasty in China

After Kublai Khan became leader of the Mongols, he moved his capital to the city of Beijing, thus confirming the central importance of China in his empire. Even before the final defeat of the Song Dynasty in 1279, Kublai Khan proclaimed the start of a new, Mongol-led dynasty, the Yuan (you-EN).

In an effort to reconcile the Chinese to his rule, Kublai Khan adopted the dress and customs of a Chinese emperor. He ordered literary classics and dynastic histories translated from Chinese to Mongolian. He enforced religious tolerance, and encouraged scientists and artists. He built roads and hospitals, and extended the Grand Canal so that it reached all the way to Beijing.

But Kublai Khan never forgot that he was a Mongol ruling a conquered people. Out of fear of rebellion, he prohibited the Chinese from owning weapons. He discouraged intermarriage between

A Yuan Dynasty painting on silk shows Kublai Khan hunting. The ruler, who adopted the ways of a Chinese emperor, is shown wearing a white ermine coat.

Mongols and Chinese. He reserved the top posts in his government for Mongols. All these actions bred resentment among the Chinese.

Marco Polo

At the same time, Kublai Khan remained curious about the world. He welcomed foreigners to his court. His most famous visitor was an Italian named Marco Polo, who on his return to Europe wrote a celebrated book describing his travels across Asia. (Historians have noted that some of his accounts are wildly exaggerated secondhand reports rather than direct observations.)

Marco Polo describes Kublai Khan in awestruck terms: "Everyone should know that this Great Khan is the mightiest man, whether in respect of subjects or of territory or of treasure, who is in the world today or who ever has been." According to Polo, the khan's palace was so huge that six thousand men could dine in its main hall. Exotic trees transplanted from all over the world grew in the surrounding gardens. Presiding in the palace, the khan and his high officials wore robes studded with jewels and fastened with golden belts.

Polo's description of China's astounding wealth and splendor entranced his European readers. His book inspired generations of merchants and adventurers to seek their fortunes in trade with Asia.

Mongol Decline and Legacy

Despite Kublai Khan's energies as a ruler, the dynasty he founded, the Yuan, would prove to be the shortest-lived of China's major dynasties. After Kublai's death in 1294, Mongol leaders quarreled over the need for further expansion of the empire. Confucian scholars were angered by their exclusion from high political office. Among the general population, heavy taxes fueled a growing discontent. Floods and other natural disasters increased the misery of the peasant class.

By the 1350s, rebellions flared in various parts of the country. As in the declining years of previous dynasties, regional warlords took advantage of growing political and social instability to increase their power. In 1368, the Yuan Dynasty finally collapsed.

By then, Mongol rule in Persia and central Asia was also coming to an end. Only the khanate of the Golden Horde, centered in Russia, managed to hold on to power for another century.

The Mongols left a mixed legacy. Tens of millions of people died in the course of their conquests, and millions more migrated, fleeing the Mongols' fierce advance. Some historians think that Mongol armies carried the bubonic plague westward, where it would surface in Europe as the Black Death of the fourteenth century.

Despite the devastation of their conquests, Mongol rule encouraged widespread cultural diffusion, including the introduction of Islam into central Asia. Above all, the Mongols increased trade and communication between East and West. Europe especially benefited from the introduction of Chinese inventions such as printing, gunpowder, and the compass—technologies that Europeans would eventually employ to dominate much of the rest of the world, including China itself.

The Palace of the Great Khan

Marco Polo, a merchant from Venice, introduced Europeans to Kublai Khan and China's Yuan Dynasty. In 1271, a teenage Marco Polo set off with his father and uncle on a trading expedition. A few years later, the young man was a guest of Kublai Khan. Polo became one of the emperor's favorite courtiers. More than two decades later, when Polo finally returned to Europe, he found Venice at war with another Italian city-state, Genoa. The Genoese captured and imprisoned Polo. While in jail, Polo related his experiences and adventures to a fellow prisoner who had been a professional writer.

Marco Polo's story of his journeys, published in the late thirteenth century, became immediately popular, despite, or perhaps because of, some wildly exaggerated passages. Polo's *Description of the World*—known in English as the *Travels of Marco Polo*—captured the imagination of the West and was largely responsible for accelerating trade and commerce along the Silk Road.

These walls enclose the palace of that mighty lord, which is the greatest that ever was seen. The floor rises ten palms above the ground, and the roof is exceedingly lofty. The walls of the chambers and stairs are all covered with gold and silver, and adorned with pictures of dragons, horses, and other races of animals. The hall is so spacious that 6,000 can sit down to banquet; and the number of apartments is incredible. The roof is externally painted with red, blue, green, and other colors, and is so varnished that it shines like crystal and is seen to a great distance around. It is also very strongly and durably built.

Between the walls are pleasant meadows filled with various living creatures, as white stags, …deer, wild goats, ermines, and other beautiful creatures. The whole enclosure is full of animals, except the path by which men pass. On the other side, towards the south, is a magnificent lake, whither many kinds of fish are brought and nourished. A river enters and flows out; but the fish are retained by iron gratings.

Towards the north, about a bowshot from the palace, Kublai has constructed a mound, full a hundred paces high and a mile in circuit, all covered with evergreen trees, which never shed their leaves. When he hears of a beautiful tree, he causes it to be dug up, with all the roots and the earth round it, and to be conveyed to him on the backs of elephants…. The trees are so lovely that all who look upon them feel delight and joy.

Rising Cultures in East Asia

In the history of Asia, the huge and populous country of China exerted great influence on its neighbors. To the east of China, the people of two smaller countries, Korea and Japan, felt the influence of Chinese civilization even as they developed their own distinct cultures.

Key Questions

- How were Japan and Korea shaped by their geography?

- What influence did China have on the cultures of Japan and Korea?

- What were the main features of the government in feudal Japan?

Korea

In northeastern Asia, the Korean Peninsula juts out into the Yellow Sea. Bordered to the north by China, Korea has always lived in China's shadow. While borrowing much from its giant neighbor, Korea nevertheless evolved its own distinct culture.

In 108 B.C., the armies of the powerful and expansionist Han Dynasty overran northern Korea. The Chinese would rule the north for several centuries, building cities in the Chinese style and importing Chinese goods.

With the decline of the Han in the third century A.D., Chinese control of Korea loosened. By the following century, Korea had split into three kingdoms ruled by native kings. Even during this era of the Three Kingdoms, as early Korean historians called it, the cultural influence of China remained strong.

To strengthen their hold on power, the Korean rulers borrowed the political ideas of Confucius. Meanwhile, Buddhist monks from China spread their religion to the peninsula, and Korean scholars adapted the Chinese system of writing to the Korean language.

The period of Korea's Three Kingdoms came to an end in the seventh century A.D., when one of the kingdoms, Silla, conquered the others and united most of the peninsula under its rule. Silla allied itself with the Tang Dynasty in China. This alliance protected Silla from foreign invasion and increased China's influence on Korea. The city of Kyongju, Silla's capital, was built to resemble the Tang capital, Chang'an.

Korean merchants traveled extensively through China. So did Korean scholars, many of whom passed the demanding Chinese government examinations and went on to hold civil service positions in the Tang government.

A stone figure, c. 600–800, stands guard over the Silla kingdom.

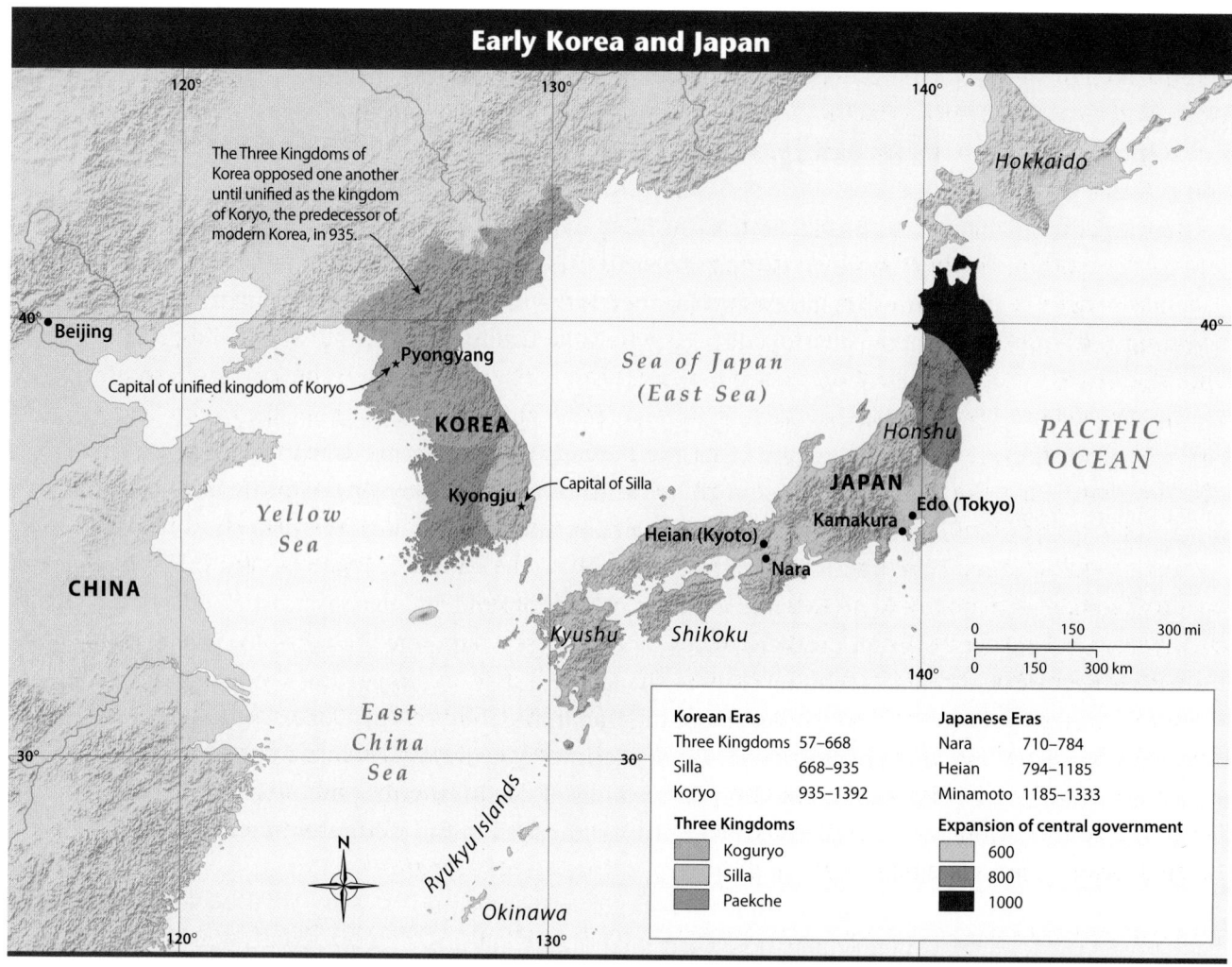

Early Korea and Japan

The Three Kingdoms of Korea opposed one another until unified as the kingdom of Koryo, the predecessor of modern Korea, in 935.

Beijing

Capital of unified kingdom of Koryo

Pyongyang

KOREA

Sea of Japan (East Sea)

Hokkaido

Honshu

PACIFIC OCEAN

Kyongju — Capital of Silla

Yellow Sea

CHINA

Heian (Kyoto)

Kamakura

Edo (Tokyo)

JAPAN

Nara

Kyushu *Shikoku*

East China Sea

Ryukyu Islands

Okinawa

Korean Eras		Japanese Eras	
Three Kingdoms	57–668	Nara	710–784
Silla	668–935	Heian	794–1185
Koryo	935–1392	Minamoto	1185–1333

Three Kingdoms
- Koguryo
- Silla
- Paekche

Expansion of central government
- 600
- 800
- 1000

Japan and Korea, once divided into rival clans and kingdoms, eventually became centralized empires under the rule of powerful families.

The Koryo Dynasty

In the ninth century, when the Tang Dynasty fell, the kingdom of Silla also declined. Competing warlords wrestled for control of Korea until, in 935, one of these generals united the country under a new dynasty he called the Koryo—the origin of the name "Korea."

Koryo rulers set up a highly centralized government on the Chinese model. They also established a civil service examination system based on that of China. In theory, the system was open to all, but in practice the examinations were held so rarely that power mostly remained in the hands of a hereditary upper class.

The Koryo Dynasty would remain in power for more than four hundred years. Beginning in the early thirteenth century, its power was weakened by a series of Mongol invasions. By the time the Mongol Kublai Khan became emperor of China, Korea had become a subject state. Members of the Koryo royal family intermarried with the Mongol ruling class and adopted Mongol customs.

After the Mongols were driven out of China in 1368, the Koryo Dynasty declined. The last Koryo king was overthrown in 1392.

Japan

About five hundred miles (805 km) off the east coast of China lies Japan, a country made up of four large islands and thousands of smaller ones. The islands are located along the Circum-Pacific Belt, a zone of frequent earthquake activity bordering the Pacific

Ocean. This belt is also known as the Ring of Fire, because it coincides with the borders of tectonic plates, segments of the earth's crust whose sudden movements can cause not only earthquakes but also volcanic eruptions.

Throughout its history, Japan has been subject to devastating earthquakes and tsunamis (tsou-NAH-meez), enormous waves generated by undersea earthquakes. When a tsunami crashes onto the shore, it can cause great destruction.

Japan's highest mountain, Fujiyama (foo-jee-YAH-mah), or Mount Fuji, is a volcano that has been dormant since the early 1700s. Its outline has become a symbol of Japan.

Japan's volcanic soil is highly fertile, but the country's terrain is so mountainous that less than 20 percent of its land can be farmed. To supplement the rice grown by its farmers, Japan had to turn to the surrounding sea. Fish, shellfish, and seaweed have always been staples of the Japanese diet.

For most of Japan's history, the sea also protected the country from invaders. Because of its isolated location, Japan would not be successfully invaded until World War II, in the middle of the twentieth century.

In their myths and traditions, the Japanese stressed their uniqueness as a people and told stories of their country's sacred origins. According to legend, two gods stirred the ocean with a jeweled spear and the drops falling off the weapon became the islands of Japan. Japanese tradition holds that the country's ruling family began with the goddess of the sun. Modern historians think that this long-lived dynasty began around 500 A.D., when a clan of warriors known as the Yamato gained control of the large southern island of Kyushu (KYOO-shoo) as well as much of the largest of Japan's islands, Honshu (HAWN-shoo).

Borrowing from China

Japan's early culture, like Korea's, was influenced by China. The Korean Peninsula—separated from southern Japan by only a hundred miles of sea—became the bridge by which Chinese goods and ideas passed to Japan.

Once an active volcano, the snowcapped Mount Fuji has become a symbol of Japan.

Early in the Yamato period, Korean missionaries brought their form of Buddhism, shaped by Chinese thought, to Japan. Buddhism gradually found favor among the Japanese ruling class, who hoped that it would create a more orderly, disciplined society. But it did not replace the country's native religion, called Shinto. Instead, many Japanese mingled Buddhist and Shinto beliefs and practices.

Shinto in Japan

The native Japanese religion, Shinto, holds that everything in nature contains sacred powers called *kami* (kah-mee). Followers of Shinto believe the kami are everywhere in nature—in the sun, the sea, mountains, animals, trees, and the spirits of the dead.

The kami are worshipped at shrines throughout Japan. Large shrines have a sacred entrance gate called a *torii* (tor-EE-EE). These beautiful wooden gates have become symbols of the Shinto religion. Joyful festivals in honor of the kami are held at special times, such as the New Year.

Unlike many other religions, Shinto has few rigid teachings. This allows the Japanese to combine Shinto practices with those of other faiths, especially Buddhism.

A Shinto sacred gate is believed to welcome the *kami*.

Japan's Yamato rulers and officials adopted the Chinese writing system for their written records and laws. One ruler of the early seventh century, Prince Shotoku, built strong relations with the rulers of the Sui Dynasty in China. He started the custom of sending large groups of scholars, artists, and officials to the Chinese capital, not only to gain cultural knowledge but also to learn to protect Japan from China. One of the prince's letters to the Sui ruler begins, "The Emperor of the sunrise country [that is, Japan, to the east of China] writes to the Emperor of the sunset country." Later Japanese monarchs would also refer to themselves as "emperors," even though they rarely ruled territory outside the Japanese islands.

Japan especially felt the influence of China during the Tang Dynasty, when China was the most advanced country on earth. In the early eighth century, the Yamato rulers built a new capital city, Nara, modeled on the Tang capital at Chang'an. Elegant Buddhist temples, modeled after Chinese pagodas, graced the capital. The Japanese royal court followed highly formal rules of etiquette, copied from China. Chinese forms of music and dance became fashionable.

The Japanese also adapted Chinese ways to their own traditional culture. For example, they used Chinese characters to write the first books in Japanese. In some of these early books, scholars recorded the traditional myths of the Shinto religion.

The Heian Period

In 794, the imperial court moved from Nara to a new city called Heian (hay-ahn), the "Capital of Eternal Tranquility." Heian, later renamed Kyoto, would remain Japan's capital for over a thousand years. In its first four centuries, the emperor's court at Heian developed a highly refined and creative culture.

Heian aristocrats lived in large houses surrounded by gardens. Their furniture was decorated with carvings of flowers, trees, and butterflies. They dressed in expensive robes scented with

Murasaki Shikibu wrote *The Tale of Genji*, considered by many scholars to be the first novel.

incense and carefully designed to please the eye. One writer describes the clothing of young aristocrats at a banquet: "The color combinations of the jackets were glossed silk, willow, cherry, grape, and, in the case of the younger men, red plum—a most delightful and glittering array." In order to succeed at court, Heian aristocrats had to show themselves skillful in a variety of endeavors, including poetry, music, and dancing, as well as archery, one of the few sports considered fit for a gentleman.

Aristocratic women also took part in this elegant but competitive life. Women made their greatest contribution in the field of literature, producing poems, stories, and collections of witty or thoughtful sayings, such as the *Pillow Book* of Sei Shonagon. (A "pillow book" was a notebook that a lady might keep by her pillow to jot down thoughts that came to her at night.)

Shortly after the year 1000, Murasaki Shikibu (mou-roh-SAH-kee shee-kee-bou), who served as lady-in-waiting to the empress, wrote the long prose work called *The Tale of Genji* (gehn-jee), focusing on the many love affairs of a fictional prince. Her book—crammed with hundreds of characters and thousands of details of life at the Heian court—is considered one of the greatest masterpieces of Japanese literature. Many scholars also consider it the first novel ever written.

Feudalism in Japan

The rich culture of Heian Japan centered on the emperor's court. Most of the real political power, however, was not held by the emperor but by a powerful clan called the Fujiwara, who had married into the royal family. The people revered the emperor as the "Son of Heaven" and symbol of the country, but in reality he was more of a figurehead—a leader with little real authority. Over the centuries, a number of different groups wielded power in the emperor's name, a pattern that would last through much of Japanese history.

In the twelfth century, the Fujiwara began losing power to landowning warriors in the provinces far from the capital. In 1180, a civil war broke out between two especially powerful warrior clans. The war ended in 1185, with the victory of the Minamoto clan. Although the emperor in Kyoto (as Heian was now called) still

Civil war raged outside the palace in Kyoto. At war's end in 1185, the Minamoto clan emerged victorious.

295

A samurai suit of armor was light and folded easily.

ruled in name, real power shifted to the city of Kamakura, the headquarters of the Minamoto. In 1192, the head of the Minamoto clan took the title of *shogun*, or "military commander."

Over the next six centuries, Japanese society would be organized according to the principles of **feudalism** (FYOO-duh-lih-zuhm). A feudal society is one in which land is held by members of a noble class, with less powerful nobles pledging their loyalty to more powerful ones. (In a later chapter, you will read about another form of feudal society that prevailed in Europe at this time.)

In Japan's feudal society, the military commander, or shogun, awarded land to local lords, known as *daimyo* (DIY-mee-oh). In exchange, the daimyo were obligated to provide soldiers to fight the shogun's wars. Thus, instead of a national army, feudal Japan had hundreds of private armies, each controlled by a daimyo. Frequently, these armies battled each other.

Leading these private armies were an elite group of professional warriors known as *samurai* (SA-muh-riy), meaning "those who serve." From childhood, samurai trained to fight skillfully with the bow and sword. They rode horses into battle and held much higher social status than the foot soldiers drawn from the peasantry. They pledged to follow a demanding code of conduct, called *Bushido* (BOU-shee-doh), or "the way of the warrior." The code required absolute bravery and unquestioning loyalty to the samurai's lord.

Minamoto, the first shogun of Japan, ruled from 1192 to 1199.

Many samurai practiced **Zen**, a form of Buddhism imported from China. Zen Buddhism grew popular during the thirteenth and fourteenth centuries. The religion appealed to warriors because it stressed discipline, self-control, and self-reliance. Such qualities were important to the samurai, who fought not only for the spoils of battle but also for honor and glory.

The Divine Wind

In 1274, many samurai fought to protect their country against a Mongol invasion. With nine hundred ships, twenty-five thousand soldiers, and several thousand sailors, the Mongol leader Kublai Khan invaded Japan. When the khan's troops landed, they were met by only a few thousand Japanese soldiers. By sunset, the Mongol warriors had killed most of the Japanese.

But then help came to the Japanese in the form of a force that even Kublai Khan could not

A Woman Warrior

A Japanese epic about the wars of the feudal period describes a warrior-woman named Tomoe Gozen, who fought alongside her samurai husband. It is said that, after a battle in which her husband was defeated, she rode off the field carrying the head of an enemy samurai.

Tomoe Gozen, woman warrior

defeat—the weather. As night fell, the island on which the khan's troops had landed was struck by the lashing winds and driving rain of a typhoon (a hurricane). The storm churned the sea and smashed the Mongols' ships to pieces. By the next morning, the fury of the typhoon had driven the Mongols out of Japan.

The shogun ordered new defenses in case of another Mongol attack. Workers built many small, fast ships, as well as a long stone wall to protect the coastline of the island of Kyushu.

In 1281, Kublai Khan launched his second attack on Japan, with some 140,000 soldiers and about 4,400 wooden ships. On land and sea, the Japanese fought the Mongols for almost two months. Then one August night, the clouds darkened and the winds began to howl. Once again, a typhoon came to the aid of the Japanese. The storm sank perhaps as many as four thousand of the Mongol ships, and the rest sailed back to China in defeat.

The Kamikaze in WWII

In 1945, near the end of World War II, Japan was at war with the United States. When the United States attacked Japan, Japanese suicide pilots smashed their planes into American ships in a last-ditch attempt to halt the invasion. The pilots called themselves *kamikaze*, in memory of the seemingly miraculous typhoons that had helped their ancestors defeat the Mongols.

The Japanese people came to call typhoons the "kamikaze" (kah-mih-KAH-zee), which means "divine wind." (Kami, you recall, are the spirits of the Shinto religion.) Thanks to the kamikaze, the Mongols gave up trying to conquer Japan. For the Japanese, the thwarted invasions strengthened their view of Japan as a sacred country, protected not just by the surrounding ocean but by the gods themselves.

Kublai Khan's marauding Mongol fleet was devastated by wild typhoon winds as it failed, for a second time, to conquer Japan.

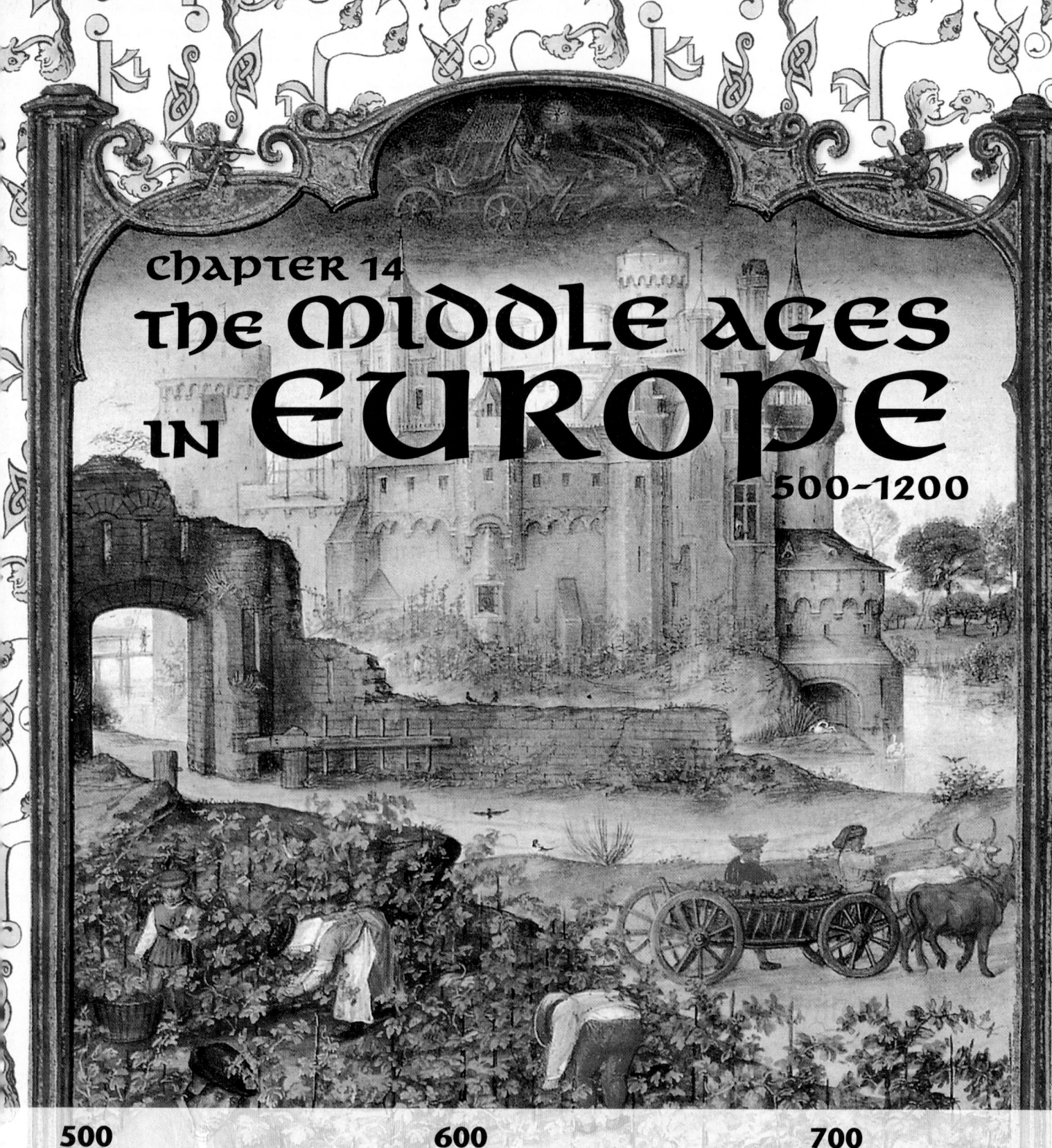

CHAPTER 14
THE MIDDLE AGES
IN EUROPE
500–1200

500

600

700

c. 500
King Clovis unites rival
tribes to form a Frankish
kingdom.

732
Charles Martel's armies
stop the Muslim advance
into western Europe at
the Battle of Tours.

Illustrations from a book, c. 1515—at left, peasants harvesting grapes; at right, lords and ladies celebrating springtime

800

900

1000

Pope Leo III crowns
Charlemagne
emperor of Rome.

c. 850
Europe enters
a feudal age in
response to outside
invasions.

c. 950
Attacks decline as
Vikings settle and
convert to Christianity;
monasteries revive.

c. 1000
Christianity has
become so pervasive
in western Europe
that the realm is
commonly referred to
as Christendom.

*B*y the fifth century, the Roman Empire was crumbling, giving way to a long and varied period that later came to be known as the Middle Ages. This time, from the late fifth century to the late fourteenth century, is also referred to as the medieval era, from the Latin words *medius* ("middle") and *aevum* ("age"). Medieval means "relating to the Middle Ages."

Because Europe went through many significant changes during the Middle Ages, many historians organize the period into three phases: early, from 476 to about 1000; High, from 1000 to 1300; and late, from about 1300 until a period of social and cultural revival known as the Renaissance (which you'll read about in an upcoming chapter).

This chapter focuses on western Europe in the early Middle Ages, as numerous tribes and rulers competed for territory, while the Christian church provided a source of social unity and took on increasing political power.

New Forces in Western Europe

Historians often date the beginning of the Middle Ages from the year 476, when Germanic tribes displaced the last Roman emperor—a mere boy named Romulus Augustulus—from the throne. The date serves as a convenient marker, though in fact the transition from Rome's long decline and fall in the late 400s to the beginning of the Middle Ages was a gradual one.

Tumultuous Times

Before 476, many parts of the Roman Empire had been under attack for centuries as land-hungry neighbors pressed its borders and weakened its outposts. Around 375, the Huns, fierce nomads from central Asia, began moving steadily westward, causing upheaval among the Germanic tribes already settled near the Roman Empire. When the Huns reached the Danube River valley, the Germanic people living there surged southward across the border of the Roman Empire in search of new land.

The Romans both feared and loathed these newcomers, whom they called "barbarians." These barbarian invasions took a heavy toll on the empire. Roman law and administration, which had brought order to a far-reaching empire, weakened under wave after wave of attacks. The fighting disrupted trade routes and scared off the merchants upon whom Rome's wealth depended. Much of what Rome had built—paved roads, aqueducts, and reservoirs—began to crumble. Malaria and other diseases swept through Roman cities, causing people to flee to rural areas.

By the fourth century, disease, war, and natural disaster had drastically reduced Rome's population, further weakening the empire. Western Europe became a dangerous and troubled place, so much so that in later years people sometimes called the period from the fall of Rome to the 900s the Dark Ages.

The Germanic Tribes

"Germanic" peoples existed long before the modern-day nation of Germany was founded. *Germani* is the Latin name that Romans gave to warlike tribes on the Roman Empire's northern frontiers. The region of northern and central Europe they inhabited was known as Germania (much of which is now part of the country we know as Germany).

Fierce Germanic tribes known as Goths had pushed into mainland Europe from Scandinavia, in search of warmer climates. By the year 500, the Ostrogoths pressed south into Italy, while a related tribe, the Visigoths, sacked Rome and then headed west into Spain. Another Germanic tribe, the Franks, invaded Gaul. The Franks eventually gave their name to the country we now call France.

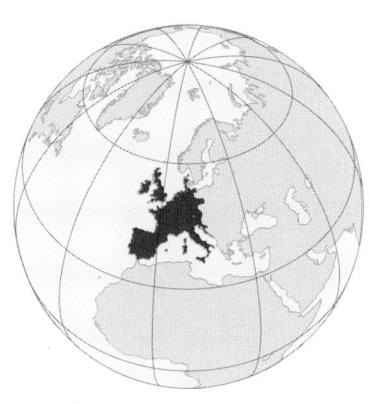

Western Europe in the Middle Ages

A seventh-century Anglo-Saxon warrior's helmet

Tribes known as the Angles, Saxons, and Jutes sailed from northern Europe to the former Roman colony of Britain. They arrived as invaders but put down roots as settlers. The land of the Angles became "Angleland," or as it is known today, England.

Other Germanic tribes, such as the Lombards, Burgundians, and Vandals, left their homelands to occupy former Roman lands. Each of these tribes had its own customs, its own rulers, and its own traditions. The Germanic tribes were governed not by written laws or ideals of citizenship, but rather by personal loyalty to a king. As the Roman Empire collapsed, western Europe became a fractured land of warring chieftains, small kingdoms, and marauding tribes.

The Franks

Of all the Germanic tribes in Europe, the Franks emerged as the strongest. Their kingdom at its height stretched from the Atlantic Ocean to the Rhine River, and south to the Pyrenees Mountains.

From about the late 400s to the mid 700s, the Franks were ruled by a succession of kings called the Merovingian (mehr-uh-VIN-jee-uhn) Dynasty, after an early leader named Merovech. In 481, when the king of the Franks died, the throne went to his fifteen-year-old son, Clovis. Clovis set about defeating rival Franks in Gaul and expanding his kingdom. He booted the Visigoths to Spain.

Clovis grew to be the most powerful of the Germanic kings. Around 500, he became the first Germanic ruler to convert to Catholicism. The support of the church in Rome added to Clovis's power. Clovis formed a united Frankish kingdom with its center in Paris. In this large and diverse kingdom, the people from once-distinct Germanic tribes gradually began to view themselves as one people—as Franks.

Missionaries and Monasteries Spread Christianity

Clovis and his successors helped spread Christianity among the Germanic tribes. Christianity also spread because of the work of monks, men who separated themselves from society to lead holy lives. You have learned about the beginnings of monasticism in the Eastern Church in the third and fourth centuries, when some Christians chose to renounce worldly activities and devote themselves to the contemplation of God. Some monks lived in isolation, but most lived, prayed, and worked in small communities called monasteries.

Benedict of Nursia

The father of monastic communities in the West was named Benedict of Nursia (NOUR-see-uh). Born around 480 into nobility, Benedict was a pious child who worked hard in his studies. His parents sent him to Rome to be educated, but he was dismayed by the rowdy behavior of his fellow students. He left Rome for the mountains of Italy. For three years he lived in solitude, praying and studying.

Clovis, pictured here with his wife and four sons, was a major force in the spread of Christianity among the Germanic tribes.

Benedict then decided to form a new monastic community, guided by the principle expressed in the Latin motto, *Ora et labora* (OR-ah et lah-BOR-ah)— "prayer and work." In Monte Cassino (MAWN-tay kah-SEE-noh), southeast of Rome, Benedict founded a monastery with twelve monks and himself as the **abbot** (the leader of the monastery).

In about 520, Benedict wrote a book that guided monks in how to live a life devoted to prayer and hard work. The book, known as *The Rule of Saint Benedict,* also gave detailed instructions about the organization of a monastery and a daily schedule of prayer services called offices. Benedict's *Rule* became a model for other monasteries and convents.

Around the year 600, Pope Gregory I dispatched many Benedictine monks to spread their faith. One of the most successful of the missionaries was Augustine of Canterbury, who converted Angles and Saxons in Britain around 600. The monks carried out their missionary work among other Germanic tribes across Europe.

Monks Preserve Learning

In addition to spreading Christianity, the monasteries helped preserve learning. Monks spent hours bent over religious manuscripts, painstakingly hand copying works thousands of pages long. They copied texts about medicine, astronomy, and law, as well as religious works.

Monasteries also became important centers of learning, attracting scholars from throughout the land. Many monasteries ran schools for children from neighboring towns. At first, these schools focused almost entirely on Christian teachings, but many soon taught other subjects as well.

By the year 800, there were Christian monasteries all over western Europe. As people came to them, monks taught about their religion, which helped convert many among the Germanic tribes to Christianity.

At the same time that Islam was gaining followers in Arabia and North Africa and advancing into southern Spain, Christianity was spreading

Among ruins of an Irish monastery, a Celtic cross, c. 545, still stands.

Patrick in Ireland

In the early Middle Ages, Irish monasteries became important homes for missionaries and scholars. In the 400s, a missionary from Britain named Patrick had spread the Christian faith to Ireland, which was never part of the Roman Empire. Patrick and other early missionaries incorporated pagan practices into the church's rituals, enabling people to make a gradual transition.

By the sixth century, monasteries dotted the Irish countryside. The monks of Ireland copied the Bible and other books. The Irish monks were among the most skilled in the art of creating illuminated manuscripts. They used gold and silver to decorate the pages with magnificent letters and beautiful designs. Sometime around 800, Irish monks at a monastery in Kells, northwest of Dublin, produced an illuminated manuscript of a Latin text of the Gospels. The Book of Kells, as it is known, is a masterpiece of medieval art.

The Book of Kells, created by Irish monks, includes exquisite artwork.

across the European continent. By 1000, the dominant religion in western Europe was Christianity—specifically, the western branch of the faith, which would become known as the Catholic Church. (The term *catholic* means "universal, all-inclusive.") The Christian faith became so deeply integrated into the life and thought of western Europe that people began to refer to the realm as **Christendom** (KRIH-suhn-duhm).

Charlemagne Unites Western Europe

When Clovis died in 511, his kingdom was divided among his four sons, which was standard practice among the Germanic kings. Over the next several generations, each time a king died, the land was further divided among his sons. The result was predictable. The Frankish kingdom declined into a patchwork of small kingdoms with bitter rivalries among their leaders.

Charles Martel

After Clovis, the power of the Frankish kings greatly diminished. To compensate, the king's chief household official, known as the mayor of the palace, took on increasing authority. By the eighth century, the power of these mayors surpassed that of the kings themselves.

One mayor, Charles Martel, whose name means "Charles the Hammer," proved to be an able leader and a brilliant general. In 732, he led Frankish troops in defeating Muslim troops at the Battle of Tours, halting the Muslim advance into western Europe.

Martel died in 741, and his two oldest sons, Carloman and Pepin (known as Pepin the Short), became mayors of the palace. Carloman soon decided to enter a monastery. With the support of the pope, Pepin was named king of the Franks.

It was Pepin to whom the pope turned for support when the Lombards, a Germanic tribe that had seized territory in Italy, threatened Rome itself. The Frankish king answered the pope's call for aid. Pepin and his army drove off the Lombards,

thus further reinforcing the bond between western Europe and the Roman Church.

The Emperor Charlemagne

Pepin's reign began the Carolingian (kair-uh-LIN-jee-uhn) Dynasty. The Carolingians would rule the Franks for more than two hundred years. The dynasty gets its name from its greatest ruler, Pepin's son, Charlemagne (SHAHR-luh-mayn), whose name means "Charles the Great"—in Latin, *Carolus Magnus*.

At six-feet-four-inches (2 m) tall, Charlemagne towered above most men of his day. Everything about him was large, including his feet. According to legend, our one-foot measure comes from the length of Charlemagne's foot. Charlemagne's abilities were equally huge. He was a skilled hunter, a lover of music and learning, a powerful athlete, and a shrewd military leader and politician.

Charlemagne greatly enlarged the Frankish kingdom. For more than a quarter century, he waged war against the Saxons in what is today northern Germany. When the Saxons finally surrendered, Charlemagne, a devout Christian,

A fifteenth-century manuscript illustration shows Charles Martel in action at the Battle of Tours in 732.

insisted they accept Christianity. He gave them a stark choice—convert or die. When the Lombards again threatened Rome, Charlemagne defeated them. He also waged war against the Muslims in Spain, known as Moors.

By 800, Charlemagne ruled most of western and central Europe—the largest kingdom since the height of the Roman Empire.

The New Emperor of Rome

In 799, Pope Leo III was under attack in Rome—not from Germanic tribes, but from Roman nobles who charged the pope with tyranny and corruption. Charlemagne came to the pope's defense. On Christmas Day in the year 800, the pope presided over a church service in Rome, with Charlemagne in attendance. As Charlemagne knelt in prayer, Pope Leo approached and placed a jeweled crown on the kneeling king's head. The pope proclaimed Charlemagne the new "emperor of the Romans."

Charlemagne claimed to be surprised and not entirely pleased. He later said that he preferred the title "king of the Franks," and that he would have stayed away from the church that day if he had known the pope's intentions.

Historians have long debated Charlemagne's claim, but much evidence suggests that the Frankish king helped plan his coronation as emperor. He and the pope had been talking about trying to revive the glory of the old Roman Empire. And Charlemagne had already taken great strides toward that goal. He had united a vast realm under the Christian faith and brought order to the empire. In later years, Charlemagne would come to be known as the first emperor of the Holy Roman Empire.

Maintaining the Empire

Governing such an immense territory was challenging, but Charlemagne, with his boundless energy, was up to the task. He divided his realm into counties—local districts run by an official called a count. To keep a controlling hand on the local counties, several times a year Charlemagne

Pope Leo III, shown here placing a crown on Charlemagne's head, proclaimed him the new "emperor of the Romans."

sent out his own royal officials, called *missi dominici* (miss-ee doh-MIHN-ih-chee), Latin for "envoys of the lord." These envoys inspected the work of local officials and reported back to the emperor. The *missi dominici* served as Charlemagne's eyes and ears throughout his empire.

Although Charlemagne could be brutal in war, he valued the blessings of peace. Among his greatest legacies was renewed interest in learning. He was himself an eager student of Latin, Greek, logic, astronomy, and mathematics. He established a palace school for members of his court and for his children and grandchildren. He also provided funds to monasteries to build and operate schools. To meet the demand for teachers, Charlemagne imported scholars from England, Ireland, and Italy. From these early schools grew some of the great universities of Europe.

Throughout his life, Charlemagne supported monasteries in their efforts to preserve learning. He gave them funds and instructed them to care for the great classical works that they held in their libraries. With renewed vigor, monks set about their task, painstakingly copying old manuscripts

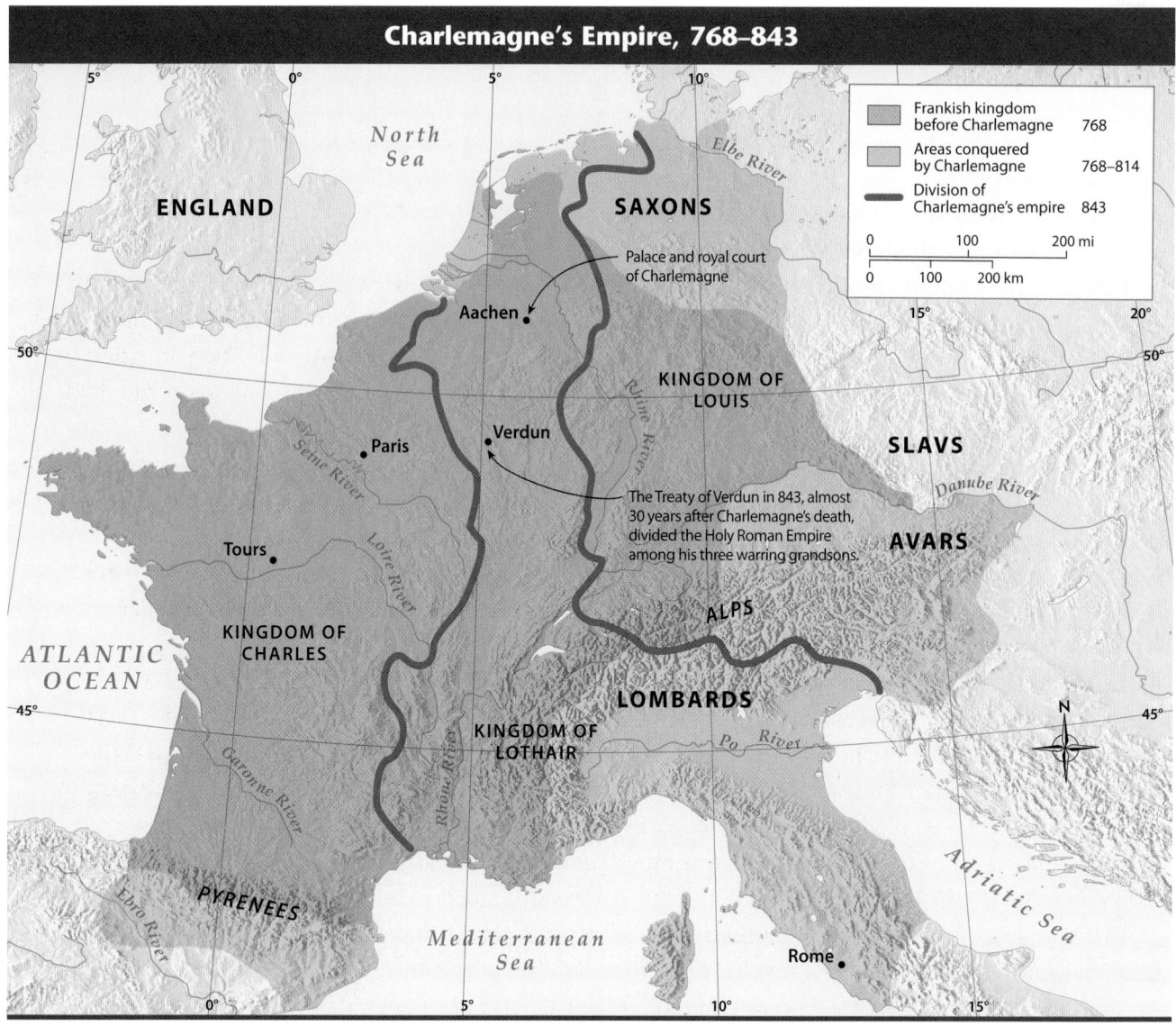

Charlemagne ruled a vast Holy Roman Empire, but little more than a quarter century after his death, civil war among his three grandsons broke the empire into three separate kingdoms.

and preserving them for the ages. Much of the classical literature we have today comes to us from copies of books made in Charlemagne's time.

Charlemagne also approved the use of a new writing style that took up less space on the page and was easier to read. This kind of writing, which mixes uppercase (capital) and lowercase (small) letters, is the basis for the combination of large and small letters we use today.

When Charlemagne died in 814 at the age of seventy-two, which was very old for the time, he left the empire to his only surviving son, Louis. Sometimes called Louis the Pious, Louis lacked his father's dominant personality, military prowess, and administrative ability.

When Louis died in 840, the empire was divided among his three sons. One took charge of western lands that make up much of present-day France. Another took the eastern lands that make up modern Germany. The third ruled the lands in between, which stretched from Italy to the North Sea. The brothers were bitter rivals. Their constant feuding sapped the once-mighty empire of its strength and unity. Worse, the kingdoms were under attack by land-hungry invaders. Within a century, Charlemagne's great empire had all but disappeared.

Feudalism and the Manor Economy

Key Questions

- Why did feudalism and the manor system emerge in western Europe?

- What were the key social, political, and economic elements of feudalism and the manor system?

By the tenth century, Charlemagne's empire was no more. The central government had broken down in the lands that now make up France, Germany, and Italy. Armed bands roamed the countryside. New invaders threatened from all sides. Who or what could provide safety and order in this dangerous time?

An answer emerged, but not in the form of one all-powerful leader. Instead, what developed was a western European form of the system of social, political, and economic relationships known as feudalism.

Before we examine the rise of feudalism in western Europe, we will learn more about the invasions that spurred the rise of the new social order.

A New Wave of Invasions

Between about 800 and 1000, as Charlemagne's empire weakened, western Europe faced constant threats. The Moors, as Europeans called the Muslims in Spain, did not see their defeat at Tours in 732 with the finality that Europeans did. Taking advantage of the empire's weakness, Muslim forces invaded southern France and captured Sicily in southern Italy. Meanwhile, the Magyars, nomads who had settled in present-day Hungary, attacked from the east. They invaded and eventually settled in parts of what now makes up eastern France, southern Germany, and northern Italy.

The Vikings

The most serious threat came from the Varangians, known to western Europeans as Vikings, and also called Norsemen (or men of the North). The Vikings came from the mountainous lands of Scandinavia. Most of Viking society hugged the Scandinavian coastline, where people eked out a living from the rocky soil. As the population of Scandinavia increased, farmland became

This illuminated manuscript, c. 1130, depicts seaborne Vikings nearing Britain.

307

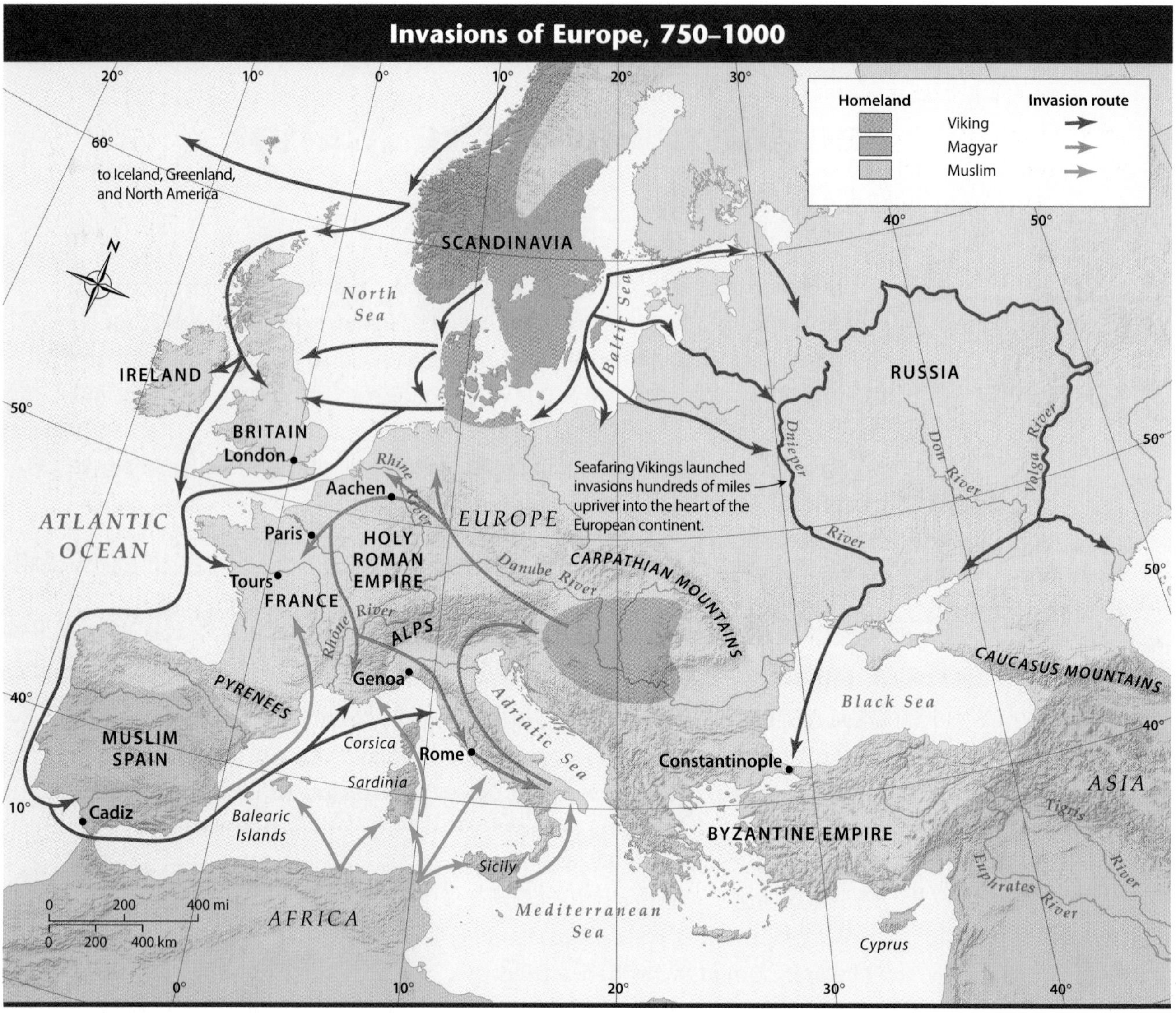

Invasions of Europe, 750–1000

Homeland		Invasion route
	Viking	→
	Magyar	→
	Muslim	→

to Iceland, Greenland, and North America

SCANDINAVIA

North Sea

IRELAND

BRITAIN
London

Rhine River
Aachen

Paris

Tours
FRANCE
HOLY ROMAN EMPIRE

ATLANTIC OCEAN

EUROPE

Seafaring Vikings launched invasions hundreds of miles upriver into the heart of the European continent.

RUSSIA

Baltic Sea

Dnieper

Don River

Volga River

River

CARPATHIAN MOUNTAINS

Danube River

ALPS

Rhône River

PYRENEES

Genoa

Corsica

MUSLIM SPAIN

Cadiz

Balearic Islands

Sardinia

Rome

Adriatic Sea

Black Sea

CAUCASUS MOUNTAINS

Constantinople

ASIA

Tigris River

BYZANTINE EMPIRE

Euphrates River

Sicily

Mediterranean Sea

Cyprus

AFRICA

0   200   400 mi
0   200   400 km

Christian Europe was invaded repeatedly by land and sea during the early Middle Ages.

scarce, so the Vikings set sail from their homes in search of new lands and riches. Their travels took them across the North Sea and down rivers into Europe's interior lands.

At first, the Vikings traded with the settlers they encountered, but they soon turned from trading to raiding. From ships positioned along the shore, gangs of men armed with battleaxes plundered towns and set fire to villages. They sought out churches and monasteries and carted off golden crucifixes, silver chalices, and gem-encrusted holy books.

Viking raiders initially traveled back and forth from Scandinavia, but over time many decided to camp closer to their prime plundering spots. From the rich river valleys of southern England and northern France, they could set forth on their next raiding missions, following the rivers far inland. Eventually, some Vikings put down roots and set up permanent colonies in the lands they had once raided.

Recognizing the futility of trying to uproot these fierce

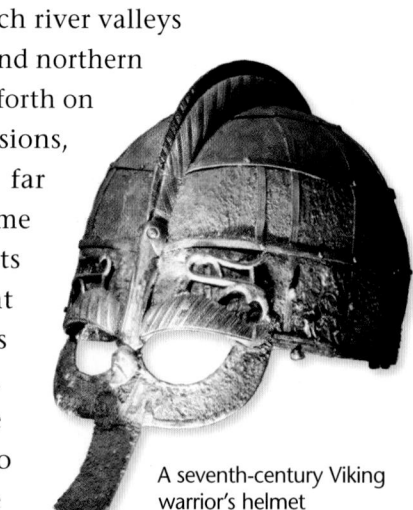

A seventh-century Viking warrior's helmet

Norse Gods and Myths

The early Viking raiders believed in gods who were as warlike as the Norsemen themselves. Viking warriors made sacrifices to Odin, the father of the gods and the spear-wielding god of battle, creator of the earth and the human race. For good luck, the Vikings looked to Thor, the hammer-wielding god of thunder who rode across the heavens in his goat-drawn chariot.

The Vikings believed their gods lived above the earth in a land called Asgard (AS-gahrd). In Asgard lay Valhalla (val-HA-luh), the Hall of the Slain. This great palace was set aside for worthy humans who fought and died bravely in battle. The hope of every Viking warrior was to spend eternity in Valhalla with Odin, Thor, and the other gods.

Viking poets recited stories of the gods from memory and passed down these tales from generation to generation. Eventually the stories were written down in two collections known as the Eddas. Much of what we know about Norse mythology and Viking beliefs comes from the Eddas.

Hammer raised, the Viking thunder god Thor rides in his goat-drawn chariot.

warriors, some local leaders paid tribute to appease their new neighbors or to enlist their support in defending against other Vikings. In 911, King Charles, a descendant of Charlemagne, forged an alliance with Rollo the Walker, a Viking leader said to be so large that no horse could carry him. Charles made Rollo the duke of what is now called Normandy—the very name of the region, Normandy, came from the name of the conquering Norsemen. In return, Rollo swore allegiance to Charles and helped the Franks fend off other Viking attackers.

Rollo accepted Christianity and married a French woman. His men did the same. The Norsemen of France were gradually transforming themselves from Vikings into Normans. A century later, Normandy would be one of the most powerful states in Europe. (And, as you'll learn, a Norman duke named William the Conqueror would invade England and make it his own.)

Viking Expeditions

At a time when few European sailors ventured far from land, the Vikings made bold journeys. Daring, determined, and hungry for land, the Vikings sailed into uncharted waters.

One of the most fearless Vikings was Erik the Red, whose hot temper often got him into trouble. Sometime around 980, when Erik was banished from his homeland of Iceland, he decided to explore the seas. Heading west from Iceland, Erik and his band of adventurers spotted a forbidding coastline covered by sheets of ice. The men set up camp on the southern part of the island and

Viking Longships

The Vikings built strong and swift longships that skimmed the ocean waves. The Viking longship was lighter, slimmer, and faster than other European vessels of the day. A typical longship, about seventy feet (21m) long and sixteen feet (5m) across, could carry nearly a hundred men, with plenty of space to hold plunder taken in raids. The ships were strong enough to withstand Atlantic storms, thanks to overlapping curved planking that would "give" in a pounding sea. The longships rode high in the water, which allowed the Vikings to sail up the rivers of Europe. On the prows of their vessels, they carved figureheads of lions, serpent heads, and especially dragons. To the Vikings, the longship was a prized possession, a useful weapon, and a symbol of freedom.

On the prows of their longships, Vikings carved figureheads, often of dragons.

sailed back to Iceland to recruit settlers for the colony. To attract potential settlers, Erik gave the new land a flattering name—Greenland.

Erik's son Leif (leef) grew up in Greenland and inherited his father's adventurous spirit. About the year 1000, Leif Erikson, with a band of thirty-five men, sailed from Greenland westward across the North Atlantic into the unknown. Leif described the land he found as warmer than Greenland and rich with timber. Because the land had vines bearing what Leif said were grapes, he named it Vinland, the land of grapes.

Historians are not certain where Leif Erikson landed, though some think he came ashore in what is today Newfoundland, Canada (though this area lacks the grapes Leif claimed to have seen). Leif and his men spent the winter there before returning home. Although their colony did not survive, Leif Erikson's voyage marked the first time a European had reached North America.

As Leif Erikson was making his voyage across the Atlantic, Viking attacks in Europe gradually dropped off as the raiders found lands where they could build farms and settle permanently. As missionaries arrived, many Vikings gave up their Norse gods and accepted Christianity.

The Rise of Feudalism

While the Vikings and other groups raided western Europe, people lived in constant fear of attack. The kings who reigned in Europe were not powerful enough to fend off the invaders and restore order and safety.

Throughout Europe, the power of kings had been giving way to the increasing power of noblemen, princes, barons, dukes, and counts who ruled the regions they had gained by combat or inheritance. These powerful landowners, called **lords**, often acted as if each ruled his own little kingdom. While technically a king ruled over a lord, a lord might own more land than the king and command a larger army.

Although lords pledged loyalty to the king, few kings had enough wealth to keep a standing army. In general, in the early Middle Ages in Europe, a king had little power outside his own domain, that is, outside the realm of his direct control.

Land for Loyalty

The lords gained much of their power from the land they owned. In exchange for loyalty, lords granted land to lesser nobles or knights. This land grant was called a **fief** (feef). A noble or knight who received a fief became the lord's **vassal** (VA-suhl).

A vassal owed his lord certain obligations, including loyalty and the promise of military service. He swore to fight for the lord if needed. In return, he owned the fief and profited from farming the land.

Giving land in exchange for loyalty became the foundation of western Europe's social, political, and economic system during the ninth century, a system that came to be known as feudalism, from the French word for "loyalty." (You have already read about an example of a feudal society in early Japan.)

Feudal Classes and Obligations

The feudal system was like a chain of interlocking loyalties. By exchanging land, service, and protection, the nobility gained some security and order in uncertain times.

In medieval Europe, feudal society was organized in a pyramid-shaped class system. At the top, barons, the most powerful and wealthy noblemen, received their fiefs directly from the king. Those barons with large tracts of land sometimes granted fiefs to hundreds of nobles. These nobles,

Lesser lords pay homage to the Duke of Burgundy seated on his throne, as shown in a fifteenth-century illustration.

Illustrations from a fifteenth-century French calendar show medieval peasants laboring in the fields.

in turn, might divide their land among lesser lords and knights. These lesser lords, too, might have vassals of their own. In this system, a lord could have vassals while he himself might be a vassal to another lord.

Feudalism was not an entirely rigid class system. An ambitious vassal who served his lord well could climb the pyramid of power.

The vassal's principal obligation to the lord was to provide military service when called upon. During the 800s and 900s, lords regularly fought each other for more land. Skilled knights became important members of the lord's army, and lords often gave them a portion of any land they acquired in battle. The knights supplied their own horses, weapons, and armor. More land meant more income to purchase better horses and equipment.

Other duties of a vassal varied from one place to another. In some courts, vassals served as advisers to the lord, providing counsel about whether to go to war or how to divide the land.

Near the bottom of the social pyramid, the peasants spent most of their time working the land. Most peasants owned only a small strip of land and had no vassals of their own. Peasants made up by far the largest class of people during the Middle Ages. Some were free men who owned or leased small plots of land. But many were **serfs**—peasants who were tied to the land they worked, and could not leave it without the lord's permission.

The Feudal Life

During the early Middle Ages, there were few towns in western Europe. Most people lived in the countryside, often on a large estate called a **manor**. Each manor was controlled by a lord. In fact, there was a saying in medieval times: "No land without a lord, and no lord without land."

The Castle

Powerful lords who controlled large manors often lived in castles that provided safety in times of danger. To protect themselves and their possessions from Viking raids, feudal lords in northwestern France built some of the earliest castles. A castle served as the home for the lord's knights when they were not engaged in battle and as a place of refuge for peasants in times of war.

The earliest castles were made of wood and surrounded by wooden fences or mounds of packed earth. By the 1100s, powerful lords were building castles of stone, which was stronger and less vulnerable to fire. Most of these stone castles were built on high ground— the better to spot approaching enemies—and surrounded by a deep ditch called a moat. Some moats held water diverted from a nearby river, but most were dry. Even a dry moat provided a tough

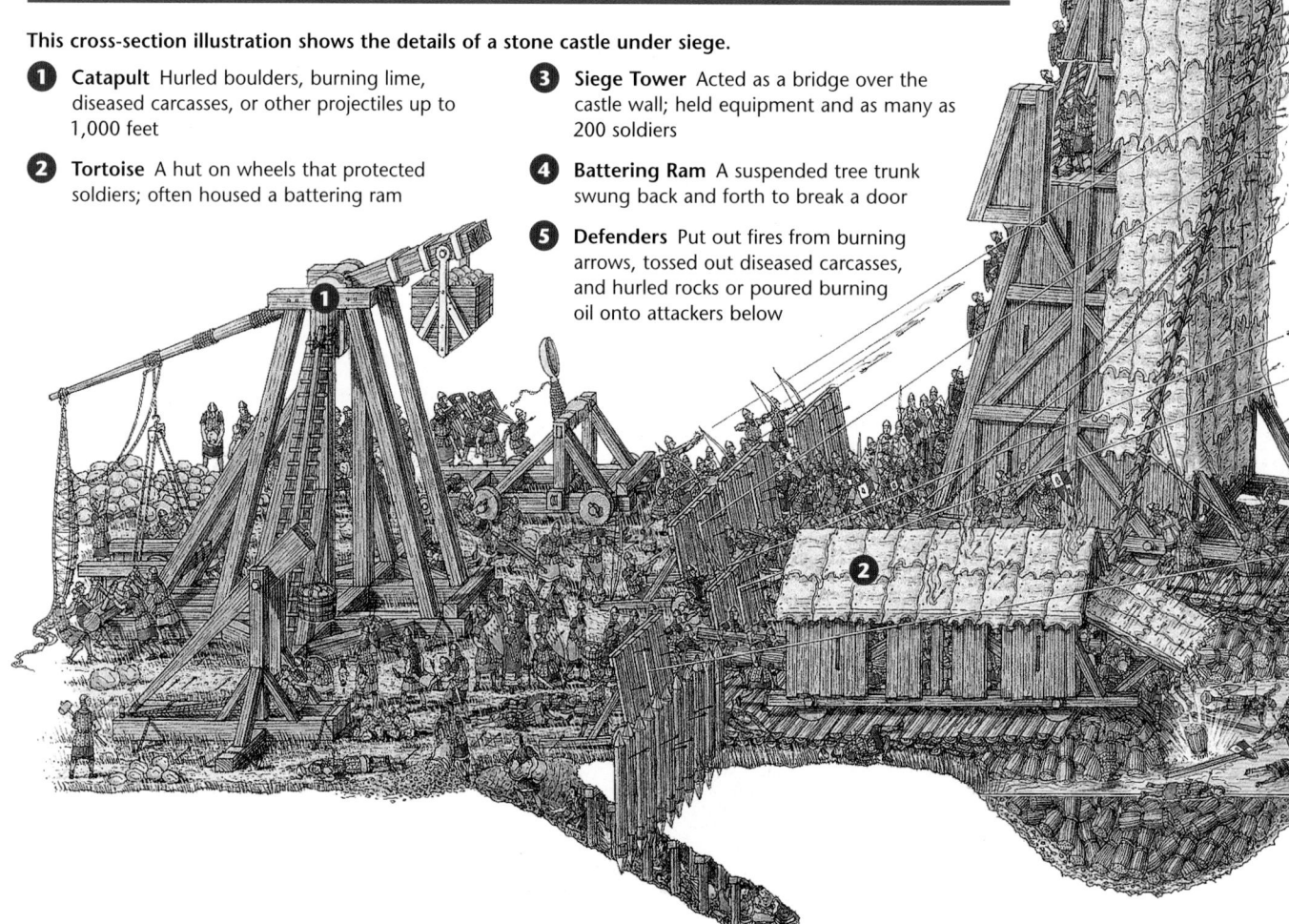

This cross-section illustration shows the details of a stone castle under siege.

1 **Catapult** Hurled boulders, burning lime, diseased carcasses, or other projectiles up to 1,000 feet

2 **Tortoise** A hut on wheels that protected soldiers; often housed a battering ram

3 **Siege Tower** Acted as a bridge over the castle wall; held equipment and as many as 200 soldiers

4 **Battering Ram** A suspended tree trunk swung back and forth to break a door

5 **Defenders** Put out fires from burning arrows, tossed out diseased carcasses, and hurled rocks or poured burning oil onto attackers below

challenge for an attacking force. The only access over the moat was a bridge, which could be drawn into the castle.

In the design of castles, protection took precedence over comfort. Guards looked out from small towers, called turrets. Narrow slits in the thick walls provided the only ventilation and natural light. These windows remained uncovered even on the coldest winter days. Through these slots, archers could shoot at approaching enemies.

In the strongest part of the castle was a stone tower called the keep. If the castle came under

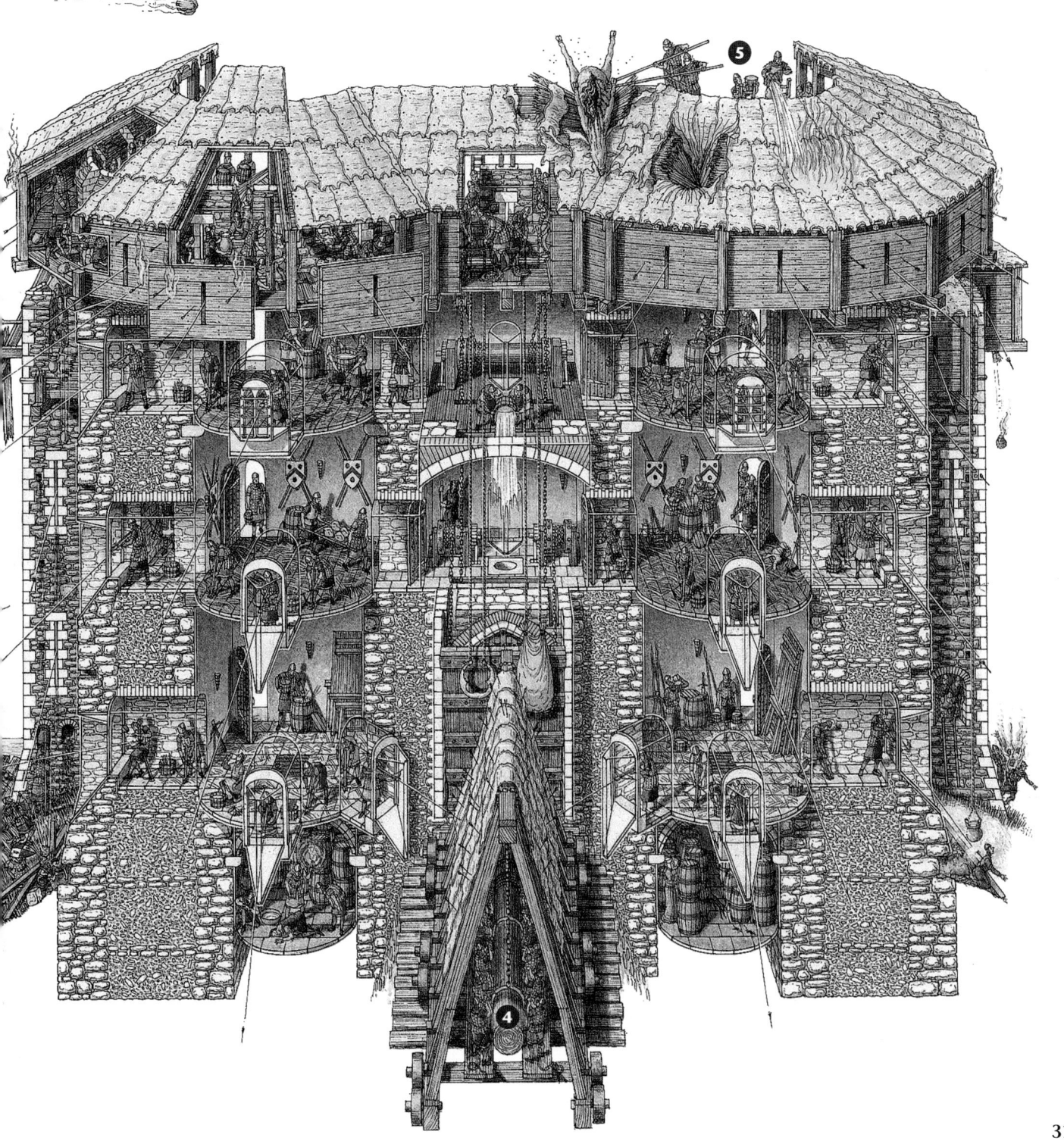

A medieval noblewoman stands at the center of this wool and silk tapestry known as *The Lady and the Unicorn.*

attack, its inhabitants could fall back to the keep. Here the castle's valuables were stored, along with supplies of food and water. Sometimes an attacking army would lay siege to a castle, lying in wait for months or even years in an attempt to starve out those trapped inside. But in a well-stocked keep, the castle's inhabitants could endure for many months and hope that the attackers would at last lose interest.

The Noblewoman

Women in medieval society had little power to make important decisions for themselves. A girl was expected to obey her father; after marriage, a woman submitted to the will of her husband. Among noble families, marriage was often not a matter of individual choice but a means to strengthen ties between families.

Despite these restrictions, noblewomen played an important role in medieval society. The lady of the manor managed household affairs and directed house servants. When her husband was away at war, the noblewoman often assumed his responsibilities for managing the finances of the manor and its estates, collecting rents, supervising farming operations, and settling disputes.

The Knight

A medieval lord often had his own army of knights on horseback. The knights defended the lord and his territory against raiders. They also took the offensive as rival lords vied for land and power.

Since ancient times, mounted soldiers had fought in battle. But before the Middle Ages, the

Medieval knights wore heavy suits of armor like this one.

soldier on horseback lacked two very important inventions—stirrups and horseshoes. The Huns or other Asian nomads may have been the first to bring stirrups to western Europe. In the 700s, Charles Martel saw the potential power of cavalry forces as he fought against Muslim forces. Stirrups helped soldiers on horseback stay on their mounts as they charged foot soldiers. Horseshoes—iron shoes nailed to a horse's hooves—helped the horse keep its footing in soft, wet ground, and gallop over hard, dry terrain. A shod horse could carry a heavy load without damaging its hooves.

A medieval knight in armor was indeed a heavy load. Early knights wore a cloak of iron links called chain mail. In time, knights replaced chain mail with full suits of armor that protected them from the blows of lances and battle-axes.

Fighting on horseback required elaborate equipment and intense training. Because both were expensive, few young men could afford to become knights. The process of becoming a knight began with apprenticeship at five or six years of age. Over the next ten to fifteen years, boys worked with an experienced knight to learn the skills they needed to defend their lord.

By the 1100s, knights were practicing their skills in mock battles called tournaments. Jousting became a popular form of entertainment—lance in hand, knights galloped toward each other, each seeking to knock the other from his saddle or pierce his armor. Over time, these tournaments became social events with more pageantry and less bloodshed.

The Code of Chivalry

In the early Middle Ages, knights often fought among themselves for land and riches. Peasants suffered from these skirmishes as warring knights trampled their fields and drove off their livestock. To curb this lawlessness, priests and bishops gradually persuaded knights to accept rules of honorable conduct known as **chivalry** (SHIH-vuhl-ree).

The code of chivalry spelled out the virtues a knight should follow. A good knight, said the code, was loyal to God, the church, and the lord he served. He fought bravely and was also expected to protect the weak, the poor, the helpless, and all women and children.

The code set high standards that few knights actually met. Many knights continued to raid and plunder. The ideal knight—charitable, kind, and generous—existed mainly in legend and in the ballads sung by troubadours (TROO-buh-dorz), poet-musicians of the late Middle Ages.

The Manor Economy

In the early Middle Ages in Europe, the lord's estate, the manor, was the center of life. Many people were born, married, had children, and died without ever venturing beyond the boundaries of the manor.

Knights honed their jousting skills in tournaments, or mock battles, a popular form of entertainment in medieval times.

Medieval manors were isolated, separated from one another by miles of dangerous, uninhabited forest. Each manor needed to be self-sufficient. The manor grew its own vegetables. It kept livestock for meat, chickens for eggs, and sheep for wool.

Usually a manor also included a blacksmith's shop, mill, bakehouse, and brewery. All these operations belonged to the lord. The peasants could use the mill or bakehouse, but they had to pay a fee to the lord to do so. The few things a lord might need to buy from the outside world included iron for forging tools, salt for curing meat, and millstones for grinding grain.

Most of the land on the manor was used for farming. It took the work of many peasants to till the soil and harvest the crops. Medieval farming tools were crude. The plows that worked well farther south barely scratched the surface of the rocky soil in northern Europe. The crops depleted the land of its nutrients, and farmers did not know how to enrich the soil.

The Hard Lot of the Serfs

Some peasants were free men who owned or leased plots of land from their lord, but most were serfs. Serfs were tied to the land and could not leave the manor without the lord's permission. Their land, their animals, their homes, their clothes, and even their food all belonged to the lord.

Serfs spent much of their time in unpaid labor for the lord. Serfs plowed the lord's fields, harvested his crops, threshed his grain, and tended his livestock. The women spent long hours cleaning the lord's house, cooking, brewing beer, spinning wool, and churning butter. In the time left over from these tasks, serfs worked small patches of land that the lord set aside for their use. By late

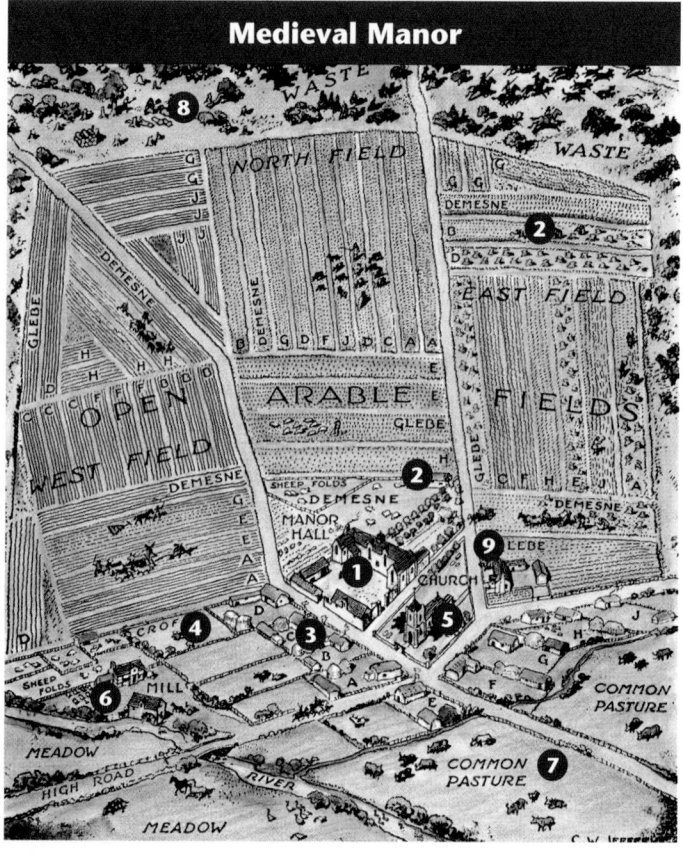

Medieval Manor

1. **Manor Hall** Residence of the lord and his family
2. **Lord's Demesne** Lord's fields worked by peasants
3. **Cottages** Peasants' homes
4. **Crofts** Peasants' fields
5. **Parish Church** Place of worship and community gatherings
6. **Gristmill** Water-powered mill (waterwheel and grindstone) for grinding grain
7. **Commons** Pasture open to all community livestock
8. **Woodland** Source of wood for fuel and construction
9. **Parsonage and Glebe** Home and farmland of the local minister

winter, hunger set in as the serfs had usually eaten all the food harvested in the fall.

Serfs weren't slaves, but they were little better off. Most who were born serfs, died serfs, after years of struggling to feed their families and fulfill their duties to their lord. It was rare for a serf to live beyond thirty-five years of age.

The Age of Faith

Historians sometimes call the Middle Ages an "Age of Faith." During this period, Eastern Orthodox Christianity flourished in the Byzantine Empire. In the powerful Islamic Empire, the Muslim faith tied together millions of people. Between A.D. 500 and 1400, the great unifying force in western Europe was the Christian church headed by the pope in Rome—what would come to be known as the Catholic Church.

The Church in Medieval Life

In western Europe during the Middle Ages, with all its hardships and dangers, the church offered hope. To those whose lives consisted of hard work and the threat of disease and hunger, the church taught that a reward waited in heaven.

The Church in Daily Life

At the head of the Christian church in western Europe stood the pope in Rome. His archbishops gave direction to the bishops. The bishops, in turn, had authority to direct the priests, who looked after individual churches.

The only church official directly known to most people was the village priest. The church was the center of village life, both literally and figuratively. It was usually the largest building on the manor. Church feasts marked sowing and reaping days, as well as religious holidays, such as Easter. These festivals offered peasants welcome relief from daily drudgery.

Village priests administered special church ceremonies, called **sacraments**, to mark important occasions in people's lives. The priest baptized infants, which assured parents that their newborn children were welcomed into the fold of the Christian community. The priest presided over marriages. He

Key Questions

- What roles did the Christian church assume during the Middle Ages in Europe? Why?

- Why do historians often call the Middle Ages the "Age of Faith"?

Peasants dance at a festival, a welcome relief from their hard daily lives.

heard confessions and forgave sins in God's name. He anointed those near death with oil, which was seen as a sign that they were free from sin and thus, they believed, prepared to enter heaven.

People were expected to attend mass, a weekly worship service. The mass and readings from the Bible were in Latin, a language most people didn't understand. Indeed, church officials were about the only people who could read and write, though some priests had little education themselves. For most people, knowledge of the faith came not through words but from rituals, traditions, statues, painted panels, frescoes depicting saints and biblical characters, and later, images in stained-glass windows.

The Power of the Church

The medieval Christian church's role went beyond spiritual matters. Indeed, the church gradually exerted great political and economic influence on European society in the Middle Ages.

After the fall of the Roman Empire, in a time of decentralized and weak government, the church increasingly assumed duties we associate with government. The church owned land, charged taxes, operated courts, and ran schools. It provided aid to those who were sick or destitute. The majority of the hospitals built during the Middle Ages were run by churches or monasteries.

The church had its own set of laws, called **canon law**. Everyone was subject to canon law, from kings to peasants. The church established courts to settle legal disputes and to try people accused of violating the law.

If an ambitious feudal lord challenged the church's authority or broke its rules, the pope could excommunicate him—that is, the pope could declare the lord no longer a member of the church. An excommunicated person lost many legal rights and couldn't participate in church services until the excommunication was lifted. The threat of excommunication gave the church power over lords who might be tempted to defy the church's authority.

Almost all high church officials were of noble birth and had their own fiefs. Wealthy noblemen who hoped to earn a place in heaven often donated huge sums of money and large tracts of land to the church. The church became the largest landowner in Europe.

During the Middle Ages, church leaders and feudal lords competed for power. Our current notions of separation of church and state did not exist. Bishops and abbots held positions in secular governments, and, as a result, bishops were often more powerful than princes, dukes, and lords.

> *Secular* means worldly, not related to religious matters.

While in principle the church had the authority to appoint its own officials, in practice kings, dukes, and other secular rulers controlled the appointment of church officials. Because the office of bishop brought power and wealth with it, a king or noble might appoint a son as bishop, even if the son had little religious interest or qualification. Secular leaders also engaged in the practice of simony (SIY-muh-nee), the selling of church offices.

Renewal and Reform

As the medieval church gained wealth and power, problems followed, including corruption among some church officials. Members of both the clergy and the laity began to call for reform.

Some monks and other church officials placed worldly wealth before spiritual matters. At the monastery of Cluny (kloo-nee) in eastern France, however, the Abbot Berno emphasized strict adherence to the Benedictine rule of obedience and poverty. He insisted that his monastery would answer only to the pope and not take orders from nobles or even from bishops. Inspired by the monks of Cluny, many monasteries and convents instituted similar reforms over the next two centuries.

In the early 1200s, groups of preachers called **friars** renewed the church in both spiritual and practical ways. In contrast to wealthy members of the clergy, the friars were **mendicant** preachers, which means they relied solely on charity to meet their worldly needs. Rather than seclude themselves in monasteries, they moved among towns and devoted themselves to helping their communities.

Two early orders of friars developed in response to the powerful examples of their founders. The Franciscans followed the example of Francis of Assisi (uh-SEE-see), who himself tried to follow the example of Jesus by living a life of poverty and service. The Dominicans, founded by a Spanish priest named Dominic, produced many leading Catholic scholars and theologians.

> A *theologian* is a scholar who studies religious faith, doctrine, and experience.

Reforms to Limit Secular Influence

Some church leaders pushed for reforms to give the church more control over its own affairs and limit the influence of secular rulers. In 1059, a church decree proclaimed that henceforth secular rulers could not choose the pope. Instead, the pope would be elected by a council of high church officials in Rome, called the College of Cardinals.

In 1073, the cardinals elected a monk to become Pope Gregory VII. Gregory worked for reforms. He attacked the practice of simony. He asserted that only the pope had the authority to appoint church leaders. This decision was unpopular among the kings of the day. Emperor Henry IV of Germany tried to organize a movement to force Gregory to give up the papacy (the office of pope). In response, Gregory excommunicated Henry (though the pope later lifted the excommunication).

The struggle over control of church offices continued for decades. It was much more than an argument over who got what job. It was, in effect, a struggle to define who had final authority in western Europe.

In 1122, religious and secular leaders met in the German city of Worms. There, they reached a compromise known as the Concordat of Worms. This complex agreement gave the church the authority to appoint bishops and abbots, but required these officials to acknowledge their status as vassals of the emperor.

The Schism of 1054

While the church in western Europe was dealing with reforms and power struggles, it was also engaged in ongoing disputes with the eastern branch of the church, based in Constantinople. As you've learned, the simmering tensions between the western and eastern churches boiled over in 1054, when the pope in Rome and the patriarch in Constantinople excommunicated each other, initiating the schism that split the church. The Byzantine branch of Christianity became the Eastern Orthodox Church, while the western branch became known as the Catholic (or Roman Catholic) Church.

Western Europe on the Eve of Change

By the middle of the eleventh century, change was sweeping through western Europe. The threat of Viking raids had ended, and most people had converted to Christianity. Although skirmishes for land continued, there began a time of relative peace and stability.

Innovations in farming, such as a new heavy plow, enabled farmers to grow more crops with less effort. The increased food supply helped people eat better and live longer.

Feudalism remained the basis of the medieval economy, but with fewer workers needed to farm, and with more goods to sell and trade, some people began to leave the manor to settle in towns. Trade flourished in western Europe as these medieval towns grew in number, population, and importance.

In this Age of Faith, the church continued to play a central role in daily life, even as reforms and power struggles began to change the church's role in the political arena. As you will see in the next chapter, the centuries ahead would be an era of sometimes wrenching transitions for the church and medieval society.

900

1000

1100

c. 900
Agricultural
advancements lead
to a population
boom in Europe.

1095
Pope Urban II calls
for a crusade to take
control of the Holy
Land from Muslims.

c. 1150
The Gothic style in
architecture emerges.

The intricate and expansive rose window of Notre Dame Cathedral in Paris, France

1200

1300

1400

1215
The Magna Carta establishes the principle of limited monarchy in England.

c. 1300
France is unified under the Capetian kings.

c. 1350
The Black Death devastates western Europe.

1453
The Hundred Years' War comes to an end.

Chapter 15
The Rise of Western Europe
1050–1500

The High Middle Ages in Europe—from roughly the eleventh through the thirteenth centuries—were a time of both upheaval and renewal. Christian armies marched east to fight the Crusades, a series of wars with Muslims over the fate of a strip of land along the eastern Mediterranean known as the Holy Land. These wars left a legacy of bitterness between Muslims and Christians. They also opened the way for exchanges of goods and ideas and a revival of learning.

Contact with Muslim and Byzantine civilizations hastened changes in Europe. New methods of trading, working, and banking spurred the growth of towns and cities. The feudal system gradually gave way to a new social order. By the early fourteenth century, strong monarchs were emerging in Europe, particularly in England and France. In England, attempts to limit royal power laid the foundation for modern democracies.

But the fourteenth century also brought devastating calamities. France and England clashed in decades of war, which took heavy tolls on both sides. Even worse, the plague spread death across Europe. In the late fourteenth century, a split within the Catholic Church led to the reshaping of political and religious institutions. In the end, these crises hastened the end of feudalism and set the stage for the rise of a dynamic new Europe.

The Age of the Crusades

During the early Middle Ages, Germanic tribes—such as the Visigoths, Vandals, Franks, and later the Vikings—plundered and pillaged throughout Europe. As people looked to the feudal lords for protection, medieval Europe became a fractured continent, ruled by many different kings, dukes, and barons. As trade, learning, and agricultural production declined, civilization itself seemed threatened.

By the mid-eleventh century, however, as the raiding tribes settled down, the people of Europe began to enjoy some peace and stability. Farmers grew more food, trade picked up, and new market towns thrived. In some parts of Europe, strong monarchs took charge, bringing order to once unruly realms. Across much of the continent, the Christian church provided a common bond of faith.

Key Questions

- What were the Crusades? Why did they begin?
- What were the lasting effects of the Crusades?
- How did economic, social, and cultural changes shape Europe during the eleventh century?

The Crusades

Great changes lay in store for medieval Europe as the people of Christendom undertook the Crusades, a long series of wars with the Muslims. The aim of the Crusades was recovering Palestine, the Holy Land in the Middle East.

Palestine had long been important to Jews, Christians, and Muslims. Jews revered it as the homeland of their Hebrew ancestors, guided to this place by the patriarch Abraham. To Christians, it was important as the land of Jesus' birth and death. For Muslims, Palestine was the site of key religious events in the life of their prophet Muhammad. Christians, Jews, and Muslims all regarded Jerusalem as the holiest city in the Holy Land.

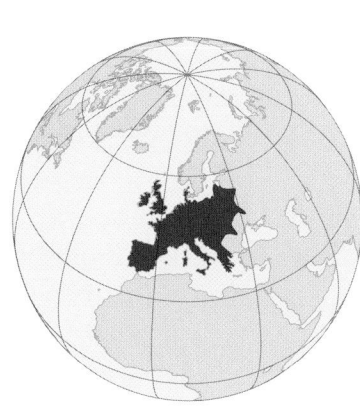

Europe, c. 1300, saw great political, social, and economic change.

The Dome of the Rock still gleams over Jerusalem, regarded by Christians, Jews, and Muslims as the holiest of cities.

323

Palestine: The Origin of the Name

Since the time of ancient Rome, a slender strip of land along the eastern Mediterranean Sea has been known as Palestine. The ancient Hebrew people, led by Abraham, settled there and called the region Canaan. Later the Philistines came from across the Mediterranean Sea and made it their home. Greek writers called this part of the world Philistia, after the Philistines. In Latin, the language of the Romans, Philistia was translated as "Palaestina" or "Palestine." The region called Palestine does not have precise borders. Over the years, it has included modern-day Israel, Gaza, the West Bank, and parts of Jordan, Lebanon, and Egypt.

A Command from the Pope

Until the seventh century, Byzantine Christians had ruled Palestine. Then Muslims conquered it, but they allowed people of other religions to visit and live there as well. Jews in Palestine could follow their faith, and Christian pilgrims were free to come and go. In the eleventh century, however, the Seljuk Turks, tribal nomads from central Asia, pillaged their way across Persia and overran the eastern Mediterranean coast. Recent and zealous converts to Islam, the Seljuks began harassing Christian pilgrims, as well as traders from the Christian West. They also surged into Asia Minor and attacked the Byzantine Empire.

Although the Byzantine Empire was by this time much reduced from its greatest extent, it was still the heart of Orthodox Christianity. In 1071, the Seljuks destroyed a Byzantine army at the Battle of Manzikert. For the next two decades, the Seljuks kept pushing closer to the Byzantine capital, Constantinople, often leaving nothing but burned villages in their wake. The Byzantine emperor finally sent a desperate message to the pope, pleading for the Christian warriors of the West to come help his empire fight the Turks.

While the Byzantine emperor was fully aware of the ongoing quarrel between the Eastern and Western branches of the church, he thought Christians of the West might be willing to defend Christians of the East against Muslim invaders. In Rome, the pope understood that if the Byzantine Empire fell, the Islamic Empire might next take up arms against the kingdoms of western Europe. Even if the Muslims didn't attack western Europe, Christians might be cut off forever from the city of Jerusalem.

So it was that on a November day in 1095, at Clermont in France, Pope Urban II stood before thousands of people and called upon the people of Christendom to prepare for a holy war. He said it would be a war to protect Christians in the East and, mainly, to recapture the Holy Land from Muslim Turks. Thousands volunteered to join the fight. Many volunteers stitched a cross on their clothes. The Latin word for cross is *crux*, and the wars that would follow came to be known as the Crusades.

Most of the Crusades were wars between European Christians and Muslims over the fate of the Holy Land. Over the next two hundred years, there would be eight major Crusades to Palestine, and many minor ones.

The First Crusade

Some of the first to respond to the pope's appeal were commoners. Crowds of peasants and urban poor joined a smattering of knights and headed for Jerusalem without much of a plan. They were marching east with many motives: to heed the pope's call, to earn salvation, to seek adventure, to gain wealth, to reap glory.

They had to walk more than 1,400 miles (2,253 km) to even reach Asia, and most had little or no money. So they tried to live off the land, which led to clashes with local people. They were eager to fight those they saw as enemies of Christianity, but most of the people they met were fellow Christians. Jews were the major exception. Christian mobs killed many Jews in towns and cities along the

Pope Urban II Calls for Crusades

When the Byzantine emperor, threatened by the Seljuk Turks, asked for help to protect his realm and safeguard the sacred sites of Christendom, Pope Urban II responded. At a church council meeting in Clermont, France, he delivered an impassioned speech to a large crowd of clergy and laity assembled in an open field. According to the later recollections of those who heard him, he urged Christians everywhere to resolve their differences and head for the Holy Land to defeat the Turks.

Impunity is freedom from punishment.

Although, O sons of God, you have promised more firmly than ever to keep the peace among yourselves and to preserve the rights of the church, there remains still an important work for you to do.... You must apply the strength of your righteousness to another matter which concerns you as well as God. For your brethren who live in the east are in urgent need of your help, and you must hasten to give them the aid which has often been promised them. For, as the most of you have heard, the Turks and Arabs have attacked them and have conquered...as far west as the shore of the Mediterranean and the Hellespont.... They have occupied more and more of the lands of those Christians, and have overcome them in seven battles. They have killed and captured many, and have destroyed the churches and devastated the empire. If you permit them to continue thus for awhile with impunity, the faithful of God will be much more widely attacked by them. On this account I, or rather the Lord, beseech you as Christ's heralds to publish this everywhere and to persuade all people of whatever rank, foot-soldiers and knights, poor and rich, to carry aid promptly to those Christians and to destroy that vile race from the lands of our friends. I say this to those who are present, it is meant also for those who are absent. Moreover, Christ commands it.

way. The pope condemned the bloodshed, but to no effect. When these ramshackle hordes arrived in Asia, the Turks quickly crushed them.

These mobs, however, were not the real crusaders. Even as the ragged crowds marched east, some of Europe's greatest dukes and counts were organizing real armies, spearheaded by thousands of Europe's most fearsome warriors, armored knights on huge horses. Each knight was a fully equipped war machine unlike anything seen in the armies of the East. These crusaders from the West made the Byzantine emperor so nervous that he arranged for them to make their way quickly past Constantinople and into Asia Minor.

In Asia Minor, the Western warriors engaged the Turks in a hard-fought battle near the city of Nicaea. The crusaders won and moved on, conquering one city after another. In 1099, the crusaders finally reached the walls of Jerusalem. After a six-week siege, they conquered the city and then massacred thousands of the city's Muslim and Jewish inhabitants. Many crusaders then went home, but some stayed on to establish Christian city-states in Syria and Palestine.

The Second and Third Crusades

Although disorganized at first, the Muslims rallied and fought back, and the struggle for the Holy Land became a deadly tug-of-war. Both sides inflicted terrible violence, with victory going first to one side, then the other. When the Muslims reconquered part of the Christian territory in Palestine, the pope called for a Second Crusade. The kings of France and Germany organized armies, but these monarchs were ineffective military leaders. In Palestine, the crusaders suffered a humiliating defeat by the Seljuks. They returned home, having accomplished nothing. The Second Crusade, which ended in 1149, was a disaster.

In the late twelfth century, a charismatic Muslim leader emerged in Egypt. Europeans called him Saladin (from the Arabic *Salah al-Din*). In 1187, Saladin's armies stunned Europeans by taking Jerusalem back from the Western knights. In response, three of Christendom's most powerful kings mounted the Third Crusade, which lasted from 1189 to 1192. Frederick Barbarossa of Germany, Philip Augustus of France, and Richard I of England assembled armies to retake Jerusalem

The First Crusade, c. 1098: Christians on the way to Jerusalem attack the city of Antioch.

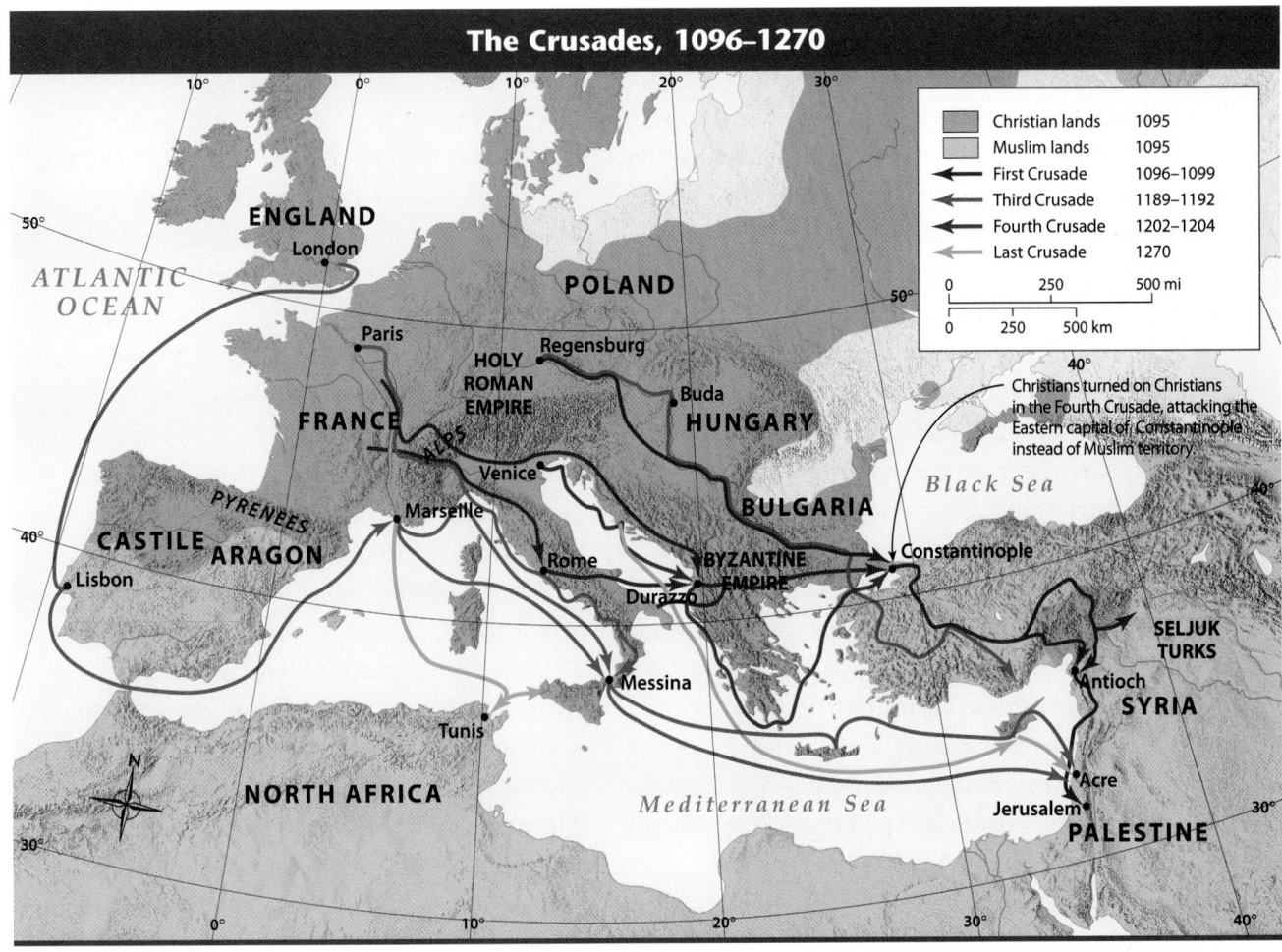

The Crusades, 1096–1270

■	Christian lands	1095
■	Muslim lands	1095
→	First Crusade	1096–1099
→	Third Crusade	1189–1192
→	Fourth Crusade	1202–1204
→	Last Crusade	1270

Christians turned on Christians in the Fourth Crusade, attacking the Eastern capital of Constantinople instead of Muslim territory.

For two hundred years, Christians and Muslims fought bitterly for control of the Holy Land.

from the Muslims. But Frederick drowned on his way east, and Philip fell ill and soon went home. The Third Crusade came down to a contest between Richard and Saladin.

Saladin was a devout Muslim, known for his wisdom, courage, and generosity. Richard was called Richard the Lion-Heart because, fierce and fearless, he plunged into battle alongside his troops. At his coronation, Richard had pledged himself to God and the Catholic Church. He aimed to redeem that pledge by recapturing Jerusalem.

Though these two great leaders, Saladin and Richard, were at war, they greatly respected each other. When a fever struck Richard, Saladin sent him fruit chilled with snow, as well as his own personal physician.

Richard won all the major battles but could not take Jerusalem. In a message to Richard, Saladin expressed his resolution to maintain Muslim control of the city:

To us Jerusalem is as precious, aye and more precious, than it is to you, in that it was the place whence our Prophet made his journey by night to heaven and is destined to be the gathering place of our nation at the last day. Do not dream that we shall give it up to you or that we can be so obliging in this matter. As to the land—it belonged to us originally, and it is you who are the real aggressors. When you seized it, it was only because of the suddenness of your coming and the weakness of those [Muslims] who then held it. So long as the war shall last God will not suffer you to raise one stone upon another.

In the end, stranded far from home without allies, Richard agreed to a compromise with Saladin. Muslims would keep Jerusalem, but Christian pilgrims would have the right to enter the city freely, visit their sacred sites, and worship at the churches.

Later Crusades

At least five more major Crusades followed the first three, but these later crusaders went east with intentions other than recapturing Jerusalem. Many had hopes of getting rich, some from plunder, and some from trade, which had thrived even amid the warfare.

The knights of the Fourth Crusade never made it to the Holy Land. Upon reaching Constantinople in 1204, they decided to sack that city instead. They destroyed buildings, set fires, and looted churches. The Fourth Crusade seriously deepened the rift that had divided the Eastern and Western branches of Christianity at least since the schism of 1054.

In 1291, the last of the Christian cities in Palestine fell. The remaining crusaders gave up and straggled home, leaving the Holy Land under Muslim rule.

Lasting Effects of the Crusades

The Crusades failed to achieve their military goal. Palestine remained under Muslim control, and the two centuries of bloodshed left bitter legacies. Muslims of the eastern Mediterranean would remain hostile to the Christian West for years. Muslims and Christians would long blame each other for the bloody struggles. The massacre of many Jews by early crusaders left Christians and Jews deeply divided. The Crusades also aggravated the mistrust between Orthodox Christians of the Byzantine Empire and Catholic Christians of the West.

But the Crusades also had positive consequences for Europe. In the East, the crusaders saw societies more advanced than their own and began to envision similar advances in their homelands. They returned to Europe with new ideas and a readiness to embrace change. European scholars learned about the libraries of the Islamic and Byzantine worlds. They began to study books like those of al-Khwarizmi, the great Arab mathematician, and Ibn Sina, the Persian philosopher and medical scholar.

The Crusades alerted Europeans to the wealth of products available in the markets of the East—lemons, sugar, rice, apricots, exotic spices, cotton cloth, and more. When merchants brought these goods into the European marketplace, they kindled tremendous interest in trade with distant Eastern lands.

The Crusades also helped hasten the breakdown of feudalism. Throughout medieval times, the feudal system had locked Europe into an

The knights of the Fourth Crusade sacked the city of Constantinople in 1204, further deepening the divide between the Eastern and Western branches of Christianity.

unchanging way of life. People were born into their stations and remained there for life. Most were tied to the land as serfs, and few traveled even so much as ten miles from home. The Crusades disrupted all this. Some kings grew more powerful as they organized great armies. Land changed hands as nobles died in battle or sold their holdings to finance their campaigns. Serfs managed to join crusading armies, and those who came back did not always return to the manor but instead found new lives in growing towns and cities.

Turning Points in Medieval Europe

When the Crusades began, great changes were already underway in Europe. The upheaval of the wars quickened those changes, leading to greater prosperity, better health, and longer life for many people.

Agricultural Improvements

In the era of the Crusades, European peasants steadily improved their harvests, thanks to some technical advances. For example, the padded horse collar allowed farmers to use fast-moving horses rather than slow-moving oxen to pull their plows. As a result, farmers could plow more land in less time.

New practices resulted in more efficient use of the land. In earlier times, serfs had divided their fields into two parts. Each year, they planted one half, and let the other half lie fallow—that is, they left it unplowed and unplanted. Leaving the land fallow allowed the soil to rest and recover its fertility. Then farmers discovered that soil did just as well if it rested only one year out of three. So peasants began to divide their fields into three parts and plant two of them each year. In effect, this three-field system increased the amount of land available for cultivation.

A Commercial Revolution

Improvements in agriculture helped peasants grow more and better food, which led to population

Agricultural advances brought surpluses of food, which contributed to the growth of markets and trade.

growth. Eventually, peasants grew more food than they needed for themselves and their manors. They took the surplus to markets in villages and towns, where they traded it for other products. Since fewer laborers were now needed in the fields, some people could spend their time making craft goods, which could also be traded. Thus trade came to play an ever larger part in European life. Commerce became so vigorous that historians speak of a **commercial revolution** during this time.

Demand built up for goods from the East, such as silks and spices from Asia. People who had tasted food seasoned with pepper or cinnamon developed a desire for such spices. Those who tried on cotton garments rarely wished to go back to wearing rough linen or scratchy wool, the two types of cloth most readily available to Europeans before the Crusades.

Several times a year, crowds gathered at great trade fairs. At the largest of these trade fairs, hundreds of merchants from across Europe came with cartloads of goods—cloth, knives, salt, porcelain, and much more.

Money, like these Italian florins, replaced barter.

The Money Economy

In village marketplaces, most people used the barter system—that is, they traded one good for another. But as markets expanded, barter proved an impractical way to do business. It was hard enough to haul great heaps of leather or huge mounds of wheat back and forth; it only made matters more complicated to have to negotiate how much of one good was worth how much of another.

The exchange of money began to replace barter as more people accepted gold or silver coins as payment for their goods and in turn used the coins to buy what they needed. Earlier, during the Dark Ages, many Europeans had almost stopped using money—on the manor, with its isolated and self-sufficient economy, there was little use for it—but now, coins began to circulate again.

Sometimes, a group of farmers or artisans would send a representative to a trade fair to sell a contract, a written promise to deliver some product in the future. Buyers of such contracts could be confident of getting what they needed when they needed it. Sellers could safely put time and money into producing the goods, knowing that they already had a buyer. Eventually, the contracts themselves became items that people bought and sold for money.

The use of money expanded trade to such a degree that some people did not have to produce anything. They could make a living as full-time merchants, buying goods from craftsmen and then traveling from market to market to sell those goods at a profit.

With traders moving through many lands, many kinds of coins began to circulate, which created a need for professional money changers. The first money changers emerged in the busy trading towns of northern Italy. They sat at benches, weighing ducats and dinars, florins and sous. When people needed to trade one kind of coin for another, they went to "the bench," as this market was called. The money changers became Europe's first bankers. In fact, the word *bank* comes from *bancus*, the Latin word for "bench."

The growth of a **money economy** further eroded the feudal system. Some serfs earned enough money to buy their freedom. Many kings, nobles, and clergymen had to sell land to raise money. The growing use of money weakened the land-for-service relationships that were the basis of feudalism.

The Growth of Towns

In the eleventh and twelfth centuries, as trade thrived in western Europe, many new towns formed, and old towns grew rapidly. Towns grew in places people could travel to easily—for example, near rivers or at convenient crossroads. Most medieval towns had about one to two thousand

As trade grew in western Europe, so did towns and cities, especially where rivers and roads met.

Crowded medieval streets bustled with commerce, but unsanitary conditions made them ripe for the spread of disease.

had a busy central square lined with the shops of tailors, furriers, barbers, and the like. Bakers, brewers, and butchers sold their breads, ales, and meats along the busy streets. In the surrounding neighborhoods, one might find cask makers, cart builders, blacksmiths, shipwrights, and the workshops of other craftsmen.

The busy, narrow lanes of a medieval town were usually noisy and dirty. Horses and oxen, drawing carts to market, left waste in the streets. People dumped their garbage and sewage into the streets as well, which led to the spread of disease.

Organizing in Guilds

inhabitants. Great cities with a population of fifty thousand or more—Venice and London, for example—were the exception. Still, more towns kept sprouting up and established towns grew bigger and busier.

The inhabitants of these medieval towns built walls around them, for these were lawless times, when criminal bands roamed the land. Most towns

During the 1100s, merchants and tradesmen organized themselves into associations called **guilds**. Merchants formed local guilds in order to restrict trade by outsiders and to set prices. Craftsmen joined guilds to protect their members and set standards for their work. Each craft guild was made up of people who followed the same occupation— for example, winemakers had one guild, cloth makers another, and druggists, shoemakers, and tanners still others.

Many medieval towns were walled in to protect inhabitants from roaming criminal bands.

Workers organized into guilds that cared for their members, set standards, and trained the next generation of craftsmen.

Guilds took care of their members. They nursed workers who fell ill, provided for orphans, arranged burials, and organized entertainments. They also trained the next generation in the ways of the craft. Youngsters started out as unpaid apprentices, helping experienced craftsmen, called masters. When they learned enough, apprentices could become journeymen, who still worked for a master but were paid for their work. Some journeymen eventually won the right to call themselves masters and open their own workshops.

A Changing Social Order

A fortified town in medieval Europe was called a *burg.* The term became part of the names of cities such as Hamburg in Germany, Edinburgh in Scotland, and Canterbury in England. The term *burg* became part of the word used to describe the craftsmen, merchants, bankers, and other town dwellers who prospered in the money economy. In Germany they were called burghers; in France, the bourgeoisie (bourzh-wah-ZEE); in England, burgesses.

In purely feudal societies, almost everyone was either upper class or lower class, but the merchants and tradesmen of the towns fit somewhere between the two extremes. These town dwellers did not fit neatly into the old feudal order of nobility, clergy, and peasants. They formed part of a rising middle class who made their living from trade and commerce.

Early medieval towns were often under the control of a king or noble and paid taxes to him. But many of the new and growing towns managed to throw off the control of the feudal lords. In some cases, kings or nobles granted charters, written agreements that guaranteed the townspeople the right to control their own affairs. Free of feudal obligations, medieval towns became more self-governing, though they were not democracies. Power was often in the hands of the wealthiest families or most influential guilds.

The upper and lower classes gave way to a rising middle class, as portrayed by this husband-and-wife team at work.

Arts and Learning in the Middle Ages

Key Questions

• What led to a revival of learning in Europe?

• How did the architecture, art, and literature of the High Middle Ages reflect medieval values?

After the fall of Rome, the learning of ancient Greek and Roman civilizations was mostly forgotten—but not entirely. Even in the darkest years of the early Middle Ages, some learning went on in the churches. Contact with Byzantine and Muslim civilizations ignited a renewed interest in learning among Europeans.

Education in Medieval Europe

In medieval Europe, most people were illiterate. The only schools were religious schools, run by the church, since the church needed clergy who could read and write. In schools run by monasteries or by the great regional churches called cathedrals, students could prepare to become monks or church officials.

In the late Middle Ages, as towns grew, so did the need for literate people. Towns needed educated officials to serve as clerks and administrators. To operate their businesses, merchants and tradesmen needed to know how to read and write. Wealthier families began sending their boys to church schools, not to prepare them for the clergy, but to gain knowledge that would help them in the family trade.

At a cathedral school, boys studied an advanced program based on a curriculum from classical times. This classical program included seven subjects called the "liberal arts," because in ancient Rome only *liberi*, or "free men," were permitted to study them. The seven liberal arts were divided into two groups. The *trivium* (meaning "three roads") included grammar, logic, and rhetoric (the art of speaking and writing effectively). The *quadrivium* (meaning "four roads") included arithmetic, geometry, music, and astronomy.

The First Universities

In towns with great cathedrals, which often had fine libraries, students could hope to learn from distinguished scholars. Some scholars, such as Peter Abelard in Paris, attracted huge audiences to their lectures. In time, communities of scholars and students in these cathedral towns organized into associations called universities. At first these universities were much like guilds, with students as apprentices who paid to learn from master scholars. Classes met in church buildings or in the open air. Those students who passed an exam in the liberal arts could then help master scholars teach other students. Eventually, some students won recognition as master scholars.

In England, Oxford, one of the world's earliest universities, dates to 1249.

The earliest universities formed in Bologna (boh-LOH-nyah), Italy; in Paris, France; and in the English town of Oxford. In 1209, a group of disgruntled Oxford professors broke away to start a university in the nearby town of Cambridge. By the late 1200s, there were universities across Europe. Some taught theology and the liberal arts, while others focused on law and medicine.

Generally, women were not allowed to study at these institutions. In well-to-do families, however, some women managed to get an education. They studied privately with family members or family friends who happened to be scholars.

Faith and Reason

As you've learned, Islamic civilization had preserved the learning of older civilizations, including the works of Greek thinkers such as Aristotle and Plato. In the part of Spain ruled by Muslims, many of these works had been translated into Arabic and then into Latin. When Christians took back parts of Spain from the Muslims—including the city of Toledo, a center of scholarship and translation—many of the Latin translations made their way into cathedral libraries across western Europe.

As some Christian scholars studied the works of the great philosopher Aristotle, they wondered if Christian thought could be reconciled with Greek philosophy. Some church leaders opposed Aristotle, whose ideas, they said, might damage a person's faith. But other churchmen tried to use Aristotle's logic to create a bridge between reason and faith. They formed a school of thought called **Scholasticism**.

The greatest Scholastic philosopher was Thomas Aquinas (uh-KWIY-nus). Born in northern Italy, he became a priest in 1250, and a few years later he took a post as professor of philosophy and theology at the University of Paris. Thomas Aquinas admired the works of Aristotle. The Greeks' confidence in the power of reason appealed to Thomas's own intellectual spirit. In his writings, he used reason, logic, and Aristotle's ideas to examine and affirm the existence of God. His most famous work was *Summa Theologica*

Venetian-born Christine de Pisan, a highly regarded poet, pursued an education, rare for women at the time.

A Medieval Experimenter

Roger Bacon, a Franciscan monk who lived in the mid-1200s, was interested in learning about the material world. Bacon anticipated modern scientific methods. To gain knowledge, he said, one must go beyond abstract reasoning and use experimentation, making observations and collecting data. Bacon performed experiments in alchemy and with light and optics. He also speculated about how to build a flying machine, though in this effort he stopped short of experimenting.

(SOO-muh thee-uh-LOH-jih-kuh), which means "summary of theology." In that work he carefully explained Christian beliefs and the logic behind such beliefs.

Medieval Language and Literature

In the early Middle Ages, most medieval literature was oral, not written. The aristocracy enjoyed listening to troubadours recite poems or sing songs, usually about a knight performing gallant deeds to honor a lady. By the High to late Middle Ages, with the gradual renewal of learning and the rise of universities, favorite songs and tales from earlier times were written down for the first time.

One of the earliest literary works from England is the Anglo-Saxon epic *Beowulf*, which survives in a single manuscript dating from about the year 1000. Scholars think the poem was composed by an anonymous poet around the year 700. It mixes historical figures with characters from Scandinavian legends. The epic's vivid verses tell the tale of the warrior Beowulf, who slew a terrible monster called Grendel, only to face (and triumph over) an even more terrible monster, Grendel's mother.

History and legend also mix in the French *chansons de geste* (shahn-SOHN duh ZHEHST), poems that celebrated Charlemagne and the knights who served him. The most famous of these epic poems, *La Chanson de Roland* (*The Song of Roland*), dates from about 1100. It tells the tale of Charlemagne's nephew Roland at the historic Battle of Roncesvalles (RAHN-suh-valz or RAWN-thays-BAHL-yays) in 778, during a war fought by Charlemagne on France's border with

Spain. When Roland and his men are ambushed and face overwhelming odds, they fight gallantly to their death.

Literature in the Vernacular

Throughout and even beyond the Middle Ages, legal documents and formal works were written in Latin, which only highly educated people could read. Much medieval literature, however, was written in the **vernacular**—that is, the native language of a place, the local language used in daily life.

One of the greatest medieval masterworks of vernacular literature is *The Divine Comedy* written in the early 1300s by the Italian poet Dante

Dante, depicted here holding his *Divine Comedy*, wrote his epic poem in the Italian vernacular.

335

From a fifteenth-century illustrated manuscript of Chaucer's *Canterbury Tales*, written in vernacular English

Alighieri (DAHN-tay ah-luh-GYEH-ree). Dante's epic tells the story of a spiritual journey, an imagined voyage from hell to heaven. While all philosophical writing of Dante's time was in Latin, he chose to write his great poem in Italian. Dante's poem thus helped shape the Italian language.

Dante was from the Italian city-state of Florence, and he wrote in a Florentine dialect. (A *dialect* is a local version of a language.) In Dante's time, the people of Italy spoke many different dialects of the Italian language. But the popularity of *The Divine Comedy* helped make the Florentine dialect into what we now know as the Italian language.

Around 1400, Geoffrey Chaucer (CHAW-suhr) wrote a vernacular masterpiece in English. *The Canterbury Tales* features a group of pilgrims traveling to a religious shrine at Canterbury. The pilgrims, whom Chaucer describes in vivid sketches, represent a range of occupations and social classes—a knight, a prioress, a carpenter, a miller, a monk, a lawyer, and many more. On the way, each pilgrim tells a story to help pass the time. These tales vary from noble to raucous, from humorous to tragic.

As the pilgrims tell their tales, we learn about the character of each teller. Chaucer goes beyond the abstract characterizations typical of early medieval literature. He presents the pilgrims as distinct individuals, each with his or her own mix of virtues and vices.

Architecture in the Age of Faith

The Middle Ages in Europe left many remarkable works of art inspired by religion. Craftsmen produced treasures expressing their faith, from the glowing pages of illuminated manuscripts to jeweled containers for the bones of saints.

Perhaps the most awe-inspiring works of medieval art are churches and cathedrals. From the eleventh century to the mid-twelfth century, Europeans built in a style called Romanesque (roh-muhn-ESK), because the structures had round Roman arches and huge Roman-style columns holding up their heavy ceilings. A Romanesque church, usually built in the shape of a cross, was meant to be a mighty fortress of God, a place of safety as well as worship.

The Spanish cathedral of Santiago de Compostela was built in the Romanesque style.

Notre Dame Cathedral in Paris, with its exterior stone supports called flying buttresses, is characteristic of the Gothic style.

Romanesque churches had thick walls and few windows. They were usually dark inside, but they made up for it with many richly colored pictures and tapestries portraying scenes from the Bible, which provided a measure of religious instruction for people who could not read.

The Gothic Style

From the mid-twelfth to the sixteenth centuries, a new architectural style emerged, called Gothic. The Gothic style began in France when builders sought ways to erect higher cathedrals. In Romanesque churches, the walls were too heavy to build very high. Then some builders realized they could push structures higher if they used steep pointed arches instead of rounded Roman ones.

The builders wanted to go even higher. They wanted tall spires and lofty towers. And they wanted to hold it all up without cluttering the inside of the cathedral with many stone supports. To give the walls extra strength, and to buttress—to support—the highest parts, they built supports outside the building. These supports took the form of stone bridges that arced through the air almost as if they were flying—which is why they are called flying buttresses.

Since the Gothic cathedrals no longer needed such thick walls, builders could open these churches to light with huge stained-glass windows. To create them, craftsmen used thousands of bits of brightly colored glass, each piece attached to the next with lead. As light came through the windows, the glass lit up like jewels.

The main architectural features of Gothic cathedrals—from their towering spires to their pointed arches to the flying buttresses—worked to lift the gaze toward heaven and fill the mind with thoughts of God. The great cathedrals—such as Notre Dame (noh-truh DAHM) in Paris, or the Cologne Cathedral in Germany, or Salisbury Cathedral in England—drew pilgrims from miles around. Both rich and poor paid what they could to finance the construction of cathedrals, and the biggest ones took generations to build. No one recorded the names of the brilliant designers or hundreds of workmen. Gothic cathedrals represent the passions and inspirations not of individual artists but of whole communities.

The Gothic arches of the Cologne Cathedral

337

The Rise of Strong Monarchs

In the early Middle Ages in Europe, political power was mostly in the hands of feudal lords—princes, barons, dukes, and counts. In a specific region, a king ruled over these lords, but sometimes the king ruled more in name than in fact. Some of the wealthiest lords with the most extensive landholdings were even more powerful than kings.

During and after the Crusades, however, as towns grew and trade thrived, the feudal system eroded. At the same time, some kings acquired more power, and strong monarchies emerged in what would become the nations of England, France, and Spain.

Strong Monarchs in England

In the medieval era, a strong monarchy emerged to unite England. The process unfolded gradually, since England was a patchwork of peoples with diverse customs and languages.

Early England

Over the years, different peoples from many places settled the British Isles. The Celts (kelts) arrived from the European continent in the 500s B.C. In the first century A.D., the Romans conquered Celtic Britain and ruled until the 400s. As the Roman Empire fell, Germanic tribes called Angles and Saxons invaded the British Isles. The areas they settled came to be known as Angle-land, or England. Their Anglo-Saxon language evolved into the earliest form of English.

In the 800s, Vikings from Scandinavia came to plunder, but some settled in and blended with the people already living in England. Other Vikings landed across the English Channel on the coast of France. At first these Norsemen, as they were called, attacked villages and burned towns. Eventually they settled down, began speaking French, and embraced Christianity. The region of France they inhabited came to be called Normandy, and its ruler the Duke of Normandy.

William the Conqueror

In 1028, a son was born to the Duke of Normandy. The boy, William, would grow up to be known as William the Conqueror.

When William was Duke of Normandy, England was ruled by an Anglo-Saxon king, Edward, who was a distant cousin of William. When Edward died in early 1066, he left no sons or daughters. The king's brother-in-law, a noble named Harold, immediately claimed the throne. But William thought he had a better claim to the English throne.

William assembled an army of more than 10,000 soldiers with 3,600 horses. On 700 ships they crossed the English Channel. Legend has it that

Key Questions

- What was the Norman Conquest and how did it shape England's development?

- How were kings in England and France able to gain and maintain power?

- What was the significance of the Magna Carta in medieval England and for the future?

as he waded ashore, William stumbled. His nobles might have seen this as an unlucky sign, but William turned it into a good omen. Grasping a fistful of sand, he rose up roaring, "Thus do I seize the earth of England!"

Harold's army tried to stop the Normans near the town of Hastings. But Harold himself was killed, and William's troops emerged victorious in the Battle of Hastings. William marched on to London, where the citizens, having no wish to put up a fight, threw open the city gates. On Christmas Day at Westminster Abbey, William was crowned William I, king of England.

William's invasion of England would come to be known as the Norman Conquest. During William's reign, England was a divided society. A Norman king and a small elite of French-speaking Norman barons ruled a great mass of English-speaking Anglo-Saxons. Gradually, however, the rulers blended with their subjects, and over time a distinctively English language and culture emerged.

Strengthening the Monarchy

About twenty years after his invasion of England, William ordered a survey to learn more about the

Defining "Monarchy"

The ancient Greek philosopher Aristotle, in his writings on different types of governments, defined *monarchy* as rule by one man. The word *monarch* comes from the Greek roots *monos* ("alone") and *archos* ("ruler"). Thus, a monarch is a person who rules over a kingdom or empire.

resources of the land he had conquered. This massive survey, known as the Domesday Book, listed every town in every shire (county) of England and calculated what each area produced. The survey enabled William to tax and govern his country effectively, making him the most powerful king England had known up to that time.

William turned England into a well-organized feudal state. He seized land from the English nobles and gave it to his Norman nobles as estates in England, but on one condition—they had to pledge their allegiance directly to him. In William's feudal system, the king could strip any noble of his lands and titles at any time. He made sure that the real power remained not in the hands of his barons or lords, but in the hands of the king.

The Bayeux Tapestry

Some of our knowledge of the Norman Conquest comes from the Bayeux (biy-YOU) Tapestry, which, around 1730, a French scholar found hanging on a wall in a cathedral in Bayeux, France. The tapestry, which dates from about 1070, is an embroidered panel of linen about 230 feet (70 m) long and 20 inches (51 cm) wide, on which pictures and words are stitched in eight colors of wool. It presents more than seventy scenes that tell a story. The story introduces Harold before the Battle of Hastings, and goes on to describe William's expedition and victory over Harold.

According to tradition, the tapestry is the work of Matilda, wife of William, and ladies of her court, but there is no firm evidence to identify who created this remarkable work of medieval art.

A segment of the Bayeux Tapestry depicts the Battle of Hastings.

While William kept a firm grip on his feudal lords, he also listened to their opinions. He formed the Great Council, a group of nobles and church leaders who met regularly to advise the king and help him make laws. The Great Council was an early forerunner of legislatures that represent the will of the people. Together, William and his nobles forged a single central government, powerful throughout the land.

Henry II

William's successors continued his work of strengthening the throne. One of the strongest was King Henry II, William's energetic great-grandson, who became king in 1154. Henry ruled for more than three decades, and during that time he turned England into one of the strongest monarchies in Europe.

Henry devoted his energies to establishing law and order in his realm. Perhaps his most lasting achievement was the change he brought to England's legal system. In the Middle Ages, ideas of justice varied from village to village. Local laws and customs determined how trials were conducted. Sometimes two knights might fight each other to decide who was right or wrong. Or people accused of crimes might be subjected to ordeals, such as being thrown into a pond to see if the accused floated or sank. Henry replaced these old feudal customs with a new system of justice.

Rather than relying on local lords to decide guilt or innocence, Henry set up courts. In many cases, these courts used juries to help make decisions. Henry sent judges traveling around the countryside to try cases and apply the law equally throughout the land. By making the laws more uniform, Henry II made England a more unified nation.

Henry made sure that the judges' rulings were written down, so that later judges facing similar cases could follow guidelines set by earlier rulings. A body of law thus emerged, known as **common law**, which reflected the practical

Eleanor of Aquitaine

During the Middle Ages, it was mostly men who held power and determined the course of nations. But in this masculine world, some women wielded great political skill and power. One such woman was Eleanor of Aquitaine (A-kwuh-tayn), who was born the daughter of the Duke of Aquitaine, a region in southwest France. In 1137, when Eleanor was fifteen, she inherited Aquitaine and married Louis VII, king of France. Several years later she and Louis parted ways, and Eleanor married King Henry II of England. Two of her sons, Richard the Lion-Heart and John, became kings of England.

Although noblewomen were expected to remain in their castles and do their husbands' bidding, in wartime Eleanor galloped around the countryside, waving her sword and calling men to battle. While her son Richard was away from the throne fighting in the Crusades, Eleanor stayed behind and helped run England herself.

In her old age, Eleanor traveled all over Europe, scheming to put her children and grandchildren on various thrones through artfully arranged royal marriages. She succeeded so well that by the time she died, people were calling her the "Grandmother of Europe."

Eleanor of Aquitaine's first marriage to King Louis of France

Despite clashes with nobility, Henry II strengthened the monarchy in twelfth-century England.

wisdom of many judges over time. English common law became the foundation of legal systems in many countries, including the United Kingdom, the United States, and Canada.

Limits on the Monarchy

Henry II strengthened the power of the throne, but not without resistance from English nobles and church leaders. The nobles clashed with the king over his right to levy taxes. Church leaders insisted that the king had no authority over church matters. Out of these struggles emerged ideas that helped lay the foundations for modern democracy.

The Tragedy of Thomas Becket

The most famous clash between king and church involved Henry II and England's leading archbishop, Thomas Becket. The two men started out as warm friends. Henry used his influence to get Becket appointed as Archbishop of Canterbury, England's highest clergyman.

Henry had reason to expect an ally in the church, but he was disappointed. As archbishop, Becket increasingly defied the king's attempts to assert power over the church. The power struggle between these two men went on for years. In 1170, four of the king's nobles, in response to hearing a furious outburst by the king against the archbishop, rode to Canterbury and murdered Thomas Becket in the cathedral.

The murder shocked medieval Europe. Although Henry probably didn't order the assassination, he was compelled to seek forgiveness from the church, which was granted only after the king walked barefoot through Canterbury as monks flogged him. Thomas Becket was later declared a saint, and his tomb became a popular destination for religious pilgrims. The tragedy damaged Henry's prestige, but it did not stop the English king from increasing his power.

The Magna Carta

In 1189, Henry's son Richard inherited the throne. He soon headed for Palestine to lead the Third Crusade. While Richard the Lion-Heart was away fighting Saladin, his brother John schemed to seize power. When Richard died in 1199, John became king of England, and some say he was the worst monarch ever to sit on the English throne.

A mean and quarrelsome man, King John clashed with the pope over the right to appoint the Archbishop of Canterbury. He quarreled with the French king over certain lands in France. He angered his nobles by arresting some of them and hanging them without trial. To finance his wars, John imposed taxes without consulting the Great Council, which infuriated the nobles.

Finally the nobles and church leaders had had enough. They raised an army and threatened rebellion. Faced with a civil war, King John backed down.

In 1215, at Runnymede (RUH-nee-meed), west of London on the river Thames (temz), the nobles forced King John to sign the **Magna Carta** (Latin for "great charter"). This document stated that even the king was bound by law and that the

341

Primary Source

The Magna Carta

In 1215, a group of rebellious barons, fed up with King John's royal abuses, forced the king to sign a "great charter." Some of the Magna Carta's guarantees have become core principles of democratic government. For example, the stipulation that noblemen could only be judged and fined by other noblemen paved the way for trial by a jury of one's peers (equals). Other parts of the Magna Carta dealt with practical demands to protect and promote commerce. For example, the lords demanded that all dams blocking England's major rivers be destroyed, to give merchant vessels access to the interior beyond London. The excerpts below suggest the range of concerns, from lofty to mundane, to which King John ("we" in the following) was compelled to agree.

John, by the grace of God, King of England, etc.

Be it known that we, looking to God, and for the safety of our soul, and those of our ancestors, and our heirs, …by this, our present charter, have confirmed, on behalf of us and our heirs forever, that the Church of England be a free church, and keep its laws entire, and its liberties uninfringed.…

We and our bailiffs [officers] will not seize any land or property for any debt, as long as the chattels [personal property] of the debtor then in his possession are sufficient to pay the debts and the debtor himself is willing to satisfy our demand out of them.…

Earls and barons shall only be fined by their peers, and then only according to the degree of their offense.…

Great Council could overrule some of his decisions. The Magna Carta said that from then on, the king would need the Great Council's consent to levy new taxes. Furthermore, the king could not arrest anyone without cause, or keep anyone secretly imprisoned, or deny a jury trial to any person charged with a crime.

The barons saw the Magna Carta as an instrument for holding onto their traditional feudal powers. Although the document barely mentioned the common people, it paved the way for protecting the rights of all people living under a king.

Over time the Magna Carta helped change the English people's ideas of justice and government.

No constable, or bailiff of his, shall take the corn or chattels of any one who does not belong to the town where the castle is situated unless he immediately pays him money, or has regard for the same at the will of the seller; but if he belongs to that town he shall pay the price within forty days....

All the weirs [dams] shall be hereafter done away with entirely in the Thames and the Medway, and throughout all England, except at the seacoast....

There shall be one measure for wine and beers, throughout the whole of our kingdom, and one measure for corn, namely, the London quarter; and one width for dyed cloths, russets [homespun cloth], and hauberjets [thick cotton garments worn under armor]...; and with weights it shall be as with measures....

No free person shall be taken, or imprisoned, or shall be dispossessed of any free tenement [property] of his, or his liberties, or free customs, nor shall he be outlawed, or be punished in any other way; nor will we come upon him, nor send him to prison, unless by legal decision of his equals, or by the law of the land....

All traders, unless openly forbidden shall have free ingress to, and egress from, England, both to stay and to go, both by land and water, to buy and sell....

The Magna Carta declared that the king had to rule within limits of the law and that the people had rights he must respect. Today the Magna Carta of 1215 is regarded as one of the great political documents of Western civilization, as well as a cornerstone of modern constitutional government.

Parliament and the Power of the Purse

In feudal times, political power belonged entirely to the church and nobles. The overwhelming majority of the population—the common people, mostly peasants—had no voice in government. By the 1200s, however, a rising middle class of merchants, artisans, and professionals lived in the growing towns. In England, while the burgesses—the prominent townspeople—lacked official powers, they did have wealth, and since the economy depended on their skills, they also had influence. The king needed their support.

In 1295, King Edward I needed to raise taxes to pay for the wars he was waging. He called for a meeting of the lords and high church leaders who formed the Great Council. But he also summoned representatives of other social groups, including members of the lower clergy, knights, and burgesses. This gathering in 1295 later became known as the Model Parliament (PAHR-luh-muhnt), because, by convening both nobles and commoners, it set a precedent for English government.

When he summoned the knights and burgesses, Edward did not have democratic motivations. He hoped to exercise control of the representatives of the lower social orders in order to weaken the influence of the most powerful lords. Over time, however, the Parliament, as the council of nobles and representatives became known, took on its own powers. Especially as it gained the **power of the purse**—that is, the authority to approve any new taxes—Parliament was able to limit the power of the monarch by, in effect, controlling his money supply.

Parliament eventually evolved into a legislative body with two houses. The knights and burgesses made up the House of Commons, while leading nobles and high clergymen made up the House of Lords.

A New Dynasty Unites France

In the medieval era, the rise of a strong monarchy in France was a long, slow process. Back in the 800s, Charlemagne had unified France, but under his successors in the Carolingian Dynasty, France dissolved into dozens of independent feudal fiefdoms ruled by dukes, counts, and other lords.

In 987, when the last Carolingian monarch died, the French lords chose a duke named Hugh Capet (ka-pay) as the new king. He had less power and land than many of the nobles who chose him, and he was probably chosen for that very reason.

While Hugh Capet ruled only a small domain, it included well-traveled trade routes and the important city of Paris. Although he was not a strong ruler, Capet insisted that the throne pass from father to eldest son. This practice helped the Capetian (kuh-PEE-shuhn) Dynasty last about three hundred years, and brought stability to France.

Philip II, better known as Philip Augustus, came to the throne in 1179. This shrewd and sometimes ruthless Capetian king worked to strengthen royal power. Philip took control of lands in Normandy that had been claimed by King John of England. Through crafty political maneuvering he seized land from his own feudal lords. He more than tripled the lands under the king's control. He bypassed nobles and appointed middle-class people to many government offices, which ensured loyalty to him. The townspeople supported Philip because his efficient government brought order.

Philip's grandson, Louis IX, who ascended the throne in 1226, further strengthened France's central government. He insisted on just relations between lords and vassals, which reduced the feuding that had long kept France in turmoil. King Louis reformed the royal courts to give Frenchmen of all stations a more nearly equal chance at justice. Like his grandfather, Philip Augustus, Louis went crusading in the East. The Catholic Church eventually named Louis a saint.

The Estates-General

In 1285, a cunning new king came to power. Philip IV was determined to make himself supreme in France. When Philip tried to tax the clergy, an outraged Pope Boniface VIII issued a proclamation declaring that the pope was superior to any king.

To gain support for his actions and to stir up sentiment against the pope, in 1302 Philip called a meeting that included representatives of France's different social orders, known as "estates." As expected, Philip called on powerful members of the First Estate (the clergy) and the Second Estate (the nobility). But he also decided to include representatives of the Third Estate, the commoners.

The gathering of representatives of the three estates became known as the Estates-General. In bringing together members of various social classes, the Estates-General was like England's Parliament, but the French body never gained authority over taxation. Without the power of the purse, the Estates-General never had real power. Its only function was to say yes to the king and make his decisions seem like the nation's decisions. In short, France developed no institution that could check the growing power of its king.

Spain: Ferdinand and Isabella

The strengthening of royal power that was unifying France and England also happened elsewhere in western Europe, but started later. In Spain, the Christian inhabitants developed a sense of national unity in the course of fighting a long war with Muslims. In 1469, two Spanish kingdoms joined together when Queen Isabella of Castile married King Ferdinand II of Aragon. Their combined forces conquered Granada, the last Muslim stronghold on the Iberian Peninsula.

Aragon and Castile became the core of the new Christian kingdom of Spain. Here, as elsewhere in Europe, the rising sense of national identity and unity went hand in hand with growing power for the monarchs. Only in England did the barons succeed in setting limits on the king's authority.

The marriage of Queen Isabella and King Ferdinand II joined two Spanish kingdoms and strengthened the monarchy.

A Century of Crises

At the dawn of the fourteenth century, medieval Europe seemed ready to thrive. There was plenty of food to support more people. There were more towns and cities in which to live, work, and do business. In some parts of Europe, strong monarchs were taking charge, bringing some order to once unruly realms.

Then a series of shocks hit the continent, beginning with famine. Starting in 1315, crops failed all over Europe. As the famine persisted, in many towns about one-tenth of the population perished. Then came decades marked by war, disease, and religious turmoil. By the end of the century, it seemed to many as though the world itself might be coming to an end.

The Black Death

In October 1347, an Italian merchant ship arrived in Sicily. It had set sail from a port on the Black Sea, loaded with cargo from China. The ill-fated ship carried not only silk and porcelain but also a hidden, deadly cargo. When the ship docked in Sicily, city residents boarded and found, to their horror, that all the sailors were dead or dying, struck down by some terrible disease.

Over the next few years, the disease spread throughout Europe. The Black Death, as the epidemic came to be known, swept across Italy. It reached France by 1348, England by 1349, and Scandinavia the following year. It spread along the countless trade routes that tied Europe together, the very routes that had given Europe such vibrant economic life.

> An *epidemic* is an outbreak of a rapidly spreading disease.

What was this disease that killed so many? Some recent researchers have suggested that it might have been a powerful virus. Other scholars think it might have been a form of anthrax (a disease that afflicts cattle and sheep, and can be spread to humans) combined with other diseases, such as a rapidly spreading pneumonia. Most historians, however, think that the Black Death was an outbreak of bubonic plague, carried by bacteria in fleas that lived on rats. The disease-carrying fleas came from China, where tens of millions of people had died of plague in the early 1300s. The fleas made their way to Europe on rat-infested ships like the one that docked in Sicily on that day in 1347.

From a docked ship, the rats scurried down mooring ropes and spread throughout filthy towns and cities. As the fleas on the rats spread the highly contagious disease, people sickened and died rapidly. Many developed oozing black boils and dark bruise-like marks on the body, from which the Black Death got its name.

Key Questions

- What major crises occurred in western Europe during the fourteenth century?
- What were the long-term consequences of these crises?

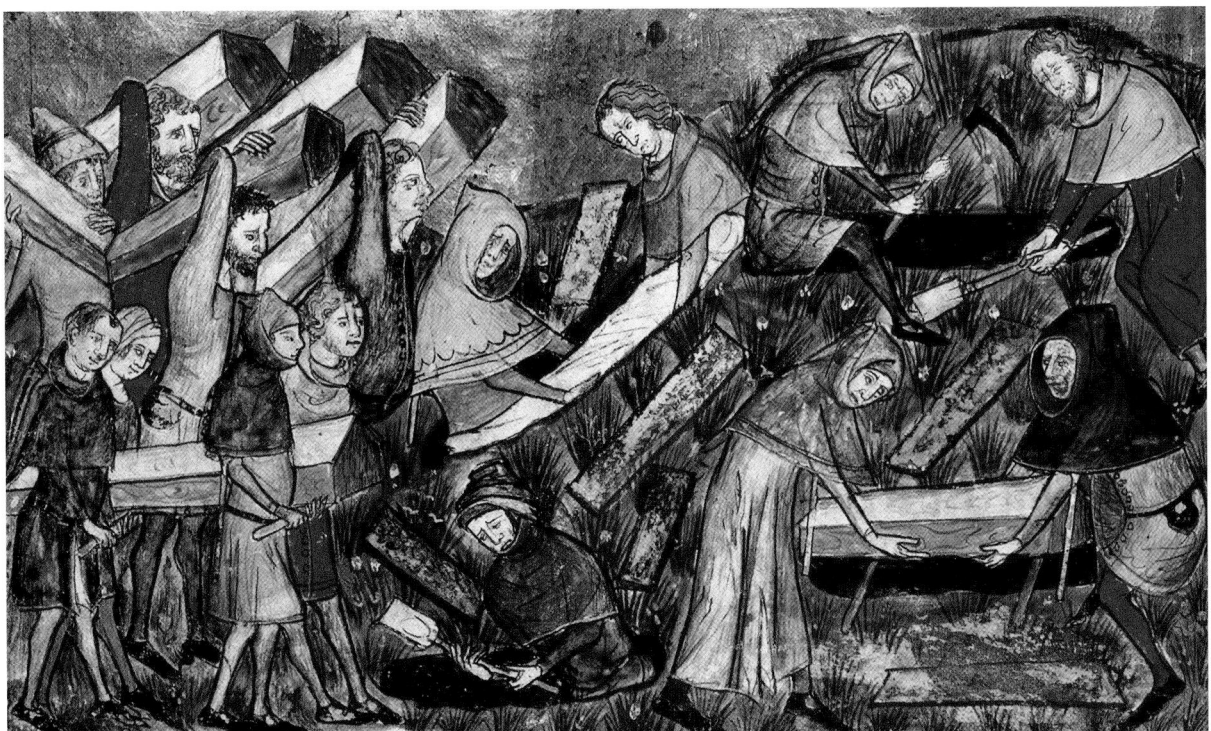

Citizens of a medieval town bury victims of the plague. The disease swept across fourteenth-century Europe and was especially deadly in cities.

Wherever the plague arrived, bodies piled up faster than survivors could bury them. Within months, large Italian cities were reduced to less than half their population. In England and France, the plague wiped out whole villages. Historians estimate that the plague killed from twenty to twenty-five million people—more than a third of Europe's population. To this day, the Black Death remains Europe's deadliest natural disaster.

The Plague Brings Social Upheaval

The Black Death plunged Europe into a period of social upheaval that lasted for decades. In the fourteenth century, scholars and doctors could not explain the plague's causes, and their medicine was powerless to stop it. Bewildered and terrified, people took desperate measures to ward off the disease.

Some who saw the plague as a punishment from God whipped themselves in public to show repentance for their sins. Others attacked convenient scapegoats. Superstitious peasants massacred many Jews, whom they blamed for causing the disease. Old women were accused of witchcraft, and many were burned at the stake.

The epidemic peaked around 1350 and then began to subside, though the plague continued to break out in various locations throughout Europe. As the death toll mounted, the normal routines of life broke down. Trade dwindled to a trickle. Food supplies ran short because there were not enough healthy people to plow, plant, or harvest.

The Black Death helped bring an end to the social order of the manor system, which had been on the wane for years. By the end of the fourteenth century, the once-tight grip that lords held on serfs was loosening. Because there was a shortage of laborers, the surviving peasants could demand higher wages. Serfdom in western Europe was on its way out, and a new class of peasant farmers was on the rise.

While peasants demanded, and sometimes got, higher wages, many landowners tried to find ways to keep wages down. Some converted farmland to pastures for raising sheep, which required fewer laborers. Some landlords still demanded high rents

Memories of the
Black Death

The Black Death struck the city of Siena in northern Italy in the spring of 1348. A resident of the city, Agnolo di Tura, survived the plague—the "Great Mortality," in his words—and wrote these recollections.

In this time began the Great Mortality, the greatest, and most obscure, and most horrible imaginable; and it lasted till October 1348. It was of such a secret character that men and women died almost without warning. A swelling appeared in the groin or the armpit, and while they were talking they fell dead. The father would not attend to his son; one brother fled from the other; the wife abandoned her husband; for it was said that to catch the disease it sufficed to look upon a victim or to feel his breath. And it must have been so indeed, since so many perished in the months of May, June, July, and August, that it was impossible to find anyone to bury the dead.

Neither relatives nor friends nor priests nor friars accompanied them to the grave.... He who lost a relative or housemate, as soon as the breath had left the body, took him by night or day, and with two or three to lend a hand, carried him to the church, and with his helpers buried the corpse as best he could, covering it with just enough earth to save it from the dogs. And in many places of the city trenches were dug, very broad and deep, and into them the bodies were thrown and covered with a little earth; and thus layer after layer until the trench was full; and then another trench was commenced.

And I, Agnolo di Tura, ... with my own hands buried five of my children in a single trench; and many others did the like.... And no bells rang, and nobody wept no matter what his loss, because almost everyone expected death.... And people believed and said: This is the end of the world.

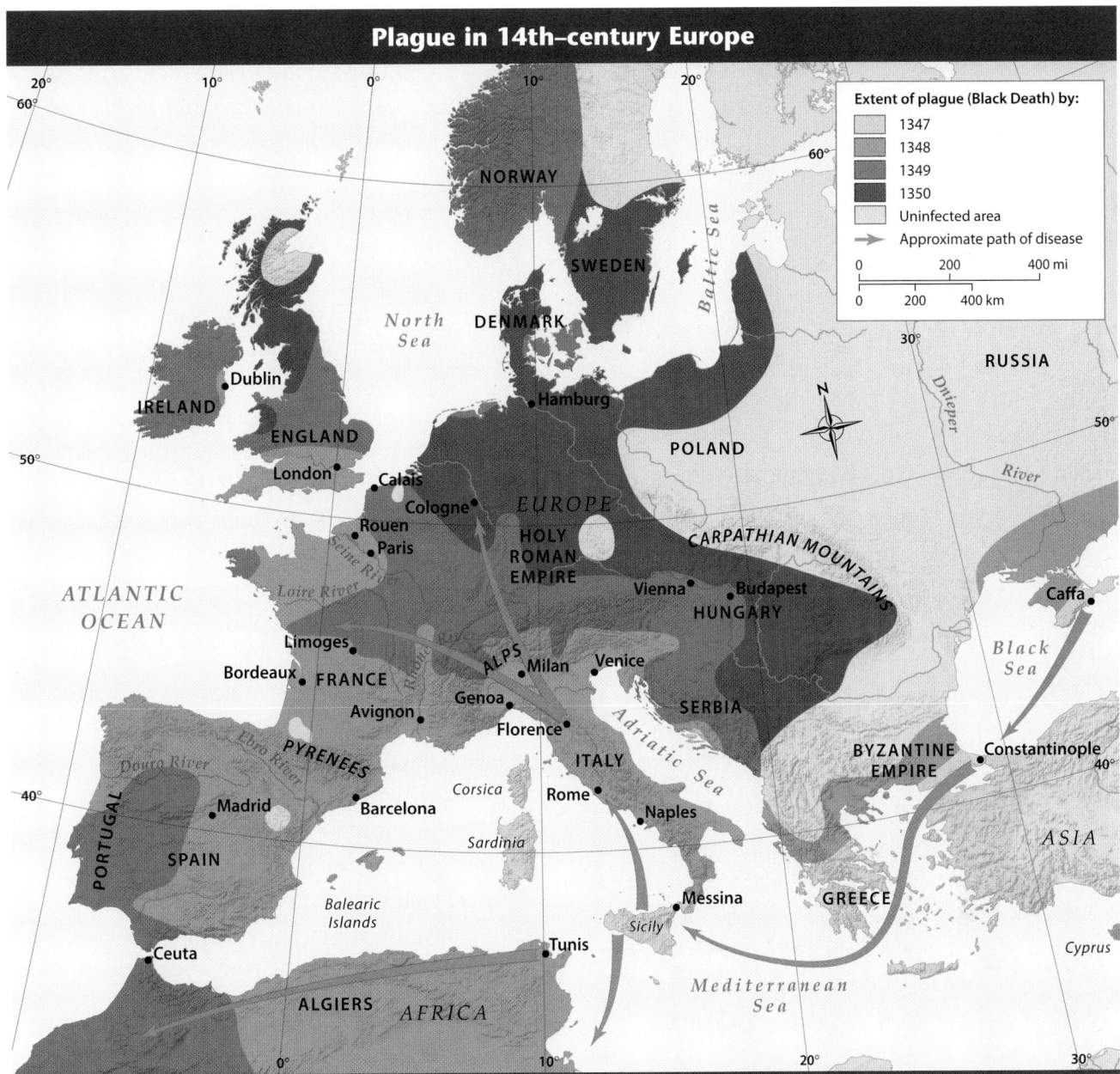

Plague in 14th–century Europe

Extent of plague (Black Death) by:
- 1347
- 1348
- 1349
- 1350
- Uninfected area
- → Approximate path of disease

0   200   400 mi
0   200   400 km

The plague, known as the Black Death, killed more than a third of Europe's people, disrupted commerce, and traumatized the entire continent.

and taxes. In many places, peasants resorted to violence. They roamed the countryside in angry bands, looting and killing.

Turmoil in the Church

Even before the Black Death struck, Christendom was a troubled realm. There was division within the Catholic Church, and tension between the church's supreme authority, the pope, and kings in the secular realm.

You have read about the tensions between France's King Philip IV and Pope Boniface VIII. Philip wanted more influence in church affairs, so he pressured Boniface's successor, Pope Clement V, to move the papacy—the office of the pope—from Rome to the city of Avignon (ah-vee-NYAHN), in southern France. It was the first time in more than a thousand years that the Christian church in western Europe was not centered in Rome.

349

For more than sixty-five years, popes resided at Avignon under the watchful eyes of the French court. During these years, many Christians lost respect for the papacy, since the popes seemed mere puppets of the French monarchy.

In 1377, Pope Gregory XI decided to move the papacy back to Rome, but he died before he could accomplish the move. When the cardinals met to elect his successor, they were split along national lines. The French cardinals wanted a French pope; everyone else supported an Italian candidate. The two factions ended up electing different popes.

For four decades, two popes—one in Avignon and one in Rome—argued about who was the real leader of Christianity in Europe. This split, called the **Great Schism** (or the Western Schism), weakened the church. A church council tried to settle the dispute and ended up creating a third challenger. Finally, in 1417, a church council reached a compromise and settled upon a single pope, with the papacy restored to Rome.

Reformers and Heresy

While the highest leaders of the Catholic Church were divided and feuding, reformers began accusing the church of corruption. They charged that too many clerics lived in luxury and failed to fulfill their spiritual role. In the late 1300s, the English theologian John Wycliffe delivered stinging criticisms of the pope, his cardinals, and other clergymen. With the help of colleagues, he undertook the first translation of the Bible into English, to bypass clergymen and make Christian doctrine available to all his countrymen who could read.

In the early 1400s, Wycliffe's writings were taken up by some priests in Bohemia (now the Czech Republic). A priest named Jan Hus (yahn hoos) criticized corruption in the church and called for reform of the clergy. Hus attracted many followers, who were called Hussites.

The church responded to Wycliffe and Hus by charging them with **heresy**, that is, with actions contrary to the teachings of the church. To stamp out heresy, as early as the 1200s the church had established the **Inquisition**, a church-run court that examined people and punished those whose beliefs went against official church teachings. In 1415, the church tried Hus. He was condemned as a heretic and burned at the stake. Some decades after John Wycliffe's death in 1384, the church condemned him as a heretic, and ordered that his remains be dug up and burned, along with his writings.

The controversies surrounding Wycliffe and Hus weakened the church's power and prestige. Although the Catholic Church forcibly tried to suppress their ideas, the influence of Wycliffe

> The word *inquisition* means "examination" or "investigation."

The Persecution of Jews in Medieval Europe

In the medieval realm of Christendom, Jews formed a visible and distinct minority. Until about the year 1000, most European Christians lived in relative peace with Jews. Although Jews could not own land, they could make a living as merchants and were allowed to lend money at interest, a practice forbidden to Christians.

During the Crusades, however, Christian intolerance of Jews spiked sharply. Crusaders marching to Asia slaughtered whole Jewish communities on the way. Some nobles and kings began persecuting Jews as well. In 1290, King Edward I expelled all Jews from England. A few years later, King Philip IV expelled them from France. In 1492, Jews were ordered out of Spain. Many fled to Muslim North Africa or into parts of what is now Turkey. As they fled the lands from which they were expelled, many Jews lost their possessions or even their lives.

and Hus lived on to motivate even more ardent reformers a century later.

The Hundred Years' War

All across Europe, the decline of feudalism sparked wars between competing kings. The worst was the Hundred Years' War, which raged between England and France from 1337 to 1453. This was not one war but a series of struggles with roots going as far back as the Norman Conquest.

Since 1066, when William, Duke of Normandy, conquered England, English kings had seen themselves as the rightful rulers not only of England but also of Normandy in northern France. In 1152, when England's King Henry II married Eleanor of Aquitaine, he laid claim to the lands in southwest France that she had inherited. As French kings grew more powerful, they sought to win back these and other lands from the English. In the early 1200s, for example, while the weak King John ruled England, Philip II of France won back most of Normandy.

English troops armed with powerful longbows battle French knights at the Battle of Crécy.

English kings fought to hold on to their feudal possessions on French soil. In 1328, the king of France died and left no sons as direct heirs to the crown. King Edward III of England, who was the son of a French princess, decided to claim the throne of France. In 1346, he triumphed over a much larger French force at the Battle of Crécy (kray-SEE) in northern France. He couldn't capture the throne but he did secure a swath of French territory.

In 1356, English forces under the command of Edward III's son, known as Edward the Black Prince (for his black armor), won a crushing victory over the French at Poitiers (pwah-tyay). In 1415, the English king Henry V, leading a force of fewer than six thousand troops, defeated a French

force of some thirty thousand at the Battle of Agincourt (A-jin-kort).

Joan of Arc

While the English won most of the famous battles of the Hundred Years' War, the French won the war. In 1429, when French spirits were low and the English occupied much of the country, including Paris, a sixteen-year-old French peasant girl, Joan of Arc, set out to save her land.

Joan claimed that heavenly voices told her she should lead French troops against the English. She met with French leaders and told them she was destined to lead her country to victory. Donning a knight's armor and waving a banner with a lily on it, this slip of a teenager routed English

New Weapons

Early English triumphs in the Hundred Years' War may be partly credited to a new technology, the longbow. With a longbow, about as tall as a man, an English archer could rapidly fire arrows with spiked tips that could pierce the armor worn by French knights. At the Battle of Crécy, as French knights advanced, the English bowmen rained arrows on them—by some estimates as many as forty-eight thousand per minute.

The technology of the longbow helped undermine the already eroding foundations of feudalism. Earlier in the Middle Ages, feudal warfare centered mostly on conflict between heavily armored, mounted knights. But if foot soldiers—many of them peasants, fighting for pay—could fire longbows and mow down knights from a distance, then the institution of knighthood seemed obsolete.

In the Hundred Years' War, both the English and the French used another new technology, the cannon. In later campaigns, the French effectively used cannons to smash the walls of castles held by the English.

invaders at the city of Orléans (or-lay-AHN). Her forces went on to win battle after battle.

Joan then marched on the French capital of Paris, which the English occupied. Her attack failed, however, and she was captured. The English used church courts to try her for heresy and accused her of witchcraft. She was convicted and burned at the stake. But the French did not forget Joan. In fact, her memory helped bring them together as one people. Inspired by her example, they continued to win battles.

The French peasant girl Joan of Arc bears a sword, and wears the armor of a knight.

Lasting Effects of the Hundred Years' War

The Hundred Years' War helped break down feudal bonds and inspire early stirrings of **nationalism**, the strong sense of attachment or belonging to one's own country. The people of France came to feel invaded by a foreign force, and they pulled together as Frenchmen. English troops fighting in France began to feel the common bond they shared as Englishmen.

The technologies of the war—cannons and longbows—hastened the end of two mainstays of the feudal world, castles and knights in armor. To wage their wars, kings now needed more than a corps of loyal vassals. They needed to raise large armies, which generally meant they had to rely on hired soldiers.

Over the course of the Hundred Years' War, French kings gained power. In England, however, power shifted to Parliament as the English kings had to keep asking Parliament to raise money to fund the fighting.

In the end, England lost almost all its land on the continent. In some ways, however, this turned out to be a good thing, as it compelled the English to expand their economy through trade. Since England is an island, to expand trade the English had to build up their sea power. Over the next few centuries, as you will see, the English used sea power to forge a global empire.

The Black Death, the Great Schism in the Catholic Church, the Hundred Years' War—all these events shook the medieval world to its core and hastened the end of the feudal way of life. All this misery and upheaval brought great change—some of it, in unexpected ways, for the better. In the fifteenth century, Europe stood poised for a time of growth and renewal such as the world had never seen.

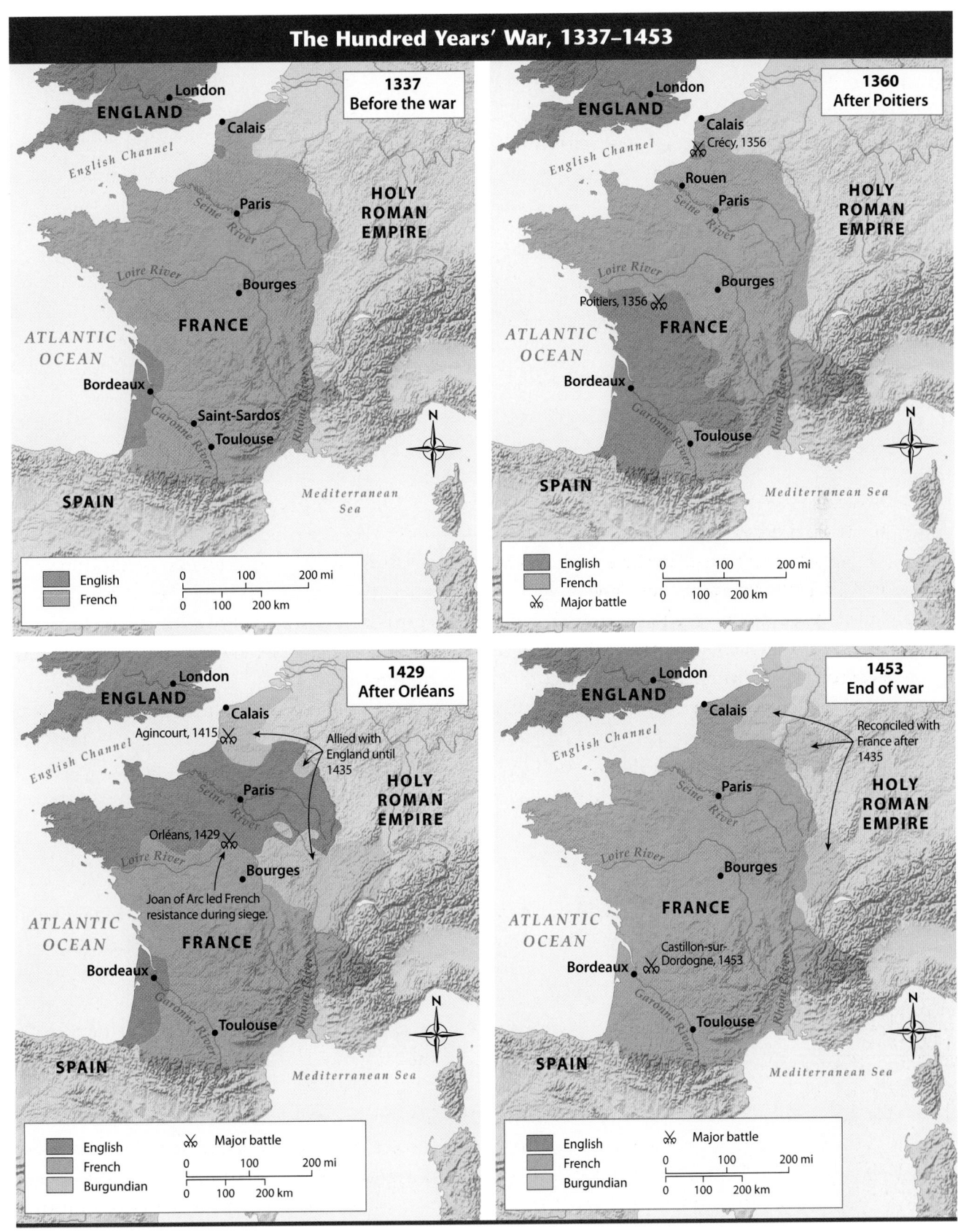

The Hundred Years' War, 1337–1453

1337 Before the war

ENGLAND · London
Calais
English Channel
Seine River
Paris
HOLY ROMAN EMPIRE
Loire River
Bourges
FRANCE
ATLANTIC OCEAN
Garonne River
Bordeaux
Saint-Sardos
Toulouse
Rhône River
SPAIN
Mediterranean Sea

English
French
0 · 100 · 200 mi
0 · 100 · 200 km

1360 After Poitiers

ENGLAND · London
Calais
Crécy, 1356
English Channel
Rouen
Seine River
Paris
HOLY ROMAN EMPIRE
Loire River
Bourges
Poitiers, 1356
ATLANTIC OCEAN
FRANCE
Bordeaux
Garonne River
Toulouse
Rhône River
SPAIN
Mediterranean Sea

English
French
Major battle
0 · 100 · 200 mi
0 · 100 · 200 km

1429 After Orléans

ENGLAND · London
Calais
Agincourt, 1415
English Channel
Allied with England until 1435
Seine River
Paris
HOLY ROMAN EMPIRE
Orléans, 1429
Loire River
Bourges
Joan of Arc led French resistance during siege.
ATLANTIC OCEAN
FRANCE
Bordeaux
Garonne River
Rhône River
Toulouse
SPAIN
Mediterranean Sea

English
French
Burgundian
Major battle
0 · 100 · 200 mi
0 · 100 · 200 km

1453 End of war

ENGLAND · London
Calais
Reconciled with France after 1435
English Channel
Seine River
Paris
HOLY ROMAN EMPIRE
Loire River
Bourges
FRANCE
ATLANTIC OCEAN
Castillon-sur-Dordogne, 1453
Bordeaux
Garonne River
Rhône River
Toulouse
SPAIN
Mediterranean Sea

English
French
Burgundian
Major battle
0 · 100 · 200 mi
0 · 100 · 200 km

To resolve a dispute over the legitimate heir to the French throne, France and England fought a series of conflicts over more than a hundred years. Burgundy, an important region in France, allied with England for part of the Hundred Years' War, but eventually reunited with France.

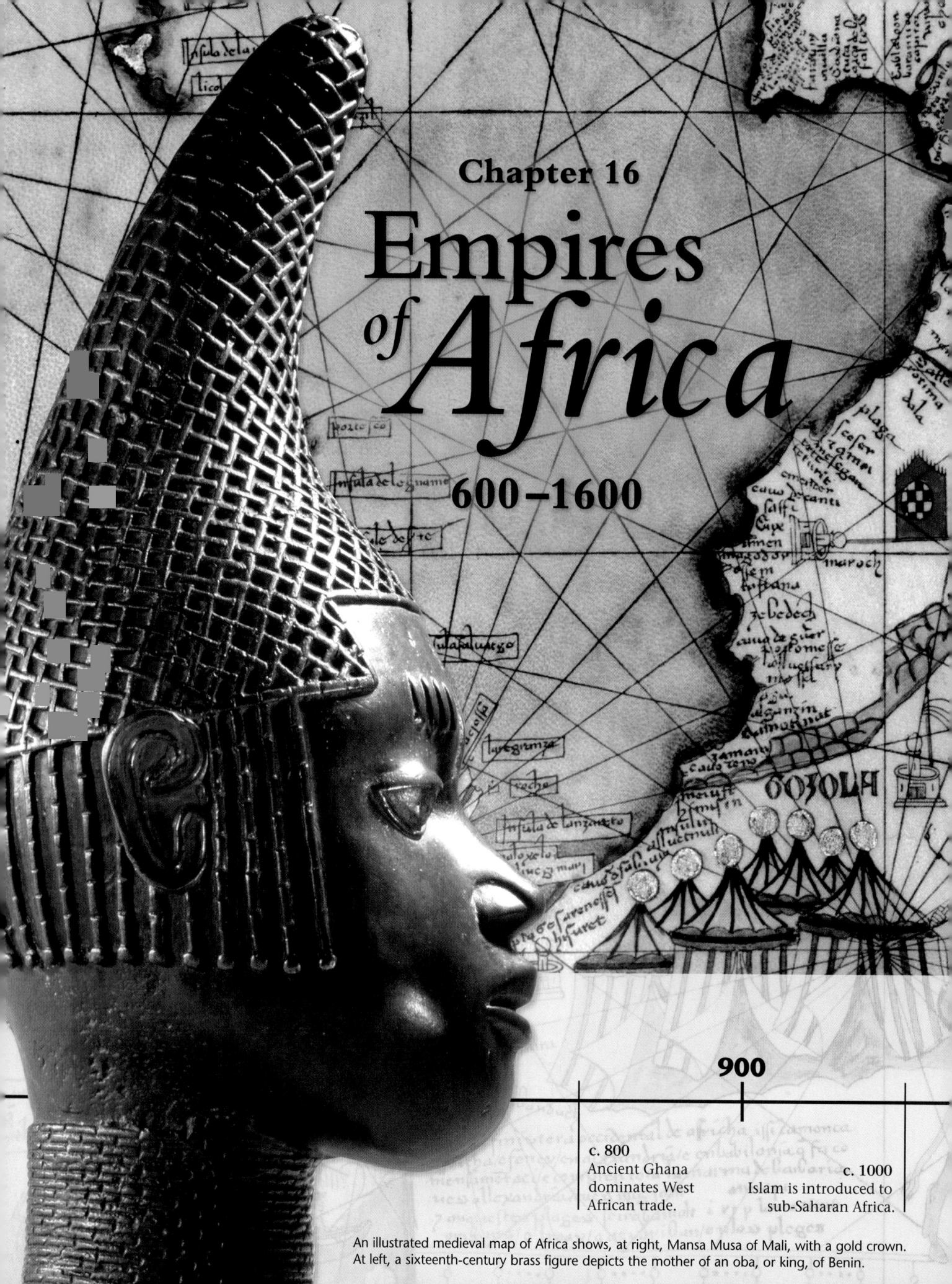

Chapter 16
Empires
of Africa
600–1600

900

c. 800
Ancient Ghana
dominates West
African trade.

c. 1000
Islam is introduced to
sub-Saharan Africa.

An illustrated medieval map of Africa shows, at right, Mansa Musa of Mali, with a gold crown.
At left, a sixteenth-century brass figure depicts the mother of an oba, or king, of Benin.

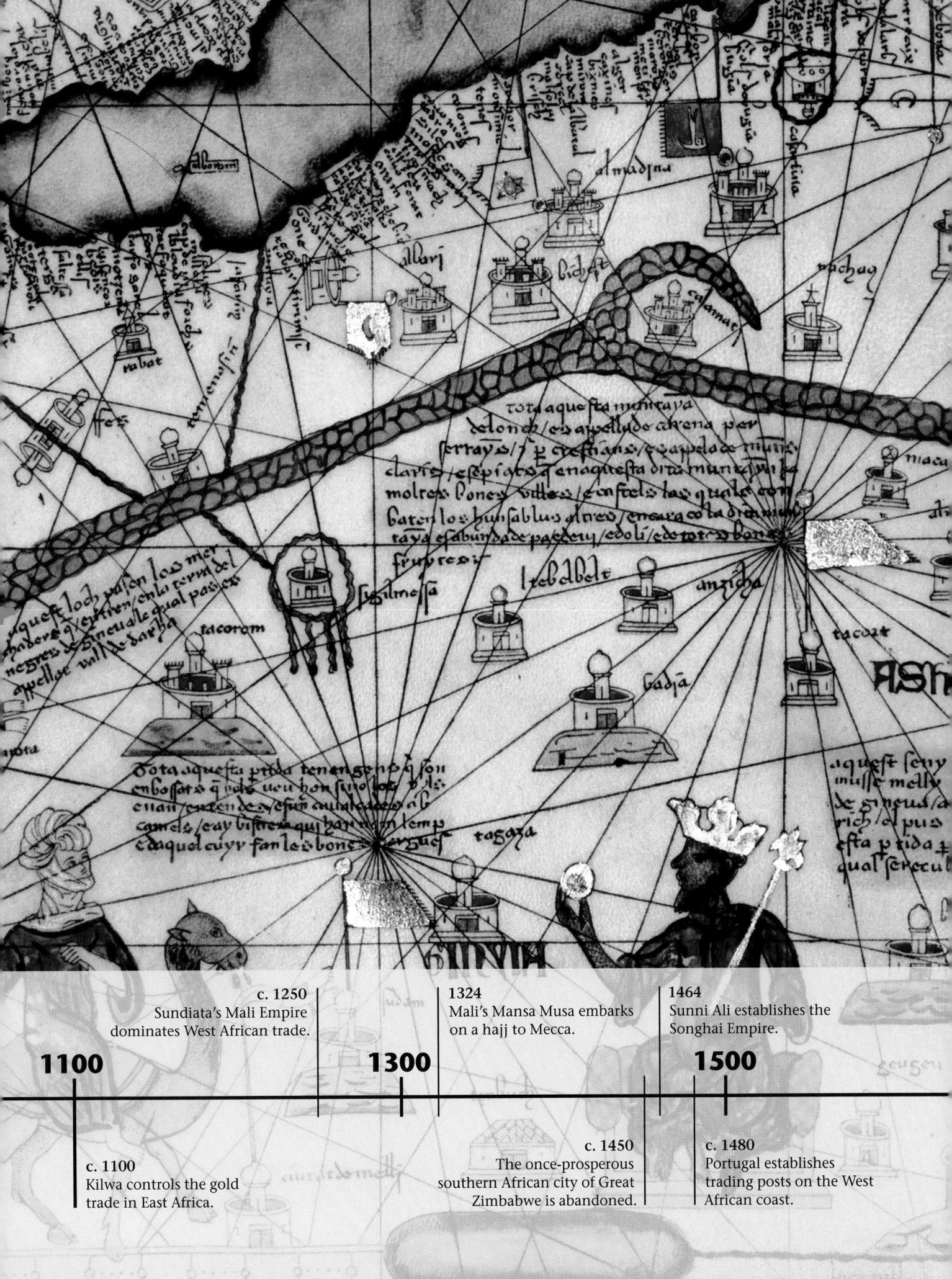

c. 1250
Sundiata's Mali Empire dominates West African trade.

1324
Mali's Mansa Musa embarks on a hajj to Mecca.

1464
Sunni Ali establishes the Songhai Empire.

1100

1300

1500

c. 1100
Kilwa controls the gold trade in East Africa.

c. 1450
The once-prosperous southern African city of Great Zimbabwe is abandoned.

c. 1480
Portugal establishes trading posts on the West African coast.

*D*uring the thousand-year period of the Middle Ages, while Europe faced invasions, famine, and plague, the Byzantine Empire was thriving and Islamic civilization expanded. In East and West Africa, prosperous trading kingdoms were growing into empires.

African gold fueled medieval trade. Luxury goods from Africa reached European princes, Arab sultans, and Chinese lords. And thousands of enslaved Africans were sold to serve as laborers or soldiers far from their homeland.

Mighty trading empires developed in West Africa—first Ghana, then Mali, and later Songhai. Muslim traders from the north spread their religion among the people of sub-Saharan Africa. Powerful African kings turned cities like Timbuktu into centers of Islamic culture.

In East Africa, cities on the Indian Ocean coast prospered through trade with merchants from faraway lands. To the south, gold helped fuel the rise of a kingdom on the savanna.

West African Kingdoms

The Sahara, the world's largest desert, covers northern Africa. For centuries, crossing it verged on the impossible. Wagon wheels got stuck in the sand. Horses and pack animals withered in the heat. Travelers faced many perils, including poisonous scorpions and snakes.

A few traders dared the crossing in search of valuable products, such as gold, to be found in Africa south of the Sahara. But such expeditions were rare. Around A.D. 300, however, the nomadic Berbers of North Africa ushered in a new era of trans-Sahara trade when they managed to domesticate the notoriously stubborn and ill-tempered camel.

Camels are well suited to desert travel. They can go without water for over a week. Fat stored in the camel's hump allows it to go without food for twice as long as a pack ox or horse. And a camel's wide feet are well adapted to plodding steadily across the sand. Camels gave Berber traders the ability to open lucrative trade routes across the desert and beyond.

In the eighth century, Arab conquerors brought Islam to North Africa, where the religion quickly spread. Among converts to the new faith were many Berber traders who had become expert buyers and sellers of sub-Saharan goods. In time, these traders introduced Islam and Arab culture to the inhabitants of lands south of the Sahara.

Key Questions

- How did the domestication of the camel and the existence of mineral resources influence the development of West African empires?

- How did Timbuktu become a center of trade, learning, and religion under Mansa Musa?

The continent of Africa was home to a series of powerful medieval trading kingdoms.

Camels, well suited to desert travel, opened up a new era of trans-Sahara trade.

The Land of Gold

By A.D. 800, Muslim traders regularly crossed the Sahara in caravans of hundreds of camels. They followed well-established routes, stopping at desert oases where freshwater springs created patches of green. The territory beyond the desert was known as the Sudan, from the Arabic phrase, *Bilad al-Sudan* or "land of black people." The Sudan began in the *Sahel*, or "shore" of the Sahara, and stretched south to the edge of the African rain forest. (Note that the region of ancient Africa called the Sudan lies to the west of the modern-day country now called the Republic of Sudan.)

Ghana, located in the grasslands of the Sahel between the Senegal and Niger rivers, became the first great empire to rise in the Sudan. Ancient Ghana (northwest of the modern-day nation of Ghana) was established by the Soninke (soh-NIN-kay) people, who had begun building small farming villages in the area as early as 3000 B.C.

Warrior Kings

The history of the Soninke people was kept alive by griots, the storyteller-poets who passed ancient legends and knowledge from one generation to the next. One ancient tale tells of the founding of a kingdom by a powerful ruler called a *Ghana*, or "warrior-king." Over time, outsiders began to refer to the land itself as Ghana. In their own language, known as Mande (MAHN-day), the Soninke called their homeland *Wagadu*.

Ghana achieved its power and wealth through two metals plentiful in the region—gold and iron. Gold brought traders from across the Sahara, whose commerce enriched a kingdom that came to be called "the land of gold." As early as 500 B.C., Soninke blacksmiths forged iron to make tools and weapons. Iron-tipped arrows helped Soninke armies subdue neighbors who fought with weapons made of wood and bone.

Gold and Salt

To the south of Ghana, prospectors collected gold dust and nuggets from streams that flowed down from the hills into the Senegal and Niger rivers. The Ghanaian kings kept the largest gold nuggets for themselves and taxed the goods for which gold was traded. The king's new title became, in the Soninke language, *Kaya Maghan*, or "master of the gold."

Ghana's rulers used the wealth they made from trade to maintain powerful armies and build majestic cities. While most native-born people of ancient Ghana held on to their traditional religious beliefs, some of their Muslim trading partners built mosques in Ghanaian cities. As these cities grew into busy centers of trade, they attracted attention from beyond the Sudan. An eleventh-century Muslim writer and geographer, al-Bakri, described Ghana as a lavish society where even the king's dogs wore collars of gold and silver.

In exchange for gold, Muslim traders brought goods from across the Islamic world—bright cloth,

A richly attired eleventh-century ruler of Ghana, with attendants behind him holding swords and shields of gold

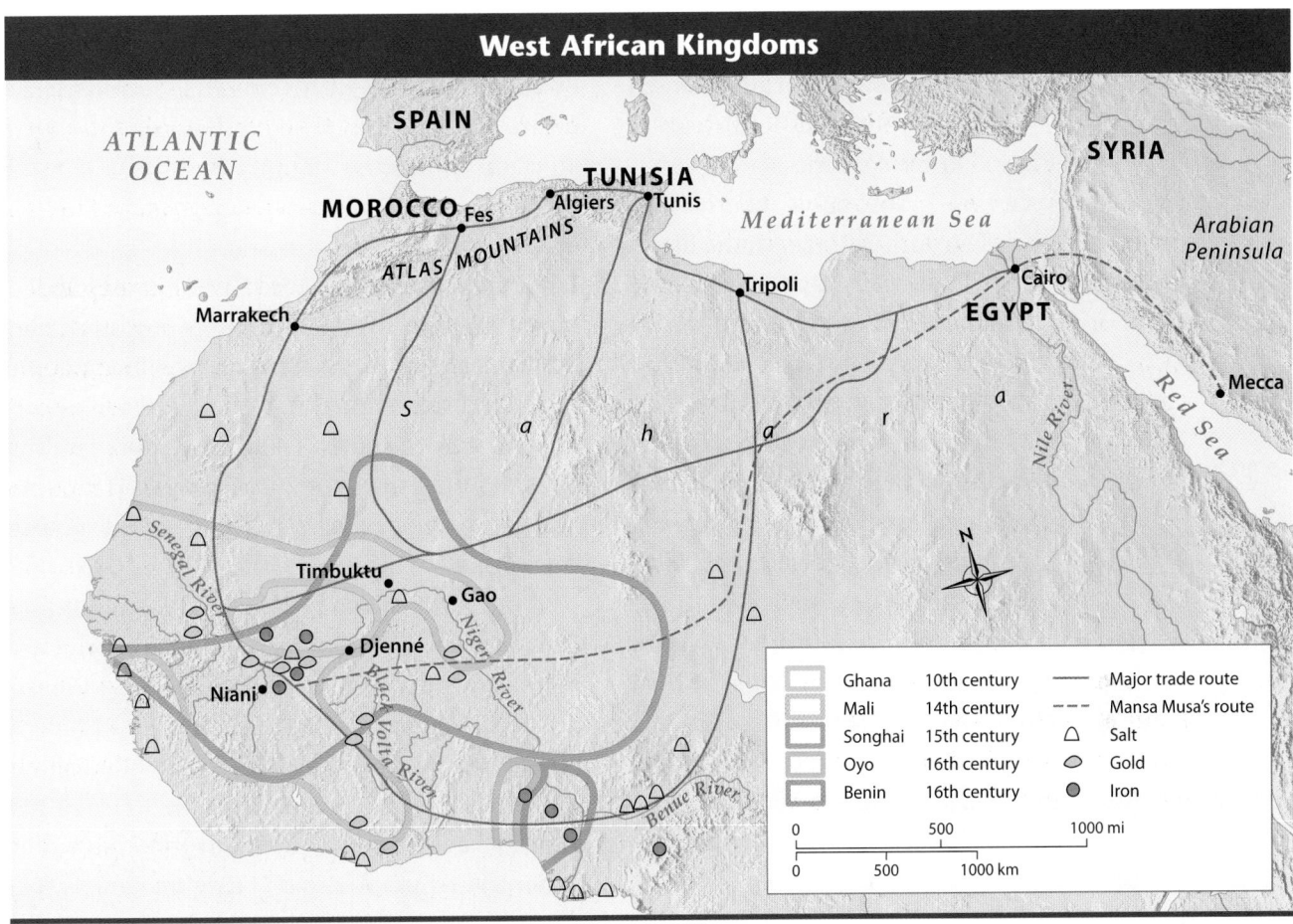

West African Kingdoms

Many powerful trading kingdoms grew and prospered in West Africa.

fine silk, copper ornaments, precious seashells, and, most important, salt. Mined from deep pits in the scorching Sahara, salt was vital to the health of the people of sub-Saharan Africa. They used salt to preserve and season their food. Salt in the diet provided essential nutrition to people who, living in a hot land, lost salt through perspiration. In West Africa, where naturally occurring salt was scarce, chunks of salt often served as a form of money.

Berber traders exchanged their salt and other goods using an unusual system sometimes called "silent barter." Traders would lay out their commodities and announce themselves by pounding a drum, and then withdraw to remain unseen by the buyers. Soon their sub-Saharan trading partners would appear and measure out a quantity of gold dust. When the sellers returned, they looked to see if the amount of gold was acceptable. If so,

they took it and departed. If not, they withdrew and waited for a counteroffer.

In the late eleventh century, the empire of Ghana slowly declined. In 1076, Ghana's largest city was plundered by a group of Muslim Berbers known as Almoravids (al-muh-RAH-vidz). They sought to control the gold trade and establish Islam as the region's major religion. Many Ghanaians fled south. Trade routes shifted, and by the thirteenth century, Ghana's glory had faded.

The Empire of Mali

Despite Ghana's decline, the demand for gold remained strong. During the thirteenth century, gold prices increased as powerful European kingdoms stockpiled the precious metal to mint coins. For a time, various peoples of the Sudan battled each other to control the gold trade. By the mid-thirteenth century, the kingdom of Mali emerged

A terra-cotta mounted warrior from Mali

victorious. By controlling the gold-for-salt exchange, Mali's rulers forged an empire that flourished for three centuries.

The name *Mali* comes from Malinke (muh-LING-kay), the name of a people who centuries earlier had settled the valleys of the upper Niger River on the edge of the rain forest. Mali, rich in gold, would eventually rival the output of the mining operations that had enriched ancient Ghana.

Griots of Mali told that, long ago, there were twelve Malinke kings who ruled twelve separate clans. Ultimately, the kings of Mali came together as a royal council and selected a single, supreme ruler, a *mansa*, or "conqueror." Sometime around 1000, a mansa of Mali converted to Islam, and many Malinke nobles followed his example.

Sundiata, the Hungering Lion

The mansa who established Mali's power in the Sudan was Sundiata (soun-JAH-tah; sometimes spelled *Sundjata*), a name that means "hungering lion." Fierce and determined, Sundiata united the Malinke people into a single kingdom. He raised an army of horse-mounted warriors. In 1235, Sundiata's army swept north and defeated Mali's enemies, a clan called the Sossos (SOH-sohz). Under Sundiata, the mounted warriors of Mali became the most feared warriors of the region. Sundiata led his forces to further victories, and took control over the remains of the old Ghanaian empire.

Sundiata quickly set about restoring the profitable trans-Saharan trade in gold. He reorganized trading routes and reestablished ties with Muslim merchants. He also converted to Islam, thus gaining favor with the Muslim merchant class. Additionally, he moved the capital of Mali to his birthplace, Niani, a town near the gold fields of

the Niger, to better control the flow of commerce. By the time of his death in 1255, Sundiata had created a large empire that efficiently managed all trade within the Sudan.

Mansa Musa and the Great Hajj

The mansas who followed Sundiata expanded Mali's domain. By 1300, the empire stretched 1,200 miles (1,930 km) eastward from the Atlantic coast, and some 600 miles (965 km) from north to south. In the early 1300s, the most famous of Mali's emperors took the throne. His name was *Musa*, which meant "Moses" in the Mande language.

Mansa Musa was a devout Muslim, and he worked tirelessly to promote his religion. One important duty of Muslim believers is to make the hajj, a pilgrimage to the holy city of Mecca in Arabia. As a powerful ruler, Mansa Musa chose to make his hajj in grand fashion. Tales of his journey later spread throughout the Arab world and into Christian Europe, bringing fame to the kingdom of Mali.

Mansa Musa's journey from Mali to Mecca covered more than 2,800 miles (4,500 km), much of it across the treacherous Sahara. With an entourage of family members, friends, doctors, teachers, soldiers, and as many as sixty thousand slaves, Mansa Musa led his caravan from atop a majestic horse. He brought a hundred camels, each laden with three hundred pounds of gold dust, while another hundred camels carried food and other supplies.

After the desert crossing, the first stop for the caravan was Cairo, the Islamic capital of Egypt. The Arab writer al-Umari reported that Mansa Musa "spread upon Cairo the flood of his generosity." By freely giving out gold in Cairo, Mansa Musa put so much of the precious metal

Mansa Musa

into circulation that, according to al-Umari, he almost "ruined the value of money."

How did Mansa Musa's generosity so severely disrupt the city's gold market? Like all commodities, the value of money is governed by the principle of supply and demand. When supplies of a commodity are low, but customers' desire for it—their demand—is high, the price of the commodity rises. But when supplies exceed demand—when there is more available than people want—prices fall. A sudden increase in the supply of money—whether gold, silver, or dollar bills—makes it less valuable.

When Mansa Musa gave out so much gold in Cairo, gold was no longer as rare a commodity as it had been, and its value plummeted. When money loses value, it takes more money to buy things, resulting in inflation, an increase in prices on all kinds of goods and services. Even a decade after Mansa Musa's visit, the gold market in Cairo had not fully recovered.

Timbuktu: The Pearl of Africa

Mansa Musa returned from his hajj inspired by the religious splendor of Mecca, and determined to make Mali a great Muslim empire. With the help of Islamic teachers, architects, and scientists, Mansa Musa began to transform Timbuktu (tim-buhk-TOO), a city on the north-south trade routes. Clinging to the edge of the Sahara, just north of the great bend of the Niger River, Timbuktu became known as the "Pearl of Africa," a city that attracted visitors from across the Muslim world.

By the late 1400s, Timbuktu featured beautiful mosques and an Islamic university that attracted scholars from far and wide. At one time, more than twenty thousand scholars studied there, and the city's population exceeded one hundred thousand.

Timbuktu was also home to many skilled artisans who created elaborately decorated volumes of Muslim scriptures. As Timbuktu's fame spread, its influence helped Islam expand throughout West Africa.

This mosque in Timbuktu, which dates to 1327, was a center of learning.

Following Mansa Musa, the empire of Mali was governed by a series of weak rulers. Gradually, the empire's power faded and trade routes shifted. In parts of the empire, people once controlled by the Mali warriors began to rebel. Invaders managed to attack Timbuktu.

By 1500, the once-great empire of Mali had been reduced to a small collection of towns in the original Malinke homeland. Trade-based power would be carried forward by the next great West African kingdom, Songhai (sahng-GIY).

Songhai: A New Empire

The Songhai heartland surrounded the Niger, south of the large horseshoe-shaped bend in the river. There the waters lay wide and flat, interrupted by small islands and banked by fertile land. The people of Songhai became experts at cruising about in long, graceful canoes. Farming and fishing helped them flourish, while trade connected them to West African kingdoms and the world beyond. Eventually, they transformed the river

The King of Timbuktu

Timbuktu, in the kingdom of Mali, sat between the thick jungles along the Niger River and the southern edge of the Sahara. The city was a center of trade between Muslims to the north and African tribesmen to the south and west. Europeans unable to penetrate the African interior to this isolated city made exaggerated claims about its fabulous wealth.

The following account, however, was written by an actual visitor, Leo Africanus, a Muslim who lived in Morocco and traveled widely throughout Africa. He was captured by pirates and taken to Rome where, in the mid-1500s, he published a book about his travels, sparking even more European interest in Africa. (Leo Africanus refers to the city we call Timbuktu as Tombuto.)

The rich king of Tombuto hath many plates and scepters of gold, some whereof weigh 1300 pounds, and he keeps a magnificent and well furnished court. When he travelleth ... he rideth upon a camel which is led by some of his noblemen; and so he doth likewise when he goeth to warfare, and all his soldiers ride upon horses.

Whosoever will speak unto this king must first fall down before his feet and then taking up earth must sprinkle it upon his own head and shoulders; which custom is ordinarily observed by them that never saluted the king before, or come as ambassadors from other princes.

He hath always three thousand horsemen, and a great number of footmen that shoot poisoned arrows attending upon him. They have often skirmishes with those that refuse to pay tribute, and so many as they take, they sell unto the merchants of Tombuto.

into a busy thoroughfare, carrying trade goods from the heart of Africa, including leopard skins, ivory, and gold.

Sunni Ali

The major city of Songhai was Gao (gow), founded around 800 along the Niger River. By 1300, during the height of Mali's power, Gao had become a bustling trade city under the control of Mali's mansa. But after decades of control by Mali, in 1375 Gao broke away from the mansa's empire. Less than a century later, Sunni Ali (sou-NEE ah-LEE), the king of Songhai, led a campaign of conquest and established his own empire.

Sunni Ali organized a disciplined army, training the troops in special military camps. He raised a large cavalry of expert horsemen from Songhai's noble families. And he created a Niger River navy with hundreds of war canoes. With this formidable force, Sunni Ali conquered Timbuktu in 1468. He allowed his soldiers to burn and loot the city. Some Muslim scholars and holy men were killed; others fled the city. Later Sunni Ali's forces occupied another important trading city of the

They exported gold and kola nuts. And the captives they took in war, they sold as slaves.

Askia Muhammad was known as a devout Muslim. Like Mansa Musa, he went on a famous pilgrimage to Mecca. In Mecca, he visited many scholars in an effort to learn more about his religion. After returning home from his pilgrimage, Askia Muhammad changed the government of Songhai to bring it closer to Islamic law. He made laws based on Islamic teaching and appointed Muslim judges to the courts. He rebuilt Timbuktu, the city that Sunni Ali had pillaged, into a center of Muslim learning.

Askia Muhammad ruled Songhai until 1528, when his son led a revolt. The empire continued to thrive for sixty more years, until a trade dispute erupted between Songhai and Morocco, which lay on the far side of the Sahara.

In 1591, a Moroccan army crossed the desert carrying weapons that used a powerful technology new to the region—gunpowder. The Moroccan firearms were crude, little more than hollow tubes that propelled some unknown form of ammunition. But the Moroccan army had also dragged six cannons across the desert, which they used to shoot large stones with a thunderous blast. The Songhai warriors, armed primarily with spears and shields, fled before the explosive onslaught.

The Moroccan army went on to conquer Timbuktu and Djenné, although they failed to maintain control of the cities. Still, the defeat crippled Songhai, and the empire never reclaimed its former glory.

Modern-day laborers stack slabs of salt. Salt was highly valued by the merchants of medieval Songhai.

old Mali Empire, Djenné, near the ancient town of Djenné-Djeno.

Griots attributed Sunni Ali's bravery, cunning, and military strength to magical powers. Arab historians, however, angered by his treatment of the Muslim scholars of Timbuktu, remembered Sunni Ali as a power-hungry tyrant.

Askia Muhammad

When Sunni Ali died in 1492, his son, Bakari, took charge. Only a year later, a rebellious general overthrew Bakari. Under this general, Askia Muhammad (as-KEE-uh moh-HAM-uhd), the Songhai empire reached its greatest size, stretching westward to the Atlantic Ocean. Askia seized former territories of Mali and turned towns of the Sahara into colonies of Songhai.

Like the old empire of Mali, the empire of Songhai grew rich by trading with lands to the north of the Sahara. Songhai's merchants imported textiles, horses, salt, cowrie shells, and other goods.

Gunpowder and Guns

The earliest form of gunpowder was developed by the Chinese in the ninth century. By the thirteenth century, the technology had spread to the Arab world. Historians believe that Arabs devised the first gun, a bamboo tube reinforced with iron that used gunpowder to shoot an arrow.

Other West African Societies

The empires of Ghana, Mali, and Songhai relied on trans-Saharan trade for their fortunes. While these three empires rose and fell, other people also thrived in West Africa. The Mossi lived north of the rain forest, and their mounted warriors were feared throughout the region. To the east, near Lake Chad, the Kanem people developed a trading empire in the ninth century. Later, the Borno established a kingdom in modern-day Nigeria.

Islam played a key role in the development of some West African city-states. But traditional religions persisted among some African people, such as the Oyo, the Nupe, and the Igala, as well as in the kingdom of Benin (buh-NEEN).

The Brass Makers of Benin

The most respected craftsmen in Benin were the brass makers, who worked exclusively for the oba himself. The walls of the king's palace were adorned with brass plaques depicting scenes of life in Benin—hunters aiming their bows, acrobats twirling on ropes, musicians playing fifes and drums. The brass makers also created remarkable freestanding statues. Some depicted animals, such as a pair of regal leopards that symbolized the oba's power. Still other statues depicted the oba himself, or his ancestors.

Brass images often showed people wearing a coral headdress with multiple coral necklaces covering their necks and chins. The Edo believed that coral had magical power to protect a person from harm. Today we recognize these richly detailed sculptures as masterpieces of art.

A brass leopard, symbol of the oba's power

Benin

Beginning in the fifteenth century, deep within the great rain forest, Benin expanded under a series of powerful warrior kings. Benin itself was a walled city of about one square mile (2.5 square km), with many homes and a large palace. The people of Benin spoke a language called Edo. They created detailed ivory sculptures and brass likenesses of their kings. Hunters were especially revered in Benin, and the bravest of them stalked elephants for their valuable ivory tusks.

An ivory mask from Benin depicts a ruler's mother.

The king of Benin was known as the *oba* (OH-buh). In the 1440s, an oba named Ewuare (eh-woo-AY-ray) built a strong army and captured nearly two hundred neighboring towns. Later rulers continued to expand the kingdom of Benin.

In the late fifteenth century, explorers from the European nation of Portugal arrived on Benin's Atlantic coast. Benin and Portugal established a trading partnership. In Benin's wars of expansion, many captives were taken in battle, and some were sold to the Portuguese as slaves. As Benin sold more and more slaves to the Portuguese, the kingdom became ever wealthier.

Slavery had existed in Africa before the Portuguese arrived in Benin. In many parts of the continent, victors in war enslaved the conquered. Throughout the Middle Ages, several African civilizations traded in slaves. Mali, Songhai, and other African kingdoms had sold enslaved people to Arab merchants from North Africa.

After the Portuguese encounter with Benin, the slave trade expanded dramatically. (In a later chapter, you will read about the development of the transatlantic slave trade.) By the eighteenth century, the kingdom of Benin was in decline as European nations asserted their authority.

Eastern and Southern African Kingdoms

In the east of Africa, the trading empire of Kush thrived for three centuries, declining around the year 350. Later, as you have learned (see chapter 10), the kingdom of Aksum in Ethiopia flourished through trade across the Red Sea to Arabia and beyond.

As Islamic conquerors took control of North Africa in the seventh and eighth centuries, they seized trade routes. As a result, the people of Ethiopia moved their capital south. While maintaining the Christianity established by King Ezana in the fourth century, Ethiopia's role in East African trade weakened for the next three centuries.

Meanwhile, Arabs and other traders looked south, along the coast of East Africa, where seasonal winds aided speedy sea travel. Over time, as more Muslim traders arrived, they helped spread Islam among the people of this coastal region.

Trade Cities in East Africa

As early as the first century, Persian traders exchanged pottery with people in what is now Somalia, just south of where the Horn of Africa juts into the Indian Ocean. Some five hundred years later, an active trading network connected the area with a string of cities that ran along Africa's east coast for some 1,800 miles (2,900 km), an area larger than the coast of the United States from Maine to Florida.

Settling the Coast

Many of the coastal cities of East Africa were founded long before the arrival of foreign traders. Some began as simple farming villages more than two thousand years ago. Others were built by Bantu-speaking people, part of the enormous human migration from West Africa that began around A.D. 100 (see chapter 10).

Bantu people brought iron tools and weapons to the coastal region. They subdued the local people, some of whom lived as hunter-gatherers, others who tended flocks. Then they settled down and built towns.

Along with farming fertile inland fields, the ancient inhabitants of the coast hunted and fished. They learned to build hardy sailing vessels of wood

Muslim merchants sailing to East Africa traded goods and spread Islam.

365

Many Languages in Africa

More than five hundred separate languages evolved out of the original Bantu spoken by the first migrants to spread across the African continent in the first and second centuries. Today, various Bantu languages are spoken throughout Africa, including Kikongo in the north, and Tswana and Zulu in the south.

Swahili, another language with Bantu origins, is the primary language of about five million people in Africa, and the official language of Tanzania. Another thirty million people speak Swahili as a second language.

and coconut-husk twine, and became expert navigators. They sailed up and down the coast, forming city-to-city connections and exchanging goods.

The Arrival of Foreign Traders

East African trade routes shifted following the Arab conquest of North Africa. Traders sought new sources of African products such as gold, ivory, leopard skins, tortoise shells, and rhinoceros horns, which were used as handles for daggers and swords and ground for medicine in distant China. From ports more than 2,500 miles (4,023 km) away in Arabia and the Persian Gulf, trading ships joined existing networks between cities of the East African coast.

In the ninth century, for example, Persian merchants founded the island city of Lamu as a trading outpost. Using large blocks of coral limestone, they built a settlement of about forty-five acres (18.2 hectares) surrounded by walls. Other traders

from Arabia, North Africa, and India also settled in East Africa and forged trading partnerships with the people of the coast.

The Swahili

Between the eleventh and fifteenth centuries, a merging of African and Arabic influences led to the development of the Swahili culture in the coastal trading cities of East Africa. The name *Swahili* came from an Arabic word meaning "people of the coast." Here, the people spoke a Bantu language that gradually absorbed many Arabic and Persian words. In time, this Swahili language became spoken by people throughout much of sub-Saharan Africa, especially in countries on the east coast.

Although ancient African religious traditions persisted on the Swahili coast, beginning in the ninth century many Swahili merchants adopted Islam. These conversions helped them create strong trade relationships and military alliances with the Muslim world. Mosques rose above thriving Swahili cities.

Located in present-day Kenya, the towering ruins of a thirteenth-century mosque stand as testament to the Swahili people who adopted Islam.

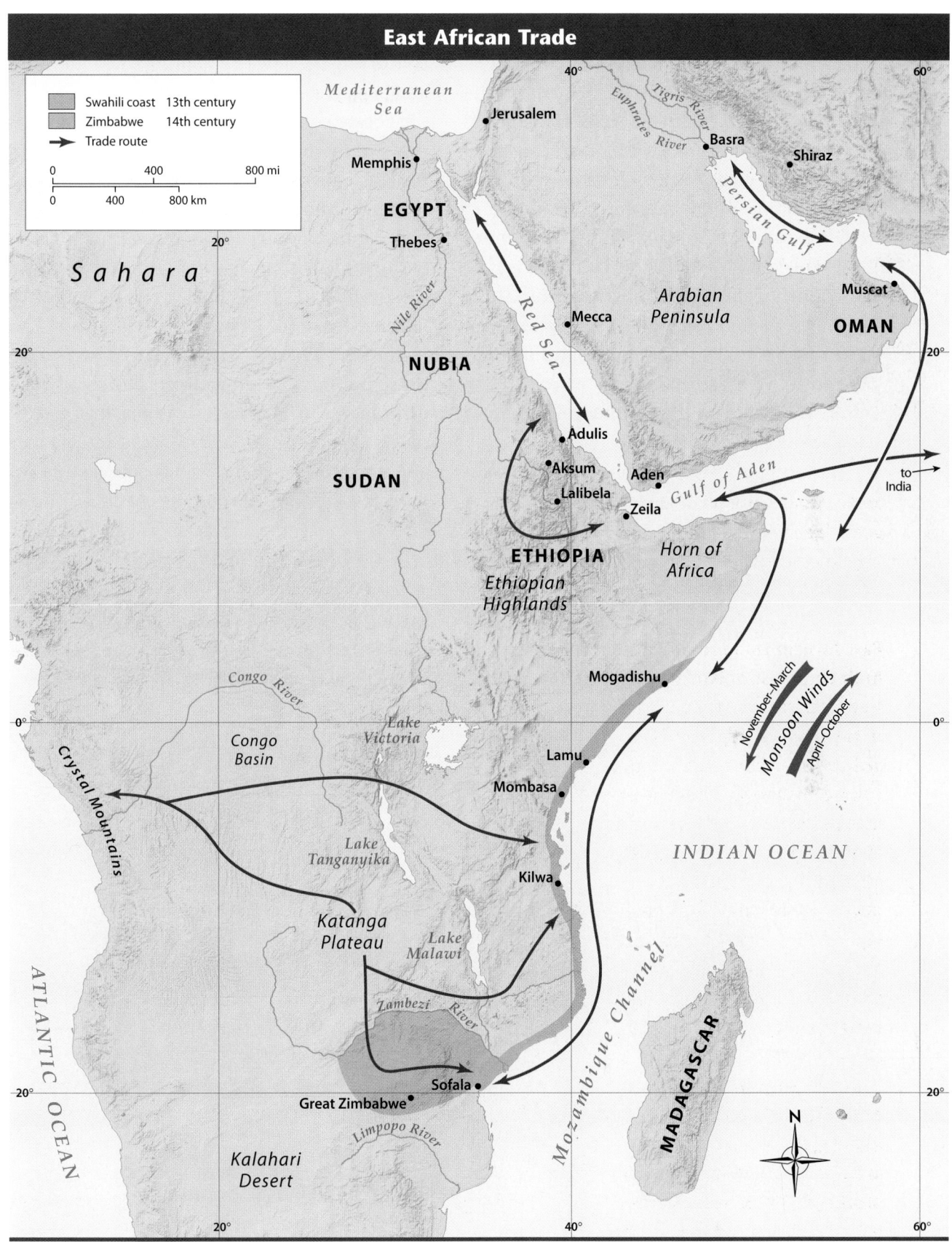

East African Trade

Legend:
- Swahili coast 13th century
- Zimbabwe 14th century
- → Trade route

Scale: 0 — 400 — 800 mi / 0 — 400 — 800 km

Mediterranean Sea

Jerusalem

Memphis

EGYPT

Thebes

Sahara

Nile River

Mecca

NUBIA

Arabian Peninsula

Muscat

OMAN

Tigris River

Euphrates River

Basra

Shiraz

Persian Gulf

Red Sea

SUDAN

Adulis

Aksum

Aden

Lalibela

Zeila

ETHIOPIA

Ethiopian Highlands

Gulf of Aden

Horn of Africa

to India

Congo River

Congo Basin

Lake Victoria

Crystal Mountains

Mogadishu

Monsoon Winds
November–March
April–October

Lamu

Mombasa

INDIAN OCEAN

Lake Tanganyika

Kilwa

Katanga Plateau

Lake Malawi

Zambezi River

Sofala

Great Zimbabwe

Limpopo River

ATLANTIC OCEAN

Kalahari Desert

Mozambique Channel

MADAGASCAR

N

Trade flourished between East African coastal cities and Muslim merchants from Egypt, the Arabian Peninsula, and the Persian Gulf.

Kilwa

About three dozen Swahili city-states developed along the East African coast, thriving from the growing commerce with traders seeking goods from deep within Africa. One of the largest of these trading cities was Mogadishu (moh-guh-DEE-shoo), just below the Horn of Africa, and now the capital of Somalia. Some 1,600 miles (2,575 km) south of Mogadishu, in what is now the country called Mozambique (moh-zahm-BEEK), lay the busy seaport of Sofala. Between these two was the city of Mombasa (in modern-day Kenya). Founded by Arab traders in the eleventh century, Mombasa grew into a busy port for trade across the Indian Ocean.

The most prosperous city on the Swahili coast was Kilwa (KEEL-wah; also spelled *Quiloa*). It grew in prosperity during the late eleventh century by controlling the flow of gold from southern Africa, and prospered for more than three centuries.

Located on an island off the coast of what is now southern Tanzania, Kilwa was founded in the late tenth century by settlers from Arabia and Persia. Ruled by a dynasty of Muslim sultans, the city featured a domed mosque and homes built of stone and decorative coral. On a tall sandstone cliff overlooking the Indian Ocean, a large palace towered above the city.

In Kilwa, wealthy city-dwellers dined on elegant porcelain tableware and wore fine silk clothing, items that came from faraway China. In exchange, they traded gold, ivory, and leopard skins. But they also sometimes sold enslaved people captured in military campaigns beyond the coastline.

An engraving details the prosperous city of Kilwa on the Swahili coast at what is present-day Tanzania.

A statue of a slave encumbered with chains stands on the site of a former slave market in eastern Africa.

In East Africa, as in West Africa, the sale of enslaved people had been going on for centuries. Captured Africans were traded to Arab and Persian merchants, who sold them as slaves throughout the Muslim world. East African slaves were also sold as soldiers to India and as laborers to China.

Still, the African slave trade remained relatively limited until European nations founded agricultural colonies in the Western Hemisphere in the 1500s. Then (as you will read about in detail in a later chapter), the slave trade expanded, especially in West Africa. Portuguese merchants continued to arrive in East Africa, seeking new sources of captives, as well as trade goods such as gold and ivory.

Intent on controlling East African trade, the Portuguese sacked the cities of Kilwa and Mombasa in 1505. They built a series of stone fortresses on the site of the Swahili cities. For the next two hundred years, the Portuguese attempted to take control of East African trade, with varying levels of success.

Great Zimbabwe

In their attempt to take over the East African gold trade in the sixteenth century, the Portuguese often sent troops into the heart of the continent to search for the source of the precious metal. During one of these expeditions to a wide plateau about 220 miles (354 km) inland from the coast, a Portuguese captain came upon

Ethiopia's Rock Churches

Though trade in East Africa was largely controlled by Muslim merchants, Ethiopia remained a Christian outpost that shipped goods to Egypt and across the Red Sea. Ethiopian merchants sold frankincense and myrrh, fragrant products made from tree resin. Ethiopians also profited by selling war captives to Arabia.

Between 1200 and 1250, during a period of great prosperity for Ethiopia, King Lalibela (lah-lee-BEL-uh) built a series of churches constructed of solid rock. To make the churches, builders excavated a giant piece of buried granite, and then carved the rock inside and out. The churches featured hollowed-out naves and vaulted ceilings. The largest of these rock churches was 109 feet (33 m) long, 77 feet (23 m) wide, and 35 feet (10 m) deep. Another was built in the shape of a cross.

This structure in Ethiopia is one of a series of Christian churches that builders carved from solid rock.

369

Fortress-like walls of Great Zimbabwe guarded the wealthy city that served as a center of power for several hundred years.

"a fortress built of stones of marvelous size... almost surrounded by hills."

The soldiers had stumbled upon Great Zimbabwe (zim-BAH-bway), a towering walled city of stone that had served as the center of a powerful kingdom for three hundred years, until it was abandoned around 1450. Great Zimbabwe, like other African kingdoms, enjoyed tremendous wealth thanks to its strategic location between rich gold fields and the trading cities of the coast.

Cities of Stone

When the Portuguese came upon the ruins of Great Zimbabwe, they were awed by the city's sheer size. They wondered if perhaps the giant stone structures were the fabled city of the Queen of Sheba, mentioned in the Bible.

In fact, Great Zimbabwe was constructed by a Bantu-speaking people who had occupied the inland plain of the Zimbabwe Plateau since the third century. These early inhabitants were the ancestors of the Shona people of the modern-day nation of Zimbabwe. They farmed the fertile soil of the region, and grazed cattle on the abundant grasslands of the savanna. Elephants provided a source of ivory, and gold came into the region from high country to the north.

In time, the kingdom of Zimbabwe controlled a vast area that included the headwaters of two important rivers, the Zambezi and the Limpopo, along which trade flowed to the coast. Kings of the plateau grew rich by demanding tribute on all ivory and gold that went to prosperous Swahili cities like Kilwa.

Throughout the Zimbabwe Plateau, wealthy and powerful people built stone enclosures

An artist's interpretation of Great Zimbabwe shows what life may have been like in the thriving city.

around their homes. Eventually they constructed some two hundred walled communities, the ruins of which still dot the region. The largest of these stone-enclosed communities was Great Zimbabwe.

Built between 1200 and 1450, Great Zimbabwe was the largest human construction in sub-Saharan Africa until recent times. Around its sprawling ruins, thick granite walls rise and fall like waves along the rolling hills. The builders of Great Zimbabwe were expert stonemasons. The walls stand more than thirty feet (10 m) high and sixteen feet (5 m) thick. At its height during the fourteenth century, Great Zimbabwe may have housed as many as eleven thousand residents, although most people lived in mud huts outside the walls.

Uncovering Great Zimbabwe

Many of Great Zimbabwe's riches were stolen by European treasure hunters in the nineteenth century. Nevertheless, recent archaeological excavations have uncovered various artifacts, including gold figurines, ceremonial weapons, and stone figures carved in the shapes of birds. Archaeologists have also found pottery, elaborate ivory carvings, golden jewelry, and the remains of a gold workshop.

Because the people who built Great Zimbabwe left no written records, historians and archaeologists don't know exactly why the city was abandoned around 1450. Some think that diseases may have devastated the population. Others suspect that trade routes shifted after the arrival of the Portuguese, ending the region's source of wealth.

Persuasive evidence suggests that the growing population of Great Zimbabwe may have depleted the area's resources. It appears likely that by the early fifteenth century, the people had created an environmental catastrophe by destroying the

Overgrazing in Africa Today

Overgrazing—allowing animals to graze to the point that they deplete the vegetation—remains a major problem throughout the African savanna today. Soils in the savanna are naturally thin, and rainfall is scattered and infrequent. These conditions create a delicate balance in which lush grasslands can rapidly become a barren landscape. When herds of cattle deplete vegetation, soils wash or blow away and the land can no longer support grasses. In Kenya, on the East African savanna, overgrazing is a serious environmental concern. In parts of Africa, overgrazing speeds up the process of desertification.

African cattle tread an overgrazed and barren landscape.

territory's grasslands through too much grazing of cattle. The inhabitants of the Zimbabwe Plateau moved on to more hospitable areas in the north. Today, their descendants live in the nations of Zimbabwe and Mozambique.

| 1300 | 1350 | 1400 | 1450 |

c. 1300
Osman establishes the Ottoman Empire.

1368
China's Ming Dynasty comes to power.

1453
Ottoman forces conquer Constantinople.

Chapter 17 Asia's New

Architecture from Asia's early empires, from left: Temple of Heaven, China's Forbidden City; Taj Mahal, India; 14th-century castle, Japan; a mosque, modern-day Iran; blue-tile dome of an Ottoman mosque, Asia Minor

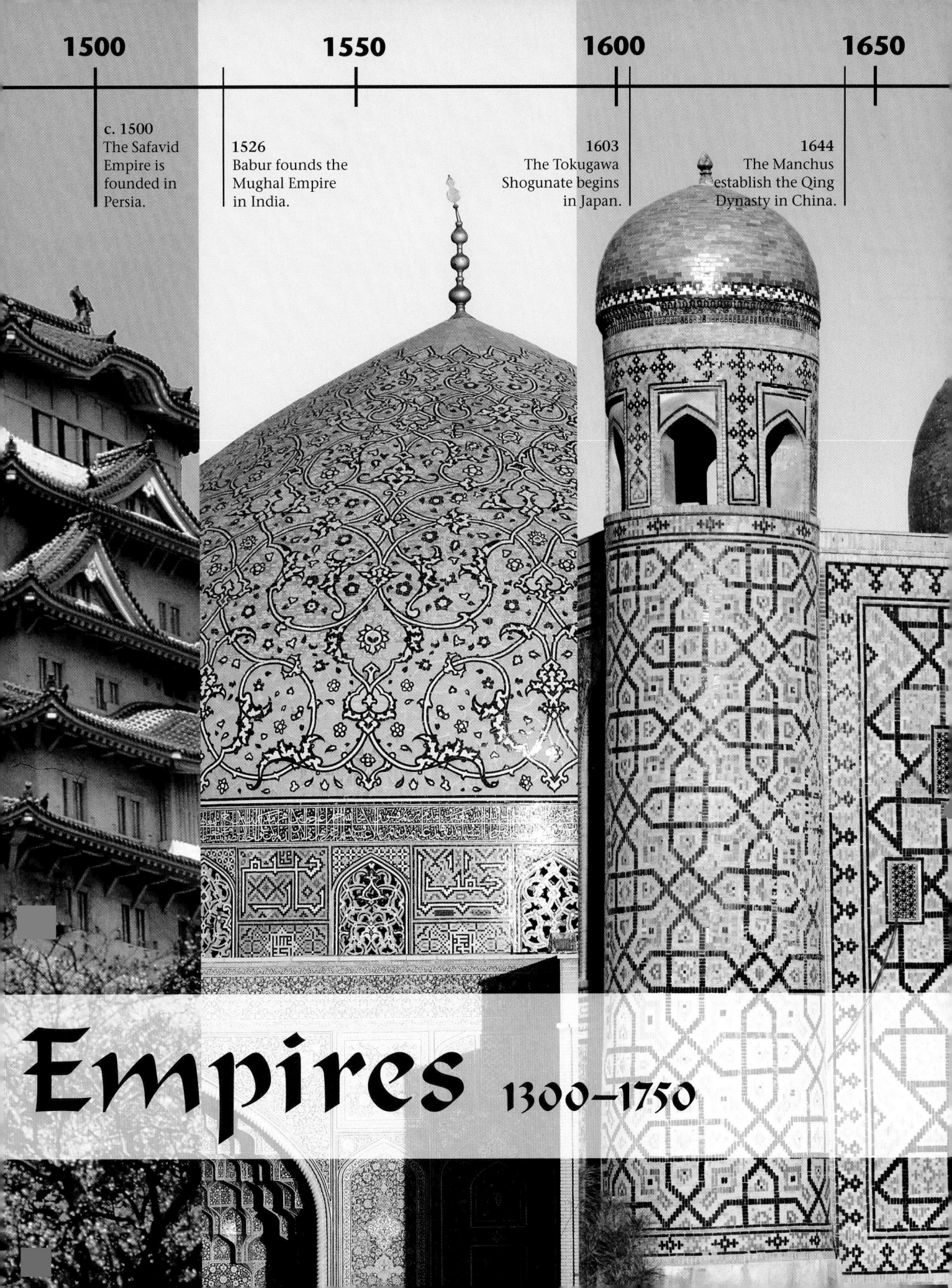

1500	1550	1600	1650

c. 1500
The Safavid Empire is founded in Persia.

1526
Babur founds the Mughal Empire in India.

1603
The Tokugawa Shogunate begins in Japan.

1644
The Manchus establish the Qing Dynasty in China.

Empires 1300–1750

*B*etween the fourteenth and seventeenth centuries, three new Muslim empires emerged to rule much of Asia. These Muslim empires—the Ottoman, the Safavid, and the Mughal—brought Islam to new levels of power and influence. In these societies, diverse cultural, ethnic, and religious groups lived together under Muslim rulers.

In China, by contrast, foreign rulers gave way to the native Ming Dynasty, which closed the empire to outside contacts, embraced China's ancient traditions, and tried to create a unified Chinese society.

Nearby, feudal Japan fragmented into a world of feuding warlords. When the Tokugawa family reunited Japan in the seventeenth century, the Japanese closed their country to foreigners and focused on developing a culture free of outside influences.

Three Islamic Empires

The Mongol conquests devastated the Islamic world, but out of the rubble emerged three vigorous new Muslim empires—the Ottoman Empire in Asia Minor, the Safavid (sah-FAH-vuhd) Empire in Persia, and the Mughal (MOO-guhl) Empire in India. Of these, the first to rise and the last to decline was the Ottoman Empire, which endured for more than six hundred years. At its peak, the Ottoman Empire stretched around the Mediterranean Sea.

The Ottoman Empire

When the Mongols erupted out of Central Asia in the mid-thirteenth century, many nomadic Turkish tribes fled ahead of them westward into Asia Minor, where they displaced an earlier wave of nomadic Turkish warriors, the Seljuks. These tribes then began raiding Byzantine territory. As recent converts to Islam, they called themselves *ghazis*, or warriors for the faith.

In about 1260, a boy named Osman was born into one such Turkish clan. He grew up to be a fierce ghazi. With other warriors flocking to his side, he built a small state in Asia Minor, bordering on the Sea of Marmara. He titled himself *emir*, an Arabic word for "prince," and his dynasty was called the Ottomans, or "Osman's line." Later Ottoman rulers would claim the exalted title of "sultan."

A series of Ottoman rulers kept expanding the empire, conquering domains in both Asia Minor and Europe. The Ottomans were among the first to use firearms in battle, including muskets and gigantic cannons. Their military success, however, was not a result of their weapons but was due to their superbly trained troops, especially the highly disciplined elite corps of **janissaries** (JA-nuh-sehr-eez).

Constantinople Becomes Istanbul

By 1450, the Ottomans had captured most of Asia Minor and extensive territory in eastern Europe. One small patch of land still eluded them, however—the city of Constantinople itself. By this time, the population of the ancient Byzantine capital had decreased from a million to about forty thousand, and the Byzantine Empire itself had shrunk to only Constantinople and its suburbs. Despite many threats, the mighty walls of the city enabled its residents to hold out against invaders.

Key Questions

- How did the Ottomans build and administer their empire? What were the Ottoman Empire's main cultural achievements?

- Why did the Ottoman and Safavid empires clash?

- What cultural achievements distinguish the Mughal Empire of India?

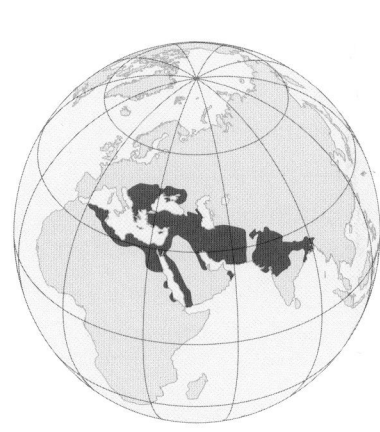

Muslim empires stretched from North Africa to India.

Osman I and his descendants established the Ottoman Empire.

375

The Janissaries: Elite Slaves

The name *janissaries* comes from Turkish terms meaning "new army." The janissaries, in their fine uniforms and tall white hats, were the best trained and most respected of all the sultan's soldiers. Yet every one of these proud soldiers was a slave. All had been taken from Christian families in conquered territories, converted to Islam as boys, and given intense military training.

Every few years, the sultan's officials toured Christian villages in eastern Europe seeking the brightest, strongest boys for the janissary corps. The chosen boys grew up in military dormitories, cut off from their families, and were instilled with fanatical loyalty to the Ottoman sultan. Janissaries were not allowed to marry or have children. Because janissaries enjoyed such high honor and privileges, some families willingly offered their boys to this form of slavery.

A soldier wearing the traditional janissary uniform, c. 1600

In 1453, a new Ottoman sultan, Mehmet II (also spelled *Mehmed*), vowed to take the city. One reason he believed he could succeed where others had failed was that he had the world's biggest cannons, including a twenty-seven-foot (8.2 m) monster that shot balls of iron weighing half a ton. To attack Constantinople by sea as well as land, Mehmet also built a powerful navy of 125 ships.

For almost two months, Ottoman cannons rained destruction on the city. Its inhabitants rallied around their leader, the Byzantine emperor Constantine XI, who battled from the city walls and refused to surrender. As the Ottoman siege continued, some of the Byzantines' European allies slipped away.

Finally, with a dwindling number of Byzantine defenders remaining to man fourteen miles (22.5 km) of walls, the Ottomans found an undefended gate and poured through. The Byzantine emperor drew his sword and led his soldiers in a hopeless charge, and the Ottoman soldiers cut him down. Soon after their emperor's death, the exhausted people of Constantinople surrendered.

Upon entering the city, the victorious sultan Mehmet went directly to Hagia Sophia. He offered thanks to Allah and gave orders that the church be transformed into a mosque. He declared that the ancient Christian city of Constantinople would henceforth be a Muslim city, the capital of an Islamic empire.

Over time, even the city's named changed. It eventually became known as Istanbul. Istanbul became a thriving, populous city with a half-million inhabitants, including people of many creeds and races, living together more or less peacefully under laws enforced by the Ottoman rulers.

Süleyman the Lawgiver

In 1520, the greatest Ottoman ruler mounted the throne. Süleyman (soo-lay-MAHN) the Magnificent, as he was later called, reigned for forty-six years. Süleyman campaigned tirelessly to expand the already vast empire that his father had conquered. Süleyman seized the cities of Tripoli and Tunis and through them took control of the trade routes into Africa. He dominated the Mediterranean with a navy led by a dreaded admiral known to Europeans as *Barbarossa* (a name that means "Red Beard").

Süleyman also pushed deep into eastern Europe, where he captured the city of Belgrade and then marched on through Hungary. In 1529,

The Ottomans, under Mehmet II, conquered Constantinople and turned it into a Muslim city, later renamed Istanbul.

his army arrived at the walls of Vienna, Austria. But winter came early that year, and Süleyman retired to his capital, vowing to conquer Vienna another year. As it happened, he never returned, and thus 1529 marked the peak of Ottoman expansion. At its greatest extent in the mid-1500s, the Ottoman Empire—the world's largest empire at the time—stretched from Algiers in North Africa to the eastern edge of Mesopotamia.

Europeans were awed by the might of Süleyman's armies, the prosperity of his realm, and the luxury and splendor of his court. In fact, it was the Europeans who called him "the Magnificent."

In his own domains, Süleyman was called "the Lawgiver" because he forged an intricate set of regulations for administering his realm. The sultan's code was needed because his subjects were diverse in both religion and geographic origin. They included Muslims, Jews, and Christians of many sects who came from Turkey, Arabia, Africa, Greece, Bulgaria, and Egypt, among other places.

Süleyman's laws improved a system the Ottomans had long been developing. The laws organized various religious groups into self-governing communities. People of all religious communities were free to worship as they pleased and live by their own religious customs as long as they paid a heavy tax imposed on non-Muslims. They also had to accept the legal authority of the sultan's chief minister, the vizier.

The vizier administered a vast bureaucratic network that controlled the empire's many provinces. All parts of the complex Ottoman Empire were thus governed by a single set of regulations that kept order while allowing many different cultures to maintain their own ways.

Ottoman Arts and Architecture

As sultan, Süleyman spent lavishly to beautify Istanbul with splendid architecture. His chief builder, a former janissary named Mimar Sinan, designed the Süleymaniye (soo-lay-MAHN-ee-yeh). From a distance, this magnificent mosque looks like a mountain of mushroom-shaped domes of different sizes. Nearby stand four graceful minarets, towers from which Muslims chant the call to prayer. Sinan perfected a distinctive Ottoman style that other architects imitated.

Ottoman craftsmen produced fine decorative art—carpets, tapestries, marbled paper, dyed silk fabrics, ornamental clothing, and pipes carved from the soft white stone called meerschaum. Court poets wrote sophisticated works in Persian, the literary language of the region. Calligraphers worked with artists to produce elaborate handmade books. Under Süleyman's rule, Islamic culture flourished.

The Later Ottoman Empire

Süleyman died in 1566. He was followed by a long line of mostly incompetent rulers who mismanaged the empire and wasted its wealth on indulgent luxuries. In trade and technology, the Ottomans began to lag behind the Europeans. Manufactured goods pouring in from Europe put Ottoman workshops out of business.

The Süleymaniye Mosque, built in the 1550s, is a splendid example of the rich architecture of Istanbul.

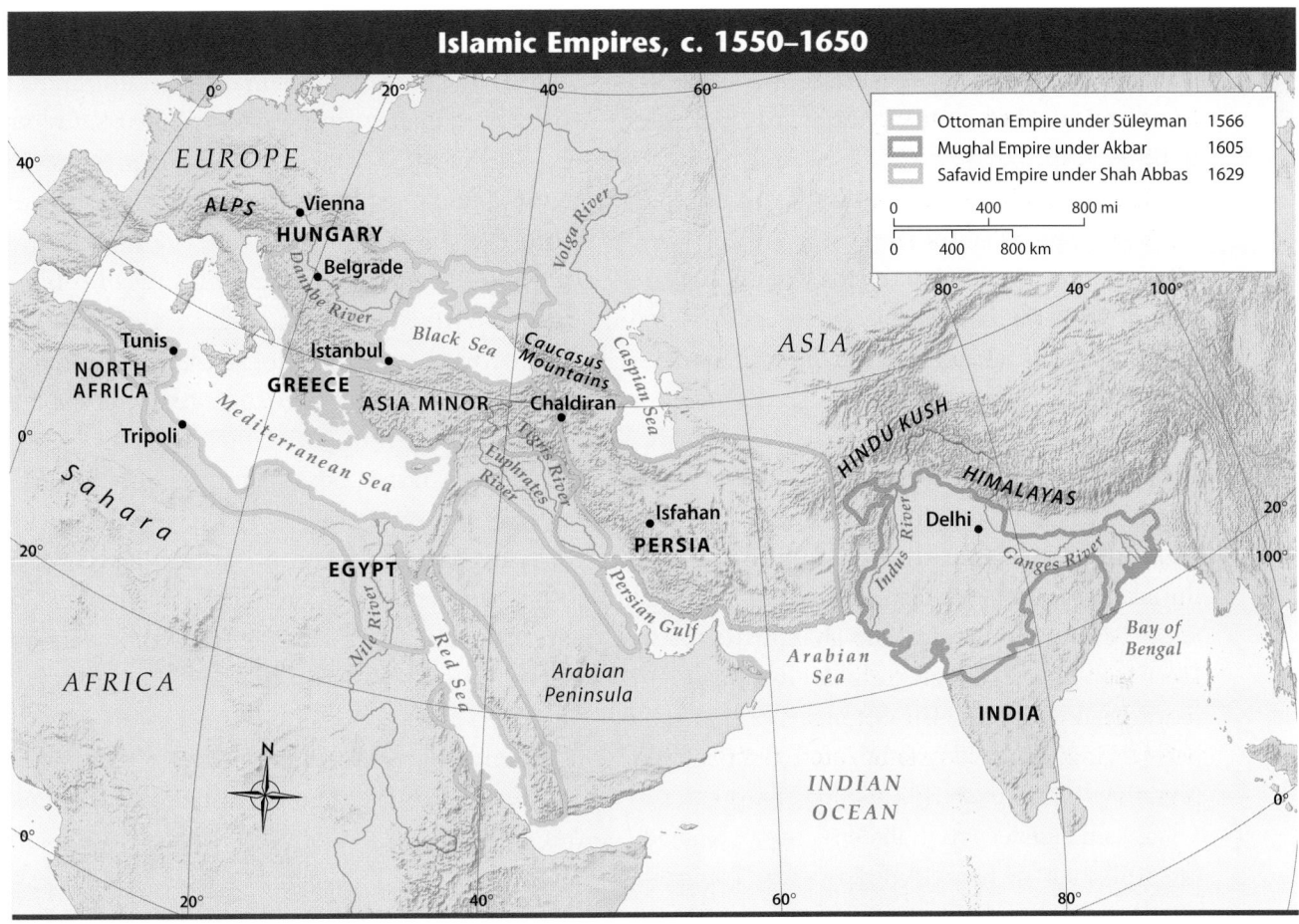

Islamic Empires, c. 1550–1650

Legend:
- Ottoman Empire under Süleyman 1566
- Mughal Empire under Akbar 1605
- Safavid Empire under Shah Abbas 1629

Three new Islamic empires exercised power in western and southern Asia for nearly five hundred years.

As the Ottoman Empire weakened, its neighbors grew stronger. In the north, the Russian Empire began expanding. In the west, Austria began to take back territory the Ottomans had conquered. In 1683, the Ottomans made a last desperate attempt to conquer Vienna, but suffered a severe defeat. The empire shrank as the Ottomans lost control of lands they had conquered in Europe and Africa. Even in its diminished state, the Ottoman Empire remained a significant political force in the nineteenth century and into the early twentieth century.

The Safavid Empire

To the east of the Ottomans, a rival Muslim empire rose in Persia. The Safavids dominated the region between the Persian Gulf and the Caspian Sea, with their power concentrated in the area now called Iran.

Ismail Establishes an Empire

The Safavids started out as a religious brotherhood whose leader was protected by a corps of bodyguards called the "Red Heads" because of the distinctive crimson caps they wore. In the late fifteenth century, when the head of the Safavids was assassinated, his son, a boy named Ismail (iss-mah-EEL), vowed to take revenge. In hunting down his father's enemies, Ismail turned the Safavid order into a political force, conquering one prince and tribe after another until he and his Red Heads controlled all of Persia. In 1501, Ismail declared himself the "shah" or king of a new Safavid Empire.

The shah made the mistake of invading Asia Minor, the heartland of the Ottoman Empire. The Ottoman sultan at the time, Selim I, sent out a great army to meet the invaders. In 1514, the two sides clashed near the Safavid capital on a field called Chaldiran (chahl-dih-RAHN). The Ottomans decisively won the battle because they had cannons and muskets while the Safavids were still fighting with spears and bows.

Safavids Versus Ottomans

The Ottomans and the Safavids were bitter enemies partly because each empire wanted to expand into the other's territory. But there was also a religious reason for the conflict.

Both the Ottomans and the Safavids were Muslims. But the Ottomans belonged to the Sunni branch of Islam, while the Safavids belonged to the Shia branch. Shah Ismail declared Shiism to be the state religion of his empire, and he persecuted Sunni Muslims who refused to change their faith. The Ottomans resented the shah's cruel treatment of their fellow Sunnis. The Ottomans retaliated by persecuting Shias, who sought refuge in Safavid Persia by the thousands.

Shiism had deep roots in Persia, so the Safavids put Shiism at the heart of their society. For example, they declared Shia holidays to be national holidays. The Safavids promoted Persian culture and customs as a way to unify their people and set them apart from their Arab and Turkish neighbors.

Shah Abbas, Warrior and Builder

Following the defeat of Ismail at Chaldiran, for the next century the Ottomans and Safavids fought an on-again, off-again war. Under Süleyman, the Ottomans seized large territories from the Safavids. But in 1587, a new leader came to power in Persia, Shah Abbas I. Abbas equipped his troops with muskets and cannons. His powerful and well-trained army won back most of the lands his people had lost to the Ottomans.

Under Shah Abbas, Persian merchants and craftsmen prospered, and trade connected the Safavid Empire to distant lands. Wealthy people in Europe eagerly purchased costly Persian carpets with intricate designs. Other Persian exports included silk and beautiful pieces of pottery.

Shah Abbas loved the arts. He supported many poets, painters, and architects. Artists illustrated illuminated books of poetry with Persian miniatures, detailed scenes painted with brush tips no bigger than a single cat hair. Architects built mosques covered with brilliant mosaic tilework and topped with shimmering pointed blue domes.

Persian Carpets

For at least two thousand years, Persia has been a source of fine, hand-knotted carpets. Muslim craftsmen turned carpets into works of art. Individual strands of wool or silk were stretched on a frame and tied together to make the carpet. Some Persian carpets have as many as three hundred knots per square inch. The carpet makers used threads of different colors to create elaborate patterns. Some carpets present realistic scenes, such as lush gardens full of flowering trees and bubbling fountains, while others feature the complex patterns known as arabesques. Fine Persian carpets grow more vivid with age and use.

Persian rugs are elaborate expressions of Islamic art.

A vibrant blue-tile dome tops a mosque in Isfahan, capital of the Safavid rulers.

The Shah's New Capital

To celebrate the glory of his empire, Shah Abbas built a new capital city, Isfahan (is-fah-HAHN). Here, public gardens dotted with fountains surrounded a huge rectangular park in the center of the city. Over one end of the park rose a magnificent mosque with a dome that glittered with colorful tiles. Trees shaded the wide boulevards running through the capital city. In Isfahan, all the wealth of Safavid culture was on display.

Travelers from all over the world came to admire the shah's beautiful, well-planned city. These visitors included many Europeans seeking opportunities for trade. Iran's exports to Europe included silk and pottery. And the intricately patterned, and expensive, Persian carpets were highly sought after by Europe's wealthy.

Under Shah Abbas, the Safavid Empire reached its peak of power and influence. Persian artistic achievements also flourished during his reign. For these reasons, he is also remembered as Abbas the Great.

India's Mughal Empire

In northern India, during the same time that Süleyman ruled in faraway Istanbul, another Muslim empire came to power. The Mughal Empire, as it was known, was very different from the Ottoman and Safavid empires. In both Asia Minor, where the Ottomans ruled, and Persia, home of the Safavids, the great majority of people were Muslims. But in India, the vast majority of people practiced the religion of Hinduism.

Babur Establishes a Dynasty

Back around the year 400, Hinduism had flourished in India under the Gupta Empire. But with the fall of the Gupta Empire around 500, India

Babur, a warrior and poet, founded an Islamic dynasty in India.

dissolved into many small kingdoms. Turkish invaders swept in from the north. One group of Muslim Turks eventually established a kingdom, or sultanate, in the northern Indian city of Delhi. Over the next few centuries, as one dynasty followed another, northern India became a society with a Muslim minority ruling a Hindu majority.

In 1526, a conqueror named Babur (BAH-bur) toppled the Delhi sultanate and founded a line of rulers known to history as the Mughals, who would establish the mightiest Islamic dynasty India had ever known.

Mughal is a Persian pronunciation of "Mongol." Among his ancestors Babur counted two Mongol conquerors, Genghis Khan and Timur. When Babur took control of Delhi in 1526, he defeated a force ten times bigger than his own. His army, equipped with guns and field artillery, had the advantage in weapons. His troops also included cavalry on horses and elephants.

Babur was a fierce warrior of legendary physical strength. But he was also a musician, a gifted poet, and a writer whose autobiography is considered one of the great works of Turkish literature.

Akbar the Great

Babur's grandson Akbar (AK-bur), who ruled from 1542 to 1605, went on to conquer most of northern and central India. Under Akbar, in the second half of the sixteenth century the Mughals built a large and powerful empire.

Akbar dealt masterfully with the central challenge of a small Muslim aristocracy trying to govern a massive population of Hindus and other non-Muslims. While earlier sultans had used force to control their subjects, Akbar practiced

tolerance and inclusion. He abolished the tax imposed on non-Muslims by Islamic law. He drew leading Hindus into his government and made alliances with Hindu princes. He took Hindu women as wives (Muslim men could marry more than one woman), and he allowed them to practice their religion in his palace.

Akbar's policies had a political purpose, but he was also genuinely curious about other religions. In his capital, Akbar built a hall for religious discussion where he had Muslim scholars debate Hindus, Zoroastrians, Christians, and others.

Akbar supported the arts, especially painting and architecture. Using his immense wealth, he lured some of the finest Persian painters away from

Akbar, shown here at center with his court, supported the arts and practiced tolerance and inclusion.

The serenely beautiful Taj Mahal, built in the 1630s as a tomb for Shah Jahan's wife

the Safavid court to found a school of miniature painting in India.

Mughal Architecture: The Taj Mahal

The Mughals respected the vibrant culture of the Safavids and learned from it in many ways. For example, Mughal architects combined Persian, Turkish, and Hindu styles. They brought the domes and arches of Islamic architecture to India to build a stunning variety of mosques, pavilions, and forts, using red sandstone, white marble, and multicolored ceramic tiles as building materials.

Mughal architecture culminated in the Taj Mahal, a mausoleum (a large, elaborate tomb) built in the 1630s by Akbar's grandson, Shah Jahan, for his beloved wife Mumtaz, who died at a young age. A perfectly symmetrical masterpiece of white marble, the Taj Mahal is surrounded by gardens that imitate paradise as imagined by Muslim tradition. An Indian poet once described this monument as "a teardrop on the cheek of time."

The Empire Declines

The India of the great Mughal rulers produced bountiful harvests and abundant handicrafts. Trade links connected India to markets from China to western Asia. In its day, the Mughal Empire was among the richest empires on earth.

The Mughals thrived while they managed to integrate different religions and peoples into a single whole. Their decline began when they abandoned policies of tolerance.

Akbar's great-grandson persecuted non-Muslim religions. He reimposed crushing taxes on Hindus and tore down their temples. He managed to suppress rebellions, but the sultans who followed him inherited a legacy of growing anger and unrest. By 1750, the Mughal Empire had splintered from within and was vulnerable to conquest.

China's Ming and Qing Dynasties

Key Questions

- What cultural achievements characterize the Ming Dynasty?

- Why did the Chinese adopt a policy of isolation from foreign trade and contact? What were the results of that policy?

In the early thirteenth century, the Mongol leader Genghis Khan conquered much of China. His grandson Kublai Khan finished the job in 1279 and established the Yuan Dynasty to rule China. For decades the Chinese suffered under Mongol rule. They paid high taxes, had little say in their government, and endured terrible famines. By the middle of the fourteenth century, the Chinese people had had enough of foreign rule. Rebellions broke out like brushfires.

The Ming Dynasty

Zhu Yuanzhang (joo you-en-jahng), a peasant from southern China, led a revolt that chased out the Mongols who had long ruled the land. For his new dynasty he chose the name *Ming*, which means "brilliant"—and brilliant it was.

Ousting the Mongols

Zhu Yuanzhang came from the humblest origins of any Chinese emperor. His parents and brothers starved to death during a famine. Zhu joined a band of rebels battling to drive the Mongols out of China. A natural leader, Zhu quickly began to recruit followers. Again and again he led his men to victory against the Mongols. In 1355, he assembled an army and conquered the southern Mongol city of Nanjing (nahn-jing), which eventually became the capital.

Zhu's army was just one of several competing rebel armies in China. Over the next decade, he fought more battles against Chinese rivals than against the Yuan rulers. By 1368, Zhu had defeated both the Mongols and his Chinese rivals in the south. He went on to capture the northern part of China and drove out the last Mongol emperor. He established a new dynasty, the Ming. For himself and his reign, he took the imperial title of Hongwu (hawng-woo), which means "vast military power."

The Hongwu emperor built an army drawn from two million households obligated to provide him lifelong military service. Soon, every neighboring country from Korea to Thailand was paying tribute to China. But the new emperor was more interested in control

China and Japan closed their borders to foreigners.

A stone Ming warrior, fifteenth century

than conquest. To have more personal control over running the empire, he did away with the office of prime minister. To prevent rebellion, he had as many as a hundred thousand of his own bureaucrats and army officers executed over the course of nearly twenty years—some on charges of thinking disloyal thoughts.

To keep order, Ming rulers revived the Confucian value system, which emphasized the need for each person to accept his or her place in the social order. Confucian values helped unify Ming China but also locked the society into a rigid order.

China Prospers Under the Ming

The Ming emperors worked hard to repair the damage the Mongols had done to their country. They restored China's irrigation systems, which had slipped into disrepair. They rebuilt the Grand Canal, which connected China's two major rivers, the Yangtze and the Huang He, and allowed crops to be transported from south to north. They reformed the tax system by surveying lands under cultivation and then adjusting taxes to match production. Most farms were small plots worked by individual families, and taxes on these families were reduced.

By the late 1300s, the amount of land under cultivation increased. Over the next century, rice harvests were bountiful. Improved roads and waterways allowed farmers to get their products

A rice harvest in China, illustrated on a silk painting

more easily to market, so they began growing profitable crops, such as tea, to sell. Market towns sprang up across the Ming Empire and China's population soared.

With cash flowing through the empire, non-agricultural industries flourished. Centuries earlier, the Chinese had invented porcelain, a ceramic as strong and thin as glass. Now, the use of new

Ming Porcelain: The World's Best

Porcelain was made of powdered stone mixed with *kaolin*, a type of clay. When heated to 1,400 degrees (760 degrees C), the clay turned hard. Under the Ming, imperial workshops perfected the use of an imported cobalt pigment, which turned blue when fired. Artisans painted delicate designs on the ceramic. Flowers, birds, phoenixes, and dragons adorned plates and vases. The elegant blue-and-white Ming Dynasty porcelain appealed to Europeans, who simply called it "china."

A Ming porcelain vase adorned with flowers

dyes, especially blue ones, allowed the Chinese to make even more spectacular pottery. The state set up huge imperial workshops to produce porcelain for sale abroad and at home, which gave rise to crowded, noisy, smoke-filled industrial cities. Ming artisans also produced rugs, lacquerware, silk, and, later, cotton cloth for export.

The Ming emperors restored the traditional Chinese civil service exams that tested candidates' knowledge of Confucian classics. Candidates who scored high could enter government service.

The Forbidden City

The Hongwu emperor's son moved the capital from busy Nanjing in the south to the old Yuan city of Dadu in the north. This new northern capital became known as Beijing. It remains the capital of China to this day.

At the emperor's command, the Chinese rebuilt much of Beijing. At the heart of Beijing, artisans and laborers built a nine thousand-room palace complex called the Forbidden City. Surrounded by walls and a moat, the Forbidden City was a private world, set apart for the imperial court. Across its 178 acres (72 hectares) spread temples, palaces, gardens, courtyards, carved stone bridges, and elaborate ceremonial halls.

The main entrance to the Forbidden City, the Meridian Gate, was taller than a twelve-story building—even the greatest king must have felt small coming to see the emperor of China. Inside, the city's seventy-five buildings all faced south, the direction from which benevolent spirits were believed to come.

Should evil forces make their way to the city, the emperor and his court had taken many precautions. On the ground, fearsome lions of gilded bronze stood guard. Carved dragons entwined themselves around tall columns. And on the rooftops sat fanciful earthenware creatures, said to protect the city.

At the heart of the Forbidden City stood the Hall of Supreme Harmony, where the emperor conducted important business. North of this building stretched the private quarters where the emperor's wives and children spent their lives.

No commoners and very few foreigners ever stepped into the Forbidden City. Only a handful of exalted officials were allowed inside. The Forbidden City was the emperor's home, office, and retreat. Everything about it was designed to show the might of the emperor, the importance of the Ming Dynasty, and the insignificance of just about everything else.

China's Great Explorer

In the early 1400s—decades before Europeans would initiate an age of exploration—the Ming

Ming emperors conducted important business in the imposing Hall of Supreme Harmony in the heart of the Forbidden City, a palace complex closed to commoners and foreigners.

emperor who ruled China from the Forbidden City dispatched great fleets of sailing ships to explore distant lands. The most renowned explorer was a Muslim-born admiral named Zheng He (choung huh), who had spent twenty years in the Chinese army.

Over the course of about three decades, Zheng He made seven journeys, each lasting about twenty months. His fleet consisted of 62 enormous ships, about 225 smaller ones, and crew of more than 27,000 men. Traveling with his fleet was like moving a small city across the waters.

Zheng He and his men made their way around Vietnam, through the islands known today as Indonesia, and around the tip of India. They explored the Persian Gulf, reached the Red Sea, traded with the Arabs at Aden, and finally sailed south along the African coast at least as far as Zanzibar.

Everywhere they went, they dropped off Chinese wares and picked up local products for

This drawing illustrates the enormity of a Ming sailing ship as compared to a typical Portuguese vessel by its side.

scholars to study. Zheng He did not see these exchanges as trade but as bestowing gifts and accepting tribute to the Ming emperor. From his seven voyages, Zheng He brought back visitors or captives from dozens of countries. Many presented the emperor with exotic gifts such as ostriches, zebras, and giraffes.

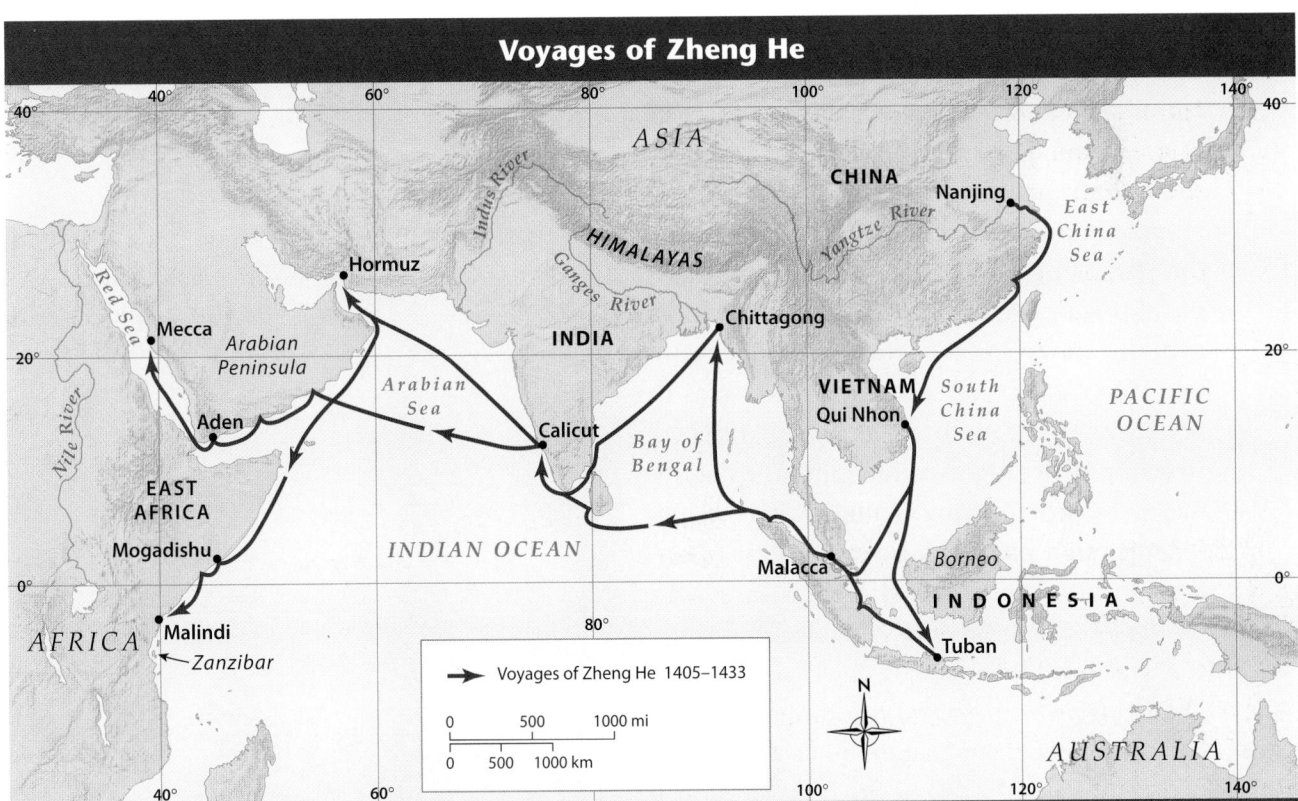

Zheng He, the grand admiral of the Chinese navy, led seven maritime expeditions during his career. His explorations dramatically expanded the commercial and political power of the Ming emperors.

Jesuits in China

European traders seeking access to China were followed by Jesuit missionaries, part of an energetic new Catholic order dedicated to spreading Christianity through education. The most influential missionary was an Italian Jesuit, Matteo Ricci (REET-chee). He arrived in China in 1582. The emperor's advisers recommended sending him home quickly, but Ricci won the emperor's favor by giving him an alarm clock, a gift that fascinated the childlike ruler.

Ricci was welcomed into the Forbidden City and permitted to discuss Christianity so long as he would also teach the Chinese about Western science. Ricci learned Chinese and not only translated Western works into Chinese but also translated Chinese classics into Latin.

A Return to Isolation

Zheng He mapped the places he visited, but when he returned from his seventh voyage, a new emperor sat on the throne. This ruler wanted to return to the closed ways of the first Ming emperor. Not only did he dismantle the fleet, he also had the navigational charts burned so no one could retrace Zheng He's journeys.

The Ming emperors turned increasingly inward. They decided that they did not need to explore faraway parts of the world. They came to distrust foreigners, whom they viewed as barbarians. Eventually they even banned the construction of oceangoing ships and forbade their merchants from leaving Chinese waters.

Although Zheng He's explorations offered opportunities for trade with the world, Ming rulers were not interested in trade. Their Confucian values led them to look down on merchants. The Hongwu emperor, who founded the Ming Dynasty, came from peasant stock and wanted to base his empire's prosperity on land and agriculture, not on trade. While China did sell silk and porcelain abroad during the Ming Dynasty,

it only accepted silver in exchange. The Chinese felt no need to buy or trade for any foreign products.

But traders from foreign countries did want Chinese goods, and they came in increasing numbers. When Europeans arrived to trade in the early 1500s, Ming officials only allowed them to dock in a few port cities, and refused to let them come inland. In 1514, a Portuguese ship docked at Guangzhou (gwahng-joh), which European traders called Canton. The Chinese called these rowdy Europeans "devils" but eventually allowed them to set up a trading post on the island of Macao (muh-KOW; also spelled *Macau*), not far from modern-day Hong Kong.

The Great Wall

In the mid-fifteenth century, in response to new Mongol raids in the north of China, Ming rulers undertook an old project with new vigor. They began to rebuild the Great Wall.

Back in the third century B.C., the Chinese had begun building walls to keep out invaders

The Ming rebuilt the Great Wall of China and its watchtowers to keep out Mongol invaders from the north.

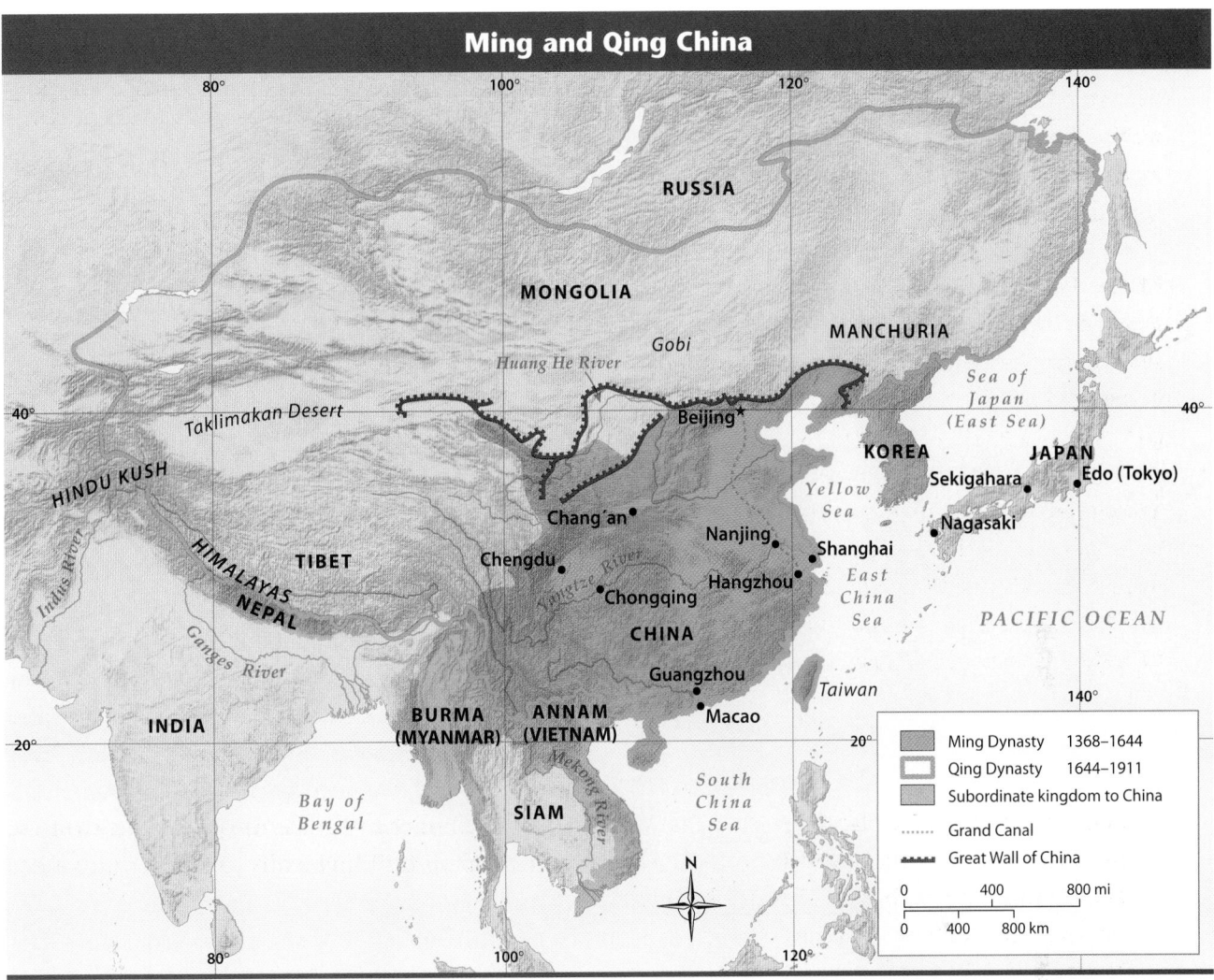

Ming and Qing China

China's final two dynasties expanded the empire and maintained power for more than five hundred years.

from the north. By the 1400s, many of these walls were in bad shape. When Mongols again threatened China's frontiers, the Ming decided to close the gaps in the Great Wall to make one continuous, impenetrable barrier against invasion from the north. They strengthened the old earthen structures with brick and granite, paved the top to support cavalry and cannons, and added watchtowers at regular intervals.

Ming rulers used countless thousands of laborers to strengthen and extend the Great Wall during their reign. Eventually the wall was some 1,500 miles (2,415 km) long, running inland from the Yellow Sea along China's vulnerable frontier. It was one of the greatest engineering feats ever undertaken.

While the Great Wall did keep the Mongols at bay, it also expressed a fundamental attitude of the Ming Dynasty—that China should be isolated, self-contained, and free from outside influences.

The Qing Dynasty

The Ming Dynasty sought to shut China off from outsiders, but by the mid-sixteenth century European traders were forcing their way into China at will, and Japanese pirates were raiding its coastal cities. The empire's northeastern borders were under attack from a new group of foreigners, the Manchu. Internally, Ming rulers tried to suppress angry peasants, who were rebelling against high taxes.

In 1644, an army of rebellious peasants seized Beijing. In desperation, the Ming emperor hanged

389

All the Tea in China

In the late 1600s, an English merchant imported a small shipment of Chinese tea. It made an immediate impression in England and quickly spread to the Americas. Over the next hundred years, English imports of Chinese tea rose to more than fifteen million pounds. Yet the Chinese still demanded silver as payment for their tea and bought virtually no products from Europe.

The Chinese grew more and more tea to satisfy increasing European and American demand.

himself. His leading general appealed to the Manchu for help. The Manchu sent troops, but promptly declared themselves China's rulers and proclaimed a new dynasty, the Qing (ching; meaning "pure"). As it turned out, the Qing would be China's last dynasty, ruling from 1644 until 1911.

Once the Qing secured full control, they began collecting all unpaid taxes. Even if a family owed as little as a small fraction of an ounce of silver, the Qing collected it. They wanted their subjects to know that the new government would not let anyone get away with anything.

Although the Qing were as foreign as the Mongols, they had been in contact with China for generations and had adopted many Chinese ways, including the Chinese writing system and Confucian values. The Qing continued using the traditional Chinese civil service exams to select government officials. Native-born Chinese were not allowed to serve in the military, but they could take the civil service exams to attain government jobs. By using China's traditional institutions to govern the country, roughly a million Manchu managed to control a nation of more than 150 million for more than two centuries.

The first four Qing emperors kept China peaceful and prosperous for about a century and a half. During these years, a great demand for Chinese tea developed in Russia, western Europe, and America. Europeans also imported porcelain, rugs, jewelry, silk, and furniture from China. Americans eagerly bought Chinese unbleached cotton. All these exports brought silver into the empire and funded improvements in agriculture.

In 1696, the Qing emperor Kangxi (kahng-shee) crushed the Mongols in a decisive battle that ended the Mongol threat to China forever and extended the empire into new territory. In fact, China reached its greatest extent under the Qing—even larger than the country's modern-day borders.

For all its prosperity and size, however, China was falling behind. In 1500, China had been ahead of Europe economically and technologically. But the Ming and Qing dynasties cut China off from the world just as Europeans were beginning to make great advances in science. In the nineteenth century, China would suffer for the isolationist policies of its final two dynasties.

Japan's Tokugawa Shogunate

The Chinese were not the only ones to turn inward. China's neighbor to the east, the island nation of Japan, also isolated itself in ways that would have long-lasting consequences.

Years of Disorder

You have learned that around the year 1000, Japan was a land divided among many different rulers. Medieval Japanese society was organized on the principles of feudalism—the system in which rulers grant land to those who pledge their loyalty and military service in return. At the top of the feudal structure stood the shogun, the military dictator, who granted parcels of land to local lords known as daimyo. The daimyo built castles on their land and pledged their political and military support to the shogun. The daimyos commanded their own private armies and often waged war with one another. To protect and control their territories, they called upon the services of the skilled professional warriors known as samurai.

For years the Japanese fended off attacks from the Mongols. Twice in the thirteenth century, Kublai Khan tried to conquer Japan, but the samurai held him off. Each time, sudden storms called *kamikaze* or "divine winds" destroyed the Mongol fleets.

Although an emperor continued to rule Japan in name, real power belonged to his military chieftain, the shogun—and even the shogun had little direct power. His might depended mainly on the number of daimyo allied to him, and since alliances kept shifting, the shogunate was passed back and forth among several powerful families. No one leader ruled the country for long. For many years, powerful warlords struggled for rule of Japan. Some managed to control particular areas, but none was ever able to dominate.

One especially violent period began around 1450 as peasants rose up against their landlords all across the islands. In this crisis, many samurai began demanding land in exchange for military service. When the fighting faded, there were no longer a few daimyos but many, most of them former

A pair of bronze figures depict fighting Japanese warriors called *samurai*.

Japanese warlords, or daimyos, built towering castles, like this one, and fought each other for control of the country.

samurai. These new warlords lived in hilltop castles that dominated just a few miles of surrounding countryside. Small towns emerged around these castles, as peasants flocked close for protection.

The Tokugawa Shogunate Unites Japan

In the mid-1500s, Europeans brought firearms to Japan. Those who took advantage of the new weapons overwhelmed those who didn't. By the early 1600s, one man vanquished all the other warlords. This fierce warrior and crafty politician came from the Tokugawa (toh-kou-GAH-wuh) family, and his name was Ieyasu (ee-yeh-yah-soo).

Tokugawa Ieyasu had himself appointed shogun and moved his headquarters to the castle town of Edo (AY-doh). In the years that followed, power passed to Ieyasu's descendants, thus forming a dynasty known as the Tokugawa Shogunate. The city of Edo would later become known as Tokyo, Japan's center of power. The Tokugawa Shogunate brought two hundred fifty years of stability to Japan.

Social Structure in Tokugawa Japan

Under the Tokugawa shoguns, local lords still ruled their own domains, but the Edo government ruled the lords with an iron hand. The Tokugawa shoguns organized Japanese society into a single chain of obedience and duty. Officially, the highest status belonged to the emperor, who was seen as the embodiment of the nation and a descendant of the gods. But the emperor's position was only ceremonial, with no real power.

The real power was in the hands of the Tokugawa shoguns. Legally, the shogun owned all the precious metal in the country and more than a quarter of the cultivated land. His spies kept close watch on the daimyos, who ranked just below the shogun.

To control the quarrelsome and often rebellious daimyos, Tokugawa shoguns required all daimyos to spend every other year at Edo. Once there, each daimyo had to send family members to the shogun's court, where they were held as hostages to ensure the daimyo's loyalty. Daimyos paid heavy taxes and also had to finance the building of the country's bridges, roads, and

Ieyasu united Japan under his rule, and founded the Tokugawa Shogunate.

other infrastructure out of their own pockets. Over time, these obligations weakened the daimyos while strengthening the shogun.

The samurai, who ranked just below daimyos, were restricted to military service. But during the period of the Tokugawa Shogunate, also known as the "Great Peace," the samurai had no way to earn a living. Masterless, out-of-work samurai, known as *ronin*, wandered in poverty, and sometimes attempted rebellion.

Although the Tokugawa government praised farmers as the foundation of society, most farmers were poor peasants who had to give up much of their harvest in taxes. Such heavy taxation sparked some two thousand peasant rebellions during the Tokugawa Shogunate, but all were quickly crushed.

Peace and Prosperity

Trade thrived during the peaceful years of the Tokugawa Shogunate. Japanese goods, such as cotton, silk, and tea, were in high demand. As trade increased, the Japanese increasingly used paper money, and prosperous banking houses were established. The flow of money enabled industries such as sword making and pottery to flourish. By the early 1700s, rich merchants enjoyed more importance than the once-powerful daimyos.

With the rise of the merchant class, hundreds of villages grew into bustling towns. Big cities like Osaka and Kyoto became sophisticated centers of art and entertainment. By 1800, Edo's population topped a million.

Culture in Tokugawa Japan

The newly rich families provided a growing market for art and entertainment. Urban audiences flocked to entertainments such as puppet plays, which featured masked operators manipulating life-sized puppets on stage. A lively new form of drama, called *Kabuki* (kuh-BOO-kee), was born in this era as well. Kabuki theater mixed highly stylized dramatic acting with singing, dancing, colorful costumes, and often sensational plots. Although a group of traveling women performers

A Kabuki actor wears an elaborate animal mask.

pioneered some Kabuki traditions, the government soon banned women from performing. To this day, Kabuki actors remain all male.

In Japan's Edo period, many people were literate, which created a wide readership for historical novels, ghost stories, and other popular fiction. Some of the new literature was more reflective. Poets such as Basho, for example, perfected *haiku* (HIY-koo), a highly compressed form of poetry. A haiku consists of only seventeen syllables divided into three lines. The first line has five syllables; the second, seven; and the third, five. A haiku captures a fleeting image, or a glimpse into a mood or emotion, as in this poem by Basho:

fu-ru-i-ke ya
ka-wa-zu to-bi-ko-mu
mi-zu no o-to

Or, translated into English:

old pond...
a frog jumps in
water's sound

393

European merchants, like these Portuguese, sailed to Japan to sell their goods in return for gold and silver.

A Return to Isolation

Shortly before the beginning of the Tokugawa Shogunate, European traders and missionaries made their way to Japan. In 1543, a Portuguese ship bound for China ran aground in Japan. The people of the island saw the sailors shooting at birds and immediately offered to buy their guns, devices they had never seen. Since the islands had plenty of gold and silver, other European merchants—Portuguese, Spanish, and finally Dutch—flocked to the islands to sell not just firearms but fabrics, glassware, clocks, tobacco, and other goods.

Among the European merchants and navigators who journeyed to Japan was the Englishman William Adams. Arriving in the islands in 1600 as the captain of a Dutch ship, Adams impressed the shogun Ieyasu and became his tutor. He taught the shogun mathematics, gunnery, and cartography, and received huge estates in return.

Cartography is the practice of mapmaking.

As in China, Jesuit missionaries followed traders into Japan. By 1600, some three hundred

thousand Japanese Christians were worshipping at two hundred churches. Tokugawa rulers grew alarmed at the number of Japanese people converting to Christianity. The shogun feared that Christianity might undermine Japanese culture and traditions. He also feared that European nations might someday threaten his rule.

In 1614, Tokugawa Ieyasu ordered all daimyos to renounce Christianity. The shogun went on to ban all trade with Europeans except through the heavily controlled port of Nagasaki. Japanese ships were forbidden to sail abroad.

These restrictions soon turned to persecutions. Christians in Japan were imprisoned—even tortured—and sometimes executed in groups. Thousands of Christians lost their lives in these persecutions.

In 1624, the Tokugawa government expelled the Spanish. Later, heavy restrictions were placed on the Portuguese and other Europeans, until at last only the Dutch remained, and they were not allowed outside Nagasaki.

In the 1630s, a new set of regulations prohibited Japanese people from leaving the country, and if they did leave, they could not come back. In 1637, Christian samurai and peasants rebelled. The Tokugawa government called in the Dutch to bombard the rebels from their ships. The brutal measures helped end Christian influence in Japan.

Even though they shut the Europeans out of their country, the Japanese were eager to keep up with European advances in science and technology. Scholars of "Dutch learning," as Western culture was called, translated manuals about gunnery, surveying, anatomy, medicine, cartography, astronomy, and other practical subjects. Still, by the late 1630s, the Tokugawa had closed Japan's borders to all but a handful of foreign traders.

Like its great neighbor China on the Asian mainland, the island nation of Japan turned its back on much of the outside world. In their isolation, the Japanese became a people devoted to nurturing all that was, in their view, most essentially and uniquely Japanese.

The Closing of Japan

Early in the seventeenth century, the Tokugawa Shogunate began to suspect that European powers might eventually try to control Japan. So Japan's rulers took steps to end all missionary efforts and restrict the movement of foreigners visiting Japan. The following excerpts are from a Japanese law known as the Act of Seclusion of 1636.

Japanese ships shall by no means be sent abroad.

No Japanese shall be sent abroad. Anyone violating this prohibition shall suffer the penalty of death, and the ship owner and crew shall be held up together with the ship.

All Japanese residing abroad shall be put to death when they return home.

All Christians shall be examined by official examiners.

Informers against Christians shall be rewarded.

The arrival of foreign ships must be reported...and watch kept over them.

The Namban people [Spaniards or Portuguese] and any other people... propagating Christianity shall be incarcerated in the Omura prison as before.

Everything shall be done in order to see that no Christian is survived by descendants, and anyone disregarding this injunction shall be put to death, while proper punishment shall be meted out to the other members of his family according to their deeds.

Children born of the Namban people [Spaniards or Portuguese] in Nagasaki and people adopting these Namban children into their family shall be put to death; capital punishment shall also be meted out to those Namban descendants if they return to Japan, and their relatives in Japan, who may communicate with them, shall receive suitable punishment.

The samurai shall not purchase goods on board foreign ships directly from foreigners.

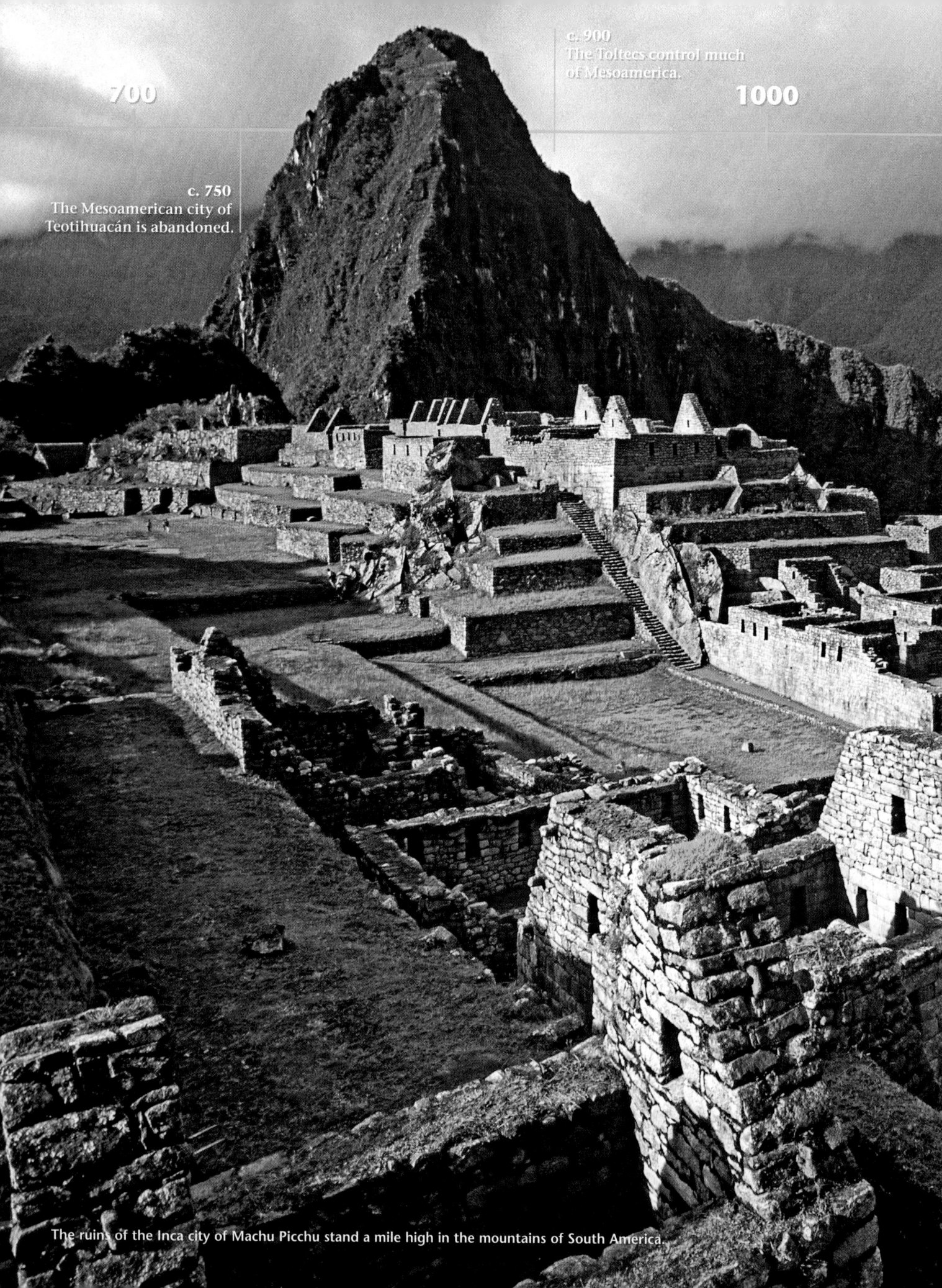

700

c. 750
The Mesoamerican city of
Teotihuacán is abandoned.

c. 900
The Toltecs control much
of Mesoamerica.

1000

The ruins of the Inca city of Machu Picchu stand a mile high in the mountains of South America.

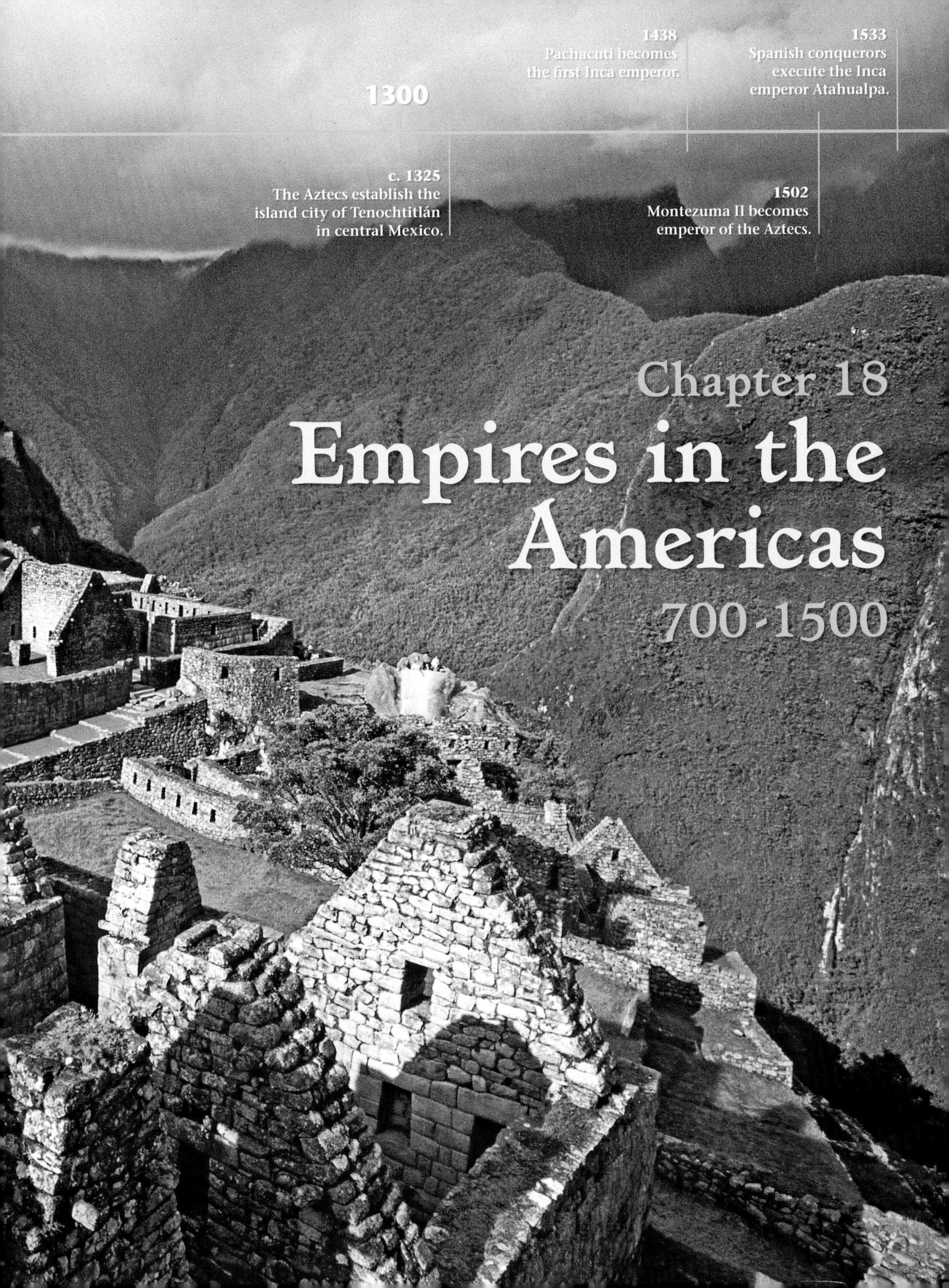

1438
Pachacuti becomes
the first Inca emperor.

1533
Spanish conquerors
execute the Inca
emperor Atahualpa.

1300

c. 1325
The Aztecs establish the
island city of Tenochtitlán
in central Mexico.

1502
Montezuma II becomes
emperor of the Aztecs.

Chapter 18
Empires in the Americas
700-1500

*B*eginning about the year 1200, two great civilizations rose to dominance in the Americas. The Aztecs established a large empire in Mexico. In South America, the Inca ruled a vast realm centered on the Andes Mountains that stretched from Ecuador to Chile.

Both the Aztecs and the Inca built magnificent cities and produced elaborate works of art. Both evolved advanced systems of government that enabled them to rule extensive territories made up of many different peoples. Then, in the early 1500s, both American empires were overthrown by invaders from Spain.

Mesoamerica's Aztec Empire

Key Questions

- What early Mesoamerican societies rose in the Valley of Mexico?

- What were the major characteristics of the Aztec society and economy?

- What role did religion play in the culture and demise of Aztec civilization?

You have read about some of the earliest civilizations in Mesoamerica, the region that includes much of Mexico and Central America. There, the Olmec flourished between 1200 and 400 B.C., and the Maya developed an advanced civilization that thrived from about A.D. 250 to 900.

The Mesoamerican civilization of the Aztecs arose in what is now central Mexico, on a high plateau where Mexico City is located today. This region, called the Valley of Mexico, centered on a series of large freshwater lakes, which swarmed with fish in Aztec times. Although located at a tropical latitude, the area's climate is mild thanks to its high altitude. Two towering volcanoes look down on the valley. When the Aztecs erected stone pyramids to honor their gods, the buildings mimicked the shape of the neighboring volcanoes.

The City of Teotihuacán

Prior to the Aztecs, between the years 150 and 750, an advanced civilization developed in the Valley of Mexico, with its center at the city called Teotihuacán, located northeast of present-day Mexico City. Around A.D. 500, at the height of its power and influence, Teotihuacán was one of the largest cities on earth. Today the well-preserved ruins of Teotihuacán make up one of the most visited archaeological sites in the Americas.

Towering over the remains of the city is a building more than two hundred feet (61 m) tall known as the Pyramid of the Sun. Like other pyramids of ancient Mexico, it has a flat top designed to serve as the base for a temple, where priests worshipped and performed sacrifices to the gods.

Most people in Teotihuacán lived in apartment buildings. The wealthy enjoyed large apartments lavishly decorated with wall paintings, while the poor survived in small, cramped rooms. The apartment buildings were connected to each other, and to the city's temples and pyramids, by streets carefully laid out in a grid pattern. The wide main street, called the Avenue of the Dead, ran for two miles (3.2 km) through the center of the city.

Teotihuacán's temples attracted religious pilgrims from as far away as today's Guatemala. The city was also a center of manufacturing and trade. Its exports included many objects, including tools and weapons made out of obsidian, a dark volcanic glass.

Around the year 750, Teotihuacán was burned, probably by invading enemies. The city never recovered its former power and influence. But hundreds of years later, its ruins so impressed the Aztecs that they gave the city the name we know it by, Teotihuacán, meaning the "Place of the Gods."

The Aztec empire stretched across central and southern Mexico.

399

The Toltec

About a century and a half after the decline of Teotihuacán, a people called the Toltec rose to power in central Mexico. The Toltec conquered and enslaved their neighbors, and practiced the cruel custom of human sacrifice. The militaristic spirit of the people is clearly visible in their art. For example, they made gigantic statues of grim-faced warriors and carved figures of eagles—the symbol of one group of Toltec warriors—devouring human hearts.

The Toltec worshipped a number of gods. One of the most important was *Quetzalcoatl* (KET-suhl-koh-AH-tl), the "Feathered Serpent." According to Toltec mythology, this deity demanded the sacrifice of birds, snakes, and butterflies, but not of human beings. The Toltec believed that when a more bloodthirsty god drove Quetzalcoatl out of the land, he sailed across the ocean on a raft made of snakes. According to legend, he would eventually return by way of the sea.

In the 1100s, the pressure of constant warfare, perhaps in combination with natural disasters such as drought and famine, led to the decline of the Toltec. The people abandoned their capital city and migrated in different directions. One group moved south to the Yucatán Peninsula, the center of the brilliant Mayan civilization. The Toltec intermingled with the Maya, bringing a more warlike spirit to that ancient culture.

The Rise of Aztec Society

In the mid-1200s, a new group migrated south to the Valley of Mexico. They called themselves the Mexica—the origin of the name *Mexico*. But we know them today as the Aztecs, after Aztlan, the name of their legendary homeland.

The warlike Aztecs at first inspired fear and hatred among the farmers and city people of the valley. Everywhere they tried to settle, their neighbors drove them off. Finally they took refuge on a deserted island in the middle of a lake, where they subsisted on fish and waterfowl.

According to Aztec legend, the war god told the people to settle in a place where they saw an

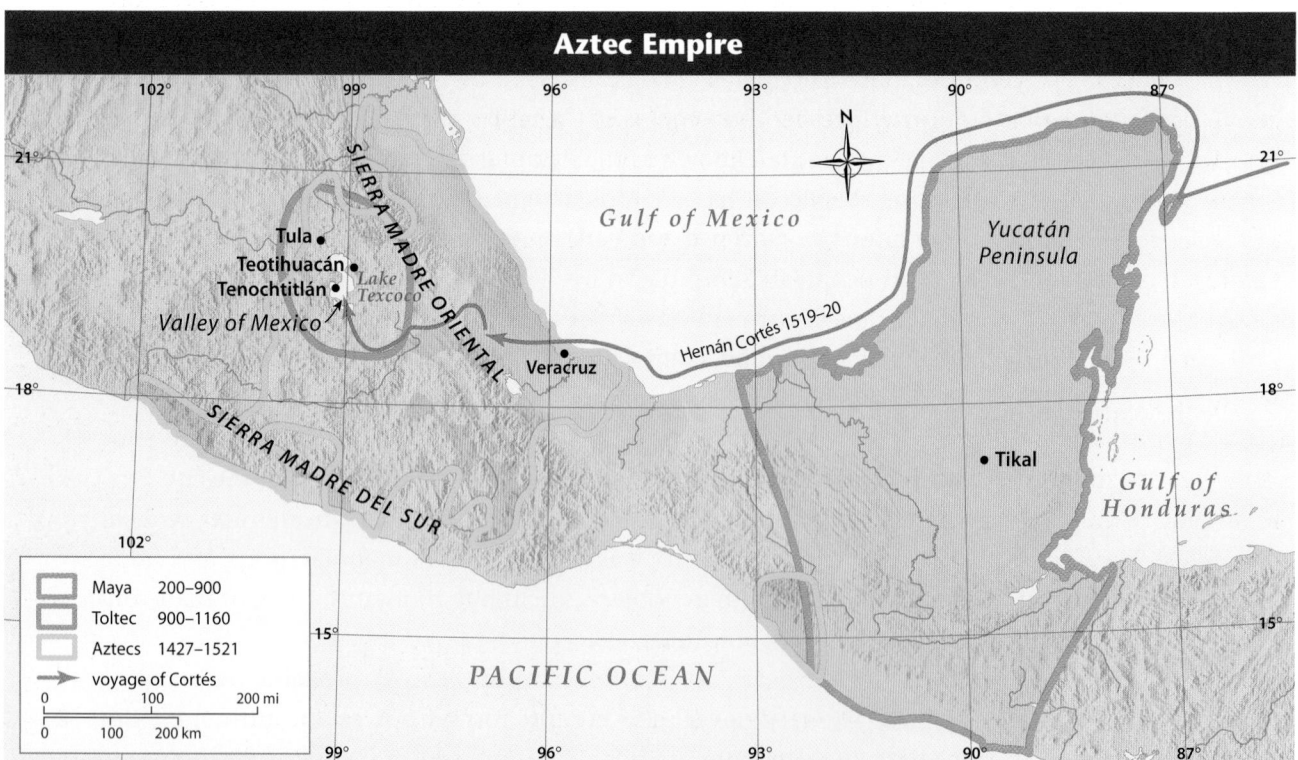

For about a century, the Aztecs ruled an empire in the Valley of Mexico, lined by the Sierra Madre mountain system (with the Sierra Madre Oriental to the east, and the Sierra Madre del Sur to the south).

This detail from a mural by the twentieth-century Mexican artist Diego Rivera depicts Tenochtitlán with its bustling markets and long causeways.

eagle devouring a snake. One day, says the legend, an eagle with a snake in its mouth descended on the barren island and perched atop a cactus. The people took this as a sign that the island, which they named *Tenochtitlán* (tay-nawch-teet-LAHN)—meaning the "Place of the Cactus Fruit"—should be the center of their new homeland.

Over the next two centuries, the Aztecs managed to turn their island home into a great city. They dredged mud from the bottom of the lake to increase the size of the island. They built dikes to prevent flooding and long causeways (bridges of earth) to connect Tenochtitlán to other islands and to the mainland.

To feed the growing population, the Aztecs developed an ingenious system of floating gardens. With mud from the lake and vegetation from nearby swamps, the Aztecs constructed small, rectangular islands in the water. Using human waste as fertilizer, farmers could grow large quantities of staple crops—corn, squash, and beans—on these small artificial islands.

By the year 1500, the population of Tenochtitlán stood at 150,000–200,000, making it one of the largest cities in the world at the time. Tenochtitlán had grown into a wealthy metropolis, crisscrossed by canals like those of Venice in Italy. Stone houses

and temples lined the streets and canals. In an expansive central marketplace, tens of thousands of people gathered to barter their wares—from building materials to jewelry to food. In a nearby plaza loomed the Great Temple, a pyramid dedicated to the gods of war and rain. The temple was said to have been built on the very spot where the eagle had perched on the cactus.

The Aztec Empire

Always short of resources on their island home, the Aztecs filled their needs by conquering some of their neighbors and forcing others into alliances. In time, Tenochtitlán became the capital of an empire encompassing some 80,000 square miles (207,200 square km) of central Mexico.

From their subject peoples, the Aztecs demanded tribute. Sometimes this tribute took the form of goods, such as crops or precious metals. Sometimes it took the form of service—for example, non-Aztecs were made to fight in Aztec armies or build the palaces and temples of Tenochtitlán.

At the top of Aztec society was the emperor, who enjoyed nearly absolute power. His vast

At the heart of Tenochtitlán lay the central plaza and the huge pyramid known as the Great Temple.

401

palace in the capital included bathing pools, sculpture gardens, and a private zoo. Despite this luxury, the emperor was expected to serve as an example to the people and lead his warriors in battle.

Beneath the emperor came the large group of noblemen who held high positions in government. Unlike the hereditary aristocracy of Europe (in which titles and positions were kept within a family, passed down from one generation to the next), the Aztec nobility was open to commoners who had distinguished themselves in battle.

Priests made up an especially powerful class of Aztec society. Thousands of priests were assigned to Tenochtitlán's Great Temple alone. Like the priests of Europe, Aztec priests were the best educated group in their society.

Merchants made up another distinct class. Less respected than the nobility, they lived in a separate part of the capital and worshipped their own special deities.

The majority of Aztecs belonged to the class of commoners that included farmers, laborers, and craftsmen. At the bottom of Aztec society came the slaves, many of whom were criminals or prisoners of war. Some slaves served for only a limited time, often to pay off a debt.

The Aztecs achieved a high degree of civilization. Their system of writing used pictures and images to represent things and ideas. Aztec historians recorded the past through pictures in vividly illustrated books. Their sculptors carved elaborate calendars out of stone, both to keep track of months and seasons and to predict the future in light of Aztec mythology. Aztec medical practices were at least as advanced as those in Europe at the same time. Aztec doctors set broken bones, filled cavities in teeth, and performed some kinds of surgery.

The Fierce Aztec Religion

The religion of the Aztecs demanded the sacrifice of human beings as offerings to the gods. Other peoples, both in Mexico and elsewhere, had performed human sacrifice, but never on the horrific scale practiced by the Aztecs. For example, during one four-day religious festival in the year 1487, the Aztecs sacrificed more than twenty thousand human victims.

The Aztecs believed their gods survived on a diet of human blood. They feared, for example, that if the rain god went unfed, the land would dry up and the people would starve. Aztecs offered a portion of their own blood to the gods, by shoving sharp thorns into their legs, arms, or tongues.

The most potent form of offering, however, was human sacrifice, usually practiced on captured warriors. While the Aztecs believed that ritual sacrifice fed the gods and preserved the order of the universe, it filled their subject peoples of the empire with dread and anguish.

Captives were put to death in a number of gruesome ways, including decapitation, drowning, and strangulation. In the most spectacular form of sacrifice, a victim was dragged to the top of a temple and stretched on a stone altar. A priest then plunged a stone knife into the victim's chest, ripped out his still-beating heart, and held it high as an offering to the sun god.

An Aztec stone calendar, carved in 1479 and nearly twelve feet (3.6 m) in diameter, depicts Aztec gods, with the sun god at center.

The Aztec emperor Montezuma II presides over his council.

Decline of the Aztec Empire

In the year 1502, a new emperor, Montezuma II, came to the throne. (His name is also spelled *Moctezuma*.) The Aztecs considered him a wise and honorable ruler. But by leading new wars of conquest and demanding ever more tribute from conquered groups, Montezuma made many more people look on the Aztecs with bitterness and hatred.

The growing ranks of enemies of the Aztecs acquired a powerful ally in the year 1519, when some five hundred Spanish soldiers landed on the Caribbean coast of Mexico. Their leader, Hernán Cortés (her-NAHN kor-TEZ), intended to claim the country in the name of Spain. He also wanted to enrich his own coffers, since the land was rumored to be full of gold. As Cortés marched his men toward Tenochtitlán, they were joined by many warriors from the peoples subject to the Aztecs, who saw in the arrival of the newcomers a hope of liberation. By the time he reached the city, Cortés was leading an army of six thousand.

The Aztecs were alarmed by the sight of Spanish soldiers wearing metal armor and riding horses, creatures they had never seen before. Some

believed that Cortés himself was the embodiment of the god Quetzalcoatl, the "feathered serpent" that, according to Toltec legend, had fled across the ocean. Stories had foretold the return of Quetzalcoatl in the form of a white-skinned, black-bearded man, like Cortés.

Within about a year, with the help of native allies and advanced European weapons, including cannons, the Spaniards conquered the Aztecs. The fallen Aztec empire became the Spanish colony of New Spain. But the legacy of the Aztecs lived on. Today's Mexico City, the sprawling capital of the modern nation, is built on the site of Tenochtitlán. The national flag of Mexico depicts an eagle perched on a cactus, holding a writhing serpent in its mouth.

Monsters with Six Legs

Fossil evidence suggests that many thousands of years ago, the animal we call the horse roamed wild in lands on both sides of the Atlantic Ocean. But some time between 8000 and 6000 B.C., the species became extinct in the Americas, perhaps because people hunted it for food rather than using it for farming and transport. Horses were not seen again in the Americas until they accompanied Spanish conquerors in the early 1500s. Some startled Aztecs at first thought that each mounted Spanish soldier was a monstrous two-headed creature with six legs.

Spanish warriors on horseback awed the Aztecs.

403

The Empire of the Inca

In the 1400s, as the Aztecs were conquering their neighbors in Mexico, another great empire developed thousands of miles to the south, in the Andes Mountains on the western edge of the South American continent. Arising in what is now Peru, the Inca Empire would eventually stretch from Colombia to Chile, a distance of some 2,500 miles (4,023 km).

The Andes are the longest and one of the highest mountain ranges in the world. Located between the equator and the Antarctic, the Andes region enjoys a relatively mild climate. Rivers cut fertile valleys through the mountains. Before the Inca rose to power, people had lived in the Andes region for hundreds of years, farming the land and fishing the seas.

A Capital at Cuzco

Some time around the year 1200, the Inca founded their capital city of Cuzco (KOOS-koh), locating it in a mountain valley about eleven thousand feet (3,353 m) above sea level. The construction of the city was a remarkable feat of engineering. Hundreds of workers, using llamas as pack animals, hauled stones up steep slopes to build walls for agricultural terraces. Other workers constructed roads and houses out of stone.

Over the next two centuries, the Inca gradually expanded their territory by conquering the lands of their neighbors. The Inca military conquests, like their building projects, relied on strong, centralized leadership.

The ruler, known as the *Sapa Inca* ("unique chief"), held ultimate authority. His people revered him as a divinity, a descendant of the sun

Key Questions

- How were the Inca able to maintain a large empire?
- How were the early civilizations of the Americas similar? How did they differ?

At its peak, the Inca Empire stretched nearly the entire length of South America.

Much of the complex stonework of the Inca capital city of Cuzco still stands today.

Inca gold figurine

god. Beneath the ruler, a class of government officials were charged with collecting taxes, assigning work, and overseeing the construction of buildings and roads. Like the position of the Sapa Inca, these government jobs were handed down from father to son.

Building a Mountain Empire

In the early 1400s, according to Inca chroniclers, an enemy people called the Chanca tried to conquer Cuzco. As the Chanca army approached the city, the elderly Sapa Inca fled in fear. He left the city's defenses in the hands of his younger son, Cusi Yupanqui (KOO-see yoo-PAHN-kee). Donning the skin of a puma—a wild cat respected by the Inca for its ferocity—Cusi Yupanqui led the Inca into battle and forced the Chanca to retreat. Inca legends later reported that the stones on the battlefield had magically turned into warriors who fought on the side of the Inca.

After saving Cuzco, Cusi Yupanqui deposed his father and declared himself the Sapa Inca. Taking the name *Pachacuti* (meaning "earthquake" or "cataclysm"), the ambitious young ruler set out to transform the kingdom of the Inca into an empire. Pachacuti had inherited a well-organized army. He increased its size by forcing the defeated Chanca to provide him with warriors. With this augmented force, he seized the lands of neighboring peoples both to the north and to the south.

Pachacuti knit his growing empire together through a combination of cruelty and diplomacy. Conquered groups who refused to submit were slaughtered. Those who submitted to the Inca were allowed to keep their own local leaders and continue worshipping their own gods.

Pachacuti brought the sons of local leaders to Cuzco to be educated in Inca ways—but also to be held as hostages if their fathers should rebel. He

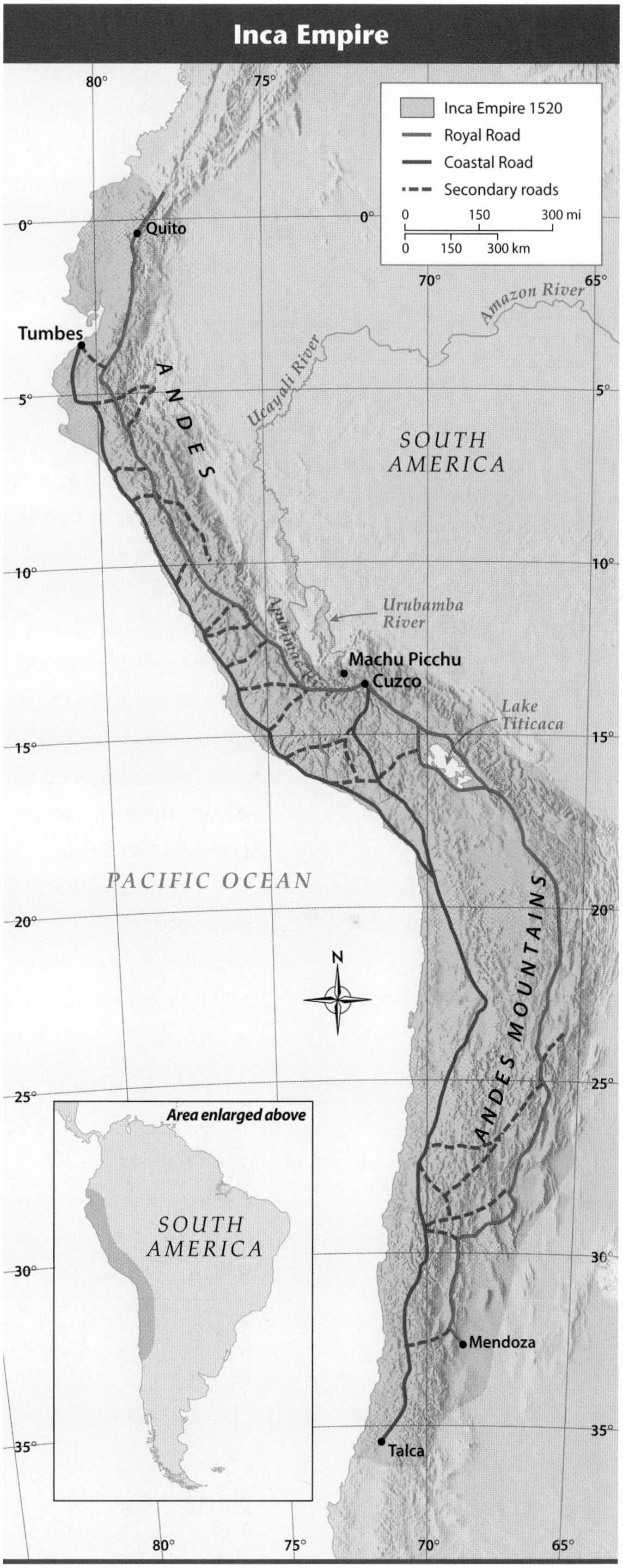

Inca Empire

Legend:
- Inca Empire 1520
- Royal Road
- Coastal Road
- --- Secondary roads

0   150   300 mi
0   150   300 km

SOUTH AMERICA

PACIFIC OCEAN

Cities and features: Quito, Tumbes, Machu Picchu, Cuzco, Mendoza, Talca, Lake Titicaca, Amazon River, Ucayali River, Urubamba River, Apurímac River, ANDES MOUNTAINS

Area enlarged above

SOUTH AMERICA

The Inca Empire united more than twelve million subjects along a 2,500-mile expanse of the Andes Mountains.

405

divided the empire into four regions, each with its own administration. This ensured that Cuzco lay at the intersection of all four and maintained the supreme authority of the Sapa Inca.

Pachacuti's son and heir came to the throne in 1471 and greatly expanded the empire, pushing it north as far as present-day Colombia and south into central Chile. Under his rule, the Inca empire reached its greatest extent, including almost the whole of the Andes as well as the Pacific coast of South America.

Unifying the Empire

The Inca ruled over millions of people of diverse origins who spoke many different languages. To strengthen their grip on power, the Incas imposed their language, Quechua (KECH-wuh), as the one official language of the realm. Because all government business was conducted in Quechua, its use spread throughout the empire. As a result, even today, centuries after Spanish became the main language of South America, millions of people from Ecuador to Chile still speak Quechua.

To further tie the empire together, Inca rulers sponsored the building of more than 15,000 miles (24,140 km) of roads. These roads ran up and down the towering peaks of the Andes. In places, stairways ascended the steep hillsides, and bridges—some made only of rope—crossed deep gorges cut by mountain rivers. Along the roads were inns to house travelers, and storehouses of grain to feed the emperor's troops.

The Inca lacked knowledge of the wheel, and unlike Europeans they had no horses to speed transportation. So to communicate across long distances they relied on the swiftness and stamina of specially trained runners called *chasquis* (CHAHS-keez), who lived in huts erected along the roads. Running in relays, the chasquis could deliver news from the far corners of the empire to Cuzco within a few days.

The Inca Economy

The Inca had no currency, so all trade was by barter. At markets, people exchanged one item for another. For example, they might trade clothing for food, pottery for jewelry, and so on.

For purposes of taxation, Inca rulers divided the population into clan groups of ten households each. Every clan group owed one-third of what it produced to the Sapa Inca and one-third to the priests for sacrifices and religious festivals. This meant that farmers, who made up the majority of the emperor's subjects, gave the government

Record Keeping with Quipu

The Inca had no written language. To maintain the records of their empire, they relied instead on *quipu* (KEE-poo; also spelled *khipu*), a word meaning "knots." Each quipu consisted of a cord with colored strings attached to it, with small knots tied in the strings. A quipu might be anywhere from a few inches to ten feet long. The larger the quipu, the more information it conveyed. The color of a particular string indicated information recorded—for example, a green string might indicate a number of soldiers, while a red one showed the size of a crop yield. The actual numbers were shown by the number of knots in the string. It required special training to make or read the quipu, and the knowledge was passed down from father to son.

A knotted Inca quipu

Primary Source

Inca Roads

In the sixteenth century, the Inca had the world's finest system of roads. Two parallel roadways, each more than 2,000 miles long, ran north to south. The roads were open to the general population, and most of their everyday traffic consisted of people on foot, often with their llamas. When the Spanish arrived, there were more than 15,000 miles of road in the network. The following description was written by Agustín de Zárate, a Spanish financial official who traveled in the Inca empire in the mid-1500s. (He refers to a now obsolete unit of distance, the league, the length of which varied in local usage. In this case, a league was probably about 2.6 miles [4.2 km].)

The road was made over the mountains for a distance of five hundred leagues. It was broad and level, rocks were broken up and leveled where it was necessary, and ravines were filled up. When the road was finished it was so level that carts might have passed along it. The difficulty of this road will be understood when it is considered how great the cost and labor has been in leveling two leagues of hilly country in Spain,… which has never yet been completely done, although it is the route by which the Kings of Castille continually pass, with their households and their court, every time they go to or come from Andalusia.

The stone remains of an Inca road

two-thirds of their harvest and kept the remaining third to feed themselves.

In addition, the government imposed a tax in the form of required labor. Every head of a household had to work for the government for a certain period each year. The work might include fighting in the army, mining gold or silver, or building roads, bridges, or temples. Within each clan group, only one head of household could be called into service at a time, which left nine others to support the group. Through this system, the Inca rulers acquired a massive pool of labor without disrupting the clans that formed the basic units of society.

Making Chuno

Potatoes were a mainstay of the Inca diet. In winter, families used potatoes to make *chuno*, a staple food since pre-Incan times. Chuno was made by leaving thin slices of moistened potato outside on cold nights. The potatoes would freeze at night, then thaw during the day. Eventually all the water in the potatoes would evaporate, leaving a dry food that resisted spoiling.

Gold and Grandeur

Today, the most impressive remains of the ancient Inca civilization are the massive stone buildings scattered around the Andean region. Inca stone-masons showed extraordinary skill in working with large stones. Using bronze chisels or the edges of other stones, they ground down the edges of stones until they fit together so tightly that not even a knife blade could pass between them. Some of the stones in a fortress at Cuzco stand over thirteen feet (4 m) tall and weigh more than two hundred tons (181 metic tons). Moving such stones must have required thousands of workers.

The most famous of all Inca ruins is the large complex of buildings at Machu Picchu (mah-choo PEE-choo), located more than a mile (1.6 km) high in the Andes, and about fifty miles (80 km) from Cuzco. Towering peaks and deep valleys surround the site, which protected its Inca inhabitants from enemies. Most archaeologists believe that Machu Picchu was built as a summer home for the Sapa Inca, perhaps by the first emperor, Pachacuti. More than a hundred steep staircases ascend the hillsides, connecting houses, temples, storage rooms, and palaces.

The massive stone monuments of Cuzco and Machu Picchu declared the glory of the Sapa Inca. So did the extraordinarily luxurious way the emperor lived and

Inca gold llama figure

dressed. He ate off gold dishes and arrayed himself with gold jewelry. Even his sandals were made of the precious metal. The Sapa Inca's use of gold—which the Inca called "the sweat of the sun"—symbolized his status as a descendant of the sun god. The Inca acquired gold by mining and by panning in streams. Although gold was abundant in the region that is now Peru, Inca rulers restricted its possession to the emperor and the nobility.

Because the Inca considered their emperor divine, they believed that, like a god, he could not truly die. Therefore, on his death a Sapa Inca was not buried but mummified, like a pharaoh of ancient Egypt. Instead of being placed in a tomb,

Stone steps lead to one of the ruined temples of Machu Picchu, the mountain city of the Inca.

Inca ruler Atahualpa bravely battled the invading Spanish forces but was overpowered and went down in defeat.

the forces of Atahualpa defeated those of his brother. But Atahualpa had little time to enjoy his victory. Within months, he was battling an invading force of Spanish soldiers, led by Francisco Pizarro, who intended to claim Peru in the name of Spain. The Inca Empire, which had been weakened by civil war, was ravaged by smallpox, a deadly disease that had traveled with the Spanish.

Disease, disorganization, and superior European weaponry soon destroyed Inca resistance. In 1533, the Spanish executed the captured Atahualpa. Little more than a decade after Cortés's conquest of Mexico, Spain had overthrown a second mighty empire in the Americas.

he remained in his palace, where his servants continued to wait on his preserved and richly dressed corpse.

Division and Decline

At the beginning of the 1500s, the Inca Empire was ruled by Huayna Capac (WIY-nah KAH-pahk), the grandson of Pachacuti. Like his grandfather, Huayna Capac was respected as a brave warrior and a wise leader. But he died suddenly in 1527, without naming an heir. Two of his sons, Atahualpa (ah-tah-WAHL-pah) and Huascar (WAHS-kahr), both claimed the kingship. War broke out between the supporters of the two princes.

The civil war lasted five years. Finally, in 1532, in a great battle fought outside Cuzco,

Hiram Bingham and Machu Picchu

At the beginning of the twentieth century, Hiram Bingham, an American archaeologist, heard rumors of a "lost city of the Incas" perched high in the Andes. In July 1911, he led an expedition to find it. In search of the city, Bingham and his group fought their way through dense jungle and clambered up tall cliffs. Finally, almost by accident, they stumbled on the ruins of Machu Picchu. "I could scarcely believe my senses," Bingham wrote. "Would anyone believe what I had found?" Bingham's accounts of Machu Picchu introduced the world to the wonders of Inca civilization.

409

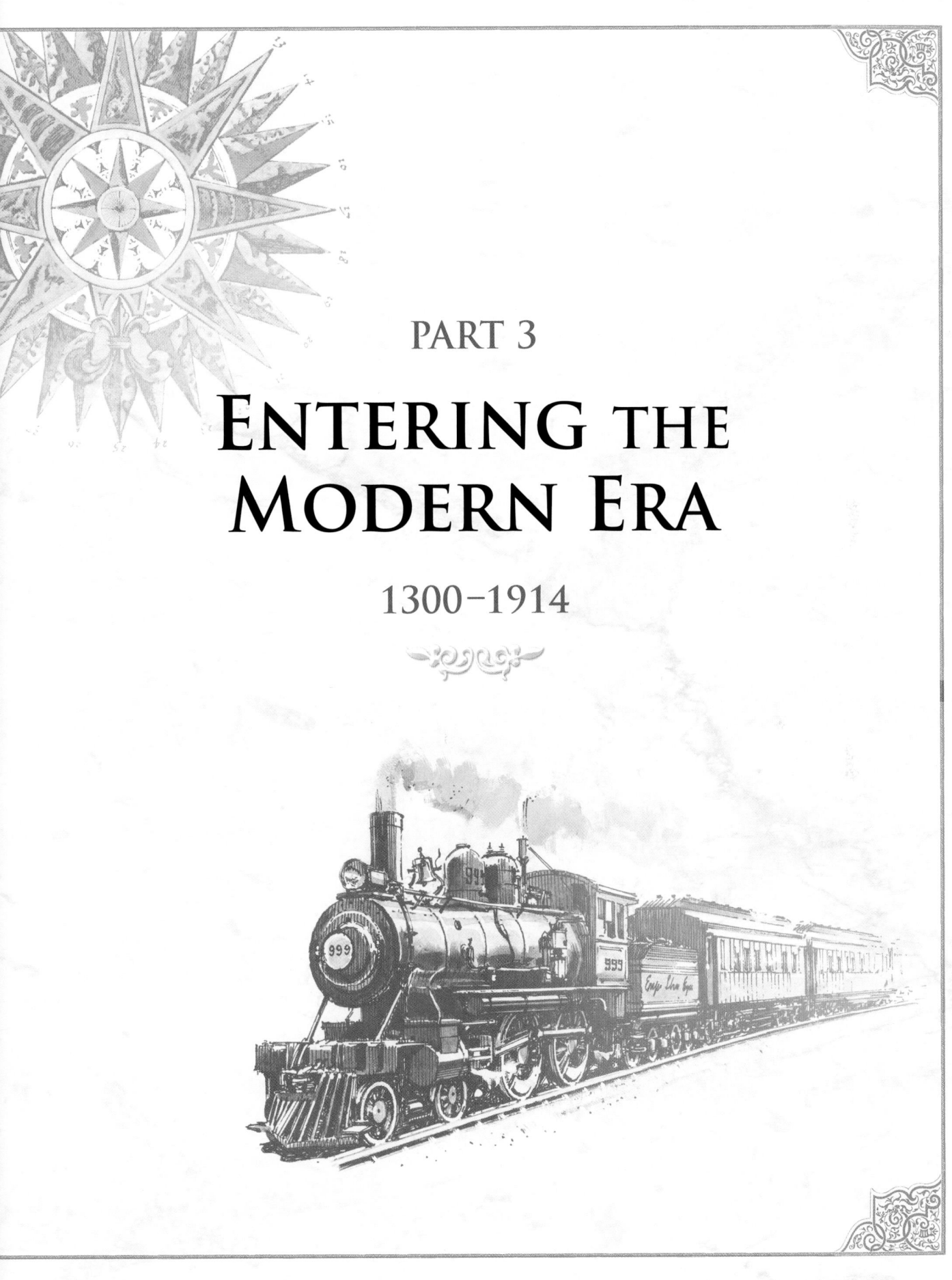

PART 3

ENTERING THE MODERN ERA

1300–1914

1300

1400

1304
Petrarch, the father of humanism, is born in Italy.

1321
Dante completes *The Divine Comedy.*

The Journey of the Magi to Bethlehem by Italian Renaissance artist Benozzo Gozzoli, 1459

c. 1455
The first Gutenberg Bibles
are printed in Germany.

1513
In *The Prince*,
Machiavelli tells rulers
how to maintain power.

1500

1600

c. 1500
Leonardo da Vinci and
Michelangelo produce masterpieces
of painting and sculpture.

c. 1600
In England, William
Shakespeare writes the great
tragedy *Hamlet*.

Chapter 19
The Renaissance in Europe
1300–1600

The Renaissance was a three-hundred-year period of tremendous cultural achievement in Europe, characterized by renewed interest in ancient Greek and Roman civilization and the new philosophy of humanism. Renaissance humanism celebrated human ability and potential, and helped inspire remarkable accomplishments in art, architecture, and literature.

The Renaissance began in Italy in the late fourteenth century, where, after the decline of the plague, city-states prospered through revived trade. Byzantine and Muslim ideas and learning made their way to the Italian city-states. The revival of trade brought a level of economic prosperity that inspired many wealthy people to support artists and writers.

Trade, warfare, and religious interactions helped spread Renaissance ideas to northern Europe and throughout western Europe. In the fifteenth century, the invention of the printing press accelerated the spread of ideas and learning.

A Renaissance in Italy

Renaissance, the French word for "rebirth," denotes a period of extraordinary enterprise and creativity in the history of Europe, from the late 1300s to the early 1600s. People living in those centuries did not call their own age "the Renaissance." Historians writing hundreds of years later coined the term as they looked back and saw how dramatically Europe had changed during that time.

What was "reborn" during the Renaissance? A revival of interest in the classical civilizations of Greece and Rome led people to learn and create in new ways. From something old, something new was born. But this newness did not happen all at once.

From Medieval to Renaissance

Momentum toward new ways of thinking and creating had been building throughout the 1300s. We can see the transition from medieval to Renaissance ways of thought in the lives and work of three brilliant individuals who lived in Italy during the fourteenth century—two writers, Dante and Petrarch (PEH-trahrk), and a painter, Giotto (JAWT-toh). Their work bridged the medieval and modern worlds, pointing back to what was old and forward to something new.

Dante's Divine Comedy

In an earlier chapter, you met the poet Dante Alighieri, from the Italian city-state of Florence. Dante wrote his great poem, *The Divine Comedy*, not in Latin but in the vernacular, the language used in daily life. For Dante, this language was the Italian of his native Florence.

The Divine Comedy tells the story of an imagined spiritual journey from hell to heaven. In it, Dante merges his Christian beliefs with his classical learning. Dante had studied not only Christian thinkers but also ancient Roman writers, including Virgil. Virgil's great epic, the *Aeneid*, was written in the first century B.C., and told of the legendary founding of Rome. Dante linked himself to the classical past by introducing Virgil as a character in *The Divine Comedy*.

In the *Inferno*—the first of the three major sections of *The Divine Comedy*—Virgil guides Dante into the Inferno, or hell. There they meet souls eternally condemned for the sins they committed during their earthly lives. They meet traitors, murderers, robbers, liars, and more, each suffering an eternal punishment suited to his or her sins.

In most early medieval poems, the characters were symbolic figures that represented virtues or vices. For example, there might be characters named Beauty and Knowledge, or Gluttony and Envy. But Dante wrote recognizable people. Some are figures from history, while some are people from Dante's

Key Questions

* What was the Renaissance? Why did the Renaissance begin in Italy?

* What questions did Machiavelli raise about politics and power in *The Prince*?

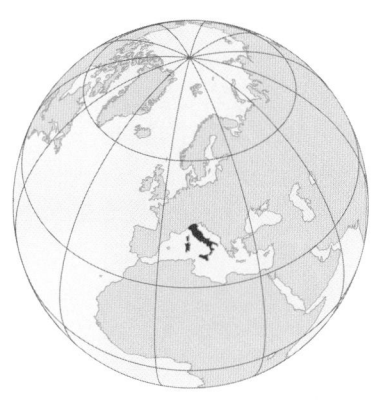

Italy was the cradle of the Renaissance.

own time, including corrupt popes, politicians, and merchants. In depicting these sinners, Dante's characters emerge as individual humans, not abstract symbols.

Like most medieval Christians, Dante saw heaven as the goal of earthly strivings. But in writing his great poem, Dante was not just looking to heaven. Dante also took earthly existence very seriously. His use of Italian, his rich portrayal of recognizable individuals, and his denunciation of the evils he saw around him were all part of a new perspective anticipating an attitude characteristic of the Renaissance—a heightened concern for this world, for the here and now.

Giotto and the Human Form

Like Dante, the artist Giotto di Bondone (JAWT-toh dee bohn-DOH-nay) stood between two eras. A fellow Florentine, Giotto painted during the same period in which Dante wrote *The Divine Comedy*.

Like most medieval artists, Giotto chose religious subject matter. But while medieval art depicted flat figures whose faces showed little personality, Giotto painted lifelike figures in natural-looking settings. He showed realistic details, such as the folds of clothing.

Giotto's subjects revealed recognizable human emotions and seemed to breathe life from the canvas. Because he celebrated nature and the human form in his art, Giotto is often hailed as the pathmaker for Renaissance painting.

Petrarch: The Father of Humanism

One name more than any other stands for the time of change in Europe between the Middle Ages and the Renaissance—Francesco Petrarca, or

Petrarch (PEH-trahrk), as the name has been translated. Petrarch was born in 1304. His family, like Dante's, was exiled from Florence during one of the city-state's many feuds.

Petrarch studied to become a priest. Even after entering the priesthood, Petrarch wrote hundreds of love poems, some in Latin but most, like Dante's verses, in Italian. Petrarch also worked as a diplomat, traveling from city to city on missions for bishops and princes. As he traveled, he visited libraries at monasteries and searched for manuscripts of ancient Latin texts. Petrarch lived in an exciting time during which scholars were discovering translations of classical works that had been lost or ignored for centuries.

Petrarch became convinced that the thinkers of ancient Greece and Rome could help restore wisdom and virtue to his troubled world. He proposed a new educational program that became known as **humanism**. Humanism emphasized the value of the classics—for example, the epics of Homer and philosophic writings of Plato. Drawing

Giotto's *Lamentation of Christ* shows realistic details and emotions.

The Rediscovery of Classical Texts

In the late 1200s and 1300s, more and more ancient Greek and Latin texts were becoming available in Europe. Where did they come from? As Spanish and Portuguese armies drove the Moors off the Iberian Peninsula, Christian scholars inherited Muslim libraries filled with classical manuscripts. As the Ottoman Turks pressed on Byzantium, Greek scholars fled west, many to Italy and especially Venice, carrying classical texts with them. Many classical works had been stored in European monasteries all along, waiting for scholars to read them with fresh and appreciative eyes.

upon insights from the classical past, humanism stressed the dignity of man and placed renewed confidence in human potential.

Petrarch saw no conflict between Christian beliefs and classical wisdom. He believed that the ancients, with their respect for human abilities and potential, could help show Christians the path to virtue. In Petrarch's humanistic view, God had endowed human beings with the ability and freedom to accomplish great things in this earthly life.

Italian City-States Spur Change

If the medieval world had been shaped by the manor, the Renaissance world was forged by cities. Most of these cities lay in northern Italy, surrounded by ruins of the ancient Roman Empire. As centers of trade and commerce, linked to distant lands by the Mediterranean Sea, these Italian city-states engaged in the exchange of both goods and ideas.

The inhabitants of the Italian city-states had never completely lost touch with Greco-Roman civilization. They were surrounded by the physical evidence of their classical heritage, including Roman roads, aqueducts, and amphitheaters. The city of Rome, headquarters of the Christian church in western Europe, had deep connections to the legacy of ancient Rome. Not far from Rome was the Benedictine monastery of Monte Cassino, with a library that by the 1300s had accumulated a large collection of works from classical times.

In the thriving city-states of Italy, the Renaissance first began to take shape.

A First Flowering in Florence

In the 1300s, the city of Florence survived fire, flood, and repeated bouts of plague to become the wealthy center of Europe's wool and silk trade. Since the late 1200s, Florence had been organized as a republic, but the political life of the city-state was controlled by the wealthiest families. Each wealthy Florentine family wanted to set itself above the others, and they all competed to display their wealth and magnificence. In some ways,

The Renaissance first flowered in Florence, which straddles the Arno River.

this competition was good for Florence because it spurred the wealthy families to fund many new buildings and artworks in their city-state.

Nurtured by wealth and ingenuity, the Renaissance came to its first full flowering in mid-fifteenth-century Florence. Florentines gloried in the classical past and embodied the humanism of their present day. They put scholarship, art, and architecture on a new course.

Rome and the Papal States

Rome lay at the heart of an area called the Papal States, a region in central Italy ruled by the pope. The Papal States included not only Rome but also such cities as Bologna (boh-LOH-nyah) and Urbino (uhr-BEE-noh). Sometimes the leading families in these cities resisted papal rule, which provoked some popes to send troops to remind these people that they lived in Papal States.

By about 1500, Rome had taken the place of Florence as the leading city of the Renaissance. The pope and his cardinals wielded great power.

Renaissance popes were often more concerned with politics, power, and luxury than with spiritual leadership. They amassed great wealth, part of which they used to finance building projects in the city and to commission artists to produce masterworks of painting and sculpture.

Venice: A Floating City

Venice is located in a sheltered lagoon at the north end of the Adriatic Sea. The city, which seems to float, was built on wooden pilings set into more than a hundred islands. Canals serve as streets.

Venice prospered as a major link for trade between western Europe and Asia. The city managed to secure a monopoly on trade with Byzantium and the Muslim world. The ruler of Venice, called the *doge* (dohj, from the Latin word *dux*, meaning "leader"), negotiated trade agreements with Byzantine and Muslim representatives. The doge commanded a trading empire that included posts all along the shores of the Adriatic and Mediterranean and stretched to the Black Sea.

Venice drew merchants, scholars, bankers, and businessmen. The grand palace of the doge, the city's ruler, stands at left.

Italian City-States, c. 1450

HOLY ROMAN EMPIRE

EUROPE ALPS

HUNGARY

Danube River

MARQUISATE OF
MONTSERRAT

Milan

Venice

REPUBLIC OF VENICE

OTTOMAN
EMPIRE

DUCHY OF SAVOY

Mantua

Padua

DUCHY
OF MILAN

Genoa

DUCHY
OF
MODENA

Ferrara

Bologna

MARQUISATE
OF
SALUZZO

REPUBLIC
OF LUCCA

REPUBLIC OF
FLORENCE

REPUBLIC
OF
GENOA

Pisa

Arno River

Florence

Urbino

Siena

Adriatic Sea

DUCHY OF
PIOMBINO

Assisi

PAPAL
STATES

Corsica

Rome

KINGDOM
OF
NAPLES

*Tyrrhenian
Sea*

Naples

Sardinia

KINGDOM OF
ARAGON

Mediterranean Sea

Sicily

AFRICA

N

0	50	100 mi
0	50	100 km

The Renaissance had its first flowering in the city-states of northern Italy. Although geographically small, these city-states were wealthy and powerful, and exerted their influence throughout Europe.

Politics of the Italian Renaissance

Beyond Italy, in other parts of Europe, strong kings were centralizing their power. France and England, for example, came under the rule of strong monarchs. But the Italian Peninsula remained a collection of independent city-states, with most led by powerful merchant families.

The new wealth produced by trade fostered a competitive, sometimes dangerous political life. Within a city-state, individuals, families, and guilds vied for power and prestige. At any given moment, people who were not in power were hatching schemes to get rid of those who were. These city dwellers didn't just fight among themselves. They fought most fiercely against other city-states. Venetians, who specialized in plotting against each other, would rapidly band together against archrival Genoa (JEH-noh-uh). Florentines

would quickly drop their quarrels with each other to respond to threats from neighboring Milan or Siena (see-EH-nah).

Each ruler wanted his city-state to outshine the others. And each ruler knew that his success greatly depended on the people who advised and served him. So rulers surrounded themselves with well-educated courtiers, advisers, and attendants, all of whom made up the ruler's court. Two Renaissance writers—Niccolò Machiavelli (neek-koh-LOH mah-kyah-VEL-lee) and Baldassare Castiglione (bahl-dahs-SAHR-ay kahs-teel-YOH-nay)—offered guidance to those who ruled and to those who maneuvered to gain the favor of the rulers.

Castiglione's Book of the Courtier

As a young man, Castiglione became a courtier to Francesco Gonzaga, the prince of Mantua. Later, he served the duke of the city of Urbino. Castiglione

Ludovico Gonzaga, ruler of the city-state of Mantua, sits surrounded by his family and courtiers.

Isabella d'Este

In a time when men held most of the power and privilege, Isabella d'Este (DES-tay) was a striking exception. She was a doer and a thinker, a true "Renaissance woman." She received an excellent education. By her mid-teens, she could read Greek and Latin. She could also play the lute, sing, dance, and discuss politics. She married Francesco Gonzaga, the ruler of Mantua.

Francesco, more soldier than politician, regularly sought his wife's advice. When her husband fell ill and retired to a country villa, Isabella governed Mantua on behalf of Francesco until his death in 1519. After that, she governed on behalf of her son.

Isabella supported the arts. Although her city-state was less powerful than Florence or Rome, Isabella made Mantua a center of learning and art.

Renaissance woman Isabella d'Este

often traveled as a diplomat on behalf of the duke. He met such figures as the king of England and Pope Julius II. In every court he visited, Castiglione carefully observed how various courtiers served their princes.

In *The Book of the Courtier*, published in 1528, Castiglione described how a courtier should act and how he could best serve his prince. Castiglione said that a good courtier needed some qualities of the chivalrous knight of medieval times, such as courage, horsemanship, and good swordsmanship. Moreover, he said, courtiers should also know how to wrestle, swim, and run. But a courtier needed to be more than a warrior or athlete. The courtier, said Castiglione, should know both Latin and Greek. He should "be versed in the poets, as well as in the orators and historians, and let him be practiced also in writing verse and prose." He should be able to discuss art and philosophy with his prince, as well as draw, paint, dance, and play some musical instruments.

Furthermore, said Castiglione, the courtier should have the quality of *sprezzatura* (spreht-zah-TOOR-uh)—that is, he should be able to display his skills with ease. "Whatever is done or said," Castiglione declared, should "appear to be without effort."

Castiglione's book, which became a favorite of rulers and courtiers throughout Europe, put forth an image of the perfect courtier, the ideal man of Renaissance times. To this day, to be a "Renaissance man" means to be a person of wide and varied knowledge and accomplishment.

Machiavelli Studies Princes

Niccolò Machiavelli of Florence lived in a time of strife and struggle, when city-states fought each other as well as forces from other countries, including France and Spain. In 1502, while on a diplomatic mission to Rome, Machiavelli met Cesare Borgia (CHAY-zahr-ay BOR-juh), a ruthless leader. The pope had given Cesare Borgia the task of crushing towns and cities that rebelled against papal rule.

Machiavelli watched the young tyrant march his army through the Papal States, seizing one mutinous town after another, not so much by military might but through trickery and sheer terror. Machiavelli left Cesare Borgia wondering if such a leader—a man who would stop at nothing to achieve his ends—could bring order to war-torn Italy.

Machiavelli's Prince
To Be Loved or Feared?

Niccolò Machiavelli's best-known work, *The Prince*, is a treatise on political leadership. While some critics attack his views as immoral and cynical, others praise his pragmatism at all costs for the sake of a secure state.

It has been sometimes asked whether it is better to be loved than feared; to which I answer that one should wish to be both. But as that is a hard matter to accomplish, I think, if it is necessary to make a selection, that it is safer to be feared than to be loved…. Men are usually more inclined to submit to him who makes himself dreaded than to one who merely strives to be beloved….

A prince, however, ought to make himself feared in such a manner that if he cannot gain the love of his subjects he may at least avoid their hatred; and he may attain this object by respecting his subjects' property and the honor of their wives. If he finds it absolutely necessary to inflict the punishment of death, he should avow the reason for it, and, above all things, he should abstain from touching the property of the condemned person. For certain it is that men sooner forget the death of their relatives than the loss of their patrimony.

Machiavelli came to believe that the time in which he lived—a time when Italy's city-states suffered invasions and war—required a leader willing to do whatever it took to protect his state and make it secure. In his book titled *The Prince*, Machiavelli laid out bold new guidelines for maintaining a secure state.

In Machiavelli's eyes, those who expected rulers to act virtuously in every instance were living in "an imaginary world." Machiavelli argued that a prince must act as circumstances required. If this meant breaking his promises, so be it. If it meant committing cruel acts, then that was the price to pay for a well-ordered and secure state. In short, the ends justified the means—a phrase often associated with Machiavelli's philosophy, though he himself never used those words.

The Prince was translated into several languages, and Machiavelli's ideas spread well beyond Italy. The book made rulers and their counselors think less about abstract ideals and more about actual human conduct. That is why many people consider Machiavelli to be the founder of modern political science—the study of politics and government.

A Flowering of Artistic Genius

The Renaissance was a time of extraordinary artistic creativity, when painters, sculptors, and architects created works of lasting beauty. These artists were inspired by the classical ideals of ancient Greece and Rome, and by the humanistic belief in human dignity and human potential. Besides inspiration, however, Renaissance artists also found ready financial support.

Key Questions

- How did wealthy families and individuals encourage the arts?
- How did the work of Italian Renaissance artists reflect Renaissance thinking and ideals?

Patrons of the Arts

Rich merchants and wealthy families in many Italian city-states became **patrons** of the arts—that is, they supported artists by buying their works or paying them to create new works. In Florence, for example, wealthy patrons hired architects to build elegant palaces, or *palazzi* (pah-LAHT-zee). Patrons paid sculptors to fill the city's public squares and guild halls with statues, and commissioned artists to create stunning paintings and frescoes.

The Medici as Patrons of the Arts

In Florence, the wealthy Medici (MED-uh-chee) family became enthusiastic patrons of art and learning. The Medici made their first fortune in cloth manufacture, and then turned their profits to another business—banking. By the 1430s, the family, led by Cosimo de' Medici (KAW-zee-moh d'MED-uh-chee), operated one of the largest banks in Europe. Cosimo spent fortunes on paintings and sculpture to adorn Florentine monasteries, convents, and chapels. He sponsored expeditions to collect classical manuscripts, statues, and coins. He also established the first public library in Italy, filled it with thousands of ancient manuscripts, and opened it to scholars and students.

Cosimo's grandson, Lorenzo, known as Lorenzo the Magnificent, brought the most brilliant painters, sculptors, and scholars to Florence. Lorenzo surrounded himself with humanists to discuss classical ideas and debate philosophical issues.

The Popes as Patrons

In 1400, Rome was in shambles. Large parts of the city had decayed during the time of the Great Schism, when French kings had forced a series of popes to live in the town of Avignon. In 1417, when the papacy officially returned to Rome, one pope after another set about to revive and beautify the city. By the mid-fifteenth century, the center of Renaissance activity had shifted from Florence to Rome as the popes called on many sculptors, painters, and architects to restore the ancient capital to its former glory.

The leader of the Christian church in Rome had more money than even the Medici family in Florence. Indeed, two popes during this period

St. Peter's Basilica, Rome, considered by Christians to be the holiest church in Renaissance Europe

(Clement VII and Leo X) were members of the Medici family. Like the wealthy merchants of Florence, Renaissance popes lived as princes and became patrons of the arts. They built magnificent new churches and palaces. They transformed the Vatican—the headquarters of the Christian church in Rome—into a vast palace complex that displayed some of Europe's finest artistic treasures. The Vatican also housed a papal library with a collection of Latin and Greek texts.

Pope Julius II was an especially fervent patron of the arts. He undertook the rebuilding of St. Peter's Basilica, which most Christians considered the holiest church in Europe.

Italian Masters

Surrounded by the remnants of classical civilization, Italian architects, sculptors, and artists were inspired to create extraordinary works of art. These masterpieces expressed not only the artist's individual genius but also the Renaissance spirit of humanism.

Brunelleschi Builds a Dome

Filippo Brunelleschi (fee-LEEP-poh broo-nehl-ES-kee), a native of Florence, was inspired by the grandeur of the ruins of ancient Rome. As a young architect, he filled his notebook with sketches of old Roman columns and arches.

In 1418, when officials in Florence announced a contest to see who could come up with a way to construct a dome for the city's cathedral, Brunelleschi leaped at the opportunity. Florentine officials knew what they wanted the dome to look like, but they didn't know how to build it. Brunelleschi built a model of brick and submitted it. Skeptics laughed and said the bricks would rain down on the heads of people below. But the judges, who included Cosimo de' Medici, gave Brunelleschi the commission.

Brunelleschi used an ancient Roman technique, building two interior shells of brick in a herringbone pattern. He used a system of rib supports to lessen the weight of the heavy dome on the building's foundation. By 1436, Brunelleschi's dome was complete. Florentines declared that not even Rome's Pantheon could compare with Brunelleschi's glorious dome.

Sculptors Inspired by the Past

In fifteenth-century Florence, sculptors revived the styles of the ancient Greeks and Romans, who

Brunelleschi's dome atop Florence's cathedral was an architectural marvel in 1436, and remains a prominent landmark today.

had sculpted in marble and bronze to express their admiration for the human form. In 1401, Lorenzo Ghiberti (luh-REN-zoh gee-BEHR-tee) won a commission from the wool merchants of Florence to adorn a church known as the Baptistery with a set of gilded bronze doors. Ghiberti spent the next two decades filling the Baptistery doors with scenes from the Bible. Just as Giotto had transformed painting, Ghiberti's work seemed to breathe life into sculpture. His rounded and natural-looking figures captured movement and individual expression, and expressed the beauty of the human form.

Another great Florentine sculptor, Donatello (dahn-uh-TEL-oh), worked as Ghiberti's assistant before striking out on his own. Donatello was hired by Cosimo de' Medici to create a bronze statue for his courtyard. Cosimo chose a subject from the Bible—David, slayer of the giant Goliath. Why David? Because the proud Florentines saw themselves as standing firm in their wars against neighboring city-states, especially their large neighbor, Milan. They saw their little city as a kind of David, a slayer of giants.

Donatello's heroic *David* was the first free-standing nude statue in western Europe since classical times. A symbol of Florentine courage, it showed the grace of the human form and breathed confidence in human abilities.

Painters Pay Tribute to Old and New

During the Renaissance, painters, too, were inspired by works from ancient Greece and Rome. They admired the proportion and graceful lines of classical sculptures. Renaissance painters tried to incorporate these elements in order to make their paintings lifelike and almost sculptural.

Lorenzo Ghiberti adorned the great bronze doors of Florence's Baptistery with lifelike figures in biblical scenes.

Like medieval artists, Renaissance painters mainly depicted scenes from the Bible or other religious subjects. But Renaissance painters treated religious topics in new ways. They focused on the beauty of creation in the here and now. They looked carefully at nature—sunlight on buildings, trees in the countryside, horses galloping in a field, the human body at rest or in motion—so they could recreate that beauty on their canvases.

The Revival of the Nude

In ancient Greece and Rome, sculptors often depicted the unclothed human body. In art, a depiction of a human figure without any clothes is called a *nude*. In the Middle Ages, artists generally did not depict nude figures because the church considered such art to be shameful. But Renaissance artists revived the nude as a proper subject for art. Like the artists of classical times, Renaissance artists saw beauty, grace, and strength in the healthy human form.

Donatello's biblical hero *David*

Masaccio's *The Tribute Money*, the first great example of the new humanism in Renaissance painting

Above all, Renaissance artists tried to represent human beings as living individuals, each figure possessing a unique identity. *The Tribute Money*, by the Florentine painter Masaccio (mah-SAHT-choh), was the first great example of this new humanism in painting. Painted for a chapel in Florence around 1425, *The Tribute Money* depicts an episode from the Bible. Masaccio set the scene in fifteenth-century Florence. He gave each biblical figure a unique face and character—Peter wary, Jesus authoritative, Judas impatient. He also gave his painting a sense of **perspective**—that is, he carefully arranged his images to make some appear closer to the viewer, and some farther away. The use of perspective, which achieves a sense of three-dimensional depth in a representation on a flat surface (such as a painter's canvas), became a distinctive feature of painting during the Renaissance and beyond.

Though Masaccio died young, he became known as the "Father of Renaissance Painting," and other artists followed his lead. One of those followers was a Florentine named Sandro Botticelli (SAHN-droh baht-uh-CHEL-ee). Botticelli often turned to classical mythology for inspiration. His *Birth of Venus*, painted around 1485, is one of the most famous paintings of the Renaissance. It shows the Roman goddess of love, Venus, rising out of the sea on a shell as two wind gods blow her to shore and a nymph waits to give her a cloak. Botticelli filled his painting with graceful lines and carefully balanced shapes that recall the harmony and beauty of classical art.

Sandro Botticelli's *Birth of Venus* was inspired by classical mythology.

Leonardo's Masterpieces

Painter, sculptor, architect, engineer, scientist, philosopher, visionary—the Florentine genius Leonardo da Vinci (lay-uh-NAHR-doh duh VIN-chee) is perhaps the most fascinating figure of the Renaissance. He carefully observed the world and kept notebooks in which he filled thousands of pages with sketches of plants and animals, plans for inventions, studies of the human body, mathematical calculations, and notes on painting and architecture. Leonardo, who was left-handed, wrote backward, from right to left. To read his famous notebooks, you must hold the pages up to a mirror.

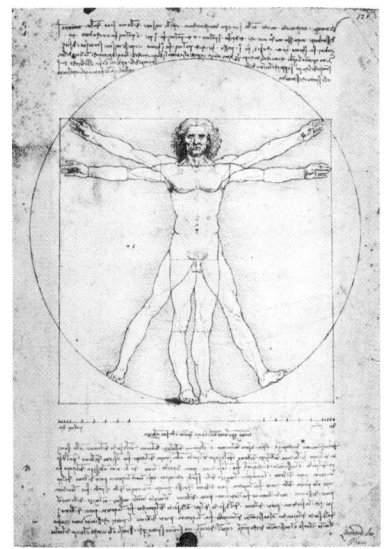 

Leonardo da Vinci's sketch of a man, at left, shows his understanding of the proportions of the human body. He drew his self-portrait, at right, in 1512.

In 1481, some monks in Florence hired Leonardo to paint a picture to hang above an altar in their monastery. He created a biblical scene of the wise men who traveled from afar to see the infant Jesus. After months of sketching and painting, however, he simply stopped. Even in its unfinished state, the *Adoration of the Magi* is one of the great works of the Renaissance.

Leonardo headed north from Florence to work for an ambitious duke in Milan. The duke commissioned Leonardo to paint a wall in the monks' dining hall in one of Milan's churches. Leonardo's painting, called *The Last Supper*, depicts the last meal that Jesus shared with his disciples. Leonardo illustrated the moment when Jesus announced that one of his followers would

Leonardo's dramatic mural, *The Last Supper*, is among the world's most famous works of art.

Leonardo, the Renaissance Man

Leonardo da Vinci was a man of many accomplishments, with a seemingly unlimited desire for knowledge. He was indeed a true Renaissance man.

While in the service of the duke of Milan, Leonardo da Vinci sang and played music at court, painted portraits, decorated the duke's castle, made cannons, built canals, and planned pageants for court celebrations. All subjects fascinated Leonardo. He spent long nights cutting into corpses in hospital morgues—in part to learn how the body worked, and in part so he could paint the human figure more accurately. In his notebooks he sketched ideas for new military machines—a tank, an exploding bomb, even a kind of machine gun. He also made studies of birds' wings and threw himself into the dream of building a flying machine.

Leonardo's mysterious *Mona Lisa*

betray him. He painted the disciples reacting with shock and despair. No artist had ever achieved such drama in a mural.

To create *The Last Supper*, Leonardo developed a new method of applying paint to the wall. The procedure proved flawed. Soon after he finished it, the painting began to show tiny cracks. Eventually it started to flake off the wall.

Leonardo returned to Florence, where, among his many and varied activities, he began work on a portrait that has become one of the best-known paintings in the world—the *Mona Lisa*. Historians were long unsure of the identity of the lady in this famous picture, but many now believe she was Lisa del Giocondo, the wife of a merchant living in Florence. Her mysterious smile and the misty landscape behind her have intrigued onlookers for centuries.

Michelangelo Masters Sculpture and Painting

One of the greatest artists of the Renaissance, Michelangelo Buonarroti (miy-kuh-LAN-jeh-loh bwaw-nahr-RAW-tee), began his career as a sculptor in Florence. Young Michelangelo lived at the Medici palace, often eating alongside the poets, philosophers, and artists whom Lorenzo the Magnificent invited to his table. From these humanists Michelangelo learned to admire human abilities and the classical past. He also made secret visits to a nearby hospital where he cut open dead bodies to study the positions of muscles and veins. He worked hard to learn to chisel arms, legs, and heads out of stone.

In 1496, Michelangelo, at age twenty-one, traveled to Rome, where an elderly French cardinal commissioned the sculptor to carve a *pietà* (pee-ay-TAH, which means "pity" in Italian), a statue of the Virgin Mary holding the dead Christ in her arms. Michelangelo worked feverishly for more than a year, hardly sleeping at all. In the finished *Pietà*, Michelangelo captured in marble the gentle folds in Mary's robe, the veins and muscles in Christ's arms, and the quiet sorrow in Mary's face. No one, not even the ancient Greeks, had sculpted with such skill.

Michelangelo's *Pietà* reveals his skill with fine detail in marble.

Michelangelo returned to Florence to take up a new challenge. The young artist had his eye on a huge block of marble that had been sitting near the city's cathedral for more than thirty years. Michelangelo persuaded the city's leaders to give him a chance to turn it into a symbol of Florentine greatness. It took the sculptor two years to produce a fourteen-foot-tall (4.25 m) statue of the biblical David about to do battle with Goliath. Michelangelo's *David* had the heroic strength and vital intensity of an ancient Greek sculpture. Florentines admired the statue and proudly displayed it in a public square.

By 1505, Michelangelo was the most famous sculptor in Italy. Pope Julius II summoned Michelangelo to Rome to design and sculpt a tomb. Michelangelo began work on the tomb. But one day Julius led Michelangelo into the Sistine Chapel and announced that he wanted the young sculptor to cover the vaulted ceiling with frescoes. Michelangelo protested that he was a sculptor, not a painter. But Julius insisted, and Michelangelo agreed to paint the chapel's ceiling.

Both Michelangelo and Julius II were temperamental, arrogant, and demanding. They often infuriated each other. But the stormy relationship between this artist and his patron led to some of the finest art the world has known.

Michelangelo's *David*

Michelangelo had to paint the curved ceiling with enormous figures that would be visible from far below. Paint dripped from his brush into his eyes. Finally, in 1512, Michelangelo declared the work complete. He had painted nearly three hundred and fifty magnificent human figures teeming with such life and energy that they looked as though they had been sculpted into the ceiling. Near the center loomed an image of God giving the divine spark of life to a near-perfect Adam. Even Julius gazed up in awe.

Raphael: The Prince of Painters

While Michelangelo was painting the ceiling of the Sistine Chapel, Pope Julius II heard of a

In the center of the great fresco painted by Michelangelo on the Sistine Chapel ceiling, God reaches out and imparts life to Adam.

Raphael painted this *Madonna* around 1505.

young genius, Raphael Sanzio (RAHF-ee-uhl SAHNT-syoh). Raphael was famous for his Madonnas, paintings of Mary and the infant Jesus. The pope summoned Raphael to Rome. Julius commissioned the young painter to decorate the walls of the pope's private rooms in the Vatican.

Julius loved the classics, so in the pope's library Raphael painted a fresco called *The School of Athens*. For this grand painting, Raphael imagined the great philosophers of ancient Greece gathered in one spot. Plato and Aristotle stand at the very center. Plato (the bearded figure with his right hand pointing up) looks very much like Leonardo da Vinci. In the foreground, looking alone and lost in thought, sits a reclusive Greek philosopher named Heraclitus. This figure, unlike others in the painting, wears leather boots and a more modern coat, and is probably Raphael's depiction of the great Michelangelo.

Raphael spent the last twelve years of his life in Rome. He lived only until age thirty-seven but left behind scores of Madonnas, portraits, and frescoes. Raphael and his paintings were so popular that he was called the "Prince of Painters."

In *The School of Athens*, Raphael depicts the great philosophers of ancient Greece gathered in the unfinished basilica of St. Peter's.

The Renaissance Beyond Italy

By the late 1400s, Renaissance ideas were spreading beyond Italy. Scholars, artists, and rulers in both neighboring and distant lands were inspired by the ideas that had sparked a rebirth in Italy—the new admiration for classics, the new confidence in human abilities, the new love of lifelike painting and sculpture, and the new principles of architecture. These ideas influenced art, religion, and thought in northern and western Europe, including Germany, Flanders, France, Spain, and England.

Key Questions

- How did Renaissance ideas spread to northern Europe?

- How did the work of Northern Renaissance artists and writers differ from Italian art and writing?

- What achievements characterized the Renaissance in England?

Monarchs as Patrons of the Arts

By 1500, France, Spain, and England had come under the rule of strong monarchs. French kings changed France from a territory of warring states into a strong monarchy. In Spain, King Ferdinand of Aragon and Queen Isabella of Castile joined their kingdoms by marrying each other in 1469. Across the English Channel, strong kings were taking charge. Beginning with King Henry VII, a royal family called the Tudors brought the English nobility under control.

In the late fifteenth century, armies from France, Spain, and Germany often invaded Italy. The invading kings and their courtiers were awed by the artwork of Milan, the gardens of Florence, and the palaces of Venice. To their homelands they took not only Italian paintings and books but also the new ideas and attitudes of Renaissance Italy.

Soon, northern European monarchs became patrons of Renaissance art. They collected Italian artwork and sent agents to Italy to buy ancient

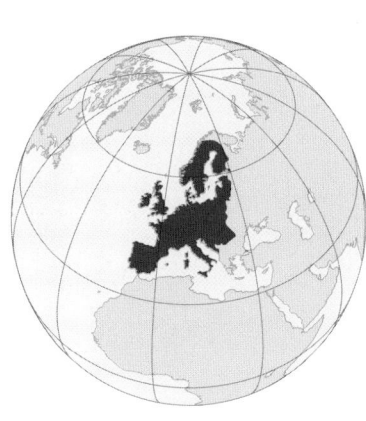

Renaissance ideas that began in Italy spread north and west.

The Renaissance-style Palace of Chambord in France was patterned on Italian design.

431

The Fragmented Holy Roman Empire

While strong monarchs ruled England, France, and Spain, other parts of Europe remained fragmented, including the vast Holy Roman Empire, covering the lands known today as Germany, Austria, and part of the Czech Republic. There a family called the Habsburgs built a powerful dynasty by marrying into other wealthy landowning families. The Habsburg ruler called himself an emperor, but his Holy Roman Empire was really a hodgepodge of duchies and city-states filled with stubborn dukes and rich merchants who ran affairs as they saw fit. (A *duchy* [DUH-chee] is a small territory ruled by a duke.)

manuscripts. In France, King Francis I brought Leonardo da Vinci from Italy for advice on architecture. Francis started a university for the study of humanist ideas, and he invited artists and scholars to live at his court. He even married his son into the Medici family.

Cities Thrive North of Italy

You have seen that in Italy, the Renaissance first began to take shape in prosperous cities such as Florence, Rome, and Venice. North of the Italian Peninsula, after the Hundred Years' War between France and England ended in 1453, important cities grew and prospered. Paris and London thrived as national capitals under strong French and English kings. Artists and merchants flocked to the city of Bruges (broozh) in Flanders, a region that contained parts of modern-day Belgium, France,

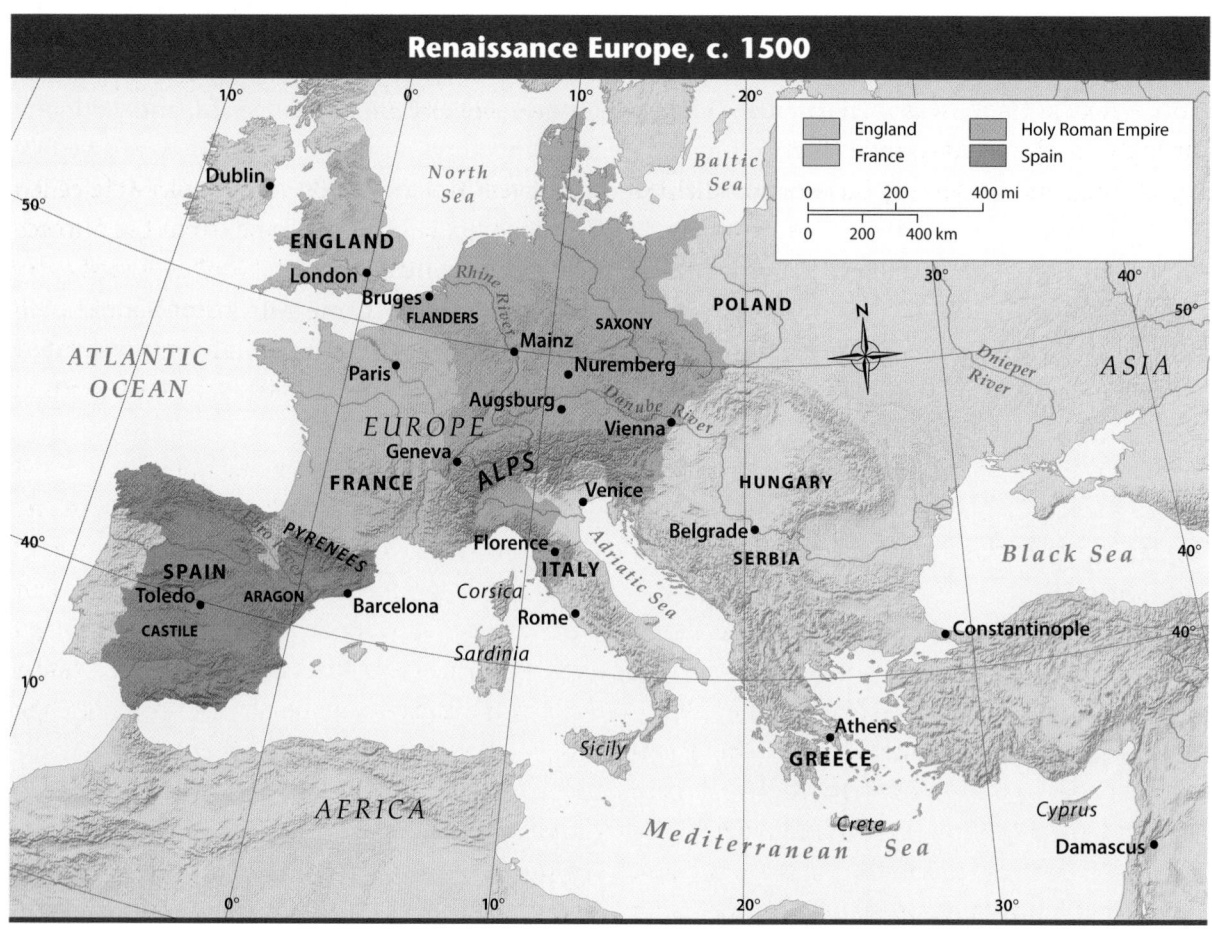

Renaissance Europe, c. 1500

By the late 1400s, Renaissance ideas were spreading north beyond Italy. European cities and city-states, such as Bruges, Augsburg, and Mainz, grew and thrived, becoming bustling centers attractive to artists and merchants alike.

and the Netherlands, and formed part of an area called the Low Countries (because much of the coastal land is at or below sea level).

In German lands near rivers, towns prospered. Population increased and trade revived after the decline of the plague. German city-states, such as Augsburg, Nuremberg, and Mainz (miynts), grew at the junctions of rivers. They were connected to each other and to the Italian Peninsula by well-traveled roads.

These self-governing, independent German city-states had their own wealthy merchant families, rival guilds, and industries. German foundries cranked out cannons and guns. Nuremberg was famous for its metalwork and toys. The city of Augsburg, which by 1400 had developed a brisk textile trade, was important throughout the Renaissance. Banking, mining, and the jewelry business also helped Augsburg prosper. Just as in the Italian city-states, the wealthiest families in the cities to the north patronized the arts and funded the construction of numerous monuments and buildings.

Gutenberg's printing press revolutionized the making of books and helped spread Renaissance culture.

The Printing Press

In the mid-fifteenth century, the spread of Renaissance culture was accelerated not only by growing prosperity but also by a new invention—the printing press.

As early as the sixth century, Chinese craftsmen had invented block printing by carving characters onto blocks of hard wood, applying ink to the raised characters, and pressing them against paper to make prints. Later, the Chinese invented an early form of movable type. By the thirteenth century, pieces of paper money and other block-printed items made their way from China to Europe. Europeans learned to block-print pages, but this method was slow.

Even into the 1400s, most books were called *manuscripts*, a term that comes from Latin words meaning "written by hand." Scribes copied every volume, word by word, with goose-feather quill pens. Copying by hand took a long time—many months for a single book. The slow process made books very expensive.

During the Renaissance, the hunger for knowledge and growth in literacy heightened the demand for books. Businesses and governments also needed a more efficient and less costly way to produce written records. Various craftsmen and inventors sought to invent a device to meet these demands. Wealthy men invested money in the efforts of inventors, hoping to profit from new methods of printing.

Johannes Gutenberg (yoh-HAHN-uhs GOOT-n-burg), a craftsman from the city of Mainz in Germany, spent years experimenting with methods to print books. He devised a way to make movable-type letters with precision, using a metal alloy that could withstand repeated printings.

Gutenberg adapted a screw-type press, like those used in winemaking, to the task of printing on paper. Gutenberg's press had a large wooden screw that, when cranked with a handle, pushed the paper onto inked type held in a boxlike frame. By about 1450, Gutenberg's machine and metal letters could make a hundred, even a thousand, identical copies of the same page.

After working on his experiments for nearly thirty years, Gutenberg was ready to print his first book. He chose the most widely read book in Europe, the Bible. Around 1455, Gutenberg printed about one hundred and eighty copies of the Bible, each with 1,282 pages.

By the end of the fifteenth century, hundreds of busy printers were churning out books across Europe. Many printers and presses went to Venice, a wealthy city that had recently welcomed many Greek scholars fleeing the Ottoman Turks in Constantinople. These scholars brought ancient texts with them. Now these texts could be printed. Books about medicine, philosophy, art, and much more traveled from one end of Europe to another. Never before had so many ideas traveled so quickly.

The Gutenberg Bible is considered the first printed book in the Western world. Many historians regard the printing press as the most important invention of the past millennium.

Innovations in Art

The artistic geniuses of northern Europe were influenced by Italian Renaissance art but developed their own distinctive styles. While Italian painters emphasized the beauty of the ideal human form—think of Michelangelo's majestic *David* or Raphael's serene Madonnas—the artists of the Northern Renaissance painted with great attention to detail, even if the detail was not flattering. If a merchant had a wart on his face, a northern European artist was likely to include that wart. For most northern European painters, capturing the ideal was less important than rendering the real in great detail.

Flemish Painters

Wealthy patrons provided generous support that helped make Flanders into a center of artistic creativity in northern Europe. One of the most influential artists working in Flanders was Jan van Eyck (yahn van IYK), who painted in the early fifteenth century. Van Eyck was one of the first artists to paint on wood panels with colors mixed in oil. One of Van Eyck's most famous paintings, *Giovanni Arnolfini and His Bride*, portrays an Italian merchant and his wife in 1434. The picture is filled with details—the glittering chandelier, the fruit sitting on the windowsill, the shoes on the floor.

The adjective *Flemish* means having to do with Flanders.

Jan van Eyck painted *Giovanni Arnolfini and His Bride* with slow-drying paints, which allowed him to add great detail.

The Flemish artist Pieter Bruegel painted many scenes from peasant life, including this work from 1568, *Peasants' Dance*.

In the mid-1500s, another Flemish master produced paintings rich in realistic detail. Pieter Bruegel (PEE-tur BROY-guhl) painted detailed landscapes but is perhaps best known for his lively and richly colored paintings of scenes from peasant life.

German Painters

From the busy German town of Nuremberg came one of the great geniuses of the Renaissance, Albrecht Dürer (AHL-brekt DYOUR-ur). As a young man, Dürer traveled to Flanders to see the paintings of Van Eyck. In 1494, Dürer made his first trip to Venice. Ten years later, he returned to Italy, where he read Latin poetry and studied with Italian painters. He took his knowledge of Italian art home to Germany and, with painstaking detail, painted remarkable self-portraits.

Dürer's most important works were not paintings but detailed engravings. To produce an engraving, an artist cut an image into a copper

The German artist Albrecht Dürer painted many self-portraits.

435

Northern Influence Spreads South

When Italian artists saw paintings by Van Eyck, Dürer, Holbein, and other northern masters, they were amazed at the lifelike details and vivid colors. Knowledge of northern techniques traveled to Italy, where artists began to experiment with oil paints and incorporate more detail. German and Flemish influences spread south, just as Italian influence had spread north.

plate. Dürer's beautiful engravings were known across Europe. By the time he died in 1528, Dürer had produced almost two hundred paintings, more than a thousand drawings, and hundreds of woodcuts and engravings.

Another great northern European artist, Hans Holbein (hahns HOHL-biyn) the Younger, was born in Augsburg in southern Germany. (He is known as "the Younger" because his father, who was also a painter, had the same name.) Like

Hans Holbein the Younger's painting of two French ambassadors to the English court includes symbols of their interests and shows how the Renaissance love of learning spread beyond Italy.

Dürer, Holbein spent time in Italy studying the works of master artists. He became known for his portraits of wealthy merchants and other important people. Indeed, King Henry VIII of England brought Holbein to London to paint portraits of the royal household.

El Greco in Spain

One of the masters of the Spanish Renaissance, the painter El Greco, used oil paints to produce detailed images that used color to convey drama and intense emotion. El Greco, whose name means "the Greek," was born Domenikos Theotokopoulos on the island of Crete, the largest of the Greek islands. His art was deeply rooted in his Catholic faith.

As a young man, El Greco moved to Venice, where he learned and adopted some of the techniques of Italian painters. In 1577, El Greco moved to Toledo, Spain, where he would spend the rest of his life. There he was commissioned to paint *The Burial of the Count of Orgaz* for the Catholic church of Santo Tomé. The painting tells the story of the miraculous appearance of Saint Stephen and Saint Augustine, who descended from on high to lower the count's body into his tomb. The figures surrounding the lifeless count—even the two saints—have naturalistic facial features and carefully detailed garments.

El Greco's dramatic *Burial of the Count of Orgaz* reveals the artist's strong religious sentiments and his ability to create natural features and detail.

Thinkers and Writers

Trade, travel, warfare, and the printing press helped spread Renaissance ideas. As humanist philosophies and attitudes spread, thinkers and writers in northern and western Europe absorbed the new influences and produced works with distinctive voices and visions.

Christian Humanism: Erasmus and More

Like the humanists of Italy, the humanists of northern Europe were inspired by the wisdom of ancient Greek and Roman writings. But compared to thinkers in Italy, northern humanists were more interested in using ancient texts to further their understanding of Christianity's teachings. The scholars of northern Europe are often known as Christian humanists. They wanted to reform the church, which they thought had become too worldly and more concerned with money, power, and land than with people's souls.

A Dutch monk, Desiderius Erasmus (DEH-sih-DEER-ee-us ih-RAZ-mus), wrote a book criticizing the pope and the church in Rome, and offering sharp observations on various failings of human conduct. In *The Praise of Folly*, published in 1509, Erasmus speaks through the voice of a character named Folly, or foolishness. "If you please," says Folly, "let us look a little into the lives of men, and it will easily appear not only how much they owe to me, but how much they esteem me even from the highest to the lowest."

Scholars, princes, courtiers, merchants, hunters—few escaped the sharp barbs hurled by Folly. But Erasmus saved his sharpest criticism for monks, priests, cardinals, and other church officials. The printing press made *The Praise of Folly* widely available. It soon became one of Europe's most read books.

Erasmus wrote *The Praise of Folly* at the London home of his good friend, and England's greatest Christian humanist, Thomas More. More translated the works of Greek authors and wrote poems in Latin. Like Erasmus and other Christian humanists, Thomas More believed that the church leaders and royalty of his day were often greedy and power hungry.

In 1516, More wrote a book to highlight the problems of Europe. The title of the book is *Utopia* (yoo-TOH-pee-uh), a word made up from the

Greek *ou-topos*, meaning "no place." More's Utopia is an imaginary island governed entirely by reason. In this perfect world, there are no rich or poor, no powerful or weak. The citizens of Utopia run their city-state not by competing for power, riches, and fame, but by cooperating, sharing, and dealing fairly with one another.

Utopia was soon translated into most European languages. The book helped some people see the wrongs of the Christian church, in which popes and bishops lived like kings and fought each other for power and wealth. The title of More's book, *Utopia*, has since become a word in the English language. People now use the word *utopia* to refer to any vision of an ideal society. Sometimes people use the adjective *utopian* to refer to ideas that seem impractical and out of reach.

France: Rabelais and Montaigne

A monk and physician deeply versed in humanist learning, François Rabelais (fran-SWAH RAB-uh-lay) wrote some of the most popular and controversial works of the Renaissance in France. Church leaders and scholars, often the targets of Rabelais' satires, condemned his writings as heretical and obscene. Rabelais stuffed his collected works, including *Gargantua* and *Pantagruel*, with fantastical characters and exuberant, often ribald, prose. His name has come to be used as an adjective, "Rabelaisian" (RAB-uh-LAY-zhuhn), which describes a literary style characterized by wicked satire and bawdy humor.

In France in the late 1500s, Michel de Montaigne (mee-shel duh mahn-tayn) turned his attention to a subject close at hand—himself. He invented a new literary form, the personal essay, in which he offered reflections on himself and his views of specific topics of his time. In the opening to his collection, titled *Essays*, he announces, "I am myself the matter of my book."

In writing about himself, Montaigne was not being boastful or egotistical. His essays, which express doubt and uncertainty, reflect his troubled times, during which France was torn by warfare and religious strife. His writings, however, are not gloomy, but show a subtle mind at work, actively probing, weighing, and questioning.

Spain: Cervantes and Don Quixote

Probably the greatest literary masterwork to emerge from Renaissance Spain was *Don Quixote* (DAHN kee-HOH-tee) by Miguel de Cervantes Saavedra (mee-GEL duh sur-VAHN-tays sah-uh-VAY-druh). *Don Quixote* was published in two parts, the first in 1605 and the second in 1615. The novel—the complete title of which is *The Ingenious Gentleman Don Quixote of La Mancha*—tells of an aging, idealistic Spanish landowner who is so deeply absorbed in medieval tales of chivalry that he imagines himself to be a brave knight. He straps on some rusty armor, mounts an aging hack of a horse, and convinces a peasant neighbor, Sancho Panza, to accompany him as his squire. Don Quixote, who tries to act by the medieval code of chivalry, finds himself out of place in his modern world. His attempts to perform noble deeds lead to a series of mostly comic misadventures.

Considered by many to be the first modern novel, *Don Quixote* contains elements of narrative fiction that would influence later generations of authors and inspire artists and composers to depict the hero in paintings and music. The novel was wildly popular in its time and has since been translated into many languages—indeed, by some accounts it is the second most-translated book in history after the Bible.

A Literary Renaissance in England

During the late 1500s and into the early 1600s, England emerged as a major European power. London became a prosperous city of merchants and shopkeepers. The island kingdom swelled with confidence and ambition. The arts thrived during the reign of Queen Elizabeth I, who ruled England from 1558 to 1603, a period often called the Elizabethan Age. This remarkable ruler (about whom you will read more in a later chapter) filled her court with brilliant artists, writers, and musicians.

A knight slays a dragon in this illustration from Edmund Spenser's *The Faerie Queene*.

One poet who greatly pleased the queen was Edmund Spenser, who blended a strong knowledge of the classics, a love of the English language, and a deep familiarity with Italian writers. Spenser wrote an epic poem called *The Faerie Queene*. The "queen" of the title was Elizabeth herself. *The Faerie Queene* was published as a series of books. In each book a knight faced a trial to master a virtue, such as temperance, holiness, or courage.

The most active parts of literary life in Elizabethan London occurred in its theaters. Theatergoers came from every walk of life, from the humblest worker to the queen herself, to view productions by a gifted generation of playwrights.

The greatest playwright of them all was William Shakespeare. Shakespeare wrote dozens of plays, thirty-eight of which survive today. His plays—including *Romeo and Juliet*, *A Midsummer Night's Dream*, *Henry IV Parts 1 and 2*, and *Hamlet*—offer something for everyone, from hilarious farce to tender romance to profound insights into human nature.

Through it all, Shakespeare demonstrated an unrivaled command of the English language. "The Bard," as Shakespeare is known, drew his inspiration from Greek comedies and tragedies, Italian romances, and English history, as well as from street ballads and folk traditions. No other work besides the Bible has had a greater influence on English language and literature than the body of Shakespeare's plays. One modern-day literary scholar has even claimed, "Shakespeare invented us."

William Shakespeare's portrait adorns the title page of a book of his plays, published in 1623.

Primary Source

"What a piece of work is a man!"

In Shakespeare's great tragedy, *Hamlet, Prince of Denmark*, written around the year 1600, Hamlet speaks words that express the essence of Renaissance humanism, the extraordinary confidence in human ability and potential. Hamlet ends this speech, however, with an expression of personal doubt, as the young prince's confidence has been shaken by immediate circumstances—the murder of his father, the king, and a visitation from his father's ghost, who has charged Hamlet with seeking revenge.

What a piece of work is a man! How noble in reason! How infinite in faculty! In form and moving how express and admirable! In action how like an angel! In apprehension how like a god! The beauty of the world! The paragon of animals! And yet, to me, what is this quintessence of dust? Man delights not me....

Renaissance Music

During the Renaissance, music, like the visual arts, underwent great changes. In medieval times, music was important in the church and in monasteries, where monks and nuns chanted praises to God. In the Renaissance, more people—courtiers, merchants and their families—wanted more music in their lives.

Sacred music—the music of the church—remained important. But secular music—music for everyday life, not for religious purposes—grew increasingly popular. Prominent composers wrote many **madrigals**, songs written usually for four or five voices, sung in **polyphony**—that is, with the voices weaving together independent melodic lines (in contrast to much medieval music, in which various voices sang the same melody). Madrigals were most often about love, sometimes romantic, sometimes bawdy. Claudio Monteverdi (KLOWD-yoh mon-tay-VAIR-dee), an Italian composer of the late Renaissance, published many collections of madrigals.

At Renaissance courts, dancing was a favorite entertainment, and composers responded by writing nonvocal dance music, usually for performance by a small consort of instruments. In England, the composer John Dowland wrote many dances for the lute, a stringed instrument

A colorful sixteenth-century Venetian painting portrays three madrigal singers.

that resembles a modern-day guitar. Dowland also composed numerous songs for a singer accompanied by the lute, which were so well loved that he became one of the most famous musicians of the Renaissance, and was known throughout Europe.

Science in the Making

The Renaissance interest in inquiry, and the focus on the here and now, opened the way to important new discoveries about the natural world and how it works. First, however, certain old attitudes had to be overcome.

While ancient Greece and Rome inspired many Renaissance artists and writers to create bold new works, the high regard for classical works and ancient philosophy discouraged original thinking about the natural world. For many centuries, people assumed that ancient Greek and Roman ideas about the physical world were correct. They unquestioningly accepted Aristotle and other ancient writers as authorities on the workings of nature. Into the early 1500s, astrologers and alchemists studied classical texts as they tried to explore what they saw as mysterious, hidden forces in nature. Astrologers watched the stars move and tried to predict the future. Alchemists tried to discover ways to turn lead into gold.

Of course the stars cannot predict the future and lead cannot turn into gold. And yet, even

A 1570 painting, *The Alchemist's Workshop*, illustrates dedicated workers in search of answers to nature's mysteries.

though astrologers and alchemists were looking for knowledge in the wrong places, they were looking—they were curious about nature. That curiosity, when combined with a new willingness to question ancient ideas, created the opportunity for scientific discovery and laid the foundation for a scientific revolution in the 1600s.

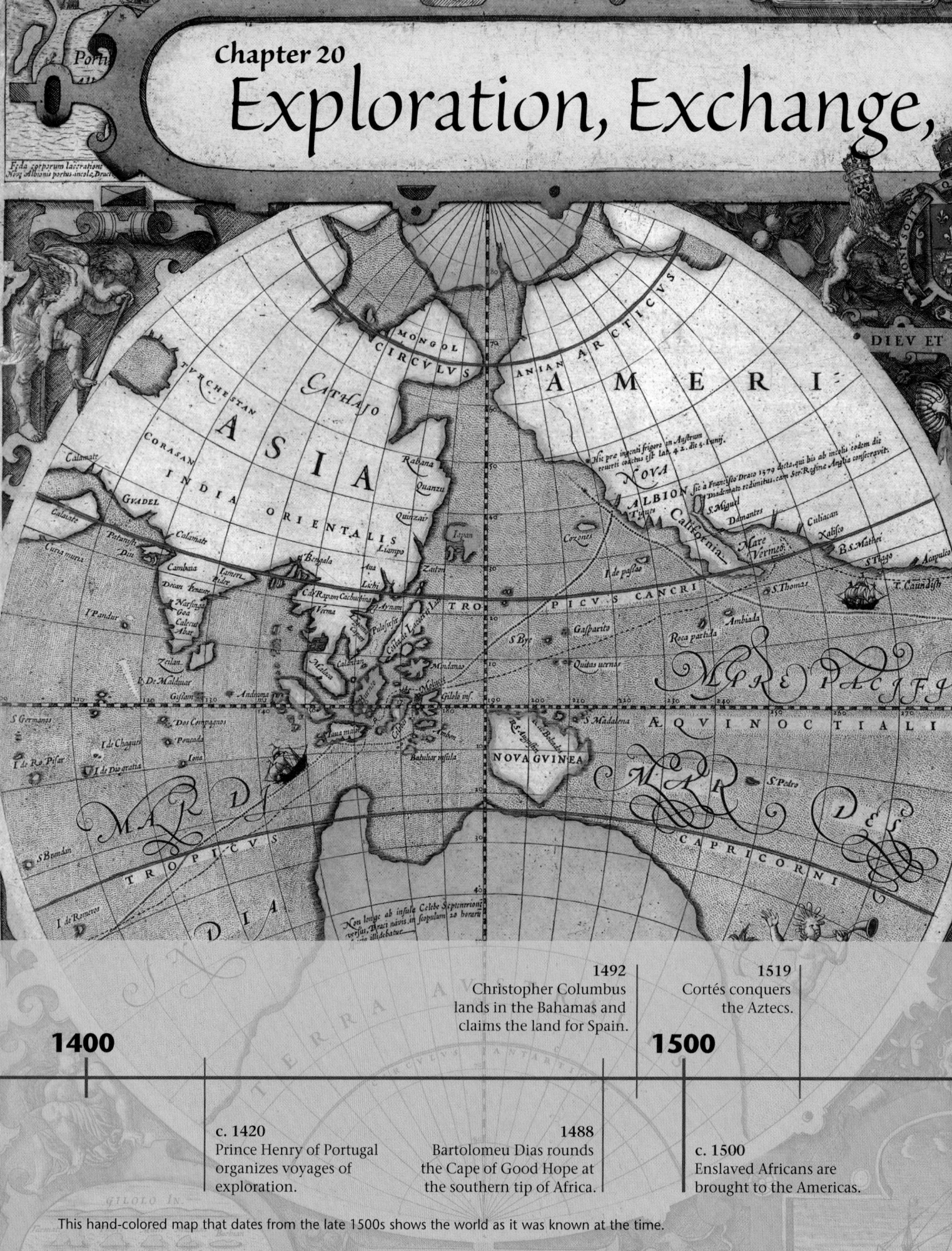

Chapter 20
Exploration, Exchange,

1400

1500

1492
Christopher Columbus
lands in the Bahamas and
claims the land for Spain.

1519
Cortés conquers
the Aztecs.

c. 1420
Prince Henry of Portugal
organizes voyages of
exploration.

1488
Bartolomeu Dias rounds
the Cape of Good Hope at
the southern tip of Africa.

c. 1500
Enslaved Africans are
brought to the Americas.

This hand-colored map that dates from the late 1500s shows the world as it was known at the time.

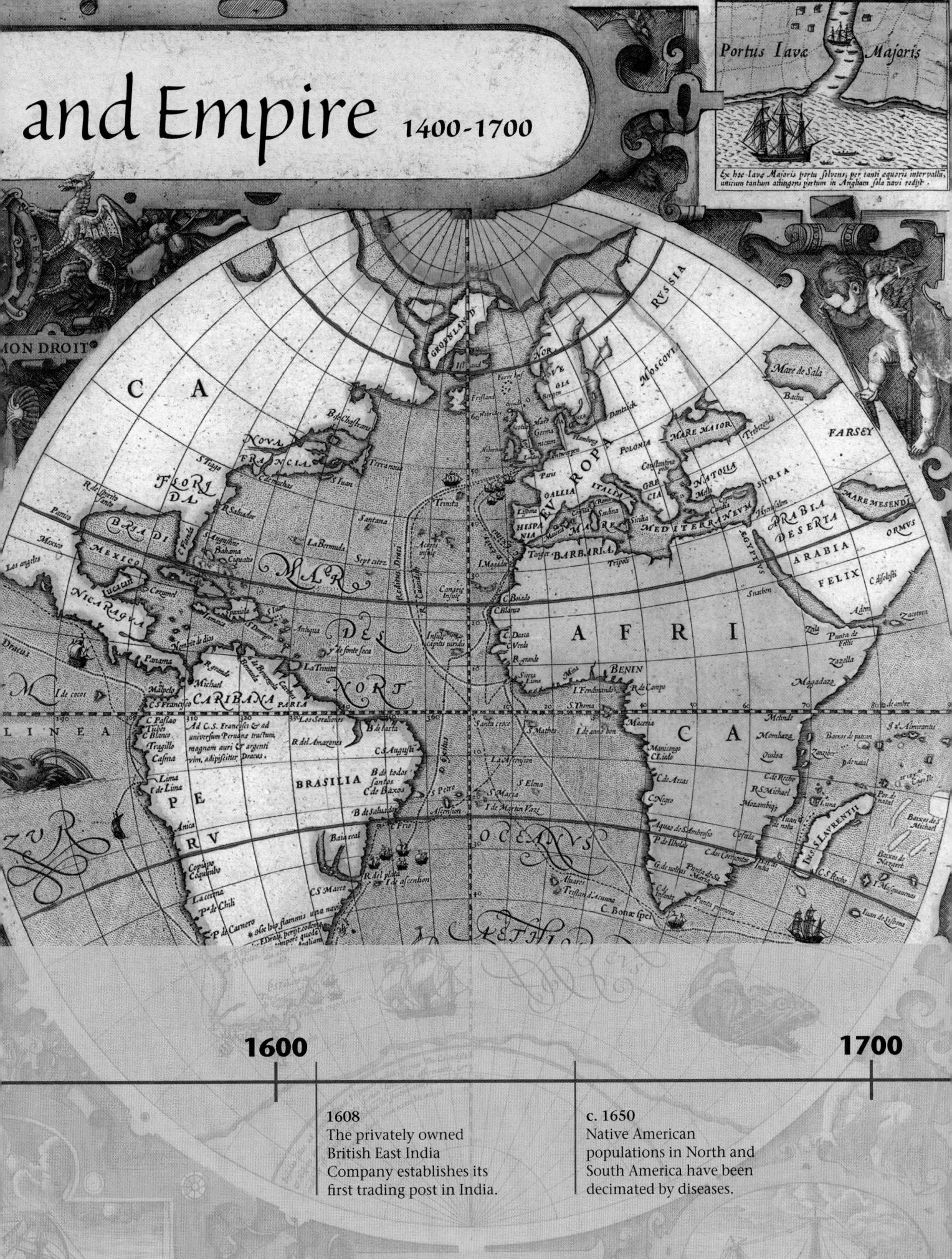

and Empire 1400-1700

Portus Iavæ Majoris

Ex hoc Iavæ Majoris portu soluens, per tanti æquoris interualla, unicum tantum attingens portum in Angliam sola naui redijt.

1608
The privately owned British East India Company establishes its first trading post in India.

c. 1650
Native American populations in North and South America have been decimated by diseases.

*I*n the late 1400s—about half a century after Zheng He, China's Ming Dynasty admiral, led his great fleets to explore distant lands—Europeans set forth on their own voyages of exploration. Seeking new water routes to the East, they were spurred by the Renaissance spirit of curiosity, a zeal to spread Christianity, and a renewed desire for trade in various goods. New ship designs and navigational aids helped explorers find their way across uncharted waters.

The explorers and those who sent them knew what they were after—spices, silk, gold, and other riches. But they had no idea that they would find whole continents previously unknown to them. The meeting of previously separated civilizations led to an exchange of peoples, plants, animals, and diseases that remains unparalleled in history.

In short order, European powers staked claims in the Americas. Economic theories and policies changed to meet new realities. Millions of Native Americans died of disease and abuse, dramatically reducing their populations within the first hundred years of contact. Millions of Africans were forced into slavery.

As people, ideas, and products moved around the globe as never before, the Age of Exploration became a time of both great progress and terrible destruction.

The Age of Exploration

In the twelfth and thirteenth centuries, Europeans returning from the Crusades brought back a new interest in the civilizations they had encountered in the East, as well as a desire for goods such as silk and exotic spices. In the fourteenth century, European trade with distant eastern lands was interrupted by the Black Death and other calamities. As the plague declined in Italy and other parts of Europe, population increased, cities grew, and trade revived. Beginning in the late fifteenth century, Europeans undertook a large-scale effort to explore faraway lands. Historians call this period the Age of Exploration.

Motivations for Exploration

What motivated Europeans to sail across uncharted seas to distant lands? In part they were driven by the Renaissance spirit of intellectual curiosity, the wish to know more about the world at large. But they were also prompted by the desire for economic gain.

As prosperity spread during the Renaissance, many Europeans were eager to buy goods from the East—silk and other cloth, pearls and gems, and, most of all, spices, including pepper, cloves, cinnamon, nutmeg, and ginger. In the days before refrigeration, spices both preserved and flavored food. Some spices were also used as medicines.

While spices were in great demand in Europe, by the 1400s it was getting harder to meet that demand. The Ottoman Turks controlled the Silk Road, a network of land routes from Europe through the Middle East to Asia, which they were determined to keep to themselves. So Europeans were motivated to find new trade routes to Asia, not over land but by sea.

On their long journeys by sea, European explorers found continents previously unknown to them. They claimed those lands for their own and settled many colonies. Eager for wealth and power, they built far-reaching empires. In some places, explorers were followed by missionaries and colonists eager to spread Christianity, partly in response to the spread of Islam and later to convert the native peoples

Some European mariners feared what they might find in unknown waters, such as the imagined sea monsters in this illustration.

Key Questions

- What motivated European exploration in the fifteenth and sixteenth centuries?
- What technological innovations aided Europeans in their voyages of exploration?

Mariner's compass,
c. 1570

in these distant lands. The mixed motivations urging Europeans to explore the world have been summed up in the phrase "glory, God, and gold."

Technologies Encourage Exploration

New or improved technologies made the Age of Exploration possible. One key innovation was a kind of ship called a *caravel*. Most ships in those days were large vessels built to carry heavy loads. But caravels could maneuver both on the open sea and in shallow waters. With their small hulls and light weight, caravels could approach unfamiliar coasts without scraping against rocks on the sea bottom. From Arab sailors, Portuguese shipbuilders adapted a triangular sail, which allowed caravels to catch the slightest breeze and even sail into the wind.

European explorers also took advantage of technologies that aided navigation. They used the magnetic compass, a tool that, as early as the twelfth century, had helped Chinese sailors find their way. European explorers also used a small round instrument from the Arab world, an astrolabe, which helped sailors estimate their latitude (their north-south position).

The Portuguese Set Sail

Portugal sits on the western edge of Europe. It is not quite one-fifth the size of Spain, its neighbor on the Iberian Peninsula. Portugal's craggy western coastline faces the vast Atlantic Ocean. In the 1400s, this tiny country launched Europe's Age of Exploration, thanks largely to the efforts of a prince who himself made only a few short sea voyages.

Prince Henry the Navigator

In the early 1400s, Prince Henry, who fervently believed in spreading Christianity, took part in a campaign that captured a Muslim stronghold in northwest Africa. As the third son of the king, Prince Henry was unlikely to become king, so he instead pursued his passion for the sea. He had both intellectual curiosity and a practical interest in seafaring. He worked with designers to improve ships. He supported voyages of exploration and enlisted mapmakers to record their discoveries. In Prince Henry's time, the Portuguese explored and colonized the islands known as the Madeiras (muh-DIR-uhz) and the Azores (AY-zohrz).

Prince Henry sponsored many expeditions, especially to Africa. He did so much to encourage exploration that, centuries after his death, he became known as Prince Henry the Navigator, the person most responsible for ushering in the Age of Exploration.

Trading in Africa

Most Europeans in the early fifteenth century knew little about Africa. European ships had sailed along the northern coastline, but no one knew the size or shape of the rest of Africa. Mapmakers did not know how far south the continent extended. Prince Henry, however, was determined to learn as much as he could about Africa and its resources, especially gold. The prince sent Portuguese explorers on more than fifty expeditions to Africa.

The Portuguese were the first Europeans to establish a large trade network in Africa in the 1400s. In 1434, Portuguese sailors sailed past Cape Bojador (boh-hah-DOHR), the farthest point Europeans had reached on the West African coast. As later voyages revealed more of the coast, the Portuguese began to trade with the local people. They bartered horses, wheat, and other products for gold. Sometimes the Portuguese took captured Africans back to Europe as slaves. (Later in this chapter you will read about the expansion of the slave trade.)

Seeking the Water Route to Asia

By the time Prince Henry died in 1460, his explorers had added some two thousand miles (3,220 km) of coastline to maps of Africa. Still, Europeans did not know where the continent ended, and had not found a way around it to Asia.

Dias Rounds the Cape

In 1487, King John II of Portugal sent Bartolomeu Dias (bahr-tou-lou-MAY-ou DEE-ahsh) to find the southern tip of Africa. Dias set sail with two caravels and a supply ship. His ships sailed south for months, when, in January 1488, they met a powerful storm. Dias left the supply ship behind, and the two caravels sailed for almost two weeks in the storm. Finally, the sea calmed. When, after days, Dias spotted land, he saw the coast was running in a new direction. His ships had accomplished the amazing feat of rounding the southern coast of Africa.

Dias wanted to push on in search of Asia but his exhausted crew demanded to return home.

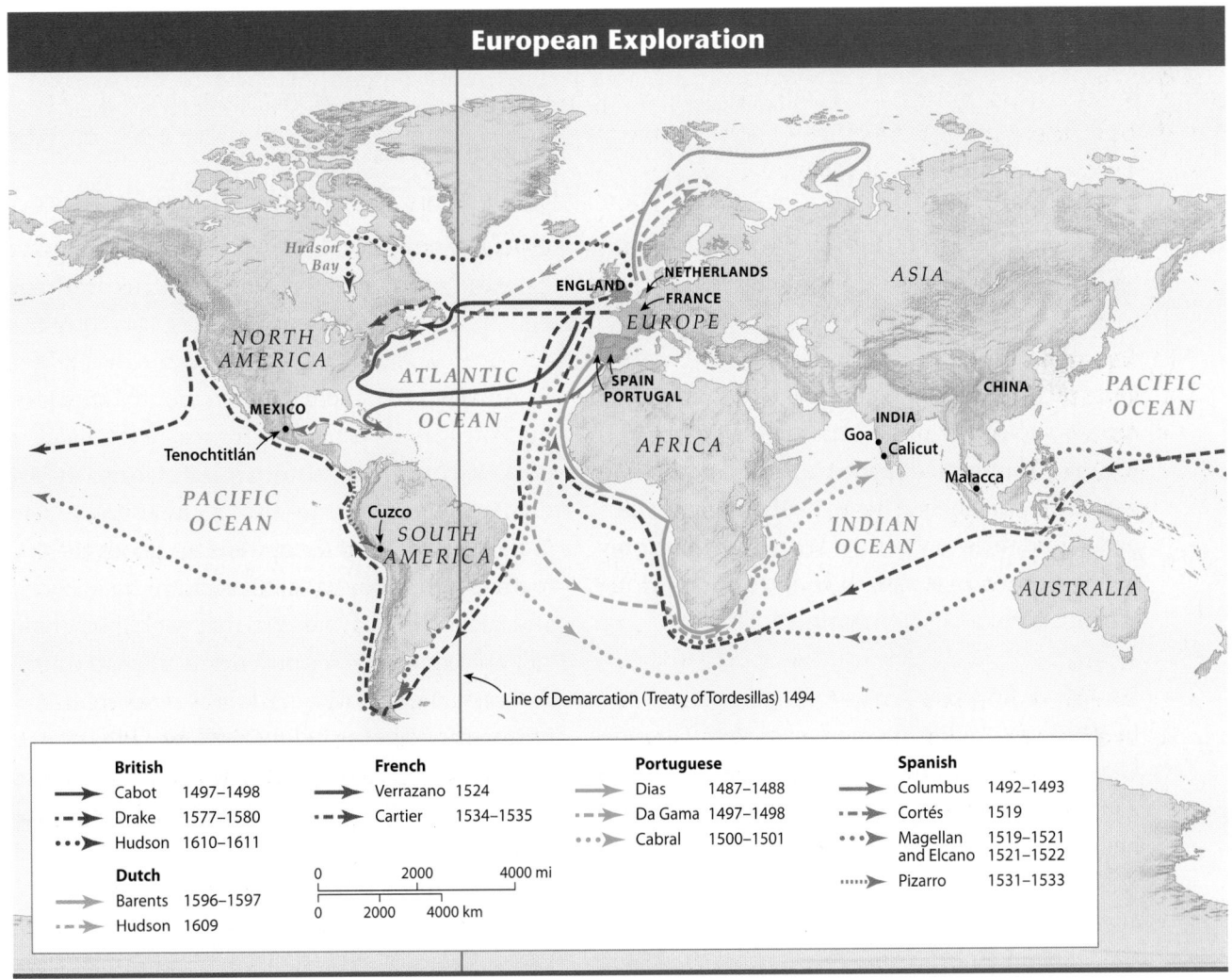

European Exploration

	British			French			Portuguese			Spanish	
→	Cabot	1497–1498	→	Verrazano	1524	→	Dias	1487–1488	→	Columbus	1492–1493
▪▪▶	Drake	1577–1580	▪▪▶	Cartier	1534–1535	▪▪▶	Da Gama	1497–1498	▪▪▶	Cortés	1519
•••▶	Hudson	1610–1611				•••▶	Cabral	1500–1501	•••▶	Magellan and Elcano	1519–1521 1521–1522
	Dutch								••••▶	Pizarro	1531–1533
→	Barents	1596–1597									
▪▪▶	Hudson	1609									

0   2000   4000 mi
0 2000 4000 km

Spurred on by Renaissance scholarship, improved maritime technology, and a growing economy, Europeans explored the globe and brought regional populations into contact for the first time.

From the Log of
Christopher Columbus

Columbus kept a daily record of his voyage of 1492. This excerpt from October 11 and 12 recounts a dramatic moment in history.

About 10 o'clock at night, while standing on the sterncastle, I thought I saw a light to the west. It looked like a little wax candle bobbing up and down. It had the same appearance as a light or torch belonging to fishermen or travelers who alternately raised and lowered it, or perhaps were going from house to house. I am the first to admit that I was so eager to find land that I did not trust my own senses, so I called for Pedro Gutiérrez, the representative of the King's household, and asked him to watch for the light. After a few moments, he too saw it. I then summoned Rodrigo Sánchez of Segovia…and asked him to watch for the light. He saw nothing, nor did any other member of the crew. It was such an uncertain thing that I did not feel it was adequate proof of land.

One early historical account says that Dias named Africa's southern tip the Cape of Storms, but that King John renamed it the Cape of Good Hope, because he finally had hope that Portuguese ships would find their way to Asia. With its often stormy weather and rough seas, the Cape of Good Hope remains a challenge for mariners.

Da Gama Reaches Asia

In 1497, another Portuguese explorer, Vasco da Gama, set sail on an expedition seeking a sea route to Asia. To avoid the coastal storms that had plagued Dias, he made a great loop south and west, out into the open sea. From there, he took advantage of trade winds that carried him around the Cape of Good Hope. The Portuguese ships rounded the cape and headed north. Along the way they stopped to explore Africa's eastern coast.

In May 1498, more than ten months after leaving Portugal, da Gama's ships reached Calicut, a port city on India's southwestern coast. At last the Portuguese were in Asia, ready to trade. The Indian merchants did not want the goods the Portuguese had brought, such as cloth, hats, corals, and sugar. Still, da Gama managed to take home valuable spices. More important, he had found the sea route to India, and he was taking useful information about trading back to Portugal.

On the trip home, approximately sixty sailors died of scurvy, a disease caused by lack of vitamin C. Of da Gama's original crew, only about one-third made it back to Portugal alive.

Columbus Sails West

In the years between the voyages of Dias and da Gama, Christopher Columbus, an Italian

The moon, in its third quarter, rose in the east shortly before midnight.... Then, at two hours after midnight, the Pinta fired a cannon, my prearranged signal for the sighting of land.

I now believe that the light I saw earlier was a sign from God and that it was truly the first positive indication of land. When we caught up with the Pinta, which was always running ahead because she was a swift sailer, I learned that the first man to sight land was Rodrigo de Triana, a seaman from Lepe....

At dawn we saw naked people, and I went ashore in the ship's boat, armed, followed by Martin Alonso Pinzón, captain of the Pinta, and his brother, Vincente Yanez Pinzón, captain of the Niña. I unfurled the royal banner and the captains brought the flags which displayed a large green cross.... After a prayer of thanksgiving I ordered the captains of the Pinta and Niña...to bear faith and witness that I was taking possession of this island for the King and Queen.... To this island I gave the name San Salvador, in honor of our Blessed Lord.

mariner from Genoa, set sail in the name of Portugal's neighbor and rival, Spain. Inspired by reading about the travels of Marco Polo, Columbus dreamed of finding a new route to the riches of China and the Indies. (When fifteenth-century Europeans spoke of "the Indies," they were referring to a large and varied group of lands, including India, China, Japan, Southeast Asia, and what they called the "spice islands" of Indonesia.)

In 1484, Columbus asked the king of Portugal to finance a voyage to find a route to Asia by sailing west across the Atlantic, rather than south and east around Africa. The king refused, as did the rulers of France and England. At last the monarchs of Spain, King Ferdinand and Queen Isabella, agreed to provide Columbus with three caravels, the *Niña*, the *Pinta*, and the *Santa María*.

In late summer 1492, Columbus's little fleet set off across the Atlantic. Columbus had seriously underestimated the distance between Europe and Asia—and he had no idea that another continent lay between. After sailing for a month out of sight of land, Columbus's men threatened mutiny. Finally, they saw land in the distance. It was a tropical island in the Caribbean, which Columbus promptly christened "San Salvador" or "Holy Savior."

The Spaniards landed and were greeted by some of the native people. Because Columbus thought he had reached the Indies, he called the native people "Indians." In reality, Columbus and his men had landed in what is now known as the Bahamas, a chain of islands off the coast of North America. And the natives he encountered were the Taino (TIY-noh) people.

Columbus and the "Indians"

When Columbus sailed back to Spain after his first voyage, he left behind a small colony of thirty-nine men on one of the Caribbean islands. In 1493, when Columbus returned to the Caribbean, he found that the colonists had been killed in a conflict with the natives. In revenge, he mounted a war against the Indians, killing hundreds, and shipping hundreds more as slaves to Spain to help pay for his expedition. The remaining natives were forced under penalty of death to hunt for gold and to provide the colonists with food. Columbus's treatment of the Native Americans set a tragic precedent for the centuries to come.

Columbus sailed home, where he received a hero's welcome from Ferdinand and Isabella. With the support of the Spanish monarchs, Columbus made three more transatlantic expeditions. On these voyages, he explored parts of the coastline of Central and South America. Columbus would die believing that he had reached Asia, never knowing that he had come upon what was, for the Europeans, a new continent.

New Lands and New Names

Columbus had happened upon a huge landmass separating the Atlantic and Pacific oceans, but these lands were not named after Columbus. That honor went to Amerigo Vespucci (uh-MEHR-ih-goh veh-SPYOO-chee), an Italian merchant with some expertise in navigation, who made an expedition across the Atlantic sponsored by Portugal in 1501.

While exploring the coast of what is now Brazil, Vespucci concluded that Columbus had not reached the Indies but instead found "a new land" that stood between Europe and Asia. Later, Vespucci wrote some widely circulated letters in which he described his voyages to the *Mundus Novus*—Latin for "New World." Vespucci's letters made their way to a German mapmaker. This mapmaker, apparently unaware of Columbus's voyages, issued a set of maps in which he labeled the new world "the land of Amerigo," or America. Later mapmakers repeated the label, and the name persisted.

Columbus's landfall in what he called the Indies did lead to a new name. Mapmakers eventually referred to the Caribbean islands off the coast of the Americas as the West Indies, to distinguish them from Columbus's original destination, which became known as the East Indies.

Magellan's Expedition Circles the World

In 1519, a Portuguese mariner, Ferdinand Magellan, led the most extraordinary voyage of the sixteenth century. Because he could not get funding

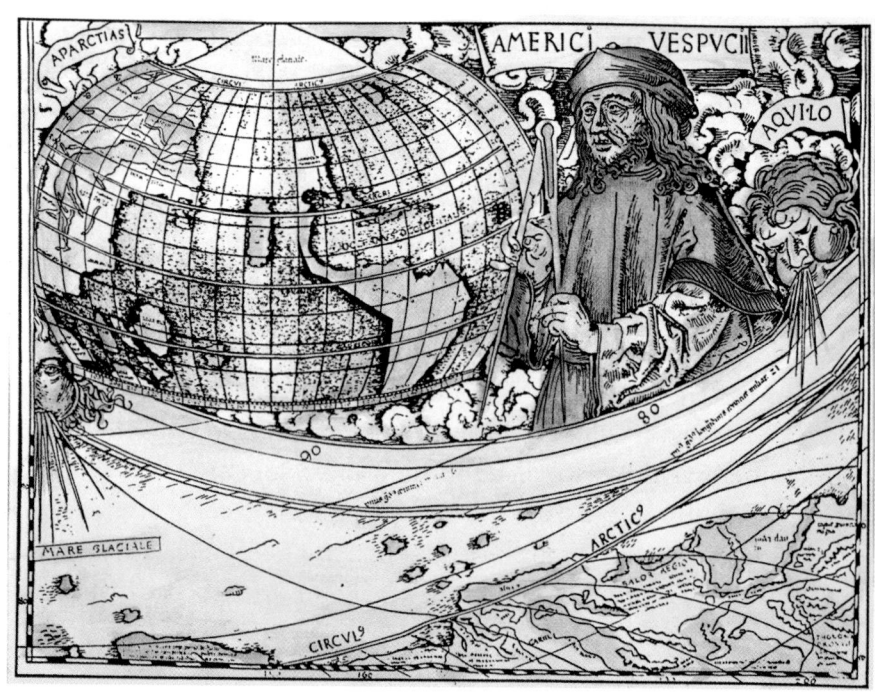

Amerigo Vespucci's widely circulated letters about the "New World" led mapmakers to name the unknown continent "America." This map dates from 1507.

Ferdinand Magellan

from the Portuguese king, Magellan sailed under the Spanish flag.

Given five ships and approximately two hundred seventy men, Magellan's task was to cross the Atlantic Ocean, find a way around South America to the Indies, and then return home. Magellan and his intrepid band rounded the southern tip of South America through stormy straits that now bear his name. When he got to the other side, he found the waters so peaceful that he labeled them "the Pacific."

Magellan and his crew sailed across the Pacific Ocean to the Philippines. There, Magellan was killed in a skirmish with native peoples. Losing ships as they went, his men sailed on, navigating through the Indian Ocean and up the west coast of Africa. Finally, three years after they had departed, they returned to their home port in Seville. Only one ship, appropriately named the *Victoria* (Victory), and eighteen of the original crew returned. Powered by nothing more than the wind, they had circumnavigated—sailed completely around—the world, and in the process claimed many lands for Spain.

Joining the Race and Seeking a Northwest Passage

News of Portuguese and Spanish successes inspired other European countries to sponsor their own expeditions. England, France, and the Netherlands all joined the race for trade and colonies. (Later in this chapter you will read more about the colonies they established.)

The English, French, and Dutch all hoped to find the Northwest Passage, a shortcut to Asia in the form of a sea route through North America to the Pacific Ocean. In 1497, the king of England sent the Italian mariner Giovanni Caboto—John Cabot to his English sponsors—to find this sea route. Cabot landed in Canada, and though he never located the Northwest Passage, England later used his trip as the basis for claims in North America.

In the 1520s, France sponsored a voyage led by another Italian, Giovanni da Verrazano, who explored the east coast of North America from Nova Scotia to the Carolinas and found what we know today as New York Harbor. A decade later, Jacques Cartier traveled along the St. Lawrence River in another fruitless search for the Northwest Passage. In doing so, Cartier established France's claim to the region.

One of Magellan's ships, the *Victoria*, safely returned to Spain after circling the globe.

451

Conquest and Colonies

Portugal and Spain were great rivals in the exploration of the seas. Both countries wanted to claim distant lands for themselves. With conflict looming, Spain and Portugal, both Catholic lands, turned to the pope.

Key Questions

- How did a small number of Spanish conquistadors manage to conquer the Aztecs and the Inca?

- What political and economic systems characterized the Spanish, French, and English colonies in the Americas?

- What was the impact of European colonization on Native Americans?

Spain and Portugal Divide the World

In 1493, Pope Alexander VI drew a line on a map of the Atlantic Ocean. He declared that anything east of the line—including lands along the coast of Africa—belonged to the Portuguese, while anything to the west—including almost all of the New World—belonged to the Spanish. The following year, Spain and Portugal signed the Treaty of Tordesillas (tor-day-SEE-yahs), which moved the line farther west, giving the Portuguese most of what would become the country of Brazil, and leaving the rest of the New World to the Spanish.

No one asked the natives of Africa and the Americas their opinion of this treaty that divided their lands and put them in European hands. Most Europeans of this time believed that European Christians had a God-given right to rule over "uncivilized" people who had not accepted the Christian religion.

Spain's New World Empire

Not long after Portugal launched the Age of Exploration, its larger neighbor, Spain, rushed to find new routes to Asia and to conquer new lands across the seas. Spanish explorers wanted to win glory for themselves and new lands for the Spanish crown. Some came to make converts to Christianity. Most of all, they came in search of gold.

In the early 1500s, Central and South America were invaded by groups of ruthless Spanish adventurers known as conquistadors (kahn-KEES-tuh-dorz). With superior weaponry and often treacherous tactics, the conquistadors conquered powerful and sophisticated native civilizations, including the Aztecs and the Inca.

Cortés Conquers the Aztecs

In Mexico, the conquistador Hernán Cortés overthrew the rich and populous Aztec Empire. The Aztecs' capital city, Tenochtitlán, boasted great temple pyramids and palaces that awed the Spaniards. One soldier later recalled, "These great towns and temple pyramids and buildings rising from the water, all made of stone, seemed like an enchanted vision."

The Spaniards had military advantages, including horses, weapons of sharp steel, and cannons. In his conquest of the Aztecs, Cortés found allies

Cortés led his Spanish troops across a causeway into Tenochtitlán, where the Spaniards eventually overpowered the Aztecs.

among the people who bitterly resented the tribute they were forced to pay to the Aztec emperor—not just corn and silver, but sons and daughters to be kept as slaves or sacrificed to the gods.

When the Spanish troops reached Tenochtitlán, the emperor himself, Montezuma II, came out to meet Cortés. The emperor welcomed Cortés with great ceremony. He lodged the Spaniards in a palace and sent servants with Aztec delicacies, such as chocolate. But Cortés, vastly outnumbered by the native population, grew worried that he had walked into a trap. He took the emperor hostage, and the Spaniards proceeded to ransack the royal treasury of Tenochtitlán, melting down priceless works of art for the gold.

Fearing for their emperor's life, at first the Aztecs did not resist. But finally they rose up against the Spaniards. In the fighting, Montezuma was killed, and Cortés lost half his troops. Ten months later, Cortés returned with a large force and laid siege to Tenochtitlán. He cut off the city's supply of food and fresh water.

The Aztecs held out for nearly four months. But the Spaniards had an unexpected ally in their fight—disease. An outbreak of smallpox had spread throughout the city of Tenochtitlán. The Aztecs had no resistance to this European plague. Thousands of people sickened and died. In the end, disease, starvation, and the steel swords of the Spaniards overwhelmed the Aztecs.

On the site of Tenochtitlán, the victorious invaders built Mexico City, the capital of New Spain. The Spaniards gained a huge empire, and the once mighty Aztec civilization was no more.

Pizarro Betrays the Inca

Far to the south, in the Andes Mountains of Peru, Francisco Pizarro led a small group of Spanish

Sculpted hands of gold, a rare surviving artifact of the Inca

soldiers who overcame the mighty Inca Empire. In 1531, when Pizarro landed on the coast of Peru, he did not find the prosperous towns he expected, but a scene of devastation. In the years since his last voyage, disease and civil war had ravaged the Inca Empire. The disease was smallpox. The Inca emperor himself may well have been one of the epidemic's millions of victims. He left behind two sons who battled each other. Years of bloody conflict had ended with Atahualpa as the emperor of the Inca.

When the Spaniards arrived, Atahualpa's control over his battered empire was still shaky. Pizarro saw his opportunity. He plunged into the mountains in search of Atahualpa. Pizarro had only a couple hundred Spanish soldiers, while the Inca emperor had eighty thousand warriors. But the Inca did not realize how treacherous Pizarro could be.

Pizarro sent messages of peace and friendship to Atahualpa. The Inca emperor, dressed in finery and surrounded by servants, ventured forth to meet the conquistador. Suddenly cannons boomed. The Spaniards emerged from hiding. Soldiers on horseback charged into the crowd, swords flashing. By nightfall, thousands of Inca lay dead, and their ruler had become a hostage.

In exchange for his release, Atahualpa offered to give his captors enough gold to fill the room where he was being held, and enough silver to fill two rooms. The Spaniards agreed. Load by load, the ransom began to arrive from the Inca capital, Cuzco. Pizarro and his men melted the jewelry and masks, more than thirty thousand pounds of gold and silver. But the Spaniards broke their promise to release Atahualpa. Instead, they executed him. When news of Atahualpa's death reached the Inca warriors, they scattered.

By 1537, the Inca Empire was in Spanish hands. Cuzco had fallen to Pizarro. The conquistador founded a new capital city named Lima (LEE-muh) near the Pacific coast.

Spanish Control in the New World

Both the Aztec and the Inca empires were rich in gold. As the Spanish pressed farther into the Americas, they discovered both gold and silver in many areas, including parts of the modern-day countries of Mexico, Peru, Bolivia, and Chile. Soon fleets of giant ships called *galleons* were crossing the Atlantic toward Spain, weighed down with the precious metals.

Conquistadors in the Southwest and Florida

Rumors of cities of gold lured the conquistador Francisco Vázquez de Coronado. In 1540, he set out to explore parts of modern-day New Mexico, Texas, and Oklahoma. While Coronado encountered such natural wonders as the Grand Canyon, he found no gold.

In 1565, Pedro Menéndez de Avilés landed in Florida with a fleet of Spanish ships and soldiers. He attacked a French settlement, killing all of its inhabitants. To defend against further challenges from the French or others, he established a fortified town that he named St. Augustine. In the decades and centuries to come, while St. Augustine would fall in and out of Spanish hands, it would persist, thus earning the distinction of being the oldest permanent European settlement in North America.

Gold and silver provided only a fraction of the wealth exported to Europe. Back in Europe, textile manufacturers wanted the blue dye from the indigo plant. Merchants wanted animal hides. And Europeans developed an appetite for food products from the New World, including chocolate (made from cacao beans), corn, tomatoes, potatoes, and, most of all, sugar (made from the juice of sugarcane, which grew well in tropical parts of the Americas).

Under the direction of Spanish conquistadors, native slaves built Mexico City on the ruins of the Aztec capital of Tenochtitlán.

The Spanish saw the Americas as an endless stream of gold, silver, sugar, and other goods, constantly flowing to fill royal purses. To ensure a steady flow of riches from the New World, the Spanish crown took steps to impose tight controls on its colonies.

Spain's rulers began by dividing their New World lands into two parts, New Spain and Peru. To rule each part, the king of Spain appointed an official called a *viceroy*, a title that means "in place of the king." Through the viceroys, the king gave orders that touched every detail of the colonists' lives. For example, the king specified that the colonists could plant lemons and oranges, but not grapes and olives (because the king wanted the colonists to keep buying high-priced wine and olive oil imported from Spain).

The king also maintained control of his New World colonies by imposing a rigid class structure. At the top were the *peninsulares* (pehn-EEN-suh-LAHR-ehs), native Spaniards born on the Iberian Peninsula. The peninsulares held all important government positions in the colonies. Beneath the peninsulares were the *Creoles* (KREE-ohlz), members of Spanish families who were born and raised in America. Many of the Creoles were grandchildren or great-grandchildren of the conquistadors. The Spaniards placed a high importance on a person's place of birth and held on to the prejudice that the Creoles were inferior because they had been born in the "savage" New World.

Beneath the Creoles were the *mestizos* (meh-STEE-zohz), people of mixed race descended from both Spaniards and native people. At the very bottom of the class structure came the Aztec, Inca, and other native peoples who had survived the Spanish conquest.

Through the *encomienda* (en-koh-mee-EHN-duh) system, the Spanish forced the native people to do backbreaking labor in mines and fields. An *encomienda* was a large grant of land from the Spanish crown. Those who received these grants, often victorious conquistadors, took "tribute" from the local Indians in the form of a large share of the crops they grew or the gold and silver they mined. For the native people, the encomienda system was little better than slavery.

"Nothing more detestable or more cruel"

Catholic missionaries came from Spain to the New World to convert the native people to the Catholic faith. Many were friars, members of religious orders who had taken vows of poverty. Some perceived that widespread mistreatment of the native people made it harder to win converts. In the 1540s, some missionaries called for an end to mistreatment of the Native Americans.

A friar named Bartolomé de Las Casas (bahr-toh-loh-MAY day lahs KAHS-ahs) wrote *A Brief Account of the Destruction of the Indies* to publicize Spanish mistreatment of the Indians. Most scholars think that while Las Casas may have exaggerated some claims in order to prompt reforms, his accounts are generally accurate. For forty years, Las Casas traveled back and forth between Spain and the Americas, addressing influential audiences in person and in writing, with the goal of ending the mistreatment of native peoples.

In this excerpt, Las Casas describes the way Spanish colonists forced natives to dive for pearls.

There is nothing more detestable or more cruel, than the tyranny which the Spaniards use toward the Indians for the getting of pearl. Surely the infernal torments cannot much exceed the anguish that they endure, by reason of that way of cruelty; for they put them under water some four or five ells [15 to 18 feet] deep, where they are forced without any liberty of respiration, to

The Portuguese in Brazil

Like Spain, Portugal kept a tight grip on its New World colonies, and compelled natives to labor in mines and fields. As a result of the Treaty of Tordesillas, in which the pope had decreed a line dividing the lands of the New World between Portugal and Spain, Portugal's only South American colony was the country now called Brazil.

At first the Portuguese did not realize they had been given Brazil. Not until 1500, when the Portuguese explorer Pedro Cabral was blown off course, did they know that New World lands existed to the east of the dividing line. When Cabral landed on the coast of what became Brazil, he planted the flag for Portugal, and Portuguese colonization followed. (To this day, while the language spoken in most of South America is Spanish, the official language of Brazil is Portuguese.)

Dutch, French, and English Ventures

During the 1600s, other European countries competed with Spain and Portugal for trade around the world. The Netherlands, France, and England

gather up the shells wherein the pearls are; sometimes they come up again with nets full of shells to take breath, but if they stay any while to rest themselves, immediately comes a hangman rowed in a little boat, who as soon as he has well beaten them, drags them again to their labor.

Their food is nothing but filth, and the very same that contains the pearl, with a small portion of that bread which that country affords; in the first whereof there is little nourishment; and as for the latter, it is made with great difficulty, besides that they have not enough of that neither for sustenance; they lie upon the ground in fetters, lest they should run away; and many times they are drowned in this labor, and are never seen again till they swim upon the top of the waves: oftentimes they also are devoured by certain sea monsters, that are frequent in those seas.

Consider whether this hard usage of the poor creatures be consistent with the precepts which God commands concerning charity to our neighbor, by those that cast them so undeservedly into the dangers of a cruel death, causing them to perish without any remorse or pity, or allowing them the benefit of the sacraments, or the knowledge of religion....

The painter symbolizes the concern of Las Casas for the native people by depicting an Indian standing at the priest's shoulder.

all sought to enrich themselves through trade and colonization.

The Netherlands: Many Dutch Colonies

Despite its small size and lack of natural resources, the Netherlands, or Dutch Republic, quickly became a power at sea. The Dutch capital of Amsterdam became a hub of commerce in Europe, and the Netherlands became one of the wealthiest countries in the world.

By 1600, the Netherlands had the biggest fleet in the world. By the middle of the 1600s, the Dutch controlled the very profitable spice trade in today's Indonesia. They also traded coffee, tea, and sugar, and controlled many of the major islands of the region.

Dutch settlers known as Boers colonized Capetown on the southern tip of Africa, where ships sailing to Asia put in for supplies. In North America, the Dutch established the colony of New Netherland, with a busy trading post, New Amsterdam, on Manhattan Island. There they enjoyed a profitable fur trade with the natives of the area. In 1664, the English gained control of

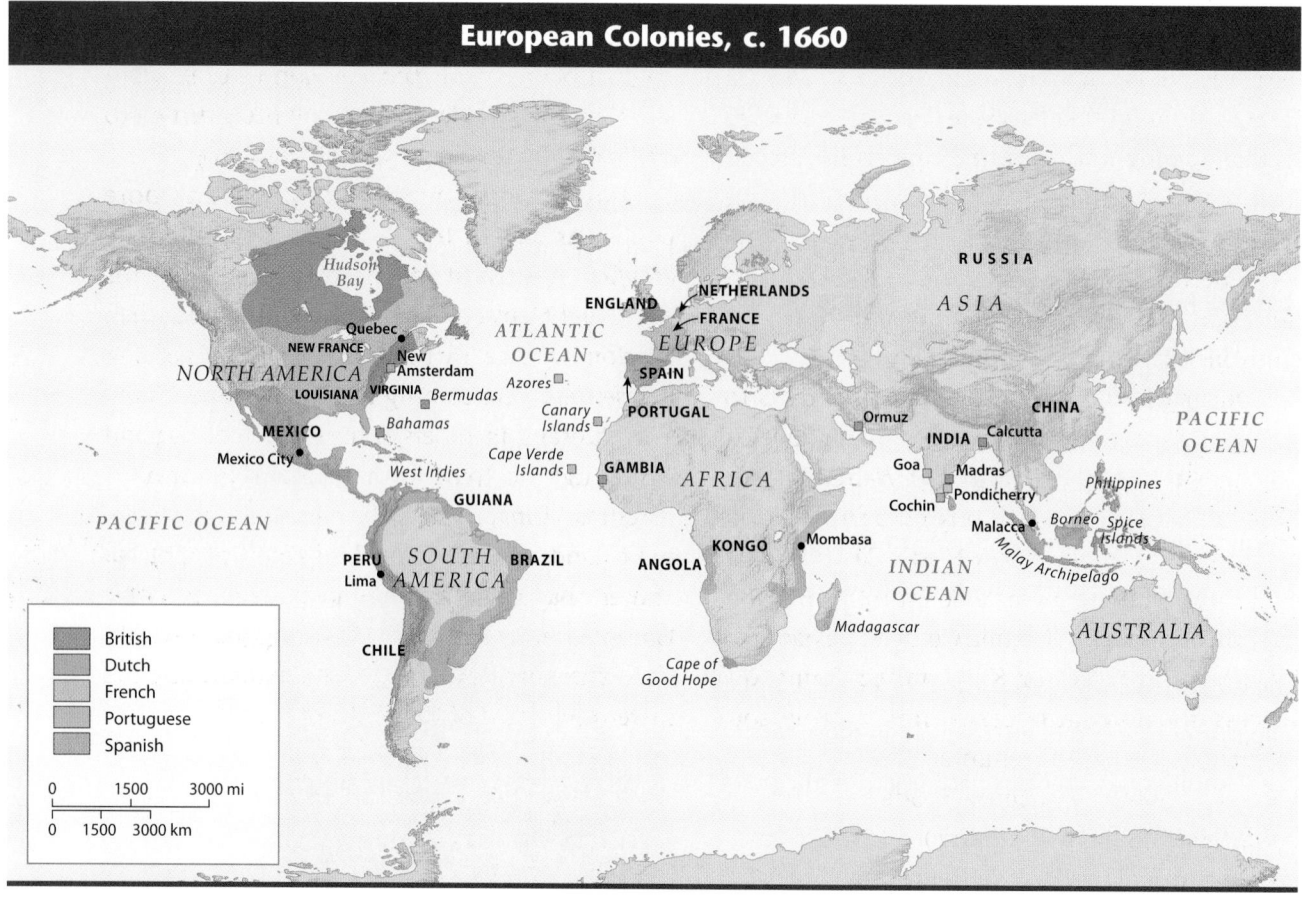

European Colonies, c. 1660

British
Dutch
French
Portuguese
Spanish

0   1500   3000 mi
0   1500   3000 km

One hundred fifty years after the first daring European voyages of discovery, five major European powers had established colonies throughout the Americas, Asia, and Africa.

New Netherland and renamed it New York, but Dutch influence can still be seen in place names throughout the Hudson River valley.

The French in North America

France, too, sought overseas trade and colonies. The French hoped to profit from the Indian Ocean trade but were unable to dislodge the Dutch. In North America, however, the French did find success. There, they established a profitable fur trade along the rivers where Verrazano, Cartier, and other early explorers had made claims for France. In 1608, Samuel de Champlain founded the settlement of Quebec (kwi-BEK) on the cliffs above the St. Lawrence River.

In the late 1600s, another explorer, Louis Joliet (LOO-ee jahl-ee-ET), and the Jesuit missionary Jacques Marquette (zhahk mahr-KET) explored the northern Mississippi River valley and the area around the Great Lakes. A later explorer, Sieur de La Salle, traveled south on the Mississippi River and claimed the region he called Louisiana in honor of France's King Louis XIV.

Though France controlled a wide swath of North America from the Gulf of St. Lawrence to the Gulf of Mexico, few French settlements grew bigger than trading posts. Most French who came to North America were Catholic priests who hoped to convert Native Americans and young adventurers hoping for profit from the growing fur-trapping and trading business.

England's North American Colonies

England's Queen Elizabeth I came to power in the 1550s as Spain, England's rival, was gaining enormous wealth from its overseas empire. Elizabeth was determined to make England an empire as well. During the late 1500s, Elizabeth sponsored many voyages, though not all were focused on exploration. Francis Drake and others attacked Spanish ships for their treasure and were rewarded by the queen. Not until the English East India Company was chartered in 1600 did England begin to compete with Portugal, Spain, and the Netherlands for territory. By the mid-1600s, England had successful trading posts in India and controlled the trade in Indian fabric.

Queen Elizabeth also sponsored attempts to establish an English colony in North America. The queen's favorite courtier, Sir Walter Raleigh, proposed to establish a colony on a small island off the coast of what is now North Carolina. The attempt to colonize there failed. In 1607, however, the privately owned Virginia Company, chartered by Elizabeth's successor, King James I, founded a successful colony at Jamestown in what is now Virginia. (Later in this chapter you will read about the business model behind the Virginia Company.)

The first English settlers at Jamestown were unprepared for the hardships they faced. Hunger and disease killed all but 38 of the 104 men. But more settlers arrived the next year, led by Captain John Smith, who took charge and set everyone to work. The outlook for the colony improved until Smith was injured and returned to England.

Many colonists died of starvation during the hard winter of 1609–10. Still Jamestown survived, in part because the Virginia Company continued to send colonists, ten thousand in all by 1622. Jamestown began to prosper when the colonists planted tobacco, a crop that proved so profitable that many settlers refused to plant food on the land they cleared. The cultivation of tobacco required intense labor. In 1619, when a Dutch ship arrived in Jamestown carrying abducted Africans, some English planters saw the solution to their labor shortage. Decades later, many planters turned to enslaved Africans to grow their cash crop.

Farther north on the Atlantic coast, more English arrived in 1620 aboard a ship called the *Mayflower*. Most of these settlers were Pilgrims who sought a place where they could practice their religion in peace. By the 1630s, thousands of English settlers were coming to New England. Many were Puritans, members of the Church of England who sought to "purify" their church of Catholic practices. Unhappy with the religious atmosphere in England, they established the colonies of Massachusetts Bay, Connecticut, Rhode Island, and New Hampshire. By the early 1700s, England would have thirteen colonies south of Canada along the eastern seaboard of North America.

Pilgrims prepare to set sail from England aboard the *Mayflower*. Many traveled to the New World seeking freedom to worship in peace. By the 1630s, thousands of English settlers were coming to New England.

Global Contact and Its Consequences

Key Questions

- What is the Columbian Exchange? What were its consequences?

- As Europeans colonized the New World, what new economic ideas guided them, and what new business organizations emerged?

- What effect did the emerging transatlantic slave trade have on Africa, on enslaved Africans, and on the Americas?

The age of European exploration and expansion marked a turning point in world history. Previously separated civilizations met, mingled, and often clashed. The transfer of plants and animals between continents changed diets and farming patterns around the world. New sources of food led to enormous population growth in parts of Europe and Asia. Colonial trade vastly increased the wealth of some European nations and gave rise to new forms of economic organization. But for non-European peoples, the consequences of these exchanges were often disastrous.

The Columbian Exchange

For most of the earth's history, the continents of North and South America remained cut off from the rest of the world by two broad oceans. Because of this isolation, American plants and animals evolved into forms very different from those of Europe or Asia. For example, South America had llamas, while Asia had camels. Bison roamed in North America, while cattle grazed in Europe. In the Old World—the parts of the world known to Europeans before their encounter with the Americas—people grew rice and wheat for food. But in the New World, they grew maize (corn) and potatoes.

The European encounter with the Americas started an enormous two-way traffic in plants and animals, as well as people and diseases, between the Old World and the New. Historians call this process the **Columbian Exchange**, named after Christopher Columbus. The Columbian Exchange would have far-reaching and long-lasting consequences for human history. To appreciate these consequences, it is necessary to look ahead to the years following the beginnings of the Columbian Exchange.

Europeans who came to conquer or settle in the New World brought domesticated animals such as horses, cattle, and sheep. The horse played an especially important role in the Spanish conquests of Mexico and Peru. Horses had once existed in the Americas, but had become extinct there centuries before the arrival of the Europeans.

At first, Native Americans were terrified by the sight of mounted Spanish warriors. Later, however, Native Americans would learn from Europeans how to domesticate

Corn originated in the Americas.

horses and other Old World animals. In the 1800s, the Comanche of North America's Great Plains became famous for their skill at hunting and fighting from horseback.

Native groups in the southwestern United States, such as the Navajo, started raising sheep for food and clothing. At the same time, in the United States, Mexico, and South America, the descendants of European settlers raised vast herds of cattle to consume as beef.

Like the exchange of animals, the exchange of plants altered the diets of people in both the New World and the Old. Wheat from Europe became a staple crop in the United States and other American countries. From the New World came tomatoes and an even more important export, the potato, long a mainstay among the Inca. Spanish soldiers brought potatoes back from Peru. At first, Europeans looked down on the potato as plain and bland. Gradually, however, they realized that potatoes were both easy to grow and highly nutritious. By growing potatoes, even a poor farmer could feed a large family. After potatoes became a staple food in Ireland, the population of that impoverished country doubled. The cultivation of the potato also led to dramatic population growth in England and France.

Tomatoes, new to the Old World

Devastating Diseases

The Columbian Exchange had tragic effects as well. It was not only plants and animals that crossed the oceans. Europeans brought several diseases to the New World, including measles, chicken pox, malaria, and yellow fever. These diseases were new to America, so the native people had not developed immunity to them.

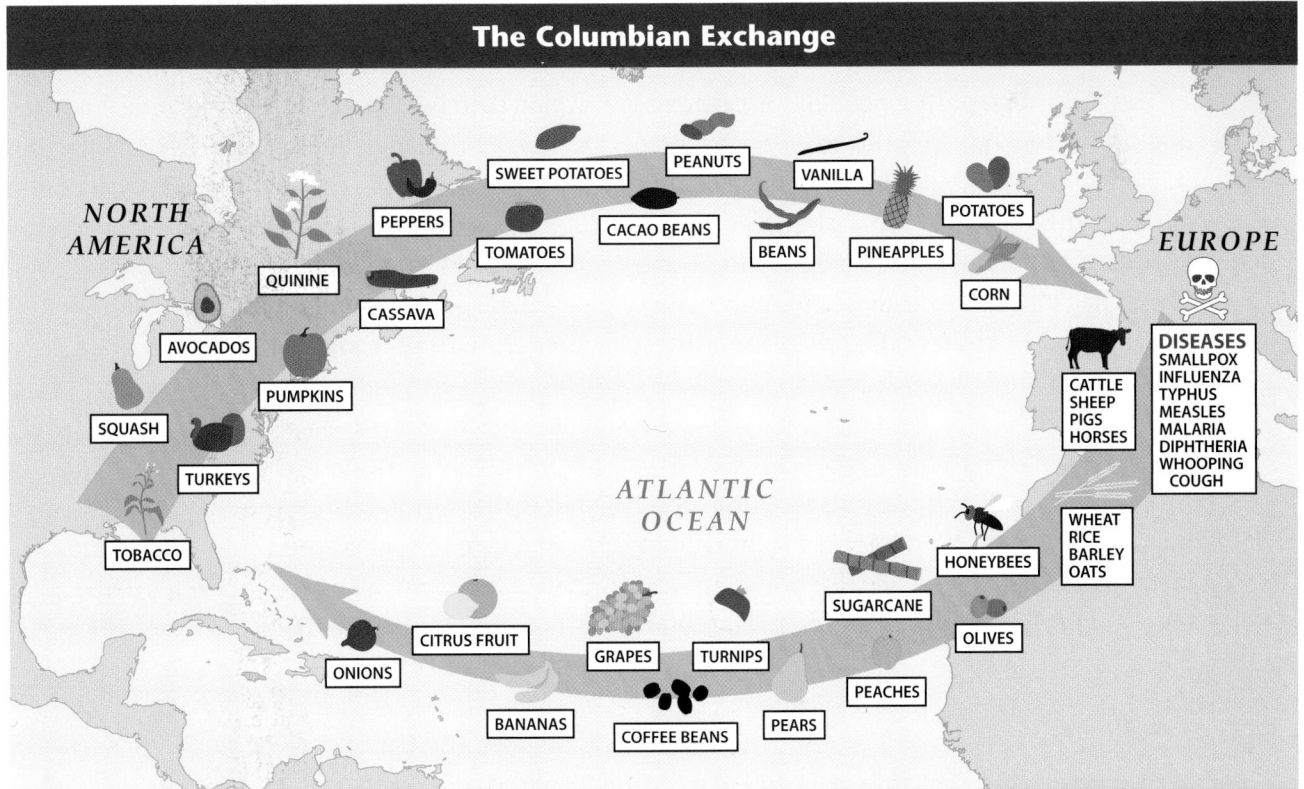

The Columbian Exchange

Movement of goods and people from Europe to the Americas and back again, by the process that came to be known as the Columbian Exchange, changed the course of human history in both the Old World and the New.

Disease and Population in Mexico

Effects of diseases on the population of native peoples of Central Mexico

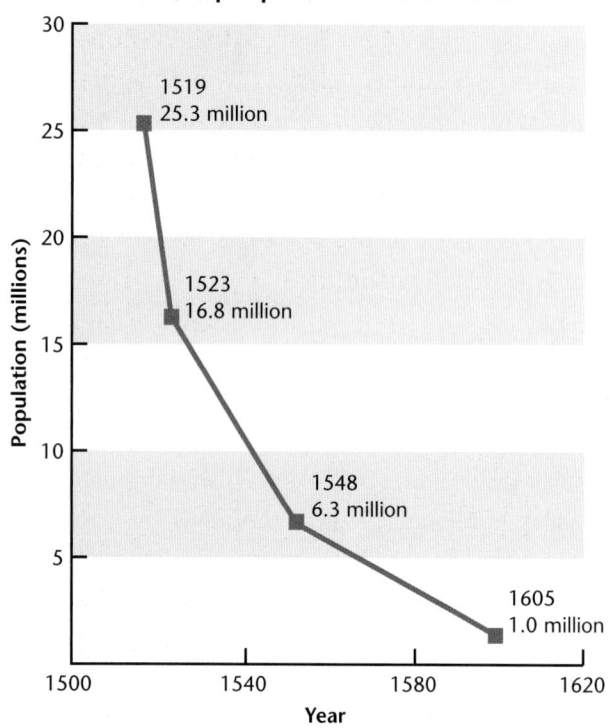

The most devastating of these diseases was smallpox, which killed millions in both North and South America. Modern historians estimate that after fifty years of contact between Native Americans and Europeans, smallpox and other diseases had killed almost 90 percent of the native people. One scholar has called this "the greatest tragedy in the history of the human species."

New Economic Arrangements

Europeans had different reasons for conquering and settling the New World. Some sought military glory, some sought a better life for themselves, and some sought to spread Christianity. The rulers of nations such as Spain and England saw their colonies, above all, as a source of wealth.

Mercantilism and Capitalism

The English soldier and explorer Sir Walter Raleigh declared, "Whosoever commands the trade of the world, commands the riches of the world and consequently the world itself." His words capture the essence of an idea called **mercantilism** (MUR-kuhn-tih-lih-zuhm). The governments of colonial nations based their economic policies on mercantilism. According to this economic theory, a nation's power was directly connected to its wealth, and its wealth depended on the amount of gold and silver it owned. Thus, colonies where these precious metals could be mined—like Mexico and Peru—were especially valuable. Colonies with other resources—for example, timber, cotton, or tobacco—were still valued, because those resources could be traded for gold and silver.

Under mercantilism, the possession of colonies was thought to increase the wealth of a nation and therefore also increase its power. Mercantilist nations profited from their colonies not only as suppliers of raw materials but also as consumers of manufactured goods. For example, a colony might produce cotton as a raw material, which would be shipped to the "mother country" to be manufactured into cloth, which the colonists would then purchase. Because mercantilist nations generally forbade colonists from manufacturing their own goods or trading with other nations, the colonies became a ready-made market for goods produced in the ruling country.

Trade between Europe and its colonies spurred the growth of **capitalism**. Under this economic system, most businesses are owned by private individuals rather than the government. Capitalism in some form had existed in Europe since the Middle Ages. But Europe's expansion into the Americas vastly increased the opportunities for its businessmen to acquire wealth through manufacturing and trade.

Tobacco could be traded for gold and silver.

Colonists load a ship with Virginia's most valuable export—tobacco. England's North American colonies were thriving by the end of the seventeenth century.

Another privately owned joint-stock company, the Virginia Company, chartered by King James I in 1606, founded the colony of Jamestown in Virginia. The investors in the Virginia Company were disappointed when no gold or silver was found in Jamestown or its surroundings. But they soon profited from the colony's growth and export of tobacco.

The Atlantic Slave Trade

As the Age of Exploration got underway in the late 1400s, the Portuguese arrived on the African coast to find an already active slave trade. African traders sold enslaved people, often captives taken in war, to eastern lands and to the Islamic world. As you've seen, the Portuguese were the first Europeans to export enslaved people from Africa. At first, in the early 1400s, these Africans were taken to Spain and Portugal to work as servants. By 1550, as much as one-tenth of the population of Portugal's capital, Lisbon, consisted of African slaves.

On the other side of the world, landowners and mine owners in Spanish and Portuguese colonies in Central and South America faced a severe labor shortage. As diseases like smallpox caused the deaths of hundreds of thousands of Native Americans, the Spanish and Portuguese had to look elsewhere for a supply of labor. They found it in Africa.

Early in the 1500s, the Spanish began importing African slaves to their colonies in the Caribbean. At first they had to buy slaves from the Portuguese, who for a while held exclusive control of the African slave trade.

The Rise of Joint-Stock Companies

When a merchant made a profit, he then had capital—money that he could invest. He could use this money to expand his business and become even more prosperous. Individual investors, however, rarely had enough capital to support very expensive ventures, such as trade with the colonies. So they pooled their capital to form **joint-stock companies**. In a joint-stock company, each investor owned a part of the company and, if the company succeeded, was entitled to a share of the profits.

Joint-stock companies played a large role in colonial trade, especially in the English colonies. In 1600, Queen Elizabeth granted a royal charter to the East India Company, giving it an exclusive right to trade with the Indies, as the lands of southern and eastern Asia were called. In 1608, the British East India Company established its first trading post in India. Over the next two centuries, the power of the East India Company would grow until this privately owned company in effect ruled large parts of India.

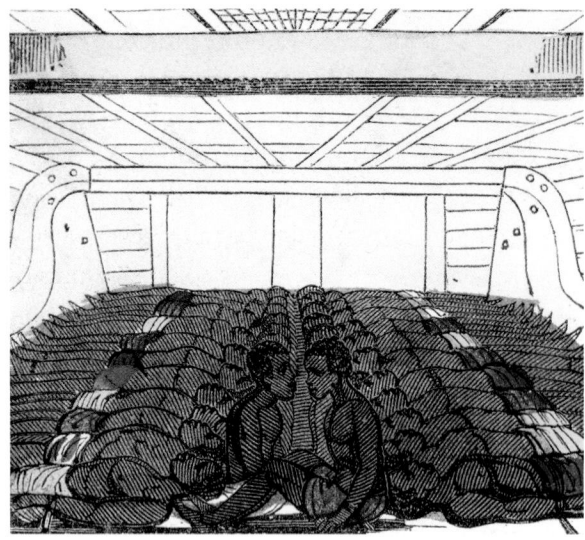

Captured Africans were chained and tightly packed below the decks of slave ships during the Middle Passage.

of a slave-trading ship, was part of a three-legged, triangular trade route that developed between western Europe, Africa, and the Americas. On the first leg of the journey, ships carried manufactured goods from Europe to Africa. European merchants sold their cargo on Africa's west coast, and bought slaves.

In the second or "middle" leg of the journey, the merchants transported the slaves across the Atlantic and sold them in the West Indies or elsewhere. Finally, the merchants purchased sugar or tobacco, and then sailed back to Europe. Because the slave crossing represented the middle leg of this triangular trade, it became known as the Middle Passage.

The transatlantic slave trade accelerated in the sixteenth century, when the Portuguese began growing sugarcane on plantations in the West Indies and in Brazil. For the slaves on sugar plantations, life was especially brutal. At harvest time, slaves worked all day in the tropical heat, cutting and lifting heavy cane stalks, driven by overseers brandishing whips. They kept working far into the night, standing over boiling cauldrons for up to twelve hours. Those who couldn't keep up were whipped or put in the stocks. To satisfy Europe's taste for sweets, tens of thousands of African slaves died in Brazil from overwork or abuse.

Far more Africans were transported to Brazil as slaves than to any other New World colony. Historians estimate that roughly 40 percent of the millions of abducted Africans who eventually crossed the Atlantic wound up in Brazil.

The Middle Passage

The voyage from Africa to the Americas, crossing the Atlantic while chained in the filthy hold

More Nations Join the Slave Trade

Portugal and Spain started the transatlantic slave trade. But soon other European nations—England, France, and the Netherlands—claimed colonies in the West Indies and joined in the grim human commerce. By the middle of the eighteenth century, British merchants were transporting more slaves than any other European nation. Most of those slaves were taken to work on sugar plantations in

African slaves work on a sugar plantation in the Americas. Slaves replaced the native peoples who died largely from diseases brought from the Old World.

Britain's island colonies in the Caribbean. The rest were taken to the British colonies in North America.

Slaves sent to the Caribbean and to South America often did not live long. A harsh climate, disease, and severe living conditions led to high mortality among these mostly male slaves. As they died, plantation owners bought new slaves to replace them.

In the early seventeenth century, the British began importing slaves into their North American colonies. There, as in the Caribbean and South America, most slaves were agricultural workers. In North America, the important crops were rice, tobacco, and indigo.

In North America, life expectancy for slaves was longer. Because many of these slaves were women, more North American slaves had children, who also became slaves. Thus, the North American slave population continued to grow.

The transatlantic slave trade resulted over time in the forced migration of as many as twelve

Where Were Transatlantic Slaves Taken?

By 1750, the Spanish, Portuguese, French, Dutch, and British all participated in the transatlantic slave trade. About 45 percent of slaves who crossed the Atlantic were sold to work in the sugar fields of the West Indies. About 40 percent were sent to the Portuguese colony of Brazil. Another 10 percent were taken elsewhere in the Caribbean and Spanish-American colonies of Central and South America. About 5 percent went to the North American colonies that later became the United States.

million Africans to the Americas. It destroyed many African families and communities, created unspeakable misery for those enslaved, and left behind a complex legacy of ongoing race and class struggles.

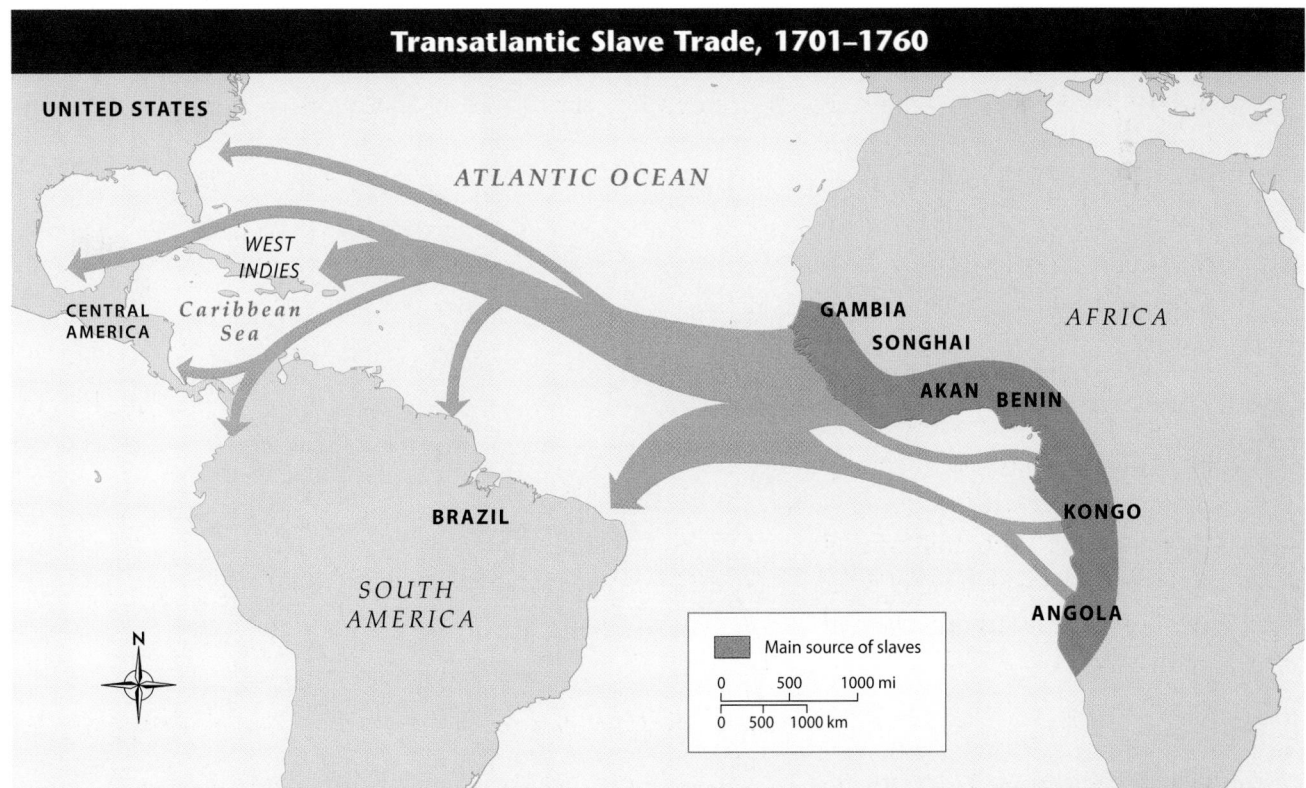

Transatlantic Slave Trade, 1701–1760

UNITED STATES

ATLANTIC OCEAN

WEST INDIES

CENTRAL AMERICA   *Caribbean Sea*

GAMBIA   *AFRICA*
SONGHAI
AKAN   BENIN

KONGO

BRAZIL

SOUTH AMERICA

ANGOLA

Main source of slaves

0   500   1000 mi
0   500   1000 km

N

Trade in enslaved people from western Africa—begun by Portugal and Spain and soon taken up by England, France, and the Netherlands—extended to much of the New World, but was concentrated in Brazil and the West Indies.

Chapter 21
Religious Reformation
and the *Rise of Monarchs*
1500–1700

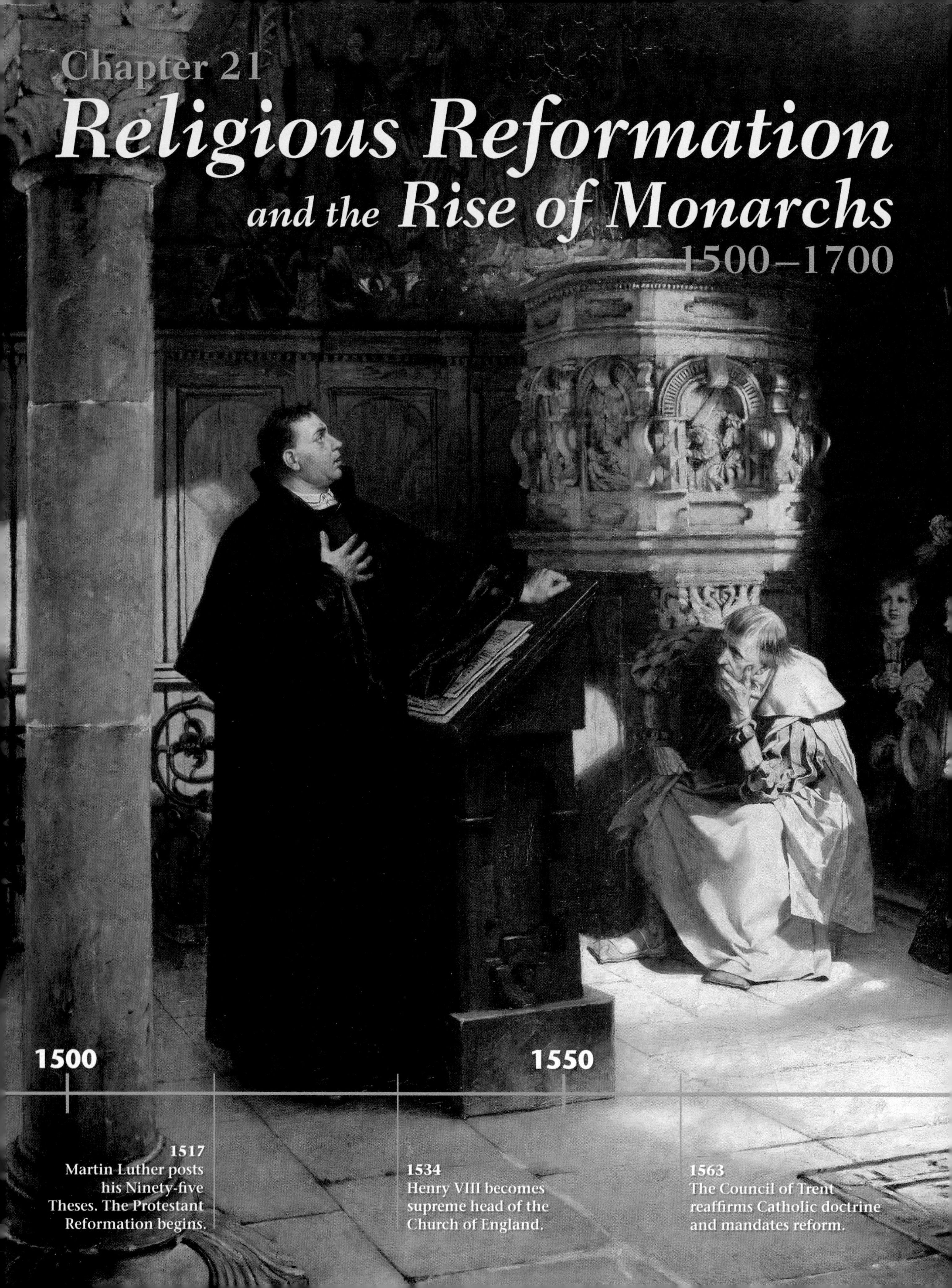

1500

1550

1517
Martin Luther posts his Ninety-five Theses. The Protestant Reformation begins.

1534
Henry VIII becomes supreme head of the Church of England.

1563
The Council of Trent reaffirms Catholic doctrine and mandates reform.

Martin Luther spoke against corruption in the Christian church, which eventually split into Catholic and Protestant.

1648
The Peace of Westphalia ends
the Thirty Years' War.

1600

1650

1643
Louis XIV, the Sun King,
becomes king of France.

1649
Oliver Cromwell and
Puritan followers end
the English Civil War by
executing King Charles I.

1689
England's monarchs
agree to a Bill of Rights.

*I*n the sixteenth century, critics within the Catholic Church launched a movement known as the Reformation. The name of the movement comes from the word *reform*, which means "to improve, to make better." The Reformation began as an attempt to make changes that would lead to a better church. But before it was over, the Reformation expanded into a vast movement that split Christianity, divided a continent, ignited bloody wars, and changed the world forever.

As the idea of a unified Christendom dissolved, ambitious kings and princes took sides, often for political rather than religious reasons. Long-standing rivalries led to wars across Europe, including the Thirty Years' War. States and their rulers gained power at the expense of the church. In the face of increasing turmoil, strong monarchs asserted their power in various lands, nowhere more clearly than in France under Louis XIV.

England, however, took a different course, not because England's monarch didn't want absolute rule, but because Parliament and the centuries-old traditions begun with the Magna Carta wouldn't allow it. It took a civil war, the execution of a king, the repressive rule of a Puritan military dictator, and the restoration of the monarchy to reach the Glorious Revolution of 1689, which confirmed England as a constitutional monarchy, with the king subject to the rule of law.

The Protestant Reformation

By the late Middle Ages, no single institution dominated life and thought in western Europe as much as the Christian church headed by the pope in Rome—what would come to be known as the Catholic Church. So deep and widespread was the influence of Christianity that western Europe became known as Christendom. Going beyond spiritual matters, the church exerted great political and economic influence on European society. Church leaders competed with secular rulers for power and wealth. Indeed, during the Renaissance, Pope Julius II—who took his name from Julius Caesar, and came to be known as the "Warrior Pope"—even led troops into battle against rebellious city-states.

Unrest in the Roman Church

Some critics of the church—for example, Erasmus and Thomas More—charged that church leaders neglected spiritual concerns in their pursuit of power, wealth, and luxury. These critics wanted to clean up the corruption they saw among greedy priests, worldly cardinals, and power-hungry popes.

Around 1500, this desire to clean up the church took on a new intensity, fueled in part by the Renaissance spirit of inquiry, which spurred some people to question the actions and authority of the church. More and more people began to talk about the need for churchmen to change their ways, especially when Julius II died in 1513 and a new pope, Leo X, took office.

The Sale of Indulgences

Pope Leo X was determined to finish a project started by Julius II, the rebuilding of St. Peter's Basilica. Construction on the grand church was proving to be very expensive. Leo proposed to raise money through the sale of **indulgences**.

An indulgence was a kind of pardon, a partial release from punishment for one's sins. Most Christians believed in purgatory, a realm where sinners were punished in order to purify their souls and ready them for heaven. The church said that people could shorten

Leo X, like other Renaissance popes, put worldly power before spiritual concerns.

Key Questions

- What was the Protestant Reformation? What caused it?

- How did Martin Luther's efforts lead to the end of Christian unity in Europe and the beginning of Protestantism?

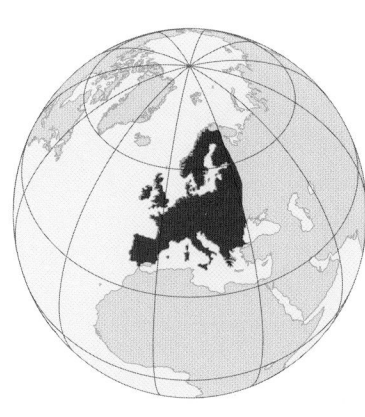

The Reformation changed the religious face of Europe.

469

their painful stay in purgatory by performing acts of prayer or charity before they died. In return for a good act, such as giving money to the church, the church could grant an indulgence. These indulgences were written on official pieces of paper and stamped with a papal seal.

In 1517, Pope Leo, seeking ways to raise money to finish St. Peter's, urged church officials to sell more indulgences than ever before. A friar named Johann Tetzel (yoh-HAHN TET-suhl) proved to be a persuasive preacher and effective showman as he rode around the countryside selling indulgences in a kind of traveling sideshow. Buy an indulgence or two, he urged, so that "when you die the gates of punishment shall be shut, and the gates of the paradise of delight shall be opened."

Martin Luther and the Reformation

No one was more repulsed by the sale of indulgences than Martin Luther, a German monk who taught university classes in the small town of Wittenberg. As a young man, Luther, urged by his father, studied to become a lawyer. But, overwhelmed by a sense of his own sinfulness, Luther decided to set aside his legal studies and instead become a monk. Although his father was furious, the young man entered a monastery.

Luther became a professor of biblical studies at the University of Wittenberg in the German province of Saxony. He continued to agonize over his sense of sinfulness. He fasted, gave alms, and kept hoping to find peace.

Then one day Luther was struck by these words of St. Paul in the Bible: "The righteous shall live by faith." Luther meditated on the words and concluded that

Martin Luther

A crowd watches as Luther nails his Ninety-five Theses to the church door in the German town of Wittenberg.

human beings were so sinful that they could never earn forgiveness by any good works of their own. Instead, he thought, Christians had to live by faith alone and depend on the mercy of God. By this reasoning, salvation could come only through God's forgiveness and could not be aided by any indulgence.

Luther's Ninety-five Theses

One day some citizens of Wittenberg came to Luther with indulgences sold by Johann Tetzel. Luther saw the sale of such indulgences as a vile moneymaking scheme. Infuriated, he took up his pen and wrote out ninety-five theses, or arguments, explaining why indulgences were wrong. He wrote, "Any true Christian, whether living or dead, participates in all the blessing of Christ and the Church; and this is granted him by God, even without indulgence letters."

Luther's Ninety-five Theses

Martin Luther once said, "I am hot-blooded by temperament and my pen gets irritated easily." You can see some of his passion in the following selections from his Ninety-five Theses concerning the sale of indulgences.

Those who believe that they can be certain of their salvation because they have indulgence letters will be eternally damned, together with their teachers. *(Thesis 32)*

Any true Christian, whether living or dead, participates in all the blessings of Christ and the church; and this is granted him by God, even without indulgence letters. *(Thesis 37)*

Christians are to be taught that he who sees a needy man and passes him by, yet gives his money for indulgences, does not buy papal indulgences but God's wrath. *(Thesis 45)*

Christians are to be taught that if the pope knew the exactions of the indulgence preachers, he would rather that the basilica of St. Peter were burned to ashes than built up with the skin, flesh, and bones of his sheep. *(Thesis 50)*

Injury is done to the Word of God when, in the same sermon, an equal or larger amount of time is devoted to indulgences than to the Word. *(Thesis 54)*

[Indulgences cause people to ask questions such as:] "Why does not the pope, whose wealth is today greater than the wealth of the richest…build this one basilica of St. Peter with his own money rather than with the money of poor believers?" *(Thesis 86)*

According to tradition, Luther nailed his Ninety-five Theses to the church door in Wittenberg on October 31, 1517. The document was soon translated from Latin into German and, thanks to Gutenberg's printing press, Luther's writings began to spread throughout Germany. Luther was openly challenging the church to reform itself.

The Reformation—the great upheaval that would change Christendom forever—had begun.

Luther Stands Firm

Although Luther was troubled by many church practices, he did not intend to break away from the Catholic Church. At first, he only wanted to end the sale of indulgences. But as he continued to think and teach, he expressed more radical ideas. He continued to insist that Christians could win salvation only by faith and through God's mercy, not through good works or indulgences. He argued that the Bible should be the authoritative basis for all church teaching and practices. Furthermore, he said that the faithful did not need priests to interpret the Bible for them. He even questioned the authority of the pope. He called on the German princes to establish a reformed church with no pope at its head.

Presses churned out pamphlets of Luther's words. These pamphlets traveled to towns across Europe, and to Rome itself. In 1520, Pope Leo X issued a papal bull, or decree, saying that if Luther did not back down, his writings would be burned. Luther and his students responded by throwing the papal bull and books of church law onto a bonfire outside the walls of Wittenberg. Leo, in turn, excommunicated Martin Luther and ordered his publications burned.

Charles V, the Holy Roman Emperor, an ally of the pope, summoned Martin Luther to a trial called the Diet of Worms (wurmz). (A general assembly of the Holy Roman Empire was called a *diet*; Worms

is a city in Germany.) Charles himself attended, along with representatives of the pope. They said Luther must recant—that is, he must admit that he was wrong and take back the heresies that he had been spreading.

At the meeting in April 1521, Luther refused to recant. "I am bound by the Scriptures," he said. "My conscience is captive to the Word of God. I cannot and I will not recant anything, for to go against conscience is neither safe nor right. God help me. Amen."

An Outlaw Translates the Bible

Luther was condemned as a heretic and an outlaw. Emperor Charles V ordered that Luther's writings be burned, and that all men shun the rebellious monk. But Prince Frederick of Saxony lodged Luther safely in a castle. There Luther lived in hiding for almost a year, during which he began translating the books of the New Testament into German, the vernacular of his countrymen. Later he also translated the Old Testament.

Before Luther's time, most Bibles were printed in Latin, which only very educated people could read. Translation of the Bible into German, combined with the printing press and the spread of learning during the Renaissance, made the Bible available to many thousands of people. Now anyone who read German could read the Bible.

As more and more people responded to Luther's message, a new branch of Christianity emerged, one that did not recognize the leadership of the pope. It came to be called Lutheranism. Some princes sided with Luther for worldly reasons. That is, they took up his cause in order to seize properties held by the Roman church and assert their independence from the Holy

In defiance of Pope Leo X, Luther burned the papal bull and books of church law.

Roman Emperor. Whatever their motivations, political or religious, people across Europe began to take sides.

Protestantism Spreads

Luther's ideas spread quickly. To the north in Scandinavia, the kings of Denmark and Norway made Lutheranism the official religion of their realms. Reformed churches, following Luther's teachings, began to spring up across Europe. They were known as **Protestant** churches because their members protested the practices of the church based in Rome. The Roman church, headed by the pope, began to call itself the Roman Catholic Church. (*Catholic* means "universal.")

John Calvin's Influence

In France, a scholar named John Calvin took up the cause of the Reformation. Because the French king, a devout Catholic, persecuted Protestants, Calvin moved to the city of Geneva in Switzerland. There, in the 1540s, Calvin and his followers ran the city with a tight hand. Citizens were required to attend classes on religion. Bright clothing and card games were forbidden. Those who broke the rules were subject to severe punishments, including banishment and excommunication.

Like Luther, Calvin asserted the authority of Scripture over any church leader. Calvin said churches should not be run by priests but instead by a group of laymen, called elders, chosen from the congregation.

Calvin's teachings spread to the Netherlands, Scotland, and central Europe. In Scotland, Calvin's followers became known as Presbyterians, from *presbyteros*, the ancient Greek word for "elder."

In England—and later in the American colonies—Calvin's followers became known as Puritans. In his homeland of France, Calvin's followers were called Huguenots (HYOO-guh-nahts).

Calvin agreed with Luther that people cannot earn salvation but can be saved by faith alone. Calvin explained that since human beings are sinful by nature, all are deserving of condemnation. But,

Protestant ideas spread through Europe. These French Huguenots followed John Calvin, a Reformation leader.

said Calvin, God has chosen to be merciful and save some people. Moreover, said Calvin, God has foreknowledge of those chosen for salvation—the "elect," as Calvin called them.

This idea of God's eternal foreknowledge of those chosen for salvation is called **predestination**. As Calvin wrote, "Predestination we call the eternal decree of God, by which He hath determined in Himself what He would have to become of every individual of mankind. For they are not all created with a similar destiny; but eternal life is foreordained for some, and eternal damnation for others." While predestination is just one among many doctrines that Calvin explores in his writings, for some of his followers—such as the Puritans in North America— it became a central focus of their beliefs.

England Champions Protestantism

In England, when King Henry VIII heard reports of Martin Luther's protests, he denounced the German monk. The pope, in turn, honored Henry with the title "Defender of the Faith." But Henry's allegiance to the Catholic faith was soon challenged by a political need—the need for a son as an heir.

As a young man, Henry had married Catherine of Aragon, a Spanish princess. Within a year the royal couple had a baby boy, but the infant died within three months. Catherine bore five girls, four of whom died. Henry wanted a son to carry on the family name and ensure a peaceful succession. So he made up his mind to take a new wife.

In sixteenth-century Europe, only the church could authorize the end of a marriage. Henry pressed the pope to annul (to set aside) his marriage to Catherine. The pope refused, since he did not want to anger Catherine's powerful relative, Charles V, the Holy Roman Emperor.

Henry's advisers suggested a solution. In 1534, Parliament passed the Act of Supremacy, declaring the king "the only supreme head on earth of the Church of England," and requiring people to accept Henry's divorce from Catherine. Anyone who disagreed with this decision to break from the pope and the Roman Catholic Church risked punishment by death. With this act, England became a Protestant nation.

The Church of England Under Henry's Heirs

Over the next several years, Henry VIII married five more times and had two more children. After Henry died in 1547, England swung back and forth between Protestantism and Catholicism.

Edward VIII, Henry's young son by his third wife, took the throne at the age of nine and was

When the pope refused him permission to divorce, King Henry VIII of England formed the Church of England.

guided by men who were fervent Protestants. Seriously ill, he was replaced by Catherine's Catholic daughter Mary. She became known as "Bloody Mary" because she ordered the execution of more than three hundred Protestants.

When Mary died without an heir, Elizabeth, the daughter of Henry VIII and his second wife, Anne Boleyn, became queen. Elizabeth asserted the status of the Church of England as the only legal church in the land. Under Elizabeth, the Anglican Church (as the Church of England is also called) tried to accommodate moderate Catholics by keeping some of the practices of Catholic services.

For Elizabeth, religion remained a cause of strife and intrigue. Some Protestants pressured

Thomas More Defies King Henry VIII

Thomas More, England's greatest Christian humanist, the author of *Utopia*, and one of King Henry's top officials, believed that the Catholic Church needed reform but still represented the only true faith. He refused to sign an oath recognizing the king as the head of the Church of England. For this defiance, he was beheaded in 1535.

the queen to make more extreme reforms. Some Catholics plotted against her and hoped to replace her with her Catholic cousin, Mary Queen of Scots. In the end, however, Elizabeth proved the greater strategist, and Mary, after long years in captivity, was executed.

The End of a Unified Christendom

The kings and nobles of Europe often fought for land and power, but for nearly a thousand years they had one thing in common—their religion.

Despite all their differences, the people of Europe thought of themselves as part of Christendom, bound by a shared religion. But in the 1500s, religious quarrels split Europe apart.

As Protestantism continued to spread, some European rulers made Protestant churches the official churches of their realms. In other lands, rulers stayed with the Roman Catholic Church. Soon the continent was divided between Protestant and Catholic states. Western Europe was no longer united by a single faith. "Christendom" was no more.

Europe's Major Religions, 1600

Legend:
- Anglican
- Calvinist
- Eastern Orthodox
- Lutheran
- Muslim
- Roman Catholic
- Holy Roman Empire

0   200   400 mi
0   200   400 km

In less than a century after Martin Luther's rebellion, most of northern Europe had rejected Catholicism in favor of a Protestant denomination.

The Catholic Reformation and Its Consequences

Key Questions

- How did the Roman Catholic Church respond to the spread of Protestantism in Europe?

- What were major long-term consequences of the Reformation and the Catholic Reformation?

The Reformation, the movement launched by Martin Luther and spread by John Calvin and other Protestant leaders, marked a crisis for the Roman Catholic Church. As many Christians turned to embrace new Protestant beliefs, the Catholic Church responded by launching its own reform movement, called the Catholic Reformation, or the Counter-Reformation. Catholic leaders set out to retain the loyalty of Catholics by correcting bad practices and clarifying the teachings of the church.

The Council of Trent

The movement to reform the Catholic Church was led by Paul III, who became pope in 1534. The pope convened a special gathering of bishops, called a council, which took place in Trent, a small city in northern Italy.

The Council of Trent, as the gathering was called, was not a single meeting but rather a series of meetings—twenty-five in all—held from 1545 to 1563. At Trent, the pope and other leaders set out to clarify the doctrines of

At the Council of Trent, Catholic leaders met to reform and strengthen the church.

the Catholic Church. Council members defended the validity of indulgences, but denounced the false selling of indulgences for money.

The council also asked: What beliefs must all Catholics share? What beliefs are heretical—that is, what beliefs violate basic Catholic teachings? The council commissioned a new catechism, or statement of beliefs, to summarize the teachings and rules of the Catholic Church.

The Council of Trent asserted the importance of the Catholic Church in guiding the lives of the faithful. The council said that Christians should be guided not only by the Bible but also by the traditions of the Catholic Church, and by decrees of gatherings such as the one at Trent. The council also insisted that only the Catholic Church had the authority to interpret the Bible. The council denounced "unbridled spirits"—for example, Martin Luther—who engaged in "distorting the Holy Scriptures in accordance with [their] own conceptions."

The Council of Trent decreed that bishops should reside closer to their congregations. Many bishops had fallen into the habit of living far away from the people they were supposed to be serving. The council told these bishops to stick close to their cathedrals and preach every Sunday.

A New Piety

By the time the Council of Trent wrapped up its work in 1563, the message of the Catholic Church was clear. Priests, bishops, and the pope needed to focus on people's spiritual needs, not on money and power. In response to the council's decrees, some priests and bishops tried to lead more devout lives. In Catholic countries, more men and women became monks or nuns.

Ignatius of Loyola and the Jesuits

Pope Paul III found a tireless ally for reform in Ignatius of Loyola (ig-NAY-shus of loy-OH-luh), so-called because he grew up in Loyola, Spain. Ignatius had dreamed of glory on the field of battle, but his dreams vanished when a cannon

Ignatius of Loyola founded the Society of Jesus. The Jesuits were known for teaching and scholarship.

blast shattered one of his legs. During his long recovery, Ignatius read about the life of Jesus and about the lives of Christian saints. He decided to devote himself to God and the church. He also began writing a book, titled *Spiritual Exercises*, which laid out a rigorous plan of daily prayer and study.

To further prepare himself for service, Ignatius studied at universities in Barcelona and Paris. A group of followers gathered around Ignatius. They vowed to pursue lives of poverty, chastity, and obedience. In 1540, Pope Paul III acknowledged Ignatius and his followers as a religious order, called the Society of Jesus. Its members became known as "Jesuits," a title first hurled at them as an insult but later embraced by the members of the order.

The Jesuits organized themselves like an army. The former soldier Ignatius called himself "the general" and his men "the Company of Jesus" who were engaged in "conflict for God." The Jesuits were highly disciplined and completely obedient to the pope. Ignatius told his followers, "We must praise all the commandments of the Church.... What seems to me white, I will believe black if the...Church so defines."

To oppose the advance of Protestantism, the Jesuits established schools to educate the young. The scholarly Jesuits also began teaching in Catholic universities. They preached and performed works of charity. Their efforts helped restore Catholicism to parts of Germany and eastern Europe.

The Jesuits also took the Christian message far beyond Europe. Thousands of Jesuit missionaries traveled to Africa, China, Japan, India, and the Americas.

Teresa of Avila

In mid-sixteenth-century Spain, a nun named Teresa, from the Spanish city of Avila (AH-vih-luh), fell gravely ill. Her fellow nuns were preparing her grave, but she slowly recovered. She began to have visions. She later wrote that she once saw an angel carrying "a long golden spear" with "a point of fire."

Teresa dedicated herself to starting a new convent at Avila. At a time when many church leaders lived in comfortable, even luxurious, surroundings, Teresa encouraged the nuns in her convent to lead lives of self-denial. Teresa and her fellow nuns wore plain robes of rough brown cloth and slept on beds of straw. They gave up all worldly possessions. They spent hours alone in prayer and silent meditation, and had almost no contact with the world beyond their convent walls.

Between 1567 and her death in 1582, Teresa traveled all over Spain. She founded more than a dozen new convents and monasteries. She wrote extensively about her life and beliefs. Her example of service and self-denial provided inspiration for a church in the process of reforming itself.

Silencing Dissent

In an age when the printing press made the writings of Martin Luther and other Protestant thinkers widely available, the Catholic Church tried to ban publications that spread Protestant ideas across Europe. Church leaders drew up an Index of Forbidden Books, a list of works that Catholics should not read. It included writings by Martin Luther, Erasmus, and Machiavelli.

To stop the spread of ideas considered heretical, the Catholic Church also arrested people and brought them before the Inquisition, the church's court that examined people and punished those whose beliefs went against Catholic teachings. The courts of the Inquisition had been around since the Middle Ages. In the fifteenth century, the Inquisition had condemned Jan Hus and Joan of Arc. But in sixteenth-century Europe, with the advance of the Reformation, the Inquisition grew more active as Catholics tried to stamp out Protestant ideas.

In France, Germany, Italy, and Spain, Catholic officials called increasingly more people to explain their beliefs to the church judges, called inquisitors. The Inquisition was most ruthless and active in Spain, where King Philip II vigorously championed the Catholic Church.

Inquisitors used cruel practices, not unique to the Catholic Church but common to European judicial systems at the time. Persons convicted of heresy were required to confess the wrongness of their beliefs. Those who refused to confess suffered terrible torture, such as being burned by

The Ursulines: Dedicated to Teaching

In the mid-1530s in Brescia, a town in Italy, Angela Merici founded an order of Roman Catholic women dedicated to teaching—in particular, the Christian education of girls and young women. The order was known as the Company of St. Ursula, or Ursulines. Its members were soon at work in Italy, France, and North America.

Those accused of heresy went before a special church court called the Inquisition. The accused wore pointed hats that were approximately three feet high. The hats, called *corozas*, were the origin of what are now called dunce caps.

red-hot irons or having their limbs agonizingly stretched on a device called the rack. Inquisitors claimed they were torturing the heretic in order to save him—unless the heretic recanted, they said, his soul could not be saved. Many people who refused to renounce their beliefs were burned at the stake.

Europe Divided

During the Catholic Reformation, the Catholic Church strove to reform itself from within, in part with the goal of halting the spread of Protestantism. But Protestantism continued to spread, and as it spread, it split into different groups, or *denominations*, including the Lutherans in Germany, the Calvinists in Scotland and Switzerland, and the Anglicans in England.

Europe split along religious lines, but when rulers chose a particular form of Christianity, their reasons were often more political than religious. For example, in a Germany divided into many

small states, those states in which Catholic officials already held much of the political power tended to remain Catholic. Some German princes became Lutherans in order to seize lands owned by the Catholic Church. In every European kingdom, the Catholic Church owned property—a lot of property. If a ruler decided to break away from the Catholic Church, then he could justify seizing Catholic properties. So these religious wars were not only about religion—a great deal of land and wealth was also at stake.

Seeking Religious Freedom

In both Protestant and Catholic lands, people were expected to adopt the religion of the ruler. Throughout Europe, those who did not follow the religion decreed by the government—whether Catholicism or one of the varieties of Protestantism—faced persecution.

In the sixteenth and seventeenth centuries, those seeking religious freedom often had to leave their homelands to find it. For example, some of England's first American colonies were founded by those fleeing persecution by the Church of England.

Two Calvinist groups, the Pilgrims and the Puritans, settled in Massachusetts. The colony of Maryland was started in part as a refuge for English Catholics. Later, members of the Society of Friends, known as Quakers—Christians who believed in following an "inner light" rather than the official teachings of a church—founded the colony of Pennsylvania.

Political and Cultural Consequences of the Reformation

The Reformation indirectly encouraged the rise of nation-states, as monarchs began to acquire more power. In France, religious divisions among the nobility increased the authority of the king. In England, Henry VIII declared himself head of the church as well as the state, making the monarchy the focus of both religious and patriotic feeling. In many places, religion became intertwined with national pride. The bitter rivalry between Catholic Spain and Protestant England for control of the seas would shape the history of the New World as well as Europe.

In another way, however, the Reformation sowed seeds that would, over time, pose a threat to the authority of Europe's rulers. These seeds were planted when Luther defied the authority of the pope and Calvin questioned the role of the clergy. Some of Luther's followers later used his ideas to question the authority of Germany's political rulers (though Luther himself rejected the application of his ideas to politically revolutionary ends). Still, Reformation ideas, abetted by the individualist spirit of the Renaissance, helped sow seeds of a new concern for political liberty.

The Reformation and the Counter-Reformation had equally broad effects on culture and politics. The Protestant emphasis on the importance of

reading the Bible encouraged translation of the scriptures from ancient languages into the vernacular languages of the time. Luther himself translated the Bible into German. French and Dutch versions soon followed. In 1604 in England, King James I authorized a historic translation of the Bible into English. The resulting translation is widely recognized as a literary masterpiece.

In Protestant countries, the importance of reading the Bible increased the importance of education and helped spread literacy. In Catholic lands, church authorities encouraged the education of young Catholics as a means to counteract Protestant ideas. The Ursuline nuns devoted themselves to the Christian education of girls, while Ignatius of Loyola, the founder of the Jesuits, set up dozens of schools to train the men who joined his order. Within a century, there were some three hundred Jesuit colleges in Catholic countries. For their devotion to rigorous education, Jesuits became known as the "schoolmasters of Europe."

Intolerance and Persecution

Despite a new emphasis on education, age-old prejudices and superstitions persisted. Indeed, under the strain of religious conflict, these prejudices often grew more violent.

Both Catholics and Protestants persecuted Jews, whom they considered dangerous unbelievers. In Spain, the Inquisition ordered thousands of people burned at the stake because they were suspected of being Jews masquerading as Christians. In 1492, the devoutly Catholic monarchs Ferdinand and Isabella ordered the expulsion of all Jews from Spain. Later, Martin Luther urged the expulsion of the "devilish" Jews from Germany.

Both Protestants and Catholics saw the work of the devil in diseases and natural disasters such as drought or crop failure. For these afflictions and calamities, they often blamed people, usually women, whom they accused of witchcraft. During the 1500s and into the 1600s, tens of thousands of suspected witches were executed in Europe.

Religious Wars and the Rise of Absolutism

Key Questions

- How did religious differences lead to conflicts in Europe during the sixteenth and seventeenth centuries?

- How did the Thirty Years' War change Europe?

- What events and conditions led to the rise of absolute monarchs in Europe? How did Louis XIV's reign in France exemplify absolute monarchy?

The war of ideas between the Catholic Church and Protestant reformers led to a split in Europe. The war of ideas eventually erupted into real and bloody wars. These wars changed the map of Europe in the sixteenth century.

Religious Wars Shake Europe

In the German lands of the Holy Roman Empire, Catholics and Lutherans took up arms. Charles V, the Holy Roman Emperor, led Catholic forces against a league of Protestant states. In France, a civil war pitted Catholics against the Protestant minority known as the Huguenots. Between 1562 and 1598, fighting repeatedly broke out across the country. In August 1572, on the day celebrated by Catholics as St. Bartholomew's Day, French Catholics killed thousands of Huguenots.

Many Huguenots left France to practice their religion in neighboring Protestant countries, including parts of the Netherlands. This region had long been ruled by Catholic Spain. But Protestants in the northern provinces of the Netherlands rose up in revolt, seeking both political independence and religious freedom. Eventually they set up an independent Protestant Dutch state, the United Provinces of the Netherlands. The southern provinces of the Netherlands—which are now the country of Belgium—remained Catholic and under Spain's control.

St. Bartholomew's Day 1572, when French Catholics slaughtered their Huguenot countrymen

Light, maneuverable English ships, shown here in the distance, approach the larger, anchored ships of the Spanish Armada.

By 1600, the Christian faith that was once a common bond in Europe had become a source of rivalry and division. The rivalry spread beyond the continent as the English, Dutch, Spanish, and Portuguese ventured across the seas. As they rushed to establish colonies, they were motivated by "glory, God, and gold" in general, but in particular by competing desires to promote either Catholicism or Protestantism.

England vs. Spain: The Spanish Armada

Protestant England and Catholic Spain became bitter enemies. Queen Elizabeth sent men and money to support the Dutch Protestants who were fighting for independence from Catholic Spain. Spain's King Philip II viewed Elizabeth's action as a declaration of war. He gathered a huge fleet to invade England. Philip, who saw himself as a defender of Catholicism, had various motivations to attack England. He wanted to get back at England for supporting the Netherlands. He wanted to overthrow Protestantism in England. And he wanted to crush England to protect Spain's merchant ships from English attack.

In late July 1588, the Spanish Armada, as it was known, sailed into English waters, with some hundred thirty ships carrying about nineteen thousand soldiers. The pope called it the Invincible Armada. (*Invincible* means "undefeatable.") Like King Philip, the pope saw the Armada as part of a holy mission to get rid of Queen Elizabeth and restore England to the Catholic faith.

As the ships of the Spanish Armada swept up the English Channel, they were met by the small, light ships of the English, which were more maneuverable than the Spanish vessels. The English raked the enemy with bursts of cannon fire. The Armada took a terrible battering. Then a fierce storm drove the surviving Spanish ships up the east coast of England toward Scotland. The English called it "the Protestant wind," and took it as a sign from God. More ships sank off the rocky coasts of Scotland and Ireland, as the remains of the Spanish Armada made its long journey home.

The English lost a hundred men and none of their ships. The Spanish lost almost two-thirds of their men and half their ships. The defeat of the Spanish Armada in 1588 weakened Spain and cleared the way for England to build its own overseas empire.

The Thirty Years' War

When Charles V, the Holy Roman Emperor, sought to suppress the German states that were embracing Protestantism, he was victorious at first. But Protestant forces quickly recovered and fought back. Soon, the battle-weary emperor put down his arms. The religious wars between the German states ended in 1555 with a treaty called the Peace of Augsburg, which allowed each German prince to choose either Lutheranism or Catholicism as the official faith of his realm.

But this peace did not last. In the early 1600s, a much longer and bloodier religious conflict began, known as the Thirty Years' War. Although this war—in fact, a series of wars—involved European

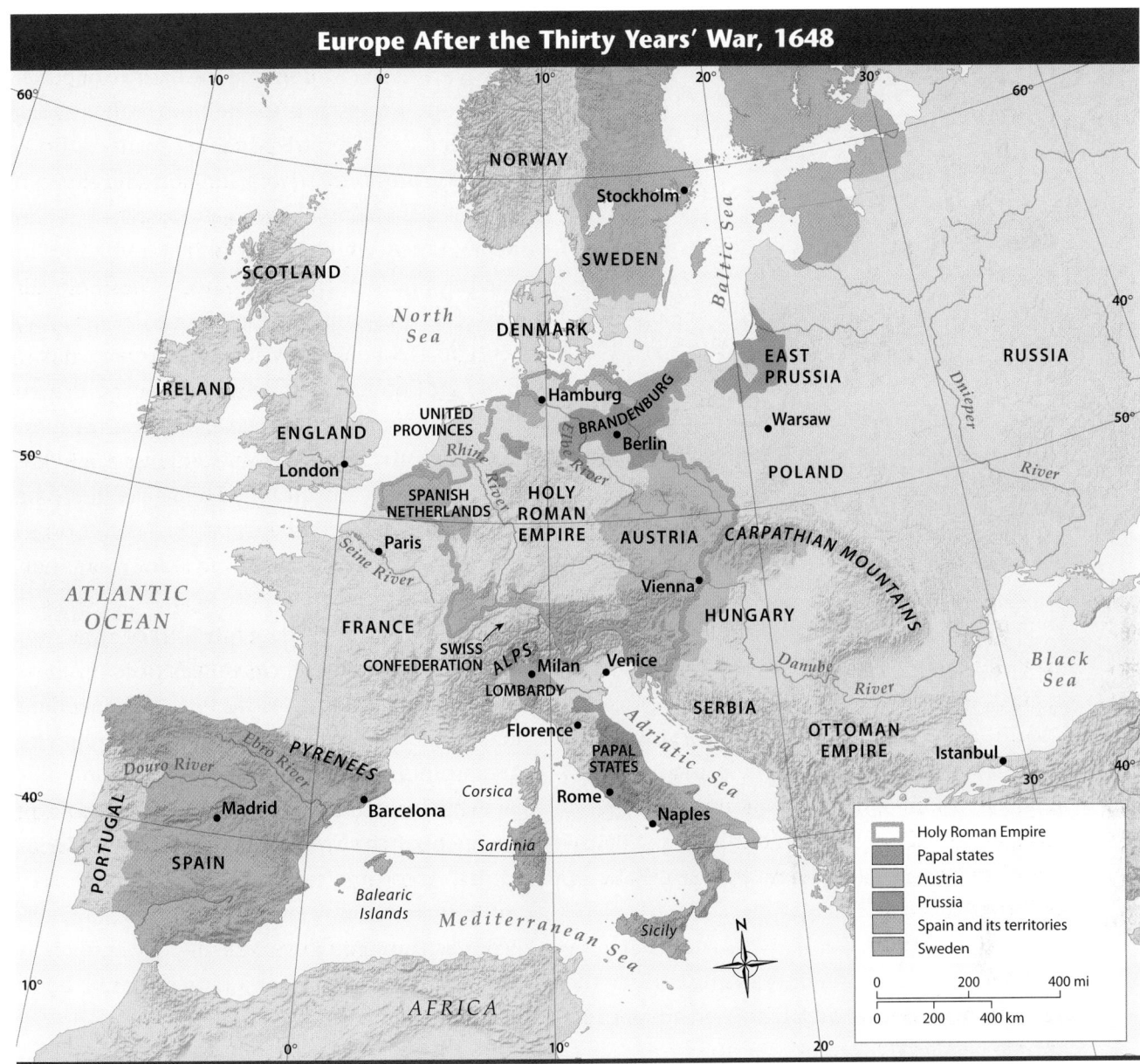

Europe After the Thirty Years' War, 1648

The hold of Catholicism and the Holy Roman Empire on Europe was broken forever as a result of the bloodshed and destruction that engulfed the continent during the Thirty Years' War.

powers from Spain to Sweden, most of its battles were fought on German soil. It was not only a war of religion, pitting Catholics against Protestants, but also a contest for power and territory among several ruling families.

The war began with an uprising by Czech Protestants in Prague (prahg) against the Catholic ruler of the Holy Roman Empire. Eventually, the Protestant rulers of Denmark and Sweden marched into Germany to fight on the side of their fellow Protestants. In response, the Spanish joined the

war on the side of the Catholics. Religious conflicts overlapped with complex political disputes. For example, France's Catholic king entered the war on the side of the Protestants in order to oppose his enemy, Spain.

The conflict raged for decades, with no side winning a decisive victory. All sides employed mercenary soldiers, who fought for pay rather than out of loyalty to their homelands. The undisciplined mercenaries considered it their right to loot and burn the farms and towns that

Most of the fighting in the Thirty Years' War—a struggle over religion, power, and land—took place on German soil.

Absolute Monarchs Reign

The Thirty Years' War shifted the balance of power in Europe. Protestants in the Netherlands at last achieved decisive independence from Catholic Spain. Spain—once so rich and powerful through its American colonies—was left weakened and in debt. France, which had won major victories in the last phase of the war, emerged as the most powerful nation in western Europe.

The Thirty Years' War left Germany devastated and fragmented. Out of more than three hundred German states, two emerged as the most powerful—the Protestant state of Prussia, and the Catholic state of Austria. Their ruling families—the Hohenzollerns in Prussia, and the Habsburgs in Austria—would remain powerful for more than two centuries.

Across Europe, the turmoil of the war prompted many monarchs to seek to consolidate their power. In Spain, Austria, Prussia, France, and Russia, rulers took charge as **absolute monarchs**. An absolute monarch is a single ruler who holds all the power in the state he or she rules. Absolute monarchs often claimed that they ruled by **divine right**. According to this concept, a monarch's authority is derived from God. Thus the monarch is not accountable to any earthly power, such as the country's nobility or a representative body like England's Parliament.

Absolutism in France

Nowhere was the power of the monarchy greater than in France. There, the authority of the king had been growing since the 1400s. In theory, he ruled with the advice of the three "estates" of French society—the clergy, the nobles, and the commoners. Especially when he wanted to levy taxes, the king was supposed to call the estates together in an assembly called the Estates-General. Beginning in the late 1500s, however, French kings acted more and more on their own, without consulting the estates.

Louis XIII, who came to the throne in 1610, further centralized power in the monarchy. By

stood in their path. Germany was devastated by battlefield slaughter, famine, and disease. By the end of the war, between a third and a half of its people lay dead.

The end came in 1648, with the Peace of Westphalia. The treaty left the Holy Roman Empire a shadow of its former self, and put an end to the concept of Europe as a united Catholic realm. The treaty in effect marked the beginning of our modern concept of Europe as a collection of independent states. The treaty affirmed the authority of the German princes to rule their domains as sovereign states, which delayed the unification of Germany as a nation.

> A *sovereign* state is a self-governing, independent state.

While Germany remained fragmented, across much of Europe a new spirit of national pride and identity was on the rise.

defeating the Spanish and Austrians during the Thirty Years' War, Louis made France the most powerful nation in Europe. With the help of his chief minister, Cardinal Richelieu (rih-shuh-loo), he subdued the French nobles by disbanding their private armies and destroying their castles. From this time on, these aristocrats would owe their loyalty directly to the French crown.

It was Louis' son, Louis XIV, who became the ultimate example of the absolute monarch. Louis XIV came to the throne as a child and ruled for seventy-two years—far longer than any other king of France. He never called a meeting of the Estates-General. He scorned the idea of sharing power. Louis is said to have declared, *"L'etat, c'est moi,"* meaning "I am the state." Louis XIV agreed with the idea of the divine right of kings. He was known as the Sun King because, according to some accounts, he believed that, in effect, the world revolved around him.

Louis was a hardworking king, devoted to his administrative duties. At the same time, he loved pleasure and luxury. Not far from Paris, in a place called Versailles (vuhr-SIY), he built the most magnificent palace in Europe. The finest tapestries, marble, and lace filled the palace. In the surrounding gardens, 1,400 ornate fountains used more water than the entire city of Paris. The nobles of France flocked to Versailles, where they entertained themselves by hunting, dancing, and gambling, always trying to flatter and please the king. By keeping the nobles close to him, Louis kept them dependent and powerless.

In the age of absolutism, artists flattered the king. Louis XIV lavished money on France's finest playwrights, poets, and painters. In return, they glorified the Sun King in their works.

For much of Louis' reign, the French economy flourished, while French armies dominated the battlefield. By invading his neighbors, Louis

The Hall of Mirrors is the most famous room at Versailles, the palace where King Louis XIV of France moved his court.

extended the borders of France to the north and east, while also expanding France's empire in North America.

Eventually, however, the heavy taxation required to support Louis' wars and building projects fueled resentment against the monarchy. Just before he died in 1715, Louis told his great-grandson, "Try to remain at peace with your neighbors. I have loved war too much. Do not copy me in this, or in my over-spending." The Sun King had brought glory to France, but many of his subjects welcomed his death.

Russia's Modernizing Monarch: Peter the Great

Russia did not get involved in Europe's conflicts, but it did experience its own troubles and setbacks, and it remained under the control of absolute monarchs. In the late fifteenth century, Ivan III, known as Ivan the Great, united Russia. His grandson, Ivan the Terrible, expanded Russia's empire and struck fear into his enemies. But then he unleashed a reign of terror in his own country, with a force of secret police killing many boyars—Russia's nobles—and their families. After the death of Ivan the Terrible, Russia suffered what is remembered as a "time of troubles," when nobles fought for power.

During Europe's Renaissance and the Age of Exploration, Russian rulers turned their backs on western Europe. But much would change when a new tsar, Peter I, took charge in 1689. For his achievements, history remembers him as Peter the Great.

Peter was a member of a family called the Romanovs, which came to power in Russia in the early seventeenth century. Peter looked beyond the boundaries of his native Russia to more technologically advanced lands. In 1697, he set off on an eighteen-month tour of western Europe—the first Russian ruler to venture abroad during times of peace. Peter recruited hundreds of European experts to follow him back to Russia—shipwrights, naval officers, navigators, doctors, mathematicians, engineers, and architects.

In order to enforce the changes he desired, Peter took steps to increase his power as an absolute monarch. He limited the power of the boyars. He also reorganized the Russian Orthodox Church to bring it more under his control. He believed that the head of the church, the patriarch of Moscow, had grown too powerful, so he eliminated that office. He found men who would obey him and put them in charge of overseeing church activities.

Peter opened secular schools for children of nobility, soldiers, and government officials. He ordered the construction of roads and canals. He built up the army, training and equipping it to fight more like the armies of western Europe.

Peter wanted his armies to expand Russia's borders, and most of all to win a warm-water outlet to the sea. At the beginning of Peter's reign, Russia had only one major port, which lay in the north, in waters that froze solid for half the year. Peter decided that he must gain more ports for Russia, by force if necessary.

He sent his army to fight the Turks to gain access to the Black Sea. Russian troops also seized part of the Baltic coastline from the Swedes. There, on the edge of a wilderness, Peter decided to build a new capital city for the Russian empire. He named the city St. Petersburg. Along the banks of the Neva River spread a new palace for the tsar, gardens modeled after parks in western Europe, dockyards to build ships for the Russian navy, and a fortress to protect the new city from attacks by sea. St. Petersburg was a magnificent city, but in building it thousands of workers died from diseases and harsh working conditions.

By the time Peter died in 1725, he had succeeded in introducing Russia to many new ideas and technological advances from the West. He had made Russia an important European power. Yet for all his efforts, when Peter died, Russia was still a feudal nation led by an all-powerful tsar, and was still dependent on the labor of downtrodden serfs.

Limits on England's Monarchs

Key Questions

- What led to civil war in England?
- How did a constitutional monarchy evolve in England?

In France, Russia, and elsewhere in Europe, absolute monarchs consolidated their power. But the political development of England took a different course.

You have seen that England rose to prominence under Queen Elizabeth I. During this Elizabethan Age, England defeated the Spanish Armada and challenged Spain for dominance of the seas. The arts thrived with the queen's patronage. England also established colonies and began to build an empire.

While Elizabeth wielded great power, her reign was also marked by frequent wrangling with Parliament, the body of bishops, nobles, and elected representatives who advised the English monarch and helped make laws. Most often the queen argued with Parliament over money. Parliament's power of the purse—its power to approve or disapprove new taxes—kept the monarch's power in check by effectively controlling the money supply.

When Elizabeth died in 1603, the queen was much loved and much mourned by her people. She left England a Protestant nation and a world power. But she also left a large debt that, for her successors on the throne, would lead to more tension and conflict between the monarchy and Parliament.

Queen Elizabeth I is shown with her hand resting on a globe. The gesture symbolizes the growing international power that was hers after England's defeat of the Spanish Armada.

The Unpopular Stuart Kings

Elizabeth came from the royal family known as the Tudors. When she died unmarried and childless, she left no Tudor heirs. Her successor was a distant cousin, King James VI of Scotland, a Protestant and a member of the Stuart royal family. He became King James I of England.

James Quarrels with Parliament

When James was crowned in 1603, for the first time in history the kingdoms of England and Scotland—two lands that had often fought in the past—were united under a single monarch. But James I did not unite much else. During his reign, the king and Parliament often quarreled over money.

England and Great Britain

Great Britain is the large island off the northwest coast of Europe. In 1603, England (which then included the western province of Wales) covered the southern two-thirds of this island, and Scotland covered the northern third. When James I came to the English throne that year to rule both England and Scotland, people began to refer to the inhabitants of this united realm as "British," and to the joined domains as "Great Britain."

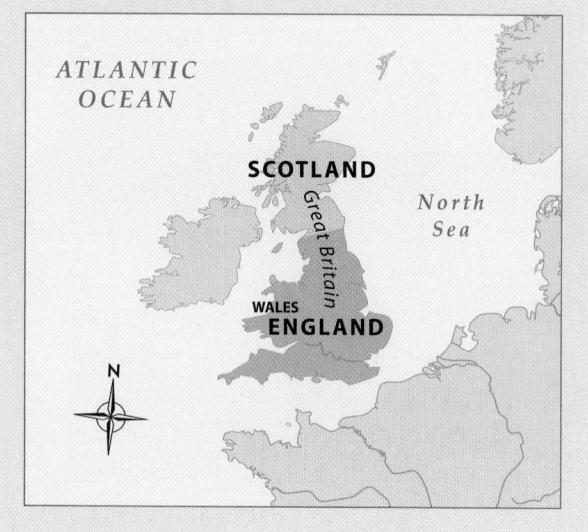

Queen Elizabeth presides over Parliament, the body that advised the English monarch and helped make laws.

James had inherited debts from England's long years of war against Spain. But by living in luxury, he almost doubled the debt left by Elizabeth.

Although he tirelessly lectured Parliament about his divine right as king, James did not like asking the governing body for money. To raise funds, he tried to go around Parliament by imposing import duties—taxes on goods entering English ports. Since import duties were not a direct tax on the people, James believed he did not need Parliament's permission. His strategy angered many of its members. More and more, the king found himself at odds with the Parliament.

King James and the Puritans

Many members of England's Parliament were Puritans, who followed the teachings of John Calvin. They wanted to "purify" many practices of the Church of England. They felt the English church was too much like the Roman Catholic Church. Because they *dissented*—which means "disagreed with"—many actions of the Church of England, the Puritans were sometimes called *dissenters*.

The Puritans hoped that King James, himself a Calvinist, would support their demands to reform the Church of England. The king agreed to only one of the Puritans' requests—he authorized a new English translation of the Bible. But James angered the Puritans by refusing to change the government of the Church of England or simplify its ceremonies and rituals.

Charles I Clashes with Parliament

After James died, his son Charles came to the throne in 1625. Like his father, King Charles I insisted on the divine right of kings. Several times, he dissolved Parliament—that is, he sent its members home—and tried to rule on his own.

Charles's father had disappointed the Puritans. But Charles himself caused great alarm among the dissenters when he married the sister of the king of France, who was a devout Catholic. During the reign of Charles I, many Puritans felt persecuted, and thousands left England to sail across the Atlantic and settle in the North American colonies of New England.

In 1628, Charles needed funds for foreign wars, so he called Parliament into session. To get the funds he needed, Charles had to bend to Parliament's demand that he sign a document called the Petition of Right. Charles agreed that he would levy no taxes without the consent of Parliament. He also agreed not to imprison subjects without just cause, and not to lodge soldiers in the homes of private citizens. Although Charles promptly broke his promises and dissolved Parliament yet again, the petition was an important statement of limits on a monarch's power.

In 1640, a war with rebellious Scots forced Charles to call Parliament back into session. Charles wanted money for the war, but the Puritan members wanted the king to accept limits on his power and admit Parliament's right to meet

The King James Bible

In 1604, King James authorized a historic translation of the Bible into English. James wanted a scholarly English translation that would closely follow the original Hebrew and Greek. Some fifty scholars undertook the task. They followed strict rules to make sure that no single translator would impose his individual beliefs or style on the text. The result, first published in 1611, is known as the King James Version of the Bible. Its stories, rhythms, and language have had a profound and lasting effect on literature written in English.

regularly. Urged on by his queen, Charles decided to take action against the leaders of the group opposing him.

On January 4, 1642, Charles did something no English king had ever done. At the head of a group of armed guards, he marched into the House of Commons and tried to arrest five members. The public was outraged. Charles had gone too far. Thousands of soldiers rushed to defend Parliament against the king. Days later, Charles fled from London.

The English Civil War

By the summer of 1642, the English people were divided between supporters of the king and supporters of Parliament. Those who backed the king were known as Royalists or Cavaliers (from the Italian word *cavaliere* for "horseman.") Parliament's Puritan supporters were called Roundheads, because some wore their hair cropped short and round against their faces.

When the English Civil War began, both sides were armed and ready. Both sides had successes on the battlefield, but gradually the Roundheads forged a well-trained army led by a Puritan general, Oliver Cromwell. Under Cromwell, the Roundheads won great victories. A devout Puritan, Cromwell said he saw "the hand of God" at work in his victories. By 1648, the Royalists were defeated.

The Roundheads captured Charles and brought him to London for trial before a special court set up by Parliament. The court declared Charles "a tyrant, traitor, murderer, and public enemy to the good people of this nation." The court sentenced him to "death by the severing of his head from his body."

On January 30, 1649, Charles stepped onto a scaffold erected outside the royal palace of White-hall. The executioner swung his axe. It was a revolutionary moment in history—the public trial and execution of a reigning king.

Cromwell and the Commonwealth

After the execution of Charles I, Parliament declared the end of the monarchy. England, they said, would no longer be ruled by a king or queen. Instead, Parliament declared England a republic, to be governed by the people's representatives. The period of the republic became known as the Commonwealth. Real power, however, was not held in common. It belonged to the army and to the man who had built that army into such a force—Oliver Cromwell.

Oliver Cromwell became England's Lord Protector and, in reality, a military dictator.

A council of officers from the Parliamentary army drew up England's first written constitution, which placed a "lord protector" at the head of the government. Cromwell became England's Lord Protector. According to the constitution, he would work with a new Parliament to make the country's laws. But Cromwell closed Parliament by force. The Lord Protector now ruled England as a military dictator.

Cromwell exercised greater power than Charles or James ever had as king. Cromwell and his Puritan supporters closed theaters and other forms of entertainment that they saw as immoral or evil. They banned Christmas and Easter celebrations, which they claimed were based in pagan traditions.

Cromwell's army invaded Ireland and Scotland, brutally crushing all resistance and bringing both under his control. Cromwell also won a war against Spain, gaining new territory for England in the Americas.

The execution of Charles I marked the first time a reigning monarch had ever been publicly tried and put to death.

Cavaliers to the Colonies

During Oliver Cromwell's rule as Lord Protector, while the Puritans held power in England, very few Puritans migrated to New England. Instead, many Cavaliers, supporters of the executed king, now fled to Virginia and the Carolinas. Unlike the Puritan colonists, these new arrivals were aristocrats and landowners. They were not driven by religious motivations. Instead, they hoped to recreate the aristocracy of old England on plantations in the New World.

The Restoration

By the late 1650s, many in England had had enough of Cromwell's military dictatorship and severe Puritan ways. When Cromwell died, Parliament met and, in 1660, decided to restore the monarchy—and thus this period in English history, from 1660 to 1685, is known as the **Restoration**.

The new king was Charles II, son of the executed Charles I. England thrived during the Restoration. Theaters reopened. Elegant buildings were constructed in the capital. Philosophers, architects, and scientists made great advances during these prosperous years.

The Reign of Charles II

Charles II had learned some lessons from his father's death. He began his reign by doing his best to maintain good relations with Parliament.

Under Charles II, in 1679 Parliament passed an act that guaranteed the right of *habeas corpus*. A Latin phrase that means "you must have [or produce] the body," habeas corpus is a legal principle that protects people from being illegally imprisoned. The principle requires that an arrested person be brought before a court, where the charges against the person must be explained. The court can then determine if the accused person is being held legally, and if not, order the person's release. The passage of the Habeas Corpus Act helped protect Englishmen from being imprisoned simply for opposing the king.

In religious matters, Charles II supported the Church of England, which did not please Puritans. During the Restoration, a number of Puritans left England. Charles II was happy to help dissenters find ways to leave, often by granting them land for settlement in North America.

In the late 1660s, Charles II presented a group of English landholders with an enormous area that includes modern-day North Carolina, South Carolina, and Georgia. The colony was named Carolina to honor the king (*Carolus* is Latin for Charles).

Who Should Be the Next King?

Because Charles II had no legitimate children, there were great concerns about who should inherit the

Crowds of cheering Londoners welcome Charles II back to the English capital. The Stuarts' return to the throne is known as the Restoration.

491

throne. Many members of Parliament were alarmed that the throne would go to Charles's brother, James, the Duke of York, who was a Catholic.

Those who opposed the idea of a Catholic king tried to pass a bill to exclude James from succession to the throne. Heated debate rang out in Parliament. On one side were the Whigs, who opposed James. On the other side were the Tories, who supported James's hereditary right to the throne despite his Catholicism.

Both labels, Whig and Tory, were first used as insults—*Whig* was a term for a horse thief, while *Tory* was a derogatory term for a supporter of the Catholic Church. Despite their original meanings, both labels persisted. The Whigs and Tories who argued over James's right to the throne were the forerunners of the first political parties in England.

The Glorious Revolution

When Charles II died in 1685, his Catholic brother inherited the throne and was crowned James II. The new monarch began to appoint Catholics to high positions in the army, government, and universities. When his subjects protested, he simply ignored them. James preferred to rule without consulting the will of Parliament.

When James's wife bore him a son, some English Protestants became alarmed that they would

In a peaceful coup called the Glorious Revolution, William and Mary replaced James II on England's throne.

be ruled by a long line of Catholic kings. English Protestant leaders decided to take action. They wanted the throne to go to James's daughter Mary, who was a Protestant, and to her Dutch husband, William of Orange, who ruled the Netherlands. So they asked William of Orange to come to England with his army.

In November 1688, supported by the English navy and army, William and his wife Mary crossed the English Channel and entered London. James II panicked and fled to France. Perhaps he recalled what had happened to his grandfather, Charles I, less than four decades before.

With almost no bloodshed, the will of Parliament prevailed, and the transition of power was complete. English Protestants called this peaceful coup the **Glorious Revolution**.

> A *coup* is the overthrow of a government by force, from the French word meaning "a blow or sudden strike."

The English Bill of Rights

When William and Mary accepted the offer to take the throne of England, they did so on the condition that they agree to accept a Bill of Rights. The Bill of Rights settled a recurring quarrel by banning Roman Catholics from England's throne.

The Toleration Act of 1689

In 1689, Parliament passed an act granting freedom of worship to Protestant dissenters from the Church of England. The law allowed dissenters to establish their own places of worship, with their own preachers. Dissenters were still subject to certain restrictions imposed by previous laws—for example, they could not hold public office. Also, the Toleration Act did not apply to Catholics, Jews, or Unitarians. Despite the limitations of the Toleration Act, it set a precedent for the legal acceptance of different religious beliefs.

More important, the Bill of Rights moved England from absolute monarchy to **constitutional monarchy**, in which a ruler's powers are limited by the nation's laws.

The Bill of Rights said that government had to be based on law, not on a king's desires. It restricted the powers of the monarch and formally increased the power of Parliament. It said that a king needed Parliament's permission to set aside laws, maintain an army in peacetime, or tax people.

In 1689, William signed the English Bill of Rights. Henceforth, kings would have to acknowledge that they held their power only with Parliament's consent, not by divine right. It was the beginning of a revolutionary era that recognized, as the English philosopher John Locke proclaimed, that it was the "natural right" of the people to oust a tyrannical ruler.

England's Legacy of Liberty

By 1700, England had moved well beyond an absolute monarch claiming to rule by divine right. Now the powers of the king or queen were limited, subject to English law and the will of Parliament. These limits on royal power were stated in the English Bill of Rights, which also guaranteed basic civil liberties to the English people.

True, there were limits to representative government in England. Only about 10 percent of the male population owned enough property to qualify to vote for members of Parliament. Elections suffered from corruption and bribery. Members of the House of Lords, who inherited their position, held as much power as the elected House of Commons. And both houses were dominated by the upper classes. Nonetheless, England's measures to limit its monarchy paved the way for great changes to come.

A fireworks display over the river Thames celebrates the coronation of William and Mary and the Glorious Revolution.

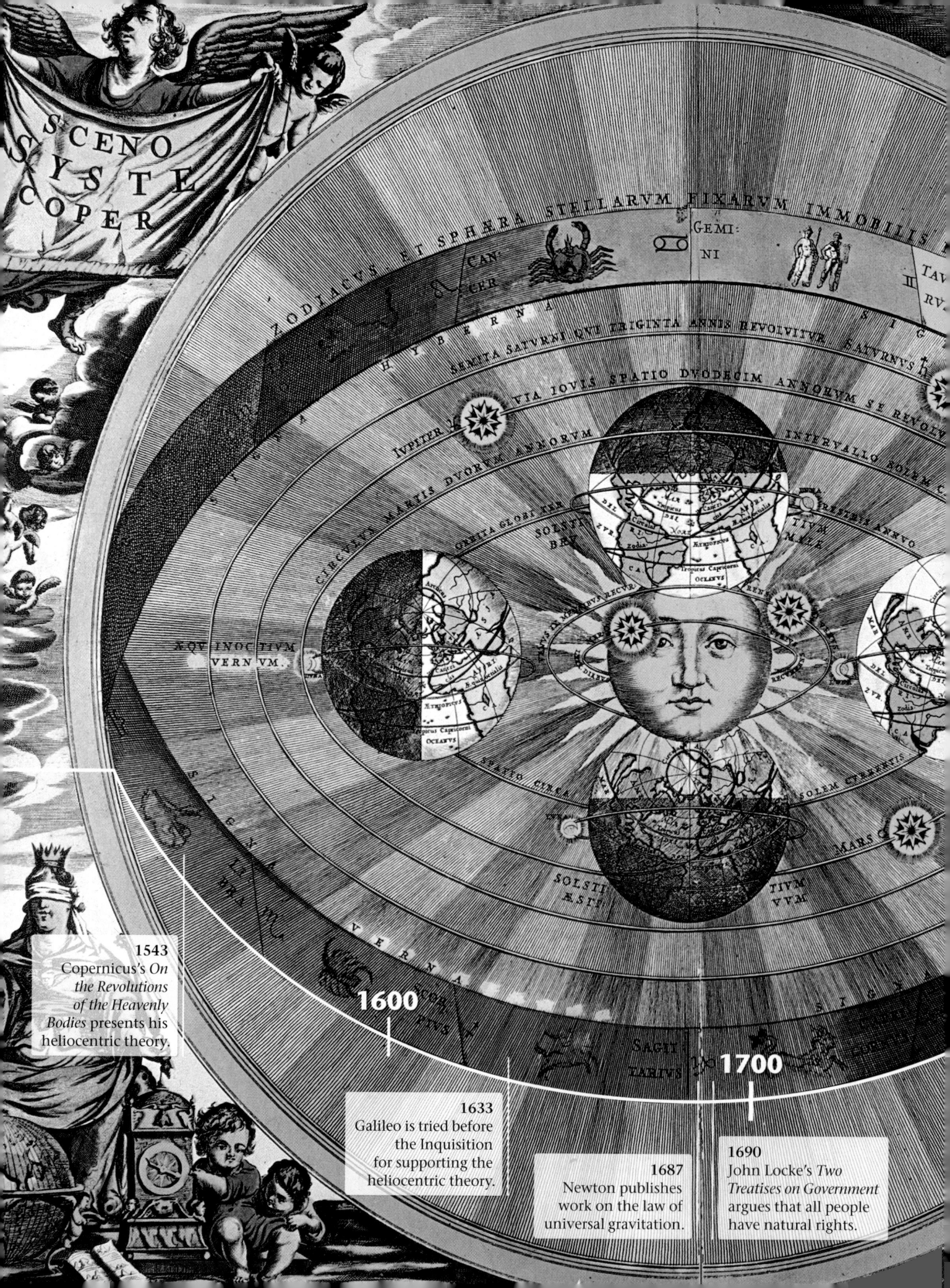

SCENO
SYSTE
COPER

ZODIACVS ET SPHÆRA STELLARVM FIXARVM IMMOBILIS

GEMI
NI

CAN
CER

TAV
RVS

ÆMITA SATVRNI QVÆ TRIGINTA ANNIS REVOLVITVR SATVRNVS

VIA IOVIS SPATIO DVODECIM ANNORVM SE REVOLV

IVPITER

CIRCVLVS MARTIS DVORVM ANNORVM

ORBITA GLOBI TER

AEQVINOCTIVM
VERNVM.

SOLSTI
BRV

SOLSTI
ÆSTI

TIVM
VM

SAGIT
TARIVS

1543
Copernicus's *On the Revolutions of the Heavenly Bodies* presents his heliocentric theory.

1600

1700

1633
Galileo is tried before the Inquisition for supporting the heliocentric theory.

1687
Newton publishes work on the law of universal gravitation.

1690
John Locke's *Two Treatises on Government* argues that all people have natural rights.

CHAPTER 22

─────

SCIENCE,

ENLIGHTENMENT,

AND

REVOLUTION

─────

1550–1790

1800

1789
The United States
establishes a federal
republic under a
written constitution.

1775
The American
Revolution begins.

*T*he spirit of curiosity that sparked the Renaissance and the Age of Exploration led in the late 1500s to the Scientific Revolution, a time when scholars made many new discoveries about the natural world. Through careful observation, experimentation, and mathematics, scholars began to realize that the universe follows certain laws, and that people can understand those laws.

As the Scientific Revolution began to reveal the natural laws governing the physical world, some thinkers concluded there must be similar laws for the world of human social activity. Moreover, these thinkers believed that these laws could be discovered through the power of human reason. Their era is known as the Enlightenment, or the Age of Reason, because of the widespread confidence in the power of reason to improve people's lives.

When Great Britain and its North American colonies ran into serious economic and political disagreements, it was, in part, the political philosophy of the Enlightenment that helped spark the American Revolution, the first successful colonial independence movement. The revolution, which resulted in the birth of the first modern republic, the United States, and the creation of the longest-lived written constitution in history, had far-reaching influence on democratic movements around the world.

The Scientific Revolution

During the Middle Ages, philosophers who studied the natural world—for example, the movements of the heavens or the workings of the human body—relied less on their own observations than on explanations that had been accepted since ancient Greek and Roman times. Medieval scholars viewed ancient thinkers, especially Aristotle (who lived in the fourth century B.C.), as authorities to be trusted, not questioned.

During the Renaissance and the Age of Exploration, Europe was charged with a new spirit of inquiry. Discoveries in the Americas—new plants and animals, new peoples, and the very existence of previously unknown continents—pushed Renaissance thinkers to question long-held assumptions. Gradually, some scholars were bold enough to question the ideas of the ancients.

In questioning accepted explanations and instead relying on firsthand observation and experience, these Renaissance thinkers paved the way for the Scientific Revolution of the 1600s. During the Scientific Revolution, scholars changed their attitudes and practices, and made great progress in understanding the workings of nature. We will look first at two figures from the mid-1500s whose work helped make the Scientific Revolution possible—the physician Vesalius (vuh-SAY-lee-us) and the astronomer Copernicus.

Vesalius Explores the Human Body

Through the Middle Ages and into the early 1500s, most doctors had little knowledge of how the human body functioned or what caused most diseases. They relied on what they read in classical texts about human anatomy,

Key Questions

- What important changes in thought occurred in Europe during the seventeenth century, and how did they constitute a Scientific Revolution?

- What were some of the key findings of Isaac Newton, and how did his work influence later scientific thought?

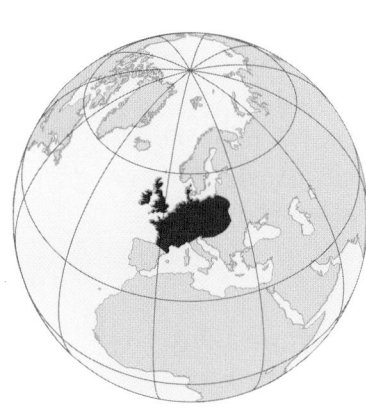

New ideas about the natural and social worlds spread across much of Europe.

Medieval scholars accepted theories of the ancient Greeks and Romans about the universe.

497

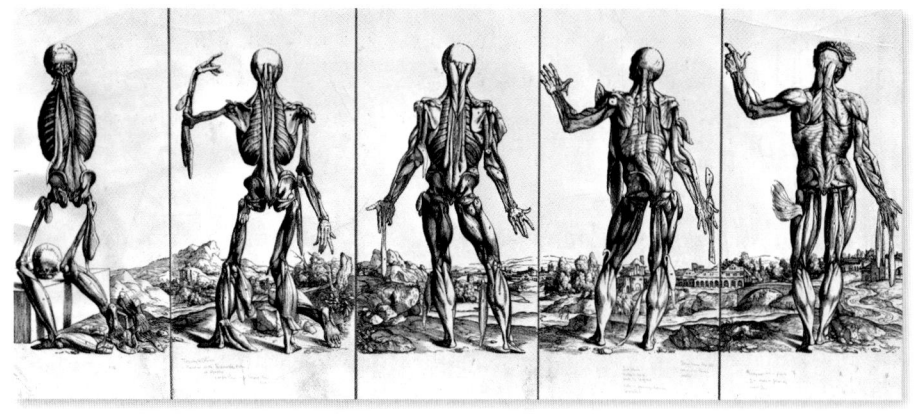

Vesalius learned about the body by dissecting human corpses.

particularly the works of Galen (GAY-luhn), a Greek physician who had lived in the second century A.D.

In the 1500s, Andreas Vesalius, a physician from Flanders, began to question what Galen had written. At the University of Padua in Italy, Vesalius taught anatomy by cutting into dead human bodies and showing his students the different organs inside. The more Vesalius peered into corpses, the more he noticed that Galen was often wrong.

Galen had dissected the bodies of dogs and pigs but probably never looked inside a human body, since dissecting human corpses was forbidden in his day. But, as Vesalius observed, despite some similarities, the anatomy of dogs and pigs differs significantly from that of humans. In 1543, Vesalius published *On the Structure of the Human Body*, a book based on his own careful observations, with illustrations by skilled Renaissance artists. This masterful work gave the first accurate and detailed picture of human anatomy.

By showing the importance of observation and experimentation—two central features of modern science—Vesalius pointed the way toward the Scientific Revolution of the 1600s.

New Views of the Universe

Since ancient times, sailors had steered their vessels by the stars. The Age of Exploration furthered the quest for knowledge in astronomy and mathematics, in part because explorers needed more

accurate ways to plot their routes. Still, around 1500, most Europeans continued to look to Ptolemy (TAH-luh-mee) as the leading expert on astronomy. Ptolemy, an astronomer and geographer of Greek descent, lived in ancient Egypt into the second century A.D. According to Ptolemy, the earth stood still at the center of the universe, and the sun and the planets revolved around it. Most people accepted the Ptolemaic (tah-luh-MAY-ik) understanding of the universe. After all, they saw the sun "come up" in the morning and "go down" at night. So it made sense that the sun moved and the earth stood still.

Copernicus Challenges Ptolemy

In the early 1500s, a Polish astronomer named Nicolaus Copernicus looked to the stars and came up with a revolutionary new view of the universe. Copernicus questioned the accepted Ptolemaic model. When Copernicus applied mathematics to the movements of the planets, he discovered that Ptolemy's ideas didn't add up. Copernicus concluded that the earth—along with the other planets of the solar system—revolves around the sun.

Copernicus replaced Ptolemy's *geocentric* (earth-centered) picture of the universe with a new *heliocentric* (sun-centered) one. But Copernicus's ideas seemed so radical that he hesitated to communicate them. His book, *On the Revolutions of the Heavenly Bodies*, was not published until just before his death in 1543.

Geo is the Greek root for "earth." *Helio* is Greek for "sun."

From Tycho to Kepler

The next major step in astronomy was taken by Tycho Brahe (TEE-koh brah) of Denmark, who studied at the University of Leipzig in Germany. Fascinated by astronomy, he traveled across Europe and collected various tools for observing the heavens and calculating their movements (though he lacked one instrument not yet invented—the telescope).

With the support of the Danish king, Tycho established an astronomical observatory. From there, he and his assistants watched the night sky for years. They recorded observations of the movements of the stars and other heavenly bodies. Their data corrected a great many errors in existing astronomical records.

When Tycho died in 1601, his assistant, Johannes Kepler, carried on his work. A German astronomer and mathematical genius, Kepler spent years applying advanced calculations to Tycho's astronomical data. Kepler found that Tycho's observations of the planet Mars did not fit with the accepted view that planets orbit in circular paths. Through careful calculations, Kepler solved this problem by showing that the

Copernicus came up with the revolutionary idea that the earth, along with the other planets, revolves around the sun.

planets do not travel in perfectly circular orbits but in elliptical (egg-shaped) ones. Kepler went on to make other important discoveries about planetary motion.

Observation, Experimentation, and Mathematics

In the early 1600s, two innovative thinkers—one British, one French—helped advance the Scientific Revolution. Francis Bacon of England and René Descartes (ruh-NAY day-KAHRT) of France both criticized the thinkers of their time for accepting without question the writings of ancient Greek and Roman philosophers. But Bacon and Descartes differed in their views about the most reliable ways to acquire knowledge about the natural world.

Francis Bacon's Empirical Approach

Francis Bacon was a man of many talents—a lawyer, statesman, writer, and philosopher. In 1620, Bacon published *Novum Organum* (Latin for "New Instrument"). In this book, Bacon asserted that to gain true scientific understanding, scholars must get beyond the habit of citing ancient authorities such as Aristotle. He wrote that the "true business of philosophy"—what we would call "science"—is "to apply the understanding…to a fresh examination of particulars."

In calling for a "fresh examination of particulars," Bacon was rejecting Aristotle's *deductive* reasoning, which moved from general premises to specific conclusions. Instead, Bacon said that the path to new knowledge is by way of *inductive* reasoning, that is, reasoning from specific facts—Bacon's "particulars"—to general principles.

In insisting on "the particulars," Bacon was taking an empirical approach to knowledge. An *empirical* approach assumes that truth is derived from experiment and observation rather than theories or generalizations. Bacon insisted on the need to conduct repeated observations and practical experiments. Moreover, he urged the careful recording, detailed description, and organized analysis of specific facts derived from observation and experiment. Bacon himself compiled many tables of data in an attempt to understand the nature of heat.

Descartes and Mathematical Reasoning

Like Francis Bacon, the French philosopher René Descartes thought that old assumptions must be questioned. Unlike Bacon, Descartes had little patience for conducting experiments or collecting data. He preferred lying in bed and thinking. In fact, he was lying in bed when he came up with one of his most famous ideas.

Looking up from his pillow, Descartes saw a fly buzz through the air and settle on the ceiling. He began to think about the best way to describe its exact location. He imagined two lines on the ceiling, one vertical and the other horizontal, each passing through the fly. He realized that if he called the horizontal line x and the vertical line y, he could describe the fly's position as "where x meets y." His idea of locating a point where two lines come together came to be called the Cartesian coordinate system, after Descartes himself (from the Latin spelling of his last name, *Cartesius*).

Descartes linked algebra and geometry to offer new insights in the field of mathematics known as analytic geometry. He also devised ways to refine mathematical proofs and simplify algebraic calculations. For his many mathematical insights and his development of the Cartesian coordinate system, Descartes is often called the "Father of Modern Mathematics." While Francis Bacon emphasized the importance of experimentation, Descartes emphasized the use of mathematics. For the French thinker, no experiment could be as reliable as the logical proofs of mathematics.

Scientific Methods

The two approaches represented by Bacon and Descartes—the experimental and the mathematical—form the basis of modern scientific methods. Modern scientists understand that observation,

careful experimentation, and mathematical reasoning are all required in the effort to understand the workings of nature. For modern scientists, these scientific methods include

- observing and gathering data
- making a hypothesis (a tentative theory) to explain one's observations
- experimenting to test the hypothesis
- collecting and analyzing data from the experiments, and, based on this data,
- drawing conclusions that may confirm or deny the original hypothesis, or lead to a revised hypothesis and further experimentation.

Galileo Explores the Heavens

Both the experimental and the mathematical approaches to science came together in the work of Galileo Galilei (gal-uh-LAY-oh gal-uh-LAY-ee), a brilliant Italian mathematician who turned to astronomy. While he was a professor of mathematics, Galileo designed scientific instruments, including a new kind of thermometer and an improved compass. Then Galileo heard about a remarkable new invention—a metal tube to look through with glass lenses inside that made far-off things seem closer. But these early telescopes were little more than toys, with weak lenses that produced blurry images.

Within a few months, Galileo managed to design a much more powerful telescope. He turned his telescope toward the sky—and what he saw changed the course of history.

Galileo saw that Ptolemy was wrong in thinking that the moon had a smooth surface. Instead, Galileo observed (as he later wrote) a "rough and uneven" surface with "lofty mountains and deep valleys." Galileo went on to describe the Milky Way as "a mass of innumerable stars planted together in clusters." He also discovered four moons orbiting the planet Jupiter.

Galileo's observations confirmed the ideas of Copernicus. Through his telescope, Galileo saw

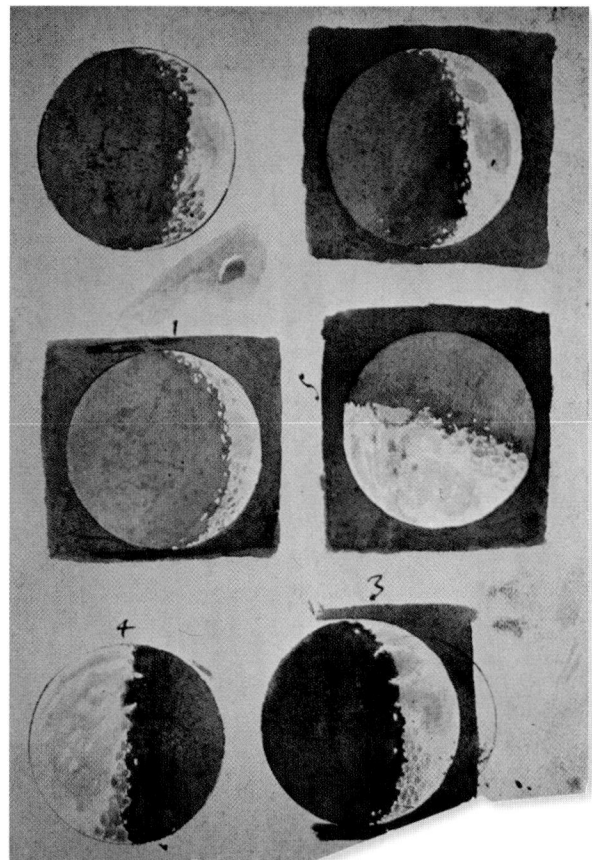

Galileo's sketches of the rough lunar surface, as he saw it through his telescope, show the earth's shadow on the moon.

that Ptolemy was wrong to say that all heavenly bodies revolved in great spheres around the earth—after all, Galileo had seen contradictory evidence in the moons revolving around Jupiter. The more Galileo observed the night sky, the more he knew that Copernicus had been right.

In 1610, Galileo published a book titled *The Starry Messenger*, which described the "great and marvelous sights" he had seen through his telescope. In the spirit of the Scientific Revolution, Galileo based his writings on observation, experimentation, and mathematics. At the end of the book, he confirmed Copernicus's idea that the earth does not sit at the center of the universe but instead "travels over a mighty orbit about the Sun."

Galileo and the Inquisition

Some officials of the Catholic Church argued that the ideas of Copernicus and Galileo went against the teachings of the Bible. Galileo responded that the Bible was not an astronomy textbook. "The Bible shows us how to go to heaven," he declared, "not how the heavens go."

In 1616, the Catholic Church condemned the ideas of Copernicus and banned any books containing the new astronomical ideas. Galileo fell silent—but only for a time. In 1632, Galileo published *Dialogue on the Great World Systems*, another book defending Copernicus's ideas. Church leaders were furious. Galileo's new book defied the church's ban. Even worse, he had written it not in Latin, the language of scholars, but in Italian, the language of the people.

Galileo was called to Rome to stand trial before the Inquisition. He knew that he faced torture and execution unless he told the inquisitors what

Honoring Early Astronomers

After learning how Galileo was using his telescope to study the heavens, the German astronomer Johannes Kepler designed an improved form of the instrument. It used a different combination of lenses to create a brighter image.

In recent years, American scientists at the National Aeronautics and Space Administration (NASA) have honored the work of Galileo and Kepler by naming missions after these pioneering astronomers. In 1989, NASA undertook the Galileo Mission by sending an unmanned spacecraft to explore Jupiter. In 2009, when NASA launched a gigantic telescope into space to study far-off planets, they called their enterprise the Kepler Mission.

Galileo demonstrates his telescope to the leading citizens of Venice.

Newton's Laws

In 1643, a year after Galileo died, Isaac Newton was born in England. As a young man at Cambridge University, Newton immersed himself in physics, mathematics, and astronomy. Many of his teachers at Cambridge still held on to old Aristotelian ideas, but Newton looked at the world with an open—and brilliant—mind. In 1665, when an outbreak of plague threatened the town, Newton left Cambridge to live in the countryside for two years. There, according to a popular legend, an apple falling from a tree started Isaac Newton thinking about gravity. Whether the legend has any grain of truth, Newton went on to develop his **theory of universal gravitation**, which revolutionized astronomy and physics.

they wanted to hear. At his trial, Galileo signed a paper taking back his ideas. He claimed to agree that the sun revolved around the earth.

In the decades after Galileo's death in 1642, scholars translated the *Dialogue* into many different languages. The printing press rapidly spread his ideas. People all over Europe began to accept the new astronomy. While the church had temporarily silenced Galileo, it did not stop the spread of his ideas.

Newton understood gravity as a force that pulls *all* objects toward each other—thus, when an apple falls, not only does the earth exert a force on the apple, but the apple also exerts a force on the earth. Newton recognized that this pull between the apple and the earth is the same force that keeps the moon in its orbit around the earth and the planets in their orbits around the

Maria Winkelmann, Astronomer

During the Scientific Revolution, scientific training was largely restricted to men. But some determined women were able to gain expertise through their own study and as apprentices to male researchers. In Germany, Maria Winkelmann studied astronomy as an apprentice. She later married the country's foremost astronomer, Gottfried Kirch, and worked as his assistant. Together, they helped produce an accurate astronomical calendar. A distinguished astronomer in her own right, Winkelmann is credited with discovering a comet in 1702. When her husband died, she applied to take over his post at the Royal Academy of Sciences, but was turned down. "It simply will not do," wrote the Academy's president. "Even before her husband's death, the Academy was ridiculed because its calendar was prepared by a woman. If she were to be kept on in such a capacity, mouths would gape even wider."

sun. Newton developed a mathematical formula to calculate gravitational force as a relationship between distance and mass.

Newton made breakthroughs in other fields. He performed experiments on the nature of light. Newton aimed a ray of white light through a prism and observed how the white light separated into rays of different colors. White light, he had discovered, was actually made up of the light from the many different colors of the spectrum.

Newton, who had carefully studied the ideas of Descartes, also invented a new branch of mathematics, now called *calculus*. Using calculus, Newton could calculate the speed, direction, and position of moving bodies such as the planets. Calculus allowed Newton to describe the movements of the planets far more accurately than they had been described before.

In 1687, Newton wrote a book titled *Philosophiae Naturalis Principia Mathematica*, or *Mathematical Principles of Natural Philosophy*. In the

Using a prism, Isaac Newton splits a ray of sunlight into the many colors of the spectrum.

William Harvey and the Circulation of Blood

About a century after Vesalius made his anatomical discoveries, an English physician, William Harvey, made new discoveries that further disproved established ideas put forth by the ancient Greek physician, Galen. In Harvey's time, most physicians believed Galen's explanation that the liver turned food into blood, which then flowed through the veins to be consumed by the body. Through experimentation—and the dissection of human and animal corpses—Harvey proved that blood circulates through the body. Harvey showed that the heart pumps blood through the arteries, and that the blood returns to the heart through the veins. When Harvey published his findings in 1628, he initially met resistance and disbelief. Within a few decades, however, Harvey's explanation of the circulatory system was widely accepted.

Principia (prin-SIH-pee-uh), as the book is often called, Newton explained, among other things, three laws of motion. Building on the work of his scientific predecessors, such as Galileo and Kepler, Newton developed his ideas about motion. Here, in simplified terms, are Newton's laws of motion:

- First law (the law of inertia): A body in motion will stay in motion, and a body at rest will remain at rest, unless acted on by a force.
- Second law: The force of an object is equal to its mass times its acceleration.
- Third law: For every action there is an equal and opposite reaction.

Newton argued that all the objects in the universe—from moons and planets to balls and apples—obey these same laws. Newton's discoveries suggested a new view of the universe, not as the mysterious working out of some divine plan, but more like an orderly machine—say, a great clock—operating precisely according to mathematical laws. Newton's ideas implied that through science and mathematics human beings could understand, and even improve on, the fundamental workings of the great machine.

Advances in Chemistry

Chemistry is the science that studies matter—its basic makeup and the changes it undergoes. It grew out of the practice of alchemy, which was pursued in the Middle Ages and the Renaissance. The alchemists followed Aristotle in holding that all matter was composed of four elements—earth,

air, fire, and water. Therefore, they believed, any one substance could be transformed into any other. Many alchemists spent their time trying unsuccessfully to transform common metals like iron or lead into silver or gold.

In the mid-1600s, a British scientist named Robert Boyle attacked Aristotle's idea of the four elements. In a book called *The Skeptical Chemist*, he argued instead that matter is made up of tiny particles called "corpuscles" that are always moving and interacting. Later scientists would build on Boyle's basic insights and reveal that atoms are the basic building blocks of matter.

Boyle also performed important experiments on gases. He established a formula known as Boyle's law—that as the volume of a gas goes up, its pressure goes down. For his contributions to the science, Boyle is often considered the "Father of Modern Chemistry."

Over the next century, other scientists would advance the field of chemistry with new experiments. In the 1770s, the Englishman Joseph Priestley discovered that, when heated, certain compounds released a gas that he suspected to be a "new species of air." Soon afterward, the French scientist Antoine Lavoisier (AN-twahn lahv-WAHZ-yay) performed more experiments on this gas, and renamed it *oxygen*. Lavoisier showed that oxygen is essential to both respiration (breathing) and combustion (burning). He also demonstrated that water is made up of a combination of oxygen and the element called hydrogen. Lavoisier was aided in his research by his wife, Marie, who translated research written in English into French, assisted him in the laboratory, and used her skill in drawing to record the results of his experiments.

Leeuwenhoek and the Microscope

A Dutchman and self-taught scientist, Anton van Leeuwenhoek (AHN-tohn vahn LAY-ven-hook) passionately pursued a hobby of grinding lenses to build a better microscope. He made nearly four hundred fifty microscopes of various types, which allowed him to see forms of life not visible to the naked eye. In 1674, while examining drops of water, he discovered tiny, wiggly creatures that he called *animalcules* ("little animals"), which we now recognize as bacteria and other simple microorganisms.

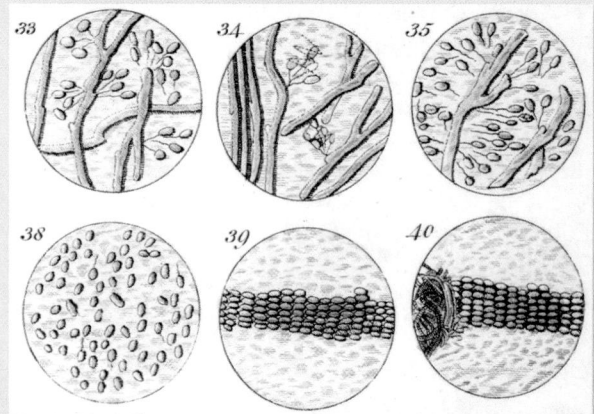

This hand-colored engraving shows bacteria, or what Leeuwenhoek called *animalcules*.

Lasting Consequences of the Scientific Revolution

Vesalius, Copernicus, Bacon, Descartes, Galileo, Newton—these are some of the most brilliant minds that contributed to that great and gradual change in thinking that we now call the Scientific Revolution. They opened the way for modern

A spectacular example of the innovations produced during the Scientific Revolution, a hot air balloon sails above an enthusiastic crowd at the Palace of Versailles in 1783.

science as we know it. Through their efforts, science became a distinct way of gaining knowledge about the natural world through careful observation, experimentation, and mathematics.

Beginning in the mid-1500s and proceeding through and beyond the 1600s, the Scientific Revolution replaced old views that characterized nature as the workings of mysterious, hidden forces. Instead, thinkers began to experiment and carefully observe. They wrote down their observations, communicated their evidence to others, and used math in new ways. They began to understand much more about the workings of nature, from the movements of the heavenly bodies to the flow of blood in the human body. Science, the organized study of how nature works, was born—and that, some would say, marked the birth of our modern world.

The Enlightenment

Key Questions

* How did the attitudes of the Scientific Revolution affect social and political thought?

* What goals did Enlightenment philosophers share? How did their political and social views differ?

* What lasting influence did the Enlightenment have?

Galileo and Newton focused on investigating the physical world. To them, nature seemed to operate in rational, orderly ways that could be explained by mathematical principles, such as the laws of motion that Newton formulated. Soon other thinkers wondered if the principles behind the Scientific Revolution might also be applied to questions of politics, economics, and society. These thinkers began to ask: If there are laws that govern the physical world, might there also be laws or principles that apply to the social world, the world of human activity and government?

To that question, many thinkers confidently answered, Yes. Furthermore, they said, we can use human reason to solve human problems. As the seventeenth-century English philosopher John Locke affirmed, reason must be "our last judge and our guide in everything." An enthusiastic optimism swept through Europe as human progress seemed a simple question of using reason to discern the principles behind social, political, and economic life. This period from the mid-1600s to the late 1700s became known as the Age of Reason. It has also been called the **Enlightenment**, because so many thinkers believed that reason could illuminate truth.

Hobbes and Locke: Two Views of Government

Some Enlightenment philosophers focused on ideas about government, particularly in England, where civil war and the overthrow of the monarchy shook the country in the mid-1600s. From their experience of the English Civil War and its aftermath, two English philosophers, Thomas Hobbes and John Locke, proposed two very different views of man and government.

Hobbes Prefers Monarchy

While many Enlightenment thinkers held optimistic views of human potential, Thomas Hobbes, an English political philosopher and scientist, came to darker conclusions. When King Charles I was at odds with England's Parliament, Hobbes wrote a widely circulated treatise justifying the king's assertion of his broad powers as monarch. During the 1640s, when civil war tore England apart, Hobbes feared for his life and went to live in France. The strife and bloodshed in England led Hobbes to think about human nature and the proper role of government. In 1651, he published his groundbreaking work of political philosophy, *Leviathan*.

Hobbes saw human beings as naturally violent and selfish. In the absence of government, he said, people live in a chaotic "state of nature." In such a state, Hobbes declared, "the life of man [is] solitary, poor, nasty, brutish, and short." Hobbes argued that people must give up some of their freedom and submit to the rule of a government, which in exchange would provide order and security.

To Hobbes, only an extremely powerful government could keep people in line and prevent them from hurting each other. Therefore, he argued, the best form of government was an absolute monarchy.

John Locke and Natural Law

John Locke was also shaped by his experience of England's profound changes, but he came to conclusions that greatly differed from those of Hobbes. Locke believed that just as certain "laws of nature" govern the physical world, there is a "natural law" at work in the universe, a moral order that existed before any king ever issued a command or any government ever exercised power.

Locke argued that people can discover this natural law by using reason. Reason, Locke argued, makes it apparent that even before any government existed, people had certain rights. Among the "natural rights" Locke specified are the rights of life, liberty, and the ownership of property.

The job of governments, Locke asserted, is to respect natural law and protect natural rights. Locke said that even kings are subject to natural law. Reason, said Locke, tells us that kings are obligated to protect the natural rights of their subjects. But if, as Locke put it, a ruler "makes not the law, but his will, the rule," then "it is lawful for the people...to resist their King."

In 1690, Locke published his essays called *Two Treatises of Government*, in which he explained his ideas about the relationship between the people and their government. Locke wrote that it is government's job to protect the natural rights of life, liberty, and property. If a government robs people of those rights, then, said Locke, the people have a right of revolution—the right to replace their government, just as the English people had replaced their king and strengthened Parliament in the Glorious Revolution.

In Locke's view, England's Glorious Revolution represented great progress. It was a sign that

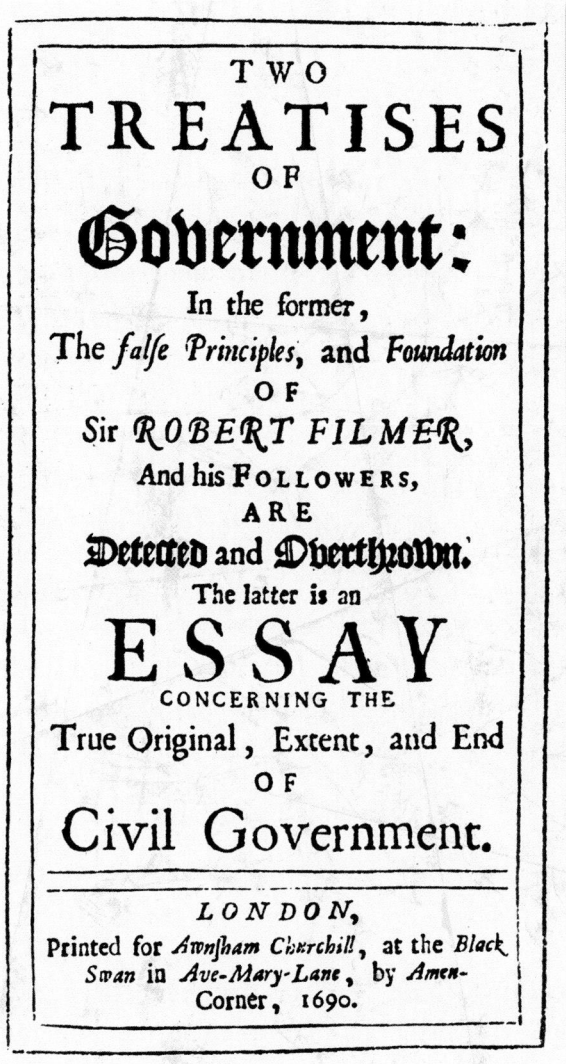

John Locke argued that people have "natural rights."

people could design governments that would protect their liberties and work for the common good. Thinkers across Europe and beyond read John Locke's essays. His writings became milestones of Enlightenment thought and influenced political thinking for centuries to come.

The French Philosophes

The keenest thinkers in eighteenth-century France were known as *philosophes* (fee-luh-ZAWFS), from the Greek for "friends of wisdom." The philosophes often criticized France's government as corrupt and unjust. They ridiculed many religious beliefs and practices as superstitions that went against reason. Behind their criticisms and

Power as a Check to Power

In *The Spirit of Laws*, published in 1748, Montesquieu argued that power should be divided such that no single part of the government could become too powerful.

Democratic and aristocratic states are not in their own nature free. Political liberty is to be found only in moderate governments and even in these it is not always found. It is there only when there is no abuse of power. But constant experience shows us that every man invested with power is apt to abuse it, and to carry his authority as far as it will go....

To prevent this abuse, it is necessary from the very nature of things that power should be a check to power. A government may be so constituted, as no man shall be compelled to do things to which the law does not oblige him, nor forced to abstain from things which the law permits.

occasional mockery was the belief that reason and knowledge could bring the justice, equality, and freedom their country needed.

Montesquieu and the Spirit of Laws

One philosophe, the Baron de la Brede et de Montesquieu (mohn-tes-kyou), was a Frenchman who had lived in England. Montesquieu admired the work of John Locke. He praised English liberties. He mocked the French court and Parisian social life.

Montesquieu asked: What can reason tell us about how people should be governed? In his work called *The Spirit of Laws*, published in 1748, Montesquieu described three kinds of government—monarchies, republics, and despotic governments. In a monarchy, Montesquieu explained, a king or queen holds limited powers. A republican government, he said, can take one of two forms. It can be an aristocracy, in which just a few people hold power. Or it can be a democracy, in which power is held by all the people. Finally, said Montesquieu, in a despotic government, a tyrant holds all the power.

Montesquieu thought that, depending on the circumstances, either monarchies or republics could be good forms of government, but he was opposed to despotic governments. He believed that the best way to protect liberty was to separate a government's powers into three branches: a legislative branch (the law-making part), an executive branch (the law-enforcing part), and a judicial branch (the courts).

With power divided among the three branches, Montesquieu explained, no single part of the government could become too powerful. Montesquieu's writings, published in 1748, influenced the creation of several constitutions in the eighteenth and nineteenth centuries, including the Constitution of the United States.

Voltaire: Champion of Intellectual Freedom

The philosophes often sharply criticized both the church and the state in France. Some discovered that it could be dangerous to criticize powerful institutions. One philosophe who learned this hard lesson was François-Marie Arouet, better known by his pen name, Voltaire (vohl-TAIR). Voltaire's writings often got him in trouble with the law. His poems poking fun at the French government briefly landed him in jail.

A hugely energetic author, Voltaire wrote works of history as well as pamphlets, poems, plays, and a novel called *Candide*. In his sharp-tongued satires, Voltaire frequently mocked the government and society of France. After quarreling with a powerful aristocrat, he fled to England, where he lived for two years.

In London, Voltaire came to admire Isaac Newton, and he was also impressed by John Locke's ideas and the English system of government. On his return, Voltaire published a book in which he praised England's laws, political liberty, and religious freedom. The French government had the book burned as a "scandalous work, contrary to religion and morals and the respect due to the established powers."

Voltaire frequently attacked organized religion, especially in the form of the Catholic Church. Like many Enlightenment thinkers, Voltaire was a **deist**. The deists believed in the existence of a creator God who had made the universe then left it to run on its own, according to the laws of nature. Deists rejected the idea—common to Christianity and other traditional faiths—that God takes part in the lives of human beings, answering their prayers and sometimes causing miracles. They dismissed all such beliefs as superstition.

Above all, Voltaire opposed organized religion for its intolerance of other faiths and ideas. He especially condemned the Catholic Church for its oppression of France's Protestant minority, the Huguenots. King Louis XIV had issued a royal decree ordering his Huguenot subjects to abandon their faith and accept the teachings of the Catholic Church. Voltaire thought it was impossible to force men and women to believe particular ideas. Rather, he said, people should be free to use reason and make up their own minds about religion, politics, and philosophy.

Although Voltaire often disagreed with the way the king ruled France, he was no enemy of monarchy. He believed that the king had too much power, but he did not recommend that the French people rid themselves of their king. Rather, he believed that the best government would be ruled by an enlightened monarch, a king who, in making policies and laws, would be guided by wise advisers. And the advisers, of course, should be guided by reason.

Voltaire's attacks on the Catholic Church and the French aristocracy helped lay the groundwork for a revolution in France in the late 1700s.

At a literary gathering in Paris, Voltaire reads from his latest writings.

More broadly, he is remembered as one of history's greatest champions of tolerance and intellectual freedom.

Diderot's Great Book of Knowledge

Just as the philosophes cherished reason, they also placed a high value on knowledge. In the mid-eighteenth century, one of the philosophes, the French writer Denis Diderot (duh-nee DEE-duh-roh), embarked on a monumental task. He decided to publish a massive collection that would organize all knowledge. He called this work the *Encyclopédie* (ahn-see-kloh-peh-DEE). (The word *encyclopedia* comes from the Greek words *enkyklios paideia*, meaning "a circle of learning," in other words, a general education.)

Diderot called on dozens of fellow philosophes to help him meet his ambitious goal. Both Voltaire and Montesquieu contributed entries. In 1751, Diderot published his first volume. He published twenty-seven more volumes over the next twenty years.

The *Encyclopédie* included a diverse range of articles, not only on big ideas of philosophy and politics, but also on practical pursuits such as swordsmanship, farming, and calligraphy. The *Encyclopédie* caused a stir. Some articles called for religious toleration, or attacked religion as superstition—no surprise, as Diderot was an atheist, someone who does not believe in the existence of God. Other articles criticized the government and called for reforms. For a time the *Encyclopédie* was banned. But the public loved it and bought every one of the four thousand sets printed. Diderot's ambitious project proved instrumental in the spread of Enlightenment ideas.

New Social Ideas

The flurry of critical viewpoints during the Enlightenment included new ideas that would echo into modern times. These included ideas about social order, education, the role of women, and economics.

Rousseau's Social Contract

Jean-Jacques Rousseau (zhahn-zhahk roo-SOH), one of the most influential thinkers of the Enlightenment, was born in Geneva, Switzerland, to French Huguenot parents. He had an unhappy childhood and suffered from many ailments. In Paris in the 1740s, he wrote articles about music for Diderot's *Encyclopédie*, and was drawn into the lively circle of writers and thinkers that made up the philosophes. But Rousseau preferred the countryside to the city, and spent many of his years living in rural homes. Rousseau called cities "the abyss of the human species."

While most Enlightenment thinkers believed in the power of reason to solve human problems, Rousseau thought that reason made people cold and unsympathetic to others. He declared that we should follow our emotions rather than our reason. Contrary to Thomas Hobbes, Rousseau believed that human beings are naturally good. By nature, said Rousseau, people are free, happy, and innocent—but then we are corrupted by society. Also contrary to Hobbes, who had justified absolute monarchy, Rousseau championed liberty and dismissed any notion of the divine right of kings.

In his *Discourse on the Origins of Inequality*, Rousseau criticized society as corrupt and hypocritical. He argued that people had given up their natural freedom and submitted themselves to laws and government in order to protect their private property, an arrangement that favored the rich and perpetuated inequality and injustice.

Rousseau was a champion of freedom. He opened his influential book of political philosophy, *The Social Contract*,

Rousseau loved the countryside and believed that many valuable lessons can be learned from nature. His writings paved the way for Romanticism.

Rousseau on Education

Rousseau criticized the schools of his time. In a novel called *Émile* (ay-MEEL), he offered his ideas on education. Students, Rousseau said, should be taught in a rural setting, where they could learn about the natural world around them. Teachers should not burden their students with tiresome lessons, but should appeal to their natural interests. Young students, said Rousseau, should be allowed to run around outside, enjoying the beauty of nature and exercising their inborn curiosity. In such circumstances, Rousseau believed, students would blossom like wildflowers.

published in 1762, with this bold assertion: "Man is born free, and everywhere he is in chains." But, argued Rousseau, people could throw off their chains by entering into a "social contract" in which they agree to subordinate their individual self-interest to the "general will." Rousseau, with his optimistic view of human nature, believed that by setting aside individual self-interest for the sake of the "general will," people would be working for the collective good of a community that would enhance rights and freedoms.

Many of Rousseau's ideas influenced the writers and artists who came after him. His beliefs about the goodness of human nature and the evil of society became a central assumption of the movement known as Romanticism (which you will read about in a later chapter).

Mary Wollstonecraft and the Rights of Women

During the Enlightenment, some upper-class women in Paris hosted "salons," gatherings in which philosophers and artists met to discuss new ideas. But very few women were educated or wealthy enough to participate in intellectual life. Even in these "enlightened" times, many male thinkers held very limited views of women's capabilities. For example, Rousseau believed that the education of women should prepare them to be supportive wives and caring mothers.

An Englishwoman named Mary Wollstonecraft strongly disagreed. In 1792, she published *A Vindication of the Rights of Women*. "When men contend for their freedom," she declared, "...it

[is] inconsistent and unjust to subjugate women." Wollstonecraft lamented that "the female mind has been...totally neglected."

The Enlightenment recognized the power of reason in all humankind, not in men alone. Thus, Wollstonecraft observed, women, who were as capable of reason as men, should have the same opportunities for education as men. Furthermore, women should be encouraged to work as doctors, politicians, businesspeople, and in other jobs assumed to be men's work.

Today Wollstonecraft's *Vindication* is seen as the first important work of feminism—the movement to secure equal rights for women.

Mary Wollstonecraft contended that women should have the same educational opportunities as men.

Adam Smith Analyzes Economics

Just as John Locke had pondered the "natural laws" that explain how governments should work, a Scottish philosopher named Adam Smith wondered whether there might be similar laws to explain how economies operate. Smith applied reason to a rethinking of the world of business, labor, and finance.

In 1776, Smith published *The Wealth of Nations*, a pathbreaking work that laid the foundation for the modern science of economics—the study of how goods and services are produced, distributed, and consumed. Smith, in fact, is often called the father of modern economics.

In *The Wealth of Nations*, Smith said that people are driven by self-interest. All of us, said Smith, have a natural desire to better our lives, "a desire that comes with us from the womb, and never leaves us until we go into the grave." Smith believed that "the market"—by which he meant the whole system of buying and selling—worked through competition among self-interested individuals. Competition, he said, helps purchasers get the best price and causes the most efficient businesses to survive.

Smith Opposes Monopolies

Adam Smith believed that competition among businesses was important. But he also recognized that true competition is hard to ensure because "people of the same trade seldom meet together" without the conversation ending in "some contrivance to raise prices." In other words, without some regulation and control, businessmen might plot to fix prices at a high level. Because he believed in the need for competition among businesses, Smith insisted that there should be no monopolies, no industries in which a single group controls all the production and prices.

Smith wrote that the market is almost like an "invisible hand" that guides the business decisions people make. This invisible hand makes sure that people produce the things and provide the services that society needs. Anyone who overcharges loses business to competitors, while anyone who undercharges goes broke.

The wealth of a nation, Smith concluded, lies in the prosperity of all its citizens. That is, it lies in their ability to produce and consume goods. To make this wealth grow, Smith recommended an economic system in which businesses produce goods and services in order to make money—in short, capitalism.

Smith insisted that government should adopt a hands-off policy and allow the invisible hand, or the natural laws of the economy, to proceed freely. In Smith's view, competition would keep prices low, and businesses that made bad decisions would go out of business. Smith's doctrine that the government should not interfere in the workings of the economy came to be known by a French term, *laissez-faire* [leh-say-FEHR], meaning "let it be."

In Smith's time, the economic policies of European governments were anything but laissez-faire. These governments based their economic policies on mercantilism, the idea that a nation's wealth consisted of its stores of gold and silver. To increase their wealth in gold and silver, European rulers passed laws to control the flow of trade. For example, the British government placed special taxes, called duties or tariffs, on cloth, wine, and other products bought from France. Because these taxes made French products more expensive, the British were encouraged to buy cloth and wine made in England. Similarly, the French government made it illegal to import printed calico, a cloth made in India, because the government wanted French citizens to buy cloth made in France.

Adam Smith concluded that all these taxes and restrictions helped no one. In his view, the proper role of government in creating wealth was to let the market regulate itself. Thus he was opposed to imposing duties or other limits on free trade. After Adam Smith died in 1790, British leaders began to follow his advice. Over the next few decades, the government lifted duties to let trade flow freely in and out of the country.

The Arts of the Enlightenment

The Enlightenment in Europe was a time of extraordinary achievement in the arts. The Age of Reason was also an age of reasonable art. Throughout most of the 1700s, the dominant style in the arts of Europe was *neoclassicism*. The name means "new classicism." The neoclassicists created art and literature that appealed to reason and the intellect.

Neoclassicists admired certain qualities of Greek and Roman art and literature, such as harmony, order, and balance. For example, neoclassical architects turned away from the ornate, dramatic style of the Palace of Versailles and instead designed stately buildings with Greek columns and Roman domes. (The style lasted long enough to influence Thomas Jefferson when he designed Monticello, his home in Virginia.)

Neoclassical poets translated and imitated the classical Greek and Roman poets. For example, the English poet Alexander Pope wrote a collection called *Imitations of Horace*, inspired by the works of the ancient Roman poet. Pope wrote many of his poems as an orderly series of rhyming couplets. In this couplet, Pope expresses his admiration for one of the intellectual heroes of the Scientific Revolution:

> *Nature and Nature's laws lay hid in night;*
> *God said, "Let Newton be," and all was light.*

Music in Eighteenth-Century Europe

Some of the best-loved music the world has known was written by composers in eighteenth-century Europe. In the first half of the century, two German-born composers, Johann Sebastian Bach (bahk) and George Frideric Handel, represent

Neoclassical Painting: Jacques-Louis David

The French painter Jacques-Louis David (zhahk-LOO-ee dah-veed) is representative of the neoclassical style and his 1784 painting, the *Oath of the Horatii* (huh-RAY-shee-iy), an example of his achievement. The painting depicts a moment in a war between ancient Rome and a rival city-state. In the painting, Horace holds up the swords of his sons (the Horatii) as the young men pledge allegiance to Rome. David's painting embodies the neoclassical traits of order and balance. The men stand in rigid poses like ancient statues. The sons on the left are balanced by the women and children on the right, who grieve for the losses to come. The figures are posed against an orderly background of massive columns and arches.

Jacques-Louis David's 1784 painting, the *Oath of the Horatii*, embodies the neoclassical traits of order and balance.

Classical Music: General and Specific

The term *classical music* has both a broad, general meaning and a specific, historical meaning. In a general sense, classical music (often contrasted with "popular music") includes music written for orchestras, choirs, string quartets, pianists, and other performers. In this broad usage, classical music includes composers from before Johann Sebastian Bach (1685–1750) to the present day. Within this general category of music, however, there is a specific period known as the *classical period*, from the mid-1700s to the early 1800s.

the peak of achievement in a musical style called the Baroque (buh-ROHK). Both wrote religious masterworks, such as Bach's *B Minor Mass* and Handel's *Messiah*. But both also wrote many works for secular performances, from Bach's works for solo violin to Handel's lavish operas.

Beginning in the mid-1700s, the greatest composers—such as Franz Joseph Haydn (HIY-dn) and Wolfgang Amadeus Mozart (MOHT-sahrt)—wrote music in what is called the classical style. Like neoclassical art and literature, most music of the classical period emphasized the values of order, balance, and clarity. Among their great musical output, both Haydn and Mozart wrote many works for a relatively new instrument at the time, the piano.

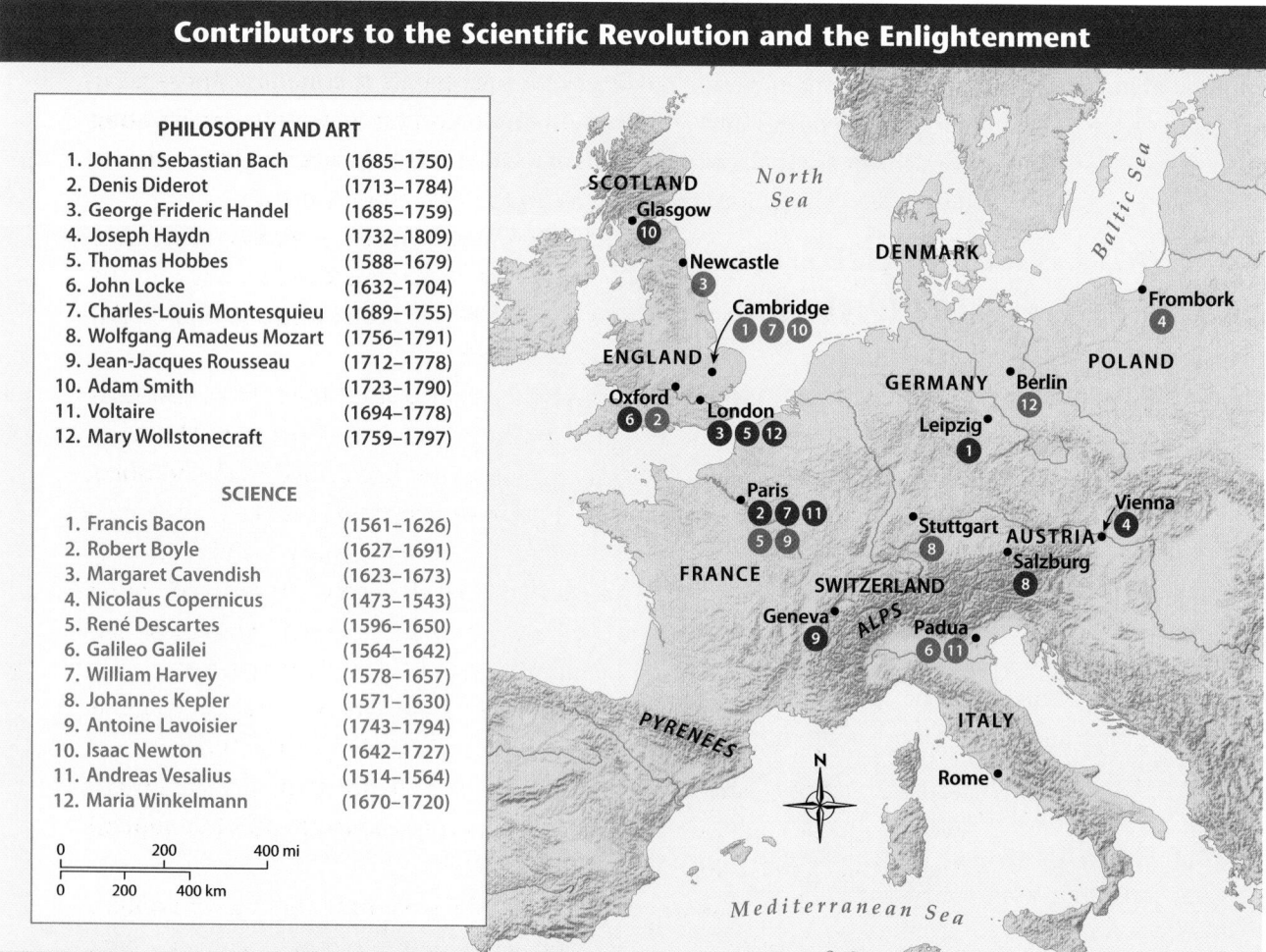

Contributors to the Scientific Revolution and the Enlightenment

PHILOSOPHY AND ART

1. Johann Sebastian Bach (1685–1750)
2. Denis Diderot (1713–1784)
3. George Frideric Handel (1685–1759)
4. Joseph Haydn (1732–1809)
5. Thomas Hobbes (1588–1679)
6. John Locke (1632–1704)
7. Charles-Louis Montesquieu (1689–1755)
8. Wolfgang Amadeus Mozart (1756–1791)
9. Jean-Jacques Rousseau (1712–1778)
10. Adam Smith (1723–1790)
11. Voltaire (1694–1778)
12. Mary Wollstonecraft (1759–1797)

SCIENCE

1. Francis Bacon (1561–1626)
2. Robert Boyle (1627–1691)
3. Margaret Cavendish (1623–1673)
4. Nicolaus Copernicus (1473–1543)
5. René Descartes (1596–1650)
6. Galileo Galilei (1564–1642)
7. William Harvey (1578–1657)
8. Johannes Kepler (1571–1630)
9. Antoine Lavoisier (1743–1794)
10. Isaac Newton (1642–1727)
11. Andreas Vesalius (1514–1564)
12. Maria Winkelmann (1670–1720)

In the 1600s and 1700s, scientists, philosophers, and artists, working in many centers of learning throughout Europe, made important contributions to society.

The American Revolution

At the dawn of the eighteenth century, the English philosopher John Locke saw great reason for hope in his country's peaceful Glorious Revolution. England was now a limited monarchy with a Bill of Rights for its people. Before the century was over, the ideas Locke had expressed in his *Two Treatises of Government* helped spark a revolution in England's North American colonies.

Key Questions

- What factors led to discontent, crisis, and rebellion in Britain's North American colonies?
- What elements of Enlightenment philosophy influenced the Declaration of Independence and the U.S. Constitution?

Proud British Colonies

In 1763, Britain's colonies in North America were celebrating, and with good reason. For almost a decade, the French and the British had been struggling for control of North America. On one side of this conflict, known as the French and Indian War, were the French and their Indian allies. On the other side were British troops and colonial militia. (A militia is made up of citizens who are not full-time soldiers but who fight as part of the army during wartime or emergencies.) One young militia commander from Virginia, George Washington, earned a reputation for bravery in battles along the western Appalachian Mountains. Other militia units fought effectively elsewhere, and colonists took pride in their accomplishments.

In the end, the British won Canada from the French, as well as the territory west of the Appalachians all the way to the Mississippi River. Throughout the British colonies, people had high hopes for the future and looked forward to settling the lush valleys of the new territory.

More than a hundred fifty years had passed since the first Englishmen arrived in Jamestown. During those decades, many people from Germany, the Netherlands, and other European countries had settled in the colonies. And nearly one-fifth of the population was made up of enslaved Africans or their descendants. Still, in 1763, the great majority of the two million people in the original thirteen colonies were of English descent. They liked young King George III, called Britain the "mother country" and, though most had never been to England, were proud to think of themselves as British.

The colonists were proud not only because of Britain's great power, but also because of their rights and freedoms as Englishmen. Nowhere else on earth did citizens have greater rights and representation than in Great Britain, whose tradition of limited government (as you read in chapter 15) went all the way back to the Magna Carta in 1215.

The colonists were pleased, too, that the government in far-off London largely let the colonies govern themselves. Most colonial governors were appointed by the king, but it was the colonial assemblies, elected by the colonists, that paid the governors. The governors, therefore, generally listened

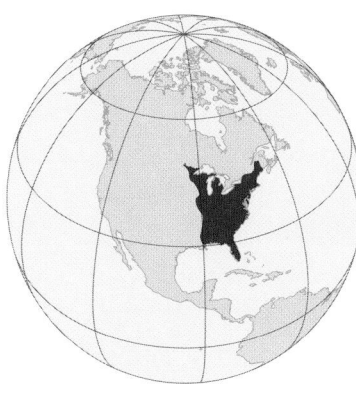

Thirteen of Britain's North American colonies formed a new nation.

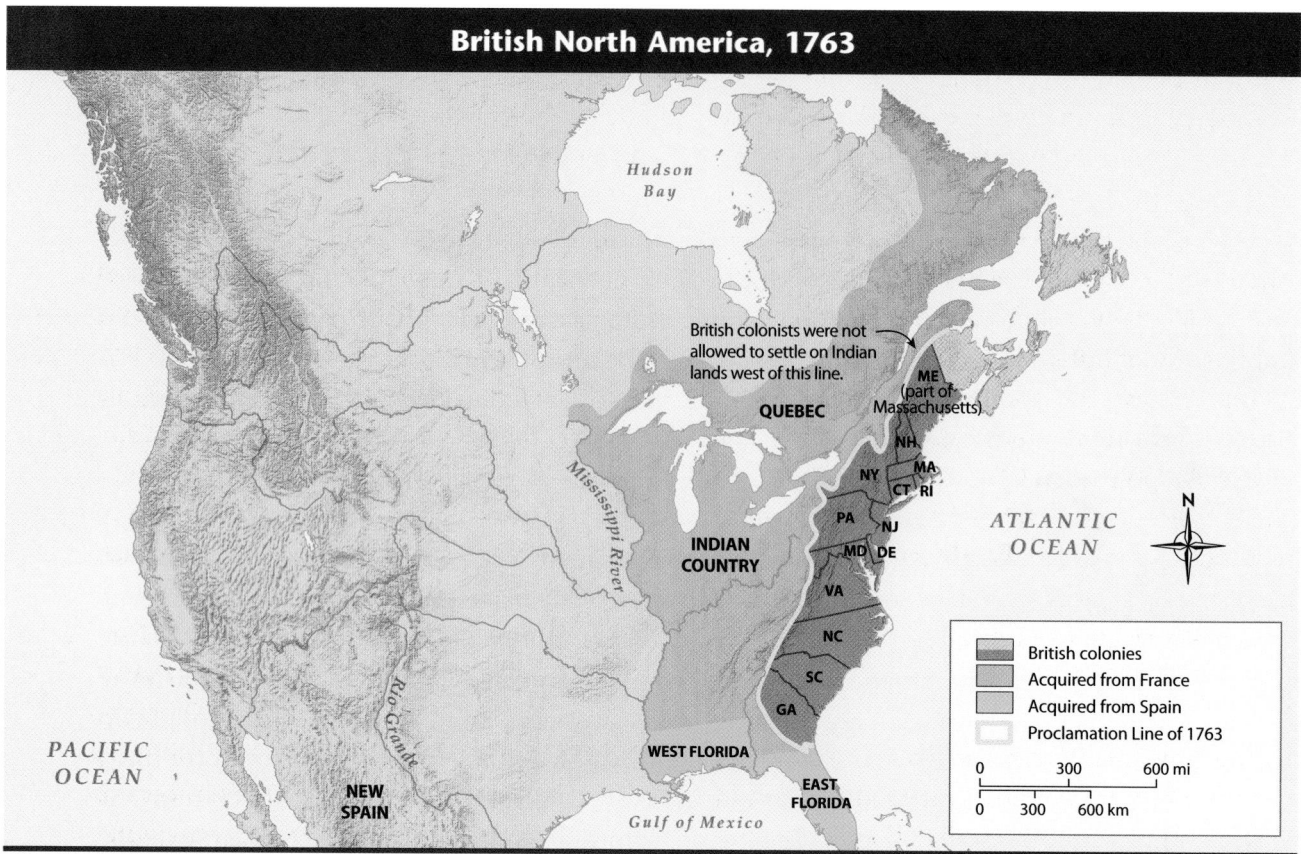

British North America, 1763

British colonists were not allowed to settle on Indian lands west of this line.

QUEBEC

ME (part of Massachusetts)

NH
NY   MA
CT   RI
PA   NJ
MD   DE
VA
NC
SC
GA

INDIAN COUNTRY

Mississippi River

Rio Grande

PACIFIC OCEAN

ATLANTIC OCEAN

N

WEST FLORIDA

EAST FLORIDA

NEW SPAIN

Hudson Bay

Gulf of Mexico

	British colonies
	Acquired from France
	Acquired from Spain
	Proclamation Line of 1763

0   300   600 mi
0   300   600 km

Confined east of the Appalachians and frustrated in asserting their rights with Britain, British colonists moved toward independence.

to the assemblies carefully. The assemblies also passed the laws that affected the daily lives of the colonists and held the "power of the purse"—only the elected assemblies could pass tax bills. John Locke had said that governments must not raise taxes "without the consent of the people," and the American colonists heartily agreed.

Moving Toward Independence

The French and Indian War had been long and expensive, and by the war's end in 1763, Britain faced an enormous debt. Thousands of British troops remained in America, primarily to protect the colonists from Indian attacks on the frontier. To keep down the cost of sustaining this protection, the government in London issued the Proclamation of 1763, which decreed that the colonists must stay east of the Appalachian Mountains. The order dashed the hopes of colonists who wanted to go west.

Parliament also decided that the American colonists should pay more to support the British troops who were protecting them. After all, it was the colonists who had gained the most from the war, and the colonists generally paid far less in taxes than people in England did. So Parliament passed laws requiring colonists to pay new taxes on goods such as sugar, paper, and tea.

"No Taxation Without Representation"

These new taxes angered the colonists. The colonists pointed out that, under British law and tradition, taxes had to have the consent of the people through their representatives. The colonists said that, because they did not elect representatives to Parliament, Parliament could not tax them. The government in London responded that Parliament represented *all* the British people, including the majority of people in England who were not allowed to vote but still had to pay taxes.

The colonists did not accept that reasoning. Tensions heightened, especially over the hated Stamp Act, a tax on printed materials from legal documents to playing cards. The act stirred up so much anger that riots broke out in some towns and cities. The British government was stunned. Parliament repealed the act, but decided to assert its authority by passing taxes on goods colonists imported from Britain.

In response, the colonists declared "No taxation without representation." Many colonists boycotted—refused to buy—the imported British goods. Merchants in England begged Parliament to repeal the taxes so the colonists would buy their products. Parliament did repeal all the taxes but one, a very small tax on tea.

The Path to Revolution

By this time, many colonists had grown openly defiant. In some colonies, groups called Sons of Liberty sprang up to organize protests. Boston, in the colony of Massachusetts, was a hotbed of agitation. When the British government sent troops to keep order there, Bostonians bitterly resented what they saw as a military occupation. Tragedy resulted on a cold night in 1770. An angry crowd began taunting a small group of British soldiers, pelting them with garbage and chunks of ice. The soldiers opened fire and five people were killed. The incident, soon known as the Boston Massacre, shocked people throughout the colonies.

Three years later, Boston was the scene of another incident. In what came to be called the Boston Tea Party, colonists disguised as Indians destroyed hundreds of crates of tea on a ship in Boston Harbor. In response, Britain sent more troops across the Atlantic to control the rebellious colonists. The colonists started organizing themselves into militias to resist the British troops.

In April 1775, British soldiers and colonial militia fired on each other near Lexington and Concord outside Boston. The American Revolution had begun.

Common Sense

For a hundred fifty years, the colonies had almost always acted independently of each other. People in New York thought of themselves both as British subjects and New Yorkers. People in Virginia thought of themselves both as British subjects and Virginians. But after the violence in Massachusetts in 1775, thirteen colonies sent representatives to Philadelphia to make decisions as a group, which they called the Continental Congress.

The Continental Congress established a Continental Army to defend the colonies against the British troops. They chose George Washington of Virginia to command the army. Still, in the summer and fall of 1775, the members of the Continental Congress were not sure what

Paul Revere, a Boston silversmith, made this famous engraving of the Boston Massacre, showing British soldiers firing on the peaceful citizens of Boston. While inaccurate, it aroused anger well beyond Boston.

to do next. Should the colonies demand their rights but remain part of the British Empire? Or, as a few voices declared, should they declare independence?

Independence from the mother country was a prospect most colonists had never considered. In early 1776, however, the tide of opinion shifted, largely because of the persuasive words of an Englishman who had come to Philadelphia seeking work, Thomas Paine.

In a pamphlet called *Common Sense*, Paine, in blunt, straightforward language, argued that it was not reasonable for a king to rule colonies three thousand miles (4830 km) away. Paine argued that it defied common sense for a small island like Great Britain to rule a huge continent like North America. "It is repugnant to reason," said Paine, "to the universal order of things, to all examples from former ages, to suppose that this continent can longer remain subject to any external power." Paine claimed that the colonies did not need a "mother country" for defense or trade. He went so far as to question the wisdom of anyone anywhere obeying a king. A king, he argued, was simply someone whose ancestors had stolen other people's land at the point of a sword.

Thousands of copies of *Common Sense* circulated quickly throughout the colonies. It was read in taverns and inns and handed from one person to another. Paine's bold words helped convince people in every colony of the need for a complete break from Britain. Many who had been proud British subjects were now agitators for independence.

Declaring Independence

On July 4, 1776, the representatives at the Continental Congress in Philadelphia voted to adopt the Declaration of Independence, which had been drafted by a brilliant young representative from Virginia, Thomas Jefferson.

Jefferson wrote with elegance and clarity. He built on the ideas of John Locke and other Enlightenment thinkers. He began by explaining that

Thomas Jefferson, a representative from Virginia, drafted the Declaration of Independence.

because the colonists were taking such a momentous step, it was necessary for them to explain "the causes which impel them to the separation."

In his explanation, Jefferson added a new, democratic dimension to Locke's argument that people have the natural rights of life, liberty, and ownership of property. While Locke had spoken of property, Jefferson offered a broader concept. It is "self-evident," Jefferson wrote, "that all men are created equal, that they are endowed by their Creator with certain unalienable rights, that among these are life, liberty, and the pursuit of happiness."

Jefferson went on to say that governments, which get their power "from the consent of the governed," exist to protect those natural rights. When a government "becomes destructive of" the people's "unalienable rights," Jefferson wrote, then "it is the right of the people to alter or abolish it, and to institute new Government."

Jefferson described in detail how the British government had trampled on the rights of the colonists. He closed by boldly declaring that "these united colonies are, and of right ought to be, free and independent states."

From the
Declaration of Independence

Inspired by John Locke and other Enlightenment thinkers, Thomas Jefferson, with clarity and power, opened the Declaration of Independence with these bold words:

When in the Course of human events, it becomes necessary for one people to dissolve the political bands which have connected them with another, and to assume among the Powers of the earth, the separate and equal station to which the Laws of Nature and of Nature's God entitle them, a decent respect to the opinions of mankind requires that they should declare the causes which impel them to the separation.

We hold these truths to be self-evident, that all men are created equal, that they are endowed by their Creator with certain unalienable Rights, that among these are Life, Liberty and the pursuit of Happiness. — That to secure these rights, Governments are instituted among Men, deriving their just powers from the consent of the governed. — That whenever any Form of Government becomes destructive of these ends, it is the Right of the People to alter or to abolish it, and to institute new Government, laying its foundation on such principles and organizing its powers in such form, as to them shall seem most likely to effect their Safety and Happiness. Prudence, indeed, will dictate that Governments long established should not be changed for light and transient causes; and accordingly all experience hath shewn, that mankind are more disposed to suffer, while evils are sufferable, than to right themselves by abolishing the forms to which they are accustomed. But when a long train of abuses and usurpations, pursuing invariably the same Object evinces a design to reduce them under absolute Despotism, it is their right, it is their duty, to throw off such Government, and to provide new Guards for their future security. — Such has been the patient sufferance of these Colonies; and such is now the necessity which constrains them to alter their former Systems of Government. The history of the present King of Great Britain is a history of repeated injuries and usurpations, all having in direct object the establishment of an absolute Tyranny over these States. To prove this, let Facts be submitted to a candid world....

George Washington (on horseback) leads his troops against the British in the Battle of Princeton, in January 1777.

Fighting a Revolution

The Declaration of Independence helped bring the colonists together as Americans. But they had to do more than declare independence—they had to win it by beating the British on the battlefield.

The British had nearly twice as many troops as the Americans. They were well-trained and included a large number of German mercenaries, or soldiers for hire. The Continental Army mostly consisted of ordinary men—farmers, merchants, fishermen, craftsmen—who had volunteered to fight but had little training or experience. Soldiers from Pennsylvania didn't want to fight beside soldiers from Georgia. Backwoods frontiersmen didn't trust sophisticated city folk. And many Americans resented taking orders, even from their own officers. They had little equipment and few supplies, and often went unpaid.

George Washington understood the challenges his army faced. He led by example, refusing to take any pay for himself. In key battles, he proved to his troops that they could stand up to the British on the field. Slowly, he turned them into a professional army.

Even so, the British won more battles than they lost. They planned to cut New England off from the rest of the states, and counted on finding support among Royalists in the south. The Royalists, also called Tories, were colonists who remained loyal to Britain and King George. British military leaders hoped many Tories would join the king's army, but fewer Tories than expected took up arms to fight against their fellow colonists.

Victory at Saratoga, Help from France

In the fall of 1777, an American victory at the Battle of Saratoga in New York helped turn the tide of the war, as it convinced the French to send troops to help the Americans.

Since their defeat in the French and Indian War in 1763, the French had longed to get back at the British. One way to do that was to help the Americans win their independence. When revolution broke out in America, the French, not wanting to risk open warfare with Britain, secretly sent money, arms, and gunpowder to the Americans. The victory at Saratoga convinced the French king, Louis XVI, that the Americans could defeat the British, so he openly proclaimed his support for the revolution and entered into an alliance with the new United States.

This alliance was especially important because the French had a powerful navy. In 1778, France sent ships to protect ports in the northern colonies. In 1778, the British, facing fierce resistance in New England and the mid-Atlantic, decided to move the war south. They captured important cities, including Charleston and Savannah, but met constant attacks on their supply lines and withdrew to the village of Yorktown in Virginia.

At Yorktown, American and French forces surrounded the British and pounded them with cannon fire, while a French fleet cut off their escape by sea. In October 1781, the British commander surrendered. A few months later, the British Parliament voted to end the war. After eight years of war and terrible human losses, a peace treaty acknowledging the independence of the United States of America was signed in 1783.

Creating a Constitution

During the Revolutionary War, the Continental Congress acted as a government for the United States. In 1781, the former colonies had agreed on a loose union governed by a document called

With his supplies dwindling and troops suffering, Lord Cornwallis realized that his only option at Yorktown was to surrender.

the Articles of Confederation. The Articles of Confederation provided for no executive—no king or president. It established a legislature, called the Congress of the Confederation, which had very little power. It could not collect taxes or force the individual states to follow laws passed by the Congress. It could not establish an army. The thirteen states acted more like thirteen separate nations than as one country. Each state printed its own money, made its own agreements with foreign countries, and levied its own taxes.

It soon became clear that such a weak central government was creating confusion and leaving the nation defenseless. Many American leaders, including George Washington, argued that the Articles of Confederation should be revised or replaced.

In the summer of 1787, delegates from all the states except Rhode Island met in Philadelphia. Almost all the men who gathered were well-educated and had studied Enlightenment philosophy. Alexander Hamilton of New York said,

"It seems to have been reserved to the people of this country to decide the important question, whether societies of men are really capable or not of establishing good government from reflection and choice."

From the start, the delegates agreed on a federal system of government, in which power is shared between a central government—the federal government—and the state governments. They also agreed that the federal government needed considerably more power than the Articles of Confederation had allowed.

The delegates followed the thinking of the French philosopher Montesquieu, who called for separation of powers among three branches of government. By distributing and balancing power among the branches of government, the delegates aimed to protect the rights of the people and the states. The delegates established a system known as "checks and balances," in which each branch of government has some control over the other two branches. The delegates established an executive branch headed by an elected president. They formed a judiciary branch, with judges appointed for life so that they would not fear for their jobs or feel political pressure.

The legislative branch proved more difficult to design. After long debate, the delegates agreed on a bicameral legislature—that is, a lawmaking body with two parts. One part, the House of Representatives, would be elected by the people, with the number of representatives based on each state's population. In the second part, the Senate,

George Washington presides over the signing of the Constitution at the Constitutional Convention.

The Preamble to the
U.S. Constitution

The United States Constitution, written in 1787 and ratified in 1788, has been in effect since 1789. The Constitution begins with a preamble, an introductory statement, which explains the general purpose of the Constitution and asserts the laws therein as an expression of the will of the people.

We the People of the United States, in Order to form a more perfect Union, establish Justice, insure domestic Tranquility, provide for the common defense, promote the general Welfare, and secure the Blessings of Liberty to ourselves and our Posterity, do ordain and establish this Constitution for the United States of America.

each state would have two senators, chosen by the state's legislature. Today, the U.S. Senate, like the House of Representatives, is directly elected by the people. Otherwise, the structure of the federal government has changed very little since the Constitution was adopted.

A Bill of Rights and a Lasting Constitution

In the spring of 1789, the United States began operating under its new government as established in the Constitution. Several leaders feared that the new government would not give enough protection to individual and state rights. To address their concerns, in 1791 ten amendments were added to the Constitution. These first ten amendments to the Constitution are known as the Bill of Rights.

The United States Constitution is a remarkable document. The framers of the Constitution established a system of republican government that has lasted for over two hundred years. They provided for a process for changing the Constitution but made it difficult enough that it cannot

be changed on a whim. Since the Bill of Rights was adopted, the Constitution has been amended only seventeen times.

The framers were not able to address every issue confronting the new nation. Long after the Constitution was ratified, debate continued over the balance of power between the states and the federal government. Debate continued, too, over the issue of slavery. These debates would be resolved only through a civil war some seventy-five years after the Constitution was first ratified (approved by the states). Nevertheless, the Constitution of the United States has endured and evolved through times of trial and crisis, and it remains the longest-lived written plan for government in history.

Many people in Europe watched the American experiment in republican government closely. Especially in France, writers and thinkers were excited by the idea that a government could be based on a constitution that reflected the will of the people. Democratic revolution was about to spread to France and beyond.

In August, 1792, French revolutionaries stormed the palace of King Louis XVI in Paris.

1790

1795

1800

1789
A mob storms the Bastille in Paris, igniting the French Revolution.

1792
The National Convention dissolves the monarchy and declares France a republic.

1793
Louis XVI is executed; the Reign of Terror begins.

1799
Napoleon Bonaparte takes control of the French government.

Chapter 23
The French Revolution
and the Age of Napoleon
1789–1815

When Europe was ruled by absolute monarchs, nowhere was the monarchy more absolute than in France. In the late eighteenth century, King Louis XVI lived lavishly, without concern for the economic, social, and political inequalities of French society. In 1789, the people of France had had enough. Suffering from hunger, motivated by the ideals of the Enlightenment, and inspired by the success of the American Revolution, they rose up against their king.

The French Revolution began with demands to limit the king's power and assign rights to the people. It then evolved into the overthrow of an absolute monarchy and the establishment of a republic—which quickly collapsed into a period of terror and bloodshed.

In this chaotic time, a brilliant military leader, Napoleon Bonaparte, rose from obscurity to become one of history's most powerful conquerors. He proceeded to enact reforms and lead his armies across Europe to build an empire. He began by claiming to embody the ideals of the French Revolution, but ended as a military dictator. He left a legacy of change that would soon pose a lasting threat to monarchies throughout Europe.

The French Revolution Begins

In eighteenth-century France, one absolute monarch after another maintained control of the government. These monarchs made the laws, and they dictated foreign policy and financial decisions. Louis XIV, the Sun King, built Versailles and demanded that his every whim be obeyed. France's next king, Louis XV, fought a number of expensive wars and seemed more interested in pleasure than governing. His grandson, Louis XVI, who became king in 1774, continued the old practices of censoring the press and imprisoning critics without trial. Like his predecessors, Louis XVI ignored France's only representative assembly, the Estates-General.

The Three Estates

In the late 1700s, French society was rigidly divided into three classes, or estates. The clergy—about a hundred thirty thousand individuals—made up the First Estate. The Second Estate included some four hundred thousand nobles. The rest of the population—about twenty-six million people—made up the Third Estate.

Members of the First and Second estates paid almost no taxes, had access to the best jobs, and received special treatment under the law. The "commoners" of the Third Estate ranged from prosperous merchants to poor rural peasants and laborers in cities. The Third Estate—some 98 percent of the population of France—in effect paid all the taxes but had no privileges. Included in this Third Estate, the increasingly prosperous French middle class, or bourgeoisie, resented shouldering so large a financial burden while having so little political power.

Most people in France at this time were overtaxed peasants. They paid taxes to the crown. To local lords they paid dues left over from feudal times, such as fees for grinding flour. And they paid tithes (usually one-fifteenth to one-twentieth of their harvest) to the Catholic Church, an immensely rich institution that was the largest single landowner in France. The poor of eighteenth-century France paid for many of the privileges and luxuries enjoyed by wealthy nobles and the church.

A cartoon depicts a peasant carrying a gray-clad clergyman and a nobleman with a plumed hat. The poor of eighteenth-century France, who paid many taxes to support wealthy nobles and the church, were bent low with economic burdens.

Key Questions

- What economic, social, and political factors led to the French Revolution?
- How did Enlightenment thinking and the American example influence French revolutionary ideals?
- What were the major accomplishments of the National Assembly?

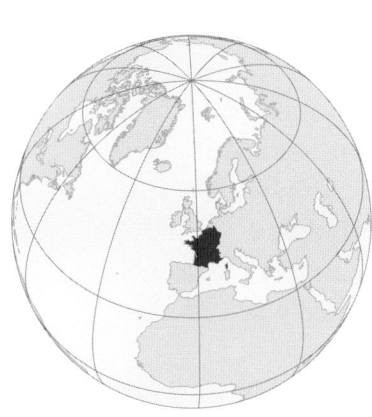

Revolution rocked France in the late eighteenth century.

527

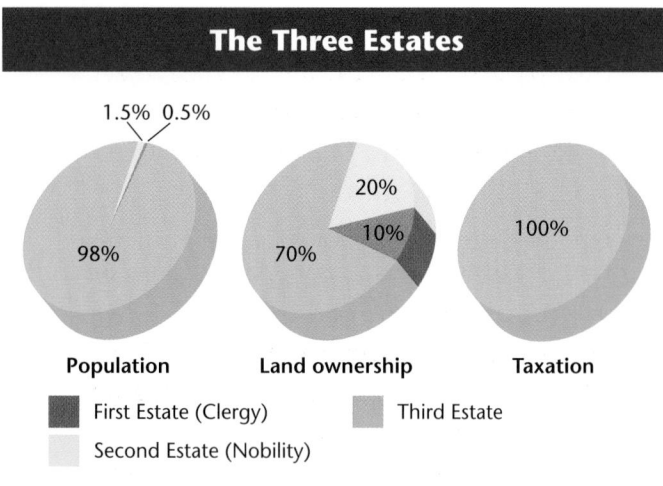

The Three Estates

1.5% 0.5%

98%

Population

20%
70% 10%

Land ownership

100%

Taxation

■ First Estate (Clergy)
□ Second Estate (Nobility)
▨ Third Estate

The Influence of Philosophy and the American Example

By the late 1780s, many people in the Third Estate were growing impatient with their king. They hoped for a different future. In Paris, the intellectual hub of Europe and home of the philosophes, dissatisfaction was especially intense. Enlightenment ideas about natural rights, representative governments, and written constitutions inspired some people in France to challenge the idea of absolute monarchy.

The notion that a king should rule with almost unlimited power seemed increasingly unreasonable to many well-educated members of the growing French middle class, who were well aware of the ideas of the Enlightenment. They had read Voltaire, who mocked the excesses of France's monarchy. They understood Montesquieu's argument that government power should be divided among separate branches. They warmed to Rousseau's call for liberty, and they shared his skepticism about the divine right of kings. Among the bourgeoisie, business leaders admired Adam Smith's *Wealth of Nations* and wanted the government to promote free trade and abandon restrictive mercantile policies.

Many people in France were also well acquainted with John Locke's arguments for natural rights, including the right of the people to replace their government. In the American Revolution, the French people saw a dramatic

and inspiring example of Enlightenment ideas turned into action. During and after the American Revolution, both Benjamin Franklin and Thomas Jefferson served as ambassadors from the United States to France, where they promoted Enlightenment ideas.

In the American Revolution, French forces fought alongside Americans against the British. Even some French nobles joined the fight. For example, the Marquis de Lafayette (mahr-KEE duh lah-fee-ET) joined the American cause of liberty and was made a general in the Continental Army. When Lafayette came home to France in 1782, like many Frenchmen who had fought on the American side, he returned excited by ideals of liberty and the rights of man.

In some European countries, Enlightenment ideas inspired monarchs to improve laws or encourage religious toleration. But no such reforms took place in France, where kings continued to claim divine right while their subjects enjoyed few rights and paid heavy taxes.

The Events of 1789

As king of France, Louis XVI devoted his days to his favorite pastimes at Versailles—eating, hunting, reading, and repairing locks and watches. Ordinary people—not the nobles, whom Louis refused to tax—continued to pay for the privileges enjoyed by the nobility and royalty.

In 1788, France suffered bad harvests that led to a sharp rise in food prices. Some laborers had to spend half their daily wages just to buy bread. Yet the king and his court continued to live in luxury that ordinary people could barely imagine. Louis and his queen, Marie-Antoinette, spent their days at Versailles surrounded by fawning courtiers and privileged nobles. Their lavish ways only added to the nation's huge debt, which Louis XVI had inherited when he came to the throne.

France's financial situation only got worse when Louis decided to help the Americans in their revolution against Britain. Louis supported

The French people disliked Louis' queen, Marie-Antoinette.

hoped the meeting would improve their lives and ease their burdens, while the middle class saw it as a chance to gain political power.

But the deputies of the Third Estate soon grew frustrated with the proceedings. Although they had more deputies in the Estates-General than the First and Second Estates combined, tradition dictated that each estate had one vote. So the First and Second Estates could outvote the Third Estate by a two-to-one margin, and force higher taxes on France's commoners.

Determined to be heard, the deputies of the Third Estate took a bold step. On June 17, 1789, they gave themselves a new name, the National Assembly. When the members of the National Assembly tried to meet on the morning of June 20, they found the door of their hall locked against them. They moved to an indoor tennis court. There, they swore an oath, now known as the Tennis Court Oath. They vowed never to disband until they had drafted a new constitution for the French government.

King Louis sent word that the National Assembly should disband, but the deputies refused. "The assembled nation cannot be given orders," they declared. It was a bold—indeed, a revolutionary—assertion.

the Americans not out of sympathy with revolutionary ideals but with the goal of weakening Britain, France's longtime rival. By 1789, France was almost bankrupt, and Louis desperately needed money.

The National Assembly

Even though Louis XVI ruled as an absolute monarch, various political pressures at the time kept him from imposing new taxes without calling a meeting of the Estates-General. A long time—indeed, one hundred and seventy-five years—had passed since the last time the representatives of the three estates gathered in the Estates-General. In 1789, ever so reluctantly, Louis once again convened the Estates-General, with the intention of raising money by creating new taxes.

In the spring of 1789, deputies representing all three estates arrived at Versailles. The event caused great enthusiasm throughout the land, especially among members of the Third Estate. The poor

"Let them eat cake."

Louis' queen, Marie-Antoinette, was a daughter of the Austrian emperor. She was widely disliked by the French people, not only because of her foreign birth but also because of her reputation for vanity and frivolity. She amused herself with fancy balls and plays while ordinary people went hungry. According to one story, the queen once asked an official why Parisians were so resentful. When told that they had run out of bread, she replied, "Then let them eat cake." The story might not have been true, but Parisians believed it and spread the tale.

Storming the Bastille and Starting a Revolution

As the National Assembly continued to meet for several days after the Tennis Court Oath, King Louis took no action. The people of France, however, were growing restless and bitter. Angry crowds thronged the roads between Paris and Versailles, just twelve miles (19 km) apart.

The king decided to order thousands of troops to Paris for a showdown with the Assembly. Rumors flew through the city. Any day now, people said, the king's soldiers would march into the city and slit their throats. On July 14, 1789, some eight thousand Parisians, seeking to arm themselves, swarmed to the Bastille (ba-STEEL), an armory in the eastern part of the city. A fortress built in the fourteenth century, the Bastille also served as a prison, though by this time it housed only a few prisoners. Above all, the Bastille was a hated symbol of royal power. The crowd demanded its surrender. The fortress's governor, backed by about a hundred soldiers, refused.

As the two sides confronted each other, a musket shot rang out. No one knows who fired it.

Hours of bitter fighting followed, in which about a hundred of the attackers were killed. When the governor of the Bastille surrendered, the enraged crowd took revenge. They killed the governor, cut off his head, and hoisted it on a pike.

In the countryside, unrest among the peasants, which had been stirring for months due to the food shortage, escalated into active rebellion. A panic broke out, known as the Great Fear, fed by rumors that foreign armies were invading and that the king and his nobles were conspiring to crush the Third Estate. Peasants attacked manor houses and destroyed documents that listed the peasants' financial obligations.

The French Revolution had begun.

The Work of the New Regime

When the Bastille fell, the National Assembly in effect became the governing body of France. No one was yet calling for a government without a king. But the National Assembly was determined to create a constitutional monarchy—a government in which laws define the powers of the king and set forth the rights of the people. As the National Assembly decreed sweeping changes, revolutionaries began to speak boldly of doing away with the *ancien régime* (ahns-yan ray-ZHEEM)—the old regime, or former order—and replacing it with a new social order.

A Declaration of Rights

To calm the rebellious peasants, in early August 1789, the National Assembly decreed sweeping changes that largely dismantled the feudal system in France. The Assembly abolished the old feudal taxes that peasants paid to their landlords and also ended the required tithes to the church.

On August 26, 1789, the National Assembly, inspired by the American Declaration of Independence, issued a document called the Declaration of the Rights of Man and of the Citizen. Like the Declaration

Parisians storm the Bastille, the hated symbol of royal power in Paris.

Declaration of the Rights of Man and of the Citizen

The National Assembly drew up the Declaration of the Rights of Man and of the Citizen in August 1789. Like the American Declaration of Independence, issued thirteen years earlier, the French Declaration expressed many ideals of the Enlightenment. Here are some of the rights stated in the seventeen articles of the French Declaration.

Men are born and remain free and equal in rights. Social distinctions can only be founded upon the general good.

The aim of all political association is the preservation of the natural and imprescriptible rights of man. These rights are liberty, property, security, and resistance to oppression.

Imprescriptible means unalienable—that which cannot be taken away.

Liberty consists of being able to do everything which injures no one else; hence the exercise of the natural rights of each man has no limits except those which assure to the other members of the society the enjoyment of the same rights. These limits can only be determined by law.

Law is the expression of the general will. Every citizen has a right to participate personally or through his representative in its formation. It must be the same for all, whether it protects or punishes. All citizens, being equal in the eyes of the law, are equally eligible to all dignities and to all public positions and occupations according to their abilities, and without distinction except that of their virtues and talents.

No person shall be accused, arrested, or imprisoned except in the cases and according to the forms prescribed by law....

No one shall be disquieted on account of his opinions, including his religious views....

The free communication of ideas and opinions is one of the most precious of the rights of man. Every citizen may, accordingly, speak, write, and print with freedom, being responsible, however, for such abuses of this freedom as shall be defined by law.

The security of the rights of man and of the citizen requires public military force. These forces are, therefore, established for the good of all and not for the personal advantage of those to whom they shall be entrusted.

All the citizens have a right to decide either personally or by their representatives as to the necessity of the public contribution [taxation], to grant this freely, to know to what uses it is put, and to fix the proportion, the mode of assessment and of collection, and the duration of the taxes.

A society in which the observance of the law is not assured nor the separation of powers defined has no constitution at all.

of Independence, the French declaration drew on the "natural law" philosophy of the English philosopher John Locke, as well as on the writings of the French philosophes. The Assembly proclaimed that "men are born and remain free and equal in rights," including the rights to "liberty, property, security, and resistance to oppression." The Declaration of the Rights of Man and of the Citizen was printed in thousands of pamphlets and spread throughout France.

The Women's March

King Louis pretended to cooperate with the Assembly, but he was simply stalling for time as he tried to figure out how to regain control of the government. Many people did not trust the king, and the longer he refused to approve the actions of the Assembly, the more public suspicion grew.

On October 5, 1789, a large crowd of women gathered in Paris, mainly to protest the high price of bread. The crowd swelled to thousands and marched the twelve miles (19 km) to the king's home in Versailles, gathering supporters along the way, including men and women armed with pitchforks, scythes, and muskets.

The Women's March to Versailles, as this event is sometimes called, forced Louis, Marie-Antoinette, and their four-year-old son to move to Paris. There the people could keep an eye on the royal family.

A New Constitution

Meanwhile, the National Assembly pressed ahead. It decreed that clergy, nobles, and local lords would have no special tax privileges—that is, they, too, would be taxed. The Assembly took away all titles of nobility and made more than half the adult male population eligible to vote. It seized the immense landholdings of the Catholic Church and sold church properties to pay some of the nation's large debt. The Assembly also decreed religious toleration for both Protestants and Jews.

In 1791, after much debate among its members, the Assembly proposed a constitution for France. The constitution provided for a limited

In October 1789, the Women's March to Versailles forced the king and his family to move to Paris, where the people could keep an eye on them.

The Politics of Left and Right

In the National Assembly, the nobles representing France's Second Estate were generally conservative, seeking to maintain traditional ways. They wanted little or no change to laws that protected their wealth and power. Representatives of the Third Estate, on the other hand, tended to be liberal, eager to reform government, law, and tradition. They hoped these changes would increase the power of the common people. In the meeting hall of the Assembly, the Second Estate sat on the right, and the Third Estate sat on the left. From this arrangement, we get the labels still used today to characterize differing political views—conservatives make up "the right," and liberals "the left." Those with moderate views are often said to be "centrists."

monarchy similar to England's, with the king's power separate from the powers of an elected legislature. Louis vaguely indicated that he would support the new arrangement, but privately he plotted to stop the revolution.

The proposed constitution of 1791 met with many objections for different reasons. Royalists, who were loyal to the king, thought the constitution went too far. Their numbers included nobles who didn't want to lose titles and privileges, as well as many Catholics who disliked the open antagonism expressed by many revolutionaries toward the church. On the opposite side were the radicals who thought the constitution did not go far enough. They called for an end to monarchy and the establishment of a republic.

Defending the Revolution: France Declares War

One June night in 1791, the royal family disguised themselves as peasants and tried to slip out of the country to join the Austrians on the eastern frontier. But they were recognized and taken back to Paris. The king's attempted flight provoked fear and anger. Many suspected that the king, had he made it to Austria, planned to lead an army back into France to crush the Revolution by force.

Their suspicions were not baseless. Some French *émigrés* (E-mih-grayz)—nobles who had fled from France—were actively trying to convince foreign monarchs to come to Louis' aid. Many of these monarchs were relatives of Louis XVI or Marie-Antoinette. The émigrés urged the leaders of Austria and various German states to stop the French Revolution in order to prevent similar revolutions in their own countries.

In France, the more radical voices in the revolutionary movement called for aggressive action against the growing threat of foreign invasion. In April 1792, France declared war against Austria. A few months later, Prussia joined the war on Austria's side.

In June 1791, an armed escort leads the royal family back to Paris after their attempt to flee was foiled.

Radical Revolution

Key Questions

- How did the Reign of Terror begin? How did it end?

- What were the accomplishments of the first French republic?

- What were the major consequences of the French Revolution?

The war with Austria and Prussia increased the strain on a people already in turmoil. In August 1792, frustrated Parisians took matters into their own hands. A well-organized group of armed citizens and soldiers stormed the palace where the king was living. They imprisoned the royal family. Radical leaders dissolved the National Assembly and replaced it with a new body called the National Convention.

The National Convention: From Monarchy to Republic

With the National Convention, the French Revolution entered a new phase, both more democratic and more violent. The National Convention decided that the country no longer needed a king. In September 1792, it declared France a republic. The streets rang with the cry of the nation's official slogan, "*Liberté, Egalité, Fraternité*" (lee-behr-TAY, ay-gah-lee-TAY, fra-tehr-nee-TAY)— "Liberty, Equality, Fraternity." (*Fraternity* means comradeship, brotherly affection.)

The National Convention put the king on trial for treason and sentenced him to death by decapitation on the guillotine (GHEE-yuh-teen). On January 21, 1793, King Louis XVI mounted the scaffold. The executioner pushed the king down onto the guillotine and placed his head inside the wooden clamp. The razor-sharp blade fell swiftly. An era ended. Shouts rang out from

January 1793: King Louis XVI is executed on the guillotine.

the onlookers: "*Vive la République!*" (veev lah ray-poo-bleek)—"Long live the republic!"

The Jacobins in Control

When news of the execution of Louis XVI spread, the rulers of neighboring countries were outraged. Fearful that revolutionary violence might spread to their own lands, European monarchs prepared their troops and joined in the campaign against France. Great Britain, Holland, and Spain joined forces with Austria and Prussia. In response, the National Convention ordered military conscription. Thousands of men were drafted into the French army.

In the spring of 1793, French forces suffered a number of defeats. With the revolutionary cause in peril, power in the National Convention shifted away from moderate middle-class members, called Girondins (juh-RAHN-dihnz), to the more radical elements, including the extremists called the Jacobins (JA-kuh-buhnz).

The Jacobins faced plenty of opposition. In western France, Catholics and royalist peasants rioted. In the cities, violent protests broke out over high prices and food shortages. Within the French government itself, the Jacobins feuded furiously with more moderate factions. In July 1793, one of the Jacobin leaders, Jean-Paul Marat, was assassinated by Charlotte Corday, a supporter of the Girondins and a royalist sympathizer.

Faced by both foreign threats and internal crises, the National Convention formed the Committee of Public Safety. From the fall of 1793 to the summer of 1794, the twelve members of the Committee of Public Safety assumed almost dictatorial control of France.

They told themselves that the goals of the Revolution—"Liberty, Equality, Fraternity"—were so noble as to justify extreme means, even violence and terror. Leading the way was Maximilien Robespierre (mahk-see-meel-yan ROHBZ-pyehr). Under Robespierre's leadership, the Revolution plunged into its bloodiest phase, known as the Reign of Terror.

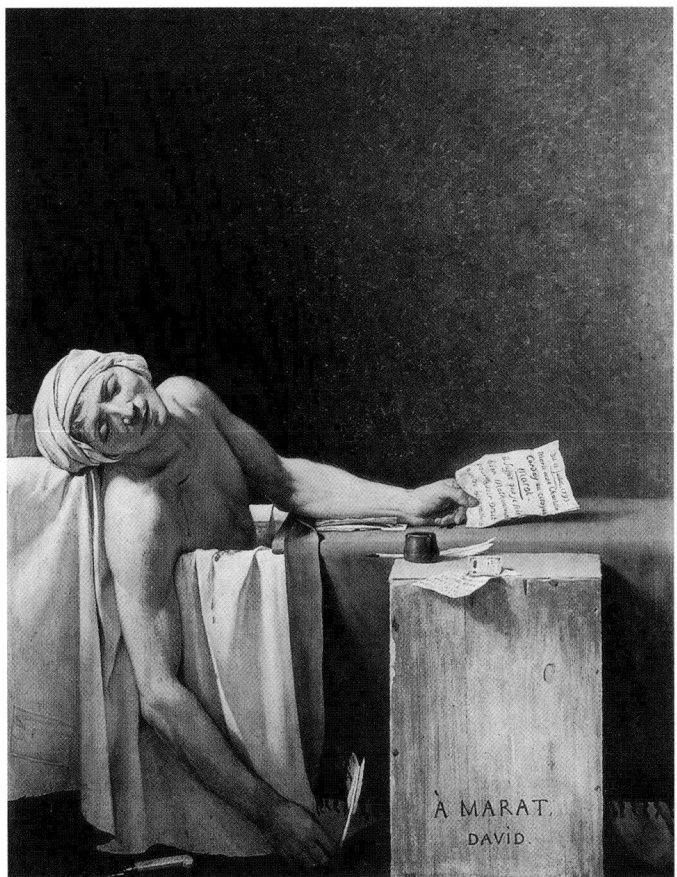

The Death of Marat, a painting by Jacques-Louis David

The Reign of Terror

During the Reign of Terror, the revolutionary government undertook a campaign to "de-Christianize" France. Many churches were closed. The National Convention adopted a new calendar, which declared Year 1 as beginning with the creation of the French Republic in September 1792. The Cathedral of Notre Dame was renamed the "Temple of Reason."

Robespierre and his supporters saw enemies of the Revolution everywhere. They passed a law that allowed the police to arrest any citizen considered a "supporter of tyranny" or an "enemy of liberty." Soon no citizen, however innocent, could feel safe from the threat of arrest.

Every day, carts rumbled through the streets of Paris, carrying condemned victims to the guillotine. Some were aristocrats. Some were nuns and priests. Others were ordinary citizens of France, workers and peasants.

The Lost Dauphin

King Louis XVI and Marie-Antoinette had a son named Louis-Charles. Louis-Charles was the *dauphin* (doh-FAN), the heir to the French throne. When the Revolution began in 1789, the boy was four years old. In 1792, revolutionaries threw him into prison with the rest of his family. The next year, guards took him away. The government reported that ten-year-old Louis-Charles died in prison in 1795.

Rumors began to fly through Europe that the young dauphin had escaped and was still alive. Over the decades, hundreds of people claimed to be the "Lost Dauphin." In 2000, scientists compared the heart of the boy who died in prison with a lock of Marie-Antoinette's hair. The boy and the queen were clearly related, so it seems that the "Lost Dauphin" died in prison after all.

Among the guillotine's victims were the former queen, Marie-Antoinette, and Georges Danton (zhorzh dahn-tohn), who had been one of the first leaders of the Committee of Public Safety, but had fallen out of favor when he voiced opposition to the Terror. During the Terror, tens of thousands of people were tried and executed, while many thousands more were killed without trial or died in prison.

Moving Toward Equality

Frenchmen put up with the bloodshed of the Reign of Terror partly because the National Convention was making progress toward one of the ideals of the Revolution, *egalité*, or equality. The Convention established free primary schooling for all boys and girls. It ended primogeniture, a long-standing legal practice in which the eldest son inherited the entire estate of one or both parents. The Convention passed new laws that required equal inheritance for both sons and daughters.

The National Convention declared slavery illegal, not only in France itself but also in France's colonies. The National Convention also granted **universal male suffrage**—for the first time, all French men could vote. Before the Revolution, men had to own property and pay taxes in order to vote.

Suffrage is the right to vote.

The Convention expanded the military draft and ordered universal conscription—now, *all* unmarried male citizens between the ages of eighteen and twenty-five were required to serve in the revolutionary forces of France. Serving in the military, the Convention proclaimed, was a patriotic duty—if a man had the right to vote, then he also had the duty to defend the republic. As in the new United States, required military service in France encouraged feelings of nationalism,

A Holiday and an Anthem

The French Revolution generated patriotic pride that lasts to this day in the form of a major holiday and national anthem. July 14—the day the Bastille fell in 1789—is now a national holiday in France, commonly known as Bastille Day, and formally as *La Fête Nationale* (The National Celebration).

In 1792, after France declared war on Austria, a captain in the French army composed a rousing marching song known as "The Marseillaise" (MAHR-suh-YEHZ). A few years later the National Convention adopted the song as the French national anthem. After the Revolution, later rulers banned the song, but in 1879 it regained its official status as the national anthem. "The Marseillaise" opens with these lines (here translated into English):

Let us go, children of the fatherland,
Our day of glory has arrived.
Against us the bloody flag of tyranny is raised....
To arms, citizens!

The Best of Times, the Worst of Times

In 1859, the great English novelist Charles Dickens published *A Tale of Two Cities*. The novel depicts events leading up to and during the French Revolution. In the novel's famous and extraordinary opening sentence, Dickens captures the contradictions of the revolutionary era in France.

It was the best of times, it was the worst of times, it was the age of wisdom, it was the age of foolishness, it was the epoch of belief, it was the epoch of incredulity, it was the season of Light, it was the season of Darkness, it was the spring of hope, it was the winter of despair, we had everything before us, we had nothing before us, we were all going direct to Heaven, we were all going direct the other way—in short, the period was so far like the present period, that some of its noisiest authorities insisted on its being received, for good or for evil, in the superlative degree of comparison only.

since citizens fought not for private ends but for the good of the country.

From the Directory to Napoleon

As the Reign of Terror continued, Robespierre acted more and more like a tyrant. He talked of plots and intrigues, and sent rivals to their deaths on the guillotine. Eventually, the National Convention turned on Robespierre. On July 28, 1794, the guillotine ended both Robespierre's life and the Reign of Terror.

After Robespierre's death, power in the Convention shifted from the radicals to the middle class. The Convention adopted a new constitution, which ended universal male suffrage and gave the vote only to those who met a requirement for ownership of property. The new constitution established a five-man body, the Directory, to run the government.

The Directory faced many enemies. On one side, Robespierre's allies plotted a return to power. On the other side, royalists schemed to restore the monarchy. Foreign armies menaced the borders.

With the economy nearly in ruins, and food shortages turning into famine, rioters filled the streets.

The desperate Directory turned to the army for help. They placed their trust in a young officer who had won victories for France on foreign fields of battle. His name was Napoleon Bonaparte (nuh-POHL-yuhn BOH-nuh-pahrt). The directors believed they could control this general and guide him to do their will. But in 1799, Napoleon took part in a *coup d'etat* (koo day-TAH)—a sudden overthrow of the government.

When Napoleon seized power, only ten years had passed since the Bastille fell. In those ten years, the French Revolution had overthrown the *ancien régime* and changed France from top to bottom. It had dethroned an absolute monarch, revoked the privileges of the upper classes, and brought new rights to workers and peasants. But Napoleon soon wielded as much power as the mightiest king. Had the French people rid themselves of one absolute ruler only to get another?

The Age of Napoleon

Napoleon Bonaparte rose from the military ranks to lead France. He was born in 1769 on the Mediterranean island of Corsica. When he was nine years old, his father sent him to military school in France. He was an average student, but he would go on to have an extraordinary career.

Once the French Revolution began, Napoleon advanced quickly in the French army. At the age of twenty-four, he won promotion to the rank of brigadier general. In 1795, he helped put down a royalist uprising in Paris. Within a year he was in command of French troops in northern Italy. There Napoleon fought brilliantly and won the devotion of his troops.

He returned to Paris in glory. In 1799, he joined the coup that overthrew the Directory. In place of the Directory, three men called consuls took over as the highest officials in France. The consuls were supposed to share power, but General Bonaparte was clearly in charge.

Stabilizing the Revolution

Napoleon became so powerful that he in effect ruled France as a dictator. He claimed that his goal was to "stabilize" the Revolution. After the bloody chaos of the Revolution, he did restore order. He reformed the French government. He enlarged the Ministry of Police. He set up a civil service system, in which citizens could be promoted based on merit rather than family background. He modernized the capital city of Paris. He improved the city's sidewalks, sewers, and water supply. Throughout the country he built a new system of roads. He also established an efficient postal service and worked to improve schools.

Though Napoleon himself was not religious, he realized that most people in France were Catholic. So he reversed the Revolution's bans and made religion legal again. Napoleon also saved the Cathedral of Notre Dame in Paris. In 1795, the Directory had sold the cathedral to a man who was going to demolish it for its stones. Fortunately, he did not act quickly, and in 1802, Napoleon stepped in and saved Notre Dame from destruction.

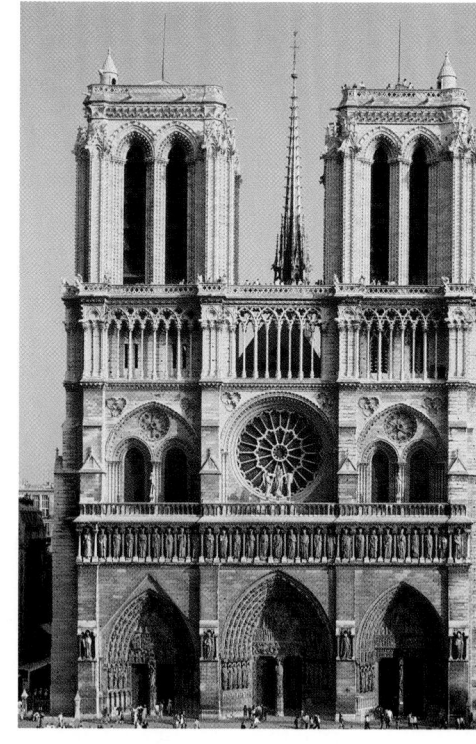

Napoleon saved the Cathedral of Notre Dame from demolition and made religion legal again in France.

Key Questions

- In what ways did Napoleon uphold and expand the ideals of the French Revolution? In what ways did he violate those ideals?

- What led to the end of Napoleon's empire?

- What is Napoleon's legacy?

Napoleon Rallies His Troops

Napoleon Bonaparte was a military genius who knew how to inspire his soldiers, as is clear in this proclamation to his troops in Italy, issued in 1796.

Soldiers:

You have won battles without cannon, crossed rivers without bridges, made forced marches without shoes, camped without brandy and often without bread. Soldiers of liberty, only republican troops could have endured what you have endured. Soldiers, you have our thanks! The grateful *Patrie* will owe its prosperity to you....

The two armies which but recently attacked you with audacity are fleeing before you in terror; the wicked men who laughed at your misery and rejoiced at the thought of the triumphs of your enemies are confounded and trembling.

But, soldiers, as yet you have done nothing compared with what remains to be done.... Undoubtedly the greatest obstacles have been overcome; but you still have battles to fight, cities to capture, rivers to cross. Is there one among you whose courage is abating? No.... All of you are consumed with a desire to extend the glory of the French people; all of you long to humiliate those arrogant kings who dare to contemplate placing us in fetters; all of you desire to dictate a glorious peace, one which will indemnify the Patrie for the immense sacrifices it has made; all of you wish to be able to say with pride as you return to your villages, "I was with the victorious army in Italy!"

Patrie is French for homeland.

Abating means diminishing, decreasing, weakening.

Fetters are chains, shackles, or other restraints.

To *indemnify* is to compensate or pay back for losses.

Napoleon did not return property that the French government had seized from the Catholic Church. He kept much of the church in France under the control of the state.

The Napoleonic Code

Napoleon reformed France's legal system. He replaced old laws that had varied by region, and sometimes contradicted each other, with a single set of laws that would apply to all citizens, no matter who they were or where they lived. His system of laws became known as the Napoleonic Code.

The Napoleonic Code preserved many of the gains of the Revolution. It protected the right to trial by jury. It affirmed equality before the law, although women lost some of the rights they had

The Discovery of the Rosetta Stone

In 1798, Napoleon led thousands of French troops into Egypt, with the goal of seizing British holdings and taking control of trade routes to the east. Along with the soldiers came many scholars and scientists. In 1799, near the town of Rashid—called Rosetta by Europeans—French soldiers noticed a black stone with ancient writing carved on it. When the symbols on the Rosetta Stone were finally deciphered, they proved the key to translating ancient Egyptian hieroglyphics.

In 1799, Napoleon left Egypt to deal with more pressing matters back in Europe. French forces held Egypt for a couple more years, but in 1801, after long battles with British and Ottoman forces, the French left Egypt. At this time, the Rosetta Stone was turned over to the British, who stored it in the British Museum, where it has remained ever since.

gained during the radical phase of the Revolution. The Napoleonic Code put a definite end to feudal practices that had reduced peasants to little more than servants.

After Napoleon's time, the Napoleonic Code lived on in France and continued to influence the legal systems of Belgium, the Netherlands, Germany, Switzerland, and Italy. Even faraway lands in the Americas adopted modified versions of the code. Napoleon considered the code his greatest accomplishment. He claimed that establishing the code gave him greater satisfaction than all of his victories in battle.

War and Empire

When Napoleon became a consul in 1799, France was still at war with the coalition of European nations that wanted to crush France's expanding Revolution. The fighting continued, with rare interruptions, for the next sixteen years.

At the head of his Grand Army, as it was called, Napoleon won a string of spectacular victories across the continent. He defeated the Austrian forces. Through diplomatic negotiations, he persuaded the Russians to withdraw from the war. Britain, whose trade suffered because of the war, also agreed to sign a peace treaty with France, though this peace would not last long.

The long string of wars, known collectively as the Napoleonic Wars, began as an effort to defend and spread the French Revolution. But as French victories mounted, Napoleon's primary goal changed from spreading the Revolution to building an empire.

In December 1804, Napoleon declared himself emperor. Thousands of dignitaries came to see Napoleon crowned as emperor. During the ceremony, the pope, who had come from Rome, anointed Napoleon with sacred oil. Then, to the astonishment of the audience, Napoleon took the

Napoleon, shown here crossing the Alps into northern Italy, forged an empire and spread revolution across Europe.

Napoleon stands in his coronation robes after being crowned emperor of France in Notre Dame Cathedral.

crown from the pope's hands and placed it firmly on his own head. With this act, he seemed to proclaim that he intended to answer to no one but himself.

Britain Resists

On the continent of Europe, Napoleon seemed almost unstoppable in his empire-building conquests. But France's old enemy, Great Britain, remained defiant. Napoleon planned to invade Britain by crossing the English Channel. But the invasion never happened. In October 1805, Admiral Horatio Nelson defeated a combined French and Spanish fleet in the Battle of Trafalgar, off the southwest coast of Spain. Nelson lost his own life in the battle, but his victory put an end to Napoleon's plans to invade Britain.

Napoleon decided on another way to defeat the British—by cutting off trade to the island nation. Napoleon devised a plan called the Continental System, in which he ordered the nations he had conquered to stop trading with Britain. For the Continental System to work, all the countries on the European continent had to keep British ships out of their ports. But even with many European ports closed to them, the British found new markets in Latin America and western Asia.

On the Iberian Peninsula, the British found ports willing to welcome their ships. The Portuguese continued to trade with Britain, and so did the Spanish, who were supposedly allies of the French. In 1807, Napoleon invaded Spain to prevent Spanish ports from allowing British ships to trade. He toppled the Spanish king and placed his brother Joseph on the Spanish throne. This act spurred resentment among Spain's American colonists, who tolerated Spanish rule but resisted the idea of being ruled by the French.

Napoleon's war on the Iberian Peninsula proved long and costly. For five years, Spanish

Selling Land to Pay for War

Wars are expensive. How did Napoleon pay for his? Partly through the sale of land. France claimed vast expanses of land in North America west of the Mississippi River. Americans were eager to own the French city of New Orleans, at the mouth of the Mississippi. In 1803, President Thomas Jefferson sent Americans to Paris to strike a deal. The Americans were shocked when Napoleon offered to sell the young United States the whole of the Louisiana Territory, from the Mississippi River to the Rocky Mountains, from the Canadian border to the Gulf of Mexico. The Americans gladly paid the price. The Louisiana Purchase, as it is called, more than doubled the size of the United States.

Napoleon's defeated Grand Army struggles through the Russian countryside.

June 1812, Napoleon invaded Russia with more than six hundred thousand troops.

The emperor hoped for a quick victory. But the tsar refused to meet Napoleon in battle. Instead, Russian troops pulled back before Napoleon's advancing Grand Army. As Russian troops withdrew, they burned their own villages and fields to prevent the invaders from finding food and supplies.

Tens of thousands of Napoleon's soldiers died from starvation, heat, and disease. The Grand Army marched on until it reached Moscow. Napoleon found the city almost deserted. Then a fire—perhaps started by the Russians themselves—destroyed two-thirds of the city.

The Russians refused to surrender. Instead they continued to strengthen their army. Napoleon, lacking supplies, realized that he could not stay in Moscow through the long, hard Russian winter. So, on October 18, he ordered a retreat westward.

Along the way his army suffered terribly in the bitter cold. Weak from hunger, the troops were barely able to march. Men and horses froze in the snow or died of starvation. Soldiers deserted by the hundreds. The Russians killed or captured those who fell behind. The Grand Army became a ragtag mob. Of the more than six hundred thousand troops Napoleon had led into Russia, fewer than forty thousand returned.

forces, with the help of the British, kept three hundred thousand French troops engaged in a long series of battles. The fighting weakened Napoleon by depriving him of soldiers he could have used elsewhere.

Catastrophe in Russia

Russia had agreed to cut off trade with Britain, but in late 1810, Russia's ruler changed his mind. Tsar Alexander I pulled out of the Continental System. Napoleon prepared to punish the Russians. He built up his Grand Army, adding soldiers from regions he had conquered—Germans, Dutch, Swiss, Italians, Poles, and Lithuanians. In

Showdown at Waterloo

Several European powers—Austria, Britain, Russia, Prussia, and Sweden—formed an alliance to defeat Napoleon while he was weakened. In 1813, the allies drove Napoleon's troops out of Germany. The following year they invaded France and marched into Paris. The once mighty Napoleon had no choice but to surrender his throne.

A Musical Tribute

In 1880, at a ceremony in Moscow, an orchestral work by the beloved composer Pyotr Ilyich Tchaikovsky (chiy-KAWF-skee) had its premiere performance. The *1812 Overture*, as it is popularly known, commemorated Russia's defeat of Napoleon's Grand Army in 1812. The overture comes to a rousing close with ringing bells and cannon fire.

The victorious allies exiled Napoleon from France. But they gave him a new territory to rule—the tiny island of Elba, less than a hundred square miles of mountainous scrubland off the northwest coast of Italy.

After just ten months on Elba, Napoleon slipped back into France, landing on the southern coast with about a thousand followers. He quickly gained the support of the French people.

The allies, alarmed by Napoleon's return, prepared to invade France again. While they made their plans, Napoleon raised another army and struck first. His targets were two allied armies—one British, one Prussian—encamped near a small town called Waterloo, in what is now the country of Belgium. He intended to defeat the allies before the British and Prussian troops could unite.

"Meeting Your Waterloo"

The Duke of Wellington and his Prussian allies dealt Napoleon a crippling defeat at Waterloo. Today, when someone suffers a complete defeat, we sometimes say he has "met his Waterloo."

But Napoleon met his match in the Duke of Wellington, commander of the British troops. On June 18, 1815, the British troops turned back the attacking French forces. When Prussian reinforcements arrived on the field of battle, Napoleon realized the end had come.

The Battle of Waterloo marked the emperor's final defeat. Napoleon fled west, to the Atlantic coast of France, where he surrendered to the Brit-

Napoleon met his match in the Duke of Wellington and an allied army of British and Prussian troops at the Battle of Waterloo.

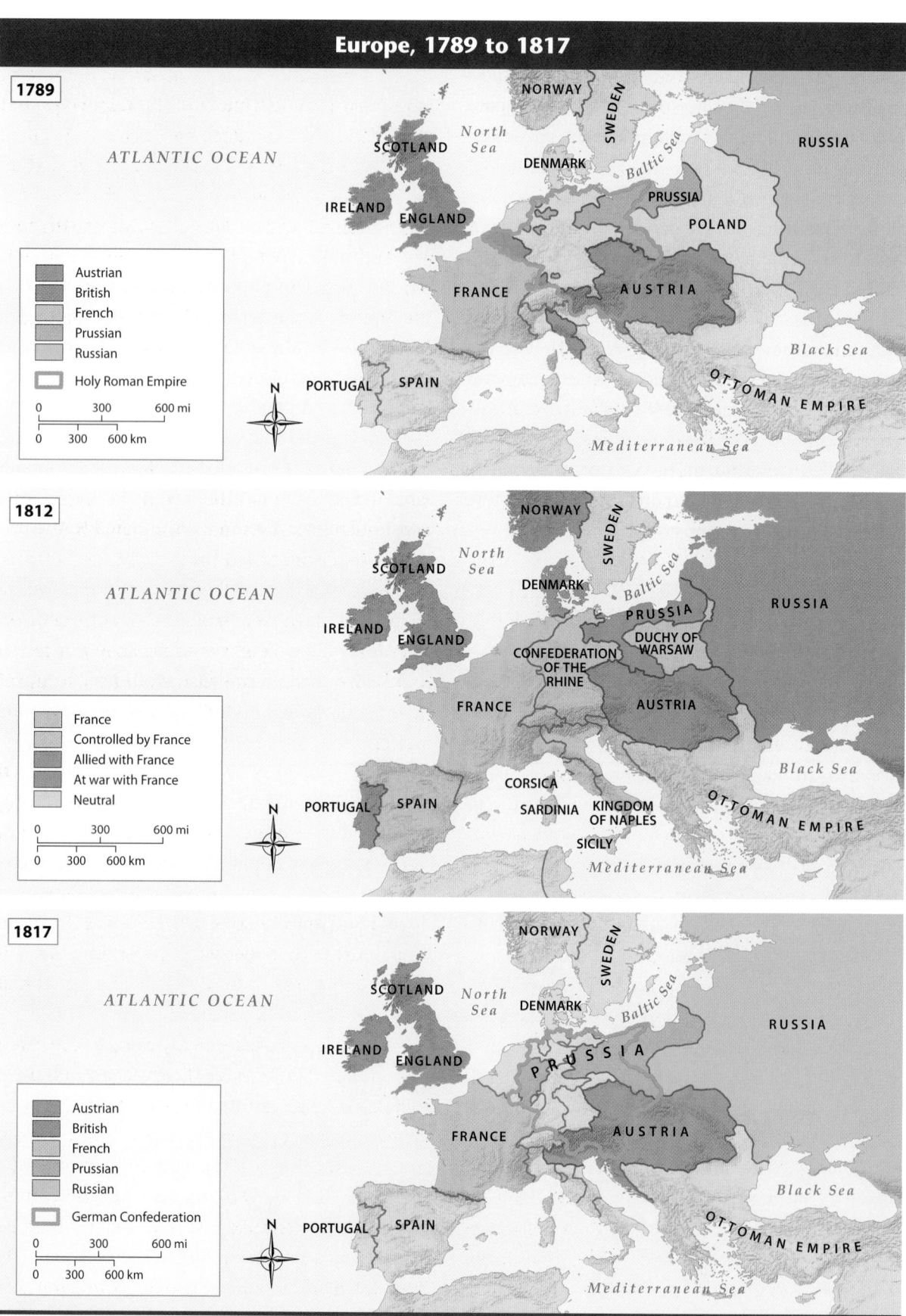

European allegiances and boundaries shifted rapidly as a consequence of the French Revolution and the Napoleonic Wars.

ish. He was exiled to St. Helena, a tiny island in the South Atlantic, 1,200 miles (1,931 km) off the coast of Africa. There he spent the last six years of his life dictating his memoirs, trying to shape the way he would be remembered—as a man of reason, genius, and action. He was such a man, but history also remembers him as a man of extreme ambition who wanted to dominate a continent.

Napoleon's Legacy

Early in his rule, Napoleon had made a grand boast—"I am the Revolution"—a boast, however, that was partly true. Wherever his Grand Army marched, Napoleon took the message of the French Revolution. "The peoples of Germany, the peoples of France, of Italy, of Spain all desire equality," he declared. In countries across Europe, he swept away old governments ruled by dukes, princes, and other nobles. In their place, he introduced constitutions and legal systems in which all were equal in the eyes of the law.

In the first decade of the 1800s, many Europeans regarded Napoleon as the heroic representative of a new era in which the power of absolute monarchs would give way to the rule of the people. Even though Napoleon became a conqueror and a military despot, he helped spread French revolutionary ideas that would continue to inspire people in various European lands to rise up against powerful monarchs.

Napoleon's most important legacy, not just to France but also to much of Europe and beyond, is the Napoleonic Code, widely regarded as one of the most important codes of law in history. Napoleon saw the code as a universal standard for all.

Napoleon's conquests changed the map of Europe. He did away with old boundaries from feudal times. He sometimes united people who shared a common language, religion, and culture. For example, in Germany, he formed the Rhine Confederation, which brought together some three hundred small German states.

Napoleon unintentionally united people who disliked his rule. He saw himself as a liberator who freed Europe from its old feudal ways, but in the lands he conquered he was often regarded as an invader and a tyrant. In Germany, Italy, Spain, and elsewhere in Europe, the presence of French rulers and French soldiers stirred a wave of nationalism, the strong sense of attachment or belonging to one's own country. With the French foreigners in charge, people began to take great pride in their own countries and traditions.

The Congress of Vienna

In 1814 and 1815, while Napoleon was in exile, representatives from Britain, Prussia, Russia, Austria, and other lands met in the city of Vienna. In this meeting, called the Congress of Vienna, the representatives of the major European powers planned how to create a stable continent on the ruins of Napoleon's empire. They wanted to make sure that no one else would try to upset their royal power. And they wanted no more wars raging across the continent.

At the Congress of Vienna, the allies agreed that France should once more be ruled by a king. They gave the throne to Louis XVIII, the brother of the executed Louis XVI. Then the monarchs of Prussia, Russia, and Austria divided some of Napoleon's empire among themselves. In those kingdoms, secret police worked to stamp out "liberty, equality, and fraternity," the ideals that had fueled the French Revolution.

After Napoleon's defeat, Europe returned to some of its old ways. Kings again asserted their power. But despite the attempts of Europe's sovereigns to suppress revolution and restore the old order, deep and permanent change had occurred. In 1820, looking on from the United States, Thomas Jefferson wrote, "We view Europe as covering a smothered fire, which may shortly burst forth and produce a general conflagration."

c. 1825
Led by Simón Bolívar and others, all of Spanish South America has achieved independence.

1820

1821
Mexico declares independence from Spain

1832
The Reform Act of 1832 doubles the number of eligible voters in Britain.

Simón Bolívar, one of the great heroes of the South American independence movements, leads his troops against Spanish soldiers.

1848
Revolutions sweep Europe, though most do not succeed.

1850

1861
Italian states unite as one nation; Russia abolishes serfdom.

1860

1867
Canada gains dominion status in the British Empire.

1870

1865
The American Civil War ends, saving the union and ending slavery.

1871
Bismarck unifies the German states under Kaiser Wilhelm I.

Chapter 24

Nationalism, Revolution, and the Growth of Western Democracies

1800–1875

*I*n the wake of the American and French revolutions, Latin Americans fought for their independence. In Europe, after the defeat of Napoleon, a wave of nationalism swept much of the continent. In 1830 and again in 1848, revolutions flared as people demanded self-determination. The spirit of nationalism also drove the unification of the Italian and German states.

In response to democratic revolutions and nationalist movements, old rulers tried to maintain their authority, while nobles sought to protect their privileges. Russia lagged behind western Europe as a series of tsars tried to bring economic change but refused to deal with the issue of serfdom.

During the 1800s, demands for reform shook Great Britain and its empire. But no violent revolution followed. Instead, Parliament gradually enacted reforms to increase voting rights at home and self-rule in some of Britain's colonies.

Sectional differences plunged the United States into civil war. The war settled the issue of slavery, addressed the question of states' rights, and, at great human cost, paved the way for a renewed sense of nationhood.

Latin American Independence Movements

Key Questions

- How did Haiti win independence from France?

- What events and ideas inspired revolutionaries in Latin America?

- Who were the major revolutionary leaders in Latin America and what did they achieve? In what ways did their efforts fail?

Historians often describe the period from the late eighteenth to the mid-nineteenth century as an age of democratic revolutions, sparked by the successful American Revolution and inflamed in Europe by the French Revolution. On both sides of the Atlantic, people spoke of natural rights. They questioned monarchy, wrote new constitutions, and experimented with representative government.

Latin America in 1800

After the revolutions in the United States and France, anything seemed possible. Thomas Jefferson wrote in 1795 that the "ball of liberty…is now so well in motion that it will roll around the globe." It would soon reach the Spanish and Portuguese colonies in the region known as Latin America.

In 1800, Spanish and Portuguese monarchs still ruled their colonies in the Americas with a tight grip. Like other European nations with colonies in the New World, Spain and Portugal followed the economic philosophy of mercantilism, which saw colonies as little more than sources of wealth for the ruling country. That wealth might come from gold and silver or from products that could be traded for gold or silver, such as cotton, tobacco, or sugar.

To ensure the flow of wealth directly from their New World colonies to the mother country, Spain and Portugal imposed harsh policies on the colonies, including a rigid class structure. Officials known as *peninsulares*, who had been born in Spain or Portugal, carried out the king's will. Some colonists began to grumble, especially the Creoles, white aristocrats born and raised in the Americas. Why should the king tell them what they could grow on their farms? Why should he tell them where they could trade their goods?

As the eighteenth century drew to a close, more and more Latin American colonists dared to speak of revolution. Inspired by events in North America and Europe, they talked eagerly about being free from the rule of kings. While many Latin American colonies would win their independence, they would face new challenges, especially because—unlike their northern neighbors in the recently formed United States—the people of Latin America had little experience with representative government.

Haiti Rising

While anger and discontent simmered in the Spanish and Portuguese colonies, the first revolution in Latin America took place in a French-ruled

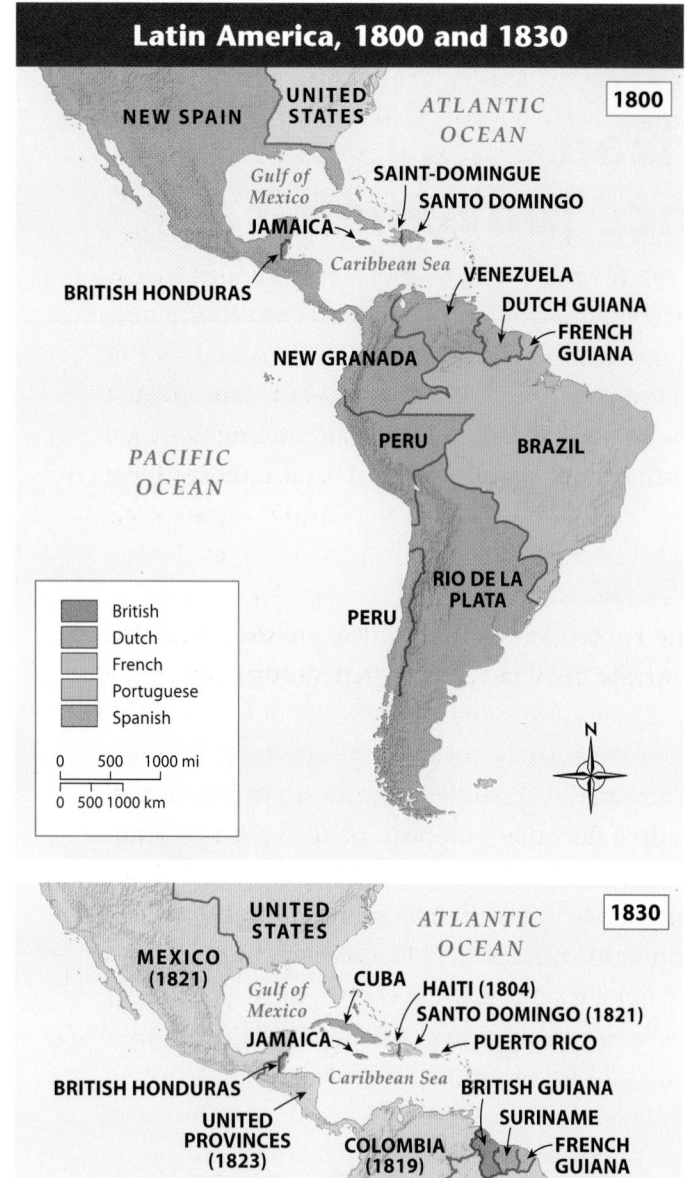

Latin America, 1800 and 1830

1800

NEW SPAIN · UNITED STATES · ATLANTIC OCEAN · *Gulf of Mexico* · SAINT-DOMINGUE · SANTO DOMINGO · JAMAICA · *Caribbean Sea* · BRITISH HONDURAS · VENEZUELA · DUTCH GUIANA · FRENCH GUIANA · NEW GRANADA · PERU · BRAZIL · PACIFIC OCEAN · RIO DE LA PLATA · PERU

- British
- Dutch
- French
- Portuguese
- Spanish

0 500 1000 mi
0 500 1000 km

N

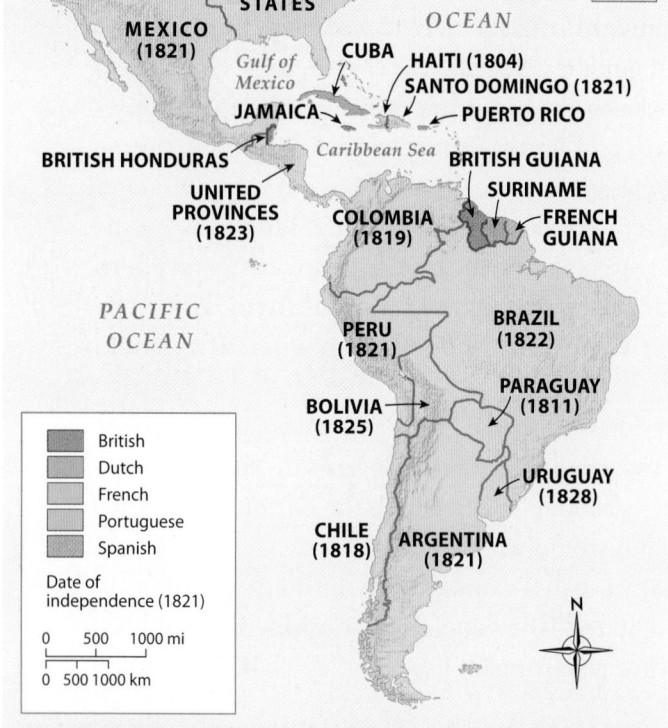

1830

UNITED STATES · ATLANTIC OCEAN · MEXICO (1821) · *Gulf of Mexico* · CUBA · HAITI (1804) · SANTO DOMINGO (1821) · JAMAICA · PUERTO RICO · BRITISH HONDURAS · *Caribbean Sea* · UNITED PROVINCES (1823) · COLOMBIA (1819) · BRITISH GUIANA · SURINAME · FRENCH GUIANA · PACIFIC OCEAN · PERU (1821) · BRAZIL (1822) · PARAGUAY (1811) · BOLIVIA (1825) · URUGUAY (1828) · CHILE (1818) · ARGENTINA (1821)

- British
- Dutch
- French
- Portuguese
- Spanish

Date of independence (1821)

0 500 1000 mi
0 500 1000 km

N

Almost all of Spain's colonies in the Americas, inspired by the American and French revolutions, gained their independence during a turbulent thirty-year period.

colony in the Caribbean Sea, Saint-Domingue (sehn daw-MEHNG), now called Haiti (HAY-tee).

In the late eighteenth century, France relied on Haiti to supply sugar, coffee, and cotton. These crops were grown on plantations, where the labor was provided by slaves. A small French minority ruled over a large population of slaves. Of the five hundred seventy thousand people living on the island, about five hundred thousand were slaves.

On the plantations of Haiti, slaves suffered brutality and severe working conditions. Those who couldn't keep up were whipped or put in the stocks. All were poorly fed. Tens of thousands died from overwork or abuse. Slaves could not own property or bring cases to court. Runaway slaves

Latin America

Latin America is a term used to describe a vast area in the Western Hemisphere south of the United States. It includes Mexico, Central America, South America, and islands in the West Indies. Beginning in the late fifteenth century, many European colonists from Spain and Portugal settled in this part of the world. Today the majority of people in Latin America speak Spanish or Portuguese. Those languages developed from Latin, which is why the area is called Latin America.

By the late eighteenth century, Spain had divided its Latin American lands into four large districts called viceroyalties, each ruled by a viceroy. The viceroyalty of New Spain included what is now Mexico and most of Central America. It also included some Caribbean islands and portions of what is now the western United States. The viceroyalty of New Granada included what is now Colombia, Venezuela, Ecuador, and Panama. The viceroyalty of Río de la Plata included what is now Argentina, Bolivia, Paraguay, and Uruguay. The viceroyalty of Peru included what is now Peru and Chile.

Toussaint-Louverture, a former slave, became leader of revolutionaries in Haiti.

Leaders for Independence in Latin America

In the Latin American colonies, the strongest push for independence came from the Creoles. Many Creoles were wealthy enough to send their sons to Europe to be educated, where they came in contact with and often adopted Enlightenment ideas.

Francisco de Miranda

One young Creole colonist from Venezuela, a wealthy merchant's son, named Francisco de Miranda (mee-RAHN-duh) read philosophical works about freedom as a natural right for all. He toured the new United States and met Thomas Jefferson, James Madison, and Thomas Paine. Miranda became inspired to work for, in his words, "the liberty and independence of the entire Spanish-American continent."

Seeking help to free Spain's colonies, Miranda traveled to Russia, France, and Britain, but all three declined. In 1806, he launched an expedition to liberate Venezuela, but he could not persuade the colonists to join him in rebellion. Instead of liberating the colony, he ended up fleeing to England.

were flogged. Some were sentenced to death by being burned alive.

During the French Revolution, slaves on Haiti heard talk of equality and liberty. In 1791, they rebelled against their French masters. A former slave, Toussaint-Louverture (too-SEHN loo-vair-tyour), emerged as leader of the revolutionaries. Toussaint's battlefield triumphs encouraged the French to abolish slavery in the colony.

Within a few years, after conflicts with various rivals, Toussaint emerged as the colony's ruler. But his victory was short lived. In 1802, Napoleon regained control of the colony and brought back slavery. Toussaint was captured and deported to a French jail. He died in prison in 1803.

After Toussaint's death, French troops occupying Haiti fell prey to a wave of yellow fever. In 1804, France gave up the colony, and Haiti declared its independence.

Yellow Fever

Yellow fever claimed many victims in Latin America, in the sub-Saharan regions of Africa, and, during periodic outbreaks, in the cities of colonial North America. The disease is caused by a virus spread by mosquitoes. Symptoms include uncontrollable shivering and fever, then intense back pain, thirst, yellow skin, and coughing up blood. In the twentieth century, when people understood the role of mosquitoes in spreading yellow fever, they controlled the disease by taking steps to eliminate pools of standing water in which mosquitoes breed. There is now a vaccine available to help prevent yellow fever.

After Miranda's attempt failed, in 1808 events took a dramatic turn when Napoleon invaded Spain. After capturing the Spanish king, the French emperor made his own brother the new king of Spain. Napoleon's actions angered most of Spain's colonists in the New World, who resented the idea of being ruled by a Frenchman. By 1810, revolts were breaking out across Latin America.

Bolívar the Liberator

Another Creole born in Venezuela, Simón Bolívar (see-MOHN buh-LEE-vahr), worked so tirelessly for Latin American independence that he became known as *El Libertador*—The Liberator. As a young man, Bolívar went to Spain and later to France, where he studied literature and read the works of Enlightenment writers such as Locke, Voltaire, and Montesquieu. The proud young Creole vowed, "I will not rest body or soul until I have broken the chains with which Spanish power oppresses us."

Bolívar returned to Venezuela in late 1810. The following year, Venezuela declared its independence from Spain. At Bolívar's urging, Francisco de Miranda, now sixty years old, took command of the rebel army. But everything seemed to go wrong. The rebels were poorly trained and ill equipped. A powerful earthquake destroyed Caracas and other cities. Then General Miranda surrendered his forces.

With Venezuela again under Spanish rule, Bolívar joined the revolutionaries in Colombia. Under Bolívar's command, Colombian forces crossed the border into Venezuela and managed to liberate Caracas, only to be pushed back by troops loyal to Spain. For several years, the fighting went on, with victory going sometimes to the rebels, sometimes the Spanish.

In the end, Bolívar's forces won independence for what are now the countries of Colombia and Venezuela. Bolívar also helped Panama and Ecuador throw off Spanish rule. A separate state, Bolivia, was named to honor The Liberator himself.

San Martín: Hero of the South

In Argentina, a very different liberator emerged—José de San Martín (hoh-SAY day sahn mahr-TEEN). Both his parents were peninsulares; his mother came from Spanish nobility, and his father was a high-ranking colonial official in Argentina. When José was a boy, his family returned to Spain. San Martín joined the Spanish army and fought heroically against Napoleon's French invaders. But when the cause was lost, he resigned his army post and traveled to London. There he came to believe that Spain's tight control of Latin America was wrong and that his rightful place lay with the rebels.

San Martín returned to Argentina, where he helped lead the fight against Spain. In 1816, at his urging, Argentines officially declared their independence. San Martín then set his sights on liberating Chile and Peru.

San Martín planned to cross the Andes Mountains into Chile, defeat the Spaniards, and then sail up the coast to free Peru. His plan, while bold, seemed impossible. The highest peaks of the Andes soared to nearly twenty-three thousand feet (7010 m). Snow and ice blocked the few passes most of the year. How could an entire army get over such mountains?

For three years, San Martín prepared his army for the mountain crossing. His closest adviser was an exiled patriot commander from Chile, a Creole of Irish descent named Bernardo O'Higgins.

In January 1817, the Army of the Andes set off on its march with more than five thousand men. By day, the troops roasted under the sun. By night, they froze. Hailstorms pelted them with ice. As the air grew thinner at high altitudes, the soldiers gasped for breath. Many did not survive.

After twenty-one days of marching, the Army of the Andes reached its destination on the other side of the mountains—Chile. With San Martín and O'Higgins in the lead, the exhausted but determined soldiers charged down on the panicked Spaniards. After a second major battle,

Simón Bolívar, who worked tirelessly for Latin American independence, became known as *El Libertador*, The Liberator.

By 1826, all of South America was free of Spanish rule. Now came a new challenge—how should the Latin Americans govern themselves?

Bolívar's wartime experiences convinced him that Latin American nations needed strong leadership. He wrote that Spanish domination "has not only deprived us of our rights but has kept us in a sort of permanent infancy with regard to public affairs."

Bolívar hoped to form a large nation covering much of South America, but by the time he died in 1830, Spain's old territories had split into several different countries. After three hundred years of strict control by the Spanish monarch, independence brought chaotic uncertainty. The people of these new Latin American nations had no history of electing representatives, passing laws, or charting their political future. This uncertainty created an opening for military strongmen called *caudillos* (kaw-DEEL-yohs).

The caudillos commanded armies held together by personal loyalties and a desire for wealth. Competing caudillos often fought each other for years on end. Governments kept changing hands until one caudillo or another gained complete victory. The victorious caudillo would then make himself a dictator and rely on force to maintain control. Through the first half of the nineteenth century, many governments in Latin America became military dictatorships.

Brazilian Independence from Portugal

About the same time that other South American nations gained independence from Spain, Brazil gained independence from Portugal. But Brazil did not go through a long, bloody revolution. Instead, events in Europe led to Brazil's independence.

Chile was liberated. The grateful citizens asked San Martín to be the head of their new government, but he passed that honor on to Bernardo O'Higgins.

San Martín remained focused on freeing Peru as well. As San Martín prepared to move north, Simón Bolívar's forces were moving south. The rebel armies of Bolívar and San Martín squeezed Peru in their grip. San Martín seized the capital, Lima, in 1821. He declared Peru independent, though forces loyal to Spain kept fighting back.

Bolívar and San Martín shared the goal of Latin American independence, but they did not agree on how to achieve that goal. San Martín, frustrated by disputes among Latin American leaders, returned to Europe and left the leadership of the revolution to Bolívar, who led the final victory over the Spaniards in Peru in 1826.

When Napoleon invaded Portugal in 1807, the Portuguese royal family quickly boarded a ship and sailed for their South American colony. They settled in the beautiful Brazilian city of Rio de Janeiro (REE-oh day zhuh-NERH-oh) and made it the new capital of their Portuguese Empire.

When Napoleon was defeated in 1815, the Portuguese royal family declared Brazil a separate kingdom under their power. A few years later, the king returned to Portugal, leaving his son Pedro to rule Brazil.

In 1822, Pedro declared his kingdom of Brazil independent of Portugal. He drew up a constitution and had himself crowned emperor. The new nation was not a republic, but it was legally independent of Portugal.

Independence for Mexico

As colonies in South America broke away from Spain and Portugal, to the north, Spain's largest colony, Mexico, went through its own struggle for independence. Creoles led the revolutionary movements in most Latin American countries. In Mexico, Indians and mestizos played a major role, especially in the early struggles.

Mexico: Father Hidalgo's Cry for Freedom

In 1810, an aging Creole priest, Miguel Hidalgo y Costilla (mee-GEHL ee-DAHL-goh ee kahs-TEE-yah), helped light the first flames of revolution in Mexico. Father Hidalgo studied the works of Enlightenment philosophers, and he admired the ideas of the French Revolution. In the dusty Mexican village of Dolores (doh-LOH-res), Hidalgo saw the suffering of his parishioners, who were mostly Indians and mestizos struggling to survive on the scraps of land left by their Spanish masters.

While Father Hidalgo worked to help his poor parishioners, Creoles across Mexico met secretly to discuss how they could

win their country's independence from Spain. The growing movement against Spanish rule rallied around the idea of "Mexico for the Mexicans." But who exactly were these Mexicans?

To the well-off Creoles, "Mexicans" meant Creoles only. They had no interest in getting rid of Mexico's class system. They just wanted to be at the top, along with the peninsulares. Better yet, the Creoles wanted to send the peninsulares back to Spain and take their place. To Father Hidalgo, however, "Mexico for the Mexicans" meant *all* Mexicans, whatever their background—Spanish, Indian, African, or mixed.

In September 1810, Spanish officials heard rumors of a revolutionary conspiracy. When Father Hidalgo learned that Spanish troops were on their

Father Hidalgo rallies his followers to fight the Spanish. He was eventually captured and executed, but Mexicans continued the fight.

way to arrest him and other suspected rebels, he rang the bell of his little village church. As a crowd gathered, he spoke out: "This new day brings us a new way of life. Are you ready to receive it? Will you free yourselves? Will you recover from the hated Spaniards the land stolen from your forefathers three hundred years ago?"

Father Hidalgo's stirring speech on the church steps eventually became known as the *Grito de Dolores*—the Cry of Dolores. His words stirred the people to revolt. The peasants armed themselves with any weapons they could find—knives and axes, miner's picks, machetes used for chopping sugarcane. Hidalgo's ragged band swelled from a few hundred to a thousand, and eventually to eighty thousand.

But this was not the revolutionary army that Creole leaders had imagined. It was a bloodthirsty mob bent on revenge for generations of Spanish oppression. Wealthy Creoles quickly realized that the Indian and mestizo rebels could see little difference between them and the peninsulares. Fearing for their lives and property, many Creoles joined forces with Spain. The two sides clashed in a civil war.

Mexico Declares Independence

Six months after the *Grito de Dolores*, the Spaniards captured Father Hidalgo. After a speedy trial, he was executed by a firing squad in July 1811. But the fighting did not end. Thousands of Mexicans kept up the battle for freedom, led by another priest, Father José María Morelos (moh-RAY-lohs). But Morelos and his troops were defeated by forces led by a Creole officer, Agustín de Iturbide (ah-goos-TEEN day ee-toor-BEE-thay).

In 1821, unrest in Spain threatened to replace the monarchy with a new government. Mexico's

The flag of independent Mexico during the reign of Agustín de Iturbide, c. 1822

wealthy Creoles feared that under this new government, they might lose their privileges in the colony. Thus Mexico's Creoles—motivated mainly by a desire to protect their status, not by a longing for liberty—decided to support the cause of independence from Spain.

So, led by the very man who had defeated Morelos and his rebel forces—Agustín de Iturbide—Mexico declared its independence from Spain in 1821. Iturbide briefly ruled as the self-declared emperor of Mexico, but he was ousted in 1823. Mexico became a republic, though for decades the new nation was torn by continuing political conflict.

Fighting also continued in the provinces of Central America, where the people struggled for independence from both Spain and Mexico. Eventually, these provinces would become the nations of Nicaragua, Guatemala, Honduras, El Salvador, and Costa Rica.

Nationalism and Disunity in Europe

Key Questions

- What were the goals of European leaders at the Congress of Vienna?

- What is nationalism? How did nationalism spur revolutions across Europe in 1848?

- Why did Russia lag behind western Europe during the early 1800s?

In the early 1800s, when Napoleon toppled old governments ruled by dukes and princes, he also spread the ideas of the French Revolution. After Napoleon's defeat, his enemies tried to put everything back the way it was before the French Revolution. Diplomats from the victorious nations met at the Congress of Vienna. Their goal was a return to peace and stability after twenty-five years of war and revolution. In 1815, hoping to achieve a balance of power in which no nation was strong enough to dominate its neighbors, they redrew the map of Europe. They also agreed to restore royal families to power in many countries where Napoleon's forces had overthrown monarchies.

The actions of the Congress of Vienna left many people in Europe dissatisfied. People of the lower and middle classes had been inspired by the democratic ideals of the French Revolution. They resented the return of monarchy. At the same time, the countries invaded by Napoleon had fiercely resisted foreign rule. Their resistance fed a growing spirit of nationalism, the strong sense of attachment or belonging to one's own country.

As nationalism grew, people felt less loyal to a monarch or empire and more loyal to their fellow countrymen. They valued the bonds created by the shared culture and language of a particular place. In the decades after the Congress of Vienna, nationalism would combine with democratic ideals to fuel a series of revolutions across Europe.

Greece Rebels Against Ottoman Rule

The first of the European nationalist revolutions broke out in Greece. Since the fifteenth century, Greece had been ruled by the Ottoman Empire, a Muslim empire centered in what is now Turkey. In ancient times, the Greeks had created the world's first democracy. As the nineteenth century dawned, the Greeks resented being ruled by a foreign power that gave them no say in their own government. Furthermore, as Orthodox Christians, they resented being ruled by Muslims.

In 1821, the Greeks rose in revolt against Ottoman rule. One of their leaders declared, "We have resolved to be free or perish." The uprising caught the country's Ottoman rulers by surprise. The rebels quickly defeated the Ottoman forces in the Peloponnese (the peninsula making up the southern half of the country). In revenge, the Ottomans carried out massacres in the parts of the country they still controlled. On the island of Chios, they slaughtered some twenty-five thousand Greek men, women, and children, while seizing another forty-five thousand as slaves.

News of the massacre at Chios shocked people across Europe. Many educated Europeans, brought up to revere the civilization of ancient Greece, rallied to the Greek cause. The English poet Lord Byron wrote these famous lines about the ancient Greeks' defeat of the Persians:

> *The mountains look on Marathon—*
>   *And Marathon looks on the sea;*
> *And musing there an hour alone,*
>   *I dream'd that Greece might still be free;*
> *For standing on the Persians' grave,*
> *I could not deem myself a slave.*

The Greek war of independence ground on for several more years. The Ottomans had far too many soldiers for the rebels to defeat. Meanwhile, the rebel leaders quarreled among themselves about their plans for an independent Greece. Eventually those quarrels erupted into civil war, with Greeks fighting Greeks as well as Ottoman Turks.

The Greek cause was saved by the help of three of the most powerful nations in Europe—Russia, England, and France. The Russians, traditional enemies of the Turks, sympathized with the Greeks as fellow Orthodox Christians. The English and the French were appalled by Ottoman cruelty and also feared the disruption of trade in the Mediterranean Sea. In 1827, the fleets of Britain, France, and Russia combined to defeat the Ottoman navy in a great sea battle. In 1830, the three powers reached an agreement guaranteeing the independence of Greece.

France: Revolution, Republic, and Second Empire

When Napoleon was in exile, the Congress of Vienna put a king back on the throne of France. The new king, Louis XVIII, was the brother of Louis XVI, who had died on the guillotine during the Revolution. Aging and unhealthy, Louis XVIII proved to be a weak ruler. A new constitution forced Louis to share power with an elected parliament. However, since only a minority of wealthy

Britain, France, and Russia joined Greek forces in 1827 to defeat the Ottoman navy.

property owners could vote in elections, France was far from democratic.

The Revolutions of 1830 and 1848

When Louis XVIII died in 1824, his energetic brother, Charles X, took the throne. Charles longed for a return to the days when the king of France was an absolute ruler. In a struggle with the parliament, he gradually tightened his grip on power. He censored books and pamphlets by his opponents and greatly reduced the number of eligible voters. While he imposed these measures, a series of bad harvests increased the misery of the poor. The population of Paris swelled with hungry, unemployed peasants.

In July 1830, Paris exploded in revolution. On roads throughout the city, rebels made barricades out of wagons, barrels, and furniture. From behind the barricades, they shot at the royal troops that were sent to put down the uprising. Soon, many of the troops themselves joined the rebels. After three days of fighting, Charles X was forced from the throne.

The new king, Louis-Philippe, was very different from the haughty Charles. Known as "the People's King," he liked to wander the streets of Paris shaking hands. His reign brought France more than a decade of prosperity. But in the mid-1840s, poor harvests once again led to widespread poverty and unrest. In 1848, another revolution broke out. Once again, the king was forced to step down. A mob invaded his palace, seized his throne, and burned it in the street.

A Short-Lived Republic

Louis-Philippe would be the last king of France. The country once again declared itself a republic. Every adult male was given the vote.

After the turmoil of the past decades, many Frenchmen looked back to Napoleon's reign as a time of national greatness. In December 1848, they elected his nephew, Louis-Napoleon Bonaparte, to the office of president.

The new French republic faced many challenges. The poor complained that the wealthy still had too much power. They called for dramatic reforms, such as guaranteed jobs and free education. The middle and upper classes feared an uprising by the poor. Taking advantage of these fears, in 1851 Louis-Napoleon overthrew the republic and began ruling as a dictator.

Louis-Napoleon proclaimed the "Second Empire," and called himself Napoleon III. The great novelist Victor Hugo mocked him as "Napoleon the Little." France would not be a republic again until 1870.

Failed Revolutions

The French revolution of 1848 inspired similar uprisings throughout Europe. In Vienna, the capital of the sprawling Habsburg Empire, mobs took to the streets, demanding a greater say in government. Soon, rebellions broke out in the other lands ruled by the Habsburgs. Fired by the new spirit of nationalism, the Czechs and the Hungarians demanded their independence. The Habsburg provinces in Italy also broke free. Meanwhile, democratic

French revolutionaries in Paris proclaim a republic after overthrowing their king in 1848. The revolt was soon crushed but such uprisings proved that democratic ideas were very much alive in Europe.

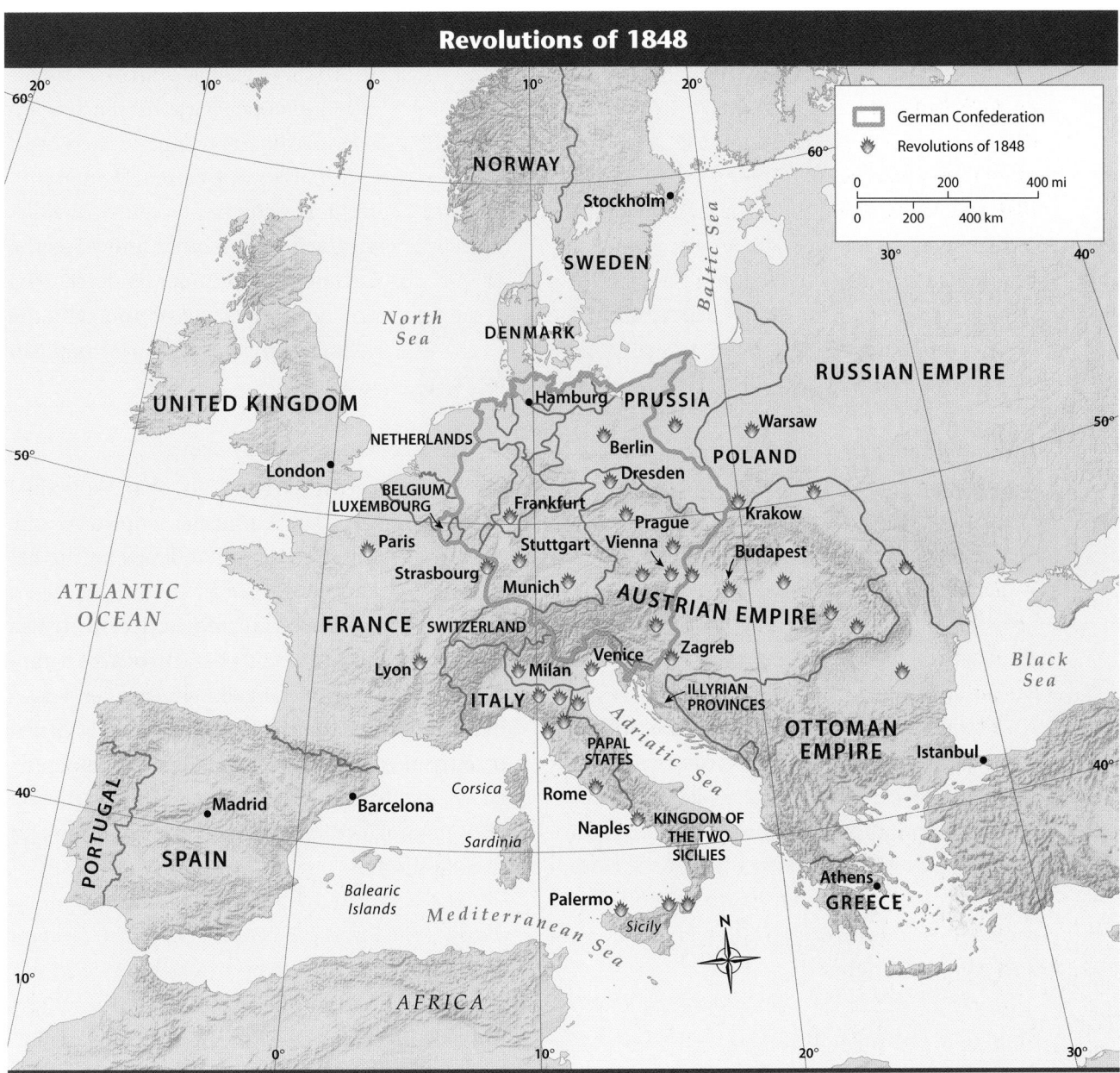

Revolutions of 1848

Legend:
- German Confederation
- Revolutions of 1848

In 1848, uprisings broke out across much of Europe, though most of these rebellions were quickly suppressed.

uprisings occurred in many of the states that made up the disunited realm of Germany.

Most of these revolutions did not succeed. The Russian tsar sent troops to Hungary to help the Austrians crush the rebellion there. In other countries, the rebels, divided by ethnicity or political ideas, failed to unite effectively. By 1849, most of the old conservative governments had returned to power. But what the Germans called "the Spring-time of Peoples" would continue to inspire democrats and nationalists in the decades to come.

Russia Lags Behind

While democratic ideals inspired revolution in western Europe, they had little effect in Russia, the vast land straddling Europe and Asia. The Russian tsar remained an **autocrat**, a single ruler who exercised nearly absolute power over his subjects. Furthermore, most of the people of Russia were serfs—poor peasants bound to the land. Little more than slaves, serfs were considered the property of the noblemen whose lands they worked.

Imperial troops crushed the Decembrist Uprising in 1825, and Russia remained a state that gave all power to the tsar and few freedoms to the people.

For centuries, Russia had lagged behind western Europe, both politically and economically. In the 1700s, two reforming tsars—Peter the Great and Catherine the Great—sought to modernize Russia by introducing Western ideas and technology. But they maintained a firm grip on power, and they did nothing to help Russia's millions of serfs gain basic rights.

In 1801, when Tsar Alexander I came to the throne, he seemed at first to be a new kind of Russian ruler. Influenced by Enlightenment ideas, he freed political prisoners, relaxed censorship, and lifted a ban on Russians traveling abroad. Alexander considered introducing a constitutional government, and he described the institution of serfdom as "a degradation."

But Napoleon's invasion of Russia in 1812 changed Alexander's views. If Napoleon's attempt to spread the French Revolution was what came of "enlightened" ideas, then Alexander wanted little to do with such ideas. The tsar played a significant role in the Congress of Vienna, joining with other monarchs in an alliance against revolutionary change.

When Alexander died suddenly in 1825, a group of army officers staged a rebellion against the new tsar, Nicholas I. They demanded a constitutional government and an end to serfdom, which they called "Russia's disgrace." The revolt, known as the Decembrist Uprising, was quickly put down by imperial troops. Again, the rulers of Russia stood firmly opposed to reform.

The Crimean War

In the early 1850s, Tsar Nicholas I tried to extend his empire by seizing some Ottoman lands on the Balkan Peninsula in the southeastern corner of Europe, between Austria and Greece. The Ottoman Empire responded by declaring war on Russia in 1853. Great Britain and France joined the war on the side of the Ottomans. The European powers wanted to halt Russian expansion and protect their trading interests in the Balkan countries and the Middle East.

The war pitted Russia against the combined forces of the British, the French, and the Ottomans, who were later joined by troops from Sardinia, an Italian kingdom. Because much of the fighting took place on the Crimean Peninsula (which juts into the Black Sea), the war is known as the Crimean War.

British and French troops were well supplied with the latest weapons, including highly accurate rifles. The Russians fought with old-fashioned muskets, and only had enough of these for about half their troops. During the severe Russian winter of 1854–55, more troops died of cold and disease than of battle injuries.

In the fall of 1855, British troops captured the key port city of Sevastopol. In 1856, the Crimean War ended. Russia suffered a humiliating defeat and was forced to give up the Ottoman territories it had taken.

The Crimean War was the first war to be covered by photojournalists. It ended with the poorly equipped Russians suffering an enormous defeat and losing Ottoman lands they had previously seized.

The End of Serfdom

Tsar Nicholas I died shortly before the Crimean War ended and was succeeded by his son, Alexander II. Alexander realized that Russia had been defeated in the Crimean War because it was so far behind western Europe, both socially and technologically.

Alexander saw serfdom as the major cause of Russia's backwardness. He knew that the free workers of Europe were far more efficient and productive than Russia's oppressed, uneducated serfs. He also feared the possibility that the serfs would rise up in bloody revolution. "It is better," he said, "to begin to abolish bondage from above than to wait for the time when it will begin to abolish itself spontaneously from below."

In 1861, Alexander II issued the Edict of Emancipation, which freed most of the country's serfs. The freed serfs gained basic rights as citizens—for example, to marry, to own property, and to go into business. Russia's farmlands were divided between the former serfs and the nobles who had owned them. But while the government gave land to the nobles, it sold land to the former serfs. Most emancipated serfs thus remained tied to the land, farming it in order to pay off their debt to the government.

Alexander also tried to modernize Russia's military and its legal system. But his reforms ground to a halt in 1881, when the tsar was assassinated. Russia remained mostly a land of impoverished peasants, lagging far behind Europe in economics and technology.

Barge Haulers on the Volga, painted by Ilya Repin in about 1870, depicts the suffering of serfs in tsarist Russia.

Nationalism and Unity in Europe: Italy and Germany

Key Questions

- Who were the key leaders in the unification of Italy, and how did nationalist sentiments shape their efforts?

- What tactics did Otto von Bismarck employ in unifying the German states?

- How did Germany's economy change after unification?

Between the days of the ancient Roman Empire and the time of Napoleon, the inhabitants of the Italian Peninsula rarely thought of themselves as "Italians." Rather, they considered themselves citizens of Florence, Genoa, Venice, or any other of the many competing city-states. In 1797, when Napoleon and his troops conquered northern Italy, the French ruler in some ways united the long-divided people.

Napoleon's conquest stirred feelings of nationalism. People began to experience a new sense of unity in their shared dislike of being ruled by French outsiders. They began to imagine an Italy that would be both unified and free from foreign rule.

Italy: From Division to Unity

Following Napoleon's defeat, the Italian Peninsula once again broke into a jumble of separate states ruled by foreign powers. Austria dominated most of the north. In central Italy, the pope ruled the Papal States, though he relied on help from Austria. Members of the Spanish royal family ruled southern Italy.

Only one major state was not dominated by a foreign power—the Kingdom of Sardinia, which included the island of Sardinia and a region near the Alps in northwestern Italy. This region was known as Piedmont, a word meaning "at the foot of the mountains." Since the capital city was located there, the entire Kingdom of Sardinia was often called simply "Piedmont."

Mazzini and Young Italy

Around 1830, in the various states of Italy, students and other young people often staged protests in the streets. They demanded a constitution to protect their rights. They called for a free press and free elections. Some of the protesters formed secret societies to fight for their causes. Among these protesters, Giuseppe Mazzini (joo-ZEP-pay maht-SEE-nee) emerged as a powerful voice for freedom and Italian unity.

In 1831, Mazzini started an organization called Young Italy. Mazzini's movement pursued both nationalist and democratic goals. Mazzini's nationalist goal was to free the Italian states from their foreign rulers and unify them as an independent republic. Mazzini argued that people who share a language, culture, and history have a common destiny to live in freedom as a single nation.

Giuseppe Garibaldi, leader of the Redshirts

Mazzini's democratic goal was to achieve a freely elected government in a united Italy. He wanted more power for the people: "Neither pope nor king," said Mazzini; "Only God and the people will open the way of the future to us."

The Young Italy movement spread rapidly. Its members tried to organize uprisings against foreign rule, but their efforts failed. In one attempt, the rebels were arrested before their revolt even began. Twelve were executed. Mazzini was not captured, but a death sentence was put on his head.

Garibaldi and the Redshirts

Although the Young Italy movement did not change things right away, its ideals inspired many Italians, including Giuseppe Garibaldi (gair-uh-BAHL-dee) of Sardinia, who joined the movement in 1833. The next year he participated in a plot to overthrow the king of Sardinia. But the plot failed at the last minute.

Garibaldi managed to avoid being captured. He made his way to South America, where the people of Uruguay were fighting for independence from Argentina. Garibaldi organized a group of Italian exiles and helped them fight. His men wore the cheapest uniforms they could get—red robes that butchers had thrown away. Garibaldi's troops thus came to be known as the "Redshirts."

In 1848, a year when revolutions were breaking out across Europe, Garibaldi sailed back to Italy with his Redshirts. When they stepped ashore in northern Italy, a crowd swarmed around them roaring, *"Evviva Garibaldi! Long live Garibaldi!"*

When the people of Rome revolted against the pope's rule in 1848, Garibaldi hurried his Redshirts to help the uprising. In Rome, the Redshirts fought hard but lost against French troops that had come to the pope's aid. Garibaldi survived and escaped to the United States. In 1854, however, he returned once more to his homeland in Piedmont.

Garibaldi Unites Italy

The Kingdom of Sardinia, or Piedmont, was the only major state on the Italian Peninsula not ruled by a foreign power. Its king, Victor Emmanuel II, longed to unite Italy under his rule. For help in running his kingdom, the king made the Count di Cavour (kuh-VUR), a shrewd politician, his prime minister. Cavour understood how valuable it would be to have the support of a popular hero like Garibaldi. So Cavour arranged secret meetings between Garibaldi and Victor Emmanuel. The rebel and the king had something in common—they both wanted foreign rulers out of Italy.

A *prime minister* is the leader of a parliamentary government.

Cavour also persuaded the French to help Piedmont if it came under attack. Then he deliberately provoked disagreements with Austria. When these disagreements erupted into war, French troops arrived to help defend Piedmont. They were joined by Garibaldi, who took charge of a Piedmontese army.

In 1859, the French and Piedmontese clashed with the Austrians. When the fighting ended, the Austrians had lost all their northern Italian states except Venice. The newly liberated states in northern Italy decided to join Sardinia. The French were alarmed to find that, right on their southern border, a united and sizable Italian kingdom was taking shape.

In a kingdom to the south, called The Two Sicilies, many people were rebelling against their rulers, who were members of the Spanish royal family. With about a thousand of his Redshirts, Garibaldi set out to help the rebels. In 1860, Garibaldi landed in Sicily and swiftly defeated the kingdom's forces. Thousands rushed to join Garibaldi's army. Garibaldi then marched on Naples. The king fled without a fight. Garibaldi now controlled all of southern Italy.

Garibaldi's success worried Cavour. But Garibaldi was not fighting for himself. He willingly handed over the newly freed territories to Victor Emmanuel, who became king of a united Italy.

Only the cities of Venice and Rome remained in foreign hands, but not for long. In 1866, Venice broke away from Austria and joined Italy. Four years later, Victor Emmanuel marched into Rome and declared it his capital. The pope refused to accept the Italian government. He retired to a small section of Rome called Vatican City.

The State of Vatican City

In 1929, the Roman Catholic Church and the Italian government finally negotiated a treaty. The pope recognized Italy as a nation with its capital at Rome, and Italy recognized Vatican City as an independent state. Vatican City, a 109-acre (44 hectare) territory in the city of Rome, is the world's smallest nation.

Vatican City, an independent state in Rome

Garibaldi was disappointed that the nation he helped create turned out to be a monarchy rather than a republic. But he was overjoyed that Italy was at last one nation. When he died in 1882, he was buried under a simple granite tombstone, revered by his countrymen as the man who had created their nation.

German Unification

To the north of Italy, feelings of nationalism were also growing among German-speaking people. Until about 1800, these people had never been united under one government. Most lived in the loose collection of states known as the Holy Roman Empire. People in these states felt loyalty to their own small kingdoms, not to the empire. They felt no sense of belonging to one nation despite their shared language and customs.

When the emperor Napoleon and his armies swept into the German states, the German people felt a new sense of unity in their opposition to the French. Napoleon's domination sparked German nationalism. Many people began to take pride in their heritage and spirit as Germans.

After the Germans drove Napoleon from their soil in 1815, they were still politically divided. Various kings, princes, and dukes ruled thirty-nine separate German-speaking states. The most powerful was Austria, whose ruling family, the Habsburgs, also controlled many non-German areas. Prussia, too, was powerful, and its people thought of themselves more as Prussian than German. Nevertheless, the campaign against Napoleon had done much to encourage feelings of nationalism and unity that lasted into peacetime.

Otto von Bismarck: Prussia's Iron Man

In the mid-nineteenth century, a strong-willed, masterful politician from Prussia did much to forge the German states into one nation. Otto von Bismarck was a huge, square-shouldered man with an enormous mustache, bushy eyebrows, and stern eyes that matched his stern words. "Not by

Prussia's Otto von Bismarck fought to unite several German states into a single German nation.

Industrial Revolution that transformed much of the Western world.)

In 1866, Bismarck put his plan in motion. First, he started a quarrel with Austria. Then he escalated the tension between Austria and Prussia. When the war he hoped for began, he directed the Prussian army to strike quickly. Prussian generals used the new railroads to move their troops faster than the Austrians could. Prussian soldiers had new guns that could fire five times a minute. Prussia's victory over a stunned Austria took only seven weeks.

Prussia became the leading German state. Bismarck used his new prestige to form a confederation of twenty-two German states. He was, of course, careful to retain the most power for Prussia.

Bismarck, known as the Iron Chancellor, knew the German people wanted a voice in their government, but he disliked democracy. So he gave all male citizens the right to vote for the lower house of a new parliament, the *Reichstag* (RIYKS-tahg). But he made sure that the king of Prussia—or rather, Bismarck acting in the king's name—could overrule the Reichstag's decisions.

Bismarck turned to his next challenge—how to draw the remaining German states away from Austria. He decided he needed another war. In 1870, he looked to France for a fight.

speeches and majority votes are the great questions of the day decided," he once said, "but by blood and iron."

Bismarck presented himself as a simple man, but he was as cunning as Cavour in Italy. In 1862, the king of Prussia, Wilhelm I, appointed Bismarck as his chancellor (a position similar to that of prime minister). Chancellor Bismarck's goal was to make Prussia a powerful state. But he knew that Germans were talking of a unified German nation. He also saw that smaller states might join Austria instead of Prussia, leaving Prussia weakened. So he decided to act quickly.

Bismarck Unites the Germans

Bismarck formed a plan to overcome Prussia's powerful rival, Austria. He strengthened the Prussian army and built up Prussia's industries, producing more iron and building more railroads. (In the next chapter, you will read about the

Bismarck's Remarks

Bismarck was famous for his pointed remarks. Here are a few that reveal his personality and aims.

"Better pointed bullets than pointed words."

"People never lie so much as after a hunt, during a war, or before an election."

"Laws are like sausages. It's better not to see them being made."

"We Germans fear God, but nothing else."

"The main thing is to make history, not to write it."

German Folktales

Two brothers, Jakob and Wilhelm Grimm, were librarians and scholars. They began collecting German folktales as a way of showing Germans their deeply rooted stories, myths, and wisdom. The Brothers Grimm published their first book of folktales in 1812. Among the stories they collected are tales we know as *Sleeping Beauty*, *Rapunzel*, and *Snow White*. They evoked a world of giants, dwarves, and wolves, and of strange sorcery unfolding in deep, dark woods. The stories reminded Germans of the land, literature, and spirit they shared.

Defeating the French and Decreeing Germany

The emperor Napoleon's nephew, Napoleon III, sat on the throne of France. Worried that a unified Germany would weaken France's power in Europe, Napoleon III sent an ambassador to meet with the Prussian king, who was vacationing in the town of Ems. After the meeting, the king sent a telegram to his chancellor, Bismarck, summarizing the talks with the French ambassador. It was the opportunity Bismarck had been waiting for.

Bismarck rewrote the telegram to make it sound as though the French ambassador and the Prussian king had insulted each other. He published the rewritten "Ems telegram," sparking outrage among both the French and the Germans.

Napoleon III fell into Bismarck's trap. He declared war on Prussia in July 1870. Nationalist feelings and the memory of the hated Napoleon Bonaparte quickly drew the smaller German states to Prussia's side. Less than seven weeks later, the French army surrendered and the Prussians laid siege to the French capital of Paris. Food and supplies in the "City of Light" dwindled as the siege went on. Reduced to eating rats, Parisians finally surrendered their capital.

Bismarck declared the birth of the German Empire. It included every German state except Austria. Prussia's king became Kaiser Wilhelm I. (*Kaiser* is the German term for "Caesar.") France was forced to pay Germany five billion francs and turn over Alsace (al-SAS) and part of Lorraine (luh-RAYN), two mostly German-speaking provinces with rich iron and coal resources that Bismarck wanted for German industry.

Bismarck continued to dominate Germany until Wilhelm I died in 1888. The new kaiser, Wilhelm II, wanted to rule without Bismarck's guidance. The Iron Chancellor resigned, leaving the country in the hands of Wilhelm II.

A New Europe

Bismarck's influence did not end with his retirement. He left Germany and much of the rest of Europe changed.

Bismarck wanted more than a unified Germany. He was determined to turn his nation into an industrial and military power as well. The Germans used the land and money taken from France to fuel this development. They introduced educational innovation with government-sponsored technical schools across the country. In these

Bismarck, in white, watches as Wilhelm is crowned kaiser of Germany. In a final humiliation for France, the ceremony took place at Versailles.

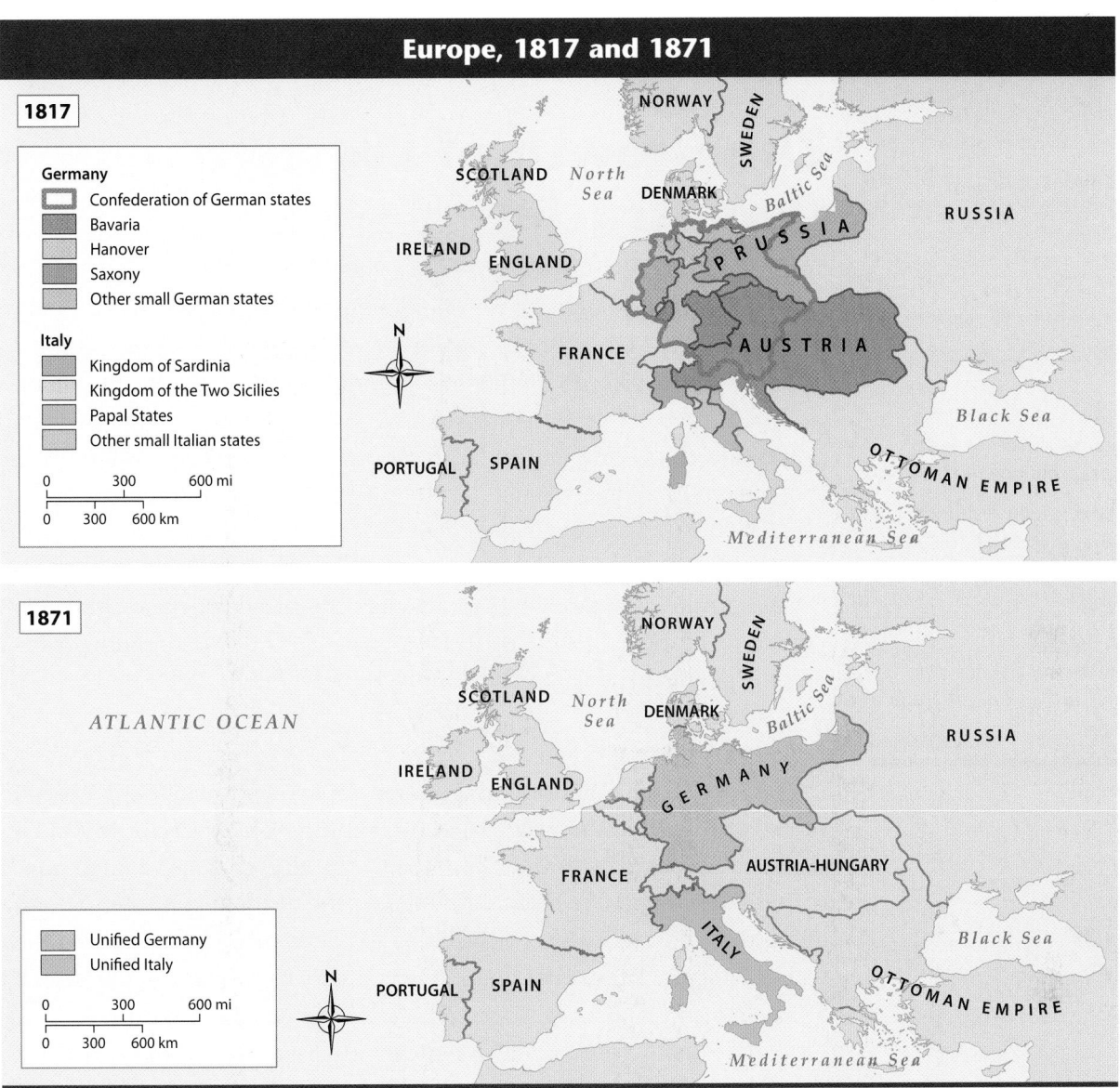

Europe, 1817 and 1871

1817

Germany
- Confederation of German states
- Bavaria
- Hanover
- Saxony
- Other small German states

Italy
- Kingdom of Sardinia
- Kingdom of the Two Sicilies
- Papal States
- Other small Italian states

0   300   600 mi
0   300   600 km

1871

- Unified Germany
- Unified Italy

0   300   600 mi
0   300   600 km

In the late nineteenth century, national unification in both Italy and Germany shaped the modern political map of Europe.

schools, German students learned to do scientific research that prepared them to develop new ideas and products. Much of the new technology was harnessed to produce new machines of war.

The desire for a strong, professional military, equipped with the most advanced weapons possible, was not new or unique to Germany. In the years after Bismarck, **militarism**—the glorification of military might—would increase across Europe, with dire consequences.

The unification of Italy and Germany changed the map of Europe. These new nations wiped away many little kingdoms, duchies, and city-states that European rulers had arranged after the fall of Napoleon. Small states that had covered much of the continent like jigsaw puzzle pieces were gone. Large, unified nations stood in their place.

Growing feelings of nationalism caused much of this change. Democratic revolutions also led to change, as people in various lands refused to be ruled by dukes, princes, or distant royal families, such as the Habsburgs of Austria.

Europe was not the only place to be changed by these forces. Nationalist and democratic movements would continue to reshape the world in the century to come.

The Growth of Western Democracies

Key Questions

- Why didn't Britain experience a revolution as other European nations did?

- How did Britain respond to demands for self-rule in Canada, Australia, and New Zealand?

- What major conflicts led to the American Civil War, and what issues did the war resolve?

During the 1800s, demands for democratic change sparked revolution in many countries. Great Britain, however, managed to avoid revolution by enacting various reforms, both at home and in its English-speaking colonies.

The United States, former colonies of Britain, grew quickly in size and power. But the young nation faced serious internal conflicts that, in the 1860s, would lead to civil war.

Democratic Movements in the British Empire

On the continent of Europe, the movement toward democracy often led to violent revolution. In the British Isles, as well as in the expanding British Empire, political change came about more peacefully.

Reforms at Home

England had a long tradition of representative government, dating back to the Magna Carta in the early thirteenth century. Since the late 1600s, England had been a constitutional monarchy. Its king or queen shared power with the representative body, Parliament. One of the two houses of Parliament, the House of Lords, consisted of aristocrats who had inherited their seats. Members of the other house, the House of Commons, were elected to office. But only 5 percent of the population—men who owned substantial property—could vote, so Parliament mainly represented the interests of aristocrats and the wealthy.

When revolution erupted in France in 1830, England's leaders worried that the unrest on the continent might spread to England. Parliament decided to try to avoid violent conflict by enacting peaceful reforms to extend the franchise—the right to vote—to more people. The Reform Act of 1832 lowered the amount of property a citizen had to own to qualify to vote. While the act more than doubled the number of eligible voters, it only extended the vote to the well-off middle class. It still left many factory and farm workers disenfranchised—without the right to vote.

Many in England remained dissatisfied with a system that gave no voice to the majority. In the late 1830s, a working-class movement rose up to demand reform. They were called the Chartists because they presented their initial demands in a statement called "A People's Charter."

The Chartists pressed for universal male suffrage, with no minimum property ownership qualifications. In 1867, Parliament passed a second Reform Act that allowed all male householders to vote. This act enfranchised (gave the vote to) the remainder of the middle class and much of the working class as well.

The extension of the franchise and many other reforms took place under Queen Victoria, who reigned from 1837 to 1901. By the late 1800s, the British monarch had largely become a figurehead. Power lay in the hands of Parliament and the prime minister. During Victoria's reign, two remarkable prime ministers—William Gladstone and Benjamin Disraeli (diz-RAY-lee)—helped guide many of the reforms that allowed British government to change through mostly peaceful evolution rather than violent revolution.

Peaceful Transitions to Self-Rule

In the early 1800s, the British ruled an empire that sprawled across the globe. Close to home, the British ruled Ireland. In Asia, they controlled most of the Indian subcontinent. In the South Pacific, they ruled Australia and the neighboring island of New Zealand. Although the British had lost the North American colonies that became the United States, they remained in possession of the country to the north, Canada.

Canada was a divided colony. Until the 1760s, when it was conquered by Britain, a large region in Canada—today, the province of Quebec—had been ruled by France. Under British rule, the people of this region clung to their French language

Slowly Extending the Franchise

In Britain in the 1860s, while Chartist reformers called for universal male suffrage, not even the most radical Chartists thought women should be allowed to vote. When Parliament passed the Reform Act of 1867, many more men gained the right to vote. Not until 1918, however, did all British men receive the right to vote. In the same year, women over thirty got the right to vote—two years ahead of women in the United States.

and culture. In 1837, rebellions broke out in both the English-speaking and the French-speaking parts of Canada, with the rebels demanding a greater say in government.

Fearful of an American-style revolution, the British government sent a representative, Lord Durham, to Canada. He reported that the main problem there was "two nations [French and English] warring in the bosom of a single state." His solution was to merge the two parts of Canada into one colony, to encourage French Canadians to learn English, and to give Canada a greater degree of self-government. In 1867, the British government gave the colony dominion status, in which Canada became largely self-governing, with its elected assembly handling

Victorian England

In 1837, eighteen-year-old Victoria became queen of England. She was strong-willed and determined to make her mark. Victoria ruled for more than sixty years and greatly influenced the values and culture of her day.

The time of her reign (1837–1901) is known as Victorian England. As queen, Victoria emphasized duty, hard work, and proper behavior. Her name has become an adjective—Victorian—that sums up the values she emphasized. In popular usage, "Victorian" sometimes implies a certain stiffness and stuffiness.

England's Queen Victoria

The Rights of Indigenous Peoples

British settlers long discriminated against Australia's indigenous people—that is, the original inhabitants—known as Aborigines. Aborigine men became eligible to vote in the 1850s, along with most other Australians. But the Aborigines, living in poor and segregated communities, seldom knew their rights, so very few voted.

The indigenous people of New Zealand, the Maoris (MOW-ur-eez), also suffered from the racist attitudes of British colonists. But they won a greater say in government than Australia's Aborigines. A law passed in 1867 reserved a number of seats in the New Zealand legislature for Maori lawmakers.

In politics, *domestic* affairs are those relating to one's own country.

domestic matters, while the British government retained some control of international affairs. (In 1931, the British Parliament recognized Canada as an independent nation.)

A similar movement toward self-rule took place in Australia and New Zealand. Australia had begun as a penal colony—a harsh land where Britain exiled many of its criminals instead of putting them in jail. Later, it also attracted free settlers who came to seek their fortunes mining gold or raising sheep. In the 1850s, most of the regions of Australia won the right to manage their own affairs through elected councils. In voting, Australians used a new system called the "secret ballot,"

under which people cast ballots without anyone finding out who they voted for. This system, now used in most democratic countries, is sometimes called the "Australian ballot."

At first, Australia, like Britain, restricted voting to the well-off. Progress toward democracy was more rapid in neighboring New Zealand. There, the Constitution Act of 1852 gave the vote to all adult males who owned even a small amount of property. In 1893, New Zealand became the first country in the world to give women the right to vote—thus granting full political rights to women nationwide, well ahead of Britain or the United States.

Difficult Transitions in Ireland

Since the Middle Ages, England had dominated its neighboring island, Ireland. In the 1600s and 1700s, the English ruled most of the island as a colony. In 1801, Ireland became part of the United Kingdom, along with England and Scotland.

Most Irish people, however, did not think of themselves as British. A minority—the descendants of Protestant English settlers—owned much of Ireland's best land and discriminated against the Catholic majority. Many Irish, especially in the south where most people were Catholic, hated their British landlords and rulers, who had passed laws restricting the rights of Catholics. It was not until 1829, after a campaign led by a Catholic lawyer named Daniel O'Connell, that Catholics received the right to sit in Parliament.

Ireland remained a mostly agricultural country where poor farmers worked small plots of land. Their staple crop was the potato—nutritious and

English, British, Irish

People often use the terms "English" and "British" as if they mean the same thing. But two major countries—England and Scotland—share the island of Great Britain. In the Middle Ages, they were often enemies. In 1707, the two countries merged into the United Kingdom of Great Britain. In 1801, the United Kingdom expanded to include the neighboring island of Ireland. But the majority of Irishmen never thought of themselves as British.

Population in Ireland, 1800–1900

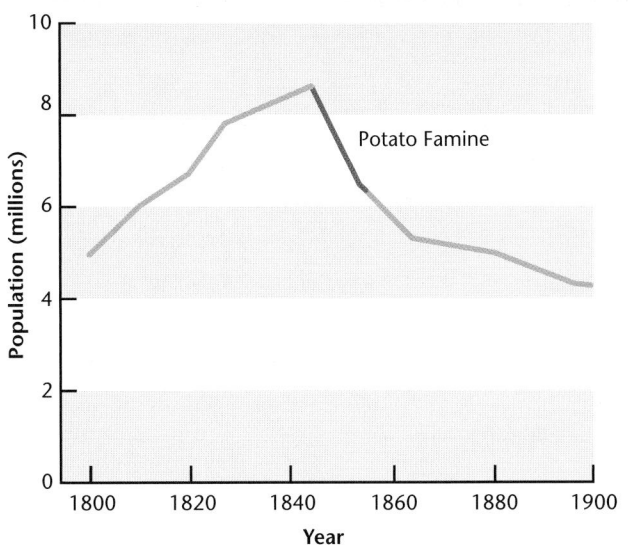

the United States generally managed to avoid the upheavals that shook much of Europe in the early 1800s. As you have learned, the United States Constitution, ratified in 1789, spelled out many details of the new nation's government. But serious questions remained about the balance of power between states and the central government, and about the economic, political, and moral dimensions of slavery. As the country expanded during the early 1800s, these issues brought the United States to a point of crisis.

Westward Expansion

The treaty ending the American Revolution in 1783 granted the United States all of North America east of the Mississippi River, roughly from the Great Lakes to Spanish Florida. In 1803, when Napoleon needed money to fund his wars against Great Britain, President Thomas Jefferson bought an enormous portion of North American territory from France. The Louisiana Purchase stretched west to the Rocky Mountains and doubled the size of the nation. Pioneers spilled into the new lands, forging new farms and towns, and often clashing with the Native American peoples who inhabited the lands the pioneers settled. But Americans wanted still more territory.

easy to grow. Along with milk, potatoes made up nearly the entire diet of the poorest Irishmen. In 1845, disaster struck when a plant disease wiped out the potato crop. Over the next four years, as many as a million Irish people starved to death in what became known as the Potato Famine. At least another million emigrated in search of new lives. The majority of these people went to the United States.

During the famine, Protestant landowners continued to export wheat, beef, and other food from Ireland, rather than using it to feed the people at home. Many Irishmen bitterly blamed both the landowners and the British government for the extent of the famine. In the 1860s, a group of Irish nationalists called the Fenians led an unsuccessful revolt against British rule. Ireland would remain a restless and turbulent part of the United Kingdom until 1921, when most of the island became independent. The northeastern counties, with a Protestant majority, remained part of the United Kingdom.

Expansion, War, and Resolution in the United States

After launching its own successful revolution to gain independence from Britain in the late 1700s,

Seeking land and opportunity, pioneers settled the American West throughout much of the nineteenth century.

In the South, cotton had become the major cash crop. But "King Cotton," as it was called, depleted the land and made the soil less productive. Many planters sought new land farther west. In the 1820s, thousands of Americans moved into the part of Mexico known as Texas. They soon outnumbered native Mexicans.

Many Americans who settled in Texas brought enslaved workers with them. When Mexico abolished slavery in 1829, these slaveholding Texan colonists were angry. Tensions escalated and violence erupted between the Americans in Texas and the Mexican army. In 1836, Americans in Texas declared their independence from Mexico and formed the Republic of Texas.

Many American settlers and politicians were eager to make Texas part of the United States. In 1845, despite opposition in the northern states, where many people did not want another slaveholding state, the United States annexed Texas and admitted it as a state.

Mexico did not recognize Texas's claim of independence or its annexation by the United States. Tensions between the two countries remained high. The next year, a skirmish between Mexican and American military forces along the disputed border resulted in war.

Most Americans saw the Mexican-American War as a contest for control of the continent. They believed in what one newspaper editor called "Manifest Destiny"—that it was the nation's God-given right and calling to settle all of continental North America.

When the Mexican-American War ended, the United States owned all the land from Texas to California. As white settlers moved into these new lands, Native Americans were pushed farther west, and many suffered deprivation, indignity, or loss of life.

A Nation Divided

After the Mexican-American War, many Americans thrilled with nationalistic pride that the nation now stretched from the Atlantic to the Pacific—in the words of the familiar song, "from sea to shining sea." While the United States had quickly become the largest republic in history, serious issues divided it.

New ways of producing goods had transformed northern cities into busy industrial centers. Smokestacks loomed and railroad tracks crisscrossed the landscape. Immigrants seeking factory work flooded into cities. By 1860, New York had over a million people.

The biggest city in America's South was New Orleans, with fewer than a hundred seventy thousand people. Tobacco and cotton plantations, rather than factories, dominated the South's economy and society. Southerners relied on slave laborers as they had since colonial times.

Great Britain and many Latin American nations had outlawed slavery by the 1830s, but in the American South, nearly four million African American people were enslaved in 1860. Northern abolitionists called for an end to the immoral practice, but exports of slave-produced cotton to British factories brought more money into the United States than all other exports combined.

As the United States expanded, decisions had to be made about whether slavery would be

Opposing the Mexican-American War

Not all Americans supported the Mexican-American War. Abolitionists—those who worked to end slavery—saw the war as an attempt to spread slavery. A young congressman named Abraham Lincoln charged that President James K. Polk had made false claims in asking for a declaration of war. In Massachusetts, the writer Henry David Thoreau refused to pay taxes that he believed would help fund an immoral war. Thoreau explained his actions in an essay known as "Civil Disobedience," which has proven a lasting inspiration for leaders of modern-day civil rights and antiwar movements.

An ironworks factory in New York, part of the northern economy that relied on industry and manufacturing

allowed in new territories. Many Northern politicians, including Abraham Lincoln of Illinois, maintained that the federal government should outlaw slavery's expansion. Southern politicians argued that each state had the right to decide on its own.

A series of compromises between 1820 and 1854 postponed conflict between the two sides. But in 1860, when Lincoln was elected president without the support of a single southern state, South Carolina seceded (formally withdrew) from the United States. Other southern states followed, and together they formed the Confederate States of America.

Civil War Tests the Nation

Lincoln believed secession was unconstitutional. He dedicated himself to preserving the Union—to keeping the United States united, as one nation. When Confederate troops fired on Fort Sumter, a federal post in Charleston, South Carolina, civil war began. On one side was the Confederacy, the southern slaveholding states. On the other side was the Union, the mostly northern states that opposed secession.

Both sides expected a short war. They formed armies, each confident they would win. The North had more than five times the number of

factories as the South. It had far more money and people, and most of the nation's railroads. Much of the grain and beef produced in the United States came from western states in the Union.

The South had its own reasons for confidence. To impose its will, the North would have to invade the South. Confederate soldiers would be fighting on familiar ground and defending their homes. The South had many of the nation's finest generals, including Robert E. Lee, a brilliant commander who took charge of Confederate forces.

The first real battle of the war, near Manassas Junction in Virginia, drove home a shocking truth—the war would not be quick or easy. Nearly five thousand men were killed or wounded. Union spectators, picnicking as they watched the battle, fled from the carnage along with panicked federal troops. For four years, the North and the South would continue the terrible struggle.

In the South, agriculture and slave labor dominated the economy.

A Nation Divided: The American Civil War

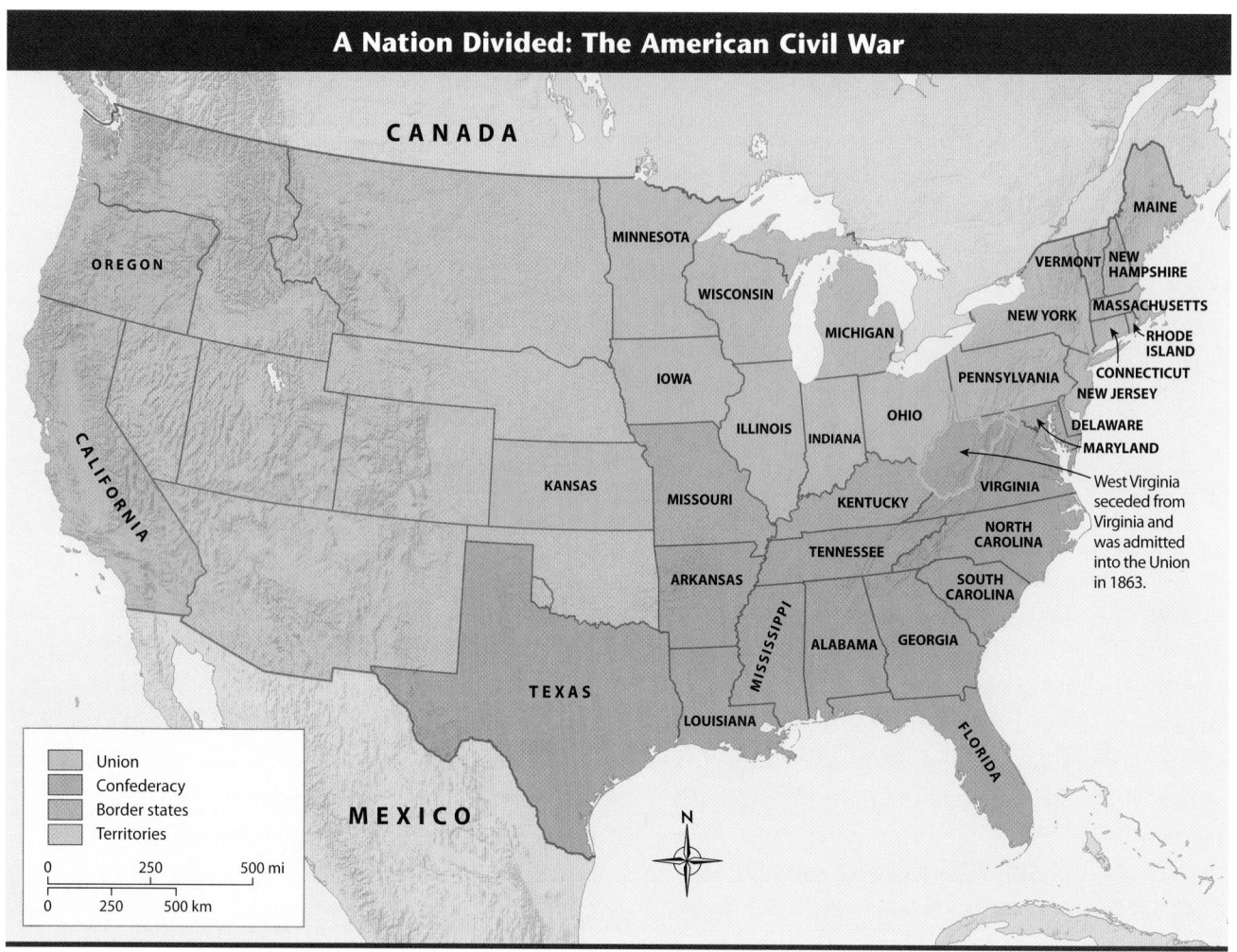

Disputes over slavery, sovereignty, and the western territories of the United States erupted in a deadly civil war.

Lincoln had begun the war determined to save the United States. He never wavered. But the South won battle after bloody battle. After two years, European nations, including Great Britain, began to consider taking sides. Some Northerners wondered if maintaining the Union was worth the human and financial cost.

From Emancipation to Appomattox

In January 1863, Lincoln signed the Emancipation Proclamation, stating that slaves in the rebellious states were free. The president was in effect declaring that the war was not only about keeping the United States together, but was also about ending slavery.

The effect of the Emancipation Proclamation was enormous. Great Britain now hesitated to aid the South. Despite its need for cotton, Britain did not want to be seen as siding with states that were fighting to preserve slavery. In the North, the war gained a moral justification that inspired federal troops and civilians. Thousands of slaves left their plantations to seek freedom in the North.

In the summer of 1863, two battles turned the tide for the Union. In Confederate Mississippi, the city of Vicksburg fell to Union forces after a long, devastating siege. In the east, Confederate General Robert E. Lee took a daring gamble and invaded enemy territory. A fierce battle raged for three days near the town of Gettysburg in Pennsylvania. Both sides suffered staggering losses—in all, some fifty thousand men were killed or wounded. But it was Lee who was forced to retreat.

The Civil War was the deadliest conflict in U.S. history. This photograph shows Confederate dead at Gettysburg.

President Lincoln visited the site of the battle four months later. He delivered a brief speech, just two minutes long. Few in the crowd recognized the significance of what they heard, but when newspapers printed the Gettysburg Address, the public realized that the president had expressed something of immense importance. He had explained the war and set forth a vision of the meaning of the United States as a country held together not by language or culture, but by a powerful idea—"the proposition that all men are created equal." Lincoln concluded,

> *...we here highly resolve that these dead shall not have died in vain, that this nation under God shall have a new birth of freedom, and that government of the people, by the people, for the people shall not perish from the earth.*

The war was not over, but slowly, Union forces under General Ulysses S. Grant pushed the Confederate armies back. The war ended with Lee's surrender to Grant at Appomattox Courthouse, Virginia, in April 1865.

A Modern, Deadly War

The American Civil War is often considered the world's first modern war. Trains moved armies to and from battlefields. New technologies had produced more deadly weapons than ever before. Cities and farms were destroyed as whole populations were pitted against each other. More than six hundred thousand people died from wounds or disease. Countless thousands were left disabled. At the war's end, much of the South lay in ruins.

While the Civil War was (and remains) the deadliest conflict in the history of the United States, the Union survived, and the country still possessed vast land and resources. The war also settled the issue of slavery. The 13th Amendment to the U.S. Constitution outlawed slavery throughout the United States. The 14th Amendment guaranteed citizenship for former slaves and "equal protection of the laws." The world's largest republic had endured a trial by fire and was ready to move forward to face new challenges.

The End of Serfdom and the End of Slavery

Tsar Alexander II freed the serfs of Russia in 1861, the year Abraham Lincoln became president of the United States and the American Civil War began. In 1863, Lincoln issued the Emancipation Proclamation, freeing the slaves held in the Confederate states. America's remaining slaves were emancipated at the end of the Civil War.

In Russia, former serfs remained tied to the land by the bonds of debt. Similarly, in the United States, many former slaves became impoverished sharecroppers, forced by poverty to work the lands of wealthy white farmers. Also, many southern states passed "Black Codes"—laws that restricted the freedoms of former slaves.

In both Russia and the United States, it would take many decades of struggle for emancipated people to make progress toward social and economic equality.

Steam locomotives revolutionized land transportation in the 1800s.

1775
James Watt perfects
his steam engine.

1793
Eli Whitney invents
the cotton gin.

1830
The Liverpool-
Manchester Railroad is
the first in the world to
link two cities.

1870
Steel, petroleum, and
electricity spur a second
wave of industrial growth.

1750

1800

c. 1760
Innovations in England's
textile industry mark
the beginnings of the
Industrial Revolution.

1908
The Ford Motor
Company introduces
the first mass-produced
automobile, the Model T.

1850

1807
Robert Fulton's steamboat
makes a successful voyage,
leading to commercial
steamboat service.

1900

1876
Alexander Graham Bell
invents the telephone.

CHAPTER 25

THE INDUSTRIAL REVOLUTION

1750–1900

*B*etween 1750 and the beginning of the twentieth century, Western societies went through an enormous transformation known as the Industrial Revolution. Beginning in England, machine production in factories replaced the making of goods by hand. As the Industrial Revolution progressed across and beyond Europe, it radically altered traditional patterns of life. In search of work, millions of people migrated from the countryside to the cities, where populations exploded.

The Industrial Revolution was accompanied by startling advances in transportation and communication. Railroads, the telegraph, and the telephone connected countries and continents as never before. Thanks to the efficiency of factory production, goods once thought to be luxuries became widely available. Rising prosperity dramatically expanded the middle class, and some businessmen made staggering fortunes.

But the benefits of these changes were not equally enjoyed by all. While the Industrial Revolution brought great progress, it also introduced many new problems and challenges.

The Industrial Revolution Begins in England

Key Questions

- Why did the Industrial Revolution begin in Great Britain?

- How did new technologies change the production of textiles in England?

- How did the factory system begin, and what were its social consequences?

Europe was still mostly a land of farmers in the year 1750. Wealth in European agricultural society was based on ownership of land. Most people lived in rural areas and worked the land, just as their ancestors had for thousands of years. Few traveled far from where they were born. At least three-quarters of Europe's population lived on farms or in small villages of two to three hundred people.

In 1750, life expectancy—the average number of years that people lived—was only about forty years. This was not because most people died at the age of forty, but because so many people died of disease in childhood or early adulthood. One of every three children died before their fourth birthday. Only half the population made it to the age of twenty-one.

Few people in 1750 owned their own land. Most rented fields from large landowners. If they owned animals, they grazed them on the village commons (an area set aside for public use). In the winter, farmers often worked in workshops or mines.

Although Europeans didn't know it, their deeply traditional way of life was about to undergo a radical change. We know this change as the Industrial Revolution.

The Gleaners by Jean-François Millet depicts the task of collecting stray grains after harvest.

The textile industry in England spurred the Industrial Revolution.

579

England's Advantages

The Industrial Revolution began in England. In the mid-1700s, Britain enjoyed natural and human advantages that set the stage for great changes to come.

Located on an island, England was spared the destruction that a series of wars had brought to the European continent. Since the late 1600s, the country had enjoyed a stable government. England also had a strong and prosperous banking system. Bankers were willing to lend money for investment in farming or manufacturing.

Britain's rulers placed few restrictions on private enterprise. They

Early factories were built near rivers, which provided water power.

tended to agree with the philosopher Adam Smith, who wrote that a nation prospers when it allows private individuals, rather than the government, to make most economic decisions.

The British had acquired an overseas empire largely by encouraging individuals to form joint-stock companies, such as the Virginia Company and the British East India Company. Though not every company succeeded, investors in the successful companies earned profits, and they used this capital to invest in new businesses.

England controlled far more overseas trade than any other European country. Its powerful navy protected its merchants at sea. Its mercantilist policies required English colonies to sell their raw materials exclusively to the mother country. In return, the colonies provided ready markets for Britain's manufactured goods. All these factors increased Britain's prosperity, while encouraging risk taking and innovation among its people.

Britain's Natural Resources

England also enjoyed the advantage of abundant natural resources. The country's numerous rivers provided the water power necessary to run mills and factories. The rivers also provided a way to

move goods across the country and down to ocean harbors for shipment overseas.

England possessed rich deposits of iron and coal. Iron was essential to the making of most tools and machines. Coal was used in many manufacturing processes, including the smelting of iron (extracting the metal from its ore). In the second half of the 1700s, new inventions improved the technologies for coal mining and ironworking. Coal output doubled between 1750 and 1800, as did iron production from 1788 to 1806.

Britain's Human Resources

In the late 1700s, England's population grew dramatically—from about 5.8 million in 1750 to around 8.0 million in 1790. This growth was largely caused by improvements in agriculture. English farmers came up with significant innovations to make farming more efficient and profitable. They doubled the size of their sheep through selective breeding. They began growing turnips, which could be used year-round as food for cattle, ensuring a constant supply of milk and butter. These and other changes led to a healthier and better-fed population.

Improvements in agriculture created a need for larger fields. Wealthy landowners demanded that the commons—the public lands—be *enclosed*, which means that they be converted to private use. Enclosure left many farmers without land on which to graze their animals. Many of these farmers left the country to look for work in the cities. There, they provided a ready labor force for the coming age of industrialization.

An *entrepreneur* is someone who operates a new business and assumes the risks of such a venture. The term comes from an old French word that means "to undertake."

As well as a plentiful labor force, England had entrepreneurs willing to invest in new businesses and inventors eager to develop new technologies. Since the late seventeenth century, with the founding of the Royal Society, a scientific organization that brought together some of the most innovative minds in England, British thinkers had actively embraced the Scientific Revolution. The English always seemed to be looking for ways to understand how things worked and how to make them work better. By figuring out how to use power-driven machines in place of human muscle, British inventors helped set off the Industrial Revolution.

A Revolution in the Textile Industry

The Industrial Revolution began in England's textile (cloth) industry. For centuries, weavers had made cloth by using a loom. A loom is a machine that weaves threads together. Looms were equipped with a wooden shuttle, a device used to carry a thread between other threads on the loom. The weaver would throw the shuttle back and forth. The work was slow and laborious, and a single weaver could only make material as wide as his outstretched arms.

In the 1730s, however, a weaver named John Kay came up with a way to speed up the process. He mounted a shuttle on wheels in a track so that a weaver could shoot the shuttle from side to side by pulling a cord. This "flying shuttle" made it possible for weavers to make wider cloth, and to make it much faster.

But Kay's invention also created a problem. Looms could now make cloth so fast that spinners—those who made thread—could not keep up with the demand for thread. They continued to twist fibers together on spinning wheels that made just one strand at a time. In the 1760s, a weaver named James Hargreaves solved the problem by inventing a machine called the spinning jenny. The spinning jenny could produce sixteen strands of thread at once.

Together, the flying shuttle and the spinning jenny made it possible to make fabric much faster and cheaper. These inventions shifted the textile industry from handmade to machine made.

As fast as flying shuttles and spinning jennies were, they required human muscle to power them, which meant they were limited by the strength of the people operating them. Then, in the 1760s, a barber named Richard Arkwright built a machine called a water frame, which used a flowing river as

Arkwright's water frame used the power of a flowing river to spin cotton into thread and wrap it around spools.

James Watt's steam engines pumped water out of mines and performed other work previously done by humans and animals. Steam power helped advance the early Industrial Revolution.

a source of power. Waterpower made it possible to spin as many as eighty strands of thread at once.

Another amateur inventor, a clergyman named Edmund Cartwright, devised a mechanical loom that could be powered by either a horse or a water-wheel. One person operating this power loom could produce as much fabric as fifteen old-style weavers working at traditional looms.

Steam Power

The most influential innovation of the textile industry was made by a Scottish inventor named James Watt. While he was a student at the University of Glasgow, Watt was asked to repair a steam engine used to power pumps that cleared water out of coal mines. The crude and inefficient steam engines kept breaking down.

As Watt worked on the broken engine, he became fascinated by the possibilities of steam as a source of power. In the 1770s, he formed a partnership with a businessman, Matthew Boulton, who ran a factory near Birmingham, England. A new steam engine, designed by Watt and produced by Boulton, was quickly adopted by mine owners because it pumped water much more quickly and efficiently than the old model.

By the end of the 1780s, Watt was building steam engines that could power the gears, belts, and pulleys in looms and spinning jennies, as well as in other machines. These steam engines revolutionized industry. Now machines could churn out fabric, thread, pins, ammunition, and much more, and at rates far faster than human muscle, or even waterpower, had ever allowed. As Boulton once told a visitor to Watt's engine factory, "I sell here, Sir, what all the world desires to have—POWER."

The Factory System Emerges

Before the Industrial Revolution, most manufacturing was done at home. A weaver, for example, would set up his loom in his own small cottage. But as the Industrial Revolution advanced, manufacturing fell under the control of businessmen who could afford to buy many machines and keep them supplied with power. Production moved from the home to the factory.

Primary Source

Adam Smith on the Division of Labor

Even early in the Industrial Revolution, the ideas of the Scottish economist Adam Smith greatly influenced businessmen and manufacturers. In *The Wealth of Nations*, published in 1776, Smith argued that the nations that produced the most goods in the greatest demand could trade their way to great wealth.

The division of labor was central to Smith's economic thinking. He understood that products could be produced more quickly and efficiently when the required labor was broken down into many tasks performed by many people. He illustrated his point by describing the manufacture of a simple object, the pin.

The greatest improvement in the productive powers of labor, and the greater part of the skill, dexterity, and judgment with which it is anywhere directed, or applied, seem to have been the effects of the division of labor.

To take an example…the trade of the pin-maker; a workman not educated to this… could scarce…make one pin in a day, and certainly could not make twenty. But in the way in which this business is now carried on, not only the whole work is a peculiar trade, but it is divided into a number of branches, of which the greater part are likewise peculiar trades.

One man draws out the wire, another straights it, a third cuts it, a fourth points it, a fifth grinds it at the top for receiving the head; …and the important business of making a pin is, in this manner, divided into about eighteen distinct operations, which, in some manufactories, are all performed by distinct hands, though in others the same man will sometimes perform two or three of them.

I have seen a small manufactory of this kind where ten men only were employed, and where some of them consequently performed two or three distinct operations…. They could, when they exerted themselves, make among them about twelve pounds of pins in a day. There are in a pound upwards of four thousand pins of a middling size. Those ten persons, therefore, could make among them upwards of forty-eight thousand pins in a day.

Eli Whitney's Cotton Gin

Before the American Civil War, American farmers faced increased demand for cotton fiber, especially from England's textile manufacturers, whose new machines enabled them to make fabric quickly and cheaply. But cotton growers faced a problem—the seeds must be removed from cotton fiber before it can be made into cloth. Picking out the seeds by hand was a slow process. In 1793, Eli Whitney, a young teacher from Massachusetts, invented a device called the cotton gin (*gin* is short for "engine"). Wire hooks mounted on a rotating drum pulled the fibers through a screen with slots big enough to accept the cotton fibers but too small for seeds to get through. With the cotton gin, cotton production soared in the United States, but so did the demand for slave labor to harvest the cotton. Thus it was that an invention changed society—the cotton gin made southern farmers more committed to growing cotton, and more dependent on slave labor.

Factories were large buildings where many workers operated machines, working together under tight supervision by the factory owner. The first industrial factories were textile mills located next to rivers and driven by waterpower. In mills like these, a single waterwheel could drive a hundred looms or other machines.

Around 1800, when steam began to replace water as the main source of industrial power, factories no longer had to be built beside running streams. Instead, more factories were built in cities, with their ready supply of workers displaced from the countryside due to the enclosure of the commons.

Factory work was very different from the work people had traditionally done as farmers or craftsmen. In the countryside, people had worked hard, but at their own pace. They lived close to nature, their work regulated by the changing of the seasons, or the transition from day to night. In factories, workers had to follow a rigid schedule. The work was highly repetitive and monotonous. Factory owners, who wanted to produce as much as possible, demanded that employees work during almost all their waking hours.

In 1818, a worker in a Manchester, England, textile factory described conditions in his workplace: "[Workers] are trained to work from six years old, from five in the morning to eight and nine at night.... If [they are] late a few minutes, a quarter of a day is stopped in wages.... The English spinner slave has no enjoyment of the open atmosphere and breezes of heaven. Locked up in factories eight stories high, he has no relaxation till the ponderous engine stops.... They are all alike fatigued and exhausted."

In some factories, like this cotton factory in England, women and children made up most of the workforce.

The Industrial Revolution Spreads

Key Questions

- How did innovations in transportation and communication advance the Industrial Revolution?

- What innovations in materials and production spurred a Second Industrial Revolution in the late nineteenth century?

In the nineteenth century, the Industrial Revolution spread from Britain to other nations of Europe and to North America. By the end of the 1800s, Germany and the United States rivaled Great Britain as industrial powers. Beginning in about 1870, new materials and methods of production led to what is sometimes called the Second Industrial Revolution, with extraordinary new inventions that would become even more important in the twentieth century, including electric lighting, the telephone, and the automobile.

Industry Spreads to New Places

The British, who had taken the lead in the Industrial Revolution, tried to maintain their early advantage over competing nations. The British government passed laws that made it illegal for textile workers to share their technical knowledge, or even to leave the country. But in 1789, a young English textile worker named Samuel Slater disguised himself and boarded a ship bound for the United States. He had carefully memorized everything he needed to know to start his own textile factory.

Slater built America's first water-powered textile mill in Pawtucket, Rhode Island. Within a few years he owned mills throughout New England. Other American businessmen copied Slater's way of running his factories, in which each task was broken down into a few simple, easily repeated steps. Slater is sometimes referred to as the "Father of the American Factory System." Other factories that made iron, guns, tools, and other goods sprang up in the United States.

The industrialization of the United States was spurred in part by the War of 1812. With Britain again at war with the United States, Americans found themselves cut off from access to British products and responded by boosting their own manufacturing. Between 1812 and 1830, production of iron in America tripled. With access to vast resources and a strong tradition of enterprise, the United States would prove to be Britain's most successful industrial competitor. By 1894, the United States ranked first in the world as a manufacturing nation, producing twice as many goods as Britain.

Other European nations weren't far behind. With the end of the Napoleonic Wars in 1815, the rest of Europe strove to catch up with the British. France and Germany made major efforts to industrialize. Like Britain, Germany had rich deposits of the coal essential to the manufacturing of iron. By the 1880s, Germany had surpassed England in coal production.

Japan Industrializes

Throughout the 1800s, the Industrial Revolution was centered in Europe and North America. Among Asian nations, only Japan successfully industrialized in the nineteenth century. In the 1860s, Japan emerged from a long period of isolation determined to catch up to the West in economics and technology. As a result, Japan entered the twentieth century as the most powerful nation in Asia.

A Revolution in Transportation and Communication

When the Industrial Revolution began in Great Britain, its first big success was in the textile industry. Inventions such as the flying shuttle, spinning jenny, and steam engine helped speed up production. But the Industrial Revolution would not have brought such huge changes to the world without a simultaneous revolution in transportation and communication.

Improving Roads

In the late 1700s, most roads in Britain were rough, muddy, and bumpy. But the new industrialists needed a way to move heavy goods quickly over long distances. In 1815, a Scotsman named John McAdam came up with a way of building better roads. He showed that by laying a foundation of crushed rock under a roadbed, the road could be raised a few inches above the surrounding ground. Roads built this way drained well and held up to heavy traffic.

After road builders began to use McAdam's system, merchants could haul heavier loads with fewer horses. Over the course of the following century, road traffic between British cities multiplied more than ten times over. Even today, many roads are made of crushed rock layered with tar—a substance known as "macadam."

Canals Extend Inland Trade

For centuries, merchants had moved heavy cargoes down the rivers of England. But the rivers did not go everywhere. In the 1700s, the increased need to move cargoes would lead to the building of a network of canals.

Francis Egerton, the Duke of Bridgewater, ordered the construction of the first important canal in Britain. The owner of a number of coal mines, Egerton needed a way to transport his coal to factories in manufacturing towns. He spent much of his fortune cutting a waterway from his estates to the city of Manchester. The Bridgewater Canal opened in 1761. By charging tolls on the boats that passed through it, the duke became one of the richest nobles in England. The Bridgewater Canal inspired a boom in canal building, with Parliament encouraging and authorizing the construction of canals by private companies.

Across the Atlantic, Americans were digging canals as well. In 1825, workers in New York completed the Erie Canal, which connected the Atlantic Coast to areas hundreds of miles inland. The Erie Canal, which extended for 363 miles (584 km), was the longest canal in the Western world at the time.

Steamboats and Steamships

In the late 1700s, inventors in both England and America sought to improve water travel by using the power of steam. Early experiments with steamboats, however, proved unsuccessful. On one early steamboat, the heavy engine broke through the deck, sinking the vessel. Another inventor's steamboat had an engine so powerful it shook the boat to pieces.

In 1807, Robert Fulton, an American inventor and businessman, successfully launched a 133-foot (41 m) steam-powered paddleboat on the waters of the Hudson River. Fulton soon had a regular steamboat service going between Albany and New

Robert Fulton's steam-powered *Clermont* carried passengers between Albany and New York City.

York City. Within a few years, steamboats were carrying passengers and cargo down the Mississippi River and across the Great Lakes.

It took longer to develop successful ocean-going steamships. Steamships had to burn wood or coal. On rivers, they could pick up fuel along the way, while an oceangoing ship would have to start out with all the fuel it needed for the long trip. Carrying so much coal or wood left little room for cargo or passengers. Gradually, however, inventors designed more powerful steam engines, propellers replaced paddle wheels, and shipbuilders began to build ships out of iron instead of wood. By 1860, a British company was offering regular steamship service across the Atlantic.

Laying Tracks: Railroads

While steamboats and steamships were changing travel by water, other inventors looked for ways to speed travel by land. One such inventor was George Stephenson, an Englishman. The son of a coal miner, Stephenson rose to be the head engineer of a mining operation. In the early 1800s, mines hauled their coal in carts on tramways. On a tramway, a horse pulled a wheeled cart on two parallel wooden tracks. Stephenson aimed to design a tramway with wagons driven by steam rather than horsepower.

Beginning in 1814, Stephenson designed several *locomotives*, steam-powered vehicles designed to pull the coal wagons behind them. Other inventors came up with their own versions of this new machine. Meanwhile, a number of English companies built tramways to move passengers and freight between English cities. These tramways became the first railroads.

Smoke billows from a steam locomotive on the railroad line between London and Bristol, England, c. 1840.

In 1829, the Liverpool and Manchester Railway decided to use locomotives instead of horses. To choose which locomotive to use, the company held a competition in the form of a race. Stephenson's machine, the *Rocket*, easily won the race, reaching a then-unheard-of speed of twenty-four miles (39 km) an hour. Afterward, railroad companies fought to hire Stephenson as their chief engineer. By the time of his death in 1848, he was known around the world as the "Father of the Railroad."

The railroad revolutionized ground transportation. Canals and roads could not compete with the railroad's ability to move goods swiftly. By 1855, more than eight thousand miles (nearly 13,000 km) of railroad track stretched across Britain, and trains were carrying more freight than passengers.

On the other side of the Atlantic, Americans were also building railroads. By the 1840s, railways connected the major cities of the East Coast and the Mississippi River valley. In 1869, the transcontinental railroad was completed, for the first time linking by rail the Atlantic and Pacific coasts of the United States.

Instant Messages: The Telegraph

The revolution in transportation was soon followed by a revolution in communication. In the 1840s, an American inventor, Samuel Morse, came up with a device called the *telegraph* (a word

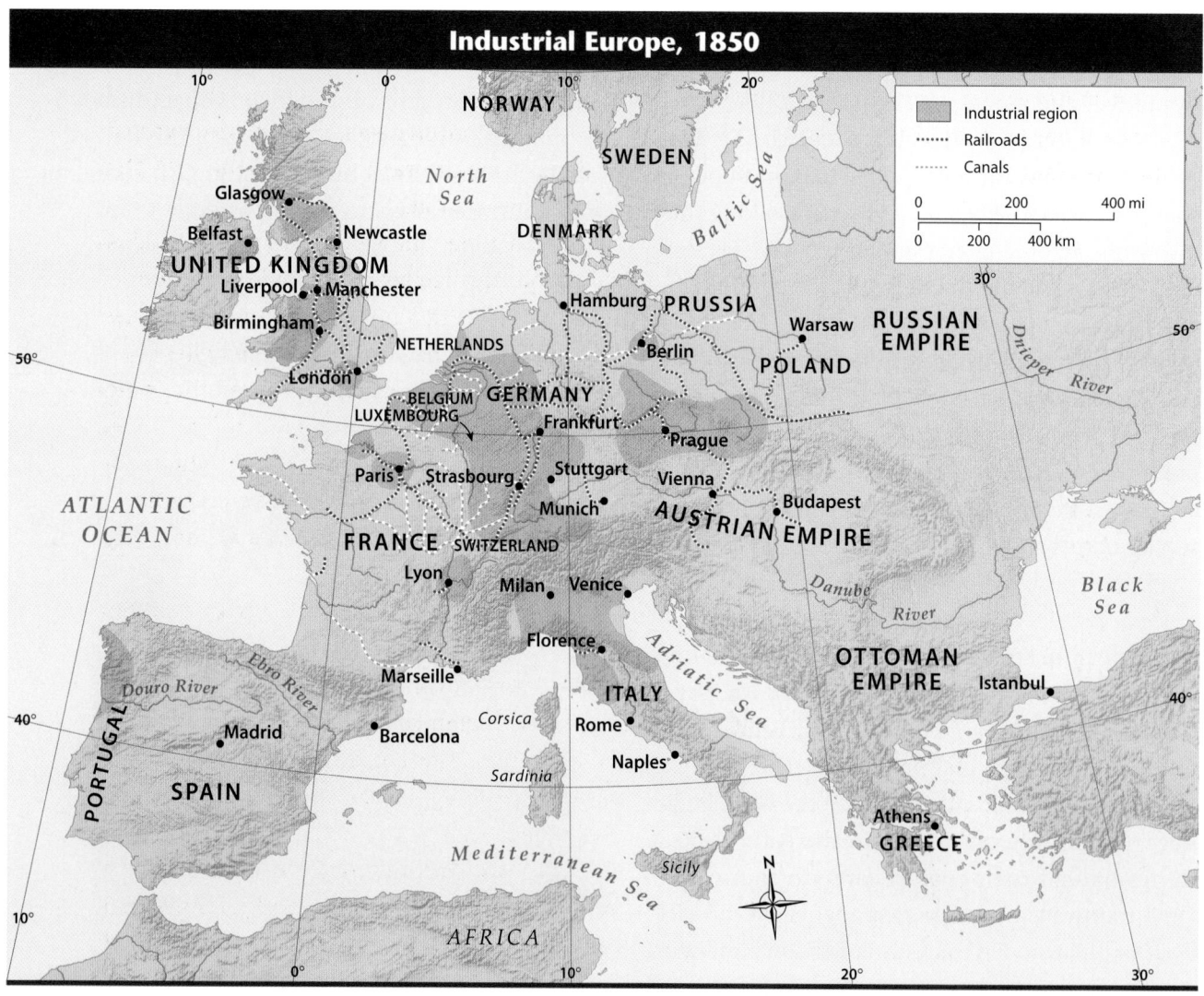

Industrial Europe, 1850

By 1850, the Industrial Revolution, which began in England, had spread to many parts of northern Europe.

derived from the ancient Greek words for "distant writing"). By pressing a key, a telegraph operator sent electrical impulses through a wire connected to another telegraph far away. Each combination of short and long clicks on the key stood for a letter of the alphabet. The person receiving a message in this "Morse code" could then assemble the letters into words.

The telegraph made it possible to send messages almost instantly over long distances. Business owners and government officials used the telegraph to send important information. Newspaper reporters sent news from one end of the country to the other. Families used the telegraph to stay in touch.

By the middle of the 1850s, twenty-three thousand miles (about 37,000 km) of telegraph wire had been strung across the United States. In 1866, a steamship succeeded in laying a telegraph cable across the bottom of the Atlantic, linking America and Europe.

A Second Industrial Revolution

By the late 1800s, the remarkable inventions of the Industrial Revolution—steamboats, railroads, the telegraph—had become part of everyday life. Scientists and engineers kept experimenting with

Bessemer's furnace made it possible for large quantities of steel to be produced faster and more cheaply.

ways to make industry even more productive and efficient. A major breakthrough came with the shift from iron to steel.

The machines and vehicles of the first Industrial Revolution had been built of iron. But iron—which is rigid, difficult to shape, and sometimes cracks—was not an ideal material for these purposes. So inventors began to look to another material—steel. Although mostly made of iron, steel is stronger, lighter, and more flexible. The art of steelmaking had been known since ancient times, but steel had always been hard to make and very expensive.

In 1856, an Englishman named Henry Bessemer invented a furnace that could cheaply turn iron into steel. Bessemer's furnace made it possible to produce steel in large quantities. The strength and flexibility of steel made it perfect for building railroads and bridges or constructing complicated machinery.

At first, England and Germany dominated the production of steel. But in the 1860s, an American businessman named Andrew Carnegie decided that steel was the industrial material of the future. He invested everything he had in the business. By

Completed in 1890, the Forth Bridge, a railway bridge in Scotland, was the first bridge in Britain to be built of steel.

1900, his company, Carnegie Steel, was outproducing all of the steel mills in Britain. Carnegie's steelworks helped the United States become the world's leading industrial power.

New Sources of Energy: Electricity and Petroleum

As steel replaced iron, industrialists also began looking for new sources of energy to run the increasing numbers of factories and machines, as well as to provide heat for homes in the growing cities. One possible source was petroleum, a liquid organic compound found underground. Petroleum could be turned into flammable liquids such as gasoline and kerosene, which could be transported more easily than solid fuels like coal. In the late 1800s, kerosene lamps became a popular source of lighting.

At first, there seemed to be little practical use for gasoline, a substance with a dangerous tendency to explode. But with the invention of the automobile at the end of the nineteenth century, gasoline became an important fuel.

In the late nineteenth century, electricity sparked the most widespread interest as a source of energy. Samuel Morse's telegraph used electricity to send messages across continents and under oceans. Soon, inventors would find even more dramatic uses for electricity.

Inventions with Electricity

In the early 1870s, an American inventor, Alexander Graham Bell, formed a partnership with a patent attorney, a specialist in the legal protection of inventions. The lawyer believed that the two could make a fortune if Bell invented an improvement to the telegraph. So Bell set to work on an ambitious project—the use of electricity to transmit the human voice itself over long distances.

The device he came up with, the telephone (from the Greek words for "distant voice"), was first successfully used in 1876. The first words spoken on the instrument were "Mr. Watson,

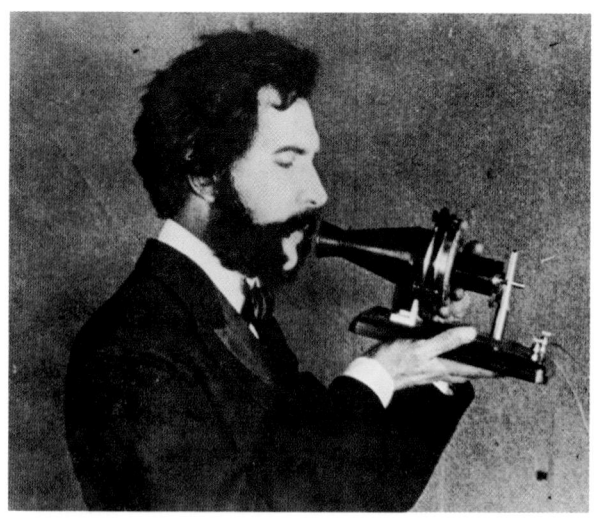

Alexander Graham Bell demonstrates his invention, the telephone, at the Philadelphia Centennial Exposition in 1876.

come here—I want you!" Bell said them to his assistant after he accidentally spilled battery acid on his clothes.

Bell presented his invention to an astonished public at the Philadelphia Centennial Exposition, a celebration of America's one-hundredth birthday. The next year, he and his partner started the Bell Telephone Company. Bell's company and others like it began stringing lines and installing telephones in offices and homes. By 1891, a phone line ran between London and Paris. The next year, phone service began between New York City and Chicago. By the beginning of the twentieth century, Bell's company had over a half million phones in operation.

Bell possessed one of the most inventive minds of his day. He worked on methods to record sounds, detect icebergs using echoes, and make fresh water from vapor in the air.

The most inspired and productive American inventor of the time, however, was not Bell but Thomas Edison. Completely focused on coming up with new ideas and devices, Edison ran a laboratory he called his "invention factory." Among other things, he invented the phonograph (a record player) and an early movie camera. When Edison died at the age of eighty-four, he held a record 1,093 patents.

Thomas Edison once said, "Genius is one percent inspiration and ninety-nine percent perspiration."

places not connected to telegraph wires, such as ships at sea.

Building on Marconi's work, other inventors learned how to send different kinds of sound, including human voices, through the air. By the 1920s, radio broadcasts were bringing news, sports, and music into homes across Europe and America. Today, Marconi is remembered as the "Father of Radio."

The First Automobiles

In 1859, a Belgian mechanic, Étienne Lenoir (luhn-wahr), invented an alternative to the steam engine. Steam engines have a separate part called a boiler, in which burning wood or coal brings water to a boil. Lenoir's engine used coal gas as fuel. The combustion—the burning of the fuel—took place inside the engine itself, not in a separate boiler, so the device was called an internal combustion engine.

In 1885, two German mechanics, Gottlieb Daimler (GAHT-leeb DIYM-lur) and Wilhelm Maybach (MIY-bahk), mounted a small gasoline-burning internal combustion engine on a bicycle, thus creating the first motorcycle. It would have been impossible to make such a device with a steam engine that needed to be fed hundreds of pounds of wood or coal.

Another German, Karl Benz, built a gas-powered three-wheeled vehicle that had a steering wheel and brakes. In response, Maybach and Daimler mounted a more powerful engine on a larger, four-wheeled vehicle. From these efforts, the automobile was born.

The companies founded by Daimler and Benz eventually merged into one company. It manufactured an automobile named after the daughter of a friend of Daimler. Her name was Mercedes. The company still uses the name—Mercedes-Benz.

Edison's most important invention was the first effective lightbulb. Other inventors had experimented with creating light inside a bulb by using electricity. But in 1879, Edison was the first to figure out how to get the filament—the wire inside the bulb—to glow brightly without getting so hot that it burned up. After perfecting the lightbulb, Edison started his own electric company, selling electrical power for people to use in lighting their homes.

In the 1890s, the Italian inventor Guglielmo Marconi figured out a way to transmit signals by creating electromagnetic waves in the air. He went on to make a device that could send and receive signals in Morse code without the use of wires. Soon people were using Marconi's wireless telegraph to transmit messages to and from

Edison's "filament lamp," or lightbulb

Business, Labor, and a New Middle Class

The Industrial Revolution spawned not only new technologies but also economic and social changes. Businessmen developed schemes to maximize production and profits. To meet the needs of the industrial economy, a new middle class of professionals and managers rose to importance. While business owners and the growing middle class enjoyed many benefits of the industrialized economy, workers often suffered in factory systems that looked upon the laborers as little more than parts of the machinery.

New Ideas in Production and Management

The factory system, which brought large numbers of workers together to operate machines under close supervision, was a far more efficient way of producing large quantities of goods than the old home-based craft system. In the 1800s and early 1900s, industrialists sought ways to make the factory system even more productive.

In 1798, the American Eli Whitney—who had become famous for inventing the cotton gin a few years earlier—was asked to manufacture muskets for the U.S. Army. Whitney pointed out that making guns by hand, one at a time, was slow and inefficient. He urged the government to use machine-made **interchangeable parts** that could then be assembled into muskets. If the parts were all exactly the same, then it would take no special skill to make a gun. A group of unskilled workers could simply assemble the pieces.

American industries quickly adopted Whitney's ideas about interchangeable parts, which became part of what was called the American system of manufacturing. Throughout the 1800s, European visitors marveled at the many high-quality, completely standardized products being made in America—everything from furniture to shoes to clocks. All were manufactured by unskilled laborers using the principle of interchangeable parts.

At the beginning of the twentieth century, the American businessman Henry Ford took further steps toward standardization and efficiency in manufacturing. Ford, an automobile manufacturer, organized his factories around the **assembly line**. Workers stood beside conveyor belts, which delivered parts to them. Each worker performed one particular task, such as adding a clamp or tightening a series of bolts. Because each worker had only one task to do, he could perform it quickly, without wasting time moving from place to place. The assembly line greatly increased speed and productivity in Ford's factories.

Henry Ford's assembly line made affordable automobiles available to the masses.

They also bought a shipping company to ensure the delivery of their products. The Krupp firm became the largest and most powerful company in Germany.

In the American oil industry, a businessman named John D. Rockefeller set out to eliminate the competition. He began by buying oil refineries. He then acquired the railroads and pipelines that transported the oil, and the companies that turned it into gasoline. By 1879, Rockefeller's conglomeration of businesses, known as Standard Oil, controlled 90 percent of oil refining in the United States. Rockefeller had effectively created a monopoly, and gained sole control of an entire industry.

Some saw men like Rockefeller as captains of industry, bringing order to the unruly business world and ensuring that a steady stream of goods

In 1908, Ford introduced a mass-produced car, the Model T. As Ford continued to improve his assembly line processes, the time required to build a Model T decreased from twelve and a half hours in 1912 to one and a half hours in 1914. Thus cars could be made more cheaply and sold for much less. Ford's assembly line method of production brought automobiles to the masses.

New Ways of Doing Business

The Second Industrial Revolution brought not only new methods of production but also new ways of organizing and conducting business. Often, companies merged into large entities called corporations. Like the joint-stock companies of earlier times, these new corporations were owned by groups of investors who stood to profit if the corporations thrived.

Some companies expanded by taking over their competitors and buying companies in related industries. In Germany, for example, a firm run by the Krupp family began by manufacturing cannons, and then branched out into the steel industry. Later, the Krupps bought mines to ensure a supply of iron to their steel mills.

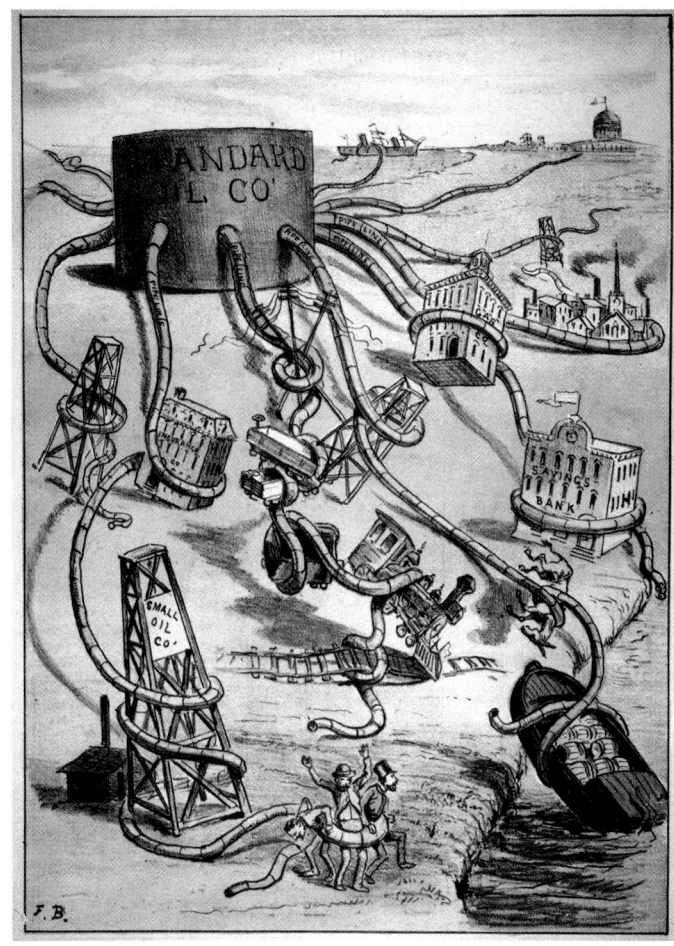
An 1884 cartoon criticizes John D. Rockefeller's oil empire.

A New Corporation

By 1890, Thomas Edison had taken steps to merge his various business efforts into the Edison General Electric Company. About this time, he was facing competition from the Thomson-Houston Company. In 1892, the two competitors merged into a new corporation, the General Electric Company, which remains one of the largest corporations in the world.

reached the public. Others saw them as robber barons, deliberately driving competitors out of business in order to fix the prices and supply of goods, and so maximize their profits.

The Human Cost of Industrialization

The wonders of the Industrial Revolution came at a high human price. Especially in the first phase of industrialization, workers lived and labored in miserable conditions.

Factories—which the English poet William Blake called "dark Satanic mills"—were usually dirty, dark, and poorly ventilated. For twelve to sixteen hours a day, six days a week, workers tended their machines in stifling heat. Factory owners didn't want their expensive machines to stand idle, so workers had to keep running them throughout the day, with only a half-hour break for dinner.

To keep everyone on schedule, factory owners imposed strict rules. A worker who arrived a few minutes late could lose a quarter day's pay. Conversations between workers were forbidden. Supervisors could fire workers on the spot any time they wanted. But if a worker tried to quit, he might find himself put in jail for "breach of contract."

Factories were unhealthy, dangerous places. The foul air made people sick. If an exhausted worker stopped paying attention for a moment,

Workers tend fires and shovel coal in a smoke-filled London factory that produced gas for lighting streets and homes.

Child labor: A child is depicted carrying clay in an English brick factory, c. 1870.

he might find his hand mangled by the machine he was tending.

Not all workers suffered such devastating injuries, but most paid a physical price for years of grueling, repetitive labor. One worker observed, "A factory laborer can be very easily known as he is going along the streets; some of his joints are sure to be wrong. Either the knees are in, the ankles swelled, one shoulder lower than the other, or he is round-shouldered, pigeon-breasted, or in some other way deformed."

Child Labor

Before the Industrial Revolution, most children had worked hard in the home or on the family farm, under the supervision of their parents. During the Industrial Revolution, millions of children became workers in factories. By 1830, two-thirds of the workers in the cotton industry were women and children. Factory owners preferred children as workers because they could be paid less than men and were less likely to break the rules.

As factory workers, children endured the same harsh conditions as adults. Children often worked from five o'clock in the morning to nine o'clock

at night and endured harsh punishments by strict supervisors. Once a young English textile worker named Sarah Carpenter was operating a machine when it suddenly stopped. Although Sarah was not at fault, her boss beat her with a stick. When she threatened to tell her mother, her boss "went out and fetched the master in to me. The master started beating me with a stick over the head till it was full of lumps and bled."

Suffering in the Cities

For workers, life at home was often as wretched as life in the factories. Many lived in tenements, which were dirty, overcrowded apartment buildings. In 1842, one government inspector described the rooms in a Manchester, England, tenement: "It seems to be the invariable practice to cram as many beds into each room as it can possible be made to hold…. The beds are filled …with men, women and children, the floor covered over with the filthy and ragged clothes they have just put off…. The suffocating stench and

A London street scene captures the poverty and hardship that many people endured during the Industrial Revolution.

595

Hard Times in England

The great mid-nineteenth-century English novelist Charles Dickens described the dehumanizing effects of the Industrial Revolution in his 1854 novel *Hard Times*. In the following passages, Dickens introduces readers to an industrial city called Coketown.

It was a town of red brick, or of brick that would have been red if the smoke and ashes had allowed it; but, as matters stood it was a town of unnatural red and black like the painted face of a savage. It was a town of machinery and tall chimneys, out of which interminable serpents of smoke trailed themselves for ever and ever, and never got uncoiled. It had a black canal in it, and a river that ran purple with ill-smelling dye, and vast piles of building full of windows where there was a rattling and a trembling all day long, and where the piston of the steam-engine worked monotonously up and down, like the head of an elephant in a state of melancholy madness. It contained several large streets all very like one another, and many small streets still more like one another, inhabited by people equally like one another, who all went in and out at the same hours, with the same sound upon the same pavements, to do the same work, and to whom every day was the same as yesterday and tomorrow, and every year the counterpart of the last and the next....

Pale morning showed the monstrous serpents of smoke trailing themselves over Coketown. A clattering of clogs upon the pavement; a rapid ringing of bells; and all the melancholy mad elephants, polished and oiled up for the day's monotony, were at their heavy exercise again....

"Serpents of smoke" rise from a nineteenth-century foundry.

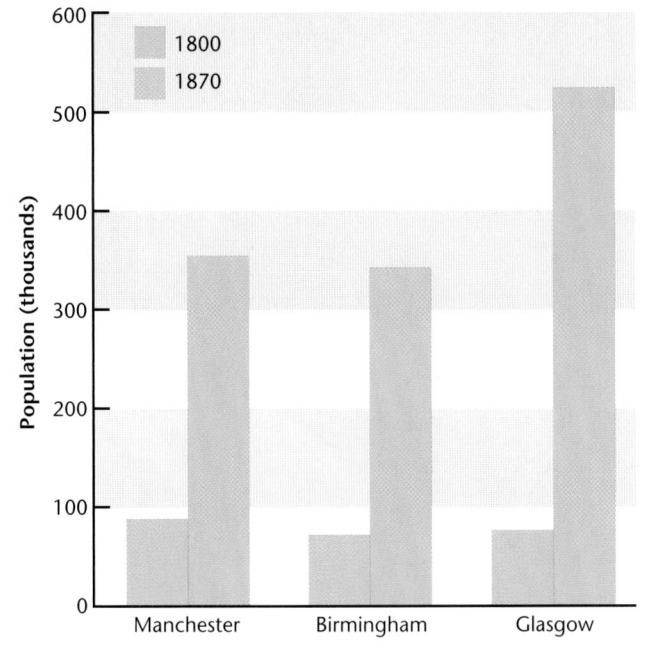

Urban Population in Britain, c. 1800–1870

typhus, yellow fever, cholera, and smallpox swept through the industrial cities. In the poor areas, one in three children died before their first birthday.

A Strong Middle Class Emerges

The Industrial Revolution brought suffering to many workers and unimaginable wealth to the most successful business owners. Between these extremes of poverty and wealth, a new middle class grew dramatically in number.

A complicated industrial society needed many skilled and educated people to keep it running smoothly. It needed doctors, lawyers, engineers, teachers, business managers, and government officials. During the Industrial Revolution, this growing sector of society—the middle class—began to assert itself as a distinct group.

Before the Industrial Revolution, wealth in European countries was based on land, which was always in limited supply. With the Industrial Revolution, money was more important than land. The business and professional world was open to those without inherited wealth. Bright, ambitious people could rise up from humble beginnings. When they reached the middle class, they could afford to have their own homes and enjoy a few luxuries. They lived in the same cities as the workers, but in much better conditions.

As time went on, the middle class developed a sense of pride in its identity. Middle-class people felt that they had earned their own success. They tended to look down on landed aristocrats as lazy and spoiled. Some members of the middle class also looked down on workers as ignorant and lacking initiative. The growing numbers and influence of the middle class would have profound effects on the development of industrialized societies.

heat of the atmosphere are almost intolerable." The overcrowding in these poor dwellings spread misery and disease.

Throughout the 1800s, millions of people left the countryside and poured into Europe's large cities, hoping to find work. Between 1800 and 1900, the population of London exploded from 900,000 to 4.7 million. But London and other cities lacked the infrastructure (the public services and facilities) to support the newcomers.

City streets were often used as open sewers or drains. Human and animal waste gave off an awful stench as it flowed through the gutters. In 1842, a British government report declared that "the annual loss of life from filth and bad ventilation is greater than the loss from wounds in any wars in which the country has been engaged." Unsanitary conditions bred deadly disease. Epidemics of

New York City and the Brooklyn Bridge, 1883

1848
Marx and Engels challenge capitalism in *The Communist Manifesto.*

1838
Charles Dickens describes the plight of the poor in *Oliver Twist.*

1833
Britain outlaws slavery in all of its colonies.

1824
Beethoven, completely deaf, composes his Ninth Symphony.

1840

1820

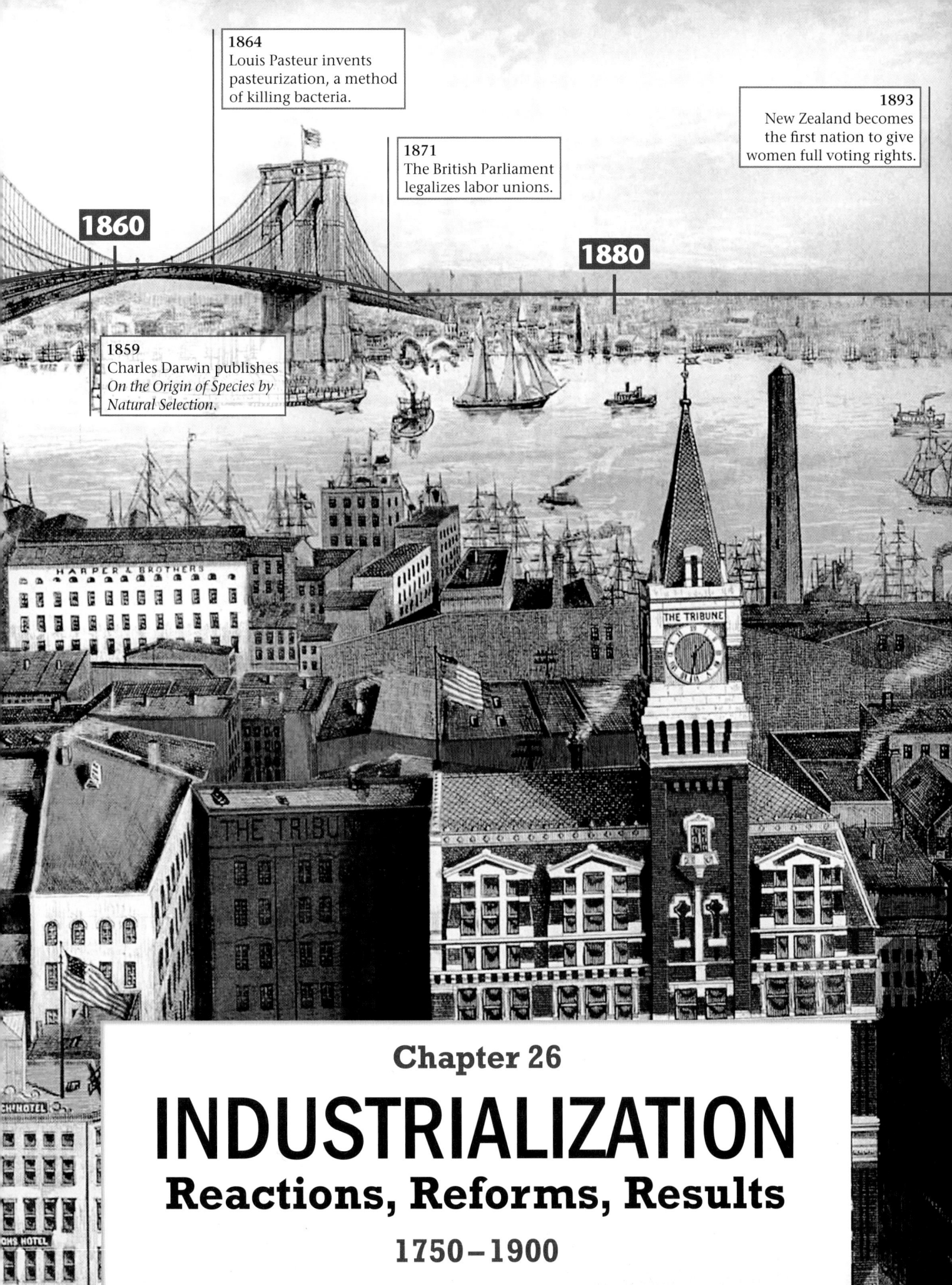

1864
Louis Pasteur invents pasteurization, a method of killing bacteria.

1871
The British Parliament legalizes labor unions.

1893
New Zealand becomes the first nation to give women full voting rights.

1860

1880

1859
Charles Darwin publishes *On the Origin of Species by Natural Selection.*

Chapter 26

INDUSTRIALIZATION
Reactions, Reforms, Results
1750–1900

The Industrial Revolution changed the way millions of people lived and worked. It also changed political and economic thought. As the working class in the industrial age suffered, some questioned the benefits of capitalism. They offered new ideas they thought would lead to a better society. Karl Marx was one who envisioned a communist society in which there would be no personal property or class struggle.

Marx predicted a comprehensive revolution, which did not occur. But workers did band together to form unions and demand better conditions. Reformers, largely from the middle class, took on a variety of social issues, including abolition (ending slavery), urban improvement, woman suffrage, and public education.

By the late nineteenth century, the Industrial Revolution helped raise the standard of living for millions of people. Medical advances, new technologies, and new economic opportunities changed the lives of a growing middle class.

Many artists and writers responded to the changes brought on by the Industrial Revolution. Artists in the Romantic movement saw industrialization as dehumanizing. In response, they stressed human emotion, imagination, and the beauty of the natural world.

New Ways of Thinking for an Industrial Age

Key Questions

- What did critics of capitalism propose as alternatives? How did they address the plight of workers?

- Why did Karl Marx believe capitalism would be overthrown?

During the Industrial Revolution, the ideas of Adam Smith, the Scottish philosopher who published *The Wealth of Nations* in 1776, greatly influenced businessmen and manufacturers. Smith advocated an economic system that came to be known as **laissez-faire capitalism**. *Laissez-faire*, you recall, is French for "let it be." Smith believed that the government should just let the economy be, and allow individuals to make their own economic decisions.

Smith believed in a **market economy**, an economy in which the forces of the marketplace—such as the division of labor, competition, and supply and demand—would determine the prices of goods and the distribution of wealth. He envisioned a future in which market forces alone would drive prices and wages.

Privately owned industries, particularly in England, benefited from growing acceptance of Smith's ideas. Entrepreneurs started new factories with little government regulation, and new industries grew and profited.

Writing at the beginning of the Industrial Revolution, Adam Smith was an economic optimist. He thought that if governments did not interfere with the economy, then the "invisible hand" of the market would benefit the greatest number of people.

But as the Industrial Revolution proceeded, workers suffered dangerous working conditions, long hours, and low pay. Industrial cities became centers of disease and crime. While a growing middle class of businessmen and managers enjoyed some benefits of the new industrialism, the gap between rich and poor widened dramatically.

In the face of these mounting social problems, some thinkers began to question the principles of laissez-faire and to offer alternative visions.

The Utilitarian Critique

In England, Jeremy Bentham, an English thinker of the late 1700s, came up with a philosophy called **utilitarianism**. According to Bentham, laws and policies should not be based on tradition but should be judged by how *useful* they are. The goal of government, he argued, should be to achieve the "greatest happiness of the greatest number." Among other things, Bentham called for the reform of England's harsh prison system. Bentham said that convicted criminals should not just be punished. They should be trained to be useful members of society.

A later utilitarian philosopher, John Stuart Mill, called for a broad range of reforms. Writing in the mid-1800s, Mill argued that the government should sometimes get involved in the economy to help the poor and powerless. For

Two images of London life, c. 1880—a study in stark contrast between rich and poor

example, he thought that the interests of the working class should be represented in Parliament, and he favored establishing government-supported schools for the poor. Mill also called for giving the vote to women. He declared that the oppression of women was both "wrong in itself" and a "hindrance" to progress because it wasted the talents of half the human race.

The Socialist Alternative

In Europe, some philosophers and economists rejected capitalism altogether. They argued that society should be radically reorganized to benefit the poor and the working classes. They believed capitalism harmed society by encouraging the huge gap between rich and poor. By 1897 in Great Britain, a nation of forty million people, two-thirds of the national income was in the hands of less than one-eighth of the population. The poor and the homeless crowded London and other cities.

As an alternative to capitalism, a growing number of European thinkers proposed **socialism**, an economic system in which the government controls property and the distribution of income. Socialists charged that in a capitalist economy, in which businesses are privately owned, owners are motivated only by profit.

Socialists argued that the government, representing the people, should own and manage the means of production, including land, raw materials, and factories. In such a society, socialists said, workers would not be mistreated or live such wretched lives. As the problems caused by industrialization grew, so did the hopes of many that socialism would replace the capitalist order.

Robert Owen, Utopian Socialist

Some early socialists put their ideas into practice in utopian communities. Robert Owen, a successful businessman from Wales, was distressed by the grim working and living conditions in industrial cities. When Owen and his business partners bought the New Lanark textile mills in Scotland, Owen prohibited labor for children under ten, set up schools for the young, built better housing for the mill workers, and encouraged cleanliness.

Owen wanted to undertake a practical social experiment based on the socialist ideals of cooperation and group effort. In 1825, he bought land in Indiana and established a community called New Harmony. New Harmony was to be a utopia—a perfect society, in which all the workers would share in the labor and profits. But harmony did not prevail. Residents quarreled over how affairs should be run, and the experiment failed after a few years. While Owen's vision of a socialist utopia did not succeed, his hope of creating better conditions for laborers endured.

Karl Marx and Class Struggle

One influential socialist thinker was a German named Karl Marx. Marx was born in 1818 to middle-class parents. His family was Jewish, but his father, a successful lawyer, converted to Christianity. As young Karl grew older and became interested in socialist ideas, he rejected both his Jewish roots and his father's Christianity. He came to believe that religion did nothing to help poor people and only dulled their senses to their misery and oppression.

Marx witnessed firsthand the suffering brought on by the rapid industrialization of his homeland. He became a journalist and wrote articles that criticized the government, condemned the powerful, and called for the overthrow of the capitalists and business owners.

Marx came to envision a kind of socialism known as communism. In 1848, the very year that revolutions were breaking out across Europe, Marx and his friend Friedrich Engels published a pamphlet called *The Communist Manifesto*. (A *manifesto* is a public declaration of beliefs, intentions, or policies.)

The Communist Manifesto said that every aspect of a society is shaped by its economic system—by its way of producing and distributing food, clothing, shelter, medical care, and other needed goods and services. Communists called for an economic system in which the wealth of a society would be shared by all—quite a contrast to capitalism, in which individuals and businesses own wealth and compete for more of it.

Every economic system, said Marx and Engels, divides people into classes. Moreover, these classes are always struggling with one another for a bigger share of economic resources. Indeed, Marx and Engels asserted, "The history of all hitherto existing society is the history of class struggles."

The Communist Manifesto predicted an unavoidable war between "two great hostile camps…two great classes directly facing each other—bourgeoisie and proletariat" (PROH-luh-TEHR-ee-uht). By the bourgeoisie, Marx and Engels meant factory owners, bankers, merchants, and the ruling classes.

The proletariat included the "working men of all countries." The two groups were on a collision course. "Let the ruling classes tremble," declared *The Communist Manifesto*. "The proletarians have nothing to lose but their chains."

Marx's Das Kapital

After the 1848 revolutions failed, the rulers of Europe were determined to stamp out radical movements. Marx fled the continent for London, where he could more safely develop his radical ideas.

Britain at that time was known as the "workshop of the world." In factory towns and crowded cities, Marx saw the misery of the laborers in stark contrast to the fabulous wealth of their capitalist bosses. He spent hours in the British Museum in London, thinking, studying, and writing. For the rest of his life, Marx worked to produce a massive work called *Das Kapital* (dahs kahp-ee-TAHL), a title that means "Capital."

In *Das Kapital*, Marx described what he believed were historical forces shaping society. He predicted the certain end of capitalism as the large class of workers would rise up to overthrow the small class of owners. The result, said Marx, would be a classless society without private property—in other words, a communist society, in which wealth would be equally shared by all.

Few people paid much attention to Marx's ideas in his lifetime, but communism did appeal to Russian revolutionaries in the early twentieth century, though under conditions very different from what Marx had envisioned. In industrial Europe and the United States, history took a different turn as workers, social reformers, and governments organized for change.

Capitalism did not collapse as Marx predicted. Since Marx's time, *communism* has come to refer to an economic system that calls for government ownership of land, factories, and resources in order to achieve a classless society. Under communism, the government controls the economy and there is a minimum of private property. Marx hoped that a communist system would provide equality and

The Communist Manifesto

The Communist Manifesto, which Karl Marx and Friedrich Engels published in 1848, became one of the most influential writings of modern times. Marx and Engels wrote that society is always divided into classes that struggle against each other. They predicted that the working class, which they called the proletariat, would eventually overthrow the bourgeoisie, the class that owns and runs businesses.

The history of all hitherto existing society is the history of class struggles.

Freeman and slave, patrician and plebeian, lord and serf, guild-master and journeyman, in a word, oppressor and oppressed, stood in constant opposition to one another, carried on an uninterrupted, now hidden, now open fight, that each time ended, either in a revolutionary reconstitution of society at large, or in the common ruin of the contending classes....

The modern bourgeois society that has sprouted from the ruins of feudal society has not done away with class antagonisms. It has but established new classes, new conditions of oppression, new forms of struggle in place of the old ones. Our epoch [EH-puhk], the epoch of the bourgeoisie, ... has simplified the class antagonisms. Society as a whole is more and more splitting up into two great hostile camps, into two great classes directly facing each other – bourgeoisie and proletariat....

With the development of industry the proletariat not only increases in number; it becomes concentrated in greater masses, its strength grows and it feels that strength more....

Of all the classes that stand face to face with the bourgeoisie today, the proletariat alone is a really revolutionary class....The proletariat, the lowest stratum of our present society, cannot stir, cannot raise itself up, without the whole...of official society being sprung into the air....

The development of modern industry, therefore, cuts from under its feet the very foundation on which the bourgeoisie produces and appropriates products. What the bourgeoisie therefore produces, above all, are its own grave-diggers. Its fall and the victory of the proletariat are equally inevitable.

Karl Marx

security for all, but communism in the twentieth century turned out very differently.

Darwin and Natural Selection

Karl Marx saw society as a fierce competitive struggle. At about the same time, an English scientist, Charles Darwin, began to take a similar view of nature. His ideas would change modern science and rock the foundations of late nineteenth-century society.

In 1831, a young Charles Darwin boarded the *Beagle* in England and set sail on a survey expedition around the southernmost tip of South America. In South America and in the Galápagos (guh-LAH-puh-guhs) Islands (off the coast of Ecuador), Darwin recorded observations of plant and animal life, and sent thousands of specimens back to England, including fossils, insects, minerals, animal skins, and plants. He puzzled over the great diversity of plants and animals he saw and wondered why some species thrived while others died out.

In 1836, the *Beagle* finally returned home. Two years after his return, Darwin read an essay that had been written in 1798 by the British economist Robert Malthus. Malthus had argued that human population grows at a rate far beyond the growth of the available food supply. Population, said Malthus, expands to the limits of the food supply, and when those limits are reached, then famine, war, and disease work to limit further population growth. Malthus—who did not anticipate the increased food production brought by the agricultural advances that took place alongside the Industrial Revolution—painted a bleak picture of society. While some predicted ever-greater human progress, Malthus saw ever-greater struggle for limited resources. This central idea in Malthus's writings—the idea of struggle for limited resources—influenced Darwin as he contemplated the workings of nature.

In 1859, Darwin published *On the Origin of Species by Means of Natural Selection*. Darwin theorized that all plants and animals had gradually changed, or evolved, over time. Darwin referred to evolution as "descent"—it was not until the sixth and last edition of *The Origin of Species*, published in 1872, that he used the term *evolution* in his book. Darwin proposed that evolution occurred through a process called **natural selection**.

In the Galápagos Islands, Darwin observed differences in the beaks of finches and theorized that natural selection explained the variations.

Darwin observed that, in a world of limited resources, species compete to survive. He concluded that species with useful traits live longer and have more offspring, and are thus more likely to survive, than species without those useful traits. For example, on an island where the plants produce many hard seeds, the species of birds most likely to survive will be those that have developed short, strong beaks capable of cracking hard seeds. A later writer who admired Darwin summarized the principles behind natural selection as "survival of the fittest."

While many scientists supported Darwin, *The Origin of Species* sparked strong opposition from many religious leaders. If a natural process could explain how species became suited to their environment, what role did that leave for God? And how could God be perceived as kind and loving if thousands of species died so that the "fittest" could survive?

Other writers took Darwin's ideas about natural selection and loosely applied them to human society. In their view, life was a struggle in which individuals or nations must compete for limited resources. These ideas, which came to be known as *social Darwinism*, applied the idea of survival of the fittest to social, economic, and political activity. In the late 1800s, some social Darwinists justified economic inequality by arguing that poverty was a sign of unfitness, while those who accumulated the most wealth were "the fittest" members of society.

605

Taking Action and Organizing for Change

During the early 1800s, a series of reform movements brought both small improvements and dramatic changes to the lives of millions of people. Reformers focused their energies on solving a variety of problems, from ending slavery to expanding access to education.

The Abolitionist Movement

Enlightenment thinkers firmly established the idea that all people have natural rights, including life and liberty. By the late 1700s, that idea helped inspire not only political revolutions but also abolitionism, the movement to end slavery. Toward the end of the Enlightenment, the antislavery movement gained strength when a widespread religious revival inspired thousands of people to embrace various forms of evangelical Christianity. Many of these people began to condemn slavery as unchristian.

Abolitionism in Britain

In the 1700s, though slavery did not exist in England itself, Great Britain was more heavily involved in the transatlantic slave trade than any other nation. Yet by 1800, the British had taken the lead in attempting to end the slave trade and abolish slavery completely.

Some of the most committed opponents of slavery were British Quakers. In 1786, an Anglican clergyman, Thomas Clarkson, joined forces with the Quakers to print and distribute pamphlets depicting the horrors suffered by enslaved people. They also organized to form abolitionist committees in many English towns.

Clarkson enlisted the aid of William Wilberforce, a young, evangelical Anglican member of Parliament. Wilberforce quickly became the most powerful voice in Britain's antislavery movement. He spoke passionately in public meetings and in Parliament, while Clarkson's group campaigned throughout the towns and cities of England. They won supporters, particularly among educated, middle-class women who took up the cause and boycotted slave-grown sugar.

To *boycott* is to refuse to do business with a group, often in order to compel them to reform in some way.

An antislavery medal, c. 1787, asks, "Am I not a man and a brother?"

In 1807, the British Parliament responded to public opinion by abolishing the slave trade. In 1833, Britain outlawed slavery in all of its colonies.

The Antislavery Movement in the United States

In the early 1800s, prior to America's Civil War, as industry grew in the northern part of the United States, slavery died out or was outlawed. In the South, however, planters continued to rely on slave labor. Abolitionists in the North began working to end slavery throughout the country.

As in England, American abolitionists organized to distribute pamphlets and make speeches wherever they could. William Lloyd Garrison, a founder of the American Anti-Slavery Society, also published an influential newspaper, *The Liberator*.

Like women in England, many American middle-class women supported abolition. The sisters Angelina and Sarah Grimké drew large audiences when they spoke at antislavery meetings, though some people came merely to see the oddity of a woman speaking in public. Former slaves, such as Sojourner Truth and, most prominently, the eloquent speaker and writer Frederick Douglass, stirred supporters to action as well.

As often as abolitionists gained support, in some places they were met with criticism, anger, and violence, especially in the South. The Southern economy depended on cotton produced by nearly four million enslaved people. Not until the Emancipation Proclamation in 1863 and the passage of the 13th Amendment to the Constitution following the Civil War in 1865 did the United States finally end slavery in all its states.

Women Seek the Vote

Many educated, middle-class women worked in the abolitionist movement, and others were inspired by women in the movement. A number of these women began to demand rights for

Frederick Douglass

themselves as well. In particular, they focused on securing the right to vote.

In 1848, women in the antislavery movement gathered in Seneca Falls, New York, for the first conference for women's rights. The conference issued a document modeled after the Declaration of Independence. It stated, "We hold these truths to be self-evident: that all men *and women* are created equal."

Declaring equal rights was one thing; gaining them was another, and much harder. Twenty-four years after the Seneca Falls convention, a leader in the woman's suffrage movement, Susan B. Anthony, tried to cast a vote in a U.S. presidential election. She was arrested and fined for casting an illegal ballot.

By the late 1800s, many women on both sides of the Atlantic were working for suffrage. Their movement sparked both ridicule and anger. Some people said giving women the right to vote would destroy the family. Others said women lacked the intelligence to vote.

In Britain, Emmeline Goulden Pankhurst became a leader of the suffrage movement. She and her husband successfully campaigned for

Suffragettes march in the United States, c. 1900. It was not until 1920 that U.S. women gained the right to vote.

the right of married women to vote in local elections. In 1903, Pankhurst, by then a widow, founded the Women's Social and Political Union (WSPU). Members of the WSPU interrupted meetings of officials in Parliament. They pelted politicians with eggs. They protested, were arrested, and went to jail for their actions.

Too Busy to Join the Campaign

The woman suffrage movement was led by a growing number of well-educated and well-to-do women. Poor and working-class women were notably absent from the campaign. Women working as domestic servants or in factories were too busy trying to earn a living to go out and fight for the right to vote.

Pankhurst staged repeated hunger strikes in jail, and as soon as she was released, she went back to organizing protests.

Gaining the Vote

Emmeline Pankhurst was not alone in her struggles. Across the Western world, woman suffragists campaigned for the right to vote. Their efforts challenged governments to live up to the promise of their ideals, and eventually led to change that affected millions of lives.

In 1893, New Zealand became the first nation to give women full voting rights. Australia followed in 1902. Finland approved woman suffrage in 1906. In 1920, the United States ratified the 19th Amendment to the Constitution, giving women the right to vote. A month before Pankhurst died in 1928, Britain extended full voting equality to women. French women had to wait until 1945 to cast their ballots.

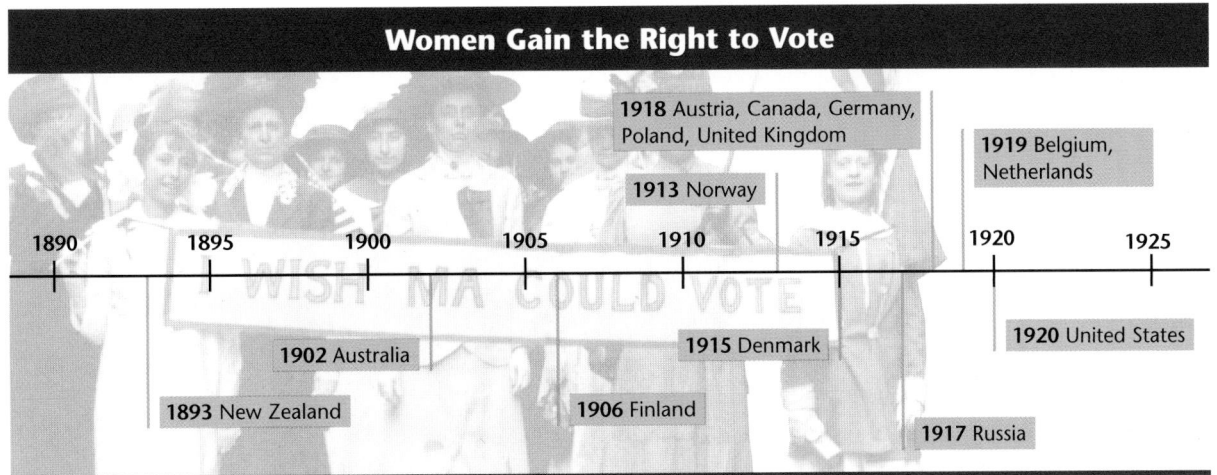

Women Gain the Right to Vote

1918 Austria, Canada, Germany, Poland, United Kingdom

1919 Belgium, Netherlands

1913 Norway

1890   1895   1900   1905   1910   1915   1920   1925

1920 United States

1902 Australia

1915 Denmark

1893 New Zealand

1906 Finland

1917 Russia

Laborers Demand Change

When the Industrial Revolution began in the early 1800s, many men, women, and children worked in miserable and dangerous conditions. In dark mines, stifling factories, or overcrowded sweatshops—makeshift factories in urban tenements—workers put in fourteen-hour days. Any worker who complained could be fired. By the mid-nineteenth century, some governments began to limit the number of hours that women and children could work. But governments hesitated to do more, believing that they should not tell industry owners how to run their businesses.

Gradually, realizing that there was strength in numbers, workers joined together. If they could speak as a group, they could hope to be heard. Workers in various trades—such as ironworkers, cotton spinners, or coal miners—organized into **unions**. Each union bargained with its employers for better hours, higher wages, and improved working conditions. The act of negotiating as a group, known as **collective bargaining**, gave workers strength that they lacked individually.

Employers had money and, often, the government on their side. Workers had only their labor. But if an employer refused to offer better conditions or higher pay, the workers could go on strike—they could refuse to work and thus force the factory, mine, or mill to grind to a halt. A strike could cost an owner millions. Workers also suffered during strikes, since they were not being paid. Still, unions found that even the threat of a strike could push an employer to meet some demands.

The Growth of Organized Labor

At first, most governments sided with business owners and banned workers' organizations. They feared that unions posed a threat to capitalism. But as unions organized and grew in strength and numbers, governments lifted the bans. By 1871, trade unions were legal in Great Britain and elsewhere.

Industrialists still found ways to fight back. Employers might fire union organizers or put their

In France, steelworkers demanding better pay march at Le Creusot in 1899.

609

names on blacklists. People named on blacklists were often fired or refused employment. Owners staged lockouts, keeping union members out of their factories. The owner might suffer losses, but the workers would suffer more. Some employers resorted to violence against unions, hiring what amounted to private armies to squash the unions.

Despite such setbacks, organized labor grew in numbers and influence. Union membership in Britain grew from 1.5 million in 1894 to 4.1 million in 1914. Similar growth occurred in Germany and the United States.

Skilled laborers continued to have more power than unskilled workers, since they could not be easily replaced. And men had more clout than women, who, no matter what kind of work they did, almost always earned less than men. Nevertheless, by the early twentieth century, working conditions were changing for the better.

Improving City Life

Despite the terrible conditions in many factories, thousands of people flocked to cities seeking work. Populations grew faster than the cities

An 1866 cartoon shows the figure of death pumping polluted water for London's poor. Outbreaks of cholera—a disease that could be spread by contaminated water from public pumps—were common among the poor.

could respond. The result, as you have seen, was overcrowded, filthy, and unsafe surroundings.

Reformers in London began to take steps to improve their city. In 1829, Sir Robert Peel urged Parliament to establish London's first police force. The bobbies, as they were called (after Sir Robert), helped make London safer. In the 1850s, a new sewer system was built to keep waste out of the river Thames in the city. And the construction of new roads improved transportation.

City officials in London tried to improve public health by tearing down buildings in the city's slums. These efforts had mixed results. Many poor Londoners lost their homes and overcrowding grew worse as more people jammed themselves into the tenements the city had left standing.

Rebuilding Paris

London was not alone in its urban problems. Paris, Berlin, and New York faced similar challenges, as did other industrial cities.

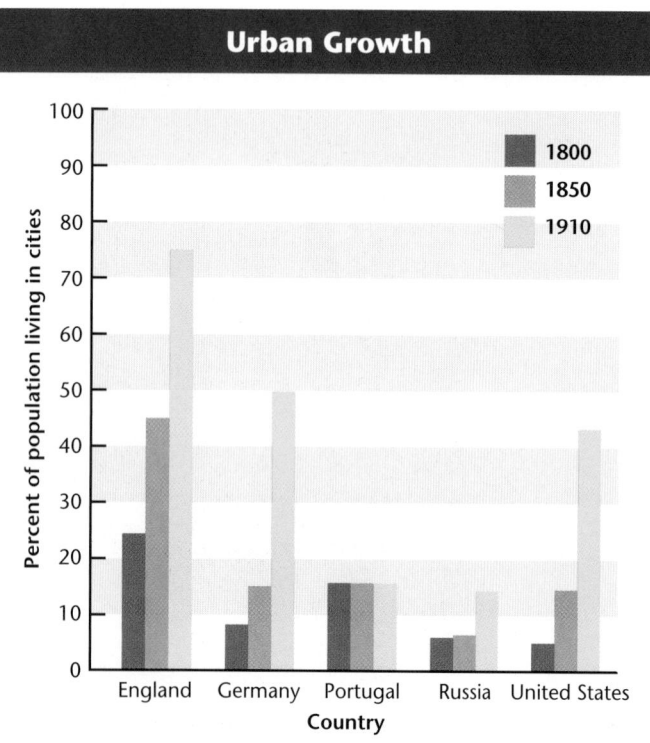

Urban Growth

Percent of population living in cities

Legend: 1800, 1850, 1910

Countries: England, Germany, Portugal, Russia, United States

In France, Napoleon III wanted to make Paris the envy of the world. To lead the effort, the emperor called on Baron Georges-Eugène Haussmann (ohs-MAHN). Together, they transformed Paris from a medieval tangle of dark, narrow, filthy streets into the "city of light" with grand, tree-lined boulevards filled with sunshine by day and gaslights by night. New aqueducts brought clean water into the city, and new sewers removed waste. By the end of the century, electric trams, trolleys, and even an underground railway system moved Parisians from one place to another.

In the process of rebuilding, so many buildings were torn down that one writer called Paris "a city without a past." The poor still lived in wretched conditions. But city dwellers around the world took note of Paris's fashionable new apartments and lovely shops. Middle- and upper-class Parisians visited museums and dined in cafés. The reconstruction of Paris marked the beginning of modern *urban planning*, the designing and organizing of all aspects of city life.

New York City Grows Up

In the United States, by the dawn of the twentieth century, New York City boasted the world's busiest ports, banks, and industries, and the world's fastest growing population. Unlike Paris, New York could not widen its streets and expand outward. The heart of New York City, Manhattan, is a small island. So New York had to grow up—literally.

In the late 1800s, a new kind of steel made it possible to erect tall buildings that would not collapse under their own weight. Another innovation—a safe, efficient elevator invented by Elisha Otis—made tall buildings practical places in which to work and live. Ten- and twelve-story buildings began to rise in New York City. Each

A mid-1800s painting, *Sunday Afternoon on the Island of La Grande Jatte* by Georges-Pierre Seurat, portrays fashionable Parisians of the time.

The Brooklyn Bridge

The island of Manhattan needed a connection to parts of New York that lay across the river. Engineers embarked on one of the most ambitious feats of the day—building the majestic 1,600-foot-long Brooklyn Bridge across the East River. The Brooklyn Bridge, completed in 1883, was the longest suspension bridge in the world, supported by thick twisted steel cables that hung from massive 275-foot towers.

New York City's 57-story Woolworth Building

year, these skyscrapers, as they were called, seemed to soar higher and higher. New York became the site of more tall buildings than any city in the world.

In 1876, New York also became home to a remarkable expanse of trees, shrubs, paths, and open space. Central Park, carefully designed by Frederick Law Olmsted, provided city dwellers an opportunity to enjoy the beauty of nature. Olmsted wanted the park to be a place of calm and harmony to restore the spirits of city dwellers. He went on to design parks for many other cities.

The Growth of Public Education

As far back as the mid-eighteenth century during the Enlightenment, some thinkers had argued for widespread public education. At the time, only children with wealthy parents could get a good education. Few poor children learned to read or write.

Under Napoleon, France managed to establish some government-funded schools and universities. Still, relatively few people received much education. In Britain, public education lagged further behind. In 1807, when a politician proposed to give two years of church schooling to penniless children, many people protested

that so much education would make the lower classes rebellious.

In the United States in the 1830s, two reformers, Horace Mann and Henry Barnard, argued for "common schools" that would help educate all children, rich or poor. They believed that state governments should set up elementary schools and require all children to attend them. In 1852, Massachusetts became the first state to pass a law requiring children to go to school. During the next few decades, the other states followed. Public high schools in the United States began to multiply after 1900.

In late-nineteenth-century Germany, where the government sponsored technical schools to train an industrial workforce, children received eight years of government-funded education. By the late 1800s, Germany surpassed England as an industrial power.

Economic competition from Germany and the United States—where, by 1890, most young children had access to free public schooling—motivated Britain to increase access to education. In 1891, Britain passed a law funding universal public education.

In the United States and western Europe, governments passed laws requiring children to attend school and forbidding them to work. By the early twentieth century, most adults in the United States and western Europe could read. In eastern Europe, where public education had not taken hold, far fewer adults were literate. As a result, the western part of the continent moved even further ahead of the eastern regions.

A Rising Standard of Living

The Industrial Revolution transformed technology, business structures, transportation, and communications. The human effects—the transformation of economies and societies—were just as dramatic and, for many in the working class, traumatic. By the end of the nineteenth century, however, millions of people were enjoying the benefits of advances in science and medicine. New means of production and new economic opportunities led to a rising standard of living, especially for the growing middle class.

Advances in Science

Throughout the 1800s, population boomed in the great cities of Europe. With so many people living in close quarters, deadly diseases such as cholera and smallpox spread quickly, killing thousands. By the 1850s, authorities in London and other cities recognized the connection between disease and overcrowding. They sought to improve public health by clearing congested slums and building better sewage systems.

The Germ Theory of Disease Revolutionizes Medicine

In the mid-1800s, the importance of sanitation was recognized in medicine as well. In 1854, during the Crimean War, the English nurse Florence Nightingale emphasized the importance of cleanliness in field hospitals. Less than a decade later, her work helped inspire the creation of the U.S. Sanitary Commission during the American Civil War.

Key Questions

- What major scientific advancements changed medicine and saved lives during the nineteenth century?

- In what ways did the standard of living for many people in the industrialized world improve by the late 1800s?

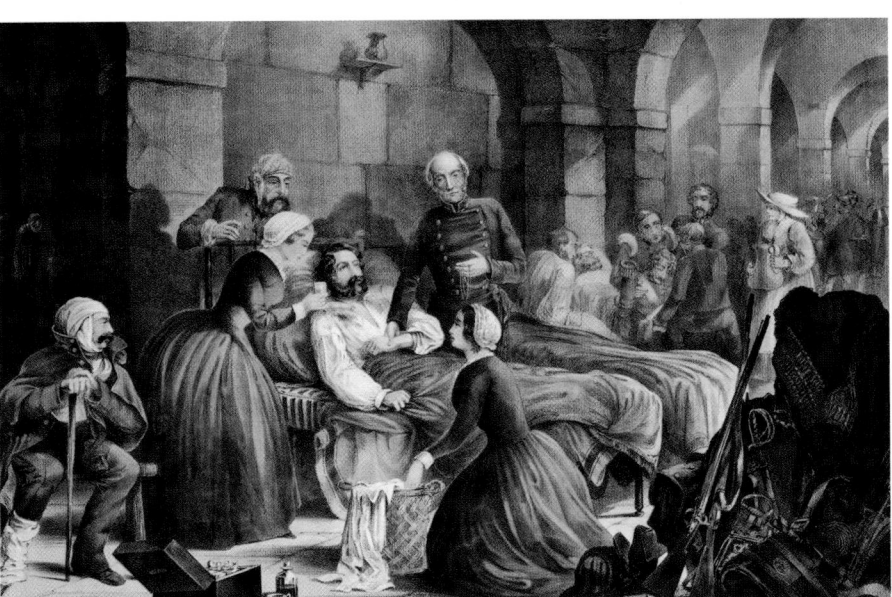

Florence Nightingale, one of the first to relate cleanliness with wellness, attends the sick.

Louis Pasteur worked tirelessly in the fight against disease, and made world-changing scientific breakthroughs.

But medical authorities could not really control diseases until they understood where they came from and how they spread. A breakthrough came in the 1860s, when a French scientist, Louis Pasteur (LOO-ee pas-TUR), discovered the link between disease and tiny organisms called microbes, or germs.

Pasteur, while studying how microbes affected French wines, had discovered that during the process of fermentation (when grape juice turns into wine) certain microbes spoiled the juice and turned it bitter. He then proved that heat can kill these harmful microbes to keep the wine from going bad. Later, scientists used Pasteur's ideas to eliminate microorganisms that cause milk and other food products to spoil. The process used to keep such products from spoiling came to be known as *pasteurization*.

Pasteur became convinced that there was a strong link between microbes and contagious diseases that made humans and animals sick. Pasteur found that if he injected microbes from diseased animals into healthy animals, the healthy ones got sick. He saw that his germ theory might provide the key to stopping the spread of disease. Pasteur discovered that if he injected weakened disease germs into animals or human patients, then their bodies would build up a resistance that protected them from the disease. This process, known as vaccination, would eventually be used to fight dozens of deadly diseases, including anthrax, rabies, tuberculosis, and cholera.

Surviving Surgery

In Scotland, a surgeon named Joseph Lister applied Pasteur's discoveries to his own branch of medicine. Surgery at the time was highly risky—nearly a third of patients died after operations, when their wounds became infected.

After reading about Pasteur's ideas, Lister figured out that these infections were caused by germs. He began treating his patients' wounds with antiseptic (microbe-killing) chemicals. When other surgeons started using Lister's methods, the surgical death rate plummeted from one in three to one in twenty.

The Science of Behavior

In the late 1800s, some scientists turned their attention to human behavior. They looked for scientific explanations for what people do and how groups of people behave. New social sciences emerged, including anthropology, the study of

What Are Vaccines?

A *vaccine* is a preparation of microorganisms (usually weakened or killed) given to patients to build up their resistance to a specific disease. A British doctor, Edward Jenner, developed the first vaccines. In 1796, he used the virus from cowpox—a cattle disease generally not harmful to humans—as a vaccine to protect against a related virus often deadly to humans, smallpox.

Sigmund Freud

the social and cultural development of humans, and sociology, the study of the organization and functioning of humans in society.

Another new social science that emerged in the late nineteenth century was psychology, the study of the human mind and behavior. Psychologists observe how people relate to each other and to their environment and try to explain and predict behavior. A major pioneer in psychology was Sigmund Freud (froyd), a physician in Vienna, Austria.

According to Freud, the mind has different parts. We think and solve problems with the conscious mind, the reasonable and reasoning part. But, said Freud, another part of the mind—the unconscious—is filled with powerful instincts and strong desires that drive us even though we are not aware of their influence. If disturbing thoughts, memories, or wishes threaten to come into our consciousness, then we try to repress them—we push them back into the unconscious. In some people, Freud theorized, the struggle to repress these feelings leads to mental illness.

Freud thought that mentally ill patients would get better only when they could understand their unconscious desires. To help his patients tap into the unconscious part of their minds, Freud developed a process called *psychoanalysis*. In psychoanalysis, Freud tried different methods with his patients. In one method, patients described their dreams, since Freud thought that dreams express hidden wishes and desires.

After 1900, Freud's revolutionary ideas spread rapidly, not only among psychologists but also to some artists and writers who embraced the idea of exploring the hidden recesses of the mind.

Abundance for Millions

Despite the continuing hardships faced by many factory and mine workers, by the mid-1800s more people could afford more food, clothing, and other goods than ever before. By the early twentieth century, that abundance was available even to many working-class people in the industrialized world.

Catering to the Middle Class

By 1900, millions of middle-class families lived in Europe and America, and their numbers were growing. Members of the middle class worked in offices, stores, factories, and other businesses. While much less wealthy than the factory owners, middle-class workers far outnumbered the rich. So businesses began to cater to the needs and wants of the growing middle class.

People in the middle class needed shirts, dresses, coats, hats, and household goods. Sometimes they wanted to buy small luxuries, such as pocket watches or jewelry. They wanted newspapers to read. In their spare time, they wanted to be entertained, by going to plays or listening to music.

In 1800, only the rich could afford many of these things. But by 1900, new products, inventions, and forms of entertainment were available

Banks of telephone operators enabled more and more people to use Alexander Graham Bell's new invention.

For the urban middle class, department stores like this one in Paris changed the whole idea of shopping.

to many more people. This period witnessed the birth of what has been called *mass society*.

By 1900, many factories were engaging in the mass production of goods. Millions of people were buying those goods, thus giving rise to mass consumerism. New forms of mass entertainment developed as people sought readily available ways to amuse themselves. Mass education made it possible for more people to read and write. Mass communication, such as the telephone and wireless telegraph, enabled more people to get in touch with each other. In this mass society, the goods and services created by the Industrial Revolution were beginning to reach millions of people.

Marketing the New Abundance

In 1869, Aristide Boucicaut (ah-ree-steed BOO-sih-koh), a former traveling salesman, borrowed some money and built an enormous new store in the heart of Paris. It was a department store, with goods sorted into separate categories, or departments. It changed the whole idea of shopping.

Boucicaut astounded Paris with new marketing ideas that consumers now take for granted.

He did away with the customary practice of haggling over the price. In his new Bon Marché (bohn mar-SHAY, French for "good buy"), Boucicaut set fixed prices and marked them on the products. He kept prices low by selling mass-produced goods at great volume.

Boucicaut displayed merchandise in clever and creative ways. He lured shoppers by holding sales. He placed advertisements in newspapers. He let people buy things on credit and pay for them over time.

Department stores similar to the Bon Marché sprang up all over Europe and the United States. They became the marketplaces of choice for many thousands of urban, middle-class consumers.

In the United States and other industrial nations, many people who lived on farms outside the crowded cities had no access to the new department stores. But their wants and needs were filled by a growing mail-order catalog business.

Merchants such as Montgomery Ward in the United States issued mail-order catalogs listing items for sale. By the 1880s, Ward's catalog offered thousands of items—clothing, jewelry, silverware, toys, medicines, tools, and more. Soon, other merchants, including Richard Warren Sears and his business partner Alvah Curtis Roebuck, issued catalogs. The mail-order industry grew steadily, feeding the increasing appetite of the middle class for an amazing assortment of products, from books to stoves to bicycles.

Leisure for the Masses

Early in the Industrial Revolution, when workers first started toiling in factories, they had little if any spare time. Many labored twelve or more hours a day, six days a week, every week of the year. But over the course of the nineteenth century, workers won shorter hours and higher wages. By 1900, the typical workday had shrunk to ten hours, with half of Saturday and all of Sunday off. So began the idea of "the weekend"—a regular weekly interval set aside for leisure. With their leisure time and spare money, millions of middle-class people sought entertainment in the evenings, on weekends, and eventually during summer vacations.

A new type of theater, the variety show, provided affordable mass entertainment. In the United States of the 1890s, these variety shows were called vaudeville (VAWD-vil). In Europe, similar shows were staged at music halls. Tickets were cheap, and people could stay as long as they liked. The shows featured many performers in a series of short acts, one after the other. People could arrive whenever they finished work. In a single visit, customers might see a trained monkey, a singer, a juggler, and a comedian. It didn't matter what they'd missed—something else would start soon.

Outside big cities, at the ends of trolley lines, streetcar companies built "trolley parks" with dance halls, picnic tables, and carnival rides such as the Ferris wheel (invented by George Ferris). Some trolley parks grew into huge amusement parks, such as New York's Coney Island and London's Blackpool Pleasure Beach.

Athens, 1896: French cyclist Paul Masson is congratulated on winning an event at the first modern Olympic Games.

Sports as Entertainment

With the growing hunger for entertainment, sports became big business. Professional rugby and soccer leagues formed in Britain. Stadiums were built to accommodate the games. In the United States, baseball became a favorite sport, with many cities forming professional teams.

The growing interest in sports gave birth to the modern Olympic Games. A French nobleman, Baron Pierre de Coubertin (koo-behr-tan), proposed to revive the games that had been held every four years in ancient Greece. The first modern Olympics were held in Athens in 1896. Amateur athletes from many countries competed in sports such as cycling, gymnastics, and wrestling.

The 1900 Olympics were held in Paris, and the 1904 games in St. Louis, Missouri. Improved transportation enabled athletes and spectators to travel across oceans and continents to attend the international games. Telegraph reports allowed newspapers to print news about how the athletes were faring in the contests. By 1908, when the games were held in London, the modern Olympics had fans all over the world.

Crowds flock to a public park in Vienna, Austria, at the turn of the twentieth century.

617

New Technologies: Phonographs and Motion Pictures

New inventions led to forms of mass entertainment that competed with vaudeville and music halls. The phonograph brought music out of the concert hall and, eventually, into the home. Thomas Edison invented the phonograph in 1877, but the foil-covered cylinders on which he recorded proved difficult to mass produce. A German-born immigrant to the United States, Emile Berliner, captured sound on flat discs. In 1901, Berliner and a partner started the Victor Talking Machine Company. They produced affordable phonographs, called Victrolas, and recordings of famous singers, such as the Italian tenor Enrico Caruso who sang with the Metropolitan Opera in New York City. For the first time in history, ordinary people could hear concert hall music.

Another invention from Thomas Edison and his engineers helped bring entertainment to millions in the form of "moving pictures," or movies. Edison's first movie, on a device called the Kinetoscope (from the Greek words *kineto*, movement, and *scopos*, to watch), showed jerky flickering images of a man sneezing—nothing more.

A dog named Nipper, Victor Talking Machine Company's trademark, became an image and symbol known worldwide.

In 1903, one of Edison's employees made an eight-minute movie that told a story. *The Great Train Robbery* ended with a man pointing a gun straight at the audience. People shrieked with delighted terror. Soon, movies moved from booths for individual viewers to rooms where the pictures were projected onto a large screen. The early movies were silent, with no words or sounds, although sometimes a piano player or organist played music to accompany a film's story.

Theaters sprang up across both the United States and Europe. In large studios in France and Italy, filmmakers produced movies about everything from ancient Rome to imaginary flights to the moon.

Mass Publishing: Pulp Fiction and Yellow Journalism

In the second half of the nineteenth century, new high-speed printing presses gave rise to mass publishing. Millions of middle-class readers bought books called "dime novels" in the United States and "penny dreadfuls" in Britain. These books usually featured a detective story, an outlaw tale, or a breathless romance.

In the late nineteenth century, magazines called *pulps* became popular. Their name came from the fact that they were printed on cheap wood-pulp paper. The magazines specialized in short, exciting stories that included science fiction and tales about cowboys in the American West.

In the United States, two publishers, Joseph Pulitzer and William Randolph Hearst, transformed the daily newspaper into a form of entertainment. Their newspapers still carried news, but they favored sensational stories about murders and scandals. The newspapers of Pulitzer and Hearst also contained sections devoted to sports and other entertainments, as well as illustrated stories called *comics*. The first comic strip featured a character called The Yellow Kid, so the sensational news reporting in the Hearst and Pulitzer papers came to be called "yellow journalism."

The Arts Respond to the Industrial Age

Key Questions

- How did the artists and writers of the Romantic movement respond to the industrial age?
- What are some of the major ideas and key works of the realists?

As the Industrial Revolution spread, it brought material abundance. For workers and city dwellers, it also brought great suffering. Many people began to ask: Is this progress worth the human and social cost? As artists and writers responded to the dramatic transformations of the industrial age, two cultural movements took shape—Romanticism and, in the later nineteenth century, realism.

The Romantic Reaction

Roughly simultaneous with the Industrial Revolution came a revolution in Western thinking—not a revolution of guns and swords, but of pens, paintbrushes, and pianos. It was a revolution in literature, painting, music, philosophy, and more—a creative revolution called Romanticism.

Romanticism was in part a rejection of the neoclassical art of the Enlightenment. Neoclassical artists valued reason, order, and balance. Romantic artists and writers, however, insisted that the deepest truths lay not in reason but in the power of emotion, the beauty of nature, and the creative potential of the free individual. As the Romantics reacted against the neoclassical values of the Enlightenment, they also responded to the social changes brought about by the Industrial Revolution.

Early Romantics

One early influence in the development of Romanticism was the French philosopher Jean-Jacques Rousseau. His beliefs about the goodness of human nature and the evil of society became a central assumption of Romanticism. Also like Rousseau, many Romantic poets and artists celebrated nature and called for people to follow their hearts rather than their heads.

Rousseau was a strong influence on a movement in German literature called *Sturm und Drang* (shturm oont DRAHNG), which means "storm and stress." The best-known work to come out of this movement was *The Sorrows of Young Werther* (VEHR-tuh), a novel published in 1774 by Johann Wolfgang von Goethe (GUR-tuh). The novel introduced a new kind of hero, a hero of strong feelings rather than bold actions. The novel was so popular that for a while a kind of "Werther fever" gripped much of Europe, as young men imitated the sensitive hero, even dressing like Werther in a blue coat and yellow vest.

Romanticism in Poetry

One of the first major statements of Romantic poetry in English was a volume called *Lyrical Ballads* by William Wordsworth and Samuel Taylor Coleridge, first published in 1798. The Preface to *Lyrical Ballads* boldly proclaimed that poetry is "the spontaneous overflow of powerful feeling."

Wordsworth celebrated the natural world. He loved to take long walks through England's beautiful Lake District. He believed that by immersing ourselves in nature, we connect to something larger and purer. He wrote:

> *My heart leaps up when I behold*
> *A rainbow in the sky.*

Wordsworth shared the Romantic faith that nature communicates a spiritual truth, and that by experiencing this truth we become more completely human.

It's no coincidence that Romantic poets celebrated the wonders of nature just when the Industrial Revolution was beginning to transform many aspects of life from rural to urban. As nations industrialized, many thousands of people moved from farms to cities, and forests and fields gave way to factories and railroads. It was in part this sense of separation from the natural world that led the Romantics to glorify nature as a source of moral and imaginative power.

The English poet William Blake attacked the dehumanizing effects of industrialization. It was Blake who described factories as "dark Satanic Mills." In his *Songs of Innocence* and *Songs of Experience*, as well as in other works, Blake evoked the poverty and misery of urban life in the industrial age. The speaker in Blake's poem called "London" says that "in every face" he sees "marks of weakness, marks of woe."

The English poet George Gordon Byron, who at age ten inherited the title Lord Byron, became a hero of Romanticism partly because he broke so many rules—not just artistic rules but also social ones.

Arm raised, Lord Byron declares his readiness to help the Greeks win independence from the Ottoman Turks.

The Hay Wain, by English landscape painter John Constable, depicts the artist's beloved countryside.

Byron lived a very different life from Wordsworth. While Wordsworth wrote about the calm beauty of his native landscape, Byron sought adventure in distant lands. He died of a fever while assisting the Greeks in revolt against their Ottoman rulers.

Romanticism in Art

Like the Romantic poets, Romantic painters celebrated the beauty and power of nature. One such artist was the English painter John Constable. Constable took his easel out of his studio and set it up in the grass to work in the open air. Constable's landscapes embrace the opposite of the industrial and the urban. Even as the Industrial Revolution pushed more and more people out of the countryside and into cities, Constable stayed focused on the forests, lakes, and fields.

The leading Romantic painter in France was Eugène Delacroix (ou-ZHEHN del-uh-KWAH). Delacroix shared the Romantics' fervent faith in the ideals of freedom and liberty. To celebrate the short, successful revolution against the oppressive policies of France's King Charles X in 1830, Delacroix painted one of his best-known works, *Liberty Leading the People*, in which a triumphant female figure, representing the spirit of liberty, leads armed revolutionaries of very different classes and backgrounds in a struggle against tyranny.

In Delacroix's *Liberty Leading the People*, the symbolic female figure of Liberty rebels triumphantly against royal tyranny.

621

Ludwig van Beethoven

Romanticism in Music

In the early 1800s, Romantic ideas began to influence music as well. One of the pioneers of the Romantic movement in music was the German composer Ludwig van Beethoven (LOOD-vihg vahn BAY-toh-vuhn).

Beethoven began composing in the classical style of Franz Joseph Haydn and Wolfgang Amadeus Mozart, whose music displayed order, balance, and clarity. As his career progressed, Beethoven was increasingly influenced by Romanticism. Like the Romantic artists, he declared his profound love of the natural world. For example, Beethoven's Sixth Symphony, known as the *Pastoral* Symphony, evokes a day in the country by using instruments to imitate the sounds of birdsong and thunder.

In his triumphant Ninth Symphony—the last he wrote, also known as the *Choral* Symphony—Beethoven expressed a dream he shared with many Romantic artists, the dream of universal brotherhood. In the symphony's fourth and final movement, Beethoven adds a full chorus and vocal soloists to the orchestra. They sing words from a poem known as the "Ode to Joy"—"All men become brothers under the sway of [Joy's] gentle wings."

Romanticism in Prose

Novelists of the early nineteenth century reflected the ideals of Romanticism in stories that often featured characters from humble origins who demonstrate heroic qualities. The works of Scotland's Sir Walter Scott, whose most famous novel is *Ivanhoe*, became immensely popular throughout Europe and the United States.

In France, Victor Hugo achieved the status of a national hero for his writing. Raised in Paris during Napoleon's reign, Hugo was a renowned writer and political activist throughout his life. His greatest success outside France came from two novels, *The Hunchback of Notre Dame* and *Les Misérables* (which means "the wretched" or "the miserable ones").

Like other Romantics, Hugo believed in the natural goodness of the common man. Some of his most memorable characters are ordinary people who demonstrate extraordinary virtue or make heroic sacrifices, such as Fantine, a young working-class mother in *Les Misérables*.

Hugo wrote about the social issues of his time. When he described the terrible working conditions in the factories of France, he inspired his readers to demand reforms. When Hugo died in 1885, he was so revered that more than two million people turned out for his funeral procession in Paris.

An 1862 engraving from Victor Hugo's *Les Misérables* depicts one of its memorable characters—Little Cosette.

A Transition to Realism

By the mid-to-late 1800s, a new movement was emerging in art and literature, known as **realism**. Realist painters and writers did not glorify either nature or humanity. They focused on the lives of ordinary people, and aimed to depict life as they saw it.

Realist Painters

In France, the painter Gustave Courbet (coor-BAY) declared, "I cannot paint an angel because I have never seen one." Instead, Courbet depicted, for example, the workers in his most famous painting, *The Stone Breakers*. Another French artist, Jean-François Millet (mee-LEH), focused on the lives of peasant farmers. In Millet's *The Winnower*, a peasant stands in a barn, shaking a basket of grain to separate the edible parts from the inedible ones.

The American artist Winslow Homer painted many works featuring sailors facing the hazards of life at sea. Another American realist, Thomas Eakins, attempted to portray modern reality in stark

The Winnower by Jean-François Millet

The Stone Breakers by Gustave Courbet

623

The Gross Clinic by Thomas Eakins portrayed a surgical operation in stark and unsentimental terms.

and unsentimental terms. Eakins's most famous painting, *The Gross Clinic*, shows a prominent surgeon, Samuel Gross, performing an operation. The realistic details—the surgeon's bloody hand, the open wound in the patient's flesh—shocked many viewers.

Realist Writers

Like realist painters, many realist writers focused on the lives of workers and ordinary people. In many great novels—including *Oliver Twist*, *Hard Times*, and *David Copperfield*—the English writer Charles Dickens depicted the lives of working-class people with great sympathy.

In 1857, the French writer Gustave Flaubert (floh-behr) published *Madame Bovary*. The novel's precise descriptions and lifelike characterizations make it a masterpiece of realistic writing. It was also controversial, as the novel's central character, Emma Bovary, a young married woman living in a small town in the French countryside, becomes bored with her husband and engages in adulterous affairs with two different men. Both affairs end unhappily. *Madame Bovary* startled many readers, and Flaubert was even tried for breaking a law against obscenity. Other writers recognized the novel as a masterpiece, and followed Flaubert in writing about the difficult lives of ordinary people.

In the 1860s, the Russian novelist Leo Tolstoy produced his great historical novel *War and Peace*. Set in the time of the Napoleonic Wars, the book swarms with hundreds of characters, from peasant women and low-ranking soldiers to Russian aristocrats and Napoleon himself.

An English writer of great moral seriousness, George Eliot—the pen name of a woman named Marian Evans—set out to realistically depict what she called the hidden life of ordinary people. Her most famous novel, *Middlemarch*, describes the interactions between people of different classes living in a small town.

In the United States, the writer William Dean Howells championed realism as "nothing less than the truthful treatment of material." His own novels condemn the corruption of American society in the so-called Gilded Age of the late 1800s. Howells's friend, Samuel Langhorne Clemens, who adopted the pen name Mark Twain, became famous for *The Adventures of Tom Sawyer* and

Realist writers Leo Tolstoy and George Eliot explored the lives of ordinary people.

other works that humorously celebrate the vitality of life in the American Midwest and West. As a realist, Twain captured the everyday language and slang of the American West.

The Impressionists

In the age of realism in the arts, painters found their task complicated by the invention of photography. By the late nineteenth century, photography had become so cheap and popular that most European homes had many family photographs. How could painters compete with the true-to-life accuracy of a photograph?

Beginning in France in the 1860s, one group of painters decided that truth in art was not a matter of trying to make their paintings depict reality with photographic accuracy. Instead, they set out to capture the changing effects of light, or the many colors of water, or the shifting shades of the evening air. Critics said these artists simply gave their impression of a scene. Thus this group of painters was called the Impressionists.

The major Impressionist painters included Edgar Degas (duh-GAH), Édouard Manet (ma-NAY),

Vincent van Gogh emblazoned *The Starry Night* with vivid colors and bold, swirling brushstrokes.

Claude Monet (moh-NAY), Pierre-Auguste Renoir (ruhn-wahr), and the American artist Mary Cassatt. Impressionism was marked by short brushstrokes and vivid dabs of color, as though the artists were attempting to capture the fleeting light of a passing moment. As Claude Monet wrote, "Other painters paint a bridge, a house, a boat…. I want to paint the air in which the bridge, the house, the boat are to be found—the beauty of the atmosphere around them."

Beginning in the 1880s, some French painters grew dissatisfied with the Impressionist style. These artists are sometimes known as the Post-Impressionists (*post* is a prefix that means "after"). The Post-Impressionists included the brilliant Dutch painter Vincent van Gogh (van GOH), who admired the Impressionists but thought their methods did not leave the artist enough freedom to express his emotions. Van Gogh's swirling brushstrokes and blazing colors reflect bouts of joy and anguish. In *The Starry Night*, he depicts the stars as whirlpools of light.

Thames at Charing Cross by the Impressionist painter Claude Monet

1842
China gives up Hong Kong to Britain after losing the first Opium War.

1850

1860

1869
In Egypt, the Suez Canal opens, connecting the Mediterranean and Red seas.

1857
Sepoys rebel against the rule of the British East India Company, sparking two years of violence in India.

British troops pose at the Great Sphinx at Giza in 1882. Egypt, though not a colony, was dominated by Britain for six decades.

1885
Belgium's King Leopold II makes the Congo in Africa his personal possession.

1890

1905
Japan defeats Russia in the Russo-Japanese War.

1900

1898
A treaty ending the Spanish-American War gives the Philippines and territory in the Caribbean to the United States.

Chapter 27

The New Imperialism

1850–1914

As the Industrial Revolution advanced, Great Britain, France, Belgium, Russia, and the new nation-states of Germany and Italy gained colonies in Asia and Africa. Later, other nations beyond Europe—including Japan and the United States—acquired overseas territories.

As many industrializing countries sought control of resources, markets for manufactured goods, and investment opportunities, they engaged in **imperialism**, the practice of extending a nation's power by taking over other lands or exerting political and economic control over them. European imperialist nations often justified their actions as a way to bring Western improvements and "civilization" to the lands they dominated. But the frenzied grab for land and resources left long-lasting anger and resentment among many peoples, especially in Africa and Asia.

A European Scramble for Empire

Key Questions

- Why did industrial nations seek to build or expand empires during the late nineteenth century?

- How did imperialism affect Africa and Africans?

In the mid-1400s, the Portuguese set up trading posts on Africa's west coast. As the Age of Exploration proceeded, European powers—including Spain, Britain, France, and the Netherlands—explored and colonized distant lands in Asia and the Americas as well as in Africa.

In the late nineteenth century, partly as a result of the Industrial Revolution, European nations' interest in overseas colonies grew. Many industrialized European nations, in an attempt to ensure their prosperity and spread what they saw as their superior civilization, set out to claim gigantic empires. The grab for empire from the 1870s to about 1910 is often called the **New Imperialism**, to distinguish it from the earlier empire-building activities of the sixteenth and seventeenth centuries.

Imperialist Expansion in the Industrial Age

In the 1800s, as trade picked up during the Industrial Revolution, European nations used their overseas colonies to provide ports where both commercial and military steamships could take on fuel and supplies. European powers also turned to their colonies for raw materials, including coal, iron, rubber, and other resources they needed to continue their relentless growth. In the late 1800s, Europeans began seizing control of large parts of Africa—a continent rich in ivory, gold, copper, and rubber, as well as foodstuffs such as coffee and fruit.

Industrialized European countries soon produced more cloth, steel, tools, and weapons than they could sell at home. They couldn't sell to other industrialized countries because all the industrialized nations restricted imports of manufactured goods. So the European nations created markets for their manufactured goods by prohibiting or restricting their colonists from manufacturing their own goods.

An 1885 cartoon depicts Germany, Russia, and Britain grabbing for territory in Africa and Asia.

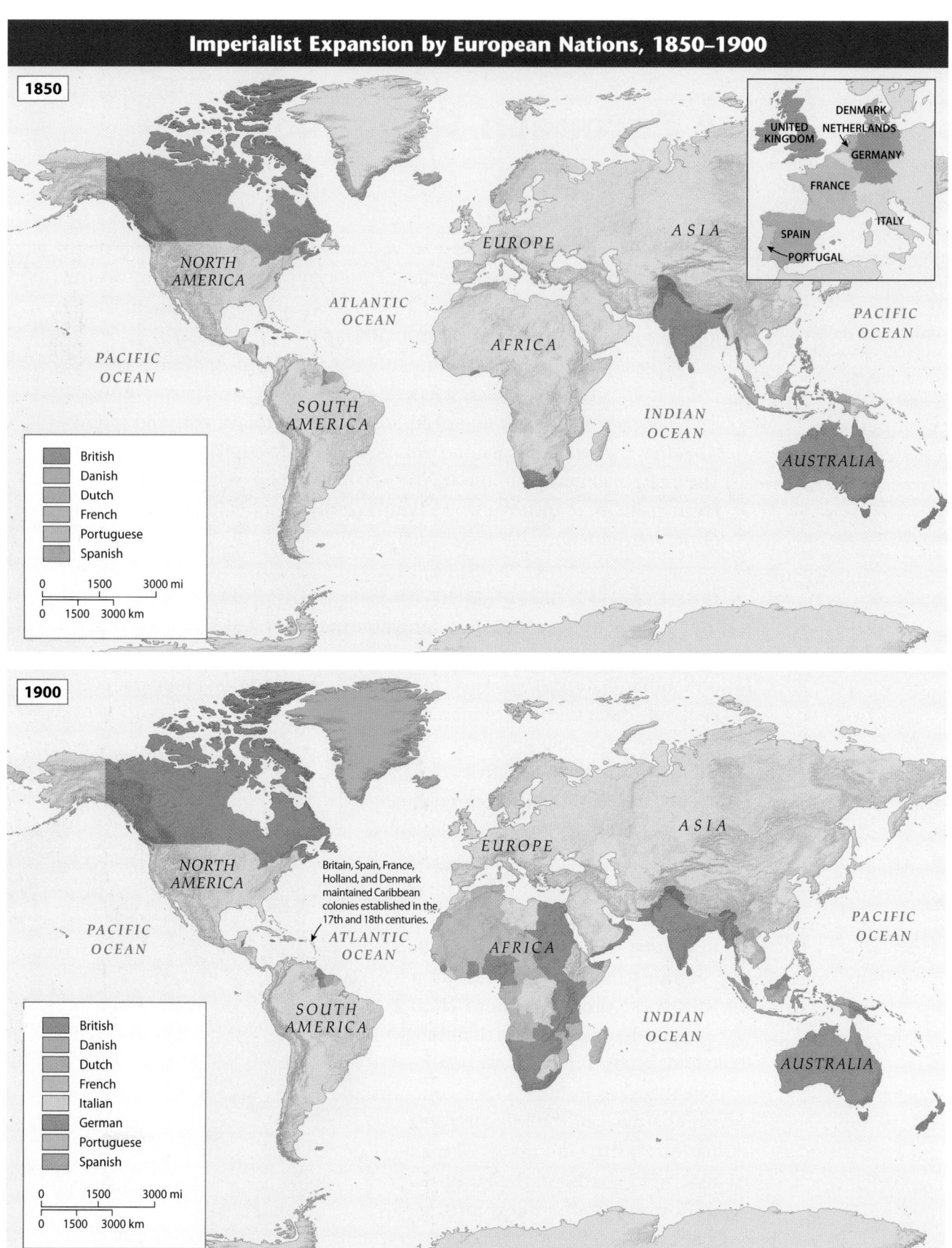

Imperialist Expansion by European Nations, 1850–1900

1850

NORTH AMERICA

ATLANTIC OCEAN

PACIFIC OCEAN

SOUTH AMERICA

EUROPE

ASIA

AFRICA

INDIAN OCEAN

PACIFIC OCEAN

AUSTRALIA

UNITED KINGDOM · DENMARK · NETHERLANDS · GERMANY · FRANCE · ITALY · SPAIN · PORTUGAL

- British
- Danish
- Dutch
- French
- Portuguese
- Spanish

0   1500   3000 mi
0   1500   3000 km

1900

NORTH AMERICA

Britain, Spain, France, Holland, and Denmark maintained Caribbean colonies established in the 17th and 18th centuries.

PACIFIC OCEAN

ATLANTIC OCEAN

SOUTH AMERICA

EUROPE

ASIA

AFRICA

INDIAN OCEAN

PACIFIC OCEAN

AUSTRALIA

- British
- Danish
- Dutch
- French
- Italian
- German
- Portuguese
- Spanish

0   1500   3000 mi
0   1500   3000 km

Between 1850 and 1900, European nations greatly expanded their overseas colonial holdings, especially in Africa and Asia.

Seeking Opportunities

European businessmen saw colonies as highly profitable places in which to invest. Companies could run farms, mines, and railroads where labor was cheap and competition nonexistent.

For many individuals, colonies also offered the promise of prosperity. Beginning in the 1830s, thousands of Frenchmen made their homes in the French colony of Algeria. The Australian gold rush of the 1850s attracted many fortune seekers from Britain.

Some Europeans emigrated to remote colonies hoping to find more success and status than they enjoyed at home. A store clerk in France, for example, might become a government official in Algeria, with authority over thousands of native people.

Seeking Converts

In the mid-nineteenth century, a wave of missionary fervor swept England and North America. Christians, many of whom had been working to abolish the slave trade, began to send missionaries to India, China, and Africa. Missionaries often set up hospitals and schools while they tried to convert people to Christianity.

Some of these missionaries—like the Scotsman David Livingstone, who traveled across Africa—earned the gratitude of native people for their efforts to treat the sick and rescue people from slavery. But many native people resented the missionaries' attempts to turn them away from their traditional faiths. The missionaries' work sometimes became a source of conflict in India, China, and parts of Africa.

Justifying Imperialism

When Livingstone returned to Britain, he gave speeches to urge the spread of the Christian faith and Western commerce across Africa. Livingstone saw Africa as a "dark continent" in need of the "light" of European civilization.

Livingstone's views were typical of his time. Most Europeans took for granted that their culture was superior. They considered Africans and Asians uncivilized and in need of Western guidance and leadership. Referring to Africa, King Leopold II of Belgium urged his fellow European rulers to "open up to civilization the only part of our globe which it has not yet penetrated, [and] to pierce the darkness in which entire populations are enveloped." This belief in Western superiority would regularly be used to justify imperialist conquests and the oppression of native peoples.

In the late nineteenth century, some Western thinkers used the new ideas of social Darwinism to justify imperialism. In their view, among nations engaged in competition for limited resources, only the fittest nations would survive. And which were those? The ones with the most factories, the biggest cities, the strongest armies, the most resources—and, therefore, the most colonies. Social Darwinist thinking spurred nations to compete ever more fiercely to build the biggest empire.

Social Darwinist justifications of imperialism often relied on racial arguments. Some so-called "social scientists" misused Darwin's ideas to claim that certain races had characteristics that made them naturally superior to others. Newspapers in England, for example, praised the superiority of "the British race" over "lesser breeds" such as Asians and Africans.

Nationalism was another force driving the New Imperialism. Countries like Britain, France, Belgium, and Germany competed to acquire colonies not only as sources of wealth but also as symbols of national pride. In the 1700s, France had lost control of its lands in North America and India to Britain. Later, rivalry with Britain helped spur France to build a new empire in Africa and Southeast Asia. In the late 1800s, a newly united Germany set up colonies in East Africa in order to show that it was the equal of Britain and France.

Africa Partitioned

European nations had explored and traded with Africa since the 1400s. For Africans, the most devastating consequence of European contact was the expansion of the slave trade. By 1870, some nine million captured Africans had been shipped across the Atlantic to labor in Europe's New World colonies. In the 1800s, various European nations, with their huge appetite for Africa's raw materials, began claiming large parts of the continent as colonies.

North Africa

The region called North Africa is the part of the continent closest to Europe. It includes farmland and cities along the Mediterranean coast, with the largely uninhabited Sahara to the south. Since the 1500s, the area had been ruled by the Ottoman Empire, centered in Asia Minor. With the decline of Ottoman power in the 1800s, European nations moved in.

France invaded Algeria in 1830, establishing a colony where French emigrants formed a ruling class. Later, the countries of Tunisia and Morocco became French protectorates. (A *protectorate* is a country that is dominated by, but not formally a colony of, a stronger nation.) Similarly, in 1912, the Ottomans gave up Libya to Italy.

Through much of the 1800s, Britain and France competed for influence in Egypt. In 1869, a French company working in Egypt completed the Suez Canal, a waterway linking the Mediterranean and Red seas. Soon after the canal opened, however, three-quarters of the ships using it were British. By dramatically cutting the sailing distance between Europe and India, the canal became a vital link between Britain and its most important colony.

In 1881, nationalist officers in the Egyptian army rose in revolt against European influence. Worried about the security of the Suez Canal, Britain sent in troops to put down the revolt and occupy the country. For the next six decades, although never officially called a colony, Egypt was dominated by Britain and was declared a British protectorate in 1914.

The Congo

North of France and west of Germany sits the small European nation of Belgium. In the late nineteenth century, Belgium's King Leopold II declared, "We must obtain a slice of this magnificent African cake." If European nations were going to carve up Africa, Leopold wanted a large piece for himself.

In central Africa, in a vast region surrounding the Congo River, Leopold set up his own private kingdom. He gave himself the title of King-Sovereign of the Congo Free State. The region was rich in resources, including ivory, palm oil, timber, and copper. But Leopold's dreams of riches focused mainly on rubber, a substance made from sap in the vines of the rubber tree. European manufacturers clamored for rubber to use in making tires, first for bicycles and later for cars.

Harvesting rubber was backbreaking work. Few of Leopold's Congolese subjects would do it voluntarily. So Leopold's forces resorted to a

The Building of the Suez Canal

Designed by the French engineer Ferdinand de Lesseps, the Suez Canal took ten years to build. No one had ever tried to construct a canal of its size, and skeptics doubted that Lesseps could succeed. To build the Suez Canal, Lesseps's company forced thousands of men into what amounted to slave labor, using picks and shovels. Later, Lesseps used machines powered by coal and steam to carve tunnels and scoop sand and mud. When the canal finally opened in 1869, it linked the Mediterranean and Red seas, and had a dramatic effect on world trade. Ships could pass from Europe to Asia without sailing around the African continent.

system of forced labor. When they entered a village, they would seize the women and children as hostages, and then march the men off into the forest. Men who failed to produce their assigned amount of rubber might be brutally flogged, or have their hands, noses, or ears sliced off. Whole villages might be massacred if they resisted.

These brutal methods succeeded in vastly increasing the export of rubber from the Congo, from a hundred tons in 1890 to six thousand tons in 1901. Leopold presided over one of the worst slaughters in human history—between eight and ten million Congolese were murdered, starved, or worked to death.

Eventually, missionaries and journalists revealed what was happening in the Congo. People in Europe and the United States reacted with outrage. In 1908, the Belgian parliament voted to remove the Congo from King Leopold's control. The worst abuses largely ended. But the Congo would remain a Belgian colony until 1960, with the Congolese people having little if any say in their own government.

Colonial bosses oversee the weighing of rubber collected by Africans in King Leopold's colony in the Congo.

Rivals for Southern Africa

In the year 1652, sailors from the Dutch East India Company built a small fort near the Cape of Good Hope, on the southern tip of Africa. Gradually the settlement expanded to become the Cape Colony and attracted colonists from Holland. They farmed the land while fighting with, and often enslaving, the native inhabitants. The colonists called themselves *Boers*, from a Dutch word meaning "farmer." (Later, they would come to be called Afrikaners.)

In the early 1800s, the British occupied the Cape Colony, in order to prevent Napoleon from taking control of the Cape of Good Hope, an important station on the sea-lanes between Europe and Asia. From the first, the Boers resented the British takeover of their colony.

In 1833, Great Britain passed a law abolishing slavery everywhere in British territory. Soon, large numbers of Boers—who believed fiercely in their "right" to own slaves—migrated northward to escape British rule. In making this migration, which they remembered as the "Great Trek," the Boers engaged in fierce battles with native tribes who stood in their path.

The Boers set up two republics of their own, known as the Transvaal and the Orange Free State. Soon after, when diamonds were discovered on British territory, immigrants from Britain flooded into the Cape Colony. The British wanted to use the native population as a source of low-paid labor for the new mines and railroads. But they feared the warlike reputation of native groups, especially the tribe called the Zulu.

When the British demanded that the Zulu army disband, the Zulu king, Cetshwayo (kech-WAH-yoh), refused. In 1879, the British invaded Zululand. Cetshwayo commented bitterly, "First comes the trader, then the missionary, then the red[-coated] soldier." The Zulu fought with determination but their short spears were no match for the rifles and machine guns of the British. After a bloody six-month war, the Zulu were defeated.

The Anglo-Boer War

In South Africa, the Boers remained at odds with the British, who insisted that Boer territories should be subordinate to the British Empire. Tension increased in the 1880s, when large gold fields were discovered in the Transvaal. Cecil Rhodes, a millionaire businessman who owned gold and diamond companies, helped spearhead the drive for British expansion.

In 1899, the long bitterness between the British and the Boers erupted into war. The vicious conflict pitted lightly armed Boer guerrillas against heavily armed British troops. The British had more manpower and better weaponry, but the Boers enjoyed a superior knowledge of the land and the belief that they were fighting for their independence. Frustrated by the success of Boer raids, the British retaliated by herding Boer women and children into camps where many died of disease and malnutrition.

Wealth and Empire: Cecil Rhodes

At the end of the 1800s, the British millionaire Cecil Rhodes controlled South Africa's rich diamond industry. He believed it was the right—indeed, the obligation—of the British to spread their way of life around the globe. "I contend," said Rhodes, "that we are the finest race in the world, and that the more of the world we inhabit, the better it is for the human race." A fervent imperialist, he dreamed of a British African empire stretching "from the Cape to Cairo" (that is, from South Africa to Egypt). When Rhodes and his company seized control of a large territory north of South Africa, they named it Rhodesia.

Cecil Rhodes, who named Rhodesia after himself, bestrides the African continent in this 1892 cartoon.

In 1902, the British won the Anglo-Boer War and established the Union of South Africa as part of the British Empire. In 1910, the colony attained self-government. But the years of imperialism left a society in which whites held most of the country's wealth and political power, while most blacks lived in poverty and had few rights. In a society whose government was based on racial separation and control, black South Africans were deprived of most of the country's land, and subjected to discriminatory laws. In the mid-twentieth century, these laws would evolve into an almost complete separation of the races, known as *apartheid* (uh-PAHR-tiyd, meaning "apartness").

Carving Up the Continent

Before the transatlantic slave trade was abolished in the early 1800s, West Africa was the center of the grim commerce. In the era of the New Imperialism, European powers sought access to West Africa not for slaves but for the region's natural

The New Imperialism in Africa, c. 1914

MOROCCO

TUNISIA

Mediterranean Sea

ASIA

Isthmus of Suez

Suez Canal

SPANISH WEST AFRICA

ALGERIA

LIBYA

EGYPT

Red Sea

FRENCH WEST AFRICA

Niger River

AFRICA

Nile River

FRENCH EQUATORIAL AFRICA

SUDAN

SIERRA LEONE

NIGERIA

SOMALILAND

GOLD COAST

ETHIOPIA

LIBERIA

CAMEROON

Congo River

Lake Victoria

BELGIAN CONGO

Lake Tanganyika

INDIAN OCEAN

GERMAN EAST AFRICA

ATLANTIC OCEAN

PORTUGUESE WEST AFRICA

NORTHERN RHODESIA

PORTUGUESE EAST AFRICA

Zambezi River

MADAGASCAR

GERMAN WEST AFRICA

SOUTHERN RHODESIA

SOUTH AFRICA

Colonies

Belgian
British
French
Italian
German
Portuguese
Spanish

N

0   250   500 mi

0   250   500 km

Cape of Good Hope

Hungry for land and resources, the European imperial powers competed for their slice of what King Leopold of Belgium notoriously described as the "magnificent African cake."

635

resources. The two major European competitors for land and influence in West Africa were Britain and France. France claimed the vast territory known as French West Africa, which stretched from the Sahara to the Atlantic Ocean. Britain established colonies along the coast—Sierra Leone, the Gold Coast (today's Ghana), and Nigeria.

In West Africa, once the center of the transatlantic slave trade, Britain and France competed for land, resources, and influence. Some African groups resisted the European invaders, but by 1900 the only West African country to remain independent was Liberia. Liberia—then Africa's only republic—had been founded by freed slaves

Ethiopian ruler Menelik II and his soldiers retained their country's independence after defeating Italian troops in 1896.

from the United States. Strong American support for the country helped discourage the French or the British from trying to take it over.

While Britain and France dominated West Africa, the countries of East Africa had been largely divided among Britain, Germany, and Portugal. In 1895, Italy tried to join the ranks of major imperial powers by launching an invasion of Ethiopia. But the Ethiopians united around their ruler, Menelik II, who had once proudly declared, "I have no intention of being an indifferent looker-on if the distant powers have the idea of dividing up Africa." In 1896, Menelik's soldiers defeated a seventeen-thousand-man Italian army. Ethiopia was the only East African country to retain its independence.

By 1900, almost all of Africa was under European control. African raw materials—rubber, palm oil, diamonds, and gold—flowed out of the continent to feed the stores and factories of Europe. To reach these resources, colonial governments built roads, railways, and bridges across Africa. In many places, they also built schools and hospitals. Efforts to eradicate disease left many Africans healthier. Between 1880 and 1935, the continent's population increased by one-third.

While modern improvements brought some benefit to colonized peoples, the Europeans continued to exploit Africans and look down on them as inferior, uncivilized, and unfit to rule themselves. The colonial powers allowed Africans few political rights and discouraged traditional customs and religions. These racist attitudes bred deep resentments among Africans. Much of Africa would remain under European dominance until the middle of the twentieth century.

Asia Divided

Since the days of Marco Polo and Columbus, Europeans had coveted the riches of Asia. In the era of the New Imperialism, European powers, especially the British, expanded their control of India and China.

India: The Jewel in the Crown

Great Britain, the nation that started the Industrial Revolution, had a head start in the race for colonies. By the mid-1800s, Britain had built a vast empire that stretched from Canada to Australia. The British navy, the largest in the world, so dominated the oceans that a popular song boasted, "Britannia Rules the Waves." By 1897, when Queen Victoria celebrated sixty years on the throne, the British could truthfully proclaim, as newspapers bragged, that "the sun never set" on their empire. The little island nation had the largest empire in the world, ruling nearly one-quarter of the land surface of the globe.

At least as early as the seventeenth century, the British had made inroads into Asia, where the British East India Company did business in the Indian cities of Calcutta, Madras, and Bombay. For many years, the British government was content to leave India in the hands of officials of the privately owned British East India Company. But in the mid-nineteenth century, the British government stepped in and took control.

Rebellion in India

Back in the 1600s, when the British East India Company established trading posts in India, company officials made arrangements with Mughal princes to get the goods the British wanted, such as spices, silk, indigo, and cotton cloth. Some company officials preferred to control the Mughal leaders rather than cooperate with them. Occasional conflicts followed, and in 1757, troops employed by the British East India Company defeated India's Mughal princes.

The British East India Company continued to expand its rule over the Indian subcontinent. It collected taxes, redistributed land, and organized Indian troops, outfitting them with uniforms and guns. Some of those troops, called *sepoys*, rebelled in 1857.

In a ceremonial procession, British colonial officials ride atop elephants in India, Britain's "Jewel in the Crown."

Key Questions

- Why did Britain seek to maintain India's colonial status? What was the Indian response to British rule?

- What methods of control did Western powers employ in China? How did the Chinese respond?

"The White Man's Burden"

Rudyard Kipling, a British poet and novelist, sometimes criticized British colonial actions, but he was also well known for many works that boosted British patriotism and pride. In a famous poem published in 1899, Kipling described empire building as a noble if thankless task. It was, as he put it "the white man's burden" to spread what he and his countrymen saw as the benefits of civilization. Here are two stanzas from the poem. In the second, Kipling suggests that efforts to bring "the light" to native people will be met by "blame" and "hate" of people who prefer to stay in "night," that is, in a supposed state of backwardness and ignorance.

Take up the White Man's burden—
Send forth the best ye breed—
Go bind your sons to exile
To serve your captives' need;
To wait in heavy harness,
On fluttered folk and wild—
Your new-caught, sullen peoples,
Half-devil and half-child.

Take up the White Man's burden—
And reap his old reward:
The blame of those ye better,
The hate of those ye guard—
The cry of hosts ye humour
(Ah, slowly !) toward the light:—
"Why brought ye us from bondage,
Our loved Egyptian night?"

The immediate cause of the Indian Rebellion (sometimes called the Sepoy Rebellion or Sepoy Mutiny) was a British demand that the sepoys use new rifles, which used greased cartridges as ammunition. To load the gun, a rifleman had to bite off the end of the greased cartridge, an act that the sepoys, who were mostly Hindu and Muslim, considered a religious insult. The grease on the cartridge was partly made from the fat of cows and hogs. Many Hindus do not eat beef, and Muslims are not supposed to eat pork.

At one military base, when a group of sepoys refused to use the new cartridges, the British sentenced them to long terms in prison. Their angry colleagues rebelled and killed the British officers. Since many other Indians resented the East India Company, the rebellion spread quickly. For years,

tension had been building up as the British tried to impose Christianity and Western ways on the Indian population. The mutiny allowed for the violent release of these pent-up tensions.

A bloody conflict followed the rebellion. It took two years for the British to restore order, often through cruel means. When the conflict ended, the British government shut down the East India Company and decided to rule India directly.

Early Stirrings of Nationalism

After the Indian Rebellion, the British pushed ahead with efforts to modernize India and spur its economic development. The British set about building railroads across India. They constructed telegraph and telephone systems. They expanded irrigation networks and established universities.

Spreading "Civilization"?

J.A. Hobson, an English economist and journalist, was an early critic of imperialism. He attacked capitalism as the driving force behind the aggression of British imperialism. In the following passage from *Imperialism*, a now-classic study first published in 1902, Hobson mocks the idea that Europeans benefit conquered peoples by "civilizing" them.

For Europe to rule Asia by force for purposes of gain, and to justify that rule by the pretence that she is civilizing Asia and raising her to a higher level of spiritual life, will be adjudged by history, perhaps, to be the crowning wrong and folly of Imperialism. What Asia has to give, her priceless stores of wisdom garnered from her experience of ages, we refuse to take; the much or little which we could give we spoil by the brutal manner of our giving. This is what Imperialism has done, and is doing, for Asia.

In 1876, Queen Victoria took the title "Empress of India." The queen proudly proclaimed India as the brightest "jewel in the imperial crown." But while the resources of India enriched the British, most Indians lived in poverty and were discriminated against by the British.

While the majority of Indians were poor, an Indian middle class emerged, though British policies kept middle-class Indians from advancing to higher positions in government or the army. Resenting British domination, many well-educated Indian lawyers, professors, journalists, and others met in 1885 to form the Indian National Congress. At first this group served mainly to communicate Indian concerns and requests for moderate reforms to British officials. Over time, as feelings of nationalism grew, the congress took on a more active role. In the mid-twentieth century, the Congress Party, as it would come to be called, helped lead the struggle for Indian independence.

China and the West

You have learned that the rulers of China's Ming and Qing dynasties worked to isolate China from the rest of the world. Like many emperors before them, they distrusted foreigners, whom they viewed as barbarians. By 1800, China, once the world's most advanced civilization, had fallen behind economically and technologically, opening the way for European domination.

The Opium Wars

Europeans had long desired Chinese goods such as silk and porcelain. During the 1700s, Chinese

639

Lin Zexu writes to Queen Victoria

In 1839, Lin Zexu wrote to Britain's Queen Victoria to remind her that China had outlawed the sale of opium and to demand that she stop British traders from selling the drug in his country. In his letter, Lin Zexu followed the Chinese practice of his time in referring to foreigners as "barbarians."

We find that your country is [far from China]. Yet there are barbarian ships that strive to come here for trade for the purpose of making a great profit. The wealth of China is used to profit the barbarians; that is to say, the great profit made by barbarians is all taken from the rightful share of China. By what right do they then in return use the poisonous drug [opium] to injure the Chinese people?... Let us ask, where is your conscience? I have heard that the smoking of opium is very strictly forbidden by your country; that is because the harm caused by opium is clearly understood. Since it is not permitted to do harm to your own country, then even less should you let it be passed on to the harm of other countries....

The barbarian merchants of your country, if they wish to do business for a prolonged period, are required to obey our statutes respectfully and to cut off permanently the source of opium.... May you, O [Queen], check your wicked and sift your vicious people before they come to China, in order to guarantee the peace of your nation, to show further the sincerity of your politeness and submissiveness, and to let the two countries enjoy together the blessings of peace.

tea gained popularity in Europe, particularly in Britain. The demand for tea was tremendous, and China was its only source.

China's rulers had limited trade with foreigners to one city. With no interest in trading for foreign products, the Chinese demanded that all payments for their goods be made in silver. This created an unfavorable balance of trade in Britain. (The *balance of trade* is the difference between a nation's imports and exports over time.)

British traders could not sell manufactured goods in China in exchange for products such as tea. Instead, British silver went to China to pay for tea and other goods. Eager to change this imbalance, in the late 1700s British traders found a product they could sell in China despite government restrictions—opium.

Opium, a drug made from poppies grown in Britain's colony of India, existed in China as a medicinal painkiller, but Europeans encouraged the Chinese masses to smoke it. Selling opium was illegal, but British traders ignored the law and bribed authorities to allow the drug into the country. Millions of Chinese became addicted to opium—so many that China's economy and society suffered serious harm.

Tensions between China and Britain increased when an imperial commissioner, Lin Zexu (lin dzeh-SHOO), traveled to the port of Guangzhou (which the British called Canton) to end the opium trade. When the British refused to cooperate, Lin closed the port to British ships and ordered all British people to leave China. Great Britain responded with gunships that forced their way into port. So began the first of two Opium Wars between China and Great Britain.

China was no match for Britain's powerful navy. When British forces captured the port of Shanghai in 1842, China signed the Treaty of Nanjing, the first of several "unequal treaties," as they were called, in which China was forced to grant trading privileges to foreign powers and exempt these countries' citizens from Chinese law. The 1842 treaty also gave Britain a new colony in China, Hong Kong.

The Chinese were humiliated by their inability to defend their own territory and regulate their own trade. Even so, Chinese officials ignored pleas to adopt the technologies of the West. Many feared that railroads, factories, and other modernization would disturb the imperial ancestors and cause unemployment. They insisted that China must build on its historic strengths, not on those of the West.

The Taiping Rebellion

By 1850, China was in crisis. Many Chinese believed that the Qing Dynasty had lost the mandate of heaven. A series of rebellions shook the country. The most significant one was led by a group called the Taipings (tiy-PINGZ).

The Taipings attempted to establish a new dynasty, the Taiping Tianguo, meaning "Heavenly Kingdom of Great Peace." They promised starving peasants land and shared property. They appealed to workers with promises of new industrial development. The Taipings took control of large regions in southeastern China, and their army swelled to over a million men and women. But China's government fought back in a brutal civil war.

The Taiping Rebellion went on for fourteen years. The strife took a staggering toll. Historians estimate that more than twenty million civilians died in the famine and epidemics that resulted from the conflict. In the end, the Chinese government, with aid from British and French armies, put down the rebellion.

Spheres of Influence

After the Taiping Rebellion, many Qing officials pushed for a campaign of reform and modernization that they called "self-strengthening." Confucian scholars and others in government opposed them or pretended to support the plan while quietly working against it. The biggest pretender was the Empress Dowager Cixi (tsuh-shee), who rose to power after her husband, the emperor, died in 1861 and left a young son on the throne.

The Empress Dowager acted as China's primary ruler for over forty years. She lived extravagantly, using funds intended for military improvements to build a luxurious summer palace. She presided over lavish dinners while peasants outside the palace gates worried that they would not have enough rice to last the winter.

Under the Empress Dowager's rule, China suffered a humiliating loss in a war with Japan (called the Sino-Japanese War, which you will read about later in this chapter). Even when China was forced to make huge payments of silver and give Japan the island

The Empress Dowager Cixi of China

German cavalry troops arrive in Beijing in response to the Boxer Rebellion.

The Boxer Rebellion

In China's provinces, several groups met secretly to plan how to drive the foreigners from their country. One of these secret societies was known as the Boxers because the movements of their ritual martial arts resembled boxing. Like many Chinese, the Boxers focused their anger on the foreigners they saw in their daily lives.

In 1900, the Boxers rose up in fury, killing missionaries, diplomats, journalists, and thousands of Chinese Christians. Six European nations with spheres of influence in China, plus the United States and Japan, joined to send a rescue force that crushed the Boxers.

With foreign forces in the provinces, even the Empress Dowager finally saw the need for change. Over the next few years, she announced a series of reforms in the military, financial, and educational institutions of China. But it was too late. China, once the center of one of the world's most advanced civilizations, was in ruins. Its people were uneducated and desperately poor, its military lacked modern equipment and training, and opium addiction plagued every level of society.

of Taiwan, the Empress Dowager refused to make changes. When her adopted nephew, who held the title of emperor, tried to modernize the country, she staged a coup and overthrew him.

During the war with Japan, desperate Chinese officials turned to Europe for aid. The Europeans helped China recover some territory from Japan, but in return they demanded even more trading rights and territories. Germany, Russia, France, and Great Britain each established *spheres of influence* in China—regions in which an industrialized nation exercises control. The European powers described their action as "carving up the Chinese melon."

As the twentieth century approached, China was crippled. Many suffering Chinese grew angrier every day. They directed much of their anger at the foreigners whom they believed had brought China nothing but trouble.

The 1911 Revolution

In 1894, a young man from southern China, Sun Yat-sen (also known as Sun Yixian), formed the Revive China Society to promote Chinese nationalism. Although born the child of peasants, Sun obtained a good education when he went as a laborer to Hawaii and then to Hong Kong, where he attended schools run by Christian missionaries. Sun became a physician and converted to Christianity. He also picked up many Western political ideas.

Sun had three goals: to expel the Manchu Qing dynasty that many Chinese

Sun Yat-sen worked to end foreign rule in China.

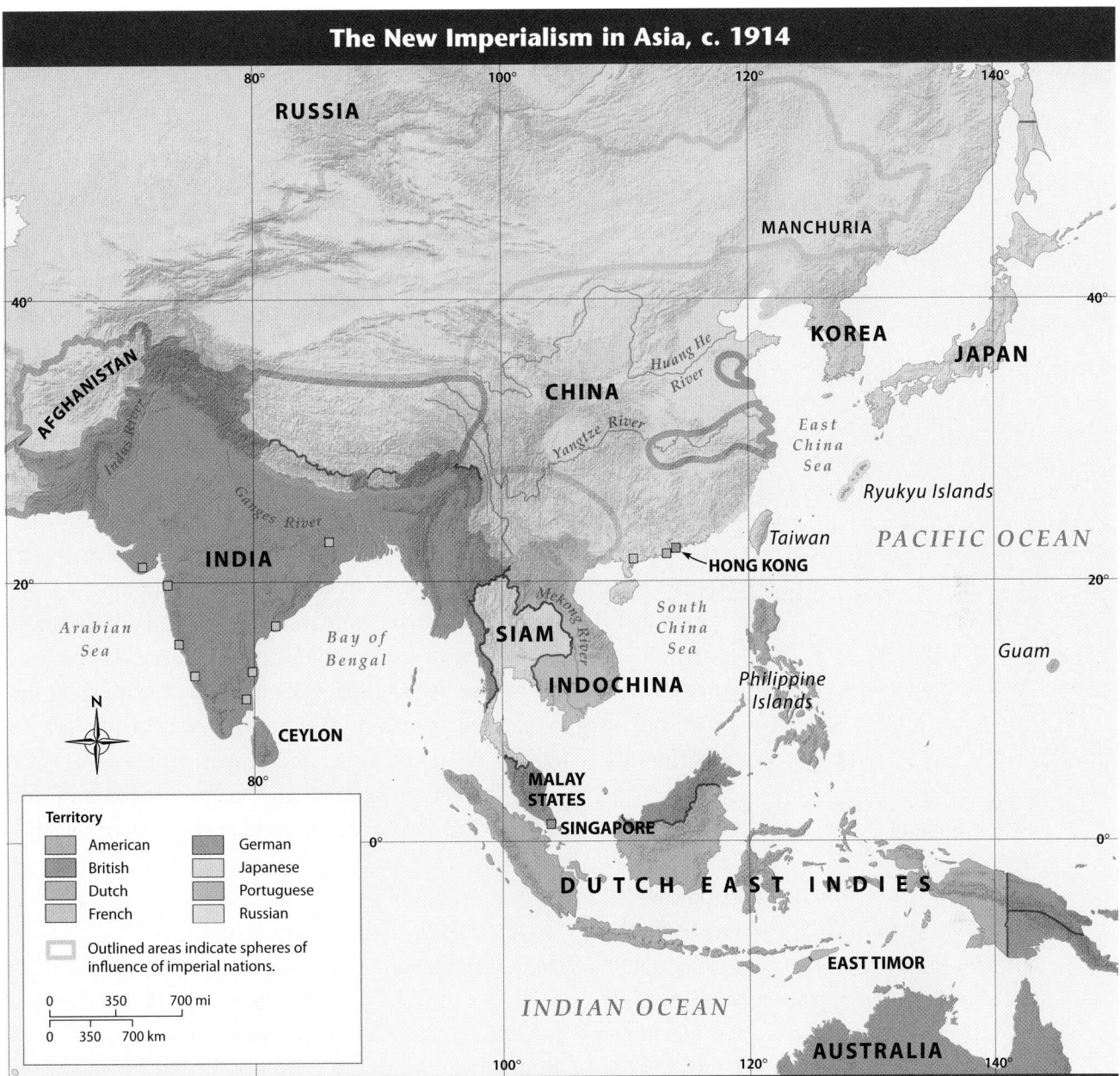

The New Imperialism in Asia, c. 1914

Territory

- American
- British
- Dutch
- French
- German
- Japanese
- Portuguese
- Russian

Outlined areas indicate spheres of influence of imperial nations.

0 — 350 — 700 mi
0 — 350 — 700 km

New territory and trade opportunities drove the swift colonization of Asia by European powers, and by Russia, Japan, and the United States.

saw as foreigners, to establish a democratic republic, and to bring economic security to the Chinese people. After organizing an unsuccessful revolt in 1895, Sun fled China and set about seeking international support for the cause of Chinese nationalism.

Sun Yat-sen was not alone in calling for the overthrow of the Qing dynasty. In 1911, while Sun campaigned for support in the United States, a group of officers of the imperial army led an uprising that quickly spread. The last emperor of China, a five-year-old boy, was forced off the throne. When Sun heard the news, he made his way home.

Greeted as a great leader of the revolutionary movement, Sun Yat-sen was made president of the new Chinese republic. His hold on power was brief. The army soon took control of the country. Still, the work of Sun Yat-sen and his supporters had ended foreign rule and set China on the path to self-government and modernization.

Non-European Nations Compete

Key Questions

- How and why did Japan become an imperial power?
- Why did the United States seek overseas territories? What territories did the United States acquire?

In the age of the New Imperialism, European powers were the most ambitious and assertive in their grab for new colonies. In the late nineteenth century, the United States, a major industrial power, took steps to acquire overseas territories. And, while much of Africa and Asia remained unindustrialized, one Asian country, Japan, quickly transformed itself from a feudal kingdom into a modern industrial nation.

A Turning Point for Japan

In the early seventeenth century, during the reign of the powerful Tokugawa Dynasty, the shogun took extreme steps to seclude Japan from foreign influence. He closed all but one port to foreigners. He decreed that any Japanese people who tried to leave the country would be put to death. He permitted only a few Dutch and Chinese ships to bring foreign goods to the country each year, and insisted that they trade only at the port of Nagasaki, hundreds of miles from the capital.

The Opening of Japan

In the 1850s, the United States began to look at Japan with new interest. American merchants, who were trading with China and other Asian lands, were eager to trade with Japan. Also, Japan's islands would provide a convenient location where American whaling vessels could restock and American naval ships could refuel.

When Commodore Matthew Perry arrived in Japan with a heavily armed American naval squadron, Japan's leaders realized that their sword-wielding samurai were no match for Western ships, cannons, and rifles. They also knew that their neighbors, the Chinese, had just been crushed by the British in a recent series of wars. So they reluctantly agreed to open their country to more trade.

Japan's proud isolation came to an end. The United States and other Western nations insisted that Japan's rulers sign trade treaties similar to those China had been forced to accept. The treaties required Japan to maintain low tariffs on goods imported from the West, and also stated that Westerners residing in Japan were not subject to Japanese law.

The Meiji Restoration

As Western powers extended their presence and influence in Japan, many Japanese noblemen lost respect for their shogun. They believed that if the

With the defeat of the shogun, Japan's Emperor Mutsuhito began an era called *Meiji* or "Enlightened Rule."

shogun could be bullied by the United States or any European power, then the country needed a more powerful government. A civil war broke out, which ended in 1868 with the defeat of the shogun's forces. The victorious rebels announced that they were restoring rule by the emperor, who in recent times had been only a figurehead with no real power.

The emperor, a boy of fifteen named Mutsuhito (mout-sou-HEE-toh), was brought from Kyoto, the ancient imperial capital in the west, to Edo. Edo, which had been home to the shogun, was promptly renamed *Tokyo* (TOH-kee-yoh), a name that means "Eastern Capital."

Japanese officials declared the reign of Emperor Mutsuhito as the beginning of a new period in their country's history, which they called *Meiji* (MAY-jee), meaning "Enlightened Rule." The 1868 restoration of the emperor as the governor of Japan is known as the Meiji Restoration, and the long period of Mutsuhito's reign (1868–1912) is known as the Meiji Era.

Modernizing Japan: The Meiji Look West

The Meiji government decided to respond to Western dominance by abandoning its feudal past and rapidly modernizing. The Japanese embraced the slogan "Prosperous Nation, Strong Military," and set out to become as wealthy and powerful as Europe and the United States.

Japanese officials traveled to Europe and the United States, where they visited shipyards, iron foundries, paper plants, cotton mills, and coal mines. The Meiji government began to invest heavily in the latest means of communication and transportation. It installed telegraph lines and laid thousands of miles of railroad track. It set up a modern banking system and invested in textile mills, cement factories, and shipyards.

Soon the smokestacks of factories towered over the countryside. The Japanese constructed a mammoth steel mill and started building steamships. Japan industrialized so successfully that by the end of the Meiji era, nearly 80 percent of the country's exports consisted of manufactured goods rather than raw materials.

As Japan modernized, leading officials understood that a modern economy relied on an educated workforce. After touring Western schools, one official wrote, "Nothing has more urgency for us than schools.... Our people are no different from the Americans or Europeans of today; it is all a matter of education or lack of education." The Meiji government ordered that schools be built in most Japanese towns and villages. By 1900, most of Japan's children were educated at least through the elementary level. Like European schools, Japanese schools taught not only reading and writing but also strong loyalty to their nation. The Japanese school system was designed to produce not only industrious workers but also loyal subjects.

The Meiji set out to build Japanese military forces organized on modern principles. As a model for their navy, Japan turned to Great Britain, which had the largest navy in the world. Japanese naval officers studied in Britain, and the ships of the Japanese navy were built in European shipyards.

The Sino-Japanese War

Japan's rapid industrial growth soon fueled the same appetite for raw materials that spurred imperialistic European nations. Between 1890 and 1910,

as trade and prosperity increased, so did Japan's population. The nation needed more coal, more iron, and more rice. And it wanted someone to buy its many manufactured wares.

Japan's western neighbor, Korea, had what Japan wanted, including iron and coal. Korea, at this time, was a poor country whose weak government had long been forced to make tribute payments to China. When Koreans started an uprising against Chinese domination in 1894, and China sent troops to Korea in response, Japan saw its chance.

Japan sent its own troops to Korea, supposedly to protect it. This action provoked a war with China. In the Sino-Japanese War, the well-coordinated forces of the tiny island nation of Japan trounced the poorly organized army and navy of China, the largest nation in eastern Asia.

> The prefix *Sino-* means "Chinese."

Japan then proceeded to dominate Korea. The Japanese also demanded that China make huge payments of silver, and turn over the island

Japanese troops overpowered Chinese forces in the Sino-Japanese War. Japan then dominated Korea and Taiwan.

Japanese troops await attack by Russian cavalry in the 1904 Russo-Japanese war over the Chinese province of Manchuria.

of Taiwan to Japan. Startled Europeans and Americans watched as Japan showed its strength in modern warfare and imperial bullying.

The Russo-Japanese War

Both Japan and Russia sought to control Manchuria, a province in northern China. The Russians wanted to control Manchuria in order to protect the Trans-Siberian Railroad, a six-thousand mile (9,656 km) railroad that, when completed, would connect Moscow to a Russian port on the Sea of Japan. Japan wanted Manchuria for its coal and rice, and to help safeguard its control of Korea.

In 1904, the Japanese, flush with confidence after defeating the Chinese in the Sino-Japanese War, decided to gamble on defeating the Russians for control of Manchuria. Fighting the Russians on the Manchurian plains, the Japanese troops made little headway. But at sea, Japan's modern navy, which included ships captured from the Chinese, easily sank Russia's vessels.

To the Western world's surprise, the Japanese defeated the Russians in the Russo-Japanese War. In a peace treaty brokered by the United States, Japan gained formerly Russian ports in Manchuria, but the Russians were allowed to keep their railroad. Japan hungrily eyed the rest of Manchuria.

A great surge of nationalist pride swept through Japan. A nation that had wanted to defend itself against Western imperialism would soon set out on its own path of imperialist conquest.

Expanding United States Interests

The aftermath of the American Civil War turned the country's attention inward, but by the 1890s, the nation's focus began to shift outward. Many of the same motivations for empire that influenced European countries also fueled imperialist ambitions in the United States. A desire for investment opportunities, new markets for manufactured goods, a nationalist urge to prove its fitness among economic competitors—these and other motivations spurred the United States in its drive to acquire overseas territories.

The Beginnings of American Empire

In 1867, the United States purchased Alaska from Russia for $7.2 million dollars. In the 1890s, the United States set its sights on the islands of Hawaii in the Pacific, where more than two-thirds of the land was owned by American and European planters and businessmen. The planters wanted the Hawaiian monarch to let the United States build a naval base at Pearl Harbor on the island of Oahu. When Queen Liliuokalani resisted, American marines advanced on the queen's palace with cannons and machine guns. To avoid bloodshed, the queen agreed to resign, and in 1900 Hawaii became a territory of the United States.

Queen Liliuokalani of Hawaii had to step down when faced with U.S. military force.

647

Nationalists in the United States supported these acquisitions, as their ancestors had supported American expansion into Mexican territory in the 1840s. But other Americans opposed the idea of an American Empire. Some objected that it was wrong for a nation born in anticolonial revolution to become a colonial power. And some expressed worries, grounded in racism, about the addition of millions of nonwhite people to American territory.

The Spanish-American War

As early as 1823, President James Monroe had announced a policy known as the Monroe Doctrine, which stated that the United States would resist any European attempts to set up new colonies in the Americas or to interfere with Latin American affairs. In Monroe's time, the United States did not have the military strength to back up its bold words. By the late 1800s, however, the United States was strong enough to take military action. In the late 1890s and early 1900s, the United States acquired several new territories in the Western Hemisphere as a result of the Spanish-American War.

The sinking of the U.S. battleship the *Maine* in Havana Harbor was a catalyst for a declaration of war on Spain.

The war began on the Caribbean island of Cuba. In the 1890s, Cuba was still part of the Spanish Empire. American businesses had invested heavily in the island's sugar and cigar industries. In 1895, José Martí led Cubans in an uprising against Spanish rule. Americans were outraged when they heard that Spanish forces were herding Cubans into overcrowded prison camps, where tens of thousands died of disease and starvation. Some politicians began calling for the United States to enter the conflict, both to assert its own interests and to help the Cubans.

In February 1898, the *Maine*, an American battleship sent to protect Americans in Cuba, blew up in Havana Harbor, killing more than 260 sailors. A New York newspaper reported that the ship had been destroyed by a Spanish mine. A banner headline in the newspaper proclaimed, "Remember the *Maine!*" The cause of the *Maine's* sinking was never determined, and many historians today blame it on an accidental explosion inside the ship. But in the spring of 1898, Congress declared war on Spain.

In Cuba, the Spanish soldiers were worn out from fighting Cuban rebels. The United States won a swift victory in what an American diplomat called "a splendid little war." Technically, Cuba gained its independence from Spain, but the United States established a naval base at Guantánamo Bay and largely controlled affairs on the island until the 1930s.

Treaty negotiations to end the Spanish-American War gave the United States the Caribbean island of Puerto Rico, as well as two Spanish possessions in Asia—the island of Guam and the Philippines, a chain of islands in the Pacific southeast of China. Reflecting on the aftermath of the war, President William McKinley said, "And so it has come to pass that in a few short months we have become a world power."

Rebellion in the Philippines

Even before the outbreak of the Spanish-American War, American expansionists had their eye on the Philippines. They wanted these islands as a base for American power in Asia. Only days after the Spanish-American War began, American warships sailed into Manila Bay and easily destroyed the old Spanish vessels. Within weeks, American troops occupied Manila, the capital city of the Philippines.

President McKinley justified the takeover of the Philippines by saying that unless the United States assumed control of the islands, they would fall into the imperial clutches of France, Britain, or Germany. Furthermore, said McKinley, reflecting the attitudes of his time, it was the duty of Americans to "uplift" and "civilize" the Filipinos.

In a 1903 cartoon, President Theodore Roosevelt throws dirt on Bogota, Colombia, which wouldn't allow the U.S. purchase of land for a canal.

Some American leaders justified the acquisition of the nation's new Pacific territories—Hawaii and the Philippines—because they provided stepping-stones to China. Many American businessmen believed that this vast and heavily populated nation could be a very profitable market for American goods.

In February 1899, a rebellion broke out against American rule in the Philippines. For the next three years, American troops battled against nationalist guerrillas in fierce and often brutal fighting. In 1901, the rebel leader Emilio Aguinaldo was captured, and the war ended by the next year. The United States would not grant the Philippines its independence until 1946.

In small, fast-moving bands, *guerrilla* fighters battle a larger army by using surprise tactics such as raids, ambushes, and sabotage.

Theodore Roosevelt and the Panama Canal

As a result of the Spanish-American War, the United States possessed territories in both the Atlantic and the Pacific. President Theodore Roosevelt wanted a way to move ships swiftly from one ocean to another to protect American colonial interests or in the event of war. Ships had to travel thousands of miles to go around South America's Cape Horn. But in Central America, at the narrowest point of the Isthmus of Panama, less than forty miles (64 km) separate the Atlantic and Pacific oceans. In the late nineteenth century, a French company had tried but failed to build a waterway across Panama. President Roosevelt was determined to pick up where the French left off.

An *isthmus* is a narrow strip of land connecting two larger land areas.

When Roosevelt took office, Panama was a colony of Colombia. In early 1903, Roosevelt tried to negotiate a treaty permitting the United States to buy a strip of land for a canal across the Isthmus of Panama. When the Colombian legislature refused, an angry Roosevelt urged a group of Panamanians to stage an uprising against Colombia.

Roosevelt sent American warships to support the revolutionaries. Colombia quickly withdrew its forces from Panama, which declared itself an independent republic. The new Panamanian government sold the United States a ten-mile-wide (16 km) strip of land for the planned canal. The agreement gave the United States the right to possess the Canal Zone "in perpetuity" (forever).

Back to Panamanian Control

The U.S.-controlled Canal Zone, which split the nation of Panama, led to resentment among Panamanian citizens. In the 1960s, Panamanians staged anti-American riots. In 1977, the United States signed a treaty giving most of the Canal Zone back to Panama, with the canal itself remaining under the joint control of the U.S. and Panama. In 1999, Panama assumed full control of the canal.

The construction of the canal, which took about ten years, was one of the greatest engineering feats in history, employing as many as fifty thousand workers at a time. Using shovels, dynamite, and rock drills, laborers dug up 338 million tons of soil and rock. Workers poured millions of yards of concrete for the locks designed to raise and lower ships as they passed through the canal.

In building the Panama Canal, more than five thousand workers died in accidents or were killed by tropical diseases. Upon completion of the canal, ships that once took weeks to travel between the Atlantic and the Pacific could make the voyage in hours. The United States now owned a waterway of immense military and economic significance.

Expanding Influence: The Roosevelt Corollary

Theodore Roosevelt extended the Monroe Doctrine to claim a more assertive role for the United States in foreign affairs. Explaining a policy known as the Roosevelt Corollary, the president declared that the United States had the right to assert "international police power" in the Western Hemisphere. Roosevelt claimed that the United States would intervene in the affairs of Latin American nations "only in the last resort." In practice, the Roosevelt Corollary led to the increasing use of "gunboat diplomacy," that is, the threat or use of military force to restore stability to governments in the region, and to make them support American interests.

The Roosevelt Corollary was used to justify numerous interventions in Latin American affairs. In 1902, when Germany and Britain mounted a naval blockade of Venezuela in a dispute over repayment of Venezuela's debts, Roosevelt lifted

The Panama Canal dramatically cut the time it took for ships to travel between the Atlantic and the Pacific oceans.

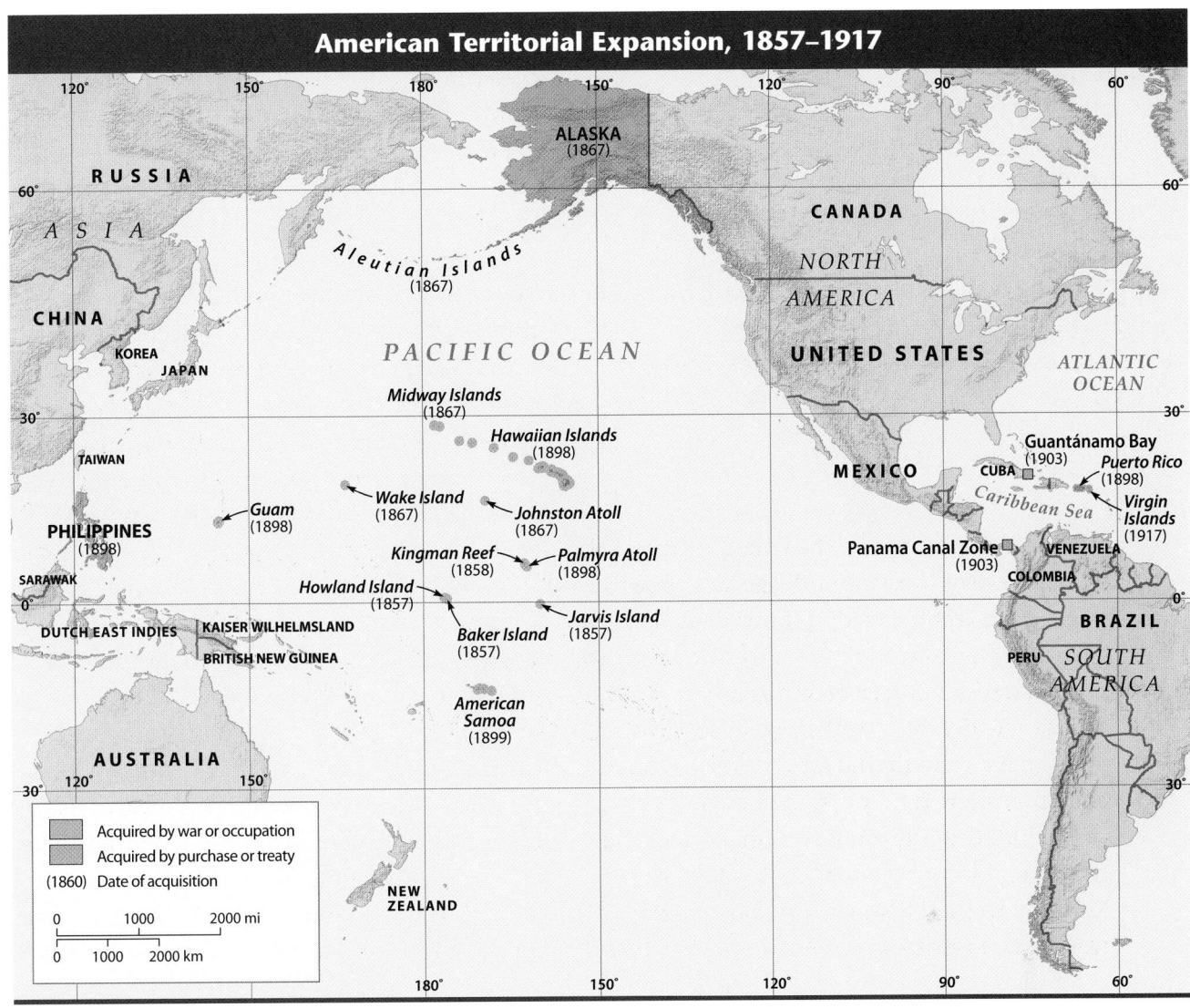

American Territorial Expansion, 1857–1917

Legend:
- Acquired by war or occupation
- Acquired by purchase or treaty
- (1860) Date of acquisition

0   1000   2000 mi
0   1000   2000 km

The United States, a rapidly emerging industrial and economic power, competed with European imperial powers by acquiring new territories in the Pacific Ocean and the Caribbean Sea.

the blockade by threatening military action. The United States intervened in a similar quarrel over debts owed by the Dominican Republic. When political unrest threatened American economic interests in Cuba, Roosevelt sent in the marines, who occupied the island from 1906 to 1909. In the following decades, the United States would use military force to intervene in Nicaragua and Haiti.

Conflict Ahead

In the late nineteenth and early twentieth centuries, the United States proved that it could compete with the empire builders of Europe. But European powers remained dominant in the New Imperialism. European countries continued to compete enthusiastically, and sometimes ruthlessly, to expand their empires by gaining more colonies.

While some in the United States protested that American imperialism was a distortion of the nation's ideals, many gloried in their country's growing power and prominence. Americans would soon find that, as a world power, they would be drawn into world conflicts.

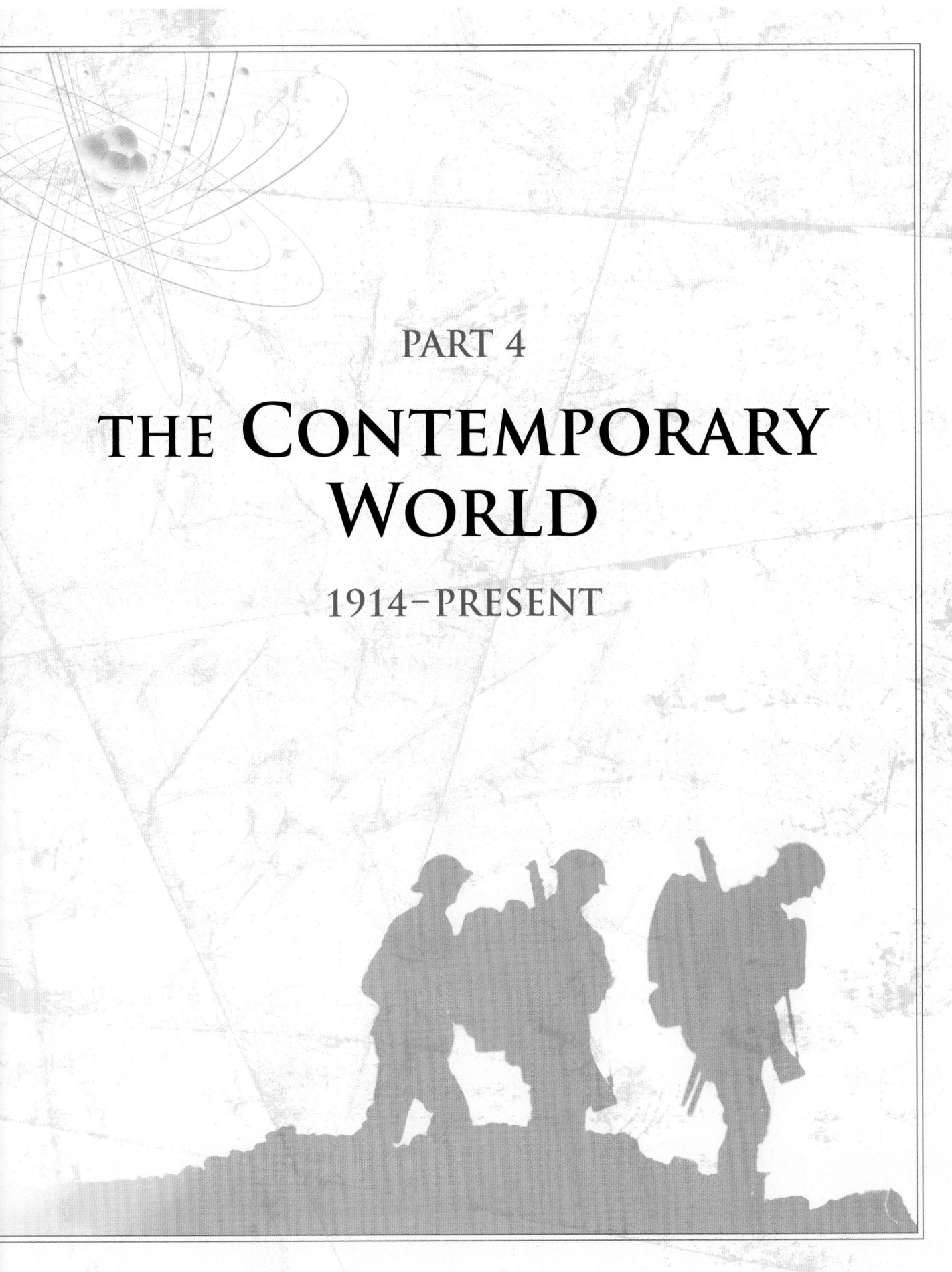

PART 4

THE CONTEMPORARY WORLD

1914–PRESENT

France, 1916: Trench warfare during the "Great War"

1904

1908

1912

1907
Europe's great powers
stand divided into the
Triple Alliance and the
Triple Entente.

CHAPTER 28

WORLD WAR I

1914–1920

1914
A Serbian nationalist assassinates Austria's Archduke Ferdinand, triggering World War I.

1916

1918
A worldwide influenza epidemic begins, killing tens of millions.

1915
In a stalemate on the Western Front, the war becomes defined by trench warfare.

1917
The United States declares war on Germany and joins the Allies.

1919
The Versailles Treaty holds Germany responsible for the war and all damages.

*I*n many Western nations, the twentieth century dawned with optimism, confidence, and a bright sense of promise. The industrial and democratic revolutions of the nineteenth century appeared to be steaming ahead into the twentieth. Factories hummed and ships weighed anchor for foreign ports. More people were taking part in the political life of their countries, helping to make laws and important decisions.

But tensions mounted as industrialized nations competed to build the most productive factories, the richest colonies, and the most powerful military. Where would this race for arms and territory lead?

Some statesmen feared that the clashing ambitions of industrialized nations would trigger what one British diplomat called a "long-dreaded European war." Indeed, war did come—and by the time it was over, more than nine million soldiers were dead, four empires lay in ruins, and the confidence with which the century began turned to despair.

The war that raged from 1914 to 1918 is called World War I, to distinguish it from a second catastrophic war that came later in the twentieth century. Of course, those who lived through World War I could not foresee future conflicts. They only knew the world had never experienced warfare on such a scale. They gave the disastrous conflict another name—the Great War.

The Great War Begins

At the beginning of the twentieth century, Europe's great powers—Britain, France, Germany, and Russia—competed fiercely to expand their empires in Africa and Asia. This imperialist competition was in part driven by strong feelings of nationalism. In the late nineteenth and early twentieth centuries, nationalism changed from a feeling of "pride in my country" to the belief that "my country, right or wrong, is superior to all others." This self-glorifying kind of nationalism fueled heated rivalries among Western nations.

Key Questions

- What circumstances, attitudes, and events led to war in Europe in 1914?

- Once the war was underway, how did it differ from popular expectations?

Military Buildups and Fragile Alliances

Such aggressive nationalism often went hand in hand with militarism—the glorification of military might. The most fervently militaristic state was Germany. One German general wrote that war "is not only a necessary element in the life of the people, but also an indispensable factor in culture, indeed the highest expression of the strength and life of truly cultured peoples."

The German government embarked on an ambitious shipbuilding program intended to challenge the British navy's dominance of the seas. France strengthened its land forces in response to the growing might of the German army.

For decades, Europe's industrialized nations built up their armies and stockpiled weapons, yet still managed to stay at peace with each other. In part, they avoided war through a fragile system of military alliances. Each nation entered into an agreement with other nations that said, in effect, "If your enemies attack you, I will come to your aid. And if my enemies attack me, you will come to my aid." Through such alliances, the European powers hoped to protect themselves and discourage each other from launching a major war.

As early as 1879, Germany made an alliance with Austria-Hungary.

The Great War involved all of Europe, and more.

This German foundry used new technologies and materials to make cannons, which added to the growing might of the German army.

657

Prewar Alliances, c. 1912

Triple Alliance
Triple Entente
Ottoman Empire
Colony (Triple Alliance)
Colony (Triple Entente)

NORWAY

St. Petersburg

Stockholm

SWEDEN

North Sea

Baltic Sea

DENMARK

Copenhagen

Minsk

GREAT BRITAIN

London

NETHERLANDS
Amsterdam

Berlin

Warsaw

RUSSIA

Kiev

Vistula R.

Dnieper River

Brussels
BELGIUM
LUXEMBOURG

GERMANY

ATLANTIC OCEAN

Rhine River

Paris

Loire River

Prague

Vienna

Budapest

SWITZERLAND

Danube River

AUSTRIA-HUNGARY

FRANCE

Belgrade

ROMANIA
Bucharest

Black Sea

BOSNIA-
HERZEGOVINA
Sarajevo

SERBIA

BULGARIA
Sofia

PORTUGAL

ANDORRA

ITALY

MONTENEGRO

Lisbon

Madrid

*Corsica
(France)*

Rome

ALBANIA

Istanbul

SPAIN

*Sardinia
(Italy)*

Mediterranean

OTTOMAN EMPIRE

Neutral when the war began in August, 1914, the Ottoman Empire was persuaded to join the Central Powers three months later.

GREECE

Athens

SPANISH
MOROCCO
(Spain)

Algiers

Tunis

*Sicily
(Italy)*

*Dodecanese
(Italy)*

*Cyprus
(Great Britain)*

*Crete
(Greece)*

MOROCCO
(France)

ALGERIA
(France)

TUNISIA
(France)

*Malta
(Great Britain)*

Sea

A F R I C A

Tripoli

LIBYA
(Italy)

Cairo

EGYPT
(Great Britain)

Intense rivalry and distrust among the imperial dynasties of Europe led to a complex web of alliances that helped trigger World War I.

Each empire pledged to fight for the other if attacked by Russia. A few years later, Italy joined the agreement, which became known as the **Triple Alliance**. Germany, Austria-Hungary, and Italy, the three members of the Triple Alliance, pledged that if any member were drawn into a war with two or more countries, the other members would come to its aid.

France, alarmed by Germany's military buildup and by the Triple Alliance, formed its own alliance with Russia. The two nations agreed to help each other if attacked by Germany.

Britain, troubled by the buildup of the German navy, decided it had better seek potential allies. In 1907, Britain, France, and Russia entered into an agreement called the **Triple Entente** (ahn-TAHNT, French for "understanding").

So, by the early twentieth century, Europe's great powers lay divided into two opposing camps—the Triple Alliance and the Triple Entente. These complicated alliances helped maintain a fragile peace. But they also meant that if one nation went to war, all might find themselves in a fight.

Tensions in Austria-Hungary

Austria-Hungary, one of the members of the Triple Alliance, was also known as the Austro-Hungarian Empire or the Habsburg Empire, after the name of the ruling family. In the mid-nineteenth century, the Habsburgs ruled the second largest empire in Europe, after Russia. The Austro-Hungarian Empire's government was centered in the Austrian city of Vienna.

The empire was made up of many different peoples and cultures, including Germans, Hungarians, and Slavs. (The Slavs, a large ethnic group with roots in eastern Europe, include the Czechs, Slovaks, Croats, Slovenes, and Serbs.)

An *ethnic group* is a group of people that share a common language and culture.

In the mid-to-late nineteenth century, nationalist movements splintered the Austro-Hungarian Empire. Urged on by Kaiser Wilhelm's chancellor, Otto von Bismarck, many German states united to become the new nation of Germany. To the south, the Habsburg's Italian provinces broke away to join the new nation of Italy.

To deal with rising nationalism in Hungary, the Habsburg emperor, Franz Josef, accepted a compromise. Hungarians got their own parliament and constitution, while Franz Josef reigned as the new king of Hungary. Franz Josef's many Slavic subjects were angered. Slavic nationalists argued that, like the Hungarians, they should have a say in governing themselves. Slavic resentment of Habsburg rule would soon flare up and have dire consequences.

The Balkan Peninsula: The Powder Keg of Europe

In the southeast corner of Europe lay the Balkan Peninsula, or "the Balkans" for short. This region was home to a number of small nations, including Serbia, Croatia, Bosnia-Herzegovina (BAHZ-nee-uh HERT-se-gaw-VEE-nah), Albania, and Bulgaria.

For centuries most of the Balkan Peninsula had been ruled by the Ottoman Empire. Once one of the world's most powerful empires, the Islamic empire of the Ottoman Turks had stretched across much of central Europe and into North Africa and the Middle East. But in the 1800s, as feelings of nationalism grew stronger, various peoples broke free of Ottoman rule. As European nations industrialized and grew strong, the Ottoman Empire grew weak.

By the early 1900s, the once-dominant Ottoman Empire was known as the "Sick Man of Europe." As the Ottomans lost their grip on the Balkan Peninsula, two other empires sought to control it. One was Russia, ruled by Tsar Nicholas II. The other was Austria-Hungary, ruled by Emperor Franz Josef.

The people of the Balkan Peninsula, however, wanted to rule themselves. The long years under Ottoman rule had stirred feelings of nationalism in the Balkans. More than once, Balkan revolutionaries had fought for independence from the Ottomans. The people of the Balkans were not willing to sit back and watch new foreign rulers take control.

One of the Balkan states, Serbia, was a hotbed of nationalism. The Serbs, a Slavic people, had won their independence from the Ottoman Empire in 1878. But in that same year, Austria-Hungary occupied neighboring Bosnia-Herzegovina. The Serbs were enraged. They had hoped to make Bosnia-Herzegovina, where many Slavs also lived, part of a larger Serbian kingdom. Likewise, many Slavs in Bosnia-Herzegovina longed to be part of a larger Serbia and free from Austrian control.

Feelings of nationalism in Bosnia and Serbia were on a collision course with Austria-Hungary's imperialist ambitions to dominate the Balkans. Such tensions earned the Balkans the nickname the "Powder Keg of Europe." Germany's Chancellor Bismarck looked at the explosive situation and predicted that "some damned thing in the Balkans" was likely to plunge Europe into its next major war.

The Powder Keg Explodes

Bismarck's prediction came true on June 28, 1914. On that day, Archduke Franz Ferdinand, heir to the throne of Austria-Hungary, was visiting Sarajevo (sar-uh-YAY-voh), the capital of Bosnia. As Franz Ferdinand and his wife, Sophie, rode through the city in an open car, a young Bosnian nationalist rushed forward, pistol in hand, and killed them both.

Austrian officials believed, correctly, that Serbians had been involved in the plot to murder the archduke. To Emperor Franz Josef and his advisers, the assassination provided the perfect excuse to crush Serbia and put an end to the Slavic independence movements at the edge of the Austro-Hungarian Empire. The Austrians promptly declared war on Serbia.

But the giant empire of Russia, home to many Slavic peoples, considered itself the protector of all Slavs. Although Russia's leader, Tsar Nicholas II, tried to avoid conflict, too many people had been whipped into a frenzy for war, and too many generals were ready to fight.

A trainload of enthusiastic soldiers leaves Paris in 1914, bound for what many thought would be a quick fight.

The system of alliances that Europeans had counted on to maintain peace now tumbled the great powers into war. To defend the Serbs, Russia mobilized its army for a fight with Austria-Hungary. That brought Austria-Hungary's ally in the Triple Alliance, Germany, into the war. France called up troops to support Russia, its ally in the Triple Entente. Germany declared war on France. Britain responded by declaring war on Germany.

> To *mobilize* troops means to assemble them and get them ready for war.

By early August in 1914, the great powers of Europe were at war. On one side were Germany and Austria-Hungary, and eventually the Ottoman Empire. (Italy, which had been part of the Triple Alliance, decided to stay neutral.) On the other side were Britain, France, and Russia. The First World War had begun.

Home by Christmas?

Waves of patriotic feeling swept through the nations on both sides. Both sides expected a short war. "You'll be home by Christmas," civilians assured troops on their way to the front.

Each side was confident of its superior military strength. The British felt sure their Royal

The assassination of Franz Ferdinand and his wife Sophie was the spark that ignited war among Europe's great powers.

Navy would easily destroy the German fleet and choke the German economy by blockading German ports. The French felt safe behind the massive barricades they had built on their eastern border. The overall strategy seemed simple—France would attack Germany from the west, while Russia attacked from the east. Then Russia, after quickly overwhelming Germany, would turn to crush the Austrians.

The Germans had their own plan for a quick victory. With about two million troops ready to fight, they planned to deliver a swift knockout punch to France and then, with their Austrian allies, dash east to deal with the Russians, who usually took a long time to get their army ready.

The War Widens on Two Fronts

The fighting began on August 4, 1914, when a million German troops surged west into Belgium, which lay between northeast France and Germany. Belgium was not their target—it was a way to get to France without having to encounter the barricades the French had built on their eastern border. German generals reasoned that their troops could quickly march through Belgium and then storm south into France and capture the capital city, Paris. They could then hurry back to Germany and arrive at the border with Russia before the Russians could put their boots on.

The Germans charged into Belgium expecting little resistance. But the Belgians cut communication lines, sabotaged roads, and blew up railway tunnels and bridges. The British, who had promised to protect Belgium, rushed to the small country's aid.

Together, the Belgian and British forces slowed the Germans but could not stop them. The Germans burned the Belgian university town of

British cavalry on horseback try to hold back heavily armed German troops advancing through Belgium.

How World War I Started

Here are the main incidents in the rapid-fire chain of events that led to the beginning of World War I in 1914.

August 1	Germany sees Russian troops mobilizing and declares war on Russia; France orders a general mobilization.
August 3	Germany declares war on France.
August 4	Germany invades Belgium; Britain, alarmed by the invasion of a neutral country, declares war on Germany.
August 5	Austria-Hungary declares war on Russia.
August 23	Japan declares war on Germany and begins to occupy German colonies in China and the Pacific.

Louvain (loo-VEN) to the ground, including its medieval library and priceless manuscripts. As German troops pushed south, they shot hundreds of Belgian civilians who resisted the invasion. British and French newspapers denounced the "barbarism" of troops they called "the Huns." Despite French and British resistance, by the end of September, German soldiers were only a two-day march from Paris.

But then the French and British forces rallied, confronting the Germans at the Marne River. In early September, two million soldiers clashed in battle, and the Germans were forced to retreat. As the Germans fell back, both sides dug long trenches and unrolled spools of barbed wire. By year's end, two parallel, opposing lines of entrenchments stretched some four hundred fifty miles (725 km), from the North Sea to Switzerland.

That line became known as the Western Front. For nearly four years, the two sides bogged down on the Western Front. To almost everyone's surprise, the anticipated short war turned into a long, bloody deadlock.

East of Germany, fighting broke out in a vast area that came to be known as the Eastern Front. Russian troops had mobilized more quickly than the Germans thought possible. Two Russian armies thrust deeply into a region of forests and marshy lakes in eastern Germany. The Germans drove the Russians back. In two battles, the Russians suffered nearly two hundred fifty thousand casualties.

The *casualties* of war include the dead, wounded, captured, and missing.

As on the Western Front, the war along the Eastern Front ground down into a stalemate. No longer was there talk of bringing troops home by Christmas.

France, 1914: Allied soldiers are silhouetted along a ridge during the Battle of Mons.

The Reality of War

As the war expanded, more nations were drawn into the conflict. On one side were the **Allied Powers**, whose principal members included Great Britain, Belgium, France, Russia, and, later, Italy. The Allies were opposed by the **Central Powers**, the alliance formed by Germany, Austria-Hungary, and eventually the Ottoman Empire.

With the opposing armies hunkered down in a huge system of trenches, trench warfare on the Western Front came to define the Great War. New military technologies would make World War I the deadliest war in history up to that time. Nations found their resources strained as they were pulled into the world's first "total war."

Key Questions

- Why did the war result in such high casualties on both sides?
- What is "total war"? In what ways was World War I an example of total war?

Horror in the Trenches

On the Western Front, both opposing armies developed complex mazes of underground shelters and communication trenches leading to hospitals, supply dumps, and railroads. On the front lines, French and British soldiers peered out of their trenches over earthen mounds and sandbags across "no-man's-land," the few hundred yards of bombed-out earth that separated them from the Germans.

Life in the filthy, narrow trenches was agony, even when there was no fighting. Rainwater collected in the trench bottoms. One soldier wrote, "The men slept in mud, washed in mud, ate mud, and dreamed mud." The air stank from human waste and decomposing bodies. Lice infested the men's hair and clothing, and rats scurried at their feet.

In trench warfare, soldiers seldom saw the enemy they were fighting. Each side unleashed powerful artillery barrages. In the trenches, the men crouched and prayed that the shells would not find them. The explosive shells ranged from the size of a fist to the size of a man, and they caused more destruction and death than any other weapon in the war.

Artillery includes any guns too large to be fired from the hand or shoulder.

When generals gave the order to attack, soldiers scrambled out of their trenches—they called it going "over the top"—and made a dash toward the enemy trenches. The odds were that they would not make it alive across no-man's-land. Trees had been blasted away, leaving no cover. Buried land mines lay waiting, and barbed wire snaked across the broken fields. Machine guns fired from enemy trenches could mow down entire lines of advancing soldiers.

Deadly Firepower

The Industrial Revolution made World War I the most deadly in history. It was the first war in which actual firepower killed more soldiers than disease.

663

U.S. soldiers wearing protective masks forge through plumes of poison gas, one of the horrors of trench warfare.

Long-range rifles were supplemented by new machine guns that could fire up to six hundred rounds per minute. Some huge artillery could loft shells as far as seventy-five miles (120 km). In World War I, on average, five thousand men died each day, most from shellfire.

The British developed an armored, gun-carrying, tracked vehicle known as a "land battleship," what we call a *tank*. Tanks could crush barbed wire and cross trench lines, impervious to machine-gun bullets. Advancing infantrymen clustered behind tanks for protection. The early tanks were clumsy vehicles and often broke down, but they represented a significant technical advance in the history of warfare.

Each side tried to invent weapons that would end the trench warfare stalemate. In April 1915, the Germans introduced a new weapon, chlorine gas. This poison crept like a stealthy fog across the trenches. It could choke a man to death in minutes. Later in the war, the Germans launched attacks with mustard gas, which blinded people and burned the

skin. Soon both sides developed and used poison gas. Factories began to churn out gas masks. When troops in the trenches saw a gas cloud approaching, they hurried to don the clumsy masks and hoped the winds would push the poison in some other direction.

The first Allied soldiers to fall to poison gas were North Africans from the French colony of Senegal, who were among the colonial divisions recruited to fight in the Great War. A British official recalled that as the doomed soldiers fell back from the gas, they "coughed and pointed to their throats." A second gas attack two days later claimed the lives of many Canadian troops.

Verdun and the Somme

In early 1916, the Germans tried to break the stalemate on the Western Front by launching a devastating artillery assault on the French city of Verdun. The French had declared they would defend the ancient fortress town at all costs. Millions of artillery shells turned Verdun into a bleak, cratered moonscape. When rains came, the muddy battlefield was clogged with corpses.

By the end of June 1916, the number of men killed or wounded at Verdun had passed four hundred thousand. In his diary, a French lieutenant,

German soldiers face French artillery fire at the Battle of Verdun. Millions of explosions turned the land into a cratered moonscape.

Primary Source

Dulce et Decorum Est

Wilfred Owen, a British officer, wrote this poem about a soldier caught in a poison gas attack. Its title, *Dulce et Decorum Est,* is from a Latin motto popular before World War I: *Dulce et decorum est pro patria mori*—"It is sweet and right to die for your country."

Five-nines were explosive shells, so-named because their caliber (diameter) was 5.9 inches.

Bent double, like old beggars under sacks,
Knock-kneed, coughing like hags, we cursed through sludge,
Till on the haunting flares we turned our backs
And towards our distant rest began to trudge.
Men marched asleep. Many had lost their boots
But limped on, blood-shod. All went lame; all blind;
Drunk with fatigue; deaf even to the hoots
Of tired, outstripped Five-Nines that dropped behind.

Gas! Gas! Quick, boys!–An ecstasy of fumbling,
Fitting the clumsy helmets just in time;
But someone still was yelling out and stumbling,
And flound'ring like a man in fire or lime…
Dim, through the misty panes and thick green light,
As under a green sea, I saw him drowning.
In all my dreams, before my helpless sight,
He plunges at me, guttering, choking, drowning.

If in some smothering dreams you too could pace
Behind the wagon that we flung him in,
And watch the white eyes writhing in his face,
His hanging face, like a devil's sick of sin;
If you could hear, at every jolt, the blood
Come gargling from the froth-corrupted lungs,
Obscene as cancer, bitter as the cud
Of vile, incurable sores on innocent tongues,
My friend, you would not tell with such high zest
To children ardent for some desperate glory,
The old Lie; *Dulce et Decorum est*
Pro patria mori.

World War I, 1914–1918

Legend:
- Allied Powers
- Central Powers
- Neutral nations
- Greatest extent of Central Powers invasion, 1918
- ····· Trench system
- ---- Armistice line, December 1917
- —— Armistice line, November 1918
- Major battles

0   200   400 mi
0   200   400 km

World War I, embroiling the nations of Europe, and later the United States and other nations around the world, was unprecedented in its carnage and destruction.

who was eventually killed by an artillery shell, wrote, "Hell cannot be so terrible. Men are mad!"

In the summer, to ease the pressure on Verdun and break through the German lines, the British launched an attack along a river called the Somme (sahm). Nearly two thousand artillery guns unleashed a week-long barrage. The barrage was designed to destroy the German positions and blast away the barbed wire that blocked no-man's-land in front of their trenches.

One summer morning along the Somme, thousands of young British soldiers went "over the top," clambering from their trenches along eighteen miles (29 km) of the Western Front.

Almost shoulder to shoulder, they stepped out across no-man's-land. Gunfire erupted from the German lines.

Soldier after soldier fell to the ground, dead or wounded. In a few hours, twenty thousand British soldiers died, and another forty thousand were wounded. The first day at the Somme was the bloodiest of the war. And still the fighting went on. By October, more than a *million* men had been killed or wounded at the Somme. And no breakthrough came on the Western Front.

The Eastern Front: Challenging the Ottomans

The Eastern Front, the scene of Russia's life-and-death struggle, was much longer than the Western Front. In October 1914, when the Ottoman Empire decided to join the Central Powers, Russia's situation became desperate.

In 1915, German and Austrian armies drove the Russians three hundred miles (483 km) back into their own territory, taking more than a million prisoners and killing or wounding as many more. Russia's leader, Tsar Nicholas II, took command of the army. He then made a series of foolish decisions that cost his nation many thousands of lives.

In 1915, the British tried to come to the aid of Russia by opening up another front in the south against the Ottoman Turks. The British sent troops to the Gallipoli Peninsula on the western shores of the Dardanelles, a strait between Europe and Turkey. The Gallipoli expedition failed, but it led some Italians to believe that the Allies could win the war.

Italy, which had stayed out of the fight, joined the Allies, hoping to grab territory from Austria and the Ottoman Empire as they fell. Italy launched a series of attacks against the Austrians in the Alps, which opened another long battlefront.

The Armenian Massacre

Armenia, situated on the Anatolian Peninsula, was ruled by the Ottoman Empire. The Armenians, who were Christians, had long endured persecution under the rule of the Ottoman Turks, who were Muslim. The Armenians hoped that a Russian victory over the Ottoman Empire would help secure the independence they had long sought from the Turks.

In the spring of 1915, the Ottomans accused the Armenians of cooperating with the Russians. The Ottomans used this as an excuse to execute tens of thousands of Armenian men and boys. Ottoman troops plundered Armenian villages, raped thousands of women, and then began the systematic deportation of women, children, and the elderly. These Armenians were herded onto trains, taken to a desert region, and left to walk to their deaths, usually by starvation. In all, more than a million people—about half of the Armenian population—perished.

> To *deport* someone is to send that person out of the country.

In 1915, a troubled American diplomat in Istanbul warned the U.S. State Department, "It appears that a campaign of race extermination is

The Anatolian Peninsula

The Anatolian Peninsula, also known as Asia Minor, is bounded by the Black Sea, the Aegean Sea, and the Mediterranean Sea. Today, most of the nation of Turkey lies on the peninsula, with a small part of the country extending into Europe. These names—Anatolia, Asia Minor, and Turkey—all refer to the same area.

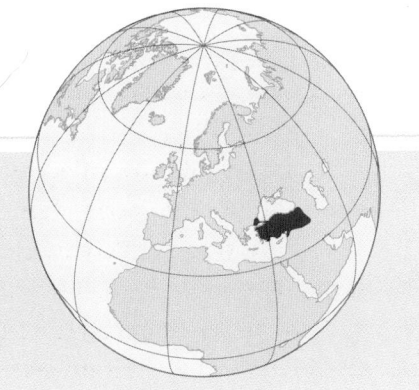

in progress." Today, historians looking back at the massacre of the Armenians in 1915 often refer to the tragedy as the Armenian Genocide. *Genocide* is the deliberate and systematic destruction of a racial, political, religious, or cultural group. (The term *genocide* had not been invented in 1915; it was first used in 1944 to describe Nazi actions against the Jews in World War II, which you will read about in a later chapter.)

War at Sea

Before the Great War began, Great Britain and Germany had raced to build up their navies. In May 1916, their warships met off the coast of Denmark in the Battle of Jutland, the greatest sea battle of the war. More than two dozen ships were destroyed. Both sides claimed victory, and both suffered high casualties—the British lost twice as many sailors as the Germans. But the Battle of Jutland left the British navy in control of European waters. The British fleet could then blockade Germany's North Sea ports, and keep out the ships trying to bring food and help to the Central Powers.

The Germans, however, had a deadly new weapon for the war at sea—submarines called U-boats. The "U" stood for *untersee*, German for "undersea." For several decades, the navies of industrialized nations had experimented with submarines as weapons. But World War I was the first war in which submarines played a significant role. Prowling the sea-lanes, lurking just beneath the surface, a submarine could launch a torpedo and destroy a ship before the crew even knew that an attack was coming.

Early in the war, in response to the British blockade of German ports, Germany used its submarines to enforce a blockade of Britain. U-boats began to torpedo vessels in waters around Britain, including neutral cargo ships. In 1915, U-boats sank at least two passenger ships that they suspected of carrying munitions.

The Sinking of the Lusitania

On May 1, 1915, the *Lusitania*, a British steamship, sailed from New York Harbor for its home port in Liverpool, England. Most of the tourists and businessmen aboard the luxurious British ocean liner looked forward to the voyage.

Some, however, were nervous. The German embassy had placed an ad in newspapers declaring, "Travelers intending to embark on the Atlantic voyage are reminded that a state of war exists between Germany and her allies and Great Britain.... Vessels flying the flag of Great Britain...are liable to destruction." But surely, most people thought, the Germans wouldn't attack an ocean liner carrying civilian passengers.

For six days, the *Lusitania* steamed across the Atlantic without incident. Then, as passengers gathered on deck to catch sight of the Irish coast, a German U-boat sent a torpedo slamming into the ship's hull. The *Lusitania* sank in 18 minutes, taking 1,198 people, including 128 Americans, to their deaths.

The sinking of the *Lusitania* turned many Americans against Germany. Up to this time, the United States had managed to stay out of the Great War. But when German torpedoes destroyed the *Lusitania*, many Americans began to think the time had come for their country to enter the war against the Central Powers.

Germany used submarines to launch torpedoes to destroy Allied ships.

French and German planes battle aloft in the first war that effectively used airpower.

War in the Skies

In the spring of 1915, German airships called *zeppelins* crossed the North Sea to bomb London and the east coast of England. Zeppelins created alarm among the British people, but only limited damage.

Another new technology, however, became a deadly instrument of warfare—the airplane. World War I broke out only about a decade after Orville and Wilbur Wright made their first flight at Kitty Hawk, North Carolina. At first, both the Allied and Central powers used planes to scout the positions of enemy armies. But by 1916, squadrons of fighter planes outfitted with machine guns were battling each other for control of the skies.

Daring pilots, known as aces, engaged in swirling aerial battles called dogfights. Germany's Manfred von Richthofen (RIHKT-hoh-fuhn), known as "the Red Baron," became the most successful fighter pilot of the war, with more than eighty confirmed air combat victories.

Total War

The Allies enlisted not only their own citizens on the home front, but many people from their dominions and colonies as well. Hundreds of thousands of Australians, Canadians, Irish, and New Zealanders fought in Europe and the Near East. Soldiers from British and French possessions in Africa and Asia took up arms—Indians, Senegalese, Algerians, Moroccans, South Africans, and others. The conflict, mostly European at first, grew into a true world war.

In 1914, most Europeans had expected a short war with few casualties. By 1916, leaders on both sides refused to seek a truce even in the face of nightmarish death and destruction. World War I escalated into the first "total war," a war in which the opposing nations used virtually every resource they possessed to keep up the fight, and involved every citizen in the effort.

Planned Economies

The demands of total war brought dramatic economic changes. European governments took charge of many aspects of their nations' economies. They devoted whole industries—steel, rubber, munitions—to war production.

Government leaders in Britain, France, and Germany brought union leaders and businessmen into the planning. Soon government agencies in both the Allied and Central powers were setting prices, determining wages, rationing food, and deciding which industries

Rationing is the planned distribution of something (such as food) in short supply.

A German airship, called a *zeppelin*, advances toward an attack on England.

669

would get what resources. Planned economies—economies largely organized and controlled by governments—temporarily replaced free-market capitalism in Europe.

Women's Changing Roles

Societies also changed dramatically during World War I, especially for women. Many women who had never worked outside the home took jobs in banking, commerce, and industry. Whereas only a small number of women held clerical jobs before the war, millions entered the workforce between 1914 and 1918. In Britain alone, more than 1.3 million women took new jobs or worked outside the home for the first time.

As men perished on the Western Front, women worked to support their families. They worked as bank tellers, telephone operators, and shopkeepers. They took jobs in the mills, factories, mines, and furnaces of Europe. Above all, they worked in heavy industry and in munitions factories. Nearly 40 percent of workers in Germany's major munitions plant were women.

War pushed women to take on tasks once reserved for men. This change led to a growing belief among women in the Western world that they could support themselves and contribute to their nations' economies outside as well as inside the home.

The War and Woman Suffrage

The Great War helped advance the woman suffrage movement in many Western nations. As millions of women went to work in jobs usually done by men, reformers insisted that women who could do such work surely deserved the right to vote.

During the war and shortly afterward, many Western governments extended the right to vote to women. Britain, Sweden, Germany, Poland, Hungary, Austria, Czechoslovakia, and Canada all approved woman suffrage. In 1920, the 19th Amendment to the U.S. Constitution gave American women the right to vote. In France and Italy, however, women had to wait until the mid-1940s to cast their ballots.

Women, like this welder, helped the war effort by taking on work once done mainly by men.

War's End and a Troubled Peace

Key Questions

- Why did the United States remain neutral in the first years of the war? How did U.S. entry into the war affect its outcome?

- What were Woodrow Wilson's goals for peace? To what extent were they achieved?

- How did the Treaty of Versailles deal with Germany, and how did many Germans respond?

Among the Allies, Russia suffered some of the war's worst blows, losing 1.7 million soldiers by 1917, with another 5 million maimed and wounded. In 1917, revolution erupted in the tsar's empire. (You will read about the Russian Revolution in the next chapter.) An exhausted Russia signed a peace treaty with Germany, which ended the Great War on much of the Eastern Front.

Now Germany was free to shift masses of troops to the Western Front. The German generals were sure they could hammer their way through the weary French and British lines. But they had to move quickly. The Allied Powers had lost Russia but gained a new and powerful partner—the United States.

The United States Enters the War

Since the start of the Great War in 1914, the United States had managed to stay out of the fighting. Most Americans saw it as a European conflict—why should they get involved? Great Britain and France put pressure on the United States to join the Allies, but Americans remained neutral. President Woodrow Wilson had even won reelection in 1916 on the slogan, "He Kept Us Out of War."

Americans found it hard to remain neutral, however, when a German submarine fired torpedoes into the *Lusitania*. Among those who died when the great ship sank were more than a hundred U.S. citizens.

When the Germans sank the *Lusitania*, the U.S. began to question its policy of neutrality.

The War of Emotions: Propaganda

As the fighting dragged on and casualties mounted, public enthusiasm for the war faded. To build support for the struggle, leaders used propaganda—biased information designed to rouse emotions.

Much wartime propaganda fueled hatred of the enemy. In Britain's new cinema industry, newsreel announcers described the Germans who carried out bombing raids on London as "baby-killers." German propaganda portrayed the Allies in similar terms, blaming the British blockade for a sharp increase in infant mortality.

Propaganda posters on both sides showed heroic soldiers defending the homeland against the enemy. Posters became recruiting tools, urging men to join the war effort.

A British recruiting poster

Initially, the Germans apologized for the *Lusitania* disaster and agreed to stop such attacks. But in early 1917, the Germans announced they would resume unrestricted submarine warfare. They proceeded to sink American cargo ships.

President Wilson realized that the United States could not avoid a conflict that was threatening to engulf so much of the world. On April 2, 1917, Wilson reluctantly went before Congress and asked for a declaration of war against Germany. Congress responded by erupting into cheers. American troops were soon on their way to Europe.

Wilson's Fourteen Points

President Wilson did not join the war just to defeat the Germans. He felt he had a higher aim. In urging Congress to declare war, Wilson said that "the world must be made safe for democracy." Wilson, the son of a Presbyterian minister, approached his task with a missionary's zeal. He had lofty goals, which some would say were unrealistic.

By early 1918, Wilson, confident of an Allied victory, was already thinking about a peace treaty that he hoped would rid the world of such catastrophic wars. On January 8, 1918, while the war still raged in Europe, the president presented to Congress his program to end the conflict and solve some of the problems that had triggered the fighting.

Wilson listed fourteen principles to help remake Europe after the war. His Fourteen Points, as they are known, called for justice, not revenge. Wilson wanted the victors of the Great War to be generous toward defeated countries. A generous peace, he hoped, would save the world from bitterness that might become the seed for future wars.

Under the Fourteen Points, Wilson stressed *self-determination*. He said the people of Poland, Romania, Serbia, Turkey, and many other lands should choose their own forms of government. Wilson hoped that self-determination would end the old imperialist system in which powerful industrial nations grabbed and ruled overseas colonies.

The Fourteen Points also included principles for easing tensions between nations. Wilson called for an end to secret treaties between countries. He urged freedom of the seas and removal of barriers to trade. He called for nations to reduce their stockpiles of arms and weapons. He also said that disputes over colonies must be resolved in ways that accounted for the wishes of the colonized peoples.

Finally, the Fourteen Points proposed the creation of a new organization composed of countries throughout the world, called the League of Nations. The League would have one major goal—to keep peace. Wilson hoped that members of the League would solve their differences through discussion rather than armed conflict. He also hoped the League's members would pledge to defend any member attacked by another nation. Wilson reasoned that even a very powerful country would hesitate to attack another if it knew it would face the united opposition of the League of Nations.

The War's End

Even as Wilson sent American troops to Europe and laid out his vision for the future, after Russia's withdrawal from the war, hundreds of thousands of new German troops were on their way from the east, rushing toward the Western Front. Germany's military leaders gambled on one last

Russia Leaves the War

Russia's poorly equipped army suffered terrible losses early in World War I. At home, the Russian people were hungry and jobless. In the next chapter, you will read about the revolution that overthrew the tsar and established the Union of Soviet Socialist Republics. When the leaders of that revolution surrendered to Germany in 1917 and withdrew from the war, German troops that had been fighting on the Eastern Front moved to the Western Front to battle the British and French.

attempt to break the stalemate in the trenches. In March 1918, German generals launched what they hoped would be a devastating final offensive in France.

They almost succeeded. The assault pushed back the British and French troops. But Germany suffered terrible casualties, while French and British forces managed to regroup. Moreover, the Allies could now count on American help. Hundreds of thousands of U.S. soldiers were arriving in Europe every month. By the fall of 1918, two million Americans had joined the Allied ranks.

By August, Germany's massive offensive had collapsed. It was then the Allies' turn to launch assaults on the German trenches. Thousands of Germans surrendered. The long stalemate on the Western Front finally came to an end.

Meanwhile, to the south, the Italians held off Austrian forces weakened by mass desertions. In the Middle East, British troops triumphed over the Ottomans.

In the fall of 1918, both the German kaiser and the Austrian emperor faced uprisings among

France, 1918: Allied soldiers advance against the entrenched Germans on the Western Front.

Woodrow Wilson's Fourteen Points

In his Fourteen Points, President Woodrow Wilson laid out his idealistic plan for lasting peace in a postwar world.

A *covenant* is a formal and binding agreement between two or more parties.

I. Open covenants of peace…no private international understandings of any kind, but diplomacy shall proceed always frankly and in the public view….

II. Absolute freedom of navigation upon the seas, outside territorial waters, alike in peace and in war….

III. The removal, so far as possible, of all economic barriers and the establishment of an equality of trade conditions among all the nations….

IV. Adequate guarantees given and taken that national armaments will be reduced to the lowest point consistent with domestic safety….

V. A free, open-minded, and absolutely impartial adjustment of all colonial claims….

In this context, to *evacuate* means to withdraw foreign military forces.

VI. The evacuation of all Russian territory and…a sincere welcome into the society of free nations under institutions of her own choosing….

their hungry people. The British had blockaded German ports, causing a shortage of food in Germany and Austria. Angry crowds rioted in Berlin and Vienna. Revolution threatened to break out all across Germany. Workers went on strike, demanding peace.

When a monarch *abdicates* the throne, he or she formally gives up power to rule.

On November 9, 1918, Kaiser Wilhelm abdicated the German throne. A new government took power. Some generals of the German army, which still held its defensive positions in France, wanted to fight on. Many German soldiers opposed surrender. But the new government called for a truce.

On the morning of November 11, 1918, the war came to an end. Representatives of France, Britain, and Germany gathered in a train car outside the French town of Rethondes (ruh-TOHND)

VII. Belgium…must be evacuated and restored, without any attempt to limit the sovereignty which she enjoys in common with all other free nations….

VIII. All French territory should be freed and the invaded portions restored….

IX. A readjustment of the frontiers of Italy should be effected along clearly recognizable lines of nationality….

X. The peoples of Austria-Hungary, whose place among the nations we wish to see safeguarded and assured, should be accorded the freest opportunity of autonomous development….

Autonomous means self-governing.

XI. Romania, Serbia, and Montenegro should be evacuated, occupied territories restored….

XII. [N]ationalities which are now under Turkish rule should be assured an undoubted security of life and an absolutely unmolested opportunity of autonomous development….

Unmolested means free from disturbance or interference.

XIII. An independent Polish state should be erected which should include the territories inhabited by indisputably Polish populations….

XIV. A general association of nations must be formed…for the purpose of affording mutual guarantees of political independence and territorial integrity to great and small States alike….

An *armistice* is a truce before the official signing of a peace treaty that brings an end to fighting.

and signed an armistice. It demanded that Germany leave the territories it occupied, surrender its arms, and allow Allied Powers to patrol the Rhineland, the land in western Germany along the banks of the Rhine, bordering France.

At the eleventh hour on the eleventh day of the eleventh month of 1918, the guns finally fell silent on the Western Front.

British and French soldiers rejoiced at the news—at last, they could leave behind the horrors of the trenches. Many German soldiers, however, felt betrayed by the armistice. Even though they had been steadily retreating, they did not believe they had been defeated by the Allies. Many felt they had been betrayed by their own government. For them, the peace did not bring joy but rage and a desire to fight again another day.

Soldiers blinded by mustard gas move past bodies of dead comrades in this painting by American artist John Singer Sargent.

The "Glorious Dead" and a Day to Remember

The world had never experienced a conflict like the Great War. About nine million combatants perished, far more than in all the wars during the previous hundred years. About twenty-one million soldiers were wounded. No one knows how many civilians died of disease, hunger, and other war-related causes. Some historians believe as many noncombatants died as soldiers.

The armistice brought World War I to an end on November 11, 1918. Along the Allied trenches, soldiers celebrated.

Germany and Russia suffered the most casualties, each with about 1.7 million dead in battle. France lost almost as many, from a smaller population. Nearly half of all French men between the ages of twenty and thirty-five at the start of the war were dead or wounded by the war's end.

Britain and its empire lost nearly a million men. Austria-Hungary lost more than a million. More than half a million Italians died, and at least 325,000 Turks perished, although their exact numbers were never counted. The United States, which had joined the fighting late, suffered much lighter losses. Still, almost 120,000 American soldiers died.

How is it possible to comprehend loss on such a scale? In some villages, all the able-bodied young men volunteered to fight alongside their hometown friends—and often they died together, sometimes in a single battle on a single day. For the women, children, and elderly left behind, waiting for the men to come home, there would be no reunions.

Two years after the armistice, the remains of an unidentified soldier were returned to Britain from a battlefield on the Western Front. The British buried the remains with full military honors at Westminster Abbey in London. Within a week, more than a million Britons came to pay their respects at the Tomb of the Unknown Soldier. King George V asked the nation to come to a standstill for two

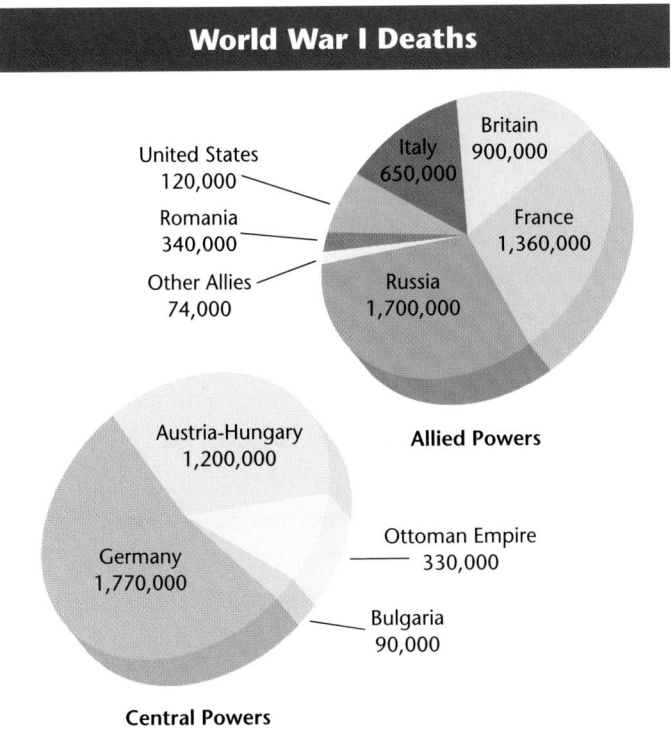

World War I Deaths

Allied Powers

United States 120,000
Italy 650,000
Britain 900,000
France 1,360,000
Romania 340,000
Other Allies 74,000
Russia 1,700,000

Central Powers

Austria-Hungary 1,200,000
Germany 1,770,000
Ottoman Empire 330,000
Bulgaria 90,000

minutes every November 11 at precisely 11 a.m. to remember the moment of the armistice. "All locomotion should cease," requested the king, "so that, in perfect stillness, the thoughts of everyone may be concentrated on reverent remembrance of the glorious dead."

For a while after the Great War, the people of Britain referred to November 11 as Armistice Day. Today they know it as Remembrance Day. In the United States, November 11 is called Veterans Day.

The Cost of Total War

In addition to the staggering human losses, the face of Europe was scarred and bruised by the war. In France and Belgium, as armies advanced and retreated, they wrecked farms, villages, and towns. Artillery fire destroyed bridges, railroad tracks, roads, factories, and homes. Whole stretches of the Western Front—pounded by shells, gouged by trenches, exposed to poison gas—were reduced to barren wastelands.

For Britain and Germany, the cost of waging total war added up to about 60 percent of each country's economic output. To pay for it all, governments raised taxes. When that wasn't enough, they borrowed money. Nations ran up huge debts, mostly to the United States.

The U.S. economy thrived during the war as Americans sold food and weapons to the combatants. In Europe, however, the fighting devastated business and trade. Many European companies went out of business, and thousands of returning soldiers could not find jobs.

For the Allies in Europe, the cost of victory was near ruin. When it came time for the victors to forge a peace settlement, the leaders of France knew whom to blame—Germany.

Versailles: A Punitive Peace

Two months after the armistice, the Allies assembled at Versailles, the lavish royal palace built around 1700 by France's "Sun King," Louis XIV. Their purpose was to agree to the terms of a lasting peace. Delegates arrived from around the world, representing the thirty-two victorious nations. The

Although France was one of the victorious nations, by war's end many French towns and villages stood in ruins.

677

The Influenza Pandemic

Day by day, month by month, year by year, the death count of the Great War increased into the millions. Even this, however, paled before the fatal power of an influenza epidemic. This disease, which raged across six continents in 1918 and 1919, was a *pandemic*, an epidemic that spread worldwide. It killed between twenty-five million and fifty million people, causing even more deaths than the Great War itself.

Japanese, who had supported the Allies, sat at the negotiating table. They had become an important power, commanding the third-largest navy in the world. India and China also sent delegates. Most decision-making power, however, lay with France, Britain, and the United States.

At this meeting to decide the fate of the defeated Central Powers, one group was notably absent—the Central Powers. They had not been invited.

Woodrow Wilson arrived in Europe to a hero's welcome. To the continent's war-weary people, he seemed a man who might create a new and better world.

But Wilson's idealism could not stop France from wanting to punish Germany. The French prime minister, Georges Clemenceau (zhorzh kleh-mahn-SOH), was determined to cripple Germany and make it incapable of striking again. "For the catastrophe of 1914," Clemenceau bluntly stated, "the Germans are responsible." He insisted that Germany make huge financial payments, called reparations, to cover the costs of the war. He also demanded that Germany be disarmed, and that French troops be stationed in the German Rhineland.

While Clemenceau longed to punish Germany, Woodrow Wilson sought a generous peace. In Wilson's eyes, the United States had fought not to save France but "to redeem the world and make it fit for free men like ourselves to live in." He argued for a peace based on his Fourteen Points and their promise of self-determination. Wilson argued that his proposals offered the best chance of helping Germans accept their defeat and get on with their lives.

Between Clemenceau and Wilson stood Britain's prime minister, David Lloyd George. Behind the scenes, he tried to find a compromise between the French and American positions.

In the end, the Treaty of Versailles included many of France's demands. It included a "war guilt" clause that blamed Germany for the war. The treaty stripped Germany of its overseas colonies and many regions along its borders. The treaty also demanded that Germany pay large reparations.

But the Treaty of Versailles also included some provisions that Wilson wanted. It partly incorporated his idea of national self-determination, the belief that nations should rule themselves. And it stated that the Allies would set up the League of Nations that Wilson so badly wanted. In the end, Wilson agreed to many French demands in order to save his cherished hopes for the League of Nations.

Allied leaders (from left) David Lloyd George of Britain, Vittorio Orlando of Italy, Georges Clemenceau of France, and Woodrow Wilson of the United States gather at Versailles. No Central Powers representatives were invited.

Redrawing the Map

The Treaty of Versailles changed the map of Europe. The Allies' peace terms dramatically altered political boundaries in eastern and central Europe.

- The empire of Austria-Hungary was split into new independent states: Austria, Hungary, and Czechoslovakia, as well as a kingdom of Serbs, Croats, and Slovenes that eventually became Yugoslavia, "the land of the southern Slavs."
- A restored nation of Poland emerged from territory previously controlled by Germany, Russia, and Austria-Hungary.
- The Ottoman Empire lost all of its territory in the Middle East and on the Arabian Peninsula.
- Greece temporarily occupied the western coast of Asia Minor until expelled by Turkish nationalists in 1923.

Wherever the Allies drew new borders, many people protested that they had been left on the wrong side of the line. Many Germans and Hungarians found themselves ruled by Italians, Poles, Czechs, or Romanians. In all, more than twenty million people in eastern and central Europe lived as minorities in nations to which they felt no allegiance. Many of those people had fought in the Great War out of feelings of nationalism and the desire for self-determination. Their anger over the new postwar borders sowed seeds for future conflicts.

Beyond Europe, many of the Arabs who had fought against the Ottomans failed to win their freedom immediately after the war. Instead, they found themselves living in territories called mandates. Britain and France administered these mandates, and were supposed to prepare the people living there for self-government. The Arab people living in these mandates resented this arrangement and longed for independence.

In southern and eastern Africa, the British took over what had been German colonies. In

A French political cartoon shows (from left) David Lloyd George, Georges Clemenceau, and Woodrow Wilson surveying a "new world" created by the Treaty of Versailles.

western Africa, formerly German possessions went to the French. These changes also sowed seeds of resentment.

German Response to the Treaty

The Germans, bitter and humiliated at their defeat, saw nothing just about the Treaty of Versailles. The Allies had not included the defeated Germans in the treaty talks. The Allies just showed the Germans the finished product and told them to sign it.

The terms dictated by the Treaty of Versailles made many Germans feel anything but peaceful. They seethed with anger and looked forward to the chance to strike back. As a German general told one of his countrymen, "We'll be able one day to resume and conclude this war.... In the final battle we shall be the victors."

Postwar Europe, c. 1923

NORWAY
SWEDEN
FINLAND
North Sea
DENMARK
Baltic Sea
ESTONIA
LATVIA
LITHUANIA
EAST PRUSSIA (Germany)

UNION OF SOVIET SOCIALIST REPUBLICS

NORTHERN IRELAND
IRISH FREE STATE
BRITAIN
NETHERLANDS
GERMANY
POLAND
BELGIUM
LUXEMBOURG
ALSACE-LORRAINE
CZECHOSLOVAKIA
SWITZERLAND
AUSTRIA
HUNGARY

ATLANTIC OCEAN

FRANCE
YUGOSLAVIA
ROMANIA

PORTUGAL
SPAIN
ITALY
ALBANIA
BULGARIA
GREECE
TURKEY

Mediterranean Sea

Black Sea

Caspian Sea

Turkish nationalist forces drove Greek occupation armies out of Asia Minor by 1923.

ASIA

SYRIA
LEBANON
PALESTINE
TRANSJORDAN
IRAQ

Persian Gulf

AFRICA

ARABIA

Red Sea

YEMEN

Legend:
- Austro-Hungarian Empire
- German Empire
- Ottoman Empire
- Russian Empire
- New nation
- British mandate
- French mandate

0   250   500 mi
0   250   500 km

N

Four European empires—Germany, Russia, Austria-Hungary, and the Ottoman Empire—were dismantled as a result of World War I.

American Isolationism

By 1920, the Great War had been over for more than a year. Yet, in many ways peace had not come. The wreckage of war left people in Europe with a deep sense of anger, loss, and failure. Disputes over power and territory often erupted into violence. Across the continent, governments faced coups, plots, and threats of revolution.

In the United States, Americans felt more disillusioned than triumphant. They opened their newspapers and saw pictures of death and devastation. They saw men come home with missing arms and legs or lungs ruined by poison gas. Veterans told horrifying stories of fighting on the front.

President Wilson had said that the United States went to war to make world "safe for democracy." But many Americans found it hard to believe the fighting had done much good. As far as they were concerned, the United States would have been better off staying out of Europe's conflicts.

Americans wanted to put the quarreling nations of Europe out of mind. Even though the United States was now one of the world's leading economic powers, with American businesses thriving in markets around the globe, the American people embraced **isolationism**, a policy of withdrawal from world affairs.

Woodrow Wilson still hoped that his League of Nations could help make a better world. In an impassioned speech, he urged the U.S. Senate to ratify the Treaty of Versailles and declared that the League of Nations was "the only hope of mankind.... Dare we reject it and break the heart of the world?"

To undermine Wilson, a Democrat, Republican senators opposed the treaty. With the treaty stalled in the Senate, Wilson took his case to the people. He traveled the country and gave many speeches, trying to persuade his countrymen that the League was a good idea. But most citizens met his appeals with skeptical stares. Already exhausted from his work at Versailles, Wilson fell ill and suffered a stroke, which left him physically incapacitated for the remainder of his presidency.

The U.S. Senate refused to ratify the Treaty of Versailles. The United States never joined the League of Nations. Without the United States, one of the leading powers in the world, the League of Nations was doomed to fail.

Consequences of the Versailles Treaty

The end of World War I saw the creation of a number of new nations, most notably in central Europe, where the Austro-Hungarian Empire fragmented into the states of Austria, Hungary, Czechoslovakia, and Yugoslavia. But the rise of small nations did not result in the peaceful cooperation Wilson had hoped for. Instead, it led to a surge in nationalist feeling and antagonism between peoples.

Nowhere was the spirit of militant nationalism stronger than in Germany. Humiliated and embittered by what they viewed as the unjust terms of the Treaty of Versailles, many Germans longed for revenge against their former enemies. Former corporal Adolf Hitler ranted, "It cannot be that two million Germans should have fallen in vain.... No, we do not pardon, we demand—vengeance!" Thus the First World War helped pave the way for a second.

At war's end, an angry German paramilitary group distributed this poster urging Germans to "Protect Your Homeland!" Many Germans, including a young former officer, Adolf Hitler, longed for revenge.

Vladimir Lenin (right of center) is depicted as a hero of the Russian people.

NATIONALISM

1900–1930

1920

1925

1930

1919
In the Amritsar Massacre, British troops open fire on demonstrators in India.

1922
Nationalists under Atatürk overthrow the last Ottoman sultan and establish an independent republic in Turkey.

Stalin comes to power in the Soviet Union.

Gandhi leads the Salt March to protest the British tax on salt and to rouse Indian nationalism.

1932
Ibn Saud establishes the Kingdom of Saudi Arabia under strict Islamic law.

When Russia entered World War I, it was already a nation in crisis. The war magnified the social and economic problems that a long line of autocratic tsars had too long neglected. In 1917, Vladimir Lenin, a fervent Marxist, helped lead an uprising that turned Russia into a communist nation. Lenin and his successors ruled as dictators and aspired to worldwide communist revolution.

At the end of the Great War, strong feelings of nationalism surged in many parts of the world. Britain's largest colony, India, began a long struggle for independence. The breakup of the Ottoman Empire at the end of World War I left people in the Middle East eager for self-rule. But the Treaty of Versailles put many Middle Eastern lands under British and French rule.

In the 1920s and 1930s, Arab nationalism became an even more potent force. In many Muslim lands, this nationalism was accompanied by another movement, Islamism, whose followers denounced Western influence and demanded that Islamic law form the basis of government. Many Arabs and Islamists were alarmed by the growth of a new Zionist movement intent on establishing a Jewish homeland in the British mandate of Palestine.

Revolution: From Russia to Soviet Union

Key Questions

- What problems did Russia face during the early twentieth century?

- How did World War I trigger revolution in Russia?

- What are the major characteristics of the political and economic system that emerged under the leadership of Lenin and Stalin?

Early in World War I, Russia suffered heavy losses. In 1917, the once-mighty empire, shaken by revolution, surrendered to Germany and withdrew from the war. While the calamity of the Great War helped push Russia into revolution, the crisis had deep roots going back many centuries. The war magnified a conflict between Russia's long feudal past and its efforts to enter the modern world.

Russia Struggles to Modernize

A huge empire straddling two continents, Russia was rich in natural resources and had an enormous population. But Russia did not begin to industrialize in earnest until the late 1800s. In the 1890s, workers embarked on the construction of the Trans-Siberian Railroad, which would become the longest rail line in the world. By 1900, Russia had become one of the world's leading producers of oil and was a major producer of iron and steel.

Still, as the twentieth century approached, Russia suffered from a stark division between rich and poor. For three centuries, Russia had been led by tsars from the Romanov (ROH-muh-nahf) family. In the years leading up to World War I, Tsar Nicholas II held the throne. He ruled with his unpopular German-born wife, Alexandra. Like previous tsars, Nicholas never doubted his right to absolute rule.

The privileges enjoyed by the small minority of Russian nobles rested on the backs of the vast majority of the people at the bottom of Russian society, the peasants who did the farmwork. Through much of the nineteenth century, most of these peasants were serfs. Technically serfs were not slaves, but they owed labor to their masters, who considered them little more than property of the estate.

Although Russia legally abolished serfdom in 1861, this did little to improve the lives of the peasants. By 1900, peasants

Tsar Nicholas II and his family sit for a portrait in 1913.

Rural peasants made up 80 percent of Russia's population in 1900. With industrialization, many moved to the cities.

made up 80 percent of Russia's population. As the twentieth century began and Russia rushed to industrialize, many peasants left the countryside for factory work in cities, where they suffered long hours, low pay, and grueling working conditions. Millions of peasants continued to work on the estates held by rich nobles.

Marxist Revolutionaries

By 1900, unrest flared in the Russian capital of St. Petersburg, and in Moscow and other cities. Students, workers, and many anti-tsarist groups demanded change. Among those demanding change were a growing number of revolutionaries who advocated the ideas of the German philosopher Karl Marx. These Marxist revolutionaries looked forward to the revolt of workers against owners, and the establishment of a communist system. They shared Marx's vision of a classless society in which all means of production—such as factories, equipment, and railroads—belonged to the people as a whole.

One of the most devoted Marxists was Vladimir Ilyich Ulyanov, who went by the name of Vladimir Lenin (VLAD-uh-mihr LEN-in). (Like

other Russian revolutionaries, he took a "revolutionary" alias.) As a young man, Lenin became the leader of the Social Democrats, a Marxist revolutionary group. In 1895, Russian authorities arrested him and later exiled him to Siberia, the northern region of Russia where winters are bitterly cold. Lenin spent three years in exile.

In 1903, when the Social Democrats divided over disagreements about revolutionary strategy, Lenin took charge of the more radical faction, the Bolsheviks (BOHL-shuh-viks). The Bolsheviks believed that a small party of full-time, professional revolutionaries was needed to bring about change. Opposed to the Bolsheviks were the more moderate Mensheviks (MEN-shuh-viks), who sought to build popular support for revolutionary change.

Marxist-Leninist Doctrine

Lenin developed his own brand of Marxism, which he explained in a famous pamphlet titled *What Is to Be Done?* Marx had predicted that in the course of time, historical forces would bring about a workers' revolution. Lenin said revolutionaries should not wait for history to take its course. Instead, they should form a disciplined party of "professional revolutionists" who could operate in secret, combat the police, and seize power on behalf of the industrial working class, the class Marx had called the proletariat.

In 1903, Russia didn't have a large proletarian class. But Lenin said that once his revolutionary party took power, it would build factories that would enlarge the proletariat, who would then create a classless communist society.

The Revolution of 1905: "Bloody Sunday"

Lenin believed absolutely in his own ideas and tolerated no differences of opinion. He surrounded himself with loyal followers, including a ruthless young disciple, Joseph Stalin (STAH-luhn), whose adopted name meant "Man of Steel." Another revolutionary, known as Leon Trotsky, noted for both his brilliance and his arrogance, stood second only to Lenin in the Bolshevik Party.

In 1905, Lenin, Trotsky, and other revolutionaries were taken by surprise when unrest in Russia suddenly turned to revolt. At the time, Russia was losing to Japan in the Russo-Japanese War. Unemployment was rising, and discontented students and workers blamed Tsar Nicholas. One Sunday in January, thousands of workers and their families poured into the streets of St. Petersburg to rally for economic improvements and democratic change. The tsar's troops responded by opening fire on the crowd, killing and wounding hundreds of men, women, and children.

"Bloody Sunday" enraged Russian workers and set off a wave of strikes. Across the country, workers began setting up revolutionary councils known as *soviets* (SOH-vee-ets). Peasants, soldiers, and students joined these soviets, or formed their own. At last Tsar Nicholas yielded to pressure and created an elected parliament called the Duma (DOO-muh)—but he then refused to cooperate with it.

After the revolution of 1905, more people organized into soviets, but the tsar's secret police hunted down the leading revolutionaries and sent them to prison or into exile. Stalin ended up in Siberia. Lenin and Trotsky fled from Russia.

War Leads to Revolution

When the Great War began, Russia was on the verge of complete social upheaval. Russian armies had little food and poor equipment. Tsar Nicholas insisted on taking charge of military affairs, though he had almost no military talent or experience. German troops pounded the Russians. By the end of 1915, some five million men had been killed, wounded, taken prisoner, or had gone missing.

As Russian soldiers suffered on the battlefields, so did the people back home. Many went jobless and hungry as factories in St. Petersburg and Moscow shut down because of a lack of fuel. Grain

On Bloody Sunday, the tsar's troops shot hundreds of workers gathered at the Winter Palace in St. Petersburg.

and other foods were scarce in inland cities. There was no general shortage of either fuel or food, but neither could get to the cities because the trains were being used to move troops and wartime supplies.

Rasputin's Strange Power

In 1915, Tsar Nicholas had moved from his palace in St. Petersburg to the war front, leaving his wife, the tsarina Alexandra, at home to reign over the government. But the tsarina had fallen under the influence of Rasputin (ra-SPYOOT-uhn), a self-proclaimed holy man with a reputation for healing powers. Rasputin had managed to bring comfort to the tsarina's young son, who suffered from hemophilia, a disease that prevents clotting of the blood. Around Alexandra, Rasputin acted like a holy mystic, but outside the royal court he led a depraved life.

While Nicholas was away at the war front, Alexandra funneled money to Rasputin and let him decide who should be appointed to high government positions. In 1916, a group of noblemen, fearing Rasputin's growing power, murdered him.

The March Revolution

In early 1917, Russia was near collapse. Millions of Russians lay dead on frozen battlefields or maimed in hospitals that lacked medical supplies. Millions more were starving. As a hard winter set in, hungry rioters clamored for bread while mobs stormed government buildings.

The soviets organized larger and angrier demonstrations. In March 1917, crowds of women, mostly textile workers, poured into the streets of the Russian capital, whose name had been changed from St. Petersburg to Petrograd

Women, for the first time in great numbers, joined the protest rally in Petrograd in March 1917 to demand "Peace and bread!"

(replacing the German *-burg* with the Russian *-grad*). The crowds chanted "Peace and bread! Peace and bread!"

Tsar Nicholas II, who had learned nothing from Bloody Sunday, dispatched troops to crush the demonstrations. But this time, after starting to follow orders to shoot the demonstrators, the soldiers joined the mobs. The uprising spread into what has become known as the March Revolution. The tsar realized he had lost control and gave up the Russian throne. Thus ended the first act in the great drama of the Russian Revolution.

Lenin and the Bolshevik Revolution

It looked as if revolutionaries had succeeded at last. But what sort of government should Russia have? No one knew, since so many differing forces had opposed the tsar. The elected representatives in the Duma hastily assembled a provisional government to run the country. They made plans to write a constitution and chart Russia's future.

Provisional means temporary. A provisional government is one set up to serve until a permanent government can be put in place.

Far away in Switzerland, the exiled Lenin seized his opportunity. The German government gave Lenin money, a railroad carriage, and guards to get him safely to Finland. From there, Lenin could easily enter Russia. The Germans helped Lenin because they liked the idea of revolutionary chaos in the country they were trying to conquer.

Leon Trotsky, who was living in New York City, also rushed back to Russia, where he took charge of the biggest workers' group, the Petrograd Soviet. This group wielded as much power as the provisional government, and for many months it wasn't clear who was in charge of Russia.

When one of the tsar's former generals led a revolt, the provisional government supplied the workers of Petrograd with guns to fight that general and his troops. Most of the arms ended up in the hands of the Bolsheviks, which set the stage for the second act in the Russian Revolution.

In the early hours of November 7, 1917, Bolshevik guards led by Trotsky seized key bridges

Bolshevik fighters pose by an armored vehicle captured in November 1917 from provisional government forces.

and government buildings throughout the capital. When morning came, Lenin announced that the Petrograd Soviet had taken charge. Since Bolsheviks controlled this soviet, Lenin and his allies were now in control. Within weeks, Lenin dissolved the Petrograd Soviet and took command.

A Humiliating Treaty and Revolutionary Terror

When the Bolsheviks took power, German armies were marching toward the Russian capital. Lenin, who firmly believed in the Marxist ideal of a unified working class worldwide, thought German communists might lead a revolution to overthrow the kaiser's government in Germany. He reasoned that a German communist state would never wage war on a Russian communist nation. He sent Trotsky to engage the Germans in peace talks until the German revolution broke out. But no revolution broke out in Germany. The talks crumbled, and the German army surged to within a hundred miles of Petrograd.

Lenin hastily moved his capital to Moscow, where he signed a treaty that gave Germany huge chunks of Russia, including more than a quarter of its best farmland, one-sixth of its population, much of its industry, and most of its coal and iron. Russia was now out of the Great War.

While the humiliating treaty crippled Russia, it left Lenin free to launch his communist program. He declared that all land, all banks, all mines, and all factories now belonged to the state. Under the Communist Party, as the Bolsheviks called themselves, peasants were forbidden to sell their crops. Instead, Lenin ordered them to give all that they produced to the government.

Lenin assembled a police force with the authority to arrest and execute anyone considered dangerous. No one knows how many thousands of people Lenin's police killed between 1918 and 1920. The casualties included the former tsar Nicholas II and his entire family—even the children and a pet dog—all of whom were murdered in a house where they had been imprisoned.

Lenin Predicts Worldwide Revolution

In March 1919, Lenin addressed the First Congress of the Communist International, an organization of communist leaders from several countries. In attendance were representatives of groups such as the Spartacus League, a Marxist faction of the German Social Democratic party. Lenin boldly predicted an unstoppable "worldwide Communist revolution."

Comrades, our gathering has great historic significance…. The bourgeois are terror-stricken at the growing workers' revolutionary movement…. Even though the bourgeoisie are still raging, even though they may kill thousands more workers, victory will be ours, the victory of the worldwide Communist revolution is assured.

No matter how the bourgeoisie of the whole world rage, how much they deport or jail or even kill Spartacists and Bolsheviks—all this will no longer help. It will only serve to enlighten the masses, help rid them of the old bourgeois-democratic prejudices and steel them in the struggle. The victory of the proletarian revolution on a world scale is assured. The founding of an international Soviet republic is on the way.

In a poster, Vladimir Lenin, leader of the Russian Revolution, urges his comrades on.

Russia fell into chaos. Gangs of bandits roamed the land. Various ethnic groups began fighting for independence. Generals who supported the murdered tsar began gathering armies at the fringes of the former empire. Since Bolsheviks had long been called "Reds," these opposing forces came to be known as "Whites."

The Communists put Trotsky in charge of fighting the Whites. In less than a year, Trotsky built an army of almost three million troops. Over the next two years, the Reds and the Whites fought one of history's most savage civil wars. In a nation already devastated by the Great War, millions were killed, and millions more died of starvation and disease.

By late 1920, the Reds routed the Whites. The Bolsheviks were in charge of a Russia reduced to rubble.

A Dictatorship Is Born

With power firmly in hand, Lenin took on the task of rebuilding the country. He reorganized the old Russian empire into independent republics under the central government. The country forged by Lenin's Communist Party became the Union of Soviet Socialist Republics (USSR).

The republics within the USSR turned out to be anything but independent. All of the soviets were controlled by Lenin's Communist Party. All but the most trivial decisions flowed from a Central Committee in Moscow. Within this central core, power was concentrated in the hands of a small ruling group called the Politburo (PAH-lut-byour-oh). This inner circle included Stalin and Trotsky. Ultimately, however, one dictator held absolute power—Chairman Vladimir Lenin.

Lenin Suppresses Religion

Lenin sought to control many aspects of people's lives, including their religious beliefs. Years before, Karl Marx had described religion as "the opium of the people." He meant that religion, like a drug, offered people an escape from the struggles and challenges of life. Lenin agreed. He thought that tsars and nobles had long used the Russian Orthodox Church as a tool to keep power. Lenin ordered the government to seize church property, and he launched a campaign to turn people against religion.

Lenin's government imprisoned many clergymen and sentenced some to death. It outlawed religious instruction for children. The Communist Party adopted atheism—the belief that there is no God—as an official policy.

Lenin and his fellow Bolsheviks saw the Russian Revolution as merely the first step in a larger drama. They considered it their duty to spread communism abroad. They expected their communist revolution to spread across Europe

From Russia to USSR

Russian revolutionaries renamed their nation the Union of Soviet Socialist Republics. English-speaking people in the West often shortened the name to the Soviet Union or the USSR. Many people continued to refer to the powerful communist country as Russia, despite the fact that the USSR included millions of non-Russians, such as Finns, Latvians, Lithuanians, Ukrainians, Poles, Tatars, and Turkic peoples, among many others.

and the world. Such beliefs made European rulers very nervous. Americans also watched uneasily.

Lenin's aspirations for worldwide communism, which he passed on to succeeding generations, made the Russian Revolution of 1917 a crucial event not just in Russian history but in the history of the world. The revolution helped shape the course of the twentieth century.

Stalin Takes Charge

When Lenin died in 1924, he distrusted most of his closest associates. Before he died, he warned against one man in particular—the general secretary of the Communist Party, Joseph Stalin.

Few in the Soviet Union saw the thickset, pencil-pushing Stalin as a successor to Lenin. But they underestimated him. By pitting one leader against another, Stalin eliminated them all. He drove Leon Trotsky, a potential rival, into exile, and later had him murdered in Mexico. By 1928, Stalin reigned as the Soviet Union's dictator.

Stalin wanted to transform the Soviet Union into an industrial power. After the devastation of World War I, Stalin faced a choice. He could concentrate the hungry people's energies either on building factories or on growing food. He chose the factories. He decided his people must starve, if necessary.

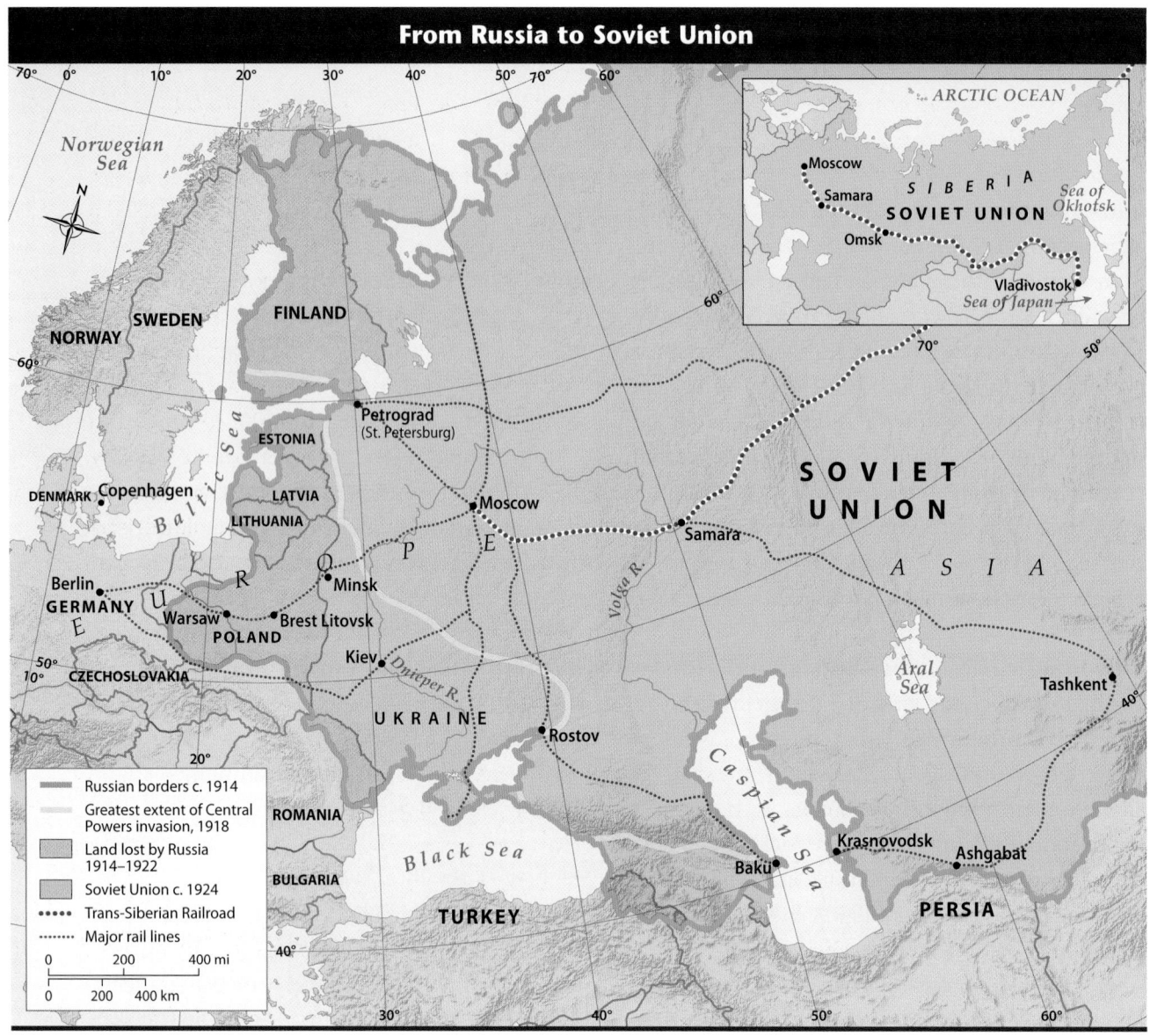

From Russia to Soviet Union

By the end of 1922, Russia had become the leading partner in a vast confederation of communist states that eventually became the world's largest country.

Five-Year Plans and Collective Farms

To accelerate industrial production, Stalin decreed the first of many Five-Year Plans, which set extremely ambitious targets for industrial production, especially of steel, coal, oil, and electricity. While industrial production did rise, people lacked basic necessities such as clothing and food.

Beginning in 1929, Stalin's troops herded some twenty million peasants into cities to work in factories. The rest were ordered onto huge "collective farms" that covered thousands of acres.

The Communist Party planners reasoned that peasants could pool their labor and use modern equipment, such as tractors, to produce more food, which the state could use to feed factory workers.

Many peasants who owned their own land and livestock resisted this drastic plan. Rather than go along, they slaughtered their farm animals, destroyed their tools, and burned their crops. Stalin declared that these troublesome peasants, mainly living in the fertile Ukraine, were capitalists who "must be eliminated as a class."

Any peasant caught eating his own produce was imprisoned or shot. Those who rebelled against "collectivization" were marched to Siberia. It has been estimated that perhaps fifteen million people were deported, and that about three million—mostly children—died along the way. The survivors ended up in brutal prison camps where many more died.

Although millions of peasants worked on the Soviet Union's collective farms, famine spread across much of the USSR. In 1932 and 1933, at least five million people in the Ukraine, once the breadbasket of eastern Europe, died of starvation.

Totalitarian Rule in the Soviet Union

Stalin tolerated no dissent and kept his eyes open for anyone who might challenge his leadership. He demanded the power to arrest anyone he deemed a threat, to try people in secret, and to execute them if he saw fit.

In the 1930s, Stalin undertook a so-called "great purge" of the Communist Party. He arrested any rivals, including close comrades from the revolutionary days. He had them tortured until they agreed to confess to treasonous crimes in open court. Then he had them killed. Under Stalin, millions of people were sent to their deaths.

Stalin had become a **totalitarian** ruler, a dictator exercising almost total control over the state and the lives of its people. Across the huge country, his Communist Party told farmers and factory workers exactly what it expected them to produce. By the 1930s, Stalin's plan to turn the Soviet Union into a worker state seemed to be succeeding. The Soviet Union was becoming an industrial powerhouse, producing steel, cars, tractors, and military goods.

Propaganda and Belief

Stalin was a master of propaganda. Government-controlled newspapers portrayed the dictator as a warm family man, the father of his people. This was a lie. But those not directly affected by Stalin's tactics were willing to close their eyes. At least

Stalin was moving the country forward, they told themselves.

Stalin, like Lenin, was hostile to religion in general and the Russian Orthodox Church in particular. He demolished churches in peasant villages, continued the persecution of priests, and used a Communist Party organization called The League of the Militant Godless to promote atheism.

Soviet propaganda painted a picture of a harmonious society of happy workers cooperating for the common good. Stalin's propaganda machine convinced many outsiders that the Soviet Union was succeeding in creating a new kind of society. In Europe and America, some intellectuals saw the Soviet Union as the future of mankind. The truth, however, was that the communist revolution had fallen into the hands of one the most brutal dictators in all of history.

A Soviet propaganda poster from the 1920s declares: "With weapons we beat the enemy, with hard work we'll get bread. All for the work, friends!"

Nationalism in India

At the end of World War I, President Woodrow Wilson, in his Fourteen Points, had urged self-determination—the idea that people have the right to determine their own fate and choose their own governments. While imperial powers were willing to acknowledge self-determination as a worthy goal, they did little to promote self-determination in their own colonies. In the decades following World War I, much of the globe remained under colonial rule. People in India, Indochina, North Africa, and elsewhere were ruled by a handful of mostly European nations, including Great Britain, France, Belgium, and Portugal.

Key Questions

- What philosophy and tactics did Gandhi advocate in India's independence movement?

India's Advocate: Mohandas Gandhi

In many colonies, nationalists stirred the desire for independence. In the world's largest colony, India, nationalists were inspired by the leadership of Mohandas Gandhi (MOH-huhn-dahs GAHN-dee), who fought British rule not with guns but with the strength of his will and the force of his ideas.

Born in 1869, Gandhi grew up during a time when Britain had a complex relationship with its most important colony. In the late nineteenth and early twentieth centuries, people called India the "Jewel in the Crown" of the British Empire. After the Indian Rebellion (1857–1858), the British government took control of India out of the hands of the private East India Company and decided to rule India directly, thus establishing what is often called the British Raj (rahj; *raj* means "reign" or "rule").

The British Raj and British companies built schools, railroads, and highways across the Indian subcontinent. A British-designed civil service, staffed mostly by Indians, ran the colony. Indian taxes paid for soldiers and policemen, most of them Indians, who worked to keep the British in power.

Gandhi in South Africa

Many Indians from upper-class families traveled to England to be educated. Mohandas Gandhi, the son of an Indian administrator, went to London in the 1880s to study law. Gandhi's family had raised him in the traditions of his native land and as a follower of Hinduism, India's majority religion. As a student in London, young Gandhi adopted British manners and dressed like a fashionable London gentleman in well-tailored suits with stiff-collared shirts. He also adopted the British liberal ideals of liberty, equality, and natural rights.

After he became a lawyer, Gandhi accepted a job with a law firm in South Africa, which was also part of the British Empire. Tens of thousands of Indians had traveled to South Africa seeking work. Many took jobs that no

The young lawyer and future nonviolent activist Mohandas Gandhi in Western-style clothing

They could be arrested for walking on the same sidewalk as white people. And, unless they were Christian, their marriages were not recognized. In response to these and other injustices, the young lawyer became an activist. He organized rallies, held protests, and wrote letters to newspapers. He challenged unjust laws in court. For twenty years, he worked for equal rights for South Africa's Indians.

Gandhi in India: Nonviolent Resistance

In 1915, Gandhi left South Africa. When he returned to India, he was celebrated as a champion of the downtrodden. He abandoned his European-style clothing in favor of the plain cotton robes and sandals worn by many poor Indians. In his homeland, he saw that most British rulers and white settlers looked down on Indians. He witnessed many of the same injustices he had seen in South Africa. He realized that as long as India remained a British colony, the injustices would continue. Gandhi then had a new cause—the independence of his homeland from British rule.

As he had in South Africa, Gandhi organized rallies against laws that treated Indians unfairly. He advocated civil disobedience—the refusal to obey unjust laws. He tried to change laws and attitudes in India the same way he had brought change to South Africa—by **nonviolent resistance**.

Even when facing guns and bayonets, Gandhi urged his supporters to meet violence with nonviolence. Nonviolent resistance, said Gandhi, demanded "the strength and courage to suffer without retaliation, to receive blows without returning any." If enough people resisted peacefully, he said, others would see their suffering and eventually be moved to correct the injustice. Gandhi himself spent several years in prison for disobeying colonial laws.

Nonviolence is a central principle in Gandhi's philosophy of *satyagraha* (suh-TYAH-gruh-huh), which may be translated as "soul force" or "truth force." Gandhi described satyagraha as the "quiet and irresistible pursuit of truth."

one else would do, such as working on farms and growing sugarcane. White South Africans, descendants of the British and Dutch, looked down on the Indians and treated them badly. As Gandhi found out, it did not matter that he was a lawyer. The white people scorned him as much as they did the poorest Indian laborer.

Soon after he arrived in South Africa, Gandhi purchased a first-class ticket and boarded a train for the city of Pretoria to start his new job. During the journey, a white passenger objected to sharing his compartment with a brown-skinned Indian. The passenger complained to a policeman, who threw Gandhi off the train. Shivering on an empty station platform at night, Gandhi considered his future. He could ignore the insults and get on with his job. Or he could fight for the rights of Indians in South Africa. He decided to fight—not with guns but with words and ideas.

Gandhi quickly learned that Indians in South Africa were denied basic political rights and subject to constant discrimination. They could not vote.

Gandhi was revered not only for his courage but also for the simplicity and purity of his life. A deeply spiritual man, Gandhi practiced the traditional Hindu disciplines of fasting and meditation. At the same time, he preached respect for all religions. Gandhi's followers began referring to him as the *Mahatma*, which means "Great Soul."

Amritsar and After

About a million Indians had fought with the British army in World War I. For this service, the British government had promised reforms and greater self-rule for Indians. But after the war ended, it quickly became clear that Britain had no intention of making any significant changes.

In 1919, in the city of Amritsar (uhm-RIT-sur), thousands of Indian demonstrators gathered to protest a decision to extend wartime measures that allowed the British to jail protesters without trial. Some of the Amritsar demonstrators turned violent—they went looking for Europeans and killed at least three of them. The mob burned buildings and attacked a woman missionary. Days later, a British general ordered his troops to fire on a largely unarmed crowd of Indians. Within minutes, hundreds were dead and many more wounded. The Amritsar Massacre, as it came to be known, increased Indians' determination to bring an end to British rule.

After the Amritsar Massacre, Gandhi stepped up his efforts for Indian independence. By this time, around 1920, Gandhi had become a leading figure in the Indian National Congress, a nationalist organization founded in the mid-1880s. Under Gandhi's leadership, the congress evolved from a small organization of mostly urban upper-class professionals to a broad-based political movement with supporters in towns and villages across India.

Gandhi persuaded the Indian National Congress to adopt a program of nonviolent noncooperation with the British. Indians were urged to refuse to pay British taxes, and to have nothing to do with various British institutions, including schools and courts. Gandhi encouraged people

Gandhi sits and reads by his spinning wheel. As part of his protest, he made and wore the cloth of a Hindu peasant.

to protest colonial rule by refusing to buy British-made products. He led a boycott of British cloth. Rather than enrich the British by buying their cloth, the people of India, said Gandhi, should make their own cloth at home. He set an example by working daily at a spinning wheel, and by wearing only homespun cloth.

In 1930, Gandhi organized a dramatic act of nonviolent resistance that came to be called the Salt March. According to British colonial law, Indians were prohibited from making their own salt. They had to buy salt from British sources and pay a tax on it. Gandhi led a 241-mile (388 km) march to the sea where, with newspaper reporters watching, he scooped up a muddy lump of salt that had been left on the beach by the waves. It was a signal for thousands to gather salt in pans and let it sit on their rooftops to dry, thus producing illegal salt. British officials arrested Gandhi and tens of thousands of other Indians, and in doing so brought worldwide attention to an unjust law.

In 1935, the British Parliament granted Indians limited self-rule. But these measures fell far short of the independence Gandhi and others sought. More struggle would be required before India would become an independent, self-governing nation.

Primary Source

Gandhi's Nonviolent Resistance

Mohandas Gandhi spent much time in jail and risked his life many times while refusing to obey unjust laws, both in South Africa and, later, in his homeland of India. Still, Gandhi insisted upon nonviolence. If enough people peacefully resisted, he said, others would see their suffering and eventually be moved to correct the injustice. Here are some of Gandhi's thoughts about the power of nonviolent resistance.

[Nonviolence] calls for the strength and courage to suffer without retaliation, to receive blows without returning any.

In the composition of the truly brave there should be no malice, no anger, no distrust, no fear of death or physical hurt. Nonviolence is certainly not for those who lack these essential qualities.

In nonviolence the masses have a weapon which enables a child, a woman, or even a decrepit old man to resist the mightiest government successfully. If your spirit is strong, mere lack of physical strength ceases to be a handicap.

The virtues of mercy, nonviolence, love, and truth in any man can be truly tested only when they are pitted against ruthlessness, violence, hate, and untruth.

Those who die unresistingly are likely to still the fury of violence by their wholly innocent sacrifice.

If freedom has got to come, it must be obtained by our own internal strength, by our closing our ranks, by unity between all sections of the community.

I know that the progress of nonviolence is seemingly a terribly slow progress. But experience has taught me it is the surest way to the common goal.

Nationalism in the Middle East

Key Questions

- How did nationalist movements influence events in the Middle East after World War I?

- What issues led to continuing tensions in the Middle East?

Since the 1500s, most of the Middle East had been ruled by the Islamic empire of the Ottoman Turks. With the defeat of the Ottomans in the Great War, however, nationalist movements emerged in the region. These nationalist movements were in part a response to decisions made at the peace treaty conference in Versailles.

The Allied leaders at Versailles decided to create new nations in the Middle East. They said that the people in these lands would eventually govern themselves. But for a time, the new nations would be *mandates*, states placed under British and French rule.

The British and French were supposed to help people in the mandates design constitutions and set up new governments. But for the people living in these mandates, European non-Muslims were now in charge of lands Muslims had ruled for centuries.

Egyptian Independence

Britain had dominated Egypt since shortly after the Suez Canal was constructed in the mid-1800s. The canal, connecting the Mediterranean and Red seas, was so important to British trade that even though the British had not built it, they maneuvered to take control of it in the 1870s. The

Camels bring trade goods to ships in the Suez Canal.

British interfered in Egyptian affairs whenever the canal seemed threatened. During World War I, Britain declared Egypt a protectorate, and exercised a strong hand in running Egypt's government.

After the war, nationalists in Egypt demanded independence, but the British refused. Egyptians, who had fought and died to cast off their Ottoman rulers, refused to accept British rule. Demonstrations in Cairo eventually gave way to three years of fighting between Egyptian nationalists and British forces.

In 1922, Britain agreed to grant Egypt formal independence. The country became a constitutional monarchy. The British, however, left troops throughout the country to protect the Suez Canal and keep watch on the region. The Egyptians had no way to force the heavily armed British to leave the country.

The Debate over Egyptian Identity

When they gained their independence in 1922, Egyptians saw evidence of Western influence all around them. Like other Middle Eastern cities—such as Baghdad, Damascus, and Beirut—Egypt's capital city, Cairo, had electric lighting, railroads, motorcars, and telegraphs. Egyptians listened to radio broadcasts and went to movies. The urban population soared as labor-saving equipment allowed farmers to grow more food. This equipment put farmhands out of work.

Western influence appeared as well in Egypt's new constitution. It separated church and state, leaving governance in the hands of political, not religious, leaders.

Egypt stood at the crossroads of the East and the West. Many voices in the newly independent nation debated Egypt's identity and the country's future. Should Egyptians embrace what the West had to offer? Or should they turn away from the West?

Many Egyptian nationalists agreed that Egypt could build on three elements for its identity: the distant past of the pharaohs, the Arab and Muslim identity from Muhammad's time, and the Western influences that had begun to shape Egypt from the times of Alexander the Great and Julius Caesar. These moderate nationalists believed Egypt could remain grounded in Islam while integrating Western learning and principles of government, including the separation of church and state.

Other Egyptian nationalists disagreed. In 1928, an Egyptian teacher formed an organization called the Muslim Brotherhood. Its members were dedicated to ending Western influence in Egypt. They denounced the idea of a secular nation that separated church and state. They called for a government run according to the Islamic legal and moral code known as Sharia. The Muslim Brotherhood demanded nothing less than complete Islamic rule.

The start of the Muslim Brotherhood marked the rise of a new movement in the Arab world called **Islamism**. Islamists called for a pure Islamic state, which they thought would restore harmony to their lands. Islamism attracted many followers, but they were often at odds with the secular nationalist movements growing throughout the region.

Ibn Saud Unites Arabia

Before World War I, the western Arabian Peninsula, where Islam's holiest cities of Mecca and Medina are located, was under Ottoman rule. Sharif Hussein (shahr-EEF hoo-SAYN), whose family claimed descent from the Prophet Muhammad, was in charge of the Ottoman territory. Hussein wanted to oust the Ottomans from Arabia and become king of the entire Arabian Peninsula and beyond. During the war, he aided the British and French. At the end of the war, his sons were made kings of Jordan and Iraq, but Hussein himself did not gain the power he wanted and soon lost even the western peninsula.

The central and eastern Arabian Peninsula, independent of the Ottomans, was ruled by Ibn Saud (ib-uhn sah-OOD), a member of a powerful rival family called the House of Saud. A strict observer of Islamic law, Ibn Saud had spent years expanding his territory, building an army, and gaining the support of Arabs who were part of an Islamic movement known as Wahhabism (wah-HAH-bih-zuhm). Wahhabists urged strict adherence to Islamic law. They believed Muslims should model their society on the way people lived more than a thousand years earlier. They saw themselves as warriors for the "true" Islam and were willing to destroy and even kill in the name of Islamic purity.

Ibn Saud wanted Sharif Hussein's kingdom because it contained the holy sites of Mecca and Medina. When Hussein declared that Wahhabi pilgrims would no longer be allowed to visit the Muslim holy sites, Ibn Saud launched an attack that caught Hussein by surprise. By 1926, the House of Saud controlled the Arabian Peninsula. Ibn Saud named his lands the Kingdom of Saudi Arabia, which he molded into a Muslim

Ibn Saud established the Kingdom of Saudi Arabia.

state demanding strict adherence to Islamic law. Unlike Egypt, Saudi Arabia would have no secular constitution.

Independence for Turkey

In Turkey, in the heart of the old Ottoman Empire, nationalists founded a country free of Western control but friendly to many Western traditions and ideas. The determined nationalist who led Turkey to independence was Mustafa Kemal (MOO-stah-fah keh-MAHL).

Mustafa Kemal and Turkish Nationalism

Kemal grew up in Greece, which was part of the Ottoman Empire. As a boy, he attended schools that exposed him to European thinking and learning. He later distinguished himself at the Ottoman War College in Istanbul where he and other young Turkish cadets started an underground newspaper. Believing the Ottoman ruler, the sultan, was weak and corrupt, they called for his overthrow.

During World War I, Kemal led the Ottoman forces that prevented an Allied fleet from sailing past the fortifications at Gallipoli and attacking Istanbul, the Ottoman capital. Kemal became a national hero, and grateful Turks pronounced him "the Savior of Istanbul." But the Allies went on to win the war, and in 1918 they established a military administration in Istanbul.

At the end of World War I, all that was left of the once-great Ottoman Empire was the city of Istanbul and parts of Asia Minor. Mustafa Kemal was sickened by his country's decline and began organizing a nationalist movement to resist the Allied occupation. He declared that the sultan was nothing more than a prisoner of the Allies. He told cheering throngs that he, Mustafa Kemal, would lead his countrymen to independence.

Over the next three years, through both war and negotiation, Kemal and his nationalist forces overthrew the sultan and drove Greek and French forces from Asia Minor. In 1923, the Allies recognized Turkey as an independent republic.

The Turkish leader known as Kemal Atatürk (center) encouraged his countrymen to embrace Western ideas and customs.

Atatürk Transforms a Nation

Mustafa Kemal came to be known as Kemal Atatürk, meaning "Father of the Turks." Atatürk looked upon his newly independent nation and declared, "The civilized world is far ahead of us. We have no choice but to catch up." He worried that a traditional Islamic nation would not be able to compete in an industrial world dominated by the West. So he took steps to transform Turkish life in both symbolic and concrete ways.

Atatürk's government changed the alphabet from Arabic letters to Latin letters similar to those used in the West. It created a public education system and prohibited most traditional Islamic schools. It decided that Islamic law would not be the basis of government, but that Turkey would be a secular nation with a constitution separating church and state.

Atatürk also urged Turks to dress more like Westerners. The government prohibited men from wearing turbans and the traditional flat-topped head covering called a *fez*. Atatürk himself discouraged women from wearing the veil used in many Muslim countries. "Let them show their faces to the world, and see it with their eyes," he said. "Don't be afraid. Change is essential."

Under Atatürk's government, women gained new rights. The Grand National Assembly forbade the old Muslim practice of marriage to more than one woman. Women gained the right to enter institutions of higher learning. Turkey awarded women the right to vote in parliamentary elections, and in 1935, Turkish voters elected seventeen women as delegates to the assembly.

Atatürk pushed hard to bring Turkey's economy into the industrial age. New state banks

701

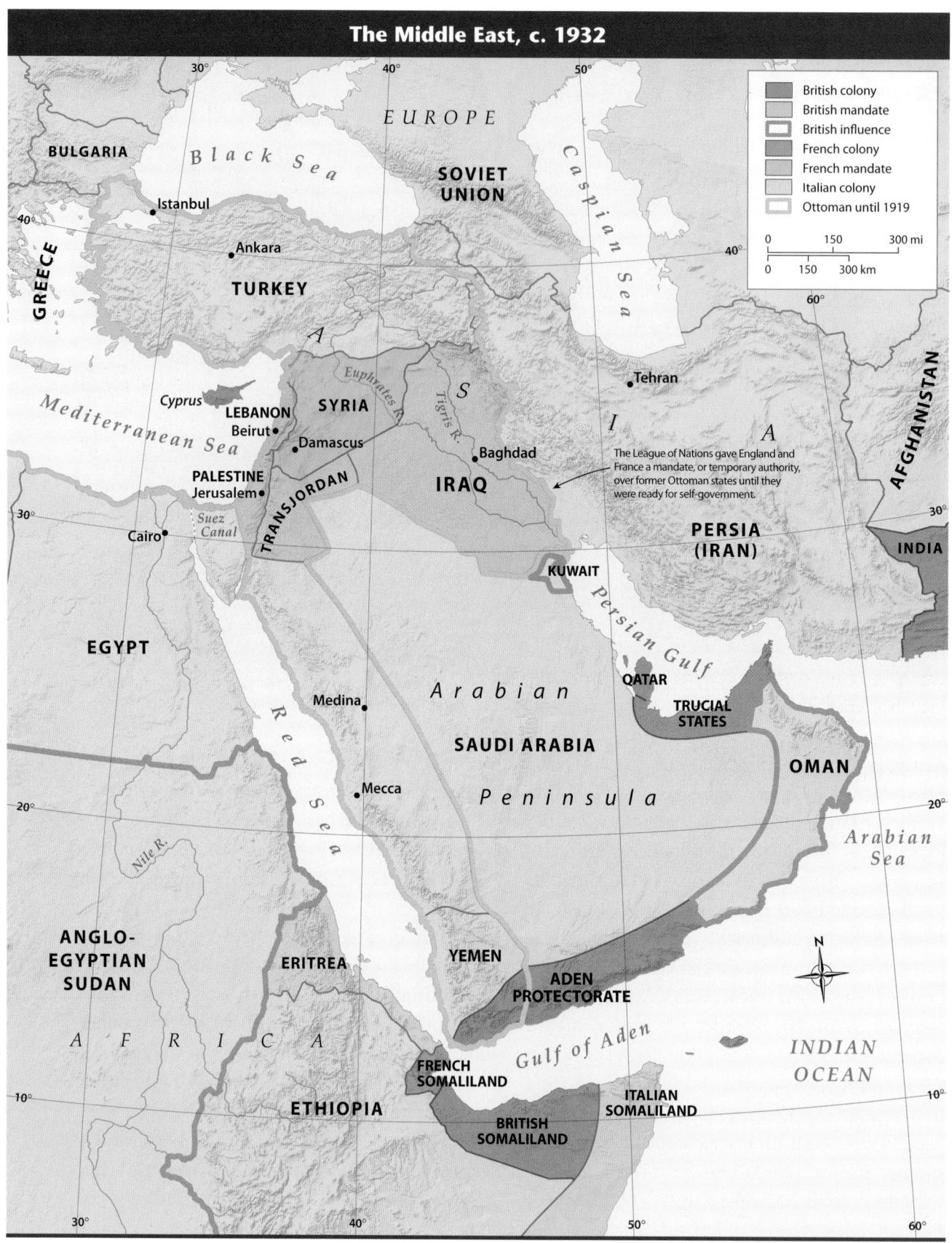

The Middle East, c. 1932

▨	British colony
▨	British mandate
▢	British influence
▨	French colony
▨	French mandate
▨	Italian colony
▢	Ottoman until 1919

0   150   300 mi
0   150   300 km

BULGARIA

Black Sea

EUROPE

SOVIET
UNION

Caspian Sea

Istanbul

GREECE

Ankara

TURKEY

Cyprus

Mediterranean Sea

LEBANON
Beirut
Damascus

SYRIA

Euphrates R.

Tigris R.

Tehran

Baghdad

IRAQ

The League of Nations gave England and
France a mandate, or temporary authority,
over former Ottoman states until they
were ready for self-government.

PERSIA
(IRAN)

AFGHANISTAN

PALESTINE
Jerusalem

TRANSJORDAN

Suez
Canal

Cairo

KUWAIT

INDIA

EGYPT

Red Sea

Medina

Nile R.

QATAR

Persian Gulf

TRUCIAL
STATES

Arabian

SAUDI ARABIA

Mecca

Peninsula

OMAN

*Arabian
Sea*

ANGLO-
EGYPTIAN
SUDAN

ERITREA

YEMEN

ADEN
PROTECTORATE

N

A F R I C A

Gulf of Aden

*INDIAN
OCEAN*

FRENCH
SOMALILAND

ITALIAN
SOMALILAND

ETHIOPIA

BRITISH
SOMALILAND

Independent nations began to emerge in the Middle East following World War I, but always under the watchful eye of European nations intent on preserving their own strategic interests.

increased loans for agriculture. Atatürk used government power and funding to build railroads and expand electric service. The state also set up factories to produce textiles, glass, and steel.

Not everyone agreed with Atatürk's changes. In 1925, Muslim Kurds in southern Turkey led a revolt to overthrow the "godless government" and restore Islamic law. Atatürk dispatched troops and declared martial law. He issued orders to shut down newspapers and disband opposition political parties. Journalists were jailed and sternly warned against treason. Some of the Muslim Kurds who had led the uprising received death sentences.

Atatürk consistently pushed for a strong, independent, and secular Turkey. At his death in 1938, the grief-stricken Turks proclaimed him "Eternal Leader."

Reza Khan: Independence for Iran

In the 1920s, another Middle Eastern nation embarked on a nationalist and secular path. Foreign powers had been interfering in Iran—or, as the Europeans called it, Persia—for centuries. At the end of World War I, Iran was an independent but weak nation. The country lapsed into chaos under the rule of an ineffective shah. (*Shah* is the traditional title for the ruler, or king, of Iran.)

A fiercely nationalist Iranian military officer, Reza Khan (RIH-zuh kahn), decided his nation must resist foreign domination and become a strong independent state. In 1921, he marched troops into Tehran and took over the capital city. For the next twenty years, Reza Khan controlled his nation's destiny.

Reza Khan thought that, like Turkey, his nation should become a modern, secular republic. But Iran's powerful clergymen did not like the idea of losing their power and influence. Reza Khan decided to meet them halfway. He would not proclaim his nation a republic. It would be a monarchy, and he would become its new shah.

Nationalist leader Reza Khan declared Iran a constitutional monarchy and ruled for more than two decades.

For his new dynasty, Reza Khan chose the name Pahlavi (PAH-luh-vee), from an old name for the Persian language. He was now known as Reza Shah Pahlavi. As shah, he attempted to foster national pride by recalling the glory of the ancient Persian Empire. He declared that Iran's official language would be the Persian language of Farsi, not Arabic, Turkish, or Kurdish, all of which were spoken in Iran. And because the Farsi word for Persia was *Iran*, the nation's name was officially changed to Iran in 1935.

Iran Expands and Modernizes

Reza Shah believed that the key to independence was military strength. He immediately set about building up the army. The shah then used his large force to conquer rivals and expand Iran's territory. He also set out to modernize its transportation system. The government built many new highways

703

and roads. A new trans-Iranian railway connected Iran from the Persian Gulf to the Caspian Sea. The railway brought down the cost of transporting goods, which spurred the economy.

Like Atatürk, the shah closed many religious schools and made education a public responsibility. The new state-run schools taught loyalty and patriotism. The shah also thought Iran's capital needed a first-rate university. In 1935, the University of Tehran opened, and it soon started admitting women. Women in Iran gained other important rights as well. The shah himself discouraged use of the veil and even outlawed it in 1936. (Later, as you'll learn, Iranian women lost many of these rights and freedoms.)

Like Atatürk in Turkey, Reza Shah in Iran held enormous power and used it to stamp out the strong dissent among those who objected to the changes he demanded. But while the shah encouraged modernization and even Westernization, he opposed foreign influence in his nation's affairs. Through the 1920s and 1930s, the powerful shah worked to minimize British profits from Iran's oil fields, and to steer those profits to Iran. To diminish Russian influence, he outlawed the Communist Party.

Palestine and the Zionist Movement

Palestine, a small strip of land bordering the eastern shore of the Mediterranean Sea, often called the Holy Land, is hugely important to the followers of three major religions—Judaism, Christianity, and Islam. In the years following the Great War, this region saw the rise of a nationalist movement for a Jewish homeland in Palestine.

In the late 1800s and early 1900s, Arabs from the land now called Syria made up most of Palestine's population. Some of those Arabs were Christians, but most were Muslim. A small number of Jews also lived in Palestine, mostly in and around cities, such as Jerusalem.

The moon over the Mount of Olives and the Dome of the Rock (at left) and in the city of Jerusalem, Israel

In the nineteenth century, European Jews bought land in Palestine and began moving there in greater numbers. They started a movement called **Zionism**, named for the historic site of Solomon's temple. Zionism aimed at establishing a Jewish state in Palestine, which Zionists considered both the Holy Land and the Jewish people's ancestral home before the Romans forced most Jews out of the region.

One strong motivation behind the Zionist movement was nationalism—the Jews, like many other peoples, wanted their own state. Another motivation was the long history of oppression of Jews. During the late nineteenth and early twentieth centuries, anti-Jewish sentiment was on the rise in Europe. Many people accused Jewish intellectuals of spreading dangerous ideas. They resented wealthy Jewish business owners such as the Rothschild family, who owned banks throughout Europe.

Sometimes the prejudice against Jews turned violent. Waves of *pogroms*—organized massacres of Jews—swept parts of Russia and Poland. Faced with such oppression, Zionists worked to establish a state in Palestine where Jews from all over the world might find refuge. The Jews' desire for their own state received support from the British. In 1917, British Foreign Secretary Arthur Balfour issued the Balfour Declaration,

In the 1920s, European Jews increasingly settled in Palestine as part of a movement known as Zionism.

which supported "a national home for the Jewish people," while also insisting that the "rights of existing non-Jewish communities in Palestine" be fully respected.

After World War I, Palestine became a mandate of Great Britain. Hopeful Zionists encouraged more Jews to move into the area. By 1922, Jews made up just over 10 percent of Palestine's population. Tensions rose in Palestine as various interests began to collide—Jewish nationalism, Arab nationalism, growing Islamism, fervent devotion to the Holy Land, age-old prejudices, and anger at old imperialist powers. As you'll read in later chapters, these tensions would lead to ongoing bitterness and violence.

1919
After World War I, the Treaty of Versailles imposes harsh terms on Germany.

1922
James Joyce's experimental novel *Ulysses* is published.

1927
Charles Lindbergh completes the first nonstop solo flight across the Atlantic.

1925

c. 1921
In the Roaring Twenties, the United States enjoys a postwar economic boom.

1926
Italy becomes a fascist state under Mussolini.

1929
The American stock market crashes. The Great Depression begins.

Adolf Hitler, Nazi Germany's leader, ascends stairs to address a rally in 1934.

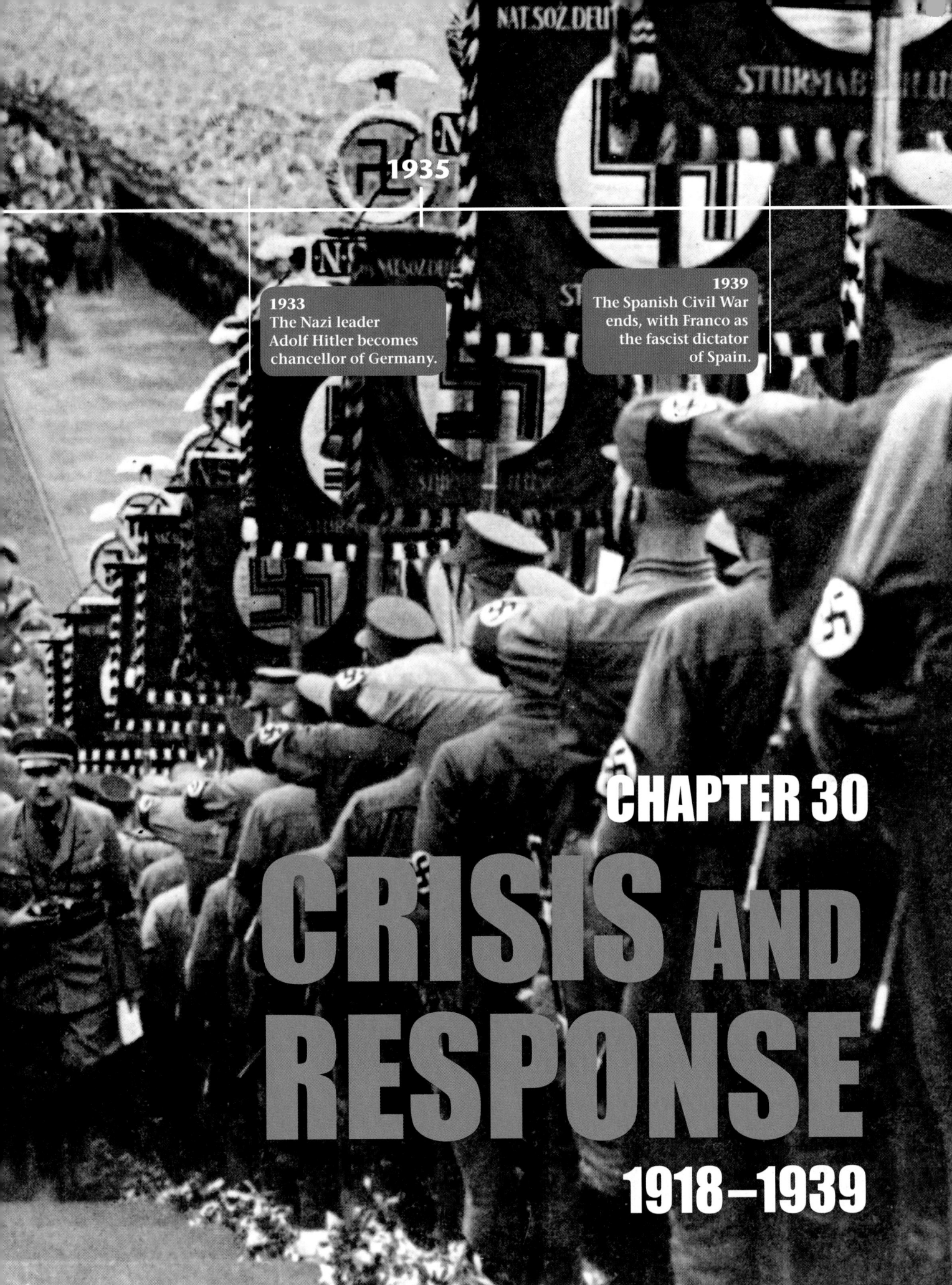

1935

1933
The Nazi leader Adolf Hitler becomes chancellor of Germany.

1939
The Spanish Civil War ends, with Franco as the fascist dictator of Spain.

CHAPTER 30

CRISIS AND RESPONSE

1918–1939

*T*he Great War and the influenza pandemic brought such widespread death and destruction that people wondered what the world was coming to. Artists, writers, and composers created new forms of expression as they struggled to find meaning in the postwar era.

After World War I, the United States experienced cultural and social shifts during a time known as the Roaring Twenties. The American economy seemed to be thriving but the prosperity hid deep problems. In 1929, the American economy collapsed.

As the economic catastrophe known as the Great Depression spread worldwide, it brought panic and suffering. In Europe in the 1930s, as people longed for economic and social stability, they turned to dictators who promised to end the hardship.

Uncertainty in the Postwar World

Key Questions

- How did artists, writers, and composers respond to the uncertainty of the postwar era?

- Why was the United States able to enjoy an economic boom after World War I?

- What characterizes the American era known as the Roaring Twenties?

The French poet Paul Valéry said this about the decades after World War I: "The storm has died away and still we are restless, uneasy, as if the storm were about to break. Almost all the affairs of men remain in a terrible uncertainty." This sense of uncertainty found expression in the works of artists, composers, and writers who explored creative paths that led in new directions—sometimes startling, sometimes disturbing.

Artists Question Reality

Even in the years leading up to World War I, some artists had begun to question the relationship between art and reality. The Spanish artist Pablo Picasso was one of the pioneers of a style called *Cubism*, which transformed modern art. Picasso was perfectly capable of painting a lifelike portrait, but in his Cubist paintings he turned his subject into an array of geometric forms on a flat surface. Cubism rejected the long-standing idea that art should mirror nature. In his Cubist paintings, it was as though Picasso held a shattered mirror up to nature, breaking reality into an array of sharp-edged fragments.

Dada Mocks Reality

After the Great War, in response to a world in which the old certainties seemed shattered, many artists altered, questioned, or simply abandoned reality in their works. The founders of the artistic movement called *Dada* looked at the ruins of World War I and responded with a bitter laugh.

Dadaists produced a kind of anti-art, intended to subvert and mock everything about modern civilization, including art itself. In response to a call for works for an exhibit, the French Dada artist Marcel Duchamp submitted one titled *Fountain*. It was a porcelain urinal, which the artist signed "R. Mutt."

In 1921, Tristan Tzara, a Dada poet, issued a manifesto in which he proclaimed,

If you make artistic discoveries
and if all of a sudden your head begins to crackle with laughter,
If you find all your ideas useless and ridiculous, know that
IT IS DADA BEGINNING TO SPEAK TO YOU.

Surrealism Taps the Unconscious

Out of the impulses behind Dada there emerged another artistic movement called *surrealism*. The term *surrealism* was coined in 1924 by the French poet

André Breton (bruh-TOHN) as a shortened form of "super realism."

The surrealists were influenced by Sigmund Freud, who argued that the unconscious mind is filled with powerful instincts and urges that shape our actions, even though we are not aware of their power. Surrealist writers and artists wanted to tap the unconscious mind for access to what they thought was a deeper, truer reality. One of Breton's surrealist poems begins, "The timetable of hollow flowers and prominent cheekbones invites us to leave volcanic salt shakers for birdbaths."

The surrealist painter Salvador Dali said he wanted his work to be like "handmade color photography of concrete irrationality." In *Persistence of Memory*, one of Dali's best-known works, pocket watches hang limply in an eerie landscape. The painting is like a glimpse into the realm of dreams and the unconscious.

The Stream of Consciousness

While the surrealists tapped their unconscious minds for dreamlike images, some writers tried to chart the flow of the mind in a technique called *stream of consciousness*. The Irish novelist James Joyce took the technique of stream of consciousness to new lengths in fiction.

Joyce's best-known novel, *Ulysses*, published in 1922, follows three central characters through a single day in the city of Dublin. In *Ulysses*, as one critic put it, Joyce used words to capture "the mind of man in all its apparent inconsequence and confusion, its mixture of memory of the past and attention to the present, of things thought, things imagined, things felt and things experienced in the subconscious." *Ulysses* ends with many pages of one character's unpunctuated and uninterrupted thoughts:

> *"...frseeeeeeeefronnnng train somewhere whistling the strength those engines have in them like big giants and the water rolling all over and out them all sides like the end of Loves old sweet sonnnng the poor men that have to be out all night from their wives and families in those roasting engines...."*

James Joyce became one of the most influential writers of the twentieth century. His example encouraged other writers to experiment with language and push the boundaries of storytelling into new literary forms.

Musical Disruptions: Stravinsky and Schoenberg

Some music historians like to say that modern music began in Paris in 1913 with the premiere of a ballet called *The Rite of Spring*, with music by the Russian composer Igor Stravinsky. When the audience first heard the music—by turns eerie, harsh, and fierce, like an eruption in sound of dark, irrational forces—some hissed and booed. When they saw the dancers leaping jerkily in response to the music's violent rhythms, some shouted and whistled. Fistfights broke out in the crowd.

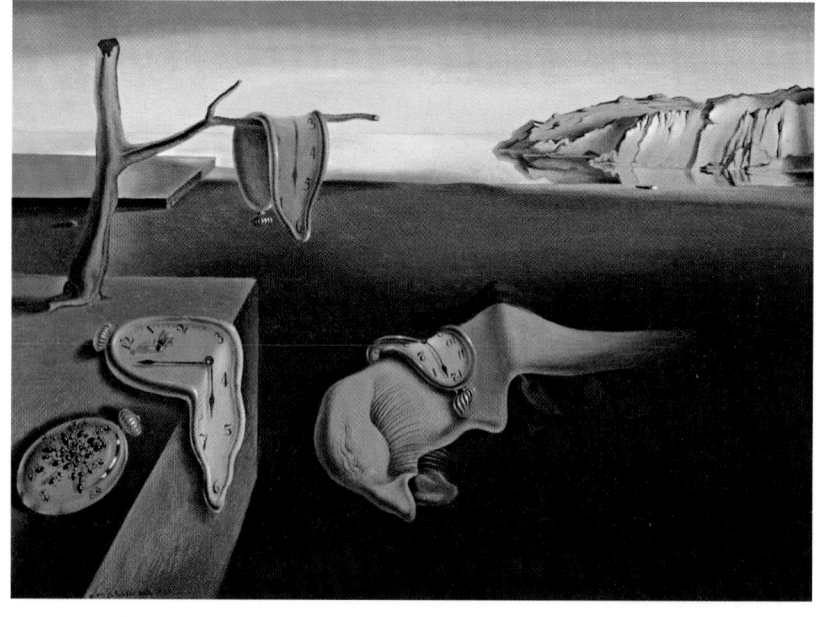

The Spanish artist Salvador Dali painted *The Persistence of Memory* in 1931. His surrealist paintings often depict dreamlike settings.

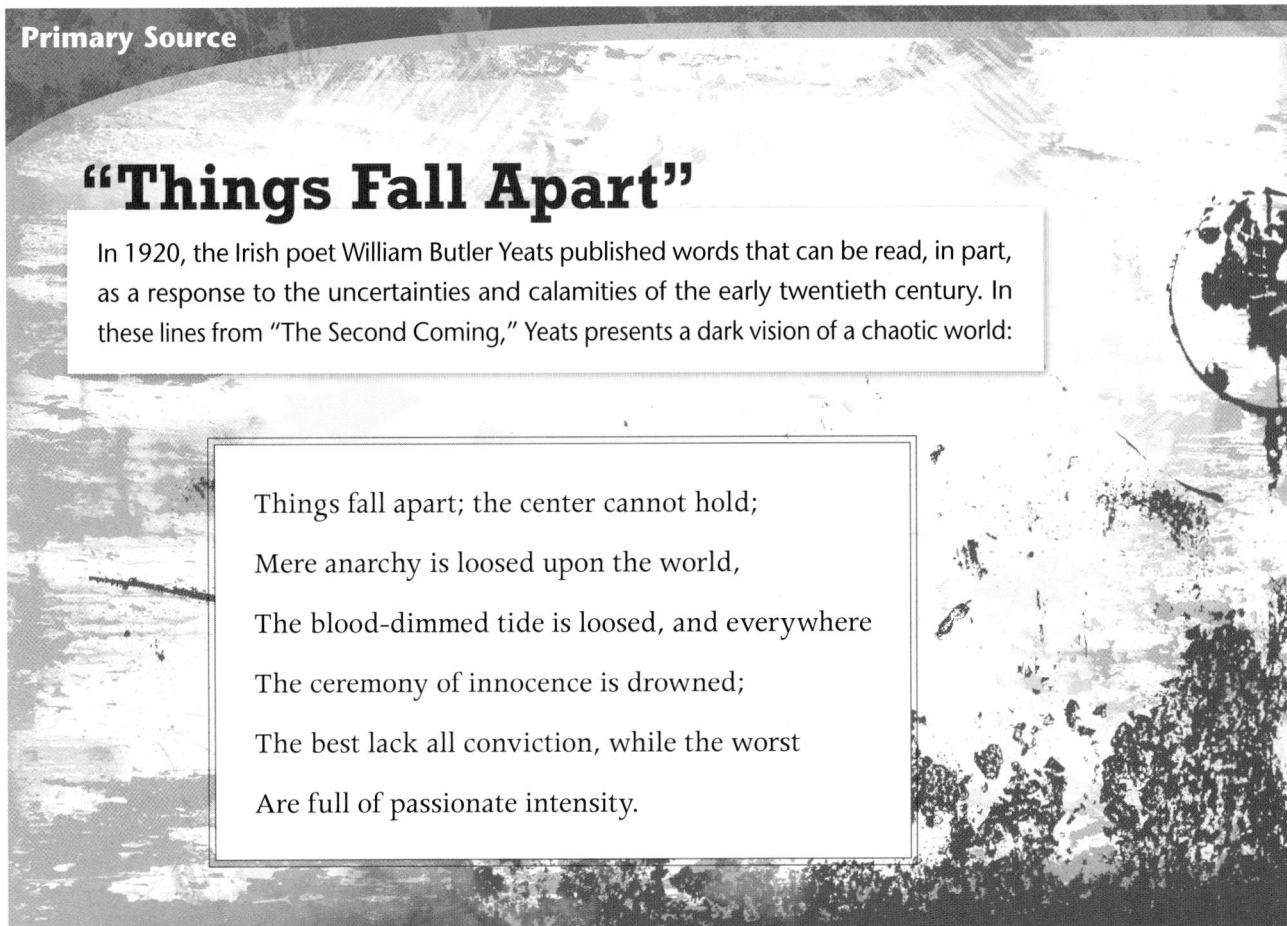

Primary Source

"Things Fall Apart"

In 1920, the Irish poet William Butler Yeats published words that can be read, in part, as a response to the uncertainties and calamities of the early twentieth century. In these lines from "The Second Coming," Yeats presents a dark vision of a chaotic world:

Things fall apart; the center cannot hold;

Mere anarchy is loosed upon the world,

The blood-dimmed tide is loosed, and everywhere

The ceremony of innocence is drowned;

The best lack all conviction, while the worst

Are full of passionate intensity.

Although many in that first audience rejected Stravinsky's *Rite of Spring*, the music strongly influenced other modern composers. And in time, people learned not just to accept but to enjoy Stravinsky's music. (Indeed, in 1940, the American filmmaker Walt Disney used *The Rite of Spring* as one of the major works in his animated film *Fantasia*.)

The musical innovations of another modern composer, Arnold Schoenberg (SHUHRN-buhrg), never achieved the same popular acceptance, although they did influence other composers. Schoenberg's music became increasingly *atonal* (ay-TOH-nuhl), which means it had no key and was not centered on any specific musical tone.

Schoenberg developed a method of composition called *twelve-tone music*, which worked through a careful arrangement of notes in numerical patterns. To many music lovers, twelve-tone music sounded discordant. But other composers, who were Schoenberg's devoted students, heard it as genius.

The challenging complexity of this modern music—and of much modern art—shrank the audience for such art. As the public turned to more popular culture, many modern artists found themselves addressing each other and a relatively small group of scholars.

America's Roaring Twenties

In Europe, the Great War left behind death, destruction, and poverty. But the United States had been spared the physical ruin of the war and enjoyed an economic boom in the decade that followed, known as the Roaring Twenties.

Prosperity and Technology

As war-torn European countries struggled to recover from the war, the United States prospered. The roots of the nation's prosperity lay mainly in the decades preceding the war, which had been filled with industrialization and technological

Postwar prosperity allowed American consumers to enjoy new products such as refrigerators and telephones.

innovation. Many businesses introduced mass production, and many industries switched to electric power. From textile mills to appliance factories, electric motors powered machines that allowed employees to produce more products in less time.

For millions of Americans, the new prosperity brought new luxuries, such as electric lighting and indoor plumbing. Many middle-class households could afford new electric appliances, such as refrigerators, vacuum cleaners, and washing machines.

The new prosperity also spurred the growth of mass entertainment. Radio came into commercial use in 1920. In 1922, there were about thirty radio stations operating in the United States; a year later, there were more than five hundred. Local stations began to link into bigger networks. The National Broadcasting Company (NBC) formed in 1926, followed the next year by the Columbia Broadcasting System (CBS).

The motion picture industry in Hollywood, California, also became big business. Crowds lined up to buy tickets at movie theaters. In 1927, Hollywood released *The Jazz Singer*, the first feature-length film with spoken dialogue. When

the film's star, Al Jolson, uttered "You ain't heard nothing yet," he made movie history.

Cars and Planes

Mass-produced automobiles dramatically transformed people's lives. By the mid-1920s, on the moving assembly line at Henry Ford's plant, workers were churning out a Model T in less than half a minute.

The 1920s were the first decade in which automobiles came into wide use. By 1929, almost one of every five Americans owned a car. In both the United States and Europe, the dramatic increase in the number of cars demanded the building of more roads. As the automobile industry boomed, so did the industries that supplied the parts and materials for cars, including rubber, glass, and steel. Oil refineries worked overtime to meet the demand for gasoline. As more people traveled by car, new businesses opened to meet their needs. Cars also allowed some people to move from the city to suburbs, since they could now drive to work.

The 1920s also saw dramatic advances in aviation. The technology of flight was still young—not many years had passed since December 1903, when the Wright brothers made their first flights

Henry Ford made cars affordable for the masses. By 1929, millions of motor vehicles were traveling America's roads.

at Kitty Hawk, in North Carolina. During World War I, both the Allied and Central powers used planes for military purposes. After the war, people began to look to using airplanes for business and personal travel.

In 1927, the American aviator Charles Lindbergh completed the first nonstop solo flight across the Atlantic Ocean. In a small, single-engine plane, the *Spirit of St. Louis*, Lindbergh flew from New York to Paris in 33 hours, 30 minutes. A year after Lindbergh's historic flight, Amelia Earhart became the first woman to fly across the Atlantic (as a passenger, not a pilot). She made her first solo flight across the Atlantic in 1932. In 1937, she set out to fly around the world, but somewhere over the Pacific her plane vanished.

The solo flights of Lindbergh and Amelia Earhart had no immediate practical consequences, but they generated tremendous public enthusiasm for aviation. They also demonstrated that the airplane had become a means of transportation reliable enough to span continents.

The Jazz Age

In the wake of the Great War, the standards of American social decorum and moral life changed. Young ladies became "flappers" who dared to show their legs, bob their hair, and drive automobiles by themselves. The spirit of the times is captured in these lyrics by the American songwriter Cole Porter:

In olden days a glimpse of stocking,
Was looked on as something shocking,
Now heaven knows,
Anything goes.

The Roaring Twenties in America are also known as the Jazz Age. The name comes from the vibrant new American music that got its start in the cultural melting pot of New Orleans. There, African American musicians mixed African

A flapper doing the Charleston, a lively 1920s dance

The blues singer Mamie Smith and her Jazz Hounds were one of the popular bands of the Jazz Age.

rhythms with European musical traditions, marching band music, the swing of ragtime, and the spirit of improvisation. As these musicians migrated north to Chicago, New York, Saint Louis, and other cities, they took jazz with them.

Jazz became the music of choice for the postwar young generation. In European cities, especially Paris, some African American musicians found less racial tension and division. They settled in Europe and took jazz with them. It wasn't long before this distinctively American music became popular on the international scene.

A "Lost Generation"

For some, the glittering festivities of the Roaring Twenties had a desperate edge, as if people were attempting to drown the sorrows of the past decade in a binge of frantic partying. Many of the young American soldiers who had gone off to fight in the Great War returned home bitter and disillusioned. They had lived through the horrors of poison gas and the carnage of trench warfare. Back home, they felt like strangers in a strange land. They asked themselves: Did their sacrifice have any meaning? What was the point of it all?

"The Waste Land"

In 1922, T.S. Eliot, an American expatriate poet living in England, published a poem called "The Waste Land." The poem depicts a postwar world that is emotionally exhausted and spiritually desolate, lacking hope or faith. In this excerpt, Eliot describes a dry, barren physical landscape that suggests his vision of the modern world as a spiritual wasteland.

> What are the roots that clutch, what branches grow
>
> Out of this stony rubbish? Son of man,
>
> You cannot say, or guess, for you know only
>
> A heap of broken images, where the sun beats,
>
> And the dead tree gives no shelter, the cricket no relief,
>
> And the dry stone no sound of water.

An *expatriate* is someone who has willingly left his or her own country to live in a foreign land.

Some American artists and writers felt so out of place at home that they left the United States to join a growing group of expatriate artists and writers in Paris and other European cities. One of these expatriates was the novelist Ernest Hemingway, who often visited Gertrude Stein, an American writer whose home in Paris served as a hub for artists and writers. It was Stein who once said in conversation, "All of you young people who served in the war, you are all a lost generation."

The name—the Lost Generation—came to characterize the generation that had survived the war only to confront the terrible uncertainties that followed. They had been changed by the war. Many of the values they had grown up with seemed to make little sense in the postwar world.

A Time of Doubt

For many people, the postwar sense of uncertainty fueled doubts about the Christian faith. If this is what the world is coming to, many in the Western world thought, then what good is religion doing for humanity? Scientists continued to make findings that did not conform to traditional Christian beliefs. As scientists explained the workings of nature, they offered rational explanations for what had once seemed miraculous. Charles Darwin's theories, in particular, seemed to undermine the idea of divine creation.

Many Europeans decided that they could lead their lives without the daily influence of Christianity. Church attendance in Europe declined as many people could no longer find in Christianity the answers they sought in a fragmented postwar world.

The Great Depression

For many nations, the two decades after the Great War were a time of political unrest and economic distress. As nations worked to recover from the war, some also struggled with new and vulnerable democratic institutions. Germany's was an especially fragile government, which from 1919 to 1933 was known as the Weimar (VIY-mahr) Republic, named for the city in which its constitution was adopted.

Efforts to recover from the Great War suffered a serious blow with the onset of the Great Depression, one of the greatest economic catastrophes the world has ever known. Beginning in the United States, it circled the globe swiftly. To understand how the Great Depression happened, we must first look back to economic conditions in Europe and the United States at the end of World War I.

European Economies in the Wake of War

Europe's Western democracies emerged from the Great War victorious but burdened with serious problems. France and Britain, in particular, had borrowed enormous amounts of money from the United States to finance their war efforts. Industrial plants in both France and Britain were out of date. Worse, both nations had lost many of the young men who would have made up a strong workforce in the postwar years. Unemployment and inflation made everyday life hard for millions. In France, where the most destructive battles of the war had been fought, farms, villages, roads, and railroads were in ruins.

In the Treaty of Versailles, the victorious Allies blamed World War I on Germany. By the terms of the treaty, Germany lost territory and most of its military, and was ordered to pay yearly reparations, large payments for war damage. British and French leaders believed that these reparations were critical to the recovery of their nations. The leaders of Germany's Weimar Republic resented the severe terms imposed by the Versailles treaty. Weimar officials said that paying the reparations would cripple their country.

Germany's economy was weak, and the German government made things worse by printing more and more money, a policy that led to wildly escalating inflation. By late 1923, a single U.S. dollar could be traded for four *trillion* German marks. (At the time, the mark was the basic unit of German money.) In German restaurants, people grimly joked that they could get a cheaper meal by eating fast, because the price was rising as they chewed.

In the end, the Weimar Republic made almost no reparations payments. Despite this, European economies did make progress toward recovery in the years after the war. But without reparations, France, Britain, and other nations across the continent faced huge debts and massive rebuilding efforts.

Key Questions

- What conditions did most of Europe face after World War I?

- What were the major causes of the Great Depression in the United States? Why did the U.S. economic catastrophe become a worldwide depression?

- How did Western democracies respond to the worldwide depression?

American Boom and Bust

In contrast, the United States came out of the war economically stronger. No battles had been fought on American soil. American farm products were in high demand in Europe throughout the war and for some years after. American businesses had prospered by producing ships, engines, guns, and other military supplies. After the war, American industries turned to the production of new goods, such as radios, automobiles, and kitchen appliances.

In the United States during the Roaring Twenties, the economy roared ahead. Between 1922 and 1929, the nation's income rose by more than 40 percent. New labor-saving devices made it possible to farm more productively, while factories manufactured goods faster and faster. The number of automobiles on U.S. roads leapt from seven million in 1919 to twenty-three million in 1929. Stores offered "buy now, pay later" options, allowing clerks and factory workers to buy a new car or refrigerator on credit and pay for it in installments.

This visible prosperity, however, hid underlying weaknesses in the American economy. Farmers faced severe challenges. During World War I, they had profited by selling crops to European countries. But after the war, as European farms recovered in the early 1920s, American farmers saw their profits decline. As their profits sank, many American farmers could not keep up payments on the farm equipment they had bought on credit. They tried to boost production to increase income, but then the supply of farm products exceeded demand and prices fell.

As American consumers bought on credit, manufacturers made handsome profits. Instead of investing the profits in new machinery or increasing their workers' wages, many business owners filled their own pockets. The nation's wealth was concentrated at the very top. By the late-1920s, a third of the country's income went to just 5 percent of families, while the bottom 40 percent struggled to get by. Manufacturers continued to increase production even as demand for their products declined. Workers began to lose

In the United States, as demand for goods declined, workers lost their jobs when factories cut back on production.

jobs when factories were forced to cut back on production.

Most middle-class Americans were unaware of these problems. Since they expected the prosperity to continue, many got into the habit of spending more than they earned, buying on credit, and investing in the soaring U.S. stock market. In the boom times of the 1920s, stock prices kept rising. To many Americans—not just the wealthy, but working people as well—the stock market seemed like a sure bet. They poured their money, sometimes their whole life savings, into stocks. All this frenzied buying pushed prices up until the stocks were valued at more than they were worth. It was a bubble waiting to burst.

The booming American economy came to an abrupt end in October 1929 when the U.S. stock market crashed—the value of stocks fell rapidly. Panicky investors scrambled to sell their stocks. But no one was buying.

Before the stock market crash, banks had made loans to investors who used the money to buy stock, a practice called "buying on margin." These investors planned to repay the banks when they sold the stocks at a higher price. When the value of the stocks fell, these investors could not repay their loans. People with deposits in banks all over the country grew nervous about their money and tried to withdraw it all from the banks. Many banks did not have that much money in their vaults and locked their doors.

As banks began to fail, countless businesses went broke, factories closed, and millions of workers lost their jobs as well as their savings. The United States entered the Great Depression, its longest, deepest economic downturn ever.

The causes of the Great Depression were many and complex, and are still debated by historians and economists. Its effects were obvious and devastating. By 1933, unemployment in the United States soared to about 25 percent, and more than one-third of the nation's banks had failed. Millions of people lost all they had. Homeless families searched for scraps of food in garbage barrels or lined up at charity soup kitchens. America had never before experienced such hard times.

Investing in Stocks

When you buy stock, you are buying a piece of ownership in a company. You invest money in the company, and the company can invest that money in expanding its business or launching new products. Each piece of stock is called a share. People who buy shares of stock are called *stockholders* or *shareholders*. They own a piece of the company, along with many other people who also own shares of the company's stock.

If the company does well, shares of stock increase in value. Shareholders can sell their stocks and make a profit, or shareholders might receive dividends, which are cash payments from the company's profits. But if the company does poorly, the value of its stock may go down, which means that shareholders may lose money.

A family stands by a car loaded with their possessions. Millions found themselves homeless during the Great Depression.

Frenchmen wait in a soup line in Paris in the 1930s when the Great Depression spread to Europe and beyond.

The Spread of the Great Depression

As factories closed and banks failed, Americans did less and less business overseas. The American government stopped loaning money to foreign countries. Thus the Great Depression spread through much of the world. Across Europe, where many economies had experienced some recovery and growth in the late 1920s, factories slowed production or shut their doors. Thousands and then hundreds of thousands of workers lost their jobs. As in the United States, banks failed and millions of people lost their life savings.

The chain reaction of failed banks, lost savings, closed factories, and unemployment swept far beyond Europe. At the worst point of the Great Depression, more than thirty million people were unemployed worldwide. The United States suffered the greatest decline in industrial production—nearly 47 percent. In Western Europe, Germany suffered most with a 42 percent decline in production. But nonindustrialized countries, especially those where poor farmers relied on a single crop for their livelihoods, also felt the crippling effects of a 50 percent drop in world trade.

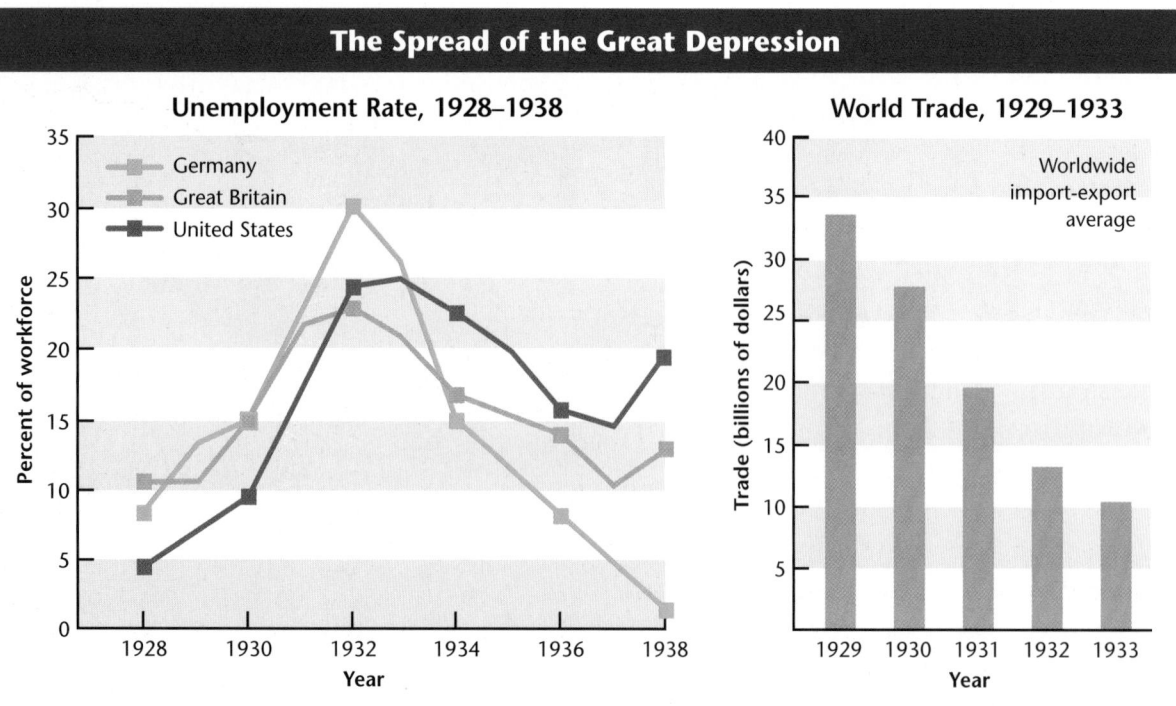

Able-bodied men across continents spent day after day searching for work or begging for handouts. On the street corners of crowded cities, from London to Berlin to Rome, unemployed workers passed the time drawing pictures on the sidewalks with colored chalk while hoping that passersby would throw a coin or two in a hat. Millions of homeless families camped in parks and stood in line for soup and bread. In many cities, frustration erupted into riots and protests.

Responding to the Economic Crisis

Governments around the world grappled with the suffering brought on by the Great Depression. At first, governments in Europe and the United States maintained their traditional economic policies. They imposed high tariffs on imports in order to encourage people to buy domestic goods (goods made in the country). They tried to balance their budgets by cutting government spending. Many governments continued the same monetary policies they had used for decades. But the Depression only deepened.

As the hard times worsened, many people grew restless and bitter. Some said the Depression was the fault of factory owners and capitalism. Others blamed the leaders they had elected. In Britain, voters turned to the Labour Party, whose platform called for full employment and public ownership of large industries. Political unrest rocked France, where by 1936 many communists and socialists won election.

Elsewhere, democratic nations such as Sweden dramatically increased their government-sponsored social programs, using tax revenues to provide all citizens with, for example, health care and unemployment insurance. In

1935, the United States implemented a program called Social Security, which taxed both employers and employees to provide temporary payments to people who had lost their jobs, as well as modest pensions to retired senior citizens.

The New Deal in the United States

In the United States, after three Republican presidents during the 1920s, a Democrat, Franklin Delano Roosevelt (FDR), won the 1932 election in a landslide. While Roosevelt believed in capitalism and free enterprise, he also believed that the Great Depression demanded bold government action rather than a laissez-faire approach.

Roosevelt implemented the New Deal, a diverse array of programs and initiatives to pull the United States out of the Great Depression. The New Deal focused on relief, recovery, and reform. Relief meant providing money to ensure that jobless people had life's basic necessities. Recovery involved national planning to get the economy moving again and put people back to work. And reform brought new laws to

Franklin Roosevelt's New Deal policies put many of the unemployed in the United States back to work.

restructure banks, change labor relations, and create new social programs.

The New Deal marked a major turning point in the political development of the United States. Historians continue to debate the extent to which Roosevelt's many programs helped to end the Great Depression. They also debate the effectiveness of similar programs adopted in Britain, France, and other democracies during the 1930s. One clear consequence of these social programs, however, was that people came to expect their governments to take a more active role in the economic welfare of individuals and their nations.

Germany's Unstable Weimar Republic

The role of government in the United States and other Western democracies changed during the Great Depression. More than ever before, the governments of Great Britain, France, the United States, and other Western countries implemented policies and programs designed to shape the economic lives of their nations. Though these nations faced unrest, fear, and the worst economic downturn in history, they had long traditions of democratic government, and they remained representative democracies.

Governments also changed in other countries, but not for the better. The situation in Germany was especially unstable. Germany had largely escaped the physical damage of World War I—no French or British bombardments had leveled German cities, the country's fields were undamaged, and its factories still functioned. Nevertheless, Germany suffered severe food shortages during the war, the nation's economy was a wreck, and its postwar government was ineffective.

After the war, the Allies had made sure that no strong kaiser was left in charge of Germany. Instead, in 1919, Germany became a republic. But the Reichstag, the elected parliament of the Weimar Republic, was paralyzed by squabbling factions—socialists, communists, republicans, and nationalists. None was prepared to deal with the economic chaos.

To the German people, the government seemed to drift aimlessly while businesses closed and people went hungry. Many Germans complained that democracy had only made things worse, splintering politicians into parties that did nothing but argue while the economy went to ruin. Resentful citizens longed for some powerful leader to take charge and set things right.

The Rise of Dictators

In Europe in the 1920s and 1930s, disillusioned survivors of the Great War struggled to rebuild their lives amid shattered economies and uncertainties about the future. More than anything else, they wanted security and a release from fear. That desire was so strong that many willingly traded freedom for security. As a result, some of history's worst dictators took charge in Russia, Italy, and Germany.

In the 1930s, Joseph Stalin ruled the Soviet Union as the dictator of a totalitarian state. A totalitarian government controls almost every aspect of people's lives, including political, economic, cultural, religious, and social activities. To maintain power, totalitarian governments try to bind their people in some shared effort, such as war. Or they may try to unify the people through fear or hatred of something, such as a foreign enemy. Totalitarian governments often maintain secret police forces to stamp out anyone who opposes them.

Mussolini's Fascism

After World War I, in parts of Europe a kind of totalitarianism called fascism (FA-shih-zuhm) was taking root. *Fascism* comes from the Latin *fasces*, a ceremonial bundle of rods wrapped around an ax, carried by officials in ancient Rome as a symbol of state power and strength through unity. Fascist governments glorified the nation above all else. They insisted that all citizens put the interests of the state ahead of their individual interests.

Fascist thinking grew out of the feelings of nationalism that had swept Europe in the decades leading up to World War I. After the chaos of the war, power-hungry leaders channeled the people's desperation into the idea of devotion to their state. Nationalism taken to an extreme became fascism.

Modern Europe's first fascist dictator was Benito Mussolini (beh-NEE-toh moos-soh-LEE-nee) of Italy. Like other European countries after World War I, Italy suffered from economic depression and social unrest. Mussolini organized discouraged Italians into the Nationalist Fascist Party.

Mussolini's Fascists dressed in black shirts and carried clubs that they used to beat up anyone they disliked. The Blackshirts, as they were known, especially hated socialists and communists, whom they blamed for Italy's economic troubles. Mussolini's Fascists attacked striking workers, trade union offices, and anyone who seemed to have Bolshevik sympathies.

In 1921, by bullying voters, the Fascist Party won a small fraction of the seats in Italy's parliament. The next year, tens of thousands of Blackshirts poured into the capital city in what Fascists called the March on Rome. They demanded that Mussolini be put at the head of the government. Italy's king hastily appointed Mussolini as prime minister.

Key Questions

- How did Italy, Germany, and Spain respond to the social instability resulting from the economic crisis?

- How do communism and fascism differ? How are they alike in practice?

- What ideas did Adolf Hitler express in *Mein Kampf*? How did he gain and maintain power in Germany?

Mussolini soon declared himself *Il Duce* (il DOO-chay). The title means "the Leader," but Mussolini was really a dictator who demanded extreme devotion to the state and to the leader who represented the power of the state, Mussolini himself.

Mussolini threw out the parliamentary system and established the Fascists as the single party in power. He outlawed all other political parties and declared trade unions illegal. He suppressed all rights to free speech. He used spies and a secret police to intimidate anyone who might object to his rule.

A clever politician, Mussolini allowed the king, whom the people liked, to remain on the throne. He cooperated with the Catholic Church and persuaded the pope to recognize the authority of the Fascist dictatorship. He worked closely with businessmen and industrialists. Unlike communists, fascists believed in an economy built on private ownership.

Mussolini used militarism—the glorification of military power—to rally his followers and divert their attention from continuing social problems. He championed war as an ennobling cause. "Fascism," he wrote, "believes neither in the possibility nor the utility of perpetual peace. War alone… puts the stamp of nobility upon the peoples who have courage to meet it."

Benito Mussolini marches with his Fascist followers, called Blackshirts, at a demonstration in Rome in 1922.

Communism vs. Fascism

Communist and fascist governments resemble each other in some ways. In both, the ruler is usually a dictator. Both suppress opposition and claim that individual liberties must be sacrificed for the greater good of society. Both tend toward totalitarian control of people's lives. But their economic policies are different, and so are their larger goals.

In a communist society, the government directs the economy and owns most or all of the land, factories, and other resources that contribute to the economy. In theory, workers control the production of goods and share property. The stated goal of communism is a world in which social classes disappear and all people are treated equally. That's the theory—in reality, leaders of communist nations usually have far more material goods and privileges than the workers, who lack both wealth and freedom.

A fascist government allows individuals to own property and businesses, but it maintains strict control over economic activity, and makes sure that private businesses serve the government's goals. Fascism glorifies the nation and its leaders, and calls on citizens to put the interests of the nation above individual interests. Fascist regimes often use war as a way to expand and strengthen the state. They reject the idea of equality for all. On the contrary, fascists often persecute minorities, and claim that their own national group is superior to others and destined to rule.

Hitler's Rise to Power

Fascism quickly spread beyond Italy throughout Europe. Mussolini's ideas appealed to Adolf Hitler, who had volunteered to serve in the German army in World War I. Hitler survived gas attacks and received honors for bravery.

Germany's defeat made Hitler bitter and angry. He lashed out against the politicians who had surrendered, for he believed Germany had been on the verge of winning the war. Soon, encouraged by army commanders, Hitler took over a tiny political party. He renamed it the *Nationalsozialistische*

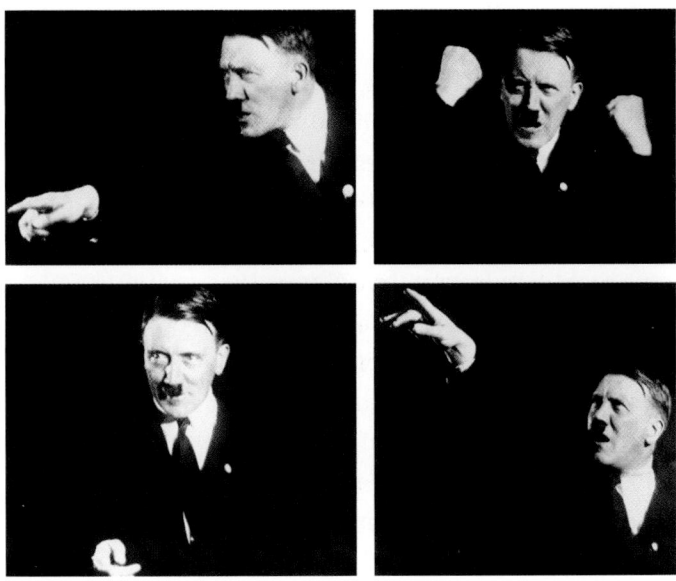

Adolf Hitler launched into tirades extolling the glories of the "Aryan" race and blaming the Jews for Germany's ills.

Deutsche Arbeiterpartei—the National Socialist German Workers Party, or Nazi (NAHT-see) Party for short. He quickly attracted thousands of followers by playing upon their sense of frustration with the Weimar government.

In 1923, with inflation soaring and the ranks of his Nazi supporters growing, Hitler sensed the time was right to start a revolution against the Weimar government. Inspired by the Italian Fascists' March on Rome, Hitler led a band of Nazis into a political meeting and seized three government officials. "The National Revolution has begun!" he screamed. A few days later, however, the police arrested him, and Hitler went to prison.

Mein Kampf and Anti-Semitism

Hitler served only nine months of a five-year sentence. While behind bars, he began writing *Mein Kampf* (miyn KAHMPF), which means "My Struggle." The book set forth Hitler's beliefs about German destiny. He claimed that the Germans were members of a so-called "Aryan" (AIR-ee-uhn) race, a master race destined to rule humanity. He expounded the self-glorifying myth that civilization grew out of the Aryan conquest and enslavement of "inferior" races, among which Hitler included the Slavs and Jews.

Hitler directed his most intense racial hatred against the Jews. "The Jew," he wrote, "offers the most striking contrast to the Aryan." Anti-Semitism, hatred of the Jews, had a long history in Europe, particularly in Germany. Hitler stoked the fires of that prejudice. He blamed all of Germany's troubles on the Jews, whom he compared to "parasites" and "vampires."

Hitler told Germans that it was their "sacred mission" to maintain racial purity. The German people, he said, must "occupy themselves not merely with the breeding of dogs, horses, and cats but also with care for the purity of their own blood." For Hitler, it was not enough to maintain the purity of the Aryan race; he also called for the elimination of what he viewed as inferior races. The elimination of the Jews, he wrote, "must necessarily be a bloody process."

Hitler as Führer

Hitler promised to lead Germans to glory by conquering new territories and giving them *Lebensraum* (LAY-bens-rowm)—"living space." He believed they would find much of this "living space" by conquering Russia, home of the "inferior" Slavs. In part, Hitler wanted to conquer Russia because it was the home of communism, a philosophy he detested.

During the 1930s, the Great Depression hit Germany hard, and Hitler's ranting appealed to many Germans. As wages shrank, prices climbed, and millions lost their jobs, Hitler offered an enemy to blame—the Jews.

With their message of anti-Semitism and promise of a glorious future for the Aryan race, Nazi candidates began winning elections. By 1932, they held 38 percent of the seats in the Reichstag, the German parliament. Early the next year, Germany's aging president appointed Hitler as his chancellor.

When Germany's president died, Hitler claimed for himself the title of *führer* (FYOUR-uhr), which means "leader." Like the leaders of Russia and Italy, Hitler, as the führer of Germany, would soon become a totalitarian dictator. Like Stalin in the Soviet Union, Hitler began to wipe out every possible challenge to his rule.

The Hitler Youth

Hitler encouraged loyalty to Nazi Germany, and to its führer, by setting up paramilitary organizations for young people of the so-called Aryan race. All qualified boys age fourteen to eighteen were expected to join the Hitler Youth. Its members wore uniforms, learned about Nazi Party beliefs, built up their physical strength, and practiced for war through exercises such as throwing mock grenades and crawling under barbed wire.

> A *paramilitary* group is a group of citizens trained and organized in military fashion.

Girls age fourteen to eighteen who fit Hitler's ideals were expected to join the League of German Maidens, which encouraged activities such as camping, playing sports, and preparing to be housewives, all while learning Nazi doctrine. Some youth groups even taught members to spy on their own families and report any anti-Nazi talk they overheard.

In Nazi Germany, Hitler encouraged loyalty by requiring boys to join paramilitary groups called Hitler Youth.

From Kristallnacht to Concentration Camps

Hitler rallied the German people by playing on their fears and keeping them focused on the idea of the Jews as a scapegoat. The führer stripped Jews of citizenship rights and removed them from public offices. He seized many Jewish families' possessions, and outlawed marriage between Jews and non-Jews.

> A *scapegoat* is a person or group blamed for the faults or misdeeds of others.

In November 1938, Hitler sent Nazis on a rampage through the streets, destroying Jewish-owned stores and beating or killing any Jews they found. Germans called this *Kristallnacht* (kris-TAHL-nackt), "The Night of Broken Glass."

Hitler organized a secret police network that rivaled Stalin's. It was staffed by over a hundred thousand spies in Germany. The Nazis also set up prison camps, not for criminals but for people who did not share Hitler's views.

The secret police began to round up thousands of people—communists, socialists, journalists, and others—and detain them without trial in the prison camps. For prisoners in these camps, which came to be known as concentration camps, there was little chance of ever leaving. Upon arrival, they were stripped and had their heads shaved. They were dressed in rough clothing, herded into bleak barracks, and given minimal rations. Many were relentlessly worked to death.

As you'll read in a later chapter, Hitler's concentration camps would become part of his campaign to eliminate Jews and other races he considered "inferior."

Franco and the Spanish Civil War

In the 1930s, a decade of widespread economic hardship and political turmoil, Spain was shaken by strikes, violent protests, and assassinations. In 1936, General Francisco Franco quickly mustered an army and moved to seize power.

A brutal civil war erupted. On one side were Franco's forces, called the Nationalists. On the

A poster urges Spaniards to join the battle against Franco.

other side were the Republicans, those who supported Spain's recently elected socialist government.

The Nationalists received help from Hitler and Mussolini, who sent money, weapons, and troops to Franco, whom they considered a fellow fascist. The Republicans received equipment and supplies from the Soviet Union's Stalin. The Republicans were also aided by the International Brigade, an army of nearly sixty thousand volunteers from many countries who wanted to stop Franco.

Germany and the Soviet Union used the Spanish Civil War to test new tanks, aircraft, and other weapons. German planes experimented with dropping bombs on cities. Both sides executed thousands of civilians.

After three years of fighting, the Republican forces could no longer hold out. The Spanish Civil War ended in 1939, with Franco as the fascist dictator of Spain. Franco ruled Spain until his death in 1975.

Militarism in Japan

As fascism spread in Europe, militarists in Asia took control of the island nation of Japan. Back in the late nineteenth century, during the Meiji Era, Japan had worked hard to transform itself into a modern, industrialized nation. The Japanese embraced the slogan "Prosperous Nation, Strong Military," and they

achieved both. But like Europe and the United States, Japan suffered during the Great Depression of the 1930s. With its scant farmland, limited resources, and exploding population, Japan plunged into economic crisis.

Some Japanese began to blame the West for their country's problems. They preached hatred of democracy, of communism, of capitalism, of all things Western. Many Japanese also blamed their own government. Military leaders saw the widespread public discontent with the Diet, Japan's parliament, as an opportunity to seize more power.

Japanese military leaders soon controlled the government. No single dictator, like Hitler or Mussolini, took charge. Instead, military leaders glorified the emperor Hirohito as a symbol of the Japanese state.

Some admirals and generals began to talk of forging a new Japanese empire that would dominate much of Asia. In the years to come, these military leaders would transform Japanese society into a machine preparing for war.

A Japanese general bows to Emperor Hirohito. The emperor was revered as the symbol of the Japanese state but the military controlled the government.

1939

Germany invades Poland; World War II begins.

1940

France falls to Germany; England stands alone in the Battle of Britain.

1941

Germany invades the Soviet Union; Japan attacks the United States at Pearl Harbor; the U.S. and USSR join the Allied Powers.

1942

U.S. victory at Midway proves a turning point in the war in the Pacific.

1943

Soviet victory at Stalingrad proves a turning point in the war in Europe.

1944

In the D-day invasion, Allied forces launch the largest amphibious attack in history.

1945

Germany surrenders; the United States drops the first atomic bombs, forcing Japan to surrender.

CHAPTER 31

WORLD WAR II
1939–1945

Soviet tanks, troops, and warplanes attack Berlin, Germany, in May 1945.

In 1939, World War II began. This second world war was clearly the unfinished business of the first. Germany, Italy, and Japan embarked on conquest and plunged the world into death and destruction that surpassed even the staggering losses of World War I.

World War II revealed both the height of human courage and the depth of human evil, particularly in Hitler's campaign of genocide known as the Holocaust. The war also brought a new weapon of almost unimaginable destructive power—the atomic bomb.

Out of the horror of the deadliest war in history came earnest efforts to ensure that such a tragedy would not be repeated. Special courts were established to try those responsible for some of the worst war crimes. The victorious nations also attempted to encourage international cooperation by establishing the United Nations.

Aggression, Appeasement, and War

Hitler. Mussolini. Stalin. In the 1930s, these totalitarian leaders held much of Europe in their grip. While they differed in philosophy and practice, all three dictators led frustrated and angry populations, many of whom were ready and willing to take up arms.

Halfway around the world, the military leaders of Japan, the most industrialized Asian nation, turned their country into a war machine. They boasted of forging a glorious Japanese empire. The major actors were in place. The stage was set for global disaster.

Japan and Italy Test the League's Limits

After the Great War, Woodrow Wilson persuaded the victorious Allies to establish the League of Nations. He hoped that every nation would join the League and work to resolve their differences peacefully. But the League's prospects for success dimmed when the United States chose not to join. The nations that did join often argued about what the League should do. The actions of aggressive fascist regimes quickly revealed the League's ineffectiveness.

In 1931, Japanese troops marched into coal-rich Manchuria in northern China. The League of Nations could do nothing to stop the aggression. Japan then conquered large areas of eastern China and slaughtered thousands in the city of Nanjing (also known as Nanking). The League protested, but was powerless to act.

In 1935, Benito Mussolini, as part of his attempt to rally his followers through militarism, pushed Italy into war by stirring up old resentments against Ethiopia. In the 1880s, when Italy had tried to colonize Ethiopia, the Ethiopians had fiercely resisted and defeated the Italians. But in 1935, when Mussolini launched an invasion of Ethiopia, the ill-equipped Ethiopian troops could not survive against Italian air strikes and poison gas.

The Ethiopian emperor, Haile Selassie (HIY-lee suh-LA-see), appealed to the League of Nations,

Key Questions

- How did Britain and other European nations respond to German aggression in the years before World War II?

- What were the major causes of World War II? What unresolved issues from World War I contributed to the start of World War II?

- How was Hitler able to take over most of Europe? Why was he unable to defeat Britain?

Poorly armed Ethiopian troops fiercely resisted but eventually fell to Mussolini's army.

saying, "I ask the fifty-two nations, who have given the Ethiopian people a promise to help them in their resistance to the aggressor, what are they willing to do for Ethiopia?" The League of Nations issued declarations critical of Italy, but with no real effect. Once again, the League's inability to stop hostilities revealed its ineffectiveness as a peacekeeping body.

Hitler's Third Reich

In Germany, Hitler, who had proclaimed himself führer, ignored the Treaty of Versailles. He said his nation bore no guilt for the Great War and would pay no reparations. In 1933, he withdrew Germany from the League of Nations. Two years later, he defiantly announced that Germany would rearm, a move forbidden by the Versailles treaty.

Factories that had stood idle during the Depression started cranking out ammunition, bombers, and tanks called *panzers*. To build the German army, Hitler renewed the practice of conscription, drafting men for required military service. Hitler announced that he was establishing a "Third Reich" (riyk), or Third Empire. The Third Reich, he claimed, would last a thousand years and outshine all previous German empires.

In 1936, Hitler and Mussolini formed an alliance known as the Rome-Berlin Axis. They chose the name "Axis" to suggest that all of Europe would revolve around a line running between those two capitals. Japan soon entered into an agreement with Germany. Together, Germany, Italy, and Japan formed the Axis Powers.

Gaining "Living Space"

One of Hitler's major objectives was to gain *Lebensraum*, the "living space" he claimed the Aryan race deserved. To gain "living space," in 1936 German troops marched into the Rhineland. This action violated the Treaty of Versailles, which had forbidden German troops to enter the Rhineland, a region intended to provide a buffer between France and Germany. France and Britain protested, but they did nothing more as they

grappled with the economic crisis of the Depression. "Above all, no war," one French newspaper pleaded.

Two years later, Hitler again violated the Treaty of Versailles. He ordered his army into Austria and announced that he was annexing it to the German Reich. The leaders of France and Britain objected but took no action. They told themselves that many Austrians supported union with Germany. The United States did not even consider getting involved because at this time Americans saw Hitler as Europe's problem.

Later in 1938, Hitler threatened to invade Czechoslovakia (cheh-kuh-sloh-VAH-kee-uh), one of the new nations created at the end of World War I. The northwestern part of Czechoslovakia, called the Sudetenland, bordered Germany and was inhabited by millions of German-speaking people. Hitler demanded that this region be turned over to Germany. Czech leaders said no. They called on France for help.

The Policy of Appeasement

As tensions mounted, European nations seemed to be heading toward another catastrophic conflict. Some leaders saw war as the only way to stop Hitler. Others argued for peace at any price.

In September 1938, leaders of France, Britain, Germany, and Italy met in the German city of Munich. The British prime minister, Neville Chamberlain, believed all differences could be negotiated. When Hitler said he would be satisfied with taking just the German-speaking parts of Czechoslovakia, Chamberlain and the French premier agreed, hoping that the führer would cause no more trouble.

The French and British pursued a policy of *appeasement*—giving in to an aggressor nation's demands in the hope of preventing war. Prime Minister Chamberlain flew home to a hero's welcome, happily claiming that he had secured "peace for our time." Others disagreed. A member of the British Parliament, Winston Churchill, addressed the House of Commons and warned,

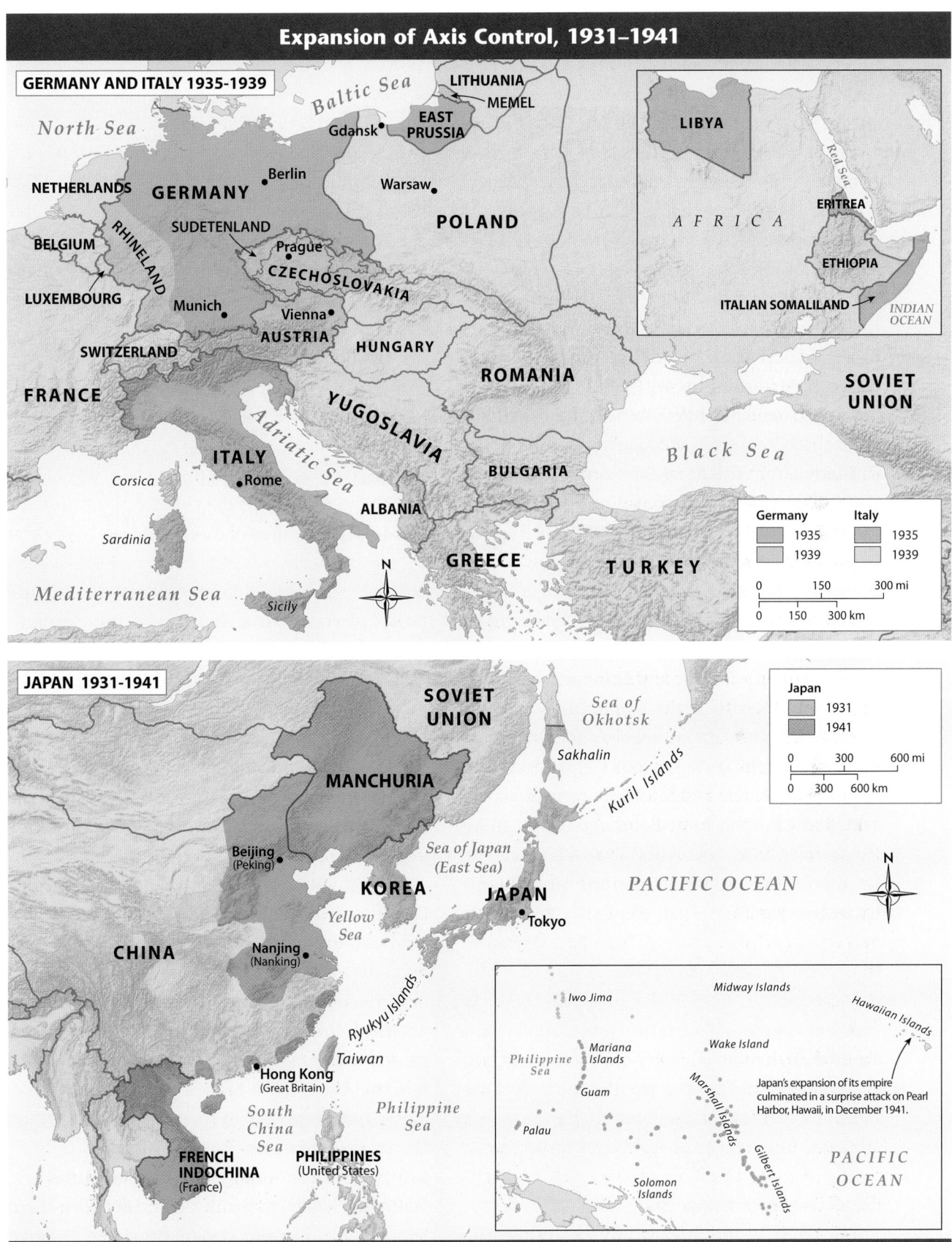

Expansion of Axis Control, 1931–1941

GERMANY AND ITALY 1935–1939

North Sea
Baltic Sea
LITHUANIA
MEMEL
EAST PRUSSIA
Gdansk
NETHERLANDS
GERMANY
Berlin
Warsaw
POLAND
BELGIUM
RHINELAND
SUDETENLAND
Prague
LUXEMBOURG
CZECHOSLOVAKIA
Munich
SWITZERLAND
Vienna
AUSTRIA
HUNGARY
FRANCE
Adriatic Sea
YUGOSLAVIA
ROMANIA
SOVIET UNION
ITALY
Rome
Corsica
BULGARIA
Black Sea
ALBANIA
Sardinia
GREECE
TURKEY
Mediterranean Sea
Sicily
N

LIBYA
AFRICA
Red Sea
ERITREA
ETHIOPIA
ITALIAN SOMALILAND
INDIAN OCEAN

Germany		Italy	
■ 1935		■ 1935	
■ 1939		■ 1939	

0   150   300 mi
0   150   300 km

JAPAN 1931–1941

SOVIET UNION
Sea of Okhotsk
Sakhalin
Kuril Islands

MANCHURIA

Beijing (Peking)
Sea of Japan (East Sea)
KOREA
JAPAN
Tokyo
PACIFIC OCEAN
N
Yellow Sea
CHINA
Nanjing (Nanking)
Ryukyu Islands
Taiwan
Hong Kong (Great Britain)
South China Sea
Philippine Sea
FRENCH INDOCHINA (France)
PHILIPPINES (United States)

Japan	
■ 1931	
■ 1941	

0   300   600 mi
0   300   600 km

Iwo Jima
Midway Islands
Hawaiian Islands
Philippine Sea
Mariana Islands
Wake Island
Guam
Marshall Islands
Palau
Japan's expansion of its empire culminated in a surprise attack on Pearl Harbor, Hawaii, in December 1941.
PACIFIC OCEAN
Solomon Islands
Gilbert Islands

Following World War I, Germany, Italy, and Japan began relentless campaigns of expansion, setting the stage for the death and destruction of World War II.

"We are in the presence of a disaster of the first magnitude which has befallen Great Britain and France.... We have sustained a total and unmitigated defeat.... This is only the beginning of the reckoning."

Appeasement Fails and War Begins

In his speech, Churchill had warned that "Czechoslovakia will be engulfed in the Nazi regime." His warning proved true.

In March 1939, to the shock of Chamberlain and those who had advocated appeasement, Hitler's troops seized the rest of Czechoslovakia. Once again, in the face of Hitler's aggression, the French and the British stood aside. They turned to their old ally from World War I, Russia, which by this time had become the Soviet Union.

French and British leaders wanted Stalin to join them in opposing Hitler. But while Stalin negotiated with Britain and France, he was also holding talks with Hitler's representatives. In August 1939, Europe was astounded when Stalin signed the Nazi-Soviet Nonaggression Pact. In this treaty, the Nazis and Communists set aside their mutual hatred and agreed not to go to war with each other. They also secretly agreed to divide the independent nation of Poland between them.

World War II Begins

On September 1, 1939, Hitler attacked Poland. As Nazi forces pounded east, the British and French abandoned their failed policy of appeasement. On September 3, 1939, some twenty-one years after the Great War had ended, both nations declared war on Germany. World War II was underway.

Blitzkrieg: Lightning War

The Second World War would be unlike the first. Hitler, who had spent time in the trenches of World War I, was determined to avoid a long

German troops march goose-step style in Warsaw, Poland. It took one month for the Nazi war machine to overtake Poland.

defensive stalemate. With the führer's modern tanks, planes, trains, and trucks, the Germans unleashed a new kind of warfare called *blitzkrieg* (BLITS-kreeg) or "lightning war," which involved surprise attacks and quickly overwhelming the enemy with massive force.

The ill-equipped Polish army was the first to experience the speed and surprise of German blitzkrieg. The Germans grouped their speedy tanks together and rolled over Polish defenses. Skimming just above the trees, Nazi planes bombed Polish soldiers. Behind the tanks and planes, German infantrymen kept up the attack. It took only a month for the Germans to sweep across Poland.

In response to these acts of aggression, France and Great Britain joined to form the Allied Powers. In the years ahead, several other nations would join the Allied effort against the Axis Powers.

Stalin Swallows the Baltic States

As part of their nonaggression pact, Hitler and Stalin had agreed to divide Poland between them. Soon after Hitler launched his blitzkrieg from the west, Stalin sent Soviet troops into Poland from the east.

Stalin then moved quickly to take over countries to the north of Poland. He met little resistance when he annexed the Baltic States—Estonia, Latvia, and Lithuania. Finland, however, surprised Stalin by putting up a fierce fight. The Finns used skis and their knowledge of the snow-covered winter landscape. In the end, however, the Soviets overwhelmed the Finns with almost a million soldiers and a thousand tanks.

In April 1940, Hitler launched another successful blitzkrieg into Finland's Scandinavian neighbors—Denmark and Norway. These conquests gave Germany access to the Atlantic Ocean and England.

The Fall of France

By the spring of 1940, German air bombardments pummeled the Netherlands and Belgium into submission. In northern Europe, refugees fleeing occupied lands clogged the roads while hundreds of thousands of British and French troops, sent to defend Belgium, retreated toward the sea.

Soon the Allied forces were trapped against the English Channel at the French port of Dunkirk. As the Germans closed in around them, the British government sounded an urgent call for help across southern England. Hundreds of military and civilian craft—Royal Navy vessels, tugboats, motorboats, fishing boats, paddle steamers, yachts—responded in what came to be known as the Miracle of Dunkirk. While German and British warplanes fought overhead, the makeshift armada ferried the more than three hundred thousand desperate soldiers across the English Channel to safety.

There would be no such miracle for France. The French military had spent years building the Maginot (MA-zhuh-noh) Line, a series of

A Frenchman weeps as Paris falls to the Nazis.

fortifications along the border with Germany. The French were certain that these defenses could repel a German attack. But Hitler's army swept around the northern end of the Maginot Line and flooded into France through Belgium. When the Nazi army reached Paris on June 14, 1940, Parisians wept as German trucks rumbled through their streets.

French Collaboration and Resistance

Some French military and political leaders managed to escape as Paris fell to the Nazis. Among them was a little-known general named Charles de Gaulle. De Gaulle refused to accept the idea of a French surrender and spoke by radio from London. Few people in France heard his broadcasts, but they soon heard reports about them.

After the fall of Paris, French officials willing to cooperate with the Nazis were allowed to set up a new government in the town of Vichy (VIH-shee) in central France. The Vichy government arrested people suspected of anti-Nazi activities. It prevented French people from leaving the country and passed anti-Semitic laws.

Many people in France were appalled at the Vichy officials who collaborated with the Nazis. They turned to the reports of de Gaulle's broadcasts:

> *Honor, common sense, and the interests of the country require that all free Frenchmen, wherever they be, should continue the fight as best they may.... I call upon all Frenchmen who want to remain free to listen to my voice and follow me.*

Thousands joined a movement called the Resistance. Resistance members secretly relayed information about German operations to the Allies, published underground newspapers, and helped Allied prisoners of war escape. Resistance fighters attacked German garrisons, derailed trains, and cut telephone wires. They were determined to assault the Germans as much as they could until the Allies could liberate their country.

German bombers rain fire over Britain.

The Battle of Britain

In May 1940, the British replaced Prime Minister Neville Chamberlain, who had advocated appeasement, with Winston Churchill. Churchill proved to be one of the greatest statesmen of all time. He knew war from firsthand experience. He had commanded the Royal Navy, and fought on the Western Front during World War I. Now in his sixties, as Churchill prepared to lead his nation, he told the British Parliament, "I have nothing to offer but blood, toil, tears, and sweat."

By June 1940, Britain stood alone against Hitler. Churchill rallied his countrymen: "Let us therefore brace ourselves to our duty, and so bear ourselves that if the British Empire and its Commonwealth last for a thousand years, men will still say, 'This was their finest hour.'"

The Battle of Britain began in the summer of 1940, in the skies of England, when Hitler launched the first massive air campaign in history. Hitler believed that if his air force, the Luftwaffe (LOOFT-vah-fuh), could eliminate Britain's Royal Air Force (RAF), then his army and navy could mount a successful invasion of the island nation.

The Germans had many more planes than the British. But the British Spitfires proved more than a match for the finest German planes. The British also had two other advantages. They had broken some of Germany's secret codes, so they could decipher German radio transmissions about

London's Tower Bridge stands amid smoke and devastation after the first German bombings of the city in September 1940.

Churchill: "Never Surrender"

British prime minister Winston Churchill, known for flashing the V-for-victory sign with his two fingers, came to symbolize Britain's defiant resistance. "We shall defend our island, whatever the cost may be," he told the British people. "We shall fight on the beaches, we shall fight on the landing grounds, we shall fight in the fields and in the streets, we shall fight in the hills; we shall never surrender."

Prime Minister Winston Churchill

oncoming attacks. And the British had radar, a recent invention that used radio waves to detect incoming enemy planes.

The Luftwaffe launched raid after raid on British air bases, ports, and docks. Royal Air Force pilots took to the skies and inflicted heavy losses on the Germans. Churchill said in tribute to the fallen RAF pilots, "Never in the field of human conflict was so much owed by so many to so few."

The Germans then expanded their air war and bombed cities such as London, Coventry, Glasgow, and Belfast. Desperate British parents put thousands of children on trains and sent them to stay with relatives in the country, where it was safer.

When air-raid sirens wailed, Londoners scurried into cellars, backyard shelters, and subway stations, where they huddled while explosions tore through the city overhead. When the all-clear siren sounded, they emerged to see which homes, schools, stores, and factories had been bombed into rubble. After every attack, rescue workers searched the ruins of buildings for survivors, as Londoners picked through the wreckage of their homes.

Churchill often appeared in the streets after these raids, inspecting the ruins and flashing the V-for-victory sign with two fingers. As he encouraged his countrymen, Churchill, whose mother was American, kept up a steady correspondence with President Franklin Roosevelt, urging the United States to join the Allies. Roosevelt was sympathetic, but Americans did not want to enter another European war. Churchill reasoned that if Britain could hold out, the United States would eventually join the fight to defeat Nazism.

By late 1940, the worst of the Battle of Britain ended as Hitler found he could not bomb Britain into submission. But the war itself was still spreading.

Mussolini Attacks, Hitler Helps

Italy's dictator, Benito Mussolini, turned his attention to North Africa. He ordered his troops in Libya to invade British-held Egypt. Whoever controlled Egypt controlled the Suez Canal, and thus controlled access to vital oil reserves in the Middle East.

Italian forces pushed into Egypt. The outnumbered British responded with superior tanks, pushing back the Italians and capturing well over a hundred thousand prisoners. Hitler was forced to send German troops to help the Italians.

Next, Mussolini decided to attack Greece. The Greeks routed the Italian invaders, driving them out in short order. Again, Hitler sent German troops to Mussolini's aid.

By the end of 1940, Hitler had wreaked terrible destruction, but he had not won the war.

The Allies Turn the Tide

In 1939, Hitler and Stalin had signed a nonaggression pact. The treaty was Hitler's way of temporarily avoiding conflict with the Soviet Union while focusing his power on other goals. Hitler knew that eventually he would fight the Soviet Union, since both he and Stalin were determined to dominate eastern Europe. Moreover, Hitler maintained a deep hatred of Bolshevism.

Hitler Turns on Stalin

In June 1941, Hitler sent more than three million German troops into the Soviet Union, which forced Stalin to join the war on the side of the Allies. Nazi tanks and trucks sped across the flat steppes of western Russia. As the Russian army retreated, its troops pursued a "scorched-earth" policy, just as they had in the early 1800s when Napoleon invaded Russia. As they fell back, the Soviet troops destroyed crops, bridges, railroad tracks, and telephone wires so that these resources would not fall into enemy hands.

The Nazis captured hundreds of thousands of Russian troops. Because they considered them "inferior" Slavs, the Nazis allowed more than half the Russian soldiers to die of starvation or disease as they were marched toward prisoner of war camps.

Pushing east, the Germans cut off the city of Leningrad from the rest of the country. The citizens of Leningrad endured a siege that lasted 872 days. Nearing starvation, they ate dogs, cats, crows, and mice. They drank water from the city's river and canals, where dead bodies floated. In all, about a million people, a third of Leningrad's population, died during the siege.

Hitler ordered his forces toward Moscow, the capital of the Soviet Union. But as the frigid Russian winter set in, the German troops began to suffer. Their generals had been so sure of a quick victory that they had provided no winter clothes for their men. Soldiers' fingers and toes turned black from frostbite. The temperature plummeted, and thousands froze to death in their trenches.

FDR and the Arsenal of Democracy

In England, Churchill read reports that the German assault against Russia had begun to stall. He took heart that Hitler now had to fight on two fronts. And again, Churchill urged President Roosevelt to join the war.

In 1940, after Franklin Delano Roosevelt (FDR) led the United States out of the crisis of the Great Depression, Americans elected him to a record third term as president. They hoped he would keep them out of the war in Europe. Privately, Roosevelt believed that the United States would have to fight or risk a world ruled by Hitler. Roosevelt began building up the American army and sent fifty aging U.S. destroyers to the British.

Key Questions

- Why did the Soviet Union enter the war in 1941?

- What were the key consequences of the attack on Pearl Harbor and the Battle of Midway?

- Why is the Battle of Stalingrad considered a major turning point in World War II?

The United States soon began selling arms to the Allies. The Lend-Lease Act initiated a program for selling, lending, and leasing arms to any nation deemed "vital to the defense of the United States." American factories turned out tanks, planes, and guns, and shipped them to Britain. President Roosevelt told Americans, "We must be the great arsenal of democracy." The United States was not yet at war, but by arming countries fighting the Axis Powers, it was edging into battle.

By late 1941, hundreds of U.S. supply ships were steaming across the Atlantic carrying war supplies to Britain. German submarines torpedoed the supply ships when they could. Many Americans believed the submarine attacks would provoke the United States to enter the war. But it was a catastrophe in the Pacific Ocean that pushed the United States into World War II.

The War in the Pacific

By the late 1930s, Japan had become a thriving industrialized nation. Japanese workers produced steel, textiles, and ships. Tokyo, the capital, bustled with seven million people. Yet Japan's success brought problems. The population was growing, but land was limited. Japan had fewer natural resources than larger countries and looked to other Pacific nations for raw materials such as rubber, metals, and oil.

Japanese military leaders, who controlled much of the government, had spent years building up the army and navy and expanding Japanese territorial claims. By the time World War II began, Japanese troops occupied Korea, Taiwan, and parts of mainland China. Japan's military leaders had visions of a grand Pacific empire. In 1940, after the outbreak of the war, Japan joined Germany and Italy as an Axis Power.

Pearl Harbor: Day of Infamy

When Japan moved into Southeast Asia in 1941, seeking more raw materials, including oil, the United States responded by banning all sales of American oil to Japan. Japanese leaders were sure that it was only a matter of time before America entered the war. They decided that their best weapon against the United States was surprise.

Sunday, December 7, 1941, began as a peaceful morning at Pearl Harbor in Hawaii, home of the U.S. Navy's Pacific Fleet. Just before eight o'clock, a swarm of warplanes dropped out of the clouds. Warning sirens began to wail. Planes with the Japanese symbol of the red sun painted on their wings screamed toward the harbor. The Japanese had caught the Americans completely off guard.

Explosions rocked the navy base as sailors ran for cover. Some reached their antiaircraft guns and began shooting, but it was too late. Ships burst into fireballs as bombs tore into their hulls. A 1,760-pound (798 kg) bomb ripped through the deck of the USS *Arizona*. Minutes later, the battleship split in two and sank to the bottom of the harbor with more than a thousand crewmen aboard. When the Japanese planes headed back to their carriers, they had destroyed two battleships and damaged six others. The remains of nearly two hundred U.S. planes littered the ground. Nearly twenty-five hundred servicemen were dead.

The USS *Arizona* burned and sank when the Japanese attacked Pearl Harbor, Hawaii, on December 7, 1941.

President Roosevelt was stunned by the news. The next day, he grimly addressed a joint session of Congress. His speech was broadcast by radio around the country. "Yesterday, December 7, 1941—a date which will live in infamy," he began, "the United States of America was suddenly and deliberately attacked by naval and air forces of the empire of Japan."

Congress overwhelmingly approved a declaration of war on Japan. Three days later, Japan's Axis partners, Germany and Italy, declared war on the United States. The United States, in turn, joined the Allies. World War II now stretched around the globe.

The Philippines Fall

Within days of the attack on Pearl Harbor, Japanese troops landed in the Philippines. American and Filipino forces had to retreat to the Bataan (buh-TAN) Peninsula. After three months of fighting, Japanese troops took the peninsula. About seventy thousand American and Filipino prisoners, already hungry and exhausted, were forced to march more than sixty miles (96 km) to a prison camp.

On the Bataan Death March, as it has become known, the Japanese treated their prisoners cruelly. Prisoners were starved and beaten. Those who could not go on were killed. The Japanese also imprisoned thousands of American, British, Australian, and Canadian civilians living in the Philippines. As the

Flags of Allied countries encircle cannons on a poster urging Americans to victory over the Axis Powers.

war dragged on, many of the interned civilians died of hunger and disease.

Interned means imprisoned.

Japan's army and navy also launched assaults across thousands of miles of land and water. Japanese troops seized the island of Guam, a U.S. possession, and the British colony of Hong Kong. They pushed into mainland China, battling both Chinese government and communist armies. Japanese forces stunned the Allies by marching across the Malay Peninsula and capturing Singapore, a British stronghold and naval base. They conquered Indonesia, invaded New Guinea, and threatened Australia. They occupied Burma and seemed ready to attack India.

By early 1942, it looked as though nothing could stop the Japanese in their drive to rule a vast Asian empire.

On to Midway

Some Japanese military leaders believed the American people would not have the stomach for a long,

The Allied Ranks

At the outset of World War II, Britain and France were the chief powers of the Allied nations. As the war spread, nearly fifty countries joined the Allied ranks. The Soviet Union and the United States were the most powerful countries to join Britain and France. The long list of Allies also included large nations such as Australia, Canada, and China, as well as smaller ones such as Liberia, El Salvador, and Panama.

hard fight in the Pacific. But the surprise attack on Pearl Harbor united Americans in support of the war. Luckily for the United States, none of its aircraft carriers were at Pearl Harbor when the Japanese attacked. Within months, the U.S. Pacific Fleet was regrouping. In the spring of 1942, American code breakers discovered that Japan's warships planned to attack the U.S. naval base in the Midway Islands, about fifteen hundred miles (2,415 km) west of Hawaii.

U.S. commanders ordered an attack on the approaching Japanese ships. American pilots roared off their carriers to strike the first blow. As they drew near the Japanese ships, they met heavy antiaircraft fire, and about one hundred fifty planes were shot down. But those that made it through pounded the Japanese ships with bombs. Within minutes, three Japanese carriers were in flames, and a fourth sank later with other ships.

The victory at Midway proved to be a turning point in the war in the Pacific. Japan was no longer in control of the seas. But the path to an Allied victory would be long and costly.

The Eastern Front

Hitler's blitzkrieg assault on the Soviet Union met with early success. Nazi forces quickly pushed east, capturing Kiev, laying siege to Leningrad, and bombing Moscow. But by January 1942, an ally came to Russia's aid—the harsh, frigid winter.

With the help of "General Winter," as they called their natural ally, the Russian army successfully drove the Germans from Moscow. But Hitler wanted to stay on the offensive. By the summer of 1942, he had a new objective—the industrial city of Stalingrad (today called Volgograd), through which Russia's oil supply flowed. Stalin gave the Soviet defenders a single order: "Not one step backward!"

The Battle of Stalingrad

The Battle of Stalingrad lasted 199 days and was the bloodiest battle in human history. The two sides often fought hand to hand, from building to

Russian soldiers advance across a field of rubble during the Battle of Stalingrad.

building, on rooftops, on staircases, and in cellars. Soviet soldiers tied grenades to their bodies and threw themselves under German tanks. A German soldier said, "Stalingrad is no longer a town...it is an enormous cloud of burning, blinding smoke...a vast furnace lit by the reflection of flames."

Time was on the side of the Russians. German supplies were running low, and another brutal winter was setting in. When the Volga River froze in November, Russian soldiers were able to push supplies across it by night. The Red Army managed to encircle the German troops and starve them into defeat. Hitler ordered his troops to fight on, but the last of them surrendered in February 1943.

In the following months, the Russians and Germans clashed repeatedly, but the Soviets, inspired by the desire to save "Mother Russia," drove Hitler's army back toward Germany. By some estimates, the battle cost more than two million lives in all.

The Battle of Stalingrad proved the turning point in the war on the Eastern Front. Some historians regard it as the most significant battle of World War II. After the Soviet forces managed to repel Hitler's army, Germany was on the defensive, and the Allies began to gain the upper hand in the war.

From North Africa to Italy

As his battered army struggled to drive the Germans out of the Soviet Union, Stalin pressured Churchill and Roosevelt to launch an Allied invasion of Europe from England. This would open a second battle front, thus pressuring the Germans to move their troops from Russia to the west. The British and the Americans agreed on the need for an invasion, but the British wanted more time to prepare. Churchill first wanted to take control of North Africa and strengthen British control of the Suez Canal.

Hitler had sent a brilliant tank commander, General Erwin Rommel, to aid the Italians in North Africa. Rommel soon became known as the "Desert Fox." At the führer's order, Rommel advanced into Egypt as far as the railway station at El Alamein (el a-luh-MAYN), though he lacked needed supplies and his troops were exhausted. There, some Egyptians who opposed British rule welcomed the Germans.

In October 1942, British forces under General Bernard Montgomery unleashed air strikes, artillery barrages, infantry charges, and the power of more than a thousand tanks against Rommel's troops. Rommel soon had to retreat to the west. Waiting for him were more than a hundred thousand Allied troops, mostly Americans, under the command of an American general, Dwight D. Eisenhower. After months of fighting, Rommel and his troops were squeezed between the forces of Eisenhower and Montgomery.

The British and Americans then finished the job of clearing North Africa of Axis troops. Then they crossed the Mediterranean and began inching their way up Mussolini's homeland, the Italian Peninsula. The people of Italy decided they had had enough of war. In July 1943, they overthrew Mussolini. The defense of Italy was then up to the Germans, who made sure that the Allied march up the Italian Peninsula was a slow and bloody struggle.

D-day

By January 1944, the Allies were focused on launching the all-important invasion of northern Europe from England. They planned to move a huge force of men and machinery across the English Channel, and then liberate western Europe and defeat the Nazis. The man responsible for making the invasion a success was General Eisenhower, who had helped defeat Rommel in Africa.

Ike, as he was known, was a mild-mannered midwesterner with an extraordinary talent for organizing armies. His job was to organize the invasion of the century. There were numerous problems to solve and questions to answer. How many men should attack? How many naval vessels? What about tanks? How many paratroopers? What kind of landing craft? Where would they invade?

Eisenhower knew he could count on the enormous American industrial machine. In 1944, assembly-line workers in the United States worked around the clock to manufacture tanks, warplanes, guns, and ammunition. Ships carried weapons and hundreds of thousands of American soldiers across the Atlantic to Britain, where Eisenhower was gathering his invasion force.

Eisenhower had to decide where to make the crossing from England. Most people thought the invasion would take place at the French port of Calais (ka-LAY), where the English Channel is narrowest. Eisenhower fooled the Germans into thinking an Allied army was amassing across

The Desert Fox

General Erwin Rommel, the Desert Fox, was a loyal German but not a Nazi. As a military commander, he refused to abuse prisoners of war or to persecute civilians. Eventually, he questioned Hitler's plans and sanity. When he was implicated in a plot to overthrow the führer in 1944, in order to protect his family and reputation, he agreed to commit suicide rather than be executed.

The D-day attack on the beaches of Normandy was an Allied operation of massive scale and complexity under the command of General Dwight D. Eisenhower.

the Channel from Calais. He even equipped this shadow army with inflatable tanks and fake landing craft, and filled the airwaves with misleading radio messages.

Meanwhile, the *real* invasion force gathered farther west along Britain's coast and prepared to strike the French region of Normandy. The size of the force was enormous: nearly 160,000 Allied troops, about 13,000 aircraft, 1,500 tanks, and 6,500 sea vessels, which included about 4,000 custom-designed landing craft.

By early June 1944, the troops, mostly British, American, and Canadian, were ready to embark. The surprise invasion had a code name—D-day. On June 6, 1944, the tides and weather were rough, but Eisenhower gave the order: "OK, let's go."

From D-day to Paris

Under cover of darkness, the great Allied armada started across the English Channel toward five Normandy beaches, code-named Omaha, Utah, Sword, Gold, and Juno. For most of the American troops, this would be their first combat.

When the fleet came within range of the French coastline, huge guns aboard the Allied warships began to pound the German defenses, while transport planes dropped paratroopers behind enemy positions. Allied soldiers clambered from the ships into flat-bottomed landing craft. As the landing craft ran close to shore, the steel doors fell forward, and the troops jumped into the water. Some struggled and drowned, but most pushed ahead to the beach.

Although the Allies took the Germans by surprise, they still met heavy gunfire from the hills beyond the beaches. On Omaha Beach, which the Americans assaulted, 90 percent of the men in some units were killed or wounded.

Despite the awful losses, Eisenhower's painstaking preparations began to pay off. More and more landing craft arrived. Tanks, trucks, and jeeps began rolling up the beaches. By day's end, all five landing sites were secured.

In the next three weeks, the Allies landed many more men and vehicles—nearly a million men, about 150,000 vehicles, and some 600,000 tons of supplies. Mile by mile, the attacking forces fought their way inland. German troops met them at every step.

The Allies advanced toward Paris. Hitler ordered his generals to burn the French capital to the ground, but the generals hesitated. On August 25, Allied troops liberated Paris, and grateful Parisians lined the streets to cheer them on.

British marines land at Juno Beach in Normandy, as part of the D-day landings.

741

Hitler's "Final Solution" and the Allied Victory

Key Questions

- What effect did the D-day invasion have on the war in western Europe?

- What role did new technologies play in the Allied victory in World War II?

In August 1944, after the massive D-day invasion, Allied troops liberated Paris. British, American, French, and Canadian forces then drove east toward Germany's great natural defense, the Rhine River. Meanwhile, Russian troops pressed west toward Germany.

Discovering the Unthinkable: The Holocaust

As Allied troops liberated German-occupied territories and began to push into Germany itself, they came across prison camps surrounded by walls, fences, barbed wire, and guard towers. In the camps were men, women, and children so thin and sick that they looked almost like skeletons. In some places, the Allies found thousands of bodies and human remains.

What had happened? For years, the Allies had heard reports that the Nazis were arresting Jews, communists, Slavs, people with physical or mental disabilities, and others considered "inferior." As the Allies pushed toward Berlin, they discovered the full scope of the Nazi campaign of mass murder known as the Holocaust. A *holocaust* is complete destruction, especially by fire. The term *the Holocaust* refers to the mass slaughter of Europe's Jews and others by the Nazis.

German soldiers round up Jews of all ages in Warsaw, Poland, in 1943.

Hitler's "Final Solution"

Hitler used anti-Semitism—hatred of Jews—to rally the German people and gain power. When the German army conquered lands where millions of Jews lived, the Nazis forced them to wear yellow Star of David badges so they could be easily identified. Specially trained death squads sought out those marked with yellow stars. The death squads murdered perhaps a million Jews, as well as socialists, Communist Party members, and others that Hitler viewed as troublemakers or as "inferior."

> Named for a king of ancient Israel, the six-pointed *Star of David*, also called the Shield of David, is a widespread symbol of Judaism.

Sometimes the Nazis forced their victims to dig trenches, and then shot them so the bodies tumbled into the shallow mass graves. Sometimes they killed people by hanging them, burying them alive, or packing them into sealed vans and suffocating them with fumes from the engine exhaust.

For Hitler, none of this was enough. He was determined to reach, as he put it, "the Final Solution to the Jewish Question"—the killing of *all* the Jews in Europe.

The Death Camps

To achieve his "Final Solution," Hitler needed a more systematic way to commit genocide. For that, he turned to his growing network of concentration camps.

Soon after coming to power in Germany, Hitler had set up prison camps for socialists, communists, and others who opposed Nazi views. The first of these concentration camps was built in 1933 near the town of Dachau (DAH-kow). In the following years, Hitler ordered more concentration camps built throughout Germany and in countries the Nazis conquered. As Nazi armies marched across Europe, they forced thousands of Jews and others onto trains, which hauled the captives, like cattle, to concentration camps.

The prisoners often spent days packed into the freight cars without food or water. Many died before reaching their destinations. Those who did reach the camps often became slave laborers, forced to mine coal or work at factories that made guns, airplanes, cement, fuel, or other products needed for the war.

Many prisoners lived only a few weeks or months. They died of overwork, starvation, or one of the diseases that frequently swept through the camps. The Nazis usually killed those who could not work fast enough.

By late 1942, the Nazis had constructed six special concentration camps in German-occupied Poland. Those camps came to be known as death camps. The most notorious of the death camps was at Auschwitz (OWSH-vitz) in southern Poland.

At Auschwitz, trains pulled straight into the camp so the prisoners, mostly Jews, could be quickly unloaded and sorted. Guards immediately divided new arrivals into two groups—those capable of slave labor, and those not.

The laborers were put into striped uniforms and tattooed on the left arm with a registration number. Then they were marched off to work in factories or mines. For many, their fate was extermination through work. By the end of 1943, at

The Ghettos

In many cities, the Nazis rounded up Jews and herded them into neighborhoods known as ghettos, sealed off from the outside world by high walls or fences, barbed wire, and patrolling guards. There were about four hundred Jewish ghettos in Poland, with the biggest in Warsaw, where about five hundred thousand Jews were isolated in overcrowded, unsanitary conditions.

At first the ghettos were intended to keep Jews separate from so-called Aryans, Hitler's "master race." Later, the Nazis used the ghettos as places to hold Jews until they could be shipped to concentration camps.

743

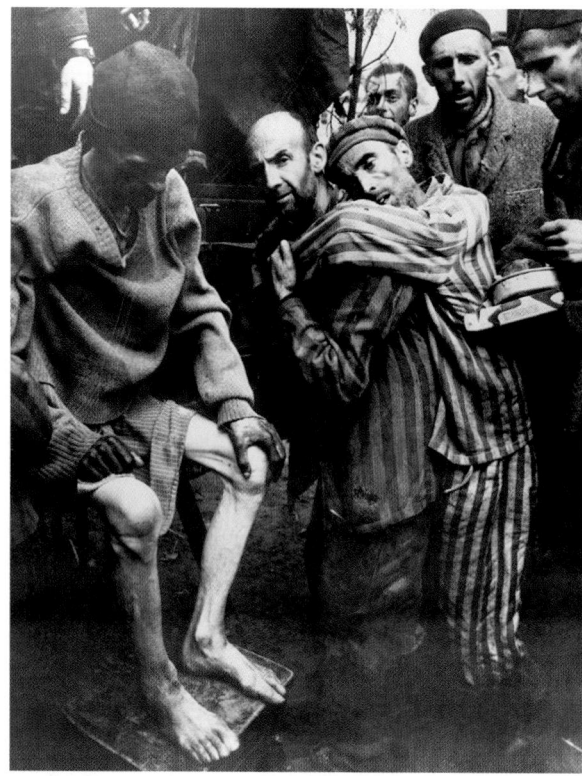

Many victims of Nazi concentration camps died of starvation.

where the prisoners were told they would shower. When the guards could squeeze no more people inside, they sealed the airtight metal doors and released poison gas, killing everyone. Afterward, prison workers removed rings from fingers and extracted gold fillings from the teeth of the dead.

At first, Auschwitz officials buried bodies in mass graves. But as the corpses piled up, Hitler's engineers designed crematoriums that could burn two thousand bodies at a time. When the crematoriums were at work, gray smoke clouded the sky over the camp.

Officials at Auschwitz and other camps used some prisoners in brutal medical experiments. They exposed inmates to intense cold, extreme pressure, drowning, burning, starvation, electric shock, and poisons to see how the human body reacted before death.

Jews from Italy, Austria, Greece, and Hungary were transported to Auschwitz. During the summer of 1944, the camp gassed and burned thousands of people a day. Historians estimate that before the war's end, some 1.5–2 million people were murdered at Auschwitz alone.

In all, the Holocaust claimed the lives of perhaps 11 million people, including about 6 million Jews—two-thirds of Europe's Jewish population.

least half a million slave laborers died of exhaustion and starvation at Auschwitz.

Those designated as unfit for work when they arrived at Auschwitz—including the sick, the elderly, pregnant women, and children under sixteen—met a much swifter death. Guards herded them into large underground chambers,

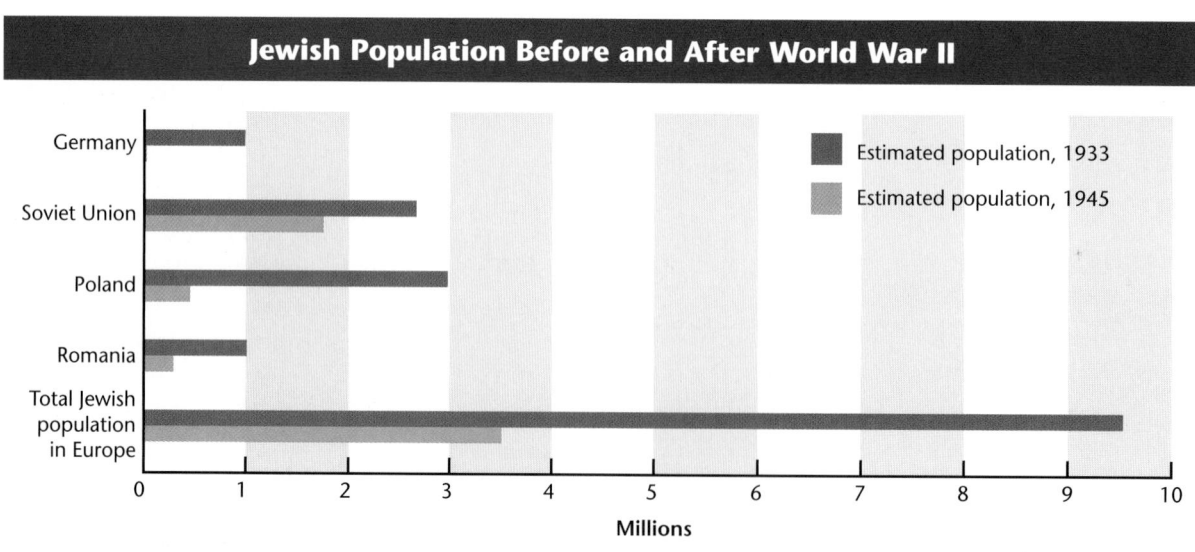

Allied Victory in Europe

Throughout the summer and fall of 1944, and into the winter, the Allies closed in on Germany. The Soviets approached from the east, and the British, Americans, and other forces from the west. In December 1944, Hitler made a desperate attempt to turn back the oncoming Allied tide. He ordered his generals to launch an assault on a thinly held American line in the Ardennes (ahr-DEN) Forest, in Belgium.

The Germans caught the Americans by surprise and forced them back, creating a huge bulge

After initial assaults deep into the heart of western Europe, Russia, and North Africa, the Axis Powers went on the defensive in 1942 as the Allies struck back with American reinforcement.

in their lines. In the Battle of the Bulge, as the fight came to be known, more than nineteen thousand American troops were killed. The American line bent, but did not break. After two weeks of fighting, the Allies managed to rally and halt the German attack.

Bombers pounded Germany's industrial and commercial centers with no regard for civilian versus military casualties. The Allies dropped hundreds of tons of bombs on the city of Dresden, setting off a firestorm that could be seen two hundred miles (322 km) away. Bombs turned much of Hamburg, Berlin, Cologne, Leipzig, and other cities to rubble.

As the Soviet army approached Warsaw, the Poles took heart and revolted against their German occupiers. The Poles expected the Soviet troops to come to their aid. But Stalin had plans to dominate Poland after the war. He held his army outside Warsaw and waited for the Germans to crush the revolt. Hitler's troops destroyed much of the city, killed as many as two hundred fifty thousand Poles, and sent hundreds of thousands to concentration camps. Only then did the Soviet army move in to capture the ruins of Warsaw. The Poles would long remember this betrayal.

By the spring of 1945, Americans advancing from the west and Soviets fighting from the east met at the Elbe River south of Berlin. Meanwhile, other Soviet troops closed in on Germany's capital, Berlin, where Hitler hid in an underground bunker. In desperation, he continued to issue impossible orders to units that no longer existed. Hitler learned that his Axis partner, Mussolini, was dead, shot by his own people. Before the Russians could capture him, the führer sat at a table and shot himself with a pistol.

Seven days later, on May 7, 1945, Germany surrendered. The Allies celebrated the next day as V-E Day—Victory in Europe Day. Churchill called it "the signal for the greatest outburst of joy in the history of mankind."

Joyous crowds greeted Soviet troops on their return home.

The Allies' Pacific Push

The war in Europe was over, but fighting in the Pacific continued. Since the Battle of Midway, the United States had pursued a strategy of "island hopping," moving toward Japan by taking one island at a time. On more than a hundred Japanese-occupied islands, American troops fought their way ashore and often suffered heavy losses.

As the Americans edged ever closer to Japan, Japanese fliers began to use a new form of air warfare—suicide attacks by pilots known as *kamikaze* (kah-mih-KAH-zee), which means "divine wind." Kamikaze pilots deliberately crashed their bomb-filled planes into American vessels.

In late 1944, Japanese fliers launched a bold attack on U.S. forces led by General Douglas MacArthur. The U.S. forces were attempting to retake the Philippine Islands. As the U.S. ships approached the islands, more than four hundred kamikaze pilots flew out to meet them. They drove their planes straight at the American vessels, sinking and damaging several. But in October 1944, MacArthur landed on the Philippine island of Leyte (LAY-tee). By February, MacArthur's troops were pressing into Manila, to the cheers of both Filipinos and Allied civilians imprisoned in the city.

U.S. troops continued to hop from island to island. After brutal fighting, they captured Iwo Jima (EE-woh JEE-mah), seven hundred miles

(1,125 km) from Tokyo. They moved on to take Okinawa (oh-kee-NAH-wah), a stepping stone to the major islands of Japan. On that small island, the Japanese lost nearly seventy thousand soldiers in fierce fighting, while thousands of Okinawan civilians died. The Americans lost more than twelve thousand men.

American pilots were soon taking off from airstrips on Pacific islands and bombing Japan itself. These raids reduced Japanese cities to ruins. Allied victory over Japan was no longer in doubt, but the Japanese refused to surrender.

The Atomic Bomb and Victory in Japan

Even before the outbreak of World War II, scientists had been exploring the structure of atoms and speculating about the possibility of splitting an atom's nucleus. They were building on the insights of a great German-born physicist, Albert Einstein.

Einstein's revolutionary theories, and his famous formula $E=mc^2$ (energy equals mass times the speed of light squared), led scientists to understand that the process of nuclear fission—splitting the nucleus of an atom—could set off a chain reaction capable of unleashing a huge amount of energy. Perhaps this energy could be used to light whole cities. Or perhaps it could be used to create a weapon, an atomic bomb of almost unimaginable destructive power.

The Manhattan Project

In 1939, Einstein was living in the United States. He wrote to Franklin Roosevelt, warning the president that the Nazis were working to build an atomic bomb. Einstein and his fellow physicists believed the United States should hurry to develop an atomic bomb before Hitler because they knew that once Hitler had the bomb, he would not hesitate to use it.

Albert Einstein

In 1921, Albert Einstein was awarded the Nobel Prize for Physics. The German physicist leapt from obscurity to celebrity.

As Hitler rose to power in Germany, Einstein, who was of Jewish descent, worked with others in the Jewish community to oppose fascism. Although Einstein headed a major research institute in Berlin, the Nazis responded by denouncing Einstein's work as "Jewish physics." The threat was clear. Einstein left Germany in 1932, never to return. He joined the Institute for Advanced Study in Princeton, New Jersey, and became an American citizen.

Albert Einstein warned of the lethal powers of the atom.

Einstein regularly spoke in support of causes that opposed fascism or sought justice for the oppressed. He also called for control of the terrible potential of atomic power. "We scientists," he said, "whose tragic destiny it has been to help make the methods of annihilation ever more gruesome and more effective, must consider it our solemn and transcendent duty to do all in our power in preventing these weapons from being used."

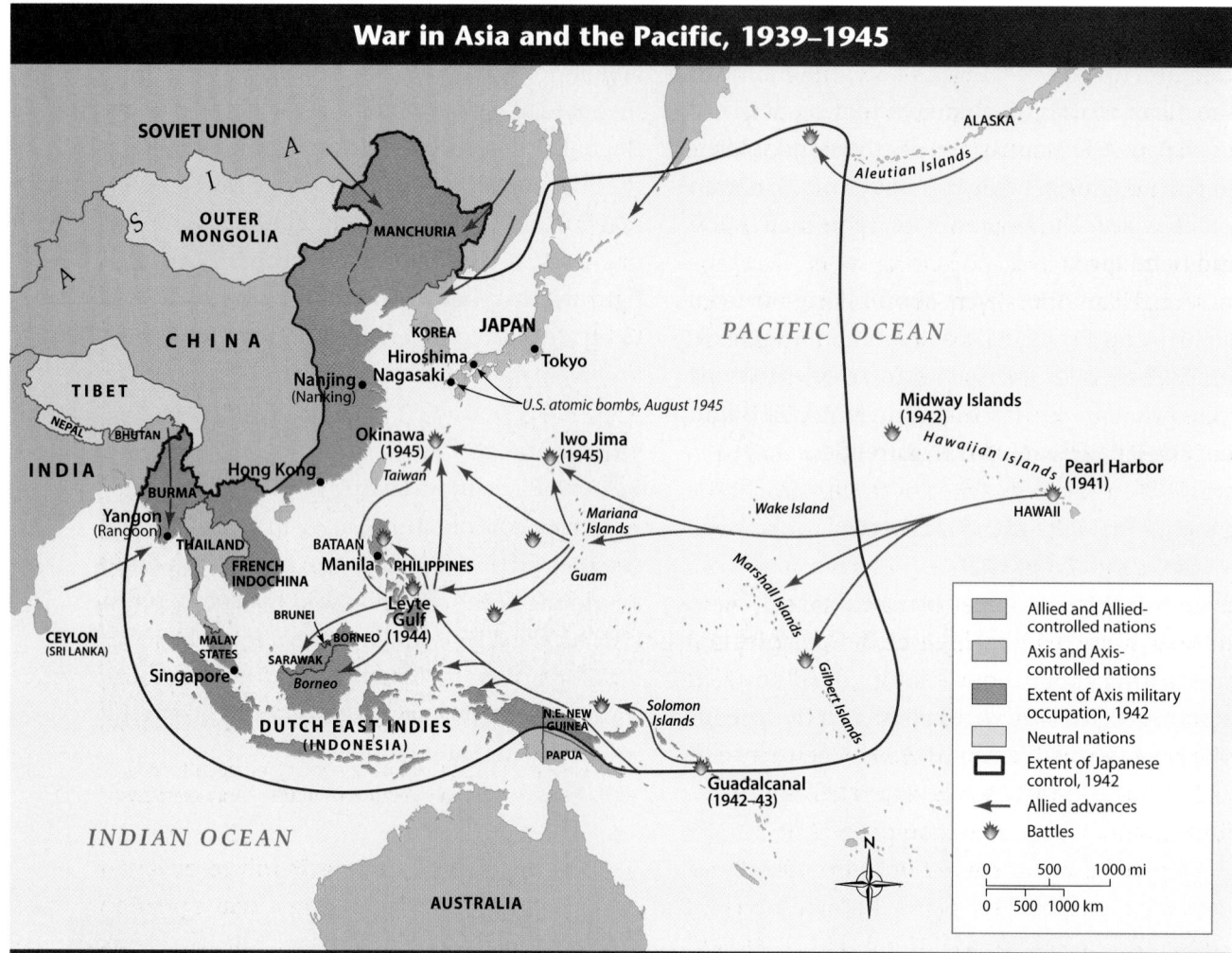

War in Asia and the Pacific, 1939–1945

After Japan's unprovoked attack on Pearl Harbor in 1941, American forces pursued a strategy of island hopping, taking one island at a time in their drive toward Japan.

President Roosevelt authorized the start of a top-secret research program that grew to include eminent scientists from other Allied nations. The program, code-named the Manhattan Project, was led by an American scientist, J. Robert Oppenheimer. The researchers set to work at secret locations across the country. Eventually some hundred twenty thousand men and women were working to win the race to develop an atomic bomb.

In July 1945, about three years after the Manhattan Project began, scientists successfully detonated an experimental atomic bomb in the New Mexico desert. By this time, the Germans had surrendered and Hitler was dead. President Roosevelt, who had set the Manhattan Project in motion, was also dead. Harry Truman, the new president

of the United States, had to decide whether to use the bomb against the Japanese.

Hiroshima and Nagasaki

The strategy of island hopping had brought the Allies close to Japan. The next logical step was to invade Japan itself. But Japan's military leaders, recalling old samurai traditions that forbade surrender, were determined to continue the fight, even in the face of inevitable defeat. Some U.S. military officials predicted that up to half a million American soldiers could die in such an invasion, and that even more Japanese would perish.

President Truman understood how costly the invasion of Japan would be. He concluded that dropping an atomic bomb on Japan could bring the war in the Pacific to a swift end. Some American officials, including scientists who had worked on the Manhattan Project, opposed using the bomb. Truman knew that dropping an atomic bomb would kill thousands of Japanese civilians, but he believed it would cost far fewer lives, Japanese and American, than an invasion of Japan.

On August 6, 1945, an American pilot steered his B-29 bomber, the *Enola Gay*, toward the Japanese port city of Hiroshima (heer-uh-SHEE-mah or hih-ROH-shih-muh). Aboard the plane was a single atomic bomb. Once over Hiroshima, the pilot dropped the bomb and turned for home.

A brilliant flash gave way to a huge mushroom cloud that bloomed over the city. The explosion unleashed an expanding fireball that flattened five miles (8 km) of downtown Hiroshima and instantly killed almost eighty thousand civilians. The nuclear blast left many more people maimed or hideously burned, while others fell victim to a more gradual killer, radiation poisoning.

Japan's government did not surrender. Three days later, another U.S. plane dropped a second atomic bomb on Nagasaki (nah-gah-SAH-kee), destroying the heart of that city and killing or injuring another eighty thousand people.

A jubilant American sailor kisses a young nurse in New York's Times Square in celebration of the victory over Japan.

On August 14, Emperor Hirohito of Japan announced that his government had agreed to unconditional surrender. The surrender ceremony took place in Tokyo Bay, aboard the battleship *Missouri*. The war was finally over.

In Allied nations around the world, crowds celebrated V-J Day—Victory in Japan Day. In New York City, two million people flooded into Times Square, where sailors embraced passing young women in what one serviceman called the "kissingest day in history." Yet behind the celebrations stood all the horror of the previous six years.

The Legacy of World War II

Exactly six years and one day after Hitler's invasion of Poland, World War II was over. But peace had come at a terrible price. World War II caused more death and destruction than any other war in history. Some twenty million soldiers died in battle. No one knows for sure how many civilians perished from disease, starvation, bombings,

The atomic bombing of Hiroshima killed tens of thousands of civilians and devastated the city and its surroundings.

and Hitler's mass murders. The total number of soldiers and civilians killed may have reached as high as sixty million.

When the war ended, cities across much of Europe and Asia lay in ruins. Millions of civilians were left hungry and homeless.

Two industrial powers, Germany and Japan, lay crippled. Britain still had its empire, but was battered and exhausted. The United States and the Soviet Union emerged from the war as two military giants, poised to dominate the postwar world. But the war had left the two nations in very different conditions.

American factories had produced many of the weapons and supplies needed for Allied victory.

World War II, Estimated War Dead		Military	Civilian
Allied Powers	**China**	1,310,000	unknown, in the millions
	France	213,000	350,000
	Great Britain	264,000	93,000
	Soviet Union	11,000,000	at least 7,000,000
	United States	292,000	5,000
Axis Powers	**Germany**	3,500,000	780,000
	Italy	242,000	153,000
	Japan	1,300,000	572,000

The United States, which saw no fighting on its mainland, emerged from the war as the richest, most powerful nation in the world.

The Soviet Union, by contrast, suffered much more from the fighting. Some twenty-five million Soviets were dead, and thousands of towns and villages had been wiped out. Yet the Soviet Union covered more territory than any other nation in the world, and Soviet troops controlled much of Eastern Europe. The United States and Britain quickly began to fear that Joseph Stalin had no intention of giving up the territory his Red Army had seized from the Axis Powers.

World War II left in its destructive wake another legacy. For the first time in history, there existed a weapon that could wipe out entire nations. Before the United States dropped atomic bombs on Hiroshima and Nagasaki, President Truman had informed Joseph Stalin about the new weapon. The Soviet dictator took comfort in the fact that his own scientists were already at work on their own atomic bombs and not far behind.

After the war, a Belgian mother and her children, left homeless, wander past ruins and rubble in search of shelter.

Securing the Peace

Early in 1945, even before World War II ended, confident Allied leaders began to plan the shape of a postwar world. Less than three decades had passed since the end of World War I, when the harsh terms of the Treaty of Versailles and other measures had deepened existing hatreds and led to even worse devastation and bloodshed. Now, with World War II drawing to a close, Allied leaders remembered the failure of the settlements following World War I. Could a lasting peace be achieved when, even among the Allied Powers, there were deep rifts and tense differences?

From Yalta to Potsdam

In February 1945, President Franklin Roosevelt, Prime Minister Winston Churchill, and Premier Joseph Stalin met at Yalta, a resort on the Black Sea. These leaders were often called the Big Three. Their purpose was to discuss the future of Europe and the world after the war.

At the Yalta summit, the Big Three met as allies. But they knew the alliance might not last. The United States and Britain were democracies that embraced capitalism, while the Soviet

A *summit* is a meeting of the heads of governments.

Key Questions

- What postwar plans did the Allied leaders make as the war came to an end?

- What was the purpose of the Nuremberg Trials, and what precedent did they set?

- What were the main goals behind the founding of the United Nations?

Prime Minister Winston Churchill (Great Britain), President Franklin D. Roosevelt (United States), and Premier Joseph Stalin (Soviet Union) met at Yalta to discuss Europe's future.

751

Union was a communist dictatorship. The United States and Britain hoped for greater democracy throughout Europe, while Stalin hoped to spread his nation's communist influence, particularly in Eastern Europe.

To prevent a clash, the Big Three agreed in principle to divide Germany and Europe after the war. Eastern Europe, including the eastern part of Germany, would fall under Soviet control, although Stalin said he would allow free elections in Poland. The United States and its allies would decide the fate of Western Europe. That was the general agreement. The Big Three decided to sort out the details at a later meeting, to be held in the German city of Potsdam, near Berlin.

The Potsdam Conference

Before the Potsdam Conference convened in July 1945, Franklin Roosevelt died. The new U.S. president, Harry S. Truman, took his place in the Big Three. Truman soon found that he would have to face Stalin without Churchill's help, because in the midst of the Potsdam Conference, British voters replaced Churchill with a new prime minister, Clement Attlee.

Truman and Attlee arrived at Potsdam concerned about what Stalin had been doing. Back at Yalta, Stalin had made vague promises about giving democracy a chance in Eastern Europe. But in the Soviet-occupied countries, he seemed determined to set up communist governments that he could control.

At the Potsdam Conference, Truman, Attlee, and Stalin disagreed about war reparations. Stalin insisted that the Germans pay huge reparations. The British and Americans believed that demands for large reparations after World War I had led to German bitterness and helped cause World War II. But Stalin kept pointing out that his country had suffered terrible destruction from the German invasion. He was determined that the Soviet Union be paid as much as possible. In the end, Stalin got many of the reparations he demanded.

Seeking Just Punishment

At the war's end, the Allies also had to decide how to treat the defeated Nazis. Should they inflict harsh punishments on German leaders? Some thought so, especially after the Allied armies found the Nazi concentration camps. For such atrocities, *someone* had to be held responsible.

Truman wanted to pursue a different course, one that Roosevelt had favored. He believed that the individuals responsible for the war should be identified, charged with specific crimes, and brought to justice through legal means.

But under what law could Nazi leaders be charged? No international legal system existed. How could people of one sovereign nation convict the leaders of another? Moreover, which leaders should be put on trial? Many Nazi leaders were dead. Hitler had committed suicide. Of the führer's inner circle, only Hermann Göring (GUR-ing), Hitler's deputy, had been taken alive. Other high-ranking Nazi officers were in captivity.

The Nuremberg Trials

The Allies decided to establish a special court, an international military tribunal, representing many nations. They appointed prosecutors and chose the German city of Nuremberg as the trial site. They also defined the crimes for which the Nazis would be tried. "Crimes against peace" included plotting and starting an unprovoked war of aggression against another country. "War crimes" included acts such as sending prisoners of war to slave labor camps. "Crimes against humanity" included murder, enslavement, and inhumane acts against civilians.

Most Nazi leaders were astounded to learn they would be tried for such crimes. They said they had not personally committed any atrocities; they were just following orders from above.

Men who had personally committed atrocities, such as concentration camp guards who had shoved children into gas chambers, were also in custody. During the trials, a psychologist interviewed some of these men and found them strangely ordinary. After a day's "work" at the camps, they went home to have dinner with their families, play with their pets, and tinker at their hobbies. Like their superior officers, they said they were just following orders.

The prosecutors at the Nuremberg Trials wanted to punish not only the guards and others who carried out the orders, but also the leaders who planned the atrocities and gave the orders. The first series of trials at Nuremberg ran for nearly a year, from November 1945 to October 1946. They focused on the most important Nazi leaders.

The prosecutors had plenty of evidence because the Nazis had kept detailed records of their crimes and conversations, which the Allies found stored in mines, tunnels, and castles across Europe. These documents proved beyond all doubt that the Nazis were guilty of unprovoked aggression, unprecedented atrocities, and an attempt to exterminate all Jewish people with their "Final Solution."

In the first year of the Nuremberg Trials, twelve of the twenty-two men on trial were convicted and sentenced to death by hanging.

Hermann Göring, Hitler's deputy, takes the oath in the witness box at Nuremberg. He showed no remorse at the trials.

The Tokyo Trials

Meanwhile, a similar trial was taking place in Tokyo. Although the Japanese had not attempted Nazi-style genocide during the war, the Tokyo Trials did expose many acts of brutality. The Japanese military had used biological weapons against Chinese civilians. In prison camps, prisoners of war were often beaten, murdered, and mutilated.

Emperor Hirohito, who had ruled Japan during the war and had full knowledge of these atrocities, was never charged with war crimes. But twenty-five military and government leaders were tried and convicted. Seven were executed.

The Tokyo Trials added weight to the judgments at Nuremberg. Together, the two trials demonstrated that the leaders of nations were accountable to the world and subject to laws that crossed international boundaries.

The United Nations

Before World War II ended, Allied leaders met to plan an international organization that would work to prevent war, promote cooperation among countries, and help settle international disputes. After World War I, the League of Nations had adopted similar goals. But this new organization—to be called the United Nations—intended to succeed where the League had failed.

The League of Nations failed in part because the United States had refused to join it. To prevent that from happening again, President Roosevelt convened a meeting in August 1944, at Dumbarton Oaks, an estate in Washington, D.C. There, delegates from the Soviet Union, the United States, Great Britain, and China hammered out a structure for the new international peacekeeping organization.

After Franklin Roosevelt died, Harry Truman continued the push to create the United Nations. In the summer of 1945, the United States hosted an international conference in San Francisco. Fifty nations sent representatives, and they filled in the plan sketched at Dumbarton Oaks. On

Flags of member nations fly at the United Nations headquarters in New York City. The building was completed in 1952.

October 24, 1945, the United Nations was born. The first meeting was scheduled for January of the following year, in London.

Human Rights for All

Today, the work of the United Nations embraces a range of goals—dealing with world health issues, working to maintain stability in the world economy, promoting free trade, providing assistance to poor countries, and much more. At its founding, the UN confronted pressing issues that grew out of World War II.

In its first year, the United Nations set up a Human Rights Commission to help prevent atrocities such as those the Nazis had committed. The commission wanted to draw the world's attention to countries that violated people's rights. But what rights belonged to all humans? Where, for example, could one draw the line between the rights of a government over its citizens and the rights of citizens against their government?

Such questions had been addressed in earlier documents. In 1776, the Declaration of Independence declared that all people are born with "certain unalienable rights, [and] that among these are life, liberty, and the pursuit of happiness." In 1789, the French National Assembly drafted a similar Declaration of the Rights of Man and of the Citizen. Franklin Roosevelt had spoken of "four freedoms" worth fighting for—freedom of expression, freedom of worship, freedom from want, and freedom from fear.

The fledgling United Nations wanted a more complete declaration of rights that everyone could embrace, regardless of culture or country. To draft such a statement, the General Assembly appointed a committee, chaired by Eleanor Roosevelt, the widow of the late president. Well-known and admired for her work on behalf of the poor and oppressed, Eleanor Roosevelt had been appointed by President Truman as a member of the first U.S. delegation to the United Nations.

Mrs. Roosevelt's warmth, good humor, and stamina helped the diverse members of the committee bridge their enormous cultural gaps and helped turn tangled arguments into a coherent set of principles.

On December 10, 1948, the United Nations adopted the Universal Declaration of Human Rights. Its first article stated: "All human beings are born free and equal in dignity and rights. They are endowed with reason and conscience and should act towards one another in a spirit of brotherhood." The declaration called for freedom of expression, for human dignity, and for safety from torture and false imprisonment. It also insisted on the rights to work, to rest, and to have food, clothing, housing, and medical care.

Of course the statement itself did not make the world a just place. But it did take a dramatic stand on rights and freedoms, in contrast to the wartime years just past, during which so many rights and freedoms had been so flagrantly violated.

New Tensions

Both the United States and the Soviet Union sat on the Security Council of the new United Nations. But tensions were pitting these great powers and former allies against each other.

Eleanor Roosevelt led the United Nations committee that drafted the Universal Declaration of Human Rights.

The Structure of the United Nations

The basic plan agreed on at Dumbarton Oaks remains in place at the United Nations to this day. The UN is divided into two chambers. One chamber, the General Assembly, includes delegates from all the member nations. Each nation, big or small, has one vote. The General Assembly democratically discusses and decides important matters.

The other chamber is the Security Council. Originally, there were five permanent members of the Security Council—China, Great Britain, France, the Soviet Union, and the United States—plus six nonpermanent members with two-year terms. Today, fifteen countries sit on the Security Council but only five—the People's Republic of China, Great Britain, France, Russia, and the United States—have permanent seats. Any one of the permanent members of the Security Council can veto decisions made by the rest of the Council.

As Churchill, Truman, and other Western leaders had suspected, Stalin had no intention of giving democracy a chance in Eastern Europe.

In the Soviet-occupied countries of Bulgaria, Romania, Hungary, Czechoslovakia, and Poland, the Soviet dictator was ready to use any means, including force, to make sure that Communist Party governments took over those countries.

Elsewhere in the world, colonized peoples began to rebel against their European rulers. Independence movements stirred in India, Indochina, and parts of Africa. As these colonized nations gained independence, would they become democracies allied to the United States, or would they join Stalin's communist camp? Could the great powers settle their differences through peaceful means, or were they headed toward yet another world war?

Chapter 32

Western Democracies

A mushroom cloud rises from a hydrogen-bomb test explosion by the United States in 1952.

troops leave Eastern Europe.

1975

1985

1995

1989
The Berlin Wall falls.

1991
The Soviet Union
dissolves.

and the Cold War 1945-1995

Two global wars in less than half a century destroyed the pre-1914 world order. As a new world order emerged, the Cold War, a struggle between the United States and the Soviet Union, spanned the globe. Many nations were drawn into conflicts with potentially catastrophic consequences as the two major powers engaged in a frenzied race to stockpile nuclear arms.

After World War II, the European powers and the United States faced very different challenges. War-ravaged European nations struggled to rebuild, and some progressed rapidly with American aid. The United States, with its industrial infrastructure undamaged by war, experienced a period of unprecedented economic growth. The nation did face new challenges as a civil rights movement emerged to push the United States to live up to its creed that "all men are created equal."

In the late twentieth century, a series of dramatic events led to the decline of the Soviet Union and the end of the Cold War. While the breakup of the USSR brought new freedom to many lands, in others it led to conflict and the violent release of pent-up tensions.

The Cold War Begins

Key Questions

- What was the Cold War, and why did it begin?

- How did Western democracies respond to the spread of communism in Europe and around the world?

The United States and the Soviet Union emerged from World War II as the world's two *superpowers*—dominant nations with the ability to influence events and project their military and economic might throughout the world. The two superpowers were increasingly at odds. Leaders of the Soviet Union suspected the United States of trying to dominate the world for the benefit of capitalists. American leaders believed that the Soviets were trying to forge a worldwide communist society ruled by a totalitarian dictatorship based in Moscow.

Because the United States and the Soviet Union did not directly engage each other in a "hot" war—a war with shooting and bloodshed—the tense forty-year standoff between the superpowers is known as the Cold War. Although the Soviet Union and the United States never fought each other directly, battles did take place in countries where people allied themselves with one superpower or the other.

The Iron Curtain: East vs. West

During World War II, the Soviets drove Nazi troops out of Bulgaria, Romania, Hungary, Czechoslovakia, and Poland. At the Yalta summit, Joseph Stalin, the Soviet dictator, had promised to let these nations hold free elections and establish democratic governments. Instead, Stalin imposed communist, pro-Soviet regimes in these lands as well as in the eastern part of Germany.

By 1946, the Soviets were refusing to allow most Western goods into the USSR or into Soviet-controlled nations in Eastern Europe. Stalin also imposed rigid censorship, with the goal of keeping out Western ideas. Stalin's actions widened the divide between his regime and his former allies.

Britain's Winston Churchill described this division between the former allies as "an iron curtain" descending across Europe. Behind this iron curtain lay the nations conquered by the Soviet Union. As the Cold War deepened, people continued to refer to the Iron Curtain dividing "the East," the communist nations led by the Soviet Union, from "the West," the United States and its allies.

The Soviet Union and its allies, both in and beyond Eastern Europe, were also referred to as the **Eastern Bloc**. Many Eastern Bloc governments were communist regimes that were manipulated or controlled by the USSR. The Eastern Bloc nations were sometimes called "satellites" of the Soviet Union.

Joseph Stalin

Following World War II, the Soviet Union tightened its grip on Eastern Europe, and the continent split into two opposing political blocs.

The United States and its allies were sometimes referred to as the **Western Bloc**, but more often as "Western nations" or simply "the West." The Western nations—such as Great Britain and France—were anticommunist. Many, but not all, were democracies. Some, such as Spain under Franco, were dictatorships. Since these dictators were opposed to communism, the United States put up with and sometimes even aided them.

The Truman Doctrine and the Policy of Containment

In the Cold War, the United States under President Harry Truman adopted a foreign policy known as **containment**. The strategy of containment aimed to prevent the spread of communism by forming key alliances and especially by strengthening noncommunist countries bordering the Soviet Union.

In early 1947, when it appeared that the Soviets were prepared to support communist uprisings in Greece and Turkey, Truman asked Congress to supply aid to both countries. He declared, "I believe that it must be the policy of the United States to support free peoples who are resisting attempted subjugation by armed minorities or by outside pressures." The president's policy, which became known as the **Truman Doctrine**, committed the United States to the containment of communism wherever it threatened to spread.

The Marshall Plan: Rebuilding Europe

As part of the strategy of containment, the United States undertook a massive effort to rebuild Europe. In the aftermath of World War II, great cities lay in ruins. Millions of homeless survivors suffered from malnutrition and disease. Winston Churchill described postwar Europe as "a rubble heap,...a breeding ground for pestilence and hate." Stalin saw a ruined Europe as fertile ground for the spread of communism. Truman also knew that poverty and chaos could lead desperate people to embrace communism, and he was determined to prevent that outcome.

Truman's secretary of state, George C. Marshall, argued for spending American dollars to help rebuild a Europe ruined by war. He proposed the European Recovery Program, which quickly became known as the **Marshall Plan**. The Marshall Plan was intended to promote a stable peace through massive American aid to rebuild the shattered economies of Europe.

Between 1948 and 1952, the United States provided $13 billion in economic aid to Europe. The money helped European nations purchase machinery, modernize factories, repair railroads, and rebuild cities. The plan offered aid to the Soviet Union and its Eastern European satellites. Stalin, however, saw the Marshall Plan as a plot to spread American influence and divide the Eastern Bloc. He rejected any aid.

The Marshall Plan was, in part, an extraordinarily generous humanitarian act by the United States. It was also a shrewd maneuver by one of the Cold War's superpowers. The United States hoped that generous aid would support capitalist economies, strengthen democratic governments, keep communism at bay, and build strong trading partners for U.S. businesses.

The Marshall Plan helped bring about a stunning economic recovery in southern and western Europe, which brought political stability to the continent. In countries such as Britain, France, and Italy, the United States earned enormous good will. And in helping Europe get back on its feet, America ensured its own prosperity by exporting goods to the newly prosperous Europeans.

The Berlin Airlift

At the end of World War II, the Soviets occupied eastern Germany while Britain, France, and the United States occupied the western portion of the country. Just as Germany was divided, so was Berlin, its capital city. The Allies controlled West Berlin, the Soviets East Berlin.

The city of Berlin was located more than one hundred miles (160 km) inside the country's Soviet-dominated zone. As Cold War tensions mounted, Stalin wanted to drive the Americans and their allies out of the western half of the city. In June 1948, he ordered a blockade of West Berlin. Without supplies, West Berlin's people would soon face starvation. Stalin hoped his blockade would bring the entire city under Soviet control.

In response to the Soviet blockade, the British and Americans organized a massive airlift of food and other supplies. In the Berlin Airlift, as the rescue operation is known, more than 277,000 flights delivered 2.3 million tons of supplies to West Berlin. At the height of the blockade, a plane touched down in the city every few minutes. Because of the difficult flying conditions, seventy-three Allied airmen lost their lives in the course of the Berlin Airlift.

Standing atop rubble, German children in West Berlin cheer a U.S. cargo plane during the Berlin Airlift.

In May 1949, Stalin lifted the blockade. In the same year, Germany itself was divided into two countries. The western part became a separate, democratic nation, the Federal Republic of Germany, which is often called West Germany. The eastern part of Germany became the German Democratic Republic, often called East Germany, with East Berlin as its capital. Despite its name, East Germany was far from democratic. The Communist Party controlled the government and took its direction from the Soviet Union.

Cold War Alliances

In 1949, twelve Western countries, led by Britain, France, and the United States, signed an agreement establishing the North Atlantic Treaty Organization (NATO). Its twelve member nations agreed that if one of them was attacked, the others would come to its defense.

The Soviet Union and its Eastern Bloc satellites eventually responded by signing their own mutual defense treaty, called the Warsaw Pact. To some observers, this new system of military alliances was a frightful reminder of the alliances that European nations formed in the years leading to World War I. They wondered if the world was heading toward yet another catastrophic conflict.

NATO and the Warsaw Pact

North Atlantic Treaty Organization: Established in 1949 to deter a Soviet attack on a member nation, its original members included Belgium, Canada, Denmark, France, Iceland, Italy, Luxembourg, the Netherlands, Norway, Portugal, the United Kingdom, and the United States.

Warsaw Pact: Established in 1955 as a Soviet-led military alliance in response to NATO, its members were Albania, Bulgaria, Czechoslovakia, East Germany, Hungary, Poland, Romania, and the Soviet Union. The pact ended in 1991.

Korean War, 1950–53

- **· · · ·** September 1950 Farthest advance of North Korean forces
- **- - - -** November 1950 Farthest advance of of UN and U.S. forces
- **– – – –** January 1951 Farthest advance of North Korean and Chinese forces
- **——** 1953 truce line

Hostilities between communist and democratic factions in Korea escalated when China and the United States entered the conflict.

Korea: The Cold War Turns Hot

Less than five years after World War II ended, a crisis broke out on the Korean Peninsula. Like Europe, the Korean Peninsula had been divided after the war. The two halves became separate nations—communist North Korea, and noncommunist, capitalist South Korea.

In June 1950, without warning, North Korean troops stormed south and seized the South Korean capital of Seoul (sohl). Their goal was to unite Korea under communism by force. Stalin supplied money, planes, and pilots to North Korea, although he refused to commit Soviet army troops.

Truman had to decide whether to risk war with the Soviet Union or let the invasion stand. He decided to take the matter to the United Nations. When the Korean crisis came up for discussion, the Soviet delegates were not present. The Security Council condemned the invasion and authorized the use of force to drive the North Koreans out of the south. Officially, it was not the United States but the United Nations that went to war with North Korea. But the soldiers fighting against North Korea were mostly Americans, though they were in Korea as "UN troops."

The Security Council approved President Truman's appointment of General Douglas MacArthur to head the UN forces. MacArthur organized an invasion that took the North Koreans by surprise and drove them northward out of Seoul. As UN troops pushed north, they drove up the Korean Peninsula, in some places coming close to the Yalu River, North Korea's border with China. MacArthur's forces captured P'yongyang, the capital, in October 1950.

MacArthur did not expect Chinese communist leader Mao Zedong to send large numbers of troops to the aid of the Korean communists. But the Chinese saw MacArthur's advance into North Korea as an invasion of a communist land by a Western army, and so a threat to China itself. In November 1950, urged on by Stalin, China sent nearly three hundred thousand troops across the Yalu River.

The army fighting against MacArthur suddenly tripled. Through the snows of a freezing Korean winter, the Chinese forced the overwhelmed UN troops to retreat into South Korean territory until they were cornered and fighting for their lives.

The fighting dragged on. The United States possessed nuclear weapons but dared not use them, because behind North Korea stood China, and behind China loomed the Soviet Union, which now had its own atomic bombs. The Korean War ground to a stalemate in which both sides suffered many casualties without gaining an inch of territory.

Stalin's Death and the War's End

There is no telling how long the war in Korea might have lasted had it not been for mysterious events that took place early in 1953. Stalin was in residence, with his inner circle of advisers, at his villa just outside Moscow. On March 1, Stalin's

P'yongyang residents and other North Korean refugees perilously cross the remains of a bridge as they flee south to escape advancing Chinese communist troops.

bodyguards found him in his bedroom unable to speak. Official reports said he died of a stroke four days later. Many historians think he was poisoned, possibly by his chief spy, Lavrenti Beria (BAIR-ee-uh). Beria, along with two others, took Stalin's place after his death.

Stalin had insisted that the Chinese continue the fight in Korea, but Beria believed that the war had gone on long enough and approved a cease-fire. On July 27, 1953, an armistice brought an end to the Korean War. It wasn't a peace treaty—nothing was settled—but at least the fighting stopped.

More than three million people were dead or missing, and millions more were homeless. North Korea remained a communist nation, its people living under totalitarian rule. South Korea remained a capitalist nation aligned with the Western democracies.

Russian tanks crush a rebellion in Budapest, Hungary, in 1956. The United States and other Western nations helped Hungarian refugees, but otherwise did not intervene because they did not want to risk war with the Soviet Union.

From Stalin to Khrushchev

After Stalin's death, a Soviet official named Nikita Khrushchev (nih-KEE-tuh kroosh-CHEHF) was elected to lead the Communist Party as its general secretary. Khrushchev seemed a likeable man, but beneath his cheerful exterior lay ruthless cunning. Khrushchev arranged to have Beria arrested and shot. By 1956, Krushchev had emerged as the USSR's dominant leader.

Khrushchev proclaimed that Stalin had committed grievous crimes, including the executions of hundreds of thousands of people for "anti-Soviet activities." Khrushchev's proclamation shocked many communists, who knew about Stalin's atrocities but didn't want to admit them to the world. In the Eastern Bloc, however, Khrushchev's words awakened hope. Leaders of some Soviet satellites thought they might have more freedom to run their states without interference from Moscow.

But when the Polish Communist Party installed a new leader without Khrushchev's approval, the general secretary flew into a rage and threatened to send Soviet troops into Poland. In the autumn of 1956, when Hungarians poured into the streets of their cities to demand more freedom, Khrushchev sent tanks into Hungary to crush the rebellion. For daring to defy the Soviets, the Hungarians suffered some twenty thousand casualties, including about twenty-five hundred deaths.

Western leaders protested but did not intervene to repel Soviet troops from Hungary. Western leaders had resolved to "contain" communism, to prevent its spread. But because Hungary was a communist country before Soviet tanks rolled into Budapest, Hungary's capital, Western leaders did not see Khrushchev's show of force as a spread of communism. While Western nations did offer help to many thousands of Hungarian refugees, they chose not to risk war with the Soviet Union.

The Cold War Spreads

During the two decades following World War II, despite the U.S. strategy of containment, communism made bold advances around the world. A revolutionary leader brought communism to the Western Hemisphere—indeed, right to the doorstep of the United States—in Cuba, an island nation only ninety miles from Florida. As communism spread, Cold War tensions heightened, and the world came perilously close to nuclear disaster.

Key Questions

• What developments and policies led to an arms race between the United States and the USSR?

• Where did Cold War conflicts erupt into fighting? What were the consequences of these conflicts?

• What was détente, and how did it affect the progress of the Cold War?

The Arms Race

One reason the United States and the Soviet Union hesitated to plunge into full-scale war was that the use of atomic bombs in World War II had dramatically increased the stakes of war. In 1949, the West was alarmed by the news that the Soviet Union had successfully detonated an atomic bomb of its own. American scientists responded by building a bomb a thousand times more powerful than the one dropped on Hiroshima. In 1952, when scientists tested the first hydrogen bomb, or "H-bomb," on an uninhabited island in the Pacific, they were stunned to find that it destroyed the island and spread deadly radiation for hundreds of miles. Within a year, the Soviets succeeded in building hydrogen bombs as well.

The two superpowers were soon engaged in an **arms race**. Both the United States and the Soviet Union built enormous arsenals of nuclear weapons that could destroy not just each other, but the entire planet many times over. Each side engaged in **deterrence**, a defensive strategy that aimed to prevent an enemy from attacking out of fear of the consequences. Each superpower understood that if it launched a nuclear attack, the other superpower would undertake "massive retaliation," that is, the other side would respond with its own devastating nuclear counterattack.

American and Soviet leaders began to speak of "mutual assured destruction" (MAD), the idea that the prospect of mutual annihilation would keep the superpowers from taking the world into nuclear catastrophe. According to this strategy, the buildup of nuclear arms was necessary to maintain a tense and fragile peace. The problem with MAD, however, was that each superpower felt it could be safe only if its military was as powerful as—or more powerful than—the other's. So each side raced to build more, and more powerful, weapons.

The Berlin Wall

In 1956, Soviet troops and tanks crushed a budding revolution in Hungary. Five years later, one of the most infamous and hated symbols of the Cold War took shape in Berlin.

In 1961, Berlin was two cities. West Berlin, which lay deep inside East Germany, was a pocket of freedom and prosperity behind the Iron Curtain. Since the end of World War II, West Berlin had been protected by Britain, France, and the United States. Most of the wreckage of war had been replaced by busy streets lined with office buildings, shops, cafes, hotels, and theaters.

In contrast, East Berlin was a drab city full of empty storefronts and buildings scarred by World War II. Refrigerators, washing machines, and cars—fairly common in West Berlin—were luxuries in East Berlin, possessed by only a few top Communist Party officials. But worse than their lack of material comforts, East Berliners had few political freedoms.

East Berliners were allowed access to the city's western sector, where many friends and family members lived. It was easy to walk into West Berlin—and, if one chose, simply not return. The East German and Soviet governments watched as, year after year, hundreds of thousands of East Germans fled to West Berlin seeking freedom and economic opportunity.

Facing the prospect of an economic collapse, with Soviet approval the East German government

A guard on the western side of the Berlin Wall looks toward his counterpart in the eastern sector.

acted out of desperation. In the early morning hours of August 13, 1961, soldiers of the East German army quietly moved up to the boundary between the eastern and western sectors of the divided city. Some began driving long metal stakes into the ground while others unrolled spools of barbed wire. By daybreak East Berliners found themselves cut off from West Berlin. Within days, the barbed wire fence had given way to a concrete barrier, a wall guarded by soldiers with orders to shoot anyone attempting to cross it.

The leader of the Soviet Union, Nikita Khrushchev, watched to see how the United States would respond. President John F. Kennedy mobilized military reserve units and reinforced the brigade of American troops in West Berlin. But he was not prepared to risk war with the Soviet Union by demolishing the Berlin Wall. The president decided that, in this case, he could tolerate the situation. "It's not a very nice solution," he said, "but a wall is a hell of a lot better than a war." Kennedy's response led Khrushchev to conclude that the American president was timid and indecisive.

Crisis in Cuba

In 1960, the Soviet Union and China were the two most powerful communist nations in the world. (In a later chapter you will read about the communist revolution in China.) Many smaller

The Berlin Wall, 1961

North Sea

NETHERLANDS

Berlin enlarged below right

EAST GERMANY

POLAND

WEST GERMANY

BELGIUM

CZECHOSLOVAKIA

FRANCE

WEST | EAST

SWITZERLAND

BERLIN

☐ Communist countries
☐ Noncommunist countries
— Berlin Wall

In 1961, the East German army built a wall to contain East Berlin, and East Berliners, cutting off access to West Berlin.

nations were also governed by communist regimes, including the Caribbean island of Cuba, ruled by a strong-willed dictator, Fidel Castro.

Castro's Rise to Power

Before Castro rose to power, Cuba had been ruled by a corrupt and brutal dictator, Fulgencio Batista (buh-TEE-stuh). The United States supported Batista because he helped protect American interests on the island. Even after Cuba gained independence from Spain in 1898, the United States maintained a dominant hand in Cuban affairs. American companies owned most of the island's arable land, as well as many of its utilities and railroads. In the 1950s, half of Cuba's sugar exports went to the United States.

Arable land is land good for growing crops.

Many Cubans resented that some Americans had become rich by doing business in Cuba while much of the island's population remained poor. These facts of Cuban life—widespread poverty under the rule of a dictator with American backing—convinced a young Fidel Castro that the solution to Cuba's problems lay in revolution. On New Year's Day 1959, the capital city of Havana fell to Castro's rebel forces and Batista fled the country.

Although Castro had fought to overthrow a dictator, he had no intention of becoming a democratic leader. He executed and imprisoned his opponents. He established a communist regime with the government controlling the economy. Castro's government seized all major companies, starting with those owned by Americans. Such actions won him the friendship of the Soviet Union, which promised economic and military aid. He won the support of many Cubans by introducing health care and schools across the island.

The Bay of Pigs

The leaders of the United States were alarmed to see a communist regime so close by. Soon after taking office, President Kennedy approved a secret plan for the invasion of Cuba. The invasion force would not consist of U.S. soldiers, because a direct American attack against Castro might provoke the Soviet Union to respond. Instead, the United States armed and trained a force of some fifteen hundred Cuban exiles who had fled Castro's dictatorship. The Americans hoped the exiles would inspire the Cuban people to rise up and overthrow Castro.

In April 1961, the small army of Cuban exiles left Nicaragua and landed on the southern coast of Cuba at a place called the Bay of Pigs. But Castro had been tipped off about their arrival. He attacked with troops, planes, and Soviet-made tanks. The United States had promised air support for the exiles, but at the last minute Kennedy changed his mind, fearing that it might expose the U.S. role. Within three days, nearly all the invaders had been killed or captured.

The Bay of Pigs disaster humiliated Kennedy and the United States. The attack caused no uprising against Castro; in fact, it had the opposite effect. Many Cubans rallied around their leader and cheered his defiance of the United States.

The Cuban Missile Crisis

Impressed by Castro's defiance of the United States, Khrushchev decided the Soviet Union should give Cuba its full support. He reasoned that supporting Cuba would help equalize the balance of power between the United States and the Soviet Union. The Americans possessed many more nuclear weapons than the

Fidel Castro led a rebel army to overthrow Cuba's U.S.-backed dictator in 1959, then set up his own dictatorship.

This photograph, taken in the fall of 1962 from an American spy plane, confirmed that the Soviets were building missile launch sites in Cuba.

Soviets, and had missiles pointing at the Soviet Union from nearby Turkey. Khrushchev decided to station Soviet nuclear missiles in Cuba, only ninety miles (145 km) from the United States.

In October 1962, an American spy plane photographed nuclear missile sites under construction in Cuba. Construction at some of the locations was just days away from completion. When finished, the sites would be able to launch nuclear missiles that could hit cities in the United States within minutes.

Some of President Kennedy's advisers urged him to bomb the missile sites before they were ready for use. Some argued that the United States should invade Cuba. Others warned that an American attack on Cuba might lead to nuclear war.

Kennedy ordered a naval blockade around Cuba to prevent weapons from reaching the island, and to pressure the Soviets to dismantle the existing missile sites. In a televised speech on October 22, 1962, Kennedy said, "I call upon Chairman Khrushchev to halt and eliminate this clandestine, reckless, and provocative threat to world

Clandestine means done in a secretive, hidden way.

peace." Khrushchev responded that the naval blockade of Cuba was "an act of aggression." He warned that while the USSR would not start a nuclear war, "if the U.S. insists on war, we'll all meet together in hell."

As the crisis deepened, Americans stocked up on food and emergency supplies. Schools held air-raid drills. Millions of city dwellers, believing they lived in a nuclear target, left their homes and fled to the countryside.

Behind the scenes, Soviet and American officials negotiated frantically. At the end of October, the Soviets backed down. They agreed to remove their missiles from Cuba if America would end the blockade and pledge not to invade the island. But Khrushchev gained something he wanted, too. Kennedy had secretly agreed to withdraw U.S. missiles from Turkey.

The tense standoff between the superpowers in the Cuban Missile Crisis had an unexpected result. It led to a thaw in relations between the

In a "duck-and-cover" drill, American schoolchildren practice how to protect themselves during a nuclear attack.

United States and the Soviet Union. Frightened by their journey to the nuclear brink, the two nations began talks to limit the use of nuclear weapons. Of those two weeks in October 1962, one historian has written, "The Cuban Missile Crisis was the most dangerous event in human history."

Cold War "Worlds"

The Cold War was waged around the world, pitting capitalism against communism, the West against the East. As the Cold War proceeded, journalists and politicians began to refer to the "first world" and the "second world." By *first world*, they meant industrialized, capitalist nations—the United States and its Western European allies. By *second world*, they meant the communist or socialist industrial states, encompassing the Soviet Union and Eastern Bloc nations.

There were also many developing nations, not yet industrialized, that generally had a low standard of living. Many of these so-called *third world* nations were in Asia, Africa, and Latin America. Many had long been colonies ruled by European nations, but after World War II, the war-ravaged European nations could no longer enforce their rule of distant territories. In many of these lands, nationalists stirred the desire for independence.

The United States and the Soviet Union began to compete for influence in third world nations. Both superpowers sought to build economic, cultural, and military ties to the countries emerging from colonial rule. Competition for their loyalty and their resources sometimes led to armed

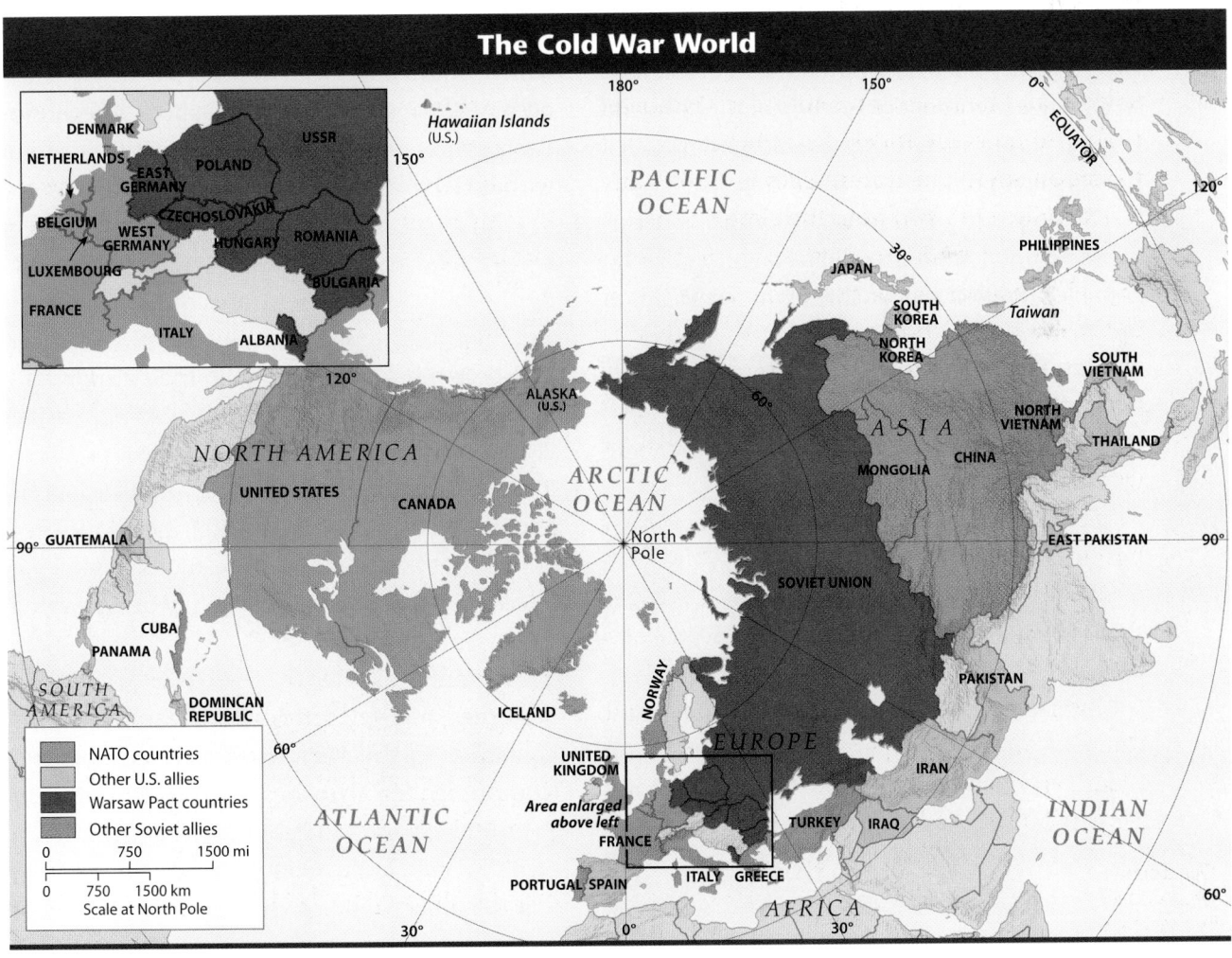

The rivalry between the United States and the Soviet Union extended to their allies around the globe.

769

conflicts among forces supported by the United States or the Soviet Union, though the two superpowers never engaged in direct, head-to-head conflict. (In later chapters you will learn how the Cold War was conducted in Southeast Asia, Latin America, and elsewhere.)

During the Cold War, some nations tried to avoid taking sides with either the United States or the Soviet Union. These nonaligned nations, as they were called, included India and Indonesia. They worked to promote the interests of poorer and developing nations.

Prague Spring

During the late 1960s, Soviet leaders faced a challenge within one of the countries behind the Iron Curtain, Czechoslovakia. In 1968, Alexander Dubček (DOOB-chek) was elected to lead Czechoslovakia. He began a program of reforms that he called "socialism with a human face." He aimed to loosen government censorship of the press and popular culture, and to increase citizens' participation in party politics.

To Western observers, Dubček's reforms appeared mild. At no time did he question Czechoslovakia's position as a satellite of the Soviet Union.

A Czech protester mounts an invading Russian tank in Prague in August 1968.

Nevertheless, his measures had an electrifying effect at home and abroad. In the Czech capital, Prague, and in other cities, students and intellectuals rejoiced at the prospect of more freedom. Some bold voices even dared to speak out against the Communist Party. The general air of excitement and optimism that swept Czechoslovakia at this time became known as the Prague Spring.

Soviet leaders were worried by what was happening in Czechoslovakia. Leonid Brezhnev (BREZH-nef), who had replaced Khrushchev as the Soviet Union's leader, said that Dubček's reforms were "a bad program, opening up possibilities for the restoration of capitalism in Czechoslovakia."

At midnight on August 21, 1968, half a million Soviet and other Warsaw Pact troops crossed the Czech border. Long columns of tanks headed for Prague. The Czech army did not put up a fight, which would have been hopeless. The Red Army occupied Prague and arrested Dubček. Czechoslovakia's brief experiment with political freedom withered, crushed by Soviet military might.

Détente and Arms Control

By the early 1970s, the strains of the Cold War weighed on the world's two superpowers. The race between them to build up their armies and nuclear arsenals had proven terribly expensive. Leaders in the United States and USSR began to look for ways to slow the buildup of nuclear arms and ease tensions between their two countries. This effort to establish better relations was known as *détente* (day-TAHNT), a French word meaning "easing" or "relaxation."

Beginning in 1969, the United States and USSR began negotiations known as the Strategic Arms Limitation Talks (SALT). Three years later, the two sides signed SALT treaties that placed limits on the numbers and kinds of nuclear missiles each country could build. Critics on each side worried that the other would not stick to its promises. But supporters of détente viewed the SALT treaties as progress in thawing Cold War tensions.

The Western Democracies in the Postwar Era

Key Questions

- What characterized the American economy and American society during the 1950s and 1960s?

- What political and economic changes shaped Western Europe in the postwar era?

Even during the tense Cold War years, the United States had much to celebrate. The 1950s and 1960s brought unprecedented economic growth that spurred tremendous national confidence. But beneath the surface of these apparent "happy days" lurked new social pressures and problems.

At the same time, European nations struggled to rebuild after the war. With American aid, many of them made quick and dramatic progress.

The United States in the Postwar Years

Just after World War II ended, the United States faced the challenge of accommodating some twelve million veterans returning home to find housing shortages, inflation, and limited job opportunities. Many Americans feared high unemployment and a possible financial crisis. But the American economy bounced back quickly and optimism replaced worry.

A Booming American Economy

There were several reasons for the postwar economic boom in the United States. While the war had devastated many industrialized nations—including England, Germany, and Japan—the United States was spared. American manufacturers soon profited from brisk international trade. At the same time, consumers were eager to buy. During the war years, rationing had placed limits on what Americans could buy. Now, with the war over, they wanted to buy cars, houses, and appliances. When factories shifted back to peacetime production, spending shot up.

During the Cold War, the U.S. government continued to fund both military and business efforts to strengthen security. The government also boosted the economy by passing what was called the GI Bill. The new law granted monetary assistance to help veterans get back on their feet. It also offered business and mortgage loans, as well as tuition money to help veterans reenter civilian life. The GI Bill helped promote the greatest expansion of the middle class in the history of the United States.

During the Great Depression and the war, many young couples had postponed starting families. After the war, however, as people felt more economically secure, the United States experienced a "baby boom," a dramatic postwar surge in population growth. Between 1945 and 1960, the U.S. population increased by almost 30 percent. New families demanded appliances, diapers, clothes, and toys, as well as schools and houses.

In the postwar United States, many families moved to suburbs, "cookie-cutter" housing developments on former farmland outside cities. Without buses or streetcars to take them to work or shopping, suburbanites met their needs by buying automobiles. In 1950, 59 percent of American families owned a car. Just five years later, that number was 70 percent. Bigger, sleeker cars became status symbols. The American car culture came to include drive-ins, motels, and interstate highways.

Cold War Fears

The economic surge of the 1950s, as well as America's new position as the most powerful nation in the world, made many Americans optimistic about the future. But the Cold War threat of nuclear war and the spread of communism stirred fear even in the midst of good times.

In 1947, President Truman ordered that all government employees undergo background checks. The investigations revealed little information of concern, but Cold War tensions still fueled widespread suspicion of communist spies in the United States. Many states required teachers to take loyalty oaths, and school materials were scrutinized for content that seemed "un-American."

Fear of communism inspired a "red scare" that infected American politics with a witch-hunt mentality. Congress began to investigate individuals and groups suspected of being communists or communist sympathizers, even though there was no law against belonging to the Communist Party. The movie industry came under intense scrutiny due to its broad influence on the public and because of widespread rumors of communist activity among many actors and screenwriters in Hollywood. During congressional hearings, several witnesses were jailed for contempt when they refused to answer questions, though they had broken no laws. Many careers were ruined by mere rumors of communist leanings, and a frightened film industry began to churn out bland but safe movies.

Senator Joseph McCarthy became famous for accusing prominent people and institutions of collaborating with communists. He called the Roosevelt and Truman administrations "twenty years of treason" and pressured many federal employees to resign. McCarthy claimed to have a list of government workers who were communists and spies. In reality, there was no such list, nor was there any evidence of widespread spying or communist leanings in the government.

In 1954, televised hearings exposed McCarthy for what he was—a fraud, a bully, and a demagogue (a politician who tries to rouse passions and prejudices). By this time, McCarthy had ruined many lives and trampled on peoples' constitutional rights. The term "McCarthyism" is still used to describe any use of reckless accusations against others for political gain.

The Power of Television

Around 1940, people stood outside store windows to watch black-and-white images on the screens of the new medium of television. In 1946, about 7,000 American homes had televisions; by 1950, there were 10 million TV sets in the United States. The few national networks broadcast news, sports, and popular shows such as *Ozzie and Harriet* and *Leave It to Beaver*. These programs spread an image of America as a land of white, middle-class, affluent families. The reality, of course, was more complex.

An American family watching television, c. 1950

With stirring words, Martin Luther King, Jr., addressed a sea of eager listeners on August 28, 1963, in Washington, D.C.

The Civil Rights Movement in the United States

Most African Americans and other minorities did not share in the postwar prosperity. Many employers refused to hire blacks. Most of the new suburban developments refused to sell homes to African Americans or other minorities. Schools across the South were segregated. Professional sports and the entertainment industry were all but closed to blacks. Starting in the late 1940s, however, some bold leaders initiated a nonviolent revolution that, in the 1950s and 1960s, brought

the United States closer to the realization of equal rights for all.

During World War II, African Americans by the thousands had left the rural South to take war industry jobs in northern cities. By the time the war was over, their expectations of their country had changed. Moreover, tens of thousands of African Americans had served honorably during World War II, though they were restricted to segregated units. After the war, President Harry Truman desegregated the armed forces.

In 1954, the U.S. Supreme Court ruled in the case of *Brown v. the Board of Education of Topeka* that segregation in public schools was unconstitutional. It would be years before employment and education throughout the nation were integrated, but the *Brown* decision set the stage for major changes.

A young African American minister, Martin Luther King, Jr., emerged as an inspiring leader of the civil rights movement in the 1950s and '60s. King came to national prominence when, in 1956, he led a successful boycott to change the segregationist policies on public buses in Montgomery, Alabama. King then took on discrimination in public facilities, jobs, housing, and

Protesters calling for voting rights marched from Selma to Montgomery, Alabama, in 1965.

773

The United States Exports Popular Culture

In the decades after World War II, technologies such as television, satellites, radio, and movies made it possible for people around the world to listen to the same music, see the same shows, share the same slang, and adopt the same styles of dress. The United States, with its booming economy, exported rock and roll, Hollywood movies, Coca-Cola, and much else that became part of a popular culture that crossed boundaries and spread around the globe.

voting rights. A brilliant speaker, he advocated nonviolent tactics and won support from whites as well as blacks.

It would take the combined efforts of remarkable black leaders, ordinary black citizens, sympathetic white citizens, and the commitment of the federal government to integrate American society. In 1964 and 1965, President Lyndon Johnson, a white Democrat from Texas, pushed Congress to pass the Civil Rights and Voting Rights acts, the most sweeping civil rights legislation in the United States since the end of slavery a century earlier.

The growing success of the civil rights movement inspired Americans of many races and backgrounds. Latinos, Asian Americans, Native Americans, and other minorities organized to demand rights and opportunities. Discrimination, though no longer legal, continued in some regions, and prejudice, poverty, and unemployment persisted. But the power of the vote and the force of law brought progress.

American women demanded equal rights as well. The women's movement of the 1960s and '70s was in part a reaction to the social pressures of the 1950s, when women were encouraged to marry and become full-time homemakers. Television, movies, and advertising reinforced conformity to this domestic ideal of the perfect middle-class housewife. Many women who had entered the workforce during World War II felt limited by the restrictions they faced in jobs and education after the war. By the 1960s, many of these women were working to achieve social and economic equality with men.

The demand for equality grew when protestors for women's rights took to the streets of New York City in 1971.

Young demonstrators raise a peace symbol at a rally against the war in Vietnam.

Decades of Unrest

By the 1960s, the United States faced economic competition as manufacturers in other countries began making cars, steel, electronics, and other goods. Inflation, the rapid rise in the cost of goods, hurt consumers' ability to buy new products. While the growing computer industry prospered, many industrial jobs in the United States were lost.

The United States was embroiled in conflict in the late 1960s. Racial and economic tensions erupted in riots in a number of cities, and thousands protested U.S. military actions in Southeast Asia (which you will read about in a later chapter).

In the early 1970s, international political conflict spurred the world's petroleum-producing nations to double the price of oil for the United States and other Western nations. The American economy, already sputtering, fell into a period of inflation and high unemployment. Economic stress, coupled with cultural and racial unrest, shook the nation's confidence.

Canada in the Postwar Years

Like the United States, Canada was spared the destruction of World War II, and like the United States experienced a postwar economic boom. Manufacturing increased, as did production of mineral resources.

Canada's population increased dramatically, partly from a postwar baby boom, and partly through immigration. New industries demanded workers, and Canada's government actively encouraged immigration from eastern and southern Europe, where war refugees were eager to start new lives. For the first time, a significant number of Canadians came from backgrounds that were not English or French.

Canada's changing cultural and political landscape presented challenges throughout the 1960s and '70s. The women's movement grew stronger. Members of Canada's First Nations, or Native Americans, demanded a greater voice in government. French-speaking Canadians demanded recognition and protection of their culture and status in a changing nation.

Western Europe Recovers

As World War II ended, Western European democracies faced a far different situation than that which confronted North Americans. Many cities, especially in Germany, had been reduced to rubble. Farmland was barren. Hundreds of thousands of people were homeless, separated from family, malnourished, and traumatized. Yet by 1960, most nations in Western Europe had not only recovered from the war, but managed to achieve a higher standard of living than ever before.

Economic Recovery

The European Recovery Program known as the Marshall Plan helped rebuild war-torn Europe. By 1951, the United States had sent $13 billion in food, fuel, machinery, and money to rebuild cities, factories, and economies across Western Europe. The Soviet Union refused to allow Eastern Bloc countries to accept any aid.

The Marshall Plan was a driving force in Western Europe's rapid economic recovery, as well as in fueling the economic boom in the United States, since American companies supplied the materials and food that went to Europe. The Marshall Plan aided U.S. allies, including France and Britain.

Even with aid, Britain faced great challenges. Its factories, mines, and railroads were outdated and in disrepair. The government had borrowed heavily to finance the war, but it had no way to repay its debt. The country could not produce enough food itself, and even with loans from the United States and Canada could not afford to import sufficient food for the British people. With aid from the Marshall Plan, Britain's economy was recovering by the mid-1950s.

The Marshall Plan also extended aid to West Germany. The newly elected democratic government of West Germany oversaw the building of modern, efficient industrial centers. In short order, West Germany was able to end rationing and put the German people back to work in what became known as Germany's "economic miracle."

The Changing Role of Government in Western Europe

Many European nations expanded their government-sponsored social welfare programs during the Great Depression. This trend continued after World War II. In Britain, the government took control of the failing railroads and coal mines. It also established a national health service that provided medical care for all citizens. France took similar measures. Most other Western European democracies also established government-supported health care systems or national health insurance. They also expanded unemployment insurance and old-age pensions, as well as aid to the poor.

Critics argued that these measures were too costly, and by the 1970s and '80s some European countries began to scale back their social programs. As the twentieth century ended, in an attempt to control government spending, some European nations also returned nationalized industries to the private sector.

The European Union

As Western Europe struggled to rebuild, several nations decided to work together for economic progress. In 1951, six nations—France, the Netherlands, Belgium, West Germany, Luxembourg, and Italy—signed a treaty eliminating trade restrictions, such as tariffs on coal, iron ore, steel, and other resources. The European Coal and Steel Community (ECSC) helped spur economy recovery.

The success of the ECSC in promoting economic growth led in 1957 to another treaty. The same six nations that had formed the ECSC organized as the European Economic Community, and agreed to eliminate most restrictions on trade among the members. They also agreed to make it easier for workers in one country to take jobs or do business in another country. During the 1970s and '80s, several more European countries, including the United Kingdom, joined what was known as the Common Market.

By the early 1990s, the Common Market had evolved to include more nations and more issues of shared concern. In 1992, those nations formed the European Union (EU). The EU eliminated tariffs and quotas on trade among member nations, set common security policies across Western Europe, and promoted shared standards for environmental protection. Despite resistance and anxiety, the EU also established a common currency for most member nations. The euro replaced Italy's lira, France's franc, and Germany's mark. In 2010, twenty-seven nations were members of the EU.

One euro, the common currency of the European Union

Beyond the Cold War

The Western democracies recovered quickly after World War II. Most experienced tremendous economic prosperity and, by the 1960s, greater political and social freedom. But the communist nations behind the Iron Curtain struggled economically and denied their people the most basic freedoms.

Key Questions

- Why was the Soviet economy failing by the 1970s?

- What key causes led to the end of the Cold War and the end of communism in Europe?

- What challenges did the former Soviet Union and the nations of Eastern Europe face after their communist regimes collapsed?

Dissatisfaction in the Communist Bloc

While West Germans benefited from their nation's "economic miracle," their neighbors and relatives in communist East Germany struggled to get by. People behind the Iron Curtain saw that communism had failed in its promise to improve workers' lives. In Poland, for example, as payment for long hours in coal mines or shipyards, workers received only ration cards to buy limited consumer goods and inadequate food.

In Eastern Europe, the struggle to get by was compounded by lack of freedom. Thousands of people across Eastern Europe and the Soviet Union were sent to prison camps on the slightest suspicion of disloyalty. Travel was severely restricted, and freedom of religion and speech were nonexistent.

Despite the risks, some dissidents boldly challenged the policies of repressive governments. One of the most powerful dissident voices was that of Alexander Solzhenitsyn (sohl-zhuh-NEET-suhn), who was imprisoned for criticizing Stalin in a personal letter to a friend. After eight years of hard labor in Siberia, he began writing novels about the abuses he had seen and experienced. In *The Gulag Archipelago* (1973), Solzhenitsyn exposed the cruelties of the Soviet police state. After the Soviet government exiled Solzhenitsyn, he lived first in Switzerland and then the United States. His writings, as well as the writings of other dissidents, were smuggled behind the Iron Curtain, where they inspired many people in the growing drive against communism.

A *dissident* is one who disagrees, especially one who challenges the government in power.

More Voices Against Communism

In 1975, representatives of the United States, the Soviet Union, and several other nations signed the Helsinki Accords. These agreements recognized the Soviet Union's control in Eastern Europe, but also required the signing nations to respect "the universal significance of human rights and fundamental freedoms."

People in Soviet-dominated nations formed "Helsinki groups" and demanded that the Soviet Union live up to the promise of "human rights and fundamental freedoms." In Czechoslovakia, a group of writers, artists, and intellectuals drafted a manifesto insisting that the Czech government honor rights of free expression. Although several members of the group were sent to prison, their efforts made the world aware that Soviet-controlled governments were flagrantly violating human rights.

In 1978, a new leader joined the Cold War struggle when the Roman Catholic Church chose Karol Jozef Wojtyla (voy-TEE-wah), an archbishop from Poland, as pope. Pope John Paul II did not directly challenge the communist authorities, but he insisted that communism should not take away people's basic rights, including the right to worship. The pope's message of freedom inspired millions living behind the Iron Curtain.

Solidarity in Poland

In the summer of 1980, Poland's communist government announced that it was raising the price of meat by as much as 100 percent. Across the country, angry workers went on strike to protest the increase. At the Lenin Shipyard in the port city of Gdansk (guh-DAHNSK), workers joined the strike, and then went further. A young unemployed electrician named Lech Walesa (lehk va-WEN-suh) announced the formation of a trade union called Solidarity.

For the first time, a worker's union had formed in opposition to the government of what was supposed to be a worker's state. Solidarity demanded increased pay and better working conditions. The union also called for political changes, such as greater freedom of worship and an end to censorship. Solidarity eventually enlisted millions of members and evolved into a home for all those who hated Poland's communist government. Lech Walesa emerged as the spokesman for a nation of Poles eager for freedom.

The Polish government banned Solidarity and proclaimed martial law. Lech Walesa and thousands of others were arrested. "This is the moment of your defeat," Walesa defiantly told the officials who arrested him. "These are the last nails into the coffin of communism."

The Decline of the Soviet Union

Soviet leaders were rattled by economic stagnation and challenges to Soviet authority in the Eastern Bloc. By 1980, the Soviet Union faced other problems as well.

South of the Soviet republics of Turkmenistan and Tajikistan lay the independent country of Afghanistan. In the late 1970s, communists in Afghanistan, with aid and support from the USSR, launched a coup and took over Afghanistan's government. The new Marxist regime adopted atheism as its official policy and imprisoned many religious leaders. Most Afghan Muslims opposed the communist government's atheistic policies, and they resented the Soviet Union's domination. Nationalist Muslim

Cheering shipyard workers at Gdansk, Poland, carry Lech Walesa, leader of the trade union Solidarity, founded in 1980.

Afghan rebels, called mujahideen, stand atop a destroyed Soviet helicopter.

rebels known as *mujahideen* (moo-ja-hih-DEEN) took up arms against the Afghan communists.

In 1979, the Soviet Union sent an army to occupy Afghanistan and battle the mujahideen. The war became a nightmare and an embarrassment for the powerful Soviet military. The Afghan rebels—supplied with weapons and money from the United States and other nations—used guerrilla tactics against the Soviet invaders. Striking from hideouts in vast, mountainous regions, they ambushed Soviet troops and bombed Soviet garrisons.

President Jimmy Carter of the United States denounced the Soviet invasion of Afghanistan. The United States cut back on trade with the Soviet Union and refused to allow U.S. athletes to take part in the 1980 Olympic Games in Moscow. Détente faltered as tensions between the two superpowers increased. Perhaps more important, the Soviet Union found itself spending vast sums of money it could not afford on a war it could not win.

Ronald Reagan Confronts Communism

In 1980, voters in the United States elected Ronald Reagan as president. Reagan had been a movie

and television actor and, for a time, president of the Screen Actors Guild in Hollywood. Eventually he entered politics and became a firm anticommunist.

As president, Reagan was determined to change the Cold War policy of détente, which he considered a failure because it had done little to halt the nuclear arms race or the spread of communism. Reagan made it clear that he wanted to do more to prevent the spread of communism. He told an adviser, "My idea of American policy toward the Soviet Union is simple.... We win and they lose."

In an address to the British Parliament in 1982, Reagan declared that the Soviet Union could not survive because its totalitarian government was crushing its own people's spirit by robbing them of their basic rights and freedoms. Britain's new prime minister, Margaret Thatcher, agreed, and the two soon worked closely to confront the spread of totalitarianism.

Reagan began a spending program to build up the military strength of the United States. The increased spending, combined with a series of tax

A budget *deficit* occurs when government spending exceeds income.

cuts, resulted in huge budget **deficits**. But Reagan's strategy put even greater strains on the much weaker Soviet economy, as the Soviets struggled to keep up with the U.S. military buildup.

Gorbachev Tries "Restructuring"

In 1985, Mikhail Gorbachev (mih-kah-EEL gawr-buh-CHAWF) took the helm in the Soviet Union as head of the Communist Party. Gorbachev was known as an energetic enemy of corruption and inefficiency. He recognized that the clumsy, government-controlled Soviet economy was in shambles, and understood that his country must either reform or collapse.

Gorbachev advocated changes to make the Soviet system work more efficiently. He called for *perestroika* (pehr-uh-STROY-kuh), a Russian word that means "restructuring." He wanted to restructure the Soviet economy to give local officials more power to make their own production decisions.

Even bolder than perestroika was Gorbachev's call for *glasnost* (GLAZ-nohst), meaning "openness, candor, transparency." In Gorbachev's view, Soviet citizens should be allowed to speak more openly about their society's problems. He believed that the government needed to stop trying to control ideas and speech. He called for an end to such practices as banning books and throwing dissidents into prison.

Gorbachev was desperate to cut back his nation's military spending. Compared to the United States, the USSR put a far greater percentage of government spending into its military, but the Soviets were still falling behind in military technology, and the ongoing war in Afghanistan continued to drain resources.

In 1986, Reagan and Gorbachev held a summit in Reykjavik (RAY-kyuh-vihk), the capital of Iceland. Gorbachev offered to make major weapons cutbacks if the United States would do the same. Reagan responded with a breathtaking proposal—that both sides eliminate *all* nuclear weapons in ten years. In the end, the two leaders left Reykjavik without an agreement, but with the beginnings of a shared vision of abolishing nuclear arms. The Reykjavik summit, said Gorbachev, "for the first time enabled us to look over the horizon."

New Directions

Reagan believed that Gorbachev sincerely wanted to reform the Soviet Union. The two men developed a solid working relationship as no other Cold War leaders had before. But the American president also realized that, despite perestroika and glasnost, the Soviet Union continued to deny basic human rights to millions.

In June 1987, near the Berlin Wall, Reagan gave a speech that was broadcast across Western Europe. "General Secretary Gorbachev," said Reagan, "if you seek peace, if you seek prosperity for the Soviet Union and Eastern Europe, if you seek liberalization: Come here to this gate! Mr. Gorbachev, open this gate! Mr. Gorbachev, tear down this wall!"

Gorbachev did not tear down the Berlin Wall. But he continued on the path of reform, and he kept talking with Reagan. Gorbachev was not looking to overthrow the Soviet regime or attack socialism. He hoped to energize the system and make it more effective in a modern setting. He

Mikhail Gorbachev, Soviet reformer and perestroika advocate, is greeted by well-wishers in Czechoslovakia in April 1987.

President Ronald Reagan's call to tear down the Berlin Wall was greeted with applause by many who heard it.

munist nations that they could make their own decisions, and even spoke of the right of all people to choose their governments.

Hungary Tests the USSR

The first country to test Gorbachev's spirit of openness was Hungary, a nation with a long history of confrontation with the Soviets. In 1956, when Hungarians had marched to demand more freedom, the Soviets had responded by sending tanks to crush the rebellion. In January 1989, Hungary's parliament voted to allow independent political parties. Such a change would bring an end to the Communist Party's lock on power. This time, the Soviet response was very different. No tanks appeared. Instead, Soviet troops began to leave the country.

The Hungarians then wrote a new constitution allowing free elections. They also opened their border with democratic Austria. Suddenly, a new way to the West and the free world was open. Thousands of East Germans began traveling to Hungary, then crossed the border into Austria, and from there made their way to West Germany. This was no mere trickle of people—it was, almost immediately, a stampede through a widening rip in the Iron Curtain.

realized that it was becoming impossible for Moscow to maintain control over so many millions of unwilling people. He wanted, he later said, to change the Soviet regime "so a human being can feel normal, can feel good, in a socialist state. So that he will feel above all like a human being."

In December 1988, Gorbachev addressed the United Nations General Assembly and delivered a stunning announcement. The Soviet Union had decided to cut its troops in Eastern Europe by half a million men. While the move would loosen the Soviet grip on its satellite states, it would also bring economic relief because, as Gorbachev saw it, the USSR was being drained by its domination of Eastern Europe. In his address to the United Nations, Gorbachev came close to telling the com-

The Fall of Communism in Europe

In November 1989, the East German government decided to relax travel restrictions to the West. At a press conference, an official read a hastily written decree announcing the changes. When surprised reporters asked when the new rules were to take effect, the spokesman, who didn't really know, stammered, "Immediately." When asked if the new rules applied to travel to West Berlin, the official shrugged, and replied that "permanent exit can take place via all border crossings."

Before almost anyone knew what was happening, word spread that the Berlin Wall was open, even though it was not. Throngs of East Berliners rushed to the Berlin Wall. Unsuspecting border guards, bewildered by the turn of events and the

An East German citizen slams a hole in the newly opened Berlin Wall, the hated symbol of communist oppression. East and West Germany were united in 1990.

huge crowd, opened the gates. Soon thousands of East Berliners stood on the west side of the wall, many for the first time in their lives. West Berliners rushed to embrace them in delirious celebration. People grabbed picks, chisels, and hammers, and began to knock away small pieces of the wall.

East German officials realized that there was no turning back. In a matter of days, bulldozers were dismantling the hated symbol of oppression. Totalitarianism in East Germany crumbled along with the wall. On March 18, 1990, East Germans voted the Communists out of office. Soviet troops began to depart.

The Cold War was over. Less than two years later, the Eastern Bloc was gone and the nations of Eastern Europe had democratically elected leaders, including Lech Walesa, the new president of Poland.

The USSR Dissolves

In most of the countries that Moscow had once dominated, Mikhail Gorbachev gained immense popularity. But in the Soviet Union itself, many viewed Gorbachev as a failure. Perestroika, his attempt at economic reform, had not created prosperity. On the contrary, the Soviet economy was in ruins as the Soviet empire fell apart.

Gorbachev's political opponents staged a coup and placed him under house arrest. He was released after three days, but he had lost much of his power. Moscow was dominated by a new figure, Boris Yeltsin, the president of the state of Russia. Yeltsin had his own goals—to abolish the Communist Party, dissolve the Soviet Union, and turn Russia into an independent, capitalist state.

By the end of the year, the Soviet Union was indeed dissolving. Regions such as Ukraine, Georgia, Armenia, and Kazakhstan broke away to become new republics, free to form their own governments.

On Christmas Day 1991, seventy-four years after the Russian Revolution brought communism to the world stage, Mikhail Gorbachev signed the decree that officially brought an end to the Union of Soviet Socialist Republics.

New Struggles

Much of the world celebrated the end of the Cold War and the collapse of communist governments in Europe. But serious challenges remained.

Among former Eastern Bloc countries, the most successful transitions to democracy were made by European countries such as Latvia, Estonia, and Lithuania, which had enjoyed democratic institutions before they were conquered by the Soviet Union at the close of World War II. In contrast, central Asian countries such as Kazakhstan, Uzbekistan, and Turkmenistan had had no experience

Collapse of European Communism, 1989–1991

Legend:
- Former Soviet republics
- Former Czechoslovakia
- Former Yugoslavia
- Former East Germany
- Other former communist countries

The collapse of the Soviet Union led to the independence of the Warsaw Pact nations of Eastern Europe and the creation of several new countries.

of popular decision making or respect for human rights. In those nations, former communist leaders persecuted their political opponents and rigged elections to keep themselves in power.

Yugoslavia, an Eastern European nation on the Balkan Peninsula, collapsed into civil war. The war was in part the result of tensions that had simmered since Yugoslavia was founded at the end of World War I, when different ethnic groups, with a history of antagonism, were yoked together to form one nation. Ethnic Serbs had dominated the country's communist government and tried to hold the nation together. But after communism fell, different parts of Yugoslavia, each with a dominant ethnic group as its majority, declared independence. In the conflict that followed, ethnic and religious groups—including Orthodox Christian Serbs, Muslim Bosnians, and Catholic Croats—attacked one another in a bloody attempt at "ethnic cleansing" to rid their states of minorities.

NATO eventually intervened to stop the warfare, and under the guidance of the United States, the rival parties signed the Dayton Accords in 1995. Violence in the region has continued into the twenty-first century. Each of these nations has achieved some form of representative government, but the future of democracy in the region is far from certain.

1960

1968
Brazil begins a period of great economic growth, but a loss of human rights.

1970

1959
Fidel Castro establishes a communist regime in Cuba.

1973
Chile's socialist government is overthrown in a U.S.-backed military coup.

Chapter 33
Contemporary
Latin America
1945–present

Sugarloaf Mountain rises above the glowing city of Rio de Janeiro, Brazil.

1983
Democratic elections return a civilian government to power in Argentina.

1990

1998
Hugo Chavez is elected president of Venezuela.

2000

Nicaragua's Violeta Chamorro becomes Central America's first woman president.

1992
Civil war ends in El Salvador.

Vicente Fox is elected president of Mexico, ending seventy years of PRI domination.

After World War II, many Latin American leaders sought to modernize their countries by industrializing. But the rush to industrialize caused wrenching social changes and greatly strained the economies of many nations.

In parts of Latin America, economic chaos helped dictators rise to power. During the Cold War, the United States, which feared the spread of communism in neighboring regions, supported dictators who claimed to be anticommunist. After the communist takeover of Cuba, the United States intervened even more heavily in Latin American affairs.

The fall of the Soviet Union and the end of the Cold War encouraged Latin Americans to seek peaceful solutions to their problems. Beginning in the late 1980s, democracy spread through much of the region. Most countries adopted free-market reforms to improve their economies. Nevertheless, Latin America remains a region with stubbornly high levels of poverty and inequality.

Latin America in the Postwar Years

Key Questions

- What economic challenges did Latin American nations face during the postwar era?
- What trends characterized social and political development in Latin America after World War II?

The area known as Latin America consists of the central and southern parts of the Western Hemisphere, including Mexico, Central America, the Caribbean islands, and the continent of South America. This vast region contains thirty-five independent nations. It is called Latin America because it was colonized mainly by two European powers, Spain and Portugal, whose languages descended from Latin, the language of ancient Rome.

The largest country in Latin America, Brazil, was colonized by Portugal. Most of the rest of Latin America was colonized by Spain. In the early 1800s, with Spain and Portugal weakened by the Napoleonic Wars, rebellions against colonial rule broke out throughout Latin America. By 1830, most of the region's countries had become independent nations. The newly independent Latin American nations struggled with problems inherited from colonial times, including poverty, inequality, and racial divisions.

Colonial Legacies

Except for Brazil, which became a constitutional monarchy, the new Latin American nations called themselves republics. They did not develop into democracies, however, in part because Spain and Portugal had never encouraged the development of representative institutions in their colonies. Most of the wealth in the newly independent nations, as in colonial times, remained in the hands of a minority of large landowners. In many countries, military strongmen known as caudillos used social unrest as an excuse to seize political power.

In most of Latin America, strong racial divisions from colonial times continued. A white minority, descendants of European colonists, dominated government and commerce. The whites discriminated against the Indians, who had been the original inhabitants of these lands. Most Indians lived in isolated, impoverished communities. Mixed-race mestizos, with both white and Indian blood, held a position between the two groups. Although discriminated against, mestizos could sometimes rise through ambition and hard work.

When they colonized Latin America, the Spanish and Portuguese brought their Catholic faith with them to the New World. (To this day, a majority of the world's Catholics live in Latin America.) In nineteenth-century Latin

From the nineteenth century on, the Catholic Church has greatly influenced Latin America.

Latin America

America, the Catholic Church wielded enormous influence. Because it possessed great wealth in the form of land, the church favored political stability. Thus, the Catholic Church often stood opposed to change in the newly independent Latin American nations.

Changes and Challenges

During the nineteenth century, the Industrial Revolution gradually helped raise living standards for many of the inhabitants of Europe and North America. Latin American nations, however, never developed a similar industrial base. Instead, agriculture remained the foundation of their economies. Because a small minority owned most of the land for farming, wealth was concentrated in the hands of a few. Thus, Latin America entered the twentieth century as a region of *developing nations*—countries with low levels of industry and commerce, where a majority of the people live in poverty.

The developing nations of Latin America exported agricultural products to the developed countries of Europe and North America. Major exports included coffee, sugar, bananas, and meat. In turn, the Latin American countries imported manufactured goods from the industrialized nations. When the worldwide Great Depression of the 1930s drove down demand for agricultural products, the value of Latin American exports fell by nearly half. Across the region, more people sank into poverty.

Consequences of Transforming from Agriculture to Industry

In the period after World War II, as the world economy recovered, Latin American leaders tried to remake their own economies. Realizing that their countries had depended too much on agriculture, they promoted the growth of industry. They believed that by manufacturing goods at home, they could end *trade deficits*—the gap between the value of a country's imports and exports—and make their nations more self-sufficient.

To get factories built, Latin American businessmen often had to look to the developed countries for technical knowledge and *investment capital*, the money necessary to start a business. Latin American economies thus remained dependent on the economies of the wealthier developed nations. Among many Latin Americans, this dependence fueled resentment and a growing sense of nationalism.

With Latin American governments encouraging industry, millions of poor people left their rural homes and flocked to the cities, hoping to find well-paying jobs in factories. In the decades after World War II, Latin American cities grew so fast that between the 1940s and the 1990s, the population of Mexico City soared from 1.6 million to 19 million, while that of São Paulo, Brazil, went from 1.4 million to over 17 million. Many migrants, from the countryside to the cities, found that not enough jobs were available, and most migrants lacked the skills to perform the ones that were.

Costa Rican workers display a bountiful banana crop. Latin America has long supplied Europe and North America with bananas, coffee, sugar, and meat.

Political and Social Turmoil

After World War II, social inequality remained the norm in most Latin American societies, with wealth concentrated in the hands of a few. Beginning in the 1950s, inequality and widespread poverty fueled political unrest in many countries.

Those in power resisted reform. In some countries, violent rebellions broke out. In Cuba, as you have learned, a revolution led by Fidel Castro swept a communist government into power. In Chile, an elected socialist government instituted reforms before being overthrown by military officers. In a number of countries, right-wing dictators used the fear of revolution to justify harsh measures to suppress all dissent.

Cold War Intervention

By far the most powerful nation in the Western Hemisphere is the United States, which Latin Americans sometimes call the "Colossus of the North." Since the nineteenth century, Latin American economies have been closely tied to the economy of the United States. In the early 1900s, the United States sometimes intervened in Latin American countries when political turmoil threatened American business interests.

During the Cold War, leaders of the United States grew anxious that the Soviets would spread communism in Latin America. Those fears seemed to come true after Fidel Castro led a successful revolution in Cuba in 1959. Castro soon allied his country with the Soviet Union. In 1962, during the Cuban Missile Crisis, the United States used a naval blockade of Cuba to force the removal of Soviet missiles from the island.

Three years later, President Lyndon Johnson sent U.S. troops to another Caribbean nation, the Dominican Republic, because he feared that fighting among political factions might bring an anti-American group to power. Johnson declared that the United States "cannot, must not, and will not permit the establishment of another communist government in the Western Hemisphere."

Allende in Chile

Cold War rivalries would have an especially dramatic impact on the nation of Chile. Unlike many other Latin American countries, Chile had a history of democratic government and free elections. But American leaders were alarmed when, in 1970, Salvador Allende (ahl-YEN-day) was elected president of the country. Allende, a friend of Fidel Castro, announced his intention to bring socialism to Chile through peaceful means.

Allende's government confiscated private property and gave it to landless peasants. It also nationalized—that is, the government took

Key Questions

- Why did the United States intervene in several Latin American nations during the Cold War era?

- Why did dictatorships rise to power in much of Latin America?

In 1973, the Chilean army laid siege to La Moneda Palace in Santiago. The coup ended President Allende's life and the country's attempt at socialism.

control of—foreign-owned mines, banks, and industries. These actions antagonized many upper- and middle-class Chileans. American businessmen, too, resented the nationalization of their companies. The United States cut off aid to Chile.

At the same time, the Soviet Union, China, and Cuba issued loans to Allende's government. When Fidel Castro paid a three-week visit to Chile, in his speeches he called for a complete communist takeover. Castro's speeches alarmed many Chileans, who bought weapons to defend their homes. The country edged toward civil war.

By 1973, Allende's policies and programs had ruined the Chilean economy. Food shortages and a 500 percent annual inflation rate plagued the country. (A 500 percent annual inflation rate means that every item a Chilean bought in 1973 cost five times what it had in 1972.)

Behind the scenes, the U.S. Central Intelligence Agency (CIA) tried to bring down Allende's government. The CIA helped engineer a truck drivers' strike that paralyzed the nation. The CIA also urged the Chilean military to stage a coup. In September 1973, the Chilean army surrounded the presidential palace with tanks while Chilean air force jets dropped bombs. Allende refused to surrender and died inside the building. Control

of the country passed to the military. Chile's experiment in socialism had come to an end.

Nicaragua: Somoza and the Sandinistas

The United States had a long history of intervening in the Central American nation of Nicaragua, where U.S. companies were heavily invested. From 1912 to 1933, U.S. troops occupied Nicaragua and controlled its government. After the troops left, power passed into the hands of a family called the Somozas. For the next four decades, the Somozas, with the support of the United States, ruled Nicaragua as dictators, tolerating no opposition.

In 1979, Anastasio Somoza was overthrown by a rebel group called the Sandinistas. The Sandinistas took their name from Augusto Sandino, a nationalist leader who had fought American occupation troops in the 1920s.

Like Allende in Chile, the Sandinistas instituted socialist reforms and accepted aid from Cuba. The U.S. president, Ronald Reagan, feared that Nicaragua would become "another Cuba."

While the Somoza family ruled Nicaragua, many who opposed the dictatorial regime were arrested and jailed.

Adoring crowds in Nicaragua surround Violeta Chamorro, who in 1990 was elected the first woman president of a Central American republic.

He ordered a trade embargo of the country. (An *embargo* is a government order to impose barriers to trade or stop trade in certain goods.) Reagan also supplied aid to the Contras, a counterrevolutionary guerrilla group fighting against the Sandinistas.

As the war with the Contras intensified, the Sandinistas imposed military rule over Nicaragua and cracked down on dissent. Many former supporters of the Sandinistas became disillusioned. In 1990, national elections brought a democratic, anti-Sandinista party to power. Nicaragua's new leader, Violeta Chamorro, was the first woman president of a Central American republic.

Civil War in El Salvador

In the 1980s, Nicaragua's smaller neighbor, El Salvador, was torn by civil war. The conflict was rooted in the country's poverty, overpopulation, and inequality. At the time, 60 percent of the land in El Salvador was owned by just 2 percent of the people. The country's government, a military dictatorship, ignored the plight of the poor.

In the 1970s, Catholic priests, practicing a form of "liberation theology," had begun demanding reform in the name of workers and peasants.

The head of the country's Catholic Church, Archbishop Oscar Romero, proclaimed the right of the poor "to organize and defend" themselves. In 1980, Archbishop Romero was assassinated while conducting a church service.

Inspired by the Sandinista victory in neighboring Nicaragua, the opponents of El Salvador's government mounted an armed rebellion. In the United States, President Reagan believed that the rebels were acting on the direction of communists in Cuba and the Soviet Union. "The government of El Salvador," he said, "is on the front line in a battle that is really aimed at the very heart of the Western Hemisphere, and eventually us." Reagan sent military advisers and helicopters to support Salvadoran troops in their fight against the guerrillas.

In 1982, the leaders of a new government in El Salvador enacted some reforms, including the redistribution of land. But the civil war still raged on, with both sides committing terrible atrocities. Many in the United States protested America's involvement.

With the collapse of the Soviet empire in the late 1980s, American leaders had less reason to fear the spread of communism. They grew more reluctant to support a costly war in El Salvador. At the same time, the Salvadoran guerrillas were shaken by the electoral defeat of the Sandinistas in Nicaragua. At the beginning of 1992, the Salvadoran government and the guerrillas signed a peace agreement, ending a civil war that had cost seventy-five thousand lives.

Liberation Theology

In the 1960s and 1970s, some Catholic priests and nuns in Latin America practiced *liberation theology*, the belief that Christians should work on behalf of the poor and oppressed. The Catholic Church, which had long opposed change in Latin America, now had within it a group working for radical political and social change.

791

President Juan Perón of Argentina (at right) waves to a crowd. His wife Eva (center) was beloved by the people.

Dictators in Control

From the middle to the late 1900s, a number of Latin American countries were ruled by dictators. Some of these rulers began by enacting beneficial reforms, but most imposed increasingly harsh and oppressive measures on their people.

Perón in Argentina

In Argentina, an army officer named Juan Perón (wahn puh-ROHN) was elected president in 1946. Perón came to power as a populist, a leader who promises to oppose the wealthy and privileged in the name of the common people. Much of his support was drawn from the country's labor unions.

Once in office, Perón made good on his promise of reform. He made sweeping changes to improve the lives of workers, including instituting a minimum wage and an eight-hour workday. He also built hospitals, schools, and shelters for the homeless.

Perón's popularity was increased by the activities of his wife, Eva Perón. Evita, as she was known, was a glamorous former actress who had grown up in poverty. Describing herself as a "humble woman of the people," Evita Perón won great affection for her charitable work with the poor. In 1947, she persuaded Perón to sign a law giving Argentine women the vote. When she died in 1952, grieving crowds mobbed her funeral.

With its rich agricultural lands, Argentina had long been the wealthiest country in Latin America.

At first, prosperity continued under Perón. But as the government tightened control of industry and agriculture, the economy faltered. Farmers and ranchers reacted to strict price controls by cutting back on production. Meanwhile, Perón ruled more and more as a dictator, censoring the press and harassing his political opponents.

In 1955, Perón was overthrown in a military coup. For the following two decades, governments in Argentina would rise and fall, as democratic governments alternated with military dictatorships.

In 1976, an especially brutal military regime came to power. Its leaders took action against all who dared to oppose their rule. In the middle of the night, soldiers broke into people's homes, taking them away to be tortured and killed. Between 1976 and the fall of the military government in 1983, between 10,000 and 30,000 Argentines "disappeared" in this way.

Pinochet in Chile

In Chile, after the fall of Salvador Allende in 1973, an oppressive military regime took charge of the country. Its leader, General Augusto Pinochet (pee-noh-CHET or pee-noh-SHAY), ordered the arrest of thousands of Allende supporters. Some

General Augusto Pinochet took charge of Chile after the fall of Salvador Allende in late 1973.

Chileans took to the streets in 1983 to protest General Pinochet's military regime, whose policies severely limited their freedom.

were tortured and executed. Tens of thousands more fled into exile abroad.

Pinochet announced that he would roll back the socialist reforms of the Allende years and make Chile a thriving capitalist nation. He declared that he wanted "to make Chile not a nation of proletarians, but a nation of entrepreneurs." Pinochet slashed government jobs, sold off nationalized industries, and reversed land reform. These changes dramatically reduced inflation and helped many Chileans enjoy a degree of economic security.

In 1982, however, the Chilean economy was hit hard by a worldwide recession. Nearly one-third of the population became unemployed. Strikes by angry workers led to further government repression. Although unconcerned with political freedom, Pinochet remained committed to free-market principles in economics. By 1985, the country was beginning to recover financially. Chilean entrepreneurs had developed a range of new products to

market around the world. Chile's rate of economic growth was the highest in Latin America.

Nevertheless, most Chileans resented the military regime for restricting their freedom. In 1988, Pinochet held a plebiscite (PLEH-buh-siyt)— a vote on an issue—asking the Chilean people whether they wanted him to continue in power. To his surprise, the vote went against him. He stepped down from office, and was replaced by a democratically elected government. The new leadership sought to restore human rights to the Chilean people, while leaving most of Pinochet's free-market reforms in place.

Brazil: A Costly Economic "Miracle"

The nation of Brazil takes up nearly half of the South American continent. Like the rest of the region, it faced challenges and conflicts as it tried to develop in the years after World War II. In 1955, Juscelino Kubitschek (zhoo-suh-LEE-noo KOO-buh-chek) was elected Brazil's president. He

793

declared an ambitious plan of modernization, promising "fifty years of progress in five."

Kubitschek realized that Brazil had become too dependent on the export of its main crop, coffee. The Brazilian economy rose and fell according to changes in world demand for coffee. Like other Latin American leaders of the time, he believed that the solution to his country's problems was rapid industrialization.

Kubitschek poured money into the nation's steel and automobile industries. As a sign of the country's modernity, he built a spectacular new capital city, Brasília, lined with gleaming buildings of concrete and glass. To finance this modernization, however, Kubitschek had to borrow heavily from foreign nations. Eventually, the heavy debt load bankrupted Brazil's economy.

In 1964, a group of military officers overthrew the democratic government. In an attempt to stabilize the economy, they cut government spending and workers' wages. Attracted by the new stability, foreign investors poured money into Brazil. Between 1968 and 1974, during what came to be known as the "Brazilian miracle," Brazil had one of the fastest-growing economies in the world.

But Brazil's economic success came at the price of human rights. The military government harshly suppressed all dissent, torturing and killing its critics. In 1973, when war in the Middle East sent the worldwide price of oil skyrocketing, Brazil faced a crisis. Brazil was importing 90 percent of the oil needed to run its factories and transport its products. The soaring prices for oil caused Brazil's economy to crash again. Many Brazilians lost confidence in their military rulers. By the 1980s, Brazil returned to democracy.

The "Shining Path" in Peru

In the 1980s, the South American nation of Peru descended into chaos. Its elected president, Alan Garcia, pursued policies that wrecked the

Brazil's president Juscelino Kubitschek built the capital of Brasília, a gleaming example of modern architecture and planning.

In the 1980s, the Indians of the Andean highlands especially suffered when high inflation wrecked Peru's economy.

economy and caused crippling inflation. Unrest spread in the country's Andean highlands, whose Indian inhabitants suffered from both desperate poverty and the racism of white and mestizo Peruvians. Indian grievances gave rise to a guerrilla movement that called itself *Sendero Luminoso*—the Shining Path.

Sendero's leader was a former professor named Abimael Guzman (GOOZ-mahn). He had studied in communist China and followed the philosophy of Chinese leaders who called for the complete and violent remaking of society.

Sendero quickly established itself as the most brutal of all Latin American guerrilla forces. It waged war not only against government troops, but also against anyone who dared to cooperate with the government. It even attacked activists who called for peace.

Sendero's campaign of bombings and assassinations alienated the Peruvian Indians that the guerrillas claimed to be fighting for. A quarter million people fled the mountains for the relative safety of coastal cities, forming the largest group of refugees in Latin America. For a time, it looked as if Sendero forces might seize the capital city of Lima.

In 1990, at the height of Sendero violence, Alberto Fujimori was elected president of Peru. Fujimori applied free-market reforms to improve the economy and tame inflation. He also stepped up the war against Sendero. The capture of Abimael Guzman in 1992 crippled the group. But Fujimori's opponents accused his soldiers of committing widespread atrocities in an attempt to defeat the guerrillas. Angered by the criticism, Fujimori disbanded the country's legislature and supreme court. A new constitution gave the president nearly dictatorial powers.

Made popular by his success in controlling inflation and defeating the guerrillas, Fujimori was elected to two more terms as president. But in 2000, charges of corruption forced him out of office. In 2009, a Peruvian court found him guilty of involvement in two massacres by military forces during the war against Sendero. The court sentenced the former president to twenty-five years in prison.

Castro in Cuba

The longest-lived dictatorship in modern Latin America is that of Fidel Castro in Cuba. In the late 1950s, Castro led a rebellion that overthrew the island's corrupt and oppressive leader, Fulgencio Batista. Once in power, Castro declared himself a communist and looked to the Soviet Union for aid.

Fidel Castro, communist dictator of Cuba, speaks as the image of Karl Marx looms in the background.

795

Under Castro, all political parties except the Communist Party were banned in Cuba. Opposition newspapers were shut down. Castro established so-called Committees for the Defense of the Revolution, which were little more than citizens' groups tasked with spying on their neighbors and reporting anyone who criticized the government. Soon, Cuba's jails were crowded with thousands of political prisoners.

Castro's government took total control of the Cuban economy. Most forms of private property were banned. The government also seized the property of foreign companies, including many from the United States. In response, the U.S. instituted an embargo of Cuba, forbidding Americans to trade with the country.

In 1961, American leaders took an even more drastic step by supporting an invasion of the island by anticommunist Cuban exiles. Castro's forces easily defeated the invaders, reinforcing nationalist and anti-American feeling in Cuba. The following year, the United States and the Soviet Union came to the brink of nuclear war over the presence of Soviet missiles in Cuba.

Many Cubans risked their lives to flee Castro's repressive regime. In desperation, some took to the open seas in makeshift rafts and boats.

While stamping out individual liberties, Castro's government did make efforts to improve the health and welfare of the people. The regime built schools throughout the island. All Cuban citizens received free medical care. They were also guaranteed work and a place to live.

Many of the homes distributed by the government had been left behind by people fleeing the island in search of freedom or greater economic opportunity. Eventually, more than a million Cubans would leave the country. Most came to the United States, where they remained vocal opponents of the communist regime. Cuban exiles strongly supported tough U.S. action against Cuba, including the trade embargo, which has remained in effect for fifty years.

From the beginning, the Soviet Union was communist Cuba's main benefactor and trading partner. The collapse of the Soviet Union in 1991 severely damaged the Cuban economy. Cuba's foreign trade plummeted. In response, Castro encouraged investment from capitalist countries. He also decreed that Cubans could set up their own small businesses. But Cuba's economy never fully recovered. Cuba remains a country of chronic shortages and strict rationing.

Those who hoped that the fall of the Soviet Union would bring political freedom to Cuba have been disappointed. In 2006, approaching his eightieth birthday, an ailing Castro handed over most of his authority to his brother, Raul Castro. Raul Castro has made dramatic changes to Cuba's economy, encouraging more privately owned businesses and ending state-guaranteed employment. But he has shown no willingness to give up the Communist Party's monopoly on power.

Directions in Latin America

During the course of the Cold War, both the United States and the Soviet Union had frequently intervened in the affairs of Latin American nations. When the Soviet Union collapsed in 1991, the Cold War ended. The end of the Cold War would have profound implications for the fate of Latin America.

With the failure of communism in the Soviet Union, leftists in Latin America no longer looked to the Soviet Union or Cuba as models for their own societies. Right-wing politicians could no longer count on the United States to support dictatorial governments that claimed to be fighting communism. In many countries, leaders on both the left and the right came to see that the only way to achieve their goals was through democratic means.

Latin America's Modern Democracies

Although dictators took charge in many Latin American nations after World War II, there were exceptions. The small Central American nation of Costa Rica established the most successful and longest-lived democracy in Latin America. For most of the twentieth century, Costa Rica has pursued a democratic and peaceful road to development. In 1949, the country's president abolished its army, declaring, "War is not a natural human condition."

In the late 1980s, another Costa Rican president, Oscar Arias, helped negotiate an end to the bloody civil wars in Nicaragua and El Salvador. His peace plan included free elections in both countries. "Only democracy," Arias declared, "can end wars between brothers." Since the fighting ended, both Nicaragua and El Salvador have experienced peaceful, democratic transitions of government. Former guerrilla groups have transformed themselves into political parties, and the people have elected their leaders.

Dictatorships Falter

In the 1980s and 1990s, military dictatorships fell in the major countries of South America. In Argentina, the military government that waged a campaign against dissidents had badly mismanaged the economy. In an attempt to win popularity and rally patriotic feeling, the government invaded the Falklands, a group of islands in the South Atlantic that were owned by Great Britain but claimed by Argentina. Britain sent a fleet to the islands and seized them back in a brief war. Humiliated, the general who headed the government resigned. In 1983, democratic elections returned a civilian government to power in Argentina.

In Brazil, mounting economic problems caused the military dictatorship to give up power in 1985. In Chile, General Pinochet stepped down in 1990,

Key Questions

- Why did many Latin American dictatorships fail in the late twentieth century?
- What have been the results of attempts at economic reform in Latin American nations?
- What challenges do Latin American nations continue to face?

The IMF and the OAS

Various international organizations have helped Latin American nations make the transition to democracy. One of them is the International Monetary Fund (IMF), an organization that helps member nations stabilize their economies. The IMF offers loans to Latin American countries that promise to make reforms that encourage free-market economies, for example, by lowering tariffs and selling government-owned industries to private investors.

As Latin American countries have made the effort to change, they have also turned to the Organization of American States (OAS) for help. The OAS was founded in the 1940s to encourage regional cooperation. In the 1990s, the OAS focused on promoting democracy. For example, the OAS sent observers to member states to see that elections were conducted fairly.

after a nationwide vote showed his lack of support from the people. For the past two decades, Argentina, Brazil, and Chile have remained functioning democracies.

Two Exceptions: Cuba and Venezuela

In recent decades, while most Latin American nations have turned to democracy, Cuba remains an exception. There, the Communist Party retains firm control. Another exception is Cuba's close ally, Venezuela. Hugo Chavez, Venezuela's socialist president, came to power through a free election in 1998, but since then he has acted more and more like a dictator.

Venezuela is one of the world's largest producers of oil. Chavez has used the country's great wealth from oil to fund programs for the poor, but also to clamp down on political opposition. Chavez has compared himself to Simon Bolívar, the nineteenth-century revolutionary who dreamed of uniting the South American countries. Chavez has often denounced capitalism and the

United States. In a speech at the United Nations, Chavez referred to then-U.S. president George W. Bush as "el Diablo" ("the Devil").

Mexico's Many Challenges

Mexico has long been a special case in Latin American politics. Between 1910 and 1920, revolution shook the country. Afterward, the nation remained relatively stable, with a government that was neither a dictatorship nor a full democracy.

The Mexican government had a democratic structure, with political parties and elections. But decade after decade, a single party, the Institutional Revolutionary Party (*Partido Revolucionario Institucional*)—called the PRI after its Spanish initials—remained in charge of the country. PRI candidates won every presidential election. Often, the voting was rigged to ensure a PRI victory. PRI candidates bribed poor citizens for their votes. Sometimes, supporters of opposition parties were murdered.

After World War II, Mexico, like other Latin American countries, pushed to industrialize. In the effort, Mexico ran up high levels of foreign debt. In the late 1970s, however, vast quantities of oil were discovered in Mexican territory. Mexico's oil exports surged from $500 million in 1976 to $13 billion in 1981.

Offshore oil derricks in Venezuela, one of the world's largest producers of oil

The PRI government quickly became dependent on oil revenues. In the mid-1980s, when the worldwide price of oil fell sharply, Mexico found itself without the money to pay its foreign debts. The country had to be rescued by loans from the IMF, which insisted on deep cuts in government spending. As the standard of living fell, the Mexican people's resentment against their government grew.

In 1992, Mexico, Canada, and the United States signed the North American Free Trade Agreement, which ended almost all tariffs (import taxes) on trade among the three countries. The goal of the agreement was to improve the economies of all three nations by encouraging commerce. But the agreement met resistance in the countries it affected. For example, in Mexico, nationalist politicians argued that the agreement weakened Mexico, while labor unions in the United States protested that their members would lose jobs because of competition from cheaper foreign imports.

In Mexico, soldiers raid an open-air laboratory that produces drugs, a source of illegal income as well as the cause of much gang violence.

Fall of the PRI

In 1995, a major scandal rocked Mexico's long-dominant political party, the PRI. The brother of the former president of Mexico was charged with murdering a rival PRI official, all while stealing millions from the government and hiding the money in a Swiss bank. Many voters were appalled by this glaring evidence of corruption in the ruling party. In the 1997 congressional elections, the PRI lost control of the lower house of the Mexican legislature.

In the 2000 presidential elections, for the first time in seventy-one years, the PRI candidate lost the presidency. Mexico's new president was Vicente Fox, from the conservative National Action Party (*Partido Acción Nacional*), called PAN after its Spanish initials. Fox improved Mexico's relationship with the United States and cut down on corruption in politics. But his ability to reform the system was limited because his party did not control the legislature.

In 2006, Fox was succeeded as president by another member of PAN, Felipe Calderón. As Mexico's president, Calderón has faced two especially severe challenges. One is the economic downturn caused by the worldwide recession that began in 2008. The other is the almost nonstop violence caused by Mexico's drug cartels. Gun battles frequently erupt in major Mexican cities as rival drug gangs fight not only each other but also the police and soldiers sent to arrest them. Between 2006 and 2010, nearly twenty-three thousand people died in drug-related violence across Mexico.

A *cartel* is a group of business interests joined together to fix prices and limit competition.

Ongoing Issues

In recent decades, Latin American nations have struggled to address a variety of economic, social, and environmental challenges. Some of the greatest challenges include urban poverty and the violence associated with the drug trade.

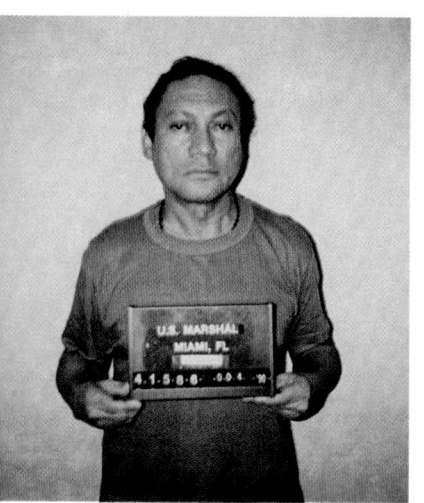

Manuel Noriega of Panama, dictator and drug trafficker, 1989

The Drug Trade

Mexico is far from the only Latin American country to be affected by the trade in illegal drugs. Colombia, Peru, Bolivia, Panama, and Brazil have all suffered from the violence and corruption associated with the trade in drugs such as marijuana, heroin, and cocaine. Part of what drives the Latin American drug trade is demand in the United States. For example, 45 percent of the world's cocaine is consumed in North America.

When the Cold War ended, the drug trade became one of the main concerns for the U.S. government in its relations with Latin America. In 1989, the United States invaded Panama to overthrow a dictator, Manuel Noriega, who engaged in drug trafficking. The American government has given Colombia some $5 billion in aid to destroy crops of coca, the plant from which cocaine is made. The United States has also provided military assistance to the Colombian armed forces to fight guerrilla groups that support themselves by smuggling drugs.

Also, since 2006, the United States has given millions of dollars to Mexico's military and police to assist in their war on drug cartels.

Problems in Agriculture

Historically, most farmers in Latin America have been landless peasants who worked the fields of *haciendas*—the large estates of wealthy landowners. In recent years, these subsistence farmers—farmers who grow just enough for their own needs—have lost their land to powerful *agribusinesses*, multinational companies specializing in high-demand products, such as beef for fast-food restaurant chains.

In Brazil, farmers desperate for farmland clear the rain forest by burning it.

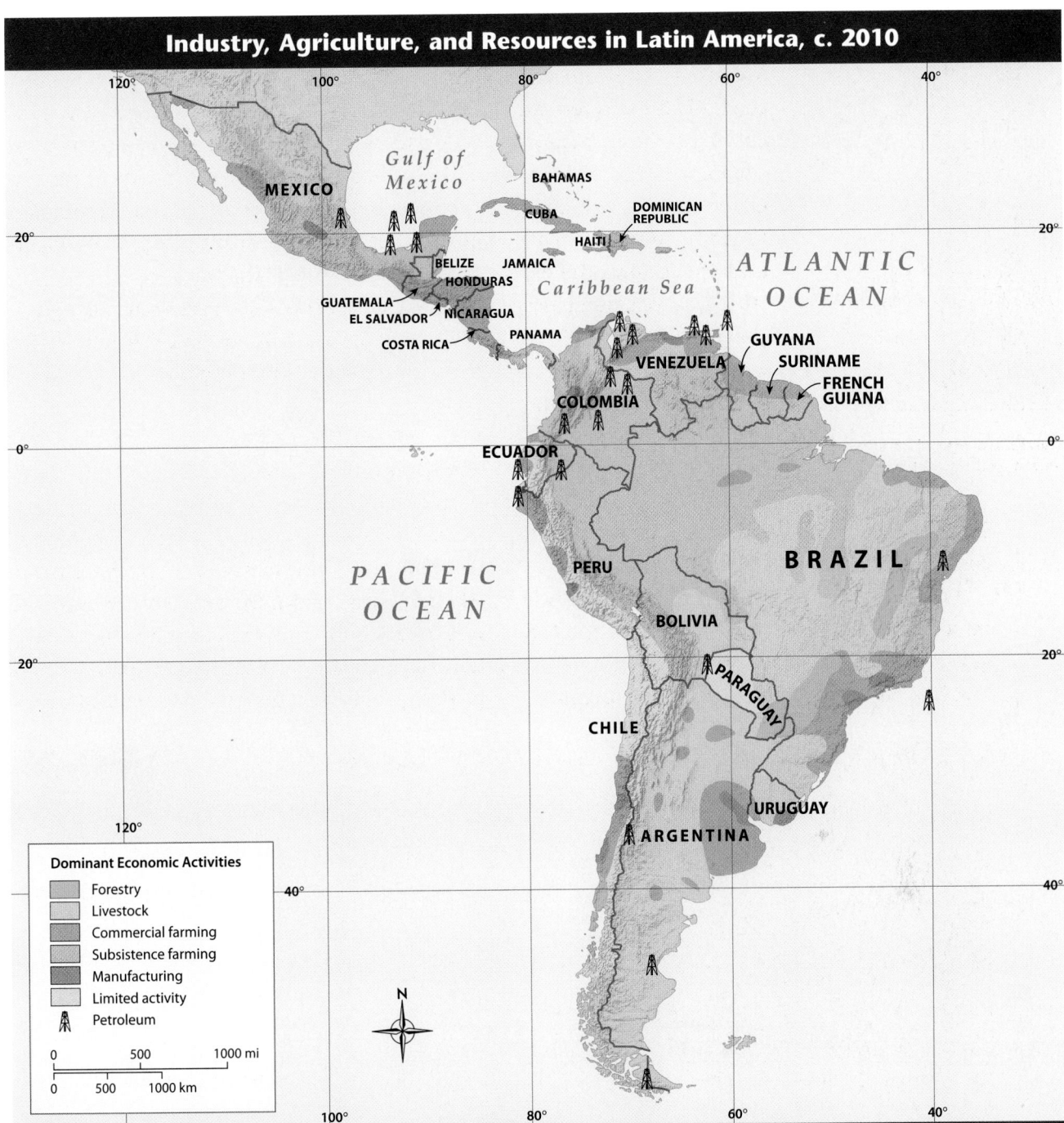

Industry, Agriculture, and Resources in Latin America, c. 2010

Dominant Economic Activities

- Forestry
- Livestock
- Commercial farming
- Subsistence farming
- Manufacturing
- Limited activity
- Petroleum

Although the economies of Latin America are diversifying rapidly, especially in urban areas, much of the economic activity in many nations is still controlled by a small minority of wealthy people.

In Peru and Brazil, poor farmers have cleared land in protected rain forests, causing severe environmental damage. As farmers turn to commercial farming, they plant crops for export and often grow fewer food crops. So local food prices rise, causing inflation. Many farmers have moved to the region's cities, in an often-unsuccessful effort to find work. Unable to find jobs, they lead lives of desperate poverty.

Rapid Urbanization

Some Latin American cities have grown too fast to accommodate their populations. Shantytowns have grown up around many of Latin America's

801

Latin America, Poverty by Country 2006

Population Below the Poverty Line

- 9–29%
- 30–39%
- 40–55%
- 56–80%
- no data

0   500   1000 mi
0   500   1000 km

Despite economic growth, poverty persists in Latin America, especially among subsistence farmers and in overcrowded urban areas.

large cities. In these areas, people live crowded together in shacks made with scraps of metal or wood. Usually, they have no running water, sewers, or electricity.

The problems caused by growing too rapidly are illustrated by Mexico City, the largest city in the Western Hemisphere, with a population of over nineteen million (including surrounding areas). Built on the site of the capital of the Aztec Empire, Mexico City boasts grand avenues lined with beautiful colonial buildings. But the city has a high crime rate. It suffers from periodic water shortages because its system of wells and reservoirs has not kept up with the growth in population. In 1992, the

Mexico City boasts wide avenues and striking buildings, but it struggles with crime and pollution.

United Nations declared Mexico City's air to be the most polluted in the world. The Mexican government has since taken steps to reduce air pollution, but on many days smog still hangs over the city.

The Gap Remains

Since the 1990s, as Latin American nations have become more democratic, most have accepted the free-market reforms encouraged by the IMF. They have cut government spending and sold off unprofitable government businesses. These reforms have attracted investment from around the world. Exports have increased, while inflation has been reined in.

While economic reforms have helped many Latin Americans become prosperous over the last two decades, there remains a wide gap between rich and poor. A third of Latin America's population lives on the equivalent of less than two U.S. dollars a day. In 2003, the top 10 percent of the region's population earned nearly 50 percent of all income. Despite the embrace of democracy and the spread of free-market reforms, Latin America continues to face stubborn problems of inequality and poverty.

Poverty remains a stubborn problem in much of Latin America, as shown on a street on the Caribbean island of Haiti.

Chapter 34 Southern and Eastern Asia:

1947
India gains independence and is partitioned into India and East and West Pakistan.

1953
Korea is divided into a communist North and a noncommunist South.

1968
Japan, democratic since 1946, has the world's second-largest economy.

1945

1955

1965

1975

1949
Mao Zedong proclaims the communist People's Republic of China.

Communist North Vietnamese forces defeat South Vietnam

With its great wealth and extreme poverty, Mumbai, India, is a city of contrasts.

Change and Challenges 1945–2010

1985

1989
In Tiananmen Square, Chinese troops kill hundreds of students demonstrating for political rights.

1995

2005

2010
Twenty years after easing controls, communist China has the world's second-largest economy.

2004
A tsunami strikes Indonesia and other areas in the Indian Ocean, killing more than 200,000 people.

*I*n the years after World War II, the nations of southern and eastern Asia struggled to free themselves from European colonial domination. Once they had achieved independence, the new nations faced great challenges. How would they govern themselves? How would they organize their economies? How would they settle internal conflicts that had been set aside during years of colonial domination?

For the new nations, independence sometimes led to democracy, but more often to war and fragmentation. India, for example, managed to establish a democratic system of government, but its neighbors saw the rise of military dictatorships. Totalitarian communist regimes came to power in China, North Vietnam, and North Korea. Japan, which had been a militaristic power, was forced by its American occupiers to democratize.

After World War II, some of the nations of southern and eastern Asia experienced dramatic economic development. Japan recovered from postwar poverty to achieve a level of prosperity comparable to that of advanced Western nations. The two giants of the region—India and China—both experienced surging growth 1980s and 1990s, after changing their economic policies.

Communist China

In earlier chapters, you read about the emergence, spread, and eventual collapse of communism in the Soviet Union. In the mid-twentieth century, another communist nation formed and quickly played a major role in world affairs—China. To understand the beginnings of communism in China, we need to look back to 1911, when Chinese revolutionaries overthrew the last Qing emperor and ended a dynasty that had ruled for more than two centuries.

Nationalists vs. Communists

As you learned, after the revolution of 1911, Sun Yat-sen became the provisional president of the new Republic of China. His party, the Nationalist Party, also known as the Kuomintang (KWOH-mihn-tahng), set out to unify and modernize China, and to end the long domination of the country by foreigners. But the collapse of the old empire left a fragmented country. Sun Yat-sen quickly gave up the presidency, as regional warlords fought among themselves.

Chiang Kai-shek and the Nationalist Party

After Sun Yat-sen's death in 1925, Chiang Kai-shek (CHANG kiy-SHEHK) took over the Nationalist Party. Chiang Kai-shek built up his Nationalist army and clamped down on the feuding warlords. He declared his intention to modernize China by adopting ideas and technology from the West. Chiang's reforms improved the lives of many Chinese, especially those living in the cities.

But most Chinese people were rural peasants living in poverty. Chiang's government largely ignored their needs. In response to the Nationalists' indifference, many peasants turned to the Chinese Communist Party, which had been founded with help from the Soviet Union.

Members of the Chinese Communist Party set out to spread the ideas of Marx and Lenin, and to organize the peasants into a revolutionary force. They demanded the redistribution of land from wealthy landlords to poor farmers.

Alarmed by this threat to his authority, Chiang Kai-shek launched a series of extermination campaigns designed to wipe out the Chinese Communist Party. By 1930, civil war raged in China, with the Nationalists battling the Red Army of the Communists. Chiang's forces were larger and better equipped. In 1934, they surrounded the main body of the Red Army in southern China. Faced with certain defeat, the Communists began a grueling, six-thousand-mile (9655 km) march to safety in northwestern China.

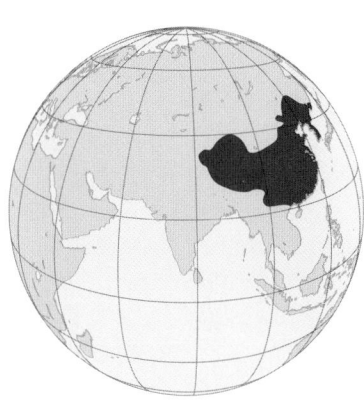

In the mid-twentieth century, China turned to communism.

This two-year journey, from 1934 to 1935, is known as the Long March. Of the hundred thousand Communist troops who started the march, only about six thousand survived. One of the survivors, Mao Zedong (MOW zuh-DOUNG), emerged as the new chairman of the Chinese Communist Party. From a base outside the government's control, Mao rebuilt the Communist forces.

Communists Gain Control

In 1937, Japan invaded China. The Communists and Nationalists formed an uneasy alliance against the common enemy. Over the next eight years, the Communists waged a guerrilla war against the Japanese in northern China, while the Nationalist army fought the invaders in the south. After the United States declared war on Japan, the American government sent nearly a billion dollars in aid to Chiang's forces. But much of the money was pocketed by corrupt Nationalist officials.

In 1945, with Japan defeated, the Nationalists and Communists resumed their civil war. Attracted by promises of land reform, poor peasants flocked to join the Communist side. As the Nationalist government became more corrupt and repressive, the Communists grew more disciplined and determined. With the support of the rural population, the Red Army soon gained control of the countryside. It moved on to surround the large cities. One by one, the cities surrendered.

In 1949, the leaders of the Nationalist government fled to the island of Taiwan (then called Formosa by Westerners). On the mainland, in the capital city of Beijing, Mao Zedong addressed a cheering crowd. He proclaimed the birth of a new communist nation, the People's Republic of China. The crowd roared back, "Long live Chairman Mao!"

China Under Mao

After the victory of his Chinese Communist forces, Mao Zedong ruled a country of more than half a billion people—nearly a quarter of the world's population. Mao's new government tried to improve conditions for China's impoverished, rural majority. The government seized almost half the land in the country and redistributed it to landless peasants. It raised literacy rates and improved public health. But Mao's Communist Party allowed no dissent. Anyone who questioned the rule of the party was declared an "enemy of the people" and either executed or sent to a labor camp.

The Great Leap Forward

Mao's regime formed an alliance with the leading communist power, the Soviet Union. With Soviet help, China began to modernize. Within a few years, Chinese factories doubled their output. In some parts of the country, people enjoyed electricity and running water for the first time. But the pace of change was not fast enough for Mao. In 1958, he announced a radical plan to modernize the country within fifteen years. He called this plan the Great Leap Forward.

To fulfill his goal, Mao declared that the Chinese people would have to work harder than ever before. Communist officials cheered workers on with the slogan "More, faster, better, cheaper." Under threat of punishment, factory managers

Mao Zedong was the first leader of the People's Republic of China, the world's most populous communist nation.

Communal farmers were forced to produce ever-larger harvests under Mao's Great Leap Forward plan.

were ordered to speed up production. Many drove both their machines and their workers to the point of breakdown.

In the countryside, Mao's government abolished private ownership of land. Almost the entire rural population was forced into gigantic farming communes of five thousand or more families. Inhabitants of a commune were forbidden to leave it and were subject to military-style discipline. With the government demanding ever-larger harvests, commune officials drove the workers mercilessly.

The commune system proved unsuccessful. Despite poor harvests, to finance the costs of industrialization, the government shipped more and more food abroad. Soon there wasn't enough food for the farmers themselves. Throughout the countryside, people began to starve. Between 1959 and 1962, at least twenty million Chinese starved to death as a result of Mao's Great Leap Forward—the greatest man-made famine in the history of the world.

The Great Leap Forward also drove a wedge between China and the Soviet Union. The Soviet leader, Nikita Khrushchev, criticized the recklessness of Mao's policies. In return, Mao dismissed Khrushchev as timid and lacking commitment to communist ideals. By 1960, the close alliance between the Chinese and the Soviets had come to an end. Mao declared himself the new leader of the communist world, which then split into pro-Soviet and pro-Chinese factions.

The Cultural Revolution

After the disaster of the Great Leap Forward, Mao moderated his policies for a time. Communes were reduced in size, and farmers were allowed to grow food for themselves. Harvests soon rebounded. Life seemed to be getting better for the Chinese people.

But by the mid-1960s, Mao had once again grown dissatisfied with the pace of change. He decided that too few of his countrymen had truly committed themselves to communism. In 1966,

Mao's Red Guards, composed mainly of students, attacked those who represented China's traditional culture and ideas.

he launched a radical new campaign called the Great Proletarian Cultural Revolution. Mao sought to stamp out any trace of capitalism in China, and to destroy the allegiance of the Chinese to their traditional culture, especially the ancient philosophy of Confucianism.

To carry out the Cultural Revolution, Mao created a new group called the Red Guards, composed mainly of high school and college students fanatically loyal to Mao himself. At mass rallies, Red Guards waved copies of *Quotations from Chairman Mao*, also known as the "Little Red Book." They cried, "We will smash whoever opposes Chairman Mao!"

When Mao unleashed the Red Guards, China descended into chaos. All over the country, radical students turned on their teachers, the men and women who passed along China's traditional culture and values. Red Guards dragged teachers from classrooms, beat them, and paraded them in front of jeering crowds. Anyone with an education became suspect. To avoid being attacked, intellectuals and artists destroyed their own libraries and artworks.

Mao ordered the closing of all schools and colleges in China. Red Guards were given free railway passes so that they could travel easily across the country. They beat, tortured, and killed people they accused of being capitalists or traditionalists. Many who were not killed were sent to work camps to be "reeducated" through heavy labor. Prominent scholars, writers, and scientists were put to work cleaning latrines and shoveling pig manure.

By 1967, some Red Guards were fighting the national army, and different Red Guard groups were fighting among themselves. Mao grew alarmed at the turmoil he had let loose. In the summer of 1968, he began to disband the Red Guards. But two years of violence had caused incalculable damage. Hundreds of thousands of people had been killed, and millions more had had their lives disrupted. Nearly an entire generation of Chinese students were deprived of an education.

The Cultural Revolution largely succeeded in one of its goals—wiping out traditional or foreign culture in China. Afterward, the only officially approved works of art and literature were those that praised communism and the leadership of Chairman Mao.

China After Mao

In 1976, Mao Zedong died at the age of eighty-two. Two years later, Deng Xiaoping (duhng show[rhymes with *now*]-ping) took over as leader of the Communist Party. Deng had been one of Mao's comrades on the Long March in 1934. During the Cultural Revolution, however, he had been attacked as a moderate, fired from his government job, and sent to work in a factory. He fully understood the destructiveness of Mao's policies.

The Four Modernizations

Deng declared that to become prosperous, China must undergo "the Four Modernizations"—of agriculture, industry, technology, and defense. Deng opened China to ideas and technology from the more advanced countries of the West. His government invited foreign companies to invest in China. At the same time, thousands of Chinese students were sent to study at universities in Europe and North America.

Deng encouraged a spirit of enterprise among the Chinese people. The government relaxed its control of the economy. Peasants were allowed to farm their own plots of land, and craftsmen could sell their goods on the open market. These changes improved the lives of many Chinese people. The country's per capita (per person) income doubled in the 1980s.

Deng's economic reforms, however, did not translate into political reforms. The Communist Party kept its grip on power and continued to suppress all dissent. In 1986, when a dissident named Wei Jingsheng (way JIHNG-shuhng) called for the government to allow a "Fifth Modernization," democracy, he was imprisoned.

Tiananmen Square and After

In the late 1980s, as communist rule weakened in the Soviet Union and Eastern Europe, China's communist leaders faced a dramatic challenge. Democratic ideas had been gradually spreading among students and intellectuals, and in the spring of 1989, thousands of students gathered in Tiananmen Square in Beijing. They called on the government to listen to the people and grant them basic rights such as freedom of speech. In the center of the square, the students set up a large statue of a woman holding a torch, which they called the "Goddess of Democracy."

Panicked by the size of the protest, the government sent in troops. Tanks smashed the statue of the goddess. Soldiers with automatic weapons opened fire on the unarmed students. Hundreds died; the rest fled the square. And so, for the time being, the government had succeeded in crushing the democracy movement in China.

Through the 1990s and into the twenty-first century, China's communist government has continued to allow greater economic freedom while severely limiting political freedom. The Chinese economy has boomed. By 2010, China had the world's largest population and the second-largest economy, after the United States. While the majority of Chinese remain poor, there is a growing middle class that dresses in Western clothes and can afford consumer goods like television sets, washing machines, and personal computers. In some ways, the lives of these Chinese people resemble those of people in Europe or the United States—except that they cannot vote in a free election, criticize their government, or worship if and as they please.

A Chinese citizen attempts to block tanks sent to drive protesting students from Tiananmen Square in Beijing.

South Asia

Before World War II, more than a third of the globe lived under colonial rule. People in India, Indochina, North Africa, and elsewhere were ruled by a handful of mostly European nations. Great Britain controlled the largest empire, but other European nations, such as France, Belgium, and Portugal, also directed the destinies of their colonies far across the seas.

During the twenty-five years following the Second World War, however, the rising tide of nationalism quickly eroded the vast European empires of the late nineteenth and early twentieth centuries. In Asia, Africa, and the Middle East, scores of new nations achieved independence. Historians use the term *decolonization* to refer to the achievement of independence by these Asian and African colonies after World War II.

In southern Asia, on the Indian subcontinent, decolonization proceeded quickly. Two years after the end of World War II, Britain's giant colony of India gained its independence. But it immediately split into two separate and hostile countries—India and Pakistan.

India's Independence Movement

India was England's largest and most important colony, often called the "Jewel in the Crown" of the British Empire. You have learned that in the early to mid-twentieth century, Mohandas Gandhi led the cause for Indian independence from British rule. Gandhi organized nonviolent protests against the British, following the philosophy of passive resistance to injustice. Gandhi became revered not only for his courage but also for the simplicity and purity of his life.

Gandhi's example inspired other prominent Indians to work for independence, including Jawaharlal Nehru (jah-WAH-hahr-lahl NAY-roo). Like Gandhi, Nehru studied law in England. On his return to India, Nehru entered politics. After meeting Gandhi, Nehru committed himself to the campaign of passive resistance. He spent more than nine years in jail for his activities in protest of British rule. In 1929, Nehru became the leader of the Congress Party, the main organization of Indian nationalists.

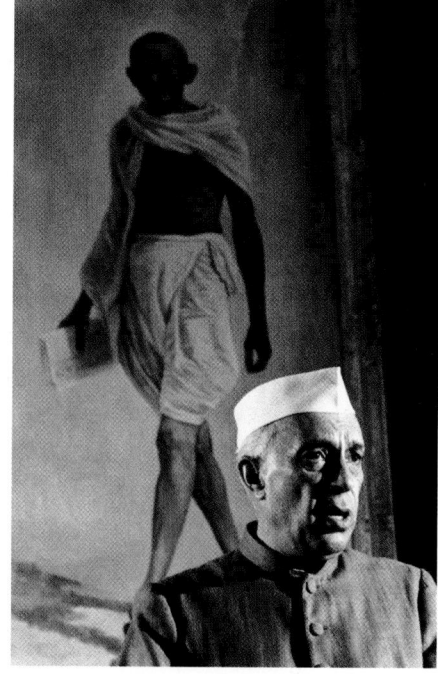
Nehru, inspired by Mohandas Gandhi, worked to free India.

Key Questions

- What role did Jawaharlal Nehru play in India's independence movement?

- Why was India partitioned in 1947? What happened as a result?

- What major political and economic changes have occurred in India since independence?

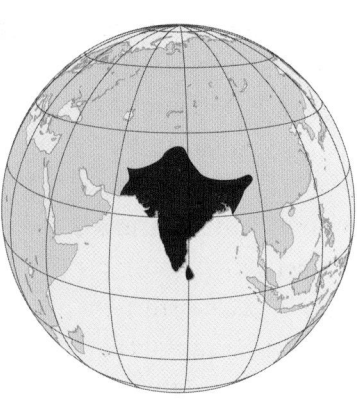
India, Pakistan, and Bangladesh in southern Asia

While the nationalists were united in their desire for independence, they were divided by religion. The majority of India's population was Hindu, but the country was also home to some 100 million Muslims. The Muslim minority feared that, with independence, the Hindus would refuse to share power with Muslims or grant them equal rights.

To safeguard their interests, prominent members of India's Islamic community formed the Muslim League. A brilliant lawyer, Mohammed Ali Jinnah (ah-LEE JIH-nuh), headed the Muslim League. At first, Jinnah and other leaders of the league called for cooperation between Muslims and Hindus in an independent India. In the 1940s, however, as the prospect of independence from Britain grew more likely, Jinnah called for the separation of India into two nations, one Hindu and one Muslim. Gandhi and Nehru strongly opposed this plan and urged that people of all faiths should live together in a single India.

Independence, Partition, and Conflict

When World War II ended in 1945, a war-weakened Britain could no longer maintain its huge overseas empire. In 1947, the British government announced that India would be granted its independence at the stroke of midnight on August 15. Nehru was selected by the Congress Party to serve as the new nation's first prime minister.

The new India did not take the shape that Gandhi and Nehru wanted. The British agreed with Jinnah to partition the country into two nations—India, with a Hindu majority, and Pakistan, which would serve as a homeland for Muslims. Pakistan itself was divided into two separate territories, one east and one west of India. As the partition occurred, fighting broke out between the two religious communities as Indians fled Pakistan and Muslims fled India. At least a million people were killed, and more than ten million became refugees.

Gandhi was heartbroken by the violence. In the months after independence, the Muslims

In August 1947, Indian citizens in Calcutta celebrated after their country won independence from Great Britain.

who had stayed behind in India were frequently attacked by their Hindu neighbors. Gandhi protested by fasting—refusing to eat until the worst of the persecution died down. Then, in January 1948, Gandhi himself fell victim to religious intolerance. He was assassinated by a Hindu fanatic who resented Gandhi's defense of the Muslim minority. A shocked Nehru lamented, "The light has gone out of our lives and there is darkness everywhere."

India: Nehru and After

Nehru would go on to become the longest-serving prime minister in Indian history. He held the office for nearly seventeen years. Nehru emphasized the need for national unity and a respect for the principles of democracy. Under his leadership, laws were passed forbidding discrimination against the so-called "untouchables," Indians born into the lowest part of the rigid caste system. His government also worked to improve the status of women, who were given the rights to vote, hold office, and inherit property on equal terms with men.

The India that Nehru took over in 1947 was a desperately overpopulated and impoverished nation. Nehru believed that the solution to India's poverty was the reorganization of the economy on socialist principles. The government took over major industries and most agricultural production. By the 1960s, India had become the world's seventh most advanced industrial nation. Still, food shortages often plagued the countryside, and most Indians remained poor.

In foreign affairs, Nehru pursued a policy of nonalignment, refusing to take sides in the Cold War between the United States and the Soviet Union. Nonalignment benefitted India because it encouraged the flow of assistance from both communist and noncommunist nations. India assumed a position of leadership among Asian and African nations that wished to remain neutral in the conflict between East and West.

Nehru was overwhelmingly popular among the Indian people. When he attempted to retire in 1958, so many people protested that he decided to remain in office. He died in 1964, still serving as prime minister. His vast popularity established his family as a political dynasty. Both his daughter and his grandson would go on to serve as leaders of India.

Indira Gandhi Leads India

Nehru's daughter Indira Gandhi became prime minister of India in 1966. (Gandhi was the family name of her husband; she was not related to Mohandas Gandhi.) Indira Gandhi continued the socialist economic policies of her father. At first, she also adhered to his foreign policy of nonalignment. But in 1971, angered by American support of India's enemy, Pakistan, Gandhi formed an alliance with the Soviet Union. In pursuit of India's security, Gandhi also pushed scientists to develop nuclear weapons. In 1974, India successfully tested a nuclear bomb.

Indira Gandhi was twice reelected to office. In 1975, however, a court found her guilty of corruption and ordered her to step down as prime

Indira Gandhi served as India's first woman prime minister and continued the socialist economic policies of her father, Nehru.

minister. In response, Gandhi accused her opponents of trying to tear the nation apart. She declared a "state of emergency" in order "to save the country from disintegration and collapse."

Instead of resigning, Gandhi assumed almost dictatorial powers. She suspended civil rights, censored the press, and jailed thousands of her political opponents. Gandhi justified her actions by saying that she was like a mother whose child, India, needed a strong dose of bitter medicine.

In 1977, confident of her popularity, Gandhi called for new elections. To her surprise, she was voted out of office. But the new government proved to be divided and ineffective. In 1980, India's voters elected Gandhi to her fourth term as prime minister.

One of the problems Gandhi faced in the 1980s was a growing independence movement among the Sikhs (seeks), a minority religious group. In 1984, militant Sikhs took over the Sikhs' holiest shrine, the Golden Temple in Amritsar. Gandhi ordered troops to drive the militants from the temple. During the assault, hundreds of people were killed. Afterward, many Sikhs bitterly resented Gandhi's action. In October 1984, the prime minister was assassinated by two of her own Sikh bodyguards.

Economic Progress in India

After Gandhi's murder, her son, Rajiv Gandhi, succeeded her as prime minister. India's new leader reversed his mother's socialist policies. Rajiv Gandhi argued that the cause of India's backwardness was government interference in the economy. His government cut taxes, reduced tariffs on imports, and encouraged entrepreneurs. The country's industrial output shot upward.

Rajiv Gandhi left office in 1989, and succeeding governments continued his pro-business policies and promoted investments in science and technology. In the 1990s, computer-related businesses boomed in India. By the year 2004, the Indian software industry was employing six hundred thousand people and exporting $13 billion worth of services. The booming

Mother Teresa

In 1948, Mother Teresa, a Roman Catholic nun, established a religious order in the densely populated city of Calcutta (now called Kolkata) in eastern India. From then until her death in 1997, she ministered to people who live in some of the worst slums on earth. Mother Teresa called her order the Missionaries of Charity. Its nuns dress in simple Indian clothes and tend to the needs of the poor and the sick. The order has grown to operate hospitals, schools, and orphanages. In 1979, Mother Teresa received the Nobel Peace Prize for her work.

Mother Teresa

high-tech industries led to the growth of a large new middle class.

Indian agriculture, however, lagged behind, and the country struggled to feed itself. Moreover, lack of education prevented millions of Indians from advancing. At the end of the 1990s, about a third of India's people remained desperately poor. Many of them lived in dismal city slums. The world's largest democracy entered the twenty-first century with its economic progress still weighed down by age-old problems.

Pakistan and Bangladesh

The partition of India in 1947 both created and divided the new Islamic nation of Pakistan. West Pakistan and East Pakistan were separated not

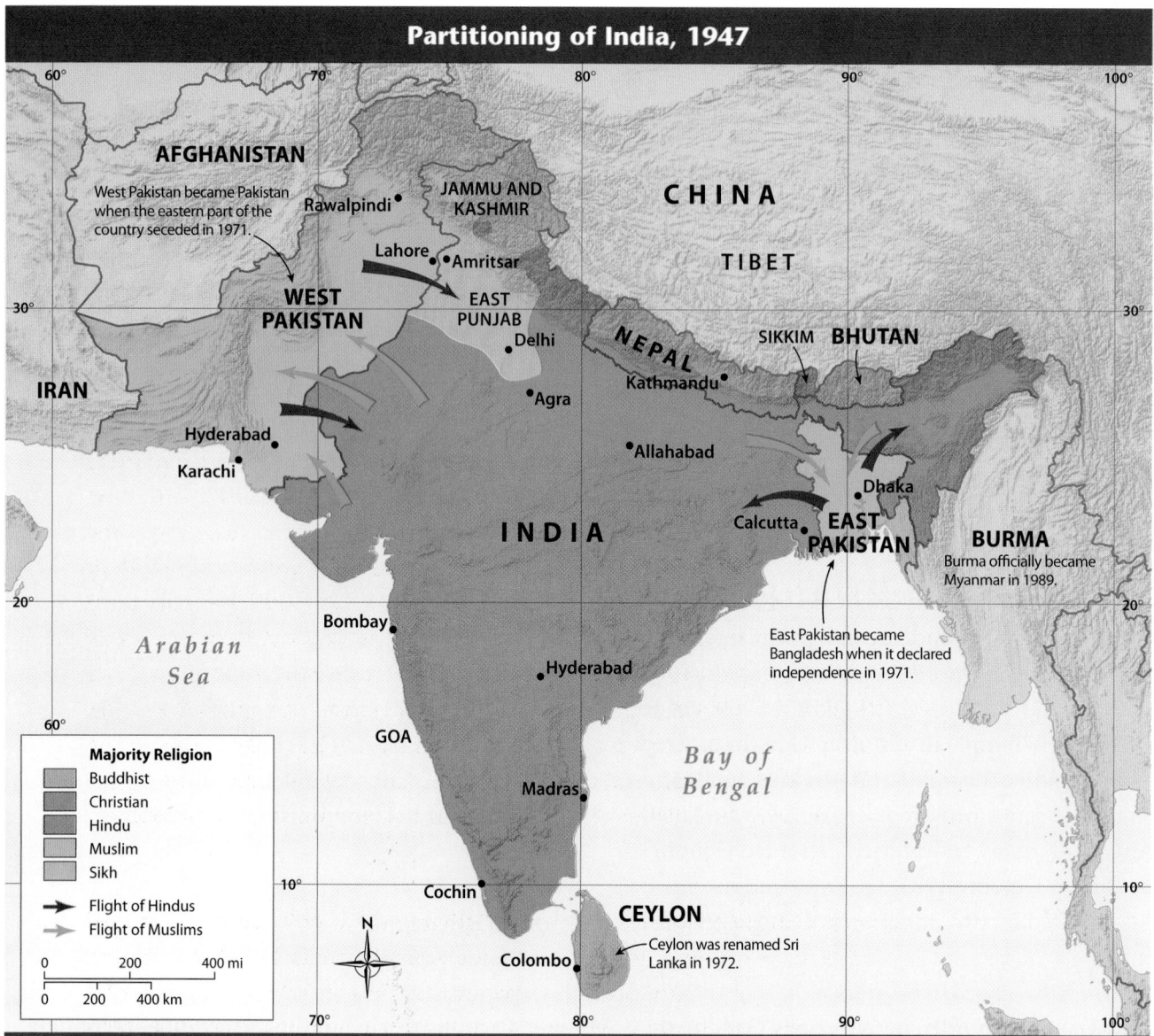

Partitioning of India, 1947

West Pakistan became Pakistan when the eastern part of the country seceded in 1971.

East Pakistan became Bangladesh when it declared independence in 1971.

Burma officially became Myanmar in 1989.

Ceylon was renamed Sri Lanka in 1972.

Majority Religion
- Buddhist
- Christian
- Hindu
- Muslim
- Sikh

→ Flight of Hindus
→ Flight of Muslims

0   200   400 mi
0 200   400 km

Intense religious differences sparked the division of British India into the independent states of India and Pakistan in 1947. Religious tensions continue to trouble the region.

only by a thousand miles of Indian territory, but also by ethnic background, language, and culture. From the beginning, power was concentrated in West Pakistan. The government devoted most of its resources to the west and largely ignored the poverty-stricken east.

In 1971, East Pakistan declared itself an independent state called Bangladesh. Civil war followed, and India sent troops to support the cause of an independent Bangladesh. In a brief yet brutal war, the Indians defeated the Pakistani government troops. Bangladesh became a

struggling democracy. It remains one of the poorest countries on earth, with few resources and many natural disasters, including devastating cyclones, floods, and tsunamis.

Democracy never fully took hold in Pakistan. Throughout its history, the military has wielded great political power. Elected governments have alternated with periods of military rule. In addition, Pakistan has experienced conflict between its various ethnic groups, and between those who want a strict Islamic government and those who favor separation between religion and the state.

Southeast Asia

The nations of Southeast Asia include the mainland countries of Myanmar (formerly called Burma), Cambodia, Laos, and Vietnam, as well as the vast island chain of Indonesia. After World War II, these nations struggled to free themselves from European colonial rule. They achieved independence, but then fell into decades of warfare and political turmoil.

Vietnam's Struggles

During the 1800s, the French gained control of Indochina, the region south of China that includes the present-day countries of Vietnam, Laos, and Cambodia. In the early 1900s, a nationalist movement took root in Vietnam. By the 1940s, the movement against French colonial rule had grown in strength. It was led by a man who would become known as Ho Chi Minh (hoh chee min).

The son of a Vietnamese scholar, Ho left home in 1912 at the age of twenty-one. He first traveled to New York, where he worked odd jobs. Later he moved to England and then to France. In France, he studied the works of Karl Marx and embraced communism. In 1920, he became a founding member of the French Communist Party. Later he traveled to the Soviet Union and China, where his commitment to communism intensified.

Ho Chi Minh Fights for Independence

In 1941, Ho Chi Minh returned to Vietnam, just after Japan had occupied parts of the country. He formed an underground organization, the Vietminh (vee-et MIN), to fight both the Japanese invaders and the French colonialists. It was during this time that he adopted the name Ho Chi Minh (which means "Illuminator").

For the next four years, the Vietminh waged a guerrilla war against the Japanese. As World War II came to an end, the Japanese retreated from Vietnam, and Ho's forces moved into the areas the Japanese had abandoned. By the time peace was declared, Ho Chi Minh was in control of the country. In 1945, he declared Vietnam an independent nation.

The French, however, were determined to keep Vietnam as a colony. For eight years, the French fought the Vietminh. Although the French sent more and more troops, they were unable to defeat Ho's determined guerrillas. In 1954, Ho's fighters defeated a large French force at Dien Bien Phu (dyen byen foo), a victory that finally ended France's rule in Indochina.

Independence and Division

At a peace conference held in Geneva, Switzerland, it was agreed that French Indochina would be divided into three countries—Laos, Cambodia, and

Key Questions

- Why did many countries of Southeast Asia gain independence after World War II?

- What events led to conflict in Vietnam after World War II? How did the United States become involved in the conflict? With what result?

- What are the key features of politics and society in modern-day Indonesia?

Southeast Asian countries sought independence after World War II.

817

Vietnam. It was also agreed that Vietnam would be temporarily divided into two parts, with the communists ruling the north and a noncommunist government ruling the south. Elections aimed at unifying the country under a single government were to be held within two years.

Those elections never took place, largely because the United States feared that Ho Chi Minh might win them. American leaders were worried by the victory of communism in China and feared its further spread in Asia. They encouraged the government in the south to ignore the requirement for nationwide elections. Vietnam became two countries—the Democratic Republic of Vietnam (also known as North Vietnam) and the Republic of Vietnam (also called South Vietnam).

Despite their names, neither country was truly democratic. In North Vietnam, Ho Chi Minh established a communist dictatorship modeled on the Soviet Union and China. His government controlled the country's economy and ruthlessly suppressed all dissent. South Vietnam was ruled by Ngo Dinh Diem (ngoh deen dee-EM), who believed his countrymen were not ready for Western-style democracy. Diem, who was Catholic, often dealt harshly with the country's Buddhist majority. But the United States supported Diem because he was anticommunist.

Colonialism had ended in Indochina, but the Cold War had arrived, with communists and anticommunists staring at each other across an increasingly hostile border. The years ahead would bring a final showdown in this ongoing struggle.

War in Vietnam

In Ho Chi Minh's eyes, the United States was, like France, a foreign power trying to dominate Vietnam. Ho regarded Diem, the ruler of South Vietnam, as a mere puppet of the United States. Beginning in 1959, Ho supported and supplied a group of southern communists, known as the Viet Cong, in their campaign to overthrow Diem. In 1961, the American president John F. Kennedy

sent American military advisers to train and assist Diem's soldiers. Despite help from roughly three thousand U.S. military advisers, the Viet Cong grew stronger.

By 1963, there were more than sixteen thousand American advisers in Vietnam. At the end of the year, Diem was overthrown and killed by some of his own generals. But the new South Vietnamese government proved just as incapable of defeating the Viet Cong.

In November 1963, only weeks after Diem was killed, President Kennedy was assassinated. He was succeeded by Lyndon Johnson, a fervent anticommunist. Shortly before he became president, Johnson had warned, "The battle against communism must be joined in Southeast Asia with strength and determination...or the United States, inevitably, must surrender the Pacific and take up our defenses on our own shores."

Johnson escalated the war—that is, he increased American involvement and commitment. He sent more American soldiers. By 1966, there were some three hundred eighty-five thousand American troops in Vietnam.

Tens of thousands of North Vietnamese soldiers surged south to join the Viet Cong in fighting the Americans and South Vietnamese. Beginning in 1966, the United States launched constant air strikes against North Vietnam. One North Vietnamese remembered, "The Americans thought that the more bombs they dropped, the quicker we would fall to our knees and surrender. But the bombs heightened rather than dampened our spirit."

In fighting the Viet Cong, Americans had the advantage of the most advanced weapons on earth. But they faced

A poster from the late 1960s depicts Viet Cong soldiers.

an elusive enemy who could strike quickly and then blend back into the countryside. Many civilians fell victim to the devastation caused by U.S. firepower, which increased support for the Viet Cong.

As the war dragged on into the late 1960s, there seemed to be no end in sight. American public opinion turned against further involvement in Vietnam. In 1969, a new American president, Richard Nixon, began withdrawing troops. He planned to turn most of the fighting over to South Vietnamese soldiers—a process he called the "Vietnamization" of the war.

In 1973, a cease-fire agreement was signed. The agreement called for the United States to pull

A Vietnamese mother and her children ford a river as they flee a U.S. bombing raid.

Vietnam Conflict, 1964–1975

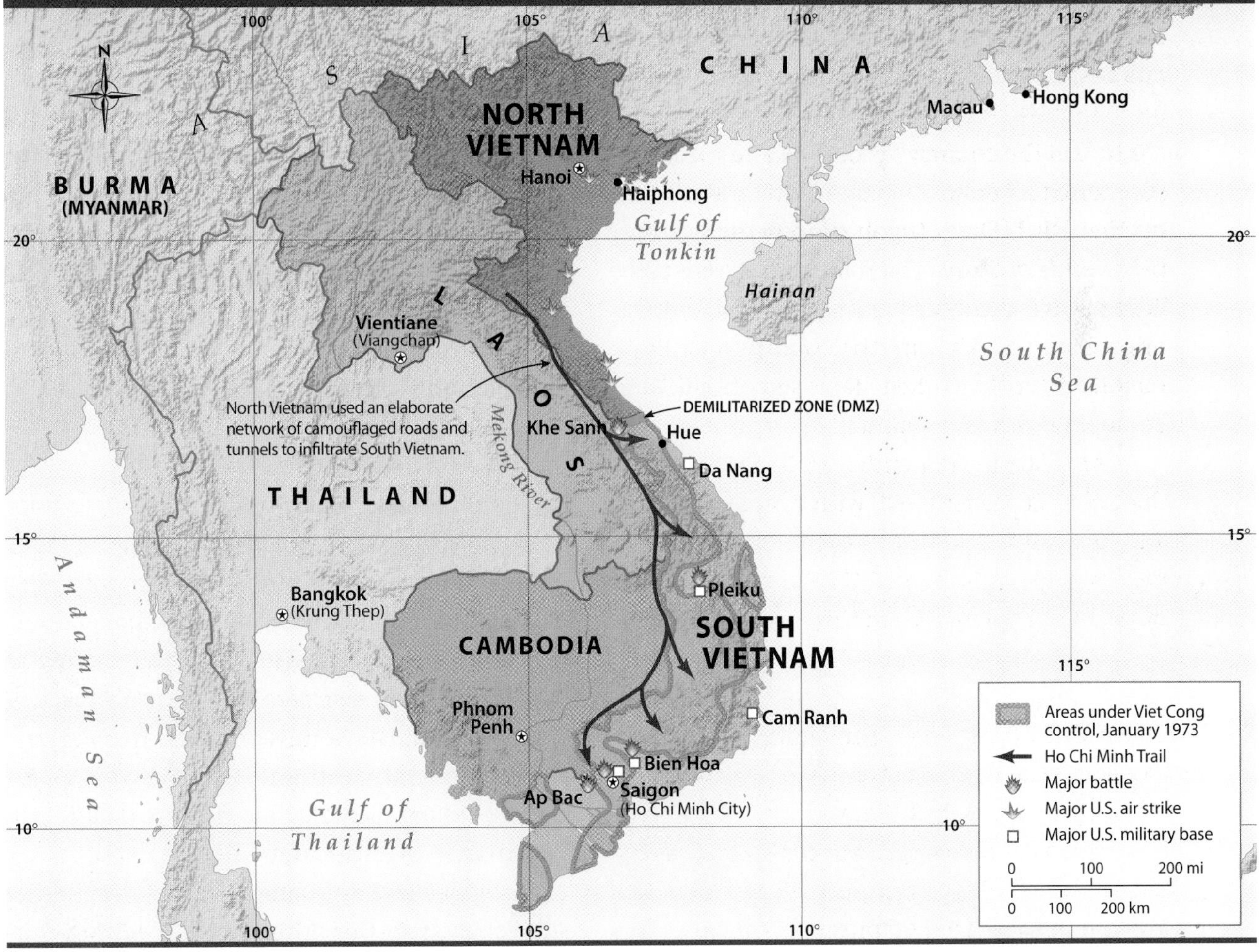

Map legend:
- Areas under Viet Cong control, January 1973
- Ho Chi Minh Trail
- Major battle
- Major U.S. air strike
- Major U.S. military base

Map labels: CHINA, Macau, Hong Kong, NORTH VIETNAM, Hanoi, Haiphong, Gulf of Tonkin, Hainan, BURMA (MYANMAR), Vientiane (Viangchan), South China Sea, LAOS, Mekong River, DEMILITARIZED ZONE (DMZ), Khe Sanh, Hue, Da Nang, THAILAND, Bangkok (Krung Thep), Pleiku, CAMBODIA, SOUTH VIETNAM, Andaman Sea, Phnom Penh, Cam Ranh, Bien Hoa, Ap Bac, Saigon (Ho Chi Minh City), Gulf of Thailand

North Vietnam used an elaborate network of camouflaged roads and tunnels to infiltrate South Vietnam.

Scale: 0 100 200 mi / 0 100 200 km

The long, deadly war in Vietnam was part of a larger Cold War struggle in the region between factions aligned with either the Soviet Union or the United States.

its troops out of Vietnam, and for South Vietnam to be ruled by a freely elected government. Nixon declared that he had achieved "peace with honor." But as the last U.S. ground forces left, the North Vietnamese violated the agreement by invading the South.

The South Vietnamese fought on for two more years. They were hampered by the cut-off of most U.S. aid and a lack of effective military leaders. In the spring of 1975, communist troops reached the capital city of Saigon, and the South Vietnamese government surrendered. Saigon soon received a new name—Ho Chi Minh City.

North and South Vietnam were now reunited by force into a single communist nation, the Socialist Republic of Vietnam. Communist leaders imprisoned thousands of people who had worked or fought for the United States. Over the next several years, more than a million people left the country, fleeing poverty and political oppression.

Communist Vietnam

After their victory, the communists instituted a harsh dictatorship throughout the country. Thousands of South Vietnamese were sent to be "reeducated" in concentration camps. No one was allowed to speak against the Communist Party. As in China, farmers were deprived of their land

A helicopter evacuates South Vietnamese from Saigon as the city falls to the communists in the spring of 1975.

and forced to work on collective farms. The state took control of industry.

Collective agriculture proved inefficient, and many Vietnamese went hungry. Faced with government takeover of their businesses, many merchants and manufacturers in the south fled the country. In 1978, a new war broke out—this time between Vietnam and its neighbor, Cambodia. The costs of the war further drained the nation's resources. By the early 1980s, Vietnam's economy was in shambles.

In the late 1980s, the government announced a new economic policy of "renovation." Collective farms were dismantled. State-owned industries were sold off, and foreign companies were encouraged to invest in Vietnam. With these reforms, the economy gained strength through the 1990s.

Today, Vietnam has a sizeable middle class that can afford to buy electronics and luxury goods made in the West. The United States, which officially recognized the communist government in 1995, is Vietnam's main trading partner. Still, poverty remains a widespread problem in Vietnam, especially in rural areas. As in China, economic liberalization has not led to political liberty. The Communist Party remains firmly in control and tolerates no dissent.

Carnage in Cambodia

In the nineteenth century, Vietnam's neighbor, Cambodia, was colonized by France. In the 1950s, under the leadership of Prince Norodom Sihanouk (NAWR-uh-dahm SEE-uh-nouk), Cambodia won its independence. During the Vietnam War, fighting between American and North Vietnamese forces spilled over into Cambodia. In 1975, the year of the communist victory in Vietnam, a communist group called the Khmer Rouge (kuh-MEHR roozh) took over in Cambodia.

Led by a dictator named Pol Pot, the Khmer Rouge set out to transform Cambodia into a communist society. They took Mao Zedong's Great Leap Forward as their model.

Armed Khmer Rouge guerrillas, directed by Pol Pot, fought to transform Cambodia into a communist society.

The Khmer Rouge abolished private property and even the use of money. They shut down schools, hospitals, and shops. Cambodia's cities emptied as their residents were forced into the countryside to work as farmers. People were arrested for the "crime" of having an education. Tens of thousands were thrown into prison, where they were tortured and executed. Many more starved to death as the country's economy collapsed.

Under Pol Pot, the Khmer Rouge undertook one of the worst mass slaughters in modern times. At least 1.5 million people died—20 percent of the country's population.

In 1979, Vietnam invaded Cambodia and drove Pol Pot from power. For the next decade, Vietnam occupied Cambodia and fought a guerrilla war with the remnants of the Khmer Rouge.

A peace treaty signed in 1991 called for democratic elections. The country's royal family returned from exile, and Cambodia became a constitutional monarchy. In the early twenty-first century, some of the surviving Khmer Rouge leaders were put on trial for crimes against humanity.

Military Rule in Myanmar

In Southeast Asia, to the east of India lies a country now called Myanmar (myan-MAR), but long known as Burma. In the 1800s, Burma was colonized by Britain. During World War II, the country was invaded by Japan. After the war, a Burmese nationalist, Aung San (awn sahn), led a movement to win the country's independence from Britain. Aung San was assassinated in 1947, just before he was set to become prime minister of the newly independent nation.

After breaking away from Britain, Burma enjoyed a few years of democracy. But in 1962, a group of army officers seized power and established a military dictatorship. In 1988, widespread demonstrations broke out against the military government. The military leaders forcefully suppressed the protests, killing thousands. But the pro-democracy movement continued to spread, led by Aung San's daughter, Aung San Suu Kyi (awn sahn soo chee).

The military government promised free elections, but it placed Suu Kyi under house arrest to prevent her from campaigning. (A person under house arrest is not allowed to leave his or her home, and contacts with the outside world are limited.) Nevertheless, when elections were held in 1990, Suu Kyi's party won four-fifths of the vote. The military leaders

Aung San Suu Kyi worked to bring democracy to Burma.

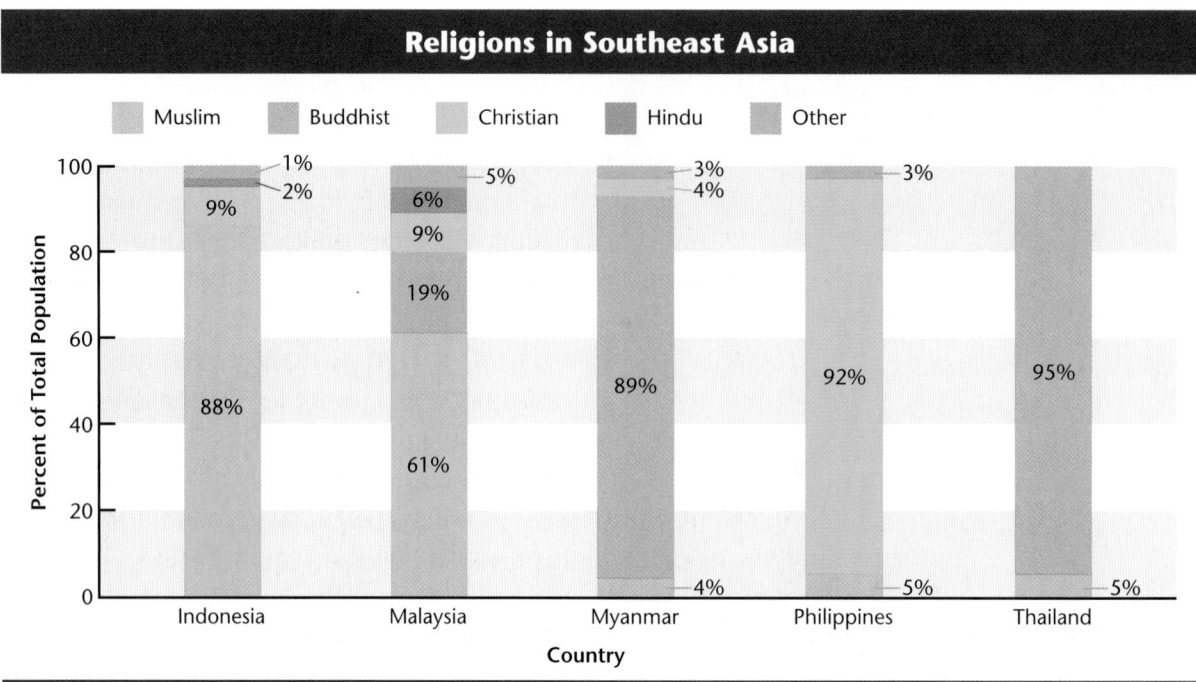

ignored the election results and refused to give up power.

By this time, Suu Kyi's brave defiance of military rule had made her an international symbol of the struggle for democracy. In 1991, she was awarded the Nobel Peace Prize. In late 2010, after seven years under house arrest, Aung San Suu Kyi was freed by Myanmar's military rulers. She continued to speak out for democracy and human rights.

Indonesia: Progress and Problems

The nation of Indonesia consists of more than seventeen thousand islands stretching from the Indian Ocean to the Pacific Ocean. A former Dutch colony, Indonesia won its independence after World War II. The leader of the independence movement, Sukarno, became the country's first president. (Like many Indonesians, Sukarno went by one name.)

In the 1960s, Sukarno adopted socialist economic policies and increasingly allied himself with Indonesian communists. By the middle of the decade, Sukarno's policies had brought the country close to bankruptcy. In 1965, a group of army officers overthrew Sukarno and took over the government. To secure their grip on power, they killed hundreds of thousands of communists or suspected communists.

The leader of the coup, General Suharto, took control of Indonesia. He ruled the country for more than three decades. Suharto's government revived Indonesia's economy by encouraging foreign investment and the development of an oil industry. But in 1997, a severe *recession* struck the country. Many Indonesians charged government leaders with corruption and blamed them for the country's economic problems. In 1998, violent protests forced Suharto to give up power. After Suharto stepped down, Indonesia adopted a democratic form of government.

Indonesia, currently the world's fourth most populous country, is home to more than three hundred different ethnic groups. Indonesia's religious makeup includes a sizeable minority of Christians alongside its Muslim majority. The country continues to experience conflict based on religious and ethnic divisions. In recent years, Indonesia has also experienced major natural disasters, including a devastating tsunami that struck the islands in 2004.

> When business activity slows down, an economy can go into a *recession*, usually marked by a drop in sales and consumer spending, and a rise in unemployment.

Change in East Asia

World War II and the Cold War had tremendous effects on various nations in eastern Asian. Japanese cities lay in ruins, and the economy was shattered, yet over the course of the three decades following World War II, the Japanese economy revived with staggering speed.

Korea, as you have learned, became a hot spot during the Cold War, as fighting left the country divided into a communist north and a noncommunist south, with tensions continuing to this day. After World War II, the former American colony of the Philippines also struggled to find its way, passing from democracy to dictatorship and back to democracy.

Japan Rebuilds and Reforms

After the defeat of Japan in World War II, American troops occupied the island nation. Just as the United States enacted the Marshall Plan to rebuild Europe, it also helped rebuild Japan, for reasons partly motivated by the Cold War. The United States wanted a stable, friendly Japan to stand as an ally against the spread of communism in East Asia. The commander of the American forces, General Douglas MacArthur, devised an ambitious plan to transform the heavily militarized country into a peaceful and democratic nation.

MacArthur disbanded the Japanese military and removed all wartime leaders from power. He also ordered top Japanese generals tried for war crimes. He left the emperor in office as a figurehead, since he knew that most Japanese revered their emperor. But MacArthur made the emperor announce that he was only a man and not, as Japanese tradition held, a god.

Most important, MacArthur forced the Japanese to accept a new constitution. One of its terms declared, "The Japanese people forever renounce war as a sovereign right of the nation…. Land, sea, and air forces…will never be maintained." Other provisions gave women equal rights with men, including the right to vote. Individual liberties listed in the United States Bill of Rights—such as freedom of speech, assembly, and religion—were guaranteed by Japan's new constitution.

Japan's Economic Revival

In the devastated landscape of postwar Japan, the Japanese people endured great hardships. Japan's economy and society had been shattered by the war. Large sections of Tokyo and other cities had been flattened by American bombs. Millions of families were homeless. Food distribution had broken down, leaving most of the civilian population malnourished. In the first years of the occupation, most Japanese people depended on emergency food aid from America.

Key Questions

- What political and economic transformations occurred in Japan after World War II? How did they occur?

- How have North and South Korea developed differently since the end of the Korean War?

- What challenges does the Philippines face?

Japan, North Korea, South Korea, and the Philippines

823

The Japanese economy began to revive in 1950, with the outbreak of the Korean War. The American forces fighting in Korea were supplied from nearby Japan. Japanese factories made vehicles, uniforms, and medicine for the troops. Japanese mechanics repaired American tanks and aircraft. Unemployment dropped and wages rose.

The Korean War helped the Japanese rebuild their factories. Through the 1950s, Japan's government encouraged the expansion of heavy industry, especially the production of steel and automobiles. Many Japanese people moved from the countryside to cities to take advantage of manufacturing jobs. Between 1950 and 1972, the proportion of Japanese living in cities climbed from 38 percent to 72 percent. Productivity soared, assisted by the strong work ethic of the Japanese.

The extent and pace of Japan's economic recovery was unparalleled. By 1968, Japan had the world's second-largest economy, after the United States. By the 1970s, the country as a whole had achieved a level of prosperity comparable to that of the United States or Western Europe. Like Americans, most Japanese considered possessions like cars, color televisions, and washing machines to be necessities rather than luxuries. People who remembered the devastation of the war years spoke with amazement of how far Japan had come.

But the new consumer society caused problems. Banks eagerly loaned money and people used the easy credit to buy things they could not really afford, especially houses and land. The price of real estate soared. Around 1990, the bubble of inflated prices burst. Japan entered a deep recession. Through the 1990s, the country experienced a stagnant economy and high unemployment.

Despite the problems of the 1990s, Japan still had the world's second-largest economy until 2010, when it dropped to third, behind China.

Mount Fuji graces the landscape near the vibrant city of Toyko, Japan.

Shoppers crowd a busy street in Tokyo. As of 2010, Japan had the world's third-largest economy.

Korea Divided and at Odds

After the Korean War, the Korean Peninsula remained divided into a communist North and a noncommunist South. The dictator of North Korea, Kim Il Sung, ruled his country with an iron fist. He executed or imprisoned all who dared to speak out against him. Kim was a megalomaniac—a person fanatically convinced of his own greatness. He ordered gigantic statues of himself built throughout the country. He insisted that people address him by titles such as "Fatherly Leader" or "Genius of Mankind."

Kim instituted a **command economy**, with all factories and farms controlled by the government. Kim's government also dictated the prices of goods. Because he wanted North Korea to be a major military power, he ordered factories to concentrate on producing arms. For a time, the economy grew because of aid from Kim's communist allies in the Soviet Union and China. But

when this aid declined in the 1960s, the focus on military spending proved disastrous for North Korea's economy.

Unlike China and Vietnam, North Korea has not moved to liberalize its economy. Since the 1960s, the regime's agricultural policies have caused periodic famines. The worst of these came in the late 1990s and led to hundreds of thousands of deaths.

Kim Il Sung died in 1994 and was replaced as dictator by his son, Kim Jong Il. Like his father, the younger Kim has been obsessed with increasing North Korea's military might. By 2005, his government had acquired nuclear weapons. Today, because of the country's aggressiveness, many consider a nuclear-armed North Korea a serious threat.

South Korea

During the Korean War, American and United Nations troops kept North Korea from imposing communist rule on the South. South Korea did not succumb to communism, but neither did it immediately become a democracy. Its wartime leader, Syngman Rhee, was a harsh authoritarian who suppressed dissent and jailed his opponents.

An enormous statue honors Kim Il Sung, who ruled North Korea with an iron fist in the years after the Korean War.

825

Prosperity in Singapore

Like South Korea, the tiny island city-state of Singapore, off the southern tip of the Malay Peninsula, has seen tremendous economic growth in recent decades. Since independence in 1965, Singapore's government has poured enormous resources into developing new industries and strengthening the nation's labor force through its education and health care systems. Today, Singapore is home to one of the world's busiest ports, and it has become a leading financial center, petroleum refiner, and exporter of electronics and technology. As a result, Singapore's standard of living and average life expectancy are among the highest in the world. While Singapore's government has promoted economic growth, it has limited some civil rights, prompting calls for reform.

Since gaining independence in 1965, Singapore has enjoyed extraordinary economic growth.

After Rhee stepped down in 1960, political power soon passed to the army. For almost three decades, South Korea was run by a series of military dictators. In 1987, massive pro-democracy demonstrations led by college students forced the last military strongman to resign. A free election followed, and South Korea became a functioning democracy.

Like Japan, South Korea has been one of Asia's economic success stories. Under both dictators and military leaders, the government strongly promoted economic growth. It encouraged savings over consumption, and emphasized the education of the workforce. As a result, the economy grew nearly as quickly as Japan's. Today south Korea has one of the twenty largest economies in the world.

Koreans on both sides of the border share a common culture and traditions. Most long to see the country reunified. But when the democratic leaders of South Korea have put forward ideas for reunification, they have been rejected by the hostile, suspicious rulers of the North.

The Philippines

The Philippines, a group of islands in Southeast Asia, was colonized by Spain in the 1500s. After the Spanish-American War of 1898, control of the islands passed to the United States. In 1946, the Philippines became an independent nation. The country adopted a democratic system of government largely modeled on that of the United States.

By the early 1970s, the unity and peace of the Philippines was threatened by two guerrilla movements—one made up of communists, and the other of Muslims who wanted to form a separate nation. In response to these threats, the elected president Ferdinand Marcos declared martial law. (Under martial law, a government can suspend civil rights and use military force to maintain order.)

Gradually, President Marcos acted more and more like a dictator. He ordered protesters to be arrested and tortured. He used his power to enrich his friends and family members. By the 1980s, the Filipino people began to turn against the corrupt and repressive Marcos regime. In 1983, a popular opposition politician, Benigno Aquino (beh-NEEG-noh ah-KEE-noh), was assassinated. Aquino's supporters suspected that Marcos had ordered the killing.

In 1986, Aquino's widow, Corazon Aquino, ran for president. Marcos rigged the election and declared himself the winner. Aquino then led a series of mass protests against the government. This "People Power Revolution," as it was called, coupled with pressure from the United States,

After the dictatorship of Ferdinand Marcos, President Corazon Aquino helped restore democratic rule to the Philippines.

drove Marcos out of office and into exile. Aquino succeeded him as president.

Since 1986, the Philippines has once again enjoyed a democratic form of government. But the country still faces many challenges, including a Muslim separatist movement. Unlike many of its East Asian neighbors, which industrialized rapidly after World War II, the Philippines has remained largely agricultural. Combined with overpopulation, the lack of economic development has kept many Filipinos trapped in poverty.

Chapter 35
CONTEMPORARY AFRICA AND THE MIDDLE EAST
1945–2010

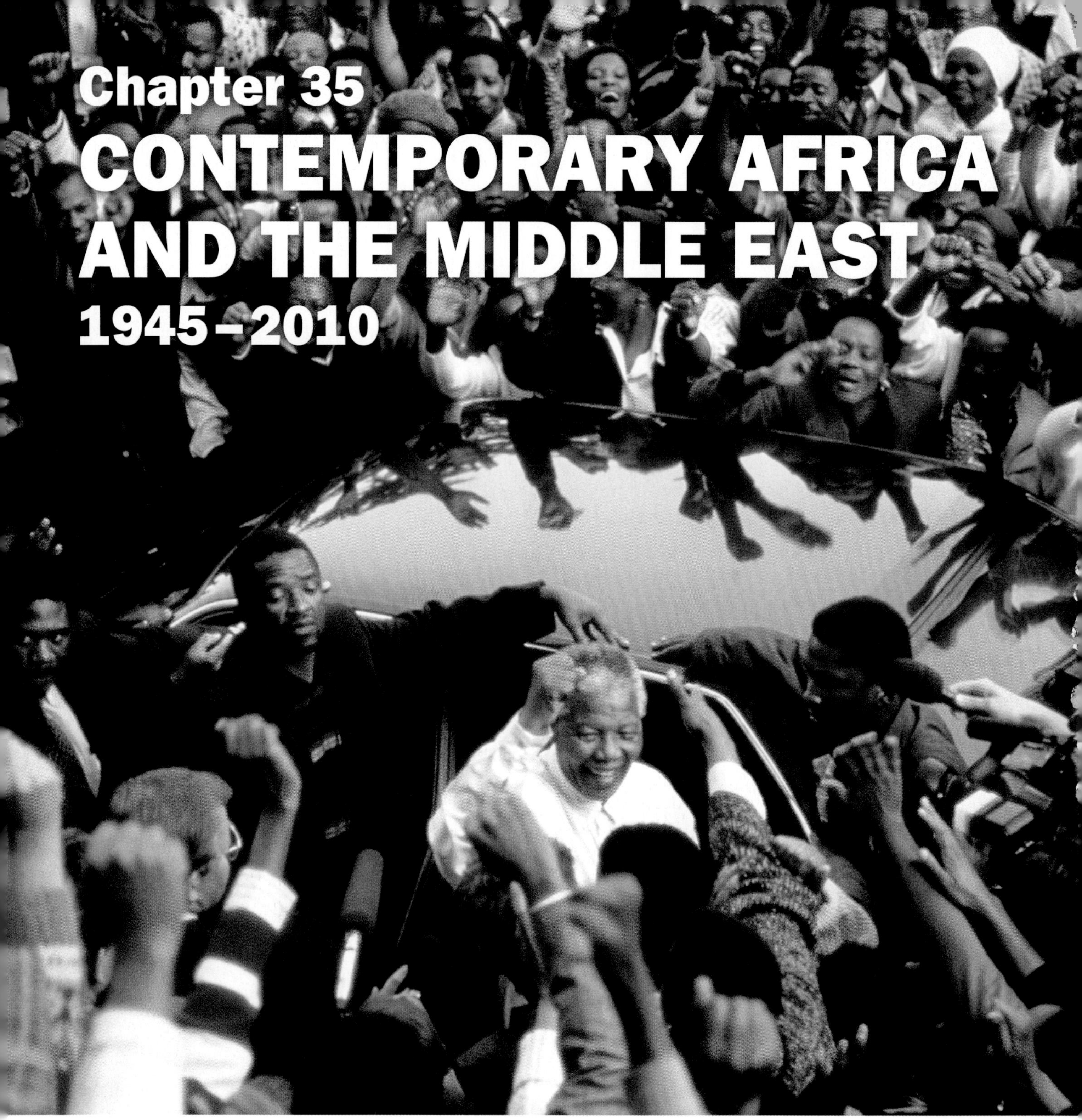

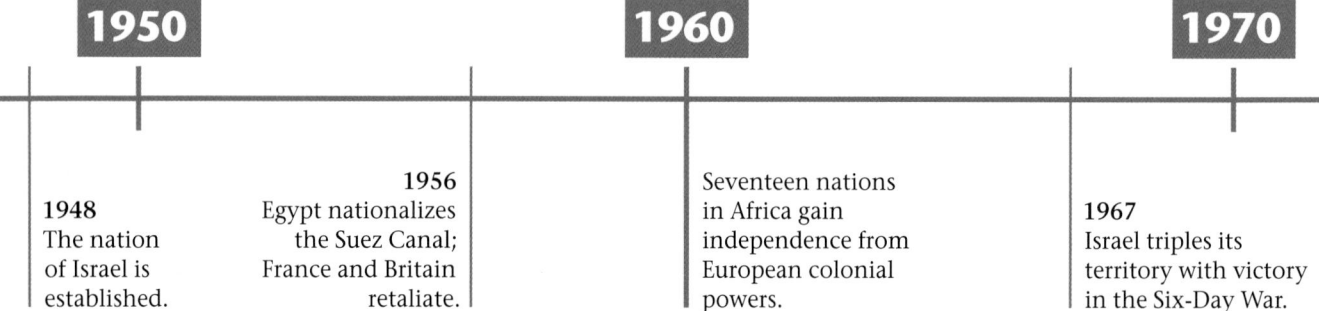

1950		**1960**		**1970**

1948
The nation of Israel is established.

1956
Egypt nationalizes the Suez Canal; France and Britain retaliate.

Seventeen nations in Africa gain independence from European colonial powers.

1967
Israel triples its territory with victory in the Six-Day War.

Left: Nelson Mandela of South Africa is greeted by a crowd in 1994. *Right:* Oil fuels development in the Middle East.

*I*n the late nineteenth and early twentieth centuries, the imperial powers of Europe dominated the countries of Africa and the region known as the Middle East. In the period after World War II, however, Europe's nations abandoned most of their colonies. African nations won independence and struggled to modernize. But they faced severe challenges that have persisted until today, including ethnic divisions, repressive rulers, and lingering poverty.

Conflicts also arose in the newly independent Muslim countries of the Middle East. Those who favored secular, Western forms of government opposed those who advocated governments based on a strict version of Islam. At the end of the twentieth century, this conflict erupted out of the Middle East and spilled across the world in acts of terrorism.

1980

1990

1979
A revolution in Iran
establishes an anti-Western,
Islamist regime.

1994
Anti-apartheid activist
Nelson Mandela is elected
president of South Africa.

830

The End of Colonialism in Africa

Key Questions

- What major challenges did African colonies experience as they gained independence from European powers?

In the 1940s, most of the African continent was still ruled by European powers. After World War II, however, nationalist leaders in dozens of countries fought to end colonial rule. Many of these leaders had been educated in Europe and challenged European governments to live up to their own principles of democracy and human rights. They invoked the UN Declaration of Human Rights, which upheld the idea that all nations should rule themselves.

Africa: Struggles for Independence

Most African nations gained their independence in the 1950s and 1960s. For some, the process was peaceful. For others, freedom came as the result of bloody rebellions. Throughout Africa, independence brought challenges. New nations struggled to achieve stable governments and economies. Many experienced conflict between rival ethnic groups. Some countries lapsed into civil war.

From Gold Coast to Ghana

The Gold Coast, as it was long known, was the most prosperous of Britain's African colonies, rich in minerals and agricultural products such as cocoa. By the early 1950s, Britain allowed the colony a measure of self-government. A nationalist leader, Kwame Nkrumah (KWAH-mee uhn-KROO-muh), who had been educated at colleges in the United States, called for total independence. Leading a peaceful campaign of strikes and boycotts, Nkrumah forced the British to give in to his demands. In 1957, the Gold Coast became the new nation of Ghana, with Nkrumah as its first prime minister.

Inspired by the example of Nkrumah, nationalists across Africa determined to end colonial rule. At a meeting called by Nkrumah in 1958, a union leader from Kenya addressed the colonial powers. "Your time is past," he declared. "Africa must be free."

Nkrumah worked to modernize Ghana. He ordered the building of schools, roads, and hospitals. However, his rule soon became more authoritarian. In 1964, Nkrumah declared Ghana a one-party state with himself as "president for life." Two years later, the army overthrew the increasingly unpopular leader. In the decades since, Ghana has alternated between periods of civilian and military rule.

Kenya: From the Mau Mau to Kenyatta

In Britain's East African colony of Kenya, independence came only after a bloody guerrilla war. Unlike Ghana, Kenya was home to many white settlers,

African nations gained independence after WWII.

831

who claimed the country's richest agricultural lands and stood opposed to independence for the colony.

In the late 1940s, a guerrilla group known as the Mau Mau began a campaign of murder and intimidation designed to drive out the settlers. The colonial authorities reacted by killing thousands they suspected of being Mau Mau and throwing many people into prison or concentration camps.

As the Mau Mau waged their violent campaign, a peaceful independence movement emerged, headed by Jomo Kenyatta. Despite Kenyatta's calls for peaceful change, the colonial authorities distrusted him. He was falsely charged with being the secret leader of the Mau Mau, and put on trial in 1953. He was sentenced to seven years in prison.

By the late 1950s, British leaders realized that they risked catastrophic bloodshed if they continued to hold on to their East African colonies by force. Between 1961 and 1964, Britain granted independence to Kenya as well as Tanzania, Uganda, Malawi, and Zambia. Jomo Kenyatta became the first president of the independent nation of Kenya.

Until his death in 1978, Kenyatta served as a democratic leader, aligning himself with the West during the Cold War. Today Kenya remains democratic, although its political system is weakened by conflict between ethnic groups.

Guerrilla War in Algeria

While Britain dominated eastern and southern Africa, France ruled vast areas in the north and west of the continent. The French treated their African colonies differently than the British treated theirs. Native leaders in French colonies could become full citizens of France and even serve in the national legislature in Paris. As a result, when the French colonies became independent nations in the late 1950s and early 1960s, their ruling classes remained strongly attached to French culture. In these countries, independence came about peacefully.

The exception was Algeria, a North African nation inhabited mostly by Muslim Arabs. There, the French faced the same problem that the British faced in Kenya—a large and powerful white minority that wanted the country to remain under colonial rule. Approximately one million Europeans owned most of the fertile farmland and dominated the government in Algeria, leaving eight million Arabs poor and powerless.

In 1954, a nationalist group known as the FLN (from the French initials for National Liberation Front) launched a guerrilla war against French rule. FLN guerrillas murdered white civilians as well as Arabs whom they regarded as government collaborators. In response, the French government sent hundreds of thousands of troops into the country. The guerrilla war raged for another eight years, with atrocities committed on both sides.

By 1962, France's president, Charles de Gaulle, decided that French rule in Algeria could no longer be justified. When he ordered his troops home, most white Algerians fled as well, fearing violence

Jomo Kenyatta, the first president of independent Kenya

Demonstrators both for and against independence from France pack a street in the Algerian capital of Algiers in 1961. After bitter fighting, France granted Algeria independence.

from the Arab majority. France's attempt to cling to a single colony had cost half a million lives or more.

The nationalists who took over the newly independent country seized the property and businesses of the departed colonists. They set up a one-party state that pursued socialist economic policies. In the late 1980s, Algeria instituted a more democratic political system. By that time, however, conflict had broken out between the government and Muslim radicals calling for Algeria to become an Islamic state—a conflict that has continued into the twenty-first century.

Struggles in the Congo

Beginning in the 1880s, the small European country of Belgium ruled the vast central African territory of Congo, a land seventy-five times the size of Belgium itself. At first, the Congo was run as the personal property of the Belgian king, Leopold II. The writer Joseph Conrad described the king's rule as "the vilest scramble for loot that

ever disfigured the history of human conscience." Leopold's officials forced millions of Congolese to labor under grueling conditions, harvesting rubber for export to Europe. Those who resisted were tortured or killed.

By 1908, after these ruthless acts had created a worldwide scandal, the Belgian government took over control of the colony from the king. Some of the worst abuses ended. But Belgium continued to treat Congo purely as a source of wealth. All political power was kept firmly in the hands of white rulers. Unlike France and Britain, Belgium never attempted to train native leaders. No Congolese were sent to Europe to be educated, and even the most talented could not enter professions such as medicine or law.

As a result, Congo was badly prepared for the independence it won in 1960. The new nation's first leader, the young Patrice Lumumba, impressed many Africans with his fiery anticolonial speeches. But the inexperienced Lumumba proved incapable

Congolese shout for joy in celebration of their country's newly won independence from Belgium in 1960.

of governing a huge country torn by ethnic divisions. In 1961, he was overthrown and murdered by his Congolese enemies, who were aided by the Belgians, who still had a large economic stake in the country.

Civil war raged through the country until 1965, when General Joseph-Désiré Mobutu seized power. For the next three decades, Mobutu ruled Congo as a dictator. He changed the name of the country to Zaire (zah-IHR), and for himself adopted the African name Mobutu Sese Seko (say-say SAY-koh). Always appearing in public wearing his trademark leopard-skin cap, he became one of the best-known of Africa's strongmen.

Because of his opposition to communism, Mobutu enjoyed the support of the United States, which feared the spread of Soviet influence in Africa. But Mobutu suppressed all dissent and plundered the country's natural resources to enrich himself and his family. In 1997, rebel forces finally overthrew Mobutu's corrupt regime, and the country's name was changed to Democratic Republic of the Congo.

The Portuguese Leave Angola

Portugal, the first European country to colonize Africa, would be the last to give up its territories on the continent. In 1960, Antonio Salazar, Portugal's dictatorial leader, mocked the European powers that were granting independence to their colonies. "We have been in Africa for four hundred years," he boasted, "which is rather more than to have arrived yesterday."

The Portuguese colony of Angola was located to the south of Congo. After World War II, the government encouraged inhabitants of Portugal to settle in Angola. By 1960, some two hundred thousand Portuguese were living in Angola, where, like the French settlers in Algeria, they dominated both the government and the economy. White landowners forced native laborers to work on plantations, which fueled the resentment of Angolan nationalists.

In 1961, several nationalist groups launched rebellions against Portuguese rule. Salazar reacted by sending troops to suppress the rebels. He also announced reforms, including the end of forced labor. But he made no move toward granting independence to the colony. Through the decade, the guerrilla war raged on. By the mid-1960s, with seventy thousand Portuguese troops in Angola, the conflict was draining the national treasury.

After Salazar suffered a stroke, another dictator took charge, but in 1974 a military coup in Portugal toppled the dictatorship. The new government recognized that Portugal could no longer afford the fight to keep its African colonies. In 1975, Angola won its independence. Nearly all the Portuguese settlers fled.

One of the rebel groups, the Marxist MPLA (from the Portuguese initials for the People's Movement for the Liberation of Angola), took over the government of the new nation. Angola soon became one of the battlegrounds of the Cold War between the United States and the Soviet Union. The MPLA pursued communist economic policies and looked to the Soviets and Cubans for support. In response, the United States financed noncommunist rebels that sought to oust the MPLA. The end of the Cold War brought no relief from the fighting. Civil war continued in Angola until 2002, when the various factions signed a peace agreement.

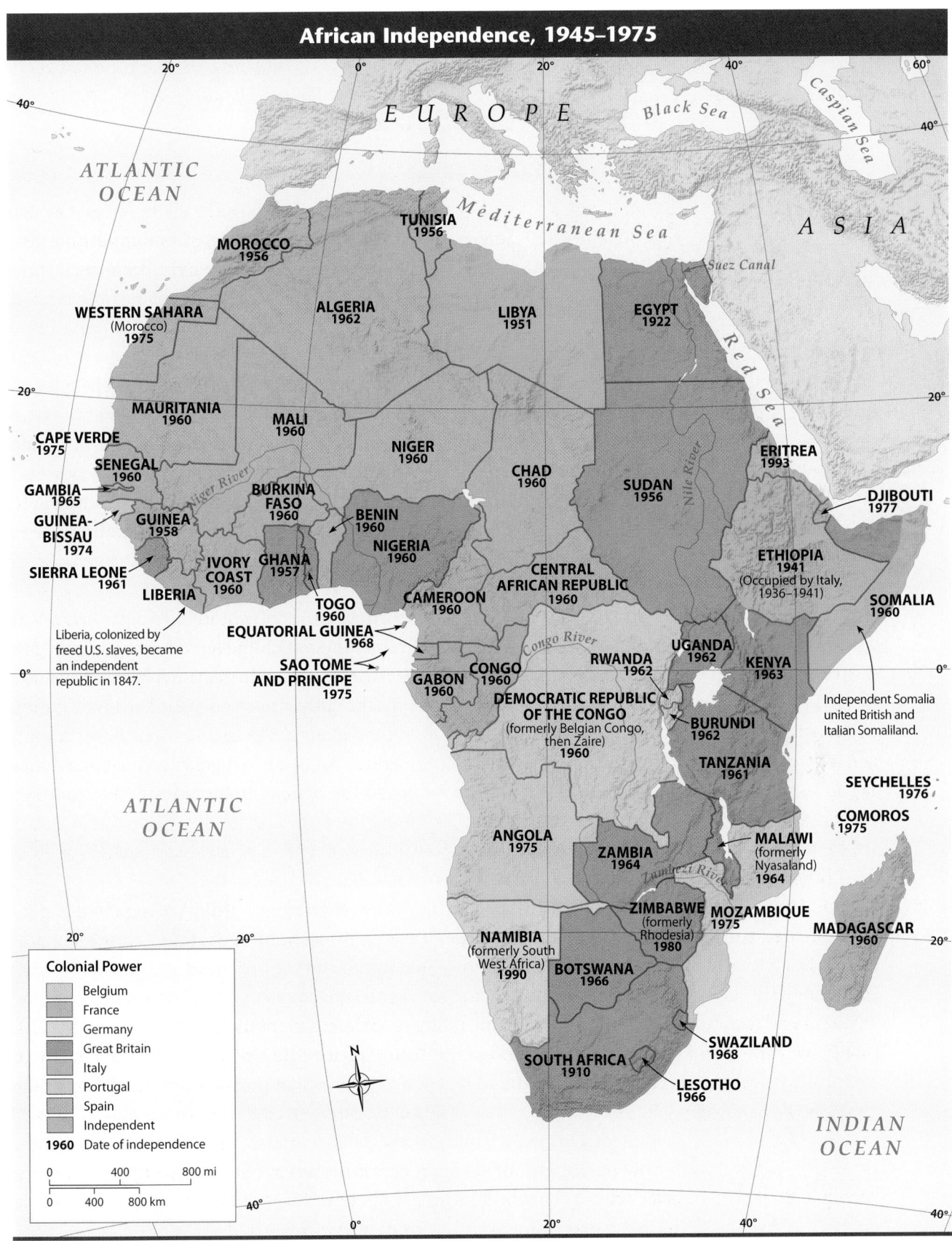

African Independence, 1945–1975

EUROPE

Black Sea

ATLANTIC OCEAN

ASIA

Caspian Sea

Mediterranean Sea

TUNISIA 1956

Suez Canal

MOROCCO 1956

WESTERN SAHARA (Morocco) 1975

ALGERIA 1962

LIBYA 1951

EGYPT 1922

Red Sea

MAURITANIA 1960

MALI 1960

CAPE VERDE 1975

NIGER 1960

CHAD 1960

SUDAN 1956

ERITREA 1993

Nile River

SENEGAL 1960

GAMBIA 1965

BURKINA FASO 1960

Niger River

GUINEA-BISSAU 1974

GUINEA 1958

BENIN 1960

DJIBOUTI 1977

SIERRA LEONE 1961

IVORY COAST 1960

GHANA 1957

NIGERIA 1960

CENTRAL AFRICAN REPUBLIC 1960

ETHIOPIA 1941 (Occupied by Italy, 1936–1941)

LIBERIA

TOGO 1960

CAMEROON 1960

SOMALIA 1960

Liberia, colonized by freed U.S. slaves, became an independent republic in 1847.

EQUATORIAL GUINEA 1968

SAO TOME AND PRINCIPE 1975

GABON 1960

CONGO 1960

Congo River

DEMOCRATIC REPUBLIC OF THE CONGO (formerly Belgian Congo, then Zaire) 1960

RWANDA 1962

UGANDA 1962

KENYA 1963

BURUNDI 1962

Independent Somalia united British and Italian Somaliland.

TANZANIA 1961

ATLANTIC OCEAN

SEYCHELLES 1976

COMOROS 1975

ANGOLA 1975

ZAMBIA 1964

MALAWI (formerly Nyasaland) 1964

Zambezi River

MADAGASCAR 1960

ZIMBABWE (formerly Rhodesia) 1980

MOZAMBIQUE 1975

NAMIBIA (formerly South West Africa) 1990

BOTSWANA 1966

SWAZILAND 1968

SOUTH AFRICA 1910

LESOTHO 1966

INDIAN OCEAN

N

Colonial Power

- Belgium
- France
- Germany
- Great Britain
- Italy
- Portugal
- Spain
- Independent

1960 Date of independence

0   400   800 mi

0   400   800 km

African independence movements gained momentum after World War II. By 1975, almost all of the continent was free from European control.

Challenges for Postcolonial Africa

Key Questions

- Why did violence and civil war erupt in many newly independent African nations?

- What economic, social, and environmental struggles do many African nations face?

Since the 1960s, many African nations have suffered violent ethnic conflicts. Tens of thousands of Rwandans and Sudanese have been the victims of campaigns of genocide (the attempted extermination of a whole people). Civil war in two of Africa's largest countries, Nigeria and Congo, caused millions of deaths.

Elsewhere, however, wise leadership averted conflict between peoples. In South Africa, where whites had long dominated blacks through a racist system known as apartheid, Nelson Mandela helped create a multicultural democracy by calling for the races to live together in equality and peace. However, in South Africa and across the continent, Africa's governments struggle to feed and house their people, as well as to fight the spread of deadly diseases.

South Africa and the End of Apartheid

At the end of World War II, the former British colony of South Africa was an independent country with a democratically elected government. But democracy applied to only its white citizens, who were mainly descendants of Dutch and English settlers. Black South Africans, who made up by far the majority of the population, were denied the vote and other basic human rights. Blacks labored for low wages in South Africa's gold and diamond mines, while the white minority enjoyed the prosperity brought by the country's mineral wealth.

After World War II, South Africa's whites grew alarmed by the growth of independence movements across Africa. They feared the loss of their wealth and privileges if the black majority gained power in their own country. To prevent this, the South African government in 1948 instituted a systematic policy of racial discrimination called *apartheid*, meaning "apartness."

Under apartheid, blacks and whites lived almost completely segregated lives. Blacks were forbidden to attend white schools, eat in whites-only restaurants, or swim on beaches reserved for whites. They were forced to live in slums on the outskirts of South African cities. While white children got good educations, black children received training only for menial jobs.

Black South Africans toiled in the gold mines. The whites reaped the benefits.

Men and children gaze from behind a barbed-wire barrier. Blacks and whites were strictly segregated in South Africa.

South African blacks began resisting the unfair laws that kept them apart and denied their rights. An organization called the African National Congress (ANC) led protest marches, boycotts, and strikes. When these tactics were met with violence from the authorities, ANC leaders turned to sabotage, attacking public buildings and railway lines.

The leader of the sabotage campaign was an ANC official named Nelson Mandela. In 1962, he was captured, imprisoned, and charged with plotting violence against the government. At the end of a long trial, Mandela was sentenced to life imprisonment. He defiantly told the court that he would continue to fight for a South Africa in which neither race dominated the other and democracy applied to all. Mandela spent twenty-six years in prison.

As the years went by, the apartheid system drew more and more attention and condemnation from the outside world. Many nations imposed economic sanctions against South Africa, refusing to let their companies do business in the country. South African athletes were barred from taking part in the Olympic Games. During his imprisonment, Nelson Mandela became an international symbol of the struggle against apartheid. Across the world, people campaigned for his release.

The End of Apartheid

The mounting protests at home and pressure from abroad forced the South African government to give in. In 1990, the new South African president, F.W. de Klerk, announced that he would work for a new constitution under which all South Africans received the right to vote. At the same time, he ordered the release of Nelson Mandela.

Many called for Mandela's freedom.

837

Nelson Mandela greets supporters at a rally in 1994, the year he was voted president in South Africa's first truly democratic elections.

Mandela emerged from prison to a hero's welcome. Upon his release, he gave a speech in which he said,

I have fought against white domination, and I have fought against black domination. I have cherished the ideal of a democratic and free society in which all persons live together in harmony and with equal opportunity. It is an ideal which I hope to live for and to achieve. But, if need be, it is an ideal for which I am prepared to die.

Four years later, in the country's first truly democratic elections, Mandela won the presidency. In his inaugural speech, he pledged to build a "society in which all South Africans, black and white, will be able to walk tall, without any fear in their hearts, assured of their inalienable right to human dignity." Mandela served as president until 1999, working hard to achieve racial reconciliation.

Today, South Africa remains a multiracial democracy, though the country still struggles with the legacy of apartheid. While the ranks of the government are dominated by black officials, poverty remains far more widespread among blacks than whites.

Ethnic Rivalry and Civil War

When the European powers divided Africa in the nineteenth century, the borders they drew had little connection with the existing cultures. Often, groups that had little in common were bound together into a single colony. For example, the British colony of Nigeria contained some two hundred fifty different ethnic and language groups. When African countries gained independence, different groups often erupted into conflict and even civil war.

Nigeria and Uganda

Nigeria, Africa's most populous country, has especially suffered from conflict between ethnic and religious groups. In 1967, a tribe known as the Igbo attempted to secede from Nigeria and form its own nation called Biafra. The resulting civil war went on for two and a half years and cost nearly a million lives. Ultimately, the national government's army surrounded Biafra and starved the Igbo into surrender. But the reunification of the country did not heal its many divisions. In recent years, Nigeria has been torn by conflict between the Muslims who inhabit the northern part of the country and the Christians in the east.

Britain's East African colony of Uganda gained its independence in 1962. Nine years later, Idi Amin (EE-dee ah-MEEN), a Nigerian who had served as an officer in the British army, seized control of the country. He went on to

Idi Amin, Uganda's brutal dictator

rule as a brutal dictator. An imposing figure always dressed in military uniform, Amin surrounded himself with loyal followers from his own part of the country and savagely repressed people from other tribes. Amin tortured and murdered anyone he feared might oppose him. Amin ruled Uganda until 1979, when he was overthrown by Ugandan rebels and an invading force from neighboring Tanzania.

Genocide in Rwanda and Its Consequences

In the former Belgian colony of Rwanda (ruh-WAHN-duh), ethnic conflict led to one of the twentieth century's worst cases of genocide. In Rwanda, the ethnic group called the Tutsi (TOO-see or TOOT-see) made up a minority of the country, but Belgian administrators favored them and used Tutsi leaders to help dominate the majority ethnic group, the Hutu (HOO-too). Tensions between the two groups simmered after Rwanda became independent in 1962.

In 1994, when a plane carrying Rwanda's Hutu president was shot down, Hutu radicals blamed the Tutsi. Allies of the dead president mounted a campaign of extermination against the Tutsi. Hutu were urged to murder their Tutsi neighbors. In the short space of four months, more than eight hundred thousand people were slaughtered, many hacked to death with machetes. The massacres ended only after a Tutsi rebel force overthrew the Hutu-dominated government. Before the end of the year, the United Nations set up a court in Rwanda to try Hutu extremists for acts of genocide.

The conflict in Rwanda led to turmoil in neighboring Congo (at the time called Zaire), where many Hutu had fled after the Tutsi victory. With the support of Congo's dictator, Mobutu, some of the refugees launched guerrilla attacks into Rwanda. In response, the new Rwandan government sent forces to Congo to support rebel forces trying to oust Mobutu.

In 1997, Mobutu's government fell. Afterward, a devastating civil war for control of the country broke out among different ethnic groups. Soon,

Rwandan children plead to be reunited with their mothers. Ethnic conflict in Rwanda caused great suffering.

Congo's neighbors—Rwanda, Uganda, Angola, and Zimbabwe—entered the war in support of one side or another. These countries intervened largely in hopes of seizing their share of Congo's vast natural resources, including diamonds, oil, and timber. By the time a shaky peace agreement was reached in 2002, at least three million people had died in what some historians call "Africa's First World War."

Massacre in Darfur

Africa's longest-running civil war was fought in Sudan, between the Muslims who dominated the northern part of the country and the Christians who inhabited the south. The conflict raged from the early 1980s to 2005. Before it was over, a new conflict broke out in the region in western Sudan called Darfur. There, a group of black Sudanese rebelled against the country's Arab-dominated government.

The government responded by sending in a brutal militia called the *janjaweed*. They destroyed hundreds of villages in Darfur and massacred thousands of people, driving hundreds of thousands more into refugee camps. Under international pressure, the Sudanese government eventually reined in the militia, and the United Nations sent troops to keep peace in Darfur.

A Botswanan woman casts her ballot in free elections. Botswana has been democratic since winning independence from Britain in 1966.

Botswana's Hopeful Example

While many of Africa's emerging nations have been torn by ethnic and religious conflicts, the example of Botswana provides a more positive and hopeful experience. Since winning its independence from Britain in 1966, Botswana has been a functioning democracy. The country is inhabited by several distinct ethnic groups, who live together without conflict.

The majority of Botswanans, who are Christians, peacefully coexist with those who practice traditional African religions. Some historians attribute the success of Botswana's democracy to native traditions of limited government that existed before the arrival of the British.

Poverty and Disease

Since independence, most African nations have struggled with the problem of poverty. Over half of the countries on the United Nation's list of least developed countries are in Africa. In the year 2005, in the parts of Africa below the Sahara, a majority of the people lived on less than the equivalent of $1.25 a day.

Africa's poverty has numerous causes. The colonial powers saw the continent solely as a source of raw materials. As a result, Africa in general did not experience the industrial revolution that brought prosperity to Europe. The

Renewing African Culture

European colonists in Africa generally brought their own cultures with them, and had little interest in or respect for Africa's traditional cultures. In the years after independence, African artists and writers began to celebrate the strength and vitality of their own cultural traditions.

Nigeria has produced two of the world's most celebrated modern writers. When he studied English literature in college, Chinua Achebe (ah-CHAY-bay) grew angry at works that depicted Africans as savages. He wrote his most celebrated novel, *Things Fall Apart*, to show the dignity and complexity of Nigerian village life in the days before colonialism. The dramatist Wole Soyinka (WOH-lay shaw-YING-kuh) has written plays depicting the arrogance and ignorance with which Europeans treated African ways of life. In 1986, Soyinka became the first black African to win the prestigious Nobel Prize in Literature.

A scene from a play by Nobel Prize winner Wole Soyinka

Famine in Sudan

economies of the newly independent nations were fragile because they usually relied on one or two exports. Some developed countries sent aid, much of which disappeared into the bank accounts of corrupt dictators. In addition, the continent's population grew so rapidly that governments everywhere struggled to feed, house, and educate their people.

Linked to Africa's poverty is its high rate of deadly disease. Lack of clean water, sanitation, and medical care mean that many Africans die of diseases that have largely been wiped out elsewhere. Ninety percent of the world's deaths from malaria, a disease spread by mosquitoes, occur in Africa.

An even more devastating disease is HIV/AIDS. AIDS (acquired immune deficiency syndrome) weakens the immune system so that it cannot fight off other diseases. AIDS is caused by HIV, the human immunodeficiency virus. Although AIDS affects people worldwide, in 2006 almost two-thirds of those infected with HIV lived in sub-Saharan Africa. In that year, more than two million Africans died of the disease.

In recent years, the United States and other developed nations have provided money for drugs that can help those who suffer from AIDS. Uganda and some other African nations have started programs to prevent the disease through better education. While AIDS continues to afflict millions of Africans, destroying families and burdening economies, individuals and governments are working hard to fight the spread of the disease on the continent.

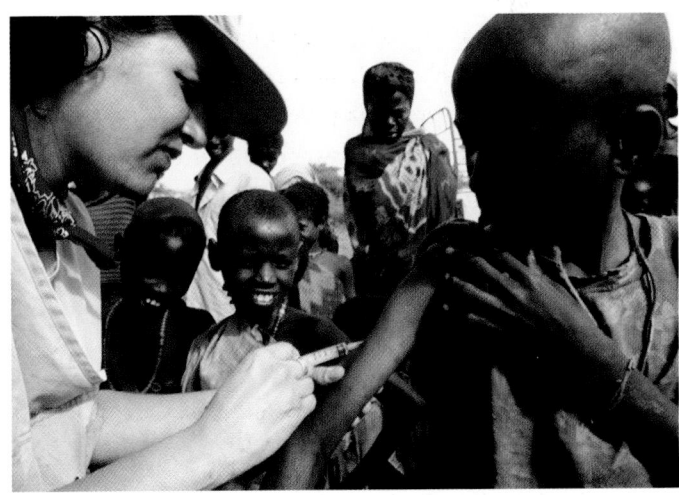

International efforts have brought hope to many Africans in the form of medical care and efforts to prevent disease.

Nationalism and Independence in the Middle East

Key Questions

- What role did nationalism play in bringing changes to the Middle East?

- What religious and ethnic conflicts present continuing challenges for the Middle East?

The Middle East generally refers to a geographic region that includes northeast Africa and southwest Asia. On a map, the arc of the Middle East swings from Egypt through the Arabian Peninsula, then up through the Fertile Crescent into Iran and Asia Minor.

The Middle East is usually considered a single region because for centuries most of its peoples have shared a common culture. Many of the region's inhabitants speak Arabic. But the people are mainly united by a shared religion—Islam. In the eighth century, Islam began to spread through the Middle East, and now the vast majority of people in this region are Muslim. Islam has provided the basis for much of the region's common culture.

Since the 1500s, most of the Middle East had been ruled by the Islamic empire of the Ottoman Turks. During World War I, nationalists in the Middle East fought alongside the British and French to help defeat Ottoman rulers who had long dominated much of the Middle East. These nationalists hoped that after the war, their homelands would become self-governing nations.

But the victorious European nations, which had long-standing interests in the Middle East, had other plans. The old imperial powers of Great Britain and France decided they should be in charge of running the affairs of many Middle Eastern countries, which became mandates under British and French rule. Thus, many people in the Middle East suddenly found themselves ruled by foreigners who were not Muslim.

Such an arrangement spurred the ambitions of nationalists in the Middle East. Shortly after World War II, Middle Eastern politics entered a state of heightened complexity and tension with the founding of the Jewish state of Israel.

The Founding of Israel

Since the days of the Roman Empire, the Jewish people had lived in scattered communities throughout Europe, Asia, and the Americas. In the 1800s, as you have learned, strong feelings of nationalism prompted some European Jews to start a movement called Zionism, with the goal of establishing a Jewish state in the Middle Eastern land called Palestine.

Zionists called for the Jews to return to their ancestral homeland in Palestine, which they called Israel. During the 1920s and 1930s, many European Jews fled the terror of the growing Nazi movement and settled in Palestine, where they sometimes came into conflict with the area's majority Arab population.

The horrors of the Nazi Holocaust, which killed six million Jews, made people around the world sympathetic to the Zionist cause. After the Second

The Middle East: northeast Africa and southwest Asia

World War, the newly formed United Nations voted to divide Palestine into two countries, one Arab and the other Jewish. Jews rejoiced at the decision, but it infuriated the Arabs of Palestine and the surrounding countries. These Arabs saw the Zionists as invaders who had stolen Arab land.

On May 14, 1948, the new Jewish state of Israel came into being. The following day, the armies of five Arab countries invaded the country. But Israel beat back these armies and conquered much of the land that the United Nations had intended for Arab Palestine. More than seven hundred thousand Palestinian Arabs who had fled the fighting became refugees.

The legacy of this conflict was lasting bitterness between Israel and its Arab neighbors. Israel refused to return lands it had seized, as the Arabs had demanded. For their part, the Arabs refused to recognize the existence of Israel. Jews were persecuted and driven out of such countries as Libya, Egypt, and Syria. Meanwhile, hundreds of thousands of Palestinians remained homeless, living in grim refugee camps just outside Israel's new borders.

Jews celebrated in Tel Aviv and other cities when the state of Israel proclaimed its existence on May 14, 1948.

Egypt and the Rise of Arab Nationalism

In the years after the establishment of Israel, a strong wave of nationalism swept through the Arab world. Its focus was the country of Egypt in northeastern Africa.

Egypt had been controlled by Britain until 1922, when it won its independence. But many Egyptians resented that British troops still occupied the Suez Canal zone, the area surrounding the critically important waterway linking the Indian Ocean to the Mediterranean Sea. Egyptian nationalists considered the country's king to be a mere puppet of Great Britain.

In 1952, a group of nationalist army officers overthrew the king. The leader of the group, Gamal Abdel Nasser, became Egypt's prime minister. He forced the British to agree to withdraw their troops from the canal zone. Then, in 1956, Nasser announced to a cheering crowd that he intended to seize control of the canal from the European company that ran it. "Tonight," he cried, "our Egyptian canal will be run by Egyptians. *Egyptians!*"

In response, Britain, France, and Israel joined forces to attack Egypt. British and French troops moved into the canal zone. But the American president, Dwight Eisenhower, was furious. He had not been consulted about the invasion, which he feared would drive Egypt and other Arab nations to ally themselves with the Soviet Union against the West. Pressure from the United States forced the invaders to withdraw.

For seizing the Suez Canal and defying the Western powers, Nasser became a hero throughout the Arab world. At mass rallies and in radio broadcasts, Nasser denounced the West and Israel. He began to call for *pan-Arabism*, the idea that Arab nations should be politically united. Although Nasser's dream of political union was never realized, he unleashed a powerful new spirit of nationalism among the Arab people.

> The prefix *pan–* comes from a Greek word meaning "all."

In the Arab-Israeli conflict, the Six-Day War of 1967 left many Palestinians homeless and living in refugee camps.

The Arab-Israeli Conflict

Since the Israeli victory in 1948, tension had been mounting between Israel and its neighbors. In the 1960s, Nasser, as the spokesman of Arab nationalism, felt increasing pressure to take action against Israel. In 1967, Nasser sent troops to the Sinai Peninsula, just west of Israel, and set up a partial naval blockade of the country. Jordan and Syria agreed to support Egypt in an attack on the Jewish state.

But the Israelis, watching the gathering forces, struck first. Israeli pilots launched surprise attacks on airfields inside Egypt, Jordan, and Syria, crippling the air forces of the Arab countries. Without planes to provide air cover, Arab tanks and troops were vulnerable in the exposed desert. In less than a week, Israel's army had smashed the Arab forces and won a stunning victory.

In the Six-Day War, as the conflict is known, Israeli soldiers seized the huge Sinai Peninsula from Egypt, as well as an area called the Golan

Heights from Syria. The Israelis also captured the West Bank of the Jordan River, and seized the eastern part of the city of Jerusalem, which had been controlled by Jordan.

The Six-Day War of 1967 had profound consequences. It more than tripled the area of Israel and brought more than a million Arabs under direct Israeli rule. It also caused a new wave of Palestinian refugees to flee into neighboring countries. When Arab nations demanded that Israel withdraw from its newly occupied territories, the Israelis refused. They believed that they needed the occupied lands as a buffer against hostile and aggressive neighbors.

The Palestine Liberation Organization

The Six-Day War showed the Palestinians that they could not rely on Arab governments for help. Many turned instead to the Palestine Liberation Organization (PLO), a group that had been founded in the early 1960s with the avowed goal of destroying the state of Israel. In 1969, the leadership of the PLO passed to a man named

Palestine Liberation Organization camps trained young men and boys to wage guerrilla warfare against Israel.

A Palestinian terrorist at the Olympic Village in Munich, Germany, in 1972

Yasser Arafat (YAH-sihr AIR-uh-fat), the head of a guerrilla group. Arafat urged his followers to engage in guerrilla warfare against Israelis, and attack not only soldiers but also civilians.

From this time on, radical Palestinians increasingly turned to the tactic called **terrorism**, the use of violence to achieve political ends by striking fear into a people. Terrorists hijacked airplanes and attacked buses and schools in Israel. People around the world reacted with horror when, in 1972, a group of Palestinian terrorists murdered two Israeli athletes and took nine others hostage at the Olympic Games in Munich, Germany. The nine Israeli athletes and five of their captors died during a failed rescue attempt.

The Yom Kippur War

In 1973, another war broke out between Israel and its Arab neighbors. It was started by the Egyptian leader, Anwar Sadat, who wanted to prove that he could do what Nasser had failed to accomplish—defeat Israel on the battlefield. In league with other Arab nations, Egypt launched its attack on Yom Kippur, the Day of Atonement, the holiest day in the Jewish calendar. In the Yom Kippur War, also called the 1973 Arab-Israeli War, the Arabs caught the Israelis by surprise and regained some of the territory they had lost in 1967.

When the United States rushed military aid to Israel, the Arab offensive stalled, and a cease-fire was signed. Even though the Yom

Kippur War ended in a stalemate, many Arabs saw it as a victory, proof that Arab soldiers could fight effectively against the Israelis.

Sadat himself, however, eventually came to the conclusion that fighting was not the answer to his country's conflict with Israel. In 1977, he astonished the Middle East by declaring, "I am willing to go to the ends of the earth for peace." Sadat backed up his words by visiting Israel—the first Arab leader to do so—where he addressed the Israeli parliament.

The Camp David Accords and After

In 1978, the American president, Jimmy Carter, brought Sadat and Prime Minister Menachem Begin (muh-NAH-kuhm BAY-gin) of Israel together at Camp David, Maryland. There, the two leaders signed the Camp David Accords. Egypt agreed to recognize Israel's right to exist, while Israel agreed to withdraw from the Sinai Peninsula and recognize the need for Palestinian self-government.

The Camp David Accords, however, did not immediately bring peace. Sadat's agreement with Israel infuriated many in Egypt and elsewhere in the Arab world. In October 1981, while Sadat was attending a military parade, he was shot dead by

Egyptian president Anwar Sadat (at left), U.S. president Jimmy Carter (center), and Israeli prime minister Menachem Begin at a 1979 treaty ceremony

845

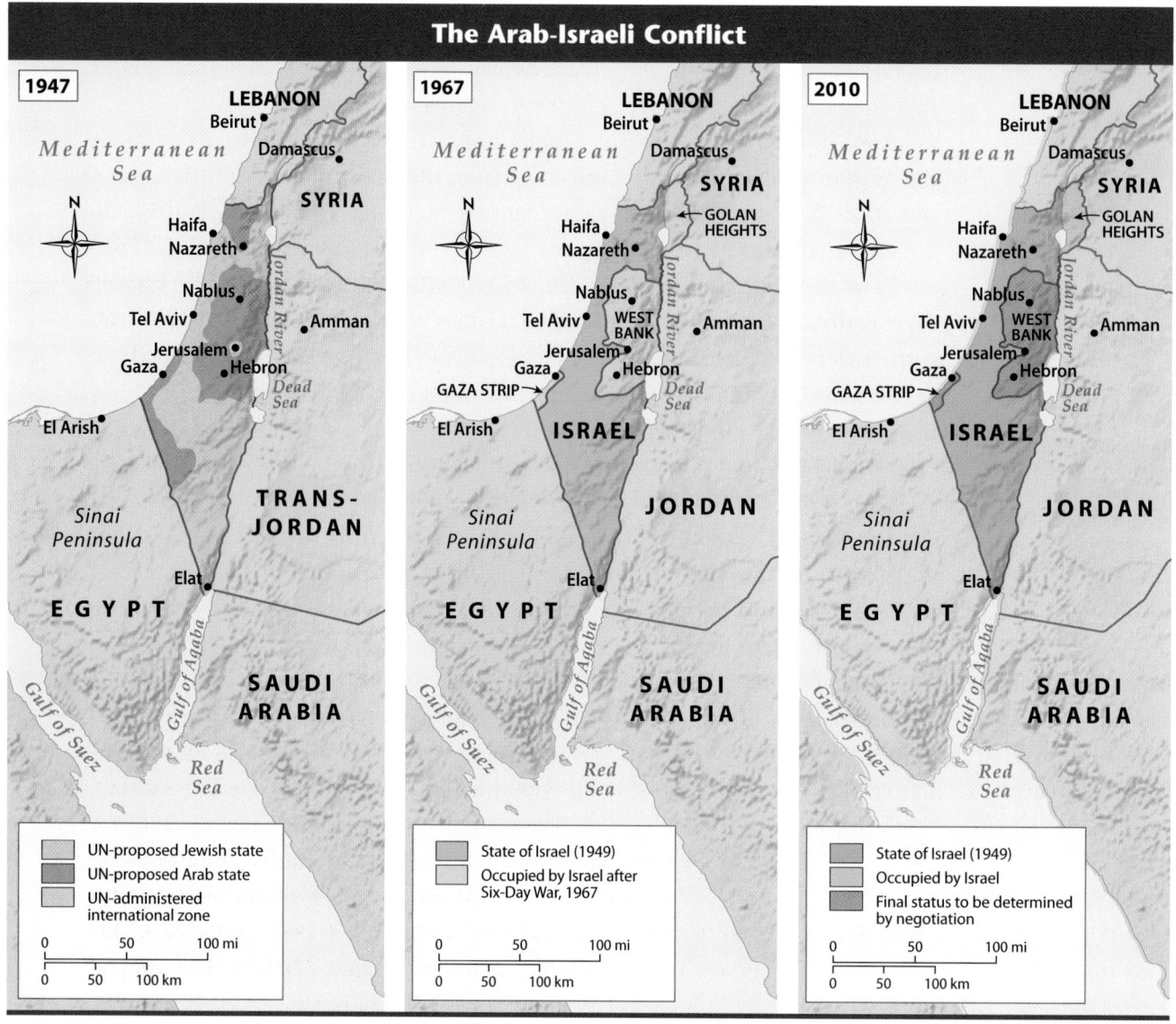

The Arab-Israeli Conflict

1947

LEBANON
Beirut
Mediterranean Sea
Damascus
Haifa
Nazareth
SYRIA
Nablus
Tel Aviv
Jerusalem
Gaza
Hebron
Jordan River
Amman
Dead Sea
El Arish
Sinai Peninsula
TRANS-JORDAN
Elat
Gulf of Aqaba
EGYPT
Gulf of Suez
SAUDI ARABIA
Red Sea

- UN-proposed Jewish state
- UN-proposed Arab state
- UN-administered international zone

0   50   100 mi
0   50   100 km

1967

LEBANON
Beirut
Mediterranean Sea
Damascus
SYRIA
GOLAN HEIGHTS
Haifa
Nazareth
Nablus
Tel Aviv
WEST BANK
Jerusalem
Gaza
Hebron
GAZA STRIP
Jordan River
Amman
Dead Sea
El Arish
ISRAEL
Sinai Peninsula
JORDAN
Elat
Gulf of Aqaba
EGYPT
Gulf of Suez
SAUDI ARABIA
Red Sea

- State of Israel (1949)
- Occupied by Israel after Six-Day War, 1967

0   50   100 mi
0   50   100 km

2010

LEBANON
Beirut
Mediterranean Sea
Damascus
SYRIA
GOLAN HEIGHTS
Haifa
Nazareth
Nablus
Tel Aviv
WEST BANK
Jerusalem
Gaza
Hebron
GAZA STRIP
Jordan River
Amman
Dead Sea
El Arish
ISRAEL
Sinai Peninsula
JORDAN
Elat
Gulf of Aqaba
EGYPT
Gulf of Suez
SAUDI ARABIA
Red Sea

- State of Israel (1949)
- Occupied by Israel
- Final status to be determined by negotiation

0   50   100 mi
0   50   100 km

In the Middle Eastern land called Palestine, the state of Israel was formed in 1948. Since then, the borders of Israel have changed as a result of conflicts with neighboring nations.

a small group of soldiers who considered him a traitor to the Arab cause. Israel remained in possession of the occupied territories and angered Palestinians by building new settlements in these lands. In the late 1980s, Palestinians in the West Bank and Gaza (an Israeli-occupied area between Egypt and Israel) launched a series of rebellions against Israeli rule.

Still, some leaders on both sides reached for peace. In 1993, the Israeli prime minister, Yitzhak Rabin (YIHT-sahk rah-BEEN), flew to Norway to meet with Yasser Arafat, the head of the PLO. There, they signed the so-called Oslo Accords. The PLO agreed to recognize Israel and renounce terrorism. In return, Israel gave Palestinians in the West Bank and Gaza limited self-rule.

However, similar to 1978 and the Camp David Accords, many in the region were hostile to the agreement. Like Anwar Sadat, Rabin paid the ultimate price for his commitment to peace. In 1995, Rabin was assassinated by a young Israeli extremist who was enraged about the Oslo Accords.

Ongoing Struggles in the Middle East

Key Questions

- What role do natural resources play in the economic and political challenges facing Middle Eastern nations?

- How have events in Middle Eastern nations affected the rest of the world?

After World War II, some Middle Eastern nations became wealthy by exploiting their most valuable resource, oil. Most of the wealth from oil remained in the hands of a powerful few, while the majority of the region's people lived in poverty. This inequality bred resentment, linked with a feeling among some Muslims that their leaders had turned away from Islam, becoming too secular and Westernized. In 1979, Islamic fundamentalists toppled Iran's pro-Western leader, and soon afterward Iran and its neighbor Iraq clashed in a disastrous eight-year war.

Oil as Blessing and Curse

The world's largest oil fields are located in the Middle East, under and around the Persian Gulf. Most of this oil lay undiscovered until after the Second World War. Its discovery coincided with a huge new demand for energy in the United States and the recovering countries of Europe. Oil-producing countries, like Saudi Arabia, Kuwait, Iran, and Iraq, quickly gained new wealth and influence.

In 1960, in order to fix prices and limit competition, the oil-producing nations joined together in a cartel known as the Organization of Petroleum Exporting Countries (OPEC). Besides enriching its member countries, OPEC allowed them to exercise a newfound political power. After the Yom Kippur War of 1973, OPEC imposed an oil boycott on the Western nations that had supported Israel, chiefly the United States. The boycott drastically raised the price of energy, and thus led to widespread inflation and unemployment in the United States and Europe.

The power and wealth of the oil-rich Middle Eastern nations did not always benefit the ordinary people of the region. Too often, oil revenues simply served to enrich a few powerful individuals and families. The rulers of oil-producing states built lavish palaces for themselves and invested their money abroad, while most people struggled to get by.

Middle East oil revenues have brought economic power and political influence to oil-rich nations.

847

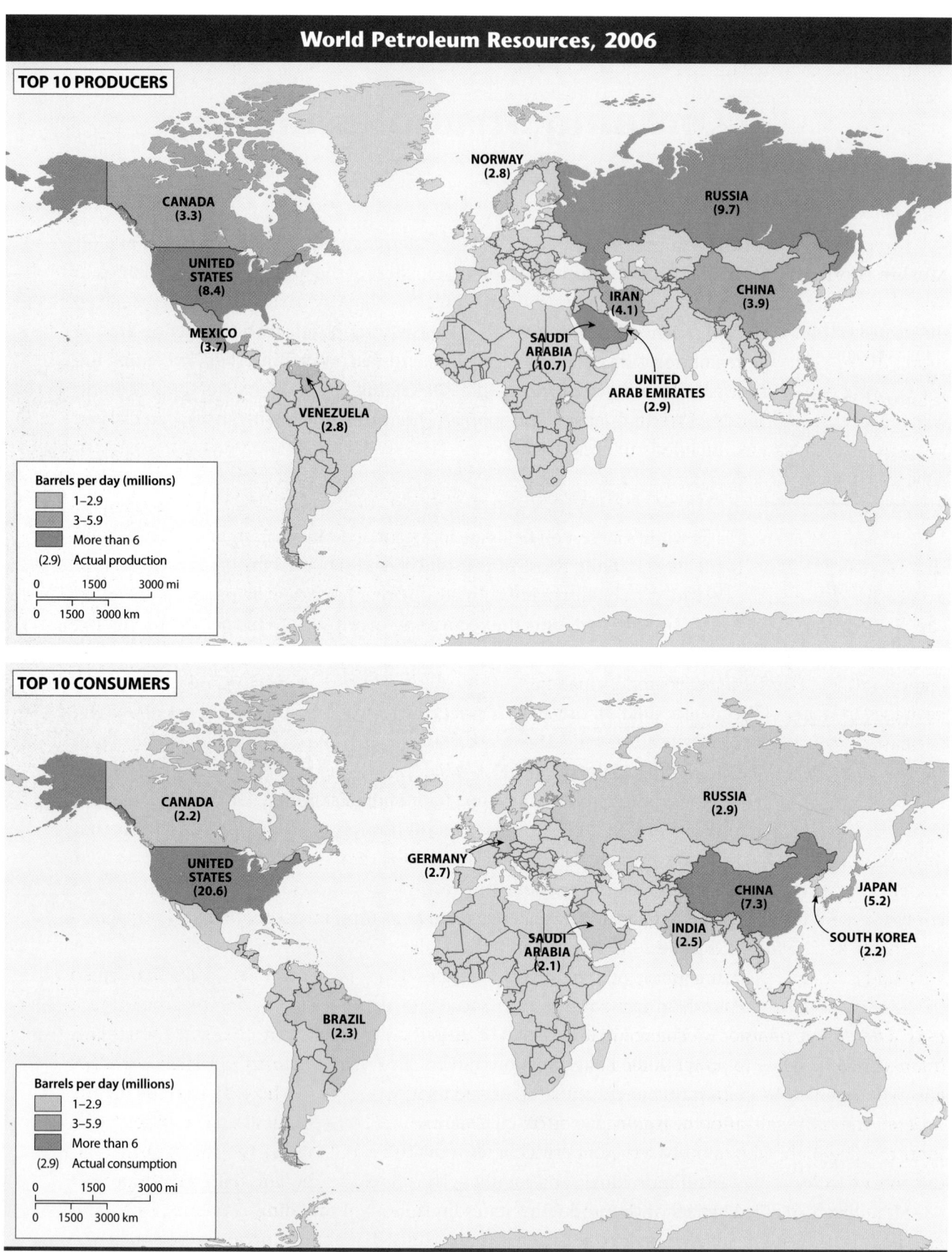

World Petroleum Resources, 2006

TOP 10 PRODUCERS

NORWAY (2.8)
RUSSIA (9.7)
CANADA (3.3)
UNITED STATES (8.4)
CHINA (3.9)
IRAN (4.1)
MEXICO (3.7)
SAUDI ARABIA (10.7)
UNITED ARAB EMIRATES (2.9)
VENEZUELA (2.8)

Barrels per day (millions)
- 1–2.9
- 3–5.9
- More than 6
- (2.9) Actual production

0   1500   3000 mi
0 1500 3000 km

TOP 10 CONSUMERS

CANADA (2.2)
RUSSIA (2.9)
GERMANY (2.7)
UNITED STATES (20.6)
CHINA (7.3)
JAPAN (5.2)
INDIA (2.5)
SOUTH KOREA (2.2)
SAUDI ARABIA (2.1)
BRAZIL (2.3)

Barrels per day (millions)
- 1–2.9
- 3–5.9
- More than 6
- (2.9) Actual consumption

0   1500   3000 mi
0 1500 3000 km

In the twenty-first century, while the search for alternative sources of energy continues, petroleum remains the lifeblood of industrialization. The production and consumption of petroleum continues to grow with the global economy.

These inequalities fueled resentment. Radical Muslim groups criticized the rulers of their nations for adopting what they saw as the decadent habits of the West. They called for the overthrow of the region's secular regimes and their replacement by governments based on Sharia, or traditional Islamic law.

Some of these radical groups, such as the Muslim Brotherhood, had existed for decades. The economic and cultural changes brought by oil wealth caused their ranks to swell. More and more, the rulers of the region felt threatened by the growing power of the Islamic extremists who wanted to rid their lands of what they saw as Western contamination and establish what they thought of as true Islamic regimes.

Iran After World War II

Iran, one of the Middle East's oil-rich states, is culturally distinct from the region's other countries. First, Iran's people are not Arabs. And second, most Iranians belong to the Shiite rather than the Sunni branch of Islam. Despite these differences, Iran has been torn by many of the same conflicts that have troubled the rest of the Middle East, especially the conflict between secularism and religion.

The Shah Toppled and Restored

At the end of World War II, Iran was a constitutional monarchy. It had both a hereditary king, known as the shah, and an elected prime minister. The shah was the eldest son of Reza Shah Pahlavi, who had modernized Iran and forged close ties to Western governments and oil companies. In 1951, a new prime minister, Mohammad Mosaddeq (moh-sah-DEK), came to power. A fervent nationalist who resented Western influence, Mosaddeq ordered the nationalization of the country's oil industry. The shah, who opposed this policy, was driven into exile.

Mosaddeq had allied himself with Iran's Communist Party. Fearful of Soviet influence over the oil-rich country, the United States intervened. In 1953, the Central Intelligence Agency engineered

The shah of Iran and family pose amid the opulent trappings of extreme wealth.

a coup that toppled Mosaddeq and reinstated the shah.

After his return from exile, the shah ruled more and more as a dictator. His government clamped down on dissent. His secret police constantly spied on the country's citizens, arresting and torturing anyone who criticized the regime. The shah used oil revenues in an ambitious plan to modernize and Westernize the country. Tehran, the capital city, became a busy metropolis of luxury apartment buildings, cinemas, cafes, and nightclubs. The shah supported the expansion of education and the granting of equal rights to women.

Ayatollah Khomeini

But the shah's reforms did little to alleviate the poverty of most Iranians. Most of the country's new wealth flowed to a small elite. Many Iranians were angered by these inequalities. Others resented some of the shah's reforms, such as the expansion of women's rights, because they went against traditional Islamic teaching.

Islamic Revolution in Iran

Perhaps the strongest opposition to the shah came from religious leaders called *ayatollahs* (iy-uh-TOH-luhz). In Shiite Islam, the title *ayatollah* indicates a religious leader who is very learned in Islamic law and other subjects. In the early 1960s, the religious opposition to the shah found a leader in Ayatollah Khomeini (koh-MAY-nee). In 1963, Khomeini was arrested and banished from Iran.

From exile, he sent tapes of his speeches back to his followers at home, calling for an Islamic revolution. In 1978, riots and demonstrations against the shah's rule broke out across Iran. The shah was forced to flee the country. Ayatollah Khomeini, nearly eighty years old, returned from exile to assume leadership of the revolution he had helped unleash. He immediately proclaimed the formation of an Islamic republic.

Iranians who had hoped that the overthrow of the shah would bring democracy were quickly disappointed. Khomeini's regime proved even more repressive than the shah's. Thousands of people were executed—not only members of the former government, but Jews, Christians, and even Muslims whose faith the new authorities deemed less than pure.

Khomeini's followers had a special hatred for the country that had most strongly supported the shah, the United States. In November 1979, a group of Iranian students seized control of the U.S. embassy in Tehran and took more than sixty

Militant Iranian students display a blindfolded American hostage at the U.S. embassy in Tehran in 1979.

Weapons in the Hands of Rogue States

In recent years, Western governments have accused Iran of secretly developing nuclear weapons. Iran has denied this, saying that its nuclear plants are designed only for the peaceful purpose of generating energy. Many believe that a nuclear-armed Iran would threaten the existence of Israel, a nation that Iranian leaders have vowed to destroy.

In the early twenty-first century, many people are concerned about powerful weapons in the hands of "rogue" nations—countries with aggressive or unstable leaders who do not obey the usual international rules, such as North Korea, a nuclear-armed nation ruled by a belligerent, egomaniacal dictator. The weapons that raise the most alarm are powerful chemical, biological, and nuclear weapons, often called "weapons of mass destruction." People remain concerned that rogue states might use the weapons themselves or sell them to terrorists.

American hostages. They announced that the hostages would be released only when the U.S. government sent the exiled shah, who had traveled to the United States for medical treatment, back to Iran to stand trial. In a speech, Khomeini congratulated the students and denounced the United States as the "Great Satan." Mobs gathered outside the embassy walls, chanting "Death to America!"

A few hostages were released shortly after the embassy takeover. The rest, however, remained in captivity. As the hostage crisis dragged on, many Americans felt increasingly frustrated, angered, and humiliated. President Carter ordered a risky rescue mission, but a sandstorm caused helicopters to crash, and the mission ended in failure. After more than a year, all the hostages were released. Khomeini's followers celebrated their victory over the "Great Satan."

Iran's Current Political Situation

The death of Ayatollah Khomeini in 1989 inspired some moderates in the Iranian government to call for more individual freedom and more pro-Western policies. In the decades since, moderates and conservatives in Iran have frequently battled over the need for reform.

Today, Iran has an elected president and parliament. But ultimate power rests with the Islamic religious figure known as the Great Leader, the successor to Ayatollah Khomeini. Traditional Islamic law is strictly enforced. People caught drinking alcohol may be whipped. Women are expected to wear clothes that completely cover their bodies. Religious police patrol the streets, looking for anyone violating the moral rules.

A Dictator in Iraq

In 1979, the same year that Ayatollah Khomeini came to power in Iran, an even more brutal dictator, Saddam Hussein (sah-DAHM hoo-SAYN), took over in neighboring Iraq. Hussein had risen through the ranks of the Baath Party, an organization that promoted Arab nationalism and a secular, socialist form of government in several Middle Eastern countries.

As leader of the Baath Party and deputy to the president of Iraq from 1968 on, Hussein led an ambitious program of modernization. He used oil revenues to build hospitals, schools, and roads. He promoted industry and brought electricity to much of the country. His government also allowed women more freedom than they enjoyed in much of the Muslim world.

Saddam Hussein became dictator of Iraq in 1979.

Underlying all Hussein's efforts, however, was a burning ambition to achieve absolute power. In 1979, he forced Iraq's ailing president out of office and then ruthlessly eliminated his rivals among the Baathists. He ordered images of himself to be plastered on walls and buildings throughout the country. His special police units tortured and murdered tens of thousands.

Although a majority of Iraq's population were Shiite Muslims, Hussein himself was a Sunni, and his regime discriminated against the Shiites. When Ayatollah Khomeini came to power in Iran, he urged his fellow Shiites across the border in Iraq to rise up and overthrow Hussein. Enraged, Hussein launched an invasion of Iran in September 1980. He intended both to overthrow Khomeini and to seize control of Iran's rich oil fields.

Hussein's troops drove deep into Iran. Both sides committed atrocities, including the use of chemical weapons, banned by international law. To prevent the spread of Khomeini's Islamic revolution from Iran, the United States and other Western nations sold arms to Iraq and gave economic aid to Saddam Hussein's government. After eight years, the war finally ended in a draw, crippling both countries' economies and leaving perhaps a million dead.

The Persian Gulf War

Saddam Hussein remained intent on expanding and enriching Iraq through conquest. In August 1990, he invaded the small, oil-rich country of Kuwait. Hussein justified the invasion by saying that since Kuwait had once been part of Iraq, it should be so again. The United States and other Western countries feared that Hussein would move on to attack Saudi Arabia, the world's largest oil producer. They knew that such an attack would have a devastating effect on the world economy.

The United States sent troops to Saudi Arabia to protect the country's borders. It also assembled a coalition of thirty-nine countries to confront Iraq and demand that it pull out of Kuwait. The coalition included such Muslim nations as Pakistan, Egypt, Syria, and Saudi Arabia, all of which felt threatened by Hussein's aggression toward his neighbors. Still, Hussein refused to withdraw from Kuwait.

In January 1991, the United States led the coalition in an air offensive against Iraq. Night after night, coalition planes rained bombs on the capital city of Baghdad as well as on military installations. At the end of February, coalition forces launched a ground attack, quickly driving Hussein's soldiers back across the Iraqi border and out of Kuwait. Only a hundred hours after the ground war began, Iraq's army was defeated.

The Persian Gulf War cost the lives of perhaps as many as a hundred thousand Iraqis, while fewer than four hundred coalition troops were killed. Yet many in the West saw this as only a partial victory. They had wanted coalition troops and tanks to roll on to Baghdad and remove Saddam Hussein from power. But the American president, George H.W. Bush, chose not to push the war into Baghdad, in large part because his Middle Eastern allies strongly opposed the idea of Western forces overthrowing an Arab government and occupying a Muslim nation.

After Saddam Hussein invaded Kuwait, the United States sent troops to the Middle East to halt the Iraqi aggression.

New Threats and Responses

The Islamic revolution in Iran helped inspire a wave of violent radicalism in the Middle East. Islamic extremists called for the overthrow of secular governments as well as the destruction of Israel. Since these groups did not have armies at their disposal, they turned to terrorism, the planned use of violence to strike fear into people or governments to obtain political goals. The victims of terrorism are often innocent civilians. Terrorists want people to live in fear. They believe that if they can create enough fear, their opponents will give in to their demands.

After World War II, a growing number of political movements turned to terrorism. For example, a group called the Irish Republican Army (IRA) wanted to end British control of Northern Ireland. From the 1960s until the 1990s, the IRA carried out a campaign of terror, shooting British soldiers, planting bombs in British cities, and assassinating British politicians. In an area of northern Spain inhabited by a people called the Basques (basks), a separatist group has used bombings and kidnappings in an effort to achieve Basque independence.

Over the past several decades, various groups have employed terrorist tactics and caused bloodshed in parts of Europe, Asia, and Latin America. In the 1970s, a new form of terrorism appeared on the world scene. It emerged as a response to deep-rooted problems in the Middle East. But it would have devastating effects far beyond the region itself.

Deep-Rooted Problems in the Middle East

The overwhelming majority of people living in the Middle East are Muslims. At the end of the twentieth century, some Muslims felt bitter and angry about the state of the region. Centuries earlier, Islamic empires had ruled vast portions of northern Africa, Asia, and Europe. But as European nations industrialized, they surpassed Muslim countries in wealth and technological advancement. In the late nineteenth and early twentieth centuries, the imperial powers of the West seized control of much of the region.

By the mid-twentieth century, most Middle Eastern countries had regained their independence. But Egyptian president Nasser's dream of a new Islamic empire founded on pan-Arabism never came to pass. Citizens in Western countries still enjoyed far higher standards of living. While wealth did come to oil-rich nations such as Saudi Arabia, it remained concentrated in the hands of a few, while across the Middle East millions lived in poverty.

One group of Muslims, known as Islamists, believed that Middle Eastern nations were in decline because their leaders had failed to follow the traditional teachings and laws of Islam. They faulted nations like Turkey, Egypt, and prerevolutionary Iran for adopting secular forms of government. Islamists

Key Questions

- What is terrorism?
- How has terrorism been used in the twenty-first century?

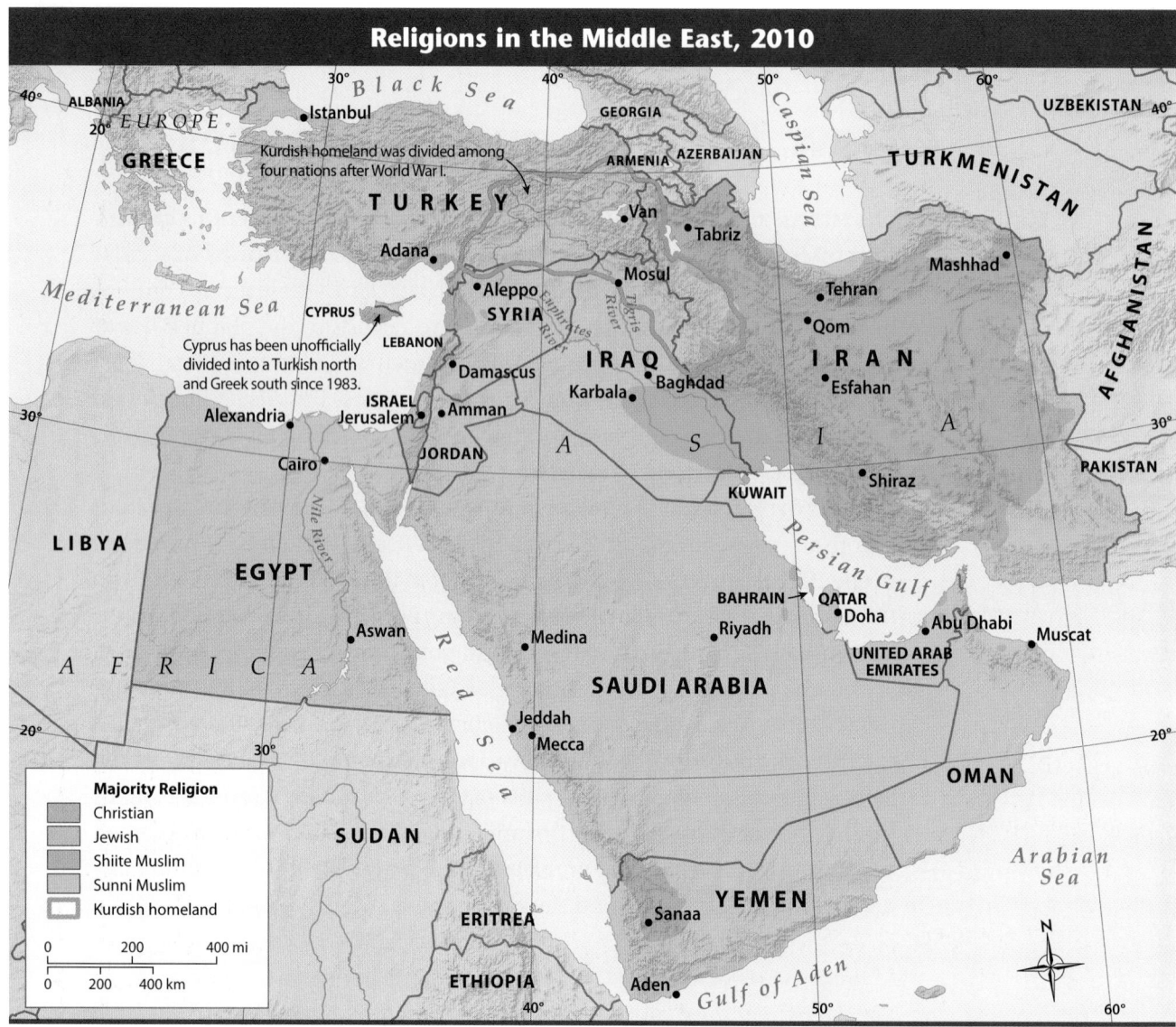

Religions in the Middle East, 2010

Kurdish homeland was divided among four nations after World War I.

Cyprus has been unofficially divided into a Turkish north and Greek south since 1983.

Majority Religion
- Christian
- Jewish
- Shiite Muslim
- Sunni Muslim
- Kurdish homeland

The volatile mix of religions and ethnicities in the Middle East continues to ignite bloody conflicts between Muslims and Jews, Christians and Muslims, and the major Islamic Sunni and Shiite sects.

believed that the leaders of those countries had been corrupted by the influence of the West.

After the Second World War, as colonies gained independence from the exhausted European powers, many Islamists focused their resentment on the United States. They accused the U.S. government of meddling in Arab affairs, supporting the Jewish state of Israel, trying to control the region's oil, and supporting tyrannical regimes (like that of the shah of Iran) that bowed to America's wishes.

Islamists mounted further grievances against the United States. They felt especially angry when, during the Persian Gulf War, U.S. troops were stationed in Saudi Arabia, the country where Islam's holiest sites are located.

Some Islamists vowed to rid the region of what they saw as Western contamination and were willing to use violence to achieve their goal. They committed themselves to the destruction of the non-Muslim state of Israel and, in the rest of the Middle East, the replacement of secular regimes with strict Islamic rule. Beginning in the 1970s, these militant Islamists attracted more and more followers. Their first major victory was the Iranian revolution led by Ayatollah Khomeini.

Extremists Organize for Violence

The success of the Islamic revolution in Iran inspired the creation of militant Islamist groups elsewhere in the Middle East. One of these was Hezbollah (meaning "the Party of God"), a radical Shiite group in Lebanon. Hezbollah was formed partly in response to a 1982 invasion of Lebanon by its southern neighbor, Israel. Israel had invaded to stop attacks launched from Lebanon by the Palestine Liberation Organization.

Hezbollah used terrorist methods, such as kidnappings and bombings, against the Israeli forces occupying Lebanon. Hezbollah also pioneered the use of a grim new terrorist tactic, the suicide bombing. Suicide bombers strap explosives to their bodies, or load them into their vehicles. They then go to a place where they will do the most damage, or kill the most people, and blow themselves up. Although the Qur'an condemns suicide, some militant Islamist clerics teach that those who kill themselves in defense of Islam will be richly rewarded in an afterlife paradise.

Like other militant Islamist groups, Hezbollah preached hatred of the "infidel" West as well as Israel. When Western nations sent troops to

Apart from terror, Hamas provided social services. Here, a student uses the library in a school supported by Hamas.

keep peace in Lebanon, Hezbollah turned its terror tactics on them. In October 1983, a suicide bomber drove a large truck filled with explosives into a compound occupied by U.S. Marines. Two hundred and forty-one U.S. servicemen were killed.

In 1987, another militant Islamist group formed among Palestinians living in the West Bank and Gaza, territories occupied by Israel since 1967. The group called itself Hamas, a name meaning "zeal." Like the main Palestinian nationalist group, the Palestine Liberation Organization, Hamas pledged itself to the destruction of Israel. But Hamas denounced the PLO for being too secular. Instead, the new organization vowed to "raise the banner of Allah over every inch of Palestine."

In pursuit of this goal, Hamas launched a campaign of terror. Hamas members fired homemade missiles into Israel. They strapped bombs to their bodies and blew themselves up in crowds of Israeli civilians. They tortured and killed Palestinians whom they accused of collaborating with Israel.

But there was another side to Hamas. In the occupied territories, Hamas acted as a social service organization. Its members spread funds donated by other Arab countries, helping to support schools, orphanages, mosques, and health care. Through such actions, Hamas gained broad popularity among Palestinians, even those not involved in its campaign of terror.

A Palestinian youth uses a slingshot to launch a stone at Israeli soldiers during a clash on the West Bank.

The Taliban and al-Qaeda

In 1996, a group called the Taliban seized power in the country of Afghanistan. The Taliban had its origins among the guerrillas fighting the Soviet occupation of the country in the 1980s. At that time, the Afghan fighters who would later form the Taliban had been armed and funded by the United States and other Western nations opposed to the expansion of Soviet communism.

About seven years after the Soviet withdrawal from Afghanistan, the Taliban shocked the West and much of the Muslim world by imposing a radically strict version of Islamic law. They banned computers and TVs, as well as a long list of apparently harmless activities—making music, playing chess, flying kites. For those convicted of crimes, they instituted harsh punishments, including flogging, amputation, and stoning to death.

The Taliban also suppressed all women's rights. Females over the age of eight were forbidden to go to school. Older girls or women who sought an education faced the death penalty. Women could not work outside the home. When a woman left her house, she had to be accompanied by a male relative. She also had to be covered from head to toe by a long cloak called a *burqa*, so that not even her face was visible.

Besides terrorizing its own people, the Taliban supported what would become the most notorious of international terrorist organizations, al-Qaeda (al-KIY-duh). This group, whose Arabic name means "the base," was founded in the late 1980s. Its leader, Osama bin Laden, was a Saudi Arabian who had fought against the Soviets in Afghanistan. The Persian Gulf War, however, persuaded bin Laden that the Americans had become the greatest enemy of the Islamic world.

After the Taliban victory in 1996, bin Laden set up his headquarters in Afghanistan. He announced that al-Qaeda's goals were to destroy Israel and topple pro-Western governments throughout the Middle East. But he reserved his special hatred for America.

To bin Laden and other militant Islamists, the stationing of American troops in the Middle East amounted to a Western invasion like the Crusades of the Middle Ages. In February 1998, an Arabic newspaper in London published bin Laden's "Declaration of the World Islamic Front against the Jews and Crusaders." The document exhorted, "We—with God's help—call on every Muslim who believes in God and wishes to be rewarded to comply with God's order to kill the Americans and plunder their money wherever and whenever they find it."

From secret locations in Afghanistan, bin Laden and al-Qaeda organized several attacks against Americans and their allies. In 1998, terrorists linked to al-Qaeda set off bombs in the U.S. embassies in Tanzania and Kenya, killing 224 people and injuring thousands. In 2000, al-Qaeda suicide bombers attacked the USS *Cole*, an American warship harbored in Yemen. The

Covered from head to foot, burqa-clad women pass by an armed patrolman. The Taliban regime completely suppressed women's rights in Afghanistan.

Rescue workers aid a victim of the 1998 terrorist bombing of the U.S. embassy in Kenya.

assault killed seventeen American sailors. But al-Qaeda members were planning an even more destructive and horrifying attack.

September 11, 2001

On the morning of September 11, 2001, thousands of people in New York City watched in horror as a disaster unfolded. A passenger plane slammed into one of the twin towers of the World Trade Center. Smoke billowed from the 110-story skyscraper. About fifteen minutes later, a second plane smashed into the second tower of the World Trade Center, setting it ablaze. Inside the two towers, hundreds lay dead from the initial explosions. Hundreds more were suffocating from the smoke, while some, seeing no escape from the flames, jumped to their deaths. Network news broadcast the scenes of horror around the country.

Less than an hour later, a third plane crashed into the side of the Pentagon, the U.S. military headquarters near Washington, D.C. Then came reports that a fourth plane had crashed in a field in Pennsylvania. That plane was likely intended to crash into either the White House or the Capitol Building, but a group of heroic passengers sacrificed their lives to bring it down. By this time, in New York, both of the burning towers had

collapsed, burying thousands of people under heaps of concrete and steel, including many firefighters and police officers who were helping to evacuate the burning buildings.

Over the next few days, U.S. intelligence agencies determined that the attacks had been planned and financed by Osama bin Laden and al-Qaeda. Four or five Islamist terrorists had boarded each plane, then hijacked it and piloted it into the target. Each target had been carefully chosen as a symbol of American financial, military, or political power. Nearly three thousand people died in the worst terrorist attack in the history of the United States.

The Response to Terror

In response to the attacks of September 11, the American president, George W. Bush, declared that America would wage a "war on terror." He said that any nation harboring terrorists would be regarded as an enemy. United States intelligence reports indicated that Osama bin Laden was in Afghanistan, where al-Qaeda's training grounds were located.

President Bush demanded that the Taliban regime hand over bin Laden and other al-Qaeda leaders. When the Taliban refused, the United States, along with several allied nations, launched

September 11, 2001: Terrorists slam passenger planes into the twin towers of New York's World Trade Center.

857

A U.S. Army soldier checks his machine gun atop an Afghan outpost in 2006.

an invasion of Afghanistan. The U.S.-led forces joined with Afghan rebels to overthrow the Taliban government. But bin Laden escaped and went into hiding.

The Iraq War

After the September 11 attacks, U.S. leaders grew concerned about future terrorist threats. They turned their attention to Iraq and its dictator Saddam Hussein. In the past, Hussein had harbored terrorists. Western intelligence agencies also feared Hussein was stockpiling chemical and biological weapons—the "weapons of mass destruction" banned by international law. He had used such weapons during the Iran-Iraq war. Now, the United Nations and the United States demanded that the dictator allow UN inspectors to examine suspected weapons sites. Hussein stalled and refused to comply.

In March 2003, the United States announced that it would use force to disarm the Iraqi regime. It was a controversial decision. Critics argued that the United States had no business launching a "preemptive war"—a war designed to head off a future threat. They pointed out that Iraq had not invaded the United States or launched the attacks of September 11. Some of America's closest allies, such as Germany and France, argued that the United States should give diplomacy time to work. The United Nations refused to approve military action.

Nevertheless, on March 20, 2003, American and British troops invaded Iraq. As in 1991, Iraqi forces proved no match for Western firepower. In early April, Baghdad was captured. Hussein's regime quickly fell apart. Hussein himself went into hiding. Later, he was captured, tried for mass murder, and hanged.

President Bush hoped that after the overthrow of Saddam Hussein, Iraq would become a stable democracy. Instead, the country descended into chaos. Long-simmering hatreds between Sunni and Shiite Muslims boiled over. Both groups formed militias to fight each other. Militant

An Iraqi youth rushes past victims and burning debris moments after a bomb blast in March 2004.

President Barack Obama visits with U.S. troops in Iraq in the spring of 2009.

Islamists from other countries, including some associated with al-Qaeda, rushed to Iraq to battle the Western occupiers. Terrorists mounted suicide bombings against U.S. troops and Iraqi civilians alike. Tens of thousands of people died.

To make matters worse, no weapons of mass destruction were found. It became apparent that American and British intelligence agencies had overestimated Iraq's military capability. Critics charged the U.S. government with using incomplete and inaccurate information to justify an unnecessary war. As the turmoil continued, support for the war effort dwindled, both within the United States and abroad.

Yet amid the bloodshed and controversy, free elections brought a democratic government to power in Iraq in 2005. In 2007, President Bush, in an attempt to quell the ongoing violence, sent many more troops to Iraq. This surge of U.S. forces succeeded in reducing the violence. But terrorist attacks continued, especially against the new Iraqi army and police force that the Americans were training.

In February 2009, the newly elected American president, Barack Obama, announced that he would begin pulling American troops out of Iraq. "Iraq's future," he declared, "is now its own responsibility." In August 2010, the last American combat forces left Iraq. But fifty thousand American military personnel stayed behind to provide security and train Iraqi soldiers. Some observers fear that when the remaining American forces leave, Iraq might descend into civil war.

Responding to an Ongoing Threat

While America struggled with its involvement in Iraq, militant Islamists continued to mount terrorist attacks around the world. In 2004, several bombs exploded aboard commuter trains in Madrid, Spain, killing nearly two hundred people. In 2005, suicide bombers with links to al-Qaeda blew themselves up in the London subway and aboard a bus, killing fifty-two people. Terrorists also murdered civilians in such Muslim nations as Morocco, Jordan, and Indonesia. In those countries, the attacks often focused on places frequented by Westerners, but the victims were mostly Muslim.

People heatedly debate the best way to respond to these attacks. Some say that Islamist terrorism is the greatest threat to the peace and stability of the world. Others argue that militant Islamists make up only a very small minority of the Muslim world, and express concerns that the terrorists will create deep divisions in Western societies by turning non-Muslim majorities against their Muslim fellow citizens. As the debate continues, what remains clear is that militant Islam has reshaped the world we live in.

Conflict in Afghanistan

As of late 2010, some 120,000 U.S. and other coalition troops (largely from the United Kingdom, Germany, France, Italy, and Canada) continued to fight in Afghanistan. Though al-Qaeda was weakened, Osama bin Laden remained at large and was thought to be hiding in the mountains of Pakistan, near the Afghan border. Coalition forces faced enormous challenges in seeking to defeat both the Taliban and al-Qaeda, protecting the Afghan people from Taliban brutality, and building basic government institutions in one of the poorest nations on earth.

1950

1960

1970

1945
The United Nations establishes the International Monetary Fund to promote economic cooperation and reduce poverty.

1957
The Soviet Union launches the first man-made satellite, *Sputnik*.

1976
Apple develops its first personal computer.

Once a crossroads of the **ancient Silk Road**, today Shanghai, China, is an urban megacity.

Chapter 36

ISSUES FOR THE 21ST CENTURY

1945 – present

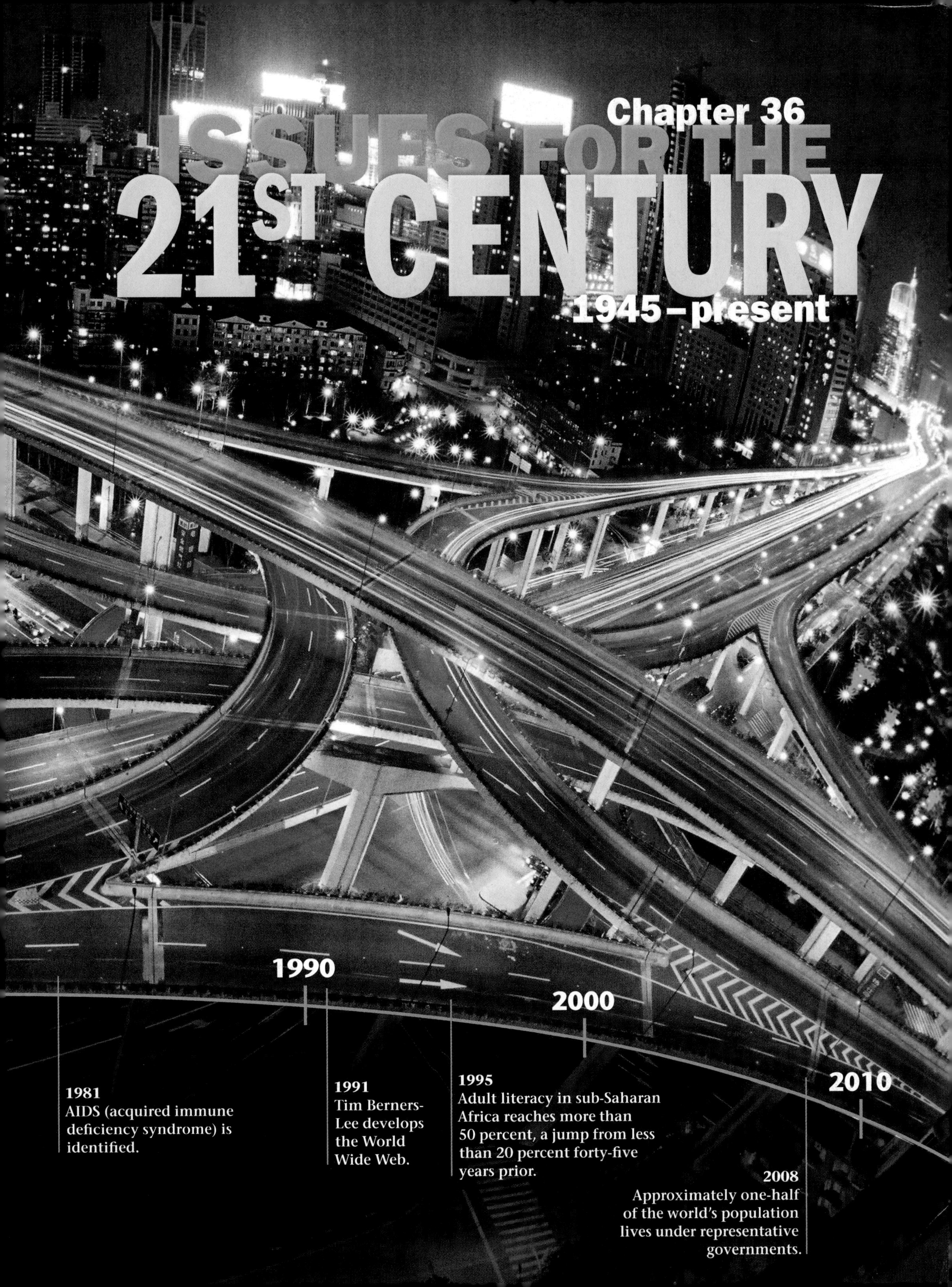

1990

2000

2010

1981
AIDS (acquired immune deficiency syndrome) is identified.

1991
Tim Berners-Lee develops the World Wide Web.

1995
Adult literacy in sub-Saharan Africa reaches more than 50 percent, a jump from less than 20 percent forty-five years prior.

2008
Approximately one-half of the world's population lives under representative governments.

We close with a brief look at the world of today and the recent past. It is too early to predict what future historians will say about our own times. But some important events and trends stand out. One of the most significant is *globalization*—the increasing interaction and integration of the world's economies and cultures.

Globalization has accelerated because of rapid advances in computer technology. The Internet allows for almost instant communication around the globe. Besides enabling companies to do business almost everywhere, the Internet plays a large role in spreading ideas from one culture to another. But this effect is controversial, with some people fearing the disappearance of traditional cultures into a single, standardized way of life.

Globalization has expanded the world's economies and lifted some nations out of poverty. But poverty, hunger, and disease remain major challenges in developing countries. In these countries, many governments continue to deny their citizens basic human rights. Yet the last half century has seen a steep rise in the number of countries with representative governments, as well as a dramatic increase in the standard of living for many of the world's people.

Global Interaction and Interdependence

Key Questions

- How have globalization and economic interdependence affected people and nations in the twenty-first century?

- How have business and culture been influenced by globalization?

Globalization is a contemporary phenomenon shaping the course of our present-day lives. But in some ways, globalization began as long ago as five centuries, with the European Age of Exploration. The Industrial Revolution also encouraged globalization, as advances in transportation and communication in the 1800s enabled industrialized nations to acquire raw materials from distant countries and ship manufactured goods around the world. As early as 1848, Karl Marx noted, "In place of the old wants, satisfied by the production of the country, we find new wants, requiring for their satisfaction the products of distant lands and climes. In place of the old local and national seclusion and self-sufficiency, we have…universal inter-dependence of nations."

In our own time—especially since 1990, with advances in computer technology—the process of globalization has accelerated rapidly. This new phase of rapid globalization has brought both opportunities and challenges. One challenge is that while the world is increasingly united *economically*, it remains *politically* divided into nearly two hundred independent nations, each with its own goals and concerns.

Economies in a Global Age

As globalization links the economies of developed nations, it has contributed to a rising standard of living. Consumers in much of the world now have access to more goods than ever before, at lower prices. But globalization has benefited some groups and nations more than others.

Free Trade

Globalization relies on **free trade**, when businesses in various nations engage in commerce with little government interference or restriction. Governments have frequently interfered with trade in an attempt to protect businesses in their own countries from competition. Often, governments have placed tariffs on foreign goods. Such taxes make the foreign goods more expensive, which encourages consumers to purchase domestically manufactured products. Governments have also enforced quotas that limit the amount of foreign goods that can be imported.

Despite diverse currencies, world economies are increasingly united.

863

Tariffs, quotas, and other barriers to free trade are all forms of the economic policy known as **protectionism**. As long ago as 1776, the philosopher Adam Smith attacked protectionism, saying, "If a foreign country can supply us with a commodity cheaper than we ourselves can make it, better buy it of them with some part of the produce of our own industry, employed in a way in which we have some advantage."

Today's defenders of free trade agree with Smith. For example, advocates of free trade say that if Chinese businesses can make clothes more cheaply than American manufacturers, then it is good for the American consumer, who saves money by buying Chinese clothes. And, with the money the Chinese make from selling clothing to America, they can buy machinery made in the United States. Advocates of free trade argue that both countries benefit by concentrating on what they do best.

Free trade can also provide a basis for cooperation among nations. After World War II, the recently formed United Nations sponsored the creation of two organizations devoted to economic matters—the International Monetary Fund (IMF) and the World Bank. The IMF was designed to stabilize the flow of money between countries. The World Bank was set up to lend money to countries in need. In the beginning, the World Bank helped rebuild war-torn Western Europe. Later, it lent money to developing nations on the condition that they follow principles of free enterprise and free trade.

In recent decades, more and more nations have made their own agreements to promote international commerce. In 1947, twenty-three countries signed the General Agreement on Tariffs and Trade (GATT). In 1995, GATT was replaced by the World Trade Organization (WTO), with more than a hundred members. The WTO was designed to encourage free trade and help settle trade disputes between nations. By 2008, 153 countries—a majority of the nations in the world—had joined the WTO.

Arguments Against Free Trade

With the spread of free-trade practices, the world's economy has grown faster than ever before. Many countries have become more prosperous. Around the world, consumers have benefited by having access to goods at lower prices.

Yet many people think that free trade does more harm than good. For example, free-trade policies allow companies in developed countries, such as the United States, to shut down factories and set them up again in less developed countries where the cost of labor is much cheaper. When this happens, American workers lose jobs. But the workers in the less developed countries may also not truly benefit, because they work for low wages, sometimes in harsh conditions that would not be permitted in a developed country. For these reasons, most labor unions in the United States and other Western countries want more restrictions on trade.

Other opponents of free trade argue that free-trade agreements restrict countries from passing laws that protect the environment or regulate labor practices. Without such laws, say the critics of free trade, businesses have free rein to pollute the environment and mistreat their workers.

Chinese workers make athletic shoes for a U.S. company because labor is cheaper In China than in the United States.

Regions Integrate for Trade

Global organizations like the World Trade Organization are not the only groups promoting free trade. Smaller groups of countries have also come together to dismantle trade barriers with their neighbors. The North American Free Trade Agreement (NAFTA) removed many trade barriers between Mexico, the United States, and Canada. Twenty-seven European nations have been integrated into the European Union (EU). Goods and people flow freely across national borders, as there are no trade barriers or passport controls between EU countries. Sixteen of the EU countries use a common currency, called the euro.

In 1999, at a meeting of representatives to the World Trade Organization in Seattle, Washington, about fifty thousand protesters took to the streets. Most came from labor, environmentalist, and anti-capitalist groups. A few protesters smashed windows, burned cars, and fought with police. While the leaders of the protest condemned these actions, the violence demonstrated the strong emotions stirred by the subject of free trade.

Businesses Go Global

Leading the trend toward economic globalization are large companies called **multinational corporations**. Many of these are headquartered in developed countries such as the United States, although they do business in rich and poor countries alike. More than half the goods the United States makes for export are produced by multinational corporations.

The revolution in computer technology and the invention of the Internet (discussed later in this chapter) have encouraged the growth of multinational corporations. Today, businesses can easily stay connected to workers abroad. Thus, for example, an American corporation can hire thousands of workers in a country like India, which has a large force of educated, English-speaking workers. As a result of this practice, known as **outsourcing**, a person in the United States might call for help with his or her computer and wind up speaking to someone at a call center in New Delhi, India.

Outsourcing is a controversial practice. Advocates of outsourcing argue that consumers at home benefit from lower prices when a corporation is able to cut costs. Besides, they say, as multinational corporations export more unskilled jobs abroad, their growing profits allow them to hire more skilled and high-paid workers at home. Critics say that outsourcing leads to a loss of jobs in a corporation's home country. After the recession of 2007 brought high unemployment to the United States, outsourcing became a hotly debated political issue. In the 2010 American congressional elections, one politician voiced a typical sentiment when he accused his opponents of supporting policies that "shipped jobs overseas to China instead of creating jobs here at home."

At an outsourcing center in Kashmir, north of India, men and women work on developing twenty-first-century software programs.

865

In Mumbai, India, a study in contrast: A billboard advertising the "Millionaire" clothing brand looms above the houses of people living in poverty. In much of the world, there remains a wide gap between the haves and have-nots.

this category is too broad because it includes nations at very different stages of development. At one extreme are what the IMF identifies as "advanced developing countries," including South Korea, Turkey, and Brazil, whose economies are rapidly growing, and which may soon qualify as "developed." These countries have benefited considerably from globalization.

At the other extreme are the "least developed nations," which suffer from widespread poverty and political instability. In 2009, the United Nations included forty-nine countries on its list of least developed nations. Thirty-three were in Africa, with most of the rest located in southern Asia. Globalization has had little positive effect on these nations. Although they make up more than a quarter of the world's countries, their combined share of world trade is only about 1 percent.

Developed and Developing Nations

Although globalization has connected the economies of different nations as never before, the wealth of the world remains very unevenly distributed. Most of that wealth is concentrated in developed countries, the industrialized nations with a high standard of living. The head of the United Nations once defined a developed country as "one that allows all its citizens to enjoy a free and healthy life in a safe environment." Fewer than 20 percent of the world's countries are considered "developed" in this sense. The developed nations are concentrated in North America and Europe, although Israel, Japan, Australia, New Zealand, and others are also among the world's most developed nations.

The rest of the world's nations are called "developing" countries, though some argue that

Economic Interdependence

As the economies of the world's nations grow increasingly interdependent, the ups and downs of one country's economy can affect the rest of the world. This fact was dramatically demonstrated by the worldwide recession that began in 2007.

The recession, a severe slowdown in economic activity, was triggered by the collapse of the U.S. housing market. Beginning in the late 1990s, the price of the average American home soared, increasing by almost 10 percent a year. The rise in prices was fueled by rising demand. Encouraged by political leaders and financial institutions, more and more people aspired to the "American dream" of owning their own homes. To make money on the interest, banks encouraged people to take out mortgages (loans to buy homes). Many buyers took out loans they could not afford to pay back. Banks and other financial institutions sold the risky mortgages to investors, who themselves hoped to make money as home prices climbed.

Easy credit and the unrealistic inflation of prices created what economists call a "bubble." In the summer of 2007, the bubble burst. House prices plummeted. People who had their life savings invested in a home were left with nothing. Banks were stuck with mountains of bad debt. Many small banks went out of business. With huge infusions of aid from the U.S. government, large banks survived, but afterward were wary of lending money. Unable to borrow from the banks, thousands of businesses failed. Millions of people lost their jobs.

Because the United States accounts for such a large share of the world's economy, the effects of the crisis were quickly felt abroad. Businesses throughout Europe and Asia suffered as demand for their exports rapidly declined. Many foreign banks that had invested in the United States lost heavily, leaving them with less money to lend at home. In stock markets from England to Japan, the price of shares tumbled.

Government economists, using standard measures of economic activity, declared in 2010 that the recession had been over for more than a year. But many people still felt caught in the economic slump. The unemployment rate remained high in most developed countries. Many developing countries suffered even more. In Africa, millions of poor people slipped even deeper into poverty as governments sliced their budgets and foreign countries cut back on aid.

Cultural Interaction

Globalization affects culture as well as economics. When consumers in a country are exposed to new products from abroad, they may change their tastes in food, music, and clothing, and even their political ideas. The United States, which accounts for almost 25 percent of world economic output, is the largest source of products that influence other cultures.

As globalization progresses, more and more people watch American movies, listen to American music, and wear American-style clothes. In some countries, people fear that their own cultural traditions will be submerged in a tide of Americanization. This fear has led to protests against some popular American companies doing business in other countries.

For example, in 1999, French protesters used tractors and crowbars to destroy a McDonald's restaurant, part of a fast-food business chain. In 2007, hundreds of thousands of Chinese signed a petition and forced the closure of a Starbucks coffee shop at the Forbidden City in Beijing.

While some worry about the Americanization of their culture, others point out that due to globalization, the culture of the United States is changing in response to influences from other lands. For example, thanks to the Internet, people in the United States can listen to music from around the world. Many American teenagers enjoy Japanese comic books called *manga*. Lively musical movies made in India—so-called "Bollywood" films—have become popular in the United States.

A Canadian writer, Marshall McLuhan, argued that thanks to electronic communications, "'Time' has ceased, 'space' has vanished. We now live in a global village." McLuhan believed that humanity would have to give up thinking on an individual, local, or even national level, and instead join a worldwide common culture. So far, his ideas have proven only partially correct. Uniquely local customs and distinctly national cultures have proven to be strong and resilient. But a new international popular culture continues to develop, connecting nations and peoples in sometimes surprising ways.

Social and Environmental Challenges

Key Questions

- What are some of the major social challenges facing the world today?

- What are some of the major environmental challenges facing the world today?

In the early twenty-first century, the people of the world continue to face severe challenges. Nearly one-quarter of the earth's population lives in extreme poverty. Hunger and disease remain widespread in many developing countries. In many lands, governments continue to deny basic human rights to their citizens. Pollution, deforestation, and other environmental threats affect the health of the planet itself. Although some developed countries have made effective efforts to protect the environment, many developing countries lag behind.

Social Challenges

Poverty, often defined as the inability to satisfy one's basic needs, remains one of the great challenges facing the world's governments. Especially in the developing world, governments struggle to improve the lives of their people by battling poverty and disease. But many of those governments deny basic freedoms to their citizens.

Poverty and Hunger in the Twenty-first Century

Over the last few decades, the most extreme poverty has declined. But nearly half the people in the world still live on less than the equivalent of two U.S. dollars a day. The gap between rich and poor nations remains huge. People in the twenty richest countries earn an average of nearly forty times as much as people in the twenty poorest.

The richest nations—such as the United States and the countries of Western Europe—are generally those that industrialized early and got a head start on development. Most are politically stable, with capitalist economic systems that encourage ambition and innovation. Poor nations, by contrast, are often located in regions with harsh climates that breed disease and make work more difficult. In many cases, these nations were colonized by European powers that plundered them for raw materials rather than encouraging them to industrialize. After gaining independence, these nations often descended into civil war or were taken over by corrupt dictators who seized the nation's wealth for themselves. Such factors help account for the persistently high poverty rate in sub-Saharan Africa.

An African woman suffers from starvation.

The HIV/AIDS Pandemic

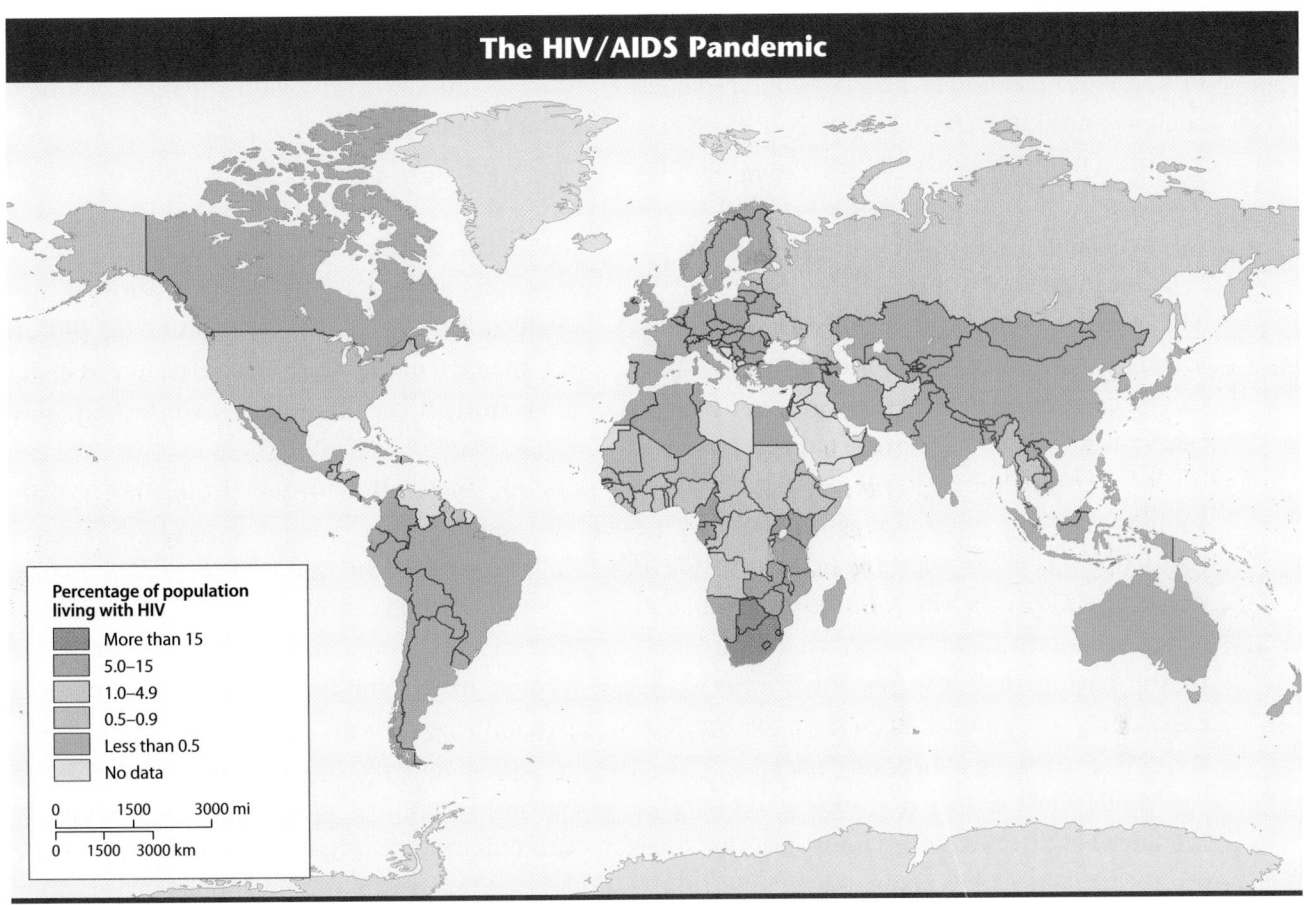

Percentage of population living with HIV

- More than 15
- 5.0–15
- 1.0–4.9
- 0.5–0.9
- Less than 0.5
- No data

```
0      1500    3000 mi
0   1500  3000 km
```

Since AIDS (caused by the human immunodeficiency virus or HIV) was first identified in 1981, millions of cases have been diagnosed around the world. The disease has taken an especially severe toll in sub-Saharan Africa.

The world's poorest people usually lack access to adequate shelter, health care, and education. All too often, they also lack sufficient food. According to the United Nations, in 2008 more than nine hundred million people were undernourished and twenty-five thousand a day died of starvation.

Famines—especially severe and prolonged shortages of food—still strike parts of our world. Famines are often caused by a combination of natural and human factors. For example, before the fall of the Soviet Union, the communist superpower sent large amounts of food aid to its ally, North Korea. In the 1990s, when the Soviet Union collapsed, Soviet aid to North Korea ended. This, coupled with natural disasters that included floods and droughts, led to the deaths of as many as a million people in North Korea.

In Africa in 2004, famine struck Darfur, a region in Sudan, when fighting between rebel groups and a government-backed militia caused farmers to flee their lands. Two years later, when a drought in East Africa led to crop failures, a civil war kept aid workers from delivering food to the starving.

Disease: The Threat of Pandemics

At various times in history, infectious diseases have caused devastating loss of life. In the 1300s, the plague called the Black Death swept through Europe, killing between a third and a half of the continent's population. Beginning in the 1500s, some 90 percent of the native populations of North and South America were wiped out by smallpox and other diseases brought by European settlers. The end of the First World War in 1918 saw the outbreak of an influenza pandemic—a worldwide epidemic. In 1918 and 1919, influenza killed 50–100 million people, more than the world war itself.

Since the early twentieth century, better sanitation and the invention of more powerful medicines, such as antibiotics, have helped control illness. Vaccination programs have largely wiped out some deadly diseases, such as smallpox. But other diseases continue to threaten large populations.

The most devastating of these illnesses is AIDS (acquired immune deficiency syndrome), an infectious disease of the immune system. AIDS can be controlled by drugs, but no cure has yet been found. Since AIDS was first recognized a quarter-century ago, it has led to the deaths of some twenty-five million people. AIDS is a true pandemic, occurring worldwide. Two-thirds of those currently living with AIDS are in sub-Saharan Africa, where the disease has taken a terrible toll. In the nation of Botswana, for example, life expectancy has tumbled from sixty-five years to thirty-five since the pandemic began.

Modern technology helps track and control the spread of diseases. But scientists fear that modern technologies may inadvertently contribute to new and worse epidemics. Already, overuse of antibiotics has made some germs resistant to drugs. About two billion people a year travel by airplane, potentially spreading diseases more rapidly than ever before. In 2002 and 2003, air travelers spread a respiratory disease called SARS (severe acute respiratory syndrome) from China

Commuters in Taiwan wear face masks to protect from the airborne respiratory disease called SARS.

to more than two dozen countries. Public health officials remain on the alert for signs of a new influenza pandemic.

Migration and Urbanization

The process of migration, in which large numbers of people move from one place to another, has accelerated in the age of globalization. In 2005, a full 3 percent of the world's population was living in a country other than the one where they were born. The world's leading host country was the United States, with thirty-eight million foreign-born residents.

People often migrate from developing countries to developed countries such as those in North America and Europe. Immigrants often seek more freedom, more stability for their families, or more economic opportunity.

But immigrants do not always find themselves welcome when they arrive. Especially in times of economic trouble, such as during the worldwide recession that began in 2007, immigrants are often accused of taking jobs away from native-born residents. In the wake of terrorist attacks by militant Islamists, many Muslim immigrants to European countries faced suspicion and hostility.

Much migration occurs not only from one country to another but within countries as well. In such cases, migration often coincides with urbanization, as many people move to cities. Rural areas in developing countries generally offer few opportunities for work, education, or health care, so people often flock from the countryside to the cities. But most cities in developing countries lack the infrastructure—housing, roads, water, sanitation systems—to support an exploding population. Often, migrants wind up living in crowded slums or in shacks in shantytowns on the outskirts of urban areas.

Recent decades have seen the growth of sprawling, densely populated urban areas sometimes called "megacities," such as Mexico City, or Lagos, Nigeria, or Mumbai, India. Mumbai, for example, draws a million new residents a year. In

Gleaming office towers rise behind modest dwellings on the outskirts of Kuala Lumpur, the largest city in Malaysia.

Mumbai, gleaming office towers loom over dismal slums where people lack toilets and running water, and where fifteen members of a family might sleep in a single room.

Democracy and Human Rights

In 1948, the newly formed United Nations adopted the Universal Declaration of Human Rights. This document asserted that "everyone has the right to take part in the government of his country." It went on to say that governments should protect such basic rights as freedom of speech, freedom of religion, and equality before the law. Despite the noble words of the declaration, in 1948 only a small minority of the world's nations had democratic forms of government that respected human rights.

In the decades since, the spread of democracy around the world has been gradual but significant.

The end of European colonial rule in the 1960s and 1970s, and the fall of the Soviet empire in 1989, helped spur democratic change on several continents.

But much of the world's population is still denied basic rights. In China, the world's most populous country, the ruling Communist Party allows its citizens considerable economic freedom but no *political* liberty. The people of China can go into business for themselves, but they cannot choose their leaders. And if they speak out against the government, they may suffer imprisonment or worse.

Most people in Africa and the Middle East still live under dictatorial regimes. On the African continent, few countries have followed South Africa in turning toward democracy. In the Middle East, Iran's Islamic rulers have brutally suppressed demonstrations against their dictatorship. In Iraq, an elected government has replaced the tyranny of Saddam Hussein, but bitter ethnic and religious divisions hamper the creation of a fully functioning democracy.

The Rights of Women and Children

Over the past five decades, a strong feminist movement has worked to improve the status of women in the developed world. Women in the United States and other Western nations have seen their opportunities increase dramatically. For example, the percentage of female students in American medical schools shot up from 6 percent in 1961 to 50 percent in 2006. But across the world, most women still lack the same rights and opportunities as men. In the words of a UN report, women "perform nearly two thirds of all working hours, receive only one tenth of the world's income, and own less than 1 percent of world property."

In many developing countries, cultural traditions discourage women from leaving the home or getting an education. Consequently, more than 60 percent of the illiterate people in the world are women. The status of women is especially low

Child labor: A boy toils in an aluminum factory in Bangladesh.

in some Muslim countries that follow a strict form of Islam. In Iran, women may be severely punished if they go out in "immodest" clothing. In Saudi Arabia, women are not allowed to vote or drive, and they must be fully covered when they appear in public.

Just as many nations deny women basic rights, they also fail to prevent the exploitation and abuse of children. Many developing countries either lack or fail to enforce laws against child labor. Worldwide, an estimated one in six children between the ages of five and fourteen is forced to work. Millions work as servants to well-off families, who treat them as little more than slaves. Millions more labor at dangerous occupations—working in mines, operating heavy machinery, handling dangerous chemicals. In recent years, Western labor unions and other groups have campaigned strongly against child labor, but their efforts run up against long-held views in some societies that it is normal for children to work.

Environmental Challenges

At least since the beginnings of the agricultural revolution—many thousands of years ago, when early humans first deliberately planted seeds—human beings have struggled to control their physical environment. Humans now have the ability to affect the natural environment in dramatic ways. With population growth and the worldwide spread of industry, the human toll on the environment has increased to the point that we can no longer take for granted such basic natural resources as clean air, clean water, and arable soil.

A polluted river in the African country of Nigeria is a source of disease and unsafe drinking water.

Desertification and Deforestation

One of the world's great environmental challenges is *desertification*, which occurs when natural or human activity causes land to become desertlike and therefore uninhabitable. The United Nations estimates that by 2017, some fifty million people may be displaced by desertification.

Desertification is especially severe in Africa. In the decades after the coming of political independence, the continent's population exploded—from 200 million in 1960 to 450 million in 1990. In many regions, there was too little good farmland available to feed the population. Farmers were forced to plant their crops in poor soil, which caused the soil to dry out. One especially hard-hit area is the Sahel, south of the Sahara. Its inhabitants are subject to frequent famines as farmland disappears and the desert expands.

Many factors lead to desertification, including climate change and poor farming practices. In some countries, environmentalists are teaching farmers techniques such as crop rotation to help preserve the soil.

Another major threat to the environment is *deforestation*, the cutting down of large forests for wood or to clear the way for agriculture or industry. The forests that are being destroyed serve a vital environmental function by removing poisonous carbon dioxide from the air and releasing life-giving oxygen. Deforestation is especially severe in tropical rain forests like those of the Amazon in South America, home to some two-thirds of the plant and animal species on earth. As habitats are destroyed, deforestation can potentially cause the extinction of many species.

In recent years, environmentalist groups have drawn attention to the dangers of deforestation. Because of their efforts, in some parts of the world, such as Europe, the amount of forestland is increasing because trees are being replanted.

Desertification in Namibia and other parts of Africa has led to the loss of valuable farmland.

Elsewhere, however, many forests are being cut down without being renewed.

The Hazards of Pollution

Over the last century, industrialization, expanding populations, and the growth of large cities have worsened the pollution of the world's water and air. Rivers, lakes, and the oceans are polluted by numerous sources, including wastewater from homes, chemicals from factories, and fertilizer from farms. Some 1.5 billion people in the world, most in developing countries, lack clean water to drink. Millions die every year of waterborne illnesses.

Many of the world's urban areas suffer from air pollution. While the burning of coal and the release of industrial chemicals contribute to the problem, the main source of air pollution is the carbon monoxide emitted by cars and trucks. Air pollution can cause severe diseases of the lungs. Today, the worst air pollution occurs in large cities in developing countries. The capitals of India and China—New Delhi and Beijing—rank as two of the most polluted cities in the world.

In recent decades, many developed countries, because of their greater resources, have taken steps to control pollution. For example, in the 1970s

873

A thick blanket of smog hangs over Mexico City. The city has recently taken steps to reduce air pollution.

the United States passed the Clean Air Act and the Clean Water Act. These laws have helped to reduce pollution. Some developing countries have also worked hard to overcome the problem. In the early 1990s, Mexico City had the world's worst air, so bad that it was said to cause birds to drop dead in flight. By moving factories outside the city, and replacing cars with buses and trains, the city's leaders have cut its level of air pollution in half.

Climate Change

In recent years, scientists have issued warnings about changes in the earth's climate caused by human activities. Many scientists link these climate changes to global warming, a gradual rise in earth's temperature that results when carbon dioxide and other gases, mainly from factories and motor vehicles, become trapped in the earth's atmosphere, causing the so-called greenhouse effect.

Some scientists argue that if current trends continue, climate patterns will change drastically, with disastrous consequences, including the melting of the polar icecaps, a worldwide rise in the sea level, flooding in some parts of the

world, and droughts in others. A small minority of scientists argue that climate change is less the product of human activity than of natural variations in the world's temperature over time. They think that predictions of potentially disastrous climate change are overstated.

Scientific evidence of the potential harm of global warming was sufficient to prompt representatives from many countries to sign the Kyoto Protocol, an international agreement sponsored by the United Nations and named for the city in Japan where the treaty was adopted in 1997. The treaty set targets for the reduction of emission levels to control greenhouse gases.

The United States was one of the few countries that refused to sign the Kyoto Protocol. President George W. Bush announced that he would not support the Kyoto Protocol because it failed to impose emissions requirements on developing countries, and because he thought it would hurt the U.S. economy. A number of states and cities responded by independently endorsing the protocol or similar programs, which illustrates how climate change remains a controversial issue among policy makers.

In China, a man walks across a dry lake bed that was once a major source of water for a nearby city.

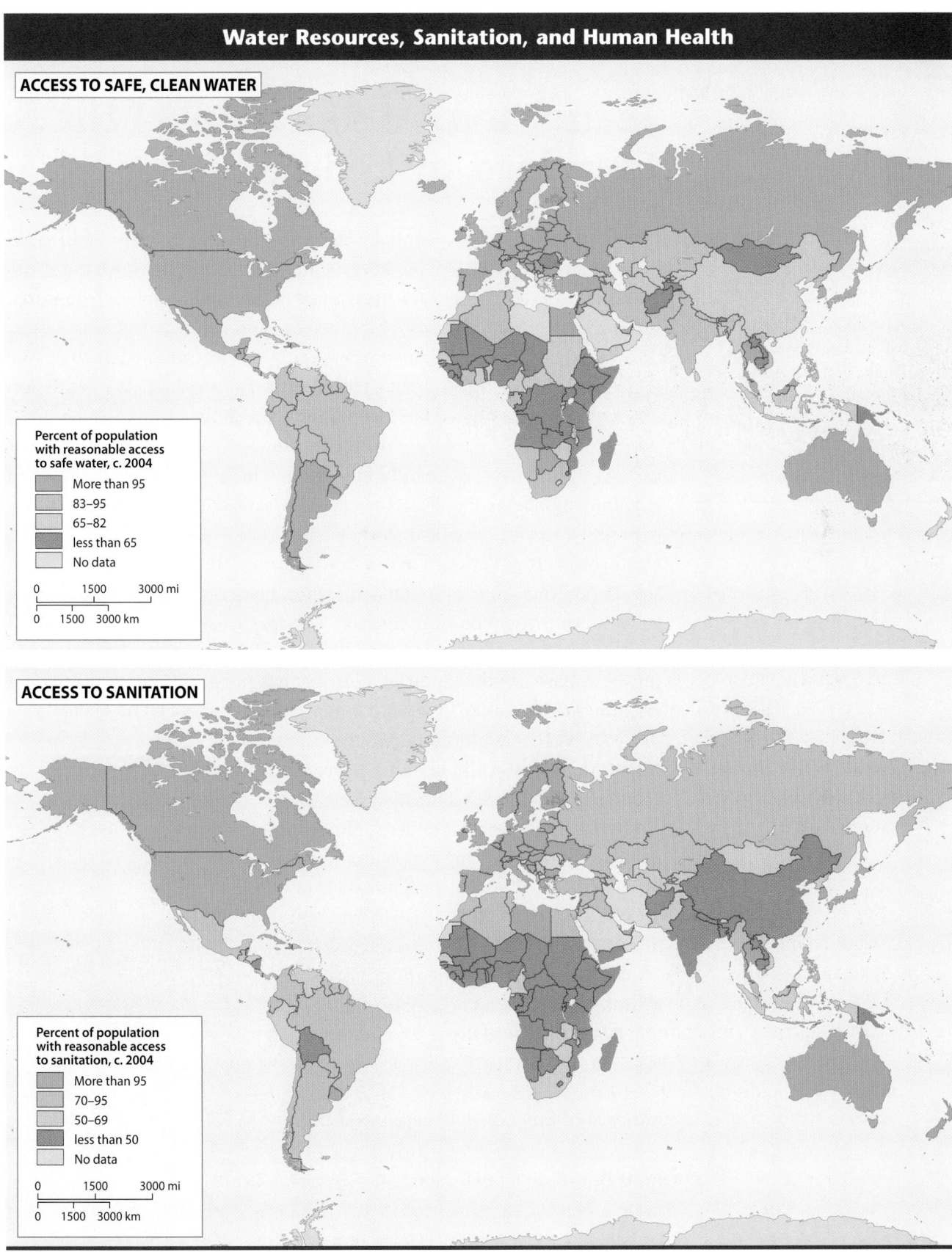

Water Resources, Sanitation, and Human Health

ACCESS TO SAFE, CLEAN WATER

Percent of population with reasonable access to safe water, c. 2004

- More than 95
- 83–95
- 65–82
- less than 65
- No data

```
0      1500      3000 mi
0   1500   3000 km
```

ACCESS TO SANITATION

Percent of population with reasonable access to sanitation, c. 2004

- More than 95
- 70–95
- 50–69
- less than 50
- No data

```
0      1500      3000 mi
0   1500   3000 km
```

The health of many people remains at risk in those parts of the world where people lack sufficient access to both sanitation and safe, clean water.

Technology, Science, and the Standard of Living

Key Questions

- What benefits and challenges have resulted from recent scientific and technological advances?

- How has the standard of living around the world changed in recent decades?

The last half century has brought extraordinary advances in science and technology. Although the benefits of this progress have spread unevenly, even the poorest nations have seen a slow but steady improvement in their standards of living.

Advances in Science and Technology

The exploration of space has led to new knowledge of the universe and spurred technical innovation on earth. New methods of diagnosing and treating disease have saved millions of lives. Underlying all this progress is an information revolution created by rapid advances in computer technology.

Exploring Outer Space

Some of the most dramatic scientific achievements of the twentieth century grew out of the exploration of space. The space age began in 1957, when the Soviet Union launched *Sputnik*, the first artificial satellite. (A satellite in this sense is an object that orbits a planet; thus, while our moon is a natural satellite, *Sputnik* was an artificial, or man-made, one.)

Cold War competition spurred the United States and the Soviet Union into a "space race." Soon both nations were launching men as well as satellites into space. President John F. Kennedy set a goal of putting a man on the moon by the year 1970. Although Kennedy himself did not live to see it, that goal was achieved in July 1969, when the American astronaut Neil Armstrong set foot on the moon. America's National Aeronautics and Space Administration (NASA) achieved five other manned moon landings, the last in 1972.

In the 1980s and 1990s, NASA concentrated on flights using space shuttles—large spacecraft that could perform a variety of functions, from launching satellites to engaging in scientific experiments. In 1990, NASA launched the Hubble Space Telescope, which is still in orbit, helping scientists on earth peer into the farthest known galaxies. In recent

Tethered astronauts work on the International Space Station.

New technologies link our world. Here, a man in a rural part of the African nation of Kenya speaks on a cellular phone.

years, NASA has joined with agencies from other nations to construct an International Space Station to be used as a platform for further voyages into space.

While broadening our knowledge of the universe, the science of space exploration has also improved life on earth. Engineering innovations designed for spacecraft have been applied to automobiles and airplanes, improving their efficiency and safety. Imaging techniques that doctors use to see into the human body were first used by NASA to study pictures of the moon. Research on nutrition for astronauts has even been used to make better baby food.

Today, some three thousand satellites orbit the earth, serving many purposes. Some satellites are used for observation, providing vital information to government officials, weather forecasters, and military planners. Others transmit television shows. Satellites linked to cell phones can send messages to points on earth where no cell towers exist. Through the Global Positioning System (GPS), satellites can help guide motorists and travelers accurately to their destinations.

Medical Breakthroughs

In the past half century, breakthroughs in medicine have helped save many lives. Advanced technology now allows doctors to diagnose and treat illness and injury more effectively than ever before.

You are probably familiar with how doctors use X-rays (beams of radiation discovered by a German scientist in 1895) to get pictures of the interior of the body, especially its bones. In the 1970s, scientists invented the CT (computerized tomography) scanner, which uses X-rays to see much more clearly inside the body. A CT scan lets doctors observe a three-dimensional image of internal bodily structures. A machine invented a few years later, the magnetic resonance imaging (MRI) scanner, uses the force of magnetism, rather than X-rays, to probe the body for disease. The images produced by MRI are even more detailed than those of the CT scanner. Doctors use both technologies in the diagnosis and treatment of various illnesses.

Some of the most astounding medical advances have been made in the field of surgery. In 1967, a South African surgeon carried out the first successful transplant of a heart from one human body to another. Today, heart transplant surgery is common, along with the transplantation of lungs, kidneys, and livers. Lasers—high-energy light beams that can cut with great precision—have made surgery safer and less painful.

In the early 1950s, a team of English scientists unraveled the structure of DNA (deoxyribonucleic acid), which contains the genetic material that

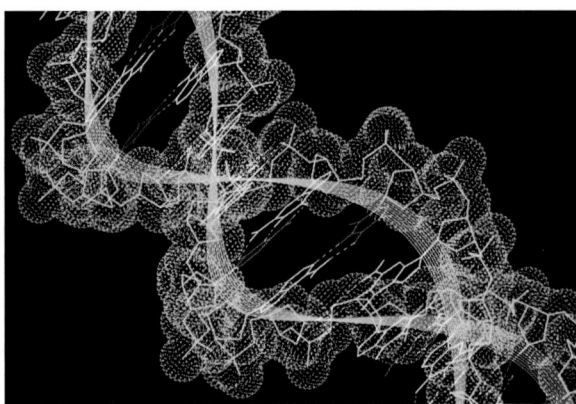

A computer-generated model of DNA, which contains the genetic blueprint of living organisms

A sheep named Dolly was cloned in 1996. Cloning creates an organism with the same DNA as another organism.

determines the formation and development of all living organisms. In 1990, an international network of scientists began collaborating on the Human Genome Project. By 2003, they had successfully identified the nearly twenty-five thousand genes in the human body. Because most disease has some connection to genetics, this information should eventually help scientists predict, prevent, and treat many diseases.

Some new medical technologies have sparked controversy. For example, cloning—creating an organism with the exact same DNA as another organism—presents ethical challenges about the role of science. Similar concerns have been raised about the use of stem cells, which can be developed into many different types of cells in the body.

Computers and the Information Revolution

During the nineteenth century, the Industrial Revolution profoundly changed the modern world. In the late twentieth century, another technological revolution, sometimes called the Information Revolution, has had similarly far-reaching consequences, as advances in computer technology have dramatically changed the way people around the world live and work.

The first modern computers, designed to perform rapid mathematical calculations, date from the 1940s. During and after World War II, these early computers were used mostly by government scientists and military planners. Early versions of the computer were huge, expensive machines. One computer used by the U.S. government weighed thirty tons and filled a large room.

A breakthrough came in the 1950s, with the invention of the transistor, a tiny device to control the flow of electrical current. With transistors, electronic devices such as radios and computers could be made much smaller. By the 1960s, engineers had designed computers small enough to fit into an elevator.

Governments and corporations proceeded to use computers for everything from tracking sales figures to guiding spacecraft to the moon. But computers were not readily available to individual

This enormous early computer, c. 1940, required operators to program it by plugging and unplugging cables and adjusting switches.

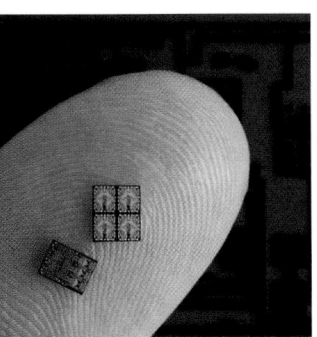

Computer microchips hold complex electronic circuits.

consumers until 1976, when two young American inventors, working out of a garage, came up with a computer small enough to fit on a desk. They called it the Apple I and put it on sale for $666.66. In 1981, the giant electronic company IBM introduced the even smaller and less expensive personal computer (PC).

The pace of change accelerated as engineers and inventors competed to produce ever more powerful computers. The speed and memory capacity of the machines doubled every two years. While a computer of the 1940s could perform five thousand operations a second, a typical computer of the early 1980s could perform five million. The laptop computer, which became widely available in the 1990s, allowed businesspeople to take computers onto airplanes and college students to tote them to class.

A significant advance in computer technology occurred when inventors figured out a way to get millions of computers talking to each other. In the 1970s, businesses, government agencies, and universities had set up networks to allow their computers to share files and programs. In the 1980s, these networks were connected to form what we now call the Internet, an interconnected network of networks.

At first, the Internet was used mainly by government officials and university researchers. Then, in the late 1980s, a young British physicist, Tim Berners-Lee, came up with the idea for software programs, called browsers, that could organize the information on the Internet. Berners-Lee did further work that led to the creation of the World Wide Web (WWW) in 1991. The Web is composed of an interconnected and highly flexible system of computer files linked together on the Internet.

During the 1990s, businesses began advertising and selling their products on the Web. Colleges

Searching the Web

From its earliest days, the Web overflowed with information. At first, users were often frustrated by the difficulty of tracking down the specific information they needed. Then, in 1998, two graduate students at Stanford University in California devised a search engine designed to guide people efficiently through the maze of the Web. They called their invention "Google," and offered it free to anyone using the Internet. They made money by selling space on their website to advertisers. Google now responds to hundreds of millions of search requests each day. Its name has even turned into a verb—when people search the Web for information on a topic, they often say they're "googling" it.

and even high schools offered courses online. Later, individuals posted their thoughts and opinions on their own "Weblogs," or "blogs." For businesses and individuals alike, e-mail (electronic mail) replaced old-fashioned letters as the preferred way of communicating.

The Internet quickly evolved from the domain of a few experts to a vast public commons for the exchange of information. Like the telegraph in the nineteenth century, and like radio and television in the twentieth, the Internet transformed the ways in which people around the world communicated and shared information.

Economic Progress and Rising Standards of Living

As you've read, the problems of poverty, hunger, and disease continue to plague millions of people in the world today. Nevertheless, over the last half century enormous progress has been made in many areas of human life. Especially in developed countries, thanks to childhood vaccines, improved sanitation, and breakthroughs in medicine, people live longer and healthier lives than ever before.

Old and New

Our world today is marked by the sometimes startling side-by-side coexistence of the old and new. Consider, for example, the crowded city of New Delhi in India, home to many young, well-educated people who perform high-tech jobs—often outsourced by Western companies—such as computer support or software programming. They live in modern apartments, and they own high-tech luxuries such as flat-screen televisions and cell phones.

In the same city, however, not far from the modern apartments, there is a slum where, every morning at dawn, women gather in a line, carrying buckets and plastic jugs. They wait, sometimes an hour, sometimes all day, for a tanker truck carrying fresh water. They have no running water. The wells are polluted or have run dry. Even in the middle-class apartments of New Delhi where the high-tech workers live, running water is available only a few hours per day. Thus, even as members of the high-tech middle-class workforce are writing computer code, they, like the women carrying plastic jugs, still struggle to get enough water, one of life's most basic needs.

In both developed and developing nations, improvements in agriculture have cut down on the prevalence of hunger. In the 1960s, scientists discovered how to alter the genes of food crops to produce hardier plants. The result was a so-called green revolution that vastly increased the productivity of farmers. In countries like China and India, terrible famines that had been recurring for centuries came to an end.

More recently, the economic growth spurred by globalization has dramatically decreased poverty in some areas of the world. China, the world's most populous country, saw its poverty rate drop from 60 percent in 1990 to 16 percent in 2005. Since globalization is so closely linked to the Information Revolution, the spread of computer technology holds the promise to lift more regions out of poverty. Already about one-third of the world can access the Internet, and even in some traditionally poor and remote areas, solar-powered computers can be used for business and education.

The United Nations, the World Bank, and other organizations have established many programs designed to alleviate poverty in developing countries. One recent, promising program involves *microloans*—small loans given to impoverished individuals, often women, so they can start their own businesses. In countries where corrupt leaders often monopolize much of the national wealth, microloans can help build prosperity from the bottom up.

The United Nations publishes a Human Development Index (HDI) that compares the standard of living among various countries worldwide. The index considers three factors: a nation's average level of education among its residents, its average life expectancy, and its gross domestic product per person (a measure of average wealth). The current HDI shows stunning gaps between the richest and poorest nations. For example, the

With the help of a microloan, this woman in India was able to start up her own grocery business.

average person in the United States is more than 150 times wealthier than the average person in the Democratic Republic of Congo in Africa.

Nevertheless, the HDI also shows that since the mid-twentieth century, the standard of living has risen most steeply in the developing world. Between 1950 and 1995, life expectancy in developed countries rose from 66 to 74 years, while in developing countries it climbed from 40 to 61 years. In the same period, the literacy rate in China increased from 48 to 82 percent. In the world's poorest region, sub-Saharan Africa, literacy rose from less than 20 to more than 50 percent.

The last facts are especially important because only literate people will be able to take full advantage of the opportunities offered by an increasingly globalized economy. Both economic and social progress rely on the spread of education. The Internet by its nature can help accelerate this

Digital audio players, cell phones, laptop computers—all part of the interconnected world of the Information Revolution

process, making more information available to more people than ever before. The human ingenuity that created the Information Revolution has the potential to help us solve some of humanity's most pressing problems.

The Standard of Living

Annual GDP per capita 2010 (in U.S. dollars)

- Under 2,500
- 2,500–9,999
- 10,000–24,999
- 25,000 or more
- No data

0   1500   3000 mi

0   1500   3000 km

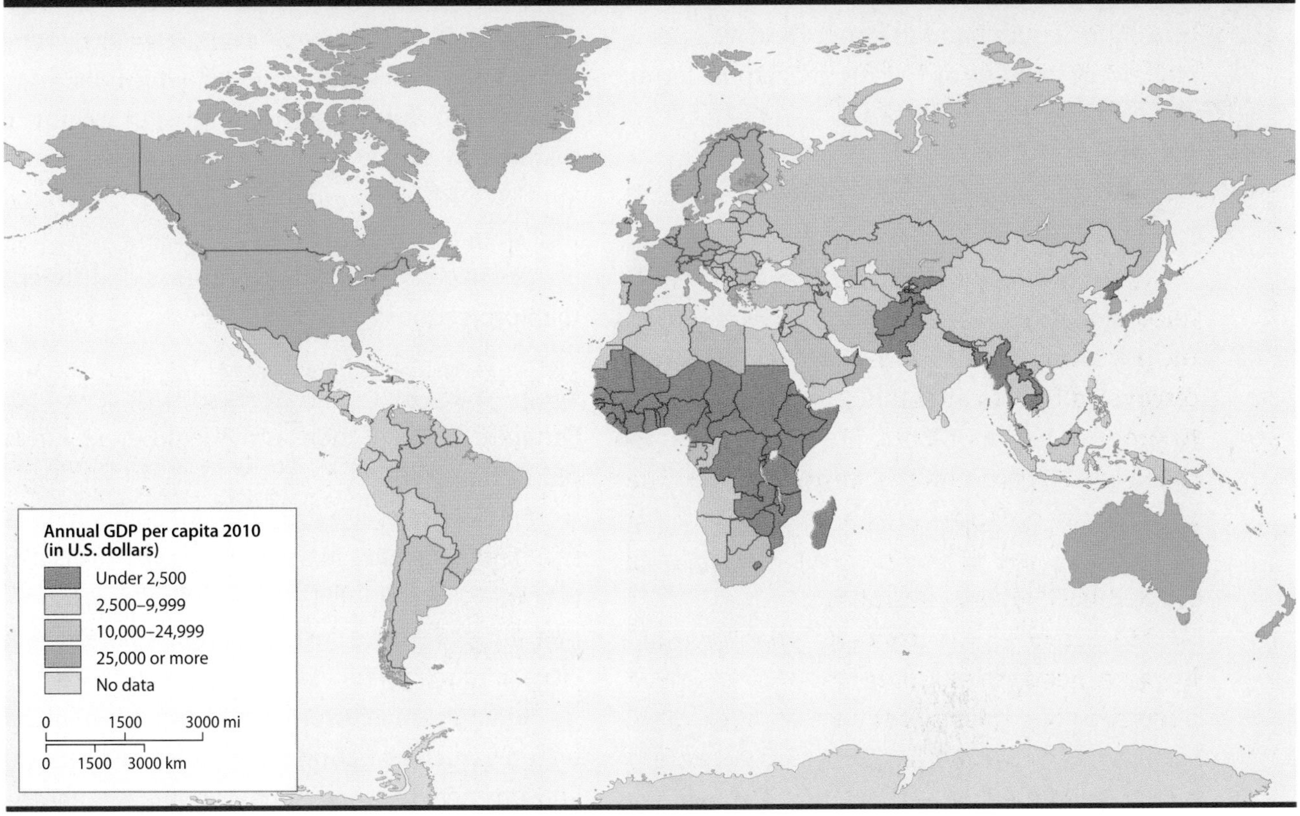

Statistics on the gross domestic product (GDP), a measure of average wealth (represented here in U.S. dollars per person), demonstrate the persistent disparities in the standard of living between developed and developing parts of the world.

Appendix: Geographic Terms and Concepts

The word *geography* comes from the Greek terms for "description of the earth." *Physical geography* concerns the natural features of the earth such as landforms and climates. *Human geography* focuses on people and how they interact with their environments.

To understand historical events, we often need to understand the related geography. Historians want to know what a place was like long ago. They look for the influence the environment had on the people who lived there. They want to know the significance of location. They make connections between where events took place and why things happened as they did.

Throughout this book, we treat historical and geographic issues hand in hand. Here we offer a brief overview of some specific geographic terms and concepts.

A map generated by a Landsat satellite shows part of the British Isles and the surrounding seas.

The World in Spatial Terms

Globes, Maps, and Map Projections

Globes and *maps* represent the earth. They are the geographer's most important tools. Since the earth is roughly sphere-shaped, globes are the most accurate way to show it. However, flat maps are more practical. Try putting a globe in your pocket or on the page of a book!

While flat maps are practical, they all share one disadvantage. It's impossible to represent a sphere on a flat surface with complete accuracy. Thus all flat maps distort the earth when they try to show it. Common distortions include distances, direction, and the shapes and sizes of landmasses.

Cartographers, or mapmakers, have developed various *map projections* as a way to minimize inaccuracies. One kind of projection might minimize distortions in the shape of landmasses, while another projection might minimize distortions in distance.

See pages 906–907 for examples of different map projections.

Types of Maps

Different kinds of maps provide different kinds of information.

Physical maps use symbols and colors to indicate natural features like mountains and rivers. For example, see pages 890–891. *Political maps* show man-made features such as national boundaries, cities, and roads. For example, see pages 892–893.

Some *general purpose maps* show both political features (such as national boundaries and cities) and physical features (such as rivers and mountains). The maps on pages 894–905 show both physical and political features.

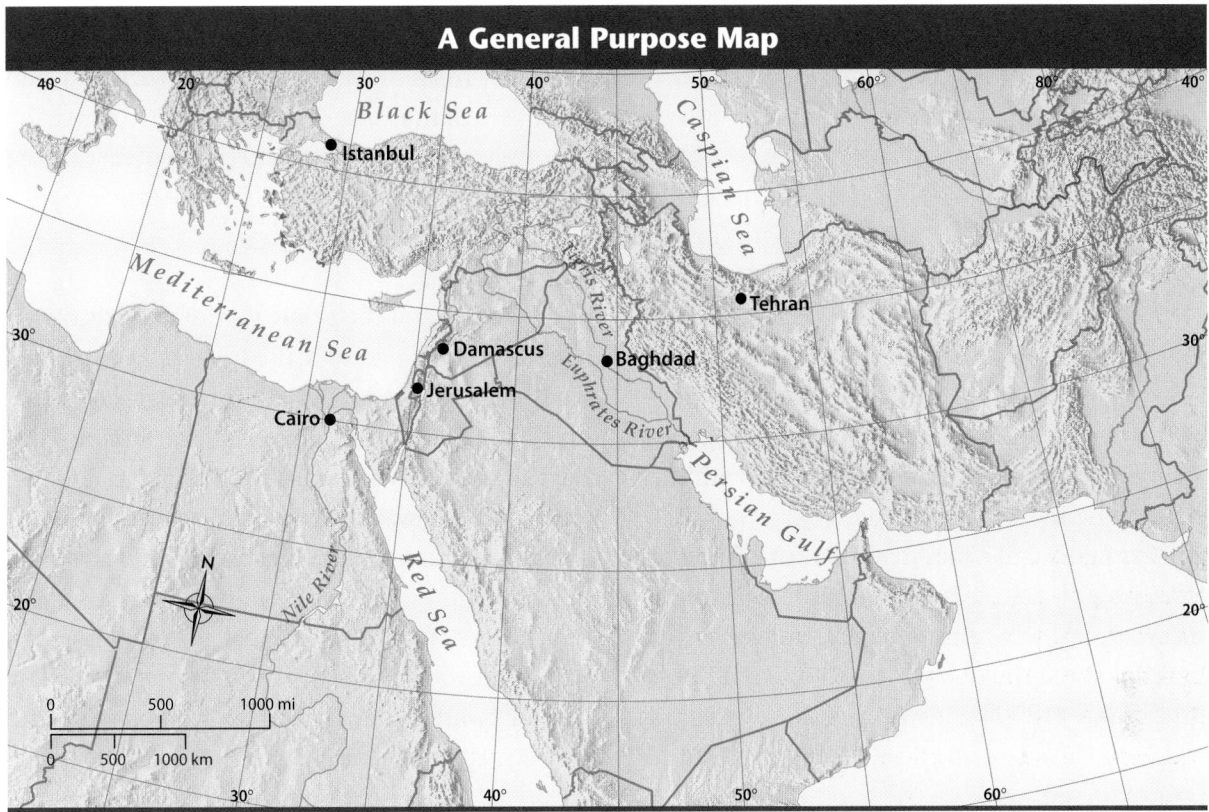

This general purpose map of the Middle East shows both political and physical features. Note the compass rose and scale on the map.

Special purpose maps focus on one type of information such as climate or population. Historical maps might show trade routes or settlements. For examples of special purpose maps, see pages 908–911.

Today, Earth Resources Technology Satellites (ERTS) allow us to make maps from photographs of energy waves. Scientists and geographers use these *Landsat* maps, as they're called, to study the earth's features and resources in greater detail than ever before.

Map Symbols

A *map key* tells you what the symbols on a map mean. For example, a road map might use red lines for two-lane roads and blue lines for highways. Political maps often use a dot to represent cities, and sometimes a circled dot for the capital city.

See the Climate Zones map on page 908. At the bottom right is a map key that explains which color stands for which climate.

Many maps identify the *cardinal directions—* north, south, east, and west—with an arrow pointing north, or in a compass rose that shows all four directions.

Scale tells us the ratio between what is on the map and what is in the real world. A large-scale map of the Egyptian city of Cairo might use one inch on the map to represent 1,000 feet in the real world. A small-scale map of Africa might use one inch to represent 500 miles.

Locating Ourselves
Latitude and Longitude

Mapmakers use a grid of imaginary lines to divide the world into sections. This grid lets us locate places on a map or globe.

Running around the middle of the globe is an imaginary line called the *equator*. The equator is halfway between the North Pole and the South Pole.

On a globe you'll see lines running around the globe parallel to the equator. We call these

883

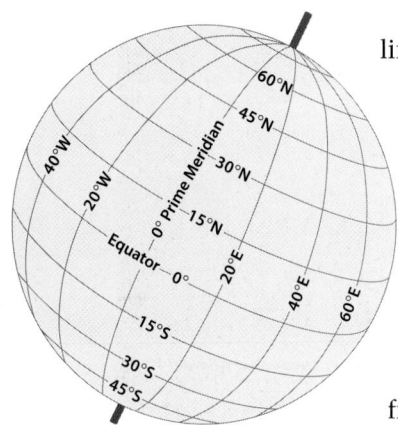

Lines of latitude and longitude

lines of *latitude*, or *parallels*. Latitude lets us identify a location north or south of the equator, measured in units called *degrees*. The latitude of the equator is 0° (zero degrees). Lines of latitude are numbered from 0° (the equator) to 90° north (the North Pole), and 0° (the equator) to 90° south (the South Pole).

On a globe, the lines that run north and south, from pole to pole, are called lines of *longitude*, or *meridians*. You'll notice that meridians are not parallel since they come together at the poles. Meridians are also measured in degrees. An imaginary line called the *prime meridian* is 0°. The prime meridian runs through Greenwich, England, at the original site of the Royal Greenwich Observatory. There are 180 degrees east of the prime meridian, and 180 degrees west.

Hemispheres

The equator and the prime meridian let us divide the earth into halves, called *hemispheres*. North of the equator is the *Northern Hemisphere*, while south of the equator is the *Southern Hemisphere*. To the west of the prime meridian is the *Western Hemisphere*, while to the east of the prime meridian is the *Eastern Hemisphere*.

Every place on earth is in two hemispheres at once. For example, the city of Chicago, Illinois, is in the Northern and Western Hemispheres. The city of Sydney in Australia is in the Southern and Eastern Hemispheres.

Absolute and Relative Location

The grid system allows us to identify any place on earth by its specific position, or what geographers call its absolute location. Often, however, we use relative location—that is, the location of a place compared to another place. For example, if you're driving, knowing that Baltimore is about 35 miles (56 kilometers) northeast of Washington, D.C., can be more useful than knowing that it is at 39° N and 77° W.

Places, Regions, and Landforms

Geographers use concepts of *place* and *region*. One way to describe *place* is to look at natural physical features, including land, water, and climate.

Geographers group places that have similar characteristics into *regions*. Regions may be defined by various characteristics—for example, by a physical characteristic such as climate, or by a cultural characteristic such as language. In the United States, the Pacific Northwest is a mountainous, rainy region. Latin America—which includes Mexico, Central America, South America, and islands in the West Indies—is a vast region where

Degrees, Minutes, Seconds

Lines of latitude and longitude are spaced in units called *degrees*. The distance between one parallel and the next (one degree of latitude) is approximately 69 miles, or 111 kilometers. The distance between one meridian and the next (one degree of longitude) varies from about 69 miles at the equator to zero at the poles.

To help pinpoint locations more precisely, each degree is divided into smaller units called minutes and seconds. These minutes and seconds are measures of distance, not time. There are 60 minutes in a degree, and 60 seconds in a minute.

You can identify a location by its coordinates—that is, by the intersection of the parallel (latitude) and the meridian (longitude). For example, the coordinates of the Emperor's Palace in Tokyo, Japan, are 35°40'45" N, 139°46'14" E. You say that as "35 degrees, 40 minutes, 45 seconds north; 139 degrees, 46 minutes, 14 seconds east."

most people speak Spanish or Portuguese, languages that developed from Latin.

Continents

About 30 percent of the earth's surface is land. The largest landmasses are continents. Most geographers identify seven continents—Asia, Africa, North America, South America, Antarctica, Europe, and Australia. Europe and Asia are part of the same landmass, called Eurasia, but are usually considered separate continents. On the map on pages 890–891, locate each of the seven continents.

Major Landforms

Landforms are natural land features. Major landforms include mountains, plateaus, and plains. We identify landforms by their relief, or shape, and their *elevation*, or height above sea level.

Mountains, sometimes called highlands, stand well above the surrounding landscape and have distinct relief, including steep slopes and peaks. They range from 2,000 feet (roughly 600 meters) above sea level, like parts of the Appalachians in eastern North America, to a high of about 29,000 feet (8,850 meters). The Himalayas in Asia are the highest mountains in the world.

Top: Canyonlands National Park in Utah
Bottom: One of the Maldive Islands in the Indian Ocean

Plateaus are areas of moderate or high elevation with little relief. They are sometimes called tablelands. The surface of a plateau may be flat or have small, rolling hills.

Plains are large areas of flat or almost flat land, usually at low elevations. Coastal plains lie near the shore at sea level.

Canyons and valleys are much lower than the land around them. *Islands* are landmasses surrounded by water. A *peninsula* is a landmass almost surrounded by water.

While those are some of the common landforms, there are others as well.

Bodies of Water

Most of the earth is covered by water. Water continually cycles from ocean to air to ground and back to ocean. Geographers identify bodies of water by their size, shape, and content.

Mountain peaks in the Himalayas, the highest mountain range in the world

885

Oceans and Seas

The body of salt water that surrounds the continents and makes up more than 95 percent of the world's water is divided into four *oceans*—Arctic, Atlantic, Indian, and Pacific. (Some geographers identify the waters surrounding Antarctica as the Southern Ocean.) The peak of the highest mountain, Mount Everest, if placed in the Pacific Ocean at its deepest spot, would lie a mile beneath the ocean's surface.

Seas are smaller bodies of salt water, almost surrounded by land. Where portions of seas or oceans extend into coastlines, we find *gulfs* or *bays*.

Lakes and Rivers

Lakes are bodies of water completely surrounded by land. Most lakes hold fresh water. Many lakes were formed by glaciers that carved deep valleys in the earth where rain and melting ice collected. The largest freshwater lake in the world is Lake Superior, one of the Great Lakes of North America.

The Atlantic Ocean extends into the Gulf of Mexico. The Gulf is bounded by the coastline of the United States to the north and Mexico to the west.

Rivers are waterways that flow through land and into larger bodies of water. Rivers usually begin as *streams* at high elevation. Streams join one another to form a river. These rivers often combine to form larger rivers. A *tributary* is a stream or river that feeds into a larger stream, river, or lake. For example, the Ohio River is a tributary of the Mississippi River.

The longest river in the world is the Nile in Africa, which begins as several smaller rivers in the East African Highlands and flows more than 4,100 miles (6,650 kilometers) north to the Mediterranean Sea.

Climate and Biomes

Weather refers to atmospheric conditions in a particular time and place—"We're having stormy weather today." *Climate* refers to the general weather patterns that occur in an area over a long time—"We live in a dry climate." Climate is determined by many factors, including distance from the equator (latitude), elevation, and proximity to water or mountains. (See page 908 for a detailed climate map.) Climate plays a large role in defining the world's different *biomes*. A biome

A River Delta

A *delta* is a triangular piece of land at the mouth of a river. It's usually laden with rich deposits of alluvial soil (that is, soil deposited by flowing water). The term *delta* comes from the fourth letter of the Greek alphabet, which looks like this: Δ.

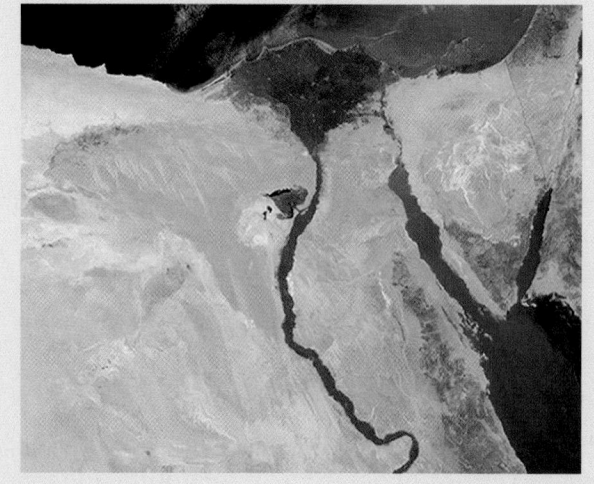

The Nile River delta in Egypt

is a large area characterized by a similar climate and similar plants and animals. (See p. 909 for a detailed map of terrestrial biomes.)

Tropical Climates and Biomes

The tropical climate zones are mainly located near the equator. Here you will find the tropical rain forest and tropical savanna biomes. Because year-round the sun's rays shine more directly on the tropics than on other regions, temperatures there are always warm.

A tropical rain forest gets rain almost daily, totaling more than 80 inches (2,000 millimeters) per year. The result is dense vegetation and a remarkable variety of plant and animal life. Tropical rain forests are home to hundreds of thousands of species of plants and animals, more than anywhere else on earth.

Tropical savannas are located farther from the equator than rain forests, but still within latitudes that are warm year-round. They experience dry and wet seasons. Savannas are grasslands with few trees.

Rain forest in northeastern Australia

Dry Climates and Biomes

Dry climates are those with little or no precipitation. They can be hot year-round, or have bitterly cold winters. Because the air in these regions is so dry, temperatures tend to fall dramatically at night. Biomes defined by dry climate include the desert and steppes. The desert biome typically receives less than 10 inches (250 millimeters) of rain per year. Steppes get 10 to 20 inches (250 to 500 millimeters) of rain annually.

Midlatitude Climates and Biomes

Farther from the equator are several climate zones grouped as midlatitude climates. While they vary in their temperatures and precipitation, they are all moderate climates that have distinct seasons. See the map on page 908 to locate some of these midlatitude climates, including Mediterranean, humid subtropical, humid continental, and marine west coast. Cooler biomes in midlatitude climates include temperate forests and boreal forests.

Dunes in the Sahara, the world's largest desert

Elephants on an African savanna with Mount Kilimanjaro in the background

High-latitude Climates and Biomes

In the polar regions, which are farthest from the equator, climates are so cold that little vegetation can survive. High-latitude biomes include the tundra, which supports short grasses and dwarf trees during brief summers, and ice cover and permanent frost at other times of the year. High-latitude conditions can also occur at very high elevations, regardless of latitude. For example, mountain peaks at high elevations are snowcapped even near the equator.

Physical Systems

Our Changing Earth

The earth's surface is constantly changing. Forces within the earth and on the surface cause much of this change. But human activity also changes earth's physical systems.

Internal Forces

The part of the earth on which we walk and on which the oceans rest is called the crust. The crust varies in thickness, but generally extends about 25 miles (40 kilometers) beneath land surface. Below the crust are the mantle, an outer core, and an inner core.

The crust is made up of plates, huge masses of rock that float on the semiliquid material in the mantle. These plates can shift position and bump or rub against each other, causing earthquakes.

Earthquakes beneath the ocean cause great sea waves called *tsunamis*. Plates pushing against each other can also build mountains. When plates pull apart, they can form gorges and valleys.

Deep in the earth flows melted rock called magma. When a volcano erupts, magma comes to the surface, where it is called lava. Volcanoes can dramatically change the earth's surface.

External Forces

Some changes to the earth's surface come from external forces such as wind and water. Weathering occurs when water breaks down the chemicals in rocks and the rocks disintegrate. When water freezes and melts, it can split rocks apart.

Flowing water, wind, and the movement of glaciers are some of the causes of erosion, the wearing away of the earth's surface.

A river of lava flows from an erupting volcano in Hawaii. Lava is melted rock. Beneath the earth's surface, it is called magma.

Ecosystems and Human Systems

Ecosystems

An ecosystem is a group of living things and the environment in which they live. Ecosystems can be as small as a tiny pond and the living things it supports, or as large as the tundra.

Small changes in factors such as climate or air quality can alter or even destroy an ecosystem. Humans can change ecosystems when they alter some element of the environment around them. Some human activity, such as digging mines or clearing forests, can have dramatic effects on the environment.

Human Systems

Historians and geographers ask questions about individuals and about groups of people. They study human settlements around the world and across time, and observe the distribution of population. See page 911 for a map of population density. They pay attention to patterns of migration—why people move from one place to another, and the results of those moves. They want to know about culture—the traditions and customs of a group of people, their ways of life and thought, and how those ways differ from the ways of other groups. Historians and geographers also look for patterns in the way groups of people trade and interact with each other, sometimes peacefully, sometimes not.

Environment and Society

Resources

Geographers examine the resources available in different areas. Renewable resources can be replenished by the earth's own processes or, in some cases, by human activity as they are used. These resources include water, forests, and solar power. Nonrenewable resources cannot be replenished once they are used. Minerals and fossil fuels like coal and oil are examples of nonrenewable resources. Because nonrenewable resources are limited, their use and distribution affect human interaction.

The specific resources that people use and value vary by place and change over time. For example, petroleum was not valued before the combustion engine was invented.

Human-Environmental Interaction

Humans adapt to their environments and change them. When we put on a winter coat, or jump into the surf to cool off, we are adapting to our environment. We change the environment every time we build a house or fertilize a lawn.

One dramatic historical example of humans adapting to and changing the environment occurred in the early 1500s, soon after Christopher Columbus came in contact with the Americas. The exchange of hundreds of species of plants and animals among continents in the years following his voyages resulted in profound changes in populations, ways of life, and ecosystems.

The geography of an area, in turn, has a huge impact on human activity in that area. People build differently in earthquake or hurricane zones than in the Amazon. Historians look at geography to explain, for example, why people in one part of the world developed farming communities while people elsewhere remained nomads. Geography affects economic, social, and political activity.

Wind turbines convert wind energy into electricity, making wind a clean and renewable source of energy.

World Physical

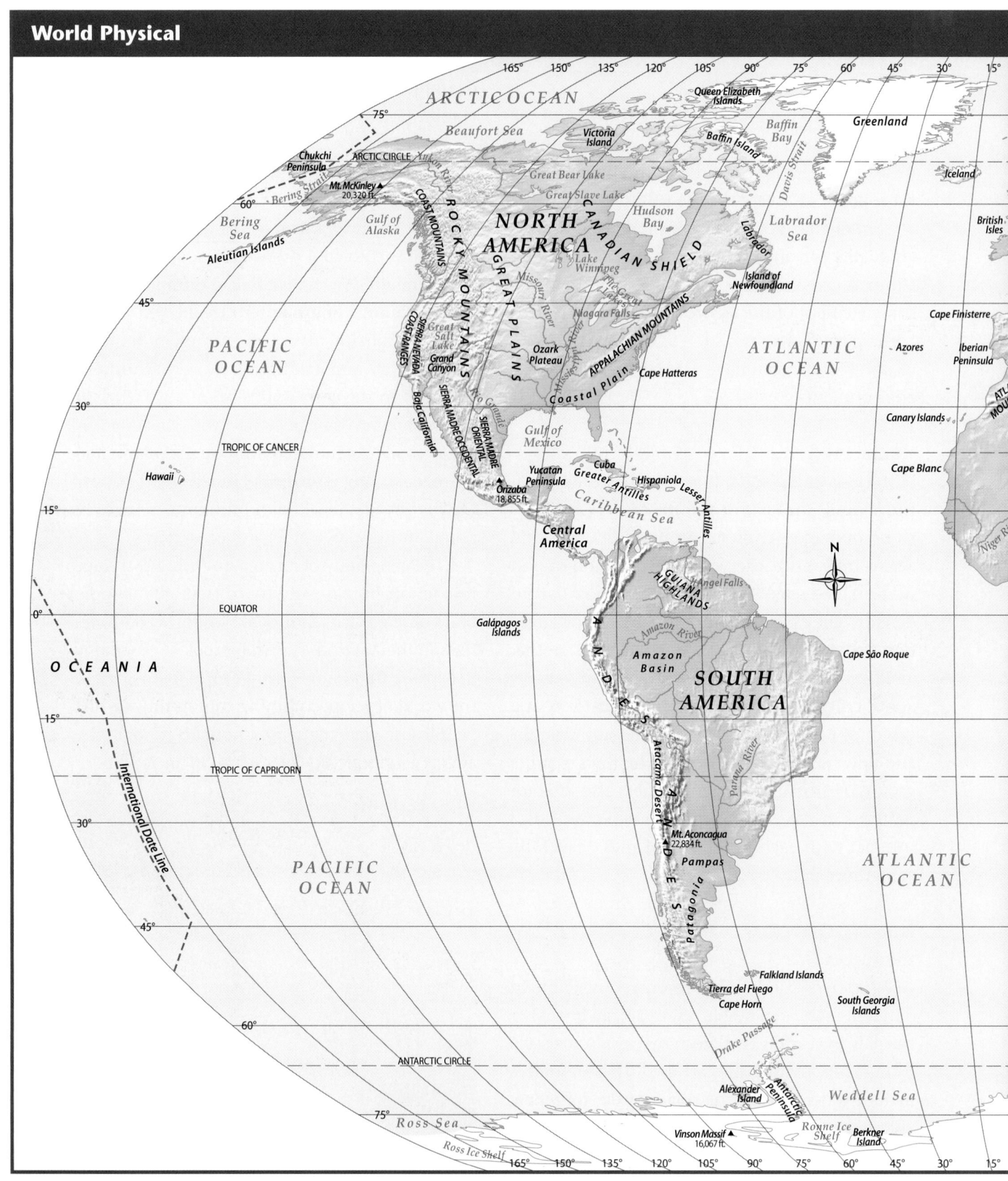

ARCTIC OCEAN

Queen Elizabeth Islands

Greenland

Beaufort Sea

Victoria Island

Baffin Island

Baffin Bay

Davis Strait

Iceland

Chukchi Peninsula

ARCTIC CIRCLE

Yukon River

Great Bear Lake

Great Slave Lake

Labrador Sea

British Isles

Bering Strait

Mt. McKinley 20,320 ft.

ROCKY MOUNTAINS

CANADIAN SHIELD

Hudson Bay

Labrador

Bering Sea

Gulf of Alaska

COAST MOUNTAINS

NORTH AMERICA

Lake Winnipeg

Island of Newfoundland

Aleutian Islands

GREAT PLAINS

Missouri River

Great Lakes

Cape Finisterre

PACIFIC OCEAN

SIERRA NEVADA COAST RANGES

Great Salt Lake

Niagara Falls

APPALACHIAN MOUNTAINS

ATLANTIC OCEAN

Azores

Iberian Peninsula

ATLA MOUN

Grand Canyon

Ozark Plateau

Cape Hatteras

TROPIC OF CANCER

SIERRA MADRE OCCIDENTAL

Baja California

Rio Grande

SIERRA MADRE ORIENTAL

Coastal Plain

Gulf of Mexico

Canary Islands

Cape Blanc

Hawaii

Cuba

Yucatan Peninsula

Greater Antilles

Hispaniola

Lesser Antilles

Orizaba 18,855 ft.

Caribbean Sea

Niger Ri

Central America

15°

Angel Falls

N

EQUATOR

Galápagos Islands

GUIANA HIGHLANDS

A N D E S

Amazon River

Cape São Roque

OCEANIA

Amazon Basin

SOUTH AMERICA

15°

TROPIC OF CAPRICORN

Atacama Desert

Paraná River

International Date Line

30°

Mt. Aconcagua 22,834 ft.

Pampas

ATLANTIC OCEAN

PACIFIC OCEAN

A N D E S

Patagonia

45°

Falkland Islands

Tierra del Fuego

Cape Horn

South Georgia Islands

60°

Drake Passage

ANTARCTIC CIRCLE

Alexander Island

Antarctic Peninsula

Weddell Sea

75°

Ross Sea

Vinson Massif 16,067 ft.

Ronne Ice Shelf

Berkner Island

Ross Ice Shelf

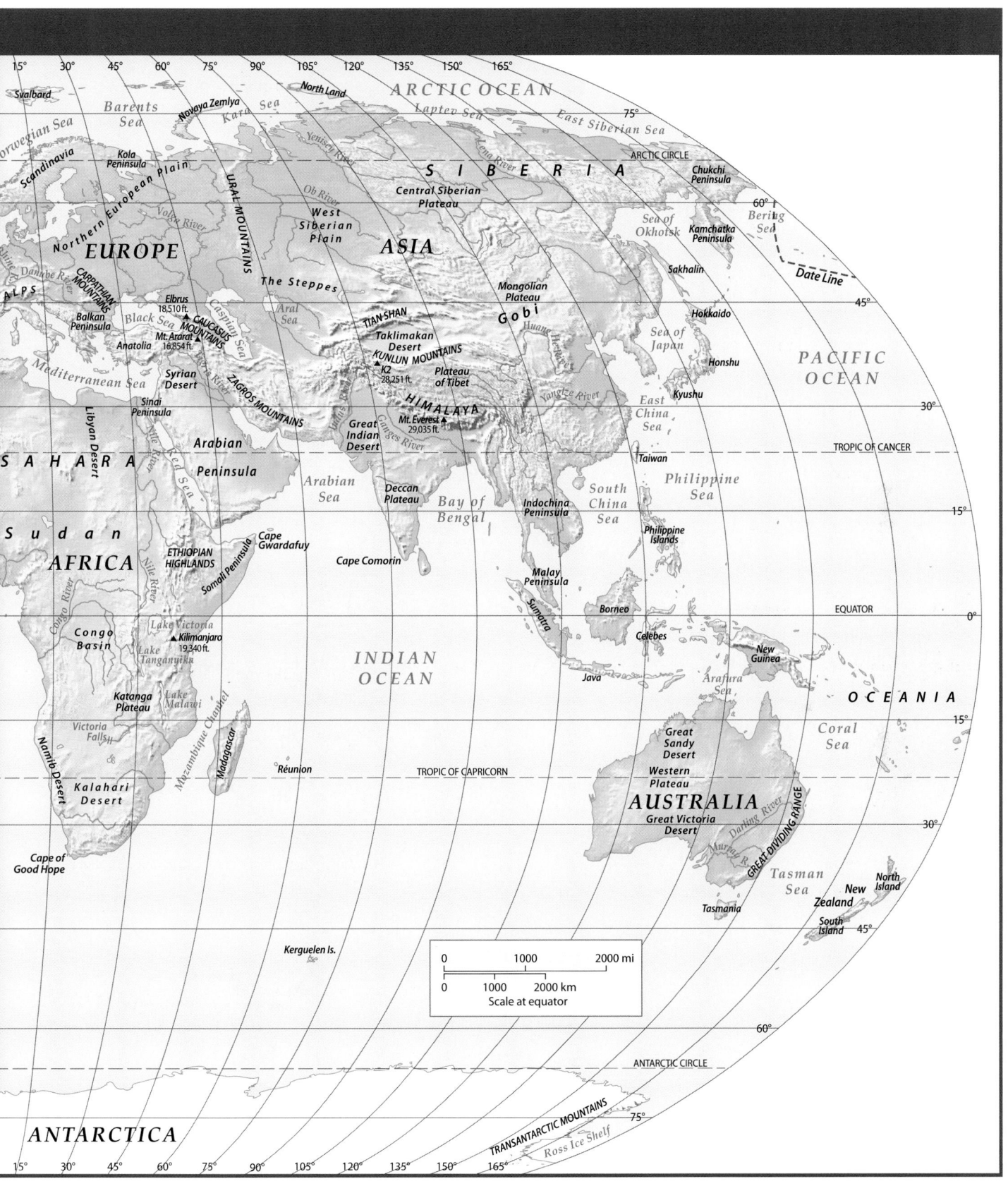

15° 30° 45° 60° 75° 90° 105° 120° 135° 150° 165°

ARCTIC OCEAN

Svalbard
Barents Sea
North Land
Norwegian Sea
Novaya Zemlya
Kara Sea
Laptev Sea
East Siberian Sea
75°
ARCTIC CIRCLE
Scandinavia
Kola Peninsula
Northern European Plain
URAL MOUNTAINS
Ob River
Yenisey River
S I B E R I A
Central Siberian Plateau
Lena River
Chukchi Peninsula
60°
Bering Sea

EUROPE
Volga River
The Steppes
ASIA
Mongolian Plateau
Sea of Okhotsk
Kamchatka Peninsula
Date Line
Sakhalin
45°

Rhine
Danube River
CARPATHIAN MOUNTAINS
ALPS
Elbrus 18,510 ft.
Aral Sea
TIAN SHAN
Gobi
Hokkaido
Sea of Japan
Balkan Peninsula
Black Sea
CAUCASUS MOUNTAINS
Caspian Sea
Taklimakan Desert
KUNLUN MOUNTAINS
Huang He
Honshu
Anatolia
Mt. Ararat 16,854 ft.
K2 28,251 ft.
Plateau of Tibet
PACIFIC OCEAN

Mediterranean Sea
Syrian Desert
ZAGROS MOUNTAINS
HIMALAYA
Mt. Everest 29,035 ft.
Yangtze River
Kyushu
East China Sea
30°

Libyan Desert
Sinai Peninsula
Red Sea
Arabian Peninsula
Great Indian Desert
Ganges River
Taiwan
TROPIC OF CANCER

S A H A R A
Nile River
Arabian Sea
Deccan Plateau
Bay of Bengal
Indochina Peninsula
South China Sea
Philippine Sea
15°

S u d a n
Cape Gwardafuy
ETHIOPIAN HIGHLANDS
Cape Comorin
Philippine Islands

AFRICA
Somali Peninsula
Malay Peninsula
EQUATOR
0°

Congo Basin
Lake Victoria
Kilimanjaro 19,340 ft.
Sumatra
Borneo
Celebes
New Guinea

Lake Tanganyika
Lake Malawi
INDIAN OCEAN
Java
Arafura Sea
O C E A N I A

Katanga Plateau
Mozambique Channel
Coral Sea
15°

Victoria Falls
Madagascar
Great Sandy Desert
Western Plateau

Namib Desert
Kalahari Desert
Réunion
TROPIC OF CAPRICORN
AUSTRALIA
Great Victoria Desert
Darling River
GREAT DIVIDING RANGE
30°

Cape of Good Hope
Murray River
Tasman Sea
New Zealand
North Island

Tasmania
South Island
45°

Kerguelen Is.

0   1000   2000 mi
0   1000   2000 km
Scale at equator

60°

ANTARCTIC CIRCLE

ANTARCTICA
TRANSANTARCTIC MOUNTAINS
Ross Ice Shelf
75°

15° 30° 45° 60° 75° 90° 105° 120° 135° 150° 165°

World Political

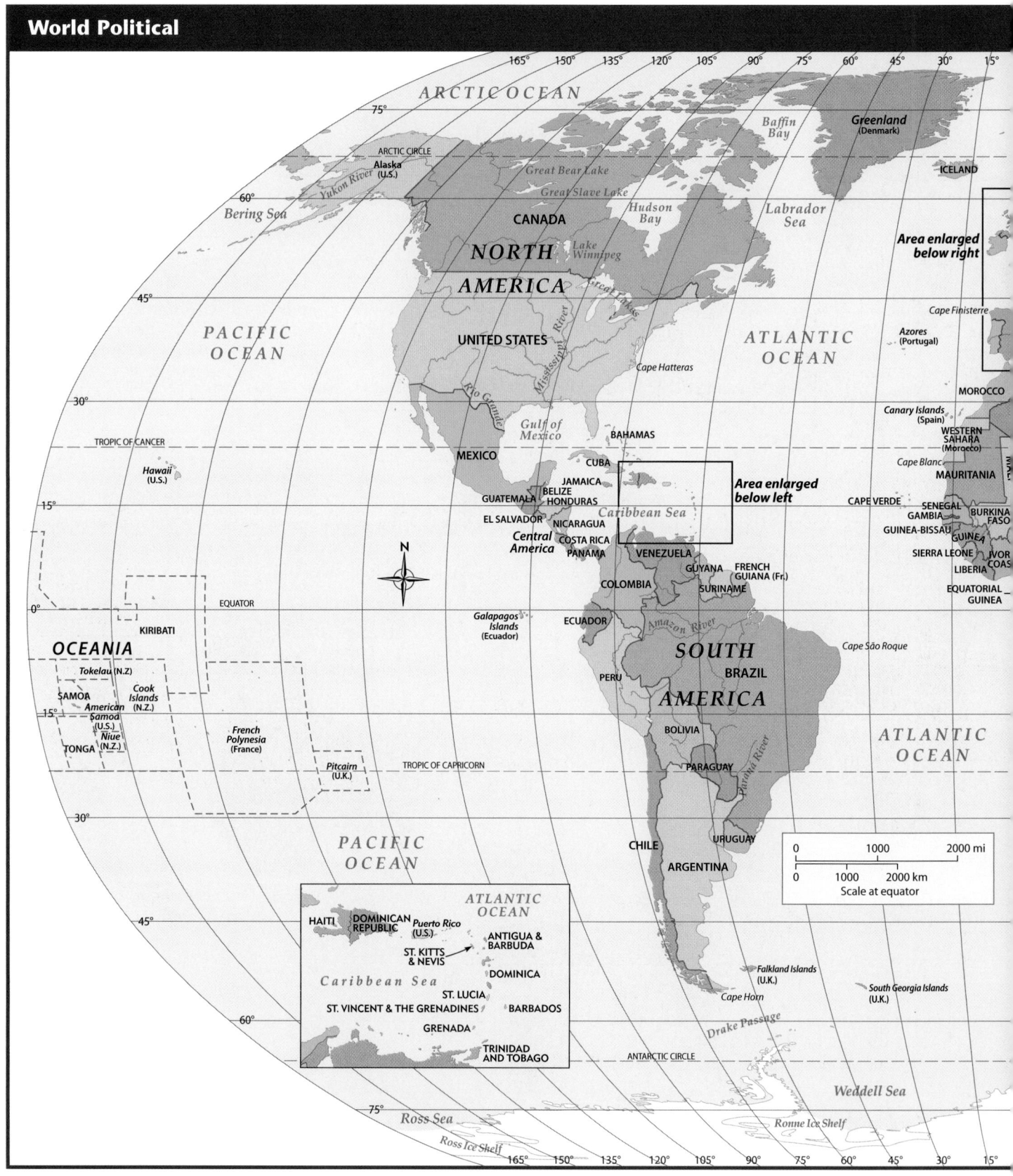

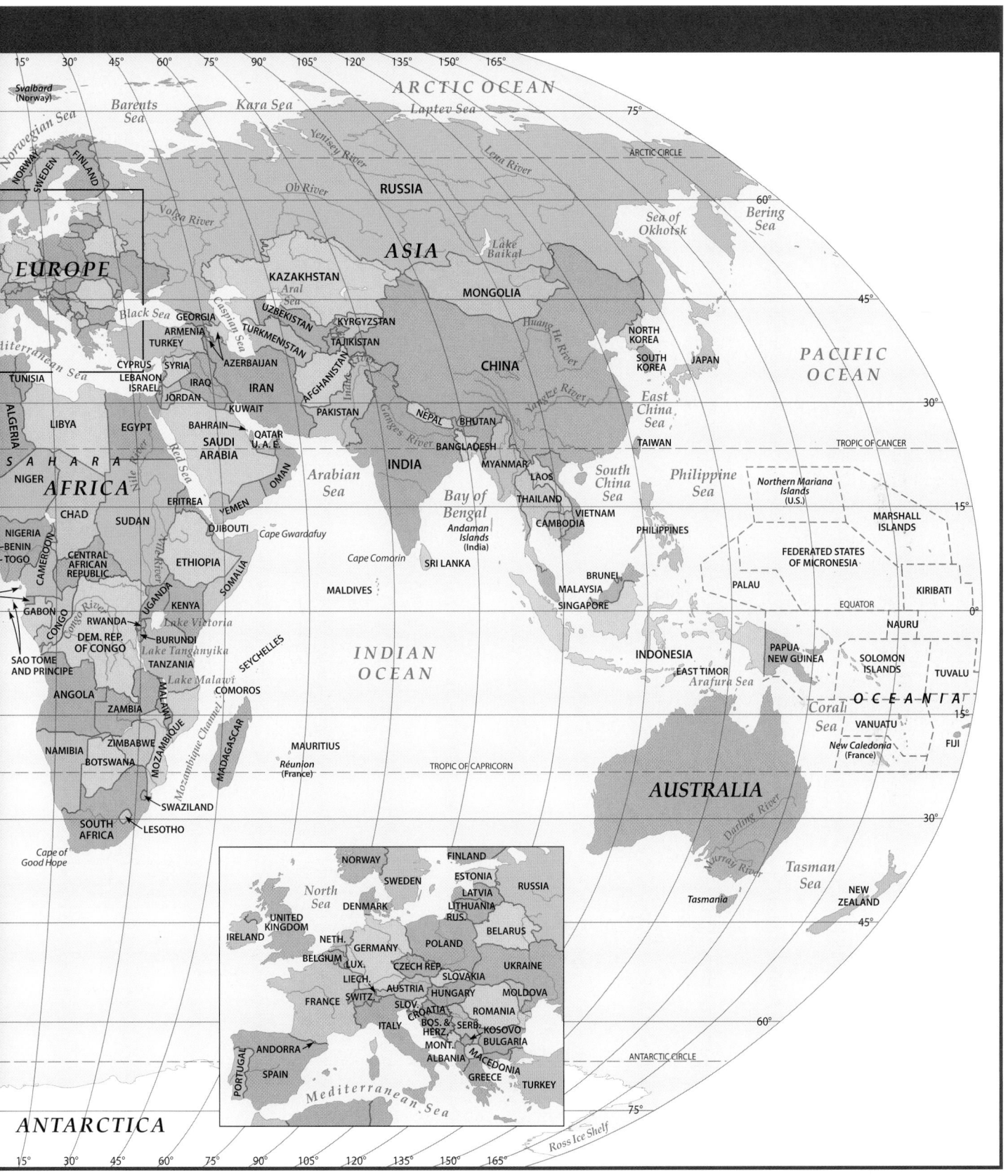

Pacific Rim

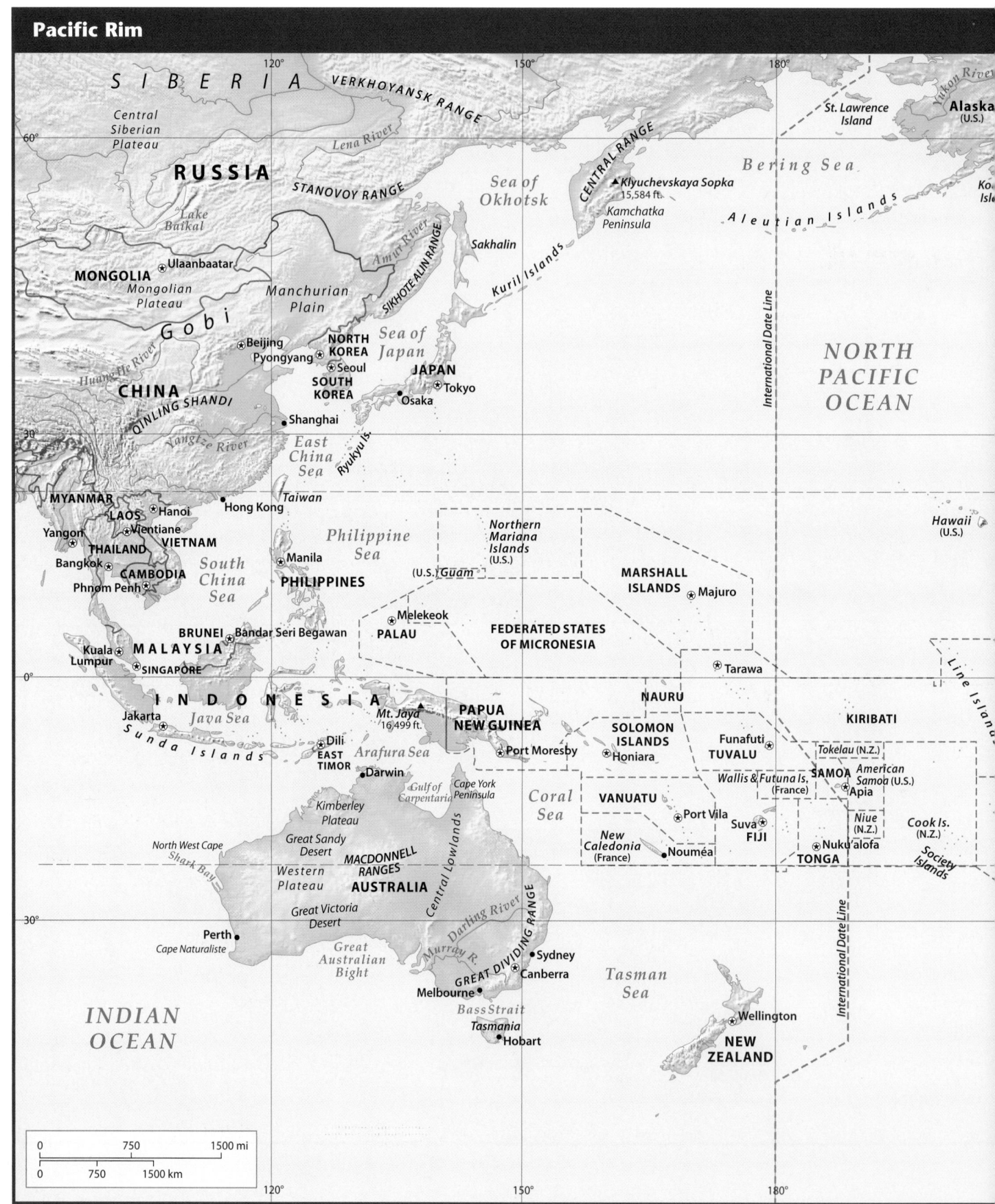

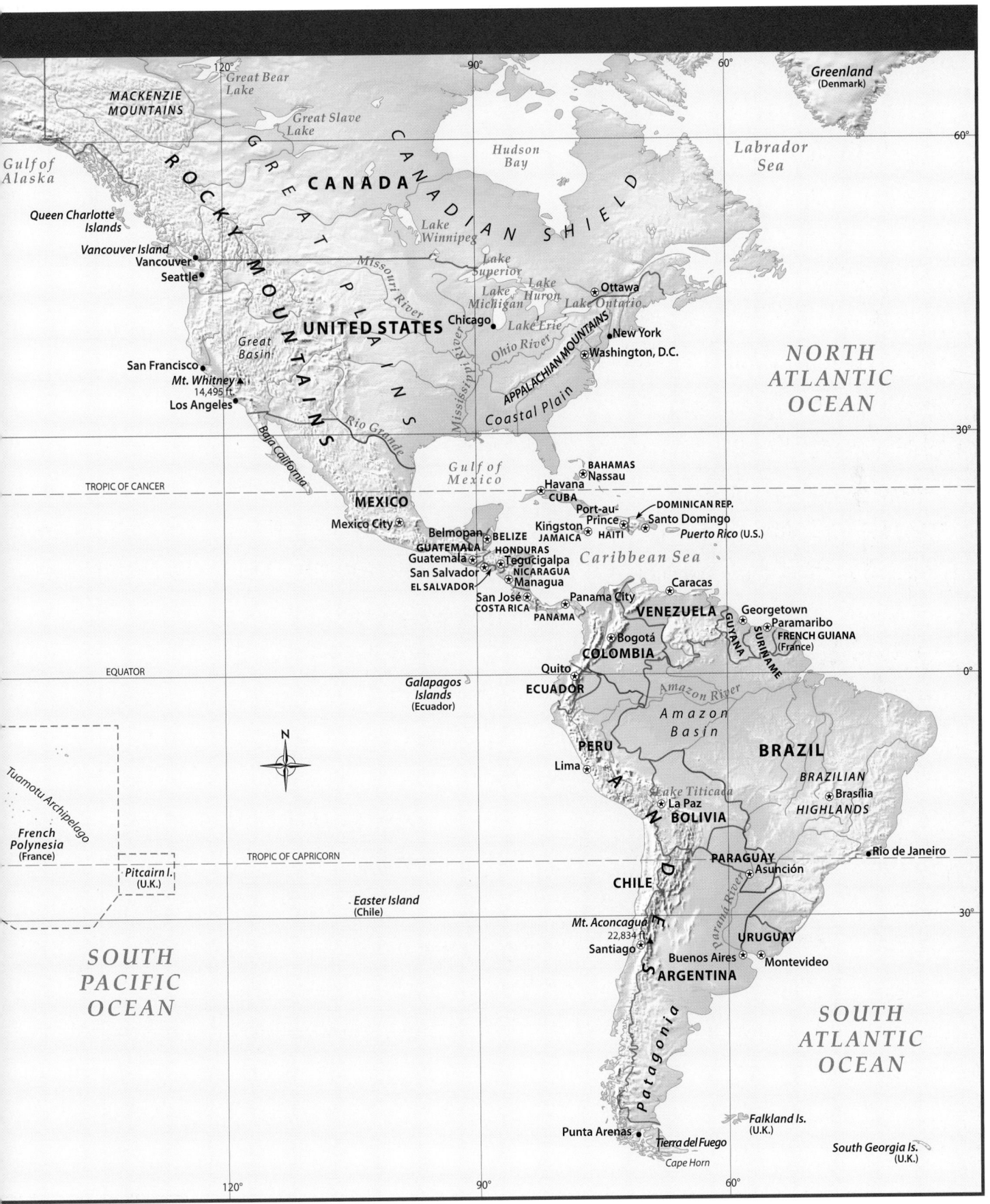

North America

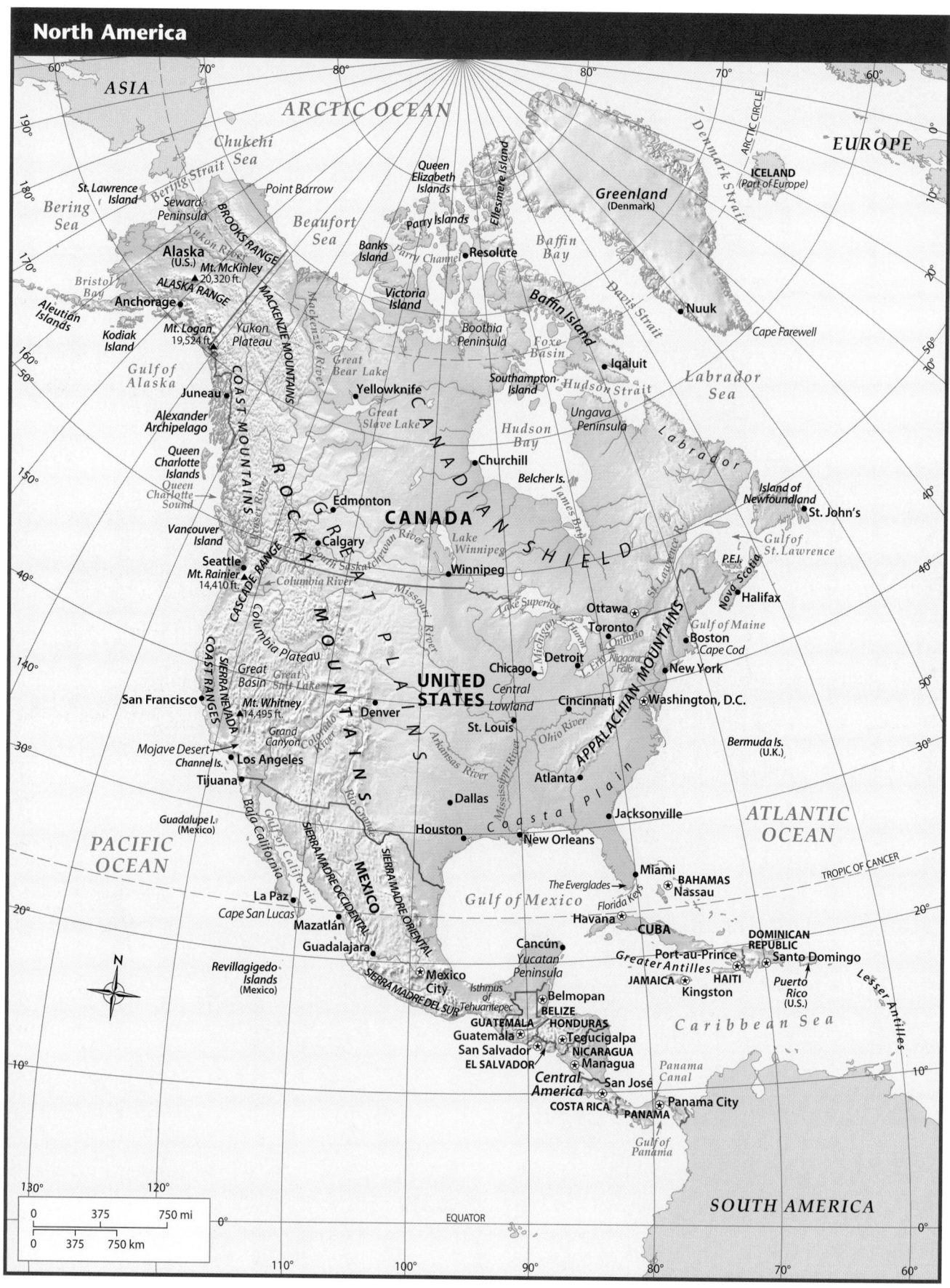

ASIA

ARCTIC OCEAN

EUROPE

Chukchi Sea

Point Barrow

Queen Elizabeth Islands

Ellesmere Island

ICELAND (Part of Europe)

ARCTIC CIRCLE

Bering Strait

Beaufort Sea

Parry Islands

Denmark Strait

St. Lawrence Island

Seward Peninsula

BROOKS RANGE

Banks Island

Resolute

Baffin Bay

Greenland (Denmark)

Bering Sea

Alaska (U.S.)

Mt. McKinley 20,320 ft.

Yukon River

Mackenzie River

Victoria Island

Boothia Peninsula

Baffin Island

Davis Strait

Nuuk

Bristol Bay

ALASKA RANGE

Anchorage

MACKENZIE MOUNTAINS

Foxe Basin

Cape Farewell

Aleutian Islands

Kodiak Island

Mt. Logan 19,524 ft.

Yukon Plateau

Great Bear Lake

Iqaluit

Labrador Sea

Gulf of Alaska

Juneau

COAST MOUNTAINS

Yellowknife

Southampton Island

Hudson Strait

Great Slave Lake

C A N A D I A N

Ungava Peninsula

Labrador

Alexander Archipelago

Churchill

Hudson Bay

ROCKY

Queen Charlotte Islands

Belcher Is.

James Bay

Island of Newfoundland

Queen Charlotte Sound

Edmonton

CANADA

S H I E L D

St. John's

Vancouver Island

Calgary

GREAT

Fraser River

Lake Winnipeg

St. Lawrence R.

Gulf of St. Lawrence

Seattle

North Saskatchewan River

Winnipeg

P.E.I.

Mt. Rainier 14,410 ft.

CASCADE RANGE

Columbia River

Missouri River

Lake Superior

Ottawa

Nova Scotia

Halifax

Columbia Plateau

MOUNTAINS

Toronto

Lake Huron

Gulf of Maine

Cape Cod

SIERRA NEVADA

Great Basin

Great Salt Lake

PLAINS

Chicago

Lake Michigan

Detroit

Lake Ontario

Lake Erie

Niagara Falls

Boston

New York

San Francisco

COAST RANGES

Mt. Whitney 14,495 ft.

Denver

UNITED STATES

Central Lowland

Cincinnati

APPALACHIAN MOUNTAINS

Washington, D.C.

Grand Canyon

St. Louis

Ohio River

Bermuda Is. (U.K.)

Mojave Desert

Colorado River

Arkansas River

Channel Is.

Los Angeles

Atlanta

C o a s t a l

ATLANTIC OCEAN

Tijuana

Dallas

Mississippi River

Rio Grande

Houston

New Orleans

Jacksonville

Guadalupe I. (Mexico)

SIERRA MADRE OCCIDENTAL

Baja California

Gulf of California

MEXICO

SIERRA MADRE ORIENTAL

P l a i n

Miami

The Everglades

BAHAMAS

Nassau

TROPIC OF CANCER

PACIFIC OCEAN

La Paz

Cape San Lucas

Gulf of Mexico

Florida Keys

Havana

CUBA

Mazatlán

Guadalajara

Cancún

Yucatan Peninsula

DOMINICAN REPUBLIC

Revillagigedo Islands (Mexico)

Mexico City

Port-au-Prince

Santo Domingo

Greater Antilles

JAMAICA

HAITI

Kingston

Puerto Rico (U.S.)

Lesser Antilles

Isthmus of Tehuantepec

Belmopan

BELIZE

SIERRA MADRE DEL SUR

GUATEMALA

HONDURAS

Caribbean Sea

Guatemala

Tegucigalpa

San Salvador

NICARAGUA

EL SALVADOR

Managua

Central America

San José

Panama Canal

COSTA RICA

Panama City

PANAMA

Gulf of Panama

N

SOUTH AMERICA

0	375	750 mi
0	375	750 km

EQUATOR

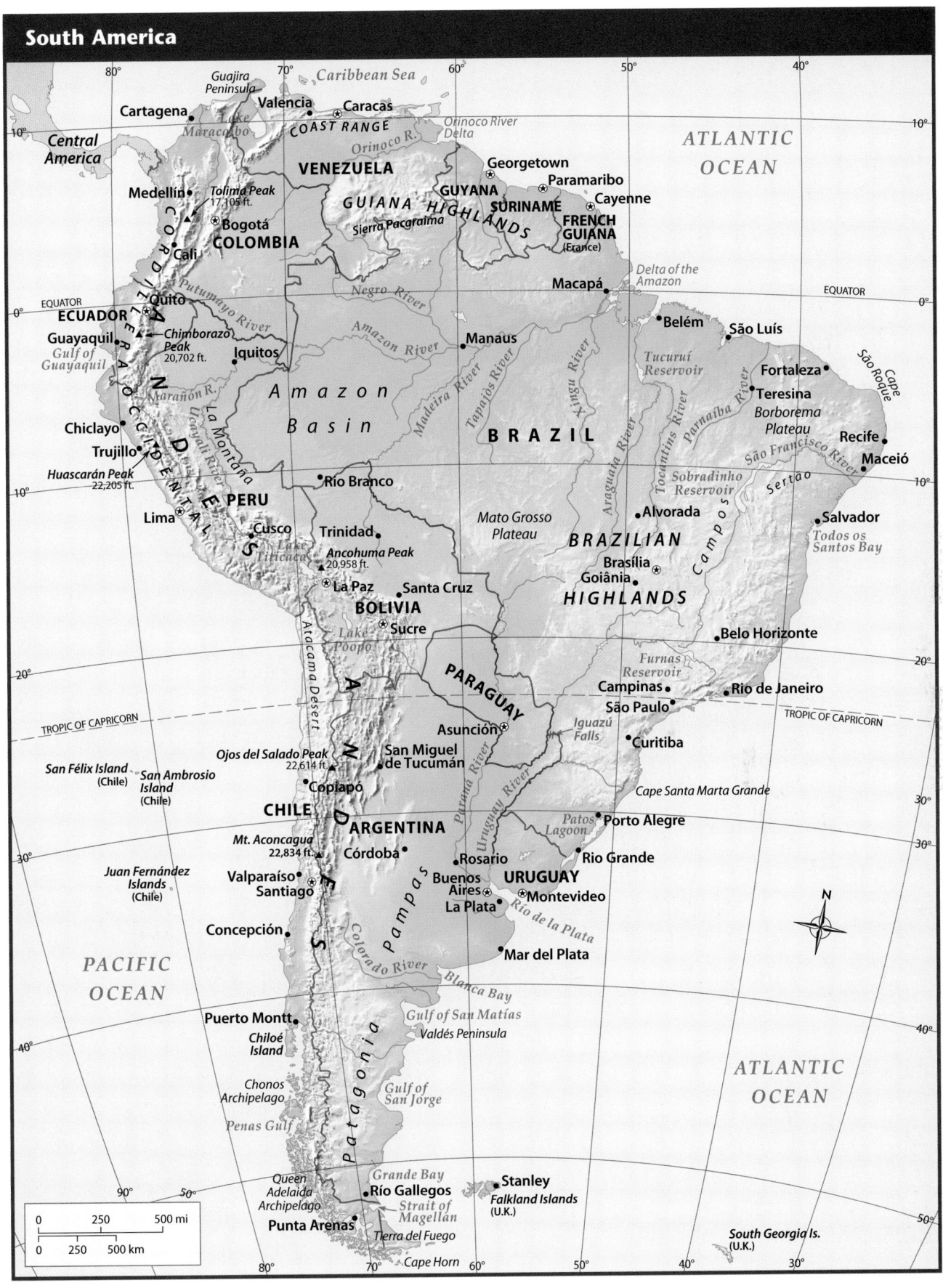

South America

Caribbean Sea

Central America

Cartagena

Guajira Peninsula

Valencia · Caracas

COAST RANGE

Lake Maracaibo

Medellín · Tolima Peak 17,105 ft.

⊛ Bogotá

COLOMBIA

Cali ·

Orinoco River Delta

Orinoco R.

VENEZUELA

GUIANA HIGHLANDS

Sierra Pacaraima

Georgetown

GUYANA

Paramaribo

SURINAME

Cayenne

FRENCH GUIANA *(France)*

ATLANTIC OCEAN

10°

EQUATOR 0°

ECUADOR ⊛ Quito

Guayaquil

Gulf of Guayaquil

Chimborazo Peak 20,702 ft.

Iquitos

Putumayo River

Negro River

Amazon R.

Manaus

Delta of the Amazon

Macapá

Belém

São Luís

Cape São Roque

Fortaleza

Teresina

EQUATOR

Chiclayo

Trujillo

Marañón R.

La Montaña

Ucayali River

Amazon Basin

BRAZIL

Madeira River

Tapajós River

Xingu River

Tucuruí Reservoir

Araguaia River

Tocantins River

Parnaíba River

Borborema Plateau

Recife

Maceió

Huascarán Peak 22,205 ft.

PERU

Lima ·

Río Branco

São Francisco River

Sertão

10°

Cusco ·

Trinidad ·

Ancohuma Peak 20,958 ft.

⊛ La Paz

Santa Cruz

Mato Grosso Plateau

Alvorada

Sobradinho Reservoir

BRAZILIAN

Brasília ⊛

Goiânia

HIGHLANDS

Campos

Salvador

Todos os Santos Bay

Lake Titicaca

Lake Poopó

BOLIVIA

⊛ Sucre

A N D E S

PARAGUAY

Belo Horizonte

Furnas Reservoir

Campinas

Rio de Janeiro

20°

TROPIC OF CAPRICORN

San Félix Island (Chile)

San Ambrosio Island (Chile)

Ojos del Salado Peak 22,614 ft.

Asunción ⊛

San Miguel de Tucumán

Paraná River

Iguazú Falls

São Paulo

Curitiba

Uruguay River

TROPIC OF CAPRICORN

Cape Santa Marta Grande

Copiapó ·

CHILE

ARGENTINA

Mt. Aconcagua 22,834 ft.

Córdoba ·

Patos Lagoon

Porto Alegre

30°

Juan Fernández Islands (Chile)

Valparaíso ·

Santiago ⊛

Rosario

Buenos Aires

La Plata

URUGUAY

Montevideo ⊛

Rio Grande

Río de la Plata

30°

Concepción ·

Pampas

Colorado River

Mar del Plata

Blanca Bay

N

PACIFIC OCEAN

Puerto Montt ·

Chiloé Island

Patagonia

Gulf of San Matías

Valdés Peninsula

40°

Chonos Archipelago

Gulf of San Jorge

ATLANTIC OCEAN

Penas Gulf

Queen Adelaida Archipelago

Grande Bay

Río Gallegos

Strait of Magellan

Stanley

Falkland Islands (U.K.)

50°

	250	500 mi
0	250	500 km

Punta Arenas ·

Tierra del Fuego

Cape Horn

South Georgia Is. (U.K.)

50°

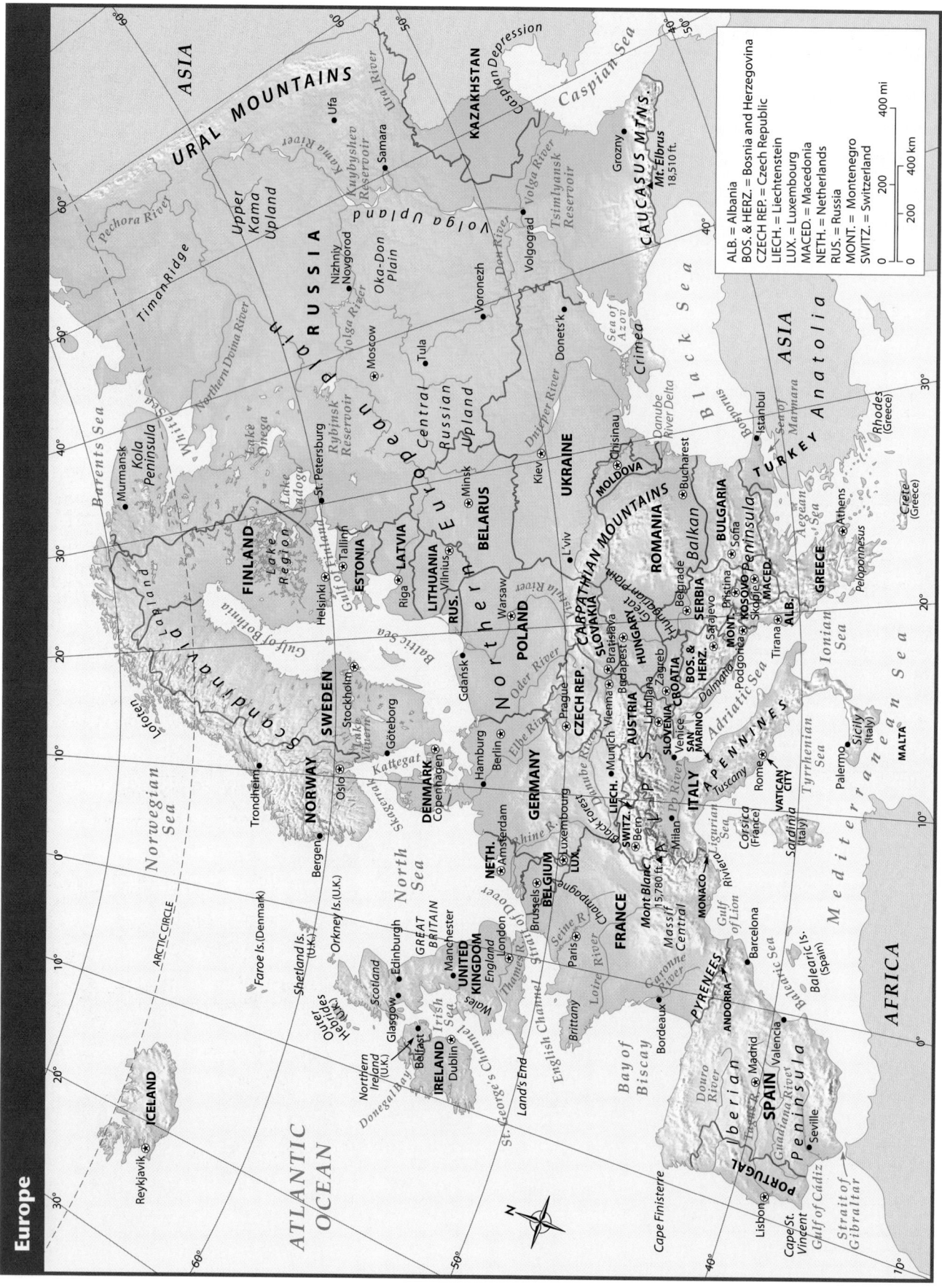

Africa

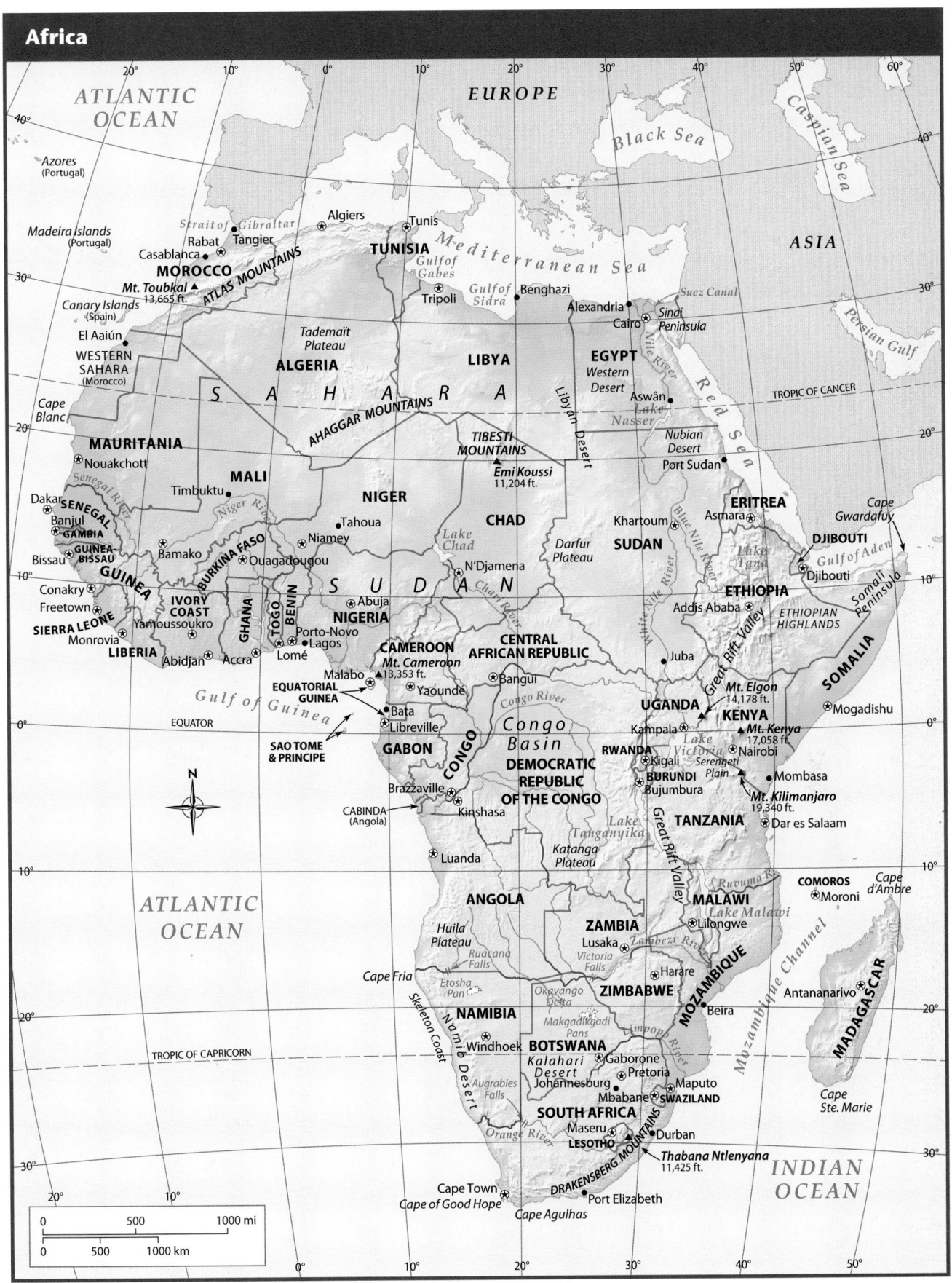

ATLANTIC OCEAN

EUROPE

Black Sea

ASIA

Caspian Sea

Azores
(Portugal)

Madeira Islands
(Portugal)

Strait of Gibraltar
Algiers
Tangier
Tunis
TUNISIA
Mediterranean Sea

Rabat
Casablanca
MOROCCO
Gulf of Gabes
Tripoli
Gulf of Sidra
Benghazi

Mt. Toubkal
13,665 ft.
ATLAS MOUNTAINS
Alexandria
Cairo
Suez Canal
Sinai Peninsula
Persian Gulf

Canary Islands
(Spain)
El Aaiún
WESTERN SAHARA
(Morocco)
Tademaït Plateau
ALGERIA
LIBYA
EGYPT
Western Desert
Aswân
Lake Nasser
Red Sea
TROPIC OF CANCER

Cape Blanc
MAURITANIA
Nouakchott
S   A   H   A   R   A
AHAGGAR MOUNTAINS
TIBESTI MOUNTAINS
Libyan Desert
Nubian Desert
Port Sudan

Senegal River
Timbuktu
MALI
Niger River
NIGER
CHAD
Emi Koussi
11,204 ft.
Darfur Plateau
Khartoum
Asmara
ERITREA
Cape Gwardafuy

Dakar
SENEGAL
Banjul
GAMBIA
GUINEA-BISSAU
Bissau
Bamako
BURKINA FASO
Tahoua
Niamey
Ouagadougou
Lake Chad
N'Djamena
Chari River
SUDAN
Blue Nile River
Lake Tana
DJIBOUTI
Djibouti
Gulf of Aden
Somali Peninsula

GUINEA
Conakry
Freetown
SIERRA LEONE
Monrovia
LIBERIA
IVORY COAST
Yamoussoukro
GHANA
TOGO
BENIN
S U D A N
Abuja
NIGERIA
Porto-Novo
Lagos
Lomé
Accra
Abidjan
CAMEROON
CENTRAL AFRICAN REPUBLIC
Bangui
Addis Ababa
ETHIOPIA
ETHIOPIAN HIGHLANDS
SOMALIA
Mogadishu

EQUATORIAL GUINEA
Malabo
Mt. Cameroon
13,353 ft.
Yaoundé
Congo River
Juba
White Nile River
Great Rift Valley
Mt. Elgon
14,178 ft.
UGANDA
KENYA
Mt. Kenya
17,058 ft.

SAO TOME & PRINCIPE
EQUATOR
Bata
Libreville
Gulf of Guinea
GABON
CONGO
Congo Basin
DEMOCRATIC REPUBLIC OF THE CONGO
Kampala
RWANDA
Kigali
BURUNDI
Bujumbura
Lake Victoria
Serengeti Plain
Nairobi
Mombasa
Mt. Kilimanjaro
19,340 ft.

Brazzaville
CABINDA
(Angola)
Kinshasa
Lake Tanganyika
Katanga Plateau
TANZANIA
Dar es Salaam

Luanda
Great Rift Valley
Ruvuma R.
COMOROS
Moroni
Cape d'Ambre

ATLANTIC OCEAN
ANGOLA
Huila Plateau
ZAMBIA
Lusaka
MALAWI
Lake Malawi
Lilongwe
Zambezi River

Cape Fria
Ruacana Falls
Etosha Pan
Victoria Falls
Harare
ZIMBABWE
MOZAMBIQUE
Beira
Antananarivo
MADAGASCAR

NAMIBIA
Skeleton Coast
Namib Desert
Windhoek
BOTSWANA
Okavango Delta
Makgadikgadi Pans
Limpopo River
Mozambique Channel

TROPIC OF CAPRICORN
Kalahari Desert
Gaborone
Johannesburg
Pretoria
Maputo
Mbabane
SWAZILAND
Cape Ste. Marie

Augrabies Falls
SOUTH AFRICA
Maseru
LESOTHO
DRAKENSBERG MOUNTAINS
Thabana Ntlenyana
11,425 ft.
Durban
INDIAN OCEAN

Orange River
Cape Town
Cape of Good Hope
Cape Agulhas
Port Elizabeth

0   500   1000 mi
0   500   1000 km

N

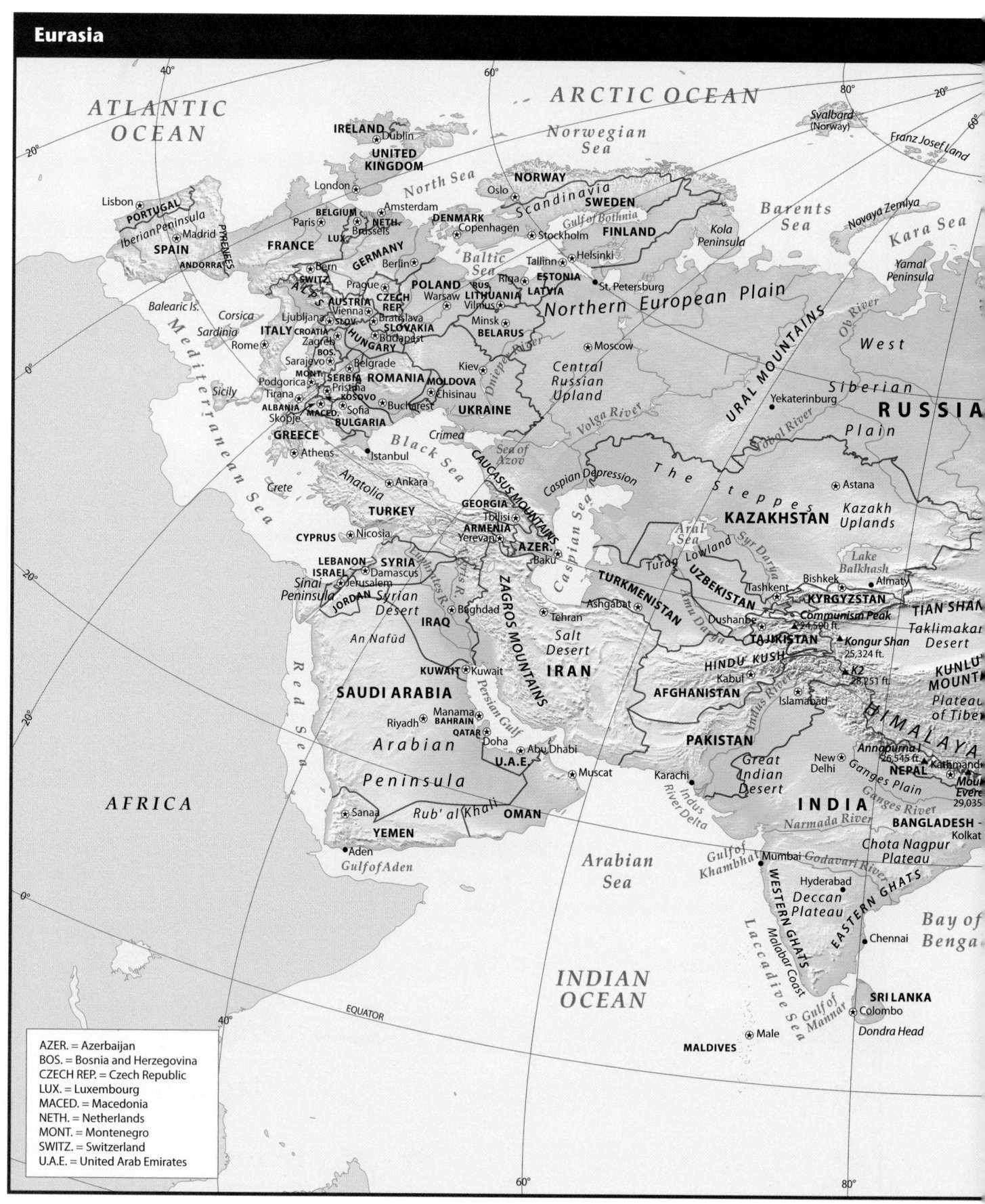

Eurasia

ATLANTIC OCEAN

ARCTIC OCEAN

Norwegian Sea

IRELAND ⊛ Dublin

UNITED KINGDOM

NORWAY

London

North Sea

Scandinavia

Oslo

SWEDEN

Gulf of Bothnia

FINLAND

Barents Sea

Kola Peninsula

Svalbard (Norway)

Franz Josef Land

Novaya Zemlya

Yamal Peninsula

Kara Sea

Lisbon ⊛

PORTUGAL

Iberian Peninsula ⊛ Madrid

SPAIN

ANDORRA

BELGIUM ⊛ Amsterdam

Paris ⊛ NETH.

LUX. ⊛ Brussels

FRANCE

DENMARK ⊛ Copenhagen

Stockholm ⊛

Helsinki ⊛

Tallinn ⊛

ESTONIA

LATVIA

Riga ⊛

St. Petersburg ⊛

Northern European Plain

Ob River

West Siberian Plain

RUSSIA

Balearic Is.

Corsica

Sardinia

ITALY

Rome ⊛

Bern

SWITZ.

GERMANY

Berlin ⊛

Prague ⊛

CZECH REP.

Vienna ⊛ AUSTRIA

Ljubljana

CROATIA

Zagreb ⊛

BOS.

Sarajevo ⊛

POLAND

Warsaw ⊛

SLOVAKIA

Bratislava ⊛

Budapest ⊛

HUNGARY

LITHUANIA

Vilnius ⊛

Minsk ⊛

BELARUS

Kiev ⊛

Moscow ⊛

Central Russian Upland

URAL MOUNTAINS

Yekaterinburg ⊛

Tobol River

Plain

Podgorica ⊛

MONT.

SERBIA

Belgrade ⊛

ROMANIA

MOLDOVA

Chisinau ⊛

UKRAINE

Dnieper River

Volga River

Caspian Depression

The Steppes

Astana ⊛

Kazakh Uplands

Sicily

Tirana ⊛

ALBANIA

KOSOVO

Pristina ⊛

Skopje ⊛

MACED.

Sofia ⊛

BULGARIA

Bucharest ⊛

Black Sea

Crimea

Istanbul ⊛

Sea of Azov

Caspian Sea

Aral Sea

Turan Lowland

Syr Darya

KAZAKHSTAN

Lake Balkhash

GREECE

Athens ⊛

Crete

Anatolia

Ankara ⊛

TURKEY

Tbilisi ⊛

GEORGIA

CAUCASUS MOUNTAINS

ARMENIA

Yerevan ⊛

AZER.

Baku ⊛

Bishkek ⊛

Almaty ⊛

Tashkent ⊛

UZBEKISTAN

KYRGYZSTAN

TIAN SHAN

CYPRUS

Nicosia ⊛

LEBANON

ISRAEL

SYRIA

Damascus ⊛

Euphrates R.

Zagros Mountains

TURKMENISTAN

Ashgabat ⊛

Amu Darya

Dushanbe ⊛

TAJIKISTAN

Communism Peak
24,590 ft.

Kongur Shan
25,324 ft.

Taklimakan Desert

Sinai Peninsula

JORDAN

Jerusalem ⊛

Syrian Desert

Tigris R.

Baghdad ⊛

IRAQ

Tehran ⊛

Salt Desert

IRAN

Kabul ⊛

HINDU KUSH

Islamabad ⊛

K2
28,251 ft.

KUNLUN MOUNTAINS

Plateau of Tibet

An Nafūd

KUWAIT

Kuwait ⊛

SAUDI ARABIA

Riyadh ⊛

Manama ⊛ BAHRAIN

QATAR

Doha ⊛

Abu Dhabi ⊛

U.A.E.

Muscat ⊛

AFGHANISTAN

PAKISTAN

Karachi ⊛

Indus River Delta

Great Indian Desert

New Delhi ⊛

Ganges Plain

Ganges River

NEPAL

Annapurna I
26,545 ft.

Kathmandu ⊛

Mount Everest
29,035

Red Sea

Arabian Peninsula

Sanaa ⊛

Rub' al Khali

OMAN

YEMEN

Aden ⊛

Gulf of Aden

AFRICA

Arabian Sea

Persian Gulf

Gulf of Khambhat

Mumbai ⊛

Godavari River

Narmada River

Hyderabad ⊛

Deccan Plateau

INDIA

BANGLADESH

Kolkata ⊛

Chota Nagpur Plateau

WESTERN GHATS

EASTERN GHATS

Chennai ⊛

Bay of Bengal

INDIAN OCEAN

EQUATOR

Malabar Coast

Laccadive Sea

Gulf of Mannar

SRI LANKA

Colombo ⊛

Dondra Head

MALDIVES

Male ⊛

AZER. = Azerbaijan
BOS. = Bosnia and Herzegovina
CZECH REP. = Czech Republic
LUX. = Luxembourg
MACED. = Macedonia
NETH. = Netherlands
MONT. = Montenegro
SWITZ. = Switzerland
U.A.E. = United Arab Emirates

ARCTIC OCEAN

Wrangel Island

Chukchi Peninsula

Cape Navarin

Bering Sea

North Land

Laptev Sea

New Siberian Islands

Lena River Delta

Kolyma Lowland

KOLYMA RANGE

Kolyma River

Taymyr Peninsula

VERKHOYANSK RANGE

Lena River

Kamchatka Peninsula

Central SIBERIA Siberian Plateau

STANOVOY RANGE

Amur River

SIKHOTE ALIN' RANGE

Sea of Okhotsk

Sakhalin

Tatar Strait

Kuril Islands

SAYAN MOUNTAINS

Lake Baikal

Lake Khanka

Manchurian Plain

Hokkaido
Sapporo

Z

MONGOLIA

Ulaanbaatar

Mongolian Plateau

Gobi

Shenyang

NORTH KOREA

Sea of Japan

JAPAN

Tokyo

PACIFIC OCEAN

ALTAY MOUNTAINS

Huang He River

Beijing

Bo Hai

Pyongyang
Seoul

Honshu

ALTUN SHUN

Qinghai Hu

Mu Us Desert

North China Plain

SOUTH KOREA

Pusan

Kitakyushu

Kyushu

20°

CHINA

QIN LIN

Yangtze River

Yellow Sea

Shanghai

East China Sea

Naha

Ryukyu Islands

160°

Saltween River

▲ Gongga Shan 24,790 ft.

WUYI SHAN

Taipei

BHUTAN

Hongshui River

Guangzhou
Hong Kong

Taiwan

Philippine Sea

Irrawaddy River

Hanoi

Leizhou Bay

Hainan

MYANMAR

LAOS

Gulf of Tonkin

Luzon

Luzon Strait

Nay Pyi Taw

Vientiane

South China Sea

Mekong River

Manila

Yangon

Indochina

THAILAND

VIETNAM

Bangkok

CAMBODIA

Phnom Penh

Ho Chi Minh City

Palawan

Mindanao

PHILIPPINES

Melekeok PALAU

0°

Andaman Islands (India)

Gulf of Thailand

Celebes Sea

EQUATOR

Nicobar Islands (India)

Malay Peninsula

Bandar Seri Begawan

BRUNEI

Andaman Sea

Halmahera

MAOKE MOUNTAINS

Medan

Kuala Lumpur

MALAYSIA

BORNEO HIGHLANDS

INDONESIA

Mt. Jaya ▲ 16,499 ft.

New Guinea

Borneo

SINGAPORE

Celebes

Torres Strait

BARISAN MOUNTAINS

Sumatra

Banda Sea

Coral Sea

Java Sea

Jakarta

Dili

Java

EAST TIMOR

AUSTRALIA

100°

120°

140°

Middle East

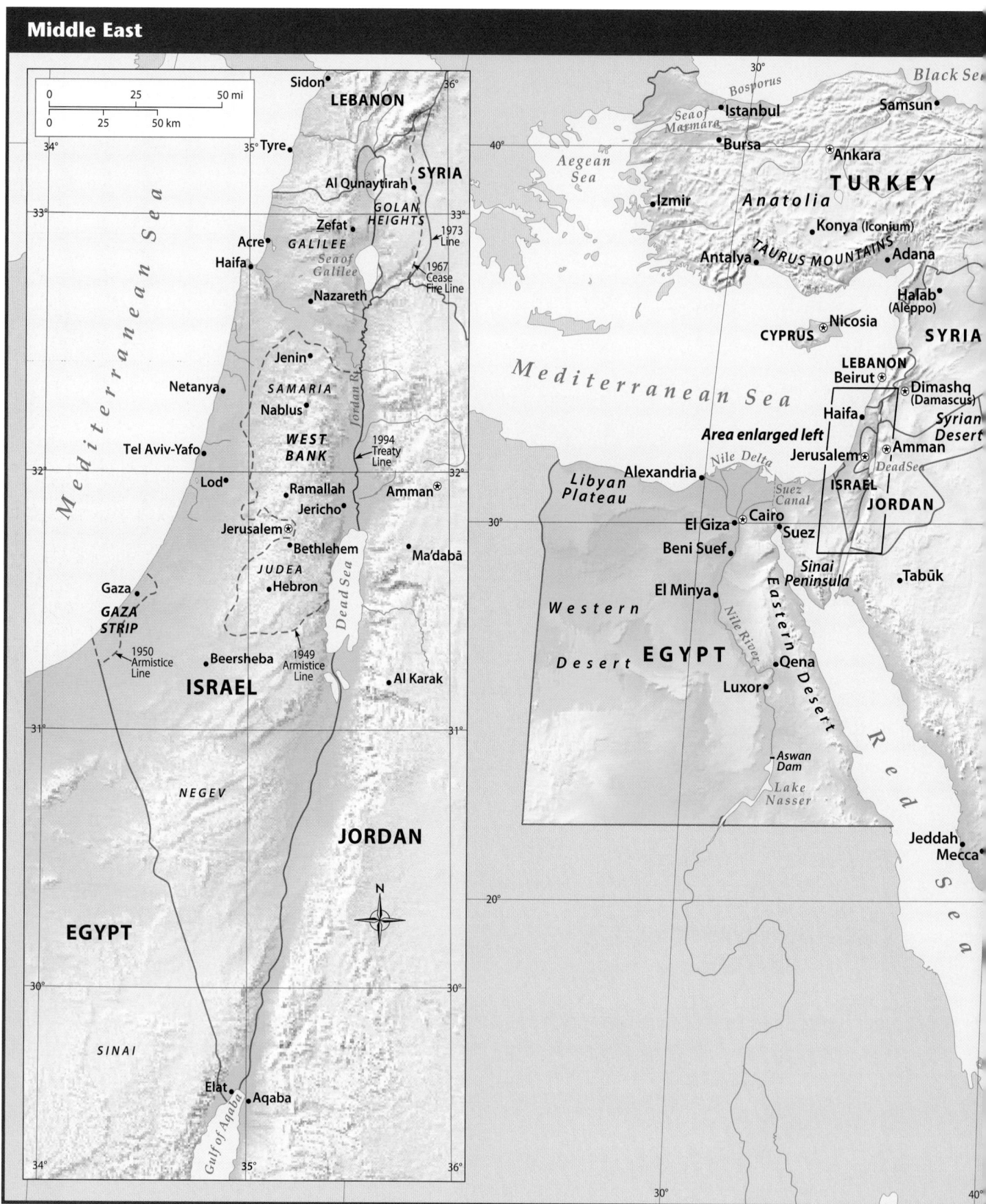

Sidon

LEBANON

Tyre

Al Qunaytirah

SYRIA

GOLAN HEIGHTS

1973 Line

Zefat

GALILEE

Acre

Sea of Galilee

Haifa

1967 Cease Fire Line

Nazareth

Jenin

Netanya

SAMARIA

Nablus

WEST BANK

1994 Treaty Line

Tel Aviv-Yafo

Lod

Ramallah

Amman

Jericho

Jerusalem

Bethlehem

Ma'dabā

JUDEA

Gaza

Hebron

GAZA STRIP

1950 Armistice Line

Dead Sea

Beersheba

1949 Armistice Line

Al Karak

ISRAEL

NEGEV

JORDAN

N

EGYPT

SINAI

Elat

Aqaba

Gulf of Aqaba

Mediterranean Sea

Jordan R.

Black Sea

Bosporus

Sea of Marmara

Istanbul

Samsun

Bursa

Ankara

Aegean Sea

TURKEY

Izmir

Anatolia

Konya (Iconium)

TAURUS MOUNTAINS

Antalya

Adana

Halab (Aleppo)

CYPRUS

Nicosia

SYRIA

Mediterranean Sea

LEBANON

Beirut

Dimashq (Damascus)

Haifa

Syrian Desert

Area enlarged left

Jerusalem

Amman

ISRAEL

Dead Sea

Alexandria

Nile Delta

JORDAN

Libyan Plateau

Suez Canal

El Giza

Cairo

Suez

Beni Suef

Sinai Peninsula

Tabūk

El Minya

Eastern Desert

Western Desert

EGYPT

Nile River

Qena

Luxor

Red Sea

Aswan Dam

Lake Nasser

Jeddah

Mecca

Scale:
0 25 50 mi
0 25 50 km

South Asia

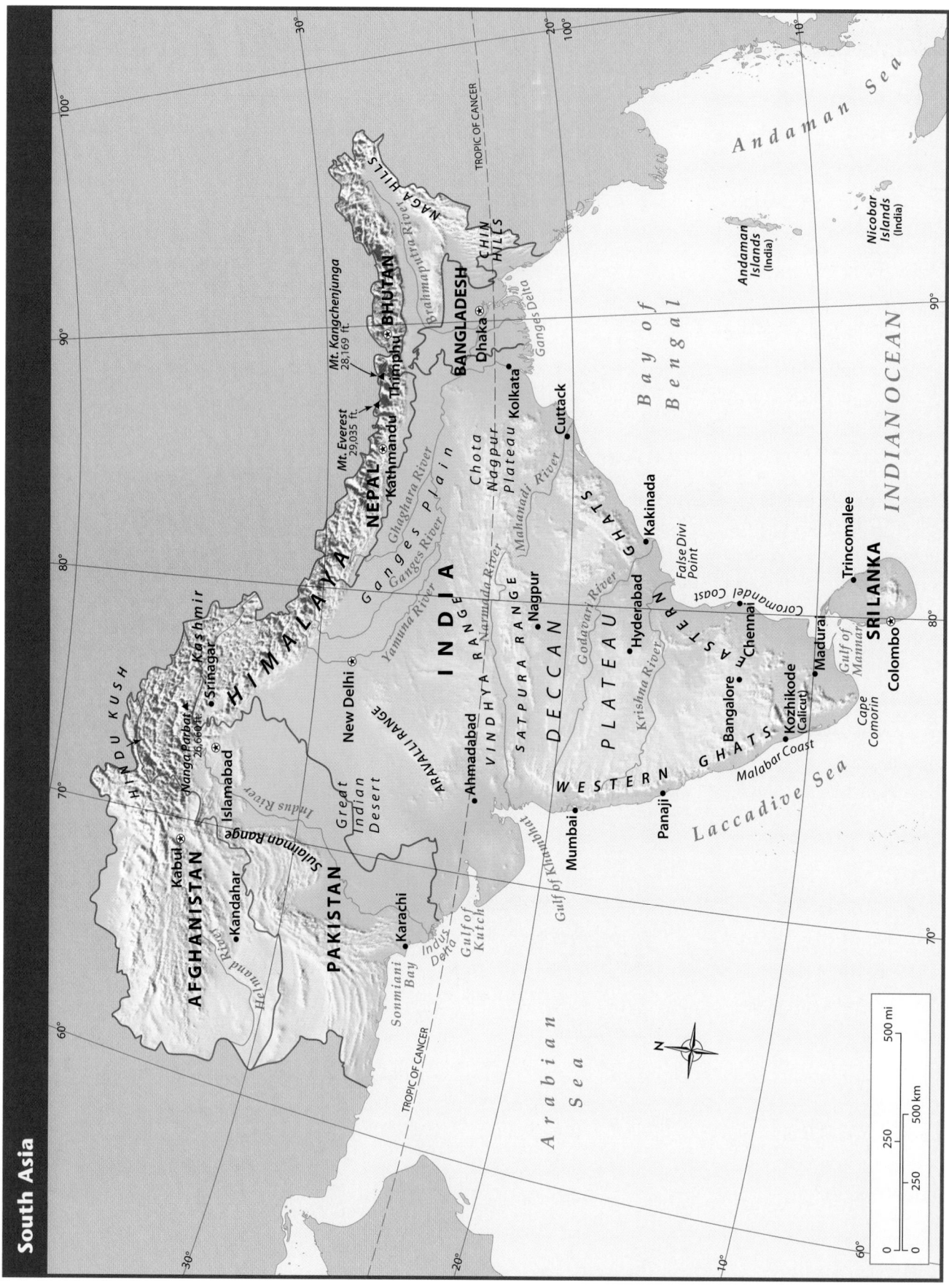

Andaman Sea

Nicobar Islands (India)

Andaman Islands (India)

TROPIC OF CANCER

NAGA HILLS

CHIN HILLS

BANGLADESH

BHUTAN

Thimphu

Mt. Kangchenjunga 28,169 ft.

Dhaka

Brahmaputra River

Ganges Delta

Ganges Plain

Kolkata

Bay of Bengal

NEPAL

Mt. Everest 29,035 ft.

Kathmandu

Ghaghara River

Chota Nagpur Plateau

Cuttack

Ganges River

Mahanadi River

INDIA

HIMALAYA

Yamuna River

Narmada River

VINDHYA RANGE

SATPURA RANGE

Nagpur

DECCAN PLATEAU

Kakinada

Godavari River

False Divi Point

EASTERN GHATS

Coromandel Coast

Trincomalee

INDIAN OCEAN

SRI LANKA

Kashmir

Srinagar

HINDU KUSH

Nanga Parbat 26,660 ft.

New Delhi

ARAVALLI RANGE

Ahmadabad

Krishna River

Hyderabad

Chennai

Bangalore

Madura

Colombo

Gulf of Mannar

Islamabad

Indus River

Great Indian Desert

Kozhikode (Calicut)

WESTERN GHATS

Cape Comorin

Kabul

Suliman Range

AFGHANISTAN

Kandahar

PAKISTAN

Karachi

Gulf of Kutch

Panaji

Mumbai

Malabar Coast

Laccadive Sea

Kabul River

Helmand River

Sonmiani Bay

Indus Delta

Gulf of Khambhat

TROPIC OF CANCER

Arabian Sea

N

| 500 mi |
| 250 |
| 0 |
| 500 km |
| 250 |
| 0 |

North and South Poles

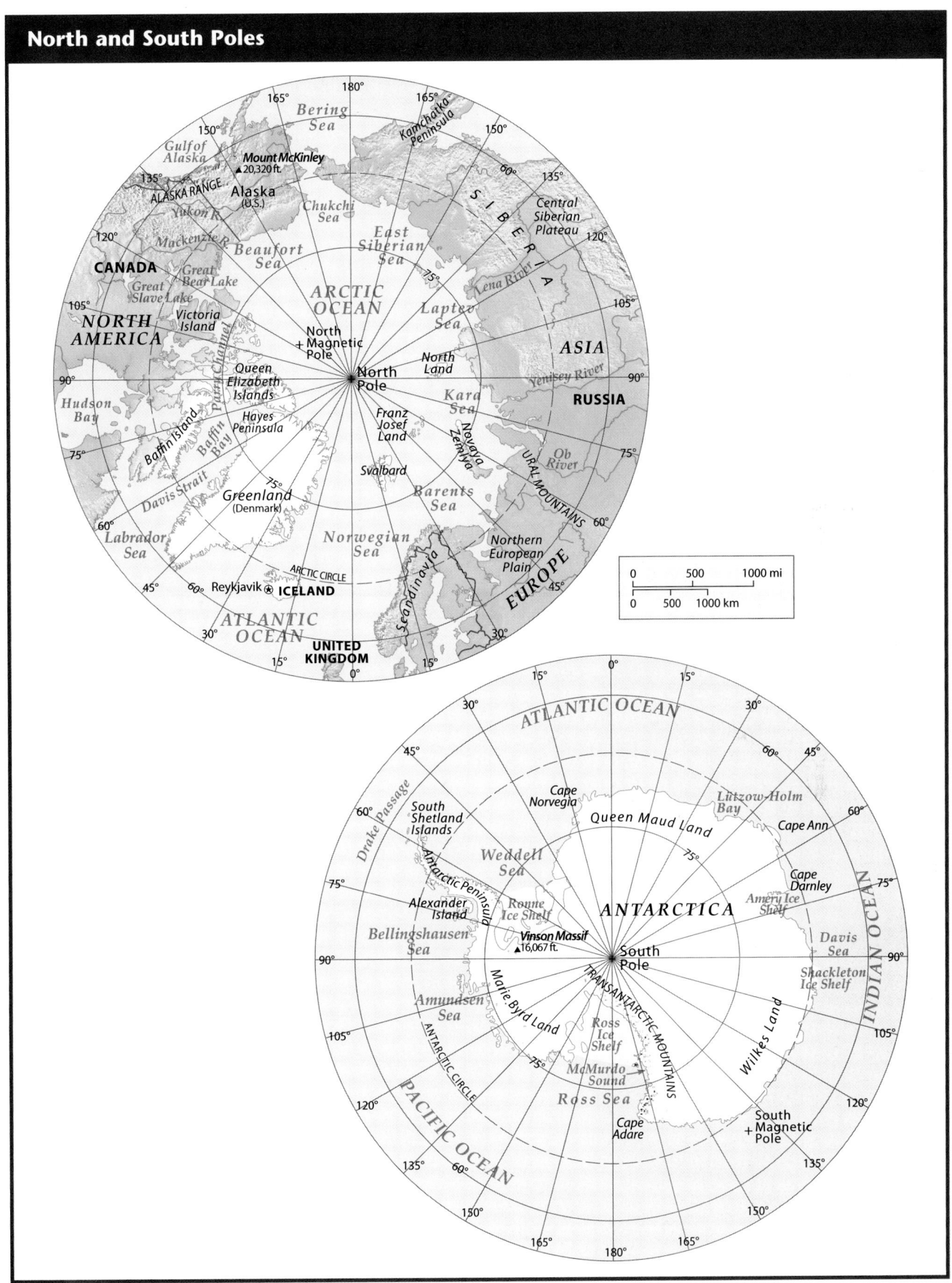

North Pole map (top):

180°
Bering Sea
165° 165°
150° 150°
Kamchatka Peninsula
Gulf of Alaska
135° 60° 135°
Mount McKinley ▲20,320 ft.
ALASKA RANGE
Alaska (U.S.)
Central Siberian Plateau
Chukchi Sea
120° 120°
Yukon R.
East Siberian Sea
S I B E R I A
Mackenzie R.
Beaufort Sea
75°
CANADA
Great Bear Lake
ARCTIC OCEAN
Lena River
Great Slave Lake
Laptev Sea
105° 105°
Victoria Island
North America
North Magnetic Pole
North Land
ASIA
90° North Pole 90°
Queen Elizabeth Islands
Yenisey River
RUSSIA
Hudson Bay
Parry Channel
Franz Josef Land
Kara Sea
Hayes Peninsula
75° 75°
Baffin Island
Baffin Bay
Novaya Zemlya
Ob River
Davis Strait
Svalbard
URAL MOUNTAINS
60°
Labrador Sea
Barents Sea
60°
Greenland (Denmark)
Norwegian Sea
45° 45°
Northern European Plain
EUROPE
ARCTIC CIRCLE
Scandinavia
60°
Reykjavik ⊛ ICELAND
30° 30°
ATLANTIC OCEAN
15° UNITED KINGDOM 15°
0°

Scale:
0   500   1000 mi
0 500 1000 km

South Pole map (bottom):

15° 0° 15°
ATLANTIC OCEAN
30° 30°
45° Cape Norvegia 60° 45°
Lützow-Holm Bay
Drake Passage
South Shetland Islands
Queen Maud Land
Cape Ann
60° 60°
Weddell Sea
75°
Antarctic Peninsula
Cape Darnley
75° 75°
Ronne Ice Shelf
ANTARCTICA
Amery Ice Shelf
Alexander Island
Bellingshausen Sea
Vinson Massif ▲16,067 ft.
Davis Sea
90° South Pole 90°
Marie Byrd Land
TRANSANTARCTIC MOUNTAINS
Shackleton Ice Shelf
Amundsen Sea
Ross Ice Shelf
Wilkes Land
INDIAN OCEAN
105° 105°
ANTARCTIC CIRCLE
McMurdo Sound
75°
120° Ross Sea 120°
South Magnetic Pole
PACIFIC OCEAN
Cape Adare
135° 60° 135°
150° 150°
165° 180° 165°

Goode's Interrupted Homoline Projection

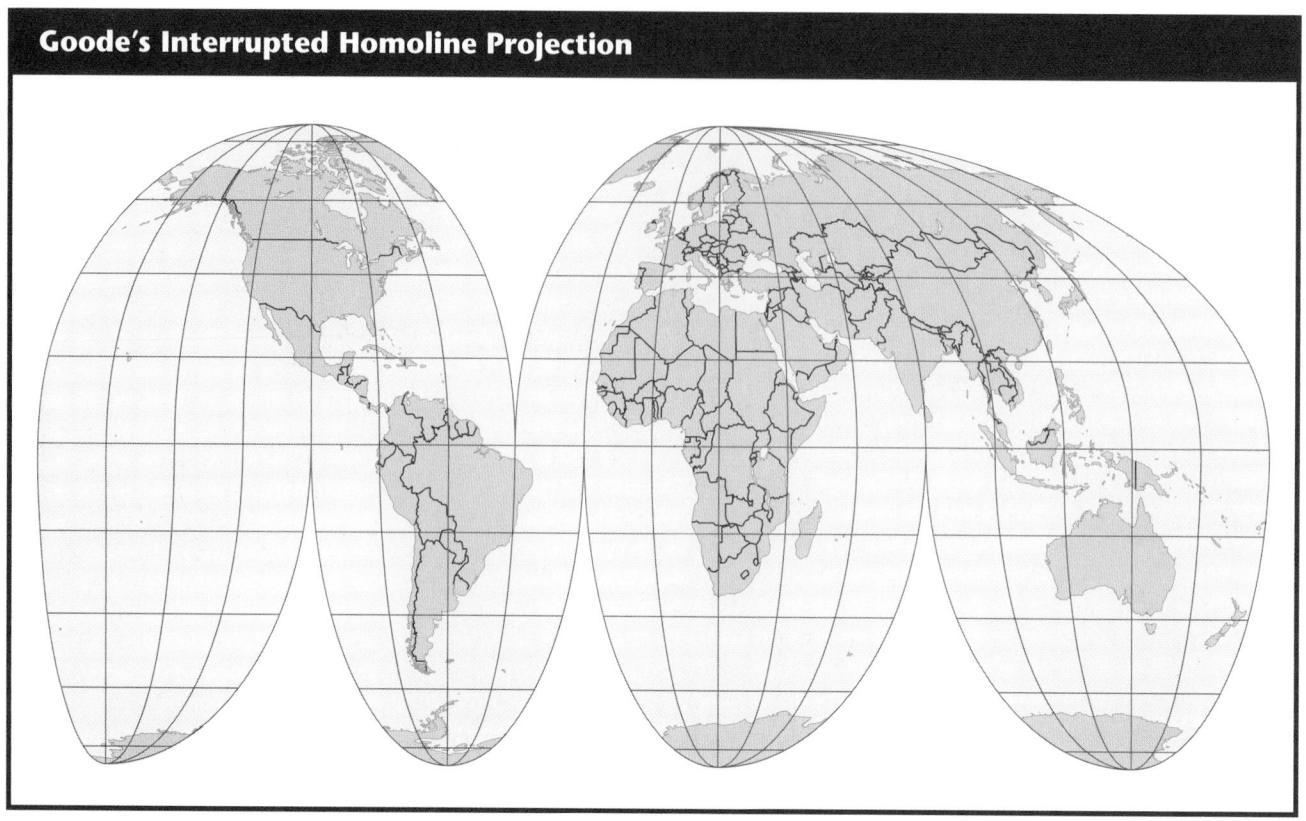

Miller Projection

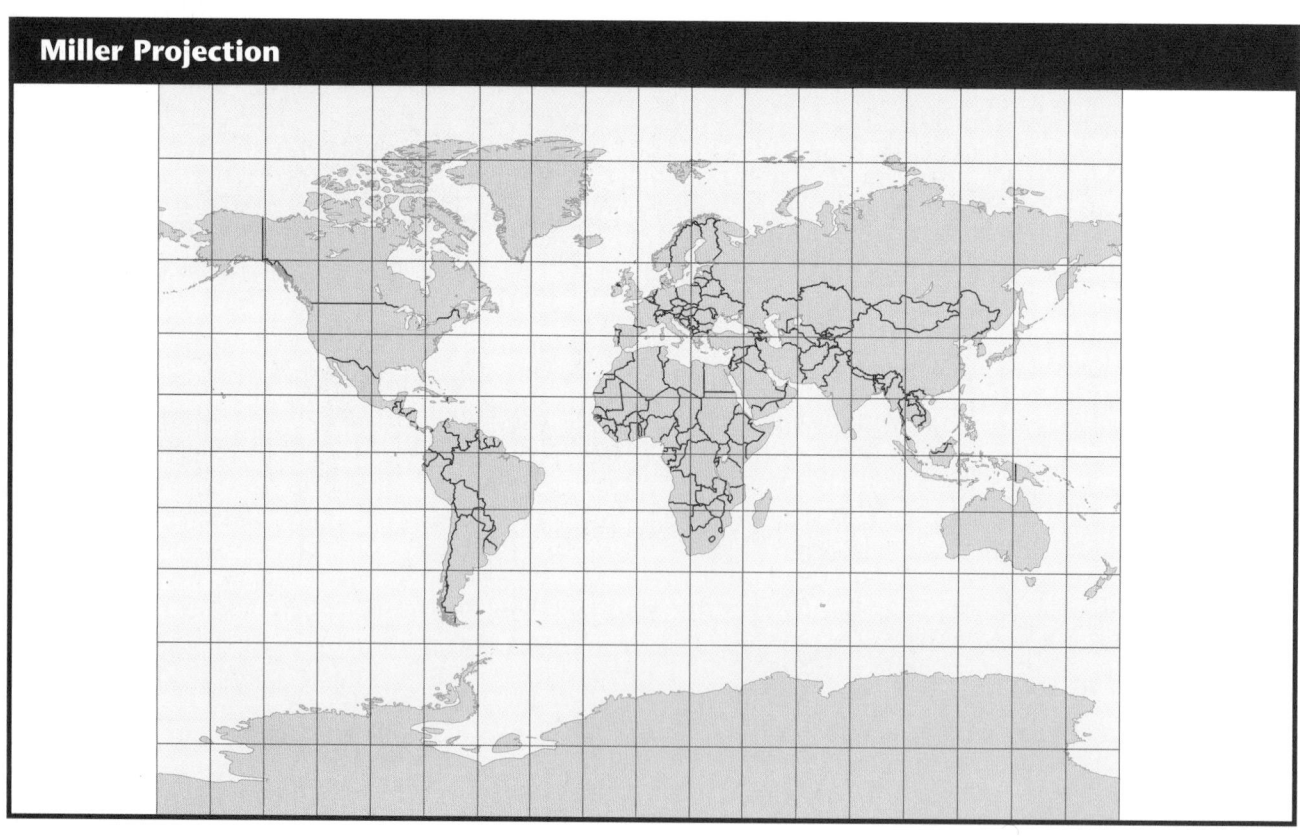

Mollweide Projection

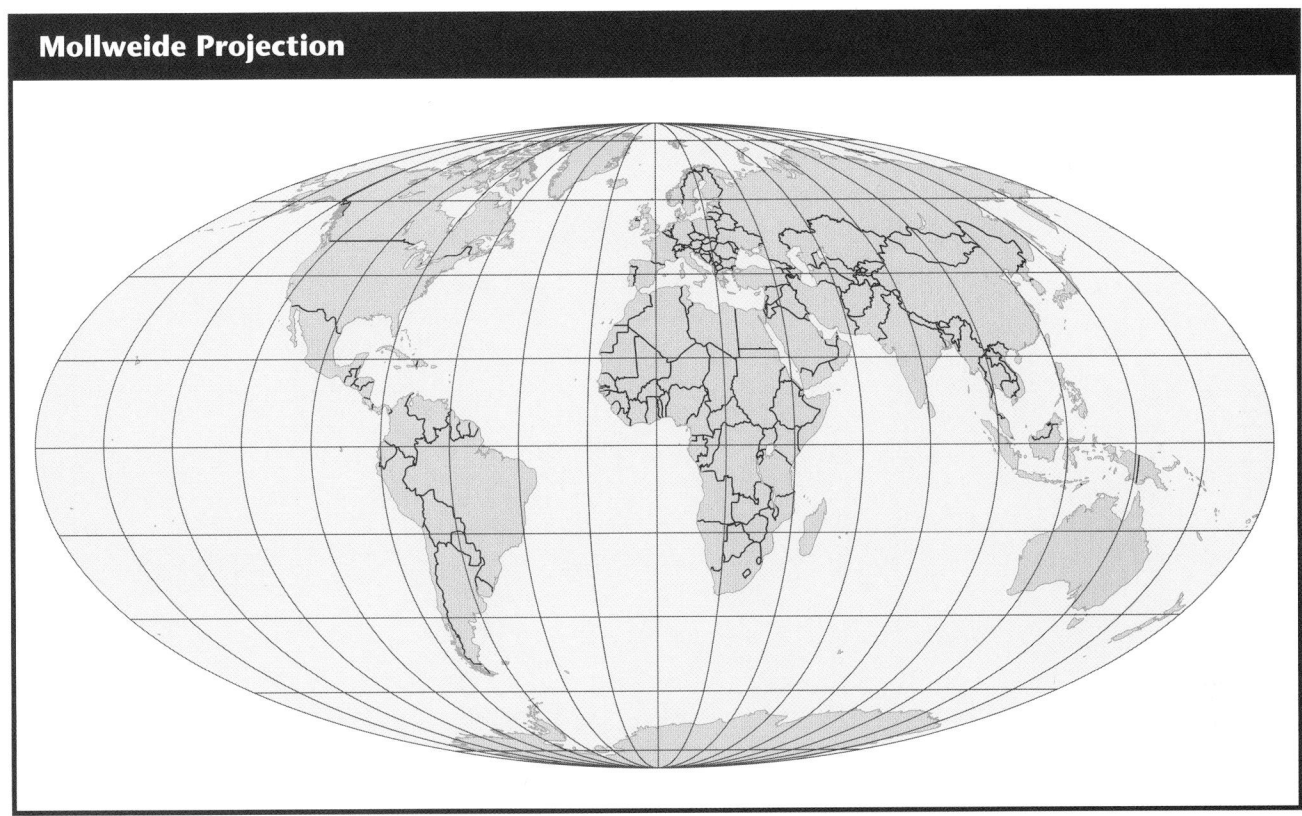

Winkel Tripel Projection

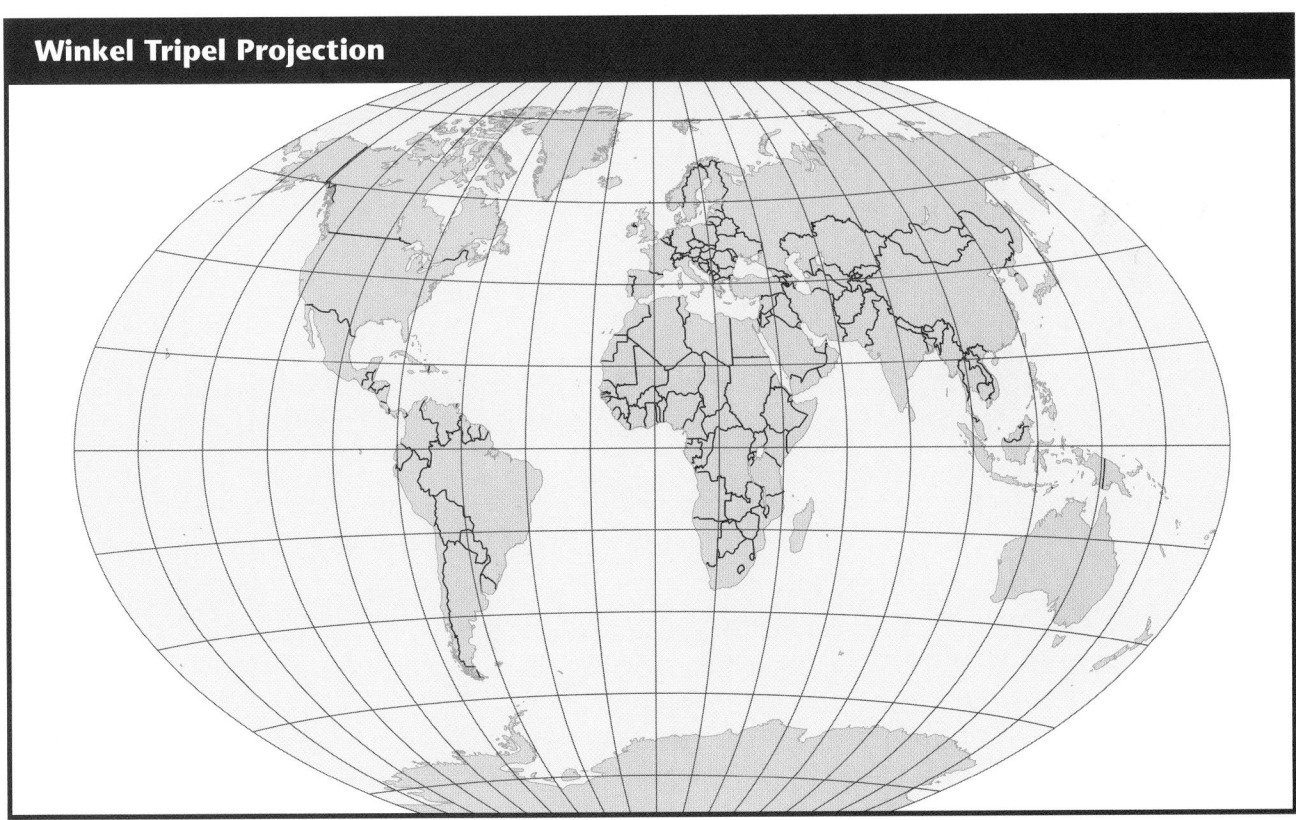

Climate Zones

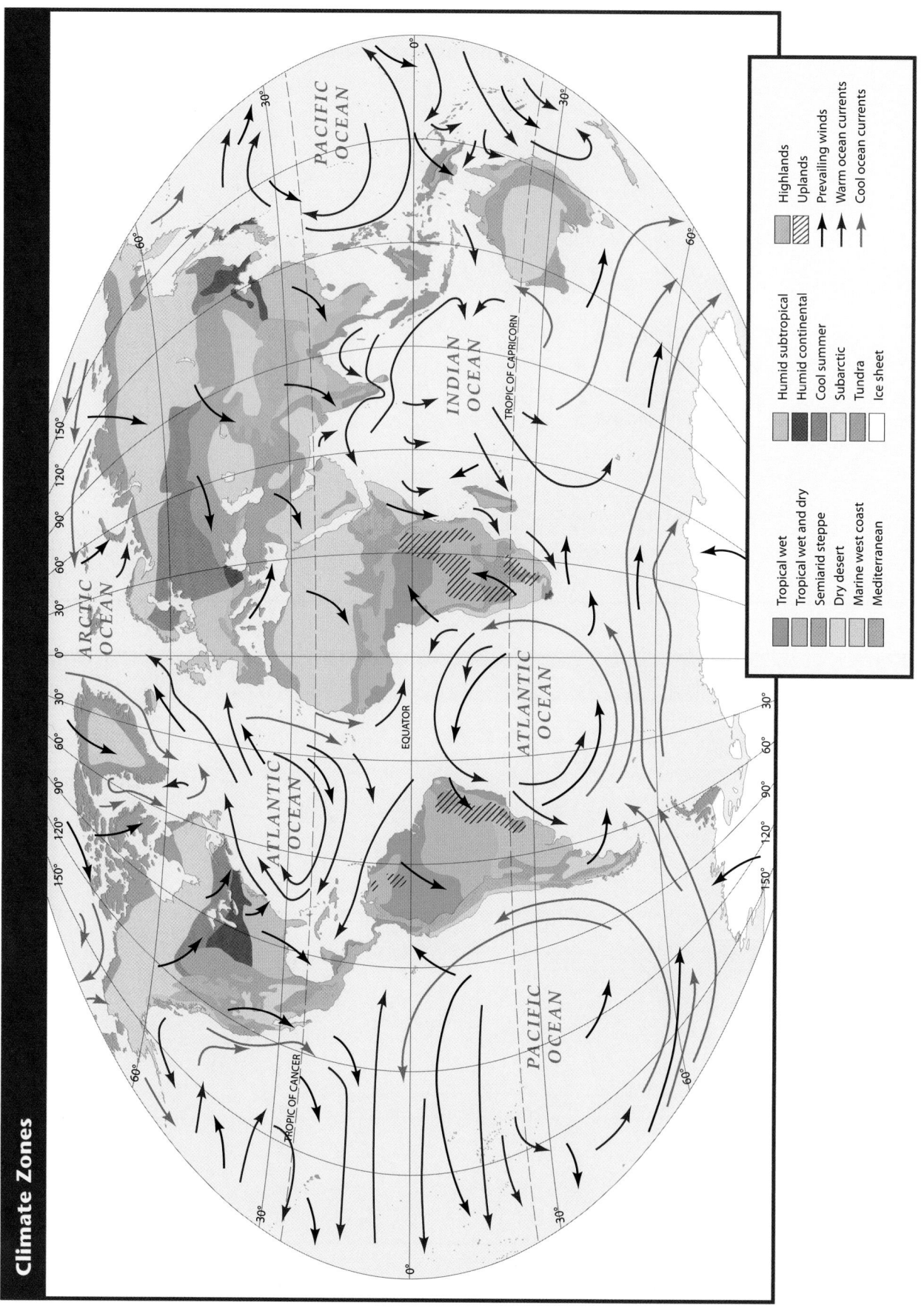

Tropical wet
Tropical wet and dry
Semiarid steppe
Dry desert
Marine west coast
Mediterranean

Humid subtropical
Humid continental
Cool summer
Subarctic
Tundra
Ice sheet

Highlands
Uplands
Prevailing winds
Warm ocean currents
Cool ocean currents

Terrestrial Biomes

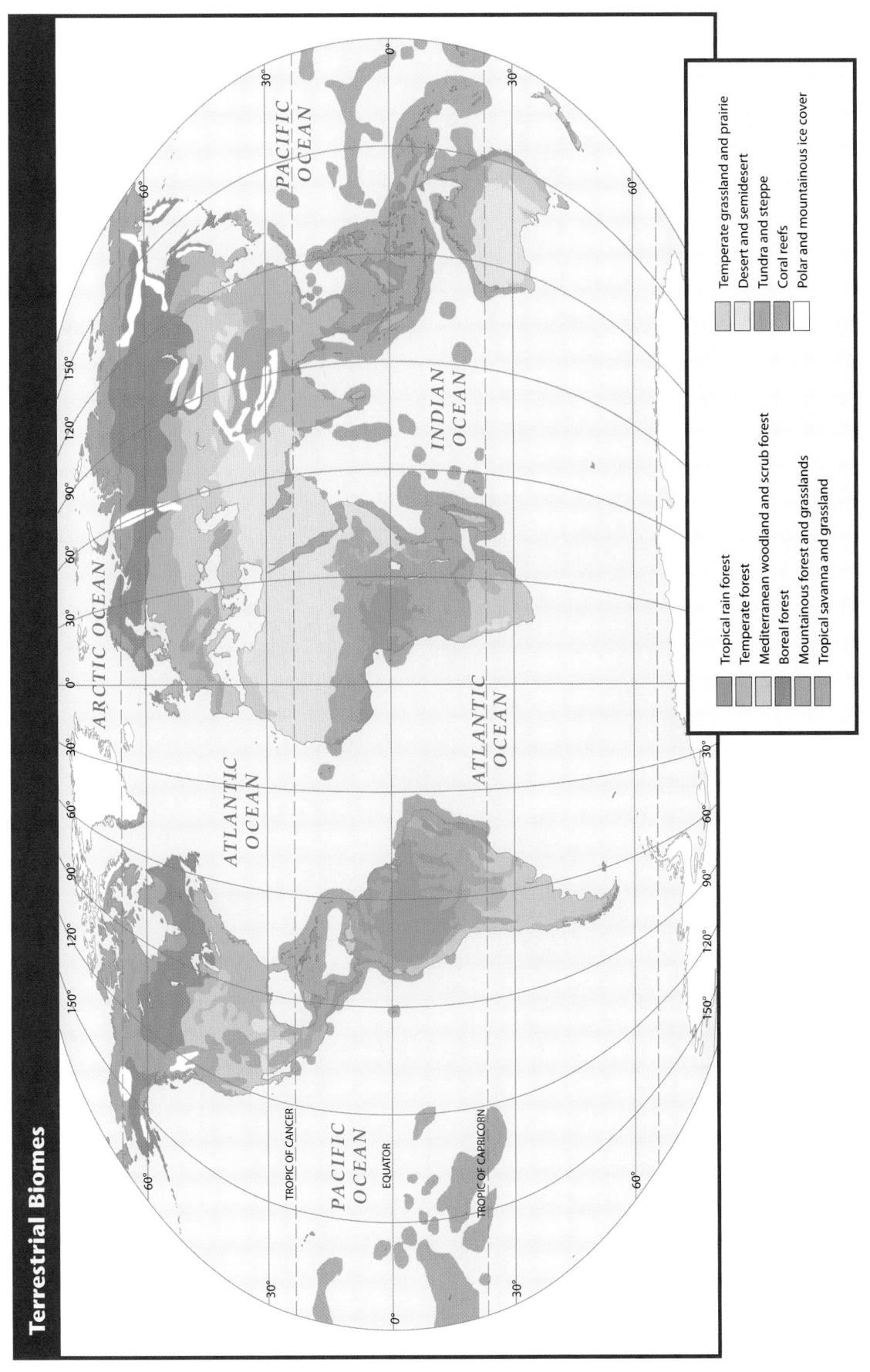

Legend:

Tropical rain forest
Temperate forest
Mediterranean woodland and scrub forest
Boreal forest
Mountainous forest and grasslands
Tropical savanna and grassland

Temperate grassland and prairie
Desert and semidesert
Tundra and steppe
Coral reefs
Polar and mountainous ice cover

Ocean labels: PACIFIC OCEAN, INDIAN OCEAN, ATLANTIC OCEAN, ARCTIC OCEAN

TROPIC OF CANCER
EQUATOR
TROPIC OF CAPRICORN

GDP (Gross Domestic Product)

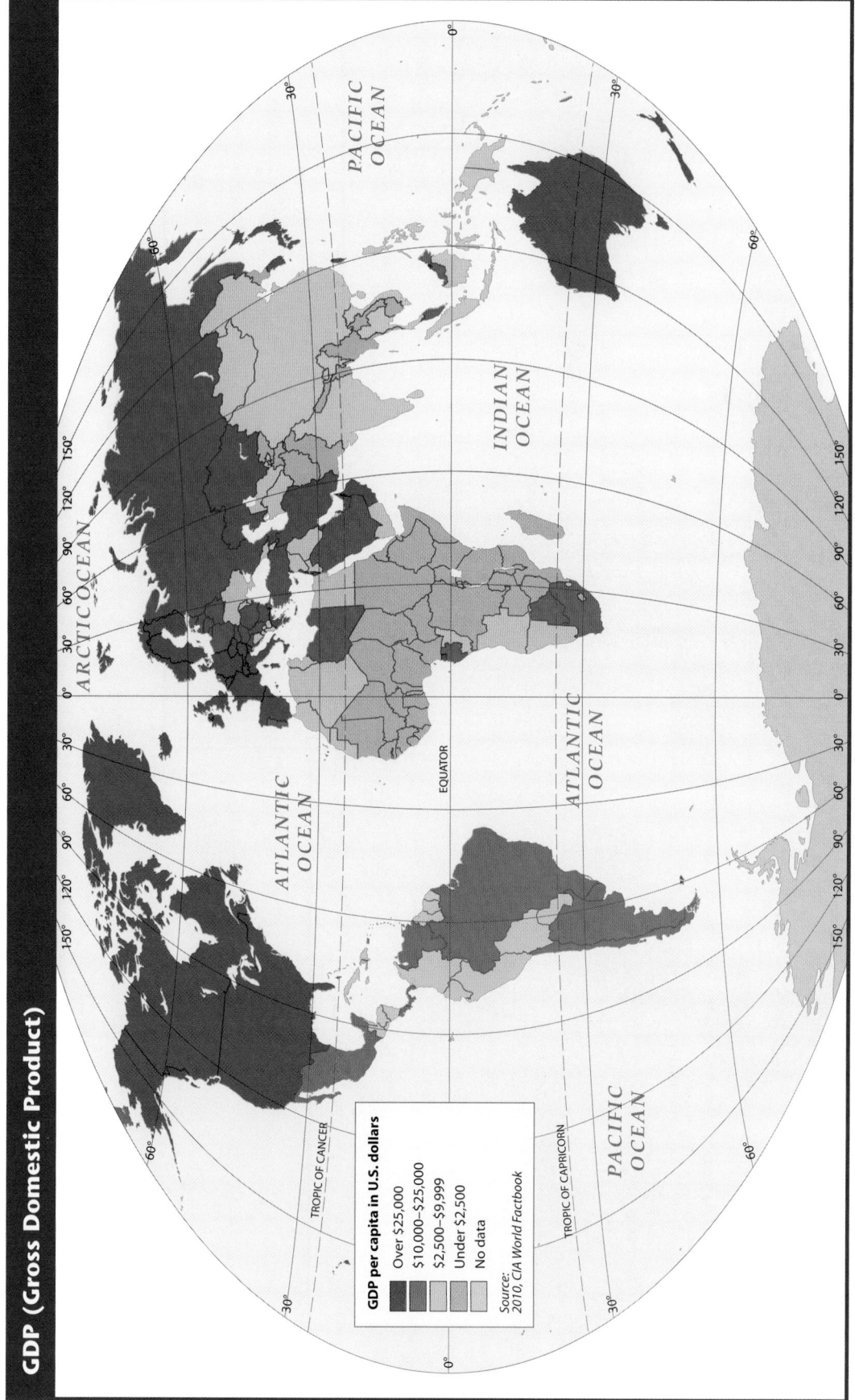

GDP per capita in U.S. dollars

Over $25,000
$10,000–$25,000
$2,500–$9,999
Under $2,500
No data

Source:
2010, CIA World Factbook

Gross Domestic Product (GDP) is the total value of all final goods and services produced in a nation in a given year. When measured in U.S. dollars, the GDP per capita (per person) is a way to compare the economic well-being of countries.

Population Density

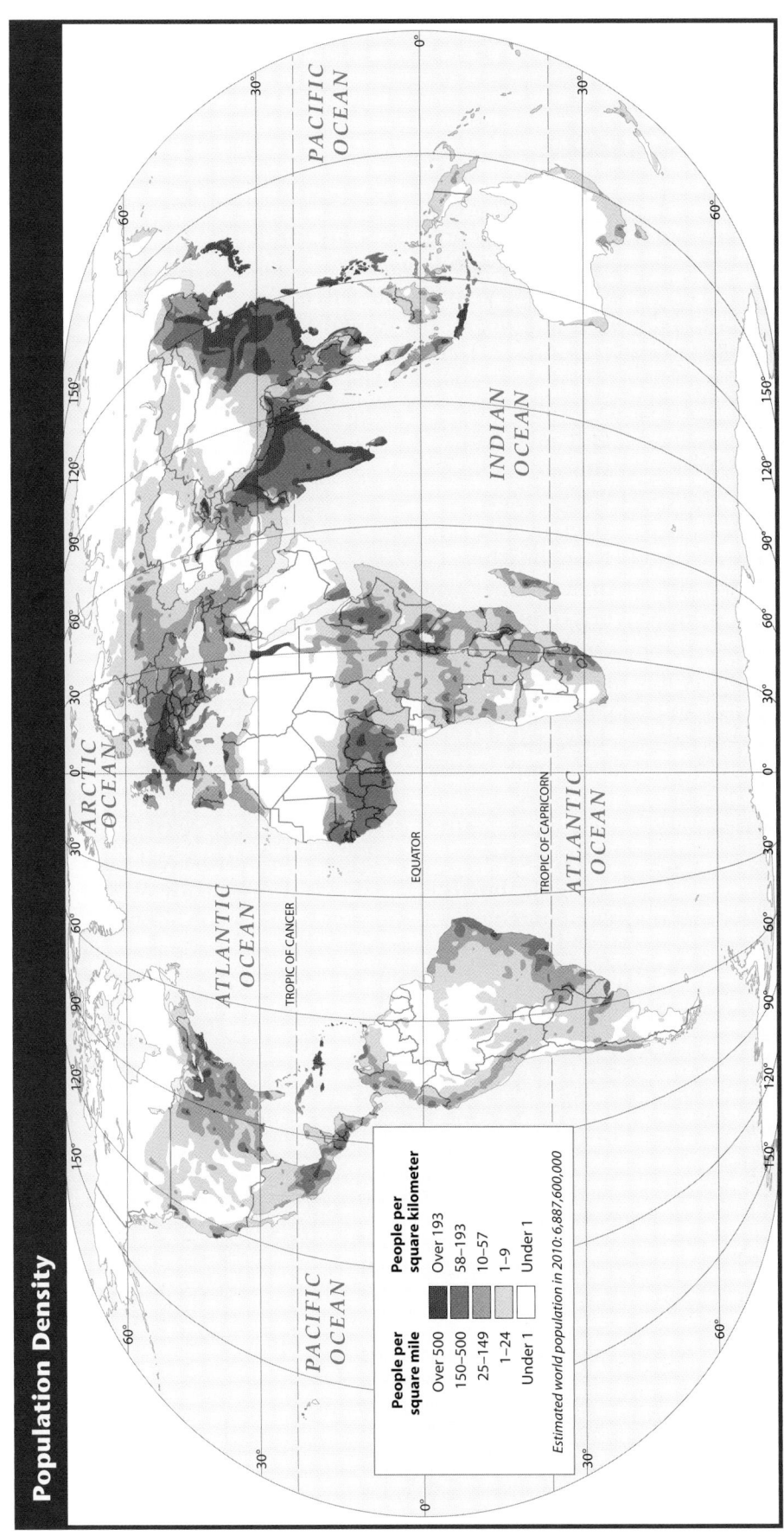

People per square mile
- Over 500
- 150–500
- 25–149
- 1–24
- Under 1

People per square kilometer
- Over 193
- 58–193
- 10–57
- 1–9
- Under 1

Estimated world population in 2010: 6,887,600,000

Pronunciation Guide

The table below provides sample words to explain the sounds associated with specific letters and letter combinations used in the respellings in this book. For example, in the respelling of *Bolshevik*—BOHL-shuh-vik—the letters OH represent the vowel sound you hear in *home* and *throw*. The capital letters indicate which syllable to accent.

Vowels

a	short a: **a**pple, c**a**t
ay	long a: c**a**ne, d**ay**
e, eh	short e: h**e**n, b**e**d
ee	long e: f**ee**d, t**ea**m
i, ih	short i: l**i**p, act**i**ve
iy	long i: tr**y**, m**i**ght
ah	short o: h**o**t, f**a**ther
oh	long o: h**o**me, thr**ow**
uh	short u: sh**u**t, **o**ther
yoo	long u: **u**nion, c**u**te

Letter combinations

ch	**ch**in, an**c**ient
sh	**sh**ow, mi**ss**ion
zh	vi**s**ion, a**z**ure
th	**th**in, heal**th**
th	**th**en, hea**th**er
ur	b**ir**d, f**ur**ther, w**or**d
us	b**us**, cr**us**t
or	c**our**t, f**or**mal
ehr	**er**ror, c**are**
oo	c**oo**l, tr**ue**, f**ew**, r**u**le
ow	n**ow**, **ou**t
ou	l**oo**k, p**u**ll, w**ou**ld
oy	c**oi**n, t**oy**
aw	s**aw**, m**au**l, f**a**ll
ng	so**ng**, fi**ng**er
air	**A**ristotle, b**a**rrister
ahr	c**ar**t, m**ar**tyr

Consonants

b	**b**utter, **b**aby
d	**d**og, cra**d**le
f	**f**un, **ph**one
g	**g**rade, an**g**le
h	**h**at, a**h**ead
j	**j**u**dg**e, **g**orge
k	**k**ite, **c**ar, bla**ck**
l	**l**ily, mi**l**e
m	**m**om, ca**m**el
n	**n**ext, ca**n**did
p	**p**rice, co**pp**er
r	**r**ubbe**r**, **fr**ee
s	**s**mall, **c**ircle, ha**ss**le
t	**t**on, po**tt**ery
v	**v**ase, **v**i**v**id
w	**w**all, a**w**ay
y	**y**ellow, ka**y**ak
z	**z**ebra, ha**z**e

Glossary

abbot   the leader of a monastery

aborigine   one of the original inhabitants of a place, such as the indigenous people of Australia

absolute monarch   a single ruler (such as a king or queen) who governs with unlimited power; sometimes contrasted with a constitutional monarch, whose power is limited by a nation's constitution

acropolis   a fortified hill in Greek city-states where people could take refuge in time of attack

A.D.   the abbreviation for the Latin words *anno Domini* ("in the year of the Lord"), used to date events that took place after the birth of Jesus Christ

African National Congress (ANC)   South African political organization founded in 1912; it became the major voice against apartheid and the nation's most prominent political party

agora   central square in an ancient Greek city where people sold goods, gave political speeches, and held athletic competitions

agricultural revolution   the shift from hunting and gathering to farming that occurred around 10,000 B.C.

Allah   the name for God in the Arabic language

Allied Powers   in World War I, the countries that formed an alliance to fight the Central Powers; the principal Allied Powers in World War I were the United Kingdom, Belgium, France, Russia, Italy, and the United States (from 1917 to end); in World War II, the countries that formed an alliance to fight the Axis Powers; the principal Allied Powers in World War II were the United Kingdom, France, the United States, and the USSR

al-Qaeda   See Qaeda, al

Analects   book containing the teachings of the ancient Chinese philosopher Confucius, who emphasized ethical behavior

anarchy   a state of lawlessness and disorder, generally due to the absence or breakdown of a functioning government

ancien régime   the old order; specifically, the political and social system of pre-Revolutionary France under the monarchy

animism   the belief that spiritual forces inhabit everything in nature

anthropology   the study of human beings, particularly their societies and cultures

anti-Semitism   hatred of or prejudice against Jews

apartheid   policy of strict racial segregation in South Africa in place from 1948 to 1991

apostle   a follower or someone sent on a mission; specifically, one of the twelve original followers of Jesus Christ

appeasement   policy of giving in to an aggressor nation's demands in the hope of preventing war; most frequently applied to the British and French response to Hitler before World War II

aqueduct   channel constructed to carry water into cities, such as those built by the ancient Romans

Arab-Israeli War of 1967   See Six-Day War

Arab-Israeli War of 1973   See Yom Kippur War

archaeology   the scientific study of ancient ruins and artifacts in order to learn about the past

aristocracy government by a privileged upper class

Armenian Massacre the forced deportation and massacre of Armenians by the Ottoman Turkish government during World War I, often considered the first genocide in history

armistice an agreement by the opponents in a war to cease fighting for a time, usually to allow negotiations for peace

Articles of Confederation 1777 agreement establishing a loose association of North American states while guaranteeing individual state sovereignty; replaced by the United States Constitution in 1789

artifact object left behind by humans or human ancestors

ascetic person who practices self-denial to attain spiritual insight

Assembly the lawmaking body of Athens, open to attendance by all the citizens of the city-state

astrolabe instrument for determining the position of the sun, moon, and stars

autocrat ruler with unlimited power

Axis Powers in World War II, the nations of Germany, Italy, and Japan; they fought the Allied Powers

ayatollah in Shiite Islam, a religious leader learned in Islamic law and other subjects

Baath Party Arab nationalist party founded in Syria in the 1940s that gained followers in Syria, Iraq, and Lebanon; it promotes Arab unity, freedom from Western influence, and economic socialism; it produced two dictators, Saddam Hussein of Iraq and Hafez al-Assad of Syria

baby boom a significant rise in the birthrate, such as in the United States following World War II

balance of trade the difference between the value of a nation's imports and its exports

barbarian a term for outsiders seen as inferior; the name the Greeks and Romans gave to the nomadic tribes on the fringes of their empire

barter system economic system in which one good is traded directly for another, rather than traded for credit or money

Bastille fortress and prison in Paris, and symbol of royal power; its fall on July 14, 1789, marked the beginning of the French Revolution

Bataan Death March the forced march of more than seventy thousand American and Filipino prisoners over sixty miles by the Japanese military in April 1942

Battle of Marathon battle on the plain of Marathon in 490 B.C. at which the Athenian army defeated the much larger Persian army, preventing Persia from conquering Greece

Battle of Midway Pacific naval battle, a turning point in World War II, in which American forces won a major victory over the Japanese

Battle of Stalingrad World War II battle between Soviet and German forces from summer 1942 to February 1943; a turning point in World War II and the most deadly battle in human history, leaving almost two million dead

Battle of Trafalgar 1805 naval battle in which British Admiral Horatio Nelson defeated a French and Spanish fleet during Britain's war against Napoleon

Battle of Waterloo 1815 battle in which Napoleon met his final defeat at the hands of the British and the Prussians

B.C. the abbreviation for "before Christ," used to date events that took place in the years before the birth of Jesus Christ

Bedouin a member of the nomadic Arab tribal people

Black Death a highly contagious plague that ravaged fourteenth-century Europe

blitzkrieg "lightning war"; a type of warfare employed by Nazi Germany in World War II, with the objective of quickly overwhelming the enemy

Boer Dutch settler of southern Africa

Bolshevik Party communist party founded by Vladimir Lenin as a party of professional revolutionaries; the Bolsheviks came to power in Russia in 1917

bourgeoisie the middle class; in Karl Marx's writings, *bourgeoisie* refers to factory and property owners, bankers, and businessmen, in contrast with the proletariat (working class)

Boxer Rebellion 1900 uprising against foreigners in China, led by a secret society known as the Boxers, who resented foreign domination of China

boyar powerful landowning noble of tsarist Russia

boycott to refuse to do business with a company or group, often to compel it to change in some way

Bronze Age period when people primarily used bronze rather than stone or iron for tools; the Bronze Age began in Sumer around 3000 B.C.

Buddhism the ideas and path set forth by the Buddha

Bushido meaning "the way of the warrior," the code of behavior of the samurai of feudal Japan, requiring devotion to duty and absolute bravery and loyalty

caliph the title for Muhammad's successors as civil and religious leaders of Muslims

calligraphy the art of fine or beautiful writing

Calvinism doctrines of sixteenth century Protestant Reformation leader John Calvin, emphasizing predestination and salvation by God's grace alone

canon law a body of laws established by a church, especially of the Roman Catholic Church

capitalism economic system based on private ownership of land and resources, in which individuals and businesses produce goods and services to make money; also known as the free enterprise (or free market) system

caravel a light sailing ship developed by the Portuguese in the fifteenth century

cartography the science of mapmaking

caste a social class in Hinduism into which a person is born; basis for India's caste system

catacomb an underground burial chamber, as in ancient Rome where early Christians sometimes met in secret

cataract portion of a river with rapids and steep waterfalls

catechism summary, in question and answer format, of basic tenets of a religion

Catholic Church the body of Christians who recognize the authority of the pope in Rome as leader of the church; also called the Roman Catholic Church

caudillo military strongman who seized power in a South American nation after its liberation from Spain

Cavalier supporter of King Charles I during the English civil war

census a count of the entire population of an area

Central Powers World War I alliance formed by Germany, Austria-Hungary, and the Ottoman Empire; the Central Powers fought the Allied Powers

Centuriate Assembly group of wealthy men in the Roman Republic who furnished armed troops and elected government officials

centurion Roman army officer commanding a group of about 100 soldiers

charter a written grant of rights from a government or ruler to a person or organization; for example, a document authorizing the establishment of a new colony

Chartism   British working-class movement in the 1830s and 1840s, supporting parliamentary reform and universal male suffrage

checks and balances   system under which each of the branches of government limits the powers of the other branches

chivalry   code of conduct for European knights during the Middle Ages

Christendom   in European history beginning about A.D. 1000, the name used to denote the idea of Europe as a realm politically and religiously united by the Christian faith

Christianity   world religion based on the life and teachings of Jesus Christ

Circus Maximus   U-shaped stadium that held the largest of ancient Rome's chariot racetracks

citadel   fortress of a city

citizenship   membership status in a nation or state, entitling the citizen to certain rights and requiring from him or her certain duties

city-state   an independently ruled city and the land around it

civil disobedience   the refusal to obey unjust laws

civil service   the administrative offices of a government

civilization   a stage of social development characterized by the building of cities and made possible when people have a surplus of food and division of labor

classical civilization   the civilization of ancient Greece and Rome between about 500 B.C. and A.D. 500

Code of Hammurabi   a set of laws assembled by the Babylonian king Hammurabi

codex, codices   a manuscript book, particularly one created by the Maya using hieroglyphs

Cold War   period of tension and rivalry between communist nations (led by the Soviet Union) and noncommunist nations (led by the United States) from 1947 to 1991; the superpowers did not fight an actual war (a "hot" war)

collective bargaining   the process by which groups of workers (such as trade unions) negotiate with employers for higher wages or better working conditions

Colosseum   the huge amphitheater in Rome where gladiator contests and other events were held

Columbian Exchange   transfer of people, animals, crops, and diseases between the Eastern and Western hemispheres as a result of European colonization in the Americas after 1492

Committee of Public Safety   group that ruled France with dictatorial powers during the French Revolution's Reign of Terror

common law   originating in England in the early Middle Ages, the body of law based on custom and precedent set by judicial decisions

communism   economic and political system based on the writings of Karl Marx and Vladimir Lenin, in which the government plans the economy and owns the means of production, and which in theory is dedicated to social equality (though in practice has often led to totalitarian rule)

Confederate States of America   nation formed by the southern states that seceded from the United States in 1861; it dissolved after being defeated in the American Civil War in 1865

Confucianism   philosophy based on the teachings of the Chinese philosopher Confucius

Congress of Vienna   series of meetings in 1814 and 1815 at which, after the defeat of Napoleon, representatives from Britain, Prussia, Russia, Austria, and other countries determined the new national borders of Europe and restored many monarchs to power

conquistador "conqueror" in Spanish; Spanish conquerors of the Americas in the early sixteenth century

conscript to force someone to do work or join a military; also, a person conscripted into work

constitutional monarchy a form of government in which a king or queen rules in conjunction with a parliament, congress, or some representative body elected by citizens as set forth in a constitution that guarantees certain rights

consul the highest magistrate in the Roman Republic, an official who oversaw most of the government and army

containment the U.S. Cold War policy of stopping the spread of communism

Continental Congress meeting of delegates from the American colonies during the Revolutionary War; the first Continental Congress met in secret in Philadelphia in 1774 to plan how to act on their grievances against the British government; the Second Continental Congress drafted the Declaration of Independence and the Articles of Confederation between 1775 and 1789

Continental System unsuccessful attempt by France under Napoleon to cut off trade between Great Britain and the rest of Europe in the early 1800s

cotton gin a machine that separates cotton seeds and hulls from the cotton fibers; invented by Eli Whitney in 1793

Council of Nicaea assembly of church leaders first convened by Emperor Constantine in A.D. 325, which set out the basic tenets of the Christian church at the time

Council of Trent 1545–1563 gathering of Roman Catholic bishops at Trent, Italy, that defined and clarified the doctrines of the Catholic Church

Counter-Reformation the Catholic Church's efforts to reverse the spread of Protestantism

and reform itself during the sixteenth and seventeenth centuries; also called the Catholic Reformation

coup d'état sudden overthrow of a government by force

covenant a solemn, binding agreement or promise

Creole during the Spanish colonization of the Americas in the sixteenth century, a person of Spanish descent born and raised in the Americas; generally, a person of European descent born in the Caribbean or Latin America

Crimean War war in the early 1850s in which Russia fought against the Ottoman Empire and its allies Great Britain, France, and Sardinia

Crusades medieval wars undertaken by European Christians to recapture the Holy Land from the Muslim Turks

Cuban Missile Crisis confrontation between the United States and the USSR in October 1962, when the Soviets secretly installed nuclear missiles on the island of Cuba; the United States blockaded the island; the crisis was the closest the world has ever come to nuclear war

Cubism artistic movement developed by Pablo Picasso and Georges Braque, in which the artist typically breaks objects into geometric shapes and imaginatively reassembles them

cultural diffusion the spread of ideas, goods, and customs from one society to another

Cultural Revolution movement for radical social change launched by Mao Zedong in China in 1966, intended to replace China's traditional order with a new revolutionary culture, during which Mao's youthful Red Guards engaged in widespread violence and terrorism

culture the traditions and customs of a people; their way of life and thought

cuneiform ancient Sumerian form of writing that used wedge-shaped marks

Cynics school of wandering ancient Greek philosophers who rejected the pursuit of wealth and power

Cyrillic alphabet writing system used mainly in Slavic languages, such as Russian

Dada a post–World War I movement in the arts that rejected tradition and convention, mocked certitude, and emphasized absurdity

daimyo in medieval Japan, a local Japanese lord who pledged to provide soldiers to the shogun in exchange for land

Daoism philosophy founded by the legendary Chinese thinker Laozi that emphasizes harmony with the mysterious order beneath things

Dayton Accords 1995 peace treaty signed by leaders of Serbia, Croatia, and Bosnia, ending the war in Bosnia and outlining the territorial divisions of Bosnia and Herzegovina

D-day a military term for the date an operation is to begin; it now generally refers to the massive Allied invasion of the European continent on June 6, 1944, at Normandy, a major turning point in World War II

Decembrist Uprising December 1825 revolt by Russian revolutionaries, many with military backgrounds, demanding reforms; the revolt was quickly put down by Tsar Nicholas I's imperial troops

Declaration of Independence document announcing the separation of thirteen American colonies from Great Britain, drafted by Thomas Jefferson and adopted July 4, 1776

Declaration of the Rights of Man and of the Citizen document drawn up by the French National Assembly in 1789 to limit royal power and list rights of the people

deforestation destruction of a region's forests, often to create farmland or harvest timber

deist person who believes in a God who created the universe but then left it to run on its own

delta triangle-shaped part of the end of a river that fans out and feeds into the sea, named for the Greek letter Δ

democracy government by the people; originated in the Greek city-state of Athens, where citizens directly took part in government and lawmaking; also used generally to refer to any representative government based on the will of the people

desertification the process by which fertile land turns into desert, often caused by climate change or by human practices such as deforestation or overgrazing

détente an effort to reduce tensions and establish better relations between the superpowers of the United States and the USSR in the 1970s; from the French word meaning "easing" or "relaxation"

dharma in Hinduism, the notion that each person has a particular religious and social duty to fulfill

dialect a regional variety of a language that differs somewhat in pronunciation, grammar, and vocabulary from the standard form of the language

Diaspora the scattering of the Jewish people throughout the world; also, the scattering of any people away from their land of origin

dictator a single ruler with absolute power

Diet of Worms meeting in 1521 of the Holy Roman Empire's assembly at Worms, Germany, at which Martin Luther was asked to recant; when Luther refused, he was condemned as a heretic

direct democracy system of government under which citizens vote on the issues themselves, in contrast to a republic or representative democracy, under which citizens vote for people who represent their interests and decide the issues

Directory group of five men who ruled France after the Reign of Terror and before Napoleon came to power in a coup

dissenter   someone who disagrees; in England during the seventeenth century, Protestants who disagreed with some beliefs and practices of the Church of England

divine right of kings   the belief that kings receive their power to rule directly from God and therefore are not answerable to the people or to parliament; used to support absolute monarchy

division of labor   the breaking of work into smaller tasks performed by various workers to increase efficiency of production

doge   formerly, leader of the Italian city-state of Venice or Genoa

Domesday Book   survey of English counties and their products under William the Conqueror

duchy   small territory ruled by a duke

Duma   legislative body of Russia, formed by Tsar Nicholas II after the Revolution of 1905

dynasty   a ruling family that remains in power for many years

Eastern Bloc   communist nations led by the Soviet Union during the Cold War

Edict of Milan   order issued by Roman emperor Constantine in 312 A.D. proclaiming religious toleration and protecting Christians from persecution

Emancipation Proclamation   order signed by U.S. president Abraham Lincoln granting freedom to Confederate slaves as of January 1, 1863

embargo   an official prohibition on trade with a particular country

encomienda   sixteenth-century Spanish American system that allowed land grantees to exploit and control the labor of the native people who lived on the land

English Bill of Rights   1689 document proclaiming the basic rights and freedoms of the British people

Enlightenment   also known as the Age of Reason, an intellectual movement in Europe and the American colonies during the seventeenth and eighteenth centuries, emphasizing a rational and scientific approach to problems, and believing that society could be perfected through the power of reason

entrepreneur   a person who organizes, manages, and takes on the risks of a new business

Estates-General   French representative assembly that met infrequently before the French Revolution; composed of three estates—the clergy, the nobility, and the rest of the people

ethical monotheism   the idea of a single God who demands just behavior of people

ethics   moral standards of behavior

ethnic cleansing   the systematic expulsion or killing of a minority ethnic group within a country

EU   See European Union (EU)

European Union (EU)   organization of European nations formed in 1992 to establish a common currency, eliminate barriers to trade, and work on common security concerns; in 2010, the European Union included twenty-seven member nations

excommunication   an official declaration barring a person from receiving Christian sacraments

executive branch   the part of government charged with implementing and enforcing laws; often headed by a president, prime minister, or head of state

Exodus   the journey of the Hebrew people out of Egypt, probably in the thirteenth century B.C.

famine   severe food shortage leading to widespread starvation

fascism   political system, usually led by a dictator, characterized by extreme national and racial pride and suppression of opposition

federal system system of government in which power is shared between a central, or federal, government and regional, or state, governments

feminism the belief, and the consequent political movement, that women should have political, economic, and social rights equal to those of men

Fertile Crescent fertile region stretching from the east coast of the Mediterranean Sea to the Persian Gulf and encompassing the land between the Tigris and Euphrates rivers where civilization began

feudalism in the Middle Ages in Europe, a political and economic system in which aristocratic landowners provide land and protection in exchange for service and loyalty

fief a grant of land by a medieval lord to a lesser noble or knight

Final Solution the Nazi plan for the extermination of all Jews in Europe, taken from Hitler's reference to the "final solution to the Jewish problem"

First Estate the clergy, one of the three social groups that made up the Estates-General in pre-revolutionary France

flapper young woman of the 1920s who asserted independence and went against conventions of dress and behavior

Forbidden City the walled palace complex in Beijing where Chinese emperors lived and imperial staff worked; few Chinese and almost no foreigners were permitted inside

Four Noble Truths four fundamental beliefs of Buddhism, that life is suffering, that suffering is caused by desire, that suffering only ends when the cycle of desire and rebirth ends, and that the way to end the cycle of rebirth is through the Noble Eightfold Path

Fourteen Points Woodrow Wilson's proposed set of principles for a World War I peace settlement; proposed in 1918, they included self-determination of peoples, removal of barriers to trade among nations, and an international organization to mediate differences

free trade the ability of businesses to engage in commerce with few government restrictions, especially the ability to conduct business across international borders

French and Indian War eighteenth-century conflict in North America in which the British and British colonists fought the French and their Native American allies; part of the larger Seven Years War, 1754–1763

fresco wall art made by painting on wet plaster

GATT See General Agreement on Tariffs and Trade (GATT)

General Agreement on Tariffs and Trade (GATT) 1947 agreement to reduce tariffs, signed by twenty-three countries; GATT went through several updates until it was replaced by the World Trade Organization (WTO)

genocide the deliberate and systematic destruction of a racial, political, religious, or cultural group

gentry aristocracy; upper class, often wealthy landowners

geocentric earth-centered; usually refers to the concept of a solar system or universe that places the earth at the center

ghetto section of a city where a minority group lives due to government restrictions or economic or social pressure

GI Bill popular name for the 1944 Servicemen's Readjustment Act, U.S. legislation that gave American soldiers returning from World War II loans, unemployment insurance, grants for education, and assistance buying homes

Gilded Age nickname for the period in the United States between the end of the American Civil War and the end of the nineteenth century, characterized by rapid economic growth, greed, political corruption, and extravagant displays of wealth by the upper class

glasnost   Russian word meaning "openness, candor, transparency"; in the 1980s, Soviet leader Mikhail Gorbachev called for glasnost, or an end to such practices as banning books and throwing dissidents in prison

globalization   trend toward increased integration and interconnectedness among nations, especially in business

Glorious Revolution   the bloodless overthrow of England's King James II in 1688, placing William and Mary on the throne; the revolution restricted the king's powers and increased Parliament's powers

Gospels   the first four books of the Christian New Testament that recount the life and teachings of Jesus Christ

Gothic   a medieval style of architecture characterized by flying buttresses, pointed arches, and soaring spires

Great Depression   severe worldwide economic decline during the 1930s, resulting in high unemployment and low business activity and contributing to political unrest in Europe

Great Leap Forward   Mao Zedong's 1958–1961 program of modernization for China, including forced industrialization and collectivization of agriculture; the process resulted in the deaths of tens of millions of Chinese due to famine, violence, and overwork

Great Schism   four decades (from 1378 to 1417) during which the Catholic Church was divided, with rival popes in Rome and in Avignon, France

Great War   original term used to describe the unprecedented conflict later known as World War I

Greco-Roman   pertaining to the mix of Greek and Roman cultures

griot   in west Africa, one whose role is to tell and pass on the traditional stories and the oral history of a people

guerrilla warfare   a strategy of fighting in which a small, unconventional force attacks a larger one using hit-and-run tactics

guild   in medieval times, an association of merchants or tradespeople organized to maintain standards and promote its members interests

guillotine   device for beheading people used for executions during the French Revolution

gunboat diplomacy   the display or threat of military force to compel another country to support a certain policy

habeas corpus   a Latin phrase meaning "you must have (or produce) the body"; habeas corpus is the legal right of an arrested person to be brought before a court to have the charges explained and thus prevents unlawful detentions

hacienda   large plantation owned by a landowner and worked by peasants, particularly in Latin America

haiku   traditional Japanese poem of three lines and seventeen syllables

hajj   the pilgrimage to Mecca that Muslims must make once before they die, if possible

Hamas   Palestinian political party and terrorist organization founded in 1987 by militant Islamists

heliocentric   sun-centered; usually refers to a concept of the solar system or universe that places the sun at the center (in contrast to geocentric)

Hellenistic Age   period during and after the reign of Alexander the Great when Greek civilization spread throughout the Mediterranean and nearby lands

heresy   a belief or practice that goes against official doctrine

Hezbollah   militant Islamist terrorist and political organization formed in Lebanon in 1982 and inspired by the Iranian revolution

hieroglyphics a form of picture-writing, particularly as used in ancient Egypt

Hijrah Muhammad's flight to Medina in A.D. 622, the first year of the Muslim calendar

Hinduism world religion and major faith of India; emerged from the beliefs of the Aryan peoples who settled in India in the 1500s B.C.

hippodrome a stadium for horse racing and, in ancient Greece and Rome, chariot races

Holocaust the Nazis' systematic mass slaughter of Europe's Jews and others during World War II; the Holocaust brought about the deaths of at least six million people, including approximately two-thirds of Europe's Jewish population

Holy Roman Empire loose western and central European empire, largely German-based and long associated with the Roman Catholic Church; established by Charlemagne according to tradition, the empire existed in some form from A.D. 962 to 1806

Huguenot French Protestant follower of John Calvin

humanism philosophy that stresses the dignity of man and places confidence in human potential

Hundred Years' War a long, destructive series of struggles between England and France that lasted from 1337 to 1453

hunter-gatherer person who obtains food by hunting animals and foraging for plants

icon painting or statue used to focus religious worship

iconoclasm literally, "icon-breaking"; a movement to ban the use of icons in the Byzantine church

illuminated manuscript handwritten book with elaborate decorations and designs

IMF See International Monetary Fund (IMF)

imperialism empire building; the policy or action by which one country controls another country or territory

Impressionism an artistic movement in which painters give an "impression" of a scene rather than depicting reality with photographic accuracy; major Impressionists include Degas, Manet, Monet, Renoir, and Cassatt

Indian National Congress political party in India, originally established in 1885 as an organization advocating greater self-government under British colonial rule and later leading the movement for India's independence

Indian Rebellion 1857 uprising of Indian troops against the British East India Company; also called the Sepoy Rebellion or the Sepoy Mutiny

indigo plant that produces a blue dye, or the dye from those plants

indulgence in Roman Catholicism, a partial pardon for sins

Industrial Revolution great technological and economic changes brought about in the late eighteenth and nineteenth centuries, when power-driven machinery began to produce many goods, which were assembled in factories

inflation rapid rise in prices associated with an increase in the supply of currency or credit

Information Revolution dramatic increase in the availability of information, made possible by enormous advances in electronics in the late twentieth century

infrastructure the fundamental structures and systems of transportation, communication, etc., needed for the functioning of a society

Inquisition a court of the Roman Catholic Church that examined and punished those whose beliefs were thought to go against Church teachings

International Monetary Fund (IMF) an organization that helps member nations stabilize their economies through loans in return for market reforms

Iron Curtain term coined by UK prime minister Winston Churchill in 1946 in reference to an imaginary dividing line between the Soviet-dominated, communist nations of Eastern Europe and the capitalist, democratic nations of the West

irrigation   bringing water to dry land using channels and canals, usually for agricultural purposes

Islam   world religion based on the teachings of Muhammad; followers are called Muslims

Islamism   a political and social movement that insists Islamic law (Sharia) and Islamic teachings must govern all aspects of life

isolationism   a national policy of withdrawal from world affairs

isthmus   a narrow strip of land connecting two larger land areas

Jacobin   member of the radical faction during the French Revolution

janissary   soldier in an elite corps of troops in the Ottoman Empire

Jesuit   member of the Catholic order the Society of Jesus, devoted to missionary and educational work

jihad   literally translated, "struggle"; in Islam, moral striving or the struggle for goodness; also sometimes used to refer to armed struggle against nonbelievers in the Muslim faith

joint-stock company   an organization in which every investor owns part of the company and is entitled to share in any profits

journeyman   someone who has completed an apprenticeship and is employed usually by a master craftsman

Judaism   religion of the Jews, descendants of the ancient Hebrews; first major religion to teach belief in one God

judicial branch   part of government charged with interpreting laws; may consist of a Supreme Court and lower courts

Justinian's Code   the collection of Roman laws commissioned by the Byzantine emperor Justinian; the Code of Justinian is a basis for legal codes in many modern nations

Ka'bah   cube-shaped shrine in Mecca considered the most sacred site in Islam and the center of Muslim worship

Kabuki   type of Japanese drama with highly stylized acting, singing, dancing, elaborate masks and costumes, and often sensational plots

kamikaze   Japanese for "divine wind"; the term can refer either to typhoons that destroyed two separate Mongol fleets invading Japan in the thirteenth century, or to Japanese suicide bombers who rammed their planes into enemy ships in World War II

karma   in Hinduism and Buddhism, the principle that one's actions, good or bad, will have corresponding effects in this life or in later reincarnations

khan   a Mongol ruler or chief

Khmer Rouge   communist group led by Pol Pot that took over Cambodia in 1975 and caused widespread suffering and death among the population

Kyoto Protocol   1997 agreement among signing nations at the UN Conference on Climate Change held in Kyoto, Japan, to set targets to reduce greenhouse gas emission levels; the U.S. Senate refused to ratify the agreement

laissez-faire   a French term meaning "let it be," used to describe an economic policy of minimal government interference in business and economic affairs

laity   the members of a church who are not part of the clergy

League of Nations   international organization formed after World War I to maintain peace among nations; the United States did not join the League, which was unsuccessful in deterring fascist aggression in the 1930s

legislative branch   part of government charged with making laws

Lend-Lease Act   program proposed by U.S. president Franklin D. Roosevelt to provide arms and supplies to Britain in exchange for long-term leases on British military bases in the period before the United States joined the fighting in World War II

Little Red Book   informal name for *Quotations from Chairman Mao*, a collection of speeches and sayings by Mao Zedong; all Chinese citizens were required to own and read the book during the Cultural Revolution

liturgy   rites used in public worship

loess   yellowish brown soil deposited by the wind

Long March   1934–1935 retreat of the Chinese Communist Red Army to safety in northwestern China to avoid defeat by Chiang Kai-shek's Nationalist Army; Mao Zedong's leadership during the Long March led to his rise to power within the Chinese Communist Party

Lost Generation   generation that fought and survived World War I, many of whom were disillusioned by the war and its aftermath; American writers such as Ernest Hemingway and F. Scott Fitzgerald were part of the Lost Generation

Louisiana Purchase   1803 acquisition by which the United States, under President Thomas Jefferson, bought the Louisiana Territory from France, which included lands from the Mississippi River to the Rocky Mountains

Lutheranism   Protestant Christian denomination that grew out of the reforms and teachings Martin Luther

macadam   an early road paving material made from crushed rock layered with tar

MAD   See mutual assured destruction (MAD)

Maginot Line   ultimately unsuccessful fortifications built by France along its border with Germany between the two world wars

Magna Carta   document signed in 1215 by England's King John recognizing the rights of England's nobles and church leaders

maize   corn, from the Taino language

mandate of heaven   ancient Chinese belief that a ruler's authority was granted by the gods while the ruler governed well

mandate   after World War I, a territory administered by Great Britain or France

Manhattan Project   secret research program launched by the U.S. government during World War II to develop the first atomic bomb

Manifest Destiny   the mid- to late-nineteenth century idea that it was the inevitable fate of the United States to expand its territory west to the Pacific

manor   the large estate of a medieval lord

Maori   indigenous person of New Zealand

market economy   economic system in which individuals and businesses control production, and decisions are based on supply and demand and competition

Marshall Plan   U.S. program that supplied billions of dollars in aid to help rebuild Europe after World War II; named for Secretary of State George Marshall

martial law   military rule, often involving the suspension of civil rights

mass production   the use of factories, assembly lines, and other efficiency-promoting technologies and practices to make more products in less time

medieval   of or relating to the Middle Ages (in Europe from about 500 to about 1500)

megacity   enormous, densely populated area

mercantilism   economic system dominant in sixteenth to eighteenth century Europe that emphasized precious metals such as gold and silver as essential to a nation's wealth, promoted policies to encourage more exports than imports, and saw colonies as suppliers of raw materials and markets for the mother country's manufactured goods

mercenary   professional soldier for hire

meritocracy   government or society where advancement is determined by abilities and effort rather than through family connection or wealth

Mesoamerica   the narrow southern portion of North America, including much of Mexico and Central America, where civilizations (including the Olmecs, Maya, and Aztecs) flourished before the arrival of Europeans

Messiah   the expected king or deliverer of the Jews; the term comes from ancient Hebrew and means "anointed one"

mestizo   during Spanish colonization of the Americas, a person of mixed European and Native American descent

Mexican-American War   1846 to 1848 war between Mexico and the United States sparked in part by the annexation of Texas by the United States; the victorious United States acquired lands that now make up parts of California and the southwestern United States

microloan   small loans to poor people, often women, to start their own businesses; microloans are used as an antipoverty program in many poor countries

Middle Passage   the second, or middle, leg of the three-way transatlantic slave trade between Europe, Africa, and the Americas, during which slaves suffered, and often did not survive, terrible conditions on overcrowded ships

migration   mass movement from one place to another

militarism   the glorification of military might; also, a policy of maintaining strong armed forces to gain political advantage

militia   citizen-soldiers not part of a regular army

minaret   a tower, part of a mosque, where the Muslim call to prayer is issued

mobilize   to assemble troops in preparation for war

monarchy   rule by one person who holds sovereign power over a kingdom or empire

monopoly   control over a particular industry, product, or service without competition

monotheism   belief in one god

Monroe Doctrine   U.S. president James Monroe's foreign policy asserting that the United States would resist any further colonization of the Western Hemisphere by European states

monsoon   wind that changes direction with the seasons; in India, winter monsoons blow dry air from the northeast while summer monsoons bring moist air and heavy rains from the Indian Ocean

mosaic   artwork made of pieces of colored tile arranged to form a picture or design

mosque   a Muslim place of worship

movable type   blocks with letters or characters carved into them, which can be arranged and rearranged to make printed pages

mujahideen   Islamic guerilla fighters, such as the nationalist Muslim rebels in Afghanistan who took up arms against the Soviet invasion and Afghan communists in the 1980s

mummification   the process of preserving a dead body by removing internal organs and moisture

mutual assured destruction (MAD)   a Cold War strategy to avoid nuclear war; the United States and the USSR each understood that to launch a nuclear attack on the other would result in a nuclear retaliation, resulting in the destruction of both countries

NAFTA   See North American Free Trade Agreement (NAFTA)

Napoleonic Code   code of civil law commissioned by Napoleon; it organized the many regional laws of France into a single code and became a model for the legal systems of many nations

National Assembly   revolutionary governing body formed in France in 1789 by representatives of the Third Estate

National Convention   governing body during the French Revolution that replaced the National Assembly and declared France a republic

nationalism   strong sense of attachment or belonging to one's own country; at its extreme, nationalism means glorifying one's own nation over all other countries, even at the expense of other countries

nationalization   government takeover of private business or industry

NATO   See North Atlantic Treaty Organization (NATO)

natural selection   sometimes called "survival of the fittest," according to Charles Darwin's theories, the process in nature by which organisms best suited to their environments will survive, reproduce, and pass their traits to their offspring

Nazi Party   National Socialist German Workers' Party, the German political party led by Adolf Hitler before and during World War II; Nazi goals included eliminating races they viewed as "inferior," especially Jews

Nazi-Soviet Nonaggression Pact   August 1939 treaty between Nazi Germany and the Soviet Union agreeing to not attack each other and secretly dividing the country of Poland between them

neoclassicism   art inspired by classical models of ancient Greece and Rome; specifically, an eighteenth-century movement in art and literature that emphasized harmony and order

Neolithic period   the New Stone Age, a period between the Paleolithic and the Bronze Age when people made advanced stone tools

Neolithic Revolution   the agricultural revolution, the period when the development of farming allowed humans to shift from food gathering to food production

New Deal   a wide range of government initiatives offered by U.S. president Franklin Roosevelt as a response to the Great Depression

New Imperialism   nineteenth century effort by major powers to obtain overseas colonies, particularly in Africa and Asia

New Testament   the second part of the Christian Bible, including work on the life and teachings of Jesus Christ and other early Christian writings

Ninety-five Theses   Martin Luther's arguments against the sale of indulgences by the Catholic Church; according to tradition, Luther nailed them to a church door in Wittenburg, Germany, in 1517

Nirvana   the state of freedom and peace; in Buddhism the release from the continual cycle of rebirth

nomadic   wandering, particularly moving around in search of food

nonalignment   policy of avoiding alliance with either of the world's two Cold War superpowers, the United States and the Soviet Union

nonviolent resistance   the use of peaceful protest to achieve a political or social cause

North American Free Trade Agreement (NAFTA)   1993 treaty creating a free-trade zone among the United States, Mexico, and Canada

North Atlantic Treaty Organization (NATO)   Cold War military alliance established by the United States, Britain, and other Western nations in 1949 to deter a Soviet attack on a member nation

Northwest Passage   a navigable waterway leading from the North Atlantic across North America to the Pacific Ocean, sought but not found by European explorers during the Age of Exploration

OAS See Organization of American States (OAS)

oasis, oases a small area with water and vegetation within a desert

occupation the control of an area by a foreign military

oligarchy a system of government in which power is held by a small group

OPEC See Organization of Petroleum Exporting Countries (OPEC)

Opium Wars two mid-nineteenth-century wars, the first fought between China and Great Britain, the second pitting Britain and France against China, over the illegal sale of opium by British merchants to the Chinese, and ending in expanded trading privileges for Western nations in China

oral tradition knowledge or lore passed down by word of mouth rather than being written down

Organization of American States (OAS) international organization of countries in North, South, and Central America; the OAS's goals include working for mutual security, resolving disagreements, promoting democracy, and reducing poverty in the region

Organization of Petroleum Exporting Countries (OPEC) cartel of oil-producing countries, established in 1960, that seeks greater control over the supply and price of oil

Paleolithic period the Old Stone Age, a period from about 2,000,000 B.C. to 11,000 B.C. when people made primitive stone tools

paleontology the study of fossil remains of plant and animal life

Palestine Liberation Organization (PLO) organization established by Arab leaders in 1964 to represent Palestinians and help them regain lands they lost in 1948 with the creation of Israel; has often conducted guerilla attacks against Israel, although it negotiated for peace with Israel in the 1990s

pan-Arabism movement that promoted the idea that the Arab world could act with unity for a common purpose

pandemic disease that spreads over a large geographical area and affects a high percentage of the population, such as the worldwide influenza outbreak of 1917 to 1920

papyrus a paperlike writing material made from pounded reeds, used in ancient Egypt, Greece, and Rome

parliament a national legislative assembly made up of representatives of the people, such as the British Parliament

Parthenon the temple to Athena that stands atop the Acropolis in Athens, Greece

passive resistance nonviolent opposition to a government policy or an occupying force

paterfamilias literally, the father of the family; the male head of household in Roman society

patriarch male leader of a tribe or nation; literally, a father

patrician member of one of the aristocratic ruling families of early Rome

patron person who supports an activity, in particular, one who provides financial support for artists and the arts

Pax Romana the "Roman Peace" or period of stability in the Roman Empire, lasting nearly two centuries, usually dated from 27 B.C. to A.D. 180

Peace of Augsburg 1555 treaty that allowed each local German prince to choose either Lutheranism or Catholicism as the official religion of his realm

Peace of Westphalia 1648 treaty ending the Thirty Years' War

Peloponnesian War a war fought from 431 to 404 B.C. between two leagues of Greek city-states, one headed by Athens and the other by Sparta

peninsulare   native Spaniard born on the Iberian peninsula who emigrated to Spain's colonies in the New World

perestroika   economic reforms in the Soviet Union instituted by Mikhail Gorbachev; the word literally means "restructuring"

Persian Gulf War (1991)   war in which a coalition of thirty-nine countries led by the United States and Great Britain quickly defeated Iraq, which had invaded the neighboring country of Kuwait

Persian Wars   a series of wars between Greek city-states and the Persian Empire that lasted from about 492 to 449 B.C.; also known as the Greco-Persian Wars

perspective   a mathematical or scientific system artists use to show depth in a two-dimensional artwork, that is, a technique of depicting depth on a flat surface, so that some objects appear closer to the viewer and some farther away

phalanx   tight formation of ancient Greek foot soldiers armed with spears and shields

pharaoh   the title for rulers of ancient Egypt

philosopher-king   according to Plato in *The Republic*, the ideal ruler, guided by knowledge of eternal truths

philosophes   from the Greek for "friends of wisdom," the political thinkers of eighteenth-century France who believed that reason and knowledge could bring justice, equality, and freedom

philosophy   the study of truth, knowledge, and the things of fundamental importance in life

pictogram   a picture of symbol representing a thing or concept; pictograms evolved into early writing

pietà   from the Latin word for "pity," a representation of Mary, the mother of Jesus, mourning over the body of her dead son

plateau   high, flat area of land

plebeian   commoner of ancient Rome

plebiscite   a vote by the people directly on an issue

PLO   See Palestine Liberation Organization (PLO)

pogrom   organized attack against or massacre of a targeted group, especially Jews

polis   city-state of ancient Greece

polytheism   belief in many gods

pope   title for the spiritual leader and head of the Christian Church in western Europe until the fifteenth century; head of the modern Roman Catholic Church

porcelain   a type of ceramic made from powdered stone mixed with clay

Potato Famine   massive failure of the potato crop in Ireland between 1845 and 1852, leading to widespread starvation and mass emigration

power of the purse   the ability to influence government policy by controlling taxes and funding

predestination   the idea that God has already determined who will be saved and that human beings cannot influence their own salvation

prehistory   the period of time before the invention of writing

prime minister   chief executive of a parliamentary government

primogeniture   by law or tradition, the right of eldest son to inherit the entire estate of his parents

Proclamation of 1763   British royal decree banning colonial settlement west of the Appalachian Mountains

proletariat   factory laborers and others who work for wages; according to Karl Marx, the huge proletariat class would someday overthrow the wealthy owners of businesses

propaganda information, often biased and distorted, used to influence public opinion

protectionism policies such as tariffs and quotas that are designed to prevent foreign companies from competing with a country's domestic industries

protectorate a country that, while not formally a colony, is largely controlled by a stronger nation

Protestant a member of one of the Christian churches that rejected the authority of the pope during the Reformation, such as the Anglican, Lutheran, Calvinist, and Presbyterian churches

Punic Wars a series of three wars between ancient Rome and the north African power of Carthage, lasting from 264 to 146 B.C. and ending with the destruction of Carthage

purgatory mainly in Roman Catholic teaching, the realm or condition in which sinners experience suffering to purify their souls in preparation for heaven

Puritans followers of the teachings of John Calvin in England and the American colonies; English Puritans wanted to purify the Church of England

Qaeda, al Islamist terrorist organization founded by Osama bin Laden in the late 1980s

Qu'ran the sacred book of Islam

Quaker member of the Protestant Christian religious sect known as the Society of Friends, which does not have formal ceremonies or ministers

quipu knotted cords used by the Inca to keep records

realism beginning in the mid-to-late nineteenth century, a literary and artistic movement emphasizing the portrayal of life as it is, often with subject matter drawn from lower- and middle-class life

recession a slowdown in business activity, leading to increased unemployment

Reformation religious movement of the sixteenth century that rejected the authority of the pope and led to the formation of Protestant churches; the Reformation split Christianity in Europe into Catholic and Protestant branches

refugee a person who flees a country, often to escape persecution

regent person who governs a country in place of the actual ruler, usually because the ruler is absent, incapacitated, or too young to govern the country

Reichstag German legislative body, 1871–1945

Reign of Terror the bloodiest phase of the French Revolution, in 1793 and 1794, when thousands were guillotined as enemies of the Revolution

reincarnation belief common to Hindus and Buddhists that at death the soul is reborn in the form of another living being

relativism belief that truth is subjective and changes according to the perspective of the individual

Renaissance period of great European cultural achievement that lasted from the late fourteenth to the early seventeenth century; the term *renaissance,* which means "rebirth," refers to a renewed interest in classical civilizations

reparations payments to make up for some wrongdoing, especially war damages

representative democracy system of government in which citizens elect those who make laws and decisions on their behalf, in contrast with direct democracy, under which people vote on the issues themselves

republic a government in which citizens elect leaders who rule on behalf of the people

Restoration the period of English history following the return of the royal family to power in 1660; the reign of King Charles II marked the end of the English Commonwealth and restored the monarchy

Ring of Fire zone encircling the Pacific Ocean that experiences frequent earthquakes and volcanic activity

Romanesque style of medieval architecture prominent in western Europe from the ninth to the twelfth centuries

Romanticism a movement in literature and the arts that emphasized an appreciation of nature, feeling, and emotion over reason and intellect, and celebrated the artist as an individual creator

Roosevelt Corollary President Theodore Roosevelt's extension of the Monroe Doctrine, arguing that the United States had the right to assert "international police power" in the Western Hemisphere

Rosetta Stone a stone found near the Egyptian city of Rosetta that helped modern scholars decipher Egyptian hieroglyphs

Roundheads Puritan followers of Oliver Cromwell in the English Civil War, so called because of their close-cropped haircuts

royalist supporter of a king, particularly a supporter of Charles I during the English Civil War

Russo-Japanese War 1904–1905 war in which Japan defeated Russia for control of parts of Manchuria

sacrament Christian rite, such as baptism or the Eucharist, believed to transmit God's grace

Sahel the band of semiarid lands forming the southern border of the Sahara in Africa

salon informal gathering of philosophes, writers, artists, and others to discuss ideas

SALT See Strategic Arms Limitation Talks (SALT)

samurai professional Japanese warriors who served feudal lords

savanna grassland dotted with scattered trees

Scholasticism intellectual movement of the Middle Ages that attempted to reconcile classical ideas and Christian tradition

Scientific Revolution era of great progress in understanding the workings of nature that occurred during the sixteenth and seventeenth centuries; during this period, modern science emerged as a distinct discipline

scorched-earth policy military tactic of destroying crops and infrastructure so that those resources cannot be used by an advancing military

scribe one who keeps public records

secede to withdraw, as from a nation; in 1860 and 1861, southern states seceded from the United States, setting off the American Civil War

Second Estate the nobility, one of the three social groups that made up the Estates-General in prerevolutionary France

Second Industrial Revolution social and economic transformations in late nineteenth and twentieth centuries spurred by the development of steel and electrical power

secular not related to religious matters

self-determination the belief that nations should rule themselves; the idea that people have the right to determine their own future and choose their own government

Senate a legislative body; in the Roman Republic, the most powerful branch of the government, made up of wealthy landowners; in the United States, the upper chamber of the legislature

Sepoy Mutiny See Indian Rebellion

serf peasant obliged to remain on the land of a lord and pay him with labor and rents

shah a king in the Safavid empire of Persia and later in Iran

Sharia legal and moral code of Islam

Shia member of the smaller of the two major branches of Islam (from Shia Ali, "the party of Ali"); often referred to as Shiites; distinguished from Sunni Muslims by differences in belief over leadership in Islam, the two branches share most religious beliefs but have a long history of conflict

Shinto religion native to Japan, whose followers worship spirits, especially in nature, known as kami

shogun title of the military ruler of Japan from the late twelfth century to mid-nineteenth century

Sikhism monotheistic religion founded in India and blending elements of Hinduism and Islam

Silk Road network of ancient overland trade routes stretching from eastern China to the Mediterranean Sea, linking East and West

Sino-Japanese War 1894–95 war in which Japan defeated the forces of China, marking the emergence of Japan as a world power

Six-Day War one of a series of Arab-Israeli military conflicts; in this June 1967 clash, Israeli forces, using swift air strikes, shocked the Arabs and made significant gains in territory, including the Sinai Peninsula, the Gaza Strip, and the West Bank; Israel also gained control of all of Jerusalem

slash-and-burn agriculture the practice of clearing land for farming by cutting down and burning trees

smelt to refine metals by heating them in order to remove impurities

social Darwinism the view that applies Charles Darwin's ideas of natural selection to society, seeing human interaction as driven by fierce competition and survival of the fittest

socialism an economic and political system emphasizing government control of productive property (such as factories and land) and regulation of the distribution of income; community ownership is preferred to private ownership, and government control often replaces the free play of market forces

sociology the study of the organization of humans in groups

Socratic method technique of teaching that involves asking questions of the student

Sophists school of ancient Greek philosophers who emphasized skepticism about traditional ideas

Soviet Union See Union of Soviet Socialist Republics (USSR)

Spanish-American War 1898 war between the United States and Spain over Cuba's attempt to gain independence from Spain and resulting in the United States' acquisition of territories including Hawaii, Guam, Puerto Rico, and the Philippines

sphere of influence region where trade is controlled by a foreign power that enjoys special economic privileges, particularly in China in the late nineteenth and early twentieth centuries

Stalingrad See Battle of Stalingrad

Stamp Act British legislation that required American colonists to pay for special stamps on most printed documents; the law was extremely unpopular in the American colonies

stele, stelae commemorative stone monument, particularly one built in the kingdom of Aksum in what is now Ethiopia

steppe dry, treeless land blanketed by short grasses

stock shares in a company signifying partial ownership of that company

Stoics school of ancient Greek philosophers who believed that suffering is caused by emotion and that people should accept whatever happens

Strategic Arms Limitation Talks (SALT) negotiations that began in 1969 between the United States and the Soviet Union to slow the buildup of nuclear arms

stupa   Buddhist place of worship

Sturm und Drang   German for "storm and stress"; a German literary movement that rejected the Enlightenment emphasis on reason and instead emphasized nature and strong feelings

suffrage   the right to vote, as in the movement for women's suffrage

summit   a meeting of the heads of governments

Sunni   member of the larger of the two major branches of Islam; distinguished from Shia Muslims by differences in belief over leadership in Islam, the two branches share most religious beliefs but have a long history of conflict

superpower   nation powerful enough to project military and economic power around the world

surplus   more than what is needed, such as the production of more resources than needed

surrealism   short for "super realism"; term coined in 1924 by André Breton to describe the exploration by writers and artists of the deep reality of the unconscious mind

synagogue   house of worship for Jewish people

Taliban   extremist Islamist regime that came to power in Afghanistan in the mid-1990s after the Soviet withdrawal and demanded strict adherence to Islamic law, banned many so-called Western behaviors, and brutally suppressed women's rights

Talmud   collection of ancient writings by Jewish religious teachers

telegraph   device for sending messages by electrical impulses sent along a wire

Ten Commandments   according to the Torah, the ten laws given by God to Moses for every Hebrew to obey

tenement   a large, usually overcrowded, urban apartment building

terrorism   the planned use of violence to strike fear into people or governments to obtain political goals

theocracy   government by a religious leader or leaders

theology   the study of god and the nature of the divine

Third Estate   professionals and laborers, one of the three social groups that made up the Estates-General in prerevolutionary France

Third Reich   official Nazi title for the German regime from 1933-45; literally, "the Third Empire," it refers to the Holy Roman Empire and the modern German Empire of 1871–1918 as the first and second reichs

Thirty Years' War   series of religious wars between European Protestants and Catholics in the early 1600s

tithe   percentage of income given to a church, either voluntarily or as a requirement

Toleration Act of 1689   British legislation allowing some freedom of religion for dissenting Protestants

Torah   the first five books of the Hebrew Bible; sometimes also used to refer to the whole Hebrew Bible, or what Christians call the Old Testament

Tory Party   British political party from the seventeenth through the nineteenth centuries that supported the power of the monarch and the Church of England; precursor to the modern-day Conservative Party

totalitarianism   a form of government that controls almost every aspect of people's lives, including political, economic, cultural, religious, and social activities

trade deficit   the difference in value between a country's exports and its imports

transcontinental railroad   a railroad line that spanned North America, connecting the East Coast to the West Coast, completed in the spring of 1869

Trans-Siberian Railroad   6,000-mile railroad connecting Moscow to a Russian port on the Sea of Japan

Treaty of Nanjing   1842 treaty ending the first Opium War, giving Great Britain trading privileges in China, and establishing Hong Kong as a British colony

Treaty of Tordesillas   agreement dividing the New World between Spain and Portugal, giving Portugal most of what later became Brazil and giving Spain the rest of the New World

Treaty of Versailles   1919 agreement ending World War I, establishing the League of Nations, and blaming Germany for the war, stripping it of overseas colonies and requiring war reparations

trench warfare   warfare closely associated with World War I in which enemy forces attack and defend from long ditches

tribunal   a court of justice

tribune   in ancient Rome, a magistrate elected to represent and protect the plebeians

tribute   payment given by a conquered people to its conquerors

Triple Alliance   the late nineteenth-century alliance between Germany, Austria-Hungary, and Italy

Triple Entente   the early twentieth-century alliance between France, Russia, and Great Britain

Trojan War   legendary war between the city of Troy and the city-states of Greece recounted in the *Iliad* and *Odyssey* and possibly based on historical events

troubadour   wandering poet-musician of the late Middle Ages in Europe

Truman Doctrine   U.S. president Harry Truman's policy committing the United States to providing economic and military aid to any country resisting communist takeover

tsar   title for ruler of Russia (sometimes spelled czar); from the Latin word caesar

tsunami   enormous sea wave caused by an undersea earthquake

Twelve Tables   the first set of written laws in ancient Rome, compiled around 450 B.C.

typhoon   a hurricane, especially one occurring in the region of the western Pacific Ocean

U-boat   German submarine; the U stands for *untersee,* German for "undersea"

UN   See United Nations (UN)

Union of Soviet Socialist Republics (USSR)   communist country made up of Russia and fourteen other socialist states; established in 1922, it dissolved in 1991; often known as the Soviet Union

United Nations (UN)   international organization with representatives from almost all countries in the world, established in 1945 to prevent war, promote cooperation among countries, and help settle international disputes

Universal Declaration of Human Rights   document written by a United Nations committee led by Eleanor Roosevelt and committing nation-states to key principles of human dignity and rights

Upanishads   philosophical writings of Hinduism compiled around 1000 B.C.

urban planning   the design of aspects of city life, including architecture, landscaping, zoning, and economic development

urbanization   mass movement of people from rural to urban areas

USSR   See Union of Soviet Socialist Republics (USSR)

utilitarianism philosophy that holds that policies should be judged on how useful they are, particularly in how likely they are to achieve the greatest amount of happiness for the greatest number of people

utopia an ideal, perfect society

vaccination the injection of weakened disease-causing germs to cause a body to develop immunity to a particular disease

vassal in medieval Europe, one who received land in exchange for loyalty

Vatican Vatican City, or "the Vatican," both the headquarters of the Roman Catholic Church and the smallest independent country in the world

vaudeville inexpensive form of entertainment in the United States in the late nineteenth and early twentieth centuries, which featured musicians, dancers, comedians, and other performers in a series of short acts

V-E Day Victory in Europe Day, proclaimed by U.S. president Harry Truman on May 8, 1945, marking Germany's surrender

Vedas the first sacred writings of Hinduism

vernacular the native language of a place; for example, Martin Luther translated the Bible from Latin into German, the vernacular of Germany

Versailles suburb of Paris, site of a lavish palace used by the last few French kings; See also Treaty of Versailles

veto the power to make invalid a legislative act

viceroy government official who acts for and rules in the name of the king, such as the official ruling some of Spain's colonies, or the British viceroy in India

Viet Cong communist guerrilla force in Vietnam, also known as the National Liberation Front

Vietnamization U.S. president Richard Nixon's effort to transfer the fighting of the Vietnam War from American forces to South Vietnamese soldiers by providing the Vietnamese with equipment and funding

V-J Day Victory in Japan Day; August 14, 1945, the date Emperor Hirohito of Japan surrendered, ending World War II

war crime an action that is illegal under international law and is committed in connection with a war, such as torture or enslavement of prisoners of war

War of 1812 war between the United States and Great Britain fought over trade restrictions, the impressment of American merchant sailors into the British navy, and British support of Native American tribes

Warsaw Pact 1955–1991 Cold War military alliance between the USSR and its eastern European nations, established in response to the NATO alliance of noncommunist nations

weapons of mass destruction weapons that have the potential to kill large numbers of people, such as nuclear, chemical, and biological weapons

Western Bloc during the Cold War, the countries made up of the United States and its democratic allies in Europe

Westernization the process by which a person or people adopts Western culture and values, sometimes abandoning traditional native customs or values

Whig Party British political party of the late seventeenth through early nineteenth centuries favoring a strong Parliament, limited power for the monarch, and toleration for Protestant dissenters; also, an American political party of the early nineteenth century in favor of modernization and economic protectionism

World Bank organization established after World War II to extend loans and grants to countries ravaged by war

World Trade Organization (WTO) international organization set up to promote free trade; most of the world's countries are members

World War I initially called the Great War, fought from 1914 to 1918 mainly between the Allied Powers of France, Russia, and Great Britain and the Central Powers of Germany, Austria-Hungary, and the empire of the Ottoman Turks; in 1917 the United States entered the war on the side of the Allies, who emerged victorious

World War II war fought from 1939 to 1945 mainly between the Axis Powers of Germany, Italy, and Japan, and the Allies, consisting of France, Britain, the Soviet Union, and later the United States; it was the most destructive war in human history, involving massive genocide and the first use of atomic weapons against an enemy

WTO See World Trade Organization (WTO)

yellow fever viral disease of the tropics whose symptoms include fever, headache, jaundice, and bleeding

Yom Kippur War also known as the Arab-Israeli War of 1973, a conflict launched in 1973 on Yom Kippur ("the day of atonement," the holiest of Jewish holidays), starting with surprise attacks by Egypt and Syria that took a heavy toll on Israeli troops; Soviet aid to Egypt and Syria spurred the United States to send aid to Israel; the war ended in a stalemate but, after Israel's swift defeat of Arab forces in the Six-Day War of 1967, restored Arab confidence

Young Italy nineteenth-century nationalist movement that sought to free Italy from foreign rulers

yurt domed tent used as a movable dwelling by Mongol nomads

Zealot Jewish rebel against Roman rule and Greek influences in Palestine

Zen form of Buddhism that uses meditation as a means of attaining enlightenment

ziggurat a stair-stepped temple built by Sumerians

Zionism Jewish nationalist movement based on the belief that the Jews should have their own nation, and specifically aiming to establish a Jewish state in Palestine (which occurred when the state of Israel was proclaimed in 1948)

Zoroastrianism religion founded in the Persian Empire; Zoroastrianism sees the world as a battleground between forces of good and evil

Illustration Credits

Key: t=top; b=bottom; c=center; l=left; r=right

Images/Corbis; (r) Vanni/Art Resource, NY; (background) © Fotosearch Stock; (background) © pic-a-boo/iStockphoto.com; **102** akg-images/Visioars. **103** (t) © Photodisc/Getty Images, Inc.; (b) Xinhua/Landov **104** © Burstein Collection/Corbis. **105** © The Trustees of The British Museum/Art Resource, NY. **106** Jean-Baptiste Rabouan/Hemis.fr/Aurora Photos. **107** (t) The Art Archive/Golestan Palace, Teheran/Gianni Dagli Orti; (b) Keren Su/Getty Images. **108** Xinhua/Landov. **109** Erich Lessing/Art Resource, NY.

Chapter 6: 110 The Art Archive/Bibliothèque des Arts Décoratifs, Paris/Gianni Dagli Orti. **113** Peter Horree/Alamy. **114** © Schmitz-Söhnigen/Corbis. **115** © Nimatallah/Art Resource. **116** © Scala/Art Resource. 117 © Yann Arthus-Bertrand/Corbis. **119** © Christophe Boisvieux/Corbis. **120** Erich Lessing/Art Resource, NY. **121** © Birmingham Museums and Art Gallery/ The Bridgeman Art Library. **123** akg-images/Peter Connolly. **124** © Bettmann/Corbis. **125** akg-images. **127** Vatican Museums and Galleries, Vatican City, Italy/Alinari/The Bridgeman Art Library; Dover Publications; (background) © Fotosearch Stock; (background) © pic-a-boo/iStockphoto.com.

Chapter 7: 128 Sitki Tarlan/Panoramic Images. **132** (tl) akg-images/Peter Connolly; (tr) Guy Vanderelst/Getty Images; (b) © Dorling Kindersley. **133** (tl) Scala/Art Resource, NY; (tr) © Araldo de Luca/Corbis. **134** (t) Paul Souders/World Foto/Aurora Photos; (bl) Vanni/Art Resource, NY; (br) The Art Archive/Museo Nazionale, Taranto/Alfredo Dagli Orti. **136** © Mary Evans Picture Library/The Image Works. **138** © Francis G. Mayer/Corbis. **139** Dover Publications; (background) © Fotosearch Stock; (background) © pic-a-boo/

iStockphoto.com. **140** © Scala/Art Resource. **142** The Granger Collection, New York. **144** © Araldo de Luca/Corbis. **145** Tom Lovell/National Geographic Stock. **147** Matthew Weinreb/Getty Images.

Chapter 8: 148 Scala/Art Resource, NY. **151** © Panoramic Images/John Rizzo 2010. **152** The Granger Collection, New York. **153** The Art Archive/Gianni Dagli Orti. **154** Scala/Art Resource, NY. **156** (background) akg-images/Gerard Degeorge; (background) © Fotosearch Stock; (background) © pic-a-boo/iStockphoto.com. **157** © Dorling Kindersley. **158** akg-images/Peter Connolly. **159** Bridgeman-Giraudon/Art Resource, NY. **161** Gilles Mermet/Art Resource, NY. **163** (tr) John Ross/Robert Harding; (background) © Massimo Listri/Corbis; (background) © Fotosearch Stock; (background) © pic-a-boo/iStockphoto.com. **164** Scala/Art Resource, NY. **165** (t) © Bettmann/Corbis; (b) Erich Lessing/Art Resource, NY. **166** © Panoramic Images/Frank Chmura 2010. **168** (t) © Juliane Jacobs/iStockphoto.com; (b) The Art Archive/Museo Capitolino, Rome/Gianni Dagli Orti. **169** © Kalkriese Museum/akg-images/The Image Works.

Chapter 9: 170 © Sites and Photos/HIP/The Image Works. **173** Rob Wood, Wood Ronsaville Harlin, Inc. **174** (b) Archives Larousse, Paris, France/Giraudon/The Bridgeman Art Library; (t) © akg-images. **176** (t) The Granger Collection, New York; (b) Réunion des Musées Nationaux/Art Resource, NY. **177** Louis S. Glanzman/National Geographic Stock. **178** © The Metropolitan Museum of Art/Art Resource, NY. **179** (t) © Masterfile; (b) © Panoramic Images/Bo Brannhage 2010. **180** © vito

arcomano/Age Fotostock. **183** The Bridgeman Art Library/Getty Images. **184** (t) The Art Archive/Musée Archéologique, Naples/Alfredo Dagli Orti; (background) © Fotosearch Stock; (background) © pic-a-boo/iStockphoto.com; (b) The Trustees of The British Museum/Art Resource, NY. **186** © AISA/Everett Collection. **187** The Art Archive/Museo Capitolino, Rome/Alfredo Dagli Orti. **190** (background) akg-images/Electa; (background) Gilles Mermet/Art Resource, NY; (background) © Fotosearch Stock; (background) © pic-a-boo/iStockphoto.com. **194** Vanni/Art Resource, NY. **195** © Topfoto/The Image Works.

Part 2
Part opener: 196 © beboy/Shutterstock. **196–197** 2011/Steve Estvanik/BigStockPhoto; (border) Dover Publications; (border) © Getty Images. **197** (t) © The Trustees of The British Museum/Art Resource, NY; (b) © INTERFOTO/Alamy.

Chapter 10: 198 (tl) Robert Caputo/Aurora Photos; (tc) Kenneth Garrett; (tr) Werner Forman/Art Resource, NY; (bl) Werner Forman/Art Resource, NY; (c) Kenneth Garrett/National Geographic Stock; (bc) © Jon Arnold Images/DanitaDelimont.com. **199** (tl) Kenneth Garrett/National Geographic Stock; (tr) The Art Archive/Archaeological Museum Lima/Gianni Dagli Orti; (bl) © Ancient Art and Architecture/DanitaDelimont.com; (br) © Russell Gordon/DanitaDelimont.com. **201** Ariadne Van Zandbergen/Lonely Planet Images. **204** © Pierre Colombel/Corbis. **205** Marvin E. Newman/Getty Images. **206** Musee di Quai Branly/Scala/Art Resource, NY. **207** Paul Harris/JWL/Aurora Photos. **208** Kenneth Garrett. **209** Michael Freeman/Aurora Photos. **210** © Jon

Maria Cuellar/Getty Images; (b) © Trevor Wood/Stone/ Getty Images. **425** (t) © Scala/ Art Resource; (b) © Scala/Art Resource. **426** (t) © Scala/Art Resource; (b) Dover Publications. **427** (tl) © Sqback/Dreamstime. com; (tr) Dover Publications; (b) Dover Publications. **428** (t) Dover Publications; (b) © Araldo de Luca/Corbis. **429** (t) © Super-Stock; (b) Dover Publications. **430** (t) Dover Publications; (b) Vatican Museums and Galleries, Vatican City, Italy/Giraudon/The Bridgeman Art Library International. **431**(b) Robert Harding Images/Masterfiles. **433** The Art Archive/Galleria d'Arte Moderna Rome/Gianni Dagli Orti. **434** Dover Publications. **436** (t) Erich Lessing/Art Resource; (b) Dover Publications. 436 Erich Lessing/ Art Resource. **437** © The Gallery Collection/Corbis. **439** (t) The Granger Collection, NYC. All rights reserved; (b) British Library, London, UK/Giraudon/ The Bridgeman Art Library International. **440** (background) Dover Publications; (background) Dover Publications; (background) Ryan McVay/Thinkstock; (background) Dover Publications; (b) © Lebrecht/The Image Works. **441** Palazzo Vecchio (Palazzo della Signoria) Florence, Italy/The Bridgeman Art Library.

Chapter 20: 442–443 Library of Congress, Prints and Photographs Division, G320.S12-1595.H6. **445** © British Library Board. All Rights Reserved/The Bridgeman Art Library International. **446** © National Maritime Museum, Greenwich, London. **448** (background) © Corbis. **448–449** (background) Private Collection/Index/The Bridgeman Art Library; (background) Ryan McVay/Thinkstock. **449** (background) © Mike Agliolo/ Corbis. **450** The Granger Collection, NYC. All rights reserved.

451 (t) © Getty Images; (b) © Erich Lessing/Art Resource. **453** Private Collection/The Bridgeman Art Library. **454** The Art Archive/ Museo del Oro Lima/Gianni Dagli Orti. **455** © The Print Collector/ Age Fotostock. **456–457** (frame) The Granger Collection, NYC. All rights reserved; (background) © art12321/iStockphoto; (background) Ryan McVay/Thinkstock. **457** Architect of the Capitol. **459** © ARPL/HIP/The Image Works. **460** The LuEsther T. Mertz Library, NYBG/Art Resource, NY. **461–462** The Granger Collection, NYC. All rights reserved. **463** © MPI/Stringer/Getty Images. **464** (t) © World History/Topham/The Image Works; (b) The Granger Collection, NYC. All rights reserved.

Chapter 21: 466–467 Bildarchiv Preussischer Kulturbesitz/ Art Resource, NY. **469** Galleria degli Uffizi, Florence, Italy/The Bridgeman Art Library. **470** (t) akg-images; (b) © Erich Lessing/ Art Resource, NY. **471** (background) Ryan McVay/Thinkstock; The Granger Collection, NYC. All rights reserved. **472** akg-images. **473** © The Art Archive/University Library Geneva/Gianni Dagli Orti. **474** (frame) © Photodisc; © NTPL/Derek Witty/The Image Works. **476** © Alfredo Dagli Orti/Art Resource, NY. **477** The Granger Collection, NYC. All rights reserved. **479** © Scala/ Art Resource. **481** © The Art Archive/Musée des Beaux Arts Lausanne/Gianni Dagli Orti. **482** © Erich Lessing/Art Resource, NY. **484** The Granger Collection, NYC. All rights reserved. **485** © Réunion des Musées Nationaux/ Art Resource, NY. **487** (frame) © ElementalImaging/iStockphoto; © Topham/The Image Works. **488** The Granger Collection, NYC. All rights reserved. **490** (t) © Philip Mould Ltd, London/The Bridgeman Art Library International;

(b) akg-images. **491** The Granger Collection, NYC. All rights reserved. **492** © British Library, London, Great Britain/HIP/Scala/ Art Resource **493** The Granger Collection, NYC. All rights reserved.

Chapter 22: 494–495 The Granger Collection, NYC. All rights reserved. **495** (background) The Granger Collection, NYC. All rights reserved. **497** © The British Library/HIP/The Image Works. **498** © Bettmann/ Corbis. **499** Jean-Leon Huens/ National Geographic Stock. **501** The Granger Collection, NYC. All rights reserved. **502** The Granger Collection, NYC. All rights reserved. **503** The Granger Collection, NYC. All rights reserved. **504** © World History Archive/ Alamy. **505** Library of Congress, Prints and Photographs Division, LC-DIG-ppmsca-02472. **507** The Granger Collection, NYC. All rights reserved. **508** (background) Ryan McVay/Thinkstock; (background) (detail) The New York Public Library/Art Resource, NY. **509** Réunion des Musées Nationaux/Art Resource, NY. **510** The Art Archive/Private Collection/Gianni Dagli Orti. **511** Private Collection/The Bridgeman Art Library International; (frame) © Michal Rozanski/iStockphoto. **513** © Réunion des Musées Nationaux/Art Resource, NY. **517** © Massachusetts Historical Society, Boston, MA, USA/The Bridgeman Art Library International. **518** Delaware Art Museum, Wilmington, USA/Howard Pyle Collection/The Bridgeman Art Library International. **519** (background) The Granger Collection, NYC. All rights reserved; (background) Ryan McVay/Thinkstock. **520** © Francis G. Mayer/Corbis. **521–522** © Architect of the Capitol. **523** © Marcopolo9442/ iStockphoto; (background) Ryan McVay/Thinkstock.

Chapter 23: 524–525 Erich Lessing/Art Resource, NY. **527** The Art Archive/Musée Carnavalet Paris/Marc Charmet. **529** © Réunion des Musées Nationaux/ Art Resource; (frame) © subjug/ iStockphoto. **530** © Bridgeman-Giraudon/Art Resource, NY. **531** (background) Ryan McVay/Thinkstock. **532** Giraudon/Art Resource, NY. **533** The Granger Collection, NYC. All rights reserved. **534** Giraudon/Art Resource, NY. **535** Dover Publications. **537** (background) Ryan McVay/Thinkstock; The Granger Collection, NYC. All rights reserved. **538** © Scala/ Art Resource. **539** (background) Ryan McVay/Thinkstock; © Bill Noll/iStockphoto. **540** © David, Jacques Louis/Musee Nat. du Chateau de Malmaison, Rueil-Malmaison, France/Lauros/Giraudon/ The Bridgeman Art Library International. **541** © Getty Images/ Thinkstock; (background) © Eliza Snow/iStockphoto. **542** FORBES Magazine Collection, New York, USA/The Bridgeman Art Library. **543** Victoria and Albert Museum, London/Art Resource, NY.

Chapter 24: 546–547 The Art Archive/Simon Bolivar Amphitheatre Mexico/Gianni Dagli Orti. **551** The Granger Collection, NY. **553** © Luis Marden/ National Geographic Stock. **554** © The Art Archive/National History Museum Mexico City/ Gianni Dagli Orti. **555** The Granger Collection, NY. 557 Bildarchiv Preussischer Kulturbesitz/Art Resource, NY. **558** © Roger-Viollet/The Image Works. **560** The Granger Collection, NY. **561** (t) Réunion des Musees Nationaux/Art Resource, NY; (b) State Russian Museum, St. Petersburg, Russia/Giraudon/ The Bridgeman Art Library. **563** The Granger Collection, NY. **564** © Cotton Coulson/ National Geographic Stock. **565** Time and Life Pictures/Getty

Images. **566** The Granger Collection, NY. **569** © Getty Images/ Thinkstock; (frame) louoates/ Bigstock. **571** The Art Archive/ Gift of Ruth Koerner Oliver/Buffalo Bill Historical Center, Cody, Wyoming/6922.1. **573** (t) The Metropolitan Museum of Art/ Art Resource, NY; (b) © Christie's Images/SuperStock. **575** Library of Congress, Prints and Photographs Division, LC-DIG-cwpb-00831.

Chapter 25: 576–577 © E.O. Hoppe/Corbis. **579** Dover Publications. **580** The Metropolitan Museum of Art/Art Resource, NY. **581** © SSPL/The Image Works. **582** The Granger Collection, NY. **583** © Private Collection/The Bridgeman Art Library International; (background) Ryan McVay/Thinkstock. **584** © Bettmann/Corbis. **587** (t) The Granger Collection, NY; (b) © NRM/Pictorial Collection/SSPL/ The Image Works. **589** (t) © SuperStock; (b) The Granger Collection, New York **590** The Granger Collection, NY. **591** (t) The Granger Collection, NY; (b) © SSPL/The Image Works. **593** (t) © Mary Evans Picture Library/The Image Works; (b) The Granger Collection, NY. **594** © ARPL/HIP/ The Image Works. **595** (t) The Granger Collection, NY; (b) © Getty Images/Thinkstock. **596** © The Art Archive/Bibliothèque des Arts Décoratifs Paris/Dagli Orti; (background) © Getty Images/ Thinkstock; (background) © Jonathan Larsen/iStockphoto; (background) Ryan McVay/Thinkstock.

Chapter 26: 598–599 © Topham/The Image Works. **602** (t) Pope Family Trust/The Bridgeman Art Library; (b) Royal Holloway, University of London/ The Bridgeman Art Library. **604** The Art Archive; (frame) © CatNap72/iStockphoto; (background) Ryan McVay/Thinkstock;

(background) The Granger Collection, NY. **605** © Mary Evans Picture Library. **606** © National Maritime Museum, London/The Image Works. 607 The Granger Collection, NY; (frame) © Tim Mainiero/iStockphoto. **608** © A.H.C./Age Fotostock. **609** (t) © A.H.C./Age Fotostock; (b) © 2010 Artists Rights Society (ARS), New York/ADAGP, Paris/ Réunion des Musées Nationaux/ Art Resource, NY. Reproduction, including downloading, of Jules Adler works is prohibited by copyright laws and international conventions without the express written permission of Artists Rights Society (ARS), New York. **610** The Granger Collection, NY. **611** © Dover Publications, Inc. **612** Library of Congress Prints and Photographs Division, LC-USZ62-100109. **613** Florence Nightingale Museum, London, UK/The Bridgeman Art Library. **614** The Art Archive. **615** (t) akg-images; (frame) © gbrundin/ iStockphoto; (b) akg-images. **616** © Stefano Bianchetti/Corbis. **617** (t) Victoria and Albert Museum, London/Art Resource, NY; (b) Private Collection, © The Fine Art Society, London, UK/The Bridgeman Art Library. **618** Private Collection, Archives Charmet/The Bridgeman Art Library. **620** The Art Archive. **621** (t) Dover Publications; (b) Dover Publications. **622** (t) The Art Archive; (frame) © Eliza Snow/iStockphoto; (b) akg-images. **623** (t) Réunion des Musées Nationaux/Art Resource, NY; (b) © Staatliche Kunstsammlungen Dresden/The Bridgeman Art Library. **624** (t) Jefferson College, Philadelphia, PA, USA/The Bridgeman Art Library; (cl) The Granger Collection, NY. **624** (bl) The Granger Collection, NY; (cr) © ARPL/HIP/The Image Works; (br) Lebrecht Authors; (t) Dover Publications; (b) Giraudon/The Bridgeman Art Library.

Index

Page references in bold refer to maps and titled works of art.

O